Hayner Public Library District-Alton
P9-DZN-972

ENCYCLOPEDIA OF AMERICAN LIVES
CSS

The SCRIBNER ENCYCLOPEDIA *of*

AMERICAN LIVES

The SCRIBNER ENCYCLOPEDIA *of* AMERICAN LIVES

VOLUME TWO

1986–1990

KENNETH T. JACKSON
EDITOR IN CHIEF

KAREN MARKOE
GENERAL EDITOR

ARNOLD MARKOE
EXECUTIVE EDITOR

CHARLES SCRIBNER'S SONS
AN IMPRINT OF MACMILLAN LIBRARY REFERENCE USA
NEW YORK

Charles Scribner's Sons
An imprint of Macmillan Library Reference USA
1633 Broadway
New York, NY 10019

Library of Congress Cataloging-in-Publication Data

The Scribner encyclopedia of American lives / Kenneth T. Jackson, editor in chief ; Karen Markoe, general editor ; Arnold Markoe, executive editor.
p. cm.
Includes bibliographical references and index.
Contents: v. 1. 1981–1985
ISBN 0-684-80492-1 (v. 1 : alk. paper)
1. United States—Biography—Dictionaries. I. Jackson, Kenneth T. II. Markoe, Karen. III. Markoe, Arnie.
CT213.S37 1998
920.073—dc21 98-33793
CIP

ISBN 0-684-80491-3 (v. 2 : alk. paper)

1 3 5 7 9 11 13 15 17 19 20 18 16 14 12 10 8 6 4 2
PRINTED IN THE UNITED STATES OF AMERICA

The paper in this publication meets the minimum requirements of the American National Standard for Information Services—Permanence of Paper for Printed Library Materials, ANSI Z39.48-1992.

EDITORIAL *and* PRODUCTION STAFF

Managing Editor
TIMOTHY J. DEWERFF

Editorial Assistant and Photo Editor
ALEXANDER GOLDMAN

Editorial Assistants
AMELIA DEREZINSKY MARCIA B. HAHAM ANDREW MCCARTHY

Editors
HANNAH BORGESON JEFF CHEN JOHN FITZPATRICK LAURA SMID STEPHEN WAGLEY

Copy Editors, Researchers
MELISSA A. DOBSON LOUISE B. KETZ MICHAEL LEVINE
CHRISTINE M. GROVE JEAN F. KAPLAN MARTHA SCHÜTZ ELIZABETH I. WILSON
BRIGIT DERMOTT GEOFFREY GNEUHS JOSEPH GUSTAITIS BERNARD JOHNSTON
LINDA SANDERS JOHN M. SICILIANO SARAH VALDEZ

Proofreaders
GRETCHEN GORDON CAROL HOLMES EVANGELINE LEGONES

Production Manager
ROSE CAPOZZELLI

Designer
BRADY MCNAMARA

Executive Editor
SYLVIA K. MILLER

Publisher
KAREN DAY

PREFACE

This second volume of the *Scribner Encyclopedia of American Lives* (*SEAL*) contains the biographies of 506 persons who left their imprint on history and who died between 1 January 1986 and 31 December 1990. With its publication, three months after the appearance of Volume 1, the number of subjects in the *SEAL* series increases to exactly 1,000; future volumes will cover persons who died in subsequent five-year periods. Wherever possible, each biography includes the names and occupations of parents, the number of siblings, the names of spouses and dates of marriages, the number of children, places of residence, cause of death, and place of burial. The authors of the essays have also endeavored to discuss the formative influences on the subjects and the lasting significance of their achievements.

The 334 contributors to this volume are biographers, journalists, academics, and others with a passion for history who possess well-honed skills in research and writing. Many had written entries for the *Dictionary of American Biography,* an earlier biographical reference work published by Scribners that remains in print. The writers have been resourceful in completing their biographies, many of them conducting original research and interviewing family members and professional associates of their subjects to gain previously unrecorded insights.

In contrast to the *Dictionary of American Biography,* which was produced under the auspices of the American Council of Learned Societies, *SEAL* is being produced independently by scholars working with the Scribner editorial staff. *SEAL* also introduces a number of new features. First, almost every entry included in this volume is accompanied by a photograph of the subject. Second, each biography alerts readers to the significance of the subject's life at a glance by encapsulating his or her most important achievements in the opening paragraph. Third, an index listing the subjects by occupation is printed in the back matter of the volume that includes their biographies. Fourth, all the authors are identified at the end of the book along with their institutional or occupational affiliations and a listing of the articles for which they were responsible.

The process of selecting a few hundred subjects from the nearly 10 million Americans who died between 1986 and 1990 necessarily involved many people. Specialists in numerous fields were enlisted to nominate those Americans who would likely have the most enduring legacies. These names were submitted to an advisory board consisting of Stuart W. Bruchey of Columbia University, Joshua Lederberg of Rockefeller University, Vivian Perlis of Yale University, and Arthur M. Schlesinger, Jr., of the City University of New York. The final list, however, is solely the responsibility of the editors, who weighed the relative significance of particular politicians and poets, chemists and criminals, business leaders and baseball players. The subjects represent a multiplicity of races and ethnic backgrounds, some born to privilege, others to poverty. Some, such as British-born Cary Grant, were included because most of their important work was done in the United States. Many were famous during their lifetimes, some were infamous, and others were quietly important, but all the persons included clearly lived extraordinary lives, winning fame on the battlefield or in the laboratory, writing great books, or governing cities and states.

The subjects in this volume represent many professions, including the writers James Baldwin, Mary McCarthy, Robert Penn Warren, Bernard Malamud, and Barbara Tuchman; musicians Irving Berlin, Aaron Copland, Leonard Bernstein, and Pearl Bailey; dancers and choreographers Bob Fosse, Alvin Ailey, and Robert Joffrey; politicians Claude Pepper, Harold Washington, Averell Harriman, and Jacob Javits; military commanders Curtis LeMay and Hyman Rickover; artists Georgia O'Keeffe and Andy Warhol; performing artists Greta Garbo, Bette Davis, James Cagney, and Fred Astaire; sports figures Sugar Ray Robinson and Billy Martin; business leaders William Paley and Henry Ford II; scientists and inventors William Shockley and An Wang; and physicians Howard Rusk and Karl Menninger.

Others memorialized herein are Mel Blanc, the voice of Bugs Bunny and other memorable Warner Brothers cartoon characters; Christine Jorgensen, who underwent the first widely publicized sex-change operation; Laurence Peter, creator of the "Peter Principle"; comedian Gilda Radner, whose struggle with breast cancer heightened national awareness of that disease; divorcée Wallis Warfield Simpson, for whom King Edward VIII of England gave up his throne; and Frank Zamboni, whose eponymous invention smooths the ice for hockey rinks worldwide. We hope that readers intent on finding out about the life of one subject will be tempted to stay and browse through the lives of others who until that moment may be names but dimly remembered.

As is the case in any large-scale research effort, *SEAL* depended on the hard work and cooperation of hundreds of persons, many new to this effort. We acknowledge again the diligent research efforts undertaken by our writers. Resourceful photo editors located photographs for almost every subject. Happily, the editors of this volume all had worked together on similar ventures and chose to do so again. The result of this collaboration is a book that we trust will be useful, reliable, and enjoyable.

We especially praise Timothy J. DeWerff, managing editor, who took charge of the project for Charles Scribner's Sons and whose judgment, perseverance, and good humor were essential for seeing the volume through to publication. We are indebted to our colleague Richard H. Gentile, who offered invaluable help throughout the project, and to William Gargan, who provided thoughtful and extensive counsel on literary subjects. A team of copy editors and proofreaders, too numerous to name here, were guarantors of quality and were immensely valuable to the enterprise. Finally, we wish to acknowledge the deep commitment of Karen Day, the publisher of Charles Scribner's Sons, who was the guiding inspiration of *SEAL* from conception through publication.

Kenneth T. Jackson, Editor in Chief
Karen E. Markoe, General Editor
Arnold Markoe, Executive Editor

CONTENTS

The SCRIBNER ENCYCLOPEDIA *of*
AMERICAN LIVES

ABBEY, Edward Paul (*b.* 29 January 1927 in Indiana, Pennsylvania; *d.* 14 March 1989 in Tucson, Arizona), novelist and essayist best known for his depiction of life in the stark landscape of the U.S. Southwest in *Desert Solitaire* (1968).

Raised on a remote farm in the Allegheny Mountains near Indiana, Pennsylvania, Edward Abbey was the oldest of five children born to Paul Revere Abbey, a farmer, and Mildred Postlewaite, a teacher. Abbey first encountered the deserts of the Southwest when he hitchhiked across the country in the summer of 1944, the year before his graduation from high school. He served with the U.S. Army in Alabama and Italy from 1945 to 1946, then attended the University of New Mexico, where he studied English and philosophy from 1947 to 1951, receiving a B.A.; he also edited the student literary magazine. In 1950 he married Jean Schmechal; they divorced in 1952. From 1951 to 1952 Abbey was a Fulbright fellow at the University of Edinburgh in Scotland. He returned to the University of New Mexico from 1954 to 1956 to study philosophy; his M.A. thesis was titled "Anarchism and the Morality of Violence." In 1952 Abbey married Rita Deanin; they had two sons and were divorced in 1965.

Abbey's first novel was *Jonathan Troy* (1954), the story of a self-involved young man who yearns to escape his Pennsylvania home for the open spaces of the West. Although Abbey later called it "a very poor book," the novel anticipates the conflict between wilderness and civilization that appears in his subsequent works. *The Brave Cowboy* (1956) enjoyed a greater success and became the basis for the film *Lonely Are the Brave* (1962), starring Kirk Douglas and Walter Matthau. Subtitled *An Old Tale in a New Time,* the novel features Jack Burns, a nineteenth-century-style cowboy whose rugged individualism has become anachronistic in modern New Mexico. *Fire on the Mountain* (1962) similarly explores the struggles of John Vogelin as he unsuccessfully attempts to prevent the White Sands Missile Range from encroaching on his ranch land in southern New Mexico. Abbey married his third wife, Judith Pepper, in 1965; she died in 1970. They had one daughter.

Abbey worked as a seasonal U.S. Park Service ranger and U.S. Forest Service fire lookout from 1956 to 1979. *Desert Solitaire* (1968), his best-known work, grew out of the three seasons he spent as a ranger at Arches National Monument (now a national park) near Moab, Utah. In eighteen nonfiction essays in which he utilized novelistic techniques, *Desert Solitaire* explores the significance of the arid southwestern landscape. Edwin Way Teale, writing in the *New York Times,* described the work as "a voice crying in the wilderness, *for* the wilderness." Abbey's arguments against the spread of "industrial tourism" and for the preservation of wilderness as a "refuge from authoritarian government" are the book's most important contributions. In 1973 Abbey married Renee Downing; they had no children.

Abbey also wrote commentaries for several large-format

Edward Abbey performing on the Outlaw Trail near Lake Powell, Utah. JONATHAN BLAIR/CORBIS

photography books. *Appalachian Wilderness* (1970), with Eliot Porter, explores the Great Smoky Mountains of North Carolina and Tennessee; *Slickrock* (1971), with Philip Hyde, describes the red rocks and canyons of southeastern Utah; *Cactus Country* (1973), with Ernst Haas, captures the Sonoran Desert of southern Arizona and northern New Mexico; *The Hidden Canyon* (1977), with John Blaustein, recounts a river trip through the Grand Canyon of the Colorado River; and *Desert Images* (1979), with David Muench, ranges widely throughout the Southwest. Portions of these essays were collected in *Beyond the Wall: Essays from the Outside* (1984).

Abbey's four other nonfiction books mix essays on travel, politics, and personal history. *The Journey Home* (1977), Abbey's angriest book, includes an examination of what he calls "the second rape of the West." *Abbey's Road* (1979) extends his travels to such places as Australia and Mexico. *Down the River* (1982) intersperses river narratives from Alaska, Colorado, and Utah with book reviews, personal profiles, and political diatribes. *One Life at a Time, Please* (1988) reprints some of Abbey's most notorious essays, including those defending anarchy and "ecosabotage" and others attacking immigration, feminism, and the livestock industry.

Abbey's later fiction reflects his love of the deserts of the Southwest as well as his frustration with their "development." In the somber *Black Sun* (1971), which Abbey considered his finest novel, a middle-aged fire lookout falls in love with a teenage girl, only to have their idyllic relationship cut short when she mysteriously disappears into the Grand Canyon. *The Monkey Wrench Gang* (1975) is a fast-paced adventure story, part melodrama, part survival manual, which popularized the term "monkeywrenching"—committing nonviolent sabotage in the name of environmental protection—and inspired the radical environmental group Earth First! *Good News* (1980), a grim, futuristic western set in and around the wasteland of Phoenix, Arizona, dramatizes the devastating consequences of unbridled growth and "progress." *The Fool's Progress* (1988) chronicles the comical cross-country journey of the Abbey-like Henry Lightcap from Tucson to his ancestral home in West Virginia. *Hayduke Lives!* (1989), published posthumously, is a sequel to *The Monkey Wrench Gang*. After his divorce from Downing, in 1982 Abbey married Clarke Cartwright, with whom he lived until his death. They had two children.

Abbey's awards included a Wallace Stegner Creative Writing Fellowship at Stanford University (1957), a Guggenheim Fellowship in fiction writing (1974), and a Creative Achievement Award from the American Academy and Institute of Arts and Letters (1987, declined). From 1981 onward he taught creative writing at the University of Arizona, where he became a full professor in 1988. Abbey died of internal bleeding due to a circulatory disorder at age sixty-two and was buried, according to his wishes, in an unmarked grave in or near Saguaro National Monument in southern Arizona, near Tucson.

The author of eight semiautobiographical novels and eleven works of personal nonfiction, "Cactus Ed," as Abbey was known, explored the social, political, and environmental landscape of the twentieth-century American West with a highly distinctive combination of irreverence and lyricism.

In the essay "A Writer's Credo," Abbey declared, "I write to entertain my friends and exasperate our enemies. I write to record the truth of our time as best I can see it. To investigate the comedy and tragedy of human relationships. To oppose, resist, and sabotage the contemporary drift toward a global technocratic police state, whatever its ideological coloration. I write to oppose injustice, to defy power, and to speak for the voiceless. I write to make a difference."

★

The University of Arizona at Tucson holds Abbey's papers. From these David Petersen assembled *Earth Apples: The Poetry of Edward Abbey* (1994) and *Confessions of a Barbarian: Selections from the Journals of Edward Abbey, 1951–1989* (1994). James Bishop, Jr., *Epitaph for a Desert Anarchist* (1994), is a popular biography. Critical discussion of Abbey's writing appears in Garth McCann, *Edward Abbey* (1977); Ann Ronald, *The New West of Edward Abbey* (1982); James Hepworth and Gregory McNamee, eds., *Resist Much, Obey Little: Remembering Edward Abbey* (1996); Peter Quigley, ed., *Coyote in the Maze: Tracking Edward Abbey in a World of Words* (1998); and in the journal *Western American Literature*. John Elder, ed., *American Nature Writers* (1996), contains a detailed biographical treatment. An obituary is in the *New York Times* (15 Mar. 1989). A video documentary, *Edward Abbey: A Voice in the Wilderness* (1993), contains valuable source material.

DANIEL J. PHILIPPON

I. W. Abel. UNITED STEELWORKERS OF AMERICA ARCHIVE, THE PENNSYLVANIA STATE UNIVERSITY

ABEL, I(orwith) W(ilbur) ("Abe") (*b.* 11 August 1908 in Magnolia, Ohio; *d.* 10 August 1987 in Malvern, Ohio), founder of the United Steelworkers of America and its international president from 1965 through 1977.

One of four children, Abel was raised in a town about twelve miles from Canton, Ohio. His father, John Franklin Abel, was a blacksmith, and his mother, Mary Ann Jones, was born in Wales, the source of Abel's first name. During the 1920s, Abel attended high school for two years and then Canton Actual Business College in preparation for office work. In 1925 he landed a job in the office of the American Sheet and Tin Mill Works in Canton. Because clerical workers did not earn much, he transferred to the company's foundry, where he learned the molding trade. Abel found better jobs at the Canton Malleable Iron Company (1927) and then at the Timken Malleable Iron Company. In June 1930 he married Bernice Joseph; they had two children. Six months after Abel's marriage, as the economy worsened, Timken shut down for a time, and Abel was out of work.

Like that of many other trade union leaders of his day, Abel's social ideology was shaped by the Great Depression. After six months of unemployment, Abel found a job firing kilns for a tile-making company, where he worked twelve hours a night, seven nights a week for 16 cents an hour. Abel's boss had rejected the workers' demand for 5 cents more, claiming that he would have to close the plant if he had to pay 21 cents an hour. But six months later, under the National Recovery Administration, Abel's wages rose to 37.5 cents an hour. He learned a valuable lesson about corporate behavior and government potential. By 1936 he was back at Timken, and he joined the Steel Workers Organizing Committee (SWOC), which was created in that year by John L. Lewis, head of the United Mine Workers, and was led by Philip Murray. Abel was first a voluntary organizer, then the plant steward, grievance committeeman, and vice president. In 1938 he was elected president of Local 1123 at Timken. When SWOC became the United Steelworkers of America (USWA) in 1942, Abel was first appointed and then elected the director of District 27, with a seat on the union's international executive board. From 1942 to 1945 Abel also served on regional boards for the War Manpower Commission and the National War Labor Board.

Murray, who was USWA president, died in 1952, and David McDonald became the union's president. The executive board chose Abel to replace McDonald as secretary-treasurer, and he moved to Bethel Park, Pennsylvania, outside of Pittsburgh. During the 1950s, the USWA gained pensions and other fringe benefits as well as good wage packages, but with the recession of 1957 and 1958, the sluggish economy and automation produced dissatisfaction among steelworkers. In addition, President McDonald maintained an expensive lifestyle and became increasingly aloof from members and other officers. In 1965 the economic and democratic issues proved to be a potent brew. Abel, muscled, stocky, and plainspoken, challenged McDonald, charging him with "tuxedo unionism" and "contempt" for the rank and file, and beat the manicured, nightclubbing incumbent by ten thousand votes.

Under Abel's presidency, the USWA became more democratic and visible in labor and public affairs. Where McDonald had been inactive in the American Federation of Labor and Congress of Industrial Organizations (AFL-CIO), Abel became its vice president and head of its Industrial Union Department. He was in the forefront of fights for social legislation, especially Medicare. On 27 July 1967 President Lyndon B. Johnson named Abel one of eleven members of the National Advisory Commission on Civil Disorders (Kerner Commission). Although Abel and the USWA were attentive to broad public policy, during the 1960s they were confronted with civil rights challenges and the steel industry's mounting economic difficulties.

Abel's greatest challenge was the economic condition of the industry, which was undergoing extensive and expensive modernization at the same time that it faced rising imports from America's cold war allies. The USWA, like most of the labor movement, had supported free trade. As the U.S. market became an outlet for the excess production of Europe and Japan, Abel reluctantly advocated temporary limits on steel imports. In 1971, when the United States suffered its first merchandise trade deficit, he became the primary labor spokesperson for the proposed Burke-Hartke law. That law would have created a tripartite body, including representatives of business, labor, and government, to regulate both the movement of U.S. capital abroad and the quantity of imports to the United States, which Abel believed were reducing the standard of living of American workers. Instead, in 1974, Congress passed the Trade Reform Act, which continued past policy. That year, largely owing to USWA urgings, Congress created the Pension Benefit Guaranty Corporation to protect employee pensions at bankrupt firms.

Failing to change overall U.S. trade policy, Abel attempted to tackle the economics of the steel industry through collective bargaining. The USWA and Big Steel signed the Experimental Negotiating Agreement (ENA) in 1973. In return for guaranteed wage increases, the union promised not to strike during the 1974 contract talks and to submit differences that could not be solved at the bargaining table to arbitration. The purpose of the agreement was to prevent stockpiling of steel from domestic and foreign sources in anticipation of a potential steel strike. Although no national steel strike had occurred since the walkout of 1959, the memory of that strike, which had lasted for 116 days, affected corporate buying patterns in contract years. By ending the resulting "boom-bust" cycle, Abel hoped to stabilize production in the industry. The ENA was used in the 1977 and 1980 negotiations but was scrapped by the industry during the hard times of the later 1980s.

Responding to the civil rights movement, Abel in 1974 signed consent decrees with the industry and the federal government that changed steel seniority from job or department to plant calculation. The agreement broadened opportunities for blacks, who had been initially assigned poor jobs, and it aided disadvantaged whites and other ethnic groups as well.

Abel retired from the USWA presidency in 1977 and threw his weight behind Lloyd McBride, who was challenged for the position by Edward Sadlowski, the district director from Chicago. McBride won a closely contested election to face the worsening economic conditions that Abel had attempted to control. In 1982 Abel's first wife died; he married Martha L. Turvey in 1984. He died of cancer in Malvern, Ohio, where he is buried.

Abel represented the generation of unionists who created the new CIO during the 1930s. When he assumed the presidency of the USWA during the 1960s, the industry and the American social climate were rapidly changing. He successfully responded to civil rights challenges but could not alter the nation's economic policies, which had devastating effects on the steel industry and its workers. Before globalization became a household word, Abel confronted the issue and sought to alter its impact on American workers.

★

Abel's official records and a few of his personal papers are in the collections of the United Steelworkers of America in the Historical Collections and Labor Archives at Pennsylvania State University, which also holds three oral history interviews conducted in 1970, 1979, and 1980. John Herling, *Right to Challenge: People and Power in the Steelworkers Union* (1972), is a thorough analysis of Abel's election in 1965. Judith Stein, *Running Steel, Running America: Race, Economic Policy, and the Decline of Liberalism* (1998), addresses many of the substantive issues Abel confronted as president. Obituaries are in the *New York Times* (11 Aug. 1987); the *Washington Post* (11 Aug. 1987); *Newsweek* (24 Aug. 1987); and *Time* (24 Aug. 1987).

JUDITH STEIN

ABERNATHY, Ralph David (*b.* 11 March 1926 in Hopewell, Alabama; *d.* 17 April 1990 in Atlanta, Georgia), minister, civil rights leader, and confidant of the Reverend Martin Luther King, Jr.

One of twelve children, Abernathy was the son of William L. Abernathy and Louivery Valentine Bell, farmers in Marengo County, Alabama. His parents were Baptists, and his father was active in the local black community. Abernathy attended high school at Linden Academy.

Abernathy joined the U.S. Army in 1944 and served in France and Germany, achieving the rank of platoon sergeant. After the war he completed the high school equivalency examination and, although he had no formal training for the ministry, was ordained a Baptist preacher in 1948. He received a B.S. degree in mathematics from Alabama State University in 1950. He then studied at Atlanta University, where he received an M.A. degree in sociology in 1951. While in Atlanta he met Martin Luther King, Jr., who was a guest preacher at the Ebenezer Baptist Church.

In 1951 Abernathy became pastor of the First Baptist Church in Montgomery, Alabama. In August 1952 he married Juanita Odessa Jones; they had five children. In the meantime King became pastor of the Dexter Avenue Baptist Church in Montgomery. As respected religious leaders of Montgomery's black community, Abernathy and King rose to prominence during the Montgomery bus boycott, sparked by the refusal in December 1955 of Rosa Parks to relinquish her seat on a bus to a white man and move to the rear seats. Abernathy became King's assistant and ally.

The Reverend Ralph Abernathy eulogizing Martin Luther King, Jr., in Atlanta, 9 April 1968. ARCHIVE PHOTOS

In January 1957 Abernathy and King founded the Southern Christian Leadership Conference (SCLC). King assumed the presidency of the SCLC and Abernathy was secretary-treasurer. The SCLC advocated direct action based on Christian nonviolence to promote civil rights for black Americans. Abernathy's high profile in the founding of the SCLC catapulted him into national prominence. He was an outspoken leader, calling for "frontal attacks" on segregation. Not only did he and King shape SCLC's overarching strategy of civil disobedience, but the two of them shared the same southern jails seventeen times in such cities as Selma, Alabama, and Albany, Georgia.

At the urging of King, Abernathy resigned as pastor of the First Baptist Church of Montgomery and accepted a position as pastor of the West Hunter Baptist Church in Atlanta in 1961. The move placed Abernathy near the headquarters of the SCLC in Atlanta. In 1965 Abernathy assumed the newly created position of vice president at large of the SCLC, a move that indicated that he was King's "heir apparent." In the mid-1960s Abernathy and King came under attack from the the more radical Black Power movement, which rejected integration in favor of separation. To partially blunt the strident attacks of these Young Turks, Abernathy sought to mold old-line civil rights policies into a new strategy of demanding immediate economic opportunity and gain for America's black dispossessed, and in 1967 he began formulating plans for a massive march of poor people on Washington, D.C. The assassination of King in Memphis, Tennessee, on 4 April 1968 temporarily placed Abernathy's Washington protest on hold. Abernathy delivered the eulogy at King's funeral. In his remarks, he recalled their long friendship and sacrifices in the cause of human rights. Abernathy ended his eulogy with a magnanimous statement about how proud yet never envious he had been to spend fifteen active years in the shadow of King.

Abernathy then assumed the presidency of the SCLC. With approval of its board, he pursued the Memphis strike of sanitation workers as a tribute to King. Within days the Memphis workers had won concessions from the city, and Abernathy became America's most visible civil rights leader. In characteristic fashion, he chose not to dwell on the Memphis victory but rather to fast and pray for new guidance in the cause of civil rights. He emerged from this period of abstinence by announcing a new commitment to social activism and a renewed pledge to complete the Poor People's Campaign.

Dressed in the traditional bib overalls of a southern field hand, Abernathy presided over the inauguration of the Poor People's Campaign in Washington on 13 May 1968. At that time he secured a pledge from the National Park Service to allow a shantytown to be built in park grounds near the Lincoln Memorial. This village of the poor, which Abernathy dubbed Resurrection City, U.S.A., eventually attracted some 50,000 protesters to Washington, but when Abernathy failed to dismantle Resurrection City as he had agreed with the Park Service, the police moved in on 24 June 1968 and forced the people to leave. Abernathy's refusal to acquiesce in this action led to his arrest and eventual twenty-day jail sentence. His incarceration simply punctuated the failure of his Poor People's Campaign to ignite public opinion and mass support nationally in the wake of King's death.

Abernathy returned to Atlanta and for a brief time directed the SCLC's Operation Breadbasket in an attempt to bring pressure to hire and promote black employees on companies that discriminated against blacks. Through 1977 he concentrated his efforts on the SCLC's economic thrust and on his own ministry in Atlanta. Also in 1977 he resigned his unpaid, full-time position at the SCLC, ostensibly to run for a congressional seat from Atlanta, which he lost in the Democratic primary to Wyche Fowler. Rumors persisted, however, that he was forced out of the SCLC position because he had become an ineffectual leader and had led the organization into serious indebtedness. After his defeat Abernathy returned to his pastorship at West Hunter Street Baptist Church.

In 1980 Abernathy estranged himself from the black community when he endorsed the Republican candidate, Ronald Reagan, for president. Later, he conceded that he had no special, even limited, entrée into the Reagan White House, and many of his longtime associates and supporters distanced themselves from him. In 1983 Abernathy suffered the first of two debilitating strokes and subsequently contracted glaucoma.

In 1989 Abernathy published *And the Walls Came Tumbling Down,* his autobiography and personal reminiscences of the civil rights movement. Although a moving account of his years in the civil rights movement, the book's references to King's marital infidelity caused a controversy. Abernathy reacted to the criticism of such black leaders as Joseph Lowery, his successor as president of the SCLC, by stating in *Time* magazine, "I am not a Judas. I have written nothing in malice and omitted nothing out of cowardice." Abernathy died of cardiac arrest at Crawford W. Long Hospital at Emory University and was buried at Lincoln Cemetery in Atlanta.

Abernathy was one of the nation's best recognized civil rights leaders, who was willing to speak out and take stands regardless of their unpopularity.

★

Paul Good, "No Man Can Fill Dr. King's Shoes—But Abernathy Tries," *New York Times Magazine* (26 May 1968), provides a good assessment of Abernathy's early civil rights career and his heightened visibility after King's death. David J. Garrow, *Bearing the Cross: Martin Luther King, Jr., and the Southern Christian Leadership Conference* (1986), and Adam Fairclough, *To Redeem the Soul of America: The Southern Christian Leadership Conference and Martin Luther King, Jr.* (1987), describe the King-Abernathy relationship in the founding and conduct of the SCLC. David J. Garrow, ed., *We Shall Overcome: The Civil Rights Movement in the United States in the 1950s and 1960s* (1989), is a useful overview of the civil rights movement. Obituaries are in the *New York Times* (18 Apr. 1990) and *Washington Post* (21 Apr. 1990).

IRVIN D. SOLOMON

ADAMS, (Llewellyn) Sherman (*b.* 8 January 1899 in East Dover, Vermont; *d.* 27 October 1986 in Hanover, New Hampshire), politician who served as governor of New Hampshire and assistant to the president during the Eisenhower administration; he is best known for establishing the modern "chief of staff" position during his five years in the White House.

The son of Clyde H. Adams and Winnie Marion Adams, grocers, Sherman Adams graduated from Hope High School in Providence, Rhode Island. After serving in the U.S. Marine Corps in 1918, he received a B.A. in economics from Dartmouth College in 1920, where he was president of the Outing Club. Adams then worked as a forester for the Black River Lumber Company in Healdville, Vermont, and then for two decades as a lumber industry executive at the Parker-Young Company of Lincoln, New Hampshire, where he served as corporate treasurer. On 28 July 1923 he married Rachel Leona White (who affectionately referred to him as the Great Stone Face); they had three daughters, Marion, Jean, and Sarah, and a son, Samuel.

While working in the lumber industry, Adams entered the state legislature as a Republican in 1941. He was elected speaker of the New Hampshire house the following year. Adams secured passage of a bill creating forestry advisory boards to give the industry better access to state officials. He was a delegate to the Republican National Convention in 1944 and supported Thomas Dewey. He served as a U.S. representative from New Hampshire's Second District from 1945 to 1947, and compiled a record as an internationalist on reciprocal trade issues and a moderate on labor-management relations.

Adams was elected governor of New Hampshire in 1948, after losing his first try for the office in 1946 by only 157 votes in the Republican primary. As governor he cut state expenditures, consolidated state departments and

Sherman Adams. ARCHIVE PHOTOS

agencies from eighty-three to forty-three, and opposed Democratic plans for higher taxes. He was reelected in 1950. In his second term he created the New Hampshire Business Development Corporation, which made loans to new enterprises. He served as chairman of the Conference of New England Governors in 1951 and 1952.

In September 1951, at the governors' conference in Gatlinburg, Tennessee, Adams became one of the first Republican politicians to call for the nomination of General Dwight D. Eisenhower for the presidency. In 1952 Adams chaired the Eisenhower for President Committee in New Hampshire, where the first primary in the nation was held, and was largely responsible for Eisenhower's victory over Senator Robert A. Taft. He engineered the adoption of the Houston Manifesto at the June 1952 Republican Governors Conference, which condemned Taft for challenging southern delegates won by Eisenhower. At the Republican National Convention the following month, Adams served as floor manager of the Eisenhower delegates. After the convention he became the chief of staff for the successful national election campaign.

In 1953 Adams joined the new administration with the title of assistant to the president. "I think of Adams as my chief of staff," Eisenhower later wrote, "but I don't call him that because the politicians think it sounds too military." Eisenhower told Adams that "I am looking to you to coordinate this office," and he gave Adams vast powers. Adams ensured that only issues that had been presented to him through proper channels were brought to Eisenhower's attention. Adams forced cabinet secretaries to settle their differences without bothering the president and he kept secondary issues away from the Oval Office. He had the final say about who could see the president and about what briefing papers the chief executive would read.

Critics charged that Adams was an "assistant president" who ran domestic policy making and insulated the president from legislators, party politicians, and governors. This was untrue, but because Eisenhower wished to appear above partisan politics, he was happy to foster the impression that he was passive and that Adams was highly influential in making policy. The joke in Washington among Democrats was that it would be too bad if Eisenhower died and Vice President Richard Nixon entered the Oval Office, but that it would be a disaster if Adams died and Eisenhower became president. Adams became aligned with the Modern Republican faction in the party, which emphasized internationalism, free trade, and reduced spending and lower taxes without completely dismantling the welfare state. He alienated conservative Republicans, who called him "the abominable no man" and blamed Adams rather than Eisenhower for domestic policies and lack of access to the president.

Adams resigned under fire following a June 1958 investigation by the House Special Subcommittee on Legislative Oversight, which revealed that he had accepted a $700 vicuña overcoat, payment of hotel bills totaling $2,000, and an oriental rug valued at $2,400, all from Boston financier and textile manufacturer Bernard Goldfine, on whose behalf Adams had intervened with the Federal Trade Commission and the Securities and Exchange Commission to determine the status of matters pending. It appeared as if Adams was exerting influence in exchange for these gifts, though there was no direct evidence that Adams had attempted to circumvent the regulatory process. Republicans in Congress, worried about the 1958 midterm elections, pressured Eisenhower to remove Adams, as did the party's financial backers, who withheld contributions until the president acted. At a press conference on 18 June 1958, Eisenhower initially refused, saying that "no one has believed that he could be bought," adding that although Adams had acted imprudently, "I need him." Republican leaders finally persuaded Adams to resign rather than harm the party, and he did so on 22 September 1958, charging that he was leaving because of a "campaign of vilification."

After leaving public service, Adams developed a ski resort on the same mountain he had once worked as a forester, serving as president of the Loon Mountain Recreation

Corporation from 1966 to 1980 and as its chairman of the board between 1980 and 1986. In his memoirs he refused to admit wrongdoing in the Goldfine affair, only admitting that he had made "mistakes in judgment." These mistakes extended to his personal affairs. In 1965 President Lyndon Johnson, at the request of Eisenhower, directed the Internal Revenue Service not to bring charges of tax evasion against Adams, who had failed to report $300,000 in income. The back taxes were paid through a fund set up by Adams's friends. (His associate Goldfine served a year in prison and paid $110,000 for tax evasion.) Adams died at age eighty-seven of respiratory arrest and renal failure in Hanover and was buried in Lincoln, New Hampshire, near his beloved forests.

Neither Kennedy nor Johnson appointed anyone to serve as chief of staff in their administrations, in part due to the perception that such a strong official would act as "assistant president." The position was revived in the Nixon presidency, with similar results: the first assistant to the president since Adams, Chief of Staff H. R. Haldeman was also forced to resign because of a scandal, Watergate, involving the abuse of presidential powers.

Adams was a brusque man who was capable of reducing subordinates to tears. He typically treated members of the cabinet and Congress with contempt. In Washington he had the reputation for being arrogant and power hungry. When he wound up in trouble, no one in his party except the president and vice president was willing to defend him. Here, too, Sherman Adams set the pattern for subsequent chiefs of staff.

★

Sherman Adams, *Firsthand Report: The Story of the Eisenhower Administration* (1961), provides Adams's account of key decisions in Eisenhower's presidency. Rachel White Adams, *On the Other Hand* (1963), discusses the Adams family's life in Washington. Dwight Eisenhower, *The White House Years,* vol. 1 (1963), contains a discussion of Adams's role in the White House. Fred Greenstein, *The Hidden-Hand Presidency: Eisenhower as Leader* (1982), offers an analysis of Eisenhower's role as party leader that sheds new light on the limits of Adams's influence. Samuel Kernell and Samuel L. Popkin, *The Chief of Staff: Twenty-five Years of Managing the Presidency* (1986), describes Adams's role in creating the modern chief-of-staff system. James Pfiffner, "The President's Chief of Staff: Lessons Learned," *Presidential Studies Quarterly* 23 (winter 1993): 77–102, discusses how a chief of staff can succeed by avoiding Adams's mistakes. An obituary is in the *New York Times* (28 Oct. 1986). Interviews of Sherman Adams are in the John Foster Dulles Oral History Collection, Seeley G. Mudd Manuscript Library, Princeton University.

RICHARD M. PIOUS

ADDAMS, Charles Samuel (*b.* 7 January 1912 in Westfield, New Jersey; *d.* 29 September 1988 in New York City), cartoonist who was the premier pictorialist for the *New Yorker* and who is known for his artistic technique and macabre originality.

Born to Charles Huey Addams and Grace M. (Spear) Addams, Charles Addams was the only child of a well-to-do family. Addams's father was trained as an architect and had tried to work in ship design, but settled into a managerial job with a piano company.

During grammar and high school in Westfield, Addams began drawing by copying favorite comic strips, such as *Krazy Kat*. He contributed illustrations to his high school paper and won a monetary prize for a public service poster in a magazine contest. His reading included Grimm's fairy tales and Edgar Allan Poe's fiction and he enjoyed stories of knights and chivalry.

Addams spent one year apiece attending Colgate (1929–1930), the University of Pennsylvania (1930–1931), and the Grand Central School of Design in New York City (1931–1932). At Colgate he studied architecture, training that can be seen in his command of perspective and in the well-wrought settings of his cartoons. His first professional drawing was published in the *New Yorker* in February 1932; his first cartoon appeared there a year later.

Charles Addams, 1950. AP/WIDE WORLD PHOTOS

In the early 1930s Addams spent two years at his first and final full-time job: lettering, drawing, and retouching photos for Macfadden magazines, including true-crime titles, for $15 a week. He quit as soon as his cartooning income allowed him to support himself. By 1935 he had a contract with the *New Yorker;* he had also sold cartoons to *Life, Collier's,* and *Cosmopolitan*. His early work featured unshaded line drawings, but he quickly developed his characteristic wash technique, using a wide variety of monochrome shades to provide the solidity and impact of a color drawing.

Addams secured public attention when the *New Yorker* (13 January 1940) published his cartoon of a woman skier whose tracks pass on either side of the tree behind her; an observer stares back in disbelief while the woman glides nonchalantly on. Purportedly, this cartoon has been used in psychiatric and intelligence tests. Certainly, it demonstrates the inimitably odd world of Addams's cartoons.

From the late 1930s to the late 1940s Addams developed the darkly comic and ghoulishly amiable cast of characters that came to be known as the Addams family. A famous 1946 drawing shows the monstrous family, on the roof of its crumbling mansion, ready to greet Christmas carolers below by tipping a vat of boiling oil.

Addams served as a private in the U.S. Army from January 1943 to February 1946, assigned to a division of the Signal Corps in New York City (operating in Manhattan and in Astoria, Queens) that produced illustrated manuals and animated educational films.

Addams enjoyed both his work and the rewards it brought. On 29 May 1943 he married Barbara Day, a former model who resembled the dark-haired femme fatale of Addams's cartoons. They had no children and were divorced in 1952. The first of a dozen collections of Addams's work, *Drawn and Quartered,* appeared in 1942; other titles, such as *Addams and Evil* (1947) and *Monster Rally* (1950) sold well. Galleries and leading museums, including the Metropolitan Museum of Art in New York City, began to show his work.

His fame, success, and enjoyable personality made Addams popular in high society. He liked to dress well and he was known for giving and attending the best parties. His many friends described him as easygoing and urbane, elegant and uncontrived, charming and levelheaded. Addams loved automobiles; he collected vintage cars and drove the fastest sports cars.

Addams cultivated the macabre persona that fans of his cartoons expected. Rumors spread that he produced his drawings from his experiences in a psychiatric ward, and that his editor would have him committed periodically; in fact, Addams was never treated for a mental disorder—he had never even seen a psychoanalyst. He did collect morbid bric-a-brac in both his Manhattan apartment and Long Island house, as interviewers loved to report: included among his household items were an embalmer's rack used as a coffee table and a collection of crossbows, which he kept oiled and ready for action.

Addams married again, to Barbara Barb, on 1 December 1954; they had no children and were divorced in 1956. In addition to further collections of his artwork, Addams compiled *Dear Dead Days* (1959), an odd omnibus of weird pictures from various sources.

When ABC broadcast *The Addams Family* television series, from September 1964 through September 1966, Addams's fans increased from thousands to millions. NBC aired an animated version of the series from 1973 to 1975. Ironically, as part of negotiations for the television show, editor William Shawn barred "Addams family" cartoons from the pages of the *New Yorker.*

Addams married Marilyn Matthews Miller, a widow, on 31 May 1980. Eight years later he died of a heart attack while sitting at the wheel of his Audi 4000 prior to setting out for a drive. He was declared dead at St. Clare's Hospital in Manhattan. *The Addams Family* movie of 1991 and its 1994 sequel brought the sinister, perverse, yet endearingly affectionate family to a new generation. The New York Public Library held a comprehensive Charles Addams exhibit in 1994. *Creature Comforts* (1982) was his final collection; *The World of Charles Addams* (1991) provides an overview of his career.

Addams's work is sui generis, morbid but undeniably funny, outrageous without offending. His style is unmistakable, and his best work is unforgettable. Before black humor became popular, when Disney and sanitized suburban families dominated popular art, Addams brought out a dark side of the human, or inhuman, condition and showed that we could laugh at it. His cartoons contributed something irreplaceable to the *New Yorker* and deeply influenced many artists, such as Gahan Wilson.

Most writing about Addams's work does not analyze it, since the meaning of any cartoon is self-evident, often with no need of a caption, let alone a critical explication. Nor is there a debate on the quality of the work, which is undeniable. Many critics instead discuss why Addams's work is so popular. Is it catharsis for a fear-ridden age? A healthy antidote to idealization of the family? Or an expression of the American love of violence? Perhaps there is no mystery, after all, in why people respond to well-drawn, creative work that shocks even as it delights.

★

John Kobler, *Afternoon in the Attic* (1950), a study of eccentrics, takes Addams as the subject of its first chapter and is illustrated by Addams. Marjorie Dent Candee, ed., *Current Biography 1954* (1954), contains a biographical sketch with a wealth of information and references. Mort Gerberg, *The Arbor House Book of Cartooning* (1983), uses Addams's work for examples of how to write and draw cartoons and provides indispensable analysis of his technique. Charles Addams, *The World of Charles Addams* (1991), contains an introduction by Wilfrid Sheed that is a good depiction by an insightful friend of Addams and his work. Lee Lorenz, *The Art of the New Yorker 1925–1995* (1995), helps place Addams's work in context and also discusses his often-neglected magazine covers. John Mason Brown, "Welcome Horrors," *Saturday Review of Literature* (11 Nov. 1950), reviews *Monster Rally* in depth. Dwight Macdonald, "Charles Addams, His Family, and His Fiends," *Reporter* (21 July 1953), contains both biographical information and an analysis of Addams's popularity. Brad Darrach, "The Addams Family Loses Its Father, Charles, the Great Cartoonist Who Taught America to Love the Macabre," *People* (17 Oct. 1988), is well written and informative. An obituary in the *New York Times* (30 Sept. 1988) is rich in anecdotes and information regarding his life and death in the New York City area.

BERNADETTE LYNN BOSKY

AILEY, Alvin (*b.* 5 January 1931 in Rogers, Texas; *d.* 1 December 1989 in New York City), choreographer who founded a leading American dance company and school and created *Revelations* (1960), a popular and frequently performed modern dance piece.

Ailey was the only child of Alvin Ailey, Sr., and Lula Elizabeth (Cliff) Ailey and was born in his paternal grandfather's primitive wooden cabin in a farming village in southeast Texas. His father deserted his wife and son a few months after Alvin's birth and remained a distant, little-known figure in Ailey's life. His father attempted to reunite with the family a few years later, but he was rebuffed by his independent-minded and ambitious young wife. Ailey did not have any contact with his father until the senior Ailey initiated a brief telephone conversation a year before he died.

Ailey's early life was a series of uprootings. His mother took her toddler son with her when she went into the fields to pick cotton. As he grew older, he was left alone or deposited with relatives when his mother traveled to nearby towns looking for better jobs. Ailey's feelings of loneliness and not belonging colored his entire life, as did his difficult relationship with his mother. Lula Ailey had little formal schooling. She drank at times, beat him when tiredness overtook her, and was a rough, outspoken woman. She was, however, the major influence of his life as an artist and was a beautiful, imaginative woman who gave her little son her undivided attention and encouragement during their happy times together.

Another important early influence was Amos Alexander, a black businessman in Navasota, Texas, who was in love with Lula Ailey and opened his home to her and young Alvin after they moved to that town in 1937. Alexander, a surrogate father, lavished attention and love on Alvin and offered him a measure of stability he had never before known. In Navasota, Ailey was exposed to a rich and exciting black world in which men and women, somewhat more cosmopolitan than in Rogers, thought nothing of partying hectically in smoky bars on Saturday night, then turning up to repent the next morning in long, drowsy church services filled with religious music as sensually charged as what had come out of the jukebox the night before. Ailey was known to his schoolmates as a genial but rather prim loner, but the dances he would later create made it plain that this quiet child was an intent observer of the life around him.

Alvin Ailey, 1988. AP/WIDE WORLD PHOTOS

In 1942 Ailey's mother departed for Los Angeles, hoping to find a good job in the wartime aircraft industry there. She left her son behind with Alexander, but Ailey followed his mother to Los Angeles at the end of the school year.

He refused to stay in the white school where his mother had enrolled him, preferring, he said, to be with his own kind. Because of the kindness and high expectations of teachers in the two ghetto schools he attended, Alvin became interested in music and dance. He explored the theater life of Central Avenue, a busy and alluring center of black popular culture in the 1940s, and the major theaters in white downtown Los Angeles.

Two of Ailey's fellow students, one of them Carmen de Lavallade, who became a dancer and actress in the East, studied with an intriguing-sounding modern dance choreographer and teacher named Lester Horton, one of the few white teachers who accepted students of all races in his classes. Intensely private and a bit of a prude, Ailey resisted studying dance at first but in 1949 finally succumbed to Horton's charisma. Ailey came and went at the struggling but vital school, dropping out periodically to take courses at the University of California at Los Angeles and to perform as a nightclub dancer in San Francisco. He always returned, however, and Horton welcomed him back unconditionally.

Horton believed that dancers must know not only about dance but about all the arts and societies of the world. His dancers and students found themselves helping to dye costumes, playing musical accompaniment at performances, building and painting sets, and even choreographing. After Horton died suddenly of a heart attack late in 1953, Ailey volunteered to create dances to help the company survive. His first efforts, prolix and weighted with literary symbolism, received mixed reviews from newspaper critics in Los Angeles. In 1954 the Horton company's performance drew exasperated anger from Ted Shawn, director of the Jacob's Pillow Dance Festival in the Berkshires of Massachusetts.

While in the East, Ailey and de Lavallade were noticed by Arnold Saint-Subber, who invited the two dancers to join the cast of his next Broadway production, *House of Flowers,* a lush Caribbean musical that starred Pearl Bailey. They declined, eager to return to Los Angeles and resume work with the Horton company. The atmosphere at home was tense, however, as the company struggled to keep going. Ailey and de Lavallade left for New York in December.

Ailey was a featured dancer in the critically praised but short-lived *House of Flowers* (1954) and soon after in *Jamaica* (1957), which starred Lena Horne, but he did not attract individual attention in either. Nevertheless, he soon became immersed in the dance and theater life of New York. He acted in several plays, including *Call Me by My Rightful Name* (1961), in which he performed with a young, unknown actor named Robert Duvall, and *Tiger, Tiger, Burning Bright* (1962). In the latter play, a Broadway production, Ailey was mercilessly upstaged by Claudia McNeil and other experienced cast members, and he gave up acting. He attended many dance performances and observed up-and-coming dancers at a variety of dance studios. While performing in *Jamaica,* Horne encouraged the dancers to work on their own choreographic projects, and Ailey began to create his first masterwork, *Blues Suite,* in 1958. *Revelations* followed two years later and established Ailey as a choreographer of major powers and potential.

Ailey had entered dance at an advantageous time, when black modern dancers and choreographers were coming into their own. He followed in the wake of Katherine Dunham, Talley Beatty, Pearl Primus, and Donald McKayle, all established in the field. An accomplished poet who wrote for his own eyes alone, Ailey had an interest in American literature and music that made him a favorite of theater literati. His exotic good looks and deceptive social ease drew dancers to him. Through sheer luck, he acquired a home base for his collection of dancers, who were fast becoming a company. In 1960 Ailey was invited to settle into a new YWCA facility in the Broadway theater district, where a visionary white couple named Edele and Al Holtz took the moody but obviously gifted young man under their wings.

Engagements began to flow in steadily. In 1962, a time of rapidly growing racial unrest in America, Ailey and his troupe, the Alvin Ailey American Dance Theater, were invited to perform in Southeast Asia as American cultural ambassadors on a government-sponsored tour. The thirteen-week tour was the first of many for the Ailey company, which in 1997 toured more than any other American dance group. The tour also marked the beginning of a pattern for Ailey and his dancers, who worked steadily in the United States but were far more celebrated in other countries.

By the late 1960s, the demands of running a company and creating dances for it had begun to wear Ailey down, but out of his exhaustion and anger came a masterpiece, the seething *Masekela Language* (1969). Set to the music of the South African jazz trumpeter Hugh Masekela, the piece featured brooding, hostile men and women trapped in a dusty café that could have been in a small town in either South Africa or America.

By the 1970s, Ailey had also taken on the job of building an institution, the Alvin Ailey American Dance Center, and much of his energy went into fund-raising, budget balancing, and dealing with boards. The Ailey school was consolidated, and a junior company was formed, in part as a workshop group for new choreography by Ailey and young artists he wished to encourage, among them Donald Byrd and Ulysses Dove.

The little family of dancers Ailey had begun with was now an internationally celebrated troupe, and commissions flowed in from abroad. Ailey created several classics during the decade, among them *The River,* choreographed for the American Ballet Theatre; *Cry,* a solo that made a star of Judith Jamison; and *Night Creature,* a shimmering, playfully witty celebration of the music of Duke Ellington.

Ailey had begun to drink and take drugs to escape the pressure of work and personal problems that sprang, in part, from his fairly open homosexuality. Success had come to him too early. He was haunted by the feeling that he would never again create a dance as popular as *Revelations,* and he found himself increasingly in opposition to his own board of directors. In 1980 he had two public nervous breakdowns that resulted in arrests. Hospitalized, he was diagnosed as manic-depressive. The rest of the 1980s was a relatively quiet time, during which several senior dancers and board members took over many of the burdens of running the Ailey company. Ailey found it hard to devote himself to the studio and created only a few notable works during the decade, among them *For Bird—With Love,* a portrait of Kansas City jazz in the 1940s and particularly the troubled jazz saxophonist Charlie "Bird" Parker.

Beginning in 1987, Ailey received many important honors, including the Samuel H. Scripps American Dance Festival Award (1987), a Kennedy Center honor (1988), and the Handel Medallion, New York City's highest cultural award (1988). In failing health for several years, he began to feel seriously ill while in Washington, where he had gone with his jubilant mother to accept the Kennedy Center award. Several days later, he was rushed to a hospital and diagnosed with pneumonia and cytomegalovirus, manifestations of acquired immunodeficiency syndrome (AIDS).

Ailey continued working but was hospitalized again in September 1989. He died at Lenox Hill Hospital in New York City two and a half months later. He was given the equivalent of a state funeral at America's largest church, the Cathedral of St. John the Divine in Manhattan. Government figures, the poet Maya Angelou, and the singers Ashford and Simpson spoke and performed, and the Ailey company danced excerpts from Ailey's *Revelations, Cry,* and *A Song for You.* A smaller service followed in Artesia, just outside Los Angeles. Ailey is buried in Rose Hills Memorial Park in Whittier, California.

Ailey choreographed to a wide range of music in a variety of styles, including ballet, jazz, and modern dance. His two greatest dances were the early *Blues Suite* and *Revelations,* which universalized black life experiences and culture so that audiences all over the world identified with them. Ailey dreaded choreographing, and some of his works appear to have been created primarily to fill a requirement for new repertory each season. Most of his pieces, however, from dances that address social issues to celebrations of musical scores or the sheer power of dance itself, share a simplicity and immediacy that draw the viewer irrevocably into the piece. He was, in the words of the dance writer Robert Greskovic, "an amazingly truthful artist."

★

Peter Bailey, *Revelations* (1995), tells in Ailey's words of the darker sides of the choreographer's life. Jennifer Dunning, *Alvin Ailey: A Life in Dance* (1996), is a critical biography. Kathilyn Solomon Probosz, *Alvin Ailey, Jr.* (1991), is a children's book that provides a clear distillation of Ailey's life and work. An obituary is in the *New York Times* (2 Dec. 1989).

JENNIFER DUNNING

ALBRIGHT, Horace Marden (*b.* 6 January 1890 in Bishop, California; *d.* 28 March 1987 in Los Angeles, California), cofounder and second director of the National Park Service.

In January 1890, Mary Marden Albright traveled from Candelaria, Nevada, to Bishop, California, to have her baby under the care of a physician there. Mary's husband, George L. Albright, a native of Canada who had traveled to the West in 1873 to work the Comstock Lode, stayed behind in Candelaria to work as a carpenter and engineer at the Northern Belle mine. After Horace, the first of three boys, was born, mother and son returned to Candelaria. The Panic of 1893 hurt the Candelaria mine where George Albright worked, and the family moved to Bishop, where

Horace M. Albright. UPI/CORBIS-BETTMANN

he opened a milling business and later started a contracting business that put up many of the homes and churches in Bishop. He also established a mortuary firm.

Horace's parents were instrumental in exposing him to the wonders of California's Owens Valley. George enjoyed taking his three sons on fishing trips to Mammoth Lake, where Horace came to know a Forest Service ranger who took him on horseback rides through the Sierra Forest Reserve.

In 1903 Horace accompanied his mother on a summer trip to San Francisco, where she stayed because of health reasons. As planned, Horace traveled as far as Sacramento with her and then continued north to Shasta to visit his grandfather's logging camp. His grandfather discussed effective conservation logging practices with him as well as those techniques that damaged the land. His grandfather also took him on a journey to the top of Mount Shasta. Horace would remember that view of the upper Sacramento Valley for the rest of his life and regarded that summer as influential in the development of his conservation and preservation philosophy.

Albright graduated from Bishop High School in 1908 and entered the University of California at Berkeley. There, he concentrated his studies in the fields of economics and pre-law. When he graduated with his bachelor's degree in May 1912, he had already decided he would enter law school in the fall. To pay his college expenses Horace worked for Professor Adolph C. Miller, chairman of the Department of Economics and a noted financial expert. When Miller became assistant secretary of the interior, he asked Albright to join his staff in Washington. Despite doubts about leaving Grace Noble, with whom he had developed a close relationship, Albright accepted the clerk's position in the Department of the Interior in 1913. Upon arrival, he enrolled in Georgetown University Law School and completed the requirements for his degree the following year.

As assistant secretary, Miller was responsible for the national parks and the task of trying to organize their administration. In 1914, however, President Woodrow Wilson appointed Miller to the Federal Reserve Board and Stephen T. Mather took over Miller's job. Albright immediately became part of his staff. In July 1915 Mather and Albright arranged a successful two-week camping tour of western parks for congressional representatives, members of the press, and railroad executives to gather support for the pending legislation that would create a national park service. *The Mather Mountain Party of 1915* (1990), cowritten by Albright and his daughter, Marian Albright Schenck, relates the adventures of this two-week trip.

Albright married Grace Noble on 23 December 1915 in California. They traveled by train to Washington, D.C., stopping at the Grand Canyon for a brief honeymoon. They had two children. Meanwhile, Albright's success in lobbying Congress resulted in President Wilson signing a bill on 25 August 1916 that authorized the creation of the National Park Service. Unfortunately, no funding was appropriated for the new agency.

In January 1917 Mather suffered a nervous breakdown, and Albright became acting director of the service; he was also promoted to assistant director of the National Park Service. The task of securing the necessary appropriation for the new agency fell to Albright. He successfully testified before Congress, and the National Park Service received its first appropriation in April 1917.

Albright soon had to oversee the administration of seventeen national parks and twenty-two national monuments. During World War I there were pressures to open the parks to cattle and sheep grazing, and although Albright permitted some cattle grazing, he drew the line at the more destructive sheep grazing, preventing damage at parks such as Yellowstone. Albright made another important contribution to the management of the park service in 1917, when he drafted a set of three key management principles: national parks must remain unimpaired for future generations; national parks are to be set aside for public enjoyment; and "national interest must dictate all decisions affecting public or private enterprise in the parks."

Mather returned to the directorship of the park service in June 1918. After Albright's son was born in February 1919, Horace and Grace agreed that it was time to resign and return to California. Fortunately, Mather offered Albright the superintendency at Yellowstone National Park, with the condition that he also assist him with budget and congressional concerns.

Holding the dual title of superintendent of Yellowstone and field assistant from 1919 to 1929, Albright worked to protect the park from dams and irrigation projects. He instituted naturalist interpretive programs and coauthored a book, *Oh, Ranger* (1928).

In 1924 the businessman and philanthropist John D. Rockefeller, Jr., visited Yellowstone with three of his sons. Albright desperately wanted to share with him his dream to add the Grand Tetons and the northern part of Jackson Hole to Yellowstone, but he was under strict orders not to raise these issues with Rockefeller. On a subsequent Rockefeller visit, however, Albright told Rockefeller of his wish, and Rockefeller asked him to put together a cost estimate regarding the amount of land required. A company was formed that purchased the land for Rockefeller, who remained a silent partner. Over the years this partnership resulted in the addition of lands to the National Park Service.

After Mather suffered a stroke in the winter of 1928, Albright was sworn in as director of the National Park Service on 12 January 1929. As director, Albright oversaw the addition of several parks into the system, including Grand Teton National Park. He worked hard to raise the status of the service from one that was considered a major bureau to one that was classified as one of the largest and most important bureaus in government. The reclassification resulted in more positions and better salaries for employees.

In 1933 President Franklin Roosevelt ordered a reorganization of the executive branch of the federal government, including the Department of the Interior. Albright successfully lobbied Roosevelt to transfer War Department battlefields, parks, and monuments to the National Park Service. The executive order, signed on 10 June 1933, accomplished three things for the Department of the Interior and the National Park Service. It made the service the primary federal agency responsible for the management of historic and archaeological sites across the United States. It established the service as an agency that had interests in virtually every state in the union. (Prior to the reorganization the service's interests were concentrated in the West.) Third, it entrusted the service with unique responsibilities, thereby reducing the chance that it would someday be consolidated into another agency.

The executive order became effective on 10 August 1933. The day before, Albright resigned his position as director of the National Park Service to become vice president and general manager of United States Potash Company in New York City. Albright expanded the company and his efforts earned him a promotion in 1946 to the position of president and general manager.

In 1956 Albright retired from United States Potash, but he never retired from being an advocate for the National Park Service. He continued his efforts to add property to various parks, especially his favorite areas, the Grand Tetons and Jackson Hole. He chaired the Presidential Commission on Organization of the Executive Branch of Government for natural resources (1948–1949), was a member of the advisory council on Outdoor Recreation Resources Review Committee (1959–1962), and a founder of Resources for the Future, an organization committed to natural resource problems and research.

The Albrights returned to California in 1962, and Albright wrote a booklet, *Origins of National Park Service Administration of Historic Sites* (1971). He also wrote, with the assistance of Robert Cahn, *The Birth of the National Park Service* (1985). In 1981 he was given the Medal of Freedom, the nation's highest civilian honor. He died of heart failure.

Horace Albright was instrumental in creating the National Park Service and formulating the policy that still guides the service. His advocacy to add the administration of historic sites to the National Park Service solidified the service as the leading government agency responsible for the preservation and use of not only America's national parks but also America's premier historic sites.

★

Material on Albright can be found in the records of the National Park Service, Record Group 79, National Archives, and the records of Yellowstone National Park. Horace M. Albright and Robert Cahn, *The Birth of the National Park Service: The Founding Years, 1913–1933* (1985), is based on interviews conducted by Robert Cahn in which Albright explains his role in the creation of the National Park Service. Donald C. Swain, *Wilderness Defender: Horace M. Albright and Conservation* (1970), is the only scholarly biography published on Albright's role in the creation of the National Park Service. See also Robert Shankland, *Steve Mather of the National Parks* (1951). An obituary is in the *New York Times* (29 Mar. 1987).

JON E. TAYLOR

ALLEN, George Herbert (*b.* 29 April 1918 in Detroit, Michigan; *d.* 31 December 1990 in Palos Verdes Estates, California), professional football coach with a reputation for turning losing organizations into winners.

The only son of automobile plant worker Earl Allen and Loretta (Hannigan) Allen, George Allen was born in 1918, although he often gave the year as 1922, in the Grosse Pointe Woods suburb of Detroit. He was raised in the Catholic faith with his sister in the St. Clair Shores district. After graduating from Lake Shore High School, where he had a perfect attendance record and lettered in basketball, football, and track, Allen attended Alma College in Alma, Michigan, and Marquette University as an officer trainee in the U.S. Navy's wartime V-12 program. He then served as athletic adjutant at the Farragut, Idaho, navy base until his discharge in 1946, when he enrolled at the University of Michigan, where he received a B.S. degree (1947) and a M.S. degree (1948) in education. His thesis was "A Study of Outstanding Football Coaches' Attitudes and Practices in Scouting." As a graduate student at Michigan, Allen was an assistant to head football coach Fritz Crisler.

Allen began his head coaching career in 1948 at Morningside College in Sioux City, Iowa, and then was head coach at Whittier College in Whittier, California, from 1951 to 1956. While at Whittier, Allen spent much of his free time observing professional football's Los Angeles Rams and their coach, Sid Gillman, who eventually hired him to be the Ram's offensive end coach in 1957. Allen, however, lost his position in a staff shakeup. After running a car wash in the San Fernando Valley for a year, Allen was hired by George Halas, owner-coach of the Chicago Bears, as chief scout (1958) and then as personnel director. In 1963, Allen became the Bears' defensive coach and helped guide them to the National Football League (NFL) championship, receiving the game ball from the players.

The first of many controversies involving Allen revolved around his decision to accept the head coaching position

Washington Redskins football coach George Allen. WALLY MCNAMEE/CORBIS

from the Rams in 1966 while still under contract with the Bears. Halas filed a breach of contract suit, proved his point in court, and then released Allen from the contract. During his five years with the Rams, Allen gave the team its first winning season in eight years, won his division twice, and compiled the best record in the NFL. A personality conflict with team owner Daniel Reeves led to Allen being fired the morning after Christmas 1968. One week later, after pressure from players and fans, Reeves rehired Allen, but he let the coach's contract expire after the 1970 season.

Allen's coaching philosophy involved heavy motivation and bringing in tested veteran players in exchange for future draft choices. When he was hired to be coach and general manager of the Washington Redskins in 1971, he adopted the motto The Future Is Now, and he immediately began to acquire (expensive) proven veterans, including many of his former Rams, guiding the Redskins into the playoffs for the first time since 1945. Although they were derided as the Over-the-Hill Gang, Allen led the Redskins to the Super Bowl after the 1972 season. After they lost to the Miami Dolphins, 14–7, he commented, "Losing is like death." His overall record as Redskins coach was 67–30–1, but he was only 4–7 in the playoffs.

Allen married Henrietta ("Etty") Lumbroso on 26 May 1951, and they had four children; George, Jr., the oldest child, was elected governor of Virginia in 1993. Believing strongly in physical conditioning, Allen jogged three miles a day and was named chairman of the President's Council on Physical Fitness in 1981, serving in that capacity during Ronald Reagan's administration. Tall and lean, Allen was considered to be the best-conditioned coach in the NFL. He continued to run at least 3 miles a day, do 101 sit-ups, and 51 push-ups into his seventies. He wrote or coauthored fourteen books on football and motivation. Allen founded the Red Cloud Athletic Federation for the purpose of providing athletic equipment for Sioux children and was made an honorary Sioux chief for his longtime dedication to that cause.

Allen's critics claimed that he had an "end justifies the means" philosophy, and, indeed, he was fined the (then) league maximum of $5,000 in 1973 for trading away the same draft choices twice, which he attributed to an oversight. Described by some as eccentric, manipulative, and ruthlessly pragmatic, Allen was a master motivator who instilled an us-versus-them mentality in his players. Fearing potential spies, Allen would have his team practice behind high chain-link fences surrounded by tarpaulins. A fierce competitor, he believed in time management; he insisted on a chauffeured limousine so he could work instead of drive and usually subsisted on ice cream and milk (supplemented by vitamin tablets), in order to not waste time chewing. He once wrote, "Every day you waste is one you can never make up. Winners don't waste time, and that applies in every walk of life."

His free spending with the Redskins led team owner Edward Bennett Williams to remark shortly after his arrival, "When Coach Allen came to Washington, we agreed he had an unlimited budget. He's already exceeded it." Although the Redskins made the playoffs five times in his seven years, the owner and the coach disagreed over the terms of a new contract, and Allen was fired. Hired in 1978 to again coach the Rams, Allen was quickly fired by owner Carroll Rosenbloom after losing the first two exhibition games.

Allen went on to work as a CBS Sports commentator and briefly worked for the Montreal Alouettes of the Canadian Football League before coaching the Chicago Blitz (1983) and the Arizona Wranglers (1984) in the fledgling United States Football League (USFL). After retiring from coaching for five years and again working for CBS, Allen accepted the head coaching position at California State University, Long Beach, in December 1989. After an 0–3 start, Long Beach finished the season at 6–5, and Allen called it his "most gratifying year in coaching." He died of cardiac arrest in the kitchen of his home six weeks after the end of the season and was buried in Green Hills Cemetery in suburban Rancho Palos Verdes. Although he never felt completely well after being doused with ice water after the school's season-ending victory, it did not contribute to his death, according to the pathologist who performed the autopsy.

Innovative and defense-oriented, Allen was the first head coach to employ a special-teams assistant and was one of the first to emphasize situation substitutions on defense. He was named NFL Coach of the Year four times, and never had a losing record in his fourteen professional seasons, including with the USFL. At the time of his death, his career NFL winning percentage (.705) was the third highest in history, and he was the winningest coach in team history for both the Rams and Redskins. Fourteen of his assistants went on to become NFL head coaches.

★

Allen interspersed reminiscences of his career with advice on how to survive being unemployed in his book *Merry Christmas—You're Fired!* (1982), written with Charles Maher. An early biography of Allen is William Gildea and Kenneth Turan, *The Future Is Now: George Allen, Pro Football's Most Controversial Coach* (1972). Another early source is John Underwood, "The Ice-Cream Man Cometh," *Sports Illustrated* (25 Oct. 1971).

Obituaries are in the *Washington Post* and the *New York Times* (both 1 Jan. 1991). Several informative articles (with many anecdotes) appeared in the *Washington Post* after his death, including Leonard Shapiro, "Allen: Motivator and Innovator" (1 Jan. 1991); Richard Justice, "He Wasn't Like Anyone You'd Ever Met in Your Life" (2 Jan. 1991); and Ken Denlinger, "When the Sun Comes Up, You'd Better Be Running" (6 Jan. 1991).

JOHN A. DROBNICKI

ALLISON, Fran(ces) (*b.* 20 November 1907 in La Porte City, Iowa; *d.* 13 June 1989 in Sherman Oaks, California), radio and television performer best known for the children's show *Kukla, Fran, and Ollie*.

Fran was one of two children born to Jess Allison, a grocer who died young, and his wife. The children had a modest upbringing, supported by their mother's cooking meals for teachers at Fran's school, La Porte City School, which housed kindergarten through twelfth grade. Allison attended Coe College in Cedar Rapids, Iowa, graduating in 1928 with a two-year teaching certificate in music. After teaching for four years in Schleswig, Iowa, and Pocahontas, Iowa, she was invited through her brother, a musician, to sing background music with the orchestra on radio station WMT. Pleased with her work, the program director hired her as a singer and advertising salesperson. She also sang as a soloist from time to time; this led to a job with NBC Radio.

By 1937 she had moved to Chicago, where she became a staff singer for various shows on NBC Radio. Allison became a familiar voice of the airwaves, singing on such programs as *Smile Parade* and *Uncle Ezra's Radio Station* (also known as *Station EZRA*), as well as playing the gossipy Aunt Fanny on the radio (and, later, television) show *The Breakfast Club,* with Don McNeill. For twenty-five years Aunt Fanny would dish about her neighbors Bert Beerbower, Orphie Hackett, and Ott Ort, characters Allison had created for local Iowa radio. In 1939, banking on the popularity of *The Breakfast Club,* the Aunt Fanny character was briefly spun off into her own radio show, *Sunday Dinner at Aunt Fanny's.*

Fran Allison. ARCHIVE PHOTOS

Allison married Archie Levington, a representative for a music publisher, in 1942. They had no children. While her husband served in the army during World War II, Allison traveled the country on bond-selling tours, where she met and became good friends with the puppeteer Burr Tillstrom. Tillstrom had performed with his puppets Kukla and Ollie at the RCA Victor exhibit at the 1939 World's Fair and at United Service Organizations shows and army hospitals. It was their natural rapport that prompted Tillstrom to choose Allison as his sidekick in 1947 when network executives at local Chicago station WBKB hired Tillstrom and his puppets, dubbed the Kuklatopians, to create a show that would increase the station's hours of family programming. Creative and spontaneous, Allison was the perfect "straight man" to Tillstrom's host of unique characters.

Thin and pretty with large, wide-set eyes and a big smile, she could sing and improvise along with Tillstrom in the show's informal structure. With only an enthusiastic handshake between the two performers, *Kukla, Fran, and Ollie* was born. Musical director and pianist Jack Facianato was an essential part of the mix that made the show a success.

Episodes aired daily on WBKB from four to five in the afternoon beginning on 13 October 1947. The station was acquired by NBC in 1948 and *Kukla, Fran, and Ollie* began to be broadcast nationwide. It soon attracted an adult audience as well as children and was moved to a half-hour time slot at 7 P.M. In its third season the show was drawing 6 million viewers with ratings that rivaled programs featuring Milton Berle and Ed Sullivan. The show was always live and never scripted, with Allison helping to spontaneously create a make-believe world in which she interacted with the puppets, creating detailed personal histories, families, and distinct personalities for each character. The group was led by Kukla, the gentle clown with a perpetually worried expression, and Oliver J. Dragon ("Ollie"), the mischievous, buck-toothed dragon whose family's fire-breathing ability had been doused when his great-great-great-great-grandfather swallowed water while swimming the Hellespont. Others included Fletcher Rabbit, Ophelia Oglepuss, and Beulah Witch, who was named after the show's producer Beulah Zachary and flew around on a jet-powered broomstick. Allison used a simple, conversational style to draw out the characters, whose human qualities and idiosyncracies endeared them to audiences. The show created larger productions such as musicals, satires, and operettas including *Martin Dragon, Private Tooth,* and *The Mikado.* As the only live character on the show, Allison laughed with and sang songs to the captivated characters; she was once referred to by Tillstrom as "big sister, favorite teacher, baby-sitter, girlfriend, and mother" to his band of "kids." Allison also was responsible for the creation of many characters, such as Ollie's ancient mother, Olivia.

The show was cut to fifteen minutes in 1951, which sent the ratings even higher as people diligently tuned in to see their favorite characters. It was shifted to a weekly spot on Sunday afternoons and became a daily show again when it moved from NBC to ABC in 1954. After running for ten years, *Kukla, Fran, and Ollie* was canceled in 1957. The show was resurrected in 1961 (without Allison), then ran, with Allison as host, from 1969 to 1971 on PBS and as the connecting segments between films on the *CBS Children's Film Festival* between 1971 and 1978.

Over the course of its run *Kukla, Fran, and Ollie* received six Emmy nominations for best children's program, winning the award in 1952. The show also garnered a Peabody in 1949 for outstanding children's program.

Allison's career continued through the late 1950s with the *Fran Allison Show,* a panel-discussion program on local Chicago television. She also appeared in TV musicals such as *Many Moons* (1954); *Pinocchio* (1957), with Mickey Rooney, in which she played the Blue-Haired Fairy Queen; *Damn Yankees* (1967); and *Miss Pickerell* (1972).

Much of her later career was spent as a TV pitchwoman for various products and as a guest on TV interview and variety shows. Her marriage to Archie Levington lasted until he died in 1978. In the 1980s Allison hosted a local program, *Prime Time,* for senior citizens on KHJ-TV in Los Angeles. She was inducted into the Miami Children's Hospital's Ambassador David M. Walters International Hall of Fame to honor her work contributing to the health and happiness of children. Allison died in Sherman Oaks from bone-marrow cancer at the age of eighty-one. She is buried at Mount Cavalry Cemetery in Cedar Rapids, Iowa.

★

For additional reading on Allison and *Kukla, Fran, and Ollie,* see Stuart Fischer, *Kids' TV: The First Twenty-five Years* (1983); Lester L. Brown, *Les Brown's Encyclopedia of Television,* 3d ed. (1992); Tim Brooks and Earle Marsh, *Complete Directory to Prime Time Network and Cable TV Shows 1946–Present,* 6th ed. (1995); and Horace Newcomb, ed., *Encyclopedia of Television* (1997).

MATTHEW HUNTINGTON

ALLOTT, Gordon Llewellyn (*b.* 2 January 1907 in Pueblo, Colorado; *d.* 17 January 1989 in Englewood, Colorado), Colorado attorney and public official whose long career included three terms in the U.S. Senate.

Allott was one of four children of Leonard J. Allott, a federal meat inspector, and Bertha L. Reese, a high school teacher. After attending Central High School in Pueblo he attended the University of Colorado, earning a B.A. degree in 1927 and an LL.B. degree in 1929. During his time at the university, Allott participated in class elections and other forms of school politics. While pursuing his law degree he ran the 400-meter hurdles in the 1928 Olympic tryouts but did not make the U.S. team.

Upon graduation and admission to the bar he returned to southern Colorado, where he involved himself in law, business, the military, and politics. He practiced law in the cities of Pueblo and Lamar for several years and on 15 May 1954 married Welda O. Hall; they had two children. That year he became a director of Lamar's First Federal Savings and Loan Association. During this period Allott's opposition to the policies of the Democratic president, Franklin D. Roosevelt, motivated his growing involvement in politics. As Allott explained, "I was absolutely convinced that the course he [Roosevelt] was pursuing was going to break down the moral fiber of the people of this country in the sense that they would no longer have to look out for themselves." In 1934 he served as county attorney for Prowers

Gordon Allott. ARCHIVE PHOTOS

County, a position he would hold again from 1941 to 1946. From 1937 to 1941 he was city attorney for Lamar. As the national chairperson of the Young Republicans from 1941 to 1946, Allott often clashed with the leaders of the old guard of the GOP in Colorado. After serving in the U.S. Army Air Forces in the Pacific (although not as a combat pilot) during World War II he became district attorney for the Fifteenth Judicial District, a position he held from 1946 to 1948. In 1950 Allott was elected lieutenant governor of Colorado. Despite his numerous professional activities, Allott found time for a personal life. When not working, he enjoyed fishing. After his World War II experience he became interested in flying. At one point he even owned his own small airplane. Broad-shouldered with wavy salt-and-pepper hair, Allott was a distinguished-looking man.

In 1954 Allott was elected as a Republican to the U.S. Senate, where he served from 1955 to 1973. After an initial stint on the Labor and Public Welfare Committee and District of Columbia Committee, he gained a seat on the Interior and Insular Affairs Committee in 1956 and the Appropriations Committee in 1959. He served on these committees for the rest of his time in the Senate. He eventually became the ranking Republican member of a defense appropriations subcommittee, and from 1969 to 1972 he was the ranking Republican member on the Interior Committee. He chaired the Republican Policy Committee from 1969 to 1972, making him the third-ranking Republican in the Senate.

As a senator the Colorado Republican often crossed ideological and partisan boundaries. He frequently clashed with Democratic senator Clinton P. Anderson over conservation legislation that would limit development on public lands by classifying them as wilderness, but in 1963 Allott himself called for setting aside 6 million acres as wilderness area. He often criticized antipoverty and other social welfare programs of the 1960s. Nevertheless, he favored the Civil Rights Act of 1964 and argued that the federal government needed to do more to address inequities in the educational system. He supported the space program, as did liberal Democratic presidents John F. Kennedy and Lyndon B. Johnson. Allott's strong interest in water issues led him to work closely with Colorado Democrat and House Interior Committee chair Wayne N. Aspinall to pass the Colorado River Basin Storage Act of 1968, which provided for the construction of five Colorado water projects and the Central Arizona Project. Allott helped secure funding to build the National Center for Atmospheric Research (NCAR) in Boulder and the Air Force Academy in Colorado Springs.

Allott's interests were not limited to domestic policy. He was a "cold warrior" and an anticommunist. He supported a resolution calling on the Soviet Union to grant the Baltic states independence and (like many members of his party) favored a strong stand against North Vietnam in the 1960s. He served as the Senate delegate to the United Nations and the Interparliamentary Union (a worldwide organization of legislators). He belonged as well to the Institute Politique, a private international think tank that met in Liechtenstein.

Despite his credentials and experience Allott lost his 1972 reelection bid to Floyd Haskell, a former Republican who had switched parties in protest against the Vietnam War. The historian Robert Athearn has attributed the defeat to the widespread perception among young people and newcomers to the state that Allott was out of touch with the voters and unsympathetic to the concerns of the budding environmental movement. (The same election saw Aspinall lose his House seat after serving twenty-four years.)

After his loss Allott and his wife moved to Denver, where he practiced law. He was appointed by President Richard M. Nixon to the General Advisory Commission to the Arms Control and Disarmament Agency. In 1981 President Ronald Reagan appointed Allott to the National Park System Advisory Board. Allott's long and distinguished career ended when cancer took his life at age eighty-two. He is buried in Fairmount Cemetery in Denver, Colorado.

Allott stands out as an important figure both for what he did and what he represented. He played a key role in the development of Colorado's water resources. He helped ensure federal support for educational and scientific endeavors. He spoke out in favor of racial equality and against communism. Although a conservative in many ways, his brand of conservatism was one that allowed him to cross partisan and philosophical lines for the benefit of his nation and his state.

★

Allott's papers are housed in the Archives of the University of Colorado Libraries in Boulder, Colorado. His 1954 election to the U.S. Senate and 1972 defeat are touched on in Robert G. Athearn, *The Coloradans* (1976). References to Allott's positions on conservation issues can be found in Richard Allan Baker, *Conservation Politics: The Senate Career of Clinton P. Anderson* (1985). Allott's views on the Vietnam War and other aspects of foreign policy are addressed in Robert V. Hunt's 1987 dissertation "Colorado and the Vietnam War, 1964–1974: A Study in the Politics of Polarization" (University of Colorado). Short but useful summaries of Allott's life appear in the obituaries in the *Rocky Mountain News* and *Denver Post* (both 18 Jan. 1989). Selected aspects of Allott's career are explored in a 17 January 1979 oral history interview conducted by Nancy Whistler for Former Members of Congress, Inc.; a transcript of the interview can be found in the University of Colorado Archives.

CHRISTOPHER K. RIGGS

ALSOP, Joseph Wright, V (*b.* 11 October 1910 in Avon, Connecticut; *d.* 28 August 1989 in Washington, D.C.), newsman, author, and confidant of presidents.

Alsop was the son of Joseph Wright Alsop IV, an insurance executive, and Corinne (Robinson) Alsop. Both of his parents had served in the Connecticut legislature. Joseph was educated at the Groton School in Massachusetts and at Harvard, where he studied English literature and gained a reputation as something of a raconteur. After graduating from Harvard in 1932, he landed a job, through family connections, with the *New York Herald Tribune*. For that newspaper he wrote features on New York City life and produced literary pieces for the newspaper's Sunday book review section. But he hungered to write about politics and to get to Washington, where his "Cousin Franklin" (his mother was Eleanor Roosevelt's first cousin) was ensconced in the White House. In late 1935 Alsop was transferred to Washington to cover the U.S. Senate. Soon he teamed up with Turner Catledge of the *New York Times* to produce numerous freelance pieces for the *Saturday Evening Post,* and with Catledge he wrote *The 168 Days* (1938), a book recounting Roosevelt's failed effort to enlarge the U.S. Supreme Court. The book, based largely on three articles Alsop and Catledge had written for the *Saturday Evening Post,* received favorable notices.

The success of Alsop's writing led to the offer of a column from the North American Newspaper Alliance, a leading syndication service. In 1937 Alsop joined with fellow *Herald Tribune* reporter Robert Kintner to write the column, called "The Capital Parade." The two men quickly become well known for getting behind the story to break news and force into the open matters that policy makers wished to keep behind closed doors. They also collaborated on two books: *Men Around the President* (1939), a look at the Roosevelt brain trust, and *American White Paper: The Story of American Diplomacy and the Second World War* (1940), a dramatic rendition of Roosevelt's diplomatic maneuvering in the year leading up to the September 1939 outbreak of war in Europe.

In mid-1941, with the country moving toward war, Alsop quit the column and joined the U.S. Navy as a lieutenant junior grade. He shipped out to the Far East, where he was slated to become a forward intelligence observer in Bombay, India. But while traveling through China, he encountered General Claire Chennault, the flamboyant former U.S. military aviator who was leading the American Volunteer Group (better known as the Flying Tigers), an aviation combat unit seeking to protect the regime of China's Nationalist leader, Chiang Kai-shek, from the Japanese invaders. Taking advantage of U.S. military rules designed to bolster the Flying Tigers and assist the Chinese Nationalists, Alsop resigned his commission in September 1941 and joined Chennault as aide and "odd job man."

While traveling around Asia trying to cadge spare parts for Chennault's ragtag air force, Alsop found himself flying from the Philippines to Burma via Hong Kong on the morning of the Japanese attack on the U.S. naval base at Pearl Harbor, Hawaii. He was trapped in Hong Kong as the Japanese laid siege to it, and a few weeks later was captured and incarcerated by the invading forces. He spent eight months at Stanley Prison with other Westerners caught in the Japanese advance across the Pacific, and suffered nutritional deprivation there that he later termed "slow starvation." By passing himself off as a newsman, rather than the combatant that he was, he managed to get repatriated with other civilians when prisoner exchanges were negotiated by the American and Japanese governments. Upon his release, in July 1942, he immediately returned to China and worked in a number of capacities before landing a commission in the U.S. Army Air Corps and joining Chennault's Fourteenth Air Force as plans officer.

In 1945 Alsop resumed his column, now titled "Matter of Fact" and produced under the banner of the New York Herald Tribune Syndicate. He also acquired a new partner—his brother Stewart, four years his junior and something of a war hero (he had fought in Italy as a platoon leader in the British army and parachuted into France,

Joseph Alsop. ARCHIVE PHOTOS

behind German lines, in July 1944). The brothers emerged as two of the leading journalists of the postwar era. Their column, syndicated in nearly 200 papers, reached 25 million readers, and their frequent contributions to the *Saturday Evening Post* were read by upwards of 20 million. The column was based upon a sharp insight—that America was about to embark on what the Alsops considered a grand adventure as the world's great power. They welcomed this development and championed it in the column, which often was written from major world capitals and diplomatic hot spots.

During the early cold war, the Alsops traveled the globe like panjandrums, dining with prime ministers and kings; enjoying social prominence in London, Paris, Tokyo, and Rome; and stirring up international diplomacy with their relentless news coverage. They quickly identified the Soviet Union as a major threat to world peace and became known as ardent cold war hard-liners. They championed the efforts of the leading American diplomats and government officials of the day—James Forrestal, George Kennan, Charles Bohlen, Dean Acheson, Robert Lovett, John McCloy, David Bruce, Averell Harriman. These and lesser lights were their friends as well as their sources, and the Alsops enjoyed ready access to their offices as well as their dinner tables. In 1950 and 1952 the Alsops received the Overseas Press Club's award for best interpretation of foreign news. The brothers wrote two books together—*We Accuse!* (1954), an angry account of the fall of prominent nuclear physicist J. Robert Oppenheimer, and *The Reporter's Trade* (1958), a collection of columns along with a portrayal of inside Washington journalism.

In 1958 the brothers' partnership ended, and Stewart pursued magazine journalism at the *Saturday Evening Post* while Joseph wrote the column by himself. Without Stewart's leavening sensibility, Joseph's work became sharper and more pointed; he wrote with ever greater self-assurance and less balance. He also used the column increasingly to push pet causes, particularly the presidential candidacy of his best friend in the Senate, John F. Kennedy. After Kennedy's election, Alsop frequently interviewed the new president and his closest advisers, enjoyed intimate dinners at the White House, and had President and Mrs. Kennedy to his home for dinner parties on numerous occasions. He was devastated by the president's death and afterward never seemed to enjoy Washington or his job with the same intensity as before.

Alsop and the new president, Lyndon Johnson, were close friends, and his easy access to the White House family quarters continued. But soon Alsop stirred Johnson's ire, and his invitations ended abruptly. The reason: Vietnam. Throughout the election year of 1964, Alsop wanted Johnson to take dramatic steps to blunt communist advances in South Vietnam, a virtual American protectorate at the time. Johnson shared Alsop's concern but wanted to avoid any provocative actions in an election year. After the election he followed the Alsop prescriptions and got himself and the United States mired in a war that proved to be his political undoing and a source of intense anguish for the country.

The war also left its mark on Alsop's career. After the Tet offensive of early 1968, when America's resolve to fight the war weakened, Alsop became fair game for writers and commentators bent on attacking his hawkish views. Whereas for years he had been written about with respect, he now became a "figure of fun," as economist and Alsop detractor John Kenneth Galbraith put it. Numerous magazine articles ridiculed his elaborate mannerisms, his furious temper, his zest for high living, and his tendency to get stormy when defending his ironclad convictions.

Meanwhile, Alsop's marriage to Susan Mary Jay Patten was coming apart. She had been married to Alsop's closest friend from Harvard, William Patten. Shortly after Patten's death in 1960, Alsop proposed to his widow, and after several months of wavering, she accepted. Alsop was homosexual, and the marriage he was proposing was to be a platonic one. After their marriage on 16 February 1961, the couple quickly joined the top ranks of social Washington, their home in Georgetown becoming a leading salon. But it was a stormy marriage, largely because Alsop felt constricted by the relationship and did not want his beautiful young wife to outshine him socially. In 1973 she left him. Though they remained good friends, and she often served as his hostess on social occasions, the breakup devastated the aging columnist.

An even more painful blow came in May 1974 when his brother Stewart died of leukemia. Alsop told friends that the loss was like "an amputation," and it sapped his zest for the reporter's trade. Within six months of Stewart's death, Joseph announced his retirement. He sold his big house on Dumbarton Avenue in Georgetown, rented a smaller house down the block, and dropped from prominence. He still hosted dinner parties that continued to draw the city's high and mighty, but he ceased all polemical writing and devoted his last years to a major book on the history of art collecting. He died of lung cancer fifteen years after his retirement.

★

The Joseph W. Alsop Papers are in the Library of Congress. See also the Stewart Alsop Collection, Special Collections, Mugar Library, Boston University; and the Robinson/Alsop Papers, Theodore Roosevelt Collection, Houghton Library, Harvard University. Further works by Alsop are *From the Silent Earth* (1964), a study of the Greek Bronze Age; *The Rare Art Traditions* (1982), a history of art collecting; *FDR: A Centenary Remembrance* (1982); and *I've Seen the Best of It* (1992), his memoirs, written with Adam Platt. He also figures in Stewart Alsop, *Stay of Execution: A Sort of Memoir* (1973). An obituary is in the *New York Times* (29 Aug. 1989).

ROBERT W. MERRY

ALVAREZ, Luis Walter (*b.* 13 June 1911 in San Francisco, California; *d.* 1 September 1988 in Berkeley, California), experimental physicist who was awarded the Nobel Prize in physics for his participation in the construction of the hydrogen bubble chamber.

Luis Walter Alvarez was one of four children. His father, Walter Alvarez, was a research physiologist who worked as a private physician in order to earn money for his family. His mother, Harriet Smyth, graduated from the University of California at Berkeley and prepared for a career as a grammar school teacher.

In his childhood Alvarez showed a strong curiosity about science. As the son of a physician, he was exposed to the machines and methods of the laboratory. He took little interest in the medical nature of his father's occupation but, as he boasts in his autobiography, "By the time I was ten, I could use all the small tools in my father's little shop, measure resistances on a Wheatstone bridge, and construct circuits." At the age of eleven, with some help from his father, Alvarez built his own crystal radio set, the beginning of a lifelong engagement with scientific equipment.

In 1924, because his father had noticed young Luis's affinity for mechanical devices, Alvarez was enrolled at Polytechnic High School in San Francisco. There he learned mechanical and freehand drawing. The following year Alvarez's father went to work as a full-time researcher at the Mayo Clinic, and the family relocated to Rochester, Minnesota, where Alvarez continued his studies at Rochester High School. Although he found his science courses "not very interesting," it was during these years that Alvarez, through the help of his father, was able to see professional physicists engaged in their daily work. His father even arranged for a machinist at the Mayo Clinic to give young Luis private lessons in cutting gears and in working with clinic instruments.

Alvarez gained a great deal of technical knowledge during the summers he spent working at the Mayo Clinic, but he also gained something that he considered equally valuable: "a characteristic . . . that has been important to my scientific career. . . . All the scientists I know . . . have a healthy skepticism about authority. We are trained to ask 'Why?' continually."

Despite the expectation that he follow the family tradition of attending the University of California, Alvarez decided that the University of Chicago would better prepare him for a scientific career. He took courses in chemistry and mathematics, disciplines in which he did respectable but not brilliant work. It was not until his junior year, when he studied experimental physics for the first time, that Alvarez discovered the work he loved. He was inspired by his teacher, George Monk, who noticed Alvarez's keen fascination with physics and allowed him to perform optical experiments using equipment built by Nobel laureate Albert Michelson's technicians. Alvarez considered Michelson his "first scientific hero."

Alvarez received his B.S. degree from Chicago in 1932. In 1934 he paid a visit to the Berkeley laboratory of Ernest Lawrence, the inventor and developer of the atom smasher known as the cyclotron. Although brief, the visit would influence the direction of his career. Alvarez was awarded his Ph.D. in physics, also from Chicago, in 1936. His thesis, a diffraction-grating experiment, was published in the *Journal of the Optical Society of America.*

Also in 1936, on 15 April, he married Geraldine Smithwick, with whom he would have two children. After their marriage the couple moved to Berkeley, where he began working as an assistant to Lawrence. Two years later he joined the Berkeley faculty.

Alvarez spent the rest of his career at Berkeley, although he took a leave during most of World War II to work at the Radiation Laboratory of the Massachusetts Institute of Technology (MIT) and at the Los Alamos Laboratory in New Mexico. At the MIT Radiation Laboratory, from 1940 to 1943, Alvarez worked on the development of radar,

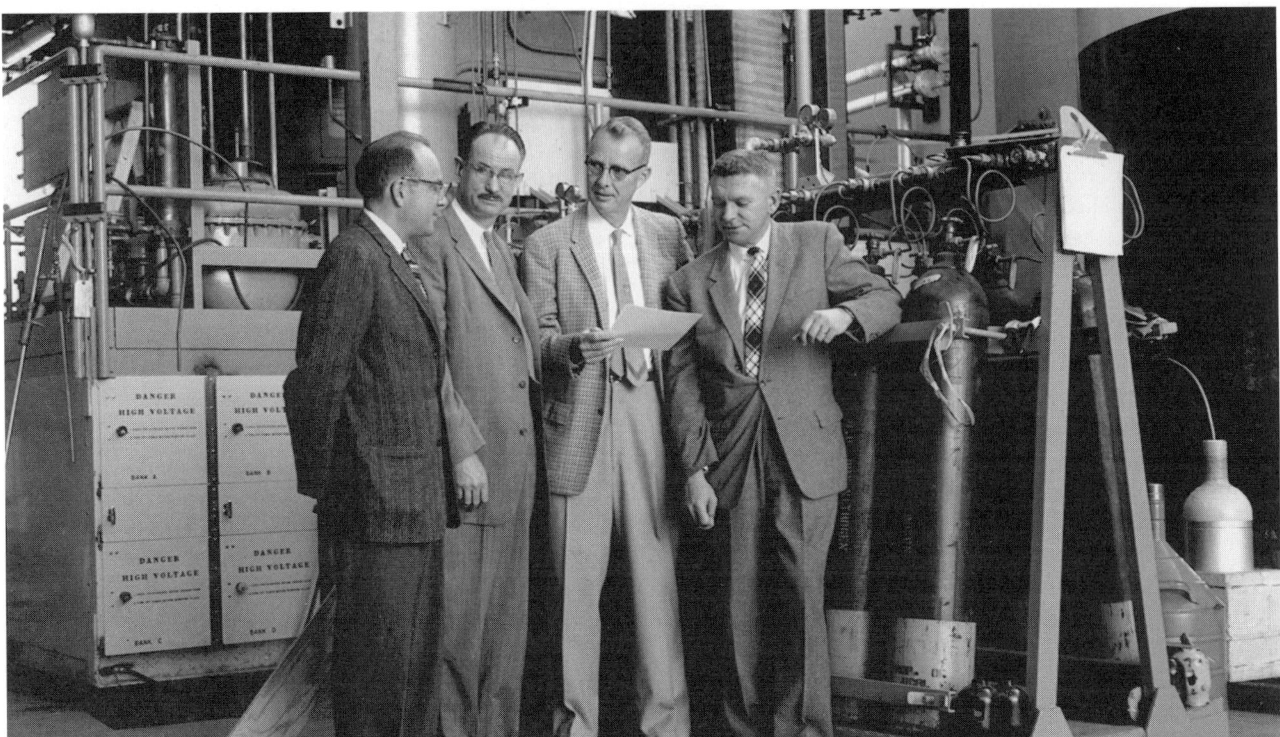

Luis Alvarez (*second from right*) with Paul Hernandez, Edwin McMillan, and Don Gow in front of the seventy-two-inch bubble chamber at the Lawrence Berkeley National Laboratory. ERNEST ORLANDO LAWRENCE BERKELEY NATIONAL LABORATORY

including Ground Control Approach, a system to help land aircraft, and microwave radar equipment for locating airplanes. From 1944 to 1945 he was one of a select group of physicists chosen to work at Los Alamos during the development of the first atomic bomb. He not only observed the test detonation of the first atomic bomb on 16 July 1945 but also flew in an airplane accompanying the *Enola Gay* when it dropped the atomic bomb on Hiroshima. Although several of his fellow scientists expressed guilt at having developed such a destructive weapon, Alvarez recalled disagreeing with his colleagues: "I could muster very little sympathy for their point of view; few of them had any direct experience with war and the people who had to fight it." After the war Alvarez returned to Berkeley's physics department as a professor.

The crowning achievement of Alvarez's career was the development of the hydrogen bubble chamber, a tank filled with a heavy liquid (hydrogen) used to detect subatomic particles. The chamber began yielding significant pictures during the summer of 1957. After shooting electrically charged particles through the liquid, Alvarez and his colleagues photographed the vapor trails they left. From these trails, they determined the mass, momentum, and electric charge of the particles. Alvarez pioneered the use of liquid hydrogen as the best medium to use in a bubble chamber. His device allowed him to discover seventy subatomic particles. For this research, Alvarez was awarded the 1968 Nobel Prize in physics.

Meanwhile, Alvarez and his first wife divorced in 1957. The following year, on December 28, he married Janet Landis, with whom he had two children. In his later years Alvarez teamed up with his son from his first marriage, Walter Luis Alvarez, a geologist, to produce several fascinating and controversial theories. When he discovered an iridium-rich layer of soil in a sample from Walter's geological excavation site in Gubbio, Italy, Alvarez helped his son construct the theory that the iridium, which is rare on Earth, had been deposited during an asteroid or comet impact and that the dust cloud caused by the impact had changed the Earth's climate, leading to the extinction of dinosaurs. Despite criticism that the element iridium is also deposited in the Earth's soil during volcanic eruptions, the scientific community did not dismiss the Alvarez theory about these mass extinctions. Some scientists even presented data that the traces of a "smoking-gun" crater exist beneath the Yucatán Peninsula in Mexico.

Alvarez, who retired in 1978, died of complications resulting from cancer of the esophagus. He was buried in Berkeley.

Luis Walter Alvarez is credited with many inventions and insights besides his bubble chamber, including the development of a color television system, the use of X rays to search for hidden chambers in the Chephren pyramid at Giza in Egypt (there were none), the discovery of the first nonradioactive observations of an artificial isotope, the spectral analysis of mercury, and the first time-of-flight neutron spectrometer—eventually used to measure neutron emissions during the development of the atomic bomb. He obtained at least twenty-two patents in his lifetime. His place in the pantheon of American physicists would have been secured by his development of the bubble chamber alone, but his indefatigable creativity and willingness to take risks solidified his reputation as a pivotal—if not sympathetic—participant in some of the most critical events in the history of science.

★

Alvarez's autobiography, *Alvarez: Adventures of a Physicist* (1987), describes his life and career. His contribution to the asteroid/dinosaur extinction theory is discussed in detail in *T. Rex and the Crater of Doom* (1997), by his son Walter Alvarez. An obituary is in the *New York Times* (2 Sept. 1988).

LEROY GONZALEZ

ANDERSON, Robert Bernerd (*b.* 4 June 1910 in Bartleson, Texas; *d.* 14 August 1989 in New York City), government official who served as secretary of the navy (1953–1954), deputy secretary of defense (1954–1955), and secretary of the treasury (1957–1961).

Anderson was the son of Robert Lee Anderson, a farmer and sometime mayor of Bartleson, and Elizabeth (Haskew) Anderson. After a local public school and junior college education, he graduated first in his class in 1932 with an LL.B. from the University of Texas Law School. Following his election to the state senate during his senior year, he began a law practice in Fort Worth. In 1933 he became an assistant professor of law at Texas, and then was appointed to the State Tax Commission, which made him an ex-officio member of the State Racing Commission. In 1936 he became executive director of the Texas Unemployment Commission. On 10 April 1935 Anderson married Ollie Mae Rawlings; they had two sons. In 1937 Anderson became general attorney and manager of the huge W. T. Waggoner farm and range estate and later of many other domestic and international banking ventures.

Polio left Anderson with a slight limp that prevented him from serving in the armed forces during World War II, but throughout this period he worked as a civilian adviser to the secretary of war. In 1949 he was appointed chairman of the Texas Board of Education and was subsequently elected twice to the post. He was also deputy chairman of the Federal Reserve Bank of Dallas and a director of several commercial and philanthropic organizations.

Robert B. Anderson. PAOLO COLETTA, U.S. NAVAL INSTITUTE IN ANNAPOLIS, MD

While president of Columbia University, Dwight D. Eisenhower met Anderson and found him to be "intelligent, articulate, broadly experienced and educated, and, at forty-two, still a relatively young man." As U.S. president, Eisenhower told Secretary of Defense Charles Wilson that he could use Anderson elsewhere if the Pentagon could spare him. Democrats objected when Eisenhower nominated the "Democrat-for-Eisenhower" as secretary of the navy, but he was easily confirmed by the Senate on 19 June 1953.

An early problem for Anderson was how to handle attacks on the navy for its failure to utilize the talents of the atomic specialist Captain Hyman G. Rickover, twice passed over by selection boards prior to his retirement in 1953. Anderson called for a special board to select engineering officers for retention on active duty and to specify that one "be experienced and qualified in the field of atomic propulsion machinery for ships"; Rickover became a rear admiral on 10 July 1953. Anderson was thus responsible for promoting the man who would launch the first atomic-powered submarine, the *Nautilus,* on 21 January 1954, and until the 1980s head the navy's nuclear power program.

A second problem Anderson faced was how to follow

President Eisenhower's directive for the fiscal year 1954 budget, which was to provide maximum safety at least cost, or what became known as the New Look. With his budget lightly cut, Anderson obtained a third Forrestal-class carrier, but it was oil fired rather than nuclear powered. Funds for other new construction, aircraft, and naval and marine personnel were deeply cut, however.

While a Department of Defense reorganization plan removed the Joint Chiefs of Staff from the command structure, it made Anderson the executive agent for the unified commands, thus strengthening civilian control over the military. Eisenhower was pleased when Anderson successfully eradicated almost all remaining racial segregation in naval installations in the South.

Greatly interested in personnel, Anderson worked to improve conditions in the services so that they could retain talent. He also, unavailingly, called for improving the merchant marine and reviving the shipbuilding industry so that it could produce ships to replace the obsolescent ones of World War II. To improve his department's organization, he had his assistant, Thomas Gates, chair a board to offer recommendations. The result in part added the posts of assistant secretary of the navy for personnel and reserve forces and assistant secretary of the navy for fiscal management to his office.

Anderson disagreed with Secretary of State John Foster Dulles about the doctrine of massive retaliation, because he believed that a future war would be fought with conventional weapons. But Anderson was forced to adopt ballistic missiles for submarines. Lessons learned from the explosion of two hydrogen bombs in 1954 rested with his successors.

Anderson suffered personnel cuts in the fiscal year 1955 budget, but the small 3.5 percent increase in construction funds permitted the building of the fourth Forrestal-class carrier, a third nuclear submarine, two conventional submarines, five destroyers, eight destroyer escorts, and various auxiliaries.

From 1954 to 1955 Anderson served as deputy secretary of defense. On the evening of 3 September 1954 he informed President Eisenhower that the Chinese had begun shelling Quemoy Island, off the Chinese coast. For nine months Anderson stationed American naval forces in the Formosa (later Taiwan) Strait to prevent war between Communist China and Chiang Kai-shek's Nationalist government in Taiwan. As Eisenhower ordered, he avoided getting bogged down in a land war in Southeast Asia.

Anderson left the Pentagon in July 1954, only to be recalled in November 1956 by Eisenhower and Dulles and given plenipotentiary power to attempt to bring peace between Egypt and Israel. Egypt's Gamal Abdel Nasser balked at the initiative, but Anderson's shuttle diplomacy set the pattern for Henry Kissinger's diplomatic efforts in the early 1970s and for the peace accords of Camp David in 1978.

Anderson declined Eisenhower's offer to become undersecretary of state with the possibility of succeeding Dulles and also to become secretary of defense. He agreed, however, to be secretary of the treasury and served from 1957 to 1961. In this capacity he advised Eisenhower to accept rising unemployment rather than devalue the dollar during recessions. Eisenhower thought Anderson to be "just about the ablest man that I know. He would make a splendid President." But Anderson declined Eisenhower's three offers to run for vice president. His last service as secretary of the treasury was to give the incoming president, John F. Kennedy, a forty-five-minute briefing on the United States' balance-of-payment problems.

Late in his career Anderson served as counsel for the sultan of Oman and the Reverend Sun Myung Moon's Unification Church, and as adviser to the Phillips Petroleum Company, Texaco, and other large oil companies. He was also a limited partner in the New York City investment banking firm of Leb, Shoades Company. In 1987, after pleading guilty to federal income tax evasion and the illegal operation of an offshore bank, Anderson was sentenced to a month in prison and five months of house arrest. In January 1989 he was disbarred by the Appellate Division of New York State Supreme Court. He died in New York City of multiple causes.

★

Dwight D. Eisenhower, *The White House Years,* vol. 1, *Mandate for Change, 1953–1956* (1963), and vol. 2, *Waging Peace, 1956–1961* (1965), contain high praise for Anderson. See also U.S. Department of Defense, *Semi-Annual Report of the Department of Defense* (1953–1960), and William Bragg Ewald, *Eisenhower the President: Crucial Days, 1956–1961* (1981). A character sketch is in Paolo E. Coletta, ed., *American Secretaries of the Navy,* vol. 2. (1981). Stephen E. Ambrose, *Eisenhower,* vol. 2, *The President* (1984), gives Anderson high marks. An obituary is in the *New York Times* (16 Aug. 1989).

PAOLO E. COLETTA

ANGLETON, James Jesus (*b.* 9 December 1917 in Boise, Idaho; *d.* 11 May 1987 in Washington, D.C.), first chief of counterintelligence at the Central Intelligence Agency (CIA), for more than twenty years heading the office whose purpose is to protect the agency from infiltration by foreign agents.

One of four children of James Hugh Angleton, who worked for the National Cash Register Company, and Carmen Mercedes Mareno, Angleton entered Yale University in 1937. There he roomed with E. Reed Whittemore, Jr., a poet. They founded the literary magazine *Furioso,* a reflection of Angleton's lifelong interest in letters. On 17 July

James Jesus Angleton at the CIA, 1979. WALLY MCNAMEE/CORBIS

1943 he married Cicely d'Autremont; they had three children.

In 1943, two years after graduating from Yale, Angleton joined the Office of Strategic Services. He directed agents working against Nazi Germany, and in 1944 he traveled to Rome, where he conducted operations aimed at the Italian Fascist intelligence service.

After World War II, Angleton worked closely with Italian counterintelligence to uncover data about Soviet operations. When he returned to the United States, he began to specialize in the workings of the Soviet secret police (KGB). After compiling huge files on Soviet espionage operations, Angleton was authorized in 1954 by Allen W. Dulles, then the director of the CIA, to set up the first counterintelligence staff. His office became one of the most secret in the agency. The mere suspicion that a Soviet defector might be a double agent convinced Angleton that a mole had burrowed into the CIA's top levels, and for years he involved the agency in what was seen then as a fruitless search.

Angleton's view of the world was characterized by a never-ending suspicion about the Soviet Union's motives and maneuvers. When the Soviet Union and China split over ideological differences in the early 1960s, Angleton was convinced that the widely reported antagonism was a clever ruse concocted by the two communist powers.

In 1974, when the CIA was under fire for domestic spying, Director William Colby decided Angleton had to go. He fired him at a Christmas Eve meeting and cut the counterintelligence staff from 300 to fewer than 80. Subsequent events, however, lessened the disgrace of the ousted counterspy. When several devastating spy cases involving the CIA came to light in the 1990s, analysts noted that such things had not occurred on Angleton's watch. Ironically, in 1975 Angleton was awarded the CIA's Distinguished Intelligence Medal, its highest award.

On 24 September 1975 Angleton was questioned by the Senate committee headed by Frank Church about the CIA's counterintelligence section and the official in charge of the mail-intercept program from 1955 to 1973. He acknowledged the program was illegal but defended it as vital to U.S. security. It was "inconceivable," Angleton stated, "that a secret [covert] intelligence arm of the government should have to comply with all the government's overt orders." The interception of mail to and from communist countries, particularly the Soviet Union, produced a number of items that were of great intelligence value, he insisted. It appeared that the Soviet officials had decided to communicate openly with political sympathizers and agents in the United States because they believed their communications would not be opened before they reached their destination. Asked who had known of the intercept program, Angleton listed former CIA director Richard Helms, J. Edgar Hoover, and William C. Sullivan, former head of the FBI's domestic section. He said he could not refute an assertion by Senator Church that President Richard Nixon had not known of the intercept program, although it had existed fifteen years before Nixon took office.

Angleton handled one of the CIA's most sensitive relationships with an allied intelligence service, Israel's Mossad. He personally oversaw this function, called "the Israeli Account," for more than a decade beginning in the mid-1950s, until William Colby insisted that Angleton give up his oversight. A plain stone monument in Angleton's memory was erected in Israel; it lists none of his activities—merely his name.

On 27 February 1979 the CIA stated that it had thoroughly examined and rejected an accusation that Angleton was himself a Soviet spy. Agency spokesman Herb Hetu confirmed that in the mid-1970s an employee had accused Angleton of working for the Soviets. An investigation had been carried out and had found the charge groundless. Former CIA Director Colby said he never had any doubts about Angleton's loyalty. He had removed Angleton because his long search for a possible spy or spies in the CIA had failed to produce results.

Tall, stooped, and professional, Angleton was a student of Dante, a poet, an orchid grower, a fly fisherman, and, not suprisingly, a poker player. He died of lung cancer and was buried in Arlington National Cemetery in Virginia. Even following his death, and the subsequent unsealing of U.S. documents relating to the cold war, it is difficult to compile a reasonably certain account of Angleton's intelligence successes, which largely remain classified. For instance, by one account he was instrumental in obtaining the text of Nikita Khrushchev's secret denunciation of Stalin in 1956, although it is now believed that this was provided by the Mossad.

Former U.S. Senator Malcolm Wallop, a strong defender of Angleton, said at his death: "James Angleton lived long enough to serve his country before, during, and after World War II. He was the architect of the best counterintelligence the United States ever had. In the mid-1970s, Angleton went out of fashion, but he lived long enough to see time and events vindicate him and show how little his accusers understood the difficult and inherently thankless business of counterintelligence."

★

Information on Angleton is in David Martin, *Wilderness of Mirrors* (1980); *U.S. News and World Report* (25 May 1987); G. J. A. O'Toole, *Encyclopedia of American Intelligence and Espionage* (1988); Tom Mangold, *The Cold Warrior: James Jesus Angleton, the CIA's Master Spy Hunter* (1991); G. J. A. O'Toole, *Honorable Treachery: A History of U.S. Intelligence, Espionage, and Covert Action from the American Revolution to the CIA* (1991); and Pat M. Holt, *Secret Intelligence and Public Policy: A Diplomatic Dilemma* (1995). An obituary is in the *New York Times* (12 May 1987).

MARK SOMMER

ARDEN, Eve (*b.* 30 April 1907 in Mill Valley, California; *d.* 12 November 1990 in Beverly Hills, California), actress who appeared in over sixty films, most often as a caustic, wisecracking woman; she is best remembered for her role as the wry but good-hearted high school teacher Connie Brooks in the late 1940s and early 1950s radio and television series *Our Miss Brooks*.

Born Eunice Quedens, the only child of divorced parents (her mother Lucille Quedens was a stage actress who became a milliner), Arden spent several of her early years in a convent and then lived with an aunt in Mill Valley. She displayed an early interest in acting and performed while a student at Tamalpais High School in Mill Valley. After working with stock and touring companies for several years and appearing in bit movie parts, she won a role in a Pasadena Community Playhouse revue called *Lo and Behold*. There she was noticed by producer Lee Shubert, who cast her as a showgirl in the 1934 edition of *Ziegfeld Follies* in New York City. At that time she took the stage name of Eve Arden, claiming later that the name came from cosmetic jars on her dressing table: "I stole my first name from Evening in Paris and the second from Elizabeth Arden." She also appeared in the musical revue *Parade* (1935) with comedian Jimmy Savo and in the 1936 *Ziegfeld Follies*, in which she sang "I Can't Get Started" with Bob Hope. As Fanny Brice's understudy, she starred in several *Follies* performances.

Eve Arden with Brooks West on the day of their marriage, 1951. AP/WIDE WORLD PHOTOS

After the death of her mother in 1937, Arden returned to California, where she began to seriously pursue a motion picture career. Her first film of this period was *Oh, Doctor* (1937), but it was in her second, *Stage Door* (1937), that she attracted attention, playing an aspiring actress who strode through the Footlights Club, a theatrical boardinghouse, with a cat draped over her shoulders. Many films followed, in which she was usually cast as the friend of the heroine or a girl Friday, always ready with a quip or a wisecrack. In 1939 she married Edward Bergen, a literary agent; they adopted two daughters and were divorced in 1948.

Arden's more conspicuous roles over the years included a circus aerialist in *At the Circus* (1939), with the Marx Brothers; a Russian sniper in *The Doughgirls* (1944); the bored wife of Paul Douglas in *We're Not Married* (1952); secretary to lawyer James Stewart in *Anatomy of a Murder* (1959); and (in a rare change of pace) a frustrated wife in *The Dark at the Top of the Stairs* (1960). However, she was most frequently cast as an acerbic ballast to the tempest-tossed heroine. She won an Academy Award nomination for playing the straight-talking friend of beleaguered Joan

Crawford in *Mildred Pierce* (1945). In the film, Arden's character comments on the protagonist's selfish daughter with typical sarcasm: "Veda's convinced me that alligators have the right idea. They eat their young." Arden was also actress Eleanor Parker's breezy confidante in *The Voice of the Turtle* (1947), wisecracking secretary to stagestruck heiress Doris Day in *Tea for Two* (1950), and all-knowing assistant to Joan Crawford's congresswoman in *Goodbye, My Fancy* (1951). In later years she had roles in such films as *Grease* (1978) and *Under the Rainbow* (1981).

On several occasions Arden returned to New York City and the Broadway stage, appearing in 1939 in the Jerome Kern–Oscar Hammerstein musical *Very Warm for May*, and in 1941 in the Cole Porter musical *Let's Face It*, with Danny Kaye, Nanette Fabray, and Vivian Vance. Her later theater work included starring in the West Coast company of *Auntie Mame* and the national company of *Butterflies Are Free*. She also briefly replaced Carol Channing in *Hello, Dolly*.

In 1948 Arden made her debut on CBS radio as English teacher Connie Brooks, cheerfully if a bit sardonically coping with her students at Madison High School, especially the punctilious Walter Denton (Richard Crenna). Frequently, she was obliged to cross swords with the crusty principal, Osgood Conklin (Gale Gordon). She also endured an unrequited passion for shy biology teacher Philip Boynton (Robert Rockwell). The show received mixed reviews and moved to television in 1952, lasting four seasons, and Arden was awarded an Emmy in 1953 for her performance. Arden married actor Brooks West on 25 August 1951; they had one son, adopted one son, and would remain together until West's death in 1984.

In 1956 *Our Miss Brooks* was made into a theatrical film, with Arden and the other principal players repeating their television roles. The following year Arden attempted to repeat her Miss Brooks success on television with *The Eve Arden Show*, playing author Liza Hammond, but the program lasted only one season. Ten years later, in 1967, she costarred for two seasons with Kaye Ballard in the comedy series *The Mothers-in-Law*. Over the years she also appeared in a number of television films.

At the time of her death from heart disease in 1990 Arden had been in failing health for over a year, suffering from cancer and heart problems. She is buried in Westwood Memorial Park in Los Angeles.

Over a career that spanned more than five decades, Eve Arden was a consummate professional who brought a crisp style and a sharp-edged wit to her many acting roles. Her entrance onto the screen signaled that a note of bracing candor was about to be introduced into the story. And always, she was a pleasure to see.

★

Eve Arden's autobiography is titled *Three Phases of Eve* (1985). Obituaries are in the *New York Times* (13 Nov. 1990) and *Variety* (19 Nov. 1990).

TED SENNETT

ARLEN, Harold (*b.* 15 February 1905 in Buffalo, New York; *d.* 23 April 1986 in New York City), composer who wrote music for songs used in stage productions and motion pictures, many of which became popular standards.

Arlen, born Hyman Arluck, was the older of two surviving sons of Samuel S. Arluck, a cantor, and Celia (Orlin) Arluck; he was the younger of twins, the elder of whom died shortly after birth, and he had a brother, Julius, seven years his junior. He first sang in public in the choir at his father's synagogue. He began piano lessons at nine, and his parents hoped he would become a concert pianist. He grew interested in popular music, however, especially ragtime, and formed Hyman Arluck's Snappy Trio in 1919. The group expanded to a sextet called the Southbound Shufflers and found work on excursion cruises across Lake Erie. Arlen stayed with the group until 1925, when he joined the Yankee Six, who subsequently added instruments and became the Buffalodians. The group moved to New York City in 1926 but broke up soon after. Arlen stayed in the city and joined Arnold Johnson's band. In July 1928 he left Johnson and briefly tried to launch a career as a singer-pianist. In 1929 he was cast in the Broadway musical *Great Day*, and though his part was cut, he stayed with the show as musical secretary to composer Vincent Youmans.

Although he had already written songs, Arlen envi-

Howard Arlen, 1965. ARCHIVE PHOTOS

sioned himself as a performer, not a composer. But the songwriter Harry Warren heard him improvising a tune while serving as rehearsal pianist for *Great Day*, and he introduced Arlen to Ted Koehler, who wrote lyrics to it. The result was "Get Happy." Koehler arranged for the song to be used in the *9:15 Revue* in February 1930. The show was a flop, but "Get Happy" became a hit. The newly formed team was hired to write songs for the 1930 edition of another revue, the *Earl Carroll Vanities*, which had a successful run of 215 performances. Then they replaced Hollywood-bound Jimmy McHugh and Dorothy Fields as principal songwriters for the revues mounted by the Cotton Club in Harlem. Arlen also found time to collaborate with Jack Yellen on the Broadway musical *You Said It*, which ran 192 performances following its January 1931 opening.

At the Cotton Club, Arlen and Koehler proved particularly adept at writing appropriate material for African-American performers in productions with such names as *Brown Sugar* and *Rhythmania*. Arlen's background in jazz and dance music, as well as a noticeable affinity for blues, enabled him to turn out a series of memorable songs, such as "Kickin' the Gong Around," "Between the Devil and the Deep Blue Sea," and "I Love a Parade" for such performers as Cab Calloway and Louis Armstrong in 1931. He and Koehler produced similar material when they returned to Broadway in September 1932 for the annual edition of the *Earl Carroll Vanities*, to which they contributed "I Gotta Right to Sing the Blues." A month later, back in Harlem, they placed "I've Got the World on a String," among other songs, in the *Cotton Club Parade*. In December, working with a new lyricist, E. Y. ("Yip") Harburg, Arlen had a song in the Broadway play *The Great Magoo*. Initially called "If You Believed in Me," it was retitled "It's Only a Paper Moon" and acquired a second lyricist in Billy Rose when it was used in the national tour of Rose's revue *Crazy Quilt of 1933*. It later was recorded and included in films on its way to becoming another Arlen standard.

Arlen and Koehler scored the biggest hit of 1933 with "Stormy Weather," written for another *Cotton Club Parade* in which it was sung by Ethel Waters. The most successful recording was by Leo Reisman and His Orchestra, with Arlen himself singing. The songwriters' next hit was the title song for the 1934 film *Let's Fall in Love*, which marked Arlen's first trip to Hollywood. They had only a one-picture deal, however, and returned to New York to write a final Cotton Club revue, which included "Ill Wind." They then broke up their partnership amicably so that Arlen could collaborate with Harburg and Ira Gershwin on the Broadway revue *Life Begins at 8:40*, though they sometimes worked together later on. *Life Begins at 8:40*, opening in August 1934, had a successful run of 237 performances and included the hit "You're a Builder-Upper."

Arlen spent his first extended period in Hollywood in 1935 and 1936, writing songs for the films *Strike Me Pink* (starring Eddie Cantor), *The Singing Kid* (starring Al Jolson), *Stage Struck*, and *Gold Diggers of 1937*, all released in 1936. On the last three his lyricist was Harburg, and the two returned to New York to write the Broadway musical *Hooray for What!* Arlen married Anya Taranda on 8 January 1937. They remained married until her death in 1970 and had no children.

Harburg had intended *Hooray for What!* as an antiwar satire, but the show was watered down considerably before it reached Broadway on 1 December 1937, where it lasted a respectable 200 performances. It also led to Arlen and Harburg's being hired for the plum assignment of writing songs for the fantasy movie musical *The Wizard of Oz*. Starring Judy Garland, the film was a box office flop when released in August 1939, though the score featured "Over the Rainbow," which topped the Hit Parade and won the year's Academy Award as best song. Eventually the film was recognized as a classic, not least because of Arlen and Harburg's songs, which also included "If I Only Had a Brain" and "Ding Dong! The Witch Is Dead."

Surprisingly, Arlen found little work for a couple of years. He finally returned to the movie theaters and the record stores in late 1941 with the Oscar-nominated, chart-topping title song from the otherwise forgotten film *Blues in the Night,* a song he wrote with new collaborator Johnny Mercer. A year later Arlen and Mercer enjoyed the same success with "That Old Black Magic," written for the film *Star Spangled Rhythm*. Arlen had a second Academy Award nomination in 1943 with "Happiness Is (Just) a Thing Called Joe," from *Cabin in the Sky*, written with Harburg, and a third the same year with "My Shining Hour," from *The Sky's the Limit*, again with Mercer. *The Sky's the Limit* also featured "One for My Baby (and One More for the Road)," which went on to become a signature song for Frank Sinatra, who called it the ultimate saloon song.

Arlen's next Oscar nomination came for "Now I Know," from the 1944 film *Up in Arms*, which reunited him with Ted Koehler. He next joined with Harburg for the Broadway musical *Bloomer Girl*, which opened 5 October 1944 for a healthy run of 654 performances. At the end of the year, in the film *Here Come the Waves*, star Bing Crosby sang the Arlen and Mercer song "Ac-Cent-Tchu-Ate the Positive," another chart-topper and Academy Award nominee. Six months later came the film *Out of This World*, with a title song that became a hit for Jo Stafford. Arlen and Mercer then tried Broadway, writing songs for the musical *St. Louis Woman* in 1946. It failed despite a much-admired score that included "Come Rain or Come Shine."

The late 1940s and early 1950s were slower for Arlen, though he earned another Academy Award nomination with "For Every Man There's a Woman" (lyrics by Leo Robin), from the 1948 film *Casbah,* and wrote songs for other films with Mercer, Ralph Blane, and Dorothy Fields. But he had a number of projects in release late in 1954: he collaborated with Ira Gershwin on songs for *A Star Is Born*, starring Judy Garland and featuring "The Man That Got Away," and *The Country Girl*, starring Bing Crosby; he also wrote the music for the Broadway musical *House of Flowers,* with Truman Capote doing the book and lyrics. It turned out to be another financial failure with an excellent score. In contrast, the musical *Jamaica* (1957) became a Broadway hit with a run of 557 performances, credited more to star Lena Horne than to the music. Arlen's last Broadway musical, *Saratoga* in 1959, failed.

Arlen contributed to the films *Gay Purr-ee* in 1962 and *I Could Go On Singing* in 1963; both gave him the opportunity to write again for Judy Garland. Among the many other singers who regularly performed his songs, he was particularly championed by Barbra Streisand, and in 1966 she joined him on several tracks of his album *Harold Sings Arlen (With Friend)*. He was in ill health in his later years due to Parkinson's disease and died at age eighty-one. He is buried in Ferncliff Cemetery in suburban Hartsdale, New York.

Harold Arlen was the first major American songwriter of the twentieth century to be inspired primarily by ragtime, dance music, and jazz rather than Tin Pan Alley and show music, and this showed in the vibrancy and rhythmic appeal of his music. A compelling melodist who also had a well-developed dramatic sense, he wrote songs that fit effectively into musicals and films while also independently conquering the airwaves to become hits and infiltrating the public consciousness to become standards. Such songs as "Over the Rainbow," "It's Only a Paper Moon," "I've Got the World on a String," "Stormy Weather," "Blues in the Night," and "That Old Black Magic," have been performed regularly since they were first introduced and remain instantly familiar to generations of listeners, thus marking their composer as one of the greatest songwriters of his century.

★

The standard biography of Arlen is Edward Jablonski's *Harold Arlen: Rhythm, Rainbows, and Blues* (1996), a complete rewrite of his earlier *Harold Arlen: Happy with the Blues* (1961). There is a chapter about Arlen in Alec Wilder's subjective, but nevertheless useful, book of musical analysis, *American Popular Song: The Great Innovators 1900–1950* (1972). Max Wilk, in *They're Playing Our Song* (1973), effectively interviews and profiles Arlen. An obituary is in the *New York Times* (24 Apr. 1986).

WILLIAM J. RUHLMANN

ARMOUR, Richard Willard (*b.* 15 July 1906 in San Pedro, California; *d.* 28 February 1989 in Claremont, California), writer, humorist, and professor of English, famous for his comic and satirical verses, of which over 4,000 appeared in the *New Yorker, Saturday Evening Post,* and other national magazines, and for sixty books of prose and poetry.

Born in San Pedro, California, the port city of Los Angeles County, Armour was the only child of Harry Willard Armour, a pharmacist, and Sue (Wheelock) Armour. In 1912 Harry Armour moved his family from San Pedro to Pomona, where he took over the family drugstore. Richard attended Pomona city schools, working evenings and weekends in the drugstore and as an usher in the Pomona movie theater. He entered Pomona College, in nearby Claremont, in 1923. He was elected to Phi Beta Kappa and graduated with a B.A. degree in 1927. In the fall of that year Armour enrolled as a graduate student at Harvard University, where he received an M.A. degree in 1928. The next year he taught English at the University of Texas at Austin; in 1930 and 1931 he was an instructor at Northwestern University.

With a Dexter fellowship from Harvard, Armour spent parts of 1931 and 1932 doing research at the John Forster Library of the Victoria and Albert Museum in London; in 1932 and 1933 he was professor of English at the University of the Ozarks in Clarksville, Arkansas. He received his Ph.D. in English philology from Harvard in 1933. On 25 December 1932 Armour married Kathleen Fauntleroy Stevens. They had one son, Geoffrey Stevens, and one daughter, Karen Elizabeth.

Armour's first two books, drawn from his Harvard dissertation, were biographical and critical studies of Barry Cornwall (pseudonym of the prolific nineteenth-century English poet Bryan Waller Procter), published in 1935 and 1936. They were followed by *Coleridge the Talker* (1940), which he edited with Raymond F. Howes. From 1934 to 1944 Armour was professor of English at Wells College in Aurora, New York, where he edited *Young Voices: A Book of Wells College Verse* (1941). A reserve officer in the U.S. Army, he was called to active duty in 1942 in the antiaircraft artillery, in which he served through the end of World War II, receiving the Legion of Merit with oak leaf cluster. One of his wartime assignments was to the army general staff. When he was discharged in 1946, he kept his reserve commission, and in 1950 he was recalled to active duty during the Korean War. He subsequently retired as a colonel.

In 1945 Armour was appointed professor of English at Scripps College in Claremont and began his most productive period as a poet and an author. From 1961 to 1963 he was dean of the Scripps College faculty. He also taught English in the Claremont College Graduate School from 1945 until his retirement in 1966.

Among Armour's early books were *Yours for the Asking: A Book of Light Verse* (1942), *Private Lives* (1943), *Golf Bawls* (1946), *Leading with My Left* (1946), and *Writing Light Verse* (1947). He collaborated with Bown Adams in writing a play, *To These Dark Steps* (1943), for the Institute

Richard Armour, 1953. AP/WIDE WORLD PHOTOS

for the Education of the Blind in New York City. Some years later he wrote *For Partly Proud Parents: Light Verse About Children* (1950).

In the early 1950s Armour began a series of best-selling books of light verse and satirical prose, beginning with *It All Started with Columbus: Being an Unexpurgated, Unabridged, and Unlikely History of the United States from Christopher Columbus to the Present* (1953). Avoiding the verbose and pedantic style often found in textbooks, he wrote briefly and simply, spoofing traditions and clichés, and taking ingenious liberties with names of people, such as American Vesuvius (for whom Columbus named America) and Lewis N. Clark, and of places, such as the Eeerie Canal, and ships, such as Sir Francis Drake's *Golden Behind*. Frequently reprinted, a 1975 edition was titled *It All Would Have Startled Columbus*.

In *Light Armour: Playful Poems on Practically Everything* (1954), Armour published a collection of whimsical verse, which became a best-seller and which ended with a double quatrain on gossips:

> When gossips die, as mortals must,
> And leave their earthly home,
> Their punishment will be, I trust,
> Eternally to roam
> Down dismal paths and darkened pits
> And empty halls of hell
> With heads crammed full of juicy bits,
> And not a soul to tell.

It All Started with Europa, spoofing continental history, appeared in 1954. It was followed in 1956 by *It All Started with Eve: Being an Account of Certain Famous Women Endowed with Some Quality Which Drives Men Mad.* Armour's *Twisted Tales from Shakespeare: In Which Shakespeare's Best-Known Plays Are Presented in a New Light,* was published in 1957. *It All Started with Marx: A Brief and Objective History of Russian Communism,* a facetious history of the Russian Revolution, appeared in 1958.

Armour's *Drug Store Days: My Youth Among the Pills and Potions* (1959) was published in England as *Pills, Potions, and Granny* (1959). He followed this book with *The Classics Reclassified: In Which Certain Famous Books Are Not So Much Digested as Indigested* (1960) and *A Safari into Satire* (1961).

In 1962 Armour's *Golf Is a Four-Letter Word: The Intimate Confessions of a Hooked Slicer,* and *Armour's Almanac; or, Around the Year in 365 Days,* were published. In 1963 his *Through Darkest Adolescence: With Tongue in Cheek and Pen in Checkbook* appeared, followed by *American Lit Relit: A Short History of American Literature.* His *Going Around in Academic Circles: A Low View of Higher Education* (1965) contained incisive caricatures of colleagues and acquaintances in higher education.

Armour's first children's book, *The Year Santa Went Modern* (1965), was followed by *The Adventures of Egbert the Easter Egg* (1965), *Animals on the Ceiling* (1966), *A Dozen Dinosaurs* (1967), and *Odd Old Mammals: Animals After the Dinosaurs* (1968). Later children's books were *All Sizes and Shapes of Monkeys and Apes* (1970), *Who's in Holes?* (1971), *The Strange Dreams of Rover Jones* (1973), *Sea Full of Whales* (1974), *Strange Monsters of the Sea* (1979), *Insects All Around Us* (1981), and *Have You Ever Wished You Were Something Else?* (1983).

Later books of adult humor and whimsy were *It All Started with Hippocrates: A Mercifully Brief History of Medicine* (1966); *It All Started with Stones and Clubs: Being a Short History of War and Weaponry from Earliest Times to the Present* (1967); and *A Satirist Looks at the World* (1967). Following soon after were *My Life with Women: Confessions of a Domesticated Male* (1968); *A Diabolical Dictionary of Education* (1969); *English Lit Relit: A Short History of English Literature* (1969); and *A Short History of Sex* (1970).

During the 1970s he wrote *Out of My Mind* (1972); *It All Started with Freshman English* (1973); *Going Like Sixty: A Lighthearted Look at the Later Years* (1974); *The Academic Bestiary* (1974); *The Spouse in the House* (1975); *The Happy Bookers: A History of Librarians and Their World* (1976); and *It All Started with Nudes: An Artful History of Art* (1977).

Armour wrote a syndicated newspaper column, "Armour's Armory," and appeared on national television shows. By his own estimate he lectured at some 200 colleges and universities in the United States, Europe, and Asia. Most notably, Armour was a visiting lecturer in 1933 and 1934 at the University of Freiburg in Germany; Carnegie Visiting Professor at the University of Hawaii in 1957; Chancellor's Lecturer at California State University and Colleges from 1964 to 1989; Author of the Year at Stanford University in 1965; writer-in-residence at Redlands University in 1974; and visiting professor at Whittier College in 1975.

One of his best-known couplets is "Shake and shake the catsup bottle. / None will come, and then a lot'll." Another favorite is "The older I get the less I pine for / Things I have to stand in line for."

Richard Armour suffered during his last few years from complications due to Parkinson's disease. He died in a Claremont convalescent hospital.

Substantial collections of Richard Armour's papers are in the Denison Library at Scripps College in Claremont, California, and in the Department of Special Collections of the Boston University Library. Among his books containing personal reminiscences are *Drug Store Days* (1959), *My Life with Women* (1968), and *The Spouse in the House* (1975). Biographical sketches appear in the *Saturday Evening Post* (28 Jan. 1950) and in Marjorie Dent Candee, ed., *Current Biography* 1958 (1959). Obituaries are in the *Los Angeles Times* (1 Mar. 1989) and the *New York Times* (2 Mar. 1989).

DAVID W. HERON

ARMSTRONG, Herbert W. (*b.* 31 July 1892 in Des Moines, Iowa; *d.* 16 January 1986 in Pasadena, California), founder of the Worldwide Church of God, whose Pasadena, California, headquarters continues to oversee hundreds of churches around the world.

Armstrong was the first of four children of Quakers Horace Elon Armstrong, a businessman, and Eva (Wright) Armstrong. As a youth he showed little interest in religion. He attended North High School in Des Moines. Ambitious and intellectually aggressive, he sold display ads for the *Des Moines Daily Capital* and the *Merchants Trade Journal.* In January 1917 he met Loma Dillon, and they were married the following July; they had four children. According to official church writings, shortly after their marriage, Loma had a dream of three angels, one of whom embraced the Armstrongs and told them Christ was coming shortly and had "important work for them to do in preparing for His coming." Armstrong reportedly dismissed the dream as insignificant.

The Armstrongs settled in Salem, Oregon. In 1926 a friend convinced Loma Armstrong, a Methodist, that Christians should observe the Sabbath on Saturday instead of Sunday. Herbert Armstrong, alarmed at what appeared to be religious fanaticism and gullibility, vowed to study the issue to set his wife straight. Exhaustive research in primary sources, however, convinced him of the legitimacy of observance of the Sabbath on Saturday. The Armstrongs thereafter affiliated themselves with the sabbatarian Church of God, headquartered in Stanberry, Missouri. As a layman, Armstrong studied the Scriptures assiduously between 1926 and 1931, developing understandings that would become the foundational doctrines of the church he would eventually found.

With the encouragement of the Oregon Conference of the Church of God, Armstrong preached his first sermon in 1928 near Jefferson, Oregon, and by June 1931 he was an ordained minister of the church. Preaching tours in tent meetings that year established his reputation as a pulpiteer. When the Church of God suffered an internal organizational schism in 1933, Armstrong established his own Radio Church of God.

Armstrong started broadcasting a Sunday morning radio program over tiny, 100-watt radio station KORE in Eugene, Oregon, a program that cost $2.50 in broadcasting fees at a time when Armstrong's salary as a minister was only $3.00 a week. The success of his Radio Church of God encouraged him to add stations in Portland (KXL) and Salem (KSLM) in 1936. He stepped up to a more powerful broadcaster, KWJJ, in 1937, thus establishing a broadcasting network that soon carried his message across the United States and into Canada and Alaska. In his program, "The World Tomorrow," he avoided overt preaching, offering instead news analysis with religious comment. At its peak the program aired over 374 radio stations and 165 television stations worldwide; in 1968 the organization was renamed the Worldwide Church of God.

Always the gifted advertising salesman with a love of the printed page, Armstrong initiated a church bulletin in April 1933. This quickly grew into a weekly magazine titled the *Plain Truth,* distributed worldwide with a peak printing run of 7.5 million in 1985. By 1946 the church had relocated to Pasadena, California, was operating its own printing plant, and was broadcasting internationally in prime-time radio slots. In 1947 Armstrong founded Ambassador College to train leaders for the church. (The college became Ambassador Center, located at Azusa Pacific University, and provides Worldwide Church of God men and women with an accredited Christian education.) Meanwhile, he was writing and publishing prolifically and crisscrossing the country on baptizing tours. Self-appointed the pastor general, he and the Worldwide Church of God became a phenomenon on the American religious scene, preaching a message that was, in his words, "radically different from what mainstream Christianity teaches."

Herbert W. Armstrong. WORLDWIDE CHURCH OF GOD

According to Armstrong, the Worldwide Church of God restored eighteen essential truths that Christianity had either lost or ignored, including the church's proper name, Sabbath keeping, baptism by immersion, faith healing, three levels of tithing, the ministry of angels, the adoption of Jewish feast days, and the indissolubility of marriage. Armstrong accepted the divinity of Christ but rejected trinitarian language. He condemned any reliance on medical science, revised the commonly accepted understanding of the Passion Week calendar, and declared that British-Israelism—the theory that Anglo-Saxons are the descendants of the "lost" ten northern tribes of Israel—was the key to understanding biblical prophecy.

In the 1970s scandal rocked the church. The former wife of a church executive won a $1.26 million libel suit, claiming that Armstrong and other church leaders had tried to smear her reputation after her divorce in 1976. When several former church members charged that Armstrong and other leaders had diverted millions of dollars in church money for their own use, the California attorney general placed the church's finances under control of a court-appointed receiver. The state eventually dropped the charges, but not before nationwide press coverage brought the church and Armstrong unwanted publicity. In 1977, ten years after the death of his wife, Armstrong married Ramona Martin. Their marriage ended in an acrimonious divorce in 1984. Armstrong's son Garner accused his father of violating the doctrine of the indissolubility of marriage. Armstrong died in his sleep in Pasadena and was buried at Mountain View Cemetery in Altadena, California.

Armstrong's handpicked successor, Joseph Tkach, gradually led the church away from most of the unique doctrinal and operational positions that were originally a part of Armstrong's message, so that relatively little remains of "Armstrongism" in the Worldwide Church of God.

★

Armstrong wrote a two-volume *Autobiography* (1986–1987). His successors have written favorably of him in Joseph Tkach, *Transformed by Truth* (1997), and Stanley Rader, *Against the Gates of Hell* (1980). Criticism appears in Roger R. Chambers, *The Plain Truth about Armstrongism* (1972); Marion J. McNair, *Armstrongism, Religion or Rip-off?* (1977); and Robert L. Sumner, *Armstrongism: The "Worldwide Church of God"* (1974). J. L. F. Buchner published a bibliography on Armstrongism in Australia in 1983, which is in the Library of Congress. An obituary is in the *New York Times* (17 Jan. 1986).

THEODORE N. THOMAS

ARNAZ, Desi (*b.* 2 March 1917 in Santiago, Cuba; *d.* 2 December 1986 in Del Mar, California), musician, bandleader, actor, and television producer who is best known for his portrayal of Ricky Ricardo opposite Lucille Ball on the long-running television comedy *I Love Lucy*.

Born Desiderio Alberto Arnaz y de Acha III, Arnaz was the only child of Desiderio Alberto II, a mayor of Santiago, and

Lolita (de Acha) Arnaz y de Acha, an heiress to the Bacardi Rum fortune. Arnaz attended Colegio de Dolores in Santiago until the 1933 Batista revolution forced the family to immigrate to the United States. He briefly attended St. Patrick's High School in Miami and worked at several menial jobs. Describing these years in his autobiography, *A Book* (1976), he stated: "Exile in Miami was a time for survival, when I perfected many interesting trades such as mobile canary-cage cleaner and broken-mosaic-tile salesman."

In 1934 he began working as a guitarist and singer with a hotel rhumba band. He later joined Xavier Cugat's orchestra as a drummer and featured singer, eventually leaving to form his own band, the Desi Arnaz Orchestra.

Arnaz performed on Broadway in the Rodgers and Hart musical *Too Many Girls* in 1939. The next year RKO Studios made a movie based on the play and brought Arnaz to Hollywood to reprise his stage role as a Cuban football player. The film starred the comedy actress Lucille Ball, with whom Arnaz began a much-publicized romance. They were married on 30 November 1940 and would have two children, both of whom would become actors: Lucie Désirée Arnaz and Desiderio Alberto Arnaz IV ("Little Desi").

Arnaz was drafted into the U.S. Army in May 1943 and served in the Medical Corps. He was discharged in 1945 with the rank of staff sergeant and returned to work as a bandleader and occasional movie actor. His accent and appearance kept him limited to specialty musical numbers in a Hollywood that generally required Latin actors to conform to a "colorful" stereotype. According to Kathleen Brady's book *Lucille,* studio head Louis B. Mayer once compared Arnaz to Mayer's racehorse, who "looks very common when he's around the barn, but when they put a saddle on him, and he goes out onto the track, you know he's a champion. The same thing happens to you when they hang that drum around your shoulder. Up to that point you're just another Mexican."

Arnaz's musical tours and Ball's acting career kept the couple apart most of the time, which strained their marriage. Ball filed for divorce in 1944 but reconciled before the decree became final. In order to work together they formed Desilu Productions in 1950 and tried to interest television executives in a comedy series starring themselves. The networks initially rejected the idea, believing audiences would not accept the idea of Ball married to a Cuban. To refute this prejudice, Arnaz and Ball developed a husband-and-wife comedy act entitled "Sally Sweet–Cuban Pete" and successfully toured the East Coast vaudeville circuit.

The comedy act's popularity prompted the Philip Morris Company to sponsor Desilu's comedy series, *I Love Lucy.* Arnaz and Hollywood cinematographer Karl Freund developed production plans using three cameras and a live audience. Arnaz and Ball accepted salary cuts in exchange

Desi Arnaz. ARCHIVE PHOTOS

for ownership of the recorded programs. *I Love Lucy* first aired on CBS on 15 October 1951 and soon became one of the nation's most popular shows. Arnaz played a character based on himself, a successful nightclub bandleader, but in the show he was constantly befuddled, if not tormented, by his wife's perpetual high jinks (often in conspiracy with the Mertzes) and frantic attempts to break into show business. Differences in their cultural backgrounds inevitably created humorous tensions, but audiences could also closely identify with the ongoing development of their onstage marriage: the young couple's initial adjustment to married life in the first television season, and then, in later seasons, their experience of parenthood, increased prosperity, and eventually their move to the suburbs. After the series went off the air in 1957, CBS purchased the rights to the recorded shows for $4 million.

Shortly after that sale Arnaz purchased RKO Studios, not telling his wife until after he closed the deal. They renamed it Desilu Studios and used its sound stages for the production of numerous other shows, including *Our Miss Brooks, The Texan, The Ann Sothern Show,* and *The Untouchables,* as well as diversifying into motion pictures, records, music publishing, and real estate development.

Arnaz played a crucial role in Desilu's growth and expansion, particularly in his selection of talented executives.

He had a phenomenal memory for scripts and business details and could be charming to peers and subordinates. His obsessive perfectionism, however, became counterproductive as the firm expanded. Needing to maintain constant hands-on control, he was unable to delegate authority and found himself under increasing stress. He began alienating many associates by his abusive language and behavior during his periods of drinking, which increased in the late 1950s. His daughter recalled, "He always drank—I think from a young guy on the beach, for all the stories he told, it was part of his upbringing."

Having been raised in a culture of machismo, Arnaz made no effort to restrain his drinking or womanizing. Both addictions increased in direct proportion to his ever-growing management duties at Desilu. Not surprisingly, Ball became increasingly critical of her husband's behavior, and even as the couple accumulated millions of dollars from their Desilu Productions, their marriage deteriorated. Arnaz and Ball finally divorced in May 1960, with each retaining 25 percent ownership of Desilu Productions. Arnaz ceased his involvement with the company and Ball bought out his share in 1962 for $3 million, taking over as Desilu's president.

Ironically, Ball (who disclaimed any particular business talent) turned out to be a better manager than Arnaz, having no problem with delegating authority to competent managers. She expanded Desilu operations and later sold the company to Gulf and Western Industries in 1967 for $17 million.

After leaving Desilu, Arnaz tried breeding and training Thoroughbred racehorses at his ranch in Corona, California. He married Edith ("Edie") Mack Hirsch, the former wife of Kal-Kan pet food magnate Clement Hirsch, on 2 March 1963. The couple had no children

Arnaz later returned to television to produce and appear in *The In-Laws.* The comedy series was broadcast on NBC from 10 September 1967 to 7 September 1968. After an unsuccessful attempt to produce another show, he appeared as a guest star on a 1970 Western, *The Man from Shiloh,* and made several other unsuccessful comeback attempts. He told reporters, "The simple truth is I was getting tired of seeing Ricardo Montalban and Fernando Lamas in all these Mexican roles." But his daughter later explained, "He was depressed and disappointed in later life that that was all there was, *I Love Lucy,* and when it was over, the industry didn't trust him the way they used to."

Arnaz chaired the Viva Nixon Committee, composed of Hispanic supporters of Richard Nixon, in 1968. His final acting role was a small part in a Francis Ford Coppola film, *The Escape Artist* (1982). He was hospitalized for lung cancer in 1986 and died on 2 December of that year. Danny Thomas, whose comedy series *Make Room for Daddy* had been produced by Desilu, delivered the eulogy at the funeral. His remains were cremated and the ashes scattered at sea.

Playing a successful businessman and perennial straight man in the most popular comedy show of the 1950s, Arnaz stood out in a period when television usually portrayed "ethnics" (if they showed them at all) in cruel stereotypes. Arnaz had the talent not only to become a major television star but also to develop his own television studio and become one of the most important players among the independent production companies. Arnaz was an acknowledged genius in the new television industry—but one with severe flaws. These eventually led both to the breakup of his marriage and to an undesired early retirement, although the image that remains forever in the public's mind is that of the exasperated, but warm and loving, husband of Lucille Ball.

★

Many of the papers of Arnaz and Ball have been published by their daughter as a CD-ROM, *Lucy and Desi: The Scrapbooks, Vol 1: Made for Each Other* (1977). Arnaz is frequently mentioned in the numerous biographies of his wife: Joe Morella and Edward Epstein, *Lucy: The Bittersweet Life of Lucille Ball* (1973, revised as *Forever Lucy,* 1986); James Gregory, *The Lucille Ball Story* (1974); Kathleen Brady, *Lucille: The Life of Lucille Ball* (1994); and Lucille Ball's memoir, *Love, Lucy* (1996), which was written in the early 1960s and published posthumously. Bart Andrews, *The "I Love Lucy" Book* (1985), and Jim Brochu, *Lucy in the Afternoon* (1990), are studies of Desilu television shows. The memoir of Robert Stack, *Straight Shooting* (1980), written with Mark Evans, describes the work of Desilu on its early series, and the production company is also covered in Coyne Steven Sanders and Tom Gilbert, *Desilu: The Story of Lucille Ball and Desi Arnaz* (1993). An obituary is in the *New York Times* (3 Dec. 1986).

STEPHEN MARSHALL

ASCH, Moses ("Moe") (*b.* 2 December 1905 in Warsaw, Poland; *d.* 19 October 1986 in New York City), record company executive and founder of Folkways Records, best known for his efforts to propagate international folk music.

Moses ("Moe") Asch was one of the four children of Sholem Asch, a renowned Yiddish writer, and Madja Spiro; the family came to the United States from Poland in the last major wave of Jewish immigration in 1915. Brought up in Brooklyn, Moe showed an early talent in electronics and was a full-fledged radio ham at the age of fourteen. Shortly after the end of World War I his father sent him to Germany to study electronic engineering.

On his return to the United States in about 1926, Asch embarked on a career as a sound engineer in New York. He had a letter of introduction to David Sarnoff, head of the new Radio Corporation of America. Sarnoff, using his

Moe Asch. J. MANNING/NYT PERMISSIONS

personal telegraph key, sent a message to RCA's engineering division: "Put this young man to work." Asch's employment at RCA involved cataloging circuits for Radiolas, the first mass-produced radio sets. In this capacity, he created the nomenclature for some of the first radio components.

After leaving RCA, Asch worked with Lee DeForest in Jersey City, New Jersey. DeForest had pioneered loudspeaker technology and won the patent for the feedback circuit process. His discoveries made possible the use of sound in motion pictures. Asch worked with DeForest for a short period on transformers and later became the eastern repair representative for Stromberg-Carlson, the elite company in radio. Using what he had learned in working with DeForest, Asch built the loudspeakers for President Franklin Delano Roosevelt's second inaugural speech at Madison Square Garden in New York City in 1937. He also installed sound equipment in Yiddish theaters on Manhattan's Lower East Side.

Asch began making records to supply radio stations like WEVD-New York (named after socialist leader Eugene V. Debs), which needed recordings of foreign and ethnic material. He entered the recording business in 1939 when RCA and Columbia dropped their international series, leaving radio stations without ethnic records for immigrant audiences. Specifically, WEVD needed Jewish records. Asch's first recording was *In the Beginning,* his father's Bible stories for children. He released it in 1939 under the label Asch Records, which he founded that year at 117 West Forty-sixth Street in Manhattan.

The first commercial issue of the Asch label was *Jewish Folk Songs* by the Bagelman Sisters. Then Asch made a record of the Kol Nidre, the holy song of the Jewish people, with Cantor Waldman, who was a regular on WEVD. Asch credited this record with getting his foot in the door, as RCA took its best-selling recording of Cantor Rosenblatt singing the Kol Nidre off the market just when Asch's was issued.

In determining the international recording focus for Asch Records, Asch was encouraged by his father and many other people, including Albert Einstein, who was a friend of his father. In 1941 Asch branched out beyond ethnic recordings when Si Rady, an off-Broadway producer, introduced him to the blues singer Huddie Ledbetter, known as Leadbelly. John Lomax had discovered Leadbelly and made recordings of him singing southern folk songs for the Library of Congress. Asch had Leadbelly record children's songs for Asch Records. These recordings led to great controversy, as Leadbelly was a twice-jailed convict and murderer.

In 1944 Asch Records became Disc, and in 1947 the name of the company changed again, to Folkways. The name was coined by Harold Courlander, a shrewd businessman, novelist, and maverick scholar who joined Asch in 1947 and traveled the world recording folk music for him. The name Folkways reflected Asch's philosophy, which saw culture as an outgrowth of folk art.

Folkways Records survived for four decades despite erratic distribution and cash flow. Over that time Folkways issued as many as forty titles a year, encompassing a wide range of musical, literary, political, religious, instructional, and experimental recordings. To Asch, sales were necessary but irrelevant. This utter disregard for the demands of the marketplace mystified many industry peers, but Asch clearly made records for posterity, not prosperity. When asked to describe his theory of recording, he replied, "What I'm interested in is what intellectual knowledge do we get from a record, rather than is this super high fidelity or does it reach 10,000 cycles."

Asch had a strictly utilitarian view of recording as a means of documentation, which explains why a steady stream of sociologists, anthropologists, and musicologists beat a path to his door. Asch cultivated a worldwide network of traveling scholars. He saw himself as a conduit, not an interpreter, and he accepted the rough edges and mistakes of field recordings as the price of authenticity. Moreover, he viewed the artist as a transmitter of cultural information rather than as an individual working in a creative vacuum. He viewed such techniques as multiple takes and overdubs as indulgences that threaten honesty and spontaneity. He incorporated cassettes into his catalog grudgingly; he would not have welcomed CDs.

Although best known for folk recordings by Woody Guthrie and Pete Seeger, Folkways produced ethnic, country and bluegrass, blues, spoken word, classical, children's, and sea chantey recordings, as well as an extensive repertoire of electronic digital computer compositions. While labels came and went with the tides of fashion, Folkways continued on. Soon after Asch died, the Smithsonian Institution acquired the Folkways collection. Moses Asch had amassed some 5,000 reels of master tapes and an equal number of acetate disks from his Asch, Disc, and Folkways labels. Asch was survived by his wife, Frances, and their son, Michael.

★

A number of articles contain information about Asch's life and career. They include: "Music: Offbeat," *Time* (25 Feb. 1946); "Scholastic's Remarkable Man of Sound," *Senior Scholastic* 89, no. 9 (11 Nov. 1966); Tony Scherman, "This Man Captured the True Sounds of a Whole World," *Smithsonian* (Aug. 1987); Gary Kenton, "Moses Asch of Folkways," *Audio* (July 1990); Tom Piazza, "Pure Roots: The Smithsonian Has Reawakened Folkways Records, a Peerless Repository of Our Native Music," *Atlantic Monthly* (Apr. 1995); and Gene Santoro, "Smithsonian CDs," *Nation* (14 Aug. 1995). An obituary is in the *New York Times* (21 Oct. 1986).

KAREN M. VENTURELLA

ASTAIRE, Fred (*b.* 10 May 1899 in Omaha, Nebraska; *d.* 22 June 1987 in Los Angeles, California), actor and dancer whose peerless artistry kept him at the forefront of American theater for many years; his grace, elegance, and urbanity, coupled with his innovative approach to the depiction of dance on film, established him as an icon of the film musical.

Born Frederick Austerlitz II, Astaire was the son of Frederick E. Austerlitz and Ann (Geilus) Astaire, a schoolteacher. A Viennese emigrant, Astaire's father had traveled to the United States in 1895, settling in Omaha, where he eventually worked for a brewery; Astaire's mother was a native Nebraskan. Astaire's sister, Adele, was born in September 1897, twenty months before Fred. The family lived in a wooden frame house near downtown Omaha.

Early on it was clear to Astaire's parents that Adele had an unmistakable gift for performing. When their father lost his job after Nebraska banned alcoholic beverages, Fred and Adele traveled to New York City with their mother and were enrolled in the Claude Alvienne Dancing School.

Fred Astaire, 1949. JERRY VERMILYE

Adele was considered the more talented of the two. Around this time, the decision was made to change the family name. (Astaire later commented that the name may have been derived from an Alsace-Lorraine uncle named L'Astaire.)

To showcase the young Astaires, Claude Alvienne devised a wedding cake routine that eventually won them a coveted spot on the Orpheum vaudeville circuit. Following a two-year hiatus, during which the Astaires attended a school in Highwood Park, New Jersey, Fred and Adele, with the help of dance instructor Ned Wayburn, created a new, more mature act, which was disappointingly received. All the while it was assumed that Adele was the principal attraction, surpassing her brother Fred in expertise and professionalism.

Under the tutelage of a new teacher named Aurelia Coccia, the Astaires, although still in their teens, finally developed into seasoned professionals who toured the top vaudeville circuit. In 1917 they were offered a spot in a Shubert revue called *Over the Top,* and after appearing in *The Passing Show of 1918,* they became a popular attraction in such musicals as *Apple Blossoms* (1918), *For Goodness Sake* (1922), and *The Bunch and Judy* (1922). By 1924 they were established theater stars, performing in *Lady, Be Good!* which featured a score by George and Ira Gershwin. Another Gershwin score enhanced their musical hit, *Funny*

Face (1927). At this point Adele's star continued to shine a little more brightly than her brother's; her saucy charm enchanted audiences, while Fred remained the callow young sophisticate.

The year 1930 proved to be personally significant for the Astaires. During the short run of their musical *Smiles,* Astaire managed to meet and occasionally date a pert young redhead named Ginger Rogers, who was appearing in *Girl Crazy.* Meanwhile, Adele fell in love with a young Englishman named Lord Charles Cavendish and decided to marry him and retire from the stage. The Astaires' last show together, *The Band Wagon* (1931), featured a tuneful Howard Dietz–Arthur Schwartz score. That year also marked Fred's meeting with a Long Island socialite named Phyllis Baker Potter, whom he married on 12 July 1933. They had two children, Fred, Jr., and Ava, and Potter brought to the marriage a son, Peter, by a previous union. The marriage lasted until her death in 1954.

After starring without Adele in Cole Porter's *Gay Divorcée* (1932), Astaire went to Hollywood, where he signed a contract with RKO Studios. He was assigned a role in the musical *Flying Down to Rio* (1933), but first he was loaned to Metro-Goldwyn-Mayer, where he made his film debut in *Dancing Lady* (1933), performing in two musical numbers with the studio's glamorous but musically inexperienced star Joan Crawford.

When it was finally filmed, *Flying Down to Rio* turned out to be an infinitely more auspicious showcase for Astaire. Although he was relegated to a secondary lead (the stars were Gene Raymond and Dolores Del Rio), Astaire had the singular good fortune to be partnered with Ginger Rogers, the young actress he had known in New York. When they came together in a Latin-oriented number called "The Carioca," something miraculous occurred: her down-to-earth brashness blended with his airy man-about-town sophistication, and when they danced, their pleasure in each other was palpable.

When audiences responded enthusiastically to their teaming, the studio lost no time in putting them together again in a film version of Astaire's Broadway musical, now renamed *The Gay Divorcée* (1934). Seldom has film history arrived in so lighthearted a package. The film's story was flimsy, but the Astaire-Rogers dances to the Cole Porter music were not only sublime, they were also revolutionary. Ever the perfectionist, Astaire insisted on showing the full figures of the dancers and gave the musical numbers an emotional center, even an erotic charge. The couple never kissed (at least not until years later), but they were clearly making love on the dance floor, especially in their exquisite duet to "Night and Day." (It was also clear that Astaire's light, unassuming voice was the perfect instrument to express his ardor.)

After returning briefly to secondary leads in *Roberta* (1935), Astaire and Rogers evolved into Astaire-and-Rogers, an entity whose charm, grace, and style would never be surpassed on screen. Musical after musical, embellished with songs by such master composers as Irving Berlin, George Gershwin, and Jerome Kern, displayed their matchless appeal. *Top Hat* (1935), arguably their best film, found them dancing incomparably to Berlin songs in art deco settings and also gave Astaire his quintessential solo dance to "Top Hat, White Tie, and Tails." *Follow the Fleet* (1936) had sailor Astaire wooing dance hall hostess Rogers to Berlin melodies, while *Swing Time* (1936) delighted audiences with musical numbers (score by Jerome Kern and Dorothy Fields) that ranged from Astaire's astonishing tribute to dancer Bill Robinson ("Bojangles of Harlem") to the climactic duet that summed up the team's film-long relationship ("Never Gonna Dance"). By the time of *Shall We Dance* (1937), it was clear that some of the bloom was off the rose, and despite a good Gershwin score, the movie did not fare particularly well at the box office. After a change of partners (with pallid Joan Fontaine substituting for perky Ginger Rogers) in *A Damsel in Distress* (1937) and two more movies with Rogers (*Carefree* in 1938 and *The Story of Vernon and Irene Castle* in 1939), the two went their separate ways.

The six years in which Astaire danced with Rogers had been richly rewarding, for the team itself and for all those who took pleasure in their rapport on screen. Still, there were those whose contribution to the success of the Ginger-and-Fred musicals cannot be overlooked: producer Pandro S. Berman; Mark Sandrich, who directed five of the films; Allan Scott, who coauthored most of the films; and especially choreographer Hermes Pan, who codesigned and rehearsed Astaire's dances with the star.

In the years just after the team parted company, Astaire's film career was at a low ebb. Without the matchless give-and-take of Ginger Rogers, he was partnered in inferior films with actresses who could not measure up as dancers (Paulette Goddard in *Second Chorus,* 1940; Joan Leslie in *The Sky's the Limit,* 1943), or with an expert dancer who was not entirely suited to his style (Eleanor Powell in *Broadway Melody of 1940*). He had a ravishing partner in Rita Hayworth in two musicals (*You'll Never Get Rich,* 1941; *You Were Never Lovelier,* 1942), but her film-goddess hauteur was somewhat at odds with his lighter-than-air sophistication. Brought to Paramount for two Irving Berlin musicals opposite Bing Crosby (*Holiday Inn,* 1942; *Blue Skies,* 1946), he was obliged to play Crosby's diffident pal and, despite a few brilliant dancing turns, he seemed somehow diminished. Yet he remained personally active during the war years, touring to sell war bonds, or opening the first of a chain of dance studios under his name on Park Avenue.

Luckily, Astaire was now offered a long-term contract

by MGM, which was establishing an enviable reputation for stylish musical films. These films may have lacked the intimacy and romantic aura of the best Astaire-Rogers vehicles, but they allowed Astaire to experiment with his dancing skill. In the star-laden revue *Ziegfeld Follies* (1946), his first for the studio since *Dancing Lady,* his numbers included the dazzling "Limehouse Blues," an exotic minidrama staged by the director Vincente Minnelli, with Astaire as an ill-fated Chinese coolie in a London slum.

For the balance of the 1940s and into the 1950s, Astaire found a compatible home for his art at Louis B. Mayer's studio. Teamed for the first time with Judy Garland in Irving Berlin's *Easter Parade* (1948), he was charged by her energy and ebullience, and their best numbers together, especially "A Couple of Swells," are pure exhilaration. When Garland was unable to return for a rematch in *The Barkleys of Broadway* (1949), the studio summoned Astaire's old partner Ginger Rogers for one last turn together around the dance floor. (That year Astaire was awarded a special honorary Oscar.) He played songwriter Bert Kalmar in the enjoyable musical biography *Three Little Words* (1950), and he costarred with young Jane Powell in *Royal Wedding* (1951). The latter film featured Astaire's gravity-defying dance on the walls and ceiling of his hotel room.

Following a misstep with the leaden musical *The Belle of New York* (1952), Astaire starred in his most memorable MGM effort, *The Band Wagon* (1953). This effervescent musical borrowed some of the songs from the 1931 revue of the same name, but most of the movie created its very own sparkle, with stylish direction by Vincente Minnelli, a witty Betty Comden–Adolph Green screenplay that fleshed out the standard backstage plot, and a talented cast that included the lithe dancer Cyd Charisse and the British musical comedy star Jack Buchanan. Musical highlights included a rapturous Central Park duet by Astaire and Charisse to "Dancing in the Dark," and a satiric "Girl Hunt" ballet that spoofed Mickey Spillane's hard-boiled mystery novels.

By this time Astaire, now in his fifties, was ready to wind down (or at least slow down) his film career, but there was one more superb effort in the offing. After a middling *Daddy Long Legs* (1955), with Leslie Caron, Astaire costarred with the exquisite Audrey Hepburn in *Funny Face* (1957), one of his very best late-career musicals. Directed at Paramount by Stanley Donen, the film had Astaire as a high-fashion photographer who turns bookish sparrow Hepburn into a glamorous swan and model. The movie's virtues, however, were mainly in the splendid Gershwin score (with some songs from the 1927 stage musical of the same name), a visually stunning production, and top-notch musical numbers.

After dancing with Cyd Charisse in *Silk Stockings* (1957), a moderately pleasing musical adaptation of the 1939 comedy *Ninotchka,* Astaire turned his attention from film to television, starring from 1958 to 1960 in three highly acclaimed musical specials. For the most part, however, his dancing shoes were set aside for dramatic roles on the small screen, turning up again for two television specials in 1968 and 1972. He danced one last time on screen as the Irish codger Finian McLonergan in *Finian's Rainbow* (1968), adapted from the long-running stage musical. For the balance of his career, Astaire confined himself to dramatic roles in such films as *On the Beach* (1959), *The Pleasure of His Company* (1961), and *The Towering Inferno* (1974); for his performance in the last of these he received an Oscar nomination as best supporting actor.

In his later years Astaire was often honored by his peers. In 1978 he was among the first to receive the Kennedy Center Honors for lifetime achievement, and in 1981 he was given the ninth Life Achievement Award from the American Film Institute. On a personal note, Astaire, who had always been a horse-racing enthusiast, had married former jockey Robyn Smith on 24 June 1980. After years of quiet retirement, he died of pneumonia at age eighty-eight. He is buried in Oakwood Memorial Park in Chatsworth, California.

Moving from the nimble-footed if slightly callow young man of his early stage years, to the supremely elegant, extraordinarily graceful man-about-town who romanced and danced with Ginger Rogers, to the mature figure who brought class and style to the golden era of MGM musicals, Fred Astaire secured a lasting place in film history. It is reassuring to know that somewhere, at any given moment, even if only on a television screen, this marvelous performer continues to dance blithely down the corridors of time.

★

Fred Astaire, *Steps in Time* (1959), is his autobiography. Books on his life and career include Stanley Green and Bert Goldblatt, *Starring Fred Astaire* (1973); Stephen Harvey, *Fred Astaire* (1974); Michael Freeland, *Fred Astaire* (1976); Bob Thomas, *Astaire: The Man, the Dancer* (1984); John Mueller, *Astaire Dancing: The Musical Films* (1985); Tim Satchell, *Astaire: The Biography* (1987); and Sarah Giles, *Fred Astaire: His Friends Talk* (1988). The best book on Astaire's films with Ginger Rogers is Arlene Croce, *The Fred Astaire and Ginger Rogers Book* (1972). Obituaries are in the *New York Times* (23 June 1987) and *Variety* (24 June 1987).

TED SENNETT

ASTOR, Mary (*b.* 3 May 1906 in Quincy, Illinois; *d.* 25 September 1987 in Woodland Hills, California), actress who appeared in more than 100 movies, as well as on stage and television; she is best known for her portrayal of beautiful, sophisticated women in films of the 1940s, including *The Great Lie* and *The Maltese Falcon*.

Mary Astor in *The Maltese Falcon,* 1941. POPPERFOTO/ARCHIVE PHOTOS

Born Lucile Langhanke, Astor was the only child of Helen de Vasconcellos and Otto Ludwig Wilhelm Langhanke, a German émigré who worked as a teacher of his native language. Astor later wrote that her father "ruled his little family with an iron hand."

In the summer of 1913 the family moved to a farm. Astor attended Highland School, a two-room schoolhouse where she enjoyed history, reading, and spelling. In 1917 she was one of eight winners of a beauty contest sponsored by *Motion Picture Magazine*. Her father decided to move the family to the South Side of Chicago, where he could groom his attractive daughter for movie stardom. Astor graduated from the Kenwood-Loring School for Girls in 1919, a beautiful but painfully shy young woman.

By June 1920 her parents had saved enough money to move to New York City to seek their daughter's fame and fortune. In September, Lucile Langhanke was hired for six months at $60 a week by Famous Players–Lasky (later part of Paramount) and her name was changed to Mary Astor. The movie studios were in the Astoria neighborhood of the borough of Queens in New York City, and Astor found them fascinating. Her first bit part was in *Sentimental Tommy* (1920), but her scene ended up on the cutting room floor. Her second film was never released. When Astor's six months with Lasky had come to an inauspicious end, Charles Albin, a prominent photographer, got her a screen test with an artist, Léjaron Hiller, who gave her a part in a successful two-reeler titled *The Beggar Maid* (1921). After appearing in six two-reelers, Astor made *John Smith* (1922) for Selznick Brothers. In April 1923 she signed a one-year contract with Famous Players for $500 a week and moved to Hollywood two weeks before her seventeenth birthday.

The actor John Barrymore, then in his early forties, saw a picture of Astor, captioned "On the brink of womanhood," in a magazine and was captivated. At their first meeting, Astor said, they fell in love. She became Barrymore's protégée, acting opposite him in *Beau Brummel* (1924). "He gave me love, affection, humor, and above all, beauty," she recalled. Barrymore also taught her about acting and the theater. Astor's hard work produced enough money so that in 1925 her parents were able to buy a home on Temple Hill Drive in Hollywood with a maid, a gardener, a Pierce-Arrow, and a chauffeur. In the fall of that year she worked with Barrymore on *Don Juan* (1926). By the following May the affair was over.

In 1926, after breaking her engagement to Bill Glass, Astor began dating Kenneth Hawks, who later became a director at Fox. The following year she starred in *Two Arabian Knights*. On 24 February 1928 Astor married Hawks, and later that year she signed a forty-week contract with Fox for $3,750 a week. When the contract ended in April 1929, the silent era was over. About to be renewed at $4,000 a week for fifty-two weeks, she was asked to take a test for Fox's Movietone newsreel division. The test did not go well, and her contract was not renewed. She turned to the theater and appeared in *Among the Married* with Edward Everett Horton in Los Angeles; within a week she received an offer from Paramount.

Astor's exile from the studios had lasted ten months. But before she could begin again, her husband was killed in an airplane crash on 2 January 1930. She then made *Holiday* (1930) with Ann Harding, moved to RKO, and fell in love with her physician, Franklyn Thorpe, whom she married on 29 June 1931. On 15 June 1932 a daughter, Marylyn, was born. That same year, she made *Red Dust* with Clark Gable and Jean Harlow, and in 1933 she starred in *The World Changes* with Paul Muni.

After having an affair with playwright George S. Kaufman, Astor was divorced from Thorpe in 1935. In 1936 she became the center of a lurid custody battle in which Thorpe charged that she was "a person of continuous, gross, immoral conduct." She was eventually given custody of Marylyn for nine months out of the year.

After signing a two-year contract with Columbia, Astor made several movies and became a driving force in the formation of the Screen Actors Guild. At age thirty she fell in love with twenty-four-year-old Manuel del Campo, whom she married on 18 February 1937. They had one child, Antonio. After acting in *Dodsworth* (1937), *Prisoner of Zenda* (1937), and *Brigham Young: Frontiersman* (1940), Astor created her two most famous movie roles: as an egocentric, ambitious pianist in *The Great Lie* (1941), with Bette Davis, at Warner Brothers, for which she received an Academy Award for best supporting actress in 1942, and as Brigid O'Shaughnessy in John Huston's *The Maltese Falcon* (1941), also made at Warner Brothers. At the same time she worked in the theater and on radio. Around this time she sought help for an alcohol problem from a priest, Father Augustin O'Dea, and converted to Catholicism.

Late in 1941 Astor made *The Palm Beach Story* (1942), with Claudette Colbert. She and Manuel divorced in 1942. She learned to fly and joined the Civil Air Patrol. But along with her accomplishments, her drinking problem worsened. In 1944 she signed a long-term contract with Metro-Goldwyn-Mayer. On 24 December 1945 Astor married Thomas G. Wheelock.

Mary Astor's movie roles changed in the 1940s from glamorous, sophisticated women to caring mothers in *Thousands Cheer* (1943), *Meet Me in St. Louis* (1944), *Cynthia* (1947), and *Little Women* (1949). In 1949, as a result of her alcoholism, she entered a sanatorium. In 1951 she overdosed on sleeping pills, an event that she characterized as accidental. Believing that she was through in Hollywood, Astor turned to the theater, but that also proved unfruitful. In 1954 she filed for a divorce from Wheelock, which was granted the following year. She had hit bottom.

Her climb back to the top began in 1955 in television. Among the dramatic television plays in which she performed were a *Producer's Showcase* production of *The Philadelphia Story; The Thief,* for *The U.S. Steel Hour; The Hickory Limb* for Pond's Theatre; and a *Producer's Showcase* presentation of *The Women.* She then toured in George Bernard Shaw's *Don Juan in Hell;* the rigors of being on the road resulted in physical and emotional exhaustion. A Chicago priest, Father Peter Ciklic, encouraged Astor to make notes for an autobiography. His counsel and friendship enabled her to complete *My Story: An Autobiography* (1959). It sold well and opened up a new career for her as a writer.

While making eight more movies, including *Return to Peyton Place* (1961), again in the role of a mother, and *Hush, Hush, Sweet Charlotte* (1964), with Bette Davis, Astor also went on to write five novels: *The Incredible Charlie Carewe* (1960); *The Image of Kate* (1962); *The O'Conners* (1964); *Goodbye Darling, Be Happy* (1965); and *A Place Called Saturday* (1968). Of these, the first and last are considered her best. Her final book, the autobiographical *A Life on Film* (1971), is considered an excellent study of the movie industry and the art of acting.

In 1974 Astor retired to the Motion Picture Country Home in Woodland Hills, California. She considered herself a "loner," and that is the way she lived out her last years. She died in the Motion Picture Country Hospital of respiratory failure due to pulmonary emphysema and is buried in Holy Cross Cemetery in Culver City, California.

Mary Astor worked in the movies for forty-three years; her film roles ranged from a peasant girl in *The Beggar Maid* (1921), in which she received her first movie kiss, to a murderous old lady in *Hush, Hush, Sweet Charlotte* (1964). In all, she acted in 109 movies, creating memorable roles and earning critical acclaim. Her two autobiographical works are honest, well-written reminiscences of a woman who lived a difficult life with courage and, finally, dignity. Some say that she wasted her talent on insignificant roles, but most critics agree that her place in Hollywood history is secure. Even if she had made only *The Maltese Falcon,* she would always be remembered for her portrayal of Brigid O'Shaughnessy. Her second career as a writer revealed her as a person of intelligence and sensitivity who tried to make sense of a complex and tumultuous life.

★

Mary Astor, *My Story: An Autobiography* (1959), is a detailed and well-written account of her life from childhood until age fifty-three, an honest portrayal of her personal and professional life that is very revealing. Mary Astor, *A Life on Film* (1971), is a comprehensive history of her acting career offering valuable insights into the movie industry and the art of acting. Obituaries are in the *Los Angeles Times* and *New York Times* (both 26 Sept. 1987).

MARVIN J. LAHOOD

ATTWOOD, William Hollingsworth (*b.* 14 July 1919 in Paris, France; *d.* 14 April 1989 in New Canaan, Connecticut), correspondent, ambassador, publisher, and chronicler of the cold war era.

Attwood was the son of American parents, Frederic Attwood, a business executive, and Gladys Hollingsworth. When Attwood was eight years old his family returned to the United States. He attended the Choate School in Wallingford, Connecticut, and graduated in 1917. He then studied at Princeton University, where he received a B.A. degree in 1941. He began law studies at Columbia University the following fall but withdrew after three months to enlist as a private in the U.S. Army. He served four years in the Middle East and the Pacific and was discharged in December 1945 with the rank of captain.

Attwood—five feet, eleven inches, with brown hair and eyes and an affable manner—began work as a copy editor

William Attwood, 1961. AP/WIDE WORLD PHOTOS

in February 1946 at the *New York Herald Tribune.* He then had a brief stint as a correspondent in the *Herald Tribune*'s Washington, D.C., bureau. He recalled years later that "the cold war started for me on March 27, 1946, and has dominated most of my professional life ever since." That date marked his assignment to Paris, where he covered postwar developments for the *Herald Tribune* and also did freelance writing for *Life,* the *Nation,* and the *New Yorker.* Between 1949 and 1951 he continued to track the developing phases of the cold war for *Collier's* before beginning his ten-year association with *Look* magazine, where he served as European editor, national editor, and foreign editor. On 22 June 1950 he married Simone Cadgene; they had three children.

Attwood accompanied Adlai E. Stevenson, who lost the presidential election in 1952, on a five-month *Look*-sponsored world tour in 1953 to oversee the bimonthly articles submitted by Stevenson to the magazine. Upon his return to the United States in December 1954 after a ten-year absence, Attwood embarked on a three-month cross-country road trip with his wife before settling in New Canaan, Connecticut. Their tour, outlined in a series of articles for *Look* and detailed in *Still the Most Exciting Country* (1955), covered 12,000 miles and twenty-eight states and included hundreds of conversations and informal interviews with Americans from all walks of life. Having written a few speeches for Stevenson's presidential campaign in 1956, Attwood took a leave from *Look* in 1960 to prepare speeches in case Stevenson made a third try for the presidency. When John F. Kennedy received the Democratic nomination, he asked Attwood to join his own speech-writing staff.

Chester Bowles, undersecretary of state in the Kennedy administration, suggested Attwood for a position in the State Department. Attwood declined but proposed himself as a candidate for a diplomatic assignment to Guinea. Confirmed by the Senate in March 1961, he began his ambassadorship to this recently independent (1958) West African nation. Despite suffering an attack of paralytic polio shortly after his arrival (leaving him with a permanent limp), Attwood committed himself to establishing lines of communication and trust with President Sékou Touré. At a time when Guinea was seen as particularly vulnerable to communist influence, Attwood used patience, tact, and respect to convey U.S. support of Guinea's independence and economic development. He returned briefly to the United States in 1963 to serve as the president's adviser on African affairs to the United Nations. President Lyndon B. Johnson then appointed Attwood ambassador to Kenya, another newly independent nation that was struggling to achieve economic and racial stability; the Senate confirmed him in February 1964. Attwood encouraged an open dialogue and an exchange of views with President Jomo Kenyatta, a marked contrast to the more aggressive, sometimes clumsy tactics of the Soviet Union and China. His diplomatic tenure ended in the spring of 1966, when Gardner (Mike) Cowles offered him the position of editor in chief of Cowles Communications.

Attwood presided over the Cowles periodicals: *Look, Family Circle, The Insider's Newsletter, Venture,* and *Accent on Leisure.* During the next four years, however, he suffered two heart attacks and a period of clinical depression. These physical hardships, coupled with the decline of *Look,* led to Attwood's departure in 1970 to become publisher of the nation's largest suburban daily newspaper, *Newsday,* located in Long Island, New York. The diplomatic skills he honed in Africa served him well during his nine years with the paper. He instituted regular staff meetings to integrate the departments, prevailed on writers to keep the emotional tone of editorials calm, and ended *Newsday*'s practice of endorsing presidential candidates. He also launched the Queens and Sunday editions and oversaw the building of a new printing plant.

When Attwood retired from *Newsday* in September 1978 to pursue teaching, lecturing, and writing, he had written six books and contributed to approximately twenty-five periodicals. His childhood wish of being an explorer was satisfied by his travels in eighty-one countries, including twenty-one in Africa. His global reporting, which included interviews with many prominent world figures, including Fidel Castro, Indira Gandhi, David Ben-Gurion, Jawaharlal Nehru, and Gamal Abdel Nasser, helped earn him the National Headliners Award (1955 and 1957), the George Polk Memorial Award (1956), and the New York Newspaper Guild's Page One Award (1960). He died of heart failure.

Attwood's experiences and observations as a journalist and diplomat make his books and articles valuable primary sources for understanding the cold war and its aftermath, especially the struggle for influence over the newly independent nations of Africa.

★

Attwood's papers are in the State Historical Society of Wisconsin. His books include *The Reds and the Blacks: A Personal Adventure* (1967), which details his years as an ambassador to Guinea and Kenya; *Making It Through Middle Age: Notes While in Transit* (1982), which provides a summary of his life and career with an emphasis on his health; and *The Twilight Struggle: Tales of the Cold War* (1987), a "part memoir, part essay, and part history." See also Robert F. Keeler, *Newsday: A Candid History of the Respectable Tabloid* (1990), especially chap. 31, "Enter the Ambassador." Obituaries are in the *New York Times* and the *Washington Post* (both 16 Apr. 1989).

CARRIE C. MCBRIDE

AXIS SALLY. *See* Gillars, Mildred Elizabeth Sisk.

B

BACKUS, James Gilmore ("Jim") (*b.* 25 February 1913 in Cleveland, Ohio; *d.* 3 July 1989 in Santa Monica, California), stage, television, radio, and motion picture actor and author.

Backus was the son of Russell Backus, an engineer and wealthy industrialist who founded the Russell Backus Company, which manufactured metal stamping and other heavy machinery for factories throughout the world. His mother was Daisy Taylor Gilmore. The Backus family resided in the exclusive Cleveland suburb of Bratenahl, where Jim and his sister were raised. Backus attended the local schools but was not a good student. Golf was more interesting, and he became a proficient player at the local country clubs, so good that he entertained thoughts of becoming a professional. The theater was also an attraction, and in the summer of 1927 he worked for a Cleveland stock theater company. Among his minor roles that season was one as a native bearer in the play *White Cargo.* A then unknown actor, Clark Gable, played the lead.

Backus's parents, concerned that golf, the theater, and other distractions were becoming a detriment to their son's education, decided he should attend military school, where he would learn some discipline. In January 1928 he was sent to Kentucky Military Institute outside of Louisville. In his senior year Backus changed schools again, this time to the University School in Shaker Heights, another suburb of Cleveland. This school prided itself in placing its graduates in Ivy League colleges, but despite tutoring, it was unsuccessful in Jim's case. Backus persuaded his father to let him attend the American Academy of Dramatic Arts in New York City, where he could pursue his love of acting. His father reluctantly sent him off with the encouraging words, "If you fail, you can always go to work in my factory."

Backus was successful at the American Academy of Dramatic Arts and graduated in 1933. With the Great Depression in full swing, stage acting parts were hard to come by, but he found a few jobs in the rapidly growing medium of radio. Radio needed actors with varied voices who could read the many parts that the emerging serials, soon to be called soap operas; dramas; and comedy sketches required.

This same year Backus met Keenan Wynn, the son of Ed Wynn, the vaudeville headliner who had become one of the top radio personalities of the day. Ed Wynn's show, *Texaco's Fire Chief,* was one of the most popular programs on radio. Keenan Wynn was an aspiring actor like Backus, and they struck up a friendship that lasted throughout Backus's life. Through Keenan, Backus became friends with his famous father. Backus said that he learned more from Ed Wynn about acting and timing than he learned at the academy, but he did not follow Wynn's advice to base his career on one recognizable character.

In the winter of 1934 Backus became seriously ill, and his parents insisted he return to Cleveland. After Backus's recuperation, his father got him a job as an announcer for

Jim Backus with a Mr. Magoo doll. CORBIS-BETTMANN

radio station WTAM, the National Broadcasting Company's station in Cleveland. He introduced programs such as band music emanating from local hotel ballrooms and man-in-the-street interviews.

Backus did not want to remain an announcer, so in the fall of 1936 he returned to New York to resume his acting career. In April 1937 he appeared in the play *Hitch Your Wagon* and that fall in *Too Many Heroes,* but he found steady employment in radio. His ability to create different voices and characterizations put him much in demand, as radio's anonymity enabled one actor to play a number of parts on one program. Backus became a recurring actor on soap operas, such as *Stella Dallas, Society Girl,* and *Second Husband.* In addition, he was a comic character on the nighttime comedy-variety programs, including the *Kate Smith Hour, Rudy Vallee Show,* and *Edgar Bergen–Charlie McCarthy Show,* where songs were interspersed with comedy sketches. Backus became so busy that, as he told it, "I had a taxi waiting at Rockefeller Center with its meter running so that I could get to CBS for my next show."

In March 1941 Backus visited his agent, who was ill, in his room at the Royalton Hotel. Henriette "Henny" Kaye, an actress, brought a hot bowl of soup to the ailing agent on that day, and it was love at first sight. Backus and Kaye married on 14 January 1943 in Philadelphia, Pennsylvania, at the home of Henny's parents. The following week the ceremony was repeated in Cleveland at Jim's parents' home. They had no children.

In 1944 Backus joined the cast of the *Alan Young Show,* a situation comedy. With the help of the show's writers, he developed the character of Hubert Updyke III, "the richest bachelor in the world," which greatly enhanced the show's popularity. In 1946, when the show was moved to Hollywood, California, Backus went along to continue his role of the pampered playboy. He proved so popular that in 1947 he was given his own radio program, the *Jim Backus Show.*

Being in Hollywood and having many friends from his New York and academy days, Backus had no trouble obtaining movie roles. His first film was *Easy Living* for RKO in 1949. He went on to appear in more than eighty motion pictures. His most prominent roles were in *Bright Victory* (1951), *Androcles and the Lion* (1952), *Above and Beyond* (1952), and *Rebel Without a Cause* (1955).

Backus's voice, honed by his radio experience, was ideal for animated cartoons. In 1949 United Productions of America, a new cartoon production company founded by former Walt Disney employees, needed a voice for a nearsighted bumbler for a cartoon short titled *Ragtime Bear.* Backus made this character, named Quincy Magoo, a hit and continued to make more than fifty shorts, three television series, an hour-long television special, and a full-length feature, *1001 Arabian Nights* (1959). In a *New York Times* interview in 1958 Backus said: "Magoo's appeal lies in our hostility toward an older generation. . . . He's not only nearsighted physically; his mind's selective . . . too. That is where the humor, the satire lies, in the difference between what he sees and reality as we see it."

Backus moved quickly into television. In 1949 he hosted a half-hour variety show for the American Broadcasting Company. In 1952 he starred with Joan Davis in the situation comedy *I Married Joan,* which ran three years on the National Broadcasting Company. Backus played Judge Bradley Stevens; Davis played his wacky wife. Backus was also cast in anthology and drama series, including *Lux Video Theater* (1950), *Conflict* (1958), and *Maverick* (1960). He had his own situation comedy in 1960, *Hot off the Wire.*

In 1964 Backus again created a character that would leave a lasting impression, that of Thurston Howell III on the situation comedy *Gilligan's Island.* Howell was a pompous, blustery Harvard-educated millionaire, one of the seven castaways on a desert island. This series, criticized as inane by some critics, remained in syndication long after it ceased production in 1967.

Backus continued to work in the movies. Among his important roles were *Wonderful World of the Brothers*

Grimm (1962), *The Wheeler-Dealers* (1963), *Don't Make Waves* (1967), and *Crazy Mama* (1975). His last feature was *There Goes the Bride* (1980). On television he appeared as Mr. Dithers in an adaptation of the comic strip *Blondie,* with his wife, Henny, in 1968 and 1969. He reprised the parts of Thurston Howell III and Mr. Magoo as these characters' voices for Saturday morning cartoons in *The New Adventures of Gilligan* (1974–1976) and *What's New, Mister Magoo* (1977–1978). He was also the voice in many commercials and the popular emcee of numerous charity events.

In addition to his acting work, Backus wrote four books with his wife: *Rocks on the Roof* (1958), *What Are You Doing After the Orgy* (1962), *Backus Strikes Back* (1984), and *Forgive Us Our Digressions* (1988). All the books are anecdotal and contain humorous accounts of incidents in their lives.

In 1978 Backus's legs gave way, and, according to his version, firemen had to rescue him from a hot tub. He was diagnosed with Parkinson's disease. Backus had difficulty in accepting this diagnosis and fought valiantly for a cure. None was forthcoming, and in 1989 he died of pneumonia at St. John's Hospital in Santa Monica. He is buried in Westwood Memorial Park in Los Angeles. Backus created two memorable characters, the myopic curmudgeon Mr. Magoo and the self-indulgent patrician Thurston Howell III, who have made their stamp on American culture. Their names have become catch phrases for persons with their traits and mannerisms.

★

Clippings files on Backus are in the Margaret Herrick Library of the Academy of Motion Picture Arts and Sciences, Beverly Hills, California. His *Forgive Us Our Digressions* (1984) is his autobiography. Obituaries are in the *Los Angeles Times* and *New York Times* (both 4 July 1989).

KELLAM DE FOREST

BACON, Ernst (*b.* 26 May 1898 in Chicago, Illinois; *d.* 16 March 1990 in Orinda, California), conductor, composer, and pianist who won the Pulitzer Prize in 1932 for his Symphony in D Minor and is known for his lyric songs.

Bacon was one of four children of Charles S. Bacon, an obstetrician-gynecologist, and Vienna-born Maria von Rosthorn, a descendant of the Esterhazy family who taught piano to her children. Ernst showed an early interest in painting and writing poetry. He graduated from Lane Technical High School in Chicago in 1915, then attended Northwestern University, where he studied music theory with P. C. Lutkin (1915–1918) at the Lewis Institute. It was during these years that Bacon wrote his first book, *Our Musical Idiom,* a study of the new harmonies in 1918, published when he was just nineteen years old.

Ernst Bacon. ROBERT S. PHILLIPS

Bacon left Northwestern in 1919 and enrolled at the University of Chicago, where he studied with Narne Oldberg and T. Otterstroem (1919–1920). He also received private piano instruction from Alexander Raab in Chicago (1916–1921). In 1924 Bacon moved to Vienna, Austria, where he studied piano under Glenn D. Gunn and Malwine Bree; composition under Ernest Bloch, Franz Schmidt, and Karl Weigl; and conducting under Eugene Goosens.

Bacon's concert career began in 1922 with appearances in Germany and throughout the United States. In 1925 he made a concert tour of Europe. He cut an impressive figure at the podium. Barrel-chested and a handsome man, with a jutting lantern jaw and full bushy brows, he would conduct by planting one hand on his hip and waving the other clenched in a fist. From 1923 to 1926 he was assistant conductor of the Rochester Opera Company under his mentor, Goosens, and taught the piano at the Eastman School in Rochester, New York. In 1927 he married Mary Prentice Lillie, the first of four wives; they had two children. His first symphony, for piano and orchestra, was performed to acclaim in 1932 and won the Pulitzer Prize.

Bacon was conductor of the Civic Junior Orchestra in San Francisco from 1934 to 1936; founder and director of the Bach Festival at Carmel, California (1935); superviser and symphony conductor of the Federal Music Project in San Francisco (1935–1937); and superviser pro tem for the same project in Los Angeles. His Symphony no. 2 was completed in 1937.

In addition to composing, teaching, conducting, and administrating, Bacon also was an editor during this productive period. He served as musical editor of the periodical *The Argonaut* from 1934 to 1936. He also completed his education, receiving an M.A. degree in 1935 from the University of California. He relaxed by hiking and painting.

The year 1936 was especially productive for Bacon's composition. He completed two orchestral works (*Bearwalla*; *Country Roads, Unpaved*); a vocal work (*On Ecclesiastes*, a cantata); and a dramatic work (*Take Your Choice,* in collaboration with Phil Mathias and Kaish Stroll). In that same year he set music to *Yours, A. Lincoln* by Paul Horgan. In 1937 Bacon married his second wife, Analee Camp, with whom he had two children.

In 1938 Bacon became acting professor of music at Hamilton College in Clinton, New York. He then moved on to become dean of the School of Music at Converse College, Spartanburg, South Carolina, from 1938 to 1945. He also directed the Spartanburg Music Festival. In 1939 he received the first of three Guggenheim Fellowships. In 1942, in collaboration with Horgan, he completed the musical play *A Tree on the Plains*.

In 1945, in an important career move, Bacon left Spartanburg to join the faculty of Syracuse University in New York, where he would hold his longest appointment. During the first two years, he served as director and professor of the School of Music. He then stepped down and became composer-in-residence, a post he held until 1964, when he was made professor emeritus. His second wife divorced him in 1951. While at Syracuse he married his third wife, Moselle ("Peggy") Camp, on Easter Sunday of 1952. They had one child.

Bacon's Syracuse years were active ones. He collaborated again with Horgan, producing *Ford's Theater* (1946), a depiction of Lincoln's assassination and the aftermath. It became one of his most enduring musical suites. Bacon's *Cello Sonata* also was completed in 1946. He produced a work for women's chorus, *From Emily Dickinson's Diary* (1947); a folk opera, *A Drumlin Legend* (1949); a cantata, *The Lord Star* (1950); a suite, *From These States* (1951); the *String Quintet* (1951); and a work for narrator and orchestra, *Fables* (1953). He was awarded the Campion Citation for achievement in the field of the song in 1952.

Later works from the Syracuse years include music for *The Tempest* (1955); the orchestral *Concerto Grosso* (1957); *By Blue Ontario's Shores,* an oratorio set to words by Walt Whitman (1958); *Erie Waters* (1961); and a concerto for piano and orchestra in short movements, *Riolama* (1964). In the early 1960s he engaged Aaron Copland to conduct at Syracuse.

While these are among Bacon's major large compositions, he never lost interest in writing individual songs or song cycles. In 1932 he had composed *Songs of Eternity; Black and White Songs* for baritone and orchestra; and *Twilight,* three songs for voice and orchestra. Over his career he composed more than 200 songs. "Poetry is the basis of musical melody," he once said, and his highly American work was influenced and shaped by the works of Emily Dickinson and Walt Whitman. Twenty-two of his Dickinson adaptations were recorded by Helen Boatwright, with Bacon at the keyboard. In all he did more than seventy Dickinson settings. A collection of his songs for soprano, alto, and piano, *Grass Roots,* was published in two volumes in 1976. Other published collections of songs include *Tributaries, Dragon's Teeth,* and *Quiet Airs*.

In addition to composing, Bacon wrote poetry and fables and published two additional books—*Words on Music* (1960) and *Notes on the Piano* (1963). In 1964 he moved to Orinda, California, an area he knew well from his Civic Junior Orchestra days in San Francisco. Peggy, his third wife, died on 30 December 1966. Bacon married his fourth wife, Ellen Wendt, in 1972; they had one child.

Bacon's later works include the suite *A Life* (1966); the cycle *Spirit and Place* (1966); the ballet *Jehovah and the Ark* (1968); *The Last Invocation* for chorus and orchestra (1968); *Nature,* a cantata cycle (1968); *Saws,* a suite of canons for chorus and piano (1971); the ballet *The Parliament of Fowls* (1975); *Dr. Franklin,* a musical play for the Bicentennial (1976); *Over the Waters* for orchestra (1976); *Violin Sonata* (1982); and *Concerto No. 2* (1982).

When Bacon was eighty-eight years old and nearly blind, he composed his sonata for violin. He continued to compose and write about music nearly to the day he died of heart failure at his home in Orinda. His ashes were spread under a special California oak tree along one of the trails in the Briones Hill of Briones Regional Park, where he had walked for twenty-five years, often stopping to write in his notebooks.

Despite his enormous outpouring of orchestral works and many arrangements of American folk music, Bacon is best known for his songs, which reflect his sensitivity to the meanings and colorations of American speech. It has been noted that his lively use of syncopation actually imitates speech patterns. His most successful songs are based upon short poems by Dickinson, Whitman, and A. E. Housman.

★

Primary holdings of Bacon's literary manuscripts are at the Library of Congress and of musical manuscripts at Syracuse University Library, Department of Special Collections. There are smaller collections in the Department of Special Collections, Stanford University Libraries; the Music Division of the New York

Public Library for the Performing Arts; and the Virgil Thomson Papers in the Music Library of Yale University. Bacon's autobiography, *Ernst Bacon* (1974), includes a bibliography, discography, and a tribute by Paul Horgan. See also J. St. Edmunds, "The Songs of Ernst Bacon," *Shawnee Review* (Oct. 1941); and W. Fleming, "Ernst Bacon," *Musical America* 69, no. 36 (1949): 8. Obituaries are in the *New York Times* (18 Mar. 1990) and *Los Angeles Times* (19 Mar. 1990).

ROBERT PHILLIPS

BAILEY, Pearl Mae (*b.* 29 March 1918 in Newport News, Virginia; *d.* 17 August 1990 in Philadelphia, Pennsylvania), singer, actress, and author.

Of Creek Indian and African-American ancestry, Bailey was the youngest of four children. Her brother, Willie ("Bill") Bailey, enjoyed a successful tap-dancing career before becoming a minister and was briefly considered the protégé of Bill ("Bojangles") Robinson. Close to her siblings, Bailey, known to her friends as "Pearlie Mae," was also extremely fond of her parents, the Reverend Joseph James and Ella Mae Bailey, who strongly supported her desire to perform. Although she received no formal musical training, she began dancing and singing at the age of three in her father's Holy Roller–style church. After her father's death in 1966, Bailey recalled, "From him I got the wisdom, the philosophizing, the soul." From her mother she learned how to act: "Mama, she could say more with a flick of a wrist . . . than any words."

Pearl Bailey, 1988. UPI/CORBIS-BETTMANN

Bailey's family moved from Virginia to Washington, D.C., in 1922. Four years later, when she was just eight years old, her parents divorced. Initially, Bailey and her siblings remained in Washington with their father, while their mother married again and moved to Philadelphia. In 1928 Bailey, her sister Eura Bailey, and her brother joined their mother in that city, where Bailey attended public schools and began to cultivate a maturing passion for music and dance. An eager student, her initial desire to become a schoolteacher was sidetracked in 1933, when she entered an amateur contest at Philadelphia's Pearl Theater, where her brother had been performing regularly. For her impressive renditions of "Poor Butterfly" and "Talk of the Town," Bailey won first prize, which carried with it $5 and the promise of a two-week engagement at $30 per week. She was never paid for these subsequent gigs, however, as the theater closed down shortly thereafter. Nonetheless, success was swift for Bailey. Within the next few months, she won first prize for her buck-and-wing dance routine at the Jungle Inn in Washington, D.C., and again for her performance on amateur night at the world-famous Apollo Theater in Harlem. Her appetite for a life in entertainment sufficiently whetted, Bailey dropped out of high school at the age of fifteen to pursue a full-time musical career.

At first Bailey worked as a chorus girl on the vaudeville entertainment circuit in Philadelphia-area nightclubs. One summer in the late 1930s, following her successful debut at the Apollo, she toured with Noble Sissle's band as a specialty dancer. During the hardest days of the Great Depression, Bailey earned $15 a week plus tips as a vaudeville entertainer in tough Pennsylvania coal-mining towns like Scranton, Wilkes-Barre, and Pottsville.

Although only in her late teens, she met her first husband, a traveling drummer, with whom she had a tumultuous marriage that lasted just eighteen months. They had no children. From industrial Pennsylvania Bailey returned to Washington, D.C., in 1940, where she enjoyed explosive success as a big-band vocalist for pianist-composer Edgar Hayes. With Hayes, and later with the Sunset Royal Band (1943–1944), she sang and danced in places like New York City, Baltimore, and Washington, D.C., most notably at the famous Savoy Ballroom and Apollo Theater, both in Harlem, and on U Street, N.W., the heart of Washington's black elite entertainment district.

When the United States entered World War II in 1941,

Bailey continued her ascent to stardom during a cross-country tour with the United Service Organizations (USO), the first of many such tours she made during her long career. Able to taste some of the privileges that the vast majority of black Americans were legally denied as a result of Jim Crow segregation, she played to both black and white audiences. After her USO tour (1941–1943), she moved to New York City, where she performed as a featured vocalist with Charles ("Cootie") Williams and Count Basie. Her successful debut as a soloist came at New York's Village Vanguard in 1944, where artists such as Huddie Ledbetter and Richard Dyer-Bennett were also performing. Shortly thereafter her manager, Chauncey Oldman, lined up an eight-month solo stint at the Blue Angel, another popular New York nightclub, during which Bailey also served as a replacement for featured singer Sister Rosetta Tharpe in Cab Calloway's act at the Strand Theater in 1945. Owing to Tharpe's prolonged illness, Bailey was able to work with Calloway for three weeks and then again for sixteen weeks in his late show at Broadway's Zanzibar nightclub. Though she always prided herself foremost on being a vaudevillian, Bailey used her early big-band and nightclub experience to cultivate her distinctive style, later described by one reviewer as "a warm, lusty singing voice accompanied by an easy smile and elegant gestures that charmed audiences and translated smoothly from the nightclub stage and Broadway to film and television." A good thing, too, because Bailey was headed for both the Broadway stage and the Hollywood screen.

On 30 March 1946 Bailey made her Broadway debut at the Martin Beck Theatre, where she appeared in the role of Butterfly opposite Nat King Cole in *St. Louis Woman,* an all-black musical produced by Johnny Mercer and Harold Arlen. Modestly successful, *St. Louis Woman* ran for 113 performances, earning Bailey critical acclaim for her show-stopping renditions of "Legalize My Name" and "A Woman's Prerogative." In a *New York Herald Tribune* review of the show's opening, Howard Barnes wrote, "Pearl Bailey pulls the show up by its shoestrings every time she makes an entrance." In fact, her stirring performance, which upstaged the celebrated tap-dancing duo, the Nicholas Brothers, won her the 1946 Donaldson Award as Broadway's best newcomer. The next year she appeared in her first motion picture for Paramount, *Variety Girl,* in which she introduced "Tired," a song that would become one of her trademark hits. She followed this up in 1948 with another Paramount film, *Isn't It Romantic,* after which she returned to her true love, the Broadway stage.

From 2 February through 27 May 1950 Bailey brought a passionate integrity to the role of the runaway slave girl Connecticut in *Arms and the Girl,* a Theater Guild operetta, at the Forty-sixth Street Theater. In the winter of 1950–1951 she appeared in all eighty-four performances of the musical revue *Bless You All.* In 1948 Bailey married John Randolph Pinkett, Jr., with whom she had two children. After divorcing Pinkett in 1952, she married Louis Bellson, a white jazz drummer, that year. Though controversial in the time of Jim Crow laws, this third marriage, which lasted until her death in 1990, was by far Bailey's happiest.

By the early 1950s Bailey had become an American icon, famous for her disarming physical style, magnificent voice, and stirring performatory intensity. Throughout the 1950s and 1960s she moved effortlessly between stage, screen, and television. In 1954 she scored her first Broadway solo role in *House of Flowers,* the extravagant musical produced by Arlen and Truman Capote. During the show's successful run of 165 performances at New York's Alvin Theater, she won critical acclaim for her portrayal of Madame Fleur, the matriarch of a West Indian bordello. One reviewer characterized Bailey's performance as "easily raffish, demonically secure, justifiably confident." Performing intermittently in nightclubs, Bailey also starred opposite Harry Belafonte and Dorothy Dandridge in *Carmen Jones* (1954), Otto Preminger's film version of the all-black Broadway hit by Oscar Hammerstein, set to the music of Georges Bizet's *Carmen.* In addition, she played Gussie in the comedy *That Certain Feeling* (1956), with Bob Hope and Eva Marie Saint, and Aunt Hager in *St. Louis Blues* (1958), the film biography of the life of the blues legend W. C. Handy. In 1959 Bailey garnered accolades for her performance as Maria, the cookshop woman, in Metro-Goldwyn-Mayer's *Porgy and Bess,* also featuring Sammy Davis, Jr. In fact, it was at her insistence that the director, Preminger, and the producer, Sam Goldwyn, decided to avoid what Bailey considered to be the "exaggerated Negro dialect" called for by the script. Following this, Bailey delivered the only notable performance in *All the Fine Young Cannibals* (1960).

In addition to her stage and film work, Bailey made regular appearances on television variety shows, including the *Perry Como Show, Ed Sullivan Show, What's My Line?, Mike Douglas Show,* and *Toast of the Town.* She also released a number of fast-selling albums with the Coral, Mercury, Columbia, and Decca labels, for which she recorded many of her personal trademarks, including "Bill Bailey, Won't You Please Come Home?," "Saint Louis Blues," "Row, Row, Row," "Tired," "Toot, Toot, Tootsie, Goodbye," and "Takes Two to Tango."

After two extremely prolific decades as an entertainer, the pinnacle of Bailey's success came in 1967, when she appeared opposite her old friend Calloway as the titular lead in David Merrick's all-black production of *Hello, Dolly!* The show had been a hit since 1964, when Carol Channing delighted Broadway audiences with her portrayal of the husband-hungry Yonkers widow. Following the acclaimed performances of well-known white actresses like Channing, Betty Grable, Martha Raye, and Ginger

Rogers in the role of Dolly, Bailey knew the risks involved in her decision to take on the lead role in an all-black version of the popular musical. Dismissing vocal objections to a racially segregated production, she offered this prescient quip to a *New York Times* reporter: "I'm part Indian. And we've got two redheads and a blonde with freckles in the show. How integrated can you get?" Indeed, when she assumed the stage as Dolly in the show's opening at New York's St. James Theater on 12 November 1967, Bailey received a rousing standing ovation. By the next day critics, too, were gushing with superlatives. "Dolly is the highest office to which the American woman can aspire," one *Newsweek* reviewer erupted, "and Miss Bailey has been elected to it by acclamation." Acknowledging the unprecedented nature of her performance, the *New York Times* wrote: "For Miss Bailey this was a Broadway triumph for the history books.... She took the whole musical in her hands and swung it around her neck as easily as if it were a feather boa.... The audience would have elected her governor if she'd only named the state." Describing it as a "fantastic emotional experience," Bailey expressed her own gratification at finally being able to "sing, dance, say intelligent words on stage, love and be loved and deliver what God gave me."

At the 1968 Tony Awards ceremony, Bailey was given a special award for her "sensational" performance in *Hello, Dolly!* Following her portrayal of Dolly, underscored with the publication of her candid autobiography *The Raw Pearl* (1968), Bailey won numerous awards for her sweeping talents. Voted Entertainer of the Year in 1967 by the editors of *Cue,* she was the recipient of the 1968 March of Dimes annual award, was named USO Woman of the Year in 1969, and was presented with a special citation by New York mayor John V. Lindsay at a festival at city hall.

A beloved performer, Bailey was not embraced as universally in her role as a public figure during the heyday of her career. In 1957, as the civil rights movement began to crystallize, she was one of the featured entertainers at Dwight D. Eisenhower's second presidential inauguration. Many civil rights leaders considered that public appearance ironic at best, given Eisenhower's resistance to Court-imposed federal desegregation ordered by the 1954 *Brown* v. *Board of Education* Supreme Court decision. A frequent guest at the White House during the Eisenhower, John Kennedy, Lyndon Johnson, and Richard Nixon administrations, Bailey was dubbed "Ambassador of Love" by Nixon in 1970. In 1975, when President Gerald Ford made Bailey a special adviser to the U.S. mission of the United Nations, her appointment was sharply criticized by many black leaders, including the Harlem congressman Charles Rangel, who considered it an insult to better-qualified African Americans.

Responding to criticisms that she was insufficiently active in civil rights agitation, Bailey had this to say in a 1967 *New York Times* interview: "I belong to nothing except humanity. I hate labels and I wear no labels. ... People ask me, why don't I march. And I say, I march every day in my heart. When I walk in the street with humanity I am marching, and you know, my feet are killing me all the way." Her stubborn idealism may have seemed moderate, even naive in the context of the modern civil rights revolution, but it did not reflect a disavowal of its central charge. Indeed, when she was invited in March 1966 to give her first concert appearance at Philharmonic Hall in New York's Lincoln Center, Bailey told the audience: "You know, honey, I've never been in this place before. Why, they phone up for you to come to the stage—before, it was always up from the basement for me!" If Bailey's impulse was to respond to the serious concerns of racial and gender discrimination with a trademark throwaway style, it was not because she lacked a serious commitment to justice. On the contrary, her spectacular and widespread successes had a shattering impact on the color line in the United States, even as she herself tried to transcend it.

After starring in her own short-lived ABC-TV series, the *Pearl Bailey Show,* which started its run in 1971, Bailey began a twenty-year career as an author. She wrote another autobiographical book, *Talking to Myself* (1971), then followed with *Pearl's Kitchen* (1973), *Duey's Tale* (1975), and *Hurry Up, America, and Spit* (1976). Her last book, *Between You and Me: A Heartfelt Memoir on Learning, Loving, and Living* (1989), was published shortly before her death.

Bailey announced in 1975 that she was retiring from show business, but she remained a fixture on television commercials, game shows, and situation comedies. She co-starred with the comedian Redd Foxx in the film comedy *Norman ... Is That You?* (1976) and was the voice for Big Mama, the owl, in the animated film *The Fox and the Hound* (1981). Meanwhile, Bailey continued to rack up awards, including an honorary degree in the arts from Georgetown University in 1978, a Britannica Life Achievement Award in 1978, an "all-star" television tribute in 1979, and the Presidential Medal of Freedom in October 1988. By far her proudest accomplishment, however, came in 1985, when, fifty-two years after dropping out of William Penn High School, Bailey finally earned her B.A. degree in theology from Georgetown University. In retirement she lived in Havasu, Arizona.

At the age of seventy-two, in Philadelphia, Pennsylvania, Pearl Mae Bailey succumbed to heart disease, from which she had suffered since the early 1960s. At her funeral, attended by more than 2,000 people, her longtime friend and collaborator Calloway remembered her, appropriately, with words from *Hello, Dolly!:* "You'll always be here in our hearts where you belong." She is buried in Rolling Green Memorial Park, West Chester, Pennsylvania.

★

Books that discuss Bailey and her work include Leonard Feather, *The Encyclopedia of Jazz* (1966); Eileen Southern, *Biographical Dictionary of Afro-American and African Musicians* (1982); John Chilton, *Who's Who of Jazz* (1985); Donald Bogle, *Blacks in American Film and Television* (1988); Bogle, *Toms, Coons, Mulattoes, Mammies, and Bucks* (1989); Jessie Carney Smith, ed., *Notable Black American Women* (1992); Darlene Clark Hine, ed., *Black Women in America: An Historical Encyclopedia* (1993); and Jack Salzman, David Lionel Smith, and Cornel West, eds., *Encyclopedia of African-American Culture and History* (1996). An obituary is in the *New York Times* (19 Aug. 1990).

TIMOTHY P. MCCARTHY

BAIRD, William Britton ("Bil") (*b.* 15 August 1904 in Grand Island, Nebraska; *d.* 18 March 1987 in New York City), world-renowned puppeteer who created thousands of puppets and was one of the first people to bring puppets to television, helping to popularize the art form.

The son of William Hull Baird, a chemical engineer and playwright, and Louise Hetzel, Baird moved to Mason City, Iowa, as a child and attended the local high school. He graduated from the University of Iowa with a B.A. degree in 1926 and the Chicago Academy of Fine Arts in 1927. He traveled in Europe in the early 1920s, sketching during the day and playing the accordion at night for money.

Blessed with a creative mind and a keen interest in puppetry as a child, Baird in 1928 teamed up in New York City with the leading puppeteer of his time, Tony Sarg. Baird worked with Sarg on numerous projects, including designing and building puppets for the Chicago's World Fair in 1934 and the construction of the original balloons for the Macy's Thanksgiving Day Parade. Baird married Evelyn Schwartz in 1932; they divorced in 1934.

During 1936 and 1937 Baird appeared in several Works Progress Administration productions and met Cora Burlar, who was also a puppeteer. They were married in 1937 and had two children, Peter and Laura. In 1943 the two started the Bil and Cora Baird Marionettes and performed in the *Ziegfeld Follies* on Broadway in Manhattan.

The advent of television opened new avenues for Baird's puppets, which appeared on the programs of Ed Sullivan, Jack Paar, and Sid Caesar. From 1951 to 1953 Bil and Cora Baird had their own shows. One of these, *The Whistling Wizard* (1952–1953), was about a child named J. P. who was transported to a fantasy island to search for the "Whistling Wizard." *The Bil Baird Show* (1953) was broadcast by the Columbia Broadcasting System on Tuesday and Thursday mornings. *Life with Snarky Parker* (1949–1950) was a Western children's show directed by Yul Brynner and starring the characters Snarky Parker and his sidekick horse, Heathcliffe. Baird received an Emmy nomination in 1958 for *Art Carney Meets Peter and the Wolf.* In the late 1960s and early 1970s he worked with the National Aeronautics and Space Administration to provide a simulation of astronauts during the moon landings for national television audiences. Baird also performed in more than 400 commercials.

Bil Baird with his puppet Charlemane, 1953. ARCHIVE PHOTOS

Baird's puppets appeared in several films, including *Lili* (1952) and *The Sound of Music* (1965). Baird's real affection, however, was for live performances, which were laced with humor for both children and adults. The range of his audience was extraordinary. In 1962 and 1963 he toured India and the Soviet Union as a State Department cultural ambassador. He gave performances for Presidents John F. Kennedy and Lyndon B. Johnson in the White House, and in 1966 he and Cora launched the Bil Baird Theater in New York City by giving free performances to children in Project Headstart. Cora Baird died in 1967.

The Bil Baird Theater was a 194-seat theater in the Greenwich Village section of New York. It remained open through 1976 and proved to be a training ground for a new generation of puppeteers that would later gain international reputations. Jim Henson, creator of the Muppets, worked with Baird for a year and later credited him for much of his success. Many of Henson's puppeteers learned their craft under Baird's direction.

Baird was legendary for the care that he applied to his

puppets. He would have his carvers sculpt and sand puppet arms and legs for hours on end only to place clothes on top of the finely honed wooden muscles. When carvers complained, he explained that the detail would show through when the puppets moved. Baird treated puppetry as an art and puppet shows as entertainment for adults as well as children. In all, Baird designed and made more than 3,000 puppets, including the popular Charlemane the Lion and Jackson, the tightrope-walking hobo. In 1965 Baird wrote *The Art of the Puppet,* which became a classic in the field.

Innovation was a by-product of Baird's work. He invented new ways to manipulate marionettes with string, as well as a mechanism that preceded teleprompters to rotate scripts so puppeteers could read their lines without having to let go of the puppet strings.

Baird was a versatile musician, voracious reader, and avid artist. He drew almost every day of his adult life. Friends, family, and neighboring children would frequently let him draw animals and imaginative creatures as temporary watercolor tattoos on their arms, legs, and torsos. Baird played several instruments, among which his favorite was the bagpipe. It was not unusual during the summers for neighbors on Martha's Vineyard to see and hear him play the bagpipe in the early evening to the setting sun. Baird and Brynner were known to walk the streets of New York City playing musical instruments for the fun of it.

After Cora's death in 1967, Baird married Patricia Courtleigh in 1969. Their marriage lasted only a few years, and in 1974 he married Susanna Lloyd, with whom he had one child, Madeleine.

Baird received numerous awards, including an honorary degree from the Parsons School of Design; a Distinguished Achievement Award from the University of Ohio; and, with Cora Baird, the Outer Circle Award for their permanent puppet theater.

★

Among Baird's other publications are *Schnitzel, the Yodeling Goat* (1965) and *Puppets and Population* (1971). Secondary sources include Alan Stern and Rupert Pray, *Bil Baird's Whistling Wizard* (1952), and Richard Leet, *Bil Baird: He Pulled Lots of Strings* (1988). An obituary is in the *New York Times* (19 Mar. 1987).

ERIK BRUUN

BAKER, Carlos Heard (*b.* 5 May 1909 in Biddeford, Maine; *d.* 18 April 1987 in Princeton, New Jersey), educator, novelist, and literary critic, best known for his biographies of Percy Bysshe Shelley, Ernest Hemingway, and Ralph Waldo Emerson and as an authority in the related fields of modern American and English literature.

Baker was the son of Arthur Erwin Baker, a farmer, hardware store manager, and bank manager, and Edna (Heard) Baker, a homemaker. He attended local schools and enrolled at Dartmouth College in Hanover, New Hampshire, in 1931. It was during his junior year at Dartmouth that he made his first literary effort, a collection of poems entitled *Shadows in Stone*, which he and a fellow student printed in the basement of the Dartmouth library. He won scholastic honors at Dartmouth, receiving his B.A. degree in 1932, and on 22 August of that year married Dorothy T. Scott of Asheville, North Carolina; they had three children. Baker received his M.A. degree from Harvard University in 1933 and then taught in high schools in Maine and in Buffalo, New York, until he became an instructor in Princeton University's English Department in 1938. He also continued his studies at Princeton, where he received his Ph.D. in 1940.

Baker remained at Princeton for the remainder of his career, becoming a full professor in 1951 and Woodrow Wilson Professor of Literature in 1953, a title he held until his retirement in 1977. He also served as chair of the English Department from 1952 to 1958 and directed Princeton's Special Program in the Humanities, a pioneering venture for honors students.

The first of many works that Baker edited was the two-volume *American Issues* (1941), with Willard Thorp and Merle Curti, an anthology of American history and literature. He next edited *The American Looks at the World* (1944), a collection of readings for freshman English classes. He went on to edit volumes of prose and poetry by Henry Fielding (1959), John Keats (1962), and Samuel Coleridge (1965), among others. The year 1948 was an especially prolific one for Baker the literary critic; in addition to editing a collection of Wordsworth—*Wordsworth "The Prelude," with a Selection from the Shorter Poems and the Sonnets* (revised and enlarged in 1954)—Baker contributed a chapter on the fiction of the Reconstruction period to *Literary History of the United States,* edited by Robert E. Spiller and others, and wrote *Shelley's Major Poetry: The Fabric of a Vision,* a biography in the form of a literary chronology that uses Shelley's chief poems to trace his personal changes and intellectual development.

In 1950 Baker began his critical study of Hemingway, which was published in 1952 as *Ernest Hemingway: The Writer as Artist.* The work won high praise, such as that of Vance Bourjaily in the *New York Times Book Review* ("for scholars, the book is bedrock; on it will rest all future Hemingway studies"), and went through three more editions (1956, 1963, and 1972). Thus began Baker's reputation as one of the world's preeminent Hemingway scholars. His review of Hemingway's *The Old Man and the Sea* in 1952 in a national literary magazine was declared the best book review of the year, and his books of Hemingway criticism, *Hemingway and His Critics: An International Anthology*

Carlos Baker, 1976. PHOTO BY ULLI STELTZER. AP/WIDE WORLD PHOTOS

(1961) and *Ernest Hemingway: Critiques of Four Major Novels* (1962), were also acclaimed works.

Baker was also a popular lecturer, speaking at the Library of Congress, the Universities of Wisconsin and Virginia, Dartmouth, Bucknell University, and other schools. In 1956 he delivered an address at the Grolier Club in New York City, *Forty Years of Pulitzer Prizes,* to open the club's exhibition of books, manuscripts, and other material representing the Pulitzer Prizes for fiction, drama, and poetry.

In the 1957–1958 academic year Baker was a Fulbright lecturer in American literature at Oxford University, and when he returned to the United States, his first novel, *A Friend in Power,* was published (1958). Baker published two more novels, *The Land of Rumbelow: A Fable in the Form of the Novel* (1963) and *The Gay Head Conspiracy* (1973), and in 1963 his second volume of poems (which followed the 100 copies of *Shadows in Stone*) was published as *A Year and a Day.* A collection of short stories, *The Talisman and Other Stories,* was published in 1976. Those stories and his poetry, along with many essays and book reviews, had appeared in such periodicals as the *Nation, New Republic, New York Times Book Review, Modern Language Notes,* and *Saturday Review.*

In 1962 Baker began work on *Ernest Hemingway: A Life Story* (1969), the definitive biography of that author. Hemingway's widow, Mary Welsh Hemingway, gave Baker access to unpublished letters, papers, and manuscripts, and Baker interviewed hundreds of people who knew the author. His purpose, he stated, was "to set the record straight about the facts of Hemingway's life and exploits." The work received critical acclaim upon its publication: Granville Hicks wrote in the *Saturday Review* (19 April 1969), "A superb job of research. [Baker] has, moreover, organized his book in such a way that it can be enjoyed by the general reader and at the same time used by scholars"; Christopher Lehmann-Haupt, writing in the *New York Times Book Review* (27 April 1969), said the work was "a life-size replica of Ernest Hemingway." Lehmann-Haupt also commented on the book's wealth of detail: "Reading Carlos Baker's long-awaited biography is hugely exasperating. But then so, apparently, was Ernest Hemingway. And that's the clue to how the whole thing fits together." The biography was eventually translated into twelve languages.

Meanwhile, Baker held Guggenheim fellowships in 1965 and 1967 and completed, with Jacques Barzun and others, the 1966 edition of Wilson Follett's *Modern American Usage: A Guide.* He also worked on the 1980 edition of that text.

Baker continued to write and edit after his retirement in 1977 from Princeton as professor emeritus, beginning with the selection of about 600 letters for *Ernest Hemingway: Selected Letters, 1917–1961* (1981), working again with Mary Hemingway and with his publisher, Charles Scribner, Jr. Editors at Charles Scribner's Sons recall Baker as a short, informal, and nonprofessorial man with an attention to detail and phenomenal recall. His last work of literary criticism was *The Echoing Green: Romanticism, Modernism, and the Phenomena of Transference in Poetry* (1984). Baker died of cancer at his home on Allison Road in Princeton and was buried in Princeton Cemetery.

At his death Baker was completing a biography of Ralph Waldo Emerson, which he had begun in the early 1970s and set aside to edit the Hemingway letters. He poured his resources, wisdom, and affections into *Emerson Among the Eccentrics: A Group Portrait,* which appeared posthumously in 1996, and the laudatory reviews the work received indicate that it will stand as the definitive Emerson biography. *Emerson Among the Eccentrics* is a group biography and detailed reconstruction of the American Renaissance and the Concord Group. James R. Mellon wrote in the introduction, "[The work] brings to life Emerson and his circle of friends—Hawthorne, Thoreau, Bronson Alcott, Walt Whitman, and others. The result is a vivid and textured mosaic of not just their interrelationships, but of their daily lives. . . . It alters one's sense of Emerson the man; it revives one's appreciation of Emerson the observer and thinker."

Throughout his more than fifty years at Princeton University, Baker inspired many students to continue their studies of modern American and English literature. He left a literary legacy of more than a dozen works of criticism, and his biographies of Shelley, Hemingway, and Emerson remain the standard works on those literary giants.

★

Some manuscripts of Baker's works published by Scribners and correspondence relating to those works are in the Princeton University Library, Department of Rare Books and Special Collections. The bulk of his papers are held by his estate, which is overseen by his daughter Elizabeth Baker Carter of Ridgewood, New Jersey. There is no biography. An obituary is in the *New York Times* (21 Apr. 1987).

LOUISE B. KETZ

BAKER, Chesney Henry ("Chet") (*b.* 23 December 1929 in Yale, Oklahoma; *d.* 13 May 1988 in Amsterdam, the Netherlands), jazz trumpeter, singer, and bandleader who personified the "cool" sound of West Coast jazz; his romantic persona and the restrained lyricism of his music made him one of the most popular performers in jazz history.

Born in the first year of the Great Depression, Chet Baker's earliest memories were of his parents struggling to find work. To this end, the Baker family moved from Yale to Oklahoma City in the early 1930s and stayed with Baker's aunt, Agnes Baker, and her family for the next seven years. During this period, Baker's father was employed through the Works Progress Administration and his mother, Vera, had a job in an ice cream factory. Baker's father was an amateur musician who passed on his love of music to his son. While living in Oklahoma City, Baker attended the Culbertson Grammar School.

In 1940 the Baker family moved to Glendale, California, where Baker attended Glendale Junior High School. Baker's mother became aware of his ability to sing, and she took him to several singing competitions, but he never placed better than second. During 1941 and 1942 he sang in a church choir. When he was thirteen his father gave him his first musical instrument: a trombone. The trombone proved to be too unwieldy for Baker and it was quickly replaced by a trumpet. He took music instruction at school and played in the school's marching and dance bands. Baker completed one year of high school in Glendale before his family moved again, this time to North Redondo Beach, where they initially stayed with a family they knew from Oklahoma. Baker attended Redondo High School but quickly became restless. In 1946, during his junior year, he dropped out of high school and enlisted in the U.S. Army.

While Baker was stationed in war-ravaged Berlin, he tried out for the 298th Army Band. He was accepted as the main trumpet player and for the next two years he played in the band and performed at various official functions. It was during this time, while listening to the radio, that he experienced what he called "the first modern music I'd heard," that of Stan Kenton and Dizzy Gillespie. Kenton and Gillespie were creating the first bebop recordings, and Baker was fascinated by the new sound.

After Baker's discharge from the army in 1948, he returned to California, where his parents had purchased their first house. In 1949 Baker enrolled in El Camino Junior College in Lawndale. His major was music and his minor was English. During this period he played in various bands and began to experiment with drugs. In 1950 Baker dropped out of El Camino (his music teacher informed him that he would never have a career in music), and he reenlisted in the service, joining the Sixth Army Band in San Francisco. He played in the army band during the day and in area clubs at night. He married a woman named Charlaine, and they lived in a bungalow behind her parents' house.

Distressed after he was transferred to Arizona and separated from his wife and the California jazz scene, Baker went AWOL (absent without leave). He was given a second army discharge in 1951, after which he concentrated solely on playing in various combos around Los Angeles.

The next three years proved to be the most important in his early career. Throughout 1951 Baker played with

Chet Baker. METRONOME/ARCHIVE PHOTOS

Stan Getz. Although Baker had played with Dave Brubeck and Cal Tjader, his stay with Getz's band was his first extended employment with a jazz great. During his stay with Getz he perfected the restrained trumpet playing that would become his trademark.

Baker's trumpet work slowly became famous in the Los Angeles area, and when he tried out for a band Charlie Parker was putting together for a 1952 West Coast tour, he played only two songs before being hired. Playing with Parker was a formidable experience for Baker, who adapted his "soft" sound to the often ferocious speed of Parker's saxophone. Baker was also following in the footsteps of Miles Davis: Davis had played with Parker before moving to New York City to work with a celebrated nonet that featured arrangements by Gil Evans and Gerry Mulligan. Davis and the nonet "cooled" down bebop, exploring its complexities in a deceptively "static" or minimalist manner. The origins of this new jazz sound first appeared on Davis's *Birth of the Cool* (1949), an album Baker treasured and reportedly played throughout his life.

After his tour with Parker, Baker stayed in Los Angeles and completed the path laid out by Davis. Davis's innovation of cool jazz owed a debt to the arrangements and saxophone playing of Gerry Mulligan and, as soon as Baker learned that Mulligan was in Southern California looking to put together a band, he arranged a meeting. The result of their collaboration was one of the most famous postwar jazz units: Gerry Mulligan's "pianoless" quartet. It was at this point in his career that Baker solidified his signature style of romantic softness, of reticent phrasing, that became the hallmark of West Coast cool jazz. Baker rarely ever played louder than mezzo-forte and often held his melodic span to less than an octave. This sound was a stunning complement to Mulligan's baritone sax, and the band was an almost immediate critical and popular success. It was recorded by Pacific Jazz in 1952.

In 1953 Baker won the New Star award in *Down Beat's* first International Jazz Critics Poll. The sound of the Mulligan Quartet became internationally known. A series of other awards were given to Baker, and he quickly became the most talked about trumpet player in the country, overshadowing even Davis. Baker's detractors claimed that it was his good looks and his James Dean–like brooding that made him popular with audiences.

Just as the Gerry Mulligan Quartet was at the height of its popularity, both Mulligan and Baker were arrested for possession of drugs. Baker got off, but Mulligan spent time in jail, which effectively ended the quartet. After a short reunion with Parker, Baker went on to form his own band and toured for the next three years. Baker's singing became a consistent part of his performance, and in 1954 he released the first of his vocal-dominated recordings, *Chet Baker Sings and Plays.* The same year saw him named as the number-four male vocalist by *Down Beat.*

In 1955 he took his band to Europe for an eight-month tour, the longest taken by a jazz musician up to that time. He made his film debut in *Hell's Horizon*, the first of many film appearances, including in many Italian B pictures. However, at the height of his popularity in both the United States and Europe, heroin addiction started to show in his performances and emerging legal problems. He divorced Charlaine and married a woman named Halema, with whom he had a son in 1958. But Baker was arrested again for drug possession that same year, and in 1959 he spent four months in the New York City penitentiary on Rikers Island.

As soon as he emerged from prison he left for Europe, where he attempted to get his band back into touring form. He divorced Halema and married Carol Jackson. But his addiction and legal trouble followed. In 1960 he was arrested in Italy and spent sixteen months in prison there; it was an early tabloid scandal, and legal problems followed him throughout Europe. He was subsequently deported from Germany, Switzerland, and Great Britain.

The late 1960s were marred by lackluster performances and throwaway recordings as Baker struggled with addiction. The nadir came in 1968, when he was attacked in San Francisco by muggers for his drug money: he was severely beaten and his front teeth were knocked out. Unable to play the trumpet, Baker went into seclusion for two years and learned to play with just his lips and tongue.

The 1970s were an erratic period due to his struggle with drugs—he had been off and on methadone for years—and his attempt to relearn how to play his instrument. But the 1980s marked Baker's big comeback in jazz circles and in popularity. He recorded a series of critically lauded albums for the Danish label Steeplechase and played on a record of the pop singer Elvis Costello. In 1986 he was featured on the soundtrack to the jazz film *'Round Midnight,* and two years later he became the subject of a biographical film by Bruce Weber called *Let's Get Lost*, which was released a year after his death.

By the time of his death Baker's famous good looks had been exchanged for a mask of wrinkles he jokingly referred to as "laugh lines." He was beginning another comeback when he fell from a second-story window of an Amsterdam hotel. The circumstances surrounding the fall were mysterious: some claimed that he had committed suicide while others maintained that the fall was an accident, possibly brought on by intoxication. He is buried next to his father in Inglewood Park Cemetery in Inglewood, California. The mystery of his end has become emblematic of the romantic struggle he waged through his music and his life.

★

Baker's diary of his life in jazz and in trouble was discovered after his death and published in 1997 under the title *As Though I Had Wings: The Lost Memoir.* Two important accounts of Baker's career and struggles appeared in *Down Beat*: Ira Gitler, "Chet Baker's Tale of Woe" (30 July 1964), and Maggie Hawthorne, "Chet Baker" (14 Oct. 1981). Obituaries are in the *New York Times* and *Washington Post* (both 14 May 1988) and in *Esquire* (Dec. 1988).

JOHN ROCCO

BAKER, Ella Josephine (*b.* 13 December 1903 in Norfolk, Virginia; *d.* 13 December 1986 in New York City), community organizer and civil rights activist whose lifelong commitment toward working for social change led to a political career that spanned more than fifty years.

Baker was the second of three children born to Blake Baker, a steamship waiter, and Georgianna (Ross) Baker, a schoolteacher and community leader. Baker's parents were the educated children of former slaves, who insisted that their children receive the benefits of a formal education. As a young girl, Ella Baker grew up in Littleton, North Carolina, where the experiences and teachings of her parents and maternal grandparents played a critical role in her earliest understandings of oppression, resistance, and communal strength. Baker's grandfather was a minister who eventually bought a portion of the land on which he had toiled as a slave. Baker's grandmother had defied her white mistress by refusing to marry a man chosen for her. Baker was raised to believe in the benefits of communal responsibility, sharing, and cooperative economics. This egalitarian upbringing became her earliest example of a nonhierarchical community and laid the foundation for her social and political ideology.

Ella Baker. PHOTOGRAPHS AND PRINTS DIVISION, SCHOMBURG CENTER FOR RESEARCH IN BLACK CULTURE, THE NEW YORK PUBLIC LIBRARY. ASTOR, LENOX, AND TILDEN FOUNDATIONS

After attending primary school in Littleton, Baker moved to Raleigh, North Carolina, in 1918, to attend Shaw boarding school, because there were no secondary schools in Littleton. In 1923 Baker graduated from high school with dreams of becoming a medical missionary, but the cost of such an education was prohibitive. She enrolled instead at Shaw University in 1923 as a sociology major and graduated four years later as the class valedictorian.

Unable to afford graduate studies in sociology at the University of Chicago, in 1927 Baker moved to New York City, where she worked as a waitress and factory worker despite her college education. Baker rejected the option of becoming a schoolteacher because that was the expected career choice for educated black women at that time. She lived in Harlem during the late 1920s and early 1930s and witnessed firsthand the dehumanizing nature of poverty and hunger during the Great Depression. Simultaneously, however, New York City's burgeoning radical political culture was gaining popularity and provided forums for debate and potential organizing. One such organization with which Baker became involved was the Young Negroes Cooperative League (YNCL), whose mission was to gain economic power by forging consumer collaboration. The YNCL emphasized grassroots involvement, nonhierarchical leadership, and the full inclusion of youth and women. In 1931 Baker became the organization's first national director.

During this time, Baker was hired by the Works Progress Administration to implement a consumer education project. Baker also worked with the WPA's Workers Education Project, where she conducted literacy classes and educated workers about pertinent labor issues. At the same time, Baker joined the editorial staff of *American West Indian News* and *Negro National News.* About 1938 Baker married her longtime friend T. J. Roberts, but she never took his name.

In 1938 Baker began to work for the National Association for the Advancement of Colored People (NAACP) as a field secretary. She traveled extensively throughout the South, fund-raising and enlisting members for the organization. She visited churches and schools to speak with community members about how the NAACP could affect positive changes in their lives. Baker became known for her steadfastness and conviction and for her fearlessness in an atmosphere of racist violence where black people could be killed for simply registering to vote. Baker's dedicated canvasing laid the groundwork for her later work during the civil rights movement of the 1950s and 1960s.

In 1943 Baker returned to New York City and was appointed national director for the NAACP branches, although she questioned the organization's commitment toward gaining legal and legislative victories while ignoring a need for the meaningful involvement of its members. She recruited low-income members, who had been formerly overlooked by the NAACP, and continued to support campaigns that would engage the masses of the NAACP's membership by linking the organization's qualitative and practical goals. Following several years of internal discord, Baker formally resigned from the NAACP in 1946 because she was unable to see the organization realize its potential as an instrument for more grassroots community-building. That same year Baker became guardian to her niece, Jacqueline Baker Brockington, which hindered her ability to travel on behalf of the NAACP, and became a fund-raiser for the National Urban League Service Fund. Throughout the late 1940s she maintained an association with the NAACP on the local level by becoming an adviser to its Youth Council.

In 1953 Baker campaigned unsuccessfully for the New York State Assembly as a Liberal party candidate. The following year she became president of the New York City branch of the NAACP and chaired its education committee. When the Supreme Court in *Brown* v. *Board of Education of Topeka* (1954) ruled segregation in public schools unconstitutional, Baker dealt with the complicated social issues surrounding de facto segregation. In 1956 she and two of her political allies in New York founded the northern-based organization In Friendship to raise funds for the southern civil rights struggle. After significant fund-raising and the formation in 1957 of the Southern Christian Leadership Conference (SCLC), In Friendship ceased activity.

At the encouragement of her colleagues who were advisers to Martin Luther King, Jr., Baker moved to Atlanta to coordinate the SCLC's Crusade for Citizenship. Under Baker's leadership, this voter rights project registered 13,000 new voters. Two years later Baker became executive director of the SCLC. Although King was the leader and spokesperson for the SCLC, Baker ran its office and coordinated all of its programs. Under Baker's leadership, the SCLC grew into an organization with sixty-five affiliates in various southern cities. Although Baker was responsible for both the SCLC's community-based success and its national notoriety, the same problems of hierarchical leadership and centralized decision-making that characterized the NAACP during her years there were present within the SCLC. Baker's beliefs in group-centered leadership and participatory democracy were at odds with what became the organization's mission to promote one leader. Even though Baker had greater organizing experience than the ministers for whom she worked, her policy suggestions regarding the inclusion of young people and women were ignored. Instead, Baker and many other women who were the backbone of the movement were expected to focus on completing administrative tasks.

During a wave of sit-ins by black college students in the winter of 1960, Baker saw an opportunity to harness the students' dedication and enthusiasm for social activism. She organized the Student Nonviolent Coordinating Committee (SNCC), a conference of student leaders at Shaw University, her alma mater. At that time Baker insisted that the student movement determine how it would pursue civil rights without the governing influence of the SCLC. Baker taught SNCC members how to conduct their own Freedom Rides and coordinate voter registration drives that would reach people in the untapped southern hinterlands. She was an adviser to SNCC until 1964.

That same year Baker helped launch the Mississippi Freedom Democratic Party (MFDP), a grassroots political organization that threatened the all-white Mississippi Democratic party. Baker relocated to Washington, D.C., to manage the MFDP's national office. At the Democratic party convention of 1964, the MFDP urged Democratic leaders to refuse seats to the white Mississippi delegation because they had discriminated against Mississippi's black electorate. The Mississippi delegates were seated anyway, but the MFDP's actions were the catalyst for future anti-discrimination reforms within the Democratic party and local primaries.

In 1967 Baker joined the Southern Conference Educational Fund (SCEF) and traveled the country speaking about the need to link the fight for civil rights with the fight for civil liberties. Baker believed that this would encourage coalition-building between black civil rights activists and white liberals. In 1972 she moved back to Harlem and served as the vice chair of the Mass Party Organizing Committee. She also sat on the national board of the Puerto Rican Solidarity Committee. Throughout the 1970s and 1980s, despite failing health, Baker continued to lecture and advise various political organizations around the country, particularly regarding apartheid in South Africa. Baker continually reminded those around her that the liberation struggles of all people must never cease until equal rights are guaranteed to all.

Following a lifelong battle with asthma, Baker died in her New York City home.

★

Joanne Grant, *Ella Baker: Freedom Bound* (1998), is a full biography. Further information about Baker can be found in Gerda Lerner, *Black Women in America: A Documentary History* (1973) and Ellen Cantarow, *Moving the Mountain* (1980), a social history. See also Paula Giddings, *When and Where I Enter: The Impact of*

Black Women on Race and Sex in America, 2d ed. (1996), and Vicki Crawford, Jacqueline Rouse, and Barbara Woods, eds., *Women in the Civil Rights Movement: Trailblazers and Torchbearers* (1990). Darlene Clark Hine, *Black Women in America,* 2d ed. (1994), gives encyclopedic treatment. Baker is profiled in Jean Wiley, "On the Front Lines: Four Women Activists Whose Work Touched Millions of Lives," *Essence* (Feb. 1990): 75–79. An obituary is in the *New York Times* (16 Dec. 1986).

LaRose T. Parris

BALDRIGE, (Howard) Malcolm (*b.* 4 October 1922 in Omaha, Nebraska; *d.* 25 July 1987 in Walnut Creek, California), businessman and U.S. secretary of commerce (1981–1987).

The quintessential cowboy who lived and died a maverick, Malcolm was born into an upper-class Omaha family. As the oldest child and firstborn son, he was named for his attorney father. His mother was Regina (Connell) Baldrige. Of his two siblings, his sister, Letitia, achieved a degree of fame as First Lady Jacqueline Kennedy's social secretary. The family's initial involvement in politics dated from the 1920s, when the senior Baldrige ran successfully for the Nebraska legislature. From 1931 until 1933, Baldrige, a Republican, was a member of the U.S. House of Representatives. While his father pursued a political career, Malcolm attended school in the Midwest and then enrolled in the Hotchkiss School in Connecticut. Summer vacations were spent working on a Nebraska ranch, where he learned to rope cattle, something that became a passionate avocational pursuit. Baldrige next attended Yale University, where, as an English major, he wrote his senior thesis on Chaucer. Prior to receiving his B.A. in 1944, Baldrige was inducted into the U.S. Army. Although his initial rank was that of private, he was discharged as a captain in 1946, having served in the Twenty-seventh Infantry Division's field artillery brigade in the Pacific theater of operations during World War II and as a member of the occupation forces in Honshu, Japan.

Malcolm Baldrige, 1985. AP/Wide World Photos

In 1947 Baldrige's business career began rather inauspiciously when he accepted a position as a foreman at the Eastern Malleable Iron Company's foundry in Naugatuck, Connecticut. By 1951 he had risen to the position of managing director of the company's Frazer and Jones division, and that same year, on 31 March, he married Margaret Trowbridge Murray in Pittsburgh, Pennsylvania. The couple had two daughters. In 1957 Malcolm Baldrige was named vice president of Eastern Malleable Iron, and in 1960 he became president. Two years later he accepted the position of executive vice president of the Scovill Manufacturing Company, a Waterbury, Connecticut, brass company plagued by mounting losses.

Within a year Baldrige was president and chief executive officer of Scovill. By then he had restructured Scovill's management. According to a *Time* magazine piece (30 Aug. 1968), this was accomplished by "offering numerous vice presidents line jobs or early retirement. Baldrige eliminated committee meetings altogether, cut reports down to the bare minimum, and held his eight division managers answerable for unnecessary accumulation of statistics." Given the cyclical nature of brass manufacturing, Baldrige diversified the company. In addition to turning out aluminum products, Scovill began to market electric carving knives and other consumer items through its Hamilton Beach appliance division. Scovill also acquired other companies, including NuTone, a chimes manufacturer, in 1967, and Caradco, a door and window frame maker, in 1968. These and other Scovill products, such as Yale locks, were sold internationally. So successful was the company's expansion that by 1980 it had a presence in twenty-three countries and annual sales of $1 billion.

Although Baldrige served on the boards of a number of other companies, including IBM, Uniroyal, AMF, Inc., Bendix Corporation, the Swiss Reinsurance Company, and the Connecticut Mutual Life Insurance Company, he remained active in community organizations in Waterbury, Connecticut, where Scovill was headquartered. The Red Cross, Waterbury Hospital, the Greater Waterbury Chamber of Commerce, and the Easter Seal Society all benefited from his presence on their boards. On the local level, one of Baldrige's most noteworthy achievements was his role in establishing the Waterbury Non-Profit Development Corporation, which provided housing and recreational and job opportunities for African Americans. In the midst of racial upheaval in 1967, Baldrige, a member of the National Association for the Advancement of Colored People, personally visited minority neighborhoods in an attempt to calm tensions. When the Reverend Martin Luther King, Jr., was assassinated in 1968, Baldrige used his corporate jet to fly Waterbury's African-American community leaders to Atlanta for King's funeral.

While remaining committed to community service, Baldrige became increasingly involved in government and politics on the state level in the 1960s and 1970s. He served on the Governor's Commission on the Status of Women, a logical appointment in view of his wife's trailblazing achievements as the first female member of the volunteer Waterbury fire department. He was also a member of the Citizen's Commission on the State Legislature and a delegate to the Connecticut constitutional convention. An active Republican, Baldrige included among his party activities chairmanship of the Republican budget committee for the state of Connecticut (1969–1972) and platform committee membership and participation in Republican national conventions as a delegate from 1964 through 1980. As state campaign manager for his old friend George Bush, Baldrige was the architect of Bush's victory in the 1980 Connecticut primary in Bush's bid for the Republican presidential nomination. Although Ronald Reagan won the nomination, during the campaign Baldrige served as a member of the national Republican finance committee and as national vice chairman of the Business for Reagan-Bush Committee and cochairman of the Connecticut Reagan-Bush for President Committee. A month after his election, Reagan nominated Baldrige for the position of secretary of commerce.

Sworn in as secretary in January 1981, Baldrige immediately set out to reduce governmental regulations and to increase both productivity and U.S. exports. "As a nation we have to regain the competitive edge at home and abroad that we formerly had," Baldrige declared in the *Wall Street Journal* (12 Dec. 1980). As commerce secretary, Baldrige grappled with the challenge posed by Japanese imports, particularly automobiles. Voluntary restraints on Japanese exports was the solution he envisioned. In his efforts to boost U.S. exports, the secretary was nearly thwarted by David Stockman, director of the Office of Management and Budget, who in 1981 proposed major cuts in the Commerce Department's spending in precisely those areas directly involved with exports. Ultimately, the cuts that were made were only a fraction of those proposed by Stockman.

Although he was unalterably opposed to budget cuts that he believed would compromise his department's effectiveness, Baldrige wholeheartedly endorsed other types of reductions. A longtime opponent of unnecessary meetings (going back to his first year at Scovill), as commerce secretary Baldrige attempted to reduce the number of committee meetings, only to eventually concede that meetings were necessary to ensure involvement by interested groups and individuals. He had greater success in his efforts to promote within the department the use of precise language devoid of bureaucratic phraseology and the adoption of a goal-setting, management-by-objectives administrative strategy.

Throughout his business and government careers, Baldrige, a trim six feet, one inch, stayed in shape by pursuing his hobby of steer roping. Enamored of the American West, Baldrige adorned his library with a saddle he had won in a California team-roping contest. At Scovill he kept steer horns in his office, wore a Western-style leather belt with a large silver buckle, and always had a lasso on hand to be used while pondering difficult business problems. At his Woodbury, Connecticut, estate Baldrige was able to lasso real steers. Approaching his avocation with the same seriousness evident in his business and governmental careers, Baldrige attained the designation of professional steer roper in the 1960s. In 1981 the Professional Rodeo Cowboys Association conferred its Man of the Year award on Baldrige.

While serving as secretary of commerce in President Reagan's second administration, Baldrige died after suffering massive injuries to his heart and pancreas after a horse reared and fell on him while he was practicing for a rodeo event. Following services at the National Cathedral in Washington, D.C., and at the North Congregational Church in Woodbury, Connecticut, Baldrige was buried in Woodbury. In addition to numerous commerce department employees and high-ranking government officials, including President Reagan, the 2,000 mourners at the Washington service on 29 July included a delegation from the Professional Rodeo Cowboys Association. Addressing those assembled, President Reagan praised Baldrige for his simplicity: "He never judged a man or woman by rank or trappings." The president also noted what he called perhaps the least recognized of his major achievements—the securing of trade ties with China.

A tough but fair negotiator, Secretary Baldrige won the respect of his opponents. Despite the Reagan administration's imposition of high tariffs on Japanese imports, a move advocated by Baldrige, Nobuo Matsunaga, the Japanese ambassador to the United States, declared a few months before the secretary's death: "Our differences are never an obstacle. I have been admiring his personality. Mac Baldrige is full of cowboy spirit. I like him." Ambassador Matsunaga was not alone. The witty, incisive Baldrige was "long on candor," according to a *New York Times* editorial published after his death which noted that he "brought decency and a cool head to the upper reaches of politics."

Baldrige's admirers, both in and out of government, viewed him as an American original, a rugged individualist who set goals for himself, for Scovill, and for the Department of Commerce and then did his utmost to achieve them. Although his sudden death prevented him from surpassing Herbert Hoover's record length of service as commerce secretary, seven years and five months, he clearly left his mark on the department and on the nation. In recognition of Baldrige's commitment to excellence, in 1987 the Department of Commerce established the Malcolm Baldrige National Quality Awards to foster greater efficiency while enhancing the global competitiveness of American companies.

★

The papers Baldrige generated while he was secretary of commerce are in the National Archives, Washington, D.C. Papers relating to his business career are in the archives of the Smithsonian Institution, Yale University, and Harvard University. Information about his business career can be found in *Time* (30 Aug. 1968), *Forbes* (1 Apr. 1972), and the *Wall Street Journal* (12 Dec. 1980). Baldrige's role as commerce secretary is discussed in *Financial World* (27 Nov. 1985) and *Business America* (11 May 1987). Obituaries and other articles appearing at the time of his death include those in the *New York Times* (26–28 July 1987).

MARILYN E. WEIGOLD

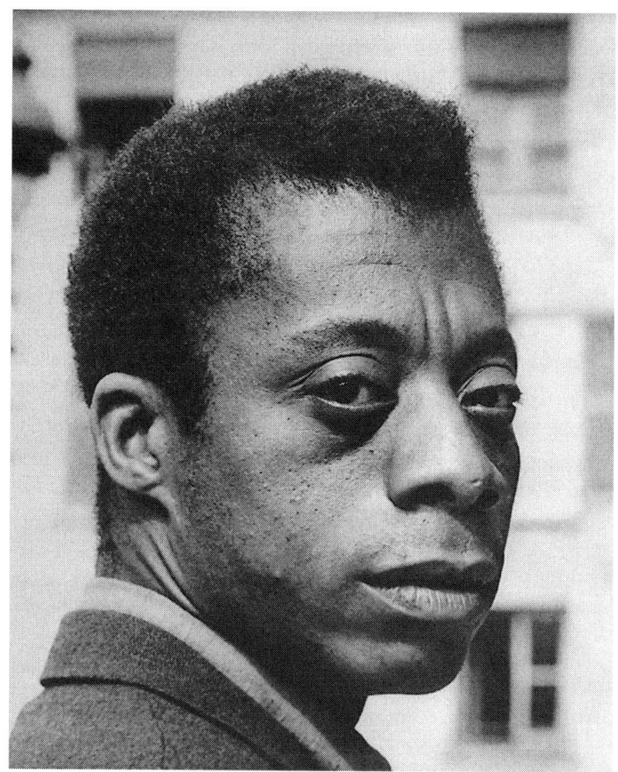

James Baldwin, *c.* 1964. UPI/CORBIS-BETTMANN

BALDWIN, James Arthur (*b.* 2 August 1924 in New York City; *d.* 30 November 1987 in Saint Paul de Vence, France), fiction writer, playwright, and essayist who was, in the 1950s and 1960s, a passionate and eloquent spokesman for the legitimacy of racial, ethnic, and sexual diversity and a summoner of humanity's conscience in the United States and the Western world.

The illegitimate child of Emma Berdis Jones, a domestic worker from Maryland, Baldwin acquired his surname from his stepfather, David Baldwin, a factory worker and lay preacher from New Orleans who married Jones in 1927 and died of mental illness in 1943. Baldwin had eight younger siblings, three brothers and five sisters, for whom he felt familial devotion. His mother heavily relied on his assistance at home, where poverty was the predominant condition. Baldwin's relationship with his stepfather was difficult, ambivalent, and painful. He craved his stepfather's love, friendship, and recognition, which his rigid and domineering stepfather was unwilling and perhaps unable to give. "My childhood was awful," Baldwin later remembered.

Baldwin's mother recalled that the boy "lived in books." Baldwin realized that reading and writing would be his escape from the menacing streets of the ghetto. Smart, tiny, and shy, with protruding eyes, he found school unpleasant because his schoolmates called him "Bug-eyes" or "Froggy." In 1938 Baldwin graduated from Frederick Douglass Junior High School in Harlem, where he had served as editor of the school paper, the *Douglass Pilot.* His interest in writing and literature was further encouraged by Countee Cullen, a poet, who was one of Baldwin's teachers. Baldwin continued his education at DeWitt Clinton High School in the Bronx. In this predominantly white and Jewish school, he established a number of lasting friendships and contributed to the school magazine, the *Magpie.* Baldwin's grades were inconsistent, partly because of his social background and partly because of his preference for the humanities over the sciences.

Baldwin spent the years from 1938 to 1941 in an intensively religious mode, possibly in defiance of his stepfather and in competition with him. He underwent a dramatically emotional conversion at Mount Calvary of the Pentecostal Faith church, and then he became a junior preacher at the Fireside Pentecostal Assembly, a small storefront church in Harlem. There he practiced his rhetorical talent and became passionately articulate in elaborating on biblical texts, inspired by the cadences of the King James version. He never lost that ability, even after he left the church. He received his high school diploma in January 1942.

During the summer of 1942 Baldwin joined his school friend Emile Capouya in searching for a job that would enable him to support his family and leave Harlem. Granted a hardship deferment from military service, he spent a year working on the construction of an army depot in Belle Mead, New Jersey, which placed him in a confrontation with segregation. In his refusal to comply with the role-playing expected from blacks in those days, Baldwin came to the brink of self-destruction. Yet he refused to give in to the hatred for whites that his stepfather preached.

Baldwin was fated to live his books before he could write them. In 1943 he moved to Greenwich Village in New York City to pursue a writing career, while making his living as a busboy, dishwasher, and waiter. By this time, he had accumulated enough life experience for his earliest fiction, essays, and plays. A full decade before his semiautobiographical novel would be published, he produced the first draft, which he initially called "Crying Holy" and somewhat later renamed "In My Father's House." Both of the earlier titles reveal more about the contents of the book, but the final title, *Go Tell It on the Mountain* (1953), casts the experience as a poetic revelation. During this decade, Baldwin journeyed from referential storytelling to the creation of literary texts that were testimonies of a witness who exhibited a deep understanding of the world.

Baldwin's public literary life began in 1947, when he sold his first reviews to the *Nation* and the *New Leader* magazines. He entered the world of polemics with a piece on black-Jewish relations, "The Harlem Ghetto," which appeared the following year in *Commentary.* His friendship with Richard Wright, the renowned author of *Native Son* (1940), aided in bringing Baldwin a Eugene F. Saxton Memorial Trust Fellowship (1945), which enabled him to devote more time to writing. He also won a Rosenwald Foundation Fellowship in 1948 but decided to use that money for a one-way airplane ticket to France, which became his other home for the rest of his life. He maintained that his transatlantic commuting was the only way for him to survive and remain sane. In 1949 he wrote a controversial essay, "Everybody's Protest Novel," for *Zero* magazine in Paris; in this article he tried to liberate himself as an artist from his own earlier obsession with *Uncle Tom's Cabin* (1852) by Harriet Beecher Stowe and the writings of his mentor Wright. After Baldwin experienced a breakdown in Paris and brief imprisonment for "stealing" a bedsheet, Lucien Happersberger, a Swiss painter he met in 1949 who became a lifelong friend, took care of him at an isolated chalet in the Swiss Alps.

In the Alps, Baldwin finally brought his struggle with the manuscript of his first novel to successful completion. *Go Tell It on the Mountain* received enthusiastic reviews that confirmed the author's literary power and skill. Retelling his Harlem childhood and adolescence in a carefully structured narrative, Baldwin parted from the writing tradition of black protest literature with its limitations, an intention he had pronounced in "Everybody's Protest Novel." "I wanted my people to be people first, Negroes almost incidentally," he declared. However, Baldwin's first collection of essays, *Notes of a Native Son* (1955), proved that no one could compete with him as a writer on black issues. In incisive, beautiful language, he clarified his views on the issues of black and American identity, the use of history and the concept and consequences of pluralism, the terror of racial hate in society and within individuals, and the meaning and lessons of suffering and love. In 1955 Howard University produced his play, *The Amen Corner,* based on his teenage experiences, in a Harlem storefront church. The play was published in 1968. In 1956 Baldwin published his second novel, *Giovanni's Room,* a sensitively told story of an ordeal concerning the protagonist's sexual identity and orientation. Although the characters are white, critics stated that the issue of homosexuality could also be read as an alternative for racial problems. For Baldwin, both subjects were personal. He decided to return to the United States in 1957. That year he published a moving short story, "Sonny's Blues," in *Partisan Review.* It tells of a dead artist-musician who is brought back into existence through his brother's intense reveries, empathy, and attempts to understand.

In the 1960s Baldwin's writings changed from a religious to a secular mood and from the aesthetics of the spirituals to those of the blues. His essays showed growing anger and heat, and his collection *Nobody Knows My Name: More Notes of a Native Son* (1961), which became a best-seller, includes strong pieces about his trips to the American South. Race and sex were dramatically linked in his third novel, *Another Country* (1962), in which black and white characters, mostly artists, grope through the chaos of their lives in search of love. In another volume, warningly called *The Fire Next Time* (1963), he confessed to his fascination with the Black Muslim ideology of racial hatred and supremacy. At the time, Baldwin served as a public intellectual in the media and was perceived by many as a prophet of his race. His presence in the historic March on Washington on 28 August 1963 was considered important.

The tension between the roles of artist and activist was not easy to bear, as his play *Blues for Mister Charlie* (1964) illustrates. Based on the lynching of Emmett Till, which Baldwin investigated with black activist Medgar Evers in Mississippi, the story is intended to test the limits of non-violent resistance and rebellion. He refused to let director Elia Kazan and the Actors Studio stage it as a grand premiere in the Lincoln Center Repertory Theater, and the play opened on Broadway in April 1964. Although drama was not the most natural literary form for Baldwin, the play added to his reputation and fame, as did *Nothing Personal* (1964), a book in which he wrote prose to accompany the photographs of Richard Avedon, an old school friend. Also in 1964, Baldwin became a member of the National Institute of Arts and Letters. He published a collection of short fiction, *Going to Meet the Man,* in 1965. His personal argument over how a famous artist might best serve his or her community and people is reflected in *Tell Me How Long the Train's Been Gone* (1968). In this novel, the loss of artistic control over the body of the work and the sentimentalizing of political attitudes suggest how difficult it is to produce relevant art. His essayistic *No Name in the Street*, offering a rather apocalyptic and militant vision of the West in general and the United States in particular, was published in 1972, when the civil rights movement was receding and even strong expressions had begun to lose their forcible touch.

Baldwin's novel *If Beale Street Could Talk* (1974), however, was another critical and commercial success. Although it is a story of a judicial system that is insensitive to truth, especially in the cases of minority people, it is also one of the very first all-black love stories. At the time that he published his last novel, *Just Above My Head* (1979), Baldwin had, in his own words, "come full circle." Many of his typical themes, motifs, tensions, and conflicts reappeared in a complex plot in which music plays a key role. Critics were reminded of the author's earlier short story "Sonny's Blues." Death was a phenomenon that permeated Baldwin's writings and a dread he contended with throughout his life. In the 1980s he published some of his poetry and two books of nonfiction, *The Evidence of Things Not Seen* (1985) and *The Price of the Ticket: Collected Non-Fiction. 1948–1985* (1985), a summarizing volume.

Baldwin, who never married, died from stomach cancer in southern France, where he spent most of his last years. He left unfinished a play, "The Welcome Table," and a biography of Martin Luther King, Jr. Baldwin was eulogized at a huge memorial service at the Cathedral of St. John the Divine in New York City. He is buried in Ferncliff Cemetery in Hartsdale, New York.

Along with Ralph Ellison and William Demby, James Baldwin contributed in the 1950s to the liberation of African-American fiction from stereotypical protest writing. *Go Tell It on the Mountain, Giovanni's Room,* and "Sonny's Blues" remain texts valued by both critics and readers for their emotional and aesthetic power. Baldwin's earlier essays offer a sharp analysis of the human condition and its social and racial dimension, and his later, more militant pieces are charged with prophetic wisdom informed of an apocalyptic vision. His statement, "This world is white no longer, and it will never be white again," is of such a nature. Baldwin's appeal to human tolerance and love is a challenge to nations and individuals. Not surprisingly, that appeal lost some effect when it assumed a more political tone and form.

★

James Baldwin's papers are at the Schomburg Center for Research in Black Culture, New York City. Fred L. Standley and Louis H. Pratt, eds., *Conversations with James Baldwin* (1989), contains interviews that span more than a quarter of a century. Fern Marja Eckman, *The Furious Passage of James Baldwin* (1966), is based on personal interviews with Baldwin and many individuals in his life. Book-length biographies include Quincey Troupe, ed., *James Baldwin: The Legacy* (1989); James Campbell, *Talking at the Gates: A Life of James Baldwin* (1991); and David Adams Leeming, *James Baldwin: A Biography* (1994). Stanley Macebuh, *James Baldwin: A Critical Study* (1973), and Carolyn Wedin Sylvander, *James Baldwin* (1980), combine biographical and critical approaches in lucid survey treatments. Fred L. Standley and Nancy V. Burt, eds., *Critical Essays on James Baldwin* (1988), is a collection of reprinted and new criticism. Jakob Köllhofer, ed., *James Baldwin: His Place in American Literary History and His Reception in Europe* (1991), confirms Baldwin's national and international reputation and relevance. An obituary is in the *New York Times* (2 Dec. 1987).

JOSEF JAŘAB

BALDWIN, Raymond Earl (*b.* 31 August 1893 in Rye, New York; *d.* 4 October 1986 in Fairfield, Connecticut), governor of Connecticut, state supreme court justice, and U.S. senator.

Baldwin was seven years old when his father, Lucien Earl, his mother, Sarah Emily Tyler, and his sisters returned to the state where Baldwins, "Connecticut Yankees and proud of it," had lived for eight generations. They settled in Middletown, where Lucien worked with a wholesale grocery firm. Baldwin spent several happy summers on the Beacon Falls farm of his grandfather, who instilled in him the idea that in a democracy every citizen should devote some time to public service. Other summers he worked in the Connecticut Valley tobacco fields with boys from local Polish, Italian, and Swedish families or in the Colt Patent Fire Arms factory.

Baldwin attended Middletown's public schools and Wesleyan University. He graduated from Wesleyan in 1916 and, with his heart set on becoming a judge, entered Yale Law School. Baldwin became increasingly concerned about the war in Europe, however, and the day after the United States entered the war, he enlisted in the navy. He soon won a commission and served as a lieutenant on a destroyer escort. Baldwin returned to Yale in the fall of 1919 to complete his law studies and was admitted to the bar in 1921. He married Edith Lindholm, a Middletown high school teacher, in 1922; they had three sons.

Baldwin worked briefly in a New York City law office, then practiced in New Haven with well-known trial lawyer Philip Pond. In 1924 he joined Pullman and Comley, a

Raymond E. Baldwin. UPI/CORBIS-BETTMANN

leading firm in Bridgeport, and within four years became a partner. Baldwin remained with the firm until he was elected governor of Connecticut in 1939.

Baldwin began his career in public service in the office of the public prosecutor of the Stratford Town Court in 1927. He became judge of that court in 1931. As he prosecuted numerous violations of the Volstead Act, the difficulty of obtaining evidence and securing convictions of Prohibition violators convinced Baldwin that the act and the Eighteenth Amendment were unenforceable and should be repealed. In 1931, as a Republican legislator in the Connecticut General Assembly, he supported a resolution calling for state conventions to repeal the Eighteenth Amendment. Reelected to the 1933 session, he was chosen majority leader of the Republican state house, but Republican power was dwindling, and Democrats soon controlled the state senate and the governor's office. After the 1933 session, Baldwin returned to his legal practice and gained distinction as one of Connecticut's outstanding trial lawyers.

Acting on his belief that a political party survives on strong local organizations, Baldwin served as Stratford's town chairman from 1935 to 1937. He also worked with other Connecticut Republicans to rejuvenate the party. They encouraged younger persons to join them in discussion groups (the Beefsteak Clubs) throughout the state and to become candidates for public office. As strict constitutional constructionists, they denounced the federal government's growing power and the use of relief programs to win votes. They also disassociated themselves from the old Republican state party leadership. By the 1938 state convention, Connecticut Republicans were ready to reverse eight straight years of defeat and nominated Baldwin to run for governor. Campaigning as a reformer (both parties had been tainted with scandals) and on the theme of friendly but not paternalistic government, Baldwin won over popular incumbent Wilbur Cross and socialist challenger Jasper McLevy, mayor of Bridgeport.

Achieving most of his campaign platform, Baldwin established a job-training program for paying jobs to replace federally funded New Deal relief projects. The program became a model for other states and readied Connecticut to handle the growth of its huge World War II armament and aviation industries. He established uniform court procedures and compulsory annual audits of state and town books, and he supported progressive labor legislation. The Connecticut National Guard was reorganized and strengthened, so that, when it was called into service for World War II, it was a superior unit. By slashing spending, but without raising taxes, Governor Baldwin turned the state's deficit into a surplus and balanced the state budget.

Having gained nationwide attention for his success as campaigner and governor, Baldwin was presidential candidate Wendell Willkie's favorite for his running mate, but, unfortunately for Baldwin, the Republican ticket had to be "balanced" with a westerner. In the Democratic sweep of 1940, Governor Baldwin narrowly lost reelection but was returned to office in 1942. In 1944 he alone survived as Democrats took all the other state offices and the Senate, which made for a tempestuous and frustrating term. As wartime governor, he sought and received an extension of his powers to deal with the industrial expansion complicated by labor and fuel shortages. With reconversion to peacetime, he organized retraining programs for veterans and war workers facing severe unemployment.

In June 1945 Baldwin surprised Connecticut by announcing he would retire from politics at the end of his term in January 1947. "I do not think any governor should serve more than two consecutive terms," he said. Baldwin had already been elected a vice president, general counsel, and a director of Connecticut Mutual Life Insurance Company, but prominent Republicans in Connecticut and the nation were pushing him toward the U.S. Senate race, saying his name would strengthen the entire ticket. In the fall of 1946, Governor Baldwin reluctantly ran to fill the unexpired term of the late senator Francis T. Maloney. Baldwin was easily elected. With an impressive administrative record, he resigned the governorship on 27 December 1946 to begin a short Senate career.

Baldwin was one of the Young Turk Republicans seeking

a role in policy making, an internationalist who believed in bipartisanship, and a proponent of labor-management cooperation. He insisted that the Republican Congress should address the needs of the American people with progressive legislation but not excessive regulation. The conservative party leadership, however, bypassed him as the logical chairman of a subcommittee to investigate soaring postwar prices, and his advice for attracting young and independent voters was disregarded.

In the Eighty-first Congress, Baldwin was made chairman of an armed services subcommittee investigating the trial of German troops sentenced for the Malmedy Massacre of American soldiers in 1944. While serving as chairman, he became the victim of personal attack by Senator Joseph McCarthy. When Baldwin's subcommittee upheld the findings of the original trial, McCarthy, siding with the German soldiers, charged Baldwin as "criminally responsible" for a miscarriage of justice. This clinched the senator's decision to leave politics. Baldwin had already been consulting with Connecticut governor Chester Bowles on his lifelong desire to be a judge. When the Democratic governor Bowles appointed Baldwin associate justice of the state's supreme court (then called the supreme court of errors), he resigned as senator on 16 December 1949. Ten years later Democratic governor Abraham Ribicoff appointed him state chief justice. Judge Baldwin overhauled court rules, lessened congestion in lower court dockets, developed stricter legal ethics, and simplified citizen complaint procedures. He participated in nearly 3,000 cases and wrote more than 350 opinions. After mandatory retirement from the bench in 1963, at age seventy, Baldwin worked for the next two decades as a referee of the Middlesex Superior Court, hearing civil cases that did not require a jury trial. He also continued his lifelong activity in Connecticut's Episcopal diocese. When the state's constitutional convention met in 1965, he was its chairman. Baldwin died at a Fairfield convalescent home and is buried at Middletown's Indian Hill Cemetery.

Baldwin was a large, affable gentleman, stubborn at times, with a rich voice and an eloquent manner of speaking. Always professional in action, he was also hospitable and friendly. His sense of loyalty to the Republican party included the obligation to criticize and correct its faults. In a congressional tribute to him, U.S. Representative Barbara Kennelly described Baldwin as a "bedrock Yankee conservative—in the noblest sense of that oft-misunderstood term."

★

Baldwin's papers are in two collections at the Connecticut State Archives, located in the Connecticut State Library: Records of the Governor, 1939–1941, which includes correspondence; and Papers of Raymond E. Baldwin, 1938–1974, which includes correspondence, personal files, scrapbooks, speeches, and court administrative files. *Connecticut Reports,* vols. 97–125, contain cases argued by Baldwin as an attorney; his deliberations and findings while on the state court are in vols. 136–151. *American Law Reports* cites twelve of Baldwin's opinions as noteworthy cases. Baldwin's series of lectures on the practical side of politics at Wesleyan University (1947, 1948, 1949) are compiled in his book *Let's Go into Politics* (1952). Curtiss S. Johnson, *Raymond E. Baldwin* (1972), is a detailed biography by someone close to his subject for more than fifty years and who had access to a variety of sources. State Historian Albert E. VanDusen, *Connecticut: A Fully Illustrated History of the State from the Seventeenth Century to the Present* (1961), places Baldwin's importance within the perspective of the state emerging from depression and into its role as the "arsenal of democracy" during World War II. Chester Bowles, *Promises to Keep* (1971), describes the nuances of his appointment of Baldwin to the Connecticut supreme court. Robert Griffith, *Politics of Fear: Joseph R. McCarthy and the Senate,* 2d ed. (1987), details Baldwin's experience with Senator McCarthy and cites congressional sources for the Malmedy Massacre investigation. Charlotte Crystal, "Many Join in Farewell to Baldwin," is a front-page feature in the *Middletown Press* (9 Oct. 1986). An obituary is in the *New York Times* (5 Oct. 1986).

SYLVIA B. LARSON

BALL, Lucille Désirée (*b.* 6 August 1911 in Jamestown, New York; *d.* 26 April 1989 in Los Angeles, California), film actress, comedienne, and television producer whose television persona of Lucy Ricardo was one of television's most popular characters.

Lucille Ball was one of two children of Henry Dunnell Ball, a telephone lineman, and Désirée ("DeDe") Evelyn Hunt, a pianist who encouraged her daughter's acting ambitions. When Henry Ball died in 1915, the family moved into DeDe's parents' home, where "Grandpa Hunt," an ardent socialist, became a father figure for Ball and encouraged her acting ambitions by taking her to vaudeville shows and films. Ball interrupted her high school education at the age of fifteen to enroll in an acting school in New York City but returned home after six weeks with the school's advice that she give up her stage aspirations.

She continued to return to New York for casting calls and rehearsals, using the stage name Diane Belmont, while she supported herself with jobs as a drugstore soda jerk, dress model, and nude model for artists and photographers. She contracted rheumatoid arthritis at the age of seventeen and was incapacitated nearly three years, but she returned to modeling after her recovery.

Ball eventually gained nationwide exposure in advertisements as the Chesterfield Girl in 1932. This led to movie roles with United Artists (she moved to California in the spring of 1933), first a brief walk-on in *Broadway Thru a*

Lucille Ball. ARCHIVE PHOTOS

Keyhole (1933), then as a Goldwyn Girl in *Roman Scandals* (1933).

Ball spent eighteen months under contract with Goldwyn–United Artists then joined the Columbia Pictures stock company, where she gained her first screen credit in *Carnival* (1935) and appeared in several comedies with the Three Stooges. She later recalled: "It was one continuous shower bath of Vichy water and lemon-meringue pie. I was the 'she-Stooge' to the Three Stooges, and I loved every minute of it."

She then went to RKO studios, where she had her first speaking role, in *I Dream Too Much* (1935), and over the course of the next seven years her weekly salary went from $50 to $3,500. During the following decade she appeared in dozens of films and eventually obtained top billing in *The Big Street* (1942), *Du Barry Was a Lady* (1943), and *The Dark Corner* (1946). For a time she shared an office with the comedian Buster Keaton, to whom she attributed much of her later success at slapstick and pantomime routines. Ball also made appearances on several radio programs during the late 1930s and early 1940s, including the *Phil Baker Show, Wonder Bread Show, Lux Radio Theatre,* and *Screen Guild Playhouse.*

During the filming of *Too Many Girls* (1940), Ball became attracted to one of the actors, a Cuban bandleader named Desi Arnaz. The couple married on 30 November 1940; they had two children, both of whom would become actors: Desiderio Alberto Arnaz IV ("Little Desi") and Lucie Désirée Arnaz.

As the business fortunes of Hollywood moviemakers began to decline in the post–World War II era, Ball and her husband explored other media. She starred in the CBS radio series *My Favorite Husband* from July 1947 to March 1951. During 1947 and 1948 she also toured in the stage play *Dream Girl.* In 1949 and 1950 she returned to films, starring in the comedies *Sorrowful Jones* (1949), *Easy Living* (1949), *Miss Grant Takes Richmond* (1950), *Fancy Pants* (1950), and *The Fuller Brush Girl* (1950).

During this period Ball and her husband tried to persuade television executives and advertisers to support their idea for a comedy series starring both of them. The executives were skeptical that audiences would accept the "mixed marriage" of an Irish wife and a Cuban husband, so Ball and Arnaz went on a vaudeville tour, performing slapstick comedy and a "Cuban Pete–Sally Sweet" song medley.

Vaudeville audiences loved the Ball-Arnaz comedy team. CBS was persuaded to contract for the proposed television series, although the performers largely financed the initial programs of *I Love Lucy.* Ball and Arnaz hired two vaudeville veterans, Vivian Vance and William Frawley, to play their second bananas (and landlords) Ethel and Fred Mertz. The contract with Vance, who was several years younger than Ball, stipulated that she would gain enough weight for her character to look frumpy and appear considerably older than Ball's character.

Ball and Arnaz set up Desilu Productions, Inc., in 1950 to film and finance the episodes of *I Love Lucy,* thereby retaining substantial control over their product and introducing a number of innovations into television production. Unlike most programs, which were produced and televised in New York City, *I Love Lucy* was shot with three cameras on movie film in Hollywood. The innovative technique was devised by Arnaz in collaboration with Karl Freund, an Academy Award–winning MGM cinematographer, whom Arnaz affectionately called "Papa." Desilu retained ownership of the programs, which would bring the stars further revenues when the programs were later rebroadcast as syndicated reruns.

Within a short time after its premiere on 15 October 1951, *I Love Lucy* became one of the most popular programs on television. It was nominated for twenty-three Emmy awards, winning five times. When Ball was expecting her second child, her pregnancy was written into the script. The two birth dates coincided (on 19 January 1953), and more viewers watched that show than viewed the televised inauguration of President Dwight Eisenhower the following day. Ten years later Arnaz and his son happened to meet Eisenhower at the El Dorado Country Club, where the former president asked Arnaz, "Is that the little fellow who knocked me off the front pages the day before I was inaugurated?"

Most of the *I Love Lucy* plots were built around a common theme, deriving from Lucy's dissatisfaction with a life limited to cooking and housework. Her continuing attempts to enter show business, make money on her own, or otherwise circumvent the traditional feminine restrictions imposed upon her by her husband, inevitably led to chaos, embarrassment, and a return to the ever-frustrating domestic status quo.

Her television producer, Jesse Oppenheimer, later recalled: "The entire project rode on the radiant talent of that woman. . . . In every sense she was a star. Unexpected qualities appeared out of nowhere. Little human, ordinary, recognizable values. Inflections that were exactly the way your sister or your mother or the lady bus driver used to sound. She was everywoman."

The only threat to the show's success came from revelations by the media in September 1953 that Ball had been a member of the Communist party during the 1930s. In a secret hearing she told congressional investigators that she had briefly held nominal party membership, solely at her grandfather's urging, but was basically apolitical. Arnaz announced to the public that "Lucy has never been a communist. Not now, and never will be." Her popularity was not harmed and *I Love Lucy* remained a hit.

Ball and Arnaz also used Desilu to diversify into films, producing and starring in two films distributed by MGM, *The Long, Long Trailer* (1954) and *Forever, Darling* (1956). Lukewarm reviews scotched the idea of any more films.

I Love Lucy ran until 6 May 1957, and Desilu sold the rerun rights of the program to CBS for the then-unheard-of sum of $4 million. This allowed Desilu to purchase RKO Pictures, whose main asset was its film and television production lot. Arnaz soon began production of numerous other programs, including *Our Miss Brooks,* the *Ann Sothern Show,* and *The Untouchables.*

Desilu financed these new productions with income from televised "specials" of the *Lucille Ball–Desi Arnaz Show,* also called the *Lucy-Desi Comedy Hour,* thirteen hour-long comedy shows featuring prominent celebrities as guest stars. These shows appeared from 6 November 1957 through September 1958.

The couple's marriage was under constant pressure, due in part to their completely different temperaments. One friend recalled an incident that illustrated their divergent personalities: "We'd be down at Del Mar at their little house on the beach. Late in the afternoon, Desi would be looking at the ocean, and she'd say, 'What are you looking at?' 'The ocean. It's beautiful with the sunset and all.' She'd say to him, 'Why do you want to waste your time? C'mon, there's a gin game down the street.'" Unfortunately, this sensual aspect of Arnaz's personality also manifested itself in extensive womanizing, which, together with his increased drinking and extreme high-stakes gambling, caused severe disputes in his marriage. Tensions mounted after he was arrested for being drunk after leaving a notorious Los Angeles brothel. Ball wrote in her memoirs, *Love, Lucy,* that, by the late 1950s, "I realized that we never really liked each other. We had a great attraction going for each other in the beginning, but we didn't approve of each other. He disapproved of my moderation and my conservatism. . . . I disapproved of the way he worked too hard, played too hard, and was never moderate in anything. It was like living on top of a volcano; you never knew when it would erupt or why."

In 1958 Arnaz moved into the family's guest house, and the two divorced on 4 May 1960, each retaining 25 percent ownership of Desilu Productions.

Ball decided to return to the stage and starred in the musical *Wildcat,* which premiered in Philadelphia on 29 October 1960, then moved to Broadway on 16 December 1960. She initially played her role of the oil driller Wildy Jackson as originally written, but audience expectations gradually compelled her to transform it into an *I Love Lucy* persona. Critics gave the show only lukewarm reviews but the public continued to love Lucy. The show had 171 sold-out performances until its early closing on 3 June 1961 owing to Ball's illness and physical exhaustion.

After her divorce she began dating Gary Morton, a former television talk-show host, and they were married on 19 November 1961. Morton became her business adviser and the unofficial coproducer of her subsequent television shows. The couple had no children.

Deciding to return to television, Ball bought out Arnaz's share of Desilu in 1962 for $3 million (thereby becoming the first female president of a major television production company) and began production of *The Lucy Show,* with costars Vance and Gale Gordon. The show ran from 1 October 1961 to 16 September 1968 and showcased her daughter's television debut in the episode "Lucy Is a Soda Jerk."

Unlike Arnaz, Ball did not hesitate to delegate management duties to the competent core of executives at Desilu. Under Ball's leadership, Desilu experienced further expansion and profitability. She later sold the company to Gulf and Western Industries in 1967 for $17 million. As the major stockholder she received $10 million. She then formed Lucille Ball Productions, the main program of which was another reprise of her standard comedy routines, *Here's Lucy,* again costarring Vance and Gordon. The series ran from 23 September 1968 to 2 September 1974.

Ball had starred in several film comedies during the 1960s, including *The Facts of Life* (1960), *Critic's Choice* (1963), *A Guide for the Married Man* (1967), and *Yours,*

Mine, and Ours (1968), which were popular hits with the public if not with the critics. But her 1974 appearance in *Mame* was disastrous, and the film flopped at the box office.

She then made two televised films in which she played characters with a sharper, more bitter edge, *Happy Anniversary and Goodby,* which aired 19 November 1974, and *What Now, Catherine Curtis?,* which aired 20 March 1976. On 28 November 1976, CBS presented a televised tribute, *CBS Salutes Lucy: The First Twenty-five Years.*

Ball made few comedy appearances during the remainder of the decade, as her comic persona was perceived as old-fashioned. However, she starred in a dramatic role as a homeless person in *Stone Pillow,* a 1985 televised film. The filming of winter scenes on the streets of New York during summer resulted in her being hospitalized for dehydration, but the show's critical acclaim allowed her to find the financial backing to begin production of another comedy series.

In 1986 Ball starred in *Life with Lucy,* a coproduction with Aaron Spelling, who had been an actor in *I Love Lucy* productions and a screenwriter for *Desilu Playhouse.* ABC dropped the show after only eight episodes. A critic for *Channels* complained: "That wasn't Lucy up on the screen. It was some elderly imposter. Caked with makeup, she looked mummified. . . . She gamely attempted her old style of slapstick but her impeccable timing had fled. Worse, what used to be cute and girlish in a younger woman turned out to be embarrassing in a senior citizen today."

Despite her marital difficulties with Arnaz, the two had maintained a friendly relationship, and she was emotionally devastated when he died on 2 December 1986. Later that week Ball flew to Washington, D.C., to receive the Kennedy Center Award from President Ronald Reagan.

The failure of *Life with Lucy* killed any hope for a comeback. "Retirement is death itself," she told a friend. "There's a limit to how many drawers you have to straighten." Her final public appearance was with Bob Hope at the 29 March 1989 Academy Award ceremony. Three weeks later breathing problems prompted her to enter Cedars of Lebanon–Mount Sinai Medical Center. Doctors diagnosed an aortal aneurysm and replaced her aortic valve, but she experienced cardiac arrest several days later. After her death, in late April, her ashes were interred at Forest Lawn Memorial Park in Los Angeles, next to her mother's.

During a compilation of *I Love Lucy* clips televised after Ball's death, the narrator, Charles Osgood, stated: "We did love Lucy. She could make us laugh until we hurt, she was just so funny. But there was more to Lucille Ball than comic instincts and timing. Like Charlie Chaplin, her funniness was art. And it came out of being like us—human and vulnerable."

Lucille Ball was the most important woman in the history of early television. Using the acting and comedy skills she developed in her B movies during the 1930s and 1940s, Ball and her husband made their first television program, *I Love Lucy,* the nation's most popular show. Ball and Arnaz also used the series as a stepping-stone to make Desilu Productions, Inc., one of the preeminent and most profitable independent television production companies. After her marriage ended and Arnaz left Desilu, Ball became the first woman to head a major production studio. Not only did her company continue to produce successful programs, but Ball also starred in numerous other comedy series and television specials. Her combination of good looks, comic genius, capacity for hard work, and ambition allowed her to rise from an impoverished background in upstate New York to become one of the nation's wealthiest and most beloved television personalities.

★

Lucille Ball's memoir, *Love, Lucy,* was written in the early 1960s and published posthumously in 1996. Her daughter, Lucie Arnaz, has published many of her papers and much of her photograph collection as a CD-ROM, *Lucy and Desi: The Scrapbooks, Vol 1: Made for Each Other* (1997). Ball was the subject of several biographies, including Joe Morella and Edward Epstein, *Lucy: The Bittersweet Life of Lucille Ball* (1973, revised as *Forever Lucy* 1986); James Gregory, *The Lucille Ball Story* (1974); and Kathleen Brady, *Lucille: The Life of Lucille Ball* (1994). Desi Arnaz also wrote an autobiography, *A Book* (1976). Her early movies are covered in James Robert Parish, *The RKO Gals* (1974). Bart Andrews, *The "I Love Lucy" Book* (1985), and Jim Brochu, *Lucy in the Afternoon* (1990), are studies of her television shows. Robert Stack's memoirs, written with Mark Evans, *Straight Shooting* (1980), describes the work of Desilu on its early series. Desilu and its programs are also covered in Coyne Steven Sanders and Tom Gilbert, *Desilu: The Story of Lucille Ball and Desi Arnaz* (1993); Thomas Schatz, "Desilu, *I Love Lucy,* and the Rise of Network TV," in Robert J. Thompson and Gary Burns, eds., *Making Television: Authorship and Production Process* (1990); and Patricia Mellancamp, "Situation Comedy, Feminism and Freud: Discourses of Gracie and Lucy," in Tania Modelski, ed., *Studies in Entertainment* (1986). Obituaries are in the *New York Times* and *Washington Post* (both 27 Apr. 1989) and *Time* (8 May 1989).

STEPHEN MARSHALL

BARNETT, Ross Robert (*b.* 22 January 1898 in Standing Pine, Mississippi; *d.* 6 November 1987 in Jackson, Mississippi), governor of Mississippi from 1960 to 1964 and a hard-line white supremacist who came to loggerheads with federal authorities in 1962 over the integration of the University of Mississippi.

Barnett's father, John William Barnett, was a Confederate veteran who became a cotton farmer and sawmill operator. His mother, Virginia Ann Chadwick, was a schoolteacher.

Governor Ross Barnett testifying on civil rights before the U.S. Senate, 1963. ARCHIVE PHOTOS

Ross Barnett, the youngest of five boys and five girls, later recalled that "we were poor, poor."

While attending Agricultural High School in Lena, Mississippi, Barnett worked as a barber and a janitor. He served in World War I. In 1922 Barnett graduated from the prelaw program at Mississippi College in Clinton with a B.A. degree. He then worked for two years as a teacher and basketball coach at Ponotoc High School before entering the University of Mississippi School of Law at Oxford.

Soon after obtaining his LL.D. in 1926, Barnett began practicing law in Jackson, the state capital. There he met Mary Pearl Crawford in 1928 at the Calvary Baptist Church; they married in August 1929 and would have one son, Ross, Jr., and two daughters, Virginia and Quida. An outstanding trial lawyer, Barnett built up a highly successful practice, specializing in damage suits. In 1943 and 1944 he was president of the Mississippi State Bar Association.

In 1951 and 1955 Barnett finished fourth in Mississippi's Democratic gubernatorial primaries. Running for governor again in 1959, Barnett claimed that he was the most ardent white supremacist in the field. He declared that "the Negro is different because God made him different to punish him." Barnett denounced then-governor J. P. Colemen—who under state law could not succeed himself—as a moderate on segregation and promised that he would close Mississippi's schools rather than see them integrated.

Barnett finished first in the August 1959 Democratic primary but failed to win a majority. In the runoff three weeks later, he defeated the second-place finisher, Lieutenant Governor Carroll Gartin, with 230,557 votes to Gartin's 193,706. Barnett ran unopposed in November and was inaugurated on 19 January 1960.

Barnett's two predecessors had declined to support the extremist White Citizens' Councils, which defended segregation through propaganda and economic retaliation. Barnett, however, was a member of the organization and saw to it that the group received state funding. Its Mississippi leader, William J. Simmons, played an influential role in Barnett's administration.

In all matters, large and small, Barnett defended white supremacy. In 1960 he backed an unpledged slate of Mississippi presidential electors in retaliation for the national Democratic party's support of racial equality. In 1963 he persuaded the University of Mississippi's band leader not to drop the Confederate motif from the band's uniforms, Confederate symbols being a banner of southern resistance to racial equality.

In 1961, Freedom Riders seeking to integrate interstate bus terminals were attacked by whites in Montgomery, Alabama. On their arrival in Jackson, Barnett ordered the Freedom Riders' peaceful arrest before any similar violence could take place. For this, Barnett briefly won an inaccurate reputation as a racial moderate.

Any such standing, however, went up in smoke, as the following year Barnett resisted the efforts of James Meredith to become the first black student at the University of Mississippi. A long legal battle came to an end on 13 September 1962, when a U.S. district court issued a sweeping injunction against efforts by the board of trustees and university officials to block Meredith's admission. On the same day, Barnett went on television to read an interposition proclamation that rejected federal court rulings. "We must either submit to the unlawful dictates of the federal government, or stand up like men and tell them 'Never,' " he asserted. For the remainder of the month he promoted a spirit of illegal defiance, urging state officials to be prepared for arrest and threatening to arrest federal officials.

Appointed a special registrar by the state's Board of Trustees for Institutions of Higher Learning, Barnett on 20 September went to the university's campus at Oxford to personally turn back Meredith's attempt to register. On 24 September, the trustees, having been hauled into federal court, agreed to register Meredith. The following day, however, the governor physically blocked Meredith from entering the trustees' office in Jackson.

During the last days of September, Barnett spoke by

telephone several times with U.S. attorney general Robert F. Kennedy and with President John F. Kennedy. Despite his public defiance, Barnett seemed willing to retreat if he could do so without appearing weak. The three agreed that Meredith would be sneaked onto the Oxford campus on 30 September and quickly registered; then Barnett could claim he had been forced to accept a fait accompli.

Meredith's arrival on campus Sunday afternoon was kept secret. But federal marshals arrived there at about the same time, and a crowd of students and nonstudent vigilantes and extremists gathered. After state highway patrolmen left the campus area at around 7:30 P.M., members of the crowd began pelting the marshals with objects, which led to full-scale rioting. About two hours later, Barnett declared that he had no choice but to submit to the federal government, and he urged an end to violence. Nevertheless, state troopers on the scene did not act against the rioters, and violence continued until nearly noon on Monday, 1 October, by which time the U.S. Army and federalized National Guardsmen restored order.

Although Meredith was registered that day and the U.S. Court of Appeals levied fines against the governor for his part in the affair, Barnett remained hugely popular in Mississippi. But elsewhere, including some parts of the South, Barnett's die-hard defiance was blamed for the rioting, in which two persons were shot dead and some 375 were injured.

Barnett believed that his greatest accomplishment was bringing industrial jobs to his mostly rural state. He traveled some 50,000 miles around the country to attract business and, in this, is generally believed to have been more successful than most previous Mississippi governors. Much of Mississippi's appeal lay in its low wages, however, and to keep them that way, Barnett urged workers to reject trade unions.

An imposing figure, Barnett stood at over six feet tall and spoke with a deep, throaty voice. He was widely admired among Mississippi's whites for his speaking ability, humor, and guitar playing, all of which he demonstrated annually at the Neshoba County Fair.

Not eligible to succeed himself as governor, Barnett returned to private law practice in 1964. After finishing a weak fourth in the 1967 Democratic gubernatorial primary, he continued to practice law until his retirement in March 1984. He died of heart failure and was buried in the Barnett family cemetery in his native community of Standing Pine.

Barnett was in the final generation of Deep South politicians, politicians in a tradition dating back to the turn of the twentieth century, who combined fervently racist views with a colorful populist flair. By the late 1960s, the Voting Rights Act of 1965 had made his type of political leadership obsolete. But as part of the South's last-ditch struggle against desegregation, he created what was perhaps the most serious federal-state confrontation since the end of Reconstruction.

★

James W. Silver, *Mississippi: The Closed Society* (enl. ed., 1966), is an often derisive examination of Barnett's views and of his actions as governor. Erle Johnston, *I Rolled with Ross: A Political Portrait* (1980), is a rare defense of Barnett's governorship, written by a former aide. Taylor Branch, *Parting the Waters: America in the King Years, 1954–1963* (1988), contains a detailed account of Barnett's telephone conversations with the Kennedys. Obituaries are in the *Clarion Ledger/Jackson* (Mississippi) *Daily News* (7 Nov. 1987) and the *New York Times* (8 Nov. 1987).

MICHAEL L. LEVINE

BARON, Salo Wittmayer (*b.* 26 May 1895 in Tarnow, Austria [now Poland]; *d.* 25 November 1989 in New York City), leading scholar in Jewish history whose views and writings influenced generations of scholars.

Salo Baron was born Sholom Baron, the second of three children of Elias Baron, a banker with interests in real estate, lumber yards, mills, and oil fields, and Minna Wittmayer, who came from a wealthy family of commodity brokers. Elias Baron was an Orthodox Jew, educated in the traditional Jewish manner as well as in secular subjects; Minna Baron was fluent in French, Polish, and German as well as Yiddish and Hebrew. When very small, Sholom was in the charge of a Polish nursemaid, and his first language was Polish. At the age of four, when he started his formal Jewish studies with a tutor, he learned Yiddish and Hebrew simultaneously.

A more learned tutor was hired when Baron was ten, and they focused for eight years on the Talmud and Jewish religious literature. At the same time Baron was an "external student" at the local gymnasium, passing his periodic examinations with ease. He was also inducted into his father's business at age ten, and by the age of fifteen he would at times be left in charge while his father traveled. He decided against a business career and entered the University of Vienna, from which he received three doctorates, in philosophy (1917), in political science (1922), and in law (1923). At the same time he attended the Jewish Theological Seminary in Vienna, receiving an M.H.L. and ordination in 1920. He married Jeanette G. Meisel on 12 June 1934; they had two children.

Baron's first position was that of lecturer in history at the Juedisches Paedagogium (Jewish Teachers College) in Vienna, Austria, where he taught from 1919 to 1926. Upon the invitation of Rabbi Stephen S. Wise, he came to the United States as a visiting lecturer at the Jewish Institute of Religion in New York City, where he remained until 1930 as professor of history and director of the department of advanced studies. In 1930 he was appointed to a newly created chair in Jewish literature and institutions at Columbia University. This was the first appointment in Jewish studies to the history faculty of any American university, and Baron held the position until 1963, when he retired and became professor emeritus. He retained the directorship of the Center for Israel and Jewish Studies (founded by him in 1950) until 1968.

Baron lectured at many universities in the United States and Israel, including Colgate-Rochester Divinity School (1944), Jewish Theological Seminary of America (1954–1972), Hebrew University in Jerusalem (1958), Rutgers University (1964–1969), and Brown University (1966–1968). He also received numerous awards and honors, among which are the Knight of the Order of Merit (Italy), a D.H.L. from Hebrew Union College (1944), an LL.D. from Dropsie University (1962), a Litt.D. from Rutgers University and another from Columbia University (1963), a Golden Doctorate from the University of Vienna (1969), and a Ph.D. from Tel-Aviv University (1970). Columbia University created a new chair in Jewish history named in Baron's honor.

Baron's scholarly writings are impressive both in terms of quantity and breadth of knowledge. His bibliography consists of more than 500 items, including dozens of books. In his first monograph, *Die Judenfrage auf dem Wiener Kongress* (1920), he discussed the relationship of Jewish needs and rights to the Gentile society. His two major works are the three-volume *The Jewish Community* (1942, reprinted 1972) and the eighteen-volume *A Social and Religious History of the Jews,* which first appeared in 1937 in three volumes and was then revised and enlarged (1952–1983). He was editor of *Jewish Social Studies* and a coeditor, with Joseph Blau, of the three-volume work *The Jews of the United States, 1790–1840: A Documentary History.*

The central thesis of Baron's view of Jewish history is that the Jewish experience was part of the larger historical experience in which the Jews lived. Contrary to the prevailing approach that Jewish history was totally apart from the Gentile world and therefore no knowledge of the larger world was necessary in order to understand Jewish history, Baron declared that at every point in the Jewish experience there was a serious encounter with other cultures. Even in the almost sealed environment of ghettos, the Jews were interacting. He argued that because the cultures of the Gentile worlds differed throughout the long span of Jewish history as well as throughout the geographic dispersion of the Jews, Jewish history can only be understood as part of world history.

Baron's views have had important consequences, because he wrote not only of the tragic dimensions of Jewish history but also of the cooperation between Jews and Gentiles. He increased the load on scholars of Jewish history, who now had to understand both the Jewish and Gentile worlds. Baron's ideas on the uniqueness of the Jewish people were based on his view of the Jews as bearers of a monotheistic messianic religion that manifests itself through a particular way of life, intertwined with a culture of landlessness.

In addition to writing, teaching, and editing, Baron was active in many academic organizations. He was a four-time president of the American Academy for Jewish Research, president of the American Jewish Historical Society (1953–1955), and cofounder and twice president of the Conference of Jewish Social Studies. In 1952 he became a corresponding member of UNESCO's International Commission for a Scientific and Cultural History of Mankind. In 1961 he was called by the prosecution in the Adolf Eichmann trial in Jerusalem to deliver a historical account of anti-Semitism. His account had personal overtones because both his parents had been killed by the Nazis in 1942.

Baron died of congestive heart failure. He is credited with broadening and modernizing the historic view of the Jewish experience and redefining the field of Jewish history.

★

Biographical information may be found in Saul Lieberman and Arthur Hyman, *Salo Wittmayer Baron Jubilee Volume on the Occasion of His Eightieth Birthday* (1974), and Arthur Hertzberg, "Baron, Salo Wittmayer," *Encyclopedia Judaica* (1971). An obituary is in the *New York Times* (26 Nov. 1989).

SARA REGUER

BARTHELME, Donald, Jr. (*b.* 7 April 1931 in Philadelphia, Pennsylvania; *d.* 23 July 1989 in Houston, Texas), leading writer of contemporary fiction.

Donald Barthelme was the oldest of the five children of Donald Barthelme, Sr., and Helen Bechtold. In 1933 the family moved to Houston, where Barthelme's father embarked on a long career as a professor of architectural design at the University of Houston and opened his own architectural firm. The family was Roman Catholic, and Donald and his siblings attended parochial school. His first byline was "literary reporter" for the *Eagle,* the St. Thomas School newspaper. For his efforts on the Lamar High School literary magazine, the *Sequoyha,* he received both poetry and short-story awards.

Barthelme enrolled at the University of Houston in 1949 as a journalism major and joined the staff of the *Daily Cougar*. By his sophomore year, he had become, at twenty years old, the youngest student to head the *Daily Cougar* as editor. In 1953 his college career was cut short when he was drafted by the army to serve in Korea. No sooner did he arrive in Korea than military action ended. He soon found work on the army newspaper, however, and continued with it until his return to Houston in 1955. Later that year, he began a professional career as a journalist, taking a position as a reporter for the *Houston Post.* By 1955, he was again affiliated with the University of Houston, where he worked with Farris Block at the university's public relations office, writing speeches for the university president. He succeeded Block as editor of *Acta Diurna,* a weekly newsletter published for the university's faculty and staff. In 1956 Barthelme began publication of *Forum,* a quarterly journal featuring articles in the humanities, arts, and sciences, which he edited until 1960. The following year, at just thirty years of age, he became director of the Contemporary Arts Museum in Houston. He held this position until a job opportunity led him to New York City, where he moved in 1962 to embark on a career as a writer.

In 1963 Barthelme assumed the position of managing editor of *Location,* an art and literature journal published by Harold Rosenberg and Thomas Hess. He stayed with *Location* until 1964. In the same year his first short story, "L' Lapse," was published in the *New Yorker* magazine. Roger Angel became his editor and mentor at the *New Yorker,* where many of Barthelme's short stories appeared first. In 1964 he impressed the literary world with the publication of his first collection of short stories, *Come Back, Dr. Caligari.*

After spending a year in Denmark, Barthelme returned to New York and began publishing frequently. In 1966 he received a Guggenheim Fellowship. Barthelme's first novel, *Snow White,* appeared initially in the *New Yorker* in 1967 and was published that same year by Atheneum. This parody brought him critical acclaim and national recognition. He was awarded the National Institute of Arts and Letters Zabel Award in 1972 and also that year won the National Book Award for his children's book, *The Slightly Irregular Fire Engine; or, The Hithering Thithering Djinn* (1971), penned especially for his daughter Anne. He was again nominated in 1974 for *Guilty Pleasures* (1974), a collection of parodies. Among his other honors are the Texas Institute of Arts and Letters Award in 1976 and the Rea Short Story Award. In 1975 he published a second novel, *The Dead Father.* His other short-story collections are *Unspeakable Practices, Unnatural Acts* (1968); *City Life* (1970); *Sadness* (1972); *Amateurs* (1976); *Great Days* (1979), which was adapted for an Off-Broadway production in 1983; *Sixty Stories* (1981); *Overnight to Many Distant Cities* (1983); and *Forty Stories* (1987). His nonfiction includes *Here in the Village* (1978), as well as film reviews, essays, and Japanese translations.

Barthelme's brand of fiction was labeled postmodern, avant-garde, and experimental in his treatment of language. He all but abandoned the traditional and linear conventions of plot and characterization and focused instead on language, subverting and exploiting its typical forms. His fiction is postrealist in that it relies not on the mimetic impulse but on the actual words on the page—the metaphors, the clichés, the literary conventions—and considers them literally for a moment, drawing attention to the absurdity of traditional usage. Barthelme played with language, and the result is often comic. He explained the origins of this late-twentieth-century style—practiced by John Barth, William Gass, and Robert Coover, among others—in "A Symposium on Fiction" (in *Shenandoah*): "Painters had to go out and reinvent painting because of the invention of photography, and I think films have done something of the sort for us," implying perhaps that film conveys realism better than words, forcing writers to go beyond realism. Alfred Kazin has branded Barthelme an "anti-novelist," which seems suitable.

Barthelme was married four times. He had two daughters with his first wife, Birgit. In 1978 he married Marion Knox, with whom he shared the rest of his life. They lived in Greenwich Village in New York City, where Barthelme wrote and taught at City College of the City University of New York in the post of distinguished visiting professor. In 1980 he began living in both New York and Houston so that he could direct the creative writing program at the University of Houston.

In 1982 Barthelme was honored with the PEN/Faulkner Award for fiction for his short-story collection *Sixty Stories.* He published another novel, *Paradise,* in 1986. Barthelme died of cancer in Houston. His last work, *The King,* based

Donald Barthelme. AP/WIDE WORLD PHOTOS

on the Arthurian legend, was published posthumously in 1990.

★

Barthelme's papers are in the University of Houston Libraries Special Collections. A biography is Lois Gordon, *Donald Barthelme* (1981). See also Stanley Trachtenberg, *Understanding Donald Barthelme* (1990). An obituary is in the *New York Times* (24 July 1989).

JENNIFER FARTHING

BASQUIAT, Jean-Michel (*b.* 22 December 1960 in Brooklyn, New York; *d.* 12 August 1988 in New York City), African-American artist who achieved international fame with his visceral, "neoexpressionist," graffiti-inspired paintings.

Basquiat was raised with his two younger sisters in Boerum Hill, a middle-class Brooklyn neighborhood. His father, Gerard Basquiat, was Haitian and worked for an accounting firm; his mother, Matilde (Andradas) Basquiat, was of Puerto Rican descent. Encouraged by his mother, Basquiat began drawing at the age of four. In 1968 his parents separated, and for the next ten years Basquiat lived with his father, who moved the family several times, including once to Puerto Rico in 1974. Attending several public and private schools, Basquiat was a difficult student. His last formal schooling was at the progressive City as School in Brooklyn (1976–1978), where he illustrated the school paper.

While at City as School he met Al Diaz, a graffiti artist from the Lower East Side of Manhattan. Together they formed a graffiti team called SAMO (their graffiti "tag," which stood for "same old shit"). Diaz and Basquiat worked together for two years, spray painting such SAMO graffiti messages as "Pay for Soup," "Build a Fort," and "Set It on Fire" in the Manhattan subways. SAMO's social message was critical of mainstream culture; the style was poetic with an intellectual edge.

Basquiat left home in 1978 and moved to lower Manhattan, where he stayed with friends. He became part of the East Village art scene, frequenting places such as the Mudd Club and Club 57, where he socialized with other young artists and musicians. He supported himself by selling postcards, T-shirts, and drawings. The SAMO project continued, and its writings appeared on the walls outside East Village galleries. Basquiat was hoping to be noticed, and eventually SAMO was written up in the *Village Voice* late in 1978. After 1979 Diaz and Basquiat went their separate ways, and Basquiat formed an experimental and short-lived band called Gray that was dedicated to making "noise music." Also in 1979, Basquiat met Kenny Scharf and Keith Haring, artists who would become associated with the graffiti movement.

Jean-Michel Basquiat. PHOTOGRAPHER JAMES VANDERZEE. COPYRIGHT © BY DONNA MUSSENDEN VANDERZEE.

In 1980 Basquiat had his first break when he was invited to participate in the Times Square Show, organized by Haring and held at Club 57. The exhibition featured several young artists and received an excellent review in *Art in America,* where the critic Jeffrey Deitch singled out Basquiat in particular. Also in 1980, Basquiat starred in a never-to-be-released film about graffiti art, called *New York Beat.* In that year, Basquiat also met a personal hero, the famous pop artist Andy Warhol.

Early in 1981 Basquiat exhibited several paintings and drawings in the New York/New Wave Show. His raw and gestural works drew the interest of several dealers. The art market was then bullish, and fortune and fame could come quickly. Basquiat's paintings suddenly became hot commodities. In 1981 Basquiat had his first one-artist show at the Gallerie d'Arte Emilio Mazzoli in Modena, Italy. Annina Nosei became his first American dealer, and he had his first one-artist show in the United States early in 1982 at Nosei's gallery. Critics admired the "aggressively handmade look" of his paintings and soon their prices topped the $10,000 mark.

At the age of twenty-two, Basquiat became the youngest artist ever to participate in the important international invitational Documenta 7 exhibition held in Kassel, West Germany. Also in 1982 he had successful one-artist exhibitions in Zurich and Rotterdam. Among the paintings he exhibited were some in which he eulogized African-American heroes, such as the boxer Sugar Ray Robinson. Basquiat gained even more financial success and critical acclaim in 1983. Among his shows was a one-artist exhibition at the Larry Gagosian Gallery in Los Angeles and an invitation to the prestigious Whitney Biennial in New York. Basquiat also worked on a series of collaborative paintings with Warhol.

Basquiat's rise to fame had a downside. His lifestyle became excessive, and he spent thousands of dollars on parties and unnecessary household appliances. He bought expensive tailor-made suits, only to ruin them by wearing them while he painted. Worst of all, he developed a $2,000-a-week cocaine and heroin addiction.

In 1984 Basquiat began showing at the Mary Boone Gallery in New York City. In his emotionally charged paintings the influences of jazz, black culture, graffiti, and abstract expressionism were merged. Although spontaneously executed, his paintings showed sophistication in the way he arranged and layered his symbolic primitive figures and fragmented words and texts. Exhibitions of his work continued to be front-page news, but the critics felt that his paintings were becoming "stylized." Basquiat's drug use escalated and his health began to decline.

In 1985 there were shows and sales but also unfavorable reviews. An exhibition of the Basquiat/Warhol paintings at the Shafrazi Gallery in New York City was not well-received by the critics. In the years that followed, Basquiat became increasingly reclusive and emotionally unstable. Warhol's death in February 1987 greatly affected him. At times, his works conveyed a violent and socially critical message, as in the painting *Victor 25448* (1987), where the struggling, stick figure of a black man, mouth taped shut and feet tied, is menaced by the word "IDEAL," which Basquiat painted to look like a logo. In a corner of the painting is written, "Nothing to be gained here."

Basquiat had three shows in 1988, and they all received good reviews. His future was beginning to look brighter, when he died suddenly, of a cocaine and heroin overdose, in his Grey Street loft. He is buried in Greenwood Cemetery in Brooklyn.

Many critics claim that Basquiat was a revolutionary painter with a universal message, while others attempt to reduce his artistic achievements, calling him a fame-hungry pawn of the white gallery establishment. Although the art market helped Basquiat, ultimately it was his talent and his desire that brought him international recognition achieved by few African-American artists.

★

Phoebe Hoban, *Basquiat: A Quick Killing in Art* (1998), is a full-length biography of the artist. Examples of Basquiat's work are in John Cheim, *Jean-Michel Basquiat: Drawings* (1990), and Richard Marshall, *Jean-Michel Basquiat* (1992), the catalog that accompanied the 1991–1993 Basquiat retrospective at the Whitney Museum. Suzi Gablik, "Report from New York: The Graffiti Question," *Art in America* (1982), discusses Basquiat's work within the larger context of New York graffiti art. Cathleen McGuigan, "New Art, New Money: The Marketing of an American Artist," *New York Times Magazine* (10 Feb. 1985), is a cover story on Basquiat. Anthony Haden-Guest, "Burning Out," *Vanity Fair* (Nov. 1988), discusses Basquiat's last days in detail. Trevor Fairbrother, "Double Feature," *Art in America* 84, no. 9 (1996), is an article about the Warhol-Basquiat collaboration. An obituary is in the *New York Times* (27 Aug. 1988).

PETER SUCHECKI

BAUER, Eddie (*b.* 19 October 1899 on Orcas Island, Washington; *d.* 18 April 1986 in Bellevue, Washington), outdoorsman, merchant, and inventor who designed quilted down clothing and popularized sports and sporting goods through retail and mail-order sales.

Bauer was one of six children of Jacob and Marie Kathriene Bauer, German-speaking Russian immigrants who had built a cabin at the foot of Mount Constitution on Orcas Island in the San Juan Islands off the northwest coast of Washington State. Jacob Bauer, a farmer and orchard man, also butchered game for hunters. Marie Bauer was a farmwife who helped her husband supply hunters and fishermen with provisions and a place to stay. The family moved in 1904 from Orcas Island to Yarrow Point on Lake Washington, where Bauer's father established a dairy. Eddie Bauer learned to fish and accompanied sportsmen on hunting trips. In 1909 he began to caddie at the Seattle Golf Club, where he met wealthy sports enthusiasts who hired him for odd jobs. When his parents separated in 1913, Bauer, having completed the eighth grade, moved to Seattle with his mother.

Preferring hunting and fishing to being in school, Bauer found a part-time job at Piper and Taft, a Seattle sporting goods store. He opened the store, ran errands, and did chores for $18 a month. Capitalizing on his skill as a fisherman, the store promoted its fishing gear by displaying Bauer's catches in the front window. His reputation as a guide and sportsman benefited the store and provided Bauer with friendships and connections with wealthy sportsmen. Because salaries were meager, he later said, "I made it a must to build personal and name value to assure . . . employment and increased income." At Piper and Taft, Bauer learned to split bamboo to make fishing rods, to tie lures, and to customize golf clubs and rifle stocks.

In 1917 Bauer became the manager of three departments—outdoor camping, clothing, and footwear. In addition, he was given responsibility for advertising, promotion, and window displays. Responding to the national

Eddie Bauer, 1920. EDDIE BAUER ARCHIVES

enthusiasm of the time for tennis, Bauer, wearing white flannels, positioned himself in the store's window where he strung racquets on a vise of his own design. As he entertained Seattle pedestrians, the ploy indelibly connected Eddie Bauer's name and face with personalized service in sporting equipment and supplies.

In 1920 Bauer rented space in Bob Newton's gun repair and sporting goods shop for $15 per month. His new business, Eddie Bauer's Tennis Shop, began with $25 in capital and a $500, four-month note cosigned by a family friend, Rolland H. Denny. Bauer drew on his acquaintances among well-to-do Seattle sportsmen, his name recognition as a sportsman, and his unequivocal promise of service and quality. After his first year in business for himself, Bauer had made a $10,000 profit, established a $10,000 line of credit, and built a commitment for dealer credit among his suppliers. When Newton raised the rent in the store's second year, Bauer moved his business down the block, renamed the store Eddie Bauer's Sporting Goods, and expanded the tennis business to customized golf clubs and fishing tackle.

Bauer kept his overhead low and his visibility high by closing his shop every Labor Day and taking the next five months off to go hunting, fishing, trap shooting, and mountaineering. He organized and participated in clubs centered on different sports. He brought expert craftsmen and coaches into his store to introduce novel sporting equipment to his customers. In an early direct-mail advertising piece, Bauer introduced saltwater game fishing. He and Bill Lindbergh, a childhood fishing companion, formed a club, Sockos, for new enthusiasts of saltwater salmon fishing. Much of Bauer's early success was connected to his ability to introduce a sport, create excitement, and sell the equipment. The image Bauer created underlined the quality of the goods he sold and validated his promise of absolute customer satisfaction.

Bauer, who had been married and divorced briefly in the early 1920s, married Christine Heltborg on 2 February 1927; they had one son, Eddie Christian. Bauer's wife, known as "Stine," shared his enthusiasm for outdoor activities. She joined the business, oversaw the introduction of women's clothing and equipment into Bauer's inventory, and became a model of the modern sportswoman. In 1934, financed by a Seattle friend, Dan Smith, Bauer moved to his third and largest store. He began to promote and sell ski equipment and mountain climbing gear. That same year, Bauer patented standard-sized shuttlecocks for badminton, forming a new company, Bauer's Shuttles, Inc. The shuttlecocks, made from goose feathers, cork, kidskin and lead shot, were in demand by recreational and championship badminton players.

The idea for a quilted down jacket, which Bauer designed in 1935, came from a near-fatal winter fishing expedition in 1923, during which Bauer, soaked and freezing, nearly died from hypothermia. As a child, Bauer had also heard stories from his uncle Lesser, a soldier in Manchuria during the 1904 Russo-Japanese War. Bauer's uncle credited the quilted down lining of his coat with saving his life. Goose down, lighter in weight than wool or leather, holds air as insulation, prevents loss of body heat, and wicks away perspiration. The Eddie Bauer Blizzard-Proof jacket was manufactured for Bauer by Ome Daiber, a skier and mountain man recruited to run the store's mountaineering department. Bauer formed another company to import feathers, Arctic Feather and Down, and financed the manufacture of the jackets. Quilted down clothing was sold through advertisements placed in sport magazines.

Bauer patented his quilted down jacket, the Skyliner, in 1936; it and his down pants and sleeping bags were prized not only by sportsmen but by anyone living or working in extreme cold climates. Expanding his direct-mail business, Bauer organized Bauer Expedition Outfitters. Between 1934 and 1937, he was issued more than twenty patents, giving him a virtual monopoly on quilted down clothing. In 1938 he moved his store to Seattle's Washington Athletic Club Building. His holdings included the retail store, a growing mail-order business, and the feather import company. In 1941 Arctic Feather and Down began to supply the U.S. Army Air Forces with quilted down flight suits and sleeping bags, snowshoes, snow harnesses, and backpacks. Because it was increasingly difficult to import quality goose down, Bauer established Ducks Unlimited, a volunteer organization of sports hunters who contributed waterfowl feathers for down clothing to be manufactured as part of the war effort. Bauer also developed a process for converting chicken feathers into a downlike substitute. During World War II, Bauer's feather factory, Feathers, Inc., washed and dried more than 14,000 pounds of curly chicken feathers daily.

After the war, Bauer, suffering from debilitating back pain, experienced his first, serious financial reverses. Although the demand from returning soldiers for Eddie Bauer's quilted down clothing inspired the first Bauer catalog in 1945, by 1946 his retail businesses were losing money, and Bauer had overextended his bank credit. In poor health, he sold his shares of his sporting goods businesses and liquidated Feathers, Inc., and Arctic Feather and Down to pay bank loans. Left with a license to operate Eddie Bauer, Inc., the umbrella company for Eddie Bauer Mail Order and Eddie Bauer Expedition Outfitters, Bauer turned to William Niemi, a Seattle saloon keeper, hunter, and fisherman, whose wife, Louise, was a friend of Stine Bauer. Niemi bought Bauer out for one dollar in 1949 and began negotiations to restore Bauer's credit and credibility.

In 1953 Bauer and Niemi became equal partners in a manufacturing and mail-order company that was profitable from their first year in business. As he had in the past, Bauer guaranteed his sporting goods and his quilted down garments unconditionally. Eddie Bauer Outfitters supplied equipment and clothing for the 1957 expedition by the United States First Geophysical Year scientists to Antarctica. Bauer also supplied clothing and equipment for James Whittaker, the first American to reach the top of Mount Everest (1963). Bauer sold equipment and clothing designed for extreme climates and strenuous, demanding activities with the belief that through specialized production he could manufacture superior clothing and equipment for ordinary consumers who might themselves face challenging or life-threatening situations. In 1968, with sales near $5 million, Bauer and his son, Eddie C., sold their shares to William Niemi, Jr., and his father for $1.5 million in cash and retired from the sporting good business.

In retirement, Bauer and his wife continued to enjoy outdoor sports and camping. Bauer, who had introduced black Labrador retrievers to the Seattle area, was named Retriever Breeder of the Year in 1974. Two weeks after his wife died of pancreatic cancer, Bauer died of cardiac arrest at Overlake Hospital in Bellevue.

Eddie Bauer was a man whose hobbies generated a multimillion-dollar business, whose enthusiasms opened up cold-weather sports for many Americans, and whose quilted down designs and patented innovations made comfort in extreme temperatures possible. Bauer's signature, the symbol of his good word, appears on his equipment and clothing labels and continues to guarantee quality for consumers.

★

A 1983 manuscript by Bauer, describing his early business career, is in the Seattle Museum of History and Industry. The museum's collections also include clippings from Seattle-area newspapers detailing the growth of Eddie Bauer, Inc. Rebecca Case, "Eddie Bauer Parlayed $25 into $10 million," *Journal American* (Bellevue, Washington; 26 Sept. 1982), emphasizes Bauer's youthful industry and how he used feathers to build his business and make his fortune. Steve Netherby, "The Old Man and the Boy," *Field and Stream* (Oct. 1982), describes Bauer's sports equipment innovations. Joseph J. Ficini and Suzi Ficini, *The Entrepreneurs: The Men and Women Behind the Names and How They Made It* (1985), offers a brief description of Bauer's career. Robert Spector, *The Legend of Eddie Bauer* (1994), is available through Eddie Bauer stores and is valuable for corporate information and photographs. Obituaries are in the *Seattle Post Intelligencer* (25 Apr. 1986), *New York Times* and *Los Angeles Times* (both 26 Apr. 1986), and *Chicago Tribune* (27 Apr. 1986).

WENDY HALL MALONEY

BEADLE, George Wells ("Beets") (*b.* 22 October 1903 near Wahoo, Nebraska; *d.* 9 June 1989 in Pomona, California), geneticist, university president, and Nobel laureate whose work showed how genes control the chemical reactions in living cells through enzymes and inaugurated the field of biochemical genetics.

Beadle grew up on a farm set on forty acres of rolling prairie land just outside the town of Wahoo in eastern Nebraska. His parents, Chauncey Elmer Beadle and Hattie Hendee Albro, raised field and truck crops, kept livestock, and sold produce, including apples and potatoes purchased out-of-state by the carload. The Beadle farm, selected as a model small farm by the U.S. Department of Agriculture in 1908, supported the family (Beadle had an older brother, who died in 1913 after being kicked by a horse, and a younger sister) and turned a profit. His mother died when George was four and a half. As a youth, Beadle split his time between working on his father's farm and learning to hunt and fish, make tools, and plant a garden; gardening remained his lifelong passion. He attended public schools expecting to become a farmer like his father. But Bess MacDonald, a young physics and chemistry teacher in his high school, talked him into going to college first.

At the University of Nebraska College of Agriculture, where he received a B.S. degree in 1926 and an M.S. degree

George Wells Beadle. COURTESY OF THE ARCHIVES, CALIFORNIA INSTITUTE OF TECHNOLOGY

in 1927, Beadle studied English and then entomology and plant ecology, before Frank D. Keim, a professor of agronomy, introduced him in 1924 to genetics. That summer he collected data for Keim on the offspring of wheat hybrids. Beadle's first paper, published jointly with Keim in 1927, involved the development of grass roots. He wrote his master's thesis, under Keim's direction, on the identification of local prairie grasses. By then, Keim had persuaded Beadle to continue his education in the East and had obtained a teaching assistantship for him at Cornell University in agronomy.

In 1927 Beadle entered Cornell planning to work on the ecology of the pasture grasses in New York State. But his thesis adviser, H. P. Cooper, and he did not agree on the research, and Beadle resigned his assistantship. Instead, he started working with Rollins A. Emerson, a plant geneticist, on the cytogenetics and origin of the corn plant. While studying for his doctorate, Beadle discovered that certain types of genetically determined chromosomal behavior caused different cases of inherited sterility in corn. Out of that work came a series of papers—on chromosomal asynapsis, genes for pollen sterility, supernumerary cell divisions, failure of cytokinesis, and sticky chromosomes—which he published between 1929 and 1932. Beadle married Marion Cecile Hill in 1928; they had one son.

After receiving his Ph.D. from Cornell in 1931, Beadle moved to the California Institute of Technology in Pasadena, where as a National Research Council Fellow, he worked in the genetics laboratory of Alfred H. Sturtevant. There his interest shifted from corn to the fruit fly, *Drosophila melanogaster*. Beadle's fruit fly investigations at Caltech involved intricate analyses of the results of the interchange of genes within various chromosomal rearrangements. This second phase of Beadle's research career culminated in 1936 in a notable publication, in collaboration with Sturtevant, of the first systematic study of crossing-over and disjunction in chromosomes with inverted gene sequences.

Meanwhile, Beadle began a friendship with Boris Ephrussi, an embryologist who had come to Pasadena from Paris as a Rockefeller Fellow in 1934 to work in the genetics laboratory. In 1935, Beadle teamed up with Ephrussi in his Paris laboratory at the Institut de Biologie Physico-Chimique to study larval development in *Drosophila*. They tried and failed to culture *Drosophila* tissue, whereupon they switched to transplantation; together they devised a method of transplanting *Drosophila* tissue from one larva to another. The first transplant to develop fully was an embryonic eye disc that had been transplanted into the body cavity of another fly. Applying this technique to the determination of eye color in the adult *Drosophila,* Beadle and Ephrussi identified a sequence of two successive reactions controlled by genes. Beadle later said that this finding marked the beginning of the one-gene, one-enzyme theory that he later brought to fruition.

Late in 1935 Beadle returned to Caltech. In 1936 he moved east to take a position as assistant professor of biology at Harvard University, where he lectured on botany and continued research on eye pigment in collaboration with Kenneth Thimann. The following year (1937), Beadle accepted a position at Stanford University as professor of biology, with the promise of research support. With funds supplied by the Rockefeller Foundation, he built laboratories, furnished them, and hired biochemist Edward L. Tatum as a research associate.

At Stanford, Beadle's interest shifted toward biochemistry. Between 1937 and 1940, Beadle, Tatum, and others struggled to work out the identification of the two eye-color substances in *Drosophila*. During this period, Beadle also taught genetics and wrote an important textbook together with Sturtevant, *An Introduction to Genetics* (1939).

In 1940 Beadle switched from *Drosophila* as an experimental organism to the microorganism *Neurospora crassa,* the red bread mold, whose genetics and growth requirements were well understood. The inspiration for reversing the approach, namely to start with known nutritional requirements and then work out the biochemical role of the genes, Beadle later said, came to him during a lecture he heard Tatum give in a course on comparative biochemistry. After confirming the organism's nutritional requirements, Beadle and Tatum put the new method to the test. After exposing the bread mold to X rays to induce mutants, they studied the growth of the mutants on a culture medium containing the minimum nutrients that the normal wild-type mold required and on media with known supplements.

Success came on the 299th culture, which failed to grow on the minimal medium unless pyridoxine, a B vitamin, was administered, suggesting that the growth requirement was inherited as a single-gene trait. Beadle's *Neurospora* work demonstrated the contention that all biochemical processes in an organism are under genetic control, an idea that was first outlined in a brief research paper with Tatum (1941). The one-gene, one-enzyme theory was summarized by Beadle in the landmark paper "Biochemical Genetics," published in *Chemical Reviews* 37 (1945), and brought him a share, with Tatum and Joshua Lederberg, of the 1958 Nobel Prize in physiology or medicine.

Meanwhile, in 1946, Beadle returned to Caltech as a professor of biology and chairman of the biology division. The chemist Linus Pauling played a key role in recruiting Beadle. Together at Caltech, Beadle and Pauling established a new program in chemical biology. Beadle and his first wife divorced in 1953; he married Muriel Barnett that same year.

Soon Beadle stopped doing laboratory research and became a full-time academic administrator as chairman of the Caltech Division of Biology. In 1961 Beadle accepted a job as president of the University of Chicago; while in this position he stanched the loss of faculty caused by urban decay in the university neighborhood and saved the neighborhood through urban renewal. He retired from the university in 1968 and next served briefly as director of the American Medical Association's Institute of Biomedical Research (1968–1970). He then returned to the University of Chicago, where for some years he engaged in research on the origin of corn. Beadle died of Alzheimer's disease. His ashes were scattered at the University of Chicago.

Beadle's enduring reputation as a scientist rests not only on his development of the one-gene, one-enzyme concept—which cemented the idea that genes control enzymes, the chemical stuff of life, and thus ignited the science of biochemical genetics—but also on the inspired method he and Tatum devised to initially produce the *Neurospora* mutants they used to demonstrate their Nobel-honored theory.

★

Beadle's papers are at the California Institute of Technology in Pasadena, California. There are no book-length biographies of Beadle. His autobiographical writings include "Mendel to Watson and Crick," in his *Genetics and Modern Biology* (1963), pp. 1–28; "Biochemical Genetics: Some Recollections," in John Cairns, Gunther S. Stent, and James D. Watson, eds., *Phage and the Origins of Molecular Biology* (1966), pp. 23–32; and "Recollections," *Annual Review of Biochemistry* 43 (1974): 1–13. Norman H. Horowitz, Beadle's longtime colleague and coworker, provides reminiscences of Beadle in "*Neurospora* and the Beginnings of Molecular Genetics," *Neurospora Newsletter* 20 (1973): 4–6, and a memoir in National Academy of Sciences, *Biographical Memoirs* 59 (1990): 27–52. A discussion of his scientific research is in Robert E. Kohler, "Systems of Production: *Drosophila, Neurospora,* and Biochemical Genetics," *Historical Studies in the Physical and Biological Sciences* 22 (1991): 87–130. An obituary is in the *New York Times* (12 June 1989).

JUDITH R. GOODSTEIN

BEARDEN, Romare Howard (*b.* 2 September 1912 in Charlotte, North Carolina; *d.* 12 March 1988 in New York City), painter, author, and songwriter best known for his collages of New York City and the rural South and his encouragement of other African-American artists.

Bearden was the only child of college-educated parents, Howard Bearden, an employee of the New York City De-

Romare Bearden. MANU SASSOONIAN

partment of Health, and Bessye Johnson Banks, a political organizer and leader in the Democratic party and in African-American organizations. Although the family moved to New York City in 1915 and settled in Harlem in 1920, Romare continued to have deep ties to his grandparents in the South and summered there until 1925. One of his early influences was a crippled playmate, Eugene Baily, who showed him how to draw. In New York City he enjoyed the Harlem Renaissance of artists and musicians and the interesting and famous people attracted to his mother's wide social circle.

After attending New York City public schools, Bearden enrolled in Boston University in 1931. After two years he moved to New York University, from which he graduated in 1935 with a B.S. degree in mathematics. In college he drew cartoons for the school newspapers, *Medley* and the *Afro-American.* From 1936 to 1938 he attended the Art Students League and studied under the German Expressionist painter George Grosz, who encouraged him to learn composition by examining the great masters and to continue expressive line-rendering of figures. In 1938 he became a full-time caseworker at the New York City Department of Welfare. He continued to paint African-American social genre in gouache and watercolors and held his first solo show at Ad Bates's "306" Studios in Harlem in 1941.

From 1942 to 1945 Bearden served in the U.S. Army as a sergeant in a cannon company of an all-black infantry. While still in the army, he was introduced to Caresse Crosby, a well-known art patron, who arranged two exhibitions for him at the G. Place Gallery in Washington, D.C., and who introduced him to Samuel M. Kootz, a New York art dealer. By 1944 Bearden had changed to modernist painting, producing semiabstract watercolors inspired by the Bible and Greek myths and legends. He was included in more Kootz exhibitions, and the Museum of Modern Art in New York purchased *He Is Arisen* in 1945.

In 1950, taking advantage of the GI Bill, Bearden studied philosophy at the Sorbonne in Paris. He did no painting but met many important artists, including Georges Braque, Constantin Brancusi, and Pablo Picasso. He then toured Italy and in 1952 returned to New York, where he tried his hand at songwriting and returned to his job at the Department of Social Services. In 1954 he married Nanette Rohan, a dance teacher; the couple had no children. Bearden's wife persuaded him to again take up painting, and he produced a small body of abstract expressionist work, which was shown at the Barone Gallery and met with favorable reviews. He was included in more Kootz exhibitions and five annual exhibitions at the Whitney Museum of American Art. A number of successful shows followed at the Barone, Arne and Ekstrom, ACA, and Cordier galleries. In 1955 his "World at Work" was sponsored by the American Federation of Arts in Chicago. In 1956 he moved with Nanette into a studio on Canal Street in lower Manhattan and started experimenting with collage.

The civil rights movement of the 1960s gave rise to politically oriented artists, composers, and writers who inspired Bearden. With two dozen black artists he formed the Spiral Group to help black artists win recognition. When the group abandoned a planned collaborative collage, Bearden completed it himself. He developed the "projection" technique, a process of making a collage in color and then enlarging it to create a photomontage. These tableaux of Bearden's life in the South marked a return from abstractions to representational figures. They were shown to great acclaim at Cordier and Ekstrom, and in 1965 the Corcoran Gallery in Washington put the "Projections" on display. Thereafter he worked primarily in the medium of collage.

In 1966 Bearden found he could earn a living as an artist and retired from New York's Department of Social Services. His *Painter's Mind: A Study of the Relations of Structure and Space in Painting* (1966), written with Carl Holty, treated the study of structure and what vision means in art. In 1969 he and Holty established the Cinque Gallery, a nonprofit showcase for young African-American artists. Recognition and fame came copiously to Bearden in the 1970s. His painting "Patchwork" was acquired by the Museum of Modern Art; he published, with Harry Henderson, *Six Black Masters of American Art* (1972); he designed "Ancestral Voices" for the front curtain of the Alvin Ailey Dance Theatre (1977); and he painted the Odysseus Series, based on the Iliad but with an Odysseus from ancient Africa (also 1977).

In 1980 the Mint Museum in Charlotte, North Carolina, held a retrospective of Bearden's work, "Romare Bearden 1970–1980." He was the recipient of numerous honorary degrees and awards, including the Frederick Douglass Medal, given by the New York Urban League in 1978, and the National Medal of the Arts (1987). He died after struggling with cancer for several years. A memorial service at the Cathedral of St. John the Divine included contributions by artists and musicians and a song of Bearden's own composition, "Seabreeze."

Bearden was a prolific painter whose works have appeared in exhibitions worldwide and in the permanent collections of major museums in the United States. He designed sets and costumes, painted murals on subway stations and civic centers, and produced cover art for *Time, Fortune,* and the *New York Times* magazines. His work, a combination of collage and paint, emphasized color. He called his philosophy the "prevalence of ritual" because he felt that ceremony and ritual are common to all cultures. He loved jazz and the blues and saw connections between them and his painting. His work relayed his love of guitar players, roosters, bathing women, and Obeah women and his dedication to and love of black culture.

★

Collections of Bearden's personal papers are in the Archives of American Art at the Smithsonian Institution, Washington, D.C.; the Archives of American Art, New York City; the Museum of Modern Art, New York City; the New York Public Library Schomburg Center for Research in Black Culture; the Romare Bearden Foundation, Staten Island, New York; the Whitney Museum of American Art, New York City; and the Hatch-Billops Archives, New York City. Bearden's writings include the posthumously published *A History of African-American Artists, from 1792 to the Present* (1993), written with Harry Henderson. Biographies include Myron Schwartzman, *Romare Bearden: His Life and Art* (1990), which contains interviews with Bearden and many color plates; Theresa Dickason Cederholm, *Afro-American Artists* (1973), which includes a lengthy bibliography and list of exhibitions; Elton C. Fax, *Seventeen Black Artists* (1971); and *Memory and Metaphor: The Art of Romare Bearden, 1940–1987,* an exhibition catalog from the Studio Museum in Harlem with introductions by major Bearden scholars. See also Avis Berman, "Romare Bearden," *Art News* 80 (Dec. 1980): 60–67; and a profile by Calvin Tomkins in the *New Yorker* (29 Nov. 1977). Obituaries are in the *New York Times* and *Newsday* (both 13 Mar. 1988); *Los Angeles Times* (14 Mar. 1988); *Jet* (28 Mar. 1988); and *Art News* (summer 1988).

PATRICIA BRAUCH

BECHTEL, Stephen Davison, Sr. (*b.* 24 September 1900 in Aurora, Indiana; *d.* 14 March 1989 in Oakland, California), builder who transformed Bechtel Corporation from a regional construction firm into one of the world's largest and most influential contractors and participated in many of the twentieth century's major engineering projects, from the Hoover Dam to the Trans-Arabian Pipeline.

Stephen Bechtel was the second of four children of Warren A. Bechtel and Clara (West) Bechtel. His father, who had gotten his start grading railroad routes with his own mules, was by that point known as an innovative contractor specializing in road building. As a child, Bechtel moved with his family from one construction camp to another.

During World War I, Bechtel served in France as an army motorcycle dispatch rider. After the war, he enrolled in the University of California at Berkeley but dropped out in 1920 after killing two pedestrians in an automobile accident. Bechtel then joined the family business, becoming a vice president of W. A. Bechtel Company in San Francisco in 1925. In 1928 he took charge of the company's first pipeline, built in California.

In 1923 Bechtel married Laura Adaline Peart; they had two children: Stephen, Jr., who became president of Bechtel Corporation in 1960, and Barbara. Laura Peart Bechtel died in 1992. In 1931 the W. A. Bechtel Company joined with seven other contractors, including Henry J. Kaiser, to submit a bid to dam the Colorado River for the federal government. When the bid was accepted, Stephen Bechtel was put in charge of administration, including responsibility for materials. In 1933, in the middle of the project, Warren Bechtel died during a trip to Russia, and Stephen and his two brothers took charge of the company in his place. In 1935, following the completion of the Boulder (later Hoover) Dam, Stephen Bechtel was named president of the W. A. Bechtel Company, and in 1936 he and his younger brother founded a new firm, the S. D. Bechtel Company, later renamed the Bechtel Corporation. Soon after, the company helped build part of the San Francisco–Oakland Bay Bridge.

In 1937 Bechtel teamed up with his college friend John A. McCone, who had supplied steel to the Boulder Dam, to form the Bechtel-McCone Corporation in Los Angeles. Bechtel proposed that rather than bidding for individual parts of a project, such as just a pipeline, the company should offer clients an entire package—design and construction of a pipeline, tanks, and refinery—for which nothing but a "turn-key" was required to start the whole operation rolling. This concept of a "turn-key solution" was later widely imitated, especially in the computer industry.

During World War II, Bechtel moved into shipbuilding, constructing the enormous Calship and Marinship yards (in Los Angeles Harbor and San Francisco Bay, respectively), which together turned out 560 ships, making the Bechtel-McCone Corporation the nation's third-largest wartime shipbuilder. He also continued oil-related work. Bechtel and McCone grossed more than $100 million during the war.

After the war, Bechtel briefly retired, but was soon back to work, forming the Bechtel Corporation and pursuing his interest in pipelines in particular. In 1949, during a lunchtime conversation with a Mobil Oil Company executive, he took pen to tablecloth and sketched out what would become the Canadian Trans-Mountain Pipeline. Becoming operational in 1953, the 718-mile line carried oil from Edmonton, Alberta, across the Rockies to Vancouver, British Columbia. The company also built several pipelines and refineries in the Middle East, including the 1,068-mile Trans-Arabian Pipeline (Tapline), which carried Saudi Arabian oil from the Persian Gulf to the Mediterranean Sea. By 1955, pipelines accounted for a third of the company's contracts and 22 percent of its annual $250 million in revenue. Bechtel also built oil refineries, including the Aden Refinery for the Anglo-Iranian Oil Company. That project, completed in 1954, was notable for the speed with which it was completed. After negotiating a contract in which he would pay a penalty for delays but be paid a bonus for finishing on time, Bechtel opened the refinery four months before deadline.

Stephen Bechtel with a Bay Area Rapid Transit (BART) train. COURTESY OF BECHTEL CORPORATION

Bechtel helped pioneer nuclear power. During World War II, his company helped in the Manhattan Project, building parts of the "heavy water" storage plant at Hanford, Washington. In 1951 Bechtel built Experimental Breeder Reactor No. 1 for the Atomic Energy Commission, the first nuclear reactor to generate electricity. In 1953 he approached the chairman and chief executive officer of General Electric, Ralph H. Cordiner, with the idea of taking nuclear power beyond its experimental and military stages. The result was the Dresden Power Station in Illinois, the world's first commercial nuclear power plant, which went on line in 1959. Bechtel built parts of many of the nation's subsequent nuclear plants and also built hundreds of millions of dollars' worth of conventionally powered plants, both in the United States and abroad.

Bechtel enjoyed close ties with the U.S. government, especially during Dwight D. Eisenhower's administration, when he golfed with the president. His friend John McCone served under President Eisenhower as chief of the Atomic Energy Commission and under President John F. Kennedy as director of the Central Intelligence Agency, with which Bechtel cooperated, sharing intelligence and providing cover for agents. Bechtel also served as a liaison between the government and major businesses as a member of the National Committee for a Free Asia, the Business Advisory Council, and other organizations. He was one of five members of the President's Advisory Committee on a National Highway Association, which helped plan the interstate highway system. During Richard Nixon's administration, he served on the advisory committee of the Export-Import Bank.

Bechtel was described as his company's "star salesman," boasting "We'll build anything for anybody" and personally negotiating deals with CEOs, government officials, and even royalty. He preferred to deal with a few large, reliable customers, so that 85 percent of his business was done for seventeen clients, and he himself decided whether to work with a new customer. Bechtel personally visited many of the company's job sites, traveling more than six months and 50,000 miles in a year, often accompanied by his wife and children. Daily operations in the San Francisco headquarters were left to top executives.

By the mid-1950s, Bechtel's personal fortune was estimated at $250 million, only one-third of which was invested in Bechtel enterprises. The Bechtel Corporation under his leadership had become one of the United States' largest privately held firms. Bechtel made major donations to Oakland's Merritt Hospital and to several universities, including Berkeley, Stanford, and the American University in Beirut. By the 1970s, his net worth of $700 million made him one of the richest people in the United States. Bechtel received many honors, including several honorary degrees (among them a degree from Berkeley in 1954), the John Fritz Medal, given by a group of engineering societies (1960), and induction by the editors of *Fortune* magazine into the Hall of Fame for Business Leadership (1976).

Stepping down from the presidency of Bechtel Corporation in 1960, Bechtel passed that position on to his son,

Stephen Bechtel, Jr., but remained active in the company as chairman and then, after retiring from that position in 1965, as senior director. He personally helped negotiate deals for large projects, such as the Bay Area Rapid Transit (BART) system and the building of the industrial city of Jubail, Saudi Arabia. In 1985, at the age of eighty-four, he traveled to China to negotiate a joint engineering deal. Only when hospitalized for what proved his final illness did he stop going into the office. He is buried in Oakland, California.

★

Robert L. Ingram, *The Bechtel Story: Seventy Years of Accomplishment in Engineering and Construction* (1968), commissioned by the company, chronicles and celebrates major projects and executive appointments. Laton McCartney, *Friends in High Places: The Bechtel Story: The Most Secret Corporation and How It Engineered the World* (1988), is written in the muckraking tradition, weaving charges of fraud and favoritism into a lively narrative history of the Bechtel family and companies. The book prompted the Bechtel Group to issue a sixteen-page rebuttal. Robert Sheehan, "Steve Bechtel: Born to Build," *Fortune* 52 (Nov. 1955): 142–146, 148, 150, 153–154, profiles Bechtel at the peak of his career. The *Bechtel News Memorial Edition* (1989) includes a complete list of Bechtel's honors. An obituary is in the *New York Times* (15 Mar. 1989).

ZACHARY M. SCHRAG

BELVIN, Harry J. W. (*b.* 11 December 1900 in Boswell, Indian Territory [now Oklahoma]; *d.* 21 November 1986 in Durant, Oklahoma), principal chief of the Choctaw Indian Nation from 1948 to 1975.

Belvin, the oldest of six children, was born on a ranch. His mother was Irish, and his father, Watson J. Belvin, was a full-blooded Choctaw who was a member of the Choctaw Tribal Council. Belvin graduated from high school in Durant, Oklahoma, and received a B.A. from Southeastern State College (now Southeastern Oklahoma State University) in Durant, Oklahoma, majoring in history and English. He then earned a master's degree in education from the University of Oklahoma at Norman.

On 21 December 1922 Belvin married Lucille Brightwell, a non-Indian; they had one daughter. He started his professional career as a public school teacher in Bryan and Choctaw Counties (1926–1941). In 1941 he was elected superintendent of the Bryan County public schools, a position he held until 1952.

In 1948 Belvin was elected chief of the Choctaw Nation. There had been no principal chief of the Choctaws since Oklahoma became a state on 16 November 1907. At that time Congress had abolished traditional tribal governance for all the Indian tribes in the state, allowing only a "chief" appointed by the Bureau of Indian Affairs. This chief was perceived as having primary loyalty to the federal government rather than to his tribe. Belvin had been selected as chief in 1946, but the Bureau of Indian Affairs refused to approve his selection. He then went to Washington, D.C., and met with Bureau of Indian Affairs officials to propose a detailed plan for Choctaw governance, and was successful in gaining the Choctaws a referendum on self-governance within two years. After this referendum President Harry S. Truman appointed Belvin principal chief of the Choctaw Nation. The Choctaws thus became the first tribe to have an independent voice in their own governance.

Belvin's term as principal chief (18 August 1948 to 25 August 1975) is the longest of any Choctaw chief. From 1954 to 1964 he also served in the Oklahoma state legislature: six years in the house of representatives and four years in the senate.

Belvin was instrumental in helping to resolve longstanding issues connected with 400,000 acres of mineral-rich lands (primarily coal and asphalt) that were held jointly by the Choctaw and Chickasaw tribes. The federal government, via the Atoka Supplemental Agreement of 25 September 1902, was supposed to coordinate the sale of this land and distribute the proceeds to the two tribes, but this had not been done. By 1942, ravaged by the effects of the Great Depression, many Choctaws were almost destitute. Four delegates from the confederation of the Choctaw and Chickasaw tribes—Hollis Hampton, Henry Gooding, Houston Hickman, and Harry Belvin—went to Washington to attempt to resolve this issue. The representatives were given five minutes to state their case, and the government made them an offer of $3.5 million for the land in question. Belvin stated that this offer would undoubtedly be refused by his tribe, and the government made a second offer of $8.5 million. The coal and asphalt fields were sold for this amount, and the tribe later won an additional $4 million in a further lawsuit. The per capita payment to the Choctaws that resulted from these negotiations was $511. Additional land sales were made during the 1950s, providing further payments and contributing to Belvin's early popularity with his people.

Belvin was also involved in the Choctaws' ongoing quest for self-governance. The Choctaw Termination Act of 25 August 1959, proposed as a self-rule plan for the tribe, was supposed to end federal supervision of Choctaw affairs. Belvin had been assured that this act would not undermine individuals' abilities to participate in federal health, education, and welfare programs, but it quickly became clear that it would have a devastating impact upon individuals' rights regarding government support. Belvin fought to have the bill repealed. Representative Carl Albert was instrumental in having the bill repealed hours before it was to be signed into law by President Dwight D. Eisenhower.

During Belvin's leadership, the Choctaws made major strides in attaining self-governance and improved economic conditions. Among his accomplishments were the establishment of more than 1,300 units of low-rent housing; the development of an industrial park on tribal land just outside of Talihina, Oklahoma; the establishment of health clinics; and the construction of a quarter-million-dollar Choctaw Cultural Center, a joint project involving the Choctaw Nation, the city of Hugo, Oklahoma, and the U.S. Department of Housing and Urban Development. Belvin was instrumental in establishing and advancing other cultural and educational programs, and as times changed, he also worked to block the sale of valuable Choctaw Nation lands.

By 1973 some Choctaws were complaining that Belvin did not allow for wider participation in decisions concerning tribal money and other areas. Belvin argued that he was not in charge of the Choctaw Nation but served as a liaison between the tribe and the federal government. The role of the chief, as well as tribal and governmental relations, changed over the course of Belvin's tenure, and in 1975 he was defeated by David Gardner. Belvin retired, dividing his time between Durant, Oklahoma, and his ranch about twenty miles away. He died on 21 November in Durant.

★

The Carl Albert Congressional Research and Studies Center at the University of Oklahoma in Norman has a collection of papers relating to Belvin's career. Belvin's *Choctaw Tribal Structure and Achievement, August 18, 1949, to August 25, 1974* (1981), gives an excellent summary of his accomplishments and concerns. W. David Baird, *The Choctaw People* (1973), provides a detailed history of the Choctaw people; there is also a detailed biographical essay on Belvin at the conclusion of the book. Vivian McCullough, "A Good Chief, This Belvin of Choctaws," *Daily Oklahoman* (29 May 1955), gives a good basic summary of his early life and accomplishments. An obituary is in the *New York Times* (22 Nov. 1986).

MARTHA E. NELSON

BENDER, Lauretta (*b.* 9 August 1897 in Butte, Montana; *d.* 4 January 1987 in Annapolis, Maryland), child neuropsychiatrist best known as the creator of the Bender-Gestalt Visual Motor Test.

Bender was the daughter of John Oscar Bender, an attorney, and Katherine Parr (Irvine) Bender. She attended Leland Stanford University for two years (1916–1918), then transferred to the University of Chicago, from which she earned a B.S. degree in 1922 and an M.A. degree in neuropathology in 1923. In 1926 she received a Ph.D. from the State University of Iowa.

Bender did her residency in neurology at Billings Hospital at the University of Chicago (1928) and her psychiatric residency at Boston Psychopathic Hospital (1928–1929). She spent 1929 to 1930 as a research associate at the Phipps Clinic at Johns Hopkins Hospital in Baltimore.

Lauretta Bender (*center*) receives an Elizabeth Blackwell Citation from the New York Infirmary, 1949. UPI/CORBIS-BETTMANN

The majority of Bender's professional career was spent at Bellevue Hospital in New York City, where she worked as a senior psychiatrist from 1930 to 1956 and was in charge of children's services from 1934 to 1956. While at Bellevue, she fostered the development of the Bellevue School for inpatients, as well as the provision of tutoring services for children with language disabilities in the clinic, services that were innovative at the time. She also used electroconvulsive therapy (ECT) in treating one hundred children at Bellevue. Patients showed no improvement or got worse, and Bender abandoned this controversial method in the 1950s.

Early in her career, working with children from foster homes, Bender noticed that the institutional environment led to emotional problems. In 1934 she developed the Bender-Gestalt Visual Motor Test, which became a widely used diagnostic instrument for children with learning difficulties. The test consists of nine geometric patterns comprising dots, lines, angles, and curves. The designs are presented singly in a specific order to the subject, who is asked to copy each of them. The patterns were borrowed from Max Wertheimer's classic study on the theory of Gestalt psychology. Bender originally conceptualized the test as a maturational measure for use with children and as a device for exploring regression or retardation and detecting possible brain damage. Later, it was used predominantly for detection of organic cerebral damage. The test's name derived from Bender's advocacy of Gestalt psychology and her use of Gestalt principles in the construction of the test. In 1938 Bender published the monograph *A Visual Motor Gestalt Test and Its Clinical Use*. The test was later abandoned when positive results proved to be fleeting.

In 1936 Bender married Paul Ferdinand Schilder, a prominent Viennese neurologist and psychoanalyst; they had three children. In December 1940 Schilder had just visited his wife in the maternity ward when he was struck and killed by a truck as he crossed the street outside of the hospital. Bender married Henry B. Parkes in 1967.

Bender taught from 1930 to 1958 at New York University, where for seven years (1951 to 1958) she was a professor of clinical psychiatry. She taught as a professor of clinical psychiatry at Columbia College of Physicians and Surgeons from 1959 to 1962 and, after moving to Maryland, at the University of Maryland School of Medicine from 1974 to 1987. In clinical practice, after leaving Bellevue, Bender served as the director of research in child psychiatry at Creedmoor State Hospital from 1959 to 1967 and attending psychiatrist at New York State Psychiatric Institute from 1969 to 1974. During this time she also worked (from 1969 to 1973) as an attending psychiatrist at the New Jersey State Neuropsychiatric Institute. She continued to teach, consult, lecture, and write until her death.

In addition to her clinical work, Bender belonged to numerous professional organizations. She was a consultant for various state, federal, and academic programs in the field of psychiatrics and mental health from the 1940s to the end of her career. In 1955 she became New York State's principal research psychiatrist, and in 1958 New York State named her "Medicine's Woman of the Year." She edited *Bellevue Studies in Child Psychiatry* (1952–1955), and throughout her life she served on the child-welfare committees of various civic organizations. She received numerous honors for her wide-ranging contributions in psychiatry and the understanding of human development and learning. Most notably, she was the first recipient of the Samuel Torrey Orton Award (named for the neuropsychiatrist who pioneered the study of dyslexia).

Near her eightieth birthday, the Orton Dyslexia Society produced a videotape about Bender's work in which her colleagues describe her legacy. Neuropsychiatrist Rosa A. Hagin states that "Dr. Bender's approach demonstrated for generations of clinicians the richness of developmental, longitudinal, motility, and graphic techniques in understanding the problems of children and youth." Bender's colleague Ralph D. Rabinovitch notes that "for so many of us, perhaps especially her students, she was concerned, giving, loyal, and a wonderful friend."

Bender's earliest professional studies were laboratory studies in basic biology. This approach continued to influence her later work. Her highly respected research focused on the causes of childhood schizophrenia and other children's psychiatric illness; she published numerous books and articles on the topic of child suicides and violence. A pioneer in identifying learning disabilities in preschool children, she used the concept of the plasticity of the human organism to describe the ability to adapt to change, and she contributed to the understanding of developmental lag. Bender was herself dyslexic, a fact that contributed to her longtime interest in language disorders. Her writings, whether focused on brain-behavior relationships or the emotional components of language impairment, consistently focused on the whole child.

★

Biographical sources include Sally Elizabeth Knapp, *Women Doctors Today* (1947), pp. 81–93, which includes an artist's drawing of Bender; Gwendolyn Stevens and Sheldon Gardner, *Women of Psychology* (1981); Archie A. Silver, "Lauretta Bender (1897–1987): An Appreciation," *Learning Disabilities Focus* 2 (1987): 72–74; Arthur S. Reber, ed., *The Penguin Dictionary of Psychology* (2d ed., 1995), p. 91; and Stella Chess, "Images in Psychiatry," *American Journal of Psychiatry* 52, no. 3 (Mar. 1995): 436. Bender summarized some of her contributions in "Highlights in Pioneering the Understanding of Language Disabilities," *Annals of Dyslexia* 37 (1987): 10–17. An obituary is in the *New York Times* (17 Jan. 1987).

KAREN M. VENTURELLA

BENNETT, Joan (*b.* 27 February 1910 in Palisades, New Jersey; *d.* 7 December 1990 in White Plains, New York), actress in films, stage, and television whose movie career stalled in 1951 when her husband, the film producer Walter Wanger, shot and wounded her agent, Jennings Lang.

Bennett was the third acting daughter (the others were Constance, who was a leading film star in the 1930s, and Barbara) of matinee idol Richard Bennett and actress Adrienne Morrison. As a child, she appeared briefly in two of her father's pictures, *The Valley of Decision* (1916) and *The Eternal City* (1923). She attended St. Margaret's, a boarding school in Waterbury, Connecticut, and a French finishing school, L'Ermitage, in Versailles, before making her stage debut with her father in *Jarnegan* (1928). That year Bennett played her first significant film role in *Power,* and she soon became a star in *Bulldog Drummond* (1929), with Ronald Colman.

Joan Bennett. AMERICAN STOCK/ARCHIVE PHOTOS

Bennett's career languished through roles in *Moby Dick* and *Scotland Yard* (1930), then picked up with *The Trial of Vivienne Ware* in 1932. Playing a hash slinger, she exchanged snappy repartee (including a takeoff of the interior monologues in *Strange Interlude*) with Spencer Tracy in *Me and My Gal* (1932). She then starred as the selfish, pretentious Amy, one of the four March sisters, in *Little Women* (1933). Her best films of the mid-1930s were *Private Worlds* (1935), one of the earliest films to deal with psychological problems, in which she plays the wife of a mental institution director who herself goes insane; and *Big Brown Eyes* (1936), a clever comedy-mystery with Cary Grant. Bennett later commented on Hollywood in the 1930s: "The industry held a combination of nuts, talents, charlatans, and geniuses, all of whom were learning, bumbling and creating with fury and innocence. The colorful types had a passionate love for the business, not just for the money. Today, it seems to me, it's strictly a big business, based on dollars and cents."

Bennett was a down-to-the-wire contender for the role of Scarlett O'Hara in *Gone with the Wind* but lost the part to Vivien Leigh. Raven-haired Hedy Lamarr had just come to Hollywood to make *Algiers;* she was all the rage, so producer Walter Wanger turned Bennett into a brunette for *Trade Winds* (1938). "They always told me I looked like Hedy Lamarr," she said. "God knows where they got that idea. To me I always looked like plain old Joan Bennett." Her new hair color changed her image completely and went well with her husky voice and come-hither eyes. Wanger guided her career from that point on, and her best pictures were made under his aegis. They married in 1940 and had two daughters, Stephanie and Shelley, but were divorced in 1965. (From 1926 to 1928 Bennett had been married to John Marion Fox, with whom she had a daughter, Diana; from 1932 to 1937, to the screenwriter Gene Markey, with whom she had another daughter, Melinda.)

Bennett starred in four films directed by Fritz Lang. In *Man Hunt* (1941) she plays a Cockney tramp—a seamstress, as opposed to the streetwalker of Geoffrey Household's book, *Rogue Male* (1939), from which the movie was adapted. Trying to escape the Nazis in London, Walter Pidgeon, as the male lead, picks her up. Bennett is by turns tough, pathetic, and wistful, and her accent slips noticeably, but she is very sweet. Lang later described her as wonderful to work with, an actress who understood her character very well.

In two films noir with Edward G. Robinson, the women Bennett plays lure him to his doom—an imaginary doom in *Woman in the Window* (1944) and a real one in *Scarlet Street* (1945). In the latter, an adaptation of Jean Renoir's film *La Chienne* (The Bitch, 1931), Bennett plays a penthouse vamp kept by Robinson, a Sunday painter who allows her to take credit for his works. Cold and calculating, Bennett plies her womanly wiles to their best advantage but winds up murdered in her boudoir. Under Lang's direction, Bennett discovered a dynamic combination of corrupted morality and natural sensuality. Before working with Lang she was often cast as a wisecracking blonde; in *Scarlet Street* she plays a dark, smoldering bombshell. *Secret Beyond the Door* (1948) has none of the virtues of Bennett's first three films with Lang and is merely a tiresome variation on Alfred Hitchcock's *Suspicion,* wherein Bennett suspects her husband of being a lunatic killer.

The Macomber Affair (1947) is based on an Ernest Hemingway short story about a weak man (Robert Preston) who takes his wife on an African safari led by a respected white hunter (Gregory Peck). Bennett (as Mrs. Macomber) despises her husband, flirts with Peck, and manages to kill Preston in an ambiguous hunting accident. She is tough, flirtatious, and dripping with scorn.

Woman on the Beach (1947) is a nonsensical, brooding story about the wife (Bennett) of a blind painter (Charles Bickford) who falls for a Coast Guard officer (Robert Ryan). Inasmuch as it was directed by Jean Renoir during his exile in Hollywood during World War II, the film has a certain interest, with Bennett occasionally struggling to cool the melodrama down.

Under the direction of Max Ophuls, in *The Reckless*

Moment (1949) Bennett plays a chic matron, still beautiful, but older. She is blackmailed by James Mason after she disposes of the body of a man whom her daughter (Geraldine Brooks) has accidentally killed. Mason and Bennett develop a certain sympathy for each other's plights, and their furtive meetings, in which Bennett pleads for time and Mason for money, take an almost romantic turn. Ophuls uses close-ups in a film noir style to make the two stars look like desperate halves of the same person.

In Vincente Minnelli's *Father of the Bride* (1950) and *Father's Little Dividend* (1951), Bennett plays Ellie Banks, the mother of the bride, to Spencer Tracy's "Pops" Stanley; Elizabeth Taylor plays Kay, the bride. Commenting on her portrayal in his book *Directed by Vincente Minnelli,* Stephen Harvey observes: "Bennett brings real individuality to the part, effortlessly segueing from acidulous sangfroid to dervish-like industry in the flick of a mascaraed eyelash. There's tenderness behind Bennett's brittle chic, as well; early in the film, her hushed reverie on the pleasures of having grandchildren is one of the picture's quiet highlights."

Bennett's personal life and her career intersected in 1951 when her third husband, producer Walter Wanger, shot her agent, Jennings Lang, in the groin. Wanger claimed that Lang was breaking up his home and served 100 days in prison for the assault. The scandal brought Bennett's career to a virtual halt. In 1981 Bennett laughingly contrasted the rigid 1950s with the freer 1970s and 1980s: "It would never happen that way today. If it happened today, I'd be a sensation. I'd be wanted by all studios for all pictures." In 1970, divorced from Wanger and asked if she would marry again, Bennett said, "No, what's the point? I'm a three-time loser. I started out at sixteen." Nevertheless, she married the critic David Wilde in 1978.

We're No Angels (1955), with Humphrey Bogart, was the last picture of interest that Bennett made; she had a nonstarring role as Leo G. Carroll's wife. Bennett made a few more movies, then took to the stage and television, touring the country in *Susan and God; Bell, Book and Candle; Once More with Feeling;* and other plays. From 1966 to 1971 she lent her name and presence to *Dark Shadows,* television's gothic soap opera. "I wasn't too eager for the series," she admitted in 1970. "I always had the idea that TV actors were inferiors, especially on the soaps—oh, they hate that word, I'm supposed to call it 'daytime'—but the cast is very capable and it's great fun." When she starred in *House of Dark Shadows* (1970), a feature film based on the series, she commented, "I'm not too anxious to be identified with that." Her last film was *Suspiria* (1977), an Italian horror film directed by Dario Argento, in which she played the headmistress of a ballet school that also happens to be a witches' coven.

One mark of Bennett's rehabilitation over the years, and of changing mores, was that she was asked to write a monthly column called "Equal Time by Joan Bennett" for the magazine *Girl Talk,* which was distributed in beauty salons. In it she recounted her life in Hollywood and offered her opinions on life in general. It was through the magazine that she met her last husband, to whom she remained married until her death.

Joan Bennett made a sixty-year career of playing femmes fatales, both good-hearted and bad-hearted, smart-mouthed babes, and harassed housewives. In 1986 she said, "I don't think much of most of the films I made, but being a movie star was something I liked very much." She died of cardiac arrest and is buried in Old Lyme, Connecticut.

★

An autobiography is Joan Bennett and Lois Kibbee, *The Bennett Playbill* (1970). Nicholas Thomas, ed., *International Dictionary of Films and Filmmakers: Actors and Actresses* (1992), lists Bennett's films and gives a brief biography. See also Ephraim Katz, ed., *The Film Encyclopedia* (2d ed., 1994), and David Shipman, *The Great Movie Stars: The Golden Years* (1979). Obituaries are in the *New York Times* and *Los Angeles Times* (both 9 Dec. 1990) and *Variety* (17 Dec. 1990).

JUDITH M. KASS

BENNETT, Michael (*b.* 8 April 1943 in Buffalo, New York; *d.* 2 July 1987 in Tucson, Arizona), dancer, choreographer, director, coproducer, and script developer who gave show dancers a voice, largely through his best-known production, *A Chorus Line* (1975), and transformed old-time Broadway dance "arrangers" from silent into full partners in shaping Broadway musicals.

Bennett was born Michael ("Mickey") Bennett DiFiglia, one of two children of Salvatore DiFiglia, a machinist, and Helen (Ternoff) DiFiglia, a secretary. His mother encouraged him to develop his dance talent, first with local tap lessons and then with further study in New York City during summer vacations from school. While attending Hutchinson Central Technical High School (1957–1960), he was active in the dramatic society, producing, directing, and choreographing. His driving ambition to work on a professional level quickly became apparent, and he dropped out of school to follow his career.

Bennett was initially aided by Jack Lenny, a local producer who ran Melody Fair, a summer theater dedicated to musical revivals. Lenny secured for the seventeen-year-old, who at five feet, five inches barely looked teenaged, the part of Baby John in a touring production of Jerome Robbins's *West Side Story.* Experiencing Robbins's work in the production was a turning point in Bennett's life. Robbins, who choreographed and directed the show, was a role model for him. Bennett eloquently outlined his dream life in 1983, saying, "I wish I was born in a trunk of a Broadway theater,

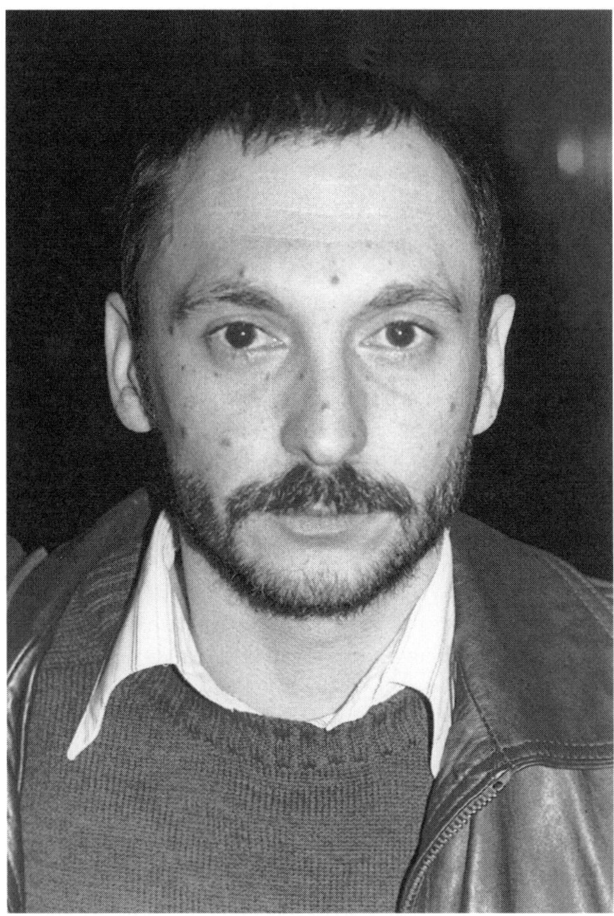

Michael Bennett, 1977. UPI/CORBIS-BETTMANN

and I crawled into the pit and looked up and there was Julie [Jule] Styne conducting the overture to *Gypsy,* and I heard Ethel Merman sing, and the first moment of life was experiencing a Jerry Robbins musical."

When *West Side Story* returned from Europe, the stage manager recommended Bennett to choreographer Michael Kidd, who was auditioning dancers for *Subways Are for Sleeping* (1961). That show did not last long, nor did Kidd's *Here's Love,* in which Bennett appeared two years later. Choreographer Peter Gennaro's *Bajour* (1964) was the last Broadway show in which Bennett worked as a gypsy, or chorus dancer. He continued to dance on television shows, of which NBC's *Hullabaloo* was the most important. At NBC he met Donna McKechnie, who subsequently became his most expert interpreter. Bennett stated, "Bob [Fosse] had Gwen [Verdon] and Carol [Haney], Jerry [Robbins] had Chita [Rivera], and I had Donna."

During the summer, Lenny hired Bennett to choreograph shows booked into Melody Fair. Bennett's first opportunity to choreograph a Broadway show was the short-lived *A Joyful Noise* (1966). Amazingly for a show that sank after twelve performances, Bennett's choreography received a Tony (Antoinette Perry) Award nomination. He had been noticed favorably amidst the wreckage. The same thing happened after his second show, *Henry, Sweet Henry* (1967), which closed after eighty performances. What was most significant was the development of a lifelong professional relationship with dancer Bob Avian, who became his assistant and a sensitive editor on every subsequent show. Such long-term commitments marked Bennett's career. Lenny, who had secured for him his first professional job, was retained as his manager until Bennett died. His design team, Robin Wagner (sets), Tharon Musser (lighting), and Theoni V. Aldredge (costumes), worked with him as often as conflicting professional commitments permitted. They all worked on *A Chorus Line.*

How Now, Dow Jones (1967) was experiencing troubles in out-of-town tryouts when producer David Merrick hired Bennett as a "show doctor" to fix it. It, too, failed, but Merrick hired Bennett again to choreograph Neil Simon's *Promises, Promises* (1968), which was Bennett's first hit after four misses. For that show, Bennett devised choreography that was not dancing per se but another form of less overt but real movement design. He developed the form further in his next show, *Coco* (1969). Director Hal Prince recruited him to arrange *Company* (1970) and then *Follies* (1971), in which he became even more involved in blending direction with choreography.

Seesaw (1973) was a large show mired in directorial, choreographic, and book difficulties when Bennett was called to Detroit to "doctor" it back to health. The job had appeared hopeless to the professionals approached before Bennett, who demanded and received complete control. He ruthlessly pruned the cast as well as the artistic staff and had himself billed as author-director-choreographer by the time the show opened on Broadway. Bennett received a Tony for his choreography. *Seesaw* proved to be a dress rehearsal for his landmark production *A Chorus Line* (1975).

Bennett had been obsessed with success long before he danced in his first Broadway show. He wanted to make a musical about his own successes and failures and the real life of a chorus dancer, the Broadway gypsy. He had worked within the system that basically allotted two months of rehearsal with last-minute changes by producers and directors to ready a show to open. Now, sixteen productions later, he needed complete control, more time, and freedom from economically driven artistic decisions. He got it from the nonprofit New York Shakespeare Festival. He employed the workshop format.

Producer Joseph Papp put the cast on survival salary for the months necessary to shape a production from twenty-four hours of tapes of ruthlessly probing, confessional gypsy reminiscences. Bennett led off the first session with his own story. In the final production, a character commented,

"When I was living in Buffalo, I considered suicide but realized it was redundant."

In addition to musicals, Bennett directed a handful of straight dramas, also bringing to them the eye of a choreographer who moves people smoothly from scene to scene. The method was honed from his first big opportunity to apply it in *Promises, Promises.* The style totally flowered in *A Chorus Line,* which won nine Tony Awards, including best direction and best musical for Bennett; the Pulitzer Prize, which Bennett shared; and the New York Drama Critics Circle Award. What gave *A Chorus Line* special resonance to the public was its "documentary" look at the human side of the Broadway musical. The performers were people with emotional and work needs that were universal. In the show's finale number, "One Singular Sensation," their anxieties and efforts were rewarded with the glamorous cloak of theatrical success.

After *A Chorus Line,* which ran on Broadway for more than 5,000 performances over twelve years, Bennett's productions included *Ballroom* (1978), a middle-aged romance; *Dreamgirls* (1981), loosely based on the Supremes singing group and for which he won a Tony Award for choreography; *My One and Only* (1983), an adaptation of George and Ira Gershwin's *Funny Face* (1927); and *Sunday in the Park with George* (1987), with music by Stephen Sondheim.

On 4 December 1976, Bennett married Donna McKechnie, but the marriage ended a few months later. They had no children. Bennett died in Tucson, Arizona, from AIDS. Bennett was not interested in dance steps and abhorred the idea of being asked to revive a musical of the era that thought only of steps. He was interested in character development through movement. His was a style that only a choreographer could evolve but only a director could permit to happen. Bennett knew that he had to be both to fulfill his need to tell the story in the right way, so that dancers were people with whom everyone could identify.

★

For information on Bennett, see Ken Mandelbaum, *"A Chorus Line" and the Musicals of Michael Bennett* (1989), and Kevin Kelly, *One Singular Sensation* (1990). An obituary is in the *New York Times* (3 July 1987).

DON MCDONAGH

BERGMAN, Jules Verne (*b.* 21 March 1929 in New York City; *d.* 12 February 1987 in New York City), reporter and broadcast journalist who specialized in science stories and was best known for his on-camera live broadcasts of U.S. space missions from the 1960s to the 1980s.

The son of New York storekeepers Irving and Ruth B. Bergman, Jules Bergman studied journalism at City College of New York (1946), Indiana University (1947), and Columbia University School of Journalism (1948–1950), where he received his bachelor's degree. Even before completing his B.A. degree, Bergman was a CBS news desk assistant from 1947 to 1948 and a writer-trainee with *Time* magazine between 1948 and 1950. These internships paved the way for Bergman's entry into journalism after graduation from Columbia. He worked as assistant news director, writer, and newscaster for the short-lived WFDR-FM radio station in New York City from 1950 to 1951.

After army service during the Korean War, Bergman returned to New York City in 1953 and became a newswriter with ABC Television and Radio. On 11 January 1953 Bergman married Joanne Skowron of Nyack, New York; they had three children. He remained with ABC news for the rest of his career, progressing from a junior staff writer to reporter to science editor. When he was named science editor for ABC in 1961, Bergman became the first network correspondent in the United States assigned to report exclusively on the subject. It was a recognition of the significance of science in American life, but it was also an opportunity for Bergman, as a relatively young beat reporter, to carve an important niche for himself in the journalism community.

Bergman made his reputation covering the nascent U.S. space program. He focused on the activities of the astronauts, helping to put a human face on a highly technological endeavor. Early on, Bergman went on location for his reports in order to give his audience "not an ivory-tower discussion of science, but an on-the-spot report of discoveries, which are changing the lives of human beings daily." He covered all fifty-four human spaceflight missions in the United States between the launch of Alan Shepard on 5 May 1961 and the *Challenger* disaster of 28 January 1986, many of them from the launch site at Cape Canaveral, Florida, or from mission control in Houston, Texas.

Bergman brought a special zest to space program reporting by traveling with the astronauts and participating in their training and exercise regimens. In one report he rode a centrifuge to the sustained force of five gravities (Gs) to demonstrate how astronauts prepared for launches, and in his on-camera wrap-up he called the experience "exhilarating." During the Mercury program flight of M. Scott Carpenter in 1962, Bergman reported on the biomedical monitoring of astronauts by having himself placed in a harness with sensors to record vital signs. The instruments showed that he was under as much stress during his twelve hours on the air as the astronaut in orbit.

Bergman's linkage to the space program proved a symbiotic relationship. His reporting helped to make the U.S. space program one of the best-known and best-liked activities of the federal government. At the same time, the space program helped to make Bergman a household name in

Jules Bergman. UPI/CORBIS-BETTMANN

the United States of the 1960s. Officials in charge of the space effort solicited his assistance to explain both their complex technologies and the rationale for their program. In turn, Bergman sought their support to give his reporting more credibility, insight, and excitement.

Bergman also developed a series of award-winning documentaries for ABC News during the 1960s and 1970s. In 1962 he developed the special "Ninety Seconds to Space" about Project Mercury, and in 1965 "Anyone Can Fly." In 1974 he wrote and narrated the documentary "Fire," which received an Emmy Award. He produced "Weekend Athletes" (1975), "Danger in Sports" (1975), "Crashes, Illusions of Safety" (1975), "Asbestos, the Dusty Way to Death" (1978), and "DuPont" (1982).

In the late 1970s Bergman was diagnosed with a meningioma, a benign brain tumor, which was removed. He was plagued for the rest of his life with malignant growths in his skull and had several operations to remove them. He also developed epilepsy during this period and took medication to control seizures. These health problems slowed Bergman's career significantly in the 1980s. He died of an apparent seizure in his Manhattan apartment.

★

There is no formal collection of Bergman's papers, but there are scattered materials at the NASA Historical Reference Collection, NASA Headquarters, Washington, D.C. Bergman's comments on space exploration can be found in *TV Guide* (2 Mar. 1974); Senate Committee on Commerce, Science, and Transportation and House Committee on Science and Technology, *Next Steps for Mankind: The Future in Space* (1979); "NASA and the Press: The Whole Truth," *Columbia Journalism Review* (summer 1968): 58–60; and *The Impact of Science on Society* (1985). Obituaries are in the *New York Times* and *Philadelphia Inquirer* (both 13 Feb. 1987).

ROGER D. LAUNIUS

BERLIN, Irving (*b.* 11 May 1888 in Tumen, Siberia; *d.* 22 September 1989 in New York City), the most successful, long-lived, and influential songwriter in American history and composer of many American standards, including "Alexander's Ragtime Band," "Blue Skies," "God Bless America," and "White Christmas."

Born Israel Baline, "Izzy" was the youngest of eight children of Moses and Leah Baline. When the boy was five the Baline family emigrated to the United States as part of a massive wave of Jewish immigration in the late nineteenth century. Settling his family in a teeming immigrant community on the Lower East Side of Manhattan, Moses Baline gave up his prestigious position as a cantor and took up work first as a kosher meat inspector and then as a house painter. Leah supplemented the family income as a midwife. The children worked as well. Izzy hawked newspapers and sold "junk," including the dismantled parts of a family samovar, a prized possession in many Russian households. When his father died in 1901, Izzy dropped out of school to earn more money for the family. As a teenager he became a singing waiter in a Lower East Side saloon called the Pelham Cafe, also known as "Nigger

Irving Berlin. CORBIS-BETTMANN

Mike's" after its dark-complected Russian-Jewish proprietor. Izzy won a reputation as a sly, bawdy parodist of popular songs, which were issuing by the hundreds from Tin Pan Alley, New York's famous music publishing district. He also earned money as a song plugger, promoting new songs in vaudeville theaters. Although he could not read or write music, Berlin had a keen ear, and with pianist Mike Nicholson he collaborated on his first song, "Marie from Sunny Italy" (1907). This bright, gently syncopated love song remains unremarkable but for one thing: on the sheet music, the publisher printed the lyricist's name as "I. Berlin." Keeping the new surname, Izzy adopted the new first name "Irving" and thereby stripped away the ethnic resonance of his given name.

Berlin's songwriting career blossomed quickly. On the strength of a comic song about a Jewish burlesque dancer entitled "Sadie Salome (Go Home)," he got a job as a staff lyricist for the Ted Snyder Company, at $25 per week plus royalties. Meanwhile, he was becoming well-known on vaudeville and Broadway, where his songs were regularly interpolated into the period's loosely plotted shows. In a 1910 revue called *Up and Down Broadway,* Berlin and Snyder performed a few of the songs they had written together. That same year, the showman Florenz Ziegfeld began using Berlin's songs in his annual Follies production, a practice that would continue intermittently over the next two decades. Two other events would enlarge Berlin's musical life in 1910: he acquired a transposing piano, which allowed him to play in any key with the shift of a lever under the keyboard; and he traveled with Ted Snyder's business partner, Henry Waterson, to England. There, the songwriter met the British publisher Bert Feldman, who helped establish Berlin's reputation overseas by featuring Berlin's songs in his "song annuals."

In 1911 Berlin's international reputation soared with the publication of "Alexander's Ragtime Band." Although Berlin had already published several ragtime songs, "Alexander's Ragtime Band" secured his international fame as the "Ragtime King," with estimated sheet-music sales of 2 million copies in 1911 alone. It also won him a partnership with his publisher; in 1912 his songs began to be issued by the firm known as Waterson, Berlin, and Snyder Company. In February 1912, now at the height of fame and prosperity, Berlin married Dorothy Goetz, the sister of his friend and fellow songwriter E. Ray Goetz. Shortly after the couple's honeymoon in Cuba, Dorothy contracted typhoid fever or pneumonia. Her health deteriorated rapidly and she died on 17 July. Berlin paid homage to his deceased wife in a gentle, mournful waltz called "When I Lost You."

Personal loss seems to have driven Berlin to new professional heights, because he consolidated his success with a string of Broadway hits, working with many of the musical theater's leading figures. *Watch Your Step* (1914), starring the popular dance team of Irene and Vernon Castle, marked the first time Berlin had written a complete Broadway score; this "syncopated musical show" became the hit of the season. *Stop! Look! Listen!* appeared the following year with two hit songs, "I Love a Piano" and "The Girl on the Magazine Cover." In 1916 Berlin collaborated with Victor Herbert on a lavish Ziegfeld production called *The Century Girl.* He worked with George M. Cohan on the *Cohan Revue of 1918.* He then contributed several songs to the *Ziegfeld Follies of 1919,* including his sentimental standard, "A Pretty Girl Is Like a Melody."

This period also marked the crucial final stage of Berlin's naturalization. He had begun the process of seeking U.S. citizenship by filing a declaration of intention in 1915; he took the oath of allegiance on 6 February 1918. Soon thereafter he was drafted into the U.S. Army and assigned to Camp Upton in Yaphank, Long Island. Berlin's genuine patriotism did not mitigate his distaste for army life, and, with the comic irreverence he had brought to his early work as a singing waiter, he composed "Oh! How I Hate to Get Up in the Morning." Berlin himself introduced the song in his new show called *Yip! Yip! Yaphank* (1918), a Broadway revue about army life with a cast featuring his fellow soldiers from Camp Upton. Berlin's winning performance—enhanced by his shy, aw-shucks stage persona, Lower East

Side accent, and diminutive size (about five feet, six inches, and less than 125 pounds)—helped make the song the hit of the show.

Berlin's business acumen also came to the fore during this period. He had joined with Herbert and others in the music business to form the American Society of Composers, Authors, and Publishers (ASCAP) in 1914, ensuring that they would earn royalties for performances of their songs. In 1918 Berlin confirmed his allegiance to Broadway by opening his own publishing house on West Forty-fifth Street, in the theater district north of Tin Pan Alley. In 1921 he moved his residence as well, buying an entire building a few blocks away on West Forty-sixth Street. That same year he crowned his Broadway success by building a theater, the Music Box Theatre, down the street from his publishing house. For the next four seasons Berlin's new theater featured a *Music Box Revue,* another in a long line of annual shows inspired by the Ziegfeld Follies. The revues launched several hit songs, including "All Alone," "All By Myself," "Everybody Step," "Pack Up Your Sins and Go to the Devil," "What'll I Do?," and "Say It with Music," which became the theme song of the series.

The early 1920s brought significant changes in Berlin's personal and social life. His mother, having watched her son's rapid climb from Lower East Side obscurity to international celebrity, died in 1922. The same year Berlin was absorbed into the tight-knit social group of the Round Table at the Algonquin Hotel. This voluble, witty circle of writers, actors, and musicians met regularly under the informal leadership of theater critic Alexander Woollcott. There Berlin formed several important professional and personal relationships. Playwright George S. Kaufman, for example, wrote scripts for the Music Box shows, and in 1925 he collaborated with Berlin on a new musical, *The Cocoanuts,* starring the Marx Brothers. Woollcott himself wrote the first biography of the songwriter. By the mid-1920s Berlin had befriended Ellin Mackay, daughter of the Postal Telegraph Cable tycoon Clarence Mackay. The upright businessman, a devout Catholic, bitterly opposed the courtship between his daughter and the self-made Jewish entertainer, and the press covered every twist in the romance. Ellin and Irving finally married over Mackay's objections on 4 January 1926. As a wedding gift Berlin presented his new wife with a tender waltz about enduring love, "Always," and assigned its copyright to her.

By the mid-1920s the music industry had undergone a major change, thanks to the emergence of radio and the proliferation of sound recordings, and Berlin was in a strong position to benefit from these developments. For example, in 1925, when the Irish tenor John McCormack sang Berlin's "All Alone" on radio, orders for both the recording and the sheet music soared. Recording sales had now supplanted sheet-music sales as the chief measure of popularity. The same year Warner Brothers developed the "vitaphone" system, which revolutionized film with synchronized sound. Just two years later the Warner Brothers studio scored an international hit with *The Jazz Singer,* featuring vaudeville star Al Jolson singing Berlin's new song "Blue Skies." With film as a new way to plug his wares, Berlin devoted his attention to Hollywood. From 1928 to 1930 eight films featured his music, including a screen adaptation of *The Cocoanuts,* again starring the Marx Brothers; *Mammy,* another Al Jolson vehicle; and *Puttin' on the Ritz,* named after its featured Berlin song. Hollywood did not entirely distract him from the stage, however. In 1933 he scored another Broadway hit with a revue called *As Thousands Cheer,* featuring the songs "Easter Parade" and "Heat Wave." Berlin's growing family also absorbed him. A daughter, Mary Ellin, was born in 1926, and it was to her that Berlin dedicated his cheerful, optimistic love ballad "Blue Skies." A son, Irving, Jr., was born in 1928, but died in infancy. A second daughter, named Linda, arrived in 1932, and the last Berlin child, Elizabeth, was born in 1936.

In late 1934 Berlin traveled to California by airplane and signed a contract with RKO Pictures for a film score. The contract granted him a large sum, plus a percentage of the movie's profits and the unusual privilege of retaining the music copyrights. The movie, *Top Hat* (1935), was Berlin's first entry in a successful series featuring Fred Astaire and Ginger Rogers and helped establish a new standard for the Hollywood musical. The film featured several hit songs, including "Cheek to Cheek" and "Top Hat, White Tie, and Tails." Two more collaborations with Astaire and Rogers followed in close succession: *Follow the Fleet* (1936), featuring "Let Yourself Go" and "Let's Face the Music and Dance"; and *On the Avenue* (1937), featuring "I've Got My Love to Keep Me Warm" and "This Year's Kisses." Berlin and his music thrived in this milieu. He later said that "I'd rather have Fred Astaire introduce one of my songs than any other singer I know—not because he has a great voice, but because his diction and delivery are so good that he can put over a song like nobody else."

Back in New York after a trip to England in September 1938, Berlin declared his interest in writing a "great peace song." His initial attempts failed, so he pulled from his files an unpublished song he had discarded from the show *Yip! Yip! Yaphank* two decades earlier. He changed a few words and published it as "God Bless America." On 11 November 1938 the popular radio singer Kate Smith performed it on an Armistice Day broadcast, then sang it again on Thanksgiving Day. By the end of the year she was singing the song to sign off her weekly broadcast. Since then it has often been referred to as the unofficial national anthem. Such was its popularity that Berlin felt obliged to deny any attempt to replace "The Star Spangled Banner." In 1940 it was sung at both the Republican and Democratic national conventions, and Berlin established the God Bless America Fund to distribute the song's profits to the Boy and Girl Scouts of America. By this time, Berlin, anticipating U.S. involvement in the war that had broken out in Europe in 1939, "seemed to be spending all his time singing 'God Bless America' at civic events and writing war-related songs," as his daughter Mary Ellin Barrett has recalled.

After the Japanese bombed Pearl Harbor on 7 December 1941 and the United States entered the war, Berlin arranged with the Department of War to revive *Yip! Yip! Yaphank* to benefit Army Emergency Relief. Working at Camp Upton, where he had been a recruit almost a quarter-century earlier, Berlin revised and rehearsed his show. Now entitled *This Is the Army,* it opened on Broadway on 4 July 1942. Berlin himself again sang "Oh! How I Hate to Get Up in the Morning," with a voice Mary Ellin has described as "high, with a slight rasp, familiar, sweet," and with his "impish," winning stage persona. The show also produced a new Berlin hit—"I Left My Heart at the Stage Door Canteen." In early 1943 Berlin and the show's cast went to Hollywood to make a film version starring George Murphy and Ronald Reagan. From fall 1943 through summer 1945, *This Is the Army* played overseas, first in England, then, after General Dwight Eisenhower, the Supreme Allied Commander in Europe, recognized the show's morale-boosting potential, in Italy and the South Pacific for enthusiastic audiences of thousands of Allied troops. For Berlin's contribution to the war effort, President Harry Truman presented Berlin with the army's Medal of Merit in 1945.

Although *This Is the Army* was Berlin's principal focus during the war, it barely interrupted his tenure as a leading Hollywood composer. After the three Astaire-Rogers movies, Hollywood continued to issue a string of new films with Berlin's music, including *Alexander's Ragtime Band* and *Carefree* (1938), *Second Fiddle* (1939), *Louisiana Purchase* (1942, based on a Broadway show of 1940), and *Holiday Inn* (1942). *Holiday Inn* featured Bing Crosby singing "White Christmas," for which Berlin won an Academy Award. After the war came *Blue Skies* (1946), featuring Crosby and Astaire and using Berlin's 1926 ballad as its title and theme song; *Easter Parade* (1948), starring Astaire and Judy Garland and reviving the lilting holiday song featured fifteen years earlier in *As Thousands Cheer;* and *Annie Get Your Gun* (1950), the film version of Berlin's most popular Broadway musical (1946). With Ethel Merman, as Annie Oakley, singing Berlin's proud paean to entertainment, "There's No Business Like Show Business," the show had enjoyed a Broadway run of 1,147 performances. *Miss Liberty* (1949) had a much less successful run. Another Broadway hit starring Merman, *Call Me Madam* (1950), became a movie in 1953. The following year *White Christmas* brought back Crosby singing Berlin's award-winning song in a film derived from *Holiday Inn.* Published estimates of record sales of "White Christmas" vary, but by all accounts it sold more records than any other song in the era before rock.

After *White Christmas* two more films featured songs by Irving Berlin: *There's No Business Like Show Business* (1954) and *Sayonara* (1957). Dwight Eisenhower, now U.S. president, presented Berlin with the Congressional Gold Medal in 1955. By then, however, Berlin had begun to sink into a severe depression, as his daughter Mary Ellin Barrett has put it, which led to semiretirement and intermittent hospitalization. In 1962, now recovered, he attempted to capture the spirit of the administration of John F. Kennedy in what would be his last Broadway musical, *Mr. President* (1962). The show ran for eight months on the strength of advance ticket sales, but critical reaction to the musical suggested that Berlin had missed the mark. For a 1966 revival of *Annie Get Your Gun,* Berlin composed "An Old Fashioned Wedding," the last song ASCAP lists for him. One last film project, dubbed *Say It with Music* after the theme song of the *Music Box Revues,* percolated through the 1960s, but finally fell through in 1969. At that point, as Mary Ellin Barrett has written, "he really did retire." Even though Berlin no longer went to his office, he continued to dictate song ideas over the telephone to his assistants until two years before his death.

After his retirement Berlin remained a private man, but he did make a few more public appearances. His last was in 1973, when he sang "God Bless America" at the White House before a group of former prisoners of war back from Vietnam. In 1977 President Gerald Ford gave Berlin the Medal of Freedom. Meanwhile, many of Berlin's songs assumed new lives. In the late 1970s and early 1980s two songs that Berlin had written a half century earlier once again became hits: country singer Willie Nelson's version of "Blue Skies" and the Dutch pop singer Taco's revival of "Puttin' on the Ritz" to a disco beat. In his last years Berlin became more and more reclusive, never leaving his home on Beekman Place and refusing to receive visitors; he kept in touch with friends by telephone. He turned 100 years old in 1988, and the occasion was marked by celebrations throughout the world. ASCAP held a birthday celebration at Carnegie Hall in New York City with a diverse array of musicians, including Frank Sinatra, Isaac Stern, Willie Nelson, and Leonard Bernstein; Berlin himself did not appear. Quoting the song Berlin had given to his wife Ellin six decades earlier, ASCAP president Morton Gould announced that "Irving Berlin's music will last forever. Not for just an hour, not for just a day, not for just a year, but always." Later that year, after a series of strokes, Berlin died at home and was buried in Woodlawn Cemetery in the Bronx.

In Berlin's obituary in the *New York Times,* Marilyn

Berger wrote that "his was a classic rags-to-riches story that he never forgot could have happened only in America." Over a musical career spanning seven decades, Berlin wrote songs that distilled the musical, social, or political spirit of the times. He consistently engaged with—and helped to define—the principal forums and media of musical entertainment, beginning with the bustling world of Tin Pan Alley, to the Broadway musical, then to Hollywood. He worked with a veritable who's who of popular entertainers. His music has been reinterpreted and revived in virtually every style of American music, including jazz, barbershop, cabaret, marching band, and chorus. His enterprising musicianship, industrious work habits, irrepressible optimism, and strong patriotism seemed to grow from a single impulse. Like Stephen Foster and Cole Porter, Berlin was one of the few songwriters who wrote both words and music in the age before rock. For his songs and their symbolic resonance, Berlin stands as perhaps the most powerful force in twentieth-century American music. It was the songs that led composer Jerome Kern to make his famous declaration, in a letter to Alexander Woollcott, that "Irving Berlin has *no* place in American music. He *is* American music."

★

A collection of Berlin's papers is at the Library of Congress; the Rodgers and Hammerstein Organization in New York City also has records of the Irving Berlin Music Company. Every generation gets a new biography of Irving Berlin. The first posthumous biography was Laurence Bergreen, *As Thousands Cheer: The Life of Irving Berlin* (1990), although its many inaccuracies have been widely noted. Mary Ellin Barrett, *Irving Berlin: A Daughter's Memoir* (1994), is a clear-eyed account that offers an indispensable complement to Bergreen's book, especially for the period after 1925. Also see Philip Furia, *Irving Berlin: A Life in Song* (1998), the first biography of Berlin to discuss his life and works based on new documents from the Berlin archives at the Rodgers and Hammerstein Organization. The fount of all Berlin biography for the period before 1925 has been the biography written by Alexander Woollcott, *The Story of Irving Berlin* (1925), which stresses Berlin's raw, untrained talent and the ethnic Jewish sources of his musical style. Subsequent biographies include David Ewen, *The Story of Irving Berlin* (1950), and one by Michael Freedland, *Irving Berlin* (1974), and its revision as *A Salute to Irving Berlin* (1986). Ian Whitcomb, *Irving Berlin and Ragtime America* (1987), offers a chatty account of Berlin's early career. In the 1990s Berlin began to attract serious music scholars. Charles Hamm, *Irving Berlin: Songs from the Melting Pot, the Formative Years, 1907–1914* (1997), the first study of Berlin by a musicologist, offers a vivid, compelling interpretation of Berlin's early songs as revealing documents of early twentieth-century immigrant culture in New York. *Irving Berlin: Early Songs* (1994), three volumes edited by Hamm, presents a substantial introductory essay followed by the music and lyrics to more than 200 songs that Berlin wrote before 1915, including several that were previously unpublished. An elegant analysis of Berlin's lyrics appears in a chapter of Philip Furia, *The Poets of Tin Pan Alley: A History of America's Great Lyricists* (1990). In Alec Wilder, *American Popular Song: The Great Innovators, 1990–1950* (1972), a composer-critic offers vivid commentary on Berlin's music. An obituary is in the *New York Times* (23 June 1989).

JEFFREY MAGEE

BERLIN, Richard Emmett (*b.* 18 January 1894 in Omaha, Nebraska; *d.* 28 January 1986 in Rye, New York), chief executive officer of the Hearst Corporation for more than two decades, nurturing the Hearst media empire through the turbulent shakeouts of the newspaper and magazine industries after World War II.

Berlin's father, Richard E. Berlin, was an unsuccessful stockbroker who relocated the family to Oakland, California, when the young Richard was nine years old. His father's death two years later fostered Berlin's deep devotion to his mother, Sara Noonan Berlin, and his two sisters and his strong drive for success in order to overcome the difficulties of his youth. He may have studied for a time at the University of California, Berkeley, but when World War I broke out in 1914, Berlin made a fateful choice to go to officer candidate school. While serving as a naval officer (through 1917) he was invited to a party hosted by one of San Francisco's leading citizens, Millicent Hearst, the wife of the publisher William Randolph Hearst. Berlin was "charming to good purpose," and she gave him an introduction to the sales department of the Hearst Corporation.

In 1919 Berlin began his lifelong tenure at Hearst by selling magazine subscriptions. He quickly moved to selling advertising space, and his abilities soon attracted the attention of the "Chief," Mr. Hearst. The Hearst Corporation was headquartered in New York City, and it was there in 1930 that Berlin became general manager of the magazine division. Hearst magazines included several profitable titles, including *Cosmopolitan, Good Housekeeping,* and *Motor Boating*. The division remained a profit center during the Great Depression of the 1930s, and Berlin felt successful enough to marry Muriel Johnson on 21 December 1938. They had four children. Other sections of the overextended media empire, however, were financial drains, and the company found itself fighting off dismemberment. In 1939 Berlin proved his worth by securing new loans for the Hearst Corporation (thus thwarting Joseph P. Kennedy's attempt to buy the magazine division) and strong-arming the company's Canadian paper suppliers into accepting an extended schedule of payments.

Hearst elevated Berlin to the presidency of the corporation in 1943. The two men had a close, almost paternal-filial relationship, which brought Berlin into conflict with Hearst's sons, but Berlin proved to be a master of office politics and continued to accumulate power. His nonfamily rivals were older and had either fallen out with the Chief or had faded away over the years. Berlin took full control of the company when Hearst died in 1951. He not only became the CEO but also had effective control over eight of the thirteen board members in the privately held corporation. William Hearst, Jr., in particular, felt thwarted by Berlin's power.

In the 1950s the Hearst newspaper chain began to decline as its traditional base of readers was relocating from the inner city to the suburbs and giving up its tabloid habits. In addition, advertisers were losing interest in the type of lower-income readers that the Hearst papers attracted with their fiercely partisan campaigns and reactionary editorials. Despite the opposition of the younger Hearsts, Berlin responded to these circumstances by selling off various newspapers, beginning with the *Chicago American* in October 1956. He admired and sought to emulate the strategy of the rival Gannett organization, which avoided head-to-head competition and went after newspapers with monopoly status in midsized towns. The Hearst Corporation closed down most of its big-city newspapers, with the exception of the *San Francisco Examiner,* the *Los Angeles Herald-Examiner* (closed in 1989), and the *Boston Herald-American* (sold in 1982). A particularly traumatic closure was the merger of Hearst's New York flagship newspaper, the *Journal-American,* with the short-lived *World-Journal-Tribune* in 1966. The *WJT* went out of existence a year later, and the corporation was left without a daily in America's largest city.

Richard Berlin. UPI/Corbis-Bettmann

Although Berlin was personally uninterested in the new medium of television, a chance conversation with Leonard Goldenson, the head of the American Broadcasting Companies, convinced him to purchase a Pittsburgh television station in 1956. The Hearst Corporation acquired a few more stations over the years—a time in which advertisers were abandoning general-interest magazines because they felt that television was a more efficient way of reaching a mass audience. Advertisers preferred magazines that could deliver special-interest readers, and Hearst magazines continued to be cash cows because they were targeted at "niche" readers, such as single career women for *Cosmopolitan* and household shoppers for *Good Housekeeping*.

Berlin retired in 1973 owing to declining health. Alzheimer's disease afflicted him in later years. He is buried in Kensico Cemetery, Valhalla, New York. He was a Knight of Malta and a Roman Catholic.

Berlin's career in the publishing industry rarely involved him in editorial decisions. He did agree with the Hearst papers' editorial passion for anticommunist crusades and was a drinking pal of the red-baiting senator Joseph McCarthy. During the height of Berlin's power in the 1940s through the end of the 1960s, most prominent politicians made the pilgrimage to his office. One liberal Democrat who did manage to win his support at the beginning of his national career was future president Lyndon Johnson. Berlin was a master of extracting strategic favors in exchange for timely political support. This practice was rendered possible by the decline in the fiercely partisan journalism that had been a trademark of William Randolph Hearst since the era of yellow journalism in the 1880s and 1890s and that had continued through the controversies and libel suits of the 1950s engendered by Westbrook Pegler and Walter Winchell (both Hearst columnists). The Hearst corporate image after Berlin's tenure was perhaps kinder and gentler, although this was more the result of a generational change than any specific corporate decision. On one occasion, Berlin cut back on the sexual provocations of *Cosmopolitan* during Helen Gurley Brown's editorship, although he basically took a hands-off approach to her profitable refitting of the magazine.

Berlin was able to steer the Hearst Corporation away from tabloid journalism. In 1940 the Hearst chain had seventeen newspapers and was number one in total circulation. By 1976 only eight Hearst papers remained, and the total circulation of the chain was ranked eighth in the United States. Berlin may have given up the already waning influence of the Hearst papers, but in exchange he had eliminated many losing operations. His downsizing was financially successful, and the Hearst company started to expand again in the 1980s under the leadership of Frank Bennack (who was able to buy the *Houston Chronicle,* now the largest Hearst daily). Richard Berlin had presided over a transition in the purpose and style of journalism in the age of television and suburbanization.

★

The most informative book about Berlin and the later history of the Hearst Corporation is Lindsay Chaney and Michael Cieply, *The Hearsts: Family and Empire, the Later Years* (1981). A more selective and pointed narration of those years is provided by a second-generation Hearst in William Randolph Hearst, Jr., with Jack Casserly, *The Hearsts: Father and Son* (1991). The context of newspaper publishing in the era of downsizing is given in Benjamin M. Compaine, *The Newspaper Industry in the 1980s: An Assessment of Economics and Technology* (1980). An obituary is in the *New York Times* (29 Jan. 1986).

FREDERICK WASSER

BERNHARD, Arnold (*b.* 2 December 1901 in New York City; *d.* 22 December 1987 in New York City), investment company head and author who founded the investment advisory publication *Value Line Investment Survey.*

Arnold Bernhard. COURTESY OF MS. JEAN BUTTNER

The son of immigrants—his father, Bernhard Bernhard, was Austrian and his mother, Regina (Steigelfest) Bernhard, was Romanian—Arnold Bernhard grew up with his younger siblings, Cecilia and Harold, in New York, New Jersey, and Delaware. His father, who had become a successful businessman as a partner in a company that manufactured infantware in New York City, died at about the time of Bernhard's graduation from military high school in 1919. Although Bernhard finished school with high marks, he was not interested in a military career. Instead, equipped with a scholarship, he entered Williams College, from which he graduated with a bachelor's degree cum laude in English in 1925.

Between 1926 and 1928 Bernhard was involved in newsprint journalism in New York City. He worked three jobs simultaneously: writing theater reviews for *Time,* covering movies and nightclubs for the *New York Post,* and syndicating his own column for several other papers. At this same time he was also courting his high school sweetheart, Janet Marie Kinghorn, a Skidmore graduate who had become a high school English teacher; they married in 1929 and had two children (twins, born in 1933). The couple would often go to the nightclubs and plays that Bernhard was reviewing for the papers. Despite this busy schedule, he found time to read books, especially on the stock market. Living in New York City during the Roaring Twenties, Bernhard was predictably attracted to the glamour of the market, especially since a major portion of his father's legacy was invested in it.

While in college, Bernhard had become well versed in classical works of philosophy and logic. As a result, when he later began educating himself about the stock market, he was uneasy with the lack of any firm rules or principles explaining stock-market fluctuations and guiding investment decisions. In the fall of 1928 he accepted a job with the legendary speculator Jesse Livermore, and he immediately found himself even more astonished at the extent to which stock-market transactions were influenced by individual and social whim.

In late 1928 Bernhard switched to Moody's Investors Services, a specialist in bond transactions. He began as an "analyst," analyzing the price movements of individual bond issues vis-à-vis the market, and the circumstances of the corporations issuing those bonds.

Bernhard's fear about a market that seemed able to plunge on a whim was finally realized in October 1929. The stock-market crash made a deep impression on him. His analytical mind operated on the notion that each event should have a precise cause. The fact that no one was yet able to pinpoint with certainty whether the market was undervalued or overvalued greatly bothered him. The October crash caused his mother to lose the life insurance money she had received after his father's death, and Bernhard thus gained a personal as well as a professional interest in finding the golden formula of value that would tell when to buy and when to sell.

In 1933 Moody's concluded that Bernhard's ideas on portfolio management were too revolutionary, and Bernhard found himself out of a job. Fortunately, several Moody's clients who were pleased with Bernhard's advice had asked him to continue managing their portfolios. At about this time, the idea came to Bernhard of publishing a weekly stock-portfolio-management bulletin and selling it to the public. Based on the performance of his clients' portfolios, he thought he had finally found the formula of stock valuation—a sound formula based on facts rather than emotions.

In 1937 the first issue of *Value Line Ratings of Normal Value* made its way out of Bernhard's house and into the market. For a $200 subscription fee, the publication offered "buy or sell" advice on 120 companies. The advice was based on a simple but powerful formula. A stock was undervalued if its current price-to-earnings and price-to-book-value ratios were markedly below their twenty-year averages, and vice versa for overvaluation. Because this type of statistical analysis was new at the time, the bulletin did not immediately find an enthusiastic market. However, as the investment community began to realize the utility of Bernhard's advice, both the number of subscriptions to *Value Line* and the number of clients held by its parent company, Arnold Bernhard and Company (incorporated in 1935), started to increase.

Over time, Bernhard's formula for determining stock values became more sophisticated to reflect the current market conditions and the development of better statistical techniques. By the late 1950s, Bernhard's *Value Line Investment Survey* had become an investing guide for millions of American investors. For those who were skeptical about his methodology, Bernhard published a comprehensive book, *The Evaluation of Common Stocks,* in 1959. Meanwhile, Bernhard's portfolio-management business had also prospered, and the company now had four successful mutual funds with various objectives.

Throughout the 1960s, 1970s, and 1980s, as his business continued to prosper, Bernhard devoted more and more of his time and wealth to philanthropic endeavors, particularly the causes of higher education, the improvement of health care, and the development of the arts, especially theater. With his increased involvement in these matters, Bernhard decided to retire from the active management of his company at the age of eighty-one. His daughter, Jean, who had been working with the company since the 1970s, took over a public company with a market capitalization of more than $200 million. Bernhard died at the age of eighty-six.

Bernhard is remembered as the person who introduced common sense and quantitative analysis to the average investor in the stock market. Over a sixty-year period, those who followed Value Line's recommendations on stock purchases beat the average market return by a wide margin, a fact that remains a thorn in the side of those who hold that no one can consistently outperform the market.

★

Quentin Reynold and Wilfrid S. Row, "The Search for Underlying Causes" in their *Operation Success* (1957), provide a good account of the earlier part of Bernhard's life. "Value Line's Arnold Bernhard," *Financial World* (15 Jan. 1979): 70, gives a brief evaluation of Arnold Bernhard's management of his company. "Value Line Figures It's Time to Go Public," *Business Week* (24 Jan. 1983): 72, contains a brief history of the Value Line Company. "Order in the Ranks," *Barron's* (3 June 1985): 6–7, offers an assessment of Bernhard's achievements as an investment adviser. Obituaries are in the *New York Times* (23 Dec. 1987) and *Time* (4 Jan. 1988).

MOJTABA SEYEDIAN

BERNSTEIN, Leonard (*b.* 25 August 1918 in Lawrence, Massachusetts; *d.* 14 October 1990 in New York City), composer, conductor, pianist, and educator best known for his successful incorporation of popular and art music idioms in his compositions, typified by his Broadway musical *West Side Story*.

Bernstein was one of three children born to Russian-Jewish émigrés Samuel Joseph Bernstein, a hairdressing supplies wholesaler, and Jennie Resnick. Bernstein first showed musical talent at the age of ten, when he began taking piano lessons. From 1929 to 1935 he attended Boston Latin School, where he also participated in glee club and the school orchestra. Bernstein entered Harvard College as a music major in 1935, studying harmony with Walter Piston, history with Arthur Tillman Merritt, and orchestration with Edward Burlingame Hill. It was during his Harvard years that he met Dimitri Mitropoulos, Adolph ("Al") Green, and Aaron Copland, three men whose friendships had lasting influences on Bernstein.

He graduated from Harvard cum laude in 1939, writing a senior honors thesis entitled "The Absorption of Race Elements into American Music." His last two musical projects at Harvard both involved music theater. In April 1939 he conducted his own incidental music for a production of Aristophanes' *The Birds.* The next month Bernstein supervised a production of Marc Blitzstein's overtly political work *The Cradle Will Rock*. Bernstein invited the composer to attend, and the resulting relationship lasted until Blitzstein's death in 1964.

Leonard Bernstein, 1966. HULTON-DEUTCH COLLECTION/CORBIS

In the fall of 1939 Bernstein began postgraduate work at the Curtis Institute of Music in Philadelphia, studying conducting with Fritz Reiner. After the relaxed, interdisciplinary environment of Harvard, the rigorous musical focus forced upon him at Curtis came as a shock. The long days spent practicing and the lack of an active social life made his stay in Philadelphia particularly dreary. Regardless, his study at Curtis prepared him for Tanglewood's first educational program in the summer of 1940, where Serge Koussevitzky, music director of the Boston Symphony Orchestra, accepted Bernstein into his conducting class. Bernstein found both a conducting mentor and surrogate father in Koussevitzky, whose influence lasted well beyond his death. Although Koussevitzky invited him to continue studying through the winter, Bernstein returned to Curtis for another year, earning a diploma in May 1941.

Shortly before returning for Tanglewood's second year he made his professional debut leading the Boston Pops in a July 1941 concert on the Esplanade. The summer of 1941 went much as the previous season had, with Bernstein enjoying more conducting opportunities and increasing critical acclaim. For Tanglewood's 1942 session he was appointed Koussevitzky's assistant.

Bernstein moved to New York City in August 1942 to pursue his conducting career. (Classified 4-F because of an asthmatic condition, he did not serve in the military during World War II.) As he struggled to earn a living as a conductor, he turned to composition, completing his first published work, the Clarinet Sonata, in 1942. After this he wrote his First Symphony, the "Jeremiah" (1942), and a brief song cycle, *I Hate Music* (1943).

The year 1943 was a landmark one in Bernstein's life. On 30 March he made his New York debut, conducting the world premiere of Paul Bowles's *The Wind Remains* at the Museum of Modern Art. This performance brought Bernstein to the attention of the conductor of the New York Philharmonic, Artur Rodzinski, who was searching for an assistant. After a summer of anticipation, Bernstein was appointed assistant conductor of the New York Philharmonic on 25 August, his twenty-fifth birthday. He then acquired a drab, one-room apartment in Carnegie Hall, which made him readily available to Rodzinski and the Philharmonic. On 13 November, the mezzo-soprano Jennie Tourel performed *I Hate Music* as part of her New York debut recital. Although the concert went off flawlessly, the events of the next day eclipsed news of Bernstein's compositional debut. On Sunday, 14 November, Bernstein replaced the guest conductor Bruno Walter for a Philharmonic subscription concert that was also a national radio broadcast. With no opportunity for rehearsal, Bernstein led the Philharmonic through the program, conducting most of the works for his first time. Initially greeted with only polite applause, he so electrified the audience that the concert ended with shouts for repeated curtain calls. He suddenly found himself in demand as a guest conductor across the country.

Throughout 1943, Koussevitzky and Reiner bickered over whose ensemble would premiere Bernstein's "Jeremiah" symphony. Reiner prevailed, and Bernstein conducted his work with the Pittsburgh Symphony in January 1944. It was well received and had additional performances in Boston and New York, eventually winning the 1944 New York Music Critics Circle award for outstanding new classical work. During this same period, Bernstein was also beginning a career in professional musical theater, working with choreographer Jerome Robbins on the one-act ballet *Fancy Free* (1944). Robbins believed that the story of three sailors on a one-day leave in New York would be best conveyed by a composer such as Bernstein, who was familiar with popular musical idioms. Glowing reviews stressing the ballet's comedic aspects led Bernstein and Robbins to accept a proposal to turn it into a musical. Bernstein's friends Betty Comden and Adolph Green wrote the book and lyrics, and six months later *On the Town* (1944) was playing on Broadway. The creators worked hard to craft the show so that music, book, dance, and lyrics all contributed to telling the story. *On the Town*'s success brought Bernstein's name before the public in yet another capacity, that of composer of musical comedy.

After the 1943–1944 season, Bernstein left his position with the Philharmonic, earning his living solely through guest conducting. In 1945, on his twenty-seventh birthday, he was appointed principal conductor of the New York City Symphony Orchestra, which allowed him to expand his repertoire and refine his conducting. In the summer of 1946 he returned to Tanglewood to give the American premiere of Benjamin Britten's opera *Peter Grimes.* Amid this flurry of activity, Bernstein completed a second ballet with Robbins entitled *Facsimile* (1946). With a scenario influenced by the creators' experiences with psychotherapy, *Facsimile* was not well received and has seen few performances since its premiere.

Halfway through his third season with the City Symphony, Bernstein announced he would resign his post at the end of the year. He was a finalist to succeed Koussevitzky in Boston and had been offered the post of artistic adviser to the Palestine (now Israel) Philharmonic, having first conducted there the previous year. Passed over by Boston, Bernstein accepted the Palestine position, which he held for two years. During this period, he wrote his Second Symphony, "The Age of Anxiety" (1949); at its premiere, the composer played the prominent solo piano part under Koussevitzky's direction.

In January 1951 he signed his first recording contract, beginning a twenty-five year relationship with Columbia Records. In February 1951, Bernstein conducted and recorded *The Age of Anxiety* with the New York Philharmonic and Robbins presented a ballet choreographed to the score. On a summer holiday in Mexico, Bernstein began composing his opera *Trouble in Tahiti,* but progress stopped when Koussevitzky died on 4 June 1951. Less than one month before instruction was to resume at Tanglewood, responsibility for its conducting program fell to Bernstein. During all this he found the time to marry the Chilean actress Felicia Montealegre Cohn on 9 September 1951. The two had met in 1946 and announced an engagement at that time. They broke it off the following year but renewed the relationship in 1950. The couple spent an extended honeymoon in Mexico, where Bernstein returned to his opera. In January 1952, the opera still unfinished, the Bernsteins returned to the United States, announcing that Felicia was pregnant. Anticipating a family, the Bernsteins moved into an apartment in the luxurious Osborne Building (catercorner to Carnegie Hall) in August 1952. The couple had three children, Jamie, Alexander, and Nina.

Bernstein slowed his conducting schedule in 1952 in order to devote more time to composition. He finished *Trouble in Tahiti* in time for a premiere at the Brandeis Festival of the Creative Arts, a four-day survey of modern arts coordinated by Bernstein. Though *Trouble in Tahiti* was not well received at Brandeis, after some revision it was staged with more success at Tanglewood that same summer and was broadcast on television later that fall. Before the end of the year he completed the musical *Wonderful Town,* which opened in 1953 and reunited the creative team behind *On the Town* in another musical portraying life in New York. Although he often had great difficulty completing compositions, he wrote *Wonderful Town* in five weeks—a remarkable accomplishment that reflected his comfort with creative collaborations. For Bernstein the high point of 1953 was his debut at La Scala, conducting Maria Callas in Cherubini's *Medea.* He briefly considered turning to opera conducting and did return to La Scala in 1954, but after that he did not return to the opera theater for ten years.

The 1950s were Bernstein's most productive years for composition. In addition to *Wonderful Town,* he scored Elia Kazan's film *On the Waterfront* (1954), considered one of American film's finest soundtracks; wrote his violin concerto, *Serenade* (1954), which has proven to be Bernstein's most popular orchestral work; and produced incidental music for *The Lark* (1955, Lillian Hellman's translation of Jean Anouilh's *L'Alouette*). On 1 December 1956 one long-standing project came to fruition with the Broadway opening of his musical *Candide,* an adaptation of Voltaire's satire, written with Lillian Hellman and Richard Wilbur. The show received strongly divided criticism at its premiere. Bernstein's score was praised for its wit and brilliance, but Hellman's book was seen as too heavy-handed, and the production closed after two months. Although *Candide* was a financial failure, Bernstein's score was so strong that the show would be frequently revised over the next thirty years in hopes of arriving at a book equal to the music. (In 1989 the Scottish National Opera, with Bernstein's blessing and a thoroughly revised book produced the composer's "final revised version.") *Candide* also contributed to Bernstein's growing national celebrity. On 14 November 1954 he gave the first of a series of musical lecture-demonstrations on the *Omnibus* television program, proving so charismatic a teacher that in 1956 the New York Philharmonic, where he made frequent guest conducting appearances, put him in charge of its educational Young People's Concerts. Excitement over Bernstein would reach its peak in 1957. In February *Time* magazine ran a cover story on him focusing on his multifaceted talent, even before the opening of his next major project, a theatrical piece he called a "tragic musical comedy." *West Side Story,* written in collaboration with Arthur Laurents (book), Jerome Robbins (choreography), and Stephen Sondheim (lyrics), had its Broadway opening on 26 September, earning extremely favorable reviews from the critics. Transferring the story of Romeo and Juliet to the streets of New York, *West Side Story* has become a classic of American popular culture, in large part due to Bernstein's successful incorporation of Latin and jazz elements into a score that included such songs as "Tonight," "One Hand,

One Heart," "Maria," and "America." While the show was an unquestionable success, it was not until the release of the film version in 1961 that it gained its widespread popularity. (The soundtrack to the film version would become one of the best-selling albums of all time.)

Less than two months after *West Side Story*'s New York opening, Bernstein became a household name on yet another musical front. Long-standing rumors of Dimitri Mitropoulos's departure from the New York Philharmonic were confirmed when, on 20 November 1957, it was announced that Bernstein would become joint principal conductor with Mitropoulos for the 1957–1958 season and thereafter, effective in September 1958, would take over the Philharmonic as music director, becoming the first American-born and -trained conductor to lead a major U.S. orchestra. Thus began a legendary association between conductor and ensemble that would last to the end of Bernstein's life, as music director until 1969 and as conductor laureate thereafter. On his first tour with the orchestra Bernstein included at least one American work in each concert, and his subscription programs showed a similar emphasis. Bernstein had finally become the champion of American music Aaron Copland had always envisioned.

In addition to his season schedule, Bernstein led fifteen years of televised *Young People's Concerts,* which were among his favorite endeavors. Bernstein was a natural educator, and many of his television scripts are included in his books *The Joy of Music* (1959), *Leonard Bernstein's Young People's Concerts* (1962), and *The Infinite Variety of Music* (1966). Bernstein also led the Philharmonic on a series of successful national and international tours, including trips to Japan, Latin America, the Middle East, and the Soviet Union.

With such a rigorous conducting schedule, Bernstein lamented that he had little opportunity for composition. From 1957 to 1969 he completed only two major works. His Third Symphony, "Kaddish" (1963), is an eclectic mix of musical styles and techniques. Scored for speaker, chorus, and orchestra, *Kaddish* emphasizes a recurring theme in Bernstein's serious compositions, the quest for faith—which he later identified as the fundamental issue of the twentieth century. The theatricality and questioning of religion in this work, a triple setting of the Jewish prayer for the dead, foreshadows Bernstein's similar treatment of Catholicism in *Mass* (1971). The eclecticism of *Kaddish* also highlights a crisis in Bernstein's "compositional faith" concerning his own musical language. Hoping to settle this internal debate, he took a sabbatical from the Philharmonic during the 1964–1965 season. After an aborted collaboration with Robbins, Comden, and Green, and many unfinished compositions using then-popular serial or experimental techniques, Bernstein ended his sabbatical by composing the unabashedly tonal *Chichester Psalms* (1965).

A lifetime of involvement with political causes had given Bernstein some notoriety—he had been temporarily denied a passport in the 1950s because of his pro-Russian stance during World War II—which came to a head on 14 January 1970, when Felicia hosted a fund-raising party in their fourteen-room Park Avenue apartment for the criminal defense of a group of Black Panthers, apparently with little or no knowledge of this militant group's politics, particularly their anti-Semitic views. The event became a symbol of effete social activism after the journalist Tom Wolfe coined the term "radical chic" in his account of the evening for *New York* magazine (8 June 1970). Bernstein missed much of the resulting furor while away on conducting engagements in Europe. Nevertheless, negative reaction to his political activities surfaced in criticism of *Mass,* with accusations that its juxtaposition of classical, folk, rock, and blues idioms merely represented Bernstein's attempt to prove he was still in touch with popular culture.

Bernstein returned to a university environment for his most substantive work as an educator when he accepted the Charles Eliot Norton Professorship at Harvard for 1972–1973. The resulting lectures, published in 1976 as *The Unanswered Question,* presented Bernstein's personal philosophy of music, its meaning, and its communicative ability. During this decade Bernstein finally attained a balance between his desires to conduct and to compose. Although he led his thousandth New York Philharmonic concert in 1971, he took on fewer conducting assignments, focusing his efforts in New York, Vienna, and Israel. In addition to *Mass,* he completed a ballet for Robbins, *Dybbuk* (1974); the musical *1600 Pennsylvania Avenue* (1976); and the symphonic song-cycle *Songfest* (1977).

In 1974 the Bernstein's moved from their Park Avenue apartment across Central Park to a slightly smaller apartment in the Dakota. This move represented a turn away from family life, as only Nina still lived at home, but the rupture of the Bernstein marriage still seemed abrupt. Bernstein and Felicia separated in May 1976 when, after decades of brief extramarital homosexual affairs on his part, she gave him an ultimatum to quit or leave. He lived the next year with Thomas Cothran, his assistant in preparing the Norton lectures, but found the loss of domestic stability too disturbing after so many years with Felicia. In the summer of 1977 the Bernsteins reconciled, although sadly, their reunion would be brief. Both Bernstein and Felicia were notoriously heavy smokers, and in 1977 Felicia was diagnosed with lung cancer. She died on 16 June 1978.

In his final decade Bernstein was a man obsessed with his legacy. He yearned to write the great American opera, and a final opportunity came in a commission from the Houston Grand Opera. *A Quiet Place* (1983, rev. 1984) continues the story of the dysfunctional family of *Trouble in Tahiti,* a story that has many parallels to Bernstein's own relationships with his parents, wife, and children. For various reasons, ranging from a lack of dramatic and stylistic coherence to the excessively earnest treatment of the subject, it was not the work he had hoped to create.

His last book, *Findings,* a collection of disparate essays including his Harvard thesis, was published in 1982. The final highlight of his conducting career was a memorable performance of Beethoven's Ninth Symphony in East Berlin on Christmas Day 1989, celebrating the fall of the Berlin Wall. Bernstein made a slight alteration to the text of the finale, changing it from an "Ode to Joy" to an "Ode to Freedom." During the summer of 1990, in addition to conducting at Tanglewood, Bernstein presided over the first Pacific Music Festival, a summer musical training institute in Sapporo, Japan. In early October, citing failing health and a desire to have more time for composition, writing, and teaching, Bernstein retired from conducting; his last performance had been in August, leading the Boston Symphony in Tanglewood's annual Koussevitzky Memorial Concert. On 14 October 1990, Leonard Bernstein died in New York of a heart attack brought on by complications from emphysema. He was buried two days later in Brooklyn's Green-Wood Cemetery next to his wife.

Although Leonard Bernstein is best known as a conductor, he primarily thought of himself as a composer. Yet, arguably, Bernstein made his greatest mark on American musical culture through education and outreach. Through his work at Tanglewood and similar institutions he inspired and influenced generations of musicians, and his innovative educational use of television conveyed that same love of music to countless people who possessed little or no formal training. Through the New York Philharmonic tours he became America's musical ambassador to the world. He created a distinctly American compositional voice during a period when avant-garde techniques dominated art music.

At the same time, Bernstein did not escape criticism. His detractors found fault with his conducting, citing overly romanticized interpretations and his flamboyant podium manner. His compositions were attacked for their eclecticism of style and genre, and his educational work was dismissed as patronizing popularization. At heart is the accusation, perhaps a just one, that Bernstein sought the limelight at every opportunity. He craved celebrity but bemoaned the lack of private time. He was a man who could be both petty and magnanimous, egocentric and selfless. Still, Bernstein's influence on generations of Americans has left an indelible mark on modern American culture.

★

Bernstein's papers and manuscripts are in the Music Division of the Library of Congress. Joan Peyser, *Bernstein: A Biography* (1987), is infamous for its emphasis on the darker sides of Bernstein's personality. Amid much speculation, the book contains some valid insights. Humphrey Burton, *Leonard Bernstein* (1994), is the best available in-depth Bernstein biography. While it is not an authorized biography, Burton had access to much personal material, revealed in the book's depth of detail. Meryle Secrest, *Leonard Bernstein: A Life* (1995), was researched at the same time as the Burton biography and thus contains discussions that are underdocumented due to Burton's exclusive access to the material. Forced to draw from alternative sources, Secrest provides a complementary perspective. Paul Myers, *Leonard Bernstein* (1998), is a good brief introduction to the composer's life and contains thoughtful, critical discussions of individual compositions. Jack Gottlieb, *The Music of Leonard Bernstein: A Study of Melodic Manipulation* (1964), is the first single-author study of Bernstein's compositional technique. The author, one of Bernstein's assistants, also compiled *Leonard Bernstein: A Complete Catalogue of His Works,* 2d ed. (1988). John Gruen, *The Private World of Leonard Bernstein* (1968), contains abundant photographs of the Bernstein family during his time with the Philharmonic. The accompanying text has been criticized for being too light and adoring. Burton Bernstein, *Family Matters: Sam, Jennie, and the Kids* (1982), the memoirs of Bernstein's brother, gives valuable commentary on the difficult relationship between the composer and his father. Steven Ledbetter, ed., *Sennets and Tuckets: A Bernstein Celebration* (1988), commemorates Bernstein's seventieth birthday. Its contents range from reminiscences by friends and students to excellent critical essays on Bernstein's music. William Burton, ed., *Conversations About Bernstein* (1995), contains transcriptions of interviews, some extremely candid, with Bernstein friends, students, and colleagues.

MICHAEL W. SUMBERA

BETTELHEIM, Bruno (*b.* 28 August 1903 in Vienna, Austria; *d.* 13 March 1990 in Silver Spring, Maryland), psychologist and prolific author widely acclaimed in the 1950s, 1960s, and 1970s for his work with and writings on mentally troubled and especially autistic children.

One of two children of Anton Bettelheim, a lumber merchant, and Paula Seidler, Bruno Bettelheim grew up in Vienna in a secular Jewish upper-middle-class home darkened by his father's latent syphilis. Bettelheim was an insecure, bookish child afflicted with poor eyesight and a sense of homeliness that plagued him all his life, as did depression. He attended the Realschule in the Albertgasse, achieving high marks and graduating in 1921. That year he entered both the University of Vienna and the Hochschule für Welthandel, a business school where he took two semesters of commercial courses. He studied the humanities at the university until his father's death in 1926 forced him to drop out and reluctantly enter the family lumber business, Bettelheim and Schnitzer.

On 30 March 1930 Bettelheim married Regina Altstadt

in Vienna. They had no children but took in a mentally troubled seven-year-old American child named Patricia Lyne, who would live with them under Gina Bettelheim's care for seven years while the child was in therapy with the psychoanalyst Editha Sterba. In 1936 Bettelheim resumed studies at the University of Vienna while continuing in the lumber business. His doctoral thesis was "Das Problem des Naturschönen und die modern Ästhetik" (The Problem of Nature's Beauty and the Modern Aesthetic) and he received his degree in February 1938. When the Nazis annexed Austria the following month, Gina took Patsy to the United States, but Bettelheim stayed behind to try to settle his business affairs. On 2 June the Nazis imprisoned him in Dachau; in mid-September they transferred him to Buchenwald but, on 14 April 1939, freed him during a general release of inmates.

Bettelheim arrived in New York City on 11 May 1939 and by that fall had moved to Chicago. On 7 May 1941 he and Gina divorced, and a week later he married Gertrude Weinfeld, a Montessori School teacher whom he had known in Vienna and who also had fled the Nazis. They eventually settled in the University of Chicago neighborhood of Hyde Park, where they raised three children: Ruth Colette, Naomi Michele, and Eric Christopher. Bettelheim became a U.S. citizen in November 1944.

Bruno Bettelheim. ARCHIVE PHOTOS

Bettelheim worked as an art researcher in the months immediately after emigrating and from 1941 to 1944 taught art history, psychology, and other subjects at Rockford (Illinois) College. In 1943 he attracted considerable attention in the intellectual community with "Individual and Mass Behavior in Extreme Situations," an essay on concentration camp psychology, which, he said, was based on scientific research he had gathered in Dachau and Buchenwald. Published in the *Journal of Abnormal and Social Psychology,* the article maintained that most prisoners reverted to childlike behavior and took on the characteristics of the SS guards. He expanded on the essay in *The Informed Heart* (1960) and *Surviving and Other Essays* (1979), books in which he advanced one of his most controversial positions—that the European Jews were complicit in their own destruction because they failed to fight back during the Holocaust.

In 1944 the University of Chicago appointed Bettelheim director of the Orthogenic School, its home for emotionally troubled children. He often said that he saw the school as the reverse of the concentration camp, a place where children could feel loved and safe instead of threatened and imprisoned, and, spurred by his love of art, he created a treatment center unique in the warmth of its physical embrace. Bettelheim was director for nearly thirty years, achieving international stature, particularly for his treatment of children with autism. He believed that the children he took in could only be helped if separated from their parents and was particularly vocal in blaming mothers for causing autism by rejecting their infants, a view he held tenaciously despite mounting evidence in the 1960s and beyond that autism was a neurological disorder.

Bettelheim wrote four books about his work at the school: *Love Is Not Enough* (1950), *Truants from Life* (1955), *The Empty Fortress* (1967), and *A Home for the Heart* (1974). What helped make these books popular was Bettelheim's gift for storytelling, for riveting the reader with case histories of children he said were "hopeless" when they entered the school and much better when they left. He maintained that he returned upward of 85 percent of these residents to full functioning in society, although he offered no hard evidence to support the claim and undertook no follow-up studies.

During Bettelheim's three decades at the school, he taught at the university, his courses packed with students at once drawn to and frightened by his confrontational style, one he often employed in staff meetings at the Orthogenic School and one that, in both venues, sometimes left young women in tears. Although often pugnacious and dogmatic, he could also be empathic, caring, and generous. He urged his classes and staff not to seek answers in psychology texts but to observe the patients and to try to understand from their own experiences what caused the patients' behavior. By the time Bettelheim retired from the Orthogenic School in 1973, he had achieved the rank of Stella M. Rowley Distinguished Service Professor of Education.

In 1973 Bettelheim moved to Portola Valley, near Palo Alto, California. Despite severe health problems and growing depression, he taught at Stanford University and continued to write, most notably *Freud and Man's Soul* (1982), a critique of James Strachey's standard English translation of Freud, and *The Uses of Enchantment* (1976), about the psychological meaning of fairy tales. In 1977 *The Uses of Enchantment* won both the National Book Award (for contemporary thought) and the National Book Critics Circle Prize (for criticism), and in 1995 the New York Public Library named it one of the 159 most influential and requested "books of the century." In 1983 he received the Goethe Medal. Bettelheim grew increasingly suicidal in his later years, especially after 1984, when his wife died and his sister committed suicide. In early 1990 he entered the Charter House, a home for the elderly in Silver Spring, Maryland. He committed suicide by swallowing drugs and whiskey and tying a plastic bag over his head. He was buried in Skylawn Memorial Park in San Francisco.

In his final book, *Freud's Vienna and Other Essays* (1990), Bettelheim wrote that his reading of the German philosophers Theodor Lessing, Hans Vaihinger, and Friedrich-Albert Lange as a young man had convinced him "that we must live by fictions—not just to find meaning in life but to make it bearable." After his death, it became clear that he had lived by fictions for much of his adult life. Soon after emigrating, for example, he began maintaining that Patricia Lyne was autistic and that he, not his first wife and Editha Sterba, had cared for her in Vienna. He also concocted a four-page curriculum vitae making many false claims, among them that he had attended the University of Vienna for fourteen years and graduated summa cum laude in philosophy, art history, and psychology; had taught several courses in psychology at the university; and had belonged to a Vienna organization that studied the developmental problems of children. These fabrications, combined with his intelligence and capacity for hard work, helped persuade the University of Chicago to hire him as director of the Orthogenic School.

Bettelheim's reputation suffered further after his death when former patients at the school described how he had hit them, despite his oft-stated insistence that such behavior should never be tolerated. An analysis of school records also revealed that he had overstated his cure rate, especially with autistic children; and close examination of his works, including his Holocaust writing, disclosed that his research and anecdotal material was often exaggerated and sometimes invented. He also borrowed from works without crediting the authors, most dramatically for *The Uses of Enchantment,* much of which was plagiarized from Julius Heuscher's *A Psychiatric Study of Fairy Tales* (1963). By the time of Bettelheim's death many of his professional colleagues were openly criticizing what one called his "often freewheeling reflections, and extravagant speculation." For these reasons, and also because of his abrasive personality, Bettelheim was never invited to join the Institute for Psychoanalysis in Chicago or its American and international counterparts.

At the height of his career, Bettelheim was among the best known and widely read psychotherapists in the world. By the time of his death, however, his views on the psychogenic etiology of autism had been rejected, his Holocaust writing had come under attack for its victim-blaming, his books (with the exception of *The Uses of Enchantment*) were no longer much read, and his reputation in general was diminished.

★

Bettelheim's papers are in Special Collections, Regenstein Library, University of Chicago. A Festchrift was published by the University of Chicago in 1986. Studies include Nina Sutton, *Bettelheim: A Life and Legacy* (1996), translated from the French by David Sharp in collaboration with the author; and Richard Pollak, *The Creation of Dr. B: A Biography of Bruno Bettelheim* (1997). See also David Dempsey, "Bruno Bettelheim Is Dr. No," *New York Times Magazine* (11 Jan. 1970); Terrence Des Pres, "The Bettelheim Problem," *Social Research* (winter 1979): 619–647; David James Fisher, "An Interview with Bruno Bettelheim," *Los Angeles Psychoanalytic Bulletin* (fall 1990): 3–23; D. Patrick Zimmerman, "The Clinical Thought of Bruno Bettelheim," *Psychoanalysis and Contemporary Thought* 14, no. 4 (1991): 685–721; Paul Roazen, "The Rise and Fall of Bruno Bettelheim," *Psychohistory Review* 20, no. 3 (spring 1992): 221–250; and Paul Marcus and Alan Rosenberg, eds., "Bruno Bettelheim's Contribution to Psychoanalysis," *Psychoanalytic Review* 81, no. 3 (fall 1994). Obituaries are in the *New York Times* and *Washington Post* (both 14 Mar. 1990).

RICHARD POLLAK

BIBLE, Alan Harvey (*b.* 20 November 1909 in Lovelock, Nevada; *d.* 12 September 1988 in Auburn, California), U.S. senator who steered the Southern Nevada Water Project through Congress and played an influential role in the expansion of the national park system.

Bible was born in Lovelock and grew up in Fallon, towns in northern Nevada where grazing occurs largely on the public domain and agriculture relies on federally financed irrigation projects. Bible's father had come to Nevada from Ohio to mine gold but found the grocery business in Lovelock a more reliable source of income. His mother was born

Alan Bible, 1968. UPI/CORBIS-BETTMANN

in Unionville, Nevada, a dying mining town; her parents moved to Lovelock to take up ranching. Jacob Bible and Isabel Welch were married in 1909 and had two sons. When the family home was destroyed by fire in 1919, Jacob purchased a grocery in Fallon, in an agricultural valley that had better access to water and where he enjoyed considerable prosperity. Alan was an outstanding student in high school, attended the University of Nevada in Reno, received a B.A. degree in economics in 1930, and after a year of work in his father's store moved on to Georgetown University Law School in Washington, D.C.

While at Georgetown, Bible needed a part-time job and sought help from Nevada's senior senator, Patrick McCarran, who obtained for him a position as an elevator operator in the U.S. Capitol. From then on, Bible was associated with McCarran's Democratic organization. After receiving his law degree in 1934, he worked for McCarran's law firm in Reno. Within six months he was appointed district attorney of Storey County. Bible learned a lot about mining law in Virginia City, the county seat and the site of the Comstock Lode. In 1938 his faithful efforts for the McCarran organization were rewarded with appointment as deputy attorney general of Nevada. On 17 November 1939 he married Loucile Jacks; they had four children. Denied military service because of his poor eyesight, Bible was elected attorney general in 1942 and reelected in 1946. Bible retired in 1950 to enter private practice, but his most important legal work continued to be representing Nevada's interests in the crucial water-rights litigation, *Arizona* v. *California*. In 1952 he ran for the U.S. Senate but lost in the Democratic primary. When McCarran died two years later, however, Bible easily won election to the remaining two years of his term. He was reelected in 1956, 1962, and 1968.

Bible quickly established close ties to Senator Lyndon B. Johnson of Texas and the Senate's southern establishment. He was a shy man with a strong work ethic and preferred committee work to making speeches. He also recognized that what mattered most to citizens of Nevada was the growth of the local economy, which in turn depended heavily upon federal largesse. Bible immediately obtained appointment to the Senate Committee on Interior and Insular Affairs, where he could involve himself in issues affecting the public lands, especially grazing rights, mining, water, and public power. Johnson put Bible on the Committee on Appropriations in 1959, and ten years later Bible used his seniority to become chairman of the subcommittee that controlled funds for the Department of the Interior. His knowledge of the inner workings of Congress made it possible for him to serve his constituents in the way they wanted. He was the primary architect of the legislation in 1965 that authorized and funded the Southern Nevada Water Project to bring 300,000 acre-feet per year from Lake Mead to the Las Vegas Valley. By freeing Las Vegas from dependence upon a diminishing supply of groundwater, this project made possible the desert city's spectacular expansion as a mecca for gambling, entertainment, light industry, and retirement.

As chairman of the Senate committee on the District of Columbia, Bible presided over the hearings that led to construction of the Capital Beltway, Dulles International Airport, Robert F. Kennedy Stadium, and the John F. Kennedy Center for the Performing Arts. Three times he guided bills through the Senate to provide home rule for the District, only to see them die in the House of Representatives.

During his twenty-year career in the Senate, Bible became increasingly aware of the importance of using the public lands as a recreational resource and in time began to work for the federal acquisition of privately held lands to preserve open space and scenery. The subcommittees he chaired played a key role in the creation of a dozen national seashores and lakeshores (beginning with Cape Cod National Seashore in 1961), the first national scenic river (the Ozark, in Missouri, 1964), and several national parks, including Canyonlands (1964), Redwood (1968), North Cascades (1968), and Voyageurs (1970). He was a leading contributor to the Wilderness Act of 1964. He made sure that the Nevada shore of Lake Mead was fully developed for boating and other recreational uses. Ironically, he failed to obtain congressional approval of the Great Basin National Park, proposed for his own state; it was not created until 1986. Bible's greatest achievement was the insertion of section 17(d)(2) into the Alaska Native Claims Settlement Act of 1971; this was the provision that required a survey of Alaska to identify areas that should be set aside as national parks and monuments, wildlife refuges, and forests. It made possible the Alaska National Interest Lands Conservation Act of 1980. Altogether, Bible was involved in the establishment of eighty-six units of the national park system.

Bible declined to run for reelection in 1974 because of health problems. In retirement he taught political science at the University of Nevada. Bible died of pneumonia in Auburn, California, where he had been living since 1983. He is buried in the Masonic Memorial Gardens Cemetery in Reno.

Alan Bible's reputation for integrity was unquestioned. He was a loyal Democrat but never an ideologue. He was basically a moderate who voted for most of the Great Society legislation of the 1960s (Medicare, aid to education, civil rights) but never took any role in the discussion of these issues. Instead, he focused on the economic needs of his sparsely settled, arid state. When campaigning for reelection he pointed to his accomplishments in bringing federal money for reclamation, flood control, power, mining, and tourism. Through his diligent committee service, the senator, who had been taught the pleasures of the out-of-doors by his father but who was reputedly too physically lazy to take advantage of them, became aware of the need to preserve outstanding fragments of the American wilderness and to provide for the recreational needs of urban dwellers. By pragmatically seeking common ground between preservationists and developers, he helped break congressional deadlocks that would only have benefited those who sought to profit from the status quo. As a legacy to the American people, his efforts in behalf of the national park system transcend in importance the gaudier growth of the Las Vegas Valley.

★

The Alan Bible Papers are preserved in the Special Collections Department of the Getchell Library at the University of Nevada. Gary E. Elliott, *Senator Alan Bible and the Politics of the New West* (1994), is an able account focusing on Bible's interests in federal natural resources policies and wilderness preservation. Bible never attempted to write anything autobiographical, but he did participate in a lengthy oral history interview, "Recollections of a Nevada Native Son: The Law, Politics, the Nevada Attorney General's Office, and the United States Senate," University of Nevada Oral History Project (1981).

KEITH IAN POLAKOFF

BINGHAM, (George) Barry, Sr. (*b.* 10 February 1906 in Louisville, Kentucky; *d.* 15 August 1988 in Glenview, Kentucky), owner, publisher, and editor of the Louisville *Courier-Journal,* one of the leading liberal newspapers in the South.

Bingham was the third child of Robert Worth Bingham, a lawyer, judge, and diplomat, and Eleanor Everhart Miller. When Barry was seven, he and his mother were in an automobile accident that killed his mother and left Barry unable to speak or walk for months. In 1917 his father married Mary Lily Kenan Flagler, one of the richest women in the United States. She died within the year, and Robert Bingham inherited $5 million, part of which he used to purchase the *Louisville Times* and the *Courier-Journal.* He later bought a printing company and started WHAS, Kentucky's first radio station.

His mother's death cast the only shadow upon Barry's otherwise happy childhood. He began his education at Louisville Country Day School, then he attended the Bingham Military School in North Carolina, which was founded by his great-grandfather, and Middlesex School in Concord, Massachusetts. He returned to Louisville to finish his last German credit, entered Harvard University in 1924, and graduated magna cum laude in 1928.

After a tour of Europe and writing a novel that was never published, Bingham joined the family business in 1930. He worked first as continuity writer for WHAS radio station, then as a police reporter for the *Louisville Times* and Washington, D.C., correspondent for the *Courier-Journal.* On 9 June 1931 he married Mary Clifford Caperton, a Radcliffe graduate. They had three sons and two daughters. In 1933 President Franklin D. Roosevelt appointed Bingham's father U.S. ambassador to the Court of St. James's, and Barry Bingham, at age twenty-seven, consequently became head of the Bingham media empire. He endeavored for the next half century to publish the best possible newspapers. He put most of the profits back into the papers and surrounded himself with talented people, such as the experienced journalist Mark Ethridge, who shared his view of a newspaper's responsibility to the reader.

Bingham believed that anyone who owned a city's only newspapers had a greater than usual obligation to present the news in an unbiased manner. In his view, newspapers were a public trust, and the business should be conducted in a way that would render the greatest public service. But he also believed that editorials should take a strong stand on issues of the day, and he was never afraid to take an unpopular stance. The *Courier-Journal* was an early advocate of American participation in World War II.

In 1941 Bingham joined the U.S. Navy. He left Ethridge in charge of the *Courier-Journal* but delegated some of the editorial writing to his wife, Mary Bingham, because she shared his ideas on most issues. During the next four and

Barry Bingham, Sr. COURTESY OF THE COURIER-JOURNAL. PHOTO BY JAMES N. KEEN.

a half years, Bingham served in both theaters of war and earned two Bronze Stars. He headed a group of correspondents aboard the battleship *Missouri* when the Japanese came on board to sign the surrender document that ended the war. He also served as chief of mission for the Marshall Plan in France in 1949 and 1950.

Returning to Kentucky in 1950, Bingham that year expanded the family's communications interests by starting WHAS television station. He also continued to support liberal causes and politicians. He endorsed Adlai Stevenson for president in 1952 and in 1956 and crusaded for civil rights, education reform, and conservation. His *Courier-Journal* editorials were largely responsible for stricter strip-mining legislation. Two of his sons died in accidents, in 1964 and in 1966.

Bingham turned the *Courier-Journal* over to his son Barry Bingham, Jr., in 1971 but remained head of the board of directors. He also placed his daughters on the board of directors, an action that ultimately caused problems. In the next few years, the *Courier-Journal* earned three more Pulitzer Prizes, bringing the total to eight since 1918. By the mid-1980s, Bingham's son and daughters were fighting over how the companies should be run. In 1986 Barry Bingham, Sr., decided that the only way to bring peace to his warring children was to divest the family of the cause of the conflict. The Bingham newspaper dynasty ended when he sold all of the family enterprises. The *Courier-Journal* and *Louisville Times* were purchased by Gannett Company, helping to make Gannett the largest newspaper group in the country.

Before taxes, Bingham and his wife received approximately $115.7 million of the $442.75 million sale. They immediately established the Mary and Barry Bingham Senior Fund to disperse the money. By 1988, the Bingham Fund had given away over $30 million in grants to education, the arts, and health care. Diagnosed in 1987 with a malignant brain tumor, Bingham died of cancer at his home in Glenview, near Louisville. He is buried at Cave Hill Cemetery in Louisville.

Barry Bingham, Sr., was a good citizen, a generous benefactor, and an outstanding editor. He was not afraid to stand up and be counted. He fought for better mental and physical health care, civil rights, and conservation. His newspapers were models of honest reporting and were consistently ranked among the top ten in the United States. The demise of the Bingham newspaper dynasty was the end of one of the last great family-owned newspapers in the United States. In an era of growing public distrust of the news media, the Bingham *Courier-Journal* was a beacon of integrity.

★

Correspondence between Bingham and his wife is in the Schlesinger Library at Radcliffe; a large collection of family papers is at the Filson Club Historical Society, Louisville, Kentucky. Samuel W. Thomas, ed., *Barry Bingham: A Man of His Word* (1993), is a compilation of oral history interviews and personal letters that includes letters never intended for publication. Marie Brenner, *House of Dreams: The Bingham Family of Louisville* (1988), is a somewhat romanticized biography of the Binghams. A more realistic treatment is Susan E. Tifft and Alex S. Jones, *The Patriarch: The Rise and Fall of the Bingham Dynasty* (1991). Joe Ward, "The Binghams: Twilight of a Tradition," *Courier-Journal Magazine* (20 Apr. 1986), details the family conflict and the sale of the newspapers. Obituaries are in the Louisville *Courier-Journal,* the *Lexington Herald-Leader,* and the *New York Times* (all 16 Aug. 1988). Oral history interviews are housed at the Kentucky Historical Society.

ANNA BEATRICE PERRY

BINGHAM, Jonathan Brewster ("Jack") (*b.* 24 April 1914 in New Haven, Connecticut; *d.* 3 July 1986 in New York City), lawyer, diplomat, and congressman from New York who was deputy director of President Harry S. Truman's Point IV program, a delegate to the United Nations, and an eighteen-year member of the House of Representatives, where he was a legislative leader in limiting nuclear weapons and in restricting the president's authority as commander-in-chief.

Born into an old New England family whose Puritan ancestors crossed the Atlantic in the first waves of settlement in the seventeenth century, Jack Bingham was the last of Hiram and Alfreda (Mitchell) Bingham's seven sons. His father was a noted South American explorer and professor of history who discovered the Inca ruins at Machu Picchu, Peru, in 1911 and represented Connecticut in the U.S. Senate from 1925 to 1933. Jack graduated summa cum laude from Groton in 1932 and went on to a distinguished undergraduate career at Yale University (class of 1936), editing the college's daily newspaper while earning a B.A. degree in economics and membership in Phi Beta Kappa. Three years later he received his LL.B. from Yale Law School, where he was note editor of the *Yale Law Journal.* He was a member of the Congregational Church.

Bingham spent the summer months of 1939 traveling in Europe and Asia as a freelance correspondent for the *New York Herald Tribune,* and on 20 September 1939 he married June Rossbach, a writer, with whom he had four children. Bingham was admitted to the New York bar in 1940, briefly practicing law as an associate at Cravath, de Gersdorff, Swaine, and Wood in Manhattan before entering public service, first as counsel for the New York State Labor Relations Board and then on the legal staff of the Office of Price Administration, following America's entry into World War II.

Jonathan Brewster Bingham, 1964. UPI/CORBIS-BETTMANN

In 1943 Bingham enlisted as a private in the army. Assigned to army intelligence in Washington, D.C., he mustered out in 1945 with the rank of captain. He remained in the nation's capital until the spring of 1946 as a special assistant in the State Department. Returning to New York in June of that year, he became a partner in the law firm of Cohen and Bingham and, despite his family's staunch Republican background, took an active role in the Democratic party at both the state and local levels, building a solid reputation for political liberalism and personal integrity and serving as New York State chairman of Americans for Democratic Action (1948–1950). In April 1951 he was back in Washington with the State Department as the assistant director of the Office of International Security Affairs.

Six months later Bingham was appointed deputy director of the Technical Cooperation Administration, the agency established by Congress on 27 September 1950 to carry out Truman's Point IV program—so named because it was in the fourth section of the president's 1949 inaugural address—which offered U.S. technical assistance and investment capital to the world's underdeveloped areas. In the next year and a half, Bingham traveled regularly to South America, Africa, and the Middle East to oversee, as he once put it, "the workings of the whole thing" and emerged as a leading spokesman for foreign aid in a series of articles for the *New York Herald Tribune* (20 March 1952), the *Department of State Bulletin* (29 December 1952), the *New York Times Magazine* (10 May 1953), and the *Foreign Policy Bulletin* (15 June 1953). In 1954, after he had returned to private law practice, he published *Shirt-Sleeve Diplomacy: Point IV in Action,* a firsthand account of his travels and a defense of the program as "a necessary and noble experiment" in combating worldwide social and economic inequities. He coauthored a second book, *Violence and Democracy,* with his brother Alfred in 1970.

From 1955 to 1958, Bingham was secretary to W. Averell Harriman, governor of New York, leaving that position to run unsuccessfully for the state senate. He next joined the New York City law firm of Goldwater and Flynn, and in 1961 he was named by President John F. Kennedy as U.S. representative to the Economic and Social Council of the United Nations with the rank of ambassador, a post he held until 1964. In that year, running as a reform candidate in the Democratic primary, he defeated Charles A. Buckley of the Bronx, a deeply entrenched party boss who was seeking his sixteenth term in the House and who had once described Bingham to his working-class constituency as "a big stiff." (This was a reference to Bingham's privileged background and his height—he was a trim six feet, two inches tall—but also a bemused comment on his campaign tactics. As an accomplished pianist and string player, he delighted in performing chamber music with his wife and children and made it a habit, while seeking office, to invite potential voters to his home in the Riverdale section of the Bronx for tea and a family concert.) His winning margin in the 1964 primary was only 4,000 votes, but Bingham won an easy victory over his Republican opponent in November and was never seriously challenged in any of the eight races that followed.

Once in Washington, Bingham joined the liberal wing of the Democratic caucus and became a blunt-spoken champion of congressional reform. He was one of the leading strategists in securing the House rules changes in 1974 that democratized the choice of committee chairmen (notably through the introduction of a secret ballot) and gave greater power to subcommittees. He was unsuccessful in an ongoing effort to effect controls on campaign spending. He took a particular interest in foreign policy and especially in foreign aid, both of which he believed had been seriously mishandled in recent years by Congress and the executive branch. As early as 1976 he urged President Gerald Ford to normalize relations with Cuba, and in February 1977 had an eight-hour interview with Cuban president Fidel Castro in Havana in the hope of finding grounds for reconciliation. Neither Congress nor the newly elected president, Jimmy Carter, was prepared to meet Castro's demand that the Cuban embargo be lifted before serious discussion between the two governments could commence.

As a member of the Foreign Relations Committee and a strong supporter of Israel, Bingham drafted the Soviet Jewish Assistance Act of 1972. He was the chief author of the War Powers Act of 1973, which reduced the president's power to send U.S. military forces overseas without the consent of Congress. He is best known as a vigorous opponent of nuclear power and especially for his role in the passage of the Nuclear Non-Proliferation Act of 1978, which sharply restricted the export of materials used in producing nuclear power or nuclear weapons.

In 1982 Bingham's Bronx congressional district was divided in three as part of a redistricting brought on by the 1980 census. Rather than run against a younger Democratic colleague (Ted Weiss) who was also affected by the change—"I have no quarrel with him," Bingham said—he chose not to seek a tenth term and returned to New York, where he remained active in a number of civic groups. He died of pneumonia four years later, after an illness of more than six weeks, in Columbia Presbyterian Hospital in New York City.

★

Bingham's papers are uncollected. Some of his correspondence is included in the Lubin Papers and in the Harriman Papers, both of which are at Syracuse University. Several taped interviews are available in the Oral History Collection at the John F. Kennedy Library in Boston. His early career is profiled in *Current Biography* (1954). His public career can be traced through the *New York Times, New York Herald Tribune,* and *Congressional Record.* Obituaries are in the *New York Times* and *Washington Post* (both 4 July 1986).

ALLAN L. DAMON

BISHOP, James Alonzo ("Jim") (*b.* 21 November 1907 in Jersey City, New Jersey; *d.* 26 July 1987 in Delray Beach, Florida), newspaper columnist and novelist best known for his terse, Hemingwayesque prose and "you are there" best-sellers about Abraham Lincoln's assassination, John Fitzgerald Kennedy's White House routine, and the crucifixion of Jesus Christ.

Bishop was one of three children of John Michael Bishop, a Jersey City police lieutenant, and Jenny Josephine Tier. Bishop claims that he got his inspiration to write from watching his father fill out police reports. "I'd be doing my homework and Dad would be sitting across the kitchen table making out his report. He'd start at the beginning where he'd spotted the suspect, Bostwick and Jackson Avenues, 9:40 A.M., and tell his story so neatly and concisely that he made it sing for me."

Formal education ended in the eighth grade for Bishop,

Jim Bishop. ARCHIVE PHOTOS

although he did attend Drake's Secretarial College in Jersey City in 1923. The writer's last nonwriting job was delivering milk in Jersey City from a horse-drawn wagon. He left to become a $12-a-week copy boy for the *New York Daily News* in 1929. His journalism career advanced, and he was a reporter for the *New York Daily Mirror* from 1930 to 1932 and then a rewrite man for *Mirror* theater columnist Mark Hellinger.

As Hellinger's assistant on a daily column, Bishop learned his rewrite skills. Instructed to write short sentences and to use short words, he made it a practice to read a few pages of Ernest Hemingway's novel *The Sun Also Rises* before he wrote his own copy. He stayed at the *Mirror* until 1943, ultimately becoming a feature writer. He was assistant editor at *Collier's* magazine from 1943 to 1944 and the magazine's war editor from 1944 to 1945. He became executive editor of *Liberty* magazine in 1945. In 1947 he became director of the literary department of the Music Corporation of America. He left two years later to become founding editor of Gold Medal Books, and in 1953 he moved on to become executive editor of *Catholic Digest.* In 1954 he created the Catholic Digest Book Club and served as founding editor until 1955.

During his early journalism career, Bishop began writing books. He published a tale about a fictional alcoholic entitled *The Glass Crutch: The Biographical Novel of William Wynne Wister* in 1945 and a biography of his mentor, Mark Hellinger, in 1952. The first of his many best-selling successes came at a low point in his career. Three thousand dollars in debt, he finished a project he began on off-hours at the rewrite desk. Although he had been researching the book for years, it took him six months to write about the final hours of the sixteenth president. *The Day Lincoln Was Shot* became a best-seller in 1955 and prompted an invitation from the television comedian Jackie Gleason to write his biography.

Bishop's biography of Gleason, *The Golden Ham,* won a Benjamin Franklin Magazine Award from the University of Illinois and excerpts from the book, published in 1956, were printed in *Life* magazine. In 1958 Bishop claimed that he had told Gleason to find another writer. "I reminded him that if I wrote the book it would be the truth as I saw it. He insisted that I write the book." He did as promised, and the candid result supposedly caused a split between the two men, although Bishop christened his boat *Away We Go II,* after the comedian's signature phrase.

With his career secure again as a best-selling author, Bishop signed with King Features Syndicate to pen three columns a week. His column, "Jim Bishop: Reporter," ran for twenty-seven years in as many as 200 newspapers. In addition to his column, which he claimed averaged about thirty-five minutes to write, Bishop continued to publish books, many of them following "a day in the life of" format. Among them are *The Day Christ Died* (1957), *A Day in the Life of President Kennedy* (1964), *A Day in the Life of President Johnson* (1967), *The Day Kennedy Was Shot* (1968), *The Days of Martin Luther King, Jr.* (1971), and *FDR's Last Year* (1974). During his lifetime Bishop published twenty-one books.

Bishop married Elinor Margaret Dunning on 14 June 1930. At the time, she was a twenty-year-old Wall Street secretary who made more money than he did, but he was a handsome, five-foot, seven-inch Irish Catholic charmer out to conquer the newspaper world. They had two daughters. Elinor Bishop died in October 1957. Bishop married again on 19 May 1961, to Elizabeth Kelly Stone. She had two daughters from a previous marriage.

For five years in the late 1950s and 1960s, Bishop lived with his family in the New Jersey seaside resort of Sea Bright. About sixty miles south of New York City, the shore residence fulfilled a boyhood dream of the author to live by the water. The columnist created a stir in the community by writing unfavorable pieces about the residents and life in a small town. The relationship improved and Bishop was invited to attend a "Jim Bishop Day" in July 1984, when a time capsule that included some of his predictions was opened on the silver anniversary of its burial. The writer declined. Bishop moved to Florida from Sea Bright in 1964 and died of respiratory failure in Delray Beach in 1987.

Bishop's career was distinguished by its longevity and variety, but he prided himself on being a good reporter first. His demand for the truth often incurred the wrath of his subjects. In his career as reporter and author he was challenged by the NAACP, Jacqueline Kennedy, and the town of Sea Bright. Bishop was a product of the early-twentieth-century urban school of journalism. With little formal education, he honed his skills on the daily tabloids of New York City and never lost that punch. Even his longer works reflected the in-the-moment style of his columns. Bishop credited his grandmother for advice that sustained him through a long and productive career: "Thy will be done."

★

Bishop's autobiography, *A Bishop's Confession* (1981), offers good insight into his Irish-Catholic background, his home and personal life, and his experiences in the world of big city newspapers; the style is breezy and informal. For insight into Bishop's relationships with his subjects, in particular his feud with the town leaders of Sea Bright, see the *Journal American* (12 Nov. 1958); *Asbury Park Press* (15 May 1957, 19 June 1957, 8 Dec. 1958, 15 Feb. 1959, 31 Oct. 1959, 20 May 1959, 15 May 1960, 17 Jan. 1966, 16 Sept. 1966, 10 Sept. 1981, 2 July 1984, and 15 July 1984); and *Editor and Publisher* (11 Oct. 1958). For biographical details, achievements, and career history, obituaries in the *New York Times* and *Asbury Park Press* (both 28 July 1987) are good sources.

LINDA DOWLING ALMEIDA

BLAIK, Earl Henry ("Red") (*b.* 15 February 1897 in Detroit, Michigan; *d.* 6 May 1989 in Colorado Springs, Colorado), college athlete and football coach best known for coaching the U.S. Military Academy at West Point to consecutive national football championships in 1944 and 1945.

Blaik, one of three children of William Douglas Blaik, a home builder, and Margaret Jane Purcell, graduated in 1914 from Steele High School in Dayton, Ohio, where he lettered in football, basketball, and baseball, and in 1918 from Miami University of Ohio with a B.A. degree. At Miami he played end on the undefeated 1916 and 1917 Ohio Conference championship football teams, captained the baseball squad, and served as president of the student body.

After being appointed to the U.S. Military Academy in 1918, the six-foot, two-inch, 190-pound Blaik made third team All-America as a football end in 1919 and played center-forward in basketball and outfield in baseball. He was awarded the saber as the outstanding athlete of his class and earned a B.S. degree in 1920, ranking 108 in a class of 271.

Blaik graduated from Cavalry School at Fort Riley, Kansas, as a first lieutenant in 1921 and spent several months with the First Cavalry Division at Fort Bliss, Texas. After resigning from the U.S. Army in 1923 with the rank of colonel, he worked in his father's home-building business in Dayton from 1923 to 1934. Blaik married Merle J. McDowell on 20 October 1923. They had two sons, William and Robert.

Blaik served as a part-time assistant football coach at the University of Wisconsin in 1926 and at the U.S. Military Academy from 1927 to 1933. In 1934 he became head football coach at Dartmouth College and quickly rebuilt its program. Darmouth produced a 45–15–4 record in his seven seasons, three times ranking among the top twenty. After finishing 6–3 in 1934 and 8–2 in 1935 under Blaik, the Indians compiled a twenty-two-game undefeated streak from 1936 to 1938. Dartmouth defeated Yale University in 1935 for the first time since 1884 and captured unofficial Ivy League championships in 1936 and 1937.

Blaik's greatest football moment came in November 1940, when Dartmouth ended Cornell's undefeated streak at eighteen games. The Indians led, 3–0, until Cornell scored as the final gun sounded. Cornell, however, forfeited the game to Dartmouth the next day after discovering referee Red Friesell mistakenly had given Cornell an extra down on the final drive.

In 1941 Blaik became the first civilian head football coach at the U.S. Military Academy in thirty years, inheriting a nearly winless squad. Superintendent Robert Eichelberger lured him back to the academy by promising to liberalize the Cadets' recruitment policy, build a new house for the head coach, and keep the line of command clear and streamlined. Army's fortunes soared during World War II as the service academy attracted more students. Blaik transformed the Cadets into the nation's top team in just three years, attaining records of 5–3–1 in 1941 and 1942 and 7–2–1 in 1943. Army switched from a single-wing back formation to a T-formation in 1943.

Army compiled among the most impressive records in college football history from 1944 to 1950, finishing with an astonishing 57–3–4 mark. Blaik guided the Cadets to a thirty-two-game undefeated streak, including two scoreless ties, from 1944 to 1947. Army won national championships with 9–0 records in 1944 and 1945, outscoring opponents 917–81 and conquering the University of Notre Dame and the U.S. Naval Academy both seasons. Halfback Glenn Davis, whom Blaik considered his greatest player, and fullback Felix ("Doc") Blanchard spearheaded the phenomenal Army offense. Davis scored 51 touchdowns and averaged 9.9 yards per carry from 1944 to 1946, while Blanchard tallied 38 touchdowns.

The American Football Coaches Association named Blaik coach of the year in 1946, having voted him second the previous two seasons. After Columbia University and Notre Dame triumphed over Army in 1947, Blaik masterminded another remarkable twenty-eight-game undefeated string. Navy ended that streak, 14–2, in the 1950 season finale.

Ninety Cadets, including forty-four football players, were expelled from the U.S. Military Academy in 1951 for violating the Honor Code in a cribbing scandal. Blaik's son Robert, the starting quarterback, was one of those dismissed. Army, completely decimated, suffered ten defeats in 1951 and 1952 combined. Blaik then accomplished an amazing rebuilding feat, steering Army in 1953 to fourteenth nationally with a 7–1–1 record to earn the Washington Touchdown Club Coach of the Year Award. The Cadets rose to seventh nationally in 1954 with a 7–2 mark.

Blaik's final campaign in 1958 saw him direct the 8–0–1 Cadets to third place nationally and receive the Touchdown Club of New York's annual award. He devised the "Lonesome End" strategy to spread out defenses, using brilliant receiver Bill Carpenter as a flanker near the sideline. The strategy opened up the running game for Pete Dawkins and helped Army's passing game enormously because more than one defender usually was needed to cover Carpenter. Blaik, who also served as athletic director, led Army to a 121–33–10 mark in eighteen seasons with thirteen top-twenty teams.

Blaik served as vice president and chairman of the executive committee of Avco Corporation and of the Blaik Oil Company. He also helped solve racial problems in Birmingham, Alabama, in 1963 and participated on the Clark Board that rewrote the draft laws in 1966. He retired to Colorado Springs, Colorado, and authored two books, *You*

Earl Blaik and his son Robert. ARCHIVE PHOTOS

Have to Pay the Price (with Tim Cohane, 1960) and *The Red Blaik Story* (1974). In 1986 President Ronald Reagan presented him with the Presidential Medal of Freedom, the nation's highest civilian award. Blaik died from complications after breaking his hip in a fall.

Blaik compiled a 166–48–14 career record for a .759 winning percentage at Dartmouth and Army, producing two national championship squads; two second-ranked teams; and three undefeated, untied aggregates. Under Blaik, seven Army teams won the Lambert Trophy as eastern champions. Contemporaries regarded him as dignified, reserved, diplomatic, calm, dedicated to leadership, and a brilliant tactician. Blaik inspired players to believe in themselves and give their best performance. His honors included being named to the Helms Athletic Foundation College Football Hall of Fame and in 1965 to the National Football Foundation's College Football Hall of Fame. In 1966 the National Football Foundation presented him with its Gold Medal Award for "significant contributions and highest ideals."

Blaik coached forty-three All-Americans, with Doc Blanchard, Glenn Davis, and Pete Dawkins winning both the Heisman Trophy and Maxwell Award and guard Joe Steffy garnering the Outland Award. Nineteen former players and assistants, including Vince Lombardi, Andy Gustafson, Stu Holcomb, Sid Gillman, Paul Dietzel, and Murray Warmath became head college or professional football coaches.

★

Earl H. Blaik with Tim Cohane, *You Have to Pay the Price* (1960), and Earl H. Blaik, *The Red Blaik Story* (1974), provide autobiographical accounts of his life and career. Jim Beach and Daniel Moore, *Army vs. Notre Dame: The Big Game, 1913–1947* (1948), reviews games against a major West Point rival. Tim Cohane, *Gridiron Grenadiers: The Story of West Point Football* (1948), features Blaik's early Army teams. Edwin Pope, *Football's Greatest Coaches* (1956), reviews his career. Jack Clary, *Army vs. Navy: Seventy Years of Football Rivalry* (1965), is about the renowned annual interservice game. Tim Cohane, *Great College Football Coaches of the Twenties and Thirties* (1973), covers his pre–West Point coaching career. Joe Hoppel, Mike Nahrstedt, and Steve Zesch, eds., *College Football's Twenty-five Greatest Teams* (1988), deals with his early West Point clubs. Stanley Woodward, "The Man Behind the Army Team," *Sport* (Nov. 1950), surveys his Army coaching career. An obituary is in the *New York Times* (7 May 1989).

DAVID L. PORTER

BLAISDELL, Thomas Charles, Jr. (*b.* 2 December 1895 in Pittsburgh, Pennsylvania; *d.* 27 December 1988 in Berkeley, California), government employee who was assistant secretary of commerce (1949–1951) and helped formulate the economic policies of the Marshall Plan.

Blaisdell was one of four children born to Thomas Charles Blaisdell, Sr., a teacher, and Kate Christy, a homemaker. Around 1907 the family moved to East Lansing, Michigan, where Blaisdell's father taught at the Michigan Agricultural College (now Michigan State University) and later became president of Alma College. Blaisdell attended Lansing High School and graduated at the age of sixteen in 1911. He entered Alma College the following year and then studied at the Konigstadtische Oberrealschule in Berlin, Germany (1913–1914). He returned to Alma College for his junior year in 1915 but transferred to Pennsylvania State College in 1915, when his father accepted the position of dean at Penn State. Blaisdell received a B.A. degree in 1916.

Blaisdell then taught British, European, and Indian history at Ewing Christian College in Allahabad, India (1916–1919). In 1919 he returned to the United States to serve as traveling secretary for the Student Volunteer Movement (1919–1920). Based in New York City, the organization recruited students for missionary work. As secretary, Blaisdell traveled to different universities describing his experiences in India and encouraging students to become missionaries. Completing his one-year appointment in 1920, he accepted a scholarship to study at the Columbia University School of Social Work.

On 27 December 1921 Blaisdell married Catherine Maltby; they had one child. He received an M.A. degree from Columbia in 1922 and moved to Peking, China, where he taught at Yenching University under the direction of the International Young Men's Christian Association (1922–1925) and worked with famine relief efforts. The Blaisdells returned to the United States in 1925 and he began teaching economics at Columbia University (1925–1933) and work on his Ph.D., concentrating on the study of economics. In 1932 he received his doctorate and became an assistant professor. His dissertation was titled "The Federal Trade Commission: An Experiment in the Control of Business."

Thomas C. Blaisdell, Jr., 1950. UPI/CORBIS-BETTMANN

Rexford Tugwell, who had been chairman of the Economics Department at Columbia and was now assistant secretary of agriculture in the Roosevelt administration, lured Blaisdell to Washington, D.C., where Blaisdell served as assistant director and consumers counsel in the Agricultural Adjustment Administration (1933–1934) and as executive director of the Consumers Advisory Board, for the National Recovery Administration (1934–1935). Blaisdell also worked with Tugwell in his next assignment, as economic adviser to the administrator of the Resettlement Administration (1935–1936), which involved the Tennessee Valley Authority and the Bureau of Reclamation. From 1936 to 1937 he was assistant director of the Bureau of Research and Statistics for the Social Security Board. In this capacity he researched European social security systems, studying their organization and general principles.

Blaisdell joined the Securities and Exchange Commission in 1938, where he directed a study on monopolies. He had differences of opinion with William O. Douglas, the SEC chairman, and left to become the assistant director for the National Resources Planning Board (1939–1943), which was part of the Executive Office of the President. He also served as chairman of the Industrial Committee of the Natural Resources Planning Board investigating industries such as oil and steel and was a planning member of the War Production Board (1942–1943).

After serving briefly as director of the Orders and Regulations Bureau (1943–1944), Blaisdell moved to London, England, where he became the chief of the Mission for Economic Affairs, with the rank of minister (1945–1946). Afterward, he went to work for the Foreign Economic Administration, which was separate from the State Department and had the task of overseeing the last days of the lend-lease program.

From 1947 to 1951 Blaisdell worked in the Department of Commerce, first as director of the Office of International Trade (1947–1949) and then as assistant secretary of commerce (1949–1951), during which time he was involved in the Marshall Plan, developed by Secretary of State George Marshall to aid in the economic recovery of Europe in the aftermath of World War II. He also supervised the Office of International Trade, which created licensing procedures for exporters selling commodities overseas, and worked on a team that reviewed the relationship between the appropriations for the newly formed North Atlantic Treaty Organization (NATO) and the Marshall Plan.

Blaisdell retired in 1951 and moved to Berkeley, California, where he was professor of political science from 1951 until his retirement in 1963. However, he resumed teaching there in 1964, before finally retiring in 1967. He coauthored *The American Presidency in Political Cartoons* with Peter Selz (1976).

Blaisdell held many positions in his long career of public service. His expertise in economic policy as assistant secretary of commerce made a substantial contribution to the effectiveness of the Marshall Plan. In his later years as professor of political science he drew upon his eighteen years of public service as he taught students about international affairs and politics.

★

Blaisdell's papers as well as an oral interview (26 Mar. 1971) are in the Harry S. Truman Library, Independence, Missouri. Michael J. Hogan, *The Marshall Plan: America, Britain, and the Reconstruction of Western Europe, 1947–1952* (1987), mentions Blaisdell's support for a coordinated effort to address the economic devastation of Europe after World War II. An obituary is in the *New York Times* (31 Dec. 1988). See also Thomas C. Blaisdell, Jr., "India and China in the World War I Era; New Deal and Marshall Plan; and University of California, Berkeley," an oral history by Harriet Nathan, Regional Oral History Office, Bancroft Library, University of California, Berkeley (1991).

JON E. TAYLOR

Art Blakey. BILL SPILKA/METRONOME/ARCHIVE PHOTOS

BLAKEY, Arthur ("Art"; Abdullah Ibn Buhaina) (*b.* 11 October 1919 in Pittsburgh, Pennsylvania; *d.* 16 October 1990 in New York City), musician and bandleader long acknowledged as a jazz immortal for his drum virtuosity, his influence on other jazz musicians, and his innovations in hard bop jazz.

Blakey's early years in Pittsburgh are clouded. According to him, his mother, Marie Roddericker, died when he was six months old. Raised with his two brothers by a woman variously referred to as a friend or as his mother's first cousin, whom he called "Mrs. Parran," Blakey recounted that the relatives of his father, a mulatto, shunned his mother because of her dark complexion and that his father abandoned her shortly before he was born.

Blakey's years of schooling were erratic, and he had problems with his schools' administration and teachers. Pittsburgh schools were lawfully integrated even in the 1920s, but Blakey believed that because "most of the teachers were white," they were bigots, "and I couldn't learn anything."

As a youngster Blakey began playing piano by ear in his foster mother's home. By the age of thirteen, he considered himself a man, because he was working outside the home, had a girlfriend, and had learned how to survive in the streets. At the age of fourteen, he dropped out of school and married his girlfriend. By age fifteen, he was a father who supported his small family first by working in the Pittsburgh steel mills, then by trying his hand as a professional musician. Blakey pursued his interest in music with determination. He had gained proficiency on the piano, though unable to read music, and had some skill playing other instruments. Forming a band made up of his school friends, he began playing at local affairs. During Prohibition, despite their youth, the band members played occasional gigs in bars and at speakeasies.

In 1936, at age seventeen, Blakey experienced one of the first turning points in his life as a musician. Blakey's band was booked in a Pittsburgh club called the Ritz. The band was to accompany a traveling Broadway show scheduled to perform at the club. Blakey's inexperience and his inability to read music nearly turned the gig into a tragedy. He was saved by another young man, who had been sitting at the rear of the club listening to the band rehearse and who offered his piano-playing services to Blakey. The young man was Erroll Garner, also formally untrained, but whose uncanny ear enabled him to go on to a remarkable career as a jazz pianist. After listening to Garner, the club's owner suggested that Blakey turn his attention to the drums. As he says, "So that's how I started playing drums—I had to survive." In 1939 Blakey was still supporting his wife and their young son, Art Blakey, Jr., but it was difficult, and Blakey began to experiment with drugs.

Big breaks occurred in 1941 and 1942, when Mary Lou Williams, an accomplished jazz artist, was recuperating in Pittsburgh after an extended illness. She heard of young Blakey and employed him as part of a combo she had formed, taking him with her for an engagement in Kelly's Stable in New York. When Blakey returned to Pittsburgh, he resumed playing with his own band and caught the eye of the legendary New Orleans jazz musician Fletcher Henderson, who was traveling across the country and who hired both Blakey and his band to travel and perform with him. Traveling was a new experience for Blakey, a tough kid of Pittsburgh streets, who had trouble with the restrictions and racism of the South. A confrontation with an Atlanta, Georgia, policeman resulted in a struggle in which Blakey was badly beaten.

While playing in Boston in 1944, Blakey became ill and left the Henderson band. He soon met a fellow Pittsburgh native, singer Billy Eckstine, whose gifted band of musicians, including Dizzy Gillespie, Dexter Gordon, Charlie Parker, and Miles Davis, would forge some of the greatest careers in music. Blakey recalls that traveling with Eckstine and being among such first-rate musicians was "the most fascinating time of my life." One such performer, Gillespie, helped Blakey perfect his drumming style, raising the drum virtuoso's talent to the next pinnacle of mastery. Dizzy literally put his ears to the drums while Blakey played and, in his inimitable fashion, sang the beats so that Blakey understood exactly what he had to do.

For Blakey, his three years with Eckstine were equal to attending a music university. On his "graduation" in 1947, Blakey had become associated with the new jazz sound known as "bebop."

After the Eckstein band broke up, Blakey played with assorted small groups. In 1954 he joined a group of five musicians that included trumpeter Kenny Dorham, tenor saxophonist Hank Mobley, bassist Doug Watkins, and pianist Horace Silver. The group became the "Jazz Messengers," a phrase coined by Horace Silver, but it was Blakey who held the group together, becoming bandleader in 1956.

The late 1940s and early 1950s were also years of frustration for Blakey. His marital relationship appears to have been troubled and his drug problems increased. Experiencing a spiritual and emotional crisis, he sought renewal by going in 1947 to Africa, ostensibly to "study drums," he recounted, but "I went to Africa because there wasn't anything else for me to do. I couldn't get gigs, and I had to work my way over on a boat. . . . I went over there to study religion and philosophy." According to a friend, who accompanied Blakey on his first trip to Africa, "Smoking, drinking, loving, and testing the limits of the human body were all matched by expanding the limits of his music." While in Africa in the 1950s, Blakey underwent a spiritual awakening and adopted the Islamic name Abdullah Ibn Buhaina.

Blakey's personal popularity waned somewhat during the 1970s, when pop/rock music eclipsed jazz and rhythm and blues. But his place as jazz guru to aspiring jazz musicians never wavered. In the 1980s a jazz renaissance occurred, sparked by younger musicians, many of whom came under Blakey's tutelage. Included among them were Wynton and Branford Marsalis, Billy Pierce, Donald Harrison, Terrence Blanchard, Freddie Hubbard, and Benny Green.

Blakey's life was consumed by his music, but his private life, while guarded, was not without its problems and tragedies. His love of children was almost as significant, if less public, as his love of music. Married at least three and possibly four times, and the father of ten children, he adopted several others. In 1988 Blakey's son Art Blakey, Jr., died at age forty-seven.

Blakey's masterful recordings as leader of the Jazz Messengers are vast. Among his notable were *The Complete Black Lion and Vogue Recording of Thelonius Monk* (1954); *A Night at Birdland, Volumes 1 and 2* (1954); *Drum Suite: Art Blakey and the Jazz Messengers* (1956); *Album of the Year* (1981); and *One for All* (1990). Blakey also won awards as best drummer and as the leader of the best combo in the *Down Beat* magazine polls, as well as awards in Japan and elsewhere. He was the recipient of a Grammy Award in 1984 for best jazz instrumental performance group. In 1985 Blakey summed his life up with the following comment: "That's my life up there on the bandstand." He died five days after his seventy-first birthday, from lung cancer, in St. Vincent's Hospital and Medical Center in New York City.

★

Biographical accounts include Wayne Eustace and Paul Rubin, "Art Blakey," in *Reading Jazz: A Gathering of Autobiography, Reporting, and Criticism from 1919 to Now,* ed. Robert Gottlieb (1996); Herb Nolan, "New Message from Art Blakey," *Down Beat* 61 (June 1994): 34–35; Art Lange, "Wynton Marsalis. Chuck Mangione. Kenny Garret. . . . ," *Down Beat* (Jan. 1991); Terrence Cook, "Art Blakey: Fifty Years with a Message," *Jazz Education Journal* (1990); Judge Bruce McM. Wright, "Recalling Art Blakey—Abdullah Buhaina—The Indestructable," *Amsterdam News* (3 Nov. 1990); and Zan Steward, "Art Blakey: In His Prime," *Down Beat*

52 (1985): 20–22. Obituaries are in the *New York Times* (17 Oct. 1990), and *Down Beat* 58 (Jan. 1991): 30.

WILLIAM F. BROWNE

BLANC, Mel(vin) Jerome (*b.* 30 May 1908 in San Francisco, California; *d.* 10 July 1989 in Los Angeles, California), voice actor in radio, film, and television best known as the voice of many Warner Brothers cartoon characters.

Blanc was born Melvin Jerome Blank, the younger of two children of Frederick Blank and Eva Katz, who together ran a ladies' clothing shop in San Francisco. Soon after Mel's birth, the Blanks moved the family to Portland, Oregon.

As a child, Mel was fascinated by the foreign accents of the immigrants he heard in Oregon. He was a grammar school class clown, and the encouragement of his classmates steered him toward performing. His penchant for answering questions in class with different voices earned Blank the scorn of one teacher, who told him, "You'll never amount to anything. You're like your last name: blank." From age sixteen on, he spelled his name with a "c." Later, he changed it legally.

From early childhood, Blanc loved vaudeville, movies, and radio. Shortly after his graduation from Lincoln High School in 1927, radio station KGW in Portland gave Blanc his first on-air exposure when he sang a parody of the Spanish ballad "Juanita" on *The Hoot Owls* radio program. His appearance was a hit, and he was hired to perform on a regular basis. He also played the tuba with a series of small, local orchestras. During the 1930s he moved back and forth between cities in California and Oregon, taking various positions in orchestras. In 1930 (at age twenty-two), Blanc became the youngest musical director in the country when he was made pit conductor at the Orpheum Theater in Portland. The end of vaudeville steered Blanc toward Hollywood, where he hoped for a future in radio. There he worked, uncredited, for the National Broadcasting Company doing comedic voices for variety programs.

Blanc married Estelle Rosenbaum, a legal secretary, on 4 January 1933 before a justice of the peace in Riverside, California. Because it had not been a formal, Jewish wedding, they lived apart until May 1933, when they went through the traditional religious ceremony. Two days later, Mel accepted an offer to produce his own radio show in Oregon. Estelle worked uncredited with Mel, who, operating on a small budget, developed a wide repertoire of voices for the daily hour-long show, *Cobwebs and Nuts*. The show was not a success, however, and the Blancs returned in 1935 to Los Angeles, where Mel would spend the rest of his life.

At first he found only limited roles on various radio shows, but in December 1936, after eighteen months of trying, Blanc succeeded in getting an audition at Warner Brothers. He was immediately hired to provide the voice of a drunken bull for the 1937 Porky Pig short "Picador Porky." Soon Blanc was asked by cartoon producer Leon Schlessinger to replace actor Joe Dougherty in performing Porky's voice as well. Porky's tag line, "That's all, folks!" was originally a Blanc ad-lib, as was Bugs Bunny's catchphrase, "What's up, Doc?" It was also Blanc's idea to name the cartoon rabbit after Ben ("Bugs") Hardaway, his creator.

Blanc changed the way cartoons were produced when he suggested that instead of recording the entire dialogue track all the way through, each character's voice be recorded separately and the lines edited together later. Blanc found this easier to do, since occasionally his was the only voice heard in a cartoon. He once played fourteen different characters in a single short. Between 1936 and 1969, Blanc provided the voices in 848 Warner Brothers animated shorts. Besides Bugs Bunny and Porky Pig, he was the voice of Daffy Duck, Elmer Fudd (Blanc took over after Arthur Q. Bryan died in 1959), Yosemite Sam, Foghorn Leghorn, Pepe Le Pew, the Road Runner, Sylvester the Cat, and Tweety Pie, as well as a host of others. Blanc was the first cartoon voice actor to receive on-screen credit. He was also the original voice and laugh of Walter Lantz Production's

Mel Blanc. ARCHIVE PHOTOS

Woody Woodpecker. Over the course of his career, Blanc was heard in more than 3,000 cartoons.

During his years working in cartoons, Blanc continued to appear on nationally broadcast radio shows such as *The Great Gildersleeve*, *Amos 'n' Andy*, and *Blondie*. Blanc's schedule was so busy that he frequently had to run from one studio to another. The Blancs' only child, their son Noel, was born in 1938.

In 1939 Blanc joined Jack Benny's radio program, where he started as Carmichael, the polar bear who guarded Benny's vault, and Benny's car, a 1924 Maxwell. Gradually, he was allowed speaking roles, most famously the train caller who announces trains leaving for "Anaheim, Azusa, and Cuc-amonga!" and as Professor LeBlanc, Benny's French violin instructor. Later, when the Benny show moved to television, Blanc made appearances there as well.

In 1946 the Columbia Broadcasting System gave Blanc his own radio program, *The Mel Blanc Show,* which lasted only one year. While continuing his cartoon and other radio appearances, Blanc appeared in small roles in films, including *Neptune's Daughter* (1949) and *Kiss Me, Stupid* (1964), but he preferred to work behind the scenes. He frequently coached other Warner Brothers stars on the accents their roles required. Blanc also recorded novelty songs. His performances of "The Woody Woodpecker Song" and "I Tawt I Taw a Puddy Tat" sold millions of copies.

In 1960 Blanc received a star on the Hollywood Walk of Fame, and Hanna-Barbera Productions asked him to provide the voice of Barney Rubble on the first prime-time animated television series, *The Flintstones*. Blanc was also the voice of Dino the dinosaur and, later, the Rubble's son, Bamm-Bamm. That year, Blanc and Warner Brothers executive producer Johnny Burton founded a commercial production business, Mel Blanc Associates. The company had only been in business a few months when an automobile accident on 24 January 1961 left Blanc in a coma for three weeks. At one point, Blanc's doctor asked, "How are you feeling today, Bugs Bunny?" Still comatose, Blanc replied in the cartoon character's voice, "Eh, just fine, Doc. How're you?" Soon after, he regained consciousness. After three months, Blanc was released, but was in a body cast and confined to bed for the next seven months. His bedroom was converted to a ministudio, and Blanc recorded for television lying flat on his back.

When Blanc's son, Noel, took over Mel Blanc Associates in 1961, business started to boom. The company, which innovated the use of humorous and entertaining commercials—voiced by Mel and other voice actors like Daws Butler and June Foray—was renamed the Blanc Communications Corporation in 1973.

During the 1970s and 1980s, Blanc lectured at colleges and performed such cartoon voices for Hanna-Barbera as Secret Squirrel, Captain Caveman, and Magilla Gorilla. In 1984 the Smithsonian Institution asked Blanc to donate memorabilia from his career to its entertainment collection.

In 1987 Blanc provided the voices for Warner Brothers' first all-original animated theatrical release in eighteen years, *The Duxorcist*. Blanc also performed many of his classic characters in the feature film *Who Framed Roger Rabbit* (1988). That year he published a memoir, *That's Not All, Folks!: My Life in the Golden Age of Cartoons and Radio,* written with Philip Bashe. Blanc died in Los Angeles of heart disease and emphysema. He is buried at Hollywood Memorial Cemetery in Hollywood, California.

★

Mel Blanc and Philip Bashe, *That's Not All, Folks!: My Life in the Golden Age of Cartoons and Radio* (1988), is a detailed autobiography. Blanc's entry in *Current Biography* (1976), pp. 46–48, is a lengthy distillation of many sources. Obituaries appear in the *Los Angeles Times, New York Times,* and *Washington Post* (all 11 July 1989).

KEVIN LAUDERDALE

BOLET, Jorge (*b.* 15 November 1914 in Havana, Cuba; *d.* 16 October 1990 in Mountain View, California), pianist acknowledged as one of the great interpreters of the romantic piano repertoire, especially the works of Franz Liszt.

Bolet was the son of Antonio Bolet, an insurance salesman, and Adelina Tremoleda. Reared in a staunch Protestant household of six children, Bolet at age five began taking piano lessons from his older sister Maria, who had studied with Alberto Falcon, graduate of the Paris Conservatory and instructor at the Havana Conservatory. A few years later the precocious youth's playing at a soirée so impressed an American visiting from Erie, Pennsylvania, that she arranged an audition for Bolet for the scholarship-only program at the Curtis Institute of Music in Philadelphia. After his parents received confirmation of a September 1927 audition with Josef Hofmann, director of the Curtis Institute, and Mary Louise Curtis Bok, the institute's founder, a fund-raising concert with the Havana Sinfonica, at which Bolet performed, helped finance the trip. He was accepted as a student and began studying with David Saperton. On 29 January 1932 Bolet was among the students to perform at Carnegie Hall with the Curtis Symphony, under the baton of Fritz Reiner. He graduated in 1934.

During the year following graduation, Bolet traveled to Europe on a trip financed by the Cuban government. He attended as many concerts as possible for nine months before beginning his own concert tour in Amsterdam in 1935. He then went to London, Paris, Vienna (where he took a few lessons during the summer of 1935 with Morz Rosenthal), Berlin, Milan, and Spain. Upon his return to the United States, Bolet coached with Abram Chasins and

Jorge Bolet. UPI/CORBIS-BETTMANN

engaged in part-time studies at Curtis between 1936 and 1939, including some conducting with Reiner and additional coaching with Saperton. He was one of four young artists—out of 123—to win the Walter W. Naumburg Memorial Foundation Award (April 1937), which included a New York Town Hall debut. In 1940 he received Curtis's Josef Hofmann Award.

Summoned home for training with the Cuban army, Bolet was then assigned to the Cuban embassy in Washington, D.C., as assistant military attaché in 1943. Because of a 1944 change of regimes in Cuba, Bolet decided to enlist in the U.S. Army. After attending Officer Candidate School, Bolet served as musical director of Special Services with the American occupation forces in Tokyo. Responsible for providing musical entertainment to soldiers, he performed as pianist and also produced and conducted the Japanese premiere of Gilbert and Sullivan's *The Mikado* in 1946.

Discharged from the army that same year, Bolet became an American citizen in 1947 and resumed his professional career. He had signed a contract in March 1944 with Columbia Artists Management, with which he remained until 1973. During the late 1940s and 1950s he performed across the United States and in Europe, South America, and Cuba (where his brother Alberto conducted the Havana Sinfonica). Bolet looked back upon this period as "terrible years" of "half-starvation," where the remunerative recognition fell far below the rigorous routine and ambitious repertoire that he was building and refining. Bolet's recitals sometimes opened with Haydn or Mozart and then concentrated upon Beethoven, Schubert, Schumann, Liszt, Chopin, Franck, Debussy, Rachmaninoff, or Prokofiev, as well as certain contemporary works and premieres. His concerto repertoire included Beethoven, Schumann, Liszt, Tchaikovsky, Grieg, Rachmaninoff, and Prokofiev. His early recording contracts were with Remington Records and Boston Records. With rare exceptions, he played exclusively on the Baldwin piano throughout his professional life.

Hollywood supercharged his name recognition with screen credit for performing the piano music in *Song Without End* (1960), a film about Liszt, played by Dirk Bogarde. In the fall of 1961 Bolet engaged in a ten-concert, twenty-six-day tour of Poland. On 31 October 1962, he celebrated the silver anniversary of his New York debut with a Carnegie Hall concert. He became a professor at Indiana University's School of Music in 1968, where he taught until 1977, when he became head of the piano department at Curtis.

One particularly memorable Bolet appearance took place when he was asked to stand in for a performance of Liszt's *Totentanz* for the 1971 gala opening of the New York Philharmonic's season under the baton of Pierre Boulez. Bolet's outstanding performance boosted his already secure reputation. He received recording contracts with RCA and London-Decca; RCA recorded his concert at Carnegie Hall on 25 February 1974. At the end of that year he appeared in the eight-piano gala at London's Festival Hall (9 December) to assist in fund-raising for New York's International Piano Library.

Despite his many performances, Bolet remained dedicated to teaching piano students, to whom he felt a moral obligation to hand down the romantic tradition. He continued giving master classes (frequently televised on closed circuit) across the country, arranging recording sessions, performing on foreign radio stations, and maintaining his rigorous national and international tours (which, even up through his final years, averaged about 100 to 150 concerts yearly). He also played chamber music.

During the 1980s Bolet toured in South Africa, the Far East, and Australia and gave two five-part series of performances and master classes for BBC-TV with the BBC Scottish Symphony. His final recording sessions took place in March 1989; his last Carnegie Hall concert was on 16 April; and his final public performance was on 8 June in West Berlin. During the summer, he underwent brain surgery, from which he never fully recovered. He died at home of heart failure. He never married.

Bolet's death represented the passing of an era, because he was one of the last of the titan romantics. His numerous Liszt recordings testify to his reputation as a master interpreter of that composer; three times he earned the Grand Prix du Disque.

Bolet was a princely poet of the piano, who created an aura of sublime magnificence during his performances. With his imposing but elegant six-foot, two-inch physique, huge hand extension, and formal white-tie-and-tails attire, he had a colossal presence, counterpoised with refined delicacy of musical interpretation. He epitomized the ideal of artistic moderation; he tried to make the music "sing," as he used to say, by use of his pianistic palette of warm tones, a wide range of nuances preferred over abrupt tempo changes, clear delivery of line, controlled pedal application, and tasteful flamboyance, especially in the most frequently abused passages of Liszt. His stated artistic vision was to convince his audience that his performance at any given time was the only interpretation possible and that the performer and the composer seemed to be one and the same person.

★

Articles by Bolet include "You Need More than Talent! Courage and Tireless Effort Are Necessary to Complement the Talent of the Artist in Public Life," *Etude* 69 (Nov. 1951): 23, 56; "Impersonating a Great Pianist" (about performing for *Song Without End*), *Music Journal* 17 (Oct. 1959): 16–17; and "Judging a Piano Competition," *Music Journal* 21 (May 1963): 24–26. Interviews include Bryce Morrison, *Music and Musicians* 24 (May 1977): 16, 18, 20; Dean Elder, *Clavier* 22 (Oct. 1983): 14–17; Robert J. Silverman, *Piano Quarterly* 34 (spring 1986): 15–16, 18–21; and Vincent Alfano, *Fanfare* 9 (July/Aug. 1986): 332–339.

Detailed entries on Bolet are in David Ewen, comp. and ed., *Musicians Since 1900* (1978); Harold C. Schonberg, *The Great Pianists* (rev. ed. 1987); Elyse Mach, "Jorge Bolet," *Great Pianists Speak for Themselves*, vol. 2 (1988); and Stephen Husarik and Marilyn J. Joyce, eds., *American Keyboard Artists* (1989), which includes a listing of London/Decca recordings. Obituaries are in the *New York Times* (17 Oct. 1990), the *Washington Post* (18 Oct. 1990), and the London *Times* (18 Oct. 1990).

The Indiana University School of Music, William and Gayle Cook Memorial Library, has a collection of sound recordings. The Curtis Institute has a small collection of photographs, programs, recordings, and reviews.

MADELINE SAPIENZA

BOLGER, Ray(mond) Wallace (*b.* 10 January 1904 in Dorchester, Massachusetts; *d.* 15 January 1987 in Beverly Hills, California), lanky, loose-limbed actor, comedian, and dancer who starred in Broadway musicals, in films, and on television; he is best remembered for his role as the awkward, "brain"-less, but endearing Scarecrow in the classic 1939 film version of *The Wizard of Oz*.

The son of James Edward Bolger and Annie C. (Wallace) Bolger, Ray Bolger attended Dorchester High School. From an early age, he worked at after-school chores, selling newspapers, caddying, or delivering groceries or coal. At age sixteen, he attended dancing school and even learned a few routines from a former vaudeville performer who was working in Dorchester as a night watchman. For several years, Bolger worked variously as a bank clerk, a vacuum cleaner salesman, and a bookkeeper for an insurance company. All the while he took dancing lessons and performed in amateur shows.

After being dismissed from the insurance company, allegedly for dancing in the corridors, Bolger decided to become a professional dancer. In 1922 he joined the Bob Ott Musical Repertory Company, which toured small New England towns. He left the company to play vaudeville, performing with a partner, Ralph Stanford, in an act called "Stanford and Bolger: A Pair of Nifties." He finally won a small role in the Broadway musical *The Merry Whirl*, which later became *The Passing Show of 1926*. While with this show, Bolger was seen by producer-composer Gus Edwards, who hired him to tour the Orpheum circuit for two years. During this time, he met Gwendolyn Rickard, a fellow vaudevillian, whom he married in 1929; they had no children.

Bolger's unique dancing style—his air of amiable goofiness, his flapping arms, his rubbery legs—soon made him a valuable performer in musical comedy. In 1929 he appeared in *Heads Up!*, by Richard Rodgers and Lorenz Hart, and in 1931 he joined a stellar cast, which included Ethel Merman, Rudy Vallee, Willie Howard, and a chorus girl named Alice Faye, in a new edition of the revue *George White's Scandals*. Three years later, he starred with Bert Lahr and Luella Gear in a revue called *Life Begins at 8:40* (1934).

Bolger finally achieved major stardom when he appeared in the 1936 Rodgers and Hart musical *On Your Toes*. The show made full use of his talents as a comedian and dancer and also achieved landmark status with the ballet sequence "Slaughter on Tenth Avenue." Created and choreographed by the eminent George Balanchine to Richard Rodgers's music, the sequence showed, for the first time, that a dance could be both a separate entity and an integral part of the story line.

Although he had achieved star status in the theater, Bolger made only a few films in the 1930s, usually in supporting roles. Under contract to Metro-Goldwyn-Mayer, he had been featured in *The Great Ziegfeld* (1936), *Rosalie* (1937), and *Sweethearts* (1938). In 1939, however, he won the screen role that guaranteed him a measure of immortality. As the scarecrow in search of a brain, who joins Dorothy and her friends in a journey to the land of Oz, Bolger displayed a knockabout charm that endeared him to audiences. Many years later, Bolger remembered *The Wizard*

Ray Bolger. JERRY VERMILYE

of Oz as "a great experience . . . the most satisfying piece of work I've ever done."

Bolger's work in the theater continued into the 1940s. He starred in *By Jupiter* (1942), Rodgers and Hart's ribald musical set in ancient Greece; performed "The Old Soft Shoe" memorably in the musical revue *Three to Make Ready* (1946); and enjoyed a substantial hit with *Where's Charley?* (1948), Frank Loesser's sprightly musical version of the perennial farce *Charley's Aunt*. It was in *Where's Charley* that Bolger performed "Once in Love with Amy," which became his signature song for the rest of his career. (Bolger also appeared in the 1952 film version of the musical.) Bolger's later attempts to return to the musical stage, first in *All American* (1962) and then in *Come Summer* (1969), were not successful.

Over the years, Bolger continued to make occasional movies. He was featured in the Western musical *The Harvey Girls* (1946); costarred with June Haver in *Look for the Silver Lining* (1949), ostensibly about the dancing star Marilyn Miller; and played the leading role opposite Doris Day in *April in Paris* (1952). In 1961 he was the villainous Barnaby in Walt Disney's version of Victor Herbert's *Babes in Toyland*. Many years later, in 1979, he took on his first dramatic role, as an elderly priest in *The Runner Stumbles*.

On television, Bolger made his debut in 1952 on *The Colgate Comedy Hour*, then, in 1953, he starred for two seasons in a situation comedy first called *Where's Raymond?* and then *The Ray Bolger Show*. In 1976 he made an unusual dramatic appearance on television as Jack Lemmon's father in an American reworking of John Osborne's *The Entertainer*. His last performance in films was as a narrator in the 1985 dance anthology, *That's Dancing*, which included a dance by the Scarecrow that had been cut from the original release of *The Wizard of Oz*.

In the last years of his life, Bolger performed one-man shows, but he finally had to stop dancing in 1984 when a hip gave out as he stepped down from a stage in Coronado, California. He was elected to the Theater Hall of Fame in 1980. Bolger died of cancer and is buried at Holy Cross Cemetery in Los Angeles.

Nimble dancer, affable actor, and engaging comedian, Ray Bolger brought a special joy to whichever medium he graced with his talent. For audiences everywhere, the image endures of his Scarecrow, dancing merrily and hopefully down the road to Oz.

★

See Ray Bolger, "*The Wizard of Oz* and the Golden Era of the American Musical Film," *American Cinematographer* (Feb. 1978). An "Interview with Ray Bolger," by Mark Hagen, appears in *Films and Filming* (July 1985). Aljean Harmetz, *The Making of "The Wizard of Oz"* (1977), contains comprehensive information on the production of the film. Obituaries are in the *New York Times* (16 Jan. 1987) and *Variety* (21 Jan. 1987).

TED SENNETT

BOUDIN, Leonard B. (*b.* 20 July 1912 in Brooklyn, New York; *d.* 24 November 1989 in New York City), civil liberties lawyer who defended a number of controversial clients, including Paul Robeson, Julian Bond, Benjamin Spock, and Daniel Ellsberg.

Leonard Boudin was born into a family of lawyers. His father, Joseph Boudianoff Boudin, specialized in real estate law, and his uncle, Louis Boudin, was a constitutional and labor lawyer, an international Socialist, and a friend of Vladimir Lenin and Leon Trotsky. Boudin's parents were Russian-Jewish immigrants; his father was born near Kiev and his mother, Clara Hessner, came from the Buchawina region. The family lived in the East New York section of Brooklyn until the birth of Leonard's brother Arthur in 1920, when the Boudins moved to Richmond Hill, Queens. Leonard Boudin graduated from Richmond Hill High School in 1929. He majored in sociology at City College of New York, graduating in 1933 with a bachelor of social science degree.

Boudin earned his law degree in 1935 from St. John's Law School in Queens. He was admitted to the bar in January 1936 and joined Louis Boudin's firm. Leonard

Boudin married Jean Roisman, a clerical supervisor, on 20 February 1937. They had two children. From 1947 to the end of his life, Boudin's home was a duplex in a brownstone at 12½ St. Luke's Place in the Greenwich Village section of Manhattan. In 1947 Leonard Boudin and Victor Rabinowitz, another young attorney from Louis Boudin's law firm, established their own firm, and they remained in partnership until Boudin's death in 1989. Initially, they concentrated on labor law, representing the more aggressive of the left-wing unions.

Boudin first drew national attention in 1950, when he successfully argued the appeal for Judith Coplon, a Justice Department analyst convicted of espionage for passing secret documents to a Russian agent. He established that government prosecutors had illegally recorded Coplon's telephone conversations with her first attorney. In the fall of 1951, a group that included Corliss Lamont and Boudin's brother-in-law, I. F. Stone, founded the National Emergency Civil Liberties Committee, and in 1952 Boudin became the committee's general counsel. As a specialist in constitutional law, he defended hundreds of NECLC clients for alleged communist affiliation before House and Senate investigating committees.

Boudin often stated that his most important contribution to the law came in 1958, when he persuaded the Supreme Court that travel abroad was a fundamental right protected by the due process clause of the U.S. Constitution. In *Kent* v. *Dulles,* the Court, in a 5–4 decision, ruled in favor of the artist Rockwell Kent and against the State Department, which had denied Kent a passport on the suspicion that he was a communist. This achievement represented the culmination of eight years of work on behalf of several clients, including the actor and singer Paul Robeson, whose passport had been invalidated in 1950 for political reasons. Beginning in 1959, Boudin represented Cuba's interests in the United States as well as people who were criminally prosecuted for travel to Cuba.

During the 1960s, Boudin won several significant court victories based on the First Amendment. In 1965 he persuaded the Supreme Court to invalidate a statute that required the post office to obtain a signed receipt from an individual before delivering "foreign Communist propaganda." In 1966 Boudin represented Julian Bond before the Supreme Court. Bond had been refused his seat in the Georgia legislature when he issued a statement endorsing draft resistance. The Court ruled that such speech did not constitute "incitement" and was therefore constitutionally protected.

Boudin viewed the trial in 1968 of Benjamin Spock, the noted pediatrician, in Boston as the "showpiece" of intellectual opposition to the Vietnam War. Spock and three others had been indicted for conspiracy to counsel young men to evade the draft. Boudin argued that Spock's actions

Leonard Boudin at the time of the Benjamin Spock case, 1968. UPI/ CORBIS-BETTMANN

arose from a profound belief that the war was unconstitutional. After the four defendants were found guilty, the U.S. Court of Appeals for the First Circuit reversed the convictions on 11 July 1969 and stated that "vigorous criticism of the draft and of the Vietnam War is free speech protected by the First Amendment."

Boudin again tested the legality of the Vietnam War along with the issues of free press and access to government information in a case related to the Pentagon Papers. In 1971 Daniel Ellsberg and Anthony Russo were indicted for conspiracy, theft, and espionage for making available to the *New York Times* a study of U.S. involvement in Vietnam that had previously been secret. On 11 May 1973 Boudin's motion for dismissal of all charges was granted after it was disclosed that the White House and other government agencies had engaged in a series of illegal actions against the defendants, including a wiretap and a break-in of Ellsberg's psychiatrist's office.

Boudin tried to remain detached from his often controversial clients, but he had difficulty being objective when the client was his daughter, Kathy Boudin. Long active in civil rights causes and Vietnam War protests, Kathy Boudin had become a member of the Weather Underground, a militant offshoot of the Students for a Democratic Society. On 6 March 1970, she was seen crawling from the rubble of a townhouse in Greenwich Village that had been destroyed in an explosion in which three members of the Weather Underground were killed. Kathy Boudin remained in hiding for the next twelve years, during which time she joined a group committed to the black liberation struggle. On 20 October 1981, she was arrested in Nyack, New York, after the group attempted to rob an armored truck. A guard and two police officers were killed. As a participant in a crime that resulted in homicide, she was sentenced to a twenty-year prison term on 3 May 1984.

After 1971, Boudin took periodic leaves from his law practice to teach at Harvard, Yale, the University of California at Berkeley, and Stanford Law Schools. A dedicated legal scholar, he wrote scores of book reviews and articles on the courts and law. For several years after 1979, he acted for the Central Bank of Iran in a suit to recover Iranian government assets from the shah of Iran. Boudin died of a heart attack in St. Vincent's Hospital in Manhattan. His remains were cremated.

Boudin was a man of the left, as were most of his associates, clients, and friends, but as one stated, "his passion was the law, not politics." In nineteen cases before the Supreme Court and dozens at the appellate level, Leonard Boudin dedicated his skill as a litigator and his knowledge of constitutional law to protecting the individual's freedoms as guaranteed under the Bill of Rights.

★

Informative works about Boudin are Marlise James, "Leonard Boudin and the National Emergency Civil Liberties Committee," in *The People's Lawyers* (1973), pp. 15–23; and Paul Wilkes, "Leonard Boudin: The Left's Lawyer's Lawyer," *New York Times Magazine* (14 Nov. 1971). Four of his colleagues at New York University Law School wrote brief essays on his career after his death; see Norman Dorsen et al., "Leonard B. Boudin," *New York University Law Review* 64 (Dec. 1989): 1225–1238. An obituary is in the *New York Times* (26 Nov. 1989). Boudin produced a comprehensive oral history from 1980 to 1983 and in 1987 for the Columbia University Oral History Project, Columbia University, Butler Library.

KENNETH R. COBB

BOWLES, Chester Bliss ("Chet") (*b.* 5 April 1901 in Springfield, Massachusetts; *d.* 25 May 1986 in Essex, Connecticut), advertising executive, government administrator, diplomat, U.S. congressman, governor of Connecticut, and author whose inventiveness, liberal idealism, and capacity for public service helped direct American foreign policy toward a broader, more inclusive worldview.

Chester ("Chet") Bowles. ARCHIVE PHOTOS

Bowles was the youngest of three children of Charles Allen Bowles and Nellie (Harris) Bowles. His father, a sales agent for the wood pulp industry and a partner in a paper mill, was the son of Samuel Bowles, the publisher and editor of the Springfield *Republican,* whose liberal editorials in support of the Union during the Civil War and the opening of the American West influenced his grandson's thinking about American ideals, public service, and the role of government. Chester's mother was a homemaker. Bowles attended Springfield public schools through the tenth grade, when he was sent to Choate, in Wallingford, Connecticut. There he was a classmate of Adlai Stevenson and first met John F. Kennedy. From Choate, Bowles went to the Sheffield Scientific School at Yale University. A better golfer than an engineering student, Bowles regretted not pursuing a liberal education and took pains to educate himself about history, literature, art, and music.

After graduating from Yale in 1924 with a B.S. degree, Bowles worked for a year at the family-owned Springfield newspapers. His eagerness to restore the Springfield *Republican* to the status bestowed by his grandfather's liberal intellectual prominence ran counter to Bowles's cousin's view of how to best make the paper profitable. In 1925 Chester Bowles sought to begin a career in the Foreign Service, but his father's illness caused him to take a $25-per-week job as a copywriter at a New York City advertising agency, the George Batton Company, later Batton, Barton, Durstine, and Doyle. William Benton, also from Yale and subsequently Bowles's partner in Benton and Bowles, the advertising agency they founded in 1929, said, "Bowles came to the agency without the most elementary knowledge of how to write." His skill at writing advertising copy quickly improved, and Benton found in Bowles, given his enthusiasm, imagination, and inventiveness, a brilliantly creative partner in a business that grew through the Great Depression from an initial investment of $12,000 to a billing of more than $15 million in 1935.

Bowles was skillful at reading the temperament of the American public. He did his own market surveys, visiting low- and middle-income families that were coping with the financial strains of the period. That experience helped cement his liberal political ideology. Listening to American families tell him their daily experiences, and his belief in the quality of the products he was advertising, led Bowles to recommend to such major clients as Maxwell House, Bristol Myers, and Procter and Gamble that they lower their prices and improve the quality of their consumer goods in order to win a larger share of the market. Bowles made effective use of radio advertising. He introduced musical jingles and connected products to radio shows that had a continuity of character, setting, and theme.

Shortly after beginning his career in New York City, Bowles married Julia Mayo Fisk on 25 July 1925; they had two children and were divorced in 1933. On 22 February 1934 Bowles married Dorothy Stebbins; they had three children.

By 1941 Bowles was earning more than $250,000 annually and was searching for another career. Although he had been an early supporter of the America First Committee, Bowles volunteered for the navy when Japan bombed Pearl Harbor. Rejected from active service because of an ear injury, Bowles was recruited by Connecticut governor Robert A. Hurley to take over the administration of the Connecticut bureau of the Office of Price Administration (OPA), a war rationing effort established by President Franklin D. Roosevelt. From the beginning of his work for OPA, Bowles used his skill with the media, broadcasting regular radio spots to educate the public as well as politicians and businessmen about price controls as protection against inflation and profiteering. He advocated reasonable use by both manufacturers and consumers of such critical supplies as rubber, gasoline, fuel oil, sugar, canned foods, and meat. In 1943 President Roosevelt appointed Bowles director of the OPA. There, Bowles was responsible for overseeing more than 70,000 employees and 500,000 volunteers.

In February 1946 President Harry S. Truman named Bowles the director of the Office of Economic Stabilization, which was created to manage price controls against postwar inflation. Bowles submitted his resignation to Truman in April to protest congressional passage of the Price Control Act, which Bowles believed "would serve to legalize inflation."

Bowles turned to writing, service to the United Nations, and to state politics. In 1946 he ran unsuccessfully for the Democratic nomination for governor of Connecticut. Two years later Bowles again ran in the Democratic primary, this time winning the nomination and then the general election against Governor James C. Shannon. Governor Bowles, acting on his liberal, New Deal beliefs, was able to achieve reforms in Connecticut in the areas of housing, welfare, and child care. He was defeated by John Davis Lodge in his bid for reelection to a second term in 1950.

In 1946 Bowles went to Paris as a delegate to the first conference of the United Nations Educational, Scientific, and Cultural Organization (UNESCO). He continued to serve American interests in the United Nations both as a member of the American Commission for UNESCO and as a consultant to Secretary General Trygve Lie. In 1948 Bowles chaired a $2 million fund-raising drive for the United Nations Appeal for Children and made a fact-finding tour of Europe on behalf of the United Nations Children's Fund. The activities he undertook for the United Nations reflected and strengthened his beliefs that the United States would continue to prosper and democracy would flourish only if the wealth, know-how, and power of the United States were shared with those countries whose people had been ravaged by war or oppressed by colonialism.

In 1951 Truman appointed Bowles ambassador to India and Nepal. Bowles enthusiastically engaged in a campaign to " 'sell democracy' by practical demonstration—by American technical skills, American dollars, and American idealism." Bowles was impressed by Mohandas Gandhi and Jawaharlal Nehru's success at achieving democratic independence from Great Britain through nonviolence. While ambassador, Bowles and his family lived outside the official U.S. residence. The family learned Hindi, the ambassador rode a bicycle to his office, and his three youngest children attended Indian public schools. Bowles traveled throughout India, and his understanding of traditional village life influenced his advocacy for other developing nations in Asia and Africa.

Bowles resigned his position in 1953 when Dwight D. Eisenhower became president, and he returned to the United States to write and lecture, from a liberal Democratic perspective, on what he saw as America's obligation to provide economic and educational support to other countries. In 1958 Bowles ran and was elected to the U.S. House of Representatives from Connecticut's second district. He served on the House Foreign Affairs Committee.

In 1959 Bowles agreed to support John F. Kennedy's bid

for the Democratic nomination for the presidency and became the chief foreign policy adviser for Kennedy's 1960 campaign. He was also chair of the Democratic Platform Committee. Bowles was eager to educate Kennedy and to be named to the Kennedy cabinet as secretary of state, but the position was awarded to Dean Rusk, with Bowles nominated as undersecretary in 1961. Bowles took on the job of managing Foreign Service officials and replaced career staffers with outsiders and younger, liberal-minded diplomats sympathetic to the governments of the Asian and African nations where they were posted.

International crises plagued the first six months of the Kennedy administration. Bowles, who was increasingly concerned with what he perceived to be unethical, short-term, militaristic responses to serious international situations, was a clear dissenting voice in the 1961 Bay of Pigs fiasco, a CIA-backed attempt to overthrow Fidel Castro's regime in Cuba. When he countermanded Attorney General Robert Kennedy's directive for military action against the Dominican Republic the same year, Bowles became expendable. Tall and heavyset, Bowles, with his rumpled demeanor and his lengthy explanations of his liberal views on foreign policy, had little currency among the slick, pragmatic, tough young men of the Kennedy administration. In the "Thanksgiving Massacre" of 1961, Bowles was removed from his position in the State Department, but he was asked to represent the administration as the president's special representative for Asian, African, and Latin American affairs.

In 1963 Bowles was again made ambassador to India and served until 1969. He was diagnosed with Parkinson's disease while serving there. After returning to the United States, Bowles continued to study and write. *Promises to Keep,* a memoir of his public life, was published in 1971. Bowles retired to his home in Connecticut, where he died a week after suffering a stroke. A memorial service was held at Yale University's Battell Chapel on 6 June 1986. He is buried in Essex, Connecticut.

Chester Bowles was a man of many talents and enthusiasms. Sheldon Rodman wrote, "Next to courage and charm, stubbornness was the most dominant note in his character." An optimistic, liberal humanist; a master at administration; a best-selling author, Bowles, in David Halberstam's words, "truly believed in the idea of the Republic, with an expanded Town Hall concept of politics. . . . It was his view not just of America but of the whole world." A member of the Unitarian-Universalist church, Bowles taught Americans how to make the best of the Great Depression, of shortages during World War II, and of their emerging sense of world community.

★

Collections of the papers of Chester and Dorothy Stebbins Bowles are in the Manuscript and Archives Division, Sterling Memorial Library, Yale University. Chester Bowles, *Promises to Keep: My Years in Public Life, 1941–1969* (1971), is a memoir of Bowles's work in government and in the United Nations. Two of his other books, *Ambassador's Report* (1954) and *The Conscience of a Liberal* (1962), reveal episodes in his personal life and his thinking about world affairs. Cynthia Bowles, *At Home in India* (1956), is a description by his daughter of life in Delhi. Howard B. Schaffer, *Chester Bowles: New Dealer in the Cold War* (1993), is a thorough account of Bowles's ten-month tenure as undersecretary of state in 1961. Biographers and historians of John F. Kennedy include analyses of Bowles's politics and policies in their works, as in Deane Heller and David Heller, *Kennedy's Cabinet: America's Men of Destiny* (1961); Arthur Schlesinger, Jr., *A Thousand Days: John F. Kennedy in the White House* (1965); and David Halberstam, *The Best and the Brightest* (1969). Sheldon Rodman, "Chester Bowles," *Harper's* (Apr. 1946), gives an account of Bowles's work for the OPA and of his earlier work in advertising. Harris Wofford, "You're Right, Chet. You're Right. And You're Fired," *Washington Monthly* (July/Aug. 1980), discusses Bowles's positions on foreign policy and his stand against military intervention in Cuba, Laos, the Dominican Republic, Berlin, and Vietnam. An editorial by Roger Wilkins on Bowles written after his death is in the *Nation* (14 June 1986). Obituaries are in the *New York Times* and *Washington Post* (both 26 May 1986).

WENDY HALL MALONEY

BOWMAN, Thea Bertha ("Sister Thea") (*b.* 29 December 1937 in Yazoo City, Mississippi; *d.* 30 March 1990 in Jackson, Mississippi), the only black member of the Franciscan Sisters of Perpetual Adoration, who urged the Catholic church to embrace African-American culture.

Bowman was the only child of Theon Edward Bowman, a physician, and Mary Esther (Coleman) Bowman, a homemaker. Her Protestant parents sent her to a Catholic school, Holy Child Jesus, in Canton, Mississippi, because it offered the best education available to an African-American child in that part of Mississippi. The school was administered by the Franciscan Sisters of Perpetual Adoration, an order of nuns based in La Crosse, Wisconsin. Bowman converted to Catholicism when she was twelve.

Feeling called to religious life, she entered the novitiate in La Crosse in 1956, taking the name Sister Thea (she took her final vows in 1963). She studied at Viterbo College in La Crosse, where she received a B.A. degree in English literature in 1960. The next year she returned to Mississippi to teach at the Holy Child Jesus High School in Canton. Beginning in 1968 she studied English literature at the Catholic University of America in Washington, D.C., focusing on William Faulkner and on African-American literature. She received an M.A. degree in 1970 and a Ph.D. in 1972.

Sister Thea Bowman. ARCHIVES OF THE FRANCISCAN SISTERS OF PERPETUAL ADORATION

Sister Thea then returned to Viterbo College, where from 1972 to 1978 she taught African-American literature and was chair of the English Department. She also founded and directed the Hallelujah Singers. Known for its singing of spirituals, the group performed regularly throughout the United States.

In 1978 Sister Thea returned to Canton to help care for her sick and aging parents. She also became the head of the Office for Inter-Cultural Awareness for the Diocese of Jackson. In this position, she created programs that allowed Catholics of different cultural backgrounds to share their cultural traditions and to use them in worship. She encouraged African-American children to learn about their history and traditions and worked to make those traditions an integral part of the Catholic church.

Sister Thea also taught at Xavier University in New Orleans, where she was on the faculty of the Black Catholic Studies Institute. Her essay "Black History and Culture" was published in the *U.S. Catholic Historian* in 1988; in it she argues that "where Black culture is alive in our Churches, its vitality spills over into our communities." She thought that black culture could revitalize both the churches and poor urban or rural communities. During the 1980s Sister Thea participated in the National Black Catholic Congress, where she gave speeches and helped to formulate the group's national agenda. She explained that "when we understand our history and culture, then we can develop the ritual, the music, and the devotional expression that satisfy us in the Church." With this goal in mind she published a collection of black spirituals called *Songs of My People* (1989), in which she explicated each spiritual, tying its biblical themes to African-American history as well as spirituality.

In the article "Let the Church Say 'Amen!' " (*Extension,* March/April 1987), Sister Thea highlighted a particularly vital African-American congregation, the Holy Ghost Parish in Opelousas, Louisiana. As the largest and most active black parish in the nation, she presented it as a model for incorporating black spirituality into the Catholic church. A typical Sunday mass at the church was attended by some 3,000 people, and the congregation, led by the choir, readers, servers, and celebrant, sang and "moved in rhythms held sacred for generations." She argued that this type of physical and psychological engagement with religion was a gift and a lesson that could be imparted by African Americans to the wider Catholic community in America.

Sister Thea wore African-style gowns and wore her long hair in elaborate braids. She asked the church to adapt itself culturally to other peoples in order to retain its vitality and grow. In 1984 she began a six-year struggle with cancer. Despite chemotherapy, constant illness, and confinement to a wheelchair, she continued to be a spokeswoman for intercultural and interracial awareness. She battled her debilitating disease with grace and courage, asking only "Lord, let me live until I die."

Sister Thea Bowman gained a national reputation among Catholic leaders, convincing many to make their religious services reflect different cultural styles of music and worship. The innovations at the Holy Ghost Parish in Opelousas, Louisiana, and in Jackson, Mississippi, which Sister Thea lauded, have been adopted by other Catholic parishes whose revitalization is tied to building up new membership and generating commitment among African Americans.

★

Articles about Sister Thea include John Bookser-Feister, "We Are All Children of God," *Extension* (Apr./May 1989); Fabvienen Taylor, "Lord, Let Me Live Till I Die," *Praying* (Nov./Dec. 1989); and Mary Queen Donnelly, "Nun Brings Black Roots into Church," *Xavier Gold* (spring 1989). Obituaries are in the *New York Times* (1 Apr. 1990) and *America* (28 Apr. 1990).

ALISON M. PARKER

BOYINGTON, Gregory ("Pappy") (*b.* 4 December 1912 in Coeur d'Alene, Idaho; *d.* 11 January 1988 in Fresno, California), World War II Pacific naval air ace and recipient of the Medal of Honor.

Of mixed American Indian parentage, Boyington graduated from high school in Tacoma, Washington, and received a B.S. degree in aeronautical engineering from the University of Washington in 1934. He excelled in college wrestling and swimming. Having served in the Reserve Officers Training Corps as an undergraduate, he was commissioned a second lieutenant in the Coast Artillery Reserve, then enlisted in Volunteer Marine Corps Reserve while working full time as an engineer for Boeing Aeronautics in Seattle. From February 1936 to March 1937 he underwent flight training at the Naval Air Station in Pensacola, Florida. He then transferred to the regular Marine Corps and served with Aircraft One, Fleet Marine Force, at Quantico, Virginia, in fleet problems off aircraft carriers in the Pacific. After attending the Basic School at Philadelphia (1938–1939), he joined Marine Fighting Two at Naval Air Station, North Island, California.

On 26 August 1941, while serving as a flight instructor at the Naval Air Station at Pensacola, the brash, pugnacious, rebellious, and hard-drinking Lieutenant Boyington agreed to serve with the American Volunteer Group (General Claire Chennault's Flying Tigers). His contract read that he would be well paid and then reinstated in his service at the end of his tour. The good pay would be helpful because he and his wife had divorced, and he had three children to support (they lived with Boyington's mother and stepfather, Mr. and Mrs. Ellsworth J. Hallenbeck). At that time Boyington was horribly in debt, with a booze bill that was higher than his rent. He joined Chennault's corps near Rangoon, Burma. After the Japanese attack on Pearl Harbor, Chennault moved his group to Kunming, China. On Christmas Day, while flying over Rangoon, Boyington shot down six of the Japanese Army's Nakajima Ki-97 aircraft with his American P-40s.

Gregory Boyington. PAOLO COLETTA, U.S. NAVAL INSTITUTE IN ANNAPOLIS, MARYLAND

Despite Chennault's opposition and in violation of the Volunteer Group contract, Boyington was inducted into the U.S. Army Air Corps in July 1942. Wounded in a crash, he was evacuated to New York in July 1942. He then tried to get back into the Marine Corps, but because he had been charged with desertion, he was sent home to await orders. Only after telegraphing the assistant secretary of the navy did he receive orders to return to active duty in the Pacific as a major.

After serving as the assistant operations officer on a fighter strip on Espiritu Santo, in New Hebrides (west of Fiji), Boyington in May 1943 became the executive officer of Marine Corps Air Group 122 on Guadalcanal. Having broken an ankle in some free-for-all tumble, he was hospitalized in Auckland, New Zealand, in June. After passing two flight physicals, in December he was made the commander of six fighter squadrons, operating out of Guadalcanal, Vella Lavella, the Russell Islands, and Munda. With his planes being destroyed by enemy action, he obtained permission to gather pilots and planes into Fighter Squadron 214. Considered "ancient" at age thirty, Boyington acquired from his young colleagues the nickname "Grandpappy," soon shortened to "Pappy." Because reporters would not print the name given by his men to squadron 214, "Boyington's Bastards," he convinced them to change the name to the better-sounding "Baa Baa Black Sheep." His leadership principle was similar to that of his idol, "Chesty" Puller: "You can get along fine with the American boy if you show him and lead him and do not try to order him or drive him."

While flying the passageway between islands from Guadalcanal to Bougainville known as "the Slot," Boyington's squadron escorted bombers or flew alone. While flying alone, Boyington destroyed twenty-five Japanese Zero fighters and needed only one more to beat the world record, set by Captain Eddie Rickenbacker in World War I. He brought down his twenty-sixth while over Rabaul on 3 January 1944—and eventually destroyed twenty-eight—but then, shot down and wounded, he parachuted into Rabaul Harbor. Picked up by a Japanese submarine, he suffered privations, physical labor, and tortures for the next twenty-two months in captivity near Tokyo. Blindfolded, he was moved about frequently but managed to survive American aerial destruction visited on Truk and later on Saipan. He spent his last months of the war near Yokohama, where he restored his weight from 110 to 190 pounds by working in a kitchen and by being denied alcohol. Only after American B-29s dropped atomic bombs on Nagasaki and Hiroshima was he transferred to a prisoner of war camp and treated decently. He was rescued on 28 August 1945. He did not criticize the Japanese for their mistreatment of him but, rather, thanked them for keeping him off booze for a year and predicted that Japan would be a friend of the United States in the postwar years.

Upon his return as a war hero to San Francisco, Boyington kept his earlier promise to aviator friends to have a party in San Diego six months after the war ended. Held in San Francisco instead, the event garnered media attention, with *Life* magazine carrying full-page pictures of the drunken brawl. He nevertheless received the nation's two highest awards for valor, the Congressional Medal of Honor (5 October 1945) and the Navy Cross (1946), and then was ordered to speak at war-bond rallies for three months. He was given parades in Seattle, San Francisco, New York, and Chicago but felt that he was being used by the Marine Corps for publicity and, in his last speech, called his audience "slobs." An aerial artist with fighter planes, he had skillfully led the Black Sheep in downing ninety-six Japanese planes in eighty-six days, becoming the Marines' most flamboyant aviator. He was retired on 1 August 1947 with the rank of colonel because of his injuries, but without a pension except for the small stipend given to Medal of Honor holders.

During the postwar years Boyington worked as a beer salesman and refereed wrestling matches until the fans turned on him for his drunkenness. His hobbies included writing and painting. Although short, cocky, and homely, he was attractive to women and married four times, the last time to Josephine Wilson Moseman, who survived him. Friends auctioned off some of his paintings—mostly desert landscapes—to clear up his debts. He died of cancer and is buried at Arlington National Cemetery.

★

Boyington's autobiography, *Baa Baa Black Sheep* (1958), became the basis for a 1970s television series starring Robert Conrad. His experiences with Chennault are described in an autobiographical novel, *Tonya* (1960); Charles R. Bond, Jr., and Terry H. Anderson, *A Flying Tiger's Diary* (1984); and Daniel Ford, *Flying Tigers: Claire Chennault and the American Volunteer Group* (1991). A description of some of Boyington's aerial victories is in Robert Sherrod, *History of Marine Corps Aviation in World War II* (1952). His strategy and tactics are described in Office of the Chief of Naval Operations, Air Intelligence Group, Division of Naval Intelligence, *The Combat Strategy and Tactics of Major Gregory Boyington USMCR* (15 Feb. 1944). A sympathetic sketch is in *Leatherneck* 71 (Mar. 1988): 5. An obituary is in the *New York Times* (12 Jan. 1988).

PAOLO E. COLETTA

BRADSHAW, Thornton Frederick ("Brad") (*b.* 4 August 1917 in Washington, D.C.; *d.* 6 December 1988 in New York City), Harvard Business School professor who left academia to become president of Atlantic Richfield (ARCO) and chairman of RCA.

Bradshaw was the elder of two sons of Frederick Bradshaw, a bookkeeper, and Julia V. See. Raised in New York City, he graduated from Phillips Exeter Academy in New Hampshire in 1936 and enrolled in Harvard College, where he received his A.B. degree in 1940, in the same class with John F. Kennedy. That year Bradshaw married Sally Davis, with whom he had three children. He then attended Harvard Business School and obtained his M.B.A. in 1942. During World War II he spent three years in the Pacific theater, rose to the rank of lieutenant, and earned seven battle stars. He taught at Harvard Business School until 1952, rising to associate professor (he concurrently received a D.C.S. degree from Harvard in 1950). He shared an office with Robert S. McNamara before McNamara went to the Ford Motor Company. After McNamara left, Bradshaw

Thornton Bradshaw. COURTESY OF THE BRADSHAW FAMILY

noticed that a student parking facility was being constructed. When he realized he owned no car, he decided it was time he made some money.

In 1952 Bradshaw became a management consultant at Cresap, McCormick and Paget Company. One of his clients was Atlantic Refining, which hired Bradshaw as its treasurer in 1956. Atlantic Refining bought Hondo Oil Company, headed by Robert Anderson, who became chairman of the new company. Atlantic Refining then bought Richfield Oil Company to form Atlantic Richfield, known as ARCO. In 1966 Bradshaw became president of ARCO, where he remained until 1980. At ARCO, he presided over the discovery of the massive Prudhoe Bay oil field in 1967 and the construction of the Alaska pipeline. The legend in the oil business is that geologists had given up on Prudhoe Bay, but Bradshaw and others decided to try once more. Finally, they made the great find.

Bradshaw took pleasure in sending his photographer with infrared film to take pictures of the caribou frolicking and jumping over the pipeline. In fact, he took many positions portraying his concern for the environment. Under his leadership, ARCO developed a carpooling program that, in the mid-1970s, was used by 60 percent of its employees, and the ARCO Foundation gave $1 million for the purchase of Santa Cruz Island as a wildlife preserve. Bradshaw personally advocated a gasoline tax of twenty-five cents a gallon to foster conservation and to pay for further research into alternative energy resources, including solar energy and fusion energy. To the dismay of his oil industry peers, he favored long-range energy planning by the federal government, explaining, "Someone has to ensure the country has a long-term energy supply, and industry is not doing it."

In fact, Bradshaw took a wide perspective on business leadership in general. In an internal ARCO memo, he wrote that while the basic goals of private enterprise are to turn out needed products and earn a fair return, "the new dimension for business . . . is social approval. Without it economic victory would be Pyrrhic indeed." Bradshaw attracted attention in the oil industry and from the public at large by suggesting that the industry give up the oil depletion allowance of 27.5 percent in return for decontrol of oil prices. His successor, William F. Kieschnick, Jr., rightly typified Bradshaw's position as "unthinkable" to his colleagues.

A leading philanthropist, Bradshaw served as chairman of the John D. and Catherine T. MacArthur Foundation and as a board member of the Conservation Foundation. Under Bradshaw, the ARCO Foundation gave $75 million a year to hospitals, museums, and environmental organizations, among others.

Bradshaw's last challenge came in 1981, when he was chosen as chairman of the board of Radio Corporation of America (RCA). Under his leadership, RCA's earnings went from $41 million in 1981 to $369 million in 1985, and its stock quadrupled. Most of the increase was the result of the rebound of NBC, an RCA subsidiary, orchestrated by Grant Tinker, whom Bradshaw hired.

In 1985 Bradshaw closed the chapter at RCA by engineering a controversial buyout of the company, then earning $9 billion a year, by a larger corporation, General Electric. He believed the sale offered the best hope for preserving RCA's semiconductor and consumer electronics businesses. Bradshaw retired in 1986 but remained on the board of General Electric until his death.

A soft-spoken man who often appeared tousled, he made his home in Manhattan and also had a house on Martha's Vineyard, Massachusetts. Bradshaw and his first wife had divorced in 1974, and on 11 May of that year Bradshaw married Patricia Salter West, a writer; they had no children. He died of a stroke in New York City and is buried at West Tisbury, on Martha's Vineyard.

Brad Bradshaw's life was a seamless piece of industrial statesmanship. His academic training at Harvard University laid the foundation for a career that was capped as chairman of RCA. His high ethical standards and social concerns propelled him toward business leadership. It is fitting that the one-time business school professor became a model for business accomplishments and concern for the public interest.

★

An obituary is in the *New York Times* (7 Dec. 1988).

TOM FORRESTER LORD

BRATTAIN, Walter Houser (*b.* 10 February 1902 in Amoy, China; *d.* 13 October 1987 in Seattle, Washington), industrial physicist, inventor, educator, and cowinner of the Nobel Prize for physics in 1956; as part of a scientific team at Bell Telephone Laboratories, Brattain conducted semiconductor research that led to the invention of the transistor, a device that revolutionized electronic communications and decisively advanced the development of computers.

Brattain was the first of five children born to Americans Ross R. Brattain and Ottilie Houser. At the time of Walter's birth, Ross Brattain was employed as a teacher in a private school for Chinese boys. While Walter was still of preschool age, his parents moved back to their native state of Washington. His father then worked as a farmer, cattle rancher, and flour miller in the small town of Tonasket, Washington. Walter attended the Tonasket public schools, then enrolled in 1920 at Whitman College in Walla Walla, Washington, an institution from which both his parents had graduated. At Whitman, Brattain majored in mathematics and physics, graduating with a B.S. degree in 1924 and with election to

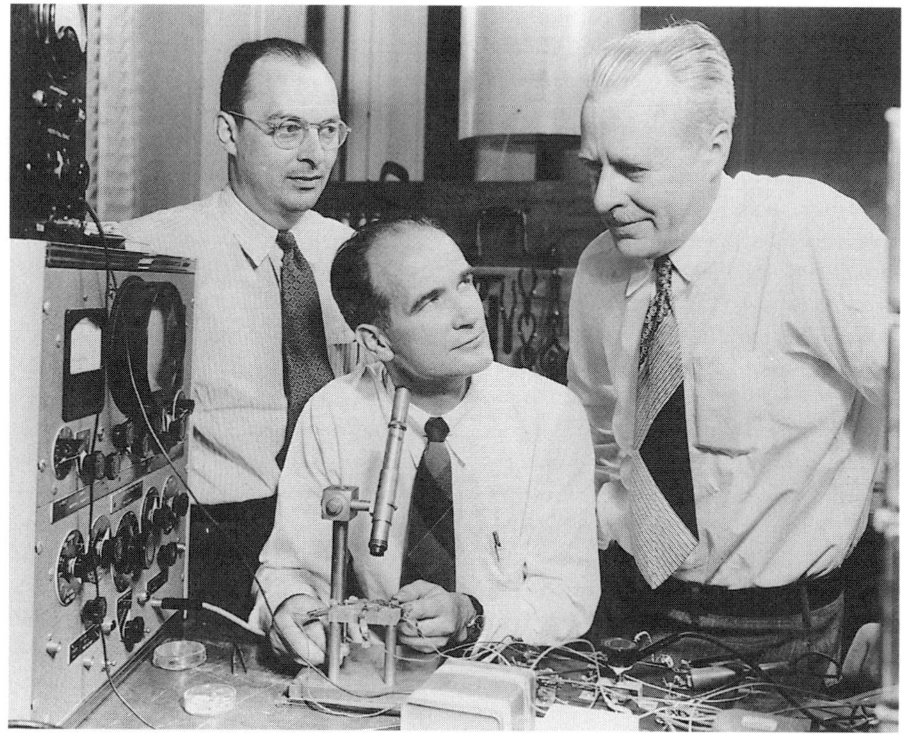

Walter Brattain (*right*), John Bardeen (*left*), and William Shockley (*center*) with transistor research equipment at Bell Labs in New York City, 1948. UPI/CORBIS-BETTMANN

Phi Beta Kappa and Sigma Xi, the scientific honor society. He then began graduate work in physics at the University of Oregon, receiving an M.A. in 1926. Continuing graduate work at the University of Minnesota, he received his Ph.D. in physics in 1929.

As he neared the completion of his doctoral program, Brattain applied for and received an appointment to the National Bureau of Standards in Washington, D.C. While finishing his doctoral dissertation, he participated as a member of the bureau's radio section in projects that included improvement of precision time measurements and design of a portable radio frequency oscillator.

After receiving his Ph.D., Brattain left the Bureau of Standards, and in 1929 he began his distinguished thirty-eight-year career as a research scientist with the Bell Telephone Laboratories in Murray Hill, New Jersey. Bell Labs was the most important nonacademic industrial center of advanced physics research at the time. During his initial years at Bell Labs (1929–1936), Brattain contributed to a variety of programs, including studies of infrared phenomena, thermionic emissions from incandescent surfaces, radio frequency standards, and general investigations of surface phenomena in solids under electromagnetic field excitation.

Brattain's most important experimental work began in 1936, when William Shockley, primarily a theoretical physicist, came to Bell Labs as the scientific head of the physics group concerned with semiconductor research. As its name suggests, a semiconductor is a substance the electrical conductivity of which is intermediate between that of excellent conductors like metals (such as copper or silver) and insulating substances that have extremely low conductivity (that is, high resistance to the flow of electric current). Shockley envisioned a device using semiconductors that would replace the large vacuum-tube three-electrode triode amplifier that had been invented in 1907 and that was found in nearly every radio set in the world. Triodes and related vacuum-tube devices with more than three electrodes were then widely used in the many systems in which electromagnetic wave generation, detection, and control were required.

At the time the group under Shockley initiated its work, a good deal was already known about many aspects of semiconductor behavior. For example, the practice of adjusting conductivity by temperature and illumination had already been established. The most important control, altering the conductivity by introducing a current (which in essence was the basis of the transistor) awaited difficult, frequently unsuccessful, efforts by the Bell Labs scientists.

Initially, the group decided to concentrate on silicon and germanium rather than on the semiconducting materials studied earlier—oxides of copper and zinc. They had determined that the silicon in which the flow of current at a point contact occurred in either a negative or positive direction could be prepared with attention to trace materials carefully introduced into pure silicon. Rectifying solid-state devices, analogous to vacuum-tube diodes, were built of silicon and germanium, but the important objective was to achieve current amplification, as in the vacuum-tube triode. Efforts in this direction were interrupted during World War II, during which Brattain and Shockley undertook military research assignments in New York City at Columbia University's Division of War Research. Brattain's activities involved developing technical methods to combat the German submarine threat to Allied ships.

Resuming research at Bell Labs after the war, Brattain worked on many experimental arrangements suggested by Shockley to create the semiconductor amplifier. These were unsuccessful until John Bardeen, a theoretical physicist, joined the group in 1946. Bardeen concluded that the earlier failures were attributable to insufficient attention to the buildup of electrons on the semiconductor surfaces. This insight led to an accelerated experimental program by Brattain to study semiconductor surfaces and confront the electron accumulation problem.

In 1947 the experimentalist Brattain and the theoretician Bardeen constructed a device consisting of a germanium crystal with two closely spaced gold contacts on one side and a third terminal contact on the opposite side. When an input electrical signal was introduced into one side of the crystal, an outgoing signal was obtained from the output terminal with an amplification factor of eighteen. This arrangement, subsequently designated by the inventors as the transistor (for *trans*fer res*istor*), was soon to be greatly improved. By 1950 Brattain, following a suggestion by Shockley, built the first junction transistor in which the point contacts were replaced by electron-deficient semiconductors on one side and electron-surplus semiconductors on the opposite side.

Although Shockley did not include himself among the transistor inventors, in 1956 the Nobel Prize committee for the physics award properly recognized Shockley's essential early and later contributions to transistor development, and included him in the 1956 award along with Brattain and Bardeen.

Brattain continued his semiconductor research at Bell Labs until 1967, when he reached the mandatory retirement age of sixty-five. In that year he returned to Whitman College, where he taught undergraduate physics and undertook exploratory research on the surface physics of biological cells until his retirement in 1972.

On 5 July 1935 Brattain had married Keren Gillmore, a physical chemist; they had one son. Keren died in April 1957, and on 10 May 1958 Brattain married Emma Jane Kirsch Miller.

Brattain received honorary doctorate degrees from his two alma maters, Whitman College (1955) and the University of Minnesota (1957). Other academic honors included degrees from Union College, the University of Portland, Gustav Adolphus College, and Hartwick College. He also received the Stuart Ballantine Medal of the Franklin Institute (1952) and the John Scott Award of the City of Philadelphia (1956), and in 1974 he was elected to the National Inventors Hall of Fame.

On 14 October 1987 Brattain died of Alzheimer's disease in a Seattle nursing home.

★

Three of Brattain's most important papers are "The Transistor: A Semi-Conductor Triode," *Physical Review* 74 (1948): 230–231; "Nature of the Forward Current in Germanium Point Contacts," *Physical Review* 74 (1948): 231–232 (both with John Bardeen); and "High Energy Electron Scattering and the Distribution of Selected Nuclei," *Physical Review* 101 (1956). His Nobel lecture, "Surface Properties of Semiconductors," can be found in *Nobel Lectures, Physics, 1942–1962* (1964). See also William Shockley, "Holes and Electrons," *Physics Today* 3, no. 10 (1950): 16–24; George L. Trigg, *Landmark Experiments in Twentieth-Century Physics* (1975); and Emily J. McMurray, ed., *Notable Twentieth-Century Scientists* (1995). An obituary is in the *New York Times* (14 Oct. 1987).

LEONARD R. SOLON

BREWSTER, Kingman, Jr. (*b.* 17 June 1919 in Longmeadow, Massachusetts; *d.* 8 November 1988 in Oxford, England), president of Yale University and ambassador to Great Britain.

Brewster was the son of Kingman Brewster, Sr., a lawyer and a direct descendant of William Brewster, who settled in the Massachusetts Bay Colony in 1620, and Florence Foster (Besse) Brewster, a housewife. He had two sisters. When Brewster was six years old, his parents divorced. His mother married Edward Ballantine, a Harvard University music professor, in whose home Brewster met such luminaries as Felix Frankfurter and Rudolf Serkin. Brewster spent his summers in Martha's Vineyard, where he developed a lifelong love for sailing.

After graduating from Belmont Hill School, Brewster in 1937 entered Yale. As an undergraduate, he founded a chapter of America First, and he was selected by his classmates as the student who had done the most for Yale. After graduating in 1941 with a B.A. degree in history, he worked for Nelson Rockefeller, coordinator of the Office of Inter-American Affairs. On 30 November 1942 Brewster married Mary Louise Phillips, a Vassar graduate, with whom he had five children. From 1942 to 1946 he served as an aviator in the U.S. Navy with the rank of lieutenant and flew patrols

Kingman Brewster, Jr., 1977. UPI/CORBIS-BETTMANN

looking for submarines in the Atlantic Ocean. In 1946 he enrolled in Harvard Law School, where he was note editor and treasurer of the *Harvard Law Review.* He graduated magna cum laude with an LL.B. degree in 1948.

Following graduation from law school, Brewster went to Paris as assistant general counsel to Milton Katz, U.S. representative in Europe for the Economic Cooperation Administration. Returning to the United States in 1949, he was a research associate in the Massachusetts Institute of Technology Department of Economics. In 1950 he accepted a position at Harvard as an assistant professor of law, and he was promoted to full professor in 1953, at age thirty-four. His areas of expertise were antitrust laws, international relations, and international commerce. During his Harvard years, Brewster published *Anti-Trust and American Business Abroad* (1958), which he coauthored with Katz, and *The Law of International Transactions and Relations: Cases and Materials* (1960).

In 1960 Yale University president A. Whitney Griswold, whom Brewster knew from his summers at Martha's Vineyard, invited Brewster to join the Yale faculty. From 1960 to 1963, Brewster was professor of law and provost, the second highest university official. Upon Griswold's death in 1963, Brewster became president of Yale, the first lawyer to hold this post.

As president, Brewster upgraded the graduate science and medical faculties, and he employed a committee of outside scholars to advise the university on curriculum changes. He revised the admission policies to decrease the number of sons of alumni admitted from 30 percent to 15 percent of the entering class. He also raised the ratio of public school graduates to private school graduates admitted and increased the enrollment of blacks from 2 percent in 1963 to 12 percent in 1977. In 1967 Harold Howe, U.S. commissioner of education, called Brewster "one of the most lively voices in higher education today." In 1969 women were admitted to the Yale undergraduate college.

Brewster, who did not avoid controversy, criticized administrators "who shrink like prunes in happy ideological conformity." He publicly opposed U.S. involvement in Vietnam and flagrant inequities in the military draft. In 1970, when Black Panthers were tried for murder and kidnapping, Brewster expressed his skepticism that they could receive a fair trial anywhere in the United States, drawing a virulent attack from Vice President Spiro Agnew. As student protests disrupted universities across the United States during the late 1960s and early 1970s, Brewster maintained relative peace at Yale with "a shrewd blend of diplomacy and discipline" (*Newsweek,* 18 Apr. 1977). He refused alumni demands to dismiss the Reverend William Sloane Coffin, Jr., the university chaplain, who was indicted for conspiring to counsel draft evasion, and Staughton Lynd, assistant professor of history, who traveled to Hanoi, North Vietnam.

Garry Trudeau, a Yale graduate, created in his "Doonesbury" comic strip a character, President King, who was based on Brewster. To the faculty, Brewster was, according to William Zinsser, "a hero for his defense of the democratic decencies in the late 1960s and for holding his university together when others were cracking throughout the Ivy League." He was also popular with the students. When Brewster received an honorary degree during the 1977 Yale graduation ceremonies, the students shouted, "Long live the King." However, toward the end of his presidency, financial support from alumni had dropped sharply and operating losses had increased.

Subsequent Yale presidents were highly complimentary of Brewster. A. Bartlett Giamatti said: "He was an immensely distinguished educational leader. He had an extraordinary sense for the values of the university and for how they meshed with the public good." Benno C. Schmidt added, "Kingman Brewster was the preeminent university president of his day—a man who stood for equity as well as excellence, change as well as continuity, and understanding as well as courage."

Although Brewster, who was six feet tall, was considered a colorless public speaker, he was admired for his skill in private dialogue. Proclaiming the merits of a liberal arts education, he said: "Perhaps the most fundamental value of a liberal education is that it makes life more interesting. It allows you to think things which do not occur to the less learned, and it makes it less likely that you will be bored with life."

In 1977 Brewster left Yale when President Jimmy Carter appointed him ambassador to Great Britain. In a speech, he explained his sophisticated opinion of British-American relations, saying: "It is the natural desire of each nation to use the other as an instrument of its own purposes and policies. By dint of our mutual dependence, your influence is amplified by our power. Our power is made more responsible and more effective by your influence." He believed that the special relationship between the United States and Great Britain was conditioned by a mutual tradition of common law. Traveling widely in Great Britain, he made opportunities to encounter people of various backgrounds, including workers, the aged, and the influential.

Leaving the ambassadorship in 1981, Brewster became chairman of the English Speaking Union of the United States. From 1981 to 1983, he was counsel to the New York City law firm of Winthrop, Stimson, Putnam, and Roberts. He was resident partner of that firm's London office from 1984 to 1986 and remained a counsel until his death. In 1985 he was elected to a five-year term as master of University College, Oxford University, an almost unprecedented position for an American. He held that office until his death.

Brewster served on numerous presidential commissions, including the National Commission on the Humanities (1963) and Law Enforcement and Administrative Justice (1965–1967). He was active as a trustee of the Carnegie Endowment for International Peace, the Saltzburg Seminar in American Studies, and the Reuters news agency and as a director of the American Council of Learned Societies. He was president of the board of directors of the Buckingham Society and a member of the International Board of the United World College, the Population Institute, the Council on Foreign Relations, the American Philosophical Society, the American Council of Education, and the American Academy of Arts and Sciences. He was an honorary bencher, Middle Temple; an honorary fellow, Clare College, Cambridge University; a fellow, American Bar Association; and a commander of the French Legion of Honor. His club memberships included Metropolitan (Washington), Athenaeum, Buck's (London), Tavern (Boston), Yale, and Century (New York). Brewster died of a brain hemorrhage.

★

Information on Brewster is in the *New Yorker* (11 Jan. 1964). An obituary is in the *New York Times* (9 Nov. 1988).

HENRY WASSER

BRICKER, John William (*b.* 6 September 1893 near Mount Sterling, Ohio; *d.* 22 March 1986 in Columbus, Ohio), lawyer, governor, and U.S. senator whose conservative Republican efforts to roll back the New Deal and Fair Deal while limiting the White House's power to shape foreign policy through treaties and executive agreements failed during the presidency of Dwight D. Eisenhower.

Born and raised in a farming community twenty-five miles from Columbus, Bricker and his twin sister, Ella, were the children of Lemuel Spencer Bricker and Laura King. While the family's commitment to farming never generated more than an adequate income, the children nevertheless enjoyed a comfortable, middle-class upbringing. After graduating from the Mount Sterling public schools and teaching for a year to help finance his college education, Bricker enrolled at Ohio State University in 1912. He served as president of his class and was president of the student Young Men's Christian Association, captain of the debating team, and first-string catcher for the varsity baseball team.

Although Bricker was offered an instructorship in the English Department upon his graduation in 1916 with a B.A. degree, he decided to enter Ohio State's law school. Admitted to the bar in 1917 even though he had yet to complete the program, Bricker interrupted his career at the start of World War I. He was rejected for the Officers' Train-

John W. Bricker. UPI/CORBIS-BETTMANN

ing School at Fort Benjamin Harrison in Indianapolis, Indiana, because of a heart condition. As a last resort to get overseas, he applied for and obtained a commission as chaplain with the rank of first lieutenant, but the war ended before he was ordered to Europe. Although his lack of participation in World War I was an opportunity lost in Bricker's eyes, it was not an absolute disappointment. He first met Harriet Day when he stepped off a troop train in Columbus, and the two were married on 4 September 1920. The couple adopted one son.

After graduating from Ohio State's law school in 1920, Bricker launched a lifelong career in public service. In 1920 he was first appointed public solicitor of Grandview Heights, a Columbus suburb. Three years later he was tapped to be assistant attorney general of Ohio, and in 1929 he was assigned to Ohio's Public Utilities Commission. Buoyed by his increasing stature and driven by an ambition typical of a politician on the rise, Bricker ran for the Republican nomination for attorney general in 1928. He fell short by nine thousand votes. Unbroken, he ran unopposed for the nomination four years later. Although a Democratic governor was elected and President Franklin D. Roosevelt carried Ohio, Bricker prevailed in his race for attorney general. He was reelected in 1934. In the Depression years Bricker redoubled his commitment to a tight-fisted budget. As attorney general he took great pleasure in sending $45,000 of unspent appropriations back to the state.

His ambition still unquenched, Bricker made an ill-fated run at the Ohio governorship in 1936. Roosevelt swept the state, and Bricker lost his bid to the incumbent governor, Martin L. Davey. Beaten but unbowed, he completed his comeback and claimed the state house in 1938, when Ohio went strongly Republican as a result of the 1937 recession, Roosevelt's efforts to reform the Supreme Court, and Democratic factionalism. Once inaugurated, Bricker made good on his campaign commitments to reduce the size of government and tackle public corruption. In addition to passing highly publicized antigraft legislation, he won acclaim for balancing the state budget and producing a surplus by the end of 1939. Believing that welfare was primarily a local responsibility, Bricker held state relief appropriations steady at $20 million for his first two years as governor. His austerity infuriated needy Ohioans and provoked the ire of national Democrats. Bricker appeared unmoved, lambasting the New Deal for "unblushing political immorality."

By 1940 Bricker had found his stride as a promising politician. His admirers dubbed him "Honest John." Standing six feet tall with a sturdy and healthy frame, his most prominent physical features were his shock of white hair and bright blue eyes. His demeanor was quiet and reflective, but he enjoyed the company of others and relished the opportunity to tell stories with political allies and college friends. While he forbade alcohol at the executive mansion, he smoked a pipe and appreciated a highball on special occasions. In addition to his unbroken passion for sports and the Cincinnati Reds and Ohio State Buckeyes, his hobbies included golf and fishing.

Bricker's life, however, was politics. Winning reelection in 1940 and 1942, he launched a brief campaign for the presidency in 1944 but never threatened the eventual nominee, New York governor Thomas E. Dewey. To balance the ticket with a midwesterner and to reward Bricker's steadfast opposition to the New Deal, the Republican national convention nominated the Ohio governor for vice president, but the Dewey-Bricker team fell to Roosevelt in the general election.

Bricker revived his political career in 1946 by embarking on a successful campaign for the U.S. Senate. Even though he called himself a "middle-of-the-roader," he based his platform on conservative Republican notions of antilabor legislation and the imminent danger of a leviathan executive committed to stripping the Congress of its rightful place within the national framework. Elected with fellow stalwarts Richard Nixon of California, Joseph McCarthy of Wisconsin, and William Jenner of Indiana in what was dubbed the "Class of '46," Bricker became an active member of the conservative Old Guard wing of the Republican party. Eager to whittle down the size of the national government and return power to individual states, he supported efforts to reduce taxes and tore into Democratic and Republican plans to provide federal subsidies for public housing. He voted against the Taft-Ellender-Wagner housing bill in 1947 and fought the National Housing Act of 1949.

Bricker matched his enthusiasm for an unfettered economy with an unbroken fervor to rid the nation of communist and radical tendencies. He supported the 1948 Mundt-Nixon bill, which required all communist and communist-front organizations to register with the federal government. Bricker gave unflinching support to McCarthy's campaign to expose and eliminate domestic communists and radicals. "Joe," he once told his Senate colleague, "you're a real SOB. But sometimes it's useful to have SOBs around to do the dirty work." In the field of foreign policy Bricker, like many of his midwestern constituents, was an unabashed isolationist. Part of his ideology was driven by his disdain for what he called "world government." A second variable in his thinking was his passion for smaller government. Although he was a devoted anticommunist at home, he battled efforts to extend federal dollars to noncommunist regimes abroad. He opposed the Truman Doctrine in 1947 and voted against the creation of the North Atlantic Treaty Organization in 1949.

Bricker's signal importance to post–World War II political history revolved around his campaign to strip the

White House of unilateral power in the realm of foreign policy. He carried his disgust for Truman's prosecution of what Bricker called a "one-man war" in Korea into the Republican administration of Dwight D. Eisenhower. Bricker alienated Eisenhower by launching a crusade to restrict the federal government's treaty-making powers. Reported favorably by the Judiciary Committee in June 1953, the Bricker Amendment contained several important provisions. First, it voided any part of a treaty that violated the Constitution. Second, it insisted that treaties, executive agreements with foreign powers, and international organizations had no power to dictate domestic policy without accompanying federal or state legislation. Third, the amendment mandated that all executive agreements be subject to Senate ratification.

Bricker's amendment won the backing of a wide array of conservative groups. Outside the Senate, the campaign was overseen by Frank Holman, the former president of the American Bar Association. Other interested associations that devoted unwavering support for the cause included the American Farm Bureau, American Legion, Daughters of the American Revolution, and Vigilant Women for the Bricker Amendment. Sensing that the amendment was a useful weapon in defense of states' rights and one more way to block national civil rights legislation, southerners endorsed the measure enthusiastically.

Determined to protect the power of the presidency from Republican isolationists, Eisenhower lobbied against the amendment. Privately, he described Bricker as "almost psychopathic" on the issue and sensed that the Ohioan was driven by "his one hope of achieving at least a faint immortality in American history." In January 1954 the White House committed its every resource to blocking the amendment. Eisenhower told the public that the amendment would alert allies and foes alike that America had decided "to withdraw from its leadership in world affairs." The president's efforts paid off. Battling from behind against heavy odds, the White House won a major victory on 26 February 1954, when the Senate failed to ratify a milder version of Bricker's amendment by a single vote. Just two days before the Senate had defeated the original text by the more resounding tally of 42–50. Bricker rightly blamed Eisenhower for the result, later telling his principal biographer that "Ike did it! He killed my amendment!"

Even though he was a prominent Republican who served as chairman (1953–1955) and ranking Republican (1955–1959) on the Interstate and Foreign Commerce Committee, Bricker's domestic record was unexceptional. In 1954 he betrayed the White House and voted against the extension of social security benefits to 10 million additional Americans and opposed the construction of the Saint Lawrence Seaway. His critics pointed to the fact that his Columbus law firm represented the interests of the Pennsylvania Railroad, one of the principal opponents of the project.

Bricker was contemplating retirement in 1958 when Eisenhower urged his former nemesis to run for a third Senate term. Expecting to prevail and encouraged by the president's support, Bricker declared his candidacy for reelection. Few observers gave his unknown Democratic opponent, Stephen M. Young, much of a chance. Young, however, highlighted Bricker's questionable dealings with his Columbus law firm and began to make up ground in the race. Young was helped most of all by a group of Ohio business leaders that met in June 1958 and decided to place a right-to-work referendum on the November ballot. Believing that the ploy was likely to inspire a heavy labor turnout, Bricker tried and failed to convince his allies to postpone the referendum. He lost the election by 155,000 votes and struggled to control his bitterness. Annoyed that Eisenhower had decided not to travel to Ohio to campaign for him and disgusted with the antics of the state's business leaders, Bricker wrote, "It is hard to take a licking, but it is worse when your friends do it to you."

In retirement Bricker devoted the bulk of his time to his law firm, of which he was now a senior partner. He also continued his service on Ohio State's board of trustees, to which he was appointed in 1948. Far removed from the political world, he attended his last Republican convention in 1976, where he supported President Gerald Ford against challenger Ronald Reagan. More and more his health failed him. Circulatory problems forced him into a wheelchair, and a series of small strokes resulted in the employment of a full-time nurse at his Columbus home. After Harriet Bricker died in 1985 he lost the will to live. In early 1986 he moved to a Columbus nursing home, where he died of congestive heart failure. Bricker was buried in Greenlawn Cemetery.

Bricker was representative of those conservative midwestern Republicans who tried and failed to reverse the accumulation of presidential power through the New Deal's reforms and the nation's commitment to a worldwide policy of containment. Many contemporary observers sensed that the downfall of the Bricker Amendment and his 1958 defeat signaled the erosion of conservative Republicanism, but it later became clear that the party's conservative wing had merely shifted from the Midwest to the South and the West. Bricker's ultimate place in the nation's political history remains contentious. Some assert that his greatest shortcoming was an inability to shuck off the norms of the 1920s and embrace a more modern America. Others argue that Bricker's contempt for an unbridled executive might have tamed the excesses of the imperial presidency and perhaps saved the nation from the tragedies of Vietnam and Watergate.

★

The bulk of Bricker's papers are housed at the Ohio Historical Society in Columbus. The best full-length biography is Richard O. Davies, *Defender of the Old Guard: John Bricker and American Politics* (1993). The most scholarly treatment of the senator's amendment is Duane Tananbaum, *The Bricker Amendment Controversy: A Test of Eisenhower's Political Leadership* (1988). For Bricker's views on the amendment, see Marvin R. Zahniser, ed., "John Bricker Reflects upon the Fight for the Bricker Amendment," *Ohio History* 87 (summer 1978): 322–333. Some historians have examined the amendment in article form. See Gary W. Reichard, "Eisenhower and the Bricker Amendment," *Prologue* 6 (summer 1974): 88–99; Terence L. Thatcher, "The Bricker Amendment: 1952–1954," *Northwest Ohio Quarterly* 49 (summer 1977): 107–120; and Cathal J. Nolan, "The Last Hurrah of Conservative Isolationism: Eisenhower, Congress, and the Bricker Amendment," *Presidential Studies Quarterly* 22 (spring 1992): 337–349. For Bricker's obituary, see the *Columbus Dispatch* (23 Mar. 1986). Bricker provided oral histories to the Columbia University Oral History Project in New York City and to the Dwight D. Eisenhower Library in Abilene, Kansas.

BYRON C. HULSEY

BRICO, Antonia Louisa (*b.* 26 June 1902 in Rotterdam, the Netherlands; *d.* 3 August 1989 in Denver, Colorado), pianist, teacher, and the first woman conductor to achieve international fame.

Antonia Brico at home rehearsing for the Metropolitan Opera, 1932. UPI/CORBIS-BETTMANN

Brico was the daughter of Johannes Brico and Antonia Shaaken, but nothing is known about her parents except that they died when Brico was two. In April 1907 she immigrated with her foster parents, Mr. and Mrs. John Wolthuis, to Oakland, California, where she attended school as Wilhelmina Wolthuis, the name her foster parents had given her.

When she was ten, Brico began piano lessons after a doctor suggested this remedy to overcome her nail biting. Soon she was performing at local churches and club meetings. Her original ambition to become a concert pianist changed after she heard an orchestral concert at a park in Oakland. Rather than limit herself to a single instrument, she decided to become a conductor because, as she later said: "The orchestra to me is the greatest instrument. It is to the musician what the palette is to a painter."

In 1919 Brico learned that her foster parents were not her birth parents, and she moved out of the Wolthuis home. That year she graduated from Technical High School in Oakland and enrolled at the University of California at Berkeley, where she received a B.A. degree with honors in music in 1923. Officially reclaiming her birth name, Antonia Brico, she moved to New York City, where she studied piano with Sigismond Stojowski for two years.

Armed with a letter of introduction to Karl Muck, the legendary former conductor of the Boston Symphony, Brico moved to Hamburg, Germany, in 1926. For the next four years, she served as Muck's apprentice, the only student he ever accepted. During this time she also attended the Master School of Conducting at the Berlin State Academy of Music, from which she graduated in 1927. In December 1930 she made her conducting debut with the Berlin Philharmonic, becoming the first woman ever to lead that orchestra. Of her performance, the *Allgemeine Zeitung* critic said: "Miss Brico displayed unmistakable and outstanding gifts as a conductor. She possesses more ability, cleverness, and musicianship than certain of her male colleagues who bore us in Berlin."

After a brief return to the United States to conduct the Los Angeles Philharmonic and the San Francisco Symphony, she toured Europe for two years, conducting concerts in Germany, Latvia, and Poland. A document from this period indicates that Brico was not then a U.S. citizen; no further evidence of her citizenship is available.

In 1932 Brico returned to the United States and settled in New York City. In 1933 she conducted the Musicians' Symphony Orchestra in two concerts at the Metropolitan Opera House, but she was denied a third when a male soloist refused to perform with her. Unable to obtain a conducting position with an established orchestra, she founded in New York the Women's Symphony, which she conducted from 1934 until 1938, garnering excellent reviews. For the 1938–1939 season, the orchestra included male musicians and was renamed the Brico Symphony Orchestra, but financial difficulty forced that group to disband after one season.

In 1938 Brico became the first woman to conduct the New York Philharmonic Orchestra. Of her concert at Lewisohn Stadium, the *New York Times* critic said her interpretation of Jean Sibelius's First Symphony "brought one of the most spontaneous and sustained outbursts of approval of the Stadium season." The review went on to praise the "life, color, and sanity of her readings [which were] expressed with effective verve and intensity."

Despite such positive reviews, Brico was unable to obtain a conducting job. In 1942 she moved to Denver, Colorado, where she taught piano and guest conducted. In 1945 she applied for but was denied the Denver Civic Orchestra conducting post. In 1946 Brico went to Europe to conduct concerts in Sweden, Austria, and Holland. At the invitation of Sir Adrian Bolt, she led the London Philharmonic in a concert in Royal Albert Hall. In Finland, Sibelius saw her at the podium and deemed her "a conductor of flame and fire." After discussing his compositions with her, he invited her to conduct an all-Sibelius concert in Helsinki.

Upon Brico's return to Denver in 1947, a group of amateur musicians invited her to lead the Denver Businessmen's Orchestra, the only permanent conducting post she ever held. From 1947 until 1985 she led the orchestra in five performances each year. In 1967 the musicians renamed the orchestra the Brico Symphony in her honor. Throughout the 1950s and 1960s, Brico toiled in obscurity in Denver, but a turning point came in 1971, when the folk singer Judy Collins decided to film a documentary about her. As a teenager, Collins had studied piano with Brico in Denver, and in 1952, Collins had been a piano soloist with Brico's Denver orchestra.

Antonia: A Portrait of the Woman, codirected by Collins and Jill Godmilow, was released in 1974. The film gives a picture of Brico's indomitable will, unshakable determination, and healthy sense of humor. However, in one scene Brico laments: "I have five performances a year, but I'm strong enough to have five a month! It's like giving a starving person a piece of bread." The film won critical acclaim and an Academy Award nomination, and it also briefly revitalized Brico's career. During the 1975–1976 season she conducted two concerts at the Mostly Mozart Festival in New York City and guest conducted other prominent orchestras.

After retiring from conducting in 1985, Brico continued to teach. She never married. In 1988 she broke her hip in a fall and was bedridden for the final year of her life. She died of natural causes in a Denver nursing home. Her body was cremated.

During Brico's lifetime, symphonic conducting was a male preserve. Arthur Judson, who managed the New York Philharmonic and the Philadelphia Orchestra, told her she had been born fifty years too soon, yet Brico felt the prejudice came from management, not musicians. "If the leader knows her business," she said, "the orchestra doesn't care whether it is a man or a woman." Early in her career Brico mastered the standard orchestral repertoire and won the support of the conductors Karl Muck and Sir Adrian Bolt and the composer Jean Sibelius. Reviews of her concerts were overwhelmingly positive. Nevertheless, after an auspicious start, Brico sank into obscurity in midcareer and regained brief prominence only in the twilight of her years.

★

The Antonia Brico Collection at the Library of the Colorado Historical Society in Denver, Colorado, contains Brico's personal papers, concert programs, news articles, an oral history collection, and audio and video materials. A catalog is available. Other material, primarily Brico's letters to Sibelius, is at the University of Helsinki Library in Helsinki, Finland. Informative magazine articles include L. Morris, "Pace of the Arts," *Pictorial Review* (May 1933); M. Rosen, "Antonia Brico: The Orchestra Is Her Instrument," *Ms.* (Dec. 1974), a review of Collins's documentary film about Brico; H. Saal and A. Kuflik, "Music, Maestra," *Newsweek* (18 Aug. 1975), an article about the Mostly Mozart Festival; and "Wielding Their Batons Too," *Opera News* (14 Feb. 1976). A review of her New York Philharmonic concert is in the *New York Times* (26 July 1938), and an interview is in the *Christian Science Monitor* (13 Nov. 1946). Obituaries are in the *New York Times* and the *Rocky Mountain News* (both 5 Aug. 1989).

SUSAN FLEET

BRIDGES, Harry (*b.* 28 July 1901 in Melbourne, Australia; *d.* 30 March 1990 in San Francisco, California), leading figure in the American labor movement.

Born Alfred Bryant Renton Bridges in the Melbourne suburb of Kensington, Bridges was the son of Alfred Ernest Bridges, a prosperous Australian real estate agent, and Julia Dorgan. Harry, as he was called, dropped out of school at sixteen and took a job as a clerk in a stationery store. It was the adventure novels of Jack London that drew him to the sea. He began his lifework in shipping as a merchant seaman.

In April 1920, while at port in San Francisco, California, Bridges left his ship and permanently entered the United States. He joined the Sailor's Union of the Pacific. While in New Orleans in 1921 during a dockworkers strike, Bridges joined the picket line and soon thereafter was arrested for his activism. Rather than serving to diminish his growing radicalism, his arrest spurred him on. Shortly after

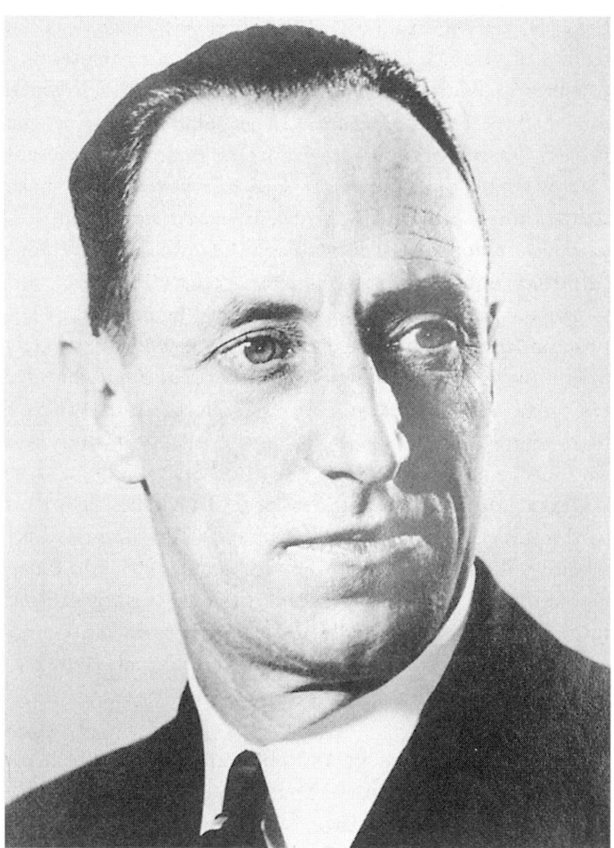

Harry Bridges, 1970s. ARCHIVE PHOTOS

the strike he joined the Industrial Workers of the World, or Wobblies, a radical union that followed an anarchistic doctrine that was anticapitalist.

In October 1922, having drifted away from the Wobblies but still a radical, Bridges returned to San Francisco and began to work as a longshoreman. Bridges had a hard time, as did many others, obtaining work on the docks. In order to obtain work, dockworkers needed to join the Longshoremen's Association, known as the "Blue Book Union," which was dominated by the large Pacific Coast shipping companies. Workers showed up each morning before dawn with their blue books paid up to join the "shape up," those waiting in line. The gang bosses would then pick the workers who were given work that day. Many found work only if they "kicked back" some of their wages to the hiring bosses, or otherwise ingratiated themselves to them. If the workers complained, or if they were known as agitators, as Bridges was, they were blacklisted. In 1923 he married Agnes Brown; they had one child, Jacqueline, before their marriage dissolved.

In 1924 and again in 1926, Bridges tried to form a local of the International Longshoremen's Association (ILA) to fight for workers' rights. But fear of the blacklist kept many workers away. The Great Depression of the 1930s only exasperated the conditions under which longshoremen worked. From 1933 to 1935 Bridges was one of the editors of the *Waterfront Worker,* a newsletter started by the Marine Workers Industrial Union, where he kept the idea of unionization alive.

In 1933 Bridges was instrumental in the birth of an ILA local in San Francisco. Employers retaliated with their blacklist, but the new labor policies of President Franklin D. Roosevelt (especially his 1933 National Industrial Recovery Act and the 1936 National Labor Relations Act) gave workers a much-needed edge. By 1934 Bridges had become the leader of the militant rank-and-file workers of the Pacific branch of the ILA. In 1934 Bridges led a general strike of the Pacific dockworkers. Bridges demanded union recognition, higher wages, and a coast-wide labor agreement. When Bridges's rank-and-file group received support from the Teamsters and dozens of other unions, employers and conservatives began to accuse him of communist intentions. Although the strike was a failure, most of Bridges's demands were met within the following eighteen months. The repressive actions—police use of gas, batons, and bullets—taken against his union and the public attacks aimed at him proved to be precursors of the McCarthyite attacks Bridges would endure in the coming decades.

Starting in 1934, after the strike, Bridges began "the march inland," as he called the organizing drive among the warehouse workers. Bridges believed that only if all workers who toiled on the ships, docks, and warehouses were organized would workers have the bargaining power they needed. His philosophy of industrial unionism was opposed in his own national union and within the American Federation of Labor. In 1937 Bridges brought the Pacific branch of the ILA, which he headed, out of the AFL and into the Congress of Industrial Organizations (CIO), then headed by John L. Lewis of the United Mine Workers. He reorganized the Pacific unions into the International Longshoremen's and Warehousemen's Union, of which he was president until he retired in 1977. He also became CIO director of the West Coast in June 1937, as well as a member of the CIO National Board.

As a spokesperson for the rank and file and an outspoken opponent of conservative craft unionism, Bridges found many allies among American communists. Because of this alliance and his status as an immigrant alien (Bridges did not become a U.S. citizen until 17 September 1945), conservatives and businessmen on the West Coast demanded his deportation as an enemy alien and a radical. Bridges was in and out of court for nearly twenty years. His enemies were never able to deport him, but their actions obviously sidetracked him at an important time in his union's history.

During World War II, Bridges, along with other CIO leaders, pledged unity for the war effort. The ILWU issued a nonstrike pledge in exchange for union security and wage increases. This unity lasted until 1948, when Bridges led the ILWU in a massive strike. The contract that the union signed retained the gains the union had made during the war. That Bridges was able to produce results while being attacked by the government, accused of communism, and confronted by a strong, unified employers group demonstrated his ability as a labor leader. The 1948 contract cemented his leadership among the union members. Bridges had married Nancy Fenton Berdecio in 1946; they had two children, Julie and Robert. After this marriage ended, he married Noriko Sawada in 1956, and the couple had one child, Katherine.

In the 1960s Bridges negotiated "mechanization and modernization" agreements. These agreements were the most controversial of Bridges's career. The contracts were prompted by a need to reduce labor costs and increase productivity. Bridges accepted mechanization—mechanical loading and unloading of the ships—as well as containerization—the use of prepacked containers. Rather than hand-loading cargo, workers would now load ships with containers, which could then be hauled on semitrailers. In exchange for this concession, Bridges received wage increases and higher pension guarantees. These contracts spelled the end to a way of life on the docks. When Bridges retired in 1977, the union he had founded was much reduced, and his acceptance of containerization had tarnished his reputation as a great man of labor since many workers blamed him, rather than the technology and changes in the industry and economy, for the downturn in their union and in their jobs. He died of emphysema at the age of eighty-eight; his ashes were scattered in the San Francisco Bay.

★

A biography is Charles P. Larrowe, *Harry Bridges: The Rise and Fall of Radical Labor in the United States* (1972). Other sources include Charles Madison, *American Labor Leaders: Personalities and Forces in the Labor Movement* (1962); Maud Russell, *Men Along the Shore* (1966); Bruce Nelson, *Workers on the Waterfront* (1988); and Robert W. Cherny, "The Making of a Labor Radical; Harry Bridges, 1901–1934," *Pacific Historical Review* 64 (Aug. 1995): 363–388. An obituary is in the *New York Times* (31 Mar. 1990).

RICHARD A. GREENWALD

BROYARD, Anatole Paul (*b.* 16 July 1920 in New Orleans, Louisiana; *d.* 11 October 1990 in Boston, Massachusetts), critic, columnist, editor, and essayist who, as a longtime book reviewer for the *New York Times,* helped shape the contemporary literary canon, and who in the last years of his life brought his critical faculties to bear on his own mortality.

Broyard, known familiarly as Buddy in his youth, was the second of three children of Paul Broyard, a carpenter and construction worker, and Edna Miller. In 1926 the Broyards moved from a predominantly black neighborhood in the French Quarter of New Orleans to the Bedford-Stuyvesant area of Brooklyn in New York City. His parents were both light-skinned African Americans, as was Anatole. Paul Broyard was able to pass for white and join the New York carpenters' union, which discriminated against black applicants; Anatole would, after his death, be accused of appropriating his father's racial subterfuge when he undertook a literary career. The family was a close one, but did not nurture Broyard's burgeoning intellectualism. As a teen he developed a fierce attraction to the European films and art then being imported to the United States.

After graduating from Boys High School in 1938, Broyard enrolled in Brooklyn College, which he attended for several semesters. In 1942 he married a black Puerto Rican woman, Aida; they had one child. In 1943 Broyard enlisted in the army, leaving his wife and daughter with his parents in Brooklyn. After attending officers' training school he was made the captain of a stevedore battalion based in Yokohama, Japan.

After his discharge in 1945 Broyard returned to New York City and, with money he had made in Tokyo's black market, opened a secondhand bookstore on Cornelia Street in Greenwich Village. In his memoir about this period, *Kafka Was the Rage: A Greenwich Village Memoir* (1993), Broyard described the postwar period in New York City as being "like Paris in the twenties." A devotee of postmodern culture, he immersed himself in the intellectual life of Greenwich Village, in what he called "the movements toward sexual freedom and toward abstraction in art and literature, even in life itself." His shop became a center of bohemian life, offering rare translations of European writers such as Louis-Ferdinand Céline, Paul Valéry, and Franz Kafka in the days before paperback reprints. Broyard and his wife separated in the late 1940s and were later divorced.

Taking advantage of the GI bill, Broyard attended the New School for Social Research on West Twelfth Street three nights a week. The New School in the years following World War II was a hotbed of European intellectual activity, as many of its staff were European émigrés; Broyard's professors included the existentialist psychiatrist Erich Fromm, who taught a celebrated class on the psychology of American culture, and the Gestalt psychologist Max Wertheimer. Broyard himself underwent psychoanalysis in 1946, but his preoccupation with literature undermined his progress: "I wanted to discuss my life with him not as a patient talking to an analyst," he later wrote, "but as if we were two literary critics discussing a novel."

Broyard began to achieve recognition as a writer beginning in the late 1940s, publishing essays of cultural criticism in such intellectual journals as *Commentary* and *Partisan Review.* He also contributed short stories to literary magazines; one of these, "What the Cytoscope Said," an autobiographical piece about his father's illness and death from cancer, published in 1954, garnered the attention of the publishing community, in which it was expected that Broyard was on the verge of a promising career as a novelist.

The expected novel did not materialize, however, and Broyard ended his association with the bookstore so that he could concentrate on an exhaustive regimen of reading, supporting himself through the 1950s by freelancing for advertising agencies and book publishers, and as a copywriter for the Book-of-the-Month Club. In 1958 he became a lecturer in sociology and literature at the New School for Social Research, where he taught an occasional class until 1979.

In 1961 Broyard married Alexandra ("Sandy") Nelson, a dancer of Norwegian descent who was just under half his age; they had two children. Sandy Broyard had a later career as a psychotherapist. In 1963 the couple moved to Fairfield, Connecticut, and Broyard took a full-time job as a copywriter with a Manhattan advertising agency, Wunderman, Ricotta, and Kline, commuting into the city on a daily basis. He remained with this company until 1970.

In 1971 Broyard was hired as a book reviewer for the *New York Times,* on the strength of several front-page reviews he had contributed to the *New York Times Book Review* in the late 1960s. His "Books of the Times" column showcased his knowledge of world literature; his vivid, exhilarating prose style; and his neoconservative views. He influenced the public reception of such authors as V. S. Pritchett, Anthony Powell, Paul Theroux, John Cheever, John Updike, and Eudora Welty. His emphasis was on literary quality and language. He was always emphatic and idiosyncratic in his opinions, and he could be brutal in his assessments, as when he wrote of Christy Brown, an Irish writer with cerebral palsy, "He is said to have typed his highly regarded first novel . . . with his left foot—but I don't see how the badness of his second novel can be blamed on that."

From 1978 to 1980 Broyard taught a creative writing class at Columbia University. In 1986 he became a senior editor at the *New York Times Book Review,* a position he held until 1989, when he was diagnosed with prostate cancer. It was at this time that he moved with his wife to Cambridge, Massachusetts, to undergo hormone therapy in Boston. After his retirement Broyard continued to contribute the monthly column "About Books" and the weekly unsigned column "Noted with Pleasure" to the *Book Review* up until his death. He had begun writing his Greenwich Village memoir in the late 1980s but shelved that project to focus on the subject that had become most vivid to him—his cancer. *Intoxicated by My Illness* (1993), a collection of essays that first appeared in the *New York Times,* rests on the premise that seriously ill persons must develop a "style . . . a narrative, a story" to cope with their disease. "Illness is primarily a drama," Broyard wrote, "and it should be possible to enjoy it as well as to suffer it."

Anatole Broyard died at the Dana Farber Cancer Institute in Boston. He was cremated, and a memorial service was held at the Congregationalist Church in Southport, Connecticut.

In his writing as well as in his life, Broyard was a consummate stylist. Associates described him as charming, handsome, and a brilliant conversationalist. His book reviews, erudite, lively, driven by metaphor and allusion, were sometimes criticized as being hyperbolic tours de force that called more attention to Broyard than to the books under review. The critic Ernest van den Haag wrote that Broyard frequently made "a tedious book appear less tedious—even when its tediousness is scrupulously remarked on."

Broyard's love of literary fiction was thought by some to extend to his personal life. Wanting to be known as a writer rather than as a black writer, Broyard, who for much of his life identified himself with the gentrified WASP culture of Connecticut, dissociated himself from his past and from his African ancestry, something for which he was criticized after his death, when the writer Henry Louis Gates, Jr., revealed Broyard's history of dissembling in "White Like Me," an article published in the *New Yorker* in 1996. Whatever judgment can be made about Broyard's life, however, does not negate the fact that his writing, what Alfred Kazin called his "grasping insistence upon recalling the immortal life in . . . books," points to inclusiveness, to his commitment to literature as a way of revealing the possible, of uncovering universal truths.

★

Anatole Broyard, *Men, Women, and Other Anticlimaxes* (1980), contains brief personal essays published between 1977 and 1979 about his life as an "exurbanite" in Connecticut. Henry Louis Gates, Jr., "The Passing of Anatole Broyard," in his *Thirteen Ways of Looking at a Black Man* (1997)—a reprint of "White Like Me," *New Yorker* (17 June 1996)—analyzes the implications of Broyard's efforts not to be ghettoized as a "black writer." Alfred Kazin, "Anatole Broyard, 1920–1990," *New York Times Book Review* (25 Nov. 1990), is a tribute. An obituary is in the *New York Times* (12 Oct. 1990).

MELISSA A. DOBSON

BRUHN, Erik Belton Evers (*b.* 3 October 1928 in Copenhagen, Denmark; *d.* 1 April 1986 in Toronto, Canada), one of the greatest ballet dancers of the twentieth century.

Bruhn was the only son of five children of Ernst Emil and Ellen Evers Bruhn. His father, who had worked as a civil engineer in prerevolutionary Russia, never had any real occupation in Denmark. His mother owned and operated a successful hairdressing establishment in Copenhagen. The couple separated when Erik was five. A serious child, Bruhn became withdrawn when he entered public school, and his mother felt he needed some outside activity. She enrolled him in the local dancing school that his sisters attended, and he excelled in his lessons. When he was nine, his teachers encouraged his mother to have him try out for the Royal Danish Ballet School, where successful applicants received both dance and academic training for free. In May 1937 he passed his audition and entered the school that fall.

The Royal Danish Ballet, part of the Royal Theatre, had been in existence for 200 years. For much of this time, it had specialized in the Bournonville style, named after its great ballet master August Bournonville. Children accepted in the school were often used in Royal Theatre productions as well as in ballets, and those who successfully passed the annual exams were eventually accepted as apprentices with the opportunity to join the company for life.

Despite a disastrous formal debut in the Tivoli Gardens on 4 May 1945, Bruhn became a member of the Royal Danish Ballet in 1947. That summer he traveled to London to study at the Metropolitan Ballet and so impressed the ballet's management that he was offered a contract as a principal dancer. Obtaining a leave of absence from the Royal Danish Ballet, he danced with the Metropolitan for six months.

In 1948 Bruhn returned to the Danish Ballet. Dancing the role of James in Bournonville's *La Sylphide* in 1949, Bruhn was noticed by Blevins Davis, president of the Ballet Theatre Foundation in New York. Davis persuaded Bruhn to dance in the United States, where he initially performed very little. Bruhn returned to the Ballet Theatre for the 1951–1952 season as a second soloist but received only lukewarm reviews from John Martin, the dance critic for the *New York Times.*

Bruhn, who had been granted several leaves of absence from the Royal Danish Ballet, was torn between feelings of obligation to the company that had trained and educated him and a hunger to learn dance styles other than the Bournonville system. Martin's criticism alerted Bruhn that he needed to go beyond technique in his performances, and he returned to the Danish Ballet to study with its new artistic adviser, Vera Volkova. He later said Volkova taught him that "technique was only a means to an end" and called her his "primary influence."

In 1953 Bruhn created his first choreography, *Concertette,* but the Danish management, objecting to his frequent absences, asked Bruhn either to stay permanently or to resign. He resigned in 1953 and joined the Ballet Theatre, which was soon renamed the American Ballet Theatre (ABT).

Erik Bruhn and Nadia Nerina in *Swan Lake* at Covent Garden, London, 1962. POPPERFOTO/ARCHIVE PHOTOS

In New York for the 1954–1955 season, Bruhn was scheduled to dance Albrecht in the ABT's *Giselle* with Alicia Markova. The performance on 1 May 1955 was a sensation. William Como of *Dance* magazine wrote that Bruhn had to be "considered the quintessential classical male dancer of his generation," and Martin, enthusiastic this time, said Bruhn's "dancing was like velvet." Bruhn was now a star. From the fall of 1955 to June 1957, he danced almost every night for the American Ballet Theatre, generally with Nora Kaye or Lupe Serrano. In May 1957, he created a second ballet, *Festa.*

Unfortunately, the ABT was in financial disarray by 1958, and for the 1959–1960 season Bruhn joined George Balanchine's New York City Ballet, where he danced with Maria Tallchief. In 1959, Bruhn showed a small choreographic study by Bournonville to Lillian Moore, an American critic. Moore convinced Bruhn to collaborate with her on a book, *Bournonville and Ballet Technique,* which was published in 1961. By the spring of 1960, the ABT was functioning again, and Bruhn and Tallchief joined its summer tour of Europe, which included the Soviet Union. The Soviets were so struck by Bruhn's dancing that the Bolshoi Theater Ballet directors asked him to dance with that company in an upcoming season. During the tour, the young Rudolf Nureyev, unable to see Bruhn himself, had a friend film Bruhn's performance. When Nureyev saw the film, he said that Bruhn was the "only dancer who could impress me out of my wits." The next year, Nureyev defected to the West and, introduced to Bruhn by Tallchief, lived with Bruhn in Copenhagen for several months in 1961. The Soviets, learning of the association, canceled all plans for Bruhn's visit.

In early 1962 Bruhn left the ABT to dance with Nureyev and the Royal Ballet in London. Although Bruhn and Nureyev were frequently compared, the critic Clive Barnes called them "very, very different dancers. . . . [Every] dancer and . . . the elite critics knew that Erik was the world's greatest male dancer." But Bruhn was devastated when the Royal Ballet finally hired Nureyev, and not himself, and he abandoned England.

In 1963 Bruhn was invited back to the New York City Ballet by Balanchine, who personally taught him the role of *Apollo,* but Bruhn never did perform the work, and he left New York shortly thereafter. In late 1964 Bruhn was invited to stage his first full production of *La Sylphide* for the National Ballet of Canada. He subsequently staged three other major works for the National Ballet, including a controversial *Swan Lake* in 1967. The company retained in its repertoire all of Bruhn's works. In 1967 Bruhn returned to the ABT as a guest artist with his longtime partner, Carla Fracci. Also that year he accepted the post of artistic director of the Royal Swedish Ballet, where he remained until 1970.

For many years, Bruhn had been plagued by severe stomach pains. In 1971 the pains were so serious that, after performing a final *La Sylphide* with the ABT, he officially retired from dance on 8 January 1972. He returned to Europe, where his health deteriorated further. During surgery, the doctors discovered that Bruhn had a perforated ulcer, which was ultimately treated successfully.

Following his recovery, Bruhn in 1974 joined the National Ballet of Canada for his annual teaching visit. The company appeared in New York that summer, with Nureyev performing as James in Bruhn's staging of *La Sylphide.* Bruhn, at age forty-six, danced the character role of Madge the Witch in this production, a performance that literally "stunned" Barnes. Despite his age, Bruhn danced Dr. Coppélius in his own production of *Coppélia* for the National Ballet (1975) and the title roles of *Petrouchka* (1976), José Limón's *The Moor's Pavane* (1977), and James Clouser's *Rasputin* (1978). He may have retired from the traditional classical roles, but for many years he continued to learn and dance major character parts.

From 1983 until his death, Bruhn was the artistic director of the National Ballet of Canada. He never married and had no children. He died in Toronto of lung cancer and was cremated. His ashes were returned to Denmark.

Erik Bruhn was a dancer's dancer. Handsome in a Nordic way, his technique was flawless, elegant, precise, and aloof, but when Nureyev first saw Bruhn, he found him "cool, yes—so cool that it burns." *New York Times* critic Anna Kisselgoff wrote at Bruhn's death that "passion was at the heart of every Bruhn performance." He was a highly intelligent and articulate man who constantly studied and restudied his roles, "destroying" himself so that he could become whatever persona the role demanded. He retained the acting tradition of his early training, and many observed that he created a powerful presence on stage without even moving. John Gruen, his biographer, noted that Bruhn was possibly the only male dancer to have successfully "bridged the gap between the *danseur noble* and the character dancer."

Kisselgoff found it "unjust" that Bruhn's name was never as well known outside the dance world as that of Nureyev, to whom Bruhn taught the role of James in his own *La Sylphide,* or Mikhail Baryshnikov. Yet almost every dancer who worked with him could not praise his abilities enough, and his partners often used the word "love" to describe their feelings for him on stage. Made a knight of the Order of Daneborg in 1963, he won numerous dance awards, including the Nijinsky Prize in Paris in 1963 and the Dance Magazine Award in 1969. Kisselgoff remarked that "paradoxically" the fact that Bruhn was not publicly well known gave him "a special and assured place in dance history. For anyone who claims to have a serious interest in dance is aware of Erik Bruhn's greatness as a dancer."

★

Erik Bruhn's "My Bournonville Background," the introduction to *Bournonville and Ballet Technique* (1961), describes his early training. John Gruen, *Erik Bruhn: Danseur Noble* (1979), is the best biography and is based on extensive interviews with Bruhn. Gruen's *The Private World of Ballet* (1975) includes another interview, in which the dancer discusses his relationships with Rudolph Nureyev and George Balanchine. Journal articles useful for an understanding of the young Bruhn and his dance background are Emily Coleman, "Ballet's Bruhn, a Rare Bird," Jerome Robbins, "Reflections on the Royal Danish Ballet," and Walter Terry, "The Royal Danish Ballet: Blithe Spirit and the Bournonville Bounce," *Theatre Arts* (Sept. 1956). In Eugene Palatsky, "Conversation with Erik Bruhn," *Dance* magazine (Feb. 1962), and Olga Maynard, "Erik Bruhn," *Dance* magazine (Jan. 1966), the dancer reflects on preparing for roles and on Balanchine as a choreographer. William Como, "A Tribute to Erik Bruhn," *Dance* magazine 55 (May 1981), and Anna Kisselgoff, "Erik Bruhn: Epitome of the Danseur Noble," *New York Times* (13 Apr. 1986), are excellent analyses of Bruhn's contributions to dance. An obituary is in the *New York Times* (2 Apr. 1986). The archives of the National Ballet of Canada are also an invaluable source.

SANDRA SHAFFER VANDOREN

BUBBLES, John William (*b.* 19 February 1902 in Louisville, Kentucky; *d.* 18 May 1986 in Baldwin Hills, California), vernacular dancer credited with creating a new style of tap dance known as rhythm tap.

One of eight children, Bubbles was born John William Sublett and attended primary school in Louisville. He received the nickname "Bubber" in childhood and began performing as a singer at the age of seven. He never learned to read music, and learned his songs by ear. By age eight, he had worked up a routine of the song "Walking the Dog" with one of his seven sisters. He was thirteen when he met Ford Lee Washington, four years his junior, who had already started out on his own career in show business. "Bubber" Sublett and Washington, whose nickname was "Buck," teamed up in an act called "Buck and Bubbles." Bubbles sang, and Buck accompanied him on the piano, standing up.

The two young entertainment prodigies performed in and around Indianapolis and between engagements worked at a bowling alley and, later, sold candy in theaters. After winning several amateur-night contests in Indianapolis, they began to perform in Louisville and Detroit, and finally, in New York City.

John Bubbles, 1980. UPI/CORBIS-BETTMANN

Bubbles arrived in New York City in September 1919, at the age of eighteen. His voice had changed in puberty, and he had begun practicing tap dance steps in order to add dancing to his repertoire. Full of confidence, he visited the Hoofers Club in Harlem, where all the great dancers met to jam and show off. When space opened up on the floor, Bubbles did his fledgling "strut and turn" dance step and was laughed out of the club.

Buck and Bubbles soon left New York, joining the Orpheum theater circuit and performing in the West. While Bubbles continued to sing on stage, in his spare time he practiced tap dancing with great determination. After a year with the Orpheum circuit, the team returned to New York. This time, when Bubbles showed off his routine at the Hoofers Club, he was greeted with hooting approval and applause.

Around 1920 Buck and Bubbles made their New York City debut at a Sunday afternoon benefit at the Columbia Theater on Broadway. That brief gig earned them a booking in 1922 at the Palace Theater on Broadway, then the most famous vaudeville theater in the nation. Many dancers came to watch them, for although their act included singing, music, and comedy, it was their tap-dancing skill that shone through.

The two wore ill-fitting stage costumes—shoes that were too big and trousers that were too short on one man, too long on the other. As the act opened, Buck sat at the piano and Bubbles walked onstage singing. Charging that Bubbles was not singing the song properly, Buck would bang out a stomping, up-tempo tune, whereupon Bubbles would launch into a voice version, adding tap steps. Buck would then rise from the piano and ask suspiciously, "What was that?" Bubbles would show him, and Buck would imitate the step, in lazy fashion. Bubbles would then launch into an energetic, complicated routine, in which the variations were endless, and which attracted the other dancers, who realized he was on to something new.

Bubbles's new style, which became known as rhythm tap, involved cutting the tempo in half, changing from two-to-a-bar to four-to-a-bar, giving himself twice as much opportunity to add new steps. The actual steps combined elements from traditional tap, including the Lancashire Clog and Buck dancing, but Bubbles accented the steps in an unusual fashion, creating offbeats with his heels and toes.

While the team performed to great demand at New York's vaudeville theaters, the heyday of black Broadway following the stunning success of *Shuffle Along* (1921) virtually passed them by, as it did most of the other great black dancers of the time. Their "eccentric" style of dancing was not in vogue. Buck and Bubbles were hired, however, for the *Ziegfeld Follies of 1931,* taking a salary cut from $1,750 to $800 per week for the privilege. After a rocky start in tryouts in Pittsburgh and elsewhere, the team became so popular that no one else in the show wanted to follow their act. When the *Follies* reached New York, the team augmented their income by performing concurrently at the Lafayette Theater in Harlem.

As their fame grew, Buck and Bubbles changed their act, dispensing with the comic garb. Billed as the stars of the 1939 World's Fair Edition of the Cotton Club Parade at the famed Harlem nightclub, they performed in white tuxedos. They were, as Bubbles put it, an "uptown [act] in a downtown style" (Fox, *Showtime at the Apollo,* p. 103). They never discarded their comic style, however. Wearing white tails, Buck would play stop-time piano in such a lazy fashion that he would fall off the piano stool, remembering to reach up from the floor just in time to plunk one note every sixteen bars. Bubbles's nonchalant manner contradicted the incredibly complicated routines performed by his feet.

Composer George Gershwin chose Bubbles for the part of Sportin' Life in the Broadway production of *Porgy and Bess,* which opened in 1935 and ran for eighteen weeks. Still unable to read music, Bubbles learned his songs by ear. He later went to Hollywood, where he did a stick-and-stair routine in the all-black film *Cabin in the Sky* (1943) and appeared in *A Song Is Born* (1948) and a few other films.

Although Bubbles's film career was a solo one, he remained with the Buck and Bubbles act until Ford Lee Washington died in 1955. After Washington's death, Bubbles virtually disappeared from show business until 1961, when he performed in a revue titled "Le Jazz Hot" at Carver House, a fledgling black nightclub in Las Vegas. Many blacks objected to Bubbles's singing "Shine," pointing out that the word was an epithet for "Negro." According to Marshall and Jean Stearns, authors of *Jazz Dance: The Story of American Vernacular Dance,* Bubbles responded indignantly, "Who's kidding? There really are people like that and at least it helps one colored man—myself—make a living" (p. 218). Carver House soon folded, but Bubbles's comeback had begun. In 1964 he joined the singer Anna Maria Alberghetti in a successful nightclub act. He made numerous television appearances on *Tonight* and several variety shows, toured Vietnam with Bob Hope's Christmas show, and made a record album, *Bubbles, John W., That Is* in 1964. In 1967 he suffered a stroke and was forced to curtail his career once more.

Twelve years later, at the age of seventy-seven and partially crippled by the stroke, Bubbles recreated his characterization of Sportin' Life for a one-night show titled "Black Broadway," produced by Bobby Short at Avery Fisher Hall at New York City's Lincoln Center for the Performing Arts. The show was repeated in 1980 for a limited run at Town Hall in New York City. That same year, Bubbles received the Lifetime Achievement Award from the American Guild of Variety Artists. He died at his retirement home in the Baldwin Hills section of Los Angeles, California.

Known as the greatest ad-lib dancer of his time, Bubbles was also widely regarded as one of the best all-around entertainers. During the heyday of tap he influenced a score of young dancers, notably Chuck Green of the Chuck and Chuckles team and Honi Coles.

Biographical information is provided in Donald Bogle, *Toms, Coons, Mulattoes, Mammies, and Bucks: An Interpretive History of Blacks in American Films* (1973); Ted Fox, *Showtime at the Apollo: Fifty Years of Great Entertainment from Harlem's World-Famous Theatre* (1983); James Haskins, *The Cotton Club* (1994); and Marshall Stearns and Jean Stearns, *Jazz Dance: The Story of American Vernacular Dance* (1994). An obituary is in the *New York Times* (20 May 1986).

JAMES HASKINS

BUHAINA, Abdullah Ibn. *See* Blakey, Arthur.

BUNDY, Theodore Robert ("Ted") (*b.* 24 November 1946 in Burlington, Vermont; *d.* 24 January 1989 in Starke, Florida), serial killer who murdered at least twenty-six women over a five-year period (1973–1978).

Bundy was the son of E. Louise Cowell, who gave birth to him in a home for unwed mothers when she was twenty-two. There is no official record of his father, a returning war veteran who abandoned Louise when she became pregnant. Bundy spent his early years in Philadelphia at the home of his maternal grandparents. In 1950 he moved with his mother to Tacoma, Washington, where they lived for a time with the family of Ted's great-uncle. That year his surname was changed to Nelson to disguise his illegitimacy.

Bundy's mother went to work as a church secretary and in 1951 married John C. Bundy, a cook at a veterans' hospital outside of Tacoma; he adopted Ted, who by 1961 had two half-sisters and two half-brothers. The family lived in a working-class neighborhood and regularly attended Methodist church services; according to Bundy he grew up in "a fine, solid, Christian home." Ted, described by those who knew him at the time as studious and somewhat aloof, graduated from Woodrow Wilson High School in Tacoma in 1965. An above-average student, he received a scholarship to the University of Puget Sound, where he studied for one year, commuting from home. In 1966 he transferred to the University of Washington at Seattle and lived in a dormitory, working in a series of jobs to pay his way through college.

He began as an Asian studies major and in 1967 took a summer course in Chinese at Stanford University, where

Ted Bundy in a Florida prison, 1986. UPI/CORBIS-BETTMANN

he struggled both academically and socially. In 1968, following a failed romantic relationship with a fellow student, Stephanie Brooks, Bundy dropped out of college and traveled across the country, briefly attending Temple University in Philadelphia in early 1969. He returned to Seattle and reentered the university there in 1970, living in a rooming house in the University District, where he would reside for four years. It was at this time that he began a seven-year romantic relationship with Beth Archer, who worked as a secretary at the university. She recounted their time together in *The Phantom Prince: My Life with Ted Bundy* (1981), under the pseudonym Elizabeth Kendall. In 1971 Bundy was employed by the Seattle Crisis Clinic as a work-study student. In 1972 he graduated with a B.A. degree in psychology.

Rejected from several law schools because of his low aptitude-test scores, Bundy went to work as an outpatient counselor at Seattle's Harborview Hospital and was briefly employed by the Seattle Crime Commission, where he coauthored a pamphlet on rape prevention. He was also involved in Republican politics, a longtime interest—in 1968 he had attended the Republican National Convention in Miami as a state organizer for the Nelson Rockefeller campaign. He was active in the reelection campaign of Washington governor Daniel J. Evans, and on the basis of Evans's letter of recommendation, Bundy was admitted to the University of Utah College of Law in 1973. Harboring political ambitions of his own, Bundy instead entered the University of Puget Sound night school, where he hoped to meet local power brokers. He became a salaried aid to the head of Washington State's Republican Central Committee and also worked for the King County Office of Law and Justice Planning. In the summer of 1974 he went to work for the Washington State Department of Emergency Services in Olympia, and in September of that year he moved to Salt Lake City after transferring to the University of Utah College of Law. Outward appearances suggested that Bundy, tall, slender, handsome, and articulate, had a bright career ahead of him.

Bundy's successful public image, however, was eventually overwhelmed by a highly secretive and compartmentalized aspect of his personality, which he later referred to as "the entity." This private self surfaced in pathological behaviors such as compulsive shoplifting and voyeurism, and in 1973 Bundy began to stalk and murder women. By August 1974 eight women, all but one of them college students, were missing in the Seattle area. That fall, the skeletal remains of the victims began to be found in remote locations throughout the region. In October 1974 similar disappearances began to be reported in Utah, coincident with Bundy's move to Salt Lake City, and in Colorado. All of the women were young and attractive; later their resemblance to Bundy's first girlfriend was remarked upon.

The crimes were dubbed the "Ted Murders"—one of the victims had last been seen in the company of a man calling himself by that name; this man reportedly drove a Volkswagen. Bundy was in fact implicated in the murders as early as July 1974, when Beth Archer anonymously tipped off police after seeing a composite sketch of the suspect. Bundy's carefully groomed public image, however, dissuaded authorities from pursuing the lead. In August 1975 Bundy was arrested for evading a police officer who had attempted to pull him over on a traffic violation; a search of his 1968 Volkswagen yielded items such as a ski mask, an ice pick, and handcuffs. In October 1975 he was identified in a police lineup by Carol DaRonch, whom he had attempted to abduct. He was found guilty of aggravated kidnapping on 1 March 1976 and sentenced to one to fifteen years in Utah State Prison.

In January 1977 Bundy was extradited to Colorado to stand trial for the murder of Caryn Campbell, who had disappeared from the Snowmass ski resort in January 1975. Her body was found the following month in a wilderness grave; she had been raped and beaten to death. Bundy had been linked to this murder through gas station receipts and travel brochures that put him at the scene. In June 1977, while representing himself at his trial, Bundy escaped through a second-floor window of the Aspen, Colorado, courthouse; he was captured after a week on the run. Six months later, in December 1977, he escaped again, this time from the Garfield County jail in Glenwood Springs, Colorado. He was named as one of the FBI's ten most wanted fugitives.

Bundy fled to Tallahassee, Florida, where he took a room on the campus of Florida State University (FSU) under the name Chris Hagen. Two weeks after the escape, in the early morning hours of 15 January 1978, he broke into the Chi Omega sorority house at FSU, murdering two women and seriously injuring two others; the women were beaten with a club, and one was sexually assaulted. He attacked another woman in a house blocks away. The following month Bundy abducted a twelve-year-old girl, Kimberly Leach, from her school in Lake City, Florida. Her mutilated body was found under an abandoned hog shed in April 1978. Bundy was apprehended in Pensacola on 16 February 1978 and charged with three counts of murder.

The Chi Omega trial was the first nationally televised murder trial in the United States. Throughout the week-long, highly sensational deliberations, Bundy, who again took part in his defense, maintained his innocence, claiming he was the victim of mistaken identity and a police conspiracy. He was convicted on 24 July 1979 and sentenced to death a week later. The key evidence was a bite mark on one victim's body that forensic experts matched to a cast of Bundy's teeth. On 7 February 1980 he was convicted in a separate hearing for the murder of Kimberly Leach. During the penalty phase of this trial, on 9 February 1980 in an Orlando courtroom, Bundy married Carole A. Boone, with whom he had worked in Washington State in 1974; they had one child.

Bundy maintained his innocence through ten years of appeals, during which his legal maneuverings continued to keep him in the news. In January 1989 he confessed to thirty-two murders in what some felt was a last-minute attempt to obtain yet another stay of execution. Twenty-six murders were officially attributed to Bundy; investigators believe he may have been responsible for many more. He was put to death in Florida's electric chair as a crowd of 300 people outside the prison cheered. His body was cremated.

In 1986 a New York City psychologist, Dorothy Lewis, diagnosed Bundy as having bipolar mood disorder, or manic depression. In interviews with Bundy's relatives, she found that Bundy's grandfather, with whom he had lived until the age of four, had been emotionally and physically abusive and that his grandmother had been treated for psychotic depression. On the eve of his execution in an interview with the Christian commentator Dr. James Dobson, Bundy said that in addition to having a "predisposition" to violent behavior, he had been "deeply influenced and consumed by violent pornography" beginning in his early twenties. This revelation was immediately taken up by conservative critics as proof that violence in the media influences criminal behavior.

★

Numerous true-crime books of a pulp nature were written about Bundy after his murder conviction; the best of these is Stephen G. Michaud and Hugh Aynesworth, *The Only Living Witness: A True Account of Homicidal Insanity* (1983; rev. ed. 1989), based on a series of interviews in which Bundy agreed to speculate, in the third person, on the mind of the perpetrator of the crimes of which he stood accused. Many popular magazines covered the Bundy story. See especially Jon Nordheimer, "All-American Boy on Trial," *New York Times Magazine* (19 Dec. 1978), and David Gelman, "The Bundy Carnival," *Newsweek* (6 Feb. 1989). Malcolm Gladwell, "Damaged," *New Yorker* (24 Feb. and 3 Mar. 1997), provides information on Dorothy Lewis and her dealings with Bundy, and on the neurological approach to the study of criminal behavior.

MELISSA A. DOBSON

BUNSHAFT, Gordon (*b.* 9 May 1909 in Buffalo, New York; *d.* 6 August 1990 in New York City), architect who was a leading exponent of modernism and who is best known for his glass and steel structures in the International Style.

Gordon Bunshaft was the first of two children of David and Yetta Bunshaft, emigrants from Russia who had settled in Buffalo, New York, the year before his birth. David Bunshaft was a furniture dealer. Gordon's parents doted on him; when he decided in 1929 to attend Massachusetts Institute of Technology and study architecture, they gladly paid his way; they even denied themselves a car in order to buy him one. Bunshaft received a B.A. degree in 1933 and an M.A. degree in 1935 and then proceeded to repay his parents many times over for their investment in him.

Bunshaft obtained work with a Boston architect, Harold Field Kellogg, who recommended him as a candidate for the prestigious Rotch Fellowship. Bunshaft's designs, through two rounds of competition, won him the fellowship, and in 1936 he began to explore Europe, learning about both traditional architecture and the new International Style. He returned to the United States when his money ran out and went to work in New York City, first for Edward Durell Stone, a previous Rotch Fellowship winner, then for the industrial designer Raymond Loewy, and finally, in 1937, for Louis Skidmore, another Rotch Fellowship holder. Skidmore, in partnership with Nathaniel Owings, was working on designs for the 1939 New York World's Fair. Bunshaft would stay with Skidmore and Owings for forty-two years.

Gordon Bunshaft. ARCHIVE PHOTOS

Bunshaft's first work for the partnership (which became Skidmore, Owings, and Merrill in 1939, when John O. Merrill joined the pair) was the Venezuelan Pavilion at the World's Fair, which shared with Bunshaft's next design, a hospitality building at the Great Lakes Naval Training Center, sheer glass walls and a dramatic slab canopy. When the United States entered World War II in 1941, Bunshaft enlisted first in the Signal Corps and then in the Corps of Engineers, where he designed field hospitals. In December 1943 he married Nina Elizabeth Wayler, a dancer; they remained together for the rest of his life. They had no children.

Bunshaft's first mature work was Manhattan House, a block-long apartment complex in New York City completed in 1950. It featured a glass-enclosed lobby, which had by this time become a Bunshaft trademark, and offered prospective tenants large rooms with both traditional amenities, like fireplaces, and contemporary touches, like full electrical service for air conditioners. Perhaps Bunshaft, a burly, pipe-smoking man, designed the space and amenities to suit his own preferences, for he and his wife were among the first to move in. Over the years they would fill their apartment, and the country house Bunshaft later designed for them on Long Island, with the contemporary art of which they were passionate collectors.

Two successful projects, the Fort Hamilton Veterans' Hospital in New York City and the H. J. Heinz Vinegar Plant in Pittsburgh, followed Manhattan House, and then his first masterpiece, Lever House (1952). Located on Park Avenue in Manhattan, its serene, blue-glass tower—heat-absorbing glass came only in limited colors—and garden courtyard—New York City zoning laws granted more space to developers whose buildings covered only 25 percent of a site—became integral parts of the modern architect's vocabulary.

Bunshaft followed this triumph with a series of magnificent structures that were described as glass boxes: the Manufacturer's Trust building on Fifth Avenue in Manhattan (1954), with its massive bank vault used as sculpture; the Connecticut General Life Insurance headquarters in Bloomfield, Connecticut (1957), his first exercise in designing a large-scale site; the Union Carbide headquarters in Manhattan (1960), as massive as Lever House is delicate; the Chase Manhattan (1961) and Marine Midland (1967) bank buildings, which together carve out a sculptural pathway through lower Manhattan's crowded alleyways; and, farther uptown, Nine West Fifty-seventh Street (1974), whose sloping sides outraged conservative architects and critics.

Meanwhile, Bunshaft was exploring new territory with a series of libraries and museums. Greatest of these was his design for the Beinecke Rare Book and Manuscript Library at Yale University (1963), where the structure that houses the books is encased in a windowless vault, described as a jewel box, which in turn glows as the sun penetrates its translucent marble walls. He also designed the Lincoln Center Library-Museum in New York City (1965), the Lyndon B. Johnson Library in Austin, Texas (1971), and the Hirshhorn Museum and Sculpture Garden in Washington, D.C. (1974). These museums were controversial, because when building them, Bunshaft consciously decided to set the needs of his clients first and therefore designed his buildings from the inside out. This decision produced buildings that fulfilled their primary goals but ignored certain outside demands: they were considered too aggressively modern for their sites, or they failed to mesh with neighboring buildings. It was a charge Bunshaft faced throughout his career, beginning with Lever House, when his design broke the traditional wall of masonry facades that marched up Park Avenue. For the taciturn and plainspoken Bunshaft, his defense then and every time was simple—the client came first.

Although Bunshaft formally retired from Skidmore, Owings, and Merrill in 1979, he continued to obtain commissions. He ended his career with two designs in Saudi Arabia: an air terminal that was to be used only one month a year, during the pilgrimage season, and a bank building in Jeddah. In these last projects his growing love of monumentality yielded both triumph and controversy. For the

Haj Terminal (1981), he constructed a series of bedouin tents, re-created in twentieth-century fiberglass and steel; the result is airy and traditional, yet functional. For the National Commercial Bank building (1983), he constructed a triangular monolith, forty stories high, with three 100-foot openings that let sun and air into a complex series of light shafts and garden platforms without exposing any offices to the heat and light of the Arabian sun. Like the nearly windowless Hirshhorn Museum, the result is magnificent within but controversial from without. Bunshaft was awarded the Pritzker Prize, the most prestigious in architecture, in 1988. He died of heart failure in his Manhattan House apartment two years later.

Gordon Bunshaft's career can be defined in one word: modernism. He brought the International Style to the United States, and he perfected it in a series of magnificent structures using the simplest post-and-beam construction and the purest of materials, glass and steel. Then, most effectively, he went beyond his high-rise and suburban triumphs to build a series of buildings unique in architecture, growing not out of convention but out of each client's desires and the possibilities of each site: the Beinecke Library, the Hirshhorn Museum, the Haj Terminal. Although these buildings did not share the unanimous triumph of his conventional designs, they helped to push back the horizon of what an owner can dream and what an architect can build.

★

Much has been written about both Bunshaft and Skidmore, Owings, and Merrill. Most useful are Carol Krinsky, *Gordon Bunshaft of Skidmore, Owings, and Merrill* (1988), and A. Drexler and A. Menges, *Architecture of Skidmore, Owings, and Merrill 1963–1973* (1974). An obituary is in the *New York Times* (8 Aug. 1990).

HARTLEY S. SPATT

BURNS, Arthur Frank (*b.* 27 April 1904 in Stanislau, Austria [now Ukraine]; *d.* 26 June 1987 in Baltimore, Maryland), economist and adviser to post–World War II U.S. presidents.

Born Arthur Frank Burnseig, Burns was the only child of Eastern European émigrés Nathan Burnseig and Sarah Juran, who settled in Bayonne, New Jersey. His father was a paint contractor, and young Burns received a tuition scholarship at Columbia University, working his way through college as waiter, shoe salesman, house painter, postal clerk, and summer sailor. Burns received an A.B. degree in 1921 and an A.M. degree in 1925 from Columbia. He began teaching in 1927 at Rutgers University, where he became an associate professor by 1933. He married Helen Bernstein on 25 January 1930; they had two sons. He received his Ph.D. from Columbia in 1934 and moved there in 1944 as a professor of economics.

Burns became a disciple of Wesley Clair Mitchell at the National Bureau of Economic Research in New York City, where Burns had begun studies of business cycles and their supposed regularity in the 1930s. In 1946 he published an important critique of the theories of British economist John Maynard Keynes. The economics profession had adopted a generally Keynesian outlook by the end of World War II, seemingly representing a validation of Keynes's *General Theory of Employment, Interest, and Money* (1936). Whereas most Keynesians were predicting a serious postwar recession, Burns emphasized the pent-up demand for consumer goods built up during the war and more correctly predicted relatively minor transition problems for the postwar years.

Burns acquired national prominence during the 1950s. President Dwight D. Eisenhower, whom Burns had met when the general was president of Columbia, had originally wanted to abolish the Council of Economic Advisers, which had developed into an active arm of the Truman administration after Leon Keyserling became its chairman in 1950. Instead, Burns convinced the president in 1953 to retain the council, with Burns as his first chairman. In this role, Burns presided over the first Eisenhower recession, recommending a fiscal stimulus (removal of the Korean War taxes), and by 1955, the brief post–Korean War recession had been turned around.

Burns warned Vice President Richard Nixon in March 1960 of an impending recession before the November election, and he recommended a tax cut of $5 billion to prevent the recession. Burns was overruled by Eisenhower, and the subsequent recession, producing an unemployment rate of 7 percent, may have cost Nixon the election to John F. Kennedy.

Burns resigned as council chairman at the end of Eisenhower's first term to return to academia as professor of economics at Columbia University and to serve as president of the National Bureau of Economic Research. He remained in policymaking under the Kennedy administration as a part-time member of the Advisory Committee on Labor-Management Policy. As the only conservative on the committee, he supported the Kennedy-Johnson tax cut in 1964 and went so far as to propose annual tax cuts thereafter.

Burns's most important policymaking role came in the Nixon administration, when he served as chairman of the Federal Reserve System ("Fed") from 1970 to 1978. In a speech given in 1970, Burns recognized the stagnation that was taking place in the late 1960s along with continued inflation—a development that was referred to as "stagflation" (see his *Reflections of an Economic Policy Maker,* 1978). As a result, he recommended a return to an incomes policy to confine wage increases to increases in labor productivity, similar to that introduced by President Kennedy in 1962. This idea was later incorporated into the New Economic

Policy that Nixon announced after a summit meeting at Camp David on 15 August 1971. Burns and all economists present were opposed to "closing the gold window," which in effect represented a partial devaluation of the dollar, particularly in relationship to the Japanese yen and the West German deutsche mark.

The devaluation of the dollar and its three-month downward float before the Smithsonian Agreement in December 1971 were engineered largely by Secretary of the Treasury John Connally and Nixon himself as a political move designed to ensure Nixon's reelection in November 1972. The plans for the devaluation were worked up in the Treasury by the so-called Volcker group, headed by undersecretary of the Treasury Paul Volcker, and the float represented a significant victory for the monetarist University of Chicago professor Milton Friedman, who had sent a secret memo to Nixon before the 1972 election recommending a float, rather than a system of fixed exchange rates. This action signaled the end of the central purpose of the International Monetary Fund, established as a result of the Bretton Woods Agreement. While fixed rates of exchange were temporarily patched up at the Smithsonian Agreement conference, the preceding events really represented the end of fixed exchange rates and the beginning of the era of "managed" floating exchange rates.

Burns's monetary policy before the Nixon reelection has been criticized as being responsible for serious inflation in the 1970s, but this seems doubtful. Burns was always militantly vigilant against inflation, and it seems likely that the stimulative effect of the devaluation and its pricing of U.S. products back into world markets account for the rapid growth, including a largely endogenous 9 percent increase in the money supply, before the 1972 election.

Burns left the Federal Reserve Board in 1978 when President Carter declined to reappoint him. He then established a base at the American Enterprise Institute, where he became a distinguished scholar. Burns criticized the early supply-siders and their tax reduction plans between 1981 and 1983 by stating that concrete action to reduce the budget deficit was more important than tax reductions aimed at "expectations" for future growth. Just as Kennedy had sent John Kenneth Galbraith to India to achieve his tax reductions, President Ronald Reagan dispatched Burns to West Germany in order to remove him from domestic economic-policy decision making.

Burns closed out his public service in the Reagan administration, serving as ambassador to the Federal Republic of Germany (1981–1985). He had a close relationship with West German chancellor Helmut Schmidt and resigned in 1985 after Reagan's first term. In April 1987 Burns underwent triple-bypass heart surgery, which was followed by complications and, eventually, his death at Johns Hopkins Hospital several weeks later. A memorial service was held under the aegis of the American Enterprise Institute on July 22.

Arthur F. Burns. CAMERA PRESS LTD./ARCHIVE PHOTOS

Arthur Burns can be classified a "pragmatic conservative." Although nominally a Democrat, he served primarily in Republican administrations. Nevertheless, he frequently advised moves that were against the grain of traditional Republican policy. He also opposed the "fixed throttle" of Milton Friedman—a steady growth of the money supply without Federal Reserve Board discretion—which would have neutralized monetary policy. Instead, he preferred that the Fed "lean against the wind," as practiced by his predecessor, William McChesney Martin. Because of his early work studying business cycles, Burns felt that a function of the Fed would be to reduce the amplitude of business fluctuations. As chairman of the Federal Reserve Board, he proposed that the chairman vote first rather than last, as evidence of "leadership." He opposed Supersonic Transport flights to the United States and assisted in rescuing Penn Central Railroad and the "Big Mac" bailout of New York City. Washington lawyer John Hawke, who served as Burns's general counsel at the Federal Reserve, claimed that Burns "had this pathological concern about compromising the integrity and secrecy of the Federal Open Market Committee debate." The FOMC was, in Burns's eyes, "the holiest of holies" in the Federal Reserve temple, according to his congressional liaison from 1971 to 1975.

★

Burns's publications include *Production Trends in the U.S. Since 1870* (1934); *Economic Research and the Keynesian Thinking of Our Time* (1946); *The Frontiers of Economic Knowledge* (1954); *The Management of Prosperity* (1966); and *The Business Cycle in a Changing World* (1969). An interview with Burns is Richard D. Bartel, "An Economist's Perspective over Sixty Years," *Challenge* 27 (Jan.-Feb. 1985): 17–25. An obituary is in the *New York Times* (27 June 1987).

LYNN TURGEON

BUSCH, August Anheuser, Jr. ("Gussie") (*b.* 28 March 1899 in Affton, Missouri; *d.* 29 September 1989 in Affton, Missouri), leading brewer and president of the St. Louis Cardinals baseball club.

The son of August Anheuser Busch, Sr., and Alice Edna Zeismann, August, Jr., had one brother and four sisters. His father was the son of Adolphus Busch, the founder of Anheuser-Busch, which at the time of his birth was an important although not the largest brewery in St. Louis. Gussie, as he was known, married four times. He married his first wife, Maria C. Church, in 1918; she died in 1930. In 1933 he married Elizabeth Overtown Dozier, who died in 1952. His third wife was Gertrude Buholzer, whom Gussie married on 22 March 1952; they were divorced in 1980. On 11 March 1981 he married Margaret Mary Rohde; she died in 1987. All together, Gussie had eleven children.

August Anheuser Busch, Jr. LIBRARY OF CONGRESS/CORBIS

Gussie attended the Fremont Public School and then the Smith Academy, a private school, but dropped out before graduating from the latter to take a job at the Manufacturers Railway Company and then the Lafayette South Side Bank and Trust Company of St. Louis, a small institution in which the family had an interest. Perhaps he would have gone to work at the family brewery had it been in operation, but during Prohibition Anheuser-Busch manufactured such products as soft drinks (including Bevo), yeast, ice cream, and refrigerated truck bodies. The company also owned coal mines, a small railroad, and the Adolphus Hotel in Dallas.

Gussie was twenty-two years old, recently married, and expecting his first child when in January 1922 he indicated his willingness to accept almost any kind of work at the company. He was told he would have to literally start at the bottom, washing bottles at the Bevo plant, driving trucks, and sweeping out.

After this combination indoctrination-hazing, perhaps imposed to see if he truly was serious about entering the business, Gussie was elevated in turn to the posts of assistant plant superintendent and then superintendent in 1924. In 1926 he was elected sixth vice president and general manager and joined the board of directors.

When Prohibition ended in 1933, Gussie was at the reopened brewery, which sent the first case of beer to President Franklin D. Roosevelt at the White House and the second to former New York governor Al Smith, both opponents of Prohibition. August, Sr., died in 1934, and as eldest son and first vice president, August's brother, Adolph, took his father's place as president of Anheuser-Busch. He would be responsible for overall leadership of the corporation, with special emphasis on the yeast business. Gussie, as the new first vice president and general manager, became the effective chief operating officer, primarily responsible for brewing and marketing operations.

Around the brewery, old-timers remarked that while Adolph was very much like his father in temperament, Gussie resembled his grandfather in approach and outlook. Both men were outgoing, enjoyed life, were optimistic about the nation and the business, and were natural showmen. They were gregarious and truly enjoyed the social whirl of their respective periods.

Gussie's major task was to reestablish the company's

leading brand, Budweiser. While there never was any doubt that it would survive, only a few brewers were prepared to stake everything on beer. Most intended to retain at least some of the profitable enterprises they had developed in the 1920s; others would be divested.

Anheuser-Busch's ice cream business was sold after repeal was certain, but the company retained the coal mines, railroads, and other properties, including the Adolphus Hotel. Indeed, the company even entered a new enterprise in 1935, producing a line of table syrups—Bud Waffle, Bud Crystal White, Bud Golden, and Delta. This was a logical outgrowth of its corn syrup business. The syrups were produced in New Orleans and sold in eight southern states.

Six months after the Pearl Harbor attack, Gussie entered the army with the rank of major in the Ordnance Department and spent the war working for the Pentagon on coordination of military procurement. He rose to the rank of colonel. His aides took over the brewery and executed orders communicated to them by Gussie. Adolph directed the company into war-related businesses, such as the creation and supplying of yeast for field rations. The firm also increased its sales of corn syrup, starches, and dextrines, especially to the armed forces. In addition, Busch-Sulzer, which manufactured truck parts, became part of Anheuser-Busch's War Work Division, which converted the vehicle department to the manufacture of glider fuselages, wing assemblies, and sheet metal parts for army field kitchens. Of critical importance was the production of apparatus used in the creation of antiaircraft guns. Busch-Sulzer also developed devices used on large warships to bring shells from magazines to guns, known as ammunition hoists, as well as many kinds of diesel engines.

The war had a major impact on the beer market. Although few within the industry seemed to appreciate it, the potential for national brands had been enhanced by the wartime experience. Ten million young American soldiers were taken far from their homes, and they came into contact with products little known in their parts of the country, including different brands of beer. This was particularly true for those servicemen who went overseas. The nationals—Anheuser-Busch, Schlitz, and Pabst being the most important—had the canning lines to produce beer for the armed forces, and the locals lacked such facilities. This meant that a soldier from Detroit, where the beers tended to be dark, and a sailor from Pittsburgh, where strong, bitter brews were preferred, spent a few years drinking and becoming accustomed to the lighter brands produced in St. Louis and Milwaukee. Many did not return to their old beers and sought out Budweiser, Schlitz, and Pabst. This tendency, together with the growth of packaged beer and new forms of advertising and promotion, revolutionized the industry.

Upon his brother's death, Gussie became president of Anheuser-Busch in 1946, chairman of the board in 1956, and chief executive officer in 1971, but the latter two titles were not as consequential as might appear. Even before Adolph's death, Gussie was the dominant force at the company. After the war he rose to industry leadership as well. The largest American brewer, Anheuser-Busch still had only 4 percent of the market and was sold in relatively few states. Busch set out to make Anheuser-Busch the dominant force in the field.

In this period few breweries had more than one site. This was acceptable at a time when local beers predominated, but Busch decided to open a second brewery to serve the East Coast. Newark, New Jersey, was ideal. It was on U.S. Highway 1, not far from New York City, and just across the road from the Newark Airport, which meant that communications between a new brewery and the home office would be relatively easy. It was decided that the St. Louis brewery would service the area west of Columbus, Ohio, while Newark would take care of those markets east of the city. The new brewery was opened in 1952. The following year Gussie made his second important move, the purchase of the St. Louis Cardinals National League baseball club for $3.7 million.

What Anheuser-Busch obtained was a second division team, nine minor league teams, and working arrangements with twelve others. Although Busch purchased the Cardinals primarily as a gesture of goodwill and for promotional reasons, the investment turned out well. The baseball team's worth grew as media sales became an important source of revenues. Most important was the goodwill generated by the move and the matter of imagery. Were it not for Busch's swift action, the Cardinals doubtless would have departed the city, a not insignificant matter for the people of St. Louis. There was a bonus in the regional effect. At the time of the purchase the Cardinals were the westernmost team in major league baseball and the only one in the region. (The St. Louis Browns left town at the end of the 1953 season.) In addition, its games were carried on three radio stations, which enabled fans throughout the region to hear them, along with Budweiser commercials.

Originally, Busch had intended to rename Sportsman's Park the Budweiser Stadium, but he settled for Busch Stadium. Soon after, he announced that a new, modern facility would be erected in downtown St. Louis, to be called Busch Memorial Stadium. It was a popular move and would later be considered a fitting monument to Busch in the center of the city.

Soon after acquiring the Cardinals, Busch opened to visitors his home, Grant's Farm, a 281-acre estate with a thirty-four-room French Renaissance chateau. By 1963 Grant's Farm was attracting 250,000 persons a year, especially for the remarkable collection of flora and fauna that Bush had accumulated. Busch was then planning a new brewery to be located in Tampa, Florida, with an adjacent "garden." His reasoning was fairly traditional. After touring the plant visitors could go to the garden, stroll through the "hospitality house," which was erected over a lagoon, look at tropical birds Busch planned to bring in, and see other attractions. The two projects were contiguous; one entered the garden through the brewery.

Busch Gardens was an immediate success, soon drawing two million visitors a year as it expanded to include animals. By the end of the 1960s the company had poured more than $38 million into the project, creating an African veldt with freely roaming elephants, zebras, giraffes, and other indigenous animals, and even erecting a miniature Mount Kilimanjaro, on the side of which was a Swiss chalet, from which diners could view it all. Other gardens followed. By the 1980s Busch Gardens was drawing more visitors than any other attraction of its kind except for the Walt Disney parks.

On 8 May 1975 Gussie resigned as chief executive officer, to be succeeded by his eldest son, August III. By then Anheuser-Busch had 23 percent of the beer market, a vast increase over the immediate postwar 4 percent. Gussie Busch retired to Grant's Farm and died fourteen years later after going into the hospital with pneumonia. He is buried at the Sunset Hills Memorial Park in St. Louis.

★

There is no biography of Gussie Busch. An unpublished history of Anheuser-Busch, "King of Beers" by Robert Sobel, is in the company's archives. The Anheuser-Busch official history, Roland Krebs with Percy Orthwein, *Making Friends Is Our Business: 100 Years of Anheuser-Busch* (1953), contains little on Gussie. Ronald Plavchan, *A History of Anheuser-Busch, 1852–1933* (1976), is the best history of the company. Among the more important magazine articles dealing with Busch are "Budweiser East: Purchase of 18½-Acre Site for Postwar Brewery at Newark, N.J.," *Business Week* (27 Jan. 1945); "The Brotherly Brewers," *Fortune* (Apr. 1950); "Selling Beer with Baseball," *Business Week* (27 Feb. 1954); "Promotional Flair Keeps Busch on Top," *Business Week* (13 Apr. 1963); "Budweiser Pulls Ahead," *Forbes* (1 Mar. 1968); "First in Brewing," *Business Week* (24 Mar. 1973); "Busch Ends 50 Years with his 'Second Love,'" *St. Louis Post Dispatch* (9 May 1975); and Thomas O'Hanlon, "August Busch Brews Up a New Spirit in St. Louis," *Fortune* (15 Jan. 1979). An obituary is in the *New York Times* (30 Sept. 1989).

ROBERT SOBEL

CAGNEY, James Francis, Jr. (*b.* 17 July 1899 in New York City; *d.* 30 March 1986 in Millbrook, New York), film actor noted primarily for his vivid portrayal of criminals.

Born on the Lower East Side of Manhattan, the son of James Francis Cagney, an alcoholic bartender and saloon proprietor, and Carolyn (Nelson) Cagney, a housewife, James was one of seven children, two of whom died in infancy. When he was eight, his family moved uptown to the Yorkville section, then a melting pot, working-class neighborhood of Germans, Irish, Italians, and Jews. Cagney credited his mother for the fact that, unlike a number of his childhood friends, neither he nor his brothers slipped into a life of crime. Nevertheless he learned to use his fists in street fights and even achieved a modest success as an amateur boxer. Wearing a mask of toughness for self-protection, the young Cagney was in fact a thoughtful, keen observer of life in the teeming city streets. He later drew on his recollections to create the screen roles that earned him worldwide fame. He was also a hard worker who took on a variety of odd jobs to help his struggling family and a dedicated student. Among his siblings he was closest to William, who was later his associate and adviser in Hollywood, and Jeanne, who acted in a number of his films. After graduating with honors from Stuyvesant High School in 1917, Cagney enrolled in Columbia University, but he had to withdraw after a year when his father died, at age forty-one, from Spanish influenza.

Cagney was working as a package wrapper at Wanamaker's Department Store when a fellow clerk told him about an opening in the chorus of a revue at Keith's 86th Street Theater. Cagney had no formal training as a dancer, but he moved well and learned quickly. He was hired, and, ironically, the future tough guy of gangster pictures first appeared on stage in drag. Cagney made his Broadway debut on 29 September 1920 in the chorus of a revue called *Pitter Patter.* Also in the chorus was a young woman named Frances Willard Vernon, who was called "Billie." She and Cagney married early in 1922 and they were happily wedded for the rest of Cagney's life. They adopted two children. In an abortive first attempt to try his luck in films, Cagney moved to Los Angeles, where he and Billie opened a dance studio. When that failed, they toured for three years on the small-time vaudeville circuit as a song-and-dance team called Vernon and Nye.

In September 1925 Cagney made his debut on the legitimate stage as a hobo in the play *Outside Looking In.* Impressed with Cagney's performance, George Abbott cast him as the lead, a hoofer in a speakeasy populated with Runyonesque guys and dolls, in the London production of a big hit, *Broadway.* Although Cagney was fired when he refused to simply provide a copy of Lee Tracy's original performance, he went on to understudy the lead in the Broadway production and eventually played a small role. His major break came in 1929, when the esteemed playwright George Kelly chose him to play a swaggering urban

James Cagney. ARCHIVE PHOTOS

roughneck in *Maggie the Magnificent.* Cagney and Joan Blondell, as a wisecracking, gum-chewing flapper, received positive reviews, and later the same year both were cast again as colorful lowlifes in *Penny Arcade,* a melodrama about murder in a carnival setting. After a screen test, Warner Brothers hired Cagney and Blondell to recreate their roles in the film adaptation, *Sinner's Holiday* (1930). Cagney was thirty when he arrived in Beverly Hills, Los Angeles, in April 1930 to launch a career that would endure for more than three decades.

Cagney was in exactly the right place at the right time. Unlike well-spoken stage actors who were imported to Hollywood in the first years of talking pictures, Cagney had an unreconstructed city-streets accent, and his natural speech and movement proved to be ideally suited to the new medium. The moviegoing audience could more readily identify with Cagney's proletarian image than with actors who had immaculate diction and a patrician manner. Short, decidedly ethnic in face and voice, he lacked the glamour and sex appeal of romantic leading men. Rather, he inaugurated a new film persona, a city boy with a staccato rhythm who was the first great archetype in the American talking picture. Quick, savvy, and feisty, he bristled with urban energy, swinging his arms when he walked and jabbing the air with his fists.

Cagney became a star in his fifth film, *The Public Enemy* (1931), a landmark gangster saga that chronicles the rise and fall of a daredevil kid from the slums who slugs his way to the top of the underworld. As Tom Powers, Cagney is subversively charismatic. Playing a ruthless, misogynistic hoodlum, his most famous gesture is shoving a grapefruit in the face of a nagging mistress. Cagney is both brutal and appealing, a combustible combination that incited the disapproval of censors.

Following *The Public Enemy,* Warner Brothers exploited their new star by assigning him to a succession of low-budget films with urban settings. He was not always cast as a criminal. For instance, in *Taxi!* (1932), he is the leader of independent cabbies in a taxi strike; in *The Crowd Roars* (1932), he appears as a self-destructive race-car driver; and in *Winner Take All* (1932), he is a prizefighter. But he was slotted into the mold of a fast-talking proletarian with a touch of the con artist, and only a few films in this hectic phase of his career offered relief from routine roles, which Cagney increasingly resisted. In *Footlight Parade* (1933), as a hard-driving impresario who stages splashy theatrical prologues for film palaces, he at last demonstrated the musical skills he had honed in vaudeville. In Max Reinhardt's spectacular version of *A Midsummer Night's Dream* (1935), a unique departure for Cagney as well as his studio, Cagney delivers a vigorous low-comedy performance as Bottom, but in the same year, he was forced to appear in five other films cut to the measure of conventional studio formulas.

By the end of 1935, Cagney was drained from overwork, complaining about the recycled scripts he was handed, and bruised from fighting with Jack Warner, his intransigent boss, for a higher salary. Determined to exert greater creative control over his career, Cagney left Warner Brothers and, with his brother William, set up a small, independent company, Grand National Pictures. While the two films Cagney made under this new arrangement were neither commercial nor artistic successes, they clearly indicated how he wished to present himself. In the revealingly titled *Great Guy* (1936), he plays a staunch crusader determined to correct fraud in the weights and measures bureau. In *Something to Sing About* (1937), he is a bandleader who engagingly sings and dances his way to Hollywood stardom. In 1938, Cagney returned to Warner Brothers, where, playing a fast-talking screenwriter, he costarred with his good friend Pat O'Brien in *Boy Meets Girl.* He and O'Brien eventually made eight films together. Later in 1938, Cagney achieved one of his greatest successes, as a recidivist hoodlum in *Angels with Dirty Faces.* Returning to his old neighborhood, Cagney's character, Rocky Sullivan, is idolized by a local youth gang. After he is sentenced to death, his boyhood pal, now a parish priest played by O'Brien, urges him to sacrifice his "honor" by pretending to walk the last mile as a coward, thereby demolishing his image as a hero in the eyes of the gang. Cagney's virtuoso shrieks and screams leave the viewer uncertain whether the character is faking, as the priest requested, or is truly frightened. In *The Roaring Twenties* (1939), he plays another criminal with an atavistic drive to conquer the underworld, and again he has a bravura death scene, this time enacted in snow on the steps of a church. Both *Angels with Dirty Faces* and *The Roaring Twenties* have a valedictory aura while casting a nostalgic glance at the roles he played early in the decade, but Cagney was fated to return on-screen to a life of crime.

Throughout the 1930s, as he animated a series of antisocial characters and fought for his independence from the studio system, Cagney maintained an active profile in politics. A staunch Franklin D. Roosevelt Democrat, he was a prominent and often outspoken Hollywood liberal. Although Cagney never joined the Communist party, from time to time the right-wing press painted him red. In the early 1940s, long before the McCarthy era, when actors were branded for their real or imagined political derelictions, Cagney and his brother felt the need to establish his patriotism. The project they selected to "cleanse" his image was a highly sanitized portrait of the fabled entertainer and true-blue American George M. Cohan. In *Yankee Doodle Dandy* (1942), Cagney sheds all vestiges of his psychotic crime-movie persona to give a sentimental, charming, high-spirited performance in which he sings and dances with a captivating verve. He won the Academy Award for best actor and regarded the film as both a personal and a professional vindication. Buoyed by his triumph, he departed Warner Brothers for the second time.

Cagney and his brother established William Cagney Productions, and their films were distributed by United Artists. As in his first hiatus from studio domination, Cagney's second group of independent works is revealing and disappointing. In *Johnny Come Lately* (1943), he plays a journalist at war against corrupt small-town politicians. In *Blood on the Sun* (1945), he is another crusading reporter, determined to thwart Japan's plans for world conquest. In marked contrast to his hyperactive performances in urban pictures, he is a sedentary barroom philosopher in William Saroyan's *The Time of Your Life* (1948).

Devoting most of his time to farming on Martha's Vineyard and in Dutchess County, New York, Cagney made few films during the World War II years. Eager to abandon his con man persona, he was unable to create a potent new image, and he began to resemble an actor from another era who had settled into comfortable semiretirement, working only when it suited him. Then, at the end of the decade, he returned again to Warner Brothers to make yet another crime picture. In *White Heat* (1949), as a trigger-happy, mother-dominated outlaw who suffers from blinding headaches, he gives the most intense performance of his career. Grown stout and homelier than ever, Cagney is electric, the performing energy unaccountably held in reserve since *Yankee Doodle Dandy* released at fever pitch. Curling up on his mother's lap, slugging his greedy, two-timing mistress, barking orders to his dim-witted henchmen, dodging the law as if in retreat from the Furies, he proffers his most physical performance. The role afforded him his two most bravura acting moments: in prison, when he learns of his mother's death, he cracks up operatically, and at the end, just before the gas tank he has climbed upon explodes apocalyptically, he exultantly shouts, "Made it, Ma! Top of the world!"

White Heat inaugurated a final Cagney renaissance, during which he freelanced among a number of major studios. As in his heyday in the 1930s, the quality of his material varied, but Cagney was clearly eager to accept challenges. He appeared in musicals, including *West Point Story* (1950), *The Seven Little Foys* (1955), and *Never Steal Anything Small* (1958); war comedies, including *What Price Glory?* (1952) and *Mister Roberts* (1955); Westerns, including *Run for Cover* (1955) and *Tribute to a Bad Man* (1956); a soap opera, *These Wilder Years* (1956); and biographical dramas, playing Lon Chaney in *Man of a Thousand Faces* (1957) and Admiral William F. Halsey, a World War II hero, in *The Gallant Hours* (1960). During the 1950s, he portrayed villains in only two films, *Kiss Tomorrow Goodbye* (1950), a strikingly mean-spirited film noir, and *Love Me or Leave Me* (1955), in which he is a tyrannical racketeer with a limp. Tellingly, these are his most persuasive performances of the decade. His final reprise of the sharp, bracingly confident persona he created in the 1930s is an effulgent display in *One, Two, Three* (1961), in which he appears as a take-charge representative of American capitalism in postwar Berlin. Along with Howard Hawks's *His Girl Friday,* this movie is among the fastest talking of American films, and in his ebullient staccato delivery, Cagney concedes nothing to his advancing age and weight.

After *One, Two, Three* was completed, Cagney at long last did what he had intermittently threatened throughout his career—he hung up his hat and retired to the life of a gentleman farmer in Dutchess County. As ever, he avoided publicity and fanfare, becoming increasingly reclusive and rarely venturing into public for fear of being recognized. He continued to receive acting offers but was tempted only once, when he was asked to play a cockney, Alfred P. Doolittle, in *My Fair Lady.* When he declined, the role was given to Stanley Holloway, who recreated his original Broadway performance.

In 1974 Cagney reemerged to accept the Life Achievement Award of the American Film Institute and, engagingly unassuming, claimed that acting was simply a job at which he had done his best. In 1976 he published *Cagney by Cagney,* a casual, sketchy account of his life and career in which he distanced himself from his crime-movie persona. Unable or at least unwilling to be articulate about technique, he maintained that he worked purely by instinct and that, to enliven the routine material he was often required to perform, he frequently improvised dialogue and behavior. For the first time, he addressed his political commitments and his gradual shift to the right.

In 1980 Cagney made the mistake of returning to films. Visibly aged, heavyset, and with a vacant look in his eyes, he gives an all but immobile performance as the sheriff in *Ragtime* (1981), an adaptation of E. L. Doctorow's novel (1974). Cagney died of heart failure.

Although he often tried to prove otherwise, Cagney, like most film stars, had a limited range. He could not sound or move like anyone other than James Cagney, city boy, but like most performers who attained his stature, in his own line he was definitive. He was a true prototypical American icon, and his essential integrity illuminated and deepened even the most depraved of his characters. He thought of himself as a humble song and dance man and an urban populist. The central irony of his career is that he is best remembered as a supremely skillful delineator of criminal psychopaths. Fittingly, his obituary in the *New York Times* (31 March 1986) hailed him as "a master of pugnacious grace."

★

James Cagney, *Cagney by Cagney* (1976), is a chatty but guarded and incomplete overview of the actor's on- and off-screen lives. Michael Freedland, *Cagney: A Biography* (1975), is superficial and entirely undocumented. Patrick McGilligan, *Cagney: The Actor as Auteur* (1982), offers a shrewd appraisal of the actor's imprint on his films along with a few biographical details. Richard Schickel, *James Cagney: A Celebration* (1985), is a thoughtful critical study in which the author attempts to reconcile the contradictions between the actor's personae on and off the screen. Robert Sklar, *City Boys: Cagney, Bogart, Garfield* (1992), perceptively defines the types the three actors incarnated and explores connections in their careers and iconography. An obituary is in the *New York Times* (31 Mar. 1986).

FOSTER HIRSCH

CALDWELL, Erskine Preston (*b.* 17 December 1903 in White Oak, Georgia; *d.* 11 April 1987 in Scottsdale, Arizona), novelist and short-story writer whose straightforward prose focused attention on the Depression-era South; combined social concern, rollicking humor, and a daring sexual frankness; and earned him a huge audience and acclaim from literary and social critics.

The only child of Ira Sylvester Caldwell, a minister in the Associate Reformed Presbyterian Church, and Caroline Bell Preston of Staunton, Virginia, Erskine (called "Skinny" or "Red" for the hair he inherited from his

Erskine Caldwell, 1938. LIBRARY OF CONGRESS/CORBIS

mother) traveled with his parents from one small southern town to another before the family settled in Wrens, Georgia, in 1919. There his home teaching ended when the Caldwells took possession of the parsonage and Erskine was enrolled in the Wrens Institute, where both his parents taught. Erskine did not distinguish himself at the all-white school, even in his rather prissy and strict mother's Latin class. He found employment briefly on the night shift at a cottonseed oil mill, where he came in contact for the first time with black workers and heard their stories of raw life, "some scandalous, some tragic, others humorous." Also during this time he began chauffeuring his father and a local doctor on visits to white tenant farmers.

He came face to face with people previously seen only at a distance. The tenant farmers lived in ramshackle wooden shacks, spread far apart, some on the "tobacco road," where heavy hogsheads of tobacco had once been rolled down to the Savannah River. He saw the desperate poverty and empty lives he would later depict in his books that seared America's conscience.

Although Caldwell fell short of his high school's graduation requirements, he enrolled at Erskine College in Due West, South Carolina, his father's alma mater. The strict religious school, affiliated with the Associated Reformed Presbyterian Church, did not suit the awkward teenager whose academic performance continued to be marginal.

Having limped through his first year, Caldwell returned home to Wrens, where he briefly found employment at the *Jefferson Reporter;* he also hoped to be paid for his sports reports as a "stringer" for several Augusta and Atlanta papers. Neither job worked out. He claimed later in his unreliable autobiography, *Call It Experience* (1951), that the owner-editor failed to pay him and he quit, but more objective sources reveal that Caldwell was fired for general incompetence.

Caldwell's second year at college was his last by his and the school's mutual agreement. With the aid of a scholarship offered by the United Daughters of the Confederacy he managed to transfer to the University of Virginia, where he continued to do badly. In the summer of 1924 he enrolled for courses at the Wharton School of the University of Pennsylvania, passing two and failing one. Instead of returning south, he stayed on in Philadelphia, supporting himself with a variety of jobs, including sweeping out the Trocadero Burlesque Theater, an experience that fueled his raging hormones. Although lonesome and generally dissatisfied with life, he pushed farther north to Wilkes-Barre, Pennsylvania, where he scraped by for a few more months, discovering that football at Erskine College had not prepared him for the semiprofessional Anthracite League and longing for the sort of anything-goes woman that the Jazz Age promised was readily available. His impressionistic, autobiographical prose-poem, *The Sacrilege of Alan Kent,* written some years later, chronicles the throbbing presence of his libido in these lonely years.

In the winter of 1925, again at the University of Virginia, Caldwell, now a sturdy six-foot-tall man, met in his English class eighteen-year-old Helen Lannigan, daughter of the school's popular track coach. One month later the two eloped to begin a stormy thirteen-year marriage that ended in divorce. By spring Caldwell and Helen had left Charlottesville for Atlanta, where he spent a year as a reporter and book reviewer for the *Atlanta Journal.* He returned briefly to the University of Virginia before leaving for Maine, where his wife's father owned a sprawling house used as a training camp for athletes. In rural Maine, Caldwell, now the father of two, began to work seriously at becoming a writer. Although he had labored tirelessly reviewing books in Atlanta in addition to carrying out his onerous reporting duties, and had started writing stories while his wife edited his tortured spelling and syntax, it was in Maine that his first fiction was accepted for publication. Also in Maine he established the nearly obsessive habits of a lifetime, writing hour after hour, brooking no interruption, and showing impatience for his family's needs, becoming a remote figure whose dedication to his craft made him irascible and inapproachable.

Uncertain about the method and subject of his writing, Caldwell experimented with genre and subject matter. He wrote two embarrassingly bad novelettes, *The Bastard* (1929) and *Poor Fool* (1930), both influenced by lurid pulp magazines. In the spring of 1929, with a small bequest from his grandmother, Caldwell opened a bookstore in Portland, Maine, and ran it with his wife and a woman named Margaret Montgomery. He encountered the first of many censorship battles when he attempted to publicize *The Bastard* in the bookstore. In "The Bogus Ones," a never-published short novel, he fictionalized his struggles against puritan Portland.

At this time Caldwell was also writing short stories, both about his new home and the South he had left behind. He did not immediately discover that the South and rural Georgia were to be the shaping factors of his creative imagination and at first the results were extremely uneven. He was attracted to the naive narrator, a legacy of Sherwood Anderson and Mark Twain. He tried both first- and third-person narrations to depict the poor and the oppressed and the influence of sex in human lives, never in a strictly realistic fashion but rather with imagination, symbols, and humor.

In July 1929, for the first time, one of Caldwell's stories was accepted for publication. The appearance of "Midsummer Passion" in the *New American Caravan* suddenly opened doors. Soon his stories were appearing in America's "little magazines" in the company of established writers, drawing the attention of F. Scott Fitzgerald, who in turn recommended Caldwell's work to the famed Scribner editor Maxwell Perkins. Although Caldwell had previously sent stories to *Scribner's* magazine without result, this time Perkins published his collection of stories, *American Earth* (1931), but advised Caldwell to return to the novel. Leaving his family in Maine—a habit he had already begun—Caldwell headed for New York City to write most of *Tobacco Road* (1932).

Tobacco Road depicts the life of Jeeter Lester, a destitute sharecropper, who faces ruin while a lecherous woman evangelist schemes to marry his son Dude. The deaths of Jeeter and his wife, Ada, give a grim naturalistic twist to a book in which laughter mixes with tears. In 1933 Caldwell quarreled with Scribner's and moved to Viking, which published *God's Little Acre.*

About this time the young playwright Jack Kirkland got Caldwell's grudging permission to dramatize *Tobacco Road.* The play opened on the night Prohibition ended, 3 December 1933, and although it got off to a slow start it soon became one of the biggest hits in the history of the Broadway stage, where it ran for 3,180 performances. This success not only improved Caldwell's finances but also made a celebrity of the young writer, who was about to become a father for the third time. (*Tobacco Road* was made into a motion picture in 1941.) Kirkland's play also drew readers to *God's Little Acre,* another story of backcountry Georgia, which, like its predecessor, was a collection of little episodes, similar to short stories, united by their common setting. This novel, however, takes a new and more serious direction as it shifts away from the largely comic antics of Ty Ty Walden, a none-too-honest farmer, to the struggle of his charismatic and macho son-in-law, Will Thompson, to organize striking South Carolina mill workers. (The film version of *God's Little Acre* was released in 1958.)

Now recognized as a social progressive, Caldwell undertook new projects with the photographer Margaret Bourke-White, first a photoessay volume of the Depression-era South, *You Have Seen Their Faces* (1937), followed by similarly formatted books about Nazi-threatened Europe. In 1939 Caldwell and Bourke-White married, but their union did not survive World War II, a conflict that gave new impetus to Caldwell's career as he reported by radio and dispatch from Russia while service editions of his racy novels reached American fighting men across the world. The end of the war, however, marked the end of Caldwell's critical acclaim, although his popular decline came much more slowly. Throughout the 1950s and 1960s he turned out novels whose suggestive covers, displayed in paperback editions, still attracted readers. He married June Johnson in 1942, fathering a son; they divorced, and in 1957 he married Virginia Fletcher. During these years, Caldwell moved restlessly throughout the West.

By the 1970s, although he continued to write an autobiography and travel sketches in addition to novels, he was largely forgotten. His election to the American Academy of Arts and Letters in 1984 was an attempt to make up for years of neglect. He died from lung cancer, the result of years of heavy smoking. His ashes are in a mausoleum on a hillside in Ashland, Oregon.

The author of two fine novels and a number of accomplished short stories, Erskine Caldwell remains an important, if minor, figure in American literature who succeeded in depicting human irrationality with both sympathy and humor in a fashion millions of readers found irresistible. With his emphasis on sex, injustice, and the poor, his voice was vigorous and clear.

★

The Erskine Caldwell Collection, Baker Library, Dartmouth College, holds everything from letters to nightclub match books. The Margaret Bourke-White Collection, George Arendt Research Library, Syracuse University, contains detailed information on Caldwell's relationship with the noted photographer. Erskine Caldwell, *Call It Experience: The Years of Learning How to Write* (1951) and *With All My Might: An Autobiography* (1987), leave out as much as they include. The first full-length biographies, Harvey L. Klevar, *Erskine Caldwell: A Biography* (1993), and Dan B. Miller, *Erskine Caldwell: The Journey from Tobacco Road* (1994), make clear just how difficult and contradictory Caldwell was. James E. Devlin, *Erskine Caldwell* (1984), the first book-length study of Caldwell, is still useful, while Wayne Mixon, *The People's Writer: Erskine Caldwell and the South* (1995), depicts Caldwell enthusiastically as a southerner embraced by the northern left. The *Pembroke Magazine II* (1979) and Scott MacDonald, ed., *Critical Essays on Erskine Caldwell* (1981), offer access to a large number of provocative essays on Caldwell. An obituary is in the *New York Times* (13 Apr. 1987).

JAMES E. DEVLIN

CAMPBELL, Joseph (*b.* 26 March 1904 in New York City; *d.* 30 October 1987 in Honolulu, Hawaii), scholar, teacher, and popularizer of mythology who became familiar as the subject of six hour-long Bill Moyers interviews broadcast by the Public Broadcasting Service (PBS) in 1988 as *The Power of Myth*.

Campbell was the oldest of three children of Charles William Campbell, who imported and sold hosiery, and Josephine Lynch, who encouraged her children to learn from a variety of experiences. Joseph Campbell traced his interest in myth to seeing Buffalo Bill's Wild West Show when he was about seven. The Native Americans in the show inspired in Campbell a lifelong fascination with comparative culture—particularly comparative religion and mythology. The family moved to New Rochelle, New York, when Jo-

Joseph Campbell, *c.* 1972. UPI/CORBIS-BETTMANN

seph was nine, and he pursued this interest in the local public library, where he devoured information on Native Americans, and at the American Museum of Natural History in New York City.

By the time he enrolled in the Roman Catholic Canterbury School—a private secondary school in New Milford, Connecticut—Campbell had already been struck by the similarities between the patterns of Native American myths and those of his own Christian tradition. In 1921 he graduated from Canterbury and entered Dartmouth College, but he grew dissatisfied at Dartmouth and transferred in 1922 to Columbia University, where he majored in English and concentrated on playing saxophone in a jazz band and on running track. After he earned his A.B. in 1925, he worked briefly for his father and then continued to play in the band and run track while he worked toward a master's degree in medieval literature, pursuing his early interest in Arthurian legend. Rounding out his education, Campbell traveled with his mother, brother, and sister on a series of summer trips, including a 1924 journey to Europe on which he met Indian theosophist Jiddu Krishnamurti and was introduced to Hinduism and Buddhism through Edwin Arnold's *The Light of Asia.*

Columbia granted him an M.A. in 1927, and his thesis earned him a Proudfit Fellowship, which enabled him to attend the Sorbonne in Paris (1927–1928), where he studied Old French and Provençal, and the University of Munich (1928–1929) where he studied Sanskrit. In Paris he also encountered modern art and literature for the first time, most significantly James Joyce's *Ulysses* and early sections of *Finnegans Wake,* both works alerting Campbell to the potential for the application of myth to the modern world.

Just before the stock market crash of October 1929, Campbell returned to New York City, where, on discovering that Columbia considered mythology to be an unacceptable subject for academic work, he dropped his plans to pursue a Ph.D. Without an income, Campbell lived off savings from his undergraduate jazz band earnings and wrote short stories. In 1931 he traveled by car to the West Coast, where he met the novelist John Steinbeck and his wife, Carol, and then by boat to Alaska. Over the next three years he taught for a year at the Canterbury School (1932–1933); sold a story, "Strictly Platonic," to *Liberty* magazine for $350; moved to Woodstock, New York, to read, study, and write; immersed himself in the writings of Carl Jung, Oswald Spengler, Thomas Mann, James Joyce, and Ferdinand Georg Frobenius; and turned his attention to mythology. In 1934 he accepted an offer to teach at Sarah Lawrence College, where he remained for thirty-eight years, teaching courses in comparative literature and mythology, formulating his mythological theories, and publishing a variety of scholarly works.

Jean Erdman was a junior at Sarah Lawrence when Campbell took her on as a private student in aesthetics; when she left to travel around the world with her missionary father and family, Campbell courted her in a series of letters. They were married on 5 May 1938 in New York City and settled in Greenwich Village, where they lived until 1982. Jean became a dancer (with Martha Graham) and choreographer. They had no children.

As soon as *Finnegans Wake* was published in 1939, Campbell and Henry Morton Robinson began writing a guide to reading and understanding Joyce's difficult work. Their guide was published five years later as *A Skeleton Key to "Finnegans Wake"* (1944). In 1943 Heinrich Zimmer, an Indian Studies specialist at Columbia University whom Campbell had admired, died unexpectedly, and Campbell was asked to edit Zimmer's notes and papers into a coherent work. These appeared as *Myths and Symbols in Indian Art and Civilization* (1946), *The King and the Corpse: Tales of the Soul's Conquest of Evil* (1948), *Philosophies of India* (1951), and *The Art of Indian Asia* (1955; repr. 2 vols., 1960).

In 1949 Campbell published the book that established his reputation as a mythologist and that many regard as his masterpiece—*The Hero with a Thousand Faces* (rev. ed., 1980). In this work Campbell argues that all heroes are essentially the same, facing the same ordeals, and that all hero myths can be subsumed in the "monomyth," a pattern in which the hero heeds the call to adventure, crosses the threshold, descends into an underworld (or another world or an inner world), finds and obtains the boon he has been seeking (often with help), and then returns, sometimes with and sometimes without the boon, but always enlightened. The broad knowledge of the myths of many cultures that informed *The Hero with a Thousand Faces* also provided the foundation of and illustrative material for Campbell's next major work, *The Masks of God,* an ambitious four-volume work resulting from Campbell's 1953–1954 trip to the Middle East and Far East, from Lebanon to Japan. The work explains the origin and nature of three sweeping categories of myth and asserts that the twentieth century demands new myths derived from individual experience and expressed in the creative works of great artists. The four volumes of *The Masks of God* appeared over a ten-year period: *Primitive Mythology* (1959); *Oriental Mythology* (1962); *Occidental Mythology* (1964); and *Creative Mythology* (1968).

Two more ambitious and widely admired works followed. In 1974, two years after Campbell retired from Sarah Lawrence, he published *The Mythic Image,* a demonstration of the visual dimension of myth and its connection to dreams, for which he received the 1976 Melcher Award from the Unitarian-Universalist Association for his contribution to religious liberalism. Campbell's last major project, the planned six-volume *Historical Atlas of World Mythology,* began appearing in 1983 but was left unfinished at the time of his death.

During the last fifteen years of his life, Campbell created, with his wife, the Theater of the Open Eye in 1971, attended conferences, lectured widely, and became a favorite figure in the New Age movement, teaching regularly at the Esalen Institute, at which he had first participated in 1966. He and Jean moved to Hawaii in 1982. During this period he also collected and published his lectures and talked with Bill Moyers for twenty-four hours at filmmaker George Lucas's ranch in 1985 and 1986 to produce the six-hour program aired on PBS as *The Power of Myth* in 1988. Meanwhile, he and his work were recognized with a Distinguished Scholar Award from Hofstra University in 1973, an honorary degree from Pratt Institute in 1976, a National Arts Club Medal of Honor for Literature in 1985, and election to the American Academy of Arts and Letters in 1987.

Campbell died of a heart attack at the age of eighty-three; he had been undergoing radiation treatments for esophageal cancer. He is buried in Oahu Cemetery. Immediately following his death, he and his work were widely praised, his *Hero with a Thousand Faces* became a bestseller, and Sarah Lawrence College raised money to endow a chair in his name. In 1989, however, Campbell was accused by former students and colleagues of having been a "crypto-fascist," an anti-Semite, and a racist. He was also accused of having promoted a kind of selfish materialism with his oft-repeated encouragement to "follow your bliss." In the fall of 1989 and spring of 1990, these accusations led to a lively debate in the New York press, and the Joseph Campbell Foundation was established in 1990 to defend and extend Campbell's work. Although his biographers subtly refute the charges, these accusations and the ensuing debate make it more difficult to assess Campbell's contributions to mythological scholarship and understanding.

Clearly, Campbell's breadth of knowledge and his ability to see parallels where none had been seen before led to new mythological insights and prompted unprecedented interest in and excitement about comparative myth and religion. His application of Jungian ideas to mythological matters established the significance of the inner truth of myth and explored the important connection between myths and dreams. His theories about the myths of agricultural societies and hunting societies shed light on differences between mythological systems. More obviously, the fact that Campbell's description of the hero and his monomythic quest inspired the *Star Wars* films and that the Campbell-Moyers television broadcasts reached an immense audience gave the study of myth power and currency beyond the confines of the classroom and the scholarly press.

Ironically, Campbell's particular strengths aroused the suspicions of his academic detractors. Those strengths included his facility for citing examples from a wide variety of cultures, his quickness at drawing parallels between such examples, his ease in telling an apparently infinite repertoire of stories, his lively style of writing about serious academic subjects, and his charm, with which he entranced Moyers, television viewers, lecture audiences, and four decades of Sarah Lawrence students.

★

The Joseph Campbell Foundation is collecting and cataloging Campbell's works and papers and plans to publish a collected works. Stephen Larsen and Robin Larsen, members of the board of directors of the foundation, have produced the only full-length biography, *A Fire in the Mind: The Life of Joseph Campbell* (1991). John Lobell, *Joseph Campbell: The Man and His Ideas* (1993), which includes a brief biographical sketch by the Larsens, is rather adulatory, Lobell also being a director of the Campbell Foundation. Robert A. Segal, *Joseph Campbell: An Introduction* (1987), examines Campbell's philosophical antecedents and takes him to task for inconsistencies. *Joseph Campbell: The Power of Myth* (1988), presents an edited version of the television interviews and contains an introduction by Bill Moyers. Sharon Winters, "Joseph Campbell: Prophet for a New Age" (master's thesis, Univ. of Texas at Dallas, 1993), looks at Campbell as a New Age religious visionary. A short source of biographical details is provided by Donald Newlove, "The Professor with a Thousand Faces," *Esquire* (Sept. 1977). Florence Sandler and Darrell Reeck review Campbell's contributions to religious scholarship in "The Masks of Joseph Campbell," *Religion* 11 (Jan. 1981): 1–20. The controversy over Campbell's prejudices is ignited by Brendan Gill in "The Faces of Joseph Campbell," *New York Review of Books* (28 Sept. 1989), and continues raging in the letters of Joan Konner and others, "Joseph Campbell: An Exchange," *New York Review of Books* (9 Nov. 1989). Obituaries are in the *New York Times* (3 Nov. 1987), *Washington Post* (4 Nov. 1987), *Chicago Tribune* (5 Nov. 1987), and *Los Angeles Times* (30 Nov. 1987).

PETER P. CLARKE

CAMPION, Donald Richard (*b.* 29 August 1921 in Brooklyn, New York; *d.* 11 December 1988 in the Bronx, New York), priest, writer, and editor in chief of the Jesuit weekly magazine *America*.

Campion was the elder of two sons of Josephine (Gayne) Campion, a homemaker, and Richard Campion, a World War I veteran, New York City firefighter, and longshoreman. He attended Holy Name of Jesus and St. Savior parochial schools in Brooklyn and Jesuit-run Regis High School in Manhattan, from which he graduated in 1939.

Shortly before his eighteenth birthday, Campion joined the Jesuits and spent two years of novitiate training as well as his first two years of college at St. Andrew-on-Hudson in Poughkeepsie, New York. After earning an A.B. in 1945 and an M.A. in sociology in 1946 at St. Louis University, he taught Latin and English to seniors at Xavier High School in New York City for one year. He then taught

Donald Campion. FUNERAL CARD, NEW YORK PROVINCE ARCHIVES

sociology and economics for two years at the newly founded Le Moyne College in Syracuse, New York. In 1949, he went to Woodstock College in Maryland for four years of theology studies. There he was ordained a priest in 1952 and earned an S.T.L. in 1953. After a year of prayer, study, and ministry at Xavier Hall in Pass Christian, Mississippi, he attended the University of Pennsylvania, where he was awarded a Ph.D. in sociology in 1960. The title of his dissertation, which, he is said to have conceded, would have drawn sardonic comment from W. C. Fields, was "Patterns of Suicide in Philadelphia, 1948–1952."

From 1957 to 1965 Campion was an associate editor of the Jesuit periodical *America,* during which time he covered the Second Vatican Council in Rome. His accounts and interpretations of the council's events and issues in the pages of *America* and elsewhere were influential within and without the American church. When the documents of Vatican II were published in English (1966), he wrote the introduction to the "Pastoral Constitution on the Church in the Modern World," perhaps the most important of the council documents. In that essay, he wrote approvingly, "Time and again, even the most casual reader must be struck by the document's evident openness to fundamental elements in the intellectual climate of twentieth-century civilization, to the dimensions of human culture opened up by advances in the historical, social, and psychological sciences."

In 1965 Campion left *America* to direct the Fordham/Nativity project, a socio-pastoral experiment in a mostly Latino parish on Manhattan's Lower East Side. A few months later, his Jesuit superiors also named him coordinator of the North American portion of a worldwide self-study of the Society of Jesus, an assignment that once again required his shuttling back and forth between Rome and the United States.

In June 1968 Campion returned to *America* as editor in chief. At that time, Catholics were struggling to understand what had happened at Vatican II and to figure out what it meant for the daily life of the church. Under Campion's direction, *America* magazine played a leadership role in this process. Joseph O'Hare, S.J., Campion's associate editor and his immediate successor as editor in chief, later said of Campion, "As editor in chief of *America* from 1968 to 1975, his original experience of the Council as it took place informed his perceptive judgments on the applications of the Council in the decade following its conclusion." Campion wanted *America* to be a model and force for the generous, open approach to the modern world that he admired in Vatican II.

From 1975 to 1978, at the request of Pedro Arrupe, head of the Jesuits, Campion served as director of the Jesuit Press and Information Office in Rome. From 1979 to 1984, he was secretary for communications at the American Jesuit headquarters in Washington, D.C. He moved in 1984 to Fordham University in the Bronx and joined the staff in charge of training young Jesuits. Four years later he died in the Bronx of Parkinson's disease, from which he had been suffering for about a decade. His grave is at the Jesuit Retreat House in Auriesville, New York.

Campion was a portly man of medium height. He had great energy, could stay up late into the night to work or party, and loved to laugh and tease. His most prominent physical feature was a broad, toothy smile set in a strong jaw. The recurring theme in the tributes at the time of his death and in interviews with those who knew him was his capacity for friendship. In the sermon at Campion's funeral mass, his editorial colleague O'Hare said, "To say that Don Campion had a gift for friendship is a bland understatement; he had a genius for friendship." Perhaps the secret to this genius is contained in these words of another close friend, "I never saw Don angry or in any mood even close to ugly."

What stands out in Campion's life is the volume and variety of his writings, service, and relationships. He contributed scores of articles to both religious and secular publications on topics ranging from capital punishment to ecumenism to social justice. He lectured widely, participated on panels, and frequently was interviewed on radio and television. He was a trustee at colleges including Fordham, St. Peter's, Boston College, and Holy Cross and served on the boards of ecumenical organizations and human rights groups. As vice president of the Appeal of Conscience Foundation, set up by his friend Rabbi Arthur Schneier of the Park East Synagogue in New York City, Campion traveled to Eastern Europe, North Africa, and China to discuss human rights and promote religious freedom. Throughout his career, journalists, Jesuits (especially younger ones), churchpeople, intellectuals, and public servants trusted his judgment, sought his advice, and enjoyed his company. Especially in the 1960s and 1970s, Campion was a major influence within the Jesuit order and the American Catholic church, and he was an important presence and voice in many of the church's post–Vatican II dialogues with the modern world.

★

Campion's papers are in the Georgetown University Library, Washington, D.C., and the New York Province archives at 39 East Eighty-third Street, New York City. See also G. W. Hunt, "In Memoriam," *America* (24–31 Dec. 1988). An obituary is in the *New York Times* (14 Dec. 1988).

JAMES N. LOUGHRAN, S.J.

CANIFF, Milton Arthur (*b.* 28 February 1907 in Hillsboro, Ohio; *d.* 3 April 1988 in New York City), creator of the classic comic strips *Terry and the Pirates* and *Steve Canyon.*

Caniff was the only child of John William Caniff, a printer, and Elizabeth Burton. The family moved from Hillsboro to Dayton, Ohio, in 1919. As a teenager, Caniff worked as an artists' helper at the *Dayton Journal.* He graduated from Stivers High School in 1925 and entered Ohio State University, where he majored in fine arts. While there, he was a part-time retoucher at the *Columbus Dispatch* and served as the art editor of both the college humor magazine and his class yearbook. After earning his B.A. degree in 1930, he worked full time at the *Dispatch.*

On 23 August 1930 Caniff married Esther Parsons, whom he had known since grammar school; they had no children. When the Great Depression forced the *Dispatch* to make cutbacks in 1932, Caniff lost his job. Three months later he landed a job with the Associated Press and moved to New York City; for the rest of his life he and his wife lived in the city or its environs to the north. At the Associated Press, Caniff worked as a general illustrator and did a one-column panel, *Puffy the Pig;* a three-column panel, *The Gay Thirties;* and an adventure strip, *Dickie Dare.*

In 1934 Joseph M. Patterson, publisher of the *New York Daily News,* asked Caniff to submit samples for a new adventure strip. The premise was Patterson's: the strip would be set in China, "the last outpost of adventure," and would be centered around a boy (to attract youngsters), a handsome young man (to provide romantic interest), and a daffy sidekick. It was to have a hard edge; Patterson asked for "blood and thunder." Three days later Caniff turned in his samples. They featured Tommy Tucker, a blond American boy; Pat Ryan, a dark-haired young man; and George Webster Confucius, a Chinese guide. The villainess was a Caniff original—the Dragon Lady, a ruthless and gorgeous Eurasian leader of a band of river pirates. Patterson changed the boy's name to Terry Lee, and the strip was ready to run.

Terry and the Pirates made its debut on 19 October 1934 and was an immediate success. Caniff, who had never been to the Far East, acquired an extensive research library and began to develop a formidable reputation for accuracy. His drawing also matured. Caniff drew all of his female characters from models, and dangerous women with knockout figures became his trademark. He inked his drawings with a brush rather than a pen, and the darker look gave his strip an aura of danger. The creative cinematic angles of his drawings owed much to his lifelong interest in movies and were, in turn, widely studied by filmmakers. He also gained a reputation as a formidable storyteller, noted for his complex plots and sophisticated character development.

"[Caniff] has invented in all, forty-five characters who have played sufficiently important roles in the strip to be remembered by regular readers," said the *New Yorker.* "Some of the people who show up in 'Terry' are . . . calm, well-adjusted types, but many are bundles of emotional quirks. One character is troubled by an anxiety neurosis, another with nymphomania, and still another with transvestitism. . . . It is inevitable that a few of the kiddies who read 'Terry' may miss some of the Krafft-Ebing undertones, but this doesn't worry Caniff. 'I'm interested in pleasing their daddies,' he says simply."

By the late 1930s *Terry* was paralleling actual events. Japanese troops were shown as early as 1937, and the Dragon Lady and her river pirates, who proved to be patriotic as well as ruthless, turned their attention to fighting "the invaders." *Terry and the Pirates* was never the most popular comic strip in terms of total readership, but it was the favorite of sophisticates, the one comic strip that those who claimed they did not read the comics would admit to reading. In 1941, when Caniff took the unusual step of killing off a major character, Raven Sherman, 450 students at Loyola University paid tribute by facing east for a minute of silence.

A childhood leg injury barred Caniff from military service when the United States entered World War II in December 1941, but he threw himself into the war effort. He

Milton Caniff, 1985. UPI/CORBIS-BETTMANN

wrote a special weekly comic strip for the service, *Male Call;* illustrated various service handbooks; and put both Terry (by now a young man) and Pat Ryan into uniform. In his effort to make sure that *Terry* accurately portrayed the war effort, Caniff developed an impressive array of military informants, and many of them became *Terry* characters: Terry's commanding officer, Flip Corkin, for example, was Philip Cochran, whose real-life war record was even more distinguished than that of Flip.

In July 1945, with *Terry* at peak popularity, Caniff shocked the newspaper world with the announcement that he would be leaving *Terry* at the conclusion of 1946 to launch a new strip for the Field Syndicate. He was the first creator ever to voluntarily leave a successful strip to start a new one, and with the new strip he became the first comic-strip author ever to completely own his creation.

Caniff incorporated the most successful elements of *Terry* (which was continued by the Chicago Tribune–New York News Syndicate under the authorship of George Wunder) into his new creation—the picaresque-novel character of the strip, the huge cast of recurring characters, and the intricate plot lines. Steve Canyon, a blond, curly-haired World War II veteran heading a flying service teetering on the brink of bankruptcy made his debut in early 1947. His profession enabled Caniff to place Steve anywhere in the world, so he was not locked into one locale, as Terry had been; furthermore, his precarious financial situation forced him to take unusual jobs. Caniff carried the trademark characteristics he had developed in *Terry* into *Steve Canyon:* fast-moving and complex plots; characters in which good and bad are intermingled; and striking, resourceful, and often deadly villainesses. Just as *Terry* had reflected world events prior to and during World War II, *Steve Canyon* soon began to reflect cold war politics.

With the entrance of the United States into the Korean War, Steve went back into uniform. After the war Steve chose to stay with the air force, and the military cast of the strip was set. Paradoxically, although *Steve Canyon* was viewed by the air force as a propaganda strip, it never lost its independent slant. In fact, even though it dealt extensively with cold war issues, few out-and-out errors or misguided premises can be spotted in the strip, even with the benefit of forty years of hindsight, a tribute to the extensive background research Caniff never stopped doing on each and every story.

Steve Canyon hit an impressive stride in the 1950s and early 1960s, with Steve serving as a troubleshooter for the air force. He was frequently called upon to calm skittish civilians who wanted military installations moved elsewhere; ferret out spies; or, occasionally, save the world (by preventing a wildcat invasion of China that could set off World War III, for example).

When a backlash against the military began to develop during the Vietnam War, however, *Steve Canyon*'s military orientation started to alienate what should have been the strip's natural audience. At the same time, the public's attention span for long, complex stories began to wane, and adventure strips went into serious decline. Then, as disillusionment with the war grew, heroes of any sort fell into disfavor. Caniff, who always kept a finger firmly on the public pulse, responded by reducing the length of his average episode from thirteen to nine weeks, increasing the percentage of episodes with comic elements, and having Steve's sidekicks, who tended to fall into the antihero category, take the lead in many episodes.

The quality of Caniff's work was not fully appreciated toward the end of his career, when gags were honored more than storytelling, limited space made it impossible for newspapers to reproduce Caniff's best artwork, smaller dialogue balloons forced him to leave out some of the nuance that placed his dialogue in a class by itself, and lingering hostility toward the military kept sophisticates from realizing just how flip, cynical, and on the cutting edge *Steve Canyon* really was.

Caniff died of lung cancer and was buried in Mt. Repose Cemetery in Haverstraw, New York. *Steve Canyon* continued two months longer, ending its run on Sunday, 5 June 1988.

Caniff's peers considered him the finest adventure-strip cartoonist ever. A few may have approached Caniff's level in artwork, storytelling, creativity, or verve, but no one else has combined all of these elements at such a high level over such a long period of time.

★

Caniff's papers, which include tear sheets, proofs, and a good deal of original artwork, are at the Cartoon Research Library of Ohio State University in Columbus, Ohio. For a full-length study of Caniff, see John Paul Adams, *Milton Caniff: Rembrandt of the Comic Strips* (1946). See also Milton Caniff, "Comic Strips at War," *The Magazine of Sigma Chi* (Feb.-Mar. 1944). Other articles of interest include John Bainbridge, "Significant Sig and the Funnies," *New Yorker* (18 Jan. 1944); "Not for Kids," *Time* (2 Dec. 1946); "Escape Artist," *Time* (13 Jan. 1947); "Caniff, Canyon, and Calhoon," *Newsweek* (20 Feb. 1947); and William Zimmer, "Art: A Classic, Heavily Shadowed Style," *New York Times* (20 Jan. 1985). An obituary is in the *New York Times* (4 Apr. 1988).

LYNN HOOGENBOOM

CANUTT, Enos Edward ("Yakima") (*b.* 29 November 1896 near Colfax, Washington; *d.* 24 May 1986 in Los Angeles, California), national rodeo champion, movie actor, stuntman, and noted second-unit director of motion pictures.

Yakima Canutt, one of the five children of John Lemuel Canutt, a rancher, and Nettie Ellen Canutt, grew up in eastern Washington on a ranch founded by his grandfather and operated by his father, who also served a term in the state legislature. During Canutt's professional career, many thought him descended from various Native American tribes, but his ancestry was Scotch-Irish and German.

Canutt's formal education was limited to attending an elementary school in Green Lake, Washington, a suburb of Seattle. He gained the education for his life's work on the family ranch, where he learned to ride. By the age of thirteen, he rode unbroken horses, and within three years he began to compete in area rodeos. After his parents divorced, Canutt devoted his full time to the rodeo circuit. In 1916 he married Kitty Wilks, who was also a rodeo performer. They had no children, and their stormy marriage ended quickly. He became proficient at saddle-bronc riding and bulldogging and was named a world champion for the first time in 1917. He won that designation three times more before he abandoned rodeo riding for work in the motion picture industry.

Canutt claimed that he received his nickname, Yakima, while performing in a rodeo in Pendleton, Oregon. After drinking with two friends from Yakima, Washington, he competed in the bronc riding. His two companions demanded difficult horses to show the others how expertly riders from Yakima could perform, but both riders were thrown. To support his friends' claims, Canutt also asked for a difficult horse so the fans could have another chance to see how well persons from Yakima could ride—even though he was from Colfax. But he also was thrown, and a picture of him in the air above the horse ran in several newspapers. Thereafter he was called Yakima, which was frequently shortened to Yak.

Canutt joined the U.S. Navy in 1918 and trained in gunnery in Bremerton, Washington. He was released when World War I ended in November of that year. In 1919 he returned to the rodeo circuit and traveled to Los Angeles, California, for the first time. There he met Tom Mix, a Western movie actor, who offered him a job in films. Canutt's first brush with moviemaking was unpleasant, so he returned to the rodeo. In 1923 Ben Wilson offered him an opportunity to appear in eight motion pictures. Canutt experienced such stage fright in the first film, *Branded a Bandit* (1924), a silent Western, that he doubted he would be able to continue. However, reassurances from Wilson and others convinced Canutt to remain in the business, and he completed nearly twenty motion pictures before 1930. In these silent features, he played the lead role, and since he was an experienced horseman and athlete, he did not use a "double," or stuntman, during action scenes. Probably his best-known film from this era is *The Devil Horse,* produced by Nat Lavine in 1926.

In the 1930s Canutt moved more completely into planning and performing stunt work. His voice was unsuited to the movies, so once sound revolutionized the industry, he felt more comfortable doing the "gags," or stunts, in action scenes. At that time, stuntmen often made more money than the lead actors in the B Westerns. On 12 November 1931 he married Minnie Audrea Rice. They had

Yakima Canutt poses with rodeo trophies, including four Police Gazette buckles, *c.* 1923. UPI/CORBIS-BETTMANN

three children, including two sons who followed Canutt into stunt work.

Canutt continued to appear in films in nonspeaking roles, but mostly he doubled for lead actors, especially John Wayne in the Westerns and Clark Gable in his major films, such as *Gone with the Wind* (1939). In *Gone with the Wind*, Canutt doubled for Gable driving the horse and wagon through Atlanta as the city burned, and he was the ruffian who accosts Scarlett (Vivien Leigh) on a bridge before she is rescued by Big Sam (Everett Brown).

Canutt's best-known work of the 1930s is in *Stagecoach* (1939), directed by John Ford. Dressed as an American Indian, he mounts the lead horse in a "six-up," or team of six horses, pulling a stagecoach at high speed. Wayne shoots him, and Canutt drops to the tongue of the stagecoach. Wayne shoots again, and Canutt drops to the ground. He is dragged by the coach until he lets go and passes between the horses and under the stagecoach. In later films, he perfected the gag sufficiently to complete the circle; that is, he jumps from the seat to the rear team, leaps eventually to the lead team, passes under the vehicle, grabs a bar on the rear of the coach, climbs over the top, and resumes his seat in the driver's box.

Canutt sustained multiple injuries while performing stunts, including six broken ribs while filming *San Francisco* (1936) and multiple injuries during the filming of *Boom Town* (1940), which caused him to restrict his activities to directing and intensified his determination to make stunt work as safe as possible. As a second-unit director for action sequences, he made scores of films during the 1940s, 1950s, 1960s, and 1970s, but his best-known work is the chariot race in *Ben-Hur* (1959), starring Charlton Heston and Stephen Boyd. Canutt improved upon the previous version of the film, made in the 1920s by Reeves Eason, and took greater safety precautions. In 1966 Canutt won an Academy Award for his stunt work, and the citation included his inventions that had increased the safety of stuntmen. In 1976 he was inducted into the National Cowboy Hall of Fame.

Perhaps the many injuries, some of them life threatening, that Canutt suffered while doing stunt work made him conscious of the safety of the stuntmen and stuntwomen he directed. In his autobiography, *Stunt Man: The Autobiography of Yakima Canutt* (1979), he claimed more pride in his safety record than all of his other accomplishments. He died of natural causes in Los Angeles, where he is buried.

★

The best source on Canutt's career is his autobiography, *Stunt Man* (1979), in which he describes in detail his stunts, injuries, business activities, and associations with movie producers, directors, and actors. This work also contains a list of motion pictures in which Canutt appeared. For a discussion of stunt work in motion pictures in general, Arthur Wise and Derek Ware, *Stunting in the Cinema* (1973), is informative. "A Tribute to Yakima Canutt," a transcript of an event produced by the Academy of Motion Picture Arts and Sciences on 11 September 1978, contains testimonies of fellow stuntmen and Charlton Heston to Canutt's achievements. An obituary is in the *New York Times* (27 May 1986).

ARCHIE P. MCDONALD

CARNEY, Robert Bostwick (*b.* 26 March 1895 in Vallejo, California; *d.* 25 June 1990 in Washington, D.C.), naval officer best remembered for his service during World War II in the Pacific theater and as a chief of naval operations in the 1950s.

Carney, the eldest of three children of Robert Emmett Carney, a naval officer, and Bertha V. H. Bostwick, attended Central High School in Philadelphia, Pennsylvania, and was appointed to the U.S. Naval Academy in 1912. He graduated in 1916 with a B.S. degree and was commissioned an ensign. During World War I, Carney, with the rank of lieutenant, served as gunnery and torpedo officer on the destroyer *Fanning,* which assisted in the sinking of the German submarine *U-53,* and at the Bethlehem Shipbuilding Corporation in Squantum, Massachusetts, helping to outfit the destroyer *Laub.* On 7 September 1918 he married Grace Stone Craycroft; they had two children.

Between the world wars Carney rose to the rank of commander while holding a variety of shore and sea assignments. His sea assignments included the command of four destroyers; a tour as plotting room officer on the battleship *Mississippi;* duty on the staffs of Destroyer Squadron 11, Commander Battleship Division 4, and as commander in chief of the Battle Fleet; service as gunnery officer on the cruiser *Cincinnati;* command of the cargo ship *Sirius;* and duty as executive officer of the battleship *California.* Carney also taught navigation at the Naval Academy, served in the Division of Fleet Training in the Office of Chief of Naval Operations, commanded the Receiving Station of the Washington Navy Yard, served as war plans officer of the Naval Gun Factory and the Washington Navy Yard and District, and had a tour in the Shore Establishments Division of the Office of the Assistant Secretary of the Navy from 1938 to 1940. When the United States entered World War II in December 1941, Carney was chief of staff to Vice Admiral Arthur L. Bristol, Jr., commander of the Support Force of the Atlantic Fleet. In this post Carney earned a reputation as an expert in antisubmarine warfare for helping to organize a special surface-air convoy task force that escorted more than 2,600 ships across the North Atlantic from September 1941 to April 1942, with the loss of only six vessels to German submarine attack.

From October 1942 to July 1943, Carney, with the rank of captain, commanded the light cruiser *Denver,* seeing considerable action in the Solomon Islands campaign. Recognized as an able tactician and strategist, Carney in July 1943 was appointed chief of staff to Admiral William F. Halsey, Jr., commander of the South Pacific Force and later commander of the Third Fleet, which brought promotion for Carney to rear admiral. As Halsey's chief of staff, he was a major figure in the planning and implementation of several major operations in the Pacific war, including the landing at Bougainville Island in November 1943, the Battle of Leyte Gulf in October 1944, the landing at Lingayen Gulf on Luzon Island in the Philippine Islands in January 1945, and the navy's air strikes against the Japanese homeland in the summer of 1945. When Japan surrendered in August 1945, Carney was engaged in the planning for the first proposed landing on the Japanese mainland.

In the postwar period, from 1946 to 1950, Carney, with the rank of vice admiral, was deputy chief of naval operations for logistics. He then served for five months as commander of the Second Fleet, which operated in the Atlantic. Later in 1950 Carney, now a full admiral, was named commander of United States naval forces in the Eastern Atlantic and Mediterranean. In June 1951 General Dwight D. Eisenhower, Supreme Allied Commander, Europe, appointed him commander in chief, Allied Forces, Southern Europe. Headquartered at Naples, Italy, Carney was responsible for U.S. naval forces in the eastern Atlantic and the Mediterranean Sea and all North Atlantic Treaty Organization units in southern Europe. In these assignments Carney impressed Eisenhower with his "global" outlook, based on his experience in both the European and Pacific theaters, his abilities as a planner and as an administrator, and his reputation for forthrightness in expressing his views, leading Eisenhower, now president, to name him chief of naval operations in 1953.

Carney publicly supported Eisenhower's New Look defense strategy, which placed emphasis on nuclear weapons as a deterrent to aggression by the Soviet Union and called for reduced defense expenditures for conventional forces. Privately, Carney questioned the wisdom of overreliance on nuclear weapons and complained that reductions in defense spending could leave the nation with inadequate ground and naval forces to meet a conventional threat. Within the navy Carney struggled to reconcile Eisenhower's austere defense budgets with a growing Soviet naval threat and sought to encourage new thinking by naval officers about the missions of the aircraft carrier and the nuclear submarine.

Carney's relations with his civilian superiors gradually soured. He feuded with Secretary of Defense Charles E. Wilson and Secretary of the Navy Charles S. Thomas over the chain of communications between the chief of naval operations and the president and between the chief of naval operations and the fleet commanders. Carney preferred to deal directly with both Eisenhower and the fleet com-

Robert Carney in his office with a map of North Africa behind him, 1953. UPI/CORBIS-BETTMANN

manders, while the two civilian secretaries insisted that they should be included in all communications. By the spring of 1955 Carney's relations with Eisenhower also were strained. During the crisis with Communist China over the Chinese Nationalist–held offshore islands in the Taiwan Strait, in comments that he thought were off the record, Carney told reporters that the Joint Chiefs of Staff had advised Eisenhower to use nuclear weapons if China attacked the islands of Quemoy and Matsu and that war was nearly inevitable. These comments aroused a storm of protest when published and enraged the president, who had been complaining about the penchant of the service chiefs to make public statements without administration approval. As a result, Eisenhower did not reappoint Carney to a second two-year term as chief of naval operations, prompting him to retire when his first term expired in August 1955.

In retirement Carney was a director on the boards of several corporations in the defense sector, a consultant to the Westinghouse Electric Company, and a two-time president of the U.S. Naval Institute. He died of cardiac arrest and was buried at Arlington National Cemetery, Virginia.

Slight of frame, Carney excelled as a naval planner during World War II and was a capable chief of naval operations who was noted for his readiness to express strong views and his determination to strengthen the navy.

★

Carney's papers and interviews are in the U.S. Naval Historical Center in Washington, D.C. Betty C. Taussig, *A Warrior for Freedom: Admiral Robert B. Carney* (1995), is an affectionate biography by Carney's daughter. Carney's tenure as chief of naval operations is examined in Paul R. Schratz, "Robert Bostwick Carney, 17 August 1953–17 August 1955," in *The Chiefs of Naval Operations,* edited by Robert William Love, Jr. (1980). References to Carney's service during World War II are in E. B. Potter, *Bull Halsey* (1985). Obituaries are in the *Washington Post* (26 June 1990) and the *New York Times* (27 June 1990).

JOHN KENNEDY OHL

CARPENTER, Robert Ruliph Morgan, Jr. (*b.* 31 August 1915 in Wilmington, Delaware; *d.* 8 July 1990 in Montchanin, Delaware), sportsman and philanthropist who owned the Philadelphia Phillies National League baseball club for twenty-nine years.

Carpenter was one of four children born to Robert R. M. Carpenter, Sr., an executive of the DuPont Company, and Margaretta Lammot du Pont. The grandson of Pierre S. du Pont, Carpenter was raised in the genteel tradition and was educated privately. He developed an interest in sporting and outdoor activities at an early age, and those activities remained central themes throughout his life. At Tower Hill School in Wilmington, Delaware, he lettered in baseball, basketball, and football. Following graduation in 1933, Carpenter entered Duke University, where he earned a berth on the varsity football team before leaving school in 1935 to pursue other interests.

Finding little solace after two years in the public relations department of the DuPont Company, Carpenter resigned from the family business and turned his full atten-

Robert Carpenter, Jr. © THE PHILLIES

tion to the avocation of an active yet leisured lifestyle. Besides team and individual sports, he enjoyed hunting on the family's estate in South Carolina and raising champion Chesapeake Bay retrievers. One of his kennel garnered recognition from *Field and Stream* magazine as the outstanding retriever for 1937. That same year Carpenter won the Delaware state badminton title. Although he was a talented athlete, his professional interests increasingly turned toward sports management. In 1938 he married Mary Kaye Phelps; they had four children.

Carpenter's first experience administering a professional sports team came as president of the Class B (AA) Interstate Baseball League's Wilmington Blue Rocks, which was co-owned by his father and Connie Mack, the manager of the American League's Philadelphia Athletics (A's). The Blue Rocks served as a farm team for the Athletics and later for the Phillies before being dissolved in 1952. In addition, as president of the Wilmington Sportsmen's Club, Carpenter brought professional boxing and basketball to the city. His Wilmington Bombers won the 1941–1942 American Basketball League championship. In recognition of his efforts, the Wilmington Junior Chamber of Commerce presented Carpenter with its Distinguished Service Award for 1943.

Later in 1943, the baseball commissioner, Kenesaw Landis, banned the Phillies owner, William Cox, from baseball for gambling on his team. Carpenter's father bought the troubled Phillies National League franchise, naming his son as president. At twenty-eight years of age, the junior Carpenter found himself the youngest club president in league history. The task was daunting. The Phillies had long been overshadowed by the rival Athletics and had, as one local sportswriter lamented, "a perpetual lease on last place." Nonetheless, this ball club, which had won only one league pennant, in 1915, became Carpenter's professional passion for the remainder of his life.

Inexperienced at operating a major sporting franchise, Carpenter hired a family friend, Herb Pennock, who was also a former big league pitcher and a farm director for the Boston Red Sox, as the Phillies general manager. The two then developed a five-year plan to make the club competitive. The plan called for the establishment of a strong farm system, to which Carpenter unreservedly applied his wealth to sign promising young players. To break away from the team's dismal heritage, the management sponsored a contest to rename the ball club, which briefly became known as the Blue Jays. In March 1944, just as his first major league campaign was set to begin, Carpenter was drafted into the U.S. Army. Discharged from the army as a staff sergeant in January 1946, he returned to the baseball club and hired Edith Houghton, possibly the first female scout in professional baseball, as part of his ongoing blueprint for developing homegrown talent.

By 1949, Carpenter's strategic plan began to bear fruit. The club's third-place finish was the best in more than thirty years, and as a result, Carpenter was named major league executive of the year. The new team name, the Blue Jays, garnered little enduring fan support, and the team officially reverted to the Phillies in 1949. His young team, dubbed the "Whiz Kids," captured the National League crown the following season but were swept by the New York Yankees dynasty in the 1950 World Series. Unfortunately, the team that had quickly captured the hearts of Philadelphia baseball fans was unable to repeat its miracle season and, in fact, failed to capture another league pennant during Carpenter's remaining two decades of ownership. The Phillies' near-success, however, spurred the Athletics, who were much maligned, to move to Kansas City in 1954.

More troubling for Philadelphia than the loss of the A's was a growing postwar racial antagonism, which smoldered for decades but found early manifestation in its professional baseball teams. The Phillies became the last National League club to sign a black player, in 1956, fully ten years after Jackie Robinson broke the color barrier. Such inaction did little to cultivate positive relations with the neighborhood population, increasingly made up of minority groups, surrounding the stadium, Shibe Park. During the civil rights movement of the 1960s, the City of Brotherly Love's race problems were encapsulated in microcosm in the saga of Dick Allen, the first black player to become a Phillies star. Controversy engulfed the power hitter both on and off the field, and he was ultimately traded to the St. Louis Cardinals in 1969 for another black standout, Curt Flood. Flood was reluctant to play daily under such openly hostile conditions, and he challenged professional baseball's reserve clause in court. The resulting advent of free agency ultimately changed the very nature of the game.

In 1971, following a long campaign for a better ballpark, the Phillies moved to a new home in Veterans Stadium. Carpenter, wearied by decades of organizational details and unhappy with the new relationship between players and owners, turned team operations over to his son Ruly Carpenter in November 1972. The elder Carpenter became chairman of the Phillies organization but spent most of his time serving the state of his birth. As a member of the University of Delaware Board of Trustees, a position he held since 1945, he sought to improve the quality of the school's athletic department. In recognition of Carpenter's yeoman work and philanthropic support, the university broke ground on the Bob Carpenter Sports/Convocation Center less than a month before his death. Additionally, he remained a strong supporter of the Delaware Association for Retarded Children, an organization he helped establish in the early 1950s. Carpenter died of lung cancer in Montchanin, Delaware, and was buried in the du Pont family cemetery there.

Bob Carpenter brought long-term stability to a poorly managed, second-rate baseball franchise that had foundered for decades in the shadow of Mack's mighty Athletics. With few professional skills but plenty of enthusiasm, he provided both the vision and the wealth to build an organization that, at its best, could compete with any the league had to offer. Unpretentious by nature, Carpenter overcame his initial insensitivity to league integration to become one of baseball's most beloved owners. Even Dick Allen lamented Carpenter's loss. In the end, although the club rarely finished above the .500 mark, Carpenter's diligence and sense of civic duty ensured that the Phillies remained Philadelphia's professional baseball team.

★

Many of Carpenter's business records as owner of the Philadelphia Phillies are maintained at the Hagley Museum and Library in Wilmington, Delaware. Bruce Kuklick, *To Every Thing a Season: Shibe Park and Urban Philadelphia, 1909–1976* (1991), examines the complex social dynamics surrounding the "house that Mack built." Rich Westcott and Frank Bilovsky, *The New Phillies Encyclopedia* (1993), includes a concise discussion of Carpenter's front-office reign. Rich Ashburn, "As Owners Go, 'Bob' Was One in a Million," *Philadelphia Daily News* (11 July 1990), is a tribute by one of the "Whiz Kids," while Kevin Mulligan, "Carpenter a Phillie Until End," *Philadelphia Daily News* (11 July 1990), includes several reflections by Whiz Kids. Obituaries are in the New Castle (Delaware) *News Journal* (10 July 1990); *Philadelphia Inquirer* (11 July 1990); and *New York Times* (11 July 1990).

WILLIAM E. FISCHER, JR.

CARRADINE, John (*b.* 5 February 1906 in New York City; *d.* 27 November 1988 in Milan, Italy), noted character actor of stage, screen, and television for more than fifty years.

Born Richmond Reed Carradine in the Greenwich Village neighborhood of New York City, Carradine was the son of William Reed Carradine, an attorney, poet, and Associated Press correspondent, and Genevieve W. Richmond, a surgeon. After attending the Episcopal Academy and the Graphic Art School in Philadelphia, young Carradine hitchhiked through the South, supporting himself as a scenery painter and sketch artist.

In 1925 Carradine abandoned the canvas for the stage, making his acting debut in *Camille* at the St. Charles Theatre in New Orleans. After a stint with a traveling Shakespearean troupe, he hitchhiked in 1927 to Hollywood, where he appeared in stage productions while attempting to break into films. He finally made his film debut under the name John Peter Richmond in *Tol'able David,* a 1930 remake of a successful silent feature. Two years later he landed his first important role as leader of the gladiators in Cecil B. DeMille's epic *The Sign of the Cross.*

In 1935 Carradine married Ardanelle McCool Cosner; they had one son and adopted another, both of whom entered the acting profession. Signing with Fox in 1935, he adopted the name John Carradine and began a distinguished career as one of Hollywood's leading character actors. As one critic noted in 1936, Carradine's "air of idealism, his projection of character-integrity, of wholesouledness" made him particularly convincing in villainous roles.

The tall, raw-boned actor's dour features and rich baritone voice earned him a lasting place in the informal stock company maintained by the legendary director John Ford, particularly after the favorable notices Carradine received for his portrayal of the sadistic prison guard in *The Prisoner of Shark Island* (1936). Appearing in more than ten Ford films between 1936 and 1964, Carradine gave impressive performances as the ruthless Tory in *Drums Along the Mohawk* (1939), as a gallant southern gambler in *Stagecoach* (1939), and most memorably as the itinerant preacher Casey in *Grapes of Wrath* (1940).

Nunnally Johnson, the famed screenwriter, recalled that Carradine was one of the few actors that Ford could never intimidate. Ford was often enraged by what he regarded as Carradine's absentminded approach to acting. Carradine always weathered Ford's torrents of abuse with a gentle smile. Then after a pleasant "You're okay, John," he would

John Carradine. COLUMBIA PICTURES/ARCHIVE PHOTOS

pat the sputtering director on the shoulder and calmly walk away.

While Carradine was winning critical and popular acclaim in early Ford classics, he joined the spirited circle of misfits that surrounded a fading Hollywood legend, John Barrymore. Despite the fact that a lifetime of drinking had destroyed his career, Barrymore was still loved by old friends like W. C. Fields and worshiped by young admirers such as Carradine, Errol Flynn, and Warren William. Carradine, as one Barrymore biographer noted, was one of several young actors who emulated his idol's style both on the screen and in private life. Barrymore, who shared Carradine's love of Shakespeare, clearly influenced the persona the young actor adopted that earned him the reputation of being a bit of a ham and an eccentric. Sporting a satin cape with a red lining and a wide-brimmed hat, Carradine, who was sometimes called the "Bard of the Boulevard," often wandered the streets of Los Angeles and New York reciting Shakespearean verse.

Carradine nonetheless remained a solid professional on the stage. Forming his own repertory company at the Geary Theatre in San Francisco, he enhanced his reputation as a keen Shakespearean stage actor through his portrayals of Hamlet, Othello, and Shylock in 1943. He and his wife divorced in 1944, and in 1945 he married Sonia Sorel, an actress who appeared with him on the stage. They had four sons, two of whom became actors. Carradine made his New York stage debut in 1945 as Allan Manville in *My Dear Children,* a role popularized by Barrymore in his last years. In 1955 Carradine's second marriage ended in divorce, and two years later he married Doris Irving Rich; they had no children. Carradine appeared on Broadway only a few times, and he played his last major stage role in 1962 as Lycus in the Stephen Sondheim musical *A Funny Thing Happened on the Way to the Forum.* His last major theatrical tour was in 1966 as Fagin in *Oliver.*

Throughout the same period, Carradine remained a familiar figure on the screen. Although he continued to make his mark in supporting roles, such as Aaron in DeMille's *Ten Commandments* (1956), Carradine starred in dozens of B movies, particularly in the horror genre. In all, he made some forty horror and science-fiction films, many of which he admitted were second-rate, shoddy productions. In many cases, he took such roles to finance his stage career. Nevertheless, many film buffs regard his portrayals of Count Dracula in *House of Frankenstein* (1944) and *House of Dracula* (1945) as second only to Bela Lugosi's interpretations. Furthermore, his role as the gentleman murderer in *Bluebeard* (1944) has often been regarded as one of his better performances.

Television offered Carradine yet another medium for his craft. In 1949 he made his television debut on *NBC Repertory Theater* as Malvolio in *Twelfth Night.* He then hosted the syndicated television series *Trapped* (1951) and appeared as a regular, Mr. Corday, in the series *My Friend Irma* (1953–1954). Carradine made appearances in dozens of major network programs, including such popular series as *Gunsmoke, Alfred Hitchcock Presents, The Twilight Zone, Bonanza, The Rifleman,* and *The Beverly Hillbillies.* In 1985 he received an Emmy for best performer in a daytime children's program, *Umbrella Jack.* When not appearing on stage, screen, or television, Carradine performed readings throughout the United States. In 1952 he gave a one-man recital at a nightclub in Greenwich Village, the Village Vanguard. In addition to his beloved Shakespeare, he quoted passages from Bernard Shaw, Rupert Brooke, and the Bible.

Carradine's was an acting family. His son John adopted the name David Carradine and emerged as a major television star in the 1970s. Father and son appeared together in two episodes of *Kung Fu,* David's internationally popular television series that aired from 1972 to 1975. Not surprisingly, the elder Carradine often urged his actor sons to study Shakespeare, maintaining, "If you play Shakespeare, you can play anything." His son Keith recalled, "He was a unique father who invested us all with a great sense of honor and integrity and professionalism in whatever we did." In an interview in 1986, Carradine summed up his career: "I never made big money in Hollywood. . . . I was paid in hundreds, the stars got thousands. But I worked with some of the greatest directors in films and some of the greatest writers. They gave me freedom to do what I can do best and that was gratifying."

Following the death of his third wife in 1971, Carradine in 1975 married Emily Cisneros. While traveling in Italy, he died in Milan of pneumonia and kidney and heart failure. A trouper to the end, Carradine's last words were: "Milan. What a beautiful place to die."

One of the most prolific actors of his generation, Carradine appeared in more than 220 films during a career that spanned half a century. While some critics derided his cheap-horror-movie roles, Carradine's talent graced some of the finest classics of Hollywood's golden era.

★

Carradine is the subject of entries in numerous standard biographical reference works, including David Ragan, *Who's Who in Hollywood* (1962); Walter Rigdon, ed., *Biographical Encyclopaedia and Who's Who of the American Theatre* (1966); and *Who's Who in Entertainment* (1988). Related sources include James Vinson, ed., *The International Dictionary of Films and Filmmakers,* vol. 3, *Actors and Actresses* (1986); and Ephraim Katz, *The Film Encyclopedia* (1994). John Kobler, *Damned in Paradise: The Life of John Barrymore* (1977); John Kotsilibas-Davis, *The Barrymores: The Royal Family in Hollywood* (1981); and Tag Gallagher, *John Ford: The Man and His Films* (1986), offer colorful glimpses of Carradine during Hollywood's golden era. A lengthy tribute is in *People* (12 Dec. 1988). Detailed obituaries are in the *New York Times* (29 Nov. 1988) and *Variety* (30 Nov. 1988).

JAMES M. PRICHARD

CARVEL, Thomas Andrew (*b.* 14 July 1906 in Athens, Greece; *d.* 21 October 1990 in Pine Plains, New York), entrepreneur who built a large franchise system of ice cream stores and invented numerous devices related to the manufacture of ice cream.

Thomas Carvel was one of seven children born to Andreas Carvelas and Christina (Triandefilou) Carvelas, who emigrated from Greece to Stratford, Connecticut, when Thomas was five years old. Carvel's father was an agriculturalist and wine chemist who changed the family name to Carvel in 1920. Thomas Carvel became an American citizen in 1918. He lived and went to school in Stratford and Bridgeport, Connecticut, as well as on the Lower East Side of New York City.

Carvel began his working life as a drummer for a Dixieland jazz band, the Georgia Melodians, and later became a fullback for a semiprofessional football team. Hoping for steadier employment, Carvel became a test driver for Studebaker automobiles in 1925. A misdiagnosis of tuberculosis caused him to leave the automobile industry for outdoor work. Borrowing $15 from his girlfriend, Agnes Stewart, Carvel purchased ice cream, which he sold from the back of a vending truck, in 1932.

With his brother Bruce, Carvel developed a machine that created a soft ice cream by instantly freezing cream and creating a fresh product, for which he obtained the first of more than 300 copyrights, patents, and trademarks. In 1934 his ice cream trailer blew out a tire in suburban Hartsdale, New York, en route to Kensico Dam, a popular picnic area. Lacking the money to fix the trailer, he moved the vehicle to a lot owned by a local pottery shop and sold ice cream there until he could raise the money to pay for repairs. The venture was a success, and on that site in 1937 the first Carvel store opened. On 22 May of that same year he married Stewart. They had no children.

Carvel started to sell his soft-ice-cream machines to other entrepreneurs in the early 1940s. Many purchasers had difficulty operating the devices and defaulted on the loans used to buy them. To protect his investments, Carvel began to sell his expertise and trademark in addition to the machines for a fee and a percentage of the profits, establishing one of the earliest and most successful franchises in America. The franchise training soon grew into a two-week course at the "Carvel College of Ice Cream Knowledge" in Yonkers, New York, where Carvel himself sometimes taught and always gave the graduation address. The franchise agreement fixed the Carvel Corporation as the sole supplier of equipment, ingredients, and other items for the individual stores, and franchisees were forbidden to form dealer organizations.

In 1954 Carvel was investigated by the Federal Trade Commission for his franchising practices, having been charged by several franchise owners with illegally restricting their supply sources, prices, and products. Carvel countered that he was indeed harsh in his management, but that in a franchise chain strict quality control was essential for the survival of the business. The case was settled in Carvel's favor in 1965 by the U.S. Supreme Court, which awarded Carvel $10.5 million, to be paid by the plaintiffs' lawyers for provoking the litigation. The suits drove the Carvel Corporation to near-bankruptcy, and the company lost about 70 percent of its stores during the affair as franchisees split away. The chain rebounded from the crisis quickly and started to expand internationally. In order to raise money, the company went public in 1969, but the stock did not rise appreciably. Carvel and his wife bought back about 90 percent of the stock in the late 1970s.

In 1955 a radio advertisement for the opening of a new Carvel store neglected to mention the borough of New York where the store was located, and Carvel drove to the radio station that same day and recorded a new commercial by himself without a script, leaving his grammatical mistakes and hesitations in the final tape. Carvel's gravelly voice and unrehearsed style made the ads memorable and thus suc-

Tom Carvel. CARVEL CORPORATION

cessful. This campaign helped make the chain (and Carvel himself) famous, and he continued to record his own advertisements at the corporation's Yonkers, New York, headquarters for the next thirty years.

The New York State Attorney General's office brought antitrust charges against Thomas Carvel and the Carvel Corporation in 1979, accusing them of using "fear, threats, harassment, extortion, coercion, and repressive measures, as well as fraud, fraudulent concealment, misrepresentation, and deceit" against the franchise owners. The charges were quickly pared down to one relating to purchasing restrictions. In 1985 the suit ended, with the final settlement not awarding damages to either side. The Carvel Corporation nevertheless relented, allowing the franchisees to purchase some products from other sources, provided they met Carvel's specifications.

Carvel himself was a firm believer in capitalism, and he received the Horatio Alger Award in 1957 for his success in business. He was the author of an article for the *New York Times* titled "Land of Opportunity? Damned Right!" (4 April 1973). In 1976 he set up the Thomas and Agnes Carvel Foundation, which grants money for medical research, rehabilitation, and scholarships. The foundation also funded a family health center for St. Joseph's Medical Center in Yonkers and a children's rehabilitation center at St. Agnes Hospital in White Plains, New York.

After resisting retirement for decades, Carvel finally sold control of the company in 1989 to Investcorp, an international investment bank, for more than $80 million and remained as a consultant with the company. He died of undetermined causes.

Thomas Carvel was a successful businessman and inventor who ran his corporation with a personal style. By creating the machines that made his different form of ice cream, recording his own commercials, and maintaining tight controls over his franchise owners to the point of litigation, he took a $15 loan and became the head of a multimillion-dollar international corporation.

★

Media coverage of Carel includes "Carvel's Recipe for Success," *New York Times* (26 Aug. 1973); "Carvel Going Stronger near Seventy," *Fort Lauderdale News* (31 Mar. 1975); "They're Making Their Own Pitch—And Loving It," *New York Times* (30 Aug. 1977); "A Voice Terrible, Yet Mouthwatering," *New York Times* (25 July 1978); "State Suit Accuses Carvel and Nineteen of Conspiracy to Seek Monopoly," *New York Times* (19 Aug. 1979); "The Trials of an Ice Cream Man," *New York Times* (26 Aug. 1979); "A Sweet Job with Sour Notes," *New York Times* (1 Dec. 1985); and "Meet the Presidents #4," *Good Housekeeping* (Nov. 1986). Obituaries are in the *New York Times* and the *Wall Street Journal* (both 22 Oct. 1990).

BRADLEY F. REED

CARVER, Raymond Clevie (*b.* 25 May 1938 in Clatskanie, Oregon; *d.* 2 August 1988 in Port Angeles, Washington), short story writer and poet celebrated for his portrayal of blue-collar American life.

Carver was the first of two children born to Clevie Raymond Carver, a saw filer, and Ella Beatrice Casey, a sometime waitress and store clerk. In 1941 the Carvers moved to Yakima, Washington, where Carver's father found employment in a lumber mill. Raymond and his brother were raised in a lower-middle-class household where money was always tight but the woods and streams of the Pacific Northwest provided hunting and fishing opportunities that enriched their young lives.

After graduating from Yakima High School in June 1956, Carver followed his father to work in a sawmill in Chester, California. He returned to Yakima and married Maryann Burk on 7 June 1957; they had two children. Moving to Paradise, California, Carver enrolled part-time at Chico State College, where he studied with the novelist John Gardner. The responsibilities of early parenthood weighed heavily on the Carvers as they struggled both to support a family and complete their educations. Hired at the Georgia-Pacific sawmill in Eureka, California, in June 1960, Carver transferred to nearby Humboldt State College, where he earned an A.B. degree in English in 1963 and

Raymond Carver, 1983. TESS GALLAGHER/ARCHIVE PHOTOS

received a $500 scholarship to the prestigious Iowa Writer's Workshop. Unable to support his family, he left Iowa to take a janitorial job at Mercy Hospital in Sacramento, California, without completing his M.F.A. degree.

By then Carver had begun to publish in small magazines and literary reviews. "Pastoral," his first work in a legitimate journal, appeared in the *Western Humanities Review* (winter 1963); the *Carolina Quarterly* featured two stories: "The Night the Mill Boss Died" (winter 1963) and "The Student's Wife" (fall 1964). "Will You Please Be Quiet, Please?," originally published in *December* magazine (1966), was selected for *The Best American Short Stories 1967.* In 1968 the English Club of Sacramento State College issued *Near Klamath,* Carver's first book of poems.

Carver's writing career was blossoming, but he and Maryann still had to worry about paying their bills. Overburdened with debt in 1967, they declared bankruptcy. In July, Carver became a textbook editor for Science Research Associates (SRA) in Palo Alto, California. When Maryann received a scholarship to Tel Aviv University, however, he took a leave of absence to accompany her to Israel. The family left in June 1968, planning to remain a year, but they returned in October, unable to cope with housing and schooling problems.

Back at SRA, Carver was named advertising director, a position he held until he was laid off in the fall of 1970. His dismissal proved a godsend. His unemployment benefits, coupled with a grant from the National Endowment for the Arts, freed Carver to devote himself exclusively to writing for the first time. Meanwhile, Gordon Lish, a friend from Carver's SRA days, became fiction editor at *Esquire.* He published Carver's story "Neighbors" in June 1971 and was instrumental in bringing out *Will You Please Be Quiet, Please?* (1976), Carver's first short story collection with a mainstream publisher, McGraw-Hill.

If Carver had not yet arrived in the 1970s, he was well on his way. His work was beginning to appear in the top commercial magazines, and he had contributions included in the O. Henry Awards *Prize Stories* in 1973, 1974, and 1975. His growing reputation also garnered him several teaching opportunities. In the early 1970s, Carver taught at the University of California, both at Santa Cruz and Berkeley, and at the University of Iowa Writer's Workshop. An essentially shy person whose voice often trailed off into a whisper when he read his poems, Carver found teaching painful but financially necessary. During this period Carver, in his own words, "took to full-time drinking as a serious pursuit." At Iowa, he later admitted, he and John Cheever "did nothing but drink." In 1975 Carver was teaching at the University of California, Santa Barbara, but he left early because of his alcoholism. Over the next fifteen months, Carver was hospitalized four times for alcohol abuse or rehabilitation before he stopped drinking on 2 June 1977.

This date marked a watershed in Carver's life. In May 1977 he and Maryann had separated. An attempt at reconciliation failed in July 1978, and they divorced officially on 18 October 1982. In the fall of 1977, Carver met the poet Tess Gallagher at a writer's conference in Dallas, Texas. Their paths crossed again in 1978, when, after being awarded a Guggenheim Fellowship, Carver went to teach at the University of Texas at El Paso. They began living together in 1979, forming a loving and supportive relationship that carried over into each other's work.

During the 1980s Carver was showered with success. In 1980 he and Gallagher joined the English department at Syracuse University. In 1981 Knopf published *What We Talk About When We Talk About Love,* the same year Carver broke into the *New Yorker* (30 November) with his story "Chef's House." *Cathedral* (1983), Carver's next collection, sold more than 20,000 copies after a front-page review in the *New York Times Book Review* (11 September 1983) and was nominated for the National Book Critics Award as well as a Pulitzer Prize. In May 1983 Carver received the American Academy and Institute of Arts and Letters Mildred and Harold Strauss Livings Award. The prize carried a $35,000 annual stipend for five years, provided that Carver give up teaching, a condition he enthusiastically embraced.

In January 1984 Carver left for Port Angeles to work without distraction. Although he intended to write stories, he found himself producing poems, most of which appeared in *Where Water Comes Together with Other Water* (1985) and *Ultramarine* (1986). In September 1987, at the height of his career, Carver, a heavy cigarette smoker, was diagnosed with lung cancer. He underwent surgery and radiation treatments, but by spring 1988 the cancer had reappeared in his lungs and had spread to his brain. On 17 June 1988 Carver and Gallagher were married in the Heart of Reno Chapel in Nevada. They continued to work on Carver's last book of poems, *A New Path to the Waterfall* (1989), until his death. After a wake, held in his living room at Ridge House, Carver was buried in the Ocean View Cemetery in Port Angeles on 4 August 1988.

Dead at age fifty, Carver was hailed as "America's Chekhov" and the best American short story writer since Ernest Hemingway. His reputation was based primarily on four collections: *Will You Please Be Quiet, Please?* (1976), *What We Talk About When We Talk About Love* (1981), *Cathedral* (1983), and *Where I'm Calling From* (1988). Carver's stories gave voice to the plight of America's working class and are generally credited with the revival of the short story in the United States during the 1980s, despite detractors who labeled his work "K-Mart realism" and "freeze-dried fiction." In his brief career, Carver received numerous awards, including a Wallace Stegner Creative Writing Fellowship (1972), *Poetry* magazine's Levinson Prize (1985), and an honorary doctorate from the University of Hartford (1988). Shortly before his death, Carver was inducted into the American Academy and Institute of Arts and Letters.

★

Carver's papers from 1978 to 1984 are on deposit at Ohio State University. Later materials are in the hands of Tess Gallagher. While there is no full-length biography, there are several volumes containing interviews and reminiscences, including Marshall Bruce Gentry and William L. Stull, eds., *Conversations with Raymond Carver* (1990); William L. Stull and Maureen Carroll, eds., *Remembering Ray: A Composite Biography of Raymond Carver* (1993); and Sam Halpert, *Raymond Carver: An Oral Biography* (1995). Adam Meyer, *Raymond Carver* (1995), primarily a critical survey, also contains biographical material. *Carver Country: The World of Raymond Carver* (1990) uses Carver's own writings and photographs by Bob Adelman to provide an impressionistic tour of the writer's life and times. An obituary is in the *New York Times* (3 Aug. 1988). Film and video presentations include "Dreams Are What You Wake Up From," a BBC *Omnibus* documentary appearing on English television on 22 Sept. 1989, and *To Write and Keep Kind* (1992), a PBS documentary done at KCTS, Seattle.

WILLIAM M. GARGAN

CASEY, William Joseph (*b.* 13 March 1913 in Queens, New York; *d.* 6 May 1987 in Glen Cove, New York), director of the Central Intelligence Agency (CIA) from 1981 to 1987, one of the most controversial figures in the Reagan administration, and a principal force in shaping that administration's anti-Soviet foreign policy during the final phase of the cold war.

Casey, one of five children, was raised in a solidly Catholic, middle-class Irish family in the borough of Queens in New York City. His father, William Joseph Casey, who began his career as a street cleaner with political connections, was a supervisor of the New York City employees retirement system. His mother, Blanche (Lavigne) Casey, was a housewife. Casey attended both parochial and public elementary and high schools before entering Fordham University in the Bronx, from which he graduated in 1934. At first intending a career in social work, Casey studied briefly at Catholic University in Washington, D.C., before returning to Queens to study law at St. John's University, graduating in 1937. He married Sophia Kurz on 22 February 1941; they had one child.

In 1938 Casey joined Leo Cherne's Research Institute of America, where he revealed a prodigious talent for absorbing and boiling down complicated government regulations into guidebooks for doing business with the government. After the Japanese attack on Pearl Harbor, Casey

William J. Casey testifies before the U.S. Senate Foreign Relations Committee, *c.* 1981. RICARDO WATSON/ARCHIVE PHOTOS

worked for the Bureau of Economic Warfare before obtaining a commission as a navy lieutenant, junior grade, in the navy's Office of Procurement and then transferring to William Donovan's Office of Strategic Services (OSS), the forerunner of the CIA. He served in Donovan's London station, eventually heading the OSS Secretariat for the European Theater of Operations, in charge of spy networks in occupied Europe and Nazi Germany.

After the war Casey founded his own research firm, the Institute for Business Planning, and he made a fortune producing how-to texts to guide lawyers and accountants through tax laws and government regulations. One of these guides, *Tax Sheltered Investments* (1952), has been credited with popularizing the idea of tax shelters. He also became a highly successful venture capitalist, and by providing seed money for fledgling enterprises he gained an interest in many profitable companies, including a major media empire, Capital Cities Broadcasting. From 1957 to 1971 he practiced law in New York City as a partner in the firm of Hall, Casey, Dickler, and Howley.

After working for the candidate Thomas Dewey during the 1948 presidential campaign, Casey remained active in Republican party politics, and in 1966 he ran unsuccessfully for a Long Island seat in Congress. After working for Richard Nixon's campaign in 1968, Casey was confirmed as chairman of the Securities and Exchange Commission in 1971. He resigned in December 1972 to become undersecretary of state for economic affairs, and in 1974 moved to the presidency of the Export-Import Bank. In 1974 Casey left government to resume his law practice, quickly establishing himself as one of the country's top corporate lawyers. President Gerald Ford appointed him to the Foreign Intelligence Advisory Board in 1976, and that same year Casey drew on his lifelong interest in the history of the American Revolution and of intelligence to write *When and How the War Was Fought: An Armchair Tour of the American Revolution.*

When Ronald Reagan's campaign for the Republican presidential nomination faltered during the 1980 primaries, Casey took over as his campaign director. After the election Reagan nominated Casey to be director of central intelligence. Assuming that office on 28 January 1981, Casey set himself the task of rebuilding and reenergizing the CIA, which he felt had been devastated under President Jimmy Carter's director of central intelligence, Stansfield Turner. Casey's excellent contacts in the White House enabled him to win significant increases in the agency's budget, with an emphasis on acquiring human intelligence sources in hostile countries (HUMINT). During the 1980s the Soviet Union also increased the tempo of its espionage operations against the United States, and Casey and the CIA were greatly embarrassed when a Soviet mole, Edward Lee Howard, was discovered within the ranks of the CIA. (The FBI shared in the embarrassment when Howard managed to elude FBI surveillance and flee to the Soviet Union.)

As director of central intelligence Casey was instrumental in shaping the aggressive anti-Soviet policies that became known as the Reagan Doctrine, which included, in addition to a renewed arms race and policies designed to destabilize the Soviet Union's Yalta empire in Eastern Europe, support for anticommunist insurgencies in Central America, Africa (especially Angola), and Afghanistan. Casey searched the world for opponents of Soviet-sponsored Marxist regimes and was indefatigable in efforts to aid them, most notably the Muslim rebels opposed to the communist regime in Kabul, where American-furnished weapons, including Stinger surface-to-air missiles that wreaked havoc on the Soviet air force, helped defeat the Soviet army that had invaded Afghanistan in 1979.

Casey's Afghan operations enjoyed bipartisan support in Congress. The situation was different in Latin America, where Casey's efforts to topple the communist regime in Nicaragua and to aid anticommunist governments despite congressional opposition eventually led to the greatest political crisis of the Reagan administration. By 1982 liberals in Congress were becoming worried that the CIA's aid to anti-Sandinista insurgents (Contras) in Nicaragua might involve the United States in a Vietnam-style quagmire, and an amendment sponsored by Representative Edward P. Boland of Massachusetts was attached to the defense appropriations bill for 1983 prohibiting funds for overthrowing the communist government in Nicaragua. President Reagan signed the legislation on 21 December 1983, but determined, at Casey's behest, that the Contra aid was not for the purpose of overthrowing the Sandinista government but was intended to encourage the Managua government to hold elections and to discourage it from furnishing arms to Marxist insurgencies in the region. Under this tortured logic the CIA continued its aid to the Contras.

The CIA's continued support for the Contras became a political issue in April 1984, when the *Wall Street Journal* revealed that the mining of three harbors in Nicaragua on 7 January 1984, which the Reagan administration had credited to the Contras, had actually been done by the CIA. It was further revealed that Casey had not informed (or at least not adequately informed) the ranking members of the Senate Select Committee on Intelligence, as required by law. Senator Barry Goldwater of Arizona, chairman of the Intelligence Committee, notified Casey in a letter that he was "pissed off"; this document was promptly and, in view of Goldwater's choice of words, appropriately, leaked to the press. When Casey claimed that he had actually mentioned the mining in an obscure reference during his committee testimony, the committee's vice chairman, Senator Daniel Patrick Moynihan of New York, resigned in protest, returning only when Casey apologized and signed the "Casey

Accords," which bound the director to inform the committee of any presidential findings for covert operations. Casey was now thoroughly distrusted by most Democrats, and some Republicans as well.

A second Boland Amendment was signed on 12 October 1984. It prohibited the CIA from providing any military or paramilitary support to the Contras for any reason. Boland and Congress believed that the amendment clearly prohibited any U.S. support for the Contras, but the administration, determined to maintain pressure on Soviet-supported regimes throughout the world, but particularly in Central America, embarked on an elaborate plan of deception to circumvent the Boland Amendment, an operation that eventually became known as the Iran-Contra affair. The Boland Amendment prohibited aid by any "agency involved in intelligence activities." The National Security Council (NSC), the administration reasoned, was not engaged in intelligence activities and furthermore did not require a presidential finding to launch a covert operation, nor did it report to a congressional oversight committee. Thus, support for the Contras was passed off to the NSC. Because the NSC had no money to give the Contras, Casey and the CIA helped guide the NSC toward third-party funds from sympathetic governments in Israel, South Africa, and Saudi Arabia. The plan eventually involved arms sales by the Israelis to the Iranians (which, it was hoped, would lead to the release of American hostages held by Iranian-influenced guerrillas in Lebanon); the profits from the sales, after the Israelis replaced the weapons with new purchases from the United States, were deposited in Swiss bank accounts for Contra arms purchases.

The need for this elaborate subterfuge passed in June 1986, when Congress once again authorized aid for the Contras, but in November 1986 a Beirut periodical published an account of the Iran-Contra operation during the prohibited period. This quickly escalated into a major constitutional crisis, with congressional hearings, the resignation and convictions (both overturned) of the director of the National Security Council, Admiral John Poindexter, and his aide, marine Colonel Oliver North, and the possibility of the impeachment of President Reagan. Long before the scandal reached this point, however, Casey had become deathly ill from a brain tumor. He resigned on 29 January 1987 and died of pneumonia. He was buried in Westbury, New York, on Long Island.

Debate still rages about whether, as director of central intelligence during some of the most critical years of the cold war, William J. Casey posed an even greater threat to his own country's constitutional system than he was to the enemy. Legendarily untidy, his mumbling almost impossible to decipher, his bald head fringed with unmanageable wisps of white hair, his hooded eyes peering suspiciously through owlish glasses, Casey looked like the stereotype of a James Bond movie spymaster. His days working for Wild Bill Donovan in the OSS had convinced him that intelligence and covert operations could change history, and his prodigious research in the history of intelligence led him to the same conclusion, which he thoroughly tested during his tenure as director of central intelligence.

Throughout his government career, Casey's reputation as a Wall Street wheeler-dealer surrounded him with an aura of distrust. This, combined with his natural secretiveness and his preference for a deceptive operating style, caused him to be regarded even by supporters as a man not particularly to be trusted. By liberal opponents of the administration's aggressively anticommunist foreign policies, Casey was regarded as a menace devoid of concern for the U.S. Constitution. His behavior in office reinforced their suspicions. This essential ambiguity is dramatized in Casey's purported deathbed interview with Bob Woodward. (Whether that famous encounter actually took place is denied by some authorities, notably Casey's biographer Joseph Persico and Casey's family.) After an admission by Casey that he knew about the diversion of arms sale funds to the Contras, Woodward asked him why he had done it. With speech almost beyond his physical capacities, Casey gasped out an answer that could be taken either as a confession of delusion or a final testimony of his anticommunist faith: "I believed."

★

There is no scholarly biography of Casey, but Joseph E. Persico, *Casey: From the OSS to the CIA* (1990), and Bob Woodward, *Veil: The Secret Wars of the CIA, 1981–1987* (1987), both contain a wealth of information based on interviews with Casey, his family, and his associates. Theodore Draper, *A Very Thin Line: The Iran-Contra Affairs* (1991), is the definitive account of the scandal. An obituary is in the *New York Times* (7 May 1987).

RICHARD GID POWERS

CHASE, Lucia Hosmer (*b.* 24 March 1897 in Waterbury, Connecticut; *d.* 9 January 1986 in New York City), dancer and codirector and chief financial support of the American Ballet Theatre for many years.

Chase was one of five daughters of Elizabeth Hosmer Kellogg and Irving Hall Chase, president of the Waterbury Clock Company and manufacturer of Ingersoll watches. From 1903 to 1913 she went to St. Margaret's School in Waterbury. She then attended Bryn Mawr College from 1913 to 1917 but did not take a degree. In a 1975 interview in *Dance* magazine, Chase admitted that "from the time I was three, I always wanted to be an actress." Her family, both wealthy and socially prominent, supported her early endeavors in theater, music, and dance. She moved to New York City in 1923 to study drama at the Theatre Guild

Lucia Chase with a sketch from *La fille mal gardée*. JOHN ORRIS/NEW YORK TIMES CO./ARCHIVE PHOTOS

School. She also took piano, voice, and tap dance lessons and received ballet instruction at the Vestoff Serova School from Mikhail Mordkin. In 1926 she married Thomas Ewing, Jr., vice president of the Alexander Smith and Sons Carpet Company in suburban Yonkers, which he had inherited from his uncle.

In 1933 Chase's husband died of pneumonia, leaving her with two sons. Although Chase had continued with her dramatic studies after her marriage, she did not consider a professional career in ballet, which she had taken up at sixteen, until after her husband's death, when she started to study seriously with Mordkin. Mordkin had been a premier danseur with the Bolshoi Theater Ballet in Moscow, partnering Anna Pavlova in the United States from 1910 to 1911. He had left Russia permanently in 1924. He taught in New York City and in the mid-1930s was operating several ballet schools, which gave performances featuring himself and Chase.

By 1935 Mordkin was organizing a new Mordkin Ballet Company, which opened at the Majestic Theatre in April 1937, with Chase in the lead role in *Giselle* and a principal role in Mordkin's *The Goldfish*. The reviews were sufficiently favorable to convince management of the need for a full-time administrator, and Richard Pleasant was hired. Despite the reviews and the personnel changes, the company lost money and would have had to close without a new infusion of cash. Unbeknownst to most, its principal backer was Lucia Chase, who with her children had inherited approximately $4.5 million from her husband. Her desire for anonymity was partly inspired by her wish to retain her comradeship with the other dancers and her integrity as a bona fide company member and, partly, as Charles Payne later observed in his *American Ballet Theatre* (1978), to obscure the fact of her continued investments in what appeared to be a failing enterprise.

By March 1939, influenced by Chase, the company's activities had been curtailed, while at the same time Pleasant was presenting "fantastic" plans to its directorate for a "ballet theater," which would be like a "museum," exhibiting different dances, old and new, the way museums exhibited art. As Chase said later, "it was [his] great wish that Ballet Theatre would always be a gallery of dance . . . a great international company, but American in spirit." Chase and the others were soon persuaded, and in the summer of 1939 Pleasant became the de facto executive secretary of the revised organization.

One of Pleasant's other ideas was to invite various choreographers to work on different dances, rather than have a resident choreographer. This led to disputes with Mordkin, but it also provided an early forum for some of the best dances created by Agnes de Mille, Jerome Robbins, Michael Kidd, Antony Tudor, and Michel Fokine.

In July 1939, when Pleasant asked Chase if she could underwrite some of the new organizational costs, she agreed to contribute $25,000, possibly annually, and Pleasant indicated he would seek other backing equal to hers. Ballet Theatre's opening at Radio City's Center Theatre in New York City on 11 January 1940 was highly acclaimed—John Martin of the *New York Times* dubbed it the "beginning of a new era." By the end of that month, however, the new enterprise had lost $200,000 and Chase remained the only backer. She later confessed that "if I had to do it all over again, I wouldn't stick my neck out," but as Payne noted, "Miss Chase [had] enthusiastically approved of and supported the project," with Pleasant on hand to "lead the not too unwilling but fiercely resisting lamb to the slaughter."

Largely because of his inability to find other funding, Pleasant resigned at the end of the 1940–1941 season. He was followed by German Sevastianov (1941–1943), who contracted with Sol Hurok, the impresario, to guarantee Ballet Theatre a weekly fee, and then by John Alden Talbot (1943–1945). Under Hurok, company performances came to be advertised as "S. Hurok Presents the Greatest in Russian Ballet," thus minimizing the Ballet Theatre's role and its original American focus. Despite the guarantee, Chase became increasingly convinced that the majority of the profits were going to Hurok. After a number of financial clashes between Hurok and Chase, Talbot resigned, and Hurok's influence was soon diminished.

Chase still continued to be Ballet Theatre's major financial source, and after Talbot's failure to find other backing and subsequent resignation, she and Oliver Smith (a fellow director who had designed Robbins's *Fancy Free*) were appointed its administrative directors on 21 April 1945. Although Chase said she only meant the appointment to last a year, "until they could find somebody else," she remained a director until 1980.

During most of the Hurok years, Chase was able to concentrate on her dancing, performing in a number of new ballets created by Fokine and Tudor, among others. She once said that she had been drawn to Mordkin as a teacher because "he was such a marvelous actor," and later critics of her own performances praised her as a "superb dramatic dancer and a brilliant comedienne." Indeed, she excelled in certain roles, especially as the Eldest Sister in Tudor's *Pillar of Fire,* which she performed with Nora Kaye for eighteen years and with which they both officially retired from dance in 1960, and as Fourth Song in his *Dark Elegies.* Other prominent roles included her performances as Queen Clementine in Fokine's *Bluebeard,* the Greedy Virgin in de Mille's *Three Virgins and a Devil,* and the Stepmother in *Fall River Legend.* After her retirement she continued to appear occasionally in character roles in *Swan Lake, Pillar of Fire,* and *Fall River Legend* and even took on a new role in Kenneth MacMillan's *Las Hermanas* in 1967 at the age of seventy.

Under the Chase-Smith leadership Ballet Theatre (renamed American Ballet Theatre in 1956) vacillated in terms of quality, size, and, always, funding, once having to disband entirely. Nevertheless, it built up a reputation as a "great artistic institution . . . a major force . . . in the entire world of international dance." Chase continued to contribute sizable amounts of money to keep the company alive. At the same time, as artistic director, she was responsible for selecting the dancers for the company itself as well as program casts and, with Smith, the repertory and choreographers; negotiating contracts with dancers and choreographers; and handling problems with subscribers and the press. Not everyone uniformly admired her decisions, and John Martin excoriated her in 1960 for being "devoted, determined and wrong-headed." Nevertheless, when she retired in September 1980, William Como, the editor of *Dance* magazine, wrote that Chase's years had been spent "intelligently and successfully . . . [forming] an unparalleled dance company . . . and we shall remember her as . . . willing to dare everything to make her company into a glorious reality." During those years she had been elected to the Grand Council of the (British) Royal Academy of Dancing (1946) and had received the Dance Magazine Award (1957), the Capezio Award (1968), the New York City Handel Medallion (1975), the U.S. Medal of Freedom (1980), the North Carolina School of the Arts Norman Lloyd Award (1981), and honorary degrees from Long Island University (1979), Yale University (1980), and the University of Wisconsin.

Chase died after a long illness and was buried in the family plot in Waterbury. Almost all the speakers at a memorial program in her honor that April extolled her refusal ever to be defeated, and all agreed that it was this quality especially—as "an indomitable woman" with a "granite will"—that allowed this tiny, extremely private lady to make Dick Pleasant's dreams of a great American ballet company with international fame come true.

★

Charles Payne, *American Ballet Theatre* (1978), contains a wealth of material on both Chase's association with the Ballet Theatre and her personal life, including an essay by Chase entitled "Directing a Ballet Company." The best biographical information is in interviews with Emily Coleman, "Lucia Chase: Director in Spite of Herself," *Theatre Arts* 42 (Sept. 1958): 63–65, 80; Olga Maynard, "Lucia Chase: First Lady of American Ballet," *Dance* (Aug. 1971); and John Gruen, "Close-Up: Lucia Chase," *Dance* (Jan. 1975), reprinted in Gruen, *People Who Dance* (1988). Over her long career *Dance* published other articles about Chase, most notably when she received the Dance Magazine Award of 1957 (Feb. 1958); the editorial by William Como when she resigned as American Ballet Theatre director (Sept. 1980); and the article at the time of her death (Mar. 1986). A controversy about her age is conclusively resolved by records found in the Bryn Mawr Archives. An obituary is in the *New York Times* (10 Jan. 1986).

SANDRA SHAFFER VANDOREN

CHASE, William Curtis (*b.* 9 March 1895 in Providence, Rhode Island; *d.* 21 August 1986 in Houston, Texas), army general best known for his role in the American recapture of Manila in the Philippine Islands during World War II.

Chase was the older of two children of Ward Beecher Chase, a real estate agent, and Dora Evelyn Curtis. He enrolled at Brown University in 1912 with the intention of becoming a lawyer, and the following year he enlisted as a private in the Rhode Island National Guard, serving in a field artillery battery. He graduated from Brown in June 1916 with a B.A. degree. During the next months, after President Woodrow Wilson mobilized the National Guard as a result of troubles along the Mexican border, he was on active duty as a sergeant with his battery at Fort Bliss, Texas.

In January 1917 Chase accepted a commission as a second lieutenant in the cavalry of the regular army, serving initially with the Third and Sixth Cavalry Regiments in

Texas. After the United States entered World War I in the spring of 1917, Chase, now a captain, attended the machine gun school at Fort Sill, Oklahoma, and then was assigned to the Fourth Infantry Division. A company commander in the Eleventh Machine Gun Battalion, which was attached to the Thirty-ninth Infantry Regiment, Chase saw action in France in 1918 in the Aisne-Marne, St. Mihiel, and Meuse-Argonne offensives and served with the occupation army in Germany until his division returned to the United States in the summer of 1919.

Between 1919 and 1941 Chase held a variety of line and school assignments while rising to the rank of lieutenant colonel. After serving with the Sixteenth Cavalry Regiment in Texas from 1919 to 1921, he taught military science and tactics at Michigan Agricultural College (now Michigan State University) until 1925. In 1922 he married Dorothea Marie Wetherbee; they had no children. From 1925 to 1927 Chase attended the Cavalry School at Fort Riley, Kansas, and the Infantry School at Fort Benning, Georgia; he was promoted to major in 1928. Following a stint with the Fourteenth Cavalry Regiment at Fort Sheridan, Illinois, he attended the Command and General Staff School at Fort Leavenworth, Kansas, from 1929 to 1931. For the next three years Chase was stationed at Fort Stotsenburg in the Philippines with the Twenty-sixth Cavalry Regiment. He returned to the United States in 1934 to attend the Army War College in Washington, D.C., and from 1935 to 1940 he was an instructor in tactics at the Cavalry School and the Command and General Staff School. By the fall of 1940, when he was appointed intelligence officer of the VIII Corps, Chase had earned a reputation as a skilled and energetic officer who combined an ability to command troops with a sound grasp of tactics.

Shortly after U.S. entry into World War II in December 1941, Chase was given command of the 113th Cavalry Regiment, and in March 1943 he was appointed commander of the First Cavalry Brigade in the First Cavalry Division with the rank of brigadier general. The following summer Chase went to Australia with his division, and after extensive training in jungle warfare and amphibious landings, he led a one-thousand-man reconnaissance force that captured the Japanese air strip at Momote on Los Negros Island in the Admiralty Islands on 29 February 1944. Later that year Chase led his brigade in the fierce battle for Leyte Island in the Philippines.

On the evening of 1 February 1945, just days after the First Cavalry Division had landed at Lingayen Gulf on Luzon Island in the Philippines, Chase was assigned command of a special motorized task force drawn from the division, dubbed the "flying column," that had orders to race to Manila as quickly as possible and free American internees who had been imprisoned by the Japanese at Santo Thomas University since 1942. Assuming command

Major General William C. Chase, commander of the U.S. First Cavalry Division, *c.* 1945. U.S. ARMY MILITARY HISTORY INSTITUTE, CARLISLE BARRACKS, PENNSYLVANIA

at Cabanatuan, about seventy miles north of Manila, Chase dashed south with his left flank open, and with speed and surprise his men were the first Americans to enter Manila, crossing the city lines in the evening of 3 February and liberating 3,700 internees, a feat that earned Chase front-page newspaper coverage around the world.

Several days later Chase was appointed commander of the Thirty-eighth Division. During the next months it participated in the capture of the Bataan Peninsula and Corregidor Island and other fortified islands in Manila Bay and in the bitter fighting east of Manila that lasted through the spring of 1945, helping to ensure a fresh water supply for Manila by seizing the critical Wawa Dam. In July, now a major general, Chase was named commander of the First Cavalry Division, and on 5 September units from his division were the first Americans to enter Tokyo, after the Japanese surrender in August.

Chase remained in command of the First Cavalry Division during the occupation of Japan until February 1949, when he returned to the United States to serve as chief of staff and later deputy commander of the Third Army at Fort MacPherson, Georgia. In May 1951 he became head of the Military Advisory and Assistance Group for Generalissimo Chiang Kai-shek's Nationalist Chinese army on

Formosa. Over the next four years Chase, an outspoken anticommunist and a fervent supporter of Chiang's regime, worked tirelessly to upgrade Chiang's understrengthed, underequipped, and poorly trained army. Despite delays created by the demands of the Korean War, Chase instituted programs to reorganize, reequip, and retrain Chiang's army, and by February 1955, when he retired, Chase had helped effect a marked improvement in its equipment, efficiency, and morale.

Following his retirement from the army, Chase attended Trinity University in San Antonio, Texas, earning an M.A. degree in history and political science in 1957, and then taught political science at the University of Houston until his retirement in 1965. His first wife having died in 1957, Chase married Hallie Barlow Olcott, a widow, in 1961. He died of undisclosed causes.

An unpretentious soldier of slight build who was popular with his troops, Chase was one of the outstanding combat commanders in the Southwest Pacific in 1944 and 1945 and an effective military adviser to Chiang Kai-shek.

★

A collection of Chase's papers is in the U.S. Army Military History Institute, Carlisle Barracks, Pennsylvania. William C. Chase, *Front Line General: The Commands of Maj. Gen. Wm. C. Chase* (1975), is an autobiography that provides extensive discussion of his service during World War II and on Formosa. References to Chase's service during World War II are in Benjamin C. Wright, *The First Cavalry Division in World War II* (1947); Peyton Hoge, Thomas J. Hopper, and Victor H. Lott, *Thirty-eighth Infantry Division* (1947); M. Hamblin Cannon, *Leyte: The Return to the Philippines* (1954); John Miller, Jr., *Cartwheel: The Reduction of Rabaul* (1959); Robert R. Smith, *Triumph in the Philippines* (1963); and D. Clayton James, *The Years of MacArthur, 1941–1945* (1975). References to his work with Chiang Kai-shek are in Karl Lott Rankin, *China Assignment* (1964). An obituary is in the *Washington Post* (25 Aug. 1986).

JOHN KENNEDY OHL

CHILDRESS, Alvin (*b.* 1908 in Meridian, Mississippi; *d.* 19 April 1986 in Los Angeles, California), African-American stage and screen actor and director best known for his role as the good-natured cabdriver Amos Jones in the highly controversial *Amos 'n' Andy* television series of the early 1950s.

The son of a dentist and a schoolteacher, Childress received a B.S. degree from Rust College in Holly Springs, Mississippi, in 1927. Although he first envisioned a medical career, Childress discovered at Rust his passion for theater and, after graduation, made his way to New York City and his Broadway debut in the 1932 show *Savage Rhythm.* The play soon folded, and Childress began working at Columbia University's Service Bureau for Education in Human

Alvin Childress (*left*) and Spencer Williams in the televised version of *Amos 'n' Andy,* 1951. ARCHIVE PHOTOS

Relations, a depression-era project of the Works Progress Administration (WPA). While there, Childress penned twenty playlets that illuminated for students the cultural contributions of various racial groups in the United States.

In 1935 Childress joined the Federal Theatre Project's Negro Theatre Unit in New York, established by the WPA to provide training and experience to actors and technicians. A drama coach for two years, Childress expanded his acting portfolio with appearances in Federal Theatre productions of *Sweet Land* (opening January 1937), *Haiti* (February 1937), and *The Case of Philip Lawrence* (June 1937), all at New York's Lafayette Theater. Childress's talents were equally suited to motion pictures. His first film, the 1932 musical *Harlem is Heaven,* was followed by *Crimson Fog* that same year; from 1933 to 1938 Childress was an actor and director with the Harlem-based Paragon Pictures Corporation. In 1940 he began an eight-year association with the American Negro Theatre (ANT), a New York company best known for its 1944 production of Philip Yordan's *Anna Lucasta,* in which Childress played the role of Noah. First presented at the Harlem Branch of the New York Public Library, *Anna Lucasta* went on to a two-year run on Broadway, and Childress later directed one of the show's touring productions. Childress also developed and oversaw ANT's training program, which offered workshops for community and theater members, and he appeared in company productions, including *Natural Man* (1941) and the Harlem comedy hit *On Striver's Row* (1946).

In the mid-1940s, Childress married fellow ANT actor and playwright Alice Childress, later highly acclaimed for her contributions to African-American theater; they had one child. The family fared well; in addition to his blossoming New York stage career, Childress also owned a successful radio and record shop at 155th Street and Amsterdam Avenue in Manhattan.

Childress's greatest, albeit short-lived, fame came with the role of Amos Jones, the philosophical cabdriver in the television spinoff of the popular *Amos 'n' Andy* radio show. The radio show, featuring two white men playing a range of African-American comedic characters, had first aired in 1928 and had quickly become a national sensation. During a yearlong talent search that began in 1948, Childress was the first actor cast; he and costars Spencer Williams and Tim Moore were among the first African Americans with starring roles in prime-time television. Although most of the show's other characters were broadly drawn, with caricatured speech and mannerisms, author and historian Melvin Patrick Ely noted that Childress played his own noncomedic role "calmly, with dignity and intelligence." The Christmas episode featuring Amos (Childress) explaining the meaning of the Lord's Prayer to his young daughter, Arbadella, is consistently cited as an example of *Amos 'n' Andy* at its finest.

The series was roundly denounced by the National Association for the Advancement of Colored People (NAACP), which complained that the show perpetuated negative racial stereotypes and called for a boycott of the program's sponsor, Blatz Beer. Opposing camps argued that the show was no different than "white" situation comedies that relied on formulaic misunderstandings and crazy antics by tried-and-true character types. Although dissension within the African-American community undercut NAACP efforts and prevented a successful boycott, the show was canceled after its second season despite initially solid ratings and a 1952 Emmy nomination for best comedy series. Reruns of *Amos 'n' Andy* were broadcast on local television stations and remained popular until the mid-1960s, when civil rights groups pressured Columbia Broadcasting System (CBS) to withdraw the series from syndication.

The cancellation of the show vitually sounded the death knell for Childress's acting career, which he felt had been sabotaged by the NAACP. Childress told the *Los Angeles Times* in 1964, "I don't feel it [the series] harmed the Negro at all. . . . The series had many episodes which showed the Negro with professions and businesses like attorneys, store owners, and so on which they never had in TV or movies before." To add insult to injury, Childress and his costars received virtually no residual payments, because their contracts had been written prior to the development of modern television syndication practices. Disillusioned by the experience, divorced from his wife Alice, and typecast as Amos while reruns of the show aired, Childress was not seen on television again until 1964, when he appeared in an episode of *Perry Mason,* and later in cameo roles in *Sanford & Son* (1972), *Good Times* (1974), and *The Jeffersons* (1975). He returned briefly to the stage in *The Amen Corner,* a 1966–1967 production of Los Angeles's Theatre of Being. On the big screen, he appeared in an all-black version of *Anna Lucasta* (1958), *The Day of the Locust* (1975), and *The Bingo Long Traveling All-Stars and Motor Kings* (1976).

Childress worked at various temporary jobs and eventually found a position with the Los Angeles County Civil Service Commission. He settled into a modest life with his second wife, Sophie, and died at St. Erne Sanitarium after suffering from a variety of illnesses, including Parkinson's disease, pneumonia, and diabetes.

Amos 'n' Andy ushered in—then quickly ushered out—a brief period of ethnic diversity not seen again on prime-time television for two decades. Another show featuring a cast of African Americans did not appear until 1971 (*Sanford & Son*). In 1983 the NAACP restated its opposition to *Amos 'n' Andy* in response to plans for a nostalgic retrospective, calling the show a "scurrilous stereotypical treatment of blacks." Despite the ongoing criticism, videocassettes of *Amos 'n' Andy* television episodes retained a following among viewers of all races. Scholars and legions of fans, both black and white, remain divided on whether *Amos 'n' Andy* was, in fact, damaging to the public image of African Americans or simply all-around good television comedy.

★

Information on Childress is in John E. O'Connor, ed., *American History/American Television: Interpreting the Video Past* (1983); J. Fred MacDonald, *Blacks and White TV: Afro-Americans in Television Since 1948* (1983); Melvin Patrick Ely, *The Adventures of Amos 'n' Andy: A Social History of an American Phenomenon* (1991); S. Robert Lichter et al., *Watching America* (1991); and Edwart T. Clayton, "The Tragedy of Amos 'n' Andy," *Ebony* (Oct. 1961). An obituary is in the *Los Angeles Times* (29 Apr. 1986).

RACHEL SNYDER

CHILDS, Marquis William (*b.* 17 March 1903 in Lyons, Iowa; *d.* 30 June 1990 in San Francisco), Pulitzer Prize–winning journalist and author widely respected for his thoughtful commentaries on domestic and international politics from the New Deal to the 1980s.

Childs was the son of William Henry Childs, an attorney occasionally active in local Republican politics, and Lilian

Marquis Childs. ST. LOUIS POST-DISPATCH

Malissa Marquis Childs. He had one younger brother. Both parents had deep roots in Lyons, a Mississippi River town later absorbed into neighboring Clinton; their families had farmed their extensive landholdings for generations. Despite a continuing decline in economic status, they ranked among the locality's top families socially. Childs's early years were happy, although somewhat clouded by his father's failures in politics and business. Later, he recalled the joyous freedom of outdoor life, especially the hours spent riding his pony along the riverbank. In his teens he participated in the formal social events sponsored by the town's handful of lumber millionaires. A peripatetic "cousin" encouraged his reading and his curiosity about faraway places. In 1918 Childs graduated in a class of eighteen from the local high school.

By the age of thirteen, Childs knew he wanted to be a writer, but his father insisted that he study medicine. He thus spent three restless years doing poorly in premedical courses at the University of Iowa before dropping out after a few agonizing months of anatomy lab. When his outraged father refused further assistance, Childs left abruptly for Chicago. For the next eight months he clerked at the huge Marshall Field's department store. The following year, with an uncle's financial help, Childs was at the University of Wisconsin studying journalism. He still longed to be a writer, but after getting his B.A. degree in 1923 he headed the tiny United Press (UP) bureau in Madison, Wisconsin, for the next year and a half. Because Wisconsin was then a laboratory for progressive social legislation, Madison was an exciting place. For the first time Childs could share his innermost thoughts with like-minded people.

Somewhat later, Childs received word of his father's apparent suicide. The family home was sold, and in 1924 Childs moved to Iowa City, Iowa, doing graduate work and some teaching in the University of Iowa's English Department. It was a time rich in friendships, mentors, and intellectual stimulation. In 1925, with an M.A. degree in hand, he went to New York City as a UP reporter, delighting in the ferment of Greenwich Village life. The following year UP asked him to take over their bureau in St. Louis, where his fiancée, Lu Prentiss, was teaching. They were married on 26 August 1926 and had two children. Before year's end, Childs convinced the prestigious *St. Louis Post-Dispatch* to hire him as a feature writer for their Sunday magazine. From 1926 to 1931 he crisscrossed the United States seeking stories.

It seemed Childs would never find the time to write fiction, but an unanticipated anonymous gift of $2,500 allowed him to obtain a leave of absence from the *Post-Dispatch* and to attempt a first novel. Discouraged by the difficulties of creating convincing characters, however, he abandoned the project partway through. *The Cabin,* a second attempt at fiction written in the winter of 1932, was rejected as "not significant" by Simon and Schuster. The book, which Childs considered his best, was published by Harper's in 1944. His other novels were *Washington Calling* (1937) and *The Peacemakers* (1961), the latter drawing very effectively on his direct knowledge of cold war diplomacy. Meanwhile, Childs's career had taken a significant turn toward political journalism. A 1930 visit to Sweden aroused his interest in progressive social legislation. After a second visit he published "Sweden: Where Capitalism Is Controlled" (*Harper's,* Nov. 1933) and *Sweden: The Middle Way* (1936), his first major literary success. The latter work stimulated President Franklin D. Roosevelt's interest in cooperative movements.

In early 1934 Childs was appointed to head the *Post-Dispatch* Washington, D.C., bureau. It was the heyday of the New Deal, a time of experimentation, invention, political debate, and bubbling energy. Producing column after column, as well as books and articles, he loved it all and got to know everyone. In 1936 he traveled 15,000 miles covering Roosevelt's reelection campaign. Two years later he completed *This Is Democracy: Collective Bargaining in Scandinavia.* Another series for the *Post-Dispatch* included reports on the Spanish Civil War and the social and economic status of Mexico. His account of corrupt commercial dealings between the United States and Mexico was bitterly attacked by Senator Joseph Guffey. A subsequent congressional investigation vindicated the accuracy of Childs's report. The senator apologized publicly and retracted his charges. In 1943 Childs spent three months in Europe as a war correspondent.

Over the years Childs's acquaintances came to include presidents, Supreme Court justices, members of the cabinet, diplomats, generals, and European leaders. He continued as Washington correspondent for the *Post-Dispatch* until 1944. He then joined United Features Syndicate as a columnist, returning to the *Post-Dispatch* as special correspondent in 1954. In 1962 he was named chief Washington correspondent, and from 1968 until his retirement from the paper's staff in 1974, he held the title of contributing editor. In August 1969, a year after the death of his wife, he married Jane Neylan McBaine. In 1970 he was awarded his first Pulitzer Prize for distinguished commentary. Childs's syndicated columns—five a week for many years—appeared in more than 150 U.S. and international newspapers. He also contributed essays to leading magazines, such as *Harper's,* the *Saturday Evening Post,* and the *New Republic,* and lectured, taught, and wrote many books.

In the 1940s Childs was primarily concerned with the New Deal and the effects of World War II. His books *This Is Your War* (1942) and *I Write from Washington* (1942) were highly praised. His interests expanded, with particular attention given to civil rights, U.S.-Soviet relations, and the prevention of nuclear war. Whatever the subject, he drew on his deep fund of knowledge and experience. Noteworthy titles include *The Ragged Edge* (1955); *Eisenhower: Captive Hero* (1958); *Taint of Innocence* (1967); *Witness to Power* (1975); *Sweden: The Middle Way on Trial* (1980); and, in a different vein, *Mighty Mississippi: Biography of a River* (1982). He also coauthored *Ethics in Business Society* with Douglass Cater (1954) and coedited *Walter Lippmann and His Times* (1959) with James Reston.

Between 1974 and 1981, Childs continued to write two or three columns a week for the *Post-Dispatch.* Fair and close to six feet tall, he lived with his second wife in San Francisco for several years. He died there after a prolonged illness and was buried in Clinton, Iowa.

Childs believed wholeheartedly in his obligation to help Americans understand and think about the important issues of public life in a democracy. For him, facts had to be accurately reported in context and presented from a clearly articulated point of view. The range of his influential contacts in Washington and his reputation for trustworthiness gave him extraordinary access to events and ideas. His liberal sympathies never distorted his balanced presentations. He had, as his friend and colleague James Reston once said, a fine sense of history and of humor. When he criticized, he did so constructively, conscious of the harm done "in this bloody century" by ideologues. His 28 May 1981 column announcing his retirement identified the questions that had consistently guided his thinking and writing about politics: Was a proposed action likely to work and at what cost? Would the action—would his commentary—help to lessen human suffering?

★

Two columns in the *St. Louis Post-Dispatch* (28 May 1981) give a sense of Childs the man: Thomas Ottenad's "News Columnist Childs 'Winding-Down' Career" and Childs's own "Thirty-five Years of Deadlines." An obituary is in the *New York Times* (2 July 1990). "The Reminiscences of Marquis William Childs," recorded in 1957, were transcribed as pt. 1, no. 34 of Columbia University's Oral History Collection (1972).

URSULA SYBILLE COLBY

CIARDI, John Anthony (*b.* 24 June 1916 in Boston, Massachusetts; *d.* 30 March 1986 in Edison, New Jersey), poet, translator, essayist, editor, lexicographer, and author of more than forty books who is best known for his translation of Dante's *Divine Comedy.*

Ciardi was the son of Carminantonio Ciardi, an insurance salesman, and Concetta DiBenedictis, a homemaker. In 1921, two years after the death of his father, Ciardi moved with his mother and his three sisters from Boston to Medford, Massachusetts. After his graduation from Medford High School in 1933, he entered Bates College in Lewiston, Maine, in 1934. In 1936 he transferred to Tufts College in Boston, from which he graduated magna cum laude with an A.B. degree in 1938. Enrolling at the University of Michigan, he received an M.A. degree in 1939 along with the Avery Hopwood Award for poetry.

Ciardi's first poetry collection, *Homeward to America,* was published in 1940, when he also was hired as an instructor at the University of Kansas City. During World War II, from 1942 to 1945, he served in the Pacific as a gunner on a B-29 heavy bomber. While in the military, he sent poems to the magazine *Poetry,* from which he received prizes in 1943, 1944, 1946, and 1955. On 28 July 1946 he married (Myra) Judith Hostetter, a journalist, with whom he had a daughter and two sons. They lived in Metuchen, New Jersey, and had a second home in Key West, Florida. In the fall of 1946, he became an instructor of English at Harvard University. His book *Other Skies,* based on his military experience, was published in 1947 and was followed by *Live Another Day* in 1949, the same year he became poetry editor for Twayne Publishers.

Mid-Century American Poets (1950), his first publication for Twayne, includes an essay by each poet on his or her working principles. The book fulfilled a major objective of

Ciardi's career, to make clear to "an audience of general culture" the way poets approached the creative process. Taking a leave from Harvard from 1950 to 1951, he lectured on poetry at the Salzburg Seminar on American Studies. In 1953, he was appointed associate professor of creative writing at Rutgers University.

The most active and controversial period of Ciardi's career was from the mid-1950s to the early 1970s. In 1954 he published a verse translation of the first part of Dante's *Divine Comedy*. Ciardi's rendering of the *Inferno* into idiomatic American English received critical praise and was also a commercial success, selling more than a million copies during his lifetime. In 1955 Ciardi authored *As If,* and that year he became director of the Bread Loaf Writers Conference, operated by Middlebury College in Vermont. Further recognition came in 1956, when he was promoted to full professor at Rutgers, he took the post of poetry editor of *Saturday Review,* and he was awarded the Prix de Rome of the American Academy of Arts and Letters in Rome. In 1957 he was elected a fellow of the National Institute of Arts and Letters.

On 12 January 1957 Ciardi wrote a controversial review of Anne Morrow Lindbergh's *The Unicorn and Other Poems* (1956) in the *Saturday Review.* Responding to the considerable reader protest, he wrote "The Reviewer's Duty to Damn," which asserted that negative evaluations were appropriate if they followed stated principles. Although Ciardi nearly resigned over the dispute, the ability to arouse such furor over poetry was considered by Ciardi and Norman Cousins, an editor and colleague at the *Saturday Review,* as a major accomplishment. After publishing *I Marry You: A Sheaf of Love Poems* (1958) and *Thirty-nine Poems* (1959), many of which were about artists, Ciardi ended the decade with *The Reason for the Pelican* (1959), his first publication of poetry for children.

In the 1960s Ciardi published twelve juvenile collections, of which the most popular were *The Man Who Sang the Sillies* (1961); *John J. Plenty and Fiddler Dan* (1963), for which a ballet was choreographed in 1986; and *The King Who Saved Himself from Being Saved* (1965), which became the text for an operetta in 1986. For an adult audience, he produced *In the Stoneworks* (1961), *In Fact* (1962), and *This Strangest Everything* (1966). Also devoting his time to translating Dante's *Purgatorio* (1961); hosting the television show *Accent* (1961–1962), where he interviewed writers and artists; his editorship at *Saturday Review;* and numerous lecturing engagements, he decided to give up his tenured professorship at Rutgers in 1961.

Ciardi's teaching of prosody continued, however, through his participation in writers' conferences and his books and essays, especially *How Does a Poem Mean?* (1959), *Dialogue with an Audience* (1963), *On Poetry and the Poetic Process* (1971), and *Manner of Speaking* (1972). Ciardi wrote, "A poem is never about ideas: it is always and only about the experience of ideas. . . . Whatever emerges in a piece of writing emerges as words, forms, images, and rhythms. . . . A good poem has dramatic structure. . . . Metaphors . . . must perform very much as a scene in a play . . . [with] the sense of entrance, development, and motion toward a climax." Ciardi wanted to express the universal through the personal: "What I am, you are" and "evil, like innocence . . . must be accounted for in any man's psyche before he has faced himself fully. No man knows himself until he has been embarrassed by what he knows of himself." The poem "Tenzone" was Ciardi's own internal debate between the poet he aspired to be and all the other talents to which he directed his energies.

John Ciardi. ARCHIVE PHOTOS

Although through the 1960s and early 1970s Ciardi was awarded seven honorary doctorates, his coerced resignation as director of the Bread Loaf conference in 1972 was the signal of his falling out of favor. He rejected the notion of "relevance," which had become the buzzword of the decade. He resisted being classified as an Italian-American poet, despite numerous references to his roots, and he refused to categorize poets by ethnicity, race, or gender. His translation of *Paradiso* (1970) was not as well received as the *Inferno* had been, although in 1977 his complete translation of *The Divine Comedy* appeared in hardcover and for at least the next two decades was widely viewed as the standard text in English of Dante's fourteenth-century allegory. *Lives of X* (1971), a collection of autobiographical poems that he thought innovative in their use of narrative detail, received no reviews at the time. He left *Saturday Review* in 1972 and followed Cousins to *World Magazine,* where Ciardi was contributing editor until 1973. He published *The Little That Is All* in 1974 and *For Instance* in 1979.

Selected Poems (1984), which includes a reprint of *Lives of X,* was Ciardi's effort to select for the public the best of his entire opus. But his poem "A Trenta-Sei of the Pleasure We Take in the Early Death of Keats," from *Birds of Pompeii* (1985), introduced a new structure that may prove to be his most significant contribution to poetry. The *trenta sei* is six stanzas of six lines each, in which the second stanza begins with the second line of the first stanza, the third stanza begins with the third line, and so forth. In response to earlier criticism that he was not able to develop longer poems or a new structure, his last collections were usually of long, unrhymed, but clearly rhythmed stanzas.

Among Ciardi's best poems are "The Evil Eye," "To Judith Asleep," and especially "Most Like an Arch This Marriage," which consists of four stanzas of embraced rhymes. The arch provides a perfect structure for the theme of two people building a marriage: "Most like an arch—two weaknesses that lean / into a strength."

The last two decades of Ciardi's life were devoted to his new interest in limericks and etymologies. He produced two collections of limericks, *Limericks: Too Gross* (1978) and *A Grossery of Limericks* (1981), both coauthored with Isaac Asimov, and two volumes of *A Browser's Dictionary* (1980 and 1983). He was working on the third volume of the dictionary at the time of his death. The self-portrayed poet, "That affable, vital, inspired even, and well-paid / persuader of sensibility with the witty asides / but at core, lucent and unswayed— / a gem of serenest ray—besides being the well-known poet, critic, editor, and middle-high / aesthete of the circuit," died of a heart attack at the John F. Kennedy Hospital in Edison, New Jersey, on Easter Sunday. He is buried in Metuchen, New Jersey.

Ciardi's place in twentieth-century poetry is defined by what he did not write as well as by what he did. His poetry did not espouse causes, except against censorship. He opposed the Vietnam War but did not write about it. Accused of being a radical in 1950, he insisted he was a moderate liberal and was henceforth apolitical. Whereas many of the "new" poets were either Christian mystics or Zen-Buddhists, he was a self-described secularist. His poetry does not fit easily into any of the categories that describe the works of his contemporaries, such as objectivist, psychoanalytic, existential, abstract expressionist, or beat. He liked to cite a line of Wallace Stevens, "What has there been to love that I have not loved?" to which he responded, "Well, for one thing, categories."

The poet Kenneth Rexroth described Ciardi as one who "wrote about himself, loving his wife and children, always located in a very concrete poetic situation, poems with definite location and occupied with tangible objects, animals, stars, people . . . [poems] clear, intimate, and living . . . simple, sensuous and passionate." Many of his contemporaries admired him, as did John Updike, more for his "robust personality" than for his poetry.

★

Collections of Ciardi's papers are in the Library of Congress, the Lockwood Library of the State University of New York at Buffalo, and the Wayne State University Library. Edward M. Cifelli, *John Ciardi: A Biography* (1997), is the definitive biography. Cifelli, ed., *The Selected Letters of John Ciardi* (1991), includes Ciardi's correspondence from the age of nineteen until shortly before his death. Ciardi's *Dialogues with an Audience* (1963), mostly comprising his reviews in *Saturday Review,* gives a good sense of his sensibility. See also William White, *John Ciardi: A Bibliography* (1959), and Edward Francis Krickel, *John Ciardi* (1980), a study of Ciardi's works until 1980 that includes biographical information and an updated selected bibliography. An obituary is in the *New York Times* (2 Apr. 1986).

BARBARA L. GERBER

CLARK, Joseph Sill, Jr. (*b.* 21 October 1902 in Philadelphia, Pennsylvania; *d.* 12 January 1990 in Philadelphia, Pennsylvania), U.S. senator and mayor of Philadelphia.

One of two children born to Joseph Sill Clark, a lawyer, and Kate Richardson Avery, Clark grew up in Chestnut Hill, an upper-class neighborhood in the northwestern part of Philadelphia. He attended Middlesex School in Massachusetts, where he played football and baseball and graduated first in his class in 1919. At Harvard College, he studied history, government, and economics; competed on the baseball and track teams; and received his B.A. degree magna cum laude and with Phi Beta Kappa honors in 1923. He returned home to attend the University of Pennsylvania Law School, where he was an editor of the law review and from which he graduated with a law degree in 1926.

Clark was admitted to the Pennsylvania bar in 1926 and joined his father's law firm. Although he had been raised as a Republican, he broke with family tradition in 1928 and supported Democrat Alfred E. Smith for the U.S. presidency. With another young Philadelphia lawyer, Richardson Dilworth, Clark founded the Warriors, a Democratic

Joseph S. Clark, Jr., *c.* 1967. COURTESY OF STEVE NEAL

reform group. He ran unsuccessfully for the Philadelphia City Council in 1933. Dilworth managed his campaign. In 1934 Clark ran Dilworth's losing bid for the state senate.

During the Great Depression, the elder Clark lost most of his law clients, and Joseph, Jr., left his father's firm in 1934 to serve as deputy attorney general of Pennsylvania, handling trial work in connection with bank closings. Clark joined the firm of Dechert, Bok, Smith, and Clark in 1935. In 1941 he entered the U.S. Army Air Forces as a captain. He served as director of the AAF organizational planning headquarters and, later as General George E. Stratemeyer's deputy chief of staff in the India-China-Burma theater. During twenty-three months in this theater, Clark earned the Bronze Star and was promoted to full colonel.

On his return to Philadelphia, Clark joined forces with Dilworth to challenge the Republican machine. Clark managed Dilworth's campaign against Republican mayor Bernard Samuels. Although Dilworth lost, he made a surprisingly strong showing.

Clark made his second political race in 1949, for city controller, while Dilworth ran for city treasurer. Both won by large pluralities. As controller, Clark exposed graft and corruption in other city departments, including the embezzlement of amusement taxes and court funds and falsification of records in the purchasing and water departments. A patrician in politics, he was highly principled, thoughtful, and reflective but could also be self-righteous in his dealings with other elected officials.

Using a broom as his symbol, Clark ran for mayor in 1951 and pledged to sweep out corruption. Republicans slated a noted Protestant clergyman, Reverend Daniel A. Poling, as Clark's opponent in an attempt to offset the corruption issue. Clark was elected by a vote of 442,133 to 319,923 as the city's first Democratic mayor in sixty-seven years. Dilworth was elected district attorney in the same election, and Democrats won all but two of the seventeen city council seats.

Clark, who proclaimed his election a triumph for "all decent people in Philadelphia," took office on 7 January 1952 with a new city charter that consolidated city and county government, extended civil service, and increased the power of the mayor's office. He took charge by scrapping the city's spoils system and hiring lawyers, business executives, and academicians on the basis of their skills, not their political affiliations. With professional economists and accountants, Clark overhauled the city's financial structure, opened its books, and modernized its system of keeping records. He introduced data processing to replace the unreliable recording methods of the ward heelers.

"A good political leader must have the ability to look ahead for the best way to the ideal future of his city and try to lead his community a short distance in the right direction," Clark said. He sought to deal with long-range problems, including urban renewal, traffic congestion, reviving neighborhoods, and affordable housing. His biggest regret, Clark said years later, was allowing an expressway to run through the city's largest park. Clark claimed that his major achievements as mayor were "the reform of the police—taking them out of politics" and "the opening of a career service in city government to blacks." He pushed through a $20 million tax increase and put the city on a pay-as-you-go fiscal system that enabled him to increase and improve many city services that had been neglected by previous administrations. He reorganized the fire department, increased city support to schools and cultural institutions, improved street cleaning, and modernized street lighting.

Clark did not seek reelection, stepping down in January 1956 to run for the U.S. Senate. After narrowly defeating Republican incumbent James Duff, Clark spent twelve years in the Senate, where he was a fighter for progressive causes. He clashed with Senate majority leader Lyndon B. Johnson and sought to reduce the influence of southern conservatives over the Democratic caucus. Clark urged Johnson to pursue a liberal agenda as outlined in the 1956 Democratic platform, but Johnson spurned his advice.

With the election of John F. Kennedy to the presidency in 1960, Clark became one of the administration's key legislative allies. He wrote the draft of Kennedy's first proposed civil rights legislation but cautioned that the votes were not yet there for passage. Clark, who was among the first senators to call attention to the plight of the nation's inner cities, was the major architect of the Accelerated Public Works Act of 1962, which was signed by Kennedy. Clark was also the author of the Manpower Development and Training Act of 1962. He had focused on job retraining because of the shutdowns of coal mines and steel mills in his home state. As a member of the Senate's Subcommittee on Education, Clark helped to shape the Higher Education Facilities Act of 1963.

Clark had never liked Johnson, who moved up to the presidency following Kennedy's assassination. In 1964, however, Clark was among the floor leaders in the passage of Johnson's Civil Rights Act, and he managed the fair-employment practices provision. In 1965 Clark became a member of the Senate Foreign Relations Committee, and that same year he broke with Johnson over the Vietnam War. As one of the Senate's leading doves, he was also an advocate for arms control. Clark was defeated for reelection to a third term in 1968 by Republican Richard Schweiker.

Clark was married three times. In 1926 he married Elizabeth Jenks; they had no children and were divorced in 1934. In 1935 he married Noel Hall, with whom he had two children. They were divorced in 1967. He married Iris Cole Richey in 1968.

After his Senate defeat, Clark served for two years as president of World Federalists U.S.A. He was also chairman of the Coalition on National Priorities and Military Policy. Although he never ran for office again, Clark remained active in Philadelphia's liberal Democratic politics. He was a bitter opponent of conservative mayor Frank L. Rizzo in the 1970s. Clark died at his home in Chestnut Hill after a long illness and complications of old age. He is buried at Saint Thomas Cemetery in Whitemarsh, Pennsylvania. At the time of Clark's death, Mayor Wilson Goode said, "No public servant has done more for the city than Joe Clark."

★

Clark's papers, including an unpublished autobiography, are kept at the Pennsylvania Historical Society. The most authoritative accounts of Clark's Philadelphia administration are Kirk R. Petshek, *The Challenge of Urban Reform: Policies and Programs in Philadelphia* (1973), and James Reichley, *The Art of Government* (1959). Clark's *Congress: The Sapless Branch* (1964) is partly a memoir of his Senate years and is also a sprightly polemic. His role in the Civil Rights Act of 1964 is described in Robert Mann, *The Walls of Jericho: Lyndon Johnson, Hubert Humphrey, Richard Russell, and the Struggle for Civil Rights* (1996). Clark's relationship with John F. Kennedy is chronicled in Irving Bernstein, *Promises Kept: John F. Kennedy's New Frontier* (1991). Obituaries are in the *Philadelphia Inquirer* (15 Jan. 1990) and *New York Times* (16 Jan. 1990).

STEVE NEAL

CLIFTON, Nat(haniel) ("Sweetwater") (*b.* 13 October 1922 in England, Arkansas; *d.* 31 August 1990 in Chicago, Illinois), basketball player who was the first African American to sign a contract with the National Basketball Association (NBA).

Clifton got his nickname "Sweetwater" shortly after his family moved to Chicago when he was eight years old. He loved to drink soda pop, but his family often could not afford soft drinks. He thus developed a habit of filling up a jar with water and pouring sugar in it. Clifton was a resident of Chicago's South Side throughout his life. When he was thirteen, he was recruited by a neighborhood softball team that played in an otherwise all-white citywide semiprofessional league. Although not yet of high-school age, he was a star. Despite tough competition and frequent fights in the league, Clifton is reported never to have fought. He was always known as the strong, silent, diplomatic type.

Basketball, however, was his first love. His DuSable High School basketball team was the first black team to win the Public League's Stagg Tournament. He scored a then-record forty-five points in a tournament game. He continued his basketball career at Xavier College in New Orleans after high school, spending a year there before being drafted into the army in 1943. He served in Europe through 1946. After being discharged, Clifton played semiprofessional basketball because the established professional

Nat ("Sweetwater") Clifton. UPI/CORBIS-BETTMANN

leagues had not yet begun admitting African Americans as players. He played with the New York Rens and integrated the Dayton Metropolitans.

Clifton signed with the Harlem Globetrotters in 1948, which led to two years of travel and entertaining with what was then the most famous basketball team in the world. He was not a "comic" Trotter, but during his NBA career he was stereotyped as such by some. During the spring and summer months of 1949 and 1950, Clifton was a baseball-slugging first baseman in the Cleveland Indians farm system. Then, in June 1950, a day after the annual NBA draft of college players, the New York Knickerbockers signed Clifton to a contract, the first ever with an African American by an NBA team. He was one of three blacks to play in the NBA when the season began in the fall. (He missed training camp his first season in the NBA because he was still playing minor-league baseball.) Chuck Cooper of Duquesne University was the first black drafted, by the Boston Celtics. Also drafted, by the Washington Capitals, was Earl Lloyd of West Virginia State, who, because the Capitals played their first game of the season on 31 October 1950, was the first African American actually to play in the NBA. Cooper played the next day for the Celtics, and Clifton debuted three days later with the Knicks. There was little mention in the press of the first blacks in the NBA. Lloyd later theorized that basketball was different from baseball, which had been integrated by Jackie Robinson in 1947, in that baseball had more players from the South and basketball had more players who were college graduates.

Clifton played with the Knicks for seven seasons, from 1950 to 1957, averaging 10.3 points and 8.5 rebounds per game in 476 games. He helped the Knicks reach the NBA finals three times and was a crowd favorite because of his strong, steady play and his unique nickname. He was listed at six feet, seven inches and 225 pounds, played both forward and center, and had a reputation as one of basketball's best rebounders. In the 1956–1957 season, he was named to the NBA Eastern Division All-Star team. He scored 8 points and grabbed 11 rebounds in that year's All-Star game. His best season was probably in 1954–1955, when he averaged 13.1 points.

Clifton was twenty-eight years old when he signed with the Knicks and often said that his best playing years had been with the Globetrotters. He said he could have scored more and been more colorful (palming and passing behind the back, Globetrotters style), but his team wanted him to stick to fundamentals. He was a tenacious defender and rebounder, but not a shooter at first. Later he developed an outside set shot. He was a tremendous clutch player and wanted the ball at the end of close games. Although only a 60 percent foul shooter, he was known for not missing important free throws.

Meticulous on and off the court, he brushed his teeth at halftime of each game and personally washed his own uniform. He wore expensive, carefully tailored clothes and cologne. A stickler for hygiene, he would shower two or three times a day. Clifton projected a distinguished image and was respected by the entire league as much for his character as for how he played. He was a gentleman who could physically dominate games. Back in Chicago, Clifton provided a role model for youngsters. During the off season he lived near his old neighborhood, where he was like a pied piper to children. It was not uncommon to see him lead groups of youths into the local sweetshop and buy them all candy.

Clifton played his final NBA season in 1957–1958 with the Detroit Pistons. A year later he retired at age thirty-six, seven years before the league instituted a pension plan. Clifton played two seasons with Globetrotter spinoffs, the Harlem Magicians and the Harlem Americans. After injuring his knee in 1960 while playing for the Magicians, he left basketball and returned to Chicago. Clifton was such a popular figure in his hometown that he could have easily found a regular job with the city. Some friends urged him to explore various business plans that would draw on his fame. Instead, he bought a taxi and was a cab driver until his death, suffering a fatal heart attack while at the wheel.

★

See Terry Pluto, *Tall Tales: The Glory Years of the NBA in the Words of the Men Who Played, Coached, and Built Pro Basketball* (1992). See also "NBA Pioneers Encountered Own Barriers," *USA Today* (25 Feb. 1991), and "Sweetwater: The Nobility of Simplicity," *New York Times* (4 Sept. 1990). Obituaries are in the *Chicago Tribune, New York Times,* and *New Orleans Times Picayune* (all 2 Sept. 1990).

CHARLES A. BURNS

CLUBB, O(liver) Edmund, II (*b.* 6 February 1901 in South Park, Minnesota; *d.* 9 May 1989 in New York City), a China specialist in the U.S. Foreign Service who became a target of the anticommunist hysteria of the late 1940s and 1950s.

Clubb grew up in Minnesota. His father, Oliver Edmund Clubb, a cattle rancher, died when Clubb was five years old. Clubb's mother, Lillian May Nichols, had to struggle to make ends meet. One of three children, Clubb enlisted in the army at the age of seventeen and was discharged in 1919. He held a variety of jobs before entering the University of Washington and then the University of Minnesota. Clubb graduated from Minnesota in 1927.

Clubb qualified for the U.S. Foreign Service in 1928 and quickly decided to become a China specialist. That same year he married Mariann Smith, who in 1929 accompanied him to China, where he took a two-year course in

O. Edmund Clubb before the U.S. House Un-American Activities Commitee, 1951. UPI/CORBIS-BETTMANN

Chinese history and language offered at Peking (Beijing). During this period, the Clubbs had two children. In mid-1931 Clubb started his first assignment, as vice consul in Hankow.

While in Hankow, Clubb began to submit reports on the possibility of social revolution in China. In this connection, he was one of the first non-Russian Occidentals to take a long and hard look at communism. (His 1932 impressions were published in 1968 under the title *Communism in China, As Reported from Hankow in 1932*.) Although not accurate in all particulars, Clubb's reporting represented a serious effort to understand an emerging social revolution in China and the relationship of communism to this process.

Reassigned to Peking in 1934, Clubb's political reporting concentrated on the ebb and flow of the Chinese Communist–Chinese Nationalist rivalry, set against the background of increasing Japanese aggression toward China. In July 1937 full-scale war broke out between Japan and China. Clubb's activities turned to the task of protecting American life and property in China while reporting on the extensive gains of the Japanese. Following home leave in 1940, Clubb returned to China without his family. After a brief stint in Nanking, he was dispatched to Hanoi, Vietnam, an area nominally under Vichy French control but in fact controlled by Japan. Clubb was in Hanoi when the Japanese attacked Pearl Harbor. He was taken prisoner by the Japanese and interned by them under harsh conditions for close to eight months.

When he was released by the Japanese, Clubb declined to return to the United States, serving first in the Chinese wartime capital of Chungking and then in Luchow, in Kansu province. Clubb was then dispatched to open a consulate in Tihwa (Urumchi), in the northwestern province of Sinkiang. The State Department commended Clubb for the excellent quality of his work in Tihwa, but illness at the end of 1943 forced him to return to the United States, where he saw his family for the first time in more than three years.

In mid-1944 Clubb became consul general in the Soviet maritime city of Vladivostok. After the Soviet victory over Japan, Clubb was assigned to the consulates in Mukden and Changchun in Manchuria. These postings placed him in the center of the emerging postwar struggle between the Chinese Communists and the Nationalist government of Chiang Kai-shek. Clubb's reporting by 1945 warned that serious weaknesses were apparent in Chiang's government, and the Chinese Communists had to be treated as serious contenders for power in China. Clubb maintained these themes when civil war broke out between the competing Chinese factions in 1946. Clubb returned to Peking in late 1947 to take charge of the U.S. consulate. As he left Manchuria, he observed that the Nationalist cause there was bleak, and this precarious position in Manchuria did not bode well in general for the Nationalists. By the end of 1948, Manchuria was under Communist control. At the end of January 1949, Peking fell to Chinese Communist troops.

Clubb maintained the U.S. consular presence in Peking in the face of increasing harassment from Communists. Following the formal establishment of the People's Republic of China in October 1949 and U.S. refusal to recognize the new government, Communist pressure on the consulate in Peking increased. By April 1950 the situation was intolerable, and Clubb supervised the closing of the consulate. With that closing, the formal diplomatic presence of the United States in China came to an end.

Clubb returned to the United States to assume the position of director of the Office of Chinese Affairs. His new position as head of the China desk at the State Department was a clear indication of the high regard in which he was held. The United States, however, was in the midst of a growing anticommunist hysteria, and conservative officials wanted to discover who was responsible for the "loss" of China to the Communists. Anyone connected to American

China policy in the 1930s and the 1940s was a possible target for this harmful inquiry. Initially, Clubb managed to stay out of the line of fire, but early in 1951 he was informed that he was under investigation by the State Department's Loyalty-Security Board (LSB).

The catalytic agent that made Clubb a target was testimony provided to the FBI and the House Un-American Activities Committee by Whittaker Chambers, the accuser of alleged spy Alger Hiss. Chambers testified that in 1932 Clubb had appeared at the office of the leftist *New Masses* magazine with a sealed envelope intended for Grace Hutchins, a reported communist employed by the Labor Research Bureau. Chambers did not emphasize this incident in his testimony, nor did he ever accuse Clubb of being a member of any communist organization, but this testimony, in combination with Clubb's former criticism of Chiang's government, was sufficient to bring about the LSB inquiry. Such were the times.

Once he recalled the *New Masses* meeting, Clubb was unable to convince the LSB that it was a case of an ambitious young Foreign Service officer trying to become an expert on communism in all of its national manifestations. The board was also unsympathetic to Clubb's contention that his reports from China were simply his best assessments of the situation there. He was suspended from his job in June 1951, pending a formal investigation by the LSB.

Clubb's cause was not helped by the direction taken by the loyalty program of President Harry Truman's administration. Before 1951 the government took disciplinary action only when substantial evidence clearly demonstrated disloyalty. By an executive order of April 1951, however, a new standard was invoked, requiring only that reasonable doubt as to loyalty be established. In an age of demagogic attacks, the convening of an investigation in and of itself became grounds for doubting loyalty.

In December 1951 the LSB ruled that Clubb was a security risk and should be dismissed from the Foreign Service. He was never given a detailed explanation as to why he was deemed a risk. Clubb appealed this decision and was reinstated in February 1952. He was assigned, however, to the Historical Research Bureau in the State Department. This assignment was a clear signal to Clubb that he would never be allowed to work again on East Asian affairs, a subject to which he had devoted his entire professional life. Clubb chose to retire from the Foreign Service.

Following his retirement, Clubb began a productive career as a writer, lecturer, and teacher. He wrote *Twentieth Century China* (1970) and *China and Russia: The "Great Game"* (1971). He also became associated with the East Asian Institute of Columbia University. Clubb died of Parkinson's disease in Manhattan. He was cremated and his ashes were scattered in the area of Palenville, New York.

★

Clubb's account of his experience before the Loyalty-Security Board is in his *The Witness and I* (1974). E. J. Kahn, Jr., *The China Hands: America's Foreign Service Officers and What Befell Them* (1975), places Clubb's troubles in the context of the purge of several State Department China hands. Earl Latham, *The Communist Controversy in Washington: From the New Deal to McCarthy* (1969), and Richard Freeland, *The Truman Doctrine and the Origins of McCarthyism* (1972), provide solid accounts of American anticommunist hysteria. Obituaries are in the *New York Times* (11 May 1989) and the *Chicago Tribune* and *Washington Post* (both 12 May 1989). The Harry S. Truman Library in Independence, Missouri, has an oral history interview with Clubb.

JAMES FETZER

COHEN, Wilbur Joseph (*b.* 10 June 1913 in Milwaukee, Wisconsin; *d.* 17 May 1987 in Seoul, South Korea), secretary of health, education, and welfare, father of Medicare, and draftsman of social welfare legislation.

Cohen was the first child of Aaron Cohen and Bessie (Rubenstein) Cohen, who shared the work in several small grocery stores that they owned. Wilbur and his brother lived with their parents over a store in a mixed working-class neighborhood of Milwaukee. An honors student at Lincoln High School in Milwaukee, Cohen was amiable, witty, and popular, serving on the student council, managing the football team, and editing the senior yearbook. At the Univer-

Wilbur Cohen before the U.S. Senate Select Committee on Nutrition, 1969. UPI/CORBIS-BETTMANN

sity of Wisconsin, which he attended during the depths of the Great Depression, Cohen majored in economics, studying under pioneer institutional reformers John R. Commons, Selig Perlman, and his senior adviser, Edwin E. Witte.

In 1934, Cohen's senior year, U.S. Secretary of Labor Frances Perkins and her Committee on Economic Security outlined the proposed contents of the Social Security Act of 1935. Hired as technical director, Witte selected Cohen as a personal assistant on a staff of experts preparing a draft bill. During the six-month drafting stage of the Social Security Act, Cohen prepared short reports on European social welfare, clipped newspapers and magazines, and searched the libraries for answers to the senior staff's questions. Once the bill came before the House Ways and Means Committee, Cohen sat behind Witte, the government's principal witness, listening and taking notes.

Shortly after President Franklin Roosevelt signed the Social Security Act into law on 15 August 1935, Cohen went to work in the Bureau of Unemployment Compensation. When Arthur Altmeyer became head administrator, Cohen joined his office, having moved up the civil service ladder sufficiently to save some money. On 8 April 1938 he married Eloise Bittel, a nonreligious Baptist from Texas. Like Cohen, Eloise, a graduate of Baylor College, was from a modest background and had an avid interest in the politics of social reform. They had three sons, Christopher, Bruce, and Stuart.

Following passage of the 1939 amendments to the Social Security Act, a process in which Cohen demonstrated his growing usefulness, social reform entered the doldrums during World War II and after the defeat of President Harry Truman's plan for universal health care. When, unexpectedly, the Republicans under President Dwight Eisenhower supported social insurance, Cohen aided them by answering technical questions and even suggesting and drafting legislation, but no tangible credit was forthcoming from the Republican officials at the Department of Health, Education, and Welfare (HEW).

In 1956 Cohen left his government position in Washington for the University of Michigan School of Social Work, where, to no one's surprise, he proved to be an outstanding teacher. Meanwhile, Cohen continued to work on social security legislation through frequent phone calls and personal contacts with liberal activists in Washington. Soon he began to wonder whether instituting a counseling process for recipients might be helpful in attacking "the welfare mess"—chronic dependency, runaway fathers, illegitimacy—that characterized the Aid to Dependent Children program of the Social Security Act.

With the return of the Democratic party to the White House in 1961, President John Kennedy appointed Cohen the assistant secretary for legislation (14 April 1961). Cohen was behind one of the more expensive reforms of the short Kennedy presidency—the social services amendments applicable particularly to the problem-riddled Aid for Families with Dependent Children (AFDC) program. These amendments raised the federal share of matching grants from about 50 to 75 percent, with the expectation that counseling would bring the rolls down. In 1965 President Lyndon Johnson moved Cohen up to undersecretary (30 May 1965), then to secretary (16 May 1968) of HEW. By the mid-1960s, HEW had earned the dubious distinction of closely approaching the federal expenditures of the Department of Defense. Cohen was the single individual most responsible for this phenomenon.

On 30 July 1965, Cohen stood behind President Johnson at Harry Truman's Missouri home as Johnson signed into law the programs known as Medicare (health insurance for persons age sixty-five and older, with the elderly sharing the costs, as in social insurance) and Medicaid (free health care for the poor with federal-state sharing of costs, as in public assistance). On 30 May 1968, members of the Poor People's Campaign occupying the HEW departmental auditorium shouted for Cohen's appearance. He and other departmental officials listened to their grievances and subsequently agreed, for example, to give representatives of the Poor People the right to review research and demonstration projects in AFDC. Even before Johnson's decision not to seek reelection in 1968, Cohen saw some of his and Johnson's liberal actions branded as failures. The use of counseling in AFDC not only failed to lower the public assistance rolls, but, partly because of higher payment standards, created an unpopular "welfare explosion." Johnson's War on Poverty—justly or not—was also condemned a failure.

Cohen left the federal government in 1969 with the beginning of President Richard Nixon's first term. Cohen, however, supported the enactment of Nixon's Family Assistance Plan (FAP), designed by Democratic bureaucrats for Democrat Daniel Patrick Moynihan, who was then working at the White House. FAP, which would gradually have abolished AFDC in favor of income subsidies, failed to pass the Senate.

At age fifty-five Cohen returned to the University of Michigan as dean of the School of Education. Meanwhile, after a series of disagreements with President Jimmy Carter over Carter's establishment of a Department of Education separate from HEW and what Cohen perceived to be a chipping away at the foundations of social security, Cohen organized a pressure group called Save Our Security (SOS). A voluntary lobbying organization, SOS was dedicated to the preservation of Social Security programs as they existed and the exclusion of alternative means of funding, public or private. Cohen left Michigan in 1978 to become a professor at the Lyndon B. Johnson School of

Public Affairs at the University of Texas at Austin, where he taught until his death.

In his book *The Politics of a Guaranteed Income,* Daniel Patrick Moynihan described Cohen's career as reaching "the level where men consider seeking the presidency and some attain it." Although Cohen had seen a Roman Catholic become president (Kennedy), he firmly believed that a Jewish president was far in the future. Whatever his political dreams, he buried them early. He did believe, as he expressed it to Johnson upon retirement, that "public service was the greatest privilege and the highest duty," a conviction he instilled in coworkers and students. In reply to liberal activists who faulted him as overly cautious and too ready to compromise, Cohen referred to himself as "the old salami slicer" and pointed to the pile of legislation he had helped transform into law. While on a trip to South Korea with his wife and friends, Cohen suffered a fatal heart attack before delivering a speech on social security.

On 17 June 1987, at a memorial service held in the hearing room of the Ways and Means Committee, some 300 persons—family, former HEW secretaries, senators, congressmen, and numerous bureaucrats—paid tribute to Cohen for more than three hours. A *New York Times* editorial concluded that Cohen left his own memorial, "the fruits of a half-century of energetic effort . . . to help people in need and pain." The Wilbur J. Cohen Federal Building, which was dedicated on 28 April 1988, is just down the hill from the U.S. Capitol. Cohen was buried in Milwaukee, Wisconsin.

★

Cohen's papers are located in the Wisconsin State Historical Society; the Lyndon Baines Johnson Library, University of Texas at Austin; the Bentley Historical Library, University of Michigan; and the University of Wisconsin Memorial Library. On his life, see Edward D. Berkowitz, *Mr. Social Security: The Life of Wilbur J. Cohen* (1995). Other useful sources include Blanche D. Coll, *Safety Net: Welfare and Social Security, 1929–1979* (1995); Blanche D. Coll, "Public Assistance: Reviving the Original Comprehensive Concept of Social Security," in Gerald D. Nash, Noel H. Pugach, and Richard F. Thomasson, eds., *Social Security: The First Half-Century* (1988); and Daniel Patrick Moynihan, *The Politics of a Guaranteed Income: The Nixon Administration and the Family Assistance Plan* (1973). Obituaries are in the *Washington Post* (18 May 1987) and *New York Times* (19 May 1987).

BLANCHE D. COLL

COHN, Roy Marcus (*b.* 20 February 1927 in New York City; *d.* 2 August 1986 in Bethesda, Maryland), prominent New York attorney and chief counsel to the Permanent Subcommittee on Investigations of the Senate Committee on Government Operations during the McCarthy era.

Roy Cohn. ARCHIVE PHOTOS

Cohn, the only child of Dora Marcus and Albert Cohn, grew up in a spacious apartment on Manhattan's Park Avenue. His father, a protégé of the Bronx Democratic party boss Ed Flynn, was a justice in the Appellate Division of the State Supreme Court. Both parents were protective and domineering and treated Roy as a little adult. Cohn recalled, "I didn't hang around arguing with my buddies about whether DiMaggio was better than Mel Ott." In fact, Roy had few friends and spent his time with older people. When a nervous condition forced his departure from the Community School for gifted students, he attended the Fieldston Lower School in the Riverdale section of the Bronx and then Horace Mann Prep School. After skipping his senior year of high school, he went on to Columbia College, graduating with a B.A. degree in 1945, and Columbia Law School, receiving an LL.B. in 1947, all before his twentieth birthday. His father had exerted his considerable influence to keep Cohn out of the army during the final months of World War II.

Cohn was admitted to the New York bar in 1948 and was sworn in as an assistant U.S. attorney. His first cases were routine, ranging from stamp and currency violations to drug trafficking, but he quickly made a name for himself by bombarding newsmen with reports of the "biggest," "most sensational," "worldwide" vice operations in the history of organized crime. Before long, Cohn moved into the glamorous internal security field, specializing in subversive activities. He played a prominent role in the 1949 conviction of eleven top communist leaders for violating the Smith Act. In 1950 he became the confidential assistant to U.S. Attorney Irving Saypol. A celebrity at twenty-three, Cohn spent his evenings at New York's plush Stork Club, where, according to friend and journalist Walter Winchell, he moved "from table to table, greeting friends of his family and people he knew—lawyers, judges, politicians, et al."

Cohn further enhanced his reputation during the sensational 1951 trial of Julius and Ethel Rosenberg, who were accused of spying and conspiring to transmit atomic secrets to the Soviets. His interrogation of witnesses was forceful, focused, and relentless. In *The Autobiography of Roy Cohn* (1988), Cohn alleged that he pulled strings to make certain that federal judge Irving Kaufman, a family friend, presided at the trial and that he and Kaufman engaged in ex parte (private) communications about the case, particularly on the sentencing issue, which was a clear violation of the law. Cohn noted, correctly, that such practices were not uncommon in the 1950s.

While Judge Kaufman portrayed himself as a man wrestling with his conscience over the death penalty for the Rosenbergs, according to Cohn, the judge had made up his mind to execute Julius Rosenberg before the trial even began. As for Ethel, when Kaufman asked Cohn for his opinion, the young prosecutor replied: "She engineered the whole thing, she was the mastermind of the conspiracy. So unless you're willing to say that a woman is immune from the death penalty, I don't see how you can justify sparing her." The terrible irony is that Ethel Rosenberg was at most a peripheral member of the spy ring.

In 1952 Cohn arrived in Washington, D.C., to become a special assistant to Attorney General James McGranery. At the Justice Department, he prepared a seven-count perjury indictment against Owen Lattimore, a China specialist at John Hopkins University, who was falsely accused by Senator Joseph McCarthy of being the "top Russian espionage agent in the United States." (The charges were eventually dismissed or dropped.) A few months later, Cohn alienated his superiors by charging that they had blocked his efforts to investigate American communists on the United Nations staff. The dispute grew so ugly that a congressional committee looked into the matter, exonerated the attorney general, and noted that Cohn, who testified before the committee, left the impression that he was "aggressive in the performance of his duties and probably not free from the pressure of personal ambition."

In 1953 McCarthy became chairman of the Senate Committee on Government Operations. One of his first moves was to select Cohn as chief counsel for its Subcommittee on Investigations. Cohn's contacts within the FBI increased the subcommittee's access to confidential files. His purported photographic memory and aggressive and arrogant manner dominated most hearings. Before long, McCarthy came to rely on Cohn for almost everything—contacts, information, ideas, scheduling, briefings, and political advice. "He's a brilliant fellow," the senator told a friend. "He works his butt off and he's loyal to me. I don't think I could make it without him."

With Cohn leading the way, McCarthy's subcommittee investigated communist infiltration of the federal government, including the State Department, the Voice of America, and the Foreign Service. While uncovering no communists, the hearings undermined government morale, damaged numerous reputations, and made the United States look sinister in the eyes of the world. At Cohn's request, Senator McCarthy created a nonsalaried subcommittee post, chief consultant for psychological warfare, for Cohn's best friend, G. David Schine, a strikingly handsome young man who was the son of Meyer Schine, multimillionaire hotel owner. Schine's credentials rested on a six-page pamphlet he had written ("Definition of Communism") that managed to get Lenin's first name wrong, misdate the Russian Revolution, and butcher Marx's theory of revolution.

In 1953 Cohn and Schine journeyed to Europe to investigate the overseas libraries of army bases, embassies, and the U.S. Information Service (USIS) to "sniff out communism." The trip, which included stops in Austria, France, England, Germany, Greece, and Italy, was a colossal blunder. The press wanted to report the worst, and Cohn and Schine rudely obliged. In Vienna they visited the USIS library and the Soviet Union's House of Culture, searching for books on the shelves of both places. They found several, including the works of Mark Twain, and dutifully wrote down the titles. In Munich they loudly demanded separate rooms, explaining none too subtly that "we don't work for the State Department," where charges of homosexuality were currently under investigation. In Paris they went on a huge buying spree at government expense and then ran out on their hotel bill.

Although Cohn and Schine were both young, single, and Jewish, they also were a study in contrasts. Cohn was short, dark, intense, and abrasive; Schine was tall, fair, frivolous, and complacent. There were rumors of a homosexual relationship, which both men denied. As Vermont Senator Ralph Flanders, a prominent Republican, put it, "Anybody with half an eye could see what was going on."

In the fall of 1953 the Subcommittee on Investigations opened hearings into subversive activities in the U.S. Army. The first allegation—that a communist spy ring existed at Fort Monmouth, New Jersey, headquarters of the Army

Signal Corps—led to the suspension of several dozen top engineers as security risks, although no credible evidence was presented and all the suspended workers eventually were cleared. Meanwhile, Schine got his draft notice in November 1953. For months thereafter, Cohn demanded—and received—preferential treatment for Private Schine from high-ranking military officials, who feared that Cohn would, as he threatened, "wreck the army" by escalating the subcommittee's investigation. On 11 March 1954, the army released a detailed chronology of Cohn's pressure tactics. The report listed dozens of phone calls and meetings—with Cohn ordering that Schine be transferred to a desk job in New York, excused from long marches and guard duty, and given extra passes for weekends and holidays. In response, Cohn and McCarthy accused the army of raising false allegations to block the subcommittee's probe.

In April 1954 the Senate began a televised investigation of these charges and countercharges, known as the Army-McCarthy hearings. As one of the central figures in the controversy, Cohn temporarily stepped down as chief counsel. According to his account of the hearings, he struck a private deal with army counsel Joseph Welch, in which the McCarthy forces agreed not to mention that a young attorney in Welch's Boston law firm, Fred Fisher, had once joined a communist-front group, and Welch promised not to mention that Cohn had managed to avoid military service in both World War II and the Korean War. On 9 June, McCarthy broke the pledge with a televised assault on Fisher. Cohn sat in silence, eyes lowered, slowly shaking his head. He even scribbled a note to McCarthy: "Please respect our agreement . . . because this is not going to do any good." As McCarthy raged on, Welch rose up in defense. "Until this moment, Senator, I think I never really gauged your cruelty or your recklessness. Have you no sense of decency, sir? At long last, have you left no sense of decency?" The audience burst into applause.

Cohn resigned as chief counsel a few weeks later. "It has been a bitter lesson," he said, "to come to Washington and see a reputation, gained at some effort, torn to shreds because I was associated with Senator McCarthy, who has become a symbol of hatred for all who fear the exposure of communism." Cohn's friends threw a banquet in his honor at New York's Astor Hotel. The guest list read like a who's who of the American right: Westbrook Pegler, Fulton Lewis, Jr., William F. Buckley, Senator McCarthy. There were delegations from the Catholic War Veterans and the Minute Women of America. At the end, toastmaster George Sokolsky praised the child-rearing habits of Dora and Albert Cohn in remarkably ironic terms. "Your son," said Sokolsky, "represents something in American life that we did not know existed."

Cohn returned to New York City. Joining the law firm of Saxe, Bacon, and Bolan, which Cohn was associated with until his death, he defied those who predicted his swift demise. Cohn parlayed his celebrity, killer instinct, and political contacts into a high-powered, wildly controversial legal career. On three different occasions—in 1964, 1969, and 1971—he was tried and acquitted on federal charges of bribery, fraud, and income tax evasion. He blamed his troubles on a political vendetta orchestrated by Attorney General Robert F. Kennedy, his longtime rival, and U.S. Attorney Robert M. Morgenthau.

In 1973 Cohn was implicated in a plot to scuttle the charter yacht *Defiance* in order to collect a $200,000 insurance policy. The yacht burned at sea in a mysterious fire, killing a crew member whose father publicly blamed Cohn for his son's death. Investigators could find no evidence linking Cohn to the fire itself, but they did uncover a series of connections between Cohn's law firm and a dummy corporation known as Pied Piper that collected the bulk of the insurance payment. In addition, Cohn received an insurance settlement for personal property he claimed to have lost on the yacht. Although no criminal charges were filed against Cohn, the *Defiance* incident would play a prominent role in his disbarment thirteen years later.

Not surprisingly, Cohn became the symbol of invincibility, a man the system could not beat. His law practice boomed. Clients ranged from Francis Cardinal Spellman and developer Donald Trump to Mafia boss "Fat Tony" Salerno. A lifelong bachelor with extravagant tastes, he made the rounds of New York's trendiest nightclubs, such as Studio 54, and threw lavish parties at his suburban Greenwich, Connecticut, home and Upper East Side apartment in Manhattan for such notable personalities as Barbara Walters, Norman Mailer, William Safire, and Ronald Reagan. His homosexuality became an open secret, with young men constantly at his side.

By the early 1980s, Cohn's legal skills had diminished. He knew how to intimidate and how to sidetrack a case he could not settle, but once a matter got to litigation, he seemed to falter. He did not stay current on laws or precedents, and he hated to prepare. His style, quite simply, was to take a cash retainer from a client and then do as little as possible.

In 1986 Cohn learned that he had AIDS. On 23 June of that year, he was disbarred from practicing law in New York State. A unanimous five-judge panel ruled that his conduct in representing several clients (who had charged him with fraud) was "unethical," "unprofessional," and "reprehensible." To the end, Cohn remained defiant, protesting his innocence, refusing to admit his homosexuality, even claiming that he had liver cancer and not AIDS. Asked by reporters for a comment about his disbarment, he said, "I couldn't care less." He died at Warren Grant Magnuson Clinical Center of the National Institutes of Health of

AIDS-related cardiopulmonary arrest, with his friend and aide Peter Frazier at his bedside.

★

Cohn's autobiography, *The Autobiography of Roy Cohn* (1988), was completed by Sidney Zion and published posthumously. Cohn himself wrote two popular books, *A Fool for a Client: My Struggle Against the Power of a Public Prosecutor* (1971), and *How to Stand Up for Your Rights* (1981). Nicholas von Hoffman, *Citizen Cohn: The Life and Times of Roy Cohn* (1988), is a useful biography. For information on Cohn during the McCarthy era, see his own work, *McCarthy* (1968), and David M. Oshinsky, *A Conspiracy So Immense: The World of Joe McCarthy* (1983). An obituary is in the *New York Times* (3 Aug. 1986).

DAVID M. OSHINSKY

COLLBOHM, Franklin Rudolf (*b.* 31 January 1907 in New York City; *d.* 12 February 1990 in Palm Desert, California), aviation engineer best known for his work on the DC-3 transport plane and his role as head of the RAND Corporation (1948–1967), which he formed into a nonprofit, interdisciplinary research center.

Frank Collbohm spent his early childhood in Madison, Wisconsin. He moved to Swissvale, Pennsylvania, with his father, Max Herman Collbohm, an electrical engineer for Westinghouse Electric; his mother, Adelheid Michelson; and three younger siblings. When Collbohm was ten his father died from food poisoning, and the family returned to Madison. In 1925 he entered the University of Wisconsin on an academic scholarship to study electrical engineering. Following his sophomore year he worked for one year for Westinghouse before returning to college.

After his junior year Collbohm entered the fledgling aviation industry, moving to southern California, where the Douglas Aircraft Company hired him as an engineer in 1928. For the next twenty years Collbohm played a key role in research and development at Douglas Aircraft. In the 1930s he was one of the nation's top flight test engineers. As special assistant to the vice president and head of engineering, he often assisted Donald Douglas, the company founder, and Arthur E. Raymond, the vice president, with special projects, including flight testing of the now famous DC-3 transport airplane. On 15 November 1934 he married Kathryn Louise Pierce; they had two children.

During World War II Collbohm participated in several military projects. He worked closely with the Massachusetts Institute of Technology and had an informal position in the Office of Scientific Research and Development within the War Department. Both positions brought him in contact with most of the important men in the applied science fields; he later recruited many of them into RAND. He also became a consultant to Secretary of War Robert Patterson from 1944 to 1946 and met the Boeing Aircraft Company's chief engineer, Edward Wells, while working on a project to improve the B-29 bomber.

In this environment the idea for RAND took root. Collbohm, Wells, and Raymond created an Army Air Corps program, known as Project RAND, in 1946 to solve defense-related problems. Initially under the auspices of Douglas Aircraft with Collbohm as project head, RAND in 1948 became an independent corporation in Santa Monica with him as president shortly after the Army Air Corps became the U.S. Air Force in 1947. RAND's first project was a feasibility study of space flight. The report "Preliminary Design of an Experimental World-Circling Spaceship" concluded that satellites could be placed in orbit. The report also highlighted the military value of satellites as reconnaissance and communications platforms. On 2 May 1946 Collbohm presented this report to the Army Air Corps; ultimately it benefited the U.S. space program. RAND played a key role in the development of nearly every U.S. orbital satellite project over the next twenty years.

Collbohm maintained an open-minded attitude at RAND, allowing researchers a free hand with projects. Above all, he emphasized that the product had to be an honest assessment rather than what the customer wanted to hear. He also stressed interdisciplinary work in his research sections, with social and physical science specialists teaming together. He preferred a fully empowered section head steering the project as opposed to voting committees.

Franklin Collbohm, 1959. RAND CORPORATION

Although a self-taught aviation engineer, he maintained interests in other sciences, referring to himself as a "generalist." Partly as a result, RAND conducted studies in computer technology, space exploration, systems analysis, and eventually, foreign policy.

As corporation president from 1948 to 1967, Collbohm rarely involved himself with details of projects, asking instead for occasional updates and screening the final written product before presentation. He was directly involved with RAND's studies on intercontinental ballistic missiles (ICBMs). The final report, circulated in 1954, called for more emphasis on ICBM development and was critical of air force bureaucracy. As a result, the air force doubled ICBM development efforts.

Although the air force provided most of RAND's business in the first twenty years, Collbohm stressed independent research. These independent projects were diverse and included studies of the Russian economy and the use of computers in the development of cancer treatments. Collbohm maintained the principle that 20 percent of the company's time and funds be devoted to subjects of general relevance as opposed to solutions of specific problems.

Collbohm was quiet and serious. Five feet, ten inches tall, with a slight build and blue eyes, his tight blond crew cut supported a businesslike demeanor, but he often revealed a congenial and modest side. He especially enjoyed the company of family and friends and sailing his boat in the waters around Santa Monica, where he made his residence shortly after starting work with Douglas Aircraft.

Collbohm retired as president of RAND in 1967. Some of his commendations included the Defense Department's Distinguished Public Service Medal (1967) and the U.S. Air Force's Exceptional Service Award (1967). He was named one of the National Space Club's space pioneers (1989). He died of a stroke and his ashes were spread over the Pacific Ocean.

During his career Collbohm made significant contributions to aviation and the defense industry. His work with the DC-3 marked a revolution in the civil aviation industry. As the first modern passenger airplane, it facilitated the growth of the airline industry. His greatest contribution, though, was molding RAND in its early years. Collbohm's vision of a nonprofit organization, utilizing associates with varied specialties divorced from the research laboratory, served as a model for several nonprofit research and advisory corporations. Collbohm moved RAND beyond just an air force project to an organization providing a wide range of scientific and scholarly research. Within such an environment, ideas concerning space flight, advanced aviation technology, and foreign policy could develop.

★

The RAND Corporation archives are not cataloged but contain many of Collbohm's memoranda and policy letters. Useful sources for information on Collbohm's work at RAND are Rand Corporation, *The RAND Corporation: The First Fifteen Years* (1963); Bruce L. R. Smith, *The RAND Corporation: Case Study of a Nonprofit Advisory Corporation* (1964); Paul Dickson, *Think Tanks* (1972); and Harold Orlans, *The Nonprofit Research Institute: Its Origin, Operation, Problems, and Prospects* (1972). For his work on the ICBM program see Edmund Beard, *Developing the ICBM: A Study in Bureaucratic Politics* (1976), and Paul B. Stares, *The Militarization of Space: U.S. Policy, 1945–1984* (1985). An obituary is in the *Los Angeles Times* (14 Feb. 1990). An oral history interview with Collbohm, conducted by Martin Collins and Joseph Tatrewicz, is at the National Air and Space Museum in Washington, D.C.

CRAIG A. SWAIN

COLLINS, J(oseph) Lawton ("Lightning Joe") (*b.* 1 May 1896 in New Orleans, Louisiana; *d.* 10 September 1987 in Washington, D.C.), army officer, commander of VII Corps in the Normandy invasion of 1944 and the subsequent campaign into Germany, and chief of staff of the U.S. Army from 1949 to 1953.

The tenth of eleven children born to Jeremiah B. Collins, a Union veteran of the Civil War and grocer, and Catherine Lawton, Joe Collins graduated from Boys' High School in New Orleans and attended Louisiana State University for a year before enrolling in the U.S. Military Academy at West Point. Graduating in 1917, he saw no action during World War I, remaining at Fort Jay in New York harbor. Promoted to major in September 1918, he joined the small U.S. army of occupation in the American Zone of Germany centered on Koblenz. There he met Gladys Easterbrook, the daughter of a Protestant chaplain. Their marriage on 15 July 1921 required three ceremonies—civil, Protestant, and Catholic (Collins was Roman Catholic). They had three children.

After returning from Germany in 1921, Collins had a series of assignments, including instructor at West Point, 1921–1925; infantry school at Fort Benning, Georgia, 1927–1931; and attendance at Command and General Staff School at Fort Leavenworth, Kansas, and at the Army War College in Washington (obligatory for most officers who achieve high rank). At Fort Benning, Collins met the commandant, Colonel George C. Marshall, and when Marshall became chief of staff of the army in 1939, it was clear that Collins would have a bright future in the military.

Days after the disaster at Pearl Harbor in 1941 and the U.S. entry into World War II, Collins was sent to Hawaii, and within a few months he became a major general, commanding the Twenty-fifth Infantry Division, which post he held for a year and a half until reassignment early in 1944. His division saw serious action in the Guadalcanal and

J. Lawton Collins. National Archives

New Georgia campaigns. Collins's chief in the Southwest Pacific, General Douglas MacArthur, refused to advance him to corps command. "But Collins is too young!" he informed Marshall. The army chief of staff then sent Collins to the European theater, where General Dwight D. Eisenhower gave him command of the VII Corps in preparation for the Normandy invasion.

The VII Corps was one of the two U.S. corps to go in on D day, being assigned to Utah Beach. Thereafter, Collins was in his element, and on 1 July his three divisions captured Cherbourg, much needed as a port to supplement supplies brought in over the Normandy beaches. Collins led in the breakout from Normandy at St.-Lô and took his corps into Germany, meanwhile taking part in the Ardennes counteroffensive during the Battle of the Bulge. Early in March 1945, when the VII Corps had just taken Cologne, Eisenhower stopped by, spoke to Collins in private, and told him he had been "the ace corps commander" since D day.

During the first years of the post–World War II army, Collins, like other wartime commanders, found himself underemployed, occupying such posts as chief of staff of army ground forces and chief of information. But then came appointment to the Office of Army Chief of Staff, in succession to Generals Marshall, Eisenhower, and Omar N. Bradley, in August 1949. Collins's tenure, which lasted until 1953, covered the critical period of the Korean War, which began in June 1950. Before that war the army had become almost the stepchild of the military services, with money going to the more glamorous proposals of the air force and navy. Rivalry between the latter two services was epitomized in their fight for appropriations for, respectively, the huge B-36 propeller-driven bomber and the proposed supercarrier USS *United States,* a fight that the navy lost. The onset of the Korean War brought the army the appropriations it needed.

Prior to the Korean War, Collins had visited General MacArthur in Japan but failed to bring closer relations between that general's command and Washington, and in April 1951 Collins joined his fellow service heads in advising President Harry S. Truman to remove the Far East commander. Other issues Collins confronted involved desegregation throughout the army and, in Western Europe, the army's reinforcement of the North Atlantic Treaty Organization, including the controversial equipping of field units with nuclear artillery.

After stepping down as army chief of staff, Collins had three years until retirement. He spent part of that time in a mission to Vietnam (1954–1955), where he examined the military-political situation, including the abilities of the then-president of Vietnam, Ngo Dinh Diem. With reluctance Collins advised Washington that Diem could not handle his country's problems.

Retiring in 1956, after forty-three years of army service, Collins became vice chairman of the board of the pharmaceutical and chemical concern Pfizer and Company and for twelve years took a leading part in its international operations.

Collins spent his retirement years in Washington, the confines of the nation's capital made easier by trips to a cottage on Chesapeake Bay, Jayhawk Rest. He died of heart failure and was buried in Arlington National Cemetery.

Throughout his military assignments the able Collins radiated both energy and thoughtfulness, and these qualities brought him to the attention of such higher commanders as Marshall. Slightly above average in height, squarely built, and handsome, with straight mouth, snub nose, quiet and sharp eyes, and straightly brushed hair, he instilled trust. Behind the appearance was a cultivated intellect, for he was well-read and versed in classical music. At West Point he found the technical courses uninteresting and made no large effort to excel in them, preferring to spend his time reading. During his first assignment, at Fort Jay, he frequented New York City's concert halls, among other things attending the debut of the young violinist Jascha Heifetz in Carnegie Hall. With such qualities he could act imaginatively, the prime necessity of a great field commander, but he also possessed another essential. In France and Germany he often stopped his jeep and had his driver plug into telephone lines so he could listen in and see what units were doing. The large issues fascinated him, yet no details escaped his attention.

★

The Collins papers are in the National Archives. His autobiography, *Lightning Joe* (1979), is a subtle and highly literate account of his military career. His part in the Korean War appears in his *War in Peacetime* (1969). Martin Blumenson, *European Theater of Operations: Breakout and Pursuit* (1961), details the Normandy and subsequent campaigns.

ROBERT H. FERRELL

CONIGLIARO, Anthony Richard ("Tony") (*b.* 7 January 1945 in Revere, Massachusetts; *d.* 24 February 1990 in Salem, Massachusetts), baseball player known for having been the youngest home run champion in major league history and for having suffered a severe beaning that shortened his promising career.

Conigliaro was the eldest of three sons of Salvatore P. ("Sal") Conigliaro and Teresa Maria Martelli, first generation Italian Americans who had married during World War II. His father worked in a zipper factory and engaged in a number of mostly unsuccessful small business ventures before landing a substantial position as plant manager of a tool and die company in Lynn, Massachusetts. In 1953 the Conigliaros moved from Revere, Teresa's native city, to East Boston, where Sal had grown up. Ten years later they settled in Swampscott, a coastal town north of Lynn.

Tony Conigliaro. NATIONAL BASEBALL HALL OF FAME LIBRARY, COOPERSTOWN, N.Y.

Young Tony, slow in school and often truant, found his salvation in sports. A natural athlete, he was encouraged by his father to play baseball at an early age. His maternal uncle, Vinnie Martelli, a former semipro third baseman, pitched to the boy and tutored him in the fundamentals of the game. Batting and throwing right-handed, Conigliaro developed into the dominant hitter and pitcher in East Boston's Little League and Pony League.

At St. Mary's High School in Lynn, Conigliaro starred in football and basketball in addition to playing every position but catcher and first base in baseball. He drew the attention of major league scouts in his junior year by lashing three sharp hits off a rival pitcher who had been viewed as a leading prospect. After compiling a .560 batting average as a senior in 1962, he was offered $22,000 to sign a contract by both the Baltimore Orioles and the Boston Red Sox. He chose the Red Sox because Fenway Park, where the team played its home games, was only a fifteen-minute drive from his home and because the park's left-field wall (known as the Green Monster) was just 310 feet from home plate and ideally suited for a right-handed power hitter.

Owing to his success at every level, Conigliaro was supremely confident about his abilities (both teammates and opponents thought him cocky). A fierce competitor, his style was to lean out over home plate and challenge pitchers. Though occasionally hit by inside pitches, he would more often turn and drive them hard to left field. Already possessing a fluid, uppercut swing, Conigliaro made himself even more of a home run threat by working out with weights and swinging a leaded bat at home. Standing six-feet, three inches tall and weighing 185 pounds, he also became a capable outfielder with better than average speed and a strong, accurate throwing arm.

Before reporting to his first minor league assignment at Wellsville, New York, Conigliaro broke his thumb in a fistfight with a youth who had made a pass at his high school girlfriend. The injury forced him to miss the first six weeks of the season. Playing center field for the last eighty-three games, Conigliaro batted .363, with twenty-four home runs and seventy-four runs batted in (RBIs). He was chosen Most Valuable Player in the New York–Pennsylvania League and given a place on Boston's spring training roster in 1964.

Although most observers predicted the brash nineteen-year-old Conigliaro would be farmed out for another year of seasoning, he outplayed his outfield rivals at the Red Sox camp and won the starting center field job (he later moved to right field). Although hampered by injuries caused mostly by pitched balls, he played in 111 games, batted .290, with twenty-four home runs and fifty-two RBIs, and was runner-up to Tony Oliva of the Minnesota Twins in American League Rookie of the Year balloting.

Even as Conigliaro's batting average dropped in the next two years, he established himself as one of the premier power hitters in baseball. With thirty-two home runs in 1965, he became the youngest to lead a league in that offensive department. A year later he was voted Boston's Most Valuable Player after hitting twenty-eight homers and driving in ninety-three runs (up from eighty-two in 1965). Commensurate with his growing star status, Conigliaro's salary increased from $7,500 in 1964 to $55,000 in 1967.

In addition to being one of the few productive players on a weak Boston team that finished near the bottom of the American League from 1964 through 1966, Conigliaro emerged as a celebrity off the field. A handsome, charismatic, outspoken, and free-spirited child of the early 1960s, he was idolized by New England teenagers and considered good copy by the Boston press. Accustomed to winning, Conigliaro made waves in the clubhouse by loudly criticizing what he viewed as the losing attitude of his teammates. At the same time, his penchant for late-night partying often antagonized Red Sox management, resulted in substantial fines, and earned him a reputation as a "playboy." Conigliaro, who never married, was also frequently mentioned in gossip columns for his romantic involvement with a dazzling array of beautiful women. Nonetheless, he resented the playboy label because he was a light drinker and was never out of playing shape.

With left fielder Carl Yastrzemski, Conigliaro (twenty home runs, sixty-seven RBIs, and a .287 batting average) formed a powerful hitting combination that kept the Red Sox in the thick of the pennant race in the summer of 1967. He made the American League All-Star team and, in July, became the second youngest player to reach 100 career home runs in major league history (Mel Ott had been the youngest). But on 18 August, Conigliaro's season abruptly ended when he was struck in the left eye and cheek by a fastball thrown by Jack Hamilton of the California Angels. A fractured cheekbone, a dislocated jaw, and a badly bruised eye kept him on the sidelines as Yastrzemski led the Red Sox to the pennant and the World Series, which they lost to the St. Louis Cardinals in seven games.

In 1968 Conigliaro's troubles continued. When he tried to return to action, blurred vision impeded his hitting. A cyst that had formed on the macula of the retina of his injured eye burst, leaving a blind spot at the center of his vision. He was forced to sit out the entire season, and his career seemed in jeopardy. A few months later, however, his eye showed substantial improvement, and he was cleared to play again.

In an effort to reduce the strain on his eye, Conigliaro attempted to come back as a pitcher in 1969. But when he returned to form as a hitter in the Florida Instructional League, the Boston front office convinced him to give up pitching. Back in right field for the Red Sox, he hit a respectable .255, with twenty home runs and eighty-two runs batted in, and won the major league Comeback Player of the Year award.

In 1970 Conigliaro had his best offensive year ever, hitting thirty-six homers and driving home 116 runs. His performance was even more remarkable because his eyesight had again begun to deteriorate. His great concentration and intense study of opposing pitchers enabled him to succeed at the plate. But he faltered noticeably in the field, misplaying a number of routine fly balls. Perhaps as a consequence, the Red Sox sent him to the California Angels in a six-player trade in the off-season.

Conigliaro was devastated psychologically by the trade. He also found Anaheim Stadium far less congenial than Fenway Park to his hitting style, and the bright California sun only added to his worsening vision problems in 1971. Batting only .222, with four homers and fifteen RBIs at midseason, Conigliaro opted to leave baseball. He and his brother Billy (who also spent time in the major leagues) subsequently operated a combination cocktail lounge and golf course in Nahant, Massachusetts.

In 1973 the American League adopted the designated hitter rule, which allowed a team to use a batter in place of the pitcher in the regular lineup. Since the DH was not required to play a position in the field, Conigliaro saw the rule as his ticket back to the big leagues. Invited to spring training by the Red Sox in 1975, he made the team. But his second comeback was short-lived. He was plagued by minor injuries, batted .123 with two home runs in just twenty-one games, and was sent to the Red Sox farm club in Pawtucket, Rhode Island. There he hit only .203 before retiring in August to take a sportscasting job in Providence.

Conigliaro remained in Providence for a year before he was hired by a TV station in San Francisco. Although at first handicapped by a pronounced Boston accent, he had some success as a West Coast sports anchor from 1976 to 1981. In December 1981 he returned home to audition for the job of color commentator for televised Red Sox games.

After apparently winning the Red Sox post, Conigliaro was felled by a heart attack in Boston in January 1982. He lapsed into a coma that lasted for three weeks. The resulting brain damage left him in need of around-the-clock nursing care for the rest of his life. He died of kidney failure and pneumonia and was buried in Holy Cross Cemetery in Malden, Massachusetts.

Tony Conigliaro is mainly remembered as a star player whose career was thwarted by injuries, and remains the object of much speculation as to what might have been. Even Yastrzemski, a Hall of Famer who hit 492 runs in twenty-three years with the Red Sox, opined that Conigliaro might have hit 500 or more home runs with good health and a long career at Fenway Park.

★

Seeing It Through (1970), an autobiography written with the assistance of Jack Zanger, is a frank, if not always accurate, account of Conigliaro's first twenty-five years, with particular emphasis on his beaning and return to baseball in 1969. A full-length biography is David Cataneo, *Tony C: The Triumph and Tragedy of Tony Conigliaro* (1997). Peter Golenbock, *Fenway: An Unexpurgated History of the Boston Red Sox* (1992), discusses Conigliaro and contains additional observations and quotes from teammates and fans. The National Baseball Hall of Fame Library in Cooperstown, New York, has a file of clippings on Conigliaro. The statistics of his career are in the *Baseball Encyclopedia*. Obituaries are in the *Boston Globe* and the *Boston Herald* (25 Feb. 1990) and the *New York Times* (26 Feb. 1990).

RICHARD H. GENTILE

CONLAN, John Bertrand ("Jocko") (*b.* 6 December 1899 in Chicago, Illinois; *d.* 16 April 1989 in Scottsdale, Arizona), baseball player, National League umpire for twenty-five years, and a member of Major League Baseball's Hall of Fame.

"Jocko" Conlan. COURTESY OF THE NATIONAL BASEBALL HALL OF FAME

Conlan was the youngest of nine children born to Irish parents on Chicago's South Side at Twenty-fifth and Butler, within walking distance of Comiskey Park, home of the Chicago White Sox. Andrew Conlan, his father, was a stockyards policeman who died when John was three. His mother, Mary Ann O'Connor Clayton, was determined to keep the family together. She washed, cooked, cleaned, and mended to make ends meet. At the age of seven Conlan could be found at the neighborhood baseball diamond, affectionately called the Stinkbuck because it was surrounded by a brewery, a barrel factory, a candle factory, and a gashouse. He played on a team with his brothers Pete, Joe, and Heinie. He spent hours before and after games throwing a taped ball against the brewery wall to study hops off a rock-pile ballfield. At twelve he was a barefoot batboy for the White Sox. He remembers stealing the glove of Kid Gleason of the Sox and taking it home. Gleason was a righty and the young Conlan a lefty, but that did not stop him from wearing the glove. "I said to myself this is the greatest thing that ever happened to me," he recalled.

Conlan managed and pitched his All Saints Parochial School team to a Catholic League championship despite his frequent run-ins with umpires. During his two years at De La Salle Academy, his last years of formal education, he played first base and outfield with semiprofessional teams around Chicago, including teams in the highly respected Midwest League. In 1918 he enlisted in the navy. After his release a year later, Conlan continued his career in baseball. He played unspectacularly with Tulsa and Wichita in 1920. At five feet, seven inches and 160 pounds, he was a good contact hitter and an even better fielder with a surprisingly strong and accurate arm. Ten days before the end of the 1920 season, in a characteristic fit of impetuosity, he broke his contract and headed back to Chicago homesick. On 12 January 1921 he married Ruth Anderson, a Chicago sweetheart. They had two children; one of them, John, became a congressman. Suspended by Wichita for having broken his contract, he played the 1921 season for the Chicago Pyotts in the Midwest League. When Wichita found out he had returned to semiprofessional ball, it suspended him for the 1922 season as well. He effectively argued his case and was reinstated by Wichita for 1923. At the end of that season he was sold to the Rochester club of the International League.

Over the next twelve years Conlan proved to be an excellent minor-league ballplayer. He hit over .300 six times in the high minors and never batted lower than .283. He averaged twenty assists a year, frequently a league high for an outfielder. His top salary in the minors was $5,500, and he received that only after leading the league in hits, runs, triples, and stolen bases, while leading outfielders in putouts and assists. It took a ten-day contract holdout to win the raise, which added to Conlan's reputation as a determined, and often fearless, competitor. During the off season he boxed in the ring, getting his nose broken more than once, and judged bouts. His only opportunity to crack the major leagues as a young player was shattered when he tore up a knee in 1925, the day before he was to have reported to the Cincinnati Reds. He would wait nine more years before the Chicago White Sox agreed to take a chance on him.

Conlan got his nickname "Jocko" from a minor-league sportswriter, because of the way he jockeyed opposing players. It stuck and became one of the most famous names in baseball history. An on-the-field fight with an umpire in Jersey City and a winning run he scored on a broken ankle for Casey Stengel in Newark solidified the impression that few could match Conlan's grit. Conlan was a part-time outfielder for the White Sox in 1934 and 1935, hitting .263 in 128 games and 365 at bats. It was in 1935, during the first game of a doubleheader in Sportsman's Park between the White Sox and the St. Louis Browns, that Red Ormsby, one of two umpires working that day, passed out in 114-degree heat. Conlan, who could not play because of a broken finger, volunteered to replace him. Rogers Hornsby, the manager of the Browns, agreed. Umpiring the bases in his White Sox uniform, Conlan's impartiality was tested when he called teammate Luke Appling out in a critical play at third. White Sox manager Jimmie Dykes complained, but Appling admitted Conlan had made the right call. Conlan umpired the remainder of the series in St. Louis and at year's end agreed to try his hand at minor-league umpiring.

Conlan worked the New York–Pennsylvania League for three years at $1,500 a year. He was quick, active, showed good judgment, and could run faster than most ballplayers. He was also fearless, throwing a prize Yankee farmhand out of an important game before he had tossed his first pitch because he had cursed at Conlan. After the game Conlan went into the pitcher's team clubhouse to fight it out, but cooler heads prevailed. Conlan's motto was, "You've got to have and command respect. Without them, you're nothing." He said this at a time when umpires did not get much respect. When Conlan entered umpiring, umpires were expected to dress for games "in a toilet under the stands," as he put it. Nine innings of insults were part of the job description. Many an umpire was pelted by fans or embarrassed by managers after an unpopular call. Some were beaten up by players after games that had not gone their way.

In 1938 Conlan was promoted to the American Association, where he stayed for three years. When he was hired by the National League before the 1941 season, he had served twenty years in the minor leagues, fourteen as a player and six as an umpire. It was a remarkable apprenticeship. He knew the game and the rules of the game as well as any umpire ever had. He was also about to change the way that fans, sportswriters, managers, and players looked at umpires.

Over the course of the next twenty-five seasons, Conlan umpired six World Series, six All-Star games, and all four playoff games to decide pennants in the National League. A glimpse of what was to come came in his first game behind the plate. The Pittsburgh Pirates were hosting the world champion Cincinnati Reds when a Pirate batter hit a ball down into the dirt. It came back up, hit him in the leg, and rolled out in front of the plate in fair territory. The Reds catcher pounced on the ball and threw to first base, where the first-base umpire signaled out. Conlan, however, had called a foul ball, and Bill McKechnie, the Reds manager who had a reputation with umpires, raced out of the dugout to do battle. Conlan spun around, ripped off his mask, and stuck out his hand, like a policeman directing traffic. He shouted to McKechnie, "Don't you come up here! I don't need you. That was a foul ball." McKechnie, shocked, stopped and looked at Conlan, took off his cap, and a bit embarrassed, bowed before meekly returning to the dugout. "That's the kind of umpire I like," McKechnie later told reporters, "one who can run a ball game."

Conlan's feel for the game and presence on the field made him a legendary umpire. "Right or wrong the umpire's always the villain," Conlan observed. "That's the way it's been for 100 years and you learn to take it," but Jocko learned to dish it out, too. In an infamous kicking match with Leo Durocher in 1961, Conlan ejected the Los Angeles Dodgers third-base coach after Durocher argued a call. Durocher kicked dirt over Conlan's trouser legs and Conlan did the same to Durocher's uniform. One kick led to another, and, when separated by other umpires and players, the two combatants were working over one another's ankles. "The worst thing in this world is a weak umpire," Conlan told interviewers afterward, sorry only that he and Durocher did not finish their fight with fists.

"Everyone liked and respected Jocko," said Bill White, future president of the National League, who remembered that Conlan gave him a hitting tip when White was breaking in with the St. Louis Cardinals. Conlan knew the old umpire's rule of never talking to players or fans on the field, but he was too loquacious to listen. White was certain that Conlan's advice on being aggressive as a hitter when ahead in the count helped make White a .300 hitter. When singles specialist Richie Ashburn, a Philadelphia Phillies outfielder, complained once too often, Conlan had him call his own balls and strikes. Ashburn, flabbergasted, promptly struck out, and left the umpiring to Conlan. When Dodger catcher Jeff Torborg dislocated a finger behind the plate, Conlan called time out and fixed it for him. "Jocko Conlan was a living work of art," observed New York sportswriter Robert Creamer. A jutting jaw, flashing eyes, and a penetrating glance became his signature. "The little blue hat, the bow tie, the cocky walk," Creamer noted, became legend, too.

Conlan was not merely the quintessential umpire, he was an actor playing the part of the quintessential umpire. There was no one tougher on the field or more congenial off it, recalled fellow umpire Shag Crawford. "He had fans in every city," observed Augie Donatelli, who worked with Conlan for eight years. "Wherever we'd go there were always people waiting to see Jocko." He was also admired by other umpires. "He helped all the young umpires," Donatelli recalled. "He helped me believe in myself," reported Bruce Froemming. Conlan saw it as a way of giving back to the game that had given him so much. "Hang with 'em kid," he'd often say. "You'll get 'em next time."

Bone spurs on his heel forced Conlan's retirement after the 1964 season. His farewell tour across the country led to an outpouring of affection and support rarely seen for anyone associated with the game. After retiring, he moved from Chicago to Paradise Valley, Arizona. Conlan returned to the game for two weeks in 1965 to help out a sick friend. Two years later Conlan wrote *Jocko,* a highly popular autobiography. He served as a consultant to the National League president Warren Giles and in 1974 became only the fifth umpire elected into the Baseball Hall of Fame. He died of a heart attack fifteen years later. Conlan was buried in Scottsdale, Arizona.

"I was a strong umpire," he once said, reflecting on his storied career. "And I was a good umpire. I always respected the ground that a ballplayer walked on, and I respected the player himself. But, in turn, I demanded respect from every player that I came across. And I got it."

★

A file highlighting Conlan's career is available at the Major League Baseball Hall of Fame in Cooperstown, New York. His career is chronicled in Jocko Conlan and Robert Creamer, *Jocko* (1967). A biographical sketch appears in David L. Porter, *Biographical Dictionary of American Sports: Baseball* (1987). Arthur Daley of the *New York Times* wrote an appreciation for Conlan's career, "How Jocko 'Broke' In," that appears in the *Baseball Writers of America Scorebook* (1965). An appreciation by veteran sportswriter Jerome Holtzman appears in the *Chicago Tribune* (18 Apr. 1989). Richie Ashburn's tribute appears in the *Philadelphia Daily News* (11 May 1989). An obituary is in the *New York Times* (17 Apr. 1989).

BRUCE J. EVENSEN

COPLAND, Aaron (*b.* 14 November 1900 in Brooklyn, New York; *d.* 2 December 1990 in North Tarrytown, New York), composer, writer, conductor, teacher, and vigorous proponent of twentieth-century American music.

Born over the fair-sized Brooklyn department store that his parents owned and ran, Copland was the last of the five children of Harris Morris Copland and Sarah (Mittenthal) Copland, Russian immigrants. Although Aaron's two brothers and two sisters were not near him in age, he was not a lonely child. His extended family included fifteen aunts and uncles, and he apparently had a relatively happy and comfortable childhood in this generally nonmusical, commercially successful Jewish family.

Copland showed an early interest in music. By age eight and a half, he was making up songs, and at the age of eleven he ambitiously produced seven measures of an opera he called *Zenatello*. At about this time, he persuaded his sister Laurine Copland to give him piano lessons. He soon advanced beyond his sister's level of expertise, however, and from 1914 to 1917 he studied piano with Leopold Wolfsohn. Copland decided to devote his life to music, and from 1917 to 1921 he took serious composition and theory lessons with Rubin Goldmark in Manhattan. Although Goldmark, a traditionalist, was unsympathetic with contemporary musical ideas, he was an excellent teacher who counted

Aaron Copland, 1962. HULTON-DEUTSCH COLLECTION/CORBIS

George Gershwin among his pupils at this same time. Copland also took piano lessons with Victor Wittgenstein for a couple of winters.

Upon graduation from Boys' High School in Brooklyn in 1918, Copland decided to study music full-time instead of attending college. He took various part-time jobs playing piano with small ensembles for dances at such places as the Finnish Socialist Hall in New York and, during the summers of 1919 and 1920, at resort hotels in the Catskill Mountains. From 1919 to 1921 he studied piano with Clarence Adler. Intrigued by reports of a new American Conservatory that was being organized in Fontainebleau, just outside Paris, Copland set sail for France in June 1921 and became the first student to enroll. There he worked with Nadia Boulanger, the famous composition and theory teacher, and had his first taste of conducting. He also came into contact with Jacques Durand, the distinguished Parisian publisher who in 1922 issued Copland's first published piece, *The Cat and the Mouse* (1920), after hearing it at a conservatory concert.

In September 1921 Copland moved to Paris, where he spent three exciting and important years (1921–1924) immersed in the vitality and innovation of writers, dancers, and artists from France and around the world. The young Copland drank in the heady cosmopolitan atmosphere and continued his composition, orchestration, and theory studies with Boulanger, who was demanding, insightful, and lively and who encouraged new musical ideas, techniques, and expression. At her studio, he met famous composers, such as Igor Stravinsky, Darius Milhaud, Francis Poulenc, Maurice Ravel, Heitor Villa-Lobos, and Camille Saint-Saëns.

Living in Paris also afforded Copland the chance to travel to England, Belgium, Germany, Austria, and Italy, where he listened to as much music as he could. American jazz was popular in Europe in the 1920s, and he heard jazz and ragtime rhythms in the concert works of European composers such as Claude Debussy and Stravinsky. It occurred to the expatriate Copland that here was a deeply American vein into which he could tap, and he awakened a desire to write music that would be unmistakably American, to put American music on the map.

Copland blossomed as a composer during his years in Paris. Working with Boulanger, who encouraged his exploration of unusual rhythms and use of dissonance, he composed vocal, choral, instrumental, and orchestral pieces, including his most ambitious work of the time, the ballet *Grohg* (1922–1924). He formed work habits that served him well for the rest of his life. Ever a meticulous craftsman, he explained in his autobiography (written with Vivian Perlis) that the peaceful hours of night always seemed most conducive to composing and most "appropriate for a slow worker like myself—I have never dashed anything off in a burst of inspiration, even when very young. I tend to work carefully, put things aside, and then take them up again for a fresh look."

Before Copland returned to the United States in June 1924, Boulanger invited him to compose an organ piece for her first American tour. The *Symphony for Organ and Orchestra,* which Boulanger premiered with the New York Symphony in January 1925, introduced Copland's music to the American public. While it has no jazz quotations, the three-movement work has some raw jazz elements disguised in concert silk, and it received good to excellent reviews. Nearly all critics admitted it was a powerful, dramatic work by a talented new artist. Serge Koussevitzky, conductor of the Boston Symphony Orchestra and a champion of new music, played the symphony in the same year and became an avid and lifelong supporter of Copland's work.

Copland spent the years from 1924 to 1926 mainly in New York City. At first he received much-needed financial support from Alma Wertheim, a wealthy patron of the arts, then he won Guggenheim Fellowships for the years 1925 to 1927. Copland was a member of the League of Composers, an association based in New York that was devoted to the promotion of new music, and while in New York City he began writing for the organization's quarterly journal, *Modern Music*. An eloquent and often bold contributor, he was fervent about the cause of new music and its part in America's search for an artistic identity.

Copland spent the summer of 1925 at MacDowell Colony, a tranquil and secluded retreat for artists in Peterborough, New Hampshire. He devoted this, the first of his eight stays at the colony, to working on a five-part suite called *Music for the Theatre,* which was premiered by Koussevitzky in Boston on 25 November 1925. Written with no particular story in mind, it is by turns brash and lyrical, full of jazzy rhythms and unconventional harmonies. Even though critics did not care for it, the piece became popular during the 1920s, the era when jazz boldly entered the concert halls of the United States.

In March 1926 Copland returned to Paris. After quickly completing *Two Pieces for Violin and Piano* for a concert in Paris, he settled in a villa on the western coast of France for the summer. There he wrote *Concerto for Piano and Orchestra,* his last piece that explicitly uses jazz materials. The concerto has a blues opening, slow and lyrical, that is followed by a fast, rhythmically interesting section. Copland played the piano part himself at the concerto's premiere in Boston in January 1927. The critics were harsh, calling it "a harrowing horror" and "poor stuff," but Copland, who was never hamstrung by bad reviews, maintained his typical quiet confidence and good sense. He wrote in his autobiography that he "composed out of real conviction" and that "there was a lot of fun in bucking the tide and feeling part of the avant-garde out there fighting new battles." Less than one month later, the piece was received as a success in New York City, but already Copland was turning away from the frank use of jazz idioms and was looking elsewhere for inspiration and musical ideas.

New opportunities presented themselves to Copland in the late 1920s. In the autumn of 1927, he began a ten-year stint as a lecturer on modern music appreciation at the New School for Social Research in New York City. His classes, which met once a week, allowed him to organize his thoughts on the subject and to view his own compositions in historical perspective. When he returned later to teach a general music appreciation course at the school, he published his notes in *What to Listen for in Music* (1939), which was eventually translated into eleven languages and reissued in a revised edition in 1957. Ever an energetic champion of modern music, Copland worked with fellow composer Roger Sessions to organize a series of concerts to give new composers a chance to be heard and Americans a chance to hear them. Between 1928 and 1931, ten concerts, mostly in New York City, provided members of the League of Composers with a venue for their works.

Copland devoted himself in the 1930s to composing, writing, giving lecture recitals around the country, and traveling. In addition, he helped organize Cos Cob Press, an early effort to help American composers publish their music, and in 1932 and 1933 he directed the Festival of Contemporary Music at Yaddo, the artists' colony in Saratoga Springs, New York. During 1932, he spent five months in Mexico, where the first all-Copland concert was held at the Conservatorio Nacional de México on 2 September 1932. It was a "rich time" for him, he wrote to a friend. He found that "Mexico offers something fresh and pure and wholesome." Inspired by a visit to a colorful dance hall in Mexico City, he wrote one of his most popular pieces, *El salón México* (1936), in which he used a variety of themes and fragments from Mexican music.

Copland accepted a teaching position at Harvard University in 1935. During 1936 and 1937, he wrote music for the Columbia Broadcasting System radio network, and in 1937 he created an opera for high school use, *The Second Hurricane.* He helped organize the American Composers Alliance (ACA) in 1937 and served as its president from 1937 to 1945. The goals of the ACA were to protect the economic rights of composers and to stimulate interest in the performance of American music.

In 1938 Lincoln Kirstein, the American dance impresario and director of the Ballet Caravan, persuaded Copland to help move ballet away from the Russian tradition and toward a new American expression. In response, Copland wrote *Billy the Kid,* incorporating material from such tunes as "Git Along Little Dogies," "The Old Chisholm Trail," and "Bury Me Not on the Lone Prairie." This ballet became another of Copland's popular pieces and was widely recorded and praised. In addition, Copland wrote two more quintessentially American ballets in the 1940s. *Rodeo,* commissioned by the Ballets Russes de Monte Carlo, premiered in October 1942 and starred Agnes de Mille. *Appalachian Spring,* a landmark piece performed by Martha Graham and her dance company in 1944, earned a Pulitzer Prize for the composer.

In 1939 Copland's score for a film documentary titled *The City* captured the interest of Hollywood producers. Later that year he was invited to the West Coast to compose music for a feature film, *Of Mice and Men,* directed by Lewis Milestone. Copland went on to produce scores for the films *Our Town* (1940), a version of a play by Thornton Wilder; *North Star* (1943); *The Cummington Story* (1945), a documentary for the U.S. Office of War Information; *The Red Pony* (1948), based on the story by John Steinbeck; *The Heiress* (1950), based on the novel *Washington Square* by Henry James; and *Something Wild* (1961). For *The Heiress,* Copland won an Academy Award for best film score in 1950.

In 1940 Koussevitzky established the Berkshire Music Center (renamed Tanglewood Music Center in 1985), a summer music school affiliated with the annual Berkshire Music Festival at the Tanglewood estate near Lenox, Massachusetts. Koussevitzky recruited Copland as a composition teacher and lecturer, and Copland later served as chairman of the faculty. From 1940 until 1965, except for the years 1943–1945, during World War II, Copland lectured, performed, composed, and worked with serious young composers each summer at Tanglewood, which would become one of the most important musical institutions in the world.

In the autumn of 1941 Copland published *Our New Music: Leading Composers in Europe and America,* a guide to understanding musical developments from the nineteenth century to 1940 (it was later revised and reissued as *The New Music: 1900–1960* in 1968). Also in 1941, the U.S. State Department designated Copland as a member of the President's Advisory Committee on Music. In this capacity, he promoted Pan-American relations during a four-month tour of South America, where he met with local composers, gave lectures in Spanish, and conducted and played his own music. He taught at Harvard again in 1943 and 1944 and made another tour of South America with the State Department in 1947.

Busy as he was with all these activities, Copland did not fail to compose. In 1941 he completed the Piano Sonata. In 1942 André Kostelanetz commissioned *Lincoln Portrait,* which included passages from Abraham Lincoln's writings and speeches, to encourage war-weary Americans. In 1943 Copland produced perhaps his most popular piece, the stirring *Fanfare for the Common Man,* which has accompanied television coverage of Olympic games, was played at a presidential inauguration, and was arranged by Mick Jagger for the Rolling Stones. Copland's longest orchestral work, the Third Symphony, premiered in 1946 after nearly two years of composition.

The 1950s started out promisingly for Copland. Benny Goodman, the clarinetist, commissioned and premiered the Clarinet Concerto in 1950. Also that year, Copland produced *Twelve Poems of Emily Dickinson* and *Old American Songs,* a setting of five folk songs. In 1951, a Fulbright Fellowship allowed him to work at the American Academy in Rome and then to make his first visit to Israel, where he gave lectures and conducted. In the 1951–1952 academic year he wrote and delivered the prestigious Charles Eliot Norton Lectures at Harvard University, which were collected and published in 1952 under the title *Music and Imagination* (reprinted in 1959).

In May 1953 Copland, whom fellow composer and critic Virgil Thomson once called "the President of American Music," was summoned before Senator Joseph McCarthy's infamous Senate subcommittee investigating communist and subversive activities. Copland's association with musicians and artists who appeared questionable to this reactionary and paranoid committee had made him suspect as well, but he handled himself with aplomb and was not blacklisted. Nevertheless, he found the whole episode nerve-racking, infuriating, and wasteful, and he experienced lingering repercussions as late as 1967. In his autobiography, Copland lamented the time and energy lost during this period, but with his typical pragmatism, he asked, "What can one do but go through it and carry on?"

Carry on he did. During the remainder of the 1950s, Copland completed his opera *The Tender Land,* on which he had worked for over two years and which the New York City Opera Company premiered in April 1954. He was named a member of the American Academy and Institute of Arts and Letters in 1955 and was awarded its Gold Medal in Music in 1956. He received thirty-two honorary degrees from universities around the country. He also made two more trips to South America, in 1954 and 1957, and sojourned for six months in Europe in 1955, where he visited with friends and fellow composers, conducted, gave lectures, and composed.

During the late 1950s, as his compositional production began to slow down, his conducting career took flight. In 1958, he made two conducting tours, one in the United States and one in Europe. In 1960, he took part in a State Department trip to the Soviet Union, where he conducted and lectured. Later in the 1960s, he guest conducted the British Broadcast Corporation Orchestra, the London Symphony Orchestra, and the Boston Symphony Orchestra, among many others around the world.

The turbulent 1960s were busy for Copland in other ways as well. In 1960 he published another book, *Copland on Music,* and in 1962, President John F. Kennedy and his wife chose Copland's ballet *Billy the Kid* for a performance at the White House. During 1965 and 1966, Copland wrote the scripts, conducted the music, and served as host for a television series, *Music in the Twenties,* produced by WGBH in Boston. He continued to compose, two of his major works of the decade being *Connotations* (1962) and *Inscape* (1967).

During his long career, Copland appeared on television as conductor, lecturer, or pianist nearly sixty times. In his later years, his birthdays were often celebrated with galas and concerts in his honor. The tall, lanky, blue-eyed composer was the recipient of many honors, including the Presidential Medal of Freedom in 1964, the Kennedy Center Honor in 1979, and both the Medal of the Arts and the Congressional Gold Medal in 1986.

Copland, who kept his homosexuality from the public eye as much as possible, spent his last years at his home, Rock Hill, in suburban Peekskill, New York. During the last three weeks of his life, he suffered two strokes. He finally succumbed to respiratory failure brought on by pneumonia. His ashes were enshrined in the Tanglewood Music Center Garden in Massachusetts.

Copland was a successful and accessible American composer with a strong, distinct voice who, as Leonard Bernstein once said, led "American music out of the wilderness." He was also a conductor dedicated to taking new music, his and others', to the world. He was a practical man, who organized large-scale musical events, helped other composers get their works into print and into concert halls, and worked as a faculty member or officer for a variety of musical schools, institutes, and associations. He was a writer, teacher, and lecturer who reached out to his peers, to several generations of composers, and to anyone interested in music. Copland's myriad and monumental achievements make it impossible to gauge the full extent of his influence on twentieth-century American music and culture.

★

Copland's manuscripts and personal papers are in the Music Division of the Library of Congress. Aaron Copland's own *Our New Music* (1941) and *The New Music: 1900–1960* (1968) offer valuable information not only on his life and career but also on his perceptions of music in the twentieth century. His autobiographies, *Copland: 1900 Through 1942* (1984) and *Copland: Since 1943* (1989), both written with Vivian Perlis, are eminently readable and well-illustrated. Arthur Berger, *Aaron Copland* (1953), is a dated but still important resource by a fellow composer and friend. Detailed studies of his style and work are Julia F. Smith, *Aaron Copland: His Work and Contribution to American Music* (1955), and Neil Butterworth, *The Music of Aaron Copland* (1985). JoAnn Skowronski, *Aaron Copland: A Bio-Bibliography* (1985), includes bibliographies of writings by and about Copland, a discography, and a detailed, chronological list of his works. William W.

Austin with Vivian Perlis, "Aaron Copland," in *The New Grove Dictionary of American Music*, vol. 1, edited by H. Wiley Hitchcock and Stanley Sadies (1986), provides a concise discussion of the life, works, and style of Copland as well as a full list of his works and a selected bibliography. Obituaries are in the *New York Times* (3 Dec. 1990), *Time* (17 Dec. 1990), and *Clavier* 30 (Feb. 1991).

MICHAEL MECKNA

COTTON, Norris Henry (*b.* 11 May 1900 in Warren, New Hampshire; *d.* 24 February 1989 in Lebanon, New Hampshire), lawyer and congressman whose experience in the U.S. Congress extended over half a century.

Norris and his half-sister and brother grew up on a farm on a "hemmed-in plain, encircled by hills." His mother, Elizabeth Moses, a homemaker, and his father, Henry, were Warren natives, used to a hard life. Henry Cotton worked at numerous trades and upheld the family tradition of civic duty, serving as deputy sheriff in the local court, where the argumentation of country lawyers sparked Norris's interest in oratory. When Norris entered the one-room Maple Grove schoolhouse, he was already an avid student, thanks to his parents and to the family mentor, "no-nonsense uncle" Horace Abbott. At Phillips Exeter Academy in Exeter, New Hampshire (1916–1918), Cotton developed his public speaking skills. As a student at Wesleyan University in Middletown, Connecticut, he became a great storyteller and mimic. He financed his own education, working as a waiter, dishwasher, and bellhop and using his oratorical skills as a lay preacher to earn $5 per sermon. He graduated from Wesleyan in 1922.

Norris Cotton. ARCHIVE PHOTOS

Cotton returned to New Hampshire and became editor of the *Granite State Monthly*. The people of Warren elected him in 1922 to the New Hampshire House of Representatives, where he served one term. Cotton supported legislation to replace the Agriculture College with the University of New Hampshire, commencing a lifelong concern for that university. His oratorical skills were noticed by his party's leaders, who chose him at age twenty-three to be president of the 1924 Republican state convention and secretary of the state committee for the fall election.

After the 1924 campaign, Cotton went to Washington to take up an appointment to the staff of New Hampshire Republican senator George H. Moses. He attended George Washington University Law School at night and observed the workings of the U.S. Senate by day. As a clerk to the Committee on Post Offices and Roads, his job included submitting to the senators for their rejection or approval the names of nominees for postmasters in their respective states. Thus Cotton had personal contact with every member of the Senate. Also, as a Senate clerk he was privileged to be on the floor of the Senate at all times, and he spent hours listening to such "blunt and ruthless" debaters as Senators William Borah and Robert La Follette. The law student studied Senate procedure and learned its traditions, and he observed senators as a collegial body and as individuals, noting how they remained in contact with their constituents.

While in Washington, Cotton met Ruth Isaacs from Lynville, Tennessee, a member of the staff of Senator Kenneth McKellar, the ranking Democrat on the Committee on Post Offices and Roads. They married on 11 May 1927 and had no children.

In 1928 Cotton was admitted to the New Hampshire bar and left Washington, not expecting to return to the Senate except as a gallery visitor. For nearly twenty years he devoted himself to the law in New Hampshire, first with the Concord firm of Demond, Woodworth, Sulloway, and Rogers. Cotton also worked as clerk of the New Hampshire Senate (1927–1929), a period overlapping his clerkship in the U.S. Senate, inasmuch as the then briefer U.S. Senate sessions enabled senators and their staff to spend much time back home. In 1933 he moved to his home county of Grafton and established the firm of Cotton, Tesreau, and Stebbins in Lebanon. He was elected county solicitor in 1933, 1935, and 1937. Appointed justice of the Lebanon

Municipal Court, he held that position from 1939 to 1943. Cotton was elected to the state House of Representatives and chosen majority leader for the 1943 session. He was reelected in 1944 (despite Democratic president Franklin Roosevelt's sweep of the state), with the double endorsement of the Democratic and Republican organizations, and chosen speaker for the 1945 session.

In 1946 an unexpected development changed the course of Cotton's life. New Hampshire's politically powerful Sherman Adams gave up his congressional seat to run for governor, and Cotton was elected to represent the state's Second District in the Eightieth Congress. He was sworn in on 3 January 1947, reelected three times, and resigned on 7 November 1954. He went to Washington with principles ready to apply and a moral code intact but found that "one is constantly compelled to settle for the best of several unsatisfactory substitutes." Thus, he said, he voted, in one month, for "a compulsory Selective Service bill I disliked, a tax bill I detested, and a price-and-wage control bill I abominated." To explain the issues and the reasoning behind his votes, he began writing "Reports" (weekly, then biweekly), which for twenty-five years he sent back home to his constituents.

In 1954 another unexpected event affected Cotton's career. New Hampshire's senator Charles Tobey died in office, and Cotton was elected to the Senate, where he had served as a committee clerk a quarter of a century earlier. He was sworn in on 8 November 1954 to fill Tobey's unexpired term and was subsequently reelected for three full terms. Senator Cotton's first vote was to censure Senator Joseph McCarthy. He introduced an amendment to the Social Security Act in 1955, lowering the eligibility age to sixty-two. He also helped draft the Interstate Highway System Act and pioneered the idea of federal revenue sharing with the states. As a fiscal conservative, however, his focus was always an "unremitting fight against excessive federal expenditures and the ballooning federal bureaucracy." In 1973, wanting to be with his ailing wife, he announced he would not run for reelection in 1974; his own regret was shared by constituents and colleagues. He returned briefly to the Senate (8 August to 18 September 1975), while the disputed election of his successor was resolved.

Retirement gave Cotton the time to lecture at Plymouth State and Dartmouth Colleges and to fulfill his dream of writing a book on the Senate he had loved and respected for half a century. *In the Senate: Amidst the Conflict and the Turmoil* was published in 1978, the same year his wife died. In 1980 Cotton married Eleanor Coolidge Brown. He continued his interest in Republican politics and his intense support of what became in his words "the apple of my eye"—the Norris Cotton Cancer Center at Dartmouth. He died of pneumonia at his home in Lebanon and is buried in Lebanon's First Congregational Church Cemetery.

A tall New Englander of commanding presence, Cotton was a self-described "rock-ribbed" Republican. For him, however, political parties had a deeper purpose, as organizations for government, and his main concern was for those whom government exists. Colleagues in both parties praised Cotton's independent thinking, exemplified by his colorful assertion on the Senate floor, in 1970, that, if necessary, he would "invade the sacred precincts of the White House" to discover suspected administration tactics behind the stalled vote on the Cooper-Church Amendment prohibiting further U.S. involvement in Cambodia. His book is the legacy of a concerned, astute senator. His most important legacy may be his example as a legislator who never lost touch with his constituents back home.

★

Norris Cotton's papers are at the archives of the University of New Hampshire Library; they include each letter he received and, stapled to it, a copy of his reply. Norris Cotton, *In the Senate: Amidst the Conflict and the Turmoil* (1978), records scenes and people and explains trends and traditions from the perspective of a Yankee senator. Roland Bixby, *Standing Tall: The Life of Senator Norris Cotton* (1988), is valuable for its insight into the townspeople of Warren, New Hampshire, who took part in the author's reconstruction of Cotton's life story. A detailed résumé of Cotton's public career was prepared by New Hampshire legislative historian Leon W. Anderson and is included in "A Salute to Norris Cotton," published by the state in 1973. Charles T. Morrissey, "Memory, Like Congress, Is a Forest Full of Trees: The Recollections of Two Hampshiremen in Washington—Norris H. Cotton and Chester E. Merrow," *Historical New Hampshire* 33 (1978): 246–257, discusses Cotton's book. Thomas J. McIntyre, "A Tribute to My Colleague, Norris Cotton, Upon Announcement of His Retirement at the End of His Term," *Congressional Record* (21 June 1973), S11646–11647, includes Cotton's "Report" to his constituents concerning his retirement. Warren Rudman, "The Death of Former New Hampshire Senator Norris Cotton," *Congressional Record* (1 Mar. 1989), S1905–1906, is a tribute with biographical content. Obituaries are in the *New York Times*, *Washington Post*, and *Manchester Union Leader* (all 25 Feb. 1989); *Boston Globe* (26 Feb. 1989); and *Concord Monitor* (27 Feb. 1989).

SYLVIA B. LARSON

COURNAND, André Frederic (*b.* 24 September 1895 in Paris, France; *d.* 19 February 1988 in Great Barrington, Massachusetts), physician and medical researcher who was a recipient of the 1956 Nobel Prize for physiology or medicine for implementing the use of catheterization to examine the interior of the human heart.

Cournand was one of three children born to Jules Cournand, a dentist, and Marguerite (Weber) Cournand. At the age of five he began his education at the Lycée Condorcet,

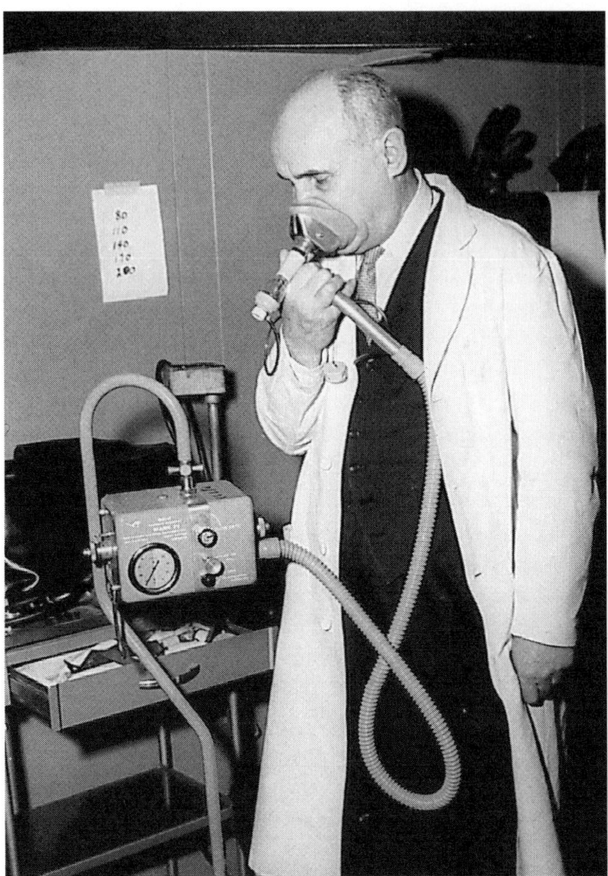

André Cournand demonstrates the use of a residual breather, 1962. ARCHIVE PHOTOS

and in 1913 he received a B.A. degree from the University of Paris (the Sorbonne). He continued his studies there and received a certificate in physics, chemistry, and biology from the Faculté des Science in 1914. Cournand next entered the university's medical school, adhering to a career goal made at the age of nine. However, World War I interrupted his studies; in 1915 he entered the French army as an infantryman and medical corpsman. Near the end of the war, he was gassed and wounded, and he convalesced in Paris before resuming his medical studies in the spring of 1919. For his war services he received the Croix de Guerre with three stars.

In 1924 Cournand married Sibylle Blumer; they had four children, Muriel, Marie-Eve, Marie Claire, and an adopted son, Peter, from Sibylle's previous marriage. In 1926 he became a medical intern at the Hôpitaux de Paris, where he received training in internal medicine and chest diseases. He earned his medical degree, with a thesis titled "Acute Disseminated Sclerosis," in 1930.

Cournand was attracted to hospital medicine rather than private practice, and before taking a position at a Paris hospital, he decided to spend a year in the United States as a resident in the Chest Service of the Columbia University Division of Bellevue Hospital in New York City. He ultimately stayed on at Bellevue, after being offered a full-time research post, advancing from assistant to senior and then to chief resident by 1933. In 1934 Cournand started doing research on respiration in the cardiopulmonary laboratory at Bellevue, of which he became director in 1935. Also in 1935 he became an instructor in medicine at the College of Physicians and Surgeons of Columbia University.

That same year Cournand began a collaboration with Dickinson W. Richards, an assistant attending physician at the Columbia-Presbyterian Hospital, which eventually led to their sharing the Nobel Prize. In seeking an answer to the question of why some individuals survived a therapeutic lung collapse in the treatment of tuberculosis and others did not, the two men realized that a method of monitoring blood pressures, flow, and gas concentrations in the heart and pulmonary artery was essential. They turned to the work of Dr. Werner Forssmann performed at the Eberwalde Surgical Clinic in Germany in 1929. Using his own arm in the experiment, Forssmann had been the first to show that a long thin tube, a catheter, could be inserted into a vein and moved along for some two feet to the right side of the heart without doing damage to this organ. Cournand and Richards first worked with this technique in 1936 on dogs and chimpanzees, developing a suitable catheter, and were able to measure blood pressure in the heart.

In 1941, after a discussion with Homer W. Smith and with the assistance of Hilmert Ranges, physicians associated with New York University, Cournand and Richards undertook the first cardiac catheterization on a human being since Forssmann's experiment. They were able to measure the subject's blood's pressure, amount, flow, and oxygen content within the heart. They also demonstrated that a catheter could stay in the blood system up to seven hours without the development of clotting. This information was especially valuable for patients with diseased hearts and lungs, as well as for determining if operations could be safely performed. By the late 1940s, cardiac catheterization had become a standard technique in a number of academic medical facilities.

Also in 1941, Cournand became a U.S. citizen. During World War II, he was a member of a Bellevue Hospital team, which, at the request of the U.S. government, studied the treatment of shock. He also did work for the Chemical Warfare Service. During the 1940s, his academic career at the Columbia College of Physicians and Surgeons advanced; he became assistant professor in 1942, associate professor in 1945, and professor in 1951. Cournand continued his studies of the lung, using the cardiac catheterization methodology, and was the first individual to push a catheter into the pulmonary artery and measure the blood pressure in this vessel. In this research he also showed that an increase or decrease in pulmonary blood pressure was due to the amount of oxygen in the smaller arteries of the pulmonary blood system. He worked with infants and children with different kinds of congenital heart disease, and, in the treatment of the atrial septal defect, he was able to insert a catheter into the left heart chamber and calculate the blood pressures there. In 1956 the Nobel Prize for physiology or medicine was awarded jointly to Cournand, Richards, and Forssmann for their discoveries with respect to heart catheterization.

Cournand retired in 1964 from his positions at the College of Physicians and Surgeons and in Bellevue's Cardiopulmonary Laboratory. His wife died in 1959, and in 1963 he married Ruth Fabian, a former laboratory assistant; she died in 1973. Two years later he married Beatrice Bishop Berle, the widow of Adolph Berle, a political adviser.

During his youth, Cournand had been a championship soccer player. He later became an avid mountain climber and enjoyed playing tennis. In matters of faith, he was an agnostic, and in appearance, he possessed an oval face with Gallic features.

Cournand received many honors and awards, including the Lasker Award of the U.S. Public Health Service in 1949. His articles appeared in many medical periodicals, such as the *American Journal of Medicine* and the *Transactions of the American College of Cardiology.* He possessed an affinity for the humanities, and during the 1920s he became acquainted with many artists and authors, including the artist Jacques Lipschitz. As a scientist he has been described as "intellectually rigorous"; his research and discoveries helped greatly to advance modern medicine. He died of pneumonia and is buried in the Great Barrington (New York) Cemetery.

★

The Archives and Special Collection Room of the Columbia University Health Science Library houses a considerable collection of Cournand's papers. Cournand's *From Roots—to Late Budding: The Intellectual Adventures of a Medical Scientist* (1986), is an autobiographical memoir that discusses Cournand's parents, education, acquaintances, and career, as well as his views on various areas of science, including the "responsibility of scientists." The end of *A Life in Two Worlds: The Autobiography of Beatrice Bishop Berle* (1983) contains a brief account concerning Berle's acquaintance with Cournand and their decision to marry. Tyler Wasson, ed., *Nobel Prize Winners: An H. W. Wilson Biographical Dictionary* (1987), presents a detailed account of Cournand's life and is especially good in describing his scientific accomplishments. Allen B. Weisse, *Conversations in Medicine: The Story of Twentieth-Century American Medicine in the Words of Those Who Created It* (1984), contains a useful interview between the author and Cournand and a historical background essay on the cardiac catheterization process. Obituaries are in the *New York Times* (20 Feb. 1988) and *Time* (7 Mar. 1988).

ALLAN NELSON

COUSINS, Norman (*b.* 24 June 1915 in Union City, New Jersey; *d.* 30 November 1990 in Los Angeles, California), longtime editor of the *Saturday Review* and author of *Anatomy of an Illness,* a landmark book about the body's power to heal itself.

Cousins was the second of four children of Samuel Cousins, a builder of apartment buildings in New York City, and Sara (Miller) Cousins, an interior decorator. An early misdiagnosed illness set the tone for much of Cousins's later work. At the age of ten he was sent to a sanatorium for six months after a false positive reading for tuberculosis. The experience had a profound effect on him, and it was at the sanatorium that he first became aware—through observation—of the influence of emotions and attitude on the body's healing process. He went to public high school in the Bronx, New York, and then attended Teachers College of Columbia University for three semesters. To pay for his education he worked from 1934 to 1935 as a night-shift reporter covering the education beat at the *New York Post,* but he was not able to complete his degree in philosophy

Norman Cousins. PHOTO COURTESY OF ELEANOR COUSINS

and social sciences because of the financial burden. In 1935 he joined the staff of *Current History* magazine, where he soon became managing editor. During World War II he was a member of the editorial board of the Office of War Information's Overseas Bureau and edited *U.S.A.*, a government journal that was sent overseas. He married Eleanor Kopf on 23 June 1939. They had four children.

Cousins joined the staff of *Saturday Review* (then *Saturday Review of Literature*) in 1940 and two years later, at the age of twenty-seven, became its editor. In his long relationship with *SR* he worked with writers of great renown, including Cleveland Amory, Judith Crist, John Ciardi, and Goodman Ace. Under his leadership, the magazine moved from a narrow focus on literature to a broad range of articles, essays, and criticism about current events, the arts, science, education, and travel. Circulation increased from 20,000 to 600,000. In 1958 the wealthy industrialist Everette L. De Golyer, the owner since 1942 and long an admirer of Cousins, transferred ownership to him.

During his tenure at *SR,* Cousins wrote some 1,200 editorials, most chronicling what he termed "basic lessons of the learning experience." He championed nuclear controls, believing in this cause so strongly that he helped to arrange for the "Hiroshima Maidens"—victims of the bomb dropped on the Japanese city at the end of World War II—to come to the United States for medical treatment. He and his wife adopted one of these young women. Under his leadership, *SR* railed against pollution, cigarette advertising, and violence in the performing arts. Critics sometimes took him to task for his liberalism, but he had a strong national following of well-educated, well-read people. He left *SR* in 1972 and founded the magazine *World.* He returned to *SR* in 1973, the year he was named publisher of the year by the Magazine Publishers Association, and was named editor emeritus in 1980. For the last twenty-five years that he worked in New York City, he and his family lived in New Canaan, Connecticut.

Cousins, who long maintained his youthful looks, vigor, and optimism, was a creative thinker who wrote or edited twenty-seven books, many of them on health and healing, including the best-selling *Anatomy of an Illness as Perceived by the Patient* (1979) and *Head First: The Biology of Hope* (1989). *Anatomy of an Illness,* written after he retired from *SR,* dealt with his recovery from a near-fatal paralysis in 1965. The book's premise was that every person should accept responsibility for recovery from illness, and Cousins astounded doctors and entranced readers by documenting how a patient with a life-threatening illness could mobilize the body's natural healing abilities. The book went through thirteen printings in its first year, was a Book of the Month Club selection in 1980, and was serialized in several magazines the same year. Cousins used the same approach after a serious heart attack at the age of sixty-five, and he made a video called *The Healing Force* (1982) to talk about the unconventional methods he used to achieve full recovery.

The idea of writing a "genuine autobiography," Cousins said, terrified him. Many of his books were what he termed "autobiographical notebooks"; they assemble "the details that went into my learning adventure," he wrote in *Human Options* (1981). "What is of greatest consequence in a person's life is not just the nature and extent of his or her experiences but what has been learned from them." He may have eschewed strict autobiography, but his books paint a picture of a man who was both passionate and compassionate. Largely self-educated, he was often a step ahead of the times, as was evident in his work with the body's ability to heal itself. He is frequently cited in contemporary books about healing. His own experience with healing led to his appointment to the UCLA Medical School staff in the department of psychiatry and biobehavioral sciences—the only lay member of the staff. Thus, in 1977 he began a new career and moved to Beverly Hills, California. Until this time, he wrote in *Head First*, his entire career had been spent writing and editing, with brief interludes in college teaching and government service.

Cousins joined a staff of teachers and researchers of national caliber, including Herbert Weiner, a pioneer in mind-body research. He was attracted to the position for three reasons: UCLA had one of the top medical schools in the country; it had broad research capabilities; and it was interested, as he was, in humanistic medical education. "I was ushered into a new arena in which knowledge seemed to be accumulating faster than it could be recorded or absorbed," he wrote of those years. His particular area of interest was how the human body responded to challenges, particularly serious illness. In 1984 he founded the Norman Cousins Program in Psychoneuroimmunology at UCLA, dedicated to research and education in the field.

While at UCLA, Cousins worked with patients, bolstering their will to live and chronicling their success. Over and over, he emphasized the combination of psychological and physiological factors involved in combating illness. His alternative views on medicine had their roots in his childhood misdiagnosis. Even at the age of ten he recognized the influence of the will to live on a person's ability to recover: "There were 'realists' and 'optimists' at the sanatorium, and optimists seemed to do better." When he suffered a life-threatening paralysis at the age of fifty, one that threw him into a world of pain, he pursued this early discovery and found that laughter provided him with pain-free sleep. "At that time," he wrote, "nothing was known about the ability of the brain to produce endorphins that have painkilling abilities. We also didn't know about the effect of words, attitudes, and emotions on the immune system." He discovered that if he watched a show like *Candid Camera* and laughed for ten minutes, he would be able to have an hour of painfree, drug-free sleep. *Anatomy of an Illness* helped people realize they played an integral part in their own healing process.

Cousins's other books include *Present Tense: An American Editor's Odyssey* (1967), *The Celebration of Life* (1974), *The Healing Heart: Antidotes to Panic and Helplessness* (1983), *Albert Schweitzer's Mission* (1985), *The Pathology of Power* (1987), and *The Republic of Reason* (1988). He was the recipient of many honorary degrees and several awards, including the Albert Schweitzer Prize for Humanitarianism and Japan's Niwano Peace Prize in 1990.

Cousins died of a heart attack at UCLA's Medical Center after collapsing at a hotel. He is buried in Union City, New Jersey.

Cousins was at the forefront of the holistic health movement in the United States, helping to bridge the gap between physicians and the public. He was respected by both groups, and his popularity as a magazine editor allowed him to bring an important message to a wide audience. In her book *A Gift for Healing* (1996), Deborah Cowens quotes a simple declaration from *Anatomy of an Illness:* "Drugs are not always necessary. Belief in recovery always is." It was revolutionary thinking in the United States in 1979, but time has shown that Cousins was on the right path.

★

A number of Cousins's books are autobiographical in nature, including *Present Tense: An American Editor's Odyssey* (1967); *Anatomy of an Illness as Perceived by the Patient* (1979), an autobiographical account of Cousins's recovery from a life-threatening disease using the body's internal ability to heal; *Human Options* (1981), an autobiographical notebook that offers details on his life as well as philosophical views; and *Head First: The Biology of Hope* (1989), another autobiographical notebook that discusses Cousins's career at UCLA School of Medicine and his findings on the way emotions affect the body and the role of attitude in combating serious illness. An obituary is in the *New York Times* (2 Dec. 1990).

TERRY ANDREWS

COWLEY, (David) Malcolm (*b.* 24 August 1898 in Belsano, Pennsylvania; *d.* 27 March 1989 in New Milford, Connecticut), literary historian, editor, and poet who significantly influenced the course of American writing before and after World War II and chronicled the history of the Lost Generation of the 1920s.

Cowley was the only child of William Cowley, a homeopathic physician, and Josephine Hutmacher. His early years were marked by loneliness, a profound sense of separation, and a deeply rooted love of nature, all of which became recurring themes in his poetry and prose. Kept at arm's length by his parents and usually without playmates, he found solace wandering in the woods and fields that bordered the family farm in Belsano, seventy miles east of Pittsburgh, where he spent his childhood summers. Such rambles continued into adulthood, and even late in life Cowley often took to the woods to tramp for miles in solitude, working out the intricacies of an essay, a poem, or a book. Throughout his career he saw himself as "a country man" and held to an Emersonian belief that nature was the empowering force that gave his writing its elegiac quality and its moral core.

Malcolm Cowley. UPI/CORBIS-BETTMANN

With his father usually busy at his medical practice in Pittsburgh, and often left alone by his emotionally unsettled mother, Cowley retreated into a world of books, in which all things were possible and which bred in him, he wrote, a fierce desire to rise "by force of ability." From his earliest years he excelled as a student in Pittsburgh's public schools. He graduated in 1915 from Peabody High School, where he formed a lifelong friendship with Kenneth Burke and where, like Burke, he determined to be a writer.

A member of Harvard University's class of 1919, Cowley interrupted his studies in April 1917 for six months of service as a munitions truck driver with the American Field Service in France. Back in Cambridge (1918), he was sent to officers' training camp a week before the November armistice ending World War I, and after mustering out, he lived for a time in New York City's Greenwich Village as a struggling freelance writer. On 12 August 1919 he married

Marguerite ("Peggy") Frances Baird. Returning briefly to Harvard to complete his degree requirements, he received a B.A. degree cum laude (1920) and membership in Phi Beta Kappa.

After a year in New York copywriting for *Sweet's Architectural Catalogue,* Cowley sailed with his bride to France, where an American Field Service fellowship provided him with two years of study, first at the Université de Montpellier (1921–1922), where he earned a diploma in French studies, and then at Giverny and Paris (1922–1923) for independent research. In France he met a number of the expatriates whose lives he would come to chronicle in his literary histories, as well as such leading French dadaists as Tristan Tzara and Louis Aragon, and contributed articles and editorial services to *Broom* and *Secession,* two of the "little magazines" then in vogue.

Back in New York, he again worked at *Sweet's Architectural Catalogue* (1923–1925), but finding the job intolerable, he moved to Staten Island and cut himself loose from the constraints of the commercial world to become an independent man of letters, living solely on the income of his writing. Over the next three years he strung together a number of freelance assignments that gave him a steady, if precarious, existence. In 1926 he returned to country living, renting a small farmhouse in Sherman, Connecticut, for $10 a month. Two years later, with a $100 prize from *Poetry* magazine as a down payment, he bought an abandoned seventy-acre farm in Patterson, New York. When he and Peggy divorced in 1931—there were no children—he deeded the property to her.

The experience of writing for publications of every stripe allowed him to find his literary voice and led him to those elements of style that became his hallmark in the years ahead. Influenced in part by French classicism, he wrote precise but supple prose of great clarity, the whole undergirded by a well-honed intelligence notable for its breadth and depth. He became a master of the informal essay but was expert as well in nearly every literary form except the novel. As a critic and essayist, he held himself and others to uncompromisingly high standards, but he also took it as his responsibility to encourage emerging writers in whatever ways he could. He saw his readers as "intelligent but unspecialized" and his task as introducing them to new books, authors, and ideas, which he would set in historical context.

Drawn early in his intellectual development to French symbolists like Baudelaire and Rimbaud and to modern voices like Paul Valéry, Cowley established himself as one of America's principal explicators of post–World War I French literary thought and, in this period of freelancing, published a number of translations from the French, including Pierre MacOrlan, *On Board the Morning Star* (1924); Joseph Delteil, *Joan of Arc* (1926); Paul Valéry, *Variety* (1927); Marthe Lucie Bibesco, *Catherine-Paris* (1928) and *The Green Parrot* (1929); Maurice Barrés, *The Sacred Hill* (1929); and Raymond Radiguet, *The Count's Ball* (1929). He later translated *Imaginary Interviews* by André Gide (1944); *Aragon: Poet of the French Resistance* with Hannah Josephson (1945); and Paul Valéry's *Leonardo Poe Mallarmé* with James R. Lawler (1972).

Cowley's own literary career, as he saw it, began with the publication of *Blue Juniata: Poems* (1929), a slim volume of fifty-six autobiographical meditations that won him enthusiastic praise for his craftsmanship, lyricism, and emotional range. Reissued in 1968 as *Blue Juniata: Collected Poems*—an edition that included *The Dry Season* (1941), his only other volume of poetry—it remained Cowley's favorite among his many books.

In 1929 he was selected to replace Edmund Wilson as the literary editor of the *New Republic.* Over the next eleven years, he produced what many intellectuals believed was the foremost literary journal in America, its pages a major forum for new writing and the chief source of the critical vocabulary and aesthetic standards by which the techniques and formalisms of modern writing could be judged. Throughout this period, Cowley wrote the lead page of the book section, and after his resignation as editor in 1944 to accept a five-year study grant from a private benefactor, continued as a principal reviewer until 1948. Indeed, the greater part of the 1,400 or so essays and book reviews he wrote in his sixty-year-long career appeared in the *New Republic.* Some of them were collected by Henry Dan Piper in *Think Back on Us . . . A Contemporary Chronicle of the 1930s* (1967) and in *A Many-Windowed House: Collected Essays on American Writers and American Writing* (1970). A third collection, edited by Donald W. Faulkner, was published as *The Flower and the Leaf: A Contemporary Record of American Writing Since 1941* (1985).

From 1936 until his death, Cowley lived on a seven-acre farm in Sherman, Connecticut, with his second wife, Muriel Maurer, whom he had married on 18 June 1932. Their only child, Robert, was born in 1934, the year in which Cowley completed *Exile's Return: A Narrative of Ideas,* his most famous book and the basis for his reputation as a literary historian. An autobiographical account of his generation's experiences in Paris and Greenwich Village in the 1920s, the book found immediate favor among his contemporaries, but it was cruelly dismissed by older critics in reviews so devastating, Cowley later said, that he was unable to write another book for nearly twenty years.

In the interim, he turned to editing. He wrote introductions to two collections: *After the Genteel Tradition: American Writers Since 1910* (1937, reissued in 1964 as *After the Genteel Tradition: American Writers 1910–1930*) and, with Bernard Smith, *Books That Changed Our Minds* (1939). During this same period, he broke his earlier vow to eschew politics for art and in the midst of the Great Depression and the international unrest associated with the Spanish Civil War, entered openly into what he later called his "Red romance." Never a member of the Communist party, he was nonetheless its most prominent fellow traveler and was embroiled in a number of public controversies because of his strong support for Stalinism, a position he abandoned in 1939, when the Soviet Union signed a nonagression treaty with Germany and then invaded Finland. In 1942 he resigned from the Office of Facts and Figures, a wartime agency headed by Archibald MacLeish, after he had been targeted by the Dies Committee, which Congress had empowered to investigate communists in government.

After 1944 Cowley was associated with Viking Press, first as a freelance editor and (after 1948) as a literary adviser, encouraging the development of young writers and overseeing such projects as Viking's famed Portable Library. He edited *The Portable Hemingway* (1944) and *The Portable Hawthorne* (1948). In 1946 his brilliant introduction to *The Portable Faulkner*—and his skillful selection from Faulkner's prose, all of it previously out of print—rekindled national interest in a major writer who, Cowley wrote, had been "scandalously neglected." Within months Faulkner's career took on new life, and he later said that he owed Cowley "the kind of debt no man could ever repay."

Cowley's own reputation as a literary historian was revived in 1951 with the republication of *Exile's Return,* bearing the new subtitle *A Literary Odyssey of the Twenties* and some revisions. An immediate success, the book became the standard introduction to the literary renaissance spawned by the Lost Generation and to Cowley's thesis—the basis for his later histories—that outstanding writers appear in generational clusters, identified by their revolt against established literary (and moral) norms and by the commonality of their technical experimentation with language and literary form.

Over the next decade Cowley edited three books by F. Scott Fitzgerald: *Stories* (1951), *Tender Is the Night* (1951), and *Three Novels* (1953). In 1954 he wrote *The Literary Situation,* an examination of American writing at midcentury, which, in turn, led to *Writers at Work: "The Paris Review" Interviews* (1958). A critical edition of *Whitman's Leaves of Grass* (1959) was followed by Sherwood Anderson's *Winesburg, Ohio* (1960). He and Daniel P. Mannix wrote *Black Cargoes: A History of the Atlantic Slave Trade, 1518–1865* (1962). He printed his correspondence with William Faulkner in *The Faulkner-Cowley File* (1966) and joined Robert Cowley in editing *Fitzgerald and the Jazz Age* (1966).

Until the middle of the century, Cowley had avoided university teaching because it interfered with his writing, but after 1948 he took on what he called "knockabout" jobs. He was a visiting professor or lecturer at the University of Washington (1950), Stanford University (1956, 1959, 1960–1961, and 1965), the University of Michigan (1957), the University of California at Berkeley (1962), Cornell University (1964), the University of Minnesota (1971), and the University of Warwick, England (1973). In addition, he served as president of the National Institute of Arts and Letters from 1956 to 1959 and 1962 to 1965 and as chancellor of the American Academy of Arts and Letters from 1967 to 1976.

As he entered his late seventies, Cowley published the first of three major books on twentieth-century American writers, *A Second Flowering: Works and Days of the Lost Generation* (1973). This was followed by *And I Worked at the Writer's Trade: Chapters of Literary History, 1918–1978* (1978) and *The Dream of the Golden Mountains: Remembering the 1930s* (1980). His vivid assessments of his contemporaries and of his own life sparked extended debate among academics and in popular journals, especially among neoconservatives, who accused Cowley of distorting his communist sympathies in his recollections of the *New Republic* years. Cowley defended himself in a foreword to Karen Lane Rood, ed., *American Writers in Paris, 1920–1939,* volume 4 of the *Dictionary of Literary Biography* (1980), and in "Hemingway's Wound—And Its Consequences for American Literature," *Georgia Review* 38 (summer 1984): 223–239. His final book was a series of observations on old age, *The View From 80* (1980). Cowley continued to write articles and book reviews until his death from a heart attack in New Milford Hospital nine years later.

★

Cowley's papers are in the Newberry Library, Chicago. His correspondence with William Faulkner is at the Bienecke Library, Yale University. The most complete bibliographic guide is Diane U. Eisenberg, *Malcolm Cowley: A Checklist of His Writings, 1916–1973* (1975). Donald W. Faulkner offers a selection of his writings in *The Portable Malcolm Cowley* (1990). Cowley's years at Viking are described in Louis Sheaffer's interview of Marshall Best, general editor of the Portable series, in a Columbia University Oral History Interview (22 Apr. 1976). In addition to the autobiographical material in his later books, Cowley wrote several self-revealing articles; three of consequence are "Privatation and Publication: A Memoir of the Year 1934," *Sewanee Review* 83 (winter 1975): 139–148; "Mother and Son," *American Heritage* 34 (Feb. 1983): 28–35; and "Looking for the Essential Me," *New York Times Book Review* (17 June 1984). His son, Robert Cowley, interviewed him at age eighty-five for "Malcolm Cowley: Countryman," *Country Journal* (Oct. 1983): 62–70. Thomas Daniel Young, ed., *Conversations with Malcolm Cowley* (1986), is a collection of radio, television, and printed interviews. See also Paul Jay, ed., *The Selected Correspondence of Kenneth Burke and Malcolm Cowley: 1915–1981* (1988). An introductory biography, James Michael Kempf, *The Early Career of Malcolm Cowley: A Humanist Among the Moderns* (1985), is superseded by Hans Bak, *Malcolm Cowley: The Formative Years* (1993). See also *Visionary Company* (summer 1987), a special issue devoted to Cowley. A perceptive assessment of Cowley's career is made by Lewis P. Simpson in "Malcolm Cowley and the American Writer," *Sewanee Review* 84 (spring 1976): 221–247. Cowley's principal neoconservative critics are Robert Alter, "The Travels of Malcolm Cowley," *Commentary* 70 (Aug. 1980): 33–40; Joseph Epstein, "The Literary Life Today," *New Criterion* 1 (Sept. 1982): 6–15; and Kenneth S. Lynn, "Malcolm Cowley Forgets," in *The Airline to Seattle* (1983), 163–171. The work of Cowley's critics is assessed in Sanford Pinkser, "Revisionism with Rancor: The Threat of the Neoconservative Critics," *Georgia Review* 38 (summer 1984): 243–261. See also the review of Cowley's political and literary life by Irving Howe, "Critic's Return," *New Republic* (30 Apr. 1990). An obituary is in the *New York Times* (29 Mar. 1989).

ALLAN L. DAMON

CRAWFORD, (William) Broderick (*b.* 9 December 1911 in Philadelphia, Pennsylvania; *d.* 26 April 1986 in Rancho Mirage, California), actor who is best known for his Oscar-winning performance in *All the King's Men* (1949) and for his portrayal of the gravel-voiced, no-nonsense police chief in the 1950s television series *Highway Patrol*.

Crawford was born into a show-business family. His mother, Helen Broderick, was the daughter of opera singers and had a long career in musical comedy on both stage and screen. His father, Lester Crawford, was a vaudeville song-and-dance man. In his childhood Broderick Crawford toured with his parents, and his early schooling was sporadic. He was eventually enrolled at Dean Academy in Franklin, Massachusetts, where he excelled at sports, winning letters in football, baseball, and swimming. Although he wished to rejoin his parents on the vaudeville circuit, they insisted that he attend college. After only three weeks at Harvard, however, he dropped out to seek a theatrical career. He went to New York City, where he supported himself by working as a stevedore and a merchant seaman.

Broderick Crawford. ARCHIVE PHOTOS

In the early 1930s Crawford appeared on several radio programs, playing a second-banana stooge to the Marx Brothers and taking the lead dramatic role in the radio production of Warden Lawe's *Twenty Thousand Years in Sing-Sing.* His first major part was as a football player in the London production of Howard Lindsay's *She Loves Me Not.* Noël Coward chose Crawford to appear with Alfred Lunt and Lynn Fontanne in the 1935 production of *Point Valaine.* Other minor Broadway roles came in *Punches and Judy* and *Sweet Mystery.*

The tall, husky, almost hulking Crawford emerged to wider notice in the role of Lenny, a half-witted laborer who accidentally commits a murder, in the Broadway production of John Steinbeck's *Of Mice and Men* (1937). His ability to imbue the physically powerful yet emotionally fragile man-child with a convincing sense of decency and humanity was credited as a factor in the play's success. However, when Lon Chaney, Jr., was chosen for the screen adaptation, Crawford realized that Hollywood was not likely to call him, and he moved to Los Angeles to refocus his career on screen work.

Under contracts to Paramount and Warner Brothers, he appeared in minor roles during the late 1930s in such pictures as *Submarine D-1, Ambush, Undercover Doctor, Beau Geste,* and *Eternally Yours.* He moved on to three featured character roles in films of 1940: *Slightly Honorable,* a murder mystery; *When the Daltons Rode,* a Western; and *Seven Sinners,* a romantic war story starring Marlene Dietrich and John Wayne. His ability to play hard-bitten characters in an intelligent, engaging style won him several leading roles as a kind-hearted tough guy in comedies. These included *Tight Shoes* (1941), based on a Damon Runyon story, and *Butch Minds the Baby* (1942). Meanwhile, in 1940, he married the actress Kay Griffith. They had two children.

Crawford joined the U.S. Army during World War II, achieving the rank of sergeant and seeing combat during the Battle of the Bulge. Upon his return to Hollywood, he again appeared in minor roles in mostly undistinguished pictures, including *The Runaround* (1946), *Slave Girl* (1947), and *The Time of Your Life* (1948), before winning the part that would prove the highlight of his artistic career.

Director Robert Rossen cast Crawford in the difficult lead role of Willie Stark in *All the King's Men* (1949). The character was a thinly veiled portrait of Huey Long, the controversial populist governor of Louisiana who was assassinated on the steps of the state capitol. In the *New York Times* review of the film, Crawford's performance was described as "magnetic, compelling, and part of the moxt exciting film to come out of Hollywood this year." *All the King's Men* won the Academy Award for best picture, and Crawford received the best actor award.

Under contract to Columbia Pictures in the early 1950s, Crawford made a number of middling pictures, none of which did much to capitalize on the stardom afforded by his Oscar. These included *Anna Lucasta, Cargo to Capetown, New York Confidential,* and *Stop, You're Killing Me,* the latter another Damon Runyon–inspired gangster comedy. A break came, however, when he was called upon by the Italian director Federico Fellini to play a rakish con man in *Il Bidone* (1955), a performance that won him international recognition.

That same year Crawford signed a deal with the independent television producer Fred Ziv to star in a half-hour weekly police series, *Highway Patrol.* The show was sold directly to local TV stations for broadcast, rather than broadcast over one of the national networks, which was a somewhat unusual arrangement at that time. Crawford, as Chief Dan Matthews, was the only regular cast member in the formulaic shoot-'em-up. It ran in production for four years and was the most highly rated nonnetwork dramatic series of the late 1950s. In his most characteristic pose, the hard-boiled police chief is seen leaning over the door of a squad car barking "10-4, 10-4" and other two-way radio lingo into a handset.

A drinking problem was blamed for the slide that Crawford's career took during the 1960s. The actor spent much of the next two decades appearing in low-budget European pictures, ranging from an Italian muscle epic, *Goliath and the Dragon* (1960), to a Spanish Western, *El Tejano* (1966). Two attempts at new television series, *King of Diamonds* (1961) and *The Interns* (1970–1971), failed to win renewal. During these years he married again (his first marriage had ended in divorce in the mid-1950s), to Mary Adams and then Joan Tabor, from both of whom he was divorced, and in 1973, to Mary Alice Michaels. In 1976, largely on the basis of the evolving cult popularity of *Highway Patrol,* he was asked to guest-host the TV show *Saturday Night Live.* The following year he gave one last memorable performance in the lead role of *The Private Files of J. Edgar Hoover* (1977). He died from complications of a series of stokes and was buried in Ferndale Cemetery, north of Johnstown, New York.

Failing to fit the Hollywood mold of either a leading man or a comic character actor, Broderick Crawford remains the quintessential example of an actor whose full potential could be tapped only sparingly by the huge commercial entertainment establishment. When given the opportunity to play extraordinary roles, he proved himself beyond doubt; such roles, however, are by nature few and far between. Crawford was acutely aware of this. "Oscar winner? Big deal," he told an interviewer. "Cukor wants you, Fritz Lang, Fellini—and still you spend your life waiting for another phone call."

★

There is no autobiography or biography of the actor, and relatively little has been written about him beyond the reviews. A thoughtful and factually comprehensive sketch of his career appears in David Shipman, *The Great Movie Stars: The International Years* (1970). An obituary is in the *New York Times* (27 Apr. 1986).

DAVID MARC

CRAWFORD, Cheryl (*b.* 24 September 1902 in Akron, Ohio; *d.* 7 October 1986 in New York City), prominent theatrical producer and cofounder of the Group Theatre, the American Repertory Theatre, and the Actors Studio.

Crawford was the eldest of four children and the only daughter of Robert Kingsley Crawford and Luella Elizabeth (Parker) Crawford. The owner of a real estate company, her father also served as superintendent of the Congregational church. His strong religious beliefs created a

Cheryl Crawford. AP/WIDE WORLD PHOTOS

puritanical atmosphere in the home. In her autobiography, Crawford states that her greatest love was for her maternal grandmother, Lavinia Lynn Parker, who lived with the family and who entertained her granddaughter with tales of the Civil War, a possible Cherokee heritage, and a love of movies.

After a healthy, happy childhood, Crawford graduated from high school in Akron and entered Smith College in Northampton, Massachusetts, in 1921. Without forethought she claimed "the theater" as her major extracurricular activity and embarked on a series of roles in college plays. With that decision, her commitment to the stage was sealed. Although her grades were outstanding after her freshman year, Crawford was denied a Phi Beta Kappa key because of questionable morals—she drank and smoked and was generally an unconventional Smith student. Her alma mater eventually awarded her an honorary doctor of fine arts degree in 1962.

Even before she left Smith, Crawford knew that her theatrical aspirations were not as an actor but as a producer. Following graduation in 1925 with a B.A. degree, she moved to New York City, where she entered the Theatre Guild's prestigious acting school and became a protégée of Theresa Helburn, one of only a few women in an executive position in the theater at that time. As assistant stage manager of Theatre Guild productions, Crawford gained experience in casting and directing. Most significantly, she formed relationships with playwright Clifford Odets, director Harold Clurman, and acclaimed teacher Lee Strasberg. She also developed a strong desire to form a repertory company.

In early 1931 Crawford left the Guild and with Clurman and Strasberg formed the Group Theatre, using the acting principles of Konstantin Stanislavsky. Although the Great Depression presented the fledgling company with financial difficulties, there was no shortage of actors and playwrights who wanted to join. Members included John Garfield, Luther Adler, Franchot Tone, Lee J. Cobb, Elia Kazan, and Stella Adler. Plays of social significance became the company's signature; among the playwrights were Odets, William Saroyan, and Irwin Shaw. Sidney Kingsley's *Men in White,* the Group's first hit, won a Pulitzer Prize. Crawford, who acted as chief fund-raiser for the organization, was coproducer or codirector of many productions.

Lack of funds and misjudgments about plays led to dissension within the Group. Hollywood also lured writers, in particular, away with large salary offers. Worn out by attempts to keep the company going, Crawford resigned in March 1937 and launched a career as an independent producer. According to her recollections, she presented five failures in succession and, at the end of that period, had exhausted her access to investors. Crawford, however, never lost her determination or unadulterated love of the theater.

A proposal to produce plays in summer stock at a defunct theater in Maplewood, New Jersey, induced her to cross the Hudson River to carry out her profession. One of the largest stock companies of that time, the Maplewood Theatre drew such performers as Helen Hayes, Ethel Barrymore, Paul Robeson, Tallulah Bankhead, and Ingrid Bergman. Crawford stayed through three seasons, but by 1942 wartime gas rationing curtailed patronage. Wanting to close on a triumphant note, she chose to revive *Porgy and Bess.* Not only was it well received, but *Porgy and Bess* went on to a very successful Broadway run, a cross-country tour, and two return Broadway engagements.

Crawford decided then that her fortune lay with musicals. She had successes with *One Touch of Venus, Paint Your Wagon,* and, perhaps her biggest hit, *Brigadoon,* but her real desire was to promote repertory theater and serious plays. In 1945 she cofounded the American Repertory Theatre with Eva Le Gallienne and Margaret Webster. Dedicated to both modern plays and classics, the American Repertory Theatre lasted until 1948. During the same period Crawford became involved with the American National Theatre and Academy (ANTA) and served as vice president of its board of directors. By the end of the 1940s, she had also established the Actors Studio with Elia Kazan and Robert Lewis; they were later joined by Lee Strasberg.

Over the years Crawford alternated affiliations with theater groups with stints as an independent producer. A close working relationship with Tennessee Williams led to independent productions of *Camino Real, The Rose Tattoo, Sweet Bird of Youth,* and *Period of Adjustment.* Although she created many successes, her errors of judgment were no less notable. She declared her five major mistakes to be rejecting *Member of the Wedding, Cat on a Hot Tin Roof, Threepenny Opera, Death of a Salesman,* and *West Side Story.*

Crawford, who never married, described her private life as having been lived "in passing," admitting it was a high price to pay for unwavering commitment to work. Her personal finances fluctuated widely, as she was generally more concerned with raising money for productions than with her own checkbook. She took delight in her getaway home, Eastham, in Connecticut, and was devastated when it was consumed by fire in 1969; fortunately, the insurance saved her from financial disaster. A devoted resident of New York City, she died in New York Hospital in Manhattan from complications from a fall.

During more than a half century in the theater, Crawford was both a trailblazer for women in a man's domain and the producer of some of the most noteworthy shows of her time. The Theatre Guild, the Group Theatre, the American Repertory Theatre, ANTA, and Actors Studio all served as fertile training grounds for actors and playwrights, enriching American theater in the process.

★

Cheryl Crawford, *One Naked Individual: My Fifty Years in the Theatre* (1977), traces the author's life from childhood until ten years before her death and is the only substantive work about her. An obituary is in the *New York Times* (8 Oct. 1986).

MYRNA W. MERRON

CREMIN, Lawrence Arthur (*b.* 31 October 1925 in New York City; *d.* 4 September 1990 in New York City), eminent historian of education in the United States and president of Teachers College, Columbia University, from 1974 to 1984.

Cremin was one of the two children of Arthur T. Cremin and Theresa Borowick, who together founded and operated the New York Schools of Music. He graduated from Townsend Harris High School in New York City in 1942 and entered the City College of New York. His studies were interrupted for nineteen months during World War II, when he served in the U.S. Army Air Forces. He graduated from City College in 1946 with a B.A. in social sciences. Enrolling in Teachers College, Columbia University, he received an M.A. in 1947 and a Ph.D. in 1949. His dissertation, published in 1951 as *The American Common School: An Historic Conception,* demonstrated his ability to find and review formidable amounts of material. Although he pointed out that children "learned" in many settings, such as the family and the church, his conclusion—that the public school was "the only means potentially capable" of providing the education nineteenth-century American culture had demanded—fit nicely into the triumphalism characteristic of contemporary educational history.

Portrait of Lawrence Cremin by Everett Raymond Kinstler, 1985. SPECIAL COLLECTIONS, MILBANK MEMORIAL LIBRARY, TEACHERS COLLEGE, COLUMBIA UNIVERSITY

In 1948 Cremin's former teacher, R. Freeman Butts, helped found the History of Education Section of the National Society of College Teachers of Education. In 1950, Cremin was placed on the coordinating committee of the section. He collaborated in 1953 with Butts in writing *A History of Education in American Culture,* a companion to Butts's work, *A Cultural History of Education* (1947). Butts, like most contemporary "progressives," believed that the history of education should be "functional" to the needs of its principal audience: prospective teachers. Rather than learning "straight history," students should try to understand the "social foundations" of intellectual and institutional developments. Rather than memorizing chronology, they should investigate how history illuminated the most pressing contemporary educational "problems." On 19 September 1956 Cremin married Charlotte Raup; they had two children. Cremin served as president of the History of Education Section of the National Society of College Teachers of Education from 1959 to 1960. He early made clear, however, that he was not wholly committed to functionalism. For him, history was always an essential part of the liberal arts—something to be studied in its own context, rather than as background to a contemporary problem. In 1955 he responded to the publication of Arthur Bestor's highly controversial attack on progressivism, *The Restoration of Learning,* with qualified endorsement.

Cremin most eloquently declared his independence from the dogmas of the recent past in 1961, when he published *The Transformation of the School: Progressivism in American Education, 1876–1957.* Some years later, in the course of insisting that only a fraction of education took place in "schools," he admitted that the subtitle promised more than the book delivered. He devoted the first half of the book to a review of nineteenth-century "traditions of popular education" and to masterful, wide-ranging surveys of the ways in which industrialization, urbanization, immigration, and revolutionary developments in science and philosophy in the years before World War I were to be understood not as "the background" or the "social foundations" of educational change but as the warp and weft of the "progressive impulse." The second half of the book, in which Cremin focused on the history of the Progressive Education Association, was a sympathetic exposition of the "polyglot" assumptions and practices that constituted "progressive education" and a brilliant analysis of the reasons why, by the 1950s, the movement had atrophied. *The Transformation of the School* was not the kind of book functionalist historians most admired, but historians in the arts and sciences were impressed. Cremin was awarded the prestigious Bancroft Prize in 1962. Thenceforth, he was both Frederick A. P. Barnard Professor of Education at Teachers College and professor of history at Columbia University.

In the 1950s, a group of scholars, prompted by the Ford Foundation's Fund for the Advancement of Education, secured financial backing to encourage historians of the United States to assume the obligation—too often, they regretted, surrendered to professors in schools of education—to study the history of education, "not in its institutional forms alone, but in terms of all the influences that have helped shape the mind and character of the rising generation." In 1964, at a conference of historians sponsored by the Ford Foundation, Cremin derided the "wonderful world" of Ellwood Patterson Cubberley, whose best-selling book *Public Education in the United States* (1919) epitomized the limited perspectives of the "old" history of education. Furthermore, Cremin lamented, "there has been no overall rethinking of our educational history" since. Rather than criticize directly his contemporaries, he confessed that his "own work of the late 1940s and early 1950s . . . represented a refinement of Cubberley rather than a fundamental revision." Cremin concluded by stipulating the "marks" of a more adequate educational history: a recognition of the many agencies that made up the "architecture of contemporary education," the mass media, for example; the use of the insights being developed by the social sciences and contemporary historiography; and a comparative dimension. Cremin's essay, the historian Sol Cohen would write ten years later, "signaled both his own and his generation's break with the past."

Shortly thereafter, the executive secretary of the American Historical Association and the U.S. commissioner of education persuaded Cremin to prepare a modern, sophisticated history of American education. With generous funding from the Carnegie Foundation, he expected to complete the task in seven years. In fact, it took him twenty-three years to complete the three volumes of *American Education* (1970–1988), with nearly 2,000 pages of text and more than 225 pages of bibliographical suggestions. He viewed "education" as "the deliberate, systematic, and sustained effort to transmit or evoke knowledge, attitudes, values, and skills." This definition comported with his felt obligation to deal with educative institutions as various as the family, the newspaper, and the county fair.

The Colonial Experience, 1607–1783, published in 1970, surveys the transplantation and modification of European ideas and institutions. *The National Experience, 1783–1876,* published in 1980, describes the emergence of an "authentic American vernacular" of education that proffered a "popular *paideia* compounded of evangelical pieties, democratic hopes, and utilitarian strivings" and was manifest especially but by no means exclusively in the growing importance of schools. He was concerned in *The Metropolitan Experience, 1876–1980,* published in 1988, with the impact of such modernizing forces as industrialization, urbanization, immigration, and secularism on the configuration of educative institutions, including such powerful agents as radio, film, and television.

Cremin was awarded a Pulitzer Prize in 1981 for *The National Experience*. Most historians praised all three volumes, admiring Cremin's comprehensive vision, his erudition, and his energy in seeing through to completion this highly ambitious undertaking. Some believed that his notion of education was so all-embracing as to compel him to write an encyclopedia rather than a master-narrative of an American *paideia*. Other historians complained that Cremin, all too willing to celebrate the pluralism of American educational enterprises, failed to recognize that most of these enterprises were, essentially, engines of bourgeois hegemony. Cremin, in fact, had always rejected such "reductionism." Acknowledging that all institutions, even schools, were somewhat constraining, he was convinced that "on balance" they were "more liberating than not."

Cremin assumed steadily heavier responsibilities as a spokesman for education. He lectured at major universities, such as Wisconsin, Harvard, and Stanford. He helped found the National Academy of Education and served as its president from 1969 to 1973, and he did many jobs for the U.S. Department of Education. From 1974 to 1984 he served as president of Teachers College, the nation's most prominent such institution and one he hoped would play a key role in restoring "the richness and complexity" that he believed had been missing from the public discussions of the problems of education. He shied away from controversy, professing himself a "latitudinarian" of the same disposition as he had been in 1965, when he wrote that "we are all Essentialists—we are all Progressives." What was needed, Cremin believed, was much more first-class scholarship, so he was understandably frustrated by the "financial downturn" in what both universities and the federal government in these years were spending on research. After resigning the presidency of Teachers College, he became president of the Spencer Foundation, where he systematically encouraged innovative research.

Cremin's last book, *Popular Education and Its Discontents* (1990), celebrated the achievements and the potential of American education. Instead of bewailing a "rising tide of mediocrity," the United States had every reason to be proud, he declared, of the range and variety of its educational institutions. Cremin was at work on a biography of John Dewey when he died suddenly of a heart attack across the street from his Teachers College office in New York City. He was buried in Beth Israel Memorial Park in Woodbridge, New Jersey.

An enterprising, hard-working, and gregarious man,

Cremin was well-liked by students and colleagues at Columbia, and by scholars across the country. Effective as an administrator, Cremin was happiest as a teacher and a scholar. His books on the progressive-education movement and on American education demonstrate that the study of history could emancipate friends of education from the orthodoxies based on misleading stereotypes of the past.

★

Cremin's personal papers, deposited at Teachers College, are closed until further notice. Two useful articles are Sol Cohen, "The History of the History of American Education, 1900–1976," *Harvard Educational Review* 46 (Aug. 1976): 298–330; and Jennings L. Wagoner, Jr., "Historical Revisionism, Educational Theory, and an American *Paideia,*" *History of Education Quarterly* 18 (summer 1978): 201–209. Ellen Condliffe Lagemann and Patricia Albjerg Graham, both colleagues and former students, wrote "Lawrence A. Cremin: A Biographical Memoir," *Teachers College Record* 96 (fall 1994): 102–113, an affectionate and judicious article. Diane Ravitch's memorial in *American Scholar* 61 (winter 1992): 83–89, stresses Cremin's commitment as a teacher and mentor. See also John H. Fischer's testimonial, "Lawrence A. Cremin (1925–1990)," *Century Association Yearbook, 1992.* An obituary is in the *New York Times* (5 Sept. 1990).

ROBERT D. CROSS

CROTHERS, Benjamin Sherman ("Scatman") (*b.* 23 May 1910 in Terre Haute, Indiana; *d.* 22 November 1986 in Van Nuys, California), singer, songwriter, and actor who was one of the first African-American performers to cross entertainment lines and become a star of both the big and small screens.

One of five children, Crothers took to music early, teaching himself to play the drums and guitar. By the time he was fourteen he was singing and playing the instruments in speakeasies after school and on weekends. He attended Booker T. Washington School and Wiley High School in Terre Haute but dropped out before earning his degree. Instead, in the 1930s he formed a band and toured the area. At one point the band won a five-year contract to appear on the *Amos 'n' Andy* radio program. "We played jazz, blues, dixie," Crothers said, "and it all came from the church. When I went to church, I would see all the sisters and brothers doing the same beat."

In 1932 Crothers moved to Dayton, Ohio, to do his own radio show. The program manager told him he needed a gimmick, so Crothers responded, "Call me Scatman because I do quite a bit of scat singing." Scattin', in which nonsense lyrics are improvised to a melody, had been popularized a few years before by Louis ("Satchmo") Armstrong and was also used frequently by jazz star Ella Fitzgerald. Crothers's radio show was short-lived, but the nickname stuck. He and his band continued touring the Midwest, at times playing clubs that had never featured a black person before. During a gig in Canton, Ohio, in 1936, he met nineteen-year-old Helen Sullivan, a white Hungarian woman who had come to the club with a girlfriend. "We moved on to another booking, and when we returned to Canton I thought, 'doggone, I hope those two little girls come in the club again,' " he said in an interview in 1981. They did meet up again, and they married in 1937, at a time "before [interracial] marriage was fashionable." Crothers and his wife experienced only one racially based "incident" because of the marriage, and Crothers insisted that it lasted "about five minutes."

In 1948 Crothers, Helen, and the band moved to Los Angeles, where they enjoyed hit records like *The Dead Man's Blues, On the Sunny Side of the Street,* and *Chattanooga Shoe Shine Boy.* In 1949 Crothers was signed to a four-week appearance at the Bingo Club in Las Vegas. After a few shows he was stopped by an employee who told him that he would no longer be able to enter through the front door. In 1981 Crothers recalled: "I said, 'look man, I use the front door just like everybody else.' And I did. So they cut me from four weeks to two weeks, but I still walked in that front door. I didn't use no back door. They thought I was crazy, but hell, I wasn't working in the kitchen." Also in 1949 Helen gave birth to the couple's only child, Donna. Later that year Crothers was tapped for his first television job as a character on *Dixie Showboat,* making him the first African-American actor on a regular television series. That performance won him a part on the *Colgate Comedy Hour,* which he held while also acting on *Dixie Showboat.* During that time he made guest appearances on the *Steve Allen Show,* the *Jack Benny Show,* and the *Jerry Lewis Show.* He made the jump to movies in 1952 with a supporting role in *Meet Me at the Fair,* which was followed by *Walking My Baby Back Home* (1953) and *The Sins of Rachel Cade* (1961).

In 1970 Crothers added another line on his resume—cartoon voice-overs. That year he was the voice of Scat Cat in the Disney film *The Aristocats,* and he played Meadowlark Lemon in the cartoon series *The Harlem Globetrotters.* From 1974 through 1976 he was the voice of the crime-fighting mutt *Hong Kong Phooey.* He lent more than his voice to other projects. He was a regular cast member on the NBC-TV hit *Chico and the Man* (1974–1978), in which he played a garbage man named Louie. He had guest spots on the miniseries *Roots* and on *Hill Street Blues, Hotel,* and *McMillan and Wife.*

Crothers won critical acclaim for his role as Orderly Turkle in the 1975 Academy Award–winning movie *One Flew over the Cuckoo's Nest* and for his portrayal as a psychic cook in *The Shining* in 1980. He was honored with a star on the Hollywood Walk of Fame in 1981. Although he had long since passed retirement age, Crothers kept working.

He appeared in *The Twilight Zone: The Movie* and *Two of a Kind* in 1983, among several other projects. For relaxation, he played golf.

In 1985 Crothers learned that he had a cancerous tumor behind a lung that was inoperable. Following surgery in July 1985 he received a get-well letter from "another recuperator," President Ronald Reagan, who had undergone cancer surgery shortly before Crothers. Reagan wrote to him: "I hope that you have as comfortable and as speedy a recovery as I am experiencing. We both have bookings to keep and I know you are anxious to get back on the golf course just as I can't wait to get on horseback."

Following his release from the hospital, Crothers returned to work. He starred in the CBS-TV series *Morningstar, Eveningstar,* which was about a group of senior citizens who adopt a group of orphans. He played Excell Dennis, a retired actor working as a lounge pianist.

By 1986 the cancer had spread to Crothers's esophagus. Crothers died in his sleep with Helen at his bedside in Van Nuys, California. He is buried at Forest Lawn Memorial Park in Los Angeles. James Komack, producer of *Chico and the Man,* said of Crothers, "He never saw himself as a star." At Crothers's funeral, Komack recalled that Crothers once told him, "We're all God's children, we just happen to be doing different jobs."

★

Informative articles about Crothers include Frances E. Hughes, "Local Man on Television Every Week," *Spectator* (26 Apr. 1975); Bob Lucas, "Scatman Crothers: 56 Years of Show Biz, 44 Years of Marriage," *Jet* (11 July 1981); and "Terre Haute's Scatman Doesn't Talk of Success," *Terre Haute Tribune-Star* (9 Jan. 1981). Obituaries and related articles are in the *New York Times* and *Terre Haute Tribune-Star* (both 23 Nov. 1986).

JONATHAN TAPPER

CROWN, Henry (*b.* 13 June 1896 in Chicago, Illinois; *d.* 14 August 1990 in Chicago, Illinois), shrewd sand and gravel man, entrepreneur, and philanthropist with vast holdings in the construction business, real estate, mining, and transportation.

Henry Crown was the third of seven children of Arie Crown (formerly Krinsky) and Ida Gordon. Crown's father, who immigrated to the United States from Lithuania, worked at times as a suspender maker, a foreman in a sweatshop, a pushcart peddler, and an agent for the Diamond Match Company. Henry Crown attended Barr Elementary School in Chicago but left school in 1910, after the eighth grade. Like his older brothers, Sol and Irving, he went to work to help support his family. At fourteen, he was fired from his $4-per-week job as a dispatcher for the

Henry Crown. COURTESY OF LESTER CROWN

Chicago Firebrick Company by his brother Sol, the office manager, for sending the wrong order to a customer. By 1912, Henry Crown was working as a traffic manager for Union Drop Forge Company, learning the wrought-iron business, and taking night-school classes in bookkeeping.

In 1916 Sol Crown organized S. R. Crown and Company, a steel brokerage, with help from his brothers Henry and Irving, who each invested several hundred dollars. When big steel companies like Inland Steel or U.S. Steel took major orders, they routinely rolled steel in excess of what was ordered to allow for any possible defects in the product. S. R. Crown located small forges that would be willing to buy the overruns for the same discounted price as the major purchasers. Although the brothers had little capital, Henry Crown persuaded Chicago banks to extend him credit, using the money he was promised from small forges for the delivery of steel mill overruns as collateral. In 1919 Henry and his brothers invested $10,000 to reorganize their business as Material Service Corporation, a sand and gravel building supply company. As the company's treasurer, Henry Crown negotiated $218,000 in sales for a $7,000 profit in their first year in business. With Crown's careful research, shrewd negotiation, guaranteed bank credit, and commitment to absolute trustworthiness, qualities that continued as the hallmarks of his future business deals, Material Service grew to dominate the construction industry in the Midwest. On 12 August 1920 Crown married Rebecca Kranz; they had three sons.

In 1921, following Sol Crown's death from tuberculosis, Henry Crown became the president and chief executive of Material Service Corporation, and the company's success continued. When freight costs rose, Crown shifted from surface to canal transportation, investing in towboats and barges that were designed to make unloading sand and gravel more efficient. Diversifying his markets, he sold limestone and clinker dolomite to steel manufacturers from his Lockport, Illinois, gravel pit. When Chicago winters limited canal access, Crown invested in building a fleet of trucks to haul his building supplies to contractors. During the Great Depression, Crown won a number of government contracts for Material Service Corporation. Continuing to draw on credit from Chicago banks, he expanded his company by purchasing additional sand and gravel quarries, taking control of cement production, and making an initial move into the purchase and mechanization of coal mines.

In 1941 Crown resigned from active leadership of Material Service Corporation to serve in the U.S. Army during World War II. A lieutenant colonel, he was assigned to duty as a procurement officer for the Western Division, Corps of Engineers. Crown's service took him first to Los Angeles, where he directed the purchasing of military supplies. Eventually reassigned to the Great Lakes Division as chief of procurement, he was stationed near Chicago and promoted to full colonel. Crown's wife died on 31 October 1943, and on 28 May 1946, he married Gladys Kaye. They had no children.

Returning to his business in 1946, Colonel Crown further diversified his holdings by buying controlling interests in railroads, hotels, banks, and real estate. With a $2 million share, he joined a group of investors in New York City who bought and sold the site of the United Nations Building. Crown bought the Chicago, Rock Island, and Pacific Railroad Company and, with Conrad Hilton, negotiated the sale of the Palmer House and the Stevens Hotel in Chicago and the Waldorf-Astoria in New York City to the Hilton Corporation. He eventually converted his profit from the Palmer House sale into 150,000 shares, or 8.7 percent of Hilton's stock. In the early 1950s, Crown bought the Mercantile Building in Chicago to house the offices of Material Service Corporation, which had expanded into mines that produced coal, lime, and clinker dolomite. In 1952, with an investment of $3 million, Crown joined a partnership to buy the Empire State Building. He used his earnings to buy out other shareholders, reduce the mortgage, and improve the property to draw new office tenants to the landmark skyscraper at Fifth Avenue and Thirty-fourth Street. When he sold the building in 1961 for $65 million, his profit amounted to nearly $50 million.

In 1959 Crown negotiated the merger of Material Service Corporation as an autonomous division with General Dynamics Corporation, a huge military contracting firm that was experiencing an erosion of profits and market confidence. Crown's shares, $116 million worth of preferred stock, gave him a controlling interest in the company, and he assumed the position of chief executive officer. Over the next several years, in spite of his reputation for negotiation and efficiency, he was unable to persuade the board of directors to centralize the management of the many autonomous divisions of General Dynamics, nor could he control duplication and waste. In 1966 Crown's opponents on the General Dynamics board voted to call up all of the company's preference stock and, with more than $100 million in cash, bought Crown out of the company. He had lost both his job and his Material Service Corporation, so he turned his attention to organizing new firms. In addition to investing in banks, railroads, meatpacking, and mining, Crown began to buy back the depressed General Dynamics stock. In 1970, he announced that he owned 18 percent of General Dynamics. He was offered a seat on the board of directors and was named chair of the executive committee. He reorganized the company and revitalized its divisions. By 1971, General Dynamics was again showing a profit.

Crown's pleasure was in creating profitable and efficient businesses. He believed that a deal was successful only if those negotiating the transaction left the table as friends and was proud of his reputation for truthfulness, his ingenuity as a trader, and his prodigious memory. He spent some of his fortune supporting universities and colleges, and by the last decade of his life, he had donated hundreds of millions of dollars to schools, museums, and medical centers. He joked that he always tried to have less money at the end of every year than he did the year before.

In 1986, at the age of ninety, Crown retired from his position as director and chair of the executive committee of General Dynamics and was replaced by his son Lester Crown. Colonel Crown served as honorary chairman until his death from natural causes in Chicago. His funeral was held at Temple Shalom in Chicago; he is buried in Rosehill Cemetery in that city.

★

Notes on Crown's tenure at General Dynamics are at the corporate headquarters in Falls Church, Virginia, and the corporate offices of Material Service in Chicago. Charles Moritz, ed., *Current Biography Yearbook* (1972), and John N. Ingham, ed., *Biographical Dictionary of American Business Leaders* (1983), provide overviews of Crown's personal and business lives. A chapter in *The Art of Success* (1956), by the editorial staff of *Fortune* magazine, and a chapter in Michael Patrick Allen, *The Founding Fortunes: A New Anatomy of the Super-Rich Families in America* (1987), analyze

Crown's financial successes. Crown's business career is recorded in "Man on the Empire State," *Business Week* (20 Nov. 1954); "Colonel Crown Revisited," *New Yorker* (18 Feb. 1956); R. A. Smith, "Henry Crown: Sand, Gravel, and Money," *Fortune* (Apr. 1956); and "Henry Crown: Chicago's Ubiquitous Capitalist," *Business Week* (22 Dec. 1975). Obituaries are in the *Chicago Tribune* (15 Aug. 1990), *Los Angeles Times* (16 Aug. 1990), *New York Times* (16 Aug. 1990), and *Current Biography* (Oct. 1990).

WENDY HALL MALONEY

CUGAT, Xavier (*b.* 1 January 1900 in Gerona, Spain; *d.* 27 October 1990 in Barcelona, Spain), bandleader best known for popularizing Latin American music and Latin American talent.

Xavier Cugat was born Francisco de Asís Javier Cugat de Bru Mingall Deulofeo, the son of Juan Cugat de Bru, a handyman and inventor, and Avila Mingall, a seamstress. He had three brothers. His family visited Havana, Cuba, in 1904, eventually settling there; Juan Cugat was credited with introducing the acetylene welding torch in Cuba. Cugat began violin lessons at age five. As a teenager his musical interests led him to Berlin, Germany, where he studied with Carl Flesch, Willy Hess, and Franz Kneisel. During the mid-1910s he toured North America with Enrico Caruso, who featured him as violin soloist. Caruso and his young protégé spent much of their travel time drawing cartoons and caricatures; drawing and painting were interests that Cugat maintained for the rest of his life.

Xavier Cugat and his second wife, Abbe Lane, in Rome, *c.* 1958. HULTON-DEUTSCH COLLECTION/CORBIS

Cugat's broadcast debut was on 28 December 1921 in Camden, New Jersey, on WDY; some media historians consider this to be the first solo performance on radio. After being featured with the Los Angeles Philharmonic during the late 1920s, and receiving a lukewarm review for his solo performance, Cugat turned to cartooning, working in this capacity for the *Los Angeles Times* for over a year. Meanwhile, he organized a six-piece band to play rumbas, tangos, and other Latin American dances. This group began working at Hollywood's Cocoanut Grove in 1928 as the relief band; in the same year they appeared in the film *Cugat and His Gigolos,* Cugat's first appearance on screen.

By the late 1920s North Americans had developed a strong interest in Cuban dance music; this was both symbolized and fueled by the runaway success in 1930 of the popular Cuban composer Moises Simón's *El Manisero* (The Peanut Vendor), which became an integral part of the international "rhumba craze" that characterized the era. Cugat realized the commercial potential of Latin American music in general and Cuban music in particular and moved his band to New York City. In 1933 Cugat's band opened the new Starlight Roof of the plush Waldorf-Astoria Hotel. During its sixteen years at this location it became the hotel's highest-paid band at $7,000 a week plus a percentage of the cover charges. That year Cugat and his band began appearing on New York radio, with a half-hour time slot on WEAF. Such broadcasting ultimately won the Cugat band a reputation comparable to the greatest American bands of the swing era. In 1941, when the American Society of Composers, Authors, and Publishers (ASCAP) refused to let its music be aired on radio after a dispute with the networks over fees, orchestras were limited to broadcasting public domain material. But Cugat could draw on a library of more than 500 non-ASCAP tunes. As a result, he was signed to *The Camel Caravan,* a radio program that brought him a national following.

During the 1940s Cugat's recordings on the RCA and Columbia labels were best-sellers and his radio transcriptions were a staple of the broadcasting industry. In addition to his hotel work and long-term engagements at movie palaces such as New York's Strand, Paramount, and Roxy Theaters, Cugat played for the large New York Latino community at dance halls such as the St. Nicholas Arena, the Odd Fellows' Temple, and the Audubon Ballroom. His orchestra was presented in feature films such as *Luxury Liner* (1948); *Go West, Young Man* (1936); *Neptune's Daughter* (1949); *Bathing Beauty* (1944); *This Time for Keeps* (1947); and *On an Island with You* (1948). Cugat toured both nationally and internationally; his tours of the Far East in the 1950s helped establish Latin music in Japan and paved the way for its later popularity in that country. A master showman, Cugat had a command of lighting, timing, pacing, programming, and comedy that was unsurpassed in Latin musical circles. The sounds of his orchestra were enriched by talented singers whose careers were in turn enhanced by exposure via the Cugat organization. Some of the most outstanding were Carmen Castillo, Lina Romay, Desi Arnaz, Miguelito Valdés, José Luis Moneró, Dinah Shore, Buddy Clark, Luis del Campo, and Abbe Lane.

Cugat's public image was based largely on his association with beautiful women; in some cases his personal and professional involvements were intertwined. His first wife was Carmen Castillo, a singer; they were married in 1929 and divorced in 1946. His marriage to the model Lorraine Allen lasted from 1947 to 1951. In 1951 Cugat and his featured singer, Abbe Lane, were married; this marriage ended in divorce in 1964. Cugat and singer-guitarist María Rosario Pilar Martínez Molina Baeza (known as Charo) were married in 1966; by the mid-1970s the couple had separated. No children resulted from any of Cugat's marriages.

By the 1980s Cugat had retired from performing and his artistic activities focused on cartooning and painting. He moved to Barcelona, where he participated in the film *Una rosa al viento* (his last) in 1983. He died of heart failure during a stay at Barcelona's Quiron Clinic.

Purists have criticized Cugat's musical interpretations for their commercial orientation. Nevertheless, he was an international popularizer of dance rhythms of the Hispanic world. With the aid of the singer Miguelito Valdés, Cugat brought elements of Afro-Cuban music before a public that had never been exposed to this culture. The Cugat band played a major role in exposing the conga drum in a period when this instrument was virtually unknown outside of Cuba. His theater performances as well as his appearances on radio and television and in films paved the way for many younger Latino bandleaders and entertainers.

★

Cugat wrote two autobiographies, *Rumba Is My Life* (1948) and *Yo, Cugat: Mis primeros 80 años* (1981). Biographical studies include Juan Poch Soler, *Cugat vivió* (1990), and Charles Garrod, *Xavier Cugat and His Orchestra* (1995), a discography. See also Joseph J. Ryan, "Good-Will Set to Music," *New York Times* (20 July 1941). Information on Cugat can also be found in Desi Arnaz, *A Book* (1976), esp. pp. 45–66; Vira Liebling, "The King of Rhumba at Home," *Musical Courier* (5 Feb. 1944); and Rudolfo C. Quebleen, "Xavier Cugat, pintor y caricaturista," *ABC de las Américas* (10–16 Feb. 1973). An obituary is in the *New York Times* (28 Oct. 1990).

DAVID M. CARP

CUNLIFFE, Marcus Falkner (*b.* 5 July 1922 in Rochdale, England; *d.* 2 September 1990 in Washington, D.C.), scholar who authored books on American history and helped to pioneer the American Studies movement in the United States and Great Britain.

Cunliffe came of age in the middle-class world of a Northlander from England. His parents, Keith Harold Cunliffe and Kathleen Eleanor Falkner, managed laundry and dry cleaning businesses when they moved the family to Newcastle-upon-Tyne in 1930. After attending Newcastle's Royal Grammar School, Cunliffe attended Oriel College, Oxford, from 1940 to 1942 and 1946 to 1947. He earned the B.A. in 1944, M.A. in 1946, and B.Litt. in 1947, but his sense of education ostensibly derived from his voracious reading habits. Even during his early years at Oxford, Cunliffe demonstrated the eclectic interests of a Victorian man of letters. He neither needed nor wanted a Ph.D., though Cunliffe continued his studies while a Commonwealth Fund Fellow at Yale and the University of Chicago from 1947 to 1949 and in 1954.

During an educational interregnum from 1942 to 1946, Cunliffe served as an intelligence officer in the British army and as a lieutenant on a tank crew. He learned much from his personal experiences during World War II, discovering a new world that included the significant presence of the United States. After seeing the sacrifice of U.S. soldiers at Normandy, the Netherlands, and Ardennes, Cunliffe came to admire America without forgetting England. "We knew how vast and omnipresent the American contribution had been," Cunliffe recalled. "We were predisposed to agree that the United States was different from, and in important respects, better than Europe: exceptional, and exceptionally good." In effect, his lifelong fascination for American exceptionalism remained grounded in his British sense and sensibilities, which accentuated a particular Cunliffian paradox: unity in diversity.

For much of his career Cunliffe imagined himself as a kind of New World missionary to Great Britain. He held an appointment to the University of Manchester, England, as a lecturer from 1949 to 1956 and as senior lecturer from 1956 to 1960, then as professor of American history and institutions from 1960 to 1964. Thereafter, he moved to the University of Sussex, England, to become professor of American Studies from 1965 to 1980. In 1980 Cunliffe became University Professor at the George Washington University in Washington, D.C., where he taught graduate and undergraduate courses. In his forty years as an academician, Cunliffe was a visiting professor and scholar at many institutions, including Harvard University, Mount Holyoke College, Washington State University, the University of Michigan, City College of New York, the University of California at Berkeley, and Mercer University. He provided active leadership in the British Association of American Studies, which included service in the chairmanship and development of the *Journal of American Studies.*

Cunliffe claimed to be dedicated to the pursuit of happiness, a Jeffersonian phrase that undoubtedly held special meaning for a British Americanist. On 3 July 1949 he married Mitzi Solomon, a distinguished American sculptor who accentuated his developing passion for the New World. They parented a son, Jason, and two daughters, Shay and Antonia; the marriage ended in divorce in 1971. On 18 November 1971 Cunliffe married Lesley Hume, a journalist, although they too divorced, in 1979. In 1984 he married historian Phyllis Palmer, with whom he shared his last years in Washington, D.C. Cunliffe enjoyed the cinema, theater, and literature and maintained an elegant style and gentlemanly character. He enjoyed opening professional doors for others, at the same time evincing a keen distaste for administrative duties and office politics. Cunliffe was remembered for his warm conversations colored by word games and ironic speculations. He once quipped that his interest in America emerged through his own Lincolnesque physique, that is, big feet and gangling arms. With a playful sense of humor, wit, and imagination, he enjoyed the lighter absurdities of life.

Cunliffe's legacy included books, essays, and articles that earned the respect and praise of scholars on both sides of the Atlantic. His first major book, *The Literature of the United States* (1954), became not only a standard text on the subject but also a popular work among nonexperts. Other notable studies by Cunliffe included *George Washington: Man and Monument* (1958); *The Nation Takes Shape, 1789–1837* (1959); and *American Presidents and the Presidency* (1969). Despite his own gentle, disarming character, Cunliffe also delighted in American military history, which he described in *Soldiers and Civilians: The Martial Spirit in America, 1775–1865* (1968). As with a number of his titles, he juxtaposed the elements of a complex American civilization. In his work Cunliffe also revealed an ability to bridge the Atlantic through comparative history, and *Chattel Slavery and Wage Slavery: The Anglo-American Context, 1830–1860* (1979) underscored external unity between the Old and New Worlds.

While he enjoyed exploring the American past, Cunliffe epitomized the mid-Atlantic intellectual eschewing the specialization of the academic world. Indeed, he produced an exceptional yet broad body of historical literature that explored nationalism and identity in American culture and reflected his own sense of irony. In short, he never limited himself to a single subject, or to any kind of bland theorizing, but preferred instead to remain a pragmatic dilettante.

Cunliffe died at the George Washington University Hospital following complications from leukemia. His body was cremated and his ashes were scattered at Rock Creek in Washington, D.C.

★

Cunliffe's papers reside in the special collections of the Melvin Gelman Library at George Washington University in Washington, D.C. His last book, *In Search of America: Transatlantic Essays, 1951–1990* (1991), demonstrates the remarkable intellectual journey of a scholar of American Studies on both sides of the Atlantic. Brian Reid and John White, eds., *American Studies: Essays in Honour of Marcus Cunliffe* (1991), is a Festschrift that includes a concise biography of Cunliffe. Professional biographies appear in Michael Heale, "Marcus Cunliffe, 1922–1990," *Journal of American Studies* 24 (Dec. 1990): 477–478; John Higham, "Marcus Cunliffe," *American Quarterly* 43 (June 1991): 255–258; and Lawrence S. Kaplan, "Marcus Cunliffe Remembered," *Journal of the Early Republic* 12 (spring 1992): 1–9. Obituaries appear in many newspapers, including the *Times* (London) (4 Sept. 1990), *New York Times* (5 Sept. 1990), and *Washington Post* (5 Sept. 1990).

BRAD D. LOOKINGBILL

CUNNINGHAM, Glenn V. (*b.* 4 August 1909 in Atlanta, Kansas; *d.* 10 March 1988 in Menifee, Arkansas), track and field athlete known as the Kansas Flyer and the Kansas Ironman who held several world mile and 1,500-meter records and won a silver medal in the 1,500-meter event at the 1936 Olympic Games in Berlin.

Cunningham, the son of Henry ("Clint") Cunningham, a farmer, well driller, and odd-jobs man, grew up in Elkhart, Kansas, with three brothers and three sisters. At age seven Cunningham was severely burned when his older brother, Floyd, started a fire in the potbellied stove of their schoolhouse. Because the kerosene container had been accidentally filled with gasoline, the stove exploded and Floyd was killed. Glenn's left foot was burned so badly that the transverse arch was destroyed, and his right leg was shriveled by scar issue, leaving it shorter than the other. The doctors, who nearly amputated his left leg, feared he would never walk again. Cunningham spent several months in a hospital while skin was grafted to his scarred legs; he then hobbled on crutches for three years. His tenacious spirit, the loving care of his mother, and the hard-nosed "never quit" philosophy of his father sparked his miraculous recovery. Cunningham not only learned to walk again, but he also became a champion runner.

The courageous Cunningham took up running in an effort to lessen his pain. At age thirteen he defeated a high school miler in his first race and ran the mile in 4 minutes, 36.5 seconds as a junior at Elkhart High School. His coach timed him during practice at 3 minutes, 58.9 seconds in 1930, twenty-four years before Roger Bannister officially broke the four-minute barrier in the mile. He set a high-

Glenn Cunningham finishes fourth in the 1,500-meter race at the 1932 Olympic Games in Los Angeles. ARCHIVE PHOTOS

school record of 4 minutes, 24.7 seconds for the mile at the 1929 National Interscholastic meet in Chicago in his last race before graduating from Elkhart High School.

Cunningham enrolled at the University of Kansas in 1929. Because of circulation problems, he had to warm up for about an hour before each race. The 179-pounder with no transverse arch on his left foot, scarred legs, and eight abscessed teeth won the mile in 4 minutes, 14.3 seconds, and the 880 yards in 1 minute, 53.5 seconds, at the Big Six Conference championships in May 1932. The following month he set an American record in the 1,500 meters with a 4 minute, 11.1 second clocking at the National Collegiate Athletic Association (NCAA) championships. After winning the 1,500 meters at the Amateur Athletic Union (AAU) championships, he finished fourth at the 1932 Olympic Games in Los Angeles.

Cunningham dominated U.S. middle-distance racing from 1933 through 1940. He scored a rare double at the 1933 AAU championships, taking the 800 meters in 1 minute, 51.8 seconds and the 1,500 meters in 3 minutes, 52.3 seconds. Besides capturing the mile in 4 minutes, 9.8 seconds at the NCAA championships, he earned the Sullivan Memorial Trophy as the nation's outstanding amateur athlete for 1933.

In 1934 Cunningham and Bill Bonthron of Princeton University, the world-record holder in the 1,500 meters, engaged in several exciting mile duels. After splitting two close indoor races, Cunningham defeated Bonthron by forty yards at the Princeton Invitation meet on 16 June to set a world outdoor record of 4 minutes, 6.7 seconds. He deliberately ran the second half faster than the first, clocking laps of 61.8 seconds, 64.0 seconds, 61.8 seconds, and 59.1 seconds. His record lasted for three years. Bonthron, however, defeated Cunningham in the mile at the NCAA championships and in the 1,500 meters at the AAU championships that summer.

Cunningham captured the 1,500 meters in 3 minutes, 52.1 seconds at the 1935 AAU championships and in 3 minutes, 49.9 seconds at the 1936 AAU championships. A silver medalist at the 1936 Olympic Games, he recorded his second fastest 1,500 meters with a time of 3 minutes, 48.4 seconds. He tried to break away from the field on the third lap, but Jack Lovelock of New Zealand outsprinted him in a world record 3 minutes, 47.8 seconds. Two weeks later, Cunningham set a world record of 1 minute, 49.7 seconds for the 800 meters in Stockholm, Sweden.

Cunningham triumphed in the 1,500 meters at both the 1937 and 1938 AAU championships, giving him four consecutive titles. In March 1938 officials at Dartmouth College invited him to try for a world mile record on a new high-banked indoor track. Six Dartmouth runners paced him, enabling him to clock an unbelievable 4 minute, 4.4 second mile. Although not surpassed indoors until 1955, his time was never officially recognized because pacing runners had aided him. Cunningham clocked 3 minutes, 48.0 seconds for his fastest 1,500 meters at the 1940 AAU championships in his last major race, but Walter Mehl defeated him. Because World War II forced cancellation of the 1940 Olympic games, he retired from athletic competition.

Throughout his career, Cunningham performed exceptionally well at Madison Square Garden in New York City, where he won twenty-one of thirty-one races and set six world indoor records in the mile and 1,500 meters. In 1934 he established a world indoor mile mark with a 4 minute, 8.4 second clocking, and his best indoor mile at Madison Square Garden came in 1938 with another world record time of 4 minutes, 7.4 seconds. He won six Wanamaker Miles at the Millrose Games, a record finally broken by Eamonn Coghlan of Ireland in 1987. Cunningham, a member of the Helms Athletic Foundation Hall of Fame and the National Track and Field Hall of Fame, was honored in 1979 as the most outstanding track performer in the 100-year history of Madison Square Garden.

Because of circulation problems, Cunningham never

ran smoothly, but he compensated with tremendous endurance and strength. Although not especially fast for short distances, the chunky, barrel-chested Kansan ran with almost scientific precision against the era's best runners in events from 800 yards to two miles. His thrilling races against Bonthron, Lovelock, Gene Vensky, Archie San Romani, Don Lash, and Chuck Fensky remain legendary.

Cunningham graduated with a B.S. degree from the University of Kansas in 1934 and earned an M.A. degree from the University of Iowa in 1936. After receiving a Ph.D. in physical education from New York University in 1940, he served as director of athletics and physical education at Cornell College in Mount Vernon, Iowa, from 1940 to 1944 before spending two years in the U.S. Navy during World War II.

Cunningham married Margaret Speir of Peabody, Kansas, in August 1934. They had two daughters and were divorced. In the summer of 1947 Cunningham married Ruth Sheffield, a schoolteacher. They had ten children. The couple established the Cunningham Youth Ranch on an 840-acre spread in Cedar Point, Kansas, for troubled and underprivileged children; nearly 10,000 youths passed through the center. They sold farmland and livestock and spoke at commencements, clubs, churches, and schools across the nation to support the ranch until it closed in 1978. They then operated a farm near Menifee, Arkansas, where Cunningham died of an apparent heart attack.

Cunningham's heroic achievement in overcoming his grave injuries to become one of the world's greatest middle-distance runners conspicuously raised the profile of track and field—and especially the mile—in the United States. In addition, his innovative warm-up and pacing techniques paved the way for the sub-four-minute milers who came after him. Finally, Cunningham performed even more valuable work with troubled and underprivileged youth.

★

Information on Cunningham can be found in the Glenn Cunningham file at the National Track and Field Hall of Fame, Indianapolis, Indiana. The fullest account of his life is his autobiography, Glenn Cunningham with George X. Sand, *Never Quit* (1981). Edwin V. Burkholder, "Glenn Cunningham and the Four-Minute Mile," *Sport* (March 1950); William Herman, *Hearts Courageous* (1949); David K. Boynick, *Champions by Setback* (1954); Mel Allen with Frank Graham, Jr., *It Takes Heart* (1959); Vernon Pizer, *Glorious Triumphs* (1980); and Craig Morton and Robert Burger, *The Courage to Believe* (1981) recount how he overcame enormous adversity to become one of the world's greatest middle-distance runners. An obituary is in the *New York Times* (11 Mar. 1988).

DAVID L. PORTER

D

DACHÉ, Marie-Louise ("Lilly") (*b.* 1892 in Bèigles, France; *d.* 31 December 1989 in Louvecienne, France), America's foremost milliner, whose trendsetting hats were worn by the most famous women of stage, screen, and society over a span of forty years.

Daché was born in the south of France near Bordeaux, where her parents (whose full names are not known) were grape farmers. She was the sixth of eight children. Her mother dressed elegantly and would sometimes travel to Paris, where she opened a short-lived shop, where Daché had her first experiences selling ribbons and laces and learned to distinguish good from poor quality materials. Daché made hats and gloves from scraps, and when she was six, she cut up her mother's best blouse to make a hat. Because she was not beautiful like her mother and sisters, who thought it doubtful that she would find a husband, Daché was encouraged to learn about colors and fabrics and to do fine needlework. At fourteen Daché quit school to begin apprenticeships in Paris in the salons of Suzanne Talbot and Georgette. For four years she was apprenticed to the famous milliner Caroline Reboux. When still a teenager, Daché designed a hat with a visor, based on a boy's bicycling cap, a shape she would use again.

In 1924 Daché went to the United States. After unhappy experiences in New Jersey and Philadelphia, she discovered New York City on 13 September 1924. With only $13 in her pocket, she fell in love with the sights, smells, and excitement of the city, and from that day she considered thirteen her lucky number. After brief unsuccessful stints as a millinery saleswoman in department stores, Daché found work in a small hat shop on Broadway at Seventy-seventh Street. In 1928 she bought out her partner. Developing her sales ingenuity, she charmed her customers into leaving $2 deposits for hats she would design right on their heads after carefully studying their features. She rushed out to purchase materials with the deposits and completed the hats for pickup the next day.

During a time of mass-produced cloche hats, Daché provided her customers with personalized assistance and one-of-a-kind hats. As word spread, women from the nearby theater district became her avid customers, and the movie star Marion Davies was one of her first. Daché opened two branches, one on West Eighty-second Street and another on West Fifty-seventh Street. In 1928 she consolidated the three stores into one at 485 Madison Avenue. While she continued to make uniquely trimmed cloches in the fashion of the day, one of the first hats she made on her own was, significantly, a velvet turban, which became a Daché signature. Her customers in the 1930s were a "who's who" of stage and screen, including Dolores Del Rio, Jean Harlow, Helen Hayes, Gertrude Lawrence, Carole Lombard, Marilyn Miller, Merle Oberon, Mary Pickford, Norma Shearer, and Sylvia Sidney.

On 13 March 1931 Daché married Jean Desprès, an executive with Coty's American operation. They adopted

Lilly Daché, *c.* 1943. ARCHIVE PHOTOS

one daughter. Daché continued her career but made time to have lunch, evenings, and weekends with her family. Her "smart" hats could cost as much as $165, but most sold for a minimum of $25. Besides masses of silk roses or carnations, Daché used more unusual flowers, such as gladioli, sometimes accented with tiny jeweled insects. Some of her hats were antique, ethnic-inspired, or caps with generous veiling attached. She believed that women purchased hats for emotional reasons, to feel better, to look prettier or more glamorous, or to catch and keep a husband. "A woman's hat is close to her heart," she explained. On weekends Daché and her family relaxed in their country home in Pound Ridge, New York, which they purchased in April 1935. There they attended mass on Sunday mornings, and Daché loved to work in her garden.

On 13 April 1937 the cornerstone for a new Daché building was laid at 78 East Fifty-sixth Street, off Park Avenue. Aware of the power of the press, Daché announced that a live horned toad would be buried inside the cornerstone. Secretly she had a friend call the American Society for the Prevention of Cruelty to Animals (ASPCA), which organized highly publicized protests of animal cruelty. The toad was removed, and Daché made the news. The modernistic nine-story building was capped by two floors of penthouse apartments for Daché and her family. The lower seven stories included leopard-skin upholstery, reception rooms with mirrored walls, salons, showrooms, workrooms, and circular fitting rooms with satin walls, gold for blondes and silver for brunettes. She eliminated display windows to prevent piracy of her designs. In addition, each Daché hat design was photographed and numbered to discourage imitations.

Daché created the draped toques Marlene Dietrich wore in the film *Desire* (1936), and by 1938 she was collaborating with Travis Banton, a film costume designer. Daché showed her designs two to four times a year and gave speeches at fashion shows, where her accent was considered exotic. In June 1939 she showed millinery at the World's Fair in New York City. That summer, before war broke out in Europe, she took a trip to Paris to buy materials, a practice she resumed after the war ended.

In 1940 Daché introduced the half-hat, which left the back of the head bare. Worn by the famous New York debutante Brenda Frazier and, with a snood, by the actress Betty Grable, the half-hat became very popular with the mass market. For this creation, Lord & Taylor presented Daché with a $1,000 American Design Award, citing her for "outstanding achievement in the field of design in 1940." She was also credited with boosting the millinery industry at a time when women were beginning to go without hats.

In August 1940 Daché opened a shop in Chicago, and that year Neiman-Marcus presented her with an award. In 1941 she faced a highly publicized strike by the United Hatters, Cap, and Millinery Workers' Union of the American Federation of Labor (AFL), which claimed her wages were well below the millinery industry standards of $35 for a thirty-five-hour week. By that time, Daché, who designed three-quarters of the hats herself, and her staff of milliners, who finished the hats, were producing 9,000 hats per year for her own store and for forty-seven department stores.

Socialites and actresses continued to favor Daché hats. She created turbans piled high with flowers and fruit for "Brazilian bombshell" Carmen Miranda. For the mass-market *Collier's* magazine, Daché explained how to update hats for several years by wearing them different ways and changing the trim. In 1942 she introduced two fragrances she called "Drifting" and "Dashing." In response to shortages during World War II, she experimented with ordinary materials, such as mop strings, wooden beads, dyed chicken feathers, glass, and Lucite. In January 1943 she received the Coty American Fashion Critics special award for millinery.

Daché's autobiography, *Talking Through My Hats* (1946), became a best-seller. Although later criticized as more opinion than fact, it gives a good picture of her energy, personality, and beliefs. Daché seemed the epitome of the excitable, heavily perfumed, energetic Frenchwoman: she wore her auburn hair piled high (with the help of hair pieces) and favored black dresses on her five-foot, two-inch, 140-pound frame, along with colorful high-heeled platform shoes and masses of jangling jewelry. Of course, she wore her own hats, sometimes even in the bath. By 1946 she employed 150 milliners and Lilly Daché hats were sold around the world. Rosalind Russell, Sonja Henie, Joan Crawford, and Clare Boothe Luce joined the list of Daché customers, and Daché designed Paulette Goddard's hats for the historical film *Kitty* (1946).

In January 1947 Daché donated millinery supplies to be used for vocational training in a displaced-persons camp in Hanau, Germany. By 1949 Lilly Daché hats were produced at the rate of 20,000 a year and were sold in 500 specialty and department stores. The gross income of her New York salon exceeded $500,000 a year. She called hats that sold for $85 to $150 each "terrific creations." They featured seasonal decorations such as flowers for spring and summer, feathers or stuffed birds for fall. Turbans or pillboxes covered in gold or silver embroidery served for dressy occasions. Her less expensive models, at $59.50 to $79.50, were the "molded-like-sculpture" hats, which were simpler, emphasized the line, often asymmetrical, and sometimes decorated with bits of embroidery or light feather accents. In 1949 Daché presented her first collection of dresses coordinated with her hats.

In the early 1950s Daché introduced ready-to-wear hat lines, "Mlle. Lilly" and "Dachettes," and she further diversified into suits, shoes, stockings, gloves, furs, foundation garments, costume jewelry, cosmetics, and a beauty salon. In 1954 she became president of General Beauty Products, handling her own perfumes and those of Lucien Lelong. Daché owned a boutique in Paris and a Lucien Lelong salon on the Place Vendôme. She timed the introduction of her "Glampoo" shampoo to coincide with the publication of *Lilly Daché's Glamour Book* (1956).

During the late 1950s Daché hired a design assistant named Roy Halston Frowick; "Halston" later became famous as a dress designer. In the 1960s Kenneth Battell joined her beauty shop, where he created elaborate coiffures that, ironically, contributed to the demise of the hat. While public interest in hats was waning, Daché became even more innovative, creating tiny pillboxes, space-age helmets, lampshades, cartwheels, and feather poufs. By 1965, however, production was down to only 9,000 hats a year. In 1968 Daché retired. Just before she closed the House of Daché, her longtime fan Loretta Young purchased the last thirty hats.

On 9 August 1988 Daché's husband died. Daché lived in retirement in Delray Beach, Florida, and in a nursing home in Louvecienne, France, where she died. She was buried in Meudon.

Lilly Daché brought European hatmaking techniques to American millinery. Because of her brilliant ability to flatter her customers and promote an aura of exclusivity, her designs had snob appeal. Yet by writing articles and books aimed at all readers and by keeping her name in the news, she appealed to most women in an era when hats were chosen with as much care as the costume. Her designs set trends and were carefully made, epitomizing the milliner's craft and leaving a lasting legacy in fashion. Still sought after by collectors, Daché's hats show up at auctions, in vintage clothing shops, and antique shows.

★

Caroline Rennolds Milbank chronicled Daché's career in *New York Fashion: The Evolution of American Style* (1989). Alan J. Flux captured the essence of Daché's genius and personality in his critical essay in *Contemporary Fashion,* edited by Richard Martin (1995). A lengthy profile is Margaret Case Harriman, "Hats Will Be Worn," *New Yorker* (4 Apr. 1942). An obituary is in the *New York Times* (2 Jan. 1990).

THERESE DUZINKIEWICZ BAKER

DANGERFIELD, George (*b.* 28 October 1904 in Newbury, Berkshire, England; *d.* 27 December 1986 in Santa Barbara, California), historian whose publication *The Era of Good Feelings* (1952) won the Columbia University Bancroft Prize and the Pulitzer Prize.

Dangerfield was the youngest of the four children of Ethel Margaret Tyrer, a homemaker, and George Dangerfield, an Anglican clergyman. His father had changed his surname from Bubb to Dangerfield to show his gratitude to his aunt of that name for paying the expenses of his university education and his training at a seminary in the cathedral town of Wells. His father became rector of Mixbury-cum-Finmere, in the diocese of Oxford. Dangerfield grew up in a middle-class family and attended a preparatory school in Wiltshire. From 1916 to 1922 he went to the Forest School, a private boarding school in Walthamstow, Essex. He entered Hertford College at the University of Oxford in 1923, studied classics, and graduated in 1927 with a B.A. degree and honors in English literature. (In 1968 he received an M.A. degree from Oxford, which he would have received pro forma after earning his B.A. degree had he been able to pay the fee at that time.) He taught English at the English Institute in Prague, Czechoslovakia, in 1928 and 1929 and at the English College in Hamburg, Germany, in 1929 and 1930. On 28 June 1928 the good-looking and cultivated Englishman married Helen Mary Deey Spedding. They had no children; Helen died in 1935.

Immigrating to the United States in 1930, Dangerfield readily adapted. He worked in New York City as an assistant editor with Brewer, Warren, and Putnam, a publishing firm, from 1930 to 1932 and as a literary editor of *Vanity*

George Dangerfield, 1980s. COURTESY OF ANTHONY DANGERFIELD

Fair magazine from 1933 to 1935. He supplemented his income in the 1930s by speaking on the lecture circuit in various parts of the country. On 29 June 1941 he married Mary Lou Schott; they had three children. From 1942 to 1945 Dangerfield, who had been drafted by both the British and American armies and who had chosen the latter, served in the Ninth Army, 102d Infantry Division (the Ozark Division), where he achieved the rank of technical sergeant. He became an American citizen in 1943 while stationed in Paris, Texas. He later served in France and Germany, but as a staff sergeant he was never in combat. In 1951 the family moved to Carpinteria, California, a suburb of Santa Barbara. Some ten years later they moved to Toro Canyon Road on the outskirts of Santa Barbara, where Dangerfield lived for the rest of his life.

Reading widely, Dangerfield turned to the study of history, whose function, he believed, was "to engage and even to delight the intellect." Virginia Woolf was a special favorite of his, and in a crucial essay, "The Insistent Past," he asserted that the popular historian

> will maintain that [the past] can invigorate the present, enable it to transform itself. . . . If the past is to have a more popular life, it cannot depend on the novel. . . . But if the novel can go to history, history can go to the novel, at least to the extent of bringing a creative imagination to bear upon its characters. . . . History, which reconciles incompatibles, and balances probabilities, by its very nature eventually reaches the reality of fiction. And that is the highest reality of all. (*North American Review,* 1937, pp. 141; 151–152)

Dangerfield's first popular interpretive historical work was *Bengal Mutiny: The Story of the Sepoy Rebellion* (1933). A review in the *Spectator* said of Dangerfield, "He is fair-minded and feels the intense pity of the story." Dangerfield perceived "a considerable hiatus in English [political] history" between the death of Edward VII in 1910 and the onset of World War I in 1914, which prompted him to write his pioneering narrative on rebellion and protest, *The Strange Death of Liberal England* (1935). The book went through nineteen editions, and Peter Stansky of Stanford University attributed this popularity to "the brilliance of the writing" and its being "an example that history can be abiding literature." The book was also controversial and became a pivotal point in the continuing historiographical debate on early twentieth-century England.

Dangerfield was partial to biography because he could "tie it up with a period" and "a large field of untouched material" existed. Out of his reading he produced *Victoria's Heir: The Education of a Prince* (1941), a political study of the life and times of Albert Edward, who was Prince of Wales from 1841 to 1901 and who reigned as Edward VII from 1901 to 1910. Dangerfield's book *Chancellor Robert R. Livingston of New York: 1746–1813* (1960), resulting from research at the New-York Historical Society, won both the California Literature Silver Medal Award and the Marquis Biographical Award in 1961.

In 1952 Dangerfield published *The Era of Good Feelings,* which focuses on the presidential administrations of James Monroe and John Quincy Adams (1817–1829) during an important and largely overlooked period. In 1953 this work was awarded the Columbia University Bancroft Prize and the Pulitzer Prize, both for American history. Arthur M. Schlesinger, Sr., a member of the Pulitzer Advisory Committee, commented that the book "perhaps comes closest to being a work of literary art" and "should be of as much interest to the layman as to the professional historian." The Columbia University historian Richard Hofstadter viewed the book as "one of the solidest works of historical writing in years," adding that Dangerfield had produced "a general synthesis of the history of the period that is almost certain to endure as a standard work."

Dangerfield, with Otey S. Scruggs, a colleague, edited a two-volume abridgment of Henry Adams's *History of the*

United States During the Administrations of Jefferson and Madison (1963), choosing from Adams's masterful and enduring nine-volume *History of the United States of America* (1889–1891) his examples of momentous events in the movement of democratic nationalism. *The Awakening of American Nationalism, 1815–1828* (1965), a perceptive and absorbing volume in the New American Nation series, established Dangerfield as a political historian. In *Defiance to the Old World: The Story Behind the Monroe Doctrine* (1970), a short work for schoolchildren, he explained how three paragraphs from President Monroe's seventh State of the Union address (1823), which came to be known as the Monroe Doctrine, could be understood only in terms of the dramatic events then taking place in Europe.

The Guggenheim Fellowship that Dangerfield received for 1970 and 1971 enabled him to do research in London, Dublin, and Oxford for *The Damnable Question: A Study in Anglo-Irish Relations* (1976), his last book. Exploring the course of those relations, he wrote that "the strangeness and variety of the human condition" is the stuff of history. The book was a runner-up for the National Book Critics Circle Award.

Dangerfield was an intellectual who extended himself to the public. He taught at the University of California at Berkeley in the 1950s, served as Benjamin D. Shreve Fellow at Princeton University in 1957 and 1958, and was a lecturer in British history at the University of California at Santa Barbara from 1968 to 1972. Dangerfield's modesty, gentle demeanor, vibrant personality, fine speaking voice, and breadth of knowledge made him an impressive teacher. When his friend and colleague Alfred Gollin asked one of Dangerfield's former students at the University of California at Santa Barbara what it was like when he first met Dangerfield, the undergraduate replied instantly, "It was magic."

A fellow of the Society of American Historians and a member of the American Historical Association, Dangerfield was a Democrat who belonged to Americans for Democratic Action, the American Civil Liberties Union, the National Association for the Advancement of Colored People, and Common Cause. Absorbed in the study of current history, he asked, "Doesn't the spirit of our times express itself in a tendency to question and to protest?" Beginning in the 1930s he wrote numerous articles and reviews on literature and history in such periodicals as *American Heritage, Commonweal, Harper's, Nation, New Republic, North American Review, Saturday Review of Literature,* and *Scribner's.* He continued to review history books after his retirement from book writing.

Dangerfield's impact on British historians was enormous. Once during his retirement, when Dangerfield had returned to Santa Barbara to deliver a talk to graduate students, Gollin introduced him as a speaker, saying, "As long as people are interested in English history, they will have to read George Dangerfield's *The Strange Death of Liberal England.*" In March 1985, upon the occasion of the fiftieth anniversary of that publication, the Pacific Coast Conference on British Studies held a symposium in California to honor him and to analyze his famous work. In the new paperback edition of that book, published in 1997 by Stanford University Press, Stansky wrote, "Now, more than sixty years later, the book is as vital, if not more so, as when it was first published."

Dangerfield died of leukemia. His remains were cremated, and his ashes were scattered at sea off Santa Barbara.

★

John A. Garraty, ed., *Interpreting American History: Conversations with Historians* (1970), contains an interview with Dangerfield in a chapter titled "The United States in World Affairs: 1790–1860." A biographical essay is in Marjorie Dent Candee, ed., *Current Biography 1953* (1954). Michael Tratner, *Modernism and Mass Politics: Joyce, Woolf, Eliot, Yeats* (1995), discusses Dangerfield and scrutinizes *The Strange Death of Liberal England* alongside the writings of four other modern authors. "George Dangerfield," *Wilson Library Bulletin* 16 (Nov. 1941): 202, is a brief biographical sketch. Peter Stansky et al., "George Dangerfield and *The Strange Death of Liberal England:* Fifty Years After," *Albion* 17, no. 4 (winter 1985): 401–447, is a symposium that also includes biographical information. Charles Poore reviewed *Victoria's Heir* in the *New York Times* (13 Sept. 1941). Reviews of *The Era of Good Feelings* are by Poore in the *New York Times* (3 Jan. 1952) and by Henry F. Graff in the *New York Times Book Review* (6 Jan. 1952). Obituaries are in the *Times of London* (29 Dec. 1986), which is the best and most accurate; the *New York Times* (6 Jan. 1987); and *Washington Post* (10 Jan. 1987).

BERNARD HIRSCHHORN

DANIEL, Price Marion (*b.* 10 October 1910 in Dayton, Texas; *d.* 25 August 1988 in Liberty, Texas), governor of Texas, justice of the Texas Supreme Court, and U.S. senator.

One of three children of Marion Price Daniel, a real estate dealer and newspaper editor, and Nannie Partlow, Daniel was raised in Liberty, Texas, until the age of fourteen, when his father decided to attend the Southwest Baptist Theological Seminary and moved the family to Fort Worth. Finishing his high school education in just three years, he then entered Baylor University in Waco, Texas, where he majored in journalism. Energetic and ambitious, he was president of his college class, organized and played saxophone in a jazz band known as the Varsitonians, and worked as a reporter for the *Waco News-Tribune*.

After receiving an A.B. degree from Baylor in 1931, Daniel entered Baylor University Law School, from which

Price Daniel, 1952. UPI/CORBIS-BETTMANN

he earned an LL.B. in 1932. Also in that year he made the fateful decision to become a member of the speaker's bureau for the Democratic national campaign. He said, "I'm pretty sure I would have become a Baptist minister if I hadn't gone into politics. . . . I'll tell you this—there must be something besides the law that makes people want to live under the law, and that thing is religion. It just must have a place in our government." Admitted to the Texas bar in 1932, Daniel began his law practice in Liberty. He remained active in politics and was elected in the fall of 1938 to the first of three consecutive terms in the Texas House of Representatives in Austin. In 1943 he was unanimously chosen as speaker of the house. Daniel married Jean Houston Baldwin, a great-great-granddaughter of former Texas governor Sam Houston, in 1940; they had four children: Price, Houston, John, and Jean.

After serving a brief stint in U.S. Army intelligence during World War II, rising from private in 1943 to the rank of captain by 1946, Daniel announced his candidacy for attorney general of Texas. Running without Republican opposition, he was elected in 1946 and then reelected in both 1948 and 1950. He was considered an effective and aggressive attorney general. According to *Newsweek* magazine, Daniel won admiration by "smashing the Maceo gambling syndicate in Galveston, closing down the Continental Press race-wire service in his state, shuttering the horse parlors, and wiping out the slots" (28 Apr. 1952).

Daniel was popular with the electorate, chiefly as a result of his folksy style, support of segregation in education, and defense of states' claims to offshore oil reserves. In fact, the defeats that he endured at the hands of President Harry Truman in the matter of the offshore oil reserves were the impetus for his decision in 1952 to seek a seat in the U.S. Senate. He won the election (running unopposed), and his voting record in his first year in the Senate helped to solidify his image, which the *Saturday Evening Post* called "an economy-conscious middle-of-the-roader" (2 Jan. 1954). Daniel described himself privately as a "Texas" rather than a "national" Democrat. As a senator, he voted repeatedly against pay raises for federal employees and opposed foreign aid bills and funding for public housing. As chairman of the Senate Judiciary Committee subcommittee on narcotics, Daniel favored mandatory sentences for drug dealers, and advocated the death penalty for drug dealers "when warranted."

In 1957 Daniel resigned his Senate seat to run unopposed for governor of Texas. He served three two-year terms as governor, from 1957 to 1963, then lost a bid, to John B. Connally, for an unprecedented fourth term. Following this loss, he headed the Texas Library and Historical Commission and then served as an assistant to President Lyndon B. Johnson for federal-state relations and was a member of the National Security Council from 1967 to 1969.

Daniel was appointed in 1971 to the Texas Supreme Court and served on the bench for eight years before returning in 1978 to private law practice and his ranch in Liberty, Texas. A major factor in his decision not to continue on the court was his desire to assist his eldest son, Price, Jr., who was running for attorney general that year. Price, Jr., was shot to death in his home in Liberty in 1981. Although his wife was charged with his murder, she was later acquitted.

On Daniel's death, of a stroke at his ranch in Liberty, Governor Bill Clements observed in a statement, "No man has done more for our state than Price Daniel. He will be remembered as a great patriot, a great American, and most of all, a great Texan." He is buried in Liberty, Texas.

A classic Texas-style Democrat who at the national level sought compromise and reconciliation rather than confrontation and conflict, Price Daniel became a symbol of his time and place—a gentleman whose conservative views on segregation would fall out of favor but whose views on law and order remained popular.

★

Daniel's papers are kept in his former residence, located next to the Sam Houston Regional Library and Research Center in

Austin. A biographical account is in Kenneth E. Hendrickson, Jr., *The Chief Executives of Texas: From Stephen F. Austin to John B. Connally, Jr.* (1995), pp. 217–222. See also the *New York Times* (23 Mar. 1953); *Newsweek* (28 Apr. 1952); and the *Washington Post* (30 Jan. 1953). An obituary is in the *New York Times* (27 Aug. 1988).

DANIEL BARWICK

DANIELS, William Boone ("Billy") (*b.* 15 September 1915 in Jacksonville, Florida; *d.* 7 October 1988 in Los Angeles, California), nightclub performer, actor, and big-band singer best known for his hit recording of "That Old Black Magic."

Although they were of African-American ancestry, Billy Daniels's family claimed the famed American woodsman Daniel Boone as a member of their family tree. Daniels, whose father worked as a railway mail clerk, sang as a child with street singers for coins thrown by passersby. By the time he was a teenager, he was performing on local radio stations WJAX and WMBR in Jacksonville. Daniels began prelaw studies at Florida State Agricultural and Mechanical College but dropped out to help support his family.

Visiting New York City in 1934 for the first time to see his grandmother, Daniels was taken to Harlem's Hotcha Club, where a college classmate insisted that he "give the Harlem folks a load of Florida talent." Daniels sang two songs and was hired on the spot as a singing waiter at twenty-five dollars a week. Other New York City establishments where he developed his craft were Dickie Wells's, the Ubangi, the Black Cat, and Mammy's Chicken Koop. By the mid-1930s he was traveling as a vocalist with Erskine Hawkins and his 'Bama State Collegians. In 1936 he recorded "Until the Real Thing Comes Along" and "I Can't Escape from You" with this band for the Vocalion label; these were his first recordings. By the late 1930s, Daniels was a fixture of the nightclub scene on Manhattan's Fifty-second Street, then the center of jazz life. He was engaged for long periods at the Three Deuces, the Yacht Club, and Kelly's Stables; his performances of the ballad "Intermezzo" were often accompanied by soulful obbligatos from jazz violinist Stuff Smith.

After serving in the merchant marine during World War II, Daniels returned to New York City in 1945, when he made his Broadway debut in the musical *Memphis Bound* with the celebrated dancer Bill ("Bojangles") Robinson. It was during an engagement at a club in Atlantic City, New Jersey, that Daniels is said to have first sung "That Old Black Magic." Written by Harold Arlen and Johnny Mercer for the 1942 film *Star Spangled Rhythm,* this song was also recorded by such artists as Frank Sinatra, Keely Smith, and Sammy Davis, Jr., but it was Daniels's version that became the most celebrated. Daniels's 1948 recording eventually sold more than 15 million copies; near the end of his life, he estimated that he had performed the number more than 25,000 times over a forty-year period.

The late 1940s and early 1950s were marked by long engagements for Daniels at posh New York City area nightclubs, such as Bill Miller's Riviera, the Copacabana, and Club Ebony, and at movie palaces, including the Capitol Theatre. At the same time, he maintained his popularity with the African-American audiences that patronized such uptown locations as Club 845 and Hunts Point Palace in the Bronx. In 1950 Daniels began his movie career with an appearance in *When You're Smiling;* other film performances included roles in *Sunny Side of the Street* (1951), *Rainbow 'Round My Shoulder* (1952), *Cruisin' Down the River* (1953), *The Big Operator* (1959), and *The Beat Generation* (1959). The success of his "Black Magic" recording along with his stage presence led to wide exposure; in 1956 his engagements included Philadelphia's Latin Casino, the Beachcomber and Ciro's in Miami Beach, Florida, and the Tropicana Club in Havana, Cuba. He was the first black nightclub performer to have his own weekly radio show, and in 1952 he became one of the first black entertainers

Billy Daniels. PHOTOGRAPHS AND PRINTS DIVISION, SCHOMBURG CENTER FOR RESEARCH IN BLACK CULTURE, THE NEW YORK PUBLIC LIBRARY, ASTOR, LENOX, AND TILDEN FOUNDATIONS

to have his own television variety program, which played for thirteen weeks on ABC.

In March 1952 Daniels was hired to play two weeks at the London Palladium; the engagement was extended, and he was a regularly featured performer there during the 1950s and 1960s. Daniels was also frequently booked into Las Vegas hotels such as the Flamingo; he was such a success in the resort city that his salary reached as much as $26,000 a week. He took fourteen months out of his tour schedule to costar with Sammy Davis, Jr., in the Broadway play *Golden Boy* (1964). Daniels's first wife, Florence Clotworthy, committed suicide in 1946. In 1950 he married Martha Braun, a white socialite from Lowell, Massachusetts; the marriage received front-page coverage throughout the United States. By 1954 Braun and Daniels were divorced. In 1955 Daniels married a Frenchwoman named Pierrette Cameron. During this period Daniels's nonmusical activities began to receive as much attention as his performances, especially his association with various underworld figures. Daniels was found guilty of violent behavior several times; on one occasion he was stabbed and on another he was found guilty of shooting a man. In 1956 his cabaret license was suspended by the New York Police Department, and he was unable to perform in New York City nightclubs again until 1959.

By the 1970s the Daniels persona was mellowness personified; he captivated audiences in the award-winning show *Bubbling Brown Sugar* (1977), a nostalgic evocation of 1930s Harlem. During the 1980s, however, his theatrical and club activities were increasingly interrupted by ill health. Daniels died of stomach cancer at the Kenneth Norris, Jr., Cancer Hospital and Research Institute at the University of Southern California in Los Angeles. He was buried in the cemetery of the Church of the Good Shepherd in Beverly Hills, California.

In addition to his smooth vocal style, Daniels was celebrated for his ability to impart the meaning of a song's lyrics. By the late 1940s he was known as "The Voice You See." He was a natural for the emerging medium of television and made an effortless transition from nightclubs to TV studios. A handsome and very light-skinned African-American who could have passed for white, he was respected by black colleagues and fans for his honesty regarding his race. Daniels's box-office power led to engagements at rooms such as Bill Miller's Riviera, which had previously been unwilling to hire black entertainers, and his popularity made it easier for other black artists to find work in nightclubs catering to American high society.

★

For further information, see: "Billy Daniels, Veteran Night Club Tenor with Remarkable Voice," *Ebony* (Sept. 1950); "Mr. Black Magic," *Our World* (Apr. 1951); "Cruisin' Down the River," *Our World* (June 1953); and Bruce Chadwick, "Bubbling, White-haired Daniels," *New York Daily News* (17 Jan. 1986). Obituaries are in the *New York Times* (10 Oct. 1988), the *Daily Telegraph* (10 Oct. 1988), and the *New York Amsterdam News* (29 Oct. 1988).

DAVID M. CARP

DAUGHERTY, Hugh ("Duffy") (*b.* 8 September 1915 in Emeigh, Pennsylvania; *d.* 25 September 1987 in Santa Barbara, California), football coach who, in nearly two decades as head coach at Michigan State University (1954–1973), led the MSU team to national prominence and two Big Ten titles.

The son of Joseph Daugherty, a coal miner and owner of a small grocery store, and Elizabeth Daugherty, a homemaker, Duffy was raised with his siblings in football-mad west-central Pennsylvania. As a youngster he played amateur football for the "Alley Eleven" in Barnesboro, Pennsylvania. He played center for the Barnesboro High School football team, and after graduating from Barnesboro in 1932 he worked for two years in the Phillips-Jones Shirt Factory, then for two more years in the coal mines of Arcadia, Pennsylvania. Weary of getting up at 4:30 each morning to go to work in the cold, dark mines, Daugherty decided that there had to be a better way to earn a living.

Duffy Daugherty, 1957. UPI/CORBIS-BETTMANN

Fortunately, he met Jim Rorapaugh, a former Syracuse University football player, who saw Daugherty play amateur football and recommended him to Syracuse University's head football coach, Vic Hansen. After receiving an academic scholarship, Daugherty agreed to attend Syracuse and play on the football team as an offensive lineman. Although he broke his neck during his junior-year season, he came back his senior year in 1939 as captain of the team.

Upon graduation Daugherty stayed at Syracuse to coach the offensive and defensive lines for the freshman team. He joined the U.S. Army in 1940. In 1942, before being shipped overseas to serve in World War II, Daugherty married Francie Steccati; they had two children. He received the Bronze Star for his service during the war. After his discharge, with the rank of major, Daugherty was asked by Clarence "Biggie" Munn, head football coach at Syracuse, to sign on as assistant coach. After one season with the Orangemen, in 1947 Daugherty followed Munn to Michigan State University, where he served as assistant coach for seven years before replacing Munn as head coach in 1954. Munn's teams at MSU went 54–9–2, and Daugherty's offensive and defensive lines earned the name Duffy's Toughies for their aggressive and effective play.

During his nineteen-year tenure as head football coach at Michigan State, Daugherty became known for his dry wit and bone-crushing defensive teams. A self-described realist who believed a successful football program was essential for raising money to support nonrevenue sports and other university programs, Daugherty directed much of his humor—and anger—toward those who did not appreciate the demands of coaching a top-level National Collegiate Athletic Association (NCAA) college football team. He believed that a "football coach's main problem is that he is responsible to irresponsible people." The irresponsible people he referred to included Big Ten conference officials, university administrators, and boosters. At one time or another he thought that each of these groups had prevented him from accomplishing the job he was hired to do. "Winning is the name of the game," he said.

Despite his complaints that antiquated Big Ten conference rules tied the hands of football coaches and prevented their teams from keeping pace with those of other conferences, Daugherty was successful at his job. In addition to winning two conference titles and finishing second four other times, MSU finished among the top ten teams in the nation seven times during his nineteen seasons. In 1965 MSU had a 10–0 record during the regular season and included on its roster such greats as Gene Washington, Bubba Smith, and Clint Jones. MSU's impenetrable defense held three teams, Notre Dame, Ohio State, and Michigan, to minus rushing yardage, while two others, Northwestern and Iowa, could manage only seven and one yards on the ground, respectively. Despite its loss to UCLA in the Rose Bowl in January 1966, MSU's 1965 team is ranked as one of the greatest teams ever to play college football. The nucleus of this team returned in 1966 and completed a successful 9–0–1 season. The second-ranked Spartans played the top-ranked Irish of Notre Dame to a nationally televised 10–10 tie in the last game of the season. Despite outplaying Notre Dame in almost every facet of the game, both offensively and defensively, MSU lost the top spot to the Irish in the polls at season's end.

For most of his career at MSU, Daugherty had the advantage of working for a football-friendly university president, John Hannah. Daugherty believed a strong football program required a supportive administration. He attributed much of the success of MSU football up until 1969 to the "gung-ho interest and aggressive support" of President Hannah. Daugherty became increasingly disenchanted with Hannah's successor, Clifton R. Wharton, Jr., during the 1970, 1971, and 1972 seasons. In Daugherty's mind, Wharton did not appreciate the needs of a winning football program. He pointed to Wharton's cuts in the athletic budget as evidence of this. Wharton wished to make academics a priority over athletics and to spend money to expand the school's educational mission to the underprivileged. By 1972 MSU's athletic budget, football coaches' salaries, and athletic facilities had declined to ninth in the Big Ten.

When not holding Wharton responsible for his teams' troubles, Daugherty often aimed his criticism at MSU alumni. Instead of griping about poor-performing teams, Daugherty believed, the alumni should get more involved in the recruitment of blue-chip players. "Now, if Michigan State is once again to excel as a national football power . . . the alumni and friends of the school are going to have to get their feet wet and their hands dirty," he said. Exactly what he wanted the alumni to do was unclear, but consistent with his narrow-minded focus on victories, he seemed to encourage the sort of involvement that has since put many schools, including MSU, in trouble with the NCAA for providing illegal incentives to get prospects to commit to the school.

After placing the blame for the mediocrity of his teams during the early 1970s on President Wharton, the alumni, and Big Ten regulations, Daugherty resigned in 1973. Shortly after his resignation he said, "Maybe things were too sweet too long at Michigan State while Dr. Hannah was president. I had hoped to coach a few more years, but when he left the downhill slide began."

Following his retirement Daugherty worked for a short time as a television commentator on college football games for the American Broadcasting Companies. He then retired to Santa Barbara, California, with his wife, Francie, where he died at Santa Barbara Cottage Hospital from heart and kidney failure. He is buried in Santa Barbara.

Daugherty is best remembered as a hardworking man of Scotch-Irish descent who learned his work ethic, love of football, and sense of humor while growing up amid the coal mines of Pennsylvania. While innovative in his coaching, Daugherty's progressive ideology could best be witnessed in his vision for the future of college football, which he saw as a business; as such he believed that college officials should think of how best to attract fans to the stadium or their television sets to watch games. For example, he argued in the 1960s for a football playoff to determine a national champion. He was also instrumental in convincing the Big Ten to do away with the no-repeat rule, which prevented a team from going to the Rose Bowl two years in a row, and the no-redshirt rule, which prevented coaches from sitting players out one year to extend their eligibility.

Daugherty was effective at concealing his obsessive drive for victories behind his homespun humor. Players, coaches, fans, and the media were so taken by his charm that they seldom appreciated the underside of his intense competitiveness. While his wit had served him well through the 1960s, by the 1970s he was finding it increasingly difficult to persuade people to his point of view with a few well-timed jokes. In the context of a politically charged atmosphere, Daugherty was an anachronism, preaching the value of competitive sports on a university campus mired in social and political problems. While other coaching legends of this time, such as Bear Bryant, benefited from sympathetic administrations, Daugherty found himself out of the mainstream at a university that for a time tried to focus its attention on the pressing issues confronting its community and the nation.

★

The best anecdotal information about Daugherty can be found in his autobiography, *Duffy* (1974), which includes an introduction by Howard Cossell. Feature articles on Daugherty appeared in popular magazines during his more successful seasons. Most of these focus on his working-class background and dry wit. The three best examples are in *Time* (8 Oct. 1956) and the *Saturday Evening Post* (17 Nov. 1956 and 4 Nov. 1967). Obituaries are in the *New York Times* (26 Sept. 1987) and *Time* (5 Oct. 1987).

TROY D. PAINO

DAVIS, Bette (*b.* 5 April 1908 in Lowell, Massachusetts; *d.* 6 October 1989 in Neuilly-sur-Seine, France), Academy Award–winning film star.

Born Ruth Elizabeth Davis, she was the elder of the two daughters of Harlow Morrell Davis, a patent lawyer, and Ruthie Favor. Her parents divorced when Davis was seven. She and her sister were raised, often in trying circumstances, in New England by their devoted mother, who became a portrait photographer. Davis attended several boarding schools and, in her teens, began calling herself Bette after Honoré de Balzac's nineteenth-century novel *Cousin Bette.* She acted in school plays and in semiprofessional stock productions and, in the summer of 1925, studied interpretive dance at New Hampshire's Mariarden artists' colony. After graduating from Cushing Academy in Ashburnham, Massachusetts, in 1927, she studied acting in New York City at the John Murray Anderson–Robert Milton School, where her dance teacher was Martha Graham.

Bette Davis, 1962. JOEL KUDLER/ARCHIVE PHOTOS

Davis got a small role in a Rochester stock company production of *Broadway* (1928), acted and ushered on Cape Cod, and then rejoined the Rochester company. She made her New York City debut off Broadway at the Provincetown Playhouse in *The Earth Between* (1929), after which she toured with Blanche Yurka's repertory company, appearing in two plays by Henrik Ibsen, *The Wild Duck* and *The Lady from the Sea*. Davis then acted on Broadway in *Broken Dishes* (1929) and *Solid South* (1930). Failing her first screen test for Samuel Goldwyn that year, she passed her second for Universal Pictures and signed her first Hollywood contract.

Davis eventually made eighty-seven movies. Her first was as the good sister in *Bad Sister* (1931), and, with her natural ash-blond hair considerably lightened, she was soon churning out four to six mostly disposable films a year. On 18 August 1932 Davis married her high school boyfriend Harmon ("Ham") Oscar Nelson, Jr., a musician. They had no children. Her career was boosted when she played opposite George Arliss in *The Man Who Played God* (1932). That year she signed a long-term contract with Warner Brothers, with whom she made many of her most memorable films. In a series of nasty battles with the studio head Jack Warner over her roles, scripts, salary, directors, and contractual restrictions, she complained that stars at Metro-Goldwyn-Mayer (MGM) were given the royal treatment, while Warner Brothers' stars were treated like factory workers. Nevertheless, she was so successful for the studio that she was labeled "the fourth Warner brother."

By the end of the 1930s Davis was known as "First Lady of the American Screen" and was the industry's top-ranked female draw. Among her most important performances in that decade were *So Big* (1932), with Barbara Stanwyck; *The Cabin in the Cotton* (1932), in which she captured the bitchiness of a teenage slattern so well that roles with similar qualities became identified with her; *Ex-Lady* (1933), an inferior work in which she first had star billing; and *Fog over Frisco* (1934), junk kept afloat by Davis's excellence. In 1934 she won a fight with Warner Brothers for permission to film *Of Human Bondage* on loan-out to RKO, and her role as the ruthless cockney waitress Mildred, opposite Leslie Howard, established her, after twenty-two tries, as a major actress. In *Bordertown* (1935) she had a powerful mad scene. Playing an actress on the skids in *Dangerous* (1935), she won her first Academy Award, which she and others claimed she had deserved for *Of Human Bondage.* Upon accepting the award, she quipped that its backside resembled her spouse's, which led to its nickname, "Oscar." *The Petrified Forest* (1936) revealed her strength in a subdued dramatic role.

Davis's biggest conflict with Warner Brothers was a dispute over a role in 1936 that led to her suspension and stopped her salary of $5,000 a week. She was offered $50,000 to make two films in Europe for the British filmmaker Ludovic Toeplitz, but Warner Brothers issued an injunction while she was in London. Davis took the studio to court, but her contract was upheld. She was also liable for all court costs, but in 1938 the studio agreed to cover a generous portion of them. This did not, however, end the star's frequent hostility toward management, which often prompted her to walk off sets claiming illness or exhaustion, sometimes feigned, sometimes real.

She appeared in *Marked Woman* (1937); and in *Kid Galahad* (1937) as Edward G. Robinson's moll. For *Jezebel* (1938), as a headstrong southern belle under William Wyler's brilliant direction, she snared her second Oscar. That year Davis and Nelson divorced. Davis's other films of the 1930s include *The Sisters* (1938); *Dark Victory* (1939), a favorite in which she played a dying society lass and for which she won an Academy Award nomination; *The Old Maid* (1939), costarring with her contemporary rival, Miriam Hopkins; *The Private Lives of Elizabeth and Essex* (1939), her first Technicolor movie; and *All This and Heaven Too* (1940). *The Letter* (1940) was another Wyler coup, of which the critic Pauline Kael later wrote that Davis, who had earned her fourth Oscar nomination, gave "what is very likely the best study of female sexual hypocrisy in film history." Most of Davis's other films of the period were less than mediocre. Among her costars were Humphrey Bogart, Spencer Tracy, Paul Muni, James Cagney, Henry Fonda, Errol Flynn, George Brent, and Charles Boyer, yet she always resented that the studio system prevented her from acting with Clark Gable and Gary Cooper. On 31 December 1940 Davis married Arthur Austin Farnsworth, a hotel manager and an alcoholic, who died mysteriously in 1943. They had no children.

During the 1940s, despite some of her strongest efforts, Davis grew less busy. In 1948 she earned $385,000 and was filmdom's best-paid star. One of her greatest roles was in Wyler's *The Little Foxes* (1941), made when she was on loan to MGM. In that movie, as the grasping Regina, she earned her fifth Oscar nomination despite a quarrel with Wyler, who refused to let her copy Tallulah Bankhead's stage interpretation. Other notable films include *The Man Who Came to Dinner* (1941), one of her few comedies; *Now, Voyager* (1942), a grand tearjerker in which she and costar Paul Henreid popularized the romantic practice of a man lighting two cigarettes and passing one to his lover (she was again nominated for an Oscar); *Thank Your Lucky Stars* (1943), in which she sang and danced; *Watch on the Rhine* (1943); *Old Acquaintance* (1943); *Mr. Skeffington* (1944), which costarred Claude Rains and gained Davis a seventh Oscar nomination; *Hollywood Canteen* (1944), a picture glorifying the eponymous United Service Organizations (USO) center she helped to found; and *The Corn Is Green* (1945). On 30 November 1945 she wed William Grant Sherry, an artist. They had one daughter. *A Stolen Life* (1946), her only film produced under the aegis of her own company, B.D., Inc., allowed her to play dual roles. In the same year she appeared in *Deception* with Rains and Henreid. *Beyond the Forest* (1949) was her last Warner Brothers film, notable mainly because of her often-quoted line "What a dump!" She divorced Sherry, a physically abusive alcoholic, in 1950. Her final film of the decade was the outstanding *All About Eve* (1950), in which she replaced Claudette Colbert, who was ailing, in the role of the aging Broadway star Margo Channing (a character portrayal based on the actress Elisabeth Bergner) and landed her eighth Oscar nomination for what many consider her finest role. This was the first of several films she made with her fourth spouse, Gary Merrill, whom she married that year.

She and Merrill adopted two children, one of whom was retarded and eventually institutionalized.

During the 1950s, Davis made nine movies, two of which she filmed abroad. Her best work was seen in *The Star* (1952), for which, in a role based on her rival Joan Crawford, Davis received Oscar nomination number nine. In *The Virgin Queen* (1955) she portrayed Elizabeth I for the second time. *The Catered Affair* (1956), with the role of Aggie, was her favorite, despite critical disapproval. Some critics reprimanded her for selecting scripts designed more to showcase her performances than to create quality films. She returned to the stage in 1952 with *Two's Company* (1952), a revue, and *The World of Carl Sandburg* (1959), a program of readings in which she performed with Merrill and other actors. She and Merrill, an alcoholic who was also physically abusive, divorced in 1960.

Davis appeared on Broadway in the supporting role of Maxine in Tennessee Williams's play *The Night of the Iguana* (1961), but she was unhappy and departed after four months. She made eight movies in the 1960s, of which *Pocketful of Miracles* (1961) and *The Nanny* (1965) were second-rate offerings. However, she had good material in *Whatever Happened to Baby Jane?* (1962); *Dead Ringer* (1964), in which she played twins; and *Hush, Hush Sweet Charlotte* (1964). In *Baby Jane,* one of several macabre horror flicks she starred in, Davis played an unbalanced former child star opposite Joan Crawford as her sister, and their rivalry afforded journalists a field day. It also inspired Davis's tenth Academy Award nomination and became an international smash. Despite having signed on to the film for a small fee of $25,000, Davis earned more than $1 million from *Baby Jane* because she owned a percentage of the take. In early 1962, before the movie was released, Davis, unaware of the movie's potential, took out a controversial, self-mocking advertisement in *Variety,* noting that she was "mobile still and more affable than rumor would have it. Wants steady employment in Hollywood." Davis's work in *Sweet Charlotte,* which costarred Olivia De Havilland and was of the same genre as *Baby Jane,* was considered her best of the decade.

Davis had been acting on major television programs, such as *General Electric Theatre* and *Perry Mason,* since the 1950s, but in the 1970s, she also began to make television movies on a regular basis, commencing with *Madame Sin* (1971). During the 1970s and 1980s, she made stage appearances in *Bette Davis in Person* (1973), in which she chatted about her career with fans, and starred in *Miss Moffat* (1974), an unsuccessful musical version of *The Corn Is Green* that folded in Philadelphia. In 1977 Davis was the first woman to receive the American Film Institute's Lifetime Achievement Award. She also acted in seven movies, playing secondary or cameo roles, as in *Death on the Nile* (1978). In 1979 she won an Emmy for *Strangers: The Story of a Mother and a Daughter*. Her final film of note was *The Whales of August* (1987), costarring Lillian Gish, in which her talent remained luminous despite the obvious effects of a recent stroke. During her last film, *The Wicked Stepmother* (1989), she was so dissatisfied with the direction, script, and photography that she quit midway.

Davis was a heavy drinker and a five-pack-a-day chain smoker whose filmic way with a cigarette was famous. She was involved in a series of love affairs and had three abortions. Biographers also note her obsessive-compulsive tidiness. Her daughter, B. D. Hyman, wrote two tell-all books about her mother's destructive behavior that led to the pair's estrangement. Davis told her own story in several books, one of which responded to her daughter's charges.

Davis suffered from numerous ailments in her later years. She succumbed to cancer in Neuilly-sur-Seine, France, after being honored at a film festival in Spain. She is buried in Forest Lawn Memorial Park in Los Angeles.

Davis's strong will was reflected in her many roles as fiercely independent women, and she acquired an often justified reputation as a willful, bellicose, and impossible-to-work-with virago. Still, many thought her a consummate professional who was always prepared, thoroughly knowledgeable about what was best for her, and simply unwilling to brook anything less from her coworkers.

Although Davis often fought for better roles and wasted time in feeble films, her biographer Barbara Leaming insists that, once she was established, she rarely made the best choices, even when she briefly headed her own company. Nevertheless, she played an unusually wide range of demanding characters, from drunks to glamour queens to retiring old maids to lunatics, which made her difficult to type. Even with her commanding versatility, she was best suited for characters, good and bad, who required a brassy but controlled edge, emotional intensity, and depth. Only five feet, two inches tall, she was noted for her unusually large eyes, and in 1982 a hit song was titled "Bette Davis Eyes." Although physical beauty was not her strong point, she could seem strikingly attractive. Upon meeting her, Carl Laemmle of Universal Pictures thought she had "as much sex appeal as Slim Summerville," referring to a homely actor of the day. Unlike most other stars of her generation, she was willing to let herself look unglamorous and even shaved her eyebrows and the front of her scalp to play Queen Elizabeth. Frequently speaking in a clipped and emphatic manner, she possessed physical grace and an ability to make gestures and movements emotional—attributable, perhaps, to her training with Martha Graham. These traits grew mannered and even baroque as her career progressed, and Davis has been much imitated by campy female impersonators. But she could provide electrifying performances when given the right material and direction, and during her declining years, she was honored at many film festivals. During Davis's era, only Katharine Hepburn won more Academy Award nominations.

★

Davis's autobiographies are *The Lonely Life* (1962; rev. ed. 1990) and *This 'n' That* (1987). She contributed significantly to Whitney Stine, *Mother Goddam* (1974). Her daughter's accounts are B. D. Hyman, *My Mother's Keeper* (1985), and B. D. Hyman and Jeremy Hyman, *Narrow Is the Way* (1987). Her former husband described their relationship in Gary Merrill, *Bette, Rita, and the Rest of My Life* (1988). Revealing interviews with and about her are in Boze Hadleigh, *Bette Davis Speaks* (1996). Biographies and career overviews include Jerry Vermilye, *Bette Davis* (1973); Charles Higham, *Bette: The Life of Bette Davis* (1981); Jeffrey Robinson, *Bette Davis: Her Film and Stage Career* (1982); Christopher Nickens, *Bette Davis* (1985); Gene Ringgold, *Bette Davis: Her Films and Career* (1985); Lawrence J. Quirk, *Fasten Your Seat Belts: The Passionate Life of Bette Davis* (1990); Alexander Walker, *Bette Davis* (1986); Roy Mosley, *Bette Davis: An Intimate Memoir* (1990); and Barbara Leaming, *Bette Davis: A Biography* (1992). Obituaries are in the *New York Times* (8 Oct. 1989) and *Variety* (11–17 Oct. 1989).

SAMUEL L. LEITER

Sammy Davis, Jr. NEIL PRESTON/CORBIS

DAVIS, Sammy, Jr. (*b.* 8 December 1925 in New York City; *d.* 16 May 1990 in Beverly Hills, California), variety artist known for his impressions, tap dancing, and singing, who performed in nightclubs, films, television, recording studios, and on Broadway.

Sammy Davis, Jr., was born in a Harlem tenement at 140th Street and Eighth Avenue, to parents who were both in show business. His mother, Elvera ("Baby") Sanchez, was a chorus girl; his father, Sam Davis, Sr., was the chief dancer in the vaudeville revue *Will Mastin's Holiday in Dixieland.* Because his parents were constantly on the road, young Sammy was left to the loving care of his paternal grandmother, Rosa B. Davis, whom Davis would always refer to as Mama. When Sammy was two, his parents had a daughter, Ramona (Sammy's only sibling), whom they sent to live with his mother's family. Six months later his parents separated. His mother joined another traveling show while his father, who had gained custody of the boy, came home only long enough to take Sammy on the road.

Sammy was a talented youngster, constantly mimicking the singing and dancing of his father and Will Mastin, who became Sammy's second parent. Recognizing the precocious abilities of the youngster, who had won a dance contest when he was three, Mastin created a spot for the boy in the renamed revue, *The Will Mastin Trio,* featuring himself, Sam, Sr., and Sammy. Because of the itinerant nature of the vaudeville revue, the boy never spent a day of his life in a formal school setting, receiving a haphazard academic education from occasional tutors. He also obtained a great deal of show business education from Mastin, whom Sammy called Uncle Will. Mastin taught him that there are only two things to remember in show business: making an impression on members of an audience and leaving them with it.

Pearl Harbor was bombed the day before Davis's sixteenth birthday. He wanted to sign up for the service but was turned down because of his age. Turning eighteen, he was drafted, but because of an enlarged-heart condition, he could not be shipped out for duty overseas. He requested special services, but the army had few openings for variety artists. Davis was recycled through basic training several times in Cheyenne, Wyoming, while the army tried to figure out what to do with him. During this time he suffered harsh treatment because of his race. Small and frail, five feet, six inches in height and never weighing more than 130 pounds, Davis fought back futilely with his fists, a response which resulted in a broken nose and even more humiliation.

A black platoon leader admired his courage and tried to help the recruit. He introduced Davis to the world of books, giving him remedial reading lessons and lending him books. Having finished *Cyrano de Bergerac,* Davis realized that violence would not help him and that his talent was the best weapon with which to fight racism and hatred.

Discharged from the army, Davis rejoined his father and Will Mastin, who were struggling more than ever because the film industry had all but killed theatrical vaudeville. The trio managed to book opening acts at Las Vegas even though they had to sleep in the Negro section of the city, on the outskirts of town. In their act, Davis did Louis Armstrong and Stepin Fetchit impressions but really wowed the nightclub crowds by being the first black impressionist to do white stars such as Jimmy Cagney, Edward G. Robinson, and Jimmy Durante.

During this time Davis met Frank Sinatra, who was singing with Jimmy Dorsey's band. Sinatra and another show business friend, Mickey Rooney, helped the trio with bookings. Their first major breakthrough came in 1951 on Academy Awards night at Ciro's, a Hollywood nightclub where the trio opened for Janis Paige. Davis's performance earned him instant stardom, and shortly thereafter, offers for appearances flowed in. The trio's appearance on Eddie Cantor's *Colgate Comedy Hour* led to a contract as the show's summer replacement. Decca Records signed Sammy, and in 1954 he recorded his first album, *Starring Sammy Davis, Jr.,* which gained the number-one chart position of 1955.

On 19 November 1954, while driving from Las Vegas after a big finish with "Birth of the Blues" at the New Frontier Hotel, Davis was involved in an automobile accident; his face smashed into the cone in the center of his Cadillac convertible's steering wheel, resulting in the loss of his left eye. At the time Davis was making $7,500 a week and was on his way to record his first movie sound track in Los Angeles. While convalescing at Community Hospital in San Bernardino, Davis felt the need for spiritual strength. His father was a Baptist, and his mother had been a Catholic, but Davis had never practiced any formal religion. Influenced by the hospital visits of a rabbi, he converted to Judaism and often joked afterward that he was the only "colored, one-eyed Jewish entertainer" in the history of show business.

When released from the hospital, Davis received tremendous media coverage. Thereafter, he would use any means to keep his name before the public, confident that this was the secret of making money in the entertainment world. The constant publicity worked, earning for the Will Mastin Trio, now headlined "Featuring Sammy Davis, Jr.," offers averaging $15,000 a week. Davis's eye patch for a while was a trademark of the act, even after his doctors had implanted a realistic-looking plastic eye (he stopped using the patch in 1956).

Although critics raved about Davis's dynamic talents, they were not so enthusiastic about his father or Will Mastin, many of them claiming that the two old vaudevillians were hampering the young performer. Sammy, however, refused to abandon the two, splitting the net proceeds from even his solo performances three ways.

Davis sought new outlets for his indefatigable energy. In 1955 his recording "Black Magic" was the number-one radio song in the country. The trio made its Broadway debut in 1956 in Jule Styne's *Mr. Wonderful,* Broadway's first fully integrated play. The play ran for 383 performances. Afterward, Davis turned to television, viewing the medium as yet another way to remain before the public eye. In 1958 he became the first black to star in episodic television when he appeared on the *General Electric Theatre,* receiving an Emmy nomination for his performance. At the same time he enhanced his movie career, appearing in *The Benny Goodman Story* (1956), in *Anna Lucasta* (1958) as a down-to-earth sailor, and in the role of Sportin' Life in the screen version of *Porgy and Bess* (1959).

In the early 1960s Davis became a permanent member of the infamous Rat Pack, the closely knit clique of fast- and loose-living entertainers consisting of Frank Sinatra, Dean Martin, Joey Bishop, and Peter Lawford. The Pack made six movies together: *Ocean's Eleven* (1960), *Sergeants Three* (1962), *Johnny Cool* (1963), *Robin and the Seven Hoods* (1964), *Salt and Pepper* (1968), and *One More Time* (1970). The movies were very popular because the five stars had great drawing power. When the Rat Pack went to Las Vegas to shoot scenes for *Ocean's Eleven* at the Sands Hotel and Casino while simultaneously performing together at the hotel's nightclub, they created a media sensation resulting in sold-out shows for their "Summit at the Sands."

Membership in the Rat Pack brought Davis wealth and publicity but it wreaked havoc on his personal life. His relationship with Loray White, a black dancer whom he had married on 1 January 1958 to show the public that he was willing to settle down to family life and abandon his free-living style, ended in divorce the following year.

On 13 November 1961 Davis married May (pronounced "My") Britt, a Swedish actress. The interracial marriage resulted in hate mail and so many death threats that Davis had to hire personal bodyguards. To protect his wife from accusatory stares and racial epithets, he refused to take her out, remaining at home or in a hotel room while on the road. The couple had two children and adopted a third. May gave up her film career to care for the children. The pressure of bringing up interracial children in an age of rampant racial prejudice—plus the fact that Davis yearned more than ever for the public's adulation and sought to obtain it through a frenzied marathon of performances—would lead to another divorce in 1968.

Davis engaged in one such frenzied marathon in 1966 when he was simultaneously involved in three projects. He performed on Broadway in *Golden Boy,* by Clifford Odets, portraying a young black man involved in an interracial love affair who has to decide between a career as a rich prizefighter or a poor violinist; Davis won a Tony Award for his dramatization. He was also doing his own one-hour television variety program, *The Sammy Davis, Jr., Show,* which premiered 7 January 1966 with guest stars Elizabeth Taylor and Richard Burton. In addition, he somehow found time to make a movie, *A Man Called Adam* (1966), the story of the rise and fall of a black jazz musician.

On 11 May 1970 Davis married Altovise Gore, a black dancer whom he had met while doing *Golden Boy* in London. The couple later adopted a son, Manny.

The 1970s were prolific years for the indefatigable performer, who no longer shared the spotlight with his father and Mastin. In frequent appearances on Rowan and Martin's hit television program, *Laugh-in,* he immortalized the line "Here come de judge" (borrowed from an old routine by "Pigmeat" Markham). When he appeared as the first guest star in a 1972 episode of *All in the Family* and planted a kiss on the cheek of the bigoted character Archie Bunker, the show broke all previous Nielsen ratings. In the same year he recorded "Candy Man," his all-time best-selling record and one of his signature songs, along with "I've Gotta Be Me," "Mr. Bojangles," and "What Kind of Fool Am I?"

While his popularity as an entertainer was at its peak, he was attacked by the black press on the charge of trying to be white. Accusations increased when, at a Young Voters for Nixon rally during the August 1972 Republican Convention in Miami Beach, Davis suddenly hugged President Richard M. Nixon, who had appeared unannounced and made some flattering remarks about Davis, a loyal supporter of John F. Kennedy in the 1960 campaign. Photos of the hug appeared in newspapers across the country, setting off a wave of attacks against the performer by the black and the liberal press.

Eventually, years of easy living and chronic drinking and smoking caught up with Davis. He developed liver and kidney problems, and in 1974 suffered a mild heart attack. After a short recovery period, Davis returned to an energetic performance schedule. A new television variety show, *Sammy and Company,* ran for two seasons, from 1975 to 1977. He continued his recording and film career, making the highly successful *Cannonball Run* movies in 1981 and 1984. His last movie, *Tap* (1989), was a tribute to the great tap dancers of the past.

In his final concert, appearing with Frank Sinatra and Liza Minnelli in "The Ultimate Event" at the Brendan Byrne Arena in New Jersey in 1988, Davis stole the show with his effervescent entertaining, even though hip-replacement surgery three years earlier curtailed his dancing. He was scheduled to go on another tour with Sinatra and Minnelli when, in September 1989, during his annual medical examination, Davis was diagnosed with cancer of the throat. He began eight weeks of radiation treatments. In November, a benefit for the United Negro College Fund held in Los Angeles celebrated Davis's sixty-year-long show business career. Saluted by celebrity friends such as Frank Sinatra, Dean Martin, Bob Hope, and Michael Jackson, Davis managed a very slow tap dance with Gregory Hines, his costar in *Tap*.

In January 1990 Davis was admitted to Cedars-Sinai Medical Center in Los Angeles for treatment of a gum infection, but doctors found a recurrence of throat cancer. He was released on 13 March and died two months later at the age of sixty-four. At his funeral service on 18 May at Forest Lawn Memorial Park in Los Angeles, Frank Sinatra, Dean Martin, Michael Jackson, and Bill Cosby served as pallbearers. The Reverend Jesse Jackson said in the eulogy, "He has answered the curtain call over and over and over again, and now we want an encore. Encore, encore no more. Let him rest. Let Mr. Bojangles rest. He has earned it."

★

Sammy Davis, Jr., with Jane and Burt Boyar, *Yes I Can* (1965), the starting point for anyone wishing to learn more about the celebrity, covers everything from Davis's birth to the birth of his daughter in 1964. Sammy Davis, Jr., *Hollywood in a Suitcase* (1980), is a mixture of personal anecdotes about the entertainment business and political observations that do not contribute a great deal to understanding the entertainer himself. Sammy Davis, Jr., with Jane and Burt Boyar, *Why Me? The Sammy Davis, Jr., Story* (1989), condenses most of the material in *Yes I Can* and adds details of the performer's life in the 1970s and 1980s. Tracey Davis with Dolores A. Barclay, *Sammy Davis, Jr.: My Father* (1996), is a somewhat sentimental look at the performer from his daughter's point of view. A biographical sketch is in Charles Moritz, ed., *Current Biography 1978* (1979). Lerone Bennett, Jr., "Sammy Davis, Jr., 1925–1990: The Legacy of the World's Greatest Entertainer," *Ebony* (July 1990), is a picture-filled biography of the celebrity's personal and professional lives. Obituaries are in the *New York Times* (17 May 1990), *People Weekly* (28 May 1990), and *Time* (28 May 1990).

JOHN J. BYRNE

DAVISON, William Edward ("Wild Bill") (*b.* 5 January 1906 in Defiance, Ohio; *d.* 14 November 1989 in Santa Barbara, California), jazz cornetist whose original style was a dominant force in traditional "hot" jazz from the 1920s through the 1950s.

Davison's father, Edward Davison, an itinerant worker, and his mother, Anna (Kreps) Davison, left him in 1913 to be raised by his maternal grandparents. His natural musical ability quickly became apparent, and he easily mastered the mandolin, banjo, and guitar. He joined the Boy Scouts in order to play the bugle as a step toward the cornet, which he took up at age twelve. Davison so admired its rich sound that he never sought to play the sharper-toned trumpet, nor did he ever take lessons. With perfect pitch and a flawless musical memory, he could master the melody, chord

"Wild Bill" Davison. METRONOME/ARCHIVE PHOTOS

progressions, and harmony of any tune after only one hearing. Although he eventually developed some music-reading skills, they were never strong—or necessary for his unique approach to jazz.

As a member of the home-based Ohio Lucky Seven, from 1919 to 1923, Davison matured rapidly. He scrutinized the trumpet solos of Louis Panico on records made by the Isham Jones Orchestra and, after hearing the pure tones of the widely influential cornetist Bix Beiderbecke in 1923, Davison abandoned the use of mutes in favor of an open bell. The driving power that characterized Davison's solos was inspired by Louis Armstrong, who Davison first heard in Chicago in 1927. Although Davison was the featured soloist with the Cincinnati-based Chubb-Steinberg Orchestra from 1923 to 1925 and the Detroit-based Seattle Harmony Kings from 1926 to 1928, he occasionally fronted his own small jazz bands. His big, colorful, individual sound, which was made possible by his strong lip, led to a starring role in the Benny Meroff Orchestra, Chicago's leading dance band, between 1928 and 1931. Because Davison and many contemporary white jazz bands in Chicago played their own brand of hot, four-beat swinging jazz, its admirers dubbed it "Chicago-style" jazz, erroneously linking it with two-beat New Orleans (or Dixieland) jazz. Nevertheless, when these players, who later became identified with the jazz guitarist Eddie Condon, migrated, like Condon, to New York City during the 1930s, this fairly meaningless term traveled with them.

Davison, lacking both initiative and the prospect of employment in New York City, remained behind in Chicago. He formed his own twelve-piece band in 1931, built around his cornet and the clarinet and alto saxophone of Frank Teschemacher. Once, when he arrived at Chicago's Savoy Ballroom for a "battle" with the black band of Tiny Parham, Davison was surprised by the effusive sign, "Wild Bill Davison, the White Louis Armstrong." The promoter had clearly likened Davison's powerful playing to that of Armstrong, but the "wildness" also reflected Davison's reputation for alcoholic consumption, sexual appetite, a playful kleptomania, and general antics, traits that rarely affected his playing or his immaculate attire. Davison's casual attitude toward women was reflected by his many marriages, the first four of which ended in either annulment or divorce. He had one child—by his third wife, Vera Milton—but the baby died in infancy. In 1954 he married starlet Anne Hendlin McLaughlin, who went by the stage name Anne Stewart. This fifth and final marriage gave him stability for the rest of his life.

Davison's fortunes suffered a severe setback in March 1932. His car was hit broadside by another vehicle, his passenger, Teschemacher, was killed, and some musicians unfairly blamed Davison for Teschemacher's death. His big band also suffered from labor union troubles and soon folded. Employment opportunities lured Davison in 1933 to Milwaukee, where he played in several bands and led others until 1941, when a wealthy, admiring widow financed his move to New York City. His reputation as an outstanding cornetist preceded him, and he quickly asserted his musical authority as a member of Condon's "gang." By this time, his nickname had become firmly established.

Davison led the band at Nick's nightclub in Manhattan's Greenwich Village from 1941 to 1942 and at Jimmy Ryan's club on Fifty-second Street ("Swing Street") in 1943. Although he had participated in several unremarkable recordings, beginning in 1925, his first major records were cut in November 1943 with Condon's musicians, but under Davison's name, for the Commodore label. Drafted into the army the next month, he spent most of his military duty leading the band at the Grove Park Inn in Asheville, North Carolina, for convalescing soldiers. Weekend liberties enabled him to play gigs and make records in New York City until his discharge in September 1945. When Condon's own club opened three months later, Davison became its musical leader and major attraction until the club relocated in 1957. Davison's musical powers peaked in the postwar era, a time that included his appearance at the first Newport Jazz Festival in 1954 and his first two

European tours in 1957. Except for his Giants of Jazz group, which performed in 1968 and 1969, after 1962 Davison starred with local bands instead of leading his own. He spent his final two decades playing mostly in Europe, where he was revered. He died following surgery for an abdominal aneurysm shortly after playing a tour in Japan. He was cremated and his ashes were buried in Defiance.

Davison's unique cornet style emanated from boundless energy, optimism, and raw, almost primitive, emotion. In hot numbers, his playing could be searing, in ballads gorgeous and sensual. His solos also displayed humor, which could be biting and even vulgar, like his manner of speaking. When he blew, he angled his horn to the left to force the air past a tooth misaligned by a flying beer bottle sometime in the late 1930s. He suffered from acute stage fright, an inhibition that may have prevented him from rising to star status. As much as any musician, however, Wild Bill Davison epitomized hot jazz during the 1940s and 1950s.

★

The Wild Bill Davison Archives are located at Bowling Green State University, Bowling Green, Ohio. They formed the basis for an exhaustive candid biography, Hal Willard's *The Wildest One: The Life of Wild Bill Davison* (1996), although it contains no discography and very little discussion of the final decade of Davison's life. Davison is also the subject of the 1991 videotape *Wild Bill Davison: His Life, His Times, His Music.* Of some 800 Davison recordings, the most important are those made for Commodore between 1943 and 1950; they were included in boxed LP sets *The Complete Commodore Jazz Recordings* from Mosaic, with explanatory booklets on the musicians. The major recordings under his name are in *Commodore Master Takes,* on CD. Among LP albums of live performances from the same years and the early 1950s are *Wild Bill Davison: Ringside at Condon's* and *The Individualism of Wild Bill Davison,* both on Savoy records, and *"Wild Bill" Davison* on Aircheck. In the mid-1950s Davison was successfully matched with strings in several albums for Columbia, including *Pretty Wild* and *With Strings Attached* and on the single "Yesterdays," released by Circle, which is considered by his biographer to be his greatest recording. Davison appeared in the 1961 film short *Eddie Condon,* in which he is featured on the tune "Blue and Brokenhearted." An obituary is in the *New York Times* (16 Nov. 1989).

CLARK G. REYNOLDS

DAWIDOWICZ, Lucy Schildkret (*b.* 16 June 1915 in New York City; *d.* 5 December 1990 in New York City), Jewish historian and author best known for her examination of the Holocaust in *The War Against the Jews, 1933–1945* (1975).

Dawidowicz was one of two children of Max and Dora (Ofnaem) Schildkret, Polish Jews who had immigrated to New York City and who worked as shopkeepers. She grew up and was educated in New York City.

Lucy Dawidowicz, 1977. NYT PERMISSIONS

In 1936 she received her B.A. degree in history from Hunter College in New York City. She accepted a postgraduate research fellowship at the Yivo Institute of Jewish Research and in 1938 went to live in Vilna, Poland (later Vilnius, Lithuania), remaining there into 1939. As she told *Publishers Weekly* in 1989, "There was a certain irony to my trip to Vilna. I went there with the romantic belief that it might become the world center for a self-sustaining Yiddish culture." Instead she witnessed the beginning of the end of Jewish life and culture in much of Europe and particularly in Poland. Having observed at first hand the growth of European anti-Semitism and the intricate and all-encompassing architecture of the Nazi program concerning the Jews, including the planned extermination of European Jewish culture, she saw ahead to the necessity of reestablishing and preserving that culture after the war. With this goal in mind she took a position as assistant research director of the Yivo Institute in New York City from 1940 to

1946 and immersed herself in studying Yiddish literature and Jewish history and culture.

After World War II, Dawidowicz returned to Europe, where she worked as an education officer in the displaced-persons camps with the American Jewish Joint Distribution Committee in 1946 and 1947. She helped Jewish survivors of the Holocaust to re-create schools and libraries. She also helped the Allies to recover and catalog vast collections of books that had been seized by the Nazis.

After returning to the United States in 1947, she met Szymon Dawidowicz, a political refugee from Poland, through the American Jewish Committee. She married him on 3 January 1948; they had no children. That same year she took a position as a research analyst for the committee. She remained with the organization until 1969, eventually becoming its research director. Earning an M.A. degree from Columbia University in 1961, she served on the faculty of Yeshiva University from 1969 to 1978, where she was named the Paul and Leah Lewis Professor of Holocaust Studies (1970–1975) and the Eli and Diana Zborowski Professor of Interdisciplinary Holocaust Studies (1976–1978). She was a member of the President's Commission on the Holocaust in 1978 and 1979.

Throughout her career, as Dawidowicz published and edited numerous articles and books, sometimes in collaboration with other scholars and historians, her own focus as a historian held fast to a central question: whether the Holocaust was a central or secondary policy of the Nazi war effort. *The War Against the Jews, 1933–1945* (1975), the work that established her preeminence as a Jewish historian, was the culmination of firsthand observations of the Third Reich's policy toward European Jewry, her postwar work with survivors in the displaced persons camps, and her subsequent research. *The War Against the Jews* caused a controversy within the historical community because of its contention that the planned annihilation of European Jews was always a central element of the Nazi ideology, was always one of the major war objectives of the Third Reich, and was just as important as the territorial objectives of the war. Other historians disagreed, taking the stance that the Holocaust evolved in response to setbacks in the war or as a way to deal with the large Jewish population the Nazis had acquired in Eastern Europe.

The War Against the Jews remains a standard work on the Holocaust, comprehensive and painstakingly researched. It examines the Final Solution in a nonemotional manner, allowing the facts to create their own emotional impact as it describes the detailed and deliberate engineering of the Holocaust, from the laws restricting movement and trade, to identification of Jews, to, finally, the creation of the camps and their evolution into places of technological genocide. Dawidowicz does not debate but allows the details to make her argument regarding the way the Third Reich used its entire bureaucratic apparatus and its best technological resources to achieve its goals. At the same time she chronicles the efforts of the Jewish community to hold on to fragments of normal life and culture.

In *The Holocaust and the Historians* (1981), Dawidowicz takes issue with those such as Hannah Arendt, Raul Hilberg, and Bruno Bettelheim who had described the European Jews as cowardly, passive, and even identifying with their Nazi captors. Building on the conclusion she had demonstrated in *The War Against the Jews,* this volume argues essentially that Jewish resistance was futile given the Jews' isolation and lack of arms.

Dawidowicz's research and books refocused how some scholars viewed the evolution of the Holocaust, the response of the Jews, and the effects on European Jewry. She demonstrated that the Final Solution was not a secondary issue to the Third Reich but was planned and executed with the same commitment as the territorial war, a perspective that gave subsequent historians and students deeper insight into both the Jewish response and the Nazi worldview.

Dawidowicz died at age seventy-five and was buried in New York City.

★

Lucy S. Dawidowicz, *From That Place and Time: A Memoir, 1938–1947* (1989), is her only memoir and concentrates solely on her experiences and work during and after World War II. *The War Against the Jews* also gives insight into Dawidowicz's experience in World War II–era Poland. *Who Was Who in America with World Notables,* vol. 10, *1989–1993* (1993), gives a succinct synopsis of Dawidowicz's academic and publishing career. An obituary is in the *New York Times* (6 Dec. 1990).

LISA R. PERRY

DAY, Dennis (*b.* 21 May 1917 in New York City; *d.* 22 June 1988 in Brentwood, California), singer on the Jack Benny radio and television programs, whom Benny called his "smiling Irish songbird."

Dennis Day was born Owen Patrick Dennis McNulty in the Bronx. His father worked in the New York City civil service as an engineer. Day was educated at St. Benedict's parish school in the Bronx, and in 1934 he graduated from Cathedral High School in Manhattan. In 1939 he graduated second in his class at Manhattan College, where he was president of the glee club. He was planning to enter Fordham University Law School when he got his first radio job as an announcer at station WNYC, where he initiated his use of his grandmother's maiden name, calling himself "Dennis Day." He first sang on the radio for Ray Bloch's *Varieties* on the Columbia Broadcasting System.

In October 1939 Day auditioned for the singer's slot on Jack Benny's radio program. When Benny's wife, Mary

Dennis Day. ARCHIVE PHOTOS

Livingstone, began to question him with a "Now, Dennis," he responded "Yes, please?" and got the job on the spot, establishing his persona as the dim-witted Irish tenor. He said in 1946 that he pitched his speaking voice four notes higher than his normal range. In addition to singing, Day filled other roles on the program, particularly as a comic foil to other cast members, and his talent as a mimic served him well in skits and sketches. His outrageous entry lines, such as, "If I have nothing better to do tomorrow, I'm going to join the Foreign Legion," his naive non sequiturs that echoed the lines of Benny and others on the program, and his deference to his overbearing radio mother, played by Vera Felton, drove Benny to comic frustration and the audience to appreciative laughter.

In 1940, in his first appearance in films, Day sang "My Kind of Country" in a spoof Western, *Buck Benny Rides Again.* Between 1940 and 1953, he appeared in six other live-action films and two animated features. He supplied all ten voices in the Johnny Appleseed episode for Walt Disney's cartoon *Melody Time* (1948). In 1944 and 1945, during World War II, Day served in the U.S. Navy, where he organized an entertainment unit with the bandleader Claude Thornhill and performed in 300 shows for the troops in the South Pacific. After legally changing his name to Dennis Day in 1944, he changed it back to McNulty in 1947 "just to keep the Ancient Order of Hibernians happy."

Day's return to Benny's program on 17 March 1946 illustrates his roles as singer, comic foil to Benny, and mimic. When Benny reminisced that he was tossed overboard during his own navy service in World War I, Day responded, "Oh, I was tossed overboard lots of times . . . but the captain made the fellows cut it out." Benny asked, "The boys kept throwing you overboard?" Day replied, "Oh, it wasn't so bad; the Japs kept throwing me back." When Benny asked for a song, Day announced in an obviously fake Irish brogue that he would sing "Danny Boy," which he did in a clear, high tenor, holding the notes firmly with a slight vibrato. His singing was straightforward, well phrased, and free of sobbing or a catch in the throat. In the skit that followed, a takeoff on Fred Allen's program, Day mimicked Allen's farmer, Titus Moody, employing a lower-pitched voice and a New England drawl while trading snappy comebacks with Benny. Day starred as a soda jerk in *A Day in the Life of Dennis Day* on National Broadcasting Company (NBC) television from 1946 to 1951. In 1948 he married Margaret Ellen Almquist; they had ten children. Day's successful recordings for Radio Corporation of America include *Mam'selle* (1947) and *Christmas in Killarney* (1950). His next television role was in the *RCA Victor Show,* and in the autumn of 1952 he became the sole star of the show. In 1953 the name was changed to *The Dennis Day Show,* on which he played a young singer trying to break into show business.

Day's business acumen belied the naïveté of his character. He acted as producer of his shows, he owned the production company, and he delivered the programs to his sponsor on NBC. When in 1953 he realized how much NBC had budgeted for the sets of *The Dennis Day Show,* he had the sets built and saved the difference in cost. He conducted audience testing to develop his character, who was not as simple as the one he played on Benny's program. He stated: "The tests showed that the audience was displeased whenever I got stupid—the Benny type joke, I mean. The most favorable response came when I do something for somebody." Day also owned the building in which the show was filmed and rented out stores on the ground floor to pay his overhead and make a profit. In the 1950s he appeared on Milton Berle's *Texaco Star Theater* and in dramatic anthology series.

Day spoke the penultimate line on Benny's last radio program on 22 May 1955. As Benny gushed appreciation to his cast, writers, and producers, Day cut in, saying: "How can you read that stuff? Doesn't it make you sick?" He carried his role to Benny's television show, which ran from 1950 to 1965, and impersonated the comic actors of other programs, including Cliff Arquette's character, Charlie Weaver, on Jack Paar's *Tonight Show* and Art Carney's character, Ed Norton, on *The Honeymooners.* Day's wife and nine of his children appeared on Benny's television program on 25 September 1964, as Day attempted to rebut the notion that he was just a silly kid. Day appeared on Benny's birthday special in 1969 and on "Jack Benny's Twentieth Anniversary" special in 1970. He returned to television to do voice-overs for animated Christmas specials in 1976 and 1978. He made investments in his television production company, a restaurant chain, oil wells, and the stock market and continued to appear at conventions, fairs, churches, and clubs, performing from a wheelchair after he contracted amyotrophic lateral sclerosis (Lou Gehrig's disease). He died in Brentwood, California, following brain surgery to control bleeding that resulted from a fall.

★

No book-length biography of Day has yet been written. A chapter on Day is in Milt Josefsberg, *The Jack Benny Show* (1977), and numerous references to Day are in Museum of Television and Radio, *Jack Benny: The Radio and Television Work* (1991). Obituaries are in the *Los Angeles Times* (23 June 1988), *New York Times* (24 June 1988), and *Variety* (29 June 1988).

STEPHEN WAGLEY

DEAN, Arthur Hobson (*b.* 16 October 1898 in Ithaca, New York; *d.* 30 November 1987 in Glen Cove, New York), lawyer, diplomat who negotiated some of the most intractable problems of the twentieth century, and adviser to Presidents Roosevelt, Eisenhower, Kennedy, and Johnson.

Arthur H. Dean. ARCHIVE PHOTOS

Arthur Hobson Dean was one of two sons of Maud Campbell Egan and William Cameron Dean, a professor at Cornell Law School. An enterprising youth, Arthur worked as a newspaper delivery boy for the *Ithaca Journal* and later as a stack boy at Cornell University's main library. After graduating from Ithaca High School in 1915, he enrolled at Cornell University for his undergraduate studies. He met college expenses by working as a night clerk at the Ithaca Hotel and as a bookkeeper in the First National Bank of Ithaca. World War I interrupted his studies, however. Dean served with the U.S. Navy in 1918 and returned to Cornell after the armistice in 1919. He was awarded an A.B. degree in 1921 and then earned an LL.B. degree from Cornell Law School in 1923. While at the law school, he became managing editor of the *Cornell Law Quarterly* and was elected to Phi Delta Phi, a legal fraternity.

Dean was admitted to the New York bar in 1923. In the same year, he secured a position with Sullivan and Cromwell, a prestigious law firm in New York City that specialized in international law. John Foster Dulles, the future secretary of state, was a partner in the firm at the time. Dean had opportunities to attend to several important and interesting legal matters while employed by Sullivan and Cromwell. In 1927 and 1928 he collaborated with lawyers from Tokyo to offer the first Japanese open bond issue to the American public, and he frequently acted as counsel for English and American banking firms in corporate reorganizations. In addition, he represented industrial firms, public utilities, and railroads in the United States, Germany, Japan, France, and Italy. In 1929 Dean became a full partner in Sullivan and Cromwell. On 25 June 1932 he married Mary Talbott Clark Marden. They had two children and lived in Oyster Bay, Long Island, New York.

Dean had his first taste of government service during the administration of Franklin D. Roosevelt. In 1933 Roosevelt named him to the Dickinson Committee, formed by the Department of Commerce, which recommended the creation of the Securities and Exchange Commission. Dean also had a hand in preparing the materials that were used in drafting the Securities Exchange Act of 1934, which created the Securities and Exchange Commission, and he helped draft the Bankruptcy Act (1938), the Trust Indenture Act (1939), and the Investment Company Act (1940).

During World War II, Dean served as an officer in the Coast Guard Reserve, instructing and supervising classes in navigation and piloting. In 1945, at the end of the war, Governor Thomas E. Dewey appointed him a trustee of Cornell University. For the rest of his life, Dean remained a committed supporter of Cornell, to which he provided a great deal of financial support. In 1949 he became senior partner at Sullivan and Cromwell.

Representing his clients, Dean acquired a legal knowledge of the Far East, and in 1953 the administration of President Dwight D. Eisenhower invited him to begin talks to end the Korean War. He served as U.S. negotiator, with the rank of ambassador, during seven weeks of negotiations with North Korea and China in an attempt to set up a political conference as envisaged by the cease-fire agreement. During the summer of 1953, Syngman Rhee, president of South Korea, ordered the release of 27,000 anti-Communist prisoners of war. The Chinese responded with accusations of perfidy, and in December 1953 Dean broke off negotiations. After leaving Korea, Dean stated that the "Chinese Communists are determined to keep North Korea politically and economically integrated into their own economy" (*New York Times,* 22 December 1953).

In January 1954 Dean was accused of believing that the United States should recognize the People's Republic of China. Ardent anti-Communists in the House and the Senate attacked Dean for collaboration with China, and Dulles asked him to resign from the Korean negotiations in March 1954. Nonetheless, Dean continued to advise Dulles and President Eisenhower on the political situation in Korea. In fact, Dean did believe that the United States should recognize China. He maintained that acceptance of Britain's two-China idea would bolster the international position of the United States. Despite his unpopular ideas, he represented the United States in Geneva at the 1958 Conference on the Law of the Sea, which was attended by eighty-eight nations.

In 1961 President John F. Kennedy appointed Dean U.S. representative to the Conference on Discontinuance of Nuclear Weapons Tests, which met in Geneva during 1961 and 1962, and U.S. representative to the United Nations General Assembly. In these positions, Dean served as American spokesman at the many unproductive test-ban meetings held between the United States, the Soviet Union, and Britain in Geneva and at the United Nations. Dean was a presidential adviser on disarmament, and he wrote several of the important weapons-limitation proposals for the international conferences.

In September 1961 Dean helped President Kennedy draft his "Proposal for General and Complete Disarmament in a Peaceful World." The plan called for nuclear disarmament and for the eventual reduction of conventional weapons. In recognition of his public service, Dean was awarded the Theodore Roosevelt Distinguished Service Medal in 1962 and the National Institute of Social Sciences Gold Medal in 1963. In June 1963 Soviet premier Nikita Khrushchev accepted President Kennedy's proposal to carry out future arms talks through the leaders' personal emissaries in Moscow. W. Averell Harriman, undersecretary of state for political affairs, replaced Dean as head of the U.S. delegation, and in August 1963 a partial nuclear test-ban treaty was signed.

In July 1964 Dean was appointed chairman of the National Citizens Committee for Community Relations, in which position he oversaw community compliance with the Civil Rights Act of 1964. Also in 1964 he became a member of a nonpartisan panel of citizens formed to advise President Lyndon B. Johnson on foreign affairs, and in the same year he joined another panel created to study ways of halting the spread of nuclear weapons.

In March 1968 President Johnson asked Dean to become a member of the Senior Advisory Group on Vietnam, convened to consider the military's request for over 200,000 additional troops for the Vietnam War. The group ultimately recommended rejection of the request and the deescalation of the war, and Johnson announced this change in policy on 31 March 1968. Dean's fact-finding missions were credited with helping to persuade President Johnson to stop bombing North Vietnam and with convincing Johnson not to seek reelection.

Dean wrote *The Federal Securities Act* (1933); *Economic and Legal Aspects of the Federal Securities Act* (1933); "An Analysis of the Amendments to the Federal Securities Act of 1933," *Fortune* (September 1934); *The Lawyer's Problems in the Registration of Securities* (n.d.); *A Review of the Law of Corporate Reorganizations* (1941); *An Inquiry into the Nature of Business Income* (1949); "Amending the Treaty Power," an address delivered before the Southern Regional Meeting of the American Bar Association (March 1954); "Extraterritorial Effects of the U.S. Antitrust Laws: 'Advising the Client,' " a paper delivered at the annual meeting of the Section of Antitrust Law, American Bar Association, London (July 1957); *William Nelson Cromwell, 1854–1948: An American Pioneer in Corporation, Comparative, and International Law* (1957); *John Foster Dulles, 1888–1959: An Appreciation* (1959); *The Lawyer and the Courts* (1963); and *Test Ban and Disarmament: The Path of Negotiation* (1966).

An Episcopalian, Dean was a member of the Cold Spring Harbor Beach, Lloyd Neck Bath Inc., Piping Rock, the Century Association, and the Lunch, Recess, University, and Metropolitan clubs. He collected rare books, primarily in the field of French history, and acquired books in French history for Cornell's library. In 1976 he retired from Sullivan and Cromwell. He died of pneumonia in a hospital in Glen Cove, New York, and is buried in St. John's Cemetery, Cold Spring Harbor, New York. A heavyset, deep-voiced man, Dean was a gregarious and jovial lawyer and diplomat. He could be endlessly patient when necessary, so he often was called upon to serve as a negotiator in trying situations.

★

Dean's work is covered in "People of the Week," *U.S. News*

and World Report (6 Nov. 1953); "Wall Street Lawyer," *Time* (21 Dec. 1953); "People of the Week," *U.S. News and World Report* (21 Mar. 1958); "Our Man in Geneva, Durable," *Newsweek* (13 Aug. 1962); and D. Cook, "He Argues for Peace," *Reader's Digest* (Dec. 1962). Obituaries are in the *New York Times* and *Washington Post* (both 1 Dec. 1987).

MICHELLE C. MORGAN

DEGAETANI, Jan (*b.* 10 July 1933 in Massillon, Ohio; *d.* 15 September 1989 in Rochester, New York), mezzo-soprano, best known for her definitive interpretations of the work of contemporary composers.

DeGaetani was born Janice Ruetz, one of four daughters of Earl D. Ruetz, a lawyer, and Cora Eleanor Hayman, a nurse. As a child, Jan sang in a local church choir and from a very early age was determined to be a musician. After graduating in 1951 from Washington High School in Massillon, she won a scholarship to the Juilliard School of Music in New York City, where she studied under Sergius Kagen and developed her interest in twentieth-century music. She received her B.S. degree summa cum laude in 1955 and then taught sight singing at Juilliard.

Over the next two years she sang contemporary music with the Gramercy Chamber Ensemble, operatic roles in workshop productions of Mozart and Rossini, and medieval and Renaissance music with the New York Pro Musica Antiqua and the Waverly Consort. Upon joining the Contemporary Chamber Ensemble (CCE) in 1957, she met the pianist Gilbert Kalish, who became her accompanist and collaborator; for the next thirty-two years they gave joint recitals throughout the United States and abroad and made more than a dozen recordings of their collaborations. In 1958 she married Thomas DeGaetani, a stage manager; they had two children. After their divorce in 1966 she retained DeGaetani as her professional name.

Preparing to record Arnold Schoenberg's *Pierrot lunaire* with the CCE, DeGaetani devoted a full year (1958–1959) to mastering the difficult score, which calls upon the soprano soloist to deliver the mordant verse setting in a combination of speech and song (*Sprachgesang*) that involves abrupt leaps between high and low notes. DeGaetani's seamless articulation of these leaps was acclaimed. As she once noted, the work "opened my mind to endless kinds of beauty, and music hasn't been the same to me since." From then on she began to establish close professional relationships with composers of the "new music," who recognized and were inspired by her musical intelligence and the technical virtuosity she brought to bear upon their work—her ability to produce clear, creamy tones over a two-and-a-half-octave range, perfectly placed and always on pitch.

In 1965 DeGaetani met the composer George Crumb, who wrote one of his best-known pieces for her, *Ancient Voices of Children* (1970), a setting of poems by Federíco García Lorca. DeGaetani gave the work its world premiere with the CCE in 1970 at the Library of Congress in Washington, D.C.; three years later she sang it in New York, on the occasion of her first appearance with the New York Philharmonic and under the baton of Pierre Boulez. Others who composed for her were Jacob Druckman, György Ligeti, and Peter Maxwell Davies. The latter's *Stone Litany,* a setting of twelfth-century Old Norse inscriptions, with gong and Chinese cymbal accompaniment, was dedicated to her in 1976; her performances of this haunting score, first with the New York Philharmonic, later with the Scottish National Orchestra, received glowing critical reviews.

Teaching was always as central to DeGaetani's musical life as concertizing. After stints at Bennington College and the State University of New York College at Purchase, she joined the faculty of the Eastman School of Music in Rochester, New York, in 1973. Concurrently, she frequently gave master classes at other American schools and universities, and served as artist-in-residence at the Aspen (Colorado) Music Festival. As a teacher DeGaetani made use of a system of yogalike exercises she had developed in the course of her own performing, believing that this method of relaxing and releasing feelings opened up a channel—the voice—through which "your whole sensibility is available."

During the 1976–1977 season, with funds from the Kilbourn professorship she had been awarded at the Eastman School, DeGaetani organized a series of three chamber music concerts at the Metropolitan Museum of Art in New York City. Among the eighteen musician friends she gathered to join her was her husband, Philip West, oboist and fellow member of the Eastman faculty, whom she had married in 1969. The music selected for these concerts reflected the breadth of her repertory, from John Dowland to Luigi Dallapiccola and including Bach and Mozart, Robert Schumann and William Schuman, French art songs, Stephen Foster, and Charles Ives. In the words of Harold C. Schonberg, the *New York Times* music critic, the soloist's performances demonstrated her ability to move through musical epochs and moods with "absolute finesse." A radiant onstage presence, she nonetheless was "an artist . . . more interested in making music than in showing off her voice."

In the course of her career, DeGaetani sang with chamber groups and orchestras across the United States and throughout the world. Her discography (dating back to the 1960s) amounted to more than sixty recordings, among them the award-winning *Songs of Stephen Foster,* chosen by *Stereo Review* as Record of the Year in 1972, and performances of Crumb's *Ancient Voices* and songs by Hugo Wolf (from his *Spanisches Liederbuch*), both of which were chosen by *High Fidelity* in 1974 as among the best recordings of the previous twenty-five years. One of DeGaetani's last recordings was the highly praised *Songs of America* (1988), and just before her death (she was stricken with leukemia in 1986), she completed a compact disc of interpretations of Hector Berlioz's *Nuits d'été* and songs by Gustav Mahler.

In tribute to her distinction as artist and teacher, the Fritz Reiner Center for Contemporary Music (which she had inaugurated in January 1989) presented a series of three memorial concerts at Columbia University in 1992. Honoring her musical legacy, her colleagues and former students, among them such luminaries as Dawn Upshaw and Renée Fleming, performed music of four centuries—compositions DeGaetani had herself sung as well as pieces composed for the occasion.

★

The Complete Sightsinger: A Stylistic and Historical Approach (1980), written by Jan DeGaetani and Norman and Ruth Lloyd, is a detailed textbook with musical examples, giving instruction on reading music from plainsong to twentieth-century scores. *A Tribute to Jan DeGaetani* (1992), the program for the memorial concerts performed at Columbia University, includes a biographical note and critical appreciation, a discography, and a listing of DeGaetani's premiere performances. A review of the third of her Metropolitan Museum of Art concerts by Harold C. Schonberg, *New York Times* (21 Feb. 1977), provides his assessment of her artistry. Obituaries are in the *New York Times* (17 Sept. 1989) and *Opera News* (9 Dec. 1989).

ELEANOR F. WEDGE

DE KOONING, Elaine Marie Catherine (*b.* 12 March 1918 in New York City; *d.* 1 February 1989 in Southhampton, New York), artist, teacher, and critic whose art reflected her grounding in abstract expressionism and whose writings helped define postwar contemporary art.

The oldest of four children, Elaine de Kooning was born Elaine Marie Fried to Charles Frank Fried, an accountant, and Mary Ellen (O'Brien) Fried. Elaine was raised as a Roman Catholic in the Sheepshead Bay section of Brooklyn. Her interest in art stemmed from childhood, when her mother took her to museums, encouraged her artistic efforts, and instilled in her a strong will to succeed. She recalled that by age eight, her friends began to request her work, so she "began to have a little ego about it."

After her graduation in 1935 from Erasmus Hall High School in Brooklyn, where she excelled in both mathematics and writing, Elaine Fried entered Hunter College to study mathematics. She dropped out in 1937 to enroll in the Leonardo da Vinci Art School, then transferred to the American Artists School, because, as she recalled, she "couldn't stand not having a paintbrush in [her] hand." She was living in Manhattan by 1938, sharing an East Village studio. Around this time Elaine met the Dutch-born artist Willem de Kooning, who invited her to paint in his Chelsea studio under his guidance. By 1939 she had moved in with him; they married on 9 December 1943. They moved to a Greenwich Village apartment in 1944, and spent the next thirteen years as active participants in the social and artistic milieu of the New York School. They had no children.

In their art, Elaine and Willem de Kooning served as inspirations for one another. Elaine became his initial subject for his images of women, which he had begun shortly after meeting her, and in her own work Willem was the subject of numerous paintings and sketches that led to her "faceless men" series (1949–1956). In these portraits of people she knew in the New York art world, Elaine de Kooning captured the sitter through a stance or position, honing her abilities with gesture and line. Her recognition as a portraitist led to a commission in 1962 to paint President John F. Kennedy.

Between 1944 and 1945 Elaine de Kooning began to accompany Edwin Denby, the music critic for the *New York Herald Tribune,* to dance productions. Soon she began writing her own reviews (signing them with the initials E. de K.), which led to a position in 1948 as editorial associate for Thomas Hess, the editor of *Art News*. Assigned to review art exhibitions, de Kooning stated that she labored over each, striving to evaluate the work. Her articles were often among the first to appear on recent developments, to the extent that in 1963 the *New York Times* critic John Canaday called her the "mascot, Sybil, and recording secretary" of abstract expressionism.

The next decade saw greater involvement by the de Koonings in the art world. In the summer of 1948 Elaine accompanied Willem to Black Mountain College, the famed art school in North Carolina where he was to teach; she painted seventeen enamel abstractions. (*Untitled #15* is now in the Metropolitan Museum of Art in New York.) In 1949 the de Koonings were included among other famous artist couples in a Sidney Janis Gallery exhibition entitled *Artists: Man and Wife*. In 1951 they spent the first of many summers in East Hampton on Long Island, where they both eventually settled year-round. In 1954 the Stable Gallery in New York City gave Elaine de Kooning her first solo show. She received her first museum exhibition, a retrospective, in 1959 at the Lyman Allen Art Museum in New London, Connecticut.

By 1957 the de Koonings had decided to live apart, and Elaine accepted her first teaching position as visiting professor at the University of New Mexico in Albuquerque, where she began her bullfight series (1957–1963). For the next twenty years Elaine de Kooning continued to paint and write while teaching at numerous schools, including Pennsylvania State University (1960), the University of

Elaine de Kooning. COPYRIGHT © BY THE ESTATE OF ELAINE DE KOONING, SALANDER O'REILLY GALLERY, NEW YORK CITY

California at Davis (1963–1964), Yale University in New Haven, Connecticut (1967), Parsons School of Design in New York City (1974–1976), and the University of Georgia (1976–1978). In 1964 she received from Western College, Oxford, Ohio, the first of five honorary doctorates. (Her last was in 1988 from Long Island University in Southampton, New York.)

In 1975 Elaine de Kooning reconciled with Willem, and purchased an East Hampton home and studio near his on Alewive Brook Road. She provided him with a stable environment and promoted his work and reputation. During this time Elaine continued her own activities of writing, teaching, and painting. She also began to travel. In 1976, during a visit to the Luxembourg Gardens in Paris, Elaine saw a nineteenth-century statue of Bacchus, which motivated her to produce some sixty paintings and numerous sketches over the next seven years.

In 1983, during a trip to Europe, Elaine de Kooning saw the Lascaux Paleolithic cave paintings in the French Pyrenees, inspiring her to produce her cave paintings series (1983–1988). She followed this trip with one to the Altamira caves in the Spanish Pyrenees in 1984 and 1985. Elaine found potent material in these paintings by the earliest humans, producing large-scale canvases, as well as a number of watercolors and sketches. Of more than forty solo exhibitions, at least ten were of her cave paintings. The last exhibition of these works during her lifetime was held in November 1988 by the Fischbach Gallery in New York City. Included was her final large painting, a massive triptych, *High Wall,* that she had completed in the summer of 1988. After attending the opening of the exhibition, she entered a hospital in Southampton, where she died of lung cancer. She was buried in Green River Cemetery in the Springs area of East Hampton, Long Island, New York.

Elaine de Kooning received the greatest recognition for her work during the 1980s. Although she sought in her art the tension between abstraction and figuration, her style and approach essentially originated in abstract expressionism. Standing in an active pose with her arms outstretched, she would begin to paint, often working on as many as eight canvases at once. She described her process as "Trust," stating that "when I start, I don't know what's going to happen. . . . I want something there that's more than just the visual."

★

Most of Elaine de Kooning's papers, including notebooks kept by her from the early 1940s through 1989, are with her sister, Marjorie Fried Luyckx, in New York City. An unpublished interview of de Kooning in her studio, conducted by Claude Cowles, 29 Mar. 1972, is in the Claude Cowles Papers, Archives of American Art, Smithsonian Institution, Washington, D.C., reels 2802–2803. One of the most valuable published sources on the artist is Marjorie Fried Luyckx and Rose Slivka, *Elaine de Kooning: The Spirit of Abstract Expressionism, Selected Writings* (1994). For other published primary source material see statements and comments by the artist in *It Is* (spring/summer 1958): 19; (autumn 1958): 72; (winter/spring 1959): 59–62; and (autumn 1959): 29–30, and Robin White, "Elaine de Kooning," *View* 5 (spring 1988): 2–23, an interview. A valuable source of information is Jane K. Bledsoe, *Elaine de Kooning* (1992), a catalog of an exhibition held at the Georgia Museum of Art, University of Georgia. For an anecdotal, though gossipy, account of the de Koonings' social scene, see Lee Hall, *Elaine and Bill, Portrait of A Marriage: The Lives of Willem and Elaine de Kooning* (1993). Amei Wallach, "The Art and Energy of Elaine de Kooning," *Newsday* (2 Feb. 1989), is an appreciation. An interview of Elaine de Kooning, 27 Aug. 1981, conducted by Phyllis Tuchman, is part of an oral history project, *Mark Rothko and His Times*, in the Archives of American Art, Smithsonian Institution, Washington, D.C., sound cassette and transcript (partially microfilmed). An obituary is in the *New York Times* (2 Feb. 1989).

LEIGH BULLARD WEISBLAT

DIVINE (Harris Glenn Milstead) (*b.* 19 October 1945 in Baltimore, Maryland; *d.* 7 March 1988 in Los Angeles, California), actor, singer, and nightclub entertainer best known for his colorful, often outrageous, female roles in John Waters's comedies of the 1970s and 1980s.

Divine, the only child of Harris Bernard Milstead and Diana Frances Vukovich, grew up in the Baltimore suburb of Towson. He and his conservative Baptist parents, who ran a nursery school, lived in a mansion once occupied by F. Scott Fitzgerald. In 1958 the family moved to the nearby town of Lutherville, into a house on the street where John Waters's family lived.

An effeminate child, Glenn, as he was known, was the target of verbal and physical abuse in school, to the extent that police escorts between home and school were sometimes necessary. He became acquainted with Waters while attending Towson High School. Glenn worked as a hairdresser for several years, but his budding partnership with Waters led him to underground filmmaking. The pair's first collaboration was *Roman Candles* (1966), which also features some of Waters's other regulars, collectively called the Dreamlanders. Glenn Milstead was transformed into Divine by Waters (who came up with the stage name—"probably something from my Catholic upbringing," he has said) and the makeup artist Van Smith. Divine's garish look, flamboyant female costumes, brash on-screen personality, and sheer size—his weight vacillated between 240 and 375 pounds—won him instant recognition and frequent mockery (some of which was invited or at least not unwelcome). In his obituary, *People* magazine described Divine as "a Miss Piggy for the blissfully depraved"; *Time* magazine simply called him "freaky." In a review of *Polyester* (1981) in *New York* magazine, David Denby wrote, "Divine doesn't have a trace of delicacy—she's a squalling big mama with a bullhorn voice, wallowing in put-on degradation."

Divine at the premiere of the film *Female Trouble,* 1975. TIM BOXER/ARCHIVE PHOTOS

The roles Waters created for Divine range from mild send-ups of suburban stereotypes (a suicidal teenager in the 1969 short *The Diane Linkletter Story*, a loving mother in the 1988 nostalgic comedy *Hairspray*) to the grotesque and deliberately offensive, calculated to shock. Divine gave his most notorious performance as Babs Johnson, the "filthiest person alive," in *Pink Flamingos* (1972). In the closing seconds of a film that is already suffused with all manner of human indignities, Divine tops it off by picking up a fresh piece of dog excrement (no prop) and putting it in his mouth. *Pink Flamingos* has remained a cult favorite and was re-released in 1997, its twenty-fifth anniversary, with thirteen and a half minutes of footage cut from the original version.

Divine's other roles in Waters's films include Jackie Kennedy (in a fantasy sequence that re-creates the John F. Kennedy assassination) in the short *Eat Your Makeup* (1967); Dawn Davenport, disturbed teenager turned crazed criminal, in *Female Trouble* (1974), Divine's favorite of his own films; and a besieged housewife in *Polyester* (a film that is also known for its marketing gimmick, the "Odorama" scratch-and-sniff card). Divine had male parts in *Female Trouble* (in which he played two roles, with his male character assaulting his female one) and *Hairspray*. His other films with Waters were *Mondo Trasho* (1969) and *Multiple Maniacs* (1970).

Although Divine is remembered chiefly for his performances in Waters's films, the actor also enjoyed a considerable career as stage actor, recording artist, and nightclub performer. In 1973 Divine performed with the Cockettes, a San Francisco cross-dressing troupe, in shows such as *Divine and the Stimulating Studs*. He acted in two off-Broadway farces in New York, *Women Behind Bars* (1976) and *The Neon Woman* (1979), both by Tom Eyen. Divine also acted in films not directed by Waters: Paul Bartel's *Lust in the Dust* (1985), Alan Rudolph's *Trouble in Mind* (1985), in which he plays a male gangster, and Michael Schroeder's *Out of the Dark* (1988). He appeared on many television talk shows and in a 1987 episode of the television series *Tales from the Darkside*.

Divine's career as a recording artist of dance music was more successful in Europe than in the United States. His record *Shoot Your Shot* sold more than 100,000 copies in the Netherlands in 1983. The most successful single of his career was "You Think You're a Man," released in 1984. After his disco-club debut in October 1979 at the Copa Disco in Fort Lauderdale, Florida, Divine toured extensively and internationally, entertaining both gay and straight audiences. Between the numbers Divine usually traded good-natured obscenities with audience members.

Divine's personal life was marred by financial trouble (thanks to his lavish spending habits) and heavy use of marijuana. A gay man, Divine had a few intimate relationships, but in public he declared his aversion to being in love. Between his filming and touring engagements, he lived mostly in New York City, but he also spent time in Provincetown, Massachusetts; San Francisco; and Key West, Florida. Divine returned to Baltimore to act in several of Waters's films.

Divine did not consider himself a transvestite or a female impersonator, preferring to be called an actor. "I only put [women's clothes] on when someone pays me to," he said. He had an ambition to become a character actor out of drag. Ironically, just as a Hollywood career appeared within his grasp, following the positive reviews of his performance in *Hairspray*, Divine died suddenly of heart failure in his sleep at the Regency Plaza Suites Hotel in Los Angeles. He had been scheduled to film an episode of the Fox television sitcom *Married . . . with Children*, in which he was to play a potentially recurring male role, Uncle Otto.

Divine was buried at the Prospect Hill Park Cemetery in Towson, Maryland. On his tombstone is a sign of reconciliation between Divine and his straitlaced parents, with whom he had had a sometimes rocky relationship: "Divine" is inscribed below his birth name, acknowledging the singular career the actor had made for himself.

★

Not Simply Divine (1993), by Divine's personal manager, Bernard Jay, is a lively if biased chronicle of Divine's career. Books by and about John Waters, as well as numerous interviews with and articles about Waters and Divine, give insights into the working relationship between the director and actor. A recording of one of Divine's club appearances, on 16 February 1983 in Manchester, United Kingdom, is available on videocassette (*Divine Live at the Hacienda*). Obituaries are in the *New York Times* (8 Mar. 1988) and *Rolling Stone* (21 Apr. 1988).

JEFFREY H. CHEN

DODD, Robert Lee ("Bobby") (*b.* 11 November 1908 in Galax, Virginia; *d.* 21 June 1988 in Atlanta, Georgia), one of only two men enshrined in the College Football Hall of Fame as both a player and coach and the top winning football coach in Georgia Tech history.

Bobby Dodd was the youngest of four children of furniture factory manager Edwin Dodd and Susan (Nuckolls) Dodd. He attended public schools in Kingsport, Tennessee, and acquired sixteen letters in football, baseball, basketball, track, and gymnastics. In 1926 Bobby enrolled at the University of Tennessee, after being denied a scholarship to his first choice, Georgia Tech. His lanky build and bowleggedness belied his ability as a natural athlete. He earned nine varsity letters, participating in football, basketball, and baseball. With Dodd as quarterback, his football teams compiled a 27–1–2 record, with Dodd earning All-American honors in 1930. He married Alice Davis of Atlanta in 1933. They had two children; his son, Bobby, Jr., went on to play quarterback and safety at the University of Florida.

After graduating from Tennessee in 1931, Dodd served as an assistant coach for fifteen years at Georgia Tech. He became head coach in 1945, a position he held until his resignation in 1967. He continued as athletic director until 1976. From 1952 to 1956, his teams won six consecutive bowl games: three Sugar Bowls, one Orange Bowl, one

Bobby Dodd, *c.* 1931. GEORGIA TECH ATHLETIC ASSOCIATION, 150 BOBBY DODD WAY, N.W., ATLANTA, GEORGIA

Cotton Bowl, and one Gator Bowl. Overall, his teams won nine of thirteen postseason bowl games. From 1951 to 1953, his teams had a thirty-one-game unbeaten streak, including a 12–0 season and a national championship in 1952 (he was named coach of the year by the New York *Daily News* for this achievement). His overall record of 165–64–8 is one of the best in college history. Considered by many to be one of the best sideline coaches of his time, his coaching style emphasized craftsmanship, finesse, and on-the-field execution and adjustment.

Dodd employed numerous routines and held many beliefs that were considered odd and iconoclastic. He avoided the regimented, overwork routines followed by many of his contemporaries and implemented his view that football should be fun for the players by conducting short, noncontact practices. He emphasized thinking on the field and preferred that his players spend more time studying rather than practicing. He voiced a desire to abolish spring football practices, in exchange for an extra week of practice in August before school opened. Determined to have his players graduate, Dodd led Georgia Tech to withdraw from the Southeastern Conference in 1965, due to his disagreement with the conference on grants-in-aid. He did not believe in enforced dropouts, preferring to evaluate academic as well as athletic abilities prior to selecting candidates for athletic scholarships. Dodd believed if a mistake was made in evaluating talent, and a player could not make the grade either athletically or academically, the fault was with him and his staff. Other universities commonly withdrew scholarships or forced recruiting failures to drop out. Once committed, Dodd made every effort to provide assistance to those who needed tutoring, or to allow those who could not compete on the varsity level to retain their athletic scholarship.

Dodd treated his athletes more like sons than football players. He used praise as the principal form of motivation, but he was a strict disciplinarian. He insisted that they attend church on Sundays, often taking them himself. He did not allow his players to smoke or drink, although he was not puritanical with his rules. He believed in allowing "boys to be boys," but at one point in his career he kicked his star player off the team for repeatedly violating team rules. He approved of marriage for his players, another renegade idea at the time. "Keeps them off the streets. You know where they are at night," he expressed.

Dodd's ideas and values were formulated from personal experience. He was well known for his gambling at golf, poker, and pool. In fact, police in Kingsport removed Bobby from a pool hall at age twelve, the summer before he tried out for the high school football team, for hustling adult gamblers. At one point, golf was Dodd's main diversion. After a particularly bad day, he wrote a check to cover his losses and said he would never play golf again. He kept that promise until just a few years before he died, when he played one last time but stopped after only four holes. He put his clubs away, grumbling, "Now I know why I quit this game," and walked the rest of the round with his companions. Bass fishing and tennis were other pastimes. Although he had a reputation for flamboyance early in his career, Dodd controlled his passions.

Dodd was known for his good luck. Once when a magazine was preparing a story on Dodd's fishing, an accompanying photographer asked him to "throw out a line so I can see if I'm in focus." Dodd made a relaxed cast and immediately had a strike, reeling in a six-pound bass. His cross-state rival in the 1950s at the University of Georgia, Wally Butts, once complained: "If Bobby Dodd were trapped at the center of an H-bomb explosion, he would walk away with his pockets full of marketable uranium." Dodd and Georgia Tech beat archrival Georgia eight consecutive times from 1949 to 1956. Alabama's great coach, Paul ("Bear") Bryant once said, "Nobody else in the country can coach like Dodd and win." Dodd readily acknowledged his good fortune, even entitling his autobiography *Dodd's Luck* (1987).

Dodd's activities and influence extended far beyond the football field. He earned the first Big Heart Award in Georgia for significant long-term contributions. For thirty years, he led charity work for mentally retarded children and the Shriner's Crippled Children's programs. In 1956, his team played an integrated University of Pittsburgh team in the Sugar Bowl. This violation of the Southeastern Conference's "gentleman's agreement" caused an uproar and infuriated politicians by helping to break the resistance to the civil rights movement in the South. He was universally respected for his outstanding ability in handling and understanding people, inspiring confidence, and representing the highest standards.

Georgia Tech renamed its football stadium for Bobby Dodd. Similarly, the American Sportsmanship Council's national Coach of the Year award is named in tribute to Dodd, who died from lung cancer.

★

Dodd's autobiography, written with Jack Wilkinson, is *Dodd's Luck: The Life and Legend of a Hall of Fame Quarterback and Coach* (1987). Biographical information may also be found in David L. Porter, ed., *Biographical Dictionary of American Sports: Football* (1987), and Ralph Hickok, *A Who's Who of Sports Champions: Their Stories and Records* (1995). An obituary is in the *New York Times* (22 June 1988), and an obituary and a tribute are in the *Atlanta Constitution* (22 June 1988).

BRIAN CRADDOCK

DOISY, Edward Adelbert (*b.* 13 November 1893 in Hume, Illinois; *d.* 23 October 1986 in St. Louis, Missouri), internationally acclaimed biochemist who shared the 1943 Nobel Prize in physiology or medicine for his discovery of the chemical and physical nature of vitamin K.

Edward A. Doisy. NANCY HERRINGTON

Doisy was one of two children of Edward Perez Doisy, a traveling salesman, and Ada (Alley) Doisy. His parents had a strong interest in education. His father served on the school board and was instrumental in bringing a stimulating new principal to the Hume High School; shortly afterward the school became fully accredited by the University of Illinois. Doisy attended the high school, where he was both a good student and an athlete. He was one of a class of seven when he graduated in 1910.

The Doisys moved to Champaign, Illinois, and in the fall of 1910 Doisy entered the University of Illinois at Champaign, where he continued to pursue his interests in sports and academics. He played both basketball and baseball and was a staff member of the college yearbook. A science major, he was elected to Phi Beta Kappa and the honorary scientific fraternity Sigma Xi. Doisy received a B.S. degree with honors in 1914.

In 1916 Doisy earned an M.S. degree, also from the University of Illinois. Writing his master's thesis, which dealt with the lipids of the brain, increased his interest in biochemistry. While pursuing his master's he also was an assistant in biochemistry at Harvard Medical School from 1915 to 1917. World War I interrupted his studies, and from 1917 to 1919 he served in the U.S. Army, primarily at the Walter Reed Research Institute in Washington, D.C. He was discharged with the rank of second lieutenant in the Sanitary Corps. Following his army service he returned to Harvard, where in 1920 he earned a doctoral degree under the supervision of Otto Folin, professor of biological chemistry at the Harvard Medical School. His doctoral dissertation was entitled "Determination of Sodium, Potassium, and Chlorine in Small Samples of Tissue."

In Atlanta, on 20 July 1918, Doisy married Alice Ackert, a teacher from Dixon, Illinois, whom he had met at the University of Illinois. They had four sons.

In 1919 Doisy became an instructor in biochemistry at Washington University School of Medicine in St. Louis. His first major long-term research project, on which he collaborated with his good friend, biologist Edgar Allen, concerned ovarian function in rats and mice. The two later extended their research to humans and the nature of ovarian hormones. In 1923 Doisy became an associate professor and helped to establish the St. Louis University School of Medicine's biochemistry department, which in 1955 was named the Edward A. Doisy Department of Biochemistry and Molecular Biology. He was appointed professor and chairman of the department in 1924, a position he held with distinction until his retirement in 1965. He continued his research concerning ovarian function and in 1929 succeeded in purifying estrone to a pure crystalline substance. By the time his research was completed in 1935 he had isolated two other important hormones, estriol (1930) and estradiol-17 beta (1935).

After the Danish scientist Henrik Dam discovered vitamin K, a fat-soluble compound that promotes coagulation of blood, Doisy began his research on the isolation of this lipid from various natural products. The cost of the research project was shared by St. Louis University and Parke-Davis and Company. Doisy later stated, in an article in *Science Illustrated* (January 1948), that this financial arrangement could be a model for university-industry relations.

By 1939 Doisy had succeeded in crystallizing vitamin K from alfalfa meal and fermented fish meal. As a result of this research, in 1943 Doisy and Dam were jointly awarded the Nobel Prize in physiology or medicine. (A description of his prize-winning work is contained in volumes 130 and 131 of the 1939 issues of the *Journal of Biological Chemistry.*) One of the benefits of this important work was the establishment of the value of vitamin K as an antihemorrhagic agent in surgery. Vitamin K deficiency is seen in newborns, and low levels of prothrombin, which is needed for the clotting of blood, may be raised by vitamin K. The resulting product of Doisy's research, called Menadione, was patented by St. Louis University. All profits from its use went to further research in the field.

During World War II, Doisy engaged in research for the Office of Scientific Research and Development. Working with his wife, Alice, he isolated and tested several new antibiotics. This research, which continued after the war, concerned the metabolism of steroids, including the estrogenic hormones, cholesterol, and the bile acids.

A prolific writer, Doisy published many papers on vitamin K, as well as on metabolism, insulin, blood buffers, theelol, dihydrotheelin, ovarian hormones and estrogenic substances, and other aspects of endocrinology. He was active in several professional associations and served as president of the American Society of Biological Chemists in 1945. He also served on the League of Nations Committee on Standardization of the Sex Hormones.

Among his many awards and honors were the Gibbs Medal from the Chicago section of the American Medical Society (1945), and honorary degrees from Yale University (1940), Washington University (1940), the University of Chicago (1941), the University of Paris (1945), St. Louis University (1955), the University of Illinois (1960), and Gustavus Adolphus College (1963).

In 1964, after forty-six years of marriage, Alice Doisy died. A year later, Doisy married one of her best friends, Margaret McCormick. He also retired that same year as professor and chairman of the Department of Biochemistry and Molecular Biology at the St. Louis University School of Medicine. Doisy died of heart disease at the St. Louis University Hospital at the age of ninety-two. He is buried in St. Louis.

Robert E. Olson, one of the seventy or more graduate students who received their doctorates during Doisy's tenure as department chairman, expressed the sentiments of many former students and associates in an obituary in *Nature* (15 January 1987), stating: "His many students and associates remember Edward Doisy as a single-minded and astute judge of research problems that could be solved with the techniques available, and an excellent mentor who both recognized scientific skills in young people and helped to develop them to the utmost."

★

Edward A. Doisy, "An Autobiography," *Annual Review of Biochemistry* 45 (1976): 1–9, provides insight into Doisy's early years in Hume, Illinois, the reasons why his life took the path it did, and an expression of appreciation to the people who influenced his life. Robert E. Olson, ed., *Perspectives in Biological Chemistry* (1970), is a volume prepared by fifteen of Doisy's colleagues during the sesquicentennial celebration of St. Louis University to honor him on the occasion of his retirement. It contains several pages of biographical reference, essays on biochemistry, and six pages of reminiscences by Doisy. Lloyd G. Stevenson, *Nobel Prize Winners in Medicine and Physiology, 1901–1950* (1953), contains a substantial amount of information about the research that led to the Nobel Prize in 1943. In addition to brief biographical sketches of Doisy and Henrik Dam, there are reprints of the two articles from the 1939 volumes of the *Journal of Biological Chemistry* that delineate the prize-winning work at the St. Louis University School of Medicine. Obituaries are in the *New York Times* and *Boston Globe* (both 25 Oct. 1986). Harriet A. Zuckerman, *Reminiscences of Edward Adelbert Doisy: Oral History* (1964), is an interview conducted as part of the Columbia University Oral History Project: Nobel Laureates on Scientific Research Projects. Written permission is required from the interviewer for access to this material.

NANCY J. HERRINGTON

DOLGUN, Alexander Michael (*b.* 29 September 1927 in New York City; *d.* 28 August 1986 in Gaithersburg, Maryland), government official who wrote about his eight-year confinement in a Soviet prison camp in *Alexander Dolgun's Story: An American in the Gulag* (1975).

Dolgun was the son of Michael Dolgun, an auto mechanic and engineer, and Anna Katrynick Dolgun. Because jobs

Alexander Dolgun, 1974. AP/WIDE WORLD PHOTOS

were scarce in the United States during the Great Depression, his father accepted government-sponsored work as a technician in a Soviet trucking company in the early 1930s. Soon after, Alexander and his mother and sister, Stella, moved to the Soviet Union, which was then under Joseph Stalin's dictatorial rule.

At the age of seven, Dolgun entered the Anglo-American school in Moscow. While he was a student there, anti-foreign campaigns raged in the Soviet Union and Dolgun was beaten regularly by his Russian schoolmates. These incidents of abuse caused him to develop strength in his identity as an American, which would prove instrumental to his survival in the years to come.

Following his graduation in 1943 Dolgun was hired by the United States Embassy in Moscow to work as a file clerk. After a few years, he was promoted to head the consular section's file division. On 13 December 1948 Dolgun, aged twenty-one, left the embassy for lunch at one o'clock in the afternoon. While on his way to meet his date on Gorky Street—Moscow's main thoroughfare—he was arrested by a major in the Ministry of State Security (MGB), who had approached him as though he were an acquaintance. Dolgun was informed that he was wanted by the MGB for questioning. After presenting his identification card and explaining that his status as an American citizen did not allow him to talk to Soviet officials, Dolgun was forced into a car and taken to Lubyanka, the secret police headquarters in Moscow.

At Lubyanka, Dolgun was assigned to a cell. For eighteen months, he was brought before an interrogator, six days a week, eighteen hours a day, and questioned about his alleged anti-Soviet activities and espionage. Dolgun steadfastly maintained that a mistake had been made and reminded his captors of his American citizenship. He was sentenced to twenty-five years of hard labor. Meanwhile, the United States Embassy suspected that Dolgun had been arrested and filed a complaint with the Soviet foreign ministry.

After his sentencing Dolgun was transferred to Lefortovo, where he was kept in solitary confinement for one year. He later referred to his prison room, which was painted black, as a "psychic cell" that was designed to break the will of its inhabitants. Sleep deprivation and a diet of weak soup, porridge, and sour bread caused him to hallucinate. He retained his sanity by never giving up hope that he would be freed; he entertained himself by singing the popular American songs of the day. "Don't Fence Me In," "Pardon Me, Boy, Is That the Chattanooga Choo Choo?," and "The Marine's Hymn," were among the tunes that kept Dolgun's memory for his country alive. His daily dreams of returning to the United States were manifest in fantasies in which he pictured himself, as he paced the length of his cell, walking through the prison walls, out to the streets of the Moscow suburbs, across Europe and the Atlantic, and onto American soil.

While Dolgun was imprisoned at Lefortovo, his sister returned to the United States to plead her brother's case before the State Department. After a few perfunctory inquiries, the State Department dropped the matter because United States–Soviet relations were tense. The State Department believed that any attempt to extricate Dolgun or even inquire about him could lead to his death. Richard H. Davis, a State Department official who knew Dolgun in Moscow, urged that there be no public outcry, as it could lead to severe implications.

Next Dolgun was transferred to Sukhanovka, near Moscow, where he was continually beaten and tortured. The beatings were so severe that he suffered internal abdominal injuries that resulted in his having to undergo surgery. It was at this time, with the threat of further physical violence, that Dolgun "confessed" to various charges of espionage. In 1951 he was resentenced without trial to a twenty-five-year term of hard labor at Dzhezkazgan in Kazakhstan.

Although the United States and the Soviet Union were in the midst of the cold war, and the paranoia of McCarthyism was consuming American society, Dolgun's sister persisted in her quest to free her brother. Her calls for help fell on deaf ears, however, as U.S. officials were reluctant to involve themselves in a potentially volatile political case.

During his years of confinement, Dolgun worked in the labor camp's rock quarries, in its copper mines, as a welder, as an electrician, and as a hospital assistant. In 1956 Soviet premier Nikita Khrushchev granted general amnesty to political prisoners. Dolgun was released, but only after being forced to sign a statement attesting to his naturalization as a Soviet citizen. The statement also held that if he attempted to contact the United States Embassy in order to leave the Soviet Union, he would be imprisoned for life without the right to a trial. He would also be under constant KGB surveillance. At the time of Dolgun's release, he was twenty-nine years old.

Once out of prison, Dolgun found a job as a typist with the Ministry of Health in Moscow and moved into a small apartment with his mother, who had been released from a psychiatric hospital following her arrest by the MGB. Dolgun's responsibilities at the Ministry of Health increased and he began to translate many English-language books into Russian. Later he acquired freelance work as a translator with Moscow publishing houses.

In the early 1960s Dolgun was introduced to Aleksander Solzhenitsyn, who was writing a book about his experience in the Soviet Union's labor camps. Solzhenitsyn interviewed Dolgun about his years in prison and included some of Dolgun's experiences in his book *The Gulag Archipelago*. In 1963 Dolgun met a Russian woman, Irene Knysh, whom he married on 23 January 1965; they had one son. Meanwhile, Dolgun's sister, who had relocated to Vienna, enlisted the support of the American ambassador, John P. Humes, to investigate her brother's case. Humes pressured the State Department and sought the help of President Richard M. Nixon. Finally, in December 1971 the Soviet Union granted Dolgun permission to return with his family to his homeland.

Once back in the United States, Dolgun was unable to get a job with the State Department because his wife could not get government clearance. From 1975 until the mid-1980s, he held positions with the U.S. Public Health Service; the Health, Education, and Welfare Department, and the National Institutes of Health.

On 27 January 1972 Dolgun was honored in a State Department ceremony, and in 1975 his personal story was published by Knopf. He died of kidney failure in his Maryland home.

★

Several articles and reviews discussed Dolgun's *An American in the Gulag* (1975), including Sal Moloff, "Alexander Dolgun's Story," *New York Times Book Review* (25 May 1975); S. Wagner and J. F. Baker, "Story Behind the Book," *Publisher's Weekly* (26 May 1975); and M. Maddocks, "Dear America," *Time* (2 June 1975). See also Alexander Solzhenitsyn, *The Gulag Archipelago: 1918–1956* (1974). An obituary is in the *New York Times* (29 Aug. 1986).

LaRose T. Parris

DONNER, Frederic Garrett (*b.* 4 October 1902 in Three Oaks, Michigan; *d.* 28 February 1987 in Greenwich, Connecticut), chairman of General Motors through years of its great prosperity.

Donner was raised in a small town in southwestern Michigan, the son of Frank Donner, an accountant, and Cornelia (Zimmerman) Donner, a homemaker. He had one younger brother. A brilliant student with a quiet personality, he graduated from local schools in Three Oaks and the University of Michigan in 1923 with a B.A. degree in economics. He worked for three years as an accountant for Reckitt, Benington, and LeClear in Chicago until he was recruited as a financial analyst for General Motors (GM) at its financial headquarters in New York City. Although he traveled often to Detroit over the next forty-one years, he always maintained his home in New York.

Donner's rise through the executive hierarchy was swift, even during the depression years. He was made assistant treasurer in 1934, general assistant treasurer in 1937, and vice president in charge of the financial staff in 1941. In January 1942 he was named to the board of directors, where he remained for thirty-two years. At age thirty-eight Donner was remarkably young for a vice president at GM, but

Frederic G. Donner. Archive Photos

he distinguished himself by close attention to detail and a remarkable talent for cost analysis. He was strictly a finance expert and was never directly involved with automobile manufacturing or marketing. His assignments included raising capital, managing benefit programs, and negotiating defense contracts. He played a major role in reviving GM's automobile production in postwar Germany. In 1956 he achieved what he expected to be his final promotion, executive vice president for finance.

The automotive industry was surprised when General Motors named Donner chairman of the board and chief executive officer in 1958. A small board committee led by chairman emeritus Alfred P. Sloan, Jr., decided that the size and complexity of GM required a full-time employee as chairman and chief executive officer in New York City, with a president and chief operating officer at the manufacturing headquarters in Detroit. Donner worked closely with John F. Gordon, named president at the same time, and the new management system was highly successful.

Donner disliked personal publicity, but as head of GM he was inevitably a public figure. In 1962 he was featured in a cover story by *Time* magazine. GM dominated the automotive industry during his nine years as chairman, and he was deeply concerned by the threat of antitrust actions or any other federal regulations. Unfortunately, he resisted the required installation of automobile seat belts. A strong opponent of corporate support for auto racing, he kept GM out of the sport throughout his chairmanship. Under Donner's leadership, GM achieved record high levels of vehicle sales, revenues, and profits. When the consumer advocate Ralph Nader accused GM in 1965 of knowingly manufacturing a dangerous car, Donner defended the Corvair before Congress. He was traveling overseas when GM was discovered to have hired detectives to investigate Nader's private life, and company president James Roche had to face harsh congressional criticism when he offered the company's official apology.

When Donner retired as chairman in 1967, GM was at the peak of its prosperity and power, manufacturing more than half the automobiles in the United States. Government "interference" was a growing concern but not yet a serious threat. Criticism of Donner's leadership emerged only years later, when GM had lost its dominance of the U.S. automobile market. He was the epitome of the GM "system" of divisional autonomy coupled with strict financial controls that had been devised by Sloan and Donaldson Brown in the 1920s. Donner was later blamed for allowing the financial staff to pinch pennies in manufacturing while spending heavily on marketing. The long-term result was a reputation for poor-quality automobiles, many of which were too large for changing consumer tastes.

Donner traveled widely for both business and pleasure and took a strong interest in GM's international operations. His most extensive public speaking was a series of three lectures at Columbia University in 1966, published as *The World-Wide Industrial Enterprise: Its Challenge and Promise* (1967). He reaffirmed the GM tradition of full ownership of its European subsidiaries but called for maximum employment of local citizens in management as well as production. He showed no concern about foreign cars entering the U.S. market or the growth of automobile manufacturing in Japan.

In retirement Donner cherished his privacy and avoided any public comment about the automobile industry. He remained a GM director until 1974. President Lyndon Johnson named him to the board of the new Communications Satellite Corporation in 1964. He chaired the Alfred P. Sloan Foundation from 1968 to 1975 but accepted no other directorships.

Donner married Eileen Isaacson, a high school teacher from Three Oaks, Michigan, in 1929, and they had two children. For relaxation he enjoyed travel and reading, particularly Civil War history and mysteries, as well as an occasional round of golf. Although he was the highest-paid corporate executive in the United States, he continued to live in the upper-middle-class neighborhood of Port Washington on Long Island. He commuted to his Manhattan office by railroad and subway because he found this more efficient than driving through traffic. Close associates enjoyed his sense of humor, but to others he always appeared as the stern accountant. Donner was of moderate height, wore heavy glasses, and favored gray suits. On occasion he joked about his reputation: "I am not taciturn, I am not shy. I am not afraid of people, and I don't even own a slide rule." Donner died of pneumonia following a stroke. His body was cremated and the remains buried at Nassau Knolls Cemetery in Port Washington.

★

There is a small collection of Donner papers in the Bentley Historical Library at the University of Michigan, but it is not yet open to researchers. The corporate archives at General Motors are entirely closed. There is as yet no biography. Major stories about Donner appeared in *Time* (18 May 1962) and in *Automotive Industries* (15 Aug. 1967). Donner is subjected to harsh criticism in Ed Cray, *Chrome Colossus: General Motors and Its Times* (1980), and Maryann Keller, *Rude Awakening: The Rise, Fall, and Struggle for Recovery of General Motors* (1989). There is a clippings file at the Automotive History Collection at the Detroit Public Library. Obituaries are in *Automotive News* (9 Mar. 1987) and the *Detroit Free Press, Detroit News,* and *New York Times* (all 1 Mar. 1987).

PATRICK J. FURLONG

DONOVAN, Hedley Williams (*b.* 24 May 1914 in Brainerd, Minnesota; *d.* 13 August 1990 in New York City), editor in chief of Time, Inc., who was best known for his managing skills and for his journalistic abilities with regard to national, political, and social issues.

The son of Percy Williams Donovan and Alice Dougan, Hedley Donovan moved to Minneapolis at the age of two with his parents, his brother, and his sister. Percy Donovan worked as a mining engineer for Longyear, and Alice Donovan taught high school English and Latin. The Donovans raised their children in the Protestant tradition and with Republican values in a middle-class neighborhood in Minneapolis. Hedley Donovan learned to read at a young age and developed a passion for language. He began his journalistic forays at the age of ten, when he started writing for his junior high school paper, the *Jeffersonian,* which he eventually edited. In 1930 he graduated from West High School in Minneapolis.

In September 1930 Donovan enrolled at the University of Minnesota, where he pledged Delta Upsilon and was inducted into Phi Beta Kappa. Through his studies, he developed a keen interest in history, and he decided to become a history professor. His interest in politics led him to compose numerous editorials for the campus paper, the *Minnesota Daily.* Donovan rose to assistant editor, and in 1934 he became editorial chairman of the *Daily.* In 1934 Donovan earned a B.A., magna cum laude, and won a Rhodes Scholarship for study at Oxford University in England. At Oxford, he was a fellow of Hertford College, and he served as a stringer for the United Press. He graduated from Oxford in June 1937 with a B.A. in modern history.

Hedley W. Donovan, 1964. ARCHIVE PHOTOS

On returning to the United States, Donovan settled in Washington, D.C., where from 1937 to 1941 he worked as a reporter for the *Washington Post.* His reputation for honest reporting and timeliness grew, and he was promoted to the national desk in 1939 to cover President Franklin Delano Roosevelt's politics. On 18 October 1941 Donovan married Dorothy Hannon, a bacteriologist; they had three children. Donovan remained at the *Washington Post* until 1942, when he left to serve in naval intelligence during World War II. His wife, who maintained her medical job for a few years, worked for the ladies auxiliary during Donovan's tenure with the navy. From 1942 to 1945 Donovan was responsible for reading classified files and producing the *Office of Naval Intelligence Weekly.* He achieved the rank of lieutenant commander.

After his time with the navy, Donovan left Washington for New York City, where he became a political and financial writer for *Fortune.* During his years there, 1945 to 1959, Donovan developed a reputation for being honest, stubborn, and an exceedingly proficient yet heavy-handed editor. He was promoted to the board of editors in 1950, to associate managing editor in 1951, and to managing editor in 1953. In recognition of his achievements, the University of Minnesota in 1956 awarded Donovan the Outstanding Alumni Achievement Award.

Concurrent with his time at *Fortune,* Donovan also worked for the State Department. As a result of his many positions, he was widely respected, a fact that was not lost on Henry R. ("Harry") Luce, editor in chief of Time, Inc. Luce was a savvy businessman with a smart eye for magazines and an incredible sense of the public's wants. He valued Donovan as a writer, manager, and friend, and in 1959 he asked Donovan to assume the position of editorial director, the first step to succeeding Luce as editor in chief.

Donovan officially succeeded Luce in May 1964. When he took control, Time, Inc., was the largest publishing company in the United States, producing magazines such as *Time, Life,* and *Sports Illustrated* as well as Time Life Books. Donovan managed all divisions and built such a reputation that President Lyndon Johnson appointed Donovan to his task force on education in 1964. In later years, President Richard Nixon also requested Donovan's presence on several presidential committees. Donovan was also a trustee of the Carnegie Endowment for International Peace, and he served on the Council for Foreign Relations from 1969 until 1979.

Donovan's most important career decisions revolved around the creation and dissolution of the company's magazines. In 1972, for example, he recommended that Time, Inc., cease publication of *Life,* a weekly magazine. Although he eventually helped make *Life* a monthly, he had had the foresight to realize that as a weekly, the magazine was becoming a victim of time's passage. Donovan also influenced the creation of two new magazines, *Money,* in 1972, and *People,* in 1974.

During his tenure at Time, Inc., Donovan divided his time between residences in Manhattan and in suburban Sands Point on Long Island. His wife was diagnosed with cancer, and she died in 1978. In 1979 Donovan retired from his position as editor in chief, but he remained with the company as a consultant. Also that year, he served as President Jimmy Carter's senior adviser.

In retirement, Donovan continued to write articles for *Time* and *Fortune.* Returning to his original career ambitions, he taught at the Kennedy School of Government, Harvard University, from 1980 to 1987; served as the Leslie Moeller Distinguished Lecturer at the University of Iowa in 1985; and was a visiting resident fellow at Oxford University in 1986.

In 1985 Donovan chronicled his working years in *Roosevelt to Reagan: A Reporter's Encounters with Nine Presidents.* He was awarded honorary degrees of Litt.D. from Pomona College, Boston University, and Mount Holyoke College; L.H.D. from Southwestern at Memphis, Rochester University, and Transylvania University; and LL.D. from Carnegie-Mellon University, Lehigh University, and Allegheny College. He died at New York Hospital after a long battle with lung problems.

Donovan's life was filled with challenges, famous people, interesting assignments, and intense responsibilities. During his fifteen-year tenure as editor in chief at Time, Inc., he created new readership, appointed several managers, and produced new magazines. Because of his managerial abilities, Time strengthened its reputation as a company dedicated to producing top-quality magazines that covered economic, political, and social news in an unbiased, honest, and interesting fashion.

★

Hedley Donovan, *Right Places, Right Times: Forty Years in Journalism, Not Counting My Paper Route* (1989), is an autobiographical work that traces his life from his early days in Minnesota through his schooling and then focuses on his various assignments and his leadership at Time, Inc. *Time, Inc.: The Intimate History of a Publishing Enterprise,* vols. 1 and 2 by Robert T. Elson, vol. 3 by Curtis Prendergast and Geoffrey Colvin (1968, 1973, 1986), is an official company history documenting the writers, reporters, and managers at Time, Inc., which details Donovan's relationships with several people in the company, especially Luce. Daniel Bell et al., *Writing for "Fortune": Nineteen Authors Remember Life on the Staff of a Remarkable Magazine* (1980), is a nostalgic look at the workings, leadership, and ideological slants of *Fortune* from its creation in the research and development phase, through its rough launch, and into its 1980s status as a respected publication. Richard M. Clurman, *To the End of Time: The Seduction and Conquest of a Media Empire* (1992), chronicles the beginnings, successions, and growth of Time, Inc., as a media force to emulate and respect. An obituary recalling Donovan's achievements, career changes, and history, and containing several quotes from esteemed journalists and colleagues, is in the *New York Times* (14 Aug. 1990).

SHARON L. DECKER

DORATI, Antal (*b.* 9 April 1906 in Budapest, Hungary; *d.* 13 November 1988 in Gerzensee, Switzerland), prominent conductor and composer.

Dorati was one of two children of Sándor (in English, Alexander) Doráti, an orchestral violinist, and Margit Kunwald, a self-taught musician on the piano, violin, and viola. His family's comfortable middle-class life included summers at a country house near Lake Balaton. Taught early at home how to read and write, Dorati skipped the first

Antal Dorati. ARCHIVE PHOTOS

two grades when he entered school at age seven. He received his first piano lessons from his mother when he was five; she taught him Hungarian and German folk songs. His next piano teacher was Paula Brown, and he also began cello studies, so that by thirteen, he could join the family string quartert with his father, mother, and her brother, Caesar Kunwald.

Dorati entered the gymnasium (secondary school) in the fall of 1917, where he earned the *matura,* or certificate, upon completion of studies in 1920. That year he passed the challenging musical examinations for admittance to the Franz Liszt Academy of Music in Budapest and became its youngest student. Among his professors at the academy were Zoltán Kodály and Leo Weiner. After graduation in 1924, Dorati accepted a salaried position as an opera coach, rehearsal pianist, and sometime conductor at Budapest's Royal Opera House. He worked with Fyodor Chaliapin, Matteo Battistini, and Maria Jeritza.

In 1928 Dorati started a one-year term as special assistant to Fritz Busch, the general music director of the Dresden State Opera. In 1929 he began conducting at the Münster Opera House. On 14 July 1929 he married Klári Kórody in their native Hungary, and they honeymooned in Italy; they had one child. In 1933 Dorati and his wife left for Paris, where he coached vocal students and organized music (including an orchestra) at the new state radio station. In December he agreed to conduct in England three performances with the Ballet Russe de Monte Carlo; this first-time experience conducting ballet led immediately to his accepting a permanent post as second conductor. Dorati left that December with the company for a tour in the United States, first in New York and then other cities. As conductor from 1938 to 1941 of what became known as the Original Ballet Russe, Dorati was part of their tours, which included England, Australia, New Zealand, Europe, Cuba, and the United States.

In 1941 Dorati moved to New York City and accepted two contracts: one as music director of the Ballet Theatre (eventually known as American Ballet Theatre), the other as director of the New Opera Company. Dorati worked with Michel Fokine and David Lichine developing new arrangements of Offenbach's *Bluebird* and *La Belle Hélène,* as well as a medley of Johann Strauss, Jr., waltzes for Lichine's *Graduation Ball* (1940). The New Opera Company requested that Dorati conduct Offenbach's *La Vie parisienne* in English, with his newly arranged overture. When the company's board rejected Dorati's suggestion in 1942 to produce the highly acclaimed work on Broadway, Dorati severed his affiliation.

Dorati resigned from the American Ballet Theatre in 1945 and became chief conductor of the Dallas Symphony Orchestra. His first public performance with the Dallas Symphony Orchestra, on 15 December 1945, was soon followed by a concert at Carnegie Hall, whereupon RCA Victor signed a recording contract with Dorati and the Dallas Symphony. He commissioned and conducted world premieres of compositions by Walter Piston, William Schuman, George Antheil, and Paul Hindemith. He became an American citizen in 1947.

In 1949 Dorati succeeded Dmitri Mitropoulos as conductor and music director of the Minneapolis Symphony Orchestra, a position he held until 1960, and conducted works by Stravinsky, Bartók, and Menotti, as well as Dorati's own compositions, including *The Way of the Cross,* a cantata based on a poem by Paul Claudel and one of several musical expressions of Dorati's Catholic faith, presented on Good Friday, April 1957. He also conducted the Minneapolis Symphony in more than one hundred recordings, first with RCA and thereafter with Mercury Records, including a series of complete ballets and his own *Symphony* and *Nocturne and Capriccio, for Oboe and String Quartet* (composed in 1957 and 1926, respectively). The acclaimed interpretations of these high-quality Mercury Living Presence recordings secured the international reputation of the Minneapolis Symphony and of Dorati as orchestral conductor.

In the early 1950s, Dorati was diagnosed with Menière's disease (an inner ear nerve imbalance, potentially leading to permanent deafness) and considered it "a near miracle" when the disease failed to develop. He maintained an active schedule of conducting, including work with the London Symphony Orchestra, and a summer conducting course at Salzburg's Mozarteum in 1959.

In 1960 Dorati left the Minneapolis Symphony Orchestra and moved to Rome, where he focused on guest conducting. He was especially proud of conducting Verdi's *Simon Boccanegra* (1960), for which his daughter, Antonia, had prepared the scenery and costumes. In 1962 he made his Covent Garden conducting debut with Rimsky-Korsakov's opera *The Golden Cockerel.* He then served as chief conductor of the BBC Symphony Orchestra in London (1963–1966). His marriage ended in divorce in the late 1960s. On 16 December 1969 he married Ilse von Alpenheim, an Austrian pianist; Switzerland became their permanent residence. During a period of several years Dorati undertook a monumental, highly successful project with Decca to record all of Haydn's 104 symphonies with the Philharmonica Hungarica. The recording sessions were completed in December 1972.

From 1966 to 1974 Dorati was principal conductor of the Stockholm Philharmonic (conductor laureate, 1981–1988). He was also the music director of the National Symphony Orchestra (1969–1977) in Washington, D.C. He had made his American debut as a symphonic conductor in

Washington with the National Symphony Orchestra in December 1937, and on 9 September 1971 he inaugurated the Concert Hall of the new John F. Kennedy Center for the Performing Arts in that city. He served as principal conductor of the Royal Philharmonic Orchestra in London from 1975 to 1978 (conductor laureate, 1978–1981) and as music director of the Detroit Symphony Orchestra from 1977 to 1981. His second symphony, titled *Querela Pacis,* received its premiere on 24 April 1986. He died of undisclosed causes at his home at Gerzensee, near Bern.

Dorati considered himself a "renaissance man"—a conductor capable of superior readings of totally different types of works and composers, from the classical structures of Haydn through the new tonal expressions of the twentieth century. He believed that vocal works should be performed in the native tongue of the audience and tried to cultivate new audiences with special attention to the young. He was respected for his scholarly musicianship, the molding of colorful vibrant sound from his different orchestras, and the precision of his rhythmic attacks. Most of the time he committed the scores to memory. A striking figure at five feet, eleven inches, with penetrating gray eyes, Dorati frequently spoke against bombastic histrionics of musicians at the podium, and he conducted with minimal, self-contained movements of the baton. During rehearsals he treated the members in a polite professional manner, and when warranted only rarely demonstrated short-tempered reactions. Dorati earned international recognition as an orchestra builder and stimulated musicians and audiences alike with interesting programming (including gradual exposure to contemporary compositions), challenging national or overseas tours, and prestigious recordings. His recording legacy includes more than 500 titles and twenty-nine Grands Prix du Disque.

★

Dorati's *Notes of Seven Decades* (1979; rev. 1981) contains autobiographical episodes of his professional and sometimes personal life as well as discussions on conducting and composing, with about three dozen photographs. For extensive discussions by him on performing musical texts in translation, certain recording projects, and the conductor-audience relations in regard to contemporary music, see his articles, "Non-Traveling Opera," *Opera News* (Apr. 1965); "Next—the Haydn Operas?," *High Fidelity Magazine* (Aug. 1973); and "I Am Pleading for the Works I Perform," *Symphony News* (June 1975). See also E. Ruth Anderson, comp., *Contemporary American Composers: A Biographical Dictionary* (1982), for a generic grouping of some of his compositions through 1979. For a chronological cataloging of Dorati's compositions from the 1920s through his final works, see Calum MacDonald, *Tempo* (Dec. 1982, June 1986, and Mar. 1989).

Important interviews include Shirley Fleming, "Antal Dorati: The Ability to Compose Matches the Ability to Command," *High Fidelity* (June 1963); and Richard Lee, "Musician of the Month: Antal Dorati," *High Fidelity* (Sept. 1971). Obituaries are in the *New York Times* (15 Nov. 1988) and London *Times* (15 and 16 Nov. 1988).

MADELINE SAPIENZA

DRAKE, (John Gibbs) St. Clair (*b.* 2 January 1911 in Suffolk, Virginia; *d.* 15 June 1990 in Palo Alto, California), sociologist, cultural anthropologist, and educator best known for coauthoring *Black Metropolis* (1945), a groundbreaking analysis of African-American life in Chicago.

Drake was the son of a Barbados immigrant who became a Baptist minister and Bessie Lee Bowles, a schoolteacher from Virginia. He grew up in Pittsburgh, Pennsylvania, then Staunton, Virginia, when his parents separated. He graduated from Booker T. Washington High School in Staunton in 1927, then attended Hampton Institute's School of Education, majoring in biology and graduating with honors and a B.S. degree in 1931. From 1931 to 1932 he attended the Pendle Hill School, a Quaker graduate center in Wallingford, Pennsylvania. During this period he participated in a pacifist tour through the South with

St. Clair Drake, 1966. AP/WIDE WORLD PHOTOS. COURTESY NYT PERMISSIONS.

Quaker activists. His travels with these "peace caravans" nearly got him lynched by angry southerners on several occasions (he was one of three blacks among 200 whites). He was a high school teacher in Cambria, Virginia, from 1932 to 1935, then taught at Dillard University in New Orleans until 1937, while also doing field research in Mississippi for Allison Davis's book *Deep South.*

In the summer of 1937 Drake went to Chicago on a Rosenwald Fellowship, and under the auspices of the Works Progress Administration (WPA) and the Illinois State Commission on the Conditions of the Urban Colored Population, he and another researcher, Horace R. Cayton, began a study of blacks in Chicago. This study was submitted in 1940 as "Churches and Voluntary Associations in the Chicago Negro Community." From 1937 to 1943 he was also enrolled as a graduate student in anthropology and sociology at the University of Chicago. In September 1941 he returned to Dillard to teach social anthropology, but the school's president dismissed him in 1942 for supporting a student bus sit-in. In June of that year Drake married a white sociologist, Elizabeth Dewey Johns; they had two children. Although he had been raised in mixed neighborhoods and had rarely encountered prejudice as a youth, his experience in raising an interracial family in a segregated society later influenced his academic interest in race relations. From 1943 to 1945 he served as a statistician in the Medical Division of the U.S. merchant marine.

In December 1945 Drake and Cayton published the two-volume *Black Metropolis: A Study of Negro Life in a Northern City.* This work, which grew out of their WPA research, analyzed the black section of Chicago's South Side, popularly referred to as Bronzeville. Drawing on hundreds of interviews and other sociological data, *Black Metropolis* examined the migration of blacks to Chicago from other states; the development of local churches, newspapers, and other establishments; and the relationships among upper-, middle-, and lower-class blacks. Drake and Cayton also investigated the impact of the New Deal and World War II on the economy of the South Side and how those changes created a "new Negro mentality" that accelerated the fight against segregation. In his introduction to the book, the author Richard Wright called *Black Metropolis* the "definitive study of Negro urbanization." Wright praised Drake and Cayton for combining sociology and anthropology to reveal how industrialization, secularization, urbanization, and social differentiation shaped relations between blacks and whites in Chicago. The study won the 1945 Wolf Award for being a landmark in American urban scholarship.

In September 1946 Drake was appointed assistant professor of sociology at Roosevelt University in Chicago. He returned to the University of Chicago that year to complete his graduate studies. He passed his doctoral qualifying exams in 1947, earning his master's degree in anthropology, and left Roosevelt to research his dissertation in Cardiff, Wales. While conducting his dissertation research on British race relations, Drake became involved with the Pan-African Federation and began a longtime political collaboration with Kwame Nkrumah, who became prime minister of Ghana. During this same period, he published articles on race relations in such journals as *Crisis, Ebony, Negro Digest, Phylon,* and the *Journal of Negro Education.* In June 1954 he received his Ph.D. in social anthropology, with a concentration on African studies, from the University of Chicago. His dissertation, which he never published, was entitled, "Value Systems, Social Structure, and Race Relations in the British Isles."

From 1954 to 1955 he researched West Africa under a Ford Foundation Fellowship, and from 1958 to 1961 he headed the University of Ghana's Sociology Department. In 1961 Drake returned to Roosevelt to teach full-time and became a supporter of the Student Nonviolent Coordinating Committee. During the summers of 1961, 1962, and 1964, Drake helped train Peace Corps volunteers heading for Africa. In 1963 he started to teach part-time at Roosevelt, so that he could also teach at Stanford University in Palo Alto, California. In April 1965 Drake left for Ghana on a Social Science Research Council Fellowship. However, when Nkrumah's government was overthrown that year by the first of a series of military regimes, Drake returned to the United States and joined civil rights marches in Chicago and in Jackson, Mississippi, in 1966. He also became involved in protests against the Vietnam War.

During the next two years Drake published *Race Relations in a Time of Rapid Social Change: Report of a Survey* (1966) and *Our Urban Poor: Promises to Keep and Miles to Go* (1967). He was in the Caribbean from the summer of 1967 to the winter of 1968, researching and writing a study to be called "Africa and the Black Diaspora." The study was never published in its complete form. In 1969 Drake became a full-time professor at Stanford University. He organized and directed the innovative and imitated African and African-American studies program there, in addition to teaching anthropology and sociology, until he became professor emeritus in 1976.

In 1970 Drake published *The Redemption of Africa and Black Religion,* which represented the first chapter of his projected study of the black diaspora. Three years later, while working as a fellow of the Center for the Study of Multi-Racial Societies at the University of the West Indies, he was given the Du Bois–Johnson–Frazier Award by the American Sociological Association. During his final years at Stanford, Drake found it necessary to put aside his initial studies of the black diaspora in order to address attitudes among his colleagues and students that racial differences were due to heredity and that racial prejudice was a natural and inevitable part of human society. Drake published *Black Folk Here and There: An Essay in History and Anthropology* in 1987, after a decade of research and writing, in response to these controversies. In this work, Drake distinguished between slavery, skin-color prejudice, and racism, arguing that these three concepts had existed independently of each other before the sixteenth century, and that the concepts only came together in an interdependent framework after Europeans began to use African slaves in their expansion into the New World.

Drake died of a heart attack at his home in Palo Alto.

★

The Schomburg Center for Research in Black Culture in New York City has many of Drake's personal papers (1935–1990), correspondence, unpublished writings, and several biographical and autobiographical sketches. The introductions to *Black Metropolis* (1945; rev. and enlarged, 1993), and *Black Folk Here and There* (1987) contain further biographical information, particularly about the research that led to the publication of each work. An obituary is in the *New York Times* (21 June 1990).

DURAHN TAYLOR

DUNCAN, Robert (*b.* 7 January 1919 in Oakland, California; *d.* 3 February 1988 in San Francisco, California), poet and author known for his dynamically innovative poetry, which concentrates on the individual creative process and its vital connections to European poetic traditions, world mythologies, religious and mystical lore, and twentieth-century science.

Robert Duncan. COURTESY OF NEW DIRECTIONS. PHOTO BY KELLY WISE

After the death of his natural mother, Marguerite Wesley Duncan, the infant Duncan, born Edward Howard Duncan, was put up for adoption by his father, Edward Howard Duncan, a day laborer, in 1920. His adoptive parents renamed him Robert Edward Symmes, a name he kept until 1942, when he resumed his original surname.

Raised in Bakersfield, California, by an upper middle-class family (his adoptive father was an architect), Duncan was deeply influenced by his family's commitment to Christian theosophy and hermetic beliefs, instilling in him at an early age a spiritual perspective on language. An accident in 1922 left him cross-eyed, causing a "vertical and horizontal displacement of vision," which he frequently cited as critical to his own complex notions of human perception. As a boy, he was also drawn to fairy tales and myths, further cultivating a deeply felt sense of what he himself later called the fertile "confusions" of daily life, literature, and the subconscious.

Encouraged to write poetry by a high school teacher, Edna Keough, Duncan went on to study from 1936 until 1938 at the University of California at Berkeley, where he published many of his earliest poems. After leaving Berkeley in his sophomore year, he went to New York City, where he mingled in avant-garde art circles that included, among others, Anaïs Nin and Henry Miller. With Sanders Russell in Woodstock, New York, he edited *Experimental Review* (1938–1940), and after a very brief period of military service, he was discharged, on psychiatric grounds, in 1941.

Duncan's private conflicts with his emerging homosexuality reached a crisis point in 1943 after a failed one-year marriage to Marjorie McKee. In his groundbreaking essay "The Homosexual in Society" (1944) he indicted both the insularity of the homosexual community and the insidious suppression of homosexuality from mainstream literary study. Although the landmark essay was a personally liberating experience for Duncan, it caused his poetry to be rejected by many of the leading magazines of the time. Throughout his life Duncan was to claim that it was his sexuality that ultimately determined his poetic vocation and his wholesale rejection of the "paradigms of the Protestant ethic" and the banality of a commodity-driven, capitalist culture. Although never a political activist, he became an ardent pacifist, and his poetry often exhibits a sophisticated and often embittered awareness of postwar American militarism.

By 1945 Duncan had resettled in California and was already associated with the poet Kenneth Rexroth and the movement known later as the San Francisco Renaissance. His *Heavenly City, Earthly City* (1947) and symphonic

"Venice Poem" (1948) represent the best of his earliest poetry. He reenrolled at Berkeley in 1946 to study medieval and Renaissance literature while completing *Medieval Scenes* (1950), a collection of poems about the dynamics of sexual desire, religious worship, poetic practice, and pagan and Christian symbol-making.

In 1950 Duncan met painter Jess Collins (who went by only his first name), and the two became lifelong partners. The couple set up a home and artistic salon in the Potrero Hill section of San Francisco, and Duncan's new relationship expanded his interests in contemporary art, especially the art of collage, of which Jess was a leading practitioner. Duncan consciously adopted collage as a model for his own derivative and open-ended poetic style, and he published a book of poetic imitations of Gertrude Stein and established personal relationships with the prominent American poets and literary icons Ezra Pound and Hilda Doolittle (H.D.).

From 1954 to 1956 Duncan taught at Black Mountain College in North Carolina, in a program run by the avant-garde poet Charles Olson, whose essay on projective verse and "field" poetry had been a deep influence on an emerging generation of postwar American poets, particularly Duncan. Still, his artistic openness led to his association with many different schools of poetry of this period: back home in the Bay Area he was, by the late 1950s, frequently grouped with the Beat Movement, which included poets Allen Ginsberg and Lawrence Ferlinghetti, and in 1957 he and poet Jack Spicer organized a "Poetry as Magic" workshop at San Francisco State College. Increasingly, Duncan's poetry began to reflect a self-conscious fascination with the primal sources and unpredictable currents of the creative impulse. As he writes in "Source" (1956), "In this I am not a maker of things but, if maker, maker of a way."

Duncan's breakthrough came in 1960 with the critically acclaimed *The Opening of the Field,* a volume that combined the influence of Walt Whitman's upbeat American vernacular tone with Duncan's own Modernist reverence for the godlike calling of the artist and the need for new poetic visions. As he had in his early volumes, Duncan stresses in *The Opening* the inherent music of free verse as well as its formal possibilities, writing that he "saw a snake-like beauty in the living changes of syntax." In poems energized by shifting, elliptical sequences and verbal tapestries, Duncan weaves references to the Old Testament and ancient Greek and Egyptian mythologies into imagistic, dreamlike meditations on the creative will—from the determination in "The Structure of Rime" to the quietly organic outlook of "Poetry a Natural Thing," as well as the personal, historical and political perspectives of Duncan's most famous poem, "A Poem Beginning with a Line by Pindar."

Roots and Branches (1964) continues his focus on transcending artificial boundaries between the physical life and the spirit world, celebrating a poetry written on the margins of consciousness and beyond the limits of conventional thinking. Its follow-up, *Bending the Bow* (1968), contains poems rich in allusions to ancient and Renaissance artistry as well as increasingly angry refrains about the American involvement in Vietnam—in "Up Rising Passages 25" the speaker compares President Lyndon Johnson to Hitler and Stalin.

Duncan announced in 1968 that he would not publish work again for fifteen years, and although he made occasional public appearances, his artistic withdrawal during most of the 1970s cost him considerable long-term recognition. His final volumes, published as his health began to fail, extend the ambitious serial poems of earlier collections, while also paying homage to the visionary poetry of the ancient Persian poet Rumi and medieval Italian poet Dante, as Duncan's meditations attempt to place his infirmity and impending death within the poetic lifework of the universe. After a long struggle with kidney failure, Duncan died in San Francisco.

Even today, Duncan's poetry is often harshly criticized for its deliberately derivative and allusive qualities. Yet he remains a widely anthologized if often overlooked figure in twentieth-century American letters, distinguished by his commitment to a poetry that is at once refined and colloquial, deeply rooted in learning and tradition while branching out to undiscovered art forms, and ever alive with an unfashionably romantic faith in the mythic sources and energies of poetic creation.

★

Ekbert Fass, *Young Robert Duncan: Portrait of the Poet as Homosexual in Society* (1983), is the only biography of the poet. *Robert Duncan: Selected Poems* (1993) and *A Selected Prose* (1995), both thoughtfully edited by Robert J. Bertholf, provide the best introductions to the important poems, lectures, and essays of Duncan's career. Other important collections of Duncan's writing are *Ground Work: Before the War* (1984), *Fictive Certainties* (1985), and *Ground Work II: In the Dark* (1987). Robert J. Bertholf and Ian W. Reid, eds., *Robert Duncan: Scales of the Marvelous* (1979), contains interviews with close friends, testimonials by fellow poets (including poet and close friend Denise Levertov's invaluable and moving autobiographical essay), as well as thorough scholarly assessments of Duncan's poetics. An obituary is in the *New York Times* (4 Feb. 1988).

TIM KEANE

DUNNE, Irene Marie (*b.* 20 December 1898 in Louisville, Kentucky; *d.* 4 September 1990 in Holmby Hills, California), film actress whose reputation for ladylike behavior onscreen and off-screen earned her the nickname "first lady of Hollywood."

Dunne was born Irene Marie Dunn, the elder of the two children of Joseph John Dunn, a riverboat engineer, and

Irene Dunne. ARCHIVE PHOTOS

Antoinette Henry, a musician. She added the *e* to her last name when she became an actress. She went to elementary school at St. Benedict's Academy in Louisville and transferred to the Loretto Convent School in St. Louis when her father became a supervisor of steamboat inspectors for the federal government in that city. Joseph Dunn died when Irene was eleven, and his widow moved to her parents' home in Madison, Indiana. Irene graduated from Madison High School in 1916. She also studied voice and piano, first with her mother and later at the Oliver Willard Pierce Academy of Fine Arts in Indianapolis. She earned a teaching certificate from Webster College in St. Louis in 1918, but she also won a scholarship contest at the Chicago Musical College in September of that year and decided to pursue her vocal studies instead. She studied there for two years, hoping to become an opera singer.

In 1920, after an unsuccessful audition with the Metropolitan Opera, Dunne began auditioning for musical comedies in New York, where she landed a role in the touring company of *Irene,* a popular play. Dunne's first Broadway part was a minor one in *The Clinging Vine* (1922). This led to other, bigger roles. She replaced stars in leading roles until 1928, when she got her first original leading role in *Luckee Girl.* In July 1928 she married Francis Griffin, a dentist. In 1929, shortly after her marriage, Dunne found her best role yet as Magnolia in the touring company of the musical *Show Boat*. Dunne later recalled, perhaps apocryphally, that she got the part by accident. She happened to ride in an elevator with Florenz Ziegfeld, the showman, who was apparently so impressed with her slender, ladylike looks that he sent his secretary scouring the building for her. The performance that resulted from this meeting gleaned Dunne a movie contract with RKO Studios.

Although Dunne was hired in large part for her musical skills, by the time she arrived in Hollywood in 1930, musical films had lost much of their initial popularity. Her debut for RKO, *Leathernecking* (1930), was, therefore, a minor, nonmusical comedy. Her next film, *Cimarron* (1931), a saga of the land rush in Oklahoma based on a novel by Edna Ferber, was a tremendous success and earned Dunne an Academy Award nomination. She would be nominated for four other Academy Awards over the course of her career. After a few more light roles at the studio, Dunne made *Symphony of Six Million* (1932), based on a novel by Fannie Hurst. This was her first "weepie," a genre for which she would become well known. Also in 1932, she was loaned to Universal for *Back Street,* another Hurst adaptation, in which Dunne played the long-suffering mistress of John Boles. The movie broke box-office records for Universal.

Dunne continued alternating between light comedies and dramas through the mid-1930s. In 1934 she was finally allowed to sing on-screen in *Stingaree,* which was followed by *Sweet Adeline* and *Roberta* in 1935. After *Roberta,* Dunne left RKO, preferring to sign short-term contracts with a variety of studios. The financial security offered by her husband aided Dunne in her decision to leave RKO. Her career continued to flourish, and in 1935 she worked with Columbia on a new type of film for her, the screwball comedy. In *Theodora Goes Wild* (1936), her ladylike persona added an amusing touch to her character, a proper spinster who writes a scandalous novel. In 1936 Griffin moved to California, where he managed a number of lucrative real-estate holdings and helped Dunne's agent, Charles Feldman, manage her career. In December 1936 Dunne and Griffin adopted a daughter. Dunne was one of the few major stars who avoided being tied down to one employer in the 1930s and 1940s.

In 1936 Dunne reprised the role of Magnolia on-screen for Universal's production of *Show Boat*. In 1937 she co-starred with Cary Grant, one of her favorite leading men, in another screwball comedy, *The Awful Truth.* Dunne always maintained that she was prouder of her comedy work than her drama. She told an interviewer: "An actress who can do comedy can do drama, but the vice versa isn't necessarily true. Big emotional scenes are much easier to play than comedy. An onion can bring tears to your eyes, but what vegetable can make you laugh?"

Dunne continued to make films in the late 1930s and

the 1940s. Among the best-known are *Love Affair* (1939), one of Dunne's personal favorites, with Charles Boyer; *My Favorite Wife* (1940), a screwball tale of accidental bigamy; *Anna and the King of Siam* (1946); *Life with Father* (1947); and a nostalgic film, *I Remember Mama* (1948).

In the 1950s Dunne retired from films and made various television and radio appearances. She was an enthusiastic Republican, and in 1957 President Dwight D. Eisenhower appointed her an alternate delegate to the United Nations. She received a number of honors during this decade, including the Lateran Cross from the Catholic Church in 1951, the Award of Merit from the Sister Elizabeth Kenny Foundation in 1953, an honorary doctorate from Notre Dame in 1958, and numerous retrospective film showings.

After her husband's death in 1965, Dunne took over his business interests and continued to be active in charities, Hollywood organizations, and politics. In 1985 she was named by her friend Ronald Reagan as a recipient of a Kennedy Center Honor. After suffering for some months from heart trouble, Dunne died of heart failure in her home at Holmby Hills, California. She is buried in Calvary Cemetery in Whittier, California.

Although she was never a flashy star, to many fans and to many of her fellow professionals, Irene Dunne exemplified the best of Hollywood. Whether suffering nobly through a weepie, trilling her light soprano voice blithely through a musical, or moving archly through a screwball comedy, she symbolized beauty and class to millions of Americans.

★

Dunne's scripts and scrapbooks as well as a number of other papers are at the University of Southern California Cinema-Television Library. The Billy Rose Theater Collection of the New York Public Library also has a number of clippings files on Dunne. The best book on her life and career is Margie Schultz, *Irene Dunne: A Bio-Bibliography* (1991). Also helpful is James Robert Parish, *The RKO Gals* (1974), which features extensive commentary and a filmography. Obituaries are in the *New York Times* (6 Sept. 1990) and *Film Comment* (Mar.-Apr. 1991).

TINKY "DAKOTA" WEISBLAT

E

EAKER, Ira Clarence (*b.* 17 April 1896 in Field Creek, Texas; *d.* 6 August 1987 in Camp Springs, Maryland), aviation pioneer and air force general who commanded U.S. Army air forces in Europe and the Mediterranean during World War II.

Eaker was the oldest of five sons born to Young Yarcy Eaker, a tenant farmer, and Donna Lee Graham. A drought forced the family to move to Oklahoma when Eaker was a young boy. Eaker later said that the hardships of farming taught him toughness and self-reliance. He was a voracious reader and excelled at debating in school.

Eaker graduated from the Southeastern Normal School (now Southeastern Oklahoma State University) in the spring of 1917 with a degree in journalism. He wanted to attend law school, but his plans changed abruptly on 6 April 1917 when the United States declared war on Germany. On 8 May 1917, Eaker enlisted in the army.

While waiting to begin officer training school, Eaker chanced to meet a pilot recruiting for the aviation section of the Signal Corps. He quickly signed up for flight training. After earning his pilot's rating, Eaker was assigned to Rockwell Field near San Diego. His commander was Colonel Henry A. ("Hap") Arnold, who later commanded the U.S. Army Air Corps in World War II. With Arnold, Eaker cowrote and published three books: *This Flying Game* (1936), *Winged Warfare* (1941), and *Army Flyer* (1942).

After World War I ended, Eaker was sent to the Philippines to join the Second Aero Squadron, and later he was given command of the Third Aero Squadron. In July 1920 he was promoted to captain and named executive officer in the air office of the Philippine Department.

Eaker returned from a two-year tour in the Philippines still yearning to study law. He nearly left the army in 1922, but instead enrolled in a program that allowed him to attend Columbia University Law School and at the same time remain in the army.

After one semester at Columbia, Eaker was summoned to Washington, D.C., to become assistant executive officer to Major General Mason Patrick, chief of the air service. He remained in this position until October 1926.

In 1923 Eaker married Leah Chase. They had no children and were divorced in 1930. He married Ruth Huff Apperson on 23 November 1931. His second marriage also produced no children.

In 1926 Eaker was made second in command of a Pan-American Flight that was designed as a goodwill trip around South America. The trip, in which five planes participated, was to cover the length of South America and back. During the 133-day trip, two of the planes were lost in a midair collision, and Eaker himself survived several close calls. He was awarded the Distinguished Flying Cross for his part in the flight and returned to Washington as executive officer in the office of the assistant secretary of war.

In 1929 Eaker became chief pilot of the *Question Mark,* the plane with which he set a world endurance record of 150 hours, 40 minutes, and 15 seconds with refueling in

Lieutenant General Ira C. Eaker. AMERICAN STOCK/ARCHIVE PHOTOS

the air. In 1930 he completed the first transcontinental flight to use in-flight refueling, and in 1936 he became the first person to cross the United States using only his plane's instruments. In between his record-setting flights, Eaker earned a degree in journalism from the University of Southern California in 1932.

Eaker was promoted to major in 1935. In the following months, he attended the Air Corps tactical school at Maxwell Field, Alabama, and the Command and General Staff School at Fort Leavenworth, Kansas. In 1937 he returned to Washington as chief of the public relations section of the Air Corps. When war broke out in Europe in 1939, he was stationed at Mitchell Field, New York. In 1940 he was promoted to lieutenant colonel and was sent to Hamilton Field, California, as commander of the Twentieth Pursuit Group. He spent the summer of 1941 in England as an observer with the Royal Air Force.

Shortly after the attack on Pearl Harbor, Eaker was promoted to colonel and sent back to California to head up fighter defenses for the West Coast. In July 1942 Eaker, now a brigadier general, was sent to Great Britain as commander of the U.S. Eighth Bomber Command. Upon his arrival in England, the husky, balding, cigar-smoking pilot with a soft-spoken Texas drawl said, "We won't do much talking until we've done more fighting. We hope that when we leave you'll be glad we came."

On 4 July 1942 Eaker was ordered by Washington to lead his men on their first mission against targets in Europe. Though largely a failure, the "first American mission" did make headlines at home, which was its intention. "I never thought 'morale bombing' made much sense," wrote Eaker to General Carl A. Spaatz in 1943. "We must never allow the record of this war to convict us of throwing the strategic bomber at the man in the street."

More encouraging was the raid on Rouen, France, on 17 August 1942. Eaker led a group of American B-17s that destroyed German railroads, freight yards, and roadhouses. A week later Eaker was awarded the Silver Star for his "planning, organizing, and participation in the attacks on the enemy." In July 1942 he was given command of the entire Eighth Air Force, and in September of that year was promoted to major general.

While planning air strategy, Eaker became a proponent of precision daylight bombing of German industrial targets. The Combined Bomber Offensive (or "Eaker Plan") commenced in January 1943, with the Americans bombing by day and the British bombing by night.

In 1944 Eaker took over as commander in chief of Mediterranean Allied air forces in Italy. He flew the first bombing raid into Germany from Italy in June 1944, and he flew a fighter plane during the invasion of southern France on 15 August 1944. Near the end of the war, Eaker was summoned back to Washington and named deputy commander of the army air forces and chief of the air staff. He served in that position until his retirement as a lieutenant general on 31 August 1947.

Eaker joined the Hughes Tool Company and the Hughes Aircraft Company in 1947. In 1957 he became a vice president of the Douglas Aircraft Company, but in 1962 he returned to Hughes as an adviser. Between 1962 and 1980 Eaker wrote a syndicated column on military affairs that appeared in 180 newspapers. In 1985, with the approval of Congress, President Ronald Reagan bestowed upon Eaker the fourth star of a full general.

In 1987 Eaker died of heart failure at Malcolm Grow Medical Center at Andrews Air Force Base, in Camp Springs, Maryland. He was buried with full military honors in Arlington National Cemetery.

★

James Parton, *Air Force Spoken Here: General Ira Eaker and the Command of the Air* (1986), is a detailed biography written by Eaker's aide through most of World War II. Articles on Eaker's life appear in *Time* (30 Aug. 1983) and the *Washington Post* (10 Apr. 1985). Obituaries are in the *Washington Post* (7 Aug. 1987) and *New York Times* (8 Aug. 1987).

ERNEST A. MCKAY
ELLEN FRENCH MCKAY
STEPHEN MCKAY

EAMES, Ray (*b.* 15 December 1912 in Sacramento, California; *d.* 21 August 1988 in Los Angeles, California), artist, designer, and filmmaker who with her husband, Charles, created some of the most famous furniture of the twentieth century, large-scale exhibitions, and award-winning films.

Born Bernice Alexandra Kaiser, Eames was the third child of Alexander Kaiser, a theatrical manager who later became an insurance salesman, and Edna Burr, a housewife. She had at least two siblings and was called "Ray-Ray" as a child, which she later shortened to Ray. After graduating from Sacramento High School in 1931, she attended Sacramento Junior College for a term, then went to the May Friend Bennet School in Millbrook, New York (1931–1933). From 1933 to 1939 she studied painting with Hans Hofmann in New York City and Provincetown, Massachusetts. In 1940 and 1941 she attended Cranbrook Academy of Art, Bloomfield Hills, Michigan, where she met Charles Eames, head of what later became known as the Department of Industrial Design. She helped him prepare drawings and models for the molded plywood chairs that were winning entries (shared with Eero Saarinen) in the Organic Design in Home Furnishings competition sponsored by the Museum of Modern Art in 1940. Ray and Charles Eames married on 20 June 1941, beginning a design partnership that lasted until Charles's death in 1978. They had no children.

After marrying, Ray and Charles Eames moved to Los Angeles in 1941. During World War II they set up a workshop in Venice, California, where they experimented with molded plywood, developed leg splints and stretchers for the U.S. Navy (with John Entenza, Gregory Ain, and Griswald Raetze), and later made plywood parts for aircraft. Their home, Eames House, which they built as "Case Study House #8" for *Arts and Architecture* magazine, in Pacific Palisades, California, was considered a classic in architecture. Begun in 1945 in collaboration with Saarinen and finished in 1949, Eames House had prefabricated, standardized parts used previously only in industrial design, an exposed steel framework, alternating glass and solid color panels, light-filled open interiors, and a high view of the ocean. Utilizing technologies developed during the war, Eames House was intended to be one solution to the postwar housing shortage and was featured in a short film produced by Ray and Charles Eames, *House after Five Years of Living* (1955). In 1978 the American Institute of Architects gave Eames House its twenty-five-year award, calling it a "merger of technology and art, transcending mere construction and avoiding sterility by combining elegance and utility."

Ray and Charles Eames focused on furniture in the 1940s and 1950s and are best remembered for their chair designs. In 1946 they created the molded plywood chair, one version with wooden legs and another with metal legs, copies of which were widely used. They designed the Plastic Armchair in 1950 and the Wire Mesh Chair and the Plastic Side Chair in 1951. A version of the latter became the famous plastic Stacking Chair of 1954. In 1956 they produced the Lounge Chair or Eames Chair, made for the film director Billy Wilder and arguably their most famous creation. This handsome black leather chair and ottoman

Ray Eames (*left*) with her husband and collaborator Charles Eames. LIBRARY OF CONGRESS/CORBIS

with molded plywood frame is a classic and was produced by the Herman Miller Furniture Company, with whom the Eameses worked for many years. Throughout their careers, they continued to design chairs, tables, and sofas, for which the Eames firm won numerous awards.

Ray Eames was especially fond of filmmaking, which she and Charles began as a way of recording objects that filled their home and studio. They continued to develop their talent as commissions for instructional films came from CBS, Boeing, the U.S. government, and other clients. Their films, which were both educational and aesthetically superb, won many international awards, including the 1957 Edinburgh International Film Festival Award for *Toccata for Toy Trains* (1957, fourteen minutes). An Eames trademark was creative design in films, including multiscreen presentations such as *IBM at the Fair* (1965, eight minutes), shown at the 1965 New York World's Fair; and *The Powers of Ten* (1968, eight minutes), which introduced relativity to American schoolchildren of the 1960s and 1970s. They also designed toys, including The Toy (1951), House of Cards (1952), and the Coloring Toy (1955).

Ray and Charles Eames produced major exhibitions and originated the idea of the "history wall," a type of exhibition employing photographic images, short films, interesting objects, and games to contextualize a given subject over time. In creating such history-wall exhibitions about topics as diverse as mathematics, computers, and the life and times of Jawaharlal Nehru, the Eameses were brilliant organizers who connected the disparate threads of modern life to make art. While the exhibitions were criticized by some for being "information overload," they were loved by others for the same reason.

In the 1940s the petite Ray wore long hair and tight-bodiced, full-skirted dresses, her characteristic style, which made her look younger than she was. Although she was described as "sweet smiling," she and her husband did not separate their private lives from their work and may not have been easy people for whom to work. Charles said of Ray:

> She has a very good sense of what gives an idea, or form, or piece of sculpture its character, of how its relationships are formed. She can see where there is a wrong mix of ideas or materials, where the division between two ideas isn't clear. If this sounds like a structural or architectural idea, it is. But it comes to Ray through her painting . . . any student of Hans's [Hofmann's] has a sense of this kind of structure.

When discussing a stool made in 1960 for the lobby of the Time-Life Building in New York City, Ray Eames said: "People still call it 'Ray's stool.' That implies Charles had nothing to do with it—which was not so. It also implies that I had nothing to do with all [those] other chairs." Esther McCoy, a longtime friend of Ray Eames, said, "That was the thing about Ray, the infinite number of variations that sprang from those square fingered hands." While it is impossible to tell what work was done by whom in the Eames partnership, Charles was the one in the forefront. They jointly received the first Kaufmann International Design Award in New York City (1960), but in 1967, when Charles was awarded the Design Medal by the British Society of Industrial Artists and Designers, Ray was presented with only a red rose. Ray Eames died of cancer in Los Angeles.

★

The Eames Archive in the Library of Congress in Washington, D.C., houses design drawings, photographic prints, negatives, transparencies, and numerous manuscripts. The Vita Design Museum in Weil am Rhein, Germany, has numerous examples of experimental objects and prototypes. Books on Eames are Frederick S. Wight Art Gallery, *Connections: The Work of Charles and Ray Eames* (1977); James Steele, *Eames House, Charles and Ray Eames* (1994); and Pat Kirkham, *Charles and Ray Eames: Designers of the Twentieth Century* (1995). Kirkham, "Introducing Ray Eames," *Furniture History* (1990), is a useful article. Obituaries are in the *New York Times* (23 Aug. 1988); *Architecture* (Oct. 1988); and Esther McCoy, "Ray Eames, 1913–1988," *Progressive Architecture* (Jan. 1989).

CAROL TONER SHANE

EASTLAND, James Oliver (*b.* 28 November 1904 in Doddsville, Mississippi; *d.* 19 February 1986 in Greenwood, Mississippi), lawyer, planter, and U.S. senator who was the dominant influence in Mississippi politics during the racially turbulent 1950s and 1960s and one of the most formidable congressional defenders of racial segregation.

James was the only child of Alma Austin and Woods Caperton Eastland. His father, a successful lawyer and influential state politician, was part of the powerful cotton planting aristocracy of the Mississippi Delta. When James was an infant the Eastlands moved from the Sunflower County family plantation at Doddsville to Forest in Scott County, where James grew up and went to school. In 1922 he enrolled at the University of Mississippi. After three years he transferred to Vanderbilt University, but he spent only a semester there before switching to the University of Alabama. He attended Alabama from the fall of 1926 through the spring of 1927, when he passed the bar exam and returned to Mississippi without graduating.

At his father's urging, Eastland ran for and won a seat in the Mississippi House of Representatives in 1927. In the same election Democrat Theodore G. Bilbo became governor of Mississippi. While in the legislature, Eastland was

James Eastland. LIBRARY OF CONGRESS/CORBIS

a strong Bilbo ally, and he tried unsuccessfully to marshal the votes to pass the governor's progressive program, which included free textbooks for schoolchildren and paved highways. Eastland left the legislature in 1932 after two terms.

On 6 July 1932 Eastland married Elizabeth Coleman of Doddsville. The newlyweds lived in Forest until 1934, when they moved permanently to Doddsville. Eastland took over management of the family plantation and opened a law office in nearby Ruleville. Through the worst years of the Great Depression, when cotton brought only pennies a pound, he supplemented his meager farm income with legal fees. In 1941 Governor Paul B. Johnson appointed him to the vacancy caused by the death of U.S. senator Pat Harrison. In Washington, Eastland blocked an attempt by the Office of Price Administration to establish a ceiling price on cottonseed oil, a move that would have cut cotton farmers' profits in half. This endeared him to cotton farmers everywhere and made him a hero back home. Constituents urged him to enter the upcoming special election.

Honoring a promise to Governor Johnson, Eastland did not run. Wall Doxey replaced him and served the remainder of Harrison's term. Eastland's eighty-eight day sojourn in Washington whetted his appetite for national political office, however, and he decided to challenge Doxey for the Senate post in 1942. Although Doxey had the backing of Bilbo, who was now Mississippi's other senator, Eastland won the contest on an anti-Roosevelt platform. He began a thirty-six-year Senate career on 3 January 1943.

During his first decade in the Senate, Eastland accomplished nothing especially noteworthy. A conservative Democrat, he favored low tariffs, supported the Marshall Plan, opposed organized labor, and voted consistently for cotton subsidies and other programs to aid farmers. He served on six different standing committees during the decade, including the Agriculture and Forestry Committee and the Judiciary Committee. The longtime chairman of the Subcommittee on Soil Conservation and Forestry, he promoted important conservation legislation. He became a respected authority on a wide range of farm issues. Appointed to the Judiciary Committee in January 1945, Eastland chaired two of its subcommittees, one on immigration and naturalization, the other on internal security, before gaining seniority to chair the whole committee. In March 1956 he became the youngest senator ever to become chairman of the Judiciary Committee. He retained his subcommittee chairmanships.

For twenty-two years Eastland chaired the Judiciary Committee, one of the Senate's most powerful committees and where more than half of all legislation considered by the Senate, together with all federal judicial appointments, were first considered. As chairman, Eastland exercised tremendous political power. An astute politician who knew how to amass and use power, he exercised virtual veto power over presidential judicial nominations and civil rights legislation. His arbitrary style of leadership and heavy-handed control of the committee angered liberal colleagues who decried the fact that during the first decade of his tenure as chairman he bottled up in committee more than 120 civil rights bills. More than one president learned that the best way to get an appointment or bill through the Judiciary Committee was not to challenge "the Chairman," but to court him by sharing a drink of scotch and branch water in his office.

During the 1950s and 1960s Eastland became the foremost champion of what he termed "the southern way of life." That way of life, with racial segregation at its core, was being attacked on one front, he asserted, by communists who had infiltrated civil rights groups, and on another by Supreme Court justices, who under Chief Justice Earl Warren had become the "brainwashed victims of Red plotting." Linking communism with the civil rights movement, Eastland, in his capacity as chairman of the Internal Security Subcommittee, conducted extensive hearings to ferret out communist influence wherever he suspected it existed. A great admirer of Senator Joseph McCarthy, he became the Senate's most ardent patriot and communist hunter after the Wisconsin senator died in 1957. Eastland charged that communist subversives conspired to destroy states' rights as a first step toward the eventual overthrow of the United States government. In numerous investigations and hearings he attempted to discredit civil rights groups and leaders by showing that communists were behind the black protest movement. He denounced the Supreme Court's historic 1954 *Brown* v. *Board of Education* decision banning racial segregation as a monstrously "illegal, immoral, and sinful doctrine" that the people of Mississippi and the South would fight to the end. "The Negro race is an inferior race," he asserted, warning that his constituents would "protect and maintain white supremacy throughout eternity."

Shortly after the *Brown* decision, a group of Eastland's Sunflower County constituents founded the White Citizens' Council, a group that Mississippi newspaperman Hodding Carter called "the uptown Ku Klux Klan," to fight integration. The council movement spread rapidly, soon numbering half a million members. Eastland, whose Senate denunciation of the school desegregation decision had made him a favorite of diehard segregationists, became the council's icon. Moreover, he gave the organization a voice, not just in the Senate, but at frequent council gatherings across the South, where he was a popular speaker. His message was always the same—the South must defend its way of life. He called on white citizens to defy the law and do everything possible to resist court-ordered desegregation. He preached state sovereignty and urged state legislatures, employing "authentic acts of interposition," to challenge the Supreme Court's right to "interfere with, or place a limitation on, the authority of the state to regulate health, morale, education, marriage, and good order." For most of the decade following *Brown,* Eastland was the South's champion of racial apartheid and its most vehement critic of school desegregation. Some of his most inflammatory exhortations preceded violent racial outbreaks in Little Rock, Arkansas, and at the University of Mississippi.

The stranglehold that Eastland's committee had on civil rights legislation was broken during 1964 and 1965, when the Senate invoked cloture and passed the Civil Rights Act and the Voting Rights Act. Thereafter, Eastland and other inveterate segregationists could only fight a rearguard action in a losing cause. Eastland's influence, although diminished, was not ended. He continued to wield exceptional power over judicial appointments. In addition, he was elected president pro tempore of the Senate in 1972, a position he held for six years. Twice during this period, after the resignation of Vice President Spiro Agnew and the elevation of Vice President Gerald Ford to the presidency, Eastland became acting vice president of the United States, thereby achieving the highest national office ever held by a Mississippian.

A taciturn, gruff, stoop-shouldered man with an ever-present cigar in his mouth, Eastland shunned the Washington social scene, preferring to spend evenings with his wife and four children at their modest Washington home. His real home was back in Mississippi, where he spent as much time as he possibly could on his 5,800-acre cotton plantation. A hands-on manager, he was a successful and wealthy planter who grew corn, soybeans, grains, and other crops. His principal money crop was cotton, on which he collected hundreds of thousands of dollars in government subsidies. His liberal critics noted that he accepted this government assistance while opposing almost every form of government aid to the poor.

Eastland decided not to seek reelection in 1978. Changes he had fought hard to prevent during his six terms in the Senate had transformed the political landscape of his state and the nation. His loyalty to the Democratic party had been severely strained over the years. With the ranks of that party now being swelled by the influx of newly enfranchised black voters, he decided it was time to retire. He spent his last years doing what he enjoyed most—managing his plantation, dispensing hospitality to friends and neighbors at his Doddsville home, participating in activities of the Methodist church, of which he was a lifelong member, and spending quiet evenings with his family. He died of multiple medical problems complicated by pneumonia and was buried near his parents in the Forest Cemetery in Scott County.

Asked in retirement what he hoped to be remembered for, Eastland cited constructive legislation he had sponsored or supported—a national disaster loan program, agricultural legislation, and the Marshall Plan for the reconstruction of Europe. These were constructive programs, but the positive elements of the Eastland legacy are completely overshadowed by the negative. He is remembered mainly not for what he built but for what he opposed—equality for African Americans. His intransigence on the race question made him a symbol of the unreconstructed segregationist South. His racism may have mirrored the sentiments of the majority of his white constituents, but almost half of Mississippi's population was black. When they acquired the ballot, he never accepted them as constituents. The tremendous power he commanded afforded him exceptional opportunities to lead. After the Judiciary Committee's power was curtailed, he might have bowed to the change he knew was inevitable and used his great personal influence to lead his state and region to accept the new political reality. That he failed to do so was a tragic squandering of power.

★

The major collection of Eastland's papers is housed at the Law Archives at the University of Mississippi. It consists of 1,600 linear feet of material, including correspondence, speeches, political files, material relating to his Senate assignments and activities, and an assortment of photographs, cartoons, and political memorabilia. The most complete collection of papers relating to his role as chairman of the Judiciary Committee and various subcommittees, including the Internal Security Subcommittee, is in the National Archives in Washington, D.C. The Mississippi Department of Archives and History in Jackson has four boxes of Eastland Papers consisting mainly of campaign material, speeches, and printed matter from the Judiciary Committee. Eastland's personal and business papers remain in the possession of the family.

There is no biography of Eastland. His early life and career before 1942 are covered by Dan W. Smith, "James O. Eastland, Early Life and Career, 1904–1942" (master's thesis, Mississippi College, 1978). The significance of his fight against the Supreme Court is examined in Nick Walters, "The Repairman Chairman: Senator James O. Eastland and His Influence on the U.S. Supreme Court" (master's thesis, Mississippi College, 1992). Wolfgang Schlauch, "Representative William Colmer and Senator James O. Eastland and the Reconstruction of Germany, 1945," *Journal of Mississippi History* 34 (Aug. 1972): 193–213, examines Eastland's support of the Marshall Plan. The most extensive analysis of Eastland's public persona before 1968 is the chapter "Jim Eastland, Child of Scorn," in Robert Sherrill, *Gothic Politics in the Deep South: Stars of the New Confederacy* (1968). *Time* magazine (16 Mar. 1956) did a cover story on Eastland and his Senate role. An obituary is in the *Jackson Clarion Ledger* (20 Feb. 1986).

CHARLES D. LOWERY

Douglas Edward. CBS TELEVISION/ARCHIVE PHOTOS

EDWARDS, Douglas (*b.* 14 July 1917 in Ada, Oklahoma; *d.* 13 October 1990 in Sarasota, Florida), radio and television journalist who was the first anchor of a daily television news program for the Columbia Broadcasting System.

Douglas Edwards was the son of teachers, Tony and Alice (Donaldson) Edwards. His father died of smallpox when Douglas was a baby. His mother moved Douglas and his older half brother from Ada, Oklahoma, to Troy, Alabama, where Douglas spent his high school years. Growing up in a small town, he was fascinated by the ability of radio to bring news of world events into American living rooms. As a boy he read stories from the newspaper into the telephone mouthpiece, and his first radio job came at the age of fifteen, when he became a junior announcer at WHET, a 100-watt station begun by some older friends in Troy.

Edwards enrolled at the University of Alabama in 1934 with hopes of studying medicine. To pay for his college tuition and pursue his interest in radio, he took a summer job as a news reporter at WAGF in Dothan, Alabama, before moving to Atlanta the following year to enroll at Emory University. In Atlanta, Edwards began working at the *Atlanta Journal* as an assistant news editor and as an announcer at its radio station, WSB. His interests increasingly shifted from medicine to journalism, and the growing responsibilities of his job forced him to leave Emory and enroll in evening journalism courses at the University of Georgia. In 1938 he decided to gain some "northern experience" by taking an announcing job at WXYZ in Detroit, Michigan. As he grew more serious about news reporting, he set his sights on joining the Columbia Broadcasting System (CBS), whose news reputation was solid and established. He returned to WSB and the *Atlanta Journal* in 1940 to strengthen his writing and announcing skills before applying for a job at CBS. On 29 August 1939 Edwards married Sara Byrd. They had three children and were later divorced.

Edwards began his forty-six-year association with CBS in December 1942, when he was hired as a radio staff announcer. Within six weeks he was not only filling in as a news reporter for Mel Allen, the future sportscaster, but also understudying and writing for John Daly's fifteen-minute nightly show, *The World Today,* and his Sunday afternoon show, *World News Today.* When Daly was assigned overseas in 1943, Edwards eagerly replaced him, and also began work on *Report to the Nation,* which reenacted wartime events using actors accompanied by an orchestra. He was thrilled to have regular reporting duties, but like most newsmen of the time dreamed of a European assignment. His wish was answered in 1945 when he was sent to London to cover the last months of World War II under the direction of the famed newsman Edward R. Murrow.

Edwards spent fourteen months in Europe, where he was named chief of the CBS Paris News Bureau in 1945. In the course of this assignment, he completed an 8,000-mile roving assignment across Europe and the Middle East. Upon his return to New York City in May 1946, he was invited to describe his adventures overseas on a weekly CBS news show. Network executives were impressed by this telegenic, five-foot, nine-inch man whose rich, warm voice and innocent good looks conveyed a mixture of sincerity and authority. They offered him a permanent position doing news for television.

In 1946 television was an unproven, uncharted medium for imparting the news. Edwards was understandably hesitant to leave the establishment of radio news, recalling that "I was leery, to say the least. Back then, radio was the dog. TV was the very tiny tail." While continuing his radio commitments, he began *The CBS Television News,* which was expanded to two nights a week. On 15 August 1948 *Douglas Edwards with the News* became the first CBS news show to air Monday through Friday. Initially, it had an audience of 30,000 viewers in five eastern cities. The challenge facing Edwards and his colleagues was to create a format for news on television that went beyond "radio with pictures." There were no TelePrompTers from which anchors could read the news script, and Edwards rejected producer Don Hewitt's suggestion of learning Braille, so cue cards and ad-libbing became the standard. As many visual aids as possible were utilized, including Associated Press wirephotos, film footage from Telenews or local camera crews, maps, graphs, charts, cartoons, stock film, and still pictures. At first only in-studio interviews were used, but soon it was possible to take cameras into the field and to switch to other cities for breaking news.

Douglas Edwards with the News was the most popular national evening newscast for most of the fourteen years it aired. Edwards had many "firsts" and "bests" including anchoring CBS News's first gavel-to-gavel coverage of the national political conventions in 1948 (Democratic, Republican, and Progressive National), on-location live coverage of the Missouri River at flood stage, and exclusive eyewitness coverage of the 1956 sinking of the ocean liner *Andrea Doria* off the Nantucket coast. He interviewed such prominent figures as Eleanor Roosevelt, Winston Churchill, Herbert Hoover, and John F. Kennedy. After the show began losing ratings points to the National Broadcasting System's *Huntley-Brinkley Report* in the early 1960s, CBS decided to replace Edwards with Walter Cronkite.

Edwards's disappointment at losing the evening news show did not keep him from working for CBS. For several years he anchored CBS News's daytime broadcasts and the late-night local news on WCBS-TV in New York City. Upon his retirement in April 1988, he was the anchor of *Newsbreak* on CBS television and *The World Tonight* on CBS radio. During his career Edwards also worked on such television shows as *Armstrong Circle Theatre, Celebrity Time, F.Y.I., Masquerade Party, Youth Takes a Stand,* and *For Our Times.* His radio programs included *World News Roundup, Wendy Warren with the News, CBS Views the Press, Newsmakers,* and *A Trip to the North Pole.* His many awards included the George Foster Peabody Award (1955), the first Freedom of Speech Award from the Georgia Association of Broadcasters (1975), the Lowell Thomas Award from Marist College (1986), and the Paul White Award from the Radio and Television News Directors Association (1988). He was inducted into the Broadcast Hall of Fame in 1986 and 1991.

Edwards had married his second wife, May H. Dunbar, on 10 May 1966. After his retirement in 1988, they lived in Sarasota, Florida, where Edwards died of cancer at the age of seventy-three.

Edwards is justly regarded as one of the pioneers of broadcast journalism, anchoring a daily network television news broadcast without interruption for forty years. Fellow CBS journalist Charles Kuralt was one of many journalists who remembered Edwards's contributions: "He helped establish the credibility of news on the air. Viewers found him trustworthy; they were correct in their judgment of him. All of us who followed owe Douglas Edwards much gratitude for getting broadcast news off to such a good start."

★

A biographical file on Edwards is at the CBS News Reference Library in New York City. See David Schoenbrun, *On and Off the Air: An Informal History of CBS News* (1989); Thomas Fensch, ed., *Television News Anchors: An Anthology of Profiles of the Major Figures and Issues in United States Network Reporting* (1993); and Tim Brooks and Earle Marsh, *The Complete Dictionary to Prime-Time Network and Cable TV Shows, 1946–Present* (6th ed., 1995). Periodical articles include Haskel Frankel, "Profile: Douglas Edwards," *Connecticut Magazine* (May 1982), and Earl Schwed, "CBS' Original Anchor Signs Off," *Los Angeles Herald Examiner* (31 Mar. 1988). An interview by Spencer Kinard is in *RTNDA Communicator* (Dec. 1988). An obituary is in the *New York Times* (14 Oct. 1990).

CARRIE C. MCBRIDE

ELDRIDGE, (David) Roy ("Little Jazz") (*b.* 30 January 1911 in Pittsburgh, Pennsylvania; *d.* 26 February 1989 in Valley Stream, New York), jazz trumpeter who is credited for supplying the artistic link between Louis Armstrong's New Orleans–style "hot jazz" and Dizzy Gillespie's "bebop" innovations, and who also established a vital legacy of his own.

Eldridge was born to Alexander Eldridge and Blanche (Oakes) Eldridge in Pittsburgh, where he began playing

Roy Eldridge. METRONOME/ARCHIVE PHOTOS

the drums at age six. He took up the bugle and then the trumpet by age ten, receiving instruction on that instrument from his older brother Joe, who was himself an accomplished musician who played the alto saxophone and violin. From an early age, Roy also tried his hand at singing, composing, and playing the piano. As a trumpet player, Eldridge looked to brass players, such as Rex Stewart, Red Nichols, and Jabbo Smith, for stylistic guidance, though his style was also influenced early on by his brother. Eldridge would come to be influenced by other saxophonists, such as Lester Young, Chu Berry, Benny Carter, and, especially, Coleman Hawkins, prompting Eldridge's later remark, "I play nice saxophone on the trumpet."

Eldridge began his career playing in carnivals (the Greater Sheesley Shows band, the Nighthawk Syncopators), hired reputedly for his ability to replicate on the trumpet Coleman Hawkins's popular saxophone solo on Fletcher Henderson's recording of "Stampede." As a teenager, Eldridge toured with his own band under the pseudonym Roy Elliott and His Palais Royal Orchestra, which performed for the "Rock Dinah" show in 1927. In 1928 he toured with Horace Henderson's Dixie Stompers, then with Zach White and Laurence ("Speed") Webb, mostly in the Midwest.

In 1930 Eldridge moved to New York City to join some of the finest ensembles then playing jazz: groups led by Cecil Scott, Charlie Johnson, Teddy Hill, and Elmer Snowden, among others. In 1931 Eldridge was dubbed "Little Jazz" by Otto Hardwick, a reed player with Duke Ellington's orchestra. The nickname became permanent, though the only thing "little" about Eldridge was his stature of five feet, three inches. By 1935 Eldridge had carved out his own musical niche and come to national prominence, appearing as a featured solo trumpeter in Fletcher Henderson's orchestra.

In 1936 Eldridge took up a two-year residency at Sam Beer's Three Deuces Club in Chicago, where his band included his brother Joe on alto sax; the ensemble broadcast from the club on the radio seven nights a week. During this time, Eldridge recorded what became popular renditions of "After You've Gone" and "Wabash Stomp," both of which featured Roy's fiery, crackling solos. Eldridge would later remark that this was "the best little band I ever had." Back in New York City, Eldridge had regular gigs at the Famous Door and debuted at the Savoy Ballroom in Harlem in 1938. He married Viola Lee Fong in 1936; they had one daughter, Carole Elizabeth.

In the 1940s, Eldridge joined two famous bands, each led by a well-known white director: Gene Krupa, with whom he recorded one of his best-known pieces and his own personal favorite, "Rockin' Chair" in 1941, and with whom he performed in the Hollywood movie *Ball of Fire* (Eldridge was edited out of the film, told, disingenuously, that he was "too tall"); and Artie Shaw. Eldridge was one of the first black musicians to attain a permanent seat in the brass section of a white orchestra.

Integrated bands at this time created controversy, and while Eldridge's presence in both of these groups represented progress, Eldridge still experienced the exclusion that celebrated baseball player Jackie Robinson had endured. He was often humiliated by club owners and by restaurant and hotel personnel. In one episode, Eldridge, while on tour with Shaw's orchestra in San Francisco, was not allowed in the front door of the performance hall on whose very marquee Eldridge's name appeared. (He was told to enter through the back door.) Tears rolling down his cheeks while performing, Eldridge found himself too upset to play well that evening; the incident also reinforced his sentiment, expressed in 1944, that "as long as I'm in America, I'll never in my life work with a white band again."

This period in Eldridge's life was difficult for him artistically as well. His own band folded ("they couldn't hold their whiskey" he said later), and Eldridge questioned his own artistic identity as a swing player while the more modern bebop style had burst on the jazz scene. In 1949 bebop trumpeter Howard McGhee taunted Eldridge for his swing-influenced playing style, making him feel "out of step." "I was torn whether I should do that sort of thing [bebop], or go for myself. It stopped being fun anymore," Eldridge later remarked. He decided to take a long sabbatical in France. In contrast to his experiences in America, during the two years he lived and performed in Europe, Eldridge found immense audience appreciation with relatively few racial prejudices and little artistic competitiveness. There he played with other jazz greats, such as clarinetist Benny Goodman, tenor saxophonist Zoot Sims, and pianist Dick Hyman. Eldridge recorded a version of "Fireworks" in a duo with Claude Bolling in which the two musicians reworked the ideas and melodies of Armstrong and Earl Hines.

Returning to New York in 1951, Eldridge proceeded to play with Norman Granz's Jazz at the Philharmonic for much of the 1950s. Eldridge also played regularly with jazz singer Ella Fitzgerald's ensemble through the 1950s and 1960s; he worked with vocalist Billie Holiday at this time, as well as with Count Basie in 1966. In 1970 Eldridge began a ten-year stint at Jimmy Ryan's, a New York club featuring Dixieland-style jazz music, which to many less-sensitive ears sounded old-fashioned and archaic. In fact, Eldridge brought originality, ingenuity, and novelty to this popular playing style.

In the decade before he suffered a debilitating heart attack in 1980, Eldridge also had steady club dates at Eddie Condon's in New York and at Rick's Café American in Chicago. While continuing to suffer from heart disease after his attack, Eldridge performed only a few times, and then not as a trumpeter, but as a singer, drummer, and even pianist; he also offered trumpet lessons and served as an important spokesman for jazz. In his seventies, Eldridge was tired of living the life of the full-time musician and welcomed spending more time with his wife and working on hobbies such as carpentry and electronics. His heart weakened both physically and emotionally, Eldridge died three weeks after his wife, to whom he had been married for fifty-three years.

Described by the jazz scholar Phil Schapp as a "tireless jazz maniac," Eldridge was also said, paradoxically, to "sound relaxed at any tempo." Eldridge played up-tempo numbers with an extroverted force verging on the "mad" and the "demonic," yet he was sensitive and emotional. He was competitive, known to challenge his best trumpet-playing colleagues to "cutting contests," which he often won, but remained less well-known to the general public than some of these colleagues, such as Dizzy Gillespie. Eldridge's slightly abrasive edge as a person was a sign of his deep sensitivity, which came across in his music, said by drummer Phil Brown to go "directly to the heart."

Eldridge contributed an important element in the history of jazz, creating transition and artistic links between swing and bebop, but he also shone, in his own right, as an electrifying, "emotionally compelling, versatile, rugged, and far-reaching" player. He was said to have "an unprecedented dexterity, particularly in the highest register" of his trumpet as well as an easy mobility over a range of nearly three octaves. The unforgettable tone he created on the trumpet was utterly his own, described as having "an urgent, human roughness that gave his music an immediacy" yet also said to be "joyful." Eldridge left dozens of sparkling recordings that set new standards for jazz soloists. As Ella Fitzgerald remarked of Eldridge, "He's got more soul in one note than a lot of people could get into the whole song. . . . God gives it to some and not others."

★

Biographical sources include Nat Shapiro and Nat Hentoff, *The Jazz Makers: Essays on the Greats of Jazz* (1957); and Whitney Balliett, *American Musicians: Fifty-Six Portraits in Jazz* (1986). See also Whitney Balliett, "Jazz," *New Yorker* 61 (16 Dec. 1985); Gunther Schuller, *The Swing Era: The Development of Jazz, 1930–1945* (1989); and Daniel Okrent, "Brothers in Brass," *Esquire* 114 (Nov. 1990). Obituaries are in the *New York Times* (28 Feb. 1989) and *Down Beat* 56 (May 1989): 11.

SARAH MARKGRAF

ELIADE, Mircea (*b.* 9 March 1907 in Bucharest, Romania; *d.* 22 April 1986 in Chicago, Illinois), historian of religion and writer of serious fiction who is credited with rehabilitating the religious and existential meaning of myth and symbol for Western audiences.

The second of three children born to Gheorghe Eliade, a Romanian army captain, and Ioana Arvira, Eliade began his research and writing at an early age. He was given great freedom to pursue his interests, both scientific and literary,

Mircea Eliade. COURTESY UNIVERSITY OF CHICAGO PRESS

and at age fourteen published his first full-length article, "How I Found the Philosopher's Stone," in the *Newspaper of Popular Science* (1921). The attic of his family home in Bucharest became his personal preserve, stocked with books, prints, and scientific collections. Within its confines his spiritual world expanded to embrace the languages and literature of Italy, the Orient, and the Near East, to name but a few of his many interests. While still at the Lycée Spiru-Haret, a high school in Bucharest, Eliade contributed to numerous magazines on a rich variety of topics, and in 1925 he completed a sustained piece of autobiographical fiction, "Novel of a Nearsighted Adolescent" (unpublished). Having graduated from the *lycée* that year, he enrolled at the University of Bucharest, where he contributed twice weekly to a daily newspaper known as *Cuvantul* (the Word) under the tutelage of the philosopher Nae Ionescu.

In 1927, while still a student, Eliade undertook his first trip to Italy to inspect its libraries and there met several famous philosophers and men of letters, including Giovanni Papini and Giovanni Gentile, among others. A second trip to Italy the following spring gave his life a decisive turn. While working on his master's thesis on the hermetic undercurrent in Renaissance philosophy, he read *A History of Indian Philosophy* (1922), by Surendranath Dasgupta. Intrigued and motivated, Eliade determined to petition Dasgupta and his patron, the Maharajah of Kassimbazar, for a scholarship to study at the University of Calcutta. The maharajah granted his request, and upon receiving the M.A. degree from the University of Bucharest in October 1928, Eliade left for India, where he spent the next three years in a variety of intellectual and personal adventures.

For the first six months of 1929, Eliade lived in a boarding house at 82 Ripon Street in Calcutta and devoted his major effort to learning Sanskrit under Dasgupta's guidance and attending his lectures at the university. His focus of study became Tantric Yoga. The impulse to write, however, soon overtook him, and he produced *Isabel and the Devil's Waters* (1930), a novel set in India and modeled loosely on his own experience. In 1930 Eliade went to live in Dasgupta's house in Bhawanipore, entering into a promising collaboration that ended with a falling-out over Dasgupta's daughter, who became the title and subject of Eliade's next novel, *Maitreyi* (1933). In October 1930 Eliade took up residence in a Himalayan ashram, where he practiced yoga under Swami Shivananda, but it became clear that the life of a Himalayan hermit was not his destiny. At his father's urging, he returned to Bucharest in December 1931 and completed his military service in the Romanian army from January to November 1932.

Eliade returned to the University of Bucharest in 1932 and in June 1933 received his Ph.D. from that university. His dissertation, in expanded form, was published jointly in Paris and Bucharest as *Yoga: An Essay on the Origins of Indian Mysticism* (1936). In 1933 he began teaching philosophy at the University of Bucharest as an assistant to his former mentor Ionescu and took his place as a prominent member of the Criterion group, a fellowship of writers and scholars of the young generation of Romanian intellectuals. In January 1934 he married Nina Mares, a divorced woman with one daughter. Around this time Eliade initiated a steady stream of publications, culminating in 1939 with the first issue of *Zalmoxis: A Review of Religious Studies,* an international journal of the history of religions. For a brief but telling moment in the growing domestic upheavals of 1938, he became a political detainee on account of his international contacts and close association with Nae Ionescu; Eliade, however, considered himself and his work to be "nonpolitical."

Following the outbreak of war in Europe in 1939, Eliade served as cultural attaché to the Romanian legation in London, where he survived the beginning of the Luftwaffe blitz and was evacuated to Oxford in September 1940. In January 1941 he became cultural adviser to the Romanian legation in Lisbon. During the family's stay in Lisbon, his wife died of cancer. Also while living in Lisbon, Eliade completed the greater part of his famous work, *Patterns in Comparative Religion,* which was published in Paris in 1949 and in New York in 1958.

With the ascendancy of the communist government in Romania, Eliade immigrated with his stepdaughter to Paris in September 1945 rather than return to Bucharest. In November 1945 he accepted an invitation to present a course of lectures at the École des Hautes Études of the Sorbonne and shortly thereafter took up residence at the Hôtel de Suède on the rue Vaneau, where he lived and worked for some four and a half years. On 9 January 1950 he married Georgette Christinel Cottescu. Also in 1950 Eliade attended his first Eranos Conference at Ascona, Switzerland, where he began an association with Carl Jung that continued over many summers.

During this period Eliade lived in relative poverty until he finally received a research grant from the Bollingen Foundation in New York City for the years 1951 to 1955 and began to give lectures throughout Europe. Meanwhile, his fame spread with the publication of *Cosmos and History: The Myth of the Eternal Return* (Paris, 1949; New York, 1959), *Shamanism: Archaic Techniques of Ecstasy* (Paris, 1951; New York, 1964), *Images and Symbols: Studies in Religious Symbolism* (Paris, 1952; New York, 1961), *Yoga: Immortality and Freedom* (Paris, 1954; New York, 1958), and *The Forge and the Crucible* (Paris, 1956; New York, 1962). During his Paris years he also completed *The Forbidden Forest* (1955; Notre Dame, 1978), his most important novel.

After delivering the 1956 Haskell Lectures at the University of Chicago, Eliade became chairman of the

Department of History of Religions at that university and a professor on the Committee on Social Thought. In 1962 he became the Sewell L. Avery Distinguished Service Professor at the University of Chicago. Over the next several years, Eliade accepted a succession of honorary doctorates while popularizing the discipline of the history of religions in the United States. In 1970 he became a U.S. citizen. Carrying on his work, he published the three volumes of *A History of Religious Ideas* (1978, 1982, 1988) and undertook the editorship of a sixteen-volume *Encyclopedia of Religion* (1987). During his years in Chicago he published in English a great wealth of autobiographical material and a number of novellas, including *Two Tales of the Occult* (1970), *The Old Man and the Bureaucrats* (1979), *Tales of the Sacred and the Supernatural* (1981), and *Youth Without Youth and Other Novellas* (1988).

Eliade retired from the University of Chicago in 1983. In 1986 he was hospitalized after suffering a stroke and diagnosed with inoperable lung cancer. He died of the stroke two weeks later, and his ashes were interred in Chicago's Oakwood Cemetery. While he had no children of his own, he left a train of distinguished students and personal admirers, a thousand of whom gathered in the university's Rockefeller Chapel on 28 April 1986 to pay him a final tribute.

As a historian of religion, Eliade made it his task to decipher the myths and symbols of ancient and archaic religions, as against the strong modern tendency to demystify them. As such, he was a great opponent of the various reductionisms of his time, such as Marxism and Freudianism. Moreover, he believed, in parallel with Teilhard de Chardin, that cosmic religion could hold a place even in an age that prided itself on technical mastery of nature. In this Eliade considered Goethe his intellectual next of kin—a protean talent, a "naturalist" and writer, and one whose views on religion were apparently not unlike his own. Nevertheless, although Eliade was widely considered the foremost religious expert of his time, he had little to say about God. In *Ordeal by Labyrinth* (1982) he stated: "I made the decision long ago to maintain a kind of discreet silence as to what I personally believe or don't believe. But I have striven all my life to understand those who do believe in particular things: the shaman, the yogin, the Australian aborigine, as well as the great saints" (p. 132).

Although Eliade considered his vocation to be culture rather than sainthood, he could not escape a lifelong contest between "science" and literature, everyday life and paradisial escape, historical conditioning and absolute freedom. In his novels and novellas, no less than in his scholarly work, Eliade plied these themes as a man of his time who nevertheless sought to exist in a transhistorical realm, a realm both ancient and new that belongs to the secret heritage of our age.

★

Eliade's journal, which covers most of his adult life, is in the Special Collections section of the Regenstein Library at the University of Chicago. He told his life story in *Autobiography*, vol. 1, *Journey East, Journey West (1907–1937)* (1981), and *Autobiography*, vol. 2, *Exile's Odyssey (1937–1960)* (1988). Journal selections from his years of exile have been republished in the United States as *Journal I (1945–1955),* translated from the Romanian by Mac Linscott Ricketts (1990); *Journal II (1957–1969),* translated from the French by Fred H. Johnson, Jr. (1989); *Journal III (1970–1978),* translated from the French by Teresa Lavender Fagan (1989); and *Journal IV (1979–1985),* translated from the Romanian by Mac Linscott Ricketts (1990). An obituary is in the *New York Times* (23 Apr. 1986).

KENNETH M. BATINOVICH

ELLIS, Perry Edwin (*b.* 3 March 1940 in Churchland [now Portsmouth], Virginia; *d.* 30 May 1986 in New York City), leading American sportswear designer.

The only child of Edwin L. Ellis, owner of a fuel company, and Winifred Alene (Roundtree) Ellis, a homemaker, Ellis grew up in Virginia. He attended the College of William and Mary in Williamsburg, Virginia, where he received a bachelor's degree in business in 1961. He fulfilled his military obligation by serving in the U.S. Coast Guard in 1961 and 1962, then continued his education at the graduate school of business at New York University, where he earned a master's degree in retailing in 1963.

Ellis's first position in retail was as a sportswear buyer at the Miller and Rhoads department store in Richmond, Virginia. His background in retail operations was augmented by his talent as a designer, and he developed a conceptual appreciation for the stores where his apparel was sold. Understanding the pricing systems, store layout, and gross margins gave him a solid grounding in the volatile business of fashion. Ellis continued at Miller and Rhoads until 1967, when he left Virginia for Norwich, Connecticut, to join the John Meyer Company as a merchandiser. A conservative sportswear firm, John Meyer relied on Ellis to advise on which styles would sell, and while he worked there, he began to learn about fabrics and to experiment in pattern making and sketching.

After seven years Ellis left John Meyer to work in merchandising for Manhattan Industries, specifically in the subsidiary known as the Vera sportswear line. Before long he began designing for Vera, entering the fashion design industry fairly late in his career with his signature line, known as Portfolio. Interested in creating a relaxed look for women, he coined the term "the slouch look," which the emerging Portfolio line epitomized. He designed clothes to reflect ease and comfort and did not want his fashion or

Perry Ellis at the Metropolitan Museum of Art, New York City, 1984. ROBERT MAASS/CORBIS

the shaping world of fashion to be viewed too earnestly. "I think fashion dies when it is taken too seriously," he said.

In 1978 Manhattan Industries organized a separate company called Perry Ellis Sportswear, which Ellis chaired. As his designing responsibilities grew, he formed his own licensing company, Perry Ellis International, which shared royalties with Manhattan Industries. His women's designs became more sophisticated, including furs and shoes, and he began to design men's clothes, accessories such as scarves and leg wear, and even sheets and blankets.

Ellis's success story continued through the early 1980s, as domestic shoppers became attentive to American designer brands. He never married, but in 1984 he and a friend, Barbara Gallagher, had a daughter. Also in 1984 Perry Ellis International revived the Portfolio label for men and women. This line was more classic and inexpensive than Ellis's signature collection and was directed at upper-middle-class consumers who sought designer names but without the prohibitive price. The oversized "slouch" look again gained popularity, and Portfolio found an eager audience. Ellis was even able to use some of his early designs in this new mid-1980s fashion moment.

As designers created more casual looks, sportswear giants came to designers. Ellis was contracted by Levi Strauss and Company to design active leisure wear for the whole family. His sportswear gravitated toward a very relaxed look, and at the same time his couture collection became elegant and extravagant as he branched out into dresses, skirts, and formal evening wear. His fresh attitude and sense of adventure triggered an opening up of the skirt-length issue. Once Ellis began designing skirts, hemlines stopped conforming to short one year, long the next. He believed in an "anything goes" and "freedom of choice" attitude for the female consumer that emphasized what looks best on the individual.

In May 1986 Ellis was reelected to a third term as president of the Council of Fashion Designers of America, a well-established organization of creative people in the fashion industry. A week later he died of viral encephalitis, a complication of acquired immunodeficiency syndrome (AIDS), at the New York Hospital–Cornell Medical Center in Manhattan. He is buried in a family plot in Portsmouth, Virginia. In his honor, the Council of Fashion Designers of America established the Perry Ellis Award, which is given annually to the most promising new designer of menswear, womenswear, and accessories.

Ellis won the Neiman Marcus Award in 1979, and he won eight Coty American Fashion Critics' Awards, including the Winnie in 1979, the Return Award in 1980, the Hall of Fame citation in 1981, the Special Award (menswear) in 1981, the Hall of Fame citation (womenswear) in 1983, the Men's Wear Return Award in 1983, the Hall of Fame citation (menswear) in 1984, and the Hall of Fame citation (womenswear) in 1984. He also captured the Council of Fashion Designers of America (CFDA) awards as Outstanding Designer in Women's Fashion in 1981 and Outstanding Designer in Men's Fashion in 1982 and 1983. The Cutty Sark Men's Fashion Award for Outstanding Menswear Designer went to Ellis in 1983 and 1984. Perry Ellis International remained a privately held, successful company that by the mid-1990s licensed products in thirty-seven categories. The Perry Ellis brand continued to grow and accounted for more than $800 million in worldwide retail sales in 1996. Perry Ellis's credo, courtesy of Perry Ellis International, stated, "I was determined to change the course of fashion . . . to move away from what I call the pretentiousness of clothes . . . to design clothes that are more obtainable, more relaxed, but ultimately more stylish and witty."

★

Jonathan Moor, *Perry Ellis* (1988), is the most substantial source of information. See also Anne Stegemeyer, *Who's Who in*

Fashion, 3d ed. (1996). An obituary is in the *New York Times* (31 May 1986).

JENNIFER FARTHING

ELLMANN, Richard David (*b.* 15 March 1918 in Highland Park, Michigan; *d.* 13 May 1987 in Oxford, England), educator, literary critic, editor, translator, and author, who is best known for his critical studies of Irish literature; his masterwork, *James Joyce* (1959), set the standard for subsequent literary biographies.

Ellmann was the son of James Irving Ellmann, an attorney, and Jeanette Barsook Ellmann. His parents hoped he would study law. Although his brothers became attorneys, Richard chose a different path. He studied literature at Yale University, where he received a B.A. degree in 1939. Interested in the poetry of William Butler Yeats, he continued his studies at Yale and received an M.A. degree in 1941. He taught at Harvard from 1942 to 1943. During World War II, Ellmann served in the U.S. Navy. He was assigned to the Office of Strategic Services and was briefly stationed in London. While there he visited Yeats's widow in Dublin. She loaned him Yeats's personal letters and papers and assisted Ellmann by interpreting confusing passages in letters or explaining unfamiliar events in Yeats's life.

Richard Ellmann. NORTHWESTERN UNIVERSITY ARCHIVES

At the end of the war in 1945, Ellmann returned to Yale for doctoral studies. He won the John Addison Porter Prize in 1947 for his dissertation on Yeats, which was published in 1948 as *Yeats: The Man and the Masks.* Also in 1947, Ellmann pursued studies at Trinity College in Dublin, on a Rockefeller fellowship, and earned a B.Litt. degree.

Ellmann then returned to Harvard, where he was the Briggs-Copeland Assistant Professor of English Composition from 1948 to 1951. He married Mary Donahue, a writer, on 12 August 1949; they had three children. In 1951 Ellmann published a translation of the works of Henri Michaux titled *Selected Writings.* He had met the French poet while in Paris during the war.

In 1951 Ellmann left Harvard to become a professor of English at Northwestern University in Evanston, Illinois. In 1954 he published a critical analysis of Yeats's poetry, *The Identity of Yeats.* Intrigued about the first meeting between Yeats and Joyce and their ensuing relationship, Ellmann next decided to undertake a biography of Joyce.

His *James Joyce,* published in 1959, was immediately regarded by scholars as the preeminent Joyce biography, although Hugh Kenner in the *Times Literary Supplement* criticized the wide use of the term "definitive" in describing the work, citing that a biography by its very nature is "a narrative form . . . a mode of fiction" (17 December 1982). Nonetheless, *James Joyce* set a new standard for literary biography with its meticulous research and masterly prose style. It won the National Book Award in 1960 and, according to Richard B. Kershner, "established Ellmann's reputation as probably the greatest literary biographer of our time."

In 1963 Northwestern appointed Ellmann to the Franklin Bliss Snyder Professorship. He edited a number of works, including *My Brother's Keeper: James Joyce's Early Years* (1958), the memoirs of Joyce's younger brother, Stanislaus, volumes 2 and 3 of *Letters of James Joyce* (1966), and a corrected edition of Joyce's *Portrait of the Artist as a Young Man* (1968).

After seventeen years at Northwestern, Ellmann returned to Yale as a professor in 1968. Then in 1970 he accepted an appointment to teach English literature at Oxford University as Goldsmiths' Professor of English Literature, a position he held until 1984. He was also named a fellow to New College at Oxford.

In 1972 Ellmann published *Ulysses on the Liffey,* a critical interpretation of Joyce's *Ulysses.* The following year he published *Golden Codgers: Biographical Speculations,* a compilation of biographical essays that he had published earlier in his career, including his inaugural lecture at Oxford in 1970. He coedited, with Robert O'Clair, *The Norton An-*

thology of Modern Poetry (1973), and edited a compilation of American poetry, *The New Oxford Book of American Verse* (1976). *The Consciousness of Joyce,* Ellmann's review of Joyce's personal library with an analysis of its impact on Joyce's prose, appeared in 1977.

Ellmann's scholarship continued to flourish into the 1980s. He published a revision of *James Joyce* (1982) to coincide with the Joyce centenary. The new edition contained more than 100 pages of material Ellmann had collected during the twenty years following the publication of the first edition. He also published two monographs, *Oscar Wilde at Oxford* (1984) and *W. B. Yeats' Second Puberty* (1985), and *Four Dubliners: Wilde, Yeats, Joyce, and Beckett* (1986).

Ellmann had become interested in Oscar Wilde while conducting research for his Joyce biography in the 1950s, and he continued to collect information about the Irish playwright over the years, although after completing his Joyce biography in 1959, he had written: "There really aren't any other modern writers that measure up to Yeats or Joyce. I can't think of anyone else I'd want to work on the way I've worked on them." In the meantime, he was diagnosed in 1986 with amyotrophic lateral sclerosis (Lou Gehrig's disease), a degenerative nerve condition. The illness, however, did not daunt Ellmann's enthusiasm for writing and research. He completed his biography on Wilde during the remaining weeks of his life. He died in Oxford from pneumonia.

A talented teacher, Ellmann throughout his career received numerous awards and fellowships. He was the Frederick Ives Carpenter Visiting Professor at the University of Chicago and the Woodruff Professor of English at Emory University. He was a Fellow of the American Academy of Letters, the British Academy, and the Royal Society of Literature. He posthumously received the National Book Critics Award in 1988 and the Pulitzer Prize in 1989 for *Oscar Wilde.*

A Long the Riverrun, a collection of twenty of Ellmann's essays, was published in 1989. The title, taken from James Joyce's *Finnegans Wake,* is intended to convey the great span of Richard Ellmann's literary career. Ellmann achieved new heights in biographical scholarship and rekindled interest in Irish literature. James Joyce had called the biographer a "biografiend." Oscar Wilde once stated that "every man has his disciples, and it is usually Judas who writes the biography." Ellmann was neither a fiend nor a Judas in his biographies. He had the ability to combine painstaking research with a captivating narrative style.

★

Ellmann's papers are in the University of Tulsa (Oklahoma) Library. For a critical review of Ellmann's writings, see R. B. Kershner, Jr., "The Achievement of Richard Ellmann," *Georgia Review* 42 (fall 1988): 617–623. Obituaries are in the *New York Times* (14 May 1987) and the *Times* (London) (15 May 1987).

LOIS CHEREPON

ERTESZEK, Olga Bertram (*b.* 15 June 1916 in Cracow, Austria-Hungary [in present-day Poland]; *d.* 15 September 1989 in Los Angeles, California), intimate-apparel designer and manufacturer who, as one of the best-known and most highly regarded women in her field, revolutionized women's undergarments.

Born Olga Bertram, Erteszek was the second daughter of a watchmaker and a corsetiere, whose full names are not known. Olga completed gymnasium in her native Cracow, which became part of Poland after World War I. She fled war-torn Poland late in 1939 with her fiancé, Jan J. Erteszek, a lawyer, whom she married hastily that year as they traveled to the United States.

Erteszek and her husband arrived in the United States with hope, talent, and ambition. The couple continued

Olga Erteszek. NYT PERMISSIONS

westward, settling in 1941 in southern California, around Los Angeles, with little money but ready to begin work. They invested $5 in a sewing machine rental and spent another $5 on fabric and sewing materials. What later became known as the Olga Company started out as a $10 investment and a good idea. Using herself as a model, Erteszek fashioned a garter belt that was both lighter and prettier than the norm. After long hours of sewing and critiquing, she turned over her finished product to her husband, who promised to sell her designs. Jan Erteszek's first sale was to Bullocks-Wilshire, an upscale department store whose intimate apparel buyer ordered two dozen. Other buyers followed suit, and the Olga Company was launched in 1941. Before long the Olga line of garter belts was well known in the United States, and the company was able to produce quality undergarments during World War II despite the unavailability of certain fabrics.

Olga Erteszek followed a principle that she called the three F's: fit, fashion, function. She approached design as architecture and continued to use her own body as her model. From garter belts the company quickly branched out into other undergarments, such as the first Olga girdle, then brassieres, slips, camisoles, panties, and sleepwear. Erteszek received dozens of patents as she experimented with Lycra and fashioned a version of the seamless bra. Her reputation for beautiful products equaled her renown for lightweight, uncomplicated, functional pieces. She believed that one should dress attractively from the inside out and that pretty undergarments give a woman a psychological lift, a boost in morale, and self-esteem. She was committed to outfitting her customers with a high-quality, comfortable product, complete with soft lace, pretty trims, and tiny bows known as "Olga touches."

In the 1940s Olga and Jan Erteszek became U.S. citizens and started their family. They had three daughters and lived in Brentwood, an upscale section of Los Angeles. Their ever-expanding, successful company had factories in suburban Van Nuys, California, and later pioneered the fashion-factories movement across the border into Mexicali, Mexico. In the 1970s the Olga Company tried another innovation—setting up a factory on a Hopi Indian reservation. Olga and Jan Erteszek stressed Christian values in the workplace and established a charity called the Erteszek Foundation. They also employed many modern business-management techniques that helped foster a loyal workforce. For example, instead of "employees," workers were called "associates," and associates were encouraged to join in a Creative Meeting, a brainstorming gathering in which ideas were shared with management. Free English language classes were scheduled on-site, and a generous profit-sharing program was implemented in 1954. As a personal touch, Olga made fruitcakes for every associate at Christmastime.

The Erteszeks learned early on the marketing value of showing the real person responsible for the product. Olga Erteszek's face appeared in the Olga Company's advertisements with the slogan "Behind every Olga there really is an Olga." Women trusted the face that made a revolutionary garment without sacrificing a fine attention to detail. Olga touches appeared in unlikely places, such as a California warehouse sign that read, "Olga: the first lady of under fashion."

Olga Erteszek received the fashion industry's prestigious FEMY award. She continued to work for the company as a consultant into the early 1980s, when her daughter Christina Erteszek became the vice president of design. By 1984 the company had annual sales of $67 million, and that year it was sold to Warnaco. Both Olga and Jan Erteszek were known for their philanthropy and humanitarian efforts. In 1985 the couple received the California Industrialist of the Year Award for lifetime achievement. Also that year they renewed their wedding vows before family and friends. In 1986 Jan Erteszek died. Three years later Olga died of breast cancer at her home. A memorial service was held for her on 20 September 1989 at Forest Lawn Memorial Park in Glendale, California, where she was buried.

★

The benevolent policies of the Olga Company are discussed in Robert Levering et al., eds., *The 100 Best Companies to Work for in America* (1984). An obituary is in the *New York Times* (19 Sept. 1989).

JENNIFER FARTHING

EVANS, Gil (*b.* 13 May 1912 in Toronto, Ontario, Canada; *d.* 20 March 1988 in Cuernavaca, Mexico), arranger, composer, and bandleader whose record-album collaborations with Miles Davis (*Miles Ahead, Porgy and Bess,* and *Sketches of Spain*) are generally considered to be some of the best jazz music ever written and performed.

Christened Ian Ernest Gilmore Green, Gil later in life chose to take a stepfather's surname, Evans. His father, Ian Ernest Green, was a doctor, and his mother, Margaret Julia McConnachy, a homemaker. The Green family, including Gil's two siblings, Jean and Montgomery, moved from Toronto to western Canada, then to Washington State, and finally to California. Evans graduated from Stockton High School and Modesto Junior College, both in California. He was, a self-taught musician who learned by listening and transcribing into musical notation the records of Louis Armstrong, Duke Ellington, Don Redman, Red Nichols, and the Casa Loma Band. Out of school, he led and wrote for his own band, which lasted from 1933 to 1938. His singer, Skinny Ennis, took over the band in 1938, and Evans stayed on as the band's arranger. That year, the band

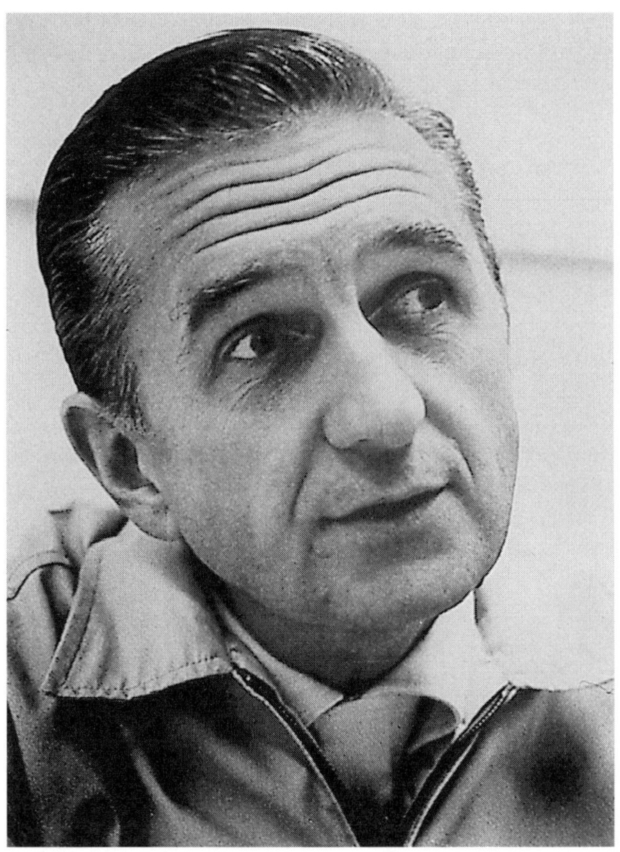

Gil Evans. METRONOME/ARCHIVE PHOTOS

began working on the Bob Hope radio show. Also writing for the band was Claude Thornhill, who left in 1939 to form his own group. Thornhill had a distinctive sound: he used French horns and integrated a tuba into the standard big-band instrumentation. Because this band offered new creative challenges, Evans joined it as arranger in 1941.

Although a Canadian citizen, Evans joined the U.S. Army during World War II (thereby gaining U.S. citizenship) and worked again with Skinny Ennis, who was leading a band at the Santa Anita Army Ordnance Base in California. He later directed a band at Fort Lewis, in Washington State. After his discharge from the army in 1946, Evans moved to New York City and rejoined Thornhill. He wrote arrangements of such modern jazz pieces as *Donna Lee, Anthropology, Robbins' Nest,* and *Yardbird Suite.* Evans's work was recognized by many innovative jazz musicians for his individualistic use of orchestration, form, and harmony. Leonard Feather wrote in the 1960 edition of the *Encyclopedia of Jazz* that Evans's arrangements "showed more originality in their variety of tonal texture than anything else that was then being created in either the dance band or the jazz field." Evans left Thornhill's band in 1948.

Evans's one-room basement apartment on West Fifty-fifth Street in New York City—a few blocks away from the jazz clubs on Fifty-second Street—became a hangout and informal workshop for such young musicians as Gerry Mulligan, John Lewis, Dave Lambert, Charlie Parker, and Miles Davis. Composer and educator George Russell, one of the regulars there, said it was "like a school in a way . . . an esoteric school." Evans, older than the rest of the group, was the central figure; Mulligan nicknamed him "Svengali" because of his enormous influence.

The group eventually crystallized into a nine-piece band, led by Miles Davis, beginning with an engagement at a New York nightclub, the Royal Roost, in August and September 1948. The Miles Davis Nonet recorded Evans's arrangements, *Boplicity* in 1949 and *Moon Dreams* in 1950. The Davis Nonet recordings—collectively called *Birth of the Cool*—are generally recognized as a high point in the history of jazz. As French critic André Hodeir wrote, "*Boplicity* is enough to qualify Gil Evans as one of jazz's greatest composer-arrangers." Although critical opinion was favorable, the public ignored the band. Still, a new style of jazz had been created, called "cool." For three generations, its leading practitioners would be Miles Davis, Gerry Mulligan, John Lewis, and Gil Evans.

From 1950 to 1957 Evans did freelance arranging for the saxophonist and bandleader Charlie Parker and for the singers Pearl Bailey, Johnny Mathis, Tony Bennett, and Peggy Lee. In 1957 he was reunited with Miles Davis for the album *Miles Ahead.* Critic Max Harrison wrote of the album, "In elaboration and richness of resources they [Evans's arrangements] surpass anything previously attempted in big band jazz." Davis and Evans returned to the studios in the summer of 1958 to record George Gershwin's opera *Porgy and Bess.* Evans did more than simply orchestrate the melodies. Gunther Schuller called Evans's work "complete transformations." Evans also introduced Davis to "modal jazz," where the improvisations are based on scales rather than chord sequences. Their next collaboration, *Sketches of Spain,* released in 1960, used themes from Spanish classical and folk music. The album won a Grammy in 1961.

Evans also appeared on albums under his own name, including *Gil Evans and Ten* (1957), *Old Bottle New Wine* (1958), *Great Jazz Standards* (1959), and *Out of the Cool* (1960). In a characteristically selfless gesture, he used one of his albums, *Into the Hot* (1961), to showcase the work of John Carisi—a friend from the Fifty-fifth Street apartment days—and Cecil Taylor.

Individualism of Gil Evans was recorded in 1963, the same year that Evans married Anita Cooper. They had two sons: Noah, who became a sound engineer, and Miles, who became a trumpet player in his father's band. (Little is known about Evans's first marriage, to Lillian Grace.) Evans arranged albums for guitarist Kenny Burrell (1964) and singer Astrud Gilberto (1965–1966). In 1968 he received a Guggenheim Fellowship for composition. In 1972 he became a founding artist of the John F. Kennedy Center for the Performing Arts, and in 1973 was named an artistic director of the New York Jazz Repertory Company.

Evans led a band throughout the 1970s and 1980s that played New York City nightclubs and gave concerts in Europe and Japan. His group now included electronic instruments and used rock rhythms. There were plans for an album with rock superstar Jimi Hendrix, but a few weeks before they were to meet, Hendrix died. Evans went on to record *The Gil Evans Orchestra Plays the Music of Jimi Hendrix* (1974). To the critics of his new jazz/rock fusion music he replied, "Current jazz, now jazz, uses the rhythm of the time." He also wrote film music for Julian Temple's *Absolute Beginners* and Martin Scorsese's *The Color of Money,* both released in 1986.

Evans was creatively active until the end of his life. He underwent prostate surgery early in 1988 and went to recover in Mexico, but there he contracted peritonitis and died. His remains were cremated, and his ashes were scattered in the Caribbean.

Upon Evans's death, Miles Davis commented: "He and Duke Ellington changed the whole sound. There's no way to describe it, because there's nobody on this earth that can do that anymore. What he did to the texture of an orchestration, what he did with pop songs was like writing an original piece. Students will discover him. They'll have to take his music apart layer by layer. That's how they'll know what kind of a genius he was."

★

Joe Muccioli, ed., *The Gil Evans Collection: Fifteen Study and Sketch Scores from Gil's Manuscripts* (1977), includes musical manuscripts from Evans's entire career. Jack Chambers, *Milestones 1: The Music and Times of Miles Davis to 1960* (1983), provides invaluable information about Evans's early career. Other useful sources of information include Raymond Horricks, *Svengali; or, The Orchestra Called Gil Evans* (1984), and Gene Lees, "He Fell from a Star," *Jazzletter* 14, nos. 6, 7, and 8 (June, July, and Aug. 1995), consisting of eight-page newsletters that deal exclusively with Gil Evans. Nat Hentoff, *Gil Evans: A List of Compositions Licensed by B.M.I.* (1961), provides outstanding critiques of Evans's compositions. Max Harrison, *A Jazz Retrospect* (1977), is a collection of articles about a number of great jazz musicians, including Evans. See also Fernando Gonzalez, "In the Key of Evans," *Boston Globe Magazine* (10 May 1987). An obituary is in the *New York Times* (22 Mar. 1988). *The Complete Columbia Studio Recordings: Miles Davis and Gil Evans* (1996), compiles all of the albums *Miles Ahead, Porgy and Bess, Sketches of Spain,* and *Quiet Nights. Gil Evans and His Orchestra,* VIEW (1987) is a video made during a late 1980s tour of Japan.

JOHN VOIGT

F

FAIN, Sammy (*b.* 17 June 1902 in New York City; *d.* 6 December 1989 in Los Angeles, California), composer for films and the stage whose works include numerous popular-music standards.

Fain was born Samuel Feinberg in New York City, the son of Abraham Feinberg, a prominent rabbi, and Manya (Glass) Feinberg. Growing up in New York City and, later, on a farm in the Catskill Mountains, Fain attended public schools and taught himself to play the piano. Early on he began writing music, and as an adolescent he made attempts to sell his compositions by mail. After finishing high school, Fain moved to New York City, where he became a pianist for Jack Mills, Incorporated, a leading popular-music publishing company. Fain's first published song, with lyrics by Al Dubin and Irving Mills, was "Nobody Knows What a Redheaded Mama Can Do," in 1925. The song was recorded by Sophie Tucker. Also in 1925, Fain's music was heard by Broadway audiences for the first time when he contributed songs to the revues *Chauve Souris* and *Sky High.*

In 1927 Fain began a lengthy partnership with lyricist Irving Kahal. One of their first collaborations, "Let a Smile Be Your Umbrella," soon became a national hit. The song's peppy melody and optimistic lyrics had successfully captured the self-consciously carefree mood of the Roaring Twenties. In 1929 another Fain and Kahal composition, "Wedding Bells Are Breaking Up That Old Gang of Mine," was a success.

Fain was among the many composers drawn to Hollywood by the advent of sound motion pictures. Although he returned to the stage frequently throughout his career, Fain made his biggest mark in films. Continuing to work with Kahal, he wrote songs for pictures produced by Paramount in the early 1930s, most significantly "You Brought a New Kind of Love to Me," sung by Maurice Chevalier in *The Big Pond* (1930). Moving to Warner Brothers Pictures, where major songwriting chores were entrusted to composer Harry Warren, Fain contributed songs to numerous B-level films, including "By a Waterfall" to *Footlight Parade* (1933), "Lonely Lane" to *College Coach* (1933), "Spin a Little Web of Dreams" to *Fashions of 1935* (1934) and "Ev'ry Day" to *Sweet Music* (1935). Fain contributed the song "When You Were a Smile on Your Mother's Lips and a Twinkle in Your Daddy's Eye" and made a brief on-screen appearance as a songwriter in *Dames* (1934).

Leaving Warner Brothers, Fain (with lyricist Lew Brown) earned his first Academy Award nomination for the song "(I Saw You Last Night and Got) That Old Feeling," which premiered in the United Artists release *Vogues of 1938* (1937). The song eventually became a "standard" recorded by numerous vocalists over the years. Fain devoted the late 1930s and early 1940s to composing for Broadway, contributing songs to *Right This Way* (1938), *Hellzapoppin'* (1938), *George White's Scandals* (1939), *Blackbirds* (1939), *Boys and Girls Together* (1940), and *Sons o' Fun* (1941). Only *Hellzapoppin'* was a major box-office success, running for 1,404 performances, but no songs from the comedy-oriented show made any impression. The much-shorter-lived *Right of Way* featured two songs that have entered the popular music canon—"I'll Be Seeing You (In All the Old Familiar Places)" and "I Can Dream, Can't I?" The hopeful yet melancholic "I'll Be Seeing You" became one of the most frequently heard ballads during World War II. "I Can Dream, Can't I?" was a hit for the Tommy Dorsey Orchestra and, later, for the Andrews Sisters. Fain married Sally Fox in 1941; they had a son, Franklin. The couple divorced in 1949.

Returning to Hollywood in 1943, Fain went to work for Metro-Goldwyn-Mayer Pictures, writing songs for *Presenting Lily Mars* (1943), starring Judy Garland; *Two Girls and a Sailor* (1944), starring June Allyson; *Weekend at the Waldorf* (1945), starring Lana Turner; and *Holiday in Mexico* (1946), starring Jane Powell. Irving Kahal had died in 1942, and Fain now collaborated with a number of lyricists. With Ralph Freed, he wrote "The Worry Song," to which Gene Kelly danced (partnered with animation character Jerry the Mouse) in *Anchors Aweigh* (1945). For the next few years, Fain continued to compose for quickly forgotten films. A Fain song not connected with a film or stage show, "Dear Hearts and Gentle People," with lyrics by Bob Hilliard, was a best-selling recording for singer Bing Crosby in 1949.

Fain reached the height of his success in the 1950s. He wrote the scores for two popular Walt Disney–produced animated features—*Alice in Wonderland* in 1951 (lyrics by Hilliard) and *Peter Pan* in 1953 (lyrics by Sammy Cahn). Also in 1953, Fain's composition "Secret Love," sung by Doris Day in the film *Calamity Jane,* won the Academy Award for best song. Lyrics were by Paul Francis Webster, who was influenced by William Wordsworth's celebrations of love and nature. Fain and Webster provided a similarly Wordsworthian effort with the title song to the drama *Love Is a Many Splendored Thing* in 1955. The soaring, declamatory song won Fain and Webster a second Academy Award. Both of Fain and Webster's Academy Award–winning songs became best-selling recordings. Six other Fain and Webster songs earned Academy Award nominations: "April Love," from the movie of the same name starring Pat Boone in 1957 (Boone's recording of the song was a top hit); the title song from the drama *A Certain Smile* and "A Very Precious Love," the theme song for the drama *Marjorie Morningstar,* both in 1958; the title song from *Tender Is the Night,* a screen version of the F. Scott Fitzgerald novel, in 1962; "Strange Are the Ways of Love," from *The Stepmother* in 1971; and "A World That Never Was," from *Half a House* in 1976. With lyricists Carol Connors and Ayn Robbins, Fain earned a final Academy Award nomination for "Someone's Waiting for You," from *The Rescuers* in 1977. His last screen work was "Katie," for *Just You and Me, Kid* in 1979.

Sammy Fain. ARCHIVE PHOTOS

Fain found success on Broadway elusive. His efforts at writing a "book musical," in which songs establish characterization and advance the plot, were all short lived. These are *Toplitsky of Notre Dame* (1946), lyrics by George Marion, Jr.; *Flahooley* (1951), lyrics by E. Y. ("Yip") Harburg; *Ankles Aweigh* (1955), lyrics by Dan Shapiro; *Christine* (1960), lyrics by Webster; and *Something More* (1964), lyrics by Marilyn and Alan Bergman. Fain thought the key to good songwriting was simplicity. "Take a great painting: it's usually simple. When it gets cluttered up it isn't so great," Fain told *Time* in 1950. He was named to the Songwriters Hall of Fame in 1971. From 1979 to his death, Fain was a member of the board of directors of the American Society of Composers, Authors, and Publishers, from which he received a lifetime achievement award in 1989. He died of a heart attack at the University of California Medical Center in Los Angeles.

Trained in the Tin Pan Alley school of "for hire" songwriting, Fain is notable for the wide variety of his styles, ranging from snappy, optimistic ditties of the 1920s to wistful World War II–era ballads to florid 1950s romantic anthems, which brought him success and recognition over a period of half a century.

★

There are short essays on Fain and lists of his compositions in *Sweet and Lowdown: America's Popular Songwriters* (1978) and *The Great Songwriters of Hollywood* (1980), both by Warren Craig, and in David Ewen, *American Songwriters* (1987). A short interview with Fain is in *Time* (23 Jan. 1950). Obituaries are in the *New York Times* (7 Dec. 1989) and *Variety* (13 Dec. 1989).

MARY KALFATOVIC

FAULK, John Henry (*b.* 21 August 1913 in Austin, Texas; *d.* 9 April 1990 in Austin, Texas), humorist and political activist whose successful lawsuit against Aware, Inc., et al., in 1962 helped end the political blacklisting system in the broadcasting industry.

Faulk was the fourth of five children of Henry Faulk and Martha ("Mattie") Downs. His mother was a homemaker, his father a prominent lawyer and democratic socialist who played a leading role in the successful effort in 1906 to break up the Standard Oil Trust in Texas. John Henry was educated in Austin public schools and at the University of Texas, where he earned a bachelor's degree in 1939 and a master's degree in 1940. At the university Faulk's views were shaped by the liberal, pro–New Deal ideas and teachings of folklorist J. Frank Dobie, historian Walter Prescott Webb, and naturalist Roy Bedichek. His master's thesis was an analysis of sermons that he transcribed during field trips to African-American churches in central Texas. As a doctoral student at the university from 1940 to 1942 (although he did not complete his degree), Faulk taught a class on Texas folklore. In 1940 Faulk married Hally Wood, a fellow student, with whom he had one child. The following year he received a Julius Rosenwald Foundation scholarship. Rejected for military service because of blindness in one eye, Faulk entered the merchant marine in 1942. After a year working on transatlantic routes, he served with the Red Cross in Cairo, Egypt. In 1944 he joined the U.S. Army as a psychiatric social worker and served the rest of the war at Camp Swift, Texas.

In 1945 musicologist and fellow Texan Alan Lomax introduced Faulk to CBS management in New York City, and he was signed to a radio contract. In April 1946 Faulk premiered *Johnny's Front Porch,* a weekly program broadcast on WCBS Radio, and when that went off the air he worked as a disk jockey for WOV Radio. During this period Faulk and his wife formed friendships with several folk singers, including Pete Seeger and Woody Guthrie. Faulk became well known to social and political protest activists in Greenwich Village, serving as a master of ceremonies at folk music concerts and at fund-raising events in support of causes associated with the political left.

Faulk divorced Hally in 1947 and on 28 June 1948 he married Lynne Smith; they had three children. Also in 1948 he campaigned for Progressive presidential candidate Henry Wallace, serving as an entertainer at rallies in Texas and other southern states. In 1949 he was employed by WPAT Radio in Paterson, New Jersey. Known on the air as "Pat the Rancher," Faulk hosted a variety of radio shows. He returned to WCBS Radio in September 1951. The *John Henry Faulk Show* featured a mix of music, humorous political commentary, and folksy stories about rural characters whom Faulk had known in Texas. It soon became one of the most popular radio programs in New York City. After his return to WCBS, Faulk made appearances on a variety of CBS television programs, including game shows produced by Mark Goodson and Jerry Todman. His broadcasting career reached its peak in the summer of 1955, when he hosted the CBS network television program *The Morning Show* and his local radio program was rated second in popularity among sixteen radio programs.

In December 1955 Faulk was among the leaders of a successful effort to gain control of the American Federation of Television and Radio Artists (AFTRA). The union had been dominated by associates of Aware, Incorporated, a New York–based organization that ran a blacklisting "clearance" system for media advertisers and radio and television networks. For a fee, Aware investigated the backgrounds of entertainers to determine if they had any communist sympathies or affiliation. On 10 February 1956 Aware retaliated against Faulk for his involvement in the AFTRA election by issuing a bulletin accusing him of procommunist activities. When his radio program lost commercial sponsors as a result of these accusations, Faulk hired attorney Louis Nizer, who filed a suit against Aware and others on 26 June 1956, charging defamation of Faulk's professional reputation. CBS fired Faulk in August 1957 and he spent the next five years on the blacklist, unable to secure employment in the broadcast industry. Aware's lawyers, led by former McCarthy Committee counsel Roy Cohn, were able to delay

John Henry Faulk, *c.* 1964. ARCHIVE PHOTOS

trial of the suit until April 1962. On 28 June the jury awarded Faulk the largest libel judgment in history to that date—$3.5 million. An appellate court later reduced the amount to $500,000. Faulk's legal fees and other related debts exceeded the amount finally awarded.

In 1963 Faulk wrote *Fear on Trial,* his memoir of life on the blacklist and his legal case against Aware. Despite his victory and the widespread publicity it generated, CBS did not rehire Faulk. He had small roles in the movies *All the Way Home* (1963) and *The Best Man* (1964), but his career as an entertainer never regained its earlier momentum. His marriage to Lynne ended soon after the conclusion of his trial, and in 1965 he married Elizabeth Peake, with whom he had one child. In 1968 he moved back to Austin, where he earned a living as an after-dinner speaker at business conventions and political events. He was a vocal critic of the Vietnam War, and he toured the country in support of the presidential bid of Senator George McGovern.

In 1974 CBS television broadcast its movie version of Faulk's book, *Fear on Trial.* From 1975 to 1983 he was on the syndicated television program *Hee-Haw,* and he served occasionally as a commentator on National Public Radio. During the 1970s Faulk wrote a one-man play, *Pear Orchard, Texas,* in which he used folksy rural characters to express his views on social and political matters. He revised the play in the late 1980s and renamed it *Deep in the Heart.* In 1983 Faulk waged a campaign for Congress in a special election won by Republican Phil Gramm. He spent the last years of his life as a First Amendment activist. His friends established an endowment at the University of Texas Center for American History to support a biennial conference on the First Amendment. The main building of the Austin Public Library is named in his honor. Faulk died of cancer and was buried in the Texas State Cemetery in Austin.

★

The John Henry Faulk Papers and the *John Henry Faulk* v. *Aware, Inc., Laurence A. Johnson, and Vincent Hartnett* case files, at the Center for American History, University of Texas, Austin, provide valuable documentation on Faulk's fight against the blacklist as well as his political activities. John Henry Faulk, *Fear on Trial* (1963), is a firsthand account of Faulk's legal battle against Aware. John Henry Faulk, *The Uncensored John Henry Faulk* (1985), is a collection of Faulk's essays, commentary, and stage scripts rich in autobiographical information. Michael C. Burton, *John Henry Faulk: The Making of a Liberated Mind* (1993), concentrates on Faulk's formative years. Louis Nizer, *The Jury Returns* (1966), includes an in-depth chapter on the Faulk case. An obituary is in the *New York Times* (10 Apr. 1990). The John Henry Faulk Oral History Collection at the Center for American History, University of Texas, Austin, consists of interviews with several of Faulk's family members and professional associates.

DON E. CARLETON

FELDMAN, Morton (*b.* 12 January 1926 in Queens, New York; *d.* 3 September 1987 in Buffalo, New York), composer who created a unique experimental music, including new forms of notation.

Feldman was one of two children of Irving Feldman and Francis (Breskin) Feldman, who ran a garment business. One of his first memories was of his mother holding his finger and picking out the Jewish folk song "Eli Eli" on the piano. By the age of eight he was composing his own music. He attended the High School for Music and Art for a time, and in 1941 he began composition lessons with Wallingford Riegger. Three years later Stefan Wolpe became his teacher. Both men had outstanding international reputations as composers, but Feldman was not happy with Riegger, and Wolpe rejected Feldman's music as purposely undeveloped and esoteric. Feldman stopped paying him, but the lessons continued.

Late in 1949 Feldman went to Carnegie Hall to hear

Morton Feldman. NYT PICTURES/NYT PERMISSIONS

Anton Webern's Symphony. At the concert Feldman first met the experimental composer John Cage. At their subsequent meeting Feldman showed Cage a score of a string quartet he had written. Cage asked, "How did you make this?" Thinking of the quarrels with Wolpe, Feldman weakly answered, "I don't know how I made it." Cage jumped up and down and screeched, "Isn't that marvelous. Isn't that wonderful. Isn't that beautiful, and he doesn't know how he made it." With that Cage gave him permission to have confidence in his own artistic instincts.

Early in 1950 Feldman rented an apartment in the building in which Cage lived, on the corner of Grand and Monroe Streets on Manhattan's Lower East Side. There he associated with Cage and other composers, including Earle Brown and Christian Wolff. Feldman introduced pianist David Tudor to the group. But the main source of inspiration for all of them was the frequent contacts with the abstract painters Philip Guston (Feldman's closest friend), Willem de Kooning, Robert Rauschenberg, Jackson Pollock, Mark Rothko, Franz Kline, and Jasper Johns. Feldman later wrote, "The new painting made me desirous of a sound world more direct, more immediate, more physical than anything that had existed heretofore." Throughout this period, until 1967, Feldman supported himself by working in his parents' business.

In 1950 Feldman created graph notation while visiting Cage for dinner. He began doodling on a piece of note paper and intuitively made a freehand graph that designated high, middle, and low pitches. This was the beginning of a new form of musical notation in which only approximations of pitch are given. The new system helped free Feldman from any unwanted past musical references, which he called "rhetoric." The *Projection* series (1950–1951) was the first music written in this "indeterminate" style.

In 1951 Feldman completed two orchestral graph pieces, *Intersection I* and *Marginal Intersection,* in which he used his mother's plastic dishes and aluminum pots and pans because he "wanted percussion to sound like noise." But he was not getting what he wanted from the graphs: he wanted the music to be free, not the musicians. Nevertheless, he continued the graph technique with such compositions as *Atlantis* (1958) and *Out of Last Pieces* (1960).

Feldman used traditional notation in *Structures,* for string quartet (1951), and *Extensions 1* (1951), but he found that notation also too restrictive, calling it "one dimensional." With *Intermission VI* (1953) for one or two pianos, he created the first work in "open form," in which the performer is presented with musical elements from which he may freely choose. This concept, like others of Feldman's, was quickly adopted by avant-garde European composers, such as Karlheinz Stockhausen. In the *Durations* series (1960–1961) Feldman developed another approach by writing precisely notated parts but allowing the musicians the freedom to choose their own pace of execution; he called it a "race-course" notation.

Feldman continued to use graph and graphlike constructions in *Straits of Magellan* (1961) and *In Search of an Orchestration* (1967). He used traditional notation in *On Time and the Instrumental Factor* (1969). No matter what notation scheme he used, Feldman's music always has his sound—usually very quiet with little melodic movement, producing an almost out-of-time meditative state. He defined it once as "like a bug under a microscope—unmoving to the naked eye, it is in fact quivering with activity." *Why Patterns?* (1978), *The Viola in My Life* series (1970–1971), *False Relationships and the Extended Ending* (1968), and *Rothko Chapel* (1971) are his only major works that even suggest a traditional classical music contrast and development.

In 1966 Feldman won a Guggenheim Fellowship. He also received awards from the National Institute of Arts and Letters (1970) and the Koussevitsky Foundation (1975). In 1972 he was appointed to the faculty of the State University of New York at Buffalo, where from 1976 to 1979 he was also the director of the Center of the Creative and Performing Arts. From 1976 Feldman began an intimate relationship with the composer Bunita Marcus. In her words, "for the next ten years we would discuss and work with his music for three to four hours a day." The piano piece *For Bunita Marcus* was published in 1985. In 1984 he went to Germany and lectured at the Darmstadt Internationale Ferienkurse für Neue Musik. During the last years of his life he created pieces of extreme length. String Quartet no. 2 (1983) is about six hours long. *For Philip Guston* (1984) lasts more than four hours. He admitted that such pieces were not geared for performance.

Even with the continued growing recognition of his work, Feldman in his last years felt separated from the musical world. In 1985 he ironically said, "My own students think I'm a cross between Wittgenstein and Zero Mostel." About his personality, John Rockwell wrote, "Despite the ethereal quality of his music Mr. Feldman in person was an almost Rabelaisian figure, with a pungent Brooklyn accent and an undisguised appetite for sensuous pleasure." Feldman married the composer Barbara Monk in June 1987 shortly before his death from pancreatic cancer. He is buried in Beth Moses Cemetery in Farmingdale, New York.

★

The Morton Feldman Archive is at the Music Library of the State University of New York at Buffalo. C. F. Peters published his music from 1949 to 1969, as did Universal Editions from 1967 to 1987. Interviews with Feldman are found in "I Met Heine on the Rue Fürstenburg," in *Buffalo Evening News* (21 Apr. 1973); Peter Gena and Jonathan Brent, *A John Cage Reader in Celebration of His Seventieth Birthday* (1982); and in Cole Gagne and Tracy

Caras, *Soundpieces: Interviews with American Composers* (1982). *Feldman Essays,* edited by Walter Zimmermann (1985), captures Feldman's encyclopedic aesthetic opinions. Thomas DeLio, *The Music of Morton Feldman* (1996), has three essays by Feldman. Analysis of his music is found in Reginald Smith Brindle, *The New Music: The Avant-Garde Since 1945* (1975), and Benjamin Boretz and Edward T. Cone, *Perspectives on Notation and Performance* (1976). An obituary is in the *New York Times* (4 Sept. 1987).

JOHN VOIGT

FESTINGER, Leon (*b.* 8 May 1919 in New York City; *d.* 11 February 1989 in New York City), social psychologist best known for his work published as *A Theory of Cognitive Dissonance* (1957).

Leon Festinger, son of Alex Festinger and Sarah (Solomon) Festinger, grew up in New York City and attended the City College of New York. By his own admission, Festinger would have been quite content to have made his living playing chess, and actually spent his first two years of college "mainly inhabiting chess clubs." Science also fascinated him, but early courses in physics and chemistry left the impression, he later said, that there was "no room left for any new discoveries." Eventually he turned to psychology, his interest aroused by an early work by Clark Hull, *Hypnosis and Suggestibility* (1933), which revealed to him a field "that was scientific and still had questions to be answered." He received his B.S. degree in psychology from City College in 1939.

Leon Festinger. FROM BENTLEY HISTORICAL LIBRARY, UNIVERSITY OF MICHIGAN

Festinger was intrigued with the work of psychologist Kurt Lewin, in whose ideas he saw "creativity, newness, and a sense of importance," and he eagerly looked forward to graduate study with Lewin at the University of Iowa. But by 1939, when Festinger arrived in Iowa City, Lewin had shifted his focus to social psychology, particularly the study of group behavior. Festinger preferred more scientific rigor than the new study offered, and so pursued work that ranged from aspiration theory to a mathematical model of decision making, to statistics, and even to a study using laboratory rats. He received his M.A. degree from the University of Iowa in 1940 and stayed on to complete his doctoral program. After receiving the Ph.D. in 1942, he went to the University of Rochester, where he worked as a senior statistician for the Committee on Selection and Training of Aircraft Pilots. On 23 October 1943 Festinger married Mary Oliver Ballou; they had three children.

In the early 1940s Lewin had left Iowa and gone to the Massachusetts Institute of Technology, where he had established the Research Center for Group Dynamics. Still Lewin's student, Festinger joined him there in 1945 as an assistant professor at the center, "by fiat" a social psychologist. There he immersed himself in the field, drawn in by Lewin's innovative approach. Lewin investigated actual problems using methodology that tried to "create, in the laboratory, powerful social situations that made big differences." Festinger felt strongly that he and his colleagues were at the beginning of something momentous and groundbreaking.

Not everyone, however, shared this view. When Lewin died in 1947, the Research Center lost the leadership and prestige that had secured its place at MIT. Likely it would have folded, but in 1948 Rensis Likert and Donald Marquis of the University of Michigan moved the facility, including its faculty and students, to Ann Arbor. There the center joined the existing Survey Research Center to constitute the newly formed Institute for Social Research. This move made Michigan central to the field of social psychology and engendered a healthy interchange of ideas. Appointed associate professor of psychology and program director of the Research Center, Festinger coedited *Research Methods in the Behavioral Sciences* (1953), a cooperative venture that involved the entire institute.

The field of social psychology grew rapidly in the 1950s. Festinger left Michigan in 1951 to become professor of psychology at the University of Minnesota, and four years later he took a similar appointment at Stanford University. While in Palo Alto, California, Festinger became interested in what makes people so ready to accept rumors, even those that promote anxiety and distress. This work, reported in the field study *When Prophecy Fails* (1956), eventually led Festinger to the theory of cognitive dissonance, which asserts that when people hold conflicting attitudes, ideas, or beliefs, they will adjust their beliefs in an attempt to decrease the resultant psychological discomfort. Published in 1957, *A Theory of Cognitive Dissonance* proved to be Festinger's most significant and enduring contribution to the field of social psychology. In 1959 he received the American Psychological Association's Distinguished Scientific Contribution Award for his work.

By the mid-1960s Festinger was feeling personally restless, and in 1964 he left social psychology in pursuit of "intellectual stimulation from new sources." Although Festinger stayed at Stanford until 1968, he turned his attention to the study of perception and consciousness. Through a careful technical analysis of eye movements, Festinger hoped to discover how an internal readiness to receive visual information combined with the incoming visual input to produce the conscious experience of visual perception.

Festinger married his second wife, Trudy Bradley, on 7 September 1968; they had no children. In that same year Festinger returned to New York City to become the Else and Hans Staudinger Professor of Psychology at the New School for Social Research. There, he said, research and science became a pleasure again. He thoroughly enjoyed learning the background and techniques of perception study, an endeavor that he described as "like being a graduate student again on a professor's salary." In 1975 the American Association for the Advancement of Science elected Festinger a fellow, declaring that his "work in social psychology has placed him in the front rank of that discipline, and his recent work in perception has received substantial and merited recognition." Around 1978 his interests turned again, this time to anthropology, specifically the study of the social organization of prehistoric groups. His research, based largely upon archaeological sources, was published in *The Human Legacy* (1983).

In the 1990s Festinger's cognitive dissonance theory was still being widely critiqued and cited. Upon his death from cancer in 1989, Festinger's colleagues admired him as a man who had been a scholar "until his final breath"; the European social psychologist Serge Moscovici also acclaimed Festinger's contributions to the development of international research, particularly the Committee of Transnational Social Psychology, with which he worked from its inception in 1964 well into the 1970s. He was buried in New York City.

★

The Leon Festinger Papers, 1939–1988, Bentley Historical Library, University of Michigan, Ann Arbor, Michigan, are an especially good source for his post–social psychology career but reveal very little of Festinger's personal life. The Director's Files (1940s–1950s) in the Research Center for Group Dynamics series, in the Institute for Social Research Records (1936–1992), at the Bentley Historical Library, University of Michigan, Ann Arbor, Michigan, offer a look into this phase of Festinger's career. David Cohen, *Psychologists on Psychology: Modern Innovators Talk About Their Work* (1977), contains an interview and discussion showing Festinger as theorist and methodologist. Leon Festinger, "Looking Backward," in *Retrospections on Social Psychology,* edited by Leon Festinger (1980), takes a "personal view" of trends begun by the Research Center for Group Dynamics and contains insights into Festinger's professional development. Eliot Aronson, *Leon Festinger and the Art of Audacity: An Appreciation* (1989), is the transcript of an address given at a symposium on Festinger's contributions to social psychology for the Society of Experimental Social Psychologists. Roger R. Hock, *Forty Studies That Changed Psychology: Explorations into the History of Psychological Research* (1992), is a summary and review of cognitive dissonance theory. Serge Moscovici, "Obituary: Leon Festinger," *European Journal of Social Psychology* 19 (1989): 263–269, is a retrospective analysis of Festinger's work and its continuing decisiveness for social psychology. Another obituary is in the *New York Times* (12 Feb. 1989).

MARILYN SAUDER MCLAUGHLIN

FEYNMAN, Richard Phillips (*b.* 11 May 1918 in New York City; *d.* 15 February 1988 in Los Angeles, California), theoretical physicist and educator who shared the Nobel Prize for physics in 1965 and became a public figure as a member of the commission that investigated the fatal explosion of the space shuttle in 1986.

Feynman was the oldest of three children of Melville Feynman and Lucille (Phillips) Feynman. Both of his parents were children of Jewish families who had emigrated from Europe. Although Melville Feynman was only intermittently successful in his various business enterprises, he did communicate his enthusiastic amateur interest in science to his son, and at an early age Richard demonstrated exceptional interest and ability in science and mathematics. In his senior year at Far Rockaway High School in Queens, New York, in 1935, Feynman placed first in the citywide mathematics contest held annually at New York University.

Following his graduation from high school in 1936, Feynman entered the Massachusetts Institute of Technology (MIT), having been rejected by Columbia University, probably on account of a restrictive Jewish quota. At MIT he became a brilliant student both in his initial major, mathematics, and his ultimate career choice, theoretical physics. In his senior thesis, Feynman elegantly solved a problem proposed by his thesis adviser—why does quartz

Richard Feynman. COURTESY OF THE ARCHIVES, CALIFORNIA INSTITUTE OF TECHNOLOGY

expand so little when heated compared to metals? His paper became the basis for an article in *Physical Review* under the abridged title "Forces in Molecules." Such publication by an undergraduate physics student, although not altogether without precedent, was certainly unusual. As a senior, Feynman was one of four entrants from MIT for the Putnam Fellowship in advanced undergraduate mathematics, with the winner offered a full graduate scholarship at Harvard University. Feynman won decisively but turned down the Harvard offer in favor of pursuing his graduate studies at Princeton. Despite some apparent reluctance by the chairman of the Princeton physics department to admit Feynman because he was Jewish, in 1939 Feynman enrolled for graduate work toward a Ph.D.

In his first year, Feynman was assigned to Professor John A. Wheeler, who had come to Princeton in 1938 after studying for four years in Copenhagen with the great physicist Niels Bohr. Wheeler, only seven years older than Feynman, was initially Feynman's supervisor, but the relationship rapidly became one of colleagues. Using as a starting point the difficulties recognized in the existing theory of quantum mechanics, Feynman began work on his dissertation, "The Principle of Least Action in Quantum Mechanics." He explored new mathematical approaches toward applying quantum mechanics to advanced classical electrodynamics, and the result was recognized by his examiners as an important step forward. Feynman received his Ph.D. in theoretical physics in June 1942.

Even before completing his doctoral work, Feynman had been invited to join a group of Princeton scientists in 1941 for confidential work on the atomic bomb. As a result, Feynman shortly became part of the large group of scientists assembled for this project at Los Alamos, New Mexico. Later in 1942 he became a group leader under the supervision of the head of the theoretical division, Hans Bethe, and he rapidly became one of the most important theoreticians on the project.

Among the most important problems that Feynman solved was the probability of potentially hazardous predetonation as the result of cosmic-ray neutrons acting on a nearly critical bomb mass of uranium or plutonium. Another result of his work, which became known as the Bethe-Feynman formula, predicted the explosive yield of a fission weapon. Feynman was one of those present at the test of the first atomic bomb at Alamogordo, New Mexico, on 16 July 1945. Consistent with his not infrequent unorthodox behavior, he elected to view the detonation without wearing the recommended protective glasses for eye safety.

J. Robert Oppenheimer, the scientific director at Los Alamos, had already said in November 1943 that Feynman "is by all odds the most brilliant young physicist here, and everyone knows this." Oppenheimer had expressed his desire to have Feynman eventually join him at his own institution, the University of California at Berkeley. Feynman, however, had developed a warm friendship with Hans Bethe and elected to join him at Cornell University in Ithaca, New York, at the war's end.

At Cornell from 1945 to 1951, Feynman performed most of the principal work that was to be recognized with the Nobel Prize in 1965. Among his theoretical investigations was a renewed approach to his earlier work in quantum electrodynamics. His formulations made use of a new perspective involving the relative probabilities of an atomic particle interaction with another particle along a space-time path. Calculation of these interaction probabilities required difficult mathematical analysis, which Feynman worked out with the assistance of ingenious graphic representations of his own creation. These are now known as Feynman diagrams and have found wide application in many areas of nuclear physics.

Using different theoretical approaches and working independently, Julian S. Schwinger of Harvard and Sin-Itiro Tomanaga of Tokyo University also reformulated aspects of quantum electrodynamics. The combined Feynman-Schwinger-Tomanaga theory is among the most successful scientific constructs of the twentieth century, with strong experimental verification in particle physics, solid-state physics, and statistical mechanics.

In 1951 Feynman left Cornell and moved to the California Institute of Technology in Pasadena, where he became Richard Chase Tolman Professor of Theoretical Physics. He remained in Pasadena for the remainder of his career. While continuing his research on quantum electrodynamics, Feynman also worked on the theory of superfluidity of liquid helium developed by the Russian physicist Lev Landau. Feynman furnished the basic atomic explanation for the anomalous behavior of liquid helium as it approaches the temperature of absolute zero. Along with his fellow professor in Pasadena, Murray Gell-Mann, Feynman made important contributions to the theory of radioactive beta decay and its relation to one of the fundamental parameters in nature, the electroweak force.

In February 1986 Feynman was named as one of the thirteen members of a commission appointed by President Ronald Reagan to investigate the cause of the space shuttle *Challenger* explosion of 28 January 1986, in which all seven crew members were killed. Feynman, in his typical fashion, independently traced the cause of the disaster to a failure of O-rings inadequately tested for elasticity changes caused by low temperatures. He dramatically demonstrated the validity of this hypothesis by placing O-ring material in a glass of ice water, thus demonstrating its brittleness for National Aeronautics and Space Administration officials and, later, on national television—an act that made him a celebrity. At the time of his service on the presidential commission, Feynman was already afflicted with the abdominal cancer that would cause his death.

Feynman was married three times. Arline H. Greenbaum, whom he married in 1941, died of tuberculosis four years later. His marriage to Mary Louise Bell in 1956 ended the same year in divorce. In 1960 he married Gweneth Howarth; they had one child and adopted another.

In addition to the Nobel Prize, Feynman also received the Albert Einstein Award of the U.S. Atomic Energy Commission and the Niels Bohr Gold Medal from the government of Denmark. He was esteemed by his colleagues not only for his contributions to science but also for his ebullience and good humor—traits that made him one of the outstanding personalities of twentieth-century science.

★

Among the more accessible of Feynman's works are *The Feynman Lectures on Physics* (1963); *QED: The Strange Theory of Light and Matter* (1985); *"Surely You're Joking, Mr. Feynman": Adventures of a Curious Character* (1985); *Elementary Particles and the Laws of Physics* (1987); and *Six Easy Pieces: Essentials of Physics Explained by Its Most Brilliant Teacher* (1994). *"What Do YOU Care What Other People Think?": Further Adventures of a Curious Character* (1994) presents Feynman's analysis of the *Challenger* disaster. On his life, see James Gleick, *Genius: The Life and Science of Richard Feynman* (1992). An obituary is in the *New York Times* (17 Feb. 1988).

LEONARD R. SOLON

FIDLER, James Marion ("Jimmie") (*b.* 24 August 1900 in St. Louis, Missouri; *d.* 9 August 1988 in Westlake, California), gossip columnist who was widely syndicated in radio and newspapers; at the height of his popularity in the late 1940s he was broadcast on 486 radio stations and printed in 360 newspapers.

Jimmie Fidler was the son of William Porter Fidler and Belle Wrinkle. Soon after Jimmie's birth, the family moved to Memphis, Tennessee, where his father worked for the American Snuff Company. Jimmie attended local public schools. He dropped out of high school and joined the U.S. Marine Corps on 26 September 1918; he was dispatched to Parris Island and then to Quantico. After his discharge in June 1919 he reenlisted in the service with a new commission as a second lieutenant.

An infatuation with the movie actress Betty Compson then led Fidler to Hollywood. He had started a correspondence with Compson during his enlistment, and she had answered his letters. Upon meeting the actress, however, Fidler learned that she had answered his letters at random from the many she had received from servicemen and that she had done so only to boost morale. Remaining in Hollywood, Fidler won a contest, hosted by the magazine *Film*

Jimmy Fidler, 1938. UPI/CORBIS-BETTMANN

Fun, for young men who wanted to act. After a brief apprenticeship in one picture, Fidler was laid off during the 1920 recession in the film industry. He was then hired as Sid Grauman's assistant at the Million-Dollar Theatre in Los Angeles.

Fidler's first job in journalism was as movie critic and city editor of the *News,* Hollywood's first daily newspaper; because of this job, Fidler was able to claim that he was Hollywood's first gossip columnist. In 1922 he became a press agent and worked for Famous Players–Lasky (which later became Paramount Pictures); the following year he opened his own publicity office, managing the press of such celebrities as Janet Gaynor, Gloria Swanson, Wallace Reid, Lilyan Tashman, Edmund Lowe, Rudolph Valentino, and Cecil B. DeMille. By distributing such unlikely stories as that DeMille was hunting cannibals in Mexico while sailing on his yacht, Fidler ensured that his clients were always in the limelight. He continued with his independent publicity business until 1933, when his client Dorothy Jordan asked him to help her prepare for an interview on the radio program *Hollywood on the Air.* Fidler prepared Jordan for the interview and then conducted it himself; he was such a success that he appeared regularly on the show for a year.

Jimmie Fidler's Hollywood, a five-to-fifteen-minute spot scheduled between news and prime-time programming, was broadcast for sixteen years in the 1930s and 1940s after it moved from West Coast coverage to the full National Broadcasting Company network in 1934. The show featured Fidler's high-pitched voice acerbically dispersing Hollywood's gossip, and at the height of his success, Fidler attracted an audience of approximately 40 million; he was second in popularity only to Walter Winchell in the gossip trade. Fidler reviewed movies with a four-bell rating system, and he also broadcast "open letters" in which he admonished movie stars for their immoral behavior. Fidler always ended the show with his catchphrase, "Good night to you . . . and you . . . and I do mean you!"

On his radio shows and in his news columns Fidler often berated celebrities for their divorces, but he himself was married four times and divorced three times. His first wife was Dorothy Lee, whom he married in March 1931 and divorced in 1932. He married his second wife, Roberta Law, on 22 March 1936; they had a daughter. He married his third wife, Adeline Cox McKnight, in June 1947; they had three children. Fidler's final marriage was to Darrow Davenport in December 1960. Fidler responded to criticism about his hypocritical stance on divorce by declaring, "Why shouldn't I knock [divorce]? I've had more experience with it than most people."

In addition to his radio and newspaper work, Fidler was also a television personality as the host of *Hollywood Opening Night,* a dramatic anthology that aired on the Columbia Broadcasting System from July 1951 to March 1952 and on NBC from October 1952 to March 1953. On CBS the dramas were thirty-minute films made for television, while on NBC the productions were telecast live. NBC's broadcast of *Hollywood Opening Night* was both the first live dramatic program telecast from the West Coast and the first program staged in NBC's new Burbank studios. Fidler introduced each production in a simulated theater lobby and invited the television audience to watch the show with him; he offered a brief preview of the next week's show at the end of the program.

Also in the early 1950s Fidler was implicated in a fraudulent charity scandal in his position as president of the National Kids' Day Foundation. The charity collected nearly $4 million for the goal of promoting a National Kids' Day for underprivileged children, but only $302,000 went to the explicit purpose of the group while more than $3.2 million was allocated to fund-raising costs, including salaries. The charity was also accused of using Bing Crosby's name without permission, and Bob Hope's wife withdrew her support as a sponsor. Los Angeles officials shut the foundation down. Fidler's reputation escaped mostly unharmed because his position was not a salaried one.

Fidler continued to produce his radio show until 1983 and his syndicated newspaper column until shortly before his death. He died of natural causes at Westlake Community Hospital in Westlake, California.

With Hedda Hopper, Louella Parsons, and Walter Winchell, Jimmie Fidler ruled the gossip world in Hollywood's early years. Both a hypocrite and a moral crusader with his on-air tirades, Fidler provided information to his radio, television, and newspaper audiences about their favorite celebrities for more than fifty years.

★

See the Jimmie Fidler clipping file, Billy Rose Theatre Collection, Lincoln Center Library for the Performing Arts, New York City. George Frazier, "Open Letter to Jimmie Fidler," *Collier's* (29 May 1948), provides an interesting critique of Fidler's practice of writing "open letters" by turning the focus of scrutiny on Fidler himself. Obituaries are in the *New York Times* (12 Aug. 1988) and *Variety* (17 Aug. 1988).

WILLIAM WHITE TISON PUGH

FLESCH, Rudolf Franz (*b.* 8 May 1911 in Vienna, Austria; *d.* 5 October 1986 in Dobbs Ferry, New York), writer, lecturer, and editorial consultant whose book *The Art of Plain Talk* (1946) emphasized the writing of "readable" English, which he defined as prose that is readily understood by the average American.

Rudolph Franz Flesch, the son of Hugo Flesch and Helene (Basch) Flesch, attended public schools in Vienna, and like his father became a lawyer, graduating in 1933 from the

Rudolf Flesch. ARCHIVE PHOTOS

University of Vienna. He had one sister. In 1938 he fled Vienna as a refugee, arriving in New York City in October 1938.

In 1939 Flesch was granted a refugee scholarship by Columbia University. He graduated from the School of Library Service in 1940 with highest honors and a B.S. degree. While at Columbia he worked as a research assistant in the Readability Laboratory, sponsored by the American Association for Adult Education, where he worked with Lyman Bryson. Flesch credited Bryson with helping him tremendously in his career and in the development of his thinking. On 6 September 1941 Flesch married Elizabeth Terpenning. The couple had six children. While busy with family life, Flesch continued at Columbia, receiving an M.A. degree in adult education at Teachers College in 1942 and a Ph.D. in educational research there in 1943. From 1942 to 1944 he worked at the Columbia Broadcasting System, where he prepared educational programs and analyzed scripts for readability.

As part of his doctoral thesis, Flesch developed a statistical formula to help writers determine the "readability" of their work. His thesis, "Marks of Readable Style: A Study in Adult Education," was published in 1943 with the same title by Columbia Teachers College as part of its Contribution to Education series. Because of its readability formula and ideas for clearer writing, Flesch's thesis enjoyed an unusual sales success. This was gratifying but also somewhat embarrassing to Flesch, who said *Marks of Readable Style,* originating as a Ph.D. thesis, was not a very readable book. He rewrote it, adding some new ideas that were published as articles in popular magazines and educational and professional journals. The result of the rewrite, *The Art of Plain Talk* (1946), achieved widespread success. One critic said that Flesch wrote easily, delightfully, and with humor, adding that Flesch's examples showed that plain talk made for good reading as well as good understanding.

After graduating from Columbia, Flesch taught at New York University, and then became a freelance writer, lecturer, and editorial consultant. He served as a consultant on readability for the Associated Press and many publishers, government agencies, educational organizations, and corporations. He continually lamented the state of literacy in America, targeting for criticism what he called "Federalese," the language of bureaucrats, and "gobbledygook," a description of meaninglessness. He said government writings were "incomprehensible, not only to the average American with an eighth-grade education but also to the better-educated government employee."

In 1944 Flesch became a United States citizen. As a participant in a democracy as well as a literary expert, he would later say that "colloquial, easily understandable language is the outward sign of democratic, peaceful methods of settling disputes. This holds true in domestic as well as in international affairs: in fact democracy could be defined as government by plain talk."

Flesch and A. H. Lass wrote *The Way to Write* (1947), a high school textbook on composition. This was followed by Flesch's *The Art of Readable Writing* (1949), *How to Test Readability* (1951), and *How to Make Sense* (1954). He edited *Best Articles: Most Memorable Articles of the Year* (1953).

In 1955 Flesch targeted the nation's schools for what he contended was a decline in the state of literacy in the United States. In his *Why Johnny Can't Read, and What You Can Do About It* (1955), he contended that the way schools taught reading was totally wrong, and against all logic and common sense. In the book he advised parents to teach their children reading at home, using phonics, which is a method of teaching that stresses the phonetic values of letters. The book's specific instruction and seventy-two phonics exercises were based on an alphabetic-phonetic primer designed in the 1930s by Leonard Bloomfield, a professor of linguistics at Yale University. Flesch had used this method to teach his oldest daughter to read when she was five years old, and he would go on to use it to teach all of his children.

Flesch argued against the schools' use of reading series like *Fun with Dick and Jane,* which utilized the "look and see" method, focusing on the memorization of whole words rather than the sounds of the letters. Flesch's view was that these books were "stupid, emasculated, pointless, and tasteless little readers, prepared by the tireless teamwork of many educational drudges."

In later decades Flesch continued to be scornful of the "look and see" books and of the educational profession that promoted them. In the early 1980s he wrote *Why Johnny Still Can't Read: A New Look at the Scandal of Our Schools* (1981). By the mid-1980s Flesch was teaching his six-year-old grandson Luke to read. No matter the prevailing mode of thought, Flesch continued to insist that phonics was the only way to teach children reading.

Other books by Flesch include *The Book of Unusual Quotations* (1957), *A New Way to Better English* (1958), *How to Write, Speak, and Think More Effectively* (1960), *How to Be Brief* (1962), *The ABC of Style* (1965), *The Book of Surprises* (as editor, 1965), *The New Book of Unusual Quotations* (1966), *Say What You Mean* (1972), *Look It Up: A Deskbook of American Spelling and Style* (1977), *How to Write Plain English: A Book for Lawyers and Consumers* (1979), and *LITE rpt LITE English: Some Popular Words That Are OK to Use* (1983).

Flesch was a member of the American Library Association, the American Association for Adult Education, the American Psychological Association, the American Association for the Advancement of Science, the Linguistic Society of America, and the National Council of Teachers of English. In his early seventies Flesch began to suffer from coronary heart disease, and he died of congestive heart failure in Dobbs Ferry, New York.

★

Anna Rothe, ed., *Current Biography 1948* (1949), comments on the impact and the critical reaction to Flesch's early work, including *The Art of Plain Talk*. A brief personal and educational background and a list of Flesch's publications can be found in *Contemporary Authors on CD* (1996). An obituary is in the *New York Times* (7 Oct. 1986).

JULIANNE CICARELLI

FLEXNER, Stuart Berg (*b.* 22 March 1928 in Jacksonville, Illinois; *d.* 3 December 1990 in Greenwich, Connecticut), lexicographer, writer, lecturer, and editor in chief of the second edition of the *Random House Dictionary of the English Language* (1987).

Flexner was the son of David Flexner, a clothing retailer, and Gertrude Berg. He had one sibling and grew up in Louisville. His first monograph, *A Glossary of Racetrack Terms,* was published while he was still in high school. In 1944 Flexner enrolled at the University of Louisville, where he majored in American history. After receiving his B.A. degree in 1948 and his M.A. degree in 1949, he moved on

Stuart Berg Flexner with several Random House dictionaries, 1987. NYT PERMISSIONS

to Cornell University in 1950 as a doctoral candidate. After two years there, he left academia for a job as executive editor at Verlan Books in New York City, where he worked from 1952 to 1957. He subsequently served as managing editor in the College Textbook Division at Macmillan (1957–1958) and as president of the publishing house Jugetas, S.A., in Mexico City (1958–1964) before accepting the first of two tours (1964–1972 and 1980–1989) in the Reference Books Division of Random House.

Flexner's first major contribution as a lexicographer was the *Dictionary of American Slang* (1960), which he coedited with Harold Wentworth. Flexner served as the volume's specialist on military, jazz, teenage, and criminal argots, in the latter case drawing upon an expertise he first honed by interviewing thieves, pickpockets, and prostitutes while he was a graduate student at Louisville. Praised in the *New York Times Book Review* as "a proving ground for words and a mirror of the American mind which no student of that mind will want to neglect," the volume moved a reviewer in the *London Times Literary Supplement* (25 November 1960) to express a hope that he would never "have to use or hear a great deal of the vocabulary assembled for our enlightenment here." Edmund Wilson, writing in the

New Yorker (18 February 1961), commended it for offering "a very full vocabulary of the jive-junky-beatnik lingo." On 21 November 1967 Flexner married Doris Louise Hurcombe; they had two children.

In his preface to the second edition of the *Dictionary of American Slang* (1975), Flexner stated his argument for a less prescriptive approach to language: "Standard words do not necessarily make for precise, forceful or useful speech. . . . There is no reason to avoid any useful, expressive word merely because it is labeled 'slang.' Our present language has not decayed from some past and perfect King's English. . . . All languages and words have been, are and can only be but conventions mutually agreed upon for the sake of communicating." He adhered to this premise in compiling *I Hear America Talking* (1976), which William Safire of the *New York Times* (12 December 1976) found particularly praiseworthy for demonstrating how "spoken English, especially the words considered non-standard by lexicographers, is the well-spring of American expression." Safire singled out for special mention in this regard Flexner's entries on "huh?" "uh-uh," and "um." A companion volume, *Listening to America* (1982), followed a similar formula. Though dismissed by linguistic purists as entertainments rather than reference books, these two works helped solidify Flexner's reputation as a new kind of lexicographer, "a derivation detective," who, according to William Cole in a review of the latter volume in the *New York Times Book Review* (16 January 1983), tried to "show us how society has changed old words and brought new ones in."

Well-schooled in the history of the English language, Flexner was unapologetically upbeat in his assessment of its past evolution and his predictions about its future. In 1973, as a senior editor of the *Random House Dictionary of the English Language*, he was quoted in the *New York Times* to the effect that a resurrected Shakespeare would understand only five of every nine words of the English he heard spoken on the streets of present-day London or New York. But Flexner was far from sharing the concerns widely held by those who, feeling that things had indeed gotten "out of hand" linguistically speaking, longed for the authority of an Anglo-American counterpart to the French Academy. In fact, he regarded the lack of such an official body in the United States as a decided advantage in an increasingly globalized society. The very flexibility and friendliness to change inherent in English-speaking society's traditionally laissez-faire attitude toward its mother tongue, including its ready incorporation of useful foreign terms; a tendency toward grammatical simplicity, unlike Old English, which, he pointed out, had five cases and three genders; and in the case of American English, a constitutional guarantee of free speech made English a better candidate for adoption as a second language than those languages that were rigid, rule bound, and culturally exclusive. The political and economic advantages promised by that adoption could be incalculable.

Between his two tours at Random House, Flexner lectured frequently on language; helped to found the Hudson Group, a publishing operation based in Pleasantville, New York; and wrote *The Family Word Finder* (1975) and *I Hear America Talking* (1976). From 1981 to 1990 he hosted a widely syndicated radio spot called "The Random House Dictionary Word for the Day."

In 1982 Flexner succeeded Jess Stein as editor in chief of the second edition of the *Random House Dictionary of the English Language* (1987), which was Flexner's crowning achievement. This work served as the ultimate statement of Flexner's case for treating language as the reflection of culture, high as well as low. "It sounds silly, because a dictionary doesn't sound exciting," he told an interviewer in 1987, "but it's almost like working on a newspaper, because you feel you have a sort of hot line to the world." Among those frequently at the other end of that hot line, he noted, were respondents such as the scientists at the Centers for Disease Control in Atlanta, who shared with the dictionary's medical editors their latest research on acquired immunodeficiency syndrome (AIDS). "Long before the drug AZT hit the headlines," Flexner recalled, "one of our consultants was telling us 'Be sure it's in there. It's going to be a biggie.' " Of the 315,000 entries, 50,000 were words not included in the dictionary's first edition, published in 1966. Some 75,000 new meanings of old words were also added. For example, a writer noted in *People,* "RHD-II must have been a *mother* to proofread."

Not surprisingly, such inclusiveness exposed Flexner to criticism from more traditionalist scholars. The tenor of their complaints was probably best represented by a rather sharply worded front-page appraisal of the dictionary by William Arrowsmith, a professor of classics at Boston University. Arrowsmith wrote:

> Real authority, argues Stuart Berg Flexner, . . . belongs not to those who use English with sensitivity, elegance and precision, but to lexicographers whose decisions are purely descriptive. . . . Usage here is not so much the king, a constitutional monarch whose power is limited and legitimated by the consent of the governed and the parliament of literary tradition and educated speech, but simply God. . . . To whom does this god reveal himself? Apparently only to a lexicographical pollster like Mr. Flexner. If misuse and verbal blurring are frequent, their very frequency legitimates the usage. (*New York Times Book Review,* 3 January 1988)

In his preface to the second edition, "Essay on Usage," Flexner asserted that so long as it has hundreds of millions of speakers and writers, "English will remain alive and well." Arrowsmith dismissed such thinking as "pernicious drivel" and observed: "That English is alive and kicking is abundantly evident in this dictionary's record of our demotic practice; that it is well (in top expressive shape) is anything but evident. The slippage of meaning and the explosion of cliché, buzzwords and phrases, and the cant of the half-educated show all too clearly that those writers who struggled so hard 'to purify the language of the tribe' may have labored in vain."

In a larger sense, the differing philosophies embraced by Flexner and Arrowsmith were rooted in the ongoing and historic clash between the competing claims of public order and individual liberty peculiar to American culture. To his critics Flexner represented the forces of linguistic anarchy that abandoned all prescriptive discretion in favor of a dangerous, potentially debasing permissiveness, while in Flexner's own judgment, he was only acknowledging reality. "It [the English language] was never perfect, never followed unchanging rules," he told an interviewer for *U.S. News and World Report* in 1985, observing further that "in the search for simpler, more direct communication, the human mind is always going to ignore or break some of them, whether we like it or not. That's how language evolves." In this very linguistic evolution, he argued in his preface to *I Hear America Talking,* one could trace the parallel evolution of a distinctive American culture, and in so doing come to understand "that our language is an integral part of our history . . . [and] that history resides in the legacy of our language long after the battles and the events, great and small, are over, the fads and fashions spent."

Flexner never subscribed to the traditional view of dictionary editors as guardians of linguistic purity and enforcers of strict usage. Instead he regarded language, particularly the English language, primarily as a tool shaped by society at large to reflect its own continuing cultural evolution. "The charge that English is degenerating into a sloppy and ungrammatical language is not new," he observed in *U.S. News and World Report* in 1985, replying obliquely to critics of his approach. "It has been made since the 17th century—but English is still alive and growing, and we communicate as well as any people ever have. Those who feel the language is declining just don't know much about its history."

Flexner retired from Random House in 1989. He died of bone cancer in Greenwich, Connecticut. A memorialist in *Publishers Weekly* (21 December 1990) described Flexner as a "precocious lexicographer."

★

Posthumous publications include, with Doris Flexner, *The Pessimist's Guide to History* (1992) and *Wise Words and Wives' Tales* (1993), and with Anne H. Soukhanov, *Speaking Freely: A Guided Tour of English from Plymouth Rock to Silicon Valley* (1997). Flexner commented on language in *U.S. News and World Report* (18 Feb. 1985). Biographical information and critical assessments of Flexner's work are in Ann Evory and Linda Metzger, eds., *Contemporary Authors,* New Revision Series, vol. 11 (1984). See also "All the Words That Are Fit to Print—and Some That Aren't," *People* (23 Nov. 1987). Obituaries are in the *New York Times* (5 Dec. 1990) and *Publishers Weekly* (21 Dec. 1990).

RICHARD B. CALHOUN

FOLSOM, James Elisha ("Big Jim") (*b.* 9 October 1908 near Elba, Alabama; *d.* 21 November 1987 in Cullman, Alabama), two-term governor of Alabama who provoked the ire of segregationists for his moderate stance on racial issues and his attempts to help the poor and the disenfranchised.

James Elisha Folsom was one of seven children of Joshua Marion Folsom and Eulala Cornelia (Dunnevant) Folsom. His father served as a deputy sheriff for many years, was a member of a county commission, and had three terms as a tax collector. James attended the Coffee County High School at Elba, graduating in 1927. He enrolled in the University of Alabama in 1928 and the following year transferred to Howard College in Birmingham. Folsom's education was interrupted in 1930, when a flood severely damaged the family farm, which necessitated spending the money he had saved for tuition. In 1931 he joined the merchant marine and served for twenty months. He returned to Alabama in 1933, when he secured a supervisory position

Governor James Folsom at the U.S. Senate office building, 1948. UPI/CORBIS-BETTMANN

in the Alabama Relief Administration in Guntersville. For a time, Folsom was assigned to the Works Progress Administration in Washington, D.C., where he worked with the Alabama congressional delegation. This provided him with the opportunity to attend George Washington University, where he studied political science and public speaking. On 25 December 1936 he married Sarah Carnlay, who left him a widower with two small children in 1944.

Folsom's first three bids for political office were unsuccessful: in 1936 he lost to incumbent Democratic congressman Henry B. Steagall; two years later he was again defeated by Steagall; and in 1942 he ran against incumbent Democratic governor Channing Sparks and lost in a runoff in a primary. Folsom finally won the Democratic gubernatorial nomination in 1946 on a populist platform that advocated an $1,800 minimum annual wage for public school teachers, a $50-a-month old age pension, the paving of rural roads, the repeal of the poll tax, reapportionment of the legislature, and free textbooks for public school students. Folsom gave 350 speeches in the campaign that preceded the general election. On this sojourn across the state, he was accompanied by a country band called the "Strawberry Pickers." At each rally, Folsom waved a homemade mop that symbolized his determination to clean up the legislature. Folsom spurned the support of the Democratic establishment and financed his campaign by collecting money in a scrub bucket from his largely rural constituency. Folsom was inaugurated as governor on 20 January 1947.

A rift soon erupted between Folsom and the state legislature over his appointment of four members to the board of trustees of the Alabama Polytechnic Institute (now Auburn University). Folsom intended that his appointees would reduce the influence of the State Farm Bureau, the agency that had traditionally controlled the board of trustees. His appointments, however, were not confirmed. Further, the legislature proposed, in January 1948, an amendment to the state constitution to give the legislature the authority to call itself into emergency session, thereby overriding the governor's authority. Folsom campaigned against the proposed amendment, and it was defeated in the general election of November 1948. The upshot, for the duration of Folsom's first administration, was an obstreperous legislature that continued to oppose the platform on which he was elected in 1946.

The election of 1946 that sent Folsom to the statehouse also ratified the Boswell amendment, the intent of which was to prevent African Americans from voting. The amendment stipulated that all prospective voters had to comprehend and be able to explain any section of the U.S. Constitution to the satisfaction of the county boards of voter registrars. Folsom opposed the amendment and called on the legislature to repeal it. The legislature, however, refused to honor Folsom's request. In January 1949 Folsom made a proposal to establish a state university for African Americans that would be backed by a $5 million building program; in addition, he proposed an increase of $835,000 a year in appropriations for African-American colleges. In May 1949 Folsom recommended the abolition of the poll tax, the simplification of voter registration, and the construction of additional state parks and recreational facilities for African Americans. All of these proposals were rejected by the legislature. On 5 May 1948 Folsom married Jamelle Moore, an employee of the Alabama State Highway Department; they had one son.

State law prohibited Folsom from serving consecutive terms, so he could not run in 1950. But, in 1954, he again sought the governorship and was easily reelected. Folsom's second administration was even less successful than his first. He was severely criticized by his white constituents for inviting Adam Clayton Powell, Jr., an African-American congressman from Harlem in New York City, to the Alabama statehouse. During the Montgomery bus boycott of 1956, Folsom met secretly with the Reverend Martin Luther King, Jr., and white city officials in an attempt to mediate the crisis. In 1958 Folsom again incurred the wrath of white Alabamians when he commuted the death sentence of Jimmy Wilson, an illiterate fifty-five-year-old African American who had been sentenced to death by an all-white jury for robbing an elderly white woman of $1.95.

After he left the governorship in January 1959, Folsom ran for office five more times. In 1968 he ran unsuccessfully for the U.S. Senate. His last bid for political office was in 1982, when he was defeated by George C. Wallace, who won his fourth term as Alabama's governor. By that time, Folsom was legally blind and nearly deaf and was not considered a serious contender. Folsom died at his home in Cullman, Alabama, where he was interred.

Folsom was anathematized in segregationist Alabama in the 1950s and 1960s because of his moderate stance on racial issues. He fought to change the status quo, which denied the vote to African Americans on account of their race. In his two administrations, Folsom urged the legislature to appropriate funds for the construction and maintenance of decent schools for African-American children, but few of his proposals were enacted. He contended that desegregation was inevitable and that violence toward African Americans was unconscionable. Folsom was later vindicated by the U.S. Supreme Court, which outlawed the poll tax and upheld the principle of one man, one vote.

★

William D. Murray, *The Folsom Gubernatorial Campaign of 1946* (1949), consists of research notes compiled by the University of Alabama on the election of 1946. Donald S. Vaughan, *Administrative Responsibility in Alabama* (1967), details the gubernatorial actions of the Folsom administration. *Current Biography 1949* presents an account of Folsom's life through the midpoint of his first term as governor. Carl Grafton, "James E. Folsom and Civil Liberties in Alabama," *Alabama Review* 32 (Jan. 1979): 3–27, looks at Folsom's career as an advocate of the poor and the disenfranchised. William D. Barnard, *Dixiecrats and Democrats* (1974), focuses on the postwar politics of New Deal Democrats and populist politicians. Earl Black, *Southern Governors and Civil Rights* (1976), discusses political and administrative changes introduced by governors in the postwar period. Carl Grafton and Anne Permaloff, *Big Mules and Branchheads* (1985), explores Folsom's personal and political beliefs and evaluates his impact on Alabama. Sheldon Hackney, *Populism to Progressivism in Alabama* (1977), delineates the history of populism in Alabama in the nineteenth century to the rise of progressivism a century later. An obituary is in the *New York Times* (22 Nov. 1987).

P. DALE ROREX

FORBES, Malcolm Stevenson (*b.* 19 August 1919 in Brooklyn, New York; *d.* 24 February 1990 in Far Hills, New Jersey), chairman and editor in chief of Forbes Magazines, Inc.

Malcolm Forbes, 1980. BOB KRIST/CORBIS

Forbes was the third of the five sons of Albert Charles Forbes, a Scottish immigrant who had founded *Forbes* magazine in 1917, and Adelaide Stevenson. Intimations of his drive to accomplish manifested as early as 1937, when he graduated cum laude from the Lawrenceville School in New Jersey. In 1941, having studied at the Woodrow Wilson School of Public and International Affairs, he received an A.B. degree in politics and economics from Princeton University, where he was awarded the Class of 1901 Medal as "the member of his class who contributed the most to Princeton as an undergraduate." Immediately thereafter he entered the newspaper business, becoming owner and publisher of the *Lancaster (Ohio) Fairfield Times;* in 1942 he founded the weekly *Lancaster Tribune.*

In 1942 Forbes enlisted as a staff sergeant of a heavy-machine-gun section in the 334th Infantry, 84th Division. In December 1944 he was leading a patrol that discovered a gap in the American lines on the German-Belgian border; unfortunately, a German patrol made the discovery at the same time. In the firefight that ensued, Forbes was struck twice in the left leg. For nine months he recuperated in American military hospitals, and was awarded the Bronze Star and Purple Heart.

On 21 September 1946 Forbes married Roberta Remsen Laidlaw. They had four sons and a daughter and were divorced in 1985.

In 1947 Forbes became a vice president of Forbes, Inc., serving as associate publisher of *Forbes* magazine. A year later he launched the award-winning *Nation's Heritage,* a bimonthly publication presenting a pictorial record of American history; it ceased publication in 1949. Nearly forty years later Forbes returned to his interest in publishing American history when he acquired *American Heritage,* a magazine founded in 1954.

Forbes began his political career in 1949 by winning a seat on the Bernardsville (New Jersey) Borough Council. In 1951, the same year he was named New Jersey's "Young Man of the Year" by the New Jersey Junior Chamber of Commerce, he was elected to the New Jersey State Senate by a record plurality. One of the first Republicans to back Dwight Eisenhower for president of the United States, he founded and chaired the New Jersey "I Like Ike" clubs.

In 1953 Forbes made an unsuccessful bid for the New Jersey gubernatorial nomination. Four years later he won the nomination but lost the race to incumbent governor Robert B. Meyner. He penned a wry account of his political experiences in his "Fact and Comment" column in *Forbes* magazine, accompanied by a photograph of himself as candidate for the New Jersey governorship, standing in an open car and waving to an unseen crowd. The reason the crowd was unseen, he explained, was that "there wasn't one; the only soul in sight [was] the photographer"; he further wrote that he was "nosed out by a landslide." Forbes continued to serve in the New Jersey State Senate until he resigned in 1958. In 1960 he was a delegate-at-large to the Republican National Convention.

In 1957, the year of Forbes's defeat in the New Jersey gubernatorial election, he became editor in chief of *Forbes,* inaugurating at the magazine a spiral of growth in size and circulation that continued for decades.

In 1969 Forbes began to diversify his business interests by purchasing the 260-square-mile Trinchera Ranch in Colorado, 200 miles south of Denver; 140 adjacent square miles were acquired in 1981. The property was developed, subdivided, and marketed as Sangre de Cristo Ranches, Forbes Park, and Forbes Wagon Creek Ranch. Land Forbes acquired in Missouri was similarly developed and marketed.

In 1987 Forbes, Inc., bought Somerset Press, a six-paper weekly group in Somerville, New Jersey, consisting of the *Somerset Messenger-Gazette, Middlesex Chronicle, Bound Brook Chronicle, Piscataway-Dunellen Review, Metuchen-Edison Review,* and *South Plainfield Reporter.* Subsequently Forbes founded or acquired the *Green Brook–North Plainfield Journal, Highland Park Herald, Hills-Bedminster Press, Franklin Focus, Cranford Chronicle, Scotch Plains–Fanwood Press, Somerset County Shopper,* and *Middlesex County Shopper.*

A flamboyant exemplar of what the *New York Times* in his obituary termed "gleeful capitalism," Forbes once told an employee that he owed his position to "sheer ability, spelled i-n-h-e-r-i-t-a-n-c-e." Adept at publishing and promotion, he was even better known for savoring life on an epic scale. On his seventieth birthday he flew 1,000 guests and relatives, including the actress Elizabeth Taylor, a family friend, to Morocco to celebrate with an opulently festive $2 million party.

Forbes owned homes, estates, and ranches in London, New Jersey, Colorado, and Missouri; a palace in Tangier; a château in France; and the island of Laucala in Fiji. He also owned a world-renowned collection of toy soldiers and a 151-foot yacht. In addition, between 1950 and 1980 Forbes accumulated the most distinguished collection in America of eggs crafted by the Russian jeweler and goldsmith Peter Carl Fabergé. Twelve imperial Easter eggs, including the "Coronation Egg" (1897) and the "Lilies of the Valley Egg" (1898), highlight this collection, which is on permanent display at the Forbes Building on Fifth Avenue in New York City. It was loaned in 1996 to the Metropolitan Museum of Art for an exhibit marking the 150th anniversary of Fabergé's birth.

In addition to being a successful entrepreneur, Forbes was an author, sometime rancher, record-holding hot-air balloonist, motorcycling and bridge enthusiast, and the recipient of sixty-five honorary degrees. His publications included *Fact and Comment* (1974); *The Sayings of Chairman Malcolm* (1978); *Around the World on Hot Air and Two Wheels* (1985); *The Further Sayings of Chairman Malcolm* (1986); *They Went That-a-Way* (1988); *More Than I Dreamed* (1989); *Women Who Made a Difference* (1990); and *What Happened to Their Kids?* (1990).

During his first ride in a hot-air balloon in June 1972, Forbes became so enthusiastic that he turned the ride into a piloting lesson; five months later he received a commercial balloon pilot's license. In 1973 he set six official world records in hot-air ballooning. In October of that year he became the first person to fly successfully from coast to coast across the United States in a hot-air balloon. His specially designed blue-and-gold craft safely transported him from the Oregon coast to a landing in Chesapeake Bay. For this achievement President Gerald Ford awarded Forbes the Harmon Trophy as Aeronaut of the Year in 1975. In 1985 he was inducted into the Aviation Hall of Fame. Founder of the world's first balloon museum, at his Château de Balleroy in Normandy, Forbes received from the French association Les Aéronautes the Charles Dollfus Medal for his outstanding achievements in ballooning.

Another of Forbes's recreational enthusiasms, motorcycling, triggered a change in state traffic regulations. Brendan T. Byrne, former governor of New Jersey, recalled: "As a footnote to history, Malcolm Forbes in 1974 talked me into changing the rules on the Garden State Parkway so that motorcyclists could ride it." Byrne claimed he had to fire three commissioners to make the change.

The day before he died, Forbes—who rated himself an enthusiastic rather than a world-class bridge player—played the British House of Lords as a member of the Corporate America bridge team that included Laurence Tisch, president of CBS, who partnered Forbes in the tournament. Forbes then hosted a dinner at Old Battersea, his seventeenth-century London home, for the two bridge teams, friends, and members of the press, after which he flew home to New Jersey. The cause of Forbes's death was listed as cardiac arrest, though Malcolm ("Steve") Forbes Jr., revealed that his father had battled cancer in the past, and "for two years underwent painful treatments, but never lost his exuberance." In accordance with his wishes, Forbes's body was cremated and his ashes were interred on Laucala, his island in the South Pacific.

Forbes amassed a fortune estimated at his death to be between $400 million and $1 billion. Court records show that his heirs paid $16.9 million in estate taxes in 1992; in 1994, at the request of Malcolm Forbes, Jr., a New Jersey tax court permitted the value of his father's estate to be lowered via federal interest deductions. Lawyers familiar with the case then estimated the estate's worth at about $100 million for tax purposes.

★

The official biography and papers of Malcolm Forbes are in

the archives of Forbes, Inc., 60 Fifth Avenue, New York City. An obituary is in the *New York Times* (26 Feb. 1990). Posthumous tributes and articles include Malcolm S. Forbes, "The Spirit Remains," *Forbes* (19 Mar. 1990); "Letters of Tribute," *Forbes* (2 Apr. 1990); James W. Michaels, "With All Thy Getting, Don't Take Yourself Too Seriously," *Forbes* (19 Mar. 1990); and Jeannie Williams, "Remembering the Magic of Malcolm Forbes," *USA Today* (2 Mar. 1990). See also "Forbes Given Major Tax Break, New Jersey Records Show," *USA Today* (1 May 1996).

DEBORAH AYDT MARINELLI

FORD, Henry, II ("Hank the Deuce") (*b.* 4 September 1917 in Detroit, Michigan; *d.* 29 September 1987 in Detroit, Michigan), director, president, and chairman of the board of Ford Motor Company who revived the company founded by his grandfather and namesake, Henry Ford.

Ford was the first of four children of Edsel Ford and Eleanor Clay and the first grandson of Henry Ford. At age two, in perhaps his first company activity, he helped light the new blast furnace at the Ford Motor Company's Rouge Plant in Dearborn, Michigan. He often played at the factory as a boy, even driving Model Ts. Raised in the staid Detroit suburb of Grosse Pointe, with summers in Seal Harbor, Maine, and winters in Hobe Sound, Florida, he led a life of privilege through inheritance. He went to Detroit University School up to eighth grade, then to Hotchkiss School in Lakeville, Connecticut, from 1933 to 1936. From 1936 to 1940 he attended Yale College, where he was not a distinguished student and did not graduate. But the Ivy League could not have taught him much that he already did not know from watching his father and grandfather at work and his mother, whom he resembled, everywhere. What he knew only obliquely at that time, however, was the true situation of his father within the company. His grandfather was unceasingly determined to withhold power and to treat Edsel Ford with condescension and cruelty.

Henry Ford II. ARCHIVE PHOTOS

In 1938, at age twenty-one, Ford was made a director of the Ford Motor Company. On 13 July 1940 he married Anne McDonnell, whom he had met four years before aboard the *Normandie* after a European grand tour. He was always attracted to the Old World's style of life. On the morning of the wedding he was baptized a Catholic by Bishop Fulton Sheen, who also presided at the nuptials. Henry and Anne Ford had three children. His father gave him a house in Grosse Pointe and 25,000 shares of Ford stock. Returning from his honeymoon in Hawaii, he got his hands dirty working as a mechanic in the dynamometer room of Ford Motor. His grandfather, extending his dislike, anger, and jealousy from son to grandson, tried to bar him from the premises.

World War II intervened, and in 1941 Ford was appointed an ensign in the U.S. Navy and was stationed at the Great Lakes Naval Station in Chicago. In July 1943, two months after his father's death from cancer at the age of forty-nine, he was returned to civilian life by Secretary of the Navy Frank Knox and came home to the shambles that Harry Bennett had made of the family company as his grandfather sat by. Bennett had begun work as an enforcer, had instigated the violent response to unionization at Ford, and was the subject of a probably unenforceable codicil to the will of Henry Ford I that would have given him control of the company. Eleanor Ford forced a momentous change by threatening her father-in-law with the sale of her 41 percent of the family stock if her son were not made president of the company. Henry Ford II took control of Ford Motor Company on 21 September 1945 and together with John Bugas, a friend and former Federal Bureau of Investigation (FBI) agent who now worked for the company, immediately fired Bennett and his network of cronies and allies. Ford Motor, which at the time of Ford's birth in 1917 had manufactured 60 percent of the cars purchased in the United States, had by 1945 seen its share slip to 20 percent. Two years later Ford's grandfather died.

Ford always worked long hours. He began a program that brought college graduates to the company, and he hired the brilliant "whiz kids," ten former U.S. Air Force officers, including Robert McNamara, who did not know cars but were managerial wonders. Ford pulled in several executives, including Ernest Breech and Lewis Crusoe, from General Motors, the largest industrial company in the world, whose calm, stratified, extremely organized image he often dreamed of recreating at Ford Motor. General Motors, among others, was building the cars Americans wanted; Ford Motor Company was not. Ford built the new world headquarters in Dearborn, called "the Glass House," which was completed in 1957. Prior to construction, he had the contractors put a pole as high as the building would be to demonstrate to his grandmother that its height would not impair her view from "Fairlane," the home where she lived. However, she died in 1950 and thus did not live to see the building. Ford Motor Company maintained Fairlane for several years and then gave it to the University of Michigan. Ford disliked the house immensely and rarely went there. Partly owing to their temperaments and partly owing to his own ambition, he muscled aside his brothers, Benson Ford and William Ford. Because of the times, his sister, Josephine Ford, was never in contention for a position. Reviewing his father's papers in 1952, he destroyed practically all of them, as he would his own years later.

By 1953, the fiftieth anniversary of its founding, the Ford Motor Company had passed Chrysler in sales and had introduced the much admired Thunderbird. Meanwhile, Ford himself became a strong although iconoclastic spokesman for American business. President Dwight Eisenhower named him an alternate delegate to the United Nations, but Ford disliked Richard Nixon and did not care for John Kennedy, in part because Kennedy tapped McNamara for secretary of defense just after McNamara had been named president of the Ford Motor Company. Ford came to support and like Lyndon Johnson, another powerful, earthy man. In the 1960s Ford created a program to encourage hiring of African Americans as well as a program to hire the hard-core unemployed, firsts in the industry.

Entranced by the infamous "Big Plan," developed quickly in 1955 by F. C. Reith, another "whiz kid," and Crusoe, with its goal to surpass General Motors by offering many new models in higher price ranges, Ford gave the go-ahead to create separate Mercury, Lincoln, Continental, and Special Products divisions, out of which came the Edsel in 1957. The Edsel and its name were large mistakes and sank, despite the efforts of enthusiasts, into derision. Within another two years Continental was folded back into Lincoln and then combined with Mercury. The Mustang, introduced in 1964, electrified the country. Consumers who wanted sensible cars could buy the Falcon or Fairlane, also major sales successes, but all of these models were in the less profitable lower price ranges.

Ford bought a big house in Southampton, Long Island, a manor in Henley-on-Thames, England, and moved to a mansion on Lakeshore Drive in Grosse Pointe in 1955. In 1964 he and his first wife divorced. On 19 February 1965 he married Maria Cristina Vettore Austin, with whom he had been involved since 1959. They had no children.

The Ford Foundation, which owned more than 80 percent of the company's nonvoting stock and was initially conceived by Ford's father and grandfather as a refuge from taxes, became a large part of the reason the company went public in 1956. The foundation wanted more money and control than it had from its dividends. The Ford Company's move was one of the biggest stock offerings of all time. The Ford family retained control of 40 percent of the voting stock. The foundation, with Henry Ford II on its board, eventually sold its stock and pursued ends that Ford did not always agree with. For instance, in 1973 he had to fight to get financing from the foundation for the Henry Ford Hospital in Detroit, which his grandfather had founded in 1915. Ford resigned as chairman of the foundation's board in 1956 to devote his time to the company, but he remained a foundation trustee until 1976. Later he regretted that the family had lost control of the Ford Foundation.

Determined to restore the city of Detroit, Ford conceived of the Renaissance Center, a glass-towered edifice unfortunately isolated from the rest of downtown, which was dedicated on 21 April 1977. Ford employees were dutifully moved in. Twenty years later General Motors bought the building and moved its headquarters there.

Executives flowed in and out of the Ford Motor Company as Henry Ford attempted to balance the daring of engineers and marketing and the caution of the finance department. Lee Iacocca, who had come into the company as a young engineer, rose to the position of president in 1970 and fought to oust Ford. In response, Ford fired the "father of the Mustang" on 15 October 1978 with the words, "I just don't like you." The 1970s brought the oil crisis and the advent of pollution standards accompanied by a general decline in the public's confidence in American cars, particularly the Ford Pinto. In March 1980 Ford turned to Philip Caldwell, who had made a success of Ford International, to succeed him as chairman of the company. Caldwell, the first person who was not a Ford family member to run the company, contributed to its great success in the 1980s with the Taurus, and in 1986 Ford Motor's profits exceeded General Motors for the first time in sixty-two years, the first time since Henry Ford II was seven years old.

At midnight on 22 February 1975, Ford was pulled over for going the wrong way on a one-way street in Santa Barbara, California. He was drunk and in the company of a young former model, Kathy DuRoss. At the Detroit Economic Club shortly thereafter he told the press, "Never complain, never explain." He and his second wife divorced in 1980. On 14 October 1980 Ford married DuRoss, with whom he had no children, and two years later he retired as a company officer and employee, although he remained a member of the board of directors. Ford died of a heart attack in Henry Ford Hospital in Detroit. His remains were cremated.

In many ways Henry Ford II was the Ford Motor Company. "My name is on the ship," he once said. Broad, even coarse, gregarious, with a high voice, and hefting a big belly, perhaps his purest moment came when he wrested control of the company from Bennett. As Ford made the company his own, he saved it and the Ford family from ruin. All events afterward, including the hirings and firings, were secondary. He was a legendary big businessman when most were anonymous figures, and he loved the good life. He was an ambitious yet cautious man in work and life who was given to the occasional creative and daring lunge.

★

Ford's papers are in the Ford Industrial Archives, Ford Motor Company, Dearborn, Michigan, and the Edison Institute, Henry Ford Museum, Dearborn, Michigan. Biographies include Victor Lasky, *Never Complain, Never Explain: The Story of Henry Ford II* (1981); and Walter Hayes, *Henry: A Life of Henry Ford II* (1990). See also Peter Collier and David Horowitz, *The Fords: An American Epic* (1987); Robert Lacey, *Ford: The Men and the Machine* (1986); and David L. Lewis, "'A Super Existence': The Boyhood of Henry Ford II," *Michigan Quarterly Review* 25, no. 2 (spring 1986): 195–203. An obituary is in the *New York Times* (30 Sept. 1987).

MARK ZADROZNY

FOSSE, Robert Louis ("Bob") (*b.* 23 June 1927 in Chicago, Illinois; *d.* 23 September 1987 in Washington, D.C.), dancer and one of the foremost Broadway and film director-choreographers, who was honored with a Tony, an Oscar, and an Emmy in the same year (1973).

Fosse, named for Robert Louis Stevenson, was the son of Cyril K. Fosse, a salesman, and Sarah Alice Stanton, a homemaker. He and his five siblings grew up on the North Side of Chicago. His father was a former vaudeville entertainer, and his mother played piano and acted in community light operas. When he was nine Fosse went to study at the Chicago Academy of Theatre Arts, where for ten years he studied tap under Frederick Weaver, who prepared him to dance professionally in area nightclubs. He and Charles Grass performed as the Riff Brothers. Although he was small and suffered from asthma, Fosse was considered a child prodigy. He attended Roald Amundsen Senior High School from 1941 to 1945, where he danced in school variety shows and also professionally in area nightclubs. Graduating as an honor student, he was president of his class, won letters in swimming and track, and was voted most likely to succeed. After graduation he enlisted in the U.S. Navy and served in the Special Services entertainment division, performing in musicals throughout the Pacific with Joseph Papp.

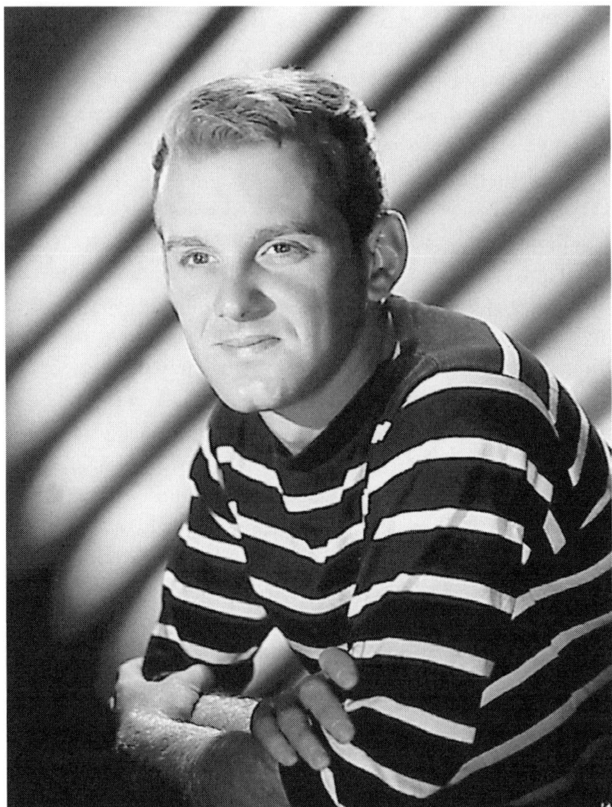

Bob Fosse. JOEL KUDLER/ARCHIVE PHOTOS

In October 1946 Fosse went to New York to study at the American Theatre Wing. He met Mary Ann Niles while in rehearsals for *Call Me Mister.* They were married in 1947; they had no children. Fosse and Niles performed at the major hotels in New York and Chicago and on Sid Caesar's television program *Your Show of Shows.* Both were featured dancers in the Broadway revue *Dance Me a Song* (1950).

In 1951 Fosse divorced Niles and married Joan McCracken; they had no children. Fosse then studied with Anna Sokolow, José Limon, and Charles Weidman. He choreographed numbers and danced in the films *Kiss Me Kate* (1953) and *Give a Girl a Break* (1958). Next, he choreographed the Broadway hit *Pajama Game* in 1954. "Steam Heat," his most famous Broadway dance number, won him a Tony for best choreography. He choreographed the film version of *Pajama Game* in 1957.

In 1955 he choreographed and danced in the film musical *My Sister Eileen* and worked with George Abbott and Jerome Robbins on the Broadway show *Damn Yankees,* starring Gwen Verdon. *Damn Yankees* earned him a Tony

Award (and Verdon three), and it was the first of many Fosse shows with controversial sexy dance numbers, such as "Whatever Lola Wants." Fosse worked with Verdon on the successful *New Girl in Town* (1957), based on Eugene O'Neill's *Anna Christie* and written for Judy Holliday, whose most popular dance was "Mu Cha-Cha." Verdon requested Fosse as choreographer and director for *Redhead* (1958), the first show ever to credit an entire production, direction, and choreography to one person. Fosse borrowed heavily from music hall and vaudeville and earned five Tony Awards.

Fosse, who suffered from epilepsy and severe bouts of insecurity, fear of failure, and depression throughout his life, spent five years in analysis. He and McCracken divorced in 1960. That year he married Gwen Verdon; they had one daughter.

The musical *The Conquering Hero* (1961) was Fosse's first failure. He was fired as director and choreographer because the soldiers looked effeminate; his work was included but uncredited, and the show closed after eight performances. In 1961 Fosse was headliner, director, and choreographer in a revival of *Pal Joey* with the New York City Center Light Opera Company. He also staged musical numbers ("Coffee Break" and "A Secretary Is Not a Toy") for *How to Succeed in Business Without Really Trying* (1961), one of Broadway's most successful shows. It won its authors (Frank Loesser and Abe Burrows) a Pulitzer Prize and also received seven Tony Awards and the Drama Critics Circle Award. In *Little Me* (1962), with Sid Caesar, Fosse's "Rich Kid's Rag" was one of his finest creations.

Sweet Charity (1966), the most enduring of Fosse's fourteen stage musicals, featured Verdon in her most spectacular role and represented a turning point choreographically and thematically for Fosse. The dances became more fractured ("Hey, Big Spender" and "The Rich Man's Frug"), and Fosse began experimenting with smaller groups of dancers. He wrote the first draft (under a pseudonym), although his friend Neil Simon was credited as author. The film version of *Sweet Charity* (1969), starring Shirley MacLaine, while not as well received, established Fosse as a film director.

Fosse's film musical *Cabaret* (1972), starring Liza Minnelli, was a smash hit in the United States and Germany and won eight Academy Awards, including best director. *Pippin* (1972), a rock opera about the son of Charlemagne, was Fosse's longest-running show on Broadway and won him Tony Awards for best direction and choreography. At this time Ann Reinking, who danced in both *Cabaret* and *Pippin,* became Fosse's girlfriend in a much publicized five-year relationship; in the meantime he and Verdon separated. In 1972 Fosse also directed *Liza with a Z,* a television variety special starring Liza Minnelli, for which he won three Emmys, for producing, directing, and choreographing.

Following these successes Fosse experienced depression and breakdown and stayed briefly at the Payne Whitney Clinic in New York. In 1974 he performed a dance cameo as the snake in *The Little Prince;* it was the highlight of the film and his definitive film performance as a mature dancer. *Lenny* (1974), his first nonmusical project, was a stark biographical film about Lenny Bruce in black and white and utilizing interview-style scriptwriting. Starring Dustin Hoffman and Valerie Perrine, it was nominated for Academy Awards for best director and best picture. In 1974, during rehersals for the Broadway musical *Chicago* (1975), Fosse had a massive heart attack. Bypass surgery did not prevent a second heart attack. Nevertheless, he continued smoking four packs of cigarettes a day.

Dancin' (1978) was a smash Broadway hit, and earned Fosse a Tony for best choreography. Reinking was a "star" in the chorus of this grueling show for dancers. Fosse next directed the semiautobiographical film *All That Jazz* (1979), about a Broadway and film director-choreographer who chases pills, liquor, and skirts. The film *Star 80* (1983), about the life and murder of the *Playboy* centerfold Dorothy Stratten, was rejected by critics because of its shocking content. The Broadway musical *Big Deal* (1986), based on an Italian movie, concerned a Chicago gang of ineffectual burglars in the early 1930s; it earned Fosse a Tony Award for best choreography but closed after seventy performances.

Fosse next collaborated with Verdon on a revival of *Sweet Charity* (1987), starring Debby Allen and later Ann Reinking. He was production supervisor/director and choreographer, and Verdon helped reconstruct dances. The show won three Tonys, including one for the year's best revival, and the Fred Astaire Award for the year's best dances on Broadway.

During the 1980s Fosse often retreated to a summer home at Quogue on Long Island. He died of a massive heart attack at George Washington University Hospital, in Washington, D.C., having just left the last rehearsal of *Sweet Charity* before its opening night. Verdon was at his side when he collapsed near the theater. By the time of his death he was stooped and gaunt. He was cremated at the Trinity Church Crematory in New York City. A public memorial was held on 30 October 1987 at Broadway's Palace Theatre, at which Verdon showed her film retrospective on his life and career. A dinner for seventy-five people was held that night at the Tavern on the Green restaurant, as requested in Fosse's will.

Bob Fosse transformed musicals and films using sensual dance numbers influenced by jazz dancing. He redefined the role of dance on stage as a narrative device, from which the score and book extended. He revolutionized not only stage but screen musicals by experimenting with how dance was filmed, how to integrate it into a story line, and how to present nonformulaic dances. A man of great energy and talent, he created a large body of work that inspired a generation of dancers and performers.

★

Studies of Fosse's life include Kevin Boyd Grubb, *Razzle Dazzle: The Life and Work of Bob Fosse* (1989), and Martin Gottfried, *All His Jazz: The Life and Death of Bob Fosse* (1990). See also Ronna Elaine Sloan, "Bob Fosse: An Analytic-Critical Study" (Ph.D. diss., City College of New York, 1983), and James Winston Challender, "The Function of the Choreographer in the Development of the Conceptual Musical: An Examination of the Work of Jerome Robbins, Bob Fosse, and Michael Bennett on Broadway Between 1944 and 1981" (Ph.D. diss., Florida State University, 1986). An obituary is in the *New York Times* (24 Sept. 1987).

PHYLLIS BADER-BOREL

FREDERICK, Pauline (*b.* 13 February 1908 in Gallitzen, Pennsylvania; *d.* 9 May 1990 in Lake Forest, Illinois), pioneering woman broadcast journalist and international affairs analyst in radio and television news, best known for covering the United Nations with distinction for nearly three decades.

Pauline Frederick grew up in Harrisburg, Pennsylvania, in a middle-class, staunchly Methodist family with agrarian roots. She was the second of three children born to Susan Stanley and Matthew P. Frederick, a postmaster involved in union affairs and local politics who also served as an official of the Pennsylvania State Department of Labor.

Pauline Frederick in front of the United Nations in New York City. ARCHIVE PHOTOS

While attending Central High School, Frederick wrote stories on school and social events for the local newspapers. After graduation in 1926, she was offered the job of society editor of the *Harrisburg Evening News,* but turned it down to attend American University in Washington, D.C., where she earned a B.A. in political science in 1930 and an M.A. in international law in 1931.

Unable to bear children because of an emergency hysterectomy when she was only seventeen years old, Frederick felt a career was her only choice in life. She thought of going to law school, but a favorite professor urged her to try journalism because he believed law was an overcrowded field. At his suggestion, she interviewed three diplomats' wives in Washington, D.C., and promptly sold the pieces to the *Washington Star.* The first of what became a weekly series in the *Star* was published in October 1931, launching a freelance career that over the next eight years included writing for *U.S. News and World Report, Uncle Sam's Diary,* and the North American Newspaper Alliance. The Alliance syndicated her interviews with diplomatic and political wives, and they also appeared in the *New York Times* on Sundays. Her work came to the attention of the head of women's programming for NBC Radio, who asked Frederick to do interviews on the air.

The first time Frederick's rich contralto voice was heard on network radio was during an interview for NBC with the Czech ambassador's wife in 1939, in the aftermath of Hitler's takeover of Czechoslovakia. Similar freelance broadcasts continued until World War II news pushed women's features aside.

From 1938 until 1944, Frederick worked as a part-time assistant to H. R. Baukhage, an old-time commentator at ABC Radio. She complained that he never let her write and discouraged her from visiting war zones. She briefly became a freelance war correspondent anyway, touring China and Burma from May to August 1945. She made her first overseas broadcast from Chungking, China. Frederick later reported from Europe for the North American Newspaper Alliance, the Western Newspaper Union, and ABC Radio and covered the Nuremberg war trials into 1946.

Back home, Frederick discovered that women were still unwelcome in broadcast news. She auditioned for CBS and had the distinction of being turned down by broadcast titan Edward R. Murrow, who penned a now-famous memo of rejection. After noting her pleasant voice and good reading ability, he wrote: "I would not call her material or manner particularly distinguished." He mentioned a long list of women applicants and "little opportunity to use them," adding that Frederick's name would not be high on the list.

By the time ABC in New York City hired her as a staffer in June 1946, she was thirty-eight years old and a seasoned reporter, but one news director told her she could not do hard news on the air because "a woman's voice just does not carry authority." She was aggravated at being sent to cover fashion shows and similar events, such as, in one case, a forum on "how to get a husband." "I had to make my own opportunity to cover real news," she once said. That opportunity came when an editor informed her he had orders not to use her for serious issues, but that if she got an exclusive, he would have to use her. Frederick decided her best chance lay at the United Nations, where few journalists received regular assignments and those who did lacked her background in international affairs. She began sharing the UN beat with a male reporter in September 1947 and worked long hours to get exclusives that sometimes attracted wire service coverage.

With the advent of television and its immediate need for female faces, Frederick suddenly found herself assigned to help cover the first televised national political conventions in the summer of 1948. The ABC network attempted to make the bespectacled five-foot-nine-inch-tall Frederick into a glib glamour girl with contact lenses and bleached blond hair. She preferred going back to more conservative straight news reporting, even if it was primarily on radio. By October, at age forty, she at last had her first full-time network contract. For the next dozen years, Frederick was the only woman in hard news on any radio or television network.

Of the many world crises she reported, she was most proud of her coverage of the outbreak of the Korean War in 1950, when she broadcast live from the UN Security Council for six weeks, day and night, seven days a week. By the time NBC hired her in 1953 when she was forty-five, she had her own early-morning show at ABC in addition to regular reporting assignments. At NBC, she was to keep the UN beat for the next twenty-one years, building a reputation for tact, integrity, and lucid reporting while covering the complex world affairs of the cold-war era. She explained the Korean truce, wars in the Middle East, and the Cuban missile crisis mostly on radio, although she also became a regular on television's *Today Show*. It was her thorough coverage of the United Nations' attempt to restore peace to the Congo in 1960 that made her perhaps the best-known woman broadcaster in the country at the time.

By the middle of the 1960s, Frederick was also the highest paid broadcast newswoman. Her salary peaked at the rather modest sum of $50,000 a year, augmented by fees for lectures on world peace and disarmament. She published *Ten First Ladies of the World* in 1967, a book of short biographies with subjects as varied as Indira Gandhi of India and Imelda Marcos of the Philippines.

Despite several romantic involvements, Frederick remained single most of her life. She lived alone for years with a poodle named Patrick in an apartment on the East Side of Manhattan, just a fifteen-minute walk from the United Nations. But in 1969, at age sixty-one, she became the wife of a former *Wall Street Journal* managing editor she had known for fifteen years, Charles Robbins, who had recently headed the Atomic Industrial Forum. The couple lived in suburban Westport, Connecticut. In 1974, at age sixty-six, Frederick was forced to retire from NBC. "I read about my retirement one morning in the *New York Times,*" she later told a *Washington Star* reporter. "They had me announcing it myself; I was hurt, I have to admit."

Frederick's long career, however, was not over. National Public Radio in Washington, D.C., quickly hired her in 1975 as a foreign affairs analyst, and in that capacity she became in 1976 the first woman to moderate a presidential debate, that between President Gerald R. Ford and Democratic candidate Jimmy Carter. She retired in 1980, and died of a heart attack in 1990 while visiting relatives in Lake Forest, Illinois, less than a year after her husband's death.

Frederick was the first woman elected president of the UN Correspondents Association (1959) and was the recipient of many national awards, including the Alfred I. DuPont Award (1954), the George Foster Peabody Award (1955), and the Paul White Award of the Radio-Television News Director's Association (1980). She was named to the Hall of Fame of Sigma Delta Chi, the formerly all-male journalists' professional organization (1975), and received more than twenty honorary degrees.

For millions of American listeners and viewers, however, Pauline Frederick was simply the voice of the United Nations. For the broadcast industry, she was much more. *Television Digest* pointed out in her obituary that Frederick "achieved success when the broadcasting field was nearly closed to women." She proved that women could be well-prepared, intelligent, and outstanding reporters even under the greatest pressure. Her extraordinary perseverance paved the way for greater acceptance of serious women broadcast journalists.

★

The Pauline Frederick Papers, in the Sophia Smith Collection, Smith College, Northampton, Massachusetts, consists of thirty-three linear feet of correspondence, writings, printed material, broadcast scripts, broadcast and press conference transcripts, notes, photographs, memorabilia, and audiovisual materials spanning the subject's lifetime; it also includes a forty-eight-page finder's aid. The Pauline Frederick Files, located in the Broadcast Pioneers Library of American Broadcasting, University of Maryland at College Park, Maryland, consists largely of secondary sources that distill the essence of Frederick's career and personality. Most valuable is an unpublished M.A. journalism thesis that consists of an oral history interview made for the collection (see below). The files also contain transcripts of speeches Frederick made late in her career, such as an address to the New York City Women in Communications (20 Sept. 1983), in which Frederick recounts her early career experiences, including details of her first foray into television in 1948 and how poorly women were treated in the business; and "A Broadcaster in Search of Peace" (speech to Women in Communications, Washington, D.C., 22 May 1984), in which Frederick discusses her coverage of world crises and her commitment to the UN. Gioia Diliberto, "Ladies in the Mensroom: Three Profiles of Female Journalists," University of Maryland at College Park, Maryland, is an unpublished M.A. thesis (1975). A forty-page section devoted to Frederick is based on two extensive interviews held in August 1974 following her retirement from NBC that year. It includes personal information, a full accounting of Frederick's career, and a description of the subject. Anita Kleever, *Women in Television* (1975), contains a brief but valuable section in which Frederick recounts her struggle for acceptance by the networks and details of her career at the UN. Marion Marzolf, *Up from the Footnote: A History of Women Journalists* (1977), is a well-documented classic work that contains a short but expert account of Frederick's career highlights and an important analysis of her significance as a woman journalist. Judy Flander, "Pauline: Still Dean of the Newswomen," *Washington Star* (29 Apr. 1977), is an excellent interview with Frederick after she had retired from NBC and gone to work at National Public Radio; it includes reminiscences of her early career and many revealing first-person quotes. An interview of Pauline Frederick by Carol Bennett (8 Sept. 1984) can be found in the Broadcast Pioneers Library of American Broadcasting Oral History Project, University of Maryland, College Park, Maryland; the eighteen-page transcript is in question-and-answer format and emphasizes Frederick's work at the UN. Obituaries are in the *New York Times* (11 May 1990), *Broadcasting Magazine* (14 May 1990), and *TV Digest* (14 May 1990).

MARY-MARGARET S. PATTERSON

FREDERICKS, Carlton (*b.* 23 October 1910 in New York City; *d.* 28 July 1987 in Yonkers, New York), radio broadcaster, writer, educator, and consultant who was a pioneer in using the popular media to increase public awareness of proper nutrition.

Fredericks, whose original name was Harold Carlton Caplan, was the son of David Charles Caplan, a pharmacist in Brooklyn, New York, and Blanche (Goldsmith) Caplan. He was raised in the Flatbush section of Brooklyn and attended the New York City public schools. In 1931 he received an A.B. degree from the University of Alabama, and during the subsequent decade he was employed by several manufacturing firms. Among them were the National Phenochrome Corporation in Oxford, New York, where Fredericks served from 1933 to 1937 as a manufacturing chemist in germicides and testing; McKesson and

Carlton Fredericks. ARCHIVE PHOTOS

Robbins in Bridgeport, Connecticut, where he worked in 1938 in the vitamin section; and the Milk Minerals Company in New York City, where he conducted research on nutrition from 1938 to 1939. From 1939 to 1944 Fredericks worked for the U.S. Vitamin Corporation, where he was put in charge of disseminating data to professional and popular audiences. While thus employed, he gave a talk to a medical society in 1941; his success led to his being asked to consider presenting information on nutrition to a larger public audience. Following this suggestion, he soon began broadcasting talks over radio station WMCA in New York. The next year his broadcasts were presented on WJZ and other radio stations on the Blue Network, and by the 1960s Fredericks's programs were being carried by approximately 300 stations around the United States.

At the beginning of his radio career the budding star decided to change his name to the more harmonious Carlton Fredericks. He possessed a fine "silky and exquisitely articulated" voice and spoke in a crisp tone. Beginning in 1957 and continuing for the following thirty years, Fredericks presented a program entitled *Design for Living,* which at the time of his death was being broadcast six days a week, in addition to being syndicated.

In 1949 Fredericks received a master's degree from New York University, and in 1955 he received a Ph.D from the same institution. The subject of his dissertation was the eating practices of a representative number of his listeners. Between 1956 and 1959 he taught nutrition and health education at Fairleigh Dickinson University in Teaneck, New Jersey. (He also taught there between 1974 and 1982.) Fredericks and his first wife were divorced in 1945; in 1946 or 1949 he married Betty Schachter, and in 1962 the couple and their children moved from New York to Miami Beach, where Fredericks taped his broadcasts. He later lived in Spring Valley, New York.

Early in his career Fredericks began to write books on nutrition, starting in 1943 with *Lessons in Living: A Guide to Sane Eating and Buoyant Health,* which was reissued in 1945 as *Living Should Be Fun.* His other books include *Eat, Live, and Be Merry* (1951), later published in a 1964 revised edition as *Nutrition: Your Key to Good Health; The Carlton Fredericks Cook Book for Good Nutrition* (with Hazel Meyer, 1960); *Low Blood Sugar and You* (with Herman Goodman, 1969); *Psycho-Nutrition* (1976); and *Eat Well, Get Well, Stay Well* (1980). He also wrote a syndicated newspaper column on nutrition, as well as one for *Prevention* magazine.

During his long career, Fredericks sought to help prevent disease by educating the public and the professions about nutrition and by disseminating information and research through the media. His aim was to reduce the "cultural lag" between discoveries in "nutritional science" and their acceptance and use.

Fredericks's activities were not always viewed favorably, and his methods became controversial. In 1944, for example, the New York State Education Department, Division of Professional Conduct, undertook an investigation and charged him with illegally practicing medicine; Fredericks declared his guilt rather than endure the notoriety of a trial that might have injured his broadcast career. In November 1961 the U.S. Food and Drug Administration (FDA) accused Fredericks of employing "false labeling" in his book *Eat, Live, and Be Merry,* charging that the work advocated "vitamins and mineral supplements" to treat certain disorders, such as cancer and peptic ulcers, for which they were of no proven benefit. Some copies of this book were confiscated from an Illinois distributor. The FDA also questioned the description of Fredericks as "America's leading nutritionist" and said that he lacked "formal training" and credentials in the field. Fredericks denied the charges and argued that the FDA was trying to silence him for an earlier criticism of the agency. In February 1962 the FDA charged that Fredericks in his radio broadcasts had "misbranded" forty-three vitamins and supplements produced by Foods Plus, a corporation for which he was a consultant. The government charged that these products were not correctly labeled for treating the disorders for which they were recommended. Fredericks quickly responded that the agency's accusations were "a threat to every commentator on any subject interpreting the news on any station."

In May 1962, at a lecture sponsored by a chapter of the American Academy of Applied Nutrition, Fredericks told an audience of 1,200 that regulatory agencies were trying to stop his radio broadcast through the "dangerous device of publicity." He characterized himself as a "reporter" who examined scientific data on nutrition and who presented his findings to the public in order to keep it informed about the field.

In November 1965 the U.S. Federal Trade Commission accused Fredericks of false advertising for claiming that the Library of Congress printed his radio scripts, for asserting that he taught at other institutions besides Fairleigh Dickinson, and for advertising his book *Nutrition: Your Key to Good Health* as a new book when it was originally published in 1951. These charges were dismissed in February 1967 because of the incompleteness of the official record. Fredericks continued his broadcasting and writing into the 1980s. He died as a result of a heart attack.

★

John Kobler, "Radio's Pill Pusher," *Saturday Evening Post* (16 June 1962), contains material on Fredericks's radio career as well as details on his confrontations with the government. *The National Cyclopedia of American Biography* (1967) discusses his early life and career, as well as his start in radio. *Contemporary Authors,* New Revision Series, vol. 7 (1982), contains data on Fredericks's life and a listing of his writings. Barbara Nykoruk, ed., *Authors in the News* (1976), contains a few biographical details and discusses Fredericks's views as found in his book *Eating Right for You.* Obituaries are in the *New York Times* (31 July 1987) and the *Newark Star Ledger* (29 July 1987).

ALLAN NELSON

FREDERICKS, Sara (*b.* 19 March 1903 in Boston, Massachusetts; *d.* 8 April 1986 in Palm Beach, Florida), fashion designer and retailer whose chain of expensive specialty shops catered to America's wealthiest women for nearly fifty years.

Fredericks was born Sarah Rebecca Borofsky, the only child of Etta Borofsky and Samuel Borofsky, whose legal career led him to become the first Jewish Massachusetts state senator. She attended the prestigious Girls Latin School in Boston, where she was voted best dressed in her class. A newspaper interview once quoted her as saying, "From that moment I felt I had to live up to this image." Even as a child, Fredericks believed that a fashion career was her destiny. She had a fascination for fabrics at the age of six, began designing women's clothing while still a child, and wore a gown she had designed to a ball when she was eighteen years old. That same year, 1921, she married Frederick Cohen, a shoe manufacturer, and borrowed his first name for

Sara Fredericks, 1967. NYT PICTURES/NYT PERMISSIONS

professional purposes. For the rest of her life she was known as "Miss Fredericks." She was divorced from Cohen in 1930 and married Harold Rudnick, a real estate businessman, in 1937. She had one daughter, Dorothy.

In 1940, after selling dresses out of her home, Fredericks opened her first salon at 77 Newbury Street, just a stone's throw from the Ritz-Carlton Hotel in Boston's fashionable Back Bay section. There she offered the beautiful, expensive designer clothes and accessories that later earned her the title "the doyenne of Boston couture." It has been suggested that a defining moment for her success came in the mid-1940s, when the daughter of Mayor James Curley spent her entire wedding budget of $28,000 at Fredericks's shop.

Fredericks and Rudnick moved to Palm Beach, Florida, where Fredericks opened her second salon, on Worth Avenue, in 1952. She continued to hone her successful business formula, which relied on impeccable taste plus a commitment to consummate customer service. It was said that Sara Fredericks would stop at nothing to meet her client's needs. Her personal style was reflected in the decor of her shops, which featured mirrored walls, marble floors, and vases filled with the long-stemmed red roses she loved. Amid this opulence customers purchased gowns and dresses with price tags up to $10,000. Her business is reported to have made $12 million in 1984, the year that the chain of ten shops was sold to Baltimore-based Hutzler Brothers Company. Fredericks retained control of her salons, however, and continued to be active in business until her death.

Fredericks lived as many of her clients did, surrounded by beautiful clothing, furnishings, and antiques. She was known for her lavish apartments: an antique-filled, 4,000-square-foot apartment above her Palm Beach boutique and her former apartment on Commonwealth Avenue in Boston, which was elegantly appointed with Baccarat chandeliers, marble and parquet floors, and eighteenth-century paneling. As her business grew, Fredericks acquired an apartment in New York City's Beekman Hotel.

Many of the world's most famous designers enjoyed Fredericks's friendship and loyalty: Geoffrey Beene ("[Fredericks] bought from my first collection and she bought from my last. Her selectivity and good taste never erred."), Pauline Trigère, Mary McFadden, Bob Mackie, Oscar de la Renta, Bill Blass, and James Galanos. Asked by a journalist to describe her greatest pleasure, Fredericks responded without hesitation, "Working. I will never retire." Her daughter, who bought sportswear for the Palm Beach shop, confirmed her mother's consuming passion: "Retailing was her whole life. She devoted all her time and energy to it and loved every mintue."

A full-figured woman with perfectly coiffed snow-white hair, Fredericks was characterized as someone who would work all day and go to parties all night. No mere social butterfly, however, she practiced an active and generous philanthropy that reflected the sentiment "to care is fashionable." She organized numerous high-profile events supporting charities including the American Cancer Society, the Heart Association, STOP!Children's Cancer, Bonds for Israel, and the American Jewish Federation. The American Jewish Committee presented Fredericks with its National Human Relations Award on 31 January 1986, acknowledging her "dynamic spirit and dedication to the public welfare" and describing her as a "distinguished figure in the women's fashion industry . . . and an even more distinguished human being." When Fredericks opened a new salon in Boston's prestigious Copley Place in 1985, the gala opening benefited the Greater Boston Youth Symphony Orchestra and the Boston School of Ballet. That same year, Senator Paula Hawkins of Florida selected Fredericks as one of two Florida residents honored as Women of Achievement at a White House luncheon. Said Fredericks, "I will wear Reagan red."

True to her vow that she would never retire, Fredericks died of pneumonia at St. Mary's Hospital in Palm Beach, just ten days after returning from Paris, where she had selected the dresses, gowns, and sportswear her stores would sell in the fall.

★

See Julie Hatfield, "A Copley Opening," *Boston Globe* (11 July 1985). Obituaries are in the *Boston Globe, Miami Herald,* and *New York Times* (all 9 Apr. 1986).

RACHEL SNYDER

FRIEND, Charlotte (*b.* 11 March 1921 in New York City; *d.* 13 January 1987 in New York City), medical microbiologist who pioneered in linking viruses to leukemia and cancer, providing a model that other researchers employed to gain greater knowledge in the fight against cancer.

The third of four children and the youngest of three daughters, Charlotte Friend was born on Houston Street in Manhattan to Russian immigrant parents, Morris Friend, a businessman, and Cecilia Wolpin, a pharmacist. Charlotte was only three when her father died. After his death the family moved to Boston Post Road in the Bronx to be closer to her mother's relatives and lived on the inheritance Morris Friend had left. Following the stock market crash of 1929, the inheritance funds diminished, and the family existed on relief from the city. Despite such conditions, Charlotte's mother urged the children to continue their education.

Charlotte Friend, 1963. ARCHIVE PHOTOS

As a child Charlotte loved to read books about bacteriologists such as Louis Pasteur. She dreamed of working at the Pasteur Institute, a dream that came true later in her life. At the age of ten she wrote a homework composition titled "Why I Want to Become a Bacteriologist." Science continued to draw her interest when she attended Hunter College High School on a scholarship.

After graduation Friend worked at a doctor's office during the day and attended night classes at Hunter College, receiving a B.A. degree in 1944. Following graduation she enlisted in the U.S. Navy and in April 1944 was commissioned as an ensign. Promoted to lieutenant junior grade, she served as second in charge in the hematology laboratory of the naval hospital in Shoemaker, California. Laboratory exposure convinced her to pursue a career in microbiology. After her discharge in 1946, she enrolled as a graduate student in microbiology at Yale University, where she received her Ph.D. in 1950.

Accepted for a postdoctoral position at Sloan-Kettering Institute for Cancer Research by the director, Cornelius P. Rhoads, Friend worked under the virologist Alice Moore. In 1952 Friend entered a joint program of the institute and Cornell University in Ithaca, New York, where during the same year she became an associate professor of microbiology. While examining carcinoma cells of a mouse under a microscope, she unexpectedly saw particles that had a similar appearance to small sections of what she called "virus-infected cells." This prompted Friend to delve deeper over the next four years.

Friend had only a few studies to guide her, since little research on a link between viruses and cancer had been done. Peyton Rous, the one scientist who had written a paper on the subject, had been ridiculed. Starting without much prior documentation, Friend took tissue from leukemia-infected mice, removed the cells, and injected the tissue into healthy adult mice. The mice developed leukemia. Under the high magnification of an electron microscope, Friend found the virus she thought had caused the leukemia and photographed it.

Friend recorded her discovery in the *Journal of Experimental Medicine* and prepared to present her findings to the annual meeting of the American Association for Cancer Research in 1956. Her conclusions met with a furious outburst and ridicule from the scientific audience, which called her conclusions "absurd." She stood her ground, however, convinced that her research was correct.

After the initial controversy, Friend's arguments gained credibility when a renowned scientist, Jacob Furth, found her experiment to be correct. In 1957 Rous helped Friend carefully document her research and present a paper, which met with approval from the scientific community. Friend at last gained recognition, and the Friend virus became a model that benefited research and researchers in numerous fields. Twenty years later she addressed the American Association for Cancer Research as its president, telling her audience that she had been one of the "surfers on the tide of history," experiencing each day as a "new adventure."

In 1962 Friend received the Alfred F. Sloan Award for Cancer Research, which allowed her to spend three months at a time visiting various institutes all over the world. The same year she also received the American Cancer Society Award, and in 1970 she was awarded the Hunter College Presidential Medal Centennial Award. Elected to the Hunter College Hall of Fame in the same year, she received the Virus-Cancer Progress Award from the National Institutes of Health in 1974. In 1976 she was elected to the National Academy of Sciences, and in 1978 she became president of the New York Academy of Sciences.

In 1966 Friend left Sloan-Kettering and became director of and professor at the Center for Experimental Cell Biology at the Mount Sinai School of Medicine in New York City. A laboratory for research into viruses and tumors, the center had many specialists working as a team. By 1972 Friend had made another dramatic discovery: when she used certain drugs on a mouse leukemia cell, it then differentiated, becoming nearly normal. Friend's test-tube cells became another model in the study of cancer.

Friend's laboratory was her playground, where she often lingered in the evening to speak to colleagues about work or personal affairs. She never married, nor did she have children. She loved the Manhattan skyline and her vantage point from her apartment in the Stuyvesant Town complex on East Fourteenth Street in Manhattan, where she lived for most of her adult life. Visitors called it "the Friend Hotel" because Friend always welcomed anyone who needed a place to stay. A soft-spoken, fair-haired woman, she surrounded herself with friends and family. Her leisure was spent in the classical pursuits of theater, music, opera, and reading. She also loved to travel.

In 1981 Friend was diagnosed with lymphoma. While undergoing extensive treatment, she kept researching, writing, and sending out grant applications. During her career Friend was rarely exposed to sex discrimination and was respected for her opinions. She stood by her convictions, even when they were unpopular. A firm believer in the women's movement, she readily agreed to speak out when asked. She wrote extensively, publishing 49 abstracts and 113 original papers, reviews, and book chapters, many of them composed on her own rather than collaboratively. Friend finally lost her battle with lymphoma in New York City. She is buried in New Montifiore Cemetery in Farmingdale, New York.

Described by associates as a woman with a "brilliant and imaginative mind," Charlotte Friend provided pathways to new discoveries. She laid the groundwork for studies that assisted in the development of cancer research, the characterization of the human immunodeficiency virus (HIV), and the explanation of how viruses can interrupt the process of cell growth. She encouraged young scientists and inspired many young women scientists by sharing her knowledge of viruses and cells without hesitation. The Friend virus contributed to the search for the causes of cancer, and her legacy lives as a new generation of scientists continues to probe the Friend virus under the microscope.

★

Friend's papers are at the Mount Sinai Medical Center in New York City. Her works are too numerous to list, but an interesting example is "Presidential Address: The Coming of Age of Tumor Virology," *Cancer Research* 37 (1977): 1255–1263. Leila Diamond, "Charlotte Friend 1921–1987," in *Biographical Memoirs,* vol. 63 (1994), is a composite of personal and highly technical information. Iris Noble, *Contemporary Women Scientists of America* (1979), includes a biography of Friend; and Leila Diamond and Sandra R. Wolman, eds., *Viral Oncogenesis and Cell Differentiation: The Contributions of Charlotte Friend* (1989), synthesizes the research findings of numerous scientists who used Friend's research as a basis for their own and includes a brief biography of Friend. Greer Williams, *Virus Hunters* (1959), is a history of the developments that have occurred in virus research. Leila Diamond, "Charlotte Friend (1921–1987)," *Nature* (23 Apr. 1987), is a short memorial to a fellow scientist. An obituary is in the *New York Times* (16 Jan. 1987).

MARILYN ELIZABETH PERRY

FRIENDLY, Henry Jacob (*b.* 3 July 1903 in Elmira, New York; *d.* 11 March 1986 in New York City), federal appeals court judge who is widely considered one of the most distinguished judges in the history of the federal bench.

The son of Myer H. Friendly and Leah Hallo, Friendly was raised in a small-town environment in western New York. He entered Harvard College in 1919 and graduated summa cum laude with a B.A. degree in European history, under the guidance of renowned Harvard professors William Langer and Charles McIlwain, in 1923. He graduated number one in his class from Harvard Law School in 1927, with the highest grades in the history of the school, and was head of the *Harvard Law Review.* While at the law school, he established a relationship with Professor Felix Frankfurter, later a dominant figure of the U.S. Supreme Court from the Franklin D. Roosevelt to the John F. Kennedy years. With the support of Frankfurter, Friendly was selected by Justice Louis D. Brandeis to serve as the latter's law clerk during the 1927 term of the Court.

After his clerkship, Friendly joined the New York Wall Street law firm of Root, Clark, Buckner and Ballantine, the predecessor firm to Dewey Ballantine. There he met and worked with another future Supreme Court justice, John

Henry J. Friendly, 1971. UPI/CORBIS-BETTMANN

Marshall Harlan. In 1930 he married Sophie M. Stern, beginning a fifty-five-year partnership notable for its mutual devotion and happiness. The couple had three children: David, Joan, and Ellen. Friendly quickly established a reputation as an able corporate lawyer, specializing in railroad organizations and air transportation. Although he did not litigate, he achieved particular prominence as the legal strategist who cleared the way for international commercial air traffic free of the threat of local chattel attachments and debt and claim proceedings. His success led to his designation as director and general counsel of Pan American World Airways, the leading global carrier of the day.

In 1946 Friendly joined the firm in which he would practice for the next thirteen years, Cleary, Gottlieb, Friendly, and Hamilton. In this period he firmly established himself as one of the most respected corporate lawyers in the nation and became an influential figure in the progressive, eastern establishment wing of the Republican party, which was dominated by New York governors Thomas E. Dewey and Nelson A. Rockefeller.

Through the unrelenting support of Justice Frankfurter and Learned Hand, then a legendary figure on the U.S. Court of Appeals for the Second Circuit in New York, Friendly was appointed to that court by President Dwight D. Eisenhower in 1959. He then began a twenty-seven-year tenure as a federal appeals court judge in the second circuit, hearing appeals from federal trial courts in New York, Connecticut, and Vermont. Over that period, he demonstrated a brilliance in legal analysis, reasoning, explication, and discourse that raised him above virtually every other American judge of his generation. Indeed, he was routinely referred to as Learned Hand's true successor. He established a primacy of intellect in virtually every field of federal law, including securities, trademark, copyright, antitrust, environmental, and criminal law; evidence, tax, administrative, and contract law; bankruptcy, admiralty, jurisdiction, and constitutional law.

Judge Friendly nonetheless labored largely in obscurity and never established a public persona, as did Justices Hand, Brandeis, Benjamin Cardozo, and Oliver Wendell Holmes. He did not, as the *New York Times* editorialized at the time of his death, synthesize his legal brilliance into mere epigrams. Indeed, he never became identified with a primary judicial philosophy, as had, for example, Frankfurter, for judicial restraint, or Brandeis, for governmental intervention in private-sector economics. Nor did he ruminate on and write elegant generalizations about, for example, the spirit of liberty, as did Hand. Friendly was a meticulous craftsman of intricate and convincing solutions to legal problems exposed by litigants in the thicket of the law. His opinions became markers and signposts that illuminated the way for judges and lawyers decades after he wrote them.

In one area, Friendly did prefigure a seismic change in federal jurisprudence. For twenty years after the Supreme Court's landmark decision in *Mapp v. Ohio,* which applied the exclusionary rule to illegally seized evidence in state criminal prosecution, the federal courts broadly enlarged the constitutional rights of criminal defendants. Judge Friendly, almost alone, insistently argued against the illogic inherent in much of the prevailing legal doctrine of the day in the field of crime control, police power, and due process in criminal law. He argued that the constitutional principle of suppressing otherwise credible and probative evidence before juries in order to coerce proper police conduct was a judge-made gloss on the Constitution without foundation in the text of the Fourteenth Amendment. More to the point, in an era of ad hoc constitutional law regnant, he insisted that such a work of judicial activism did not and could not succeed. He reasoned that federal judges' attempts to rationalize the general principle in thousands of varying specific cases, with the outcome often being the release of apparently guilty defendants, could not possibly be understood, and therefore followed, by the nation's rank-and-file police officers. By the early 1980s his view on the ineffectiveness of the exclusionary rule became widely accepted, and suppression of evidence in federal criminal cases became a far less common event. Friendly was also a notable critic of the Miranda warnings, another constitutional innovation during Earl Warren's years as chief justice, which called for the suppression of confessions and incriminating statements if suspects had not been warned ahead of time by police about the risks of making such statements.

Friendly served as chief judge of the second circuit from 1971 to 1973 and during that time presided over the hearing and resolution of one of the most important First Amendment cases in the history of the United States. The "Pentagon Papers" case (*New York Times Co.* v. *United States*) in which the government sought to have the *New York Times* enjoined on national security grounds from publishing articles based on a secret and classified Pentagon study of the origins and policies underlying U.S. involvement in the Vietnam War, riveted the attention of the nation and the world in June 1971. Chief Judge Friendly, with a majority of the appeals court agreeing with him, ruled on a procedural point in favor of the government, allowing it to make an *in camera* (secret) disclosure to the trial judge on the grave security dangers to the nation attendant on publication. The Supreme Court, however, heard an emergency appeal and ultimately ruled in favor of the *New York Times.*

Friendly was a longtime adviser to the American Law Institute, and he presented the most cited summary analysis of jurisdiction of the federal courts in his widely heralded Carpentier Lectures at Columbia Law School in 1972. He received the presidential Medal of Freedom from President Jimmy Carter in 1977. In remarks at a memorial meeting at the New York City Bar Association at the time of Judge Friendly's death, the chief justice of the United States, Warren Burger, observed that in surveying his own fifty years of practice, he could not identify "any judicial colleague more highly qualified to have come to the Supreme Court of the United States than Henry Friendly."

Friendly's death was ruled a suicide by the New York police. The judge ended his life, according to notes left by him, because of loneliness after the death of his wife and failing health.

★

Friendly's *Collected Legal Papers,* at the Harvard Law School, is a compilation of case and opinion records that will be made accessible to the public in 2006. His works include *Federal Jurisdiction: A General View* (1973). "In Memoriam: Henry J. Friendly," Harvard Law Review 99 (1986), contains an extraordinary array of tributes from the leading figures of the American bench and bar. An obituary is in the *New York Times* (12 Mar. 1986).

KENNETH CONBOY

FROWICK, Roy Halston. *See* Halston.

FULLER, S. B. (*b.* 4 June 1905 in Monroe, Louisiana; *d.* 24 October 1988 in Blue Island, Illinois), businessman who was the first African-American member of the National Association of Manufacturers.

S. B. Fuller, no relation to Alfred C. Fuller, founder of the Fuller Brush Company, was born into a sharecropper's family in Louisiana and raised in Memphis, Tennessee. He had only a sixth-grade education. As a schoolboy in Memphis he started selling soap to neighbors, convinced by his mother, who died when he was seventeen, that door-to-door sales was the best way out of poverty. In 1928 Fuller, already married and a father, hitchhiked to Chicago and found work in a coal yard. Eventually, he became an agent for and then manager of an insurance company, but he always knew that sales held the key to his future.

In 1935, in the middle of the Great Depression, he borrowed $25 on his car and used the money to purchase a load of soap from Boyer National Laboratories.. He began selling door-to-door and had, by 1939, a dozen sales representatives peddling thirty items from a little-known cosmetics line he produced in his small factory on Chicago's South Side.

As Fuller's business grew he acquired several companies, including, in 1947, the company that had become Boyer International Laboratories, manufacturer of Jean Nadal Cosmetics. The company's clientele was predominately white and located in the South. Other acquisitions included the Courier Newspaper Group, which owned the *New York Age,* the country's oldest black newspaper, and the *Pittsburgh Courier,* the black newspaper with the largest circulation in the United States. Fuller's other businesses included the South Center Department Store and the Regal Theatre in Chicago and financial interests in farming and beef cattle production. By the early 1960s, Fuller Products had sales of more than $10 million and employed 5,000 workers, and Fuller was widely regarded as one of the wealthiest African Americans in the country. In the midst of his prosperity, Fuller in the late 1950s had a $250,000, twelve-room ranch house built for himself and his wife, Lestine, and their five children. Located in Robbins, Illinois, forty-five minutes from Chicago, it had 4,000 feet of floor space and included a patio and greenhouse.

Fuller's troubles began as he found himself under attack from both blacks and whites. In the late 1950s the White Citizens Councils, a white racist southern group, learned that an African American owned Jean Nadal Cosmetics. The council organized a successful boycott of Nadal merchandise at a time when Boyer products accounted for 60 percent of Fuller Company business. In 1963, when he became the first African American inducted into the National Association of Manufacturers, Fuller said in his acceptance speech that "a lack of understanding of the capitalist system and not racial barriers was keeping blacks from making progress." He expressed similar sentiments in a

1963 interview in *U.S. News and World Report* in which he said, "Negroes are not discriminated against because of the color of their skin. They are discriminated against because they have not anything to offer that people want to buy." This apparent Uncle Tom attitude angered black nationalists, who boycotted Fuller Products and its owner's gospel of black entrepreneurship.

The combined effects of the two boycotts plus some poorly timed business decisions put financial pressure on the continued viability of Fuller Products. In 1968, in an effort to bail out his company, Fuller sold promissory notes in interstate commerce without registering them. For this action he was charged in 1968 with violating the Federal Securities Act. He pleaded guilty, was placed on five years' probation, and was ordered to repay $1.6 million to creditors. Faced with a severe cash crunch, Fuller Products entered bankruptcy in 1971. After reorganization the company reported profits of $300,000 in 1972, and Fuller successfully ran the cosmetics portion of the old company for several years, though never at the firm's previous levels of size or profitability.

On the occasion of his seventieth birthday, Fuller, a Baptist, was the guest of honor at a special tribute organized by John H. Johnson, publisher of *Ebony* and *Jet,* and other prominent black Chicago entrepreneurs whom Fuller had mentored. Besides the compliments and cake, Fuller was given the net proceeds of the dinner, some $70,000, plus $50,000 worth of stock certificates. Nearly 2,000 guests attended the event, including Illinois governor Dan Walker and the Reverend Jesse Jackson, head of Operation Push.

On 15 June 1985 more than 2,000 people, including Chicago mayor Harold Washington, Jesse Jackson, and Illinois governor James Thompson, gathered at a Chicago hotel to honor Fuller on his eightieth birthday. The celebration was the last major public event of his life. Just over three years later, the Godfather of Black Business died of kidney failure at the age of eighty-three.

★

Pamela Sherrod, "S. B. Fuller: The Dean of Black Entrepreneurs," *Chicago Tribune* (9 June 1987), and "S. B. Fuller: A Man and His Products," *Black Enterprise* (Aug. 1975), are the closest things to a biography of S. B. Fuller in print. Other items concerning Fuller's life and work include "Genius of Direct Selling," *Ebony* (Nov. 1957), and "Suburban Showplace," *Ebony* (Feb. 1959), a pictorial essay about Fuller's newly constructed home. "A Tribute to a Black Business Pioneer," *Ebony* (Sept. 1975), is a pictorial essay on Fuller's seventieth birthday bash. An appreciation of Fuller's "economics" is in Don Wycliff, "Civil Rights and Sacred Cows," *New York Times* (7 Nov. 1988). Obituaries are in the *Chicago Tribune* (26 Oct. 1988), *New York Times* (28 Oct. 1988), and *Jet* (7 Nov. 1988).

JAMES CICARELLI

G

GABEL, Hortense Wittstein (*b.* 16 December 1912 in New York City; *d.* 6 December 1990 in New York City), lawyer, public official, and New York State judge whose acclaimed career on the bench was ended by charges of conspiracy and fraud.

Gabel was one of two daughters of Reuben J. Wittstein, a lawyer, and Beth Goldberg, a bookkeeper. She attended public schools in the Bronx and then went on to Hunter College of the City University of New York, receiving a B.A. degree in 1934. Gabel, who was known as Horty to her friends, received her LL.B. degree in 1937 from Columbia University Law School. She went to work in her father's law firm and left in 1942 to begin her career in public service, becoming assistant corporation counsel for the City of New York. In 1944 she married Milton Gabel, an army dentist, and moved to Fort Hood, Texas, where she worked as a reporter; they had one daughter.

Gabel, a reform Democrat, in 1949 became a founding director of the National Committee Against Discrimination in Housing, serving until 1954. She exposed abuses in the New York City urban renewal program and was critical of the slum-clearance programs of the popular city planner Robert Moses. She went on to hold several state and city positions, all related to housing, including administrator of the state Temporary Housing Rent Commission (1955–1959); assistant to the mayor of New York City for housing (1959–1962); and commissioner of the city's Rent and Rehabilitation Administration (1962–1965), in which position she saved tenants millions of dollars in rent by enforcing the rent-control laws and by discovering overcharges. Further, she helped plan rehabilitation programs for slum sections of Harlem and the Lower East Side.

On the federal level, from 1960 to 1966 Gabel was a consultant to the U.S. Housing and Home Finance Agency and the Department of Housing and Urban Development, and she wrote the influential report "A Proposal for a Nationally Based Private Non-profit Urban Development Corporation to Rehabilitate and Replace Substandard Urban Slum Dwellings" (1966). She then returned to New York and resumed her work for improvements in state and city housing. From 1968 to 1971 she was vice president of the Center for Community Change and wrote the reports "The New York City Rehabilitation Experiments" (1970) and "Counties, Towns, and Special Improvements in New York State" (1971).

In 1970 Gabel was appointed to the New York State Civil Court and served as secretary of the court's Board of Judges from 1972 to 1973. In 1973 she also became cochair of the Hunter College Institute for Trial Judges, of which she was a founder. After serving as an acting judge in family court in 1974 and early 1975, Gabel wrote an article critical of the city's family court system and affiliated agencies that appeared on the op-ed page of the *New York Times* (7 May 1975), taking its title, "In Darkness, and with Dangers Compass'd Round," from Milton's *Paradise Lost*. It was

Hortense Gabel, 1988. UPI/CORBIS-BETTMANN

a chilling account of a boy who first encountered the city's court system at the age of ten. Gabel's enumeration of the many misleading and contradictory diagnoses of and recommendations for this youngster by various education, hospital, probation, and court officials was an indictment of the city's system of dealing with juvenile delinquents.

In 1975 Gabel was appointed by Governor Hugh L. Carey to fill a vacancy on the state supreme court; she assumed office in 1976. While on the bench she was considered a compassionate judge and a strong supporter of women's issues and civil rights. A short woman who wore thick-lensed glasses, Gabel had a no-nonsense presence on the bench during criminal trials, meting out admonitions to both prosecutors and defense attorneys. In 1979 she helped found the National Association of Women Judges and in 1986 was named judge of the year by that organization.

Gabel was a board member of the New York Women's Bar Association, the Legislative Committee on Crime, Committee on Housing and Urban Development, and the American Jewish Congress. She also served on the board of directors of the Columbia Law School Alumni Association and was elected to the Hunter College Hall of Fame in 1972.

Her career as a jurist came to an end in 1987, when she resigned from the bench during criminal and misconduct investigations. She was implicated in what became known in New York City as the "Bess Mess" case, which involved Bess Myerson, a former Miss America who headed the city's Department of Cultural Affairs, and Carl ("Andy") Capasso, owner of a plumbing and sewer construction company that held several contracts with the city and who was dating Myerson. Gabel, Capasso, and Myerson were charged with conspiracy, fraud, and bribery; Gabel allegedly abused her powers in 1983 by lowering Capasso's alimony payments to his former wife in exchange for a position for her daughter, Sukhreet, with the Department of Cultural Affairs. The trial was headline news in New York City for two months, especially during nine days of damaging testimony from Sukhreet Gabel. In December 1988 the three defendants were acquitted of all charges, but the trial brought an ignominious end to the career of a woman referred to as one of the "grandes dames" of New York's legal system.

Gabel died of heart failure in her Manhattan apartment on the Upper East Side. She is buried in Military Cemetery, Riverhead, New York.

★

The records of the cases presided over by Gabel while she was a judge in the various New York State courts are in the courthouse records in New York City. Biographical details can be found in the articles that appeared in New York City newspapers during her trial in October and November 1988. An obituary is in the *New York Times* (8 Dec. 1990).

LOUISE B. KETZ

GARBO, Greta (*b.* 18 September 1905 in Stockholm, Sweden; *d.* 15 April 1990 in New York City), film actress known for her well-guarded privacy as well as her unique artistry in films such as *Queen Christina* (1933) and *Camille* (1937).

Garbo was born Greta Lovisa Gustafson, the youngest of three children of Anna Lovisa Karlsson, a homemaker, and Karl Alfred Gustafson, a landscaper. Her father suffered from delicate health, a serious drinking problem, and a melancholy disposition. To help her struggling family Greta left school when she was fourteen and took a job as a soap-lather girl in a neighborhood barbershop. Shortly thereafter, in June 1920, her father died, leaving her devastated. She then worked as a salesgirl in the millinery section of the Paul U. Bergström department store. Despite her physical flaws—at the time she was a plump young woman with broad hips, a flat chest, sloping shoulders, and large feet—she had a presence that set her apart from her coworkers. Enhanced by unusually long lashes, her luminous eyes contained more than a hint of the sophisticated allure that would become part of her star iconography.

Greta was soon chosen to appear as a model in promotional films for the department store. Soon afterward Erik Petschler, the so-called Mack Sennett of Swedish films,

Greta Garbo. ARCHIVE PHOTOS

cast her as a bathing beauty in his comedy *Peter the Tramp* (1922). Sensing her promise, Petschler advised her to apply to the state-run, tuition-free Royal Dramatic Theater Academy. The competition was intense, but she was admitted in 1922. At the end of Greta's first year of training, Mauritz Stiller, a prominent director in the Swedish film industry who was casting his film *The Saga of Gösta Berling,* asked Gustaf Molander, head of the academy, to send him his two prettiest students. Stiller immediately chose Greta to play the Countess Elisabeth Dohna, a noble and demure young woman who redeems an alcoholic minister. Imperious, profligate, willful, and homosexual, Stiller, a Russian Jew born in 1883, became the young actress's surrogate father and mentor and was largely responsible for transforming an awkward, provincial salesgirl named Greta Gustafson into Garbo, the incomparably glamorous film star. (He changed her last name in 1923.) Garbo's relationship with Stiller was among the closest, most intense, and most significant of her life.

In August 1924 Garbo and Stiller went to Berlin to attend the premiere of *The Saga of Gösta Berling.* During their prolonged stay in Berlin, where their film had been received more enthusiastically than in Sweden, Stiller tried and failed to secure financing for a new project for his new star; he also met Louis B. Mayer, who offered him and Garbo contracts with his recently formed studio, Metro-Goldwyn-Mayer (MGM). Before Garbo's departure for Hollywood, Austrian director G. W. Pabst asked her to star in *The Joyless Street* (1925) as an innocent young woman forced into prostitution. It is in this film, where she radiates an aura of exquisite world-weariness, that Garbo emerges as a potent, immensely subtle film actress. *The Joyless Street* suggests the kind of career in European art films that she might have had if Stiller had not committed her to Mayer.

Stiller and Garbo arrived in New York City on 6 July 1925. In the subsequent weeks, as the studio seemed to have no plans for her, Garbo sat for the noted photographer Arnold Genthe, who published his study of the new Swedish import in *Vanity Fair.* Genthe's alluring photographs reawakened interest at MGM, which summoned Garbo to Los Angeles, where she and Stiller arrived on 10 September 1925.

In her first two films, *The Torrent* (1926) and *The Temptress* (1927), both based on steamy novels by Vicente Blasco Ibáñez, Garbo played an exotic sensualist, a woman who lives for love. She modernized the role of vamp, already an outmoded type, but her male costars, Ricardo Cortez in *The Torrent* and Antonio Moreno in *The Temptress,* were less successful in renovating another Hollywood stencil, that of the Latin lover popularized by Rudolf Valentino in the early 1920s. Stiller was assigned to direct *The Temptress,* but the studio found him to be extravagant and insubordinate, and he was replaced by Fred Niblo. Garbo was crushed, but at Stiller's insistence she remained on the job. After directing two films for Pola Negri at Paramount, Stiller returned to Sweden, frustrated by his inability to adapt to the Hollywood system. He died soon after, in November 1928, at age forty-five.

For her third film, *Flesh and the Devil* (1927), Garbo was paired with an actor she respected. Fresh from his triumph in *The Big Parade* (1925), John Gilbert was at his peak as a romantic hero. Attracted by her leading man's gregarious, fun-loving, impulsive style, Garbo began a highly publicized affair with Gilbert. On screen their mutual attraction is potent: Garbo's first look at Gilbert sizzles with erotic promise, and a later scene in which she fondles her lover's communion cup is a sly aria of smoldering passion. By now Garbo was firmly set in the mold of an outsider, a femme fatale whose desire was dangerous both to the men she ensnared and to herself. She was the woman who knew too much—her ability to project carnal knowledge was a threat to the patriarchal status quo—and her worldly, amoral characters were either banished or, as in *Flesh and the Devil,* killed. Garbo's characters rarely participated in Hollywood's ritualistic happy endings.

In her first few years at MGM, Garbo reluctantly consented to be interviewed and to pose for publicity photographs, but as she cultivated an austere and formidable offscreen persona, she became increasingly inaccessible. She protected her privacy to a degree no other celebrity of her magnitude has ever sought. To little avail she complained about being typecast—as a temptress with secrets, a woman of affairs destined for extinction or ennobling self-sacrifice. As the eponymous heroine of *Anna Karenina,* retitled so that marquees could announce Garbo and Gilbert in *Love* (1927); as the errant woman of the world in *A Woman of Affairs* (1927), a censored version of Michael Arlen's best-selling novel *The Green Hat;* and as a woman with a romantic and sexual mind of her own in *The Single Standard* (1929), opposite fellow Swede Nils Asther, Garbo performs the rituals of doomed romance. Using veiled glances, by turns amorous and melancholy, raised eyebrows, and charged off-screen looks in which her characters commune with an apprehension of their awaiting destinies, she eloquently expresses the tumult or the ecstasy of her characters' private feelings. In an exquisite scene in *A Woman of Affairs,* an example of the kind of privileged moment that occurs throughout Garbo's work, her character embraces a bouquet of roses with an impassioned sensuality. Only rarely did Garbo perform with theatrical overemphasis, as in the scene in the same film in which she runs her hands through her hair to express anxiety.

In the last few years of the silent era Garbo was one of MGM's most valued players. Because of her accent, the studio kept her in silent films as long as possible; her final silent, *The Kiss* (1929), was the last the studio produced. The new talking picture proved a death sentence for a number of foreign as well as American stars with thick, unmusical accents or voices inconsistent with their image, and both the studio and Garbo were concerned that she might be among the fatalities. But when Garbo spoke the famous first line in Eugene O'Neill's *Anna Christie* (1930)—"Gimme a viskey, chincher ale on the side, and don't be stingy, baby!"—it was clear that her voice would not betray her. At once sultry, haughty, husky, and deep, hers was the voice of a foreigner, to be sure, but her accent and cadence complemented her appearance. Her rich, resonant tones, capable of evoking both irony and mystery, enhanced her haunting beauty. Although her performance as Anna Christie was uncharacteristically stilted, the lure of a talking Garbo made the film a hit.

Throughout the 1930s Garbo remained one of MGM's most prized and pampered players, an artist so revered that she came to be billed by her last name only. As in the silent period, she worked mostly with impersonal contract directors—Clarence Brown, an efficient craftsman with no discernible style, was her most frequent director—and with leading men such as Robert Taylor, George Brent, Melvyn Douglas, Robert Montgomery, and Fredric March, who lacked her stature. By far her most important creative partner was cinematographer William Daniels, who shot nineteen of her twenty-four American films. With his elegant handling of light and shadow, Daniels was essential in enthroning the star as the ultimate auteur of her films.

As in the 1920s, her career alternated between prestige projects and ephemeral entertainments. She followed *Anna Christie* with two mediocre, desperately titled films, *Romance* (1930) and *Inspiration* (1931). In *Susan Lenox: Her Fall and Rise* (1931), she is cast against type as a woman in pursuit of a swaggering hero played by Clark Gable, Garbo's only leading man who exuded a sexual confidence commensurate with her own. Her first indelible performance in talking films, a small role she invests with eloquent highlights, is as a prima ballerina past her prime in *Grand Hotel* (1932). At one point in the film, she cradles the phone after she has spoken with her lover, looking off-screen with an incandescent gaze of romantic bliss. At the end of the picture, she walks through the lobby as she is about to rendezvous with him; she does not know that he has been killed, but she senses that something is wrong and her face and body speak a dual language of elation shadowed by fear. The scene is an example of Garbo's extraordinary ability to convey two contrasting emotions at once.

Her role in *Queen Christina* (1933), her second landmark performance in sound, had strong autobiographical overtones for Garbo. While the film takes liberties with history, downplaying the seventeenth-century Swedish monarch's lesbianism and indeed having her forsake her throne for the love of a Spanish count (John Gilbert in his only secure talking-picture performance), Garbo nonetheless introduces a bisexual subtext, slyly flirting with a lady-in-waiting. Christina's withdrawal from public life echoed Garbo's own desire, often announced as a threat when she was displeased with management, to "go home." The film contains two of Garbo's most celebrated acting moments: in a scene at an inn after she has spent a night with the Spanish count, she touches each of the items in the room as if wanting to memorize them; and in a long final close-up she palpably conveys the flicker of thought and feeling behind her character's eyes. During this period Garbo had an intense though short-lived affair with Mercedes de Acosta, a failed writer who believed in astrology and Eastern mysticism and whose only distinction seems to have been her ability to ingratiate herself with famous bisexuals like Garbo and Marlene Dietrich.

In *Anna Karenina* (1935), playing against the terminally frostbitten Fredric March as her lover, Garbo shrewdly and subversively transfers her sensuality to her character's son, enacted by the formidably precocious Freddie Bartholomew. Tenderly, yearningly leaning over her son as he reclines in bed, Garbo infuses their relationship with a startling subtext. As the self-sacrificing prostitute in *Camille* (1937), her ultimate romantic-martyr role, she gives what is often considered her finest performance. Her Camille is wonderfully commonsensical, dry and witty, and surprisingly lighthearted until the final crescendo of sacrifice and death. The performance is suffused with moments to savor: her insouciant laughter in the opening scenes at the opera; her mask of indifference, beneath which she reveals the intensity of her feelings when her new lover knocks at the door as she entertains an old client; her array of reactions, as anger modulates into a sly smile, after her patron pays and then slaps her; her transcendent gaze at the moment of death when her eyes seem to leave her body.

Ninotchka (1939) marked a necessary change of pace. As a Russian commissar who melts under the twin seductions of capitalism and a debonair American (Melvyn Douglas), Garbo gallantly dismantled her ice-queen image. "Garbo laughs," the film's advertising promised, and sizable audiences turned out to witness the phenomenon. But the humanized, democratized Garbo was not to enjoy a flourishing career. Her last film, *The Two-Faced Woman* (1941), in which she was again asked to soften her image, was a calamity, the only full-scale failure of her career.

Even so, Garbo did not intend to retire, but a variety of circumstances seemed to ensure that she would never appear in film again. Because her domestic box-office appeal had been declining, the studio depended on foreign markets, which were closed during World War II, for her films to make a profit. After the war, she began to seem retrograde, a reminder of a bygone era. In 1949, after financing could not be raised for a project intended for her based on Honoré de Balzac's *La Duchesse de Langeais,* Garbo withdrew from moviemaking. For the remaining four decades of her life she drifted. Although she had no enduring intimate relationships with men or women, she had an affair of sorts with set and costume designer Cecil Beaton, who was homosexual; and she had a series of friends who acted as financial advisers, walking companions, and protectors. These carefully chosen comrades were subject to Garbo's strict house rules: they were never to question her about her film career and they were never to speak or write about her for public consumption. If, like Mercedes de Acosta or Cecil Beaton, they could not respect the vow of silence she exacted, they were banished.

For decades she lived in Manhattan, at 450 East Fifty-second Street, in an elegant apartment overlooking the East River from which she ventured for long daily walks. Garbo-spotting was a popular New York activity; but, respecting the star's legendary wish to be left alone, fans rarely disturbed her.

For the last fifty years of her life Garbo made no professional public appearances; no tribute or financial offer could entice her, however briefly, into the limelight she had forsaken. Some critics speculated that it was her desire to protect the public's image of an eternally youthful screen icon that explained her elaborate efforts to conceal her aging image from prying photographers. Other observers suggested that her lesbianism created in her a deep need for privacy. Whatever the reasons for the absoluteness of her withdrawal, she remained to the end of her life a woman of mystery who may have preserved her legend in a purer form than any other Hollywood star. She never compromised her sense of dignity. Garbo died in New York City at the age of eighty-four. Her funeral was private and, at her request, she was cremated and her ashes interred at an undisclosed location.

However reserved the private Garbo may have been, for the camera she was intimate and soulful, and in her best work she created the illusion of sharing with the audience her characters' deepest secrets, which seemed to merge with her own. Her reputation as an actress of remarkable subtlety and depth is certain to endure.

★

Rilla Page Palmborg, *The Private Life of Greta Garbo* (1931), is an early biography based on contemporary interviews in which Garbo's dual legend as a great actress and a private enigma is already in place. John Bainbridge, *Garbo* (1955), was the only full-length biography for many years. Antoni Gronowicz, *Garbo: Her Story* (1990), is a largely discredited work by a writer who falsely claimed to have had access to, and the cooperation of, the star. Barry Paris, *Garbo: A Biography* (1995), is a thorough, perceptive, and reliable account of her life and career.

Alexander Walker, *Garbo: A Portrait Authorized by Metro-Goldwyn-Mayer* (1980), offers revealing details of Garbo's business relations with her studio. Raymond Daum, edited and annotated by Vance Muse, *Walking with Garbo: Conversations and Recollections* (1991), shares snatches of the wit and wisdom, and paranoia, of Garbo gleaned during strolls around New York City. Sven Broman, *Conversations with Greta Garbo* (1992), provides glimpses of Garbo in her later years by a journalist whom Garbo befriended during her annual pilgrimages to Klosters, Switzerland. Hugo Vickers, *Loving Garbo: The Story of Greta Garbo, Cecil Beaton, and Mercedes de Acosta* (1994), is a chatty peek at Garbo's love affairs. An obituary is in the *New York Times* (16 Apr. 1990).

FOSTER HIRSCH

GARDNER, Ava Lavinia (*b.* 24 December 1922 in Grabtown, North Carolina; *d.* 25 January 1990 in London, England), actress whose beauty and allure in such films as *Show Boat* (1951) and *The Night of the Iguana* (1964) secured her position as a movie star for more than thirty years; offscreen, her stormy personal life kept her in the public eye, where she was perceived as an earthy, hard-living, and outspoken woman.

Ava Gardner was the youngest of the seven children of Jonas Bailey Gardner and Mary Elizabeth ("Molly") Gardner. Her father was a tobacco and cotton farmer who eked out a living in Grabtown, a small community outside of

Smithfield, North Carolina. After he lost his property, he worked at a sawmill, while Molly Gardner took a job cooking and cleaning at a teachers' dormitory. Later, to improve their fortunes, the family moved to Newport News, Virginia, where Mrs. Gardner managed a boardinghouse for shipyard workers. Two years later, they returned to North Carolina. Jonas Gardner died of tuberculosis when Ava was sixteen.

After graduating from Smithfield High School, Gardner briefly attended Atlanta Christian College in Wilson, North Carolina, where she took secretarial courses. In the summer of 1941 she visited her sister Bernice (known as "Bappie") in New York City. Bappie's husband worked for a photography studio on Fifth Avenue, and, intrigued by Gardner's beauty, he took many pictures of her. Some of these photographs found their way to the head of talent at Metro-Goldwyn-Mayer, who asked Gardner to take a silent screen test, in order to conceal her heavy Southern accent. Although she had no experience as an actress, Gardner impressed MGM executives with her stunning good looks, and she was signed to a contract. She moved to Hollywood with her newly divorced sister and began a regimen of acting, diction, and makeup lessons.

After making her debut as a walk-on in *We Were Dancing* (1942), Gardner had bit roles in a number of MGM movies over the next few years. Occasionally, she was given a more substantial part, as in *Three Men in White* (1944), in which she appeared as a vamp attempting to seduce a doctor, played by Van Johnson. Her first major role came while Gardner was on loan to United Artists, when she appeared opposite George Raft in a minor melodrama, *Whistle Stop* (1946).

While Gardner's career appeared to be progressing slowly, her personal life was on a faster track. On 10 January 1942, at age nineteen, she married the actor Mickey Rooney, then the top-ranking male movie star in the country. The marriage lasted only sixteen months, as Rooney continued the fast-paced style of living he had enjoyed as a bachelor, leaving a homebound Gardner in his wake. Years later she remarked, "We were a couple of kids. We didn't have a chance." On 17 October 1945 Gardner married the bandleader Artie Shaw, but their marriage also ended in divorce after about a year. An erudite man, Shaw insisted on educating Gardner on a variety of subjects, and their conflicting careers made it difficult to sustain a relationship.

Gardner's first break came in 1946, when MGM loaned her to Universal to play a leading role in Robert Siodmak's *The Killers*. Using Ernest Hemingway's short story as a jumping-off point, this brooding, skillfully made melodrama cast Gardner as Kitty Collins, the nightclub singer whose treachery leads inexorably to the killing of her lover Swede (played by Burt Lancaster in his film debut). Alluring in black, her voice a throaty whisper, she riveted attention with such lines as "I'm poison to myself and everyone around me."

Ava Gardner. PHOTO ARCHIVES

Her success in *The Killers* ensured that she would continue to be cast in seductive roles. In *The Hucksters* (1947), a satire on radio advertising based on Frederic Wakeman's best-selling novel, Gardner starred opposite her onetime idol Clark Gable as his good-time ex-girlfriend. Again on loan-out from MGM, she played the goddess Venus in a mediocre film version of the stage musical *One Touch of Venus* (1948). Gardner cut a beautiful figure as the goddess who comes to life when her statue is kissed by an impulsive department store window-washer (Robert Walker). Back at MGM, she continued to play roles that drew on her image as a glamorous seductress—in *The Great Sinner* (1949), she portrayed a sumptuously gowned compulsive gambler in nineteenth-century Russia, and in *East Side, West Side* (1949), based on Marcia Davenport's novel, she was the selfish former flame of James Mason, who ends up a murder victim.

Gardner had one of her best roles in 1951, when she starred as Julie La Verne in MGM's Technicolor version of the classic stage musical *Show Boat*. As the song-and-dance star who comes to tragedy when it is revealed that she has "Negro blood," making her marriage to a white man illegal, she gave a genuinely touching performance. To Gardner's chagrin, the studio insisted on dubbing her singing voice with that of Annette Warren. On 7 November 1951, after a headlined courtship, Gardner married Frank Sinatra. Their relationship was explosive, alternately loving and embattled, until their divorce in 1957.

Gardner had some of her best and most interesting roles in the 1950s. In the self-consciously arty *Pandora and the Flying Dutchman* (1951), her first movie made abroad, she played a willful nightclub singer who has a tragic love affair with a mysterious artist (James Mason). In *Mogambo* (1953), she costarred with Clark Gable in a colorful remake of *Red Dust* (1932, also with Gable). Her performance as Honey Bear Kelly, a jaded lady stranded in Africa, won her an Oscar nomination. During the decade, she also played two Hemingway heroines: first in *The Snows of Kilimanjaro* (1952), as Gregory Peck's ill-fated first wife and true love (a character not in the original story), and then in *The Sun Also Rises* (1957), as the hedonistic Lady Brett Ashley. Her films of the 1950s also included *The Barefoot Contessa* (1954), in which she played a doomed Spanish-peasant-turned-movie-star, and *Bhowani Junction* (1956), set in India in 1947, in which she appeared as an Anglo-Indian woman whose love for three men mirrors the country's social and political turmoil. She ended the decade costarring with Gregory Peck in the apocalyptic drama *On the Beach* (1959), based on Nevil Shute's best-selling novel about the aftermath of a nuclear holocaust.

Gardner's personal life during this period was centered in Madrid, Spain, where she had moved in 1955 and where she enjoyed the frequent company of bullfighters, especially the celebrated matador Luis Miguel Dominguin. She ended her MGM contract in 1958 after appearing as the Duchess of Alba, lover of the artist Francisco Goya, in *The Naked Maja*. Her films in the 1960s were not as frequent as they had been in earlier years, nor were the roles as large, but occasionally she was given the opportunity to extend her acting range. She was especially effective as Maxine Faulk, the raucous, blowsy owner of a shabby Mexican hotel in the film version of Tennessee Williams's play *The Night of the Iguana* (1964). Other movies she made in the 1960s are *Fifty-five Days at Peking* (1963), *Seven Days in May* (1964), and John Huston's *The Bible* (1969), in which she appeared as Sarah, loyal wife to the God-fearing Abraham, played by George C. Scott. During the filming of *The Bible,* Gardner had a tempestuous affair with Scott. She closed out the decade appearing as Empress Elizabeth of Austria-Hungary, mother to Prince Rudolf (Omar Sharif), in *Mayerling* (1968), a remake of the 1936 romantic drama.

That same year, disillusioned with Spain, Gardner moved to London, where she lived in her final years. She continued to appear in films, usually in cameo or supporting roles—she turned up as the actress Lillie Langtry at the close of John Huston's *The Life and Times of Judge Roy Bean* (1972), played Charlton Heston's wife in the disaster epic *Earthquake* (1974), and joined Elizabeth Taylor and Jane Fonda in a heavy-handed adaptation of Maurice Maeterlinck's fantasy *The Blue Bird* (1976), the first Russo-American film production. Her last picture, before settling down to a reclusive life in London, was *The Sentinel,* released in 1977. She died of pneumonia in her London apartment in 1990 and was buried next to her parents at Sunset Memorial Park in Smithfield, North Carolina.

Throughout her life, Ava Gardner claimed to be contemptuous of her career and to know little or nothing about her profession. Although she denigrated her work, her best performances offer proof of her effectiveness on-screen. Apart from her incandescent beauty, she was skilled at playing strong, feisty women who could be either vulnerable or treacherous but who were always fascinating. A film goddess with both feet on the ground, she belied her own words to become an actress, after all.

★

Gardner's autobiography is *Ava: My Story* (1990). Other books on the actress include Charles Higham, *Ava: A Life Story* (1975); Judith M. Kass, *Ava Gardner* (1977); John Daniell, *Ava Gardner* (1982); Roland Flamini, *Ava: A Biography* (1983); and Karin J. Fowler, *Ava Gardner: A Bio-Bibliography* (1990). Obituaries are in the *New York Times* and the *New York Daily News* (both 26 Jan. 1990). References to her life can also be found in biographies of Frank Sinatra.

TED SENNETT

GAVIN, James Maurice (*b.* 22 March 1907 in Brooklyn, New York; *d.* 23 February 1990 in Baltimore, Maryland), diplomat, business executive, and general who pioneered airborne warfare and helped prepare the United States Army for tactical nuclear warfare.

Gavin's mother was Katherine Ryan, originally of County Clare, Ireland; his Irish father is unknown. On 26 February 1909 Martin Thomas Gavin and his wife, Mary, adopted James, who was raised by them in Mount Carmel, Pennsylvania, where Gavin's adoptive father was a coal miner. Gavin received eight years of schooling in both parochial and public schools. Having an unhappy childhood, he worked at various jobs before joining the army on 1 April 1924, never to return to Mount Carmel to live.

Posted to Panama, Gavin rose from private to corporal in six months and attended school to prepare him for the entrance examination to the U.S. Military Academy at West Point, New York. Gavin passed and was admitted in 1925. Upon graduation in 1929, he ranked 185 out of 299 students and was commissioned in the infantry. On 5 September 1929 Gavin married Irma Baulsir of Washington, D.C. They had one child, a daughter.

James Gavin, commanding officer of the 82d Airborne Division, drives a tracked vehicle out of an assault glider during Operation Market Garden, near Arnhem, the Netherlands, September 1944. THE NATIONAL ARCHIVES/CORBIS

Gavin's first assignments were at Brooks Field, Texas, where he washed out of flight school, and Camp Jones, Arizona, where he served with the 25th Infantry, an African-American unit. In 1932 and 1933 Gavin attended the Infantry Officers' Course at Fort Benning, Georgia, where he learned that a leader must be tougher than his followers. At Fort Sill, Oklahoma, Gavin served in the 38th and 29th regiments and began the serious study of military history. There, he and Lieutenant Maxwell Taylor began a lifelong rivalry that was sparked by Gavin's belief that Taylor was uncaring toward his troops. After serving with a Filipino scout unit from 1936 to 1938, Gavin became a company commander at Fort Vancouver, Washington. Following a year on the faculty at West Point, where he instructed students in the blitzkrieg tactics that had recently been perfected by the German army, Gavin volunteered to serve in the army's first parachute battalion at Fort Benning in August 1941. There General William C. Lee became his mentor, and Gavin formulated the doctrine for American airborne operations, drawing upon the German and Russian experiences in airborne warfare. He served as operations officer and was promoted to major.

The entry of the United States into World War II provided Gavin a chance to demonstrate his proficiency in airborne warfare. After completion of the Command and General Staff School in April 1942, he was promoted to colonel in August 1942 and given command of the 505th Parachute Infantry Regiment. In May 1943 the 505th arrived in North Africa to join the 82d Airborne Division and prepare for the invasion of Sicily. Gavin commanded the reinforced 505th that jumped into Sicily on 9 July to block Axis armor from reaching U.S. troops landing near Gela. Scattered by high winds, the 505th still accomplished its mission in small-unit actions. Gavin's leadership at Biazza Ridge won him the Distinguished Service Cross.

After the Allied invasion of the Italian mainland, German pressure on the Salerno beachhead caused General Mark Clark to request airborne reinforcements. On 14–15 September 1943 Gavin and the 505th jumped at Paestum and became corps reserve. The 505th spearheaded the attack into Naples and beyond toward the Volturno River. In October, Gavin was promoted to brigadier general and made assistant division commander of the 82d.

On 18 November 1943 Gavin began serving in London as senior airborne adviser to the Chief of Staff, Supreme Allied Commander, to plan airborne actions for the upcoming invasion of France. He supported the use of American airborne forces to open inland paths for seaborne troops and protect them from German counterattack. The planning done, Gavin returned in February 1944 to the 82d at Leicester, England, to conduct preinvasion training. His leadership principles included moving among the troops to locate trouble spots and putting their needs before his own.

In the early hours of D day, 6 June 1944, Gavin jumped into Normandy in command of a three-regiment airborne task force. His primary task was to seize control of two bridges over the Merderet River in order to prevent German counterattacks toward Utah Beach. These bridges were secured four days later, and thereafter until the 82d returned to England in mid-July, the division fought as infantry to sever the Cherbourg peninsula and break out to the south.

After being promoted to major general and made commander of the 82d on 16 August 1944, Gavin next led the division in Operation Market-Garden. His assignment was to seize bridges over the Maas and Waal Rivers and the Maas-Waal Canal around Nijmegen, the Netherlands. British forces then were to attack across the bridges toward Arnhem on the Rhine. From 17 to 20 September Gavin's men achieved all of their objectives despite strong German counterattacks. The overall operation failed, however, because British parachutists were unable to capture the Arnhem bridge.

After going into reserve at Sisonne, France, the 82d's next action was the Battle of the Bulge. On 17 December 1944 Gavin was acting commander of the XVIII Airborne Corps in General Matthew Ridgway's absence. Informed of the German breakthrough in the Ardennes, he put the 82d and 101st airborne divisions in motion toward Bastogne, Belgium. Gavin then met with General Courtney Hodges at Spa, Belgium, and Hodges asked Gavin to hold the shoulders of the breakthrough. On 18 December Gavin sent the 82d to the northern shoulder at Werbomont and the 101st to the southern shoulder at Bastogne. After Ridgway returned to command the XVIII Corps, Gavin led the 82d Airborne Division and repulsed three Panzer division attacks. The northern shoulder held, and in January the 82d counterattacked. In April 1945 the 82d crossed the Elbe River to unite with the Red Army. At Ludwigslust, Germany, Gavin was so sickened by conditions in a nearby concentration camp that he forced civilians to bury the dead.

The 82d Airborne Division, which Gavin continued to command until 1948, participated in the occupation of Berlin until it returned home in December 1945 to Fort Bragg, North Carolina. There Gavin racially integrated the division and experimented with helicopters. Gavin also divorced his wife after having had affairs with the actress Marlene Dietrich and with Martha Gellhorn (Ernest Hemingway's wife) during the war. On 31 July 1948 he married Jean Emert Duncan of Knoxville, who had a daughter by a previous marriage. Three daughters were born to them.

Physically, Gavin was tall and lean with a ramrod-straight posture that caused his men to call him Slim Jim. These characteristics belied his sinewy physical toughness. He had penetrating gray eyes and was fastidious in his dress. Gavin's favorite activities were tennis, handball, horseback riding, and oil painting.

In early 1949 Gavin joined the Weapons Systems Evaluation Group at Fort Monroe, Virginia. His assignment was to assess the use of tactical nuclear weapons in ground warfare. Gavin supported the development of these weapons and the use of atomic bombs during the Korean War to repel the Chinese. This interest in tactical nuclear weapons followed him to his next assignment with the North Atlantic Treaty Organization at Naples, Italy, in 1951 and 1952. He traveled across southern Europe examining potential sites for the use of tactical atomic weapons in case of war. As VII Corps commander in southern Germany from 1952 to 1954, Gavin simulated tactical nuclear war, using conventional tactics. He discovered that VII Corps could not function properly when dispersed to defend against nuclear attack.

As a result of this experience with VII Corps, Gavin spent the remainder of his military career urging greater mobility for the army so that dispersed units could fight a nuclear ground war. His appointment in March 1954 as assistant chief of staff for plans and operations enabled him to push the rapid development of army aviation and a new concept called "sky cavalry." This concept entailed the use of troop-carrying helicopters, short-takeoff and -landing aircraft, and missiles to wage ground nuclear war. Gavin also wanted the air force to procure more tactical and strategic airlift to support army operations. The administration of President Dwight D. Eisenhower would not fund these projects fully, and Gavin opposed Eisenhower's New Look policy that cut army budgets and relied more on massive retaliation with nuclear bombs than on conventional warfare. Although promoted to lieutenant general and appointed chief of research and development in 1955, Gavin found it difficult to function on the army staff because of his opposition to administration policy. In December 1957 Army Chief of Staff Maxwell Taylor asked Gavin publicly to defend the army's new budget, which had been cut 10 percent. Gavin refused and announced his retirement effective 31 March 1958.

After leaving the military, Gavin went to Boston, where he headed the Arthur D. Little Company, an industrial research and management consultant firm. From 1959 to 1960 Gavin was an adviser to John F. Kennedy's presidential campaign, urging the establishment of the Peace Corps. After he was elected, Kennedy appointed Gavin ambassador to France to try to improve relations with French President Charles de Gaulle. Gavin served from 1961 to 1963 and established cordial relations, but de Gaulle would not adapt to U.S. policy. When the Vietnam War intensified, Gavin opposed American involvement. In 1965 he urged a coastal enclave strategy and a negotiated withdrawal. Gavin died of Parkinson's disease and was buried at West Point.

James Gavin rose from poor circumstances to make major contributions to his country. He contributed significantly to the Allied victory in World War II and emerged from the war as one of the world's expert practitioners of airborne warfare. After the war he pushed the army to procure tactical nuclear weapons and to devise new organizations and tactics for their use. His work ultimately enabled the army to organize airmobile divisions.

★

A major source of biographical material exists in Gavin's writings. *Airborne Warfare* (1947) covers his experiences in Europe, airborne operations in the Pacific, and the future of airborne operations. *War and Peace in the Space Age* (1958) recounts Gavin's life and critiques national defense policy. *Crisis Now* (1968) boosted Gavin as presidential material and included his views on U.S. defense policies of the 1960s. *On to Berlin: Battles of an Airborne Commander, 1943–1946* (1978) presented his World War II experiences in greater detail. Bradley Biggs, *Gavin* (1980), gives a brief account of Gavin's career. It is superseded by T. Michael Booth and Duncan Spencer, *Paratrooper: The Life of Gen. James M. Gavin* (1994). An obituary is in *Army* (Apr. 1990).

JOHN L. BELL

GIAMATTI, A(ngelo) Bartlett ("Bart") (*b.* 4 April 1938 in Boston, Massachusetts; *d.* 1 September 1989 in Oak Bluffs, Martha's Vineyard, Massachusetts), Renaissance scholar and president of Yale University who, as commissioner of baseball in 1989, permanently suspended Pete

Rose, manager of the Cincinnati Reds and holder of the lifetime record for base hits, for gambling on games.

The second of three children, Giamatti was the son of Valentine Giamatti, a professor of Italian language and literature at Mount Holyoke College, and Mary Claybaugh Walton, a graduate of Smith College (1935). He grew up in the college town of South Hadley, Massachusetts, where, he recalled, dinner table conversation often centered on the seemingly incompatible topics of Dante and baseball.

After briefly attending South Hadley High School, Giamatti was enrolled in the International School in Rome while his father spent a sabbatical year in Italy. He completed preparatory school at Phillips Andover Academy before entering Yale in 1956. He graduated magna cum laude in 1960, the year he married Toni Smith, a graduate of Yale Drama School and a teacher of English; they had three children. He went on to graduate school at Yale, receiving his doctorate in comparative literature in 1964. In September of that year Giamatti became an instructor in Italian and comparative literature at Princeton.

Clearly, the influence of his father determined his early career. As he later remembered, "I think I learned all my real lessons from my father. He really was the person who taught me about teaching and, by watching him, about scholarship. I saw him teach all the time, not just in the classroom."

In 1966 Princeton University Press published a revised version of Giamatti's doctoral dissertation, *The Earthly Paradise and the Renaissance Epic*. The book's opening chapter, "Gardens and Paradise," described the longing in Western tradition for a place of repose, a blessed garden. This was a theme that he returned to in his later musings on baseball. In "Baseball and the American Character" he wrote, "We can still find, if we wish to, a moment called a game, when these best hopes, those memories for the future, have life; when each of us, those who are in and those out, have a chance to gather, in a green place around home."

Giamatti became an associate professor of English at Yale in 1966 and by 1968 had become a full professor of English and comparative literature. His scholarly work kept pace with his promotions. He edited *The Songs of Bernart de Ventadorn* (1965), was a coeditor of *Orlando Furioso* (1968), and authored *Play of Double Senses: Spenser's "Faerie Queene"* (1975).

Giamatti, who taught freshman survey courses as well as graduate seminars, was a popular professor. A colorful figure with an engaging personality, he was made an honorary member of the Whiffenpoofs singing group and often made impromptu appearances with the troupe during his years at Yale. He served as master of Ezra Stiles College, one of Yale's twelve undergraduate colleges, from 1970 to 1972. In 1976 he was named Frederick Clifford Ford Professor of English and Comparative Literature. He became John Hay Whitney Professor in 1977.

Giamatti's experience in administration consisted solely of brief stints as director of the humanities division in the Faculty of Arts and Sciences and as associate director of the National Humanities Institute at Yale. Thus, considerable surprise greeted the announcement in December 1977 that A. Bartlett Giamatti would assume the presidency of the university the following summer. At forty years of age when elected, Giamatti became Yale's youngest president in two centuries. His style differed so notably from his predecessors' that one member of the faculty remarked, "A human being as president of the university—my God, what will that be like?"

Giamatti's predecessor, Kingman Brewster, had presided over increasing unrest as a declining national economy created grave problems at Yale, including budget deficits, a stalled capital fund-raising drive, and a deteriorating infrastructure. Giamatti's tenure as head of Yale proved to be largely successful. The endowment increased from $544 million to $1.3 billion, and the deficits disappeared. He gave a great deal of attention to improving the physical plant, so much so that he once remarked that he would be remembered as "Bart the Refurbisher." There were difficulties, however. In 1984 the university received bad publicity during a ten-week strike by the clerical and technical workers union.

An academic traditionalist, Giamatti believed writing instruction to be an absolutely essential ingredient in any curriculum, citing the need of education to teach people to write clearly and effectively. He approved funds for undergraduate composition courses and persuaded the faculty to restore a foreign language requirement.

In 1985 Giamatti announced his intention to leave the presidency the following year, stating that he wished to take the time to write a major book on the Renaissance. His return to scholarship did not occur, however, for the baseball club owners of the National League, undoubtedly impressed by Giamatti's keen interest in the sport—he had written a widely read *Harper's* essay on New York Mets pitcher Tom Seaver in 1977—offered him the presidency of the league. Although many of his friends and professional colleagues expressed shock, even dismay, that he would abandon academic life for sports, Giamatti did not hesitate. In December 1986, six months after leaving Yale, he assumed his new job, remarking: "I've been a lover of baseball for as long as I can remember. I've always considered it the most satisfyingly nourishing thing outside of literature. My sense of excitement is high."

As chief of the National League, he gained attention for the severe penalty he meted out to Pete Rose in April 1988 for bumping an umpire in a dispute over a call. Rose's action almost touched off a riot in the stands, and Giamatti,

Bart Giamatti. NATIONAL BASEBALL HALL OF FAME LIBRARY, COOPERSTOWN, N.Y.

clearly intending to send a message to other players, suspended Rose for thirty days and fined him $10,000. Many fans and some sportswriters disapproved of the penalty imposed on the popular player, nicknamed Charlie Hustle, and crowds at some games booed Giamatti. Still, in April 1989, he received the unanimous vote of all twenty-six owners to succeed Peter Ueberroth as commissioner of baseball. Some observers believed Ueberroth resigned in order to avoid supervising an investigation into allegations that Pete Rose gambled on baseball games. (The danger of gambling-inspired corruption has been feared by baseball management since the "Black Sox" scandal of 1919.)

By April 1989 the rumors about gambling by Rose could no longer be ignored. Giamatti conducted a thorough inquiry that ended in the lifetime suspension of Rose from baseball. Although the commissioner's official statement did not include a formal finding that Rose had bet on games, Giamatti in a press conference stated he was convinced by overwhelming evidence that Rose had done so. He further declared: "Baseball is an important, enduring American institution. It must assert and aspire to the highest principles—of integrity, of professionalism, of performance, of fair play within the rules. . . . Let it be clear that no individual is superior to the game."

On 1 September 1989, eight days after his decision, Giamatti died of a heart attack at Martha's Vineyard, Massachusetts, where he had maintained a summer home. Burial was in the Grove Street Cemetery in New Haven. He had served as commissioner for 154 days. President George Bush stated that despite his brief tenure, Giamatti had made an important contribution to the game, setting the highest possible standards.

Giamatti combined in his person the introspective and individualistic world of academia with the often raucous and rough-edged world of professional sports. A short, stocky, bearded man with an affable personality—one friend remarked that he never knew anyone who did not like Bart Giamatti—he had become in a very short time baseball's poet laureate. In an essay titled "Green Fields of the Mind," he wrote "It breaks your heart. It is designed to break your heart. The game begins in spring when everything else begins again, and blossoms in the summer, filling the afternoons and evenings, and then as soon as the chill rains come, it stops and leaves you to face the fall alone."

★

Giamatti's ruminations about baseball and leisure, *Take Time for Paradise: Americans and Their Games* (1989), was published shortly after his death. See also Anthony Valerio, *Bart: A Life of A. Bartlett Giamatti By Him and About Him* (1991), and James Reston, *Collision at Home Plate: The Lives of Pete Rose and Bart Giamatti* (1991). Obituaries are in the *New York Times* (2 Sept. 1989) and *Sports Illustrated* (11 Sept. 1989).

JOHN B. DUFF

GILFORD, Jack (*b.* 25 July 1907 in New York City; *d.* 4 June 1990 in New York City), actor and comedian whose buoyant manner and quick wit enlivened many plays, films, and television shows.

Gilford was born Jacob Gellmann on Manhattan's Lower East Side, the middle child of three sons of Aaron Gellman, a furrier, and his wife, Sophie (Jackness) Gellman. During Prohibition his mother, a Romanian immigrant, divorced her husband and moved her children to the Williamsburg section of Brooklyn, where she set up a bootlegging operation in their apartment. In the 1920s, after attending Commercial High School in Brooklyn, Gilford began entering amateur shows at movie houses around New York City while managing a cosmetics shop in Manhattan. One day in 1934, according to *170 Years of Show Business,* a memoir written by Madeline Gilford and Kate Mostel, the comedian Milton Berle came into the store with his mother. Gilford ran through his routine for Berle, who eventually hired him as a sidekick in his vaudeville revue. Berle insisted that his new performer change his Jewish name, suggesting "Guilford" but agreeing to Gilford's demand to drop the "u." Nevertheless, over the decades of their friendship Berle always called Gilford "Gellmann."

Jack Gilford in *Save the Tiger.* FOTOS INTERNATIONAL/ARCHIVE PHOTOS

In 1938, after four years playing the "borscht belt"—the Jewish resorts located in the Catskill Mountains region of New York State—and vaudeville one-nighters, Gilford signed on as the master of ceremonies and house comic at Barney Josephson's new nightclub, Café Society. The Greenwich Village hotspot was a place where blacks and whites could mix—both on stage and off—and Gilford's fame grew as he mingled with the likes of singers Lena Horne and Billie Holiday. At Café Society, Gilford developed some of his famous skits, including "The Butler Did It," a phrase he invented, and his impersonation of a man on a subway who cannot stay awake.

Gilford's New York Broadway debut took place in 1939 when he performed in a revue at the Music Box Theater. During World War II he toured with the military entertainment group, United Service Organizations, in the Pacific. On 6 April 1949 he married Madeline Lee Fein, a producer, writer, and actress. They had three children.

Gilford was among the actors to be blacklisted during the Red scare of the early 1950s. Although he began his television career in 1948 as a featured performer on comedian Phil Silvers's *Arrow Show* on NBC, by 1950 Gilford was unable to find employment. For about three years the only work he could get was the role of the drunken jailer Frosch in the Metropolitan Opera's production of *Die Fledermaus.*

In 1956, when the blacklist was no longer a major threat, Gilford was called before the House Un-American Activities Committee. Asked, "Do you believe in the overthrow of the United States government by force and violence?" he answered, "No, just gently."

On Broadway, Gilford played Mr. Dussel in the original production of *The Diary of Anne Frank* (1955) and created the role of Hysterium in Stephen Sondheim's musical *A Funny Thing Happened on the Way to the Forum* in 1962, a role for which he received his first Tony nomination. His second came for the role of Herr Schultz in the musical *Cabaret* in 1966. Gilford's other stage performances included *Alive and Kicking* (1950), *Once over Lightly* (1955), *Romanoff and Juliet* (1957), *Once upon a Mattress* (1959), *The Tenth Man* (1959), *Three Men on a Horse* (1969), *The Sunshine Boys* (1972), and *Sly Fox* (1976).

He reprised his role in *A Funny Thing Happened on the Way to the Forum* in the 1966 film, again with his old friend Zero Mostel. Gilford's other films include *Main Street to Broadway* (1953), *Enter Laughing* (1966), *Who's Minding the Mint?* (1967), *Catch-22* (1970), *They Might Be Giants* (1971), *Harry and Walter Go to New York* (1976), *Cocoon* (1985), and *Cocoon II* (1988). He received an Academy Award nomination as best supporting actor for his role in *Save the Tiger* (1973).

On television, Gilford appeared on variety shows hosted by such stars as Gary Moore, Milton Berle, Jack Carson, and Frank Sinatra. Other television appearances included *Cowboy and Tiger* (1963), *Once upon a Mattress* (1964), *Wholly Moses* (1979), *Cheaper to Keep Her* (1979), and *Caveman* (1980). He also was a guest on such series as *The Defenders, All in the Family, Rhoda, Soap,* and *The Love Boat.* In 1983 he starred in *The Very Special Jack Gilford Special.*

Jack Gilford's acting career began with mimicry. "I would do people of my time, John D. Rockefeller, Sr., Jimmy Walker, Calvin Coolidge," he once said. "I was very influenced by silent movies, particularly Laurel and Hardy, even before they were partners." His first dramatic role, in *The World of Sholom Aleichem* (1953), had a single line; it invariably floored the audience and it became associated with him for years. His long-suffering, silent character, told by heaven that he can ask for anything, replies, "In that case, if it's true, could I have, please, every day, a hot roll with butter?"

The actor's routines included a day in the life of a golf ball, an impression of a surrealistic movie, pea soup coming to a slow boil, a conductor afflicted by an errant clarinetist, and a drowsy subway rider struggling not to sleep past his station. His performances consistently earned acclaim, with Frank Rich of the *New York Times* concluding in 1982 that "no Broadway season should lack Jack Gilford."

Although Gilford was an accomplished performer on stage and screen for more than half a century, he was perhaps best known for his television commercials for the candy Cracker Jack, which ran from 1962 to 1972 and gathered many accolades, including an award at the Cannes Film Festival. In January 1990, just a few months before he died, Gilford received the Arnold Weissberger Lifetime Achievement Award at the Gershwin Theater's Hall of Fame. Gilford died of stomach cancer and was buried in Mount Hebron Cemetery in Queens, New York.

Jack Gilford was in the tradition of the great silent clowns and comic masters of the early days of film. His mobile face, which changed shape like a ball of dough being kneaded, and his eyes, which would range from blazing to blank, were the key to his changes of character.

★

Entries on Jack Gilford may be found in Ian Herbert, ed., *Who's Who in the Theatre,* 17th ed. (1981); Ephraim Katz, ed., *The Film Encyclopedia,* 2d ed. (1994); and Larry Langman, ed., *The Encyclopedia of American Film Comedy* (1987). See also Kate Mostel and Madeline Gilford, with Jack Gilford and Zero Mostel, *170 Years of Show Business* (1978). An obituary is in the *New York Times* (5 June 1990).

MARK SOMMER

GILLARS, Mildred Elizabeth Sisk ("Axis Sally") (*b.* 29 November 1900 in Portland, Maine; *d.* 25 June 1988 in Columbus, Ohio), provocative German-radio hostess who tried to wear down American morale in World War II, and who was later convicted, fined, and imprisoned for treason.

Mildred Elizabeth Gillars ("Axis Sally"), *c.* 1949. THE NATIONAL ARCHIVES/CORBIS

Gillars was the only child of Vincent Sisk and Mae Hewitson. After a 1907 divorce, Mae married Robert Bruce Gillars, a dentist, and Mildred Elizabeth took her stepfather's surname. The family eventually settled in Conneaut, Ohio, where Mildred Gillars graduated from high school.

Gillars spent her young adulthood as a struggling actress. Mixing odd jobs with incomplete studies at Ohio Wesleyan University in Delaware, Ohio, and Hunter College in New York City, her career languished through her twenties and thirties. In 1929 she spent six months in Paris with her mother studying music. She returned to Europe in 1933, working variously as salesclerk, governess, and English instructor before breaking into German radio. Her career blossomed in 1940 when Max Otto Koischewitz, her former Hunter College professor and lover, hired her to work with the German Radio Broadcasting Company in Berlin; as a radio personality, Gillars enjoyed sudden popular acclaim along with a lucrative income of 3,000 deutsche marks a month.

In December 1943, at Koischewitz's urging, Gillars launched *Home, Sweet Home,* a program of nostalgic American music interspersed with morale-bruising comments directed at American soldiers. She aired the names of prisoners of war and mused aloud whether the soldiers' sweethearts were still faithful or were "running around with 4-Fs back home." Gillars embarrassed U.S. military security by exposing supposedly secret Allied plans. She inveighed against President Franklin D. Roosevelt, Jews, and the British: "Damn Roosevelt! Damn Churchill! Damn the Jews who made this war possible!" She tantalized American families with vague reports on POWs, and addressed American women with, "Well, girls, I'm on the German side because it's the gentile side. You must think I'm a little traitor." Gillars defended herself as a patriot trying to deter America from the wrong path, saying, "I love America, but I do not love Roosevelt and all his kike boyfriends." Though Gillars introduced herself as "Midge at the mike," American GIs dubbed her "Axis Sally."

In addition to the military intelligence supplied by the German army, Gillars personally gathered some program data herself. During June 1944, in the guise of an International Red Cross volunteer, she visited POW hospitals in France, recording messages that, she said, she would send home to the soldiers' anxious families. She then used the recordings for propaganda purposes.

The broadcast that became Gillars's undoing was the 11 May 1944 drama "Vision of Invasion," which was beamed to Allied troops preparing for D day. In the radio play written by Koischewitz, Gillars played an American mother who dreamed about her son's death on a ship just off the French coast. Against an audio background of anguished cries from wounded soldiers, an announcer intones, "The D in D day stands for doom . . . disaster . . . death . . . defeat . . . Dunkirk . . . Dieppe."

Gillars continued her propaganda broadcasts up to the fall of Nazism, when she tried to disappear. In 1946 the U.S. Army captured, arrested, and subsequently released her. In 1947 she was rearrested, and in August 1948 she was sent to Washington, D.C., where on 10 September 1948 federal prosecutor John M. Kelley, Jr., pressed charges of treason against her in the U.S. District Court. The government charged that Gillars "did adhere to the enemies of the United States," and supported "psychological warfare of the German government against the United States . . . with the intention of weakening civilian support of the war effort." Because she was indigent, Gillars was represented by a public defender, James J. Laughlin.

When the trial began on 24 January 1949, Gillars's defense consisted of six points. First, she claimed that she had continued working for Radio Berlin after war broke out only because she was "in constant fear of her life" and under "threat of the Gestapo." Second, she maintained that she was not responsible for her decisions because she had been under the uncanny charismatic influence of her lover and professional superior, Koischewitz. Third, her contributions to German propaganda notwithstanding, Gillars insisted that she had remained a loyal and patriotic American. She reminded the court that on her 8 December 1941 program she roundly denounced the Japanese attack on Pearl Harbor. For this act, she explained, she had come under special Gestapo scrutiny. She had publicly excoriated Japan, not knowing that a treaty bound Berlin to Tokyo. Frightened that she might be punished by being sent to a concentration camp, she ran to an immediate superior to ask what she should do. He allegedly scrawled on a piece of paper, "I hereby renounce my American citizenship," and said, "Sign this!" She explained that she had signed only under duress and in fear for her safety.

Fourth, Gillars offered a positive interpretation of her broadcast interviews of wounded POWs. Those programs, she said, comforted American and Canadian parents by letting them know which of their sons were alive. Fifth, she dismissed the charge that her radio work was treason. Her programs consisted of "mere words," she said, arguing that mere words cannot constitute treason because the Bill of Rights guarantees freedom of speech and expression. Sixth and finally, when it appeared to attorney Laughlin that the defense was not persuading the jury, Gillars tried a final ploy: since she had, on 8 December 1941, renounced American citizenship, she could not be tried for treason against a country of which she was not a citizen.

The verdict came in on 10 March 1949. The jury acquitted her of all but one count, finding her guilty on the single charge of participating in "Vision of Invasion." On 25 May 1949 federal judge Edward M. Curran passed sentence: $10,000 and from ten to thirty years in the women's federal prison in Alderson, West Virginia.

The *New York Times* editorially supported the sentence. For the "supposedly glamorous radio siren" who tried to sell American GIs "war-weariness and homesickness," jail was a better sentence than death, because it would keep her from becoming a martyr. Gillars described her life as a "chronicle of hunger, hardship, and frustration." She seemed a victim of ambition, love, psychological manipulation, and fear. Said the *Times,* "It is a story one would like to forget."

Gillars served twelve years in Alderson. Released in 1961, she moved to Columbus, Ohio, where she taught in a Catholic girls' school under the name Mildred Gillars Sisk. She earned a degree in speech in 1973 at Ohio Wesleyan College. She never married and had no children. She died of colon cancer.

★

Primary biographical information on Mildred Elizabeth Gillars, née Sisk, is included in the court records of her trial, *The United States of America vs. Mildred E. Sisk, also known as Mildred Elizabeth Gillars,* available in two formats. The first is *Federal Reporter 2d Series,* vol. 182 (1950), cited as 182F.2d 962. The second is at the Washington National Record Center (WNRC), Case File Number 1111CU48; Accession Number 21 70 B 5426; Box Number 75; Location Number: 16–7–8–6–5; pp. 3609–3617; 3706–3715. The *New York Times* covered the trial extensively with running reports in 1949. The *Times* also covered the legal appeal (20 May 1950) and Gillars's release from prison (8 Apr., 20 June, 11–12 July 1961). Popular treatments of her life include Masayo Duus, *Tokyo Rose: Orphan of the Pacific* (1979), and Dale P. Harper, "American-Born Axis Sally Made Propaganda Broadcasts for Radio Berlin in Hitler's Germany," *World War II Magazine* (Nov. 1995). Obituaries are in the *New York Times* (1 and 2 July 1988).

THEODORE N. THOMAS

GLEASON, Herbert John ("Jackie") (*b.* 26 February 1916 in New York City; *d.* 24 June 1987 in Fort Lauderdale, Florida), comedian of stage, screen, and television, best known for his broadly played comic characters, including Brooklyn bus driver Ralph Kramden of *The Honeymooners* television series and southern sheriff Buford T. Justice of the *Smokey and the Bandit* film series.

Jackie Gleason was born to a poor Irish-Catholic immigrant family in the Bushwick section of Brooklyn. His father, John Herbert Gleason, an insurance clerk, abandoned the family when Jackie was eight. Subsequently, his mother, Mae Kelly Gleason, worked as a subway token booth agent;

Jackie Gleason in *The Honeymooners.* ARCHIVE PHOTOS

she died when Jackie was sixteen. His only sibling, Clemence, had succumbed to tuberculosis in early childhood, when Jackie was three. Gleason attended Public School 73 in Brooklyn but dropped out of high school before his sixteenth birthday. He spent much of his time with the Nomads, a Brooklyn "athletic club," an organization that differed little from a street gang. He was a familiar figure in the neighborhood, well known for a sharp tongue, "dandy" dressing, and virtuoso pool playing, qualities that would be features of his professional persona. Though a voracious eater as a teenager, he excelled at football and boxing and did not then sport the heavyweight "spare tire" that would eventually become his trademark.

Early in life Gleason displayed a flair for the rough verbal play of the Brooklyn streets, and he seems to have set his sights on a career built around that talent. After appearing in several grade school and church plays, he took first prize with an original comedy routine in a neighborhood talent contest; this in turn led to a stint as master of ceremonies at the Folly Theatre, a Brooklyn vaudeville house. Upon leaving school in 1932 he began traveling around the New York metropolitan region, finding work as an emcee at amateur shows, as a carnival barker, and as a house comic at resort hotels in New Jersey and Pennsylvania.

In 1935, now known as "Jumpin' Jack" Gleason for the frenetic style of his presentation, he was hired to work as both an emcee and a bouncer at the Miami Club, a rough-and-tumble Newark saloon. There he gained notoriety for handling hecklers, both verbally and physically. He also got his first job in broadcasting, working as a part-time disc jockey at Newark radio station WAAT.

Gleason married Genevieve Halford, a dancer, in Newark in 1936; the couple had two daughters, Linda and Geraldine, his only children. The marriage was a rocky one, resulting in several legal separations and reconciliations. A permanent separation agreement was made in 1954; a final divorce would not take place until 1971.

The pace of the young comedian's career accelerated in 1938, when he won several bookings at Manhattan nightspots. This exposure brought a role in the 1940 Broadway musical *Keep Off the Grass.* In 1941 the film mogul Jack Warner caught Gleason's act at the Club 18. Responding to the comedian's loudmouthed, off-color performance, Warner signed him to a contract on the spot. At age twenty-five Gleason pulled up stakes and headed for Hollywood.

This early encounter with the movies proved disappointing. Warner could not even remember who the 250-pound comic was, attributing his signature on Gleason's contract to drunkenness. During a year as a studio player at Warner Brothers, Gleason was cast in minor roles in three films: *Navy Blues* (1941), *Larceny, Inc.* (1942), and *All Through the Night* (1942). His option was not renewed. Signing on with Twentieth Century–Fox, he appeared in *Springtime in the Rockies* and *Orchestra Wives* during 1942 but was again let go. This bitter experience in Los Angeles was never quite forgotten. Gleason would prefer to live and work on the East Coast, first in New York and later in Florida, for the balance of his career.

Returning to nightclub work, he took whatever stage roles he could get, and also tried his hand at radio, several times substituting for host Bob Crosby on the *Old Gold Hour,* a National Broadcasting Company variety program. Broadway appearances included *Artists and Models* (1943) and *Follow the Girls* (1944). In the latter he won some notice for his drag impersonation of a Navy Wave. He nonetheless found himself unable to gain a starring role on Broadway, and though he worked regularly at Manhattan cabarets, his career had reached a kind of plateau. As the *New York Mirror* columnist Jim Bishop wrote, "He was not big enough for the $5,000-a-week places."

In 1948 George ("Bullets") Durgom took over management of Gleason's career, thus beginning a mutually profitable long-term association. Within a year he had placed Gleason in a featured role with Nancy Walker in the musical *Along Fifth Avenue* (1949). But Durgom was looking beyond Broadway. At a time when many show business pundits had doubts about television, he saw the medium, with its overabundance of close-ups, as a natural showcase for the comic's extravagant mugging and gesturing.

Gleason's first encounter with television, however, was less than auspicious. In 1949 he was cast in the title role of the TV adaptation of a popular radio situation comedy, *The Life of Riley*. The Riley character was something of a kind-hearted blockhead, a role very much out of character for the quick-witted smooth talker. The show received poor notices and the series was quickly canceled, marking another West Coast failure. (It was later revived successfully with its radio star, William Bendix, in the title role.)

A far more advantageous genre for the display of Gleason's talents was the comedy-variety format. Vaudevillians and nightclub stand-ups, such as Milton Berle, Jack Carter, and Eddie Cantor, were achieving spectacular TV successes with this type of programming. Gleason got a key break in 1950 when he was signed by the Dumont Network as summer host of *Cavalcade of Stars*. Here he began to find a path to the stardom that had thus far eluded him. Making grandiose gestures at the camera, gawking at a continuous parade of long-legged showgirls, he moved seamlessly between stand-up sets and comedy blackout sketches, exhibiting what the critic Gilbert Seldes saw in him as "the traditional belief of heavy men in their own lightness and grace." After two episodes he was signed as permanent host of the show.

It was during his two years on *Cavalcade* that Gleason created and developed the repertoire of famous and beloved characters that he would reprise throughout most of his career. These included Ralph Kramden, a boisterous, blundering déclassé bus driver, eternally frustrated in his twin efforts to get rich quick and to assert dominance over an implacable wife; Reginald Van Gleason III, a vainglorious millionaire, conspicuously flaunting his worldly advantage with every facial expression and body movement; and the Poor Soul, a pantomime character wandering the streets of the city, inviting the world to make him its doormat. Lesser *Cavalcade* creations included Joe the Bartender, the fussbudget Fenwick Babbitt, and Loudmouth Charlie Bratton.

Dumont soon found itself hard-pressed to compete for the services of its biggest star. Gleason began to moonlight as an occasional host for other shows, including NBC's *Colgate Comedy Hour*. In 1952 the chairman of the Columbia Broadcasting System, William S. Paley, personally courted the star and signed him to an exclusive contract. The network agreed to cover production costs for a new Saturday night comedy-variety hour, the *Jackie Gleason Show,* and to pay the star a salary of $10,000 per week, which put Gleason among the elite performers in the new medium. CBS also built him a circular mansion in Peekskill, New York, costing hundreds of thousands of dollars; this was just one of a number of extravagant residences Gleason owned during his lifetime, reflective of his generally extravagant tastes. He would enjoy an exclusive relationship with CBS for the next eighteen years.

Given full authorial control of the program and a lavish budget to mount it, he honed the formula that had worked so well for him. Each week the star's royal entrance was preceded by a chorus-line number performed by the June Taylor Dancers, featuring a signature overhead kaleidoscope shot. His opening monologue included a visit from one of the "Glea Girls," who delivered his cup of "coffee," one sip of which would lead him to exclaim, "How sweeeeeeet it is. . . ." Asking the bandleader for "a little travelin' music," he danced wildly across the screen, freezing stage right to announce, "And awa-a-ay we go," leading the viewer off into an hour of sketch comedy and guest appearances by top musical acts.

"The Honeymooners" was the show's most popular sketch. Ralph's closed-fisted threat to send wife Alice (Audrey Meadows) "to the moon" during the couple's ritualistic arguments became a household phrase. The pairing of the nervous, quick-tempered Ralph with his dim-witted upstairs neighbor Ed Norton (Art Carney) yielded one of television's first great original comedy teams. The radical contrasts between Gleason's ostentatious, volatile gyrations and Carney's methodical, deliberate stylings suggest comparison with Laurel and Hardy.

During the 1955–1956 season, Gleason repackaged the sketch into a filmed half-hour situation comedy format so that he could reduce his hectic production schedule and pursue other projects. The thirty-nine episodes made for that season became one of the most successful commercial properties in show business history, continuing to air widely in reruns a half-century later. In 1985 dozens of the old "Honeymooners" skits from the Gleason comedy-variety shows were re-edited and released as *The Honeymooners: The Lost Episodes*.

As a television superstar Gleason attempted to rectify what he felt had been his less-than-grand treatment as a stage and screen performer. In 1959 he won a Tony Award for his performance in the stage musical *Take Me Along*. In the film *The Hustler* (1961) he was cast as the legendary pool player Minnesota Fats, performing his own pool shots for the camera; the role earned him an Academy Award nomination. *Gigot* (1962) was his most artistically ambitious project. He wrote, scored, and starred in this Chaplinesque film about an unkempt, deaf-mute Parisian street tramp who befriends and protects a prostitute and her young daughter. He also starred in *Papa's Delicate Condition* (1963). Gleason's finest dramatic work, however, was in *Requiem for a Heavyweight* (1962), in which he portrays Maish Rennick, a boxing manager caught between gambling debts to the mob and loyalty to a punch-drunk fighter.

Several new television projects were attempted as well. A 1961 game show, *You're in the Picture,* designed as a Groucho Marx–like showcase for his off-the-cuff wit, was canceled after just one episode, forcing the star to make an on-air apology. He then tried a half-hour prime-time talk program, interviewing such stars as Mickey Rooney and Jayne Mansfield, but it too failed in the ratings.

Gleason's least remembered but perhaps most remarkable achievement was in the record business. Although he did not read a note of music, he composed many songs (including his trademark television theme, "Melancholy Serenade"), humming the melodies for transcribers. In 1955, at his own expense, he assembled a large orchestra and, personally wielding the baton, recorded his syrupy arrangements of such standards as "I'm in the Mood for Love" and "My Funny Valentine." Unable to sell the album to a major company, the comedian paid Capitol to manufacture it for him. *For Lovers Only* sold more than half a million copies and became the first of some thirty-five popular Gleason "romantic music" LPs.

In 1962, after a short hiatus, he came back to television with *Jackie Gleason's American Scene Magazine,* which was supposed to break new ground in topical satire. This innovation, however, never materialized. Instead, Gleason returned to his comedy-variety formula, complete with the opening dance number and his old repertoire of sketch characters. The title soon reverted to the *Jackie Gleason Show*. In 1966 he was rejoined by Art Carney and Audrey Meadows for new hour-long episodes of *The Honeymooners*. These had little of the verve of the originals, but their nostalgic appeal to older viewers kept the show on the air through 1970, making Gleason one of the longest-lasting of the pioneer TV comedy stars. A second marriage, to Beverly McKittrick, on 4 July 1971, ended in divorce in 1974. The next year Gleason wedded choreographer Marilyn Taylor, the sister of June Taylor.

After spending much of the 1970s in enforced retirement, Gleason successfully returned to feature films as Sheriff Buford T. Justice in the Burt Reynolds comedy *Smokey and the Bandit* (1977), reprising the role in the 1980 and 1983 sequels it spawned. A new generation was introduced to Gleason as a cantankerous, drawling redneck lawman in a squad car. If Ralph Kramden had been culled from Gleason's Brooklyn childhood, Sheriff Justice was a comparable product of his later years in Florida. Following the success of these films, he began to work regularly in movies again, appearing in *The Toy* (1982), *The Sting II* (1983), *Nothing in Common* (1986), and *Izzy and Moe,* the latter a 1985 television movie that reunited him with Art Carney. Gleason died of heart failure and is buried at Our Lady of Mercy Catholic Cemetery in Miami, Florida.

★

Jim Bishop, *The Golden Ham: A Candid Biography of Jackie Gleason* (1956), is a worshipful fan piece written for maximum publicity at the height of Gleason's popularity but nevertheless contains many colorful anecdotes. Critical evaluations of Gleason's work appear in Gilbert Seldes, *The Public Arts* (1956), and David Marc, *Demographic Vistas* (1982). Donna McCrohan, *The Honeymooners' Companion: The Kramdens and the Nortons Revisited* (1978), is comprehensive to say the least. See also Bosley Crowther, review of *Gigot, New York Times* (28 Sept. 1962), and Richard Gehman, "The Great One," *TV Guide* (13, 20, 27 Oct. 1962), a three-part retrospective of Gleason's career. An obituary is in the *New York Times* (25 June 1987).

DAVID MARC

GODDARD, Paulette (*b.* 3 June 1905 [1911?] probably in Whitestone Landing [or possibly Great Neck], Long Island, New York; *d.* 23 April 1990 near Ronco, Switzerland), actress known for her glamorous lifestyle and versatility in Hollywood films of the 1930s and 1940s ranging from sophisticated comedies to popular melodramas.

Goddard, who was born Marion (or Pauline Marion) Levy, was the only child of Alta Hatch and Joseph Russell Levy (a drifter whose name was sometimes spelled Levee). She later claimed that her mother's maiden name was Goddard or that her father was a man named J. R. Goddard. However, Joseph Levy, who abandoned the family when she was

Paulette Goddard in *Vice Squad,* 1953. ARCHIVE PHOTOS

very young, was later able to prove that he was her father and even gain a weekly support check from his famous daughter. The girl briefly attended Mount Saint Dominic High School. While still quite young, she made important show business contacts at the posh Great Neck home of Charlie Goddard, whom she later identified as her uncle. After working as a fashion model, she landed a job as a Ziegfeld girl (billed as "Peaches") and adopted the name Paulette Goddard.

In 1927 Goddard briefly retired from show business to marry Edgar W. James, a wealthy lumber executive. However, life in Asheville, North Carolina, did not suit the vivacious Paulette and she filed for divorce in Reno, Nevada, in 1929. A $100,000 divorce settlement enabled her to move to Hollywood in style, driving a showy Dusenberg roadster.

She soon landed bit parts in a number of movies, but her 1932 introduction to Charlie Chaplin, the world's most renowned moviemaker, launched her career. The forty-three-year-old Chaplin, coming off two disastrous marriages, was enchanted by the beautiful, independent, and witty actress. The couple became inseparable and eventually married, possibly in 1936. (The date and even the fact of the marriage have been questioned.) Chaplin featured Goddard in his last silent film, *Modern Times* (1936). Her character, a waterfront waif, is the perfect counterpoint to Chaplin's tramp, who would otherwise break under the oppression of the modern industrial system.

Hollywood quickly took notice of the enchanting young actress and cast her in leading comedy roles. She played an adventuress in *The Young in Heart* (1938), a combative wife in 1939 in the all-star female cast of *The Women,* and Bob Hope's romantic foil in two popular comedy-mysteries, *The Cat and the Canary* (1939) and *The Ghost Breakers* (1940). In 1940 she again played a gamine, the innocent young Jewish laundress Hannah, in Chaplin's controversial *The Great Dictator.* As the film was being made, her marriage to Chaplin was breaking up. The couple divorced in 1942. Thirty years later, a silent film accompanist spotted her in a theater. "Miss Goddard," he called, "you must come to the Modern Art . . . I'm playing a series of Chaplin shorts." "Thank you," she replied, "but I've seen all I want to of Chaplin's shorts."

Goddard's career continued at full tilt. She was even featured in musicals. Paramount boasted that *Second Chorus* (1940) was "the first picture in which Paulette Goddard *dances*!" She gamely attempted to keep pace with her costar, Fred Astaire, in the production number "I Ain't Hep to That Step, But I'll Dig It." The studio's advertisements declared, "Fred's Best Yet! 'Cause He's Got Paulette!" Goddard was featured in *Pot o' Gold* the following year, opposite James Stewart, and reprised her partnership with Hope in *Nothing but the Truth.*

Goddard also starred in a number of adventure films, some directed by Cecil B. DeMille. The first was *North West Mounted Police* (1940). In 1942 DeMille cast her as a lusty Southern belle in *Reap the Wild Wind,* a role considered a consolation prize for her greatest disappointment: losing the role of Scarlett O'Hara to Vivien Leigh, after making it to the final round of the highly publicized *Gone with the Wind* competition. The 1943 war drama *So Proudly We Hail* featured Goddard as a worldly army nurse who finds true love with a Kansas farm boy.

In 1944 Goddard married the stage and film actor Burgess Meredith; they divorced in 1949. Meredith wrote and produced *Diary of a Chambermaid* (1946), directed by Goddard's good friend Jean Renoir. Many critics consider her role as a witty social climber in this film to be the best of her career. In that same year, *Kitty,* a sultry melodrama, was one of the top-grossing films and she was able to renegotiate her Paramount contract. A shrewd businesswoman, Goddard was one of the few stars who never used an agent.

In 1947 Goddard starred in her last DeMille role in *Unconquered.* On the set, conflict erupted with the director. Some observers believe that DeMille's lasting enmity helped short-circuit her career. Another problem arose as a result of her association with Chaplin and her open opposition to the House Committee on Un-American Activities. When challenged to admit to alleged communist leanings, Goddard retorted, "If anyone accuses me of being a Communist, I'll hit them with my diamond bracelets." In the early 1950s Goddard was reduced to a series of B movies, such as *Babes in Baghdad* (1952), with Gypsy Rose Lee. Her career, already declining, had ended by the mid-1950s.

Goddard was almost as famous for her personal life as she was for her roles. Her admirers included Clark Gable, Howard Hughes, and George Gershwin, who tried to win her away from Chaplin. Many presented her with fabulous jewelry, enabling her to amass a substantial fortune in gems since, as she noted, "I never give anything back." The writer Anita Loos, Goddard's close friend, claimed that she based the gold-digging Lorelei Lee of *Gentlemen Prefer Blondes* on Paulette. Loos later quipped, "Gentlemen prefer blondes until they get a load of Paulette." Robert Benchley added, "Here was a woman who could charm a rock."

In 1958 Goddard married the novelist Erich Maria Remarque, author of *All Quiet on the Western Front*. She lived in retirement with him until his death in 1970, except for appearing in an Italian film, *Gli indifferenti* (*Time of Indifference,* 1963). It was the forty-second—and final—film in which she appeared. Goddard was also a close friend of many artists. She often posed for the famed Mexican muralist Diego Rivera and, in the mid-1970s, became, for a brief time, a part of Andy Warhol's group. She emerged briefly from her private world in 1979 to sell the Impressionist art she had collected, explaining that she was tired of carting the works between her residences in Switzerland, New York, and California. The paintings sold for $3.1 million at a Sotheby's auction.

In the last twelve years of her life, Goddard was known for her philanthropies. She gave more than $3 million in scholarships to theater and film students at New York University's Tisch School of the Arts. She had earlier presented the university with the papers of Erich Remarque. John Brademas, the university's president, lauded "the vision and continued generosity" of "this remarkable actress." Goddard died of heart failure. Once described by Oscar Levant as "the most attractive and desirable woman in the world," she also possessed intelligence and vivaciousness that made her a successful movie star.

★

Joe Morella and Edward Z. Epstein, *Paulette: The Adventurous Life of Paulette Goddard* (1985), and Julia Gilbert, *Opposite Attraction: The Lives of Erich Maria Remarque and Paulette Goddard* (1995), are two chatty and gossipy biographies. An obituary is in the *New York Times* (24 Apr. 1990).

LOUISE A. MAYO

GOLDBERG, Arthur Joseph (*b.* 8 August 1908 in Chicago, Illinois; *d.* 19 January 1990 in Washington, D.C.), lawyer, government official, and U.S. Supreme Court justice.

Arthur J. Goldberg. ARCHIVE PHOTOS

Born in Chicago, Goldberg was the youngest of eight children of Joseph Goldberg and Rebecca Perlstein, immigrants from the Ukraine. His father, who died when Goldberg was eight, had come to the United States via Siberia before settling in Chicago, where he peddled produce from a horse with only one good eye. The family lived in a typical immigrant neighborhood, teeming with labor unrest and left-wing politics. Goldberg worked from the time he was twelve. After spending two years at Crane Junior College in Chicago and attending evening classes at De Paul University, he transferred to Northwestern University Law School. There he served as editor in chief of the *Illinois Law Review* and received a bachelor of science in law (B.S.L.) degree in 1929 and a J.S.D. in 1930, with the highest grades in the law school's history. On 18 July 1931 he married Dorothy Kurgans, an artist; they had two children.

Goldberg began his practice at a corporate law firm, but the work did not excite him. In 1933 he started his own firm, representing small manufacturers, and he became active in labor and liberal circles. Goldberg came to view employer-union agreements as a kind of "social contract." In 1938 he defended the Chicago Newspaper Guild, which had struck the Hearst papers. He gained an injunction, preventing the publisher from using violence against the strikers. When Hearst ignored the order, Goldberg brought contempt charges against him. The victory brought Goldberg wide attention, and he soon began to represent the Steelworkers Organizing Committee.

The advent of World War II aroused Goldberg's patriotic ardor. Because he did not meet the physical requirements for joining the U.S. Marine Corps, he instead served in the Office of Strategic Services (1942–1944). His labor contacts helped Goldberg organize anti-Nazi transportation workers behind enemy lines into a vast espionage network across Europe. He also recruited disaffected Germans as spies when the Allies invaded France, and he carried on intelligence work in Spain. The chief of Secret Intelligence wrote in recommending Goldberg for the Legion of Merit citation in 1945: "His most important contribution was getting organized labor, both in the United States and in Europe, actively participating in the unique undertaking of collecting intelligence and fomenting resistance to the enemy."

Shortly before the war ended, Goldberg returned to his Chicago practice, representing many labor unions affiliated with the Congress of Industrial Organizations. In 1948 he was appointed general counsel of the CIO and of the United Steelworkers of America. As a steady-tempered negotiator, Goldberg sensed when a specific position had lost its steam and a substitute must be found. He won many court cases, including a 1949 case that made pension rights a matter of contract negotiations. Goldberg was one of the chief architects of the CIO's merger with the American Federation of Labor. His suggestion of the new organization's name, American Federation of Labor–Congress of Industrial Organizations (AFL-CIO), broke the impasse to the merger. Goldberg was the chief drafter of its ethical practices code in 1955, which required annual audits of all funds and the adoption of rules governing local units' activities. This led to the expulsion of the Teamsters and other unions. In 1956 he published *AFL-CIO: Labor United,* which gave the official version of how the two sides reached agreement.

In 1958 and 1959 Goldberg worked closely with Senator John F. Kennedy in Kennedy's efforts to pass labor-reform legislation. Goldberg strongly supported Kennedy for the presidency in 1960, and upon his election, Kennedy appointed him secretary of labor. In his first day on the job, Goldberg settled a tugboat strike in New York Harbor. He went on to settle twelve national emergency labor disputes while secretary, many after all-night bargaining sessions at the Labor Department or the White House. He led the administration's initiative to expand substantially the coverage and raise the level of minimum wages. Viewing the "public interest" as his mandate, Goldberg pressed for a broad array of domestic programs—the training and relocation of workers, housing, a youth corps, and public facilities.

In early April 1962 both the union and the steel industry accepted a noninflationary settlement that Goldberg had helped negotiate. Then, without warning, on 10 April, the United States Steel Corporation announced it was raising prices $6 per ton. Other companies followed, and President Kennedy reacted angrily. Goldberg also felt he had been double-crossed. "You kept silent, and silence is consent," he told U.S. Steel head Roger Blough in the White House. Goldberg was one of Kennedy's leading advisers and negotiators as the administration applied pressure to force steel companies to roll back prices on 14 April.

Goldberg's Inauguration Day observation of the sordid condition of Pennsylvania Avenue in Washington, D.C., led to the establishment of the Council on Pennsylvania Avenue and the gradual improvement of the thoroughfare. At Kennedy's request, he served, in a rare procedure for a labor secretary, as arbitrator to resolve the Metropolitan Opera strike in New York in late 1961. "If the arts are to flourish, they must be relieved of total dependence upon the market place," Goldberg wrote Kennedy. This gave impetus to the establishment of the National Endowment for the Arts in 1965. Goldberg was active across so many fronts, ranging from increasing social security benefits to foreign policy with Italy, that he was called the "Davy Crockett of the New Frontier."

Kennedy appointed Goldberg to the U.S. Supreme Court on 29 August 1962 to replace Justice Felix Frankfurter, who had retired after suffering a stroke. Goldberg was the only candidate "really" considered, Attorney General Robert F. Kennedy said later, adding that he was "so broad-minded" and "understanding." "I gave away my right arm," President Kennedy wrote.

Goldberg's appointment shifted the balance on the Court from those led by Frankfurter, who held a restrictive belief of judicial power, to those who held an expansive view of the Constitution's mandates. His most important opinion for the Court was *Escobedo* v. *Illinois* (1964), in which the Court held that the admission of an incriminating statement by a defendant during the course of police questioning violated the Sixth Amendment's guarantee of right to counsel. Goldberg's reasoning foreshadowed the Court's decision two years later in *Miranda* v. *Arizona* that defendants had to be informed of their right to remain silent upon being arrested. In concurring opinions Goldberg often staked out new ground. In *Griswold* v. *Connecticut* (1965), he wrote that the Ninth Amendment expanded the concept of "liberty" in the due process clauses of the Fifth and Fourteenth Amendments beyond those rights specifically enumerated in the Constitution and the Bill of Rights. This opinion reflected his enthusiasm for new ideas and it remains the leading judicial exposition of that amendment. Goldberg called for an unconditional privilege to criticize the conduct of public officials in *New York Times* v. *Sullivan* (1964).

Goldberg abhorred capital punishment, and in his second term on the Court, he circulated a memorandum within the Court stating that the "institutionalized" taking of life by the state was "barbaric and inhuman." He analyzed application of the death penalty by type of crime and offender to suggest categories of cases in which its imposition might be found unconstitutional. Goldberg also wrote a brief dissent from the Court's refusal to hear *Rudolph* v. *Alabama* (1963), a case involving the death penalty. The effect, as he hoped, was to goad the civil liberties community to move to eliminate capital punishment.

In July 1965 Goldberg resigned from the Court to become U.S. ambassador to the United Nations. It ranks among the greatest personal blunders made by a public figure in American history. Although Goldberg had become somewhat restless on the Court ("The Justice's phone never rings," he complained), he did not yearn to abandon the bench and, in fact, hoped to be able to return eventually to the Court. Goldberg had earlier rejected President Lyndon B. Johnson's offers to become attorney general or secretary of health, education, and welfare. By persuading Goldberg to vacate his seat, Johnson achieved his goals of finding a

UN ambassador acceptable to liberal critics and of naming his old friend and adviser Abe Fortas to the Court.

Shortly before the death in 1965 of UN ambassador Adlai Stevenson, Johnson appealed to Goldberg's self-worth and assured him that he would have a key role in Vietnam decision-making. Goldberg acceded. "I had an exaggerated opinion of my own capabilities," he later said. "I also had the egotistical feeling . . . that I could influence the President to not get overly involved." Soon after coming to the UN, Goldberg had advocated a complete bombing halt in Vietnam in the hope it might lead to negotiations. Johnson turned him down, ignored his memoranda, and began to restrict his contacts with him. By May 1967 Goldberg was "most unhappy" at the UN and was ready to resign, but stayed on only because of the outbreak of the Middle East War that June. He was the principal draftsman of UN Resolution 242, which called for the withdrawal of Israeli armed forces from occupied territories and the recognition that every state in the area has a "right to live in peace within secure and recognized boundaries." It passed unanimously.

Goldberg resigned from the UN post in April 1968 and joined a New York law firm. In 1970, at loose ends, he ran as the Democratic candidate for governor of New York against Republican incumbent Nelson Rockefeller. Goldberg was an inept campaigner and lost by nearly 700,000 votes. "He just couldn't loosen up," noted one reporter. "He was a nice man, but a terrible candidate—dull and a bit pompous." In 1971 he published *Equal Justice: The Warren Era of the Supreme Court*. Goldberg represented the United States at the Belgrade Conference on Human Rights in 1977, after which he received the Presidential Medal of Freedom. He occasionally practiced law but mainly taught at many law schools after he left the UN; his exceptional drive and energy remained intact. Warm but direct, he was always sympathetic to "down-and-outers." "The copy of the Constitution, ever present in his breast pocket, fails to conceal the heart underneath," one student wrote. Goldberg died of a heart attack and was buried in Arlington National Cemetery, Arlington, Virginia.

★

Goldberg's papers are at the Library of Congress. His Supreme Court papers, at the Northwestern University Law School, will be available in the year 2000. Other material is at the John F. Kennedy and Lyndon B. Johnson Libraries. *The Defenses of Freedom: The Public Papers of Arthur J. Goldberg,* ed. Daniel Patrick Moynihan (1966), contains selections from Goldberg's writings, speeches, and opinions. David L. Stebenne, *Arthur J. Goldberg: New Deal Liberal* (1996), is a biography. See also Dorothy Goldberg, *A Private View of a Public Life* (1975); and Robert Shaplen, "Peacemaker," *New Yorker* (7, 14 Apr. 1962). His role in the Kennedy administration is treated in Theodore C. Sorensen, *Kennedy* (1965); Arthur M. Schlesinger, Jr., *A Thousand Days* (1965) and *Robert Kennedy and His Times* (1978); and Herbert S. Parmet, *JFK: The Presidency of John F. Kennedy* (1983). On Goldberg's appointment to the Court, see Edwin O. Guthman and Jeffrey Shulman, eds., *Robert Kennedy in His Own Words* (1988). On the Court during Goldberg's tenure, see Roger K. Newman, *Hugo Black: A Biography* (1994), and Bernard Schwartz, *Super Chief* (1983). Goldberg's resignation from the Court is discussed in John Kenneth Galbraith, *A Life in Our Times* (1981); Robert Dallek, *Flawed Giant* (1998); and Lyndon Johnson, *The Vantage Point* (1971). Obituaries are in the *New York Times* and *Washington Post* (20 Jan. 1990), and the *Chicago Tribune* (21 Jan. 1991). Oral history memoirs are at the Johnson Library and the George Meany Memorial Archives, Silver Spring, Maryland.

ROGER K. NEWMAN

GOLDMAN, Eric Frederick (*b.* 17 June 1915 in Washington, D.C.; *d.* 19 February 1989 in Princeton, New Jersey), historian and presidential adviser whose *Rendezvous with Destiny* (1952) won a Bancroft Prize.

Goldman was the only child of Harry Goldman, a fruit and vegetable salesman, and Bessie (Chapman) Goldman.

Eric F. Goldman, 1964. UPI/CORBIS-BETTMANN

His parents divorced when he was very young, and he was raised by his father in Baltimore. During an impoverished childhood, Goldman worked as a soda jerk, had a newspaper route, and served as a library page boy. In 1931 he graduated from Baltimore City College (actually, a public high school) and enrolled at Johns Hopkins University. A superior student in college, he skipped the B.A. degree entirely; Johns Hopkins awarded him an M.A. in 1935 and the Ph.D. in 1938, both in American history. While he lived in Baltimore, he was befriended by two prominent intellectuals, the journalist-pundit H. L. Mencken and the historian Charles A. Beard, both of whom gave hours of their time to advise the budding scholar.

From 1938 to 1940 Goldman held the rank of instructor at Johns Hopkins. In 1942 he joined the history faculty at Princeton University, where he became full professor in 1955 and was awarded the Philip and Beulah Rollins Chair in 1962. In the early 1940s he was a contributing editor for *Time* magazine; in the mid-1940s he reviewed regularly for the *New Republic*. In 1942, after two brief failed marriages, he married Joanna Ruth Jackson, a New York editor who proved to be a valuable assistant in his research and who died in 1980. He had no children.

Goldman began producing books early in his career. In 1941 he edited *Historiography and Urbanization: Essays in American History in Honor of W. Stull Holt,* paying tribute to his Johns Hopkins mentor. In 1943 both his M.A. and Ph.D. theses were published. The M.A. thesis, *John Bach McMaster, American Historian,* both traced and evaluated the career of a prominent pioneer in social history. The doctoral dissertation, *Charles J. Bonaparte, Patrician Reformer: His Earlier Career,* covered the life of a wealthy Baltimore aristocrat who was prominent in civic reform and Indian affairs and who held two posts in President Theodore Roosevelt's cabinet. Goldman collaborated with a former Johns Hopkins colleague, Frederic C. Lane, and with Erling M. Hunt of Columbia University Teachers College on a widely used high school textbook, *The World's History* (1947). Goldman's *Two Way Street: The Emergence of the Public Relations Counsel* (1948) gave special prominence to the role of Edward L. Bernays, the nation's leading figure in the field of public relations.

In 1952 Goldman's most illustrious work appeared. Recipient of Columbia University's Bancroft Prize for distinguished writing in American history, *Rendezvous with Destiny: A History of Modern American Reform* covered the great variety of reform thought manifested from the Gilded Age of the late nineteenth century to the presidency of Harry Truman. While highly appreciative of the reform tradition, the book's triumphalist tone was tempered by Goldman's concerns about liberalism's ethical relativism and special-interest politics.

Goldman's next book, *The Crucial Decade: America 1945–1955* (1956; enlarged edition, *The Crucial Decade—And After,* 1960), was contemporary history of the liveliest sort, showing the permanence of liberal reform—"the half century of revolution," he called it—and a newly developed internationalism that broke with the nation's penchant for quick foreign policy solutions. All during this time, and indeed until the last decade of his life, Goldman wrote frequently for popular magazines—for example, on seminal books in American history for the *Saturday Review of Literature* (1955), the follies of the 1950s for *Harper's* (1960), the pseudoemancipation of the American woman for *Holiday* (1961), and dilemmas of contemporary liberalism for *New Times* (1978).

In 1959, at the peak of his career, he began moderating a television forum called *The Open Mind,* a program first broadcast to New York and Boston NBC affiliates and then in 1960 over the entire network. The show was widely respected because of its prominent guests and lively conversation; Goldman stayed with it until 1967. In 1962 and 1966 it won the Emmy award of the New York Academy of Television Arts and Sciences.

In December 1963 Goldman informally began working for the administration of President Lyndon Johnson, and two months later he was appointed special consultant to the president. The post was an amorphous one; he possessed no specific responsibilities, but supposedly acted as "idea man" or "intellectual-in-residence." Goldman drafted countless memoranda, wrote speeches, and spearheaded a presidential scholars program. He promoted a White House Festival of the Arts, held in June 1965, that inadvertently turned into a forum for dissent against the Vietnam War. Afterward, official Washington virtually ignored him. Upon resigning in September 1965, Goldman returned to Princeton, where he wrote a memoir of his experience, *The Tragedy of Lyndon Johnson* (1969). He retired in 1985 and died of a stroke four years later; he was buried in Princeton Cemetery.

Goldman received many honors, including a Guggenheim Fellowship (1956–1957); an appointment as State Department lecturer in Europe (1953–1954) and India (1957); and designation as a McCosh Fellow (1962), the highest honor Princeton can bestow upon a professor. His commitment to reaching a wide public led to his serving as commentator on the *CBS Morning News* in 1975 and 1976. From 1962 to 1969 he was president of the Society of American Historians, cosponsor of the magazine *American Heritage.* In his prime he was five feet, nine inches, stockily built, and possessed brownish-gray hair.

Goldman was one of the leading intellectual and social historians in the United States. His work inspired several generations of scholars to conduct research in such areas as patrician reform, minority ethnic groups, "Asia-firstism" in foreign policy, the increasing prominence of science, and various aspects of popular culture. His unfinished projects included a work on race relations just before World War I and a four-volume history of the United States after 1900. Goldman was a man who always wore his learning lightly, and his greatest gift undoubtedly lay in his ability to convey complicated ideas and movements with clarity and vigor. Although often voted "best lecturer" by Princeton undergraduates, he never grandstanded, much less pandered to student prejudices. Viewing history as a high form of art, he possessed a superb literary style, a genius for interviewing, a knack for the revealing anecdote, and above all the capability of critiquing a nation and a tradition (that of liberalism) he deeply loved.

★

The papers of Eric F. Goldman are located in the Manuscripts Division of the Library of Congress. They contain a series of rough autobiographical notes dictated in the late 1980s. For a superior memoir by one of his former students, see Daniel J. Kevles, "Eric Frederick Goldman," in Patricia H. Marks, *Luminaries: Princeton Faculty Remembered* (1996). For Goldman's Washington service, see Donald R. Palm, "Intellectuals and the Presidency: Eric Goldman in the Lyndon B. Johnson White House," *Presidential Studies Quarterly* 26 (summer 1996): 708–724. An obituary is in the *New York Times* (20 Feb. 1989).

JUSTUS D. DOENECKE

GOODMAN, Benjamin David ("Benny") (*b.* 30 May 1909 in Chicago, Illinois; *d.* 13 June 1986 in New York City), clarinetist and orchestra leader who revolutionized jazz music, racial integration in music, and popular entertainment, becoming known as the King of Swing.

Goodman was the eighth of twelve children of Russian-Jewish immigrants, David Goodman, a factory tailor and stockyard worker, and Dora Grunzinski Goodman. Enrolled for music lessons at Kelelah Jacob Synagogue, ten-year-old Benny learned to play the clarinet because he was too small to hold a brass instrument. He took more lessons at Jane Addam's Hull House and with classical clarinetist Franz Schoepp of the Chicago Symphony Orchestra. At age twelve Goodman won a theater contest by imitating popular clarinetist Ted Lewis but probably was most influenced by the black New Orleans jazz clarinetists Jimmie Noone and Johnny Dodds. He and several friends imitated recordings of white clarinetists Leon Ropollo, of the New Orleans Rhythm Kings, and Doc Berendsohn, of Bailey's Lucky Seven. During his only year at Harrison High School (1922–1923), Goodman received his first union card (at age thirteen) and played jazz with boys from Austin and other Chicago high schools; they came to be labeled the Austin High Gang.

Late in 1923 Goodman left school to become a full-time

Benny Goodman. FRANK DRIGGS COLLECTION/ARCHIVE PHOTOS

musician, playing at Chicago ballrooms. His musical skills improved rapidly as he worked with other developing jazzmen, notably cornetist Bix Beiderbecke, whose crisp solos inspired him. Goodman's clarinet virtuosity led Ben Pollack to summon the sixteen-year-old to join his new band—the first large white jazz orchestra—at the Venice Ballroom in Los Angeles in August 1925. After the band returned to Chicago in 1926, Goodman made his first recordings with it. His reputation spread so quickly, through his work with the Pollack band and independent gigs, that in 1927 he was asked to record 100 jazz clarinet solo breaks that were transcribed and published. Moving with Pollack to New York in 1928, Goodman played at the Park Central Hotel and in the pit of the Broadway musical *Hello, Daddy* (1929). Occasionally playing alto or baritone saxophone, as well as clarinet, he also recorded with Red Nichols and pickup groups, sometimes accompanying vocalists and sometimes under his own name.

The twenty-year-old Goodman left Pollack in September 1929, but the onset of the Great Depression did not hurt him economically, as it did most other musicians, because of the great demand for his talents. Based in New York between 1930 and 1933, he performed popular, theater, dance, and jazz music for radio stations, motion picture sound tracks, recordings, and college dances, and in the pit band of *Girl Crazy* (1931). He provided accompaniment on recordings of the white female singers Lee Morse, Ruth

Etting, and Annette Hanshaw. Goodman accompanied some male vocalists on records; the most popular one he backed (not on records) was Russ Colombo, for whom he organized a band in 1932. Goodman made more than 200 recordings in 1931 alone, the most productive recording year of his career. Jazz remained his first love, and among many particularly noteworthy jazz recordings are several from a 1931 session with violinist Joe Venuti, guitarist Eddie Lang, and trombonist Jack Teagarden.

During the autumn of 1933 Goodman made several exceptional recordings, mostly under his own name. Jazz impresario John Hammond, Jr., persuaded him to assemble all-star groups of black and white jazzmen to accompany black female singers. In November he participated in such a group on the last recordings of blues giant Bessie Smith. Three days later he led a white band behind the singing of popular vocalist Ethel Waters and on the first recording of jazz singer Billie Holiday. In February 1934 Goodman added black saxophonist Coleman Hawkins to a band he formed to accompany white vocalist Mildred Bailey. In May he used black pianist Teddy Wilson on recordings that featured Teagarden. A projected European tour of a racially integrated all-star band failed to mature in the fall. Goodman was not a social reformer; he simply had great admiration for many black musicians, and in his youth he had been impressed by his teacher, Franz Schoepp, for accepting students regardless of race.

Assisted by Hammond, Goodman organized a thirteen-piece orchestra that played at Billy Rose's Music Hall in New York City from June to October 1934. The instrumentation of the sections became the norm after Goodman achieved success: three trumpets; two trombones; four reeds; and four in the rhythm section—piano, guitar, string bass, and drums. Unlike the leaders of the few white dance bands, Goodman wanted the arrangements, rhythms, and solos of his band to be rooted in jazz. For arrangements he relied mostly on black jazzmen, especially Fletcher Henderson but also Benny Carter, Edgar Sampson, and Jimmy Mundy. The band was one of three hired for a new nationwide radio program, *Let's Dance,* that began in December 1934. It was the "hot" band, the others being "sweet" and Latin American orchestras. Goodman hired Helen Ward as vocalist and Gene Krupa as the jazz beat drummer. The show was broadcast weekly until May 1935.

The Goodman band also made several recordings, as did Goodman independently, with small, integrated jazz groups. In July 1935 he was the only white musician in a Teddy Wilson septet that accompanied vocalist Billy Holiday on three records, and eleven days later he cut four sides with Wilson and Krupa as the Benny Goodman Trio, playing a unique type of chamber jazz. With Bunny Berigan on "hot" trumpet and Jess Stacy on piano, the full Goodman band then made a cross-country tour and received a mostly indifferent reception, forcing the band to play stock dance arrangements. Discouraged, Goodman decided to go down in glory when the tour reached the West Coast. On opening night, 21 August 1935, at the Palomar Ballroom in Los Angeles, he let the band loose with hot Henderson and Sampson numbers and was stunned by the wild response of the dancers. As a result of being in different time zones, the youthful clientele had heard the *Let's Dance* program earlier in the evenings than eastern radio listeners and, unknown to Goodman, had been eagerly anticipating his arrival.

Most jazz historians regard that night at the Palomar as marking the beginning of the Swing Era, despite the fact that several black big bands had been playing similar jazz for years—but without wide exposure among white audiences. In November 1935 the Goodman band opened at the Joseph Urban Room in Chicago's Congress Hotel for a monthlong engagement that proved so successful it was extended five more months and included live broadcasts. At the Congress the word "swing"—long used by jazz musicians—came into vogue in association with Goodman's music, and Goodman was popularly crowned its "king." Fans also began to refer to their idol as "BG," the initials painted on Krupa's bass drum. The swing craze was on, and other big bands quickly followed Goodman's example. Devotees danced the jitterbug and other jazz-inspired steps in response to the new music.

While at the Congress the Goodman orchestra played the first true jazz concert (no dancing allowed) on a Sunday in December 1935. Its success was repeated the following April, when Goodman brought Teddy Wilson from New York to reconstitute the Benny Goodman Trio. This first racially integrated public performance was such a musical triumph that Goodman hired Wilson and made the trio a permanent feature of the orchestra at dances and on records, thus inaugurating the band-within-a-band, which would be imitated by other orchestras. After a month in New York, the band went to Hollywood in June 1936 to appear in the motion picture *The Big Broadcast of 1937.* There Goodman discovered and hired black jazz vibraphonist Lionel Hampton for the Benny Goodman Quartet. Goodman had permanently broken the racial color line in music.

The band returned to the East Coast in September 1936 for several engagements, culminating in a several-month stay at the Hotel Pennsylvania's Madhattan Room in New York, plus weekly *Camel Caravan* broadcasts. Goodman added Ziggy Elman to the trumpet section, and he was joined by Harry James in January 1937. With Krupa laying down a solid drumbeat, reinforced by Stacy's piano, each hot number—"killer diller"—featured the highly disciplined brass and reed sections, each playing like a soloist, often juxtaposed against one another in riffs. Goodman,

James, and Elman blew their searing solos on the top of these riffs, between them, or backed only by Krupa's tom-toms, as on the showpiece tune "Sing, Sing, Sing." The excitement that this formula generated among listeners was not fully realized until the band played a Wednesday morning concert at New York's Paramount Theater on 3 March 1937. From the moment the band blasted "Bugle Call Rag," teenagers screamed and danced in the aisles—over 21,000 of them during several sets that day. Such ecstatic mob scenes, a first in American musical history, became the norm for the Benny Goodman Orchestra, which achieved the pinnacle of its form in the memorable Carnegie Hall concert of 16 January 1938. This first jazz program at the venerable hall gave jazz unprecedented respectability.

Goodman, a perfectionist and taskmaster, was so completely absorbed in his music that he was regarded by his sidemen variously as aloof, rude, preoccupied, insensitive, tactless. As a consequence the turnover in personnel was continuous; he settled for nothing but the very best from his musicians—and himself. When Krupa, James, Wilson, Hampton, and his recently hired vocalist Martha Tilton left during 1938–1940, he struggled to find musicians of equal caliber. The first major addition, the innovative Charlie Christian (a John Hammond discovery) on electric guitar in August 1939, resulted in the creation of the Benny Goodman Sextet. Its recordings often included bandleader Count Basie on piano. Trumpeter Cootie Williams and pianist Mel Powell played in the band and the sextet. (Christian, Basie, and Williams were black.) Arranger Eddie Sauter gave the orchestra a much more studied though no less swinging sound, enriched by vocalists Helen Forrest and Peggy Lee.

Between hotel and ballroom dates, many of them broadcast, and recordings, Goodman appeared with his band and/or combos in the motion picture *Hollywood Hotel* in 1938 and five more movies between 1943 and 1948, often with speaking roles. He and they also played on the sound track of a Disney cartoon feature, *Make Mine Music* (1946). Benny led combos in the Broadway musicals *Swingin' the Dream* (1939) and *The Seven Lively Arts* (1944–1945). In March 1942 he married Alice Hammond Duckworth, John Hammond's sister; she had three daughters from a previous marriage, and the Goodmans had two daughters of their own.

In 1938 Goodman began a concurrent career in classical music, performing in a recital at New York's Town Hall and recording a Mozart album with the Budapest String Quartet. He and violinist Joseph Szigeti commissioned a clarinet work from Bela Bartók, with whom they performed it at Carnegie Hall, Bartók on piano. In 1940 Goodman performed and recorded with the New York Philharmonic-Symphony; in 1947 he commissioned Aaron Copland and Paul Hindemith, and in 1954 Morton Gould, to write clarinet pieces for him. For the rest of his life Goodman occasionally played with symphony orchestras, usually performing works of twentieth-century composers, including Igor Stravinsky and Leonard Bernstein, with whom he appeared. Private study with several classical clarinetists culminated in lessons with Reginald Kell in 1949–1950. But Goodman never achieved the perfection in playing the classics that he had attained in jazz.

During his peak years Goodman had record contracts with Victor (1935–1939), Columbia (1939–1946), and Capitol (1947–1949), most of which were thereafter reissued on long-playing record format (LP). After 1950, labels varied between these and other recording companies, according to specific sessions and live performances.

Goodman disbanded his orchestra as a result of a back ailment in late 1942 and again over a contractual dispute in early 1944. He lectured at New York's Juilliard School of Music; led an exceptional combo with vibraphonist Red Norvo, pianist Wilson, and bassist Slam Stewart; and with another big band had his own weekly radio show in 1945 and 1946. The Swing Era had ended, so from 1947 through 1949 Goodman sought to emulate the new bebop sound with a big band and combos, mainly highlighting saxophonist Wardell Gray. He disliked bop, however, and abandoned the generally unsuccessful experiment in 1949, thereby marking the end of his permanent big band. Henceforth he organized an orchestra or a small jazz group only for specific gigs.

Goodman's musical reputation preceded his first performance abroad, at the London Palladium in 1949, and it continued to be enhanced until 1982: in western Europe, notably the 1958 World's Fair in Brussels; Southeast Asia, where he jammed with the saxophone-playing King Bhumibol Adulyadej of Thailand; South America; the Soviet Union in 1962, as the first jazz band officially invited to perform there; Japan; and Australia. At home his reputation was sustained by numerous concert, radio, and television appearances. The motion picture *The Benny Goodman Story* was released in 1956, with Steve Allen in the lead role. Goodman toured and performed until he made the last of his several thousand recordings in January 1986; he played his final concert the month before his death. He died of a heart attack and was buried in Stamford, Connecticut.

Benny Goodman elevated jazz music to widespread respect and acceptance because of his musical integrity, courage as a musical innovator and racial integrator, and pure clarinet genius. Even the casual listener was (and is) struck by the exuberance and happiness of his solos and the playing of his fellow musicians. His insistence on excellence gave jazz quality and dignity. His total absorption in the music made him serious, even shy, seemingly unapproachable; his absentmindedness was legendary. The only contemporary clarinet player to rival Goodman's command of the instrument was Artie Shaw, whom the public regarded as a challenger to Goodman's crown between 1938 and 1942 but who must be appreciated for his own genius. The first and quintessential purveyor of the swing idiom, Goodman produced a playing style on which no performer could improve, which proved to be a factor in the demise of the clarinet as a dominant instrument in jazz after the 1940s. The many Goodman recordings, preserving his freshness, creativity, and high artistry, are regarded as musical masterpieces.

★

The Benny Goodman archival collection of papers, arrangements, and recordings is deposited at Yale University. An early autobiography, written with Irving Kolodin, is *The Kingdom of Swing* (1939). The major biography is James Lincoln Collier, *Benny Goodman and the Swing Era* (1989). A popular account is Ross Firestone, *Swing, Swing, Swing: The Life and Times of Benny Goodman* (1993). Comprehensive biodiscographies are by D. Russell Connor, *Benny Goodman: Listen to His Legacy* (1988) and *Benny Goodman: Wrappin' It Up* (1996). Gunther Schuller devotes the first chapter of his authoritative *The Swing Era* (1989) to Goodman, whose orchestras are covered in George T. Simon, *The Big Bands* (1967). A tribute by Herb Caen, "Let's Dance, Sadly," from the *San Francisco Chronicle,* is reprinted in the International Association of Jazz Record Collectors *Journal* (Oct. 1987). Parts of Goodman's six motion pictures and several concerts are included on the 1993 biographical videotape *Benny Goodman: Adventures in the Kingdom of Swing* (Columbia) and the 1991 videotape *Benny Goodman USA-Europe* (VIDJAZZ). A detailed obituary is in the *New York Times* (14 June 1986).

CLARK G. REYNOLDS

GOODMAN, Percival (*b.* 13 January 1904 in New York City; *d.* 11 October 1989 in New York City), architect, author, educator, city planner, book illustrator, painter, and sculptor best known for his designs of numerous synagogues and public structures throughout the United States.

Percival Goodman, the son of Barnett Goodman and Augusta (Goodman) Goodman, was born into a middle-class family of German-Jewish origins. After failing in business, Barnett Goodman deserted his pregnant wife and three children in 1911. Augusta Goodman, often absent from home, supported her family as a traveling saleswoman in ladies' wear.

Despite his early poverty, Percival Goodman rose quickly to success in his chosen fields. He studied in Paris, France, at Beaux Arts Institute de Design, École Nationale Supérieure des Beaux Arts, and the American School of Fine Arts. From 1930 to 1933 he was a partner in the architectural firm of Whitman and Goodman. From 1933 on he was the head of his own architectural firm. On 28 Sep-

Percival Goodman, 1950s. PHOTO BY ARNOLD NEWMAN

tember 1944 he married Naomi Ascher; they had two children, Rachel and Joel.

In 1945 Goodman became a professor at Columbia University's School of Architecture and Planning; he was named professor emeritus on his retirement in 1972. He lectured at numerous colleges and universities. Beginning in 1930, he was an adjunct professor at New York University's School of Architecture. He was a lifelong member of the American Institute of Architecture.

In his lectures, as in his writings, Goodman stressed the importance of the role of architecture in improving society. As well as being public-spirited, he was devoted to his Jewish faith, and his architectural achievements can be roughly divided between structures designed for various Jewish organizations and for the general public. An innovator in the design of the modern synagogue, he produced more than fifty religious and community buildings for Jewish organizations throughout the United States, as well as houses, schools, and numerous bridges for his native city and the state of New York.

Goodman wrote numerous articles on art, architecture, and city planning for magazines and encyclopedias. In 1977 he published *The Double E,* a book stressing the need for city planners to be sensitive to ecology. Around 1986, apparently, Goodman completed *Choisy's Rationale of Architecture,* but this long translation and adaptation of the work of Auguste Choisy, a nineteenth-century French engineer, archaeologist, expert on classical architecture, and professor at École des Ponts et Chauseés (School of Bridges and Causeways) in Paris, was never published and remains in typescript.

Goodman's most famous publication, *Communitas: Means of Livelihood and Ways of Life* (1947; rev. eds., 1960 and 1990), coauthored with his brother, the writer Paul Goodman, became a seminal work of utopian city planning. Certain authors and reference works discussing Paul Goodman, author of the best-selling *Growing Up Absurd: Problems of Youth in the Organized Society* (1960), incorrectly either downplay the elder brother's contribution to *Communitas* or fail to cite him entirely when discussing the book. Therefore it must be emphasized that Percival Goodman, the professional expert in city planning, is *Communitas*'s primary author. Many ideas regarding utopian city planning later attributed to Paul Goodman first saw light in collaborative work with Percival Goodman. (This includes the often-cited 1961 essay "Banning Cars from Manhattan," anthologized in Paul Goodman's *Utopian Essays and Practical Proposals,* 1962.)

Communitas, a series of extended essays, considers city planning as "a choreography of society in motion and in rest." Part I, "A Manual of Modern Plans," reviews and critiques major contemporary city planning schemes. The Goodmans see these schemes as lacking in philosophical perspective and, therefore, in thinking that is "concrete and central." By this they mean "directly attending to the human beings, the citizens of the city, their concrete behavior and their indispensable concerns, rather than getting lost in traffic problems, housing problems, tax problems, and problems of laws enforcement. It is concrete to plan work, residence, and transit as one problem."

Percival and Paul Goodman viewed the city from an almost classical Greek perspective, seeing community as based on the symmetry of self-containment. Part II of *Communitas* offers "Three Community Paradigms," which the authors emphasize are not plans but models. "A City of Efficient Consumption" satirizes mass consumption capitalism but still suggests how it could be managed with more practicality (namely turning the city into a vast department store). "A New Community: The Elimination of the Difference Between Production and Consumption" is the Goodmans' own utopian scheme "where the producing and the product are of a piece and every part of life has value in itself as both means and end." "Planned Security and Minimum Regulation" is concerned with "the direct production of subsistence goods" and "has obvious applications to regions that are poorly industrialized but densely populated."

The appendix to *Communitas,* originally published in the *New Republic* in 1944, is a radical scheme for transforming New York City into a self-contained community. In it Percival and Paul Goodman propose, among other things, the redevelopment of waterfront areas for swimming and other recreations. As a practical city planner, Percival Goodman conducted many studies around riverfront improvements in New York City.

In the posthumously republished 1990 edition of *Communitas,* Percival Goodman reflects on his and his brother's ideas and their book's impact in the afterword, "Communitas Revisited."

Besides contributing his substantive expertise, Percival Goodman illustrated *Communitas.* He also illustrated a number of his younger brother's books, including *Don Juan: Or, the Continuum of the Libido* (1979) and *Parents' Day* (1985). Also a painter and a sculptor, Goodman exhibited many of his creations.

Goodman died of lung cancer; he was buried at Salem Fields Cemetery in New York City.

★

A collection of Percival Goodman's papers, including original manuscripts, drawings, and photographs of Goodman, is at the School of Architecture, Planning, and Preservation, Columbia University. Biographical information is in Kingsley Widmer, *Paul Goodman* (1980). See also George H. Godwin, "Design of a Modern Synagogue: Percival Goodman," *American Jewish Archives* 45 (spring-summer 1993): 31–71. An obituary is in the *New York Times* (12 Oct. 1989).

ALEX SHISHIN

GORDON, Dexter Keith (*b.* 27 February 1923 in Los Angeles, California; *d.* 25 April 1990 in Philadelphia, Pennsylvania), jazz saxophonist, composer, and actor who was a major figure of influence during the bop era.

The only child of Frank Alexander Gordon, a physician, and Gwendolyn Gordon, he was sometimes referred to as Long-Tall Dexter because of his adult height of six feet, five inches. The elder Gordon, whose patients included Duke Ellington and Lionel Hampton, was a jazz fan who took his son to concerts and arranged for him to study music.

Beginning at age thirteen, Gordon took up music theory and harmony as well as the clarinet. At age fifteen he began taking lessons on the alto saxophone, and in 1940 he withdrew from Jefferson High School in Los Angeles to pursue a career in jazz music. He joined a local band, the Harlem Collegians, playing tenor saxophone, before going on the road with Lionel Hampton's group for a three-year stint beginning in December 1940. Following this, Gordon re-

Dexter Gordon, *c.* 1979. JANET SOMMER/ARCHIVE PHOTOS

turned to Los Angeles, where he joined Lee Young's band. (Lee was the brother of saxophonist Lester Young, who was a major influence on Gordon's playing style.) He then spent six months in 1944 with the big band of trumpeter Louis Armstrong. While employed with this group, Gordon appeared briefly in the movies *Atlantic City* (1944) and *Pillow to Post* (1945).

After playing with Armstrong, Gordon next spent eighteen months in 1944 and 1945 with Billy Eckstine's big band. During this time he performed his first recorded solo, "Blowing the Blues Away." Subsequently, he appeared with Charlie Parker in New York City, with Cee Pee Johnson in Honolulu, and on the West Coast with various small groups, including that of Wardell Gray, an important saxophone player in the late 1940s and early 1950s.

At this point in his career, Gordon's swinging style of playing was out of favor, having been replaced by the so-called cool jazz of the West Coast in the 1950s. This factor, together with Gordon's heroin addiction, plunged him into obscurity as a musician, especially when he was sent to prison for heroin possession from 1952 to 1954 at Chino, a minimum-security facility in California. However, he continued to perform and appeared in a movie about prison life called *Unchained* (1955), in which he was filmed playing the tenor saxophone, although the sound of the instrument was dubbed. He had just been released from Chino when his friend Wardell Gray died. In 1955 Gordon recorded again for the first time in three years.

In 1960, through the help of playwright Carl Thaler, Gordon became part of the Los Angeles company of a play called *The Connection*, about heroin addiction. For this, Gordon wrote the score, led an on-stage quartet, and had a speaking role. In the same year, he recorded for Jazzland Records, his first such appearance in five years. In the following year, he went to New York City to record for the Blue Note label. He was, however, still on parole, and so was limited in the amount of time that he could spend away from Los Angeles. His parole period ended in 1961. In August 1962 Gordon traveled to London, opening at Ronnie Scott's famous jazz club the following month. This marked the start of a much more prosperous period in his life, when he began to receive critical recognition for his work.

Gordon moved from London to Paris, and then to Scandinavia, finally settling in Denmark, where he lived for several years. He became a resident of Valby, a suburb of Copenhagen, and married a local woman, Fenja, with whom he had a son, Benjamin. Not only did he travel and perform widely in Europe, but he made regular trips to the United States in the 1960s and early 1970s to record and to see his family. A 1964 production of *The Connection*, staged in Copenhagen, was canceled after four performances.

The period from 1962 to 1976 was musically rewarding for Gordon, despite his arrest in Paris during 1966 on a charge of peddling drugs. His Danish friends backed him in his successful defense against the charge, enabling him to return to Copenhagen. In 1971 Gordon was honored with the Down Beat Critics' Poll award for tenor saxophone.

In October 1976 Gordon returned to New York City and began a period of touring and recording. He went back to Denmark early in the following year and then to London. In the 1980s he made regular trips between the United States and Europe. By 1982, although he had not entirely severed his European connections, his plans to live with his Danish wife and son in the United States did not work out. He obtained a divorce, and his wife and son returned to Valby. In the meantime, he continued to reap public recognition. In June 1978 he was invited by President Jimmy Carter to perform at a "Jazz on the White House Lawn" program in the company of other major jazz figures. He also appeared on National Public Radio.

In the latter part of 1984, Gordon became gravely ill and was hospitalized. This condition was largely a result of his years of abuse of drugs and alcohol. At this time, he was cared for by Maxine Gregg, who had become his personal manager upon his return to the United States. They were married shortly before Gordon's death.

While recovering from this near-fatal illness, Gordon was approached by the director Bertrand Tavernier and producer Irwin Winkler to star in the movie *'Round Midnight*, a true-to-life depiction (not a romanticized view) of the life of a jazz musician. Although not fully recovered from his illness, during July and August 1985 Gordon taped music for the film. In 1986 an international team of critics unanimously picked *'Round Midnight* as the best entry at the Venice Film Festival. In 1987 Gordon was nominated for an Academy Award for best actor for his performance in the film.

Gordon received many other honors toward the end of his life. In 1987 he was the featured soloist at a performance with the New York Philharmonic Orchestra, following his receipt the previous year of a United States Congressional Commendation. Gordon also was awarded a National Endowment for the Arts grant for lifetime achievement. The College of Medicine at Howard University established a Frank Alexander Gordon Scholarship honoring the elder Gordon, who was one of California's first African-American physicians. The university's Department of Fine Arts paid Dexter Gordon tribute with a concert performance by the institution's Jazz Ensemble, and the National Endowment for the Arts presented him with a Jazz Masters Award.

While at the height of his popularity as a performer, Gordon died as a result of kidney failure (he was being treated for cancer of the larynx at the time). His body was cremated and the ashes scattered in the Hudson River by his widow, Maxine Gregg. A "Eulogy in Jazz" was held in Harlem in the musician's memory.

Gordon's stage performance was as distinctive as his playing style. He often held his saxophone horizontally in both hands, as if presenting it to the audience, and he would introduce numbers by reciting the song's words with his deep-voiced, slow delivery. As other bop musicians sometimes did, he often interpolated phrases from other songs into the one he was playing: for example, a phrase from "Blues in the Night" would find its way into "Society Red"; a segment of "Five O'Clock Whistle" would slip into "Three O'Clock in the Morning." His style of playing notably influenced such reed players as Sonny Rollins and John Coltrane.

★

Stan Britt, *Dexter Gordon: A Musical Biography* (1989), is the only full-length study of the subject and contains an extensive discography by Don Tarrant. Ira Gitler, *Jazz Masters of the Forties* (1966; rev. ed. 1983), contains a segment on Gordon, as does Michael Ullman, *Jazz Lives: Portraits in Words and Pictures* (1980), which also contains a chapter on Maxine Gregg. Ira Gitler, *Swing to Bop: An Oral History of the Transition in Jazz in the 1940s* (1985), contains many quotations from interviews with Gordon. Jenny Armstrong, "Dexter Gordon: Transcontinental Tenorist," *Down Beat* (22 June 1972), is an interview with the musician emphasizing his 1971 Down Beat Critics' Poll honor; it was reprinted in *Down Beat: Sixty Years of Jazz* (1995). Burt Korall provided a cover story on Gordon for the *International Musician* (Apr. 1977): 10, 22–23. Robert Palmer, "Gifted Saxophonists Reveal Bebop as an Evolving Idiom," *New York Times* (2 Feb. 1986), contains an analysis of Gordon. An obituary is in the *New York Times* (26 Apr. 1990), as is an account of the memorial service (8 May 1990). Some of Gordon's performances may be found on compact disc: *Billy Eckstine: Mr. B. and the Bebop Band* (1996); *The Best of Dexter Gordon: The Blue Note Years* (1988); and *Dexter Gordon: The Other Side of "'Round Midnight"* (1986). Dexter Gordon appeared in concert on *Harvest Jazz* (1983), broadcast on the Arts and Entertainment Television network in 1985. This provides excellent coverage of the subject's style, music, and appearance.

BARRETT G. POTTER

GOULDING, Ray(mond) Walter (*b.* 20 March 1922 in Lowell, Massachusetts; *d.* 24 March 1990 in Manhasset, New York), entertainer who was one half of the comedy team of Bob and Ray, who appeared on radio and television as well as in motion pictures and on Broadway for more than forty years.

The son of Thomas M. Goulding, a textile mill worker, and Mary Philbin, Ray Goulding had two older brothers, an older sister, and a younger sister. After graduating from Lowell High School in 1939, he obtained a job as an announcer at a local radio station, where for $15 a week he performed under the name Dennis Howard. The next year, he moved to WEEI in Boston as Ray Howard (to distinguish himself from his brother who was working in Boston radio as Phil Goulding). In 1942 Ray joined the U.S. Army and served as an instructor at the Officer Candidate School at Fort Knox, Kentucky, where he was promoted to captain. He married Mary Elizabeth Leader, a dietician, on 18 May 1945; they had four sons, Raymond, Jr., Thomas, Bryant, and Mark, and two daughters, Barbara and Melissa.

On leaving the service after World War II in 1946, Goulding obtained a job at Boston's WHDH. Now using his real name, Goulding read the hourly news reports on disc jockey Bob Elliott's morning show. Elliott later recalled that he and Goulding had not planned on becoming a comedy team or a team of any sort. But "we started bantering from time to time and it got longer and longer." Finally they joined together to produce *Matinee with Bob and Ray* on WHDH, where they developed their many characters and unique satirical repertoire.

In July 1951 Charles C. Barry, a National Broadcasting

Ray Goulding (*right*) and Bob Elliott, *c.* 1951. UPI/CORBIS-BETTMANN

Company vice president, brought Goulding and Elliott to New York City, where the *Bob and Ray Show* soon appeared in several radio time slots, both locally and nationally, for up to seventeen hours a week. They took New York by storm with their vast array of odd characters and their gentle satires of the media, advertising, and the human condition in general. Goulding, whose voice was deeper than Elliott's, nonetheless generally played the women characters in their sketches, as well as most of the peculiar assortment of reporters who "called in" to Bob from all over the world.

Bob and Ray poked fun at soap operas with their long-running show within a show, "Mary Backstayge, Noble Wife," a play on the popular serial *Backstage Wife,* which featured the character Mary Noble. They also created "Mr. Trace, Keener than Most Persons," based on the radio mystery *Mr. Keen, Tracer of Lost Persons.* Ray's Mary Magoon often presented recipes to listeners, including her singular frozen-ginger-ale salad. Among other famous bits were the periodic offerings of bizarre items from the Overstocked Warehouse and advertisements for a restaurant in Skunk Haven, Long Island, that offered only toast. Occasionally, they ventured into serious politics, most notably with a devasting critique of Senator Joseph R. McCarthy.

The writer Kurt Vonnegut, Jr., wrote of their humor in his preface to the duo's *Write if You Get Work: The Best of Bob and Ray* (1975), "They feature Americans who are at most fourth-rate or below, engaged in enterprises which, if not contemptible, are at least insane. . . . Man is not evil, they seem to say. He is simply too hilariously stupid to survive."

The team worked on several other New York radio stations, including WINS and WHN, before becoming critics at large for the *Monitor* weekend radio show on the NBC network in 1956. They became regulars on National Public Radio in 1981.

In 1954 Bob and Ray branched out by taking their act on ABC television, a medium that did not suit them as well as radio. Many of their routines played better when the visuals were left to the imagination. Their television show featured most of the radio gang, along with a new soap opera, "The Life and Loves of Linda Lovely," which featured Audrey Meadows and Cloris Leachman.

The team earned even more renown as Bert (Elliott) and Harry (Goulding) Piel in a series of witty commercials for the Piels Beer company, beginning in 1956. Their path-breaking approach to humorous and sometimes self-deprecating advertising earned them so much acclaim that the company took out newspaper advertisements to inform readers when its spots would be aired. Unfortunately for Piels, the advertisements were more popular than the beer, whose sales remained flat despite the popularity of Bert and Harry.

Bob and Ray also appeared in the motion pictures *Cold Turkey* (1969) and *Author! Author!* (1982), performed on Broadway in *Bob and Ray, the Two and Only* (1970), produced several recordings, and wrote *Bob and Ray's Story of Linda Lovely and the Fleebus* (1960), *From Approximately Coast to Coast: It's the Bob and Ray Show* (1983), and *The New! Improved! Bob and Ray Book* (1985).

The team won a George Foster Peabody Award as the "foremost satirists in radio" for their work in 1951 and a second Peabody for their 1956 shows. In 1981 they were inducted into the National Broadcasting Hall of Fame.

During their last decade together in the 1980s, Bob and Ray performed two Carnegie Hall shows (1984) and produced commercials for such corporations as Hartford Insurance Company and IBM. They were less successful at finding work on the commercial networks, where Ray complained that "the people in power are twenty-eight years old . . . [and] don't know us from a hole in the wall" and wanted the team to add off-color material to the duo's always literate and polite comic inventions. Their legions of devoted fans have never forgotten the way they signed off their shows, with Ray saying "Write if you get work" and Bob saying "Hang by your thumbs."

Ray Goulding retired because of ill health in 1988 and died two years later at his home in suburban Manhasset,

New York, of kidney failure. He is buried in Locust Valley, New York.

Bob and Ray constituted a rare show-business duo who seemed to genuinely like one another and who apparently had no interest in performing separately. Elliott recalled, "I think the main reason we worked well together was that we really appreciated each other, as opposed to some comedy teams. We had no rivalry, just great mutual respect. We always got along well." Their relationship stood the test of endless hours spent creating a unique style that attracted a wide following for more than four decades.

★

No full-length biographies of Goulding have been written, and there are no family archives or papers. The most useful articles are George Sessions Perry, "Are They the Funniest Pair on the Air?," *Saturday Evening Post* (25 Dec. 1954); "The Boys from Boston," *Newsweek* (10 Sept. 1951); and Leonard Skenazy, "Pair for Parody," *Advertising Age* (9 Mar. 1987). An obituary is in the *New York Times* (26 Mar. 1990).

MELVIN SMALL

GRAHAM, Sheilah (*b.* 15 September 1904 in Leeds, England; *d.* 17 November 1988 in Palm Beach, Florida), Hollywood gossip columnist whose 1958 best-seller, *Beloved Infidel,* described her three-and-a-half-year love affair with the writer F. Scott Fitzgerald.

The daughter of Jewish immigrants, Sheilah Graham was born Lily Shiel and changed her name around the time of her first marriage in 1923. The youngest of six children, she moved with her family to the East End of London when she was a child. The death of her father, a tailor, impoverished the family, and she spent eight years in the Jews Hospital and Orphan Asylum at Norwood, becoming head monitor and captain of the girls' cricket team. Offered a scholarship to attend high school and college, she returned home instead to nurse her mother, who was dying of cancer. This missed opportunity caused her to feel intellectually inferior (and may indirectly explain why the two children born to her in the 1940s became an English professor and a professional writer, respectively).

After her mother's death and her employment in various menial jobs, Lily, at seventeen, moved to the West End of London, where the Savoy Hotel had long symbolized worldly glamour. She became a toothbrush demonstrator at Gamage's department store and met John Graham Gillam, twenty-five years her senior. Lily's first Pygmalion, he corrected her manners and cockney speech. They married in 1923.

The newly named Sheilah Graham auditioned before Charles B. Cochran (known as the British Ziegfeld), then appeared in *One Dam Thing After Another* (1927). Blond and green-eyed, with high cheekbones, she was soon voted "the Most Beautiful Chorus Girl in London." Her career as a journalist commenced when the *Daily Express* published "'The Stage-Door Johnny' by a Chorus Girl." Then, after a nervous breakdown in 1929, she gave up the stage for writing, soon persuading the *Saturday Evening Post* to commission her to interview William M. Aitken, the British politician and newspaper magnate. Graham's "society period" followed, and she became friendly with, among others, the Marquess of Donegall. She reinvented herself, telling stories about a refined bohemian childhood in the London district of Chelsea with her parents John Lawrence and Veronica Roslyn Graham.

Sheilah Graham. ARCHIVE PHOTOS

On a 1931 trip to New York she met John Wheeler, publisher of the North American Newspaper Alliance, and four years later she became his Hollywood columnist. Years later she would write that she sometimes had to laugh as she sat at her typewriter banging out her column, "a witch's brew . . . to give indigestion to people I don't like or to those who I think have slighted me, the great me. It all seems quite absurd and unreal." Nevertheless, she was soon well-established as part of an "unholy trio" of Hollywood gossip columnists (with Hedda Hopper and Louella Parsons), whose barbs and potshots were seen as part of the price of fame.

Graham and her first husband were divorced in 1937 (although she would continue to send him monthly checks until his death in 1965). In that same year, on Bastille Day, 14 July, while celebrating her engagement to Lord Donegall at Robert Benchley's bungalow at the Garden of Allah Hotel in Hollywood, Graham met F. Scott Fitzgerald. Subsequently that summer, she told Fitzgerald (whose wife, Zelda, had been institutionalized) her well-rehearsed lies. But the truth that followed elicited his sympathy, for in Fitzgerald's acclaimed novel *The Great Gatsby,* James Gatz had become Jay Gatsby, just as in real life Lily Shiel had become Sheilah Graham; Gatsby sprang from the "Platonic conception of himself" just as Graham claimed, *"Je suis mon ancêtre."* "Orphans" both, they rose from impoverished obscurity to opulent eminence via a process of transformation involving powerful personages. Eventually, Graham would appear as the heroine Kathleen in Fitzgerald's final, fragmentary novel, *The Last Tycoon.*

Graham broke her engagement soon after meeting Fitzgerald, and they began the love affair that would last until his death. The affair is depicted more accurately in an account by her son, *Intimate Lies,* than in *Beloved Infidel,* thanks to handwritten annotations she made in a copy of the latter, in which she finally addressed "omissions," "inaccuracies," and "lies." Graham regarded Fitzgerald (whom she would later call her children's "spiritual" father) as a "split personality"—Dr. Jekyll when sober, Mr. Hyde when drunk. *Intimate Lies* recounts numerous binges during which the usually fastidious novelist exhibited "the sly leer, the unshaved face, filthy clothes, and occasional four letter word." The worst behavior toward Graham occurred about a year before his death, when he slapped her, then exposed the secrets of her past to his nurse, chanting "Lily Shiel" and "She's a Jew." The long separation that took place following this and other incidents deeply affected Fitzgerald.

Although Fitzgerald was a puritan and a hypochondriac as well as an alcoholic, the Jekyll side manifested itself often enough to merit the repeated forgiveness of Graham, who could not resist his "all-pervasive charm." A gentle and attentive lover, he called her pet names, sent flowers, wrote funny notes, read poetry aloud, and created their "college of one," in which he drew up for her a list of the books she should read to fill the gaps in her education.

On 21 December 1940 Fitzgerald suffered a fatal heart attack in Graham's Hollywood apartment at 1443 North Hayworth Avenue. After his death, she "had no status in his life, no legitimacy; she could not even go to his funeral." Upon returning to that apartment nearly half a century later, the eighty-two-year-old Sheilah Graham would discover that she still "had not gotten over the death of Scott Fitzgerald."

After Fitzgerald's death Graham returned to England to work as a World War II correspondent. On 9 January 1941 she married Trevor Westbrook, an Englishman; they were divorced in 1946. Both of Graham's children were born during this marriage and thought that Westbrook was their father. Although Graham was ultimately unsuccessful in disguising their Jewish heritage from her children, she almost succeeded in hiding their paternity. Years later, in *One of the Family,* Wendy Fairey, Graham's daughter, traced hers to the British philosopher A. J. ("Freddy") Ayer; Robert Westbrook's father remained unknown.

Meanwhile, Graham resumed her Hollywood column after the war ended in 1945. She also wrote for magazines and had a radio show, and then a television show. On Valentine's Day 1953 she married Stanley ("Bow Wow") Wojtkiewicz; they were divorced after three years. In the 1960s, in her heyday, her column was syndicated in 178 newspapers, more than either of her rivals, Hopper and Parsons. During these years she also wrote a number of books. She died of congestive heart failure, and her ashes were scattered over the Atlantic.

★

Except for an early mystery novel titled *The Gentleman Crook* (1933), all of Graham's works are autobiographical, focusing for the most part on her relationship with Fitzgerald or Hollywood. They are *Beloved Infidel: The Education of a Woman,* with Gerold Frank (1958), *The Rest of the Story* (1964), *College of One* (1966), *Confessions of a Hollywood Columnist* (1969), *The Garden of Allah* (1970), *A State of Heat* (1972), *How to Marry Super Rich* (1974), *The Real F. Scott Fitzgerald* (1976), *The Late Lily Shiel* (1978), and *Hollywood Revisited* (1984). Both her children wrote books that throw new light on her life and career: Wendy Fairey, *One of the Family* (1992), and Robert Westbrook, *Intimate Lies: Her Son's Story: F. Scott Fitzgerald and Sheilah Graham* (1995).

JOHN KUEHL

GRANT, Cary (*b.* 18 January 1904 in Bristol, England; *d.* 29 November 1986 in Davenport, Iowa), actor who epitomized elegance and sophistication; his extraordinary good looks and peerless comedic flair made him a major film star for more than three decades.

Born Archibald Alexander Leach, Grant was the only surviving child of Elias J. Leach, a presser in a clothing factory, and Elsie (Kingdom) Leach. The family was poor. His father was a drinker and a womanizer, and his mother, who had never emotionally recovered from the death in infancy of her first son, in 1899, was both overly harsh and overly protective of her son Archy. When he was nine or ten, his father moved to Southampton for six months, ostensibly to take a higher-paying job; soon after he returned, Grant's mother vanished. Twenty years later, Grant learned that she had been confined in a sanatorium for the mentally ill. He also discovered, long after the fact, that he had a half-brother named Eric Leslie Leach, born to his father and a woman named Mabel Bass.

Cary Grant. TED SENNETT

Grant was raised in Bristol and attended the Bishop Road boys' school in Bristol before winning a scholarship to the Fairfield secondary school in Somerset in 1915. Increasingly enchanted by the theater, especially by the music hall performers he saw at Bristol's Hippodrome, he never completed his schooling. In 1918, at age fourteen, he joined Bob Pender and his troupe of knockabout comedians. After ten days, his father temporarily reclaimed him and brought him back to Bristol. However, he was soon expelled from school for disciplinary problems and returned to the Pender Troupe, where he proved adept at dancing, tumbling, and stilt walking.

In 1920 the Pender Troupe traveled to the United States to appear at New York City's Globe Theatre in a Charles Dillingham revue entitled *Good Times*. After the show closed in 1921, the troupe appeared with Ringling Bros. and Barnum & Bailey Circus for three months, then toured the vaudeville circuit throughout the East. Deciding to stay in the United States, Grant worked for a while as a stilt walker for Steeplechase Amusement Park at Brooklyn's Coney Island, then resumed performing in vaudeville across the United States and Canada for several years. In the mid-1920s he returned to England for two years, touring the English hinterland with a minor repertory company.

In 1927 Grant sailed back to New York, where he met a number of show-business personalities and won a role in his first Broadway show, a musical called *Golden Dawn*. Other roles followed, in *Boom Boom* (1929), with a young Jeanette MacDonald; *A Wonderful Night* (1929), based on *Die Fledermaus;* and *The Street Singer* (1930). He also appeared with Fay Wray in *Nikki,* a 1931 musical stage version of the film *The Last Flight*. He failed his first screen test: the reviewer's report described him as bowlegged and thick-necked.

In May 1931 Grant was engaged by Paramount to appear in a short film called *Singapore Sue*. A long-term contract followed soon afterward, and it was at this time that he began using the name Cary Grant. His feature-film debut came in a 1932 romantic comedy called *This Is the Night,* in which he played the athletic husband of blonde Thelma Todd. For the next few years, he was confined largely to leading or supporting roles that relied more on his charm and good looks than on his acting ability. Typically, he was one of the men amorously involved with Tallulah Bankhead in *Devil and the Deep* (1932). In *Blonde Venus* (1932) he appeared as a playboy who starts Marlene Dietrich on her path of sin and degradation. Many of the movies in which he appeared during the early to mid-1930s, such as *Thirty-Day Princess* (1934), *Kiss and Make-Up* (1935), and *Wedding Present* (1936), were frivolous romantic comedies. Occasionally he was given a dramatic role, as in *The Eagle and the Hawk* (1933), *The Woman Accused* (1933), and *Born to Be Bad* (1934). In February 1934, Grant married the actress Virginia Cherrill; they separated after seven months and were divorced in March 1935.

Grant's most notable appearances in the early 1930s were in two films starring Mae West. The actress had seen Grant on the Paramount lot and insisted on casting him as her leading man in *She Done Him Wrong* (1933), the film version of her stage hit, *Diamond Lil*. As a secret agent posing as a Salvation Army officer, Grant made a good foil to West's bawdy Bowery saloon entertainer. (He was the target of her often-misquoted line, "Why don't you come up sometime and see me?") Later that year, he repeated as her leading man in the rowdily entertaining *I'm No Angel* (1933), as a playboy amorously involved with a circus lion-tamer, played by West. Grant also made an impression as a cockney con man in George Cukor's offbeat comedy-drama *Sylvia Scarlett* (1936), but the film was not well received.

By 1937 Grant had severed his relationship with Paramount, and his status as a free agent proved beneficial to his acting career. After appearing opposite the opera star Grace Moore in Columbia's *When You're in Love* (1937), he was signed by producer Hal Roach to play the lead in the whimsical comedy *Topper* (1937). As a mischievous ghost who joins his wife (Constance Bennett), also a ghost, in bedeviling the very proper Cosmo Topper (Roland Young), Grant began to establish his reputation as a major actor in comedy films.

Grant was assigned roles that took full advantage of his ability to play suave, sophisticated men who sustain comic assaults on their dignity. He scored an enormous hit with *The Awful Truth* (1937), as a divorcing husband who goes to great lengths to win back his wife, played by Irene Dunne. The movie fully revealed his deftness at playing both the romantic lead and the buffoon. He also found one of his most compatible costars in Katharine Hepburn, balancing his wry, lightly ironic style against her more aggressive approach in three first-rate comedies: *Bringing Up Baby* (1938), *Holiday* (1938), and *The Philadelphia Story* (1940). In *The Philadelphia Story,* a sparkling adaptation of Philip Barry's Broadway play about high society on the Main Line, he plays haughty heiress Hepburn's suave ex-husband, who reclaims her after she has acquired a degree of humility and humanity.

The actor's succession of hit films reached a peak at the close of the 1930s. He starred in two of the best films of 1939, first in George Stevens's rousing adventure film *Gunga Din,* as a swaggering English soldier battling a native uprising in colonial India, and then as the boss of a ramshackle South American airline in Howard Hawks's aviation drama *Only Angels Have Wings.* Here the cool cynicism that sometimes hovered at the edge of his performances was very much in evidence. He also gave a fine performance as a husband trapped in a loveless marriage in the 1939 drama *In Name Only.*

Grant's films in the 1940s varied in quality, but several of them gave him the rare opportunity to forgo comedy for drama. In 1941 he played opposite Irene Dunne in the tearjerker *Penny Serenade,* in which his performance as a beleaguered husband and father won him his first Oscar nomination for best actor. A key scene in which he pleads to be allowed to keep his adopted daughter showed an emotional core that seldom surfaced in his acting. In Alfred Hitchcock's *Suspicion* (1941), he portrayed a charming bounder who may or may not be planning to murder his wife (Oscar-winner Joan Fontaine). He was also notable (and again Oscar-nominated) as a restless cockney drifter in *None but the Lonely Heart* (1944), and as an American agent stalking Nazis in postwar Rio in Alfred Hitchcock's *Notorious* (1946). Although these roles allowed him to expand his acting range, he continued to hone his comedic skills, especially in such movies as *My Favorite Wife* (1940), *His Girl Friday* (1940), *The Talk of the Town* (1942), and *Mr. Blandings Builds His Dream House* (1948). When he was miscast, however, the strain showed, as in *Arsenic and Old Lace* (1944) and *Night and Day* (1946), in which he seemed uneasy as composer Cole Porter.

Grant became an American citizen in June 1942 (and legally changed his name from Archibald Leach to Cary Grant). That year he also married Barbara Hutton, an heiress who had been reviled by the public for her spendthrift ways during the Great Depression. The marriage was an unhappy one, and after a series of separations and reconciliations they were finally divorced in 1945. Four years later, on Christmas day in 1949, Grant married the actress Betsy Drake, with whom he had costarred in *Every Girl Should Be Married* (1948).

Grant's films of the 1950s were variable in quality. They included the requisite number of comedies that made full use of his still-considerable charm: *Monkey Business* (1952), with Ginger Rogers; *Houseboat* (1958), with Sophia Loren; and *Indiscreet* (1958), with Ingrid Bergman. He found a felicitous costar in Deborah Kerr, particularly in *An Affair to Remember* (1957), a smoothly rendered remake of the 1939 film *Love Affair.* Twice during the decade, he was directed by Alfred Hitchcock, first opposite Grace Kelly in *To Catch a Thief* (1955), a lightweight but visually stunning comedy-thriller, and then in *North by Northwest* (1959), a hugely entertaining melodrama in which Grant plays a hapless advertising executive who is caught up in a spy plot that has him fleeing across the country. In a celebrated sequence, Grant, alone in a cornfield, tries to elude a crop duster that repeatedly swoops to hit him. The equally famous climax finds him and Eva Marie Saint pursued across the stone faces of Mount Rushmore.

Late in the 1950s, Grant underwent a crisis in his personal life. His on-screen image radiated charm and self-assurance, but he was, in fact, a complex, often troubled man who was forever searching for inner peace. His apparently ambivalent nature made him generous and loving at one time and selfish and even brutal at another. He also appears to have been deeply conflicted about his sexuality, and most of his biographers assert that he was probably bisexual. Over a two-year period, he spent hundreds of hours at a psychiatric institute, undergoing controversial therapy utilizing LSD. During the filming of *Operation Petticoat* in 1959, Grant went public about his use of LSD, describing in candid interviews how the drug had changed his life. About this time, he separated from Betsy Drake, and they were divorced in 1962.

In the 1960s Grant's films were less frequent as he began to consider retirement. He costarred with Doris Day in the romantic comedy *That Touch of Mink* (1962) and enjoyed two successes, first opposite Audrey Hepburn in a sleek, Hitchcock-like melodrama, *Charade* (1963), and then opposite Leslie Caron in *Father Goose* (1964), in which he played the uncharacteristic role of a scruffy beachcomber. His final film, *Walk, Don't Run*, a remake of *The More the Merrier* (1943) set in Tokyo during the Olympic Games of 1964, appeared in 1966.

Early in the 1960s, after his divorce from Betsy Drake, Grant met the actress Dyan Cannon; they were married on 22 July 1965. Their daughter, Jennifer (Grant's only child), was born in February 1966 and became the center of the actor's world. His marriage, however, ended in divorce in 1968. At the divorce hearing, Cannon related lurid stories of Grant's aberrant and abusive behavior.

At the same time, Grant's public persona remained intact. In April 1970 he received an honorary Academy Award for "his unique mastery of the art of film acting," and in December 1981 he was one of the recipients of the prestigious Kennedy Center honors. Earlier that year, after a four-year affair with a British reporter named Maureen Donaldson, he met and married Barbara Harris, a twenty-five-year-old woman who worked in public relations for the Royal Lancaster Hotel in London. In 1984, now eighty years old, Grant devised a ninety-minute one-man show called *A Conversation with Cary Grant*. It was while he was touring with this show that he suffered a stroke in Davenport, Iowa, and died soon afterward. His cremated remains were scattered in California.

Whatever private demons may have haunted Cary Grant, he was, and remains, the screen's most elegant star, a gifted actor whose comic finesse has never been duplicated. Dapper, debonair, and enormously skilled at his craft, he looms large in the annals of film history.

★

Books on Grant include Jerry Vermilye, *Cary Grant* (1973); Lionel Godfrey, *Cary Grant: The Light Touch* (1981); Richard Schickel, *Cary Grant: A Celebration* (1984); Geoffrey Wansell, *Haunted Idol: The Story of the Real Cary Grant* (1984); Warren G. Harris, *Cary Grant: A Touch of Elegance* (1987); Charles Higham, *Cary Grant: The Lonely Heart* (1989); Maureen Donaldson and William Royce, *An Affair to Remember: My Life with Cary Grant* (1989); and Nancy Nelson, *Evenings with Cary Grant: Reflections in His Own Words and by Those Who Knew Him Best* (1991). An obituary is in the *New York Times* (1 Dec. 1986).

TED SENNETT

GRAZIANO, Rocky (*b.* 1 January 1921 in New York City; *d.* 22 May 1990 in New York City), professional boxer who overcame poverty, child abuse, and numerous brushes with the law to become a middleweight champion and popular television performer.

Graziano, whose original name was Thomas Rocco Barbella, was the second of two sons born to Italian-born former welterweight boxer Nicholas Barbella and his wife, Ida, on New York City's tough Lower East Side. Three other Barbella children died in infancy. Graziano's father, who fought under the name "Fighting Nick Bob," had an undistinguished boxing career and after his retirement became bitter, drank heavily, and was frequently out of work. Barbella introduced the five-year-old Rocco to boxing, forcing him to fight his older brother in their apartment to entertain friends. Bloodied, confused, and angry after each affair, Graziano would often run out of the house and not

Rocky Graziano. ARCHIVE PHOTOS

return for days. Often sleeping in abandoned buildings or on rooftops, he quit school in the sixth grade and began running with a gang. Graziano, the leader, was a ferocious brawler. "I was the best street fighter in history. Hell, I never lost a street fight," he recalled years later.

In 1931 Graziano was arrested for the first time when he broke into a subway gum machine. By 1938 he had already served three terms in reform school. Nicknamed Rocky Bob at the time, he led a group that raided rival gangs and stole virtually anything they could. "We stole offa trucks, outa warehouses, stores, an' garages, anything we could get our hands on that we could sell for a few bucks," he later wrote.

Rocky began to box in 1939, when several friends and gang members coerced him into taking part in the Metropolitan Amateur Athletic Union championships. He won the middleweight championship and began to change his attitude about boxing. Graziano had previously disliked the sport because of his "old man and all the old-time fighters he got drunk with. . . . My father and his friends were all a bunch of washed up bums," wrote Graziano.

Encouraged by his Metropolitan title and by getting his name in the newspaper "for something good for a change,"

Graziano began to take boxing more seriously. His career was interrupted in 1940, however, when he was imprisoned for a parole violation. In 1942 Graziano's promising young career was interrupted again by World War II. Drafted into the army and sent to Fort Dix, New Jersey, he lasted less than a day. First he punched out his corporal for yelling at him, and then, when brought before his captain for discipline, he punched him. Graziano went AWOL and returned to boxing as Tommy Rocky Graziano (a name borrowed from a friend) to avoid detection by the army. Short of cash, he began fighting for small purses until he was caught by the military police in late 1942. He was court-martialed, dishonorably discharged, and sentenced to nine months in the federal penitentiary at Leavenworth, Kansas.

Released in 1943, after being an undefeated member of the prison boxing team, Graziano began to change his perspective. Before his court-martial, Graziano had met Norma Unger, "a nice Jewish girl from Brooklyn." In love and eager to make an honest living, he took up boxing with a new vigor. He married Unger on 10 August 1943. They had two daughters. His career began to take off in 1943. Fighting as a welterweight under the name Rocky Graziano, he fought eighteen times and lost only twice with one draw. In the ring Graziano was much like the brawler he had been on the New York streets. His fights were action packed and made him a favorite in New York boxing clubs.

In November 1944 Graziano hit the big time with a main-event bout at Madison Square Garden against a wily veteran. Harold Green won the ten-round decision, by sidestepping Graziano's uncontrolled rushes with constant movement and a steady diet of left hooks. A month later the pair met again, and Green won another decision. Critics were prepared to write off Graziano when he met a rising star, Billy Arnold, at Madison Square Garden on 9 March 1945. Arnold, with a record of 32–1, was a 10–1 favorite. From the first two rounds and into the third, Graziano endured a merciless pounding. Then the tide changed. "All of a sudden, as if from nowhere, Rocky fired a right to the jaw. It caught Arnold flush," wrote radio announcer Don Dunphy. "He measured Arnold again and again and pounded him with both hands. Arnold was counted out—clear into obscurity."

The Arnold fight catapulted Graziano's career. Now a huge gate attraction, he lured fight fans with his exciting style and his personality. Graziano then prepared to take aim at the middleweight championship and launched a rivalry that is among the most storied in boxing history.

The first of three championship bouts against "The Man of Steel," Tony Zale, occurred on 27 September 1946 at Yankee Stadium. For the opening three rounds, Graziano, a 2–1 favorite, and Zale "battled each other with the greatest display of fistic fireworks I have ever seen," wrote Dunphy. Although Graziano took command of the fight, Zale found an opening in his midsection in the sixth round that knocked Graziano out for the first time in his career. Zale and Graziano split $350,000 for the fight, but Rocky was inconsolable for weeks. His wife urged him to quit. "But how she gonna know what I need," wrote Graziano. "That championship fight was gonna wipe my whole rotten slate clean, and I could get even for all the grief my early years brung me."

Graziano found more grief on 7 February 1947, when his license to box in New York was suspended for failure to report a bribe. Although his license was restored three months later, his scheduled rematch with Zale had been canceled. Graziano got his chance for revenge on 16 July 1947 at Chicago Stadium. Although clearly outboxed for the first five rounds, Graziano wrested the middleweight title from Zale with a sixth-round knockout. In their anticlimactic third bout on 10 June 1948 in Newark, New Jersey, Zale took back the title with a third-round knockout. Graziano had held the title for just eleven months.

Toward the end of his career, Graziano took his last shot at the middleweight championship in April 1952 against Sugar Ray Robinson, who knocked out Graziano in the third round. Five months later Graziano fought his last bout, losing a ten-round decision. His lifetime record was 67 wins, 10 losses, and 6 draws, with 52 knockouts.

When Graziano retired he had no clear plans. Although he considered opening a bar or becoming a fight manager, fate seemed to determine Graziano's path again. During the next few years, he made a number of personal and television appearances around the country. One of them, on the *Nick Kenny Show,* caught the eye of television producer Nat Hiken, who persuaded Graziano to do a one-time appearance on the *Martha Raye Show.* His performance was a hit, and Graziano became a regular, playing the part of Raye's boyfriend, "Goombah," until 1956. He was a natural for the part because he was playing himself—a lovable ex-champ who spoke in his native Lower East Side tongue, complete with "dese, dose, and dem."

In 1954 Graziano began to work with sportswriter Rowland Barber on a book about his life. *Somebody Up There Likes Me* soon became a best-seller, and in 1956 production began on the movie version. The then relatively unknown actor Paul Newman played Graziano, and the film was a huge success.

After his run on the *Martha Raye Show,* Graziano continued in show business through radio and television commercials and personal and television appearances. He also appeared in several movies, including *Mr. Rock and Roll* (1957) and *Country Music Holiday* (1958). Graziano made a healthy income endorsing products like foot powder, yogurt, and automobile mufflers. On television, he appeared many times on the *Steve Allen Show,* the *Mike Douglas Show,* the *Merv Griffin Show,* and the *Tonight Show Starring*

Johnny Carson. In 1971 he was voted into the Boxing Hall of Fame.

When Graziano first entered show business, he asked Martha Raye if he should take acting and diction lessons. Raye replied, "If you do, you'll be out of a job." Graziano caught on. In the end he made millions just being himself. From poverty and child abuse he went on to meet presidents and movie stars. Most important, he said, was his family life. He often said of himself, "What else can they remember me as but the luckiest bum dat ever lived."

He died of cardiopulmonary failure at New York Hospital.

★

Rocky Graziano with Rowland Barber, *Somebody Up There Likes Me* (1954), traces Graziano's childhood and fight career. His second autobiography, with Ralph Corsel, *Somebody Down Here Likes Me Too* (1981), is most useful in following his postfight career. Don Dunphy, *Don Dunphy at Ringside* (1988), gives detailed coverage of Graziano's bouts with Zale and Arnold. Peter Walsh, *Men of Steel* (1993), is useful for biographical information. Obituaries are in the *New York Times* and *New York Post* (both 23 May 1990).

STEPHEN MCKAY

GREEN, Edith Starrett (*b.* 17 January 1910 in Trent, South Dakota; *d.* 21 April 1987 in Tualatin, Oregon), congresswoman who became a force in the Democratic party in the 1950s and played a key role in passing legislation designed to fight poverty, aid education, and mandate equal pay for women.

Green was one of five children of James Vaughn Starrett and Julia Hunt, who were both teachers. At the age of six, she moved with her family to Roseburg, Oregon, where her father became a school principal. She attended high school in Salem, Oregon, graduating first in her class in 1927. Her ambition was to become a lawyer, but her parents discouraged her because most law firms discriminated against women. She then chose to enter the same profession as her parents. They also inspired her early interest in politics. "I grew up in a home where politics was discussed at the dinner table," she later recalled.

From 1927 to 1929, she studied at Willamette University and paid her tuition by working double shifts in a Salem cannery. She dropped out of the private college and obtained a teaching certificate in 1930 from the Oregon Normal School, which later became Western Oregon State College. She taught elementary and junior high school in Salem from 1930 until 1941 while continuing her studies, receiving a B.S. degree from the University of Oregon in 1939. She married Arthur N. Green, a building contractor, on 19 August 1933; they had two sons and were divorced in 1962.

After graduate study at Stanford University in 1944, Green quit teaching and went into broadcast communications as a commentator and announcer for Portland radio station KALE. Until 1948 she also did freelance work for several other Oregon radio stations. In 1946 she was selected as the state legislative chairman for the Oregon Conference of Parents and Teachers. She served for three years in this position and then became the group's lobbyist at the 1951 session of the biennial Oregon legislature. In 1952 she chaired a committee that held education conferences across the state, and from 1952 to 1955 she was the public relations director and chief lobbyist for the Oregon Education Association, representing the state's teachers. Green, who was short, slender, and had dark eyes, was an eloquent and forceful public speaker. She was a member of the Christian Church.

In her first bid for public office, Green was the Democratic nominee for Oregon secretary of state in 1952. Although she lost to the Republican incumbent, Early Newbry, Green made the strongest showing by a Democrat for the office since 1874. Two years later Green was elected to the U.S. House of Representatives from Oregon's Third District, which included most of the city of Portland and its eastern suburbs. Running on a platform of increased federal aid to schools, conservation of natural resources, and opposition to the Eisenhower administration's "partnership" with private utilities, she defeated Republican Tom Lawson McCall, a future Oregon governor, and became the first Democrat in eighteen years to win the congressional seat.

In Washington, Green was elected president of the Eighty-fourth Club, an organization of the new Democratic members of the Eighty-fourth Congress. In the changing of the guard as Democrats regained control of the House, she quickly made her mark as one of the party's emerging leaders. She was tough, tenacious, intelligent, and idealistic, but also pragmatic. Senator Mark O. Hatfield, a Republican who knew Green for forty years, said at the time of her death that "she was probably the most powerful woman ever to serve in the Congress."

When she first came to the House, Green was among the more liberal Democratic members. In the late 1950s she was one of the founders of the Democratic House Study Group, a liberal counterpoint to the southern conservatives and old guard regulars from big-city machines who then dominated the congressional leadership. In 1955 she introduced legislation to require equal pay for women, and eight years later, her Equal Pay Act was signed into law. She was also a strong advocate of ethics legislation but Congress failed to pass a 1963 measure that would have required all House members and their spouses to make full disclosure of their income.

Edith Green. OREGON HISTORICAL SOCIETY, NEGATIVE NUMBER ORHI98587

Green was also active in presidential politics, and her seconding speech for Adlai E. Stevenson at the 1956 Democratic convention was the first by a woman at a major-party convention. She worked with Senator John F. Kennedy in promoting labor reform legislation and as an early supporter of his 1960 presidential campaign managed his victory over favorite son Wayne Morse in the Oregon primary. When Green chaired the Oregon delegation to the 1960 Democratic convention, she became the first woman to lead a state delegation at a major-party convention. Kennedy, who regarded her as "the top woman politician of his administration," according to the *New York Times,* offered to nominate her as ambassador to Canada. Green, however, preferred her congressional role.

After Kennedy's assassination in 1963, Green was unable to forge a warm relationship with the new president, Lyndon Johnson. An early opponent of the Vietnam War, she supported Robert F. Kennedy's presidential bid in 1968, when Johnson was still presumed to be a candidate for reelection. In endorsing Kennedy, Green described Johnson's Vietnam policy as "a ruinous course that has stalemated our progress toward justice and poverty at home." Nevertheless, she helped Johnson win passage of antipoverty legislation in 1967 by drafting an amendment that was acceptable to southern Democrats.

Green, who served for eighteen years on the Education and Labor Committee, where she rose to the second-ranking position, made her largest contribution in higher education. A key proponent of the Higher Educational Facilities Act of 1963, which helped U.S. colleges and universities expand with federal aid, she also wrote, sponsored, and guided through Congress the Higher Education Act of 1965, which provided federal student aid. Another important piece of educational legislation that she helped guide through Congress was the 1972 bill that became known as Title IX. It included a provision that barred federal aid to any educational institution that discriminated against women, and the law is now credited with greatly expanding the number of women participating in college sports. "No one else in Congress had a comparable grasp of education problems or equal skill in committee and floor debate on the subject," the journalist Neil Peirce wrote of Green.

She could, however, be critical of the American system of higher education. Green proposed legislation that would have established more state and local control over federal education aid. Deeply offended by the student protest movement of the 1960s, she recommended cutting federal aid to universities that failed to thwart campus uprisings. In the early 1970s, Green lamented that colleges and universities were becoming "degree mills," and she called for a new emphasis on vocational and technical training. In 1973 she quit the Education and Labor Committee, giving up her chairmanship of the higher education subcommittee, and took a junior slot on the Appropriations Committee.

After Green did not seek reelection in 1974, President Gerald Ford nominated her to be director of the Legal Services Corporation, but she asked Ford to withdraw the nomination in the face of opposition from Democrats who pointed out that she had been an outspoken critic of legal services. Green was a national cochairman of Democrats for Ford in the 1976 presidential election. She became a professor of government at Warner Pacific College in 1975 and was named to the Oregon Board of Higher Education in 1979. She died of cancer and is buried at a pioneer cemetery in Corbett, Oregon.

★

The Oregon State Library in Salem and the Oregon Historical Society in Portland have papers related to Green's political career. Her years in the House are chronicled in Marie C. Barovic Rosenberg, "Women in Politics: A Comparative Study of Congresswomen Edith Green and Julia Butler Hansen," (Ph.D. diss., University of Washington, 1973). See also "Women in Politics: An Interview with Edith Green," *Social Policy* 2 (1972): 16–22. Obituaries are in the *Portland Oregonian* (22 Apr. 1987) and *New York Times* (23 Apr. 1987).

STEVE NEAL

GREENBERG, Henry Benjamin ("Hank") (*b.* 1 January 1911 in New York City; *d.* 4 September 1986 in Beverly Hills, California), major league baseball player and owner who was the American League's Most Valuable Player (MVP) in 1935 and 1940 and the first Jewish American to be elected to the Baseball Hall of Fame.

Greenberg was one of four children of Romanian immigrants. His father, David, owned a small textile firm in the garment district of Manhattan; his mother, Sarah, was a homemaker. Born in the immigrant melting pot of lower Manhattan, Greenberg initially lived in Greenwich Village tenements on Barrow and then Perry Streets.

At age six, Greenberg and his family moved to the Crotona Park section of the Bronx, where he attended P.S. 44 and led James Monroe High School to the New York City basketball championship in 1929. Spending hours honing his baseball skills in Crotona Park, Greenberg developed a reputation as a "bum" among neighborhood Jewish mothers, who preferred young men to devote more time to academic pursuits and more respectable professional careers. Playing baseball for coach Tom Elliffe at Monroe, Greenberg teamed with future major league pitcher Izzy Goldstein. He graduated from James Monroe in 1929. Having been an all-city center there, Greenberg won a coveted athletic scholarship to New York University (NYU).

Hank Greenberg. NATIONAL BASEBALL HALL OF FAME LIBRARY, COOPERSTOWN, N.Y.

In 1929 Greenberg played semipro baseball for the Red Bank (New Jersey) Towners and later with Brooklyn's Bayparkways. In September he signed with the professional Detroit Tigers, with an annual salary of $9,000. He invested most of his signing bonus on Wall Street, only to see it wiped out in the October stock market crash.

Having entered NYU in the fall of 1929, Greenberg left in 1930, never to return to college. He worked his way through Detroit's minor league affiliates, toiling at such outposts as Hartford, Connecticut, and Raleigh, North Carolina. At Evansville in the triple-I league in 1931, he hit .331 and led the league with forty-one doubles. The following season his reputation as a feared power hitter developed when he hit thirty-nine home runs for Beaumont in the highly respected Texas League.

As a rookie first baseman with Detroit in 1933 (he had one time at bat with the Tigers in 1930), Greenberg hit an impressive .301 with a dozen homers while driving in eighty-seven runs. He hit at least .300 for his first eight seasons, but it was his power numbers that opened eyes, as he became the most dangerous slugger of his generation. In 1934 the Tigers were in a close pennant race as Greenberg tore up American League pitching at a .339 clip, with twenty-six home runs and a league-leading (and fourth all-time) sixty-three doubles.

Having been raised in an observant Jewish home, he faced a dilemma as the pennant-chasing Tigers wound down the 1934 season and Rosh Hashanah (the Jewish New Year) approached. Seeking rabbinical guidance, he was cleared to play and hit two monster round-trippers. Ten days later, however, he spent the day in synagogue on Yom Kippur (the Day of Atonement). This episode made national news in the heyday of the notorious anti-Semitic radio priest, Father Charles E. Coughlin, who openly accused Jews of causing the nation's economic problems.

At six feet, three inches and 220 pounds, Greenberg evoked what historian Peter Levine called an image of a "tough physical player who openly defied anti-Semitic bigots," whether in the stands or opposing dugouts. Actor Walter Matthau, later a close friend of Greenberg, recalled that he "put to rest the stories of Jewish pants pressers." Greenberg wrote in his autobiography that "after all, I was representing a couple of million Jews . . . against Hitler." As one of the most visible Jewish Americans, he felt the "added pressure of being Jewish. How the hell could you get up to home plate every day and have some son of a bitch call you a Jew bastard and kike and sheenie?" Feeling a special responsibility in the anti-Semitic 1930s, he "came to feel, that if I, as a Jew, hit a home run, I was hitting one against Hitler."

In this atmosphere Greenberg approached the mythic

record of sixty home runs in a season, held by his boyhood idol, Babe Ruth. With five games to go in the 1938 season, Greenberg hit his fifty-eighth homer, tying the 1932 record for right-handers held by Jimmy Foxx. Old-timers recall persistent rumors of a conspiracy among anti-Semitic players to deprive Greenberg of a new record by not giving him any good pitches to hit. To his death Greenberg denied any collusion, simply stating "I ran out of gas." The record would stand until Yankee slugger Roger Maris broke it in 1961.

Greenberg was consistently effective at the plate. In 1935 (another World Series year) he hit .328 with 46 doubles, 36 homers, and a league-leading 170 runs batted in (RBIs). After appearing in only twelve games in 1936 because of an injury, Greenberg bounced back in 1937, hitting .337 with 49 doubles, 40 homers, and an incredible 183 runs knocked in, one shy of Lou Gehrig's American League record. Greenberg always believed RBIs were the most telling statistic, claiming more disappointment over not tying Gehrig rather than in failing to break Ruth's home-run record.

A first baseman for his entire career, Greenberg voluntarily relinquished his infield position in 1940, moving to left field to accommodate the power-hitting but weak-fielding Rudy York. This would be Greenberg's most productive season, with the Tigers winning the pennant (and only narrowly losing the World Series in seven games to the Cincinnati Reds). With 50 doubles, 41 home runs, 150 RBIs, a .340 batting average, and boasting a monumental .670 slugging percentage, he won his second American League MVP award. Greenberg was notoriously slow of foot, and it was said that home run balls were returned to the dugout well before he completed his trot around the bases. He was a committed student of the game; thus, his lack of speed never hindered him defensively, as the cerebral Greenberg always seemed to play in the correct position.

In 1941 all eligible men were required to register for the draft. Originally classified 4F for having flat feet, Greenberg denied rumors that he had bribed doctors. He was reclassified 1A soon after and was called up in May 1941. At the apex of his career, he saw his league-leading salary of $55,000 shrink to Uncle Sam's buck private rate of $21 per month. He attended Officer Candidate School at Fort Worth, Texas. Rising to captain in the Army Air Corps, he conducted speaking tours, rooming with screen actor William Holden. Wanting to see action, Greenberg requested a transfer and became a B-29 pilot, serving in combat in the China-Burma-India theater. Discharged during the summer of 1945 after having missed four and one-half years during his prime, the thirty-four-year-old hit a grand slam home run on the final day of the 1945 season to clinch the pennant for the Tigers, who then defeated the Chicago Cubs in the World Series.

Waived by Detroit following the 1946 season because his salary demands were too high, Greenberg became baseball's first $100,000-per-year player when he signed with the Pittsburgh Pirates of the rival National League. Pirates owner John Galbreath, head of the Darby Dan Thoroughbred stable, convinced Greenberg to play for the Pirates by moving in the left field wall of Forbes Field. The area became known as Greenberg's Garden. Future Hall of Famer Ralph Kiner, for whom Greenberg's Garden was eventually renamed Kiner's Korner, became Greenberg's roommate in 1947. Greenberg's dedication to his craft was well demonstrated by Kiner's tales of the older man's expert guidance and nurturing of the young player on the infamously carousing postwar Pirates club. Under Greenberg's watchful eye and influence, Kiner developed proper work habits, watching his mentor taking "hours of extra batting and fielding practice. Hank taught me that hard work was the most important thing."

In 1947 Jackie Robinson broke the color barrier in baseball by signing with the Brooklyn Dodgers. Robinson would later recall that Greenberg was the first opposing player to offer encouragement, telling him "don't let them get you down, you're doing fine, keep it up." Robinson further noted that "class tells. It sticks out all over Mr. Greenberg."

Retiring from active play in 1948, Greenberg was recruited by the iconoclastic Cleveland Indians owner Bill Veeck, first as administrative assistant and in 1949 as a minor league director. When the team came under new ownership, he became the Indians' general manager in 1950. Released by the owners in 1957, he again teamed up with Veeck as part-owner of the Chicago White Sox from 1959 to 1961. Selling his holdings in the Sox, Greenberg made a fortune in the Wall Street bull market of the early 1960s. In 1974 he moved from his New York City townhouse to a life of leisure in Beverly Hills, California.

Greenberg, who had long been one of baseball's most eligible bachelors, married department store heiress Caral Glazier Gimbel on 18 February 1945. The couple had three children and divorced in 1958. In 1966 Greenberg married a minor film actress, Mary Jo DeCicco (known on screen as Linda Douglas).

As one of baseball's most highly paid players and later a team owner and executive, Greenberg was partially responsible for the creation of the player pension plan and organized the split of World Series and All-Star game receipts on the basis of 65 percent for the owners and 35 percent for the players. In addition, he testified for Curt Flood in his landmark, but unsuccessful, antitrust case against Major League Baseball. He died of cancer and was buried in Hillside Memorial Park, Los Angeles.

A prodigious right-handed power hitter, Greenberg had a .313 lifetime batting average and led the American League in both home runs and runs batted in four times. He led the Detroit Tigers to four World Series (winning twice, in 1935 and 1945). His most notable statistics are hitting fifty-eight home runs in 1938 and being second only to Lou Gehrig as the all-time leader in runs batted in (1,276) per games played (1,394) for a .915 average. A hero to many Jews, he helped to break down anti-Semitic stereotypes.

★

Greenberg's autobiography, *The Story Of My Life* (1989), was cowritten with sportswriter Ira Berkow. It contains several interviews with family members and fellow ballplayers as well as complete career statistics and many photos. Ralph Kiner, *Kiner's Korner* (1987), offers personal reminiscences. Robert Creamer, *Baseball in 1941* (1991), covers the military draft episode in detail. A short biographical sketch along with useful analysis of Greenberg's historical significance is in Peter Levine, *Ellis Island to Ebbets Field: Sport and the American Jewish Experience* (1992). William M. Simons, "The Athlete as Jewish Standard Bearer: Media Images of Hank Greenberg," *Jewish Social Studies* 44 (spring 1982): 95–112, recounts many stories. An obituary is in the *New York Times* (5 Sept. 1986).

JEFFREY S. ROSEN

GREENE, Lorne (*b.* 12 February 1915 in Ottawa, Ontario, Canada; *d.* 11 September 1987 in Santa Monica, California), actor especially noted for the television series *Bonanza* (1959–1973), in which he starred as Ben Cartwright, the kindly father figure who set a high moral tone for his family of young TV sons.

Lorne Greene in a publicity photo for the television show *Bonanza,* 1970. NBC/ARCHIVE PHOTOS

Greene's parents were Daniel Green, a saddlemaker who developed his own business in corrective boots, and Dora Green, a homemaker. He grew up as an only child after an older brother died in infancy. Greene was introduced to the theater in high school, where he first learned to project his distinctive deep voice. He studied drama at Queen's University in Kingston, Ontario, which he attended from 1932 to 1937, and where he first studied chemical engineering but then switched to languages; meanwhile he produced, directed, and acted in school plays. After graduating with a B.A. degree, he took a position in radio with the Canadian Broadcasting Corporation (CBC) in Toronto. Shortly before the outbreak of World War II, Greene went to New York City to attend the Neighborhood Playhouse School of the Theatre and the Martha Graham School of Contemporary Dance (1937–1939). He then returned to work for the CBC, where he became greatly admired and was dubbed the "voice of Canada." Late in the war, he served a tour of duty with the Canadian Army and then returned to Canada to found two organizations to assist veterans to find positions in radio or the theater: the Academy of Radio Arts and the Jupiter Theatre.

One of the teachers at Greene's Academy of Radio Arts later invited him to appear in a play on *Studio One,* a live televised theater program produced by CBS. Greene went on to have a series of successes in this medium. He also performed on the Broadway stage and was a Shakespearean actor in Ontario. In 1940 he married Rita Hands in Toronto, with whom he had twins, Charles and Belinda Susan. The couple divorced in 1960, and Greene married Nancy Anne Deale in 1961; they had one daughter, Gillian.

Although he remained a Canadian citizen, Greene moved permanently to the United States in the early 1950s. In 1954 he appeared in the film *The Silver Chalice,* for which he received excellent reviews for his role as the apostle Peter. He next appeared in *Tight Spot* in 1955, a Columbia Pictures film based on Leonard Kantor's Broadway play *Dead Pigeon.* The *New York Times* praised Greene as "first-rate" in his supporting role as a racketeer. He was also strong in supporting roles in the films *Autumn Leaves* (1956), *Peyton Place* (1957), and *Gift of Love* (1958). In 1958 he also appeared in *The Buccaneer,* in which Yul Brynner played the pirate Jean Lafitte who aided General Andrew Jackson (Charlton Heston) at the Battle of New Orleans;

Greene played a buccaneer named Mercier. In 1959 Greene appeared in *The Trap*.

Over the course of the 1950s, Greene appeared on such television programs as *The Elgin Hour, Omnibus, Folio, Playhouse 90,* and *Producer's Showcase.* In 1959 he played in the Western series *Wagon Train,* in which he portrayed a strong, authoritative man. Stardom came after Greene was tapped for *Bonanza,* the central character of which was Ben Cartwright of the Ponderosa Ranch. The episodes usually taught a moral lesson and the importance of strong family values. Cartwright's sons were Hoss, a burly, affable character (Dan Blocker); Adam, the reader and thinker (Pernell Roberts); and Little Joe, the handsome and sensitive youth (Michael Landon). The program won many awards and was honored by the U.S. Congress in 1966 for its dedication to high moral values and family entertainment.

Greene also became a recording artist, singing such Western songs as "Five Card Stud," "Destiny," and "Ringo." He was closely associated with the Boy Scouts and often spoke or performed at fund-raising benefits. In 1964 he was master of ceremonies on Prince Edward Island for a performance of the Canadian Royal Variety Group staged for Queen Elizabeth II. In 1965 he was selected Canada's man of the year.

Following *Bonanza,* Greene appeared in such films as *The Errand Boy* (1961), *Earthquake* (1974), *Tidal Wave* (1975), *Klondike Fever* (1977), *Battlestar Galactica,* based on the TV series (1979), and *Conquest of the Earth* (1980). His television series included *Griff* (1973–1974), *Battlestar Galactica* (1978–1980), and *Code Red* (1981–1982). He also enjoyed prestige as the narrator of the documentary nature series *Lorne Greene's Last of the Wild.* Greene died in Santa Monica, California, from pneumonia, following surgery for a perforated ulcer. He is buried in Hillside Memorial Park in Culver City, California.

Lorne Greene was the master of four mediums: theater, radio, film, and television. His specialty was communication, and many praised his deep, rich speaking voice. He was a large, robust man (over six feet tall and over 200 pounds) whose love of life spilled over into his multitude of roles.

★

Current Biography 1967, pp. 149–152, gives an account of Greene's career. For other profiles see *Look* (1 Dec. 1964), *Maclean's* (23 Apr. 1960), *New York Post* (26 Apr. 1964 and 25 Mar. 1965), *Parade* (31 Jan. 1965), and *Saturday Evening Post* (4 Dec. 1965). For some film reviews see the *New York Times,* "The Silver Chalice" (27 Dec. 1954), "Tight Spot" (19 Mar. 1955), "Autumn Leaves" (2 Aug. 1956), "Peyton Place" (13 Dec. 1957), "Gift of Love" (12 Feb. 1958), "Buccaneer" (24 Dec. 1958), and "The Trap" (29 Jan. 1959). Obituaries are in *Maclean's* (21 Sept. 1987) and *People* (28 Sept. 1987).

BARBARA BENNETT PETERSON

H

HAGEN, John Peter (*b.* 31 July 1908 in Amherst, Nova Scotia, Canada; *d.* 26 August 1990 in Las Vegas, Nevada), physicist and radio astronomer who headed Project Vanguard, one of the United States' first successful civilian satellite programs.

The son of John T. Hagen, a contractor who traveled extensively, and Ella Bertha Fisher, Hagen enjoyed building model airplanes and furniture as a child, and he prided himself on having excelled academically despite moving often from one school to another.

Upon enrolling at Boston University, Hagen originally wanted to become a lawyer, but he did so well in his undergraduate science courses that in his senior year he was offered an assistantship at Wesleyan University in Connecticut. "That paid money. Law school didn't. So I became a scientist," Hagen said. He graduated from B.U. with a B.A. in 1929, and while at Wesleyan (where he earned an M.A. in 1931) he simultaneously attended graduate courses at Yale University. He subsequently earned a doctorate in astronomy from Georgetown University in Washington, D.C., in 1949.

Meanwhile, Hagen had joined the staff of the U.S. Naval Research Laboratory in Washington. From 1935 to 1954 he served as head of the laboratory's Radio Frequency Section. During World War II he worked on the development of radar and an automatic ground-speed indicator for aircraft, for which he was awarded a Distinguished Service Medal from the navy and a Presidential Certificate of Merit in 1946. After the war he headed development of a highly precise radio telescope.

In 1954 Hagen was named the superintendent of the Naval Research Laboratory's new Atmosphere and Atmospherics Division. About the same time, scientists around the world were preparing for the International Geophysical Year, which had been declared for 1957–1958 as a time of concentrated scientific observation of the Earth and its environs. In 1954 the International Scientific Radio Union and the International Union of Geodesy and Geophysics produced resolutions calling for the orbiting of an artificial satellite during the IGY. On 29 July 1955 President Dwight D. Eisenhower announced that the United States planned to orbit small satellites as part of its IGY activities.

On that same day, Hagen was appointed director of Project Vanguard, one of several proposed Defense Department satellite programs. Vanguard envisioned using a three-stage rocket to place a twenty-pound nose cone into orbit. In September 1955 the Defense Department selected Vanguard as the program that would place at least one satellite into orbit during the IGY. Congress was not asked to provide any new funds for the Vanguard project; rather, Vanguard's money was to be diverted from other Pentagon projects, placing Vanguard on an austerity footing.

One of Hagen's first decisions was to extend close supervision over the Martin Company, an aerospace firm that had done previous work for the navy on the Viking rocket,

John P. Hagen holding a scale model of a three-stage satellite-launching vehicle, 1957. ARCHIVE PHOTOS

the basis of the Vanguard rocket. Ordinarily, the government would have given Martin wide latitude in its work, but Hagen insisted that he and other NRL officials be enmeshed in the day-to-day workings of Vanguard. This set a pattern for collaboration between government and aerospace contractors that persisted in other U.S. space and missile programs.

Hagen's original plan was for six experimental launches that would test the rocket, to be followed by seven rocket launches that would loft a satellite. Meanwhile, Hagen's group developed a worldwide network of tracking stations, called Minitrack, that could receive radio transmissions from the satellites. In the spring of 1957 his group had two successful rocket tests on trajectories that did not go into orbit. These were followed by a third successful suborbital test on 23 October 1957.

This test did not occur, however, until after the Soviet Union's historic launching of *Sputnik 1* into orbit on 4 October 1957. To Hagen's dismay, on 11 October 1957 the White House issued a statement promising that the United States would place a satellite into orbit in the near future. The announcement created enormous public expectations for a subsequent Vanguard launch on 6 December 1957, which had been intended as only a test launch of the rocket but which was reconceived as an attempt to orbit a satellite. Hagen later would say that the White House announcement was "a rude shock" for those in the program. Unfortunately for Hagen and his coworkers, the launch produced the most spectacular failure of the Vanguard program: at liftoff, the rocket climbed about four feet in the air before it fell back to the ground in a fiery crash.

Although the U.S. Army beat Vanguard to orbit by launching *Explorer 1* on 31 January 1958, the Vanguard project had its moment of glory on 17 March 1958, when its three-and-a-quarter-pound satellite, *Vanguard 1,* was placed into orbit. As late as 1998, *Vanguard 1* remained the oldest artificial object in orbit. Hagen transferred with Project Vanguard to the National Aeronautics and Space Administration (NASA) when that agency was created in October 1958. Of seven additional Vanguard launches conducted through September 1959, two were successful in lofting satellites into orbit.

After Vanguard, Hagen was NASA's assistant director of space flight development (1958–1960), directed NASA's Office for the United Nations Conference (1960–1961), and then served as assistant director of NASA's office of plans and program evaluation (1961–1962). In 1962 he left government service, becoming a professor of astronomy at Pennsylvania State University in University Park, where he established a graduate program in radio astronomy. He chaired the astronomy department from 1966 until his retirement from the university in 1975. Hagen died of heart failure in a convalescent home in Las Vegas, Nevada.

Hagen was known for an informal management style. "He would putt-putt into the lab early in the morning in an old weather-beaten English auto and drive to his little covered parking spot, the prerogative of government managers above a certain grade, and then come quietly up the stairs with his dented tin lunch box," Vanguard engineer Kurt Stehling recalled.

But this informal air masked a keen intellect and a firm resolve. In many quarters, Vanguard was regarded as a failure and Hagen with it, having lost the race to the Soviets. However, Hagen and his associates had no previous experience to guide them in the technical task of designing a satellite, placing it into orbit, and communicating with it. Given the fiscal and political constraints within which Hagen operated, his leadership of Vanguard can be seen as one of the triumphs of aerospace history.

★

Hagen's papers are at the National Aeronautics and Space Administration, Washington, D.C. His writings include "The Exploration of Outer Space with an Earth Satellite," *Proceedings of the Institute of Radio Engineers* 44 (1956): 744, and "The Viking and the Vanguard," a paper presented to the American Association for the Advancement of Science (28 Dec. 1962). Biographical sources include John G. Rogers, "Man to Watch: John P. Hagen—

Heads Project Vanguard," *New York Herald Tribune* (2 Dec. 1957), and John Lear, "The Moon That Refused to Be Eclipsed," *Saturday Review* (5 Mar. 1960). See also Constance McLaughlin Green and Milton Lomask, *Vanguard: A History* (1971), and Kurt R. Stehling, *Project Vanguard* (1961). An obituary is in the *New York Times* (1 Sept. 1990).

VINCENT KIERNAN

HAGGAR, Joseph Marion (*b.* 20 December 1892 in Jazzin, Lebanon; *d.* 15 December 1987 in Dallas, Texas), businessman and philanthropist who founded the Haggar Apparel Company, which was until 1992 the largest privately owned clothing manufacturer in the United States.

Haggar's father, Khalil Hajjar, a tanner, died in Lebanon after falling from a horse when Haggar was two. One of five children, Maroun, as he was then called, left the impoverished family's one-room home in a sparse farming community just outside the mountain village of Jazzin at age thirteen. Haggar in 1906 boarded a cattle boat bound for Torreón, Mexico, to join an older married sister. He traveled from Beirut to Barcelona to Veracruz, enduring a fierce Atlantic storm on the last leg of the journey. He spent nearly three years with his sister, who taught him to speak Spanish fluently, and he contributed to the household income by peddling small goods to the natives.

At age sixteen, Haggar traveled to the Laredo border, paid the $2 head tax to enter the United States, and crossed the Rio Grande. He joined a gang of Mexican railroad workers and worked his way north to the town of Elgin, Texas. In Elgin he found a job with a cotton farmer, a prosperous German whose wife Haggar later remembered as a wonderful cook. At the end of the cotton season, Haggar moved on, hitchhiking to New Orleans. In 1910 he took a job washing dishes in the Grunewald Hotel. Some months later he moved again, this time to St. Louis, where he became a window washer at the Planters Hotel. He worked alongside the Skouras brothers, who invested in movie theaters in St. Louis. For $200 he could have joined them, but he did not have the cash. Spyros Skouras later became president of Twentieth Century–Fox.

A stocky, handsome, vibrant man, Haggar joined the Lebanese community in St. Louis and attended St. Anthony's Maronite Church, where he fell in love with the organist, Rose Mary Wasaff. He rented a room in the Wasaff home and courted Rose Mary. When the Wasaffs moved to Bristow, Texas, around 1913, Haggar quickly followed.

In Bristow, Haggar went to work as a cotton weigher for Joe Abraham, a Lebanese businessman he had known in St. Louis, who taught Haggar how to buy cotton in the seed and classify it. Haggar took a second job as a grocery clerk and paid the rent on a house in Bristow by selling the

Joseph M. Haggar. COURTESY OF THE HAGGAR FAMILY

peaches that grew on the property. In 1914 he applied for his first citizenship papers. In August 1915 Haggar married Rose Mary Wasaff. She died in 1966, shortly after they celebrated their fiftieth anniversary.

In 1916 Haggar bought and sold an oil lease, a transaction that earned him enough money to move back to St. Louis. It was the heyday of the wholesale dry-goods industry, of which St. Louis was the center. Haggar went to work for Ely and Walker, one of the nation's largest dry-goods companies, supplying retailers throughout the United States, Mexico, and Central America. He worked on commission there for five years, dealing in cotton yardage by the belt.

In 1921 Haggar moved to Dallas and began traveling throughout Texas, Louisiana, and New Mexico as a salesman for the King Brand Overall Company based in Jefferson, Missouri. On 22 January 1923 he became a U.S. citizen. In 1926, when the overall firm's owner, D. H. Oberman, dropped Haggar's territory, Haggar rented small quarters in the Santa Fe Building in Dallas and went into business for himself, selling Oberman work pants and taking out in trade the commission owed him. Within a year he was buying his own piece goods and contracting with factories in the North and East to make the pants. Not satisfied with the quality of the workmanship, he persuaded the make-and-trim team of Harry Vogel and John Sidor to move from St. Louis to Dallas. In 1928 he bought them out and moved into the eighth floor of the Santa Fe Building with a handful of sewing machines and four full-time employees. By 1929 Haggar had established the Dallas Pant Manufacturing Company, inhabiting 6,000 square feet on two floors and employing 250 workers. In the early 1930s the Haggars lived on Lakewood Boulevard in Dallas with their three children: Edward, Joseph, Jr., and Rosemary; later they moved to North Garrett Street. By 1941 the renamed Haggar Apparel Company moved into a ten-acre site on Lemmon Avenue with a building of nearly 100,000 square feet, completed at a cost of $450,000.

Haggar revolutionized the menswear industry, introducing a "one price policy" (establishing a fixed price for an item in every retail outlet nationwide, eliminating the tendency for haggling) and a system of assembly-line production. He worked eighteen hours a day, valued his employees, bought the best materials at a competitive price while maintaining good relationships with his suppliers, appreciated his retailers, sensed what the average man wanted to wear, and made the best quality product possible. In addition, Haggar maintained a state-of-the-art textile laboratory. The Haggar Company popularized the word "slacks," coined the term "wash and wear," applied the term "double knit" to material used in slacks for the first time, and introduced prefinished bottoms for dress trousers. Haggar treated his employees so well that the company was unionized only once, and then for a short time. His salesmen were typically the best paid in the apparel field.

In the early 1940s Haggar began advertising slacks nationally, through the firm of Tracy-Locke—another first in the apparel industry. He started with *Collier's, True,* and *Esquire* magazines, and by the late 1940s and early 1950s had added *Life, Saturday Evening Post,* and *Look*. Later, Haggar moved on to *Sports Illustrated* and added endorsements from such superstars as Mickey Mantle, Arnold Palmer, and Roger Staubach. By 1976 the company employed 150 sales representatives and operated out of sixteen facilities with 7,000 employees.

Haggar's two sons, both University of Notre Dame Business School graduates, contributed greatly to the success of the company and formed with their father a dynamic triumvirate. They gradually took over the company's operations as their father grew older, but Haggar went to his office every day until the time of his death.

In 1972, on Haggar's eightieth birthday, the J. M. and Rose Haggar Foundation, of which Haggar's daughter served as executive director, distributed $3 million among various academic and civic institutions, including the University of Dallas, Southern Methodist University, St. Mary's College in South Bend, Indiana, the University of Notre Dame, the city of Dallas, communities in Texas and Oklahoma with Haggar facilities, and St. Jude's Research Hospital in Memphis, Tennessee. Haggar was named a Knight of Malta and a Knight of the Grand Cross and was presented with the Golden Torch of Hope Award (1971), an honorary doctor of law degree from the University of Notre Dame (1976), and the Horatio Alger Award (1976).

J. M. Haggar died of heart failure in Dallas and was buried in Hillcrest Cemetery in that city. A Lebanese immigrant with no formal education, Haggar had created the largest privately owned apparel manufacturing company in the nation and a foundation that gave more than $1 million a year to charity. His innovations in the menswear industry were widely adopted by other clothing manufacturers. Haggar Apparel Company went public in December 1992.

★

Joy G. Spiegel, *That Haggar Man: A Biographical Portrait* (1978), is a detailed and loving biography, full of anecdotes and reminiscences of and by J. M. Haggar. A tribute by Carol Luker is in the *Texas Catholic* (16 Jan. 1987). Obituaries are in the *Dallas Morning News* and *Dallas Times Herald* (both 16 Dec. 1987).

MARVIN J. LAHOOD

HALLECK, Charles Abraham (*b.* 22 August 1900 in DeMotte, Indiana; *d.* 3 March 1986 in Lafayette, Indiana), lawyer, politician, and Republican leader in the U.S. House of Representatives.

Halleck was one of five children of Abraham Lincoln Halleck and Lura (Luce) Halleck, who were both successful lawyers in a small-town practice. His mother was also a music teacher, and his father served several terms in the Indiana state legislature. A modest success in high school, Halleck served briefly in a student military training program and entered Indiana University in 1918, graduating with an A.B. degree in 1922. He won admission to Phi Beta Kappa but failed in his ambition to win a Rhodes Scholarship. He graduated first in his Indiana University law school class in 1924 and joined his parents' law firm in Rensselaer, Indiana. Nominated as the Republican candidate for circuit court prosecutor a few weeks before finishing law school, he won by campaigning for vigorous enforcement of the antiliquor laws. Despite pressure from party members, he refused to join the Ku Klux Klan, which was then at its peak of influence in Indiana.

Halleck was effective in his part-time service as prosecutor and also maintained a successful law practice. On 15 June 1927 he married his college sweetheart, Blanche White; they had two children. Halleck was widely admired as a public speaker in a culture that still considered oratory a fine art. In 1934, nine days after Republicans regained the rural and small-town Second Congressional District in northwestern Indiana, the successful candidate died. A special election was called to fill the seat, and Halleck won the Republican nomination in a closely contested party convention. He then waged a vigorous campaign to defeat the lame-duck Democratic representative by a modest margin. Halleck was the only Republican from Indiana when he took his oath of office on 5 February 1935, and for fifteen of his seventeen terms in the House of Representatives his party was in the minority.

As a traditional midwestern Republican, Halleck was an isolationist in foreign policy and a firm opponent of most New Deal measures, although he did vote in favor of social security. He was reelected by a modest majority in 1936, once again the state's only Republican in Congress. By the end of the decade he was working closely on the Rules Committee with Democrat Howard Smith of Virginia, the beginning of a long and fruitful association with conservative southern Democrats. His nominating speech for the then relatively unknown Wendell Willkie in 1940 startled many Hoosiers, and he was among the few professional politicians in the Willkie campaign.

Halleck gained influence as the Republicans increased their strength in the House, but he was always more respected than well-liked within the party. From 1943 to 1947 Halleck led the Republican Congressional Campaign Committee, speaking widely in support of Republican candidates. When the Republicans won control of the House in 1946, Halleck was chosen as majority leader. He successfully opposed many of President Harry Truman's domestic policies, but he led the Republicans in support of the Truman Doctrine, a multimillion-dollar aid package meant to keep Greece and Turkey out of the communist orbit, and the Marshall Plan, a vast program of American aid to war-torn Europe. He played an important but behind-the-scenes part in shaping the labor reform bill that became the Taft-Hartley Act.

At the 1948 Republican convention Halleck was courted by Thomas E. Dewey's campaign managers, and he believed that he was promised the vice-presidential nomination in return for persuading the Indiana delegation to vote unanimously for Dewey on the first ballot. Once nominated, Dewey himself told Halleck he would not be on the ticket, but Halleck loyally campaigned for Dewey. "If he'd taken me and made a fight," Halleck said years afterward, "he'd have been president." In 1952 he was on Dwight Eisenhower's secret short list of vice-presidential possibilities. Determined that the Republicans should nominate a winner, Halleck was an early and outspoken Eisenhower supporter, despite strong Hoosier sentiment for Robert Taft.

Halleck was at his best serving as House majority leader from 1953 to 1955, when the Republicans controlled both Congress and the White House. Although he occasionally differed with President Eisenhower, he agreed generally with his moderation and fiscal restraint. Their personal relations were excellent, and Halleck was often invited to join the president on the golf course. After the Republicans lost control of the House in 1954, Halleck was bitterly disappointed when Joseph Martin, who had been House Speaker, decided he would continue to lead the Republicans, as minority leader, after promising to give way for Halleck. After four years of frustration with Martin's weakness, Halleck successfully challenged him for the minority leadership and entered into a new political role in 1958.

Halleck and Senate Republican leader Everett Dirksen spoke regularly with reporters after their meetings with the president. When highlights from their remarks were filmed by television news cameras, the "Ev and Charlie Show" emerged. Dirksen was more colorful, but Halleck held his own before the cameras and effectively presented the Republican view. The "Ev and Charlie Show" continued through the presidency of John F. Kennedy and into that of Lyndon B. Johnson. As leader of the minority party in the House of Representatives, Halleck's chief objective was to maintain Republican unity against the growing challenge of extreme conservatives. No Republican would be rejected, not even outspoken liberals like John V. Lindsay of New York. Halleck himself became a somewhat reluctant but effective supporter of civil rights legislation from 1963 to 1964.

Against his better judgment, Halleck delivered a seconding speech for conservative Republican Barry Goldwater at the 1964 national convention, while surviving a conservative challenge in the Republican primary at home. In the aftermath of Goldwater's disastrous showing in the presidential election and huge losses among Republicans, Halleck was rejected by the greatly diminished Republican minority and replaced by Gerald R. Ford. Halleck remained in Congress until 1968, but his heart was no longer in the political struggle. In politics, he said, there are just three things to do: "You can either quit, get beat, or die. I wanted no part of the last two. So I quit before they beat me." Not at all bitter toward Ford, Halleck retired to practice law in Rensselaer, teaching occasionally at St. Joseph College, finding time for outdoor pursuits—he was an avid hunter and fisherman—but avoiding political activity. Halleck died of pneumonia and is buried at Weston Cemetery in Rensselaer.

Never a vicious partisan, Halleck got on well with powerful Democrats such as Sam Rayburn. He was a skilled debater—clear but never colorful—and a master of House rules, but he enjoyed only one session of Republican dominance. He never lost an election in a political career of forty-four years, stretching from the last days of torchlight parades into the television era. The chief symbol for his district of his long congressional service was Burns International Harbor on Lake Michigan, constructed over the objections of conservationists.

★

The Lilly Library at Indiana University has a large collection of Halleck's papers, uncataloged as of the late 1990s. Henry Z. Scheele, *Charlie Halleck: A Political Biography* (1966), is a straightforward account. Halleck did not write a memoir, but he gave a deatiled account of his career in a long interview for the Indiana University Oral History Research Center, Bloomington, in 1969. There are also brief interviews at the Oral History Program of Columbia University in New York City and at the Dwight D. Eisenhower Library, Abilene, Kansas. Obituaries are in the *Indianapolis Star* (4 Mar. 1986), the *Lafayette Journal and Courier* (3–4 Mar. 1986), and the *New York Times* (4 Mar. 1986).

PATRICK J. FURLONG

HALSTON (Roy Halston Frowick) (*b.* 23 April 1932 in Des Moines, Iowa; *d.* 26 March 1990 in San Francisco, California), international fashion designer and businessman known as the American designer of the 1970s for his luxurious women's sportswear.

Roy Halston Frowick spent his childhood in Des Moines, Iowa, the son of James Edward Frowick, an accountant, and Hallie May Holmes, a housewife with a penchant for sewing and crocheting. The second of four children, Halston showed an early talent for design, making his first hat as an Easter present for his mother in 1945, according to his older brother, Robert Holmes Frowick. The family moved after World War II to Evansville, Indiana, where Halston graduated from Bosse High School. He attended Indiana University for two years, then enrolled for two semesters at the Art Institute of Chicago as a fine arts major.

Never completing college, Halston designed hats while at the Art Institute, selling them in a hairdresser's salon in the Ambassador Hotel. When the hats caught on, the outgoing designer opened his own milliner's salon in Chicago, where he made his first major sale to television performer Fran Allison of the *Kukla, Fran, and Ollie Show.* He stayed in Chicago for several years, building a loyal clientele, but in 1958 he gravitated to New York City, to become the hat designer for the milliner Lilly Daché. The following year Halston joined the millinery salon of the clothing store Bergdorf Goodman, where he later became head milliner. He designed the pillbox hat worn by Jacqueline Kennedy at her husband's presidential inauguration in 1961 and later created others for the First Lady. The dark-haired, handsome designer acquired a following among fashionable women, including Mrs. Henry Ford and Carol Channing. He also attended several European designers' shows with a store buyer, where he saw such designer collections as Chanel and Balenciaga. In 1962 his hat collections earned him his first major award, the Coty Award for Fashion.

Halston, 1976. TYRONE DUKES/NEW YORK TIMES CO./ARCHIVE PHOTOS

In 1966 Halston created his first clothing line for Bergdorf Goodman; with it he attempted to bridge the gap between couture lines and ready-to-wear clothing. His boutique provided the success he needed to launch his own house in 1969 in Manhattan, where he designed ready-to-wear clothing and sold licenses to product manufacturers for his label. His first solo collection for his new fashion house earned him a second Coty in 1969 for the "total look." While only six stores carried it, that collection launched his designing successes, as he turned to budget knits and a line called Halston Originals that sold in department stores nationwide. His innovative use of Ultrasuede (Halston called it "leatherette") in shirtdresses increased his popularity, and he reintroduced cashmere sweater-sets and well-tailored clothing in luxury fabrics, which became a staple of every well-dressed woman's wardrobe in the 1970s. His trendsetting sense earned him two Coty "Winnies," in 1971 and 1972. The success of Halston's collections made him America's most recognized designer among European fashion critics, and it led to the presentation of his clothing, along with that of four other American designers, at a benefit in Versailles, at which the American designers appeared much more fashion-forward than their more conservative French counterparts.

Halston's casual chic brought him customers who had tired of the early 1970s trend toward gypsyish clothing, microminis, and low décolletages; while he produced some clothing along this line, he used plush fabrics and luxury materials, such as chiffon, and introduced the matte jersey, floor-length halter-dress. Various rich and famous women sought out his clothing for its simplicity and comfort. Among them were Liza Minnelli, Lauren Bacall, Naomi Sims, Jacqueline Kennedy Onassis, Bianca Jagger, and Betty Ford. To capitalize on his considerable success, Halston sought ways to increase profits and improve his accessibility to customers, expanding into more product lines, such as his Halston fragrance, launched in 1975, in a bottle designed by Elsa Peretti. His boutique at 813 Madison Avenue in New York, opened in 1972, became one of the centers of the fashion world.

The success of his company, Halston Limited, attracted the interest of Norton Simon, Incorporated, whose chairman David J. Mahoney offered him what seemed like an excellent arrangement. Already used to licensing companies to produce merchandise under his name, Halston signed over to Norton Simon the ready-to-wear line, his couture line, and the Halston trademark; further, he agreed that he would not use the Halston name on products without the corporation's express agreement. Halston Enterprises was renamed as a division of Norton Simon in 1973. Halston trusted Mahoney's judgment and set about licensing more products, producing more perfumes and clothing designs. He designed costumes for productions by Martha Graham and Liza Minnelli; his future appeared enviable to many designers.

Introduced in the 1970s to the nightclub scene at Studio 54 in New York, Halston began to lead an active nightlife and became less involved in the division he headed for Mahoney. Halston engaged in casual, homosexual affairs with a variety of young men in the club scene, which led to his contracting the AIDS virus. He still participated in design and development projects, but his lifestyle inevitably affected his work. Halston's development of a line for the department store J. C. Penney in 1982 caused Bergdorf Goodman to drop him because his name lost its exclusiveness. Then, Esmark, Inc., acquired Norton Simon in 1983 in a hostile takeover, and Halston became unhappy working with their representatives. Finally, Revlon, Inc., purchased the Halston company name; he fought for its possession in 1984 but never reacquired it. After 1984, he stopped designing and looked only to his business interests. He eventually died of AIDS-related cancer in San Francisco in 1990, and his family cremated his remains.

Being tall, dark-haired, and physically attractive helped Halston's status as a designer; his striking appearance in a black turtleneck became almost as identifiable in the American fashion world as did his designs. Halston's achievement—his introduction of luxury sportswear for the American woman—contributed to the later successes of Ralph Lauren and Calvin Klein. His experiences also influenced other designers to strictly limit their licensing agreements. Despite his problems, Halston is remembered for introducing casual fashion to the American woman, with classic designs that reemerge year after year in modern fashion collections.

★

The best account of Halston's design impact is in Richard Martin, ed., *Contemporary Fashion* (1995). The only full-length biography is Steven Gaines, *Simply Halston: The Untold Story* (1991), which zealously covers the details of his adventures at Studio 54. For information on the loss of control of his company, see Lisa Belkin, "The Prisoner of Seventh Avenue," *New York Times Magazine* (15 Mar. 1987). An obituary is in the *New York Times* (28 Mar. 1990).

JENNIFER D. SCHWAB

HAMMER, Armand (*b.* 21 May 1898 in New York City; *d.* 10 December 1990 in Los Angeles, California), industrialist, art collector, and philanthropist who earned fortunes in whiskey and oil and, at least during his early career, facilitated financing of Soviet espionage.

Born in Manhattan's Lower East Side, Armand Hammer was the son of Julius and Rose (Lipschitz) Hammer, Russian Jews who had emigrated in the decade before his birth. Julius Hammer was a militant leader of the Socialist Labor party, and later of the U.S. Communist party, and he named his son after the party's arm-and-hammer symbol. Hammer and his siblings—a half-brother Harry, born to his mother in 1894 in a previous marriage, and Victor, born in 1902—were raised in the Bronx, where their father practiced medicine and ran a pharmaceutical company. They were nonobservant Jews, and religion never played a large role in Hammer's life.

Hammer attended Columbia University and began medical studies there in 1917. In the same year, his father fell ill and management of the pharmaceutical company fell to Armand. Midway through medical school, Hammer also helped his father by secretly attending to patients. In 1919, either Hammer or his father performed an abortion that resulted in a patient's death. Although Hammer later claimed that he had performed the operation, his father assumed responsibility at the time and was convicted of manslaughter. He was imprisoned until 1923; the truth behind the operation was never established.

Armand Hammer. ARCHIVE PHOTOS

Hammer completed his medical degree in 1921 and, although planning to begin a residency that winter, traveled to the Soviet Union at his father's behest, bearing medical supplies to ease a typhus epidemic and planning to establish business connections with Bolshevik friends of his father. Just emerging from the upheavals of revolution, the nation badly lacked basic supplies. Hammer met with Soviet leaders, including Lenin and Trotsky, and founded the Allied American Corporation, a trade firm to export furs and minerals in exchange for American wheat, tractors, and machinery. In 1925 Hammer expanded into manufacturing, founding the Soviet Union's first pencil factory, which produced some 45 million pencils a year by 1928. Though Hammer later described his Soviet years as a time of capitalist enterprising, his success owed much to the sponsorship of the Soviet state which, in turn, depended on the use of Hammer's firms as conduits for payments to espionage agents in America. Hammer's father orchestrated these connections. Although these seditious affairs never became public during Hammer's life, beginning in the 1920s, the U.S. Department of State, the Federal Bureau of Investigation, Britain's MI-5, and the Soviet KGB assembled voluminous files documenting his family's ties to international communism.

Hammer met his first wife in the Soviet Union, a singer named Olga von Root who left her husband to marry Hammer in March 1927. They had a son, Julian, in May 1929, Hammer's only child born in wedlock. Forced out by Stalin's program of nationalization, Hammer sold his businesses to the government in 1929. Although he maintained a lavish image, historians later determined that Hammer probably stood at least half a million dollars in debt. His next venture, the sale of Russian artwork, aimed to cancel this debt while continuing his furtive connections with the Soviet state. Strapped for currency, the Soviets had approached Hammer in 1925 with plans to sell artwork abroad, and for this purpose he established L'Ermitage Galleries in New York City, but the undertaking failed. Hammer resumed this plan when he returned to New York in 1931. He published *The Quest of the Romanov Treasure* (1932), in which he claimed to have spent vast fortunes in Russia acquiring Romanov artifacts. In fact, he received the artwork from the Soviet state, which had confiscated it during the revolution, and Hammer knew that among his "treasure" was much kitsch and some forgeries. Following a nationwide sales tour, he installed the collection at the Hammer Galleries in New York City. Although Hammer received commissions, he remitted the bulk of the proceeds to the Soviets.

Simultaneous with these art transactions, and perhaps as a means of justifying his ongoing payments to the Soviet Union, Hammer began importing Soviet barrel staves to the A. Hammer Cooperage Company in Brooklyn. Though Hammer maintained extravagant airs, depressed markets and problems of loan management kept his profits low. Hammer and his first wife separated during the mid-1930s, beginning Hammer's lifelong estrangement from his son. The two divorced in November 1943, and three weeks later, Hammer married Angela Carey Zevely, an opera singer whom he had been seeing since the late 1930s.

Beginning in the spring of 1940, half a year following the outbreak of World War II, Hammer devoted himself to building support for American aid to Britain. He donated money to pro-British organizations, took out full-page newspaper advertisements, and, most important, created the idea of exchanging American military equipment for leases on British naval and air bases, a concept that President Franklin D. Roosevelt adopted as the basis for America's lend-lease policy.

Hammer made his first fortune beginning in 1944. Although wartime rationing had ended most production of beverage alcohol, Hammer purchased a defunct New Hampshire distillery and, through contacts with New England senators and a handful of presidential officials, gained permission to produce whiskey. Within two years,

Hammer built a liquor empire, United Distillers of America, which owned distilleries in nine states and had revenues of $40 million. Hammer advertised his wealth in the purchase of artwork, an immense yacht, an award-winning herd of cattle, and the Roosevelt home at Campobello, an island estate off the Maine coast which he renovated and donated as a U.S.-Canadian park in 1962. He sold United Distillers in 1953.

In 1953 Hammer began an affair with a Florida waitress named Bettye Murphy, with whom he made vague plans for marriage. After divorcing his second wife in January 1956, however, Hammer married Frances Barrett Tolman, a wealthy California widow. He moved to Los Angeles and relocated Murphy to Mexico City, where, in May 1956, she gave birth to Hammer's child, a daughter named Victoria. Hammer supported the two but hid their existence to his death. Though he had other affairs, Hammer remained married to his third wife until her death in December 1989.

Hammer's final and largest venture began in 1956, when he invested in Occidental Petroleum, a small California oil firm. Within a year, through strength of finance and personality, he was elected president and chief executive officer. He hired a new head geologist, who struck oil at several domestic sites. In the 1960s, through a combination of daring expenditures, intensive lobbying, and selective bribery, Hammer succeeded in winning two of the first and largest oil concessions in Libya. From 1967 until the overthrow of Libya's royal family in 1969, the Libyan reserves built Occidental into a titan.

Libyan colonel Mu'ammar al-Gadhafi's seizure of power threatened to end the nation's oil exports. Unlike the older and larger firms, the so-called Seven Sisters, Occidental would have collapsed without Libyan oil. Thus, while the others maintained solidarity against Gadhafi's ultimatum for greater commissions, Hammer relented in late 1970. His concession forced the Seven Sisters to follow suit, immediately emboldening other petroleum-rich nations to revise their own contracts. None of Hammer's activities was so widely criticized during his lifetime as his Libyan dealings, which many believed responsible for the loss of the Seven Sisters' power over oil pricing, the strengthening of the Organization of Petroleum Exporting Countries (OPEC), and a subsequent rise in global energy prices. Hammer suffered another setback in 1976, when he was convicted of making illegal contributions to President Richard M. Nixon's 1972 campaign; President George Bush pardoned him in 1989.

During the last two decades of Hammer's life, Occidental Petroleum grew to become the eighth largest oil company in the United States, controlling diverse mineral reserves throughout the world. Hammer won praise as a capitalist extraordinaire, yet within Occidental, where he maintained an iron grip over leadership, critics charged him with recklessness and egotism: he planned billion-dollar Soviet developments, despite the tenuous cold war climate; he committed the company to a massive speculative coal venture in China; he left a path of bribery through Africa, Asia, and Latin America; he summarily fired executives who voiced dissent; he appropriated and spent millions amassing his collection of artwork and, in the 1980s, constructing the Armand Hammer Museum in Los Angeles. Such practices prompted numerous shareholder lawsuits and Security and Exchange Commission investigations.

Hammer increasingly dabbled in public and international affairs. He met with Soviet premiers and hoped that his business there might forge international understanding. He arranged for Occidental to endow the Armand Hammer United World College, establish an annual Armand Hammer Conference on Peace and Human Rights, organize international art exchanges, donate to the cause of cancer research, and finance relief efforts following the 1986 Chernobyl nuclear power plant disaster. In an autobiography, *Hammer* (1987), he proclaimed two goals for his remaining years: to cure cancer and promote world peace. He lobbied vigorously but unsuccessfully to be awarded a Nobel Peace Prize.

Hammer died of cancer at the age of ninety-two. He was interred in a family mausoleum at the Westwood Village Cemetery in Los Angeles.

At his death, Hammer was praised as an ingenious capitalist. As sources opened within Occidental, the U.S. government, and the former Soviet Union, however, this view unraveled. Hammer's career, it became apparent, included a foundation of espionage, bribery, and bullying. Hidden facts of manipulation and adultery came to light, and with them the image of a man consumed by hubris. Hammer's long-suspected connection to Soviet communism was definitely established by the historian Edward Jay Epstein in 1996, and it is thus possible that Hammer's most novel contribution—the lend-lease concept—was less an effort to protect Britain than one to delay Hitler's aggression against the Soviets. Yet Hammer himself was no communist. Rather, his work for Lenin in the 1920s seems akin to his donations to Roosevelt in the 1930s, to Ronald Reagan in the 1980s, or to his habitual contributions of money and artwork to leaders through his career, all the actions of one fascinated with power and determined to ingratiate himself to those wielding it. Indeed, Hammer's life is a study in the reaches and limits of power. He created a global financial empire and mixed in the destiny of nations, yet, despite assiduous efforts, Armand Hammer could not conceal his own past from posterity.

★

Hammer's portrayal of his career begins with Armand Hammer, *The Quest of the Romanov Treasure* (1932), resumes in an authorized biography, Bob Considine's *The Remarkable Life of Dr.*

Armand Hammer (1975), and culminates in Armand Hammer with Neil Lyndon, *Hammer* (1987). Critical accounts of his life and dealings are provided in Steve Weinberg, *Armand Hammer: The Untold Story* (1989), and Edward Jay Epstein, *Dossier: The Secret History of Armand Hammer* (1996), both works of professional historians. James Cook, "Smoke, Mirrors, and Armand Hammer," *Forbes* (18 Nov. 1996), demonstrates the nuanced view of Hammer that emerged in the years following his death. An obituary is in the *New York Times* (12 Dec. 1990). The Arts and Entertainment documentary *Armand Hammer* (1996) provides a balanced and interesting look at Hammer's public successes and hidden misdeeds.

DAVID DIAZ

HAMMOND, E(dward) Cuyler (*b.* 14 June 1912 in Baltimore, Maryland; *d.* 3 November 1986 in New York City), epidemiologist who made the first connection between cigarette smoking and lung cancer, heart disorders, and other serious diseases, and was involved in many other studies, including those of asbestos and cancer.

Hammond was the only child of Edward Hammond, Jr., an attorney, and Agnes (Cuyler) Hammond, a homemaker. He had an older half sister, Emily. Hammond's father afforded his son a first-rate education at the Boys Latin School, the Tome School, and later the Gilman Country School for Boys in Baltimore, from which he graduated in 1931.

In September 1931 Hammond entered Yale University's Sheffield Scientific School, where he majored in biology. He graduated with a B.S. degree in 1935 and that year was presented with the William R. Belknap Award for excellence in biological studies. Hammond went on to Johns Hopkins University, where in 1938 he received his Sc.D. from the School of Hygiene and Public Health.

Hammond then joined the Industrial Hygiene Division at the National Institutes of Health, where, as associate statistician from 1938 to 1942, he concentrated on studies of fatigue in interstate truck drivers. He served as consultant in the U.S. Navy's Medical Research Section, Bureau of Aeronautics, in 1941 and 1942, and in 1942 worked in the Civilian Requirements Branch of the U.S. Army's Office of the Quartermaster General. On active duty from 1942 to 1946, he rose to the rank of major in the Army Air Forces. In the statistics divisions of the School of Aviation Medicine and later at the Office of the Air Surgeon, Hammond researched causes of airplane accidents and medical reports of atom bomb survivors.

In the autumn of 1946 Hammond began a forty-year career with the American Cancer Society, the first twenty years as director of statistical research and the second twenty as vice president for epidemiology and statistics. His developing interest in neoplasms and the number of people afflicted by them made his choice of organization an ideal one. The death of his mother from cancer also motivated him to delve into the field. Hammond married Marian Elizabeth Thomas on 3 January 1948, and over the next seven years they had three sons. He and his family lived at 164 East Seventy-second Street in Manhattan, where Hammond spent the rest of his life.

In the early 1950s Hammond noticed that growing numbers of men were dying from lung cancer, and he decided to study the possible connection to smoking. Together with Daniel Horn, he enlisted the assistance of 22,000 American Cancer Society volunteers across nine states. Each volunteer, in turn, recruited several men, aged fifty to sixty-nine, from whom they secured the answers to specific questions about their smoking habits. In total, 187,783 men participated in the study. At intervals of one year the volunteers reported the number of men who died. In all cases Hammond and his team obtained death certificates and then wrote to the doctor, hospital, or tumor registry for more detailed information whenever cancer was the cause of death.

Between 1952 and 1955, 11,870 men died, of whom 7,316 (nearly 62 percent) were smokers who died of heart

E. Cuyler Hammond. COURTESY OF ELIZABETH MCKAY

disease or cancer. Due to the high mortality rate, Hammond decided to publicize the findings earlier than planned in the hope of saving lives. His presentation, with Horn, to the annual convention of the American Medical Association in June 1954 made front-page news around the country.

The impact was so great that cigarette sales dropped by 6 percent that year, and continued to decline for several more years. Hammond, who himself had smoked four packs of cigarettes a day, stopped not long after the results were evident. He continued to smoke a cigar "now and then," he said. Later, he took up a pipe. (His studies revealed a much lower association between cigar or pipe smoking and disease.)

The success of the Hammond-Horn study, published as "Smoking and Death Rates: Report on Forty-four Months of Follow-up of 187,783 Men" in the *Journal of the American Medical Association* in 1958, encouraged Hammond to design and engineer the largest of all of his studies. In late 1959 and early 1960 he engaged 68,116 volunteers across twenty-five states. The volunteers submitted reports each year for six years.

The results were reported in 1966 in a National Cancer Institute monograph titled *Smoking in Relation to the Death Rates of One Million Men and Women.* The statistics disclosed higher death rates among those who started smoking earlier rather than later in life. Cigarette smokers of both sexes died far more often from emphysema, lung cancer, cancer of the larynx, aortic aneurysm, pancreatic cancer, and cirrhosis of the liver than did nonsmokers, though more men than women died overall. Hammond expanded his epidemiological work to include autopsy studies of more than a thousand people.

In 1963 Hammond embarked on a long-term partnership with Irving Selikoff. Hammond's analytic skills and experience with sophisticated studies paired with Selikoff's medical background and connection with a union of asbestos workers made for a productive alliance. The two men developed a study of 17,800 insulation workers and traced them from 1967 to 1976. They encountered a significant cause-and-effect relationship between asbestos and various kinds of cancer, most remarkably, mesothelioma. The results were reported in "Latency of Asbestos Disease Among Insulation Workers in the United States and Canada," published in *Cancer* (15 December 1980).

Hammond generated other large-scale studies involving roofers, who in using hot pitch inhaled above-normal amounts of benzoapyrene. Again, he discovered a high death rate among the workers from lung cancer. His studies of uterine cancer enabled women to assess whether or not they were at risk of getting the disease.

Occasionally facing criticism, particularly from tobacco companies, Hammond was scrupulous in his replies. To critics claiming that subjects might have died from causes other than smoking, his response was to utilize a method called matched-pairs analysis. He matched two groups of men, smokers and nonsmokers, who shared the same age, race, community, history of certain illnesses, and so on. Nineteen variables that related to death rates were selected. In the final analysis more than twice as many smokers died, and heart disease and lung cancer were the primary causes. These facts upheld the results of his larger studies. This study was reported in *Matched Groups Analysis Method,* a 1985 monograph published by the National Cancer Institute.

Hammond's wife died of cancer in 1970. On 23 September 1972 he wed Katharine Sergeant Redmond Evans. For the next fourteen years Hammond continued his investigations into cancer and its connection to environmental factors among various populations of laborers. He also taught at the Mount Sinai School of Medicine as an adjunct professor from 1966 to 1986. Previously, he had been professor of biometry at Yale University from 1953 to 1958. He enjoyed mentoring a few students at a time more than teaching in large lecture halls where, he was convinced, students learned relatively little.

During his career Hammond was the author or coauthor of nearly one hundred articles, and he worked until his last days. In the end Hammond succumbed to the very disease he spent his life exploring, dying at his home of cancer of the lymphatic system. He was buried at St. John's Cemetery in Ellicott City, Maryland.

Hammond's extraordinary ability to design studies of mammoth proportion and to think practically and logistically were assets which led to discoveries that saved a multitude of lives. He was known among his peers as a serious-minded and fiercely honest intellectual. Tall and patrician in bearing, he exuded confidence. Hammond was the recipient of honors and awards, including an honorary doctorate from Johannes Gutenberg University in Mainz-am-Rhein, Germany, in 1969, and the Hodgkins Medal of the Smithsonian Institute in 1976.

★

Hammond's papers are in private hands. A biographical essay is in Marjorie Dent Candee, ed., *Current Biography 1957* (1957). See also E. Cuyler Hammond, "Prospects in Cancer Epidemiology, and a Theory on Carcinogenesis," *Environmental Research* 1 (June 1967), and Lawrence Garfinkel, "Classics in Oncology: E. Cuyler Hammond, Sc.D. (1912–1986)," *Ca: A Cancer Journal for Clinicians* 38 (Jan.-Feb. 1988). An obituary is in the *New York Times* (4 Nov. 1986).

ELIZABETH MCKAY

HAMMOND, John Henry, Jr. (*b.* 15 December 1910 in New York City; *d.* 10 July 1987 in New York City), writer, recording director, music talent scout, disc jockey, critic, and jazz concert promoter who changed the complexion of American popular music by promoting jazz and blues music and elevating it from the category of racially segregated music to a legitimate place in the concert hall.

Hammond was born into a socially prominent family. His father, John Henry Hammond, Sr., was a director of ten corporations and senior member of the law firm Hires, Rearick, Door and Hammond. His mother, Emily Vanderbilt Sloane, was heir to the Sloane furniture fortune and, as a granddaughter of William H. Vanderbilt, to that family's railroad fortune as well. Hammond had four older sisters.

As a child of extreme privilege, Hammond grew up in an eight-story mansion at 9 East Ninety-first Street. He attended Froebel League and Saint Bernards, both exclusive private schools. After graduating from the Hotchkiss School in 1929, he entered Yale University but left in 1931. Obsessed with the music of black Americans, Hammond was indulged by his parents, who financially supported his weekend forays into Harlem in the late 1920s. Rejecting his elite white Protestant background, he demonstrated his social consciousness by having his name removed from the New York Social Register and by moving downtown to the bohemian enclave of Greenwich Village when he reached twenty-one. Regarding his musical explorations, Hammond wrote in his autobiography, *John Hammond on Record* (1977): "I got to know Harlem. Upper class white folks went to Harlem in the twenties slumming. I went out of passion." As a fervent believer in racial equality, he would commit his life, and substantial inherited wealth, to promote both black music and more harmonious race relations.

John Hammond at the 1985 Songwriters Hall of Fame dinner and awards ceremonies. ARCHIVE PHOTOS

Evidence of his support for the oppressed began to emerge in 1929, when Hammond took a summer job as an apprentice reporter for the *Portland (Maine) Evening News* covering the local labor situation. In 1932 he worked as a radio announcer on the left-leaning New York City radio station WEVD (named for Socialist party presidential candidate Eugene V. Debs), where Hammond broadcast live, mixed-race jazz combos, an unheard-of practice at the time.

Contracted by the liberal journal *New Republic,* Hammond journeyed to the Deep South in 1933 to cover the infamous Scottsboro boys trial in Alabama in which nine black youths, accused of raping two white girls, faced a legal lynching. Hammond later claimed he used the occasion to scour the South for authentic jazz and blues artists.

Hammond began to write jazz columns for several British music publications, including *Gramophone* (1931–1933), *Melody Maker* (1933–1937), and *Rhythm* (1937–1939). He was music critic for the *Brooklyn Daily Eagle* from 1933 to 1935 and wrote for the jazz magazine *Down Beat* from the 1930s until his death. At times Hammond wrote under the pseudonym Henry Johnson.

Having established a reputation for an ear for unknown talent, Hammond began a career as a talent scout and recording director. The long list of prominent record labels he worked for include British Columbia and Parlophone (1933–1942); Keynote (1946); Majestic (1946–1947); Mercury (1947–1952); the legendary Vanguard (1953–1958), whose standards of high fidelity were unsurpassed in the record industry; and his most lasting and fruitful association, Columbia (from 1958 until his death).

Hammond later held the unofficial title of "jazz impresario." His initial concert promotion was in 1932, when he acquired the old Public Theater on Fourth Street and Second Avenue in lower Manhattan. It was there that he staged the concerts of his first protégé, Fletcher Henderson. Hammond and Chicago clarinetist Benny Goodman (later his brother-in-law) went on nocturnal excursions into Harlem foraging for new talent.

In 1933 Hammond made his first great discovery, the extraordinary songstress Billie Holiday, "the best jazz singer I've ever heard." Writing in liner notes on Holiday's Columbia reissues (which Hammond produced) in the 1970s, he claimed, "I first stumbled upon Billie Holiday over forty years ago, when she was singing at Monette Moore's speakeasy on West 133rd Street. She was just seventeen . . . she sang as if she really lived. She struck me with an impact rivalled only by Bessie Smith." Dragging a reluctant Goodman "to hear this extraordinary girl who sounded like an instrument and who had a style utterly unlike anyone else's," they became in 1933 the first to record the precocious Holiday. It would take several years for her revolutionary style to gain public acceptance, for as Hammond noted, "innovators were frowned upon in the thirties . . . musically she was way ahead of the times." Hammond supervised her extensive recording dates with Teddy Wilson for the Vocalion and Brunswick labels from 1935 to 1937. These were the recordings that propelled Holiday to international fame, especially in Europe.

One of Hammond's most enduring legacies was convincing Goodman to organize a band in the mid-1930s. It included the brilliant black pianist Teddy Wilson. The trio, with Gene Krupa on drums (later a quartet, with the black vibraphonist Lionel Hampton), was the first interracial jazz group to perform and record for paying audiences.

Hammond's second great discovery was the swing band of Count Basie. A chance hearing of Basie in 1935 over the radio (listening in his car in Chicago) soon had Hammond driving south to the second-floor Reno Club in Kansas City, Missouri. This amazingly creative nine-piece all-star band featured Lester Young on tenor sax, Walter Page on bass, drummer Jo Jones, and blues belter Jimmy Rushing. Hammond brought the Basie band to New York City in 1936, but he later would lose Basie to a more aggressive scout from Decca.

What established Hammond's reputation as a jazz impresario were the two Spirituals to Swing concerts that he organized and presented at Carnegie Hall in New York City in 1938 and 1939. Attempting to legitimize long-stigmatized musical forms, the concerts "brought the full breadth of American black music" to a white public. In 1959 recordings of the concerts were released on the Vanguard label, containing blues, gospel, boogie-woogie, New Orleans style, and contemporary jazz. The roster of artists included "primitive" blues singer Big Bill Broonzy and harmonica player Sonny Terry; black church singer Sister Rosetta Tharpe and the Mitchell Christian Singers; the quartet of boogie-woogie pianists Albert Ammons, James P. Johnson, Pete Johnson, and the form's ultimate practitioner, Meade Lux Lewis. Boogie-woogie, the craze of 1938, was a piano style from the 1920s, rhythmically complex, with eight-note bass patterns. New Orleans style jazz was represented by unparalleled soprano saxophonist Sidney Bechet, and contemporary dance music and swing by the bands of Count Basie and Benny Goodman.

In 1939 Hammond discovered the electric guitarist Charlie Christian. Tipped off by pianist Mary Lou Williams, Hammond traveled west to the Ritz Cafe, a small honky-tonk outside Oklahoma City, searching for Christian. As one of the earliest practitioners of the electrified amplified guitar, Christian was a brilliant innovator whose records (reissued under Hammond's production) continue to dazzle. Recommended to Benny Goodman, Christian joined his band.

Drafted during World War II, Hammond served in the U.S. Army's Information and Education Departments (1943–1946), promoting concerts for the troops. In the 1940s the new jazz style, bebop, flourished. Hammond never had much influence in the new idiom, claiming "bop lacks the swing I believe is essential." As one of the founders of the Newport Jazz Festival, Hammond served on its board from 1956 to 1970. A member of the NAACP from 1935 to 1967 Hammond, who served on its board of directors and as its vice president, resigned in protest over his criticism of a right-wing shift in the organization, specifically its refusal to denounce the Vietnam War.

As director of talent acquisition for Columbia Records in the 1960s and 1970s, Hammond again unearthed a trove of musical stars. As an arbiter of the public's taste, he helped mold another generation of American popular music. Chiefly responsible for bringing folk revivalist Pete Seeger to Columbia in 1959, Hammond withstood considerable corporate resistance over a second folk artist, Bob Dylan, whom he discovered in 1961. Dubbed "Hammond's Folly" after poor sales of his first two LPs, Columbia tried to jettison Dylan. The unique singer and songwriter, whose uncompromising lyrics would change a silent generation into an activist one, broke out in 1963 with his third album, *The Freewheelin' Bob Dylan*, and the huge (and political) hit "Blowin' in the Wind".

After listening to a poorly made demo tape of an obscure songwriter's work, Hammond became determined to sign the unknown female vocalist, who he claimed possessed "the most dynamic jazz voice since Billie [Holiday]." This "untutored genius" was Aretha Franklin, who Hammond signed and recorded with the gospel-inspired jazz pianist Ray Bryant in 1960. Franklin's early Columbia work did not sell well; she would leave for Atlantic Records, where Jerry Wexler made her a giant star in the late 1960s.

Other 1960s artists Hammond worked with included the experimental jazz saxophonist John Handy; smooth guitarist Herb Ellis; Canadian folksinger Leonard Cohen; and the brilliant guitarist George Benson, who became hugely popular as a ballad singer in the late 1970s.

The second "Hammond's Folly" was his early 1970s discovery of Bruce Springsteen. Hammond wrote that "The Boss" was the "greatest talent of the decade." Corporate types again wanted to rid Columbia of a Hammond protégé after disappointing early album sales. Springsteen's *Born to*

Run LP in 1975, however, launched an enormously successful series of albums. Hammond's last great find was the sizzling Texas blues guitarist Stevie Ray Vaughn.

On 13 March 1941 Hammond married his first wife, Jemison McBride. They moved into his Greenwich Village apartment on Sullivan Street. The couple had three children, one of whom, John Paul III (named "Paul" for Paul Robeson), became a noted blues singer and recording artist. The marriage ended in divorce in 1948. He married again on 8 September 1949, to Esmé O'Brien Sarnoff, former daughter-in-law of RCA's chairman David Sarnoff. They lived in an apartment on Fifty-seventh Street in Manhattan.

In the 1970s honors for Hammond poured in. He was named Man of the Century by the recording industry in 1974. In 1975 an educational television program, *A Tribute to . . .*, was produced. Hammond received a Grammy for producing the Columbia reissue series of Bessie Smith recordings in 1971 and *Down Beat* magazine bestowed upon him its Lifetime Achievement Award.

Ill for several years after a series of heart attacks in the 1980s, Hammond passed away at home. The cause of death was undisclosed.

Noted jazz historian Leonard Feather wrote that Hammond "was the most effective catalyst in the development of jazz, as well as its most important writer." The music critic Dave Marsh called him "the greatest talent scout in history." John McDonough observed that "music wasn't just an artistic pursuit in his view, it was a social force—both an agent and expression of broad social and political meaning."

★

Hammond's autobiography, *John Hammond on Record* (1977), is an informative and breezy account of his career. It contains a selective discography with recording dates, selections, and labels from 1931 through 1977 (including the many reissue series he produced). For a deeper musicological analysis of Hammond's contributions, as well as more detailed accounts of Goodman, Holiday, Basie, and Christian, see Gunther Schuller, *The Swing Era: The Development of Jazz, 1930–1945* (1989). Extensive information is in three volumes by Leonard Feather: *The Encyclopedia of Jazz* (1960); *The Encyclopedia of Jazz in the Sixties* (1966); and *The Encyclopedia of Jazz in the Seventies* (1976). Brian Case, *The Illustrated Encyclopedia of Jazz* (1978), has a plethora of anecdotes regarding Hammond in more than twenty separate articles on selected musicians. Colin Larkin, ed., *The Guiness Encyclopedia of Popular Music* (1992), contains much factual data. Insightful observations appear in an obituary by Dave Marsh in the *Village Voice* (21 July 1987). Another obituary is in the *New York Times* (11 July 1987).

JEFFREY S. ROSEN

HANCOCK, Joy Bright (*b.* 4 May 1898 near Cape May, New Jersey; *d.* 20 August 1986 in Bethesda, Maryland), naval officer who in 1948 became one of the first women commissioned into the U.S. Navy; she served as director of the women's reserve (Waves) and as assistant chief of naval personnel for women.

Joy Bright Hancock was one of ten children, eight of whom lived to maturity. Her father, William Henry Bright, was a carpenter, real estate and insurance man, developer, and local and state official, who taught her how to work on a farm, handle tools, and repair bicycles and automobiles. Her mother, Priscilla Buck Bright, taught her how to sew and paint. In her high school at Wildwood, New Jersey, the red-headed, blue-eyed Hancock was the center on her basketball team, president of her sorority, and class historian.

In 1918 she enlisted in the Navy Coast Guard Defense Reserve and served as a yeoman in communications. After attending a business school in Philadelphia, she was assigned to the navy superintending constructor at the New York Shipbuilding Corporation in Camden, New Jersey. Her next assignment was to the Naval Air Station, Cape May, New Jersey, as a stenographer and naval court reporter. Remaining there as a civilian after World War I, she married Navy Lieutenant Charles Gray Little, a blimp pi-

Portrait of Joy Bright Hancock by David Komuro, 1955. COURTESY OF THE U.S. NAVAL INSTITUTE AT ANNAPOLIS, MARYLAND

lot, on 9 October 1920; Little was killed in the crash of the rigid airship R-38 in England on 24 August 1921.

Qualified for the civil service, Hancock next maintained files on aviators for the Bureau of Aeronautics, then transferred to the helium recuperation and storage plant at the Naval Air Station in Lakehurst, New Jersey, where the rigid airship *Shenandoah* was being assembled. On 3 June 1924 she married the ship's executive officer, Lieutenant Commander Lewis Hancock; Hancock was killed in a crash of the airship in 1925. Ill for a year after her husband's death, Joy recovered and traveled around the world with her sister Eloise. After she failed to pass the oral examination for the foreign service, she returned to the Bureau of Aeronautics, and as general information secretary from 1934, she dealt with the press and edited the bureau's newsletter, which later became *Naval Aviation News* magazine. In 1937 she traveled around the world again. In 1942 she became head of the editorial research section at the Bureau of Aeronautics.

Federal law prior to U.S. involvement in World War II specified that only males could serve in the Naval Reserve, but after the creation of the Women's Auxiliary Army Corps in the fall of 1941, the Bureau of Aeronautics asked the Bureau of Navigation (Naval Personnel after 1942) to change the law so that women could serve in a similar corps in the navy. Asked to report on how women could serve in such a force, Hancock investigated how the Royal Canadian Air Force employed women. On 2 January 1942 the Bureau of Navigation finally recommended approval of a wartime women's reserve force by the secretary of the navy. President Franklin D. Roosevelt signed the necessary bill later that year, establishing Women Accepted for Volunteer Emergency Service (Waves). Hancock had to overcome two hurdles to be accepted into the women's reserve: the Bureau of Navigation disqualified her because she was too old—thirty-five—to enlist and lacked college credentials, and the Bureau of Medicine and Surgery disqualified her because she was thirty-three pounds underweight and had a history of gastroenteritis. However, high-ranking officers in the Bureau of Aeronautics obtained waivers for her, and on 15 October 1942 she was commissioned a lieutenant junior grade in the reserves and began serving as the women's representative to the chief of the Bureau of Aeronautics and to the deputy chief of naval operations (air). In this capacity, she was invited to christen the new blimp K-X and also to sponsor a new destroyer, the *Lewis Hancock*, named after her second husband. She also concentrated on women in aviation. (Specifically to overcome her own fear of flying, she had completed her pilot's training in 1928.)

Appointed on 24 February 1946 to the position of assistant director (plans) of the women's reserve in the Bureau of Personnel, Hancock was asked to determine how many women the navy needed to serve in the Waves after the war. By the end of the war there were 8,000 women officers and 78,000 enlisted, with 8,000 in training, 18 percent of the navy's total personnel assigned to the shore establishment in the United States. These women released 50,500 men for duty afloat or overseas and filled 27,000 jobs in the shore establishment.

On 26 July 1946 Hancock was named director of the Waves; she served in this capacity until 1948, the year in which the Women's Armed Services Integration Act abolished the women's reserves. Hancock was one of the first women to receive a commission in the regular navy. She was accorded the permanent rank of lieutenant commander and the temporary rank of captain, and named assistant to the chief of naval personnel, a position she held until her forced retirement at age fifty-five in May 1953. In this position she directed the selection of female naval candidates, their schools and curricula, housing, and recreation, and inspected servicewomen's installations and employment. Upon her retirement she was awarded the Legion of Merit by Secretary of the Navy Robert B. Anderson.

While living in St. Croix, Virgin Islands, Hancock was visited by Vice Admiral Ralph Ofstie, whom she had first met twenty-eight years earlier in Cairo, Egypt, during her trip around the world. They were married in 1954, and Hancock accompanied her husband overseas when he was given command of the Sixth Fleet. Ofstie died in the spring of 1956. Hancock lived in the Washington, D.C., area during the 1960s, then moved to Cape May Courthouse, New Jersey. In 1972 she moved to Carl Vinson Hall, in McLean, Virginia. She died of respiratory arrest at the National Naval Medical Hospital, Bethesda, Maryland, at the age of eighty-eight.

★

Hancock's autobiography is *Lady in the Navy: A Personal Reminiscence* (1972). Nancy Wilson Ross, *The Waves: The Story of the Girls in Blue* (1943), and Virginia Crocheron Gildersleeve, *Many a Good Crusade: Memoirs* (1954), deal with the creation and early work of the Waves. Dan Kasperich, "Women Celebrate Two Decades in the Navy," *All Hands* (July 1962): 8–22, provides text and pictorial coverage. For the Navy Department, Hancock wrote *Waves in World War II,* 2 vols. (1971–1979). U.S. Department of the Navy, *U.S. Naval Administration in World War II: Bureau of Naval Personnel, Women's Reserve* (1976), microfilm, bears the official imprint. Much can be learned from Regina T. Akers, "Female Naval Reservists During World War II: A Historiographical Essay," *Minerva: Quarterly Report on Women and the Military* 8 (summer 1990): 55–61. An oral interview by John T. Mason, "The Recollections of Captain Joy Bright Hancock, U.S. Navy (Retired)" (1979), is at the U.S. Naval Institute. Hancock's work in World War II is given high marks in the oral history of the first head of the women's reserve, Mildred McAffee Horton, "Recollections of Captain Mildred McAfee (Horton), USNR (Ret.)"

(1987), also at the U.S. Naval Institute. An obituary is in the *Washington Post* (22 Aug. 1986).

PAOLO E. COLETTA

HARING, Keith Allen (*b.* 4 May 1958 in Reading, Pennsylvania; *d.* 16 February 1990 in New York City), painter, sculptor, and performance artist, a star of the 1980s New York City art scene known best for his cartoon-like, graffiti-inspired artworks.

The son of Allen Haring, a foreman for Western Electric, and Joan Haring, a housewife, Keith Haring was the eldest of four children. He drew a lot as a child, encouraged by his father, an amateur cartoonist. His adolescent illustrations were humorous narratives peopled with his own characters. As a teenager, Haring was "obsessed by Walt Disney," and his other influences were the author-illustrator Dr. Seuss, the cartoonist Charles Schulz, and such animated television series as *The Flintstones*. In high school Haring began making all-over semiabstract drawings filled with Christian symbolism. (The term "all-over" refers to a type of drawing, painting, or design in which the marks, lines, or shapes are evenly applied throughout the surface of the picture.) It was Haring's ambition to become a professional cartoonist, and after graduating from Kutztown High School in 1976, he moved to Pittsburgh to study at the Ivy School of Professional Art.

Keith Haring in his Pop Shop, 1986. GENE MAGGIO/NEW YORK TIMES CO./ARCHIVE PHOTOS

Haring's stay in Pittsburgh was only six months, but it was decisive for his future. He attended lectures and exhibitions by internationally renowned artists such as Christo and Pierre Alechinsky, read extensively, and studied the art of other cultures, becoming particularly attracted to Aztec design. In 1978 he had his first one-artist show at the Pittsburgh Center for the Arts. In the same year he put aside his commercial ambitions and moved to New York City, where he enrolled in the School of Visual Arts (SVA). His first residence in the city was at the McBurney YMCA on Twenty-third Street near Seventh Avenue.

At SVA, Haring studied abstract expressionist painting, film, performance art, and semiology. Among his teachers were the conceptual artists Keith Sonnier and Joseph Kosuth. Haring also immersed himself in the liberal East Village art scene where he was able to be open about his homosexuality for the first time. He participated in spontaneous art events and "theme nights" at Club 57 in the East Village, where he met other young artists, including Kenny Scharf and John Sex. The early 1980s were an uninhibited, drug-filled, and promiscuous time for Haring.

The subway graffiti of New York and Haring's studies in semiotics inspired him to create his own pictographic street language. In 1980 his signature icons—the flying saucer, a barking dog, and the "radiant" child—began to appear in his paintings. Haring combined and recombined these icons in a series of colorful mazelike paintings, confidently executed in a bold and simple style.

In June 1980 Haring participated in the Times Square Show along with other "underground" and graffiti artists, such as Jean-Michel Basquiat and Fab Five Fred. His works were critically well received, and in the fall he decided not to return to SVA. By 1981 Haring had moved into his own downtown studio on Broome Street and was beginning to make a living as an artist. A catalyst in the graffiti movement, he organized shows at the Mudd Club and Club 57. In 1981 his icons began appearing in unused ad spaces in the New York subways. Between 1981 and 1986 Haring executed nearly 5,000 chalk subway drawings. With these drawings Haring achieved considerable notoriety. Art critics approved but the city police saw his subway drawings as examples of unlawful vandalism. In the early 1980s he was arrested several times and charged with criminal mischief.

In 1982 Haring had his first major exhibition at the Tony Shafrazi Gallery at 163 Mercer Street. In the same year he was invited to participate in the prestigious Documenta 7 exhibition in Kassel, West Germany. In 1983 he was represented in the Whitney Biennial in New York City. The scope of his work had become vast and his energy was seemingly inexhaustible. Along with the subway drawings, his studio work was prolific. His studio pieces tended to be more personal and filled with homoerotic imagery in addition to his standard icons. He often used unconventional materials for his paintings and sculpture—plastic, tarpaulins, and found objects.

In 1981 Haring painted his first mural, in a Lower East Side schoolyard. Virtually every year thereafter until his death Haring was involved in mural projects and public works that took him around the globe; his travels included visits to Sydney (1984), Rio de Janeiro (1984), Amsterdam (1986), Paris (1986), Berlin (1986), Washington, D.C. (1988), and Pisa (1989). Haring's murals often addressed social issues, such as drug addiction and AIDS awareness.

By the mid-1980s Haring had become something of a pop figure. His art could be found in many contexts: on walls, in public spaces, in galleries, on T-shirts, and on buttons. Haring opened two Pop Shops, one on Lafayette Street in New York City (1986) and another in Tokyo (1988), where multiples of his art could be purchased. Haring also painted sets for theater and television, designed album covers, did animated commercials, and created logos for social programs, such as the 1984 "Anti-Litterpig Campaign" for the New York City Department of Sanitation. He also printed and distributed thousands of free posters.

In the late 1980s Haring saw his paintings sell for more than $20,000 each. His yearly group and solo exhibition record was extensive, if not breathtaking, and it indicated his immense popularity and accessibility. Among the last of his philanthropic ventures was the establishment, in 1989, of the Keith Haring Foundation, which sought to raise money to fight AIDS and child drug abuse, and the creation of a United Nations stamp commemorating 1990 as Stop AIDS Worldwide Year. Haring died of AIDS complications in New York City and was cremated.

Haring felt that his goal as an artist was communication. In his brief and successful career, a career that coincided with the bullish 1980s art market, Haring achieved what can only be called mass communication. To do so he planted his feet firmly in both "the street and the gallery," crossing the boundary between fine art and popular commercial art. His visual narratives were poignant and modern; they were at once critical and celebratory of the urban condition. Although Haring never felt that his works had exact definitions, it remains clear that he was addressing the major social concerns of his time: urban alienation, industrial overproduction, racism, and nuclear holocaust.

★

Keith Haring, *Keith Haring Journals* (1996), is a posthumous publication of Haring's personal diaries. John Gruen, *Keith Haring: The Authorized Biography* (1991), contains statements and interviews by Haring, his family, friends and fellow artists. Keith Haring, *Art in Transit: Subway Drawings* (1984), is a collection of photographs of Haring's chalk drawings by the photographer Tseng Kwong Chi. Keith Haring, *Keith Haring: Future Primeval* (1990), contains a comprehensive bibliography and exhibition listing. Germano Celant, ed., *Keith Haring* (1992), contains four critical essays on Haring along with many excellent reproductions of Haring's works. See also Keith Haring, *Keith Haring: Editions on Paper 1982–1990, the Complete Printed Works* (1993). An obituary is in the *New York Times* (17 Feb. 1990). *Drawing the Line: A Portrait of Keith Haring* (1989), is a thirty-minute videocassette portrait of Haring distributed by Kultur.

PETER SUCHECKI

HARLOW, Bryce Nathaniel (*b.* 11 August 1916 in Oklahoma City, Oklahoma; *d.* 17 February 1987 in Arlington, Virginia), presidential adviser who served as the chief White House liaison to Capitol Hill during the Eisenhower and Nixon administrations.

Born to Victor Harlow and Gertrude (Gindling) Harlow, Bryce was raised in Oklahoma City. Interested in public

Bryce Harlow, 1953. ARCHIVE PHOTOS

service, he attended the University of Oklahoma to study political science, graduating with a B.A. degree and a Phi Beta Kappa key in 1936. Harlow continued his studies at the University of Texas, where he served as a graduate assistant in 1937.

In 1938 Harlow left the southwest for Washington, D.C., and secured a job as an assistant librarian in the House of Representatives. In 1940, with war approaching, he left his job on Capitol Hill to join the army, in which he served as part of the congressional liaison staff of the army chief of staff, General George C. Marshall. In the five years Harlow remained on Marshall's staff he rose from lieutenant to lieutenant colonel.

Also in 1940, Harlow married his sweetheart from Oklahoma, Elizabeth ("Betty") Larimore, on 25 September. Two years his junior, Betty had attended the University of Oklahoma, earning a B.A. degree in journalism. She shared Harlow's commitment to public service and served as a Republican precinct captain in both Oklahoma and Virginia. The couple had three children, including a son who also pursued a career in public service.

Harlow returned to civilian life in 1947 as director of the professional staff of the House Armed Services Committee. He held this position until he joined the administration of President Dwight D. Eisenhower in 1952 as an administrative assistant. Eisenhower was the first president to dispatch an official White House lobbyist, General Wilton Persons, to Capitol Hill. Persons had two main assistants, one being Harlow, who concentrated his efforts on the House of Representatives. By the end of Eisenhower's eight years, Harlow was considered the most knowledgeable man in Washington on the legislative process. His courtly manner and low-key style earned him bipartisan respect. Although himself a Republican, Harlow was successful in soliciting the aid of the two most influential Texan Democrats on Capitol Hill in the 1950s, Speaker of the House Sam Rayburn and Senate Majority Leader Lyndon B. Johnson.

Harlow quickly became a vital staff member in the Eisenhower White House. He authored many State of the Union addresses for the president and established himself as Eisenhower's favorite speechwriter. So closely had Harlow worked with Eisenhower during his administration that he served as the general's counselor and confidant during his retirement.

With the election of Democrat John F. Kennedy to the White House in 1960, Harlow joined Procter and Gamble in 1961 as director of government relations. Utilizing the skills he acquired as White House liaison to Congress, Harlow was an effective lobbyist for the manufacturer. However, when Eisenhower's former vice president, Richard Nixon, made a bid for the Republican presidential nomination, Harlow took a leave of absence from Procter and Gamble in 1968 to travel with Nixon during his campaign. Having been Eisenhower's favorite speechwriter and having helped author Republican platforms at the past four national conventions, Harlow became President Nixon's first appointee, announced only a week after the election. Nixon soon made Harlow a counselor to the president in all fields of national affairs.

Harlow left the Nixon administration in December 1970 to rejoin Procter and Gamble, but after many of Nixon's key staff members resigned following the Watergate break-in, Harlow reluctantly agreed to return to the White House in the summer of 1973. He attempted to convince Nixon not to withhold any tape recordings of White House conversations, but to no avail. Frustrated with Nixon's unwillingness to listen to his counsel, Harlow left the White House again in the spring of 1974. Tennessee governor Lamar Alexander, who had worked for Harlow early in his career, once said, "If people had listened to him [during the Watergate scandal], maybe things would have worked out a little better."

Although Harlow ceased to be a political adviser after Gerald Ford's presidency, he remained an astute observer of the Washington scene and occasionally offered advice to President Ronald Reagan. In 1982 President Reagan awarded Harlow the Medal of Freedom, the nation's highest civilian honor, and in June of that year a dinner was given in honor of Harlow by his friends who wished to salute his integrity, humor, and leadership. A scholarship fund was set up that evening for students of business-government relations at Georgetown University. Every year the Bryce Harlow Foundation sponsors an award to recognize an individual who has made an outstanding contribution to the field of business-government relations.

Harlow's wife, Betty, died of cancer in November 1982. Harlow married Sarah Jane Studebaker in July 1983 and lived out the rest of his life in Harper's Ferry, West Virginia. Suffering from chronic lung disorders, Bryce Harlow succumbed to emphysema and diabetes at Arlington Hospital in Arlington, Virginia.

The next day Senate Republican leader Bob Dole remembered Harlow on the Senate floor as "a political activist who spent a lifetime in service to his country." Richard Nixon credited Harlow as being "the ideal presidential assistant, politically astute and totally selfless." Bryce Harlow brought honesty and dignity to the career of public servant. Harlow once described the position of White House liaison with Capitol Hill as "an ambulatory bridge across a constitutional gulf"; Harlow was himself that bridge for nearly fifty years. A humorous man with a slight southern drawl and a short stature of five feet, four inches, Harlow had an immense knowledge of politics and human nature that made him one of the most influential lobbyists of the post-war era.

★

Bradley H. Patterson, Jr., *The Ring of Power: The White House Staff and Its Expanding Role in Government* (1988), although not exclusively on Harlow, serves as an excellent source for the workings of the White House staff. See also "Key Men at White House Now," *US News and World Report* (17 Nov. 1969). Obituaries are in the *Washington Post* and the *New York Times* (both 18 Feb. 1987).

VALERIE L. DUNHAM

HARMON, Thomas Dudley (*b.* 28 September 1919 in Rensselaer, Indiana; *d.* 16 March 1990 in Los Angeles, California), football player and sports broadcaster whose career at the University of Michigan (1937–1941) earned him recognition as one of college football's greatest players.

The youngest of six children of Louis A. Harmon, a police officer, and Rose Harmon, a homemaker, Harmon moved with his family to Gary, Indiana, in 1924. His three brothers were outstanding athletes, and Tom followed in their footsteps by earning fourteen varsity letters in four sports at Horace Mann High School in Gary. During his senior year (1936–1937), he was state champion in the 100-yard dash and 220-yard low hurdles and the nation's leading scorer in interscholastic football, amassing 150 points. One of the most heavily recruited high school football players of the era, Harmon chose to attend the University of Michigan, which at the time did not offer athletic scholarships. He helped pay for his education by doing odd jobs on campus and working in a Gary steel mill during the summers. A serious student, Harmon majored in English and speech in order to prepare himself for a career as a radio sports broadcaster.

Tom Harmon. AMERICAN STOCK/ARCHIVE PHOTOS

In his first year at Michigan, Harmon became an immediate sensation by leading the freshman football team to three victories over the varsity in scrimmage games. He also developed a reputation among his teammates as egocentric and boastful. As a sophomore Harmon was a starter as a blocking back in the Wolverines' single-wing offense. At six-foot-one and 199 pounds, Harmon, called "Old 98" after his jersey number, was a superb blocker and defensive player, but it was his running, passing, and kicking abilities that most impressed Coach Fritz Crisler and Michigan fans. Featured more as a runner and passer as the season progressed, Harmon helped lead Michigan to a 6–1–1 record, the Wolverines' first winning season since 1933.

In 1939 Harmon was switched to tailback and, at the receiving end of quarterback Forest Evashevski, became one of the premier running backs in the nation. Against a powerful Iowa team led by Nile Kinnick, Harmon scored all of Michigan's points in a 27–7 victory. He was a consensus All-America selection that season. Harmon enjoyed his best season in 1940, leading Michigan to a 7–1 record with a number of extraordinary games, including a four-touchdown performance against the University of California. After the season, Harmon was again a consensus All-America choice, won the Heisman Trophy and Maxwell Award, and was voted the Associated Press Athlete of the Year. He finished his collegiate career with thirty-three touchdowns, breaking the Big Ten record held by Red Grange; amassed 2,134 yards rushing; completed 101 passes for 1,396 yards; and scored 237 points. Harmon was elected to the College Football Hall of Fame in 1954. Veteran coach Amos Alonzo Stagg rated him the best all-around college back he had ever seen. Stagg remarked simply that "I'll take Harmon on my team, and you can have the pick of the rest of the backs."

After his last college game, Harmon received numerous offers to play professional football. He was selected by the Chicago Bears in the 1941 National Football League (NFL) draft, but announced that he was not interested in a career in pro football. He did, however, play one game for the New York Americans of the upstart American Football League in the fall of 1941. That same year Harmon earned $25,000 for starring in a Hollywood film, *Harmon of Michigan,* which was neither a financial nor a critical success. In later years he appeared in more than two dozen films, mainly playing bit roles as a sports broadcaster. After graduating from Michigan with a B.A. degree in speech in 1941, Harmon took a job as a sports announcer at radio station WJR in Detroit, beginning a career to which he had long aspired. He broadcast the 1941 Michigan football games with Harry Wismer.

During the fall of 1941 Harmon joined the U.S. Army Air Corps; he received his wings in October 1942. The following April a bomber Harmon was piloting crashed in a South American jungle, and he was the only survivor. Transferred to a P-38 fighter squadron, Harmon served in North Africa early the next year before volunteering for an assignment in the Pacific. He was shot down by a Japanese Zero in November 1943 on a mission in China and was missing for thirty-two days before making his way to safety. Harmon was promoted to captain and awarded the Silver Star and a Purple Heart. When he returned to the United States, he married movie actress Elyse Knox on 26 August 1944 in Ann Arbor, Michigan. They had three children.

After his discharge from the service in 1945, Harmon resumed his sports broadcasting career, doing a nationally syndicated radio program on KFI, the NBC affiliate station in Los Angeles. While continuing in broadcasting, he signed a two-year, $25,000-per-season contract in 1946 to play football with the Los Angeles Rams (NFL). In two seasons with the Rams, Harmon showed flashes of his prewar brilliance, but leg injuries sustained in combat limited his effectiveness, and he retired as a player in 1947. He scored only nine touchdowns in two years, but averaged more than five yards per carry rushing.

As a sports broadcaster, Harmon rose to national prominence and served in a variety of roles. He worked in both radio and television and at one time or another was employed by the National Broadcasting Company, the Columbia Broadcasting System, and the American Broadcasting Companies. Harmon was involved in the writing and production of shows as well as in the announcing of sports events ranging from major college bowl games and the Kentucky Derby to Gaelic football. He maintained that "sports broadcasting was the only job I ever wanted. It was the thing I loved because it put me among people I knew and wanted to be with." After completing a round of golf at the Bel Air Country Club on 15 March 1990, Harmon suffered a heart attack at a nearby travel agency and died of cardiac arrest. He was buried in Los Angeles.

Harmon was one of the outstanding players in college football history. Experts rate him as one of the most versatile backs ever to play the game. He was an outspoken individual whose readiness to admit to his talent was perceived by many as arrogance. One of the pioneers in sports broadcasting on television, Harmon displayed a versatility as a radio and television commentator that matched his multiple talents as a football player. He was as tenacious a competitor in broadcasting as he was on the football field: during the 1960s he sued NBC for trying to ban him from covering sporting events that NBC had exclusive rights to cover. A sometimes controversial figure, Harmon will be remembered both as a football player and for his contributions to the development of sports broadcasting.

★

A file on Harmon that includes newspaper clippings is in the Pro Football Hall of Fame in Canton, Ohio. Secondary works include Albert Hirshberg, *The Glory Runners* (1968); John D. McCallum, *Big Ten Football Since 1895* (1976); Mervin D. Hyman and Gordon S. White, Jr., *Big Ten Football* (1977); and Dave Newhouse, *Heismen: After the Glory* (1985). See also Cameron Shipp, "The Truth About Tommy Harmon," *Sport* 1 (Dec. 1946): 30–32, 90–93; Ed Fitzgerald, "Tom Harmon of Michigan: The Running Story of 'Old 98'," *Sport* 22 (Dec. 1956): 52–62; and Larry Reich, "How Tom Harmon Proved He Wasn't Washed Up," *Great Moments in Sport* 2 (Nov. 1961): 16–20. An obituary is in the *New York Times* (17 Mar. 1990).

JOHN M. CARROLL

HARRIMAN, W(illiam) Averell (*b.* 15 November 1891 in New York City; *d.* 26 July 1986 in Yorktown Heights, New York), financier, sportsman, federal government official, governor of New York, and diplomat best known as a special envoy for Presidents Roosevelt, Truman, Kennedy, Johnson, and Carter.

W. Averell Harriman was the oldest surviving son of Edward Henry Harriman and Mary (Williamson) Averell. His mother, from an upstate banking and railroad family, was a philanthropist, and his father, a self-made millionaire, was a Wall Street financier and a titan of the American railroad industry in the late nineteenth and early twentieth centuries.

A political feud with President Theodore Roosevelt put E. H. Harriman in national headlines, while his predatory railroad deals led to a highly publicized Interstate Commerce Commission investigation and a landmark case before the United States Supreme Court. In the press he was scorned as a ruthless monopolist.

Averell was the fifth of E. H. and Mary's six children. The others were Mary, born in 1881; Henry Neilson, 1883 (who died of diphtheria at the age of five); Cornelia, 1884; Carol, 1890; and Edward Roland, 1895. The children were reared in an atmosphere of extraordinary privilege and fatherly pressure to achieve. Throughout Averell's childhood the family divided its time between a four-story mansion near St. Patrick's Cathedral on East Fifty-first Street in Manhattan and its 20,000-acre Arden estate in the Ramapo Mountains northwest of New York City. During summers there were trips to Europe and transcontinental journeys aboard E. H.'s private railway car. In 1899 Harriman chartered a steamship with a sixty-five-man crew and took the entire family on a two-month expedition along the coast of Alaska. They were accompanied by several in-laws, friends of the Harriman daughters, a party of two dozen scientists,

W. Averell Harriman. COURTESY OF THE LIBRARY OF CONGRESS

a physician, and various servants, camp hands, hunters, and packers. Altogether the party numbered 126. During the 9,000-mile journey, they explored fjords, collected specimens of Alaskan flora and fauna, visited native villages, and crossed the Bering Sea to visit Siberia. In 1905 the family accompanied E. H. to Japan. While the party was in Tokyo the U.S.-sponsored Portsmouth Peace Conference concluded with results bitterly disappointing to the Japanese public, and anti-American riots erupted in the streets of Tokyo. For Averell, the frightening experience stirred an interest in international relations.

In the fall of 1903 Averell entered the Groton School in Massachusetts, where young gentlemen from America's first families were prepared to assume their places as leaders. E. H. Harriman died of cancer in 1909. He was sixty-one years old and at the peak of his career. Averell graduated in the spring of 1909, a few weeks after his father's death, and that autumn he entered Yale.

At the university, as at Groton, Averell was an ordinary student much interested in extracurricular affairs. He was tapped for membership in Skull and Bones, the most prestigious of Yale's secret societies, and he undertook a crusade to restore Yale's fading prestige in intercollegiate rowing, ultimately becoming coach of Yale's varsity oarsmen during his senior year. He graduated with a B.A. from Yale in 1913.

Although Harriman made his name in government, politics, and international diplomacy, he was for twenty years a conspicuous businessman and international financier. Like his father, he succeeded best at the Union Pacific Railroad Company. He joined the railroad immediately upon graduation and was assigned to seek out wasteful practices in its operations. For two years he traveled its rail network from Omaha to the West Coast, inspecting shops, visiting offices, and looking over books. In 1915, still only twenty-four years old, he was named vice president for purchasing.

Harriman opted not to enter the military service in World War I, but feeling an obligation to contribute to the war effort, he resigned from Union Pacific and entered the shipbuilding business, beginning a career marked by bold initiatives and well-publicized reverses. During the 1920s his firms, W. A. Harriman and Company and Harriman Brothers and Company, invested in shipping, mining operations, steel mills, motion pictures, aviation activities, and a host of other projects in America and across Europe. In 1917 he acquired a shipyard at Chester, Pennsylvania, and won a contract to build oceangoing freighters and to construct a new government shipyard on the Delaware River near Bristol, Pennsylvania. By the time the first freighter was launched, the war in Europe was nearing its end, however, and Harriman began moving from ship construction into shipping operations.

In the early 1920s, operating in a partnership with Germany's Hamburg-American Line, Harriman controlled the largest merchant fleet under the American flag, operating freighters in both the Atlantic and Pacific, steamers transporting European immigrants to America, and three luxury liners. Unfortunately, the American shipping industry was left with a huge surplus of cargo ships from World War I; passenger ships sailing under the American flag lost business because they were subject to the U.S. prohibition against alcohol; and American cargo vessels found it increasingly difficult to compete against foreign-flag carriers that paid crews a fraction of U.S. wages. Harriman sold his Pennsylvania shipyard and put his ocean freighters on the market. In the spring of 1925 he and Hamburg-American dissolved their joint operation.

As he withdrew from shipping, Harriman negotiated a twenty-year deal to mine and export manganese from the Soviet republic of Georgia. With exclusive rights to deposits near the Black Sea, Harriman projected his profits at $120 million, but the project soon encountered serious trouble. His experts had badly underestimated the cost of modernizing the mines and the railroads leading to ports. There were disagreements with labor unions and with Georgians who had owned the mines prior to the Soviet revolution. Most seriously, world manganese prices dropped sharply.

In November 1926 Harriman traveled to Moscow, hoping to get more favorable terms. Negotiations with Leon

Trotsky, chairman of the Soviet Concessions Committee, and subsequent talks with lesser officials proved fruitless. Two years later the agreement was terminated. When he pulled out of Georgia he provided the Soviets a $1 million loan and accepted $3.45 million worth of Soviet bonds in payment for his capital investment.

In early 1929 Harriman and former Yale classmate Robert Lehman raised $35 million to underwrite a new corporation called the Aviation Corporation of America (AVCO), with Harriman as chairman of the board. Using the stock of the publicly owned corporation to acquire small companies, they quickly turned AVCO into a conglomerate of manufacturing concerns, passenger lines, air-mail services, airfields, and flying schools. On 24 October 1929, the first day of the stock market crash, AVCO's shares lost more than half their value, and the plunge continued. For the rest of Harriman's tenure as chairman, shares that had opened at twenty dollars traded between two dollars and four dollars on the New York Stock Exchange. In 1932, amidst a battle for control of the company, he stepped down from the chairmanship and became chairman of the board of Union Pacific.

Despite his many high-profile business ventures, Harriman was equally well known as a sportsman and socialite. He hosted huge weekend and holiday parties at Arden House, the mountaintop mansion constructed by his father and given to him by his mother. He played polo with a passion and commitment that carried him into international competition. In 1928 he was one of the stars of the United States' victory over Argentina in the America's Cup matches, then tantamount to the world polo championship. Harriman also bred and trained champion Labrador retrievers and owned and raced thoroughbreds. For a time his racing partner was George Herbert Walker, a partner in W. A. Harriman and Company, and grandfather of President George Bush. An avid skier, Harriman created the Sun Valley resort in Idaho and made it a favorite retreat of Hollywood celebrities during the 1930s. For decades he played intensely competitive croquet and was named to the United States Croquet Hall of Fame when it was organized in 1979.

On 21 September 1915 Harriman had married Kitty Lanier Lawrance of New York and Lenox, Massachusetts, a close friend and riding companion of his sister Carol. The couple had two daughters, Mary Averell, born at the beginning of 1917, and Kathleen Lanier, born at the end of that year; they would be his only children. During much of their fourteen-year marriage Kitty Harriman was in frail health. Averell, traveling the world in pursuit of business deals, was romantically linked with Teddy Gerard, an Argentine-born singer and actress who performed in both Europe and America. The Harrimans were divorced in 1929 in Paris. On 21 February 1930 Averell married Marie Norton Whitney, twenty-seven years old and recently divorced from Cornelius Vanderbilt Whitney.

Harriman's interest in politics and public service was fostered by his sister Mary Harriman Rumsey, a social activist, friend of Eleanor Roosevelt, and founder of the Junior League. Breaking with family tradition, he and Mary voted for Democratic presidential nominee Al Smith in November 1928. Thereafter, Harriman considered himself a Democrat. In 1933 Harriman and his sister became active participants in the New Deal. The following year Mary, who had become head of the National Recovery Administration's Consumer Advisory Board, was fatally injured in a fox-hunting accident near Middleburg, Virginia.

Between 1933 and 1935 Harriman served in several posts in the short-lived National Recovery Administration. Although increasingly involved in government affairs, he continued to serve as chairman of the board of Union Pacific Railroad. He also remained active as a partner in Brown Brothers, Harriman, and Company, the bank created in the 1930 merger of W. A. Harriman and Company and Harriman Brothers and Company with the investment banking house of Brown Brothers and Company.

At Union Pacific, Harriman demonstrated boldness reminiscent of his father, launching an aggressive modernization program that included development of new diesel-powered streamline trains. Shortly after the first streamliner was delivered in 1933, it was taken to Washington, where Harriman conducted President Franklin D. Roosevelt on a personal inspection. In October 1934, aboard a more powerful Union Pacific streamliner, Harriman traveled from Los Angeles to New York in fifty-six hours and fifty-five minutes. The trip broke a 1906 cross-country record set by his father by fourteen hours and thirty-two minutes.

Besides introducing streamliners, Harriman outfitted conventional passenger trains with air conditioning, plush carpets, and comfortable new seats. Pullman cars were equipped with longer bunks and dressing rooms and painted in bright new colors. Sun Valley, Harriman's ski resort created as a destination for Union Pacific passengers, was hugely successful. The modernization stopped the decline of Union Pacific's passenger service, but only temporarily. The golden age of the passenger train had passed.

Harriman's diplomatic career was launched in March 1941, when President Roosevelt dispatched him to London to expedite the flow of Lend-Lease war materiel to embattled British forces. The assignment put him at the crossroads of wartime diplomacy. In addition to his duties as head of the supply mission, he sometimes served as a personal liaison between Roosevelt and Winston Churchill and between Roosevelt and Joseph Stalin. With the exception of a second Roosevelt-Churchill conference in Quebec in September 1944, Harriman took part in all of the wartime Allied summits. He participated in trilateral sessions of

U.S., Soviet, and British leaders at Teheran, Yalta, and Potsdam; the 1941 Roosevelt-Churchill meeting aboard ship off the coast of Newfoundland; and Roosevelt-Churchill conferences at Washington, Quebec, Casablanca, and Cairo.

Harriman became personally, as well as officially, close to the Churchill family. He and his daughter Kathleen were frequent weekend guests at Chequers, the prime minister's country retreat. During relaxed interludes Harriman often played croquet with Churchill's wife, Clementine, and bezique, a card game similar to bridge, with the prime minister. Throughout his more than two years in London, he was also a secret lover of the prime minister's young daughter-in-law Pamela, Randolph Churchill's wife.

From October 1943 until January 1946 Harriman served as the U.S. ambassador to the Soviet Union. He was a staunch supporter of the wartime alliance between Washington and Moscow, but he grew increasingly skeptical of Kremlin intentions. Angry at Stalin's refusal to honor Yalta agreements on Poland, he began to warn Roosevelt, and then Truman, of serious U.S.-Soviet difficulties ahead. In a meeting with Truman five days after Roosevelt's funeral, Harriman characterized Soviet behavior as "a new barbarian invasion of Europe." He departed Moscow five months after the war ended.

In April 1946 President Truman named Harriman ambassador to Great Britain, but Harriman remained in London less than six months, returning to Washington to become secretary of commerce in October. He emerged as one of Truman's most stalwart lieutenants. While secretary of commerce, Harriman chaired the President's Committee on Foreign Aid, which did crucial preparation for the Marshall Plan. When the European recovery program was launched in April 1948, he moved to Paris to coordinate its implementation. With the outbreak of the Korean War in June 1950, he flew home to become special assistant to the president. From 1951 until 1953 he was director of foreign aid under the Mutual Security Act.

In 1952 Harriman became a candidate for the Democratic party's presidential nomination, but he was an ineffective campaigner and did not become a serious contender. He was captivated by electoral politics, however, and in 1954 ran successfully for governor of New York. He was a progressive and modestly successful chief executive, making strides in mental health, consumer protection, and care for the elderly.

In 1956 Harriman made a second bid for the Democratic presidential nomination. He did not begin campaigning until the major state primaries had passed and inevitably he was no more successful than he had been in 1952. His poor showing weakened him in New York State. In his bid for a second gubernatorial term in November 1958, he was resoundingly defeated by Republican Nelson A. Rockefeller.

By the time John F. Kennedy recaptured the White House for the Democrats in 1960, Harriman was sixty-nine years old. Yet he became a significant player in an administration whose hallmark was youth. As ambassador-at-large his dogged pursuit of a settlement of a civil war in Laos in 1961 won the confidence of the forty-three-year-old president. He was rewarded with an appointment as assistant secretary of state for Far Eastern affairs in 1961. In March 1963 he was elevated to the post of undersecretary of state for political affairs. Four months later he led U.S. negotiators in concluding a treaty with the Soviet Union and United Kingdom banning nuclear weapons tests in the atmosphere, in space, and under water. It was the first agreement placing limits on nuclear weapons.

Harriman grew disenchanted with the war in Vietnam as Kennedy's successor, President Lyndon B. Johnson, increased the American military commitment. Replaced as undersecretary of state for political affairs in 1965, he again became ambassador-at-large (1965–1969). Described by the president as America's "ambassador for peace," Harriman traveled to both Europe and Asia in a vain effort to start negotiations with North Vietnam. When preliminary talks finally opened in Paris in May 1968 he headed the American delegation.

The discussions stalled immediately and months were taken up by public posturing and quibbling over parliamentary issues such as the shape of the negotiating table. With the presidential election drawing near, Harriman frenetically worked to arrange a U.S. bombing halt, which he believed would help Democratic candidate Hubert Humphrey against Richard Nixon.

With the Republicans back in power in January 1969, Harriman returned to private life. He traveled extensively in an effort to remain abreast of world issues. In a series of lectures, and in the 1971 book *America and Russia in a Changing World,* he spelled out his view that a peaceful relationship with the Soviet Union was the key imperative of U.S. foreign policy.

On 27 September 1971, a year after the death of his wife Marie, Harriman married his onetime mistress, Pamela Digby Churchill Hayward. Divorced from Randolph Churchill since 1945, she had been widowed by Leland Hayward, a leading theatrical and motion picture producer, the previous March. The third Mrs. Harriman became a Democratic party activist; fund-raiser; leading figure on the Washington social scene; and in 1993, U.S. ambassador to France. She joined Harriman on foreign travels and worked with him in support of nuclear arms control agreements and for ratification of the Panama Canal treaties.

In retirement Harriman made six more trips to Moscow. The last was in June 1983, fifty-seven years after he first went to the Soviet Union for his meeting with Leon Trotsky. Harriman died of respiratory arrest and the afflictions of advanced age. He was buried at the Arden estate, near Harriman, New York, beside the lake where he had learned to row.

Harriman arguably had been the most durable public servant in the history of the United States. Fifty years had passed between his first government job and his last trip to the State Department to report on his final private visit to the Kremlin. He was one of the last survivors from a generation of men from America's social and financial establishment who had played a huge role in shaping the American Century. After his death his friend Arthur Schlesinger, Jr., wrote: "No American of our age has been more identified with the rise of the United States as a force in world affairs."

★

See the Papers of W. Averell Harriman, Manuscript Division, Library of Congress, Washington, D.C. W. Averell Harriman, *America and Russia in a Changing World: A Half Century of Personal Observation* (1971), is drawn from a series of lectures in which Harriman considered the past and future of U.S.-Soviet relations. W. Averell Harriman and Elie Abel, *Special Envoy to Churchill and Stalin, 1941–1946* (1975), is a memoir chronicling his wartime career. Rudy Abramson, *Spanning the Century: The Life of W. Averell Harriman, 1891–1986* (1992), is the only Harriman biography to date, written with Harriman's cooperation. E. Roland Harriman, *I Reminisce* (1975), contains casual family remembrances of a brother. John R. Deane, *The Strange Alliance: The Story of Our Efforts at Wartime Co-operation with Russia* (1946), was written by the top-ranking U.S. military officer in Moscow during World War II. Roger Hilsman, *To Move a Nation: The Politics of Foreign Policy in the Administration of John F. Kennedy* (1967), is a State Department official's view of Vietnam mistakes. David Halberstam, *The Best and the Brightest* (1969), views an aging Harriman as one of the wiser architects of American policy. Chester L. Cooper, *The Lost Crusade: America in Vietnam* (1970), is an insider account by a longtime Harriman aide. Kemp Tolley, *Caviar and Commissars: The Experiences of a U.S. Naval Officer in Stalin's Russia* (1983), offers some of the bright moments of World War II Moscow, including life in Harriman's embassy. Maury Klein, *Union Pacific*, vol. 2, *The Rebirth, 1894–1969* (1990), is part of a railroad history that chronicles the Harriman years. Useful articles include Douglas Cater, "Averell Harriman, Portrait of a Public Servant," *Reporter* (19 Feb. 1952); E. J. Kahn, "Plenipotentiary," *New Yorker* (3 May 1952); and William V. Shannon, "Averell Harriman: The Cold Warrior," *New Republic* (16 June 1952). Obituaries are in the *Los Angeles Times, New York Times,* and *Washington Post* (all 27 July 1986).

RUDY ABRAMSON

HARRINGTON, (Edward) Michael (*b.* 24 February 1928 in St. Louis, Missouri; *d.* 31 July 1989 in Larchmont, New York), socialist leader, author, and educator best known for his book on poverty, *The Other America* (1962).

Michael Harrington was born into a middle-class Catholic family. His father, Edward Michael Harrington, was a patent lawyer; his mother, Catherine Fitzgibbon, was a schoolteacher. He attended St. Louis University High School, graduating in 1944, and the College of the Holy Cross in Worcester, Massachusetts, graduating with a B.A. degree in 1947; he was the class salutatorian at age nineteen.

In 1947 and 1948 Harrington attended Yale Law School, but the following year he transferred to the graduate division of the University of Chicago, where he received an M.A. degree in English in 1949. He wanted to become a poet, and for the next seven or eight years he worked on his poetry every day. He was only modestly successful. In 1949, in an effort to raise money to finance a move to Greenwich Village in New York City, he became a social worker in St. Louis. There he encountered the filth, degradation, and despair of people living in poverty. The experience was so shocking that it shaped his outlook for the rest of his life, throughout which he worked to eradicate such conditions.

Michael Harrington at a press conference on his return from a tour of Vietnam, April 1972. UPI/CORBIS-BETTMANN

Late in 1949 he moved to New York City. There he met nightly with various writers, painters, poets, sailors, stevedores, longshoremen, and others who drifted in and out of the White Horse Tavern in Greenwich Village. He sometimes referred to this experience as his graduate school. Early in 1951 he joined Dorothy Day's radical *Catholic Worker* as an associate editor. The *Catholic Worker* stressed pacifism, volunteerism, and radical social reorganization. He left the Catholic church in 1952 and the *Worker* in 1953, becoming a socialist lecturer and organizer who spoke at colleges all over the country.

In 1953, as McCarthyism was gaining strength in the United States and attacking left-wing groups, Harrington became organizational secretary of the Workers Defense League, a trade-union-sponsored civil liberties group. He also joined the Young Socialist League. As a socialist he soon came into contact with Max Shachtman, a Marxist veteran of many verbal battles with those who supported Stalin and Soviet communism. Harrington supported Shachtman's view that Stalinism was bureaucratic totalitarianism. Furthermore, he believed that democracy was not merely a political superstructure arising out of an economic base, but a fundamental and necessary condition for a proper, ethical social life. Democratic control, he believed, could only exist fully in a socialist society. Harrington was a democratic Marxist. In 1954 he was hired by the Fund for the Republic to study blacklisting in the entertainment industry.

Socialists were divided over the Korean War (1950–1953). Harrington claimed conscientious-objector status. Norman Thomas, the aging leader of the Socialist party, supported the war; Harrington and Shachtman opposed it. Harrington led many New York socialists into a radical antiwar group called the Independent Socialist League and served as chairman of its junior branch, called the Young Socialist League, until it and the parent group rejoined the Socialist party in 1958. Harrington then was made chairman of the Young People's Socialist League, the student branch of the Socialist party. In 1964 he became chairman of the League for Industrial Democracy, an affiliate of the party; he also served on the editorial board of the magazine *Dissent*.

During the 1950s and 1960s Harrington wrote articles for the *Nation, New Republic, Dissent, Commonweal, Commentary,* and other journals, even as he carried on a busy speaking schedule. He became a familiar figure at peace rallies, civil rights marches, and protest gatherings on college campuses. He was also building an international reputation. In 1959 he was a delegate to the International Union of Socialist Youth, which met in Berlin; four years later he was a delegate to the Socialist International Congress meeting in Amsterdam. On 30 May 1963 he married Stephanie Gervis, a writer for the *Village Voice,* in Paris. They had two sons, Alexander and Edward.

Meanwhile, in 1960 he was voted membership on the executive committee of the Socialist party. In 1961 and 1962 he was editor of *New America,* the official publication of the Socialist party. His *The Other America: Poverty in the United States* was published in 1962. This was the book that brought his name before a national public.

In the early 1960s it was widely believed that in affluent America poverty had been nearly eradicated. Harrington, citing facts from available public documents as well as evidence from his own observations, challenged this belief. He claimed that the poor constituted a quarter of the population, some 50 million people. They were, he said, "invisible." The book was credited with fostering President Lyndon Johnson's War on Poverty. Although Harrington was to write fifteen more books, none of the others received the attention of *The Other America.*

From 1968 to 1972 Harrington was chairman or cochairman of the Socialist party. Believing that it was useless for socialists to offer their own slate of candidates and often remarking that he wished to be on the "left wing of the possible," Harrington worked within the Democratic party. After George McGovern was defeated by Richard Nixon in the 1972 presidential election, the conflict between Harrington's views and those of many other socialists, particularly those who supported the war in Vietnam, was so great that he reluctantly resigned from the Socialist party. In 1973 he led anti–Vietnam War socialists into the formation of another political group, called the Democratic Socialist Organizing Committee (DSOC). This was a broad coalition of progressive groups representing labor, minorities, environmentalists, feminists, peace activists, and others. DSOC merged with the New American Movement in 1982 to create the Democratic Socialists of America, with Harrington as cochairman.

Harrington was a professor of political science at Queens College, City University of New York, from 1972 until his death. He was awarded a distinguished professorship there in 1988. A political reformer, more ethical than ideological, he was known as a warm, gentle person, seldom given to rancor, a good speaker who was both inspiring and practical. He died of cancer of the esophagus.

★

Harrington wrote two autobiographies, *Fragments of the Century* (1973) and *The Long-Distance Runner* (1988). The former deals with his religious background, bohemian life, Marxism, and struggles as a socialist; the latter with his broad spectrum of activities on the democratic left and on the international scene. In addition, *Taking Sides* (1985) contains much autobiographical material. For analysis and commentary, see Gary Dorrien, *The Democratic Socialist Vision* (1986). For a brief biographical survey see "Michael Harrington (1928–1989)," *Leaders from the 1960s: A Bio-*

graphical Sourcebook of American Activism, edited by Daniel DeLeon (1994). An obituary is in the *New York Times* (2 Aug. 1989).

ALAN P. GRIMES

HARRIS, Sydney Justin (*b.* 14 September 1917 in London, England; *d.* 7 December 1986 in Chicago, Illinois), author and prolific syndicated columnist, a master of the concise essay, whose popular newspaper column was unusual in that his focus was on morality, character, and a just society rather than on his own personality, topical issues, or politics.

Born in London, Harris was five years old when his parents came to Chicago in 1922. His father was a broker. He began reading at age five and writing regularly at about age eight. For much of his life, Harris read five books a day (eventually slowing down to about ten a week) in philosophy, theology, science, and biography, noted Robert W. Smith in the *Washington Post.* The novelist Saul Bellow, a classmate at Tuley High School, told the *Chicago Sun-Times* that he and Harris spent hours together writing articles, plays, poems, polemics, and stories. Bellow said they so exasperated Harris's mother, Lena Gold Harris, by working so long at her dining room table, that she would plead, "Why don't you go outside to play?" Harris wrote his first book at age fifteen and went to New York to find a publisher without telling his family.

Sydney J. Harris. COURTESY OF THE CHICAGO SUN-TIMES

In 1934, at age seventeen, Harris began his journalism career, working for the *Chicago Herald and Examiner,* leaving the following year. He worked briefly for the *Chicago Daily Times* in 1936. In 1937 he founded an opinion magazine, the *Beacon,* with Bellow as an assistant editor. Harris, who left high school without a diploma, attended the old Central College in Chicago and the University of Chicago, where he studied philosophy, but never received a degree from either. He served a stint in public relations for the city of Chicago from 1939 to 1941.

Harris joined the *Chicago Daily News* in 1941 as a reporter, and he was a columnist and drama critic there until the newspaper folded in 1978, when he went to work for the *Chicago Sun-Times.* His first marriage, to Grace Miller, ended in divorce in 1951. In 1953 he married Patricia Roche; the couple had five children.

Harris began his "Strictly Personal" column in 1944 at the *Daily News* and continued writing it for the *Sun-Times;* it eventually was syndicated in more than 200 newspapers across the United States, Canada, and South America. The column, a fixture for decades on many editorial pages, was a focused and concise but flowing essay of only eight paragraphs; in it, Harris found his ideal form as a writer. Ten of his books were drawn from "Strictly Personal," which was published five days a week for many years of its forty-two-year run. His books are *Strictly Personal* (1953), *A Majority of One* (1957), *Last Things First* (1961), *On the Contrary* (1964), *Leaving the Surface* (1968), *For the Time Being* (1972), *The Authentic Person: Dealing with Dilemma* (1972), *Winners and Losers* (1973), *The Best of Harris* (1975), *Would You Believe . . . ?* (1979), *Pieces of Eight* (1982), and *Clearing the Ground* (1986).

A man captivated by ideas and by the writings of Christian and existentialist philosophers, Harris's columns also featured his aphorisms (for example, "People eventually reject lies, but they embrace myths; and myths are a hundred times more dangerous than lies") and entertaining tidbits, such as "Things I Learned En Route to Looking Up Other Things."

Harris's recurrent theme was how to be fully human, despite ambiguity and difficulty. To Harris, "being and becoming" were the proper aims of life, not having possessions or status. "Our genuine needs are self-confidence, self-esteem, self-sacrifice," he wrote. "These can be achieved only by giving, not by getting." A person's lifelong task, he felt, was to remove the discrepancy between his or her inner self and outer self. "This persona is like the peeling on a banana: it is something built up to protect from bruises and injury," he wrote. "[In] many of us, the real person never comes to life at all, never reveals itself, never knows itself. It . . . dies without ever having found its true existence."

Harris's liberal, humanist views sometimes found controversial expression. He wrote against the Vietnam War in the late 1960s, an unpopular stance to many. He was ahead of his time in taking the position that homosexuality resulted from genetic difference. "Strictly Personal" generated as many as 300 letters a week. Harris said he answered the admiring ones while his secretary answered the insulting ones.

Of his books, the fullest expression of his beliefs was *The Authentic Person,* in which Harris says modern humans are living in the wake of historically crippling blows to their self-esteem and identity dealt by advances in science and psychoanalysis. "Man is uniquely a creature who *cannot* realize his spiritual nature unless and until he translates it into his social nature," wrote Harris. "There is no way to be genuinely spiritual except through one's intentions and acts toward others."

"Strictly Personal" gave Harris a forum before thousands of people. His unique contribution was as a philosopher with the ability to write clearly, concisely, and entertainingly. His column was a pulpit for exploring fundamental truths and appealing to people's better nature. Smoothly and lightly written, many of the essays nevertheless are highly distilled philosophy. Harris touched many lives; his column was cut out and carried in wallets and purses, pasted on gas station walls, and taped to professors' doors.

Recognition for his writing included the 1968 Brotherhood Award of the National Conference of Christians and Jews and the 1980 Freedom of the Press Award of the American Civil Liberties Union. Among his many honors, Harris was very proud of his election in 1982 to the Journalism Hall of Fame in Chicago. He was a member of the usage panel for the *American Heritage Dictionary* and led a "great books" class at the University of Chicago for seventeen years. From September through May he lectured once or twice a week at colleges around the nation, which led to his selection as a regular visiting scholar at Lenoir-Rhyne College in Hickory, North Carolina.

During the school year the Harrises lived on the North Side of Chicago. In the summers they lived in Fish Creek, Wisconsin, in the resort area of Door County, where they entertained friends and family. Having compiled a backlog of columns that could run during the summer, Harris cooked, played tennis, and indulged in word games. Theater, which he reviewed for newspapers for thirty years, remained a lifelong passion. He enjoyed chess and tennis.

"He was very tart and acerbic in his wit," recalled Richard Christianson, chief critic and senior writer for the *Chicago Tribune* and a former colleague of Harris's at the *Daily News.* "He did not suffer fools easily. He was a terrible chain-smoker, and proud of it. He was a nervous man, wrapped very tightly, and edgy in his conversation. But he could be quite sweet and gracious and kind. He was very encouraging to me."

After suffering a heart attack and stroke in 1986, Harris underwent heart bypass surgery in an unsuccessful attempt to save his life. His ashes were buried in Door County.

★

The papers of Sydney J. Harris are at the Newberry Library in Chicago. He has the distinction of being one of the few people treated kindly in A. J. Leibling, *Chicago: The Second City* (1952). Biographical and career information are in Ann Evory and Linda Metzger, eds., *Contemporary Authors,* New Revision Series, vol. 11 (1984). A review by Robert W. Smith in *Book World* (15 Oct. 1982) of Harris's *Pieces of Eight* (1982) examines Harris's work and philosophy and includes biographical details. Eulogies are reported in the *Chicago Sun-Times* (12 Dec. 1986). Obituaries are in the *Chicago Sun-Times,* the *Chicago Tribune,* and the *New York Times* (all 8 Dec. 1986).

RICHARD GILBERT

HART, Marion Rice (*b.* 10 October 1891 in London, England; *d.* 2 July 1990 in Berkeley, California), adventurous sportswoman and author who sailed around the world in the 1930s and piloted seven flights across the Atlantic Ocean in single-engine planes.

Marion Rice was the fourth of six children and was born in London to Isaac Leopold Rice and Julia (Barnett) Rice. Her father was an American corporate lawyer and industrialist who included his family on many trips; her mother had earned a degree in medicine in 1883. Marion Rice distinguished herself academically in 1913 as the first woman to graduate from the Massachusetts Institute of Technology with a degree in chemical engineering. She also earned a master's degree in geology from Columbia University in 1917. The following year she married Arthur Hart, a mining engineer. They did not have children, and the marriage ended in divorce within seven or eight years. Family money allowed Hart to pursue an independent life.

In 1928 Hart moved to a house she had bought near Avignon, France, and had been studying sculpting when in 1936 she bought a seventy-two-foot sailboat named *Vanora* and refit it for a circumnavigation of the world. She had almost no prior experience in sailing. Her letters to her brother I. L. Rice became the basis for her book *Who Called That Lady a Skipper?* (1938). She explained that after "four years of doing stone carving, [she] took on chipping rust"

Marion Hart with her Bonanza single-engine airplane in Dublin, Ireland, en route to Asia, 1975. UPI/ CORBIS-BETTMANN

from the old steel hull. By leading the renovation work with her crew of volunteers, she saved more than half the estimated cost of improvements necessary for such a prolonged voyage. Her "innocent crew" then set off from England on a three-year sail around the world. She commanded and navigated the ketch most of the way, after hiring and firing four professional captains from the time the yacht was preparing to leave England until it arrived in the Gulf of Suez. Her book concluded with the boat at Banda, Indonesia, for Christmas in 1937. She continued on to New Zealand, then through the Strait of Magellan, and arrived in New York City in July 1939 after 30,000 miles.

Hart combined her self-taught experience in practical navigation with her analytical approach to problems. The result was a clear, concise instruction book on celestial navigation, *How to Navigate Today* (1942), which was used by the U.S. Navy during World War II and was still in print almost sixty years later. On the advice of her publisher, she used the pen name M. R. Hart to disguise her gender. During the war she was a shortwave radio operator in the Army Signal Corps.

Hart's desire to fly developed when she was fifty-four years old, some thirty years after her sister Dorothy had taken to the air. Hart once said that she learned to fly so she could "look at the world." In a later interview she said that she liked to set her own schedule and preferred the legroom of the pilot's seat. Shortly after getting her pilot's license in New Jersey in 1946, she bought a Cessna, which she flew to Cuba for the winter, then on to California, hopping between airstrips. Her book on her early flying adventures, *I Fly as I Please,* was published in 1953 and recounts her flights through the Caribbean and South America and up to Alaska. Over the seven years covered in the book, she owned five planes and logged 1,750 hours.

Hart flew transatlantic for the first time in 1953 using her single-engine Beechcraft Bonanza. She and a navigator flew from Newfoundland to Ireland. In 1962 she crossed the Atlantic solo, having fitted her plane with extra fuel tanks. She flew by herself, she explained, to break a psychological barrier. After landing in Ireland with the 2,000-mile flight behind her, she reportedly swallowed a large glass of whiskey in the Shannon Airport lounge and said, "Now I feel better." She was seventy. In total, she flew the Atlantic seven times and ventured to Africa, the Middle East, and as far as Ceylon, Singapore, and Nepal—often flying alone. For twenty-five years her articles appeared frequently in *Air Facts* magazine.

Hart was a slight woman with alert eyes whose idea of a wardrobe was three drip-dry dresses with large zippered pockets to hold flight manuals. She never carried a purse. She easily acknowledged being little and old and a lady but dismissed the categorization. She told *Sports Illustrated* in 1975 that people who used to ask why she did not act like other women were now asking why she did not act her age. "What does age have to do with the way people act? I have no idea what other people my age are doing. I don't know any." In a White House ceremony in 1976 Hart received the Harmon International Trophy "for her consistently outstanding performance as a private pilot operating an aircraft on a global scale." She succumbed to pneumonia at the Alta Bates Hospital in Berkeley, California, and her ashes were scattered at sea as she had requested.

Hart spent much of her long life setting herself extraordinary challenges that required highly developed skills, persistence, and stamina. Sailing around the world in the 1930s was a voyage of exploration, often in isolated circumstances and with incomplete navigational references. She did it for sport. When she wanted to see more, go faster, and not rely on a crew, she took to the air. A fellow pilot who met her at an airport in Rome called her a "courageous, wonderful person who was capable technically and had an insight for instrument flying." During her career, she logged over 5,000 hours and flew solo until she was eighty-seven. Hart did not aim to break convention, and setting a record was irrelevant to this determined individualist. She simply left such things in her wake as she satisfied her peripatetic joie de vivre. During an era noted for its social conformities, she reveled in an independent and self-reliant existence, accomplishing what many might never allow themselves even to dream.

★

Marion R. Hart, *Who Called That Lady a Skipper?* (1938; repr. 1991), is a collection of letters sent to her brother during the first half of her voyage around the world on the *Vanora.* Her second book, *I Fly as I Please* (1953) is a lighthearted review of her first years of flying and adventuring by air. There is an anecdotal entry on Hart, with some insights on her character, in Deborah G. Douglas, *United States Women in Aviation, 1940–1985* (1991). A magazine article by Hart, "She Flew the Atlantic," *Holiday* (May 1953), gives her own account of preparing her plane, circumventing flight restrictions, and piloting a small plane across 2,000 miles of open ocean. Other magazine articles touch on different aspects of her life and travels. In Robert N. Buck, "The Most Unforgettable Character I've Met," *Reader's Digest* (Aug. 1957), a personal friend describes Hart's humor and zest. Diana Goldin, "Up, Up, and Away," *Newsday* (9 Nov. 1967), is an interview with Hart when she was taking a refresher course in instrument flying. She was still flying solo when she talked to Virginia Kraft for "Flying in the Face of Age," *Sports Illustrated* (13 Jan. 1975). An obituary is in the *New York Times* (4 July 1990).

SHEILA MCCURDY

HARTDEGEN, Stephen Joseph (*b.* 16 June 1907 in Philadelphia, Pennsylvania; *d.* 19 December 1989 in Ringwood, New Jersey), internationally renowned biblical scholar and an editor in chief of the *New American Bible* (1970).

Christened Joseph Ignatius, Hartdegen was the son of a German father, Joseph Hartdegen, a cigar maker, and Mary Louise Still from Alsace. He was the second youngest of nine children, and of the seven that survived childhood, five became members of the Franciscan order, including three of his sisters. The Hartdegen children were raised in a devout Roman Catholic household where prayer and spiritual reading were part of the daily routine. As early as age thirteen Joseph was interested in a religious calling. In 1920

Stephen Hartdegen with proofs of the *New American Bible,* 1970. UPI/CORBIS-BETTMANN

he entered St. Joseph's Seminary in Callicoon, New York, a Franciscan preparatory school in Holy Name Province. As he said much later, even at that age he had become "thoroughly captivated by the Bible . . . [and] through Scripture I thought I would get to know Christ better."

On 4 August 1925 Hartdegen was received into the Franciscan Order of Friars Minor in Paterson, New Jersey, and given the name of Stephen Joseph. He made his temporary profession on 5 August 1926 and his solemn profession on 5 August 1929. In 1930 he earned his B.A. degree from St. Bonaventure College (later St. Bonaventure University) in Allegany, New York. Hartdegen was ordained a priest on 14 June 1932 at the Shrine of the Immaculate Conception in Washington, D.C. When asked then about his preference of ministry for the future, he wrote that his first choice was pastoral work, but that "promotion of Bible study for the people" would be among his most important tasks.

The newly ordained priest was assigned to St. Anthony Friary in Butler, New Jersey, as master of clerics while he continued with his studies, receiving his bachelor of sacred theology degree from Catholic University of America in 1933. In 1935 the province sent him to the Pontifical Biblical Institute in Rome, where he earned his licentiate in sacred scripture in 1938, and later to Jerusalem. There he graduated summa cum laude from the Franciscan Biblical Institute in 1939, with a degree in advanced Scripture and biblical archaeology.

Upon his return to the United States, Hartdegen was assigned to the provincial Holy Name College, a Franciscan theological seminary in Washington, D.C., with which he remained until his death. From 1940 to 1968 he taught the New Testament at the college and, briefly, biblical Greek at Catholic University of America (1962–1964).

Around 1935 a group of Catholic prelates proposed a new translation of the Bible in English to replace the Rheims-Douay Version (1609), which was still the official church Bible after its only revision in 1750. In 1936 the Catholic Biblical Association was founded to promote this task, but until the 1943 papal encyclical *Divino Afflante Spiritu,* which encouraged new translations from the original languages, no major translating work was attempted except from the Latin Vulgate. The encyclical revised the terms of such work by the association, and in 1944 Hartdegen was invited to join the group of editors and translators. He became one of five editors in chief and the executive secretary of a project that would take twenty-six years to complete, resulting in the publication of the *New American Bible* in 1970. This translation, at last replacing the Rheims-Douay, became the official Bible for the American Catholic church.

The *New American Bible,* of which parts of the Old Testament translations were issued in the 1950s and 1960s as the *Confraternity of Christian Doctrine,* was based largely on original Hebrew, Greek, and Aramaic sources and on some more recently discovered documents, such as the Dead Sea Scrolls. The ancient texts were translated by American scholars into American English, with several Protestant translators participating in its final stages. In a further ecumenical spirit, proper names were standardized to follow the forms already set forth in the complete Protestant *Revised Standard Version* of the Bible with the Apocrypha (1975).

In a long review of the new Bible in *Worship,* Claude Peifer noted that "the lion's share of the work on the Old Testament was borne by the board of editors," citing Hartdegen's service as secretary, which made him responsible for coordinating the exhaustive translating and editing of the fifty-one scholars involved in the project. Other reviewers praised its "first-rate scholarship," and the editors in chief, including Hartdegen, received the Pro Ecclesia et Pontifice Cross from Pope Paul VI in October 1970 for their work.

In 1950 Hartdegen was given papal permission to found a branch of the Franciscan Secular Institute, the Missionaries of the Kingship of Christ, in the United States, and in 1953 the first five members made their professions. In 1957 he was appointed ecclesiastical assistant of the institute in Washington, D.C., a post he held for many years while membership in the institute spread throughout the country. From 1957 to 1958 Hartdegen was also president of the Catholic Biblical Association of America, the same organization that undertook the work of the *New American Bible,* and from 1964 to 1970 was chairman of the American Franciscan Liturgical Commission. In 1970 he was appointed director of Franciscan Liturgical Projects of the English-speaking Conference of Franciscans, in charge of revising calendars and other liturgy for the Order of Friars Minor. From 1971 until retiring in 1987, Hartdegen was director of the U.S. Center for the Catholic Biblical Apostolate, part of the Department of Education of the United States Catholic Conference.

Hartdegen also wrote extensively on biblical and textual subjects. His books include *A Chronological Harmony of the Gospels* (1942) and *Bible Readings and Studies* (1980). He also contributed numerous articles to the *Catholic Biblical Quarterly, Marian Studies,* and the *New Catholic Encyclopedia,* 17 vols. (1967–1979), among other publications. Finally, he not only edited the *New American Bible* but also *The Prayer of Christians* (1971), *The Lectionary for Lay Readers* (1972–1973), the *National Catholic Directory* (1975–1977), *Nelson's Complete Concordance of the New American Bible* (1977), and the *New Testament Revision of the New American Bible,* his last major work. This revision, begun in 1978 and completed in 1986, was undertaken to correct what were perceived as certain inconsistencies in the 1970 translation. Again non-Catholic scholars were included in the project and again Hartdegen served as its secretary.

In addition to the papal cross, Hartdegen was given the Presidential Award from the National Catholic Education Association in 1979 for his scholarship in Catholic scripture. He was presented with an honorary doctor of letters degree in 1982 from St. Bonaventure University and received another honorary degree from Siena College in 1987.

In 1988 Hartdegen was diagnosed with facial cancer and underwent surgery, which seemed to be successful. The cancer returned, however, impairing his abilities to speak and eat. He died from the disease in the Franciscan Provincial Infirmary. He is buried at Holy Sepulchre Cemetary in Totowa, New Jersey.

From all accounts, Stephen Hartdegen was a gentle, methodical man of absolute faith. One friend described him as "embodying everything he preached . . . his general goodness and humility were attractive and infectious," giving him a kind of "presence." She and others have testified that no matter how busy he was with his teaching and other scholarly duties, he always had time for his pastoral work. According to Flavian Walsh, the provincial vicar of Holy Name Province at the time of Hartdegen's death, "Stephen took great pride in being a friar minor. His understanding of what it means to be a *friar* and what it means to be a *minor* was the daily sermon he preached while he lived among us." Despite all his remarkable accomplishments as a scholar, Hartdegen best described his own attitude about his relation to his achievements by observing that "work gives the Friar Minor no right to claim any part of it as his own or to expect any personal benefit therefrom. God uses us as his instruments . . . we . . . must accept in gratitude whatever [He] gives us . . . [remaining] dependent on the goodness of God."

★

Very little has been written about Hartdegen. The St. Bonaventure University archives contain some biographical material not available elsewhere. The discussion in the *Provincial Annals* (1989) of the Holy Name Province is highly reliable. Interviews of Hartdegen are in *New Catholic World* 230 (Jan.–Feb. 1987): 38–41, and *Our Sunday Visitor* (31 May 1987). An article in the *New York Times* (25 Aug. 1970) on the publication of the *New American Bible* is helpful. An extensive review by Claude J. Peifer of the *New American Bible* is in *Worship* 45 (Feb. 1971): 102–113. The best obituary is in the *Washington Post* (21 Dec. 1989).

SANDRA SHAFFER VANDOREN

HARTZ, Louis (*b.* 7 April 1919 in Youngstown, Ohio; *d.* 20 January 1986 in Istanbul, Turkey), political theorist and historian whose seminal work helped to create a lasting debate about American liberalism.

Hartz was the youngest son of Max Hartz, a grocer, and Fannie Plotkin, both Russian Jewish immigrants. He grew up in Omaha, Nebraska, and graduated from Omaha Technical High School in 1936. Hartz's long affiliation with Harvard University began when he went to college in 1936. He graduated from Harvard summa cum laude and Phi Beta Kappa in 1940 and returned the following year to pursue a doctorate in political science. Hartz had not planned to attend graduate school but was invited to work with the Committee on Research in Economic History, a project of the Social Science Research Council. The committee hoped to answer conservatives' charges that the New Deal had deviated from the country's putative laissez-faire tradition by showing that the main legacy of economic policy in the United States was not laissez-faire but government regulation. Hartz's own effort at dismantling what he called "the myth of laissez-faire" was his dissertation on state economic regulation in antebellum Pennsylvania, published as *Economic Policy and Democratic Thought: Pennsylvania 1776–1860* (1948).

While in graduate school, on 3 July 1943, Hartz married Stella Feinberg, a Boston social worker, with whom he had a son. He also began his teaching career as an instructor in Harvard's Department of Government in 1945. In 1946 he obtained his Ph.D. and the following year became an assistant professor. Hartz was tenured, at age thirty-one, in 1950. He became a full professor in 1956.

Having in effect supported New Deal liberalism in his early work, in the 1950s, with the ideological rigidity of the cold war, Hartz became more critical of liberalism in general and more impressed with its power to shape American society. In this context he wrote *The Liberal Tradition in America* (1955). By far his best-known work, it sparked passionate debate over the character of American politics and helped to establish a historiographical school that emphasized the consensual and exceptional nature of these politics.

In a caustic tone, Hartz argued that the United States had always possessed a uniquely centrist political ideology—Lockean liberalism—that severely constrained politics and society. This ideology was Lockean because it celebrated individualism and private property but was also "irrational" because it was applied in unthinking and self-contradictory ways. What ensured liberalism's initial success in America was a concrete social fact: the absence of feudalism. Lacking a feudal class, Americans were without a revolutionary tradition and concomitant reactionary conservativism; could believe that they were "born equal," as Alexis de Tocqueville had said; and could more safely posit a limited role for the state.

Although interested in social origins, Hartz saw ideas themselves as the ruling force in politics. Once having invented liberalism, Americans developed an unconscious and absolute attachment to it. To analyze the latent content of political thought, Hartz teased out the implicit assumptions embedded in American political language. These assumptions explained America's uncritical embrace of capitalism and its unresponsiveness to alternative ideologies, such as socialism, qualities that distinguished the United States from Europe. In trying to demonstrate America's uniqueness, Hartz employed a comparative methodology, full of references to European thinkers and history, that would become the hallmark of his future work. Only comparison could illuminate the peculiarities of each national experience as well as the linkages among them.

The search for unanimity in American public life was a common feature of cold war scholarship. Unlike many consensus historians, Hartz did not simply use consensual liberalism as evidence for American superiority over communism. Pointing to McCarthyism, he instead warned of "the danger of unanimity" and suggested that American liberalism lacked vision, flexibility, and even tolerance of those who fell outside of it. While claiming to be universal, it was actually a nationalist ideology that was astonishingly parochial.

Hartz's argument resonated in the 1950s as scholars sought an explanation for the seemingly self-affirming character of American national politics. In subsequent decades, however, historians would come to see more diversity in American political beliefs and to question the idea of a uniform cast of mind as an explanation for American politics. Nevertheless, Hartz's book continued to set the terms of the debate.

Amid the social ferment of the 1960s, Hartz turned to the problem of revolution for newer societies such as the United States. Spurred by extensive traveling, he applied his theory of history developed in *The Liberal Tradition* to other European colonial progeny, which he now called "fragment" cultures. In *The Founding of New Societies* (1964), he argued that Latin America, South Africa, Canada, and Australia, along with the United States, were fragments of European culture. As fragments, however, they also broke from Europe in search of their own national identity, based on flight from Europe and its revolutionary conflicts.

In an increasingly interconnected world, where one nation's revolution was another's foreign policy concern, Hartz saw an opportunity for fragment societies to finally confront social revolution. Testifying before the U.S. Senate Committee on Foreign Relations in 1968, Hartz cautioned that there was no more escaping revolution for the United States. Optimistically, Hartz predicted that as a global leader the United States would be able to transcend its ideological stasis through encounters with nonliberal systems.

This visionary quality made Hartz a very popular teacher throughout the years, but in 1974 he abruptly resigned from Harvard following a mental breakdown. He left his family and spent most of the rest of his life traveling and living abroad. Whatever the nature of his affliction, it did not prevent him from continuing to write and think. As if in defiance of the American provincialism he had earlier identified, Hartz endeavored in his extraordinarily ambitious final work to devise a universal theory that could explain all forms of cultural "absolutes," or systems of thought, around the world, from religions to philosophies to political theories. This was possible because Hartz now thought that universalistic psychological rather than particularistic social causes were the main determinants of thought. *A Synthesis of World History* (1984) argued that social thought derived from an unbearable "tension" in human beings between their "active and passive impulses." Social thought repressed the tension by synthesizing these impulses. Again placing faith in cosmopolitanism, Hartz hoped that recognition of this common psychological underpinning would lead to an acceptance of moral diversity. Hartz published *A Synthesis* privately in Zurich; it remains unpublished in the United States. Hartz died of a seizure.

Hartz's distinguished career as a professor at Harvard University was cut short by an early retirement, but in his more than a quarter century of teaching and writing he gained the attention and respect of scholars from a variety of disciplines, principally for *The Liberal Tradition in America,* which remade the study of American political thought and quickly became a canonical text. In addition to two prizes from the American Political Science Association—the Woodrow Wilson Prize in 1956 and the Lippincott Prize in 1977—it earned Hartz perhaps the most coveted reward in academia, his own adjective: "Hartzian."

★

Hartz's papers are at Harvard University but remain private. There is no published biography of Hartz; the most extensive treatment of his life and work is in Patricia Eugenia de los Rios Lozano, "Louis Hartz: Political Theorist" (Ph.D. diss., University of Maryland, 1994). Biographical information can also be found in Harry Schneiderman and I. J. Carmin Karpman, eds., *Who's Who in World Jewry* (1965), and Glenn B. Utter and Charles Lockhart, eds., *American Political Scientists: A Dictionary* (1993). Articles that focus on Hartz's writings include Samuel Beer, "In Memoriam: Louis Hartz," *Political Science* 19, no. 3 (summer 1986); and Patrick Riley, "Louis Hartz: The Final Years, The Unknown Work," *Political Theory* 16, no. 3 (Aug. 1988).

Hartz's best-known work is *The Liberal Tradition in America* (1955). For more information on his ideas, see *The Necessity of Choice: Nineteenth-Century Political Thought* (1990), an edited compilation of his lectures, and "Coming of Age in America," *American Political Science Review* 51 (June 1957); "Democracy: Image and Reality," in William N. Chambers and Robert H. Salisbury, eds., *Democracy Today* (1960); and "A Comparative Study of Fragment Cultures," in Hugh Davis Graham and Ted Robert Gurr, eds., *Violence in America: Historical and Comparative Perspectives* (1969). An obituary is in the *New York Times* (24 Jan. 1986).

ANNE KORNHAUSER

HASSENFELD, Stephen David (*b.* 19 January 1942 in Providence, Rhode Island; *d.* 25 June 1989 in New York City), business executive and third-generation leader of the family-owned Hasbro, Inc., a toy manufacturer that under his direction became a Fortune 500 company.

Stephen Hassenfeld was a son of Sylvia Kay and Merrill Hassenfeld. His father was the second generation of Hasbro toy manufacturers, a company founded in 1923 by three brothers of Polish Jewish descent: Henry (Stephen's grandfather), Hillel, and Herman. The Hassenfeld brothers (thus the name "Hasbro") began as distributors of fabric remnants but soon made profits by wrapping cloth around cigar boxes to produce creative pencil cases. The brothers pur-

Stephen Hassenfeld, chairman and chief executive officer of Hasbro, Inc., with some of his company's products. AP/WIDE WORLD PHOTOS

chased a pencil-manufacturing firm and began marketing school supplies. With the outbreak of World War II, plastics became difficult to acquire, and the Hassenfeld brothers began manufacturing a line of toys—paint sets, junior-air-raid-warden sets, wax crayons, and doctor and nurse kits, marketed in the same pencil-case boxes—while continuing to produce school items.

Stephen Hassenfeld later told the *New York Times,* "I grew up with everybody's toys." The Hassenfeld children (Stephen had a brother, Alan, and a sister, Ellen, who also were later involved in the family's toy-making enterprise) were showered with factory samples, game prototypes, and salesmen's gifts, all due to their father's involvement in the toy industry. With these influences surrounding him, he knew from the time he was very young exactly what he wanted to be, and that was a toy manufacturer. As an adult, he never changed his mind. "Whenever the investment community asks what I'm going to do next," he once said, "I've replied: 'The grass isn't greener elsewhere; it's greenest right here.' "

Hassenfeld majored in political science at Johns Hopkins University in Baltimore from 1959 to 1962. He dropped out in his senior year and went to work for his family's toy business in 1964. In 1968 he became executive vice president, in charge of Hasbro corporate hiring. His assignment was to build a new management team inclined to take risks. In the early 1970s Hassenfeld led the company into day-care centers and housewares, but both ventures were utterly unsuccessful. After becoming Hasbro's president in 1975 Hassenfeld shackled the company with rigid principles, including the requirement that each proposed toy pass a return-on-investment analysis. With that standard, not many of the toys reached the production stage. In one instance Hassenfeld authorized an early monster toy called Terron the Terrible. It failed miserably, which helped push the company into the red in 1978.

At this point Hassenfeld developed a more individual management method. As he recounted for *Business Week,* his new philosophy was to "look for three traits in a toy: lasting play value, shareability, and the capacity to stimulate the imagination." While Hassenfeld still relied on conventional business techniques to run the business generally, toy selection became largely intuitive.

When Hassenfeld became chairman of the company in 1980, it was the nation's sixth largest toy manufacturer with annual sales of about $100 million. Hassenfeld methodically transformed Hasbro, once labeled "Hasbeen" by industry humorists, into the company with the broadest production line in the business. During his tenure, the company was said to have become the world's largest toy manufacturer, with sales of more than $1.3 billion. Much of Hasbro's success was attributed to Hassenfeld's enterprising acquisition of other toy producers, such as Milton Bradley, and to the dramatic growth of its GI Joe line of soldiers and of its Transformers, vehicles convertible into robot figures. Hassenfeld's first big success was his 1982 reintroduction of GI Joe. The doll was originally marketed in 1964 as a World War II–era soldier and in 1970 was reintroduced as a cadre of smaller, less militaristic adventurers. The toy was no longer billed as "a fighting man from head to toe" but as "a real American hero." The new-fashioned GI Joe doll racked up $49 million in the first year of sales. Other basic, perennially favorite toys that contributed to Hasbro's success under Hassenfeld were Raggedy Ann and Andy dolls, Mr. Potato Head, and the Playskool line of products for infants and children.

Hassenfeld was active and influential in numerous business, civic, and charitable causes. He founded the Hasbro

Children's Foundation in 1984 to help poor and homeless children, and he received humanitarian awards from the Rhode Island Council of the National Jewish Hospital and the Rhode Island Big Brothers Association. His significant memberships included the Rhode Island Jewish Federation, the National Council of Christians and Jews, the United Way, and the Rhode Island Strategic Development Committee.

Hassenfeld shared a house in Rhode Island and an apartment in New York City with his brother, Alan; neither brother was married. (Alan Hassenfeld took a leadership role in the company after his brother's death and immediately faced a hostile takeover attempt from the toymaker Mattel.) His waterfront property in Bristol, Rhode Island, as well as a home in Palm Beach, Florida, enabled him to indulge in his hobby of sailing, while the Midtown Manhattan apartment where he resided afforded access to the theater and ballet. But to all appearances, Hassenfeld's primary passion was work. His days began at 5:30 A.M. and rarely ended before midnight; his life, he told interviewers, was devoted to his dream of what Hasbro would become, and he found "his challenges and joys in generating profits for Hasbro." To him toys and games were not fun, they were part of a battle on the field of business. He died of pneumonia and cardiac arrest, complications of AIDS, at Columbia Presbyterian Hospital in New York City following four weeks of hospitalization.

Hassenfeld, a trim, dark-haired man, was once described as "the curly-haired dynamo, who relies on gestures to help make his points." His force, imagination, and genius transformed a family-owned toy company into a global, billion-dollar concern.

★

John Ingham and Lynne Feldman, *Contemporary American Business Leaders: A Biographical Dictionary* (1990), sketches Hassenfeld's career. Philip Gutis, "Trying to Run a Bigger Hasbro," *New York Times* (4 Aug. 1985), is an interview with Hassenfeld. Articles on Hassenfeld's success at Hasbro include Lois Therrien, "How Hasbro Became King of the Toymakers," *Business Week* (22 Sept. 1986); Neil Downing, "Stephen Hassenfeld, Hasbro Inc.," *Financial World* (21 Apr. 1987); Nathaniel Gilbert, "Stephen Hassenfeld: More Than a Family Affair," *Management Review* (Sept. 1987); and Richard Kindleberger, "Aftermath of a CEO's Death," *Boston Globe* (27 June 1989). G. Wayne Miller, *Toy Wars: The Epic Struggle Between GI Joe, Barbie, and the Companies That Make Them* (1998), tells the story of the Hassenfeld family with a focus on the fortunes of Hasbro after Stephen Hassenfeld's death. Obituaries are in the *New York Times* (27 June 1989) and *Chicago Tribune* (28 June 1989).

KAREN LYNN SVENNINGSEN

HAUGHTON, Daniel Jeremiah (*b.* 7 September 1911 in Dora, Alabama; *d.* 5 July 1987 in Marietta, Georgia), president and chairman of the board of Lockheed Aircraft Corporation who transformed the company from a general builder of airplanes to a major defense contractor.

One of two children of Gayle Haughton, a farmer, storekeeper, and timekeeper, and Mattie (Davis) Haughton, Daniel displayed a talent for business at age eight by loaning money to friends for two weeks and charging 20 percent interest. After spending just three years in high school, in 1929 he enrolled in the University of Alabama to study accounting. He graduated in 1933 with a B.S. degree in commerce and business administration. Like his father, he worked as a timekeeper and distribution checker from 1933 to 1934, first with the Dwight P. Robinson Construction Company, then with the American Potash and Chemical Corporation, both located in Trona, California. Setting his sights on the aircraft industry, he found a job with the Goodyear Tire and Rubber Company's "flying squadron," a production group in Los Angeles, and then he became a cost accountant with the Consolidated Aircraft Corporation in San Diego. On 28 September 1935 he married Martha Jean Oliver; they had no children.

Haughton joined Lockheed in 1939 as a systems analyst, a job that was so novel at the time that the manager of a furniture store refused Haughton credit. In 1949 Haughton was given charge of two troubled subsidiaries. Within two years he put them in the black, and Lockheed was able to sell them. In 1952 he became manager of Lockheed's giant Georgia division, and in 1956 he became a vice president of the company, at which time he returned to California and established his residence in Studio City; he eventually advanced to president of Lockheed in 1961 and chairman of the board in 1967. Courtlandt Gross, a Harvard graduate who had previously run Lockheed along with his brother, expressed confidence that Haughton, a former farmer, truck driver, and coal miner, possessed the leadership qualities and salesmanship to build up the company. In 1957 Haughton won a critical contract with the U.S. Army to build the Cheyenne, a rigid rotor helicopter. When the U.S. Army needed a helicopter to closely support combat troops, the Lockheed contract for an experimental craft capped the cost to no more than 115 percent of the bid price. In 1968 Haughton secured a contract with the army to produce the new TriStar jet.

Haughton foresaw the importance of the aerospace industry, and he transformed Lockheed Aircraft Corporation from a general builder of airplanes to a defense contractor. Under Haughton, Lockheed Missiles and Space Company, located near San Francisco, had more successful launchings than any other aerospace manufacturer. The Lockheed Agena, the "workhorse of space," was launched hundreds of times on missions for the U.S. Air Force and the National Aeronautics and Space Administration (NASA).

Daniel J. Haughton, 1961. UPI/CORBIS-BETTMANN

Other Lockheed successes included the Polaris and Poseidon missiles (introduced in 1960 and 1970, respectively), antisubmarine patrol planes for the U.S. Navy, carrier-based antisubmarine craft, the C-130 Hercules transport (first deployed in 1954), and the cargo carrier and the cargo air transport built for use in the Vietnam War. Lockheed also created gear that enabled offshore oil drilling in deeper waters and made possible the mining of minerals on the ocean bottom. However, by the late 1960s cost overruns in producing military transports began to cause financial woes for Lockheed.

Although Lockheed was the largest defense contractor, by 1970 the company appeared ready for bankruptcy, partly because of the risks Haughton took with the fixed army contracts. Technical problems with the Cheyenne made the army nervous, which led to contract cancellations and frequent appearances by Lockheed officials before Congress. Lockheed also had problems with the TriStar jet, because Rolls Royce was unable to produce the engine, the improved turbofan, as agreed. In 1971 Haughton asked Congress for $250 million to underwrite loans that banks had made to Lockheed, and he offered to step down from the company in return for approval. He won by a margin of one vote in the Senate, but the ensuing investigations revealed that many of the overseas trips he took had involved enormous payoffs to win aircraft sales. Accusations of bribery ensued.

After approaching various companies, the Lockheed directors in 1973 hired Lazard Frères and Company to advise them on their equity base. They worked out an arrangement to save Lockheed whereby G. William Miller, chairman of Textron, became chairman of Lockheed without merging the companies, and Haughton became vice chairman of Lockheed. The arrangement was contingent upon Lockheed securing forty-five additional orders for the TriStar by 30 November 1974. In 1976 Haughton resigned from Lockheed Aircraft amid charges of bribery.

Haughton liked to stress his humble beginnings, and he enjoyed showing up managers who thought little of southerners. Indeed, he cultivated the art and science of what could be called the beginning of corporate welfare and encouraged the government to support expensive research and development that had civilian applications. Called "Uncle Dan" by his employees, he was known for courtliness, loyalty, and sales leadership.

Haughton, who was thin and six feet tall, slept barely five hours a day, working from 6 A.M. to 6 P.M. He sat on the board of directors of the Southern California Edison Company, the United California Bank, and the Los Angeles World Affairs Council, and he directed the National Multiple Sclerosis Society and the American Red Cross in Atlanta and Los Angeles. George Washington University awarded him an honorary LL.D., and Clarkson College of Technology an honorary doctor of science. He spent his few days off on his 425-acre farm near Marietta, Georgia, where he bred Black Angus cattle and fished for bass and bream, which he called bluegills. He died in Marietta of complications from heart and gall bladder surgery.

Haughton embodied the Chinese written character for "change," a mixture of danger and opportunity. He recognized the necessity of taking risks to win big contracts and elevate the status of his company, and he also did whatever it took to ensure that his company survived and remained profitable. He was a business engineer who said engineering is not an exact science but rather one that has to be invented as one goes along. He was also an accountant who persuaded Congress to give millions to a private contractor in the name of public safety and national preparedness, interweaving private-sector technology, public-sector politics, and the economy.

★

Discussions of Haughton and his career are in *The Blue Book Leaders of the English-Speaking World* (1976); "Lock Step at Lockheed," *Time* (17 Feb. 1967); "Two Old Friends Who Worked Their

Way to First Class," *Fortune* (1 Aug. 1969); and "For Lockheed, Everything's Coming Up Unk-Unks," *Fortune* (1 Aug. 1969). Obituaries are in the *New York Times* (7 July 1987); *Time* (20 July 1987); and *Current Biography Yearbook 1987* (1988).

AMY AN MEI B. WONG

HAUGHTON, William Robert ("Billy") (*b.* 2 November 1923 in Gloversville, New York; *d.* 15 July 1986 in Valhalla, New York), the most successful harness racing trainer-driver in American history.

The only child of William F. Haughton, a pattern cutter in a glove factory, and Edith Greene, Haughton was raised in Fultonville, New York. Young Billy's love affair with horses began when he was about five years old, when his father gave him a pony named Betty. While attending Fultonville High School, Haughton began working as a groom in the area's harness racing fair circuit. He began driving in his late teens and had his first winner in 1942. After failing an army physical exam, Haughton enrolled at Cobleskill Agricultural College, from which he received a degree in animal husbandry in 1946.

Haughton opened a public stable in Saratoga, New York, in 1947. He quickly gained a reputation as an outstanding trainer-driver. In 1949 Haughton moved his stable to Roosevelt Raceway in Westbury, New York, on Long Island. Roosevelt Raceway would remain his summer base for the rest of his career. In his early Roosevelt years, Haughton's name became linked with that of Stanley Dancer, Haughton's longtime friend and rival. Haughton and Dancer so dominated the driver standings in the New York City area that the two became known as the "gold dust twins." Haughton's national reputation was given a major boost in 1949, when he drove Chris Spencer to victory in California's Golden West Trot, Haughton's first win in a $50,000 purse event.

By the early 1950s, Haughton's reputation as a consummate trainer-driver was firmly established. On 24 November 1951 he married Dorothy Bischoff, with whom he had five children: Peter, William, Thomas, Robert, and Holly Ann. During the 1950s Haughton would win the Cane Pace, the Messenger Stakes, and the Little Brown Jug, harness racing's premier pacing events. Haughton's win in the inaugural Messenger Stakes with Belle Acton was especially important to him because this outstanding pacing mare would always remain one of his personal favorites. Haughton was the national leader in driving wins from 1953 to 1958, the leading money-winning driver from 1952 to 1959, and Harness Horseman of the Year in 1958.

The 1960s brought continuing success to the Haughton stable, which achieved two more victories each in the Messenger Stakes and the Cane Pace, and three Little Brown Jug titles. In 1968 Haughton handled Rum Customer, who won the triple crown of pacing. Only the Hambletonian, the top event for three-year-old trotters, continued to escape Haughton's grasp. By the 1960s, Haughton had come to hold a leadership position in harness racing. He was a director of the U.S. Trotting Association and in 1968 was elected to the Living Hall of Fame of harness racing. His status as a complete horseman was underlined by the fact that he authored both the chapters on yearling selection and driving in the classic work *Care and Training of the Trotter and Pacer* (1968), edited by James C. Harrison.

Haughton's Hambletonian drought ended in 1974, when he scored an upset victory in the Hambletonian with Christopher T. After also winning the Hambo in 1976, Haughton came back in 1977 with Green Speed, who not only won the Hambletonian but was also chosen Harness Horse of the Year. By this time Haughton was supervising the training and racing careers of well over 100 horses. He managed to accomplish this task with hard work, good help, and the ability to catnap anywhere, at any time.

The 1980s began with tragedy for the Haughtons. Their son Peter, who was having an outstanding career as a trainer-driver, was killed in an automobile crash in 1980. Billy Haughton would start to deal with this incalculable loss by taking Burgomeister, developed by Peter as a two-year-old, to victory in the 1980 Hambletonian. During the

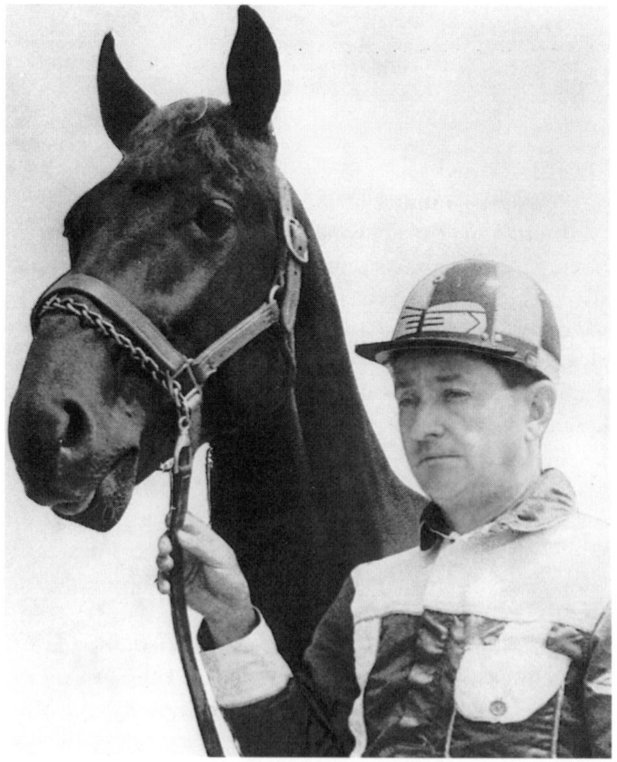

Billy Haughton with the racehorse Romulus Hanover, 1967. UPI/CORBIS-BETTMANN

1980s, Haughton started to cut back somewhat on his driving schedule. The size and quality of his stable, however, continued unabated. In 1984 and 1985, for example, the stable developed Nihilator, arguably the best pacing colt in the history of the sport.

When, on a summer evening in 1986, Haughton took his place behind the starting gate with a young pacer, he had behind him a career unmatched in harness racing. He and the sport of harness racing reasonably expected that more good days lay ahead. Both hopes were terribly dashed. On 5 July 1986 Haughton suffered fatal head injuries in a racing accident at Yonkers Raceway. He died ten days later and was buried in Westbury, New York.

As a driver, Haughton won over 4,900 races and more than $40 million in purses. As a trainer, he developed champions by the handfuls. These statistics, however, convey only a minor part of his legacy. Haughton's major contribution was as a role model. He demonstrated how to win with class. His career stands as impressive evidence that one can be both a fearless competitor and a gracious gentleman.

★

Obituaries are in the *New York Times* (16 July 1986) and *Time* (28 July 1986).

JAMES FETZER

Woody Hayes, Ohio State University football coach, on the sidelines as his team competes with the University of Southern California in the 1975 Rose Bowl. UPI/CORBIS-BETTMANN

HAYES, Wayne Woodrow ("Woody") (*b.* 14 February 1913 in Clifton, Ohio; *d.* 12 March 1987 in Upper Arlington, Ohio), college football director famed for his tenure as head coach of the Ohio State Buckeyes from 1951 to 1978.

Hayes was the son of Wayne Benton Hayes, a self-educated public school administrator, and Effie Jane (Hupp) Hayes. Woody (a nickname he acquired as a youngster) attended public schools in Newcomerstown, Ohio, where his stern but caring father served as school superintendent. Feeling less talented than his older brother, Ike, who became an All-American football player at Iowa State University, and his sister, Mary, who became New York's first female radio announcer, Woody attempted to achieve through energy and determination. His sister remembered him as "a natural leader" and the "toughest kid on the block."

Following his graduation from high school in 1931, Woody attended Dennison College, where he majored in history and English while playing football, basketball, and baseball. He graduated with a B.A. degree in 1935 and considered attending law school. Instead he settled for a teaching position at Mingo Junction High School in Steubenville, Ohio, where he also served as assistant football coach. In 1937 he moved to New Philadelphia High School as a teacher and assistant coach and the following year was named head football coach. During the 1938 and 1939 seasons, his teams won eighteen games while suffering only one loss. The next season his team lost all but one game, however, and parents and school officials began to question the coach's tough, abrasive, and demanding style. Discouraged with coaching, Hayes resigned prior to the 1940 season to enter the U.S. Navy. By this time he had begun work on his master's degree in educational administration from Ohio State University in Columbus, which would qualify him for a position as principal or superintendent. Attending summer classes and serving in the navy, he did not complete his degree requirements until 1948. In 1942 he married Anne Gross; they had one son.

In 1946 Hayes was honorably discharged from the navy with the rank of lieutenant commander, and he quickly embarked upon a college coaching career that would make him a national celebrity. In the spring of 1946 he became head coach at Dennison, which had dropped its football program during the war years. Hayes's first Dennison team posted a poor 2–6 record, but his 1947 and 1948 teams both had undefeated seasons. Success earned Hayes in 1948 the coaching job at Miami University in Oxford, Ohio, where, after a mediocre 5–4 season in 1949, his team won the 1950 Mid-American Conference with a record of 9–1. Ohio State now took note of Hayes and in 1951 named the relatively unknown coach over such nationally prominent figures as Cleveland Browns coach Paul Brown to head one of the nation's most prestigious, demanding, and troubled football programs. Ohio State was then known as "the coaches' graveyard" because of the failures of a succession of coaches to satisfy alumni and fans with conference championships and victories over the University of Michigan, the school's most despised rival. At Columbus, Hayes found himself the object of harsh criticism after his first three Ohio State teams lost to Michigan in two of three games and posted an overall record of sixteen victories and nine losses. His team's victory over Michigan in 1952 was the first by any Ohio State team in eight years, however, and his 1953 team, led by Howard ("Hopalong") Cassady, a junior, held the promise of greatness. Indeed, the following year Ohio State went undefeated, crushed the University of Southern California in the 1955 Rose Bowl, and was named the consensus national champion. Cassady received the Heisman Trophy as college football player of the year.

Hayes's tenure was now secure, and the volatile, tough, thick-bodied coach soon became known for his sideline histrionics as well as his gridiron triumphs. Over the next twenty-four years, attendance at Ohio State's football games often exceeded 85,000 enthusiastic fans. On most Saturday afternoons, the Buckeyes pounded out victories with an unspectacular but relentless running attack described as "three yards and a cloud of dust." During his twenty-eight years with Ohio State, Hayes led the Buckeyes to four undefeated seasons (1954, 1961, 1968, and 1973); three national titles (1954, 1957, and 1968); thirteen Big Ten Conference championships, six of which were shared with Michigan as cochampions; and five postseason bowl game victories, including four Rose Bowl triumphs. Yet to many Ohio State fans, Hayes's greatest achievement was his 16–11–1 record against archrival Michigan. He was named college coach of the year in 1957 and 1975, and his lifetime coaching record of 238 wins, 72 losses, and 10 ties placed him among the greatest college coaches of all time.

Hayes, who never coached for a school outside the state of Ohio, built what admirers and critics viewed as a football "machine," which included a vast network of wealthy, well-coordinated boosters, such as John Galbreath, a real estate mogul; loyal alumni; and supportive high school coaches, many of whom had played for Hayes, taken his college football courses, or attended his coaches' clinics. The machine, along with Hayes's vast network of acquaintances and his tireless efforts, produced a steady stream of high school talent for the Buckeye program.

Hayes rarely turned down an invitation to speak to a civic club or alumni group. He charmed the parents of high school prospects, demonstrated an unflinching loyalty for his players and assistant coaches, and gave his time generously in support of charitable and philanthropic causes. Hayes always considered himself an educator first and foremost. He enjoyed conversations at the faculty club with professors from diverse disciplines; encouraged his players to earn their college degrees, although many did not; and helped numerous assistants secure head coaching positions, among them Ara Parseghian, Bo Schembechler, and Lou Holtz. An avid reader of history, and especially of military history, Hayes often used military terms and anecdotes in explaining his football strategies. A lifelong Republican, he espoused a conservative political creed and developed close personal relationships with numerous like-minded politicians, particularly Ohio governor James A. Rhodes and U.S. president Richard M. Nixon.

A series of highly publicized controversies and Hayes's own pugnacious and explosive personality clouded his record in Columbus. In 1956 Robert Shaplen, a reporter for *Sports Illustrated,* wrote an article, "The Ohio State Story: Win or Else," that disclosed irregularities and Big Ten Conference rule violations, including small personal loans the coach had made to several players. Both the National Collegiate Athletic Association (NCAA) and the Big Ten Conference briefly banned Ohio State from postseason competition. Hayes retaliated a few years later by evicting Big Ten sportswriters and officials, including the conference commissioner Kenneth ("Tug") Wilson, from a preseason practice, forcing university officials to apologize for the incident. In 1959 the ethics committee of the American Football Coaches Association rebuked Hayes following a locker-room altercation with two California sportswriters, and that same year Hayes publicly challenged Forest Evashevski, the Iowa head coach, to a fistfight. Hayes's tirades were even directed against his own institution. At the end of the 1961 season, when a faculty committee voted not to accept an invitation to the Rose Bowl on grounds that the academic programs at Ohio State were being neglected because of an emphasis on football, Hayes let his anger and frustration fuel several days of student riots in protest of the faculty decision. Hayes lashed out at the director of the school's alumni association, Jack Fullen, who had become a critic of the football program, calling him a "dirty sonofabitch," a "bastard," and an "old prick."

During his final years of coaching, Hayes's boiling point seemed to lower. Before millions of shocked television viewers in 1971, he ripped up the sideline markers during the final moments of a bitter loss to Michigan. In 1973, just prior to a Rose Bowl game, he pushed and slightly injured a *Los Angeles Times* photographer, and four years later an altercation with an ABC-TV cameraman in Michigan resulted in a second probation from the Big Ten commissioner's office. In 1974 Hayes suffered the first of two heart attacks. Finally, at the 1978 Gator Bowl, his self-acknowledged inability to control his temper cost him his job when, in the waning minutes of a tough 17–15 Buckeye loss, he slugged a Clemson University player who had run out of bounds after intercepting an errant pass from Ohio State's freshman quarterback. Hugh Hindman, the Ohio State athletic director, fired the old coach within hours of the nationally televised incident.

Following his dismissal from coaching, Hayes remained on the school's faculty. His popularity with most Ohio State fans continued undiminished, and his charitable endeavors and modest personal lifestyle helped rehabilitate his image, even among former critics. His health, however, began to decline, and he suffered a stroke and his second heart attack. In 1983 he was voted into the Hall of Fame of the National Football Foundation. As the winter quarter commencement speaker at the university just a year prior to his death, Hayes received an honorary degree and told the graduating class: "There's only one thing that you cannot afford ever to do. That's feel sorry for yourself. You can't do it." He also assessed his own abilities and his approach to coaching success: "There are smarter people than I. But you know what they couldn't do: they couldn't outwork me."

Hayes died from a heart attack at his home in Upper Arlington, Ohio, a suburb of Columbus. Former president Richard Nixon delivered the eulogy at his funeral, and the following day a crowd of 15,000 attended a memorial service for the coach at the Ohio State football stadium. Hayes is buried at the Union Cemetery in Morrow, Ohio.

★

The archive at the Ohio State University library holds an extensive collection of Hayes papers and memorabilia. Hayes authored or coauthored several books: *A Survey of the Post-War Football Coach in Ohio Secondary Schools* (1948); *Football at Ohio State* (1957); *Hot Line to Victory* (1969); and *You Win with People!* 2d ed. (1973). Also see Robert Vare, *Buckeye: A Study of Coach Woody Hayes and the Ohio State Football Machine* (1974); Jerry Brondfield, *Woody Hayes and the 100-Yard War* (1974); and Timothy Weiger, *The Buckeyes: Ohio State Football* (1974). Obituaries are in the *Columbus Dispatch* (13, 14, and 18 Mar. 1987), which printed a memorial issue devoted to Hayes (2 Apr. 1987); and the *New York Times* (13 Mar. 1987), which printed related articles (18 and 19 Mar. 1987).

MICHAEL J. DEVINE

HAYNSWORTH, Clement Furman, Jr. (*b.* 30 October 1912 in Greenville, South Carolina; *d.* 22 November 1989 in Greenville, South Carolina), federal appellate judge and rejected nominee for the U.S. Supreme Court.

Clement F. Haynsworth, Jr., during his unsuccessful confirmation hearings before the U.S. Senate Judiciary Committee, 1969. ARCHIVE PHOTOS

Clement was one of three children of Elsie (Hall) Haynsworth and Clement Furman Haynsworth, a fourth-generation lawyer. Clement attended public school in Greenville and a preparatory school, the Darlington School, in Rome, Georgia. In 1933 he graduated summa cum laude with an A.B. degree from Furman University, a Baptist institution founded by his great-great-grandfather, Richard Furman, in Greenville. He then entered Harvard University's School of Law, receiving his LL.B. degree in 1936. He was awarded the Order of the Coif and ranked fifty-first in a class of 399 students.

Returning to Greenville, Haynsworth joined his family's law firm and remained until the outbreak of World War II. Haynsworth served as a lieutenant with naval intelligence in Charleston, South Carolina, and San Diego, California. On 25 November 1946 he married Dorothy Merry Barkley, a divorcée with two sons; they had no children of their own. His law practice in Greenville remained the central focus of his activities, and by 1946 he was a senior partner in the firm. Well connected socially, economically, and politically, Haynsworth identified himself as an Eisenhower Democrat, and in 1956 he was active in fund-raising for Dwight D. Eisenhower's presidential campaign. His cousins, Mr. and Mrs. Alestair G. Furman, Jr., close friends with the Eisenhowers, were personal guests of the president at the inaugural. Thus, Haynsworth's nomination for a seat on the Fourth Circuit Court of Appeals in 1957 was no surprise to those around him. The appointment made Haynsworth the youngest judge on the court, which served Virginia, West Virginia, Maryland, and the Carolinas.

Haynsworth was the epitome of South Carolina's gentry class. With family wealth rooted in the textile interests that dominated Greenville, Haynsworth's friends and associates were white, upper-class, country club aristocrats. One of his favorite pastimes was bird watching. Another was camellia growing, which he did in the greenhouse behind his Tudor home of pale gray brick. At one time he had also been an avid dove hunter, but he abandoned the sport because of his concern not to break any of the complicated legal rules governing that activity. Law became his principal absorption. Haynsworth's personality was not that of the advocate but more that of the judge. A man of medium height with an erect bearing, a heritage of his naval days, Haynsworth had a fair complexion with gray eyes and thick brownish hair that thinned with age. A heavy smoker, he had a slight lisp and stammer. Scholarly in appearance, he was shy, decorous, and retiring by nature. He possessed a ready wit and a good sense of humor; he was unemotional, almost phlegmatic, in his delivery, however, and he was not amused by any humor or wit that attorneys might display in his courtroom.

Haynsworth began his apprenticeship as a judge on the Fourth Circuit under a master, Chief Judge John J. Parker of North Carolina. Parker had been rejected for the U.S. Supreme Court in 1930 because of the opposition of labor and civil rights organizations. He had chosen to remain on the Fourth Circuit and thus became an intimate friend as well as mentor of Haynsworth. From 1957 to 1969 Haynsworth participated in a number of significant cases, many of which would be upheld by the Supreme Court, but a number of cases would be overturned, including some that involved labor and civil rights matters. Among these was *Griffin* v. *Board of Supervisors* (1963), in which Haynsworth appeared to support a plan in Virginia's Prince Edward County to close public schools that had been ordered to integrate and to subsidize private all-white schools. The Supreme Court ordered the reopening of the public schools in Virginia and in essence nullified the Fourth Circuit's ruling. Haynsworth ruled against organized labor in a 1963 case involving the Darlington plant of Deering-Milliken that was closed after the workers voted for union representation. He upheld the employer's right to close an individual textile mill for antiunion purposes, a holding reversed by the Supreme Court. This was one of seven labor cases in which Haynsworth and the Fourth Circuit's antiunion rulings were reversed by the Supreme Court. Nevertheless, Haynsworth gained the reputation of being a legal craftsman and a hardworking jurist on an efficient court.

In 1964 Haynsworth was promoted to chief judge and praised as a good administrator. It would be that attribute of administrative efficiency that Senator Ernest Hollings, Democrat of South Carolina, would stress when suggesting Haynsworth as a possible nominee to fill the Supreme Court vacancy resulting from the forced resignation of Justice Abe Fortas. President Richard M. Nixon had met Haynsworth only once, but he saw in the judicial profile presented by Hollings the type of jurist he desired for the Supreme Court. Haynsworth's opinions demonstrated that he was a judicial conservative, committed to states' rights, and clearly a law-and-order judge. Haynsworth's southern identity was seen by the president as a political plus that he could exploit to improve his standing with white voters in the South. Attorney General John Mitchell, an admirer of Senator Hollings, met with Haynsworth in March 1969 and then authorized an FBI background check to assure that Haynsworth could meet the ethical standards for the appointment. On 18 August 1969 President Nixon made the nomination public. It was a nomination doomed to failure, and Haynsworth would ultimately be defined in history by that loss.

The explanation of the failed confirmation centered on the opposition of labor and civil rights groups coupled with charges of judicial impropriety. Senators were highly sensitive to charges of ethical and judicial improprieties at this time. Justice Abe Fortas, whose seat Haynsworth was to occupy, had been forced to resign for supplementing his income with honorariums from a charitable foundation headed by a former client. The appearance of impropriety in Fortas's continuing legal relationships with former clients, including the president, led to his ruin.

In Haynsworth's case it was revealed that when he had participated in the 1963 antilabor decision clearing the Deering-Milliken textile company of unfair labor practices, he himself had been a principal shareholder in a vending machine company with business ties to Deering-Milliken. Charged with voting in another case in favor of a corporation and then buying that company's stock before the decision became public, Haynsworth had also been subjected to rumors, later proved groundless, that he had taken a bribe.

The first public response to Haynsworth's nomination had been favorable, but savage criticism quickly began. Labor and civil rights organizations approached Senator Birch Bayh, Democrat of Indiana, to lead the attack in the Senate, where leadership favorable to Haynsworth was shaken by the death of Senator Everett Dirksen, Republican of Illinois. With civil rights groups asserting that Haynsworth was seeking to hang on to segregation and labor charging a lack of ethical standards, only a strong and determined White House campaign could have saved the nomination. President Nixon at that time had an ambiguous attitude regarding how executive-legislative relations ought to be managed, and his decision at first to use indirect pressure on senators proved insufficient. As opposition mounted, the president began to personalize the conflict and Haynsworth's positive attributes were overshadowed as the crisis escalated. Pressure tactics to win Senate votes backfired. After eight days of hearings and a 10–7 vote in favor of Haynsworth in the Senate Judicial Committee, the full Senate rejected the nomination by a vote of 55–45 on 21 November 1969. On 28 November Haynsworth made public his decision to remain on the Fourth Circuit Court of Appeals, citing the example of his former mentor, Judge John J. Parker. As Parker's opinions served to surprise and confound his critics, so Haynsworth on his first day back on the circuit bench signed an order requiring total integration of five southern school districts by the beginning of 1970.

Haynsworth's reputation increased over time, and he continued to sit as presiding judge until 1981, when he took senior judge status. Haynsworth retained a heavy case load as a senior judge until his death from a heart attack shortly before he was to have left home for his chambers in the Greenville federal building named in his honor in 1983. It was almost twenty years to the day of his rejection by the Senate. Haynsworth is buried in Springwood Cemetery in Greenville.

★

Haynsworth's papers are at Furman University in Greenville, South Carolina. John P. Frank, *Clement Haynsworth, the Senate, and the Haynsworth Nomination* (1991), provides an analysis of Haynsworth's nomination to the U.S. Supreme Court. A record of his early career can be found in *Columbia State* (2 Feb. 1957); "The Supreme Court: Another Gray Man?" *Newsweek* (28 July 1969); "Haynsworth at Home," *Time* (24 Oct. 1969); and Marshall Frady, "Haynsworth of Greenville," *Life* (31 Oct. 1969). On Haynsworth's nomination, see Dean J. Kotlowski, "Trial by Error: Nixon, the Senate, and the Haynsworth Nomination," *Presidential Studies Quarterly* 26 (winter 1996): 71–91. Obituaries are in the *Greenville News* (23 Nov. 1989), the *New York Times* (23 Nov. 1989), and *Piedmont* (24 Nov. 1989).

ALICE FLEETWOOD BARTEE

HAYS, Wayne Levere (*b.* 13 May 1911 in Bannock, Ohio; *d.* 10 February 1989 in Wheeling, West Virginia), politician who, as a pragmatic New Deal liberal, served fourteen consecutive terms (1948–1976) in the U.S. House of Representatives.

Wayne L. Hays, *c.* 1970. OHIO STATE UNIVERSITY

Hays was the eldest child of Walter Lee, a grocery store owner, and Bertha Mae (Taylor) Hays, a homemaker. He had two brothers and a sister. From an early age, Hays was exposed to political rhetoric. The family was staunchly Republican in its views and voting behavior; the only known Democrat was Hays's maternal grandfather, who enjoyed taking contrary positions in family debates.

Following graduation from St. Clairsville High School, Hays entered Ohio State University in Columbus, graduating in 1933 with a B.S. degree in political science. Hays considered himself a Republican until the 1932 election. Fed up with President Hoover, he voted for Democrat Franklin D. Roosevelt. He later recalled that his decision involved no political philosophy; he simply believed that having Roosevelt in the White House would better his chances of securing employment following graduation. Hays then enrolled in prelaw at Duke University, when the country was in the midst of the Great Depression. In 1935, his funds gone, he returned to Flushing, Ohio, where he taught high school history and public speaking for the next four years. On 3 June 1937 he married Martha Judkins; they adopted a child in 1955.

In 1939, at the age of twenty-eight, Hays turned his energies toward politics. For six years, he served on the state Board of Education (1939–1940), as mayor of Flushing (1939–1945), and as an Ohio state senator (1941–1942). Two days after the Japanese bombed Pearl Harbor in December 1941, he volunteered for active duty in the U.S. Army Officers' Reserve Corps, in which he had been serving since 1933. He was honorably discharged for medical reasons in August 1942. When his mayoral term ended in 1945, Hays returned to the serenity of his Redgate farm in Belmont, where he bred cattle and Tennessee walking horses.

In 1948 at the age of thirty-seven, Hays made his first bid for national elective office, winning a seat in the United States House of Representatives from Ohio's Eighteenth Congressional District. The predominantly white, blue-collar, heavily polluted, and economically distressed region in southeast Ohio would return its favorite son to Congress with substantial majorities for the next twenty-eight years (1948–1976).

As a freshman legislator, Hays supported the Fair Deal, the social policies of President Harry S. Truman. He objected to the Reciprocal Trade Agreement on grounds that it failed to protect the pottery and glass industries so vital to his economically depressed district. A militant cold warrior, he pursued a hawkish course throughout his career. Although an ardent anticommunist, he was one of Congress's most vocal critics of political witch-hunting during the red-baiting of the 1950s.

As early as 1949, the politically savvy Hays began to amass congressional committee seniority and name recognition. He won a seat in 1949 on the House Foreign Affairs Committee; by 1972, he was its second-ranking member. In 1950 he began service on the House Administration Committee, which he chaired from 1970 to 1976. In 1955 he was selected to head the House congressional delegation to the first North Atlantic Treaty Organization Parliamentarians' Conference, serving as president of the conference in 1956–1957 and 1969–1970.

During Dwight D. Eisenhower's presidency (1953–1961), Hays remained liberal on domestic policy and fought to obtain funds for urban and public works. In foreign affairs, he preferred technical and economic aid rather than military assistance to underdeveloped countries. Under Presidents John F. Kennedy and Lyndon B. Johnson (1961–1969), Hays voted for all major civil rights legislation. He did, however, break with his liberal colleagues in the Nixon era when he opposed busing to achieve racial balance in public schools. Always attentive to the needs of his constituents, he continued to champion economic relief measures. In foreign policy, he was an outspoken supporter of the war effort in Indochina; few members of Congress denounced antiwar protesters and their congressional supporters as vehemently as did Hays.

During Richard M. Nixon's presidency (1969–1974), Hays vigorously defended the president's Indochina policy but opposed the administration's plans to financially aid reconstructing North Vietnam. Along with his colleagues, he voted to override Nixon's veto of the War Powers Bill. When the Watergate scandal unraveled in 1974, Hays called for President Nixon's resignation.

The House Administration Committee prior to Hays's chairmanship was considered by many to be a minor body that dealt with trifling housekeeping tasks. As head of this committee, however, Hays parlayed seemingly mundane chores into a personal empire, approving monies for House members and committees while overseeing 700 House employees. On 23 May 1976 this empire abruptly collapsed when the *Washington Post* reported that Hays had allegedly kept a thirty-three-year-old aspiring actress, Elizabeth Ray, on his staff payroll at taxpayers' expense for two years. Ray admitted having no secretarial skills and was in fact considered his mistress. Hays had divorced his first wife and married Patricia Peak five weeks before the scandal broke. Hays ultimately resigned from Congress on 1 September 1976 and returned to the solitude of his farm. Two years later, however, he won a closely contested election for state representative from Ohio's Ninety-ninth District. Defeated when he ran for reelection in 1980, Hays nevertheless remained active in local politics by serving on the Belmont County Board of Education and as chairman of the Belmont County Democratic party and the Citizens' National Bank.

Despite the scandal that marred his political career, Hays remained well-respected among his former constituents. Many of his neighbors led harsh lives, dwelling in a hilly land of strip mines, small farms, and unemployment. His supporters considered him an individual who accomplished things, whether pursuing pensions for black-lung victims, securing Social Security benefits for widows and children, or improving educational opportunities, as when he helped open a branch campus of Ohio University in his district.

His political views were not easily characterized. As much as he supported the Indochina war, he opposed American support for dictators. While he had sneering disdain for antiwar protesters, he could be scathing toward the Pentagon brass. He considered his coauthorship of the Fulbright-Hays Act in 1961, which increased mutual understanding between the people of the United States and other countries through cultural exchanges, to be one of his most significant pieces of legislation. Known for his acerbic tongue and lack of deference, he was widely respected as an effective legislator. Hays suffered a heart attack at his Ohio home on 10 February 1989, and later died in a Wheeling, West Virginia, hospital. Hays, age seventy-seven at his death, was interred in Union Cemetery, St. Clairsville, Ohio.

★

The Hays papers are in the Ohio University Archives of the Alden Library at Ohio University, Athens, Ohio. Ellen L. Brasel, "Wayne L. Hays: Ohio's Contentious Congressman" (1977), a thesis based on these materials, is also available in the Alden Library. See also Michael Barone, Grant Ujifusa, and Douglas Matthews, *The Almanac of American Politics 1972: The Senators, the Representatives, Their Records, States, and Districts* (1972, 1974, and 1976); Joseph Cooper, "The Origins of Standing Committees and the Development of the Modern House," *Rice University Studies*

2, no. 3 (1972): 56; "A Hurricane Blows Through the Old House," *Newsweek* (16 Dec. 1974); "Closed-Session Romance on the Hill," *Washington Post* (23 May 1976); and John Goshko, "Powerful Hays Described as 'Czar' in the House," *Washington Post* (25 May 1976). Obituaries are in the *Washington Post* and the *New York Times* (both 11 Feb. 1989).

ELLEN O'CONNELL BRASEL

HAYWORTH, Rita (*b.* 17 October 1918 in New York City; *d.* 14 May 1987 in New York City), internationally famed movie star who was noted over a long career both for her dramatic roles and for her talented dancing in musicals.

Hayworth was born Margarita Carmen Cansino. She had at least two brothers. Her father, Eduardo Cansino, maintained a family tradition of training Spanish dancers by instructing his daughter, while her mother, Volga Haworth, whose family counted among its members numerous British actors, danced for the *Ziegfeld Follies.* Vaudeville had originally attracted the Cansinos to the United States from Spain, and Eduardo Cansino became well known for this type of entertainment. After vaudeville became overshadowed by early motion pictures, the enterprising Cansino family soon found jobs in the growing industry. Margarita grew up in the milieu of entertainment, taking dancing and acting lessons while attending Hamilton High, a public high school in Los Angeles. Her father was a dance director for various film studios and, meanwhile, mentored her progress. Margarita made her stage dance debut at Cathay Circle Theatre in 1932 as part of her family's show, "The Dancing Cansinos."

Rita Cansino made her film debut in 1932 with her family in *La Fiesta.* At the age of fourteen, she danced with her father in Tijuana, Mexico, at the Foreign Club, moved on to perform in California on a riverboat, and then returned to Mexico to perform at a resort, Agua Caliente. Here she was "discovered" by Winfield R. Sheehan of the Fox film corporation, who cast her in *Dante's Inferno* (1935) when she was sixteen years old. In 1936 she received a one-year contract with Fox and in the following year a one-year contract with Columbia Pictures.

Rita's early film career consisted of a series of dancing roles in ethnic films: *Charlie Chan in Egypt* (1935), *Under the Pampas Moon* (1935), *Paddy O'Day* (1935), and *Human Cargo* (1936). In each of these films she was cast as an ethnic dancer: Egyptian, Argentine, Irish, and Russian, respectively. In 1936 she married Edward C. Judson, a wealthy Texas oilman.

In 1937 she starred in *Trouble in Texas,* the last film in which she used the name Rita Cansino. In that year she changed her name to Rita Hayworth (by adding a *y* to her mother's maiden name) and starred in *Criminals in the Air, Girls Can Play, The Shadow, The Game That Kills,* and *Paid to Dance.* In 1938 she appeared in *Who Killed Gail Preston?, There's Always a Woman, Convicted, Juvenile Court, The Renegade Ranger,* and *Homicide Bureau.* In 1939 she appeared in *The Lone Wolfe's Spy Hunt* and *Special Inspector.* Her big break came with *Only Angels Have Wings* (1939), produced by Columbia Pictures. At the suggestion of Judson, who served as her manager, she dyed her hair blond and starred in *The Strawberry Blonde* (1941). She also added singing to her list of talents, and raised her hairline by electrolysis. She had changed herself from a Latin type playing in B movies to a true starlet with whom all America could identify. She was one of the pinup favorites of GIs during World War II.

Hayworth again demonstrated her dancing abilities with Fred Astaire in *You'll Never Get Rich* (1941). This film made her a star, and she was teamed with Astaire again in *You Were Never Lovelier* (1942). Her earning power for that period was unusually high at $6,500 a week. Approaching the height of her career, she starred in *Cover Girl* (1944), with Gene Kelly, *Tonight and Every Night* (1945), *Gilda* (1946), and *Down to Earth* (1947). In *Gilda,* Hayworth played a voluptuous temptress, and for her role in *Down to Earth* she earned herself the title the "Love Goddess" (coined by *Life* magazine), as she played the role of the

Rita Hayworth surrounded by press reports about her, 1944. JOEL KUDLER/ARCHIVE PHOTOS

Greek muse of dance, Terpsichore. The image of the temptress stayed with her for the rest of her career.

Meanwhile, in 1942, she divorced Judson and, in 1943, married Orson Welles, with whom she starred in *The Lady from Shanghai* (1948). In 1948 she made *The Loves of Carmen* and divorced Welles, with whom she had a daughter, Rebecca. She married Prince Aly Khan of Pakistan in 1949. They had one daughter, Princess Yasmin.

The 1950s marked the apex of Hayworth's career, as she appeared in *Affair in Trinidad* (1952), *Salome* (1953), and *Miss Sadie Thompson* (1953). In the latter, based on the short story "Rain" by Somerset Maugham, Hayworth played Sadie, a bawdy lady and nightclub entertainer who becomes stranded on a desert island during World War II; here she meets and eventually destroys the Reverend Davidson (played by José Ferrer). In 1953 she also divorced Prince Aly Khan and married singer Dick Haymes. Her career as a major star ended in 1957, when she made *Fire Down Below* and *Pal Joey,* a film version of the Rodgers and Hart musical success based on a book by John O'Hara. The latter tells the story of a nightclub entertainer who romances a Nob Hill socialite to finance his club; Hayworth played the socialite.

In 1955 Hayworth divorced Haymes, and in 1958 she married the last of five husbands, James Hill, a producer. Also in 1958, she starred in *Separate Tables,* a serious drama that earned her high praise and excellent reviews. She played the role of Ann Shankland, a woman who preys on her former husband and brings about his downfall. In 1959, in *They Came to Cordura*—a story of American soldiers homeward bound after fighting Pancho Villa—she played an unglamorous role about which *Variety* said that "she [gave] the best performance of her career." In 1960 she appeared in *The Story on Page One* as a housewife falsely accused of murdering her husband. By the time of these two later films, she had the maturity to play older women. Throughout the 1960s and 1970s she played small roles in television films or appeared in musical dramas on stage. She retired to New York City and suffered from Alzheimer's disease for fifteen years before her death in 1987. She is buried in Holy Cross Cemetery in Culver City, California.

★

Gene Ringgold, *The Films of Rita Hayworth: The Legend and Career of a Love Goddess* (1974), is one of the best portrayals of her life. A good insider's view of Hayworth is James Hill, *Rita Hayworth: A Memoir* (1983). Christian Drea, *Rita Hayworth* (1985), provides an excellent overview of her life and loves. The actor Gary Merrill's memoir, *Bette, Rita, and the Rest of My Life* (1988), includes an account of Hayworth. Barbara Leaming, *If This Was Happiness: A Biography of Rita Hayworth* (1989), is an interesting view of the actress. Marjorie Rosen, *Popcorn Venus: Women, Movies, and the American Dream* (1974), examines how the famous faces of movie actresses mirrored and molded the fantasies of American women. Amy L. Unterburger, *International Dictionary of Films and Film Makers: Actors and Actresses* (1983), contains a good photograph and an excellent list of Hayworth's major films arranged in chronological order. Obituaries are in *Time* (25 May 1987), *People Weekly* (1 June 1987), and *McCalls* (May 1987).

BARBARA BENNETT PETERSON

HEIFETZ, Jascha (*b.* 2 February 1901 in Vilna, Russia [present-day Vilnius, Lithuania]; *d.* 10 December 1987 in Los Angeles, California), the most famous and greatest, violin virtuoso of the twentieth century.

Heifetz was born Iosef Ruvinovich Heifetz to Jewish parents of modest means in Vilna. His mother, Anna Sharfstein, was a housewife, and his father, Ruvin Heifetz, was concertmaster of the Vilna Symphony Orchestra. By the time Jascha's two younger sisters, Pauline and Elza, were born, his extraordinary musical talents were being nurtured. His father gave the three-year-old lessons on a quarter-size violin. Ruvin forbade the child to play out of tune or to bow incorrectly, and he always supervised his son's practice. Discipline and perfectionism—traits that Heifetz cherished all his life—were instilled at an age when most youngsters were learning to use a fork and spoon.

At age five he entered the Imperial Vilna School of Music to study with Ilya Malkin, a former student of the Hungarian violin virtuoso and master teacher Leopold Auer. Heifetz's public debut took place in Kovno, where, at age seven, he played the Mendelssohn Concerto. After teaching Jascha for three years, Malkin beseeched Auer to accept him as his pupil at the St. Petersburg Conservatory.

In anticipation of his son's admission to the renowned school, Ruvin gave up his job and planned to move the family to St. Petersburg. The plan was nearly derailed by the czarist ban on Jews living outside of the "pale of settlement" where they might defile great cities such as Moscow and "holy" Petersburg. However, talented Jewish students were exempt from the ban, and Auer devised a way to circumvent the law. With the approval of Alexander Glazunov, the conservatory director, Auer accepted Jascha's father as a "pupil" and thus kept the family together.

In 1910 Jascha Heifetz was admitted to the Petersburg Conservatory. He was the youngest student in Professor Auer's legendary stable of violin students, which over the years included Mischa Elman, Efrem Zimbalist, Toscha Seidel, and Nathan Milstein. After a year of study his teacher declared that Heifetz had nothing more to learn about the violin. He remained Auer's pupil for six years, however, and stated ever after that he had learned more from him than from anyone else.

Sixty years of concertizing began in April 1911 with a performance in St. Petersburg, followed by a summer en-

Jascha Heifetz. AMERICAN STOCK/ARCHIVE PHOTOS

gagement at an international exhibition in Odessa. Arriving unheralded and unknown, by season's end Heifetz nearly had been killed by wild demonstrations of adoring thousands who idolized the brown-haired and blue-eyed prodigy. He soon embarked on his first European tour, through Germany and Austria. After a sensational debut in Berlin on 23 May 1912, the conductor Arthur Nikisch invited him to play the Tchaikovsky Concerto with the Berlin Philharmonic Orchestra on 28 October 1912.

A Jewish encyclopedia published in Petersburg (1910–1912) includes an article about the "genius," commenting on the beauty and power of his sound and the ease with which he overcame extreme difficulties of technique. During World War I concertizing was curtailed throughout Europe, but Auer managed to take his star pupils, Heifetz and Seidel, on a Scandanavian tour in 1916.

The Heifetz family left Russia in the midst of the 1917 revolution. The Wolfssohn Music Bureau, New York impresarios, invited Ruvin to bring the family to the United States for a year of engagements, fifty concerts. The still-raging war, not to mention the Russian upheavals, made it impossible to travel normal routes. In June the family made a difficult journey via Siberia and the Pacific. A steamer took them to San Francisco, where they disembarked in the autumn of 1917.

Heifetz's American debut recital was played to a sold-out Carnegie Hall in New York City on 27 October 1917. His accompanist was Andre Benoist. The slender young violinist, with his grave and dignified stage manner, electrified the audience, dazzled the critics, and terrified every violinist in the crowd.

Less than two weeks later, on 9 November 1917, Heifetz made his first recording, in the Victor Studios of Camden, New Jersey. His almost exclusive association with Victor—later RCA—was to last for more than fifty years and would result in the most extensive sound-recorded legacy of any classical musician in the twentieth century.

Soon after his New York debut Heifetz began concertizing from coast to coast in grand halls and school gymnasiums, major cities and small towns. His repertoire was immense and programs were rarely duplicated. By 1920 he was commanding enormous fees for a classical musician of that time and giving a hundred concerts a year, a pace that would prevail for the next twenty years.

Despite the frenzied activity of his professional life, Heifetz enjoyed himself, bursting with vitality and enthusiasm for everything in his new country. He learned English quickly and became a citizen in 1925. He loved American movies, fast cars, and popular music. He became a "camera-fiend," learning to develop and print his own shots. A talented athlete, he excelled at tennis—winning an amateur championship in Australia while on tour there in 1921—and Ping-Pong. He took up golf, horseback riding, and target shooting. His accompanist (1919–1925) and, later, brother-in-law Samuel Chotzinoff would subsequently write that Heifetz had taken tremendous risks during the exhilarating years when he was making up for the childhood he had never had.

Collecting things had been a pastime since childhood. As he got older, richer, and more sophisticated his collections reflected interests that became lifelong passions: stamps, coins, and books. Over the years he amassed a formidable collection of first editions, mostly of English authors.

Most important was his collection of violins and bows. After his Carnegie Hall debut—played on a Tononi violin—a wealthy fan lent him a 1731 Stradivarius, which he was able to purchase from the benefactor a few years later. In 1937 he bought a second Strad. Heifetz's favorite instrument was the "David" Guarnerius (1742?), purchased by Ruvin in Germany in 1923. Through the years Heifetz steadfastly refused all offers to sell it. His handwritten will (1980) stipulated that the beloved violin was to be given to the De Young Museum in San Francisco to be cared for, displayed, and "used by playing it on special occasions—by worthy performers."

By the end of the 1920s Heifetz had concertized in almost every European country, in Australia and New Zealand (1921), in China and Japan (during the 1923 earthquake), and in Palestine (1926). During the Palestine tour he donated all of his fees to finance construction of a concert hall in Tel Aviv. The same year he was made a chevalier of the French Legion of Honor. (In 1939 he was made an officer.) He acquired a new accompanist, Isidor Achron, after Chotzinoff married Pauline Heifetz in 1925.

On 20 August 1928 Heifetz married Florence Arto Vidor in a private ceremony performed in Heifetz's penthouse apartment at 247 Park Avenue in New York City. Mrs. Heifetz, a Catholic from Houston, had divorced her first husband, American film director King Vidor, in 1925. She was a beautiful star of the silent screen who abandoned her career when she married Heifetz. The couple had two children, Josepha Anna and Robert Joseph. A year or two after their wedding the Heifetzes bought an old farmhouse in Redding, Connecticut, and the family divided its time between that home and one in Balboa, California, where Heifetz indulged his love of yachting.

Heifetz's professional life in the 1930s was characterized by heavy concertizing and repertoire expansion. In 1933 he canceled forty-five German engagements in protest against Hitler's attitude toward Jewish artists. At the invitation of the Soviet government he returned to his homeland for the first time in seventeen years in 1934. It was a profoundly emotional experience and he was especially moved to be given his first, tiny violin, which an uncle had kept for him. Heifetz never visited Russia again.

The musical marshmallows—charming salon pieces—that had dominated his programs during the carefree 1920s were giving way to more substantial fare. Heifetz championed new works such as Prokofiev's Second Violin Concerto and popularized the Elgar and Sibelius concertos. He commissioned and premiered Mario Castelnuovo-Tedesco's Second Violin Concerto and William Walton's Violin Concerto. Heifetz, who joined ASCAP in 1937, produced close to 150 transcriptions, the most popular of which were Dinicu's *Hora Staccato* and several songs from George Gershwin's *Porgy and Bess.* (This was far from his only experience as "pop" composer: In 1947 he would write, under the name "Jim Hoyl," a song entitled "When You Make Love to Me, Don't Make Believe." Bing Crosby, Margaret Whiting, and Dick Jergens, among others, recorded it, unaware of the true identity of its composer.) A good friend of Gershwin's, Heifetz asked the composer to write a violin concerto, but Gershwin died before he could comply. Arnold Schoenberg, however, did write a concerto for Heifetz, which the violinist declined to perform, saying he would need six fingers to do so.

The turbulent 1930s stimulated Heifetz's political activism. He played several benefits for refugees from fascist Europe and supported American trade-union causes in the arts. In 1936 he and Lawrence Tibbett founded the American Guild of Musical Artists. He was elected its first vice president and hoped to succeed in wooing classical musicians from the rival American Federation of Musicians, run by James Petrillo, who was quoted as saying he saw no difference between Heifetz and a "tavern fiddler." In 1937 Heifetz joined Eddie Cantor in forming the American Federation of Radio Artists and was its first vice president.

Just before World War II the country experienced a burst of pan-Americanism that was reflected in Heifetz's activities. In 1940 he, his wife, and his accompanist Emanuel Bay embarked on a goodwill tour of South America that comprised sixty concerts in thirty-five cities in ten countries. When he returned he suggested to the cultural division of the State Department that exchange fellowships be established to enable Latin American musicians to come to the United States to study and concertize. Heifetz had long been an advocate of government support of the arts. He also decried the low status accorded music education in America and the widely held belief that music study was for "sissies" and not on a par with business or sports.

Heifetz was a one-man committee to encourage modern American music and enlarge the violin repertoire. He favored lush, melodic works by his Hollywood neighbors—film composers Erich Korngold and Miklós Rózsa, for instance—from whom he commissioned concertos. Louis Gruenberg's Concerto was typical of the works written for him, in that after Heifetz stopped programming it, it disappeared from the repertoire. It was too demanding for other violinists.

With the coming of World War II, Heifetz volunteered to play in army camps and to do anything else the authorities asked of him. "If they can use me as a soldier, I'll be glad to . . . I'm a pretty good shot." He made three overseas USO tours between 1942 and 1944. Some of them were given on the Italian and North African front lines. Risk-taking was a vital component of the Heifetz personality. It was apparent in his thrilling violin playing and in his courage during the war.

Reserved and poker-faced onstage, there nevertheless burned within Heifetz a hot streak of showmanship that, together with his matinee-idol looks and a fervent desire "to spread good music among the millions," made him this century's first classical-music media star. His first radio performance was on 21 December 1930 on the half-hour "Slumber-Musical" on WJZ in New York. During the next twenty years he performed sporadically over the airwaves. He was broadcast live with conductors Arturo Toscanini and Fritz Reiner and even fellow violinist Jack Benny. In 1947 Heifetz was featured on several *Bell Telephone Hour* shows. His first film was *They Shall Have Music* (1939), produced by Samuel Goldwyn. Although its plot is dispensable, the film provides extraordinary footage of Heifetz in performance, photographed from every conceivable angle. He appeared in two subsequent Hollywood productions with similar formats, *Carnegie Hall* (1947) and *Of Men and Music* (1951). Heifetz's television debut (24 February 1952) was the opening program of a new NBC half-hour series entitled *Meet the Masters,* which featured close-up views of famous artists at home, in rehearsal, and in performance. As in all Heifetz film appearances, he was resolutely himself no matter what happened around him.

In the early 1940s the Heifetzes had moved permanently to southern California. In 1946, however, they divorced, and on 6 January 1947 he married Francis Sears Spiegelberg. They had one child, Joseph, before divorcing in 1963.

An impressive roster of European émigré artists in the Los Angeles area made for a rich cultural life. Heifetz began to play chamber music, for his own enjoyment, with an array of superb musicians who gravitated to the area. Cellists Emanuel Feuermann and Gregor Piatigorsky, pianist Artur Rubinstein, and violist William Primrose joined Heifetz in private music-making sessions that, fortunately for posterity, resulted in a great deal of recording activity and public performance. Always fond of gadgets, Heifetz designed a rubber violin mute with Henryk Kaston, which was patented in April 1949.

Heifetz was still following a grueling concert schedule through the mid-1950s. He went to Israel in 1950 and 1953 but the latter trip was a disaster. Faced with a ban on the public performance of music by composers with Nazi affiliations, Heifetz refused to change his scheduled program, which included the Richard Strauss Violin Sonata. His obstinance was not because of ideology—he had, after the war, refused to play a concert conducted by Wilhelm Furtwängler, who was accused, and later exonerated, of collaboration with the Nazis—but because the Heifetz hackles had been raised. He did not like having his programs censored. He performed the controversial work anyway, and shortly afterward a young man with an iron bar attacked Heifetz. The violinist's right hand was injured.

The 1955–1956 season was the last "regular" one in his career. He ended his annual New York recitals with a performance at Hunter College on 19 February 1956. His accompanist, Brooks Smith, had replaced Bay in 1954 and was to work with Heifetz until he retired from the concert stage permanently. It was almost four years before Heifetz played another New York engagement. On 10 December 1959 he was featured soloist with the visiting Detroit Symphony Orchestra at a United Nations Human Rights Day concert.

Teaching became the focus of his life. He was appointed Regents Professor of Music at the University of California at Los Angeles in 1958. When asked about this turn in his career, Heifetz replied that "it's a prophecy being fulfilled. My old professor put a finger on me and said that one day I would be good enough to teach. Violin playing is a perishable art . . . it must be passed on as a personal skill—otherwise it is lost."

In 1961 he was appointed Distinguished Professor of Music at the University of Southern California's Institute for Special Musical Studies. Through private teaching and master classes Heifetz hoped to attract and nurture a new generation of talented violin students. Until his affiliation with the school ended in 1983, many young instrumentalists worked with him, but ultimately he was disappointed that only two of his students—Erick Friedman and Eugene Fodor—became famous. In a poignant interview with a *New York Times* reporter in 1980, Heifetz bemoaned his lack of top-quality pupils. "I can still be of service," he said. "I have some time."

In 1966 he, Gregor Piatigorsky, and friends returned to Carnegie Hall for a series of chamber music recitals. Those appearances were his last in New York City and were held where he had made his astonishing American debut almost fifty years earlier. By 1967 Heifetz's relationship with Israel was mended; he played at an Israel Philharmonic benefit at the Hollywood Bowl, and in 1970 he and Piatigorsky made a triumphant tour of Israel. That year Heifetz was filmed in performance by the French television system. The program was later rebroadcast in the United States as a one-hour NBC special, *Heifetz.* His playing was remarkable: powerful, graceful, and technically secure.

His last public performance, on 23 October 1972 at the Dorothy Chandler Pavilion in Los Angeles, was a benefit for the University of Southern California School of Music. Heifetz played like Heifetz. The taping of it became his last recording.

In 1975 he underwent shoulder surgery, and arthritis continued to plague him. He died in 1987 at Cedars-Sinai Medical Center in Los Angeles, the result of nonrecovery from brain surgery. He had asked that there be no monuments or commemorative efforts in his memory. He wrote in his will: "I direct that my body be cremated and the ashes scattered . . . over the ocean as close as possible to Malibu Beach [near my house]."

The beauty and virtuosity of Jascha Heifetz's violin playing, consistent qualities in a career that lasted for more than sixty years, set standards that have yet to be surpassed. Commenting on the twentieth-century's greatest violinist, the critic Lawrence Gilman wrote, in 1936: "It will not be believed that music-making of so magical and conquering a sort could shape itself upon the web of time so quietly, with such patrician calm, such deep integrity, in so uncalm and brazen and treacherous an age."

★

The Music Division of the Library of Congress houses approximately 17,500 items in its "Heifetz collection," including scores, manuscripts, letters, early editions, posters, programs, and photographs. The Music Research Division of the New York Public Library possesses an extensive Heifetz clippings and programs collection. Of interest, too, is the Florence Vidor clippings file in the Theatre Research Division.

The only biography, Artur Weschler-Vered, *Jascha Heifetz* (1986), is a sober, thorough job with flashes of original insight. Dr. Herbert R. Axelrod, *Heifetz* (3d rev. ed., 1990), is a massive compendium of photographs and newspaper articles interspersed with the love-hate rantings of the author about his subject's personality. Heifetz started to sue Axelrod over a previous edition but withdrew the litigation. "Jascha Heifetz," in Gdal Saleski, *Famous Musicians of a Wandering Race* (1927), includes anecdotes of Heifetz's youth not found elsewhere; "Jascha Heifetz," in Charles O'Connell, *The Other Side of the Record* (1947), is a highly personal portrait of the artist by the former music director of RCA-Victor Corporation. "Jascha Heifetz," in Samuel Chotzinoff, *A Little Nightmusic* (1964), is a beautifully written tribute by Heifetz's brother-in-law and former accompanist. For another point of view see two of the critic Virgil Thomson's notorious Heifetz-baiting reviews, "Silk-Underwear Music" (31 Oct. 1940) and "Essentially Frivolous" (22 Nov. 1951), anthologized in his *Music Reviewed, 1940–1954* (1967). Two chapters in Schuyler Chapin, *Musical Chairs* (1977), chronicle the pains and pleasures of being Heifetz's tour manager. "The Great Auer Disciples," in Boris Schwarz, *Great Masters of the Violin* (1983), discusses, from a violinist-scholar's perspective, the Heifetz phenomenon. A rare interview, on the occasion of Heifetz's seventy-ninth birthday, was conducted by John Rockwell for the *New York Times* (31 Jan. 1980). Two articles in the same issue of *Strad* (Jan. 1995) are essential reading: Kenaway Lee, "Premier Violinist," for little-known facts about Heifetz; and Jean-Michel Molkhou, "Heifetz on Disc and Film" for its filmography. An obituary is in the *New York Times* (12 Dec. 1987).

One of the grandest undertakings in the history of recording, *The Heifetz Collection* (RCA Victor Gold Seal 09026-61778-2 ADD), consists of sixty-five compact discs arranged in forty-six volumes with generally excellent program notes by Irving Kolodin. It is virtually Heifetz's entire output. Eight half-hour sessions of the legendary Heifetz master classes at the University of Southern California are available on videocassette (vol. 1: Kultur 1266; vol. 2: Kultur 1267). The NBC television program *Meet the Masters,* featuring Heifetz and a staged encounter with some actors-as-students, offers brilliant performances by the violinist (Kultur 1101). The 1970 concert televised in the United States as *Heifetz* is available on videocassette (VAI 69026).

HONORA RAPHAEL WEINSTEIN

HEINLEIN, Robert Anson (*b.* 7 July 1907 in Butler, Missouri; *d.* 8 May 1988 in Carmel, California), science fiction writer whose popular works promoted space travel and helped lead science fiction out of the ghetto of genre fiction to commercial success in the mainstream and in Hollywood.

Born in the heart of farming country and raised a Methodist, Heinlein was the third of seven children of Bam Lyle and Rex Ivar Heinlein, an accountant. He had two older brothers, three younger sisters, and a younger brother. When he was very young, the family moved to Kansas City, Missouri, where Heinlein was an active, studious youth and an avid reader of science fiction dime novels. The strong, independent heroes of his later fiction were modeled on his maternal grandfather, Alva E. Lyle, a resourceful and morally tough "horse and buggy doctor" with whom he spent much of his youth. Heinlein was interested in science of all sorts, particularly astronomy, and planned for a time to be an astronomer.

Heinlein attended Kansas City Junior College, the local branch of the University of Missouri, in 1924. Then, on the strength of many letters of recommendation, he obtained an appointment to the U.S. Naval Academy at Annapolis the following year. Following his graduation and commissioning in 1929, he served as a gunnery officer on several ships. In 1932 he married Leslyn McDonald, apparently his second wife (their marriage certificate lists Heinlein as divorced), and later the couple bought a home in Hollywood, California. In 1934, however, Heinlein contracted tuberculosis and received a medical discharge from the navy. He would continue to think of himself as a navy officer; throughout his life friends called him "Admiral."

Robert A. Heinlein, *c.* 1985. AP/WIDE WORLD PHOTOS. PHOTO BY C. N. BROWN/LOCUS.

Heinlein, a slender, well-built six-footer with short hair and a characteristic thin mustache, then took graduate courses at the University of California at Los Angeles in physics and mathematics. He tried his hand at several careers—real estate, architecture, silver mining, and politics, running once for California state assemblyman—but all without success. Fragile health finally led him to take up writing as a career at the age of thirty-two.

An advertisement for a writing contest in a science fiction magazine provided the motivation. Drawn by the $50 prize (actually the magazine's standard rate), Heinlein wrote "Life-Line," the story of a man who invents a machine that can predict the moment of a person's death. So pleased was he with the piece that he submitted it instead to *Astounding Science Fiction,* which bought it for $70. Published in 1939, it became the first in Heinlein's Future History series, stories with a common fictional background that extrapolate a possible future of the human race. Stories that fell outside this series, or belonged in other genres, were originally published under one of his five pseudonyms: Anson MacDonald, Lyle Monroe, John Riverside, Caleb Saunders, and Simon York.

During World War II Heinlein served, beginning in 1942, as a civilian research engineer at Mustin Field, the Naval Air Experimental Station in Philadelphia. By 1947 he was back at his writing desk, beginning a series of juvenile novels—different from his adult work only by its lack of sexual content—which would draw enormous praise. That year he also divorced Leslyn, and on 21 October 1948 he married Virginia Doris Gerstenfeld, a former Wave officer, chemist, and aeronautical test engineer whom he had met at Mustin Field. They moved to Colorado Springs, Colorado, where they built a self-designed home in 1950, the year Heinlein experienced a brief relapse of tuberculosis. In Heinlein's later years, Virginia became his editor, research assistant, and manager of his voluminous fan mail and business accounts.

During the late 1940s Heinlein also managed to break into the lucrative "slicks," such as the *Saturday Evening Post,* bringing science fiction stories to a mainstream market for the first time. These stories glorified space travel and helped to win public support for America's burgeoning space efforts. The generation that grew up reading Heinlein would eventually send the first men to the Moon. In recognition of his influence, Heinlein was asked to appear as a guest commentator with television newscaster Walter Cronkite during the first manned landing on the Moon on 20 July 1969.

In 1950 Heinlein helped turn his first juvenile book, *Rocket Ship Galileo* (1947), into the first realistic space movie, *Destination Moon,* directed by George Pal. His second juvenile, *Space Cadet* (1948), became the basis of the first modern science fiction TV serial, *Tom Corbett: Space Cadet* (1951–1956). In 1956 his novel *Double Star* won a Hugo award by popular vote of science fiction fans. *Starship Troopers* (1960), *Stranger in a Strange Land* (1962), and *The Moon Is a Harsh Mistress* (1967) would also win Hugos, making Heinlein the only four-time winner in the best novel category.

By the late 1950s Heinlein's speculations began focusing more on social rather than technological change. The controversial *Starship Troopers,* with its glorification of the military and notions of a limited-franchise democracy, earned Heinlein a reputation as an extreme right-winger. But he followed this controversial book with a radically different novel that would become his best-known work. *Stranger in a Strange Land,* about a human with psychic powers who was raised on Mars and establishes a religious movement on Earth, became the first science fiction novel to make the *New York Times* best-seller list and was a "bible" of the 1960s hippie generation. The central theme of this and subsequent novels was his defense of unconventional sexual love.

Between books the Heinleins traveled widely. They spent time in Europe and South America and visited Antarctica, China, and the Soviet Union. When Virginia was diagnosed with altitude sickness, the couple moved from Colorado to Santa Cruz, California, where in 1966 they built Heinlein's beloved "Bonny Boon," a self-designed circular home with pie-shaped rooms facing a large central atrium.

Illness plagued Heinlein in the 1970s, when a case of peritonitis nearly ended his life. Recovery took two years. Still, *Time Enough for Love,* which explores varieties of futuristic incestuous relationships through a much-loved Heinlein character, the immortal Lazarus Long, appeared in 1973. Four years later Heinlein suffered a transient ischemic attack that led to surgery, which corrected the carotid blockage and brought a return of his mental acuity.

In the novels published in the 1980s, Heinlein tempered his social speculations by presenting them in the context of science fiction adventures. In 1986 the Heinleins moved to Carmel, California, to be closer to emergency medical care. His final book, *To Sail Beyond the Sunset,* was published in 1987, on his eightieth birthday. A year later he died of emphysema during his morning nap. He was cremated and his ashes were scattered at sea with military honors.

Heinlein was an influential writer whose works inspired a generation of novelists both within and outside the field of science fiction. Although some critics found his style banal, his protagonists indistinguishable, and his storytelling mediocre, Heinlein's half-century output of novels and short stories earned him legions of adoring fans who found both his narratives and characters eminently believable. His books have been translated into more than two dozen languages and have sold more than forty million copies.

Heinlein coined several words in his fiction that found their way into more general use, including the verb "grok," which means "to understand profoundly through intuition or empathy," and the noun "waldo," for a remotely operated arm and hand. In recognition of the maturity and respect Heinlein had brought to the field of science fiction, breaking down walls that had isolated the genre from the mainstream and enriching the field with new topics, Heinlein's peers—the Science Fiction Writers of America—awarded Heinlein their first Grand Master Nebula in 1974.

A bright, gracious man, usually affable and gregarious but capable of a steely chill when offended, Heinlein believed in the virtues of freedom, the uniqueness of man, and human destiny in the cosmos. In recognition of his vision, in 1988 the National Aeronautics and Space Administration posthumously awarded Heinlein its highest civilian honor, the Distinguished Public Service Medal, for "his meritorious service to the Nation and mankind in advocating and promoting the exploration of space."

★

The McHenry Library at the University of California in Santa Cruz holds the Robert A. Heinlein archive in its Department of Special Collections. It contains the author's manuscripts, outlines, proofs, and other materials related to his life and works, including books from his private and working collections and published works in various editions and languages. Robert A. Heinlein, *Expanded Universe: The New Worlds of Robert A. Heinlein* (1980), collects many of the author's stories and articles along with comments by Heinlein on their genesis. This work represents the largest single source of material about the writer by the writer. Robert A. Heinlein, *Grumbles from the Grave,* edited by Virginia Heinlein (1990), collects a small portion of the author's correspondence, mostly with his agent, Lurton Blassingame, from the beginning of Heinlein's writing career until 1970, covering such topics as juveniles, adult novels, publishers, travel, fan mail, and writing methods. Robert A. Heinlein, *Requiem: New Collected Works by Robert A. Heinlein and Tributes to the Grand Master,* edited by Yoji Kondo (1992), offers many of the author's speeches and essays, as well as memorials from several dozen friends, colleagues, and admirers. H. Bruce Franklin, *Robert A. Heinlein: America as Science Fiction* (1980), details Heinlein's early family history, but veers off into a Marxist track, using Heinlein's work as an example of everything that is wrong with the Western world. James Gifford, *Robert Heinlein: A Reader's Companion* (forthcoming), a comprehensive overview of Heinlein's work with minimal critical interpretation, provides the first authoritative view of his oeuvre. Alexei Panshin, *Heinlein in Dimension: A Critical Analysis* (1968), was the first detailed study of Heinlein. Leon E. Stover, *Robert A. Heinlein* (1987), offers a comprehensive look at Heinlein's work, though it is marred by factual errors. Obituaries are in the *Los Angeles Times* and the *New York Times* (both 10 May 1988), and *Locus* 21, no. 6 (June 1988).

PATRICK HUYGHE

HEINZ, Henry John, II ("Jack") (*b.* 10 July 1908 in Sewickley, Pennsylvania; *d.* 23 February 1987 in Hobe Sound, Florida), grandson and namesake of the entrepreneurial founder of the H. J. Heinz Company, who served as its third chief executive for twenty-five years, expanded the company internationally, and was a civic leader and major philanthropist.

Jack Heinz, born in a suburb of Pittsburgh, was the eldest of the two sons of Howard Heinz, an astute businessman who steered the H. J. Heinz Company through the Great Depression and guided its growth for twenty-two years, and Elizabeth "Betty" Granger Rust, a housewife. Jack and his brother, Rust, had a rather stern upbringing in an austere and formal Pittsburgh home. Howard traveled constantly and seemed to arouse more respect than affection from his sons. Jack, however, was considered fun-loving and outgoing by his friends. Educated at Shadyside Academy in Pittsburgh, the Choate School near New Haven, Connecticut, Yale (from which he graduated in 1931), and Trinity College, Cambridge (which he attended in 1931 and 1932), Jack was raised with every advantage of wealth and class and grew into a trim, athletic, handsome young man of great charm.

Part of Heinz's education involved following in his father's footsteps and, during summer vacations, learning the family food business from the ground up. It was understood, early on, that Rust, an artist, preferred designing cars to making pickles, and that it would be Jack who would enter and lead the family business.

After college Heinz worked with the British sales force, then returned to the United States, moving up from salesman to branch house manager, to headquarters' sales and advertising manager, and then to Howard's assistant (1937–1941) and to the board of directors. In 1934 his father had enough confidence in his judgment to send him to Australia to locate the company's first manufacturing plant in that country. By then Heinz had married Joan Diehl, an aviatrix, on 18 June 1935. They lived at Rosemont Farm, outside Pittsburgh. Their son, H. John Heinz III, was born in 1938. (Elected to the U.S. Senate from Pennsylvania in 1976, he died in an airplane crash in 1991.)

Heinz shared many family traits, including enormous energy, curiosity, a talent for advertising and promotion, and an unquenchable thirst for travel. He swam the Bosporus as a young man, toured Soviet Russia at the age of twenty-two, married three times, and, at one point later in life, owned homes in the United States, England, the Caribbean, and France, including a Manhattan townhouse on Fifty-seventh Street, the number fifty-seven having become, due to the company's "57 Varieties," its "magic" number.

The full burden of leading "the old firm" fell upon Heinz's shoulders in February 1941, upon his father's

Henry J. Heinz II. H. J. HEINZ COMPANY

death. He was only thirty-two years old, making him one of the youngest men in the United States to head a major company. He was often compared to Henry Ford II, both handsome young scions of immensely successful family-run businesses. His twenty-five years as chief executive spanned enormous changes in America, the food industry, and the H. J. Heinz Company.

When Heinz took over, World War II had begun. In London, where the company had a major facility, the German blitz bombed its Harlesden plant and killed two Heinz employees. Heinz traveled to England five times during World War II, three times at the invitation of the British Ministry of Food, which sought his advice. The company worked overtime to turn out a key wartime protein, baked beans, which remained a much-beloved staple of the English diet. (Heinz, a devoted Anglophile who socialized with the British royal family, was knighted for his contributions to British-American relations in 1979.)

Under Heinz's leadership the U.S. company threw itself into the war effort. Its Pittsburgh facilities produced K and C rations, and converted part of a baby-food factory to the production of World War II aircraft parts, accompanied by such slogans as From Beans to Bombers and From Pickles to Pursuit Planes. Heinz became a highly visible civic and business leader (as had his father during World War I). He chaired the United War Fund; received Pittsburgh's Man of the Year Award in 1942 for his leadership; and delivered speeches promoting food allocation, conservation, and rationing.

After the war Heinz took the company public. The stock offering was snapped up within twenty-four hours. His marriage to Joan Diehl had ended in divorce (1942), and in October 1947 Heinz married Jane Ewing. They divorced in 1952. On 22 August 1953 he married Drue Maher, born in England of Irish parents. They loved to entertain and led a jet-setting life, mingling with celebrities such as Aristotle Onassis, Winston Churchill, Aly Khan, Truman Capote, and Gianni Agnelli. Known for his impeccable taste in music, literature, architecture, wine, and food, Heinz was described as a man of "stratospheric elegance."

In the years following World War II, Heinz devoted himself to European recovery, food programs, and world trade issues, in addition to running the company. He testified in Congress; worked with public-private groups supporting international cooperation; attended International Chamber of Commerce and Bilderberg conferences on Europe, serving as chairman of the U.S. Council of the former organization from 1948 to 1951; assessed an economic assistance program to Pakistan for President Dwight D. Eisenhower in 1954; and continued to contribute to British recovery programs. In Pittsburgh he became a leading member of the Allegheny Conference and Community Chest (later the United Way). In 1947 the company pioneered a national campaign to help feed "the hungry children of Europe."

Between 1945 and 1965 Heinz dramatically expanded the firm in both the United States and abroad. New factories and administration offices were built in Canada, the United Kingdom, and Pittsburgh. He opened new operations in the Netherlands, Venezuela, Mexico, Portugal, Italy, and Japan. Star-Kist and Ore-Ida were acquired. Worldwide sales boomed but, with the exception of Heinz U.K., profits plummeted. Heinz was more focused on quality, taste, nutrition, advertising, and design than on the bottom line. Generations of loyal employees considered the company "a good place to work."

Although technically a public company, H. J. Heinz was still run paternalistically by an insular board. Heinz relied on a small group of self-made men to steer the ship. Financially, it began to seriously founder. Matters came to a crisis in 1963, when Heinz agreed to become nonexecutive chairman and to turn the company over to professional management. The move freed the company to succeed—and its value to shareholders, including the Heinz family, to rise—under the leadership first of R. Burt Gookin, architect of the modern Heinz, and then of Anthony J. F. O'Reilly, who transformed it into a global player. It also freed Jack Heinz to devote himself to his many interests and passions, chief among them the city of Pittsburgh and its renaissance.

The Howard Heinz Endowment, which he headed, funded the Pittsburgh Symphony, the Carnegie Museum of Art, nutrition education programs, and Heinz Hall, in downtown Pittsburgh. Heinz Hall opened in 1971 and was hailed as a stunning contribution to urban restoration and an acoustical gem. Heinz personally supervised the renovation, which transformed an old movie theater into the permanent performing home of the Pittsburgh Symphony Orchestra. In his lifetime Heinz distributed more than $300 million to philanthropic causes, both in Pittsburgh and around the world. Heinz died of cancer and was interred in Homewood Cemetery in Pittsburgh.

A Republican and a Presbyterian, Heinz presided over the H. J. Heinz Company's transition from family-run to professionally managed company with dignity and charm, ensuring its survival as an independent company bearing the family name. His civic leadership and generous support of Pittsburgh institutions contributed to the dramatic rebirth of that city, where the Heinz name, family, and company are still regarded with enormous esteem and affection.

★

Glimpses of Heinz can be found in Stephen Potter, *The Magic Number: The Story of 57* (1959), and Robert C. Alberts, *The Good Provider: H. J. Heinz and His 57 Varieties* (1973). A fuller profile is provided in Eleanor Foa Dienstag, *In Good Company: 125 Years at the Heinz Table* (1994), a company history in which Heinz is assessed within the context of company leadership as an "internationalist," and within the Heinz family context as a "gentleman" who focused more on "doing the common thing uncommonly well" than on the actual rewards. An obituary is in the *New York Times* (24 Feb. 1987).

ELEANOR FOA DIENSTAG

HELLER, Walter Wolfgang (*b.* 27 August 1915 in Buffalo, New York; *d.* 15 June 1987 near Seattle, Washington), economist and adviser to President John F. Kennedy.

Heller was the son of German immigrants Ernst Heller, a civil engineer, and Gertrude Warmburg. He graduated from Oberlin College with a B.A. degree in 1935 and received his M.A. degree and Ph.D. in economics at the University of Wisconsin in 1938 and 1941, respectively. He married Emily Karen Johnson on 16 September 1938. They had three children. Beginning in 1946 he spent most of his career at the University of Minnesota, eventually as chairman of the Economics Department from 1957 to 1960. Heller also pursued a parallel career in government and consulting, working in the Treasury Department as a tax analyst from 1942 to 1946. There he became an advocate

Walter W. Heller. ARCHIVE PHOTOS

of revenue sharing by the federal government with the states, a principle that was finally adopted by the Nixon administration in 1972. In 1947 he was chief of finance for the U.S. military government in Germany. From 1955 to 1960 Heller was an economic adviser to Minnesota governor Orville Freeman. He continued to teach and to consult for various federal organizations in Washington, including the Congressional Budget Office, until a week before his death.

In December 1960 President-elect John F. Kennedy announced that Heller was his choice to chair the Council of Economic Advisers. Early in the Kennedy administration the Soviet Union was testing the new president. After a hostile summit meeting with Nikita Khrushchev in Vienna in June 1961, Kennedy decided to follow through with his campaign promise to break out of the $40 billion annual ceiling that President Dwight D. Eisenhower had put on military spending. When the Soviet Union and East Germany constructed the Berlin Wall in August 1961, Kennedy's first impulse was to raise taxes by $3 billion. To dissuade Kennedy, Heller brought Paul Samuelson to Hyannis Port on Cape Cod to persuade the president not to raise taxes when the unemployment rate was nearly 7 percent.

One of Kennedy's first acts was to send his Council of Economic Advisers to Paris to learn the supposed secret of

European success in achieving rapid growth. Shortly thereafter, Heller came up with the concept of "fiscal drag." To measure this, a calculation was made of what the federal budget would look like at full employment, which was defined as 4 percent unemployment. This hypothetical full employment budget (later relabeled as the high employment budget) indicated that tax rates were too high and would produce a budget surplus when the economy returned to full employment.

As a result, tax cuts were devised to stimulate investment and consumption, particularly the former. Heller convinced the president that it was not necessary to plan a balanced budget at a time when the economy was weak, a state of affairs Kennedy had unveiled in his June 1962 commencement address at Yale University. On the other hand, a budget surplus might be appropriate for an overheated economy.

Heller also convinced Kennedy that it might be necessary to fight inflation coming from wages that might rise faster than productivity. In early 1962 this produced the wage-price guidelines, which linked wage increases to productivity gains, and the famous rollback of steel price increases, which occurred when the steel producers broke out of their guidelines. The same year the investment tax credit was institutionalized to subsidize private investment. Plans were also made for an across-the-board 10 percent cut in personal income taxes, but this legislation was blocked in Congress until after Kennedy's assassination. Heller remained in office to see his tax cut introduced but left the Johnson administration on 16 November 1964. Heller did not depart over policy differences, but because he had three children in college and a debt of $16,000.

Both Heller and his successor, Gardner Ackley, favored raising taxes to pay for the Vietnam War, but this did not occur until 1 July 1968. By then the wage-price guidelines had also broken down, as organized labor realized that implementing them had resulted in real wages increasing at a rate lower than expected.

Heller was a superb teacher and a frequent economic pundit on television as well as on the pages of the *Wall Street Journal.* He developed the differentiation between "active" deficits coming basically from the spending side of the federal budget and "passive" deficits arising in an underheated economy and coming primarily from the revenue side of the federal budget.

Heller initially was critical of President Ronald Reagan's supply-side economics because of the potential for unprecedented deficit financing, but he eventually came to realize that he had been the first practicing supply-sider in the Kennedy administration's decision to institutionalize the investment tax credit. Subsequently, he was invited to take part in top decision making in the Reagan administration, much to the consternation of Martin Anderson, an early Reagan supply-sider, and Milton Friedman.

Heller died of a heart attack in his vacation home near Seattle. He began having health problems stemming from rheumatic fever in the 1950s.

Walter Heller achieved prominence as the chair of the Council of Economic Advisers under President Kennedy. He is given credit for the introduction of the New Economics, which emerged from the thinking of Paul Samuelson, James Tobin, Arthur Okun, and Otto Eckstein in the years of the Kennedy New Frontier and the Johnson Great Society. The New Economics can be traced back to some of the thinking of John Maynard Keynes, particularly the role of fiscal policy, involving changes in federal spending and taxation.

Heller was widely admired by both liberals and conservatives. After his death, the conservative Alan Greenspan recognized him as "a major contributor if not the father of modern economic policymaking." Heller defined and contributed a number of economic terms that are still used by contemporary economists. Paul Sarbanes, the liberal Senator from Maryland who had once worked for the Council of Economic Advisers when Heller was chairman, recognized that he "made a major contribution to the vigor and prosperity of our society."

★

Joseph A. Pechman and N. J. Simler, eds., *Economics in the Public Service: Papers in Honor of Walter W. Heller* (1989), represents a fitting tribute to Heller's thinking. Heller's *The Economy: Old Myths and New Realities* (1976) reflects a Keynesian attempt to deal with a combination of both high inflation and unemployment, and his *New Dimensions of Political Economy* (1966) celebrates the virtues of fiscal policy, the triumph of Keynesian thinking in the New Economics of the early 1960s, and the advent of welfare capitalism. Information on Heller's invitation to join the Reagan administration can be found in Martin Anderson, *Revolution* (1988). An obituary is in the *New York Times* (17 June 1987).

LYNN TURGEON

HEMINGWAY, Mary Welsh (*b.* 5 April 1908 in Walker, Minnesota; *d.* 26 November 1986 in New York City), journalist and war correspondent and fourth wife of novelist Ernest Hemingway; after his suicide in 1961 she wrote her autobiography, largely about their fifteen-year marriage, and published three significant Hemingway manuscripts.

Mary Welsh was the only child of Thomas James Welsh, a lumberman in northern Minnesota, and Adeline Beehler, a homemaker. She grew up in and around Bemidji, Minnesota, where she attended public schools. Her fondest childhood memories were of canoe trips with her father in the lake country. "Up to the late teens of our century we

Mary Hemingway, 1962. ARCHIVE PHOTOS

lived in a world that was then remote and has now vanished at the insistence of lumbermen, plowmen, and road-builders," she wrote in her autobiography, *How It Was* (1976). "But in my childhood it was a world of forest, water-laced, where growing up was almost as untrammeled for children as for the birch trees that lumberjacks ignored."

Her father's business declined while she was in high school, and the family moved from a gracious house to an apartment. After her high school graduation in 1926, she attended classes for a year at the local state teacher's college in Bemidji. Determined to become a journalist, having been impressed with the local newspaper editor when she was a child, Mary enrolled at Northwestern University in Evanston, Illinois. She left the university in 1930 after less than two years to edit a magazine, *The American Florist,* aimed at Chicago's retail florists.

She was married briefly to Lawrence Miller Cook, whom she had known as a classmate at Northwestern and whom she divorced in 1933. In 1932 she became a reporter for a company that published five weekly neighborhood newspapers on Chicago's North Side, but later in the year she joined the *Chicago Daily News,* where she worked until 1937 as a society reporter. She longed to cover news but later was thankful she had been trained by the demanding women's editor, Leola Allard.

In 1936 Mary traveled overseas for the first time and saw London and Paris, an intoxicating vacation that made her determined to work abroad. She called the powerful London newspaper owner Lord Beaverbrook and asked for a job on his *London Daily Express,* the largest newspaper in England. She charmed the elderly man, and a year later he summoned her to New York for a meeting at which he proposed that she become his assistant. She persisted in her attempts to become a reporter in London, however, and in the summer of 1937 she started working for the *Daily Express.*

In 1938 she met and married an Australian journalist, Noel Monks, who was then covering the Spanish Civil War for the *London Daily Mail.* They lived apart for much of their marriage, their war-related assignments separating them, and the couple divorced in 1945. A highlight of Mary's work was her coverage of the Munich Agreement in September 1938, in which Great Britain and France agreed to Adolf Hitler's annexation of the Sudetenland region of Czechoslovakia. She covered Germany's march into Czechoslovakia in 1939.

In 1940 Mary was the first woman correspondent with the British Royal Air Force in France; she slipped back to London as France fell. Later that year Mary went to work for *Time* and *Life.* She wrote about, and lived through, the Luftwaffe's bombing of London that killed some 30,000 people and left more than a million homeless. Some of her war dispatches were published in *Their Finest Hour* (1941) and *I Can Tell It Now* (1946). "Whenever I was caught in the streets by bombs sounding too close for comfort, I flopped face downward with my arms around my head," she later wrote. In the whirlwind of wartime London she met and socialized with diplomats, politicians, military leaders, and famous writers, including J. B. Priestley and William Saroyan.

Mary, then thirty-six, met Ernest Hemingway, forty-four, for the first time as she lunched with Irwin Shaw at the White Tower in 1944. The next day she lunched with Hemingway, who was covering the Royal Air Force for *Collier's;* he struck her as lackluster compared with her lively friends. At their chance third meeting, in the bar of the Dorchester Hotel, she was saddened by his anger toward his mother. "In subsequent years I saw in many strangers' faces signs of the same disapproval I was feeling and not understanding," she recalled in *How It Was.* Later that night Hemingway (then married to Martha Gellhorn) visited her apartment and told her he intended to marry her.

In July 1944 she toured the Normandy invasion site and battlefields and reported on army surgeries for *Life.* On a subsequent trip for *Time* into newly liberated Paris, she reunited with Hemingway in the Hotel Ritz. They celebrated, drank with friends, and visited Pablo Picasso. One time she found herself the surprised victim of his anger, a "whipping boy" role she would play "from time to time for years," and in another incident she returned fire over his drunken friends. (In response, she said, he slapped her jaw, later sending emissaries, including Marlene Dietrich, to apologize and plead his case before showing up himself to praise her spunk.)

Despite reservations about losing her work and about the "complicated and contradictory" Hemingway, Mary decided to put her career on hold after the war and settle into Hemingway's home in Cuba. Their mutual divorces final, they formally completed a Cuban marriage contract in March 1946.

In *How It Was,* published fifteen years after Ernest's death, Mary Hemingway reconstructed from her detailed diaries and her correspondence their active social life, their Gulf Stream fishing trips and hunting trips in Africa and the American West, their rambling travels in the Alps and to Spain, their fights, and their passion for each other. She frankly reported Hemingway's periodic mistreatment (he once threw wine in her face in front of friends) as well as his tenderness (he wrote faithfully during separations, sometimes multiple letters daily). In the summer of 1946, she reported, he saved her life on the operating table during an emergency surgery in Casper, Wyoming, for a burst fallopian tube; he coolly forced plasma into her collapsed veins, although doctors had given up hope.

She was with him in his waning years, when he published his shakiest novel, *Across the River and into the Trees* (1950), nevertheless a best-seller and dedicated to her; she was his first audience when he rallied with *The Old Man and the Sea* (1952), which won the Pulitzer Prize; she was beside him when they narrowly escaped death in two back-to-back plane crashes in East Africa in 1954; and she shared his pride when he was awarded the Nobel Prize in literature that year. In her autobiography Mary chronicled Hemingway's professional decline and his paranoia and depression, which culminated in his suicide; she discovered his body in the foyer of their home in Ketchum, Idaho. (They had purchased the house in 1959 after Fidel Castro assumed power in Cuba.)

Critics were annoyed by the lack of analysis and the vast minutiae in the 537 pages of *How It Was.* Walter Clemons wrote in *Newsweek* (27 September 1976) that he felt as if he were "floundering through a giant issue of *House and Garden,*" and added, "Approximately 25 pages of *How It Was* are moving and revealing." Melvin Maddocks grumbled in his *Time* (18 October 1976) review that the book was "often as jumbled" as her marriage, although he also said that Mary Hemingway was an "indispensable witness" to Hemingway's torment and a decisive contributor to the "history of women who do time as artists' handmaidens."

Mary Hemingway comes across in her book and in other accounts as a likable, competent, and down-to-earth woman who learned to love drink, sophisticated travel, and the celebrity life during her busy reporting career and later in her equally eventful marriage to Hemingway. After his death she brought forth his three unpublished manuscripts—*A Moveable Feast* (1964), a memoir, and *Islands in the Stream* (1970) and *The Garden of Eden* (1986), both novels. These posthumous books led to a new appreciation and to critical reevaluation, especially for *The Garden of Eden,* a mammoth typescript pared down to a focused novel about a couple's sexual experimentation with another woman and with gender-role reversal. She also published three collections of Hemingway's writing: *By-Line: Ernest Hemingway* (1967), *The Nick Adams Stories* (1972), and *The Enduring Hemingway* (1974).

Mary lived in Manhattan after Ernest Hemingway's suicide. She wrote for *Vogue* and other magazines. In 1976 she established the Ernest Hemingway Foundation to give a prize for the best first novel by an American. Mary had no children. She was an invalid for several years before her death. Mary Welsh Hemingway was cremated and her ashes were buried beside those of her husband in Ketchum.

★

Mary Hemingway, *How It Was* (1976), is an autobiography with little analysis but extensive information. Various biographies of Ernest Hemingway present different views of Mary. These include Carlos Baker, *Ernest Hemingway: A Life Story* (1969), a classic biography; Robert Brainard Pearsall, *The Life and Writings of Ernest Hemingway* (1973); Anthony Burgess, *Ernest Hemingway and His World* (1978); A. E. Hotchner, *Papa Hemingway: The Ecstasy and Sorrow* (1983); and Kenneth S. Lynn, *Hemingway: The Life and the Work* (1987), a masterful work. For biographical data on Mary, see Frances Carol Locher, ed., *Contemporary Authors,* vols. 73–76 (1978). An obituary is in the *New York Times* (28 Nov. 1986).

RICHARD GILBERT

HENDERSON, Leon (*b.* 26 May 1895 in Millville, New Jersey; *d.* 19 October 1986 in Oceanside, California), economist, public administrator, and political strategist.

Leon Henderson was one of two children of Lida C. (Beebe) Henderson and Chester Bowen Henderson, an industrial worker and farmer. He graduated from Millville High School, although at one point he voluntarily interrupted his studies in favor of street life. His grandmother Beebe was instrumental in getting him to return to high school and later to college. He enrolled at the University of Pennsylvania in the fall of 1913 but the following year returned to Millville High for postgraduate work. Limited financial resources had forced him to work in many jobs,

Leon Henderson at the Waldorf-Astoria Hotel, New York City, 1943. AP/ Wide World Photos

including as a factory hand, a newspaper reporter, and a farm worker, to pay his college tuition. He remembered the period as the most miserable of his life.

At Millville he played baseball, basketball, and football, and also tried track. A dean at Swarthmore College saw him on the basketball court and offered him a scholarship. At Swarthmore he continued to work hard at various outside jobs. As a result he did not do well in his classes. His teachers, consequently, did not consider him an able student and did not believe he would have a successful professional career.

When the United States entered World War I in 1917, Henderson, then a Swarthmore junior, enlisted as a private in the Ordnance Corps. In January 1918 he was commissioned as a second lieutenant and assigned to the army's property accounting division. Henderson completed his military service as a captain, having worked in the War Department and the War Industries Board. He returned to Swarthmore in the fall of 1919 and received his B.A. degree in 1920. Henderson taught as an instructor in management at the Wharton School of the University of Pennsylvania from 1920 to 1922, then as associate professor of economics at the Carnegie Institute of Technology (now Carnegie Mellon University) from 1922 to 1923. When he granted students credit for attending a speech by socialist Eugene V. Debs, however, the institute's administrators expressed unhappiness. Henderson subsequently resigned from Carnegie Tech but reassured his students that he had not been fired for left-wing activities. The experience convinced him that he was not cut out to be a teacher.

In 1923 Henderson entered civilian public service as deputy secretary of the Commonwealth of Pennsylvania under Governor Gifford Pinchot. In that position he had diverse assignments—director of accounts, state personnel officer, and secretary of the state employment service. His pay at the time was $5,000; subsequently those jobs were established as separate entities with a total remuneration of $28,000. He quit his Pennsylvania employment in 1925 to become director of the remedial loan division of the Russell Sage Foundation in New York City. His researches into consumer credit and loan-sharking during his eight years at Russell Sage led to his successful campaign for legislation against usurious interest rates in thirty states. On 25 August 1925 he married Myrlie Hamm; they had three children.

At a consumer conference in 1934 he attracted the attention of Hugh Johnson, the first administrator of the National Recovery Administration (NRA), who had convened the conference. Henderson was openly critical of the NRA, and Johnson co-opted him by hiring him as his temporary assistant "to be purely critical." Within two months Henderson was elevated to director of the agency's division of research and planning, a post from which he criticized the behavior of many of the nation's major industries. When the Supreme Court ruled in 1935 that the NRA was unconstitutional, Henderson moved to the Senate Committee on Manufacturers.

In 1936 President Franklin D. Roosevelt asked him to become economic adviser to the Democratic National Committee. At that time his researches led him to forecast correctly the 1937–1938 economic downturn, even though the economics profession as a whole remained cautiously silent. Later, while economic counselor to the Works Progress Administration, a post he filled after the 1936 election, Henderson wrote *Boom or Bust* (1937). In 1938 he was appointed executive secretary of the newly formed Senate Temporary National Economic Committee, headed by Senator Harry Truman of Missouri. The voluminous studies of this committee, now classics, focused on the problem of concentration and monopoly in American industry. While the appointment is reputed to have "sent chills down the spine of the business community," the judgment of many was that Henderson was the guiding genius of the committee. Almost simultaneously, in the spring of 1939, he was named to the Securities and Exchange Commission, an appointment bitterly contested by the business community. Henderson's faith in competition and his animus toward monopoly did not endear him to financial and manufacturing executives.

Henderson's crowning achievement was his appointment by Roosevelt in 1941 as director of the new Office of Price Administration (OPA), the World War II agency charged with product rationing and price controls. Although Henderson was one of the important "movers and shakers" of the New Deal, he was never part of Roosevelt's "brain trust" but was a member of the "goon squad," a group of some fifteen to twenty second-line bureaucrats who met regularly but secretly to keep brain-truster Felix Frankfurter and each other informed of the work and problems of their agencies.

At OPA, Henderson tried to follow Bernard Baruch's advice to establish comprehensive rather than piecemeal price controls over labor and agricultural prices and to fight the war-related inflationary pressures. This brought Henderson into conflict with labor unions and agriculture. An unpopular government official, Henderson was realistic enough to forecast accurately that "It is only a matter of time till I shall be the most damned man in the country." After the 1942 election Roosevelt shuffled his cabinet, and presidential confidant James F. Burns advised Henderson to quit his post. Consequently, in December 1942 Henderson resigned as OPA director, citing "health reasons." *Time* magazine informed its readers that "he was pushed."

President Roosevelt did utilize Henderson's talents for a behind-the-scenes assignment to gather ideas regarding the Morgenthau Plan for reducing Germany to an agricultural nation. Emphasizing the importance of the Ruhr to the economy of Europe, Henderson submitted a report opposing the plan. In the spring of 1945, FDR asked him to visit Chungking to evaluate China's abilities to recover economically. Roosevelt died while Henderson was in China.

Leo Cherne, owner of the Research Institute of America (RIA), appointed Henderson chairman of the institute's board in the spring of 1943. Henderson kept the chairmanship for about a dozen years. During this time he was also a weekly radio news commentator for the National Broadcasting Company's Blue Network and wrote on current issues. Also during his RIA days he ventured into the private business sector, assuming leadership positions with International Hudson Corporation, United Fruit Company, and other corporations.

Henderson remained active in public affairs for a short time. He was a founding father of the liberal and anticommunist Americans for Democratic Action in 1948 and was its first head. Fearing that Harry Truman could not get elected in 1948, Henderson and James Roosevelt attempted unsuccessfully to interest first Dwight Eisenhower and then Supreme Court justice William O. Douglas to run on the Democratic ticket. One of his last public tasks before full retirement in 1960 was to conduct an economic survey for the state of Maryland.

After 1975 Henderson suffered declining health, and his last years were spent in a retirement colony in Carlsbad, California. He died in the hospital in nearby Oceanside, California. He was cremated and his ashes buried in Millville, New Jersey.

Henderson was a short man who weighed more than 200 pounds in his prime. Even as a senior administrator in Washington, he was something less than a fastidious dresser, even receiving visitors in his shorts on hot summer days. He had a mercurial and truculent personality and once, as a professor, threw a noted football player down a flight of stairs when the latter became nasty over the F grade given him. He played bridge passionately and violently, once smashing his fist through the card table when his partner made an error. Henderson's explosive personality was most apparent in his early professional life; he eventually mellowed. He worked hard but after hours enjoyed nightlife, including dancing.

★

Henderson's papers are in the Franklin Delano Roosevelt Library in Hyde Park, New York. A sketch appears in Maxine Block, ed., *Current Biography 1940* (1941). An obituary is in the *New York Times* (21 Oct. 1986).

HAROLD L. WATTEL

HENSON, James Maury ("Jim") (*b.* 24 September 1936 in Greenville, Mississippi; *d.* 16 May 1990 in New York City), puppeteer and filmmaker who is best known as the creator of the Muppets.

Jim Henson was raised in Leland, Mississippi, a small town where as a child he played by the Mississippi River. His father, Paul Ransom Henson, was an agricultural research biologist for the U.S. Department of Agriculture. His mother, Elizabeth ("Betty") Marcella Brown Henson, doted on his brother, Paul junior, who was two years older. Jim's self-confidence, creativity, and interest in the visual arts were encouraged by his maternal grandmother, known as "Dear." He was inspired by the movie *The Wizard of Oz* and hurried home from school to listen to radio shows.

When Jim was in fifth grade his father accepted a position in Washington, D.C., and the family relocated to suburban Hyattsville, Maryland. During junior high school Jim persuaded his father to purchase the family's first television set. Jim was enthralled with TV, as were many other Americans during the emergence of this new medium. But young Jim foresaw a career direction and began taking photographs, sketching, and gathering inspiration and ideas. He developed a curiosity about technical experimentation. He also had a mischievous streak and saw humor in mis-

Jim Henson with his Muppets Ernie (*bottom*) and Kermit the Frog (*top*), 1973. UPI/CORBIS-BETTMANN

haps, especially when they occurred in serious settings, such as church.

After high school Henson entered the University of Maryland in 1954 as an art major. As a freshman he took a puppetry course, where he met Jane Nebel, an art education major who would become his future wife and partner. Local television station WTOP held tryouts for a puppet show spot and Jim won the position. Although the *Junior Morning Show* was canceled after three weeks, executives at a rival network, WRC-TV, saw several episodes of his ingenious performances and hired him as puppeteer on an afternoon variety show. Jane became his assistant. Debuting on 9 May 1955, Jim's first show, *Sam and Friends,* aired for two five-minute spots and introduced Kermit the Frog. These first puppets did not speak, but Wilkins Coffee Company asked Henson to add dialogue for a series of 160 commercials, which brought Henson recognition and awards. In 1957 he and Jane did a puppet skit on Steve Allen's *Tonight Show.*

The sudden death of his brother in a car accident in April 1956 had a profound effect on Henson, who decided that he would give up puppetry after graduation for more serious endeavors. The money his puppets had helped him earn paid for a trip to Europe in 1958. While touring overseas, Henson discovered that puppetry was taken seriously there as an art form and his interest in the medium was renewed. Combining the words "marionette" and "puppet," Jim came up with the term "muppet" to describe his creations. (Henson's Muppets employed both marionette strings and hand-held puppet techniques.)

On 28 May 1959 Henson married Jane Nebel; they would have three daughters and two sons. *Sam and Friends* won an Emmy for best local entertainment program the same year. In 1960 he graduated from college with a B.A. During the 1960s Henson and the Muppets appeared on the *Ed Sullivan Show, Today Show, Jimmy Dean Show,* and other popular variety television programs.

Among key collaborators in Henson's pioneering work were Jane Henson, Jerry Juhl, Don Sahlin, and Frank Oz. Color television helped highlight the Muppets' distinctive features. Jim Henson devised the use of a monitor set below camera level and visible to the puppeteer, allowing for precise lip-synching. Transcending boundaries, he created new means of bestowing his foam-rubber creations with facial expressions, gestures, and movements. His imagination sparked unprecedented interaction between live actors and puppets, scenery, props, music, sound effects, and dialogue, with engaging results.

Under a grant from the Carnegie Institute, Joan Ganz Cooney formed the Children's Television Workshop with core writers Jon Stone and Joe Raposo, to use kids' love of slick, eye-catching commercial TV production to teach them letters and numbers. She invited Henson to join. Thereafter, *Sesame Street* used Henson's Muppets, airing continuously on a daily basis after 1969. It has been seen in more than 120 countries and translated into many languages.

Among the world-famous characters designed by Jim Henson (some with Children's Television Workshop, some as Jim Henson Productions) are Kermit the Frog, Big Bird, Ernie, Bert, Snuffleuphagus, Oscar the Grouch, Cookie Monster, Grover, The Count, Elmo, Zoe, Telly Monster, Guy Smiley, Prairie Dawn, Rowlf the Dog, Gonzo, Fozzie, and Miss Piggy. The depth and reality of such fictional characters as performed by talented puppeteers have amused, educated, and brought joy to millions of youngsters. Muppet character toys, lunchboxes, clothes, and many other items were designed and met with huge sales success.

In 1976 Henson approached various networks with the idea for a prime-time Muppet program that would appeal to adults as well as children. Rejected by the big American companies, Henson worked with Sir Lew Grade in England and introduced *The Muppet Show,* which ultimately became the top syndicated television program in the United States and the most popular first-run program in the world. It won three Emmy awards and numerous other awards during its five-year run. Henson then brought the Muppets into such feature films as *The Muppet Movie* (1979), *The Great Muppet Caper* (1981, Henson's directorial debut), and *The Muppets Take Manhattan* (1984). Henson's award-winning *Fraggle Rock*, HBO's first original children's show, aired from 1983 to 1987. In 1980 the *Sesame Street Live* arena show began touring, and the Sesame Place play park opened near Philadelphia. The Muppets comic strip was syndicated in 1981. Henson introduced *Muppet Babies,* an animated series on CBS, in 1984. Henson also conceived a series titled *Dinosaurs,* which was later produced and aired on ABC for four seasons.

Some extraordinarily creative early works by Henson include two short films, *Time Piece* (1965) and *Run, Run* (1967), as well as a documentary, *Youth '68* (1968), and a drama, *The Cube* (1969), which were both featured on "Experiment in Television." Later works included the feature films *The Dark Crystal* (1982), *Labyrinth* (1986), and *The Witches* (1990), and the television series *The Storyteller* (1987–1989). In these later works Henson developed remote-control technology for mobilizing his creatures and made many other dazzling special-effects advances. His ingenious combination of the simple, popular Muppets and this more complex, thought-provoking, technically awe-inspiring style in *The Jim Henson Hour* (1989) met with limited success and was canceled after only ten episodes. Extremely disappointed, Henson went to Los Angeles to direct a pioneer 3-D feature film attraction for Walt Disney World/MGM Theme Park titled *Jim Henson's Muppet*Vision 3D,* released in 1991.

In May 1990 Henson contracted what his doctors called a particularly virulent strain of bacterial pneumonia. His delay in seeking medical attention while energetically keeping up with the demands of a family and his many popular creations contributed to his death in a New York hospital at the age of fifty-three. His remains were cremated.

The Henson Foundation was created in 1982 to promote, develop, and encourage public interest in the art of puppetry. Jane Henson as well as Henson's children and staff continued to run Jim Henson Productions, Inc., with the Hensons' oldest son, Brian, named president in 1991. Jim Henson's Creature Workshop continued to build characters for movies, such as *Teenage Mutant Ninja Turtles* (1990) and *The Flintstones* (1994). Jane Henson created the Jim Henson Legacy, partially underwritten by Henson Productions, to preserve Jim Henson's creations and make them available to the public through schools, libraries, museums, art galleries, and other presentations. Jim Henson's vision and imagination changed people's perceptions and dramatized an optimistic interaction of fantasy and reality.

★

Useful books on Henson include Geraldine Woods, *Jim Henson: From Puppets to Muppets* (1987); Nathan Aaseng, *Jim Henson: Muppet Master* (1988); Stephanie St. Pierre, *The Story of Jim Henson, Creator of the Muppets* (1991); Christopher Finch, *Jim Henson: The Art, the Magic, the Imagination* (1993); Louise Gikow, *Meet Jim Henson* (1993); and Deanne Durrett, *Jim Henson* (1994). Articles include D. W. Samuelson and Ann Tasker, "Creating a World for the Dark Crystal," *American Cinematographer* (Dec. 1982): 1282–1289, 1316–1331; Charlene Krista, "Jim Henson: Muppet Master Breaking Ground with *Dark Crystal,*" *Films in Review* 34 (Jan. 1983): 41–44; and Carol A. Emmens, "Jim Henson and the People Behind the Muppet Mania," *School Library Journal* 31 (Sept. 1984): 27–31. An obituary is in the *New York Times* (17 May 1990).

J. S. CAPPELLETTI

HERMAN, Floyd Caves ("Babe") (*b.* 26 June 1903 in Buffalo, New York; *d.* 27 November 1987 in Glendale, California), baseball player for the Brooklyn Robins (and later the Brooklyn Dodgers), Chicago Cubs, and other clubs.

"Babe" Herman was the son of Charles Herman, a building contractor, and Rosa (Caves) Herman. The family moved to Los Angeles in 1905 and then to a home built by Herman's father in Glendale, California. Herman attended Glendale Union High School, where he won twelve varsity letters. He was ruled ineligible for baseball in his senior

Babe Herman. COURTESY OF THE NATIONAL BASEBALL HALL OF FAME LIBRARY, COOPERSTOWN, N.Y.

year because he had played for money, so he weighed scholarship offers in football from Dartmouth and Stanford. In 1921 the Edmonton baseball team, part of the Western Canada Class B League, offered him $175 a month to play first base. Herman accepted the opportunity and played 107 games during his first season, leading the league in hits and triples.

In 1922 the Detroit Tigers brought Herman to their training camp, but no opening existed at first base. Consequently, he went to the Reading team of the International (AAA) League and from there to Omaha of the Western League, where he played the outfield for the first time. On 30 October 1922 he was traded to the Boston Red Sox. Told that he would not get much playing time in 1923, he opted to join Atlanta and Memphis of the Southern League. On 9 November 1923 he married Anna Merriken; they had four children. In 1924 he played with San Antonio of the Texas League and with Little Rock of the Southern League.

While playing with Seattle in 1925, Herman was scouted by the Brooklyn National League club, then called the Robins. Herman, who was a lefty, six feet, four inches, and 190 pounds, impressed the Brooklyn scouts and finished the year with Minneapolis of the American Association. He ended his minor league apprenticeship with a batting average of .343.

Herman played his first game for Brooklyn on 14 April 1926. During his rookie season he had nine consecutive hits and placed in the top ten in the league in batting average (.319), slugging percentage, and on-base percentage. Although his hitting was not as strong the next year, it was still nineteen points higher than the team average. In 1928 Herman moved to right field and again was in the top ten in batting average (.340) and slugging percentage. His salary increased to $17,000 in 1929, and he was among the leaders in six different categories. He hit .381 and placed ninth in voting for Most Valuable Player (MVP).

Herman's best year was 1930. He began by "holding out," or refusing to sign his contract, and finally won a salary of $19,000. His 241 hits placed him ninth in that category in league history. He batted .393, which put him second in the league, and he finished in the top five in slugging percentage, home runs, runs batted in (RBIs), steals, runs, and on-base percentage.

Despite such an extraordinary year, Herman was refused any salary raise at all. When he received his contract, he ripped it in two and sent it back, but ultimately he was forced to settle for the same salary as the previous year. In 1931 he twice hit for the cycle—a single, a double, a triple, and a home run in one game—and was in the top ten of the league in six offensive categories.

In 1932, when Brooklyn tried to cut his salary by $4,000, Herman held out again, only to be traded to Cincinnati on 14 March. In 148 games, he was in the top ten in batting average (.326), slugging percentage, home runs, hits, RBIs, and on-base percentage, and he led the league in triples. In the field, he tied for the league lead for most double plays by an outfielder (six) and set a major league record for chances by a right fielder, a record that lasted forty-five years. In 1932 he received eight votes for MVP, but he was traded to the Chicago Cubs in November. Between 1928 and 1932 Herman averaged 200 hits per year, and his five-year batting average was .350. From 1926 through 1932, his average was sixty points higher than the team he played on and forty-nine points higher than the league average. An excellent base runner, Herman was never caught stealing, and he often turned doubles into triples.

Herman played 137 games for the Cubs in 1933, at a salary of $20,000. He hit for the cycle a third time, which set a record, and he hit three home runs on 20 July. Again he placed in the top ten in slugging percentage, home runs, and RBIs. The next year he was in the top twenty in batting average, slugging percentage, home runs, and RBIs, yet the Cubs traded him to Pittsburgh on 22 November. He wore a Pittsburgh uniform for about a month and a half, then Pittsburgh sold his contract to Cincinnati. With that club, he became the first player to hit a home run in a night game, and he averaged over .300 in batting again.

In 1936 Herman held out once more before playing 119 games for Cincinnati. He was released to Detroit on waivers early in the season, and Detroit sent him to a minor league team in Toledo. He also played minor league ball in Jersey City (1938) and Hollywood (1939–1944). In 1945 the Brooklyn major league club, then called the Dodgers, signed him. He played 37 games and retired in 1945.

Herman worked as a scout for the Pirates, the Phillies, the Yankees, the Mets, and the Giants from 1946 until 1964. With the advice of Ty Cobb and Casey Stengel, he made profitable investments, and he also raised avocados and prize-winning orchids. A series of strokes in 1984 limited his activities. Shortly after celebrating his sixty-fourth wedding anniversary, Herman died of pneumonia at Glendale Hospital in Glendale, California.

Herman had always cooperated with the press. He let stand stories of his errors in the field and on the base paths, a decision he later regretted. Maury Allen, who selected Herman as number 73 of all baseball players, claimed, "It is only his image . . . that has kept him from the Hall of Fame."

★

The library at the National Baseball Hall of Fame in Cooperstown, New York, has primary material on Herman. Babe Herman, *Brooklyn's Babe* (1990), is an autobiography. Joseph L. Reichler, ed., *The Baseball Encyclopedia,* 8th ed. (1990), is a good source for statistics. Bill James, *The Bill James Historical Baseball Abstract* (1985), has Herman's rankings as well as comparative statistics. An obituary is in the *New York Times* (30 Nov. 1987). Substantive

CD-ROMs include John Thorn and Peter Palmer, *Total Baseball* (1994); *Microsoft Complete Baseball* (1995); and Bill James, *Bill James Electronic Baseball Encyclopedia for Windows,* version 1.5 (1996).

THOMAS H. BARTHEL

HERMAN, Woody (*b.* 16 May 1913 in Milwaukee, Wisconsin; *d.* 29 October 1987 in Los Angeles, California), bandleader, clarinetist, saxophonist, and singer who produced innovative big-band jazz of the highest quality for a half-century.

Born Woodrow Charles Thomas Herrmann, Woody Herman was the only child of Otto C. Herrmann and Myrtle Bartoszewicz; he changed his name at an early age. His father, a master shoemaker and installer of shoemaking machinery, was also a semiprofessional singer. As Herman recalled: "My father had great interest in the theater and show biz. . . . He had a burning desire to have a son do it and that was me." Herman appeared in public as a singer and dancer from an early age. He made his first road tour at age nine and used the proceeds to buy a saxophone and a clarinet and begin lessons. He attended St. John's Cathedral Grade and High School in Milwaukee from about 1923 to 1930. He left without graduating from high school.

While in high school, Herman joined Joey Lichter's local band, playing four nights and one afternoon a week at the Million Dollar Ballroom, then went on the road with society bandleader Tom Gerun. Herman successively joined the orchestras of Harry Sosnick, Gus Arnheim, and Isham Jones, with whom he remained until Jones dissolved the band in 1936. At that point, the more jazz-oriented members of the Jones band formed a new outfit and chose Herman as their leader. They adopted a name that reflected their interests, The Band That Plays the Blues. That was "a very bad move in the early stages," according to Herman, "because nobody knew what the blues were." Initially a cooperative venture, the band gradually became known as the "Herman Herd."

Woody Herman in London, 1967. POPPERFOTO/ARCHIVE PHOTOS

Herman married Charlotte Neste, a showgirl he had met in San Francisco, in September 1936. They had one daughter. Herman's new band played its first engagement at the Brooklyn Roseland Ballroom on 3 November 1936. In 1939 the group achieved national prominence with a recording of "Woodchopper's Ball" by Joe Bishop. By 1944, Herman had purchased all the shares of the Herd. Subsequent hits in 1945 included "Bijou," "Apple Honey," and "Northwest Passage," along with novelty numbers such as "Caldonia" by Fleecie Moore. Among the band's key personnel were Neal Hefti, trumpeter and arranger; Pete Candoli and Conte Candoli on trumpet; Bill Harris on trombone; Ralph Burns, pianist and arranger; Chubby Jackson on bass; and Dave Tough on drums. In 1946 the band played a concert in Carnegie Hall in Manhattan that featured "Ebony Concerto," a nonjazz piece written expressly for the Herd by classical composer Igor Stravinsky. Later that year, Herman broke up the band, reportedly to deal with problems that had arisen in his marriage, but he and Charlotte remained together.

In 1947 Herman organized the Second Herd. This band's hallmark was the saxophone choir of Stan Getz, Zoot Sims, Herbie Steward (later replaced by Al Cohn), and Serge Chaloff, nicknamed the "Four Brothers" after the hit tune by Jimmy Giuffre that introduced the novel voicing of three tenors and one baritone. With the Second Herd, Herman explored a bebop-flavored big-band sound. That sound was epitomized in Herman's version of "Lemon Drop" (1948), by George Wallington, in which Jackson, trumpeter Shorty Rogers, and vibraphonist Terry Gibbs formed a scat vocal trio to state the theme with humorous effect. Another Second Herd landmark was Burns's "Early Autumn," with a solo by Getz that launched his career.

Subsequent incarnations of the band included the Third Herd (1950–1955), the Fourth Herd (1956–1959), and the Swingin' Herd (1960–1967). The band of later years was sometimes referred to as the Thundering Herd, although that designation is also used for earlier phases of the band's history. Among the notable members of the later band were trombonist Kai Winding and pianist/arranger Nat Pierce in the 1950s and trumpeter Bill Chase and saxophonist Sal Nistico in the 1960s. Starting in 1968, Herman experimented with jazz-rock fusion in a bid for new audiences. Recording numbers such as "MacArthur Park," "Light My Fire," and "My Cherie Amour," he concentrated on college dates in the 1970s. By 1980, he was back to straight jazz, which was enjoying a modest resurgence in popularity. Herman's wife died in 1982.

Herman delegated the money aspects of his undertakings to his business managers and paid dearly for the confidence he placed in them. From the mid-1960s onward, he was embroiled in disputes over taxes on the band's earnings that culminated in 1985, when the Internal Revenue Service seized his Hollywood residence and sold it at auction. He pursued a stiff touring schedule through the last year of his life in spite of illness, largely because of continuing financial pressure. He died in Los Angeles of cardiopulmonary arrest following a siege of heart attacks and related lung problems and was buried in Hollywood Memorial Park.

A major figure of the big-band era, Herman outlasted every working bandleader from that era except Lionel Hampton and Les Brown. Indeed, the Woody Herman Orchestra was still performing as of 1997, under the direction of saxophonist Frank Tiberi. Herman was gifted with an unusual combination of leadership ability and receptivity to other people's ideas, captured in the following story he told at his own expense (recounted in Clancy, pp. 131–132):

> [Terry Gibbs] had a thing on "What's New?," a lovely ballad, and he used mallets that in appearance and in sound were something like tongs that you would use on an anvil. So one day, casually, after a couple of shows, I said, "Terry, did you ever think about using softies, you know, mallets, for a thing like 'What's New?' " He says, "Man, you can't do that! I can't make it, man, like it's going to ruin the clank, you know?" So I said, "Forget it." P. S. That was it for the next year . . . tongs and anvils!

Woody Herman is remembered largely for creating the exacting yet supportive environment of the Herman bands, in which, over the years, large numbers of distinguished jazz performers and composer/arrangers got their start.

★

Herman's autobiography, *The Woodchopper's Ball* (1990), was cowritten with Stuart Troup. Biographies include Steve Voce, *Woody Herman* (1986); William D. Clancy, *Woody Herman: Chronicles of the Herds* (1995); Gene Lees, *Leader of the Band: The Life of Woody Herman* (1995); and Robert Kriebel, *Blue Flame: Woody Herman's Life in Music* (1995). Dexter Morrill compiled *Woody Herman: A Guide to the Big Band Recordings, 1936–1987* (1990). An obituary is in the *New York Times* (30 Oct. 1987).

JONATHAN WIENER

HICKERSON, John Dewey (*b.* 26 January 1898 in Crawford, Texas; *d.* 18 January 1989 in Bethesda, Maryland), career diplomat who played a crucial role in the establishment of both the United Nations and the North Atlantic Treaty Organization (NATO).

The son of Alva James Hickerson and Mary (Hill) Hickerson, Hickerson served in the U.S. Army in 1918. He then graduated from the University of Texas with a B.A. degree in 1920 and immediately joined the foreign service. He served in Tampico, Mexico (1920–1922); Rio de Janeiro (1922–1925); and Ottawa, Canada (1925–1930). In 1922 he married Vida Corbin; they had one son.

Hickerson was a member of the Permanent Joint Board of Defense for the United States and Canada from 1940 to 1946. During the same period he was an adviser to the U.S. delegation at the Dumbarton Oaks Conference (1944), at which the United States, Great Britain, China, and the Soviet Union drafted specific proposals for the charter of the United Nations, and at the United Nations Organizing Conference in San Francisco (1945), where the victorious Allies applied the lessons learned from the failures of the League of Nations. Hickerson was director of the Office of European Affairs at the State Department from 1947 to 1949. In this capacity he chaired the group of senior officials from foreign ministries of the United States and eleven other countries that drafted the treaty establishing NATO in 1949.

John D. Hickerson, Washington, D.C., 1960. UPI/CORBIS-BETTMANN

While serving as assistant secretary of state for United Nations affairs between 1949 and 1953, Hickerson was preoccupied mainly with events in northeast Asia—the communist triumph in China, the Korean War, and the reconstruction of Japan. Hickerson was deputy commandant for foreign affairs at the National War College (1953–1955), then served as U.S. ambassador to Finland (1955–1959) and to the Philippines (1959–1962). After his retirement from the foreign service in 1962, Hickerson became a regular lecturer at the School of Foreign Service of Georgetown University and served on the board of directors of the Atlantic Council. He died of cancer on 18 January 1989.

Perhaps most telling of Hickerson's energy and commitment as a civil servant is a story related by Walter Isaacson and Evan Thomas in *The Wise Men.* Hickerson spoke to his deputy in the Office of European Affairs, Theodore Achilles, at the end of 1947. Amid the turmoil of the cold war on the one hand and of rampant isolationism on the other, Hickerson proclaimed: "I don't care whether entangling alliances have been considered worse than original sin since George Washington's time. We've got to negotiate a military alliance with Western Europe in peacetime and we've got to do it quickly." He was particularly frustrated with the likes of George Kennan, who preferred unilateral and surgical operations by U.S. troops to a multilateral coalition with European partners who would be deemed equal to the United States. Isaacson and Thomas laud Hickerson for prodding and maneuvering his superiors—the military hero and secretary of state George C. Marshall and the personable undersecretary of state, Robert A. Lovett—into bureaucratic and programmatic action on the military side of the transatlantic relationship. This concerted operation is seen as culminating with the formation of NATO.

★

The Department of State has a collection of Hickerson's papers in its archives in Washington, D.C. Walter Isaacson and Evan Thomas, *The Wise Men: Six Friends and the World They Made: Acheson, Bohlen, Harriman, Kennan, Lovett, McCloy* (1986), is a fascinating study of the leading U.S. diplomats of the post–World War II era. An obituary is in the *New York Times* (20 Jan. 1989).

ITAI SNEH

HILDRETH, Horace Augustus (*b.* 2 December 1902 in Gardiner, Maine; *d.* 2 June 1988 in Portland, Maine), politician, diplomat, and administrator who, as ambassador to Pakistan (1953–1957), helped win that nation's alignment with the West during the cold war.

Horace Hildreth and his twin brother, Charles, were sons of Guy Hildreth, an attorney, and Florence Lawrence. Horace attended Gardiner public schools, and after graduating from Gardiner High School in 1921, he entered Bowdoin College, where he was an outstanding athlete and debater. He worked summers as a dishwasher and counselor at a boys' camp, a ranger in Yellowstone National Park, a seaman on a tramp steamer, and a YMCA traveling representative in Europe. Hildreth graduated from Bowdoin in 1925, and three years later received his LL.B. from Harvard Law School. In 1929 he was admitted to the bar in Maine and in Massachusetts, and married Katherine Cable Wing of Brookline, Massachusetts, with whom he had three daughters and a son. For eight years he practiced with the prestigious Boston firm of Ropes, Gray, Best, Coolidge, and Rugg.

Horace Hildreth after being named U.S. ambassador to Pakistan, 1953. AP/WIDE WORLD PHOTOS

Hildreth wanted a political career and sought the advice of Congressman Joseph Martin on whether to pursue it in Maine or Massachusetts. Because the veteran Massachusetts politician advised him to return to his native Maine to establish his political base, Hildreth settled his family in Cumberland Foreside and became a partner in the Portland law firm of Cook, Hutchinson, Pierce, and Connell. He served as a director of the Dorchester Mutual Fire Insurance Company, Westover Fabrics, Inc., and the company that published the Boston *Herald* and *Traveler,* and as a member of the board of two Maine wholesale hardware firms. He also founded a network of Maine radio and television stations.

Hildreth began his political career by serving on Republican town and county committees. He served in the 1940 Maine House of Representatives and was elected to the state senate in 1940. He was chosen president of the senate in 1943; as such, he became a logical candidate for the 1944 Republican gubernatorial nomination.

Hildreth won the governorship by a landslide vote. Assuming office in 1945, he led his state through the close of World War II and into the difficult postwar years. The new governor took pride in lowering the state's bonded indebtedness to its lowest point in eighteen years and in working with the executive council to enable the University of Maine to accommodate war veterans. Among the accomplishments of his second term, Hildreth took particular pride in a bond issue to finance a $150 bonus for Maine's veterans and a program for encouraging farmers from war-torn Latvia, Estonia, and Lithuania to emigrate to Maine. But he viewed the rise in state liquor tax receipts with mixed feelings: "It makes poor sense to attempt to solve our dollar problems by drinking ourselves to death," he commented.

As chairman of the New England Governors' Conference in 1947, Hildreth backed the Truman Doctrine for massive assistance to Greece and Turkey in their struggle against communism, supported universal military training, and advocated a federal government retail sales tax as an inducement for an end to taxation of gasoline, inheritance, and alcohol. In 1948 he was chosen president of the Council of State Governments. During 1948 he extended the hospitality of Blaine House (Maine's governors' residence) to such presidential hopefuls as the governor of New York, Thomas E. Dewey; Ohio senator Robert A. Taft; Speaker of the House Joseph Martin; and Hildreth's personal favorite, the former governor of Minnesota, Harold Stassen. Also in 1948, Hildreth announced his intention to seek the Republican nomination for the U.S. Senate. During the primary, Congresswoman Margaret Chase Smith, Hildreth, and two other candidates joined in several campaign debates. Hildreth was backed by the "regular" Republican organization and large corporations, including power companies. Hildreth's decision to challenge the popular congresswoman was the end of his political career, as Smith easily won the nomination.

On 15 September 1949 Hildreth became the ninth president of Bucknell University in Lewisburg, Pennsylvania. Hildreth felt strongly that private institutions of higher learning must be self-supporting and operate within their budgets, and he enthusiastically supported the drive to raise the university's endowment from $2 million to $10 million. Few thoughtful educators, Hildreth commented in a *New York Times* article (21 August 1949), want to appeal for federal funds, knowing that this would further strengthen a government "inexorably moving in to control all our educational policies and curricula."

When Hildreth left Bucknell in June 1953 to accept an appointment by President Dwight D. Eisenhower as United States ambassador to Pakistan, he announced that he would return to the university "every cent of compensation that had been paid to him," because he and Mrs. Hildreth were "so devoted to Bucknell, and so proud of it," that they would have served without compensation. He took on his new assignment in the arena of diplomacy "in a spirit of duty" and was the first person from Maine to receive the rank of full ambassador. In July 1953 Hildreth and his family moved into the American Embassy at Karachi, Pakistan.

The Muslim republic had been carved out of India in 1947, its West and East sections separated by a thousand miles of a hostile Hindu India. Prior to Hildreth's arrival, a severe drought devastated agricultural production. Pakistan's geography exacerbated the threat of starvation for the large existent population and for the refugees swarming in from India. The new ambassador oversaw the distribution of millions of dollars in American aid to the newly independent nation. In the *Department of State Bulletin* Hildreth explained how an emergency shipment of wheat would help prevent many people from starving and alleviate "what otherwise would be a grave danger to the economy and internal stability of Pakistan."

The instability of Pakistan's government was illustrated not long before Hildreth's arrival: the prime minister had been deposed and replaced by the former ambassador to the United States. Concerning Pakistan's role in the critical struggle between international communism and the West, the new prime minister, Mohammad Ali, stated that his country had little in common with the Soviet Union; by late 1954 Hildreth could write that Pakistan had "rejected communism largely on religious grounds, . . . cast its lot with the West with a degree of courage and firmness that is heartening to the entire Western world." Hildreth helped Pakistan abandon its neutrality and accept American military and economic aid, necessitated in part by distrust of India. He also, however, pointed out the risk of aggravating India, which was disclaiming any fear of international communism and already calling the agreement "provocative." During Hildreth's third year as ambassador, Pakistan's friendship with the West was further evidenced by its hosting of the Southeast Asia Treaty Organization (SEATO) conference in Karachi.

The Hildreths wrote an annual holiday letter to Maine friends describing their social, recreational, and diplomatic activities in Pakistan. Their fourth annual letter indicated that they had agreed to stay beyond the usual three years for a "hardship post," so that the United States would not have to change ambassadors during the 1956 national election.

In May 1957 the Hildreths returned home to Cumberland Foreside, and Hildreth resumed legal and business enterprises he had embarked on years earlier. He made an unsuccessful bid for the governorship in 1958, losing to a Democrat, Clinton A. Clauson. In 1977 Hildreth combined his Maine broadcasting network with the newspaper and book publishing interests of W. Russell Brace of Belfast, Maine, to form Diversified Communications, Inc., of Portland. Hildreth was chairman of the board of directors until 1980, and continued thereafter as a board member. The company remained in the Hildreth family after Hildreth died of a heart attack at Maine Medical Center in Portland in 1988.

When the former governor of Maine accepted a role in international diplomacy, he perceived that the threat to world peace was not simply a matter of East versus West or communism versus democracy. Neutralism, he explained, was the real problem. Such a status appealed to nonaligned nations but, in the context of the cold war, it drove out the forces of freedom, leaving a country ripe for communist takeover. With this subtle understanding, he guided Pakistan toward an agreement with the United States and a partnership with the West.

★

The Maine State Library and the Portland Public Library have files containing information on Hildreth. Details of his governorship can be found in Harry Draper Hunt, *The Blaine House: Home of Maine's Governors* (1974). For his appointment to Bucknell, see "Hildreth Is Named Head of Bucknell," *New York Times* (21 Aug. 1949), and "Bucknell's Ninth," *Time* (29 Aug. 1949). His tenure at Bucknell is covered in J. Orin Oliphant, *The Rise of Bucknell University* (1965). The following newspaper articles focus on his ambassadorship: "From Politician to President to Pakistan," *Portland Press Herald* (2 May 1953); Spencer W. Campbell, "Hildreth Will Have to Commute 1,000 Miles in Pakistan," *Portland Sunday Telegram* (10 May 1953); Nelle C. Penley, "Ambassadorship to Pakistan Is an Interesting Assignment Taken in a Spirit of Duty, Declares Hildreth," *Bangor Daily News* (3 July 1953); Howard Gotlieb, "Former Maine Governor Proving a Success as American Diplomat," *Bangor Daily News* (22 Mar. 1954); and "Hildreths Write News-Filled Holiday Greeting from Post in Karachi, Pakistan," *Lewiston Evening Journal* (1 Jan. 1957). See also *Department of State Bulletin* (6 July 1953 and 4 Oct. 1954) for Hildreth's remarks on U.S. wheat shipments to Pakistan and on the U.S.-Pakistani friendship. An obituary is in the *New York Times* (4 June 1988).

SYLVIA B. LARSON

HOBSON, Laura Kean Zametkin (*b.* 19 June 1900 in New York City; *d.* 28 February 1986 in New York City), writer best known for her novel on anti-Semitism, *Gentlemen's Agreement* (1947).

Laura Zametkin was the daughter of Michael Zametkin, a Russian-Jewish immigrant who edited the *Daily Forward,* a Jewish newspaper on the Lower East Side of Manhattan, and labor organizer, and Adella Kean, a writer for another Jewish newspaper, *The Day.* Although born a Jew, Laura became an agnostic. A slender woman of approximately five feet, seven inches, she had a twin sister. She also had two half-brothers, children of her father's first marriage. Laura published her first article when she was a student at Jamaica High School in New York in the *Oracle,* the school's monthly magazine. She began writing on school news for the *Evening Mail.* She entered Hunter College in New York City in 1917 and remained there until 1919, when she went to Cornell University. She graduated in 1921 with a B.A. degree.

Laura took a copywriting job in 1923 for a small advertising agency. At that time she met Thomas Mount, who was married. She lived with him and became pregnant with his child but had an abortion. She married Francis Thayer Hobson, a publisher, on 23 July 1930. They were divorced in 1935, but she adopted a child in 1936 and in 1941 bore a son. She never revealed the name of the father.

Laura Z. Hobson, New York City, 1953. UPI/CORBIS-BETTMANN

Hobson's writing career began in earnest when she became a reporter for the *New York Post* in 1926. In 1934 she worked for *Time, Life,* and *Fortune* magazines (all publications of Henry R. Luce) on the promotion staff. In 1935 she wrote a short story and then wrote for the *Ladies' Home Journal, McCall's,* and *Colliers* magazines. By 1940 she had left her position at *Time* magazine to write full-time.

Hobson's first novel, *The Trespassers,* appeared in 1943 and concerned the problems faced by World War II exiles from Europe who were not permitted in the United States. Hobson's most remembered work was *Gentlemen's Agreement,* published in February 1947. In progress for four years, the novel was about anti-Semitism in the United States after World War II, a period when a U.S. congressman could refer to a Jewish newspaperman using a vile epithet on the floor of the House of Representatives and when the general public commonly uttered anti-Jewish remarks. Hobson initially feared that magazines, movies, and the public would not be interested in the topic, but she was proved incorrect. *Gentleman's Agreement* is about a non-Jewish writer who portrays himself as Jewish while preparing a magazine article. Presumably set in the exclusive town of Darien, Connecticut, the book was banned in New York City's public high schools for almost two years because some passages were deemed immoral.

An instant hit, *Gentleman's Agreement* topped the best-seller list for nearly six months and was eventually translated into thirteen languages. It sold more than a million copies in its first year and another 600,000 afterward. A motion picture of the same name was made by Twentieth Century–Fox, starring Gregory Peck and Dorothy McGuire. The movie won the Academy Award as the best film of 1947, as well as the citation for best film by the New York Film Critics and numerous other awards.

In 1948 Hobson attended the Democratic National Convention in Philadelphia and helped write the civil rights plank in the party platform. She also wrote an advertisement sponsored by the Americans for Democratic Action (ADA) attacking the communist witch-hunts by Congress. A longtime member of the New York board of the American Civil Liberties Union, she befriended Hubert H. Humphrey. She advocated efforts to improve relations with the Soviet Union.

Hobson was an early television personality, appearing on popular game shows, including *Superghosts, Conversation,* and *I've Got a Secret.* She also wrote a screenplay, *Her Twelve Men,* and several other novels, including *The Other Father* (1950), *The Celebrity* (1951), *First Papers* (1964), *The Tenth Month* (1971), and *Over and Above* (1979), a story about her "conflicting feelings about being Jewish and her own sense of what it meant to be Jewish." Her novel *Consenting Adults* (1975) detailed the close bond between a homosexual son and his mother. Told from the point of view of the parents, it was eventually presented as a made-for-television film. She also wrote two books for children, *A Dog of His Own* and *I'm Going to Have a Baby.* She died from cancer in New York City, where she was cremated and her ashes scattered.

Hobson was a prolific author who portrayed her times in an uncompromising fashion, writing about topics and subjects that touched the lives of her readers.

★

Hobson wrote two autobiographies, *Laura Z, A Life* (1983) and *Laura Z, A Life: Years of Fulfillment* (1986). An obituary is in the *New York Times* (2 Mar. 1986).

MARTIN JAY STAHL

HOFFMAN, Abbott ("Abbie") (*b.* 30 November 1936 in Worcester, Massachusetts; *d.* 12 April 1989 in New Hope, Pennsylvania), writer, political activist, cofounder of the Youth International Party ("Yippies"), and environmental activist.

Abbie Hoffman was the son of John and Florence (Schanberg) Hoffman. He and his younger brother and sister grew up in comfortable circumstances in Worcester, Massachusetts. His father was a pharmacist who after World War II founded and ran a medical supply company. A self-

Abbie Hoffman, 1971. ANITA HOFFMAN/ARCHIVE PHOTOS

described free spirit, Hoffman was often in trouble in school. A dispute with an English teacher led to his dismissal from Worcester's Classical High School; he subsequently earned his diploma at Worcester Academy.

Hoffman studied psychology at Brandeis University, where radical social thinker Herbert Marcuse was a major influence on his thinking, especially about the role of the individual in an increasingly corporatized and repressive cold war society. In addition, the ideas of humanistic psychologist Herbert Maslow became central to his emerging concepts of personal freedom and liberation.

After completing an undergraduate degree in 1959, Hoffman earned an M.A. degree in psychology at the University of California at Berkeley in 1960. He worked as a psychologist at the Worcester (Massachusetts) State Hospital for two years and then as a pharmaceuticals salesman from 1963 to 1965. Influenced by changing views in the psychological profession about the primacy of individual fulfillment and profoundly affected by the growing activism and dissent at Berkeley (which included marches against discriminatory hiring practices in San Francisco hotels and protests in May 1960 against the presence of members of the House Committee on Un-American Activities in the city), Hoffman became increasingly active in the civil rights movement. He took part in the 1964 Freedom Summer voter-registration campaign in Mississippi, where he was arrested, and he continued to work for civil rights in Mississippi and Georgia in 1965. In 1966 he helped to found Liberty House in New York City, a store that sold handmade crafts from poor people's cooperatives in the South. Hoffman left Liberty House in 1967, but he continued to live in New York's East Village, where he identified with the emerging hippie culture. He made effective use of his imagination and lack of respect for normative standards of behavior to organize flamboyant events that highlighted his opposition to the war in Vietnam in particular and to American capitalism in general. In 1966 his six-year marriage to Sheila Karklin, with whom he had two children, ended in divorce. Hoffman married Anita Kushner on 10 June 1967; they had one son and were divorced in 1980.

Hoffman's activism in the late 1960s and early 1970s attracted attention because he was willing to engage in outrageous behavior to call attention to serious political issues. Although he was often accused of grandstanding and drawing attention to himself rather than engaging in grassroots organizing, the actualization of Marshall McLuhan's conflation of the medium and the message brought widespread attention to Hoffman's critique of capitalism, his effort to legalize recreational marijuana use, and his opposition to the Vietnam War. For example, in April 1967 Hoffman and his colleagues threw dollar bills onto the trading floor of the New York Stock Exchange from the visitors' gallery. The media coverage of the traders' mad scramble for the bills spoke for itself at a time when the Johnson administration was beginning to rethink its war on poverty in order to fight a war in Southeast Asia. In a symbolic thumbing of his nose at the "Establishment," Hoffman mailed marijuana joints to 3,000 people selected at random from the phone book. The gesture would have been meaningless without the media coverage that it attracted, along with the coverage of "be-ins" in New York's Central Park at which marijuana smoking was a prominent activity.

One of Hoffman's most outrageous media events was his plan to levitate the Pentagon as part of a major antiwar demonstration in Washington, D.C., in October 1967. Surrounded by radio and television microphones, Hoffman claimed that the mental energy of the protesters would levitate the building, raising it 300 feet in the air and causing it to vibrate in order to exorcise its evil spirits. Ludicrous though the claim may have seemed, it was Hoffman's prediction that drew attention to the protest, during which there were numerous beatings and arrests of people who hoped to stop the war. Twenty years later Hoffman maintained, in the same spirit of playful protest around serious issues, that a close look at pictures and film of the event would reveal that the building actually did rise about ten feet off the ground.

Hoffman's guerrilla-theater approach to serious political protest found organizational form in the creation of the Youth International Party on 1 January 1968. Claiming "no leaders, no members, and no organization," the group was better known by its nickname, Yippies, and for its street theater antics and the slogans of its founder, who warned young revolutionaries not to trust "anyone over thirty." In 1968 Hoffman also began his career as a writer with a pamphlet, *Fuck the System.* In his first book, *Revolution for the Hell of It* (1968), written under the nom de plume Free, Hoffman included personal anecdotes and rambling political wisdom.

Hoffman was perhaps most famous for his participation in demonstrations at the 1968 Democratic National Convention in Chicago. He was arrested outside the convention hall and several times in the succeeding months, and in March 1969 was indicted on charges of conspiracy and crossing state lines to incite a riot. He and the activists indicted with him became known as the Chicago Eight (later the Chicago Seven, after the case of Bobby Seale was separated from that of the other defendants). Hoffman turned the courtroom into a political stage, wearing a black robe to court, a gesture that Judge Julius Hoffman (no relation) did not find amusing. He called numerous celebrity witnesses who held forth on the imperative to protest the Vietnam War, and he chided the judge, often in Yiddish, calling him a "disgrace to the Jews." He and his colleagues were acquitted of the conspiracy charges, but five of the original defendants, including Hoffman, were convicted of crossing state lines to incite a riot. In addition Judge Hoffman cited Abbie for contempt 159 times and sentenced him to eight months in prison. These convictions were overturned on appeal in November 1972. Hoffman was retried and convicted of contempt, but he was not sentenced to jail.

Hoffman's celebrity resulting from the Chicago Seven trial helped sales of his second book, *Woodstock Nation: A Talk-Rock Album* (1969). He had completed the book while staying at the Ann Arbor commune organized by Beat Generation devotee and White Panther party founder John Sinclair. Like *Revolution, Woodstock Nation* was a compilation of Hoffman's thoughts on revolution with particular emphasis on the cultural upheaval promised by the famous Woodstock music festival in New York's Catskill Mountains. Hoffman was in demand as a speaker, and he continued to protest the Vietnam War even as the energy of the antiwar movement waned after the killing of student protesters at Kent State University in May 1970. In May 1971 Hoffman was beaten by Washington, D.C., police at a demonstration. He withdrew from his formerly active role in the antiwar movement with a broken nose and a bruised spirit.

Hoffman ran into difficulty with his next volume, *Steal This Book* (1971); he had to publish it himself and distribute it through an agreement with Grove Press, because Random House withdrew its support and no other publisher would accept the project. The point of contention was the book's advocacy of illegal activities such as making explosives and its instructions on how to make free telephone calls and do other things generally regarded as theft. Although *Steal This Book* sold more than 250,000 copies, it was not widely reviewed or appreciated by the mainstream press. Hoffman participated in mainstream politics by campaigning for George McGovern in 1972. *Vote!* (1972), a collaboration with Jerry Rubin and Ed Sanders, described that year's nominating conventions in Miami.

As the antiwar and student protest movements dissipated in the wake of "Vietnamization" and the Kent State deaths, Hoffman's name appeared less in the mainstream press. When Hoffman next made headlines, it was as a participant in a cocaine deal for which he was arrested on 28 August 1973. He faced a life sentence for his role in the sale of three pounds of the drug. Rather than face trial he went underground in February 1974. However, he did not quite disappear, granting interviews and publishing another book, in collaboration with his second wife. *To America with Love: Letters from the Underground* (1976) is a collection of letters to his younger son.

Hoffman had an insatiable passion for the limelight. Even in self-imposed exile, while living on an island in the Saint Lawrence River with Johanna Lawrenson, he found a cause in the Save the River Committee. He spoke out publicly against the Army Corps of Engineers' plan to dredge the river, and in 1979 he even testified before a Senate committee as "Barry Freed." When it appeared that he might receive a lenient sentence on the 1973 drug charges, Hoffman decided to come out of hiding. In a media tour de force, he appeared in an interview with Barbara Walters on 3 September 1980 that coincided with the release of his autobiography, *Soon to Be a Major Motion Picture.* He turned himself in the next day and pleaded guilty to reduced charges in January 1981. He ultimately served two months in a maximum-security facility, followed by ten months in a work-release program at a drug rehabilitation center in New York City. In 1987 he published *Steal This Urine Test* (written with Jonathan Silvers), an impassioned argument against the federal government's war on drugs.

Hoffman was plagued throughout his life by depression. He suffered more than one breakdown and expressed the fear that if people knew of his illness, they would not take his politics seriously. Of course, his craving for attention and willingness to engage in the outrageous ensured that many would think him crazy and nothing more. At the age of fifty-two, Hoffman killed himself by ingesting a variety of drugs; whether his death was intentional is still debated. His legacy is one of serious activism combined with a spirit of playfulness that, when it is not allowed to fall into cynicism, is a constructive and powerful force for social change.

★

Other works by Hoffman are *The Faking of the President: Politics in the Age of Illusion,* with Jonathan Silvers (1989), and *The Best of Abbie Hoffman,* edited with Dan Simon (1989). Biographies of Hoffman are Marty Jezer, *Abbie Hoffman, American Rebel* (1992), Jonah Raskin, *For the Hell of It: The Life and Times of Abbie Hoffman* (1996), and Larry Sloman, *Steal This Dream: Abbie Hoffman and the Countercultural Revolution in America* (1998). An obituary is in the *New York Times* (14 Apr. 1989).

BARBARA L. TISCHLER

HOFFMANN, Banesh (*b.* 6 September 1906 in Richmond, Surrey, England; *d.* 5 August 1986 in New York City), mathematician, theoretical physicist, and friend and biographer of Albert Einstein.

Hoffmann was the only child of Maurice Hoffmann, a tailor, and Leah (Brozel) Hoffmann, who were Jewish immigrants from Poland. He attended Saint Paul's School, near Richmond, before entering Merton College of Oxford University, where he earned a bachelor's degree, with first honors, in 1929. While at Oxford, he attended the lectures of Oswald Veblen, a mathematician and visiting professor from Princeton University. Hoffmann's work so impressed Veblen that Veblen invited him to become his assistant at Princeton. Veblen, who did important work in geometry

Banesh Hoffmann, 1963. AP/WIDE WORLD PHOTOS

and topology, soon became the first person appointed to the new Institute for Advanced Study at Princeton, New Jersey (1932); Einstein was the second.

After completing his Ph.D. at Princeton in 1932, Hoffmann became a research associate in theoretical physics at the University of Rochester. In 1935 he was invited to become a member of the Institute for Advanced Study and to work as an assistant to Einstein (1935–1937). Hoffmann and another assistant, the Polish physicist Leopold Infeld, worked with Einstein on an enormously complex computation in a problem in the general theory of relativity. Isaac Newton had calculated the orbit of a planet using the laws of motion and the inverse square law of gravity. In Newton's theory, these are independent laws; that is, if one turned out to be false, the other still could be valid. In the theory of general relativity, these laws are no longer considered to be independent, since the gravitational field determines motion. The paper the three scientists produced was published in 1938 in *Annals of Mathematics* as "Gravitational Equations and the Problem of Motion." Considered a classic in theoretical physics and the last major result of Einstein's work, the paper consists of thirty-five pages of computations. Not all the computations were included in the paper—the equivalent of about an additional fifteen pages of computations are on file at the institute. The results were approximate equations that are used to determine the orbits of planets and satellites.

While at the institute, Hoffmann and Einstein, who would maintain a lifelong friendship, occasionally played duets, with Einstein on the violin and Hoffmann at the piano. At about this time Hoffmann met Doris Marjorie Goodday, then a student at the Columbia University School of Social Work in New York City. They were married on 10 July 1938 and had two children, Laurence David and Deborah Ann. Doris Hoffmann quipped that the duets her husband played with Einstein were not for anyone to hear.

In 1937 Hoffmann became an instructor in the mathematics department at Queens College, newly founded as a branch of what is now the City University of New York. In 1940 he became a naturalized U.S. citizen, and in 1941 he was promoted to assistant professor at Queens College. He was concurrently an electrical engineer at the Federal Telephone and Radio Laboratories in New York (1944–1945).

About this time, Hoffmann read an article in the *American Scientist* that described how multiple-choice tests were used in selecting candidates for the Westinghouse Corporation's Science Talent Search. He wrote an article criticizing this method of testing, which led to an invitation to serve as a consultant to the Science Talent Search. He served in that capacity from 1944 to 1970, and he eventually convinced the Science Talent Search to end the use of such tests. As the leading opponent of multiple-choice tests, he published articles critical of their use in the *American Scholar*, *Harper's*, and *Physics Today*.

In 1947 Hoffmann published *The Strange Story of the Quantum,* a widely acclaimed discussion of the revolution in physics inspired by Einstein's work on the photoelectric effect, which had won a Nobel Prize; it was republished in 1959. He was once again a member of the Institute for Advanced Study from 1947 to 1948; in 1949 he was promoted to associate professor, and in 1953 to professor, at Queens College. In 1959 he was a visiting professor at King's College of the University of London, during which posting he was invited to speak at the International Conference on Relativity in France.

Hoffmann's adamant opposition to the use of multiple-choice tests for measuring scholastic achievement culminated in his second book, *The Tyranny of Testing* (1962). His thesis was that multiple-choice tests penalize the "deep student," who may choose the unwanted answer because he or she knows too much; that the tests dampen creativity since the "deep student" should realize that the wanted answer is not always the most profound one; and hence that the tests foster intellectual dishonesty. As a simple way of proving that multiple-choice tests do not give valid results, Hoffmann suggested the following experiment. Give a group of people a multiple-choice test, and afterward ask the participants to explain their reasoning. He predicted a variety of explanations, some of them extremely odd and incredible, for selecting the wanted answers.

In 1963 Hoffmann received the Distinguished Teacher of the Year Award from the Queens College Alumni Association. The author of many technical articles in professional journals, he was also a member of the American Physical Society and the American Mathematical Society and an honorary patron of the Tensor Society. He won the Gravity Research Foundation Prize in 1964 for his essay "Negative Mass as a Gravitational Source of Energy in the Quasi-Stellar Radio Sources." Hoffman also appeared on many radio and television programs. He was selected by the British Broadcasting Corporation to explain Einstein's theories of relativity in a commemorative documentary television series in 1965, the tenth anniversary of Einstein's death. In 1966 he published *About Vectors,* which includes an elementary introduction to tensors, a part of advanced linear algebra that is essential to Einstein's general theory of relativity; the book was republished in 1975. During the 1966–1967 academic year, Hoffmann was a research associate at Harvard University.

After Einstein's death in 1955, Hoffmann had become a member of the editorial advisory board of *The Writings of Albert Einstein.* With the collaboration of Einstein's secretary of nearly thirty years, Helen Dukas, Hoffmann published a popular, authoritative biography of Einstein, *Albert Einstein: Creator and Rebel* (1972). In this work, Hoffmann presented not only a view of Einstein's life but also integrated nontechnical descriptions of the physicist's major results, using appropriate analogies. The book contains family photographs of Einstein and is quoted in almost every subsequent biography of him. Hoffmann won the 1973 Science Writing Award of the American Institute of Physics and the United States Steel Foundation for this biography. In 1979 Dukas and Hoffmann published *Albert Einstein: The Human Side*, which consists of a selection of previously unpublished letters and writings of Einstein.

On the lighter side, Hoffmann was a Sherlock Holmes enthusiast and member of the Baker Street Irregulars, and he published an article, "Shakespeare the Physicist," in *Scientific American* (April 1951), in which Sherlock Holmes convinces Dr. Watson that Shakespeare had predicted both the theory of relativity and the atomic bomb. He also was an accomplished pianist who played every evening for relaxation. Hoffmann retired in 1977 and died in Flushing, Queens, of heart disease nine years later. His cremated remains were scattered on Long Island Sound.

★

Hoffmann's papers are at the Hebrew University of Jerusalem. No book-length biographies of Hoffman have yet been written, although he is mentioned in almost every biography of Albert Einstein. Biographical information is in "A Conversation with Banesh Hoffmann," *National Elementary Principal* 54 (July 1975): 30–39. Obituaries are in the *New York Times* (6 Aug. 1986) and the *London Times* (7 Aug. 1986). Hoffmann appears in stills and in brief clips of home movies in a documentary film, *Complaints of a Dutiful Daughter* (1994), written and directed by his daughter, Deborah Hoffmann. This film about Doris Hoffmann's bout with Alzheimer's disease received an Academy Award nomination in 1995.

HOWARD ALLEN

HOFSTADTER, Robert (*b.* 5 February 1915 in New York City; *d.* 17 November 1990 in Stanford, California), physicist and educator who was awarded the Nobel Prize in physics in 1961 for research addressing the fundamental properties of protons and neutrons, the basic constituents of the atomic nucleus.

Hofstadter, who was raised in Manhattan, was one of four children of Louis Hofstadter, a salesman, and Henrietta Koenigsberg. He attended elementary and high school in New York City and in 1931 entered the City College of New York, which at the time was tuition free and required superior high school grades for admission. Switching from philosophy to physics, he distinguished himself as a student

Robert Hofstadter. UPI/CORBIS-BETTMANN

and graduated magna cum laude with a B.S. in 1935. He also received the Kenyon Prize for outstanding achievement in mathematics and physics and was elected to Phi Beta Kappa and the honorary scientific society Sigma Xi.

In 1935 Hofstadter began graduate work in physics at Princeton University, where he received both an M.A. degree and a Ph.D. in 1938. His doctoral work centered on the infrared spectra of organic molecules and the clarification of specialized aspects of hydrogen atom bonding.

Hofstadter did postdoctoral work from 1938 to 1939 at Princeton University. His research during this period dealt primarily with photoconductivity, the production of electric currents in crystals by optical excitation. In 1939 he left Princeton for the University of Pennsylvania, where he contributed to particle accelerator construction, helping to build a Van de Graaff machine for positive ion production used in nuclear research.

Hofstadter returned to Princeton in 1940 as an instructor in physics; he subsequently taught at the City College of New York during the 1941–1942 academic year. On 9 May 1942 he married Nancy Givan. They had three children, Douglas Richard (who won the 1980 Pulitzer Prize for nonfiction for the 1979 book *Goedel, Escher, Bach: An Eternal Golden Braid*), Laura James, and Mary Hinda.

During World War II Hofstadter initially worked at the National Bureau of Standards in Washington, D.C., where he assisted in the development of the photoelectric proximity fuse, the critical component of an antiaircraft system used to destroy enemy planes detected by radar. Later Hofstadter worked for the Norden Laboratory Corporation in New York. There, he contributed to the construction of the famous Norden bombsight, which was employed by American aircraft against military targets.

After the war, Hofstadter was an assistant professor at Princeton between 1946 and 1950. He undertook research in conduction counters and the Compton effect concerning the scattering of electromagnetic radiation—X rays and gamma rays—by electrons. His most important research during this period led to the invention, in 1948, of a scintillation detector employing a sodium iodide crystal containing a small quantity of the element thallium. Ionizing radiation absorbed by the crystal produces light photons in the optical region of the electromagnetic spectrum that, when amplified by one or more photomultiplier tubes, permits detection and measurement of the initiating radiation with high efficiency. Applications of the sodium iodide scintillation detector include its use in medical diagnosis of cancers and heart irregularities.

In 1950 Hofstadter became associate professor of physics at Stanford University. He was promoted to full professor in 1954. In 1971 Hofstadter was named to the prestigious Max H. Stein chair of physics. After thirty-five years at Stanford, Hofstadter retired in 1985.

Hofstadter recognized that the powerful, nearly two-mile-long Stanford Linear Accelerator Center (SLAC) could be used to explore the structure of protons and neutrons, the constituents of the nuclei of all atoms. Beginning electron-scattering measurements in 1953, with a team of colleagues and graduate students, Hofstadter investigated the makeup of the positively charged proton and electrically neutral neutron. The results obtained in the years 1954–1957 established that each nucleon, whether proton or neutron, consists of a positively charged core surrounded by two shells of fundamental particles known as mesons. In the proton, the outer mesonic shell is positively charged, defining the positive charge of this nucleon. In the neutron, the corresponding shell charge is negative, making this nucleon collectively neutral.

This work, which for the first time demonstrated that nucleons have a complex structure of definite size and form, was recognized in 1961 by the awarding of the Nobel Prize to Hofstadter. (The award was shared that year with Rudolf L. Mössbauer.) In his presentation, Professor Ivar Waller of the Royal Swedish Academy of Sciences succinctly summarized Hofstadter's achievement as "fundamentally important for the understanding of these most inconceivably small systems," and credited him with stimulating "the discovery of new particles which seem to be essential for the understanding of the forces acting in the atomic nuclei."

In addition to his academic and research work, Hofstadter served as the administrative director of Stanford's high-energy physics laboratory between 1967 and 1974. He was also associate editor of the journal *Physical Review* from 1951 to 1953 and a member of the editorial boards of the *Review of Scientific Instruments* (1953–1955) and *Reviews of Modern Physics* (1958–1961). Hofstadter served on the board of governors of Israel's Technicon Institute of Technology and Weizmann Institute of Science. Among the honors he received were the Townsend Harris Medal from City College of New York (1961); the Roentgen Medal, Würzburg, Germany (1985); United States National Science Medal (1986); and the Cultural Foundation Prize, Fiuggi, Italy (1986).

Hofstadter died of heart disease at his home in Stanford in 1990.

★

Hofstadter's 1961 Nobel lecture, "The Electron-Scattering Method and Its Application to the Structure of Nuclei and Nucleons," is in *Nobel Lectures, Physics (1942–1962)* (1964), which contains a biographical sketch. The lecture is essentially a complete exposition of Hofstadter's most important work, including prior scientific history and reference to thirty papers authored by himself and others. An obituary is in the *New York Times* (19 Nov. 1990).

LEONARD R. SOLON

HOLMES, John Clellon (*b.* 12 March 1926 in Holyoke, Massachusetts; *d.* 30 March 1988 in Old Saybrook, Connecticut), novelist, poet, essayist, and teacher who chronicled the birth of the beat generation in his novel *Go* (1952) and in his essay "This Is the Beat Generation" (1952).

John Holmes was the second of three children born to John McClellan Holmes, an advertising sales representative, and Elizabeth Franklin Emmons, a professional accompanist directly descended from Benjamin Franklin. His sister Lila was two years older; his sister Elizabeth seven years younger. During the depression of the 1930s, the family moved often as Holmes's father pursued scarce job opportunities. Frequently uprooted, Holmes spent portions of his youth in Massachusetts, Long Island, New Hampshire, New Jersey, California, and Connecticut. By his sixteenth year, he had attended eighteen schools. On his own in California in the summer of 1941, he worked as a lifeguard and a movie usher. When he returned to New Jersey that fall, he learned that his parents were divorcing. He resumed his studies at Dwight Morrow High School in Englewood but dropped out after his mother moved the family to suburban Chappaqua, New York. While waiting to be drafted for military service in World War II, he took a job at *Reader's Digest,* enrolled in extension courses at Columbia University, and dedicated himself to learning the writer's craft.

In June 1944 Holmes entered the United States Navy Hospital Corps. On 30 August 1944, on leave from boot camp, he married Marian Miliambro, a young woman he had met while employed at *Reader's Digest*. He was stationed first in California, then transferred to St. Albans on Long Island. Caring for the wounded left Holmes a lifelong pacifist. Commenting later on his military experience, he stated: "I came to the conviction that though there are things worth dying for, there is nothing worth killing for."

Discharged in June 1945, Holmes resumed his studies at Columbia. His poems began to appear in the *Partisan Review, Poetry,* and other literary journals in the summer of 1948. Over the muggy Fourth of July weekend that year, Holmes accompanied Alan Harrington to a party in Spanish Harlem, where he met Allen Ginsberg and Jack Kerouac. It was a meeting that would forever change his life.

Holmes's apartment at 681 Lexington Avenue became a convenient gathering place for Kerouac, Ginsberg, and their circle. Kerouac and Holmes, both working on first novels, quickly became friends. They shared writing problems, commiserated over rejection slips, and attended courses at the New School for Social Research in 1949 and 1950. Kerouac coined the term "beat generation" in November 1948, but it was Holmes who first used the phrase in print, in his novel *Go*. More influential than his novel, however, was his essay "This Is the Beat Generation," which appeared in the *New York Times Magazine* on 16 November 1952. This essay was the first serious attempt to define the new movement, and the excitement it stirred helped pave the way for the favorable reception of Kerouac's *On the Road* (1957).

Shortly after Scribner's accepted *Go,* Holmes and his first wife divorced. Within a year, Holmes married Shirley Anise Allen. The wedding took place in East Haddam, Connecticut, on 9 September 1953. With the proceeds from the sale of the paperback rights to *Go,* the couple bought an old Victorian house at 11 Shepard Street in Old Saybrook, Connecticut. At last, Holmes had found a place to sink his roots.

The end of the 1950s was an exciting time for Holmes. Ginsberg's *Howl* (1956) and Kerouac's *On the Road* caught the media's attention and stimulated interest in Holmes's second novel, *The Horn* (1958). An article he wrote for the February 1958 issue of *Esquire,* "The Philosophy of the Beat Generation," secured his position as spokesman for the new movement. The following year, in 1959, Holmes's father died; this loss may have played a role in the writer's block he struggled with for the next eighteen months.

Holmes described his life during the 1960s as "a time of poverty" and "self-imposed exile." In order to stimulate

John Clellon Holmes. NYT PERMISSIONS

his creative powers, he began a journal, adhering to a strict regimen of daily writing. His persistence resulted in his third novel, *Get Home Free* (1964), and a well-received collection of essays, *Nothing More to Declare* (1967). Tired of living from hand to mouth, Holmes accepted an invitation to teach at the Iowa Writers Workshop in the fall of 1963. In 1966 he became the first writer-in-residence of the creative writing program at the University of Arkansas. On 1 September 1967, Holmes and his wife traveled to Europe, where they remained for four months. The trip provided Holmes with material for several articles, including "Exiles London: 1967," which appeared in *New Letters* (spring 1978) and won the Alexander Cappon Prize.

After returning home, Holmes accepted a visiting professorship at Bowling Green State University. Back in Old Saybrook, in October 1969, he learned of Kerouac's death. He traveled to Lowell, Massachusetts, for the funeral and served as one of Kerouac's pallbearers. "Gone in October," his eulogy for Kerouac, appeared in *Playboy* (February 1973) and received the magazine's award for best nonfiction of the year.

Holmes taught at Brown University from 1971 to 1972. In 1976 he was awarded a Guggenheim fellowship. In 1977, abandoning any attempt to earn a living off his writing, he accepted a permanent position at the University of Arkansas at Fayetteville. Freed from financial concerns, he turned away from commercial markets and began submitting material to alternative presses, publishing *The Bowling Green Poems* (1977), *Death Drag: Selected Poems 1948–1979* (1979), and *Dire Coasts* (1988).

Holmes spent the last decade of his life shuttling between Fayetteville, Arkansas, and Old Saybrook, Connecticut, until he was diagnosed with cancer in 1986. He returned home and worked steadily to complete several publishing projects before his death at age sixty-two. Holmes had left specific instructions that there was to be no funeral service. He was cremated at the Fountain Hill Crematory in Deep River, Connecticut, and his ashes were scattered on the waters of Long Island Sound at Peconic. Memorial services were held at the University of Arkansas on 29 April 1988 and at the St. Marks Poetry Project in New York City on 26 October 1988. He had no children.

A minor novelist, Holmes will be remembered first and foremost as an essayist and historian of the beat generation. His seminal article, "This Is the Beat Generation," prompted more than 300 letters when it appeared in the *New York Times Magazine,* and it was highlighted in the magazine's one-hundredth-anniversary issue on 14 April 1996. Early on, Holmes's insightful essays made the beats respectable, as he placed them within the larger tradition of American transcendentalism. Later, his assistance to literary scholars such as Ann Charters and John Tytell helped secure the beat generation a place in the canon. An elegant prose stylist, Holmes won *Playboy*'s award for best nonfiction three times and was a runner-up twice. At the time of his death, interest in Holmes's work was growing: his novels were being reprinted, and the University of Arkansas Press was publishing a three-volume set of selected essays as well as *Night Music* (1989), a volume of his poems. Shortly before he died, the American Academy of Arts and Letters honored Holmes with its Academy Award for Literature.

★

Holmes's papers are on deposit at Boston University's Mugar Library. His essays, particularly those collected in *Displaced Person: The Travel Essays* (1987), *Representative Men: The Biographical Essays* (1988), and the "Raw Materials" section of *Nothing More to Declare* (1967), are a good source of autobiographical information, as is *Interior Geographies: An Interview with John Clellon Holmes* (1981) by Arthur and Kit Knight. Richard Ardinger's entry in the *Dictionary of Literary Biography,* vol. 16, is the most comprehensive biography. An obituary is in the *New York Times* (31 Mar. 1988). Columbia University's Oral History Collection has a tape recording and transcript of an interview. Video clips of Holmes appear in *What Happened to Kerouac* (1985) and *Kerouac* (1985).

WILLIAM M. GARGAN

HOOK, Sidney (*b.* 20 December 1902 in New York City; *d.* 12 July 1989 in Stanford, California), philosopher, humanist, and social critic who is best known for his critiques of communism and totalitarianism.

The son of Isaac Hook and Jennie Halpern, Hook was raised in the Williamsburg section of Brooklyn, New York, and graduated from the Brooklyn Boys' High School in 1919. He then enrolled at the City College of New York, where he studied philosophy under Morris R. Cohen, who had a profound influence on the development of his thought. After graduating with a B.S. degree in 1923, Hook attended graduate school at Columbia University, studying under John Dewey, and obtained an M.A. degree in 1926 and a Ph.D. in 1927. His doctoral dissertation, *The Metaphysics of Pragmatism,* was published by Open Court Publishing Company in 1927. On 31 March 1924 Hook married Carrie Katz, with whom he had a son, John Bertrand Hook. On 25 May 1935 he married Ann E. Zinken, with whom he had a son and a daughter, Ernest Benjamin and Susan Ann.

After leaving Columbia, Hook taught for a time in the New York City public schools. In 1927 he took a job teaching at New York University, where he would spend most of his career. He served as chairman of its Department of Philosophy from 1934 to 1939 and headed the graduate department from 1948 until his retirement from the university in 1970. He also lectured, from 1931, at the New School for Social Research. In 1971 Hook became a senior research fellow at the Hoover Institution on War, Revolution, and Peace at Stanford University in California, where he died almost two decades later of congestive heart failure.

As a scholar, Hook was not afraid of controversy and might even be thought to have courted it. John Patrick Diggins, professor of history at CUNY, referred to him as the Jake LaMotta of American Philosophy. He was willing to take an extremely unpopular stand and fight for it. Though initially receptive to communism, he came to repudiate it in the 1930s, after realizing that its actual realization did not live up to its stated ideals. He became a staunch anticommunist. Marxist colleagues felt betrayed, though Hook himself viewed as primary his commitment to freedom rather than to communist dogma. Though liberal in many respects, Hook held some views that were unpopular with his fellow intellectuals on the left, especially his views on the Vietnam War. Though opposed to initial U.S. military intervention, he also opposed removing troops until North Vietnam acknowledged the independence of South Vietnam.

Hook was the author of numerous books, essays, and letters. Perhaps best known are *Toward an Understanding of Karl Marx: A Revolutionary Interpretation* (1933); *From Hegel to Marx: Studies in the Intellectual Development of Karl Marx* (1936); *John Dewey: An Intellectual Portrait* (1939); *The Quest for Being and Other Studies in Naturalism and Humanism* (1961); *Religion in a Free Society* (1967); and *Revolution, Reform, and Social Justice* (1975).

Hook's numerous honors and awards included a Guggenheim Fellowship in 1928–1929, a Ford Foundation Traveling Fellowship in 1958, a fellowship at the Center for Advanced Study in the Behavioral Sciences in 1961–1962, and a fellowship given by the National Academy of Education in 1966. He received the Presidential Medal of Freedom from Ronald Reagan in 1985. He was also a member of many committees, some of which he helped to organize, including the Congress for Cultural Freedom and the Conference on Methods in Science and Philosophy. He was president of the American Philosophical Association in 1959–1960.

Hook's commitment to freedom characterized his personal and professional life. He was famous for the stands he took in support of academic freedom. Though not on easy personal terms with Bertrand Russell, in 1940 he vigorously defended Russell's right to teach at City College in New York during the notorious incident in which Russell—one of the greatest philosophers of the century—was found unfit to teach there. The cancellation of Russell's teaching appointment at City College was probably due to his controversial views on sex and marriage, which some found offensive. Hook attributed the problem to politics. He believed that Fiorello LaGuardia, who was mayor at the time, failed to support Russell out of a concern for alienating Catholic voters. The cancellation was supported by the courts, and Russell lost. Hook viewed this as a terrible blow against academic freedom. Later, Hook was also saddened by what he believed to be the politicizing of American universities, which, he believed, damaged academic freedom by creating a climate of fear in which academics turned away from free speech so as not to become the object of student protests. His concern was not simply for academic and political freedom. In *Convictions* (1990), a collection of his essays published posthumously, Hook argued in favor of voluntary euthanasia. He believed that an individual should have the freedom to determine his own fate.

Sidney Hook. ARCHIVE PHOTOS

Hook was a secular humanist, having rejected a belief in God and religious faith at an early age. Indeed, he wrote that as a boy he had decided to forgo his bar mitzvah; he only proceeded with the ceremony to spare his family from scandal. Instead of seeking a religious basis for morals, Hook sought to ground moral value on truths of human nature, "truths that rest on scientific evidence." As a rationalist, he believed that views not based on evidence are unworthy of belief. Religion, based on faith, could not be rationally believed.

As Hook notes in his autobiography, *Out of Step: An Unquiet Life in the Twentieth Century* (1987), his life was marked by being at odds with fashionable doctrines. His unorthodox views alienated people, undoubtedly contributing to his reputation as a polemicist. Although his views on communism were consistent with the anticommunism prevalent in the United States, they did not sit well with his fellow academics. Nevertheless, through his numerous essays, articles, and books, Hook's influence in contemporary philosophy and political thought continues to be felt, as he was responsible for training a generation of New York philosophers and intellectuals including Delmore Schwartz, and Paul Kurtz.

★

There is a collection of Hook's personal papers at the Hoover Institution on War, Revolution, and Peace in Stanford, California. Biographical sources include Hook's "Memories of Yaddo: An Autobiographical Postscript," *American Spectator* (July 1988); *Sidney Hook and the Contemporary World* (1968), a Festschrift edited by Hook's student Paul Kurtz; and John Patrick Diggins, "The Man Who Knew Too Much," *New Republic* (3 Dec. 1990). An obituary is in the *New York Times* (14 July 1989).

JULIA DRIVER

HOROWITZ, Vladimir (*b.* 1 October 1903 in Kiev, Ukraine [then part of the Russian Empire]; *d.* 5 November 1989 in New York City), concert pianist widely considered one of the most influential classical performers of the twentieth century.

Horowitz was one of four children of Samuel Horowitz, an electrical engineer with his own business, and Sofia ("Sophie") Bodkik, who had studied piano at the conservatory in Kiev and gave piano lessons to all her children. Vladimir's paternal uncle had studied piano and composition with Alexander Scriabin, one of Russia's leading composers. When the boy was eleven he played for Scriabin, who told Sofia he was very gifted and that "he will definitely be a pianist." Horowitz later said, "Scriabin's verdict on my talent was very important to us." The family was fairly affluent but, being Jewish, lived in danger nonetheless. In 1905 Kiev underwent a hideous pogrom and young Vladimir just missed being shot by bullets flying through the windows.

The boy was accepted at the Kiev Conservatory in 1912 and studied with his mother's former teacher Vladimir Puchalsky, who had worked with the great teacher Theodor Leschetizky. Puchalsky was strict. Horowitz said, "He was good at screaming, not teaching." Puchalsky left the conservatory in 1915, and Horowitz next studied with the twenty-six-year-old Sergei Tarnowsky. Horowitz worked successfully with him for nearly six years, showing prodigious pianistic and musical development.

When the Russian Revolution of 1917 reached Kiev in 1919, confusion reigned. Bolshevik troops occupied the city and Samuel Horowitz's business was taken over. Horowitz recounted, "In twenty-four hours, we lost everything. Everything was different as a result of the Russian Revolution. We lost our home and all possessions." Horowitz, who had wanted to continue his studies in composition, was forced to help the family by giving concerts.

By the end of 1919 the seventeen-year-old virtuoso had begun studies with Felix Blumenfeld, who had been assistant to Anton Rubinstein, founder of Russian pianism. Horowitz always credited Blumenfeld as his chief teacher. Through him the young pianist felt a spiritual link to Rubinstein.

Within a short period in 1923, Horowitz performed twenty-two recitals with eleven different programs in Leningrad. From the beginning of his career his concerts were frenzied events. Young female piano students formed a fan club for the elegant, long-haired, slender, and pale pianist, who was thought to look like Chopin. It was quickly becoming apparent that as a pianist—with his powerful sonority, blazing technique, and musical individuality—he was unique. However, as Horowitz later said, "My Russian success was nothing at all in Europe. Germany was the citadel of music, and until the time of Hitler, everyone was there." Alfred Merovitch, an imaginative manager, realized that Horowitz—like his other young client, the violinist Nathan Milstein—must be heard in Europe.

Merovitch secured visas, and the government gave the performers a six-month leave, with Horowitz ostensibly planning to study with Artur Schnabel in Berlin. In September 1925 he left his family and his homeland. He never again saw his mother, who died in 1929 after an appendix operation, one of many tragedies that would befall the family in later years. Horowitz, whose physical health was always a barometer of emotional events, remained guilt-ridden that he had survived, prospered, and become famous.

From late 1925 until his American debut in 1928 Horowitz dazzled musical Europe. America's foremost impresario, Arthur Judson, signed Horowitz to an extensive American tour in 1928, publicizing him, much to Horowitz's embarrassment, as "the Tornado from the Steppes, a superhuman combination of Rosenthal, Paderewski, Busoni, Rachmaninoff, and Hofmann." Horowitz's sensational American debut took place on 12 January 1928 at Carnegie Hall in the Tchaikovsky First Piano Concerto. The *New York Times* wrote that "the keyboard smoked." During that first week he also met his idol Sergei Rachmaninoff and played the pianist-composer's Third Con-

Vladimir Horowitz. CORBIS-BETTMANN

certo. Rachmaninoff commented, "He swallowed it whole." From 1928 to 1932, Horowitz concertized nonstop in Europe and America. In 1930 he made a landmark recording of the Rachmaninoff Concerto no. 3 with Albert Coates conducting. In 1932 he recorded Liszt's B-minor Sonata in London. Both recordings would rock the pianistic world.

On 21 December 1933, Horowitz married Wanda Toscanini, daughter of the great conductor Arturo Toscanini. A woman of iron will, she would be an overwhelming influence on Horowitz throughout their long and stormy marriage. The couple had one daughter, Sonia, who died in 1975 at the age of forty.

From 1936 to 1938, Horowitz took a sabbatical from performing, suffering from exhaustion. After resuming his career he performed the Brahms Second Concerto with his father-in-law, Toscanini, on 29 August. Shortly thereafter the Toscanini and Horowitz families left their temporary residence in Lucerne for America because of the war. At first the Horowitzes settled in Fieldstone, New York, near the Toscanini residence in Riverdale in the Bronx; within a few years they purchased a town house at 14 East Ninety-fourth Street in New York City, which would remain their principal home. Horowitz and Toscanini recorded the Brahms Concerto in 1940 and the Tchaikovsky Concerto in 1941. The following year Horowitz gave the American premiere of Sergei Prokofiev's daunting Sixth Sonata.

Horowitz became an American citizen and displayed his patriotism musically in various ways, the most important being the war-bond concert at Carnegie Hall on Easter Sunday, 25 April 1943. At the time it was the greatest fund-raising concert in history, bringing to the U.S. Treasury Department more than $10 million. Early in 1945 he composed his dazzling transcription of Sousa's "Stars and Stripes Forever" and performed it in Central Park on "I Am an American" Day, calling himself "a one-man band." Late in 1945 he recorded the Seventh Sonata of Prokofiev. Horowitz sent the recording to the composer, who sent back the manuscript with the inscription: "To the miraculous pianist from the composer." In 1947 Horowitz gave the premiere of Kabalevsky's Third Sonata, and in 1949, at a recital in Havana, Cuba, he performed the world premier of Samuel Barber's Piano Sonata, composed for him. Horowitz returned to perform in Europe in 1951 for the first time in twelve years, and in 1953 he celebrated the twenty-fifth anniversary of his American debut in a gala concert at Carnegie Hall.

Since making America his permanent home, Horowitz had been performing nonstop for a dozen years. Now, in his late forties, he was emotionally incapacitated and physically exhausted, suffering terribly from colitis. After a concert in Minneapolis he collapsed. For twelve years (1953–1965) he was absent from the concert stage. He seldom went out, spending his time doing a small amount of teaching and a great deal of studying. Recording periodically in his home, he released important recordings of Scriabin works and the neglected sonatas of Clementi.

It was a glorious return when the sixty-two-year-old pianist once again performed at Carnegie Hall on 9 May

1965. It was an event long anticipated, and the recording of the recital proved that the artist had gained a new dimension in his art. Over the next years he played intermittently, demanding and receiving enormous fees. In 1968 he gave a one-hour concert at Carnegie Hall televised in prime time on CBS. In 1969 he performed ten recitals, then again decided to retire, the silence lasting this time for five years. Another "comeback" occurred on 17 November 1974 with the first piano recital ever given at the Metropolitan Opera House at Lincoln Center in New York City.

In subsequent years Horowitz's appearances were breathlessly awaited with long lines of admirers clamoring for tickets. The golden jubilee of his American debut was celebrated in 1978 with his first concerto performance in a quarter century, playing Rachmaninoff's Third Concerto with Eugene Ormandy conducting. That same year he performed at the White House for President and Mrs. Jimmy Carter. He accepted his eighteenth Grammy Award in 1981 and, at the invitation of Prince Charles, gave his first London recital in thirty-one years, a performance that was filmed and televised in Europe and the United States. His first concerts in Japan took place in 1983, and in 1985 he was the subject of a successful documentary film, *Vladimir Horowitz: The Last Romantic.* He made a historic return to Russia in 1985, performing concerts in Moscow and Leningrad that were seen worldwide by satellite. The video *Horowitz in Moscow* (1986) broke all sales records for a classical video. Immediately following his Russian concerts he gave recitals in Hamburg, Berlin, London, Frankfurt, Amsterdam, Paris, Milan, and Tokyo. In France he was made a chevalier of the Legion of Honor (1986), in Germany he received the Distinguished Service Cross (1986), and in the United States, President Ronald Reagan awarded him the Medal of Freedom (1988).

During his last years he was busy exploring the Mozart Piano Concerto literature. In Milan in 1987 he recorded the Mozart Twenty-third Concerto K. 488, with Carlo Maria Giulini conducting; a fascinating one-hour film, *Horowitz Plays Mozart* (1988), was made from the rehearsals.

On 5 November 1989, only days after completing what would be his last recording, he died suddenly of a heart attack while at home in his Manhattan apartment. Countless music lovers paid their respects at the funeral chapel on Madison Avenue. He was buried in the Toscanini family tomb at the famous Cimitero Monumentale in Milan.

Horowitz's influence continues to be felt in the classical music world through his recorded legacy. Few pianists attempt Liszt's *Au bord d'une source, Sonetta del Petrarca* no. 104, the second or sixth Hungarian Rhapsodies, the B-minor Sonata, or other of his works without trembling in the shade of Horowitz. It is difficult to listen to performances of a vast array of piano works—from the Schumann *Humoresque* and *Kreisleriana* to the Chopin F-sharp minor Polonaise and the Third, Fifth, Ninth, and Tenth Sonatas of Scriabin—without remembering the thrill of listening to Horowitz's recordings for the first time, or the thousandth time, for they wear so very well with the passing of time. Certainly no discography of any other artist has been so completely and consistently available. These recordings will remain precious documents of the art of piano playing. Horowitz has shown more completely than anyone else the glory of this instrument in all its range and sonority.

★

Horowitz's papers and unpublished recordings are at Yale University. Horowitz is one of the most written-about pianists in history, and there are hundreds of articles and reviews on his career. Full-length biographies include Glenn Plaskin, *Horowitz* (1983), and Harold Schonberg, *Horowitz: His Life and Music* (1992). See also David Dubal, *Evenings with Horowitz* (1991), a personal portrait, and *Remembering Horowitz* (1993), in which 125 pianists, ranging from Cliburn to Pollini, recall the Horowitz legend; the volume also contains a CD of Dubal's conversations with Horowitz. An obituary is in the *New York Times* (6 Nov. 1989).

DAVID DUBAL

HOUGHTON, Arthur Amory, Jr. (*b.* 12 December 1906 in Corning, New York; *d.* 3 April 1990 in Venice, Florida), the developer of Steuben glass, book collector, and cattle breeder.

Arthur Houghton was one of four children of Mabel Hollister and Arthur A. Houghton, a glass manufacturer. His great-grandfather, Amory Houghton, was a founder of the Corning Glass Works in 1851, and the family played a principal role in the direction of the company from that time on. After attending St. Paul's School in Concord, New Hampshire, Houghton was a student at Harvard University from 1925 to 1929. Upon graduation he joined the Corning Glass Works. In 1933 he was named president of Corning's Steuben Glass subsidiary, a position he held for forty years.

Anticipating a change in the public's taste for table crystal and decorative glass, Houghton proceeded to destroy much of the existing stock, consisting mainly of colored glass produced by Frederick Carder and his associates. Houghton was determined to establish a new image for the company, but Carder and the many admirers of his artistry regarded this action as little short of vandalism. Houghton was careful to preserve examples of the many varieties of Carder glass; years later they would form part of the collection of the Corning Museum of Glass.

Under the artistic direction of Sidney Waugh, the design and purity of Steuben glass won worldwide acclaim, and it became a frequent choice for gifts from the president of the United States to heads of state and other notables. While the sales of the glass at Steuben's Fifth Avenue store in New

Portrait of Arthur Amory Houghton, Jr., by Aaron Shikler. COURTESY OF W. R. SMITH, CORNING COMMUNITY COLLEGE

York City expanded briskly, the cost of its manufacture and marketing prevented it from being a profitable operation. The Corning Glass Company (later Corning Incorporated) valued Steuben glass mainly as a symbol of quality that added to the prestige of its other lines.

Houghton was as well known in the world of book collecting as he was in the world of glass. This passion for books began while he was still a student at Harvard, where he was profoundly influenced by the noted librarian and bibliophile George Parker Winship. Later, Houghton employed the services of the Rosenbach book firm to begin his impressive career as a collector, specializing in English literature. Beginning with seventeenth-century works, he later expanded his acquisitions to include the Romantic period in the nineteenth century. His John Keats manuscript collection was said to be the largest in private hands. Deciding to give Harvard many of the treasures of his rare book collection, he also decided that they should be housed appropriately. This led to an endowment in 1938 that was to become the Houghton Library. About twenty years later his generous gifts to Corning Community College would result in its college library also bearing his name.

Houghton left Steuben temporarily in 1940, serving as curator of rare books at the Library of Congress until 1942, when he accepted a commission in the Army Air Forces, reaching the rank of lieutenant colonel by the end of World War II. Although Harvard received Houghton's Keats collection, as well as numerous other items, there was disappointment ahead. Some of his treasures were offered for sale. Among these was a Gutenberg Bible. Houghton hated to part with this crown jewel of his library, but he could no longer insure it unless it was relegated to a bank vault, even though it was kept in a building separate from his main house at Wye Plantation, Maryland, with sophisticated fire and theft protection. Houghton also parted with the Shah-Nameh manuscript, consisting of illuminated pages from ancient Persia. The manner of disposal aroused considerable controversy because the individual pages were donated or sold separately. Many critics argued that they should have been sold as a single entity to maintain the significance of the entire work. The action was defended on the grounds that some of the pages had already been sold before Houghton acquired the remainder and that a wider population would have access to them if their ownership was diversified. Most of the rest of his library was sold at Christie's auction house in the winter of 1979–1980.

Houghton served on the board of the Metropolitan Museum of Art in New York from 1952 to 1974 and as president from 1964 to 1969. During his tenure as president he supervised the revision of the museum's charter, giving the staff a greater role in the institution's policy decisions. He then served as chairman for two years and as a board member for two more years. For thirteen years, beginning in 1952, Houghton was a member of the New York Philharmonic Symphony Society and its chairman from 1958 to 1963. It was during this period that the move from Carnegie Hall to Lincoln Center took place. In fact, Houghton was vice chairman, under John D. Rockefeller 3d, of the committee that created Lincoln Center. His style was one of active involvement in all his associations. He explained on one occasion that because he was not particularly ornamental, he thought it best to be useful.

Houghton was a director of the USX Corporation and of the New York Life Insurance Company. Among other positions held by Houghton were vice president of the Pierpont Morgan Library, chairman and trustee of the Cooper Union, chairman of the Institute of International Education, president of the English-Speaking Union of the United States, and chairman of the Parsons School of Design.

Perhaps Houghton's proudest moment was the opening in 1951 of the Corning Glass Center, which he and his cousin Amory Houghton, former U.S. ambassador to France, had conceived. From this evolved the Corning Museum of Glass, containing one of the world's largest collections of glass objects, dating from ancient times to the present, as well as popular exhibits illustrating the scientific properties of glass. With the exception of Niagara Falls, no other attraction in upstate New York consistently draws as many tourists.

Houghton donated Wye Plantation to the Aspen Institute. He had lived there in a Georgian-style manor house, complete with peacocks on the lawn, formal gardens, and a separate building housing his rare book collection. It was there that he maintained his breeding herd of Black Angus cattle, now the property of the University of Maryland. His gift of 273 acres of land on Spencer Hill, south of Corning, and his influence in obtaining a grant of more than $2 million from the Corning Glass Works Foundation for Corning Community College constituted one of the largest private gifts ever made to a public two-year college.

During his last years Houghton lived much of the time at his home in Boca Grande, Florida, with his fourth wife, Nina Rodale Houghton, whom he had married in 1973. (His three previous marriages, from which he had four children, were to Jane Olmsted in 1929, Ellen Crenshaw Gates in 1939, and Elizabeth McCall in 1944; all three ended in divorce, in 1939, 1943, and 1973, respectively.) He died of natural causes and was buried in Queenstown, Maryland.

★

There are numerous clippings about Houghton in the archives of the Corning Museum of Glass. His *Remembrances* were privately printed at Queenstown (1986). An obituary is in the *New York Times* (4 Apr. 1990).

WALTER R. SMITH

John Houseman, 1972. UPI/CORBIS-BETTMANN

HOUSEMAN, John (*b.* 22 September 1902 in Bucharest, Romania; *d.* 31 October 1988 in Malibu, California), producer and director who also achieved fame as an actor in his seventies for his portrayal of a curmudgeonly law professor in the film *The Paper Chase* (1973).

Houseman was born Jacques Haussmann, the only child of Georges Haussmann, a Jewish Alsatian grain trader, and May Davies, of Welsh-Irish descent, who married some months after the baby's birth. As a small boy, John traveled extensively with his parents, later claiming he had completed four trips on the Orient Express between Bucharest and Paris by the age of four. In this nomadic, international context he early became multilingual. When he was seven he was sent to live with a public school master at the Clifton School near Bristol, England. Regular visits to family on the Continent assuaged his loneliness but reinforced his sense of not belonging. From 1911 to 1918 he attended Clifton College, where he specialized in modern languages, edited the *Cliftonian,* and founded the Dramatic Society. He turned down a scholarship to continue his studies at Cambridge University.

Instead, Houseman moved to Argentina, where he learned Spanish and the grain business as a gaucho on a ranch and as a bank clerk in Buenos Aires. Back in England by 1921, Houseman apprenticed at an international wheat brokerage firm and wrote short stories. From 1924 on, he was in New York City, first in a job with Continental Grain Corporation, then, briefly, as head of his own grain exporting company. In 1929 he married Zita Johan, an actress. They had no children and divorced in 1931 or 1932.

When his firm collapsed in the 1929 stock market crash, Houseman decided to try his luck in the theater as a producer and director. Virgil Thomson's unconventional opera *Four Saints in Three Acts* (1934), performed on Broadway with an all-black cast, was his first directing success. Subsequent productions included a black *Medea,* as well as plays by Ibsen and Maxwell Anderson. As cofounder of the short-lived Phoenix Theatre Group, he produced Archibald MacLeish's *Panic,* starring the director and actor Orson Welles, in 1935.

That same year Houseman became head of the Federal Works Progress Administration's Negro Theatre Project in Harlem. This was the real beginning of his tempestuous partnership with Welles, which lasted until the early 1940s. Houseman's equable temperament, editorial skills, and practical competence complemented Welles's unstable genius. Later in their relationship, however, Welles tended to disparage Houseman's contributions to their joint ventures, while Houseman charged Welles with self-aggrandizement.

The plan for the Harlem project was to stage works by contemporary black writers and innovative, politically relevant adaptations of the classics. The Negro Theatre's most important production was the so-called voodoo *Macbeth,* directed by Welles. Set in nineteenth-century Haiti, the production boasted an enormous cast including native Haitian witch doctors. In 1936 Houseman and Welles added a classical theater unit to the Federal Theatre Project. Their most controversial production, Marc Blitzstein's aggressively anticapitalist opera *The Cradle Will Rock* (1937), led to a break with their federal sponsor.

The following year Houseman and Welles launched their independent Mercury Theatre, opening with a brilliant modern-dress version of *Julius Caesar.* Despite widespread critical acclaim, the Mercury, considered a milestone in American theater, was bankrupt by 1939. Houseman and Welles also collaborated on *The Mercury Theatre of the Air.* Their famous adaptation of H. G. Wells's *The War of the Worlds* (1938), broadcast on radio, had many listeners believing that a Martian invasion was actually under way. Among the partners' most notable later accomplishments were the 1941 Broadway adaptation of Richard Wright's novel *Native Son* and the screenplay, with Herman Mankiewicz, that eventually became the film classic *Citizen Kane.*

Over the next three decades, Houseman alternated work in film, live theater, and television, moving frequently between residences in California and the East. During World War II he took time to supervise news-related programs in twenty-seven languages for the Voice of America. In 1943 he changed his surname to Houseman and became a U.S. citizen. By 1962 he had produced a score of films for the major studios, which earned twenty Academy Award nominations and won seven Oscars, five of them for *The Bad and the Beautiful* (1952), starring Kirk Douglas and Lana Turner. Other well-known works include *The Blue Dahlia* (1946), *Letter from an Unknown Woman* (1948), *Executive Suite* (1954), *Lust for Life* (1956), and *Two Weeks in Another Town* (1962).

Houseman's theater productions in California included works by Thornton Wilder, Jean-Paul Sartre, and Federico García Lorca and the world premiere of Bertolt Brecht's *Galileo* (1947). In New York, Houseman directed *The Lute Song; Beggar's Holiday,* with an integrated cast and Duke Ellington's music; and highly acclaimed versions of *King Lear* (1950) and *Coriolanus* (1954). Brooks Atkinson's review of *Lear* declared simply: "This is what Shakespeare intended." Houseman and Joan Courtney, an actress, were married in 1950. They had two sons, John Michael and Sebastian.

In 1956 Houseman was named artistic director of the American Shakespeare Festival Theatre and Academy in Stratford, Connecticut, a position he held until 1959, during the latter years with Jack Landau. He succeeded in shaping his mostly young performers into a versatile repertory company, supervised an innovative redesign of the festival stage, and established an acting school in New York City. Eleven of Shakespeare's works were performed by the festival during these years; audiences and critics were enthusiastic. A legendary success was the adaptation of *Much Ado About Nothing,* set on a Texas ranch and starring Katharine Hepburn and Alfred Drake. Houseman and Landau described the festival's development in their *American Shakespeare Festival: The Birth of a Theatre* (1959). Houseman was also active in television in the late 1950s. His outstanding drama series, *Seven Lively Arts* and *Playhouse 90,* won three Emmy Awards, and *Playhouse 90* won a Peabody Award.

Houseman's next major enterprise was as director of the newly created drama division of the Juilliard School of Performing Arts (1968–1976). His charge was to design and implement a program preparing actors to work flexibly in different styles and formats. In 1972 he founded the Acting Company, a permanent repertory group of Juilliard graduates, whose artistic director he remained until 1987. Touring nationally, the company became known for faultless ensemble work in a classical and contemporary repertoire. During these years, Houseman also wrote occasional articles and book reviews and directed several contemporary works for Juilliard's Opera Theatre. From 1967 to 1970 he was producing director of the APA-Phoenix Repertory Company. Among his most noteworthy productions was *Clarence Darrow* (1974), starring Henry Fonda.

Houseman's acting career began almost by accident in 1973. His portrayal of crusty Professor Kingsfield in the film *The Paper Chase* made him a celebrity, won him an Oscar as best supporting actor, led to further acting assignments, and ultimately made him rich. His film credits include *Three Days of the Condor* (1975) and two films released in 1988: *Another Woman* and *Bright Lights, Big City.* The reprise of the Kingsfield role in the television series *The Paper Chase* and appearances in several television dramas and distinctive commercials added to his national visibility. In 1986 an off-Broadway theater in New York was named after him.

Houseman traced his experiences in four autobiographical volumes, *Run-Through* (1972), *Front and Center* (1979),

Final Dress (1983), and *Unfinished Business* (1989). He also published *Entertainers and the Entertained* (1986), a collection of essays on twentieth-century performance media. He died of spinal cancer at the age of eighty-six; despite his illness, he had continued to work up until three days before his death.

An influential producer and director for more than fifty years, Houseman had a sure sense of theater, loved to experiment, and was a gifted script adapter. The eight acting companies he founded and his many protégés speak eloquently of his lifelong faith in the importance of repertory theater in the United States.

★

Houseman's papers are in the University of California at Los Angeles Library. A piece in the *New York Times* by Chris Chase (21 Apr. 1974), based on an interview with Houseman at Juilliard just after he won the Academy Award, conveys his warm personality and huge enjoyment of fame after years of relative invisibility behind the scenes. On Houseman and Welles's joint work and background information on their projects, see Barbara Leaming, *Orson Welles* (1985), and Frank Brady, *Citizen Welles* (1989). An obituary is in the *New York Times* (1 Nov. 1988).

URSULA SYBILLE COLBY

HOVING, Walter (*b.* 2 December 1897 in Stockholm, Sweden; *d.* 27 November 1989 in Newport, Rhode Island), chairperson of Tiffany's and Company and the founder and president of the Hoving Corporation, which owned Bonwit Teller, a sophisticated department store in New York City.

Hoving was the son of Johannes Walter Wilhelm Hoving, a prominent surgeon in Helingfors, Finland, which at that time was part of the Russian Empire. His four children were all born in Stockholm because the physician did not want his heirs born under the Russian flag. Walter's mother was Helga Adamsen, a prima donna of the Swedish Royal Opera before her marriage to Johannes. She taught her children a love of music, literature, and the arts.

Walter moved to the United States with his family in 1903. He attended the Barnard School and then De Witt Clinton High School in New York City before entering Brown University in Providence, Rhode Island. While at Brown, he was a member of the Naval Reserve in 1918 and 1919. He received a Ph.B. degree in psychology in 1920.

After college, Hoving tried his hand at several fields, from accounting to publishing, ultimately landing a job at R. H. Macy's department store in the field of merchandising in 1924. At Macy's, Hoving discovered a career path in distribution that would span the rest of his lifetime. At the age of thirty, he became a vice president at Macy's and the director of merchandising. He developed a fine eye for design and attended night school at the Metropolitan Museum of Art, where he learned about furniture design, silver, rugs, and other decorative arts.

Walter Hoving, *c.* 1963. UPI/CORBIS-BETTMANN

Hoving left Macy's in 1932 to become vice president in charge of sales for Montgomery Ward in Chicago. There he redesigned the company's packaging, modernized the catalog, and hired women junior executives. Hoving was ahead of his time in demonstrating his belief that women could be valuable and innovative managers. In 1936 Hoving moved to Lord and Taylor, another New York department store, as chairman of its board of directors. The following year he became its president and established four annual $1,000 awards for outstanding work in design by his employees, asserting that "originality wore no price tags."

In 1946 Hoving resigned from Lord and Taylor and started the Hoving Corporation, which announced plans to merge specialty, department, and chain stores. One of Hoving Corporation's holdings was Bonwit Teller, the swank Manhattan specialty department store. In 1955 Hoving took over the Fifth Avenue jewelry store Tiffany's and Company, said to be on the brink of closing its doors for good. Employing his perceptive management style, Hoving reignited business at Tiffany's with an "everything goes" sale, unheard of in the store's history, marking down prices on everything from silver matchbook covers at $6.75 to an emerald and diamond brooch reduced to $29,700. Ultimately, under Hoving's leadership, Tiffany's net worth went from $7 million in 1955 to $100 million in 1980.

Hoving was tenacious about maintaining high standards at his stores. At Tiffany's, he would offer no silver plate, no diamond rings for men, and no charge accounts for patrons who were rude to the salespeople. When President John F. Kennedy asked Hoving for Lucite calendar mementos for aides who had helped him during the Cuban missile ordeal, Hoving told the president that Tiffany's did not deal in plastics. In the end, Tiffany's got the order to make the mementos in silver.

Hoving was the author of several books, including *Your Career in Business* (1940), a resource book on finding a career in business aimed at young adults just starting out in the business world, and the illustrated manual *Tiffany's Table Manners for Teen-Agers* (1961). In 1960 Hoving covered the principles of mass distribution in *The Distribution Revolution,* in which he wrote, "this revolution literally changed the world . . . not only from an economic point of view, but sociologically, physiologically, psychologically, and even spiritually." Convinced that his entire career was guided by God, he wrote in the belief that a spiritual focus could provide a life of achievement. Hoving's charitable activities included the presidency of the Salvation Army Association of New York from 1939 to 1960 and national chairmanship of the United Negro College Fund in 1944. His honors included the Legion of Honor (France) and the Order of Merit (Italy), and he was named Churchman of the Year by Religious Heritage America in 1974.

Hoving married Mary Osgood Field in 1924. They had a daughter, Petrea Field, and a son, Thomas Pearsall, who became the editor of *Connoisseur* magazine and the director of the Metropolitan Museum of Art. The couple divorced in 1936. In 1937 Hoving married Pauline Vandervoort Rogers; she died in 1976. In 1977 he married the former singer and actress Jane Pickens Langley. He died at the age of ninety-one in Newport, Rhode Island, where he had resided for about a year after a lifetime spent in Manhattan.

A business-wise entrepreneur whose dramatic sense of style and conviction blended with his passions for good taste, formalities, and spirituality, Hoving is remembered for bringing originality and the highest standards to New York City's fine specialty stores.

★

Biographical articles include "Fashion Man," *Newsweek* (29 Aug. 1949), on Hoving's career as a retailing entrepreneur; and Janet Mabie, "He Likes to Talk About Jobs," *Christian Science Monitor* (22 June 1940), on Hoving's philosophy and attitudes toward the work ethic. See also "Mr. Hoving of Fifth Avenue," *Fortune* (Sept. 1948), on Hoving's ambitious bid to create a merchandising empire, and Linda Bird Francke, "That Tiffany Touch," *New York* (22 Dec. 1980), on Hoving's impact on Tiffany's and Company at the time of his retirement. Obituaries are in the *New York Times* (28 Nov. 1989), *Washington Post* (29 Nov. 1989), and *Time* (11 Dec. 1989).

KAREN LYNN SVENNINGSEN

HUBBARD, L(afayette) Ron(ald) (*b.* 13 March 1911 in Tilden, Nebraska; *d.* 24 January 1986[?] in Creston, California), science fiction writer, author of *Dianetics: The Modern Science of Mental Health* (1950), and founder of the Church of Scientology.

Details about Hubbard's life are elusive and often filled with unprovable claims. He was the son of Harry Ross Hubbard, a commander in the U.S. Navy, and Ledora May Waterbury de Wolfe. Raised on his grandfather's ranch in Helena, Montana, he claimed he was an adventurer and traveler during this time, probably referring to trips he made to visit his father, who was stationed in Guam. At the age of twelve, Hubbard rejoined his family when his father was transferred to Washington, D.C. Hubbard enrolled at George Washington University in 1930 but left after two years because of poor academic performance. Claims that he studied mathematics at Princeton in 1945 are not confirmed by that university.

In the 1930s Hubbard began writing adventure stories. His first novel was *Buckskin Brigades* (1937), but he first gained notoriety for writing pulp science fiction stories and

L. Ron Hubbard demonstrates his "E-meter" device on tomato plants. EXPRESS NEWSPAPERS/G 907/ARCHIVE PHOTOS

novels. A prolific writer for the rest of his life, Hubbard claimed he sold more than 23 million copies of his books. He married Margaret Louise Grubb sometime before 1940.

At the beginning of World War II, Hubbard was assigned to U.S. naval intelligence in Australia as a lieutenant. He commanded two ships, but he was removed from the first for exceeding orders and from the second for firing guns in Mexican waters and creating an international incident. Although he later claimed he was crippled and blinded during the war, no naval records substantiate that he was wounded. He spent the last few months of the war in the Oak Knoll Military Hospital in California, where he was treated for an ulcer. After leaving the service, he complained to the Veterans Administration (VA) about his "suicidal inclinations." The VA decided he suffered from numerous physical ailments and awarded him a 40 percent disability pension. Hubbard married Sarah ("Betty") Northrup in August 1946, more than a year before he and his first wife divorced in December 1947. He and Sarah had a daughter, Alexis, in 1950.

Around this time, Hubbard wrote *Dianetics: The Modern Science of Mental Health* (1950), which made him a best-selling author and set the course for the rest of his life. This book outlined a form of counseling that purported to cure emotional and psychological illnesses. Through a process known as "auditing," a counselor used questions and an electronic device called an "E-meter" to help the subject increase his or her analytical mind. This therapy uncovered painful experiences, "engrams," from past lives and helped patients heal themselves. Hubbard said this process was the result of thirty years of research. The book was tremendously popular despite criticism from psychiatrists and others. Some have suggested that Hubbard developed dianetics in the hope that it would cure his own ongoing ailments.

In April 1950 Hubbard founded the Dianetics Research Foundation in Elizabeth, New Jersey, with branches in five major U.S. cities, and began giving lectures around the country. In 1951 Sarah Hubbard filed for divorce on the grounds that Ron Hubbard was suffering from paranoid schizophrenia. Ron Hubbard took their daughter with him to Cuba, where he received treatment in a military hospital. Meanwhile, the popularity of dianetics had begun to wane. He wrote *The Science of Survival: Prediction of Human Behaviour* (1951), which explained the religious background of dianetics, called Scientology. According to Hubbard, humans are eternal beings, called thetans, trapped in human bodies. Presumably, Scientology could help individuals recover memories from past lives and heal from painful experiences contained in those lives. After leaving Cuba in 1962, he began forming Scientology organizations, starting in Camden, New Jersey.

Hubbard married Mary Sue Whipp in March 1952. He opened the First Church of Scientology in Los Angeles in early 1954, and by 1959 the church had become successful, chiefly through the massive dissemination of the founder's books. Hubbard bought the Hill Manor castle and fifty-five acres in Sussex, England, to use for the worldwide headquarters of Scientology, which now had centers in England, France, South Africa, and New Zealand. The first of his two children by Margaret Grubb, Ron Hubbard, Jr., who had worked with his father from the beginning of the church, left the fold abruptly in 1959 and later changed his name to Ron de Wolfe.

In 1960 Hubbard declared that Scientology was a "new religion" that was not based on worship of a god. He began having problems with law-enforcement officials in several countries concerning fraud and other crimes. After an Internal Revenue Service ruling in 1967 stripped the mother church of its tax-exempt status in the United States, Hubbard moved the Scientology headquarters to a yacht called the *Apollo,* based in England. He lived on the yacht during much of the 1960s and 1970s. Church officials claimed that government agencies were harassing them because they did not practice a "traditional" religion. None of this apparently affected the success of the church, which in the 1970s boasted 6 million members worldwide. As his legal problems increased and the *Apollo* was denied permission to dock in many ports, Hubbard established new headquarters in Florida and in southern California.

Although Scientology continued to grow tremendously in the 1970s, the decade presented difficult times for Hubbard. In 1971 the French government found him guilty of fraud in absentia. A U.S. federal court ruled in the same year that Hubbard's medical claims were bogus, and an IRS investigation ruled that Hubbard was skimming millions from the church. In 1978 the Federal Bureau of Investigation raided Scientology offices, taking thousands of documents that purportedly showed an extensive intelligence organization engaged in burglaries and wiretapping of hundreds of government offices. Mary Sue Hubbard and other Scientology officials were convicted of these crimes. Hubbard himself could not be held liable because he had officially resigned from church management in 1966. Nevertheless, many observers felt that he had been closely involved in church affairs.

In the early 1980s the IRS challenged the tax-exempt status of the entire Scientology organization. Meanwhile, Great Britain banned Hubbard from entering the country, and Australia revoked the church's status as a religion. After further raids by the FBI, Hubbard withdrew to a ranch near San Luis Obispo, California, where he remained in seclusion for the rest of his life. He wrote and published his first science fiction novel in thirty years, *Battlefield Earth: A Saga of the Year 3000* (1982), as a commemoration of his writing career. The book rapidly made the *New York*

Times best-seller list and broke all existing sales records for science fiction.

Hubbard spent the last few years of his life researching, writing, and publishing. He officially died in Creston, California, of a stroke on 24 January 1986, although some, including Hubbard's oldest son, believed he died years earlier. No autopsy was performed, and he was cremated without ceremony. His ashes were scattered in the Pacific Ocean by Church of Scientology officials. Hubbard had two children with Margaret Grubb and four with Mary Sue Whipp. Some sources mention seven children in all.

Hubbard attracted millions of followers with his ideas, touched them with his books of fiction and nonfiction, and changed lives through the founding of dianetics and Scientology. He garnered love, hatred, loyal followers, and vehement detractors, and he lived a life of mystery, contradiction, and controversy to his end.

★

The Church of Scientology Museum in Los Angeles and the church's Web site (*www.scientology.org*) present information that often conflicts with other sources. George Malko, *Scientology: The Now Religion* (1970), written during the first surge of growth of Scientology, is a sympathetic telling of Hubbard's career and the church's growth. Stewart Lamont, *Religion Inc.: The Church of Scientology* (1986), is a more critical view. Bent Corydon, *L. Ron Hubbard: Messiah or Madman* (1987), is a harsh critique written by a former member of the church, consisting mainly of firsthand accounts from former church members and others. Russell Miller, *Bare-Faced Messiah: The True Story of L. Ron Hubbard* (1988), and Jon Atack, *A Piece of Blue Sky: Scientology, Dianetics, and L. Ron Hubbard Exposed* (1990), are attempts at fact-based critical biographies of Hubbard. L. Ron Hubbard, *Scientology: A World Religion Emerges in the Space Age* (1974), is a description of the Church of Scientology's practice, doctrines, organization, and founding. Obituaries are in the *New York Times* (29 Jan. 1986) and in *Time* and *Newsweek* (both 10 Feb. 1986).

MARKUS H. MCDOWELL

HUBBELL, Carl Owen (*b.* 22 June 1903 in Carthage, Missouri; *d.* 21 November 1988 in Scottsdale, Arizona), baseball player, executive, and scout who was one of the best left-handed pitchers in major league history and the developer of the screwball pitch.

Hubbell, one of seven children (five brothers and a sister) of George and Margaret Hubbell, grew up on a pecan farm near Meeker, Oklahoma. After graduating from Meeker High School in 1922, he worked for a year as a roustabout for an oil company, pitching for the firm's baseball team in an industrial league.

The lean, awkward, six-foot-tall, 175-pound Hubbell began his professional baseball career with Cushing of the Class D Oklahoma State League in 1923 and spent five years in the minor leagues. After dividing the 1924 season between three teams—Cushing, Ardmore of the Western Association, and Oklahoma City of the Western League—he won seventeen games for Oklahoma City in 1925. The Detroit Tigers of the American League invited him to spring training at Augusta, Georgia, in 1926 and 1927. Hubbell split fourteen decisions with Toronto of the International League in 1926 and won fourteen games for Decatur, Illinois, of the Three-I League in 1927.

Hubbell had begun experimenting with the screwball pitch, but the coach of the Detroit Tigers, George McBride, warned him that the strain of spinning the elusive pitch would ruin his elbow. The Tigers sold him outright to Beaumont of the Texas League in 1928 without having used him in a regular-season game. After the 1928 season, if he were not sold to another major league club, Hubbell planned to quit baseball and accept an oil firm's offer of year-round employment and a chance to pitch for the company team.

However, the scout for the New York Giants, Richard ("Sinister Dick") Kinsella, who was attending the Democratic Party's national convention in Houston, Texas, in June 1928, saw the quiet Hubbell hurl a 1–0 eleven-inning shutout for Beaumont against the Houston Buffs. Kinsella telephoned the manager of the Giants, John McGraw, and told him that Hubbell resembled Art Nehf, the star pitcher for the Giants, and urged him to purchase the Beaumont hurler. McGraw then acquired Hubbell for $40,000, a record price for a Texas League player.

Hubbell, who owned a 12–9 record, 2.97 earned-run average (ERA), with just forty-five walks and 115 strikeouts in 185 innings, joined the Giants, who were involved in a four-way pennant race, in the middle of the 1928 season. He garnered his first major league victory on 11 August, blanking the Philadelphia Phillies at Baker Bowl. At a critical moment, using his screwball pitch, Hubbell struck out Chick Hafey of the St. Louis Cardinals with two runners on base. The catcher Shanty Hogan encouraged him thereafter to rely on that pitch. On 26 January 1930 Hubbell married Lucille Herrington. They had two sons. After Lucille died in 1964, he married Julia Stanfield.

Hubbell spent sixteen major league seasons, 1928 through 1943, with the New York Giants, posting a losing record only in 1940. He compiled a 10–6 mark and 2.83 ERA his rookie season. Although usually weakening in late innings, Hubbell hurled a no-run, no-hit game against the Pittsburgh Pirates on 8 May 1929. This was the last no-hitter pitched by a New York Giant. Hubbell finished 18–11 with a 3.69 ERA in 1929 and blossomed after Bill Terry replaced John McGraw as manager in June 1932. Terry's cold, analytical style suited him more than McGraw's explosiveness.

Carl Hubbell. NATIONAL BASEBALL HALL OF FAME LIBRARY, COOPERSTOWN, N.Y.

Hubbell enjoyed his best season at age thirty in 1933, earning the National League's Most Valuable Player award. Besides leading the league with twenty-three victories, 308.2 innings pitched, and a brilliant 1.66 ERA, he hurled ten shutouts and lost only twelve decisions. His ERA was the lowest since Walter Johnson's 1.49 ERA in 1919. Before fifty thousand fans at the Polo Grounds on 2 July, the deliberate, businesslike Hubbell blanked the St. Louis Cardinals, 1–0, in an eighteen-inning masterpiece. He did not walk a single batter, struck out twelve, allowed only six hits, and hurled twelve perfect innings. Hubbell established a National League record by hurling 46.1 consecutive scoreless innings from 13 July to 1 August, a mark that stood for thirty-five years. In 1933 he sparked the Giants to their first National League pennant since 1924 and set a World Series record by fanning the first three Washington Senators batters, Buddy Myer, Goose Goslin, and Heinie Manush, in the first inning of the 3 October opening game. Hubbell won that game, 4–2, and defeated the Senators, 2–1, in eleven innings in the fourth game. He struck out fifteen batters and allowed no earned runs in twenty innings, establishing a World Series record for lowest ERA by a pitcher with two or more victories. The Giants vanquished the Senators in five games.

Hubbell pitched himself into American sports history in the second All-Star Game, played at the Polo Grounds on 10 July 1934. He amazed over 48,000 fans and set a standard that has never been matched by striking out five future Hall of Famers in succession with his screwball pitch. The string started after Charlie Gehringer singled and Heinie Manush walked in the first inning with two on and no one out. The catcher, Gabby Hartnett, visited the mound and persuaded Hubbell to throw just his screwball pitch. Hubbell then fanned Babe Ruth, Lou Gehrig, and Jimmie Foxx in succession. He began the second inning by striking out Al Simmons and Joe Cronin. After Bill Dickey singled sharply to center field, Hubbell fanned Lefty Gomez. His six strikeouts set an All-Star record.

Although suffering a sore elbow in 1934, Hubbell still pitched 313 innings, paced the National League with a 2.30 ERA and eight saves, and finished 21–12. The following season, he relied increasingly on a curve ball to win twenty-three of thirty-five decisions. In 1936 Hubbell led the National League with twenty-six victories, an .813 winning percentage, and 2.31 ERA, suffering only six setbacks and earning his second Most Valuable Player award. No other major league pitcher had won two Most Valuable Player awards in peacetime. Through mid-July, he compiled ten victories against six defeats. Hubbell blanked the Pittsburgh Pirates 6–0 on 17 July to launch a streak of sixteen consecutive wins to help the Giants capture the National League pennant. The victory streak spanned the rest of the 1936 season and fell just three games short of Rube Marquard's nineteen straight triumphs in 1912. Hubbell triumphed over the New York Yankees 6–1 in the opening World Series game without allowing a single outfield chance. In game four, however, Lou Gehrig belted a two-run homer to defeat him 5–2. *The Sporting News* selected Hubbell its Major League Player of the Year.

Hubbell sparked New York to another pennant in 1937, leading the National League with twenty-two victories, a .733 winning percentage, and 159 strikeouts and dropping only eight contests. He won his first eight decisions to extend his consecutive victory streak to twenty-four, a major league record. Nearly every triumph came by a low score. The Brooklyn Dodgers finally snapped Hubbell's streak with a 10–3 win on Memorial Day. The New York Yankees defeated him 8–1 in the opening World Series game and took the championship in five games. Hubbell secured the Giants' only victory, 7–3, in game four.

By 1938 Hubbell's seemingly tireless left arm began showing the ravages of the screwball pitch. His left arm was bent unnaturally around the elbow. He sought to compensate by perfecting his curve ball. Bone chips were removed from his left elbow after the 1938 season, but he averaged just eleven victories per season thereafter. Hubbell fared well against every National League club except Brooklyn but, ironically, hurled what he considered the best game of his career against the Dodgers at Ebbets Field on Memorial Day, 1940. He faced only twenty-seven batters, making only eighty-one pitches, surrendering just one hit, and allowing only three balls out of the infield. Hubbell pitched a nearly perfect game, retiring the first sixteen batters before Johnny Hudson singled in the sixth inning. The next batter hit into a double play. In 1942 Hubbell snapped a club string of four consecutive one-run losses, blanking the St. Louis Cardinals, 1–0. He recorded six straight victories, boosting the Giants to their only first-place division finish between 1938 and 1950.

After ending his pitching career, Hubbell served as farm director and director of player development for the Giants minor league system from December 1943 to 1977, helping rebuild New York into a pennant contender by 1950 with Willie Mays, Monte Irvin, Whitey Lockman, Bobby Thomson, Don Mueller, Sal Maglie, Larry Jansen, and others. He moved with the club to San Francisco in 1958 and scouted part-time after suffering a stroke in 1977. Afterward Hubbell lived on Social Security benefits in an apartment in Mesa, Arizona, and had another, less severe stroke in 1985. He died two days after suffering head and chest injuries in a 19 November 1988 automobile accident near his home. A stroke or heart attack caused Hubbell to lose control of his compact vehicle, which struck a metal pole.

In sixteen major league seasons with the Giants, Hubbell posted 253 wins, 154 losses, and a 2.97 ERA in 535 games. Over 45 percent of his victories came between 1933 and 1937. During that span, his devastating screwball pitch, remarkable concentration, and excellent control enabled him to win twenty-one or more games in five consecutive seasons. Known as "King Carl" and "the Mealticket," Hubbell struck out 1,678 batters while walking only 725 in 3,591 innings, averaging under two bases on balls per nine innings. Hubbell led the National League three times in victories (1933, 1936, 1937) and ERA (1933, 1934, 1936), twice in winning percentage (1936, 1937), and once each in innings pitched (1933) and strikeouts (1937). He compiled a 4–2 record and 1.79 ERA in 50.1 innings in three World Series, helping the Giants capture one title. He appeared in the 1933, 1934, 1936, and 1937 All-Star games, striking out ten batters in 8.2 innings. The Baseball Writers Association of America selected him on their All-Star major league clubs in 1933 and from 1935 to 1937. In 1947 he was elected to the National Baseball Hall of Fame in Cooperstown, New York. The Giants retired his uniform number, eleven.

★

Files about Carl Hubbell are at the National Baseball Library, Cooperstown, New York, and the *Sporting News,* St. Louis, Missouri. There is no full-length autobiography or biography of Hubbell, but Christy Walsh, ed., *Baseball's Greatest Lineup* (1952); Ed Fitzgerald, "King Carl: The Mealticket," *Sport* (May 1953); Robert H. Shoemaker, *The Best in Baseball,* rev. ed. (1959); and Arnold Hano, *Greatest Giants of Them All* (1967) review his baseball career. For background on the Giants, see Frank Graham, *The New York Giants* (1952); Noel Hynd, *The Giants of the Polo Grounds: The Glorious Times of Baseball's New York Giants* (1988); and Peter Williams, *When the Giants Were Giants: Bill Terry and the Golden Age of New York Baseball* (1994). An obituary is in the *New York Times* (22 Nov. 1988).

DAVID L. PORTER

HUIE, William Bradford (*b.* 13 November 1910 in Hartselle, Alabama; *d.* 22 November 1986 in Guntersville, Alabama), novelist, journalist, controversialist, and chronicler of the civil rights movement, six of whose books, including the best-selling *The Americanization of Emily* (1959), were adapted for the screen.

Huie's father, John Bradford Huie, was a railroad telegraph operator; his mother, Margaret Lois Brindley Huie, was a homemaker. There were two other children in the family, a brother and a sister. After graduating in 1930 from the University of Alabama, where he was elected to Phi Beta Kappa, Huie became a reporter for the *Birmingham Post,* where he worked from 1932 to 1936. On 27 October 1934 he married Ruth Puckett, who died in 1973. They had no children.

After several years as a freelance journalist, writing for national magazines and New York dailies, Huie became associate editor of the *American Mercury,* the magazine founded by H. L. Mencken. He held this position for two years before serving in the U.S. Navy during the last two

William Bradford Huie with his book *The Americanization of Emily,* 1964. AP/WIDE WORLD PHOTOS

years of World War II. He was discharged with the rank of lieutenant.

Huie's first novel, the semiautobiographical *Mud on the Stars* (1942), launched his career as a controversialist by depicting a family forced off its land by the New Deal's Tennessee Valley Authority. In the same year, Huie published his first nonfiction book, *The Fight for Air Power,* in which he accused the navy of neglecting aviation. Three books on the Seabees (the navy's construction battalions) were published between 1944 and 1946. In 1946 Huie again attracted controversy, with *The Case Against the Admirals: Why We Must Have a Unified Command,* in which he blamed the United States' unpreparedness at the beginning of World War II on the navy's neglect of aviation. The navy's refutation of Huie's arguments was deemed unsatisfactory by the national press.

In 1945 Huie returned to the *American Mercury* as editor and publisher. The magazine went into decline after Huie left it, in 1952, to resume his freelance career. Over the years he contributed to the *New Republic, Look,* and the *New York Herald-Tribune,* among many other publications. Huie also lectured nationwide. His novel *The Revolt of Mamie Stover* (1951) was a best-seller and was made into a film in 1956, although Huie did not consider it one of his major achievements. In 1954 the nonfiction work *The Execution of Private Slovik: The Hitherto Secret Story of the Only American Soldier Since 1864 to Be Shot for Desertion* was published after Huie's extensive research in military records. In 1974 the novel was adapted for television.

In late 1954 Huie—while doing research for a book about a black woman on trial for the murder of a white doctor in Florida—was convicted of contempt of court for attempting to influence a witness in the case. The resulting book, *Ruby McCollum: Woman in the Suwannee Jail,* was published two years later. *The Americanization of Emily* (1959), a novel about an Englishwoman corrupted by American soldiers during World War II, was a best-seller and was made into a successful film in 1964 and a Broadway musical in 1969. Huie published collections of his short stories in 1959 and 1961 and the novel *Hotel Mamie Stover* in 1962.

In 1967 the publication of Huie's historical novel *The Klansman* prompted the Ku Klux Klan to threaten his life and burn a cross on his lawn, which led Huie to ask the governor of Alabama for special protection. An earlier work, *Three Lives for Mississippi* (1965), about three civil rights activists murdered in 1964, also addressed the violence that accompanied the struggle for equality in the South. *He Slew the Dreamer: My Search, with James Earl Ray, for the Truth About the Murder of Martin Luther King* (1970; revised edition, titled *Did the FBI Kill Martin Luther King?* published in 1977) resulted in Huie's being jailed for contempt of court because he payed Ray $35,000 for information about the King assassination.

Meanwhile, in 1964, Huie published *The Hiroshima Pilot: The Case of Major Claude Eatherly,* in which he accused a U.S. military officer who had participated in the nuclear bombing of Japan of profiting financially from the event. *How America Failed Mankind,* published in 1979, also dealt with the atomic bomb, attributing the cold war to the United States' use of this weapon. A novel, *In the Hours of Night,* had been published in 1975. Other late works include *When Janet O'Barr Came to Washington* (1980), also about the cold war, and *It's Me, O Lord!* (1979), about Dan Ronsisvalle. Huie's second marriage, to Martha Hunt Robertson, took place on 16 July 1977. At the time of his death of a heart attack in Guntersville, Alabama, on 22 November 1986, Huie was working on a novel about the involvement of the Alabama National Guard in the unsuccessful Bay of Pigs invasion of Cuba in 1962.

Huie was often at odds with national opinion. He saw himself in the tradition of the crusading journalist, fighting for truth and justice, first in the cause of military reform and then of racial justice and world peace. Although often depicted as a radical, he had a deep faith in the democratic process, once asserting that "there is nothing wrong with Alabama or Mississippi that three hundred thousand votes in each state can't cure." Incurring the wrath of, at various times, the United States military, Alabama governor George Wallace, and the Ku Klux Klan, Huie had the courage of his convictions. His novels, some of which were, by his own admission, mere entertainments, are, despite narrative strengths that led to their great popularity, of lesser importance than his nonfiction works on racism and civil rights. Huie asserted that there was always a minority of southern whites who thought all people, regardless of race, deserved respect. He was their voice.

★

Obituaries are in the *New York Times* and the *Washington Post* (both 24 Nov. 1986).

STEPHEN A. STERTZ

HUSTED, Marjorie Child (*b.* 2 April 1892 in Minneapolis, Minnesota; *d.* 23 December 1986 in Minneapolis, Minnesota), home economist who directed the Home Service Program at General Mills, Inc., for twenty years (1926–1946) and was responsible for the success of the fictional Betty Crocker character.

Husted was the third of the five children of Sampson Reed Child, a lawyer and member of the Minnesota House of Representatives, and Alice Alberta (Webber) Child. She grew up in the affluent Kenwood section of Minneapolis and attended West High School. In 1909 she entered the University of Minnesota, from which she earned a bachelor of education degree in June 1913. She majored in home economics and German and belonged to the Kappa Alpha Theta sorority. In April 1914, she married Harry C. Evans; they had no children and divorced about two years later.

Marjorie Child Husted, 1950. UPI/CORBIS-BETTMANN

Husted began her career as the secretary of the Infant Welfare Society of Minneapolis. A volunteer for the Red Cross during World War I, she was appointed director of the Information and Publicity Bureau of the Northern Division, then assistant director of the Field Service Division, and was a social worker (1917–1918) with several different organizations, including the Women's Cooperative Alliance. The alliance, of which she was director of the Information Bureau, was dedicated to the prevention of juvenile delinquency. In 1923 she supervised the advertising and merchandising departments of the Creamette Company in Minneapolis. In October 1925 Husted married K. Wallace Husted, an assistant director of the Public Information Service of the American Red Cross. They had no children and would remain married until her husband's death in 1977.

In 1924 Husted was hired by the Washburn-Crosby Company to demonstrate cooking methods and recipes and to lecture on homemaking in the Kansas City region. She spoke about nutrition and child welfare, always stressing the importance of good homemaking as the linchpin of a stable family. In 1926 she started a home service department for Washburn-Crosby, which was continued by General Mills when Washburn-Crosby merged with several other milling companies in 1928 to create General Mills, Inc. In 1929 the Betty Crocker Homemaking Service was established, and Husted was named director of the Home Service Program, supervising forty people. Her duties there included verifying all advertising claims related to food and homemaking.

Husted did not invent the fictional Betty Crocker, nor was she the model for the portrait, but she was responsible for the success and influence of Betty Crocker, and the trademark handwritten signature was hers. (For years, she was often introduced as Betty Crocker.) In 1927 she became the voice of Betty Crocker on the radio program *Betty Crocker School of the Air.* In 1933 and 1934 she traveled to California and persuaded several glamorous movie stars, including Joan Crawford, Jean Harlow, Claudette Colbert, and Clark Gable, to talk about the mundane "bread-eating" side of their lives to prove that, despite popular diets, bread was not a fattening food; her efforts resulted in improved sales of General Mills baking products. The publicity was so successful that Metro-Goldwyn-Mayer Studio invited Husted back. In addition to recipes and cooking tips, the radio show highlighted new products and music; dramatized listeners' letters for on-the-air advice; interviewed men (and later women) to ascertain what qualities they looked for in future spouses; and helped homemakers with ideas for stretching food during the Great Depression and the rationing of World War II. On the air for twenty years, the program showcased Husted's pioneering ideas in advertising and product promotions.

In 1939 Husted did the first food service broadcast for National Broadcasting Company television. By 1944, 70,000 women in the United States were enrolled in the Betty Crocker Home Legion, "dedicated to good homemaking for a better world." This meant subscribing to the Homemaker's Creed, a set of eight beliefs that began with "I believe homemaking is a noble and challenging career." The creed described homemaking as "an art requiring many different skills," promoting the belief that "home must be an influence for good in the neighborhood, the community, the country." Her speeches to business, advertising, and women's groups usually included a history of women of medieval times, demonstrating that women had owned property and participated in managing households and businesses. She always stressed the importance and value of homemaking and appealed to business and advertising groups to hire women and to target women as important consumers. Husted believed that women would be responsible for the spread in use of modern appliances and food products. In the 1940s she chaired the public relations council of Home Economics Women in Business, hoping to elevate the status of home economics as a course of studies and a profession.

In 1945 Husted received a Josephine Snapp Award for outstanding achievement in advertising. In 1946 her corporate title, consultant in advertising, public relations, and home services, was equivalent to a vice presidency at General Mills, where she was the only female executive. In 1948 she served as a consultant to the U.S. Department of Agriculture in the National Food Conservation program. In 1949 she became the first businesswoman to receive the Women's National Press Club Woman of the Year Award, presented by U.S. president Harry S. Truman at the club's annual dinner on 14 May in Washington, D.C. Husted was one of six women honored, along with Eleanor Roosevelt and Grandma Moses. The award for Advertising Woman of the Year, presented to Husted on 31 May 1949 in Houston, Texas, honored her "outstanding career in advertising . . . contribut[ing] to the elevation of standards in the profession" and "her contributions to advertising in the nature of new concepts, innovations, and practices that have increased the stature of advertising as a business and a profession, and have aided in the development of other persons within and without the field." Also in 1949, she was honored by the naming of a "Marjorie Husted Day" in the Twin Cities (Minneapolis and St. Paul, Minnesota). In 1950 she was researcher, recipe tester, production overseer, and editor for the best-selling *Betty Crocker Picture Cookbook.* She ran her own advertising consulting company, Marjorie Child Husted and Associates, from 1950 to 1970.

In addition to working full-time, Husted was involved in many civic and cultural organizations during her long life in Minneapolis. She was a member of the American Association of University Women's Committee on the Status of Women (1949); president of the Women's Advertising Club of Minneapolis (1949–1950); national chair of the American Home Economists in Business (1950–1952); and president of the Woman's Board of the Minnesota Historical Society (1964–1966).

In retirement, Husted, who was five feet, seven inches tall with blue eyes and brown hair, lived in a high-rise building overlooking Lake Calhoun in Minneapolis. She jogged, played tennis, and did calisthenics. She died of natural causes and her cremated remains are buried in Lakewood Cemetery in Minneapolis.

An innovative pioneer in advertising and public relations, Husted introduced the idea of personalized company responses to consumer letters and used information and service to sell products. The idea of showing the ordinary home life of movie stars was completely original and was subsequently embraced by journalists and popular magazines. Her depression-era recipes, which were adaptable for use with rationed foods, were adopted by Hennepin County, Minnesota, and relief organizations around the United States and demonstrated Husted's scientific approach to homemaking. Using history and sociology in her speeches of the 1930s and 1940s, she foreshadowed the teachings of feminism of the 1960s and 1970s, as she spoke about the need to restore self-confidence and a sense of value and importance to women as homemakers. Convinced that homemaking had the same value as paid work outside the home, she declared: "Make no mistake about it, I'm a feminist. My object was to give homemakers a sense of recognition. . . . Women needed a champion. . . . They needed someone to remind them that they had value" (1978). Husted was a progressive thinker, leader, and innovator who addressed the civic and social problems of her lifetime.

★

The Schlesinger Library at Radcliffe College has two folders of material donated by Husted, including "The Homemakers Creed: Speeches 1948–1954"; a biographical outline from the General Mills Department of Public Services (1950); and a picture and biographical information from *Siftings,* a General Mills newsletter. The Minnesota Historical Society has notes and clippings. See also an interview with Husted by Carol Pine, "The Real Betty Crocker Is One Tough Cookie," *Twin Cities* (Nov. 1978). Other articles about and by Husted are in the *Journal of Home Economics* and *Fortune*. Obituaries are in the *Minneapolis Star and Tribune* (27 Dec. 1986); the *St. Paul Pioneer Press* (28 Dec. 1986); and the *New York Times* (28 Dec. 1986).

JANE BRODSKY FITZPATRICK

HUSTON, John (*b.* 5 August 1906 in Nevada, Missouri; *d.* 28 August 1987 in Middletown, Rhode Island), Hollywood film director whose best-known films include *The Maltese Falcon, The Treasure of the Sierra Madre, The Asphalt Jungle, The African Queen, The Misfits,* and *Fat City.*

The only child of Walter Huston, an actor, and Rhea Gore, a reporter, John Huston remained close to both parents despite their divorce in 1912. His mother worked for newspapers in St. Louis, Los Angeles, and other cities, while Walter Huston traveled about the country as an actor. John spent most of his youth at his mother's home in Los Angeles but occasionally went on the road with his father.

At Lincoln Heights High School in Los Angeles (1921–1923), Huston was an uninterested student although an avid reader. As early as 1918 his love for sketching and painting had led him to enroll in art classes; outside the classroom he became a ranking amateur lightweight boxer.

Huston first encountered serious theater in 1924 when his father brought him into the orbit of Eugene O'Neill and the Provincetown Players. He made his first stage appearances soon afterward in New York. Almost by accident he discovered that he possessed writing talent. "Fool," a short story about small-time boxing in southern California, was published in H. L. Mencken's *American Mercury* in 1929.

In 1931, at the urging of Walter Huston, director William Wyler hired John as a screenwriter. He earned his first screen credit that year for *A House Divided,* followed by *Murders in the Rue Morgue* and *Law and Order* in 1932. Wanting to make a serious film about the Great Depression, Wyler and Huston put considerable effort into a script called "Wild Boys of the Road." When Universal abandoned the project, Huston decided to go to Paris and become a serious painter. He left Hollywood after two serious car crashes, one involving a fatality and the other a conviction for drunken driving.

The mid-1930s was a critical time for Huston. In the summer of 1935 he returned to the United States to play Abraham Lincoln in a Works Progress Administration stage production of Howard Koch's *The Lonely Man* in Chicago and then to work for Warner Brothers in Hollywood. During this period he worked steadily on the screenplays of such films as *The Amazing Doctor Clitterhouse* (1938), *Jezebel* (1938), *Wuthering Heights* (1939), *Juarez* (1939), and *Dr. Ehrlich's Magic Bullet* (1940).

But Huston wanted an opportunity to direct. He followed his father to New York City in 1939 and directed him in *A Passenger to Bali* on Broadway the following year. The play closed after only four performances, but both Hustons received favorable notices. Upon his return to the West Coast, Huston received a promise from Warner Brothers that he could direct a film after he wrote one more screenplay. The script for *High Sierra* (1941) was a collaboration between Huston and W. R. Burnett, author of the novel on which the film was based.

Much of Huston's reputation as a great director stems from *The Maltese Falcon* (1941), based on Dashiell Hammett's novel. Hammett's terse writing style lent itself to films, and in writing the screenplay, Huston stuck close to Hammett's words. Huston and producer Henry Blanke put together the perfect cast—Humphrey Bogart, Mary Astor, Sidney Greenstreet, and Peter Lorre. The film, released in late 1941, achieved both commercial and artistic success.

In 1942 Huston joined the U.S. Army and was assigned to Frank Capra's documentary film unit. He made three films: *Report from the Aleutians* (1943), *The Battle of San Pietro* (1944), and *Let There Be Light* (1946; released 1980). They rank among the greatest war documentaries ever produced. The Department of Defense heavily censored *San Pietro* and would not permit the release of *Let There Be Light*—which concentrated on soldiers who had suffered psychological damage—until nearly thirty-five years had passed.

Huston returned to Hollywood as a director for *Treasure of the Sierra Madre* (1948), which reunited him with Humphrey Bogart. Huston decided to make the film on location in Mexico to obtain a realistic atmosphere. The remote setting also freed him from interference by studio executives. He received Academy Awards for screenwriting and directing, and his father earned an Oscar as best supporting actor. *Key Largo* (1948), another Huston-Bogart vehicle, soon followed.

By 1950 Huston had achieved a reputation as one of the country's best directors. His treatment of a fictional Cuban revolution, *We Were Strangers* (1949), proved unsuccessful, but *The Asphalt Jungle* (1950) was an excellent adaptation of W. R. Burnett's crime novel. Controversy surrounded Huston's next film, *The Red Badge of Courage* (1951); Metro-Goldwyn-Mayer executive Louis B. Mayer argued that the public would react negatively to a film without a standard plotline. Huston stayed true to author Stephen Crane's vision and produced an artistic film that failed to earn a profit. The entire filmmaking experience was famously documented in Lillian Ross's *Picture* (1953).

The African Queen (1952), based on C. S. Forester's novel, was Huston's most commercially successful effort. Like the *Treasure of the Sierra Madre,* much of *The African Queen* was filmed on location, this time in the Belgian Congo. *The African Queen* permitted Huston to break away from his darker films and tell a comic, optimistic story that featured two of the finest performances of the veteran stars Humphrey Bogart and Katharine Hepburn. Bogart received an Academy Award, and Huston was nominated for directing.

John Huston, 1970. ARCHIVE PHOTOS

Huston's other 1950s films included *Moulin Rouge* (1953), *Beat the Devil* (1954), *Heaven Knows, Mr. Allison* (1957), and *The Roots of Heaven* (1958). From this period only the expensive, Irish-made *Moby Dick* (1956) displayed Huston's full range of talents. The film was a critical success, although many disliked Gregory Peck's performance as Captain Ahab.

The 1960s marked Huston's directorial nadir. *The Misfits* (1961), despite a strong cast of Clark Gable, Marilyn Monroe, Montgomery Clift, and Eli Wallach, lacked focus and plot development. Both Arthur Miller's script and Marilyn Monroe's illnesses forced lengthy production delays. Eventually the story of the making of *The Misfits* became more important than the film. *The Night of the Iguana* (1964) was reminiscent of *The Misfits*—journalists wrote lengthy accounts about squabbles between cast members. Enormous effort went into *The Bible* (1966), which covered the first twenty-two chapters of Genesis (Huston played Noah), but the film was not a success.

By 1970 critics had begun to write about the decline of Huston's talents. Then, in 1972, Huston directed an adaptation of Leonard Gardner's novel *Fat City.* Filmed in a slum area of Stockton, California, *Fat City* was about struggling boxers in depression-era California. For Huston the film came close to autobiography. From the viewpoint of film critics, *Fat City* is Huston's most successful film in terms of characterization, dialogue, and cinematography.

A Huston success would often be followed by a failure, and the director now followed this pattern with two indifferent films, *The Life and Times of Judge Roy Bean* (1972) and *The Mackintosh Man* (1973). *The Man Who Would Be King* (1975) was a film version of Rudyard Kipling's short novel about two former British soldiers who embark on a grand adventure to a small kingdom in the Himalayas. By remaining true to Kipling, Huston created a fine work. Four years later he adapted Flannery O'Connor's *Wise Blood* (1979), about religious fanaticism in a small southern town. Two weak efforts started out the 1980s—*Phobia* (1980) and *Victory* (1981). Even the gigantic budget that Huston was given for the musical hit *Annie* (1982) failed to elicit any sign of his directorial genius.

In 1983 Huston received a Lifetime Achievement Award from the American Film Institute. He responded with three splendid films—*Under the Volcano* (1984), *Prizzi's Honor* (1985), and *The Dead* (1987). Scholars and critics gave high praise to the artistic achievement of *Under the Volcano,* but the viewing public was less enthusiastic. *Prizzi's Honor,* a humorous look at mob family life, was a commercial success, and it also gave Huston the opportunity to direct his daughter Anjelica, who won an Academy Award as best supporting actress. *The Dead,* Huston's last film, was based on James Joyce's short story. Despite his weakened physical condition Huston equaled his greatest films. *The Dead* also brought together daughter Anjelica and son Tony, who earned screenwriting credit with significant help from his father.

John Huston's personal life was often chaotic. He was married five times and had several affairs that were as important as his marriages. His wives were Dorothy Harvey (1927–1933); Lesley H. Black (1937–1945); Evelyn Keyes (1946–1950); Enrica ("Ricki") Soma (1950–1969); and Celeste Shane (1972–1975). Zoe Sallis, his lover for many years, was the mother of his son Danny. Huston's other biological children (Tony and Anjelica) were from his marriage to Ricki Soma, as was his adopted daughter, Allegra, from Soma's affair with the historian John Julius Norwich. Huston also adopted a boy, Pablo Albaran, while traveling in Mexico and then insisted that his third wife raise him. Huston's last companion was Maricela Hernandez. A lifelong wanderer, Huston bought a Galway country house as a retreat in 1952. He became an Irish citizen in 1964, spent much time in Mexico, and died (of complications from emphysema) in Rhode Island while helping to prepare *Mr. North,* the first film directed by his son Danny.

One of the century's greatest film directors, Huston was also a fine actor. As early as 1930 he took uncredited bit parts in various films, including *Treasure of the Sierra Madre.* In 1963 Otto Preminger cast him as a churchman in *The Cardinal,* for which Huston was nominated for a supporting actor Oscar. A decade later he gave his best-known screen performance as a criminal in Roman Polanski's

Chinatown (1974). Huston appeared in approximately thirty films or television features.

John Huston possessed extraordinary talents—as a writer, artist, and actor—as well as the ability to find the perfect actor for a particular role. Film critic Roger Ebert observed, "No one else made more great films over a longer time." And almost all of Huston's films were profitable—he knew how to stay within a budget. *Life* magazine aptly summarized his career, calling him the "most inventive director of his generation."

★

A thorough (827-page) overview is *John Huston: A Guide to References and Resources* (1997). Among the key sources are the Huston papers on file at the Academy of Motion Picture Arts and Sciences in Beverly Hills, California. John Huston, *An Open Book* (1980), is an autobiography. Novelist and screenwriter Peter Viertel described his stormy relationship with Huston in *White Hunter, Black Heart* (1953), a novel about Huston's conduct during the filming of *The African Queen,* and in *Dangerous Friends: At Large with Hemingway and Huston in the Fifties* (1992). Axel Madsen, *John Huston* (1978), is a valuable short biography. Scott Hammen, *John Huston* (1985), traces Huston's career through his films. The most complete biography is Lawrence Grobel's *The Hustons* (1989), which, despite the inclusive title, is primarily a biography of John Huston. Important works of criticism and interpretation include Gerald Pratley, *The Cinema of John Huston* (1977); John McCarty, *The Films of John Huston* (1987); Gaylyn Stendar and David Desser, eds., *Reflections in a Male Eye: John Huston and the American Experience* (1993); and Steven Cooper, ed., *Perspectives on John Huston* (1994). An obituary is in the *New York Times* (29 Aug. 1987).

GERALD THOMPSON

I-J

ISHERWOOD, Christopher William (*b.* 26 August 1904 near High Lane, Cheshire, England; *d.* 4 January 1986 in Santa Monica, California), novelist, playwright, and short-story writer best known for his stories about Berlin written in the 1930s, which served as the basis for the award-winning play *I Am a Camera* and for the popular musical *Cabaret.*

Isherwood was born at the family estate of Wyberslegh Hall in rural Cheshire, England, the elder of two sons of Francis Edward Bradshaw-Isherwood and Kathleen Machell-Smith. His father was a decorated professional soldier (a colonel at time of his death) with artistic interests, who was killed in May 1915 at the Ypres battle in France during World War I. Isherwood learned of his father's death while a student at St. Edmund's preparatory school in Hindhead, Surrey, which he attended from 1913 to 1919. His complex relationship with his mother, a forceful and traditional woman from the English upper middle class, was to be a major preoccupation throughout his life.

In 1919 Isherwood entered Repton, a prestigious public school in Derbyshire, where he formed close friendships with the poet W. H. Auden and the writer Edward Upward, whom he later joined at Corpus Christi College, Cambridge, in 1923 on a history scholarship. While at Cambridge, Isherwood and Upward collaborated on the Mortmere stories, a series of unpublished satirical critiques of English society set in a mythical land. In 1925, unprepared for his examinations and disdainful of academic life, Isherwood deliberately failed his exams by writing facetious answers to the questions. As a result he was asked to leave Cambridge.

Isherwood then moved to London, where he took a job as a secretary to the Music Society String Quartet and devoted himself to writing. In 1928 he briefly studied medicine at King's College, London University. His first novel, *All the Conspirators,* which dealt with the neuroses and tragedies of family life, was published in 1928. His second novel, *The Memorial: Portrait of a Family,* which depicted the futility of the post–World War I generation, was published in 1932.

In 1929 Isherwood left London to join Auden in Berlin. Auden soon left the German capital, but Isherwood stayed on and between 1929 and 1933 he wrote his Berlin novels, upon which his popular reputation is based. While earning a meager living as a teacher of English, Isherwood gained firsthand experience of the slums, seedy nightclubs, and decadence of pre-Hitler Germany. The awareness of these conditions was the inspiration for the development of a narrative technique that became known as the "camera eye." Through the use of this literary device, Isherwood was able to vividly portray the decaying Weimar Republic in such books as *The Last of Mr. Norris* (published in England as *Mr. Norris Changes Trains,* 1935)—considered his first success—and particularly *Goodbye to Berlin,* a collection of six short pieces, including the Mr. Norris stories, published in 1939. *Sally Bowles,* which appears as a story in *Goodbye to Berlin,* had first appeared as a novella published by the Hogarth Press in 1937. Its main character is a promiscuous English singer who works in a Berlin café. *Sally Bowles* became the inspiration for the John van Druten play *I Am a Camera,* which won the New York Drama Critics' Award in 1951, and for *Cabaret,* the Broadway musical hit (1966) and motion picture (1972).

In addition to writing the Berlin stories, Isherwood collaborated with Auden on three plays during the 1930s: *The Dog Beneath the Skin; or, Where Is Francis?* (1935); *The Ascent of F6* (1937); and *On the Frontier: A Melodrama in Three Acts* (1939). Isherwood left Berlin in 1933 amid the growing threat of Hitler's Nazi party and spent the years between 1934 and 1939 traveling and living in England and on the Continent with his German companion, Heinz Neddermeyer, who was later imprisoned for homosexuality and forced to join the German army. In 1938 Isherwood and Auden were commissioned by Faber and Random House to report on the Japanese invasion of China. This journalistic assignment culminated in the publication of the remarkable *Journey to a War* (1939). *Lions and Shadows: An Education in the Twenties,* an early autobiographical work also published in 1938, told of Isherwood's days at Cambridge and explained his need to escape England.

From China, Isherwood and Auden returned to London by way of the United States, but soon found life in England and the prospect of widespread war in Europe intolerable. It was at this time that Isherwood declared himself a pacifist, a stance for which the British press labeled him a coward. In 1939 both Isherwood and Auden immigrated to the United States. Isherwood lived briefly in New York before relocating to Southern California at the suggestion of the philosopher Gerald Heard. He wrote for the motion picture industry for the next forty-seven years from his home in Santa Monica. In 1946 Isherwood became a naturalized American citizen. He taught in the English Department at the California State College.

Through his friendship with Heard and Aldous Huxley, Isherwood became a student of Swami Prabhavananda, a Hindu monk and head of the Vedanta Society of Southern California. Isherwood was profoundly influenced by Vedanta philosophy. Swami Prabhavananda became his close friend and a cotranslator with Isherwood of several Vedanta texts, including the *Bhagavad Gita: The Song of God* (1944) and *How to Know God: The Yoga Aphorisms of Patanjali* (1953). The importance of Vedanta to Isherwood's life is clearly revealed in two books he edited, *Vedanta for the Western World* (1945) and *Vedanta for Modern Man* (1951), as well as in *A Meeting by the River* (1967) and *My Guru and His Disciple* (1980), the last of which tells of his close relationship with Prabhavananda.

Isherwood's postwar novels, written in the United States, including *Prater Violet* (1945), *The World in the Evening* (1954), *Down There on a Visit* (1962), *A Single Man* (1964), *Kathleen and Frank: The Autobiography of a Family* (1971), and *Christopher and His Kind, 1929–1939* (1976), continued to illustrate the personal style of literary autobiography for which he is best known. While these novels met with varying degrees of critical and commercial success, they are recognized as examples of Isherwood's controlled narrative style and his use of understated irony in conjunction with scrupulous honesty.

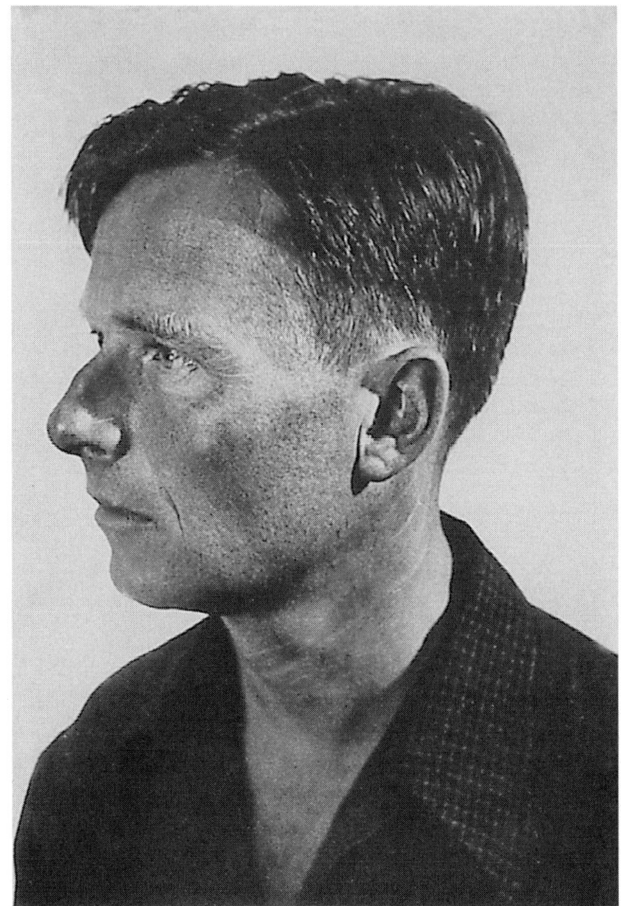

Christopher Isherwood. ARCHIVE PHOTOS

Isherwood had great personal charm, a slight but sturdy build, a distinctly boyish face, and striking blue eyes set below dark bushy eyebrows. In his later years his public activities often centered on speaking out for homosexual rights and for peace. He lived with his companion, the painter Don Bachardy, from 1954 until his death from prostate cancer in Santa Monica in 1986. In keeping with Isherwood's wishes, no funeral services were held and his body was donated to the Los Angeles Medical Center.

In the context of his time and family background, Isherwood was an unconventional author of great talent whose body of work and personal philosophy demonstrated his deep respect for human differences, individual choice, and nonviolence. His life and his books stand as enduring memorials to that philosophy.

★

Isherwood's diaries were published in 1997. Autobiographical information can also be found in *Christopher and His Kind, 1929–1939* (1976). Biographies include Jonathan Fryer, *Isherwood* (1978); Brian Finney, *Christopher Isherwood: A Critical Biography* (1979); Claude J. Summers, *Christopher Isherwood* (1980); and John Lehmann, *Christopher Isherwood: A Personal Memoir* (1987). See also Robert W. Funk, *Christopher Isherwood: A Reference Guide* (1979), and Selmer Westby and Clayton M. Brown, *Christopher Isherwood; A Bibliography, 1923–1967* (1968). Obituaries are in the *New York Times* and the (London) *Times* (both 6 Jan. 1986).

RICHARD STRINGER-HYE

JACKSON, Travis Calvin ("Stonewall") (*b.* 2 November 1903 in Waldo, Arkansas; *d.* 27 July 1987 in Waldo, Arkansas), star shortstop for baseball's New York Giants from 1922 to 1936 and a coach and manager in the minor leagues for twenty years who was elected to the Baseball Hall of Fame in 1982.

Jackson was the only child of William C. Jackson and his wife; his father was a wholesale grocer in Waldo. Jackson attended public schools in Waldo and in Memphis, Tennessee, where the family lived in 1916 and 1917. After graduating from high school in Waldo in 1921, he went to Ouachita Baptist College, in Arkadelphia, Arkansas, graduating in 1923 with a B.S. degree. Jackson married Mary Blackman, also of Waldo, on 24 January 1928; they had two children.

In a 1932 interview, Jackson said that his only ambition was to be a baseball player: "Other kids around Waldo, Arkansas, wanted to be generals and firemen and cops and the like. . . . I had heard and read about Ty Cobb, of Georgia, and I believed that to be a great baseball star was about the last word in fame and success." While in college Jackson played professional baseball in the summer; he began his career with the Little Rock Travellers, of the minor league Southern Association, in 1921. The Travellers were managed by Norman ("Kid") Elberfeld, a former standout infielder for the New York Yankees to whom Jackson had been introduced by a relative; Jackson later credited Elberfeld with teaching him the fundamentals of the game.

Jackson, a right-hander, was a slender five feet, ten and one-half inches tall, with excellent range and a great arm. He got off to a shaky start with the Travellers, batting .200 in thirty-nine games during the 1921 season. His batting improved when he became the club's regular shortstop in 1922, rising to .280 that year, but he committed seventy-three errors during his first full season.

Travis Jackson. COURTESY OF THE NATIONAL BASEBALL HALL OF FAME LIBRARY, COOPERSTOWN, N.Y.

Nonetheless, he was purchased by National League New York Giants manager John McGraw at the end of 1922. McGraw had seen the young Little Rock player during an exhibition game between the Travellers and the Giants in the spring of that year. Jackson joined the team on 16 September 1922 and played in three games during the remainder of the season, going hitless in eight times at bat. The team that Jackson joined was in the midst of its longest sustained success, winning four straight pennants from 1921 to 1924. Jackson fit the old style of baseball—of scratched-out base hits, bunts, stolen bases, and strong defense—that McGraw's team represented. (Their rivals, the New York Yankees, with the recently acquired Babe Ruth, represented the new style of baseball, swinging for the fences.)

In 1923 Jackson began his first full year with the Giants, the only team he would play with in fourteen major league seasons. Although he quickly became known as a superlative fielder, he also proved to be an excellent hitter and a skillful bunter, both moving runners and scoring base hits. During that year, he played sixty-three games at shortstop, and thirty-three at third base, batting .275 and making only twenty-three errors. Jackson had only a single at-bat in the 1923 World Series, in which the Giants played the Yankees for the third year in a row (losing after having won the first two meetings between the clubs).

Jackson replaced Dave Bancroft as the Giants' shortstop in 1924 and was a fixture there for the next ten years, under McGraw and then Bill Terry, despite frequent illnesses and injuries. Prior to joining the Giants, he had suffered a serious skull fracture in a collision with another player; he had an appendectomy in 1927 and fell seriously ill with mumps in 1930 and influenza in 1932. Knee injuries hampered him most. He tore the cartilage in his right knee while running the bases in a game on 15 July 1925 and was out for the rest of the season. In 1932 he suffered a chipped bone in his left knee, leading some to predict the end of his playing career. Following surgery on both knees in October 1932, and a year spent mostly on the bench in 1933, he made a recovery complete enough to play for three more years. Stationed at third base, Jackson had an excellent year in 1935, batting .301 in 128 games and making only twenty errors. In a 1935 article, Jackson was quoted as saying, "It's a great sensation to read your own obituary—and you baseball writers certainly wrote enough of them about me—and then figuratively to kick the top off your casket and go out to the wars once more."

Jackson retired as a player after the 1936 season. In 1,656 major league games, he batted .291 with 1,768 hits, 291 doubles, 135 home runs, and 929 RBIs. He led National League shortstops in assists four times and fielding average and double plays twice. He batted a career-high .339 in 1930, and had 101 RBIs in 1934, but he batted only .149 in four World Series (1923, 1924, 1933, and 1936). His top salary with the Giants was $14,000.

After his playing career, Jackson managed the Giants' Jersey City farm club for two years, then coached for the Giants from 1938 to 1940 and in 1947 and 1948 after a long struggle with tuberculosis. From 1949 until his retirement in 1961, he managed a series of minor league clubs, including teams in Jackson, Mississippi; Tampa, Florida; Owensboro, Kentucky; Bluefield, West Virginia; Hartford, Connecticut; Appleton, Wisconsin; Lawton, Oklahoma; Midland, Texas; and Eau Claire, Wisconsin.

Jackson was elected to the Baseball Hall of Fame in 1982 by the Veteran's Committee, after being passed over by the baseball writers during his initial fifteen-year eligibility period. Jackson died of Alzheimer's disease at his home in Waldo. He is buried in Waldo Cemetery.

Respected by players, fans, and sportswriters for his affability and consistent play, Travis Jackson was a keystone in a series of stellar Giant infields in the 1920s, which included Hall of Famers George Kelly, Frank Frisch, Heinie Groh, Fred Lindstrom, Rogers Hornsby, Dave Bancroft, and Bill Terry. Jackson was the low-key captain of one of baseball's greatest teams, in the sports-mad New York City of the 1920s and 1930s.

★

For a comprehensive history of baseball in the early twentieth century, nothing surpasses Harold Seymour, *Baseball: The Golden Age* (1971), which discusses the Giants of the early 1920s in some detail. Frank Graham, *McGraw of the Giants: An Informal Biography* (1944), deals with McGraw's managership of the team, while Peter Williams, *When the Giants Were Giants: Bill Terry and the Golden Age of New York Baseball* (1994), takes up the team with McGraw's successor, Bill Terry, and contains details about Jackson's later injuries. Also useful on the Giants are Arnold Hano, *Greatest Giants of Them All* (1967), and Fred Stein, *Under Coogan's Bluff* (1979).

In a lengthy interview in *Sporting News* (11 June 1930) by Harry Brundidge, Jackson describes his childhood and early years in baseball. He adds further details in an article published under his byline, "Here's How I Broke In," in the *New York World Telegram* (1 Apr. 1932). Joseph Durso, "Chandler, Travis Jackson Elected to Baseball Hall," *New York Times* (18 Mar. 1982), contains information about the Hall of Fame selection process. An obituary is in the *New York Times* (29 July 1987).

SAM STOLOFF

JANIS, Sidney (*b.* 8 July 1896 in Buffalo, New York; *d.* 23 November 1989 in New York City), dancer, businessman, collector, and author who founded and directed the Sidney Janis Gallery.

One of the five children of Isaac Janis, a traveling salesman, and Celia (Cohn) Janis, he attended both public and technical schools in Buffalo (1902–1914). During his senior year, Janis left school to work as a professional ballroom dancer at the Palais de Danse and then joined the Gus Sun Time vaudeville circuit. In 1917 he joined the U.S. Naval Reserve Force. He took courses in aeronautical mechanics at an Illinois naval base and earned credits toward his high school diploma, which he received in 1918. He was then transferred to San Diego, California, where he taught aeronautics. After his discharge in 1919, Janis returned to Buffalo to work with his older brother, Martin Janis, who owned a chain of shoe stores. During business trips to New York City, Sidney Janis began to visit art galleries.

At a Christmas party in the Greenwich Village neighborhood of New York City in December 1924, Janis met Harriet Grossman, known as "Hansi" to friends and family. They married on 2 September 1925, moved to Sunnyside, in the borough of Queens, and in 1926 they opened M'Lord Shirt Company (their signature item was a two-pocket shirt). The business enjoyed immediate success and helped finance Janis's burgeoning interest in art collecting. That same year, he made his first acquisition, a James McNeill Whistler etching, which he traded in 1927 to help pay for a painting by Henri Matisse.

Sidney Janis in his art gallery in New York City, 1969. In the foreground is an abstract sculpture by Jean Arp. AP/WIDE WORLD PHOTOS

The year 1928 was significant both personally and professionally for the Janises. Their first son was born, and the family moved to Mamaroneck, New York, in Westchester County. Janis's collecting became more focused in that year, when he made the first of nearly annual trips to Paris, where he met Fernand Léger and Constantin Brancusi. Returning to France in 1929, Janis purchased a 1912–1913 collage by Pablo Picasso, and in 1932 he visited Paris specifically to view an exhibition of the works of Picasso at the Galeries Georges Petit. During this trip, Janis visited the studios of and purchased works from both Picasso and Piet Mondrian, signaling his commitment to modernism.

The 1930s and 1940s were for Janis a period of expanding involvement and new experiences in the arts. In 1932, a year after the birth of their second son, the Janises moved to Manhattan. Janis was appointed to the Museum of Modern Art's advisory committee, where he served from 1934 to 1948, and learned firsthand the business of judging and exhibiting art. He began writing on art and curating exhibitions, including shows of folk art. Janis's belief in American folk art was inspired in part by his purchase in 1934 of *The Dream* (1910) by Henri Rousseau, the French naive painter. For Janis, the American equivalent was Morris Hirshfield, whom he discovered in 1939, the same year he closed his business to devote himself to writing. Janis discussed Hirshfield and other folk artists in his first major publication, *They Taught Themselves: American Primitive Painters of the Twentieth Century* (1942).

Janis collaborated with his wife on the next book, *Abstract and Surrealist Art in America* (1944), in which they recorded interviews with both European surrealists and modernists and young avant-garde Americans. The book was significant for its early recognition of emerging talent. In December 1945, Janis made his first postwar trip to Paris to work on his final book, *Picasso: The Recent Years, 1939–1946* (1946), which he coauthored with his wife. He spent nine weeks in Picasso's studio, studying and photographing work created during the German occupation. Lavishly illustrated and meticulously detailed, the book was a financial success.

At this point in his life, Janis wanted a steadier income but "decided that this time I was going to do something I loved." In 1948, after over a year of preparation, he opened the Sidney Janis Gallery at 15 East Fifty-seventh Street, New York City, with a Léger retrospective. The gallery later moved to 110 West Fifty-seventh Street. For the first few years, Janis focused on what he called "idea" exhibitions. More intellectual than commercial in purpose, these early exhibitions ranged from retrospectives of established European modernists to group shows with innovative content, and they further established Janis's reputation as a scholar. He experienced commercial success with the exhibition in 1950 called *Les Fauves,* the first of its kind in the United States.

Janis acquired his reputation as a trendsetter when he began to represent avant-garde artists who had some critical but little financial recognition. His first such success came with the abstract expressionists, many of whom he had included in another exhibition in 1950, *Young Painters of the U.S. and France*. After a well-received retrospective, *Rousseau* (1951), Janis in 1952 gave Jackson Pollock his first solo show. He then did the same for Willem de Kooning (1953) and Mark Rothko (1955), among others. By 1960, Janis had raised the desirability and price of the work of avant-garde artists to new heights. In an article in the *New Yorker* that year, John Brooks called Janis an astute and savvy dealer.

Over the next two decades, Janis continually refocused on emerging talent. In 1962, he compared styles between avant-garde Europeans and Americans in *New Realists.* This exhibition highlighted the American artists James Rosenquist, George Segal, and Jim Dine, among others, and became a touchstone for pop art. Janis held solo shows of these suddenly "hot" artists and purchased several examples for his own collection, including Claes Oldenberg's *Pastry*

Case I (1962). His 1965 exhibition *Pop & Op* contrasted the popular culture subjects of pop with the optical illusions of op art. In the 1970s, when conceptual art held sway, Janis noticed the return to the perceptual with the photorealists' urban subject-matter, and according to *Arts Magazine* (November 1973), he labeled these artists "sharp-focus realists."

In 1967 Janis donated to the Museum of Modern Art 103 works from his collection, ranging from his earliest Picasso acquisitions to three portraits of Janis created that year by the pop artists Marisol, Segal, and Andy Warhol. By designating the gift the Sidney and Harriet Janis Collection of Twentieth-Century Art, he acknowledged the vision of his wife, who had died in 1963. In the 1980s, Janis worked on his memoirs, "Keeping in Step with Art: Memoirs of an Art Dealer, 1948–1987" (never published), the title of which perhaps alludes to his love of dancing. In 1986, he retired, leaving the gallery in the hands of his sons and a grandson. He died from heart failure in New York City and was buried at Mount Hebron Cemetery on Long Island, New York.

Sidney Janis embodied the paradox of a canny dealer with the soul of a curator. He had the ability to recognize future greatness and stated: "The artist is a person of vision, ahead of his time. There is always a gap between making and appreciation. The more creative the artist, the longer the interval" (*Los Angeles Times,* 16 June 1980).

★

The Sidney Janis Papers, including his unpublished memoir, "Keeping in Step with Art: Memoirs of an Art Dealer, 1948–1987," are in the Archives of American Art, Washington, D.C. Valuable sources on Janis are Museum of Modern Art, *The Sidney and Harriet Janis Collection: A Gift to the Museum of Modern Art* (1968), and Museum of Modern Art, *Three Generations of Twentieth-Century Art: The Sidney and Harriet Janis Collection of the Museum of Modern Art* (1972). Also substantive is an exhibition catalog, La Jolla Museum of Contemporary Art and Santa Barbara Museum of Art, *Seven Decades of Twentieth-Century Art, from the Sidney and Harriet Janis Collection of the Museum of Modern Art and the Sidney Janis Gallery Collection* (1980). Biographical articles include John Brooks, "Portraits: Why Fight It, Sidney Janis," *New Yorker* (12 Nov. 1960), and Sidney Janis and Les Levine, "A Portrait of Sidney Janis on the Occasion of His Twenty-fifth Anniversary as an Art Dealer, as Taken by Les Levine," *Arts Magazine* (Nov. 1973). An obituary by Grace Glueck is in the *New York Times* (24 Nov. 1989). Unpublished interviews with Janis are by Helen M. Franc (June 1967), Museum of Modern Art Archives, New York City; Paul Cummings (21 Mar.–26 Sept. 1972), Archives of American Art, Washington, D.C.; and Avis Berman for "Rothko and His Times Oral History Project" (18 Nov. 1981), Archives of American Art, Washington, D.C.

LEIGH BULLARD WEISBLAT

JANOWITZ, Morris (*b.* 22 October 1919 in Paterson, New Jersey; *d.* 7 November 1988 in Hyde Park, New Jersey), sociologist and prolific writer well known for his works in military studies and his scholarship on various aspects of the postwar American society.

Janowitz was the second son of Samuel Louis Janowitz, a textile worker who became a silk business owner, and Rose Meyers (nee Rachel Meyerovich), both of whom had emigrated from Poland before World War I. A slim boy of medium height and an exceptional student, Janowitz attended the Eastside Paterson High School, where he distinguished himself by organizing reading and science clubs and by editing the high school newspaper. After graduating in 1937, he attended New York University, from which he received an A.B. degree in economics in 1941.

At New York University, Janowitz came into contact with the renowned political scientist Bruce Lannes Smith, who introduced him to different approaches to sociology on the one hand, and to major scholars of sociology like Harold Lasswell, on the other. These experiences paved the way for Janowitz's future career and intellectual development. Smith offered him the job of collecting tickets at public lectures, at which Lasswell was one of the speakers. Janowitz's interests were stimulated by listening to the ideas and issues in these lectures. Later in 1941, Janowitz worked as a research assistant for Lasswell's project, "Wartime Communications," a content analysis of headlines in the leading newspapers. Three months later he joined the Propaganda Analysis Section of the U.S. Department of Justice to analyze the press in order to counteract any wartime propaganda that might lead to ethnic oppression or violence in the United States.

Janowitz joined the army in 1943 and worked as a propaganda analyst until 1945 in the Psychological Warfare Division of the Supreme Headquarters, Allied Expeditionary Forces. Stationed in London, his job was to study the German broadcasts and determine the factors that contributed to the morale of the German soldiers.

After Janowitz's return from war in 1946, he entered the University of Chicago, completing his Ph.D. in sociology in 1948. During the period from 1951 to 1961, when Janowitz taught at the University of Michigan, he established himself as a pioneering scholar in sociology. Among his books, *The Professional Soldier* (1960) was pivotal in earning him recognition as an important sociologist. This book examined the transformation of military institutions during the postwar period and was considered to be the driving force behind the institutionalization of military studies and, ultimately, the development of sociological research.

On 22 December 1951 Janowitz married Gayle Arlene Shulenberger; they had two daughters, Rebecca and

Naomi. He had met Shulenberger at the University of Chicago, where she was an administrative assistant to Bruno Bettelheim, with whom Janowitz coauthored *Dynamics of Prejudice* (1950). In this work Janowitz applied psychoanalytical theory to study prejudice, arguing that people who are economically disadvantaged and experience deprivation in their childhood are likely to be prejudicial in their behavior.

Janowitz returned to the University of Chicago in 1961 and joined the Department of Sociology in 1962; he also chaired the department from 1967 to 1972. At Chicago he created two important organizations, the Center for Social Organization Studies in 1962 and the Inter-University Seminar on Armed Forces and Society in 1963. While the Center for Social Organization Studies promoted research in diverse fields, the Inter-University Seminar on Armed Forces and Society grew into an international organization. His achievements at Chicago also included the founding in 1962 of the Heritage of Sociological Series, devoted to studying the contributions of past sociologists and of which he was editor beginning in 1964.

During the last years of his career, Janowitz published three volumes in which he consolidated the major ideas and issues central to his interests and inquiry throughout his life. One of these three thematically connected books, *The Last Half-Century: Societal Change and Politics in America* (1978), examined the advanced industrial and liberal democratic societies of the West, primarily the United States, by examining the issue of how to create a society based on collective goals and civic obligation among citizens rather than on individual, selfish interests and the utilization of coercive forces. In *The Reconstruction of Patriotism* (1983), he suggested that in the fragmented society of postindustrial America, democracy can function better once citizens become conscious of their civic duties by participating in voluntary services at national and community levels. He founded *Armed Forces and Society* in 1974 and edited this interdisciplinary journal until 1983.

Janowitz held many important institutional positions, including several in the U.S. government. In addition to his wartime contributions, for which he was decorated with a Purple Heart and Bronze Star, he served as consultant to President Harry Truman's Commission on Civil Rights (1947) and consultant to the Committee on Armed Services, U.S. Senate (1961). He received a Fulbright Research professorship at the University of Frankfurt (1954–1955); the Pitt professorship at Cambridge University (1972–1973); the American Sociological Association Award for Distinguished Scholarship (1984); and an honorary doctorate from the University of Toulouse (1977). He served as the vice president of the American Sociological Association (1970–1971) and was elected a fellow of the American Academy of Arts and Sciences (1978) and of the American Philosophical Society (1983).

Janowitz worked at the University of Chicago until his mandatory retirement in 1987. A year later he died of Parkinson's disease at the age of sixty-nine in his Hyde Park home. He is buried at Fort Sheridan, Illinois.

An eminent member in the Chicago School of sociology, Janowitz pioneered the institutionalization of military studies and explored the critical issues of personal and social control in advanced capitalist countries. A friend of the city of Chicago, he helped subsidize new and used bookstores in Hyde Park and worked to improve the public schools of Chicago. As one sociologist observed, "He was not only a patriot of sociology as an intellectual undertaking; he was also a patriot of the University of Chicago, of the city of Chicago and of the United States."

★

Janowitz's papers are in the Regenstein Library, University of Chicago. James Burk's introduction to Morris Janowitz, *On Social Organization and Social Control* (1991), is a summation of Janowitz's personal, professional, and scholarly life, with an emphasis on the major themes and tendencies of Janowitz's works. Dennis Smith, *The Chicago School: A Liberal Critique of Capitalism* (1988), has a chapter on Janowitz that is a good analytical study of his work. An obituary is in the *New York Times* (8 Nov. 1988).

SAIYEDA KHATUN

JARVIS, Howard Arnold (*b.* 22 September 1902 in Mercur [near Magna], Utah; *d.* 12 August 1986 in Los Angeles, California), businessman and government reformer best known for his leadership of the "tax revolt" in California and other states in the late 1970s.

Jarvis was one of five children (four boys and one girl) of John Ransome Jarvis and Margaret McKellar, who were Mormons engaged in farming and carpentering near and in the mining town of Magna. Later, John Jarvis became a lawyer and eventually a judge and state legislator. After graduating from high school in Magna, Howard attended the University of Utah from 1921 to 1926, where he acquired both a B.A. in 1925 and graduate credentials in law. During these years he also worked in the area's mines, played semiprofessional baseball, and earned some money as a professional boxer. In 1926 he married Corinne Fickes, with whom he had a daughter, his only child.

While in college Jarvis aspired to become a lawyer like his father. But by 1926 he was also interested in journalism and decided instead to enter the publishing business. With the aid of a $15,000 loan, he purchased the local weekly, the *Magna Times,* and succeeded in turning it into a thriving enterprise. By 1932 Jarvis had acquired ten other weeklies in neighboring towns. He also became active in politics, failing in his bid for election to the state legislature but gaining recognition as a Young Republican leader, a member of state advisory commissions, and publicity director for the Republican State Central Committee. In 1932 he served as press officer on Herbert Hoover's campaign train, and in 1934, while attending a party meeting in Chicago, he met Earl Warren; through conversations with Warren, Jarvis became convinced that California offered him greater opportunities than Utah. Shortly thereafter he sold his newspapers and moved with his daughter (his wife having died earlier of cancer) to Los Angeles.

In California, Jarvis initially worked in real estate, managed a drug supplies company in Hollywood, and handled publicity for the oilman J. Paul Getty. His major business successes came in the Oakland area, where he founded a company to manufacture noise-prevention latex pads, secured wartime contracts for electrical work on government merchant ships, and acquired properties that became the basis of the Femco Corporation, a manufacturer of aircraft and missile parts. In addition, he became involved for varying periods in the manufacture of garbage disposals, electric irons, gas heaters, and car coolers. Business success did not reduce his continuing involvement in politics. He became president of the Los Angeles County Republican Assembly, a regional director in the Republican presidential campaigns of 1952, 1956, and 1960, and an unsuccessful candidate for California's Republican senatorial nomination in 1962.

Also in 1962 Jarvis decided to retire from business. He sold his holdings for approximately $750,000 and became preoccupied with the cause of lowering property taxes. Starting with a small group in Los Angeles, one of whom, Estelle, became his third wife in 1965 (his second wife had died), he subsequently founded the United Organizations of Taxpayers and combined work as its chairman with a $17,000-a-year position as executive director of the Apartment Association of Los Angeles County, a landlord lobbying group. After 1965 he became a familiar figure at tax hearings, but his successes were minimal prior to 1978. Most politicians dismissed him as part of the nuisance or lunatic fringe. He lost badly when he ran for a seat on California's Board of Equalization and in 1977 for mayor of Los Angeles, and he had no success in getting a tax amendment initiative on the ballot.

In 1978, however, Jarvis's fortunes changed. Teaming up with Paul Gann, a retired real estate salesman and head of another taxpayer association, he secured enough signatures to put Proposition 13 (the Jarvis-Gann initiative) on the ballot. Despite opposition from the state's political, media, and labor establishments, the proposition passed by nearly a two-thirds majority. In essence, its supporters had tapped both a growing revulsion against "bloated government" and increasing alarm about taxes pushed up by rapidly rising

Howard Jarvis at the polls in Los Angeles, 6 June 1978. The election revolutionized California state politics with the approval of his Proposition 13, which slashed property taxes. UPI/CORBIS-BETTMANN

housing prices. The result was a constitutional provision that reduced property taxes by some 57 percent, severely restricted future increases, and required local services to either curtail activities or rely more heavily on state funding and user fees. Almost overnight Jarvis was transformed from a perennial crank in California politics to a national figure.

Subsequently, Jarvis tried to turn his "revolution" in California into a national one. In the aftermath of his victory he founded the American Tax Reduction Movement, which pushed new anti-tax measures at the state level and urged national legislation that would cut federal spending by $100 billion and reduce federal income taxes by 10 percent a year for four years. Most of his ideas, however, were not realized. Although his followers had limited success in some states and could take some credit for helping to make President Ronald Reagan's tax cut of 1981 possible, Jarvis did not secure the federal legislation he advocated, was rebuffed by California voters when he championed new initiatives to reduce income taxes and plug court-opened loopholes in Proposition 13, and found that the public had increasingly less use for his kind of vituperative hyperbole. In his later years Jarvis lived with his third wife and his sister-in-law in a modest, two-bedroom house on North Crescent Heights Boulevard in West Los Angeles. Raised in a strict Mormon family, he said in typically blunt style, "I'm what you call a Jack Mormon. That means I'm no goddamn good. I drink vodka, smoke a pipe, and play a little golf on Sunday." He died from complications of a blood disease.

In appearance Jarvis was a burly, often rumpled figure with a bulldoggish face and prominent jowls. In personality he was gruff, cantankerous, and opinionated but also canny, often funny, and affable in a grandfatherly way. In political style he accepted the label of "right-wing populist," cultivated a homespun folksiness, inveighed against such alleged "enemies of the people" as the liberal media and the welfare state, and used an earthy rhetoric in which his adversaries were described as "popcorn balls" and their ideas a "crock of manure." He is best seen as a part of and contributor to the broad-based conservative revival that prepared the way for Ronald Reagan's election to the presidency, and the movement he helped to stimulate and direct left lasting marks on the American tax structure.

★

A collection of Jarvis's papers, dealing mostly with his involvement in the Proposition 13 initiative, is located at the California State Library in Sacramento. The longest account of Jarvis's life is the autobiographical memoir included in his *I'm Mad as Hell: The Exclusive Story of the Tax Revolt and Its Leader* (1979), valuable for elusive details but suspect in some of its claims and prone to digressive preaching and fulminating. Helpful for context are Alvin Rabushka and Pauline Ryan, *The Tax Revolt* (1982), and William C. Berman, *America's Right Turn: From Nixon to Bush* (1994). The most useful biographical sketches in periodicals are "Maniac or Messiah?," *Time* (19 June 1978); Tom Mathews and Martin Kasindorf, "Mr. Proposition 13," *Newsweek* (19 June 1978); Sally Quinn, "Proposition Man," *Washington Post* (20 June 1978); and Jack Fincher, "Cantankerous Champion of the Taxpayer," *Reader's Digest* (Aug. 1979). An obituary is in the *New York Times* (14 Aug. 1986).

ELLIS W. HAWLEY

JAVITS, Jacob Koppel (*b.* 18 May 1904 in New York City; *d.* 7 March 1986 in Palm Beach, Florida), U.S. senator from New York and a leading spokesman for liberals in the Republican party.

Jacob Javits was born in a tenement on the Lower East Side of New York City, the densely populated home of thousands of Jewish immigrants. He was the son of Morris Jawetz of Austria-Hungary (now Ukraine), a tailor and janitor, and Ida Littman of Palestine and Russia, proprietress of a series of unsuccessful small businesses. His father changed the spelling of the family name when he immigrated to the United States in 1890. Javits proudly remembered his childhood neighborhood as the urban equivalent of a frontier log cabin, where immigrants "provided much of the muscle

Senator Jacob Javits. ARCHIVE PHOTOS

and many of the brains that transformed America into an industrialized society." Growing up in poverty, Javits hawked his mother's secondhand pots and pans and credited the experience with teaching him public speaking, even before hostile audiences. His older brother Benjamin Javits, who preceded Jacob into the practice of law, was a major influence. Two older sisters died in infancy.

An excellent student, Javits attended George Washington High School then studied for three years, 1921–1923, at Columbia University. Entering law school at New York University in 1923, he graduated with an LL.B. in 1926 and was admitted to the bar the following year. He joined his brother in the firm of Javits and Javits, which specialized in business bankruptcies. Although his father had been a ward heeler for Tammany Hall, Javits was offended by the corruption of the New York City Democratic party and the influence of southern segregationists in the national party. Abandoning an early intellectual interest in socialism, he joined a local Republican organization in 1932 and had his first taste of politics in the campaigns of Fiorello La Guardia, New York City's three-term reform mayor. In 1933 Javits married Marjorie Ringling, of the circus family; they had three children. Marjorie was a Catholic, and their differing faiths proved incompatible. They divorced in 1936.

Javits attempted to enlist for military service in World War II but was rejected because of his age. He then became a civilian administrator in the Army Chemical Warfare Department and was commissioned in 1942. After attending the founding conference of the United Nations, he left the service in 1945 with the rank of lieutenant colonel. His wartime experiences were the foundation for his lifelong support of U.S. involvement in international affairs.

In 1946 Javits won the Republican nomination for the U.S. House of Representatives in a district on the West Side of Manhattan. The nomination seemed purely honorific in a solidly Democratic area, but Javits now had considerable personal financial resources, a distinctive appeal to the district's Jewish voters, and the support of the nascent Liberal party. The political environment also worked in his favor. The opposition was split between a mediocre Democratic newcomer and the leftist American Labor party, and the national tide was moving toward the Republicans. Campaigning vigorously as a liberal and protesting postwar economic dislocations, Javits won an upset victory and achieved reelection in three subsequent contests. On 30 November 1947 Javits married Marian Ann Borris, an actress and intellectual doyenne. They had no children. Marian Javits maintained her separate interests and her own residence in New York City during most of her husband's career.

In 1954, having demonstrated his vote-getting ability, Javits was nominated for New York State attorney general. Facing Franklin D. Roosevelt, Jr., the namesake of a revered president, Javits nevertheless led his ticket and achieved the only Republican statewide victory in the election. Two years later, he was elected to the U.S. Senate by a margin of 458,000 votes over New York mayor Robert Wagner, Jr. In his subsequent three reelections, Senator Javits handily defeated a gallery of prominent Democrats, including William Donovan, Paul O'Dwyer, and Ramsey Clark. In 1962, against Donovan, Javits accomplished a political miracle, as he became the first Republican to win New York City since Calvin Coolidge.

During his four terms in the U.S. Senate, Javits became an acknowledged leader of the liberal wing of the Republican party. His claim was supported by his three books on public policy: *Discrimination, U.S.A.* (1960); *The Defense Sector and the American Economy* (1968), written with Charles J. Hitch and Arthur F. Burns; and *Who Makes War: The President Versus Congress* (1973), written with Don Kellerman.

Javits's general credo was best stated in *Order of Battle: A Republican's Call to Reason* (1964), in which he presented a full exposition of his variant of Republican philosophy. Surveying American history, he defended his party's leadership in "the movement from the local to the national approach to national problems." Against the rising influence of conservatives in the party, the senator argued, "Government—which means all of us—must actively foster and preserve the conditions in which the individual will in fact remain free to make his own decisions." He implemented this philosophy through support of government programs in health, education, urban renewal, welfare, and civil rights. Javits also hoped that his prominence among liberals would lead to higher office. He vainly sought the Republican nomination for vice president in 1968 and for mayor of New York City in 1973.

In the Senate, Javits gained a bipartisan reputation for his legislative effort and expertise, first in domestic policy, then in foreign relations. He had an important role in formulating legislation to reform the budget process, to control lobbying, and to extend voting rights to southern blacks. As his interests shifted, he left his leading position on the Senate Human Resources Committee to become the ranking Republican member of the Foreign Relations Committee. He consistently supported bipartisanship in foreign policy and an active American role in world politics, including high military spending, foreign assistance to developing nations, and aid to Israel. Although initially supportive of American intervention in Vietnam, he eventually turned against the war. In reaction to the Vietnam War, he coauthored the War Powers Act of 1973, which restricted the president's use of military forces abroad. In his personal evaluation of his career, Javits considered this act among his greatest accomplishments, along with legislation to protect private pensions (Employment Retirement Income Security Act) and to create the National Foundations for the Arts and the Humanities.

In 1980 Javits lost his only electoral bid, as he sought a fifth term in the Senate. Facing both a general tide toward conservatism and personal questions about his age and health, he lost the Republican nominating primary, his only serious intraparty contest, to Alfonse D'Amato, a suburban legislator from Long Island. Rather than leave politics, Javits remained in the race as the Liberal candidate and gained 11 percent of the vote, a third-party record. Because D'Amato led the field with only 45 percent, Javits was blamed for the defeat of the liberal Democratic candidate, Elizabeth Holtzman.

After leaving the Senate, Javits served for a year as adjunct professor at Columbia University; published his memoirs, *Javits: The Autobiography of a Public Man* (1981); wrote articles; and lectured. His health was obviously deteriorating when he was awarded the Medal of Freedom by President Ronald Reagan in 1983. The following year, the new convention center in New York City was named in Javits's honor. Probably inspired by his Jewish heritage, Javits interpreted his rise from tenement poverty as an argument for active government policies to achieve wider economic opportunity and social justice.

Javits died in Palm Beach, Florida, of amyotrophic lateral sclerosis, commonly known as Lou Gehrig's disease. He is buried in New York City. The hallmarks of Javits's life were stated well in eulogies by his colleagues in the U.S. Senate. Daniel Patrick Moynihan praised his fellow New Yorker's "reverence for life" and his "quest for justice." Edward Kennedy recalled Javits's work with Robert Kennedy in "the migrant camps and a Mississippi of hunger and anguish."

Jacob Javits had a distinguished career, but it evidenced frustration as much as achievement. He was an able legislator, but because he never served in a Republican majority after his freshman term in the House, he could not author major legislation in his own name nor wield the power of a committee chairman. As an urban, Jewish, and liberal Republican, he could not rise to the highest positions in a party that was predominantly suburban, Protestant, and increasingly conservative. Outspoken, assertive, and bright, he never gained entrance to the cozy, soft-spoken dealings of the "inner club" of the Senate. Dedicated to his work, he admittedly lost some intimacy in his family life. To the end, he claimed most proudly the achievements of a public man.

★

Javits's papers are housed at the Stony Brook, Long Island, campus of the State University of New York. His autobiography was published in 1981. Nicol C. Rae, *The Decline and Fall of the Liberal Republicans: From 1952 to the Present* (1989), is a scholarly work that includes some material on Javits. An obituary is in the *New York Times* (8 Mar. 1986).

GERALD M. POMPER

JESSUP, Philip Caryl (*b.* 5 January 1897 in New York City; *d.* 31 January 1986 in Newton, Pennsylvania), jurist, scholar, and diplomat who advised both the U.S. government and the United Nations and in whose honor the premier annual international law moot court competition was named in 1959.

One of the five sons of Henry Wynans Jessup, a law professor at New York University, and Mary Hay Stotesbury, Jessup was raised with a strict Presbyterian upbringing in Manhattan. Energetic and tall, he attended the Ridgefield School in Connecticut and served in the U.S. Army during World War I in France and in Belgium (1917–1918). He earned a B.A. degree from Hamilton College in 1919 and then undertook legal studies at the Yale Law School, from which he earned an LL.B. in 1924. He was admitted to the Washington, D.C., bar in 1925 and to the New York bar in 1927, while serving as the assistant solicitor in the State Department (1924–1925). Jessup concomitantly received an M.A. degree (1924) and a Ph.D. (1927) from Columbia University, where he also taught international law. In 1921 he married Lois Kellogg, later the dean of the Berkeley School in Manhattan. The couple had one son, Philip Caryl, Jr.

From 1948 to 1952 Jessup was U.S. ambassador to the United Nations, while almost simultaneously serving as UN ambassador-at-large (1949–1953). He was credited with ending the Berlin blockade following delicate negotiations with the Soviet Union in 1949. Jessup was elected to represent the United States as a judge in the International Court of Justice in The Hague, the Netherlands (1960–1969).

During his prolonged post-retirement years, Jessup was a prolific writer of books, articles, and letters to the editor of the *New York Times.* Through the medium of the *Times,* he asked his fellow Americans not to expect too much from international associations such as the United Nations or from the International Court of Justice, calling for strong action by the member states to promote and to protect human rights, especially with respect to torture. He contested the withholding of U.S. funds from the United Nations even if Israel was to be suspended from the General Assembly (29 July 1975); intervened in the national debate concerning President Gerald Ford's pardoning of Richard Nixon (8 August 1975); contended that Iran, while not ruled by the shah, had accepted the authority of the International Court of Justice, and so was bound by the court's decision concerning the American hostages (3 June 1980); and mocked the nonconsequential U.S.-Soviet negotiations with respect to arms control (13 December 1981).

Jessup wrote several treatises on international law and a laudatory biography of the jurist and diplomat Elihu Root, *Elihu Root* (2 vols, 1938). His *The United States and the World Court* (1929), with a foreword by Root, was meticulously researched and aimed at fighting isolationism. His *Birth of Nations* (1974) analyzed the creation of new states following World War II and their admission to the United Nations.

Jessup served as a member of the board of the Center for International Policy and as a trustee of the Council of Foreign Relations, the Foreign Policy Association, and the Carnegie Endowment for International Peace. He died of Parkinson's disease.

Jessup's patriotism and character were championed by Columbia University president and future U.S. president Dwight D. Eisenhower, in response to Republican senator Joseph M. McCarthy's allegations in 1951 that Jessup had "an unusual affinity for Communist causes" (an episode that forced Jessup to devote much time to his own defense in a clash between the two cold warriors). Eisenhower wrote that "no one who has known you can for a moment question the depth or sincerity of your devotion to the principles of Americanism."

★

A collection of Jessup's papers is in the Library of Congress. Further biographical information can be found in Marshall R. Kuehl, "Philip C. Jessup: From America First to Cold War Interventionist" (Ph.D. diss., Kent State University, 1985). Jessup's article "Revisions of the International Legal Order," *Journal of International Law and Policy* 10 (1980), cites the universal condemnation of the seizure by Iran of the American hostages in 1979 as testifying to the useful role that international law has in fostering a sense of global community. Wolfgang Friedmann et al., *Transnational Law in a Changing Society: Essays in Honor of Philip C. Jessup* (1972), is a useful contribution to the body of literature that Jessup made mainstream. An obituary is in the *New York Times* (1 Feb. 1986). See also "The Reminiscences of Philip Jessup" (1959), an interview in the Columbia University Oral History Research Office.

ITAI SNEH

JOFFREY, Robert (*b.* 24 December 1928 in Seattle, Washington; *d.* 25 March 1988 in New York City), artistic director and founder of the Joffrey Ballet.

Joffrey, who at his birth was named Anver Bey Abdullah Jaffa Khan, was the only child of Dollha Anver Bey Jaffa Khan, who had emigrated in 1916 from Afghanistan to Seattle, where he opened the Rainbow Chili Parlor tavern and changed his name to Joseph Joffrey, and of Marie Gallette, an amateur concert violinist from northern Italy, whose first job in America was as the tavern's cashier. Joffrey widely publicized his birthdate as 1930, shaving two years off his age. He was born with bow legs, severely turned-in feet, and progressively worsening asthma. His early years were defined by repeated visits to doctors, braces on his feet, and strong recommendations for exercise.

In 1938, after a brief stint as a boxer, Joffrey persuaded his parents to let him study ballroom and tap dance at the school fortuitously located above their restaurant. In 1939 he took his first classical ballet lesson and was soon performing minor roles with Diaghilev's Ballets Russes de Monte Carlo, which regularly appeared in Seattle. These seminal experiences prompted him to enthuse memorably to his teacher, Mary Ann Wells, "I want someday to have my own company." He was seventeen, and no single person was to have a more profound influence on his aesthetic and ambition than Wells. She trained his creative impulses toward making ballet a quintessentially American art form, one that embraced a diversity of body types and dance philosophies.

In 1948 Joffrey and his companion, the dancer Gerald Arpino (with whom he would live for the rest of his life), moved to New York City. In 1953 they founded the American Ballet Center school in Greenwich Village. By then Joffrey had an impressive following of some of New York's most illustrious dancers and of young talented students who were acquainted with his teaching through his classes at the American Ballet Theatre school (1949–1952) and the High School of Performing Arts (1950–1955).

In 1953 Joffrey irreparably tore a ligament during a modern-dance performance with May O'Donnell and Company, ending an onstage career that had notably spanned the two conflicting disciplines of modern dance and classical ballet (the latter as a member of Roland Petit's Les Ballets de Paris in 1949). He then turned his attention solidly to choreography and the formation of a company. The original nucleus of Joffrey dancers gave its debut of an all-Joffrey program on 13 January 1952 at New York's Ninety-second Street YM-YWHA. Joffrey himself, however, marked the official start of his permanent company on 2 October 1956 in Frostburg, Maryland, where the professional troupe launched its first of seven consecutive national tours with Columbia Artists Management.

In 1962 Rebekah Harkness Kean signed on as Joffrey's patron, sponsoring the company on a tour to the Near and Far East (1962) and to the Soviet Union (1963). In 1964 Joffrey lost his company to Harkness, in a fractious battle waged in the press, because he refused to have his name removed from the troupe's title. He reconstituted the company in 1965, with Arpino as its associate director and chief choreographer. Upon acceptance of Morton Baum's invitation to reside at New York's City Center of Music and Drama the troupe became the City Center Joffrey Ballet.

Wounded by the desertion of so many of his dancers to the newly organized Harkness Ballet, Joffrey distanced himself further and further from the class studios where he had earned a nationally recognized reputation as a teacher. He also concerned himself less with his own choreography, leaving the balance of the repertoire to Arpino and a novel complement of ballet choreographers from established schools (George Balanchine, August Bournonville, Léonide Massine) and lesser-known artists working in jazz, Broadway musical, and modern-dance idioms (Eliot Feld, Anna Sokolow, Twyla Tharp). His astute eye for spotting talent and detecting trends ahead of their time produced Joffrey's greatest flourishing over the next two decades.

In 1967 Joffrey choreographed one of his few works as a mature artist, *Astarte.* A collaboration between the filmmaker Gardner Compton, the producer Midge Mackenzie, and Joffrey, *Astarte* presented a pair of dancers bombarded by dramatic color film images that were projected onto them, while an almost ear-splitting rock band accompanied them from the orchestra pit. Seen as symbolic of the new direction in modern dance and emblematic of the psychedelic, Vietnam War era, *Astarte* graced the cover of *Time* magazine on 15 March 1968. As the first ballet ever to earn that honor, *Astarte* forced the realization on Joffrey that the audience for dance was greater than most ballet pundits

Robert Joffrey. JOFFREY BALLET OF CHICAGO, PHOTO BY HERBERT MIDGALL

had previously understood. He stepped up his efforts to reach mainstream America, a goal of his since first envisioning the company in Seattle. On 21 January 1976 the City Center Joffrey Ballet reached nearly 4 million television viewers when it was the subject of the first *Dance in America* series aired by the Public Broadcasting System.

Joffrey's unabashed efforts to create repertory for a popular audience came under considerable critical attack, particularly for the sensational, sentimental, and acrobatic ballets by Arpino. When Joffrey had initially started the troupe in 1952, it was generally assumed that an American from the West Coast would have no hope of succeeding within the elite hierarchical ballet community of New York, where ballet was largely synonymous with being Russian and familiar with European academies. Joffrey's unquenchable enthusiasm, scrupulous training, and perfectionism silenced most critics then. He fell back on the same characteristics in 1969 and presented exceptionally trained artists, schooled in his methods that stressed versatility and energy over pure, classical line and proportion.

He invited Massine to stage three of his masterworks from the repertory of Ballets Russes: *Le Tricorne* in 1969, *Le Beau Danube* in 1972, and *Parade* in 1973. These Diaghilev-period revivals—culminating with Vaslav Nijinsky's *Le Sacre du printemps* in 1987—were accomplished with unprecedented attention to the original details. It is for them that Joffrey earned his permanent seat in the pantheon of great ballet directors.

The last three ballets Joffrey choreographed were *Remembrances* (1973), *Postcards* (1980), and *The Nutcracker* (1987). In 1973 the company experienced perhaps the highest peak of everything it was to be, not only creatively—Tharp choreographed *Deuce Coupe* and Frederick Ashton's *The Dream* entered the repertory—but in terms of financial stability. Joffrey, too, had met A. Aladar Marberger, an art dealer nearly twenty years younger than himself, who became a great love of his adult life. From this point on, however, Joffrey and the members of the City Center Joffrey Ballet, plagued by financial uncertainty, worried about how much longer they could support operations in New York City. In August 1979 Joffrey laid off the dancers and kept a skeletal administrative staff. Three months later the National Endowment for the Arts awarded the company a special matching grant, and Joffrey started back up with many new dancers. On 30 April 1983 the Joffrey Ballet (as it had been known since 1976) became a resident of the Music Center of Los Angeles, dividing its seasons between there and City Center in New York.

By 1985 Joffrey learned that he carried the AIDS virus and had begun to show signs of illness. By nature a deeply secretive man whose spiritual beliefs did not allow for discussion of anyone's poor health or of even remotely negative subjects, Joffrey informed no one that he was sick until he was bedridden in the summer of 1986. From his bed he carried out two of his life's ambitions, overseeing the reconstruction of Nijinsky's *Sacre* to Stravinsky's famous score and a full-length production of the *Nutcracker* set in Victorian America.

As Joffrey's death began to seem imminent, his closest colleagues and executives fought over who should take control of the company and when. One faction was set squarely against the company going to Arpino. Joffrey, earnestly believing that he would regain his health, refused to implement plans for the transition of his directorship to anyone. He never uttered the word "AIDS"; to this day, some Joffrey company officials—including Arpino—stand by Joffrey's version that he, a long-term asthmatic, suffered from respiratory, hepatic, and renal failure. Although his death certificate from New York University Hospital makes the same attribution, ample evidence points to Joffrey's fight with AIDS, which in and of itself can never be a cause of death. Joffrey's remains were cremated and his ashes divided three ways: one-third went to Arpino, one-third was scattered in Puget Sound, and one-third was buried in the Cathedral of St. John the Divine in New York City.

After his death Joffrey's company was turned over by majority vote of the board of directors to Arpino. This had been Joffrey's written wish just before his death. In 1991 the Joffrey Ballet lost its residency at the Music Center of Los Angeles. In 1996 Arpino closed the New York headquarters and, moving to Chicago, reestablished the troupe as Joffrey Ballet of Chicago.

Joffrey's name and tradition stand for a spirited comprehension of ballet that makes room for all manner of physical form and points of view. Joffrey, himself a short man at five feet, four inches in height, believed ballet could include any dancer with a fierce will to dance and could be wrenched down from its imperial European and Russian pedestal to be transformed into American entertainment, which—despite its broad, even possibly commercial, appeal—still retained integrity and classical value. His impeccable taste and unconventional vision served two disparate masters—his repertory of rock-and-roll ballets in the 1960s and 1970s attracted the broadest mainstream audience for ballet yet in America, while at the same time he was bringing back into circulation many of the so-called lost twentieth-century masterpieces from Diaghilev's Ballets Russes, thereby setting new standards for performing-arts curatorship.

★

Most of Joffrey's records and personal papers are the property of Gerald Arpino. Some of them, however, are stored at the Joffrey Ballet School, directed by Edith D'Addario, in New York City. Other papers are housed at Harvard University in Cambridge, Massachusetts; at the Newberry Library in Chicago; and in the Dance Collection of the New York Public Library for the Performing Arts. Sasha Anawalt, *The Joffrey Ballet: Robert Joffrey and the Making of an American Dance Company* (1996), is the only biography of Joffrey and is a comprehensive history of his company set in the context of America's economic and political development. John Gruen's interview with Joffrey, published in his *The Private World of Ballet* (1975), sheds light on Joffrey's mentality at the time, although Joffrey was notorious for embellishing stories from his past. Other helpful books are the collections of reviews and observations from critics, including Arlene Croce, *Afterimages* (1977), and Marcia Siegel, *At the Vanishing Point* (1972), *Watching the Dance Go By* (1977), and *The Shapes of Change* (1979). Diane Solway, *A Dance Against Time: The Brief, Brilliant Life of a Joffrey Dancer* (1994), which chronicles Edward Stierle's career and death from AIDS complications, provides a disturbing view of Joffrey from an author some of Joffrey's detractors had in their thrall. A comprehensive view of Robert Joffrey's career may be gained from *Dance* magazine's numerous critical reviews and artistic profiles by a variety of dance observers since 1952. An obituary is in the *New York Times* (26 Mar. 1988).

SASHA ANAWALT

JOHNSON, Clarence Leonard ("Kelly") (*b.* 27 February 1910 in Ishpeming, Michigan; *d.* 21 December 1990 in Burbank, California), aeronautical engineer and aviation executive.

The son of Swedish immigrants Christine Anderson Johnson and Peter Johnson, Clarence was the seventh of nine children. His father was a mason. Johnson took the nickname "Kelly" while a schoolboy, to avoid fighting with those who might make fun of his first name, he claimed. He became fascinated with aviation at an early age, and by the time he was twelve he had decided to become an aircraft designer.

In 1923 the family moved to Flint, Michigan. After graduating from high school, Johnson attended Flint Junior

Kelly Johnson. LOCKHEED MARTIN SKUNK WORKS

College and subsequently enrolled at the University of Michigan. There he became an assistant to Professor Edward A. Stalker, head of the aeronautical department, who introduced him to the more practical aspects of aircraft design.

Johnson graduated from the University of Michigan with a B.S. degree in 1932. Unfortunately, the aviation industry had been decimated by the Great Depression, and jobs were virtually nonexistent. After several unsuccessful attempts to find employment with aircraft companies in the East, Johnson headed west and contacted Lockheed Aircraft Corporation in Burbank, California. Lockheed was just emerging from receivership, however, and was in no position to hire a young engineer with only a baccalaureate degree and no experience. Nevertheless, company officials, impressed with Johnson, encouraged him to reapply the following year. In the interim he returned to the University of Michigan, secured a fellowship, and entered graduate school.

Armed with his M.S. degree, which he had received earlier that year, Johnson returned to California and on 21 August 1933 was hired by Lockheed as a tool designer. Lockheed's most successful products at this time were single-engine monoplanes of wood construction that had achieved fame in a series of record-breaking flights by well-known pilots. But aircraft design was evolving rapidly. New technologies and all-metal construction were transforming the industry, and only companies with engineering expertise would survive and prosper. In this environment, Johnson would become one of the premier aeronautical engineers.

Soon after his arrival at Lockheed, Johnson began working on a completely new design that the company had under development. The end result was the Lockheed Electra, an all-metal, twin-engine light transport that incorporated the new technologies. It first flew in early 1934 and was an immediate success. Purchased by numerous foreign and domestic airlines, it was instrumental in keeping the company solvent. In 1937 Johnson produced an improved version, which was an even greater success. Great Britain's Royal Air Force recognized its military potential and placed an order for 250 examples of a militarized version in June 1938, even before the prototype had flown. In that same year Johnson, who had risen rapidly within the company—serving as flight test engineer, stress analyst, aerodynamicist, weight engineer, and wind tunnel engineer—was named chief research engineer.

Johnson ultimately contributed to the development of some forty aircraft types, more than half of them his own creations. Outstanding examples of his genius were the P-38 Lightning, one of the best fighter aircraft of World War II; America's first operational jet fighter, the F-80 Shooting Star; the F-104 Starfighter, which was capable of flying at twice the speed of sound; the U-2 high-altitude reconnaissance aircraft (which would become embroiled in cold war politics); and, perhaps Johnson's most radical design, the SR-71 Blackbird, a strategic reconnaissance airplane capable of flying at more than three times the speed of sound at an altitude of 80,000 feet.

In addition to his aircraft design talents, Johnson was highly regarded for his organizational and managerial skills. In 1943 he organized an advanced development, design, and production team to build the XP-80 experimental prototype, which was created in the record time of 143 days. This small but highly talented and motivated team of specialists, formally known as Advanced Development Projects, became better known as the "Skunk Works," a term taken from the popular "Li'l Abner" comic strip. The managerial philosophy behind the Skunk Works was based upon the principle of strong authority with the ability to make immediate decisions and put them into rapid effect. One of Johnson's mottos was "Be quick, be quiet, be on time." Much of his success was due to his skill in choosing the right man for each job. He invariably completed his projects on or ahead of schedule, and often under budget. The Skunk Works has been described as Johnson's "most enduring legacy to the aerospace community."

Johnson was chief engineer of Lockheed from 1952 to 1959. He became vice president for research and development in 1956, and in 1958 he was named vice president for advanced development projects. He was elected to the board of directors in 1964. Johnson retired from Lockheed in 1975 as a senior vice president. He remained a director until 1980, and was a senior adviser to Lockheed at the time of his death.

Johnson married Althea Louise Young on 31 August 1937. She died in December 1969. In May 1971 he married Maryellen Elberta Meade, who died in October 1980. In addition to his home in Encino, California, where he lived at the time of his death, Johnson owned Star Lane Ranch near Santa Barbara, California. He was survived by his third wife, Nancy Powers Horrigan, whom he married in November 1980. He had no children.

Johnson received many awards, including the Collier Trophy from the National Aeronautical Association (1959, 1964), the Sylvanus Albert Reed Award of the American Institute of Aeronautics and Astronautics (1956, 1966), the Lawrence Sperry Award of the Institute of Aeronautical Sciences (1937), the Wright Brothers Medal of the Society of Automotive Engineers (1941), the Wright Brothers Memorial Trophy (1975), the Daniel Guggenheim Medal (1981), the Theodore von Karman Award of the Air Force Association (1963, 1964), and the Medal of Freedom (1964). He was a member of the American Institute of Aeronautics and Astronautics and the Royal Aeronautical Society. For "his abilities to motivate a small staff to work within a tight time frame and budget in creating revolutionary aircraft designs" he was named a fellow of the Society of Automotive Engineers.

★

The library of the National Air and Space Museum has a file on Johnson that contains information on his professional accomplishments, honors, and awards. The best source of biographical information is Johnson's autobiography, written with Maggie Smith, *Kelly: More Than My Share of It All* (1985). The story of the Skunk Works can be found in Steve Pace, *Lockheed Skunk Works* (1992); and in Jay Miller, *Lockheed Martin's Skunk Works: The Official History,* rev. ed. (1996). Numerous articles on aircraft designed by Johnson are in *Air Power* and *Wings* magazines. Also see René J. Francillon, *Lockheed Aircraft Since 1913* (1982). Obituaries are in the *New York Times* (22 Dec. 1990) and *Aviation Week and Space Technology* (7 Jan. 1991).

LOUIS R. ELTSCHER

JOHNSON, Eleanor Murdock (*b.* 10 December 1892 in Hagerstown, Maryland; *d.* 8 October 1987 in Gaithersburg, Maryland), educator and journalist who founded *My Weekly Reader,* the newspaper for schoolchildren that influenced several generations of American students.

Johnson was born on a farm in Washington County, northern Maryland, near the Pennsylvania border. Her parents, whose names are not known, were probably farmers. She attended local schools with her sister, Maria. In 1913 Johnson moved to Oklahoma to begin a career in elementary school education. She taught grade one in the Lawton, Oklahoma, public schools from 1913 to 1916 and in the Chickasha, Oklahoma, public schools from 1916 to 1917. She then taught grades one and two in the Oklahoma City public schools from 1917 to 1918. In 1918 she took a supervisory post overseeing the primary grades of the Drumright, Oklahoma, public schools, which she held until 1922. Thereafter, her positions were all supervisory. Until 1926 she was responsible for grades one through six in the Oklahoma City public schools. She simultaneously studied at the University of Chicago, where she was awarded a bachelor of philosophy degree in 1925.

Eleanor Johnson with an issue of *My Weekly Reader,* 1979. UPI/CORBIS-BETTMANN

The following year Johnson moved to Pennsylvania to supervise grades one through six at the York public schools. In 1927 she coauthored Child Story, a series of readers published by Lyons and Carnahan. While working in Oklahoma, she had conceived the idea of a weekly newspaper for schoolchildren, and when she moved to Pennsylvania, she spent a year developing the concept. Believing that "children were being given a lot of myths and folklore to read but were utterly illiterate about what was happening in the world," she saw a need for a publication that would "present selected, well-written news of interest and value to children with accuracy and fairness, colorful but uncolored." Her dream became a reality in 1928, when she met William Blakey, president of American Education Publications (AEP) in Columbus, Ohio, who liked the idea. That summer, AEP editors telegraphed her, "Ready to start your children's paper." Within a month, Johnson's first issue of *My Weekly Reader* was edited, prepared for press, and in the schools.

The first issue of *My Weekly Reader*, dated 21 September 1928, was four pages long and contained a lead article about presidential candidates Herbert Hoover and Alfred E. Smith titled "Two Poor Boys Who Made Good Are Now Running for the Highest Office in the World!" Within a year, the four-to-eight-page paper had a circulation of 100,000. While *My Weekly Reader* was finding its audience and building its circulation, Johnson continued her supervisory work in the York schools. She also advised members of Blakey's staff on how to write for the new publication, insisting on clear, straightforward prose, and supplied them with model issues for guidance and a workbook that she had developed. In 1930 she left York to take a position as assistant superintendent for grades one through twelve in the Lakewood, Ohio, public schools. While there, in 1932, she received an M.A. degree in education from Columbia University. Johnson remained in Lakewood through 1934.

By 1935, *My Weekly Reader* had become a standard element in classrooms across the country. With the success of the paper assured, Johnson moved from school administration to full-time work on the publication. She joined American Education Press in 1935 as editor in chief of *My Weekly Reader*. From 1934 to 1940 she was education director of AEP, and in 1940 she became editor in chief of AEP. Johnson moved to Middletown, Connecticut, during the 1940s, when Xerox Corporation bought her publishing company and changed its name to American Education Publications.

Johnson published more than fifty workbooks on reading, arithmetic, and geography and contributed articles to professional journals and magazines. She also developed the Spelling for Word Mastery workbooks in 1954 and coauthored the Treasury of Literature book series, published by C. E. Merrill in 1956. She served on the editorial board of *Education* magazine; held visiting professorships at Columbia University, the University of Pittsburgh, and the University of Chicago; and was a frequent lecturer. She received the Theta Sigma Phi Headliner Award in 1948. She was also awarded an honorary doctorate in literature from Hood College in Maryland.

Johnson retired in 1966 and moved with her sister to Gaithersburg, Maryland, where they lived together until Eleanor's death. Neither sister ever married. During the 1960s the name of the school newspaper was changed to *Weekly Reader,* and Johnson remained a consultant to the publication until 1978, when she was eighty-five years old. By the late 1980s, when Johnson was in her nineties, *Weekly Reader* had expanded to seven editions, one for each grade level through sixth grade, had a circulation of 13 million, and reached 60 percent of the nation's schoolchildren. Diagnosed with cancer in September 1987, Johnson died a month later of pneumonia at the Ashbury Methodist Retirement Center in Gaithersburg, Maryland.

An estimated two-thirds of American students have read *Weekly Reader* at some point during their primary school years. At its largest, the circulation of the paper was more than that of *Time* and *Newsweek* combined. Presenting news in a format children found informative, interesting, and entertaining, Johnson was one of the pioneers in the rapidly developing field of reading instruction. In response to Johnson's teachings and the scholarship of psychologists like Jean Piaget and Erik Erikson on cognitive development and the early formation of personality, the concept of age-appropriate material has gained acceptance in the field of education, and material has been aimed increasingly at well-defined, clearly targeted age groups.

★

No collection of Johnson's personal papers is extant and no full-length biography of her has yet been written. An interview with her is in the *Washington Post* (8 Oct. 1978). Additional information is in *Leaders in Education,* 4th ed. (1971), and the preface to *Weekly Reader* staff, eds., *Weekly Reader: Sixty Years of News for Kids 1928–1988* (1988). Obituaries are in the *New York Times* (9 Oct. 1987), the *Washington Post* (10 Oct. 1987), the *Los Angeles Times* (10 Oct. 1987), and the *Chicago Tribune* (11 Oct. 1987).

STEPHEN TURTELL

JOHNSON, Wallace Edwards (*b.* 5 October 1901 in Edinburg, Mississippi; *d.* 27 April 1988 in Memphis, Tennessee), entrepreneur who pioneered prefabricated housing and was a cofounder of Holiday Inns of America.

The elder son of Felix Alva Johnson and Ida Josephine Edwards, Wallace grew up on a small Mississippi farm. His mother claimed ancestry from the New England theologian Jonathan Edwards and insisted that her son finish high school. His only brother, Graves, died of malaria at the age of fifteen. Wallace married his childhood sweetheart, Alma McCool, on 10 August 1924. Their only child died in infancy.

For two decades Wallace worked for lumberyards in Itta Bena, Mississippi, Pine Bluff, Arkansas, and Memphis, Tennessee, never earning more than $37.50 a week until 1940, when he became an independent home builder. Cost control was his special concern. As a teenager he had built a luxury home only to lose $2,000 by underestimating his costs. With twenty years of experience in the lumber business and having completed a correspondence course in architecture, he was able to create a five-room home design,

Wallace Johnson. PRESS-SCIMITAR PHOTO/MISSISSIPPI VALLEY COLLECTION/UNIVERSITY OF MEMPHIS LIBRARIES

with costs figured to the last nail, permitting a $110 profit on each $2,999 house. His preparation and the Federal Housing Authority's loan guarantee for home buyers permitted Johnson to begin home building at the end of the Great Depression. His wife devoted herself to being a business partner. She completed a correspondence course in interior decorating and, in addition to managing Johnson's office, helped him design homes.

Johnson's initial resources were little more than a $250 loan, careful attention to costs, and the ebullient personality of a promoter. The six-foot, two-inch contractor boldly planted signs on five thousand vacant lots, none of which he owned, advertising, "Let Wallace E. Johnson build your home on this lot." Johnson was a devout Southern Baptist and was commonly heard reciting his favorite Scripture: "Ask and it shall be given, seek and ye shall find, knock and it shall be opened to you." The folksy salesman typically addressed associates, including his bankers, as "Sweetheart," "Honey," and "Darling."

Johnson quickly became the largest builder in Memphis, constructing 181 homes in 1940 and 360 the next year. His booster salesmanship promoted houses built by creative mass-production techniques. Johnson held construction costs down by preassembling housing parts. All studs were cut in his factory shop, and frames for doors, windows, and corners were cut and nailed together. By 1943 this "Henry Ford of Housing," as he was called by the *Memphis Commercial Appeal,* had moved on to prefabricating entire wall frames. Every month he held quality control meetings with his workers to discuss errors, possible improvements, and his own penny-saving philosophy.

Cost cutting prompted Johnson's purchase of supply companies that produced housing materials. He acquired his own sawmill, lumberyard, hardware, plumbing, electrical, brick, tile, sand, and nursery businesses. With the cheapest costs for housing, Johnson won government contracts to build homes for war workers in Tennessee, Arkansas, and Mississippi. He spoke about his success before a national audience at the National Association of Home Builders convention in Chicago.

Never one to hide his ambitions, Johnson wrote out the following prayer on 1 January 1945:

> Make me, O Lord, one of the leading Baptists in the United States, and teach me how to win souls. O Lord, help me to be one of the biggest businessmen in the United States, and if it be Thy will let me be a vice president of the Association. God, please, oh, please, let me build 2,000 units in 1945, and if it be in accordance with Thy divine purpose let me accumulate $250,000 in cash during that time.

In 1946 Johnson did become regional vice president of the National Association of Home Builders. He earned applause along with William J. Levitt as an innovator, and a reputation from a 1952 article, "That Prayin' Millionaire from Memphis," in the *Saturday Evening Post*. In 1950, a year in which he collected nearly $1 million from his rental properties, Johnson built a $65,000 mansion for himself in Memphis. In 1960 he claimed to have built 25,000 homes.

Johnson's fame brought him a second career. In 1952 Kemmons Wilson, a younger Memphis homebuilder, recognized the need for a national chain of quality motels but exhausted his credit in building three local ones. Wilson turned to Johnson for assistance in 1953. The two entrepreneurs formed a twenty-three-year partnership, creating the largest hotel-motel chain in the world, Holiday Inns of America, which had reached $1 billion in sales by 1970. Johnson held the presidency until 1969 and remained vice president of the board until 1975.

Johnson contributed his superior skill with financing and public relations to Holiday Inns, but Wilson was the dominant partner, and his more secular outlook ultimately prevailed. Johnson's open Bible might remain in every room, but his prohibition of alcohol did not last. He was eventually persuaded that the success of Holiday Inns required opening bars and taverns. The chain did not add gambling, however, until after his retirement.

Johnson managed other business enterprises, including nursing homes and hospital chains. He also devoted himself to Christian evangelism and fund-raising, cochairing a $10 million campaign for the Southern Baptist Theological Seminary in Louisville. In 1977 he sought to raise a billion dollars for the World Crusade for Christ. Contacting a thousand millionaires, he asked for $1 million each, and gained commitments of $200 million before a second heart attack forced him to drop the work in 1981. His final, fatal heart attack occurred on 27 April 1988, and he was buried in Memorial Park in Memphis.

★

A collection of newspaper clippings is in the Mississippi Valley Collection, University of Memphis library. Johnson's autobiography, written with Eldon Roark, was published twice, first as *Work Is My Play* (1973), and again as *Together We Build: The Life and Faith of Wallace E. Johnson* (1978). See also Kemmons Wilson, *Half Luck and Half Brains: The Kemmons Wilson, Holiday Inn Story* (1996). A useful article is Harold H. Martin, "That Prayin' Millionaire from Memphis," *Saturday Evening Post* (26 Jan. 1952). An obituary is in the *Memphis Commercial Appeal* (28 Apr. 1988).

DAVID M. TUCKER

JOHNSON, William Julius ("Judy") (*b.* 26 October 1899 in Snow Hill, Maryland; *d.* 15 June 1989 in Wilmington, Delaware), infielder and manager in the Negro baseball leagues who is considered one of the best third basemen of all time and was elected to the National Baseball Hall of Fame in 1975.

Johnson was the second of three children of William Henry Johnson, a merchant seaman, shipbuilder, factory worker, boxing coach, and athletic director of the Negro Settlement House in Wilmington, where the family moved when young Johnson was about five. His mother was Annie Lee Johnson. He attended Frederick Douglas Elementary School and Howard High School, from which he dropped out to work as a stevedore, factory worker, and semiprofessional baseball player. As a youngster he played on both integrated and segregated baseball, football, and basketball teams in Wilmington.

Johnson began playing semipro baseball in 1917 for five dollars per game for a number of teams in the area. His first club may have been the Chester Stars, who on Sundays traveled to Atlantic City, New Jersey, and were known as the Bacharach Giants. He soon began to play with the Philadelphia Hilldales, and their informally aligned "farm club" of younger players, the Madison Stars. From 1919 to 1921 he bounced back and forth between these two clubs, joining the Hilldales full time in 1921. It was during those years that he picked up the nickname "Judy," given to him because he resembled a veteran Hilldale player named Judy Gans.

Judy Johnson. NATIONAL BASEBALL HALL OF FAME LIBRARY, COOPERSTOWN, N.Y.

The Hilldales became charter members of the Negro Eastern League in 1922, and Johnson became their regular third baseman. He led the Hilldales to three pennants in a row from 1923 to 1925, recording stellar batting averages ranging from .280 to .392. (Negro League statistics were not recorded or published with the same precision as white professional baseball statistics.) He played in the first Negro World Series in 1924, leading all hitters with an average variously reported as either .341 or .364, but the Hilldales lost to the Kansas City Monarchs. In 1925 they beat the Monarchs in a rematch, as Johnson hit .300.

Johnson married Anita T. Irons, his childhood sweetheart, on 27 December 1923. Anita was a schoolteacher for forty-nine years, and Judy credited her income with allowing him the luxury of playing baseball. She died in 1986. They adopted one daughter, Loretta, who was Anita's niece. Loretta later married major league ballplayer Bill Bruton.

A beaning in 1926 led to lower reported batting averages for the next several years, although Johnson did continue to post averages in the .350 range while playing in the Cuban leagues during the winters of the late 1920s. In 1929 he returned to form, recording a batting average variously reported as either .383 or .416, stealing twenty-two bases, and being named Most Valuable Player by two African-American newspapers, the *Pittsburgh Courier* and the *Chicago Defender*.

In 1930 Johnson became player-manager of the independent major-league-level Homestead Grays of the Pittsburgh area. It was during this season that, with an injured catcher on his team, he invited a youngster named Josh Gibson onto the field to take over, thus launching Gibson's Hall of Fame career. For the 1931 season Johnson returned to the Philadelphia area to play for and manage the Darby Daisies, a spinoff of the Hilldale club. In 1932 Johnson returned to Homestead, now a member of the East-West League. In midseason Johnson and most of the team jumped over to the Pittsburgh Crawfords.

Johnson continued to hit and play well and in 1935 was captain of the Crawford club, which many consider to be the greatest Negro League team ever. His teammates included future Hall of Famers "Cool Papa" Bell, Oscar Charleston, Josh Gibson, and Satchel Paige. The Crawfords defeated the New York Cubans in the Negro National League playoffs that year for the championship of black baseball. Johnson played two more seasons with the Crawfords, retiring after the 1937 season.

Johnson is remembered as a fine, line-drive hitter who hit for high averages; his lifetime batting average was probably around .340. He was a slick and graceful fielder, drawing comparisons to Brooks Robinson and Pie Traynor, the best ever at third base. Johnson was known as a clutch player, able to rise to the occasion and perform well in important situations. He was considered an intelligent ballplayer, was adept at stealing signals from the opposing team, and was a student of the game. He was a leader and a steadying influence on his teammates.

The five-foot, eleven-inch Johnson weighed about 160 pounds and was a neat man and a snappy dresser. He threw and batted right-handed. He played in two East-West games, the Negro League equivalent of the All-Star Game. This game did not begin until 1933, late in Johnson's career. In 1982 he and Ray Dandridge tied for the greatest Negro League third basemen in a poll of their surviving peers.

After his playing days Johnson coached semipro baseball and basketball, drove a taxicab and a school bus, worked in a factory, and operated a general store with his brother in Marshallton, Delaware, a suburb of Wilmington. In 1951 he became a scout for the major league Philadelphia Athletics. He began scouting for the Milwaukee Braves in 1957 and scouted for the Philadelphia Phillies from 1961 to 1974. He finished out his scouting career for the Los Angeles Dodgers from 1974 to 1977. Along the way he discovered and signed Richie Allen and Bill Bruton, and could have signed Hank Aaron for the Athletics, but they reportedly balked at the $3,500 asking price.

In 1954 the Athletics hired Johnson as the first African American in a coaching role for a major league ballclub. His job was to work with Bob Trice and Vic Power, two African-American players whom the Athletics had brought aboard. This assignment apparently lasted through spring training only, and Johnson thus is not generally credited as the first black coach in the majors.

From 1971 to 1974 Johnson served as a member of the National Baseball Hall of Fame Committee on the Negro Baseball Leagues, a group that helped choose the Negro Leaguers for enshrinement at Cooperstown. In 1975 he stepped down from that committee long enough to be voted into the Hall of Fame himself, an achievement he considered the pinnacle of his successful career. Johnson was also a member of the Maryland and Delaware sports halls of fame. In retirement he lived in a modest bungalow in Marshallton.

Johnson, a member of Wilmington's Haven United Methodist Church, died of complications arising from a stroke. He was buried in Wilmington's Silverbrook cemetery.

★

A biographical clippings file for Johnson is in the National Baseball Hall of Fame in Cooperstown, New York. Art Rust, Jr., *Get That Nigger Off the Field* (1976), devotes ten pages to Johnson. Useful articles include Al Harvin, "Recognize Me Now," *Black Sports* (June 1973); David Kerrane and Rod Beaton, "Judy Johnson: Reminiscences by the Great Ballplayer," *Delaware Today* (May 1977); Frederic Kelly, "Of Greatness Confined to a Harsher Time," *Philadelphia Inquirer* (11 Sept. 1978); James E. Newton, "William 'Judy' Johnson: Delaware's Folk Hero of the Diamond," *Negro History Bulletin* (fall 1980); and Paul Green, "Baseball and William 'Judy' Johnson," *Sports Collectors Digest* (2 Sept. 1983). Obituaries are in the *Wilmington News-Journal* (16 June 1989) and the *New York Times* (17 June 1989; the *Times* gives the date of death as 14 June).

TIMOTHY J. WILES

JORGENSEN, Christine (*b.* 30 May 1926 in New York City; *d.* 3 May 1989 in San Clemente, California), entertainer who in the early 1950s underwent the first well-publicized sex-change operation.

Jorgensen, christened George William Jorgensen, Jr., grew up in a close-knit Danish-American household on Dudley Avenue in the Throgs Neck section of the Bronx. Her fa-

Christine Jorgesen, *c.* 1952. ARCHIVE PHOTOS

ther, George Jorgensen, a contractor and carpenter, her mother, Florence Davis Hansen, and her older sister, Dorothy, might not have known of young George's secret desire to become a woman, but they firmly supported her after her sex change. Until she went to Denmark for her operations in May 1950, when she was almost twenty-four, Jorgensen's life was full of frustration and doubt. Frail and effeminate, she felt trapped inside an underdeveloped male body, as Jorgensen later recounted in her autobiography. She felt attracted to men but did not identify herself as gay.

Jorgensen's career also seemed adrift after she graduated from Christopher Columbus High School. Although she would later be dubbed the GI who became a woman, Jorgensen's fourteen-month stint in the army as a private first class performing clerical duties in Fort Dix, New Jersey, could not have been less distinguished. When she was drafted in October 1945 she weighed less than 100 pounds. While she was in basic training at Camp Polk, near Shreveport, Louisiana, "target practice with a carbine ceased to be a problem of accuracy—for me, it became a challenge in weight training," she wrote. She was honorably discharged in December 1946.

Although Jorgensen had an interest in film and photography, taking courses at professional schools and holding jobs on the fringe of the film industry, her career did not take off. In 1947 she went to Hollywood but could not find a job and, disillusioned, moved back to New York City a year later.

Jorgensen was determined to find out what could be done to change her body. She sought out medical experts, read books, enrolled at the Manhattan Medical and Dental Assistant's School, and went so far as taking ethinyl estradiol tablets (a synthetic form of estrogen) without a prescription. On 1 May 1950 Jorgensen left for Denmark on the liner *Stockholm* and stayed with friends in a Copenhagen suburb.

Tests began in early August at the Statens Seruminstitut. She took female hormone injections to effect what is known as a chemical castration. She also underwent psychological evaluation, in addition to plastic surgery that had nothing to do with her sex change. (The surgery was done on her ears because she felt they were protruding.) The first sex-change operation was performed on 24 September 1951, to remove the glands that produce male hormones. In May 1952 George Jorgensen chose the name Christine, in honor of her doctor, Christian Hamburger, for her new identity. For the first time in her life, according to Jorgensen, she put on women's clothes and makeup.

In the summer of 1952 Jorgensen journeyed around Denmark, making a travel film along the way. In November she entered Rigs Hospital for the second operation, to remove her male sex organs. While she was recuperating from this operation, her sex change became public. "Bronx GI Becomes a Woman. Dear Mom and Dad, Son Wrote, I Have Now Become Your Daughter," announced a press-service wire on 1 December 1952. As soon as the *New York Daily News* broke the story ("Ex-GI Becomes Blonde Beauty" was the front-page headline), Jorgensen became a fixture in tabloid newspapers.

Initially Jorgensen was appalled by the media frenzy, but she later agreed to tell her story, for $20,000, to *American Weekly* magazine, which promoted it as "the most dramatic transformation of modern times—told by the courageous woman who was once a man." Soon after returning to New York City in February 1953, she used the money to move from the Bronx to Massapequa, on Long Island, New York. Jorgensen continued to capitalize on her celebrity and embarked on a career as an entertainer. She toured briefly with her travel film of Denmark and in August made her nightclub debut, paired with Myles Bell, at the Copa Club in Pittsburgh.

Jorgensen was regarded with curiosity, mockery, and disdain. She was voted "Woman of the Year" by the Scandinavian Societies of Greater New York in 1953. Although she toured internationally, she was banned from performing for the U.S. military personnel in Germany. In Washington, D.C., she was asked not to use women's public toilets; in Cuba, a calypso song called "Christine of Denmark" was a hit. She also performed in regional theaters. In May 1954 she underwent plastic surgery in New Jersey to give her genital area a more feminine appearance.

Jorgensen never married, but she received a proposal from John Traub, a labor-union statistician. According to Jorgensen, the marriage would have taken place had the marriage application not been rejected on the ground that her birth certificate stated her sex as male.

In 1970 Irving Rapper made a feature-length film, *The Christine Jorgensen Story,* based on Jorgensen's autobiography. Jorgensen retired to Laguna Niguel, California, in 1971 and attempted a comeback in the early 1980s. She also gave lectures on gender identity on college campuses. Jorgensen died of bladder and lung cancer.

Jorgensen never regretted her decision to change her sex. "I feel very content with what I am and who I am," she told *Newsweek* in 1981. The operations transformed her from "an inhibited, introverted half-person" to "a happy, whole human being," she wrote in her autobiography. Despite her enlightened understanding of her own sexuality, however, she seemed less sympathetic toward homosexuality and the women's liberation movement.

Jorgensen remains an icon in the transgender community, often spoken of in the same breath as the tennis player and coach Renée Richards and other pioneering transsexuals. Even though Jorgensen pursued her desire to become a woman for her personal well-being, without intending her story to become public, the massive press coverage of her case in the 1950s pushed transsexualism into the public forum for the first time. "History, for so many of us, really began with Christine Jorgensen," said Rachel Pollack of the Gender Identity Project at the Lesbian and Gay Community Services Center in New York City. In that pre–sexual revolution era, Jorgensen helped many young people confused about their sexuality realize that they were not alone.

★

Christine Jorgensen, *Christine Jorgensen: A Personal Autobiography* (1967), gives the most complete biographical information on her life. There are no book-length biographies of Jorgensen, but several books on transsexualism, such as Leslie Feinberg, *Transgender Warriors* (1996), touch on her influences. An obituary is in the *New York Times* (4 May 1989).

JEFFREY H. CHEN

K

KAHANE, Meir (*b.* 1 August 1932 in Brooklyn, New York; *d.* 5 November 1990 in New York City), rabbi, organization official, and politician who founded the Jewish Defense League and the Israeli political party Kach.

Kahane, born Martin David Kahane, began using the first name Meir after his rabbinical ordination in 1957. His father, Charles Kahane, who had emigrated from Palestine to the United States at the age of eighteen, was a rabbi in the Bensonhurst section of Brooklyn. Kahane's mother, Sonia (Trainin) Kahane, who was born in Dvinsk, Latvia, was a traditional rabbi's wife and mother. Kahane had one brother.

Kahane grew up in a middle-class neighborhood in Brooklyn and obtained both his elementary and high school education at the Yeshiva of Flatbush, a modern Orthodox day school. At Brooklyn College he earned a B.A. in 1954, and at the Mirrer Yeshiva he was ordained a rabbi in 1957. He received an LL.B. from New York Law School in 1956 and an M.A. in international affairs from New York University in 1957. He married Libby Blum in 1955; they had two sons and two daughters.

Kahane was profoundly influenced by the Nazi genocide during World War II. Through his father he was exposed to the philosophy of Vladimir (Ze'ev) Jabotinsky, founder of the Revisionist Zionist movement, and he was deeply affected by the Jews' struggle against the British policy of limiting their immigration into Palestine. In 1946 Kahane joined Betar, the paramilitary youth movement affiliated with the Revisionists. Under the leadership of Menachem Begin, the Revisionist movement eventually became Herut, Israel's right-wing nationalist political party. As a teenager Kahane participated in Zionist demonstrations.

In 1958 Kahane began serving as rabbi of the Howard Beach Jewish Center in the borough of Queens in New York City. This was a conservative synagogue, however, and Kahane had to give up the post because he was too orthodox for the community. At that time he was taken under the wing of Rabbi Sholom Klass, publisher of the *Brooklyn Daily* (soon renamed the *Jewish Press*), an English-language weekly that had a circulation of more than 200,000. Kahane started as a sportswriter in 1960 and later became editor; his byline, Michael King, enabled him to publish his evolving political ideas.

During the mid-1960s Kahane renewed his friendship with Joseph Churba, whom he had met in his Betar days, and the two became involved with federal government agencies and congressional committees (Kahane was rumored to be an FBI informant). In 1965 they founded Consultants Research Associates in New York City to do contract research for the government and the July Fourth Movement to marshal support for the war in Vietnam among college students. In 1967 they wrote a book, *The Jewish Stake in Vietnam,* advocating Jewish support for the war. But by late 1967 Kahane had abandoned these activ-

Meir Kahane in Jerusalem, 1986. ARCHIVE PHOTOS

ities, accepting the position of rabbi at the Traditional Synagogue of Rochdale Village in Queens.

The late 1960s saw an upsurge in violent crime and anti-Semitism afflicting less affluent Jewish residents in older, changing areas of American cities. Aided by two members of his congregation, Bertram Zweibon and Mort Dolinsky, Kahane founded the Jewish Defense League (JDL) in 1968 to help Jews protect themselves. Its slogan, "Never Again," was created by Holocaust survivors. Kahane left his rabbinical post and resigned his editorship at the *Jewish Press;* he devoted all his time to the JDL, which quickly became known for its militance, to the point of running into difficulties with the federal government because of its use of strong-arm and armed tactics.

In his book *Never Again!* (1971) Kahane elaborated on his ideology, predicting a huge rise in anti-Semitism in America and advocating mass emigration to Israel. He was influenced by the Black Panthers in his militant stand, and he instituted classes in karate and weapons training for JDL members. During a strike by the largely Jewish United Federation of Teachers in 1968, the JDL led confrontations with blacks who were demanding community control of schools. Kahane's flair for theatrics ensured press coverage of JDL activities, but his main arena of success was among high school and college youth. In 1970 the JDL began an intensive anti-Soviet campaign using direct confrontation against Soviet cultural, commercial, and diplomatic representatives. For these actions Kahane was arrested several times, and in July 1971 he was fined $5,000 and given a five-year suspended sentence for conspiring to manufacture explosives. He would later serve a year in prison after the United States government revoked his probation in 1975 because of letters he wrote from Israel directing his associates in America to assassinate Russian and Arab diplomats.

Mainstream Jewish organizations barred Kahane access, and most Israeli leaders shunned him. In searching for outside support, he allied himself in 1971 with Joseph Colombo, Sr., head of the Italian-American Civil Rights League, and with Dr. Thomas W. Matthew, a conservative black leader.

In September 1971 Kahane moved to Israel, where he was wooed by the extreme right-wing parties. He decided instead to form his own party, Kach, which had at the center of its platform the policy of either inducing Arabs to leave the West Bank voluntarily or expelling them. He ran for the Knesset (Parliament) unsuccessfully in 1973 and 1977, and finally won a seat in 1984. His ideas so horrified mainstream Israelis, however, that in 1988 his party was outlawed on the grounds that it was racist and "Nazi-like," and incompatible with democracy.

On 5 November 1990 Kahane was shot down in a New York City hotel, allegedly by a Palestinian Arab. He died in Bellevue Hospital and was buried in Israel. As of 1998 no one had been convicted of his murder.

Meir Kahane was one of the most controversial American Jews of his generation. Condemned as a demagogue, a racist, a charlatan, and an advocate of senseless violence, he was also praised as a man with an apocalyptic vision who took actions in confronting the Russians that did more to help free Soviet Jewry than anyone else.

★

See Robert I. Friedman, *The False Prophet—Rabbi Meir Kahane: From FBI Informant to Knesset Member* (1990). An obituary is in the *New York Times* (7 Nov. 1990).

SARA REGUER

KAYE, Danny (*b.* 18 January 1913 in Brooklyn, New York; *d.* 3 March 1987 in Los Angeles, California), comedian, actor, and singer of stage, films, and television.

Kaye was born David Daniel Kaminski (sometimes spelled Kaminsky or Kominsky), the son of Jacob Kaminski, a tailor, and Clara Nemerovsky. His parents were Ukrainian-Jewish immigrants who had two older boys. Raised in Brooklyn's East New York section, he dropped out of Thomas Jefferson High School shortly before graduation.

Tall, slim, and athletically agile, Kaye had a highly expressive face marked by a long nose and topped by wavy, red hair. He was the "Red" in Red and Blackie, a teenage duo he formed with a friend, with whom he hitchhiked to Miami Beach to perform. His most successful early endeavor was as a "tummler" (Yiddish for a kind of general entertainer) at Catskill Mountain "borscht belt" resorts; he did this for five summers. During one off-season, he was fired from an insurance firm after making a $36,000 error. Taking the name Danny Kaye, he joined a vaudeville act, the Three Terpsichoreans, in 1933, playing tank towns and eventually touring to the Far East in *La Vie Paris* (1933–1934). His funniest bit stemmed from an accident in which he split his pants. His experiences with audiences that did not speak English encouraged his aptitude at supple physicality, hand gestures, and authentic-sounding but nonsense dialects. He avoided Jewish-related material; in fact, he later disparaged Jewish comics who exploited their ethnicity. Scat singing was another of his specialties, as was his capacity for double talk, especially with the nonsense syllables "git-gat-giddle." Kaye displayed this knack in such songs as "Minnie the Moocher," encouraging his audiences to join the choruses.

Danny Kaye, *c.* 1950. HULTON-DEUTSCH COLLECTION/CORBIS

After quitting the vaudeville show in 1934, Kaye struggled. He performed under miscellaneous circumstances, such as assisting fan dancer Sally Rand and cavorting in film shorts, before he made an inauspicious London debut in 1938 as straight man to Nick Long, Jr. In 1939 he scored in New York in *Sunday Night Varieties,* a socially conscious cabaret revue. A year later he married Sylvia Fine, who had been the revue's pianist, lyricist, and composer. They had one daughter. Sylvia Fine Kaye was a powerful influence on Kaye's career, writing much of his witty special material (and often serving as his accompanist) and for many years guiding his artistic development. A journalist quipped that Kaye "had a Fine head on his shoulders." Although they never divorced, the relationship was stormy, and they often lived separately, especially after Kaye's career became bicoastal.

Kaye performed in a series of revues at Pennsylvania's Camp Tamiment in 1939. His successes included Fine's "Anatole of Paris," "Stanislavsky," and "Pavlova," which joined his permanent repertory. These shows were amalgamated on Broadway as *The Straw Hat Review* (1939).

Kaye's multiple talents made him difficult to define. He continued to develop in nightclubs, hitting it big at La Martinique in New York City in 1940. That performance led Moss Hart to create for him the role of the effeminate fashion photographer Russell Paxton in the musical *Lady in the Dark* (1941), written by Hart and Kurt Weill and starring Gertrude Lawrence. In this show, Kaye introduced "Tschaikovsky," one of the rapid-fire tongue twisters (written by his wife) that became a trademark. He continued his New York success with a held-over engagement at the Palace Theatre (1941). He also won the starring role of Jerry Walker in Cole Porter's musical *Let's Face It* (1941), in which he introduced Fine's "Melody in 4-F," another signature number. After he moved in 1943 to Hollywood to act in films, he returned to the Broadway stage only once, in 1970, for *Two by Two,* Richard Rodgers's musical about Noah and the ark.

Kaye, who could not serve in the military during World War II because of a back problem, instead sold war bonds and, with the United Service Organizations (USO), performed abroad for the armed forces. He later entertained troops during the Korean and Vietnam conflicts. He outraged an English theater company when he canceled his appearance with them in a classic comedy in order to perform for Israelis following the Six-Day War in 1967; he performed again for the Israelis during the Yom Kippur War in 1973. His humanitarian persona was enhanced in 1955, when he began traveling the globe as a goodwill ambassador for the United Nations Children's Fund (UNICEF), seeking relief for suffering children and making two well-received documentaries of his efforts. Kaye had a remarkable rapport with children, and many of his later performances were child-oriented.

Kaye made seventeen feature films, several of them highly successful, but Hollywood usually had a hard time deciding how best to use his idiosyncratic talents, and only a few films are memorable. Often he played a wimpy, sexless, "poor soul" character. In *Up in Arms* (1944), his hair was dyed blond, and he exhibited his verbal dexterity in "The Lobby Number." Other movies include *Wonder Man* (1945), the first of his several multiple-role movies; *The Kid from Brooklyn* (1946); *The Secret Life of Walter Mitty* (1947), in which he had six roles; *A Song Is Born* (1948); *The Inspector General* (1949), which featured his counterpoint number "The Gypsy"; *On the Riviera* (1951), another double-role film; and *Hans Christian Andersen* (1952), a great hit in which he sang such tunes as "Wonderful, Wonderful Copenhagen." *Knock on Wood* (1954), in which he did a comical ballet routine, was the first film produced (in collaboration with Paramount) by Kaye's own company, Dena Productions, named for his daughter. That was followed by *White Christmas* (1954); *The Court Jester* (1955), noteworthy for its hilarious "vestle with the pestle" duologue; *Merry Andrew* (1958), in which he juggled; *Me and the Colonel* (1958), a nonmusical work in which he played a rare Jewish role; *The Five Pennies* (1959), for which he mastered trumpet fingering; *On the Double* (1961), another double-role job; *The Man from the Diners' Club* (1963); and *The Madwoman of Chaillot* (1969). Most of his later films were considered failures.

Kaye had his own radio program in 1945, the *Danny Kaye Show,* but he had to be seen to be appreciated. On television, to which he came relatively late, he and his UNICEF activities were the subjects of a documentary, *The Secret Life of Danny Kaye* (1956), produced by Edward R. Murrow for the series *See It Now.* Kaye starred in a number of specials in the early 1960s and guest-starred on other programs. For four years, 1963–1967, he had his own weekly program, *The Danny Kaye Show,* which won an Emmy in 1964. Kaye was a voice for an animated version of *The Emperor's New Clothes* (1972), hosted *Danny Kaye's Look-In at the Metropolitan Opera* (1976), and had straight roles in several dramas, including *Skokie* (1980). Kaye could not read music but had an inordinate fondness for classical works, and he acquired the ability to conduct—with healthy dollops of comedy thrown in—major symphony orchestras, which he often did to raise money (eventually totaling $10 million) for musicians' welfare funds.

Kaye's versatility was amazing. Despite a lack of training, he danced with such surprising grace and technique that ballet stars were impressed, and he also became a recording star. Offstage, he was licensed to fly jumbo jets, achieved professional skill at Chinese cooking, had an inveterate interest in medicine (he would have liked to become a doctor) and psychiatry (he was a frequent analysand), was an outstanding golfer and Ping-Pong player, and made excellent investments, including part ownership of the Seattle Mariners baseball franchise. Some have attributed his diverse interests to a personality streak akin to that of James Thurber's fantasizing character, Walter Mitty. Mitty was, after all, one of Kaye's best screen roles, but Kaye did more than fantasize.

Despite his fame, his ability to make and spend money, and his loving friends, Kaye could be an insecure depressive with an ego that sometimes made him hot-tempered and difficult to work with. Perhaps most notorious of such occasions was when he appeared in *Two by Two.* Having injured a foot during the run of the play, he appeared in a wheelchair and used both this vehicle and his crutches to improvise scenes that drove his fellow players to distraction and even upset theatergoers, who thought he was destroying the integrity of the work.

After Kaye's death, Donald Spoto's 1992 biography of the actor Laurence Olivier took seriously the much-rumored speculation that the men had been lovers. Martin Gottfried's Kaye biography, while not shying from suggestions about the entertainer's heterosexual affairs, casts doubts on Spoto's allegations of homosexuality.

Kaye had a devoted international following and was intimate with notables in the highest reaches of government and society, including the British royal family. Gossip linked him romantically to Princess Margaret. The British public got to know him during his enormously successful engagements at London's Palladium from 1948 to 1952. A memorable bit saw him sitting on the edge of the stage, smoking, and casually chatting with his fans. Many thought him the most popular entertainer in postwar Britain. Kaye was especially effective in front of live spectators, where his warmth was most immediate, and he played numerous highly lucrative engagements for huge audiences.

His performing talents and humanitarian endeavors were recognized with a special Tony Award (1953), a special Academy Award (1954), the Sam S. Shubert Award for outstanding contributions to the American theater (1970–1971), the Jean Hersholt Humanitarian Award (1982), and the Kennedy Center Honors (1984).

Kaye died in Los Angeles of a heart attack brought on by hepatitis, which he contracted from transfusions following heart surgery. He was cremated; a monumental bench in his honor is in Kensico Cemetery in Valhalla, New York.

★

Kaye's papers are housed in the Music Division of the Library of Congress. A good interview with Kaye is in Roy Newquist, *Showcase* (1966). The chief biographies of Kaye are Michael Freedland, *The Secret Life of Danny Kaye* (1985), and Martin Gottfried, *Nobody's Fool: The Lives of Danny Kaye* (1994). His work is examined in Karin Adir, *The Great Clowns of American Television*

(1988), and Tom Shales, *Legends: Remembering America's Greatest Stars* (1989). See also John Culhane, "Unforgettable Danny Kaye," *Reader's Digest* (June 1988). Obituaries are in *Variety* and the *New York Times* (both 4 Mar. 1987).

SAMUEL L. LEITER

KAYE, Sammy (*b.* 13 March 1910 in Lakewood, Ohio; *d.* 2 June 1987 in Ridgewood, New Jersey), bandleader and composer most popular during the swing era of the 1930s and 1940s who survived for fifty years in the business, selling millions of records and appearing regularly on radio and television.

Sammy Kaye, born Samuel Zarnocay, was the blue-eyed, sandy-haired son of Czech immigrants Samuel and Mary Zarnocay and grew up in a suburb of Cleveland, Ohio. Excelling in track and basketball, he went to Ohio University on a track scholarship and earned a bachelor of science degree in civil engineering in 1933. He played clarinet and alto saxophone, and he earned extra money in college by forming a band. After receiving his undergraduate degree, he opened a nightspot called the Varsity Inn near the university and expanded his band's tour schedule. Although many Americans of Eastern European descent had settled in his native northern Ohio, he tried to distance himself somewhat from his heritage. Early in his musical career, he not only adopted his stage name, but he also took elocution lessons to get rid of his accent.

Sammy Kaye. COURTESY OF WHITNEY SMITH. © APA.

The Sammy Kaye Band won considerable attention in 1935 when the NBC network broadcast a performance live from the Cleveland Country Club. Early on, the ensemble became known for a soothing, reedy, "sweet band" sound, after the fashion of Guy Lombardo and marked by gentle, bubbly clarinets and saxophones. Never known as a virtuoso himself, Kaye avoided doing solos and seldom called for them from his bandsmen. He preferred featuring vocalists, sometimes employing as many as six. His vocalists often sang "song titles," meaning that they often introduced a brief phrase of the lyrics before the band came in. Fond of gimmicks, Kaye used the slogan "Swing and Sway with Sammy Kaye" for years, and he had a routine called "So You Want to Lead a Band," which involved inviting audience members to compete for a baton and the chance to use it. Music critics did not always sing Kaye's praises, and some referred to his style as "Mickey Mouse music." Big-band historian George T. Simon found the sound overly cute in the 1930s, but he considered Kaye an astute businessman, adept at setting tempos ideal for dancing and at fronting his band with finesse.

Kaye's best-known song compositions include "Daddy" and "There Will Never Be Another You" in the early 1940s and "Harbor Lights" from 1950. He also enjoyed success with "It Isn't Fair," "Penny Serenade," "The White Cliffs of Dover," "My Buddy," "That's My Desire," and "Careless Hands," among others. Kaye wrote the orchestra's theme song, "Until Tomorrow," as well as "Hawaiian Sunset" and "Tell Me You Love Me." One of his most famous original tunes was "Remember Pearl Harbor." He was conducting his orchestra live on the radio on 7 December 1941 when the announcer broke in with the news about the Japanese attack. When Kaye released the song several days later, it sold a million records.

From 1937 to 1956 the Sammy Kaye Orchestra, as it became known, performed on many radio programs for the ABC, NBC, CBS, and MBS networks. NBC's *Sunday Serenade* was one of his best-known shows; others were *The Sammy Kaye Show, Saturday Night Serenade, Sammy Kaye Showroom,* and *Your Navy Show.* In the 1950s he made the transition to television, eventually hosting programs on all three major networks. Simon, who had criticized Kaye's band years earlier, directed and produced his television programming and acknowledged that the bandleader had improved his music. Starting in 1951 *The Sammy Kaye Show* ran on CBS for about a year, then briefly on NBC in 1953, and finally on ABC in 1958 and 1959. Like several other big-band leaders on television, Kaye never equaled his radio success. Publicity shots often showed Kaye grinning, and he told the press how much he had enjoyed the swing era. He was known for paying musicians well and seeing to it that they traveled first class but also for holding long rehearsals and sometimes taking a dictatorial attitude. He continued working with the band throughout his life.

Kaye lived for years in New York City. By the time he debuted there at the Commodore Hotel in 1938, his orchestra was already known around the country. In 1940 he guest-conducted a seventeen-piece Works Progress Administration orchestra at a free dance in Central Park, where a thousand couples did the jitterbug. Kaye married Ruth Knox Elden on 2 March 1940. She was granted a divorce in Cleveland in 1956.

Over the years Kaye grew wealthy in various enterprises. He set up four music publishing firms, invested in bowling alleys, and dabbled in oil. In November 1953 a federal court granted Kaye and his manager, David Krengel, half interest in some potentially rich Kansas oil property from men who had obtained licenses on the land. The bandleader died of cancer at Valley Hospital in Ridgewood, New Jersey, after being hospitalized twice. His funeral took place at St. Jean de Baptiste Church in Manhattan.

As happened with many of his colleagues with famous dance bands, Kaye's music outlasted him. "Ghost bands," playing music from the libraries of Glenn Miller, Tommy Dorsey, and other bandleaders, continued to tour after their deaths with permission from their estates. In similar fashion, trumpeter Roger Thorpe took over the Sammy Kaye Orchestra about a year before Kaye died. Meanwhile, copies of Kaye's recordings and more than forty of his radio episodes are available, and his hit "Remember Pearl Harbor" can be heard in the 1987 Woody Allen film *Radio Days.*

★

Biographical information about Sammy Kaye can be found in Arthur Jackson, *The World of Big Bands: The Sweet and Singing Years* (1977); Leo Walker, *The Big Band Almanac* (1978); George T. Simon, *The Big Bands* (1981); Jon D. Swartz and Robert C. Reinehr, *Handbook of Old-Time Radio: A Comprehensive Guide to Golden Age Radio Listening and Collecting* (1993); and Ruth Benjamin and Arthur Rosenblatt, *The Movie Song Catalog* (1993). There are articles about Kaye in the *New York Times* (5 June 1940, 4 Sept. 1947, 1 Nov. 1953, and 21 July 1956). Obituaries are in the *New York Times* and *Chicago Tribune* (both 4 June 1987).

WHITNEY SMITH

KEELER, William Wayne (*b.* 5 April 1908 in Dalhart, Texas; *d.* 24 August 1987 in Bartlesville, Oklahoma), chief executive officer and chairman of the board of the Phillips Petroleum Company and Cherokee Nation leader.

Keeler was the son of William Keeler, a farmer and stockman, and Sarah Louisa Carr. He had five siblings, only two

William Keeler. UPI/CORBIS-BETTMANN

of whom lived to adulthood. The grandson of white businessmen who married mixed-blood Cherokee women, Keeler was one-sixteenth Cherokee. His family was involved in the oil and cattle business in the Cherokee Nation before it became part of Oklahoma in 1907. Born a year after Oklahoma achieved statehood, Keeler grew up in an upper-middle-class family in Bartlesville, a town in northeastern Oklahoma. Beginning in 1924, while still in high school, he worked during the summers for the town's major business, Phillips Petroleum Company.

After graduating from high school as valedictorian of his class in 1926, Keeler enrolled at the University of Kansas, where he studied chemical engineering on a Harry E. Sinclair scholarship. He continued working part-time for Phillips while he was a college student, but his studies were interrupted after Sinclair became embroiled in the Teapot Dome scandal and stopped funding his scholarships. In 1929 Keeler began working full-time at a Phillips refinery in Kansas City, where he earned rapid promotion and met Ruby Lucille Hamilton, a registered nurse. After their marriage in 1933, Keeler was transferred to Phillips refineries in Texas. The couple had three children: William Robert, Bradford Roger, and Kenneth Richard.

Experience in all phases of the refining process earned Keeler a job at Phillips headquarters in Bartlesville, Oklahoma, where he became the technical assistant to the vice president of the refining department in 1943. When U.S. involvement in World War II increased the need for oil, Keeler was dispatched to Mexico to supervise construction of an aviation gasoline refinery. By 1945, the young oilman had been promoted to manager of the Phillips Refining Department, and two years later he was named its vice president. Appointed vice president of the executive department and a member of the company's board of directors in 1951, he was elected to the company's executive committee three years later. Continuing to rise through the ranks of Phillips Petroleum Company, in 1956 he was named executive vice president, and in 1962 he was elevated to chairman of the executive committee. Five years later Keeler became president and chief executive officer of Phillips.

Both during and after World War II, Keeler worked closely with federal officials and served on many civilian advisory committees. Increasingly active in tribal affairs, he was named vice chairman of the Cherokee executive committee in 1948. When the appointed chief died in 1949, the executive committee endorsed Keeler to replace him. President Harry S. Truman named Keeler principal chief later that year. The government Keeler inherited was embryonic. He broadened representation of an appointed tribal council and used his own money to establish the Cherokee Foundation to stimulate economic and educational development among members of the tribe.

In the early 1960s, a legal case involving compensation for the Cherokee Outlet was settled, giving Keeler's evolving Cherokee government valuable seed money. Keeler used the money to expand tribal services. To promote pride, the chief established a national holiday, organized a national historical society, and raised funds to create a museum and cultural center on the site of the original Cherokee Female Seminary at Park Hill, Oklahoma. He secured land for a tribal headquarters complex south of Tahlequah, Oklahoma, the old Cherokee capital. Keeler's primary emphasis as chief was industrial development to improve the economic conditions of members of the tribe. Under his direction, the Cherokee Nation established a close working relationship with the federal government at a time when a new breed of militant American Indian leaders advocated confrontation.

In 1970 Congress authorized the Cherokee to elect their own leader. The next year, Keeler became the first elected chief since 1903 after receiving 75 percent of the votes. During his term as chief, he presided over the drafting of a new constitution for the Cherokee Nation. Although it did not go into effect until after his retirement, the constitution marked the final step in the reestablishment of representative tribal government.

In his dual capacities as an oilman and an Indian leader, Keeler served on national commissions and task forces, advised federal officials, and represented the government at home and abroad. During World War II he was the federal government's director of refining for the Petroleum Administration for War, and in 1952 he became chairman of the Military Petroleum Advisory Board in the U.S. Department of the Interior. President John F. Kennedy's secretary of the interior, Stewart L. Udall, appointed Keeler that June to head a task force to develop plans for reorganizing the Bureau of Indian Affairs. The following year, Keeler was called on to direct a study of BIA operations in Alaska. In 1965 President Lyndon B. Johnson appointed the Cherokee chief to the National Advisory Committee on the War on Poverty and the Presidential Committee on Economic Opportunity. President Richard M. Nixon named Keeler chairman of the President's Advisory Council on Minority Business Enterprise and a member of the National Park Service's Centennial Commission and the President's Council on Physical Fitness and Sports. Keeler was equally active in service to his community and state.

In 1973 Keeler reached the mandatory retirement age at Phillips, and two years later, after having led the Cherokee for over a quarter of a century, Keeler decided not to seek reelection as chief. When he left office, the Cherokee tribe had $50 million in assets, 65,000 acres of trust land, a staff of 700 people, and 10 business enterprises. Twice the recipient of the All-American Indian Award, Keeler was showered with recognition and honorary degrees that reflect the variety of his service. Colleagues at Phillips cited his integrity, leadership, and loyalty as well as his creative ideas and initiative. Ross O. Swimmer, his successor as chief of the Cherokee Nation, said Keeler "was the tribe" and credited him with the reestablishment of tribal government.

Keeler was not without critics, however. Some Cherokee questioned his lack of Indian heritage, claiming that their "chief" did not speak the language and was "for all intents and purposes a white man." A 1971 article in *Ramparts* suggested that Keeler used his association with the Cherokee to further the interests of Phillips and that he exaggerated the value of tribal programs in improving the incomes and living standards of poorer members of the tribe. In the mid-1960s, some Cherokee publicly questioned his administration of tribal funds, challenged his plans for representing the tribe's past, and criticized his employment of whites in key roles in preserving and interpreting Cherokee history. His critics also questioned real estate transactions, the location of funds deposited by the tribe, and Keeler's priorities. In tribal affairs, anti-Keeler sentiment went no further than protest. As chief executive officer of Phillips, however, Keeler encountered more serious charges. In December 1973 he pleaded guilty to making an illegal contribution of $100,000 to Nixon's 1972 presidential campaign, and three years later he and other former executives of Phillips were indicted for concealing $2.6 million of corporate funds from the Internal Revenue Service. This charge was dismissed when the court determined that the government had violated the plea bargain negotiated with the Watergate special prosecutor, Archibald Cox.

In 1987, after four years of failing health, Keeler died in Bartlesville, probably from Alzheimer's disease; he is buried in White Rose Cemetery in Bartlesville.

★

Keeler's career has been sketched in several anthologies of Native American leaders, including Marion E. Gridley, *Contemporary American Indian Leaders* (1972); and *Biographical Dictionary of Indians of the Americas*, 2d ed., vol. 1 (1991). Sandra Sac Parker, "William Wayne Keeler, 1908–1987: Cherokee Tribal Leader and Businessman," *Notable Native Americans,* ed. Sharon Malinowski and George H. J. Abrams (1995), raises questions about Keeler's motives. Keeler is featured in many articles, including William H. Radford, "Bill Keeler of Bartlesville . . . He's a Chief—a Big Chief—Both of Oil and Business," *Kansas City Star* (7 June 1964); and William D. Smith, "Cherokee Chief Is Phillips Man of Action," *New York Times* (13 Oct. 1968), both of which focus on Keeler's dynamic leadership of Phillips and the Cherokee Nation. Less flattering accounts of Keeler are Peter Collier, "The Theft of a Nation: Apologies to the Cherokees," *Ramparts* (Sept. 1970); and "The Shadow of W. S. Keeler . . . 'A Cherokee Watergate,' " *Akwesasne Notes* (early autumn 1975). Marjorie J. Lowe, " 'Let's Make It Happen': W. W. Keeler and Cherokee Renewal," *Chronicles of Oklahoma* 74 (summer 1996): 116–129, was written by a daughter of Keeler's first cousin and emphasizes Keeler's accomplishments. An obituary by Joseph E. Howell is in the *Tulsa Tribune* (24 Aug. 1987).

BRAD AGNEW

KEENY, Spurgeon Milton ("Sam") (*b.* 16 July 1893 in Shrewsbury, Pennsylvania; *d.* 20 October 1988 in Washington, D.C.), United Nations official who carried out family-planning and relief work in developing countries.

The son of Noah Milton and Estella (Fife) Keeny, Sam Keeny grew up in the Pennsylvania Dutch country, where his father was a farmer and flour miller. He was educated at a local Lutheran church until age twelve, when he quit and began working as a common laborer. Keeny continued studying Latin and Greek on his own, and without a high school diploma he was accepted, on special conditions, by Gettysburg College.

At Gettysburg, Keeny majored in English literature, was a member of the varsity track and tennis teams, was elected to Phi Beta Kappa, and graduated summa cum laude in

Spurgeon Keeny. COURTESY OF SPURGEON KEENY, JR.

1914. He spent the summer of 1915 at the University of Chicago and the following summer at Harvard University. From 1916 to 1920 he completed B.A. and M.A. degrees in English and social history as a Rhodes Scholar at Oxford University.

Keeny's distinguished public service career began in 1919 in Mesopotamia, where he was a volunteer for the Young Men's Christian Association. He assisted American troops in establishing order after World War I; helped repatriate Siberian, Estonian, Polish, and Czech prisoners of war; and directed delivery of relief supplies in Russia.

In 1921 Keeny married Amelia Smith; they had one son. The couple spent their honeymoon working in eastern Europe. Keeny next served two years (1922–1924) with Herbert Hoover's American Relief Administration and was responsible for delivering food and fuel to university students and teachers in the Soviet Union.

After his first stint abroad Keeny returned to America to resume work with the YMCA. For almost twenty years he held titles that included director of the association's press and executive secretary to the public affairs committee.

In 1943 the State Department invited Keeny to be chief of operations in Italy for the United Nations Relief and

Rehabilitation Administration. He worked with relocated persons and directed civilian relief after the Allies' invasions of North Africa and Italy. "I was doing the same thing I had done before," he said in an interview with the *New York Times.* "[I was] cleaning up after a war, getting people back home, rebuilding homes, and getting factories working again."

Keeny joined the United Nations International Children's Emergency Fund (UNICEF) in 1948. He worked as chief supply officer in Europe for two years, then was posted to Bangkok, Thailand, for three months. That three months turned into almost thirty years, years packed with vaccinating sick children, persuading Asian leaders to support family planning, and teaching peasants how to use contraception. Keeny documented his work in his 1957 book, *Half the World's Children,* and also wrote *Organizing National Family Planning Programs* (1972).

The man *Collier's* magazine (1955) dubbed "Asia's Best Friend" stood five feet, eight inches tall. His blue eyes, under bushy eyebrows, held an expression of friendliness. And no matter how official his duties, the broad-shouldered Keeny always dressed in old shirts and, occasionally, his only sports jacket. He was never without a pipe and hardly ever without a smile.

"You can't import enthusiasm," said Keeny. "The enthusiasm comes out of the work itself. . . . You become part of the program and are as anxious as the people themselves to see it succeed." His enthusiasm carried Keeny through dozens of Asian countries, where he fought a public health battle against malaria, yaws, and tuberculosis. On a budget of two to three cents per year per child, Keeny covered twenty-four countries and territories and traveled 100,000 miles annually from his base in Bangkok. In an article in the *Atlantic Monthly* (1955), Keeny wrote: "In Asia, with one third of the world's population, the job must be done on a gigantic scale. With penicillin costing a dime per treatment and a population willing to walk miles for it, the job will be finished."

Keeny's extensive travels, campaigns, and efforts resulted in thousands of health centers being equipped with drugs and milk, and millions of children being vaccinated with simple preventive medicines. In the *Collier's* article Howard Lewis wrote: "By the end of 1955, projects spurred by his intense drive will have brought protection against malaria to 150,000,000 people, against TB to 100,000,000 children, against yaws to 47,000,000 persons formerly menaced by loathsome skin disease." Keeny told Lewis, "I've seen enough sickness and death. . . . If we can change all that with a little effort, it would not only be absurd not to do it, it would be criminal."

But Keeny did not stop there. His next battle was overpopulation. In 1963, at the age of seventy, he moved from Thailand to Taiwan, as the Asian representative of the Population Council. "We are the last generation to have the opportunity to solve the population problem through orderly planning," said Keeny in *Life* magazine in 1967. "If we fail, it will be done with disorders, famine, and despair."

Over the course of fifteen years Keeny persuaded Asian governments to establish family-planning programs, and he trained men and women to work in clinics. His goals were twofold: distribution and education. While trying to respect taboos about sexuality, Keeny disseminated millions of condoms, loops, and pills throughout Taiwan and South Korea. Although he called himself the "roving supply man," he was also responsible for educating people about long-term birth control methods, such as sterilization and vasectomies. For several years he wrote a newsletter on his family-planning activities and distributed it throughout the countries in which he worked. In addition, he brought together public and private health organizations under the umbrella of family planning and population control.

Keeny told *Life,* "Our role is to let them know such a thing exists, make help available to them with the necessary kind of instruction, and generally to try to understand the problem from their point of view, not our own." He used pragmatism and persuasion to convince governments and families of the benefits of birth control and the necessity of smaller families. And it worked. Between 1960 and 1970 in South Korea alone, the population growth rate dropped from 3 to 2 percent per year.

After threatening to retire for more than twenty-five years, Keeny finally did so in 1978, when he returned to the United States. Even then he kept on working as a consultant to the Population Council and the World Bank, until, at the age of ninety-three, he died of a stroke.

Keeny helped millions of Asian children to reach adulthood and introduced tens of thousands of peasant women to birth control. A man whose passion for public health took him into the fields of Indonesia, the hospitals of Thailand, the governmental offices of Taiwan, and the homes of families in South Korea, he never stopped combating communicable diseases and overpopulation, treating each child in Asia as if it were his own. His work reduced annual population growth rates and cured children in substantial numbers. As he said in 1967, "What has been done is of course the merest beginning of what must be done."

★

The United Nations holds some of the papers Keeny wrote on humanitarian relief, public health, and family planning. An article by Keeny, "A Life for Ten Cents," in the *Atlantic Monthly* (June 1955), narrates his efforts in fighting tuberculosis and other diseases. Howard Lewis, "Asia's Best Friend," in *Collier's* (29 Apr. 1955), explains how Keeny achieved his public health success in Asia. "Champion of Birth Control," in *Life* (6 Oct. 1967), and "Taking On the Tide," in the *New York Times Magazine* (29 Aug.

1976), describe his family-planning work in detail. An obituary is in the *New York Times* (24 Oct. 1988).

ANNA GORMAN

KELMAN, Wolfe (*b.* 27 November 1923 in Vienna, Austria; *d.* 26 June 1990 in New York City), religious leader who was active in the Conservative branch of Judaism and in Christian-Jewish relations; he was instrumental in the modernization of the rabbinate and in extending ordination to women.

Wolfe Kelman was the second of six children (three boys and three girls) of Mirl Fish and Zvi Yehuda (Hersh Leib) Kelman, a rabbi descended from a long line of Hasidic rabbis. Wolfe's father immigrated to Canada in 1929, and Wolfe and his mother and siblings joined him there in 1930.

Wolfe attended public school in Toronto. When, at age thirteen, his father died, his mother stepped into the role of communal leader, offering religious and personal guidance. Kelman's studies at the University of Toronto were interrupted by service in the Royal Canadian Air Force from 1943 to 1945, after which he received, in 1946, his B.A. degree. He moved to the United States that year and earned his rabbinical degree and M.A. degree in Hebrew literature from the Jewish Theological Seminary (JTS) in New York City, both in 1950. He did postgraduate studies at Columbia University.

At JTS, Kelman became a disciple of Rabbi Abraham Joshua Heschel, whose dedication to Judaism, civil rights, and interfaith dialogue helped shape Kelman's professional life: "Heschel taught us that no religion has a monopoly on holiness," Kelman later wrote. He followed the advice of Heschel and JTS chancellor Louis Finkelstein, who urged Kelman not to become a congregational rabbi but rather a "civil servant" in the Conservative movement or, as he jokingly called himself, "an *un*civil servant." In 1951 Kelman became chief executive of the Rabbinical Assembly (RA), the professional association of Conservative rabbis. He then served as executive secretary, executive director, and finally, from 1951 to his retirement in August 1989, executive vice president. For many years Kelman oversaw RA publications such as the annual *Proceedings of the Rabbinical Assembly* and the *Weekday Prayer Book* (1961). On 2 March 1952 he married Jacqueline Miriam Levy, the daughter of the noted Reform rabbi Felix Levy. Their son, Levi Yehuda, was born in 1953. Their daughters were born soon after: Naamah Kathrine in 1955 and Abigail Tobie in 1956. The family lived in Riverdale in the Bronx and then moved to Manhattan, living in various apartments, including one at 210 West 101st Street, finally settling at 845 West End Avenue on the Upper West Side.

As executive vice president of the Rabbinical Assembly, Kelman presided over what he labeled "the professionalization of the rabbinate" during a period of extraordinary growth for the Conservative movement. He fought to obtain competitive salaries and benefits for rabbis, yet he personally took little credit for the reforms: "The status of rabbis improved because of the hundreds of good rabbis out there," he commented. As director of the Joint Placement Committee of the RA, United Synagogue, and JTS from 1951 to 1966, he helped more than 1,500 rabbis and rabbinical students find pulpits. Kelman mentored hundreds of rabbis, dispensing spiritual and practical advice, even occasionally counseling a rabbinical student that his talents might be better suited running a pizza parlor. During his tenure at the RA, membership grew from approximately 300 rabbis in 1951 to some 1,200 in 1989.

Kelman served on the executive council of the United Synagogue of America during the 1950s and early 1960s and on various committees of JTS. He spent 1957 and 1958 as visiting rabbi of the West London Synagogue. In 1962 Kelman became an American citizen. During the 1960s he helped revive the RA's 1930s social justice program, which led to Conservative rabbis championing civil rights on picket lines and marches, as well as from the pulpit. Joining Heschel in 1965 in Selma, Alabama, he marched with the Reverend Martin Luther King, Jr. Beginning in 1974 he served on the board of directors of the Hebrew Immigrant Aid Society. In 1986 he chaired the American section of the World Jewish Congress. He had served since 1968 on the governing council and from 1975 as chair of the cultural commission.

Kelman participated in many interfaith organizations. Serving on the International Jewish Committee on Interreligious Consultations, he represented the Jewish community with the Vatican, the World Council of Churches, and major Christian organizations in the United States, and he helped prepare Heschel for his meeting with Pope Paul VI. Kelman was a key participant in the talks that led to a Jewish delegation meeting for the first time with Pope John Paul II in Rome and Miami in 1987.

Meanwhile, Kelman taught homiletics from 1967 to 1973 at the Jewish Theological Seminary and history from 1973 to 1988. He was chair of the academic board of the Melton Research Center from 1969 to 1971. In 1976 he was invited to the Oxford Centre for Postgraduate Hebrew Studies in England as a visiting lecturer and he spent 1984 and 1985 in Israel as visiting professor of contemporary Jewish history at Hebrew University in Jerusalem.

Keenly interested in Jewish cultural, educational, historical, and sociological life, Kelman championed the writings of Elie Wiesel, Chaim Grade, and Heschel. He wrote major articles and reviews for the *American Jewish Year Book*, *Conservative Judaism* (a journal he helped found), and other publications. In 1978, to commemorate Kelman's twenty-five years of service to the Rabbinical Assembly, the

Rabbi Wolfe Kelman (*top right*) among several religious luminaries who gathered for an ecumenical service. ARCHIVE PHOTOS

RA published a Festschrift, *Perspectives on Jews and Judaism: Essays in Honor of Wolfe Kelman,* edited by Arthur Chiel. In 1986 Kelman agreed to serve on the first editorial board of the progressive journal *Tikkun*.

Kelman was most proud of his instrumental role in increasing women's participation in communal religious life, culminating in the ordination of Conservative women rabbis in 1985. "It was [my mother's] example," he explained, "that made me believe women could function as rabbis." On 24 July 1992, two years after Kelman's death, his daughter Naamah became the first woman rabbi ordained in Israel.

Maintaining an open house, Kelman was always available to his various constituencies in person or by telephone. His students joked that the afterlife had better have telephones for Kelman's use.

Diagnosed with malignant melanoma in 1989, Kelman retired from the RA that August but remained active in communal life. In 1990 he was appointed director of the Finkelstein Institute of Religious and Social Studies of the Jewish Theological Seminary and honored by New York City mayor Edward Koch at a special reception for service as a member of the informal Mayor's Advisory Board of Religious Leaders and for helping revive Jewish life on Manhattan's Upper West Side. Kelman died of cancer in 1990. He was buried in Lodi, New Jersey.

Although Wolfe Kelman worked behind the scenes, he was a major and vital force in American Conservative Judaism, helping to modernize, professionalize, and expand the rabbinate. Through an extraordinary network of contacts throughout the world, Kelman was involved in civil rights, interfaith work, and political and business affairs.

★

Kelman's papers are housed at the Rabbinical Assembly. Gerson D. Cohen, "Wolfe Kelman: A Personal Tribute," in *Perspectives on Jews and Judaism: Essays in Honor of Wolfe Kelman* (1978), edited by Arthur Chiel, is a colleague's evaluation of Kelman as Jewish scholar, organizer, leader, and mentor. A short sketch is in *American Jewish Biographies* (1982). For details on Kelman's work for the Conservative Jewish movement, see Pamela Susan Nadell, *Conservative Judaism in America: A Biographical Dictionary and Sourcebook* (1988). Entries detailing his many accomplishments appear in various editions of *Who's Who in America* and *Who's Who in American Jewry.* Ari Goldman, "Two Rabbis Leave Legacy of Change," *New York Times* (18 Aug. 1989), was written on the occasion of Kelman's retirement from the Rabbinical Assembly. A tribute is in Jules Harlow, "Rabbi Wolfe Kelman," *Jewish Spectator* (fall 1990). Kelman's obituary in the *New York Times* (27 June 1990) concentrates on his work for Conservative Judaism. Another obituary is in *Jewish Week* (29 June 1990). Two obituaries emphasizing Kelman's warmth, irreverence, and dedication appeared in England: in the *Daily Telegraph* (3 July 1990) and in the *Independent* (30 June 1990), the latter written by Hyam Maccoby. Wolfe Kelman is interviewed on the videotape *Judaism 2000: Voices and Visions: Ira Eisenstein, Wolfe Kelman, Emanuel Rackman, and Alexander Schindler* (1989).

SHARONA A. LEVY

KENT, Corita (*b.* 20 November 1918 in Fort Dodge, Iowa; *d.* 18 September 1986 in Boston, Massachusetts), artist and teacher known for merging the sacred and the secular in vibrantly colored silkscreen prints.

Born Frances Elizabeth Kent, Corita was one of the two sons and two daughters of Robert Vincent Kent, a businessman, and Edith (Sanders) Kent. While she was a baby her family moved to Vancouver, British Columbia, and later to California. She attended Catholic Girls High School in Los Angeles and, at age eighteen, joined the Sisters of the Immaculate Heart of Mary, a Roman Catholic order of nuns. Kent, who was known throughout her life as Sister Corita or Sister Mary Corita, remained with the order for more than thirty years, until 1968, and said that she probably would not have taken up art seriously had she not become a nun.

Kent received her B.A. degree from Immaculate Heart College in Los Angeles in 1941 and an M.A. degree in art history from the University of Southern California in 1951. She also studied at the Chouinard Institute. Upon graduation from college she returned to British Columbia to teach in an elementary school for Native Americans, which was run by her order. In 1946 she began teaching art at Immaculate Heart College, later becoming head of the art department there and turning it into one of the most creative in the United States. Although she had not intended to pursue a teaching career, she later said that her students were among her greatest achievements. While on sabbatical in Boston in 1968 she resigned from the sisterhood and brought her time as an art teacher to a close. She said at the time, "My reasons are very personal and hard to explain. It seems to be the right thing for me to do now. I think I've kind of reached the point where I want to do a different thing."

Corita Kent signing lithographs of her work in her home in Boston, 1985. AP/WIDE WORLD PHOTOS

Kent made her first serigraph, or silkscreen print, *The Lord Is with Thee,* in 1952. Many of her early works contain religious subject matter and abstract Byzantine figures presented in rich transparent layers of color. Examples are *At Cana of Galilee* (1952), *As a Cedar of Lebanon* (1953), *Resurrection* (1955), and *A Woman Clothed with the Sun* (1956). In the mid-1960s her work became more abstract, more colorful, and more socially conscious. She said that she felt a kinship with the artist Ben Shahn because he used line drawings and words in his pictures and took a social or political stand in his work. Her message was as important as her medium; Shahn once described her as a "joyful revolutionary." One of Kent's serigraphs quotes the playwright Samuel Beckett: "One does not have to look for distress. It is screaming at you." Another cites the poet E. E. Cummings: "Be of love (a little) more careful than anything."

Beginning in the 1950s Corita was commissioned to design advertisements for corporations such as Westinghouse and the Container Corporation of America, jackets for Spice Islands cookbooks, and Christmas boxes for Joseph Magnin stores. She created a best-selling U.S. postage stamp, "Love" (1985), and the largest copyrighted artwork at that time, a brilliant rainbow design covering a 150-foot-tall liquefied gas storage tank owned by Boston Gas Company.

Kent was petite, blue-eyed, and dynamic. She no longer wore her habit after the order made the daily wearing of religious garb optional. She traveled and lectured extensively and authored or coauthored eleven books, including *Footnotes and Headlines: A Play-Pray Book* (1967); *Sister Corita* (1968); *Damn Everything but the Circus* (1970); *To Believe in Things* (1971); and *Learning by Heart* (1992), a study of her teaching methods. *New Yorker* cartoonist James Stevenson said her work was "unique, undescribable, unpeggable" and that she was "the most extraordinary person I know. She has life in a highly concentrated form, and when she laughs—which she does easily—the effect lasts a long time." *Newsweek* reported that "in 1964 . . . she transformed Immaculate Heart College's staid religious festival, Mary's Day, into a religious happening. With black-robed nuns parading in flowered necklaces, poets declaiming from platforms and painted students dancing in the grass, Mary's Day became a prototype for the hippies' 1967 be-in in San Francisco." Along with as many as fifty students, Kent created enormous "disposable" exhibitions, such as a provocative show for the World Council of Churches Assembly in Uppsala, Sweden, in 1968. In 1964 and 1965 she executed a fifty-foot mural for the Vatican Pavilion at the New York World's Fair on the subject of the Beatitudes.

Kent was often controversial. In the late 1960s she joined liberal Protestant theologian Harvey Cox and folk singer Judy Collins in an "Evening with God," which was condemned by some as a forum for anti–Vietnam War propaganda. John Taylor, the head of the World Council of Churches' film and art department, observed that "to some her style seemed too modern for a Catholic sister, and she met with some opposition; but there were others who were deeply impressed by her vitality and originality."

Kent's work is in the collections of the Victoria and Albert Museum in London; the Art Institute of Chicago; the Museum of Modern Art and the Metropolitan Museum of Art in New York City; the Library of Congress and the National Gallery of Art in Washington, D.C.; the Philadelphia Museum of Art; and the Los Angeles County Museum of Art, among others. She designed for OxFam International, the United Farmworkers of America, Common Cause, and the Women's International League for Peace and Justice, often working for free. Shortly before her death she designed a series of billboards for Physicians for Social Responsibility that were to be erected across the United States. She was named an American Woman of Accomplishment by *Harper's Bazaar* and Woman of the Year by the *Los Angeles Times*.

Kent, who never married or had children, died of cancer at the age of sixty-seven. She was cremated. She requested that there be no formal service but said, "I wouldn't mind if my friends got together and had a party." The Corita Kent Peace Fund was established at Immaculate Heart College in her memory.

★

For the best examples of Corita's work see Mary Corita Kent, Harvey Cox, and Samuel Eisenstein, *Sister Corita* (1968). See also the Sioux City Art Center catalog *Corita Kent* (1986). Articles include "Roman Catholics: Joyous Revolutionary," *Time* (8 Sept. 1967); "The Painting Nun," *Newsweek* (4 Dec. 1967); "The Nun: A Joyous Revolution," *Newsweek* (25 Dec. 1967); "New Life Style," *Newsweek* (2 Dec. 1968); and John Taylor, "Corita," *Graphis* 26, no. 151 (1970–1971). See also Kris Hillmer-Pierson, "Artist Corita Kent Remembered for Work," *Fort Dodge* (Iowa) *Messenger* (23 Sept. 1986). An obituary is in the *New York Times* (19 Sept. 1986).

CAROL TONER SHANE

KEPPEL, Francis (*b.* 16 April 1916 in New York City; *d.* 19 February 1990 in Cambridge, Massachusetts), educator, dean of the Graduate School of Education at Harvard University, and U.S. commissioner of education.

Francis Keppel, who preferred to be called Frank, was the eldest of five sons of Frederick P. Keppel, dean of Columbia College and president of the Carnegie Corporation, and Helen Tracy Brown, a housewife. Frederick Keppel was among the first Ivy League administrators to declare that elite institutions of higher education had a public duty to admit bright but socially unprepared immigrant children. Francis attended Groton School and then received a B.A. degree in English literature from Harvard in 1938, his only earned degree. He grew up, first, in the home provided for his father as dean, and then in Montrose, New York, amid a colony of academics in what were initially summer and later permanent homes.

Keppel interrupted his academic career to enroll at the American Academy in Rome to become a sculptor. In 1939, deciding that his sculpting talent was limited, he returned to Harvard as assistant dean of freshmen. He married Edith Moulton Sawin on 19 July 1941. They had two daughters, Edith and Susan.

Francis Keppel. ARCHIVE PHOTOS

From 1941 to 1944 Keppel served as secretary of the Joint Army and Navy Committee on Welfare and Recreation, headquartered in Washington, D.C. Entering the U.S. Army's Information and Education Division as a private in 1944, he was discharged as a lieutenant in 1946. In 1950 he was made a member of the Committee on Religion and Welfare in the Armed Forces.

Keppel was assistant to the provost at Harvard from 1946 to 1948. Then, even though he had just a bachelor's degree in a milieu in which doctorates were highly valued, Keppel served as dean of Harvard's Graduate School of Education from 1948 to 1962. In that position he sponsored experimental programs in team teaching, programmed learning, and the use of television in education and curriculum reform. Additionally, he was the key figure in developing Harvard's Master of Arts in Teaching Program, which gave outstanding liberal arts graduates a year of study in education and an extended salaried internship to improve the capability of those who were to become public school teachers. He created the School and University Program for Research and Development (SUPRAD), which conducted pilot projects on such topics as the use of teaching machines and collaborative team teaching. Keppel earned the praise of Harvard's president, James B. Conant, for lessening the tension between liberal arts and education faculties.

In November 1962 President John F. Kennedy appointed Keppel, then serving on the president's Task Force on Education, as commissioner of education, the nation's highest educational post. In this position Keppel encouraged school districts throughout the country to introduce programs aimed at improving the education of those children most in need. In 1965, however, Keppel angered President Lyndon B. Johnson by targeting Chicago's elementary and secondary schools for the first cutoff of federal funds for failure to desegregate as required by the Civil Rights Act of 1964. Keppel's action had infuriated the powerful Chicago mayor, Richard J. Daley, Johnson's close ally. Johnson accused Keppel of not notifying the appropriate congressional committee thirty days before acting as required by law, and effectively demoted Keppel by replacing him as commissioner. Keppel then served as assistant secretary of education from 1965 to 1966.

Keppel left a legacy that emphasized the use of research and development in confronting the problems facing schools. Throughout his career, he always tried to bring together the factions of education and liberal arts that were feuding over the priority of methodology or content. For him the objective was the improvement of the school system; he regarded the public high school as the educational taproot of American democracy. For him, federal aid to education was all-important as a means of equalizing educational opportunities. Despite the sour termination of his service under President Johnson, Keppel took pride in his campaign to pass the Elementary and Secondary Education Act of 1965, which focused resources on classroom assistance for poor children; in his enforcement of the Civil Rights Act of 1964, which sanctioned equal access to education; and his creation of the National Assessment of Educational Progress Commission.

After leaving government service in 1966 Keppel became chairman of the General Learning Corporation, a joint venture of General Electric and Time Inc. He also participated in a number of educational review boards, including the Fleischmann and Rockefeller Commissions dealing with education in New York State. In 1967 Keppel was appointed vice chairman of the Board of Higher Education of New York City, which supervised the City University of New York. From 1967 to 1973 he was an overseer of Harvard, where he was a senior lecturer from 1977 to 1990.

Keppel's major publications were *Personnel Policies for Public Education* (1961) and *The Necessary Revolution in American Education* (1966). In these works he stressed his ideas for training teachers and reforming public education to meet the demand for equal access and to repair the educational deficiencies of the poor and dispossessed.

Among Keppel's other positions were the chairmanship of the National Student Aid Coalition (1980–1985), American trustee for the British Library (1981–1990), trustee of the Carnegie Corporation (1970–1979), and vice chairman of the Lincoln Center for the Performing Arts (1981–1984). He was also on the Board of Governors of the International Development Research Centre in Ottawa, Canada (1980–1990), and was a member of the National Commission on Libraries and the Information Society (1978–1983).

Keppel was a fellow of the American Academy of Arts and Sciences and belonged to the Cosmos Club in Washington, D.C., the Century Association in New York City, and St. Botolph's in Boston. He was elected to Phi Beta Kappa and Phi Delta Kappa. A trustee of Sarah Lawrence and Simmons Colleges, he received an honorary LL.D. from Hamilton College.

From 1974 until his death, Keppel continued to shape educational policy as the director of the education policy program of the Aspen Institute for Humanities Studies and as an adviser to libraries, art centers, the World Bank, and the governments of many developing countries around the world.

Keppel died of cancer in Harvard University's Stillman Infirmary. To the end he was a strong proponent of programs to improve learning opportunities for poor children.

★

Charles Moritz, ed., *Current Biography 1963* (1964), contains a biographical sketch of Keppel. See also *Time* (30 Nov. 1962). An obituary is in the *New York Times* (21 Feb. 1990).

HENRY WASSER

KEYSERLING, Leon Hirsch (*b.* 22 January 1908 in Beaufort, South Carolina; *d.* 9 August 1987 in Washington, D.C.), political economist and drafter of New Deal legislation.

Keyserling was the eldest of four children of William Keyserling and Jennie Hyman. His father was a partner in MacDonald-Wilkins and Company, a cotton and mercantile enterprise in Beaufort. While growing up, Leon worked on Saturdays in one of that company's stores, where he dealt with many black employees. This association with blacks and the poverty in which they lived was to influence his later life.

Keyserling enrolled at Columbia University at the age of sixteen in 1924, and graduated with a B.A. degree in economics in 1928. He then studied at Harvard Law School, receiving his LL.D. degree in 1931. He soon enrolled as a Ph.D. candidate in economics at Columbia, where Rexford Tugwell, later a member of President Franklin Roosevelt's brain trust, was a major influence on his intellectual development. By 1933 Keyserling had completed all requirements for his doctorate except the dissertation; instead of completing the dissertation he joined Tugwell in the Department of Agriculture.

In Washington, Keyserling attracted the attention of Senator Robert Wagner of New York, who offered him a job as his legislative assistant. He would work for Wagner until 1937. Keyserling helped draft a number of famous New Deal laws, including the National Industrial Recovery Act (1933), the National Housing Act (1934–1935), the Social Security Act (1935), and the United States Housing Act (1937). The centerpiece of the New Deal legislation was the National Labor Relations Act of 1935, the so-called Wagner Act. It brought the labor movement into the Democratic party's coalition and wedded unions to the entire range of New Deal laws. Keyserling wrote most of the bill, including the famous section 7a, which institutionalized collective bargaining.

Senator Wagner was chairman of the platform committee of the Democratic party in 1936, 1940, and 1944, and Keyserling wrote the initial drafts of the platform documents in each of these years. He later played a significant role in writing the Democratic platforms of 1948, 1956, 1960, and 1976.

On 4 October 1940 Keyserling, who had moved to the U.S. Housing Agency, married Mary Dublin, an economist at Sarah Lawrence College. They had no children. The couple would subsequently have trouble with the committee headed by Senator Joseph McCarthy during his anticommunist campaign in the early 1950s.

On 1 December 1943 the Pabst Beer Company announced an essay contest on how to solve the postwar employment problem. The judges included Wesley Clair Mitchell and Beardsley Ruml. Herbert Stein, who later headed the Council of Economic Advisers (CEA) during the administration of President Richard Nixon, won the first prize of $25,000, and Keyserling captured the second prize of $10,000. Some of the wording of the legislation creating the Council of Economic Advisers came directly from the Keyserling essay. Keyserling served on the CEA from 1946 to 1953.

The CEA's first chairman, Edwin Nourse, conceived of the CEA as an apolitical advisory board, whereas Keyserling felt that it should actively support the president. Prior to the 1949 recession Nourse was advocating an increase in taxes to reduce the rate of inflation while Keyserling was urging no change. When the recession proved Keyserling right, Nourse was forced out and Keyserling took his place, as acting chairman. A group of centrist economists opposed Keyserling's appointment, ostensibly because he did not have a doctorate in economics, but Democratic President Harry Truman stuck with him, and he became chairman in 1950.

To get the country out of the recession, Keyserling proposed a threefold increase in nonmilitary federal spending, basing this approach on his experience with the economics of World War II. Because the growth of federal spending during the war seemingly had validated the ideas put forward by John Maynard Keynes in his book *The General Theory of Employment, Interest, and Money* (1936), Keyserling proposed this Keynesian solution, even though he always denied Keynesian influence on his thinking. He preferred to classify himself as a "pragmatist." Eventually Paul Nitze, head of policy planning for the State Department, began to look for an economic argument for a significant increase in cold war military spending. He and Keyserling cooperated on developing such an argument in a top-secret National Security Council memorandum, NSC-68. While there was little support for this program in Congress and at the Defense Department, the Korean War, which broke out in June 1950, in effect put the military Keynesianism of NSC-68 to work.

The first year of the Korean War produced a surplus in the federal budget as previously unemployed wage earners went back to work and paid taxes. It also produced the Federal Reserve–Treasury Accord of March 1951, which returned the monetary policy of the Federal Reserve system to its pre–World War II activist role, despite Keyserling's opposition. In contrast to the situation after World War II, there was little increase in the national debt or evidence of pent-up demand after the Korean War. In fact, prices fell after the removal of wartime price controls during the administration of Republican President Dwight Eisenhower.

Keyserling left the CEA after Eisenhower's election, in line with his belief that its chairman should reflect the views of the administration in power. In 1953 he became a private

Leon Keyserling (*left*) and John J. Cassese, president of New York City's Patrolmen's Benevolent Association, for whom Keyserling conducted a study on police officers' pay. ARCHIVE PHOTOS

consulting economist. He continued to criticize U.S. economic policy in a series of books issued by his Conference on Economic Progress, a tax-exempt, nonprofit foundation he set up in 1954. When the Democrats returned to power under President John F. Kennedy in 1961, Keyserling continued to criticize the so-called New Economics of Walter Heller, whom Kennedy chose to head the CEA, as being too conservative with respect to growth and too worried about inflation. Keyserling and the economist John Kenneth Galbraith, who had been dispatched as U.S. ambassador to India, were the principal critics of commercial Keynesianism on the part of the Kennedy CEA.

Keyserling was more tolerant of the policies of Kennedy's successor, Lyndon Johnson; he resigned from Americans for Democratic Action in 1968 as a result of its criticism of Johnson and the war in Vietnam. During the administration of Democratic President Jimmy Carter, Keyserling, who had retired from private practice in 1971, helped write the Full Employment and Balanced Growth Act of 1978, usually referred to as the Humphrey-Hawkins full employment bill as a tribute to U.S. Senator Hubert Humphrey, a cosponsor of the bill, who died before it was enacted. This act set a goal of 4 percent unemployment and required a statement annually by the CEA as to when this goal could be expected to be reached. A few years later, when achieving 4 percent unemployment seemed more and more unlikely and the so-called natural rate of unemployment was considerably in excess of this target, the practice ceased. There was still a requirement that the Federal Reserve chairman report his goals for increasing the monetary supply in biannual appearances before congressional committees. But even this was vitiated by Federal Reserve chairman Alan Greenspan's decision, in the mid-1990s, to abandon monetary aggregates as leading indicators of possible inflation.

Keyserling developed liver cancer in 1987. He died in Washington and is buried in Beaufort, South Carolina.

Although Keyserling always declined to classify himself as a Keynesian, he was generally regarded as such by acknowledged Keynesians. It was mainly the stagnation hypothesis of Alvin Hansen, Keynes's foremost disciple in the United States, that he rejected. Unlike Hansen, Keyserling was convinced that rapid growth was still possible in the advanced capitalist system as a result of stimulative monetary and fiscal policies. He was always in favor of reducing the discretionary powers of the Federal Reserve system and consistently advocated lower interest rates, as had Keynes.

★

Keyserling's writings include *Toward Full Employment and Full Production* (1954), a critique of Eisenhower's non-Keynesian economic program; *Progress or Poverty* (1964), a critique of Walter Heller's "New Economics"; *The Toll of Rising Interest Rates* (1964), on the tight monetary policy under Chairman of the Federal Reserve Board William McChesney Martin, Jr.; and *Goals for Full Employment and How to Achieve Them Under the Full Employment and Balanced Growth Act of 1978* (1978), an explanation of the rationale for the Humphrey-Hawkins legislation. Robert Sobel, *The Worldly Economists* (1980), contains a long chapter on Keyserling's economics. Donald Pickens, "Leon Keyserling and the Rise and Fall of Integrative Liberalism," is the first installment of a biography of Keyserling. Keyserling's papers from the years with Senator Wagner are at Georgetown University. An obituary is in the *New York Times* (11 Aug. 1987).

LYNN TURGEON

KILLIAN, James Rhyne, Jr. (*b.* 24 July 1904 in Blacksburg, South Carolina; *d.* 29 January 1988 in Cambridge, Massachusetts), educator, journalist, and government adviser who was often described as "the father of public television."

Killian was one of two children born to James Robert Killian, Sr., a textile worker, and Jeannette (Rhyne) Killian, a homemaker. When Killian was young, the family moved twice, first to Concord, North Carolina, then to Thomson, Georgia, where Killian entered high school in 1918. He transferred two years later to the McCallie School in Chattanooga, Tennessee, where he was a member of the debating society and played in the band. He graduated in 1921 and received a scholarship to Trinity College (now Duke University) in Durham, North Carolina. He transferred to Massachusetts Institute of Technology (MIT) in 1923 and was awarded a B.S. degree in engineering and business administration in 1926. Not a stellar student, he did not complete his degree requirements on schedule.

James R. Killian, Jr. ARCHIVE PHOTOS

Killian's future success was foreshadowed in his first job after college as assistant managing editor of the *MIT Technology Review.* On the basis of his exceptional administrative and analytical abilities, he quickly rose to managing editor (1927–1930) and to editor (1930–1939) within the space of four years. At the *Review,* Killian's broad range of interests prefigured developments in his own career and U.S. culture. He carried articles on subjects as diverse as the relationship between science and the state, reduced-temperature conductivity, and the role of women in technology. He also demonstrated the collegiality that would later prove useful in his committee work for U.S. presidents Dwight Eisenhower and John F. Kennedy, among others. He worked easily with the variety of experts he asked to contribute to the magazine and exhibited equal concern with the publication's aesthetics by hiring gifted typographers and photographers. His interest in photography led to his first project in book publishing: *Flash! Seeing the Unseen by Ultra-High-Speed Photography,* a collection of detailed, close-up, stop-action photographs by science photographer Harold Edgerton. First published in 1939, it was revised in 1979 as *Moments of Vision: The Stroboscopic Revolution in Photography.* While at the *Review,* Killian met Elizabeth Parks, an English literature major at Wellesley College. They married on 21 August 1929 and had a daughter, Carolyn Makepeace, and a son, Rhyne Meredith.

Killian's rise to the presidency of MIT followed the same swift but incremental pattern as his tenure at the *Review.* In 1939, he was appointed executive assistant to President Karl T. Compton. Killian was named executive vice president in 1943, vice president in 1945, president designate in 1948, and president in 1948. In his first president's report, he advocated "better linkages between science and the humanities," which prompted him to establish several new departments at MIT, including the School of Humanities and Social Studies, the Center for International Studies, the School of Industrial Management, and the Lincoln Laboratory. He also was responsible for the expansion of graduate programs and research and for much new building, including Eero Saarinen's famous and controversial round, concrete, interdenominational chapel (1953), one of the landmarks of the post–World War II international style. He published a memoir of his tenure at MIT in 1985, *The Education of a College President.*

Killian's career as a governmental adviser coincided with and overlapped his academic life. Beginning in 1949 and continuing for the next ten years, he held many important memberships on boards and committees, including the Board of Visitors of Air University, U.S. Air Force (member, 1949–1952); President Harry S. Truman's Communications Policy Board (member, 1950–1951); the President's Advisory Committee on Management Improvement (member, 1950–1952); the Army Scientific Advisory Panel (chairman, 1951–1956); the Office of Defense Mobilization Science Advisory Committee (member, 1953–1955); the Committee for the White House Conference on Education (member, 1954–1955); and the Board of Visitors of the U.S. Naval Academy (member, 1954–1956). In the wake of the Soviet launch of *Sputnik* in 1957, the Office of Defense Mobilization Science Advisory Committee was renamed the President's Scientific Advisory Committee. Killian served as chairman from 1957 to 1959 and returned as a consultant from 1961 to 1972. The committee's mandate was "to advise [the president] on scientific and technological matters at the policy-making level." Killian designed the proposals that led to the creation of the National Aeronautics and Space Administration (NASA). After NASA was founded in 1958, he felt that his advisory work had been completed and that, in his words, "a real scientist" should continue where he left off. Killian reviewed his tenure as committee chair and described the development of NASA in *Sputnik, Scientists, and Eisenhower: A Memoir of the First Special Assistant to the President for Science and Technology* (1976), a detailed memoir of his work on the committee. In spite of his increasing fame and success, the 1950s were a difficult time for Killian personally. In 1955 his wife suffered three massive strokes, from which she never fully recovered.

In 1959 Killian left the presidency of MIT to become chairman of the MIT Corporation, a position he held until 1971, when he became honorary chairman of the corporation; he retired this post in 1979. It was during these years that he began the final phase of his career as adviser to the still relatively new medium of television. He expressed the hope that "people who are concerned about the public welfare ... [will] salvage television to serve the best in man and not the worst" and was consequently considered "the father of public television." He was chairman of the Carnegie Commission on Educational Television from 1965 to 1967 and on the board of directors of the Corporation for Public Broadcasting, serving as its chairman in 1973 and 1974.

Killian's interests were as varied as his career. An amateur ornithologist and photographer, he also enjoyed hiking, camping, and mountain climbing. Both he and his wife were avid readers and theatergoers who particularly enjoyed musical comedies and the works of Gilbert and Sullivan. Killian shared his wife's literary interests, and during the early years of their marriage they read George Meredith's *The Ordeal of Richard Feverel* aloud to each other; Killian collected Meredith's first editions. In later years, Killian claimed William Butler Yeats as "the poet of my old age" and remembered his wife quoting Robert Frost's lines about "miles to go before I sleep" to comfort herself before her death in 1986.

During his lifetime Killian was awarded nearly thirty honorary degrees, including doctorates from Harvard University, Johns Hopkins University, and Amherst College, and he held memberships in several prestigious societies. By the end of his life, he had become a fellow of the American Academy of Arts and Sciences, a member of the National Academy of Engineering, and an honorary member of Phi Beta Kappa. He remained active up to his death in 1988, from natural causes at his home in Cambridge; his body was cremated.

Killian's career illustrates the many changes in education, science, government, and electronic mass media during the middle of the twentieth century. He encouraged increased government funding of scientific research while at MIT, a trend that later broadened. He was also convinced that scientists wielding increasing power needed the humanities. In his Franklin Lecture given in 1969 at Auburn University, he asserted: "Our society is confronted with a host of problems that ... can best be solved by activists from the sciences, the social sciences, and the humanities together." His recognition of the power inherent in the relatively new medium of television was prescient, even though he was disappointed that his nation had failed to use it effectively. His career typified the rise of the technological meritocracy in the twentieth century.

★

Although there is no full-length biography, Killian published two volumes of memoirs: *Sputnik, Scientists, and Eisenhower* (1977) and *The Education of a College President* (1985). Obituaries are in the *New York Times* and *Washington Post* (both 31 Jan. 1988).

STEPHEN TURTELL

KLOPFER, Donald Simon (*b.* 23 January 1902 in New York City; *d.* 30 May 1986 in New York City), book publisher who helped to make Random House one of America's most respected imprints and to transform the book trade from a leisurely gentlemen's enterprise into a profitable, mass-market industry.

Born into comfortable circumstances, Klopfer was the son of Simon Klopfer, a businessman, and Stella Danziger. Following his graduation from Phillips Academy in Andover, Massachusetts, in 1918, he spent a semester at Columbia University before enrolling at Williams College. He left Williams in 1920, without completing a degree, to work at Sartorius, Smith and Loewi, a New York brokerage firm.

In 1921 he entered his stepfather's diamond-cutting business—the United Diamond Works in Newark, New Jersey—where he remained until 1925. Despite the financial rewards of his job (he was the company's treasurer), Klopfer was dissatisfied and restless in what he saw as intellectually unrewarding work. He eagerly accepted an offer from Bennett Cerf, whom he had known at Columbia, to purchase a half-share (for $100,000) in the Modern Library, a line of low-cost editions of English and European classics for student use, which Cerf proposed to buy from its owner (his current employer), Horace Liveright. Because the Modern Library titles were largely free of royalties, the imprint was hugely profitable, but Liveright, a notorious bon vivant and womanizer, was in desperate need of cash to finance a divorce and accepted Cerf's offer.

The new partners opened their business on 1 August 1925 in a ninth-floor loft at 73 West Forty-fifth Street in Manhattan. In all they owned 108 titles—including the only inexpensive editions of *Moby-Dick* and *The Scarlet Letter* then in print. Acting as their own salesmen, Cerf and Klopfer marketed their books with an aggressiveness unknown to the previous owner. They gave the series a distinctive colophon (a flying girl with a torch), redesigned everything from bindings to typefaces, and modernized their list. Within a year they had grossed $250,000, and within three years they had retired their start-up debts. By 1939 the Modern Library featured more than 500 titles, including contemporary fiction by Thomas Mann, André Gide, and Ernest Hemingway. Selling at ninety-five cents a volume until after World War II, when the price was raised to $1.25, the series introduced two generations of American readers to what became known as the Western canon. Its sales of more than 50 million volumes by the 1960s gave Cerf and Klopfer a solid financial foundation for all their publishing ventures.

Having agreed at the outset to plow back the greater part of their profits, the partners in 1927 decided to publish new books "at random," in addition to reprinting the classics and older fiction. Calling their firm Random House, they offered collectors elegant, leather-bound, limited editions of classic books produced in association with the English-based Nonesuch Press, which had set an industry standard for craftsmanship. Business was so brisk that Cerf and Klopfer expanded their list from seven to thirty new titles a year, and in 1928 they moved to larger quarters at 20 East 57th Street.

These were "the days of easy living," Cerf later recalled, because he and Klopfer had most of their day's work done by noon and gave over their afternoons to bridge, backgammon, and golf or, in Klopfer's case, to his family. He had married Marian Ansbacher on 14 September 1925; they had one daughter. Best of all, the business partnership was flourishing—both financially and personally—as it would until Cerf's death in 1971. For forty-five years the two men sat across from one another at matching desks, sharing the same secretary and drawing the same salary and benefits. At the outset they agreed that Cerf, as president, would handle the editorial and promotional sides of their company and that Klopfer, as secretary and treasurer, would be responsible for running the office, managing production and sales, and acting as general problem solver. In practice the lines of authority were blurred, and their roles were interchangeable. Cerf regularly negotiated business deals, and Klopfer often made editorial decisions. He was, said Cerf, "one of the nicest men that ever lived," revered by his associates for his civility, patience, and tact, and for his ability to rein in the more mercurial and emotional Cerf.

The depression of the 1930s destroyed both the easy life and the limited-edition trade, but Klopfer's business acumen, Cerf's editorial flair, and the steady sales of Modern Library books kept Random House afloat. By the mid-1930s Cerf and Klopfer were publishing thirty or so new titles a year by some of the century's leading writers. In 1933, in a landmark case that set the pattern for other First Amendment rulings in the twentieth century, they successfully challenged a federal law banning the importation of James Joyce's *Ulysses.* Three years later Cerf and Klopfer negotiated a merger with a smaller press, Smith & Haas, that brought Robert Haas in as an equal partner and added Isak Dinesen, André Malraux, William Faulkner, and others to their list. By the decade's end Random House had begun a children's line called Beginner Books (Dr. Seuss was its star) and a history series for young readers titled Landmark Books. It had established as well a reputation for producing, under Klopfer's direction, handsome books that were well designed and well made.

In the meantime Klopfer, who was divorced from his first wife in 1933, married Florence Selwyn on 30 June 1937. (She had a son from a previous marriage; they had no children of their own.) In 1942 Klopfer joined the Army Air Forces as an administrative officer with the rank of major. He spent the war years in England, returning in 1945 to Random House, which two years earlier had relocated to the Villard Mansion (designed by Stanford White) at 457 Madison Avenue. (The firm would move again in April 1969, to 201 East Fiftieth Street.)

Klopfer came back to a book trade about to undergo dramatic changes. Prior to the war and for a few years afterward, publishing was clubby and self-contained. Publishers often knew each other on a first-name basis and chose their books as a matter of personal taste. In postwar America that comfortable world was substantially altered over the course of thirty years by mergers, buyouts, and Wall Street investors, as bookselling became big business. Sales of individual titles reached into the millions of copies in hardcover, in mass-market paperbacks (introduced in

1939), and in quality—or trade—paperbacks (after April 1953). Responding to increased demand, publishers marketed their books in traditional shops and also in drugstores, supermarkets, and the franchised book outlets that appeared in suburban shopping malls across America.

Klopfer and Cerf successfully led Random House—a modest-sized operation in the prewar years—through this maze of changes and made it one of the nation's publishing giants by the late 1960s. They increased the number of titles on their annual list. They expanded existing departments and added new ones, notably a reference division. (*The American College Dictionary* [1947] and *The Random House Dictionary of the English Language* [1966] were noteworthy successes.) By 1954 they were printing the Modern Library in paperback. In October 1959 Random House was traded for the first time on the New York Stock Exchange; the partners retained control of 70 percent of the shares and delighted in discovering that, at long last, they were rich.

In 1960 Klopfer and Cerf effected a merger with Alfred A. Knopf, whose imprint was arguably the most distinguished in America. In a kind of last hurrah for traditional publishing practices, the sale was initiated by the principals over lunch at the Stork Club and sealed by a handshake in Knopf's office. In 1961 Random House acquired Pantheon (the publisher of Boris Pasternak and Mary Renault). Five years later RCA purchased Random House from Klopfer and Cerf for $40 million and a guarantee of editorial independence.

Klopfer assumed the title of vice chairman of the board of Random House in 1965, becoming chairman in 1970 when Cerf, who was four years his senior, retired. Klopfer retired in 1975 but continued to visit his office almost daily to meet with young editors and visiting writers. A widower since 1971, he married Kathleen S. Louchheim, a widow, on 19 July 1981. He remained active in civic organizations and in publishing groups until his death from a cerebral hemorrhage at Lenox Hill Hospital in New York City.

★

Klopfer's papers are in the Random House archives at Butler Library, Columbia University. Personal highlights are in the memoirs of Hiram Haydn, *Words and Faces* (1974), and of Bennett Cerf, *At Random: The Reminiscences of Bennett Cerf* (1976). See also John F. Baker, "Fifty Years of Publishing at Random," *Publishers Weekly* (4 Aug. 1975). Klopfer, Cerf, and Random House figure prominently in John Tebbel, *A History of Book Publishing in the United States* (1980), especially vol. 3, *Between Two Wars, 1920–1940,* and vol. 4, *The Great Change, 1940–1980.* An obituary is in the *New York Times* (31 May 1986).

ALLAN L. DAMON

KLUSZEWSKI, Theodore Bernard ("Ted"; "Big Klu") (*b.* 10 September 1924 in Argo, Illinois; *d.* 29 March 1988 in Cincinnati, Ohio), baseball player for the Cincinnati Reds, Pittsburgh Pirates, Chicago White Sox, and Los Angeles Angels who was noted for his ability to hit home runs.

Kluszewski was the son of Polish immigrants, John Kluszewski, a laborer, and Josephine Guntarski. One of six children, he was raised in the industrial suburb of Argo on Chicago's southwest side, where he played football, basketball, and baseball at Argo Community High School. After graduating in 1942, he worked at the Corn Products Refining Company, a starch manufacturer, and played recreational softball and sandlot football until 1944, when Indiana University offered him a football scholarship.

At Indiana, Kluszewski earned All–Big Ten Conference and Honorable Mention All-American honors. In 1945 he caught game-winning touchdown passes against Michigan and Illinois and threw a pass to defeat Northwestern. His heroics helped Indiana to an undefeated record and a Big Ten championship. Kluszewski also continued playing baseball while he was in college. He caught the attention of the Cincinnati Reds manager, Bill McKechnie, when the Reds trained at Indiana University because of travel restrictions placed on the major league clubs in the later years of World War II.

Kluszewski signed with the Reds in the winter of 1946 and left the university without a degree. On 9 February 1946, before reporting to spring training, he married

Ted Kluszewski. NATIONAL BASEBALL HALL OF FAME LIBRARY, COOPERSTOWN, N.Y.

Eleanor Rita Guckel. Called "Big Klu," he impressed the Reds organization with his hitting. He led the Sally League in 1946 with a .352 batting average, and when he was promoted to Memphis in 1947, he led the Southern Association with a .377 batting average. He made his first appearance for the Reds in 1947. In 1948 he became their regular first baseman, a position he held until he was traded to Pittsburgh in 1957.

Kluszewski's nicknames, "Big Klu" and "Muscles," came from his imposing stature. At six feet, two inches and over 240 pounds most of his career, he was seen as a gentle giant. Writers and fellow players noted the tremendous power in his wrists, arms, and shoulders, and he became the prototype of the powerful, less-mobile first basemen who played that position throughout the 1950s. Kluszewski's physique was so massive that he needed to cut the sleeves off his uniform and undershirt to allow greater freedom of motion.

By the early 1950s Kluszewski had become one of the most feared hitters in the National League, and people speculated whether he would break Babe Ruth's record of sixty home runs in one season. While he did not break that record, he did teach himself how to pull the ball to right field, and he became the most prominent power hitter in the National League. Kluszewski and his teammates, including Wally Post, Gus Bell, Frank Robinson, Ed Bailey, and Ray Jablonski, hit a major league record of 221 home runs in 1956, a record that lasted until the Baltimore Orioles combined for 257 home runs in 1996. From 1953 through 1956 Kluszewski hit 171 home runs with a high of 49 in 1954. In five seasons during the 1950s he drove in more than 100 runs, and he played in each All-Star game between 1953 and 1957.

Kluszewski worked hard to overcome fielding shortcomings, eventually making himself a solid first baseman. Though never an agile, adept fielder, he improved the quality of his fielding to the point that he led National League first basemen in fielding from 1951 through 1955. In 1957 his career was threatened by a bulging disk in his back, which the Reds manager Birdie Tebbetts believed was a result of Kluszewski's lack of conditioning and his excessive weight. Kluszewski played in only sixty-nine games for the Reds that year and was traded to Pittsburgh before the 1958 season.

Kluszewski played sparingly for the lowly Pirates throughout 1958 and into August of the 1959 season, when he was sent to the Chicago White Sox, who were in the middle of a three-way championship race. Kluszewski was a catalyst for his new team, leading them to their first American League championship since the ill-fated "Black Sox" won the American League title in 1919.

Kluszewski's greatest moment came in the first game of the 1959 World Series, when he led Chicago to an 11–0 victory over the Los Angeles Dodgers. He hit two home runs, a single, and drove in five runs. Though Chicago lost the World Series to the Dodgers four games to two, Kluszewski hit .391 with three home runs and ten runs batted in, which were then records for a six-game series.

Kluszewski played sparingly for the White Sox in 1960 and was selected by the expansion Los Angeles Angels prior to the 1961 season. At the time of his retirement following the 1961 season, he held three major league, four National League, two World Series, and three All-Star game records.

Kluszewski and his wife had no children. When he retired, they returned to Cincinnati, where Kluszewski owned three restaurants and ran a baseball school in nearby Bainbridge, Ohio. In 1970 he rejoined the Reds as the major league hitting instructor, a role he held through 1978. Many of the "Big Red Machine" members of the championship teams of the mid-1970s credited Kluszewski with improving their hitting. He finished his baseball career as the Reds' minor league hitting instructor from 1979 to 1986. He was selected to the Cincinnati Reds Hall of Fame and the National Polish-American Hall of Fame.

Kluszewski retired in 1986 after undergoing triple bypass surgery. He suffered a heart attack at his home in Maineville, Ohio, and died in Bethesda Hospital North in Cincinnati. He is buried in the Gate of Heaven Cemetery in Montgomery, Ohio.

★

The best sources for information on Kluszewski are the archives of the Baseball Hall of Fame in Cooperstown, New York, and the clippings file of the *Sporting News*, published in St. Louis. Articles on Kluszewski include Tom Meany, "Baseball Hercules," *Collier's* (26 May 1951); Earl Lawson, "The Redlegs One-Man Gang," *Saturday Evening Post* (19 Mar. 1955); and Ed Fitzgerald, "Ted Kluszewski," *Sport* (July 1956). Obituaries are in the *Chicago Tribune* (30 Mar. 1988) and *New York Times* (31 Mar. 1988).

HARRY JEBSEN, JR.

KNIGHT, Ted (*b.* 7 December 1923 in Terryville, Connecticut; *d.* 26 August 1986 in Pacific Palisades, California), actor whose portrayal of an arrogant, self-centered television news anchorman on the situation comedy the *Mary Tyler Moore Show* made a lasting impression on American audiences.

Knight was born Tadewurz Wladziu Konopka at the home of his parents, Charles W. Konopka and Sophia Kovaleski, Polish immigrants, in the mill town of Terryville, Connecticut. His father and mother made candy in their home. His father died in 1926, when Knight was just two years old, and three years later his mother married Michael Kulik. With a brother, two stepbrothers, and three stepsisters, "Tad," as he was known then, was brought up in an im-

Ted Knight (*left*) with Ed Asner and Mary Tyler Moore on the last episode of the *Mary Tyler Moore Show,* 19 March 1977. UPI/CORBIS-BETTMANN

poverished family. Knight later said, "I can remember the Depression and sleeping three brothers to a bed and no money, but I prefer to remember the family gatherings and the stuffed cabbage and the duck's blood soup and the weddings, full of drama and excitement and music and relatives and the smell of food cooking." He also recalled that in Terryville High School, "I was just an ordinary no-neck Polish kid, until one thing set me apart. I discovered I could mimic people and make people laugh."

In 1942, at the age of eighteen, Tad enlisted in the U.S. Army prior to his graduation from high school. After basic training he became a radio operator for the 296th Battalion of Combat Engineers, which was assigned to the First Army. He served from Normandy to Berlin, earning five Bronze Stars for valor. Discharged in 1945, he said: "I didn't want to go back to Terryville and work in the foundry. Acting seemed an easy way to go." He did go back home to Terryville, but he commuted to Hartford, Connecticut, where he took acting classes at the Randall School of Dramatic Arts. Between classes he did odd jobs at various radio stations.

On 14 September 1948 Knight married Dorothy May Clarke; they had three children. In 1948 he moved to Hartford, where he had a job as journeyman announcer and disk jockey at station WCCC. For three months he introduced a newscast with "This is Tadewurz Wladziu Konopka." The station manager took Tad aside and said, "By the time you tell people your name there's no time for the news." That night Tad and his wife scoured the telephone book for possible names. "Ted Knight" was their final choice.

As Ted Knight, he took a full-time job at a radio station in North Carolina, but he really wanted to be an actor. He and his wife moved to New York City, where Knight studied at the American Theatre Wing. Between classes he found bit parts in radio and live television, sometimes in dramas such as *Big Town, Lux Radio Theatre,* and *Suspense.* By 1954 he was in Providence, Rhode Island, with his own television show on WJAR-TV, *Children's Theater,* on which Knight was the puppeteer and all the voices. As Teddy the Milkman he was also the host of the station's late-night movies. He worked at various television and radio stations in the Northeast as news reader, announcer, cooking show host, and ventriloquist.

In 1957 Knight decided to try Hollywood. He moved his family there and mailed out 400 brochures to tout his talents. After a lean year he began to obtain parts, at first in commercials, then in 1958 in an episode of *How to Marry a Millionaire.* In 1960 he gained a recurring role in *The Clear Horizon,* a daytime television serial. Other one-time parts followed in programs such as *The Fugitive, Get Smart,* and *The F.B.I.* Knight appeared in small roles in twelve motion pictures. The best known were *Two Rode Together* (1961), *13 West Street* (1962), and *Countdown* (1968). He also found work as a cartoon voice for children's Saturday morning cartoons and in local legitimate theater productions.

Knight created his most memorable character in the role of Ted Baxter, the self-centered, not too bright anchorman in the fictional newsroom on the *Mary Tyler Moore Show.* The show's producers, unsure of how this person should be played, interviewed more than fifty actors for the role. Ted was the last, and after looking at the script, he asked if he could return the next day. He came back in a blue blazer and white duck pants with the character already indelibly delineated. Mary Tyler Moore starred as the associate producer of WJM-TV news under Lou Grant, played by Ed Asner, and the show was a hit. Airing from 1970 to 1977, it received three Emmy awards, and it has been described as the most literate, realistic, and enduring situation comedy of the 1970s. Knight received two Emmy awards for his role, one in 1973 and another in 1976.

When the series ended, Knight attempted to go on to other roles rather than be forever typecast as Ted Baxter. He did get a part as the lead in a Broadway play, *Some of My Best Friends* (1977), which closed on opening night. He next starred in his own series, the *Ted Knight Show* (1978), in which he headed a New York escort service, but it lasted only five weeks. He then appeared in the motion picture *Caddyshack* (1980), a mediocre comedy starring Rodney Dangerfield.

Finally in 1980 the American Broadcasting Company came up with a role that changed Knight's image. In a situation comedy entitled *Too Close for Comfort,* Knight played a cartoonist, Henry Rush, who worked out of the home he and his wife shared. The house was a duplex, and their two grown daughters lived downstairs. In this role Knight abandoned the loudmouthed buffoon character of Ted Baxter and became a caring though conservative father, reacting to the fledgling antics of his daughters. As a cartoonist on the show, he dodged the sometimes not too helpful suggestions of his wife, played by Nancy Dussault, and his boss, played by Hamilton Camp. The series was a success and continued on ABC until 1983, then as a syndicated series until 1986.

In his later years Knight was a voice on children's Saturday morning cartoons, such as *Aquaman, Batman, Super Friends,* and *Wonder Woman,* and he appeared in commercials. He was named honorary mayor of Pacific Palisades in 1981.

In 1985 Knight was hospitalized for a cancerous growth in his urinary tract. He seemed to recover, but in August 1986 the cancer returned. He died at his home in Pacific Palisades, California. He is buried in Forest Lawn Cemetery in Glendale, California.

★

An obituary is in the *New York Times* (27 Aug. 1986).

KELLAM DE FOREST

KOHLBERG, Lawrence (*b.* 25 October 1927 in Bronxville, New York; *d.* 17[?] January 1987 in Boston, Massachusetts), educator and developmental psychologist who is best known for his theory delineating the stages of moral development.

Kohlberg's father, Alfred Kohlberg, was an importer of Asian goods. His mother, Charlotte Albrecht, was his father's second wife and an accomplished amateur chemist. He had two sisters and one brother.

Kohlberg attended Phillips Academy in Andover, Massachusetts, for high school, and joined the merchant marine on his graduation in 1945. He served aboard a Jewish defense-force vessel attempting to smuggle European Jews into Palestine, and he was held in a British detention camp on the island of Cyprus after the ship's smuggling operations were discovered. This early experience focused Kohlberg's attention on the morality of disobeying authority, an issue central to the moral dilemmas he later constructed to assess moral development.

In 1947 Kohlberg entered the University of Chicago, from which he earned a B.A. degree in 1948 and a Ph.D. in psychology in 1958. In 1955 he married Lucille Stigberg. They had two sons, David and Steven, and divorced in 1985 after a long separation.

As a graduate student, Kohlberg was influenced by the work of the early-twentieth-century Swiss child psychologist Jean Piaget, who maintained that as children grew older their solutions to moral problems changed in structure. From this basis, Kohlberg's dissertation (1958) identified six successive types of moral reasoning, ranging from that based on fear of punishment, egoism, and social conformity, to principled judgments based on social utility or universal human rights. These types, Kohlberg claimed, emerged from his study of the responses of adolescent boys to hypothetical moral dilemmas, including the so-called Heinz dilemma, in which the boys were asked to decide whether a man named Heinz should steal a drug from a pharmacist, who refused to sell it at a fair price, in order to save his sick wife.

Kohlberg became assistant professor of psychology at Yale University in 1959, but returned to the University of Chicago to teach in 1962. In 1968 he became full professor of education and social psychology at Harvard University's Graduate School of Education, an appointment he accepted in part because of the mixed reception with which his moral developmental approach to psychology had been met at Chicago. At Harvard, Kohlberg established the Center for Moral Development and Education to further his research efforts.

In the first few years of his tenure at Harvard, Kohlberg published two of his most frequently cited papers: "Stage and Sequence: The Cognitive Developmental Approach to Socialization" (1969) and "From Is to Ought: How to Commit the Naturalistic Fallacy and Get Away with It" (1971). In "Stage and Sequence," Kohlberg argued that the six ideal types of moral reasoning identified in his dissertation could be called stages. Empirical evidence had shown that people do not revert to lower stages of reasoning or skip stages as they mature, and that they cannot understand the moral reasoning that occurs at stages much higher than their own. Kohlberg also cited studies showing that his six identified stages explained moral development cross-culturally. In "From Is to Ought," Kohlberg maintained that each successive stage of moral reasoning offered a more satisfying philosophic solution to moral problems than its predecessor.

Friends described Kohlberg as disheveled in appearance and as disarmingly open in manner. Although a demanding teacher and research director, he collaborated frequently with his students, many of whom went on to pursue questions posed by his research. His work absorbed him: a compelling piece of research could capture his attention even while he was driving; meals with friends would often turn into discussions of moral development.

Early in Kohlberg's academic career, his students began applying his ideas about moral development to both prisons and high schools. In the 1960s, one of Kohlberg's students studied whether high school students who discussed moral dilemmas developed more quickly as a result; in 1971, others set up a small participatory democracy at the Niantic women's prison in Connecticut. After being drawn into such endeavors by students, Kohlberg helped establish an alternative school in Cambridge, Massachusetts, in 1974. As a result of such efforts, Kohlberg came to believe that institutions that are organized as what he called "just communities" best serve the moral development of their members. He took an active part in several alternative schools until his death.

In the early 1970s, while doing a research project on moral development in Central America, Kohlberg became ill with a disease that was eventually diagnosed as giardiasis, which is caused by an intestinal parasite. Unable to build up an immunity to this parasite, Kohlberg suffered intermittent but often debilitating bouts of nausea and depression for the remainder of his life. As a result of his illness, Kohlberg depended on numerous associates to continue his work.

The interviewing of subjects over long periods of time was crucial to the confirmation of Kohlberg's theory of moral development. The results of a twelve-year study following the sample of boys Kohlberg had first interviewed for his dissertation appeared to show that some subjects, during their college years, reverted in their reasoning from a stage-four concern with social norms to the egoistic second stage of moral development. These results prompted Kohlberg and his associates to rethink their methods for coding interviewees' responses. In 1987 Kohlberg, with Anne Colby, published a revised coding manual to explicitly characterize each successive stage of development as more advanced than its predecessor. In the course of this project, Kohlberg had become convinced by 1984 that there was not sufficient evidence to claim that moral judgments made on the basis of universal human rights (stage six) constituted a discrete stage of moral development.

After having separated from his wife in the mid-1970s, Kohlberg began a relationship with Ann Higgins, a developmental psychologist. Kohlberg and Higgins were engaged but did not marry before Kohlberg's death in 1987.

According to friends, Kohlberg was physically unwell at the time of his death and slipping into another major depression. In January 1987 he attempted to take his life and was hospitalized. On 17 January 1987 he obtained a day pass from Mount Auburn Hospital in Cambridge and disappeared. His body was found on 6 April 1987 in Boston Harbor, near Logan Airport, an apparent suicide. He was cremated, and his ashes were scattered off the coast of Cape Cod, Massachusetts.

Kohlberg's theory of moral development never gained wide acceptance in the field of psychology; like Kohlberg himself, many of his students were to teach in schools of education. Although not widely accepted by psychologists, Kohlberg's approach has served as a foil for socialization theorists who deny that individuals develop along the same set of stages regardless of their social surroundings, as well as for behaviorists who deny that what people say about moral dilemmas has a bearing on how they behave. Feminists have criticized Kohlberg's conception of moral development both for its being initially drawn from an all-male sample and for its ranking moral judgments based on universal human rights above those based on care for those to whom one is closest. Although the subject of many disagreements, Kohlberg's theory of moral development is recognized as a distinctive psychological and educational philosophy.

★

Lawrence Kohlberg's papers are in the Harvard Archives, Pusey Library, Cambridge, Massachusetts. His *Moral Development and Moral Education* (1973) ranks among his most notable works. A comprehensive assessment of Kohlberg's thought and the controversies it occasioned is Sohan Modgil and Celia Modgil, eds., *Lawrence Kohlberg: Consensus and Controversy* (1986). A subsequent compilation of critiques is Bill Puka, ed., *The Great Justice Debate: Kohlberg Criticism* (1994). For an account of the relation of Kohlberg's ideas to other social psychological theories, see John C. Gibbs and Steven V. Schnell, "Moral Development 'Versus'

Socialization: A Critique," *American Psychologist* 40 (Oct. 1985): 1071–1080. For a philosophical assessment of Kohlberg's thought, see Richard Brook, "Justice and the Golden Rule: A Commentary on Some Recent Work of Lawrence Kohlberg," *Ethics* 97 (Jan. 1987): 363–373. William M. Kurtines and Jacob L. Gewirtz, eds., *Handbook of Moral Behavior and Development,* vol. 1, *Theory* (1991), begins with a number of tributes to Kohlberg from his colleagues. Obituaries are in the *New York Times* (9 Apr. 1987) and *American Psychologist* 43 (May 1988): 399–400. A tribute by Dwight Boyd is in *Journal of Moral Education* 17 (Oct. 1988).

EMILY I. HAUPTMANN

KOONTZ, Elizabeth Duncan (*b.* 3 June 1919 in Salisbury, North Carolina; *d.* 6 January 1989 in Salisbury, North Carolina), educator and government official who was the first African American to head both the National Education Association and the Women's Bureau of the United States Department of Labor.

The daughter of Samuel and Lean Duncan, Elizabeth Duncan attended public schools in Salisbury and then went on to get a B.A. degree in 1938 from Livingstone College, where she majored in English and elementary education. After graduation, she began her teaching career, instructing learning disabled students at the Harnett County Training School in North Carolina until 1940. She then entered Atlanta University, where she earned an M.A. degree in elementary education in 1941. She taught at Aggrey Memorial School in Landis, North Carolina, from 1940 to 1941, and then at the Fourteenth-Street School in Winston-Salem until 1945. Duncan received additional training in special education at North Carolina Central University in Durham and also studied at Columbia University and Indiana University.

Elizabeth Duncan Koontz, director of the Labor Department's Women's Bureau, at the White House, 1970. UPI/CORBIS-BETTMANN

While teaching at Price High School in Salisbury from 1945 to 1949, Elizabeth met Harry Lee Koontz, a math teacher, whom she married on 26 November 1947. They had no children. Elizabeth Koontz taught at Monroe School from 1949 to 1965 and at Price Junior-Senior High School from 1965 to 1968. She also joined the North Carolina Association of Classroom Teachers (NCACT), an organization founded in 1880 for the "promotion of educational progress among the Negroes of the state." This organization published a journal called the *Progressive Educator,* which called for equal funding of public schools. In 1949 the group became the first predominantly black group of classroom teachers to affiliate with the National Education Association.

During its annual meeting in 1959, Koontz was elected president of the NCACT, a position she retained until 1963. Under Koontz's leadership, the NCACT increased its funding and membership, began the publication of regionally based newsletters, and produced *Guidelines for Local Associations of Classroom Teachers* in 1961. Koontz also supervised a project, for use by teachers, that detailed Africa's contribution to world culture. Under her NCACT presidency a resolution was passed that prohibited segregated accommodations for those participating in National Education Association–Department of Classroom Teachers regional meetings in the Southeastern Region (this resolution was cosponsored by the Florida Teachers Association). Koontz participated in these meetings and was president of NEA-DCT from 1965 to 1966; in this capacity, she was the first African American to represent its 825,000 teachers across the nation.

In 1964 Koontz, along with fifteen other Americans, was chosen by the *Saturday Review* to visit the Soviet Union, where she represented and promoted the educational system of the United States and tried to improve communication between the two cold war superpowers. She was also a member of the North Carolina Governor's Commission on the Status of Women. These important positions led to her appointment in 1965 to President Lyndon B. Johnson's Advisory Council on Education of Disadvantaged Children, part of Johnson's War on Poverty program.

In 1968 Koontz was elected president of the National Education Association, becoming the first African American to serve in this post. Choosing as the theme of her presidency "A Time for Educational Statesmanship," she sought to increase the respect, professional security, and authority of teachers. Koontz asked teachers "to make use of their united power to bring about change." Attempting to bridge racial and social boundaries, she insisted in her acceptance speech in Dallas, Texas, "that educators . . . men and women . . . young and old . . . black and white . . . stand together." As NEA president Koontz also advocated dependable pension plans for all teachers and encouraged teachers to protest, organize, and even strike if their most basic demands were not met. During her tenure, the NEA did indeed strike for better conditions and pay. Koontz campaigned for higher salaries for classroom teachers so that a broader pool of talented people would choose teaching as their profession.

Koontz's prominent position as leader of the NEA attracted the attention of President Richard M. Nixon, who selected her in 1969 to be director of the Women's Bureau of the U.S. Department of Labor; she was the first African American to be named to this position. Serving for the next four years in the Women's Bureau, she spoke out for the rights and needs of African-American women. In 1975 she was appointed the U.S. delegate to the United Nations Commission on the Status of Women.

From 1975 to 1982 Koontz served as assistant state schools superintendent for the Department of Public Instruction in North Carolina. After she retired in 1982, she remained in demand nationally as a public speaker. She also served as the head of the National Council on Working Women from its founding in 1977 until 1984. In this capacity, she led a public education campaign that highlighted the problems that wage-earning women face in nonprofessional jobs—such as the need for dependable child care and pay equity. She died of a heart attack in Salisbury, North Carolina, where she was buried.

★

There is no full-length biography of Koontz. Information can be found in Hugh Victor Brown, *History of the Education of Negroes in North Carolina* (1961); Percy Murray, *North Carolina Teachers Association* (1984); "Elizabeth Duncan Koontz: Educator, Government Official," *The Black Woman* (1989); Jessie Carney Smith, ed., *Notable Black American Women* (1992); and Darlene Clark Hine, ed., *Black Women in America: An Historical Encyclopedia* (1993). A memorial is in *Journal of Home Economics* (summer 1989): 58. An obituary is in the *New York Times* (8 Jan. 1989).

ALISON M. PARKER

KRAFT, Joseph (*b.* 4 September 1924 in South Orange, New Jersey; *d.* 10 January 1986 in Washington, D.C.), journalist and nationally syndicated columnist.

Joseph Kraft, 1972. AP/WIDE WORLD PHOTOS

Sometimes called the Renaissance man of American journalism and often compared to Walter Lippmann, the legendary columnist who died in 1974, Joseph Kraft was one of two sons born to David Harry Kraft and Sophie Surasky. Educated in the public schools of South Orange, New Jersey, he began his newspaper career in 1938 at the age of fourteen, as a stringer providing high school sports news for the *New York World-Telegram.* He completed two years of study at Columbia University before being drafted into the U.S. Army in 1943; he was assigned to a Japanese language school as preparation for wartime service as a cryptographer. Restored to civilian life in 1946, Kraft returned to Columbia, graduating in 1947 with an A.B. and membership in Phi Beta Kappa. At Princeton University he enrolled as a graduate student (1948–1949) but did not earn a degree, and subsequently spent the year 1950–1951 at the Institute for Advanced Study, doing independent research. In later years he was a Ford Foundation Fellow at Harvard (1974), a Poynter Fellow at Yale (1974), and the Pringle Memorial lecturer at the Columbia School of Journalism (1974). He was Jefferson Lecturer at the University of California, Berkeley, in 1979.

From 1951 to 1952 Kraft worked as an editorial writer for the *Washington Post,* and from 1953 to 1957 he was a staff writer for the Sunday edition of the *New York Times,* producing major articles for its magazine and winning a

1958 Overseas Press Club award for distinguished reporting. (He won the award again in 1973 and 1980.) By 1958 he had established himself as a freelance journalist, contributing stories and analysis over the next twenty-seven years to national magazines like *Harper's,* the *New Yorker, Commentary,* the *New Republic,* and the *Atlantic Monthly.* On 6 January 1960 he married Polly Winton, an artist, who had two sons from an earlier marriage; they had no other children.

That same year, during the presidential campaign, Kraft was employed as a speechwriter for John F. Kennedy; after the election he returned to freelance writing. In 1961 he published the first of his four books, *The Struggle for Algeria,* an essentially analytic—though sympathetic—study of the Muslim nationalists' ongoing revolt against French colonial rule in North Africa. The next year he wrote *The Grand Design: From Common Market to Atlantic Partnership,* a powerful polemic in support of the Trade Expansion Act of 1962, a five-year plan intended to link American economic interests to the European Common Market through extensive revision of United States tariffs. His third book (1966) was generally considered his best. Entitled *Profiles in Power,* it examined, through a series of individual portraits, the political interplay between officials in the Kennedy administration (the president, several cabinet officers, and advisers) and influential institutions like the Pentagon, the Rand Corporation, the Bureau of the Budget, and the press. His fourth and final book, *The Chinese Difference,* was published in 1973 and, like its immediate predecessor, was an extensive reworking of earlier magazine essays.

For three years beginning in 1962, Kraft was Washington correspondent for *Harper's.* In 1965 he became a national columnist for the Field Newspaper Syndicate (continuing, however, to write regularly for *Harper's* and other magazines). Within a year his column, "Insight and Outlook," was appearing three times a week in seventy-five newspapers, including the *Washington Post* and the *Chicago Daily News.* By the time he joined the *Los Angeles Times* and its syndicate in July 1980, he was reaching millions of readers in more than 200 newspapers across the United States.

A wide-ranging, well-informed generalist, Kraft was a relentless researcher who burrowed deeply into public documents and traveled the globe to interview well-placed sources as background for his columns. His task, as he saw it, was first to "identify what is important" in the bewildering array of issues and events his readers confronted in their daily newspapers, and then to provide them with the means to understand the significance of what they had read by placing an event in its historical context and clarifying its complexity through careful analysis. At his best Kraft balanced scholarly detachment with strong moral conviction, the whole leavened by a gentle humor and delivered in lucid and sometimes elegant prose.

His audience included some of the most powerful figures in Washington and leading opinion makers on both coasts, but Kraft saw himself as an advocate for "middle America"—he is believed to have coined the phrase in the mid-1960s—and he consistently urged leaders in government, business, and the press not to ignore, as they often did, the traditional values of the nation's middle class. Not especially partisan in his writing—he once told an interviewer his politics were "nouvelle vague"—he nonetheless remained supportive of the political left and of liberal causes throughout his career. At the same time, he was capable of directing harsh and often unremitting criticism toward liberal legislators and government officials who appeared to be acting out of self-interest or who, as he once wrote of President Lyndon Johnson, deliberately maintained "a climate of sustained intellectual confusion" in order to mask their policies.

Kraft was an early opponent of America's military involvement in Vietnam, and in 1966 accused President Johnson of relying too heavily on force and not enough on economic and political solutions in Southeast Asia. He actively supported détente and criticized the growth of America's economic and military power worldwide. He was among the first commentators to understand the significance of the Watergate scandal that led to President Richard Nixon's resignation in 1974.

Hard-driving and intense, Kraft was beset by health problems for most of his career. He sustained at least three major heart attacks between 1961 and 1985, but they did nothing to slow his pace. Seen by his colleagues as both physically and intellectually restless, he was constantly on the go. In 1971, a typical year, he was in Santiago, Chile, in January, in Moscow in May, in Cairo in September, and in Tokyo in December. His only concession to illness was to reduce the frequency of his column to twice a week in 1985. He died of heart failure at Washington Hospital Center.

Kraft's careful reporting, extensive research, and pragmatic analysis of domestic and foreign policy in a thirty-five-year career made him one of the most respected and influential commentators of his time.

★

Kraft's papers (9,600 items from 1950 to 1986) are at Butler Library, Columbia University. An early profile, "Kraftmanship," appeared in *Newsweek* (4 July 1966). The first comparison of Kraft to Walter Lippmann was made by Henry Fairlie in "The Press: Anglo-American Differences," *Encounter* (June 1966). Obituaries are in the *New York Times* and *Washington Post* (both 11 Jan. 1986).

ALLAN L. DAMON

KRAUS, Hans Peter (*b.* 12 October 1907 in Vienna; *d.* 1 November 1988 in Ridgefield, Connecticut), rare-book dealer and publisher who achieved unmatched success by combining the talents of the collector and of the salesman.

Kraus was the only child of Emil Kraus, a physician and professor of medicine, and Hilda Rix Kraus. He was introduced to collecting through his father's passion for philately. While his father rummaged in attics for stamps, Hans was attracted by old books. By age thirteen he was buying and reselling books, including his own schoolbooks. At age sixteen he found, in a mouse-eaten atlas, an original of Mercator's 1578 map; he promptly sold it.

The choice of bookselling as a career required adherence to the rules of the guild. At age seventeen, after education at the gymnasium in Baden bei Wien and the Academy of Commerce in Vienna, Kraus was apprenticed to the Vienna bookseller R. Lechner. Later, selling in eastern Europe for the Berlin firm of Ernst Wasmuth, Kraus honed his eye for undervalued volumes with potential for appreciation in a larger market. In 1931 he joined the Leipzig firm of Karl W. Hiersemann, trading in both new and antique books.

In 1932 Kraus established his own firm in Vienna, specializing in old and rare books. His first employee was his mother, who worked for him until her death in 1969. The business grew rapidly to profitability; assistants tended the Vienna shop while Kraus traveled to acquire ever more books with ever greater resale value.

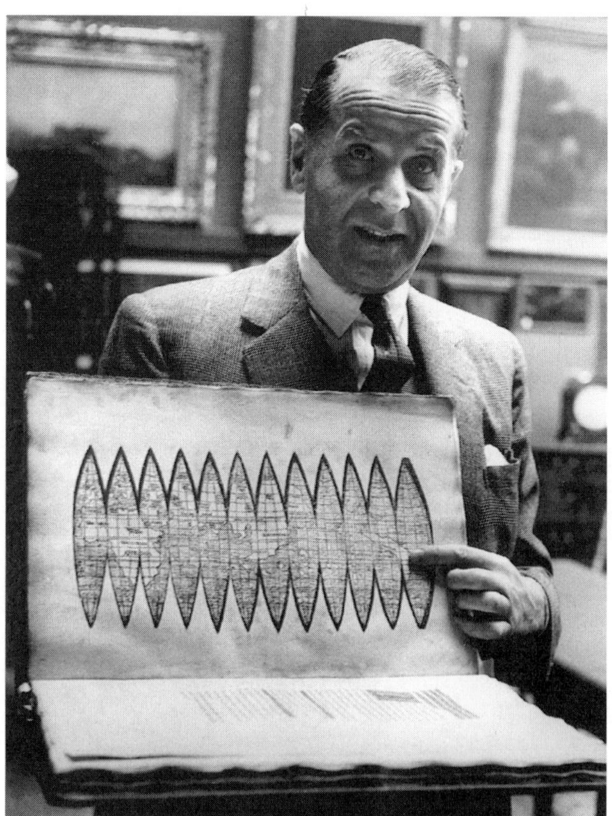

H. P. Kraus displays a book he purchased for $35,000 at Sotheby's auction house in London, 1965. UPI/CORBIS-BETTMANN

In the 1930s many Jewish families in Vienna made plans to emigrate. Kraus was able to deposit a few valuable books with friends in Switzerland, but in 1938, before he managed to leave Vienna, he was arrested and sent first to Dachau and then to Buchenwald concentration camps. In June 1939, after seventeen months of captivity, he was released but had lost everything. He was expelled from Austria and went to Sweden.

Kraus obtained U.S. visas for his mother and himself and retrieved his books from Switzerland. He then left Stockholm, arriving in New York City on his birthday, 12 October 1939.

Determined to reestablish his business in rare and antique books, Kraus rented store facilities at 21 East Fifty-seventh Street in New York City. On 27 August 1940 he married Hanni Zucker-Hale, also from Vienna; she would raise their five children as well as assist her husband in running the firm. As business flourished Kraus moved the operation to larger locations at 64 East Fifty-fifth Street and finally to 16 East Forty-sixth Street, a five-story building purchased in 1946 that eventually housed a reference library of more than 20,000 volumes. He became a naturalized U.S. citizen in 1945.

Kraus rapidly expanded his interests. Kraus Periodicals sold scholarly, scientific, and technical publications in many languages to government, corporate, and academic libraries worldwide. Kraus Reprints republished scholarly out-of-print books and periodicals.

In June 1946 Kraus made the first of many postwar trips to Europe to buy stock. Many collections, both private and institutional, were available for purchase. Kraus's strategy was to buy quickly and in volume, frequently without the opportunity to know the contents of a library fully. The strategy proved prudent; many valuable books were acquired in this way. At auctions many bidders found themselves unable to match Kraus's enthusiasm and deep pockets.

Major libraries were both the customers and beneficiaries of Kraus's unique holdings. Valuable donations found their way to the Library of Congress, the National Library of France, and the Beinecke Library at Yale. In recognition of his generosity, France made Kraus a chevalier of the Legion of Honor in 1951.

Among the masterworks that passed through Kraus's ownership were the Giant Bible of Mainz, now at the Library of Congress; the Constance Missal, purchased in 1953, at the time considered the first book printed with movable type (c. 1450) and now at the Pierpont Morgan Library, New York City; and the Revolutionary War maps of Marshal de Rochambeau, now at Yale. In 1959 he paid the highest price for a book up to that time: $182,000 for a thirteenth-century manuscript of the Apocalypse of St. Albans at an auction at Sotheby's in London.

Kraus was a gifted storyteller; his memoirs were written with both pride and modesty. He disclaimed expertise in the history of printing or in bibliography. He credited his success to many things: the scholarly knowledge of his employees, the freedom of commerce in the United States, and pure luck. (He once found a letter of indulgence printed by Gutenberg stuck into a broken binding.) Yet it was Kraus's unparalleled ability to perceive and predict value that brought him the one thing he seemed to love more than books: the companionship of his customers, rivals, and friends—his fellow bookmen.

Kraus died of pneumonia at his home in Ridgefield, Connecticut, an estate formerly owned by Henry R. Luce. His remains were cremated.

★

Kraus's personal and business papers are in the possession of the family business. Hans P. Kraus, *A Rare Book Saga: The Autobiography of H. P. Kraus* (1978), contains rich details of personal history and many colorful anecdotes. "Missal's Merchant" in "Talk of the Town," *New Yorker* (3 Apr. 1954), is a brief account of one of Kraus's deals. John T. Winterich, "The Man Who Sets Sales Records," *Publishers Weekly* (4 Jan. 1960), includes both biographical details and information on the market in old and rare books. A. Colish, *In Memoriam: Hans Peter Kraus* (1988), is a limited edition. An obituary is in the *New York Times* (2 Nov. 1988).

MICHAEL F. HAINES

L

LABOUISSE, Henry Richardson (*b.* 11 February 1904 in New Orleans, Louisiana; *d.* 25 March 1987 in New York City), diplomat and pioneer in the field of international development, best known for his distinguished leadership of the United Nations International Children's Emergency Fund (UNICEF) for nearly fifteen years.

Labouisse was the youngest of three brothers born to Frances Devereux Huger and Henry Richardson Labouisse. His father, a native of New Orleans, was descended from Huguenots who had emigrated from France in the late eighteenth century. His mother was from Charleston, South Carolina, and her ancestors were also Huguenots who had arrived from Europe at about the same time. His father was in the cotton business, and Labouisse later acknowledged that "my family was reasonably well-to-do, comfortable." Labouisse went to Woodberry Forest School in Virginia and then to Princeton University, where he earned a B.A. degree in 1926, and Harvard Law School, where he received an LL.B. degree in 1929.

The family spent summers in Westport, New York, on Lake Champlain, where Labouisse cared for a large vegetable garden. While in law school Labouisse served during summers as his father's private secretary, and he came to admire greatly his father's integrity and social concerns.

Following law school, just before the stock market crash in 1929, Labouisse started work at Taylor, Blanc, Capron, and Marsh, a New York City law office, and its successor firm, Mitchell, Taylor, Capron, and Marsh. Labouisse liked the thought processes involved in the law but was not enamored with his law practice, which involved a lot of corporate mortgage work. He stayed on, however, until he became a partner.

On 29 June 1935 Labouisse married Elizabeth Scriven Clark, who came from a well-to-do family with money from the Singer Company. Labouisse and his wife had one daughter. Living on the Upper East Side of Manhattan, they became active volunteers at a nearby settlement house, the Lenox Hill Neighborhood Association.

Shortly before the Japanese attack on Pearl Harbor, Labouisse became the U.S. Department of State's assistant chief of the Division of Defense Materials, the purpose of which was to acquire defense items abroad and to prevent such items from going to Germany. He initially thought he would stay in government service for just a few years, but he never practiced law again. He became chief of the division early in 1943 and then, after the liberation of Paris in 1944, went there as chief of the Foreign Economic Administration, concurrently serving as minister of economic affairs at the American embassy. He went without his family, and soon thereafter his wife became very ill, dying of cancer in 1945. By then Labouisse had returned to Washington, D.C., where he served as special assistant to the undersecretary of state William L. Clayton; a year later he became special assistant to the director of the Office of European Affairs.

Henry Labouisse. COURTESY OF THE LABOUISSE FAMILY

The Marshall Plan introduced Labouisse intensively to issues of foreign assistance and international development. He was part of the State Department team that formulated the plan and presented it to Congress. He also traveled often to Paris as an American observer of the creation of the Organization for European Economic Cooperation (OEEC), which later became the Organization for Economic Cooperation and Development (OECD). At the State Department, Labouisse directed a staff as coordinator for foreign aid and assistance, and he returned to Paris as head of the Marshall Plan mission to France from 1951 to 1952. When the Marshall Plan was succeeded by the Mutual Security Administration and the Foreign Operations Administration, he headed their French missions from 1953 to 1954. On 19 November 1954 he married Eve Denise Curie, the youngest daughter of scientists Pierre and Marie Curie. His new wife was an accomplished newspaper publisher and author. They had no children.

During his European missions Labouisse came to know Dag Hammarskjöld, who was then representing Sweden in talks on the Marshall Plan. In 1954 Hammarskjöld, as the recently appointed UN secretary-general, needed a head for the United Nations Relief and Works Agency for Palestinian Refugees in the Near East (UNRWA), which cared for the refugee population resulting from the tumultuous events of 1946 to 1948 in Britain's Palestine mandate and then the state of Israel. He prevailed upon Labouisse to accept the appointment. Thus began a four-year stint with UNRWA and the start of Labouisse's long association with the United Nations. Although not an expert on the Middle East, Labouisse headed for Beirut, Lebanon, and came to "face directly the problems of poverty and underdevelopment." He traveled widely in the region and visited all fifty-seven refugee camps. Throughout, he tried to stay out of political problems but recognized their importance.

About this time a journalist described Labouisse as "an easygoing, slow-speaking cigar smoker, medium-sized, florid, and Roman-nosed, who parts his iron-gray hair in the middle, in the Ivy League style of the twenties." (He soon began parting his hair on the side.) His daughter commented that despite his southern birth, Labouisse was "not of the mint-julep-and-magnolia school" but was instead a "northernized southern gentleman." His colleagues then and later noted his modesty, capacity to listen, communication skills, and warm personality.

In 1959 Labouisse joined the International Bank for Reconstruction and Development (also known as the World Bank) in Washington as a consultant. In response to a request from the government of Venezuela, he headed the bank's study of that nation's development needs. His recommendations expressed his lifelong philosophy of development, which "was to bring services closer to the people. One of the things we tried to stress was the importance of health, education, or basic services in relation with economic progress."

Hammarskjöld called on Labouisse again in 1960 for a special UN mission to the Congo, whose recent independence was fraught with strife. He was prepared to work for the World Bank in that country when the incoming Kennedy administration asked Labouisse, a Democrat, to head the International Cooperation Administration, the main foreign assistance agency of the U.S. government. President John F. Kennedy wanted to coordinate better the activities of the various foreign assistance and development agencies. The result was the creation of the Agency for International Development (AID) in mid-1961. Some White House presidential assistants wanted Labouisse to head AID but asked him to get rid of old-timers involved in the U.S. foreign assistance effort. Labouisse believed, however, that successful development programs required experienced and dedicated staff support and real teamwork rather than confrontation; when he refused to clean house, the post was given to someone else. Secretary of State Dean Rusk and Labouisse then discussed other possible appointments for him, and they agreed on the ambassadorship to Greece, where Labouisse served for three years (1962–1965).

The capstone of Labouisse's professional career was his appointment as executive director of UNICEF. The UNICEF head since 1946 had been Maurice Pate, with whom Labouisse had worked during his UNRWA days;

Pate, Hammarskjöld, his successor, U Thant, and others persuaded Labouisse to succeed Pate. Labouisse became UNICEF's executive director in 1965, a position he held until his retirement in 1979. Labouisse, "somewhat out of breath," would have preferred more time to read and study for the directorship, but he was no novice to UN development and children's issues, and he was able to draw upon his experience with children under UNRWA. (About one-half of the 900,000 Palestinian refugees were fifteen years old or younger.) One of his first duties was to accept the Nobel Peace Prize awarded to UNICEF in 1965.

One area of Labouisse's constant attention was the need for close coordination between UNICEF and the other specialized UN agencies, such as the World Health Organization, both at headquarters and in the field, as well as with nongovernmental organizations and UNICEF national committees to avoid duplication and waste of limited resources and to make the most efficient contribution to a country's development. Labouisse wanted to "focus attention on the child as a whole—as a complete human being," and thus worked to get the ministries of recipient developing governments to integrate the knowledge and skills from the health, nutrition, and education disciplines. He and his staff developed a flexible formula that gave much more money to the least developed countries. Although the total amount of assistance might be modest, he believed that UNICEF's contribution in supplies, expertise, and money could make a real difference.

Another matter was how to expand UNICEF's limited finances. UNICEF increased its total revenues by an average of nearly 15 percent annually, but Labouisse always wanted to do better. Shortly before his retirement in 1979 he told the UNICEF executive board that extension of the 15 percent growth rate over the next half decade would be "wholly inadequate." Labouisse's consistent maxim was that UNICEF's "clients are children, and children know no political barriers." Among his accomplishments, he succeeded in getting both sides in the Nigerian civil war in the late 1960s to accept UNICEF relief for children and in convincing the North Vietnamese government in 1973 to accept international aid for its children. Following the fall of the Pol Pot regime in 1979, UNICEF persuaded the government of Cambodia to accept it as the lead agency for relief of the famine there.

Labouisse was a member of the Century Association of New York City for forty-five years until his death, and earlier he had memberships in the Metropolitan Club and the Chevy Chase Club, both in the Washington, D.C., area. He was an Episcopalian, and his recreational interests included golf, tennis, and swimming. He died of cancer.

★

The Henry R. Labouisse Papers are at the Seeley Mudd Manuscript Library, Princeton University, Princeton, New Jersey. John Charnow and Sherwood G. Moe, eds., *Henry R. Labouisse: UNICEF Executive Director, 1965–1979* (1988), UNICEF History Series no. 11, contains interviews about his career, particularly about his tenure with UNICEF, with excerpts from his policy statements as UNICEF's executive director. Maggie Black, *Children First: The Story of UNICEF, Past and Present* (1996), includes coverage of Labouisse's years as executive director. Obituaries are in the *New York Times* (27 Mar. 1987) and the *Century Association Yearbook* (1988).

DAVID S. PATTERSON

L'AMOUR, Louis (*b.* 22 March 1908 in Jamestown, North Dakota; *d.* 10 June 1988 in Los Angeles, California), one of the most popular writers in American history and the best-selling Western storyteller of all time.

L'Amour, the youngest of seven children, was born Louis Dearborn LaMoore. His father, Louis Charles LaMoore, a veterinarian and farm-equipment salesman, was active in Jamestown affairs. An athletically inclined man, he taught Louis and his brothers how to box. L'Amour's mother, Emily Lavisa Dearborn LaMoore, who had studied to be a teacher, was a keen reader and, like her husband, a fine storyteller.

Though L'Amour attended the local school, his real edu-

Louis L'Amour, 1983. UPI/CORBIS-BETTMANN

cation took place outside its walls. An avid reader like his siblings, he availed himself of the 200 or more books in the family library, as well as the richer collection in the public library. He came to resent having to take required subjects, such as general science and ancient history, since, in his estimation, he had already mastered them on his own. He determined that school was interfering with his education, and at age fifteen, in the middle of the tenth grade, he quit.

In December 1923 L'Amour's father sold his business and moved with his family to the Southwest. L'Amour, already at his adult height of six feet, one inch, elected to strike out on his own. He became a hobo, roaming the West and other parts of the country, searching for work. At one time or other he was a lumberjack, longshoreman, fruit picker, miner, cattle skinner, and circus-elephant handler.

L'Amour drifted to the waterfront in his travels and wound up as a seaman. Over the years he visited the Far East, where he hiked across India and lived with bandits in Tibet and China; sailed a dhow on the Red Sea; and was shipwrecked in the West Indies. Now and then, when he needed money, he boxed, winning fifty-one of fifty-nine fights (once earning an $1,800 purse). This remarkable odyssey provided L'Amour with a wealth of experience to draw upon as a writer.

All the while L'Amour sustained his commitment to self-education through reading. Wherever he happened to be, whether in a cabin at a mining camp or on a ship at sea, he managed to find worthwhile literary fare.

L'Amour also began to fulfill his childhood aspiration of becoming a writer. He submitted stories and poetry to various magazines and received a stream of rejection slips. Concluding that he, rather than the editors, was at fault, he set out to hone his literary skills by studying the short story styles of O. Henry, Jack London, and Arthur Conan Doyle. His efforts were rewarded when he not only published some of his poetry, but in 1935 sold his first story, "Anything for a Pal," to *True Gang Life.*

In the meantime L'Amour decided that his wandering was incompatible with his goal of becoming a full-time writer, so in 1938 he rejoined his family, settling down with them in Choctaw, Oklahoma. He published his first book, *Smoke from This Altar,* a volume of poetry, in 1939. By that date his stories were appearing regularly in the pulp magazines.

In 1942 L'Amour put aside his writing because of World War II. Turned down for naval intelligence because he lacked a college degree, he ended up in the U.S. Army. He attended officers' candidate school, and he received advanced training in tank destroyers. He also taught winter survival techniques in Michigan. Subsequently he saw action as a lieutenant in the European theater and was awarded four Bronze Stars.

After his discharge in 1946 L'Amour returned to the United States and settled in Los Angeles. He resumed his writing and published scores of Western short stories in the late 1940s and 1950s. One of these, "The Gift of Cochise," which appeared in *Collier's* in 1952, was expanded into *Hondo* (1953). His eighth full-length novel, it proved to be his most popular. The story was made into a successful film, released in 1953.

In 1955 L'Amour signed a contract with Bantam Books to deliver two books a year; it was expanded later to three books. Bantam also made a clever—and for L'Amour remunerative—marketing decision to keep all his books in print.

In 1956 L'Amour married Katherine Elizabeth ("Kathy") Adams, a television actress. They had a son, Beau Dearborn, born in 1961, and a daughter, Angelique Gabrielle, born in 1964.

In the thirty-two years after his marriage, L'Amour's career blossomed. Following a demanding, self-imposed schedule, he wrote six hours a day, seven days a week. The results of this disciplined, steady effort were striking: at his death he had published 101 books. These were largely Westerns and included the multivolume Sackett family saga. He also wrote a few non-Westerns, notably *The Walking Drum* (1984) and *Last of the Breed* (1986).

Whatever L'Amour wrote was gobbled up by a huge, loyal readership. By the time of his death almost 200 million copies of his novels had been sold, and his books had been translated into some twenty foreign languages.

In 1977 the Western Writers of America recognized *Hondo* and *Flint* (1960) as two of the twenty-five best Westerns of all time. In 1981 L'Amour received the Golden Saddleman Award for his contributions to Western writing. The following year the U.S. Congress conferred on him the Congressional Gold Medal; he was the first novelist to receive this award. In 1984 he was presented with the Medal of Freedom, the highest U.S. honor for a civilian.

A nonsmoker, L'Amour died of lung cancer. He is buried in Forest Lawn Cemetery in Glendale, California.

L'Amour's immense popularity was traceable to his skill as a storyteller. Reviewers might complain that his characters were one-dimensional and his plotlines too predictable. But his novels were exciting and fast-paced, grabbing the reader on the first page and holding him to the last. Readers also appreciated the care L'Amour took in describing physical settings and historical backgrounds accurately. Ultimately, his reputation will depend on his two acknowledged classics, *Hondo* and *Flint,* and a handful of other novels.

★

The Alfred Deckey Library in Jamestown, North Dakota, has a small collection of L'Amour's correspondence. L'Amour's autobiography, *Education of a Wandering Man* (1989), unfinished at his death, is fragmentary and episodic but nonetheless useful. The best study, part biography and part literary criticism, is Robert Gale, *Louis L'Amour,* rev. ed. (1992). Two other important works are Hal W. Hall, *The Work of Louis L'Amour: An Annoted Bibliography and Guide* (1991); and Robert Weinberg, *The Louis L'Amour Companion* (1992), which contains several interviews with L'Amour, samples of his letters and short stories, and a number of articles about him. John D. Nesbit, "Louis L'Amour—Papier Mâché Homer?" *South Dakota Review* 19 (autumn 1981): 37–48, is an interesting literary critique of L'Amour's fiction. Donald Dale Jackson, "World's Fastest Literary Gun: Louis L'Amour," *Smithsonian* (May 1987), is a lively summary of L'Amour's life and career. See also Bruce Weber, "The Proust of the Prairie Gallops On," *New York Times* (10 June 1998). Obituaries are in the *Los Angeles Times* (13 June 1988); *New York Times* (13 June 1988); and *Conservative Digest* 88 (Nov. 1988): 100–104.

RICHARD P. HARMOND

LANCHESTER, Elsa (*b.* 28 October 1902 in London, England; *d.* 26 December 1986 in Woodland Hills, California), film and stage actress noted for her many eccentric and comic movie roles but best remembered for her macabre role as the intended mate of the monster in the classic horror film *The Bride of Frankenstein* (1935).

Born Elsa Sullivan Lanchester in the Lewisham district of London, the actress was the second of the two children of James Sullivan, who worked in a black lead factory, and Edith Lanchester, the daughter of a prosperous architect. Her parents, who never married, gravitated to radical causes—they were pacifists as well as ardent socialists. They managed to keep Elsa out of school until she was six and finally had her attend a private boys school where, for most of the time, she was the only girl. Later, she attended dancing classes for children conducted by Isadora Duncan's brother Raymond Duncan. She also started dancing classes of her own and then joined a dancing school as a teacher.

Elsa Lanchester with her husband, Charles Laughton, 1929. HULTON-DEUTSCH COLLECTION/CORBIS

For a while, starting in 1918, Lanchester ran a class known as the Children's Theatre, in which neighborhood youths put on programs of songs, dances, and plays. When it was closed by authorities on charges of child exploitation in violation of the child labor laws, Lanchester converted the theater into a sort of nightclub called the Cave of Harmony, where actors from the West End performed music hall turns or one-act plays after theater hours. In 1922 she made her stage debut in a play called *Thirty Minutes in a Street,* then the following year she appeared with John Gielgud in Karel Capek's play *The Insect Comedy*. After attracting attention as a leading performer in the musical revue *Riverside Nights* (1926) she played the secretary to the title character in Arnold Bennett's play *Mr. Prohack* (1927), which starred Charles Laughton, a rising actor of homely appearance but exceptional skill and power.

Lanchester and Laughton began a courtship that resulted in their marriage in February 1929. Theirs was a remarkable relationship founded on tolerance, respect, and shared interests, including art, music, and nature, rather than on sexual love. Early in the marriage, Laughton, deeply distressed, confessed to being homosexual, but Lanchester chose to stay with him until he died. Although their marriage suffered many severe strains over the years, they came to rely on each other for refuge and strength. They had no children.

While Lanchester appeared in several silent movies, including three short films written for her by the novelist H. G. Wells, Laughton's star was rising. After appearing on stage as a murderer in a melodrama titled *Payment Deferred,* in which Lanchester played his daughter, Laughton was asked to repeat his role in New York City. The enthusiastic reviews prompted film and stage offers, and he signed a contract with Paramount Pictures. His first American films, however, were on loan-out. He appeared in Universal Studios' *The Old Dark House* (1932) and in Metro-Goldwyn-Mayer's film version of *Payment Deferred* (1933), in which Maureen O'Sullivan and not Lanchester played his daughter. The couple did make one Hollywood movie together, and it proved to be a financial and critical success. Filmed in England, *The Private Life of Henry VIII* (1933) won an Academy Award for Laughton for his lusty performance as the much-married monarch. Lanchester played Anne of

Cleves, one of Henry's ill-fated wives. Around this time, Lanchester and Laughton also appeared for a full season at the Old Vic Theatre in London, where Lanchester scored a particular success as Ariel in *The Tempest*.

Back in Hollywood, Lanchester turned up in small but attention-catching roles, such as Mr. Micawber's servant Clickett in *David Copperfield* (1935) and as Frank Morgan's overbearing wife in *Naughty Marietta* (1935). Later in 1935, however, she was offered the role with which she would be forever identified—the hissing, shrieking mate of the monster in James Whale's *The Bride of Frankenstein*. Lanchester also played Mary Wollstonecraft Shelley in the movie's prologue. Wearing makeup that required three hours to complete, Lanchester managed to evoke both pity and terror with her high, electrified hairdo, scarred neck, and birdlike movements. When she screams in fright at her designated "husband," the monster proclaims, "We belong dead!" and destroys them both.

Lanchester's other film roles in the 1930s were considerably less bizarre than the "bride." She appeared with Laughton in the biographical drama *Rembrandt* (1936), playing Hendrickje Stoffels, the painter's housekeeper and, later, mistress; and again with her husband, as a prim missionary to Laughton's beach bum in *The Beachcomber* (1938), adapted from Somerset Maugham's story "Vessel of Wrath." Occasionally she returned to the stage, playing Peter Pan at the London Palladium in the Christmas season of 1936, with Laughton as Captain Hook. While Laughton prepared for the film production of *I, Claudius,* which was later aborted, she toured the provinces as Peter Pan.

In the 1940s Lanchester continued to play supporting roles in films, giving many of them the touches of wit and eccentricity that made them memorable. She was one of Ida Lupino's balmy sisters in the melodrama *Ladies in Retirement* (1941); the sympathetic wife of an orchestra conductor played by Laughton in a segment of the episodic *Tales of Manhattan* (1942); and the mother of young Roddy MacDowall in *Lassie Come Home* (1943). Somehow her persona on screen, offbeat but usually agreeable, made it inevitable that she would often be cast in lowly roles. She was a charwoman in *Passport to Adventure* (1944), a cook in *The Spiral Staircase* (1946), and a maid in *The Bishop's Wife* (1947) and *The Secret Garden* (1949). She could also project an engaging eccentricity. Her performance as a scatterbrained artist in the suspenseful melodrama *The Big Clock* (1948) diverted attention from the leading players, including Laughton, whenever she appeared. She received an Academy Award nomination for her performance as another artist in *Come to the Stable* (1949). Starting in 1941, she also enjoyed a decade-long association as a performer with the tiny Turnabout Theater in Los Angeles, California.

Lanchester became a U.S. citizen in 1950. That same year, she began a solo nightclub act with engagements in Montreal, Boston, and New York City, attracting large audiences with her diverting songs and stories. She continued her nightclub appearances throughout the decade, and also toured the country in 1952 with her one-woman stage show, *Elsa Lanchester Herself*. She continued to play colorful supporting film roles in the 1950s, including the wicked stepmother in a version of the Cinderella story called *The Glass Slipper* (1952); the officious nurse to a London barrister played by Laughton in Billy Wilder's courtroom melodrama *Witness for the Prosecution* (1957), for which both Lanchester and Laughton were nominated for Academy Awards; and a daffy witch in *Bell, Book, and Candle* (1959), a film adaptation of John Van Druten's stage comedy. In London in 1958, she appeared as a cockney shopkeeper in a play titled *The Party,* in which Laughton was the star, but the production was not well received. From 1959 to 1961 she resumed her cross-country tour with *Elsa Lanchester Herself,* ending again in New York City, where she gave seventy-five performances. In addition, she appeared frequently on television, either in variety shows or dramatic plays.

After her husband died of cancer in September 1962, Lanchester appeared in nine more films, the most notable of which was Walt Disney's delightful musical *Mary Poppins* (1964), in which she had a small role as the much-put-upon nanny who leaves her unruly charges so that Mary Poppins can take over. Her ability to combine the comic and grotesque aspects of her characters was put to good advantage in such horror films as *Willard* (1971) and *Arnold* (1973). Her final film was *Murder by Death* (1976), Neil Simon's spoof of the detective thriller, in which she played Dame Jesse Marbles, a parody of Agatha Christie's famous sleuth Miss Marple. In 1984 she suffered a stroke and became incapacitated by heart problems. She died two years later of bronchial pneumonia.

With her shock of red hair, snub nose, and air of twinkling mischief, Elsa Lanchester was not destined to play ordinary women in films or on stage. The characters she created often seemed to possess a measure of wit and audacity and more than a little looniness that set them apart from others. A consummate character actress, Lanchester brightened every film or play in which she appeared.

★

Lanchester wrote *Charles Laughton and I* (1938), a memoir about her life with the actor. Her autobiography is *Elsa Lanchester Herself* (1983). Books on Charles Laughton that contain much information on Lanchester include Charles Higham, *Charles Laughton: An Intimate Biography* (1976), and Simon Callow, *Charles Laughton: A Difficult Actor* (1987). An article on Lanchester's life and career by Florian Roberts is in *Films in Review* (Aug.–Sept. 1976). Obituaries are in the *New York Times* (27 Dec. 1986) and *Variety* (31 Dec. 1986).

TED SENNETT

LANDON, Alf(red) Mossman (*b.* 9 September 1887 in West Middlesex, Pennsylvania; *d.* 12 October 1987 in Topeka, Kansas), businessman, governor of Kansas, and 1936 Republican presidential nominee.

Landon was the only surviving child of John Landon, a Union Oil Company official, and Anne (Mossman) Landon. (Their daughter died at the age of seven.) The family moved to Marietta, Ohio, in 1891. Landon attended the local public schools and Marietta Academy, earning average grades. While in high school—a young man of average height and weight—he dislocated a shoulder while playing football against a much larger opponent, thereby ending his active sports career. In 1904, the year he graduated, Landon moved to Kansas with his parents when his father accepted a position as superintendent of field operations for the Kansas Natural Gas Company. He entered the liberal arts program at the University of Kansas that fall but soon transferred to the law school, graduating with an LL.B. degree in 1908. He was admitted to the bar but decided against a law career, instead becoming a bookkeeper for the Independent State Bank of Commerce. In 1911 he left the bank to become a full-time oilman, working with his father, with other men, and on his own. He spent much of his time bringing in oil on the Osage Indian Reservation in Oklahoma, in Kansas, and on properties elsewhere, and he enjoyed considerable success. When not working in the field he lived with his parents.

Governor Alf Landon, *c.* 1936. LIBRARY OF CONGRESS/CORBIS

Following his father's lead, Landon became active in the Progressive party in Kansas, and in 1914 he was named Progressive party chairman in Montgomery County. He followed other progressives back into the Republican party in 1916 but maintained his liberal orientation on political issues. In January 1915 he married Margaret Fleming, daughter of the president of the Ohio Oil Company. They had a son, who lived for only a short time, and a daughter. His wife died of meningitis in June 1918, and in October, Landon entered the U.S. Army as a lieutenant in the Chemical Warfare Service. Sent to Camp Humphreys, Virginia, for training, he was discharged three weeks later, following the armistice of November 1918.

Landon earned a considerable income from his oil business during the 1920s and served as a director of several organizations of independent oilmen. After taking part in H. J. Allen's successful gubernatorial campaign in 1918, he was a member of the governor's "kitchen cabinet" and served for several months as the governor's executive secretary in 1922. Active in state Republican circles, he was named chair of the Republican State Committee in 1928, following the election of Governor Clyde M. Reed, but lost that post with the failure of Reed's campaign for renomination in 1930. Throughout this period Landon strove to achieve harmony within the state party organization. In January 1930 he married Theo Cobb, daughter of a Topeka banker. They had two children; their daughter, Nancy Landon Kassebaum, was elected to the U.S. Senate in 1978.

With the decline in oil prices during the 1930s, Landon successfully pressed for passage of a state conservation and proration law, the nation's first; chaired a governors' committee seeking limits on domestic oil production and price supports for independent oil producers; and pushed for a foreign oil tariff, which Congress failed to enact (although an excise tax on imported crude oil became law in 1932).

Landon ran for governor of Kansas in 1932 on a platform of party harmony. In a difficult three-man race he defeated the Democratic incumbent and a quack doctor with a plurality of 34.8 percent of the vote, his winning margin being 5,637 votes. He was the only Republican governor elected west of the Mississippi River, and one of only seven elected nationwide. Under his leadership the legislature reduced the cost of state government, instituted an income tax, and halved the cost of most automobile license tags. With the help of the New Deal programs instituted by the government of Democratic President Franklin D. Roosevelt to counter the Great Depression, Landon took important steps in farm and unemployment relief and initiated new highway construction. The only Republican governor reelected in 1934—by a margin of more than 62,000 votes—Landon had modest legislative accomplishments in his second term despite a strong Republican majority in both houses of the legislature. He did, however, secure mandatory uniform accounting and auditing procedures in all the counties of the state. The state highway department deficit of $3 million was replaced by a surplus of $750,000, and the state prison facilities were upgraded, though not in time to forestall a major riot in June 1935. Kansas stood third in the nation in terms of federal benefits received under the Agricultural Adjustment Administration. The aggregate of federal moneys allocated to Kansas during Landon's tenure as governor came to nearly $400 million. An interstate compact providing for the conservation of oil and gas that he had diligently sought was ratified by the U.S. Congress in 1935.

Landon's position as the only two-time Republican gubernatorial winner (1932 and 1934), together with his budget-balancing record, recommended him to many Republicans as a possible presidential nominee in 1936. His party was split, however, with some supporting President Roosevelt and his New Deal while others were outspoken in their opposition. Most of the other aspirants for the nomination were too old, too conservative, or otherwise lacked broad public support. All others withdrew prior to the first ballot at the Republican National Convention, and Landon was chosen by acclamation. He selected a former Bull Moose Progressive, Frank Knox, a Chicago newspaper publisher, as his running mate. Landon was too independent and too liberal, and had too warm a personality, to fit the label of "Kansas Coolidge," which some members of the press attempted to pin on him. William Allen White, a longtime political ally in Kansas and editor of the *Emporia Gazette,* said of Landon that he "naturally believes in using the government as an agency of human welfare." "Oh, Susannah" became the Landon campaign song, and felt sunflower campaign buttons were widely distributed.

Landon faced an uphill struggle. He was not an effective speaker, though he argued that Roosevelt could be defeated by an opponent who was the president's plainspoken antithesis. He lacked the perspective, experience, and personal appeal of his opponent, and his campaign suffered from poor coordination. Landon's progressive views were often offset by the more doctrinaire conservatism of other Republican leaders. Labor gave its support to President Roosevelt. Landon's strong civil rights record was somewhat offset by his call to turn responsibility for management of relief programs over to the states. This move was opposed by the National Association for the Advancement of Colored People, which was justifiably concerned about the manner in which some states might handle that assignment.

The endorsement of wealthy, right-wing Democratic members of the Liberty League, which had been set up to rally public opinion against the New Deal, hurt Landon because of their obvious upper-class bias. Representative William Lemke's Union party candidacy received support from left and right—from such left-wing radicals as Dr. Francis Townsend and from right-wingers including the Reverend Gerald L. K. Smith and Father Charles Coughlin. Landon hoped that Lemke might help him by drawing millions of votes from Roosevelt in the three-way race, but he did not anticipate victory. On Election Day, Lemke won fewer than a million votes, while Roosevelt amassed over 27 million votes to Landon's more than 16 million votes, making the race the most one-sided contest since 1820. The margin in the electoral college was even more crushing, 523 to 8. Landon carried only Maine and Vermont, but was nevertheless cheerful and upbeat when meeting with the press. "As Maine goes," said he, "so goes Vermont." (Not until 1984 did a losing candidate, Walter F. Mondale, carry fewer states than had Landon—Minnesota and the District of Columbia.) As the 1990s came to a close, Landon's modest 36.5 percent of the popular vote had not been equaled by any losing candidate, though several had lost by larger pluralities. The *Literary Digest,* whose selective poll of telephone subscribers had suggested a clear Landon win, never recovered from this misreading of the likely outcome and soon went out of business.

During the late 1930s and early 1940s Landon continued with his oil ventures while speaking out on a variety of important issues. His views were not always consonant with those of the national Republican leadership. He unsuccessfully sought the creation of a coalition of members of both parties who would support a more strictly constitutionalist approach to political issues. He opposed the president on many domestic matters but was often supportive on questions concerning national defense. Landon was considered for a cabinet post in 1940, but in the end the appointment was not made, in large part because he strongly opposed a third term for Roosevelt and did not trust the president's integrity or judgment. Landon favored Thomas E. Dewey as the 1940 campaign opened but campaigned for Wendell Willkie, the eventual nominee. Landon opposed Willkie's effort to gain the 1944 nomination and again favored Dewey.

After World War II, Landon thought it wise to diversify his business interests by getting into radio, though he had done well because of the sharply increased wartime demand for petroleum products. Intraparty disputes effectively sidelined him in Kansas politics from the mid-1940s to the mid-1950s, but he remained active and interested while spending more time with his family and his increasingly varied business activities. At the same time he made it clear that he had no further interest in appointive or elective public office. He had little enthusiasm for many Republican or

Democratic domestic policies in his later years, but he had a keen interest in, and often spoke out in favor of, foreign policy initiatives that accorded with his views on a strong United Nations, the importance of national defense, and free trade. Less politically active after the late 1950s, Landon was regarded as an important elder spokesman by Kansas Republicans. He opposed state right-to-work legislation but was strongly supportive of improved educational facilities. Throughout his later life Landon was respected as a decent, independent-minded senior statesman, one who occasionally stated his views on important public issues without fear or favor. He died at his home in Topeka, a little more than a month after his hundredth birthday, and was buried in Topeka's Mount Hope Cemetery.

★

Landon's papers are in the Kansas State Historical Society, Topeka. The Kansas State Archives has his gubernatorial papers. Alfred M. Landon, *America at the Crossroads* (1936; repr. 1971), summarizes Landon's outlook on the issues in the 1936 campaign through some of his speeches. The standard biography is Donald R. McCoy, *Landon of Kansas* (1966). There is a briefer appreciation of Landon by McCoy in Otis L. Graham, Jr., and Megan R. Wander, eds., *Franklin D. Roosevelt: His Life and Times. An Encyclopedic View* (1985). Campaign biographies and contemporary studies include Frederick Palmer, *This Man Landon* (1936); Willis Thornton, *The Life of Alfred M. Landon* (1936); Cal Tinney, *Is It True What They Say About Landon? A Non-Partisan Portrait* (1936); and John W. Wells, *Meet Mr. Landon* (1936). William E. Leuchtenburg provides an excellent summary of the 1936 election in Arthur M. Schlesinger, Jr., and Fred L. Israel, eds., *History of American Presidential Elections* (1971), vol. 3, 2809–2849. Arthur M. Schlesinger, Jr., *The Age of Roosevelt,* vol. 3, *The Politics of Upheaval, 1935–1936* (1960), includes a comprehensive account of the campaign and the events leading up to it. See also Francis W. Schruben, *Kansas in Turmoil, 1930–1936* (1969); and George H. Mayer, "Alf M. Landon as Leader of the Republican Opposition, 1937–1940," in *Kansas Historical Quarterly* 32 (autumn 1966): 325–333. An obituary is in the *New York Times* (13 Oct. 1987).

KEIR B. STERLING

LANSDALE, Edward Geary (*b.* 6 February 1908 in Detroit, Michigan; *d.* 23 February 1987 in McLean, Virginia), military officer best known for his work in U.S. government intelligence, first in the OSS during World War II and then as a counterinsurgency expert in the Philippines and Vietnam.

General Edward Lansdale, 1975. UPI/CORBIS-BETTMANN

Lansdale was one of four sons of Henry ("Harry") Lansdale, an automobile industry executive who restructured the NAPA auto parts company into a billion-dollar-a-year business, and Sarah Frances Philips, a homemaker. The family moved often during Edward's childhood and finally settled in Los Angeles when he was fourteen. He attended Los Angeles High School, where he joined the junior Reserve Officers' Training Corps (ROTC) and attained the top student post. He graduated from high school in 1926 and enrolled at UCLA in 1927 as an English major because of his interest in journalism. He was active in campus activities, including the college humor magazine, the *Claw,* and ROTC. In 1931 Lansdale left school without graduating and headed to New York with ideas of finding newspaper work and perhaps attending the Columbia University School of Journalism. No newspaper work was available, so he obtained a job as a railroad clerk through a family friend. While in New York he met Helen Batcheller, a secretary for a hardware corporation. They married in 1933 and had two sons, Edward and Peter.

The clerk job was so unappealing to Lansdale that in 1935 he and Helen moved to California, where Lansdale took a lesser-paying job in advertising offered by his brother Phil Lansdale. Working his way up in advertising, Edward Lansdale moved to San Francisco in 1937 to work for the Segall agency, and by 1941 he was handling important accounts, such as Wells Fargo and Levi Strauss, for the Leon Livingston agency. After the Japanese bombed Pearl Harbor on 7 December 1941, Lansdale decided to join the fight for his country. When he told Livingston that he was thinking of reactivating his army commission, they quarreled, and Livingston fired him.

Originally deferred from military service because of an enlarged thyroid discovered through a routine physical, Lansdale applied for a health waiver and in February 1943 was approved for limited service as a first lieutenant in the army's Military Intelligence Service (MIS) in the San Francisco field office. Finding that positions were available in William J. ("Wild Bill") Donovan's Office of Strategic Services (OSS), Lansdale applied and was hired as a civilian worker under contract to OSS but attached to MIS in San Francisco. He thus used an intelligence position as a cover for an intelligence position.

On 22 December 1943 Lansdale was promoted to captain. He spent the last year of World War II in New York City, still doing work for MIS and the OSS. In August 1945 he was assigned to the headquarters of the Armed Forces Western Pacific in the Philippines as chief of the analysis branch of the Intelligence Division, where one of his jobs was to handle the surrender of the Japanese Ryukyu Islands. Appointed to a position in G-2 intelligence on 19 June 1947, he began to assist the Philippine government in the fight against the Communist-led Hukbalahap (Huk) rebels. Instead of staying in the office, Lansdale went out into the country to discover why the Huks were popular.

Lansdale was appointed public information officer (PIO) in the Philippines in June 1947 and was promoted to lieutenant colonel. As PIO he became close to Philippine government and military leaders, journalists, and business people and began to take on power above his rank. On 26 September 1947 he transferred from the army to the newly created air force with the rank of major. In late 1948 he was sent back to the United States and reassigned to air intelligence training at Lowry Air Force Base in Denver and then was posted as an instructor at Craig Air Force Base near Selma, Alabama. On 13 November 1949 he began another career in intelligence in the secret Office of Policy Coordination (OPC), which relied on Central Intelligence Agency (CIA) funds and personnel. Lansdale asked for a transfer to the Philippines so he could work on the Huk problem, and again using an intelligence position as cover, he returned to that country as an air force lieutenant colonel assigned as intelligence adviser to the Philippine army.

Based on his earlier experience, Lansdale believed that the Philippine government and army should combine military action against the Huk guerrillas with political, social, and economic actions aimed at winning popular support. He implemented psychological warfare or "psywar" techniques, including propaganda and dirty tricks. In addition, the army built public works, and army lawyers were assigned to help farmers. Lansdale had come to the conclusion that it was not enough for the government to be against something, it also had to be for something, and his formula was successful in defeating the Huks.

Lansdale found that a young Philippine congressman, Ramon Magsaysay, whom he had met in Washington, D.C., shared most of his views, and he supported Magsaysay's career. Magsaysay was appointed minister of defense and at one point moved into Lansdale's quarters at the Joint U.S. Military Advisory Group. In 1953 Magsaysay was elected president of the Philippines by a two-to-one margin. After the election the Indian ambassador to the Philippines told the press that a certain American colonel should change his name to "Landslide."

Even as the Philippine success story unfolded, Lansdale was called to duty in Vietnam in 1953 to assess the French situation. In June 1954 he became the head of the Saigon Military Mission, which was under the CIA but separate from the regular CIA station. The mission consisted of two teams. In the North, a team under Lucien Conein used psywar techniques to get northerners to flee to the South and attempted to destabilize the northern government in various ways, including sabotaging bus transportation by contaminating the engine-oil supply and destroying railroad engines with special coal bricks. In the South, Lansdale utilized Filipino technicians known as the Freedom Company to help the Vietnamese. He also supported Ngo Dinh Diem, who was appointed prime minister of Vietnam by Bao Dai in the summer of 1954, just as the Geneva Conference was coming to a close. Lansdale helped neutralize the opposition of powerful sect leaders from the Cao Dai, Hoa Hao, and Binh Xuyen sects, mostly through bribes, and also helped derail a planned coup by the South Vietnamese army chief of staff, General Nguyen Van Hinh.

During 1954 and 1955 Lansdale became a close and trusted adviser to Diem. When the Binh Xuyen sect tried to overthrow Diem in April 1955, Lansdale helped retain U.S. support. Lansdale thought Diem was the best hope for leadership in the South as an alternative to the Communist government of the North. However, when Diem stifled opposition and created his own party, Can Lao, Lansdale, concerned that the opposition had been forced underground, returned to the United States in 1956 to ask that Diem be pressured into reform. Unsuccessful, he asked to be assigned elsewhere.

Lansdale's next important position was in Washington, D.C., where he was assistant to retired general Graves B. Erskine in the Office of Special Operations in the Department of Defense, which kept watch over operations of the CIA involving the military. Lansdale also became chief Defense Department representative at meetings of the U.S. Intelligence Board. While in this post he was promoted to brigadier general in April 1960. He also became involved in efforts to destabilize the government of Fidel Castro in Cuba, including the assassination plots collected under the code name Mongoose. However, Lansdale antagonized CIA director Allen Dulles by opposing plans for an over-the-beach invasion, saying presciently in a special intelligence meeting, "We are going to get clobbered."

Lansdale's reputation was enhanced by two books. When Graham Greene's *The Quiet American* (1955), a novel set in Saigon, was published in June 1955, the character of Alden Pyle was perceived as based in part on Lansdale. *The Ugly American* by William Lederer and Eugene Burdick appeared in 1958 and was on the best-seller lists for seventy-two weeks. A character in that book, Colonel Edwin Barnum Hillandale, a harmonica-playing American assigned to the Philippines who was close to the Filipino leaders, had a resemblance to Lansdale as well.

President John F. Kennedy was impressed with Lansdale, especially when, after a trip to Vietnam in January 1961, Lansdale wrote a report that alerted Kennedy to the seriousness of the Vietnam problem. As a result of that report, Secretary of Defense Robert McNamara met with Lansdale. McNamara, however, was not impressed, even though he wrote in his Vietnam memoir, *In Retrospect* (1995), that Lansdale was then the only person in the Department of Defense with counterinsurgency experience in Asia. Graham Parsons, a State Department expert on Vietnam, saw Lansdale as a "flamboyant lone wolf and operator." Kennedy considered nominating Lansdale as ambassador to Vietnam but instead in April 1960 appointed him to a special task force on Vietnam headed by Roswell Gilpatrick. Lansdale went on the Maxwell Taylor assessment mission to Vietnam in 1961, but because of opposition to him in the Kennedy administration, his influence was on the decline. He was retired on 31 May 1963, while he was out of the country on a Latin American mission, although he was ordered back to extended active duty with the rank of major general until 30 October 1963. From 1965 to 1968 he served in Vietnam as special assistant to ambassadors Henry Cabot Lodge and Ellsworth Bunker and was involved in the rural pacification program. His first wife died in 1972, and on 4 July 1973 he married Patrocinio Yapcinco Kelly, a journalist whom he had met in the Philippines during the days of the Hukbalahap rebellion. In his later years he wrote and lectured on counterinsurgency. He died of a heart ailment at his home in McLean, Virginia and was buried in Arlington National Cemetery.

Lansdale's legacy, based on dirty tricks as well as good deeds, was his formulation of a response to cold war insurgency that focused on winning the hearts and minds of the people in order to create a political foundation for success. Some saw Lansdale as Greene saw Alden Pyle in *The Quiet American,* "the naive U.S. official who believed that Vietnamese peasants instilled with the precepts of town hall democracy would resist Communism." Others, especially as the United States responded to the insurgency in Vietnam with conventional warfare, agreed with Lansdale that "you don't win guerrilla wars by bombing and napalming people and then having all their relatives and tribesmen turn against you."

★

The Lansdale papers are at the Hoover Institution on War, Revolution, and Peace at Stanford University in Palo Alto, California. Lansdale's memoir of his service in the Philippines and Vietnam during the 1950s is *In the Midst of Wars: An American's Mission to Southeast Asia* (1972). Lansdale also wrote several articles, including "Viet Nam: Do We Understand Revolution?," *Foreign Affairs* 43 (Oct. 1964): 75–86; "Viet Nam: Still the Search for Goals," *Foreign Affairs* 47 (Oct. 1968): 92–98; and "Peoples' Wars: Three Primary Lessons," *Vital Speeches of the Day* 39 (1 Apr. 1973): 357–361, a speech delivered to the Air War College on 15 January 1973. Cecil B. Currey, *Edward Lansdale: The Unquiet American* (1988), is a biography that is supplemented by Jonathan D. Nashel, "Edward Lansdale and the American Attempt to Remake Southeast Asia, 1945–1965" (Ph.D. diss., Rutgers University, 1995). An obituary is in the *New York Times* (24 Feb. 1987).

ROBERT T. BRUNS

LASH, Joseph P. (*b.* 2 December 1909 in New York City; *d.* 22 August 1987 in Boston, Massachusetts), journalist, historian, biographer, and Pulitzer Prize winner.

Lash was the oldest of five children of Samuel Lash, a grocery store owner, and Mary Avchin Lash. He graduated from De Witt Clinton High School in New York City in 1927, and received a B.A. from City College in 1931 and an M.A. from Columbia University in 1932.

Lash first came to public notice as a leader of radical youth organizations during the 1930s. He joined the Socialist party in 1929 and backed its candidate, Norman Thomas, in the 1932 presidential campaign. In 1932 he became secretary of the Student League for Industrial Democracy, a socialist youth group, and editor of its publication, *Student Outlook*. In 1935, after an assemblage of socialists and communists, with a scattering of liberals and pacifists, established the American Student Union (ASU), Lash brought the Student League into the ASU and served as its national secretary between 1936 and 1939. He also wrote, with James A. Weschler (the ASU's director of publications), *War, Our Heritage* (1936), which dealt with the aims of the youth of America in the search for peace.

In 1937 Lash left the Socialist party. He regarded himself as a nonparty communist and was planning to formalize his relationship with the party. After the announcement of the Nazi-Soviet Non-Aggression Pact in August 1939, however, he gave up that idea. Indeed, the Nazi-Soviet Pact, together with the Soviet invasion of Finland in November 1939, marked a turning point in Lash's involvement with the left.

Joseph Lash with his Pulitzer Prize–winning book, *Eleanor and Franklin.* AP/WIDE WORLD PHOTOS

In November 1939, representing the American Student Union, Lash traveled to Washington, D.C., with members of the American Youth Congress to testify before the House Committee on Un-American Activities regarding communist influence in youth groups. First Lady Eleanor Roosevelt attended the session on 30 November to demonstrate her support for the young radicals. She also invited Lash and the Youth Congress delegates to the White House for lunch, dinner, and an overnight stay. The following day Lash appeared before the committee. He defended the ASU despite his own growing doubts about the role of communists in the organization. Eleanor Roosevelt, who attended the hearings, appreciated the way he handled himself in a difficult situation. This encounter between Lash and Eleanor Roosevelt began a friendship that endured until her death in 1962. Lash's trusted confidante and compassionate guide for twenty-three years, she was a major influence in his life.

In 1940 Lash broke with the American Student Union over its refusal to condemn the Soviet invasion of Finland. That fall, as director of the youth division of the National Committee of Independent Voters, he worked for the reelection of Franklin D. Roosevelt. Between 1940 and 1942 he served as general secretary of the United States International Student Service, which gave assistance to refugee students.

Failing to obtain a commission in the Naval Intelligence Service (though Eleanor Roosevelt sponsored his request), he was drafted into the Army Air Forces in 1942. He served as a weather forecaster in the South Pacific and in 1944 received the Air Medal for Meritorious Service. By the time he was discharged in 1945, he had risen to the rank of second lieutenant.

On 9 November 1944 Lash married Trude von Adam Wenzel Pratt; they had one son. His earlier marriage to Nancy Bedford Jones in 1935 had ended in divorce in 1940.

In early 1947 Lash, in cooperation with Eleanor Roosevelt and a number of former New Dealers and political independents, formed the liberal and staunchly anticommunist Americans for Democratic Action (ADA). He was its New York secretary until he resigned the post in 1948. Finding that his radical background had become a major liability to any sort of political career, Lash decided to withdraw from further involvement in politics.

In 1950 Lash accepted a position with the *New York Post* as the paper's United Nations correspondent. He became friendly with Secretary-General Dag Hammarskjöld during his years covering the United Nations, and Hammarskjöld consented to Lash's preparation of his biography. The volume, *Dag Hammarskjöld: Custodian of the Brushfire Peace,* was published in 1961 and received generally favorable reviews. That same year Lash became an editorial writer with the *Post;* he served as assistant editor of the paper's editorial page until 1966.

In 1966 Lash left the *Post* to write a biography of Eleanor Roosevelt. Given exclusive access to her extensive correspondence by Franklin D. Roosevelt, Jr., executor of his mother's estate, Lash worked on the biography for five years. He spent his winters at the Franklin D. Roosevelt Library in Hyde Park, New York, where Mrs. Roosevelt's papers were housed, and his summers writing. Published in 1971, *Eleanor and Franklin: The Story of Their Relationship Based on Eleanor Roosevelt's Private Papers* was notable for its scholarship, candor, and fairness. Not only did Lash explain Eleanor's relationship with her husband in greater depth than earlier writers had, but he described in specific detail what she was able to accomplish politically during the New Deal era. In 1972 the book won the Francis Parkman Prize of the Society of American Historians, as well as the National Book Award and the Pulitzer Prize for biography. The second volume of the biography, *Eleanor: The Years Alone* (1972), like *Eleanor and Franklin* a Book-of-the-Month Club selection, dealt with her life after the death of her husband in 1945.

Lash's other studies dealing with Eleanor Roosevelt included *Love, Eleanor: Eleanor Roosevelt and Her Friends* (1982), *A World of Love: Eleanor Roosevelt and Her Friends, 1943–1962* (1984), and *Life Was Meant to Be Lived: A Contemporary Portrait of Eleanor Roosevelt* (1984). Lash also wrote *From the Diaries of Felix Frankfurter: With a Biographical Essay and Notes* (1975); *Roosevelt and Churchill, 1939–1941: The Partnership That Saved the West* (1976), which won the Samuel Eliot Morison Award; *Helen and Teacher: The Story of Helen Keller and Anne Sullivan Macy* (1980); and, published posthumously, *Dealers and Dreamers: A New Look at the New Deal* (1988).

Lash, who suffered from heart trouble for the last fifteen years of his life, died of that affliction.

Lash was a small, shy, introspective man known for his integrity and strong convictions. He made his mark in politics as a leader of radical youth groups and a founder of Americans for Democratic Action, and in journalism as a correspondent and assistant editor of the *New York Post.* In his third career, as a biographer, Lash, particularly in his four volumes on Eleanor Roosevelt, left a significant and lasting contribution to twentieth-century American history.

★

The Franklin D. Roosevelt Library at Hyde Park, New York, has a large collection of Lash's correspondence, along with diary notes, speeches, clippings, and other writings. Lash's *Eleanor Roosevelt: A Friend's Memoir* (1964) contains numerous autobiographical references, and his *A World of Love: Eleanor Roosevelt and Her Friends, 1943–1962* (1984) includes many of Eleanor Roosevelt's letters to Lash, and some of his to her. Two articles in the *New York Post* (31 Mar. 1966 and 15 Oct. 1971); one in the *Washington Post* (16 Feb. 1977); and an interview in *Publishers Weekly* (19 Oct. 1984) are useful. His family and friends gave their views of Lash at a memorial service held at the Chilmark (Massachusetts) Convention Center on 30 August 1987. Their tribute, "Joseph P. Lash (5 Oct. 1987)," was published under the auspices of the Celeste Bartos Forum of the New York Public Library. An obituary is in the *New York Times* (23 Aug. 1987).

RICHARD P. HARMOND

LATTIMORE, Owen (*b.* 29 July 1900 in Washington, D.C.; *d.* 31 May 1989 in Providence, Rhode Island), China scholar who became a target of the anticommunist atmosphere of the late 1940s and 1950s.

Lattimore was the son of David Lattimore, a teacher, and Margaret (Barnes) Lattimore. In 1901 the family moved to North China, where Lattimore's father was a language teacher. One of four children, Lattimore spent the years 1912–1919 at boarding schools in Lausanne, Switzerland, and Cumberland, England, where he studied at St. Bees School. After failing to get into Oxford University, he returned to China and took a job with Arnhold and Company, Ltd., working in the insurance branch of the firm.

Lattimore's position afforded him the opportunity to travel widely in China. During his travels, he began to develop the intense interest in Central Asia that later became the focus of his academic work. In 1925 he met Eleanor Holgate. The two were married in March 1926; they had one son. The Lattimores spent most of the first two years of their marriage traveling in Central Asia. These travels served as the basis for Lattimore's book *Desert Road to Turkestan* (1929), which began to establish his reputation as an expert on China and Central Asia.

From 1928 to 1933 Lattimore received foundation grants that supported study at Harvard and travel and study in Central Asia, which encouraged the growth of his sympathy for Mongol nationalism. In 1933 he began his affiliation with the Institute of Pacific Relations (IPR), an international organization devoted to disseminating information and opinion about Asia. He served as editor of the IPR's journal, *Pacific Affairs,* from 1934 to 1941.

Lattimore lived in China until 1937, the year war broke out between Japan and China. Meanwhile, he completed the work for his most influential scholarly work, *Inner Asian Frontiers of China* (1940). During the 1930s he published *High Tartary* (1930), *Manchuria: Cradle of Conflict* (1932), and *The Mongols of Manchuria* (1934). In 1938 he began his long association with Johns Hopkins University. Wartime assignments aside, Lattimore taught at Johns Hopkins from 1938 to 1963; he headed its Walter Hines Page School of International Affairs from 1939 to 1953.

In 1941, as Japanese-American relations became seriously strained, Lattimore was enlisted as a political adviser to Chiang Kai-shek, the leader of the Chinese Nationalist government. Lattimore's major role in this capacity was to advise Chiang's government as to how best to gain U.S. assistance for China's war against Japan. After Pearl Harbor, Lattimore left Chiang's service and served for a time as a deputy director of the Pacific operations of the Office of War Information in San Francisco. He also accompanied Vice President Henry A. Wallace on his mission to the Soviet Union and China in 1944. By the end of World War II, Lattimore's comments about the character of Chiang's government became increasingly critical.

Lattimore's life after World War II was influenced heavily by the emerging cold war atmosphere. A growing anticommunist mobilization of American society created an environment conducive to searching out and removing any traces of communism in the United States. Moreover, the Chinese Communist victory over the Nationalist Chinese under Chiang gave impetus to a campaign to discover who was responsible for the "loss" of China. This campaign was carried out most vigorously by a loosely organized group

Owen Lattimore (*left*) meets Generalissimo Chiang Kai-shek in Chungking, China, 1942. UPI/CORBIS-BETTMANN

of pro-Chiang supporters who came to be known as the China Lobby.

During the late 1940s, Lattimore became one of the targets of the China Lobby. His contact with leftists while editor of *Pacific Affairs,* his alleged sympathy for the Soviet Union, and his critical comments about Chiang were held up for increasing criticism. Events took a still more serious turn for Lattimore in 1949, when Alexander Barmine, a defector from the Soviet Union, identified him as a Soviet agent. This accusation prompted the Federal Bureau of Investigation to tap Lattimore's phone and undertake a mail surveillance. In early 1950, Lattimore became a target for Senator Joseph R. McCarthy, who declared publicly that Lattimore was the "top Soviet espionage agent in the United States."

Lattimore's life for the next five years centered on dealing with hostile congressional committees and fending off federal indictments. His most trying experience before congressional examiners was in connection with the investigation of the IPR carried out by the Senate Internal Security Subcommittee (SISS), chaired by Senator Patrick McCarran. Lattimore was not at all submissive before his congressional interrogators and was, at times, quite sarcastic. The SISS's final report recommended that the Justice Department consider indicting Lattimore for perjury, which it did in December 1952.

In May 1953 Judge Luther Youngdahl of the U.S. District Court for the District of Columbia dismissed the most significant counts of the indictment. This dismissal was upheld on appeal in July 1954. The Justice Department then sought to reintroduce the substance of the dismissed counts by gaining a second indictment of Lattimore in October 1954. Judge Youngdahl dismissed the second indictment in toto in January 1955. Finally, in June 1955, the Justice Department announced that it was dropping the case against Lattimore.

In 1962 Lattimore published *Nomads and Commissars* and *Studies in Frontier History,* which reflected his continuing interest in Mongolia. The reaction of Lattimore's colleagues to his troubles was mixed. Some rallied to his support, while others were critical. Still others wished that he would simply go away. In 1963 he obliged his critics by leaving Johns Hopkins, accepting an offer from the University of Leeds to head a new department of Chinese studies. He remained at Leeds until 1970. His wife died not long after they returned to the United States, in March 1970.

In the 1970s Lattimore resided in the United States and Paris. A good deal of his time was spent encouraging the development of Mongolian studies. In 1972 he returned to China for the first time in twenty-seven years. This visit was followed by excursions to Mongolia. Lattimore also lectured widely in the United States and Europe. His peripatetic lifestyle began to moderate somewhat in the late 1970s. From 1979 to 1985 he resided in Cambridge, England, where he enjoyed the intellectual companionshp he found there. By 1985, poor health required Lattimore to return to the United States, and he took up residence near his son in Pawtucket, Rhode Island. He died of pneumonia and was cremated.

Owen Lattimore was an apologist for the Soviet purge trials in the 1930s; moreover, a case can be made that the aggressive and sarcastic manner he adopted before his congressional accusers was a mistake. Occasional poor judgment, however, does not constitute evidence of treason, espionage, perjury, and Communist party membership. He was accused of all of these things. None of the charges was ever supported by substantial evidence. Lattimore had it right when he described his trouble in the late 1940s and 1950s as an ordeal by slander.

★

Lattimore's account of the difficulties stemming from McCarthy's attack can be found in his *Ordeal by Slander* (1950). A full-length biography of Lattimore is Robert P. Newman, *Owen Lattimore and the "Loss" of China* (1992). Earl Latham, *The Communist Controversy in Washington* (1969), and Richard Freeland, *The Truman Doctrine and the Origins of McCarthyism* (1972), remain solid accounts of that period. An obituary is in the *New York Times* (1 June 1989).

JAMES FETZER

LAUSCHE, Frank John (*b.* 14 November 1895 in Cleveland, Ohio; *d.* 21 April 1990 in Cleveland, Ohio), U.S. senator and governor of Ohio.

Governor Frank Lausche, 1950. UPI/CORBIS-BETTMANN

Lausche was the second of ten children of Louis Lausche (Lojze Lovse), a steelworker, and Frances (Francka) Milavec, a homemaker, both recent immigrants from Slovenia. Lausche attended Roman Catholic schools in Cleveland and as a teenager displayed a talent for baseball. Starting out as a semiprofessional third baseman, he soon advanced to professional minor league teams in Lawrence, Massachusetts, and Duluth, Minnesota. Lausche's baseball career was interrupted by World War I, when in 1918 he was commissioned a second lieutenant at Camp Gordon near Atlanta. Lausche played on the camp team, and when he was discharged he received an offer to join the Atlanta Crackers of the Southern Association. Rejecting the offer, he chose instead to study law.

With no prior college education, Lausche began to study law at night at John Marshall School of Law in Cleveland. During the day, he worked as a clerk in a Cleveland law firm. In 1920 he earned his LL.B. degree, finishing second in his class, and joined the law firm of Locher, Green, and Woods. Two years later he ran unsuccessfully as a Democratic candidate for state representative. In 1924 Lausche met defeat in his campaign for state senator. Four years later, on 17 May 1928, he married Jane Sheal after a seven-year courtship; they had no children.

In 1931 Lausche became involved in Democrat Ray T. Miller's campaign for mayor of Cleveland. Following Miller's victory, he was appointed a municipal judge. A year later Lausche was elected to another term. In 1935 he was elected judge of the Common Pleas Court, gaining a reputation as a fearless, honest, and crime-fighting judge. Rejecting offers to run for mayor in 1937 and 1939, he acceded to requests in 1941, first resigning as judge and then undertaking the campaign for mayor with the support of ethnic voters. Lausche carried the election by a plurality of 50,000 votes, a record 71 percent.

After taking office Lausche demonstrated his independence from the Democratic party organization, choosing to retain the Republican safety director Elliot Ness, who Lausche felt to be highly competent. During his term as mayor, labor disputes were swiftly settled, juvenile delinquency was reduced, black marketing was curtailed, and health improvements were made for war workers and their families. Running again in 1943, Lausche was reelected to a second term with more than 70 percent of the votes. Less than a year later, he entered the Democratic primary for governor, winning it with more votes than his five rivals combined. He carried the fall election over his Republican rival by more than 100,000 votes, ignoring the national Democratic ticket and concentrating instead on sales-tax reduction, conservation, mine safety, and expanded state welfare facilities. He refused state Democratic party demands for patronage jobs and vetoed salary increases and pork-barrel legislation, to the delight of most Ohio voters.

Lausche won the Democratic primary for governor in 1946 but lost to his Republican rival in the general election by a margin of 40,000 votes. He returned to private law practice and sought the Democratic gubernatorial nomination two years later. Winning the Democratic primary, he defeated the Republican nominee in the general election by more than 200,000 votes. Following that victory he was reelected in the next three governor's races. No prior Ohio governor had been elected to more than three terms. Lausche's administrations were marked by fiscal conservatism and conflict with organized labor. Among his gubernatorial accomplishments were improvements in education funding, establishment of a state board of education, new highway construction, conservation of natural resources, and expanded services for individuals with mental illnesses. During his fifth and last term Ohio adopted a constitutional amendment increasing the governor's term from two to four years and limiting any person to two consecutive terms.

In 1956 Lausche turned his attention to the United States Senate, defeating Senator George Bender, the Republican nominee, in the general election. In the Eighty-fifth Congress, he served on the Interstate and Foreign Commerce Committee and the Banking Committee, and chaired the Subcommittee on Securities. In subsequent congresses, he served on the Foreign Relations Committee and the Interstate and Foreign Commerce Committee, and chaired the Committee on Southeast Asia. During his six-year term he supported an early civil rights act and a foreign-aid authorization bill while opposing new and expanded federal subsidies, deficit financing, and expansion of the federal bureaucracy. In 1962 Lausche ran for a second Senate term and defeated his Republican opponent by more than 600,000 votes. Returning to the Senate, he attacked federal subsidies, endorsed right-to-work legislation, opposed most antipoverty legislation, and supported the war effort in Vietnam.

In 1968, at age seventy-two, Lausche decided to run for a third term, but he ran into strong opposition in the Democratic primary and was defeated. Some attributed this defeat to his stance on the Vietnam War and the disenchantment of black voters. After leaving the Senate, Lausche, who divided his time between Bethesda, Maryland, and Cleveland, Ohio, continued to practice law, served on the boards of several financial institutions, and spoke out on political issues. His two most prominent post-Senate pronouncements were endorsements of Richard M. Nixon for president in 1968 and 1972. He died at age ninety-four and was buried in Cleveland, Ohio.

★

Lausche's gubernatorial papers are in the Manuscript Department of the Ohio Historical Society, Columbus. See also William C. Bittner, *Frank J. Lausche: A Political Biography* (1975), and Edward Gobetz, ed., *Ohio's Lincoln, Frank J. Lausche: A Tribute and Festschrift for His Ninetieth Birthday* (1985). An obituary is in the *New York Times* (22 Apr. 1990).

FRANK R. LEVSTIK

LAYNE, Robert Lawrence ("Bobby") (*b.* 19 December 1926 in Santa Anna, Texas; *d.* 1 December 1986 in Lubbock, Texas), All-American and Hall of Fame quarterback who led the Detroit Lions to four divisional and three National Football League titles in the 1950s.

Layne was one of two children of Sherman C. Layne, a used-car salesman, and Beatrice Lowe Layne, a homemaker. When he was six, his father suddenly died and his mother's financial circumstances forced her to put him up for adoption. Layne was raised by an uncle and aunt, Wade and Livinia Hampton. The family moved to Dallas, where Layne developed a fast friendship with Doak Walker. In junior high the boys were football and baseball teammates and spent the summers as lifeguards. At Highland Park High School, Layne played guard and single-wing tailback and held for Walker's kicks. He also played basketball and pitched an American Legion baseball team to the state championship.

Layne was awarded a baseball scholarship by the University of Texas in 1944 but soon left to join the merchant marine, as Walker had done. When World War II ended Layne returned to the University of Texas and guided the Longhorns to the Southwest Conference football championship. He became Coach Blair Cherry's All-American quarterback, completing eleven of twelve passes when Texas defeated Missouri in the 1946 Cotton Bowl. In 1948 Layne led the Longhorns to a 27–7 victory over Alabama in the Sugar Bowl. He meanwhile compiled a spectacular 26–0 record as a pitcher during a four-year period in which Texas never lost a Southwest Conference baseball game.

The outgoing Layne—blue-eyed, blond, six feet, one inch, and 195 pounds—became the state's glamour boy. On 17 August 1947 he married Carol Ann Krueger, a University of Texas classmate; they would have two sons. After graduating, Layne was offered a baseball contract as well as contracts with the Chicago Bears of the National Football League and the Baltimore Colts of the All-America Conference. Baltimore offered more money—an unheard-of $77,000 over three years—but Layne followed Cherry's advice and signed with the Bears. In 1948, his only year with Chicago, Layne split time at quarterback with the veterans Sid Luckman and Johnny Lujack. Reluctantly George Halas, owner of the Bears, traded Layne to the New York Bulldogs before the 1949 season.

"I learned to throw the ball from every position except standing up straight," Layne remembered after piloting the hapless Bulldogs to a 1–10–1 record. The team was owned by the singer Kate Smith's business manager, Ted Collins, who kept cutting players to make ends meet. Before the start of the 1950 season Layne was traded to the Detroit Lions, a team that hadn't won a championship since 1935. There he rejoined Doak Walker and newly emerging stalwarts such as Leon Hart, Bob Hoernschemeyer, Lou Creekmur, Thurman McGraw, and Les Bingaman under the inspired coaching of Buddy Parker. The team's 6–6 record was its best in five years. Layne threw for a league high of 2,323 yards and sixteen touchdowns. The following year the Lions swept through the regular season, but injuries cost them the conference championship by half a game. Layne's 332 passing attempts and 152 completions led the league. So did his 2,403 passing yards and twenty-six touchdowns.

After the Lions lost two of their first three games in 1952, and with Walker injured for most of the season, Layne led the team to eight victories in its last nine games—running and passing for 2,410 yards—and to a tie with Los Angeles for the National Conference Division title. Layne and the Lions beat the Rams 31–21 in a playoff game and played Paul Brown's Cleveland Browns for the championship. The four-time-champion Browns, playing at home, were a prohibitive favorite over the upstart Lions, but Layne had other ideas. He put the Lions ahead in the second quarter with a fourteen-yard sideline pass to Bill Swiacki and his own two-yard touchdown run. A fourth-quarter field goal gave the Lions a 17–7 victory and their first title in seventeen years.

The 1953 season brought an even greater personal triumph for Layne and the Lions. Buoyed by the additions of Joe Schmidt, Yale Lary, Dick Stanfel, Jack Christiansen, and Gene Gedman, the Lions swept to the Western Conference championship with a 10–2 record and a six-game winning streak. Detroit trailed the Browns 16–10 in the title game with less than five minutes to go when Layne gathered his troops on the Lions' twenty-yard line for a make-or-break final drive. "Awright, fellas," he said before they broke their huddle, "y'ull block and ol' Bobby'll pass you right to the championship. Ol' Bobby will get you six big ones." Layne then hit backup end Jim Doran with a seventeen-yard pass and after two incompletions connected with Doran again on a eighteen-yard gainer that crossed midfield. Cloyce Box hauled in a Layne bullet pass for nine yards, and when Hoernschemeyer couldn't make first down on a second-down plunge, Layne made it on a keeper. With first down on the Cleveland thirty-three, time running out, and 54,000 Lions fans screaming and on their feet, Layne hit Doran with a thirty-three-yard bomb into the corner of the end zone. Walker's extra point gave the Lions an unforgettable 17–16 victory and sealed Layne's reputation as one of the game's greatest quarterbacks.

Bobby Layne. PRO FOOTBALL HALL OF FAME

Layne's Lions teammates believed he had willed their last-minute victory and twin championships. "He hates to lose," observed the wide receiver Dorne Dibble. "And he instills that in everyone else. No matter how far we got behind, we knew with Bobby Layne we could win." Paul Brown, never profuse in his praise for opponents, thought Layne "the best third-down quarterback in football." George Halas, one of the league's founders, told reporters that if he had one game to win and could choose any quarterback, "I'd have to send for Layne." Doak Walker captured the Layne legend best when he said, "Bobby never lost a game. Some days, time just ran out on him."

The Lions repeated as Western Division champions in 1954, and Layne finished the season as the league's number-one passer. Aware of his growing reputation as a generous spender who liked to party and have a late-night drink, Layne turned in early before the title game against Cleveland. His six intercepted passes fueled his team's 56–10 pounding and led the star to swear off "too much sleep." The 1957 Lions championship, achieved with Layne on the sidelines nursing a broken ankle, was his swan song in Detroit. The camaraderie he had forged through force of personality was now giving way to bigger salaries, generated by gate receipts and television revenues, and each player looked out for himself.

In 1958, Layne joined Buddy Parker in Pittsburgh, transforming the listless Steelers into a contender by winning six and tying one of their final seven games. In 1959 Layne passed for 1,986 yards and twenty touchdowns as the Steelers continued their surge. But in the three years that followed, he was never able to duplicate the record he and Parker had produced in Detroit. Hobbled by injuries to his throwing hand and shoulder, the last man in the NFL to play without a face mask was slowing down and showing his age. He ended the 1962 season, his last, with his former brilliance, leading the Steelers to three wins and a 9–5 season, the most wins in Pittsburgh's twenty-nine-year history. Layne's 196 touchdown passes pushed him past Sammy Baugh to first on the all-time list. His 3,700 passing attempts, 1,814 completions, and 26,768 passing yards were all records at the time of his retirement. The "Gadabout Gladiator" had helped transform professional football from the trench warfare of the straight-ahead running game to the crowd-pleasing aerial spectacle of the passing game. Layne had been a league All-Pro twice and led it in scoring.

In 1967, Layne became the second player in NFL history to make the Hall of Fame in his first year of eligibility. By this time he was scouting for the Dallas Cowboys after jobs as assistant coach with Pittsburgh and St. Louis. The following year the Lions retired Layne's uniform number, 22. His successful ventures in sporting goods, real estate, and oil made him wealthy. He administered his holdings from Lubbock, Texas, wrote his memoirs, and appeared with a broad grin and ready handshake when former teammates got together to talk about old times. Cancer surgeries, liver trouble, and internal bleeding ended the life of football's beloved bad boy eighteen days short of his sixtieth birthday. He was buried in Lubbock.

Jim David, a back on Detroit's championship teams, eulogized Layne as a leader who "loved to win" and inspired teammates with the passion of his play. Pittsburgh's pro football writer Pat Livingston thought Layne the prototypical modern quarterback. "There may have been better passers," he noted, "but there was never a better strategist." Layne was a creative master of the unexpected. "My philosophy was that you've got to throw away the book or they'll read you like one," he said. The veteran sportswriter Cooper Rollow believed that Layne "left a legacy as a quarterback and popular free spirit that may never be matched in the National Football League." Other writers found him a "temperamental genius." More than one photo captures the bloodstained, broken-nosed hero leaving the field of battle, covered in grime and dirt, missing two front teeth, and holding the game ball. "There was nobody better than Bobby when the going got tough," remarked Joe Schmidt. That is what made Layne both a throwback to pro football's early days and a forerunner of the sport's future.

★

Layne's personal correspondence and related private papers are in the Detroit Lions archives in Pontiac, Michigan. A file on his career and achievements is in the Pro Football Hall of Fame in Canton, Ohio. A chronicle of his football career is his *Always on Sunday* (1962). Layne's other writings include "All Quarterbacks Are Crazy," *True* (Oct. 1957), and "This Is No Game for Kids," *Saturday Evening Post* (14 Nov. 1959). A biography is Bob St. John, *Heart of a Lion: The Wild and Woolly Life of Bobby Layne* (1991). Long interviews are in Myron Cope, *The Game That Was* (1974), and Jim Klobuchar, "Memory Layne: Life Was a Cabaret for Bobby," in *Pro!* (1975). A tribute by teammate Alex Karras, "Remembering Bobby Layne," is in Richard Whittingham, ed., *The Fireside Book of Pro Football* (1989). Harold L. Ray's appreciation appears in David L. Porter, ed., *Biographical Dictionary of American Sports: Football* (1987). Layne's career is chronicled in David S. Neft, Roland T. Johnson, Richard M. Cohen, and Jordan A. Deutsch, *The Sports Encyclopedia: Pro Football* (1974), and captured in *The Fabulous Fifties,* produced by NFL Films (1987). Obituaries are in the *New York Times, Detroit Free Press, Washington Post,* and *Chicago Tribune* (all 2 Dec. 1986).

BRUCE J. EVENSEN

LAZARUS, Ralph (*b.* 30 January 1914 in Columbus, Ohio; *d.* 18 June 1988 in Cincinnati, Ohio), retail executive largely responsible for the unprecedented expansion of Federated Department Stores between the 1950s and the early 1980s.

One of five children of Fred Lazarus, Jr., a retailer, and Meta Marx, a homemaker, Ralph Lazarus seemed destined for a career in merchandising. In 1851 his great-grandfather had founded the Lazarus Store in Columbus, Ohio, a general-goods business that Ralph's grandfather and father helped to build into a prominent department store. After graduating from Columbus Academy in 1931 and from Dartmouth College with a B.A. degree in 1935, Lazarus went to work for the family business as a salesman. He married Gladys Kleeman of Scranton, Pennsylvania, on 24 June 1939; they would have four children. Lazarus advanced rapidly to general merchandise manager and then to manager of home furnishings before receiving a commission as lieutenant in the U.S. Army Air Forces during World War II; he served a two-year stint (1941–1943) assigned to the Office of Price Administration and the War Production Board.

After completing his wartime service, Lazarus briefly headed the New York joint buying office of F. and R. Lazarus Company and Shillito's of Cincinnati. He returned to Columbus in 1945 to become manager of the Lazarus Basement Store, which under his guidance became the second-

Ralph Lazarus. ARCHIVE PHOTOS

largest store in the city. In 1947 he was named vice president in charge of merchandising and publicity for the F. and R. Lazarus Company. In that capacity he devised a sales analysis program to aid the store's transition from a wartime to a postwar economy by aiming to level off seasonal retailing peaks and reaching a broader consumer base.

In 1951 Lazarus left one family business for another, becoming executive vice president of the Cincinnati-based Federated Department Stores, a consortium of retailers his father had helped to establish in 1929. His main goal was for each member store to dominate its trading area, a concept he defined as selling "a maximum amount of goods profitably to maximum numbers of people." Always concerned about meeting customer needs, he paid attention to the smallest characteristics of merchandise, closely studying what made products popular and how to exploit that popularity in floor displays. These efforts boosted both sales and his career. In June 1957 he assumed the presidency of Federated, succeeding his father, who continued as chairman of the board and chief executive officer.

As president of Federated, Lazarus utilized his considerable skill in public relations to promote his ideas for community betterment. He turned his attention to the problems of U.S. cities, advocating tightly planned growth and local flexibility to solve urban problems. He led the record-breaking United Appeal campaign for 1959–1960 and, as chairman of the Committee for Economic Development's Subcommittee on Education, spearheaded a three-year study of public-school financing that made recommendations on efficiency, consolidation, and levels of state and federal funding. In March 1961 he was appointed to the first National Advisory Council for the Peace Corps, an appointment that President Lyndon Johnson reconfirmed in April 1964.

Throughout the early 1960s Lazarus publicly opposed suburbanization, arguing that it produced ethnic, religious, racial, and class segregation and decreased Americans' abilities to understand and deal with one another. He remained optimistic about community improvement, however, and believed that business had a large role to play by encouraging employees to give freely of their time and money to worthy causes. Lazarus offered his organizational and executive talents to many groups, including the United Community Funds and Councils of America, which he served as president from 1964 to 1966. In addition he was vice chairman of the Ford Foundation Health Committee, of the National Council of the Foreign Policy Association, and of the Committee for Postal Reform, and chairman of the U.S. Department of Commerce's Public Advisory Committee on Regional Economic Development.

On the business side, Lazarus shrugged off the growing popularity of discounters, arguing that Federated stores, as a result of local management, met customer needs better than chains did. He continued research into consumer behavior, pioneering the use of computers to reveal buying trends and to process economic and demographic data used in targeting expansion areas. He also worked to develop human capital at Federated, boasting of the company's training programs and high-quality executives, whom he gave the "freedom and authority to run their own shows." In 1964 he guided Federated through a difficult merger with the West Coast retailer Bullock's-Magnin. The process took six years and drew the scrutiny of the Federal Trade Commission, which restricted further domestic expansion and led Federated to move into European markets; in 1964 the conglomerate purchased a 10 percent interest in a Spanish department-store chain.

The last fifteen years of Lazarus's career were marked by accolades and promotions. In February 1966 the board of directors announced that Lazarus would succeed his father as chief executive officer of Federated and would join the executive committee. Nineteen months later Lazarus accepted appointment as chairman of the board. Throughout the 1960s and 1970s he served on dozens of boards of directors, including General Electric, Chase Manhattan, Scott Paper, and Gillette. In 1974 he was awarded the highest honor of the National Retail Merchants Association, a gold medal for his lifelong achievement in retailing. Lazarus retired as chief executive officer of Federated in 1981 and as chairman of the board three years later. He died after a long battle with cancer and was buried in Green Lawn Cemetery in Columbus.

Lazarus presided over the largest department-store conglomerate in the United States and oversaw its phenomenal growth. During his time as president Federated nearly tripled its number of stores and doubled its sales volume, its per-share earnings, and its dividends. Through his term as chief executive officer Federated continued to prosper; between 1966 and his retirement in 1981 annual sales rose from approximately $1.3 billion to $7.1 billion.

★

The Lazarus family papers, MSS 352, are in the Ohio Historical Society Library in Columbus. For background see Richard Michael Sabgir, "The Role of the F. and R. Lazarus Company in the Development of Columbus" (M.A. thesis, Ohio State University, 1970). Ralph Lazarus wrote an insightful piece, "The Case of the Oriental Rug," for *Michigan Business Review* (Nov. 1963), and was the subject of or featured in numerous articles, including "The Rising U.S. Economy," *Time* (31 May 1963); "Federated and the Consumer Comeback," *Dun's Review* (Dec. 1967); and "NRMA's Gold Medallist: Ralph Lazarus of Federated Department Stores," *Stores: The Retail Management Magazine* (Jan. 1974). Obituaries are in the *New York Times* and *Columbus Dispatch* (both 20 June 1988).

RAYMOND D. IRWIN

LEKACHMAN, Robert (*b.* 12 May 1920 in New York City; *d.* 14 January 1989 in New York City), college professor and left-leaning economist who authored seven books, including the 1982 best-seller *Greed Is Not Enough: Reaganomics.*

Born on the West Side of Manhattan, Lekachman was the son of Samuel Lekachman, owner of a successful printing company, and Jennie Kominsky. When Robert was five years old his father moved the family to Sea Cliff, a north shore Long Island bedroom community. The Lekachmans were relatively well-to-do, even employing a full-time maid during the Great Depression. In 1938 Robert entered Columbia University as a commuter student and earned a B.A. degree, graduating Phi Beta Kappa in 1942. For the next four years he served as a regimental clerk in the Army of the Pacific during World War II, rising to the rank of sergeant. After leaving the service in 1946, he tried his hand at the family business but proved ill suited for the task. He returned to Columbia University to work toward his Ph.D. in economics and began teaching classes at Barnard College in 1947. On 11 June 1948 he married Eva Leona Woodbrey, an attorney. Lekachman earned his degree the following year, then taught economics at both Barnard and Columbia.

Robert Lekachman. NYT PERMISSIONS

In 1965 Lekachman accepted the position of chair of the Department of Economics at the State University of New York at Stony Brook. He held the post for three years, during which he attempted to transform a mainstream economics program into an eclectic department. This, as he later acknowledged, was a mistake: "I gave that a whirl for three years and discovered that I was one of the world's worst judges of human personality. I hired some real creeps." After a Guggenheim Fellowship, Lekachman returned to Stony Brook and stayed until 1973. He then accepted the position of distinguished professor at Lehman College of the City University of New York, a post he held until his death.

A natural performer and incorrigible ham, Lekachman was an outstanding teacher who won numerous awards for his classroom effectiveness. He loved teaching, especially first-year students, no matter how ill prepared. When asked once why he had not settled in one of the country's elite institutions, Lekachman responded that his students, while not the best and the brightest, were eager to learn, and their total lack of pretension was a constant source of inspiration.

In 1986 *Change,* the magazine of higher education, selected him as one of the fifty faculty members in the United States who had made major contributions to undergraduate education. His engaging manner and quick wit made him a popular public speaker, and he appeared frequently on television and radio programs dealing with public affairs.

Why students loved him is evident in the dedication of his book *Economists at Bay* (1976), "For David Ricardo Lekachman and Samuel Bailey Lekachman." The uninitiated might conclude from this inscription that Lekachman had proudly named his sons after a pair of famous nineteenth-century economists. That was not the case, as Lekachman and his wife were childless. He had in fact dedicated the book to his two feisty cats, who squabbled as often as the famous Ricardo and his frequent critic Bailey.

A prodigious writer, Lekachman penned essays for the popular press as well as professional journals. His professional writings—that is, works intended for other academics—were published in prestigious journals, such as the *Annals of the Academy of Political Science, Political Science Quarterly,* and *American Economic Review*. His popular essays and book reviews, especially of spy novels, a genre for which he had an unabashed passion, appeared in a variety of magazines, including the *New Leader, Nation, Atlantic Monthly, Dissent, New York Times Book Review,* and *Progressive*.

Like his articles, Lekachman's books were a blend of professional texts and popular critiques. *A History of Economic Ideas* (1959) and *The Age of Keynes* (1966) were translated into several languages and were widely used as college texts. In terms of sales, his most successful works were *Greed Is Not Enough: Reaganomics* (1982) and *Visions and Nightmares: America After Reagan* (1987). Whether writing for his peers or the general public, Lekachman was always the maverick, offering a liberal point of view that clearly set him apart from mainstream economists.

The consummate crusader, in the week he died from liver cancer in New York City he published his last essay in the *Nation,* "FDR Changed, and So Can You," an open letter to the incoming U.S. president, George Bush. Lekachman is buried in New York City.

In the 1980s, when the American economics profession took a sharp turn to the right, Robert Lekachman stood almost alone as an outspoken advocate of the poor, the underprivileged, and the disenfranchised. With greater consistency than just about any other prominent contemporary economist, he took on the neoconservatives of the Ronald Reagan era with cleverly caustic, sometimes hilarious, but never nasty prose that afflicted the comfortable and comforted the afflicted. A prolific author and activist, Lekachman was a lifelong liberal and self-confessed socialist who objected to capitalism on pragmatic rather than ideological grounds. As he saw it, mainstream economics was more often irrelevant than wrong, primarily because its proponents were usually oblivious to reality.

Lekachman was forever poking fun at his colleagues because he thought their work was so removed from the real business of life. He once observed: "Ignorance of the real world is more than bliss: It is very nearly a prerequisite to a successful career in conventional economics." He had, it seemed, more confidence in those taking economics courses than in those teaching them. "It is," he said, "a tribute to the intelligent realism of most students that few of them take more than a single introductory course in economics." His disdain for his chosen profession was the hallmark of his career.

★

Robert Lekachman, "The West Side of My Youth," *Dissent* (fall 1987), is an autobiographical sketch that focuses on Lekachman's young life. Ron Chernow, "Robert Lekachman, the Irreverent Economist," *Change* 10, no. 4 (Apr. 1978): 32–37, is a detailed analysis of the life and works of Lekachman through 1978. Obituaries are in the *New York Times* (16 Jan. 1989), the *New Leader* (23 Jan. 1989), and the *Nation* (6 Feb. 1989).

JAMES CICARELLI

LEMAY, Curtis Emerson (*b.* 15 November 1906 in Columbus, Ohio; *d.* 1 October 1990 at March Air Force Base, near Riverside, California), U.S. Air Force general who directed the bombing of Japan during World War II and who fashioned the Strategic Air Command (SAC) during the height of the cold war.

The oldest of the seven children of Erving LeMay and Arizona (Carpenter) LeMay, Curtis had a difficult childhood. His father, employed sporadically as an ironworker and at odd jobs, was a poor provider for his family. The LeMays had a nomadic existence, living at different times in Pennsylvania, Montana, and California. Young Curtis worked at jobs ranging from newspaper and telegram delivery to shoveling ashes and snow in order to improve the family's circumstances. By his own admission he frequently ran away from home.

LeMay's lifelong fascination with flying dated from childhood, when he saw an airplane in the sky. Lacking political connections, he failed to win an appointment to the U.S. Military Academy at West Point, from which he hoped to launch a career in aviation. Instead, he enrolled at Ohio State University in 1924, and received a bachelor's degree in civil engineering in 1932. He worked in a steel foundry to support himself while in college, but also found the time and energy to join the Reserve Officers Training Corps unit, in hopes of ultimately securing a regular army commission. In 1928 he joined the Ohio National Guard as a stepping-stone to the Army Air Corps flying school, from which he won his commission in 1930.

General Curtis E. LeMay. Archive Photos

During the 1930s LeMay gained valuable experience in the Army Air Corps and became an outstanding navigator. He served in Michigan and Hawaii, and in 1937 he was transferred to Langley Field, Virginia, as an operations officer for the 49th Bombardment Squadron. The following year he was the navigator of one of the B-17 bombers that made a goodwill visit to South America. In 1941 he was assigned to develop ferry routes that would link the United States to Great Britain and the Middle East; he received the Distinguished Flying Cross for his efforts.

Of medium height and stocky build, the cigar-chewing LeMay earned a reputation for his unsmiling expression and no-nonsense ways. (His inability to smile was due to Bell's palsy.) Toughness notwithstanding, LeMay began courting Helen Maitland, the daughter of a Cleveland lawyer, in 1931. They married on 9 June 1934 and had one daughter.

During World War II, LeMay became one of the nation's most celebrated military heroes. In July 1942 he was put in charge of the 305th Bombardment Squadron, a unit of the Eighth Air Force that carried out strategic attacks on German cities. He was promoted to colonel that same year. Unlike their British counterparts, who opted for nighttime raids, American bomber commanders, under LeMay's direction, ordered daytime raids beginning in November 1942. To improve bombing efficacy, LeMay, personally leading his B-17 raiders, successfully initiated the practice of flying in straight and level formation rather than breaking ranks and taking evasive action. In July 1943 LeMay was given command of the Eighth Air Force's Fourth Bomb Wing. He personally led the bold attack on the Messerschmitt aircraft factory at Regensberg, Germany, on 17 August 1943 that reduced Nazi production but cost the United States sixty B-17s, which failed to return to their bases in England. For his five combat missions, LeMay earned the Air Medal and Silver Star.

In September 1944 LeMay, who was now a major general, was in charge of the Twentieth Bomber Command of B-29 Super Fortresses in the China-Burma-India theater of operations. Within a few months he had improved performance in bombing raids on Japan and Japanese-held territory through changes in both tactics and strategy.

In January 1945 LeMay was posted to Guam to head the 21st Bomber Command. Two months later he virtually staked his career on an audacious decision to fly bombers at very low levels over Japanese cities. The B-29s were stripped of defensive weapons and excess crewmen so that they could carry greater bomb tonnage. Gambling that the Japanese had not prepared for a massive aerial attack on their homeland, that they lacked effective radar, and that their fighter planes would be largely ineffective at low altitudes, LeMay sent 300 planes to firebomb Tokyo on the night of 9 March 1945. Their incendiary bombs caused the deaths of perhaps 100,000 civilians and injuries to a million more, and destroyed a huge number of homes that had become "shadow factories" for Japan's decentralized war production. Subsequent firebomb raids on Nagoya, Osaka, Kobe, and Tokyo further reduced Japan's ability to wage war, and caused thousands of civilian deaths and immense suffering. LeMay noted years later in his autobiography: "We were attacked by Japan. Do you want to kill Japanese, or would you rather have Americans killed?" And he reputedly said shortly after the war ended: "I'll tell you what war is about, you've got to kill people, and when you've killed enough they stop fighting."

When the war with the Axis powers was over, LeMay became concerned with what he deemed a new and dangerous adversary: the Soviet Union. Appointed deputy chief of the air staff for research and development in early 1946, he played an important role in evaluating new military technology and in calling for increased funding for research and development. Promoted to the rank of lieutenant general, he was appointed in October 1947 as U.S. Air Force chief of staff. Roughly six months later the Soviet Union imposed a blockade on travel between West Berlin and West Germany. As commander of the U.S. Air Forces in Europe, LeMay quickly launched Operation Vittles, which flew more than 2 million tons of supplies to beleaguered West

Berliners and, because of its success, helped convince the Soviets to lift the blockade in May 1949.

Before the Berlin airlift ended, LeMay returned to the United States as commanding general of the Strategic Air Command (SAC), the key component of the nation's deterrent force against possible Soviet attacks. Determined that the United States would maintain nuclear superiority over the Soviet Union, LeMay placed SAC bombers and bases on a global wartime alert, stating that SAC's primary mission was to be able to drop 80 percent of its total arsenal in a single mission. (By 1955 SAC virtually controlled target planning.) At the outset of the Korean War in 1950, LeMay suggested that the destruction of four or five North Korean cities would end the war, but he was reluctant to employ too many planes for fear that the United States would be vulnerable to Soviet attacks.

Having built SAC into a prodigious force, LeMay was appointed vice chief of staff of the U.S. Air Force in 1957. Four years later he received his fourth star and appointment as the air force's chief of staff, a position he held until his retirement in 1965. During his tenure LeMay espoused technological advances, notably the refinement of both offensive and defensive missiles. Nonetheless, he successfully opposed Secretary of Defense Robert McNamara's plan to do away with manned bombers and to rely on guided missiles. Less successful was his stance during the missile crisis in 1962, when he urged a military strike against Cuba that he believed would have toppled Fidel Castro's regime. In the same vein, the Vietnam War frustrated his desire for clear-cut victory. During deliberations by the administration of President Lyndon Johnson about American involvement in Vietnam, LeMay called for full-scale bombings of North Vietnam and soon became widely known for his advice to bomb the enemy "back into the Stone Ages."

After retirement LeMay briefly returned to public life in 1968 as the vice presidential candidate on the American Independent party ticket, headed by George C. Wallace, former governor of Alabama. (Wallace, while under LeMay's command, had taken part in bombing raids on Japan during World War II.) Though playing only a minor role in the campaign, LeMay damaged the ticket with his forthright, ultrahawkish statements. At a press conference he incautiously noted that Americans "seem to have a phobia about nuclear weapons. . . . I don't believe the world would end if we exploded a nuclear weapon." After the election he returned to private life and resided in California until his death from a heart attack nearly fifteen years later.

Curtis E. LeMay was one of the greatest American military leaders of the twentieth century. His military expertise, innovativeness, and daring tactics helped to achieve victory in World War II; his leadership of SAC provided a powerful deterrent to Soviet aggression during the cold war. Moreover, he was acclaimed for his willingness to lead men into battle and to inspire them to great efforts. On the other hand, critics have condemned his attacks on civilian centers and his willingness to wage nuclear war.

★

The Library of Congress houses the Curtis E. LeMay papers. Curtis E. LeMay, with MacKinlay Kantor, *Mission with LeMay: My Story* (1965), is filled with details narrated in the general's customary straight-talking manner. Curt Anders, *Fighting Airmen* (1966), contains a chapter on LeMay that is largely hagiographic but nevertheless conveys useful information. Two massive works by Richard Rhodes, *The Making of the Atomic Bomb* (1986) and *Dark Sun: The Making of the Hydrogen Bomb* (1995), offer helpful information but are more critical of LeMay. Michael S. Sherry, *The Rise of American Air Power: The Creation of Armageddon* (1987), makes use of the LeMay papers and contains an astute look at the general and his influence. An obituary is in the *New York Times* (2 Oct. 1990).

ROBERT MUCCIGROSSO

LEMNITZER, Lyman Louis (*b.* 29 August 1899 in Honesdale, Pennsylvania; *d.* 12 November 1988 in Washington, D.C.), soldier-diplomat, four-star general, and chairman of the Joint Chiefs of Staff, who during World War II helped plan the invasion of North Africa and later participated in secret negotiations that led to the surrender of German forces in Italy.

Of German Lutheran ancestry, Lemnitzer was the second of three sons of William L. Lemnitzer, a shoe manufacturer, and Hannah Blockberger. After graduation from Honesdale High School in 1917, Lemnitzer worked for a year in a machine parts factory while awaiting admission to the U.S. Military Academy at West Point. In June 1920 he graduated eighty-sixth in a class of 271 from West Point, with a B.S. degree, and was commissioned a second lieutenant in the Coast Artillery Corps.

After a year of study at the Coast Artillery School at Fort Monroe, Virginia, Lemnitzer served with coast artillery units at Fort Adams, Rhode Island, from 1921 to 1923 and at Fort Mills on the Philippine island of Corregidor from 1924 to 1926. Before departing for the Philippines, he married Katherine Mead Tryon on 6 November 1923. The couple had two children.

In 1926 Lemnitzer, who had been promoted to first lieutenant the year before, became an instructor at West Point. He left this position in 1930 to take a nine-month advanced training course at the Coast Artillery School. After a second tour of duty in the Philippines from 1931 to 1934, he again taught at West Point for a year. He was promoted to captain in August 1935 and sent to study at the Command and General Staff School at Fort Leavenworth, Kansas. After graduation in June 1936, Lemnitzer was an instructor at

Lyman Lemnitzer. ARCHIVE PHOTOS

the Coast Artillery School for three years. Between 1939 and 1940, he completed his military education at the Army War College in Washington, D.C.—the traditional stepping stone to higher command—and in 1940 he achieved the rank of major.

In May 1941, after a year of service with coast artillery units at Fort Moultrie, South Carolina, and Camp Stewart, Georgia, Lemnitzer was assigned to the War Department's war plans division. A month later he was promoted to lieutenant colonel and transferred to the plans division of Army General Headquarters.

After the entry of the United States into World War II, the army was reorganized, and Lemnitzer was assigned to Headquarters, Army Ground Forces as assistant chief of staff in the plans division from March until June 1942, when he became a colonel. Two weeks later he was made brigadier general, and soon thereafter he became the commander of the Thirty-fourth Antiaircraft Brigade, in England. Between September and December 1942, he also served on the staff of General Dwight D. Eisenhower as assistant chief of planning, where he worked with General Mark W. Clark in planning Operation Torch, the Allied invasion of North Africa in November 1942.

Robert Murphy, an American diplomat in North Africa, believed that some Vichy French commanders in the area might be persuaded not to resist the Allied landings. When General Clark volunteered to lead a top secret mission to Algeria in October 1942 to establish contact with Vichy military leaders in the hope of arranging an armistice, Lemnitzer accompanied him. Their party was transported from Gibraltar by a British submarine and landed by commandos in small boats. Although the Allied landings did not go uncontested, this was the first of Lemnitzer's forays into diplomacy.

Clark was rewarded for this effort with command of the U.S. Fifth Army, and Lemnitzer briefly served as his deputy chief of staff before leaving in February 1943 to reassume command of the Thirty-fourth Antiaircraft Brigade during the Tunisian campaign and the landing phase of the invasion of Sicily.

On 25 July 1943 Lemnitzer reported to the headquarters of the Allied Fifteenth Army Group as the senior U.S. officer on the staff of its commander, British General (later Field Marshal) Harold Alexander. In March 1944 he became Alexander's deputy chief of staff and continued in that position when Alexander was elevated to Supreme Allied Commander, Mediterranean. Lemnitzer, who became a major general in June 1944, demonstrated his diplomatic skills by lessening friction between the American military and its British ally. He also played a role in the events leading to Italy's capitulation in September 1943 and conducted secret talks in Switzerland that led to the surrender of all German forces in northern Italy and southern Austria on 2 May 1945.

In November 1945 Lemnitzer returned to Washington as an army member of the Joint Strategic Survey Committee, which advised the Joint Chiefs of Staff on strategy. He became deputy commandant of the newly established National War College in August 1947. While in that post, he headed in 1948 the American delegation to a London meeting of the military leaders of the Brussels Pact nations that helped lay the groundwork for the creation of the North Atlantic Treaty Organization.

Lemnitzer left his post at the National War College in October 1949 to become the first director of the newly created Office of Military Assistance, where he played a key role in delivering military aid to America's European allies to bolster their defenses against the possibility of Soviet aggression.

In keeping with the army's policy of rotating officers between staff work and field command, Lemnitzer in late 1950 was given command of the Eleventh Airborne Division at Fort Campbell, Kentucky, after qualifying as a paratrooper at the age of fifty-one.

In December 1951 Lemnitzer was given command of the Seventh Infantry Division in Korea. He led the unit in fighting at Heartbreak Ridge, the Punch Bowl, and the Chorwon Valley, and was awarded the Distinguished Service Medal and the Silver Star (1952) for gallantry in action.

Promoted to lieutenant general in August 1952, he returned to Washington, D.C., to serve as deputy chief of staff for plans and research.

On 25 March 1955 Lemnitzer was appointed commander of U.S. Army Forces in the Far East and the Eighth Army, with the rank of full general. In May 1955 he became commander in chief of the U.S. Far East Command and of the United Nations Command. When South Korean president Syngman Rhee threatened to disrupt the Korean armistice signed in 1953, Lemnitzer flew to Seoul in August 1955 for talks with Rhee and helped calm the situation. In 1956 Lemnitzer engaged in diplomatic efforts aimed at keeping U.S. forces on Okinawa, Japan, in the face of growing protests of American occupation by the people of the island.

In 1957 Lemnitzer became army vice-chief of staff under Maxwell Taylor. When Taylor retired from the army in July 1959, Lemnitzer succeeded him as army chief of staff and championed the creation of a mobile, hard-hitting army with airlift capabilities. As chairman of the Joint Chiefs of Staff from 1960 to 1962, Lemnitzer supervised the buildup of American forces in Europe in response to the Berlin crisis of 1961. He also organized the U.S. Strike Command (later the U.S. Central Command), which brought the U.S. Strategic Army and the Air Force Tactical Air Command under a unified command.

Lemnitzer was unfortunate in being chairman of the Joint Chiefs in April 1961, during the Bay of Pigs operation—the failed U.S. effort to overthrow Cuban leader Fidel Castro. In a search for someone to blame for the fiasco, Senator Albert Gore of Tennessee called for the ouster of Lemnitzer and the other chiefs of the military. Although President John F. Kennedy posed for pictures with Lemnitzer and his associates to show his "confidence" in them (*New York Times,* 28 May 1961), Lemnitzer was not reappointed by Kennedy to a second term.

Despite this rebuff, Lemnitzer, who was eligible for retirement, chose to remain in the army. In July 1962 he was named Supreme Allied Commander in Europe, but his assumption of the post was delayed until 1 January 1963 because of the Cuban missile crisis. When in 1966 President Charles de Gaulle formally withdrew French forces from NATO and demanded that all NATO forces and headquarters be withdrawn from French soil, Lemnitzer completely revised plans for the defense of Europe and supervised the transfer of his headquarters to Casteau, Belgium.

After retiring from the army on 1 September 1969, Lemnitzer occasionally testified before congressional committees on military matters and was a vocal critic of President Jimmy Carter's military policies during the late 1970s, because he feared Carter's cuts in military spending would make the United States militarily inferior to the Soviet Union. On the other hand, he suggested a military buildup under Ronald Reagan, who in 1987 awarded him the Presidential Medal of Freedom.

In 1982 Lemnitzer was diagnosed with prostate cancer. His health slowly declined, and he died of kidney failure at Walter Reed Army Hospital in Washington, D.C. He was buried in Arlington National Cemetery.

★

Lemnitzer's papers are in the Special Collections section of the National Defense University Library, Fort McNair, Washington, D.C. The only full-length biography is L. James Binder, *Lemnitzer: A Soldier for His Time* (1997). Clarke Newlon, "War Without Casualties," *Collier's* (12 July 1950), is a contemporary assessment of the Mutual Defense Assistance Program with reference to Lemnitzer's contribution to it as director of the Office of Military Assistance. "General Lem," *Time* (30 Mar. 1959), provides a brief discussion of the diplomatic aspects of Lemnitzer's career before his appointment as army chief of staff. "Command Shape-up," *Time* (27 July 1962), suggests why he was not nominated for a second term as chairman of the Joint Chiefs of Staff. Lawrence S. Kaplan and Kathleen A. Kellner, "Lemnitzer: Surviving the French Military Withdrawal," in Robert S. Jordan, ed., *Generals in International Politics: NATO's Supreme Allied Commander, Europe* (1987), assesses his six-year tenure as head of NATO forces. Obituaries are in the *New York Times* and *Washington Post* (both 13 Nov. 1988).

ROMAN ROME

LERNER, Alan Jay (*b.* 31 August 1918 in New York City; *d.* 14 June 1986 in New York City), lyricist, librettist, screenwriter, and author whose most successful works were collaborations with the composer Frederick Loewe.

Alan Jay Lerner was the second of three sons of Joseph J. Lerner, the wealthy cofounder of a chain of women's clothing shops bearing his name, and Edith (Adelson) Lerner. He showed an early interest in music, beginning to play the piano at five; at about the same age, his father took him to see his first Broadway musical. He attended the Columbia Grammar and Preparatory School, except for a semester spent at the Bedales School in England. He went on to the Choate School in Wallingford, Connecticut, where he wrote the football song "Gold and Blue." Although he was expelled from Choate for smoking, he was able to enroll at Harvard College in September 1936. There he joined the Hasty Pudding Club. He wrote the lyrics for and appeared in the club's musical *So Proudly We Hail* in 1938 and wrote the music, lyrics, and libretto for its 1939 show, *Fair Enough*. Lerner lost the retina of his left eye in a boxing match in college.

Lerner received a B.S. degree from Harvard in June 1940. On 26 June 1940 he married Ruth O'Day Boyd; they had one daughter and were divorced in 1947. After grad-

Alan Jay Lerner. ARCHIVE PHOTOS

uation, Lerner moved to New York City, where he wrote advertising copy and was a freelance writer for radio shows. A member of the Lambs Club, he contributed to the club's shows, the *Gambols;* his work was seen by Frederick Loewe, a fellow member. Loewe had written a couple of shows without much success. He had been approached to have the songs from one of them reused in a new show, but his lyricist partner had joined the armed services. In August 1942 he introduced himself to Lerner and proposed that they collaborate. The immediate result was a show called *Life of the Party*, for which Lerner wrote the book, based on Barry Connors's play *The Patsy,* and revised the earlier lyrics. It ran for nine weeks in Detroit, beginning in October 1942, but never reached Broadway. The next Lerner-Loewe musical, *What's Up?*, did get to Broadway on 11 November 1943, but it was a failure. Two years later they wrote *The Day Before Spring*, which managed to run 165 performances.

It was Lerner and Loewe's fourth show, *Brigadoon*, that established them as a success. Opening 13 March 1947, this fantasy about a Scottish town that comes awake only one day each 100 years featured an original book by Lerner and songs including "Almost Like Being in Love." It ran 581 performances, a substantial hit, and its cast album sold well. The show's female star was Marion Bell, who became Lerner's second wife in 1947; they were divorced in 1949.

Loewe, more than seventeen years older than Lerner, was inclined to rest on this success, so Lerner sought another collaborator. He found one in Kurt Weill, with whom he wrote the experimental *Love Life*, which opened 7 October 1948 and ran 252 performances. He then accepted an offer from Metro-Goldwyn-Mayer to go to California and write scripts and lyrics for movie musicals. On 19 March 1950 he married the actress Nancy Olson. They had two daughters and were divorced in 1957. Lerner's first completed film was *Royal Wedding*, a vehicle for Fred Astaire with music by Burton Lane. Released in March 1951, it was a box-office hit, the soundtrack album made the Top Ten, and the song "Too Late Now" was nominated for an Academy Award. Lerner wrote the script for *An American in Paris*, which used music by George and Ira Gershwin. It was released in November 1951 and went on to win the Academy Award for best picture. Lerner's script was also an Oscar winner.

Three days after the release of *An American in Paris*, on 12 November 1951, Broadway had another Lerner and Loewe musical; Lerner had lured his partner back to work on *Paint Your Wagon*, set in the California gold rush. It ran an unprofitable 289 performances, but the score, which included "I Talk to the Trees" and "They Call the Wind Maria," had better luck in record stores. The team next attempted a musicalization of George Bernard Shaw's play *Pygmalion*, but abandoned it and separated again. Lerner returned to Hollywood, where he wrote a script for a film adaptation of *Brigadoon*, starring Gene Kelly, that was released in September 1954.

Lerner and Loewe returned to work on *Pygmalion*, eventually retitled *My Fair Lady*, and finally succeeded with their adaptation. The show, starring Rex Harrison and Julie Andrews, opened on 15 March 1956 and went on to become the longest-running musical in Broadway history up to that time, playing 2,717 performances. It won the Tony Award for best musical, and the score, which featured "On the Street Where You Live," "I Could Have Danced All Night," "I've Grown Accustomed to Her Face," "With a Little Bit of Luck," and "Get Me to the Church on Time," generated a cast album that sold millions of copies.

Lerner and Loewe next wrote a musical for the screen, adapting Colette's novel *Gigi*, which was shot largely in Paris. On 29 November 1957 Lerner married French lawyer Micheline Muselli Pozzo di Borgo. They had one son and were divorced in June 1965. *Gigi* was released in May 1958 and was a box-office hit, winning the Academy Award for best picture and giving Lerner his second Oscar, for best song, the title track. The top-selling soundtrack album was a Grammy winner in its category. Despite Loewe's 1959 heart attack, the songwriters embarked on another project, their last for more than a decade. It was *Camelot*, a stage musical version of the King Arthur legend based on T. H. White's novel *The Once and Future King*. Opening on 3 December 1960 with a cast led by Richard Burton, Julie Andrews, and Robert Goulet, the show had a rocky time at first, but settled into an 873-performance run. The cast album, featuring the title song and "If Ever I Would Leave You," was a million-selling, number-one hit.

After *Camelot*, Loewe once more retired. Lerner began working with Richard Rodgers on a musical about extrasensory perception, initially called *I Picked a Daisy*. But the partnership did not work, and Lerner was forced to start over with Burton Lane. Meanwhile, he wrote the screenplay for the movie version of *My Fair Lady*, which came out in October 1964. An expensive production, it failed to make back its investment despite being one of the top-grossing films of the year and winning the Academy Award for best picture. The ESP musical, retitled *On a Clear Day You Can See Forever*, finally reached Broadway on 17 October 1965, where it ran an unprofitable 280 performances. The title song was popular, however, and the cast album was a Grammy winner.

On 15 November 1966 Lerner married his fifth wife, Karen Gundersen, a reporter; they divorced in December 1974. His next projects were both film adaptations of his shows. He wrote the script for *Camelot* (October 1967), another expensive movie that missed profitability, though the soundtrack album, featuring Richard Harris as Arthur, was a million-seller. For *Paint Your Wagon* (October 1969), coming to the screen eighteen years after it opened on Broadway, he wrote the screenplay (though Paddy Chayefsky is credited for adaptation of it) and produced the film. He also wrote five new songs with André Previn. The most expensive movie musical ever made at that time, it was disastrously unsuccessful. The month after it reached movie theaters, *Coco*, Lerner's musical about the fashion designer Chanel, starring Katharine Hepburn and with music by Previn, opened on Broadway on 18 December 1969 and ran a successful 332 performances.

Lerner continued to work steadily in the 1970s and 1980s, but none of his projects met with great success. *On a Clear Day You Can See Forever* was adapted into a film with a Lerner screenplay. Starring Barbra Streisand, it was released in June 1970 and lost money. Lerner's next musical, *Lolita, My Love*, based on the Vladimir Nabokov novel, closed before reaching Broadway, in March 1971. Lerner succeeded in convincing Loewe to join him on his next two projects, a stage version of *Gigi* with five new songs that ran only 103 performances (but won the Tony Award for best score) in 1973, and a film version of Antoine de Saint-Exupery's *The Little Prince* (1974), which brought them Oscar nominations for the title song and the score. Lerner married his sixth wife, actress Sandra Payne, on 10 December 1974; they were divorced in 1976. His next musical was *1600 Pennsylvania Avenue* (1976), which paired him with Leonard Bernstein. It ran less than a week. On 30 May 1977 he married Nina Bushkin, a college administrator and the daughter of jazz pianist Joe Bushkin; they divorced in 1980. Reuniting with Burton Lane, he wrote the musical *Carmelina*, which opened 8 April 1979 and ran seventeen performances. His eighth and last wife was Elizabeth Robertson, a singer and actress he met when she was appearing in a London revival of *My Fair Lady*. They were married 13 August 1981, and he wrote his next, and final, musical for her. It was *Dance a Little Closer*, which opened and closed on 11 May 1983. He had finished a history book, *The Musical Theatre*, and was working on a musical version of the screwball comedy film *My Man Godfrey* when he died of lung cancer in 1986, at age sixty-seven.

Alan Jay Lerner brought a high level of wit and sophistication to both his lyrics and his librettos, writing thirteen musicals that came to Broadway and the screenplays for nine motion pictures. Repeatedly he contrasted the jaded, unhappy state of contemporary civilization with youth and innocence, looking for ways by which society could be renewed through a restoration of its original ideals. He found a perfect match for his words in Frederick Loewe's neo-Viennese music but, unable to coax the composer to work at his pace, he also collaborated with other talented composers. If the results were not as satisfying, Lerner's works were always daring and challenging, the product of a restless, exploratory imagination.

★

The best biography of Lerner is Edward Jablonski's *Alan Jay Lerner: A Biography* (1996), although also to be recommended are Stephen Citron's divided account, *The Wordsmiths: Oscar Hammerstein II and Alan Jay Lerner* (1995), and Lerner's own memoir, *The Street Where I Live* (1978). Gene Lees's *Inventing Champagne: The Worlds of Lerner and Loewe* (1990) is too mean-spirited to be enjoyable, and Doris Shapiro's *We Danced All Night: My Life Behind the Scenes with Alan Jay Lerner* (1990) focuses on the drug addiction from which this former assistant says she and her employer suffered. An obituary is in the *New York Times* (15 June 1986).

WILLIAM J. RUHLMANN

LEROY, Mervyn (*b.* 15 October 1900 in San Francisco; *d.* 13 September 1987 in Beverly Hills, California), motion picture director and producer.

The only child born to Harry and Edna Armer LeRoy, Mervyn began his career when his theater-loving mother secured him the role of the papoose in *The Squaw Man* at San Francisco's famed Alcazar Theater. When he was five,

Mervyn LeRoy, producer-director of the film *Gypsy,* 1962. ARCHIVE PHOTOS

she left him and his father to live in Oakland, California, with Percy Teeple, a San Francisco newspaperman turned travel businessman, whom she eventually married. After the 1906 San Francisco earthquake, LeRoy and his father spent six months in the U.S. Army's tent city at the Presidio. Having lost home and business (an export-import department store), the elder LeRoy became a salesman for the Heinz Pickle Company.

While in grade school LeRoy sold newspapers; one day as he sold them near the Alcazar, the actor Theodore Roberts invited him to play the newsboy in Clyde Fitch's *Barbara Frietchie.* LeRoy developed a strong desire to appear in vaudeville. In his first original act, "The Singing Newsboy," he sang " 'Twas Only an Irishman's Dream." After his father died in 1915, LeRoy lived briefly with his mother and stepfather, who became his business manager in later years. LeRoy played drums in the Grant School band but preferred performing at Oakland's Ye Liberty Theater. His diligent reading in later years more than compensated for his quitting school after sixth grade.

LeRoy returned to San Francisco with a new act, "Mervyn LeRoy, the Boy Tenor of the Generation." Later that year his Chaplin imitation won first prize over a thousand contestants at the Pantages Theater on Market Street, and the impresario Sid Grauman, who was in the audience, asked LeRoy to repeat the act during the eleven-month duration of the Panama-Pacific International Exposition (February–December 1915). Following that commitment LeRoy teamed up with a young pianist-singer, Clyde Cooper; dressed in Eton suits, they were billed as "LeRoy and Cooper, Two Kids and a Piano." For three years they toured vaudeville circuits throughout the United States and Canada. When Cooper's father died the team dissolved.

For several years LeRoy was part of an act called "The Nine Country Kids" with Gus Edwards. In New York City he played a grocery boy in an episode of the popular silent-movie series *The Perils of Pauline.* Soon he approached his cousin Jesse L. Lasky at the New York office of Famous Players–Lasky (a company that combined the financial and artistic talents of Lasky, Sam Goldwyn, Cecil B. DeMille, and Adolph Zukor). The following week LeRoy went to work at the company's California studio. He folded and unfolded Civil War uniforms for *Secret Service* (1919); worked as a lab assistant responsible for "washing" (dipping the film into colored dyes); and, after taking the initiative to perfect a special moonlight effect for William C. DeMille, won promotion to assistant cameraman and, six months later, second cameraman. However, a camera error cost him his job. Decades later LeRoy compared his earliest Hollywood days to a college audit program, because he was observing outstanding directors.

LeRoy worked as an extra in Cecil B. DeMille's *Ten Commandments* (1923) and started playing bit and minor roles, including one film each with Gloria Swanson and Betty Compson. At the request of Jack L. Warner he played a horse-riding George Nelson in *Little Johnny Jones* (1923). After the director Alfred E. Green suggested that he utilize his comic flair, LeRoy became a "comedy constructor" for Green's *In Hollywood with Potash and Perlmutter* (1924) and *Sally* (1925), followed by five films with as many different directors (1925–1927) and three more with Green in 1926.

Colleen Moore, impressed by LeRoy's talents when she had starred in four of his works for Green, helped him become a director. Moore was slated to star in his first film, but the project was canceled. The studio then gave LeRoy the opportunity to direct *No Place to Go* (1927), with Mary Astor. That initial success was reinforced by the following year's release of *Harold Teen* (based on Carl Ed's comic strip), which grossed over a million dollars; *Flying Romeos*; and *Oh, Kay!* (starring Moore, with titles by P. G. Wodehouse). During 1929 LeRoy directed his first "talkies" for First National, including a remake of *Little Johnny Jones.*

Only five feet, three inches tall, with an exuberant, boyish appearance, LeRoy averaged three to six films a year during his association with First National and Warner Brothers (which bought First National in 1928), and directed more than forty of their top contract stars and featured actors. He helped initiate or advance the careers of Edward G. Robinson, Paul Muni, James Cagney, and Olivia de Havilland; his discoveries included Loretta Young and Lana Turner. He ordered and directed the first screen test for the stage actor Clark Gable, although Warner failed to sign him. Outstanding successes for First National and Warner Brothers include *Little Caesar* (1930), *Five Star Final* (1931), *I Am a Fugitive from a Chain Gang* (1932), *Gold Diggers of 1933* (with choreographer Busby Berkeley), *Oil for the Lamps of China* (1935), and a lavish, million-dollar production of Hervey Allen's popular novel *Anthony Adverse* (1936).

Little is known of LeRoy's first marriage to (in the 1920s) and divorce from (in the early 1930s) Edna Murphy, a screen actress who played in his remake of *Little Johnny Jones*. On 2 January 1934 he married Doris Warner (daughter of Harry M. Warner); they would have two children before divorcing in 1945. On 1 February 1946 LeRoy married Katherine Byfield Spiegel.

Warner Brothers released LeRoy to direct *Tugboat Annie* (1933) at Metro-Goldwyn-Mayer (MGM); there he impressed Louis B. Mayer and Irving G. Thalberg. In 1938, two years after Thalberg's death, Mayer chose LeRoy to succeed Thalberg as production head, signing him to one of the largest contracts offered up to that time ($300,000 a year). As producer, LeRoy worked on four films, including *At the Circus* (1939), with the Marx Brothers, and *The Wizard of Oz* (1939), for which he cast Judy Garland as Dorothy. Since he missed directing, he asked for a lower-salaried directorial contract. From 1940 to 1954 he directed nineteen films at MGM, including *Random Harvest* (1942), for which he was nominated for an Academy Award as best director, and war-related films such as *Waterloo Bridge* (1940); *Escape* (1940), with Norma Shearer; and the documentary-styled *Thirty Seconds over Tokyo* (1944). During World War II he also served as a consultant to Nelson Rockefeller's wartime information agency offices in Hollywood, directing brief documentaries on civilian defense and army subjects.

Even though LeRoy did not believe that films had to convey a message, he was proud of *I Am a Fugitive from a Chain Gang* (1932), *They Won't Forget* (1937), and *Blossoms in the Dust* (1941), which prompted public outcry against, respectively, inhumane prison conditions, lynching, and violation of the rights of illegitimate children. In 1945, at the urging of his friend Frank Sinatra, he agreed to direct and coproduce (with Frank Ross) a ten-minute film on racial tolerance, *The House I Live In* (RKO, 1945). LeRoy won a special Academy Award for that film.

After the war he was responsible for the first Technicolor rendering of *Little Women* (1949) and the first sound version of Henryk Sienkiewicz's novel *Quo Vadis?* (1951). LeRoy then worked on musical entertainment pieces such as *Million Dollar Mermaid* (1952); *Rose Marie* (1954) was his final MGM film. Intensifying disagreements with MGM's Dore Schary prompted LeRoy to return in 1954 to Warner Brothers, where he directed and produced (usually for Mervyn LeRoy Productions) most of his films for the next nine years. His last film at Warner, *Mary, Mary* (1963), starred Debbie Reynolds.

Memorable films from this final period were *Mister Roberts* (1955), which he took over from the ailing John Ford; *The FBI Story* (1959), with James Stewart (for which FBI director J. Edgar Hoover, LeRoy's friend, awarded LeRoy the Distinguished Service Award); and *Gypsy* (1962). One of his last professional directing projects was assisting John Wayne with *The Green Berets* (1963), at least the fifth time since the 1930s that LeRoy had refused screen credit. LeRoy received the 1975 Irving G. Thalberg Memorial Award for his career achievements. In later years he developed Alzheimer's disease. He died at his home in Beverly Hills. He is buried in Forest Lawn Memorial Park, Glendale, California.

Although his vaudeville background was not unique in Hollywood, Mervyn LeRoy was among the few to continue to embody that spirit of entertainment throughout his life, translating the instincts and abilities developed as a live entertainer into interaction, as director and producer, with screen audiences. He believed that a well-written script is the secret to success in the motion-picture business. As director of a variety of subjects and styles in his more than seventy-five films, LeRoy's primary goal was to provide entertainment—sometimes informative, perhaps even inspiring, but nearly always uplifting.

★

Legal files of contracts and memoranda, daily production sheets, scripts, and publicity materials pertaining to LeRoy's Warner Brothers years are in the Warner Brothers Archives at the University of Southern California and in the MGM Script Collection, Cinema-Television Library and Archives of the Performing Arts, University of Southern California.

LeRoy's *It Takes More Than Talent,* as told to Alyce Canfield (1953), contains basic autobiographical material. His autobiography, *Mervyn LeRoy: Take One,* as told to Dick Kleiner (1974), includes a filmography through 1965. LeRoy wrote "Motion Pictures and Pay TV," *Atlantic Monthly* (Dec. 1957). Interviews were published by Jerome Beatty, "Mervyn of the Movies," *American Magazine* (July 1938), and by Quentin Reynolds, "Shooting Stars," *Collier's* (9 Feb. 1935).

Information on LeRoy and his films is in Kingsley Canham, "Mervyn LeRoy: Star-making, Studio Systems, and Style" and "Mervyn LeRoy Filmography" (through 1965), in Clive Denton and Kingsley Canham, *The Hollywood Professionals,* vol. 5 (1976); "Mervyn LeRoy," in William R. Meyer, *Warner Brothers Directors: The Hard-Boiled, the Comic, and the Weepers* (1978); David Thomson, *A Biographical Dictionary of Film* (2d ed., rev., 1981); Charles Wolfe, in Jean-Pierre Coursodon, with Pierre Sauvage, *American Directors,* vol. 1 (1983); Ted Sennett, *Great Movie Directors* (1986); and Charles Affron, in Nicholas Thomas, ed., *International Dictionary of Films and Filmmakers,* vol. 2, *Directors* (2d ed., 1991).

Obituaries are in the *New York Times* (14 Sept. 1987), the London *Times* (15 Sept. 1987), and *Variety* (16 Sept. 1987). There is a microfilm copy (1978) of the Southern Methodist University Oral History Project on the Performing Arts, no. 45, Ronald L. Davis, interviewer (16 May 1977) in the New York Times Oral History Program on the Performing Arts.

MADELINE SAPIENZA

LEVINE, Joseph Edward (*b.* 9 September 1905 in Boston, Massachusetts; *d.* 31 July 1987 in Greenwich, Connecticut), film producer and distributor who originated the concept of saturation booking and who helped popularize foreign films in the United States.

The youngest of six children of Russian-Jewish immigrants, whose names are not known, Levine grew up in poverty in Boston's West End. His father, a tailor, died when Levine was four. His mother soon married another tailor but was abandoned when Levine was seven. To help with family finances, Levine shined shoes and sold newspapers. At age fourteen he quit school to work in a dress factory and then became a dress salesman. During his late teens, Levine joined with his brothers to open a women's clothing store, which they called LeVine's. The business prospered, but Levine grew bored after a few years. He moved to New York City, where he worked at odd jobs, such as ambulance driving, while searching for a new occupation. Drifting back to Boston in the mid-1930s, he became part owner of a nightclub, the Cafe Wonderbar.

Joseph E. Levine, *c.* 1962. ARCHIVE PHOTOS

In 1937 Levine married Rosalie Harrison, a singer with Rudy Vallee's band. The couple had a son and a daughter. Soon after his marriage, Levine left the nightclub business, which his wife considered shady, and purchased a movie theater, the Lincoln, in New Haven, Connecticut. He also founded a distribution company, Embassy Pictures, and bought local rights to second-tier attractions, primarily documentaries, sex-hygiene films, low-budget Westerns, and foreign productions. Levine showed his talent for marketing and publicity with the use of provocative advertising and clever double bill combinations. During World War II, he promoted *The Ravaged Earth* (1942), a documentary about the Sino-Japanese War, with "Jap Rats Will Stop at Nothing. See This—It Will Make You Fighting Mad." Eventually Levine operated four theaters in New England and three drive-ins and based his enterprises in Boston. He made an initial foray into motion picture production with *Gaslight Follies* (1945), a compilation of silent-era film clips.

Levine's Embassy Pictures made its first move into nationwide film distribution in 1956 with *Godzilla*, a Japanese science-fiction movie about a giant sea monster. Using borrowed money, Levine heavily promoted the cartoonlike film, which earned $1 million. Levine scored another success with *Attila*, an Italian adventure spectacle that had been ignored by American distributors because of its poor quality. Released in the United States in 1958 and accompanied by $600,000 worth of publicity, the film brought in $2 million at the box office.

Levine had even greater success with *Hercules* in 1959. He spent $1.5 million on promotion of the Italian-produced film, including comic books, chocolate novelties, and lavish dinners for potential distributors. He also employed innovative techniques, such as frequent advertising on television and opening the film simultaneously at hundreds of theaters instead of putting it into gradual release at selected sites. Widespread openings, known as "saturation booking," and television advertising eventually became standard motion picture industry practices. *Hercules*, which featured American bodybuilder Steve Reeves and a host of scantily clad women, was savaged by critics but became a box-office smash, earning $20 million. The popular appeal of *Hercules* and Levine's flamboyant showmanship helped to enliven the listless film industry of the late 1950s.

In the early 1960s, after distributing a series of unsuccessful "spear and sandal" follow-ups to *Hercules* and sensing a growing market for foreign films aimed at sophisticated moviegoers, Levine turned to more serious projects. He imported the acclaimed Italian drama *Two Women* (1961), which was directed by Vittorio DeSica and was based on a story by Alberto Moravia about a mother and daughter displaced from their home during World War II. To draw interest beyond small "art house" audiences, Levine centered publicity around the film's climactic double rape scene. He also touted the performance of Sophia Loren, enabling her to become the first performer in a foreign-language film to win an Academy Award.

Other Italian films Levine brought to the United States under the banner of Embassy Pictures, some of which he coproduced, include *Divorce—Italian Style* (1962), starring Marcello Mastroianni; *Boccaccio '70* (1962), with Loren and Anita Ekberg; *8½* (1963), directed by Federico Fellini; and *Yesterday, Today, and Tomorrow* (1964), starring Loren and Mastroianni and directed by DeSica. Levine also imported *Contempt* (1963), the French director Jean-Luc Godard's black comedy about international filmmaking that offers a scathing portrayal of an American producer said to be based on Levine, and the British film *Darling* (1965), a cynical story of a fashion model in "swinging" London that made the actress Julie Christie a star.

Levine moved into a new phase of his career when he began producing mainstream motion pictures, beginning with the popular melodrama *The Carpetbaggers* in 1964. Basing his operations in New York City, Levine traveled the world putting together deals with creative personnel and film studios. "I enter a deal on instinct. It's the only way to operate," Levine told the *New York Times* in 1965. His most significant production was *The Graduate* (1967), starring Dustin Hoffman as an aimless young suburbanite who drifts into an affair with an older woman while pondering what to do with his life. Directed by Mike Nichols, *The Graduate* was one of the most popular films of the late 1960s and was praised by critics as an insightful depiction of youthful, middle-class angst. Other noteworthy Levine productions include *The Producers* (1968), the director-comedian Mel Brooks's first feature film; and *Woman Times Seven* (1967), with Shirley MacLaine.

In 1968 Levine sold Embassy Pictures to the Avco Corporation for $40 million in stock but remained as head of the newly formed Avco-Embassy Pictures. After a major success with *The Lion in Winter* (1968), a witty tale of dynastic squabbles with Katharine Hepburn as Eleanor of Aquitaine and Peter O'Toole as King Henry II, Levine's instincts began to fail. *Carnal Knowledge* (1971), a searing look at sexual relationships directed by Nichols, was Avco-Embassy's only subsequent hit.

Finding it difficult to adapt his freewheeling style to a corporate environment, Levine resigned from Avco-Embassy in 1974 and set up his own company, Joseph E. Levine Presents. The new company's major effort was *Bridge Too Far* (1977), a big-budget World War II story. Levine personally made money from the project by selling off distribution rights to local investors, but the picture failed with both critics and audiences despite a stellar cast and a full-scale publicity buildup. His final productions, *Magic* (1978) with Anthony Hopkins and *Tattoo* (1981) with Bruce Dern, were poorly received.

Having reached the top echelon of the motion picture industry only after a long career as a local New England businessman, Levine was sometimes dismissed as a parvenu. Short, rotund, and bespectacled with an unpretentious manner and a heavy Boston accent, he made no secret of his excitement at meeting international celebrities and seeing his name on the movie screen. He was a devoted husband and father, and his wife was closely involved with his business affairs. In his off-hours he enjoyed cruising on his yacht and entertaining lavishly. He also collected art, especially the paintings of Andrew Wyeth. Levine died at his home in Greenwich, Connecticut, after being hospitalized with undisclosed ailments.

Sometimes called the last of the great "movie moguls," Levine was a major figure in the 1960s film industry. His independent, internationally oriented operating style and willingness to take financial risks enabled him to flourish amidst the chaos that resulted from the decline of the great Hollywood movie studios.

★

Donald Zec, *Some Enchanted Egos* (1972), has a short chapter on Levine. Interviews with Levine are in the following magazine and newspaper articles: "Promoters: 'A Simple Guy,' " *Newsweek* (22 Feb. 1960); Katharine Hamill, "The Supercolossal—Well, Pretty Good—World of Joe Levine," *Fortune* (Mar. 1964); "Razzle-Dazzle Showman," *New York Times* (26 Oct. 1965); "The Last of the Movie Barons," *Newsweek* (2 May 1966); and Calvin Tompkins, "Profiles: The Very Rich Hours of Joe Levine," *New Yorker* (16 Sept. 1967). Obituaries are in the *New York Times* (1 Aug. 1987) and *Variety* (5 Aug. 1987). Levine is the subject of the documentary *Showman* (1963), directed by David Maysles and Albert Maysles.

MARY KALFATOVIC

LIBBY, Leona Woods Marshall (*b.* 9 August 1919 in La Grange, Illinois; *d.* 10 November 1986 in Santa Monica, California), physicist, educator, editor, and author who was part of the Manhattan Project.

The daughter of Weightstill Woods, an attorney, and Mary (Holderness) Woods, a teacher, Leona Libby was the second child of three girls and two boys. The family lived outside the city limits of Chicago on a farm in La Grange, Illinois. Hit hard by the Great Depression, the Woods family struggled financially. Although the parents had little money, their extremely bright children were expected to attend college. Ambitious and eager to compete with her older brother, Leona won scholarship money and, in addition, worked twenty hours a week to get through the University of Chicago. She received her B.S. degree in 1938 and her Ph.D. in chemistry in 1943.

Prior to her actual graduation, Libby was hired as a research associate for the Manhattan District, later called the Manhattan Project, which developed the first atomic bomb. She worked on a team headed by the Italian Nobel laureate Enrico Fermi, and she was the only woman present for the first nuclear chain reaction, which took place under the football stands at the University of Chicago on 2 December 1942. Although Libby was the only woman on the primary team, as many as eighty-five other women served in some capacity on the Manhattan Project.

Libby was selected because her dissertation research had familiarized her with the vacuum technology needed to build boron trifluoride counters. These counters measured neutrons in a pile of graphite and uranium blocks used to create a chain reaction, a necessary step in making the atomic bomb. A sense of urgency prevailed, as the team was ever mindful that the Germans might build the bomb before the Americans. The highly classified project assumed the code name Chicago Metallurgical Laboratory. Libby explained to her family that her work was like Buck Rogers science. She worked so closely with the other physicists that she considered them family also. For leisure she swam in Lake Michigan almost daily during the summer, and she developed a friendship with Fermi, who consistently encouraged young women. In February 1943 the nuclear pile and the team were transplanted to new headquarters in Argonne, Illinois.

Extremely brilliant and attractive, the dark-haired Libby was not without admirers. John Marshall, Jr., a physicist on the project, caught her attention, and on 3 July 1943 the pair married. When Libby realized she was pregnant, she worried that she might be fired from the laboratory. She kept her pregnancy a secret by wearing loose denim overalls and jamming the pockets with tape measures, pliers, notebooks, and other necessary equipment. She worked until shortly before the birth of her son, and she returned to work within a week.

On a temporary assignment in New York, Libby was exposed to a large dose of radiation while she soldered a canister containing radium salt and beryllium metal, but the exposure was not problematic until later in her life. Leona and John Marshall's work at Argonne ended in 1944, and they went to Hanford Engineering Works in Washington State to oversee construction of artificial plutonium developed from production reactors. Libby worked with John Wheeler to help "solve the riddle of the Hanford xenon poisoning" and baby-sit the reactors, she said in an interview. Her work on the Manhattan Project from 1944 to 1946 is documented in her book *The Uranium People* (1979).

In 1946 Libby joined Fermi at the University of Chicago as a research fellow at the Institute of Nuclear Studies, where she was a member of a group of physicists researching the innovative field of fundamental particle physics. She advanced to research associate in 1947 and to assistant professor of physics in 1954. In 1949 her second son was born. She remained a consultant to Los Alamos Scientific Laboratory from 1951 until her death.

Following Fermi's death in 1954, the institute group members began dispersing. In 1957 Libby went to Princeton, New Jersey, to become a fellow at the Institute for Advanced Study, where she conducted research with J. Robert Oppenheimer. That year Libby also began work as a consultant for the Rand Corporation in Santa Monica, California, performing analysis on foreign nuclear explosions and related national defense problems. She retained this position until 1970. In 1958 she was a visiting scientist at Brookhaven National Laboratory in Upton, Long Island. She was an associate professor at New York University from 1960 to 1962 and a professor of physics from 1962 to 1963. She next became an associate professor of physics at the University of Colorado, Boulder, where she remained until 1972.

In 1966 Libby divorced John Marshall, who had been living in Los Alamos since 1957. In December of that year she married Willard Frank Libby, a Nobel laureate in physics whom she had met on the Manhattan Project. The couple had no children and alternated between their university jobs in Colorado and California. Both of the Libbys were partially responsible for developing the Environmental Science and Engineering Department at the University of California, Los Angeles, where scientists explored solutions to the effects of world pollution. A visiting professor for the department in 1970, Leona Libby became an adjunct professor in 1972. She also served as a consultant for TRW Space Systems Group, and from 1972 to 1976 she was a staff member at R & D Associates in Santa Monica.

Libby developed an interest in her husband's research of ancient climates. She studied tree rings to uncover the history of climates through the measurement of isotopes in trees and wrote *Carbon Dioxide and Climate* (1980) and *Past Climates: Tree Thermometers, Commodities, and People* (1983). Following her husband's death in 1980, she edited *Collected Papers Willard F. Libby* (1981). The author of more than 100 articles, many dealing with environmental issues and cosmology, she also published *Fifty Environmental Problems of Timely Importance* (1970).

In California, Libby lived at 129 Ocean Way in Santa Monica. Her scientific home was the Environmental Science and Engineering Department at UCLA. She enjoyed photography, swimming, and playing the piano. Although she had been raised in the Episcopal faith, she became an agnostic over the years. She died in St. John's Hospital in Santa Monica, from probable radiation-induced illness and liver failure. Her remains were cremated.

Described as having a dominant personality yet "kind-hearted," Libby had high expectations of what could be accomplished. Beginning as a chemist, she branched into physics and then high-energy physics. She contributed to environmental concerns and supported nuclear power. Leona Marshall Libby never had regrets about her work on the atomic bomb. During an interview for *Newsweek* in 1967, she emphasized that "we saved lives in the long run."

★

Richard Rhodes, *The Making of the Atomic Bomb* (1986), details the significant historical and scientific aspects of the Manhattan Project through narratives and quotes from those who participated in the project. Rachel Fermi and Esther Samra, *Picturing the Bomb: Photographs from the Secret World of the Manhattan Project* (1995), is a behind-the-scenes pictorial account of the men, women, and places involved in making the bomb. Caroline L. Herzenberg and Ruth H. Howes, "Women of the Manhattan Project," *Technology Review* 96 (Nov./Dec. 1993): 32–40, explores the contributions of the many women working on the Manhattan Project. Obituaries are in the *New York Times* (12 Nov. 1986); *Los Angeles Times* (13 Nov. 1986); *Chicago Tribune* (14 Nov. 1986); and *Washington Post* (14 Nov. 1986). Oral histories including Leona Marshall Libby and John Marshall are in Craig Wollner, ed., *Working on the Bomb: An Oral History of WWII* (1995), a collection of stories as told by scientists and construction workers regarding their work on the manufacture of plutonium in the making of the first atomic bomb. The documentary film by Robert W. Mull, *Something to Win the War: The Hanford Diary* (1985), depicts the history of Hanford through interviews and on-site footage.

MARILYN ELIZABETH PERRY

LIBERACE, Wladziu Valentino (*b.* 16 May 1919 in West Allis, Wisconsin; *d.* 4 February 1987 in Palm Springs, California), pianist, vocalist, and entertainer best known for his flamboyant showmanship in rendering classical and pop music in nightclubs and on television.

Wladziu (Walter) Liberace weighed thirteen pounds at birth; his twin brother was stillborn. His father, Salvatore Liberace, was an Italian immigrant who played the French horn but also was a grocer; his mother, Frances Zuchowski, worked in the grocery store. Beginning in 1923 they lived in Milwaukee, where Liberace attended public schools, graduating from East Milwaukee High School in 1937.

At age four Liberace demonstrated exceptional talent at playing the piano. Given lessons, he progressed so rapidly that by age seven he was recommended for a scholarship at the Wisconsin College of Music, where he received free instruction from 1926 to 1943, studying with Florence Bettray Kelly. According to family legend the young Liberace was once introduced to the Polish pianist Ignace Jan Paderewski, who was visiting Milwaukee, and the famous older musician remarked that maybe the boy would take his place someday.

The family suffered during the Great Depression: Salvatore Liberace could not find employment as a musician and took other work; the older children found part-time jobs to help out. By age eleven Liberace was playing piano accompaniment for showings of silent films, which led to offers of employment from nightspots. His mother let him accept such engagements only on the condition that he continue his classical music training: she was convinced he was destined for the concert stage. Liberace made his concert debut in 1940 in a solo performance with the Chicago Symphony Orchestra; it was reviewed favorably, but he was not convinced that his talent would bring him success in classical music. Besides, he enjoyed playing pop (and popularized classical) music, and for several years he cultivated his showmanship under the name Walter Buster Keys. He moved to New York City that year and there, exempt on medical grounds from military service, took many minor jobs; they included playing at the Persian Room of the Plaza Hotel (during intermissions).

In 1941, when Liberace's parents divorced, he blamed his father, to whom he would not speak for many years. Both parents remarried, and Frances Liberace Casadonte became the owner of an ice cream shop. (This income, plus some help from Liberace, helped her to support her youngest son, Rudy.)

While he was in New York, Liberace studied the success of other performers. In 1942 he changed his stage name to Liberace, inspired by Paderewski and the popular singer Hildegarde. (Friends, however, would call him "Lee.") He also experimented with audience participation in his act and cultivated his image (e.g., he began placing a candelabra on the piano and adopted "I'll Be Seeing You" as his theme song).

In 1943 Liberace moved to Los Angeles, and in 1945 his older brother, George, returned from military service and joined the act, playing the violin and leading the orchestra. Together they toured the United States in the late 1940s, playing at supper clubs and hotels, and occasionally appearing on local radio and television shows. These earliest television appearances, including the *Texaco Star Theatre* and *Cavalcade of Stars,* led in 1952 to his own program. *The Liberace Show,* on KLAC-TV in Los Angeles, won an Emmy as best entertainment program, and Liberace won

Liberace. ARCHIVE PHOTOS

an Emmy as TV's most outstanding male personality (both in 1953). A new version of *The Liberace Show* ran until 1956, and this success brought bookings in nightclubs in Los Angeles and Las Vegas. *The Liberace Show* appeared on 219 stations in the United States, Canada, Cuba, and Venezuela, and attracted as many as 35 million viewers.

Liberace attributed his success in part to his 1949 discovery of a book by Claude Bristol, *The Magic of Believing,* a testimony to the power of optimism. Later he wrote a foreword to a special edition of the book that advised, "To attain success, one must positively think success."

As Liberace established his image nationally, he discovered that he attracted critics as well as fans. Some considered him a handsome ladies' man while others ridiculed him as an effeminate "mama's boy" with distinctly homosexual tendencies. Not wanting to cause offense, Liberace tried to project an image of wholesome heterosexuality, denying repeatedly that he was gay. Encouraged by his agent, he appeared publicly with movie starlets and showgirls, including Betty White, Sonja Henie, and Mamie van Doren. Among these was his twenty-three-year-old neighbor Joanne Rio, a dancer at a Hollywood nightclub; they became engaged, but the relationship was brief. On two other occasions he was engaged to be married, but each time he broke it off.

The controversy over Liberace's sexual orientation fueled his popularity. He failed in several attempts to launch a career in movies—in which he usually played the part of a pianist—but his nightclub and broadcasting work improved his opportunities in the recording industry: throughout his lifetime he sold some 60 million records.

Now nationally known, in 1953 Liberace played to a sold-out house at Carnegie Hall in New York City, and in 1954 to a record crowd of 18,456 (80 percent women) at Madison Square Garden, for which he was paid a record $138,000. Of the latter performance a reviewer in *Variety* wrote: "No male attraction has devastated the opposing sex in these terms since Rudolph Valentino." Sarcastic derision of the "Candelabra Casanova" also appeared, but the entertainer himself cheerfully retorted, "I cried all the way to the bank" (a refrain he originated, according to *Bartlett's Familiar Quotations*).

In 1954 Liberace earned $2 million for a twenty-six-week season, making him the highest-paid pianist in the world. In 1955 he had 162 certified fan clubs in the United States with some 230,000 members (who wrote him 6,000 to 10,000 letters a week and sent him 27,000 valentines), and he became the highest-paid performer in the history of Las Vegas when he opened the Riviera Hotel there in April, receiving $50,000 a week.

In 1956, during his English tour, Liberace sued William Connor and the *London Daily Mirror* for printing, among other things, this statement:

> He is the summit of sex—masculine, feminine and neuter. Everything that he, she, and it can ever want. . . . [T]his deadly, winking, sniggering, snuggling, giggling, . . . fruit-flavored, mincing, ice-covered heap of mother love. . . . Without doubt, he is the biggest sentimental vomit of all time. Slobbering over his mother, winking at his brother, and counting the cash at every second.

When asked during the trial (on 23 June 1959) if he had ever indulged in homosexual practices, Liberace replied, "Never in my life." The judge ordered the newspaper and its writer to pay Liberace $22,400 and court costs. Liberace's gain was only $2,900, which he gave to charity. In 1957 he sued the tabloid *Confidential* for stating that he had propositioned a male press agent; again he won, this time a settlement of $40,000.

By the early 1960s Liberace's reputation had started to decline, and in November 1963, the day President John F. Kennedy was shot, he suffered a near fatal accident in Pittsburgh. After fainting onstage, he was diagnosed with severe nausea as a result of exposure to carbon tetrachloride, which he had used in a hotel room to clean his costumes. He recovered after nearly a month in the hospital.

In 1984, after a long absence, Liberace returned to New York City to perform. Each year until his death he appeared at Radio City Music Hall, where he set records for attendance and receipts. His act featured exuberant excess: three cars, five pianos, and ten costumes (valued at a total of $1 million). At one show, clad in a 120-pound shocking-pink llama fur coat trimmed with rhinestones and sequins, he jumped out of an Easter egg, and in another he flew across the stage dressed as a purple bird.

Liberace never admitted being a homosexual, but in his later years he was alleged to have had relationships with several young men, including Scott Thorson (1976–1982) and Cary James (1982–1987). The former, employed as a chauffeur, bodyguard, and secretary, stated he had participated in a homosexual relationship with Liberace, and in 1982 sued him for $113 million. In 1984 much of the case was dismissed on the grounds that contracts for sex are not enforceable, but Thorson was able to file other charges, including assault and battery, breach of an earlier cash settlement agreement, and loss of personal property. Finally, in 1986 he received a settlement of $95,000. Cary James was among those who contested Liberace's will. In the lawsuit he testified that he and Liberace had been "extremely close friends" and constant companions from 1982 to 1987. Both James and Thorson had been employees of Liberace and had appeared onstage in his act.

The cause of Liberace's death was reported as cardiac arrest due to congestive heart failure, but an autopsy later showed that he died of AIDS-related cytomegalovirus pneumonia; he also had pulmonary heart disease and calcification of a heart valve. Memorial services were held in Palm Springs and in Las Vegas. He was buried in Forest Lawn Memorial Park in Glendale, California.

Over the years, as he acquired wealth, Liberace became a collector of pianos, costumes, candelabra, silver, antiques, homes, automobiles, and dogs. By 1986 his six homes (in Los Angeles, Malibu, and Palm Springs, California; Las Vegas and Lake Tahoe, Nevada; and New York City), seven warehouses, and a museum (opened in 1979 in Las Vegas) were scarcely large enough to hold his possessions. In his will he provided a trust for his fifty dogs, but most of his estate was left to the Liberace Foundation for the Performing and the Creative Arts, which provided financial aid to aspiring musicians.

In April 1988, 20,000 of Liberace's belongings (except for the contents of his Palm Springs house) were auctioned off at the Los Angeles Convention Center; most items sold for four to five times their normal value. At a Palm Springs auction, also in April 1988, 2,000 items were sold.

Liberace said of his career: "Little by little [Liberace] was created by me and by the public who accepted him. . . . He's a combination of music and personality and a certain amount of shock value. It's a fantasy. . . . I'm always trying to see how far I can go."

Liberace's papers are at the Liberace Museum in Las Vegas. His writings include *Liberace Cooks! Recipes from His Seven Dining Rooms* (1970), with Carol Truax; *Liberace: An Autobiography* (1973), with Carroll Carroll; *The Things I Love,* edited by Tony Palmer (1976); and *The Wonderful Private World of Liberace* (1986). See also *Liberace: Complete Life Story* (1954), a magazine; Bob Thomas, *Liberace: The True Story* (1987); Scott Thorson, with Alex Thorleifson, *Behind the Candelabra: My Life with Liberace* (1988); and Jocelyn Faris, *Liberace: A Bio-Bibliography* (1995), with an extensive filmography. An obituary is in the *New York Times* (5 Feb. 1987).

VERNE MOBERG

LICHINE, Alexis (*b.* 3 December 1913 in Moscow; *d.* 1 June 1989 in Château Prieuré-Lichine, Bordeaux, France), winemaker and author of wine reference books who was one of the most influential promoters of wine in the United States.

Lichine, one of two children of Alexander and Alice Tseits Lichine, spent his first four years in prerevolutionary Russia. His father was a wealthy banker and lawyer who owned a dacha outside Moscow and an estate in the Crimea. Just before the Bolshevik Revolution in 1917 the family fled Moscow for Vladivostok and Japan, then settled in New York for two years before taking up permanent residence in Paris. There Lichine attended the École Alsacienne and the Cours de Droit International. At the age of thirteen the trilingual Lichine began to work on the tourist buses his father now ran in the French capital. By the time he was fifteen he was astonishing his friends with his discriminating palate.

Lichine attended the University of Pennsylvania in 1931–1932, then returned to Paris to sell advertising for the Paris edition of the *New York Herald Tribune*. Crossing the Atlantic again in 1934 he was briefly an agent for French wine merchants in New York City, then worked there as a clerk at the Cork and Bottle wine store. He became a U.S. citizen in 1936. Two years later he went to work for the most famous U.S. wine expert, Frank Schoonmaker, who sent Lichine to France in August 1939 to learn more about the trade from Raymond Baudouin, founder of *Revue de vins de France*.

The outbreak of World War II in 1939 cut short Lichine's French internship. Back in the United States he continued to work as a wine importer, traveling the country and spreading his gospel of the essential contribution of wine to fine dining. He was a tireless salesperson and pro-

Alexis Lichine (*right*) selling Château Lascombes, S.A., to Stanley Williams, managing director of Bass-Charrington Vintners. UPI/CORBIS-BETTMANN

moter who, through his demystification of wine buying and drinking, made converts wherever he went.

In 1942 Lichine obtained a commission in the U.S. Army as a first lieutenant in intelligence. Colonel John P. Ratay recruited him for his staff; Lichine spent much of his time in North Africa and Southern France, selecting the colonel's and other officers' wine. Ultimately attaining the rank of major, Lichine later prided himself in having been the first liberator to have a drink at the Hotel Carlton bar in Cannes in August 1944. His fame in the wine business eventually attracted the attention of the supreme Allied commander, General Dwight D. Eisenhower, who employed him as an aide-de-camp and sommelier. In later years the Eisenhower White House would seek his advice on wine.

Lichine returned to the United States in January 1946 and obtained a position with United Distillers. In July of that year he married Countess Renée de Villeneuve, whom he had met in Marseilles. The marriage lasted one year. Lichine left United Distillers in 1948 to create the wine list of the Waldorf-Astoria Hotel in New York City, while working for several wine importers.

In 1951, Lichine, assisted by a team of experts, published his first book, *The Wines of France,* which went through five editions. (In 1979, completely revised, it appeared as *Alexis Lichine's Guide to the Wines and Vineyards of France,* which went through three editions.) Also in 1951 he purchased, for $20,000, Château Prieuré-Cantenac in Bordeaux, which soon became Château Prieuré-Lichine. Although the 1855 Bordeaux classification designated the vineyard as a fourth growth, it had fallen on hard times. Lichine built up the château from 32 rundown acres to more than 170 acres that by the year of his death would be producing 25,000 cases a year. In 1955 he put together a syndicate that for $70,000 purchased Château Lascombes, a second-growth château. That year he also established his own wine-importing firm, Alexis Lichine and Company, which he would sell to Bass-Charrington in 1966.

Lichine, a tall, slender man with brown hair, green-blue eyes, and an elegant bearing, married Gisèle Edenbourgh in 1956; they would have two children before divorcing. He married the actress Arlene Dahl on 23 December 1965; three years later that marriage also ended in divorce.

As a château owner, Lichine became a controversial figure among Bordeaux winemakers and bottlers as he called for the modernization of what was a tradition-bound business, introducing, for example, the first tractor to Médoc wineries. For years he fought unsuccessfully to persuade the Bordeaux growers to alter their hallowed but outmoded 1855 classification list. He was more successful in leading the private and rather secretive château owners to accept modern marketing techniques, making their châteaux tourist destinations with billboards, tours, tasting rooms, restaurants, and gift shops. He also convinced many small château owners to bottle their own wines rather than selling them to shippers and collectives.

In 1967, Lichine published another reference book, *The Encyclopedia of Wine and Spirits,* which went through five editions. In 1971, during a time of severe decline in the wine industry, he and his co-owners sold Château Lascombes. He also was involved in real-estate developments in the Caribbean. During the last two decades of his life, Lichine made his home in Bordeaux but also had a residence at Fifth Avenue and Eighty-first Street in New York City, from which he traveled throughout the country, giving lectures and tastings, tirelessly promoting his own wine and wine in general. Lichine died of cancer in 1989 and was buried, following a Russian Orthodox service, in the vineyards of his beloved Château Prieuré-Lichine.

In 1958 Joseph Wechsberg referred to the larger-than-life Lichine as the Pope of Wine. This colorful, outspoken, cosmopolitan businessman, possessed of a rather large ego, was the most famous wine promoter in American history. He had much to do with the dramatic increase in interest in and sales of wine in the United States in the years after World War II.

★

There is no book-length biography of Lichine. The best article is Joseph Wechsberg, "Profiles: A Dreamer of Wine," *New Yorker* (17 and 24 May 1958). Also useful are articles by Frank J. Prial: "Wine Talk," *New York Times* (7 June 1989), and "In Possession of His Fortune," *New York Times Magazine* (21 June 1987). An obituary is in the *New York Times* (2 June 1989).

MELVIN SMALL

LICKLIDER, J(oseph) C(arl) R(obnett) (*b.* 11 March 1915 in St. Louis, Missouri; *d.* 26 June 1990 in Arlington, Massachusetts), computer scientist best known for his pioneering research in artificial intelligence and whose work established the technological basis for the concepts of time sharing and resource sharing.

Licklider was the only child of Joseph Parron Licklider, a teacher, and Margaret (Robnett) Licklider, a homemaker. After graduating from high school in 1933, Licklider enrolled at Washington University in St. Louis. He received an A.B. degree in psychology in 1937. He then matriculated in the graduate school at Washington and graduated in one year with an A.M. degree in psychology. In 1938 he entered the University of Rochester in New York, from which he received a Ph.D. in psychology in 1942. During World War II Licklider did research on hearing and speech communication in the Psycho-Acoustics Laboratory at Harvard University under the auspices of the Office of Strategic Research and Development and the National Defense Research Council.

In 1945 Licklider married Louise Carpenter Thomas; they had two children. That same year he received a nontenure appointment as a lecturer at Harvard University, where he remained until 1950. From 1948 to 1949 he was

J. C. R. Licklider. MIT MUSEUM

a consultant to the U.S. Navy Electronics Laboratory. In 1950 he was appointed as an associate professor at the Massachusetts Institute of Technology (MIT); he remained there for seven years as director of the Acoustics Laboratory. In his second year at MIT, Licklider was retained by the U.S. Air Force laboratories as a consultant in the fields of pitch perception and the intelligibility of speech. During the administration of President Dwight Eisenhower, Licklider was an adviser to the Research and Development Board (1953–1954), the Office of the Secretary of Defense (1954–1955), the committee on biotechnology and human research at the National Aeronautics and Space Administration, and the Commission on Science and Technology. In recognition of his contributions to psychoacoustics and his distinguished government service, Licklider was elected president of the Acoustical Society of America in 1958.

Licklider left MIT in 1957 and joined the computer firm of Bolt, Beranek, and Newman as vice president and director of research of the departments of psychoacoustics, engineering psychology, and information systems. In 1962 he joined the U.S. Department of Defense as director of information processing research and behavioral science and as adviser to the Advanced Research Projects Agency. In these roles he was the driving force behind the Defense Department's move to fund large-scale research projects on the potential of information science at major postsecondary institutions in the United States. The first experimental computer science research center was established at MIT and was known as Project MAC, later the Laboratory for Computer Science.

In 1964 Licklider left the Department of Defense and became a consultant to IBM, where he was the director of information sciences, systems, and applications at the Thomas J. Watson Research Center in Westchester County, New York. In 1968 Licklider returned to MIT to direct Project MAC and as professor of electrical engineering. In 1974 he took a year's leave of absence to return to Washington with the Department of Defense, as director of the Information Processing Techniques Office. Licklider returned to MIT from government service in 1975 and remained there until his retirement in 1985, when he became emeritus professor. After his retirement he was awarded the prestigious Common Wealth Award for Distinguished Service for his work in computer networking and the promotion of interaction between humans and computers.

Licklider served as president of the Society of Engineering Psychologists in 1960. He was a fellow of the American Academy of Arts and Sciences and the American Psychological Association; he held elective memberships in the National Academy of Sciences, the Association for Computing Machinery, the Commission on Science and Technological Communication, and the National Academy of Engineering. He also served with distinction on the Board of Trustees of the Interuniversity Communications Council.

Licklider died at Symmes Hospital in Arlington, Massachusetts, of complications after an asthma attack. Interment was in Arlington.

Licklider was among the first academicians in the 1960s to recognize that the fullest potential of computers would be reached only if people were able to interact and network with them and that the computer was not only a depository of data but also could assist people in thinking, understanding, and making decisions. As humans think by manipulating, modifying, and combining schemata, Licklider argued, the use of computers in the learning process would allow people to create new, complex structures by rearranging old schemata.

According to Licklider, the body of human knowledge is created in a dynamic process involving repeated examinations and comparisons of very small and disparate pieces of data; if these data remain on the shelves of libraries in the form of books, the development of new knowledge is hindered. He maintained that for work with the body of knowledge to be fulfilled efficiently, synergic action is required, in which humans and computers work together. He coined the phrase, "man-computer interaction," to indicate that the body of human knowledge is a coordinate partner of people and computers. Man-computer interaction was perceived by Licklider as consisting of three mutually related components: first, man-machine interface, the physical medium through which the interaction takes place; second, the language aspects of man-computer interaction; and third, a look at the total method as an adaptive, self-organizing process.

Licklider also made many contributions in the application of computers to libraries, introducing the concepts of digital computers and telecommunications into the process of information storage and retrieval. Shortly before his retirement, he developed a system that made it possible to construct computer programs by drawing diagrams on a computer screen instead of writing numerical and symbolic expressions.

★

Full-length works include F. S. Black, *A Question-Answering System* (1963), which reports on QAS-5; and T. Marill, *Libraries and Question-Answering Systems* (1963), which investigates the need to implement interactive libraries. J. C. R. Licklider, *Libraries of the Future* (1965), focuses on the application of computers to libraries. J. C. R. Licklider, "Panel Discussion on Man-Machine Interaction," *Gordon Research Conference on Information Problems in Research* (1962), discusses the concept of man-computer interaction. J. C. R. Licklider and W. E. Clark, "On-Line Man-Computer Communications," *Proceedings of the American Federation of Information Processing Societies* 21 (1962): 113–128, details the importance of communicating between people and computers. M. Grignetti, "A Note on the Entropy of Words in Printed English," *Information and Control* 19 (1963): 219–224, evaluates the information theory of Licklider. An obituary is in the *New York Times* (3 July 1990).

P. DALE ROREX

LINDSAY, Goldie Ina Ruby ("Eldress Bertha") (*b.* 1897 in Braintree, Massachusetts; *d.* 3 October 1990 in Canterbury, New Hampshire), the last eldress of the Shakers (the United Society of Believers in Christ's Second Appearing).

Lindsay was one of nine children of Lloyd E. Lindsay and Abbie N. (Smith) Lindsay, Baptists who were attracted to the Shaker religion and sometimes worshiped at the Shaker village at Canterbury, New Hampshire. Lindsay's parents died within a month of each other when she was four years old. In 1905 her older sister, who wanted to marry and leave New Hampshire, took Lindsay to the Shaker village for adoption. (By this time the Shaker religion was in decline but was trying, with only modest success, to increase its membership through the conversions of adopted orphans.) The Shakers took Lindsay in and provided her with a new

Eldress Bertha Lindsay in a Shaker classroom in Canterbury, New Hampshire, 1978. UPI/CORBIS-BETTMANN

extended family, including six other orphan girls. She converted to Shakerism and remained in the community for the rest of her life.

At their peak in the mid-nineteenth century, with 6,000 members, the Shakers were the largest of more than 100 utopian and religious communitarian-living experiments in the United States. To strengthen and support each other and new converts, the Shakers chose to live communally with strict obedience to confession, celibacy, and respect for the hierarchy of spiritual authority. In the twentieth century, in order for young people to learn how to live communally in a celibate religious society, each Wednesday night was devoted to religious instruction. Lindsay explained: "We had what the Shakers called a 'young people's conference.' This was given over to the instruction of the rules and regulations or laws that we would all learn together to form a well-disciplined home." These principles informed much of what she did. "The young folks," for instance, "were instructed to use everything possible and not to waste anything, as frugality was one of our instructions. Our founder, Mother Ann, said we should remember the poor and needy and give bread to the hungry."

Lindsay was taught as a young girl to cook for her community and for guests. She began to learn, at age thirteen, how to make pies and bread, and at age nineteen she was head cook at the Trustee's Office kitchen. This put her into contact with many visitors from "the World," for whom she planned and prepared meals. These outsiders included between fifteen and twenty-five men who were hired seasonally to help plant and harvest as well as to paint and maintain the buildings. The Shaker founder, Mother Ann Lee, is quoted as saying, "Prepare your food in that manner that those who partake of it may bless you with thankful hearts." Lindsay took this dictum seriously, preparing the meals as perfectly as possible.

Shaker sisters, including Lindsay, learned to sew and create handcrafted products such as cloaks and poplar boxes that were sold to the public. Trained in multiple tasks, sisters helped pick fruits and vegetables and then canned them. They made jams, jellies, pickles, and relishes to sell in the United States and as far away as England.

Lindsay admitted in an interview published in *People* magazine in 1987 that as a young woman she had experienced a spiritual crisis during which she considered leaving the Shakers: "Although I am ashamed of it now, I have to be truthful and say that I did have the desire to leave the Shakers at one time. It was during the First World War. I thought maybe I would like to marry. I loved housekeeping. . . . If I had decided to leave, I would have been permitted to go with love and a provision of money and clothing. . . . I finally decided that I would stay, that I could give my life and love here on these hundreds of acres and receive all I needed."

Just as Shaker women had done in the nineteenth century, Lindsay covered her hair with a starched white bonnet and wore simple, long-sleeved dresses. For most of her life she managed the community's fancywork trade and cooked for business leaders of "the World." In 1967 she was selected an eldress of the Canterbury community, and in 1970, a member of the Lead Ministry (governing council).

Lindsay helped make the decision during the 1960s to convert the Shakers' Canterbury settlement into Shaker Village, Inc., a nonprofit educational institution, museum, and historic site. (By the late 1990s the only active Shaker community—with fewer than ten members—was at Sabbathday Lake, Maine.) Lindsay's determination to preserve the site and the history of the Shakers stemmed from her belief that "it has been a very happy experience for me to live under the influence of such beautiful people. . . . It is my desire to further the Shaker religion in any way that I can, and if I can influence young people to take Jesus Christ as their Savior, it will be worth all the effort." This devotion to preserving the traditions of the Shakers led her to write a cookbook/memoir, *Seasoned with Grace: My Generation of Shaker Cooking* (1987). Lindsay continued to grant interviews and promote the Shakers until she died of a stroke at the age of ninety-three. She is buried in Canterbury.

★

Eldress Bertha Lindsay, *Seasoned with Grace: My Generation of Shaker Cooking* (1987), is a firsthand narrative of Lindsay's life and ideals, edited by Mary Rose Boswell; her interview, "as told to" Cable Neuhaus, is "The Shakers Face Their Last Amen," *People Weekly* (2 Mar. 1987). See also Stephen J. Stein, *The Shaker Experience in America* (1992). An obituary is in the *New York Times* (5 Oct. 1990).

ALISON M. PARKER

LIPMANN, Fritz Albert (*b.* 12 June 1899 in Königsberg, Germany; *d.* 24 July 1986 in Poughkeepsie, New York), biochemist who won the Nobel Prize in 1953 for the discovery of coenzyme A and is best known for his work in cellular metabolism.

Harvard Medical School professor Fritz Lipmann in his laboratory at the Massachusetts General Hospital on the day that he learned he had won the Nobel Prize, 1953. AP/WIDE WORLD PHOTOS

Lipmann was one of two children of Leopold Lipmann, a lawyer, and Gertrude Lachmanski, who were loving and supportive parents. Influenced by his uncle, a pediatrician, Lipmann began studying medicine at the University of Königsberg in 1917. His studies were interrupted when he was called in to the German army's medical services during the last part of World War I. After his discharge from the army in 1919, he attended the University of Munich and then the University of Berlin, where he received his M.D. degree in 1924. During his postgraduate medical training he became uneasy about "accepting its commercial aspects, to buy one's health and accepting individual payment for it." He left his training and enrolled in a three-month marathon course in biochemistry with Peter Rona in Berlin. A subsequent fellowship in a pharmacology laboratory in Amsterdam convinced him that he wanted to become a biochemist. To improve his background in chemistry, he returned to Königsberg to study organic chemistry for three years. In 1927 he was accepted as a graduate student in the laboratory of Otto Meyerhof at the Kaiser-Wilhelm Institute for Biology in Berlin. His studies under Meyerhof and Otto Warburg (Nobelists in 1922 and 1931, respectively) were influences of the "greatest momentum." He was inspired by Warburg's insistence that experiments speak for themselves and that interpretation be kept to a minimum. This, Lipmann believed, developed the foundation that allowed biology to be more of an "exact" science.

In Meyerhof's laboratory Lipmann worked on two subject areas—glycolysis (fermentation of carbohydrates) and the function of creatine phosphate in muscle contractions. Three papers in these areas served as his thesis, and he obtained his Ph.D. degree from the University of Berlin in 1929. In 1930 he was required, for the first time in his life, to find a job. He now was courting an American-born German artist, Elfreda Hall, known as Freda, and they married on 23 June 1931. They had one son.

As Lipmann later wrote in an autobiographical sketch: "I discovered that being Jewish in Germany in 1930 was already a great handicap if one was looking for a university position. Even liberal professors were reluctant to put one on their staff; they expected trouble." Fortunately, Lipmann got a job in the laboratory of Albert Fischer, who was studying tissue cultures and metabolism. Lipmann succeeded in devising a scheme of following embryonic-fibroblast growth in manometers by using carbon dioxide formation as a measure of lactic acid production.

In 1931 Lipmann went to the Rockefeller Institute for

Medical Research (now Rockefeller University) in New York City, where he worked in the laboratory of P. A. Levene on the phosphate link in phosphoproteins. That summer he spent time at the Marine Biological Laboratory at Woods Hole, Massachusetts, attending lectures and meetings and talking to scientists who came there every summer. These experiences and new and lasting friendships were very important for him.

In the fall of 1932 Lipmann rejoined Albert Fischer, who was now with the Carlsberg laboratories in Copenhagen. Lipmann resumed investigating the mechanisms by which cells produce energy for survival and growth. He studied the Pasteur effect, in which tissues with high anaerobic glycolysis (glucose metabolism without oxygen) suppress this activity in the presence of oxygen. This aerobic phase produces approximately ten times as much energy as anaerobic metabolism. Lipmann demonstrated that the change from anaerobic to aerobic metabolism involved a connection between pyruvate oxidation and thiamine (vitamin B1). His studies of pyruvic acid showed that it was metabolized to acetic acid, the main metabolic fuel, via an intermediate formation of acetyl phosphate. The process was completely dependent upon inorganic phosphate and proved true for bacteria but not for animal tissue. This work was published in 1939, a bad year for Jews in Europe. The Lipmanns, on the urging of friends, left Copenhagen in July for the United States. Lipmann went to the laboratories of Vincent du Vigneaud (a Nobelist in 1955) at Cornell University Medical School in New York City, where he started to work with Dean Burk.

An article by Lipmann in *Advances in Enzymology* (1941), "Metabolic Generation and Utilization of Phosphate Bond Energy," caused a stir because it dealt with the role of phosphate bonds as carriers of energy transportation and in biosynthesis. There was great antagonism to his theory of high-energy bonds, which he depicted as a squiggle (~). This notation is still used today.

In 1941 Lipmann went to the Massachusetts General Hospital Department of Surgery, where he obtained fellowship support from Ciba and from the Commonwealth Fund. He became a naturalized U.S. citizen in 1944. While in Boston he pursued his research on a method for determining acetyl-phosphate in the presence of inorganic phosphate, and he continued his studies of oxidation of pyruvate. Lipmann and his group found that a coenzyme was necessary for oxidative metabolism, coenzyme A ("A" for acetylation), a derivative of pantothenic acid, another B vitamin. He described this work in a landmark paper.

Lipmann's research between 1940 and 1945 clarified the understanding of cellular metabolism by identifying adenosine triphosphate (ATP), which is universally present, as the main source of energy in all living cells. Lipmann hypothesized that high-energy phosphate bonds are used to drive most of the energy requiring reactions. Coenzyme A functions in the conversion of the high-energy phosphate bonds from ATP into other forms of cellular energy. The discovery of coenzyme A enhanced the understanding of the Krebs citric acid cycle, in which food is converted into cellular energy. Following his significant research in energy metabolism and the discovery of coenzyme A, Lipmann became a full professor of biological chemistry at Harvard University in 1949. In 1953 he and Hans Krebs shared the Nobel Prize in physiology or medicine for their independent but intrinsically similar work in making "vast and significant contributions in the function of living cells."

Lipmann left Harvard in 1957 to return to Rockefeller University, where he remained active in research until 1986. He became professor emeritus in 1970. His many endeavors elucidated the application of phosphate bond energy to a number of biochemical reactions, including protein-to-protein synthesis and hormone action. His theories are also applied in cancer research.

Lipmann, an intensely dedicated scientist, was a small, very thin man, whose loose fitting and baggy clothing accentuated his thinness. His face, with its crown of brown hair and brown eyes, was heavily lined and wore a continuous look of being curious. It was remarked that one "had the feeling of talking directly to his brain." He was known to be very unaffected and friendly. He considered music his favorite recreation.

In addition to the Nobel Prize, Lipmann received the Carl Neuberg Medal in 1948, the Mead Johnson Award in 1948, and the National Medal of Science in 1966, as well as honorary doctorates from the University of Marseille in 1947, the University of Chicago in 1953, Yeshiva University in 1964, the University of Paris in 1966, Harvard University in 1967, and Rockefeller University in 1971. He died shortly after suffering a stroke at St. Frances Hospital in Poughkeepsie, New York. His ashes were scattered along his walking path in the woods surrounding his home in Rhinebeck, New York.

Lipmann thought widely on a number of issues. Colleagues and postdoctoral students appreciated his clear insights, his respect for coworkers (always giving full credit to his collaborators), and his determination. According to a friend and colleague, who regarded him both as a father and mentor, Lipmann had an uncanny sense of scientific intuition. When presented with what would later turn out to be a good idea, he would tap his nose and say, "That smells good to me."

★

Lipmann's *Wanderings of a Biochemist* (1971) is an autobiographical sketch. An entry on Lipmann appeared in *Current Biography* (1954) after he received the Nobel Prize. His short essay on the growth and uses of knowledge, "Disproportions Created by the Exponential Growth of Knowledge," in *Perspectives in Bi-*

ology and Medicine 5, no. 3 (spring 1962): 324–326, is useful. Sanford S. Singer profiled Lipmann in volume 2 of *The Nobel Prize Winners, Physiology or Medicine,* edited by Frank N. Magill (1991). An obituary is in the *New York Times* (25 July 1986).

LESLIE S. JACOBSON

LITTLE, Royal (*b.* 1 March 1896 in Wakefield, Massachusetts; *d.* 12 January 1989 in Nassau, Bahamas), industrialist and conglomerateur.

Little always refused to discuss his family and childhood. Late in his life he said he regretted having agreed to submit material for *Who's Who,* and he tried unsuccessfully to have the few uninformative lines there expunged. In his memoir, *The Royal Little Story,* privately published by Textron, Little indicated that when he was four years old his father died and his mother remarried a man who was the outcast of a prominent Boston family whose fortune was based on a printing company. The stepfather, whose name is not provided, was the head of another company that did poorly because he had no talent for business. Hoping for better things in a different locale he took the family to Buffalo, New York, where he opened a small print shop. The family left town a few steps ahead of the creditors and went successively to Cleveland, Chicago, Sioux City, Denver, Salt Lake City, and finally, in 1910, to San Francisco.

Meanwhile, in Boston, Little's uncle, Arthur D. Little, was doing quite well as a scientific consultant. Married but childless, he proposed to his sister-in-law that Royal come to live with him in the wealthy suburb of Brookline, attend private schools, and then enter Harvard. Knowing that there would be almost no chance for Royal to attend college if he stayed with her, she agreed, and Little arrived in Brookline in 1911. He attended the exclusive Noble and Greenough preparatory school and went on to Harvard as a member of the class of 1919.

Little, a poor student, was somewhat relieved when, after the United States entered World War I in 1917, he could enlist in the army. After service in France and Germany as an infantry second lieutenant he returned home in 1919. He managed to obtain a "war degree" from Harvard that year by passing a few examinations and then told his uncle he intended to go into business. Arthur Little, one of the developers of rayon, offered to help him find a position in the textile industry. He refused the offer and went to work at the Cheney Brothers Silk Company. From there he went to Lustron, which produced rayon. When Lustron failed, Little and some friends borrowed $10,000 that was used to purchase the shell of another defunct firm, Chemical Products, and then, in 1923, used one of its divisions, Special Yarns, as the basis for a new company. Special Yarns was merged with Franklin Rayon Dyeing in 1928 to form Franklin Rayon, which, as rayon use expanded, became quite successful. On 10 September 1932 he married Augusta Willoughby Gage Ellis; they had two children and were divorced in 1958.

Ever restless, Little took a sabbatical from Franklin Rayon in 1937 and joined the investment banking firm of Herrick Berg, which fared poorly in that year's recession. Chastened but with a new knowledge of finance, Little returned to what now was called Atlantic Rayon.

World War II changed the situation at Atlantic Rayon, which became an important supplier of the fabric for parachutes. Recognizing the opportunity for expansion, Little purchased other companies and facilities, in the process switching production from parachutes to hammocks. In 1944, after raising money by selling some unwanted divisions and marketing a bond issue, Little changed the company's name to Textron, a designation indicating an intention to make it an important factor in textiles.

Having had some success in acquisitions and divestitures, Little went on the prowl for underpriced companies. He had learned quite a lot about taxes during the trying 1930s, so he looked for companies with large tax losses to offset the gains he expected from other acquisitions. In

Royal Little. TEXTRON, INC. PHOTO BY TOMMY WEBER.

1944, he organized a second company, American Associates, which was to serve as the vehicle for the takeovers. These started in 1945 with Manville-Jenckes, a manufacturer of greige (unfinished cloth) with a substantial tax-loss carryforward. Using borrowed money he purchased the company and then sold some units; the selling price, together with the tax losses, came to more than what he had paid for the firm. He followed this in 1946 with the acquisitions of Lonsdale and of Nashua Manufacturing, both of which had assets valued in excess of the price Little paid for them. He then purchased twelve textile plants in the Carolinas for more than $12 million and united them in a new company, Textron Southern, a Textron subsidiary. By 1947 Textron had $125 million in sales and was paying a dividend. There was a slump in 1948, however, and Textron suffered along with the rest of the textile industry.

Around this time Little altered his approach. He had come to realize that his talents were in takeovers and divestitures, not necessarily in managing a company in the textile business. He therefore took a two-pronged approach. He would continue in textiles but also would buy just about any company on which he could turn a profit. His basic concept was to purchase "cash cows" at low prices then utilize profits from them to enhance his textile holdings. His initial acquisition unrelated to textiles was Cleveland Pneumatic Tool, a manufacturer of aircraft landing struts. Cleveland Pneumatic had substantial wartime profits on which it would have to pay an undistributed profits tax or a large dividend. Unwilling to do either, the company sold itself to Textron, which had tax losses against which to offset the profits. Next was Pathé Industries, which was in newsreels and real estate. Little continued in textiles as well, turning to American Woolen, a large, mismanaged company with $26 million in cash items. The struggle for American Woolen started in 1953 and lasted more than a year. Little won after a bruising battle, but soon found he had acquired a terminally sick concern. He then went after Robbins Mills, a manufacturer of synthetics and wool blends with a tax-loss carryforward that attracted his attention. All of these holdings were placed into a new company, Textron American, which never achieved greatness or even consistent profitability. Little had thought that three or four poorly performing companies might be combined into a single one that did well. He was wrong.

In 1955, at the age of fifty-nine, Little abandoned his hope of creating a major textile company. Now, instead of using profits from nonrelated concerns to support a textile operation, he decided to divest himself of textiles and concentrate on acquisitions. In the process he became one of the earliest conglomerateurs of the modern era.

Little's hope—shared by other conglomerateurs—was to create a balanced enterprise that would be able to withstand economic shocks. Thus he would have Textron own and manage companies in categories that complemented each other. Some would require heavy capital outlays to finance their growth, the funds obtained from "cash cows." There would be cyclical companies and growth companies. When one sector did poorly he hoped another would perform well. Little would not become dominant in any single industry so as to avoid encounters with antitrusters. He wanted leading companies in "niche" industries. "One of my particular 'no-no's,' " he told a reporter, was "never buy a company that manufactures a product with an electric wire attached—no radios, televisions, washing machines, dryers, electric stoves, or refrigerators."

Little said he preferred companies with young, competent, and hungry managements, particularly firms that were privately owned, which would ease the acquisition process. As in most aspects of his business career, all of those guidelines were breached along the way to the creation of a billion-dollar enterprise.

Little started his new campaign with Dalmo Victor, a large supplier of airborne radar antennas, followed by MB Manufacturing, which made parts for piston engines. Dozens of other small firms followed, including Kordite, Ryan Industries, Homelite, Camcar Screw & Manufacturing, and General Cement (which despite the name produced radio and television components). Little even purchased an old troop ship, which he put on the Hawaii tourist run. All of this demonstrated that what he really wanted to do was purchase a dollar of assets for 50 cents. At this stage of his career he was basically a collector of heterogeneous corporate junk. By 1960 he had purchased more than forty companies, many of them losers.

Little always seemed to be playing the corporate game by ear. In 1959, when electronics companies were popular on Wall Street, he placed several Textron firms marginally involved in high technology into a new firm he called Textron Electronics, which was then spun off. While it sported a higher price/earnings multiple than Textron, it never amounted to much.

This changed in the 1960s. In 1960 Textron purchased the helicopter division of Bell Aircraft, at a time when the company's fortunes were low. Bell became an important factor in President Kennedy's arms buildup, and Little finally had a substantial winner. Other defense firms followed, and by 1966 this sector accounted for more than 40 percent of Textron's revenues.

Little eased out of the company after 1960. While serving on the board he turned Textron over to Rupert C. Thompson, Jr. Now Little, together with his son, Arthur D. Little, started a new entity, Narragansett Capital, which invested in small, new companies. He also played golf, went on photographic safaris, and wrote a book, *How to Lose $100 Million and Other Valuable Advice*. Tall and slender, Little had a wonderful, self-deprecating sense of humor and was a fanatic regarding his privacy. He left instructions in his will that there be neither a funeral nor a memorial service after he died. "No funeral—a barbaric institution—no memorial service—hope my friends will just think I've taken a long trip."

★

There is no full-scale biography of Little, and *The Royal Little Story,* privately printed in the 1970s by Textron, is uninformative. Little's book, *How to Lose $100 Million and Other Valuable Advice* (1979), is not as frivolous as its title might indicate but contains little personal information. There is a chapter on Little in Robert Sobel, *The Rise and Fall of the Conglomerate Kings* (1984). Many magazine articles dealt with Textron and Little while he headed the company. Among the best are "Textron," *Fortune* (May 1947); "Whose Mistake at Nashua?" *Fortune* (Nov. 1948); Stanley Brown, "Textron: How to Manage a Conglomerate Making Many Products," *Fortune* (Apr. 1964); "Textron: An Orderly Conglomerate," *Magazine of Wall Street* (24 Dec. 1966). An obituary is in the *New York Times* (14 Jan. 1989).

ROBERT SOBEL

LIVINGSTON, M(ilton) Stanley (*b.* 25 May 1905 in Brodhead, Wisconsin; *d.* 25 August 1986 in Santa Fe, New Mexico), experimental physicist who was a leading scientist in the construction of the first cyclotron, an atom-smashing device.

Livingston was one of four children of Milton McWhorter Livingston, a rancher, schoolteacher, and minister, and Sarah Jane Ten Eyck, a homemaker. After the death of his mother, when he was twelve, Livingston moved with his family to Pomona, California. His father remarried and subsequently had five sons. Livingston studied at Pomona High School and then at Bonita High School in La Verne, California, graduating in 1921. The following year he matriculated at Pomona College in Claremont, California, where he majored in chemistry and physics and graduated with honors with an A.B. degree in 1926. He pursued graduate work at Dartmouth College, where he received an M.A. degree in physics in 1928. He remained at Dartmouth as an instructor until 1929, when he resumed his studies at the University of California at Berkeley under the supervision of Professor Ernest Orlando Lawrence, who had proposed the basic idea of the cyclotron. In 1930 Livingston married Lois Robinson; they had two children.

The central concept of the cyclotron involved bending the circular orbits of fundamental electrically charged particles—electrons, protons, or ions—in a magnetic field and incrementally increasing their orbit velocity and hence energy. To achieve this, two semicircular electrodes (designated "dees" because of their shape) are positioned in a vacuum chamber between the poles of an electromagnet, producing a constant magnetic field perpendicular to the dees. Electrically charged particles are introduced near the center of the vacuum chamber. In the separation between the electromagnetic dees, an alternating electric field is imposed that has the same frequency as the frequency of revolution of the charged particles. During each circuit, the particle travels in widening circles until the particle reaches the outside periphery of the dee. Each circuit results in a cumulative increase in the particle energy.

After preliminary efforts by Lawrence and another graduate student, N. E. Edlefsen, Lawrence and Livingston published the first paper on a working cyclotron, which was the basis of Livingston's doctoral dissertation, "The Production of High-Velocity Hydrogen Ions Without the Use of High Voltages," in 1931. The initial paper was published in the *Physical Review* (30 April 1931) and described "using a magnet with pole faces 10 cm (dees about 4 inches) in diameter." Three months later a larger cyclotron (dees of 9 inches in diameter) was designed by Livingston; at the beginning of 1932 he devised yet another, with 11-inch dees.

Livingston continued as a research associate, assisting Lawrence in cyclotron-related work until 1934, when he transferred to Cornell University, where he was an assistant professor from 1934 to 1938. That year he was appointed assistant professor at the Massachusetts Institute of Technology (MIT), becoming full professor in 1954. In 1939 he divorced his wife, and in 1952 he married Margaret Hughes.

In 1954 Livingston served as chairman of the executive committee of the Federation of American Scientists (FAS), publisher of the *Bulletin of Atomic Scientists,* known for its cover with the Doomsday Clock—adjusting periodically the "minutes" away from "midnight" and mankind's potential destruction by nuclear weapons. Under his leadership, FAS took strong exception to the Atomic Energy Commission's suspension of physicist J. Robert Oppenheimer from access to secret information.

Between 1956 and 1967, concurrent with his professorship at MIT, Livingston directed the construction and experimental program of the Cambridge Electron Accelerator, a joint effort of Harvard University and MIT. The accelerator became operational in 1962 with a beam of 6-GeV (billion-electron-volt) electrons.

The scientific managing consortium of Brookhaven National Laboratory (BNL) at Upton, Long Island, New York, selected Livingston to be chairman of its accelerator project, which he headed from 1946 to 1958. In addition to directing the construction of the first proton synchrotron at BNL known as the Cosmotron, he joined with his colleagues in developing the principle of strong focusing in 1952. The latter concept overcame the technical obstacles that limited energies achievable in earlier machines making use of the cyclotron principle and its advances in the later accelerator,

M. Stanley Livingston (*left*) and E. O. Lawrence stand by the first atom smasher, which weighed eighty-five tons, 1936. UPI/CORBIS-BETTMANN

such as the synchrocyclotron and synchrotron. Application of the strong-focusing principle permitted the building and operation of the alternating gradient synchrotron (AGS) at Brookhaven in 1960, with record proton energies of 33 GeV.

Between 1967 and 1970, Livingston was associate director of the Fermi National Laboratory in Batavia, Illinois. He administered the scientific effort that led to the construction in 1972 of the highest-energy particle accelerator in the United States, an alternating gradient synchrotron, reaching proton energies of 200 GeV.

He died in Santa Fe, where he had lived the last years of his retirement.

Livingston's outstanding pioneering work in the design of early cyclotrons and later administrative direction of high-energy accelerator research and development made him one of the decisive contributors to U.S. leadership in experimental nuclear science. Besides his excellence as a scientist, Livingston was a warm, enthusiastic teacher with a fine sense of humor who took a personal interest in his students.

★

Livingston's works include *High Energy Accelerators* (1954), which covers basic accelerator principles; with J. P. Blewett, *Particle Accelerators* (1962), an advanced comprehensive textbook; and *Particle Accelerators: A Brief History* (1969). He wrote scores of articles and papers, including, with E. O. Lawrence, "The Production of High Speed Light Ions Without the Use of High Voltages," *Physical Review* 40 (1932): 19; "The Cyclotron," *Journal of Applied Physics* 15 (1944): 2, 128; with J. P. Blewett, G. K. Green, and L. J. Haworth, "Design Study for a Three-BeV Proton Accelerator," *Review of Scientific Instruments* 21 (1950): 7; and with E. D. Courant and H. S. Snyder, "The Strong-Focusing Synchrotron: A New High-Energy Accelerator," *Physical Review* 88 (1952): 1190. See also Abraham Pais, *Inward Bound: Of Matter and Forces in the Physical World* (1986), and Frank Close, Michael Marten, and Christine Sutton, *The Particle Explosion* (1987). An obituary is in the *New York Times* (20 Sept. 1986).

LEONARD R. SOLON

LOEWE, Frederick (*b.* 10 June 1901 in Berlin, Germany; *d.* 14 February 1988 in Palm Springs, California), composer noted for a series of successful Broadway musicals written in collaboration with Alan Jay Lerner.

Loewe was the son of an opera singer, Edmund Loewe, and an actress, Rosa Loewe, both of whom were Austrian. His youth in Germany is subject to conflicting accounts, but he apparently attended a military academy as a child before showing a talent for music and being enrolled at Stern's Conservatory. He performed as a piano soloist with the Berlin Symphony Orchestra at thirteen, and at fifteen wrote "Katrina," which became a European hit. Probably in 1924 he moved to the United States, where he worked at a variety of occupations, including boxing and teaching horseback riding, before beginning to make a living playing piano and organ. He married Ernestine Zwerlein in 1931. They separated in 1947 and divorced in 1957. He never remarried.

Frederick Loewe. OSCAR WHITE/CORBIS

By the mid-1930s Loewe was placing songs in Broadway shows, starting with "Love Tiptoed Through My Heart," for which Irene Alexander wrote the lyrics, in the 1935 play *Petticoat Fever*. He formed a songwriting partnership with lyricist Earle Crooker, and they got "A Waltz Was Born in Vienna" into the 1936 revue *The Illustrators' Show*. Their first full-length effort was the 1937 musical *Salute to Spring*, which closed out of town; their second, *Great Lady*, opened on Broadway in 1938 but was a failure.

Loewe returned to piano playing. At the Lambs Club he met Alan Jay Lerner, a radio scriptwriter more than seventeen years his junior, who worked on some of the club's amateur shows. When he was given the opportunity to do a new musical employing some of the songs from *Salute to Spring* in 1942, Loewe turned to Lerner to write the show's libretto; Lerner also ended up rewriting some lyrics. The musical, *Life of the Party*, closed out of town, but Lerner and Loewe went on to write their own show, *What's Up?*, which opened on Broadway in November 1943 and ran an unsuccessful sixty-three performances. They tried again with *The Day Before Spring* in 1945 and were rewarded with a run of 165 performances. They finally succeeded when Lerner conceived the idea of a Scottish town that comes to life for one day every hundred years, *Brigadoon*. This charming fantasy opened on Broadway 13 March 1947 with a Lerner and Loewe score that included "Almost Like Being in Love," "Come to Me, Bend to Me," and "The Heather on the Hill," and ran 581 performances. The show's original cast album was also a popular success, as was the soundtrack album when the musical became a movie starring Gene Kelly in 1954.

The Lerner and Loewe partnership was subject to periodic interruptions as Lerner worked with others while Loewe was inactive. They next worked together on *Paint Your Wagon*, a musical of the California gold rush, which opened 12 November 1951. Its run of 289 performances was not enough to turn a profit, despite another memorable score that included the hit "They Call the Wind Maria." It took eighteen years for the show to be adapted into a film, and by the time it was, in 1969, it had been drastically altered by Lerner, who wrote a new story and added five songs with music by André Previn. Starring Lee Marvin and Clint Eastwood, the picture cost $20 million to make and lost nearly all its investment, driving another nail into the coffin of the big-budget Hollywood musical, although the soundtrack sold well.

In 1952 Lerner and Loewe embarked on the ambitious idea of trying to musicalize *Pygmalion*, George Bernard Shaw's play about the relationship between a British flower seller and the elocutionist who decides to pass her off as a lady. They failed to find an approach to the adaptation and separated, then reunited two years later and tried again. But it was not until 15 March 1956 that *My Fair Lady* opened on Broadway. Starring Rex Harrison and Julie Andrews, it was the triumph of Lerner and Loewe's career, winning the Tony Award for best musical, running an unprecedented 2,717 performances, and spawning a chart-topping, multimillion-selling cast album. The score included "Get Me to the Church on Time," "I Could Have Danced All Night," "I've Grown Accustomed to Her Face," "On the Street Where You Live," and "With a Little Bit of Luck," all of which became hits. More than eight years passed before the show came to the screen in a nearly three-hour version with Harrison re-creating his performance opposite Audrey Hepburn (whose singing was dubbed by Marni Nixon). The lavish film won eight Academy Awards but failed to break even because of its huge budget. The soundtrack album put the score high on the charts all over again.

In 1958 Lerner and Loewe followed *My Fair Lady* with their first musical written for film, *Gigi*, starring Leslie Caron, Maurice Chevalier (who sang "Thank Heaven for Little Girls"), and Louis Jourdan. Based on Colette's novel, the story of a younger woman and an older man bore some resemblance to *My Fair Lady*, which worried critics but not moviegoers, who made the film one of the year's most successful. It also won nine Academy Awards, including best picture and best song (the title song), and it generated an album that topped the charts and won a Grammy Award.

In February 1959 Loewe suffered a massive heart attack. He went on to write one more show with Lerner, then retired for more than a decade. The show was *Camelot*, based on the legends of King Arthur and the Round Table as described by T. H. White in his novel *The Once and Future King*. Starring Richard Burton, Julie Andrews, and Robert Goulet, it opened 3 December 1960 and ran 873 performances, the songwriters' second most successful show. The cast album, featuring the title song and "If Ever I Would Leave You," was another million-selling, number-one hit. The soundtrack album, released to accompany another lengthy, high-budget, low-return movie in 1967, also sold a million copies.

Loewe retired after *Camelot*, and Lerner was not able to lure him back to composing until 1973, when the two wrote some new songs for a stage adaptation of *Gigi*. It was not a financial success, despite a Tony Award for best score, nor was their film musical of *The Little Prince*, based on the children's story by Antoine de Saint-Exupery, released in 1974. Loewe resumed his retirement and died of a heart attack at age eighty-six in 1988. He is buried in Desert Memorial Park in Cathedral City, California.

After years in which the Broadway musical took its lead from Tin Pan Alley, Frederick Loewe restored it to its roots in European operetta, presenting a lush, melodic sound reminiscent of his parents' native Austria, whether the nominal setting was Scotland, London, or Paris. His music lent charm and style to his partner's wit and wordplay to create a series of delightful, stylish musicals that provided a healthy contrast, as well as competition, to their chief rivals, Richard Rodgers and Oscar Hammerstein II.

★

Gene Lees, usually thought of as a jazz critic, wrote the only full-length biography, *Inventing Champagne: The Worlds of Lerner and Loewe* (1990), which is marred by its antipathy to its subjects. Otherwise, one must rely on books by or about Alan Jay Lerner. His memoir is *The Street Where I Live* (1978), but more highly recommended is Edward Jablonski's *Alan Jay Lerner: A Biography* (1996). An obituary of Loewe is in the *New York Times* (15 Feb. 1988).

WILLIAM J. RUHLMANN

LOEWY, Raymond Fernand (*b.* 5 November 1893 in Paris, France; *d.* 14 July 1986 in Monte Carlo, Monaco), industrial designer who influenced the emergence of American designs in products, packaging, and transportation.

Loewy was the son of Maximillian Loewy, a writer and managing editor of a financial journal, and Marie Labalme, who came from a family of French landowners. Raymond and his two older brothers lived a comfortable life in the affluent Parisian suburb of Neuilly. The family spent summers in Normandy and wintered at a villa in Nice. At the age of ten, Raymond, who showed skill in drawing automobiles and trains, watched as a Brazilian inventor, Alberto Santos Dumont, flew his homemade airplanes across the polo field in the Bois de Boulogne in Paris. Five years later Raymond developed a model airplane, powered by a rubber band, that won an important competition called the James Gordon Bennett Cup. In 1908 Loewy, in a plan that would mark his life's direction, sought a design patent, registered the plane's trademark Ayrel, hired two mechanics and a salesman, and proceeded to learn all the facets of being a businessman. Sponsored by the National Aeronautical League, the fifteen year old gave lectures and demonstrated his model airplane to fascinated audiences who had never before seen anything manmade fly. The packaged models sold briskly.

Loewy's business thrived and took more and more of his time, but the young entrepreneur heeded parental advice, sold the business, and concentrated on his studies. From 1908 to 1911 he attended École de Lanneau, a preparatory school for those interested in entering École Centrale, France's prestigious technological institute. Loewy enrolled at École Centrale in 1912.

World War I interrupted Loewy's studies in 1914, when he was commissioned a corporal in the French Corps of Engineers. He was burned by mustard gas and earned seven medals and four citations for action in combat, and by the end of the war he had become a captain on the general staff of the Fifth Army. All three Loewy brothers earned the Legion of Honor. During the war both parents died in the Spanish influenza epidemic, and the family assets were lost. Finding himself penniless, Loewy nevertheless returned to École Centrale in 1917 and completed his engineering degree in 1919, at the age of twenty-six.

Following his two brothers, who had immigrated to New York City, Loewy set sail for the United States in the fall of 1919. Within the first months of his arrival, in spite of his limited English, he was able to shrewdly build up social contacts. Aided by letters of introduction, he was hired to do fashion illustrations for *Vogue* magazine and the leading New York City department stores. Loewy worked as an illustrator for ten years, and while he achieved financial success, he felt intellectually frustrated.

In 1929 Sigmund Gestetner, a British manufacturer of duplicating machines, saw a promotional card that Loewy distributed advertising his philosophy that a better-designed product would outsell one that was equal in price, function, and quality. Gestetner hired Loewy to redesign his duplicating machine in three days, in time for Gestetner's return to England. With plasticine clay, Loewy transformed the awkward-looking machine into a streamlined

Raymond Loewy, locomotive designer, March 1936. UPI/CORBIS-BETTMANN

product. Pleased, Gestetner paid the $2,000 fee, and Loewy's career as an industrial designer was born. In 1931 Loewy married Jean Thomson; they had one child.

Continuing his boyhood interest in streamlining automobile designs, Loewy signed a lucrative contract in 1931 to design the 1934 Hupmobile. Unfortunately, the company was too conservative to adopt Loewy's innovative styling and eventually ceased operations. However, Loewy was now confident enough to approach the president of the Pennsylvania Railroad with an offer to redesign its locomotives. The president countered with a challenge that he redesign the trash containers in Pennsylvania Station in New York City, and Loewy accepted the test. He was successful and won the right to design the new diesel locomotive (completed in 1937) that changed the face of American railroads. In 1933 he designed a ferryboat for the Virginia Ferry Company.

Starting in 1933, Loewy began to seek other clients and opened an office on fashionable Fifth Avenue that he staffed with two designers and a secretary. His quest for additional accounts took him across the country selling his philosophy that improved design means better sales. After two years of repeated contacts, Loewy convinced Sears, Roebuck and Company of the importance of good design in their products. He finally won a contract to redesign the 1934 Coldspot refrigerator, the turning point in Loewy's career. His modern styling and functional improvements created unprecedented consumer demand.

In 1934, five years after his first design for Gestetner, Loewy had to move into larger offices in Manhattan for his growing design staff. International Harvester and Greyhound joined his list of accounts, and he was now the central force behind the new profession of industrial design. In 1937 Loewy began an association with the Studebaker Automobile Company that lasted until 1962 and led to a streamlined look in postwar automotive design. He stated, "The keynote of my work was simplification." He became a U.S. citizen in 1938.

During World War II, when automobile production ceased and the industry concentrated on the war effort, Loewy did design work for Studebaker that would capture the postwar imagination. For the first time, auto design was not a committee effort but one man's vision. In 1945 he and his first wife divorced, and three years later Loewy married Viola Erickson, with whom he had one daughter, Laurence. During the 1950s he was able to refine his sporty auto designs into the 1962 classic Avanti, a recognized work of automotive art.

At the peak of its expansion, Raymond Loewy Associates had headquarters in New York City and branches in Chicago, South Bend, Los Angeles, and London. Near the end of his career, Loewy moved to France and opened an office in Paris. In 1979 Raymond Loewy Associates marked its fiftieth anniversary, and the following year, at the age of eighty-seven, Loewy decided to retire. He had presided over an international studio that had designed all modes of transportation, department stores, supermarkets, corporate and brand identity, packages, and the National Aeronautics and Space Administration (NASA) Skylab. In addition, the company had served as a design consultant to the Soviet Union.

After Loewy's death from natural causes in Monte

Carlo, the estate put much of his archives up for sale. A group of American designers purchased his important works and donated them to the Library of Congress.

This charismatic Franco-American, an immigrant with $40 in his pocket in 1919, became the first advocate for industrial design. He spent his life convincing manufacturers of the importance of beauty and simplicity in American products. A master of public relations and press briefings, he also trained more than 2,000 industrial designers employed in his firm. In 1975 the Smithsonian Institution paid him tribute with a one-man retrospective of his work.

★

The collection of Loewy's manuscripts and personal papers is in the Manuscripts Division of the Library of Congress, Washington, D.C. His drawings and photographs are in the Prints and Photographs Reading Room in the James Madison Building of the library. Loewy's autobiography, *Never Leave Well Enough Alone* (1951), traces his early life and his start as an industrial designer. His design principles are outlined in his *Industrial Design* (1979). Lois Frieman Brand, *The Designs of Raymond Loewy* (1975), was published in conjunction with the exhibition at the Renwick Gallery of the Smithsonian Institution, Washington, D.C. See also Angela Schönberger, ed., *Raymond Loewy, Pioneer of American Industrial Design* (1990); and Jeffrey L. Meikle, "Raymond Loewy 1893–1986," *Industrial Design* (Nov./Dec. 1986). An obituary is in the *New York Times* (15 July 1986).

ROSEMARIE S. CARDOSO

LOGAN, Joshua Lockwood, III (*b.* 5 October 1908 in Texarkana, Texas; *d.* 7 July 1988 in New York City), director of stage and screen, playwright, and producer.

Logan was one of two children of Joshua Logan II, a wealthy lumberman who died when the boy was three years old, and Susan Nabors, a homemaker whose aesthetic tastes would later be praised by her son and who raised her children in Mansfield, Louisiana. In 1917 Logan's mother married Colonel Howard F. Noble, a staff member at Culver (Indiana) Military Academy, where Logan enrolled and became active in sports and drama.

In 1927 Logan entered Princeton University, where he participated enthusiastically in the school's Triangle Club and Theatre Intime productions. He also was a leader of the University Players on Cape Cod in Massachusetts, whose members included Henry Fonda and James Stewart. During his senior year (1930–1931), Logan traveled to the Soviet Union and spent eight months at the Moscow Art Theatre, where he came under the influence of Konstantin Stanislavsky. He did not return to Princeton to graduate, but that university awarded him an honorary degree in 1953.

In 1932 the University Players moved to Baltimore,

Joshua Logan, *c.* 1969. PARAMOUNT PICTURES/ARCHIVE PHOTOS

where Logan staged various productions, but the company did not survive. After acting in a small role in a Players drama that moved to Broadway later that year, Logan focused on directing, staging two plays in London in 1933, *Champagne Sister* and *The Day I Forgot,* then directing Jane Cowl in a Boston production of *Camille* (1933). Among other theater jobs of this period, he was assistant stage manager for a play by Howard Lindsay, *She Loves Me Not* (1933), which led to jobs codirecting *It's You I Want* (1935) and directing and coproducing *To See Ourselves* (1935). He directed *Hell Freezes Over* (1935) and acted in *A Room in Red and White* (1936) before going to Hollywood, where he directed dialogue in two films and codirected and coscripted *I Met My Love Again* (1938).

Back on Broadway, Logan had his first directorial hit with Paul Osborn's *On Borrowed Time* (1938), to whose success Logan's dramaturgical revisions were crucial. It led to his directing the Richard Rodgers–Lorenz Hart musical *I Married an Angel* (1938), another hit and the beginning of Logan's close relationship with Rodgers. Logan's career moved into high gear as he directed such musicals as *Knickerbocker Holiday* (1938), by Kurt Weill and Maxwell Anderson; *Stars in Your Eyes* (1939), starring Ethel Merman; *Two for the Show* (1940), a revue; and two more Rodgers and Hart shows, *Higher and Higher* (1940) and *By Jupiter* (1942). He also offered Osborn's *Morning's at Seven* (1939) and a popular revival of *Charley's Aunt* (1940), starring José Ferrer. In 1940 he married the actress Barbara O'Neill, who had a daughter from a previous marriage; they divorced the following year.

In 1942 Logan was drafted into the army, where he assisted Ezra Stone in directing the original stage version of Irving Berlin's *This Is the Army* (1942). Having graduated first in his class of 3,000 at Officers Training School, he served in public relations and intelligence and was discharged with the rank of captain. In 1945 he married the actress Nedda Harrigan; they had two children. After the war Logan returned to Broadway with Berlin's blockbuster *Annie Get Your Gun* (1946), starring Ethel Merman. He had additional hits with the comedies *Happy Birthday* (1946), starring Helen Hayes, and *John Loves Mary* (1947). He then directed and cowrote *Mister Roberts* (1948), which starred Henry Fonda and was based on Thomas Heggen's novel. Logan's contribution in helping the author turn his work into a viable stage play led to a shared Tony Award for writing as well as one for Logan's direction. He followed up this success with his direction, coproduction, and coauthorship of Rodgers and Oscar Hammerstein's landmark musical *South Pacific* (1949), with Mary Martin and Ezio Pinza, which earned Logan his third Tony. At the time, he was wounded by oversights, such as by the Pulitzer Prize committee, concerning his coauthorship. The show had no formal choreography; all the appropriate dance movement was arranged by Logan himself, including the masterful "There Is Nothing Like a Dame." Another brilliant touch, which Logan devised in the interest of realism to short-circuit encores, was filmlike "lap dissolves," in which one scene began as the preceding one ended.

Logan's penchant for literary adaptation was evident in his revision of *The Cherry Orchard,* which he relocated to the American South and retitled *The Wisteria Trees* (1950), a failure that one critic called "Southern-fried Chekhov." Logan cowrote, coproduced, and directed the musical *Wish You Were Here* (1952), which had nearly closed before his revisions turned its fate around, an unusual feat. He scored another musical hit with *Fanny* (1954), coauthored with S. N. Behrman and with music by Harold Rome, but by now he was focusing on dramas and films. His play credits of this era include *Kind Sir* (1953); William Inge's *Picnic* (1953), for which he won his fourth Tony; Paddy Chayefsky's *Middle of the Night* (1956); *Blue Denim* (1958); and *The World of Suzie Wong* (1958). Logan's string of film successes includes *Bus Stop* (1956), *Picnic* (1956), *Sayonara* (1957), and *South Pacific* (1958). *Picnic* and *Sayonara* earned him Oscar nominations. He produced a few plays without staging them and often served as a play doctor for the productions of others.

Logan's career weakened during the 1960s, which saw his direction of the films *Tall Story* (1960), *Fanny* (1961), *Ensign Pulver* (1964), *Camelot* (1967), and *Paint Your Wagon* (1969). As before, the bulk of his film projects stemmed from Broadway shows. He also staged seven Broadway plays and musicals, among them *All American* (1962) and *Mr. President* (1962). None succeeded. The 1970s, despite a gala tribute to his career held at New York's Imperial Theatre in 1975, witnessed a major decline in Logan's career. His projects during this decade included the disastrous *Miss Moffatt* (1974), a musical version of *The Corn Is Green* starring Bette Davis, which closed out of town. His final directing effort was the meager *Horowitz and Mrs. Washington* (1980). He and his wife, who were active in New York, Connecticut, and London social events, toured in 1984 with an evening of songs and anecdotes.

The immensely energetic, deeply sensitive Logan was six feet, one inch in height and weighed more than 200 pounds, with a beautifully modulated voice. He suffered from manic depression and twice committed himself for treatment. When he discovered in 1969 that his problem could be treated with lithium, he proselytized for the drug, although he believed that the manic phase of his illness had stimulated his creativity. Late in life he fell victim to the debilitating disease of supranuclear palsy, from which he died in New York City.

To Logan the best direction was unobtrusive, and he was pleased when his work drew little attention. "When people come up and tell me the direction is wonderful," he once remarked, "then I know I have failed." His talents at combining entertainment know-how with artistic integrity gained him a niche as one of the most commercially successful Broadway directors and one of the ablest at turning theatrical material into celluloid magic.

★

Joshua Logan's correspondence is in the Special Collections Department, University of Iowa Libraries. There is also Logan-related material in the Triangle Club and Theatre Intime collections at the Seeley Mudd Manuscript Library, Princeton University. Logan's autobiographies are *Josh, My Up and Down, In and Out Life* (1976) and *Movie Stars, Real People, and Me* (1978). Logan's directing is discussed in Samuel L. Leiter, *The Great Stage Directors: 100 Distinguished Careers of the Theatre* (1994); and John W. Frick and Stephen M. Vallillo, eds., *Theatrical Directors: A Biographical Dictionary* (1994). Valuable coverage is in Norris Houghton, "B. Windust and J. Logan," *Theatre Arts* (Apr. 1937); Maurice Zolotow, "Josh-of-All-Theatre-Trades," *Theatre Arts* (Oct. 1954); Gay Talese, "The Soft Psyche of Joshua Logan," *Esquire* (Apr. 1963); and Phil Boroff, "Joshua Logan's Directorial Approach to the Theatre and Motion Pictures" (Ph.D. diss., Southern Illinois University, 1976). Obituaries are in the *New York Times* (13 July 1988) and *Variety* (20 July 1988). An oral history tape is at the Oral History Collection at Columbia University.

SAMUEL L. LEITER

LORD, John Wesley (*b.* 23 August 1902 in Paterson, New Jersey; *d.* 8 October 1989 in Wolfeboro, New Hampshire), churchman who forthrightly expressed and acted upon his deep liberal convictions on controversial political and social issues in his effort to defend the Bill of Rights, to promote social and economic justice, to improve race relations, and to advance the cause of world peace.

The second of the three sons of John James Lord, a letter carrier, and Catherine Carmichael, who wanted her son to be a minister, Lord was named after the founder of Methodism. After completing high school in suburban Montclair, New Jersey, Lord attended the New Jersey State Normal School at Montclair, from which he graduated in 1922. He was a public school teacher and principal in New Jersey from 1922 to 1924. He then entered Dickinson College in Carlisle, Pennsylvania, and received his A.B. degree in 1927. Deciding that the ministry was his true vocation, he then enrolled in Drew Theological Seminary in Madison, New Jersey, and obtained the bachelor of divinity degree in 1930. During his three years at Drew, he was assistant pastor of the Emory Methodist Church in Jersey City, New Jersey. After some graduate study in philosophy at New College, University of Edinburgh, Scotland, from 1930 to 1931, he married Margaret Farrington Ratcliffe on 29 April 1931. They had one daughter, Jean.

John Wesley Lord, 1962. UPI/CORBIS-BETTMANN

Lord's first pastorate was at the Union Community Church in Union, New Jersey, where he served from 1931 to 1934. He was then pastor of the First Methodist Church in Arlington, New Jersey, from 1935 to 1938, followed by the First Methodist Church in Westfield, New Jersey, from 1938 to 1948. One of the youngest Methodist bishops to be ordained in the United States, he was elected to the episcopacy of the Methodist church in June 1948 and served for twenty-four years. In 1948 he was assigned to the Boston area and made his home in Wellesley, Massachusetts. In 1960 he was reassigned to the Washington, D.C., area, where he remained until his retirement in 1972. From 1970 to 1971 he was president of the Council of Bishops of the United Methodist Church.

In Washington, Lord became a social activist. He upheld President John F. Kennedy's plea for the enactment of the School Assistance Bill of 1961, which provided federal aid to public schools. He explained that the public school system was the "bulwark of democracy," essentially different from the private parochial system, and that it would be unconstitutional to include the latter in the bill because of the First Amendment's strictures against the "establishment of religion." Committed to the principle of separation of church and state, Lord appeared before the House Judiciary Committee in Washington on 27 May 1964 to oppose the proposed constitutional amendment, known as the Becker amendment, that would allow doctrinal exercises in public schools. He argued that the First Amendment, as it then stood, was adequate to protect "the free exercise of religion." Further, he emphasized that the 1962 Supreme Court decision in *Engle* v. *Vitale,* which forbade a state-composed prayer and Bible reading in public schools, excluded neither teaching about religion nor studying the Bible for its "literary and historical qualities" in public schools. "The school may not pray, but it must teach," he admonished.

Dedicated to the struggle for racial equality, Lord participated in the 28 August 1963 civil rights demonstration in Washington, D.C., known as the "March on Washington for Jobs and Freedom." On 9 March 1965 he joined the abortive second attempt to stage a protest march from Selma to Montgomery, Alabama, in support of voting rights for African Americans. Motivated solely by his conscience, he demonstrated as an individual citizen and marched arm in arm with Dr. Martin Luther King, Jr. Championing racial integration in the Methodist church, Lord had, as bishop, by 1964 appointed in the Washington area black district superintendents to head predominantly white districts and churches and, beginning in 1966, black pastors to white parishes. In March 1972 he stated that "separate but equal" was the shibboleth used for many decades in some parts of the United States to defend the outrageous practice of busing black children to black schools. He favored instead busing them to better neighborhoods and better school systems, but only as a "temporary expedient." He warned that if busing were thought of simply as a means of integrating the "school," it would be a wasteful effort. The objective, in his view, was to make all neighborhoods "good" and to extend their services to all children.

A social reformer, Lord preached abstinence from alcoholic beverages and advocated penal reform and rehabilitation. As chairman of the Interreligious Committee on Race Relations from 1967 to 1969 and with the plight of America's cities in mind, he implored that "social service is not enough; we need social change" to address effectively problems stemming from poverty and racism.

A sharp critic of the Vietnam War, Lord faulted President Lyndon Johnson in December 1966 for escalating it, thus undercutting the president's call for negotiations and peaceful settlement. In May 1970 Lord accused President Richard Nixon of indifference to the moral issues of the war. He joined the Citizens Committee for the Amendment to End the War, formed in 1970, which aimed to restore to Congress its constitutional role in making war. In 1971 he served on the national committee Set the Date Now: An Interreligious Campaign to End the War and urged Congress to vote against the two-year extension of conscription that Nixon sought that year. Lord also argued that war resisters should be granted unconditional amnesty and repatriation in recognition of their right to dissent under constraint of conscience. His humanitarian efforts on the national level included accepting in 1966 an honorary chairmanship of the Committee of Responsibility to Save War-Burned and War-Injured Vietnamese Children.

Lord also disagreed with U.S. policy on China and joined the National Board for New China Policy, organized in 1970. He contended that Taiwan was historically, culturally, and linguistically Chinese and that the People's Republic of China (mainland China) was entitled to the Chinese seat on the United Nations Security Council. Concerned with the ravages caused by overpopulation, Lord explained that the Methodist (and Protestant) position was to make information and medical assistance regarding birth control available to families worldwide through public and private programs. Arguing for a more responsible attitude toward family planning, in 1972 he asked Nixon to recommend strongly to the American people his presidential commission's report *Population Growth and the American Future,* which called for a gradual stabilization of population, a national population policy, and U.S. assistance to developing countries in seeking solutions to the problem; Nixon rejected the report instead.

Lord sought a stronger United Nations. As a representative of the United States Interreligious Committee on Peace, he participated for twenty-two days in 1968 in a tour of seven countries to promote peace, calling on all nations to "surrender some of their sovereignty" to achieve a "world perspective." He pressed the U.S. Senate to reject Nixon's proposal in 1969 to deploy the antiballistic missile system.

After retiring in 1972, Lord lived in Wolfeboro, New Hampshire, and spent his winters in Lakeland, Florida. He preached often in New Hampshire and ministered around Lakeland. Lord used his mellifluous and stentorian voice both as a preacher and as a fighter for human rights. As he explained, "Methodists have a social passion." His reformist articles appeared in such Methodist periodicals as *Christian Advocate, Concern, Engage, Interpreter, Methodist Story, Together,* and *Wesley Quarterly.* As he once wrote, "In a long and arduous career, I was sustained by the thought that the work was not mine to finish, nor was I free to take no part in it." Lord died of a heart attack in Wolfeboro, New Hampshire, where he was buried.

★

Lord's personal papers and correspondence are at the Methodist Archives and History Center, Drew University, Madison, New Jersey. Biographical essays are in *Current Biography Yearbook 1971* (1971); Nolan B. Harmon, ed., *The Encyclopedia of World Methodism,* vol. 2 (1974); and Edwin Schell, "Memoir," *Minutes of the Baltimore Annual Conference of the United Methodist Church* (1990). A laudatory newspaper article is Kenneth Dole, "Search for Justice Stirs Controversy," *Washington Post* (25 Apr. 1970). Obituaries are in the *New York Times* (10 Oct. 1989); *Manchester (New Hampshire) Union Leader* (11 Oct. 1989); and *Washington Post* (11 Oct. 1989).

BERNARD HIRSCHHORN

LOVESTONE, Jay (*b.* 24 December 1898 in Lithuania; *d.* 7 March 1990 in New York City), communist leader who later became the head of the International Affairs Department of the AFL-CIO and a staunch anticommunist.

In 1907 Lovestone immigrated with his family to the United States, his father, Barnett Lovestone, having found a position as a cantor at a New York City synagogue. He became active in left-wing politics while in high school, and as a student at the College of the City of New York, he led the college's chapter of the Intercollegiate Socialist Society. Lovestone befriended the Russian Bolshevik Nikolai Bukharin when he visited the United States in 1916 and 1917, and later became Bukharin's closest American adviser. After graduating from college he briefly studied law and accounting.

Jay Lovestone testifying before the U.S. Senate Internal Security Subcommittee, 1961. UPI/CORBIS-BETTMANN

Lovestone was among the delegates who formed the Communist Labor Party in September 1919. He soon became an influential adviser to Charles Ruthenberg, the party's national secretary. He was elected to the central executive committee in May 1921 and was appointed editor of the official party newspaper, *The Communist,* the following month.

The Communist International, or Comintern, headquartered in Moscow, ostensibly led the American party, now reorganized as the Communist Party of America (CPA). In 1921 the CPA was divided between those, including Ruthenberg and Lovestone, who favored a legal political party, and those who wanted it to remain an underground organization. Lovestone believed that ultimate communist victory was possible through trade union activity and success at the ballot box rather than direct action. The Comintern favored cooperation with the mainstream labor movement, and Ruthenberg and Lovestone, having supported open-party tactics, gained favor with Moscow. Following Ruthenberg's arrest on 22 August 1921, Lovestone became assistant secretary of the party, and in January 1922, at age twenty-three, he was named national secretary.

In that capacity Lovestone continued to stress the organization of workers. He felt labor needed a political party instead of confining itself to trade union agitation. He favored the mass-strike strategy and urged that party members work for proletarian class unity. Lovestone believed that traditional communist tactics were unsuited to the American labor struggle. Because the United States would not be ripe for revolution for some time, he felt the party should focus on the workers' lot within the existing democratic system. This philosophy became known as "American exceptionalism."

The support the party enjoyed from Moscow was due in part to Lovestone's close connection with Bukharin, who was an ally of Stalin. Bukharin became leader of the Comintern in 1926. With his support Ruthenberg's and Lovestone's positions now seemed secure. After Ruthenberg's sudden death on 2 March 1927, however, a struggle ensued for leadership of the party. Lovestone, Ruthenberg's choice as his successor, enjoyed the support of the Comintern. He was confirmed as general secretary of the American Communist party in August 1927.

With the removal of Leon Trotsky and his unified opposition, Stalin turned on Bukharin in November 1927. Lovestone was in a difficult position because of his close identification with Bukharin and American exceptionalism, both of which were out of favor in Moscow. He denounced Bukharin in order to retain support in the central executive committee, but lost his position as general secretary. In April 1929 Lovestone went to Moscow to defend himself before the Comintern. Stalin rejected American exceptionalism and condemned Lovestone's leadership of the party. Upon his return to the United States, Lovestone found that the CPA remained loyal to the Comintern. He was expelled in June 1929.

In October 1929 Lovestone founded the Communist Party of the United States (Majority Group). The new organization, although communist, opposed the dominance of the Comintern in the Communist party and the undemocratic methods of Moscow. Throughout the 1930s the Majority Group, or Lovestoneites, drifted farther from the world communist movement. Lovestone, who had been allied with the communist-influenced Congress of Industrial Organizations (CIO), moved his support to the more conservative American Federation of Labor (AFL). Finally, the Moscow show trials of 1937–1938 and the execution of Bukharin in 1938 turned Lovestone completely against communism.

Following George Meany's election as president of the AFL in 1940, a long association began between Lovestone and Meany, a virulent anticommunist. Lovestone's acquaintance with prominent figures in the world communist trade union movement and his talent for intrigue and organization qualified him to establish noncommunist unions throughout the world. In 1943 Lovestone became the director of the international affairs committee of David Dubinsky's International Ladies Garment Workers Union, and in 1944 he was elected executive secretary of the AFL's newly formed Free Trade Union Committee (FTUC), the union's foreign policy arm. While directing the FTUC, Lovestone established noncommunist trade unions in postwar Germany and Japan. He used his extensive familiarity with the Kremlin to thwart the establishment of communist unions in the third world while organizing noncommunist unions in the same areas. Lovestone remained influential in the AFL-CIO International Affairs Department and in the United Nations International Labor Organization until his retirement in 1974.

Lovestone had blue eyes and fine blond hair that thinned and receded over time. He had a long, aquiline nose and a small cleft in his chin. He never married and seems to have spent most of his energy on political and union activities. He had a love and a genius for political organization and intrigue. He rose to the top of virtually every organization with which he was associated because he ingratiated himself with leaders. He succeeded in the AFL-CIO because he possessed intelligence about communists worldwide and was willing to use it for his own advantage.

Lovestone is more significant for his work with the AFL after 1944 than for his colorful career as a communist. It was not until after World War II that he wielded real power in world politics. Instrumental in the establishment of democratic unions, he clearly defined the distinction between unions in the United States, Europe, and the third world, and those in the Soviet Union.

★

Lovestone wrote numerous political pamphlets, including *The Presidential Election and the Workers* (1928); *What Next for American Labor?* (1934); and *People's Front Illusion—From "Social Fascism" to the "People's Front"* (1937). In addition, he wrote for left-wing magazines such as *The Communist* and *Worker's Age.* For background on Lovestone's early years in the Communist party, see Branco Lazitch and Milorad M. Drachovitch, *Biographical Dictionary of the Comintern* (1973); and Harvey Klehr and John Earl Haynes, *The American Communist Movement: Storming Heaven Itself* (1992). Lovestone's activities in the communist opposition are described in Robert Jackson Alexander, *The Right Opposition: The Lovestoneites and the International Communist Opposition of the 1930s* (1981). Lovestone's work with the AFL-CIO is dealt with in Alfred O. Hero, Jr., and Emil Starr, *The Reuther-Meany Foreign Policy Dispute: Union Leaders and Members View World Affairs* (1970); and Denis Macshane, *International Labour and the Origins of the Cold War* (1992). An obituary is in the *New York Times* (9 Mar. 1990).

DOUGLAS N. JONES

LOVETT, Robert Abercrombie (*b.* 14 September 1895 in Huntsville, Texas; *d.* 7 May 1986 in New York City), investment banker and federal official who served as secretary of defense under President Harry S. Truman.

Robert Lovett's mother, Lavinia Chilton Abercrombie, was the daughter of a Confederate army officer, and his father, Robert Scott Lovett, was a railroad lawyer who became E. H. Harriman's counsel in Texas in 1903 and Harriman's chief counsel in New York in 1906 and succeeded Harriman as chairman of the Union Pacific in 1909. An only child, Lovett attended the Hamilton Military Institute in New York and graduated from the Hill School in Philadelphia in 1914. That year he entered Yale College. After the United States became involved in World War I in 1917, Lovett and some friends formed the Yale unit of the Naval Reserve Flying Corps and went on active duty with Britain's Royal Naval Air Service. He flew bombing missions against German submarine bases, reached the rank of lieutenant commander, and received the Navy Cross for valor. He received his B.A. degree in absentia from Yale in 1918. Returning to the United States in 1919, he studied both law

Robert A. Lovett. U.S. ARMY PHOTOGRAPH/ARCHIVE PHOTOS

and business at Harvard University (1919–1921). On 19 April 1919 he married Adele Quartley Brown; they had two children, Robert Scott and Evelyn.

Lovett began his business career in 1921 as a clerk at the National Bank of Commerce in New York. He soon moved to his father-in-law's firm, Brown Brothers, and rose to full partnership in 1926. In 1930 Brown Brothers merged with two Harriman firms to become Brown Brothers, Harriman and Company. Lovett handled the international currency and lending operations of the company.

Lovett maintained his interest in aviation through the 1920s and 1930s, and during trips abroad he studied developments in European commercial and military aviation. In 1940 he toured U.S. aircraft manufacturers and prepared a report on the industry's organization and relationship with the War Department. Secretary of War Henry L. Stimson, who saw the report, persuaded Lovett to become his special assistant in December 1940.

In April 1941 Lovett became assistant secretary of war for air and proceeded to build up the nation's air power. He pushed for adoption of assembly line techniques in aircraft manufacturing, vastly increased the number of military aircraft, and promoted the idea of strategic bombing to destroy enemy morale. He also worked closely with the army chief of staff, General George C. Marshall. After World War II ended, Lovett organized the U.S. Strategic Bombing Survey to study the effects of strategic bombing. President Harry S. Truman noted that the air power Lovett had built up played "a large part in bringing the war to a speedy and successful conclusion."

In December 1945 Lovett resumed his position at Brown Brothers, Harriman. In February 1947 President Truman asked him to join the new secretary of state, General Marshall, as undersecretary, and Lovett assumed the post in July 1947. His earlier close relationship with Marshall blossomed between 1947 and 1949, as they agreed on policy and worked together extremely well. Lovett described himself as Marshall's alter ego. A Republican who served in Democratic administrations, Lovett was devoted to a bipartisan foreign policy.

While serving as undersecretary of state, Lovett dealt with many difficult problems. The Berlin airlift of 1948 and 1949, which transported vital supplies to the city in response to a Soviet blockade, was his idea. He feared that Truman's recognition of Israel in 1948 would alienate the Arabs and stop the flow of Middle East oil but ultimately supported the president's decision. Lovett dealt with the Soviet intervention in Czechoslovakia (1948), the development of the Marshall Plan, the drafting of the Vandenberg Resolution (1948) supporting U.S. involvement in collective defense agreements, and the creation of the North Atlantic Treaty Organization (NATO).

Lovett went back to Brown Brothers, Harriman in early 1949. In September 1950, three months after the start of the Korean War, when Truman persuaded General Marshall to become secretary of defense, Marshall insisted that Lovett become deputy secretary of defense. Upon assuming that post on 4 October 1950, Lovett assisted Marshall in building up the armed forces to meet the challenges in Korea. Lovett also supported Truman's decision to dismiss General Douglas MacArthur, the United Nations commander in Korea, when MacArthur violated policy directives and proposed military actions that threatened to bring on a full-scale war with China.

By September 1951, when Marshall resigned, Lovett carried much of the load in the Pentagon. Truman's appointment of Lovett to succeed Marshall was widely applauded. As secretary of defense Lovett continued the military buildup to strengthen both the U.S. position in Korea and prospects for the nation's long-range security. He resisted primary reliance on nuclear weapons but recognized the necessity of missile development. He urged Congress to provide adequate funding for defense, and he supported military assistance to allies and the strengthening of NATO. He made important recommendations on Pentagon reorganization, some of which were later implemented by the Eisenhower administration.

When he left the Pentagon in January 1953, Lovett again joined Brown Brothers, Harriman. During the Eisenhower administration he served as a consultant on foreign intelligence activities. In 1960 President-elect John F. Kennedy offered Lovett three cabinet positions, secretary of state, defense, and treasury. Lovett declined, but he recommended the men who eventually filled the posts. Kennedy relied on him as an unofficial adviser and used him on his executive committee during the Cuban missile crisis in 1962. Although wary about the Vietnam War, Lovett advised President Lyndon B. Johnson on war policies, including the bombing campaign against North Vietnam.

Lovett retired from participation in national affairs by the 1970s but remained active at Brown Brothers, Harriman. He had long suffered serious health problems, which intensified in his later years. At the age of ninety, he died in New York City of cancer and other ailments. He is buried in New York City.

Shy, taciturn, and plain-speaking, Lovett was one of the "wise men," along with Averell Harriman, Dean Acheson, George Kennan, Charles Bohlen, and John McCloy, who knew each other early in life and played significant roles in national security affairs from World War II through the cold war. Lovett served with distinction in both of his areas of expertise, rising to prominence in national financial circles and playing a central role in developing and leading the national security establishment of the twentieth century.

★

Much information about Lovett is in the Brown Brothers, Harriman partners' files at the New-York Historical Society, New York City. Walter Isaacson and Evan Thomas, *The Wise Men: Six Friends and the World They Made—Acheson, Bohlen, Harriman, Kennan, Lovett, McCloy* (1986), is a long book that provides a wealth of detail about Lovett's life and work. Jonathan Fanton, "Robert A. Lovett: The War Years" (Ph.D. diss., Yale University, 1978), covers Lovett's work as assistant secretary of war for air. See Alfred Goldberg, ed., *History of the Office of the Secretary of Defense,* vol. 1, Steven L. Rearden, *The Formative Years, 1947–1950* (1984), for an analysis of Lovett's role as undersecretary of state and his relationship with the Defense Department during that period; and vol. 2, Doris M. Condit, *The Test of War, 1950–1953* (1988), for a very complete history of Lovett's work as deputy secretary and secretary of defense. Forrest C. Pogue, *George C. Marshall: Statesman, 1945–1959* (1987), one volume of a multivolume set on Marshall, describes Lovett's relationship with Marshall and his work in the government between 1940 and 1953. Roger R. Trask and Alfred Goldberg, *The Department of Defense, 1947–1997: Organization and Leadership* (1997), describes Lovett's work as secretary of defense and his special contributions to defense reorganization. Obituaries are in the *New York Times* and *Washington Post* (both 8 May 1986). Lovett oral histories are at the Kennedy Library, Boston, Massachusetts (1964); the Truman Library, Independence, Missouri (1971); and the Columbia Oral History Project, Columbia University, New York City (1975).

ROGER R. TRASK

LUBELL, Samuel (*b.* 3 November 1911[?] near Sosnowiec, Poland; *d.* 16 August 1987 in Los Angeles, California), journalist and public opinion analyst who pioneered a new style of American political reporting that combined face-to-face interviews with social science analysis.

Samuel Lubell, 1968. UPI/CORBIS-BETTMANN

Lubell was born Samuel Lubelsky, the son of Louis Lubelsky and Mollie (Reitkop) Lubelsky. Lubell later wrote in the *Saturday Evening Post* that he did not know the exact date of his birth because it was difficult for his mother to travel to the city of Sosnowiec to register the births of her children. Instead, she made the trip after two children were born and registered them as twins. "Officially, all my brothers and sisters are twins except me. I was the ninth and last." Samuel's family came to the United States in steerage when he was two years old. Reared in New York City, he was an evening student at the City College of New York from 1927 to 1931 before transferring to Columbia University School of Journalism, where he earned a B.S. degree in 1933.

At Columbia, Lubell won a Pulitzer traveling fellowship, which allowed him to travel around Europe in 1934. He then began his journalism career with a stint writing obituaries for the *Long Island Daily Press.* In 1938 he took a job with the *Washington Post* as a reporter and army and navy editor. He next was a labor editor at the *Richmond* (Virginia) *Times Dispatch,* and he briefly worked at the *Washington Herald.* He also began freelancing for the *Saturday Evening Post,* a relationship that lasted for twenty-one years.

Before the United States entered World War II, Lubell developed new techniques of political reporting that would later aid him in predicting political trends. In a review of Franklin D. Roosevelt's third presidential victory in 1940, Lubell conducted interviews with voters in representative regions to illustrate how individual attitudes demonstrated broader political trends. His technique indicated that Roosevelt owed his victory to a broad and largely stable political coalition and a new generation of ethnic, urban voters. Lubell wrote that he was convinced that the people who voted for Roosevelt in 1940 would vote for him "for a fourth and fifth time as readily as a third" and that "once Roosevelt is out of the picture this vote will not slip back automatically into its former slots." Lubell's focus on long-term trends in public opinion was a distinct break from traditional political reporting, which had focused on the day-to-day machinations of politicians. His concentration on one-on-one, in-depth interviews and human anecdotes differed sharply from the statistical polling of George Gallup and others.

On 22 March 1941 Lubell married Helen Sopot; they had two sons. Also in 1941 his old friend Bernard Baruch, who headed the Office of War Information, asked Lubell to serve as his assistant. During World War II, Lubell served as Baruch's chief aide and as White House assistant to James Byrnes, director of the Office of Economic Stabilization. In addition, he did some reporting in Europe and Asia from 1944 to 1946.

After the war Lubell perfected his "door-knocking technique" and used it in his pieces for the *Saturday Evening Post* and his political column for United Features Syndicates, "The People Speak." During the 1950s he also wrote for other publications and appeared as a commentator on CBS radio and television. More broadly, his influence was evident in the dozens of acolytes he attracted to his Opinion Reporting Workshop at Columbia University and similar courses at American and Harvard Universities. Collectively, his classes changed journalism and the conduct of politics, as candidates and parties altered their practices to meet the challenges that Lubell and his followers portrayed.

In his first book, *The Future of American Politics* (1952), Lubell outlined his technique and how he had applied it to the 1948 presidential election. Analyzing election returns from across the United States, he identified trends and fluctuations, then researched "the distinctive economic, religious, cultural, and political characteristics of these major voting elements." Characteristically, he talked directly with diverse groups of voters. He wrote: "For every Presidential election really is a self-portrait of America, a self-portrait with each ballot serving as another brush stroke and through which all the emotions of the American people find expression.... I have tried to combine the crafts of both historian and reporter." The publication won an award from the American Political Science Association for the best book on political reporting that year. Living up to the portentous title of his book, Lubell predicted some of the major political developments in U.S. politics over the next two decades, from the rise of the Republican party in the South to the rupturing of the ethnic, urban-based Democratic coalition in the North.

Lubell's predictions in his next book, *White and Black: Test of a Nation* (1964), also proved true. He asserted that civil rights legislation would have only a limited effect if it were not accompanied by steps to give African Americans the opportunity to succeed as individuals within the U.S. economy. He wrote four additional books, *The Revolution in World Trade and American Economic Policy* (1955), *Revolt of the Moderates* (1956), *The Hidden Crisis in American Politics* (1970), and *The Future While It Happened* (1973). In 1976, after suffering a serious stroke, Lubell retired and moved to Los Angeles, where he died of another stroke eleven years later.

Despite the potency of many of Lubell's predictions, his greatest achievements were not of prophecy. Rather, his analytic, serious approach to journalism helped revolutionize a profession more inclined to emphasize short-term sensationalism than long-term societal trends. *Newsweek* (18 October 1954) called Lubell a model for "that relatively new newspaper phenomenon—the scholar-reporter, the eruditely backgrounded genus of newsman."

★

A brief self-portrait by Lubell is "Autobiography," *Saturday Evening Post* (20 Nov. 1940). Discussions of Lubell are "What's in Voters' Minds," *Newsweek* (18 Oct. 1954), and "Doorbell Ringer," *Time* (15 Oct. 1956). Henry F. Graff gives a scholarly review of *The Future of American Politics* in *Political Science Quarterly* (Dec. 1952). An obituary is in the *New York Times* (21 Aug. 1987).

MILES A. POMPER

LUCE, Clare Boothe (*b.* 10 March 1903 in New York City; *d.* 9 October 1987 in Washington, D.C.), journalist, playwright, congresswoman, and ambassador, known for her acerbic style, her gift for satire, and her physical beauty.

Luce was born Ann Clare Boothe, the second child and only daughter of William Franklin Boothe, an erratic musician, and Anna Clara Snyder, an occasional actress and clerical worker. The family lived on West 124th Street in Manhattan. Clare's parents never married, and they permanently separated in 1912, when Clare was nine. Her mother's main goal in life was to ensure for Clare a life of fame and fortune. Given Clare's attractiveness, a screen career as a child actress seemed a good starting point. That dream was deflated when Anna took the ten-year-old Clare to Fort Lee, New Jersey, for a screen test. "I was a born nonactress," Luce later declared. In 1915–1916 Clare attended the Episcopal School of St. Mary in Garden City, New York, and completed her formal education at the Castle School in Tarrytown-on-Hudson, where she graduated in 1919.

In 1920 Clare's mother married Albert Elmer Austin, a surgeon. He took his new wife and stepdaughter on an extended trip to Europe. Among the first-class passengers on the voyage home were Mrs. August Belmont, supporter of the Women's party and a leader in New York society, and Elsa Maxwell. These and other acquaintances made aboard the SS *Olympic* led to Clare's eventual introduction to George Tuttle Brokaw, heir to a fortune in the garment industry. They were married in Greenwich, Connecticut, on 10 August 1923. A year later, Clare's first and only child, Ann Clare Brokaw, was born. The marriage was beset with problems. The Brokaw siblings and some of their friends snubbed Clare for her modest origins and also made it clear that they thought she had married Brokaw for his money. Tension mounted as Brokaw's alcoholism worsened and he became physically abusive. After protracted discussions with her mother, who opposed her decision, Clare went to Reno, Nevada, where she was divorced in 1929.

Clare Boothe Luce. ARCHIVE PHOTOS

The divorce settlement enabled Clare to move to an apartment on the east side of Manhattan, where she was able to consider her future. Even in childhood she had been a voracious reader who had dreamed of becoming a writer, and she combined the fulfillment of this ambition with her strong interest in the theater. After a brief stint in 1929 with *Vogue,* she moved to *Vanity Fair* in 1931, where she advanced from associate editor to managing editor. Her wit and talent for satire were soon recognized when she added a new feature to the magazine, "We Nominate for Oblivion," to balance the laudatory nominations for the magazine's "Hall of Fame." A series of satirical articles on "high society" suggests that she was getting even with the snobs who had treated her badly during the years with Brokaw. The articles appeared in book form in 1931 under the title *Stuffed Shirts.*

Clare cultivated friendships with a galaxy of talented persons, especially those who appeared in the pages of *Vanity Fair.* Perhaps the most significant relationship was with Bernard Baruch, who became a lifetime friend and who introduced her to Winston Churchill and his son, Randolph, in 1933. Other friends included André Maurois, Noël Coward, Walter Lippmann, Somerset Maugham, George S. Kaufman, Joseph P. Kennedy, and Mark Sullivan. By 1934 the future of *Vanity Fair* was in doubt, and she decided to try her hand at becoming a playwright. The separation from *Vanity Fair* was amicable, however, with the magazine nominating Clare for its "Hall of Fame" with the encomium, "because she combines a fragile blondness with a will of steel."

On 23 November 1935 Clare married Henry Robinson Luce, publisher of *Time* and *Fortune* magazines, and took up residence in a fifteen-room Manhattan duplex. This alliance of power and glamour attracted public attention for three decades, as Clare expanded her activities to include the roles of war correspondent, congresswoman, and ambassador. In 1936 Henry Luce published the first issue of *Life* magazine. Clare had been a strong advocate of the photomagazine, but it was a bittersweet victory for Clare, because top management opposed her active involvement except as a correspondent and photographer, and Henry Luce did not press the case.

In December 1936, Clare's play, *The Women,* opened in New York City. Famous for its wicked dialogue and one-liners, the play's initial run enjoyed 657 performances. *The Women* was revived in every remaining decade of the twentieth century.

In 1940, with her husband's approval, Luce took a trip to the European war zone. She soon witnessed bombing in Belgium and saw terrified refugees. She became an ardent interventionist and shared (or adopted) her husband's conviction that the Republican party must not be taken over by the isolationist element. International politics and the war now became her primary interests.

Two trips to Asia in 1941 and 1942 led to Luce's meetings with Chiang Kai-shek, Madame Chiang, and General Douglas MacArthur. She wrote laudatory reports about these key figures. Fortuitously, the issue of *Life* that carried her interview with MacArthur also carried a photograph of the general on its front cover. The date was 8 December 1941, the day after the bombing of Pearl Harbor.

In 1942 Luce accepted the Republican nomination for the House of Representatives from the Fairfield County district of Connecticut. She was elected to two consecutive terms, ending her service in January 1947. Accustomed to being in the limelight, she had some initial difficulty accepting the invisibility expected of new members of the House, especially when they were members of the minority party. Her record in Congress produced few surprises. A friend of Nationalist China, she spoke in favor of repealing the Chinese Exclusion Act and surprised some of her colleagues by voting to abolish the House Un-American Activities Committee. A colorful and eloquent speaker, she attracted much attention from the press. When she referred in her first speech in the House to Vice President Henry Wallace's ideas about "freedom of the skies" as "globaloney," a great furor arose.

Known as a tough, attractive partisan, Luce was a featured speaker at the Republican National Convention in 1944. On that occasion, she referred to "GI Jims," the name she gave to the "GI Joes" who did not come back home, and blamed their deaths in part on the isolationist policies of earlier Roosevelt administrations. In October 1944 she asserted that President Roosevelt "lied us into a war because he lacked the political courage to lead us into it."

In January 1944, Luce's nineteen-year-old daughter was killed in a car accident in Palo Alto, California. Consumed with grief and remorse over not having spent enough time with her daughter, Luce suffered bouts of severe depression. The tragedy profoundly affected her and led to her conversion to Roman Catholicism in 1946, after receiving instruction from Monsignor Fulton J. Sheen. From 1946 to 1952 she divided her time between addressing Republican and Catholic audiences and writing magazine articles, film scripts, and plays. Very little came of her later film and play efforts except for the film *Come to the Stable* (1949), whose screenplay was nominated for an Academy Award.

Following the election of President Dwight D. Eisenhower, who was strongly supported by both the Luces, in 1952 Luce accepted appointment as ambassador to Italy, where she served for almost four years. Supporters praised her role in bringing about a settlement of the Trieste issue, but critics accused her of interfering in Italian domestic affairs when she tried to weaken Communist influences in the labor unions. Luce remained in her post until December 1956, when she resigned, citing health reasons.

In 1959 President Eisenhower nominated Luce as ambassador to Brazil. Opposition led by Senator Wayne Morse, a Democrat, immediately surfaced. The "globaloney" issue was revived, as was her attack on Roosevelt. Although the Senate voted to confirm by a vote of 79–11, Luce withdrew her candidacy.

In the 1960s Luce wrote magazine articles, chiefly for *McCall's* and *National Review*. She seconded Barry Goldwater's nomination for president at the Republican convention in 1964 and was a staunch supporter of Richard M. Nixon in 1968.

In 1967, following the death of her husband, Luce moved to Hawaii, where she lived for the next sixteen years. She made frequent trips back to Washington, D.C., and New York City but played a modest role in Republican affairs. President Nixon appointed her to the Foreign Intelligence Advisory Board in 1973, on which she served until 1977. In 1974 she made an unsuccessful effort to persuade the editors of *Time* to oppose the impeachment of Richard Nixon.

In 1981 President Ronald Reagan appointed Luce to serve again on the Foreign Intelligence Advisory Board. Two years later, she returned to the mainland and moved into the Watergate complex in Washington, where she died. She is buried beside her husband and daughter at a former Luce estate, Mepkin Abbey, a Trappist monastery near Monck's Corner, South Carolina.

★

The Clare Boothe Luce Papers are in the Manuscript Division of the Library of Congress. An extensive list of other collections is found in Ralph G. Martin, *Harry and Clare: An Intimate Portrait of the Luces* (1991), which is based on numerous interviews. A bibliography of many of Luce's writings, including unpublished manuscripts, with frequent citations of favorable and unfavorable reviews, appears in Mark Fearnow, *Clare Boothe Luce: A Research and Production Sourcebook* (1995). In a special category is Sylvia Jukes Morris, *Rage for Fame: The Ascent of Clare Boothe Luce* (1997), which includes extensive references to correspondence and Luce's diaries not available to other researchers. Luce included autobiographical material in her articles on the European situation in 1940, which were expanded in book form in *Europe in the Spring* (1940). There is much autobiographical material in Luce's three articles, titled "The Real Reason," in which she explains her conversion to Catholicism, in *McCall's* (Feb., Mar., and Apr. 1947). Martin, Fearnow, and especially Morris introduce materials modifying earlier standard works, such as Faye Henle, *Au Clair de Luce: Portrait of a Luminous Lady* (1943); Stephen Shadegg, *Clare Boothe Luce: A Biography* (1970); and Wilfrid Sheed, *Clare Boothe Luce* (1982). An excellent general study that includes much material on Luce is W. A. Swanberg, *Luce and His Empire* (1972). An obituary appears in the *New York Times* (10 Oct. 1987).

CHARLES E. LARSEN

LUDLAM, Charles (*b.* 12 April 1943 in Floral Park, New York; *d.* 28 May 1987 in New York City), playwright, actor, director, designer, and founder of the Ridiculous Theatrical Company.

Ludlam, the son of Joseph William Ludlam, a plasterer, and Marjorie Braun, was raised with two brothers in the suburban Long Island communities of New Hyde Park and Greenlawn. His theatrical interest was first stirred at age six, when he saw a Punch and Judy show. He later put on puppet plays in his home, and he never lost his interest in puppetry. Living across the street from a movie theater, he attended each change of bill. At the age of fifteen he apprenticed at the Red Barn summer theater in Newport, Rhode Island, and in 1959 fell under the spell of the experimental Living Theatre. In Northport, Long Island, he created the Students' Repertory Theatre in 1961, doing difficult modern plays, after which he majored in theater at Hofstra University, where he graduated with a B.A. degree in 1965.

Ludlam's career began with a role in Ronald Tavel's *Life of Lady Godiva* (1966), produced at John Vacarro's Play-House of the Ridiculous, a popular gay-oriented, experimental off-off Broadway company. Ludlam was a big suc-

Charles Ludlam, artistic director of the Ridiculous Theatrical Company, in a dressing room in New York City, 1978. AP/WIDE WORLD PHOTOS

cess in the drag role of Norma Desmond—based largely on his own improvisations—in Tavel's *Sunset Boulevard* burlesque entitled *Screen Test* (1966). Ludlam then wrote *Big Hotel* (1967), a *Grand Hotel* parody directed by Vacarro. However, during rehearsals that year for Ludlam's *Conquest of the Universe,* Vacarro fired Ludlam, who proceeded to start the Ridiculous Theatrical Company. He revised *Conquest* as *When Queens Collide* and staged it in rivalry with Vacarro's version.

Ludlam referred to this and future works as "high art" whose goal was "to provide pleasure" while serving as a "scourge of folly." For all their great variety and purpose as socially meaningful satires, they were camp-oriented, highly theatrical, low-comedy parodies either of famous plays or of film, opera, book, and theater genres and were designed to skewer modern ideas and obsessions. The uninhibited, exaggerated verbal and physical humor of these works was often scatological, and nudity was common. The early plays were crudely assembled, carelessly produced, anarchic, collagelike "epics" for a cult following, but Ludlam, having mastered dramatic structure, ultimately became a craftsman with a commitment to witty wordplay, especially in the use of puns and multiple allusions. Although unpretentious, the plays reflect intellectual depth and a strict, if eccentric, moral vision. Ludlam claimed an affinity for classic styles of theater, especially commedia dell'arte, the conventions of which he sought to restore. Many of his actors remained for years, forming an ensemble of skilled comedians.

In 1968 Ludlam's company provided midnight repertory showings of *Big Hotel* and *When Queens Collide* as well as Bill Vehr's *Whores of Babylon.* That year Vehr also collaborated with Ludlam on *Turds in Hell.* Briefly the company was the Trocadero Gloxinia Magic Midnight Theatre of Thrills and Spills. Ludlam next offered *The Grand Tarot* (1969), followed by the company's first hit, *Bluebeard* (1970), a farce inspired by H. G. Wells about a mad scientist, played by Ludlam, trying to invent a third sex. The play reflected Ludlam's interest in his own sexual ambivalence. The Ridiculous toured college campuses and added the first of several European tours to their itinerary in 1971, during which *Eunuchs of the Forbidden City* (1971) premiered in Germany. Ludlam's plays began to be published in theater journals and anthologies, and the company began to receive grant money. Ludlam wrote; directed; acted, often in drag; and occasionally designed. Cross-gender casting became a company trademark.

Ludlam's major works of the 1970s included *Corn* (1972), a country-western musical; *Camille* (1973), a travesty of the Dumas fils melodrama in which Ludlam, notably straightforward, even touching, in the title role, allowed his hairy chest to show, despite his gowns; *Hot Ice* (1974), a gangster-film spoof that featured Ludlam as a macho detective and premiered at the company's new home, the Evergreen Theatre; *Stage Blood* (1975), a *Hamlet* parody; a pair of children's puppet shows (1975 and 1976); the libretto for a never-realized Broadway musical, *Isle of the Hermaphrodites, or The Murdered Minion* (1976); the fashion-industry satire *Caprice, or Fashion Bound* (1976), which marked the debut of Everett Quinton, who became Ludlam's lover and his successor; *Der Ring Gott Farblonjet* (1977), inspired by Wagner's Ring cycle; the two-character *Ventriloquist's Wife* (1978), for which Ludlam mastered ventriloquism; *Utopia, Incorporated* (1978); *Anti-Galaxie Nebulae,* which featured Vehr and Quinton as puppets; *The Enchanted Pig* (1979); *The Elephant Woman* (1979); *A Christmas Carol* (1979); a brief opera entitled *The Production of Mysteries* (1980); and *Reverse Psychology* (1980). Beginning in 1978 his productions were at One Sheridan Square, a 166-seat basement theater in arena style. In 1988 the New York City Council renamed the street outside Charles Ludlam Lane.

Ludlam's 1980s playwriting, which focused mainly on nonparodistic farce, included *Love's Tangled Web* (1981); *Secret Lives of the Sexists* (1982); *Exquisite Torture* (1982); *Le Bourgeois Avant-Garde* (1983), a Molière takeoff on the modern art world; *Galas* (1983), a hit inspired by the opera star Maria Callas, with Ludlam as the diva; *The Mystery of Irma Vep* (1984), a highly successful, two-character "penny dreadful" exploiting quick-change artistry; the autobiographical *How to Write a Play* (1985); *Salammbô* (1986), with Ludlam as the thirteen-year-old virgin priestess of the moon; and *The Artificial Jungle* (1986).

In addition to an output of at least one new work annually, Ludlam taught at various universities, including Yale (1982–1983); filmed two underground movies (1980 and 1987); and acted in works by others. Among his many awards were six off-Broadway Obies and fellowships from the Guggenheim Foundation (1970) and the National Endowment for the Arts (1981 and 1984). Ludlam also guest-starred on several television series; played the title role in *Hedda Gabler* (1984) for Pittsburgh's American Ibsen Theatre; directed two works for the Santa Fe Opera (1985 and 1986); and acted in the mainstream movies *Forever, Lulu* (1986) and *The Big Easy* (1986). Among projects he was working on when he died of complications due to acquired immunodeficiency syndrome (AIDS) was a Central Park staging of Shakespeare's *Titus Andronicus.* His interment was at St. Patrick's Cemetery, Huntington, New York.

The bald, slightly built Ludlam, who was gifted with total recall, was described in the *Village Voice* as "a loving, generous, and joyous person" of profound intelligence. He was one of the most multitalented theater artists of his generation, a man whose combination of revolutionary freshness and respect for tradition allowed him to create one of the longest lived and most original theater companies in the United States.

★

A revealing interview with Ludlam is in Susan Shacter and Don Shewey, *Caught in the Act: New York Actors Face to Face* (1986). Selections from Ludlam's miscellaneous commentaries and interviews are in Steven Samuels, ed., *Ridiculous Theatre, Scourge of Human Folly: The Essays and Opinions of Charles Ludlam* (1992); his plays are in Samuels, ed., *The Complete Plays of Charles Ludlam* (1989), which includes a brief biographical essay. For an overview of Ludlam's work as a dramatist and a designer see Ruby Cohn, *New American Dramatists 1960–1990* (1991). Ludlam's career and a detailed production chronology are in Mark Hawkins-Dady, ed., *International Dictionary of Theatre,* vol. 2, *Playwrights* (1994). See Robert Thomas Wharton III, "The Working Dynamics of the Ridiculous Theatrical Company: An Analysis of Charles Ludlam's Relationship with His Ensemble from 1967 Through 1981" (Ph.D. diss., Florida State University, 1985). Profiles are in Calvin Tomkins, "Ridiculous," *New Yorker* (15 Nov. 1976); and Tish Dace, "From the Ridiculous to the Sublime: Charles Ludlam's Shoe-string Scenography," *Theatre Crafts* (Mar. 1986). Obituaries are in the *New York Times* (29 May 1987) and *Village Voice* (9 June 1987).

SAMUEL L. LEITER

LYONS, Theodore Amar ("Ted") (*b.* 28 December 1900 in Lake Charles, Louisiana; *d.* 25 July 1986 in Sulphur, Louisiana), baseball pitcher, manager, coach, and scout who was the winningest pitcher in Chicago White Sox history and who was elected to the National Baseball Hall of Fame in 1955.

Lyons was the son of Asa F. Lyons, a cattle rancher, rice farmer, feed store owner, and deputy sheriff. His mother's full name is not known. When Lyons was approximately one year old, the family moved to Vinton, Louisiana. Though sources are sketchy, Lyons had at least two brothers and one sister. From 1915 to 1918 he attended Vinton High School, where he played second base on the baseball team. He then entered Baylor University in Waco, Texas, in 1919 and graduated in 1923 with a B.A. degree. He was a good student and had intended to study law at Baylor, but he loved sports. He starred on Baylor's basketball and baseball teams, making All-Southwest Conference in both sports. While at Baylor he also ran track, played the trombone in the band, and was elected class president. In his senior year he led Baylor to the Southwest Conference baseball title.

Scouted early on by Connie Mack's Philadelphia Athletics, Lyons chose instead to sign with the White Sox upon his graduation. He joined the team in St. Louis in July 1923 and appeared as a relief pitcher in the first major league game he'd ever seen. Lyons is unusual among major league ballplayers in that he never played in the minor leagues.

Lyons pitched twenty-one seasons for Chicago, from 1923 through 1942 and again in 1946. The White Sox, still reeling from the decimation inflicted by baseball commissioner Kenesaw Mountain Landis, who in 1920 banned eight of the team's best players for life after they admitted

Ted Lyons. NATIONAL BASEBALL HALL OF FAME LIBRARY, COOPERSTOWN, N.Y.

to intentionally losing the 1919 World Series, was a chronically poor baseball team that never finished higher than third during Lyons's tenure.

As a young right-handed pitcher, Lyons primarily threw fastballs. In 1925 he led the American League with 21 wins and 5 shutouts. He won 22 games in 1927, again leading the league. That year he also led with 30 complete games and 307 innings pitched. In 1930 he led the American League in complete games (29) and innings pitched (297).

Between 1929 and 1931 Lyons suffered a series of arm and back injuries that limited the effectiveness of his fastball. He began to throw more slow curves and the knuckleball, a slow pitch with a tricky fluttering movement that batters found difficult to hit. Lyons's ability to modify his pitching strategy at this point in his career effectively made him a new pitcher. While he never reverted to his brilliance of 1925 to 1930, he remained a very effective pitcher for the White Sox.

Lyons threw a no-hit game against the Boston Red Sox on 21 August 1926. He had missed another no-hitter the previous season in Washington, when a batter singled with two outs in the ninth inning. Lyons also had a streak of 42 consecutive innings without yielding a base-on-balls in 1939. On 24 May 1929 Lyons pitched 21 innings against George Uhle of the Tigers but lost 6 to 5.

Extremely popular with fans, Lyons late in his career became a Sunday-only pitcher for the Sox in order to draw the biggest possible crowds. The restful routine of pitching on six days of rest may also have helped him extend his longevity. He had notable seasons in 1935, when he won 15 and lost 8, and in 1939, when he won 14 and lost 6 and made the All-Star team for the only time in his career. In 1942, at the age of forty-one, he started and completed 20 games, winning 14, and he led the American League in earned run average (2.10).

Following the 1942 season, after being summoned by a Louisiana draft board, Lyons enlisted in the Marine Corps. He graduated from Reserve Officer's School at Quantico, Virginia, and was first posted to the Marine Aviation Detachment at Chicago's Navy Pier. A later posting took him to the Marshall Islands with the Fourth Marine Air Wing. He was honorably discharged from active duty in 1945 with the rank of captain.

Lyons returned to the White Sox in the spring of 1946 at the age of forty-five. He pitched his way to a 1 to 4 record before being named manager of the Sox on 24 May 1946, succeeding Jimmy Dykes. He managed Chicago for three seasons, finishing in fifth, sixth, and last place. "I did the best I could with what we had," said Lyons. He had also never complained about the White Sox teams he played on, preferring to ascribe their poor finishes to injuries rather than incompetence.

Lyons served as a coach with the Detroit Tigers from 1949 to 1953 and as pitching coach for the Brooklyn Dodgers in 1954. In 1955 he was elected to the National Baseball Hall of Fame and returned to the White Sox as a coach and scout. He retired from baseball in 1967 because of vision problems that made the travel requirements of scouting difficult. He returned to Louisiana to manage a 760-acre rice plantation with his sister. Lyons was a member of the First Baptist Church in Vinton, Louisiana. He died in Sulphur, Louisiana, after a six-month battle with cancer and was interred at Big Woods Cemetery in Vinton.

The nearly six-foot-tall Lyons, who never married, compiled a lifetime record of 260 wins and 230 losses and pitched a total of 356 complete games. He was known as a ferocious competitor but also as a gentleman and a quiet man. He stood out as an immortal pitcher in baseball's golden age of hitting, when entire teams would sometimes bat .300. He pitched to both Ty Cobb and Ted Williams over the course of his long career. He was considered an intelligent, witty player who enjoyed the camaraderie of baseball and was well known for his practical jokes and his tall tales, usually centered around his prowess as a hitter.

Lyons was indeed a good hitter and an excellent fielder. A switch-hitter, he was often called upon to pinch-hit or pinch-run on days when he wasn't pitching. He exuded a contagious confidence and was a natural coach who helped other teams and players with their pitching mechanics. A good conversationalist and a snappy dresser, he enjoyed theater, movies, automobiles, hunting, cooking, and playing golf.

★

For information on Lyons, see the biographical clippings file, "Ted Lyons," in the National Baseball Hall of Fame Library, Cooperstown, New York, which also has an interview with Lyons conducted on 24 May 1978 (accession number BL8203.91). Donald Honig, "Ted Lyons," in *Baseball when the Grass Was Real* (1975), is informative. Other interviews with Lyons are "Ted Lyons, the Premier Pitcher of the American League," *Baseball Magazine* (Oct. 1927); and Paul Green, "Baseball and Ted Lyons," *Sports Collectors Digest* (4 Mar. 1983). See also Bill Bryson, "That Likable Lyons," *Baseball Magazine* (Oct. 1939); Thomas L. Karnes, "The Sunday Saga of Ted Lyons," *Baseball Research Journal* (1981); and Jerome Holtzman, "Lyons' Friends Recall His Special Greatness," *Chicago Tribune* (27 July 1986). An obituary is in the *Chicago Tribune* (26 July 1986).

TIMOTHY J. WILES

M

McAULIFFE, (Sharon) Christa (*b.* 2 September 1948 in Boston, Massachusetts; *d.* 28 January 1986 off Cape Canaveral, Florida), teacher chosen as the first "citizen in space," who died in the explosion of the space shuttle *Challenger*.

The eldest of the five children of Grace George Corrigan, a homemaker, and Edward Corrigan, an assistant controller for the Jordan Marsh department store in Boston, McAuliffe grew up in a middle-class, Catholic home in suburban Framingham, Massachusetts. She was called "Christa" from the time she was a baby. Only an average student, she gained recognition in school plays and on the playing fields at Marian High School in Framingham. While studying to be a teacher at Framingham State College (1966–1970), McAuliffe adopted the dress of the hippie age and most of its ideals. She considered herself a staunch feminist and protested the war in Vietnam. Personally, however, she worked toward a more traditional future, visiting Steven James McAuliffe, whom she had agreed to marry when she was sixteen, at Virginia Military Institute as often as she could.

Christa married Steven McAuliffe on 23 August 1970. The couple moved to Washington, D.C., where Steven entered Georgetown Law School. Christa taught American history for a year at Benjamin Foulois Junior High School in nearby Morningside, Maryland, and then, for the next seven years, at Thomas Johnson Junior High School in Lanham, Maryland.

A poor, predominantly black school under the pressure of a desegregation order, Thomas Johnson gave McAuliffe the opportunity to develop an unconventional teaching style. Teaching history, law, civics, and English, she enlivened her lessons with visitors from the working world: lawyers, war veterans, and politicians. Her hallmark as a teacher was her field trips. McAuliffe took her classes to watch her husband argue cases in court and to sites around Washington, D.C. She would later envision her space shuttle voyage as "the ultimate field trip" for the teachers and millions of schoolchildren worldwide who would watch the televised launch and the lessons she planned to teach from space.

In 1974 McAuliffe and her husband bought a home in Oxen Hill, Maryland. Two years later their son, Scott Corrigan McAuliffe, was born. Active in the teachers' union and frustrated with the slow pace of change in her troubled school, McAuliffe enrolled in a master's degree program in education supervision and administration at Bowie State College in Maryland, hoping to increase her influence on the district's education policy. She received the degree in 1978.

But McAuliffe longed to return to New England. In 1978 she and her husband bought a home in Concord, New Hampshire, where Steven McAuliffe was hired as an assistant state attorney general. Christa first worked as a substitute teacher in the school district and then as an English and history teacher at Rundlett Junior High School and Bow Memorial School. In 1982, three years after the birth

Christa McAuliffe, 1986. JIM WELLS/ARCHIVE PHOTOS

of their daughter, Caroline, she joined the staff of Concord High School.

In 1985 the National Aeronautics and Space Administration (NASA), eager to raise the profile of its space shuttle program, announced that it would begin its search for the first "ordinary" person in space. Its officials wanted a teacher, a person who could communicate the excitement of space exploration to the rest of the nation and bolster the program's shaky support with the members of Congress who controlled its funding. McAuliffe was one of nearly 11,500 American teachers who applied for the six-day mission, the twenty-fifth of the shuttle program. "I want to demystify NASA and space flight," she wrote. Impressed by her passion for teaching and her down-to-earth nature, a committee of New Hampshire educators picked McAuliffe as one of two state finalists who would travel to Washington, where the finalists would be reduced to ten. The committee of NASA officials who decided that McAuliffe should be the teacher in space noted that she had not been the most academically impressive of the group, but was the most likely to imbue others with her enthusiasm for space exploration.

At the White House on 19 July 1985, Vice President George Bush introduced McAuliffe to the nation. Americans saw the thirty-six-year-old on the national news that night, on the front page of their newspapers the next morning, and, soon after, joking with Johnny Carson on the *Tonight Show.*

McAuliffe spent the summer giving interviews and speeches, preparing the lessons she would teach from space, and readying her husband and children for her absence. In September she left Concord for the Johnson Space Center near Houston, to prepare for a 22 January liftoff from Cape Canaveral, Florida. Training at the space center, McAuliffe learned the basics of shuttle life: how to cook in its galley, stow her toothbrush so it wouldn't fly about the cabin, and use its high-tech toilet. NASA took her for wild rides in supersonic jets to prepare her for the *Challenger*'s bumpy liftoff and landing, and she joined the crew for sessions in the flight simulator, to practice responding to emergencies in the shuttle's electronic and mechanical systems. McAuliffe also rehearsed the two lessons she would deliver from space on live television: first a tour of the *Challenger,* and then a history of the space program followed by a few simple experiments and a question-and-answer session with high school students on Earth.

Concerns about weather and mechanical problems with the *Challenger* delayed the launch until 28 January. At 11:38 A.M. *Challenger* left the launch pad. Seventy-three seconds later it exploded, killing McAuliffe and the six others aboard. The televised picture of the rising dot of a spacecraft bursting into smoke became one of the most recognized and mournful images of the twentieth century. It was all the more poignant for its most famous passenger, the first "ordinary American in space," and for the millions of young people who had watched the launch on television.

McAuliffe's remains were buried in Concord's public cemetery on 1 May 1986. Since her death she has been memorialized in scholarship funds, as the namesake of new schools, and in the Christa Corrigan McAuliffe Center for Teaching Excellence at Framingham State College.

The report of the presidential commission that investigated the *Challenger* disaster concluded that the failure of the O-ring seals in its solid rocket boosters allowed propellant gases to leak into a tank containing liquid hydrogen and oxygen, causing the explosion. It faulted NASA officials for failing to inform those making the launch decisions of the danger posed by weak O-rings.

★

Robert T. Hohler, *"I Touch the Future . . .": The Story of Christa McAuliffe* (1986), is an account of her life and involvement with the space program by a reporter from her hometown newspaper. Grace George Corrigan, *A Journal for Christa: Christa McAuliffe, Teacher in Space* (1993), is McAuliffe's life as recalled by her mother. See also John Noble Wilford, "A Teacher Trains for Outer Space," *New York Times Magazine* (5 Jan. 1986); and *Report to the President of the Presidential Commission on the Space Shuttle Accident* (1986), which contains the conclusions of the panel appointed by President Ronald Reagan. A group obituary is "The

Shuttle Explosion: The Lost Crew Members. The Seven Who Perished in the Explosion of the *Challenger*," *New York Times* (29 Jan. 1986).

LAUREN MARKOE

McCARTHY, Glenn Herbert (*b.* 25 December 1907 in Beaumont, Texas; *d.* 26 December 1988 in Houston, Texas), oilman known as King of the Wildcatters who discovered fourteen new oil fields and whose colorful life was thought to have been the inspiration for Edna Ferber's novel *Giant* (1952).

McCarthy was one of two children of William P. McCarthy, an oil field worker, and Leah Townsend, a homemaker. Born in the heart of the greatest oil field in the United States, Spindletop, Glenn was deeply influenced by his father, whose practical and hard-won experience on the derricks created an insatiable "oil fever" in his son. He attended Tulane, Texas A&M, and Rice Universities but did not earn a degree, and in the late 1920s he founded the McCarthy Oil and Gas Corporation. On 18 June 1930 McCarthy married Faustine Lee, who came from an eminent and wealthy oil family. McCarthy allegedly insisted that he would not accept any gifts or loans from her family, however, and they led a constrained and frugal life until he made his noted discoveries in the mid-1930s. They had five children, one of whom, Glenn McCarthy, Jr., went on to succeed his father as chairman of the company.

Glenn McCarthy, 1954. UPI/CORBIS-BETTMANN

As an independent oil explorer from the mid-1930s to 1950, McCarthy drilled more than 700 oil wells with a failure rate of less than 5 percent. His discoveries produced nearly 20 billion barrels of oil and 240 billion cubic feet of natural gas. He discovered oil in fourteen new fields and extended production in twelve existing fields.

After acquiring his fortune (which newspapers quoted at $300 million) in the oil fields, McCarthy ventured into many other business ventures. He garnered international publicity with his construction of the Shamrock Hotel in Houston in 1949. As the architectural historian Stephen Fox wrote: "To Houstonians, it was astounding that a building of such size (eighteen stories) should be constructed three miles from the center of the city. McCarthy's intention was to build a downtown sized hotel that could accommodate the convention trade, imbue it with a resort atmosphere, and set it in a suburban locale." On St. Patrick's Day, McCarthy staged a gala opening that was planned for 3,000 guests, but 15,000 crashed the party. A special train from Hollywood brought Dorothy Lamour, who sang a few "dreamy" songs; Edgar Bergen; Van Johnson; Van Heflin; and McCarthy's friend Pat O'Brien. The Shamrock was demolished in 1987, but not before McCarthy, who by then no longer owned it, had joined in a march to support its preservation, calling its loss "a waste."

McCarthy's flamboyant success earned him both a cover story in *Time* in 1950 and perhaps more lasting fame as the inspiration for the character of Jett Rink in Edna Ferber's *Giant* (1952), a role played by James Dean in the 1956 screen version. Friends of McCarthy recognized in Rink something of McCarthy's legendary quick temper and scrappiness. McCarthy's biographer, Wallace Davis, for instance, chronicled a sensational battle that took place during the 1949 Houston Fat Stock Show: "Some differences between [McCarthy] and his adversary in this particular brawl led to heated words, and the two men agreed to settle the matter in privacy. They rented a downtown hotel suite and proceeded to wallop each other, toe to toe, for nearly an hour." McCarthy's reputation as a fighter was probably exaggerated, but as Davis wrote, "It would sure be wrong to say McCarthy was *not* pugnacious."

Unlike the fictional Rink, however, McCarthy learned the oil business by his own wits and hard work. He had a fierce determination and an ability to rise above failure. He had some Irish luck, but mostly he had scientific advice, practical information gleaned from long hours with the oil field roughnecks, an uncanny ability to interpret geological findings, and a rare nose for the oil. Glenn McCarthy, Jr., described his father as "probably the greatest natural oil and gas finder that ever lived." He died of multiple causes at age eighty-one and is buried in Glenwood Cemetery in Houston.

★

Wallace Davis, *Corduroy Road: The Story of Glenn H. McCarthy* (1951), is a biography of McCarthy. Jeffrey Share and Joseph A. Pratt, *The Oil Makers* (1995), provides some biographical material on McCarthy as well as a broader context for his accomplishments through interviews with his son Glenn McCarthy, Jr., and other Texas oilmen. See also Stephen Fox, *Braeswood: An Architectural History* (1988).

TOM FORRESTER LORD

McCARTHY, Mary Therese (*b.* 21 June 1912 in Seattle, Washington; *d.* 25 October 1989 in New York City), writer who for over half a century was at the center of literary and intellectual life in the United States and was often at the center of controversy as well.

McCarthy was the daughter of Roy Winfield McCarthy, who worked for his father's grain elevator business, and Therese Preston. After Mary's birth, her father, who was then thirty-two years old, entered law school at the University of Washington. McCarthy had three younger brothers and spent the first six years of her life in Seattle, where, after his graduation, her father practiced law for a while. However, her father's deteriorating health resulted in his decision to return to Minneapolis to work for his father in mid-October 1918. Within weeks after the family's arrival in Minneapolis, both parents died, victims of the 1918 influenza epidemic, leaving four orphans under seven years old.

McCarthy and her brothers were put in the care of their authoritarian great-aunt and great-uncle, who treated Mary with a harshness she never forgot. In 1923 she was rescued by her Preston grandparents and taken to Seattle, where in 1925 she finished elementary school at Forest Ridge Sacred Heart Convent. For high school she boarded at Annie Wright Seminary in nearby Tacoma, graduating in 1929. She masterfully immortalized both schools as well as her childhood years in *Memories of a Catholic Girlhood* (1957).

In 1929 McCarthy entered Vassar College, which she fictionalized in *The Group* (1963). There she majored in English and graduated with a B.A. degree in 1933. She then moved to New York City and that year married an actor, Harold Johnsrud; they had no children. Johnsrud introduced McCarthy to politically leftist circles of people in the theater and literary milieu, but the humorless dogmatism

Mary McCarthy. EDWARD HAUSNER/NEW YORK TIMES CO./ARCHIVE PHOTOS

of so many of them forestalled a serious political commitment on McCarthy's part. By the mid-1930s, however, she had become an intellectual in the French sense of that word—a literary person who is concerned with public affairs. Her interest was not with partisan politics but with larger issues like the nature of the Soviet Union, the prospects for socialism in the United States, and later, the plight of fellow intellectuals in totalitarian countries.

At the same time that McCarthy was becoming aware of these larger affairs, she set the literary world on its ear. In the mid-1930s the *Nation* published her first series of articles, "Our Critics, Right or Wrong," in which she attacked the mediocrity of America's book reviewers. Called the "Saint Valentine's massacre of reviewers and critics" by *Time* magazine, the articles made her one of New York's leading intellectual voices, both respected and feared for her ruthless wit.

In 1936 McCarthy and Johnsrud divorced, and two years later McCarthy married Edmund Wilson, the renowned literary critic. They had one child. Wilson persuaded her to try fiction, which resulted in her first novel, *The Company She Keeps* (1942), still considered by many as her finest. In it she pictured the protagonist, whose escapades are based on her own, as playing a series of roles in order to set herself "apart from the run of people." Competitiveness was deeply rooted in McCarthy's character, as a reader of any of her three memoirs, *Memories of a Catholic Girlhood, How I Grew* (1987), and *Intellectual Memoirs* (1992), can easily discern. McCarthy herself once laughingly told the political theorist Hannah Arendt that she was taking an inordinate amount of time reading page proofs of one of her short stories for the *New Yorker* because "a normal person cooperates with the checkers or uses them as a convenience, but I cannot help competing with them."

McCarthy's only child, Reuel Kimball Wilson, was born in 1938. When he was six, he and his mother left Wellfleet, Massachusetts, on Cape Cod, where they had been living with Wilson, for New York City. McCarthy and Wilson divorced in October 1945. In 1946 McCarthy married a schoolteacher, Bowden Broadwater, a union that lasted until 1960, when they divorced. During those years she published eight books, four fiction and four nonfiction.

In her novel *The Oasis* (1949), McCarthy caricatured the circle of intellectuals, including herself, centered around *Partisan Review,* the most influential literary journal of its time, of which she was a founding editor and theater commentator. "That book," said her friend and fellow writer Elizabeth Hardwick, "came about through the influence of Bowden. He thought those people were a scream." After its publication McCarthy and Broadwater moved away from New York because, McCarthy recalled, "no one was speaking to us." In 1952 she and Broadwater returned to Wellfleet to live. Later novels shone equally relentless light on other groups she had been part of, like Vassar women in *The Group;* college faculties (she had taught briefly at Sarah Lawrence and Bard Colleges during the 1940s) in *The Groves of Academe* (1952); friends and neighbors, including Wilson, in Wellfleet in *A Charmed Life* (1955); and the villagers of Stonington, Connecticut, where she and her fourth husband lived briefly, in *Birds of America* (1971). After the publication of *Birds of America,* McCarthy wrote William Jovanovich, her friend and publisher of many years, that her husband was "checking off Stonington on the map as another place we can never go back to." The nonfiction books published during her marriage to Broadwater include the two outstanding travel/art books, *Venice Observed* (1956) and *Stones of Florence* (1959).

Not until McCarthy met James Raymond West did she actually fall in love. They married in 1961. Her close friend and literary critic Dwight Macdonald told McCarthy that, after thirty years of experiment, she had found Mr. Right. That she was faithful to this husband, as she had not been to the others, and that she stayed with him until her death in 1989 provides corroboration of Macdonald's judgment. They had no children.

Life for McCarthy was very different after her marriage to West, an American diplomat and neither an intellectual nor a New Yorker. For one thing, her life became more settled; she divided her time between a spacious apartment in Paris and a capacious federal home in Castine, Maine. One of the most publicized episodes of her later life was her feud with the playwright Lillian Hellman. McCarthy, in a television interview, stated with her typical acerbic wit that everything Hellman "writes is a lie, including 'and' and 'the.' " Hellman filed a $2.25 million defamation suit, but the case never came to trial owing to Hellman's death in 1984. McCarthy died of cancer in New York City and is buried in Castine.

Toward the end of McCarthy's life many belated honors were bestowed on her, but she has never been accorded the status she deserves. Her work is less widely discussed in American colleges and universities than that of some of her contemporaries. Critic Irvin Stock thinks this is because she is a classicist in a country of romantics. She wrote in *How I Grew,* "Self-deception remains in my book a major sin or vice." The detachment of her prose, her biting, rueful indictment of human pretension, and in short, her acidulous, perspicacious examination of the American scene are not qualities that make a writer in the United States popular. Even so, millions of copies of her books have been sold in the United States as well as in the United Kingdom, Canada, Denmark, Finland, Iceland, Sweden, Norway, Holland, France, Germany, Italy, Portugal, Spain, Hungary, Poland, Romania, Israel, and Japan.

McCarthy was passionate about language and was most critical of those who composed carelessly. Those who knew her well point to the perfectionism she brought to everything in her life. She told an audience at the MacDowell Colony, "In word production, housekeeping, gardening, reading, I actually believe that the amount of labor that goes into human manufacture determines the success of the enterprise."

All of McCarthy's fiction embodies what was to her the very definition of the novel, "its concern with the actual world, the world of fact, of the verifiable, of figures, even, statistics." In her three memoirs she strove for the greatest possible factual and emotional accuracy. *Memories of a Catholic Girlhood,* her finest achievement, displays all her best literary qualities—polish, acerbic wit, candor, and at times exuberant hilarity—plus a depth of feeling Macdonald found absent in her fiction.

As the author of twenty-five books (nine fiction and sixteen nonfiction) and as an outspoken critic of Stalinism in the 1930s and 1940s and of the Vietnam War in the 1960s and 1970s, McCarthy helped shape the way Americans thought about politics, literature, and theater. In 1980 she said that Tolstoy "did not care for saviors in whatever shape they presented themselves. As is indicated in *Anna Karenina,* it is enough if a man is able to save his own soul by living for God—the rest will take care of itself." Substitute the word "ideology" for "saviors" and the titles of her own books for *Anna Karenina* in that statement for a summation of Mary McCarthy's life and work.

★

McCarthy's archives are housed at Vassar College. McCarthy wrote seven novels, including *Cannibals and Missionaries* (1979); two collections of short stories, *Cast a Cold Eye* (1950) and *The Hounds of Summer and Other Stories* (1981); and sixteen nonfiction books, including *On the Contrary* (1961), *The Writing on the Wall* (1970), *Ideas and the Novel* (1980), and *Occasional Prose* (1987). Two biographies are Carol Gelderman, *Mary McCarthy: A Life* (1988), and Carol Brightman, *Writing Dangerously: Mary McCarthy and Her World* (1994). An obituary is in the *New York Times* (26 Oct. 1989).

CAROL GELDERMAN

John J. McCloy. ARCHIVE PHOTOS

McCLOY, John Jay (*b.* 31 March 1895 in Philadelphia; *d.* 11 March 1989 in Stamford, Connecticut), lawyer, banker, diplomat, and an adviser to presidents who epitomized the conservative but nonpartisan lawyer-statesman, serving both Democrats and Republicans, particularly in the realm of foreign policy.

McCloy was the second son of a bookish Scots-Irish actuarial clerk, John Jay McCloy, and a robust Pennsylvania Dutch housewife, Anna May Snader. In 1899 the McCloys' eldest son died of a fever at age seven, and two years later John McCloy, Sr., died of heart failure at the age of thirty-nine. These events stiffened Anna McCloy's resolve to construct a new life for herself and give her son every chance at upward mobility. She became a hairdresser to several esteemed Philadelphia families, which gave her the means to educate her son. At considerable sacrifice to family finances, McCloy began attending a private academy, the Peddie Institute, in 1907. He gained entrance to Amherst College in 1912 and worked his way through with the aid of private scholarships from his mother's clients. After graduating cum laude from Amherst, McCloy entered Harvard Law School in 1916; one year later his studies were interrupted by army service during World War I, a formative experience. McCloy rose to the rank of captain in the artillery and acquired an internationalist worldview, one that saw America's rise to world power as inexorable and unavoidable.

After graduating from Harvard Law School in 1921, McCloy tried to find a position in a Philadelphia law firm, only to find his way hindered because he was considered a short, stocky scholarship boy from the wrong side of the tracks. He then headed for New York City, where talent rather than lineage was more prized. After a short stint with Cadwalader, Wickersham and Taft, in 1924 he joined the Wall Street firm of Cravath, de Gersdorff, Swaine and Moore, a prestigious firm specializing in corporate law. McCloy, while not the most brilliant lawyer, worked harder than almost anyone else. He became a full partner in 1929 and one year later married Ellen Scharmann Zinsser. They had two children.

While heading Cravath's Paris office in 1930, McCloy became enmeshed in a tangled case of international intrigue that changed his life and vaulted him to international fame. The case involved an infamous explosion of a munitions factory on Black Tom Island, New Jersey, in 1916, months before U.S. entry into the war. Bethlehem Steel claimed that German secret agents were responsible for sabotaging its munitions plant, and in 1939 McCloy won a $20 million judgment against Germany. By then, Europe was immersed in World War II, and McCloy had established himself as the leading U.S. expert on German sabotage. In 1940 he joined the War Department as a special consultant to Secretary of War Henry Stimson. McCloy soon proved indispensable to the aging Stimson. As assistant secretary of war from 1941 until November 1945, there was not a political-military decision of moment that Mc-

Cloy did not have a hand in, including the Lend-Lease Act, the internment of Japanese Americans, and the decision to drop the atomic bomb on Japan.

After the war McCloy became a partner in Milbank, Tweed, Hope and Hadley, a law firm distinguished for its ties to the Rockefeller interests. In 1947 he accepted the presidency of the International Bank for Reconstruction and Development (also known as the World Bank), and two years later agreed to become U.S. high commissioner to occupied Germany. There he oversaw the transformation of the western zone from a state of occupation to the semisovereign state of West Germany.

McCloy returned to the United States in 1952. He never held another full-time government post, and his ambition to serve as secretary of state would go unfulfilled. Still, there was scarcely an aspect of foreign policy that he did not influence privately or publicly for the remainder of the cold war. He served as a presidential envoy for the Eisenhower, Kennedy, and Johnson administrations to various countries around the world, especially the Middle East, and as a disarmament and arms control adviser from 1961 to 1974. He negotiated a new burden-sharing agreement in NATO in 1966, following France's withdrawal from the alliance. McCloy was President John F. Kennedy's special negotiator with the Soviets during the Cuban missile crisis in 1962. He also served on the Warren Commission that investigated the assassination of President Kennedy in 1963–1964. He was one of the so-called wise men who advised President Lyndon Johnson on the conduct of the Vietnam War until 1968. He played a role in the controversies over a new Panama Canal treaty and the Shah's rule in Iran during Jimmy Carter's administration.

All these involvements occurred while McCloy was either a banker (chairman of Chase Manhattan Bank from 1953 to 1960) or a lawyer (at the Milbank firm from 1961 until his death). Simultaneously, he was at the helm of several of the most influential private organizations in the nation, serving as chairman of the Council on Foreign Relations (1953–1971) and of the Ford Foundation (1953–1965). His schedule was enough to exhaust two men, but McCloy exuded physical vitality throughout his life; he died of old age, just short of his ninety-fourth birthday. He was buried near Intercourse, Pennsylvania, where he spent his childhood summers.

Other men played similar roles during this period, such as W. Averell Harriman and Robert Lovett, but no career rivaled the life's work of John McCloy in longevity and catholicity. His was a record of unmatched service to Democratic and Republican presidents alike over four decades, complemented by paid and unpaid labors for the most potent private institutions in America. His ubiquitous presence stitched together fundamental strands of American history. Most prominently, the length and breadth of his activities very nearly chronicle the key issues during America's rise from prewar provincialism to postwar internationalism.

★

The papers of John J. McCloy are in the Special Collections Department of the Amherst College Library. John J. McCloy, *The Challenge to American Foreign Policy* (1953), is a compilation of three lectures he gave at Harvard. Walter Isaacson and Evan Thomas, *The Wise Men: Six Friends and the World They Made: Acheson, Bohlen, Harriman, Kennan, Lovett, McCloy* (1986), is a group biography. Thomas A. Schwartz, *America's Germany: John J. McCloy and the Federal Republic of Germany* (1991), concentrates on his years as high commissioner (1949 to 1952). See also Alan Brinkley, "The Most Influential Private Citizen in America: Minister Without Portfolio," *Harper's* (Feb. 1983); Shepard Stone, "John J. McCloy, 1895–1989," *The Century Association Yearbook* (1990), a tribute from one of McCloy's closest colleagues; and Max Holland, "Citizen McCloy," *Wilson Quarterly* 15 (autumn 1991): 22–42. An obituary is in the *New York Times* (12 Mar. 1989).

Max Holland

MacCORQUODALE, Donald William ("Mac") (*b.* 30 June 1898 in Chicago, Illinois; *d.* 5 February 1986 in Winnetka, Illinois), biochemistry professor, researcher, head of Abbott Laboratories, and a member of one of the two research teams that won the 1943 Nobel Prize in physiology or medicine for the isolation and synthesis of vitamin K.

Donald MacCorquodale was the son of Archibald W. MacCorquodale, who worked for the publishing firm of A. C. McClurg, and Isabel Heron Lindsay, a homemaker, both immigrants to the United States from Scotland in 1893. As a teenager he was interested in architecture and worked in the office of the prominent architect Louis Sullivan, where he came into contact with Frank Lloyd Wright on a regular basis. This employment lasted through his years at Carl Schurz High School in Chicago.

At the University of Illinois at Urbana-Champaign, Roger Adams persuaded MacCorquodale to study biochemistry instead of architecture; it was the beginning of a lifelong friendship. In 1924 MacCorquodale received his B.S. degree with honors and briefly taught chemistry at the University of Tennessee.

In the autumn of 1924 MacCorquodale entered the University of Wisconsin at Madison, where he was awarded an assistantship. He acquired his M.S. degree there in 1926 and continued as an assistant while a doctoral student in organic chemistry. He worked with Harry Steenbock and Homer Atkins on the study of vitamin D until he obtained his Ph.D. in 1928. After receiving the degree he became a research associate with Atkins, who had been his dissertation adviser.

Donald M. MacCorquodale. COURTESY OF DONALD L. MACCORQUODALE.

MacCorquodale taught general chemistry from 1929 until he was awarded a Metz Fellowship in 1930 for postgraduate work at the Sheffield Scientific School of Yale University. Although he had studied medicine extensively, he decided not to pursue a medical degree because it would severely hinder his research.

MacCorquodale became an assistant professor and researcher at the St. Louis University School of Medicine in 1931. There he began his longtime collaboration with Edward A. Doisy, Sidney Thayer, Stephen Binkley, and the rest of the team that received the 1943 Nobel Prize in physiology or medicine for their groundbreaking work on vitamin K; he remained there for approximately the next ten years. MacCorquodale married Marjorie Merry in 1932; they had two children.

In 1942 MacCorquodale became head of biochemical research at Abbott Laboratories, where his research involved blood plasma, steroids, and the development of penicillin and penicillin salts. The cultivation of penicillin occurred in MacCorquodale's laboratory because research by its discoverer, Alexander Fleming, was hampered by the German bombing of England during World War II.

MacCorquodale reached the height of his achievements in 1943, when, as part of the United States team and a team from Denmark, he shared the Nobel Prize in physiology or medicine. Both groups had been successful in isolating, synthesizing, and characterizing the chemical structure of vitamin K, which led to its availability in adequate supplies for those who needed it most. Vitamin K was already known as an exceptional clotting agent, which was especially beneficial for women in childbirth and for postoperative patients.

In 1958 MacCorquodale became the coordinator of science information in the Science Information Center at Abbott Laboratories; he held this title until his retirement in 1963. For approximately the next eight years he taught general chemistry at Barat College in Lake Forest, Illinois, a school run by the Sisters of the Sacred Heart. Through the Volunteer Talent Pool he gave a substantial amount of time to the schoolchildren of Winnetka, Illinois, as well. He also became actively involved in inner city work, in teaching church school, and in gardening. MacCorquodale also enjoyed glassblowing and restoring antique furniture.

MacCorquodale participated in many learned societies and professional organizations, including the American Association for the Advancement of Science, the American Chemical Society, and the American Society of Biological Chemists. He died at his home in Winnetka of an illness triggered by a stroke three years earlier. He is buried in Winnetka.

MacCorquodale was remarkable in many respects. Although quiet and modest, he was an excellent conversationalist, often quoting Shakespeare and Robert Burns. Despite having sight in only one eye since the age of three and a half, he was able to excel in science and reach the pinnacle of success. He served as chairman of the board of trustees of the Chicago Chemical Library Foundation, and in 1944 he worked as a civilian scientist for the Office of Scientific Research and Development. What made MacCorquodale most outstanding, however, was his zest for life, his unflagging enthusiasm in the face of a challenge, the ability to help those in need, and a combination of ingenuity and the willingness to give of himself.

★

The Alumni Morgue File (Record Series 26/4/1), University Archives, University of Illinois at Urbana-Champaign, includes biographical information, a letter from MacCorquodale's wife, obituaries, and a copy of his yearbook photo. The file on MacCorquodale from the Department of Biochemistry and Molecular Biology at St. Louis University contains a letter from MacCorquodale's wife and an article by Ralph W. McKee about Doisy and his team, from the American Philosophical Society's 1988 *Yearbook*. See also Tyler Wasson, ed., *Nobel Prize Winners* (1987). An obituary is in the *New York Times* (10 Feb. 1986).

ADRIANO C. TOMASINO

McCRACKEN, James Eugene (*b.* 16 December 1926 in Gary, Indiana; *d.* 30 April 1988 in New York City), American operatic tenor best known for his interpretation of the title role of Verdi's *Otello.*

McCracken was one of two children born to John A. McCracken, who was chief of the Gary, Indiana, fire department and had a great interest in music, and Doris (Hafey) McCracken, who played the piano and acted in local amateur theatricals. Nicknamed "Moose" for his heavy stature, he attended Horace Mann High School, where he explored his talent for music by singing the lead in Gilbert and Sullivan's *Pirates of Penzance,* joining the glee club, and singing in the church choir. Upon graduating from high school in 1943, during World War II, McCracken joined the navy and became a member of the Blue Jackets Choir of the Great Lakes Training Station. In 1944, just before his eighteenth birthday, he married Shirley Fender, his high school sweetheart and a fellow performer. (The marriage would produce a son and end in divorce after six years.)

McCracken entered Columbia University in New York City on the GI bill and began to study music more seriously. He gained early experience with the Columbia Theatre Associates on various productions. To make a living he was forced to work in the chorus of the Roxy Theatre, where he sang four shows daily, sometimes singing for eighteen hours a day. Later he worked on Broadway as the offstage voice for Bert Lahr in *Two on the Aisle,* sang a small part in *A Tree Grows in Brooklyn,* and worked in a revival of George and Ira Gershwin's *Of Thee I Sing.* McCracken's life centered on these performances, auditions for larger roles, and his studies with Wellington Ezekial. In 1952 McCracken sang Rudolfo in an English version of Puccini's *La Bohème* with the Central City Opera Company in Colorado. Soon after this successful venture he auditioned for the Metropolitan Opera House in New York City and was offered a contract for the 1953–1954 season. He debuted in the minor role of Parpignol, the toy vendor in *La Bohème.* At the end of his first season at the Metropolitan he was singing a repertory of 126 small roles.

On 11 November 1954 he married the mezzo-soprano Sandra Warfield, whom he had met when they had performed the roles of Samson and Delilah in Norfolk, Virginia. Warfield encouraged McCracken to move to Europe to try for roles more challenging than those being offered at the Metropolitan. At the end of the 1956–1957 season they left the United States for Bonn, Germany, where McCracken debuted as Max in *Der Freischütz.* He also sang the leading roles of Canio in *I Pagliacci,* Manrico in *Il Trovatore,* and Radames in *Aida.*

Traveling to Verona, Italy, in 1958, McCracken was hired by Herbert Graf, stage director of the Metropolitan Opera, to understudy the leading tenor roles in *Aïda* and *Turandot* for a festival directed by Tullio Serafin. McCracken did not get the opportunity to sing any performances but Serafin recognized his talent for Italian opera and encouraged him to sing these roles. Although barely able to support himself and his wife, McCracken stayed in Verona to study voice. Their daughter was born there and the family eventually settled in Switzerland.

In 1959 McCracken made guest appearances in Bielefeld, Zurich, and Athens in the role of Samson. Back in Milan, McCracken studied for an upcoming performance of *Otello* scheduled for 1960 with the Washington (D.C.) Opera Company. The performance of 22 January was well reviewed and was the first of many in what would become McCracken's signature role.

McCracken's presence in Europe was now sought by many opera houses. In 1960 Herbert Graf, now of the Zurich Municipal Theatre in Switzerland, wanted McCracken to sing the opening performance of *Otello* for his opera house, and Herbert von Karajan invited McCracken to sing

James McCracken (*left*) and soprano Leontyne Price star in a production of *Aida* at the Metropolitan Opera, January 1985. UPI/CORBIS-BETTMANN

at the Vienna State Opera; both houses subsequently shared McCracken's talents.

At a festival in Zurich, Rudolph Bing, director of the Metropolitan Opera, heard McCracken sing Otello and invited him to repeat the role in the Met's spring 1963 production. Five years after his departure McCracken made a triumphant return to America's premier opera company. Reviews for McCracken's performances in *Otello* and *I Pagliacci* were sensational. Over the course of his career at the Metropolitan, McCracken would sing 410 performances.

Throughout his career McCracken experienced legal and artistic difficulties. He won a settlement against the Decca Record Company of England for signing him to an exclusive contract in 1964 and then refusing to allow him to record, and he often clashed with Bing over salary, contracts, and scheduling. After McCracken was denied a chance to sing a 1978 telecast performance he again left the Metropolitan. He was preparing for a return to that house in 1988 when he was taken ill and forced to cancel his performances. On 12 April he suffered a stroke and on 30 April he died at the age of sixty-one in Roosevelt Hospital in Manhattan.

Before his death, McCracken had sung leading roles in most of the major opera houses of the world and was the first American tenor to perform Otello in New York. He was sought out by directors and fans alike for the vocal power and lyricism he brought to his roles and for the dramatic and emotional intensity of his performances. His singing has been described as exact in placement and rich in color and criticized for excessive vibrato and for relying too much on falsetto. When he died, the *New York Times* called him "the most successful dramatic tenor yet produced by the United States." In his prime he was five feet, ten inches tall and weighed more than 250 pounds, a burly man who enjoyed working on his vocal technique and the rigors of rehearsals. He was a nontemperamental performer who had a great passion for his work and family and a talent that matched his love of music.

★

James McCracken and Sandra Warfield, *A Star in the Family* (1971), is a diary of one year in the personal and professional lives of the McCrackens, including flashbacks on their careers. See also the entry on McCracken in Stanley Sadie, *New Grove Dictionary of Music and Musicians* (1980); "A Day's Work," *Time* (22 Mar. 1963); and Dennis McGovern, "Singing Day to Day," *Opera News* (Oct. 1987). An obituary is in the *New York Times* (1 May 1988).

MARIA LAGONIA

McCREA, Joel Albert (*b.* 5 November 1905 in South Pasadena, California; *d.* 20 October 1990 in Woodland Hills, California), movie actor and rancher best known for his roles in Hollywood Westerns.

Joel McCrea was one of three children of Thomas P. McCrea, a public utility company executive, and Lou Whipple, a homemaker. The family moved in 1914 to Hollywood, where Joel attended Gardner Street Elementary. He had his first contact with the movie industry at the age of nine, when he delivered newspapers to his movie hero, William S. Hart, and to Cecil B. DeMille. Joel graduated from Hollywood High School in 1924 and entered Pomona State College. During the summers he worked as a lifeguard, stable boy, and ranch hand, and in 1926 he began performing as a movie stunt double. He graduated with a B.A. degree in 1928, and the following year he landed a small part in *The Jazz Age* and played a playboy gigolo in DeMille's *Dynamite*.

McCrea enjoyed his first starring role in 1930 in *The Silver Horde,* an action film. That year, following the advice of Will Rogers, whom he had met while filming *Lightnin',* McCrea borrowed money and purchased his 1,200-acre dream ranch in the Santa Rosa Valley near Camarillo, some forty miles northwest of Los Angeles. In the early 1930s he made two films with the actress Frances Dee, *The Silver Cord* and *One Man's Journey,* both released in 1933. McCrea and Dee married on 20 October 1933 and had three sons.

During the 1930s McCrea starred in nearly forty films, with roles ranging from light romantic comedy to action-adventure. He played Shirley Temple's father in *Our Little*

Joel McCrea, 1937. PHOTOFEST

Girl (1935) and the first Dr. Kildare in *Interns Can't Take Money* (1937). By the late 1930s he was starring in Westerns, including *Wells Fargo,* Paramount's biggest hit of 1937. Two years later he starred opposite Barbara Stanwyck in *Union Pacific*.

In 1940 McCrea starred in an Alfred Hitchcock thriller, *Foreign Correspondent,* which received six Academy Award nominations. The next year he played the title role in Preston Sturges's *Sullivan's Travels,* which the Library of Congress named to the National Film Registry in 1990, citing it as a movie of "cultural, historical, and aesthetic significance."

During the World War II years McCrea appeared in only six films. In 1943 he starred in *The More the Merrier,* a classic wartime comedy about Washington, D.C., that received six Academy Award nominations. He also starred in two Westerns, *The Great Man's Lady* (1942), opposite Stanwyck, and *Buffalo Bill* (1944), his first Technicolor movie, opposite Maureen O'Hara.

After the war McCrea decided to concentrate on Westerns for the remainder of his career. His decision immediately paid off with the starring role in *The Virginian* (1946). Of the two dozen movies McCrea made between 1946 and 1959, all were Westerns except *Shoot First* (1953), a spy thriller made in England. In 1959 McCrea made a foray into television, starring as the town marshal in *Wichita Town,* an NBC series in which his son Jody McCrea played a deputy. Only twenty-six episodes were shot, however, and the series was not renewed. In 1962 McCrea came out of semiretirement to costar with Randolph Scott in Sam Peckinpah's first major Western, *Ride the High Country*. The title is an allusion both to Peckinpah's coda for his outlaw heroes—they follow a higher code of honor among themselves—and for the integrity of McCrea's screen portrayals. Tony Thomas adapted the title of this film as *Riding the High Country* for the subtitle of his 1992 biography of McCrea.

McCrea's later years were filled with interests outside the movie industry. In the 1950s he began selling some of the land he had acquired over the years, including the ranch he had bought in 1930 near Camarillo, now grown to some 3,000 acres. Having bought it for $19,500, he sold most of it for a reported $1.3 million, retaining 300 acres for his home ranch. He also donated some of it as a park and facility for the YMCA, one of the organizations, along with the Boys Clubs of America, to which he gave his time. In 1969 he was named to the National Cowboy Hall of Fame, and he served as chairman of its board of directors for many years.

In 1973 McCrea narrated *The Great American Cowboy,* which won an Academy Award for best feature documentary, and in 1979 he wrote the foreword to Lee O. Miller's *Great Cowboy Stars of Movies and Television.* In 1984 McCrea was interviewed for *George Stevens: A Filmmaker's Journey* and in 1990 for *Preston Sturges: The Rise and Fall of an American Dreamer.*

McCrea's last public appearance was at a campaign dinner for Republican gubernatorial candidate Pete Wilson on 1 October 1990. The keynote speaker at the event was First Lady Barbara Bush, who immediately after her speech went up to McCrea, put her hand in his, and said, "My hero." McCrea died of pulmonary complications in Woodland Hills, California, and was buried on his ranch.

In *Western Films: A Complete Guide* (1982), Brian Garfield notes that Joel McCrea must be listed among the Western stars who truly dominated the field. Standing six feet, two inches, attractive, blond, muscular, and with a quiet, placid, confident presence, McCrea more than filled the bill for a Western star of his day. In his foreword to *The Great Cowboy Stars,* McCrea cited Tom Mix's cowboy credo: "Straight shooters always win. Those who can't shoot straight always lose." He stated, "I am proud to have been a Western actor; would be proud to act again in any good Western, as long as it represents what the Westerns of old represented: Americana." Richard Slotkin, in his *Gunfighter Nation: The Myth of the Frontier in Twentieth Century America* (1992), interprets McCrea's Westerns of the 1930s, 1940s, and 1950s as acting out the epic of American empire. Spanning the years from the silent movies of the 1920s to Sam Peckinpah's cul-de-sac cowboys of the 1960s, McCrea's movie career offers a rich overview of popular interests and concerns during the middle years of the twentieth century.

★

Tony Thomas, *Joel McCrea: Riding the High Country* (1992), is the recognized film biography on Joel McCrea. Lee O. Miller, *The Great Cowboy Stars of Movies and Television* (1979), is worthwhile both for McCrea's foreword and because Miller was a personal friend. Richard Slotkin, *Gunfighter Nation: The Myth of the Frontier in Twentieth-Century America* (1992), provides an academic critique of McCrea's films in the larger context of American history and cultural values. Frank S. Nugent, "Good Ol' Joel," *Collier's* (15 Sept. 1951), provides an interesting contemporary look at McCrea at the height of his career. Jimmie Hicks's two-part article, "Joel McCrea," in *Films in Review* (Oct. and Dec. 1991) is an accurate, useful short summary of McCrea's career.

GREGG M. CAMPBELL

McCREE, Wade Hampton, Jr. (*b.* 3 July 1920 in Des Moines, Iowa; *d.* 30 August 1987 in Detroit, Michigan), lawyer, judge, and outspoken advocate of civil rights, whose progression from private practice to the office of solicitor general of the United States, the third-highest legal position in the country, broke racial barriers and inspired generations of African Americans after him.

The second of four children, McCree lived his first four years in Des Moines. In 1924 his father, Wade Hampton McCree, who held a degree in pharmacology from the University of Iowa and owned a pharmacy in Des Moines, became the first African-American narcotics inspector for the federal Food and Drug Administration. That career change led the family to live in various locations—the territory of Hawaii (1924–1926), Chicago (1926–1930), and Boston (1930). In order for McCree to gain admittance to Boston Latin School, his mother, Lucretia (Harper) McCree, a former public school teacher of Greek and Latin, tutored him in those subjects. McCree gained from his father the pioneering spirit necessary for an African American to break racial barriers and acquired from his mother a deep respect for the liberty of all people, regardless of class status. From her teaching position in Daytona Beach, Florida, Lucretia Harper had collected money to help a sharecropper flee the state because he could not afford to pay debts imposed by his landlord.

In 1937 the University of Iowa accepted McCree's application for undergraduate studies. As he readied himself for attendance, the university informed him that he would not be allowed to live on campus. McCree, who could not afford off-campus housing, applied for and received a tuition scholarship in 1937 from Fisk University, the alma mater of his parents, in Nashville, Tennessee. While majoring in history and government and serving as president of the student council, he held several part-time jobs, including sales clerk, waiter, and bartender. In 1941 McCree graduated with highest distinction and began studies at Harvard Law School in Cambridge, Massachusetts. The following year he was drafted into the racially segregated U.S. Army. McCree was discharged four years later as a captain, having completed two years of combat duty in Italy and earning the Bronze Star. On 29 July 1946 he married Dores B. McCrary, a recent graduate of the Simmons College School of Library Science in Boston; they had three children. In December 1947 McCree completed his law degree, after which he and his wife moved to Detroit, her family's home.

Although McCree had graduated twelfth in his class at Harvard and had a letter of recommendation from the dean, one of Detroit's most prestigious law firms turned down his application for employment. A firm of African-American lawyers, Bledsoe and Taylor, did not. In 1948 Harold Bledsoe, himself a pioneer in Michigan law and politics, initiated McCree's career. McCree remained with that firm until 1952, when Michigan governor G. Mennen Williams appointed him a member of the Workman's Compensation Commission. In 1954 Williams appointed him a judge of the Wayne County Circuit Court, the first African American appointed to such a position in Michigan. In 1955, when McCree sought election to that position, he became the first person of African descent to win a judicial election in Michigan.

Wade H. McCree, Jr., 1963. UPI/CORBIS-BETTMANN

McCree remained on the Wayne County Circuit Court until 1961, when President John F. Kennedy appointed him a judge of the United States District Court, Eastern District of Michigan in Detroit, the second African-American federal district court judge in the country. In 1966 President Lyndon B. Johnson appointed him a judge of the United States Court of Appeals for the Sixth Circuit. McCree was the first black to serve as a judge on that court. Writing the majority opinion in *Davis* v. *School District of Pontiac* (1971), at a time when the nation was severely divided over school busing to eliminate segregation by race, McCree essentially upheld the U.S. Supreme Court ruling in *Brown* v. *Board of Education* (1954). In 1977 President Jimmy Carter appointed him solicitor general, at which time McCree and his wife moved to Washington, D.C.

In 1981, the first year of President Ronald Reagan's administration, McCree resigned and became Lewis M. Simes Professor of Law at the University of Michigan Law School in Ann Arbor, where he lived until his death. McCree died of cancer at Henry Ford Hospital in Detroit and was cremated. Two memorial services were held—one in Detroit at the First Unitarian-Universalist Church, of which he had been a member, and the other at the University of Michigan Law School.

As solicitor general, McCree represented the federal government in cases brought before the U.S. Supreme Court. He presented arguments in two highly publicized cases, *Nixon* v. *Administrator of General Services* (1977) and *Regents of the University of California* v. *Bakke* (1978), both cases exemplifying his general concern for the rights of all citizens. In the first case, former president Richard M. Nixon filed suit against the federal government to regain control of the private papers and tape recordings produced during his presidency. McCree urged the Court to uphold the 1974 statute that gives the federal government, on behalf of its citizens, control over former presidents' materials. Essentially, he argued that citizens have the right of access to information when its availability will not threaten national security. In the other case, the University of California at Davis sought to have overturned a lower court ruling that Allan Bakke, a Caucasian, be admitted to the university's medical school because individuals of color less qualified than Bakke had been accepted. McCree urged the Court to void the ruling that Bakke be admitted and to refer the case back to the California judicial system for development of a more complete factual record. He also argued that the U.S. Constitution permits minority status to be one of the considerations used by a school in the admissions process.

Throughout his personal life, as well, McCree was an outspoken advocate of civil rights. In 1960, when his eldest child was turned away from a private school in Detroit, he worked with a community of Quakers to establish Friends School there. In 1968, he was one of the signers of a letter to the publisher of the *Detroit News* protesting the paper's policy of identifying persons arrested by the police by race, thereby encouraging a stereotype of African Americans. In 1982 he was one of the signers of a letter to the Senate Judiciary Committee calling unconstitutional two bills that would limit court enforcement of school integration.

McCree broadened the goals to which African Americans could aspire. Like his predecessors, he had a remarkable career because he possessed outstanding qualities. He was recognized for his brilliance, his integrity, and his respect for individuals' rights, as his often reflective, candid, and compassionate expression revealed.

★

For McCree's particular role in the progression of African Americans in the legal profession, see "Black Lawyers, Law Practice, and Bar Associations—1844 to 1970: A Michigan History," *Wayne State Law Review* (1987). Two tributes to McCree, which offer a substantial amount of information on his professional and personal life, are the *Michigan Law Review* (Nov. 1987), an issue dedicated to him, and "Friends School in Detroit Honors Wade H. McCree, Jr.," a multipage brochure written for a dinner honoring him posthumously. Obituaries are in the *New York Times* and the *Boston Globe* (both 1 Sept. 1987). Also of interest is "A Tribute to Wade H. McCree, Jr.," a tape recording (1989) presented by the University of Michigan Law School Fund in support of the professorship established to honor him. A video, *Green Seedlings: The Story of Wade H. McCree, Jr., and Friends School,* includes a reading of one of McCree's many sonnets, "Green Seedlings," which he wrote at the funeral service of his first law employer, Harold Bledsoe.

CATHERINE ADAMOWICZ

MACDONALD, John Dann (*b.* 24 July 1916 in Sharon, Pennsylvania; *d.* 28 December 1986 in Milwaukee, Wisconsin), writer of hard-boiled detective fiction, most notably the Travis McGee series of novels.

MacDonald was the elder child of Eugene Andrew MacDonald, the treasurer of the Savage Arms Company, and Marguerite Dann, a homemaker. From his father, a hard-driving man, he derived a strong will and a capacity for hard work; from his mother, who read to him every day for a year when he was bedridden with mastoiditis and scarlet fever in 1928–1929, he derived a love of imaginative storytelling and a concern for those in need. MacDonald graduated from the Utica Free Academy in 1933. He studied

John MacDonald. CORBIS-BETTMANN

business administration at the Wharton School of Finance at the University of Pennsylvania but left after three semesters. He then went to Syracuse University, where he earned a B.S. degree in business administration in 1938. He married Dorothy Prentiss, an artist, in 1938; they had one son. In 1939 he received an M.B.A. degree from the Harvard School of Business Administration. After being fired from his first two jobs, he joined the U.S. Army, eventually becoming a lieutenant. When World War II began, he was sent to South Asia as an operations officer with the Office of Strategic Services, ultimately rising to the rank of lieutenant colonel.

MacDonald's writing career began out of frustration. Angered that wartime censorship would not let him tell his wife what was really happening, he wrote as a letter the story "Interlude in India" in order to get his information past the bureaucrats. His wife typed the letter and sent it off to *Story* magazine; when MacDonald returned home from the war he found himself a published short-story writer and decided to make it his career.

MacDonald approached writing the way he had learned to approach every problem—with fourteen-hour days and indefatigable will. It was five months before he sold his second story, but by the end of 1946 he had sold twenty-five stories, earning $6,000. In his peak year, 1949, MacDonald published seventy-three stories, some of which appeared in a single magazine under different pen names. The vast majority of this work appeared in the so-called pulp magazines, such as *Dime Detective,* but his work also appeared in mainstream magazines like *Cosmopolitan.*

In 1950, foreseeing the decline in pulp magazine circulation, MacDonald wrote his first novel, *The Brass Cupcake,* an original paperback published by Fawcett; three-quarters of his novels would appear as paperback originals. These works fell into many genres: fantasy, comedy, horror, and domestic drama, in addition to his forte, mystery. One of these works, *The Executioners,* was turned into the film noir *Cape Fear* (1962); another, a boardroom drama called *A Key to the Suite,* won the Grand Prix de Littérature Policière when it was translated into French in 1964. He continued to write stories, however, winning the Ben Franklin Award in 1955 for the year's best short story. His reputation buoyed by these prestigious awards, MacDonald set out to create a series character. It would prove to be his most important career move.

Travis McGee, the hero he created for the twenty-one books in the series (each one is marked by a color in the title), is a burly but sensitive boater who is regularly approached by victims of legal violence to salvage their lost money, or goods, or even reputation, in exchange for half its value. Following McGee into the complex and generally evil world of each client, readers learn about a new field—land development, electoral politics, drug smuggling—in each book. Through their identification with the never more than slightly tarnished hero, readers undergo the temptations of the corrupt world, forgive McGee's lapses into relationships that are never solely sexual, and are reassured of his essential goodness at the end. With a new title appearing approximately once each year, readers could share the hero's—and presumably his creator's—travails, admire his ability to learn from his experiences, even trace his moral development, and sense a growing mellowness, a recognition that McGee's midlife crisis was their own.

Other books MacDonald published during the last twenty years of his career included *The Last One Left,* which appeared in 1967 and won an Edgar as best mystery of the year. *No Deadly Drug,* which came out in 1968, traced the real-life trials of Dr. Carl Coppolino, acquitted of one murder only to be convicted of another. *Condominium,* a 1977 exposé of Florida real estate corruption, stayed on the best-seller list for six months. *The Green Ripper* won the American Book Award in 1979. In 1972 the Mystery Writers of America honored MacDonald with its Grand Master Award. His final volume was *Dan Rowan and John D. MacDonald: A Friendship,* an edition of his correspondence with the comedian Dan Rowan, and was published after MacDonald's death.

MacDonald maintained his energy level to the end of his life, writing as many as eighty hours a week, swimming in the Gulf of Mexico outside his home in Sarasota, Florida, playing tennis, and in his "off" hours working as a semiprofessional photographer. When he underwent coronary bypass surgery at the age of seventy he suffered complications and fell into a coma from which he did not recover.

Despite his tremendous output, MacDonald never received critical respect. The Travis McGee series attracted MacDonald because of its paradoxical ability to offer him strict limits within which he had to work, but also an openness of possibility to investigate psychology, morality, even spirituality. In an interview in 1970, he compared the McGee series to "folk dancing . . . the patterns traditionally imperative, the retributions obligatory."

★

The best source on his life and work is David Geherin, *John D. MacDonald* (1982). An obituary is in the *New York Times* (29 Dec. 1986).

HARTLEY S. SPATT

MACK, Walter Staunton, Jr. (*b.* 19 October 1895 in New York City; *d.* 18 March 1990 in New York City), president and chairman of Pepsi-Cola who is credited with being the first to put soft drinks in cans.

Born in a comfortable brownstone on West Eighty-fourth Street in Manhattan, Mack was the only son of Walter

Walter Mack, Jr., *c.* 1935. UPI/CORBIS-BETTMANN

Staunton Mack, Sr., who ran a woolens business on lower Fifth Avenue, and Alice Ranger, a housewife. In 1911 his father bought into a local cotton converting firm called Bedford Mills. His mother was the daughter of a Texan who had founded the Galveston Cotton Exchange. Mack attended Public School 87 and DeWitt Clinton High School, from which he graduated in 1913. He entered Harvard College in the fall of that year and graduated in 1917 with a B.A degree. He gave most of his attention to mathematics and economics. He completed his studies in three and a half years, just in time to enlist in the U.S. Navy when the United States declared war on Germany in 1917. After some North Atlantic service as a seaman second class, he was sent to officer's training school at Annapolis, Maryland. Graduating third in a class of 300 with the rank of ensign, Mack was assigned to destroyers and transports operating in the Atlantic. He was demobilized in 1919 and upon his return to civilian life went to work for his father. He spent nine years with Bedford Mills, beginning as an apprentice salesman in its showrooms and by 1926 rising to the presidency of the company.

In 1931 Mack entered the investment banking firm of William B. Nichols and Company as vice president. Around the same time he became president of the Phoenix Securities Corporation and vice president of Equity Corporation. As head of Phoenix, Mack deviated from the normal trends in investments—instead of investing in successful ventures, he promoted weak corporations. The ailing companies gave Phoenix options on shares, and Mack provided money and his unique management style.

In 1939 Mack announced that Phoenix had an interest in Loft, Inc., a million-dollar restaurant and candy chain in New York City. Phoenix Securities Corporation put up securities for some $400,000 in bank loans and an additional $600,000 cash. "For such help in a crisis," reported *Time,* "Phoenix got options on 300,000 shares of Loft at $1.50, on 200,000 shares at $2. However, since Loft had lost money every year since 1934, this did not look like too promising an investment." With Phoenix's financial infusion, the candy company brought suit against its former president, Charles Godfrey Guth, on the grounds that Guth had bought 91 percent of the Pepsi-Cola Company's stock with Loft's equity. The courts decided against Guth and turned the Pepsi-Cola Company over to Loft. Mack, as president of Phoenix Securities, held the major share of Loft stock and became president of the Pepsi-Cola Company. In 1938, when Mack first took over Pepsi, the net profits of the soft-drink company were less than $3 million. One year later the company's earnings had increased by 76 percent, and its stock had gone from $70 to $190 a share.

By 1939 Mack had taken active control of Pepsi's business and had made several decisions that affected the bottles, labels, and product quality control. Moreover, his influence made a major difference in the promotion and advertising campaign. One of Mack's greatest advertising success stories was his introduction of Pepsi's musical jingle: "Pepsi-Cola hits the spot. Twelve full ounces, that's a lot. Twice as much for a nickel, too. Pepsi-Cola is the drink for you." This commercial jingle made sales jump around the world. Mack also made the decision to market Pepsi at twelve ounces as opposed to Coca-Cola's soft drink at six ounces. For Mack, this decision to stick by the twelve-ounce size came with indirect advantages. No company was likely to make a bigger nickel drink, and the competition would need to justify a higher price.

During his second year with Pepsi-Cola, in 1940, Mack began the first of his educational projects. He believed that the corporation should be a good citizen and directed Pepsi-Cola into various community and philanthropic activities. As an advocate of education, he instituted the Walter Mack Job Awards for American Youth in celebration of the company's thirty-fifth anniversary. This program gave twelve college students employment at Pepsi-Cola with a salary of $1,300 annually. Another part of his educational project was a scholarship program that supported 117 college scholarships. In addition, Pepsi provided nineteen separate scholarships for African-American students. These activities were evidence of Mack's belief that a business owes more to the community than just jobs. He also began centers for military personnel in Washington, San Francisco, and New York, annual national painting contests that offered large prizes, and three recreation clubs for teenagers in New York City that opened in 1945. In announcing this project Mack said, "I am sure we all have sufficient faith in our young people . . . to feel that if they are given a place they can call their own, with games, dancing, refreshments, and activities they can enjoy, so-called 'youth problems' can be effectively met." These projects also provided Pepsi with a proven means of advertising.

As time went on Mack's colleagues at Pepsi increasingly opposed his efforts on community programs, and he ultimately resigned in 1951. After his retirement from Pepsi-Cola, Mack remained active in the soft-drink industry and went on to head several other companies, including the Nedick's chains and C and C Super, another soft-drink venture. In 1953 he was credited with being the first to put soft drinks—C and C Ginger Ale and C and C Super Coola—into cans. During his career Mack was an officer of a wide range of companies, from mining and investment corporations to consumer products. At the age of eighty-two, he came out of retirement and brought together a group of former cola executives who developed King-Cola in 1978 to compete with Coke and Pepsi. He was an advocate for older workers and in 1981 told a congressional committee, "Work keeps me alive, as it does a great many people." In 1982 Mack published his autobiography, *No Time Lost*.

Mack also had a love of politics and was actively involved at both the national and local levels. In 1932 he ran unsuccessfully for state senator as a Republican, and later he served as a fund-raiser for the mayoral campaigns of Fiorello H. La Guardia and the presidential campaigns of Wendell Willkie, Thomas E. Dewey, and Dwight D. Eisenhower. Mack achieved a level of notoriety as a New York Republican delegate at the 1940 convention, when he triggered the Willkie nomination stampede by demanding that the New York delegation be polled individually at a carefully rehearsed moment. This maneuver provided the ten extra votes needed to turn the tide for Willkie on the third ballot. In 1964 Mack returned to raise money for Lyndon B. Johnson's presidential campaign.

Mack married his first wife, Marion Reckford, in 1922; they adopted two children. After their divorce 1941, Mack married Ruth J. Watkins, who had been his secretary at Phoenix and was his personnel manager at Pepsi-Cola, in 1942. They had two children. He and Ruth lived in an expansive apartment on Fifth Avenue in New York City and had a country place at Bantam Lake, Connecticut, several hundred acres of farmland near Cooperstown, New York, and an island in Chesapeake Bay called Walrus Island.

Mack lived a bustling social life, the result of his affiliation with numerous civic and social organizations. He earned various honors for his decades of public service and community interests, particularly in New York City, where he was a trustee of Temple Emanu-El in Manhattan for fifty-six years. He died of heart disease at his home in New York City.

Walter S. Mack, Jr., was a merchandising genius remembered as the first to market soft drinks in cans and a dynamic businessperson known for his daring attitude and his ability to rescue failing companies. He proclaimed, "I'm a great guy for fundamentals," and his fundamentals were the product. Described as "an aggressive, ebullient, and public-spirited super salesman," he was much more than that; he became an elder statesman for the soft-drink industry. In 1947 *Fortune* magazine confirmed, "He's won a place for himself in the high councils of merchandising."

★

E. J. Kahn, "More Bounce to the Ounce," *New Yorker* (1 July 1950; 8 July 1950), is a two-part profile of Mack. Other useful articles are "Walter Mack," *Time* (4 Sept. 1939), and "Pepsi-Cola's Walter Mack," *Fortune* (Nov. 1947). Obituaries are in the *Boston Globe, Los Angeles Times, New York Times, Wall Street Journal,* and *Washington Times* (all 19 Mar. 1990), and *Washington Post* (20 Mar. 1990).

KAREN LYNN SVENNINGSEN

McNAIR, Ron(ald) Erwin (*b.* 21 October 1950 in Lake City, South Carolina; *d.* 28 January 1986 aboard the space shuttle *Challenger*), African-American laser physicist and astronaut.

Ronald McNair was one of three sons of Carl C. McNair, Sr., an automobile mechanic, and Pearl (Montgomery) McNair, an elementary school teacher. Ron grew up in Lake City, South Carolina, a segregated community of 12,000 residents. All three sons worked in cotton fields on farms outside the city during the summer, and at other times joined their friends to play makeshift games in nearby streets and fields. Known for his affability, Ron competed with great intensity and was determined to excel at any game. The youngster disliked idleness, sometimes keeping busy by working in his grandfather's shop. His grandmother, who never learned to write, taught him to read and to treasure books. His father preached the virtues of education, examined his sons' homework, and periodically visited their classrooms. At school, McNair's incessant quest for knowledge prompted his teachers to take note and predict good things for him.

Ron McNair at a press conference for the crew of the space shuttle *Challenger,* November 1985. NASA/CORBIS

McNair and his brothers attended all-black Carver High School. Despite his participation in many activities, he consistently made the honor roll. He loved music and played the clarinet but switched to the saxophone to which he remained faithful. Once considered too small for athletics, McNair used quickness, sharp, crisp moves, and tenacity to become a star in four sports. Occasionally McNair's obsession with extracurricular activities interfered with his class performance, but his teachers quickly countered such lapses.

McNair was especially gifted in science and mathematics. In 1967, after his graduation as class valedictorian, he entered North Carolina Agriculture and Technical (A&T) State University in Greenboro, North Carolina. He majored in physics but, surrounded by classmates from schools with stronger science programs, experienced a rare period of self-doubt. Not given to despairing, however, he emerged a top student in his class. Professor Tom Sandin, his faculty adviser, introduced him to mechanics, thermodynamics, light and optics, electricity and magnetism, and discrete matter and energy particle theories. From 1967 to 1971, McNair was a presidential scholar at the university.

Meanwhile, Shirley Jackson, who was becoming the first African-American female to earn a Ph.D. in physics (in theoretical physics from Massachusetts Institute of Technology), helped persuade university authorities to enroll more minority students. MIT initiated a program that invited promising students from "predominantly black institutions [to] enrich their undergraduate experience" at the university. Sandin and the North Carolina A&T physics chair, Donald Edwards, nominated McNair to participate during his junior year. He entered MIT a bit apprehensive, having heard that janitors held master's degrees there. Nevertheless, he benefited from his exposure to renowned scientists, the state-of-the-art facilities, and interaction with new friends.

McNair returned to North Carolina in the fall of 1970. The university conferred upon him the bachelor's degree and magna cum laude honors the following spring. Supported by a Ford Foundation Fellowship, he returned to MIT in 1971 for graduate study. McNair lived in Boston's mostly black Roxbury section, attended the St. Paul African Methodist Episcopal Church, and taught karate to neighborhood children. He found Boston's rich history, storied institutions, and famous culture impressive, but vitriolic racial slurs, threats, and skirmishes on and off campus shocked him. His tough mentality and superb physical condition enabled him to remain undeterred and without bitterness. Shirley Jackson's constant support helped forge a lifelong friendship with McNair. The National Fellowship Fund, a NATO grant, and an Omega Psi Phi scholarship provided needed financial assistance to McNair at strategic times, and Professor Michael Feld, director of the spectroscope laboratory, counseled McNair with good results.

Studying carbon dioxide and other gas-medium lasers, McNair "performed some of the earliest development of chemical hydrogen fluoride, deuterium fluoride and high-pressure CO lasers. His theoretical analysis on the interaction of intense CO_2 molecular gases with laser radiation provided new understandings and applications for highly excited polyatomic molecules" (quoted from a biographical file on McNair at the Lyndon B. Johnson Space Center). In 1975 McNair studied lasers in France on a NATO grant. Returning to MIT, he wrote his dissertation, "Energy Absorption and Vibrational Heating in Molecules Following Intense Excitation." In 1976 MIT conferred upon McNair the Ph.D. degree in physics. On 27 June 1976 he married Cheryl Moore, whom he had met at church. They later had two children.

McNair and his wife moved to Los Angeles, California, where he joined the Hughes Research Laboratory in Malibu. There he worked on laser application in isotope separation and photochemistry reactions in low-temperature liquids. McNair also investigated optical pumping techniques, electro-optic laser modulation in intersatellite space communication, and other related phenomena.

McNair turned his attention to space exploration, long

an area of fascination to him, and in 1978 was one of 8,000 applicants for astronaut training at the National Aeronautics and Space Administration (NASA). Among the thirty-five applicants accepted, he joined fellow candidates at the Johnson Space Center in Houston in arduous training; following evaluation upon his completion of the training, he was eligible for space flights as a mission specialist astronaut.

On 3 February 1984 the multipurpose orbital space shuttle *Challenger,* in flight 41B NTS, blasted off from the Kennedy Space Center in Cape Canaveral, Florida, the tenth mission of the space shuttle program. Aboard were mission commander Vance Brand, pilot Navy Commander Robert Gibson, and mission specialists Ronald McNair, Lieutenant Colonel Robert Stewart, and Navy Captain Bruce McCandless. Once in orbit each astronaut carried out numerous assignments. McNair conducted seventeen experiments involving, among other things, optical and electrical properties of arc discharge, atomic oxygen erosion, cosmic ray equipment, growth of spores, protein crystallization, and seed germination. He operated the remote shuttle arm and the new Cinema Cameras with their 180 × 360 view, launched two satellites from the payload bay, and filmed McCandless and Stewart using the manned maneuvering units for the first untethered walks in space. On 11 February 1984 *Challenger* landed at the Kennedy Space Center—a historic first, as previous flights had landed at Edwards Air Force Base in California. McNair was the second African American and third person of African descent to fly in space. After this memorable flight, honors and requests for McNair's appearance came from across the country.

On 28 January 1986 the *Challenger* again lifted off from the Kennedy Space Center carrying mission commander Frank Scobee; pilot Navy Commander Michael Smith; mission specialists Ronald McNair, Judith A. Resnik, and Ellison S. Onizuka; payload specialist Gregory Jarvis; and high school teacher Christa McAuliffe. Tragically, seventy-three seconds after liftoff, a rubber ring that sealed a joint on one of the solid rocket boosters failed, and flames reached the liquid hydrogen and oxygen propellant. A powerful explosion destroyed the shuttle; the crew cabin was severed and all the astronauts died from oxygen deficiency before impact with the ocean. This disaster left the nation in grief and prompted months of investigations that led to numerous improvements in NASA's safety procedures.

Memorial services for McNair were held on 2 February 1986 at St. Paul AME Church in Boston and Wesleyan United Methodist Church in Lake City, with South Carolina's governor, Richard Riley, attending the latter. On 12 February 1986 more than 400 people gathered in Kresge Auditorium at MIT, where the university's president, Paul Gray, eulogized McNair as "one of noble note." MIT renamed its Center for Space Research the Ronald McNair Building.

★

The Center for Space Research, Massachusetts Institute of Technology, contains valuable file papers (1978–1986) that include some McNair speeches, biographical data, newspaper articles from the Boston area, and Paul Gray's eulogy of McNair. An informative biography, Dena Shaw, *Ronald McNair* (1994), traces his life from birth to the dedication of a building in his name at MIT. J. Alfred Phelps devotes a chapter in his book, *They Had a Dream: The Story of African-American Astronauts* (1994), to Ronald McNair. NASA-TM-87454, a publication of the National Aeronautical and Space Administration, describes missions of the space program in 1984, program successes, problems, and failures.

EDWARD S. JENKINS

MACRAE, (Albert) Gordon (*b.* 12 March 1921 in East Orange, New Jersey; *d.* 24 January 1986 in Lincoln, Nebraska), singing star of stage, radio, records, television, nightclubs, and films, most notably the cinematic versions of Rodgers and Hammerstein's *Oklahoma!* and *Carousel.*

Albert Gordon MacRae was the son of William Lamount ("Wee Willie") MacRae, a self-taught inventor and radio

Gordon MacRae. ARCHIVE PHOTOS

performer, and Helen Violet (Sonn) MacRae, a concert pianist and teacher. He had one sister. By the age of two MacRae and his family moved from East Orange to Buffalo, New York, and then to Syracuse, New York, where MacRae attended the Charles Andrews School. There, two years later, MacRae led the kindergarten band. As a student at Nottingham High School, he was a charter member of the drama club. He subsequently attended and graduated from the Deerfield Academy in Massachusetts. His radio career started at age eleven as an emcee/interlocutor on a minstrel show at WBFL in Syracuse. At age nineteen MacRae entered a singing contest and won a two-week engagement with the Harry James and Les Brown bands at the New York World's Fair. In 1941 he joined the Millpond Playhouse on Roslyn, Long Island, where he played Deiphobus in *The Trojan Horse,* among other roles. There he met his future wife, Sheila Stephens, who had come from England to escape the Blitz.

Working as a page at the NBC studios in New York City in 1940, MacRae was discovered warbling in the men's room by a member of Horace Heidt's band. As one of Heidt's Musical Knights, he was given solo spots and made a few records. MacRae took over the part of Tommy Arbuckle in *Junior Miss* on Broadway in 1942. While MacRae was touring with Heidt, he and Stephens married (21 May 1941). They had four children: Meredith, Heather, William ("Gar") MacRae, and Robert Bruce. The two eldest went on to have show business careers of their own, and Sheila also made several radio, screen, and stage appearances.

MacRae served in World War II as a lieutenant navigator in the Army Air Forces. On radio, he was the host of the *Teentimers Club* (1946–1947) and starred on the *Gulfspray Show* (1945) and *Texaco Star Theatre* (1947–1948). His next Broadway role was as a singing cop in the 1946 revue *Three to Make Ready*, of which the *New York Journal American* said, "'Barnaby Beach,' sung by MacRae and Althea Elder . . . is worth waiting around for."

MacRae was then signed by Warner Brothers, where he made two nonmusical melodramas, *The Big Punch* (1948) and, with his wife, *Backfire* (1950). He made his singing debut in *Look for the Silver Lining* (1949). In 1950 he played the vaudevillian Tony Pastor in *The Daughter of Rosie O'Grady,* which gave him more songs and a showcase for his romantic charm. He sang two tunes in *The Return of the Frontiersman* (1950). MacRae made four films with Doris Day: *Tea for Two* and *The West Point Story* (both 1950), *On Moonlight Bay* (1951), and *By the Light of the Silvery Moon* (1953). His last films for the studio were *About Face* (1952), *The Desert Song* (1953), and *Three Sailors and a Girl* (1953).

MacRae sought his release from Warner Brothers and set his sights on the part of Curly in the film version of Richard Rodgers and Oscar Hammerstein's *Oklahoma!*. He tested for the role with Shirley Jones, who became his Laurey. *Oklahoma!* (1955) was a success despite the fact that the director, Fred Zinnemann, showed little affinity for musicals.

MacRae asked the Twentieth Century–Fox studio chieftain Darryl F. Zanuck for the part of Billy Bigelow in the film version of *Carousel,* but Zanuck told him the role belonged to Frank Sinatra. "I went down to Dallas to learn the part and play it there," MacRae said later. "I let my hair and sideburns grow. I had a hunch something would happen." When Sinatra bowed out, MacRae was rushed into the movie. Whereas the light and sunny *Oklahoma!* was basically Laurey's story, the more somber *Carousel* (1956) belonged to Billy. MacRae sang gloriously, but as critic David Shipman said, "It sank in a quagmire of bathos."

The Best Things in Life Are Free (1956) was a fanciful biopic about the songwriting team of Buddy DeSylva (MacRae), Lew Brown, and Ray Henderson. The film was a success, and Fox offered MacRae a contract. However, MacRae felt that movie musicals were on their way out and opted to enter television in a big way. This was a move he later said he regretted, but he was correct that the musical genre was declining. MacRae's television success was based as much on his starring role in NBC's *The Railroad Hour*, a popular radio show in which he starred from 1948 to 1954, as it was on his screen career. *The Railroad Hour* offered abridged musicals and operettas and original shows based on literature and biography. The scripts were literate, the music superb.

In 1945 and 1946 MacRae made five records for Musicraft, then signed with Capitol Records in 1947. His biggest single was "So in Love" (1948). His discs were slow, steady sellers, marked by a few hits with Jo Stafford, notably "Whispering Hope" and "Beyond the Sunset." MacRae also recorded several operettas with Dorothy Warenskjold, Dorothy Kirsten, and Lucille Norman, who starred with him on *The Railroad Hour*. In the latter years of his Capitol career his warm voice was at its richest, especially on such songs as "Only Love" and "The Long Hot Summer." In 1966 MacRae brought over forty years of experience to the album *If She Walked into My Life Today,* arguably his best work. He was one of the few pop singers who could invest a melody with emotion, singing of lost love as though his heart were breaking; becoming a bashful suitor; or sending a simple message meant for every girl listening to him. In the 1960s, when Capitol renegotiated its contracts, MacRae, like the other artists, had to sign a per-record deal.

MacRae began his television career starring on *Tune Time* in 1953 as a summer alternate for Eddie Fisher. He occasionally substituted for Ed Sullivan and hosted *The Colgate Comedy Hour* (1954–1955), on which he sang and acted. Kintail Enterprises, operated by MacRae and his wife, produced *The Gordon MacRae Show,* which ran for twenty-five shows in 1956. He was the host for *Lux Video Theatre* (1956–1957) and starred in a musical version of O. Henry's *The Gift of the Magi* (1958). MacRae starred several times on *The Bell Telephone Hour* and was one of the first nonclassical singers to appear on *The Voice of Firestone*. In 1967 MacRae and his first wife divorced. Later that year he married Elizabeth Lambert Schrafft; they had one daughter. Also in 1967 he took over the lead in *I Do! I Do!* on Broadway.

MacRae's last dramatic television appearance was as a hit man in an episode of *McCloud* (1974). He had a small part in the movie *The Pilot* (1979) and was interviewed for a television salute to Rodgers and Hammerstein (1985). By then he was clearly a singer past his prime and not very healthy. He had been a heavy smoker and alcoholic for years, confessing to *Variety* that he was habitually lazy and only worked to support his gambling habit. In 1977 he had to leave a concert in Greenville, South Carolina, because he was too drunk to remember his lyrics. The next year he sought help for his problem at the Independence Center at Lincoln (Nebraska) General Hospital. Lincoln reminded MacRae of his hometown. In 1982 MacRae suffered a stroke that paralyzed his left arm. Although he acknowledged that his voice was no longer what it had been, he continued to perform. Around that time MacRae and his family settled permanently in Lincoln, near Elizabeth's relatives.

MacRae became the honorary chairman of the National Council on Alcoholism in 1983 and made many public appearances on behalf of the council, saying, "When alcohol began to interfere with my family, my home life, and my career, I decided to call it quits." In 1984 Sheila MacRae told the *Boston Globe:* "I think he couldn't handle his success. Gordon . . . hated the confinement of making movies. He really wanted to be an opera star. Gordon couldn't take on that kind of discipline. [Opera star] Robert Merrill was one of Gordon's best friends and he told me he thought my husband had one of the great voices of all time. In opera, you're a god. Gordon would have liked to be a god."

Among MacRae's many films, only *Carousel* and *Oklahoma!* stand out. His movie career never matched his radio and television successes. MacRae's voice was more than a romantic tool. It was robust and virile, stirring followers with "Stout Hearted Men" or tripping merrily through Gilbert and Sullivan's tongue twisters. With the exception of *Carousel,* none of his screen roles mirrored the neurosis of his private life. He was always the sunny boy next door, whether the "door" was on a submarine or a vaudeville stage. Although *The Railroad Hour* was as much escapist family fare as his movies, the show occasionally allowed him to seem more real and more human than his movies did. It was the "acting school" he never attended in real life.

When his film career ended, MacRae said: "What counts is that what you're doing, you're doing well; that you're happy in what you're doing and it's not a chore. Nothing that you like is hard." He died of cancer and pneumonia in Lincoln and was buried in that city. Sheila MacRae said just before he died, "He had a wonderful time when he was here."

★

Bruce R. Leiby, *Gordon MacRae: A Bio-Bibliography* (1991), provides a brief biography and listings of MacRae's career accomplishments. Sheila MacRae with H. Paul Jeffers, *Hollywood Mother of the Year: Sheila MacRae's Own Story* (1992), details the happiness and the horrors of their life together. Information on MacRae is also in Clive Hirschhorn, *The Warner Brothers Story* (1979); Ted Sennett, *Hollywood Musicals* (1981); Ephraim Katz, *The Film Encyclopedia,* 2d ed. (1994); and John Walker, ed., *Halliwell's Filmgoer's Companion* (1997). Obituaries are in the *Chicago Tribune* and *New York Times* (both 25 Jan. 1986).

JUDITH M. KASS

MADDEN, Ray John (*b.* 25 February 1892 in Waseca, Minnesota; *d.* 28 September 1987 in Washington, D.C.), Democratic congressman from Indiana (1943–1977), best known nationally for his stalwart support of policies favorable to organized labor and for his chairmanship of the influential House Rules Committee (1973–1977), which ended decades of control of the committee by Republicans and southern Democrats.

The second of five children of John Madden and Elizabeth (Burns) Madden, Ray Madden was raised in rural Minnesota. He attended the local public schools and Sacred Heart Academy, graduating in 1910. He belonged to a staunchly Democratic farming family and expressed an interest in politics, even as a child. One of his earliest memories was the impression left by hearing the famous orator William Jennings Bryan when the Democratic presidential nominee gave a speech at a nearby community in 1900. Madden was inspired by the candidate's populism and later said that "he was the greatest orator this nation has ever seen. . . . If there was television back in those days, he would have been elected."

Madden went to Omaha, Nebraska, to study law at Creighton University. He received his LL.B. in 1913 and was admitted to the bar that same year. After a few years practicing law in Omaha, he decided to run for the position of municipal judge in 1916. During his campaign, Madden met Woodrow Wilson when the president was campaigning for reelection in Omaha. He recalled later that this was a defining moment in his early career: "The thrill I got out of that as a youngster! I always looked on Woodrow Wilson as the greatest president in this century, outside of FDR possibly." Given his youth and lack of experience, Madden

Ray Madden, Washington, D.C., 1953. UPI/CORBIS-BETTMANN

attributed his judgeship victory in part to an Omaha newspaper photograph showing him in conversation with the president's wife. It was for him, he was fond of saying, one of those "events that happened once in a lifetime."

After serving only a year as municipal judge, he resigned to join the navy when the United States became involved in World War I. After serving at the Great Lakes Naval Training Center north of Chicago, he returned to politics back in Nebraska. In 1922 he successfully managed the campaign of Charles W. Bryan (brother of William Jennings Bryan, the political hero of his youth) for governor of the state. It was his stint in the navy, however, that led Madden to continue his legal and political career in northwest Indiana. While stationed at the Great Lakes Naval Training Center, Madden viewed nearby Gary, Indiana, as a "young, thriving city ideal for a young lawyer to hang out his shingle." He opened his law office in Gary in 1927 and in 1935 was elected as a Democrat to the post of city comptroller. In 1938 he was elected treasurer of Lake County, Indiana, a heavily industrialized region of the state that included the cities of Gary, Hammond, and East Chicago. Four years later, in 1942, he was elected to the first of his seventeen terms as U.S. representative from the First Congressional District of Indiana.

Madden served on four standing committees during his tenure in the House of Representatives. His first assignment was the Post Office and Post Roads Committee. Although not generally considered to be an active committee, Madden used this assignment to push through legislation that gave postal employees their first raise in twenty-one years. Given the prevailing congressional ethic of the time, that freshmen representatives should be seen and not heard, Madden's successful initiative was noted by the party leadership.

After serving on the House Naval Affairs Committee from 1945 to 1946, Madden was able to secure appointment to the House Education and Labor Committee at the beginning of his third term (1947–1948). Given the industrial character of his home district and the union membership of many of his constituents, this was an especially attractive committee assignment. He opposed the Taft-Hartley Act, a bill that weakened labor organizations.

Madden began his long service on the influential House Rules Committee in 1949. He continued his support of labor, and during the steel strike of 1952, he voted against an amendment that would have enjoined President Harry S. Truman to invoke the Taft-Hartley Act to force steelworkers back to work. As chairman of the committee in 1975, he used his influence to eliminate the federal oil depletion allowance, a long-controversial measure that allowed oilmen to avoid paying taxes on the first 27½ percent of their earnings. According to Madden, who saw the measure as an unfair tax break for oil corporations at the expense of the individual taxpayer, elimination of the allowance despite strong pressure for its maintenance was the proudest moment of his thirty-four year career in Congress.

In addition to his service on the standing committees, Madden also gained notoriety for his chairmanship in 1952 of the special congressional committee that investigated the Katyn Forest Massacre during the winter of 1939–1940, during which 15,000 Polish army officials and intellectuals were murdered either by German or Russian forces. The investigation concluded that the evidence regarding Soviet responsibility for the incident be turned over to the United Nations General Assembly.

Madden was defeated in the Democratic primary in 1976 (at the age of eighty-four) by Adam Benjamin, Jr. He retired from Congress, having served longer than any previous U.S. representative from Indiana. He continued to live near Capitol Hill until his fatal heart attack (at the age of ninety-five) in 1987. He is buried at Arlington National Cemetery.

Madden, who never married, remained active and continued to speak out in favor of proposals and policies that were consistent with his populist principles. Thus, for example, he warned against the dangers of unfettered campaign financing and argued for congressional reform. He favored four-year terms for House members and the elimination of the filibuster in the Senate.

Madden was characterized by one of his district's newspapers as "a dyed-in-the-wool New Dealer who championed labor causes and social security throughout his career," but it was his sharp wit and good humor that were most frequently recalled. House colleague Lee Hamilton of Indiana observed that "he had a twinkle in his eye that always seemed to shine through." According to colleagues and others who knew him best, Madden's devotion to his constituency was exemplary. He loved the working class people of his district. "He was unwavering in his loyalty to labor and the cities and was a champion for civil rights and equality-in-education causes."

★

The Ray J. Madden Papers at the Calumet Regional Archives, Indiana University Northwest, contain a substantial collection of Madden's historical papers and files, ranging from speeches and reports to scrapbooks and photographs. James B. Lane, *City of the Century: A History of Gary, Indiana* (1978), provides a discussion of Madden's career in terms of interaction with local officials and politics. George C. Roberts, "A Century of Stability and Turnover in Northwest Indiana Congressional Districts," *Proceedings of the Indiana Academy of the Social Sciences,* vol. 5 (1995), discusses personnel and demographics germane to understanding Indiana's First Congressional District. An obituary is in the *New York Times* (29 Sept. 1987).

THOMAS D. KOTULAK

Cyril Magnin and a badge identifying him as chief of protocol of San Francisco, 1978. TED STRESHINSKY/CORBIS

MAGNIN, Cyril (*b.* 6 July 1899 in San Francisco; *d.* 8 June 1988 in San Francisco), retailing executive.

The son of Joseph Magnin, a merchant, and Charlotte Davis, Magnin was born on Bush Street in San Francisco, where he attended Lowell High School. He began working while still in high school, first as a barker for his uncle's carnival show at Neptune Beach in Alameda, California (for a dollar a day plus carfare), then as a barker for another show, and occasionally in his father's store, Joseph Magnin. From 1919 to 1922 he attended the University of California at Berkeley extension school in San Francisco, studying law. After attending classes during the day, he began working at night for Leon Samuels, a prominent local attorney, with whom he had a long, sustained professional relationship. Magnin left school without a degree and joined his father in managing the store. While he worked primarily in the office, Magnin found he liked selling, especially hosiery and handbags.

Magnin's work in the store soon led to the first of many buying trips. His first trip was motivated by his parents' desire to curtail his interest in a married saleswoman in the hosiery department. During a buying trip in New York, Magnin met the designer Anna Smithline. Coincidentally, they were both about to sail to Europe on the same ship. A year later, on 19 November 1925, they were married; they had three children. Anna Magnin immediately began designing dresses for Joseph Magnin and worked very effectively with her mother-in-law, a skilled milliner.

The contributions of Cyril and Anna to the store were important. Cyril's grandmother, Maryann Magnin, founded San Francisco's premier women's store, I. Magnin (named for her husband, Isaac), in 1877. Joseph Magnin had broken away from I. Magnin after he was passed over for top management and established his own store in 1913. I. Magnin systematically blocked Joseph Magnin's access to suppliers (the I. Magnin line of the family also blocked the Joseph Magnin line from membership in San Francisco's leading clubs and elite social events). Joseph Magnin responded by hiring small manufacturers to produce knockoffs of I. Magnin styles, selling them at a discount. But the Joseph Magnin store always had to struggle to get supplies, and in the years of the Great Depression, it "tiptoed around financial disaster." Indeed, the business was saved largely because Joseph Magnin had built a second business, Donner Factors, which financed manufacturers.

During the 1930s Cyril Magnin grew increasingly disenchanted with the strategy of being a second-rate I. Magnin. He argued that Joseph Magnin should focus entirely on the youth market. In 1937 Joseph tired of the arguments and gave Cyril a free hand, believing it would soon lead to bankruptcy. Cyril immediately eliminated all large sizes;

the store carried only sizes five to fourteen. To his father's amazement, business thrived. In 1940 Cyril Magnin became president of the Joseph Magnin stores, a position he held until 1975. He became chairman of the board in 1952. Anna Magnin died in 1948. On 21 June 1957 he married Lillian Ryan Helwig; they divorced in 1956.

An innovative step taken by Joseph Magnin was to open a store in the thriving suburban community of Palo Alto in 1928. Cyril Magnin recognized the value of bringing stores closer to its best customers; in 1940 he opened a third store, in Reno, Nevada; in 1942, another in San Mateo, California; and in 1946 another in Sacramento, California. By 1960, when the company went public, it had fifteen stores; by 1969 the chain had grown to thirty-two stores. Sales grew apace, to $17 million in 1947 and to $47 million in 1967.

Magnin developed an intriguing philosophy. His stores were "dedicated to trying not just the new but the unheard of." He wanted the stores to be "contemporary, trend-setting, and youthful," to be the "fastest store in the West." Joseph Magnin's was the first store in California to offer pantsuits, textured stockings, paper dresses, and the topless bathing suit. When miniskirts came into fashion, the store had miniskirted saleswomen. When Chanel introduced the straight line in fashion in the 1950s, Magnin's eliminated its belt department overnight. Later, Joseph Magnin's was the first women's specialty store to carry consumer electronics, recognizing the surge of interest among the young in such products.

Magnin aggressively offered credit, often signing up new accounts himself. He also worked at night, calling himself "Mr. Jones," trying to collect on overdue accounts. His advertising was as creative as his sales philosophy. He used color in new ways, bought the "gutter"—the space in a newspaper between two facing pages—for ads, and introduced unique gift boxes every Christmas season. The boxes were so distinctive that they became collector's items, and people would shop at the store simply to acquire one. Magnin's advertising was so influential that in 1970 *Retail Advertising Week* devoted an issue to a special twenty-year retrospective of it, and in 1985 the Fashion Institute of Design organized an exhibition, "The JM Years," in Costa Mesta, California. Magnin delighted in describing the management of his stores as "creative anarchy." Indeed, Joseph Magnin was distinctive for being the first major American retailer to focus exclusively on the youth market (as Bloomingdale's and Neiman Marcus would do later) and to rely on nimble change to accommodate the currents of youth fashion.

The success of the Joseph Magnin stores invited interest from potential buyers. Cyril Magnin insisted he would not consider an offer of less than $50 a share—25 percent more than he actually thought the chain was worth. When the Hawaii-based company Amfac met his price, totaling $30 million, in 1969, he and his family sold. They continued their affiliation with the stores until 1975, but it was an unhappy situation. Amfac was ill-equipped to run a specialty women's retailer and was soon losing money. After several further buyouts, the Joseph Magnin stores went bankrupt and closed in 1985. The same fate befell I. Magnin in 1994.

Magnin was deeply committed to his native city and served it in an extraordinary array of capacities, earning the title of Mr. San Francisco. A street and the major annual award for outstanding achievement in the arts are named in his honor. He chaired the Port Authority for nineteen years, from 1955 to 1974, playing a major role in the development of Fisherman's Wharf and the Embarcadero. He served as chief of protocol from 1964 to 1986, greeting every dignitary to visit the city. He was instrumental in bringing the American Conservatory Theater to the city and was a major fund-raiser for and contributor to the San Francisco Opera. He was also a vigorous supporter of the zany annual stage show, Beach Blanket Babylon, a production in which he himself often performed. He was a director of the city's annual film festival and served from 1969 to 1971 as president of the chamber of commerce. He used his friendship with the Egyptian president Anwar Sadat to bring the King Tut exhibit to San Francisco in 1979 and was instrumental in persuading Avery Brundage to donate his collection of Chinese art for permanent display in San Francisco.

Magnin also was a major fund-raiser for the Democratic party, beginning in 1928, and served on a multiplicity of boards, including as head of the National Conference of Christians and Jews, the March of Dimes National Foundation, and the American Cancer Society. He received more than two dozen awards in ten countries, including 1962 Retailer of the Year, the 1978 Leadership Award of the Fashion Institute for Design and Merchandising, and the 1982 Rodeo Drive Award, and honorary degrees from the University of Pacific, 1967; University of San Francisco, 1978; the American Conservatory Theatre, 1977; and the Academy of Art College, 1979.

Magnin died of a heart attack at University of California Hospital in San Francisco; Mayor Art Agnos ordered the city's flags flown at half-mast in his honor.

★

Cyril Magnin with Cynthia Robins, *Call Me Cyril* (1981), is a well-written, engaging autobiography. See also articles on Magnin in *Newsweek* (23 Oct. 1967); *San-Diego Union-Tribune* (18 Sept. 1984); and *Los Angeles Times* (27 Sept. 1985). An obituary is in the *New York Times* (9 June 1988).

FRED CARSTENSEN

MAGNUSON, Warren Grant (*b.* 12 April 1905 in Moorhead, Minnesota; *d.* 20 May 1989 in Seattle, Washington), U.S. senator for nearly four decades, one of the three most effective legislators from west of the Mississippi in the twentieth century, and primary sponsor of legislation and projects that shaped the environment and quality of life in the Pacific Northwest.

Born out of wedlock, Magnuson was adopted by William Grant and Emma (Anderson) Magnuson, who ran the Nickleplate bar in Moorhead. He was raised in a comfortable middle-class environment with the Magnusons' adopted daughter and educated in the town's public schools. He was an excellent student and a fine high school quarterback with movie-star looks. As a boy Magnuson delivered telegrams for Western Union in Moorhead and across the Red River in Fargo, North Dakota, where he became friends with the Stern family, owners of the Dakota National Bank. Bill Stern, fifteen years his senior, became a lifelong friend and adviser.

After graduating from high school in 1923, Magnuson attended the University of North Dakota, where he pledged a fraternity and made a name as a party boy. Transferring to North Dakota State in Fargo in 1924, he played a year of freshman football. In the summer Magnuson, like most of his peers, worked in the surrounding wheat fields. He dreamed, however, of distant places, moved west to Seattle, and entered the University of Washington in 1925. Undersized for the varsity, he played football as quarterback for the scout team at practice each afternoon against the Husky Eleven—rough and unrewarding sport except for the joy of physical contact. While at Washington he married Eleanor Maddieux, in June 1928. The following year he received a law degree.

Magnuson was recruited into politics while still in law school by A. Scott Bullitt, Washington State's most prominent Democrat, a candidate for governor and a "wet" in the state's battle over legal prohibition of alcohol. After graduation Magnuson became secretary of the Seattle Municipal League and in 1932 he was elected to the state house of representatives. At age twenty-eight Magnuson became floor leader for the nation's first de facto unemployment relief act. Elected King County (Seattle) prosecutor in 1934, Magnuson was a strict enforcer of the Bill of Rights but tolerant of the seaport city's red-light district, which featured gambling and prostitution. Also in 1934, he and his wife divorced. Two years later Magnuson replaced the brilliant, mentally troubled Marion Zioncheck, a college friend, as the Democratic nominee for the U.S. House of Representatives from the state's First Congressional District. He represented the district until 1944, when he was appointed to fill a Senate vacancy from Washington State. He remained a power and a fixture in the Senate until his defeat in 1980.

As noted by friends, there were "several Magnusons." One was Maggie the consummate horse player, beau to a host of Hollywood movie stars—by most common description, a man's man and a ladies' man. He had a strong taste for liquor and poker. Later he became an accomplished amateur artist, and painting almost displaced poker as his main relaxation. The best-known Magnuson was "the senator's senator," the poker-playing companion of Presidents Franklin Roosevelt, Harry Truman, and Lyndon Johnson. Johnson and Magnuson were freshmen congressmen on the House Naval Affairs Committee and friends thereafter, working closely on the 1964 Civil Rights Act and the president's War on Poverty program. Magnuson was one of the first members of Congress to enlist for active military duty at the outset of World War II. Lieutenant Commander Magnuson saw action in the South Pacific on the aircraft carrier *Enterprise* before all members of Congress were recalled to Washington. Magnuson never used his war record for campaign fodder and rarely spoke of it privately.

The congressional Magnuson was a prime mover of legislation, partly because he was a ranking member on the powerful Appropriations and Commerce committees. As important as this status was to success, his personality and way of dealing with colleagues was decisive. Warren, said

Warren G. Magnuson. UNIVERSITY OF WASHINGTON ARCHIVES

Lyndon Johnson, could pass more legislation with a smile than most senators with arm twisting. Virtually all of the federally funded dams on the Snake and Columbia Rivers, the base of the Northwest economy, came from his skills with the federal budget. He was also the sponsor and subsequent patron of the National Institutes of Health; the savior of the Boeing Company for Seattle; and the protector of Puget Sound for marine mammals as well as humans. His consumer protection legislation, including warning labels on cigarettes, raised standards for corporate accountability. He also advocated U.S. recognition of and normalization of relations with China.

In the 1950 elections Senator Joseph McCarthy moved against Democrats he regarded as "soft on communism." Eight Democratic senators fell to his attacks that year. Magnuson was reelected, however, in part because of his past friendship with the Wisconsin senator, a "grand fellow," in Magnuson's description, until he began his anticommunist crusade and "went kinda crazy." Previously, McCarthy and Magnuson drank together and sometimes shared a seaside retreat on the Virginia coast. McCarthy steered clear of Magnuson's 1950 race against Republican Walter Williams, and Magnuson continued to thrive. He also continued to drink, but liquor never impaired his Senate performance.

Magnuson's critics focused on his bachelor ways in private life and on how he earned the means to support this lifestyle. He was a lawyer-lobbyist for Northwest Airlines and the Minneapolis grain company Archer Daniels Midland while a member of Congress, creating conflicts of interest that would not pass muster under later congressional rules. One political opponent campaigned in 1956 on Magnuson's private life, describing it as "absolutely Hollywoodian with guys, dolls, and gangsters." The senator answered by saying, "My mother always said it was better to go around with girls than with boys," or, "Would you want a senator more interested in boys than girls?" In this election Magnuson carried every county in the state. Magnuson's private life was less important to his constituents than his power in bringing home federal largesse. Many years later Vice President Walter Mondale, a friend, described Magnuson's way with the federal budget as "always fair—one half for Washington State, one half for the rest of the nation." Most conspicuously, the Washington "half" included federal funds for the 1962 Seattle World's Fair, the 1974 Spokane World's Fair, Seattle's Pike Place Market, and West Seattle Bridge, but these were economic trinkets compared with the funds he brought home for construction of the Columbia-Snake River dams and for medical research.

Considered a shoo-in for reelection in 1962, Magnuson nearly lost to the Republican candidate, an unknown Lutheran minister. The result was an abrupt change in his congressional priorities and in his private life. He made Jerry Grinstein, a young Seattle attorney, his administrative aide, and on 5 October 1964 he married Jermaine Peralta, a Seattle widow with a young daughter. Grinstein switched Magnuson's attention to laws protecting consumers from fraud, shoddy products, and fly-by-night salesmen. He helped recruit new staffers, most from the University of Washington law school, eager to meet the challenge of a senior, but reinvigorated, senator. The Commerce Committee chaired by Magnuson became an initiator of legislation instead of a processor of wish lists submitted by the administration or the transportation and business lobbies. The staffers were given broad authority. They responded with legislative skill and loyalty. Magnuson's staff, by general consensus, was regarded as the best on Capitol Hill after 1962.

There is some disagreement among the staffers on Magnuson's greatest accomplishments—funding the dams, saving Puget Sound from supertankers, the railroad reorganization act, consumer protection measures, medical research, his steadfast urging for recognition of China. Each of these had enormous impact, but none so much as Title II, the public accommodations section, of the 1964 Civil Rights Act. Magnuson led its passage through the Commerce Committee, past a filibuster by southern senators (several of rank equal to his own), and to final passage. Opponents rightly charged that this measure, making public facilities open to all citizens regardless of race, altered property rights as practiced in the United States since its founding. It also made illegal racial segregation of hotels, barber shops, toilets, restaurants, and water fountains.

Magnuson's most notable failure came in the effort to secure further federal funding for a supersonic transport airplane to be built by Boeing. He teamed with his seatmate from Washington State, Senator Henry Jackson, to make this fight. At the time, 1970–1971, they were regarded as the most powerful legislative team on Capitol Hill, Jackson specializing in national security, Magnuson in domestic affairs. They lost to a Senate majority concerned about the aircraft's environmental impact. A few years later Magnuson himself was defeated in the Republican landslide of 1980. In poor health (he had been diagnosed with diabetes in 1975), he lived in Seattle until his death from congestive heart failure.

At the end of his career Magnuson was as much legend as man, the central figure of a host of political stories and quotes. One of the best, ascribed to the senator as he addressed an environmental advocate, was, "We can't all live in Walden's Pond. Walden only lived there two years." Save for his mentor, House Speaker Sam Rayburn, and his friend Lyndon Johnson, no other legislator from west of the Mississippi could match Magnuson's achievements. The difference in these great legislators, the consumer advocate Ralph Nader would note, was that Magnuson did not boast of his works. He let the record speak for itself, none of which speaks more eloquently of this man of the people than the 1964 Civil Rights Act.

★

Magnuson's papers are in the Manuscripts and University Archives Division of the University of Washington Libraries. There is a Magnuson file at the Lyndon B. Johnson Library in Austin, Texas. Shelby Scates, *Warren E. Magnuson: The Shaping of Twentieth-Century America* (1997), is an all-encompassing account of Magnuson's life and career. An obituary is in the *New York Times* (21 May 1989).

SHELBY SCATES

MALAMUD, Bernard (*b.* 26 April 1914 in Brooklyn, New York; *d.* 18 March 1986 in New York City), novelist and short-story writer widely honored for his dark yet comic fables of Jewish life.

The elder son of an immigrant grocer, Max Malamud, and his theatrically talented wife, Bertha Fidelman, Bernard Malamud absorbed the Gravesend section of Brooklyn as a youngster. "My parents worked late," he explained, "and I was allowed to stay out late and wander in the neighborhood. We skated, sledded, climbed trees and played running games." A trip across the borough to Coney Island provided him with one of his first out-of-the-ordinary encounters. "The ocean," he recalled, "especially at night, moved me."

Bernard Malamud, 1957. DAVID LESS/ARCHIVE PHOTOS

So did literature. Malamud began to take writing seriously at Erasmus Hall High School, where his compositions received high grades and his first stories and sketches appeared in the high school literary magazine. After graduating from Erasmus Hall in 1932, he entered the College of the City of New York, receiving his B.A. degree in 1936. After holding a sequence of temporary factory and sales jobs, with a stint at the U.S. Census Bureau, in 1940 he entered Columbia University, where he received his M.A. degree in literature in 1942 for a thesis on the reception of Thomas Hardy's poetry in America.

On 6 November 1945 Malamud married Ann de Chiara; they had two children, Paul and Janna. During the day he taught at Erasmus Hall; in the evenings he taught at Harlem Evening High School and wrote. Having decided on a shift of scene, he applied for a teaching post in the composition program of the English department at Oregon State College (now Oregon State University) at Corvallis. He was hired in 1949. "New York had lost much of its charm during World War II," Malamud wrote, "and my wife and I and our infant son took off for the Pacific Northwest. . . . Once there, it was a while before I had my bearings. I was overwhelmed by the beauty of Oregon, its vast skies, forests, coastal beaches; and the new life it offered, which I lived as best I could as I reflected on the old" (*The Stories of Bernard Malamud,* 1983, p. viii).

The family remained in Oregon for over a decade, returning east (to Bennington College in Vermont) in 1961. The years of high school teaching helped Malamud develop the rigor necessary for writing his fiction while meeting his academic and domestic obligations. His schedule in Corvallis was regular: composition classes on Mondays, Wednesdays, and Fridays; Tuesdays, Thursdays, Saturdays, and parts of Sunday were given over to the composition of short stories and novels, most of this work done in a World War II Quonset hut. He chafed more at the conditions of his teaching than at his schedule: "I was allowed to teach freshman composition but not literature because I was nakedly without a Ph.D." Whatever the cause of his transformation from teacher who dabbled in fiction to writer who taught for a living, the effect was noticeable. He wrote in his introduction to the 1983 volume of his stories: "One day I began to write seriously: my writing had begun to impress me."

Malamud studied short-story writers extensively, Sherwood Anderson and Anton Chekhov among them. As for subject matter, the move west seemed to have isolated his early life and turned an intense spotlight upon it. "Almost without understanding why," he said, "I was thinking about my father's immigrant life—how he earned his meager living and what he paid for it, and about my mother's, diminished by fear and suffering—as perhaps matter for my fiction. In other words, I had them in mind as I invented the characters who became their fictional counterparts."

In that statement we can hear *The Assistant* in the making. But before the novels came the stories, his first love. The stories, of course, grew out of that same Brooklyn milieu; "almost without understanding why," Malamud had what he needed. By 1950 his stories had appeared in *Partisan Review, Harper's Bazaar,* and *Commentary;* in 1958 he published his first collection, *The Magic Barrel.*

In Davidov the census taker, Feld the shoemaker, Kessler the retired egg candler, Lieb the baker, Salzman the matchmaker, and Manischevitz, a tailor in his fifty-first year "who suffered many reverses and indignities," we meet a memorable group of immigrants with one foot in the Old World, the other foot, sometimes just a toe or two, on American soil. Malamud's characters, in their representative miseries, misunderstandings, and misplaced triumphs, rise into the realm of fantasy—even, at times, allegory.

We see this in *The Natural,* published in 1952, a novel thoroughly American in its attention to the sport of baseball and yet "Old World" in its underlying fealty to myths of antique Europe, from the Grail quest back to the earliest known scenarios of vegetation kings and human sacrifice.

In *The Assistant,* published in 1957, we find a similar blending of Old World and New. In the terseness of its irony, the Malamud style embraces both the naturalness of fiction and our awareness of its artificiality. The immigrant Morris Bober opens his poor grocery store on a November morning. He has barely finished adding up the sales of the day (three cents for a roll, and a $2 purchase on credit) when, Malamud tells us, he looks down the store as if through a long, dark tunnel. "The grocer sighed and waited. Waiting he did poorly. When times were bad time was bad. It died as he waited, stinking in his nose."

Or take the case of "S. Levin, formerly a drunkard," whose tale of recuperation and reconstitution of self Malamud dramatizes in his third novel, *A New Life* (1961). Having bungled his entry into college teaching by behaving like an honorable man in his department and, in his free time, getting entangled in an affair with the wife of his department chairman, Levin seems at the end poised to leave the scene that he first entered in order to create some staying power in himself. "Flight flew in him," Malamud writes. "He wasn't fleeing yet fled, unable to determine whom he was running from, himself or her."

Malamud published a second book of stories in 1963. *Idiots First* harks back to his debut collection with its mixture of significant misfits; equally (in the story with a main character named Fidelman) it prefigures the collection of linked tales to come. There is also the seemingly anomalous "The Jewbird," wherein a talking blackbird that calls itself "Schwartz" flies to the Lower East Side apartment of a Jewish family on the mend from a mother's death; here Malamud the fabulist moves center stage.

From the heights of this sort of allegorical flight Malamud descended into the depths of czarist Russia. *The Fixer,* published in 1966 and based loosely on the historical figure Mendel Beiliss, displays the novelist's full range. *The Fixer* brought Malamud his second National Book Award and the Pulitzer Prize for 1966.

There always is an element of playfulness in Malamud's work, from the fable at the heart of *The Natural* on through the magical realism in the fables such as "The Jewbird," "Angel Levine," and "Talking Horse." In 1969 Malamud brought out *Pictures of Fidelman,* a traveler, artist, quester, and New World stranger in an old land—Italy—whose life and loves form part of an experiment in twentieth-century freedom and awareness unknown to a character such as the Fixer, Yakov Bok. Such freedom declared itself once more in Malamud's 1971 novel *The Tenants,* a fanciful yet brutal depiction of the life-and-death struggle between two writers, one white and one black, in a condemned tenement in New York City.

Malamud by this time was suffering from a heart condition that eventually resulted in his death. In his 1979 novel, *Dubin's Lives,* he focuses on how to depict a life in all its completeness, by means of the story of biographer William Dubin. This thickly textured story embraces both the traditional realism of the modern novel and the "metafictional" mode; it dances a tightrope between the two strategies and puzzled adherents of each. Malamud's last completed novel, the wildly allegorical end-world invention *God's Grace* (1982), in which atomic war has destroyed most of mankind, leaving behind intelligent apes to speak and pray, seemed to confuse critics further. Yet Malamud's persistently inventive reach is still visible in his final work. At his death he left behind the torso of and elaborate notes for a novel he had dubbed "The People." This was to be the story of a Jewish peddler named Yozip—another Easterner migrating westward—who becomes the protector of a tribe of Indians on the wane. It was published in 1989 as *The People and Uncollected Stories.*

In addition to those honors and prizes already cited, Malamud received the Jewish Heritage Award (1976), the Governor's Award of the Vermont Council on the Arts (1979), and the Brandeis Creative Arts Award (1981). He served as president of PEN from 1979 and 1981 and, in 1982, was a fellow of the Center for Advanced Study in the Behavioral Sciences at Palo Alto, California. Having been elected to the National Institute of Arts and Letters in 1964, he received its gold medal for fiction in 1983.

At Malamud's tale-telling best (and, perhaps paradoxically, most modest), the Jew becomes Everyman, and Everyman—as with "the assistant" Frank Alpine—a Jew. One hallmark of the work throughout is this seemingly seamless blend of fact and fantasy—a North American homegrown magic realism that equally obtains in ballpark and island and tenement. There is an insistent linkage of morality and art.

★

Malamud's long-term publisher, Farrar, Straus, and Giroux, produced the omnibus volume *Bernard Malamud: The Complete Stories* in 1998, with an introduction by Robert Giroux. Alan Cheuse and Nicholas Delbanco, eds., *Talking Horse: Bernard Malamud on Life and Work* (1996), provides the most sustained autobiographical overview of the author published to date. Lawrence Lasher, ed., *Conversations with Bernard Malamud* (1991), is a useful compilation of interviews and brief essays and also includes a full chronology. See also Sidney Richman, *Bernard Malamud* (1966); Leslie A. Field and Joyce W. Field, eds., *Bernard Malamud: A Collection of Critical Essays* (1975); and Edward A. Abramson, *Bernard Malamud Revisited* (1993). An obituary is in the *New York Times* (20 Mar. 1986). The Bernard Malamud Society, headquartered at Kansas State University, publishes a semiannual newsletter of items such as bibliographic data, articles, and conference abstracts.

ALAN CHEUSE
NICHOLAS DELBANCO

MALONE, Dumas (*b.* 10 January 1892 in Coldwater, Mississippi; *d.* 27 December 1986 in Charlottesville, Virginia), historian and author of the prize-winning, six-volume biography of Thomas Jefferson.

One of seven children of John W. Malone, a Methodist minister, and Lilian Kemp, a schoolteacher who hoped that all her children would become scholars, Malone graduated with a B.A. degree from Emory College in Atlanta in 1910 and taught school for several years. He entered the Yale Divinity School in 1913 and earned a B.D. degree in 1916. He taught biblical literature at Randolph-Macon Women's College and then served in the Marine Corps during World War I. In 1919 he returned to Yale, where in 1923 he earned a Ph.D. in history. On the advice of Professor Allen Johnson, Malone wrote his dissertation on Thomas Cooper, the Anglo-American friend of Joseph Priestley and Thomas Jefferson.

Malone was appointed in 1923 as associate professor of history at the University of Virginia. On 17 October 1925 he married Elizabeth Gifford; they had two children. Malone soon decided to write a major work on the university's founder, Thomas Jefferson. Before he could do more than sketch an outline, however, he accepted an invitation in 1929 to join Johnson in editing the *Dictionary of American Biography (DAB).* On Johnson's death in 1931 Malone was placed in charge of the project. By 1936 he had seen through to publication twenty large volumes in which over 2,000 scholars contributed more than 13,000 entries. Some critics complained that the choice of subjects was parochial and some of the entries unduly eulogistic. Malone contended that the *DAB* fairly represented "all the varied human elements that have made this composite America" and took pride in the fact that the *DAB* was not a mere compendium of names and dates but a collection of biographies of people who had "lived." He readily acknowledged that different historians would reach different conclusions. Indeed, fifty years after he had written the lengthy *DAB* entry on Jefferson, he revised his interpretation of Jefferson's presidency to reflect his diminished deference to the strictures of the nineteenth-century historian Henry Adams.

In 1935 Malone became director of Harvard University Press, where he was torn between the university administration's demand that the press make a profit and his desire to publish both important scholarly books and books intended for the general public, which he characterized as having "scholarship plus." Neither Malone nor the university enjoyed the discrepancy between the two outlooks, and he resigned in July 1943. With severance pay and a grant from the Rockefeller Foundation, Malone was at last able to begin work on the multivolume biography of Jefferson he had contracted to write for Little, Brown five years earlier. Malone was a member of the History Department of Columbia University from 1945 until 1959, when he returned to the University of Virginia. In 1962 he was named Thomas Jefferson Memorial Foundation biographer in residence there, a post he held until his death.

In 1948 Malone published the first of the six volumes that make up *Jefferson and His Time* (1948–1981). *Jefferson the Virginian* describes Jefferson's youth and his role in promoting American independence up to the time of his departure in 1784 for France. In *Jefferson and the Rights of Men* (1951), Malone described Jefferson's years in France and his first years as secretary of state under George Washington. Jefferson's retirement from that post and his subsequent election to the vice presidency in 1796 and to the presidency four years later are central to *Jefferson and the Ordeal of Liberty* (1962). In *Jefferson the President: First Term, 1801–1805* (1970), Malone attempted to show that Jefferson was "perhaps the most successful" party leader "in presidential history."

In *Jefferson the President: Second Term, 1805–1809* (1974), Malone wrote of Jefferson's frustration at being obliged "to reconcile the irreconcilable" on the American political scene and "to solve the insoluble" in foreign affairs. In 1981 Malone, now in his eighties and nearly blind, completed *The Sage of Monticello,* in which he described Jefferson's wonderfully active "retirement" years between 1809 and 1826.

From the time the first volume was published, Malone's biography was hailed as magisterial, partly because of his unequaled command of primary sources, such as the Jef-

Dumas Malone. BY PERMISSION OF THE UNIVERSITY OF VIRGINIA NEWS SERVICES

ferson papers, which were slowly being collected and published by Princeton University Press, but even more because of Malone's stately prose and extraordinary comprehensiveness. He had been convinced, at least since his graduate school years, that Jefferson was the most interesting of the founding fathers. But Malone's respect for Jefferson was not idolatrous, and he sedulously examined not only the gentle criticisms made by friends such as James Madison but also the scabrous attacks of political enemies such as James Callender. He made no secret of his sadness when obliged to adduce illustrations of Jefferson's financial improvidence or proclivity for devious, partisan maneuvers.

Malone readily acknowledged that every generation judges the past by its own criteria, but he was unprepared for the shift in scholarly sensibilities over the fifty years from the time he envisioned his biography to the time of its completion. To most historians in the 1920s, Jefferson seemed the peerless founding father, rational and freedom-loving. To many historians who came of age in the 1960s and 1970s, however, Jefferson seemed "a racist, logocentric representative of a discredited patriarchy that exploited women, workers, and people of color" (Shuffelton, p. 297). Scholars with this outlook were not persuaded by Malone's insistence that Jefferson could only be understood and so largely admired in the context of his times.

Nor were these readers completely satisfied with Malone's unwillingness to plumb the complications of Jefferson's personality, particularly the seeming contradiction between the strong passions often manifest in his personal letters and the cool detachment and reasonableness of his public demeanor. Malone's "verdict" that Jefferson could not have been the father of the children of his house slave Sally Hemings was less persuasive than it might have been had Malone been more willing to explore the inner character of his elusive hero. To do so would have violated Malone's conservative understanding of the biographer's proper role.

Malone's volumes won him the Jefferson Medal from the University of Virginia in 1964 for inspiring "those high ideals for the advancement of which Mr. Jefferson founded the University"; a Pulitzer Prize in 1975; the Medal of Freedom from President Ronald Reagan in 1983; and the Bruce Catton prize in 1984 from the Society of American Historians for his contributions over a long lifetime to the writing of American history. Malone died of a heart attack in Charlottesville, Virginia, where he was buried.

★

Malone's papers are in Special Collections, Alderman Library, University of Virginia. Included is his unfinished autobiographical memoir, "My Long Journey with Mr. Jefferson." Chapter four of Max Hall, *Harvard University Press: A History* (1986), deals with Malone's administration. Malone's onetime colleague, the Jefferson scholar Merrill D. Peterson, wrote the perceptive article "Dumas Malone: An Appreciation," *William and Mary Quarterly,* 3d ser., 45 (Apr. 1988): 237–252. See also Frank Shuffelton, "Being Definitive: Jefferson Biography Under the Shadow of Dumas Malone," *Biography* 18 (fall 1995): 291–304. An obituary is in the *New York Times* (28 Dec. 1986). Malone's memoir in the Oral History Collection, Columbia University, discusses his work on the *DAB*. The National AudioVisual Center of the General Services Administration recorded a nostalgic interview with Malone in his last years, *Dumas Malone: A Journey with Mr. Jefferson* (1983).

ROBERT D. CROSS

MAMOULIAN, Rouben Zachary (*b.* 8 October 1897 in Tiflis, Russia [present-day Tbilisi, Georgia]; *d.* 4 December 1987 in Woodland Hills, California), film and stage director whose innovative cinematic techniques had enormous impact on the early years of sound film; he was responsible for directing several of the landmark stage productions of the 1930s and 1940s and also some of the most memorable movies of the early sound era.

Born in the Russian province of Georgia, in the Caucasus Mountains, Mamoulian was of Armenian descent. His father, Zachary Mamoulian, was a bank president, and his mother, Virginia Kalantarian, was the director of the Armenian theater in Tiflis. As a young man Mamoulian studied in schools in Tiflis and Paris and at the University of Moscow, where he earned a law degree. In the evenings he studied acting, playwriting, and directing at the Moscow Art Theater under Eugene Vachtangov, a disciple of Stanislavsky. After directing and acting in plays in Tiflis, Mamoulian went to London in 1920, where he finally made his debut as a director in 1922.

In 1923 Mamoulian accepted the invitation of George Eastman, head of the Eastman Kodak Company, to come to Rochester, New York, to stage operas, operettas, and musicals at the Eastman Theater, which he did for three years.

Rouben Mamoulian, 1960. LONDON DAILY EXPRESS/ARCHIVE PHOTOS

At the same time he organized and became the first director of the Eastman Theater School. Eager to make his mark on Broadway, Mamoulian moved to New York City, where he was hired as a teacher at the Theater Guild's school and also staged a number of productions. His first major success came in 1927, when he directed the Guild's production of Dorothy and DuBose Heyward's all-black folk play *Porgy,* which incorporated many of his bold ideas about staging and the use of lighting and design for dramatic effect. Eight years later he directed George Gershwin's landmark musical adaptation, *Porgy and Bess.*

From 1928 to 1930 Mamoulian directed eleven plays, including Eugene O'Neill's *Marco Millions* and Ivan Turgenev's *A Month in the Country.* During this period he also decided to enter the motion picture world, making his auspicious debut as a film director with the movie *Applause* (1929). Filmed at Paramount's studio in Astoria, Queens, in New York City, it starred Helen Morgan as an aging, blowsy burlesque queen who sacrifices herself for her convent-bred daughter. Mamoulian's use of a mobile camera and his innovative sound techniques, especially a double soundtrack, turned a maudlin story into a compelling drama.

Mamoulian's subsequent films were also innovative in many ways. *City Streets* (1931), starring Gary Cooper and Sylvia Sidney, was a gangster movie with striking directorial touches, such as subjective sound, rhythmic cutting, and textural lighting. His adaptation of *Dr. Jekyll and Mr. Hyde* (1932) remains the best version of Robert Louis Stevenson's novella; audiences were startled by the sequence in which the benevolent Dr. Jekyll (Fredric March) is transformed on camera into the evil Mr. Hyde. The enchanting musical *Love Me Tonight* (1932) is probably the greatest film directed by Mamoulian. A witty, stylish tale of the romance between a jaunty Parisian tailor (Maurice Chevalier) and a love-starved princess (Jeanette MacDonald), the film expanded the boundaries of the movie musical by conceiving the material entirely in musical terms. The film is studded with exhilarating sequences, especially one in which the Rodgers-and-Hart song "Isn't It Romantic?" moves from one person or group to another, finally linking Maurice to Princess Jeanette musically, even before they meet.

After directing Marlene Dietrich in *Song of Songs* (1933), Mamoulian accepted the challenge of directing another imported screen goddess, Greta Garbo, in *Queen Christina* (1933). Garbo excelled as the seventeenth-century Swedish queen who renounces the throne out of love for a Spanish envoy (John Gilbert). In the famous ending, Christina stares enigmatically at an uncertain future from the bow of a ship carrying her dead lover. Mamoulian said he told her, "I want your face to be a blank sheet of paper. I want the writing to be done by every member of the audience." Mamoulian followed *Queen Christina* with such films as *Becky Sharp* (1935), derived from William M. Thackeray's novel

Vanity Fair (1848) and the first feature film to be made in the three-strip Technicolor process, and *The Gay Desperado* (1936), a whimsical operetta that won him the New York Film Critics Award as best director. In December 1935 Mamoulian joined other notable directors in forming the Screen Directors Guild. He was a board member of the Guild in most years through 1958, and served as first vice president for four terms.

Although Mamoulian's subsequent films were not as successful as his earlier efforts, they showed unmistakable signs of his cinematic skill. The musical *High, Wide, and Handsome* (1937) combined Jerome Kern songs with a vigorous tale of Western farmer-prospectors and their conflict with railroad tycoons. *Golden Boy* (1939) adapted Clifford Odets's Broadway drama concerning a young man, played by William Holden, torn between the career choices of prizefighter or violinist. *The Mark of Zorro* (1940), a lively remake of the silent Douglas Fairbanks swashbuckler, starred Tyrone Power as the dashing masked bandit bent on eliminating Spanish tyranny. Best of all was Mamoulian's 1941 remake of the 1922 Rudolph Valentino bullfighting drama *Blood and Sand,* with Tyrone Power as the ill-fated matador. This film's stunning color photography received an Academy Award.

During the 1940s Mamoulian had much greater success in the theater than in motion pictures. In 1943 he came to New York to direct a new Broadway musical, *Oklahoma!* At first there was little hope for this Richard Rodgers–Oscar Hammerstein II adaptation of Lynn Riggs's folk play *Green Grow the Lilacs.* But its combination of simple story, lilting songs, and sunny Americana delighted audiences and critics, and its integration of all musical elements into a seamless whole revolutionized American musical theater. *Oklahoma!* ran for 2,248 performances over five and one-half years. In 1945 Mamoulian directed a second Rodgers and Hammerstein hit, *Carousel,* which transferred Ferenc Molnar's play *Liliom* to a nineteenth-century New England setting. On 12 February 1945 he married Azadia Newman, a portrait painter; they had no children. In 1946 Mamoulian scored a moderate hit on Broadway with his direction of *St. Louis Woman.*

In Hollywood, meanwhile, Mamoulian's disagreements with Darryl F. Zanuck forced the director to resign from the mystery melodrama *Laura* (1944), which was reassigned to Otto Preminger. He directed *Summer Holiday* (1947), a musical adaptation of Eugene O'Neill's nostalgic comedy *Ah, Wilderness!* Although it received a mixed reception, it contains several diverting sequences, especially an Independence Day picnic in which Mamoulian uses color and movement with delightful results.

Back in the Broadway theater Mamoulian directed several more productions, most notably *Lost in the Stars,* a 1949 adaptation by Maxwell Anderson and Kurt Weill of Alan Paton's novel *Cry, the Beloved Country* (1948). In the early 1950s he staged new productions of *Oklahoma!* and *Carousel* and also directed one last film, *Silk Stockings* (1957), a musical version of *Ninotchka,* MGM's 1939 comedy vehicle for Greta Garbo. (The stage version had appeared on Broadway in 1955.)

Mamoulian's last two film experiences were unfortunate. In 1958 Samuel Goldwyn replaced him with Otto Preminger to direct *Porgy and Bess* (1959). Then, in 1961, after many months of work, he resigned as director of *Cleopatra* (1963), which was reassigned to Joseph L. Mankiewicz. During his last years, however, Mamoulian did not lack for honors from his peers. In 1982 he received the prestigious D. W. Griffith Award from the Screen Directors Guild. In February 1986 he accepted two awards of excellence from the Film Advisory Board, one in recognition of his outstanding career-long achievement and the other honoring the Screen Directors Guild on its fiftieth anniversary. Mamoulian died of natural causes.

In the course of an interview for *American Film* in 1983, Mamoulian reiterated the principles on which he had built his career in films and the theater. In doing so, he provided his own eloquent epitaph:

> We must all strive to elevate the quality of motion pictures. We must affirm and insist that the ultimate goal of a film, no matter what subject matter it deals with, is to add to the beauty and goodness of life, to the dignity of human beings, and to our faith in a better future.

★

Tom Milne, *Rouben Mamoulian* (1969), provides an account of Mamoulian's film career. Interviews with Mamoulian appear in Andrew Sarris, ed., *Interviews with Film Directors* (1967); Charles Higham and Joel Greenberg, eds., *The Celluloid Muse* (1969); and "Dialogue on Film: Rouben Mamoulian," *American Film* (Jan.-Feb. 1983). An article by Ken Hanke in *Films in Review* (Aug.-Sept. 1988), contains a close analysis of *Love Me Tonight.* Obituaries are in the *New York Times* (6 Dec. 1987) and *Variety* (9 Dec. 1987).

TED SENNETT

MANNES, Marya (*b.* 14 November 1904 in New York City; *d.* 13 September 1990 in San Francisco, California), essayist, journalist, and social critic known especially for her autobiography and her commentary.

Mannes was the daughter of David Mannes, a violinist and concertmaster of the New York Symphony Orchestra, and Clara Damrosch, a pianist and cofounder with her husband of the Mannes College of Music. Mannes grew up a tomboy, dramatic and emotional, with a compulsive need to write from the age of six. She had one brother, Leopold, a piano prodigy, who later created Kodachrome color film

Marya Mannes, 1968. UPI/CORBIS-BETTMANN

with Leo Godowsky, Jr., in 1935. "I found the lives led in the homes of middle-class schoolmates not only abnormal but boring. No talk, no music, no books, no funny friends, no games," Mannes recalled in her autobiography, *Out of My Time* (1971).

In 1912 Mannes went to study at Miss Veltin's School for Girls, not far from her family's Manhattan apartment. She studied French and English, classical literature, Latin, and European history. Her graduation in 1923, capped by election as class valedictorian, ended her formal education. A social rebel from an early age, she chose not to attend college, instead going to England in the fall of 1923 to write plays and take sculpture lessons for a year. During a rendezvous with her family on the Italian Riviera in June 1924, she met and became friends with F. Scott Fitzgerald and his wife, Zelda.

In the summer of 1925 her play *Foul Is Fair,* a modernization of *Macbeth,* was performed in Woodstock, New York. The beautiful Mannes later wrote that she found men a "marvelous distraction," but she learned to hide her seriousness and candor, considering them barriers to relationships with most men. In 1926, at age twenty-one, she married the scenic designer Jo Mielziner; they had no children. He was devastated in 1930 by her decision to divorce, and Mannes concluded that she should never marry again, largely because of her independent nature and her needs as a writer.

Her first professional publication was in *Creative Art* magazine, and she eventually contributed a regular column, "News of the Month." Mannes's play *Cafe* was a flop on Broadway in 1930. Her freelance work included reviewing plays for the *New Republic.* One of her short stories was published by *Harper's* in 1932. In 1933, seeking a more stable income, she became a copywriter for *Vogue* and was quickly promoted to assistant feature editor, then feature editor.

In the spring of 1936, she left *Vogue* and went to live in Florence, Italy, with Richard A. Blow, a painter. They married in 1936. She returned briefly to New York City in the fall of 1938 for the birth of their only child. In August 1939, with war imminent, they returned to New York. Mannes spent the next two years sculpting portraits, a period she described as "an escape and a self-indulgence." She and Blow divorced in 1943.

From 1940 to 1944, Mannes was an intelligence analyst for the Office of Strategic Services. In June 1944 she was sent to Portugal and Spain as a spy, with her cover that of a correspondent for the *New Yorker,* for which she wrote *Letters from Madrid and Lisbon.* Back in New York, she continued freelance writing and narrated the This Is America documentary series for RKO-Pathé. She went abroad for *Vogue* and traveled in Italy; she also went to Jerusalem and Palestine and wrote for the *New Yorker.*

Mannes served as feature editor for *Glamour* for one year, leaving in 1947 to write a novel, *Message from a Stranger* (1948). It received mixed reviews but proved popular, captivating readers with a notion of immortality in which the dead resume their conscious identities at those moments when the living think of them. The novel ultimately sold about 230,000 copies.

In 1948 Mannes married Christopher Clarkson, a British pilot and diplomat; the couple lived for four years in Washington, D.C. After yet another return to New York, in 1952, Mannes joined the *Reporter,* a liberal fortnightly. In addition to freelance work, she wrote regularly for the *Reporter* as essayist, reporter, television and theater critic, and contributor of satiric doggerel under the pen name "Sec." Mannes did much of her best work during this period, which ended in 1963 when she left the magazine over a disagreement with the editor about his support of the Vietnam War.

She attracted critical attention with her 1958 book, *More in Anger,* a collection of short essays critical of social trends, which was compiled largely from her pieces for the *Reporter.* Her satirical poems were published as *Subverse: Rhymes for Our Times* (1959). She wrote a paean to her beloved New

York, *The New York I Know* (1961), and three years later published a collection of her essays and commentary, *But Will It Sell* (1964). Mannes's novel *They* (1968) is a cautionary tale about a totalitarian state that evolves out of the public's fear of nuclear war and the fear of radical change—fear that brings on the war by giving power to reactionary leaders. In this society, old people are segregated and their cultural heritage of documents and works of art is confiscated and placed in vaults to "protect" it from destruction. The book was made into a television movie.

Mannes appeared on a variety of television shows as a commentator and interviewer in the late 1950s and early 1960s. "Her sustained acerbity is one of the attractive adornments of contemporary criticism," Jack Gould, a television critic for the *New York Times,* wrote in 1961. John Leonard called her a "good reactionary. She sympathizes with the folk singers and the flower children. She is against the war. . . . She believes in the body, the senses, animals, nature, love. But she is not willing to buy righteousness or intolerance from any source."

Her third marriage ended in divorce in 1966. Her book *Uncoupling: The Art of Coming Apart* (1973), written with Norman Sheresky, is a divorce manual and a cold-eyed look at marriage, an institution Mannes felt ill serves most people. Her book *Last Rights* (1974) is an argument in favor of euthanasia and living wills. After living most of her life in New York City, Mannes died in San Francisco after a series of strokes.

Mannes did not consider herself a "real" journalist, because she did not pursue facts single-mindedly enough, and indeed she was more noted as a commentator and for her ability to understand trends and issues. "Timing and arrogance are decisive factors in the successful use of talent," she once wrote, adding that her own timing was poor—she was too far ahead of the women's movement, for example—and that she never developed thick enough skin for her ego to be truly armored.

Mannes's nonfiction is outstanding, especially her essays. Her autobiographical *Out of My Time* is an intriguing study of an original and talented mind coming to terms with the world. Running through the book was her belief in "human duality," which holds that each person is composed of both male and female components, the proportion varying widely.

★

Mannes's final drafts and many unpublished writings, including five novels and sixteen plays, are at Boston University. David Mannes, *Music Is My Faith* (1938), originally written for his children, tells a remarkable life story and gives insight into his daughter. Robert Mottley, ed. *The Best of Marya Mannes* (1986), is an anthology of her essays, poems, journalism, reviews, and excerpted portions of her books and is an excellent introduction to Mannes and her work. An obituary is in the *New York Times* (15 Sept. 1990).

RICHARD GILBERT

MANNING, Timothy (*b.* 14 November 1909 in Ballingeary, County Cork, Ireland; *d.* 23 June 1989 in Los Angeles, California), Roman Catholic cardinal who served as archbishop of Los Angeles from 1970 to 1985.

Born to Cornelius Manning and Margaret Cronin, Timothy and his three siblings grew up in rural County Cork. His father was a blacksmith and his mother a housewife. Their financial resources were limited. Manning began his schooling in 1915 at the local National School; in 1922 he enrolled at the Christian Brothers' school in County Cork. A year later he entered Mungret College, a Limerick secondary school operated by the Jesuits, thus commencing his studies for the priesthood.

In 1928 Manning answered an appeal for priests by what was then the combined diocese of Los Angeles and San Diego, joining the student body at Saint Patrick's Seminary in Menlo Park, California. Manning thought of himself as a missionary, and was particularly concerned for Latinos who came to the area, which he called "the rim of the world," in large numbers in the 1960s.

On 16 June 1934 Manning was ordained to the priesthood by Bishop John J. Cantwell at Saint Vibiana's Cathedral in Los Angeles. His first assignment was as curate at Immaculate Conception Church, also in Los Angeles, where he served briefly before being sent to Rome the following year for studies in canon law at the Pontifical Gregorian University. In 1938 he received a doctorate. Manning returned to California and was appointed secretary to Archbishop Cantwell, a post he held for eight years. Meanwhile, in 1943, he was named a papal chamberlain by Pope Pius XII. Two years later the pope promoted him to the domestic prelacy. On 14 January 1944 he became a U.S. citizen.

In 1946 Manning was appointed auxiliary bishop of Los Angeles and titular bishop of Lesvi, Italy. He was ordained to the episcopacy on 15 October by Bishop Joseph T. McGucken. When Francis A. McIntyre of New York was named archbishop of Los Angeles in 1948, Manning became chancellor. From 1953 to 1967 he also served as pastor of Saint Gregory's, a parish four miles west of Los Angeles. He became vicar general of the archdiocese in 1955.

During this time, Archbishop McIntyre began a massive parish and school building program. Manning, known for his administrative abilities, was involved in this effort. Because of the postwar growth in population in California, the Vatican created several new dioceses in the state. Manning was named first bishop of the newly created diocese of Fresno in 1967. He was installed by Archbishop Luigi

Cardinal Timothy Manning at a press conference in Los Angeles, 29 September 1978, the day after the death of Pope John Paul I. UPI/CORBIS-BETTMANN

Raimondi, the apostolic delegate, on 15 December. During his tenure, Manning created a diocesan housing commission, directed a task force to raise funds for inner-city minorities, and established a priest's senate. Manning also started four new parishes and five new missions during his eighteen-month stay in Fresno.

Throughout his career, Manning remained committed to social justice. He was, for instance, actively involved in the struggle of farmworkers, led by Cesar Chavez, to improve their working conditions and to form a union. He headed a bishop's committee that helped resolve the impasse between the vineyard owners and the migrant pickers in the Delano labor dispute in the late 1960s. He also counseled young men during the Vietnam War on their right to be conscientious objectors based on their religious convictions.

In August 1969 Manning returned to Los Angeles as coadjutor bishop to James Francis Cardinal McIntyre. He was also vicar general and pastor of St. Brendan's Church. Upon Cardinal McIntyre's retirement in January 1970, Manning became archbishop of Los Angeles, which at the time included Los Angeles, Orange, Ventura, and Santa Barbara counties. He resided at Saint Vibiana's Cathedral, in one of the city's poor sections, until his retirement fifteen years later.

In 1971 Manning made a pilgrimage to the shrine of Our Lady of Guadalupe in Mexico, where in his words, "it all began for California." He thanked "the Mexican people for their role in bedrocking the faith" along the Pacific coast. That year, too, he was elected president of the newly created California Catholic Conference.

While en route to the archdiocesan Lay Mission Helpers in Africa in early 1973, Manning received word that Pope Paul VI had named him to the Sacred College of Cardinals. He was installed on 5 March 1973. Cardinal Manning soon formed a priest's senate in the archdiocese, a priest's personnel board, and an interparochial council. He was an enthusiastic proponent of the Cursillo movement, a program of spiritual renewal for laypeople, and a promoter of ecumenism. Locally, the Catholic church of Los Angeles, like the American church as a whole, was undergoing changes following the reforms of the Second Vatican Council. Cardinal Manning responded to the tensions and divisions caused by these changes in a conciliatory manner. With his willingness to listen and his many pastoral visits, he brought calm to the archdiocese, which, by the time of his retirement in 1985, was the largest archdiocese in the United States.

In 1983 Manning authorized the formation of the Immigration and Citizenship Department of the Catholic Welfare Bureau. He called for an end to the deportation of Salvadoran refugees who had fled their civil war–ridden homeland. He vigorously continued to support the church's teaching on social justice and abortion.

A man oriented toward public interaction, Manning did not seek to play a prominent role in the affairs of the American Catholic hierarchy. He was a popular speaker and an eloquent preacher. He served the civil community as a member of the Los Angeles Library Commission and as director for El Pueblo de Los Angeles commission.

His writings are few, but include *Clerical Education in Major Seminaries: Its Nature and Application* (1946), a treatise on the *Grey Ox,* as well as collections of homilies, including *Days of Change, Years of Challenge* (1987); *Times of Tension, Moments of Grace* 1990); and *Hours of Consecration, Minutes of Prayer* (1990).

After his retirement Manning lived at Holy Family Parish in South Pasadena, California. He died of cancer. Manning is buried at Calvary Cemetery in Los Angeles. His successor, Roger Cardinal Mahony, remembered him for "his personal spirituality, the generosity of his love and charity, and the simplicity of his humble soul." Pope John Paul II praised him for his "outstanding priestly virtues and his renowned preaching."

★

A man known for his pastoral abilities rather than for his scholarly interests, Manning wrote no major works. His personal papers are in the Archival Center of the Archdiocese of Los Angeles, Mission Hills, California. No biography has been written. Obituaries are in the *New York Times* and the *Los Angeles Times* (both 24 June 1989).

GEOFFREY GNEUHS

MAPPLETHORPE, Robert (*b.* 4 November 1946 in New York City; *d.* 9 March 1989 in Boston, Massachusetts), controversial photographer whose homoerotic pictures ignited a fierce battle over federal funding of "objectionable art."

Mapplethorpe was the son of Harry Mapplethorpe, an electrical engineer, and Joan Maxey, a homemaker, and described his childhood as "disgustingly normal." One of six children, he grew up in the middle-class neighborhood of Floral Park in the borough of Queens. "It was a good place to come from," Mapplethorpe said, "in that it was a good place to leave." He was reared in a Roman Catholic family in the shadow of his older brother, Richard, who was handsome, athletic, and clearly his father's favorite. Gawky and uncoordinated, Mapplethorpe played on his pogo stick and made jewelry for his mother. Most people in the neighborhood considered him a little "weird." He was attracted to the "magic and mystery" of the Catholic faith, and his parish priest encouraged him to draw pictures of Christ and the Blessed Mother. His creativity gave him a sense of purpose and made him feel better about himself. By the time he graduated from Martin Van Buren High School in 1963, he knew he wanted to be an artist.

During the summer of 1963 he worked as a messenger in Manhattan, where he became intrigued by the gay magazines he found in Times Square. They gave him a "powerful feeling in his stomach," yet he still could not admit the possibility that he might be homosexual. Mapplethorpe was desperate to please his father, who was firmly against his son becoming an artist, and they struck a compromise. Mapplethorpe would major in advertising design at Pratt Institute in Brooklyn so he could learn illustration and typography—skills that would help him get a job. Under pressure from his father Mapplethorpe joined the Reserve Officers Training Corps and pledged the Pershing Rifles, ROTC's military honor society, of which his brother Richard was a member.

In 1966 Mapplethorpe took his first LSD trip while working at a Catholic boy's camp in Delaware. He claimed it changed his life by opening up his senses, and he began searching for inspiration in the dreamlike eroticism of such artists as Hieronymus Bosch and Egon Schiele. He had already switched his major to the far less practical graphic arts program, and, in the spring of 1967, he purposely failed his U.S. Army physical by taking acid beforehand. No longer a member of ROTC, he let his hair grow past his collarbone. His father, angry at his son's appearance and the fact that he would not graduate with his class because he had switched majors, refused to pay Mapplethorpe's tuition thereafter.

In the summer of 1967, Mapplethorpe became involved with Patti Smith, a punk rock singer and an aspiring poet and artist. Both suffered many of the same problems concerning their parents and their sexual identities and they became inseparable. The two shared an apartment in Brooklyn, first on Waverly Avenue then on Hall Street. Two years later, they moved to Manhattan to the Chelsea Hotel. "My life began in the summer of 1969," Mapplethorpe said. "Before that I didn't exist." Mapplethorpe and Smith became regulars at Max's Kansas City, the celebrated bar and restaurant that Andy Warhol described as the "place where Pop art met Pop life." Mapplethorpe naively hoped to befriend Warhol and gain entrance to his inner circle. That never happened, although Mapplethorpe managed to meet other people at Max's who would later help him in his career. He described this part of his life as "gaining connections."

During the next two years, Mapplethorpe and Smith lived at the Chelsea and then in a loft down the street at 206 West 23rd Street. He began frequenting the gay S&M (sadomasochist) clubs, and Smith took up with the poet Jim Carroll and the playwright Sam Shepard. They were going in different directions, but both were united in their fierce desire for fame. Mapplethorpe, however, had no idea

Robert Mapplethorpe. SELF-PORTRAIT, 1986. COPYRIGHT © 1986 THE ESTATE OF ROBERT MAPPLETHORPE.

how he would achieve his goal and his early art was raw and undisciplined. He experimented with making jewelry, collages, and assemblages, all of which were heavily influenced by his nightly forays into the S&M clubs. He loved the S&M imagery—the black leather, motorcycle caps, knee-high leather boots—because it provided him with a "masculine" notion of homosexuality.

Mapplethorpe's career received a major boost when he became involved with Samuel Jones Wagstaff, Jr., a former curator at the Detroit Institute of Art and a member of an old New York family. Wagstaff bought him a loft near Soho and offered to take care of him. Intense and passionate about art and eager to play Svengali, Wagstaff became Mapplethorpe's patron and his most fervent promoter. Mapplethorpe had already been experimenting with Polaroid photography, but when Wagstaff decided to begin collecting photographs, the two men began searching for vintage photographs together. Little by little, Mapplethorpe began focusing almost exclusively on taking pictures.

In January 1973 Mapplethorpe had his first photography show at the Light Gallery in New York City, revealing the three motifs that would preoccupy him for the rest of his life: portraits, flowers, and homoeroticism. It was not until February 1977, when he had dual shows at the Holly Solomon Gallery and at the Kitchen, that he achieved instant notoriety as the art world's enfant terrible. The photographs at the Solomon Gallery comprised an eclectic mix of portraits, from Princess Margaret to Arnold Schwarzenegger, while the pictures at the Kitchen were of men handcuffed, blindfolded, and hog-tied. Mapplethorpe's pictures in the S&M milieu shocked some viewers as vicious and terrifying.

Mapplethorpe's S&M period reached a peak in 1978, when he produced thirteen graphic images that were later packaged and sold as the *X Portfolio*. The pictures included scenes of bodily mutilation and were so sexually explicit that Mapplethorpe did not know how he could top them. He had also grown bored with what he called "the same old S&M schtick" and wanted to diversify. In 1979 he began a photographic collaboration with bodybuilder Lisa Lyon that would lead to the book *Lady*. At the same time, he switched his creative focus from the largely white S&M subculture to the world of working-class black men. They became his obsession. When Mapplethorpe's nude pictures of black men first began appearing in his shows, viewers were not sure if he was exploiting or glorifying them, but the controversy only added to his growing legend.

By art photography standards, Mapplethorpe's career was an enviable one. Between 1981 and 1983, he had thirty-two shows at galleries all over the world. On 4 November 1983 he celebrated his thirty-seventh birthday with his biggest career triumph to date: the opening of a thirteen-year retrospective of his work at the Institute of Contemporary Art in London. Lines formed outside the museum to see the show. While the exhibit represented a cross-section of his work, it was Mapplethorpe's S&M pictures that attracted the crowds.

Unwittingly, Mapplethorpe had become the chronicler of a world that was dying out. AIDS had given his homoerotic photographs a broader relevance, and by 1985 he had become a considerably more respectable figure than the one who had first terrorized the art world. In November, Twelvetrees Press published *Certain People: A Book of Portraits*. It was mentioned in the *New York Times Book Review* as a possible gift idea for Christmas.

Yet Mapplethorpe could not escape the specter of death. His mother was very sick with emphysema in 1985, and in August 1986 his brother Richard died of lung and brain cancer. For years Mapplethorpe had tried to push AIDS out of his mind, but he was suffering from a bad bronchial infection. In October 1986, friends persuaded him to check into Beth Israel Hospital in Manhattan, where he was diagnosed with AIDS-related pneumonia. Two months later, in January 1987, Sam Wagstaff, his former lover and patron, died of complications from AIDS. Mapplethorpe inherited more than $7 million from the Wagstaff estate.

Contrary to Mapplethorpe's fears that AIDS would ruin his career, the disease only served to increase his sales potential. People purchased his photographs in anticipation of his demise. Another reason for this popularity was that his newer work was more obviously decorative. It was something people could hang on their walls. AIDS had diminished his sexual desire, and he had begun to photograph classical busts and pieces of statuary. Having once excelled at transforming his models into statues, he now attempted to breathe life into stone.

In July 1988 Mapplethorpe was admitted to St. Vincent's Hospital in Manhattan, where he was diagnosed with a bacterial infection that his doctor deemed "an end-stage disease." His friends did not think he would leave the hospital, but on 27 July he surprised everybody by appearing at the Whitney Museum for a major retrospective of his work. In December another Mapplethorpe career retrospective, titled "The Perfect Moment," opened at the Institute of Contemporary Art in Philadelphia. He was too ill to attend and died three months later at the Deaconness Hospital in Boston.

Mapplethorpe became even better known after his death, when in June 1989 the Corcoran Gallery of Art in Washington, D.C., canceled "The Perfect Moment." It triggered a national debate on whether federal funds should be used to subsidize "obscene or indecent art." When the exhibition arrived in Cincinnati a year later, the Contemporary Arts Center and its director were ordered to stand trial on obscenity charges—the first time a gallery in the United States faced prosecution for the material it displayed.

The question of whether Mapplethorpe was an important artist or a mediocre one has always been clouded by larger issues—the relationship between photography and art, for example, or between art and pornography. Certainly he will always be remembered for his pictures of graphic sexuality; he was a chronicler of the 1970s and 1980s, both in his sex pictures and in his numerous portraits of prominent figures in the arts and society. His great accomplishment was taking a classical approach to a previously "forbidden" subject, demonstrating that even the most shocking subject matter, when approached and treated elegantly, can be suitable for museum walls. In his wide range of subjects—flowers, portraits, and sex pictures—and his relentless quest for beauty and perfection in his art, he will be remembered as one of the key figures in the world of photography of the 1970s and 1980s.

★

Patricia Morrisroe, *Mapplethorpe: A Biography* (1995), contains a twenty-page bibliography of articles, books, and catalogs concerning Mapplethorpe. See also Anne Horton, *Robert Mapplethorpe 1986* (1987); Peter Conrad, *Mapplethorpe Portraits* (1988); Richard Marshall, Richard Howard, and Ingrid Sischy, *Robert Mapplethorpe* (1988); and Arthur C. Danto, *Mapplethorpe* (1992). Insightful essays on the photographer's work include Stephen Koch, "Guilt, Grace, and Robert Mapplethorpe," *Art in America* (Nov. 1986); Carol Squiers, "Mapplethorpe off the Wall," *American Photography* (Jan. 1988); and Dominick Dunne, "Robert Mapplethorpe's Proud Finale," *Vanity Fair* (Feb. 1989). For a general overview of Mapplethorpe's career, see Robert Hayes, "Robert Mapplethorpe," *Interview* (Mar. 1983). An obituary is in the *New York Times* (10 Mar. 1989).

PATRICIA MORRISROE

MARAVICH, Peter Press ("Pistol Pete") (*b.* 22 June 1948 in Aliquippa, Pennsylvania; *d.* 5 January 1988 in Pasadena, California), basketball player whose many collegiate records astounded the nation; some of his records remained unbroken in the late 1990s.

When Maravich was a boy, his family migrated from Pennsylvania to Clemson, South Carolina, to Raleigh, North Carolina, and then to Baton Rouge, Louisiana, as his father, Press Maravich, moved from one college coaching job to another. Pete Maravich learned to love basketball from his father, who spent countless hours teaching him the game's most important fundamentals. As the story goes, Pete had his first encounter with basketball at the age of seven, shooting hoops in the backyard with his father. Although Pete purportedly missed his first shot, he was soon hooked, practicing four to five hours per day. As a kid, Maravich was known to hustle bets from classmates by challenging them to predict how long he could spin a basketball on the tip

Pete Maravich, 1973. SPORTING NEWS/ARCHIVE PHOTOS

of his finger. Rumor has it that he once kept the ball going for fifty minutes, until one finger was bloody from having its nail worn to the nub. So obsessed with basketball was Maravich, he would even sit in the aisle seat whenever he went to the movie theater in order to practice his dribbling skills.

Maravich got his nickname, "Pistol Pete," from his father. Referring at once to the style of his shooting as a child (like most youngsters, Pete shot from his hip because the ball was too heavy) and the pace of his shooting as a high school player, Maravich quickly developed into an offensive machine with an extensive repertoire of shooting, passing, and dribbling skills. Despite criticisms that he was too greedy—Maravich shot fifty times and scored 48 points in his first varsity game—he enjoyed extraordinary success as a high school basketball player, despite playing for five different coaches in as many years. At Needham-Broughton High School in North Carolina, he captured the single-season scoring record with 735 points, the best per-game average with 32 points, and, as a senior, scored more points (47) than any other player in the North Carolina High School All-Star Game.

In 1966 Maravich enrolled at Louisiana State University (LSU), where his father had just accepted a job as head basketball coach. After nearly a decade of losing seasons,

Bayou Bengal fans, inspired by the arrival of this high school phenom, again began to flock to home games, which were still being played in a barn that belonged to the LSU School of Agriculture. Wearing number 23 (in honor of his older brother's high school jersey number), Maravich seemed up to the challenge: "If I have a choice whether to do the show or throw the straight pass, and we're going to get the basket either way, I'm going to do the show." Indeed, LSU's relatively modest facilities did nothing to stymie Maravich's audacious offensive style, nor did his father's rather permissive coaching style. "I get to the point where I don't coach him," Press once said of his all-star son, "I just watch."

During his three-year career at LSU, Maravich set countless school, Southeastern Conference, and National Collegiate Athletic Association (NCAA) records. The only college basketball player ever to become a "point-a-minute" scorer, this six-foot, five-inch guard led the nation in scoring in each of his three years, with averages of 43.8 in 1967–1968, 44.2 in 1968–1969, and 44.5 in 1969–1970. In addition, he set the following NCAA marks: most points scored in a college career (3,667) and a season (1,381); most field goals attempted in a career (3,166) and season (1,168); most field goals made in a career (1,387) and season (522); most free throws attempted in a three-year career (1,152) and game (31); most free throws made in a three-year career (893) and game (30); fifty or more points in a game within a career (28) and season (10); and best scoring average for a sophomore, junior, and senior. A three-time All-American, Maravich graduated in 1970 and was awarded the Rupp Trophy and the Naismith Award that year as the NCAA's College Player of the Year.

By the end of his illustrious career at LSU, Maravich had scored 3,667 points in 83 games for an average of 44.2 points per game, the best all-time career scoring record of any player in the history of NCAA basketball. Maravich scored more points in three years than anyone else, before or since, had scored in four. In honor of his unprecedented heroics on the court, when LSU opened its new $11.5 million, 14,000-seat sports arena in 1971, it was named for Maravich.

After being selected third in the National Basketball Association (NBA) draft in 1970, Maravich adapted swiftly to the heavy demands of professional basketball, with the Atlanta Hawks. Switching numbers from 23 to 44 (his college scoring average), he put up an impressive 23.2 points per game and was named to the NBA's All-Rookie Team in his first year with the Hawks. After his second season was crippled by mononucleosis, Maravich averaged 26.1 points a game in 1972–1973 and finished second in the league in scoring the following year, with an average of 27.7 points. In 1973, 1974, and 1977, Maravich was voted a starter on the NBA All-Star Team; he was also Second Team All-Pro in 1973.

After the 1973–1974 season, Maravich was traded to the New Orleans Jazz, an expansion team, amid mounting criticism that despite his stunning offensive accomplishments, he had never led his team, in college or the pros, to a championship. With few supporting team members during his professional career, it was all but impossible for Maravich to answer his critics, who became increasingly skeptical about his desire to win.

The absence of a championship began to haunt Maravich, so much so that he began drinking heavily to mask his deepening malaise. Nonetheless, and despite debilitating knee problems, he continued to set individual records even as his team's performance was less than noteworthy. Maravich was once again voted a starter in the NBA All-Star Game in 1977, 1978 (although a knee injury prevented him from playing), and 1979. He was First-Team All-Pro in 1976 and 1977, the same year he led the NBA in scoring with 31.1 points per game, and was Second Team All-Pro in 1978. He was released from the Jazz shortly after they moved from New Orleans to Utah in 1979, but he quickly signed with the Boston Celtics for the 1979–1980 season. After failing to win a championship in Boston, Maravich retired from the NBA at the age of thirty-three. Over the course of his ten-year professional career, he scored 15,948 points in 658 games, averaging 24.2 points, 4.2 rebounds, and 5.4 assists per game.

Maravich and his wife, Jackie, had two sons, but he was unhappy in retirement. Unable to cope with the loss of his greatest love—basketball—he became a loner, drinking heavily and dabbling in astrology, mysticism, and survivalism in an unsuccessful attempt to find inner peace. Maravich later admitted that he seriously contemplated suicide one night while driving his Porsche over a bridge at high speed. In 1982, however, during a sleepless night in suburban Metairie, Louisiana, Maravich decided that the only way to reclaim his sense of satisfaction was to embrace a Christian life. "Born again," he would later tell his former coach, Richie Guerin, that his foremost desire was to be remembered as a good Christian, a good husband, and a good father. He went on a lecturing tour to describe his newfound devotion to Christianity. Indeed, a few months before his death, he spoke to an assembled crowd of 35,000 people at a Billy Graham Crusade in Columbia, South Carolina. "Next week I'll be inducted into the Hall of Fame," Maravich said, but "I wouldn't trade my position in Christ for a thousand NBA championships, for a thousand Hall of Fame rings, or for a hundred billion dollars."

Maravich was inducted into the Basketball Hall of Fame in a ceremony in Springfield, Massachusetts, in 1987. Shortly thereafter, during a pickup basketball game in a church gym in Pasadena, California, Maravich collapsed.

He died of congenital heart failure the following morning at the age of thirty-nine.

Maravich's premature death sent shock waves through the basketball world. Following intense mourning, books, instructional videos, and memorabilia flooded the markets. *The Pistol: Birth of a Legend,* a poignant, 104-minute docudrama detailing the early relationship between Maravich and his father-coach appeared in 1990. Maravich's greatest posthumous honor, however, came in October 1996, when he was named one of the fifty best players in the first half century of the NBA and was honored at the All-Star Game in Cleveland, Ohio, on 9 February 1997.

Long considered basketball's greatest showman, Pistol Pete Maravich hardly looked like a great athlete. Lanky and slightly pigeon-toed, his body was once described by one sportscaster as "a cross between a clarinet and a filter king." With his tangled mop of brown hair, spindly legs, and floppy gray socks that he washed and hung up to dry in his college dorm room after each game, Maravich nonetheless dazzled sellout crowds with his spectacular behind-the-back passes and impossible fade-away jump shots. Teammates, too, were in awe of his seemingly endless creativity. "An American phenomenon," NBA teammate Rich Kelley once said of Maravich, and called him "a stepchild of the human imagination." Boyishly energetic and unpredictable, Maravich served as a constant reminder that driving every successful athlete was a child's dream. Indeed an original, Maravich remains one of basketball's titanic legends.

★

Biographical data on Maravich can be found in David L. Porter, *Biographical Dictionary of American Sports: Basketball and Other Indoor Sports* (1989); Peter C. Bjarkman, *The Encyclopedia of Pro-Basketball Team Histories* (1994); Alex Sachare, ed., *The Official NBA Basketball Encyclopedia* (1994); Ralph Hickok, *A Who's Who of Sports Champions: Their Stories and Records* (1995); and Mark Vancil, *The NBA at Fifty* (1996). An obituary is in the *New York Times* (6 Jan. 1988).

TIMOTHY P. MCCARTHY

MARBLE, Alice (*b.* 13 September 1913 in Beckwith, California; *d.* 13 December 1990 in Palm Springs, California), tennis champion of the 1930s known for her aggressive, athletic game.

Alice Marble was the fourth of five children (three boys and two girls) born to Harry Briggs Marble and Jessie Wood. Her father had been a "high-climber" in the logging industry in the Sierra Nevadas of California, and by the time of his marriage he owned a farm and cattle ranch near Beckwith in Plumas County, California, where Alice spent her early childhood. At age five she moved with her family

Alice Marble. ARCHIVE PHOTOS

to San Francisco, where her father worked for a lumber company. He died soon after this relocation, and Alice's mother and two older brothers worked to support the family.

Alice grew up as a tomboy. She loved sports, especially baseball, which she and her younger brother, Tim, played constantly. In her early teens she served as a warm-up player and mascot for the San Francisco Seals, a professional baseball team in the Pacific Coast League whose members dubbed her "Little Queen of Swat." At Polytechnic High School in San Francisco, she also played on the girls basketball, track, and baseball teams; she graduated in 1931.

When Marble was fifteen her oldest brother, Dan, bought her a tennis racket so she could play a more ladylike sport. Although she initially considered tennis a "sissy" sport, she started playing at the public courts at Golden Gate Park. With her natural athletic ability, she soon was winning local tournaments. During the early 1930s, while she was still a teenager and relatively new to the game, she became a highly ranked player in northern California. Through the sponsorship of tennis associations in California and an anonymous patron, she played in the Northwest and Canadian championships in 1930. Beginning in 1931 she was sent to play in East Coast tournaments and in the national championships at Forest Hills in New York City.

In 1931 her first-round loss at Forest Hills along with advice from the former national champion Mary K. Browne led Marble to seek better instruction to improve her game and make it more adaptable to the eastern grass courts. In San Francisco she worked with a professional, Howard Kinsey, but the teacher who made the difference in her career was Eleanor ("Teach") Tennant. In 1932 Marble began working with Tennant in Los Angeles and with Harwood White in Santa Barbara. Together they modified her grip and her strokes and encouraged her to use her athleticism to play an attacking game at the net. Her national ranking improved from seventh to third by 1933.

Ill health caused by overexertion nearly brought Marble's tennis career to a halt. In 1933, at a qualifying tournament before selection of the Wightman Cup team, she played 108 games in one day in temperatures over 100 degrees, causing her to have sunstroke and fatigue. She had not regained her strength when, in the following spring of 1934, she collapsed in Paris during a match between the United States and France. Back in the United States, she was diagnosed with tuberculosis and spent some time in a sanatorium. Gradually, with the financial and moral support of Tennant, Marble embarked on a rehabilitation program that enabled her to resume her tennis career.

Marble's greatest achievements as a tennis champion came from 1936 to 1940. In 1936 she beat Helen Jacobs to win the national championship and become the top female player in the United States. She won the national title again in 1938, 1939, and 1940. In 1939 she won singles, doubles, and mixed doubles at Wimbledon. When her game was at its peak, she could devastate opponents with her well-executed ground strokes, strong serves, and crisp volleys, enhanced by speed and agility around the court. In 1940 she became a professional and started playing exhibition matches on tour.

Marble was a woman of diverse interests and activities. Through her connection with Tennant, she became part of a Hollywood set that included filmdom's most glamorous couple, the actress Carole Lombard and the actor Clark Gable. She occasionally sang in New York City nightclubs and on the radio, and she served as a sports announcer for radio station WNEW in New York City. She also designed a line of tennis wear.

During World War II Marble contributed to the war effort in several ways, including entertaining servicemen by playing exhibition matches. As national director of physical training for women in the Office of Civilian Defense, she promoted the "Hale America" program to improve the physical fitness of Americans on the home front. In her autobiography Marble recounted two significant events in her life. The first was her marriage in 1942 to Joseph Norman "Joe" Crowley, an army captain whom she met at the Stage Door Canteen in New York City. They had no children, and their happiness was short-lived because he was killed in 1944 when his plane was shot down over Germany. The second was her involvement in an espionage mission to Switzerland in 1945. Through a former suitor, Hans Steinmetz, who was a Swiss banker, she obtained information about Nazi financial accounts in Switzerland. She sustained a bullet wound in the back as she was escaping.

For the rest of her life Marble maintained her involvement with tennis. She lectured, played exhibition matches, and taught, particularly after she moved back to California from New York City in 1951; her pupils included the tennis champions Darlene Hard and Billie Jean King. Her editorial in the July 1950 issue of *American Lawn Tennis* magazine attacking the whites-only policy of the U.S. Lawn Tennis Association sparked an outcry that forced the organization to change its rules and allow Althea Gibson to play in USLTA tournaments. In 1964 Marble was inducted into the International Tennis Hall of Fame in Newport, Rhode Island.

Marble continued her associations with people in the entertainment industry. She had a long-standing affair with the television writer Rod Serling and made a cameo appearance in the 1952 film *Pat and Mike,* starring Katharine Hepburn and Spencer Tracy. She coped with various health problems, including colon cancer and the loss of a lung to pneumonia. She died from pernicious anemia at Desert Hospital in Palm Springs, California, where she had lived since 1965.

Alice Marble was one of the great players of women's tennis. At five feet, seven inches and weighing 150 pounds, with golden blond hair, she had an elegant, athletic physique. With help from instructors such as Tennant, she utilized her natural athletic talents to develop a powerful, all-court game. She played tennis with the same verve, style, and daring sense of adventure that she brought to all aspects of her life.

★

The most extensive information about Marble is in her two autobiographical works, *The Road to Wimbledon* (1946) and, with Dale Leatherman, *Courting Danger: My Adventures in World-Class Tennis, Golden-Age Hollywood, and High-Stakes Spying* (1991). Several books place her in the context of the development of women's tennis. Owen Davidson and C. M. Jones, *Great Women Tennis Players* (1971), devotes a chapter to her. She also occupies an important place in Virginia Wade with Jean Rafferty, *Ladies of the Court: A Century of Women at Wimbledon* (1984); and Billie Jean King with Cynthia Starr, *We Have Come a Long Way: The Story of Women's Tennis* (1988). An obituary is in the *New York Times* (14 Dec. 1990).

KAREN GOULD

MARTIN, Alfred Manuel, Jr. ("Billy") (*b.* 16 May 1928 in Berkeley, California; *d.* 25 December 1989 in Johnson City, New York), baseball player and manager, considered among baseball's greatest managers and most controversial figures.

Of Portuguese-Italian ancestry, Martin was the son of Alfred Manuel Martin, a truck driver and musician, and Genevieve Salvini Pisani, a housewife. Martin's father deserted his wife before Martin was born. In 1929 she married Jack Downey, who held a variety of jobs but was handicapped by asthma. Martin spent much of his boyhood living with his maternal grandmother, who affectionately called him *bello* (beautiful), which eventually became "Billy," the name by which he became known.

An indifferent student, Martin avidly played all sports as a youth. Despite his frail frame he was a talented athlete and a fierce competitor with an insatiable desire to win. Martin had a violent temper and fought often, sometimes without provocation. He was strongly influenced by his mother, a diminutive woman of volcanic temperament.

Self-conscious about his appearance and socially awkward, Martin found in competitive sports an outlet for his hostility and a boost for his self-worth. He starred in baseball and basketball, but his willful nature cost him wider recognition. During a tryout with the Oakland Oaks of the Pacific Coast League, he impressed manager Casey Stengel with his energy and brash demeanor. It was the start of a lifelong friendship between the two men.

Billy Martin. NATIONAL BASEBALL HALL OF FAME LIBRARY, COOPERSTOWN, N.Y.

After graduating from Berkeley High School in 1946, Martin signed with Oakland and was assigned to Idaho Falls of the Pioneer League. With Phoenix of the Arizona-Texas League in 1947, Martin batted .393; led the league in batting, hits, doubles, and runs batted in; and was named Most Valuable Player. Playing for Oakland in 1948–1949, he learned from managers Stengel and Charlie Dressen and from other former major leaguers. In 1949 his contract was purchased by the New York Yankees.

Martin played for the Yankees on opening day of the 1950 season, and in fact established a major league record (since equaled) by getting two hits in one inning in his first major league game. He played little thereafter and was sent down to Kansas City in the American Association in mid-May; the Yankees recalled him in mid-June. He alienated many Yankee veterans with his cocky attitude but was befriended by the normally aloof superstar Joe DiMaggio. On a championship team Martin initially played little, chafing at his inactivity. On 20 October 1950 he married Lois Elaine Berndt. They had one daughter and were divorced in 1953. Shortly after his marriage Martin was drafted into the U.S. Army. Claiming to be the sole support for his parents, wife, and three younger siblings, he was granted a hardship discharge after serving five and a half months. He appeared in only fifty-one games in 1951.

A broken ankle suffered in spring training sidelined Martin for two months in 1952. Doubting his ability and fearful of being traded, he suffered from insomnia, ate little, and lost thirty pounds. Eventually regaining his weight, stamina, and emotional equilibrium, he contributed to the team's fourth consecutive world championship. In the World Series against the Brooklyn Dodgers, Martin hit a three-run home run in game 2 and saved the deciding seventh game with a running catch of Jackie Robinson's two-out, bases-loaded infield fly.

Martin had his finest major league season in 1953, batting .257 in 149 games and reaching career bests in home runs (15), runs batted in (75), hits (151), doubles (24), and triples (6). In the World Series against the Dodgers, he achieved the pinnacle of his playing career, batting .500 with twelve hits, two home runs, and eight runs batted in, including the winning hit in game 6. For his accomplishments he received the Babe Ruth Award as most valuable player.

Reclassified 1-A by his draft board in March 1954, Martin was inducted into the army in April. Not discharged until August 1955, he rejoined the Yankees and hit .320 in a losing effort in the World Series, again against the Dodgers. By 1956 Martin's playing skills had begun to fade. Years earlier he had alienated Yankee general manager George Weiss. A highly publicized incident at the Copacabana nightclub in New York City on 15 May 1957, involving Martin and a group of other Yankee players and their wives, gave Weiss the opportunity to trade Martin. Although in this instance blameless, on 15 June 1957 he was traded to the Kansas City Athletics. Between 1957 and 1961 Martin would play with six teams. His desire and aggressiveness remained, but injuries diminished his effectiveness.

On 7 October 1959 Martin married Gretchen Winkler. They had one son and were divorced in 1982. On 5 August 1960 Martin was involved in an altercation at Chicago's Wrigley Field with Cubs pitcher Jim Brewer, who suffered facial fractures. Brewer and the Cubs sued Martin for a reported $1.04 million. In 1969 Brewer was awarded a $22,000 settlement.

After being released by the Minnesota Twins in 1962, Martin became a scout for that team and, in 1965, third base coach. His teaching and motivational skills were apparent as he instilled aggressive baserunning and extracted the maximum from the team's Hispanic players. But his pugnacious independence antagonized some players, coaches, and team officials. On 27 May 1968 Martin was named manager of the Denver Bears of the Pacific Coast League. He quickly turned a losing team into a winner by demanding resourceful play, total effort, and complete player loyalty. Thus Martin was able to improve team performance while raising attendance.

Martin managed the Minnesota Twins to a division championship in 1969 but on 13 October of that year was fired, having upset the owner with his truculent off-field behavior, demands for greater authority, and conflicts with players and team officials. Managing the Detroit Tigers (1971–1973), Texas Rangers (1973–1975), New York Yankees (1975–1978, 1979, 1983, 1985, 1988), and Oakland A's (1980–1982), he achieved immediate and sustained improvement, but a combination of his insecurities, paranoia, alcoholism, brawling, and defiance of management led to his dismissals.

On 2 August 1975 Martin became manager of the Yankees, his long-desired managerial objective. His relationship with owner George Steinbrenner, an impatient, bombastic, self-promoting man, was often volatile. The two men constantly feuded, then patched up their differences, only to resume the self-destructive pattern. Under Martin's direction the team won the American League championship in 1976 and the World Series in 1977. On 24 July 1978, one day after making alcohol-fueled remarks about Steinbrenner and star slugger Reggie Jackson, Martin resigned. Five days later, in a stunning development, it was announced that Martin would return as manager in 1980, a decision prompted largely by furious fan reaction to his resignation.

Martin returned to manage the Yankees ahead of schedule in 1979 but was fired again on 28 October, shortly after an altercation in a Minneapolis lounge. Hired to manage the struggling Oakland Athletics in 1980, he led the team to a division championship in 1981. But in 1982 he encountered a difficult mix of financial, marital, and family problems, complicated by a change in team ownership. As the team's performance declined, his interest in managing waned. On 20 October 1982 he was fired. Less than three months later he returned as Yankee manager.

Martin's domestic life was convoluted. In 1975 Colombian authorities arrested his daughter for cocaine smuggling. Convicted, she was incarcerated for two years. In 1978 Martin met sixteen-year-old Heather Ervolino. They were married on 30 November 1982. Few people were aware of the marriage, which ended in divorce in 1986. In 1980 Martin met Jilluan Guiver, a twenty-four-year-old freelance photographer. For several years he maintained separate relationships with Ervolino and Guiver. On 25 January 1988 Martin married Guiver, a strong-willed woman whose expensive tastes and possessiveness antagonized Martin's family and many of his closest friends.

Managing the Yankees during the 1980s, Martin achieved winning records but no championships. In September 1985 he was embroiled in a particularly vicious fight with Yankee pitcher Ed Whitson. From then until his last stint as manager, he served the Yankees in various capacities. His final tenure as manager ended disastrously. On 7 May 1988 Martin was seriously injured in a nightclub altercation in Arlington, Texas. After a subsequent on-field tirade leading to a suspension and fine, he was fired on 23 June.

Later in 1988 the Martins bought a small farmhouse on 159 acres near Binghamton, New York. During the Christmas holidays in 1989, they hosted good friends Bill and Carol Reedy. Martin and Bill Reedy spent Christmas afternoon drinking at a Binghamton restaurant. While they were returning home in Martin's pickup truck over icy, snowy roads, the driver lost control of the vehicle, which skidded, overturned, and landed in a culvert. Martin died of internal injuries and a broken neck. Reedy survived with lesser injuries. It remains unclear who was behind the wheel. Martin was buried in Gate of Heaven Cemetery in Hawthorne, New York.

Billy Martin was a complex and controversial figure, a loyal friend and a loathsome enemy who inspired zealous fan and player loyalty and, in some quarters, equal levels of revulsion. A lifetime .257 hitter in eleven seasons, playing mainly at second base, he performed best with a championship at stake, hitting .333 with nineteen RBIs in twenty-eight World Series games. In a sixteen-year managerial career he compiled a record of 1,253 wins and 1,013 losses, winning five division titles, two American League championships, one World Series, and four Associated Press Manager of the Year awards. A peerless tactician, astute psychologist, and skilled motivator, he manipulated the tenor of a game by his force of will. Adept at winning with younger players as well as with veterans, he molded his daring style to the material at hand. No manager had a greater need to win, nor a deeper knowledge of all facets of the game. Yet his personal demons, vindictiveness, and self-destructive behavior made it impossible for him to sustain winning performances in the emotionally charged environments he created, thus limiting his long-term effectiveness as a manager. In his final years he became a sad caricature of his earlier persona, unable to focus fully on managerial tasks, ultimately destroyed in an escalating spiral of alcohol, failed marriages, family turmoil, financial problems, and self-directed rage.

★

Martin's first autobiography, *Number One* (1980), written with Peter Golenbock, is a candid, first-person account of his life in and out of baseball. *Billyball* (1987), written with Phil Pepe, continues his story through 1986, answering critics, settling old scores, offering astute observations on managerial strategy, and occasionally retracing old ground, all in typically blunt fashion. Earlier biographies of Martin include Norman Lewis Smith, *The Return of Billy the Kid* (1977); Maury Allen, *Damn Yankee: The Billy Martin Story* (1980); and Gene Schoor, *Billy Martin* (1980). Of the three, Smith is the most pedestrian, Schoor the most factually inaccurate, and Allen by far the most substantial. Two books written since Martin's death—David Falkner, *The Last Yankee: The Turbulent Life of Billy Martin* (1992); and Peter Golenbock, *Wild, High, and Tight: The Life and Death of Billy Martin* (1994)—transcend the typical sports biography genre with extensive research, interviews, and opinionated remarks from Martin's boyhood friends, family members, teammates, and management. Golenbock especially probes Martin's tangled family and sex life, and the effects of his alcoholism. Golenbock strongly contends that Martin was at the wheel in his fatal accident; Falkner tentatively concludes that Reedy was the driver.

Among the countless books written about the New York Yankees, the following have significant material about Martin: Peter Golenbock, *Dynasty: The New York Yankees, 1949–1964* (1975); Sparky Lyle and Peter Golenbock, *The Bronx Zoo* (1978); Dom Forker, *The Men of Autumn* (1989); Bill Madden and Moss Klein, *Damned Yankees: A No Holds Barred Account of Life with "Boss" Steinbrenner* (1990); and Philip Bashe, *Dog Days: The New York Yankees Fall from Grace and Return to Glory, 1964–1976* (1994). One of the best articles written about Martin during his playing days is Al Stump, "He's Never Out of Trouble," *Saturday Evening Post* (18 Aug. 1956), a frank account that touches on his emotional problems and insecurity, and the pressures facing a young baseball player. On Martin the manager see Frank Deford, "Love, Hate, and Billy Martin," *Sports Illustrated* (2 June 1975), which conveys Martin's complex personality and conflicted character. On Martin's blue-collar, West Berkeley origins, see Ron Fimrite, "Berkeley's Billy Comes Home Again," *Sports Illustrated* (10 Mar. 1980). An insightful yet sympathetic assessment of Martin and his inability to transcend the fighting reputation of his youth that indicts Steinbrenner and the media for perpetuating that feisty image is Harvey Araton, "Billy's Wrong Turn Came Years Earlier," *New York Daily News* (27 Dec. 1989). Obituaries are in the *New York Times* (26 Dec. 1989) and *Sports Illustrated* (8 Jan. 1990).

EDWARD J. TASSINARI

MARTIN, John Bartlow (*b.* 4 August 1915 in Hamilton, Ohio; *d.* 3 January 1987 in Highland Park, Illinois), prolific writer on social and political questions for mass-circulation magazines and author of more than a dozen books; he also was a speechwriter for Democratic presidential candidates and ambassador to the Dominican Republic.

Martin's father, John Williamson Martin, was a carpenter who moved his family to Indianapolis, Indiana, and became a general contractor. An infant brother died in his crib, and when another young brother, Billy, died of scarlet fever when Martin was fifteen, his father placed the blame on his mother, Laura Bartlow Martin, a Christian Scientist. An early memory was watching a huge parade of silent, white-hooded members of the Ku Klux Klan in downtown Indianapolis. Martin's father, who employed African Americans, refused to join the Klan. In high school Martin became interested in modern literature, especially Ernest Hemingway and John Dos Passos, and decided to become

John Bartlow Martin. UPI/CORBIS-BETTMANN

a writer. Although his father ridiculed Martin's bookish ways, he bought him books; he also took him hunting and fishing, which became lifelong passions. Martin hung around black ballrooms as a youth, listening to jazz with a high school friend, Francis Nipp, who became a Chicago-area book editor and Martin's longtime editorial assistant in later life. His squabbling parents separated, divorced, and eventually remarried.

At age sixteen, Martin entered DePauw University in Greencastle, Indiana, which expelled him in his first year for drinking in his room. After working as an Associated Press copyboy in Indianapolis, he reentered DePauw in 1933. He edited the college newspaper, was the local correspondent for the *Indianapolis Times,* and graduated with a B.A. degree in political science in 1937. The slim, bespectacled Martin stood out on the conservative campus with his carefully tended, red crew-cut hair, striped shirts, and yellow cardigan sweater. He cut classes and chapel and organized a campus drinking club that masqueraded as a poetry-reading society. Fellow members of the Delta Chi fraternity could hear the aspirant writer's typewriter going hours past midnight each night.

On 23 January 1937 in Greencastle, Martin married Barbara Bruce, a DePauw sorority girl from a wealthy Evanston, Illinois, family. He worked briefly as a police and city hall reporter and rewrite man with the *Indianapolis Times.* Recovering from pneumonia in 1937 and 1938, he toured the Caribbean with his wife, spending several months in the Dominican Republic. His first magazine piece, about the Dominican dictator Rafael Trujillo, appeared in *Ken,* a Chicago political magazine. Martin then decided to try full-time freelancing in Chicago. He and his wife divorced, and Martin holed up in a Rush Street hotel and wrote fact-based crime stories for Moe and Walter Annenberg's *Official Detective* and *Factual Detective* and other Annenberg magazines eight hours a day, plus pieces for *Esquire.*

On 17 August 1940 he married Frances Rose Smethhurst, of Elmhurst, Illinois. They made their permanent home in Highland Park, Illinois, and summered annually in a wilderness area near L'Anse in Upper Michigan. They had one daughter, Cynthia Ann Coleman, and two sons, Daniel Bartlow and John Frederick. Martin's book *Call It North Country,* published in 1944, was about the struggle of work-worn residents of Michigan's Upper Peninsula to survive. A long association began with *Harper's* magazine with an update of Robert and Helen Lynd's classic sociological studies of Muncie, Indiana, and a story about a Muncie Klansman who published a hate newspaper containing anti-black and anti-Semitic articles.

Martin continued writing for detective magazines and *Harper's* during army service as a criminal investigator in Arkansas and Texas during World War II. His second book, *Indiana: An Interpretation* (1947), was critical of Indiana racism and isolationism. Magazine articles in *Harper's* and elsewhere became the basis for a series of books in the 1950s about criminal psychology. *Why Did They Kill?* (1953) was termed by the *New York Times* "as smooth and gripping as a first-rate novel." It concerned three middle-class juveniles who senselessly murdered a nurse. *Break Down the Walls* (1954) explored the psychology of prison rioters. Martin was commonly called the nation's best crime reporter.

In March 1948 *Harper's* devoted most of its issue to "The Blast in Centralia #5," Martin's story about a World War II Illinois coal mine explosion that killed about 100 people. Everyone, Martin contended, knew that the mine was dangerously prone to becoming a disaster scene, but state mine supervisors and the miners' own union did little to prevent it. That year, Democrat Adlai Stevenson II, running for governor of Illinois, defeated Governor Dwight Green by a huge majority, in part by using Martin's Centralia story, which criticized the intimate relationship between Green's staff and the mine owners. The article led to a new federal mine safety code and got Martin writing jobs for the *Saturday Evening Post, Life, Look, Collier's,* and the *Atlantic.*

In 1952 Martin wrote a campaign biography of Stevenson, the Democratic candidate for president, and joined Stevenson's speechwriting staff, becoming part of a circle that met in the Springfield, Illinois, Elks Club and included David Bell, W. Willard Wirtz, Newton Minow, Arthur Schlesinger, Jr., John Kenneth Galbraith, Archibald MacLeish, and others. "Suddenly I was on the inside," Martin said. Stevenson, a fiscal conservative distrustful of big government and big labor and hesitant to discuss racism, was an eloquent speaker who became known as a liberal paladin in part because his Elks Club aides badgered him to move further to the left. For this and later presidential campaigns, Martin filled a unique niche by specializing in intensive advance canvassing of local concerns and carefully targeted courthouse speeches. His wife Frances, an Illinois board member of the American Civil Liberties Union, sometimes served as a volunteer and speaker.

Martin served from March to November 1956 in Stevenson's second campaign and helped him defeat Senator Estes Kefauver in the crucial California primary by inducing the reluctant Stevenson to take a more anti-Kefauver, pro-labor, pro-integration stance. Meanwhile, multi-issue *Saturday Evening Post* stories on southern resistance to school integration, on the mentally ill, and on the Teamsters Union became the basis of books by Martin.

Writing a *Saturday Evening Post* series about the U.S. Senate committee investigation of the Teamsters Union, Martin developed a personal association with Robert Kennedy, chief counsel of the committee. This relationship led to Martin's becoming the only Stevenson campaign aide to join John F. Kennedy's 1960 presidential campaign staff.

He performed his usual advance and speechwriting function, and advised Kennedy on Castro's Cuba and the Caribbean generally.

After Trujillo was assassinated in 1961, President Kennedy sent Martin, who had recently revisited the Dominican Republic, to study the situation. Martin advised sending a high-level negotiator, with U.S. naval vessels, to maneuver the politically and economically dominant Trujillo family out of the country and to encourage the election of a moderate anticommunist regime. Kennedy adopted Martin's advice, sent warships, and the Trujillos agreed to withdraw.

Martin, meanwhile, was writing a *Saturday Evening Post* series on commercial television. As a speechwriter for Kennedy administration officials he drafted a 1961 speech for Federal Communications Commission chairman Newton Minow that called commercial television a "vast wasteland." This phrase became Minow's most famous utterance.

In 1962 Martin successfully campaigned, with the support of Schlesinger, Robert Kennedy, and Stevenson, to be appointed ambassador to the Dominican Republic. Soon after his arrival in Santo Domingo, a leftist anti-American mob burned Martin's automobile, stoned the consulate, and invaded his sons' school. Martin worked with a temporary governing council of local oligarchs to introduce agrarian reform, a public health program, and Peace Corps economic development programs. He toured the country, trying to assure a peaceful transition to an elected government, and his wife founded a clinic for newborn children.

Juan Bosch, a noncommunist leftist, won the December 1962 election, but in September of the following year, the rightist Dominican military overthrew Bosch. Martin returned to Washington, and in 1964 he resigned his ambassadorship. He served on President Lyndon B. Johnson's 1964 campaign staff and returned to the Dominican Republic as Johnson's personal envoy. In 1965 Johnson sent U.S. troops to intervene between the rightist junta and what Martin said was a communist-influenced counterrevolution. Johnson "was running the operation like a [State Department] desk officer," Martin later reported. With the aid of economic sanctions, the Organization of American States, and gunboat diplomacy, the United States got a provisional regime that returned the Dominican Republic to representative government. On his return, Martin advised the government on Caribbean policy, turned down an ambassadorship to the Jamaican embassy, and vainly sought an appointment to the Venezuelan embassy.

In 1968 Martin joined Robert Kennedy's primary campaign, and after the assassination of Martin Luther King, Jr., advised Kennedy to adopt a law-and-order plus racial-justice strategy in conservative Indiana, whose primary Kennedy won. He was with Kennedy in Los Angeles when Kennedy was murdered. At Vice President Hubert Humphrey's invitation, he joined Humphrey's doomed presidential campaign in the fall.

Subsequently, Martin spent most of his time writing books and teaching. *Overtaken by Events* (1966) detailed his experiences in the Dominican Republic. With Newton Minow, he contributed to *Presidential Television* (1973). In the late 1960s the Martins bought a large tract of wilderness land at Smith Lake, Michigan, near their tourist-invaded Three Lakes summer home and spent four years building a new private camp. Martin did much of the carpentry himself.

Martin spent ten years writing the two-volume *Life of Adlai Stevenson* (1976, 1977), helping to pay his way with research appointments and faculty positions at Wesleyan University (1964–1965), Princeton University (1966–1967), a Rockefeller Foundation villa at Lake Como (1967), and, with the aid of Schlesinger, the City University of New York (1968). From 1968 to 1970 he was visiting professor of journalism at Northwestern University, becoming professor in 1970 and professor emeritus in 1980. In 1970 he published *U.S. Policy in the Caribbean,* and in 1980 *The Televising of Heller,* a novel about the corrupting effect of opinion polling and television on a U.S. Senate election in Illinois. *It Seems Like Only Yesterday: Memoirs of Writing, Presidential Politics, and the Diplomatic Life* (1986) appeared shortly before his death, from emphysema and throat cancer. Martin had no active church affiliation. Interment was in Herman, Michigan, near the Martin summer home.

Politically, Martin was a people-centered pragmatist; to him winning elections was more important than doctrinal purity. He said that what he wrote was carpentry, not art; he wrote stories about people, not articles. Martin's clearly illegal gunboat interventions for Kennedy and Johnson in the Dominican Republic, Martin argued, constituted a unique example of the use of U.S. military power solely to promote democracy in Latin America. As a ghostwriter, Martin saw some of his phrases ascribed to Adlai Stevenson and President Kennedy.

Martin illustrated historic events by interviewing representative citizens before Studs Terkel became famous for using the technique. His chosen subject was often an indifferent and hostile world, echoing his favorite writers, Hemingway, Franz Kafka, and Albert Camus. His novelized 1950s "heavy fact" writings on criminal behavior antedated by a decade the celebrated "nonfiction novel" *In Cold Blood* by Truman Capote, a reader of detective magazines. Denouncing commercial television, he prophesied the dumbing down of America, with its obsession with sex, celebrity, and violence. As Martin's son John Frederick said, he was lucky to live when there was a mass market for serious journalism.

★

Martin's papers are in the Manuscript Division of the Library of Congress. A special collection relating to Adlai Stevenson II is in the Seeley Mudd Library at Princeton University. Martin helped Robert Kennedy organize the John F. Kennedy oral history collection in the Kennedy Memorial Library, Boston, and conducted the tape-recorded interviews with Robert Kennedy. Arthur Schlesinger, Jr., wrote a memorial to Martin in the yearbook of the Century Association, New York (1987). John Frederick Martin's reminiscences of his father, delivered at the 1988 inauguration of Northwestern University's John Bartlow Martin public-interest journalism prize, became the basis for "John Bartlow Martin," *American Scholar* 59 (summer 1990): 95–100. See also Ray Boomhower, "A Voice for Those from Below: John Bartlow Martin, Reporter," *Traces of Indiana and Midwestern History* (spring 1997): 5–13; *Wilson Library Bulletin* 30 (Jan. 1956); and *Contemporary Authors,* New Revision Series, vol. 8 (1982). Obituaries are in the *Chicago Tribune* and *New York Times* (both 5 Jan. 1987).

JAMES STOUDER SWEET

MARTIN, Mary Virginia (*b.* 1 December 1913 in Weatherford, Texas; *d.* 3 November 1990 in Rancho Mirage, California), musical comedy star best remembered for her roles in the Broadway show *South Pacific* (1949) and the Broadway and television productions of *Peter Pan*.

Martin was the younger of two daughters of Preston Martin, a lawyer, and Juanita (Presley) Martin, a former violin teacher. Martin was attracted to the performing arts from childhood. Her formal education ended in 1930, when she left the Ward-Belmont School, a finishing school, in Nashville, Tennessee, without graduating. That same year, at age sixteen, she married Benjamin Hagman, an accountant, and opened up her own dance studio in Weatherford. She divorced Hagman in 1937. Their only child was Lawrence ("Larry") Hagman, familiar to television viewers as J. R. Ewing of *Dallas*.

After some success as a nightclub performer, Martin made her Broadway debut in Cole Porter's *Leave It to Me!* (1938), in which she introduced "My Heart Belongs to Daddy," singing it with a combination of innocence and experience that delighted audiences. Allegedly, the show's star, Sophie Tucker, had to explain the lyrics' double entendres, such as, "I'd never dream / Of making the team," to Martin. *Night and Day* (1946), a romanticized movie version of Porter's life, included Martin's rendition of the song, sanitized for the screen.

For the next five years, Martin was bicoastal, appearing in such unmemorable films as *The Birth of the Blues* (1941) and *Happy Go Lucky* (1943) and musicals that never reached New York—*Nice Goin'* (1939) and *Dancing in the Streets* (1943). In 1940 she married Richard Halliday, a story editor at Paramount who later managed her career (and whose autocratic behavior often caused friction with producers) until his death in 1973. They had one child.

Mary Martin. POPPERFOTO/ARCHIVE PHOTOS

Martin achieved stardom in the Broadway musical *One Touch of Venus* (1943), in which she sang such memorable Kurt Weill songs as "Speak Low" and "That's Him." The original cast recording reveals Martin's flawless enunciation, a quality always associated with her. Her next musical, *Lute Song* (1946), based on an ancient Chinese play, had a brief run and was significant chiefly for Yul Brynner's Broadway debut. An ill-advised venture into operetta brought her to London in Noël Coward's *Pacific 1860* (1946)—an experience that temporarily strained her relationship with Coward, with whom she later teamed up for a 1955 television special. The failure of *Pacific 1860* made her eager to tour in Irving Berlin's hit *Annie Get Your Gun* in 1947, performing the role that Ethel Merman had created. A uniquely American artist, Martin was the logical choice to play Nellie Forbush opposite opera basso Ezio Pinza in Rodgers and Hammerstein's *South Pacific* (1949). Her Broadway approach to the musical numbers complemented his operatic delivery, so that their seemingly mismatched styles actually meshed.

Understandably, Martin wanted to try a nonmusical, but *Kind Sir* (1953) was a poor choice, despite her successful attempt at sophisticated comedy. The director Joshua Logan hoped to duplicate the Martin-Pinza chemistry in a nonmusical, Norman Krasna's *Kind Sir,* by pairing Martin with movie star Charles Boyer. Martin bravely met the challenge of a romantic comedy, even holding her own against Boyer. But critics and audiences found the material too lightweight for an extended run. Her role as the title character in *Peter Pan* (1954) is the one for which she will always be remembered. Although the musical only ran for 152 performances, the 1955 and 1956 live telecasts, and the 1960 taped version that has been shown subsequently, gave Martin the kind of exposure known to few stage stars.

Martin proved to be a television favorite. Her duet with Ethel Merman on the *Ford Fiftieth Anniversary Show* (15 June 1953), made television history and is frequently requested at New York City's Museum of Broadcasting. After a State Department–sponsored tour of Thornton Wilder's *The Skin of Our Teeth,* in which Martin costarred with Helen Hayes and George Abbott, the play was telecast live (11 September 1955); Martin excelled as Sabina, the maid who delivers wry asides to the audience. Her one television blunder was *Born Yesterday* (28 October 1956), in which she played Billie Dawn, a part for which she was too old and with which Judy Holliday, who had originated the role in film, will always be associated.

Regardless, Martin had become a television name—a factor that contributed to the success of Rodgers and Hammerstein's Broadway musical *The Sound of Music* (1959), which was more operetta than musical theater, with a middle-aged Martin playing a considerably younger Maria von Trapp. Although she enunciated the lyrics with her customary clarity, her voice had begun to darken and her range to decrease. *Jennie* (1963), a musical based on the early career of the actress Laurette Taylor, was a failure that pleased neither public nor critics. Far better was *I Do! I Do!* (1966), a charming musical version of *The Four Poster,* which followed a couple from their wedding day to retirement.

Martin's last two stage appearances were in inferior nonmusicals. *Do You Turn Sommersaults?* (1978), a two-character play, barely lasted two weeks on Broadway. *Legends* (1986–1987), in which she toured with Carol Channing, never reached Broadway and included language that Martin found objectionable. Martin's failing health was much in evidence during the tour; on 3 November 1990, Martin succumbed to colon cancer, which had been detected the previous year.

The number of fans who lined up for the memorial service on 28 January 1991 at New York City's Majestic Theatre, where Martin had triumphed in *South Pacific,* attested to her popularity. The memorial was, like Martin herself, an affirmation of life. In person, Martin was diminutive with eyes that literally resembled buttons; in performance, she radiated the aura of the goddess she portrayed in *One Touch of Venus.* What she brought to the musical stage was enormous discipline that not only required her to sing but also to do whatever else was required: shampoo her hair at each performance of *South Pacific,* fly through the air in *Peter Pan,* and yodel in *The Sound of Music.* A real trouper, Martin was never averse to touring, even performing *Hello, Dolly!* in 1965 for armed service personnel in Vietnam before bringing it to London. She endeared herself to senior citizens when she cohosted the public television show *Over Easy* (1981–1983), aimed at the over-sixty viewer. Inevitably, in 1989, Martin was an honoree at the annual Kennedy Center gala in Washington, D.C. Martin epitomized both Broadway and humanity at its best.

★

Mary Martin, *My Heart Belongs* (1976), is a genial overview of her career, and *Mary Martin's Needlepoint* (1969) is part show-business memoir and part manual on the art of needlepoint. Barry Rivadue, *Mary Martin: A Bio-Bibliography* (1991), is a meticulously researched study of Martin, including a record of stage appearances, a complete discography, filmography, bibliography, and list of archival sources. An obituary is in the *New York Times* (5 Nov. 1990).

BERNARD F. DICK

MARVIN, Lee (*b.* 19 February 1924 in New York City; *d.* 29 August 1987 in Tucson, Arizona), Academy Award–winning actor known for his tough-guy roles.

Marvin was eldest of two sons of Lamont W. Marvin, an advertising executive, and Courtenay D. Marvin, a beauty consultant and fashion editor. His early life was troubled. Despite, or perhaps because of, his family's affluence and the constant travels of his parents, Marvin sought constantly to buck the system, beginning at age four, when he successfully managed to slip away from home and stay on the run for two days. His adolescence was problematic. Attending a variety of expensive prep schools, he was regularly expelled. He later claimed the number of expulsions reached a dozen—the infractions ranging from relatively ordinary (smoking cigarettes) to the more ominous (hurling a fellow student out of a second-floor window).

Marvin's parents, despairing of their son's uncontrollable, nonconformist behavior, reluctantly consented in 1942 to his leaving high school in Florida and joining the Marine Corps. (His father, in an act of contentious rivalry, joined the corps, too.) Marvin felt his life was too safe and "sheltered," and his decision to enlist in the marines and see active duty during World War II was a way to literally

Lee Marvin. ARCHIVE PHOTOS

"toughen up." He was to get his wish, as his service took him into one of the roughest arenas of the war. Participating in numerous Pacific Island landings as a scout sniper, Marvin saw horrendous action. The incredibly high casualty rates of the beach assaults introduced him to an almost unparalleled theater of blood. As he watched his friends and compatriots falling all around him, Marvin's life and attitudes were irrevocably honed and formed. He decided that the "most useless word in the world is 'Help!'" On Saipan in 1944, Marvin was shot in the lower back and incapacitated. His sciatic nerve was severed; the rehabilitation lasted thirteen months. He was awarded the Purple Heart. He would later comment that "it was nothing to shout about."

Readjusting to life in quiet Woodstock, New York, Marvin floundered. He attempted to reenlist in the marines but was reminded of his disability. He tried a succession of jobs, but none suited. He became a plumber's assistant, and in that unlikely environment he discovered an opportunity. Fixing the drains at a local repertory theater, he became enamored of the stage and tried out for a small part. Rewarded, Marvin determined to become an actor. He stayed at the theater in Woodstock until 1949, when, under the aegis of the American Theater Wing, he moved back to New York City. In 1950 he won a role on Broadway in a production of *Billy Budd.* Around this time he was scouted by the Hollywood director Henry Hathaway to appear as an extra in the film *You're in the Navy Now* (1951). Hathaway, impressed by his find, expanded Marvin's part to six lines and encouraged him to move to California. Initially recalcitrant, Marvin heeded the director's advice. Bit parts in several movies quickly followed. In California he met Betty Edeling. They were married on 5 February 1952 in Las Vegas, Nevada, and had four children.

Meanwhile, the tough-looking Marvin, with his imposing physical presence, established himself as a reliable screen villain, and the mid-1950s provided him with some memorable roles. In films such as *The Big Heat* (1953), *The Wild One* (1954), *The Caine Mutiny* (1954), *Bad Day at Black Rock* (1955), *Violent Saturday* (1955), and *I Died a Thousand Times* (1955) he was outstanding as a series of small-time lowlifes. In 1957 he graduated to leading man in the popular police television series *M Squad,* which ran until 1960. Apart from a showy supporting performance in *Raintree County* (1957), he was absent from movies during the run of the series.

The early 1960s saw Marvin's return to screen villainy, costarring with John Wayne in *The Comancheros* (1961), *The Man Who Shot Liberty Valance* (1962), and *Donovan's Reef* (1963). The film *The Killers* (1964) cemented his image as a cold, professional assassin and precipitated his jump to superstardom. Marvin's offscreen image was that of a dangerous, hard-drinking, fighting man, and the actor did nothing to dispel it. In fact, he reveled in outrageous behavior, which slowly took its toll on his health and family. His marriage ended in divorce in 1964 as his career ascended to new heights. For his dual role in *Cat Ballou* (1965), as both a drunken gunfighter and a noseless killer, Marvin received the Oscar for best actor of 1965. An impressive string of films followed: *The Professionals* (1966), *Point Blank* (1967), *The Dirty Dozen* (1967), and *Hell in the Pacific* (1968). His friendship with maverick director Sam Peckinpah led to his being offered the lead as an aging outlaw in *The Wild Bunch* (1969), which he declined, saying he'd "been there before." His drunken clowning reached its apotheosis with *Paint Your Wagon* (1969), the bloated film version of the Broadway musical. The film's tortured production history and notorious cost overruns were partially blamed on Marvin for his often alcohol-sodden unprofessional behavior. The fallout from the movie's bad notices and poor performance at the box office hurt Marvin and sullied his fading reputation. He took little consolation from the fact that his rendition of the song "Wanderin' Star" was a number-one hit in Europe.

In 1970, Marvin suddenly married again, which came as a big surprise, especially to his live-in lover, Michele Triola, who was unceremoniously cast out as a result. His bride was Pamela Feeley, whom he had met more than twenty years earlier, during his acting stint in Woodstock, and they were married on 18 October. Triola, who had changed her last name to Marvin, sued on the grounds that she had all the rights of a wife, thus setting in motion the famous Marvin-Triola "palimony" suit that would be a cause célèbre for almost a decade. Marvin had met Triola, a singer, on the set of *Ship of Fools* in 1964. Soon inseparable, they set up house together in Malibu, California. After her eviction in 1970 Triola engaged the services of Marvin Mitchelson, a prominent divorce attorney whose "pal alimony" or palimony changed the financial circumstances of unmarried couples.

Marvin remained a viable leading man during the 1970s but his career was in decline. He blamed his falling star on poor choices, and movies like *Pocket Money* (1972), *Prime Cut* (1972), *Emperor of the North Pole* (1973), *The Spikes Gang* (1974), and *The Klansman* (1974), in which he costarred with Richard Burton, did nothing to get him back on track. A brief artistic high point was his performance in the movie version of Eugene O'Neill's *The Iceman Cometh* (1973), directed by John Frankenheimer. On 9 January 1979 the palimony case came to trial. Each day the news media were filled with stories of drunken binges, gunplay, aborted pregnancies, general abuse, and mayhem. Triola was suing Marvin for half of the $3.6 million he had earned from 1964 to 1970. Judge Arthur K. Marshall awarded Triola $104,000 "for rehabilitation purposes." Both sides claimed victory. (The award was subsequently overturned.)

In 1980 Marvin appeared in Samuel Fuller's *The Big Red One,* a movie about World War II's Normandy landings and the subsequent drive across France and Germany, in which Marvin got to relive the frightening, dangerous days of his youth. Wearing a soldier's uniform, he seemed at home, fully in command, and the role fueled a change in his lifestyle. When it was over, he made a serious attempt to stop drinking, and he relocated, giving up his beloved Malibu for a ranch near Tucson, Arizona, which would be his home for the remainder of his life. In semiretirement, he lived there with second wife, Pamela, content to watch the sun rise over the mountains. He still worked, and one of his best roles of the 1980s was as the corrupt fur dealer in the movie adaptation of the Martin Cruz Smith novel *Gorky Park* (1983). Losing weight, in ill-health, and feeling old, Marvin succumbed to a fatal heart attack after a period of hospitalization in the Tucson Medical Center.

★

For biographical information see Donald Zec, *Marvin: The Story of Lee Marvin* (1980), and Pamela Feeley Marvin, *Lee Marvin: A Romance* (1997). Two articles in *Time* magazine (30 Apr. 1979) discuss the palimony case: "Man Against Woman" and J. K. Footlick and M. Kasindorf, "An Unmarried Woman." Obituaries are in the *New York Times* (30 and 31 Aug. 1987) and the *Los Angeles Times* (30 Aug. 1987).

NICK REDMAN

MATSUNAGA, Spark ("Sparkie") Masayuki (*b.* 8 October 1916 in Kauai, Hawaii; *d.* 15 April 1990 in Toronto, Canada), U.S. senator and environmentalist best known as the chief sponsor of legislation offering the nation's apology and reparations to Japanese Americans interned during World War II.

Matsunaga was one of six children of Kengoro and Chiyono (Fukushima) Matsunaga, poor immigrants to Hawaii from Japan. Economic survival compelled the family to labor in the sugarcane fields of Oahu. Matsunaga graduated from a rural high school in 1935 and enrolled at the University of Hawaii in 1936, financing his studies by holding down a plethora of part-time jobs. In 1941 he graduated with an Ed.B. degree with honors and was elected to Phi Beta Kappa.

After the Japanese attack on Pearl Harbor in December of that year and the U.S. entry into World War II, Matsunaga, although by now a second lieutenant in the U.S. Army, was, like thousands of other American citizens of Japanese ancestry, confined to an internment camp, in his case in Wisconsin. He and other Japanese-American internees petitioned President Franklin D. Roosevelt, who gave them permission to form the 100th Infantry Battalion,

Spark Matsunaga, 1974. AP/WIDE WORLD PHOTOS

which became one of the most highly decorated combat units in American history. Matsunaga was wounded twice during the war and participated in the Anzio landing in Italy in January 1944. His heroics earned him the Bronze Star with valor clasp and two Purple Hearts with oak leaf cluster. He was released from active service in December 1945 with the rank of captain. He retired from the army reserves in 1969 with the rank of lieutenant colonel.

After the war Matsunaga took advantage of the GI bill to study at Harvard Law School, graduating in 1951. He was admitted to the bar in Hawaii in 1952. While still at Harvard, Matsunaga married Helene Hatsumi Tokunaga on 6 August 1948. They had five children.

Matsunaga was the assistant public prosecutor for the city and county of Honolulu from 1952 to 1954; from 1954 to 1962 he was in private practice in the city. In 1954 he was elected to the Hawaii territorial House of Representatives; on leaving that body in 1959 he was its majority leader. In 1962 he was elected to the U.S. House of Representatives and was reelected to six terms. In 1976 Matsunaga was elected to the U.S. Senate, where he served until his death.

In Congress, Matsunaga, a liberal Democrat, was an advocate of joint exploration of space by the Soviet Union and the United States and an even stronger proponent of resolving disputes between the two superpowers by peaceful resolution. In the 1980s he was the paramount spokesperson on environmental issues in the Senate. After a fact-finding trip to Japan, he urged the federal government to explore the feasibility of developing wind power for commercial ships. He also wanted the government to fund research on the use of solar and wind power to generate electricity. He urged the administrations of Ronald Reagan and George Bush to encourage research in synthetic fuels based on hydrogen rather than continuing to use petroleum-based fuel. He was also a cosponsor of the Clean Air Act.

Matsunaga's major contribution in the Senate was as the architect of the legislation enacted on 27 July 1988 that apologized for the internment camps and authorized cash payments of $20,000 to each Japanese-American internee still living—an estimated 60,000 out of a total of 120,000 internees. While endeavoring to drum up support in the Senate for the legislation, Matsunaga drew on his experiences as an internee. At the Wisconsin camp, he told his colleagues, he saw an elderly man machine-gunned to death as he attempted to retrieve for his grandson a baseball that had rolled into a restricted zone. The final version of the bill was signed into law by President Reagan in a White House ceremony on 10 August 1988. The War Returnee Measure, as it was named, acknowledged that the U.S. government had committed "grave injustice" against Japanese Americans as a result of war hysteria in the aftermath of the Japanese attack on Pearl Harbor. The relocation and internment program was undertaken, the measure said, "without adequate security reasons and without any acts of espionage or sabotage" being recorded. President Reagan stated at the signing that "it's not for us . . . to pass judgment upon those who may have made mistakes while engaged in that great struggle. Yet we must recognize that the internment of Japanese Americans was just that, a mistake."

Matsunaga died of cancer in Toronto General Hospital, where he had gone for treatment.

It is as a humanitarian who fought hard to provide a reasonable apology to Japanese Americans from their government that Matsunaga is best remembered.

★

Lawrence H. Fuchs, *Hawaii Pono: A Social History* (1961), documents the economic plight of Japanese immigrants to Hawaii during the decades between the world wars. Tom Coffman, *Catch a Wave: A Case Study of Hawaii's New Politics* (1973), details the post–World War II politics in Hawaii. Roger John Bell, *Last Among Equals: Hawaiian Statehood and American Politics* (1984), examines the history of Hawaii's drive for statehood. Masayo Umezawa Duus, *Unlikely Liberators: The Men of the 100th and 442nd* (1987), presents the history of the 100th Battalion and 442nd Regimental Combat Team, units made up almost entirely of Japanese Americans sent into the European theater of World War II. An obituary is in the *New York Times* (16 Apr. 1990). Chuck Mau, *John A. Burns Oral History Project* (21 Sept. 1975), consists of tapes on issues of statehood and what it represented to Hawaii's Japanese people.

P. Dale Rorex

MATTHEWS, Burnita Shelton (*b.* 28 December 1894 near Hazelhurst, Mississippi; *d.* 25 April 1988 in Washington, D.C.), suffragist, feminist, lawyer, and the first woman to serve as a judge on a U.S. District Court.

Burnita Shelton was one of six children of Burnell Shelton and Lora Drew (Barlow) Shelton. Burnell Shelton was a planter and an elected official in Copiah County, Mississippi, where he served as the tax collector and sheriff and also as the clerk of the Chancery Court. Lora Shelton was educated as a musician at Whitworth College (a boarding school for young women) but stayed home to raise her children. Burnita attended the public schools and briefly attended Whitworth until the death of her mother.

From a young age Burnita wanted to pursue a legal career, but her father pushed her toward the study and teaching of music, sending her in 1915 to the Cincinnati Conservatory of Music, where she received a teaching certificate. However, Burnita never deviated from her course to become a lawyer. In 1917, against her family's wishes, she married a lawyer, Percy A. Matthews, whom she had known in high school and who by this time was planning to join the U.S. war effort in World War I. He immediately enlisted and Burnita Matthews then lived independently, supporting herself by teaching music in a small town in Georgia and later moving to Washington, D.C., to work with the Veterans Administration. She purposely chose Washington because it had one of the few law schools that would accept women. She rejected her father's offer to pay for her law school and instead sent herself at night. Attending National University Law School, she graduated with an LL.B. degree in 1919 and LL.M. and Master of Patent Law degrees in 1920.

While at law school Matthews became involved with the militant branch of the women's suffrage movement, the National Woman's Party (NWP). Although her suffrage activities were limited to weekend picketing at the White House for passage of the Nineteenth Amendment, Matthews continued with the NWP after the amendment's passage and her graduation from law school. Throughout the 1920s, as she was establishing a small legal practice, Matthews headed up the Legal Research Department of the NWP. This department engaged in a decade-long project of identifying legal discriminations against women in state laws. States passed several pieces of legislation drafted by Matthews, among them laws that removed the disqualification of women as jurors in the District of Columbia; eliminated the preference for men over women in inheritance in Arkansas, the District of Columbia, and New York; gave women teachers in Maryland and New Jersey equal pay with men teachers for equal work; and allowed South Carolina married women to sue and be sued without a husband's rejoinder. During this time Matthews also assisted Alice Paul, head of the NWP, in creating the original version of the Equal Rights Amendment and became actively engaged in the organization's effort to secure its passage. Throughout the 1920s and 1930s Matthews was the legal expert for the NWP when testifying before Congress in support of the amendment. As legal counsel for the NWP she also secured the largest government condemnation award ever granted when the United States acquired the Woman's Party house and land to build the Supreme Court building. Her success against the government in that case cemented her reputation as one of the best lawyers in Washington, and her private practice grew. She eventually joined two other women lawyers with NWP ties, Rebekah Greathouse and Laura Berrien, in the firm Matthews, Berrien, and Greathouse. As her affiliation with the Woman's Party receded during the late 1930s and 1940s, Matthews's activities gravitated toward work with legal and professional organizations such as the District of Columbia Bar Association, Woman's Bar Association, American Bar Association, and National Association of Women Lawyers. She also taught at the Washington College of Law, which later became part of American University.

In 1949 President Truman appointed Matthews to the United States District Court for the District of Columbia. She was the first woman ever appointed to a federal trial court and only the second woman ever appointed to a federal constitutional court. She hired only women law clerks and counseled them against having children if they intended a career in the law. Matthews herself had no children, never actually living with her husband, Percy, for any length of time until his retirement in 1955. During her twenty-eight-year tenure on the bench she presided over several major trials. In 1955 she refused to order the State Department to issue a passport to the African-American actor and political activist Paul Robeson, ruling that he had first to exhaust all administrative remedies. In 1957 she presided over the bribery trial of Teamsters Union president Jimmy Hoffa, in which he was acquitted. In *Fulwood* v. *Clemmer* (1962), Judge Matthews upheld the right of Black Muslims in the local prison to conduct religious services. She took senior status in 1969 and heard cases at both the district court and court of appeals (by designation) until her retirement in 1977. She died in 1988 of a stroke and was buried in the Shelton family cemetery in Copiah County, Mississippi.

Although she was undoubtedly a feminist and supporter of women and women's rights throughout her life, Matthews's true passion was the law. Her activism for the Na-

Burnita Matthews. PHOTO BY HARRIS & EWING, WASHINGTON, D.C.

tional Woman's Party always centered on legal work, and she retreated from the NWP as its activities become primarily political in nature. On the bench, Matthews's feminism was tempered by her positivist approach to the law (that is, legislatures make the law, and judges just apply it), and by her desire to be accepted and respected by other judges. Her judicial philosophy, as reflected in her written opinions, stressed an adherence to precedent and procedure rather than an emphasis on rights and freedoms. As a result her decisions were rarely groundbreaking, precedent-setting, or controversial. Yet, those who served on the U.S. District Court or who worked with Judge Matthews agreed that she was the hardest-working judge they knew, as well as a very good judge.

★

The Burnita Shelton Matthews Collection is housed at the Schlesinger Library, Cambridge, Massachusetts, and at the Mississippi Department of History and Archives, Jackson, Mississippi. Kate Greene, "Torts over Tempo: The Life and Career of Judge Burnita Shelton Matthews," *Journal of Mississippi History* 56, no. 3 (Aug. 1994): 181–210, primarily chronicles the legal career of Judge Matthews prior to her appointment to the U.S. District Court. An obituary is in the *New York Times* (28 Apr. 1988). "Burnita Shelton Matthews: Pathfinder in the Legal Aspects of Women," a transcript of a 29 April 1973 interview by Amelia R. Fry, is part of the Suffragists Oral History Project, Bancroft Library, University of California at Berkeley.

KATE GREENE

Gardiner C. Means. FABIAN BACHRACH/ARCHIVE PHOTOS

MEANS, Gardiner Coit (*b.* 8 June 1896 in Windham, Connecticut; *d.* 15 February 1988 in Vienna, Virginia), economist and public servant who coauthored *The Modern Corporation and Private Property* (1932) and originated the theory of administered prices.

One of three sons of Frederick Howard Means, a Congregationalist minister, and Helen Chandler (Coit) Means, an art teacher, Gardiner C. Means grew up in Winchester, Massachusetts, and Madison, Maine. A chemistry major at Harvard, he enlisted in the army in 1917, and following a stint at officers' training school in Plattsburgh, New York, where he met his future collaborator, Adolf A. Berle, served stateside as an aviator until 1919. Following his discharge Means worked for a year and a half with the Near East Relief effort to aid Armenians in Turkey. Upon his return to the United States, he studied at the Lowell Textile Institute in Massachusetts and then operated a wool blanket business for several years. He married Caroline Farrar Ware, a historian, on 2 June 1927. They had no children.

Means returned to Harvard in 1924 as a graduate student in economics, receiving an M.A. degree in 1927 and a Ph.D. in 1933. His observations in Turkey, as well as his experience as a businessman, contributed to his perception of crucial differences between a premodern market economy and a modern corporate economy. In granting his degree, the Harvard doctoral committee, more orthodox-minded than he, required deletion of the theoretical section of his dissertation, which was titled "The Corporate Revolution."

In 1932 Means collaborated with James C. Bonbright on *The Holding Company: Its Public Significance and Its Regulation,* but his first major impact came with publication that same year of *The Modern Corporation and Private Property,* coauthored with Berle. The project was conceived by Berle, a lawyer interested in the legal implications of the separation of ownership from management in large corporations. He engaged Means to develop the statistical economic foundations of the study. While the stylistic verve of the book was Berle's, it was Means who demonstrated the extent of corporate concentration and who fashioned the arguments as to the nature and import of corporate control. Published to much acclaim at the depth of the Great Depression, the book is now considered a classic.

In 1933 Means joined the administration of Franklin D. Roosevelt, serving as economic adviser on finance to the secretary of agriculture from 1933 to 1935. Thereafter he served as director of the industrial section of the National Resources Committee (NRC) from 1935 to 1939, and economic adviser to the National Resources Planning Board (NRPB) in 1939 and 1940. In this context Means set forth his theory of administered prices. In *Industrial Prices and Their Relative Inflexibility* (1935), published as a U.S. Senate document, Means held that, in response to reduced demand, prices controlled by the market mechanism fell, while prices in concentrated industries tended to remain relatively rigid, with production and employment reduced instead. Means identified this as the modern corporate ability to "administer" prices, and to it he attributed the exceptional severity of the Great Depression. Based upon the decline of the market mechanism as an overall coordinator of the economy, Means called for new forms of coordination via structural planning bodies, with government, business, labor, and consumer participation. His analyses were presented in popular form in *The Modern Economy in Action* (1936), coauthored with his wife, and supplemented in two NRC studies, *Patterns of Resource Use* (1938) and *The Structure of the American Economy* (1939).

Means's challenge to orthodox economic theory and policy developed concurrently with that of the British economist John Maynard Keynes. Agreeing with Means as to the existence of administered prices, but considering the phenomenon a secondary factor, Keynes focused on noninstitutional sources of the Depression and favored a fiscal rather than structural solution to it. Means's effort to find common theoretical ground with Keynes during a 1939 visit to the latter's home was rebuffed by the British economist. Bested by the leading American Keynesian, Alvin H. Hansen, and others in a struggle over future analytical and policy directions at the NRPB, Means left the agency in 1940.

Means served as a fiscal analyst in the Bureau of the Budget in 1940 and 1941 and subsequently joined the business-sponsored Committee for Economic Development as associate director of research from 1943 to 1949. He was an economic consultant to the CED from 1949 to 1958 and to the Fund for the Republic from 1957 to 1959. Means's voice was again heard prominently in economic discourse beginning in the latter part of the 1950s. In testimony before congressional committees, in *The Corporate Revolution in America* (1962) and *Pricing Power and the Public Interest: A Study Based on Steel* (1962), and as a contributor to *The Roots of Inflation: The International Crisis* (1975), Means's concepts received an encore hearing in his diagnosis of what he dubbed "administrative inflation." First briefly in the later 1950s and then powerfully in the 1970s, Means argued, there appeared a form of inflation based upon the corporate ability to administer prices rather than upon forces of supply and demand. Not remediable by conventional Keynesian fiscal techniques, the solution to this new manifestation of administered prices, Means held, required the creation of new forms of structural planning.

Means and his wife acquired a seventy-acre farm and apple orchard in Vienna, Virginia, in 1935. They lived in a clapboard house on the farm. During his later years Means became involved in conservation activities. He remained active until suffering a stroke in 1987, the complications of which led to his death six months later. He was cremated and his ashes were scattered over his property, which was bequeathed to the state and became Meadowlark Gardens Regional Park.

Means's ideas never threatened the citadel of traditional economic theory. When acknowledged at all, his points were typically dismissed by orthodox economists as reflective of deviations from the market norm. Means's influence, however, endured among heterodox economists of the institutionalist and post-Keynesian schools. He received the Veblen-Commons Award of the Association for Evolutionary Economics in 1974. Two of that organization's economists, Frederic S. Lee and Warren J. Samuels, edited *The Heterodox Economics of Gardiner C. Means: A Collection* (1992) and a previously unpublished book manuscript, *A Monetary Theory of Employment* (1994). Hence, Means's contributions continued to be valued and built upon by a significant minority of economists.

★

The Gardiner C. Means Papers are at the Franklin D. Roosevelt Library in Hyde Park, New York. Warren J. Samuels and Steven G. Medema, *Gardiner C. Means: Institutionalist and Post Keynesian* (1990), assesses his contributions to economic thought. Theodore Rosenof, *Economics in the Long Run: New Deal Theorists and Their Legacies, 1933–1993* (1997), compares Means with Keynes and Hansen. Frederic S. Lee provides detailed analyses of several key aspects of Means's career in "A New Dealer in Agriculture: G. C. Means and the Writing of *Industrial Prices,*" *Review of Social Economy* 46 (Oct. 1988): 180–202; "From Multi-Industry Planning to Keynesian Planning: Gardiner Means, the American Keynesians, and National Economic Planning at the National Resources Committee," *Journal of Policy History* 2, no. 2 (1990): 186–212; and "The Modern Corporation and Gardiner C. Means's Critique of Neoclassical Economics," *Journal of Economic Issues* 24 (Sept. 1990): 673–693. Obituaries are in the *Washington Post* (17 Feb. 1988) and the *New York Times* (18 Feb. 1988).

THEODORE ROSENOF

MEDINA, Harold Raymond (*b.* 16 February 1888 in Brooklyn, New York; *d.* 15 March 1991 in Westwood, New Jersey), federal trial and appeals court judge remembered principally for presiding over a notorious trial in which eleven leaders of the American Communist party were convicted of urging the violent overthrow of the U.S. government.

Born to Joaquin A. and Elizabeth (Fash) Medina and raised in Brooklyn, Medina had an exemplary record at Princeton University, where he was a noted classics scholar with a particular interest in the Roman poets Virgil and Horace; he graduated Phi Beta Kappa in 1909. In 1911 he married Ethel Forde Hillyer. They had two children, and lived for many years on a fifty-five-acre estate in Westhampton, Long Island. Medina received his law degree with high distinction from Columbia Law School in 1912, and he taught there periodically from 1915 to 1940.

Although highly successful as a litigating counsel in New York City for business and corporate clients, Medina first came to prominence when he took the widely unpopular case of Anthony Cramer, who was charged with treason during World War II. Cramer, a German immigrant and naturalized citizen, was convicted of giving aid to German saboteurs who in June 1942 landed on the Florida and Long Island coasts from enemy submarines to commit disruptive acts against the nation's industrial operations related to the war effort. Medina argued in the U.S. Court of Appeals for the Second Circuit in New York City that Cramer's relationship with one of the saboteurs, whom he admittedly assisted by placing a large amount of the saboteur's cash in his own safe deposit box, was innocent and without the necessary treasonable intent against the United States. Medina lost in the Court of Appeals but ultimately prevailed in the U.S. Supreme Court, where the justices ruled five to four that to be convicted of treason one must be shown to have committed an overt act that itself manifests treasonous intent. The case remains the most important analytical explication of the law of treason in the twentieth century.

In 1947 Medina left what had become an extremely lucrative law practice to accept an appointment by President Harry S. Truman as a federal trial judge in the U.S. District Court for the Southern District of New York. Two years later he presided over the case that made his name recognizable in households across the United States. *United States* v. *Eugene Dennis et al.* involved the prosecution of Eugene Dennis, head of the American Communist party, and ten other of the party's senior officials for violation of the Smith Act, a federal statute that made advocating the overthrow of the U.S. government by force and violence a crime. The law did not require that any act to effect or facilitate the overthrow be committed; proving advocacy alone was sufficient to sustain a conviction.

The trial, which was conducted in the Foley Square courthouse in New York City, lasted from 8 March to 14 October 1949 and was in constant turmoil and disorder. The defendants' lawyers, setting upon a strategy to bait the judge into committing trial error, to intimidate and confuse the jury into deadlock, and to ridicule relentlessly the procedures and dignity of the federal court, engendered unprecedented acrimony between themselves and Judge Medina. Crowds sympathetic to the defendants thronged the square outside the courthouse and chanted mocking slogans against the judge. The trial record at one point notes that Judge Medina asked one of the defense lawyers why it was that at a certain time every morning and every afternoon a member of the defense team called the judge a liar. The lawyer replied that the remark was timed to make the deadlines of morning and evening editions of the newspapers. Medina charged the jury that the right to freedom of speech granted by the First Amendment did not protect advocacy accompanied by an intent to overthrow the government "as speedily as circumstances would permit" in a period of "clear and present danger" to the government. After the defendants were convicted and sentenced to prison, the Supreme Court affirmed the convictions in 1951 on a "clear and present danger" basis.

Medina was appointed to the U.S. Court of Appeals for the Second Circuit in 1951 and served there until his retirement in 1980. His most notable decision in the Court of Appeals was a 420-page opinion that brilliantly reviewed and applied antitrust principles to a complaint brought by

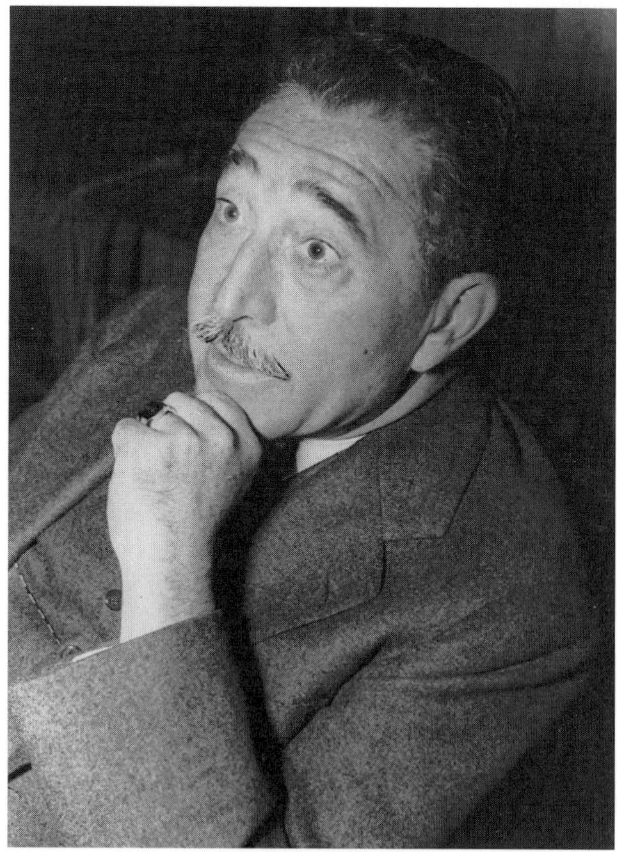

Judge Harold Medina, 1949. UPI/CORBIS-BETTMANN

the federal government against seventeen investment banking firms; he ruled in favor of the defendant firms.

During his active years on the bench, Judge Medina lectured widely and published two well-received books on free speech, freedom of the press, and constitutional values in American life. Medina died in his sleep at the age of 102 after being taken to the hospital with a slight fever. At the time of his death, the *National Review* described Medina, who read French, Latin, and Greek, as "profoundly cultivated, of impeccable manners, who presided with heroic calm. He was the sort of citizen who vitally sustains his civilization."

★

Medina's writings include *Judge Medina Speaks: A Group Address* (1954), edited by Maxine Boord Virtue, which deals with such subjects as the primacy of law in a free society, the vitality of American democratic institutions, and the values of untrammeled speech in national decisions; and *The Anatomy of Freedom* (1959), a nonscholarly review of principles of constitutional law, with emphasis on rights of freedom of speech and press.

KENNETH CONBOY

MEEKER, Ralph (*b.* 21 November 1920 in Minneapolis, Minnesota; *d.* 5 August 1988 in Woodland Hills, California), actor in theater and film known primarily for his work as the lead in the Broadway production of William Inge's *Picnic* (1953).

Ralph Meeker. ARCHIVE PHOTOS

Meeker was born Ralph Rathgeber to Ralph Rathgeber and Magnhild Senovia Haavig Meeker in Minnesota. The family moved to Chicago when he was three. An only child, Meeker attended the Leelanau School for Boys in Glen Arbor, Michigan, graduating in 1938. He then went on to Northwestern University, where he studied music composition and business administration for two years before moving into drama. Enlisting in the U.S. Navy after leaving Northwestern with "a lot of credits but no degrees" in 1942, Meeker suffered an injury on his first training cruise and was discharged. He joined the touring cast of *The Doughgirls* (1943) in a walk-on part. He later claimed to have been hired "because I fit the costume." Meeker became the understudy to the second male lead, and the play closed after nine months. He moved to New York City and worked as a soda jerk at the Whelan Drugstore across from the Roxy Theatre while searching for new acting jobs.

Meeker joined a stock company, which led to a job as a lead in *Ten Little Indians* with a touring United Service Organizations (USO) troupe in Italy for the rest of the war. Returning to New York in 1945, he gained a small part in José Ferrer's production of *Strange Fruit,* and in 1947 he became a walk-on and understudy in Ferrer's *Cyrano de Bergerac.* Meeker left *Cyrano* to join the cast of *Mister Roberts* (1947) in the part of Mannion and as understudy to Henry Fonda, who had the title role. In 1949, when Marlon Brando left *A Streetcar Named Desire* for film, Joshua Logan, the director of *Mister Roberts,* recommended Meeker as Brando's successor in the role of Stanley Kowalski. Meeker won the role and strong reviews.

His stage success led to a contract with Metro-Goldwyn-Mayer that bound Meeker for five years but allowed him to return to New York after two years to work in the theater. His first films, *Teresa* (1951) and *Four in a Jeep* (1951), met with some success. Other early films included *Shadow in the Sky* (1951), *Code 2* (1953), and *The Naked Spur* (1953). Despite his musical background and years of voice lessons, the singing for his role in his film *Somebody Loves Me* (1952) was dubbed in by another actor. "They didn't think [my voice] was romantic enough," he explained.

Meeker returned to Broadway in 1953, working again for Logan, in William Inge's *Picnic.* He was cast as the lead, a drifter and former football hero named Hal Carter who shakes up the lives of five women in a small Kansas town. Meeker became famous for his performance, for which he won a New York Critics Circle Award in 1954, and the play itself won a Pulitzer Prize. He continued in the role for more than a year and took it on the road before returning to film.

Metro-Goldwyn-Mayer bought the film rights to Inge's

play and offered the lead to Meeker on the condition that he sign a seven-year exclusive contract. He refused, explaining that "I'm living my own life. Not being a puppet is important to me. I make my own decisions and when they're wrong I have only myself to blame." The film was a hit, but the coveted role of Hal Carter was played by William Holden. Meeker made several memorable films during the mid-1950s, including the film noir *Kiss Me Deadly* (1955), directed by Robert Aldrich, and the war film *Paths of Glory* (1957), directed by Stanley Kubrick, but most of his work in Hollywood consisted of character roles in mediocre motion pictures. Tall and muscular, with an imposing presence, he was usually cast as a braggart or tough guy, and in a large number of his roles he played a sergeant in the army.

Meeker worked in television throughout the 1960s and early 1970s. *Not for Hire,* a television series in which he starred, premiered in 1960. He again played an army sergeant, this one a globe-trotting public defender for soldiers in trouble. The series lasted one season. He also worked for *Kraft Television Theater, Playhouse 90,* and as a stand-in for Ed Sullivan on the *Ed Sullivan Show* for ten weeks in the early 1960s. Meeker married the actress Salome Jens on 20 July 1964, but the relationship quickly foundered, and they divorced in Mexico in December 1966. They had no children. Meeker was married and divorced a second time, to Colleen Rose Neary.

Meeker continued to perform on stage, starring in *Cloud 7* (1958), *Rhinoceros* (1961), *Something About a Soldier* (1962), and *Mrs. Dally* (1965). He joined the Lincoln Center Repertory Theater just as it was forming under Elia Kazan and played in *After the Fall* (1964) and *But for Whom Charlie* (1965). In 1971 Meeker finally realized his long-standing dream of playing in a musical comedy, taking over the lead role in an off-Broadway production of *The House of Blue Leaves.*

Meeker retired to Sun Valley, Idaho, in the 1970s, where he owned the Cecil B. DeMille ranch, the site of many of DeMille's biblical films. He suffered a series of strokes in the last eight years of his life. He died of a heart attack at the Motion Picture and Television Hospital in Woodland Hills, California. He was survived by his third wife, Millicent Meeker.

Ralph Meeker was a dedicated actor who willingly gave up lucrative film work for chances at more fulfilling stage roles. He once said, "I want to be the best damned actor in the world, not the biggest star. I may never achieve my goal, but at least it's there for me to find the right road to it." Meeker was known for both his skill as an actor and his independence as an artist.

★

A file on Meeker that includes press releases, reviews, newspaper articles, and photographs is in the Billy Rose Theater Collection of the New York Public Library's Performing Arts Research Center at Lincoln Center. Obituaries are in *Newsday* and the *New York Times* (both 6 Aug. 1988).

BRADLEY F. REED

MENNINGER, Karl Augustus (*b.* 22 July 1893 in Topeka, Kansas; *d.* 18 July 1990 in Topeka, Kansas), psychiatrist who was one of the first physicians in the United States to receive psychoanalytic training and a founder of the world-famous Menninger Clinic and Menninger Foundation in Topeka.

Menninger's father, Charles Frederick Menninger, was a professor at Campbell University in Holton, Kansas, when he met and married Flora Knisely, a student at Campbell. Charles Menninger went on to study medicine and established a practice in Topeka, in 1890. Three years later Karl, the first of three sons, was born.

While her three sons were growing up in Topeka, Menninger's mother, a feminist for her time, taught school, organized Bible classes, and wrote her autobiography, *Days of My Life* (1939). Karl identified with his mother and behaved in a comparably strong, assertive manner all of his life. Often restless and excitable, sometimes explosive, Karl sparkled in conversation. However, Menninger labeled

Karl Menninger, *c.* 1943. UPI/CORBIS-BETTMANN

himself his mother's "oldest problem child," because he did not feel that he could measure up to her stern demands. The young Menninger respected his father's intellect and even temper but was jealous of his noticeable preference for Karl's younger brother Will. When possible, the young Menningers traveled with their father on house calls.

In their formative years stamp collecting became a serious hobby for the Menninger brothers when they formally incorporated their holdings into the KAWCEAM Company (the name was an amalgam of their initials); however, there were burdensome quarrels over the division of proceeds when the "company" was liquidated. (This was the first of many grave disagreements between the three brothers; although Karl and Will worked for the same organization throughout their careers, they continued to have many differences.)

In 1910 Menninger began his university career at Washburn College in Topeka, took some summer courses at Indiana University, and completed his B.A. degree in 1914 and M.S. degree in 1915 at the University of Wisconsin. He was awarded an M.D. degree cum laude from Harvard Medical School in 1917 and did his internship at Kansas City (Missouri) General Hospital. He served as a lieutenant, junior grade, in the U.S. Naval Reserve during World War I. In 1918 and 1919 Menninger worked with Ernest Southard, a neuropathology instructor, at Boston Psychopathic Hospital and Harvard Medical School. Southard was a major force in stimulating the young doctor's interest in helping patients with emotional problems. Menninger considered Southard his mentor, citing him as "one of the greatest inspirations of my life." Menninger also taught at Tufts Medical School during this time, but when Southard died in 1920 he returned to Topeka to join forces with his father.

On 19 September 1916 Menninger married a fellow Washburn student, Grace Gaines; they had three children: Julia, Martha, and a son, Robert, who also pursued a psychiatric career. Menninger was divorced from Gaines in February 1941, and on 9 September 1941 he married Jeanetta Lyle. They adopted a daughter, Rosemary. His second wife collaborated with Menninger on a book, *Love Against Hate* (1942).

The Menninger Clinic, established by Charles and Karl Menninger, began in the 1920s in a farmhouse and was modeled on the revolutionary concepts of the Mayo Clinic in Rochester, Minnesota. It was intended as a central group practice utilizing many types of specialists in psychotherapy. Founded on the proviso "No patient is untreatable," it provided a "total environment" where there was a family atmosphere, physical exercise, and medical doctors from various disciplines to encourage comprehensive care. The clinic utilized milieu therapy, an innovative technique centering on the relationship between patient and therapist. The original farmhouse with its thirteen patients eventually expanded to thirty-nine buildings, set on 430 acres and two campuses with a staff of 900. Karl Menninger's principal contribution was his uniquely flexible team approach to emotional treatment of patients at the family clinic. He analyzed purposes, objectives, and methods of care to try to reduce the need for extensive treatment. A colleague summarized his approach as emphasizing patients as human beings rather than bearers of bizarre diseases. Menninger sought to help troubled, isolated individuals find a caring environment in which to work out their potential for creativity and keep themselves emotionally intact. The Menninger Foundation, established in 1941, became a teaching center for psychiatrists and a model for scores of hospitals around the world. Menninger was chairman of the board of trustees until 1990.

Menninger was instrumental in establishing the Karl Menninger School of Psychiatry and Mental Health Sciences, a cooperative effort of the Menninger Clinic and Topeka State Hospital. Menninger served as dean of the school from 1946 to 1969, overseeing the training of more than 2,000 mental health professionals.

One of Menninger's main accomplishments was explaining psychiatry to the general public as an uncomplicated method of helping the mentally disturbed. A benevolent, paternalistic figure, Menninger encouraged patients to work through their problems using psychiatric techniques. His major premise was that the absence of parental love caused much individual destructiveness and mental illness. Through his writing, Menninger instilled a vital message to parents: "It is much easier, more logical, and more efficacious to help a child grow up with love and courage than it is to instill hope in a despondent soul. What mother and father mean to them is more than psychiatrists can ever mean" (quoted in the *New York Times* obituary). He advocated promoting capable schoolteachers to the lower grades so that they could exert a beneficial influence on children at an early age. These beliefs were also carried into his later studies of crime. His view was that imprisonment without psychiatric support was useless in assisting prisoners.

Menninger's list of causes was wide-ranging and eclectic. He was active in the American Indian Defense Association, the Kansas State Historical Society, the American League to Abolish Capital Punishment, the Planned Parenthood Federation, and the Council on Freedom from Censorship. Menninger's books include *The Human Mind* (1930), the first psychiatric nonfiction bestseller; *Crime of Punishment* (1966), a treatise on penal reform; and *Whatever Became of Sin?* (1973), an exploration of religion and moral values. Among the comments on his 1973 book were those of the British historian Arnold Toynbee, who wrote: "[Menninger] deals with both individual and collective sin, and at the same time shows that the distinction between the two kinds is not clear-cut, since my individual sin is partly society's and society's is partly mine." Carlylee Marney, director of Interpreter's House, a retreat for clergy added: "The full fruit of a Menninger lifetime is worth everyone's attention who cares about humanity." It has been suggested that Menninger tried in his work to address Socrates's question: "Why is it that men know what is good but do what is bad?"

Although Menninger disagreed with many of the concepts of Sigmund Freud, he was not interested in engaging in disputes with his colleagues. Instead he maintained friendships with "The Vatican," as he designated the organized school of psychoanalysts. In 1971, at the International Congress of Psychiatry in Vienna, Menninger and Dr. Anna Freud, daughter of the founder of the Freudian school, had important discussions regarding child psychiatry, their common bond.

Menninger once commented, "Nothing of human concern is really outside of psychiatry, so in a sense I have no hobbies; they are all part of my work." His primary leisure activities included farming, chess, listening to symphonies, and reading. In 1976 Menninger suffered facial paralysis after brain surgery and in 1984 he suffered a stroke complicated by bronchial pneumonia. Other, minor strokes followed. He required a pacemaker and had difficulty walking. He died of abdominal cancer four days short of his ninety-seventh birthday. He is buried in Hope Cemetery in Topeka.

In 1981 Menninger received the nation's highest civilian honor, the Medal of Freedom, from President Jimmy Carter. His most famous endowment is the Menninger Foundation. Another of his greatest legacies is the Villages, a small group of foster homes for neglected, abused, and homeless children in Topeka and other satellite sites.

★

A collection of Menninger's papers is housed at the Menninger Foundation in Topeka. His reflections, edited by Lucy Freeman, were published as *Sparks* (1973). Howard J. Faulkner and Virginia D. Pruitt, eds., *The Selected Correspondence of Karl A. Menninger,* 2 vols. (1988, 1995), cover the years 1919–1965. Lawrence J. Friedman, *Menninger: The Family and the Clinic* (1990), is a well-documented, comprehensive summary of the Menninger family and the development of the Menninger Foundation. A sketch in Anna Rothe, ed., *Current Biography 1948* (1949), summarizes Menninger's life and significant contributions to that date. An obituary is in the *New York Times* (19 July 1990).

JOAN LIZZIO

MEYNER, Robert Baumle (*b.* 3 July 1908 in Easton, Pennsylvania; *d.* 27 May 1990 in Captiva, Florida), lawyer and governor of New Jersey from 1954 to 1962.

Meyner was one of three children born to Gustave Herman Meyner, a loom repairer and silk worker, and Mary Sophia (Baumle) Meyner. His family moved to Phillipsburg, New Jersey, when he was eight years old; he attended school there, as well as in Paterson, New Jersey, where his father was employed for a short time. After graduating from Phillipsburg High School in 1926, he worked his way through Lafayette College in Easton. Majoring in government and law, Meyner also joined a dramatics group, was on the debating team, and served as editor of the college paper. In 1928 he showed his interest in politics when he organized an Al Smith for President club. Meyner received his A.B. degree in 1930 and went on to Columbia University Law School, graduating in 1933 and thus fulfilling his boyhood goal of becoming a lawyer. He was admitted to the New Jersey Bar the following year and served as law clerk with the firm of Jemil Walscheid and Milton Rosenkranz, first in Union City and then in Jersey City.

In 1936 Meyner returned to Phillipsburg to take over the practice of a lawyer who had died. The next year he became a counselor, and in 1940 he was admitted to practice law before the U.S. Supreme Court. His legal activities focused on trial work. Meyner's activity in bar associations at the national, state, and local levels, as well as his work in civic and social groups, helped him develop a political

Robert B. Meyner (*center*) and wife Helen with Irving Engel (*left*) leave for Germany for a conference on U.S.-German relations. ARCHIVE PHOTOS

base, and in 1941 he made his first bid for elective office when he ran for the New Jersey state senate. He lost by fifty votes. From August 1942 until December 1945 he was an officer in the U.S. Navy; he served as defense counsel in courts-martial and was also a commander of merchant vessel gun crews in both the Atlantic and Pacific. He was discharged with the rank of lieutenant commander.

Once back in civilian life, Meyner became active again in politics, and in 1946 he won the Democratic primary for the U.S. House of Representatives for the Seventh Congressional District but lost the general election to J. Parnell Thomas. In the following year he won election to the state senate by defeating Wayne Dumont, Jr. As a senator Meyner displayed what would become one of his basic political principles when he opposed establishing the New Jersey Turnpike Commission because it bypassed elections or referendums. In 1950 Meyner became senate minority leader, and in the next year he was made permanent chairman of the Democratic State Convention. In 1952, however, he lost his bid for reelection to the state senate to Dumont.

Meyner might have faded into political obscurity at this time, but in 1953 forces in New Jersey opposed to an attempted comeback by the once-powerful Democratic machine in Jersey City needed a primary candidate for the gubernatorial election. Virtually in a state of despair, they finally settled on Meyner. Despite the poor prospect of winning, he readily agreed. He defeated the machine-backed candidate, Elmer Wene, by 1,683 votes. Meyner's Republican opponent was Paul L. Troast, who led in the polls until a letter written by him to Governor Thomas E. Dewey of New York requesting "clemency" for Joe Fay, a convicted labor racketeer, was made public. Meyner won, and in his inaugural speech on 19 January 1954 he reiterated his views on submitting important governmental matters to the judgment of the people.

During the next four years Meyner's accomplishments included making bingo and raffles legal, increasing teachers' salaries, reorganizing Rutgers to make it a real "state university," and restructuring the state's fourteen departments to make them more effective and attuned to the populace. Meyner practiced economy in expenditures, and for his appointments he picked esteemed individuals whose qualifications were carefully checked. On 19 January 1957, at the age of forty-eight, he married Helen Day Stevenson. They had no children.

In November 1957 Meyner was elected to a second term when he defeated the wealthy publisher Malcolm Forbes by more than 200,000 votes. Meyner was the first New Jersey governor ever to serve consecutive terms. Transportation and conservation issues were among the matters on which he focused during the next four years, but he also looked ahead to a role in the 1960 presidential election contest, traveling around the country, making statements on foreign affairs, and attacking the administration of Dwight D. Eisenhower. Meyner brought a favorite-son candidacy and a slate of uncommitted delegates to the Democratic National Convention, but he did not allow the delegates to vote for John F. Kennedy on the first ballot. He thereby lost the chance to make the New Jersey vote the decisive one; the Kennedy administration was later cool to Meyner and the state.

Restricted by the state constitution to two consecutive terms, Meyner left the governorship on 16 January 1962. He resumed the practice of law in Newark and Phillipsburg, served as "national administrator of the cigarette industry's advertising code," and took well-paying jobs with insurance companies and banks. In 1969 he won the gubernatorial Democratic primary but lost the election to his Republican opponent, William Cahill. He died in his sleep after a long illness and poor health caused by a stroke in 1986; his remains were cremated.

Meyner projected an attractive physical image, which enhanced his political influence. Only forty-five when he became governor, he was almost six feet tall, possessed wavy hair, and spoke with a rich baritone voice. Besides openness to the people, he also stressed good administration, delegation of responsibility, and practicality. He was relaxed when discussing governmental matters and generally took a middle-of-the-road position in his approach to government. He developed the New Jersey Democratic party into a statewide organization rather than one dominated by Hudson County, but his appointments also included qualified Republicans. This showed his independence but annoyed some Democrats.

★

Robert B. Meyner, "From Newsboy to Governor," *American Magazine* 159 (Mar. 1955): 35–37, is an account written by Meyner describing his experiences, attitudes, and lifestyle during his first year as governor. *Three Decades of the Governor's Office: A Panel Discussion, Robert Meyner, Richard J. Hughes, William T. Cahill, Brendan T. Byrne* (1983) presents Meyner's views on government and the New Jersey governorship. William Lemmey's biography in Paul A. Stellhorn and Michael J. Birkner, eds., *The Governors of New Jersey, 1664–1974* (1982), is a comprehensive account of Meyner's life and contains many details about his political career. There are brief biographies in volume 3 of Robert Sobel and John Raimo, eds., *Biographical Directory of the Governors of the United States, 1789–1978* (1978), and in Eleanora W. Schoenebaum, ed., *Political Profiles: The Eisenhower Years* (1980). Duane Lockard, *The New Jersey Governor: A Study in Political Power* (1964), presents a brief assessment of Meyner as governor. David van Praagh, "New Jersey's Man-in-the-Middle," *Nation* 185 (7 Sept. 1957): 105–108 presents an assessment of Meyner as he completed his first term and was running for reelection; the article also contains a small amount of biographical data. An obituary is in the *New York Times* (29 May 1990).

ALLAN NELSON

MIDDLETON, Drew (*b.* 14 October 1913 in New York City; *d.* 10 January 1990 in New York City), reporter for the Associated Press and the *New York Times,* noted for his combat reports during World War II and coverage of postwar Europe and the cold war, and author of more than a dozen books on military affairs, postwar diplomacy, and foreign policy.

Middleton was the son of Elmer Thomas Middleton, the U.S. director of William Ewart and Son, Ltd., of Belfast, and Jean (Drew) Middleton. He attended elementary school in New York City and graduated from Columbia High School in South Orange, New Jersey, in 1931. He graduated cum laude from the Syracuse University School of Journalism with a B.S. degree in 1935. During his junior and senior years at Syracuse, he was the sports editor for the college paper and a correspondent for the *Syracuse Herald.*

Middleton remained in New York State after graduation, joining the *Poughkeepsie Eagle News* as a sports editor. In 1936 he became general news and sports editor of the *Poughkeepsie Evening Star.* He was hired by the Associated Press (AP) in March 1937 and in 1939 was assigned to AP's London bureau to cover sports. But with the outbreak of World War II, he instead began war correspondence, starting with coverage of Great Britain's declaration of war on Germany. In October of that year he was one of the reporters assigned to the British Expeditionary Forces and thus was able to dress in a British officer's uniform, wearing a white press armband, when he accompanied British forces to France that winter.

Middleton reported on the fall of France in June 1940 and was back in London in September, assigned to the British Home Army, just after the Battle of Britain began and the first German bombs fell on London. In 1941 he was in Iceland, reporting on U.S. troops there. He returned to London again in February 1942. In that year he won the International News Service Medal of Honor for his coverage of the failed Allied commando raid on the French port of Dieppe in August; Middleton was one of five American war correspondents chosen to accompany forces raiding the French Channel coast. On 31 March 1942, while on leave from the Tunisian front in London, he married Winifred Estelle ("Stevie") Mansel-Edwards, the daughter of a British officer; they had one child.

In October 1942 Middleton was hired as a combat correspondent by the *New York Times,* beginning a forty-two-year career with that paper. His first reports were from North Africa and the Mediterranean area. From 1943 to 1944 he accompanied the U.S. Eighth Air Force and Bomber Command, sending back to U.S. readers his interview with General Dwight D. Eisenhower and his account of the Casablanca Conference. In May 1943 he received an award from the National Headliners Club for the best exclusive foreign reporting from the North African theater.

Following his dispatches reporting on D day in June 1944, Middleton was accredited to the U.S. First Army and Supreme Headquarters, Allied Expeditionary Force, and he accompanied the First Division into the Battle of Aachen, during which the first major German city fell to U.S. forces. His firsthand accounts of that battle in September and October 1944 are representative of his factual but personal reporting throughout the war: "Machine-gun fire swept the street. Bullets hit the walls of our house and whispered as they ricocheted. This was hard, blind fighting in narrow backyards, or in steep staircases where men met unexpectedly, threw a grenade, or lunged with a bayonet."

In April 1945 Middleton covered the defeat of Germany and wrote about the meeting of U.S. and Soviet troops in Germany: "Two armies of plain men who had marched and fought from the blood-splashed beaches of Normandy and the shattered streets of Stalingrad have met on the Elbe River in the heart of Germany, splitting the Third Reich and sealing the doom of the German Army." From 1945 to 1946 he covered the peace conferences, the postwar occupation of Germany, and the war-crimes tribunals in Nuremberg. He followed postwar events from both sides of a divided Europe. In 1946 he was posted to the Soviet Union and covered the emerging cold war, and in that year he published his first volume of memoirs, *Our Share of Night: A Personal Narrative of the War Years.* Posted to Bonn, Germany, from 1947 to 1953, he covered the Berlin blockade and Berlin airlift (1948–1949). In 1947 he was awarded the Order of the British Empire and the following year the U.S. Medal of Freedom.

In 1949 Middleton published the first of his more than a dozen works of military history and historical analysis, *The Struggle for Germany.* It was followed by *The Defense of Western Europe* (1952); *These Are the British* (1957); *The Sky Suspended* (1960), about the Battle of Britain; and *The Supreme Choice: Britain and the European Community* (1963). From 1953 to 1963 he was the chief correspondent in London for the *New York Times,* and he referred to those years as his happiest abroad. He drank and dined with royalty, military officers, and political officials. After he received an invitation to tea at Buckingham Palace, his reporter colleagues began to refer to him as "Sir Drew."

From 1963 to 1965 Middleton was Paris bureau chief for the *New York Times.* He returned to New York City when he was named the paper's chief correspondent to the United Nations in 1965. In that year his books *The Atlantic Community: A Study in Unity and Disunity* and *Crisis in the West* were published. He was in Europe again from 1968 to 1970 as the European affairs correspondent, and his first

Drew Middleton. ARCHIVE PHOTOS

book on U.S. policy in Asia, *America's Stake in Asia* (1968), was published. In 1970 he returned to the United States as the Manhattan-based senior military correspondent for the *Times,* a position he held until his retirement. He covered armies, bases, conflicts, and policies and was often sought out by military and intelligence personnel. A second volume of memoirs, *Where Has Last July Gone?,* was published in 1973.

Before his retirement from the *New York Times* in 1984, Middleton wrote several more critically acclaimed books, including *Retreat from Victory: A Critical Appraisal of American Foreign and Military Policy from 1920 to the 1970s* (1973); *Can America Win the Next War?* (1975), about which national security adviser Zbigniew Brzezinski commented, "Since we desire peace, we must think about war. Middleton's provocative analysis is thus a vital contribution to peace"; *The Duel of the Giants: China and Russia in Asia* (1978); and *Crossroads of Modern Warfare* (1983).

Days after the Falklands War between Great Britain and Argentina erupted in April 1982, Middleton was on a plane to London. There he met with British officers he had known during World War II, spending evenings at his favorite hotel, the Savoy, and London's clubs, and was able to provide coverage that other reporters could not. The previous year he had been made an honorary life member of the Garrick Club in London, the first American so honored.

After his retirement as a staff correspondent in 1984, Middleton continued to write a twice-weekly column and special features for the *New York Times,* despite suffering from frail health after a heart attack in 1987. He died in his sleep at his Upper East Side apartment in Manhattan, and his remains were cremated.

Middleton, a raucous man with a cherubic face, had, as he wrote in his memoirs, "a front-row seat at the unending drama of man. I have worked in . . . the huge, changing, kaleidoscope of international affairs." From his front-line reporting of World War II up through the cold war, Middleton's articles, columns, and books provide one of the best firsthand, factual, but also personal, accounts of the twentieth century's most significant political events.

★

Correspondence concerning Middleton's books published by Charles Scribner's Sons is in the Princeton University Library, Department of Rare Books and Special Collections. See also Middleton's two volumes of memoirs, *Our Share of Night* (1946) and *Where Has Last July Gone?*(1973). An obituary is in the *New York Times* (12 Jan. 1990).

LOUISE B. KETZ

MILANOV, Zinka (*b.* 17 May 1906 in Zagreb, Croatia; *d.* 29 May 1989 in New York City), opera singer who was renowned for various Italian operatic roles, especially those performed during her three decades at New York's Metropolitan Opera.

Born Zinka Kunc (Milanov became her name in 1937) to Rudolf Kunc, a musically inclined banker, and Ljubica Smiciklas, she had one brother, Božidar Kunc, who later

Zinka Milanov as Aida, 1954. ARCHIVE PHOTOS

earned a reputation as a pianist and composer. Inspired by her father's beautiful baritone voice and her brother's precocious piano skills, Milanov began singing at age four and claimed that she sang the mezzo soprano part of Georges Bizet's *Carmen* four years later at a family gathering. Developing into a mature soprano voice, she graduated in 1920 from the Girls' Evangelical School in Zagreb, and then won acceptance to the Zagreb Royal Academy of Music, where her brother was studying. One recital there attracted the attention of soprano Milka Ternina, famed for her Wagnerian repertoire. At the academy Milanov received voice instruction first from Miss Ternina and then from her assistant, Marija Kostrenčič. She graduated with first prize from the academy.

On 29 October 1927 Milanov made her operatic debut as Leonora in Guiseppe Verdi's *Il Trovatore* with the Ljubljana Opera, where she would sing again over many seasons. In 1928 she began her long-term association with the Zagreb Opera, which ended in 1935; she sang a wide-ranging repertoire (in Croatian) in more than 350 performances. Her brother was helpful then, as in later years, as coach, musical adviser, and sometimes accompanist; she heeded his warnings not to continue certain vocally overstraining roles, such as those of Richard Wagner and Richard Strauss.

Milanov continued performing in either Croatian or German in Yugoslavia, Italy, Germany, and Austria; she became associated with the Deutsches Theater in Prague (1936–1937) and the Vienna State Opera and was excelling in some of the preferred roles of her later Metropolitan Opera career, namely the title role in Verdi'a *Aida,* Amelia in Verdi's *Un Ballo in Maschera,* Gioconda in Amilcare Ponchielli's *La Gioconda,* and Maddalena in Umberto Giordano's *Andrea Chénier*.

The year 1937 served as a turning point in Milanov's professional and personal life. Between acts of *Aida* one evening, Bruno Walter, who was conducting at the Vienna State Opera, proposed that she audition for the soprano part in Verdi's *Messa da Requiem,* which Arturo Toscanini was to conduct that August at the Salzburg Festival. After hearing her sing only twenty bars of the score, with Erich Leinsdorf at the piano, Toscanini selected her. The day following an *Aida* performance in Bratislava, 8 June, she auditioned in Prague before the trio from the New York Metropolitan Opera: Edward Johnson, general manager; Edward Ziegler, his assistant; and Artur Bodanzky, conductor. They offered her a three-year contract, stipulating that she lose twenty-five pounds within the next three months and learn several specific roles in Italian. The tenor Fernando Carpi assisted her in the Italian coaching, while bicycle exercises helped Milanov, who was a gourmet cook, to reduce. In July 1937 she married Predrag Milanov, a Yugoslavian actor and director, who assisted as her acting coach. They had no children. From then on, she generally used "Zinka Milanov" as her professional name.

Milanov's Metropolitan debut was 17 December 1937 as Leonora in *Il Trovatore*. Although she received good reviews as Leonora, her first appearance singing the title role in *Aida* there, on 2 February 1938, received a more memorable response from audience, management, and critics; many heralded her as the Metropolitan's successor to Rosa Ponselle, who had retired in April 1937. Milanov, like Ponselle, would sing Vincenzo Bellini's *Norma,* Leonora in Verdi's *La Forza del Destino,* and Elvira in his *Ernani* (29 December 1943; 9 January 1943; and 23 November 1956, her first performance dates of these operas at the Metropolitan, respectively).

There were also special concerts with Toscanini, such as the Verdi *Requiem* (in New York in March 1938; at Queen's Hall, for the London Music Festival, in May 1938; at Lucerne, in the city's first-time performance of the masterpiece, in August 1939; at a benefit concert at New York's Carnegie Hall on 23 November 1940; and in Buenos Aires in July 1941), and Beethoven's *Missa Solemnis* (in London in May 1939, and in New York City in December 1940). She sang Gilda in the Act IV presentation of Verdi's *Ri-*

goletto that Toscanini included in special wartime programming (on 25 July 1943 for a Treasury Bond NBC broadcast, and on 25 May 1944 for a Red Cross benefit at New York City's Madison Square Garden).

Other opera house appearances included San Francisco and Chicago, the Teatro Colón in Buenos Aires (from 1940 to 1942, including Puccini's *Turandot* and her first Desdemona in Verdi's *Otello* on 1 July 1941), the Teatro Municipale in Rio de Janeiro, prewar European commitments, and Milan's La Scala (in 1950 in Puccini's *Tosca,* conducted by Toscanini). Milanov did not make her debut at London's Covent Garden until 11 July 1955 (appearing in three performances of *Tosca*); she performed in another *Tosca* and in *Il Trovatore* two times the following June.

In November 1945 Milanov's husband left for Yugoslavia, reportedly for professional directing and acting commitments with the Zagreb Theater. In 1946, however, they were divorced. That same year Milanov became an American citizen. On 31 March 1947 she married Major General Ljubmir Ilič (a friend to Marshal Tito and a diplomatic minister plenipotentiary) at the Yugoslav embassy in Washington, D.C. They had no children. Ilič had to report soon to Belgrade, and his new wife was in Yugoslavia from 1947 to 1950, partly because of salary disputes with Edward Johnson. During the fall of 1949 a Soviet newspaper accused Milanov of being a cold war spy for the United States, an absurdity according to her manager, Jack Adams, in his public refutation of the story.

Returning to the United States in late November 1949, Milanov subsequently sang *Un Ballo in Maschera* at Hartford, Connecticut; there, as prearranged, Rudolf Bing, Johnson's successor, heard her live for the first time and immediately contracted her return to the Metropolitan, as Santuzza in Pietro Mascagni's *Cavalleria Rusticana* (17 January 1951). Her final years with the Metropolitan, generally considered her most glorious, included her exquisite first-time performances there of Maddalena in *Andrea Chénier* (16 November 1954) and the title role in *Tosca* (16 February 1955). When Renata Tebaldi had to cancel her first Metropolian *Aida,* Bing telephoned Milanov and, despite only six hours' notice, decided to turn the evening's performance into Milanov's Metropolitan debut as Tosca. One prominent critic, marveling at Milanov's interpretation of the role, wondered why management had deprived its audiences of such a Tosca for so long. During the 1950s Milanov made several complete opera recordings with RCA-Victor, which also reissued certain earlier performances, including some with Toscanini.

Milanov celebrated the twenty-fifth anniversary of her Metropolitan debut with *Andrea Chénier* (17 December 1962). Bing and the audience again paid tribute at her final complete opera performance of the same work on 14 April 1966. Two days later she and Richard Tucker sang a duet from *Andrea Chénier* as part of the final tribute to the "old" Metropolitan Opera House, soon to be demolished as the company prepared to open at Lincoln Center. The popular Milanov had presided over the installation of the new center's first steel beam in May 1963.

During the 1937–1941, 1942–1947, and 1950–1966 seasons, Milanov sang 417 opera performances with the Metropolitan Opera, thirteen opera roles, three Verdi *Requiems*, six galas, and nineteen concerts, either in New York or on tour. She enjoyed the special honor of opening four Metropolitan seasons, with *Un Ballo in Maschera* (2 December 1940), *Aida* (13 November 1951), *La Forza del Destino* (10 November 1952), and *Aida* again (8 November 1954, though only act 1, scene 1, and act 2 were presented during that gala devoted to operatic excerpts). Her career total of recitals (including in Japan) and such performances as Beethoven's Ninth Symphony and Dvorák's *Requiem* was at least 260.

Active during her long retirement, Milanov taught singing at the Indiana University School of Music in Bloomington (1966–1967), the Curtis Institute of Music in Philadelphia (1977–1981) as regular part-time faculty, New York University, and in Yugoslavia. She suffered a stroke on 27 May 1989, several weeks after celebrating her birthday with friends, and died at Lenox Hill Hospital in Manhattan. There were memorial services at the Frank E. Campbell Funeral Home on 8 June and New York City's Yugoslavian Press and Cultural Center on 12 June.

Milanov possessed a powerful, beautiful, and ethereal voice, rich in low tones and capable of elegant pianissimo high notes. She was a well-trained, disciplined musician and the rare timbre, earnest sensitivity, nuance, and strength of her voice were indicative of a unique instrument. During the late 1950s and 1960s, she along with Tebaldi and Maria Callas, was included in the grand rivalry among fans and critics pertaining to that great trio of divas. She remained one of the audience's favorite prima donnas; even in retirement, her entrance into the Metropolitan often evoked greater spontaneous enthusiasm than for the evening's soprano. For many, as even now her recordings prove, she projected some of the most moving and gloriously luminous vocal renderings of the mid-twentieth century.

★

Costumes, photographs, scrapbooks, contracts, as well as a Zinka Milanov exhibit cabinet and portrait are among the items on deposit at the Archives of the Metropolitan Opera. One of the best single-source collections, containing more than two dozen articles of commentary on Milanov as well as an outstanding array of photographs is *The Opera Quarterly* 7 (spring 1990): 76–170, which includes a discussion of discography and debut dates of her operatic roles. A biographical sketch is in David Ewen, ed., *Musicians Since 1900: Performers in Concert and Opera* (1978). Her career is covered in Harold Rosenthal, *Two Centuries of Opera at Covent Garden* (1958); Irving Kolodin (not always Mme Milanov's kindest critic), *The Metropolitan Opera: 1883–1966: A Candid History* (1966); Harvey Sachs, *Toscanini* (1978); and especially Gerald Fitzgerald, editor in chief, *The Annals of the Metropolitan Opera: The Complete Chronicle of Performances and Artists,* 2 vols. (1989). Alix B. Williamson, "The Singer and Specialization: A Conference with Zinka Milanov, Dramatic Soprano of the Metropolitan Opera," *The Etude* 64 (Nov. 1946): 615, and "Milanov Speaks to Gerald Fitzgerald," *Opera News* 22 (20 Jan. 1958): 8–9, 26, are interviews of Milanov. Robert Jacobson, "The Most Beautiful Voice in the World," *Opera News* 41 (9 Apr. 1977): 10–15, is an extensive cover story and interview. Another article of interest is Bruce Burroughs, "Brava Zinka!," *Opera News* 52 (Dec. 1987): 18, 20. Obituaries are in the *New York Times* (31 May 1989); the *Times* (London) (1 June 1989); and *Variety* (14 June 1989).

MADELINE SAPIENZA

MILLAND, Ray (*b.* 3 January 1907 in Neath, West Glamorgan, Wales; *d.* 10 March 1986 in Torrance, California), prolific actor and occasional director, best known for his powerful portrayal of an alcoholic writer in *The Lost Weekend,* for which he won the 1945 Academy Award for best actor.

Ray Milland. POPPERFOTO/ARCHIVE PHOTOS

Milland was born Reginald Alfred John Truscott-Jones, one of four children of Elizabeth Truscott-Jones and Alfredo Truscott-Jones, who worked in a steel mill. Welsh was his first language. As a young boy he studied at private schools and worked on his aunt's horse-breeding farm. He attended King's College at Cardiff and the University of Wales at Cardiff. There are differing accounts of how he took the name Ray Milland. In his autobiography he wrote that he wanted a name to remind him of the simple days he spent in the pools on the mill lands where he grew up. Other accounts say he took his mother's second husband's last name, Mullane, and changed it to Milland later.

After leaving school, Milland moved to London and entered the Household Cavalry, the regiment charged with guarding the British royal family. He became an excellent horseman, an expert marksman, and a boxing champion. Handsome, sharp-featured, brown-haired, blue-eyed, and tall (six feet, two inches), Milland started acting in 1929, using the name Spike Milland. He got one of his first acting jobs, in the movie *The Informer,* because of his expertise as a marksman. After roles in a few other movies he went to Hollywood in 1931 and began working under contract to Metro-Goldwyn-Mayer. In 1934 he signed with Paramount Pictures and worked for that studio for the next twenty years.

Milland met Muriel Francis Weber, nicknamed "Mal," in 1931 and married her in 1932; they had one child and adopted another. A self-described "shy homebody," Milland remained married to Mal until his death. He became a U.S. citizen in 1938. During World War II he entertained Allied troops, often in combat zones.

Milland soon graduated from small roles to roles as a debonair leading or second leading man, playing in films with such stars as Claudette Colbert, Paulette Goddard, Dorothy Lamour, Carole Lombard, Ginger Rogers, and Jean Arthur. He played Carole Lombard's fiancé in *Bolero* (1934); George Raft played the lead. He and Fred MacMurray woo Claudette Colbert in *The Gilded Lily* (1935). He falls in love with Jean Arthur in *Easy Living* (1937), an appealing comedy written by Preston Sturges. His first leading role was in *Her Jungle Love* (1938) with Dorothy Lamour. He starred in Billy Wilder's directorial debut, *The Major and the Minor* (1942), opposite Ginger Rogers. His versatility as an actor and his ability to reveal the shadow side of his attractive persona led to different kinds of roles, from his award-winning portrayal of an alcoholic in *The Lost Weekend* (1945) to his homicidal husband in Alfred Hitchcock's *Dial M for Murder* (1954).

Directing films was a dream that Milland was able to

realize beginning in 1955. He acted in them as well as sometimes producing and helping write them. Among the movies he both directed and starred in were *Lisbon* (1956), *The Safecracker* (1958), and *Panic in the Year Zero* (1962). He also starred in the television program *The Ray Milland Show* (1953–1955) and in the dramatic series *Markham* (1959–1960). In 1970 he played a memorable role as the father of one of the lovers in the movie *Love Story.* He had a role in *The Last Tycoon* (1976) and followed his part in *Love Story* with *Oliver's Story* (1978), again playing Ryan O'Neal's father. Most of his later roles were in low-budget horror films, such as *The Thing with Two Heads* (1972) and *Survival Run* (1980). He never expressed discomfort with these roles; rather, he asserted his continued interest in working. He died of cancer at Torrance Memorial Medical Center.

Milland was a competent and attractive actor who learned his profession by doing, acting in more than 150 films during his lifetime. His compelling Oscar-winning performance as a drunk in the Academy Award–winning best picture *The Lost Weekend* increased the public's awareness of alcoholism and earned Milland a place in movie history.

★

Ray Milland, *Wide-Eyed in Babylon* (1974), is his autobiography. See also Aljean Harmetz, "Ray Milland: In Coldwater Canyon with *The Lost Weekend*'s Star," *Architectural Digest* (April 1996); "Ray Milland's Adopted Child Secret for Year," *Los Angeles Times* (17 Nov. 1949); Bosley Crowther, "*The Lost Weekend,* in Which Ray Milland Presents a Study in Dipsomania, Makes Its Appearance at the Rivoli," *New York Times* (3 Dec. 1945). Obituaries are in the *Los Angeles Times* (10 Mar. 1986) and *New York Times* (11 Mar. 1986).

KAREN SHREEFTER

MILLER, Carl S. (*b.* 23 July 1912 in Edmonton, Alberta, Canada; *d.* 15 April 1986 in St. Paul, Minnesota), inventor of thermography, a duplicating process that made carbon paper almost obsolete and led to the modern copying industry.

Miller was one of five children of Alfred Dennis Miller, a professor of semantics at the University of Alberta and a Methodist minister, and Minnie Stinson Miller, a schoolteacher. When Miller was young the family moved from Edmonton to the Stoney Indian reservation town of Morley, near Calgary. His father worked as a missionary there and his mother did volunteer work.

Miller attended Calgary City Elementary School (1918–1926). When he was a teenager, the family moved back to Edmonton, and at Edmonton City High School he showed an aptitude for chemistry and other sciences. Following

Carl S. Miller. 3M COMPANY PHOTO

graduation in 1929 he entered the University of Alberta, where he majored in chemistry and earned B.S. and M.S. degrees. He completed his graduate education at the University of Minnesota in St. Paul, where he received the doctorate in physics in 1940. At the university he met Muriel Agnes Oestreich; they were married on 19 August 1944 and would have two children.

Shortly after receiving his doctorate, Miller went to work in the central research laboratories of the Minnesota Mining and Manufacturing Company (later known as 3M) in St. Paul. He had been employed there in the summers of 1938 and 1939. Now he concentrated on differential absorption, which refers to the fact that a dark object absorbs more heat than a light object. Approved by Director of Research H. N. Stephens, the idea for this project arose from Miller's experience with the hand-copying of needed materials from technical journals and other texts while he was a doctoral student. He first thought that photography might be the solution to this problem. When this proved not to be the case, he turned his attention to other methods of copying. Although many types of duplicating machines and processes were available, they were not easy to use.

According to *World of Invention,* Miller discovered the

"method of dry copying by noticing one day the way a brown leaf melted itself into a snowbank, leaving its impression in the snow. Miller, intrigued by what he saw, and mentally noting this was an example of differential absorption, also began to wonder whether the principle could be applied to copy a written image." He began trying to reproduce the process in the laboratory. In 1944 he produced a prototype of his copying machine and showed it to his superiors. They encouraged him to keep working on the invention, which eventually laid the foundation for the duplicating products division. The latter spawned other image-related products—microfilm, overhead projection transparencies, carbonless paper, fax machines and their supplies, and word-processing equipment.

Miller's first patent for heat-sensitive copying paper (2,663,654) was granted in 1953. His first two patents, in the late 1940s and early 1950s, had been for a thermoprinting apparatus (2,740,895) and for a method of using heat-sensitive copying paper (2,740,896). His partner in this invention and five other patents for heat-sensitive paper was fellow chemist, Bryce L. Clark. In 1950, 3M introduced its Thermo-Fax copier, based on Miller and Clark's original thermography ideas. In the mid-1950s Miller began working with Carl A. Kuhrmeyer, Donal G. Kimble, and Byron W. Neher. Although other duplicating processes began to replace thermography by the mid-1960s, Miller's work led to creation of a graphic systems group that by 1976 had sales that accounted for 21 percent of 3M's worldwide total. Miller continued working in 3M's central research laboratories until his retirement in 1977.

Miller was approximately six feet tall, of average build, and dark-complected, with dark receding hair and green eyes. He became a U.S. citizen in the late 1940s. After leaving 3M, Miller kept busy with various projects, including one that dealt with ceramics. He also tried his hand at photography. He died of congestive heart failure on 21 April 1986. According to his wishes, he was cremated.

★

Information on Miller's work at 3M is in *Megaphone* (Mar. 1950), the 3M employee newsletter; the 3M Annual Reports for 1952, 1954, and 1956, Graphic Products division; and 3M Corporation, *Our Story So Far: Notes from the First Seventy-five Years of the 3M Company* (1977). Bridget Travers, ed., *World of Invention* (1994), includes an article on thermography. An obituary is in the *New York Times* (21 Apr. 1986).

BRIAN CARPENTER

MILLER, William Mosely (*b.* 20 July 1909 in Pascagoula, Mississippi; *d.* 12 September 1989 in Greensboro, North Carolina), government official who served as doorkeeper of the U.S. House of Representatives; his memoirs exposed the secret lives of members of Congress.

Third of the six children born to Albert Maghus Miller, a schooner captain, and Nettie Maddox, Miller acquired the nickname Fishbait when a baseball coach told the scrawny child, who was seeking a place on the team, "You ain't even big enough for fish bait." As a child, Miller worked in a variety of jobs to help support his family, especially after his father deserted them when Miller was twelve years old. Although he was able to complete high school, further education was financially out of his reach until the Pascagoula district attorney, William M. Colmer, offered to pay for the young soda jerk, whose personality had impressed many prominent customers, to attend Harrison-Jackson-Stone County Junior College (now Mississippi Gulf Coast Community College) in 1929. He graduated in 1932.

Immediately after his graduation Miller joined Colmer's campaign for the U.S. House of Representatives. Colmer was victorious, and Miller was rewarded with a job as a clerk in the House post office in 1933. On 2 September 1937 he married Mable Breeland, a nurse whom he had met when he was hospitalized in Laurel, Mississippi. They had one daughter.

Always helpful to members of Congress, Miller won a

William ("Fishbait") Miller at the door of the U.S. House of Representatives chamber. UPI/CORBIS-BETTMANN

series of increasingly more desirable patronage jobs. In 1939 he became a messenger to the doorkeeper of the House, followed by a period as a special officer to the Capitol Police, then special assistant to the sergeant-at-arms of the House. In 1947 House Democrats elected him minority doorkeeper, and after they won majority status in the 1948 election, they elected him doorkeeper of the House, a position he held from 1949 until 1975, except for 1953–1955, when Republicans briefly controlled the House. A protégé of Speaker of the House Sam Rayburn, Miller attributed his success in Washington to the guidance of Rayburn, and to Rayburn's successor as speaker, John McCormack.

Television made Miller a minor celebrity in American homes as he announced the arrival of the president for each State of the Union Address and other appearances before joint sessions of Congress. From his position at the head of the procession of dignitaries escorting the president into the House chamber, Miller's announcement, "Mistah Speakah, the President of the United States," bellowed with an unmistakable Deep South accent, opened the proceedings for presidents from Harry S. Truman to Gerald R. Ford.

Miller's ceremonial duties included escorting visiting foreign dignitaries in the House. His folksy, informal manner was considered charming by some visitors and excessively familiar by others. After a 1952 visit by Great Britain's Princess Elizabeth and her husband Prince Phillip, during which his behavior was criticized, Miller was sent to protocol school by the State Department and afterward was issued explicit instructions on deferential behavior toward royalty.

While Miller's ceremonial duties placed him in the spotlight from time to time, his administrative duties were more important. The title of doorkeeper, which originated with the First Congress in 1789, belies the significance of the office. The doorkeeper is the chief administrative officer of the House of Representatives, not only controlling access to the floor of the House, but also supervising House pages and messengers, press galleries, cloakrooms, the document room and distribution services, switchboards, restaurants, recreational facilities, rest rooms, barber shops, police, and cleaning services. By the early 1970s Miller administered a budget of $3.5 million and supervised over 350 employees, most of them on patronage appointments from members of Congress.

Miller's goal as doorkeeper was to make the lives of individual members of Congress as comfortable as possible when they were on Capitol Hill. Observing the principle "Every congressman a king," Miller devoted his professional life to caring for the needs and desires of members, to the extent of taking constituents on tours of the Washington area, finding baby-sitters for younger members of Congress, and even doing the baby-sitting himself when necessary.

Miller's personality was well-suited to his work. Gregarious and energetic, he learned names quickly and became invaluable to congressional leaders for his ability to manage the details of social events and introduce politicians and guests. In some ways his personality complemented those of the people for whom he worked. He was modest in an environment dominated by strong egos. One member declared that Miller "turned obsequiousness into an art form." He was a faithful Baptist who abstained from alcohol, working in an institution that seemed at times to celebrate its hard-drinking members.

Miller's source of strength, his association with the Democrats' congressional old guard, unexpectedly cost him his job in 1974, after his party swept the first post-Watergate congressional elections. A large class of freshman Democrats descended on Capitol Hill determined to reform the institutions of power. Their perceived enemies were not just Republicans, but also the powerful Democratic committee chairmen, disproportionately southern and conservative, who had dominated the Congress since the New Deal. When the Democratic members caucused in December 1974 to organize the new Congress, Miller drew his first challengers for the doorkeeper position. In a runoff he lost to James Malloy, chief of the Finance Division of the House.

In retirement Miller wrote his autobiography, *Fishbait: The Memoirs of the Congressional Doorkeeper,* which attracted attention primarily for its revelations about the sexual escapades and drinking habits of members of Congress, past and present. The market was ripe for an exposé: the book was published in 1977, soon after two prominent congressmen—Wayne Hays of Ohio and Wilbur Mills of Arkansas—had been discovered in relationships with mistresses.

Miller lived quietly for the remainder of his retirement years. He and his wife moved from their Arlington, Virginia, home to Atlanta, to be near their daughter, and then to Greensboro, North Carolina, when she moved to that city. Miller died of a heart attack brought on by chronic coronary artery disease. He was buried in the Tylertown City Cemetery in Tylertown, Mississippi.

Miller's life embodied the Horatio Alger story: born to a poor family, he worked hard, and through his personality and ability attracted the support of powerful persons and achieved a position of national prominence. As a protégé of Sam Rayburn, Miller gained access to the center of congressional power and became a friend of presidents and other powerful people. His television persona confirmed the American belief in the politics of the common person. He helped to make Congress work in an era of powerful leaders, and he guided the socialization of new members to the folkways of the House. Ironically, publication of Miller's memoirs, revealing embarrassing Capitol Hill secrets, contributed to the decline of respect for Congress, but also helped to build a more realistic public assessment of the institution and its members.

★

Miller's papers are in the J. D. Williams Library of the University of Mississippi. His autobiography, *Fishbait: The Memoirs of the Congressional Doorkeeper* (1977), was written with the assistance of Frances Spatz Leighton. Obituaries are in the *New York Times* and the *Washington Post* (15 Sept. 1989). The Mississippi Department of Archives and History in Jackson has a subject file on Miller, consisting primarily of newspaper clippings. The Mississippi Oral History Program of the University of Southern Mississippi has an oral history interview with him.

VAGN K. HANSEN

MINNELLI, Vincente (*b.* 28 February 1903 in Chicago, Illinois; *d.* 25 July 1986 in Beverly Hills, California), director, known primarily for his work in film, who extended the boundaries of the Hollywood musical.

Born Lester Anthony Minnelli, he was the only one of five siblings to survive infancy. He acted in children's roles in the traveling Minnelli Brothers Tent Theater with his mother, a French-born actress named Mina Le Beau. His Italian-born father, Vincent Charles Minnelli, embittered by his lack of success as a musician, tried to discourage his son from pursuing a theatrical career. Minnelli spent his rootless childhood on the road with his parents, in various relatives' homes, and in a series of boarding schools. When the family business folded in 1915, the Minnellis settled in Delaware, Ohio. A solitary, introverted child, Minnelli insulated himself in a world of fantasy, reading and drawing. He attended St. Mary's Parochial School for three years and spent his senior year at Willis High School, from which he graduated in 1921. That same year he moved to Chicago, where he worked at Marshall Field's, decorating the department store's display windows.

This job was followed by an apprenticeship at a photographic studio. Minnelli next became chief costume designer for Balaban and Katz, Chicago's premier movie theater chain, dressing the performers in the prefeature extravaganzas. In 1931 he moved to New York City, where he designed sets and costumes for live spectaculars at the Balaban and Paramount-Publix Theater. He also worked on an operetta, *Du Barry* (1932), starring Grace Moore. In 1933 Minnelli became art director and chief costume designer of Radio City Music Hall. He then graduated to the Broadway stage, where he directed and designed the sets and costumes for *At Home Abroad* (1935), *The Ziegfeld Follies of 1936* (for which John Murray Anderson received director's credit), and *The Show Is On* (1936).

His panache and reputation as Broadway's top colorist provided his entrée to Hollywood. Unfortunately, his first experience there (at Paramount Studios) proved a frustrating ordeal. After only seven months he returned to New York City, where he directed *Hooray for What?* (1937). His last Broadway show, *Very Warm for May* (1939), closed after fifty-nine performances. In 1940 the producer Arthur Freed convinced Minnelli to return to Hollywood, where he apprenticed before directing his first movie, *Cabin in the Sky* (1943).

His next major work was *Meet Me in St. Louis* (1944). On the set Minnelli fell in love with the film's star, Judy Garland. They married on 15 June 1945 and would have one daughter, Liza. They collaborated again on *The Clock* (1945). By the time the Minnellis teamed up with Gene Kelly to film *The Pirate* (1948), Garland's addiction to alcohol and drugs was undermining their work and marriage.

Minnelli directed *An American in Paris* (1951), a groundbreaking musical that climaxed with a seventeen-minute ballet, the likes of which Hollywood had never seen. The film garnered six Academy Awards, including one for best picture, but Minnelli would have to wait until *Gigi* (1958) to win his first and only Academy Award as a director. The latter film was honored with an unprecedented nine awards, including best picture. Minnelli's other notable musical was *The Band Wagon* (1953), a witty and affection-

Vincente Minnelli. PHOTOFEST

ate satire of Broadway shows and personalities. His other musicals include *Ziegfeld Follies* (1946), *Brigadoon* (1954), *Kismet* (1955), *Bells Are Ringing* (1960), and *On a Clear Day You Can See Forever* (1970). His final film, *A Matter of Time* (1976), in which he directed his daughter Liza, was poorly received.

Though known primarily for sumptuous musicals, Minnelli handled several genres with remarkable deftness. His comedies, which deal with family life and the battle of the sexes, include *Father of the Bride* (1950), *Father's Little Dividend* (1951), *Designing Woman* (1957), and *The Courtship of Eddie's Father* (1963).

His melodramas explore frustration, obsession, and trauma. In 1952 Minnelli filmed *The Bad and the Beautiful,* widely regarded as the most compelling picture about opportunism and power in Hollywood. His favorite movie was *Lust for Life* (1956), based on Irving Stone's biography of Vincent Van Gogh. His other melodramas include *The Cobweb* (1955), *Tea and Sympathy* (1956), *Some Came Running* (1959), *Home from the Hill* (1960), *The Four Horsemen of the Apocalypse* (1962), and *Two Weeks in Another Town* (1962).

Fascinated by surrealism and preoccupied by dreams, Minnelli was a master of shifting patterns and unexpected touches. Through his sensitivity and intuition he elicited some of their best performances from Garland, Spencer Tracy, and Kirk Douglas. Unlike other directors of comparable status and achievement, Minnelli worked almost exclusively for one studio, Metro-Goldwyn-Mayer.

A perfectionist who thrived under pressure, Minnelli was obsessed by his work, often at the expense of his private life. In March 1951 Minnelli and Garland divorced. Marriages to Georgette Magnani (16 February 1954–May 1958; one daughter) and Denise Gigante (31 December 1960–August 1971) also ended in divorce. In 1980 he married Lee Anderson. France made him a member of the Legion of Honor in 1986. A lifelong smoker, he died from complications of pneumonia and emphysema. He is buried in Forest Lawn Memorial Park in Glendale, California.

Minnelli transformed the film musical by his seamless fusion of its components to advance the plot. His use of color was bold and innovative. Certain critics minimized his concern for taste, beauty, and art. His use of flamboyant costumes and decor, along with his penchant for excess, have been both exalted and criticized. Minnelli wrote in his autobiography: "I have never catered to an audience. How could I when . . . my work is lauded in one breath as mastery . . . and dismissed as mere decoration in another?"

★

The Vincente Minnelli Collection, housed in the Margaret Herrick Library at the Academy of Motion Picture Arts and Sciences, contains Minnelli's personal and professional correspondence, production files, scripts, unrealized projects, and manuscripts. Minnelli's autobiography, *I Remember It Well* (1974), written with Hector Arce, sheds light on Minnelli's personal life and recounts the making of each of his films. Stephen Harvey, *Directed by Vincente Minnelli* (1989), provides a balanced and insightful view of his life and works. James Naremore, *The Films of Vincente Minnelli* (1993), includes a close analysis of five works that represent Minnelli's full range. An obituary is in the *New York Times* (26 July 1986). Two audiovisual works written, produced, and directed by Richard Schickel are a PBS documentary, *The Men Who Made the Movies: Vincente Minnelli* (1973), and *Minnelli on Minnelli* (1987), a VHS tape that includes comments by Liza Minnelli.

DAN CHAYEFSKY

MITCHELL, (John) Broadus (*b.* 27 December 1892 in Georgetown, Kentucky; *d.* 28 April 1988 in Tarrytown, New York), economic historian, teacher, and social activist.

Broadus Mitchell was the first of five children of Samuel Chiles Mitchell and Alice Virginia (Broadus) Mitchell. Named Broadus after his maternal grandfather, John Albert Broadus, in his late thirties he entirely abandoned the use of John. Broadus was raised in an intellectual environment. His father was a college professor and later a college president who was descended from a highly religious background and was also an ordained Baptist minister. His mother was the daughter of the president of the Southern Baptist Theological Seminary. Broadus's schooling began at the Richmond Academy on the Richmond College campus in Richmond, Virginia, where Samuel Mitchell taught classical literature. Broadus's father left Richmond to attend

Broadus Mitchell. COURTESY OF CHRISTOPHER MITCHELL

the University of Chicago, where he earned his Ph.D. in 1908. Brown College hired him as a visiting professor of political science.

In Providence, Mitchell was accepted as a student at the Hope Street High School and placed somewhere between the sophomore and junior years. During his time there, Broadus traveled extensively along the East Coast, took classes at the Rhode Island School of Design, and went to museums, including the Rhode Island Historical Society. In his unpublished autobiography, Mitchell noted, "My partiality for the South was neutralized by my winter in Providence."

In 1909 Samuel Mitchell was appointed president of the University of South Carolina, and Broadus entered that university the same year. Later in life he admitted that he was ashamed of his early lack of dedication to his studies, and mathematics was his *bête noir.* He maintained that only intensive tutoring for five or six hours a day rescued him. He was active in extracurricular affairs as an undergraduate, belonging to the Southern College Press Association and the Woodrow Wilson League of College Men. The city newspaper, the *Columbia Record,* used him as its campus correspondent for most of his undergraduate years.

Mitchell received his B.A. degree in 1913, the year his father resigned from the University of South Carolina to become president of the medical school at the University of Virginia. Upon graduation, Broadus worked first as a crime reporter and later as a business reporter for the *Richmond Evening Journal.* In this occupation, which he held for a little over a year, his social awareness broadened, and he became convinced that he had to know more of economics in order to be a better journalist. He turned down a scholarship awarded him by the Columbia University School of Journalism to attend Johns Hopkins University for graduate study in economics. He had to rely upon the largesse of his father to finance the early months of his graduate study. Johns Hopkins later granted him a scholarship, and he completed his academic work and received his Ph.D. in 1918. In July 1918 he was drafted for service in World War I; upon his discharge he returned to his reporting job, but he left shortly afterward when offered a teaching post at Johns Hopkins.

Hence, in 1919 Mitchell began a twenty-year teaching career at Johns Hopkins and work on his major study, *The Rise of Cotton Mills in the South.* With its publication in 1921, he was acclaimed as the voice of the New South (that is, the newly industrialized South). In the work, he contends that community efforts led by socially minded altruistic industrialists brought the mills and jobs to the traditionally agricultural South. He was later criticized for underestimating the profit motive of mill owners.

Mitchell was a dedicated teacher with a career that stretched beyond the usual age of retirement. He resigned from the Johns Hopkins faculty in 1939 over the freedom of speech issue in the classroom and the university's unwillingness to admit an African American to their graduate program in political economy. He taught next at Occidental College (1939–1941), New York University (1942–1944), Rutgers University (1947–1958), and Hofstra University (1958–1967). Mitchell never hid his leftist political viewpoints from his students nor from the general public while an academic. It was an honest, yet potentially dangerous, stance for him to have taken in a day and environment in which such sentiments were not generally welcomed.

An experienced researcher, Mitchell accepted an invitation to serve as research director for the International Ladies Garment Workers Union (ILGWU) while still serving on the NYU faculty. As an ILGWU employee, his willingness to tolerate communists brought him into conflict with David Dubinsky, the union's president.

Mitchell's activities suggest that he was, generally speaking, a man of action. For example, he was one of the founders of the the Intercollegiate Socialist Society, which was later renamed the League for Industrial Democracy. He espoused socialism as a philosophical-economic orientation after hearing the British socialist John Spargo speak at Johns Hopkins. Mitchell, consequently, attempted to introduce a labor college at the university. In the early 1920s he conducted night courses on the history of labor for workers associated with the Workman's Circle in a Baltimore building owned by the university. Also in that decade he spent summers teaching immigrant, black, nonunion, and union activist workers in various colleges: Trinity College in Durham, North Carolina (1920); Bryn Mawr (1922–1923); and Sweet Briar (1927). Mitchell served as first president of the Baltimore Urban League, investigated the lynchings of two African Americans in 1932, and ran unsuccessfully as the Socialist party candidate for governor of Maryland in 1934. He also chaired the New Jersey Civil Liberties Committee and moderated a controversial conference on communism at Hofstra University in 1959.

Mitchell married Adelaide Hammond on 1 September 1927 and, at her wish, divorced her on 17 March 1936. They had two children. On 31 December 1936 he married Louise Blodgett; they also had two children.

Mitchell wrote or cowrote more than fifteen books and monographs. His major early works include biographies of Frederick Law Olmsted (1924) and William Gregg (1928) and a compendium of essays by his brother George Sinclair Mitchell, *The Industrial Revolution in the South* (1930). Among his later works were *American Economic History* (1947) and *Depression Decade* (1947), both written with his wife Louise, and a two-volume biography, *Alexander Hamilton* (1957). He was also a major contributor to several reference works, including entries for the *Dictionary of American Biography* and the *Dictionary of American History.*

When Mitchell turned seventy-five, he left active employment and spent his twenty-one remaining years in Croton-on-Hudson, New York, and on his farm in Wendell, Massachusetts. He continued to write, to work at carpentry, and to socialize with family and friends. He died of cancer at the Phelps Memorial Hospital in Tarrytown, New York, and is buried in Lock's Village cemetery in Wendell.

Mitchell carved out a significant place in economic history, especially by documenting and analyzing the early industrial development of the South.

★

Mitchell's papers are on file in the Special Collections of Hofstra University and Southern Historical Collections at Chapel Hill, North Carolina. His son Christopher Mitchell, a professor at New York University, is in possession of Broadus Mitchell's unpublished autobiography. Other biographical sources include Daniel J. Singal, *The War Within* (1982); John C. Presley, "Broadus Mitchell: Reflections of a Southern Activist," *Southern Studies* (winter 1986): 342–352; and Jacqueline Hall, "Broadus Mitchell (1892–1988)," *Radical History Review* (fall 1989): 31–38. An obituary is in the *New York Times* (30 Apr. 1988).

HAROLD L. WATTEL

MITCHELL, John Newton (*b.* 15 September 1913 in Detroit, Michigan; *d.* 9 November 1988 in Washington, D.C.), municipal bond lawyer, attorney general of the United States, and manager of Richard Nixon's two presidential campaigns; convicted of obstruction of justice, Mitchell became the first attorney general ever to serve time in a federal prison.

The son of Joseph Charles Mitchell, a businessman, and Margaret Agnes McMahon, a homemaker, Mitchell grew up on Long Island, New York, where he attended elementary schools in Blue Point and Patchogue. An only child, he graduated in 1931 from Jamaica High School in Queens, New York, from Fordham University in 1935, and from Fordham Law School in 1938. While in college and law school he played semiprofessional hockey for a time and was called Big John. He married Elizabeth Katherine Shine. They had two children and divorced in December 1957. On 30 December 1957 Mitchell married Martha Beall Jennings, with whom he had one child.

Mitchell became an expert on municipal bonds in the Manhattan firm of Caldwell and Raymond, becoming a partner in 1942. During World War II he commanded patrol torpedo boat squadrons in the Pacific, including the one in which John F. Kennedy skippered a PT-109. After the war Mitchell returned to his firm, now renamed Caldwell, Trimble, and Mitchell. He pioneered in new financing devices, creating separate agencies to handle bonds so as to get around state indebtedness limitations. He handled bond financing in the 1950s for New York governor Nelson Rockefeller, including college construction, housing, urban development, and hospital bond issues. Mitchell helped to draft the Housing and Urban Development Act of 1968.

Attorney General John N. Mitchell testifying before the U.S. Senate Judiciary Committee. ARCHIVE PHOTOS

In 1967 Mitchell's firm merged with former vice president Richard M. Nixon's to form Nixon, Mudge, Rose, Guthrie, Alexander, and Mitchell. Nixon asked Mitchell to become his campaign adviser and then his manager for the 1968 presidential election. Mitchell imposed organization and discipline on the candidate and became a proponent of the campaign's "southern strategy" and "law and order" themes. He also proposed that Maryland governor Spiro T. Agnew become the vice presidential candidate. After Nixon's victory, Mitchell accepted the new president's nomination for attorney general. Nixon said Mitchell had an "extra dimension" and had "coolness under fire and great judgment." Mitchell called the Justice Department "an institution of law enforcement, not social improvement."

Mitchell was the architect of the 1969 anticrime bill, which called for preventive detention by allowing federal judges in the District of Columbia to jail defendants for up to sixty days before trial if there was a "substantial probability" that they would represent a danger to the community. The bill provided for life sentences for federal offenders convicted of three felonies. It permitted "no-knock" searches by police officers and no-warrant frisking of suspects. The bill, opposed by civil libertarians, was modified by Congress. Mitchell used existing wiretapping authority to target organized crime and radical political groups, and not just for the national security matters for which that authority had originally been intended. He authorized wiretaps in 1970 and 1971 on at least thirteen members of the National Security Council staff to stop leaks to newspapers about Vietnam policy. These taps were approved without judicial clearance, in spite of procedures set forth in Title III of the Crime Control and Safe Streets Act of 1968. In June 1972 the Supreme Court ruled in *United States* v. *U.S. District Court* that the government had no power to eavesdrop without warrants unless it could show evidence of links to foreign intelligence.

Mitchell prosecuted individuals involved in civil disobedience, including the Chicago Seven, a group of activists whom he charged with organizing riots outside of the Democratic National Convention in Chicago in 1968. He ordered a conspiracy indictment against Daniel Ellsberg, a Rand Corporation analyst and former marine officer, for disseminating the Pentagon Papers, a Defense Department study detailing the history of the U.S. military involvement in Vietnam, and he brought suit to enjoin newspaper publication of the study, a case lost by the government in *New York Times* v. *United States* (1971). Based on Mitchell's advice, President Nixon approved the mass arrests of demonstrators in a march on Washington in May 1971, and 13,400 demonstrators were arrested and held at D.C. Stadium. All the arrests were thrown out of court as unconstitutional, and many of those arrested eventually won money damages.

"Watch what we do, and not what we say," Mitchell had urged civil rights leaders opposed to his appointment. But in spite of this hint that he would enforce civil rights laws, Mitchell was not prepared to enforce them vigorously, preferring to concentrate his prosecutions on organized crime and civil disobedience cases. Nixon, on Mitchell's advice, proposed modifications of the Voting Rights Act of 1965 when it was up for renewal in 1970. He wanted the act to apply nationally rather than just in the South, but in doing so he proposed to soften its provisions, particularly by eliminating the requirement of prior approval by the attorney general of any changes in voting rights laws in southern states. In spite of his proposals, the existing statute was extended with almost no modifications.

In 1972 Mitchell resigned from the Justice Department to head Nixon's reelection campaign. As a close Nixon adviser, Mitchell had already approved the appointment of G. Gordon Liddy as general counsel to the Committee to Re-Elect the President (CREEP) in December 1971. At CREEP Liddy came up with a $1 million plan for dirty campaign tricks. Mitchell ordered him to develop a less ambitious plan and approved a $500,000 budget for Liddy, according to Nixon aide Jeb Magruder. Mitchell approved the break-in of the Watergate headquarters of the Democratic National Committee. On 18 June 1972, after arrests of the burglars on the preceding day, Mitchell said that no one involved had been "operating either on our behalf or with our consent."

The White House strategy from the very beginning was to pin the blame for Watergate on Mitchell. On 1 July he resigned, and for the next two years he denied that he had any prior knowledge or involvement in Watergate, in spite of testimony by Jeb Magruder and John Dean, both of whom stated that Mitchell had approved the break-ins as part of a political intelligence operation. Dean also claimed that Mitchell had approved paying hush money to the defendants. White House aides talked in March 1973 about pinning it all on "the Big Enchilada" and of letting Mitchell "twist slowly, slowly in the wind." But Mitchell was always loyal to Nixon and he never testified against the president, though he refused to take the fall for White House aides. Martha Mitchell, his outspoken second wife, was enraged that Nixon would not defend her husband. She called on Nixon to resign, saying he had full knowledge of the break-in and cover-up. Because her husband would not denounce Nixon or provide evidence against him, Martha separated from him in 1973. She died of bone cancer in May 1976.

In May 1973 Mitchell was indicted, along with former commerce secretary Maurice Stans, by a federal grand jury in New York for perjury and conspiracy to obstruct justice. It was charged that Mitchell and Stans had obstructed a Securities and Exchange Commission investigation into the stock dealings of financier Robert Vesco in return for a $200,000 contribution to Nixon's reelection campaign. In April 1974 they were both acquitted. In March 1974 Mitchell was indicted along with several other Nixon aides for a cover-up of Watergate crimes. Mitchell pleaded not guilty, but on New Year's Day 1975 he was found guilty of conspiracy, obstruction of justice, and lying under oath. Federal district court judge John Sirica sentenced him to from thirty months to eight years. He was disbarred in July 1975. In June 1977, after losing two appeals, he began serving his term, the first attorney general ever to do prison time. He was released on parole in January 1979 after serving nineteen months and was the last Watergate defendant to be freed. After being released he served in Washington, D.C., as a consultant to business firms. He planned to write a book about Watergate but never did. He died at age seventy-five.

John Mitchell's approach to "law and order" was a fiasco. Most of the arrests he ordered and prosecutions he brought against antiwar protesters failed to win convictions. The wiretaps he authorized without judicial warrant caused sensitive cases to be lost. His attempts to put conservative justices on the U.S. Supreme Court were blocked by the Senate. Although his policies proved to be effective politically, helping Nixon to win two terms, ultimately his authorization of "dirty tricks" and attempts at a cover-up led to his own imprisonment and the resignation of the president he had served.

★

See Richard Ben-Veniste and George Frampton, *Stonewall: The Legal Case Against the Watergate Conspirators* (1977). Winzola McLendon, *Martha: The Life of Martha Mitchell* (1979), is a sympathetic biography of Martha Mitchell and an account of her marriage to John Mitchell. Stanley Kutler, *The Wars of Watergate: The Last Crisis of Richard Nixon* (1990), is a comprehensive account of Watergate crimes and Mitchell's role in authorizing them, and of the subsequent cover-up. An obituary is in the *New York Times* (10 Nov. 1988).

RICHARD M. PIOUS

MIZENER, Arthur Moore (*b.* 3 September 1907 in Erie, Pennsylvania; *d.* 11 February 1988 in Bristol, Rhode Island), educator and biographer best known for documenting the lives of F. Scott Fitzgerald and Ford Madox Ford.

Arthur Mizener was the son of Mabel Moore Mizener and Mason Price Mizener. His life was typical of his generation of American scholars—moving from school to school until he achieved tenure, then an endowed chair, and then remaining at one university for the rest of his life. He attended Princeton University, graduating with a B.A. degree in 1930. He received an M.A. degree from Harvard in 1932 and then returned to Princeton, earning a Ph.D. in 1934. That same year he became an instructor in the English Department at Yale University in New Haven, Connecticut. The following year, on 16 July, he married Elizabeth Rosemary Paris; they had two children.

In 1938 Mizener published his first book, *A Catalogue of the First Editions of Archibald MacLeish: Prepared for an Exhibit of His Works Held in the Yale University Library Beginning January 7, 1938.* Two years later the Mizeners moved to Aurora, New York, where he took an assistant professorship at Wells College. He was promoted to associate professor in 1944, but the next year he moved to Carleton College in Northfield, Minnesota, where he was named full professor and chair of the English Department. In 1946 he made one of his early contributions to F. Scott Fitzgerald scholarship by contributing a chapter to *The Lives of Eighteen from Princeton,* edited by Willard Thorp. He remained at Carleton for six years, until 1951, when he became Mellon Foundation Professor of English at Cornell University in Ithaca, New York, where he remained until his retirement.

Also in 1951 Mizener published his most famous book, *The Far Side of Paradise: A Biography of F. Scott Fitzgerald.* This was the first biography of Fitzgerald, and Mizener devoted five years to its making. He had interviewed Fitzgerald's surviving family and friends and his last lover, and had been given access to the writer's manuscripts, correspondence, ledgers, and scrapbooks (as well as the letters and manuscripts of Zelda Fitzgerald, F. Scott's wife). Mizener demythologized Fitzgerald in the biography, retrieving Fitzgerald the artist from Fitzgerald the drunkard and clown. Critics praised Mizener's honesty in dealing with Fitzgerald's drinking problems and Zelda's bouts with insanity. The reviewer for the *New York Times* said Mizener had "cut through the legend that had risen about [Fitzgerald and] helped secure his reputation."

Mizener found it difficult to drop Fitzgerald as a subject. He edited *Afternoon of an Author* (1957), an important selection of Fitzgerald's uncollected stories and essays. He then edited *F. Scott Fitzgerald: A Biographical and Critical Study* (1958) and supplied an introduction to a new edition of Fitzgerald's *Flappers and Philosophers* (1959). In 1963 he edited *The Fitzgerald Reader* and *F. Scott Fitzgerald: A Collection of Critical Essays.* He prepared a revised edition of his Fitzgerald biography for publication in London in 1969. When he was sixty-five years old he published *Scott Fitzgerald and His World* (1972). Regarded as *the* Fitzgerald expert, Mizener enjoyed many literary friendships, among them Allen Tate, Theodore Spencer, Delmore Schwartz, I. A. Richards, John Berryman, James Laughlin, and Richard Farina.

Mizener never found another project as consuming as his Fitzgerald biography. Along the way he produced numerous books of belles lettres, including a catalog of Cornell University's James Joyce Collection (1958), a literary handbook (1962), an anthology of short stories (1962), a study of twelve great American novels (1967), and an anthology on the teaching of Shakespeare (1969). A substantial contribution to the study of modern literature is his book *The Sense of Life in the Modern Novel* (1964).

In early 1966 Mizener began a biography of the British novelist Ford Madox Ford. This was an especially daunting project, because Ford was a notorious liar. Ford's literary executor, Janice Biala, deposited her Ford papers at Cornell for Mizener's research. He also had access to the best Ford collection in private hands, that acquired by Edward Naumburg, a fellow Princetonian. The Ford biography took six years to complete. *The Saddest Story: A Biography of Ford Madox Ford* appeared in 1971. This biography also was well-received. George Wickes, writing in the *Nation,*

Arthur Mizener, 1973. DIVISION OF RARE & MANUSCRIPT COLLECTIONS, CORNELL UNIVERSITY LIBRARY

called it the "best book that has been written on Ford, the one that most clearly defines his role in the world of letters." There were some complaints, however, that Mizener's book had buried Ford alive under a pile of details and facts. A far heftier tome than the Fitzgerald biography, the book was a fine capstone to Mizener's distinguished career. He became professor emeritus at Cornell in 1973. In his later years he moved to Bristol, Rhode Island, where he died of congestive heart failure.

Mizener's reputation rests upon his two biographies. *The Far Side of Paradise* was for a long time the only Fitzgerald biography, highly regarded for its clarification of issues involving the author's life and work. As the standard biography, however, it has been superseded by Matthew J. Bruccoli's *Some Sort of Epic Grandeur* (1983). On the other hand, no biography has come as close to successfully examining the life, motivations, and work of Ford as Mizener's book has. That biography is likely to remain the standard one for many years to come.

★

There are three principal collections of Mizener papers. The typescript for *The Far Side of Paradise* and all the related correspondence are at the Princeton University Library. Correspondence between Mizener and Edmund Wilson concerning the biography and a draft of the book bearing Wilson's comments are at the University of Delaware Library, Newark. The typescript of the Ford biography and all related correspondence are in the Ford Madox Ford Collection at Cornell University. The fullest account of Mizener's life and work is that by Ann W. Engar in *Dictionary of Literary Biography,* vol. 103 (1991), pp. 184–191. See also Maxwell Geismar, "And the Other Side Was Hell," *Saturday Review of Literature* (27 Jan. 1951); *New York Times Book Review* (28 Jan. 1951); and *Saturday Review* (18 Jan. 1971). Obituaries are in the *New York Times* (15 Feb. 1988) and *Los Angeles Times* (17 Feb. 1988).

ROBERT PHILLIPS

MOHR, Charles Henry (*b.* 16 June 1929 in Loup City, Nebraska; *d.* 16 June 1989 in Bethesda, Maryland), journalist whose coverage for the *New York Times,* first of the Vietnam War and later of the Strategic Defense Initiative ("Star Wars") plan, earned him fame as one of the leading reporters of his time.

Mohr was the son of a dentist. An only child, Charley, as he was known to his friends, attended public schools in Loup City and enrolled at the University of Nebraska in 1947. He began working as a reporter for the *Lincoln Star* in 1950, before he finished school, and joined the staff after he graduated in 1951. On 31 March of that year Mohr married Norma Soust. Soust had one child, Hank, from a previous marriage, whom Mohr raised as his own. The couple also had a son, Ned, and a daughter, Gretchen, and later adopted another child, Julie.

Mohr quickly moved from the *Lincoln Star* to the Associated Press bureau in Chicago. He worked there until 1954, and then joined the staff of *Time* magazine. His rise to reporting stardom began in 1962. That year, *Time* assigned him to Saigon to cover the fledgling Vietnam War. Mohr immediately began questioning the version of events put forth by U.S. military officials. Along with other reporters such as Neil Sheehan, Peter Arnett, David Halberstam, and Gene Roberts, Mohr wrote stories during those years describing Vietnam as an intractable political and military morass that was needlessly taking the lives of American soldiers.

American military officials consistently denied Mohr's accounts. Publishers at *Time* ultimately believed the military and stopped printing Mohr's stories. In 1963 Mohr resigned from the magazine in protest. Only years later did government officials concede that Vietnam was vastly more

Charles Mohr, 1972. CHARLES MOHR/NYT PICTURES

complicated than originally thought, thus indirectly supporting Mohr's initial reports.

Mohr joined the *New York Times* in 1964 as a war correspondent, continuing to report on Vietnam. He became the first reporter injured in the war in 1965, when shrapnel hit him in the leg. Three years later, during the Viet Cong's Tet offensive, he and two other reporters braved heavy enemy gunfire to try to rescue a mortally injured Marine. The military rewarded the men with Bronze Stars for their courage.

Throughout his years in Vietnam, Mohr painted gritty pictures of infantry life and picked apart the strategic plans of military forces. A front-page article Mohr wrote on 2 February 1968, the third day of the Tet offensive, was a typical example: In one sweeping piece, Mohr described the Viet Cong incursion into South Vietnam, told of a South Vietnamese army officer who discovered his entire family slain, and ended with the speculation of U.S. generals that the Viet Cong launched the Tet offensive to reestablish political prominence after the communists fared poorly in national elections.

Mohr's dispatches won praise from all corners. Tom Wicker, another renowned writer from the era and a colleague of Mohr's at the *New York Times,* said Mohr "became . . . the outstanding combat reporter of the war—militarily knowledgeable, unafraid to reach his own conclusions, unflinching under fire, filing stories of sensitivity and compassion that matched their brilliance."

Mohr spent the 1970s as a foreign correspondent for the *New York Times.* He worked in Africa for five years, covered the Middle East wars of 1967 and 1973, worked in Hong Kong, and covered Jimmy Carter's 1976 presidential campaign. At the urging of his wife, Mohr and his family settled in suburban Chevy Chase, Maryland, in the late 1970s. Mohr then joined the *Times*'s Washington, D.C., bureau.

Mohr endured five bypass surgeries in the late 1970s. He came through the operations in acceptable health, but heart problems and diabetes continued to trouble him for the rest of his life.

In Washington, Mohr turned his focus to strategic and military affairs. He helped report the Iranian hostage crisis in 1980 and contributed to the *Times*'s political coverage during the Carter administration. (Carter later called Mohr "one of the most highly professional reporters I ever met.") An avid outdoorsman, Mohr also wrote on hunting and fishing in the *New York Times*'s sports section.

No strategic issue consumed Mohr in the early 1980s more than the Strategic Defense Initiative (SDI)—more commonly known as "Star Wars"—proposed by President Ronald Reagan in 1983. SDI generated enormous controversy in military, political, and scientific circles; Mohr dutifully reported as Reagan touted SDI or various officials testified before Congress to the program's costs, usefulness, and practicality.

In 1985 Mohr led a team of eight *New York Times* reporters who wrote an exhaustive series about SDI called "Weapons in Space." The stories examined how space-based weapons systems were reshaping strategic thinking, and whether such systems would make nuclear war less likely or more probable. Stories ranged from a history of satellite technology to scientific objections to the SDI program to possible reactions from the Soviet Union. The team published a total of nine articles for the series, six in March and three in December. Mohr authored two of them, focusing on Soviet answers to America's push for SDI. The series won a Pulitzer Prize in 1986 for explanatory journalism. It also served as the genesis for a 1988 book, *The New York Times' Complete Guide to the Star Wars Debate.* Mohr served as coauthor.

In the late 1980s Mohr continued to report from Washington on national affairs, covering such topics as a proposed assault-weapons ban, health problems Vietnam veterans suffered from Agent Orange, the Exxon *Valdez* oil spill, and President George Bush's reaction to the Tiananmen Square democracy protests in China in 1989.

Mohr suffered a heart attack at his home on the afternoon of his sixtieth birthday, and died that evening at a hospital in Bethesda, Maryland.

★

An obituary is in the *New York Times* (18 June 1989). A tribute to Mohr and to journalist I. F. Stone by Tom Wicker, "Two Honorable Men," is in the *New York Times* (20 June 1989).

MATTHEW KELLY

MORRIS, Richard Brandon (*b.* 24 July 1904 in New York City; *d.* 3 March 1989 in New York City), historian of the American colonial, revolutionary, and early national periods who pioneered new areas of research and made seminal contributions to the study of legal, labor, social, economic, political, diplomatic, and constitutional history.

Morris was the only child of Jacob Morris, a supervisor in the garment industry, and Tillie Rosenberg, whose Jewish forebears had immigrated to New York City from Eastern Europe. Morris exhibited an early enthusiasm for history and debuted as a historian at age thirteen with a lively article, "The Eighth Conquest of Jerusalem," published in the *Guardian* in 1917. A prodigious reader and writer, he was quick to perceive what was central and to express it in a robust intellectual style.

After attending City College's preparatory high school, Townsend Harris Hall, Morris went on to graduate with an A.B. degree, with honors, from City College in 1924. At Columbia University, he earned both an M.A. degree (1925) and a Ph.D. (1930) in early American legal history, completing a combined program in history and law. Morris's dissertation, *Studies in the History of American Law: With Special Reference to the Seventeenth and Eighteenth Centuries* (1930), opened up the whole field of colonial law and is still an influential work. His *Select Cases of the Mayor's Court of New York City, 1674–1784* (1935) focused on labor issues and the law. His decade-long exhaustive research in legal sources yielded the monumental *Government and Labor in Early America* (1946), which brought him recognition and acclaim.

Morris rose through the ranks at City College from instructor in 1927 to professor of history in 1947. He loved teaching and encouraged his students, having himself been fortunate in his mentors, including the eminent legal philosopher Morris Raphael Cohen. He introduced courses in American legal history, organized an honors program, directed the college's Civilian Defense Council during the war, and continued his research in legal, social, and economic history. He edited with his Columbia mentor and lifelong friend, Evarts B. Greene, a *Guide to the Principal Sources for Early American History (1600–1800) in the City of New York* (1929). His recommendations as regional director in 1936 and 1937 of the Survey of Federal Archives would give rise in 1968 to the National Archives' system of regional depositories. In 1932 Morris married Berenice Robinson, a musicologist, teacher, and composer; they had two sons, Jeffrey Brandon and Donald Robinson. The family in 1950 settled in suburban Mount Vernon in Westchester County, where Morris took up the hobby of gardening.

Richard B. Morris. MANNY WARMAN, COLUMBIA UNIVERSITY

Over the course of Morris's thirty years (1946–1976) at Columbia, he trained dozens of graduate students who later became historians in their own right. He expanded his teaching and research interests to the revolutionary and early national periods. He forged abiding friendships with Columbia colleagues Henry Steele Commager and Allan Nevins. He served a term, from 1958 to 1961, as chairman of the history department. In 1959 he was named Gouverneur Morris Professor of History and, on Columbia's acquisition of the papers of American founding father John Jay, launched a program to enlarge and organize this major archive for research and publication. The project united his interests in history and exemplified his commitment to recovering, preserving, and publishing the primary source materials that are vital to the historian's task.

The wide range of Morris's interests is reflected in his associations with diverse professional organizations. As president of Labor Historians, he was a founder and the editorial board chair (1960–1976) of the journal *Labor History,* which stimulated research and writings in the field. He was also a member of the editorial boards of *New York History* and the *American Journal of Legal History,* and a council member of the American Jewish Historical Society and the Institute of Early American History and Culture.

He was a member of the American Antiquarian Society and the Massachusetts Historical Society, a fellow of the Royal Historical Society (London) and the American Academy of Arts and Sciences. He held visiting professorships, Guggenheim research fellowships, and lectureships in North America, Europe, and the Middle East. He received honorary degrees from Hebrew Union College (L.H.D., 1963) and from Columbia and Rutgers Universities (Litt.D., 1976). He was elected president of the American Historical Association for 1976 and of the Society of American Historians for 1984–1987.

Morris produced influential works on the revolutionary, Confederation, and Constitution periods. The most notable was his Bancroft Award–winning *The Peacemakers: The Great Powers and American Independence* (1965). His lectures at Boston College on *John Jay, the Nation, and the Court* were published in 1967; his monograph *Seven Who Shaped Our Destiny: The Founding Fathers as Revolutionaries* (1973) was translated and also published in France. He edited many compilations of primary sources, such as *Basic Documents on the Confederation and Constitution* (1970). Two major editorial projects were the standard reference work *Encyclopedia of American History,* first published in 1953, the updated seventh edition issued in 1996 by his son, Jeffrey B. Morris; and the multivolume reexamination of the past, the New American Nation Series, edited with Henry Steele Commager. Various writings reached a large public audience, such as his National Park Service pamphlet *Independence* (1982). Morris also produced articles on Jewish history, labor, legal, diplomatic, and constitutional history, and John Jay.

In 1982 Morris provided expert testimony for the Native American Rights Fund on behalf of the Oneida Indian Nation and for the U.S. Department of Justice on the maritime boundary case with Canada. He had earlier (1972) supported a bill to curb presidential war powers before the Senate Committee on Foreign Relations, citing Congress's constitutional authority to "declare war"; the resulting legislation was passed as the War Powers Act of 1973.

At his 1973 retirement, Morris was presented with a Festschrift: *Perspectives on Early American History: Essays in Honor of Richard B. Morris,* edited by his former graduate students Alden T. Vaughan and George Athan Billias. He continued to teach as Gouverneur Morris Professor Emeritus of History and special lecturer and remained editor of *The Papers of John Jay.* The first two volumes, *John Jay: The Making of a Revolutionary* (1976) and *John Jay: The Winning of the Peace* (1980), illuminated the period, compelling a reevaluation of Jay. He also published *Witnesses at the Creation: Hamilton, Madison, Jay, and the Constitution* (1985) and his last book, *The Forging of the Union, 1781–1789* (1987), which drew together his findings on and interpretations of the Confederation.

During the Bicentennial observations from 1976 through 1987 of the formation of the United States, Morris participated in many civic and scholarly commemorative programs. In 1976 he delivered more than fifty lectures and was the consultant to Columbia Broadcasting System Television's "Bicentennial Minutes." In 1976 he and political scientist James MacGregor Burns brought about a partnership of the American Historical Association and the American Political Science Association that sponsored Project '87—a rigorous ten-year program of scholarship, education, and public information on the U.S. Constitution. Morris worked tirelessly to assure that the Bicentennial would be an occasion for "celebration," leaving Americans a legacy of interest and inquiry about their Constitution.

In 1988 the Society of American Historians awarded Morris the Bruce Catton Prize for Lifetime Achievement in the Writing of History. A short and sprightly man of extraordinary energy and enthusiasm, at the time of his death, from skin cancer in 1989, Morris was directing the concluding Jay papers volumes, serving on the board of trustees of the John Jay Homestead in Westchester County, New York, and was in the midst of his eight-year term, to which he had been appointed by President Ronald Reagan in 1985, on the Permanent Committee for the Oliver Wendell Holmes Devise to supervise the history of the U.S. Supreme Court. Memorial services were held at Columbia University, New York City, on 11 April 1989 and at the Brookings Institution, Washington, D.C., on 8 May 1989. Morris's remains were cremated.

Morris's lifelong love for history carried a mission: "to inform students, other scholars, and the public at large." His perceptions and wide-ranging interests and commitments made him independent of any school or theory of history, and his research-based writings and teachings would strongly influence two generations of historians. Burns observed of Morris: "In Dick I felt I was coming to know not only an authority on the Founders but a Founder himself, in his learning, his vision, his public-spiritedness, his compassion. Just as the Founders are still with us, so will Dick be."

★

Columbia University's Rare Book and Manuscript Library houses the Richard B. Morris Papers, which include professional papers, correspondence, drafts of articles, and books. No full-length biography has yet been written. Two autobiographical articles are "Reflections by a Graduate Student in History After a Half Century," *Organization of American Historians Newsletter* (1983); and "History over Time," in "Early American Emeriti: A Symposium of Experience and Evaluation," *William and Mary Quarterly*, 3d ser., 41 (July 1984): 455–463. On Morris's influence, see Stephen Botein, "Scientific Mind and Legal Matter: The Long Shadow of Richard B. Morris's Studies in the History of American Law," *Reviews in American History* 13, no. 2 (June 1985): 303–

315. Memorials and tributes include Wendell Tripp, "Memorial Thoughts of Milton W. Hamilton, Mark D. Hirsch, Richard B. Morris," *New York History* 70, no. 4 (Oct. 1989): 431–443; and Harold M. Hyman, "Requiem for a Constitutional-Legal History Heavyweight: Richard Brandon Morris, 1904–1989," *Georgia Journal of Southern Legal History* 1, no. 1 (spring/summer 1991): 136–140. Obituaries are in the *New York Times* (6 Mar. 1989) and *American Historical Association Perspectives* (May–June 1989). Two oral histories are at the Rare Book and Manuscript Library, Columbia University: on the history of the Confederation and Constitution (interviewed by John A. Garraty, 1969) and on his career as an historian (interviewed by Berenice Robinson Morris, 1978).

ENE SIRVET

MULLIKEN, Robert Sanderson (*b.* 7 June 1896 in Newburyport, Massachusetts; *d.* 31 October 1986 in Arlington, Virginia), physical chemist who received the Nobel Prize for his theoretical studies of the chemical bond that holds atoms together in a molecule (the molecular orbital theory).

Robert S. Mulliken, 1962. UPI/CORBIS-BETTMANN

Mulliken was the eldest of the three children of Samuel Parsons Mulliken, professor of organic chemistry at Massachusetts Institute of Technology, and Katherine Wilmarth Mulliken (a distant relative), who had been a painter and a teacher of piano and voice before their marriage. The area in and around Newburyport was ideal for an imaginative, inquisitive boy, and Robert learned the name and classification of plants almost as well as a professional botanist. Although strong, his memory was selective. For example, he could not remember the name of his teacher of German in high school, yet in college, his knowledge of German was such that he could translate German in science and thus skip a formal course. While growing up, Mulliken had accumulated a sizable stamp collection, which he later sold to a cousin at much less than market value. He had "naively and fatalistically accepted this offer without discussion." He said that his stamps were gone but he had had fun.

When Mulliken's father was writing his four-volume *A Method for the Identification of Pure Organic Compounds,* which was a standard text for many years, Mulliken and his sister, Katherine, cut, colored, and carefully pasted the various colors in the proper places on the standard color chart. Additionally, Mulliken proofread many of his father's books. As a result he learned a substantial amount of nomenclature of complex organic compounds.

Mulliken was not skilled in sports or in the arts (though his mother tried to teach him to play the piano). While in high school he developed what he termed a deterministic point of view. He saw people as "things, coldly, cruelly," a point of view that remained with him. Mulliken took the science curriculum at the Newburyport High School and did so well that he was awarded the Wheelwright Scholarship to MIT. (His father had been a recipient of the Wheelwright Scholarship as well.) He chose to follow his father and majored in chemistry. As the second-ranking student in the 1913 graduating class, Mulliken delivered an oration titled "Electrons: What They Are and What They Do." At MIT he did his first piece of publishable research, the preparation of organic chlorides, with James F. Norris. Uncertain about what he would do later, he took some chemical engineering courses.

After receiving the B.S. degree from MIT in 1917, Mulliken took a position at American University in Washington, D.C., working under James B. Conant on the manufacture of poison gas. After nine months he was put into the Chemical Warfare Service as a private. Carelessness on his part led to serious burns that hospitalized him for about six months. Later Mulliken did work employing the Tyndall effect (scattering of light by colloidal particles in solution). He caught influenza, was hospitalized again, and was discharged as a private first class in 1918. He went to work as a chemist for the New Jersey Zinc Company, adding carbon black and zinc oxide to rubber.

In 1919 Mulliken entered the University of Chicago to study for his Ph.D. with William D. Hawkins, a physical chemist who was interested in the study of atomic nuclei. Mulliken's work entailed the separation of isotopes of mercury by nonequilibrium evaporation (the apparatus was designed so that less of the evaporated mercury returned to the original pool). The work resulted in a long publication, "The Separation of Isotopes," in *Journal of the American Chemical Society* (1922) and was accepted by the chemistry department as fulfilling the Ph.D. requirement for a piece of original research. Mulliken was introduced to the old quantum theory through a course taught by Robert A. Millikan, the 1923 Nobelist in physics. The work of Hermann I. Schlesinger on B_2H_6, diborane, got Mulliken interested in strange molecules. While still at Chicago on a National Research Council (NRC) grant, Mulliken built a six-unit device that employed irreversible evaporation followed by diffusion into separate isotopes. Due to the greater yields of separated isotopes, he called this apparatus his "isotope factory."

In 1923 Mulliken's NRC grant was renewed so that he could study the isotopic effects in boron nitride bands ($B^{10}N$ and $B^{11}N$) and other band spectra in other diatomic molecules. He went to the Jefferson Physical Laboratory at Harvard to learn the techniques of spectroscopy from Frederick A. Saunders, a well-known spectroscopist, and from E. C. Kemble, an expert on quantum theory. During his stay at Harvard, Mulliken associated with future Nobelists J. Robert Oppenheimer, John H. Van Vleck, and Harold C. Urey, as well as John C. Slate, who worked with the physicist Niels Bohr.

During visits to Europe in 1925 and 1927 Mulliken worked with the leading scientists in spectroscopy and quantum theory, many of whom later received the Nobel Prize—Erwin Schrödinger (1933), Paul A. M. Dirac (1933), Werner Heisenberg (1932), Louis de Broglie (1929), Max Born (1954), and Walther Bothe (1954)—as well as Friedrich Hund, a major contributor to the new quantum theory and an assistant to Max Born. These individuals, along with Wolfgang Pauli (who discovered the exclusion principle), had developed the new quantum theory, based on probability, that was replacing the old, deterministic quantum theory (an assumption of regularity and order in science). In 1928 Mulliken wrote a historic paper on the assignment of electronic configurations to experimentally observed states in molecules (*Physical Review,* 1928) following discussion and work with Hund in the summer of 1927. Hund had earlier applied quantum theory to the interpretation of band structures of diatomic molecules. Mulliken published several additional papers that year on his molecular orbital theory, in which the outermost electrons of a molecule are in constant motion in orbitals or a cloudlike shell over the whole molecule.

Mulliken taught physics at New York University from 1926 to 1928. On 24 December 1929 Mulliken married Mary Helen Von Noé; they had two daughters. He then moved to the University of Chicago, as associate professor; he was promoted to full professor by 1931. He continued to refine the molecular orbital theory in which the molecular orbitals were expressed in quantum-mechanical mathematical terms that gave approximate solutions to the Schrödinger wave equation. These approximate solutions gave probable descriptions of the molecules, even complex ones, whether in the ground state or the excited state.

Prior to the development of the molecular orbital theory by Hund and Mulliken, the prevailing theory was the valence-bond theory, developed by Linus Pauling (Nobel Prize in chemistry, 1954) and others, particularly Walter Heitler and Fritz London. Both the valence-bond theory and the molecular orbital theory apply quantum mechanics to account for molecular properties and structures. Although the valence-bond theory is used by many in describing molecular structures in the lowest energy state (ground state), the theory does not work well for excited states. In fact, Andrew Liehr had written that the valence-bond theory should be discarded, and he had sought experimental data that would invalidate the theory even for molecules in the ground state. Molecular orbital theory is more powerful and has applications in many types of bonding, including ionic and covalent.

During World War II, Mulliken was the director of editorial work and information for the Plutonium Project of the University of Chicago (1942–1945). After the war he contributed to the development of complex mathematical programming formulas to be used in molecular orbital theory; through them new insight was gained into the forces that hold molecules together.

Mulliken published more than 250 papers, including "The Separation of Isotopes by Thermal and Pressure Diffusion," *Journal of the American Chemical Society* 44 (1922): 1033–1051; "The Assignment of Quantum Numbers for Electrons in Molecules," *Physical Review* 32 (1928): 186–222; "Interpretations of Band Spectra III," *Review of Modern Physics* 4 (1932): 1–86; and, with C. A. Ricke, "Molecular Electronic Spectra, Dispersion, and Polarization," *Physical Society Report on the Progress of Physics* 8 (1941): 231–273. He was a Fulbright Scholar at Oxford University (1952–1953); the Ernest DeWitt Burton Distinguished Service Professor (1956–1961) and the Distinguished Service Professor of physics and chemistry (1961–1985) at the University of Chicago; and Distinguished Research Professor of chemical physics, Florida State University (1964–1971). He was also Baker lecturer at Cornell University (1960) and Stillman lecturer at Yale (1965). Mulliken was a member of the National Academy of Sciences; a fellow of the American Physical Society (first chair of the division of chemical physics); and member of the American Chemical Society, the American Philosophical Society, the American

Academy of Arts and Sciences, and the Royal Society of London (foreign member). His honors include the Theodore William Richards Gold Medal (1960), the Peter Debye Award (1963), the Willard Gibbs Medal (1965), the Nobel Prize in chemistry (1966), and the Priestley Medal (1983).

Mulliken died of natural causes in Arlington, Virginia, at the home of his daughter. He is buried in Chicago.

★

Mulliken's work is discussed in two works written with W. C. Ermler: *Diatomic Molecules: Results of Ab-Initio Calculations* (1977) and *Polyatomic Molecules: Results of Ab-Initio Calculations* (1981). There is a voluminous R. S. Mulliken archive at the University of Chicago's Regenstein Library. See also D. A. Ramsey and J. Hinze, eds., *Selected Papers of R. S. Mulliken* (1975). *Robert S. Mulliken, Life of a Scientist: An Autobiographical Account of the Development of Molecular Orbital Theory,* edited by Bernard J. Ramail (1989), includes a chronology, photographs, and illustrations. See also Tyler Wasson, ed., *Nobel Prize Winners* (1987). An obituary is in the *New York Times* (2 Nov. 1986).

SAMUEL VON WINBUSH

MUMFORD, Lewis Charles (*b.* 19 October 1895 in Flushing, New York; *d.* 26 January 1990 in Amenia, New York), cultural critic and urban planner best known for his extensive writings on cities and technology.

Lewis Mumford, *c.* 1961. ARCHIVE PHOTOS

Lewis Mumford was the illegitimate son of Elvina Conradina Baron Mumford and Lewis Charles Mack, the nephew of a man for whom Elvina served as housekeeper. "Mumford" was the name of John Mumford, Elvina's husband before her marriage was annulled some years earlier. Lewis Mumford never met his biological father and was reared by his mother. He also spent considerable time with his maternal step-grandfather, who frequently took him for long, gratifying walks in various New York neighborhoods, especially in Manhattan, where the family had relocated. Mumford also learned to savor country life thanks to rustic walks in upstate New York and through several summers of residing in the Vermont countryside. These youthful pleasures enabled Mumford to see the urban and rural experiences as not antithetical but complementary, a consideration that was to become a vital ingredient of his mature philosophy.

Interested in radio experiments and hopeful of becoming an electrical engineer, Mumford entered Stuyvesant High School in 1909. After graduation in 1912 he matriculated at the City College of New York (CCNY), where he pursued his new interest, writing. While at CCNY he encountered the work of Patrick Geddes, a British intellectual who wed his early efforts as a biologist to civic and regional planning. Geddes, whom he described as "my own master," would remain a major lifelong influence. Mumford dropped out of City College in 1916 and then took courses at Columbia University, New York University, and the New School for Social Research, returning to City College again in 1917. He never graduated from any college, however, and in 1918 he enlisted in the navy, serving as a radio technician.

After World War I, Mumford began his literary career. He briefly served as an associate editor of *Dial* magazine in 1919. The following year he relocated to London to serve as acting editor of the *Sociological Review,* only to return that same year and begin writing articles (freelance) for Albert Jay Nock's *The Freeman* as well as for other noteworthy journals, including the *American Mercury,* the *New Republic, Scribner's,* and *Harper's.* In 1922 Mumford published *The Story of Utopias,* which warned of the hopeless quest for utopia and urged reformers instead to seek a better rather than the perfect society. In this work, the first of some thirty books he wrote in his lifetime, Mumford delineated certain themes that would persistently recur in later writings, perhaps most notably what he held forth as the false equation of human progress with technological advancement. Meanwhile, in 1921, he married Sophia Wittenberg, whom he had met while working for *Dial.* Their marriage, which endured until Mumford's death, produced two children, a son, Geddes, named after his mentor, and a daughter, Alison.

Mumford's activism as an urban planner took root in 1923, when he became a founder of the Regional Planning Association of American (RPAA). Influenced by Geddes and by the nineteenth-century English reformer Ebenezer Howard, Mumford and the RPAA sought ways to prevent cities from becoming megalopolises. Their goal was to create so-called garden cities, small or medium-sized communities that would both restrain urban expansion and maintain bucolic farms and parks. This ideal community, according to Mumford, would be a balanced one, "relatively self-contained and big enough to provide out of its own resources and activities all that might be needed for the citizen's daily life." Also in 1923, the RPAA transformed theory into practice when it promoted the building of Sunnyside Gardens in Queens, New York, a small community of attached houses grouped around common gardens. Mumford moved to Sunnyside in 1925 and remained there until 1936. In 1928 he helped the RPAA plan a second and larger garden community, Radburn, located in Fair Lawn, New Jersey.

Mumford's interests in regional planning and garden city communities continued throughout his life, but his principal preoccupation and occupation was writing, and architecture was the subject that singularly engaged his earlier efforts during the 1920s and much of his career. Lacking any formal training whatsoever, Mumford brought an untutored but discerning eye and mind to the discipline. *Sticks and Stones,* his initial book on architecture, was based on his magazine articles and was published in 1924. In that work Mumford extolled modernism in architecture, particularly as it evolved in the nineteenth-century work of the Chicago School and in some of the early work of twentieth-century proponents of the International Style. Later, however, he would severely attack architectural modernism for its remoteness from human sensibilities. The book brought him widespread repute as one of the nation's finest critics. For Mumford, architecture was inextricably linked to the broader aspects of American culture, and it was a consideration of this larger continuum of history, literature, technology, and the arts that he explored not only in *Sticks and Stones* but in *The Golden Day* (1926) and *The Brown Decades* (1931) as well.

Like his friend Van Wyck Brooks and others, his interests seemed to run the gamut of American civilization. Mumford's *Herman Melville* (1929) ignited renewed interest in this largely neglected author and added luster to the biographer's already sizable reknown. In 1931 Mumford became the architecture critic for the *New Yorker* magazine. His "Sky Line" column, which appeared regularly, with some exceptions, until 1963, helped inform public opinion on matters of urban life and urban policy. Paid well for his columns, Mumford moved to Leedsville, New York, a two-hour commute from the city. In 1937 he moved to Amenia, New York, which was his residence for most of the remainder of his life. Urban congestion, which he had early warned against, had convinced him that he could best live and work in the country with occasional forays into the city.

Whatever the problems of the modern urbanism—and he considered them numerous—Mumford never lost sight of the importance of the city in human history. Indeed, the city, for him, was in many ways synonymous with human achievement. In 1931 he began his research for an open-ended project that would explore the dynamic forces of urbanism and technology as they shaped, and in turn were shaped by, the human condition. In all, this Renewal of Life series ultimately resulted in four major works completed over a nearly twenty-year period. The initial work, *Technics and Civilization* (1934), explored Mumford's long-standing interest in the decisive relationship between man and the machine. Contrasting the balanced humanistic and technological achievements of the Middle Ages with the increasingly regimented, standardized, numbing effects of technology in the modern world, Mumford reminded his readers that humans shaped technology and not vice versa. Never a Luddite, he would caution that "to preserve the efficiency of the machine as an instrument and to use it further as a work of art, we must alter the center of gravity from the external Newtonian world to that complete world which the human personality dominates and transmutes." In *The Culture of Cities* (1938), the second book of the series, he explored the genesis of the world's great modern cities and offered suggestions for dealing with their current plights. This book secured an international reputation for Mumford and enhanced his already widespread acclaim as perhaps the foremost living American architecture critic. Also in 1938, he submitted urban planning analyses for Honolulu and for the Pacific Northwest Regional Planning Commission.

Soon after World War II erupted in Europe, Mumford, convinced that Adolf Hitler had to be defeated, joined William Allen White's Committee to Defend America by Aiding the Allies. In *Men Must Act* (1939) he strongly urged military preparedness in the face of fascist aggression. During the war Mumford served an intellectually unfulfilling stint from 1942 to 1944 as a professor of humanities at Stanford University. In 1944 he published the third book in his Renewal of Life series, *The Condition of Man,* a display of encyclopedic erudition that outlined the evolution of human thought and spirit from the classical world and early Christianity to the twentieth century. That same year his son, a soldier in the U.S. Army, was killed in action in Italy.

The postwar years witnessed no abatement in Mumford's productivity. He wrote a biography of his deceased son, *Green Memories* (1947), and began actively campaigning against nuclear weapons. As he noted apropos of President Harry Truman's decision to use atomic bombs against Japan: "Apparently he did not stop to consider that it might also shorten the existence of the human race." During these years he fought against Robert Moses's ambitious projects to build urban expressways and urban renewal projects in and around New York City. The changes wrought by or proposed by Moses, complained Mumford, would destroy the human scale of living for countless urban dwellers. While he lost most of his battles with Moses, he did sometimes score an important triumph, as when he helped to lead the fight to secure New York City's famed Washington Square Park from Moses's proposed roadway incursions.

In 1951 he commenced a decade-long association with the University of Pennsylvania, where, as a visiting professor and research associate, he taught various courses on the city. As a noted authority and popular lecturer, Mumford also briefly taught and served as a research fellow at the Massachusetts Institute of Technology (1957–1960), the University of California at Berkeley (1961–1962), and Wesleyan University (1963–1964). Meanwhile, in 1951, he published the last of his Renewal of Life works, *The Conduct of Life.* The 1950s also witnessed the appearance of two other books by Mumford, *Art and Technics* (1952) and *The Transformations of Man* (1956). While neither work received extended notice, the latter presaged Mumford's final three major works.

The City in History (1961) took five years to complete and represents Mumford's most detailed observations, Cassandra-like warnings, and suggestions regarding urbanism. Received with widespread acclaim, it won that year's National Book Award for nonfiction. With age Mumford became less sanguine of humanity's ability to control technology and to preserve a civilized way of living. He ruminated at length on these themes in his two-volume *The Myth of the Machine,* the first volume of which, *Technics and Human Development,* appeared in 1967, the second, *The Pentagon of Power,* in 1970. In these volumes he warned of the "megamachine," the control of people by a power-hungry, power-driven ruler or state, and the dissipation or outright destruction of spiritual and intellectual energies and goals. During this time his bitter opposition to America's imbroglio in Vietnam intensified his growing pessimism.

His forebodings for humankind notwithstanding, Mumford continued to receive an array of accolades and honors, including the Presidential Medal of Freedom (1964), the National Medal for Literature (1972), an honorary Knight Commander of the British Empire (1975), the Prix Mondial del Duca (1976), and the National Medal of Arts (1986). During his later years Mumford wrote two autobiographical works, *My Works and Days* (1979) and *Sketches from Life* (1982). Suffering from increasing frailty and assorted illnesses associated with aging, Mumford died in his sleep at age ninety-four.

Lewis Mumford's contributions as scholar and critic helped shape twentieth-century thought and values. His earliest works were provocative, pathbreaking studies in American culture. It was as a historian of the city and critic of modern urbanism, however, that he achieved his greatest renown. While not alone among the assailants of twentieth-century cities, Mumford, through his powerful and imaginative insights gracefully conveyed, became for many the urbanist par excellence. For some, his critiques and suggestions seemed either wrongheaded or the perorations of a Jeremiah. Few, however, denied that with his broadbased concern for the quality of life, Mumford was one of the century's great humanists.

★

The Lewis Mumford Collection can be found in the Charles Patterson Van Pelt Library of the University of Pennsylvania. Other collections with pertinent Mumford material, too numerous to mention, are scattered. *My Works and Days: A Personal Chronicle* (1979) contains autobiographical matter, but *Sketches from Life: The Early Years* (1982) represents the first volume in Mumford's projected formal autobiography. The first and to date standard full-length biography of Mumford is Donald L. Miller, *Lewis Mumford: A Life* (1989). Robert Josephy, *Taking Part: A Twentieth-Century Life* (1993) is also helpful. Two collections of correspondence also help to illuminate the subject and his work: *The Van Wyck Brooks–Lewis Mumford Letters: The Record of a Literary Friendship, 1921–1963,* ed. Robert E. Spiller (1970), and *Lewis Mumford and Patrick Geddes: The Correspondence,* ed. Frank G. Novak, Jr. (1985). An obituary is in the *New York Times* (28 Jan. 1990).

ROBERT MUCCIGROSSO

MURCHISON, Clint(on) Williams, Jr. (*b.* 12 September 1923 in Dallas, Texas; *d.* 30 March 1987 in Dallas, Texas), businessman and original owner of the Dallas Cowboys football team.

Murchison was the second of three children of the wildcat oilman Clinton W. Murchison, Sr., and Anne Morris. He played halfback on the football team at the Lawrenceville School in New Jersey. In 1940 he entered the Massachusetts Institute of Technology but left in 1942 to enlist in the Marine Corps, which commissioned him a lieutenant and enrolled him in the V-12 training program at Duke University. He graduated Phi Beta Kappa from Duke with a degree in electrical engineering in 1944. After his discharge from the marines in 1945, he reenrolled at MIT and received a master's degree in mathematics. Murchison married Jane Catherine Coleman on 12 June 1945; they had four children.

In 1942 Clint Murchison, Sr., set up a partnership, Murchison Brothers, officially owned by his two sons, under whose control he placed the numerous businesses that he had purchased with profits from his lucrative oil speculations. Eventually the firm controlled more than one hundred different businesses, including a 13 percent minority interest in the publishing company Henry Holt, Inc. Murchison and his brother, John Dabney Murchison, were made members of Holt's board of directors. According to some accounts, they were responsible for the firm's expansion into the textbook market during the postwar period.

Clint, Sr., and his sons ran Murchison Brothers in a low-key manner during the 1950s. The brothers tried their hands at different types of business operations, engaging in real estate development, construction, finance, and life insurance. Eventually Clint, Jr., focused on speculative ventures involving construction and real estate development, while John concentrated on more conservative activities involving banking and insurance. One observer noted: "Clint, Jr., loved everything that had to do with construction and John liked everything that did not have to do with construction."

Clint W. Murchison, Jr. ARCHIVE PHOTOS

Murchison's father turned over control of Murchison Brothers to his sons in the mid-1950s. By the early 1960s, the firm's value had increased twofold, from an original investment of $75 million. The firm abandoned its low-profile role in the early 1960s, when the brothers initiated a hostile takeover of the Allegheny Corporation, whose assets included the New York Central Railroad. Although the brothers succeeded in winning control from the F. W. Woolworth heir Allan P. Kirby, Kirby still retained enough votes to veto most of their proposed changes. The Murchisons sold their holdings a few years later.

Clint Murchison initiated a more successful venture in professional sports in 1959. The National Football League (NFL) wanted to expand by adding a team franchise in Dallas, and on 28 January 1960 the Murchison brothers (with Bedford Wynne as a minority investor) purchased the franchise for $550,000. The team was originally named the Dallas Rangers but soon became the Dallas Cowboys. Murchison oversaw the team's operations and hired Tex Schramm as general manager and Tom Landry as head coach. The team performed dismally during its initial years (with a record of 0–11–1 the first year), but in 1966 it began an NFL record-breaking run of twenty consecutive winning seasons. In 1971 and 1977 the team was the Superbowl champion.

In 1967 Murchison announced his dissatisfaction with the Cotton Bowl Stadium, where the team played and which was owned by the city of Dallas. He designed and oversaw construction of the much larger Texas Stadium located in Irving, a Dallas suburb, which he described as "the only stadium built primarily for football since World War II." A business associate noted of Murchison that "with his engineering background, he was very much 'hands on' during its construction." Construction was completed on 24 October 1971. Murchison similarly maintained a hands-on approach regarding the team's ancillary Dallas Cowboy Cheerleaders, initially named the Cow Belles. He reviewed tryouts by the teenage applicants, dated some secretly, and obtained appointments to the squad for his lovers. He later distanced himself from the cheerleaders after the success of the football team brought him increased publicity.

After the widespread public acclaim over his success with the football team, Murchison began making business deals on his own, outside the scope of Murchison Brothers. In the 1970s he became increasingly dependent upon alcohol, cocaine, and other drugs. He also disregarded the advice of his longtime business associates and relied increasingly upon sycophants and procurers. He and his wife divorced in 1973, and in June 1975 he married Anne Ferrell Brandt, former wife of the Cowboys personnel director.

John Murchison noted the changes in his brother's behavior and began removing many of his business operations from the scope of Murchison Brothers, so that he would not be financially liable for the ever-increasing debt resulting from those bad deals which Murchison had made within the scope of the partnership. The brothers' diverging ways went unnoticed by most of their creditors until after John's death of a heart attack in 1979. John's death coincided with a collapse in oil prices and Texas real estate values. The demands of John's heirs for their remaining interests in the now-insolvent Murchison Brothers, caused Murchison to sell the firm's interest in the Dallas Cowboys to H. R. ("Bum") Bright, a Texas millionaire, for $60 million in 1984.

The profits from the team's sale did not satisfy John's heirs, and their lawsuit prompted other creditors of Murchison Brothers to examine more closely the firm's financial condition. Three creditors began bankruptcy proceedings against Murchison in 1985 and discovered his personal and business debts exceeded $400 million while his assets were only slightly more than $70 million. In 1986 the bankruptcy court approved a reorganization plan that left Murchison with approximately $3 million.

The collapse of Murchison's finances was preceded by the collapse of his health. At the time of the bankruptcy proceedings, he was debilitated and confined to a wheelchair by what was described as a degenerative nerve disorder. A friend described his postbankruptcy situation: "He no longer owned the Cowboys, he didn't have the money to make any more deals, and he was too sick for sex. What was there? Nothing. He lost his will to live." An infection from pneumonia led to his death at the Gaston Episcopal Hospital. He was buried at Hillcrest Memorial Park in Dallas.

Murchison—along with such other former Texas millionaires as John Connally and Herbert and Bunker Hunt—could be considered the living personification of arguments positing the redundancy of progressive inheritance taxes. Murchison inherited a fortune estimated at $250 million and managed to squander most of it away on drugs and bad business deals.

★

Clint Murchison's papers are in the possession of his family, but he has been the subject of numerous books and articles. The best is Jane Wolfe, *The Murchisons: The Rise and Fall of a Texas Dynasty* (1989), which contains numerous interviews with family members and business associates, and it is not superseded by her later *Blood Rich: When Oil Billions, High Fashion, and Royal Intimacies Are Not Enough* (1993). He is mentioned in John Bainbridge, *The Super-Americans: A Picture of Life in the United States, as Brought into Focus, Bigger than Life, in the Land of Millionaires—Texas* (1972); James Presley, *A Saga of Wealth: The Rise of the Texas Oilmen* (1978); Jeff Meyers, *Dallas Cowboys* (1974); Bob St. John, *Tex! The Man Who Built the Dallas Cowboys* (1988), and "Anne Murchison Found Clint, Oil Money, and the Cowboys Weren't Enough—Without God," *People* (29 Oct. 1979). The Chapter 11 reorganization plan is described in the *New York Times* (17 June 1986). Obituaries are in the *New York Times* and *Washington Post* (both 1 Apr. 1987).

STEPHEN MARSHALL

N

NAGURSKI, Bronislau ("Bronko") (*b.* 3 November 1908 in Rainy River, Ontario, Canada; *d.* 7 January 1990 in International Falls, Minnesota), All-American and professional football player and charter member of the Professional Football Hall of Fame.

One of the four children of Michael and Michelina Nagurski, Ukrainian immigrants to Canada, Bronislau was eight years old when he moved with his family over the Ontario border to International Falls, Minnesota, where they bought a farm. His first-grade teacher gave him the nickname "Bronko." In his senior year of high school he was discovered by Clarence ("Doc") Spears, the football coach of the University of Minnesota, who, after seeing him plow a field without a horse, was even more astonished when the young man picked up the plow to indicate directions. Nagurski was All-American at Minnesota from 1927 to 1929, and in 1929 the *New York Sun* named him to its All-American team, both as a defensive tackle and as a fullback. He married Eileen Kane, also from International Falls, on 10 December 1929 and moved into a home purchased from her parents along Rainy Lake, saying he had "to wake up to the sound of water." He raised his six children there, returning home to a small adjacent farm in the off-season.

After graduation in 1930 Nagurski was signed as a power runner, at a salary of $5,000, by George Halas, owner and coach of the Chicago Bears. At six feet, two inches and 234 pounds, Nagurski did not have an ounce of fat on his body. Halas found Nagurski's physique all the more remarkable because it was not the result of weight lifting, but only of farm work. Later described as "an unyielding cement block," "a bone-jarring and effective tackler," "a sensational blocker," and "a threat as a passer," the athlete confirmed Halas's good judgment by contributing to the Bears's 9–4–1 record in 1930 and their championships of 1932 and 1933, by effectively using the T formation.

Nagurski's preferred passing play was to fake a plunge forward, step back a yard or two, jump, and lob the ball to a waiting receiver. In a game between the Bears and the Portsmouth Spartans to decide the 1932 National Football League championship (needed because the teams were tied for highest winning percentage, the usual championship criterion), his use of this play to throw a pass into the end zone to Red Grange for a touchdown caused a controversy. The Spartans' coach, George ("Potsy") Clark, called the play illegal because the prevailing rule required forward passes to be thrown from at least five yards behind the line of scrimmage. Bobby Cahn, the referee, ruled in Nagurski's favor, allowing the touchdown. The controversy led to a change of rules in 1933 to allow a forward pass to be thrown anywhere from behind the line of scrimmage. In that year Nagurski used this play for two touchdowns when the Bears (10–2–1) hosted the New York Giants (11–3) at Wrigley Field in the first officially scheduled NFL championship game. With only three minutes left in the game and

Bronko Nagurski. PRO FOOTBALL HALL OF FAME

the Giants leading 21–16, two plays moved the ball to the Giants' thirty-three-yard line. Nagurski took the next snap, began to run toward the line, stopped, jumped in the air, and threw a fullback option pass over the middle to tight end Bill Hewitt, who carried the ball fourteen yards and lateraled to Bill Karr, who completed the final yards for a Bears victory of 23–21.

On Thanksgiving Day 1934 the Bears beat the Detroit Lions (formerly the Portsmouth Spartans), 19–16, when Chicago's Joe Zeller intercepted a pass and ran fifty-five yards to the Detroit four-yard line. Nagurski then faked a plunge and lobbed a pass to Hewitt. At their next meeting, on 9 December, the Giants defeated the Bears, 30–13, in what came to be known as the "sneakers game." Although the Bears were leading at halftime from a touchdown by Nagurski and a field goal by Jack Manders, with only ten minutes left to play the Giants put on sneakers to run better on the field, iced over by a temperature of nine degrees—and scored four touchdowns for the victory.

In 1937, after being turned down by Halas for a salary increase to $6,000, Nagurski played his last game of the 1930s for the Bears against the Washington Redskins, who won 21–18 in the NFL championship at Wrigley Field. The Pro Football Hall of Fame has only two games on film showing Nagurski from start to finish, both in 1937. One, on 31 October, was a tie between the Bears and the Giants. Nagurski carried only three plays and was used in less than half the game. The other, on 24 October, was a 28–20 victory for the Bears over Detroit in which, after being knocked to his knees by two backs, Nagurski crawled for five more yards, with a total gain of seventeen yards. Paul Zimmerman, who commented on these films in an article in *Sports Illustrated,* noted that, at times, Nagurski's blocking was precise, but at other times, he would throw his whole body up against the tackle. Such furious action resulted in a serious back injury during the 1935 season. Sportswriters have speculated that the injury to two vertebrae slowed down his game and accounted for his not being All-Pro beyond 1934. Even in 1937, however, Nagurski demonstrated his high energy and power by playing in five Bears games and wrestling in eight cities in one three-week period. It was for the professional wrestling circuit that he left football, enticed by the promise of more money. When the NFL named its team of the 1930s, Nagurski was among the eleven players, four of whom had played in the 1933 championship game: Hewitt, Nagurski, and Joe Stydahar of the Chicago Bears and Mel Hein of the Giants.

The advent of World War II led to the departure to the armed forces of many professional football players. As a result of weakened ankles and knees, however, Nagurski was unfit for military service. At age thirty-four, and after not playing for five seasons, he was persuaded by Halas to play in 1943. He spent most of the year at tackle but was positioned as fullback for a key game with the Cardinals, leading the Bears to the division title, and in the league championship game against the Washington Redskins at Wrigley Field he scored a touchdown and led the Bears to a 41–21 victory. This was the last season of pro football for Nagurski, but he worked full-time on the wrestling circuit until 1958. He also operated a Sun Oil filling station in International Falls until his full retirement in 1968. His career left him with severe arthritis. He made one more public appearance in 1984, when he was asked to attend the coin-tossing ceremony preceding that year's Super Bowl game in Tampa, Florida.

Official NFL records date only from 1932, after Nagurski had already played two full seasons. Including those years, he is credited with 4,031 rushing yards in 872 attempts, averaging 4.6 yards per carry in a career of nine seasons. Without the records of 1930 and 1931, he made 610 rushing attempts, totaling 2,708 yards, with 4.4 yards per carry. He scored 18 touchdowns and completed 38 of 80 passes during his Chicago career.

Any evaluation of Nagurski's performance must keep in mind that protective padding was slight in the 1930s, helmets had no face masks, and, with a team of only eighteen players, he played offensive and defensive positions, frequently in sixty-minute games, twice a week, and without substitutions, except for injuries. Playing fullback and tackle, Nagurski had to be both instinctive and forceful. All the more remarkable is that Nagurski was a quiet and shy man off the field, an all-around "good guy," who reserved his rage for the game. Nagurski ran his own interference with such enormous power that the only way to tackle him was to hit the ground right at his ankles. As teammate Red Grange said, "If you hit [him] above the ankles, you could get killed." At times, Nagurski's crashing into linebackers resulted in their being carried off the field, leading to Bunyanesque tales of this athlete, who was surely one of the "monsters of the Midway," as the Chicago Bears were called. Nagurski died of cardiopulmonary arrest at Falls Memorial Hospital in International Falls. He was buried in his longtime hometown. The Koochiching County Historical Society in International Falls houses the Bronko Nagurski Museum, a permanent record of his career in football and wrestling.

Sportswriters have speculated on Nagurski's ranking if he were playing the game in modern times. The best testimony to his standing in football history, in addition to his presence in the Pro Football Hall of Fame, is that of a fifteen-man selection committee asked in 1995 for nominees for the NFL seventy-fifth anniversary all-time team. The committee chose Nagurski for the offensive running-back position. To put his status in perspective, the other running backs chosen were Walter Payton, Gale Sayers, O. J. Simpson, and Steve Van Buren.

★

The Pro Football Hall of Fame in Canton, Ohio, has a file on Nagurski, available on request. Information about his career is in Paul Zimmerman, "The Bronk and the Gazelle," *Sports Illustrated* (11 Sept. 1989); Don R. Smith, *The Official Pro Football Hall of Fame Book of Superstars* (1990); Thomas Rogers, "Bronko Nagurski," in Joseph J. Vecchione, ed., *The New York Times Book of Sports Legends;* Denis J. Harrington, *The Pro Football Hall of Fame: Players, Coaches, Team Owners, and League Officials, 1963–1991* (1991); and Will McDonough, Peter King, Paul Zimmerman, et al., *Seventy-Five Seasons: The Complete Story of the National Football League, 1920–1995* (1994). A portrait is in Ray Didinger, *The Professionals: Portraits of NFL Stars by America's Most Prominent Illustrators* (1980). An obituary is in the *New York Times* (9 Jan. 1990).

BARBARA L. GERBER

NEF, John Ulric (*b.* 13 July 1899 in Chicago, Illinois; *d.* 25 December 1988 in Washington, D.C.), economic historian whose research into the development of the British coal mining industry yielded persuasive evidence that the Industrial Revolution had its origins in the mid-1500s rather than the 1700s; he was the founder of the elite intellectual Committee on Social Thought at the University of Chicago and a patron and benefactor of the arts.

Nef, an only child, was born into a prominent intellectual family; his father, John Ulric Nef, Sr., was a theoretical organic chemist known for his work on the carbon valence and a professor at the University of Chicago. After his mother's death, Nef and his father lived what the son described as a "cloistered life" in a Chicago hotel room. The death of Nef's father from a heart attack in 1915 led to a considerable improvement in Nef's quality of life. The philosopher George Herbert Mead became Nef's guardian and moved the teenager into his home, where he met Elinor Castle, the niece of Mead's wife and an heir to the fortune of the Castle and Cooke food products company. Although Castle was five years older than Nef, their mutual interests in the arts and scholarship produced a friendship that led to marriage in 1921.

Nef displayed academic prowess in his college preparatory work. In particular, he received high marks for his knowledge of ancient Greek history. He attended the University of Chicago but joined the army in 1918. He was discharged a year later, finished his undergraduate studies at Harvard University (1920), then spent another year doing graduate work at Harvard, studying government and American history and managing the Harvard Union. He received his M.A. degree in 1921.

In 1921 the Nefs moved to Europe, with Nef expecting to study at the London School of Economics and become an economist. Instead, they settled in France with Nef studying at the University of Montpellier's Law School, where economics was part of the curriculum. While in Europe, he and Elinor indulged their greatest mutual passion—art. They attended the great European museums and while living in Paris made daily trips to the Louvre. They collected art, acquiring several Picassos as well as paintings by Marc Chagall. Nef subsequently met Chagall, and the two became lifelong friends.

In 1922 Nef began researching the work that made his academic reputation, *The Rise of the British Coal Industry,* which took ten years to complete. It is an exhaustive two-volume treatment of the growth of English industrialism during the Middle Ages, a period not usually associated with rapid economic growth. His research showed a 25 percent increase in the amount of British coal carried by sea between 1560 and 1700, the type of economic growth that scholars had previously believed was associated with the Industrial Revolution, which was generally considered to have lasted from 1760 to the mid-1800s. Although it received excellent reviews from several academic publications—the *American Historical Review* (Jan. 1934) said it was "one of the most important contributions to the economic history of Great Britain"—Nef was disappointed to discover that the book's publication had almost no impact on the general public. Instead, he settled for the esteem it brought him in academia and a friendship it forged with

R. H. Tawney, the chief economic historian at the London School of Economics. Ironically, *The Rise of the British Coal Industry* helped emphasize a historical analysis Nef came to deplore—the use of quantitative methods to describe historical events and trends. Nef believed that a multitude of forces were at play in any development or trend and that statistics were not the best way to tell a story.

Nef and Elinor returned to the United States in 1926. He received his Ph.D. in 1927 from the Robert Brookings Graduate School, precursor of the Brookings Institution. He taught at the Department of Economics at Swarthmore College before accepting an appointment to the Economics Department at the University of Chicago. He remained disillusioned with academic specialization, believing that the world was best explained by those who had training and interests in several areas, especially in art.

Such thinking led Nef—with the enthusiastic support of Robert Maynard Hutchins, president of the University of Chicago—to create the Committee on Social Thought, a multidisciplinary graduate program. Formed in 1941, the committee was recognized for its intellectual excellence. It conferred one or two degrees a year to students who showed exceptional intellectual abilities. It drew on a visiting faculty that included Chagall, poet T. S. Eliot, violinist Igor Stravinsky, and philosopher Jacques Maritain. Philosopher Hannah Arendt and art critic Harold Rosenberg were among the committee's permanent faculty. "The proper purpose," Nef wrote, "is to offer both the young and the old opportunities to acquire a universal, a cosmopolitan, outlook in which the human being is seen as a whole and each human being is seen as a part of humanity."

Elinor died in 1953, and in 1962 Nef married Evelyn Stefansson, widow of the explorer Vilhjalmur Stefansson and best-selling author of books about Alaska and Russia. The couple settled in Washington, D.C., where they wrote and pursued their interests in art. Nef remained closely involved in the committee's affairs until the mid-1980s. He died at his Washington home following a long illness.

Within the worlds of elite academia and the arts, Nef was a formidable personality. His scholarly efforts—he wrote a dozen books, including several in French, and wrote frequently for academic journals—reshaped the views of Europe's economy during the Middle Ages. His investigations into the development of the British economy revealed the forces that ultimately shaped the economy of the United States. Meanwhile, his efforts at educational reform, symbolized by the establishment of the Committee on Social Thought, provided opportunities for scholars and intellectuals who resisted the push toward specialization. This emphasis on studies of what Nef called "the whole person" continues to influence universities and colleges throughout the world.

★

Nef's autobiography, *Search for Meaning* (1973), recounts his efforts at educational reform, the importance of art to his life, and his friendships with, among others, Marc Chagall and T. S. Eliot. An obituary is in the *Chicago Tribune* (27 Dec. 1988).

THOMAS G. GRESS

NEGRI, Pola (*b.* 31 December 1894 in Lipno or Janowa, Russian Poland; *d.* 1 August 1987 in San Antonio, Texas), silent-screen actress best known for her role in *Madam Du Barry* (1919) and as the first European actress to be offered a contract by a U.S. studio.

Pola Negri was born Barbara Apollonia Chalupec to Eleanora de Kielczeska and Jerzy Mathias-Chalupec. She had two sisters, both of whom died during childhood. Her father was involved in revolutionary activities in what was then Russian Poland. He was arrested for these activities by czarist troops in 1905 and sent to prison. After his release he did not return to the family and effectively dropped out of his daughter's life.

Negri and her mother moved to Warsaw, where the latter worked as a cook to support the family. Negri attended the boarding school of Countess Platen and the Imperial Ballet School. Her first public performance was in the role of a cygnet in the Imperial Ballet's production of *Swan Lake*.

Pola Negri. APA/ARCHIVE PHOTOS

When Negri was thirteen years old, she developed tuberculosis and had to quit dancing. At age fourteen she was cured of the disease but did not return to dance. With the help of her mother's friend Casimir de Hulewicz, Negri auditioned for and was accepted into the Warsaw Imperial Academy of Dramatic Arts. She was then briefly a member of the prestigious Little Theatre of Philharmonic Hall.

At this time she changed her name to Pola Negri: "Pola" is the diminutive of "Apollonia"; "Negri" was derived from Ada Negri, an Italian poet. Negri began her professional career with the Rozmaitoczi, a state theater. Early roles included Hedwig in *The Wild Duck* by Henrik Ibsen and the title role in *Hannele* by Gerhart Hauptmann. She became one of Poland's leading actresses, and her stage work was noticed by Alexander Hertz, a pioneer in the Polish film industry. The outbreak of World War I interrupted Negri's theater career. At the end of the war she signed with the Polish film company Sphinx and starred in her first film, *Slave of Sin* (1915). Negri came to the attention of Max Reinhardt of the Berlin Deutsches Theatre, when Richard Ordynski, a Polish director working with Berlin Deutsches, returned to Warsaw to stage the Polish premiere of *Sumurun*. Negri's success in the production led Reinhardt to urge her to go to Berlin.

In 1918 Negri went to work for Deutsches Theatre in Berlin. There, she teamed with Ernst Lubitsch, a German actor and director. Under Lubitsch's direction Negri did her strongest work. Lubitsch introduced her to Paul Davidson, head of Germany's Union Film Alliance (UFA), and Davidson hired them both. At UFA Negri and Lubitsch made *The Eyes of Mumma Ma* (1918), *Carmen* (1918), and the film version of *Sumurun* (1920). Negri also made the non-Lubitsch films *Camille* (1920) and *Sappho* (1921). However, it was the 1919 pairing of Lubitsch and Negri in *Madame Du Barry,* one of the early lavish period pieces, that led to one of Negri's biggest successes. Its popularity in Europe caught the attention of Hollywood. After the death of her first husband, Count Popper, Negri married Eugene Damski in 1919; they were divorced in 1921.

In the United States, First National bought the rights to *Madame Du Barry*, retitling it *Passion* to circumvent a ban on German movies. The company leased the Capitol Theatre on Broadway for a one-night run but the film ultimately ran for two weeks, effectively ending the ban on German films. Its success led Famous Players (Paramount) to offer Negri and Lubitsch contracts. Negri was thus the first European actress to be offered a contract by a U.S. studio. She traveled to the United States in 1922. Negri and Lubitsch were the vanguard of a wave of European film stars who left Europe for the United States, including Greta Garbo and Marlene Dietrich.

Negri's first American movie was *Belle Donna* (1923). A steady succession of films followed, including *The Cheat,* one of her best-known roles, and *The Spanish Dancer*, both in 1923; *Men, The Shadows of Paris,* and a brilliant comedic performance as Catherine the Great in *Forbidden Paradise* by Lubitsch, all in 1924; and *East of Suez* and *Flower of the Night* in 1925. Even though many felt that the caliber of her work in Hollywood was not as strong as in her German pictures, Negri worked steadily, one year turning out five movies. Her success enabled her to own a mansion in Beverly Hills, a villa on the French Riviera, and a chateau north of Paris. In 1927 she married Prince Serge Mdivani; they divorced in 1931. The advent of sound did not impact favorably on Negri's career. She made films in Germany, Austria, and England, in addition to appearing in an unsuccessful U.S. film, *A Woman Commands* (1932).

Negri's career was revived by a long-term contract with UFA in 1935. She starred in a series of strong roles, as a café singer in *Mazurka* (1935); in *Madame Bovary* (1937), directed by Gephardt Lamprecht; and as a cocaine addict in *Tango Notturno* (1938). While working in Germany, Negri was placed on the list of suspected "non-Aryans" by Nazi leader Joseph Goebbels. Adolf Hitler, a fan of her films, especially *Mazurka,* personally overrode Goebbels and allowed Negri to continue working. This later led her to make the controversial statement that Hitler was one of the people who influenced her career. The outbreak of World War II interrupted her career in Europe, and she returned to the United States in 1941, after Germany invaded France. Negri lived comfortably in New York City, then in California, and finally in San Antonio, Texas, where a friend had willed her a house. But she was no longer in demand as an actress, and her career effectively ended, except for a few roles, such as in *Hi Diddle Diddle* (1943), over the years. Her last role was in Walt Disney's *The Moonspinners* (1964). Negri, who never had children, died of pneumonia after refusing treatment for a brain tumor for two years. She is buried in San Antonio.

As the first European actress to be offered a long-term contract in the United States, Negri opened the door to a continued migration of European talent, including directors, actors, and writers, to Hollywood. This infusion led to a melding of European and American cinematic vision that changed the direction and feel of films.

★

Negri's autobiography, *Memoir of a Star* (1970), is a highly creative, often fanciful account of her life and career. Marjorie Rosen, *Popcorn Venus: Women, Movies, and the American Dream* (1973), gives a more realistic account of her career. *The International Dictionary of Films and Filmmakers,* vol. 3, *Actors and Actresses* (1990), gives a detailed listing of Negri's films. Richard Koszarski, *An Evening's Entertainment: The Age of the Silent Feature Picture, 1915–1928* (1990), is a history of the silent era including the influence of the European filmmakers on Hollywood. Klaus Kreimeir, *The UFA Story: A History of Germany's Greatest Film*

Company, 1918–1945 (1996), is a detailed look at the UFA and its stars, including Negri, and the effects Hollywood had on the European film industry. An obituary is in the *New York Times* (3 Aug. 1987).

LISA R. PERRY

NEVELSON, Louise (*b.* 23 September 1899 in Pereyaslav, Russia; *d.* 17 April 1988 in New York City), a leader of the renaissance of American sculpture during the mid twentieth century, when she developed abstract constructions assembled out of wood at a time when welded sculpture was in favor.

Louise Nevelson was born Leah Berliawsky, one of four children of Isaac and Zeisel (Smolerank) Berliawsky in a small city fifty miles southeast of Kiev. In 1905 she emigrated with her family to the United States. After they Americanized their names, Leah, now Louise, traveled with her family to Rockport, Maine, where her father held a variety of self-employed occupations. After graduation from Rockland High School in 1918, she worked briefly as a legal stenographer with plans to attend art school. Soon after, she met Charles Nevelson, a wealthy, older man also of Russian-Jewish heritage. They married on 12 June 1920, just shy of her twenty-first birthday, and moved to New York City. Louise Nevelson quickly found her marriage confining, and after the birth of her first and only son in 1922, she began to study the arts—painting, dance, voice, and drama—in an eclectic fashion.

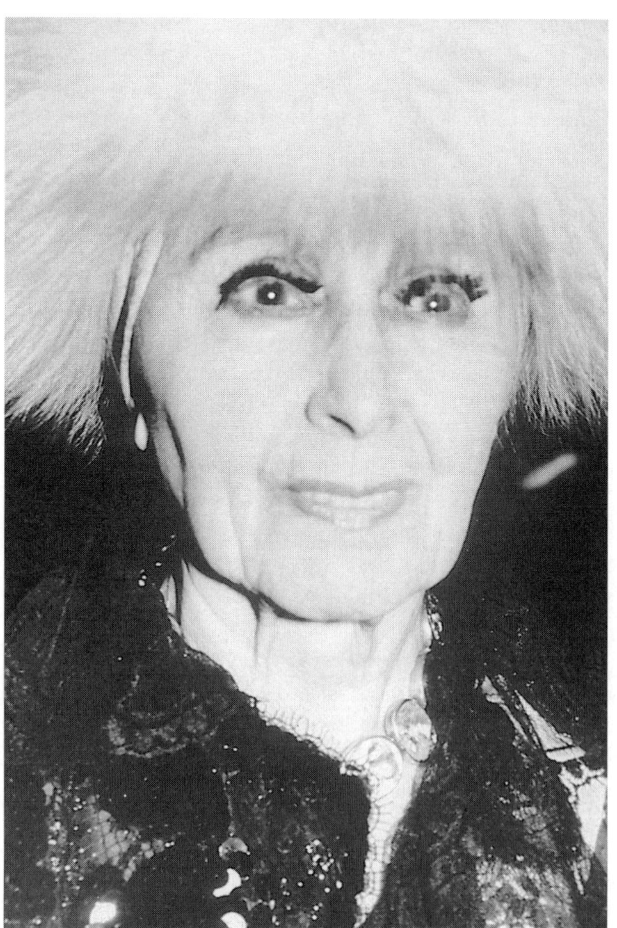

Louise Nevelson, 1981. TOM GATES/ARCHIVE PHOTOS

Nevelson's artistic explorations became more focused in 1926, when she began informal study with the painter Theresa Bernstein and enrolled for three years in the Theater Arts Institute, a laboratory for modern stage performance, organized by the avant-garde architect Frederick Kiesler and Princess Nora Matchabelli. There Nevelson received a grounding in philosophy and realized that traditional interpretations of art forms could be radically redefined. In 1929 she centered her ambitions on painting when she enrolled for full-time classes at the Art Students League under the guidance of several renowned teachers. Gaining confidence, Nevelson decided to travel in the fall of 1931 to Munich to attend Hans Hofmann's classes on cubism. In the fall of 1932 she returned to the Art Students League. For a brief period in 1933, Nevelson assisted Diego Rivera, the famed Mexican muralist, by helping prepare walls. Also that year she finally separated from her husband (they did not divorce until 1941). In 1934, after settling in a studio on West Tenth Street and studying with the sculptor Chaim Gross, Nevelson turned to sculpture.

From 1933 to 1958, Nevelson underwent a long period of maturation, drawing heavily on cubism and surrealism. At first she worked mostly in painted plaster, then other mediums, including terracotta, marble, bronze, and wood. In the 1940s her artistic vision began to emerge. After exhibiting cubist plaster pieces in her first solo exhibition in 1941 at the Nierendorf Gallery in New York City, Nevelson attempted her first thematic show, entitled *The Clown Is the Center of His World,* in 1943 at the Norylst Gallery, which comprised circus figures and animal sculptures made out of bed knobs, brackets, whiskey glasses, and other found objects.

Nevelson's style evolved rapidly from 1954 to 1958, and harbingers are found in three successive exhibitions at Grand Central Moderns in New York City. In *Ancient Games, Ancient Places* (1955), *The Royal Voyage* (1956), and *The Forest* (1957), she attempted to create unified atmospheres out of figurative and landscape and cityscape constructions. *The Forest* included totemic sculptures referring to her life experience. Nevelson achieved her breakthrough exhibition in 1958 with *Moon Garden + One,* her first fully environmental, abstract sculpture in which she sought to engage the spectator in the world of her art. The exhibition included walls, columns, and relief tablets, all stained black. The walls were built out of stacked boxes filled with relief constructions made out of found objects: newel posts, finials, pieces of molding, and other found scraps of wood; the columns were made out of three-sided boxes filled with interior reliefs and four-sided boxes with exterior reliefs. The visitor to the exhibition entered into the shadowy interior of *Moon Garden + One,* which Nevelson illuminated with a dim blue light to heighten the sense of mystery.

At its heart, *Moon Garden + One* embodied a sense of architecture and order, arising perhaps from Nevelson's anxieties about her Thirtieth Street house, which she had purchased in 1945. Although the City of New York first gave her notice in 1954 of the need for her property for urban redevelopment, the impending loss of her home provided the catalyst for Nevelson's radical redefinition of the language of constructivism. Her small circus figures made out of found materials had given way to large-scale constructions that included the concepts of environment, autobiography, and performance. As stated in her book *Dawns + Dusks* (1976), she created "a whole reality for myself," assembled out of a series of enclosures, each box filled with unique environment—an interior drama exploring her psyche.

Dorothy Miller, a curator at New York City's Museum of Modern Art, was so struck by the exhibition that she asked the artist to be in her 1959 *Sixteen Americans* show. Nevelson responded by saying, "Dear, we'll do a white show. Don't tell anybody. It will be a surprise." Entitled *Dawn's Wedding Feast,* it served in Nevelson's words as "a transition to a marriage with the world." Like her other creations, this sculpture had an ephemeral quality, in that the experience of the exhibition was as much a part of the work as the individual pieces and total arrangement. Once the show was dismantled, the complete meaning of the work was gone. As with her earlier shows, individual pieces were sold separately, although Nevelson had hoped that an institution would buy the entire work and keep it as a permanent installation. Nevelson herself often raided older pieces for wood scraps; some of the white wood from *Dawn's Wedding Feast* was incorporated into her next environment, *Voyage,* a mixture of gold, white, and black elements. It was exhibited at the 1962 Venice Biennale, where she was invited to serve as one of three artists representing the United States.

Nevelson explored new directions in her next sculptures, stating that she "was going back to the elements: shadow, light, the sun, the moon." She moved first to gold in 1961 in *The Royal Tides* at the Martha Jackson Gallery in New York City. In the mid-1960s, she turned to other mediums, using industrial materials in her *Atmosphere and Environment I,* an assemblage of black aluminum forms first exhibited in 1966 at the Pace Gallery in New York City and purchased by the Museum of Modern Art. Transparency and reflection also entered her work when she began to use clear synthetic materials—Lucite and Plexiglass—in her sculptures. She also continued to use black wood, beginning work in 1964 on a wood house environment *Mrs. N's Palace.* Completed in 1977, it was exhibited at Pace that year to rave reviews, but in order to avoid selling the sculpture to a European institution, Nevelson gave it to the Metropolitan Museum of Art.

In 1969 Nevelson received from Princeton University her first commission for a large outdoor steel piece, *Atmosphere and Environment X.* Three years later, Nevelson created for the city of Scottsdale, Arizona, the outdoor piece *Atmosphere and Environment XIII: Window to the West.* She described it by stating, "the landscape is the *atmosphere* that fills the spaces of the steel *environment.* The two together are the sculpture." She finished her masterpiece of minimalism in 1977, a white environment of low relief, created for a chapel in Saint Peter's Lutheran Church at Citicorp Center in New York City. Nevelson immediately returned to black when, from 1977 to 1978, she designed seven black Cor-Ten steel sculptures entitled *Shadows and Flags* that were installed in the Legion Memorial Square renamed the Louise Nevelson Plaza, situated in lower Manhattan at the intersection of Maiden Lane and Liberty and William Streets.

Nevelson enjoyed great success and recognition in her later years. In 1967 the Whitney Museum of American Art in New York City held her first retrospective, with a second one following in 1980. Her work was represented in major collections all over the world. In New York City alone, one can find her sculptures in the Metropolitan Museum, Museum of Modern Art, the Jewish Museum, Brooklyn Museum, and the Whitney, to name a few. Nevelson received many honorary doctorates, her first in 1966 from Western College for Women in Oxford, Ohio, and others from Smith College (1973) and Harvard University (1985). Elected in 1979 to the fifty-member American Academy of Arts and Letters, she was presented with its gold medal for sculpture in 1983. In 1985 President Ronald Reagan awarded her the National Medal for the Arts. In September 1987 Nevelson was diagnosed with lung cancer, and, after a long battle, she died at her Soho home on Spring Street (where she had been living since 1959). Her remains were cremated. In October 1989 the Metropolitan Museum held a memorial service in her honor.

Louise Nevelson saw herself as an original creation. Flamboyant, ambitious, and prolific, she made sculptures that took on greater meaning when exhibited together as an environment and that were best understood placed in the context of her life. Her work was, at its heart, autobiographical and was created for her own pleasure. In 1964 she stated: "Since art, particularly sculpture, is so living, so very living, naturally you want all of life, so you make an environment, but that environment is sculpture too. It is not really for an audience, it is really for my visual eye. It is a feast for myself."

★

Louise Nevelson's papers are located at the Archives of American Art, Smithsonian Institution of Art, Washington, D.C. Of the many excellent books on Nevelson, the following are particularly insightful and useful: Laurie Wilson, *Louise Nevelson: Iconography and Sources* (1981); Jean Lipman, *Nevelson's World,* introduction by Hilton Kramer (1983); and Laurie Lisle, *Louise Nevelson: A Passionate Life* (1990). Also useful are the two retrospective catalogs by the Whitney Museum of American Art, *Louise Nevelson* (1967) and *Louise Nevelson: Atmospheres and Environments* (1980). Of the many published books of interviews and conversations with the artist, the following are particularly good: Colette Roberts, *Nevelson* (1964); Arnold B. Glimcher, *Louise Nevelson* (1972; rev. ed. 1976); and especially *Dawns + Dusks: Louise Nevelson, Taped Conversations with Diana MacKown* (1976). For unpublished interviews, see the following Nevelson interviews, all located in the Archives of American Art: with Dorothy Seckler (June 1964–Jan. 1965), sound recordings; with Arnold Glimcher (30 Jan. 1972), sound recording and transcripts; and with Barbara Braun (1983), sound recordings and transcript. Obituaries are in the *New York Times* (18 Apr. 1988); *Art News* (Summer 1988); and the *New Yorker* (9 May 1988).

LEIGH BULLARD WEISBLAT

NEWTON, Huey Percy (*b.* 17 February 1942 in New Orleans, Louisiana; *d.* 22 August 1989 in Oakland, California), leader of the Black Panther party.

Huey Newton. CAMERA PRESS/ARCHIVE PHOTOS

Newton was the youngest of seven children of Walter and Armelia (Johnson) Newton. His father was a sharecropper, longshoreman, handyman, truck driver, and Baptist minister who moved his family to Oakland, California, during the World War II migration of blacks to the North and West from the South. Huey Newton, who had a troubled childhood, was expelled from several high schools but earned a high school diploma from Oakland Technical High School. Newton had a reputation as a street tough, but at Oakland City College (later Merritt College), a two-year school, he immersed himself in the philosophy of Camus, Sartre, Kierkegaard, Mao Tse-tung, and the black revolutionary Robert Williams. Newton also took courses at the San Francisco Law School. He dominated his classmates both intellectually and with his fists and organized a number of them into a gang of burglars and shakedown artists. In 1964 he was convicted of felonious assault with a knife on Odell Lee and was sentenced to six months in jail.

Upon his release Newton participated in the growing political radicalism of the Bay Area by joining the Revolutionary Action Movement with college friend Bobby Seale. RAM, inspired by Williams's *Negroes with Guns* (1962), encapsulated youthful dissatisfaction with the prevailing nonviolent strategy of Martin Luther King, Jr. Equally motivated by Stokely Carmichael's call for black power and rejection of integration, by Frantz Fanon's *Wretched of the Earth* (1963), and by a faith in the nobility of the poor, Seale and Newton formed the Black Panther Party for Self-Defense in October 1966. They designated Seale as chairman and Newton as minister of defense. The two issued a ten-point program emphasizing black self-determination, full employment, an end to the robbery of blacks by capitalists, decent housing, education, military exemptions for blacks, freedom for black convicts, trials of blacks only by black peers, and a United Nations plebiscite for governance of the "black colony" in the United States. Newton was influenced by his current employment in the federally inspired community action program.

Newton, Seale, and Eldridge Cleaver, who joined the party in 1967 and became its minister of information, devised a program of symbolic actions to dramatize the Panthers' demands. For example, they took advantage of a loosely written gun law that allowed public display of automatic weaponry provided the barrels were not aimed at anyone. The Panthers, garbed in black leather jackets festooned with ammunition belts, openly confronted the Oakland police force and once visited the state capitol grounds in Sacramento armed with heavy artillery. These actions made the Panthers the darlings of left-wing groups. A less pleasant consequence was increased police surveillance and, eventually, intervention by the Federal Bureau of Investigation's controversial counterintelligence program, Cointelpro. On 28 October 1967 police stopped Newton and a friend, Gene McKinney, for a traffic check. In an ensuing dispute, police officer John Frey was killed, and Newton was charged with his murder. Despite innumerable demonstrations in his support, Newton was convicted of manslaughter and sentenced to two-to-fifteen years in prison. The conviction was set aside in 1970 on procedural grounds.

After his release Newton visited the People's Republic of China and met with Chou En-lai in 1971. He published two books of essays, *To Die for the People* (1972) and *Revolutionary Suicide* (1973), and a book of poems with Ericka Huggins, *Insights and Poems* (1975). A visit to Yale University resulted in *In Search of Common Ground: Conversations with Erik H. Erikson and Huey P. Newton* (1973). He received a B.A. degree from the University of California at Santa Cruz in 1974.

Newton remained active in the Black Panther movement while in prison, but much of the organization's goals became clouded by petty criminal behavior including drug dealing, protection rackets, and abuse of female members. Newton himself, blinded by his celebrity and lionization on both coasts, became addicted to cocaine. Met with massive adulation after his release from prison, Newton soon showed signs of paranoia and power hunger, giving himself the Panther leadership title of Supreme Servant of the People. Splits wracked the movement, with East and West Coast factions severing ties.

In 1974 Newton, now heavily dependent on cocaine, was arrested for killing a prostitute, Kathleen Smith, and gun-whipping a tailor, Preston Callins, who made the unfortunate mistake of calling him "baby," a term which enraged Newton. The Panther leader then jumped bail and went into exile in Cuba. During his absence Elaine Brown took over the Panther party. By 3 July 1977, when Newton returned, the Panthers were a shadow of their former glory.

The next few years of Newton's life were a mixture of accomplishment and decline. He enrolled in the history of consciousness doctoral program at the University of California at Santa Cruz and received a Ph.D. in 1980. His dissertation was titled "War Against the Panthers: A Study of Repression in America." Beyond that achievement, his life took a downward turn because of his drug addiction. As crack cocaine became a cheap substitute for the real thing, Newton was able to maintain an addiction partly on the strength of his past reputation. In 1980 the Palestine Liberation Organization invited him to visit the Middle East, where he went while insisting upon seeing Israel in order to understand both sides of the PLO-Israeli conflict.

Newton married Gwen Fontaine, his secretary, in 1977. Gwen left him in 1982, and on 15 September 1984 he married Fredericka Slaughter. Newton had no biological children, but he adopted Gwen's two children and Fredericka's son.

Legal problems dogged his last years. His retrial for the John Frey killing ended in a hung jury in December 1971, and charges were dropped. His two trials for the murder of Kathleen Smith also resulted in hung juries. In 1985 he was arrested for embezzling funds from a nutritional program. In 1988 Newton served time in San Quentin for a parole violation. In the early morning hours of 22 August 1989, Newton was shot and killed by a gang member seeking promotion. His remains were cremated.

★

Newton's *To Die for the People: The Writings of Huey P. Newton* (1972), is a collection of Panther statements; his *Revolutionary Suicide* (1973) discusses his early life and trials of the late 1960s. Bobby Seale, *Seize the Time: The Story of the Black Panther Party and Huey Newton* (1970), is the story of Seale and Newton's meeting and political struggle in the late 1960s. A more critical approach to their unity is in Elaine Brown, *A Taste of Power: A Black Woman's Story* (1992). An interpretive history is Hugh Pearson, *The Shadow of the Panther: Huey Newton and the Price of Black Power in America* (1994). See also David Hilliard, *This Side of Glory: The Autobiography of David Hilliard and the Story of the Black Panther Party* (1993). An obituary is in the *New York Times* (23 Aug. 1989).

GRAHAM RUSSELL HODGES

NOGUCHI, Isamu (*b.* 17 November 1904 in Los Angeles, California; *d.* 30 December 1988 in New York City), artist whose sculpture, fountains, and gardens are considered landmarks of twentieth-century art.

Noguchi was the son of Yoneijiro ("Yone") Noguchi, a nationalist Japanese poet, and Leonie Gilmour, an American writer. His parents had a brief romance in New York City, but his father abandoned Gilmour before Isamu's birth and, in 1913, married a house servant to begin an entirely Japanese family. When he was two years old, Noguchi went for the first time to Japan, a place he would return to in his life and art many times. The visit to Tokyo was an effort by his mother to reestablish contact with his father, but it was unsuccessful. Noguchi and his mother remained in Japan, where his mother taught English, first in the capital and then in Omori. Noguchi had one half-sister and two

Isamu Noguchi, 1984. CHRIS FELVER/ARCHIVE PHOTOS

half-brothers. He attended a Japanese school and was apprenticed to the carpenter who built their home in Chigasaki. From 1913 to 1917 he attended a Jesuit school in Yokohama.

In 1918 Noguchi left Yokohama for Interlaken School in Rolling Prairie, Indiana, which closed several months after his arrival. Its headmaster, Edward Rumely, placed him in a La Porte, Indiana, household run by Dr. Samuel Mack, a Swedenborgian minister. Using the name Sam Gilmour, Noguchi attended the town's high school and graduated in 1922. Rumely encouraged him to become a physician, so he entered Columbia University in New York City as a premed student that fall, although Rumely had also arranged for a summer apprenticeship with Gutzon Borglum, sculptor of Mount Rushmore. In 1924 his mother returned to the United States after seventeen years in Japan and urged him to consider studying art. In the evenings Noguchi took classes with Onorio Ruotolo, a figurative sculptor, at the Leonardo da Vinci Art School. Within three months he had his first exhibition, took his father's name of Noguchi, and left Columbia.

Noguchi's first studio, set up with the assistance of Rumely, was at 127 University Place in Manhattan. Increasingly tired of formal academic styles, he admired Constantin Brancusi's abstract sculpture and, upon receiving a Guggenheim Fellowship, left for Paris in March 1927. He became Brancusi's morning assistant and began to carve in wood and stone, creating abstract forms. In late 1928 Noguchi returned to New York City, where, buoyed by his first one-person exhibition but discouraged by the lack of sales of his work, he went back to figure sculpture, making a living from portrait commissions. He made two portraits of Martha Graham, the modern dancer, whose company later performed on more that twenty sets created by Noguchi. The first, in 1935, was also the first set she ever used. After making an exhibition lecture trip to Cambridge, Massachusetts, and Chicago with R. Buckminster Fuller, the architectural visionary who had become his close friend, Noguchi left for the Far East via Paris and Moscow in the spring of 1930.

Noguchi was reluctant to go to Japan because of his emotional distance from his father, who did not want him to carry the name Noguchi, so he stayed in China for seven months, studying the techniques of ink brush on scroll with Ch'i Pai-shih. In Beijing the gardens and grand buildings, particularly the Altar of Heaven, inspired an interest in plazas and public space as sculpture on a grand scale. For eight months in 1931, defying his father's warning, Noguchi returned to Japan, where he experienced difficulties with his father but was welcomed by his uncle Totaro Takagi. In Kyoto, Noguchi made a series of ceramic figures and urns in the studio of Jinmatsu Uno. He also came upon other strong Japanese influences, especially haniwa, cylindrical clay figures that surround grave mounds, and the gardens of Zen temples.

Later in the 1930s Noguchi worked in New York, California, Hawaii, and Mexico, again earning his way by making portrait sculptures. He designed playgrounds and play equipment for New York City, but the plans were rejected by Robert Moses, the parks commissioner. The first of his playgrounds to be built was *Children's Land,* near Tokyo, in 1966. He also conceived his first monuments, including the mile-wide pyramid called the *Monument to the Plough,* designed to be placed in the geographical center of the United States but which was never built. His more successful endeavors included furniture design, produced by the Herman Miller Company and Knoll International; the *Chassis Fountain,* his first fountain, for the Ford Motor Company Pavilion at the 1939 World's Fair; and *News* (1938–1940), a sculptural relief for the Associated Press Building in Rockefeller Center.

As a resident of New York City, he was not subject to the 1942 internment of West Coast Japanese Americans, but he voluntarily entered the Colorado River Relocation Camp near Poston, Arizona. He failed to realize his plans for a recreation center and cemetery, and after six months he returned to New York City. Working with light and with a surreal sensibility, he created both freestanding biomorphic sculptures and interior wall reliefs. In 1946 his work was included in the *Fourteen Americans* exhibition at the Museum of Modern Art in New York City. In May 1949, with a travel grant from the Bollingen Foundation, he traveled to see prehistoric and ancient stone sites in Brittany, Egypt, Greece, Rome, India, Cambodia, and Indonesia. His subsequent work strongly echoes their solidity and power.

In early 1950 Noguchi returned to Japan, where he designed a memorial room and garden at Keio University in Tokyo for his father and two bridges for the Peace Park in Hiroshima. His design for the central memorial in the bomb-blasted city was rejected, however, because of his American citizenship. After a visit to Gifu, in an effort to revive Japan's traditional craftwork, he designed his first Akari lamps made of mulberry paper and bamboo. In May 1952 he married Yoshiko ("Shirley") Yamaguchi, a film actress, whom he had met in 1950 in New York. They had no children and were divorced in January 1957. Living on the property of Rosanjin Kitaoji, a potter, and using Kitaoji's kilns, Noguchi returned to ceramic sculpture.

In the 1960s Noguchi moved his studio and home to Long Island City in the borough of Queens in New York City, in an industrial building that in 1985 became the Isamu Noguchi Garden Museum, which holds more than 250 of his works. He worked on corporate projects in tandem with Gordon Bunshaft of Skidmore Owings Merrill. His largest garden, the Billy Rose Sculpture Garden (1960–1965), is in Israel. He spent ten summers in Querceta, Italy, working in marble quarries. In 1966 he built another studio in Mure, on the island of Shikoku, Japan, where for six months a year he worked in granite and basalt, often with a young stonecutter, Masatoshi Izumi. Their first project together was the granite *Black Sun* for the Seattle Art Museum (1966–1969). Two late public projects that incorporate open space, undulating columns, and water are the Philip A. Hart Plaza in Detroit (1972–1979) and the Bayfront Park in Miami (begun in 1979). Noguchi's last project was the master plan for the 400-acre Moere Numa Park in Sapporo, Japan (begun in 1988). He died in New York City of heart failure. His cremated remains were divided and interred in the Isamu Noguchi Museum garden and the Shikoku studio garden.

Intensely respectful of tradition in art yet also deeply intuitive, Isamu Noguchi created remarkable, moving forms, some quite geometric, some seemingly as natural as stones. He was influenced as much by William Blake as by Brancusi. He spoke often of wanting to create an "oasis" with his work, and much of his sculpture appearing in public spaces achieves that goal. As he aged and balded, he came to resemble the austere yet powerful sculptures he created. At times he discarded form and color. Any home with a paper lamp probably has Noguchi to thank. To truly understand his spirit and sensibility, one must, of course, experience his sculpture by being with it. The artist himself said he wanted to "make sculpture part of a large scheme."

★

Noguchi's papers are in the Archives of the Isamu Noguchi Foundation, Long Island City, New York. Noguchi published an autobiography, *A Sculptor's World* (1968), and *The Isamu Noguchi Garden Museum* (1987); further writings are collected in Diane Apostolos-Cappadona and Bruce Altshuler, eds., *Isamu Noguchi: Essays and Conversations* (1994). Books about Noguchi and his work include Sam Hunter, *Isamu Noguchi* (1978); Dore Ashton, *Noguchi East and West* (1992); and Bruce Altshuler, *Isamu Noguchi* (1994). An obituary is in the *New York Times* (31 Dec. 1988).

MARK ZADROZNY

NORRIS, Clarence (*b.* 12 July 1912 in Warm Springs, Georgia; *d.* 23 January 1989 in the Bronx, New York), the last surviving "Scottsboro Boy."

The second of eleven children, Clarence Norris was one of the nine to survive into adulthood. His father, Willie(?), who had been born in slavery, was a sharecropper, and the entire family worked in the cotton fields, including Clarence's mother, Ida. Clarence was able to attend school only sporadically and did not go beyond second grade. He hated

Clarence Norris (*fourth from left, standing*) with the other eight "Scottsboro Boys" and attorney Samuel Leibowitz, after being sentenced to death in a retrial of his case in 1933. UPI/CORBIS-BETTMANN

backbreaking farm work and did not get along with his father, who was a stern taskmaster. At age fifteen Norris left home, and he soon joined the thousands of Depression-era men and women who rode the southern railroads and who, black and white alike, were referred to as "blackbirds," because they jumped on the trains in flocks. Norris slept in empty boxcars, did occasional odd jobs in the towns through which the railroad passed, and sometimes went for days without eating. Hounded by the police, he was frequently arrested for vagrancy and jailed for ten days at a stretch, working at hard labor in a quarry.

On 25 March 1931 Norris caught a southbound train out of Chattanooga, Tennessee. The train was traveling through Alabama when, without provocation, the white hoboes on board began throwing gravel at the blacks and ordered them off the train. In the bloody battle that followed, the whites were thrown off the train instead. When the train stopped to take on water at a flag station in the small town of Paint Rock, Alabama, the blacks were surprised to see the train tracks lined with a mob of armed white men. Norris and eight other blacks were ordered off the train and taken to the nearest jail, in Scottsboro, Alabama.

The "Scottsboro Boys," as they came to be called, ranged in age from thirteen to twenty-one. Brothers Roy and Andy Wright were from Chattanooga, as were Eugene Williams and Haywood Patterson. Ozie Powell, Olen Montgomery, Charlie Weems, Willie Roberson, and Norris were from different parts of Georgia. The following day, as an angry white mob massed outside the jail and state National Guardsmen kept them back, the nine blacks were ordered into a lineup. Two white women who had been on the train were then brought in. Together, Victoria Price and Ruby Bates, seeing a chance to escape an arrest for vagrancy, accused all nine men of raping them. The men protested their innocence, but without success. Their trials began on 6 April 1931. Stephen Roddy, the local attorney hired for $50 by the Interdenominational Colored Ministers' Alliance, a group of black ministers in Chattanooga, to defend the young men, visited his clients for half an hour before the trials began. Norris and Weems were tried first; Patterson was tried by himself; Montgomery, Powell, Roberson, Andy Wright, and Williams were tried together; Roy Wright was tried alone and last. The four trials lasted three days, at the end of which all nine were convicted of rape. On 9 April 1931 Judge Alfred E. Hawkins sentenced eight of the men to die by electrocution in Kilby Prison in Montgomery, Alabama. The youngest defendant, thirteen-year-old Roy Wright, was spared the death penalty; he was imprisoned in Jefferson County Jail in Birmingham, Alabama, for six and a half years before the case against him was dropped.

National and international reaction to the case, and to the rapid convictions and harsh sentencing of the nine young men, was swift in coming. On the evening of the sentencing, the first large Scottsboro protest meeting was held at St. Luke's Hall in Harlem in New York City. By early May the protest had become international, and on 1 May workers in 300 cities around the world used their May Day demonstrations to protest what was widely seen as the frame-up of the Scottsboro Boys.

The Communist party's *Southern Worker,* based in Birmingham, had first broken the story. The party issued a statement in support of the accused on the last day of the trials, and within twenty-four hours after the death sentences the International Labor Defense (ILD) had voted to defend the nine young men. An officially noncommunist organization, but controlled by Communist party members and dedicated to the legal defense of prisoners of class war, the ILD was soon in a fight for control of the defendants' appeals with the National Association for the Advancement of Colored People (NAACP). But the more conservative NAACP was slow to act and tentative in the steps it took in the Scottsboro Boys' defense. The bitter fight between the two organizations, and the helpless defendants' switching of allegiances back and forth, dragged on until January 1932, when the NAACP finally admitted defeat and withdrew. The Scottsboro case made the Communist party and its appeal to blacks in America difficult to ignore.

National and international protests against the "legal lynching" of the Scottsboro Boys continued throughout 1932. In November, in the case of *Powell* v. *Alabama,* the U.S. Supreme Court overturned the convictions on the ground that the defendants had been denied their constitutional right to counsel. The second round of trials began on 27 March 1933. By this time Ruby Bates had recanted her testimony, but in separate retrials, both Patterson and Norris were found guilty and sentenced to death. The ILD appealed, and on 1 April 1935, in the case of *Norris* v. *Alabama,* the Supreme Court again set aside the convictions on the ground that blacks had been systematically excluded from jury service.

During 1936 and 1937 the state of Alabama dropped charges against four of the nine Scottsboro Boys: Eugene Williams, Olen Montgomery, Willie Roberson, and Roy Wright. Haywood Patterson and Charlie Weems were convicted again and given seventy-five-year sentences. Andy Wright was also convicted and sentenced to ninety-nine years. Ozie Powell, having assaulted a sheriff, pled guilty and received a twenty-year sentence. Only Clarence Norris, convicted for the third time, was sentenced to death. Norris spent two years on death row in Kilby Prison while awaiting appeal of his sentence. In July 1938 Alabama governor Bibb Graves commuted that sentence to life imprisonment.

Paroled in January 1944, Norris violated his parole by leaving Alabama and in October was returned to Kilby Prison. Paroled a second time in September 1946, Norris risked reimprisonment when he left Alabama once again. He went first to Cleveland, Ohio, then moved to New York City. He did odd jobs and was arrested numerous times—for gun possession, gambling, and once for stabbing a girlfriend. In 1960 he settled down. He married for the third time, to Melba Sanders (his first two marriages had been to Dora Lee in the spring of 1944 and to Mary Pierceson in the late 1940s), had two daughters, got a job as a maintenance worker with the City of New York, and moved his family to Brooklyn, where he lived quietly and declined all requests for interviews. As his children grew, he became concerned about clearing his name and sought the help of the NAACP, whose attorneys contacted Alabama officials about securing a pardon for him. After a flurry of national media coverage, the Alabama Pardon and Parole Board voted to grant Norris a pardon, and after Governor George Wallace approved the request on 25 October 1976, Clarence Norris was officially not guilty as well as free.

Remarkably free of bitterness, Norris declined to bring suit against the state of Alabama. He did, however, tell his story in *The Last of the Scottsboro Boys* (1979), an autobiography written with Sybil D. Washington. He outlived all the other major players in the Scottsboro case—his fellow defendants, some of whom died tragically, judges, defense attorneys, prosecutors, and Ruby Bates and Victoria Price. Norris, who suffered from Alzheimer's disease in his later years, died in Bronx Community Hospital.

Norris was an ordinary young man whose misfortune was to be born black in the southern United States at a time of rigid social inequality, who never had the opportunity to learn to read and write, and who happened to be hoboing on the same railroad train as two white women who saw an opportunity to escape arrest for vagrancy by accusing nine young black men of rape. It was his misfortune, too, that so many people saw his plight as a means of promoting their own ideologies. In the course of Norris's fight for freedom and dignity, the U.S. Supreme Court handed down two landmark decisions that reaffirmed the basic legal rights of all citizens. Those decisions helped lay the groundwork for the struggle for equality in the nation's courts that would lead to the landmark *Brown* v. *Board of Education* decision, the most crucial victory of the civil rights movement.

★

Norris's autobiography is *The Last of the Scottsboro Boys* (1979), written with Sybil D. Washington. See also Haywood Patterson and Earl Conrad, *Scottsboro Boy* (1950); Dan T. Carter, *Scottsboro: A Tragedy of the American South,* rev. ed. (1979); James Goodman, *Stories of Scottsboro: The Rape Case that Shocked 1930s America and Revived the Struggle for Equality* (1994); and James Haskins, *The Scottsboro Boys* (1994).

KATHLEEN BENSON

NORSTAD, Lauris (*b.* 24 March 1907 in Minneapolis, Minnesota; *d.* 12 September 1988 in Tucson, Arizona), four-star general who helped plan the 1945 bombing of Japan and served as supreme allied commander of NATO forces (1956–1963).

Lauris Norstad was born to Marie Johnson and the Reverend Martin Norstad, a Lutheran minister and Norwegian immigrant. When Lauris was three, his family moved to Red Wing, Minnesota, where he and his two siblings grew up. After graduating from high school in Red Wing, he attended the United States Military Academy at West Point, graduating in 1930. He ranked 139th out of a class of 241 and was commissioned in the cavalry. The following year Norstad transferred to the Army Air Corps, and from 1933 to 1936 he led the Eighteenth Pursuit Group in Hawaii. On 27 April 1935 he married Isabelle Helen Jenkins. They had one daughter.

After more than three years on the staff of the Ninth Bombardment Group at Mitchel Field, New York, Norstad entered the Army Air Corps Tactical School, graduating in 1939. The following year he was assigned to the intelligence staff at Air Force General Headquarters at Langley Field, Virginia, and served there until 1942.

After working briefly on the staff of the commanding general of the Army Air Forces, Henry H. ("Hap") Arnold in 1942, Norstad was made assistant chief of staff to the Twelfth Air Force in August of that year. Norstad served

NATO general Lauris Norstad with a map of Italy. PAUL ALMASY/ © CORBIS

with this unit in North Africa, where he attracted the attention of General Dwight D. Eisenhower. In March 1943 he was named director of operations of Mediterranean Allied Air Forces and made a brigadier general. In 1944 he returned to Washington to work on the staff of the Twentieth Air Force and helped to plan B-29 raids on the Japanese home islands, including the atomic bomb attacks on Hiroshima and Nagasaki.

In 1946 Norstad was appointed by Eisenhower as director of the Operations Division of the Army General Staff. He played a crucial role in the drafting of the National Security Act of 1947, which created an independent air force, to which Norstad transferred. In 1947 Norstad was promoted to lieutenant general and vice chief of staff for air operations. In 1950 he was named commander of the U.S. Air Force in Europe, and the following year he was put in charge of North Atlantic Treaty Organization (NATO) air forces in central Europe. Norstad's appointment to full general followed in 1952; he was the youngest American to achieve that rank. He served two supreme allied commanders in Europe, Generals Matthew B. Ridgway and Alfred M. Gruenther, as air deputy from 1953 to 1956. In November 1956 President Eisenhower appointed him supreme allied commander in Europe, the first air force officer to serve in this position.

While the post of NATO commander was held by a military officer, its functions tended to be diplomatic in nature. Because of this, Norstad saw his role as that of an international allied servant. He supported the common European belief that NATO was too dependent upon U.S. forces and nuclear weapons. In 1957 he spoke out against proposed British troop reductions. That same year he urged a five-year troop buildup in Europe and later warned that NATO states were not meeting military commitments or modernizing their weaponry. This buildup was part of a "shield theory," which emphasized the need for strong conventional forces as a deterrent to Soviet attack while at the same time maintaining nuclear weapons as a retaliatory measure. Nevertheless, Norstad felt that nuclear weapons were a critical part of NATO strategy. He believed that the deterrent effect of the weapons would be lost unless it was clear that the United States was willing to use its nuclear arsenal. In 1958 Norstad declined a Polish initiative to make central Europe a nuclear-free zone and at the same time endorsed an increase of NATO tactical nuclear weapons. By 1959 he was advocating that NATO build its own nuclear force outside of U.S. control. Norstad also felt that a rearmed West Germany was important to the strength of the alliance. His support allowed West Germany to deploy missiles capable of carrying nuclear warheads, although these remained under the supreme commander's control.

When the Soviets began constructing the Berlin wall in 1961, sparking a crisis over the city, General Norstad asked President John F. Kennedy to assure the alliance members that the United States would be willing to use nuclear weapons to defend the city. The president refused this advice, which increased the desire of Britain and Germany to build up their own European nuclear forces, a feeling Norstad shared. He wanted the United States to allow its submarine-launched missiles to be placed under a multilateral NATO command. This would allow a majority decision by the alliance's nuclear powers, France, Britain, and the United States, to decide if a nuclear strike was to be launched. President Kennedy proposed a more limited plan, which caused a split between the general and the president. Accentuating this disagreement were members of the Kennedy administration who saw Norstad as part of a dynasty of military commanders appointed by Eisenhower. These problems eventually led Norstad to resign in November 1962. However, due to the international tensions created by the Soviet deployment of missiles in Cuba, which precipitated the October Cuban missile crisis, Norstad was asked to stay on as supreme commander until 2 January 1963. Even after his retirement from the military, Norstad continued to press for an independent NATO nuclear force. He supported the Republican party on this issue in 1964 and in hearings before the Subcommittee on National Security and International Operations in 1967.

In 1963 Norstad became president of the international division of the Owens-Corning Fiberglass Corporation. From 1967 to 1972 he was chief executive officer as well as chairman of the company. In this capacity he introduced a new planning system and decentralized the corporation's organization while encouraging younger managers to take greater responsibility. From 1963 to 1972 the corporation's total sales increased from $275 million to $600 million. Later he also served as a director for United Airlines, Conoco, the Rand Corporation, and the Abitibi Paper Company. Norstad retired to Tubac, Arizona. He died at the Tucson Medical Center of cardiac arrest in 1988 and was buried in Arlington National Cemetery in Virginia.

During his term as supreme allied commander, Norstad dealt with the diplomatic problems caused by demands for greater European participation in the alliance, the shaping of U.S. nuclear policy, and the cold war. He was able to maintain allied unity partly because of his willingness to act independently of U.S. policy. His emphasis on conventional forces as a "shield" would influence the later NATO policy of "flexible response."

★

Biographical profiles are in Nelson Lichtenstein, ed., *Political Profiles: The Kennedy Years* (1976); Eleanora W. Schoenbaum, ed., *Political Profiles: The Eisenhower Years* (1977); *Webster's American Military Biographies* (1978); and Charles D. Bright, ed., *Historical Dictionary of the U.S. Air Force* (1992). "An Airman Boss for NATO," *Time* (23 Apr. 1956), covers his appointment as supreme allied commander. An obituary is in the *New York Times* (14 Sept. 1988). An oral history interview of Norstad was conducted in 1979 and is on deposit at Maxwell Air Force Base, Montgomery, Alabama.

DAVID EKBLADH

NORTHROP, John Howard (*b.* 5 July 1891 in Yonkers, New York; *d.* 27 May 1987 in Wickenburg, Arizona), biochemist who won the Nobel Prize in 1946 for identifying and proving the chemical nature of enzymes, proteins, and viruses.

Northrop was the son of John Isaiah Northrop, a faculty member in the Department of Zoology at Columbia University who was fatally injured in a laboratory accident two weeks before John's birth, and of Alice Belle Rich, who taught botany at Hunter College and introduced nature study into the curriculum of New York City public schools.

After an education in the public schools of Yonkers, Northrop entered Columbia University in 1908. He earned his B.S. degree in chemistry, with a minor in biology, in 1912 and an M.A. degree in 1913. He was a member of Columbia's fencing team (1910–1913), which won the intercollegiate championship during his senior year.

John H. Northrop, *c.* 1936. AP/WIDE WORLD PHOTOS

Northrop was a distinguished, somewhat dashing young man with a high forehead, dark hair and mustache, and an intelligent, engaging expression. Although he was dedicated to his work in the laboratory, he loved the outdoors as well; his interests ranged from horseback riding and sailing to golf and tennis. His chief hobbies were field shooting and salmon fishing, which he pursued diligently after his retirement at age seventy-one.

After working on a farm in 1913 and prospecting in Arizona the next year, Northrop returned to Columbia, where in 1915 he completed his doctorate in chemistry, based on his research with carbohydrates. He received the William Bayard Cutting Traveling Fellowship and began his scientific career at the Rockefeller Institute for Medical Research (now Rockefeller University) in New York City, in the laboratory of Jacques Loeb. There he started research into the duration of life, with special focus on the role of environmental factors in the hereditary properties of fruit flies.

Northrop's research was significant in two areas. First, he was able to cultivate fruit flies free of microorganisms—the first time this had been achieved. Second, his study invalidated the accepted hypothesis that the duration of life is regulated by an energy limit. Northrop proved that although the fruit flies' carbon dioxide output (a measure of energy expended) was greater at 15 degrees Celsius than at 22 degrees, the flies lived longer at 15 degrees than at the higher temperature.

Northrop was named an assistant at the Rockefeller Institute in 1916, an associate in 1917, an associate member in 1920, and a member in 1924. During World War I he served (1917–1918) as a captain in the U.S. Army's Chemical Warfare Service. During this period his studies of fermentation led to the development of a process for producing acetone and ethyl alcohol, chemicals of vital importance in the manufacture of war materials. On 26 June 1917 Northrop married Louise Walker; they had two children, a daughter, Alice Havemeyer, who married professor Frederick C. Robbins, the 1954 Nobel laureate in medicine, and a son, John, who became an oceanographer.

After the war Northrop returned to the Rockefeller Institute to work with Loeb on a study of enzymes essential to life processes. In 1929, using techniques pioneered by James Batcheller Sumner of Cornell University, Northrop isolated pepsin in pure crystalline form. He refined those techniques and used them later to crystallize several enzymes essential to human digestion: trypsin, chymotrypsin, carboxypeptidase, and pepsinogen.

Through the process of dissolving and recrystallizing enzymes to a high degree of chemical purity, Northrop proved his theory that all enzymes, and at least some viruses, are proteins, and that enzymatic activity is attributable to the protein molecule and not to an impurity.

In addition to his work on enzymes, Northrop teamed with Stanley to isolate a bacterial virus, and using purification through recrystallization, they proved that at least some viruses are composed of nonliving chemicals. He was particularly interested in bacteriophages, viruses abundant in the intestinal tracts of humans and animals that dissolve bacteria. In 1936 he isolated a bacteriophage from the intestines of mammals that exhibited the properties of a nucleoprotein in attacking staphylococcus. He showed that the highly purified staphylococcus bacteriophage contained nucleic acid as well as protein. He was one of the first scientists to point out the presence of nucleic acid in a virus.

In the late 1930s Northrop proposed that the nucleic acid in bacterial viruses might correspond to the free deoxyribonucleic acid (DNA) of the "transforming principle," a term used in 1928 by Frederick Griffiths to indicate the transfer of genetic information. Northrop said the protein case of the virus served to protect the DNA as it was introduced into the susceptible cell. His work on bacteriophages helped break down the distinction between living matter and "dead" crystals in the process of reproduction.

At the Nobel award ceremonies in 1946, Northrop and his Princeton colleague, Wendell Meredith Stanley, shared half of the chemistry prize (Sumner received the other half). It was acknowledged that Northrop undertook more detailed chemical studies than Sumner, and he was praised for perfecting the "art" of crystallizing enzymes and other proteins. In 1949 Northrop left Rockefeller University to become professor of bacteriology at the University of California at Berkeley; in 1958 he was appointed professor of biophysics there.

Northrop was awarded the Stevens Prize by the Columbia College of Physicians and Surgeons in 1931. He received the Charles Frederick Chandler Medal from Columbia University in 1937 and the Daniel Giraud Elliot Medal from the National Academy of Sciences in 1939. He received honorary doctorates from Harvard, Yale, Princeton, Rutgers, and the University of California.

Northrop was the author of *Crystalline Enzymes* (1939) and editor of the *Journal of General Physiology* at Rockefeller for several years, and wrote numerous papers on the physical chemistry of proteins, agglutination of bacteria, kinetics of enzyme reaction, and the chemical nature of enzymes.

Northrop died at his retirement home in Wickenburg, Arizona. He was cremated, and his ashes were scattered over the Arizona desert he loved.

Although Northrop's work was not generally known at the time he received the Nobel Prize, its value began to emerge as advances were made in the study of enzymes and viruses. In 1953 Eduard Farber praised Northrop for providing the first real proof that enzymes are chemicals by purifying them to pure substances. In 1964 Isaac Asimov credited Northrop with "breaking the back" of the enzyme controversy regarding the properties of viruses. Asimov said the controversy as to whether viruses are composed of nonliving material may have been settled in the minds of the Nobel committee, but not among investigators in the scientific community. Subsequent research confirmed Northrop's findings.

★

Northrop's writings include *The Organic Phosphoric Acid of Starch* (1915); *The Dynamics of Pepsin and Trypsin,* the Harvey Lecture (1927); and "Pepsin, Trypsin, Chymo-trypsin," *Angewandte chemische und physikalische Methoden* (1936). Nobel Foundation, *The Nobel Prize Winners* (1946), contains a comprehensive biography and discussion of Northrop's research. Eduard Farber, *Nobel Prize Winners in Chemistry, 1901–1961* (1963), explains the effects Northrop had on enzyme research. Isaac Asimov, *Asimov's Biographical Encyclopedia of Scientists* (1964), explains the importance of Northrop's research to other scientists. Roger M. Herriott, "John Howard Northrop," in *Biographical Memoirs. National Academy of Sciences* 63 (1994), covers his life and work. An obituary is in the *New York Times* (16 July 1987).

CHARLES A. ROND IV

NOYCE, Robert Norton (*b.* 12 December 1927 in Burlington, Iowa; *d.* 3 June 1990 in Austin, Texas), electronics industry pioneer who coinvented the integrated circuit and cofounded the Intel Corporation.

Noyce was the third of four sons of Ralph B. Noyce, a Congregational minister, and Harriet (Norton) Noyce. He lived in the towns of Denmark, Atlantic, Decorah, Webster City, and Rennow, Iowa, until he was twelve, when his family settled in Grinnell, Iowa. He attended local schools, where he became involved in musical groups, sports, and theater. In his senior year, he enrolled in a physics course at nearby Grinnell College and learned about the newly invented transistor, which had replaced the vacuum tube in electronic devices. He graduated first in his high school class.

In 1945 Noyce enrolled in Grinnell College as a physics and mathematics major. He studied under Grant Gale, a physics professor who created one of the first solid-state electronics courses in the United States. He graduated from Grinnell with a B.A. degree, with honors, in 1949. In September 1953 he received a Ph.D. in physical electronics from the Massachusetts Institute of Technology. That same year he married Elizabeth Bottomley, a costume director at Tufts College; the couple had four children: William Brewster, Pendred Elizabeth, Priscilla Ann, and Margaret May.

During 1953 Noyce became a research engineer at the

Robert Noyce. AP/WIDE WORLD PHOTOS

Philco Corporation in Philadelphia. By 1956 he had become dissatisfied with Philco's commitment to transistor research and development and accepted a position as research engineer at Shockley Semiconductor in Mountain View, California (in the future "Silicon Valley"). William Shockley, coinventor of the transistor and a Nobel Prize winner, headed the firm. By 1957 Noyce and seven other Shockley engineers had begun to bristle under William Shockley's restrictive management style and his concentration on diodes rather than transistors. With financial help from Fairchild Camera and Instrument Corporation of New York City, the group left Shockley and formed Fairchild Semiconductor in Mountain View. As director of research and general manager (1957–1959), Noyce steered the company toward transistor research and development and adopted a management style that was open, informal, and not bureaucratic and that promoted decentralized decision-making.

Before 1959, transistors and diodes were cut from germanium or silicon sheets, then custom-wired to form circuits. This process made mass production difficult. In July 1959 Jack Kilby of Texas Instruments theorized that all major electronic components, including capacitors and resistors, could be produced from a piece of germanium or silicon and then connected without having to cut them out. He immediately built a prototype and created the first integrated circuit. His hand-wiring of the components, however, made the circuit commercially infeasible.

In January 1959 Noyce discovered not only that all of the major electronic components could be produced from a piece of silicon, but that aluminum paths could be embedded into the silicon to connect the components. Noyce had eliminated the need for hand-wiring and had created an integrated circuit that could be mass produced. He had found a way to make components and their connections smaller, thus increasing dramatically the speeds of electrical currents flowing through them. He had made possible the placement of a virtually unlimited number of components on a piece of silicon.

Kilby and Noyce filed patent applications for the integrated circuit in February and July 1959, respectively. Because of the commercial viability of Noyce's prototype, he received the patent in 1961. From 1962 to 1969 a legal battle raged over who should get the patent; ultimately, Noyce's patent held up. However, the issue had been bypassed in summer 1966, when Texas Instruments and Fairchild Semiconductor agreed to license their integrated circuit designs to each other and to other companies.

In 1959 Fairchild Camera purchased Fairchild Semiconductor. Noyce was vice president and general manager of the subsidiary from 1959 to 1965 and group vice president of Fairchild Camera in Mountain View from 1965 to 1968. He and some of his colleagues (Gordon Moore, Andrew Grove, and Robert Graham) were uncomfortable dealing with the formal, hierarchical nature of the parent corporation and disliked the parent company's use of their profits for other than semiconductor research and development. So in 1968 they left Fairchild and founded Intel in Santa Clara, California. Noyce, Moore, and Grove once again adopted the decentralized, participatory management style that had made Fairchild Semiconductor successful. They built a corporate culture based on hard work, competition, and no frills.

From 1968 to 1975 Noyce was president and chief executive officer of Intel. Under his leadership, the company produced the first large-scale integrated memory chip (1970) and the microprocessor (1971). By 1974 the company had developed the 8080 microprocessor that became the industry standard. The heavy workload took a toll on Noyce's marriage, however, and in 1974 he and Elizabeth divorced. A year later he gave up responsibility for daily operations at Intel and became chairman of the board. That same year he married Anne Bowers, the personnel director at Intel Corporation. They had no children. In 1979 he became vice chairman of the board.

During the late 1970s and 1980s, Noyce became a spokesman for the American electronics industry and advocated strengthening it against foreign competition. In 1987 he helped found Sematech Incorporated, a consortium of businesses, educational institutions, and government agencies that subsidized research and development into semiconductor manufacturing. In July 1988 the articulate, self-effacing, and politically savvy Noyce became president and chief executive officer of the consortium when no one else would take the job. He moved to Austin, Texas, to be near Sematech's headquarters and spent the next two years lobbying for a national policy regarding competition, for education reform, for a relaxation of the antitrust laws to allow cooperation between firms, for a national emphasis on production rather than consumption, and for quicker licensing of technologies.

Noyce had a breadth of interests outside the worlds of business and technology. He loved scuba diving, underwater photography, skiing, hang gliding, piloting his own aircraft, and singing in and directing vocal groups. He was charming, soft-spoken, and introspective. Noyce died of a sudden heart attack in his home in Austin. His remains were cremated.

Labeled the "Mayor of Silicon Valley," Noyce excelled as a businessman and engineer. He coinvented the integrated circuit and made possible the manufacture of increasingly powerful personal computers. He cofounded two enterprises that became the prototypes and spawning grounds for many of the technology firms that would dot the West Coast. During his later years, as an ambassador for the electronics industry, he was considered to be one of the few who could bring the industry back to preeminence in the face of strong foreign competition.

★

Biographical sources include T. R. Reid, *The Chip: How Two Americans Invented the Microchip and Launched a Revolution* (1984); Tom Wolfe, "The Tinkerings of Robert Noyce," in Lee Eisenberg, ed., *Fifty Who Made the Difference* (1984); and Robert Slater, *Portraits in Silicon* (1987), which relies heavily on personal interviews. "Creativity by the Numbers," *Harvard Business Review* 58 (May/June 1980): 122–132, is an interview with Robert Noyce about managing a technology company. "Will the U.S. Semicon Industry Survive?: An Insider View," *Electronic News* (20 Oct. 1986): 4–17, is Noyce's conference speech about the strengths and weaknesses of America's industrial and economic system. Obituaries are in the *New York Times* (4 June 1990) and *Physics Today* 44 (Jan. 1991): 82–83.

GLEN EDWARD AVERY

O'BRIEN, Lawrence Francis, Jr. ("Larry") (*b.* 7 July 1917 in Springfield, Massachusetts; *d.* 28 September 1990 in New York City), political strategist, government official, and administrator who was the principal campaign organizer for John F. Kennedy and who served as a key aide to Presidents Kennedy and Lyndon B. Johnson; O'Brien was also U.S. postmaster general, chairman of the Democratic National Committee, and commissioner of the National Basketball Association.

O'Brien was the eldest of two children of Lawrence Francis O'Brien and Myra Theresa Sweeney, Irish immigrants from County Cork who owned and operated a rooming house and café in Springfield. His father dabbled in real estate and was a leading figure in the Democratic party in western Massachusetts. Accordingly, Larry junior was introduced to politics at an early age, gathering signatures for nomination papers and distributing campaign literature door-to-door after school. The other great enthusiasm of his youth was basketball, which had been invented in Springfield. Although O'Brien's playing aspirations were dashed by his failure to make his high school team, he remained a lifelong devotee of the game.

After O'Brien graduated from Springfield Cathedral High School in 1934, he worked in his parents' restaurant and, beginning in 1937, attended evening law classes at the local YMCA, which served as the Springfield division of Northeastern University. He received his LL.B. degree in 1942. O'Brien continued to hone his political skills as chairman of his Democratic ward committee and president of the Hotel and Restaurant Employees Union local. Poor eyesight prevented him from obtaining a commission in the U.S. Navy during World War II, but he was drafted for limited service in the army. He spent the war in Massachusetts, on Cape Cod, and was discharged with the rank of sergeant in 1945. O'Brien married Elva Lina Brassard, an office clerk from Springfield, on 30 May 1944. They had one child.

When O'Brien returned to Springfield, his father's declining health forced him to take over management of the family restaurant, a garage, and a parking lot. He resumed his involvement in politics by becoming campaign manager for Foster Furcolo, a friend who ran for Congress in 1946. O'Brien's meticulous organization helped Furcolo come within 3,300 votes of upsetting five-term Republican incumbent Charles Clason. In 1948, a better year for Democrats, Furcolo, aided by O'Brien, defeated Clason by more than 14,500 votes.

Appointed administrative assistant to Congressman Furcolo, O'Brien soon became frustrated by his lack of influence in Washington and homesick for Springfield. He managed Furcolo's successful reelection campaign in 1950 before resigning his post. According to O'Brien, Furcolo felt betrayed by his aide's departure and ended both their political association and friendship.

Although O'Brien had resolved to stay away from poli-

Postmaster General Lawrence F. O'Brien asking the U.S. Senate to approve reforms of the postal service, 1966. UPI/CORBIS-BETTMANN

tics following his break with Furcolo, he was convinced by Congressman John F. Kennedy to join the latter's campaign to unseat Republican U.S. Senator Henry Cabot Lodge, Jr., in 1952. As director of organization under campaign manager Robert F. Kennedy, O'Brien recruited 300 political neophytes who acted as Kennedy coordinators independent of the state Democratic party. In carrying out their work, they followed the teachings of the so-called O'Brien Manual, a detailed primer on political techniques; the typewritten document was revised by O'Brien for each ensuing campaign. O'Brien also lobbied successfully for the greater utilization by the Kennedy campaign of women volunteers, including the candidate's mother and sisters, who attended a highly successful series of fund-raising tea parties across the state. Kennedy's 70,737-vote victory margin over Lodge, achieved despite a landslide victory for Dwight D. Eisenhower in the presidential election that year, owed much to his campaign's smooth-running organization and its tireless director.

Following the election, O'Brien returned to Springfield, where he again ran the O'Brien Café. He also became administrator of the employee health fund for the Western Massachusetts Café Owners Association. The purchase of his family's properties by Springfield Newspapers for a substantial sum in 1953 subsequently gave O'Brien financial independence and the freedom to devote himself to political activity.

Along with Kenneth P. O'Donnell, O'Brien looked after Senator Kennedy's interests in Massachusetts, maintaining the campaign organization and preparing it for Kennedy's reelection bid. During the 1958 Senate race, O'Brien advised his candidate to undertake a grueling schedule of personal appearances instead of relying upon an expensive television advertising campaign proposed by his father, Joseph P. Kennedy. By taking O'Brien's advice, Kennedy undercut the opposition's charge that he had attempted to "buy" the election and won by an 874,608-vote plurality, a state record.

As the principal organizer of Kennedy's successful drive for the 1960 Democratic presidential nomination, O'Brien crisscrossed the country, establishing organizations for the Massachusetts senator in seven key primary states. At the Democratic National Convention in Los Angeles, O'Brien kept detailed file cards on all delegates, installed Kennedy liaisons in each state delegation, and saw to it that a modern communication system was in place to keep the candidate's headquarters informed of developments on the convention floor. As a result of these elaborate preparations, O'Brien was able to predict Kennedy's victorious first-ballot total within a half-vote. Heading the organizational effort in the fall campaign, O'Brien replicated his now-patented election formula on a national scale and played a major role in the razor-thin Democratic victory.

Upon taking office, President Kennedy, who had operated as an outsider in Congress and had weak ties to the leadership on Capitol Hill, launched an unprecedented congressional lobbying effort from the White House to promote his ambitious agenda. As the president's special assistant for congressional relations and personnel, O'Brien became the point man for this offensive. With Kennedy's backing, he transformed the Office of Congressional Relations (OCR), which the Eisenhower administration had established as a modest "buffer" between the executive and legislative branches, into something resembling a high-powered campaign operation. In addition to an eight-person OCR staff, O'Brien was given command of the personnel of the liaison offices of all of the executive departments and agencies, which had previously lobbied Congress independently, and put it to work in behalf of the Kennedy program.

Because he was often preoccupied with pressing foreign policy matters, Kennedy left much of the decision-making on domestic legislation in the hands of his energetic congressional liaison. O'Brien's careful cultivation of Democratic leaders on Capitol Hill and his deft use of persuasion and favors in lobbying the congressional rank and file helped win passage of 108 of 165 (65 percent) of the president's priority bills from 1961 to 1963. Among his more significant victories were the Omnibus Housing Act (1961), the Manpower Development and Training Act (1962), and the Mental Retardation Facilities and Community Health

Centers Act (1963). Still, the defeat of major proposals for school assistance, civil rights, and medical care for the elderly by the formidable conservative coalition of Republicans and southern Democrats left President Kennedy and O'Brien with a disappointing legislative legacy.

Anguished by the assassination of Kennedy in November 1963, O'Brien nonetheless joined other White House staffers in pledging to remain with the new president, Lyndon B. Johnson, through the 1964 election. Following his landslide triumph, Johnson convinced O'Brien to stay on and help pass what remained of the Kennedy agenda. Working with substantial postelection liberal majorities and a president who was one of the master practitioners of congressional politics in American history, O'Brien and his OCR staff participated in the most productive legislative session since the New Deal. Eighty-four of eighty-seven major bills, including the Elementary and Secondary Education Act, the Voting Rights Act, Medicare, and the many measures associated with Johnson's War on Poverty, were enacted in what *Congressional Quarterly* called "a seemingly endless stream." In 1966, 97 of 113 priority bills were approved by Congress.

With all the major bills disposed of in 1965, O'Brien tendered his resignation to Johnson. But the president again contrived to retain his key aide by appointing him postmaster general (he also kept his White House post). Upon assuming the helm at the Post Office, O'Brien found a badly floundering institution in need of change. Given low priority by the White House, stifled by congressional control over many administrative functions, hampered by outmoded facilities, and overwhelmed by an ever-increasing workload, the department he headed, O'Brien declared in February 1967, was "in a race with catastrophe." In an attempt to remedy the situation, he established an office of planning, hired college-educated managers, and substantially increased mechanization. But O'Brien came to believe that the only way to turn things around in the long term was to separate his department from politics. In April 1967 he proposed that the Post Office be removed from the cabinet and made a government-owned nonprofit corporation run by an appointed board and a professional executive. A study commission named by President Johnson came to the same conclusion a year later and a bill embodying O'Brien's original proposal became law in 1970.

Traveling across the country in his capacity as postmaster general and as Johnson's political "eyes and ears" in 1966 and 1967, O'Brien reported back to the president that the escalating Vietnam War was eroding liberal support for the administration and worrying Democratic party leaders. In 1968 O'Brien, who had previously backed the war, privately urged Johnson to consider phasing out American troops in South Vietnam, ending the bombing of North Vietnam, and seeking a negotiated settlement. Despite his misgivings about Vietnam, O'Brien supported Johnson's reelection even after Robert Kennedy announced his candidacy in opposition. It was not until the president's surprise withdrawal from the 1968 race that O'Brien resigned his cabinet post to organize the primary states for Kennedy, as he had for Kennedy's brother eight years before.

After Kennedy's assassination at a post-primary victory party in California in June, O'Brien seemed prepared to leave politics. He returned to the fray in July, however, when Vice President Hubert H. Humphrey, another close friend, prevailed upon him to manage his presidential drive. Following Humphrey's nomination at the tumultuous Democratic National Convention in Chicago, O'Brien was given the additional title of chairman of the Democratic National Committee (DNC) for the fall election effort. Heavily outspent by Republican Richard M. Nixon and trailing badly in the polls, Humphrey gained substantial support only after he heeded the advice of O'Brien and others and broke with Johnson on Vietnam. In the end, however, Humphrey's modest proposal calling for a conditional halt to the bombing of North Vietnam only helped narrow the Democrat's margin of defeat.

In November 1968 O'Brien was ready to open up a public relations and management consulting business in New York. A month later, his plans abruptly changed and he joined McDonnell and Company, a Wall Street brokerage, as president. O'Brien's career in high finance was short-lived, however, as an inflation-induced economic downturn inflicted severe damage on the investment community in general and McDonnell and Company in particular. He resigned after only seven months on the job, and the troubled firm folded shortly thereafter. He had just revived his consulting operation, O'Brien Associates, in 1970 when Humphrey persuaded him to return to the political wars again as Democratic national chairman.

In his second stint as chairman, O'Brien was faced with a debt-ridden, divided party and an entrenched, powerful Republican president. After reorganizing the DNC, O'Brien began to openly challenge Nixon administration policies and what he referred to as the president's "outrageous statements." At regular press conferences and in televised responses to presidential addresses, he launched blistering salvos at Nixon's economic policies, his conduct of the war in Indochina, and his administration's rhetorical assault on dissenters. The attacks infuriated the president, and O'Brien found himself targeted for harassment by White House operatives. His tax returns were audited three times by the Internal Revenue Service (IRS) and apartments he owned in Washington and New York were burglarized. Nixon's staff apparently sought evidence of O'Brien's financial ties to the mysterious tycoon Howard Hughes (an early client of O'Brien Associates) as well as any "dirt" the Democratic chairman might have on illegal payments made by Hughes to the president. After five men in the employ of the Committee to Re-elect the President (CRP) were arrested for breaking into DNC headquarters at the Watergate complex in Washington and planting electronic bugs in the chairman's office in June 1972, O'Brien gained a measure of revenge on his enemies. He filed a $1 million damage suit against the CRP and called for the appointment of a special prosecutor to investigate the matter. The suit was settled for $775,000 on 9 August 1974, the same day Nixon resigned his office in disgrace.

During a struggle for control of the Democratic party between party regulars and liberal activists in the early 1970s, O'Brien opted to appease the burgeoning activist faction. In an effort to achieve peace among Democrats, he embraced a party commission's recommendations to revamp electoral procedures and increase representation of minority groups, women, and young people for national conventions. The reforms instead widened the party split by reducing the influence of traditional power brokers and allowing activists to dominate the 1972 convention in Miami. At the July conclave, Senator George S. McGovern of South Dakota, an outspoken liberal who had chaired the reform commission, became the Democratic nominee for president. O'Brien was considered for the vice-presidential nomination, and McGovern later offered him another term as national chairman. But he was ultimately vetoed for both slots by the candidate's activist brain trust, which regarded him as an old-line politico. Ever the loyal Democrat, O'Brien vainly attempted to rally regulars behind the Democratic ticket as chairman of a losing campaign he later described as a "nightmare."

Back with O'Brien Associates late in 1972, he soon became bored and longed for a new challenge. It came in 1975, when he became commissioner of the National Basketball Association (NBA), which had become mired in lawsuits and labor disputes and faced a grave financial crisis. As the NBA team owners who hired him had hoped, O'Brien immediately applied his Washington negotiating experience to the difficulties that beset the league. In February 1976 he settled a five-year-old class-action suit filed by Oscar Robertson, a star player who contended that the NBA's draft system and option clause violated antitrust laws. O'Brien brought intransigent owners and NBA Players Association (NBAPA) representatives together and kept them talking until they hammered out a compromise agreement. By its terms, players were allowed to become free agents and owners were given the opportunity to match contract offers made by other teams. In similar fashion, O'Brien broke another long-standing impasse four months later by convincing NBA owners to accept a merger with the even more financially strapped rival American Basketball Association (ABA), ending nine years of cutthroat competition.

The next seven years of O'Brien's regime saw the adoption of the three-point shot, a popular innovation originated by the ABA, the doubling of gate receipts, and the tripling of television revenues. In 1983, however, a dispute over the rising costs of free agency nearly precipitated the NBA's first strike. The walkout was averted when O'Brien and the NBAPA worked out a unique revenue-sharing arrangement giving the players a percentage of gross revenues in exchange for the imposition of a cap on team salaries and benefits. Having guided the NBA successfully through one more crisis, O'Brien decided that it was time to get off the "merry-go-round." When he retired in 1984, the NBA paid tribute to O'Brien by naming its championship trophy for him. Remaining close to his favorite sport, he served as president of the National Basketball Hall of Fame in Springfield, Massachusetts, from 1985 to 1987. O'Brien died after a long bout with cancer and was buried in St. Michael's Cemetery in Springfield. His posthumous election to the Hall of Fame followed in 1991.

Called the "best election man in the business" by John Kennedy, Larry O'Brien was the preeminent campaign organizer of the second half of the twentieth century. His O'Brien Manual became the bible for grassroots campaigners, and the innovative work he did for Kennedy in 1960 set the standard for a generation of political tacticians of both major parties. As a White House aide, O'Brien helped define the Office of Congressional Relations for future administrations. And his stewardship of the Post Office, the Democratic party, and the National Basketball Association established O'Brien as the Kennedy White House adviser who had the most substantial public career after 1963.

★

O'Brien's papers, covering his career in politics and public service, are at the John F. Kennedy Library in Boston and at the Lyndon Baines Johnson Library in Austin, Texas. His NBA files are housed at Springfield College in Springfield, Massachusetts. The National Basketball Hall of Fame in Springfield has a substantial clipping file on O'Brien. His memoir, *No Final Victories: A Life in Politics—From John F. Kennedy to Watergate* (1974), is detailed and frank. Theodore H. White, *The Making of the President, 1960* (1961), provides the most vivid portrait of O'Brien as a political strategist. Patrick Anderson, *The Presidents' Men: White House Assistants of Franklin D. Roosevelt, Harry S. Truman, Dwight D. Eisenhower, John F. Kennedy, and Lyndon B. Johnson* (1968), James N. Giglio, *The Presidency of John F. Kennedy* (1991), and Irving Bernstein, *Guns or Butter: The Presidency of Lyndon Johnson* (1996), ably analyze his work as a presidential aide. Stephen E. Ambrose, *Nixon: The Triumph of a Politician, 1962–1972* (1989), and Stanley I. Kutler, *The Wars of Watergate: The Last Crisis of Richard Nixon* (1990), discuss O'Brien's role as Nixon's bête noire. Important articles include Ray Kennedy, "A Celtic Rookie Puts It Together," *Sports Illustrated* (25 Oct. 1976); and John Hart, "Staffing the Presidency: Kennedy and the Office of Congressional Relations," *Presidential Studies Quarterly* (winter 1993). Obituaries are in the *Boston Globe, New York Times,* and *Washington Post* (all 29 Sept. 1990). Substantial O'Brien oral histories are at the Kennedy and Johnson libraries and in the Columbia Oral History Collection.

RICHARD H. GENTILE

OGILVIE, Richard Buell (*b.* 22 February 1923 in Kansas City, Missouri; *d.* 10 May 1988 in Chicago, Illinois), governor of Illinois.

Ogilvie was one of two sons of Kenneth S. Ogilvie, an insurance executive, and Edna Mae Buell. The Ogilvies moved to Evanston, Illinois, when Richard was seven. He attended Lincoln Elementary School and spent his freshman year at Evanston High School. The family then moved to Westchester County, New York, where Ogilvie played tackle for the Port Chester High School football team. He graduated from high school in 1940 and entered Yale University in 1941. He became active in the Young Republicans at Yale and was a lineman on the junior varsity football team.

After the United States entered World War II, Ogilvie was initially rejected for military service because of poor eyesight, but he was accepted into the Army Enlisted Reserve Corps in 1942. Assigned as an instructor at Fort Knox, Ogilvie asked for combat duty. He became a sergeant in a tank battalion and was awarded two Bronze Stars. On 13 December 1944, while serving as a tank commander in the Alsace region of France, he was hit in the face by fragments of an exploding German shell. The left side of his face and his jaw were shattered, leaving Ogilvie with permanent scars. He was discharged with a Purple Heart and returned to Yale.

Richard Ogilvie. COURTESY OF MR. STEVE NEAL

Ogilvie began thinking about a political career while he was in college. "There was a strong emphasis that you're not just here to get an education—you're being educated to be a leader," he said in an interview. After graduating from Yale in the winter of 1947, Ogilvie worked part-time as a construction worker while attending Chicago-Kent College of Law. He and two classmates—future U.S. Senator Charles H. Percy and future Illinois Attorney General William Scott—took over the leadership of the Cook County Young Republicans.

In 1949 Ogilvie graduated from law school and joined the Chicago firm of Lord, Bissell and Cook. He married Dorothy Louise Shriver on 11 February 1950. They had one daughter.

Ogilvie took a leave from the law firm in 1954 to become an assistant U.S. attorney for the Northern District of Illinois. In 1958 he was appointed by Attorney General William P. Rogers as his special assistant in charge of the Chicago Midwest office of the Organized Crime Task Force. Ogilvie conducted federal grand jury investigations of gambling, labor racketeering, narcotics, and tax evasion. FBI special agent William F. Roemer said that Ogilvie was more effective in fighting organized crime than any federal prosecutor he had worked with. Ogilvie obtained a conviction of the mob boss Anthony Accardo on charges of tax evasion, but the conviction was reversed on appeal.

Helped by his image as a crime fighter, Ogilvie was elected Cook County sheriff in 1962, the only Republican to win countywide office that year in the traditionally Democratic stronghold. He cleaned up what had been one of the more corrupt offices in county government. Ogilvie transformed the discredited police force by hiring and promoting on a merit basis. His office conducted more than 1,800 raids on illegal activities, frequently striking at organized crime's gambling and vice operations. When it was disclosed that a top aide had ties to the crime syndicate, Ogilvie promptly fired him.

In 1966 Ogilvie was elected as the first Republican president of the Cook County Board in two decades. He increased civil service positions from 33 percent to 85 percent of county employees. Ogilvie also introduced competitive bidding on road contracts. He named a panel of civic leaders to recommend sweeping changes in Cook County government, but he did not stay in office long enough to carry out their recommendations. In a move that angered some Cook County Republican committee members who had supported him for County Board president, Ogilvie sought the governorship in 1968. When he won the election, the Democratic majority on the County Board promptly named a Democrat to serve out his unexpired term as president.

Ogilvie defeated Governor Samuel Shapiro in the 1968 general election with 51.2 percent of the vote. A tough, combative, plainspoken chief executive, Ogilvie showed political courage in pushing through the state's first income tax. When he proposed the tax on 1 April 1969, he faced opposition from both political parties. He won the support of Chicago's mayor, Richard J. Daley, by offering to share 8.5 percent of the revenue with local governments. Ogilvie also agreed to increase revenue-sharing from the sales tax. In a compromise Ogilvie won legislative approval for a 4 percent tax rate on corporations and 2.5 percent on individuals.

As governor, Ogilvie presided over the enactment of the first new state constitution in a century. He also reorganized the executive branch of the state government, reformed the budget process, and created the Illinois Department of Transportation and the Illinois Environmental Protection Agency. With increased tax revenues he promoted the state university system and increased aid to public schools. He signed the state's first minimum-wage law and increased workman's compensation. Ogilvie changed state hiring practices, resulting in the hiring of more minorities than had been hired under previous governors, and added more than 56,000 acres of state parks.

Ogilvie was defeated for reelection in 1972 by Dan Walker, a Democrat, who criticized him for the income tax. "I knew damn well that it was probably signing my death warrant as governor. But the question was: Did I want to be a mediocre eight-year governor or a really good four-year governor?" Ogilvie said in an interview.

Ogilvie was a leader of vision and courage who left a significant mark on his state by putting the public interest above his own. Neal R. Peirce, author of *The Great Lakes States of America,* wrote of Ogilvie: "Few recent American governors have demonstrated natural executive skill equal to Ogilvie's. He was a gutsy man, willing to undergo stiff criticism if he thought he was right." And Paul Simon, a Democrat, who served as Ogilvie's lieutenant governor, said, "Dick Ogilvie has been a superior and courageous public servant by any standard."

Ogilvie practiced law in Chicago after leaving office, and in 1986 he received a $3 million bonus for his work as trustee of the Milwaukee Road railroad. He died of a heart attack in his downtown law office. He was cremated and his ashes are at Rosehill Cemetery in Chicago.

★

Ogilvie's gubernatorial papers are in the Illinois State Archives in Springfield. Ogilvie discussed his career with Mike Lawrence in "Ogilvie Revisited," in *Illinois Issues* (Dec. 1982): 25–28. A biography is Taylor Pensoneau, *Gov. Richard B. Ogilvie: In the Interest of the State* (1998). See also Neal R. Peirce, *The Great Lakes States of America: People, Politics, and Power in the Five Great Lakes States* (1980); and Robert P. Howard, *Mostly Good and Competent Men: Illinois Governors 1818–1988* (1988). An obituary is in the *Chicago Sun-Times* (11 May 1988).

STEVE NEAL

O'KEEFFE, Georgia Totto (*b.* 15 November 1887 in Sun Prairie, Wisconsin; *d.* 6 March 1986 in Santa Fe, New Mexico), a first-generation American modernist painter whose aesthetic was drawn from a confluence of Eastern and Western sources, including Chinese art and photography, to create her unique approach to color and pictorial space.

O'Keeffe was the daughter of Francis Calixtus O'Keeffe, a farmer, and Ida Ten Eyck Totto. In 1903, at the age of fifteen, she followed her family east to Williamsburg, Virginia, after completing the school year in Madison, Wisconsin. In 1905 she graduated with a degree in art from Chatham Episcopal Institute in Chatham, Virginia.

Georgia O'Keefe at the exhibition of her work *Life and Death,* 1931. UPI/CORBIS-BETTMANN

Pursuing her childhood ambition to become an artist, O'Keeffe enrolled that fall at the Art Institute of Chicago, where modern architecture, Art Nouveau, and Japonisme, as well as the Arts and Crafts movement, thrived. She took top honors in the life drawing classes of John Vanderpoel. After missing the following academic year owing to illness (typhoid fever), O'Keeffe resumed her training in the fall of 1907 at the Art Students League in New York. Over the next twelve months she followed a regimen that included the study of oil, pastel, and watercolor with William Merritt Chase, Kenyon Cox, and Francis Luis Mora, as well as plein air sketching in a summer school at Lake George, for which she had earned from Chase the still-life scholarship. In 1908, like many of Chase's students, O'Keeffe visited Alfred Stieglitz's Little Galleries of the Photo-Secession, where she saw Auguste Rodin's drawings, and perhaps also Henri Matisse's work, later that spring. It was her first glimpse of the Parisian avant-garde. Very few works from the years following O'Keeffe's tenure at the Art Students League have been attributed to her. Though she corresponded with friends from the League who had studios in New York or were studying in Paris, she had, for all intents and purposes, abandoned such a career for herself. She did not paint again for four years.

For two years O'Keeffe made a living as a freelance commercial artist while staying with an aunt and uncle in Chicago. Designs of lace and embroidery for newspaper advertisements, as well as the logo for the "Dutch Cleanser Girl," have been attributed to O'Keeffe. In 1910 a severe case of measles that temporarily affected her eyesight sent her to convalesce with her mother in Charlottesville, Virginia. While attending Alon Bement's lectures at the University of Virginia summer school in 1912, O'Keeffe was introduced to Arthur Wesley Dow's method of art instruction, which had been inspired by Ernest Fenollosa's ideas on Asian art. Called the Fenollosa-Dow method, this system abandoned traditional notions of naturalism in favor of a new combination of Oriental (Zen) aesthetics with Western media. Its philosophy promised to liberate both teacher and student from slavish copyist exercises and to empower the artist to use line and color freely, according to emotional necessity, as the musician would use an instrument or the poet, words. Believing in this message, O'Keeffe began a teaching career in the fall of 1912, at Amarillo, Texas.

Each summer until 1916 O'Keeffe returned to assist Alon Bement at the University of Virginia. She spent the 1914–1915 school year at Columbia University Teachers College, where she gained firsthand experience with Arthur Wesley Dow, whose training she supplemented with painting classes at the Art Students League. Though Dow's course, which included assigned texts such as Dow's book *Composition* (1899) and Fenollosa's *Epochs of Chinese and Japanese Art* (1912), remained a primary source of inspiration for her methods, O'Keeffe experienced other influences that broadened her idea of personal expression. She joined the National Women's party and frequented Gallery 291, where she became increasingly familiar with European modernism through exhibitions of Pablo Picasso, Georges Braque, and Francis Picabia.

In the fall of 1915, while teaching in Columbia, South Carolina, O'Keeffe corresponded with classmate Anita Pollitzer, who kept her informed of activities in New York and supplied her with the latest publications. Among O'Keeffe's books were issues of Stieglitz's *Camera Work*, Jerome Eddy's *Cubists and Post-Impressionism* (1914), Floyd Dell's *Women as World-Builders* (1913), and Beatrice Irwin's *The New Science of Color* (1915). By December 1915 she had completed her second reading of Wassily Kandinsky's *Concerning the Spiritual in Art* (English, 1914) and began making her large charcoal drawings. She called them "Specials." Their vortices, V-shapes, and elipses—though restricted in color, texture, and form—remained seminal motifs for her most abstract oil paintings, as well as her later presentation of flowers, leaves, trees, crosses, and bones.

In January 1916 Pollitzer showed O'Keeffe's "Specials" to renowned photographer and dealer Alfred Stieglitz, who enthusiastically exhibited her work on at least three occasions (May–July 1916, November–December 1916, April–May 1917) before his gallery closed in June 1917. Dow, at O'Keeffe's request, visited her exhibition at 291 in May 1917. He wrote to his young protégée, then art department head at West Texas State Normal School at Canyon, to praise her harmonious rhythms. Dow may have been reassured by O'Keeffe's rippling lines, in which he may have recognized the spirit of paintings of rivers and trees from the Sung Dynasty, but his letter cautioned against her vagueness in design.

From 1917 to 1918 O'Keeffe led an increasingly divided life, residing in Texas but maintaining contact with New York through Anita Pollitzer and the photographer Paul Strand, as well as through intensely private exchanges with Stieglitz, who periodically sent her books and photographs. She enthusiastically filled her classroom with diverse materials: Strand and Stieglitz photographs, a Japanese print, reproductions of Persian textiles and Archaic Greek vases. She lectured on modern art, but met with increasing resistance from the administration, which ordered her to abandon Dow's text. Nevertheless, given the vast appeal of the western sky and canyons, O'Keeffe's painting flourished. In 1918 an episode of flu became the deciding factor in her departure from teaching. Stieglitz convinced her to return to New York in June 1918. By July he had left his wife of twenty-five years to share a studio with O'Keeffe, who, clothed and unclothed, became the subject of an extensive series of photographs that Stieglitz exhibited in 1921 in

New York as *Portrait of a Woman.* On 11 December 1924 they married.

Between 1918 and 1928 O'Keeffe lived and worked with Stieglitz among New York intelligentsia—critics Paul Rosenfeld, Waldo Frank, and Henry McBride; poets and writers Sherwood Anderson and William Carlos Williams; and painters John Marin, Marsden Hartley, Arthur Dove, and Charles Demuth. She divided her time primarily between her garden and studio at the Stieglitz family home in Lake George and apartments in New York City. During this decade she established her characteristic approach to painting. Her thinly applied oil paint adopted the resonant tonalities and reductive space of photographs. O'Keeffe used this unique conception of pictorial space as an arena for isolating detail or swelling vibrations of color. Her process of selection acknowledged practically no distinction between abstraction and representation. Contemplating the enigma of a single isolated subject—whether looking down into a plant or gazing up at the sky—was commensurate with O'Keeffe's desire to deal with colors and patterns she experienced firsthand. She rarely painted anything she did not know well. In 1924 O'Keeffe began painting magnified leaves and flowers, demonstrating the mastery of monumentality and scale that would become the hallmark of her art.

After her retrospective at the Anderson Galleries in 1923, O'Keeffe exhibited her work in New York every year until Stieglitz died in 1946. She kept pace with current developments, and on occasion—as in the cases of her skyscrapers and giant callas—her paintings garnered great attention in the New York art world. In the summer of 1928, seemingly at the height of her fame as a flower painter, a crisis in her marriage, caused in part by Stieglitz's infidelity, altered her pattern of work. Starting in 1929, O'Keeffe spent most of her summers in New Mexico, and in 1930 she began to paint the bleached animal bones and vast expanses of high desert for which she ultimately became best known (most notably her series of skulls and pelvises). In 1939 the New York World's Fair Tomorrow Committee honored O'Keeffe as one of the twelve outstanding women of the past fifty years. In 1946 she was the first woman to have a solo show at the Museum of Modern Art, a retrospective curated by James Johnson Sweeney.

In 1949, after distributing Stieglitz's estate, O'Keeffe settled permanently in New Mexico, maintaining two homes: a historic colonial adobe in Abiquiu, a village in the Chama River Valley where she kept a garden and spent winter and spring, and Ghost Ranch, north and west of Abiquiu in the high desert, where she spent summer and autumn. Abiquiu remained the primary inspiration in her late career, which included a patio series that she continued until 1960. In 1965, after undertaking a world tour, she painted her largest canvas, the culmination of a series of aerial views of clouds. In the spring of 1970 O'Keeffe was awarded the Gold Medal for painting by the National Institute of Arts and Letters, and in the fall she was the subject of a major retrospective at the Whitney Museum of American Art. Partially blind, O'Keeffe worked with assistance from 1972. Sculptor Juan (John Bruce) Hamilton assisted her during the last decade of her life and was a major heir. In 1986 she died in Santa Fe. She was cremated and her ashes scattered.

Like other artists of her generation, O'Keeffe searched for an authentic American expression through a process of self-discovery in nature. She told Sweeney, "I think that what I have done is something rather unique in my own time and that I am one of the few who gives our country any voice of its own—I claim no credit—it is only that I have seen with my own eye and that I couldn't help seeing with my own eye."

★

The Georgia O'Keeffe/Alfred Stieglitz papers are in the Yale Collection of American Literature, Beinecke Rare Book and Manuscript Library, Yale University. Among O'Keeffe's published writings are "To *MSS*—And Its Thirty-three Subscribers and Others Who Read and Don't Subscribe!" *MSS* (1922): 17–18; "About Myself," in *Georgia O'Keeffe: Exhibition of Oils and Pastels,* catalog of an exhibition at An American Place (1939); *Georgia O'Keeffe* (1976); and *Some Memories of Drawings,* edited by Doris Bry (1988).

Books that examine and reprint primary sources are Barbara Buhler Lynes, *O'Keeffe, Stieglitz, and the Critics, 1916–1929* (1989); and Clive Giboire, ed., *Lovingly, Georgia: The Complete Correspondence of Georgia O'Keeffe and Anita Pollitzer* (1990). Monographs and biographies include Roxana Robinson, *Georgia O'Keeffe* (1989); Sarah Whitaker Peters, *Becoming O'Keeffe: The Early Years* (1991); Bram Dijkstra, *O'Keeffe: New York Years* (1991); and Charles C. Eldredge, *Georgia O'Keeffe: American and Modern* (1993). Among exhibition catalogs see Lloyd Goodrich and Doris Bry, *Georgia O'Keeffe: Retrospective Exhibition* [at the Whitney Museum] (1970); Jack Cowart, Juan Hamilton, and Sarah Greenough, *Georgia O'Keeffe: Arts and Letters* [at the National Gallery] (1987); Alexandra Arrowsmith and Thomas West, eds., *Two Lives: A Conversation in Paintings and Photographs. Georgia O'Keeffe and Alfred Stieglitz* [at the Phillips Collection] (1992); Sharyn Udall, *O'Keeffe in Texas* (1998); and Ruth Fine, Elizabeth Glassman, Juan Hamilton, and entries by Sarah Burt, *Georgia O'Keeffe's Library* [at the Georgia O'Keeffe Foundation] (1997).

An obituary is in the *New York Times* (7 Mar. 1986).

ELIZABETH HUTTON TURNER

ORBISON, Roy Kelton (*b.* 23 April 1936 in Vernon, Texas; *d.* 6 December 1988 in Hendersonville, Tennessee), singer, songwriter, and star performer in early rock and roll whose haunting, ethereal voice and near operatic range have seldom been equaled in pop music.

Orbison was the elder of two sons of Depression-era refugees from Oklahoma. His father, Orbie Lee Orbison, was a peripatetic and often unemployed oil field hand, and his mother, Nadine Schultz, was a nurse who painted and wrote poetry. While the family drifted—eventually to western Texas—in search of work for Orbie, Roy spent hours listening as his father played country music in the style of Jimmie Rodgers and an uncle picked blues guitar. He was also exposed to the gospel music of the Church of Christ. These are classic rock-and-roll influences.

Presented with his first guitar at age six, Orbison soon demonstrated precocious talent and began to perform locally—live on broadcasts of radio station KVWY from Kermit, Texas, in 1944; for medicine shows two years later; and soon with his first band, the Wink Westerners, a quintet composed of members of the Wink, Texas, high school orchestra.

Roy Orbison. ARCHIVE PHOTOS

After dropping out of North Texas State University in Denton, where he studied geology for two years (a classmate was the future pop crooner Pat Boone), Orbison drove to the Clovis, New Mexico, recording studios of Norman Petty's Je-Wal label, having refashioned his band as the Teen Kings. While cutting his first single for Petty, "Ooby Dooby," Orbison met the rockabilly star Johnny Cash, who encouraged the young Texan with the clear tenor and angelic falsetto to contact the legendary Sam Phillips of Sun Records in Memphis, Tennessee.

Phillips, who had launched the careers of Elvis Presley, Jerry Lee Lewis, and Carl Perkins, recorded a grittier version of the twelve-bar rocker "Ooby Dooby" in 1956, and it became Orbison's first hit. Orbison, however, preferred to sing ballads, and a clash over stylistic differences arose between Orbison and Phillips, who demanded more rock and roll.

Moving across Tennessee to more ballad-friendly Nashville, Orbison soon penned the tune "Claudette" (named for his teenage bride, Claudette Frady, whom he married in 1957), and sold it to the Everly Brothers in 1958. Using the song's royalties to buy himself out of his Sun contract, Orbison became a staff songwriter for Nashville's powerful music publisher Acuff-Rose. There Orbison composed a series of country tunes, including the Jerry Lee Lewis hit "Down the Line."

Signing with Frank Foster's new Monument Records in 1960, Orbison soon recorded his breakthrough single, "Only the Lonely," a Latin-tinged collaboration with Joe Melson that had an initial selling of 2 million copies. Orbison's voice spans a full three octaves in this beautifully melodic ballad, at the climax of which Orbison displays a glass-shattering falsetto. Orbison and Melson teamed up again with their first *Billboard* number-one hit, the bolero-styled "Running Scared" (1961), whose paranoid lyrics were eerily prophetic of Orbison's future personal tragedy.

Dreams were a recurring motif throughout a number of Orbison's songs such as "Leah" (1962), "Dream Baby" (1962), and a pair of 1963 fantasies, "In Dreams" and "Blue Bayou." Rock critic Dave Marsh noted that on "the climactic line 'only in dreams,' " Orbison "sings somewhere between a ranchera and a cowboy yodel, the twin products of the Texas plains where he grew up." "Blue Bayou" would be covered by pop singer Linda Ronstadt in the late 1970s. A dramatic ballad, it too demonstrated Orbison's seeming obsession with isolation and longing.

The hypnotic "Oh, Pretty Woman" (1964) would reach number three on the *Billboard* charts. Cowritten by William Dees of Monument Records, it would become Orbison's all-time greatest seller (7 million copies worldwide). His last gold record in the United States, the uptempo rockabilly number has become a familiar theme on television commercials and was featured in a blockbuster 1990 film of the same name.

Orbison was a self-confessed introvert, and his black leather outfits, slicked-back pompadour, and dark Ray-Ban sunglasses presented a stark picture. His relative immobility on stage and his lack of histrionics gave him the paradoxical image of a stoic rock and roller. Orbison began wearing his trademark sunglasses almost by accident. Flying to London in 1963 to tour with the Beatles, he absentmindedly left his regular glasses home. Orbison, who was nearsighted, performed onstage and posed for photos with the Beatles wearing the dark prescription shades. His new look met with approval and he adopted it permanently.

Orbison was struck twice by extreme personal loss. On 7 June 1966 he witnessed his beloved Claudette's death in a motorcycle accident. Grief-stricken, he quit songwriting and set out on a nonstop world tour as a palliative for his anguish. While playing in England in 1968, tragedy struck again when two of his three sons (Roy, Jr., and Tony) perished in a fire in the Orbison home in Hendersonville, Tennessee, a suburb of Nashville.

Leaving Monument Records in 1965, Orbison signed with Metro-Goldwyn-Mayer, hoping for work in television or the movies, but the highly forgettable film *The Fastest Guitar Alive* (1968) was his only acting venture. Orbison married his second wife, Barbara, in 1969 and continued to perform on the rock-and-roll revival circuit. Although his career in the United States had declined, overseas his legions of fans had not deserted him, and in Europe, Asia, and Australia he continued to play to packed houses.

In 1980 Orbison teamed with Emmy Lou Harris for the hit vocal duet "That Loving You Feeling Again," recorded for the sound track of the film *Roadie.* Seven years later he was inducted into the Rock and Roll Hall of Fame, at which time the rock star Bruce Springsteen said, "In 1975 when I made *Born to Run* . . . most of all I wanted to sing like Roy Orbison."

Orbison recorded "Wild Hearts" in 1985 for the sound track of the Nicholas Roeg film *Insignificance.* His stagnant career was then revived with assistance from younger musicians whom he had influenced. A cable TV special in 1988 featured Orbison with Springsteen, Elvis Costello, and Jackson Browne. He then joined former Beatle George Harrison, Bob Dylan, Tom Petty, and Jeff Lynne of the Electric Light Orchestra to form a widely successful superstar group called the Traveling Wilburys. A posthumously released LP, *Mystery Girl* (1989), included the uplifting hit "You Got It." It has been estimated that Orbison sold 35 million copies of his songs worldwide during his lifetime. A large number were reissued after his death by Rhino Records.

Having had open-heart surgery in the late 1970s, Orbison succumbed to a massive coronary while visiting his mother, Nadine, in Hendersonville, Tennessee. He had been living in Malibu, California, and was survived by his wife Barbara and three sons (Wesley, Roy, Jr., and Alexander). Orbison is buried at Westwood Memorial Park in Los Angeles.

★

Ellis Amburn, *Dark Star: The Roy Orbison Story* (1990), is based on interviews with dozens of Orbison's contemporaries as well as family members. Another biography, Alan Clayson's *Only the Lonely* (1989), covers details of Orbison's career in Great Britain. Dave Marsh, *The Heart of Rock and Soul: The 1001 Greatest Singles Ever Made* (1989), is useful for an analysis of many of Orbison's recordings. Irwin Stambler, *Encyclopedia of Pop, Rock, and Soul* (1989), contains much detailed biographical information, and *The Billboard Book of Number One Hits* (1985), edited by Fred Bronson, is filled with anecdotes and discographical data on Orbison's singles. An article in *The Guinness Encyclopedia of Pop Music* (1992), edited by Colin Larkin, is helpful for its complete listing of album releases, labels, and dates of release. An obituary appeared in the *New York Times* (8 Dec. 1988).

JEFFREY S. ROSEN

P

PAGE, Geraldine (*b.* 22 November 1924 in Kirksville, Missouri; *d.* 13 June 1987), actress who was a preeminent force in American theater, lauded for her stage interpretations of the characters of Tennessee Williams, Eugene O'Neill, and many other playwrights; she also made her mark in television and film.

Page was the daughter of Leon Elwin Page, an osteopathic physician, and Edna Pearl Maize, a housewife. She had one sibling, a younger brother. When she was five the family moved to Chicago, where her interest in acting succeeded preoccupations with the piano and fine art. She made her first stage appearance in a church production at seventeen. Page graduated from Englewood High School in 1942, and trained at the Goodman Theatre Dramatic School from 1942 to 1945. Later she studied voice with Alice Hermes and acting with Uta Hagen and Mira Rostova, and at the Actors Studio in New York City with Lee Strasberg. Page was a cofounder of the Actors Studio Theatre, but feuded with Strasberg and quit the organization.

From 1945 to 1948 Page performed summer stock in Illinois, about thirty-five miles from Chicago, at the Lake Zurich Playhouse, of which she was a cofounder. She also played summer stock in Marengo, Illinois, in 1949 and 1950. In 1945 she made her New York City debut off Broadway at the Blackfriars Guild in *Seven Mirrors*. She also acted in winter stock in Woodstock, Illinois, from 1946 to 1948. She began her television career in Chicago when she played the Virgin Mary in *Easter Story* (1947).

Page moved to New York City and worked as a hatcheck girl, factory worker, and lingerie model. Off Broadway beckoned again, in 1951, with *Yerma* by Federico García Lorca, performed at the Circle in the Square, the theatre where a year later she made a startling breakthrough as Alma Winemiller in the landmark revival of *Summer and Smoke,* written by Tennessee Williams and directed by José Quintero. The production was instrumental in the rise of off Broadway as a postwar artistic force, and Page's performance as the repressed spinster became legendary. She ultimately played several other Williams heroines and was considered one of the author's foremost interpreters. Page's 1952 off-Broadway success led to her participation in a series of radio dramas in 1953.

Soon, Page made waves on Broadway, starting with triumphs in two otherwise forgettable plays, *Mid-Summer* (1953), by Vina Delmar, for which she won several prestigious theater awards, and *The Immoralist* (1954), based on André Gide's novel. Her first Broadway hit was *The Rainmaker* (1954), by N. Richard Nash, in which she played Lizzie, a role she later reprised in her London debut in 1956. She eventually appeared in sixteen more Broadway plays, her notable roles including Sybil and Anne in *Separate Tables* (1957), by Terence Rattigan, in which she succeeded Margaret Leighton; Alexandra del Lago in Williams's *Sweet Bird of Youth* (1959); Nina in the Actors Studio's revival of *Strange Interlude* (1963), by Eugene O'Neill; Olga in the Actors Studio's version of *The Three Sisters* (1964), by Anton Chekhov; Clea in *Black Comedy*

Geraldine Page. ARCHIVE PHOTOS

(1967), and the Baroness in *White Lies* (1967), both by Peter Shaffer; Marion in *Absurd Person Singular* (1974), by Alan Ayckbourn; Zelda Fitzgerald in *Clothes for a Summer Hotel* (1980), by Tennessee Williams; Mother Miriam Ruth in *Agnes of God* (1982), by John Pielmeier; and Madame Arcati in a revival of *Blithe Spirit* (1987), by Noël Coward.

Little is known of Page's first marriage. In 1956 she married violinist Alexander Schneider; they divorced in 1960. The following year she was married for a third time, to actor Rip Torn. They had twin sons and a daughter and remained married until her death.

Page, who toured with several of her Broadway plays, also sometimes worked in revivals outside New York City. In 1956 she played Abbie in O'Neill's *Desire Under the Elms* and Natalia in Ivan Turgenev's *A Month in the Country,* both in Chicago. Page also did a tour of three one-acters (two by Chekhov, which she also acted off Broadway) called *Marriage and Money* (1971). In Lake Forest, Illinois, and Philadelphia she played Regina (in which she succeeded Anne Bancroft) in *The Little Foxes* (1974), by Lillian Hellman, and in Lake Forest she also played Blanche DuBois in Williams's *A Streetcar Named Desire* (1976). Page also acted in numerous television roles. Her performances in *A Christmas Memory* (1967) and *The Thanksgiving Visitor* (1969), both by Truman Capote, were rewarded with Emmys.

Page made an important off-Broadway appearance in a double bill of *Creditors* and *The Stronger* (1977), both by August Strindberg. Another powerful off-Broadway role was Lorraine in *A Lie of the Mind* (1985), by Sam Shepard. This project originated with the Sanctuary Theatre, an actors' workshop that she and her husband, Torn, cofounded in 1976. Page became similarly involved as an artist-in-residence with the Mirror Repertory Company, playing various striking parts from the plays of Clifford Odets, Somerset Maugham, Robert Bolt, Jean Giraudoux, and others from 1983 onward. Devoted to the craft of acting, she enjoyed teaching, which she did during the 1970s and 1980s at the Pelican Theatre.

Page, who considered herself primarily a stage actress, made her film debut in *Out of the Night* (1947) and subsequently acted in twenty-seven movies, although she never achieved true movie stardom. Her major films included *Hondo* (1953), *Summer and Smoke* (1961), *Sweet Bird of Youth* (1962), *Toys in the Attic* (1963), *Dear Heart* (1964), *You're a Big Boy Now* (1966), *The Beguiled* (1971), *Pete 'n' Tillie* (1972), *The Day of the Locust* (1974), *Interiors* (1978), *I'm Dancing As Fast As I Can* (1982), *The Pope of Greenwich Village* (1984), and *The Trip to Bountiful* (1985), for which, after seven previous nominations, she received an Academy Award.

Page died of a heart attack. At the time of her death she was living in a brownstone on West Twenty-second Street in the Chelsea section of Manhattan.

As a believer in repertory, Page preferred interesting small roles to less well-conceived larger ones. Her selectivity sometimes led her to turn down important opportunities, though, and some critics felt her career offered her too few characters suitable to her talents. Often cast as a neurotic, the five-foot-seven-inch actress actually had a remarkable range, enjoying roles that were most unlike her personally, and finding those close to her age and personality the most difficult. She could be hilariously funny or heartrendingly tragic, believable as either a glamour queen or a dowdy frump. Offstage she was down to earth, rarely using makeup. She managed to transform her thin voice into a superbly flexible musical instrument, and to use it to invest her lines with idiosyncratic inflections and emphases that suggested unexpected meanings and feelings. This method actress's frequently eccentric readings and fluttery, compulsive gestures were considered mannered by some, but she was actually a master craftswoman who always strived to simplify her methods.

Page, elected to the Theatre Hall of Fame, became a grande dame of the American stage. Despite the unpretentious, egoless quality she projected in real life, on stage she was a larger-than-life presence who practiced her craft with the utmost seriousness and always brought imagination and joy to her multifarious roles.

★

There is no biography of Page, although her work is well documented in scattered sources. An excellent *Tulane Drama Review* interview with Richard Schechner, "The Bottomless Cup," is reprinted in Helen Krich Chinoy, ed., *Actors on Acting* (1970). For career overviews see Marjorie Dent Candee, ed., *Current Biography 1953* (1954); Gilbert Millstein, "Portrait of Miss Page, On and Off Stage," *New York Times Magazine* (29 Mar. 1959); William C. Young, *Famous Actors and Actresses on the American Stage,* vol. 2 (1975); Hilary DeVries, "Geraldine Page," *Christian Science Monitor* (25 Mar. 1986); and Vincent Canby, "Out of Marengo, Illinois, and Bound for Glory," *New York Times* (6 Apr. 1986). Obituaries are in the *New York Times* (15 June 1987) and *Variety* (17 June 1987).

SAMUEL L. LEITER

PALEY, William Samuel (*b.* 28 September 1901 in Chicago, Illinois; *d.* 26 October 1990 in New York City), business executive who in the late 1920s founded the Columbia Broadcasting System (CBS); during the six decades Paley led CBS, he wielded extraordinary influence in shaping the nature of broadcast media.

Paley's father, Samuel, who had come to the United States from Ukraine when he was nine, married a sixteen-year-old Ukrainian immigrant, Goldie Drell. With her help he built a successful cigar-making business from small beginnings in a storefront. When William was four, his sister Blanche was born. At public schools in Chicago he initially struggled, but improved academically when a grade school teacher, mistakenly thinking he had spent a recess studying, moved him from the rear where slow students were seated, to the front of the classroom, where the brighter students sat. The Paleys lived in a predominantly Jewish neighborhood of Chicago. Paley said he did not experience everyday prejudice, but recalled a terrifying episode when he was nine or ten years old: he was chased by a "Jew-hunting gang" and took refuge in a library. For his last year of high school he went to Western Military Academy in Alton, Illinois, to gain self-discipline and polish. He then attended the University of Chicago, but when the family moved to Philadelphia he transferred to the Wharton School of Finance at the University of Pennsylvania. During the summer and after his graduation in 1922, Paley worked in his father's cigar business, from sweeping floors to hiring staff, buying tobacco abroad, and supervising the construction of an eight-story plant. By 1928 the elder Paley was a multimillionaire and young William was earning $50,000 a year.

William used the fledgling medium of radio to advertise La Palina (a play on "Paley") cigars with great success. Although his father wanted him to remain in the family business, he supported William's purchase of United Independent Broadcasters, a network of struggling radio stations, for less than $500,000. Two days before his twenty-seventh birthday, in 1928, William Paley became president of UIB, which was soon renamed Columbia Broadcasting System. He then moved to New York and began adding affiliate stations. On 11 May 1932 Paley married the divorcée Dorothy Hart Hearst. They adopted two children, Jeffrey and Hilary.

Throughout the 1930s Paley brought such names as Frank Sinatra, Bing Crosby, Will Rogers, and the Paul Whiteman Orchestra to radio. But his major coups were the so-called Paley raids of the 1940s, which stole the most popular shows away from NBC by offering its stars big money and tax breaks. The roster of raided talent included Jack Benny, Red Skelton, the comedy team of George Burns and Gracie Allen, and the creators of Amos 'n' Andy, among others.

In 1930 Paley had hired Edward Klauber, a former newspaperman and adman, as his chief lieutenant. Paley agreed with Klauber's emphasis on radio news, and they fought the print media, which, fearing radio's power and immediacy, restricted stations' access to press services. Paley's policy stressed the objectivity and neutrality of broadcast journalism, in keeping with the 1929 U.S. Radio Commission's dictum for "free and fair competition of opposing views." However, conflict arose over the broadcasts of Father Charles Coughlin, a Michigan priest who voiced anti-Semitic sentiments. First, Klauber insisted on checking Coughlin's scripts before his broadcasts, then in April 1931 CBS dropped Coughlin. The priest urged his audience to complain to Paley, and 400,000 letters, mostly protests, poured in. But CBS stood firm and improvised *Church of the Air,* with clergymen of different denominations presenting their messages on a rotating basis. Coughlin raised money to continue his broadcasts on independent stations.

Controversy was also engendered by a Ford Motor Company spokesman, William J. Cameron, who espoused an anti–New Deal point of view during commercial intermissions. CBS soon removed the Ford program. Dispute again arose in 1935, when Alexander Woollcott, a distinguished critic and Paley friend, denounced Adolf Hitler's Nazi policies. In a troubled decade of ideological conflict involving fascism, communism, and democracy, the advertiser responded to listener letters protesting Woollcott's anti-Nazi comments by asking him to be more circumspect, but Woollcott refused and was dropped.

Paley adopted a policy against selling time to express a particular point of view. In a 1937 speech, he explained that selling airtime that promoted an agenda could allow a wealthy company or special interest group with deep pockets to dominate public discussion. However, the sale of time

William S. Paley. ARCHIVE PHOTOS

was allowed in election campaigns if the candidates were given equal access.

In the 1936 campaign, when President Franklin D. Roosevelt and Republican Alfred M. Landon got free time, Edward R. Murrow, then heading CBS talk programs, believed that the law required that time also be given to Communist party candidate Earl R. Browder. Paley, condemned in the sensationalist press of newspaper magnate William Randolph Hearst as a Red tool, replied that the law mandated that as a candidate Browder be heard despite his unpopular views. In the McCarthy era of the 1950s, however, CBS cooperated in blacklisting performers and writers suspected of being associated with communism. Paley knew what was being done but let CBS president Frank Stanton quietly handle the screening. Stanton later said that CBS should have been more courageous.

During World War II, with Murrow, Howard K. Smith, and William Shirer, CBS built a sterling London-based news staff. In the television era, its evening news anchor, Walter Cronkite, became one of America's most trusted figures. During the Vietnam War, CBS occasionally aired reports questioning American policy, and in retaliation, President Richard M. Nixon's aides threatened to deprive CBS of station licenses.

In a play on his name, Bill Paley was often called Pale Billy. It was an ironic reference, because his face was typically sun-bronzed and his charismatic personality was anything but colorless. A bon vivant, Paley enjoyed the nightlife of New York City, Paris, and other pleasure spots. Tall, with a winning smile, he courted beautiful women and socialized with the wits of the Algonquin Hotel Round Table. After a decade of marriage and a separation of several years, he was divorced from his first wife in 1947. On July 26 of that year he married Barbara "Babe" Cushing, the youngest of Boston's three "fabulous Cushing sisters." Beautiful and with exquisite taste, Babe headed the list of best-dressed women of the world for fourteen straight years and then was inducted into the Fashion Hall of Fame. Jet-setters, their friends included VIPs and celebrities both in the United States and Europe. The Paleys had a lively social life at their apartment on New York City's affluent Fifth Avenue, their eighty-five-acre Kiluna Farm estate on Long Island, and an estate in the Bahamas. They had two children, William and Kate. Their marriage lasted more than thirty years, until Babe died from cancer in 1978.

Although he influenced the way broadcasting covered news, Paley was more of a factor in entertainment than in journalism. In entertainment programming he had a sure sense of the public's taste. CBS's many hits included *I Love Lucy, All in the Family,* and *M*A*S*H,* as well as potboilers such as *Petticoat Junction* and *Mr. Ed.* Paley also pursued high culture. In 1935 he bought his first painting, Cézanne's *L'Estaque,* and stated that he would rather have one major piece than five mediocre works. He left one of the world's most significant private collections of twentieth-century art to New York's Museum of Modern Art (MOMA), of which he had been president and chairman. His more than eighty paintings, sculptures, and drawings included works by Picasso, Gauguin, Matisse, Renoir, and Degas.

Two edifices important to Paley are within a block of MOMA. One is the stark granite tower housing CBS headquarters, popularly known as Black Rock, designed by the famed architect Eero Saarinen. The other is the Museum of Television and Radio, which Paley founded in 1976 to house tapes and broadcasting memorabilia. Its classic building was designed by another renowned architect, Philip Johnson.

A complex individual, Paley was described by *Newsweek* as combining six personalities: Paley the Driven (as a buccaneering businessman); Paley the Careless ("disregarding new economic realities until it was too late to save his throne"); Paley the Bold (in championing broadcast news); Paley the Timorous (canceling Murrow's television documentary series *See It Now* because of the controversies it created); Paley the Charmer (in his relations with stars and attractive women); and Paley the Cruel (capable of ruthlessness in firing and cutting costs).

CBS backed Broadway musicals such as *My Fair Lady* and *Camelot,* but Paley turned down the hugely successful *Fiddler on the Roof,* a rejection that brought speculation that Paley was embarrassed by its Jewish themes. However, he maintained that he disliked the show's unhappy ending. He contributed to Jewish philanthropies while striving for acceptance in the non-Jewish social world.

Technologically, Paley made some decisions that proved costly. One was backing a system of color television that utilized a spinning disk. It had been developed by Peter Goldmark, the engineer who had invented the 33⅓-rpm long-playing record. The spinning disk was cumbersome, and its picture could not be received by the many sets already sold. By contrast, the rival RCA system was electronic and compatible with existing sets; viewers would be able to see a color program in black and white. The struggle over the two systems continued, and although the Federal Communications Commission briefly approved CBS's noncompatible system, eventually RCA's system was adopted.

Controlled understatement was part of the CBS image and reflected Paley's taste. CBS's graphics, advertising, on-air promotion, and architecture were all of a piece. Even numerals on the building's clocks conformed to the spare, dignified style of Paley's art director, William Golden, who created the network's venerable "eye" logo.

In acquiring other companies, while Paley was hungry to diversify, his commitment to quality was paramount. Acquisitions included Steinway Pianos; the publisher Holt, Rinehart, and Winston; and the New York Yankees. Unfortunately, although the Yankees had been a stellar baseball team for years, when they came under the CBS umbrella in 1964 they were about to lose several key players—and in 1966 they finished last in the American League. One CBS alumnus commented that the corporation would have been more profitable investing in troubled companies and working to turn them around.

Although CBS policy required executives to retire at sixty-five, Paley, unable to settle on a viable successor, exempted himself from the rule. In 1983 he relinquished leadership of CBS to Thomas Wyman, former chief of Pillsbury, with Paley serving as chairman of CBS's executive committee. But souring on Wyman, in 1986 Paley (who owned 9 percent of CBS stock) joined forces with Laurence Tisch (the head of Loews, who had acquired 25 percent of CBS) to oust Wyman. Paley was named acting chairman and Tisch acting chief executive, but it was Tisch who now called the tune, thus beginning a new era of "bottom line" priorities at what once was the "Tiffany network." In his late eighties, Paley's sharpness waned, although he remained in command at stockholders' meetings.

Paley died of a heart attack following a bout of pneumonia in 1990. Two thousand people attended the funeral service in New York's Temple Emanu-El. His fortune was estimated at more than $350 million. An obituary in *U.S. News and World Report* stated, "The pioneer era in the history of broadcasting dies with William Paley." The advent of cable and the impact of computers and other new technologies were ending the three major networks' dominance. But in earlier days Paley's influence was great. He had a remarkable talent for choosing talented executives and programs that would appeal to the broad public. He also had a sense of television's social responsibility and saw the need for broadcast news to be fair and balanced. And for most of his long career he flexibly adjusted policies as audience needs and media economics changed.

★

Paley's autobiography, *As It Happened* (1979), is self-justifying, although it reveals his management style and drive in overcoming obstacles. The most comprehensive biography is Sally Bedell Smith, *In All His Glory: The Life of William S. Paley* (1990). Also insightful is Lewis J. Paper, *Empire: William S. Paley and the Making of CBS* (1987). Robert Metz's gossipy *CBS: Reflections in a Bloodshot Eye* (1975) provides a critical view of Paley. Obituaries are in the *New York Times* (28 Oct. 1990), *Time,* and *Newsweek* (both 5 Nov. 1990).

BERT R. BRILLER

PALMIERI, Carlos Manuel, Jr. ("Charlie") (*b.* 21 November 1927 in New York City; *d.* 12 September 1988 in New York City), musician and bandleader who was one of the most important pianists in Latin American music and a leader in the fusion of traditional Latin styles and jazz.

During the mid-1920s Isabelle Maldonado de Palmieri and Carlos Manuel Palmieri de Villanueva, both natives of Ponce, Puerto Rico, and of Italian extraction, settled in the East Harlem area of New York City, where they opened a grocery store. Carlos, Jr., who was their first son, was born in New York's Bellevue Hospital. His precocious musical abilities were evident from an early age; at seven he was taking piano lessons with a Cuban instructor named Ramón García. In 1937 he enrolled at the New York Conservatory of Music, where his piano teachers were Ramón Zorrilla and Albert Schultz; the previous year marked the birth of his brother Eddie, who also became a trendsetting Latin pianist and bandleader.

Charlie's life as a performer began when he won numerous amateur contests held in the Spanish-language variety theaters of East Harlem. By 1941 the Palmieris were living in the Longwood section of the Bronx, an area with a tremendous concentration of Puerto Rican and Cuban musicians. Charlie made his professional debut with Osorio Selasie at the Park Plaza in 1943; while attending Sam-

Charlie Palmieri. PHOTO BY MARTIN COHEN/LP MUSIC

uel Gompers High School he performed with the bands of Bartolo Alvarez, Ramiro Medina, and Polito Galindez. After graduating from high school in 1946, Palmieri began working with Rafael Muñoz and Moncho Usera at the Tropicana, at that time the most glamorous nightclub in the Bronx. In 1948 he began a three-year engagement at the famed Copacabana in Manhattan with Fernando Alvarez, and he made his first record as a leader for the Alba label. On 2 October of the same year he married his childhood sweetheart, Esther Bartholomey; they had three children, Charlie, Nina, and Karen. During the late 1940s Palmieri maintained an active program of musical self-improvement. He further developed his piano technique and repertoire under the direction of Margaret Bonds and Claude Saavedra and studied harmony, composition, and arranging with Otto Cesana. He also attended the Juilliard School of Music in New York City for two years.

From 1951 to 1953 Palmieri performed and recorded with Tito Puente's conjunto, a percussive dance band. His expertise at sight-reading, transposition, and arranging and his organizational abilities made him an ideal bandleader for variety entertainments and for accompanying singers. He backed the famous transsexual Christine Jorgensen during her New York City theatrical debut and led the band for the Cuban singer Beny Moré during his 1958 performances at the Palladium Ballroom. After tours of South America and the United States and long-term engagements in Chicago, Palmieri organized La Orquesta Duboney in 1959. Featuring the dynamic flute playing of Johnny Pacheco, La Duboney helped create a craze in New York City for a style of Cuban dance music known as *charanga*. Palmieri maintained the flute-violin *charanga* sound for six years; by the mid-1960s he had adapted a format that included saxophones and brass instruments. His familiarity with American jazz and his facility as an improviser led to participation in a group of New York City Latino bandleaders organized by Al Santiago, owner of Alegre Records. Under Palmieri's leadership the Alegre All-Stars merged typical Latin forms with extended jazz solos; their 1960s recordings inspired countless imitators and are still highly regarded by collectors.

After a period of sparse activity in the late 1960s, Palmieri became music director of the Spanish-language television program *El Mundo de Tito Puente* in 1970, and he also began recording successful albums for Joe Cain's Tico/Alegre label. After working as a music instructor for the South Bronx Multiple Purpose Supplementary Educational Center, he was hired in 1974 as director of the Latin Ensemble and adjunct lecturer at City College of New York. Other work during this period included teaching at Brooklyn College; performing with his own orchestra at the Corso, Hippocampo, and Caborrojeño; and appearing in all-star events with his brother, Eddie.

During the 1970s Palmieri divided his time between New York City and Puerto Rico; in 1980 he moved to his ancestral homeland. Shortly after his return to New York City in 1983 he suffered a massive heart attack and stroke. In spite of his doctors' predictions that he would be unable to play again, he returned to musical performance as leader of a Latin jazz group that recorded for the Tropical Buddha label. In 1984 he became deputy director and lecturer at the East Harlem Music School; on 6 January of that year he was honored by New York City's Latin music industry at Club Broadway. In September 1988 Palmieri suffered another heart attack while flying from Puerto Rico to New York City. He died at Jacobi Hospital in the Bronx, and he was buried in Saint Raymond's Cemetery, also in the Bronx.

Charlie Palmieri's spirit of adventure and musical gifts put him on the cutting edge of Latin music for forty years; he is best known for helping popularize *charanga* and for his Latin jazz achievements, particularly with the Alegre All-Stars. Known as *el gigante de las blancas y las negras* (the giant of the keyboard), he is remembered not only for his talent but also for his warm and giving personality. This combination of qualities made him an ideal teacher and role model for developing musicians and a revered figure in the New York Latin music world.

★

Palmieri's curriculum vitae is located in the archives of the City College of New York Department of Music, New York City.

See also César Miguel Rondón, *El libro de la salsa: Cronico de la música del Caribe urbano* (1980); Max Salazar, "Charlie Palmieri: A Giant in Many Ways," *Latin Times* (Oct. 1976): 22–25; and Fernando Campos, "Habla Charlie," *Canales* (Nov. 1978): 21–22. Obituaries are in the *New York Times* (13 Sept. 1988) and *Canales* (15 Oct. 1988). A transcript of an interview of Palmieri conducted in June 1974 by René Lopez and Jorge Pérez is in the Centro de Estudios Puertorriqueños at Hunter College, New York City.

DAVID M. CARP

PARKS, Henry Green, Jr. (*b.* 29 September 1916 in Atlanta, Georgia; *d.* 24 April 1989 in Towson, Maryland), food company executive who created Parks Sausages.

Parks was the son of Henry Green Parks and Gainelle Williams. His family moved to Dayton, Ohio, where Parks's father worked as a wine steward and his mother worked as a part-time domestic. He attended Dayton public schools and in 1935 went to the College of Commerce of Ohio State University, where he roomed for a time with the Olympic sprinter Jesse Owens. Parks was an outstanding student, earning academic honors, and was the first African American on the school's swim team and the only one in his marketing classes. Despite his achievements, Parks was told he should pursue a career in South America where, regardless of his race, he "would have a real chance."

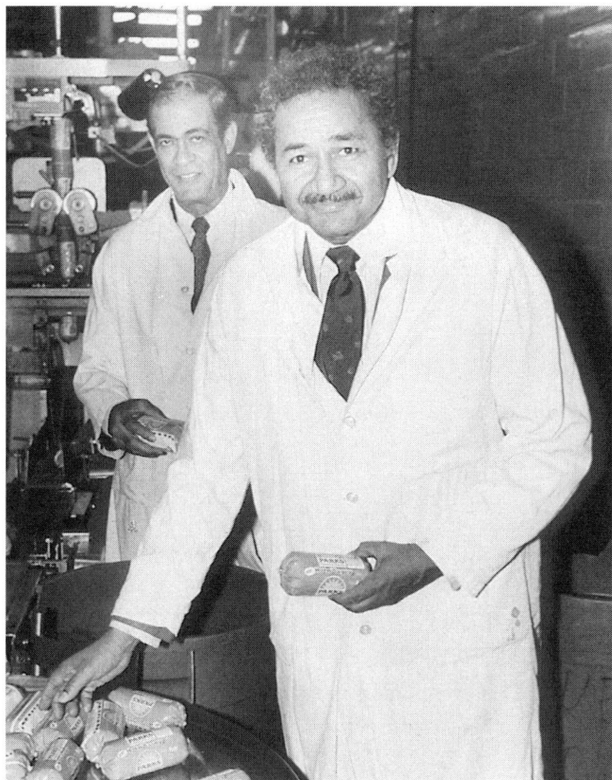

Parks Sausages Company founder Henry G. Parks, Jr. (*left*), stands behind its president, Raymond V. Haysbert, Sr., 1981. MARTY KATZ/NEW YORK TIMES/ARCHIVE PHOTOS

After completing his degree in 1939, Parks went to work in sales for Pabst Brewing Company and soon became the national representative for developing the ethnic market. He trained his own corps of salesmen and was among the company's sales leaders. His techniques included pitching Pabst beer to chauffeurs and domestics in the parking lot of a leading Beverly Hills, California, store. Parks left Pabst in 1942 to become a partner in W. B. Graham and Associates, a New York City public relations firm. Parks, however, soon settled in Baltimore, Maryland. While continuing to work with Graham, he tried selling a variety of goods, from real estate to cinder blocks. One such effort, marketing Joe Louis Punch, ended in failure.

In 1949 Parks left Graham and bought a part interest in Crayton's Southern Sausage Company in Cleveland, Ohio. Parks thought he saw a major opportunity with the company, believing there was a large potential market for foods inspired by southern tastes, especially a spicy sausage. After attempting to sell the idea of producing a spicy sausage to several major companies without success, he decided to do it himself. He sold his interest in Crayton's, mortgaged his home, and borrowed against his life insurance to raise the $60,000 with which he founded Parks Sausages Company in Baltimore in 1951. He began with just two helpers, using an abandoned dairy in a Baltimore ghetto as his factory.

Parks faced an uphill struggle. Most white-owned stores simply refused to carry his product; in those that did, the managers often put his sausages on an unrefrigerated shelf, where they quickly spoiled. When he hired white women to work on his production line, their husbands typically forced them to quit when they learned the owner was African American. Because of racial barriers, he had to train his own managers. Initially, Parks found he could sell his sausage only through six inner-city stores in Baltimore. To ensure quality and freshness, he would take orders one day, delivering just-made sausage the next. To build demand, he marketed aggressively, using a salesman to play "Parky the Pig," who marched down streets giving away samples and sending saleswomen into beauty parlors and salesmen into barbershops and shoeshine stands with more samples. Soon people were asking for Parks Sausages. Parks knew that African Americans, not trusting the stores in their own neighborhoods, frequently shopped in predominantly white areas. Their increasing demand soon persuaded these stores to carry his product; white customers then started buying Parks Sausages as well. In 1952 Parks got a Washington, D.C., supermarket chain to stock his product. By 1960 he had signed up every major chain from Virginia to Massachusetts and eventually was selling his sausages in 12,000 stores.

Aware of the need to deliver a product of consistent, assured high quality, Parks was among the first to put production dates on his products. His representatives then pulled all expired goods from the shelves so that customers always got fresh sausage. Parks also insisted on federal meat inspection, when regulations only required state inspection, to persuade consumers of the superior quality of Parks Sausages. To these approaches, Parks added his well-known radio advertising campaign, in which an obstreperous boy bleats "More Parks Sausages, Mom." It was so successful that Pulse, Inc., awarded the company a prize for the ad's high rating. Some consumers thought the boy uncivil, and, after several complaints, Parks in 1966 had a no less insistent boy add "please" to his refrain. These techniques paid off handsomely, as Parks Sausages built a large demand among both black and white consumers, even while commanding premium prices, often 10 percent above those of competitors.

By the early 1960s, with a broad customer base, rapidly growing sales, and a broadened line of products, Parks was able to secure conventional financing from an insurer and a bank to build a new headquarters and plant, where his company moved in 1964. Overall, sales during the 1960s nearly tripled, reaching about $10 million. In 1969 Parks Sausages went public, the first African-American-owned business to do so, selling two hundred thousand shares at $8 per share. By 1977, when Norin Corporation of Miami bought Parks Sausages from Parks and longtime co-owner and silent partner William L. Adams for $5 million, the company employed a staff of 300 and had sales of more than $14 million, with a fleet of fifty refrigerated trucks and distribution centers in Philadelphia; Somerset, New Jersey; New York City; and West Haven, Connecticut. Parks remained chairman of the board until 1980 and sold his last financial interests in the company in 1984. (Norin was later acquired by Canadian Pacific Railroad, which promptly sold Parks Sausages back to its management in 1981. It went bankrupt in the 1990s; Franco Harris, Pittsburgh Steelers football veteran, revived the firm, bringing it out of bankruptcy in 1996.)

Parks's only other major business activity was as an investor in Leonard Evans's *Tuesday* magazine, which was distributed by fourteen major metropolitan newspapers. Parks also served on numerous corporate boards, including those of Magnavox, W. R. Grace, Warner Lambert, and the First Pennsylvania Corporation. He also sat on the board of the Opportunities Industrial Center, Inc., and the National Interracial Council for Business Opportunity. He ran for city council in 1963, serving two terms until 1969. While in office, he pressed for open housing laws and reduced bail requirements for those accused of crimes. He also served as treasurer for the Maryland Democratic State Central Committee, as president of the Baltimore City Board of Fire Commissioners, and as a trustee of Goucher College in Baltimore. The United Negro College Fund recognized Parks in 1972 for outstanding leadership, and in 1975 Temple University awarded him an honorary degree.

Parks died of complications from Parkinson's disease in a Towson, Maryland, nursing home, the same day his company broke ground for a new $13 million plant in northwest Baltimore. He was survived by two daughters.

★

Articles on Parks and his company appeared in *Business Week* (18 May 1968) and *Black Enterprise* (June 1979). Obituaries are in the *Washington Post* (25 Apr. 1989) and *New York Times* (26 Apr. 1989).

FRED CARSTENSEN

PASSMAN, Otto Ernest (*b.* 27 June 1900 in Franklinton, Louisiana; *d.* 13 August 1988 in Monroe, Louisiana), businessman and congressman best known for his staunch opposition to American foreign aid.

Passman was one of the four children of Edward A. and Phereby (Carrier) Passman, both sharecroppers. He dropped out of school in the fourth grade and left home at

Otto Passman, 1946. UPI/CORBIS-BETTMANN

the age of thirteen. After working as a grocery store errand boy and doing odd jobs, he graduated from Baton Rouge High School by attending night classes and then Commercial Business College in Bogalusa. This was the extent of his formal education; the rest of his knowledge was acquired through practical experience.

Passman's first business venture was operating a grocery store, but the experience left him dissatisfied. Following a brief stint with a Kentucky corporation, he opened Passman Wholesale Equipment Company, a restaurant supply firm in Monroe, Louisiana, on 1 January 1930. His shrewd business sense, including an uncanny ability to cut overhead costs, enabled him to become very successful. In 1931 he married Willie Lenore Bateman; they had no children.

On 11 October 1942 Passman joined the U.S. Navy as a lieutenant and served as a procurement and matériel officer at a Florida air base. It was his military experience with the government bureaucracy that prompted his desire to decrease government expenditures and led him to run for office. After his discharge on 5 September 1944, with the rank of lieutenant commander, Passman returned to Monroe. He entered the 1946 Democratic primary and defeated Congressman Charles McKenzie, the incumbent in the Fifth District. The margin of victory was 455 votes, but his win almost assured his election to the House of Representatives through the state Democratic machine. He represented the district for thirty years.

Passman's greatest impact on policy, especially after 1955, when he succeeded to the chair of the Subcommittee on Foreign Operations of the Appropriations Committee, was on foreign aid. Something of a protégé of Congressman Clarence Cannon, who was the chair of the committee, Passman was an effective, if somewhat eccentric, chairman. A master of detail, he could be arbitrary in his conduct. He would call meetings at odd hours and cancel them without warning, was biased in favor of cutting aid, and was rude to political opponents. Although forceful, he often lost sight of the reasons behind aid policy, and his uncompromising style became known to many in Washington as the "Passman treatment."

Often successful in his battles with aid supporters, Passman trimmed approximately $17 billion from various presidential budgets, an achievement that attracted national media attention. In 1964 he suffered a political defeat when two Texans, President Lyndon B. Johnson and the new Appropriations Committee chairman, George Mahon, forced him to accept only a small percentage cut in aid. Following this setback, other congressmen led the crusade against foreign aid as the political conflict over the Vietnam War intensified. During the presidency of his friend Richard Nixon, however, Passman supported the president's requests for military aid because he was a strong backer of the military and an ardent foe of communism.

On the issue of racial equality Passman was a typical southern Democrat of the era. He opposed the civil rights initiatives of Presidents John F. Kennedy and Lyndon B. Johnson, as did the majority of whites within his district. He showed sympathy, however, when violence occurred, especially after the assassination of President Kennedy. His opposition was only in the realm of politics, and he urged others to not disrupt the peace. Only after considerable numbers of African Americans were enfranchised did he change his rhetoric from segregation and white supremacy to boasting about his contributions to the minority community.

Although probably more famous for his extensive wardrobe than for his legislative record, Passman made a considerable contribution to his district. He helped acquire almost $500 million for flood-control development and $140 million in loans to farmers. The construction of many federal buildings and of Interstate 20 through his district were at least partially a result of his influence.

Passman was also active outside Congress. He operated several businesses, including the Passman Manufacturing, Passman Equipment, Delta Furniture, and Commercial Equipment companies. By 1976, however, he owned only Passman Investment. He had been grand master of the Masons of Louisiana in 1945 and remained active in the organization throughout his life, achieving the rank of thirty-third degree Freemason in the Scottish Rite. He was also involved in charitable organizations dealing primarily with leprosy.

In the 1970s Passman's career began to decline, possibly because of his support for Nixon during the Watergate scandal. In 1974 he became involved in a sexual discrimination suit when a former employee, Shirley Davis, accused him of firing her because he felt the heavy workload of her position required a man. *Davis* v. *Passman* finally ended in 1979 when the Supreme Court overturned earlier decisions that denied Davis's right to bring suit. The two then settled out of court for an undisclosed sum. This problem was later dwarfed by other political events. In 1976, although most people felt Passman's thirty-year tenure made him unbeatable, Jerry Huckaby, an electrical engineer-turned-dairy farmer, pulled off an election upset. Passman's age, his vote against a 1971 school prayer amendment, his alleged abuse of travel vouchers, and his numerous foreign trips helped the thirty-five-year-old Huckaby defeat him.

Passman's involvement in the foreign influence scandal Koreagate posed the most serious legal threat of his life. In 1978 he faced federal charges of conspiracy, bribery, and tax evasion that were handed down by a Washington grand jury. He first asked that no trial be held, because of his advanced age and failing health, but the request was denied. He was successful, however, in having all the charges consolidated into one case tried in Monroe. Following a four-week trial the hometown jury acquitted him on 1 April 1979, after only ninety minutes of deliberation.

Passman's wife died in 1984, and the following year he married his longtime secretary, Martha Williams. He continued living in Monroe until his death from a heart attack three years later. He is buried in Mulhearn Memorial Park in Monroe.

★

Passman's papers are in Sandel Library at Northeast Louisiana University in Monroe. No full-length biography is available, but two theses—Randolph Sutton Jones, "Otto E. Passman and Foreign Aid" (1982); and Ellen Jeffrey Blue, "Congressman Otto E. Passman's Role in the 1952 Louisiana Gubernatorial Election" (1989)—contain helpful biographical information. A good summary of his early career can be found in Drew Pearson and Jack Anderson, *The Case Against Congress: A Compelling Indictment of Corruption on Capitol Hill* (1968). See also Sara Glazer, ed., *Citizens Look At Congress* (1972), Vol. 4 of the Ralph Nader Congress Project series; Glazer's volume covers Kentucky, Louisiana, Maine, Maryland, Michigan, and Minnesota. His chairmanship is treated in Rowland Evans, "Louisiana's Passman: The Scourge of Foreign Aid," *Harper's* (Jan. 1962); and Murray Kempton, "The Vanities of Otto Passman," *New Republic* (Dec. 1963). Information on his legal troubles and trial—biased against Passman—is in Robert B. Boettcher, *Gifts of Deceit: Sun Myung Moon, Tongsun Park, and the Korean Scandal* (1980). An obituary is in the *New York Times* (14 Aug. 1988).

WILLIAM TODD ALLBRITTON

PEDERSEN, Charles John (*b.* 3 October 1904 in Pusan, Korea; *d.* 26 October 1989 in Salem, New Jersey), chemist who shared the 1987 Nobel Prize in chemistry with Donald Cram and Jean-Marie Lehn for the development and use of molecules with structure-specific interactions of high selectivity.

Pedersen was the son of Brede Pedersen, a Norwegian seaman who became a mechanical engineer for an American-owned gold mine in Korea, and Takino Yasui, a Japanese silkworm trader who immigrated to Korea. He had one sister. At the age of eight he entered a Roman Catholic school in Nagasaki, Japan, and two years later, a French–American school in Yokohama run by the Marianist order of priests and brothers. Teachers at the latter institution persuaded him to go to the United States to complete his education.

Pedersen came to the United States in 1922 to study chemical engineering at the University of Dayton (Ohio), where he received a bachelor's degree in 1926. He continued his studies at the Massachusetts Institute of Technology, where he received a master's degree in organic chemistry in 1927. Urged by his professors and friends to pursue

Charles Pedersen after learning he was a cowinner of the Nobel Prize in chemistry, 14 October 1987. UPI/CORBIS-BETTMANN

a doctorate, he declined, saying that he was tired of sending bills to his father and that it was time for him to start working.

In 1927 Pedersen began his career with DuPont, at the Chambers Works' Jackson Laboratory in Deepwater, New Jersey, as a researcher. In 1946 he was promoted to research associate in the elastomer chemicals department, a post he held until his retirement in 1969. He then worked for a few months at the Agricultural Research Council's Unit of Structural Chemistry in London, until his final retirement later that year.

Pedersen's work at DuPont resulted in the publication of twenty-five technical papers and the award of sixty-five patents, mainly in petrochemical research. His patents made millions of dollars for DuPont, which was one of the main reasons for his promotion to research associate, the company's highest research position. This enabled Pedersen to choose his area of research without concern for the company's financial gain.

Pedersen married Susan J. Ault in 1947; they had two daughters. He became a naturalized U.S. citizen in 1953.

One of Pedersen's earliest accomplishments, and the one with the most commercial impact, was a dramatically improved process for making tetraethyl lead, an important gasoline additive. During the 1930s he discovered the first deactivators to counter the degradative effects of heavy metals in gasoline, oils, and rubbers, and in the space of ten years was the recipient or co-recipient of thirty patents for antioxidants and other products.

In 1961 Pedersen embarked on a systematic study of complexes of the vanadyl ion with multidentate phenolic ethers to be used as polymerization catalysts and for deactivating residual pro-oxidant vanadium in the polymers. His curiosity was sparked by a clump of crystals he found at the bottom of a beaker in a failed experiment to produce one of these vanadium-based catalysts. The clump of crystals was a small polymer with very special properties. They were determined to be macrocyclic crown polyethers or, as Pedersen called them, crown ethers. These compounds have a characteristic three-dimensional structure consisting of pairs of carbon and hydrogen atoms arranged in a ring formation, with an elevated oxygen atom between each pair, giving the molecule the shape of a crown.

Pedersen's further work allowed him to produce crown ethers containing different numbers of atoms. He found that these compounds could form complexes with a range of salts by trapping the molecules within their crown structure; this enabled them to be taken into organic solvents, in which they would normally not be soluble. In this way crown ethers mimic, in a relatively uncomplicated way, the very complicated functions of biological materials such as enzymes, and herein lay the significance of their discovery and study.

Pedersen published his work on crown ethers as a single paper in the *Journal of the American Chemical Society* under the title "Macrocyclic Polyethers for Complexing Metals" (1967). He wrote follow-up papers until his retirement in 1969.

Most of Pedersen's research was single-handed. After his retirement he enjoyed gardening, fishing, bird-watching, and writing poetry. He died at home from blood cancer and Parkinson's disease. He is buried in Salem, New Jersey.

The great significance of Pedersen's work is that it shed light on the influence of both the shape and the size of molecules on their reactivities. It became evident that a match was needed between the size of the hole in the center of the crown ether and the salt that was to be trapped. The same principle could be applied to otherwise unrelated molecules. This led to applications in many areas, such as biochemistry (to explain enzyme specificity), pharmacology (for the design of drugs with specific action), and biophysics (to explain the transport of ions through membranes). Other chemists began building on his discovery, and this new research snowballed. Among the scientists continuing this research were Donald Cram and Jean-Marie Lehn, who pioneered the field that exploits the idea that the three-dimensional shapes of molecules are vital to their chemical and biological functions. For this work Cram and Lehn shared the Nobel Prize in chemistry with Pedersen in 1987. Pedersen was the first career DuPont scientist to win a Nobel Prize.

★

Pedersen's most significant paper is the one summarizing his work on crown ethers: "Macrocyclic Polyethers for Complexing Metals," *Journal of the American Chemical Society* 89 (1967). Additional information on Pedersen can be found in Emily J. McMurray, ed., *Notable Twentieth-Century Scientists* (1995). An obituary is in the *New York Times* (27 Oct. 1989).

MARIA PACHECO

PENDLETON, Clarence Mclane, Jr. (*b.* 10 November 1930 in Louisville, Kentucky; *d.* 5 June 1988 in San Diego, California), politician, best known as the African-American conservative appointed chairman of the United States Commission on Civil Rights.

Pendleton was the only child of Clarence Pendleton, Sr., a swimming coach, and Edna Marie (Ramsaur) Pendleton. Soon after his birth Clarence and his family migrated to Washington, D.C. There they lived in the segregated middle-class neighborhood of Deanwood, and Pendleton attended city schools, graduating from Dunbar High School. Raised in an educationally progressive home, he had as role models a father who became the first swimming coach of the historically black Howard University, the assistant director of the District of Columbia's recreation center, and a lifeguard at the Banneker Recreation Center; a paternal grandfather who was one of the early law school graduates of Howard University; a maternal grandfather who was a graduate of St. Augustine College; and an uncle who was the rector at St. Luke's Episcopal Church, where Pendleton served for many years as an altar boy.

Howard University was an important part of the Pendleton tradition and Clarence, Jr., received his B.S. degree there in 1954. Later that year his graduate studies were interrupted when he began a tour of duty in the U.S. Army, serving as a specialist third class in a medical unit in Fort Monmouth, New Jersey. Upon receiving an honorable discharge in 1957, Pendleton returned to Howard, completing his master's degree in education in 1961. In the mid-1960s, following in his father's path, Pendleton also became a notable swimming coach at Howard, leading his team to ten championships within eleven years. He was also active at Howard as head coach of the baseball, rowing, and football teams. During this period he married, had two children, and divorced. In 1968 he left his post at Howard University for a better-paying position in Baltimore, Maryland. In 1970 he married Margrit Krause, with whom he had one child. Once again a Washington resident, he worked as

Clarence Pendleton, 1983. UPI/CORBIS-BETTMANN

director of the urban affairs department of the National Parks and Recreation Association.

In 1972 Mayor Pete Wilson of San Diego, a prominent and influential Republican, offered Pendleton the opportunity to direct the Model Cities program, and Pendleton moved to the West Coast to run the inner-city revitalization program. Pendleton's career took a radical turn when, guided by Pete Wilson and President Ronald Reagan's confidant Edwin Meese III, he abandoned his self-described "bleeding-heart" liberal views for a more conservative tenet and became a Republican. His advancement to the position of president of the Urban League of San Diego in 1975 was just the start of the conservative influence on his career. In 1981 Reagan fired the chairman of the U.S. Commission on Civil Rights, Arthur S. Flemming, a lifelong Republican who had strongly defended civil rights initiatives, and appointed Pendleton in his place. It was clear to many that Pendleton was to be a spokesperson for the Reagan administration's anti–civil rights policies.

As chair, Pendleton denounced issues long fought for by feminists and black leaders—affirmative action, comparable worth, hiring quotas, and school busing to end segregation. Affirmative action, he said, was a "bankrupt policy" that detracted from legitimate achievement, while hiring quotas could lead young minority group members to think they did not need to prepare themselves properly for the world of work. Busing, he held, violated the principle of neighborhood schools—and who was to say that predominantly white schools were actually better than predominantly black ones. Reflecting on his effectiveness as chair, the syndicated columnist Carl Rowan wrote that Pendleton had turned the agency into one of the most anti–civil rights units in the federal government. In fact, Pendleton established the Uncivil Rights Award for "absurdities that pass under the umbrella of civil rights." On the television program *Face the Nation* in November 1985, Pendleton, as spokesman for the U.S. Civil Rights Commission, stated that it was "going to be clear that there's going to be an order signed where there won't be any preferential treatment and where statistical imbalance in the workforce will not trigger a finding of discrimination." At a time when many black Americans struggled to defeat the dogma that the United States was and should remain a color-blind society, Pendleton diligently worked to support that idea. Outspoken to a fault, he pronounced that the best way to help poor people was "not to be one" and publicly stated that "comparable worth" was "probably the looniest idea since Looney Tunes came on the screen." A leading feminist magazine labeled him "one of the fifteen dumbest men in America."

On the issue of minority set-aside programs, which channeled governmental contracts to minority-owned businesses, Pendleton was publicly left out on a limb when he announced his intention to dismantle the programs and the White House repudiated his statement. Outraged and disillusioned by Pendleton's announcement, twenty-eight black Republicans called for his resignation as chairman of the Civil Rights Commission. Pendleton called upon the administration to "stop speaking in a double voice." In 1985, before a student audience at Cornell University, he said that abolishment of the commission when it was up for congressional reauthorization in 1989 was "not a bad idea."

Political controversy was not the only problem of Pendleton's administration. After a governmental audit covering the period from October 1982 to January 1986, the General Accounting Office, in a report to Congress in March 1986, found irregularities in hiring, travel, and record-keeping and a failure to account for $175,000 in the budget. Also in 1986, Pendleton billed the government for $70,000 in salary for what had traditionally been a part-time position. That year, Congress cut the commission's budget from $11.6 million to $7.5 million. There were even recommendations for the dismantling of the civil rights agency, and Pendleton eventually resigned.

While riding a stationary bicycle in a health club in San Diego, Pendleton died of an apparent heart attack. In 1989 his widow established the Clarence M. Pendleton, Jr., Scholarship for aspiring students.

Pendleton was once called "the most openly hated man in Washington." In choosing conservatism, he may have assumed that he could champion anti–civil rights doctrine without repercussions from other African Americans. On the firing line for the White House, however, he took many hits because the Civil Rights Commission was regarded by many as not just a governmental agency, but as the bedrock of accomplishments for millions of underclass people. Summarizing Pendleton's role as chair of the commission, Benjamin L. Hooks, executive director of the NAACP, wrote, "Too many decent Americans of every race and gender have fought and sacrificed too much to permit such a shameful retreat. The struggle before us . . . is for America's soul."

★

Biographical information about Pendleton is in *Current Biography* (1984). An obituary is in the *New York Times* (6 June 1988).

GLORIA GRANT ROBERSON

PEPPER, Claude Denson (*b.* 8 September 1900 near Dudleyville, Alabama; *d.* 30 May 1989 in Bethesda, Maryland), lawyer and U.S. senator and congressman.

Claude Pepper congratulates Rita Simon, mother of Senator Paul Simon, on her son's election victory, 1984. LAWRENCE AGRON/ARCHIVE PHOTOS

The oldest of four children of Joseph Wheeler Pepper and the former Lena Talbot, Pepper was born on a farm in the east Alabama hill country. The family's home did not have electricity or indoor plumbing, and Pepper did not see a paved road until he was seventeen, when, after graduation from high school, he taught public school for a year in Dothan, Alabama.

Pepper worked his way through the University of Alabama, graduating with an A.B. degree in 1921 as a member of Phi Beta Kappa. While serving in the army at the end of World War I, he developed a hernia. This disability entitled him to government-subsidized vocational training, and Pepper used the money to attend Harvard Law School, from which he graduated in 1924 in the top third of his class. He later wrote that "Harvard taught me the difference between a broad and narrow mind; it freed me from many prejudices." After teaching for a year at the fledgling University of Arkansas Law School, Pepper moved to the north Florida town of Perry to practice law, representing the father of a former student.

In Florida, Pepper also set about fulfilling his childhood goal of becoming a U.S. senator and, ultimately, president. He won a seat in the Florida house in 1928, only to be defeated in 1930 after having voted against a resolution criticizing the wife of President Herbert Hoover for inviting the wife of a black congressman to the White House for tea. Pepper ran for the Senate in the 1934 Democratic primary and forced the incumbent, Park Trammell, into a runoff. There was evidence that the Democratic machine stole the election. Pepper, however, chose not to demand a recount, and his good sportsmanship increased his popularity. He gained prominent attention as a fiery stump speaker, using an amplified sound truck, and as a champion of the common man. Then, in 1936, both Florida senators died within five weeks of each other. Two of the state's leading politicians quickly declared their candidacies for the first vacancy. Pepper filed for election for the other. He was not challenged and won by default.

Pepper was a New Deal stalwart in the Senate from the start. His first bill, in 1937, was to extend federal assistance to handicapped children. Later that year, he sponsored the law that created the National Cancer Institute, the forerunner of other institutes of health. Pepper introduced the first bill calling for what became, in the 1960s, the National Endowment for the Arts and the National Endowment for the Humanities. "We haven't gone far enough," he told his colleagues, chastising them for their faltering support of the Democratic platform and reciting to them the biblical story of the Israelites. "This is not the Promised Land. Are we going to commit the same folly that the children of Israel did?" Pepper was active in the passage of the federal minimum wage law in 1938, which gained him the lasting enmity of many businessmen. "The South, which I love, must grow," he wrote when the bill was before the Senate.

As a southern liberal, Pepper was forced to balance his convictions against political realities. He found it painful to recall that he spoke against a proposed antilynching bill during his first year in the Senate. Pepper's support of civil rights wavered during his close reelection victories in 1938 and 1944. He survived a runoff during the 1944 primary only after pledging to do whatever was necessary to keep blacks from voting.

Pepper advocated early military preparation to oppose Nazi Germany. In 1938, after hearing Adolf Hitler speak to a crowd in Nuremberg and seeing Nazi storm troopers march in darkness past his hotel balcony in Berlin, he warned President Franklin Roosevelt that the rise of Nazism would lead to war. In 1940 Pepper drafted and sponsored the lend-lease bill, providing supplies to Great Britain; Congress passed it the next year. His interest in international affairs increased when World War II ended, and he began to lean left on foreign policy matters. "Pray for Joe Stalin," Pepper urged Americans in 1945 after meeting Stalin in Moscow, citing the Soviet leader as "a man Americans can trust." Pepper thought that the Marshall Plan to rebuild Europe should have included the Soviet Union.

In 1944 Pepper spearheaded the losing effort to keep Vice President Henry Wallace on the national Democratic ticket. He was deeply involved in the movement of Democrats to draft Dwight Eisenhower to run for president instead of Harry Truman in 1948. When the effort failed, Pepper threw "two hats in the ring—both his own," noted the *New York Herald-Tribune*. His candidacy lasted little more than one day. Truman, who in 1940 had referred to Pepper as an "A-1 demagogue," now called him a "crackpot." In 1949, according to George Smathers, then a young, two-term Florida congressman, Truman told him, "I want you to beat that son of a bitch Claude Pepper."

Smathers ran against Pepper in the 1950 Democratic primary in what became known as one of the dirtiest campaigns in American history. *Time* reported that Smathers had told rural audiences that Pepper was a "shameless extrovert" who "practiced nepotism with his sister-in-law"; that his sister had been a "thespian" in New York; that he "vacillated one night on the Senate floor"; and that, "worst of all, he had practiced celibacy before his marriage." Smathers also emphasized race and anticommunism as McCarthyism was reaching its heights. He linked Pepper with proposals to create a Fair Employment Practices Committee. The Smathers campaign paid blacks to shake Pepper's hand, with cameras flashing, at public functions. The pictures were circulated and inflamed racist sentiment. "If they can't make a black out of me, they want to make me a Red," Pepper said. "He likes Joe [Stalin] and Joe likes him," Smathers further charged. Pepper did not help his cause when at campaign appearances he turned up his coat collar, sidled across the stage and whispered, "Joe? This is Claude. Got some secrets for ya." Smathers defeated him soundly, by a margin of 67,000 votes.

Pepper moved to Miami and opened a law practice. He was financially successful but in political exile, "like an athlete benched when he's at the top of his game," he wrote in the diary he faithfully kept. In 1958 he lost by a wide margin to Senator Spessard Holland in the Democratic primary. But a new congressional seat anchored in Miami Beach was created after the 1960 census, and in 1962 Pepper was handily elected to it. Thereafter, he routinely received two-thirds of the vote.

In the House, Pepper focused on social welfare issues and dealt with foreign policy issues only when politically necessary. As Cuban exiles streamed into his district, he attacked Cuban leader Fidel Castro whenever possible. Pepper introduced a resolution in 1971 declaring that the United States should withhold diplomatic recognition of Cuba as long as the Castro regime remained in power. In the 1980s he led the fight to arm the Nicaraguan contras.

As the first chairman of the House Select Committee on Aging from 1977 to 1983, Pepper drew much attention to the needs of elderly Americans. He was the prime mover behind the 1986 bill that outlawed mandatory retirement ages for most federal employees and raised the age for retirement in private industry from sixty-five to seventy. In 1983 he became chairman of the House Rules Committee, which controls the flow of legislation and sets rules for debate. Pepper played a major role that year in shaping legislation aimed at restoring the Social Security system's solvency, fighting against all cuts in benefits and yielding only when necessary to keep the measure alive. He became an institution within the institution and turned into a sort of national grandfather.

"I rather reproach myself that I didn't become a preacher," Pepper once wrote in his diary. But he had become a political preacher. In 1988 Pepper spoke on behalf of his bill providing for long-term home care of the chronically ill, regardless of age. Tears filled his eyes as he asked fellow members to think, when they went home at night, of what they had done to lighten the burden of the aged and sick. At least, if they approved his bill, he said, "it will give comfort, it will cool the brow of those who suffer, if we offer a little care." The House, as it hardly ever does, gave Pepper a standing ovation.

Pepper rarely saw a camera or microphone he did not manage to get in front of. His flowery oratory, sometimes with a little Ovid or other poetry casually tossed in, his courtliness, and his homely face with its red, bulbous nose became familiar to millions who ignored his two hearing aids and thick, trifocal glasses. To his party he was an institutional memory and a potent campaigner. Pepper often traveled alone, carrying his own bags and wearing his three-piece pin-striped suits, an inspiration to senior as well as younger citizens.

Pepper had married Mildred Irene Webster in 1936; they had no children, to his deep regret. She worked in his office, and her ambitiousness for both of them helped to drive him; after her death in 1979, he immersed himself even more deeply in his work. In the 1940s they spent many happy hours socializing with Supreme Court justice Hugo Black, Alabama senator Lister Hill, Washington lawyer and former White House aide Thomas Corcoran, and their wives. "Claude is very lovely with a large heavy face badly pocked by acne, black hair and has a stocky figure thickly set," Josephine Black observed. "He has a certain gentleness and sweetness entirely lacking in Mrs. Pepper. He has a splendid mind, great energy and is definitely interested in the underdog at present."

After Pepper died of cancer at Walter Reed Army Hospital, Congress voted to have his body lie in state in the Capitol Rotunda, only the twenty-seventh American to be so honored. One month earlier, President George Bush had presented him with the Medal of Freedom, inscribed with the words: "The champion of the most vulnerable among us."

★

Pepper's extensive papers, including diaries, which he started and kept at his wife's insistence, are at the Mildred and Claude Pepper Library at Florida State University. Pepper's two books, *Ask Claude Pepper* (1984) and, with Hays Gorey, *Pepper: Eyewitness to a Century* (1987), provide valuable biographical detail. See also Francis P. Locke, "Claude D. Pepper: Champion of the Belligerent Democracy," in J. T. Salter, ed., *Public Men In and Out of Office* (1946); Kenneth Stewart, "Serious Senator Pepper," *PM* (1 June 1947); Ric A. Kabat, "From New Deal to Red Scare: The Political Odyssey of Senator Claude D. Pepper" (Ph.D. diss., Florida State University, 1995); Ric A. Kabat, "From Camp Hill to Harvard Yard: The Early Years of Claude D. Pepper," *Florida Historical Quarterly* 72 (Oct. 1993): 153–179; Alexander Stoesen, "The Senatorial Career of Claude D. Pepper" (Ph.D. diss., University of North Carolina, 1965); and Cal J. Halamandaris, "Claude D. Pepper," in *Profiles in Caring: Advocates for the Elderly* (1990). See also Thomas G. Paterson, "The Dissent of Senator Claude Pepper," in Thomas G. Paterson, ed., *Cold War Critics: Alternatives to American Foreign Policy in the Truman Years* (1971). Truman comments on Pepper in Robert H. Ferrell, ed., *Dear Bess: The Letters from Harry to Bess Truman, 1910–1959* (1983). Obituaries are in the *New York Times*, *Washington Post*, *Miami Herald*, and *Fort Lauderdale Sun-Sentinel* (all 31 May 1989). George A. Smathers's oral history interviews with Pepper are in the U.S. Senate Historical Office (1989).

ROGER K. NEWMAN

PERCY, Walker (*b.* 28 May 1916 in Birmingham, Alabama; *d.* 10 May 1990 in Covington, Louisiana), writer whose highly acclaimed novels, such as *The Moviegoer* (1961), describe from a Christian and moral viewpoint the anxiety, alienation, and despair of contemporary man.

Walker Percy was the eldest of three sons of Leroy Pratt Percy, a lawyer, and Martha Phinizy Percy. When Percy was thirteen, his father committed suicide, and the family resided for a while with his maternal grandmother in Athens, Georgia. In 1931 they moved to Greenville, Mississippi, where they lived with Leroy Percy's cousin William Percy. The next year Walker's mother died in an automobile accident, and Walker and his brothers were adopted by their "uncle Will." William Percy was a writer, and his Greenville home was a meeting place for other writers. It was in this atmosphere that young Percy passed through his teens, attending Greenville High School, where he wrote a gossip column for the school paper. After graduating in 1934, he attended the University of North Carolina at Chapel Hill, and received a B.A. degree in chemistry in 1937. In college he looked to science as a discipline that could give meaning to the world.

In deference to his uncle, Percy entered the Columbia

Walker Percy. OSCAR WHITE/CORBIS

University College of Physicians and Surgeons in the fall of 1937 to study medicine; he received his medical degree four years later. While in medical school Percy showed an interest in psychiatry, and he went through three years of Freudian analysis. He began an internship in pathology at Bellevue Hospital in New York City, but contracted tuberculosis in 1942 as a result of not taking proper precautions while working on corpses. He entered the Trudeau Sanatorium in the Adirondack Mountains in upstate New York, where he spent much of his time reading. After his release Percy returned to Columbia University to teach pathology, but the tuberculosis recurred and he entered a Connecticut sanatorium. During almost three years of enforced rest, he became acquainted with Catholicism from conversations and debates with a fellow patient; he also began to read the writings of the nineteenth-century Danish philosopher Søren Kierkegaard, which were to have a great influence on him.

At the end of 1945 Percy returned to Greenville; he had decided to give up medicine as a career and was leaning toward taking up writing, although he was uncertain about what subjects and directions to pursue. In July 1946 he and his boyhood friend and confidant, the novelist and historian Shelby Foote, traveled to New Mexico; for a while he thought about residing there. Instead he went back home, and on 7 November 1946 married Mary Bernice Townsend (known as Bunt), whom he had met in Greenville in 1942. After taking instruction, he and his wife entered the Roman Catholic Church on 13 December 1947 in New Orleans. In June 1948 the couple moved to Covington, Louisiana, with their first child, Mary. They later had another daughter, Ann.

A bequest from his uncle Will enabled Percy to pursue a writing career in earnest. During the early 1950s he worked on two apprentice-type novels that were never published. In this initial stage of his fiction writing he sought the advice of the writer Caroline Gordon, a fellow convert to Catholicism. Percy continued to study Kierkegaard, and he started to read the French existentialists Jean-Paul Sartre, Albert Camus (both of whom had considerable influence on his later novel writing), and Gabriel Marcel, as well as the German philosophers Karl Jaspers and Martin Heidegger. In 1954 Percy's first philosophical essay appeared in the autumn issue of the Fordham University quarterly, *Thought,* and he published other essays on various topics during the rest of the decade, such as "Stoicism in the South," which appeared in the 6 July 1956 issue of *Commonweal.* In this article he ventured into the area of social criticism, discussing the South after the 1954 U.S. Supreme Court decision ending segregation in the public schools.

In the fall of 1957 Percy and his family lived briefly in New Orleans, where he found the motivation and environment to begin working on the novel that was to become *The Moviegoer.* He submitted it to the publisher Alfred Knopf in 1959, and after considerable editing the novel was published in 1961. The book received the National Book Award for fiction the following year. Percy wrote five more novels—*The Last Gentleman* (1966), *Love in the Ruins* (1971), *Lancelot* (1977), *The Second Coming* (1980), and *The Thanatos Syndrome* (1987). He also wrote four nonfiction books—*The Message in the Bottle* (1975), *Lost in the Cosmos* (1983), *Novel-Writing in an Apocalyptic Time* (1986), and *Signposts in a Strange Land* (1991).

Percy led a quiet life as a writer; he would typically start to write each day at 9 A.M., putting his thoughts down on Blue Horse notepaper in a three-ring binder. Usually he wrote while reclining on his bed. In the afternoons he would often walk with his wife, play golf, or visit friends. One of the themes of his writings is the search for meaning in a technological and scientific age that promotes man's physical well-being but does nothing for his spiritual yearnings. Percy, who was described as "the moralist of the deep South" and the "Dixie Kierkegaard," has been characterized as attempting to comprehend the particular anxiety of the contemporary individual "adrift in the twentieth century." Although his novels contain the serious ideas of a Christian existentialist philosopher, it was his talent as a storyteller that brought him renown.

Percy died of cancer and is buried not far from Covington on the grounds of St. Joseph's Benedictine Abbey.

★

Jay Tolson, ed., *The Correspondence of Shelby Foote and Walker Percy* (1997), contains the letters of Percy to Foote from 1970 to 1989 and the letters of Foote to Percy from 1948 to 1988. Dannye Romine Powell, *Parting the Curtains: Interviews with Southern Writers* (1994), presents interviews conducted with Percy in July 1980 and March 1987. Lewis A. Lawson and Victor A. Kramer, eds., *Conversations with Walker Percy* (1985), contains essays by authors who have spoken with Percy about his books and essays. Biographies of Percy are Jay Tolson, *Pilgrim in the Ruins: A Life of Walker Percy* (1992), and Patrick H. Samway, S.J., *Walker Percy: A Life* (1997). See also Robert Coles, *Walker Percy: An American Search* (1978); Jac Tharpe, *Walker Percy* (1983); and J. Donald Crowley and Sue Mitchell Crowley, eds., *Critical Essays on Walker Percy* (1989). An obituary is in the *New York Times* (11 May 1990).

ALLAN NELSON

PERKINS, (Richard) Marlin (*b.* 28 March 1905 in Carthage, Missouri; *d.* 14 June 1986 in Clayton, Missouri), zoologist, naturalist, and host of the acclaimed television program *Mutual of Omaha's Wild Kingdom.*

Marlin Perkins was born in rural southwest Missouri, the youngest of three sons of Joseph Dudley Perkins, a circuit

Marlin Perkins at home with a rhesus monkey named Harriet and a fennec (African desert fox) named Heime, 1985. UPI/CORBIS-BETTMANN

court judge, and Mynta (Miller) Perkins. At age six, Perkins contracted pneumonia, and although he recovered, the disease passed to his mother, whose case proved fatal. This "trauma of the first magnitude" left Perkins saddled with guilt. In the fall of 1912, Perkins's father, grieving over his wife's death, sent the boys off, the eldest two to a private school in Illinois and Marlin to an aunt in nearby Pittsburg, Kansas. Perkins lived there until the fall of 1919, when his father enrolled him in the Wentworth Military Academy in Lexington, Missouri. Two years later, his father remarried and brought his sons home. Perkins graduated from Carthage High School in 1923.

During these years, Perkins discovered his lifelong interest in animals, especially reptiles. He began catching and studying snakes and lizards as a hobby. He stashed his living collection in cellars, between walls, or in hay lofts, and sometimes he carried snakes in his pockets. In 1924 Perkins entered the University of Missouri at Columbia, where he planned to study zoology and animal husbandry. He left after two years, deciding it would be more practical to begin work in his chosen field immediately.

Perkins moved to St. Louis in June 1926 and found work as a groundskeeper at the St. Louis Zoo. Under the tutelage of the renowned zookeeper George Vierheller, he soon began tending cages and, within a year, gained charge of the zoo's small department of reptiles. Perkins expanded the reptile collection and made promotional talks at schools, churches, and clubs. An easygoing raconteur, Perkins gave regular zoo interviews on a local radio station in the early 1930s. The series ended when an electric eel demonstration went awry and blew the broadcast off the air. A more serious mishap occurred on 31 December 1928, when Perkins was bitten by a deadly gaboon viper. Perkins spent three weeks hospitalized and six months recovering; he was one of the first survivors of a gaboon viper bite.

Perkins enrolled in night classes, joined scientific societies, and conducted studies on zoo reptiles. He spent six weeks in 1927 studying at the Bronx Zoo, and he was a member of the St. Louis Zoo's first foreign expedition, a Central American collection trip, in 1929. In 1933 Perkins married Elise More of St. Louis; they had a daughter, Suzanne, in 1937 and were divorced in 1953.

In the summer of 1938, Perkins was selected to head the Zoological Gardens in Buffalo, New York. The zoo suffered chronic financial shortages, leaving Perkins to recruit volunteers, solicit donations, and teach museum classes to supplement his income. He left Buffalo in 1944, when he was named director of the Lincoln Park Zoo in Chicago, a position he assumed the following year.

Perkins oversaw numerous changes at Lincoln Park Zoo, including the construction of a children's zoo, the installation of an animal nursery, the redesign of placards to promote visitor education, and the creation of new administrative positions. As in St. Louis and Buffalo, he endeavored to raise community awareness. Between 1945 and 1947, he appeared with animals in fifteen studio broadcasts on a local television station. In 1947 he began writing a column for the *Chicago Sun-Times,* and that July he appeared on the cover of *Time* magazine, which ran a story about zoos and recognized Perkins as "one of the fastest rising zoo directors in the country."

Beginning in the spring of 1949, the National Broadcasting Company, then a fledgling television network, featured Perkins on a live series called *Visit to the Lincoln Park Zoo.* The next spring, the show was renamed *Zooparade* and appeared on nearly thirty stations. The broadcasts dealt with such topics as the physics of snake movement, the anatomy of bullfrogs, and the protective coloration of moths and lizards. *Zooparade* soon traveled into the field, first to Wyoming, then to Florida, and by 1957, to East Africa and the upper Amazon River. In 1957, however, NBC decided that the *Zooparade* program had run its course and canceled the program.

On 13 August 1960 Perkins married Carol Morse Cotsworth, a divorcée with three children. Perkins's second wife joined him on many journeys, and they remained married until Perkins's death; they had no children. Two weeks after his second marriage, he joined a three-month Himalayan expedition led by Sir Edmund Hillary. Perkins's role was to search for evidence of the yeti, the so-called Abominable Snowman. His research established that the creature was mythological and that the animals mistaken for yeti were probably blue bears.

In September 1962 Perkins left Chicago to assume the directorship of the St. Louis Zoo. He oversaw numerous renovations and expansions, including the addition of a children's zoo, the creation of an animal tissue and organ bank, the improvement of education programs, the restoration of the zoo's historic aviary, and the installation of a popular miniature railway. He is credited with guiding the zoo's growth into a modern institution for education, research, and conservation. Perkins retired from the zoo in 1970.

In the fall of 1962, when he took command of the St. Louis Zoo, Perkins also finalized plans with NBC to begin a new wildlife program under the sponsorship of the Mutual of Omaha Insurance Company. *Mutual of Omaha's Wild Kingdom* first aired in January 1963. Although early programs were filmed at the zoo, Perkins and his cohost Jim Fowler soon carried the show into the wild. For the next twenty-three years, the program filmed animal life in jungles, savannas, mountains, deserts, marshes, rivers, and ocean reefs around the globe. One of television's longest-running programs, *Mutual of Omaha's Wild Kingdom* won four Emmy Awards and scores of citations for educational and scientific merit. At its height, it was broadcast on over 200 stations, in forty nations. In the mid-1980s, animal rights critics produced evidence that at least some episodes of *Mutual of Omaha's Wild Kingdom* used faked predatory scenes, film of animals that had been captured and provoked into dramatic action. Perkins did not refute these claims.

Perkins supported conservationist causes throughout his career. In college, he authored pamphlets advising farmers not to kill snakes, which control the rodent population. In 1971 he and his wife helped establish in Missouri the Wild Canid Survival and Research Center, a laboratory and preserve for the protection of wolves. In his later years, he defended zoos as breeders of endangered animals and as wildlife emissaries to an increasingly urban world. Although never a hunter himself, Perkins accepted the hunting of healthy species. The real threat, he believed, lay in heedless global development. "In our headlong dash to maintain our economic superiority," he wrote, "we must not forget that many parts of nature are finite."

Perkins published four books: *Animal Faces* (1944), a collection of wildlife photographs taken by Perkins; *Zooparade* (1954), about animal behavior; *I Saw You from Afar* (1965), written with his wife about the Kalahari bushmen; and an autobiography, *My Wild Kingdom* (1982). He retired from television in 1985, when he fell ill with cancer. He died the following year and was buried in Clayton, Missouri, a St. Louis suburb.

★

Surprisingly little has been written about Perkins's life. Marlin Perkins, *My Wild Kingdom* (1982), provides an autobiographical overview. Articles that capture useful details about his career and personality include "By the Lake," *Time* (7 July 1947), which discusses his early accomplishments; Peter Hawthorne and Sarah Hall, "Marlin Perkins," *People Weekly* (9 Aug. 1982); and John Carey, "Life in the Wild Kingdom," *National Wildlife* (June/July 1986). An obituary with a brief review of his career is in the *New York Times* (16 June 1986).

DAVID DIAZ

PERLMUTTER, Nathan (*b.* 2 March 1923 in New York City; *d.* 12 July 1987 in New York City), lawyer and civil rights leader who was awarded the Medal of Freedom, the nation's highest civilian honor.

Perlmutter was the son of Polish Jewish immigrants, Hyman Perlmutter, a tailor and laborer, and Bella Finkelstein,

Nathan Perlmutter. NYT PICTURES/NYT PERMISSIONS

a homemaker who during summers sold ices from a pushcart. He and his brother were reared in the Williamsburg section of Brooklyn. Perlmutter studied at Georgetown University from 1942 to 1943 and at Villanova University from 1943 to 1944. He married Ruth Ann Osofsky on 2 April 1943; they had two children. Later that year he joined the U.S. Marine Corps, serving as an infantry officer in China.

In 1946 Perlmutter entered New York University Law School, where he received the LL.B. in 1949. Following graduation he took a job with the Anti-Defamation League (ADL) of B'nai B'rith, which was headquartered in New York City. Over the next several years Perlmutter served in ADL offices in Denver (1949–1952), Detroit (1952–1953), Miami (1956–1964), and New York City (1953–1956), where he later served as director of the ADL (1964–1965). He then joined the American Jewish Committee in New York City as associate national director until 1969, when he became vice president of development for Brandeis University in Waltham, Massachusetts.

In 1973 Perlmutter returned to New York and to the ADL, where he was New York regional director until 1979, when he was named national director. During his tenure at the ADL, Perlmutter established contacts with such diverse groups as the Baptists, the Mormons, the National Council of Churches, and the Moral Majority. He also reached out to blacks. He criticized President Jimmy Carter for making contacts with the Palestine Liberation Organization. In 1979 he intervened on behalf of Iranian students seeking asylum in the United States after the overthrow of the shah. In 1981, when President Ronald Reagan nominated Warren S. Richardson for a position in his administration, Perlmutter led a campaign against the nomination because of Richardson's connection with the Liberty Lobby, which Perlmutter considered antiblack and anti-Jewish; President Reagan withdrew the nomination. That year he also criticized the Reagan administration for its criticism of Israel's destruction of an Iraqi nuclear reactor. In 1984 Perlmutter denounced Jesse Jackson for calling New York City "Hymietown" during his campaign for president.

Over the years Perlmutter wrote for periodicals including *Commentary, National Jewish Monthly, Progressive,* and *National Review.* In the latter part of his life, he leaned toward neoconservatism and opposed racially based quotas. With his wife he wrote *The Real Anti-Semitism in America* (1982).

In June 1985 Perlmutter was diagnosed with lung cancer but remained active despite his illness. In November of that year he wrote an article for the *New York Times Magazine,* "Diary of a Cancer Patient." On 23 June 1987 President Reagan presented Perlmutter with the Medal of Freedom, citing his lifelong devotion to "championing human dignity." He died at Sloan-Kettering Cancer Center. His funeral was held at Temple Emanu-El in New York City. He is buried in New York City.

As a spokesman for American Jews, Perlmutter fought prejudice and confronted bigotry in its various forms, whether anti-Semitic, antiblack, or anti-Christian. Perhaps the most telling characterization of his humanitarian impact on American life is in the obituary issued by the Mormons, which praised him "for his devotion to the defense of religious liberty to which he gave outstanding leadership."

★

Besides the works mentioned above, Perlmutter wrote *How to Win Money at the Races* (1964; rev. ed. 1979) and his autobiography, *A Bias of Reflections: Confessions of an Incipient Old Jew* (1972). Obituaries are in the *New York Times* and the *Washington Post* (both 14 July 1987).

ITAI SNEH

PERLS, Laura (*b.* 15 August 1905 in Pforzheim, Germany; *d.* 13 July 1990 in Pforzheim, Germany), psychotherapist who was a codeveloper of Gestalt therapy and a cofounder and longtime president of the New York Institute for Gestalt Therapy.

Born Lore Posner, Perls was the oldest of three children in an upper-middle-class family in the Black Forest region of Germany. Her father, Rudolph Posner, was a successful businessman; her mother, Antonia (Eber) Posner, was a woman of culture and a talented musician. Lore was playing the piano by age four and at twelve she became the first girl admitted to the local gymnasium (high school) and the only Jew in her class. A brilliant student, she tried not to outshine her peers. Her first brief experience with psychoanalysis came at age sixteen as a patient of an Adlerian analyst. While studying law in Frankfurt, Germany, she became enthralled by the courses she took from the theologians Martin Buber and Paul Tillich.

In 1926 Lore met Friedrich ("Fritz") Perls, a thirty-three-year-old psychiatrist who had won the coveted Iron Cross in the German army in World War I. He had a theatrical background and excelled in physical brain neurology and philosophical psychology. They both studied with Kurt Goldstein, a philosopher who was working in the new field known as Gestalt perception, and with Adhemar Gelb. Lore was fascinated by this emerging theory, which had been formulated by the psychologists Wolfgang Köhler, Kurt Koffka, and Max Wertheimer. The school maintained that an image is perceived as a whole (a "gestalt") rather than as a sum of its component parts and that the context in which an image is perceived is crucial. As later developed by Fritz and Laura Perls, this theory was used to support the argument that the separation of mind and body is artificial and that therapists must examine both the patient's environment as well as the patient's repressed needs and emotional state. The therapeutic application of the theory was used in counseling, personal development, and psychological treatment of the individual's entire being as well as in training for theater and other arts. In response to her fascination, Lore changed majors and studied Freudian analysis with Carl Landauer. Her dissertation involved color contrast/constancy, an important subject for Gestalt theorists. She received her doctorate (D.Sc.) in psychology from the University of Frankfurt, at that time an avant-garde center of academic advancement and intellectual exchange.

Lore married Fritz Perls on 23 August 1930. A courageous, creative whirlwind, Fritz stimulated Lore's genius and relied on her to clarify his own ideas. They had two children, a daughter, Renate, and a son, Stephen. In 1933 Fritz left Germany in haste after receiving a threatening phone call from the Nazis. Lore went to Pforzheim for seven months and then joined him with the baby in Amsterdam. Without jobs, they were penniless.

In 1934 Fritz accepted a psychoanalytic position in South Africa, where the couple established practices. Lore's first article, "How to Educate Children for Peace," was published in German in 1939. During World War II, Fritz served as an army psychiatrist in hospitals far from his home; the couple had a "weekend marriage," raising the children with help from servants and working together on a book. Lore's mother and most of her relatives died in concentration camps. The Perls, who had formed an intellectual circle in Johannesburg and were acquainted with such elites as Prime Minister Jan Christiaan Smuts, left South Africa after the war because of the increasingly rigid racial segregation that would eventually culminate in apartheid.

In 1946 Fritz boarded a ship to England, went to Canada, then finally reached New York City. In 1947 Lore and the children joined him. Lore remained in New York City until just before her death, becoming an American citizen and formally changing her name to Laura in 1952. The pair collaborated on a book, *Ego, Hunger, and Aggression* (1947), but the book was published in Fritz's name. Laura was also an uncredited coauthor of *Gestalt Therapy: Excitement and Growth in the Human Personality* (1951).

Unsatisfied with traditional and Freudian psychiatry, over time Fritz and Laura developed a new approach they called Gestalt therapy. Along with Paul Goodman, the couple founded the New York Institute for Gestalt Therapy in 1952. Other prominent figures in the institute were Paul Weisz and Elliot Shapiro, and Ralph Hefferline's Columbia University students performed developing Gestalt awareness exercises.

Gestalt therapy is an experiential and existential treatment of the whole individual, as opposed to isolated symptoms or behaviors. The patient does not lie on the couch; instead posture and self-awareness are crucial. The therapist is present and encourages the patient to help himself. Unlike Freudian psychoanalysis, which emphasizes childhood experiences, Gestalt therapy focuses on the present. The patient's ailments, even those involving events from the past, are treated as occurring at the current moment. The patient-therapist relationship is seen as a "field" of flexible, creative, flowing contact, which requires complete communication.

Fritz never stopped traveling throughout his life, giving workshops, teaching, and spreading the message of Gestalt therapy, especially in California during the human potential movement of the 1960s. Laura and Fritz were instrumental in establishing the prominent Gestalt Institute of Cleveland and other centers, including the famous Esalen Institute in Big Sur, California. But over time their marriage deteriorated; Fritz retracted his earlier gratitude and criticized his wife in his book *In and Out the Garbage Pail* (1969).

For the last twenty years of the marriage Fritz and Laura lived apart. They became argumentative, which embarrassed some colleagues, but their quarrels occurred in the climate of debate about the meaning and purpose of Gestalt therapy. They never divorced. Laura was present at Fritz's death in Chicago on 14 March 1970, and after his cremation she took possession of the ashes.

Laura Perls gave up her private patients and group therapy (a fairly new concept which she had espoused vigorously) to serve full-time as president of the New York Institute for Gestalt Therapy, running weekly workshops and holding meetings in her apartment for almost forty years. She told friends that she resented Fritz for having "dumped it [the institute] in her lap," but she seemed to enjoy her work. Every summer, beginning in the mid-1950s, Laura toured Europe giving Gestalt workshops and hiking in the Alps. Unlike Fritz, she did not seek fame or recognition, which is why she is not as well-known.

Outside of her work, Laura enjoyed time alone, but some colleagues and friends worried that she was withdrawn. Throughout her life she pursued creative interests: drawing, sculpting, writing poetry, playing hours a day on her grand piano, and studying modern dance (an interest since childhood) and applying it to the "body work" aspect of Gestalt therapy.

Despite various health problems beginning around 1952, Laura worked energetically into her eighties, sharing an apartment during her last ten years with her daughter, Renate. In 1980 a Festschrift was published in the *Gestalt Journal,* in honor of her seventy-fifth birthday.

Just days before the New York Institute's commemoration of her eightieth birthday, Laura fell on a New York street and suffered a broken pelvis. She continued, however, to travel and lecture, mostly in Germany, and just before her health seriously declined in 1989 she published a collection of her writings entitled *Living at the Boundary* (1992). Due to several ailments, by 1990 she could barely stand. Renate then accompanied her to Pforzheim, where she died. At Laura's request, her ashes and Fritz's were buried together in the Posner plot in Pforzheim.

★

Information on Perls can be found in "Keeping the Flame: Laura Perls and Gestalt Therapy," special issue of *Voices: The Art and Science of Psychotherapy* 18, no. 2 (1982); Karen Humphrey, "Laura Perls: A Biographical Sketch," *Gestalt Journal* 9, no. 1 (1986); Janine M. Bernard, "Laura Perls: From Ground to Figure," *Journal of Counseling and Development* 64, no. 6 (1986); and Nijole Kudirka, "A Talk with Laura Perls About the Therapist and the Artist," in *Gestalt Voices,* edited by Edward W. L. Smith (1992). Renate Perls, *My Father's Words,* is a work in progress. Useful books on Gestalt therapy include Frederick S. Perls, Ralph Hefferline, and Paul Goodman, *Gestalt Therapy: Excitement and Growth in the Human Personality* (1951); Joe Wysong, ed., *An Oral History of Gestalt Therapy* (1982); Taylor Stoehr, *Here, Now, Next: Paul Goodman and the Origins of Gestalt Therapy* (1994); and Mitchell Ash, *Gestalt Psychology in German Culture 1890–1967* (1995). A chapter on Laura Perls is in Ilene Serlin and Paul Shane, *The Pursuit of Human Potential: A Sourcebook in Humanistic and Transpersonal Psychology,* edited by Don Moss (1997). A tribute by Ilene Serlin is in *Humanistic Psychologist* 19, no. 1 (1992). An obituary is in the *New York Times* (18 July 1990).

J. S. CAPPELLETTI

PERSICHETTI, Vincent Ludwig (*b.* 6 June 1915 in Philadelphia, Pennsylvania; *d.* 14 August 1987 in Philadelphia, Pennsylvania), composer, teacher, pianist, and conductor who produced sophisticated yet accessible statements in the realm of twentieth-century classical music in America.

One of three children of Vincent Roger Persichetti, an immigrant from Italy, and Martha Buch, an immigrant from Germany, Persichetti grew up in the Italian neighborhood of South Philadelphia. As a toddler, Persichetti listened attentively to the family's player piano, and his parents encouraged his musical talents from a young age. They enrolled him at age five in the Combs Conservatory, where he studied music theory with Russell King Miller as well as a number of different instruments, including piano (and organ, when his feet could reach the pedals) lessons with William Stanger. Considered a child prodigy, Persichetti progressed rapidly in his studies, playing on the radio at age six and composing many pieces before reaching age ten. His mischievousness, independent thinking, and good-natured rebellion against his theory teacher got him dismissed from class on occasion.

After graduating from Combs with a B. Mus. degree in 1936, Persichetti joined the faculty there (serving as conductor from 1936 to 1938), while starting his graduate work at the Curtis Institute, where he studied piano with Olga Samaroff and conducting with Fritz Reiner and received a diploma in conducting in 1939. He then attended the Philadelphia Conservatory, where he earned an M. Mus. degree in 1940 and a D. Mus. degree in 1945. During this period he also published music criticism in the *Journal of Modern Music, Musical Quarterly,* and *Notes.*

Although Persichetti's compositions had been performed locally and had even won awards, Persichetti first came to widespread public attention in 1945, when the Philadelphia Orchestra, under the direction of Eugene Ormandy, performed his "Fables" for narrator and orchestra and, two years later, his Symphony No. 3, to enthusiastic reviews. With these performances, Persichetti established and then maintained for himself a national reputation as a composer for the next fifty years.

The decade of the 1940s was also important for Persichetti for two other reasons. He took on a teaching position at the Juilliard School, offered to him by its president, the composer William Schuman, that he would hold for virtually the rest of his life. On 3 June 1941 he married the accomplished pianist Dorothea Flanagan, who would go on to serve an indispensable role in Vincent's career as performer of, and even collaborator on, his compositions. Throughout his life, he claimed she was the strongest influence on his work. The couple had two children. In 1949 they bought an eighteenth-century farmhouse outside Philadelphia, called "Hillhouse," in which they lived until both of their deaths in 1987.

In the 1950s Persichetti received a number of important commissions, including his Symphony No. 5 for the Louisville Orchestra and the Symphony No. 7 for the St. Louis Symphony. He was hired as an editorial assistant in 1952 by the music publishing house Elkan-Vogel, Ltd. (later he would be the director of publications there); this company also published much of Persichetti's own work. This decade was a productive one for Persichetti, who wrote, among other works, the Serenade No. 5 for Orchestra (1950), Symphony for Strings (1953), Concerto for Piano, Four Hands (1954), Pageant for Band (1953), and Three English Songs (1951). Some of Persichetti's best-known works, such as the Divertimento for Band (1950), were produced at this time.

In the 1960s, 1970s, and 1980s, Persichetti continued his impressive output of work, as always, spreading his talents across a diverse range of instruments, including solo harpsichord works (1982–1984), choral pieces, both sacred and secular, and his opera *The Sibyl* (1984). In 1973 Persichetti was involved in a political controversy that made him the subject of intense media attention. Commissioned by the Presidential Inaugural Committee to write a piece for

Vincent Persichetti holds the score to his composition *A Lincoln Address,* 1973. UPI/CORBIS-BETTMANN

the Philadelphia Orchestra at Richard Nixon's second inauguration, Persichetti set excerpts from Abraham Lincoln's second inaugural address to music. Committee members judged the work, titled *A Lincoln Address,* inappropriate because of references to war (in the context of Lincoln, the Civil War) as "a mighty scourge"; the United States was currently involved in the largely unpopular Vietnam War, and Persichetti was told his work might embarrass Nixon. Though Persichetti averred that the piece was not a political commentary, it was removed from the program, and instead Charlton Heston recited the Declaration of Independence to a choral setting by Roger Wagner.

Persichetti was the recipient of numerous awards, including three Guggenheim fellowships. At his death, he had completed 166 opus numbers for an astounding range of instruments (from choruses and wind ensembles to the tuba and harp) and across an impressive number of musical genres (band music, solo works for piano, an opera, and nine symphonies). He had also spent a lifetime as an influential teacher, guiding Jacob Druckman, Philip Glass, and Peter Schickele among many others. When asked to discuss his works, Persichetti preferred brevity, believing that talking about music was unnecessary. However, he often referred to his compositions as a combination of "grit" and "grazioso." Black spots were discovered on Persichetti's lungs in 1987, but he continued to work up until his death that August. Dorothea died soon after, in November.

Critics have found it difficult to delineate separate "periods" of Persichetti's aesthetic development. He has been compared to numerous prominent composers, from Scarlatti and Ravel to Tchaikovsky, Schoenberg, and Bartók. Somewhat surprisingly, many believe his compositions for wind instruments may come to be recognized as his most original musical contribution. Though unlikely to be remembered as globally as Beethoven or Stravinsky, he was, nonetheless, extraordinarily gifted in his ability to reach a general audience beyond music scholars. A gentle man of rather small stature, his face dominated by heavy glasses, Persichetti dedicated all facets of his life to music, ultimately making an enormous and lucid gift to the world.

★

An important source is Donald L. and Janet L. Patterson, *Vincent Persichetti: A Bio-Bibliography* (1988). See also Daniel Webster, "Vincent Persichetti," *High Fidelity* 35 (Apr. 1985). An obituary is in the *New York Times* (15 Aug. 1987).

SARAH MARKGRAF

PETER, Laurence Johnston (*b.* 16 September 1919 in Vancouver, British Columbia; *d.* 12 January 1990 in Palos Verdes Estates, California), author of *The Peter Principle,* which observed that "In a hierarchy every employee tends to rise to his level of incompetence."

The son of Vicenta Steves and Victor C. Peter, Laurence Peter struggled early in life. His father died in a drowning accident, and Peter had to leave school to help support his family. He subsequently suffered from tuberculosis of the spine, which put him in a hospital for four months and forced him to wear a back brace for many years.

Peter did manual labor as a young man, then taught industrial arts at a juvenile detention center. Between 1948 and 1964 he served as a teacher, counselor, and school psychologist in Vancouver schools. Peter received his bachelor's degree in 1957 and his master's degree in education in 1958, from Western Washington State College, and his doctorate in education from Washington State University in 1963. He then taught at the University of British Columbia as a psychologist and assistant professor. In 1966 he moved to California, where he was a professor of education at the University of Southern California until 1970.

Peter developed the Peter Principle while working in various bureaucracies, particularly schools, where he noticed that the best teachers were promoted out of the classroom. He frequently turned down promotions, believing that he was not up to the administrative tasks his superiors wanted to hand him. He often spoke on the subject in his classes and in lectures at teacher conferences. The idea attracted attention. Several articles about the Peter Principle appeared in the California press, including an article Peter wrote for the *Los Angeles Times* in 1967.

After attending a play with a friend, Raymond Hull, Peter explained to Hull that the reason the play wasn't very good was that the person who wrote the script also directed and played the lead. While the play may have been well written, the writer had gone beyond his level of competency. Intrigued by Peter's theory, Hull decided to collaborate with him to write a book. The book was completed in 1964, but Peter could not find a publisher. McGraw-Hill, which had previously published an education textbook entitled *Prescriptive Teaching* by Peter, rejected the proposal. "I can foresee no commercial possibilities for such a book," a McGraw-Hill editor wrote, "and consequently can offer no encouragement." All told, Peter received thirty rejection letters.

Unbeknownst to Peter, someone had sent the *Los Angeles Times* article about the Peter Principle to a British publisher, who took an immediate interest. The publisher notified a friend in New York at William Morrow and Company, who flew to California, thinking he might try to convince Peter to write a book on the Peter Principle. When it turned out that Peter had completed a manuscript, the two quickly settled on a deal with a $2,500 advance.

The 10,000-copy run of *The Peter Principle: Why Things Always Go Wrong* in 1969 was an instant success. Blending wry humor with truths that almost all people encountered in bureaucracies, the book struck a chord. The military, schools, corporations, and even churches ordered bulk quantities. The book sold more than 200,000 copies in its first year and was on the *New York Times* best-seller list through 1970. It was translated into thirty-eight languages and was on the best-seller lists in England and Germany. It is still popular in Spain, where more than thirty-five editions have been published.

Publishers Weekly wrote that the 179-page book was "precisely geared for the Age of Conglomerates." It spoofed

Laurence Peter with his book *The Peter Principle,* 1980. AP/WIDE WORLD PHOTOS

ladder climbers and the practice of rewarding people for a job well done by promoting them to the point that they could no longer handle their responsibilities. "The cream rises until it sours," Peter wrote. "In every thriving organization there is considerable accumulation of dead wood at the executive level."

Insisting that he did not want to become an example of the Peter Principle, Peter turned down several offers from companies to become a management consultant. He did, however, stick to his strengths, which were lecturing and writing. Modest, humorous, and used to speaking in front of difficult audiences from his years as a teacher of juvenile delinquents, Peter proved to be a very popular speaker.

He retired from academic life in 1970 and wrote several books, including *The Peter Prescription* (1972), *The Peter Quotations* (1977), and, with the comedian Bill Dana, *The Laughter Prescription* (1982). He also did a cartoon, "The Peter Principle," that was syndicated by United Features and appeared in about fifty newspapers.

Peter used some of the proceeds of his book to advance teacher education. He wrote four books on how to improve teacher education as part of an education project called Competency for Teaching.

Peter was married twice. His first wife was Nancy Bailey.

He married his second wife, Irene J. Howe, on 25 February 1967. He had four children, John, Edward, Margaret, and Alice.

Peter received several awards and honorary degrees for his work, including the Noble Prize, a French award that spoofs the Nobel Prize. He was a founding member of the Big Brothers Association of British Columbia and was vice president of the British Columbia Division of Canadian Mental Health. He died of complications from a stroke he had suffered in 1988.

★

An obituary is in the *New York Times* (15 Jan. 1990).

ERIK BRUUN

PIÑERO, Miguel (*b.* 19 December 1946 in Gurabo, Puerto Rico; *d.* 17 June 1988 in New York City), playwright, poet, and actor who gained fame in the 1970s as the first Puerto Rican to be accepted as a major English-language playwright.

Miguel Piñero, known as Mikey to his friends, was the first child of Adelina Piñero and Miguel Angel Gómez Ramos. At the age of four he and his four siblings and several step-siblings moved with their parents to the Lower East Side of Manhattan. His father deserted the family when Miguel was eight years old; the boy became a thief in order to help support his family and eventually developed a drug habit. He frequently got in trouble and was in and out of reform schools. He had a seventh-grade education.

After being convicted for armed robbery in 1971, Piñero was incarcerated in the Ossining Correctional Facility in Ossining, New York, better known as Sing Sing. There he began to write plays, dramatizing the things he knew: crime, street hustling, and drugs. He had been a heroin dealer and junkie until going straight in 1965. "If you see that needle in your arm, you don't like yourself," Piñero later recalled. "You're asking for death."

Short Eyes: The Killing of a Sex Offender by the Inmates of the House of Detention Awaiting Trial, Piñero's first successful drama, was begun in Sing Sing and completed after he was released on parole in July 1973. Set in prison, the play tells the story of a child molester who is ostracized and eventually murdered by other prisoners. After leaving Sing Sing, Piñero joined a theatrical group called "The Family," comprising ex-convicts and former drug addicts. *Short Eyes* was first performed in January 1974 at the Theater of the Riverside Church in New York City (where Piñero later became playwright in residence). In March it moved to Joseph Papp's Public Theater, and in May it opened at the Vivian Beaumont Theater at Lincoln Center in New York City. "If the unnerving honesty of *Short Eyes,* as well as the raw corrosive force of its language, sometimes appeared to be too much for middle class audiences," said producer Papp, who became a major supporter of Piñero, "it nevertheless won the New York Drama Critics Award for best play of the season. With this first and best known of his many plays, Miguel has probably had more impact on younger writers than any Latin playwright of his generation." The drama also won the Obie award for best off-Broadway play.

After the success of *Short Eyes,* Piñero turned to encouraging other young Puerto Rican artists, "NuYoricans" from his own neighborhood, opening up his home on the Lower East Side and offering poetry workshops to young talent. In the same spirit he gathered fifteen young hustlers from Times Square in 1974 and formed them into a theater group to perform his one-act play *Subculture,* which was about New York's gritty teenage lifestyle. His neighborhood influence was still being felt at the end of the twentieth century. The Nuyorican Poets Cafe on East Third Street continued to evoke the mood of those open-house days and provided a space for poets and artists to be heard and seen.

In 1974 Piñero was arrested for cursing at a subway attendant after the attendant shouted racial slurs at two young Puerto Ricans jumping a turnstile (the case was later dismissed). In 1977 he was arrested for allegedly robbing passengers in a cab and stealing the taxi; he was cleared of the charges a year later.

In 1975 Piñero went to Philadelphia to take a role in a Bruce Friedman play, *Steambath,* and decided to remain, in the hopes, as he put it, of "finding new energies." He set his play *Eulogy for a Small Time Thief* (1977) there and at the same time wrote *The Sun Always Shines for the Cool* (1978). Piñero married Juanita Lovette Rameize in 1977, but they divorced two years later. He had an adopted son, Ismael Castro. Piñero then moved to Los Angeles and founded the One Act Theatre Festival, where his play *Guntower* was performed. He returned to New York City in the early 1980s.

Throughout his life, Piñero's writing spanned several genres, from drama to screenplay writing (he wrote the screenplay for a film version of *Short Eyes*) to poetry. He found himself at the forefront of a movement of Puerto Rican poetry, and with his longtime friend Miguel Algarin, he coedited *Nuyorican Poetry: An Anthology of Puerto Rican Words and Feelings* (1975). Looking back on his time in Sing Sing he recalled, "As a poet I was looked on by the other prisoners with great reverence. I think it was because a man stuffed in a hole has no way of expressing his feelings. A poet does, and he expresses it for them. And when they hear his poem they have an emotional release." His collection of poems, *La Bodega Sold Dreams,* was published in 1980.

Piñero was also an actor who performed in such television shows as *Miami Vice, Baretta,* and *Kojak*. His film

Miguel Piñero (*right*) with Marvin Felix Camillo, the director of one of his plays, 1974. AP/WIDE WORLD PHOTOS

credits include *Times Square* (1980), *Fort Apache, The Bronx* (1981), *Breathless* (1983), *Exposed* (1983), *Deal of the Century* (1983), *Alphabet City* (1984), and *Pick-Up Artist* (1987). His roles, like his writing, tended to mimic his real-life experiences, as they usually dealt with the familiar topics of narcotics and hustling.

Piñero died in 1988 at the age of forty-one from cirrhosis of the liver. At the time of his death, he was completing *Every Form of Refuge Has Its Price,* a play set in the intensive care unit of a hospital.

Piñero's work captured the essence of his culture and the power of its impact on him, illuminating the realities of the tough life that he witnessed on the street. "The things that interest me," he said, "are the subtleties . . . of human relations . . . the craziness that keeps everyone from going insane."

★

Information on Piñero is in Mel Gussow, "From the Streets, a Poet of the Stage," *New York Times* (3 July 1988), and Robert Wahls, "Piñero: Prison, Parole, and Prize," *New York Daily News* (2 June 1974). An obituary is in the *New York Times* (18 June 1988).

RACHEL AYDT

POLLARD, Frederick Douglass ("Fritz") (*b.* 27 January 1894 in Chicago, Illinois; *d.* 11 May 1986 in Silver Spring, Maryland), football player and coach who is best known as the first African-American head coach in the National Football League.

The son of John William Pollard, a barber, and Catherine Amanda Hughes, a seamstress, Pollard grew up in the previously all-white Rogers Park area of Chicago, where, being black, he encountered considerable prejudice. The German and Belgian immigrants in the neighborhood gave him the nickname "Fritz."

Pollard was the seventh of eight children (five brothers and three sisters), all of whom were outstanding athletes. He attended Lane Technical High School (1908–1912), where he was a standout athlete and was named to all-county teams in track and football. Although only five feet, seven inches tall and 150 pounds, Pollard was fast, agile, and muscular. He hoped to follow in the footsteps of his older brother Leslie, who played football at Dartmouth College in 1908. Between 1912 and 1914 Pollard attended or participated in football drills at five different colleges in an effort to play college football. Boston attorney and former All-America football player William Lewis warned Pollard that he was becoming a "tramp athlete" and advised him to remedy his academic deficiencies before a further attempt to attend college. At Lewis's suggestion, Pollard attended Springfield High School in 1914 and 1915 and satisfied a foreign language requirement, which led to his acceptance at Brown University in 1915. In June 1914 Pollard married Ada Laing; they had three daughters and a son before separating in the early 1920s. Their son, Fritz Pollard, Jr., won a bronze medal in the 1936 Berlin Olympic games and was a Little All-America football player at the University of North Dakota in 1938.

Before Pollard, there had been only a handful of blacks who played Ivy League football. Pollard was initially

Frederick Pollard, 1936. AP/WIDE WORLD PHOTOS

shunned by members of the Brown football team, but he gradually won their acceptance through superior play and perseverance. As left halfback he helped lead Brown to a successful football season (6–2–1) that included an upset victory over Yale. As a result of his outstanding performance against Yale, Pollard became the best-known African-American football player in the nation. He later recalled that he was harassed and "niggerized" by fans at Yale and Harvard as well as at other schools. Pollard was also targeted by players on opposing teams. To protect himself against racially motivated aggressive play, Pollard often rolled over on his back after being tackled and pumped his legs bicycle-style to discourage opponents from piling on him. After the season, Brown was invited to play in the Tournament of Roses game in Pasadena, California. Washington State defeated an overconfident Brown team 14–0 on New Year's Day 1916. Pollard was the first African American to play in what became the Rose Bowl game.

In 1916 Pollard led Brown to its most successful season (8–1) with his spectacular running and stellar defensive play. More importantly, he had two of his best games in victories over Yale and Harvard, considered the premier teams in college football. Pollard was named to a halfback position on the 1916 All-America team selected by Walter Camp. He was the second African American selected by Camp to his first team, and the first picked for a backfield position. Camp remarked that Pollard "is hard and resilient as an india-rubber ball; but often his offensive work, on account of its very brilliancy, obscured his really sterling defense." During the spring of 1917, Pollard neglected his studies and became ineligible for the 1917 football season. In early 1918 he dropped out of school to become physical director in the U.S. Army's Young Men's Christian Association unit at Camp Meade, Maryland. As World War I neared its end in the fall of 1918, Pollard became head football coach at Lincoln University in Pennsylvania, where he coached through the 1920 season.

In 1919 Pollard played pro football for the Akron Indians in the informal Ohio league. The following year the league was reorganized as the American Professional Football Association, which was renamed the National Football League (NFL) in 1922. Along with Jim Thorpe, Pollard was one of the stars of the league and led his team to the championship in 1921. He played seven years in the NFL with the Akron Pros, Milwaukee Badgers, and Hammond (Indiana) Pros. Pollard became the first African-American head coach in the NFL (and of a major team sport) at Akron in 1921, and coached Milwaukee in 1922 and Hammond in 1924. He was also responsible for recruiting many of the African Americans who played in the early NFL. When he retired from the NFL in 1926, Pollard coached two African-American professional teams, the Chicago Black Hawks (1928–1932), which he organized, and the New York Brown Bombers (1935–1937). His main objective was to demonstrate that African-American athletes were capable of playing pro football at the highest levels, including in the NFL.

Beyond athletics, Pollard was involved in a number of business enterprises. In 1922 he established an investment firm in Chicago that served the African-American community. The firm went bankrupt in 1931 and Pollard moved to New York, where he ran a coal company. He also served as a casting agent for his friend and former Akron teammate Paul Robeson during the production of the film *The Emperor Jones* (1933). In 1935 Pollard founded the first African-American tabloid newspaper, the *New York Independent News*, which he operated until 1942. He continued to work as an entertainment agent and in 1943 headed Suntan Studios in Harlem, where he auditioned African-American entertainers and models. In 1942 Pollard began to produce Soundies, an early form of music videos, for the Soundies Distribution Corporation of America. They featured the leading African-American entertainers of the era. After obtaining a divorce in the early 1940s, Pollard married Mary Ella Austin in 1947; they had no children.

After World War II, when the Soundies Distribution Corporation was sold, Pollard continued as a booking agent for nightclubs, radio, and later television. In 1956 he produced a feature film, *Rockin' the Blues*, which showcased new African-American artists. During the early 1950s Pollard became a successful tax consultant and devoted most of his time to that enterprise until he retired in 1975. In 1954 he became the first African American elected to the National Collegiate Football Hall of Fame; he received the Whitney M. Young, Jr., Memorial Award for outstanding service to the African-American community in 1978.

Fritz Pollard was a twentieth-century African-American pioneer. He broke many racial barriers in sports while often facing stinging insults and personal injury. After his career in athletics ended, he continued to assault racial restrictions in the areas of finance, journalism, and entertainment. He was an upbeat person who used both skill and guile to further his own career and open new opportunities for African Americans. He died of pneumonia at the age of ninety-two. He was cremated, and his ashes were interred at the Fort Lincoln Cemetery in Brentwood, Maryland.

★

Materials on Pollard can be found in the Brown University Archives in Providence, Rhode Island, and at the Pro Football Hall of Fame in Canton, Ohio. A biography is John M. Carroll, *Fritz Pollard: Pioneer in Racial Advancement* (1992). Also see Carl Nesfield, "Pride Against Prejudice: Fritz Pollard Brown's All-American Pre-World War I Vintage," *Black Sports* (Nov. 1971): 16–20, 31, 53 and (Dec. 1971): 60–63, 77, 80–81. An obituary is in the *Chicago Sun-Times* (16 May 1986).

JOHN M. CARROLL

Generoso Pope, Jr. (*right*), leaving the White House with his father after visiting President Harry Truman, 1948. UPI/CORBIS-BETTMANN

POPE, Generoso Paul, Jr. (*b.* 13 January 1927 in the Bronx, New York; *d.* 2 October 1988 in Atlantis, Florida), newspaper editor and publisher whose *National Enquirer* revolutionized the reading habits of modern America.

Generoso Pope, one of three brothers of immigrant parents, was raised in the Bronx, New York. His father, Generoso Pope, Sr., embodied the idealized immigrant saga, rising from poverty to control both the largest sand and gravel corporation in New York City and the major Italian language newspaper in the United States. His mother, Catherine (Richichi) Pope, was a homemaker. Generoso was educated at the prestigious Horace Mann School in New York City and the Massachusetts Institute of Technology. He received a general engineering degree in 1946, at age nineteen, and then joined his father's enterprise. As editor of *Il Progresso* and general manager of the radio station WHOM, Pope developed a lifelong admiration for the administrative style of President Harry Truman, a personal hero. Involved with all business operations, he enjoyed making personal decisions. Although Pope dominated corporate affairs, after his father's death, in 1950, he found himself consistently outvoted by his younger siblings. Reduced to the status of a disgruntled employee, Pope quit to serve a brief tour with the Central Intelligence Agency. He found its psychological warfare section unfulfilling: "I wanted to see what it was like. . . . It was pretty bad." During his time at the agency he married Patricia McManus (25 October 1951); they had one son (Generoso Pope III) before her death.

In 1952, at the age of twenty-five, Pope returned to Manhattan without a job or a future. Drinking in a Greenwich Village cafe, he learned that the *New York Enquirer,* a failing Sunday afternoon paper with a circulation of only 17,000, was for sale. Borrowing $20,000 from friends and adding his own $5,000, he purchased the tabloid and its Tenafly, New Jersey, plant for $75,000. Pope's first editorial (7 April 1952) pledged to "fight for the rights of man" and to "champion human decency and dignity," but he rapidly discovered fine sentiments did not sell newspapers. Gradually the *Enquirer* shifted from politics and horseracing to sex, gore, and violence. Pope and one full-time employee struggled to report the "ignored" crimes of the city, and he later admitted to "kiting" a few checks to pay expenses. Only loans from William O'Dwyer; Roy Cohn, his prep-school friend; and Frank Costello, the Mafia boss, kept the tabloid alive.

Rumors that the paper depended on Mafia money intensified after Pope dined with Costello on the night the crime boss was assassinated in 1957; critics also recalled his father's Fascist leanings and purported involvement in the murder of Carlo Tresca (1943). Pope responded that only legitimate money backed his tabloid. Published as the *National Enquirer* after 1 July 1957, the tabloid began to show a profit in 1958 after Pope reduced sexual reportage. By 1968, when Pope moved the paper close to his home in Englewood Cliffs, New Jersey, newsstand circulation surpassed a million copies weekly.

A marketing genius, Pope recognized that circulation growth demanded new outlets and he targeted supermarket and drugstore sales. To attract housewife readership he mandated that "uplift" replace violence, and a new staff was hired to make the transition. During the 1970s emphasis shifted to celebrity scoops, consumerism, extrasensory experiences, medical "discoveries," diets, and "gee-whiz" stories. Frequent contributors to the *Enquirer* included Billy Graham and clairvoyants like Jeanne Dixon, and large fees were paid for stories about movie stars or UFO abductions. "Checkbook journalism" did not improve the dismal reputation of the paper and some whispered that organized crime was instrumental in the growth of Pope's expanding empire. Pope admitted only to White House connections; the Winn-Dixie supermarket chain agreed to carry the *National Enquirer* after Secretary of Defense Melvin Laird personally escorted its executives through the Oval Office.

By 1971 most major supermarkets in America stocked the *Enquirer,* and its 200 full-time and 650 part-time employees constantly filled display racks around the nation. Pope now owned one of the most profitable publications in America; its 1972 circulation of 2.6 million copies weekly was second only to *TV Guide.* On 1 July 1971 the *National Enquirer* relocated to Lantana, Florida, to take advantage of lower operating costs. It became the largest employer in town, and its annual Christmas display, boasting the world's largest Christmas tree, became a tourist attraction. Pope built a waterfront estate in exclusive Manalapan, where he indulged his passions for landscape gardening and model railroading.

Always a hands-on publisher, the chain-smoking Pope personally approved every *Enquirer* article. Public interest was "our only real rule," and to find it he worked seventy to eighty hours each week, expecting staffers to do the same. He hired journalists from London's Fleet Street tabloids by paying the highest wages in the United States, but he terrorized his workers with periodic "Friday night massacres." When the media magnate Rupert Murdoch launched the four-color *Star* in 1974 to compete with the *National Enquirer,* Pope was for once caught off guard, and profits dropped. Although the first color editions of the *Enquirer* did not appear until August 1979, the paper continued to hold circulation primacy; it sold 6.66 million papers the week Elvis Presley died by featuring a photo of the entertainer in his coffin. Two Canadian publications, the *Globe* and the *National Examiner,* soon entered America's "race to be racy," but Pope tenaciously maintained his lead. He denounced competitors who used his rejected stories and hired his dismissed writers.

When the *Enquirer* circulation peaked at 5.9 million in 1978, *Forbes* magazine proclaimed it the largest newspaper in the country. Pope relaxed pressure on employees by adopting a "thirty day improvement plan," which permitted them an extended opportunity to meet Pope's demands. Yet even as the *Enquirer* became more staid, Pope's purchase of the *Weekly World News* in 1980 created an outlet for more sensational stories. Pope's utopian goal of a circulation of 20 million was unattainable, but, in a bold effort to overwhelm his opponents, he increased the price of the *Enquirer* by 40 percent in 1982. Larger revenues financed a massive advertising campaign; Pope's many critics charged that he was attempting to buy respectability, aspiring to the credibility level of the *Reader's Digest* or attempting to become another *People* magazine. Circulation remained above 5 million but Pope was unable to shake his pursuers despite single-issue coups, such as 6.64 million copies the week Princess Grace of Monaco died. Profits remained high, distribution rights brought in $2 million weekly, and prestigious corporations like Johnson and Johnson, Kraft, and Procter and Gamble advertised in the *Enquirer.* Even with an editorial staff of more than one hundred people, final authority remained with Pope; the paper made him one of the "four hundred richest Americans." At the time of his death, circulation was 4.5 million copies weekly.

Generoso Pope altered America's reading habits, but his many critics were convinced he lowered the standards of journalism. Pope maintained that he merely found the stories people desired because, as the paper's banner declared, "Enquiring Minds Want to Know." Damage suits by entertainers such as Phil Silvers, Frank Sinatra, Shirley Jones, and Ed McMahon were settled out of court, and the *National Enquirer,* despite losing a major judgment to Carol Burnett ($800,000 in 1981), maintained domination of the tabloid marketplace. Rarely taking a vacation, Pope actively participated in community life wherever his paper was located. In New York City he served on several mayoral commissions, was a member of the Board of Higher Education, and awarded scholarships to needy youth. In New Jersey, Englewood Hospital, the police department, and children's shelters benefited from his efforts. In Florida, he donated special care units to regional hospitals and gave more than $1.5 million to the JFK Medical Center. On 29 May 1965 Pope married the *Enquirer*'s art director, Lois Berrodin Wood, a widow with two young girls. Pope suffered a heart attack at his West Palm Beach, Florida, estate and died at the JFK Medical Center in Atlantis, Florida. He was buried from Holy Spirit Catholic Church, Lantana.

★

There is no biography of Pope, but many magazine articles detail his career. See *Business Week* (7 Nov. 1983); *Forbes* (16 Oct. 1978, 19 Mar. 1979, and 14 Mar. 1983); *Newsweek* (14 Apr. 1952); and *Time* (21 Feb. 1972 and 21 Jan. 1980). Newspaper accounts of his accomplishments are found in the *Bergen Record* (3 Oct. 1988), *Chicago Tribune* (25 Feb. 1987 and 3 Oct. 1988), *Wall Street Journal* (25 Oct. 1985), and *Washington Post* (2 Apr. 1978). An obituary is in the *New York Times* (3 Oct. 1988).

GEORGE J. LANKEVICH

PREMINGER, Otto Ludwig (*b.* 5 December 1905 in Vienna, Austria; *d.* 23 April 1986 in New York City), stage and film director, producer, and actor best known for explorations of sensitive and controversial social issues in films such as *Laura* (1944), *The Man with the Golden Arm* (1955), *Anatomy of a Murder* (1959), and *Exodus* (1960).

The son of Josepha Fraenkel and Markus Preminger, Otto was six years older than his brother Ingo, his only sibling, who later became a Hollywood agent and producer of such

Otto Preminger. ARCHIVE PHOTOS

films as *M*A*S*H* (1970). Young Otto followed the example of his father, a prosperous lawyer who was once the attorney general of the Austro-Hungarian Empire, by graduating with an LL.D. from the University of Vienna in 1928. His passion for the stage, however, had already led him to study acting with Max Reinhardt at Vienna's Theater in der Josefstadt. Beginning as a scene shifter in period garb, Preminger played Lysander in a production of *A Midsummer Night's Dream* at the age of seventeen. Soon he was producing and directing plays at the Josefstadt himself, and in 1931 he directed his first film, *Die grosse Liebe* (The Great Love), in Austria. On 3 August 1932 Preminger married a young Hungarian actress, Marion Mill. They had no children. In 1933 he succeeded Reinhardt as the head of the Josefstadt theater, and his abilities led to an official offer to manage Austria's State Theatre, which he refused when learning of the requirement that he renounce his Jewish faith and convert to Catholicism.

On 21 October 1935 Preminger emigrated to the United States, reaching New York Harbor on the day he termed in his autobiography "my second birthday." Feeling himself fortunate to leave behind the mounting tensions of an increasingly anti-Semitic Europe, the director had come at the invitation of the Broadway producers Gilbert Miller and Joseph M. Schenck of the newly formed Twentieth Century–Fox to direct a production of *Libel!* on Broadway.

After moving to Hollywood and working on B pictures, Preminger was given the plum assignment of directing Fox's *Kidnapped* (1938), only to be fired by Fox head Darryl F. Zanuck over a dispute shortly after he began work on the film. His abortive career in Hollywood pointed Preminger back to New York, where between 1938 and 1941 he directed several successful plays, including *Outward Bound* (1938) and *Margin for Error* (1939). Casting himself as Rudolf Forster, a Nazi, in *Margin for Error* led to film roles for Preminger in *The Pied Piper* (1942) and *They Got Me Covered* (1943), enabling him to ease back into Hollywood as an actor during the war years. The bald, imposing Preminger, with his autocratic bearing and thick Viennese accent, was so effective in portraying German soldiers that he was asked to reprise his *Margin for Error* role in a 1943 film version of the same name, which he also directed. Ironically, that year also saw the Jewish Preminger become a naturalized U.S. citizen. The actor-director would eventually parlay his success as a cinematic Nazi into a memorably bombastic and brutal camp commandant in the Billy Wilder film *Stalag 17* (1953), a characterization Preminger's detractors came to blur with the man himself. Another instance of Darryl Zanuck's disfavor, this time falling on director Rouben Mamoulian, led to Preminger's chance to direct *Laura* (1944), a critical and commercial hit and Preminger's breakthrough. The mystery, starring Gene Tierney and Dana Andrews, earned the producer-director his first Academy Award nomination for best direction, as well as a new seven-year contract with Fox.

The period of Preminger's long-term studio contract saw an eclectic mix of productions that never seemed to equal the peak of *Laura.* These included *Royal Scandal* (1945), a disappointing costume piece with Tallulah Bankhead; *Forever Amber* (1947), a period piece set in the court of Charles II; *Daisy Kenyon* (1947), a romance with Henry Fonda and Joan Crawford; and *The Fan* (1949), a version of Oscar Wilde's play *Lady Windermere's Fan.* Perhaps most worthy of note from the immediate postwar period is the handful of thrillers and film noir pieces Preminger directed: *Fallen Angel* (1945), *Whirlpool* (1950), *Where the Sidewalk Ends* (1950), *The Thirteenth Letter* (1951), and *Angel Face* (1953). On 4 December 1951 Preminger married his second wife, Mary Gardner; they had no children. That same year, he directed several Broadway productions, including *A Modern Primitive* and *The Moon Is Blue*.

Widely considered a hot-tempered tyrant on the set, the director, sometimes referred to as Otto the Terrible, was known as a fierce disciplinarian. He also had a reputation for keeping a tight fiscal grip on productions. Largely for these reasons, and because he insisted on artistic control, Preminger was often at odds with a studio system designed to, as he saw it, undercut the authority of a film's director. His contract with Fox having expired, Preminger soon became one of the first independent producer-directors to buck the Hollywood studio system. In 1953, under his own Carlyle Productions, Preminger released *The Moon Is Blue,* igniting a storm of controversy because it lacked the approval of the Motion Picture Association, whose code had restrictions against "objectionable" material. That film became the first of several Preminger movies to challenge the institutional censorship of Hollywood. Trespassing into the forbidden territory of adultery and seduction, *The Moon Is Blue* broke convention by using the terms "virgin" and "seduce." It was followed by other films with taboo subjects: an exploration of drug addiction in *The Man with the Golden Arm* (1955); criticism of the government and the machinery of war in *The Court-Martial of Billy Mitchell* (1955); rape in *Anatomy of a Murder* (1959); the "Jewish problem" in *Exodus* (1960); homosexuality in *Advise and Consent* (1962); and racial issues in *Hurry Sundown* (1966). Preminger also took risks by hiring blacklisted talent to work on his films.

Often the controversial nature of the films helped their reception, and several garnered Oscar nominations, including, for best actor, Frank Sinatra for *The Man with the Golden Arm* and James Stewart for *Anatomy of a Murder,* which also won a best picture nomination. Preminger earned his second Academy Award nomination as best director for *The Cardinal* (1963). The director went to court several times to defend *The Moon Is Blue* and *The Man with the Golden Arm* against censorship. Eventually, the Motion Picture Association's code was liberalized, leading to the cinematic rating system. *Anatomy of a Murder* was initially banned in Chicago, and in January 1966 Preminger lost a court case to prevent gratuitous cutting and commercial interruption of the film during its television airing.

Preminger's most productive period also saw the release of *Carmen Jones* (1954), a successful updating of the Georges Bizet opera *Carmen; Saint Joan* (1957), based on the George Bernard Shaw play with newcomer Jean Seberg in the lead; *Bonjour Tristesse* (1957), with Seberg and David Niven in a south of France locale; and *Porgy and Bess* (1959), starring Dorothy Dandridge and Pearl Bailey, who had also worked with the director on *Carmen Jones.* His later work includes *Bunny Lake Is Missing* (1965), *Skidoo* (1968), *Tell Me That You Love Me, Junie Moon* (1970), and *Such Good Friends* (1971). In addition, Preminger made himself known to a younger generation of viewers by portraying the dastardly Mr. Freeze on the campy *Batman* television series. His last film was *The Human Factor* (1980).

Divorced from Mary Gardner in 1958, Preminger married his third wife, Patricia Hope Bryce, fashion coordinator on *Bonjour Tristesse*, in March 1960. Later in the year twins, Mark William and Victoria Elizabeth, were born to the couple, who remained married until Preminger's death. The family lived in a townhouse on Manhattan's East Side, where Preminger had a substantial collection of modern art. The year following the 1970 death of stripper Gypsy Rose Lee, Preminger revealed that he was the father of the burlesque star's twenty-six-year-old son, Erik Kirkland. Preminger adopted Kirkland, who then changed his name to Eric Lee Preminger. Afflicted with Alzheimer's disease and cancer in the last years of his life, Preminger died at the age of eighty at his Manhattan home.

Sometimes Preminger's large ambitions led to less than successful films. *Saint Joan* suffered from the director's misstep of casting a young Jean Seberg in the title role; *Exodus* was earnest but ultimately unsatisfying; and *In Harm's Way* (1965) was a bloated effort that had John Wayne and Kirk Douglas fighting in World War II's Pacific theater while navigating the mined straits of buried anger, father-son conflict, gender relations, sneaking politicians, and even date rape. A *New York Times* review referred to *Rosebud* (1975) as a "multi-million-dollar disaster." Preminger's explorations of vexing and complex social issues often manifested itself in a cinematically disappointing way. Stylistically, he was seen as a skilled technician who was partial to long, wide-screen takes and gradual camera movements. The long opening shot from *In Harm's Way* is a prominent example. A recurring theme in his wide range of films is the contingency and ambiguity of truth. The director, known for bringing in a production within budget and on time as well as for caustically dismantling the egos of his actors and underlings, once told an interviewer, "The actors I work with are not difficult, or I am more difficult than they are so that I don't notice!" In the end Preminger is best remembered as a producer-director who shook the Hollywood establishment by tackling difficult social issues in his films.

★

Preminger: An Autobiography (1977) is the director's story in his own words and includes many personal anecdotes. Willi Frischauer, *Behind the Scenes of Otto Preminger* (1973), is a biography written by a man who knew Preminger for more than forty years. Andrew Sarris, ed., *Hollywood Voices: Interviews with Film Directors* (1971), includes Preminger's conversations with Ian Cameron, Mark Shivas, and Paul Mayersberg. An obituary is in the *New York Times* (24 Apr. 1986).

ANDREW SMITH

PRESSER, Jackie (*b.* 6 August 1926 in Cleveland, Ohio; *d.* 9 July 1988 in Lakewood, Ohio), president of the Teamsters Union known for his connections to organized crime, to political figures, and to the Federal Bureau of Investigation, the latter as both informer and investigatee.

The first of two children of teenaged Jewish parents, Faye Friedman and William ("Bill") Presser, Jackie was born into the family business. His maternal grandfather was a bootlegger. His father, a hatmaker by trade, became a racketeer and a labor leader, as did Jackie's maternal uncle, Allen Friedman, who came to live with the Pressers as a thirteen-year-old orphan. Leaving eighth grade at age sixteen, Presser served in the U.S. Navy during World War II and received an honorable discharge in 1947. Upon his return to civilian life, he tried car thievery, the jukebox and vending machine business that his father controlled, and ownership of a bowling alley as means of making a living. As later indicated on official transcripts, his father and his Uncle Allen, who was five years older than Jackie, were often his mentors or allies in such criminal activities as kickbacks and payoffs, ghost and mob hiring, physical threats, and embezzlement.

In the 1950s Presser was employed by, but then removed from, the Cleveland hotel and restaurant employees union that was later incorporated as Local 10. The late 1950s and early 1960s was the period of investigation by the Senate Select Committee on Improper Activities in the Labor Management Field (also known as the McClellan Committee or Senate Rackets Committee). During this time, Presser became the business agent of Local 274 of the Hotel and Restaurant Employees Union, also in Cleveland. By 1956 he was elected president of the Ohio Council of the union, and in 1966 he became president and general manager of the Hotel Employees Local 10.

In 1971 Presser became a trustee of his father's Ohio Teamsters Joint Council. As an organizer for the International Brotherhood of Teamsters, he then worked at changing the image of the Teamsters Union as well as his own style. He became wealthy from his ownership of several Cleveland area businesses, including the Pavilion Wine and Spirits shop, the Forge restaurant, and the Front Row Theatre, as well as from multiple union jobs. Holding several different positions at the same time, he was one of the highest-paid union figures in America.

Also in the early 1970s, while simultaneously a confidant of labor officials and mobsters, Presser became an informer for the Federal Bureau of Investigation, a fact exposed publicly in the *Cleveland Plain Dealer* in 1981. With an FBI file of more than 2,000 pages, Presser's undercover activities

Teamster president Jackie Presser at an AFL-CIO meeting, 1987. UPI/CORBIS-BETTMANN

created jurisdictional difficulties among various federal departments and local Cleveland law officials. Testifying before the President's Commission on Crime in 1985, Presser repeatedly invoked the Fifth Amendment against self-incrimination. Although frequently investigated and sometimes indicted by the U.S. government, Presser was never jailed, unlike his father, his uncle Allen, and numerous associates. Many sources, including the *New York Times,* wondered whether this was because Presser was "innocent, too valuable an informant, or too well connected at [the] White House."

In fact, President Ronald Reagan made Presser a senior adviser on economic affairs despite his mafia connections. After more than two decades as a union official, Presser, upon his father's retirement in 1976, joined the Teamsters executive board. In 1984 he assumed the presidency of the powerful IBT—the International Brotherhood of Teamsters, Chauffeurs, Warehousemen, and Helpers of America—the largest labor union in the United States. Under his leadership, the Teamsters Union was readmitted in 1988 to the AFL-CIO (American Federation of Labor–Congress of Industrial Organizations), from which it been suspended in 1957.

As a spokesperson for American labor, Presser maintained that jobs were a major U.S. export. In *Fortune* magazine (September 1985), he wrote, "When Americans work, America works," and he went on to explain a Teamster proposal to institute financial penalties to curb the practice of American companies that hired cheap labor abroad.

A portly man, Presser was a womanizer who married five times: Pauline Wall in 1947 (one child, Suzanne), Elaine Goeble in 1949, Patricia in 1952 (two children, Bari and Gary), his longtime mistress Carmen De La Portilla in 1971 (the marriage lasted fourteen years), and Cynthia Jarabek in 1986. His first four marriages ended in divorce; his fifth wife survived him. In 1988, a few months after surgery for brain cancer, Presser, who had suffered a heart attack in 1966, died of cardiac arrest. Although he was under indictment on racketeering charges at the time of his death, elected officials and members of the U.S. Department of Labor, along with many workers, were among the more than 600 people who attended his funeral. Senator Orrin Hatch, in one of the three funeral eulogies given on 12 July, mentioned Presser's "mistakes" and "courage." Presser was buried in Mount Olive Cemetery in Solon, a Cleveland suburb. In 1994 Cynthia Presser was removed as executor of his estate and found guilty of misappropriation and embezzlement.

Starting as the son of an old-time union man, Presser gained his own place in American labor history. Alternately secretive and outgoing, he communicated with many levels of society, from known mobsters to the nation's presidents. He both perpetuated "dirty" tactics and informed on those employing them to the FBI. As president of the International Brotherhood of Teamsters, he improved benefits and conditions for millions of workers, especially retirees, and was instrumental in the realignment of the Teamsters with the AFL-CIO.

★

James Neff, *Mobbed Up: Jackie Presser's High-Wire Life in the Teamsters, the Mafia, and the FBI* (1989), is a biographical account based on court papers, transcripts of union meetings, government documents, and interviews with family members. Steven Brill, *The Teamsters* (1978), includes nine chapters on individual union leaders, including Jackie Presser. Allen Friedman and Ted Schwarz, *Power and Greed: Inside the Teamsters Empire of Corruption* (1989), is a detailed insider's view, in which Friedman, Presser's uncle, is contemptuous of his nephew. An obituary is in the *New York Times* (11 July 1988).

RACHEL SHOR

PRESTON, Robert (*b.* 8 June 1918 in Newton Highlands, Massachusetts; *d.* 21 March 1987 in Santa Barbara, California), actor who appeared in over forty films, usually in brash, energetic roles, and also on the stage and on television; he is best remembered for his performance as the breezy confidence man Harold Hill in the stage and screen versions of *The Music Man*.

Born Robert Preston Meservey, Preston moved to East Los Angeles, California, with his parents at the age of two. His father, Frank Meservey, was in the garment business and also played baseball with the Hollywood Blues of the Pacific Coast League; his mother, Ruth Rea, worked as a clerk in a Los Angeles music store. Preston attended Lincoln High School in Hollywood, where a drama teacher encouraged him in his acting aspirations and even cast him as Hamlet when he was fifteen. At age sixteen he left school to become an actor. After appearing briefly with a Shakespearean repertory company headed by the mother of the actor Tyrone Power, he joined the Pasadena Community Theatre, where he appeared in over forty productions.

While starring in a Pasadena Playhouse production of *Idiot's Delight,* by Robert Sherwood, Preston was spotted by a talent scout and signed at age nineteen to a motion picture contract with Paramount Studios. Over the next few years he appeared in dozens of minor and occasionally major films, often in supporting roles. Ruggedly handsome, with a disarming smile, he played a wide range of roles, even villainous ones. He was cast as hotheaded men in such movies as *Beau Geste* (1939), *North West Mounted Police* (1940), and *Reap the Wild Wind* (1942). He also played leading man to "sarong girl" Dorothy Lamour in *Typhoon* (1940) and *Moon over Burma* (1940). In *This Gun for Hire* (1942) he had an important role in a movie that brought actor Alan Ladd to stardom.

Robert Preston. TED SENNETT

On 8 November 1940 Preston married the actress Catherine Craig (née Feltus). They had no children. From 1950 onward the couple lived mostly on an eight-acre estate in Greenwich, Connecticut. Their marriage lasted until Preston's death.

After serving in the Army Air Forces in the European theater during World War II, Preston returned to Hollywood in 1946 and resumed making films. Few of them, however, were noteworthy and he decided to try his hand in the theater. He went to New York in 1951 to replace José Ferrer in the revival of *Twentieth Century,* then remained to star in such plays as *The Male Animal* (1952), *The Tender Trap* (1954), and *Janus* (1955).

A number of actors were considered for the role of Harold Hill in Meredith Willson's *The Music Man,* but after Preston auditioned he was endorsed by the production's organizers, including director Morton Da Costa, who admired the actor's ability to "project himself larger than life." As the good-hearted con man who sells nonexistent musical instruments to the inhabitants of River City, Iowa, circa 1912, Preston sang and acted with joyful ease. *The Music Man* opened on 19 December 1957 to enthusiastic reviews, and Preston, who received a Tony Award for his performance, settled into the part for the first two years of the run. In 1962 he reprised the role on the screen, again directed by Morton Da Costa.

After leaving *The Music Man,* Preston continued to act regularly. On film he appeared in the adaptation of William Inge's stage play *The Dark at the Top of the Stairs* (1960), as a traveling salesman with a troubled family life, and in *All the Way Home* (1963), adapted from the Tad Mosel play and James Agee novel, as an ill-fated husband. He also had a role in the star-laden epic Western *How the West Was Won* (1963). In 1974 he played Lucille Ball's adoring southern husband in the film version of the musical *Mame.* His television movies included *My Father's House* (1975), *September Gun* (1983), and *Finnegan Begin Again* (1985).

Preston's theater roles in the 1960s and 1970s kept him equally busy. He played King Henry II in James Goldman's *The Lion in Winter* (1966), and he received another Tony Award for his performance opposite Mary Martin in the two-character musical *I Do! I Do!* (1966), which followed a marriage across the years. In 1974 he starred as pioneer filmmaker Mack Sennett in the Jerry Herman musical *Mack and Mabel,* and in 1977 he replaced George C. Scott as the modern-day Volpone in *Sly Fox,* a comedy by Larry Gelbart.

In the last years of his life Preston continued to act in films and on television but he selected his parts more sparingly. Happily, he found one of his very best roles in 1983, when he appeared in *Victor/Victoria,* a comedy directed by Blake Edwards. As Toddy, a gay nightclub entertainer who turns singer Victoria Grant (Julie Andrews) into a female impersonator (a woman pretending to be a man pretending to be a woman), Preston gave a funny, touching, and irresistible performance. He won an Oscar nomination for best supporting actor, and received the best supporting actor award from the National Society of Film Critics. He also had a major role as a cheerfully corrupt Dr. Feelgood in the corrosive Hollywood satire *S.O.B.* (1981), another film written, produced, and directed by Blake Edwards. Preston died of lung cancer at age sixty-eight.

From his early years as a brash young contract player in small roles, to his portrayal of the irrepressible "music man" leading seventy-six trombones down an Iowa street, Robert Preston was an actor who projected and inspired enthusiasm. When he was at his best, audiences were delighted to march in his parade.

★

Joseph Hurley, "Robert Preston," *Films in Review* 33 (Aug.–Sept. 1982): 396–407, surveys Preston's career. Other articles on the actor include Tom Prideaux, "That Music Man Is Back on Broadway, Still Making Films and Aiming at Shakespeare," *People* (31 Oct. 1977), and D. Keith Mano, "Robert Preston," *People* (28 June 1982). Obituaries are in the *Los Angeles Times* (22 Mar. 1987), the *New York Times* (23 Mar. 1987), and *Variety* (25 Mar. 1987).

TED SENNETT

PRINZ, Joachim (*b.* 10 May 1902 in Burkhardtsdorf, Germany; *d.* 30 September 1988 in Livingston, New Jersey), rabbi, Jewish leader, and author who was a prominent opponent of the Nazi regime and a crusader for American civil rights.

Joachim Prinz was born in the village of Burkhardtsdorf in Saxony, the eldest of four children of Nani Berg and Joseph Prinz, a prosperous department store owner. He learned English as a child. Unlike most middle-class German Jews of the time, who were assimilated, he embraced Zionism, doing so at the early age of fifteen. After graduating from secondary school in Oppeln in 1921, Prinz attended the University of Breslau from 1921 to 1923 and studied for a summer at the University of Berlin in 1922. In 1923 and 1924 he attended the University of Giessen, which in 1927 conferred on him a Ph.D. in philosophy, and in 1925 he was ordained a rabbi at the Jewish Theological Seminary in Breslau. On 25 December 1925 Prinz married Lucie Horovitz.

In 1926 Prinz became the youngest rabbi to head a congregation in Berlin. For the next eleven years he was a vital force in Berlin Jewry. While many other Jewish leaders advocated further integration in German society, Prinz adhered to Zionist ideology. His book *Jüdische Geschichte* (Jewish History, 1931), a historical overview of the Jewish people, contended that despite emancipation, Jews still existed in the "twilight of the ghetto." Prinz warned against the rise of the Nazi movement.

The early 1930s was a tumultuous time for Prinz. In January 1931 his wife died of complications arising from the birth of their daughter, Lucie. (Ironically, Prinz's mother had died giving birth to his sister.) A year later, on 24 May 1932, Prinz married Hilde Goldschmidt; they had three children: Michael, Jonathan, and Deborah.

Prinz's public denunciations of the Nazi regime brought him great visibility, and he was arrested several times. "No subterfuge can save us now," he wrote in *Wir Juden* (We Jews, 1934). "In place of assimilation we desire a new concept: recognition of the Jewish nation and Jewish race." Attendance at his synagogue burgeoned. While the political environment deteriorated, Prinz's literary output flourished, with the publication of *Illustrierte Jüdische Geschichte* (Illustrated Jewish History, 1933), *Die Geschichten der Bibel* (Bible Stories, 1934), *Die Reiche Israel und Juda* (The Kingdoms of Israel and Judah, 1935), *Der Freitagabend* (Friday Night, 1935), and *Das Leben im Ghetto* (Life in the Ghetto, 1937).

After a 1937 visit to the United States sponsored by Rabbi Stephen S. Wise, a leading Jewish-American figure, Prinz decided to emigrate. His farewell meeting in Berlin, attended by 2,000 congregants, led SS officer Adolf Eichmann to report back to the Gestapo that Prinz's plan to move to the United States proved that an international Jewish conspiracy was headquartered in New York. The Gestapo briefly arrested Prinz and expelled him from Germany. Eichmann signed the order.

The Prinzes arrived in New York City on 1 August 1937. Prinz toured the United States for two years, lecturing and raising money for the United Palestine Appeal. Rabbi Wise, who thought Prinz "one of the most gifted and brilliant young men . . . in the rabbinate," was instrumental in Prinz's appointment as rabbi of Temple B'nai Abraham in Newark, the second oldest Jewish congregation in New Jersey. Prinz was installed on 9 September 1939. He became a U.S. citizen in 1944. The Prinzes lived in Newark at 49 Shanley Avenue and later moved to South Eleventh Street. Prinz and his wife unofficially adopted Jo Seelmann, a cousin of Hilde's and a survivor of Auschwitz, when she arrived in the United States in 1947. In the mid-1950s the family moved to 306 Elmwynd Drive in Orange, New Jersey.

Joachim Prinz, *c.* 1962. ARCHIVE PHOTOS

Prinz's role in Jewish organizational life expanded after World War II. In 1946 he joined the executive board of the American Jewish Congress, later serving as vice president from 1952 to 1958. He surprised many when he declared that the establishment of the State of Israel in 1948 made Zionism obsolete. He called for a new movement in which the ties between Israel and American Jews were based on the concept of Jewish "peoplehood." In 1956 Prinz became director of the Conference on Jewish Material Claims Against Germany, Inc. He joined the editorial boards of the periodicals *Reconstructionist* and *Judaism* in 1958. That same year Prinz became president of the American Jewish Congress, serving until 1966. From 1966 to 1969 he served as chairman of the Conference of Presidents of Major American Jewish Organizations. His concerns included the rise of international anti-Semitism, particularly in the Soviet Union and in Arab countries. He became well-known among Latin American Jews through the Spanish translations of his books.

Prinz's espousal of liberal causes in the 1950s led the right-wing anti-Semitic journal *Common Sense* to label him a communist. Prinz's libel suit in 1954 against the journal's editor, Conde McGinley, resulted in Prinz's being awarded $30,000 in damages, which he never collected. Still, the case was viewed as a victory for proving that courts could be an effective battleground in the fight against racial and religious libel.

Prinz was a proponent of the strict separation of church and state. Testifying before Congress in 1964 against a proposed school prayer amendment, Prinz noted that religious exercises in German public schools had failed to prevent the Holocaust. He opposed government aid to religious and private schools and called on state governments to exempt non-Christians from Sunday closing laws.

Prinz became a vocal and effective leader in the fight for civil rights and civil liberties. He took part in many demonstrations in the New York metropolitan area and in the South. In 1960 he organized a picket line at a Woolworth store in New York City to protest the company's refusal to serve blacks at its lunch counters in the South. As a founding chairman of the 1963 civil rights march on Washington, where Martin Luther King, Jr., made his famous "I Have a Dream" speech, Prinz urged Jewish participation in the civil rights movement. In his speech from the podium, he movingly denounced the "sin of silence."

Prinz, who was five feet, five inches tall, weighed 160 pounds, and had black hair and brown eyes, was a frank and direct man. He regularly worked seventeen-hour days, and enjoyed reading, gardening, and art appreciation.

Continuing to write, Prinz contributed a chapter to Samuel Caplan and Harold U. Ribalow's *The Great Jewish Books* (1952). He also wrote *The Dilemma of the Modern Jew* (1962), *Popes from the Ghetto* (1966), and *The Secret Jews* (1973).

Retired in 1977, Prinz moved to Mendham, New Jersey. He died of a heart attack at Saint Barnabas Hospital in Livingston, New Jersey, and was buried at Temple B'nai Abraham Memorial Park in Union, New Jersey.

★

Charles Moritz, ed., *Current Biography 1963* (1964), contains a profile of Prinz at the height of his career. *Encyclopedia Judaica*, vol. 13 (1971), has an entry for him. Prinz's complete speech at the March on Washington can be heard on the record *We Shall Overcome: The March on Washington, August 28, 1963*. Obituaries are in the *New York Times* (1 Oct. 1988) and *Christian Century* (2 Nov. 1988).

SHARONA A. LEVY

PRITZKER, A(bram) N(icholas) (*b.* 6 January 1896 in Chicago, Illinois; *d.* 8 February 1986 in Chicago, Illinois), iconoclastic businessman and philanthropist whose ventures placed him among the wealthiest individuals in the United States.

The second son of Nicholas J. Pritzker, from a Jewish community near Kiev, and Annie Cohen, Abram grew up hearing tales of the struggle of his father, a penniless immigrant, to become a pharmacist and lawyer. His education in Chicago public schools led to undergraduate studies at Northwestern University (1913–1914). He earned his Ph.B. degree in 1916 at the University of Chicago, then served as a U.S. Navy petty officer from 1917 to 1919. After securing an LL.B. degree at Harvard University in 1920, Pritzker joined his father and older brother, Harry, in the family practice in Chicago. He married Fanny L. Doppelt in 1921; they had three sons.

In 1936, not enjoying the practice of law, Pritzker began to make real estate investments with his younger brother, Jack. Keeping business in the family became a hallmark of Pritzker's financial dealings. Investments in small companies netted the capital to purchase the Cory Corporation in 1942, for $25,000 cash and a $75,000 promissory note. The first major investment for the brothers, the deal represented acceptance by a major bank and set standards for many years. In 1967 the Cory Corporation was sold to Hershey Foods for $23 million. Pritzker scribbled business deals on envelopes and offered terms others considered too low. His insistence on studying a deal thoroughly and negotiating fiercely for the best contract enabled his business empire to grow dramatically. In 1957 the Pritzkers purchased Hyatt House, which developed into the multibillion-dollar Hyatt Corporation with hotels and resorts around the world. Pritzker managers ran the hotels, but the corporation rarely owned the buildings. Other investments were

A. N. Pritzker, 1984. UPI/CORBIS-BETTMANN

McCall's magazine and Braniff Airlines. More than 250 companies formed the Marmon Group, established in 1964. Managers ran businesses independently; each business was expected to compete and succeed on its own merits, even against other members of the Marmon Group. Pritzker often ignored the advice of lawyers and experts. He refused to sell shares in his companies, believing that revealing information to shareholders would jeopardize chances for success. All Pritzker businesses operated under the umbrella of Pritzker and Pritzker, a legal and investment enterprise owned entirely by family members.

Pritzker, usually called A. N., believed in direct speech. Of medium height and build, he displayed a ready smile and self-deprecating sense of humor. He was extremely bright and blessed with a quick grasp of details. A benevolent patriarch, Pritzker stressed family honor and integrity. He disdained ostentatious displays of wealth. Family photographs covered his office walls, and his sons joined the family corporation after college. Family members remained close, living within a few miles of each other in Chicago and working together. To maintain privacy and avoid friction in the business, reporters rarely were granted interviews. Pritzker's wife died in 1970; on 13 January 1972 Pritzker married Lorraine Colantonio, part owner and manager of a Hyatt Chalet.

Family members benefited from a complex series of trusts established before tax law changes in 1985 ended the practice of sheltering income in that fashion. Pritzker claimed to have saved millions of dollars in taxes as a result. According to court records, his taxable personal assets totaled only $25,000. This minimized estate taxes so effectively that the Internal Revenue Service sued the family for $53 million in taxes but had to settle for less.

Pritzker donated to numerous charitable organizations. He believed Israel deserved support from the United States and founded the Israel Bond Organization in 1950, but rarely attended temple services and was emphatically not a Zionist. Though Pritzker criticized the Israeli government as too religious, he and his family actively raised funds, estimated at $500,000 per year, to support schools and other humanitarian concerns in Israel. In 1985 he received the Israel Prime Minister's Medal for his philanthropic work. The University of Chicago School of Medicine was renamed the Pritzker School of Medicine after the family donated $16 million. The Pritzker Architecture Prize honors innovative designers. Many cultural institutions in Chicago benefited from generous donations from Pritzker. His favorite philanthropic work assisted the elementary school he had attended, Wicker Park School. In 1980 an appeal from the principal inspired Pritzker to establish an annual $45,000 fund to provide after-school programs in an achievement-skills center. The school's name was changed to Pritzker Elementary to commemorate his generosity. In his last years Pritzker received honors from the National Business Hall of Fame and other organizations.

In 1975 Pritzker became the oldest man to be catapulted from an aircraft carrier in a U.S. Navy jet. Business deals faded from his life in the 1980s as failing eyesight and hearing limited his capacity for negotiating. Consequently he spent many hours on philanthropic endeavors and writing his autobiography. Following his father's example, Pritzker wrote of his youth, business dealings, and personal philosophy. The privately published book, written with historian Herman Kogan, was distributed to family members. Pritzker entered Michael Reese Hospital for abdominal surgery in January 1986; while there, he died of a stroke. Private burial in Chicago continued the family tradition of avoiding publicity.

Pritzker's business dealings amassed a fortune protected through trusts that placed him high on lists of the wealthiest Americans. Family integrity and participation built a strong corporate structure that survived him. Pritzker embodied the American ideals of hard work and striving for success. The son of a poor Jewish immigrant became one of the wealthiest men in the country through his own efforts and on his own terms. Pritzker said, "A lot of people say I brag a lot, but what the hell, I got a lot to brag about."

★

The last notable interview with Pritzker formed the basis for Jon Anderson, "Pritzker on Pritzker: A Mogul Talks About His Family Dynasty," *Chicago Tribune* (11 Nov. 1985). Ford S. Worthy, "The Pritzkers: Unveiling a Private Family," *Fortune* (25 Apr. 1988), contains information on the business dealings of Pritzker's family and a corporate history. Obituaries are in the *New York Times* and *Chicago Tribune* (both 9 Feb. 1986).

SUZANNE M. MINER

PROVENZANO, Anthony ("Tony Pro") (*b.* 7 May 1917 in New York City; *d.* 12 December 1988 in Lompac, California), a major labor racketeer in the International Brotherhood of Teamsters, believed to have been instrumental in the disappearance and murder of Jimmy Hoffa.

Anthony Provenzano was one of six sons born to Rosario Provenzano and Josephine (Dispensa) Provenzano, Sicilian immigrants living on the Lower East Side of New York City. He dropped out of school at the age of fifteen and later became a truck driver in Hackensack, New Jersey. He had aspirations of becoming a professional prizefighter and bore the scars of an amateur career.

Anthony Provenzano leaving Newark Federal Court during his extortion trial, 1963. UPI/CORBIS-BETTMANN

Provenzano's reputation for violence brought him to the attention of Anthony Strollo, better known as "Tony Bender," a *caporegime* in the Genovese crime family. With Bender's patronage, "Tony Pro," as he was known to friends and foes alike, became a member of the Genovese organization. By cunning and ruthlessness he made his way into the leadership of the International Brotherhood of Teamsters, Local 560 in northern New Jersey. By 1941 Provenzano was a shop steward, and by 1958, with the help of Jimmy Hoffa, he was elected president of the local. Provenzano was rewarded for his support of Hoffa's successful 1957 bid for the union's international presidency with an appointment to a vice presidency. At the same time he rose rapidly in the ranks of the Cosa Nostra, becoming a *caporegime* in the Genovese family.

Throughout these years Tony Pro was involved in violent union election campaigns, federal and state investigations, and the mysterious disappearances and deaths of union opponents. His influence earned him the enmity of law-enforcement officials but the homage and loyalty of Teamster rank and file.

Provenzano's leadership of Local 560 and his strategic connections with Hoffa and the international executive enabled him to embezzle funds and sign "sweetheart contracts" with trucking firms. Three of Provenzano's six brothers as well as his daughter had affiliations with Teamster Local 560.

In 1963 Tony Pro's salary of $113,000 made him the highest-paid union official in the world. However, a conviction that same year for extortion sent him to prison for seven years. During the four and one-half years he served, his brothers Salvatore and Nunzio ran the affairs of the 13,000-member Teamsters local headquartered in Union, New Jersey, and they continued doing so for the five subsequent years he was disqualified from holding union office.

Behind his rise and fall lay a shadowy world of criminal associates engaged in murder, mayhem, and corruption. In 1961 a rival, Anthony Castellito, challenged his leadership and was garroted with piano wire by unknown executioners. In 1978 Provenzano was convicted of Castellito's murder and was sentenced in Kingston, New York, to twenty-five years. Following this there were two additional convictions, one later in 1978 for which he was sentenced in Federal District Court in Manhattan to four years for arranging kickbacks on a $2.3 million pension-fund loan, and another a year later to a twenty-year prison sentence by a federal judge in New Jersey for labor racketeering. Provenzano remained in federal prison until his death.

Perhaps Provenzano's most notorious activity in a career of racketeering and murder involved the disappearance of his onetime close associate Jimmy Hoffa. The Hoffa-Provenzano alliance was typical of the bargains Hoffa struck with gangsters around the country. In return for their help in pushing him to the top, Hoffa enabled them to exploit positions of union authority by engaging in moneymaking schemes including pension frauds, loan-sharking, and employer extortion rackets.

Both Hoffa and Provenzano were serving prison terms in the federal correctional facility in Lewisburg, Pennsylvania, when bad blood between the two developed. Upon his release after serving a substantial part of his sentence and being pardoned by President Richard M. Nixon, Hoffa announced that he intended to seek the presidency of the Teamsters despite the opposition of his underworld allies. On 30 July 1975 Hoffa vanished, presumably murdered by Cosa Nostra members. On the date he was reported missing, Hoffa was on his way to what he thought was a meeting with Provenzano, who emerged as a key suspect in Hoffa's disappearance. It was widely believed that Provenzano's associates kidnapped and murdered Hoffa and disposed of his body in a garbage shredder.

In 1984 a federal judge removed Local 560's executive board and placed it in a trusteeship until such time as the membership could freely nominate and elect new officers. After more than two years, Local 560 voted in its first contested election in more than a quarter of a century. But even then scandal invalidated the outcome when the FBI disclosed that a Genovese crime family capo was promoting a Provenzano associate. Local 560 may have been rescued from mob control but the Provenzano grip on Local 84 in New Jersey and Local 522 in New York remained intact.

Late in 1988 Provenzano was admitted to the Lompac District Hospital in California, near the federal penitentiary in which he was incarcerated, for congestive heart failure. A month later he died of a heart attack.

★

A standard work on the Brotherhood of Teamsters and its mob affiliations is Steven Brill, *The Teamsters* (1978). The President's Commission on Organized Crime released two reports that provide detailed information on organized crime's penetration into the labor movement: *The Edge: Organized Crime, Business, and Labor Unions* (1985) and *Organized Crime and Labor-Management Racketeering in the United States* (1985). An obituary is in the *New York Times* (13 Dec. 1988).

ROBERT J. KELLY

R

RABI, I(sidor) I(saac) (*b.* 29 July 1898 in Rymanów, Poland; *d.* 11 January 1988 in New York City), physicist and educator who won the Nobel Prize in physics in 1944 for his invention of the molecular-beam magnetic resonance method of observing atomic spectra.

Rabi, the son of David and Sheindel Rabi, was brought to the United States as an infant. The family settled on the Lower East Side of New York City, like thousands of other Jewish immigrants from Eastern Europe. They had limited money but were not poor. In 1907 the Rabis—including a daughter, Gertrude—moved to the Brownsville section of Brooklyn, where David Rabi owned a grocery store. There young Isidor discovered the riches of the local public library. Most notably, he became acquainted with the Copernican view of the solar system—vastly at odds with what he had learned of the world of nature in his Yiddish-speaking home. "Who needs God?" he inquired of his stunned, uncomprehending parents, who were deeply wounded by his words. Although Rabi moved away from the Orthodox teachings in which he had been reared, all his life he remained a religious man deeply committed to the values and ideals of Judaism. Attending Manual Training High School in Brooklyn, he read widely, not only in science but also in psychology, history, and in the literature of socialism.

He enrolled in Cornell University in 1916 as an engineering student but shifted to the field of chemistry. After graduating in 1919, a year early, he worked at insignificant jobs for three years before returning to Cornell to do graduate work in chemistry. He later said, "I soon realized that the part of chemistry that I liked best was physics." In 1923 he entered Columbia University to do graduate work in physics. His life's work was taking shape. He organized a group of youthful physicists who like himself were smitten by the avant-garde field of quantum physics, not yet being taught at American schools. The self-appointed mission of these young men was to bring the leading edge of physics to the United States. On 17 August 1926 Rabi married Helen Newmark, whom he had met three years earlier at Cornell. They had two daughters, Nancy Elizabeth, born in 1929, and Margaret Joella, born in 1934.

After receiving a Ph.D. from Columbia in 1927, Rabi left for Europe on a two-year postdoctoral fellowship, which he spent mostly in Germany. There he met some of the luminaries of the field, including Hans Bethe, Niels Bohr, Werner Heisenberg, and Otto Stern. Upon Heisenberg's recommendation, George B. Pegram, head of Columbia's Department of Physics, offered Rabi a lectureship, to begin in the fall of 1929. Rabi thus began a career on Manhattan's Morningside Heights that would last to the end of his life. Because Jews were not generally welcome on college and university faculties, Rabi was grateful to Pegram for his appointment as the first Jewish member of the physics department. In 1964 Rabi was named Columbia's first University Professor, its highest academic distinction. The I. I. Rabi Memorial Room in Pupin Hall was dedicated in 1996.

I. I. Rabi. LOS ALAMOS NATIONAL LABORATORY/CORBIS

In 1931 Rabi began a program of molecular-beam research at Columbia. Harold Urey, who had recently won a Carnegie Foundation prize of $7,600 for his discovery of deuterium, gave half of the money to Rabi for the purchase of equipment. Undertaking what would be his seminal achievement, Rabi studied nuclear magnetic moment using a molecular-beam apparatus he had designed. He discovered that observing the behavior of molecular or atomic beams in the presence of two inhomogeneous magnetic fields yields the magnetic moment of atoms and atomic nuclei. For his work, which had been made public in 1937, he was awarded the Nobel Prize in physics in 1944. He learned later that Enrico Fermi, another nuclear pioneer, and Albert Einstein had supported his candidacy. Owing to wartime restrictions on travel, the prize was presented to him at the Men's Faculty Club on the Columbia campus by the university's president, Nicholas Murray Butler, himself a Nobel laureate. Today's MRI (magnetic resonance imaging), widely used in medical diagnosis, derives directly from Rabi's discovery.

Meanwhile, Rabi had joined the war effort, leaving Columbia to become head of research at the newly established Radiation Laboratory at the Massachusetts Institute of Technology, of which he was later associate director. A principal achievement was the perfection of radar as an essential instrument in the struggle against the Axis powers. Rabi would afterward say proudly, "The atomic bomb ended the war, but radar won it." Periodically, Rabi would absent himself from MIT to go to Los Alamos, New Mexico, where he served as a consultant to J. Robert Oppenheimer, scientific director of the Manhattan Project, which was seeking to produce an atomic weapon. Brigadier General Leslie Groves, the mission's military director, was against bringing in advisers but made an exception in the case of Rabi. Rabi was present in May 1945 for the detonation of the first nuclear test at Alamogordo, New Mexico. Earlier, Rabi had turned down Oppenheimer's offer to make him the associate director of the Manhattan Project.

At war's end Rabi returned to Columbia and became chair of the physics department. Although the department's ranks had been depleted by the war, Rabi, with his customary energy and zest, turned it in a few years into one of the best in the world. He also was a guiding spirit in creating the Brookhaven National Laboratory—a facility for the research use of physicists from nine leading universities—which opened on Long Island in 1946. Rabi was also instrumental in establishing, at Irvington, New York, the Nevis Laboratory of the Department of Physics. He was recognized as the dominating figure in the creation of CERN (the European Center for Nuclear Research) in Geneva, Switzerland, the instrument of a consortium of countries, modeled on Brookhaven.

Having become a statesman of science, Rabi served on the General Advisory Committees of the Atomic Energy Commission and the International Atomic Energy Agency and on the NATO Science Committee and the UN Committee on the Peaceful Uses of Atomic Energy. From 1952 to 1956 in the administration of U.S. president Dwight D. Eisenhower, he was a member of what became the President's Science Advisory Committee, having chaired its predecessor committee. Rabi had first met General Eisenhower in 1947, when Ike arrived at Columbia as its president. Calling together senior professors in his office, Eisenhower explained to them that he had been eager to meet "the employees of the university." Rabi interrupted immediately, chiding the novice president in a well-remembered sally: "But Mr. President, we are not employees of the university, we are the university."

A gregarious man who stood about five feet, two inches tall, Rabi was an ardent member of the Council on Foreign Relations and of the Century Association in New York. He was a good storyteller who had a distinctive, high-pitched laugh. Colleagues and students often heard him humming operatic tunes in his laboratory at Columbia. He died in

1988 after a long illness and was buried in Riverside Cemetery in Rochelle Park, New Jersey.

At his death, Rabi was considered the dean of American physics. As a young man, he had sat at the feet of the masters of his field; as an old man he was revered by a new generation of scientists, six of whom won Nobel Prizes. Rabi never regretted his role in helping to marry theoretical science to military needs during World War II. But in the postwar years he lent his prestige and immense verve to the cause of international nuclear control and the pursuit of peaceful uses of the atom. He was gratified to be in the first generation of scientists invited to share in the shaping of national and international public policy.

★

The I. I. Rabi papers, which include a tape-recorded lecture and Rabi's extensive correspondence with leading scientific contemporaries, are in the Library of Congress. Rabi wrote *My Life and Times as a Physicist* (1960) and *Science: The Center of the Culture* (1987). John S. Rigden, *Rabi: Scientist and Citizen* (1988; rev. ed. 1990), is a full-length biography. An obituary is in the *New York Times* (12 Jan. 1988).

HENRY F. GRAFF

RABORN, William Francis, Jr. ("Red") (*b.* 8 June 1905 in Decatur, Texas; *d.* 3 March 1990 in McLean, Virginia), vice admiral who from 1956 to 1959 headed the U.S. Navy's Special Projects Office, which produced the first Polaris ballistic missile submarine.

Vice Admiral William Francis Raborn, Jr. COURTESY OF THE U.S. NAVAL INSTITUTE AT ANNAPOLIS

One of the four children of William Francis Raborn, Sr., a cotton ginner, and Cornelia Victoria Moore, a housewife, Raborn went to public schools in Oklahoma before attending the U.S. Naval Academy, from which he graduated in 1928. He served in the gunnery divisions of a battleship and two destroyers before becoming an aviator in 1934. He then served on carriers and cruisers. During World War II, Raborn directed the Free Gunnery School at Kaneohe, Hawaii, then headed aviation gunnery training in the Office of the Deputy Chief of Operations (Air) in 1943 and 1944, and subsequently was executive officer of the *Hancock* while that ship was off the coast of Japan. After the war, as a captain from June 1945, he served on the staff of Commander Carrier Task Force Thirty-eight, as the operations officer of Commander Fleet Air, West Coast (1949–1950), and as the assistant director of guided missiles in the Office of the Chief of Naval Operations from 1952 to 1954. On 5 April 1955 he married Mildred T. Terrell; they had two children. Raborn was a Mason and a Baptist.

Two months before Admiral Arleigh A. Burke began serving as the chief of naval operations in August 1955, Burke stated that among the issues the navy faced was the development of a ballistic missile. With liquid-fueled, land-based missiles being vulnerable, costly, large, and dangerous for naval use, he determined that the navy must obtain its own, and he got the army's cooperation to produce an improved version of its Jupiter missile. In October 1955 Burke created the Special Projects Office to coordinate missile development, and he chose Raborn to oversee the project. This, Burke later said, "turned out to be my big contribution because [Raborn] has the driving ability, he's got a lot of energy, he's full of enthusiasm, and he can persuade people. He can get things done." In December, Raborn was given authority over a staff of forty. Another version of the story of Raborn's appointment is that because of a fire that in May 1954 had killed ninety-one men on his destroyer, the *Bennington,* he was shifted to a desk job.

Raborn enthusiastically attempted to "push back the frontiers of science" and pioneer a system in which everything was new: ship, solid-fueled missiles, nuclear warheads, guidance systems, navigation, personnel training, and logistic support. Instrumental in his success was his inventing Program Evaluation and Review Technique (PERT), a method of mapping networks; Ship's Internal Navigational System (SINS); and Pop Up, a compressed-air launching device. He made contracts with 2,000 contractors and 2,200 subcontractors, without competitive bids (Congress kept quiet), assembled his managers, and kept a tight hold on information. It greatly helped that the missile to be used had been reduced in weight by two-thirds, to 600 pounds, enabling a submarine to carry sixteen missiles.

In June 1957 Burke stopped cooperating with the army on the Jupiter project. A Polaris missile was not expected to be produced until 1963 or later. Greater construction speed was needed, however, after the Soviets in August 1957 launched an intercontinental ballistic missile and two months later shocked the world by launching the first earth-orbiting satellite.

In response Raborn had a Skipjack-class submarine cut in two and inserted a 130-foot section to hold the missiles and their controls and machinery. Renamed the *George Washington,* it was launched in June 1959 and commissioned on 1 January 1960. Burke knew of no other project that had met its initial budget and was ready three and a half years before its scheduled completion date. With the cost of his program at $1.2 billion a year, Raborn had saved from $6 to $7 billion. He left his office before all of the forty-one boats carrying 656 multiple warheads were completed in 1964. He continued to maintain that a conventional war would be the only type of war the United States would ever have to fight.

After retiring from the navy with the grade of vice admiral in 1963, Raborn directed the Central Intelligence Agency from April 1965 to June 1966. In the private sector he was the vice president of Aerojet-General in California for three years before heading his own military-related firm from 1970 to 1986. He died of cardiac arrest at his home in McLean, Virginia, and was buried at the U.S. Naval Academy in Annapolis, Maryland.

★

Admiral Arleigh Burke's conception of the Polaris project and his appointment of Raborn to head it is covered in the article on Burke in Robert William Love, ed., *The Chiefs of Naval Operations* (1980). The challenges posed by the navy's missile program are discussed in "The Development of Fleet Ballistic Missiles," in Vincent Davis, *The Politics of Innovation: Patterns in Navy Cases* (1967). Articles include "Navy Gives New Push to Polaris Program," *Army and Navy Register* 79 (25 Jan. 1958): 6; "Navy Makes Special Appeal for $1 Billion to Speed Polaris Missile-Submarine Plans," *Army and Navy Journal* 95 (8 Feb. 1958): 11; "First Polaris IRBM Submarine to Join Fleet Late 1960," *Our Navy* 53 (mid-July 1958): 5; and T. E. Shea, "Poseidon Project," *U.S. Naval Institute Proceedings* 87 (Feb. 1961): 32–41. Dr. John T. Mason's oral interviews in 1972, for the U.S. Naval Institute, of Admirals Raborn and Arleigh Burke, Under Secretary and Secretary of the Navy and Secretary of Defense Thomas Gates, and of Carleton Shugg, Jack W. Dunlap, Gordon O. Peterson, and Clement Hays Watson, workers in the Special Projects Office, provide detailed information on its top and middle managers. All had high praise for Raborn. An obituary is in the *New York Times* (13 Mar. 1990).

PAOLO E. COLETTA

RADNER, Gilda (*b.* 28 June 1946 in Detroit, Michigan; *d.* 20 May 1989 in Los Angeles, California), comedienne, actress, and writer who is best known for her work as a cast member of the television show *Saturday Night Live* from 1975 to 1980.

Gilda Radner was born into a prosperous Jewish family in Detroit. Her father, Herman Radner, began his career as a pool shark at a local billiards club, soon earning enough money to become a part owner of the club. During Prohibition he sold his share in order to buy the Walkerville Brewery in Windsor, Ontario, from which he smuggled alcohol into the United States at great profit. By the end of Prohibition, Radner had amassed considerable wealth, which he then invested in an upscale Detroit hotel called the Seville, where popular stage performers like Milton Berle, George Burns, and Frank Sinatra often stayed while playing at Detroit's major theaters, the Fisher, the Shubert, and the Riviera.

Gilda Radner and her brother, Michael, born one year apart, were raised with the help of a live-in nanny, Elizabeth Clementine Gillies, a warmhearted woman who

Gilda Radner, *c.* 1982. ARCHIVE PHOTOS

stayed with the family through Gilda's adolescence. While relations with her mother, Henrietta Dworkin, by Gilda's account an aloof woman, were often strained, she maintained a close relationship with Gillies, nicknamed Dibby, whom she often cited in later years as a strong comedic influence and role model.

Throughout most of Gilda's childhood, the Radners spent four months of every year in Florida, impeding Gilda's ability to make lasting friendships and exacerbating the social ostracism she experienced as a result of a weight problem. Facing tremendous criticism for her obesity from her peers as well as her mother, who had wanted her to be a ballerina, at the age of ten Gilda was placed on a daily regimen of Dexedrine, the first of many weight-loss medications she took in her life. In 1960, when Gilda was fourteen, her father died of brain cancer, leaving her a sizable inheritance.

At Liggett School, an all-girls high school in Detroit, Radner became active in the drama club and sang alto in a double quartet. After attaining a normal weight, she took on her classic adult look. A slight woman with a youthful face, doeish brown eyes, and a marsh of dark, loosely curled hair, she still retained the parodying, character-based sense of humor she had developed in response to the challenging years of her obesity.

After studying drama at the University of Michigan for six years, Radner left without graduating to follow her boyfriend, Jeffrey Rubinoff, to Toronto, where the two shared an opulent condominium with a Yorkshire terrier named Snuffy. Rubinoff introduced her to the *National Lampoon,* a magazine to which he subscribed, and it was during this time that she first learned of Lorne Michaels, who was then starring in the Canadian comedy revue *The Hart and Lorne Terrific Hour.*

When her relationship with Rubinoff ended in 1970, Radner began working as a clown for children's shows, a job she held for almost two years at a salary of $60 per week. Her first foray into professional theater came in the 1972 production of *Godspell,* whose cast included Paul Shaffer, Martin Short, Victor Garber, Eugene Levy, and Andrea Martin, all of whom went on to successful entertainment careers. Upon completion of *Godspell*'s successful run, Radner turned to Toronto's Second City, a comedy club with an emphasis on improvisational sketches, where she worked with Dan Aykroyd and Eugene Levy, among others.

In 1974 Radner accepted an invitation from John Belushi to work in New York for the *National Lampoon Radio Hour,* where she joined her fellow Second City alumnus Dan Aykroyd, along with Brian Murray (Bill Murray's brother), Harold Ramis, and Joe Flaherty.

Lorne Michaels had admired Radner's work at Second City in Toronto, and when he came to New York to start a live sketch-comedy television show for NBC, Radner was the first cast member to be signed. *Saturday Night Live* starred many people Gilda had worked with before; John Belushi and Dan Aykroyd both signed on to the original cast, which also included Chevy Chase, Jane Curtin, Garrett Morris, Laraine Newman, and, the following year, Bill Murray.

Over the next five years, Gilda introduced mainstream America to a bevy of comical characters, such as Emily Litella, a news commentator prone to homophonic misunderstandings, who spoke at length about "violins on television" and "Soviet Jewelry"; Roseanne Roseannadanna, a vulgar, gaudily clad, and excessively made-up caricature of American ethnicity; Babwa Wawa, a parody of TV reporter Barbara Walters; and Lisa Loopner, a gawky teenager. Many of these characters were featured in her solo Broadway show, *Gilda Radner Live from New York,* in 1979. In addition to fame and an Emmy award in 1978, *Saturday Night Live* also brought Radner her first husband, the bandleader G. E. Smith, to whom she was married from 1980 to 1982.

After leaving the show that catapulted her to stardom in 1980, Radner focused her efforts more fully on transplanting her career from television to motion pictures. To this end she accepted a part in the low-budget movie *It Came from Hollywood* (1982). On the set of her first major film, *Hanky Panky* (1982), Radner met Gene Wilder, who directed and costarred in the film. "My new 'career' became getting him to marry me," she later wrote, and she succeeded in this endeavor three years later on 18 September 1984 in a small ceremony in the south of France; her marriage to Wilder lasted until her death. Radner and Wilder divided their time between their respective homes, hers in Stamford, Connecticut, and his in Los Angeles, and they made two additional feature films together, *Woman in Red* (1984) and *Haunted Honeymoon* (1986).

Having spent years with fertility specialists in a vain attempt to conceive a child, Radner gradually developed chronic flu-like symptoms, which led to a diagnosis of ovarian cancer in 1986. Her battle with cancer brought considerable media attention and took on a national profile when she became actively involved in a cancer support group called the Wellness Community. By the time of her death she had started a support group of her own, called Gilda's Club, which was expanded posthumously by Wilder. Radner's struggle with terminal illness was outlined in a 1989 autobiography *It's Always Something*; shortly after the book's publication she died in Los Angeles. Radner is buried in Long Ridge Cemetery in Stamford, Connecticut.

In the end, Radner's innocent, plainclothes personality, reflected in her lovable characters with humorous foibles, brought her an enduring popularity and demonstrated new possibilities for women in comedy. Coupled with her active involvement in cancer causes after her diagnosis with the disease, she secured a lasting place among Americans' dearly cherished celebrities past.

★

David Saltman, *Gilda: An Intimate Portrait* (1992), is the most complete biography available, written by a reporter and longtime friend of Radner's. Obituaries are in the *New York Times* (21 May 1989) and *People* (5 June 1989).

ARI J. KAST

RAINWATER, (Leo) James (*b.* 9 December 1917 in Council, Idaho; *d.* 31 May 1986 in Yonkers, New York), physicist and educator who shared a Nobel Prize in physics for his part in formulating a new model of the atomic nucleus.

James Rainwater was the son of Edna Eliza Teague, a general store manager, and Leo Jasper Rainwater, a civil engineer. His father died during the influenza epidemic of 1918, and the family moved to Hanford, California, where his mother remarried. Rainwater was an outstanding student in chemistry, physics, and mathematics. In high school he entered a chemistry competition sponsored by the California Institute of Technology (Caltech) in which he received an outstanding score, and he was later admitted to the school as a chemistry major. He soon switched his major to physics. Rainwater obtained his B.S. degree in physics at Caltech in 1939. He then went to Columbia University in New York City to do graduate work, receiving an M.A. degree in 1941 and a Ph.D. in 1946. At Columbia he studied under such notable physicists as Enrico Fermi, I. I. Rabi, and Edward Teller.

In 1942, a year after obtaining his master's degree in physics, Rainwater married Emma Louise Smith. They had four children. Also in 1942, Rainwater began working for the Office of Scientific Research and Development (OSRD), and as a member of that office (until 1946), he took part in the Manhattan Project, delaying his thesis research in order to work on the development of the atomic bomb. Under the direction of J. R. Dunning, he studied the behavior of atomic nuclei under neutron bombardment. At the end of World War II his data were declassified, and in 1946 Rainwater was awarded his Ph.D. from Columbia University for this work.

Rainwater remained at Columbia University for the rest of his professional life, as physics instructor from 1946 to 1947, assistant professor from 1947 to 1949, associate professor from 1949 to 1952, and professor in 1952. He was named Pupin Professor of Physics in 1982.

After World War II, Columbia started building an improved particle accelerator, called a synchrocyclotron, at its Nevis Laboratory facilities. This accelerator would allow studies of other particles besides neutrons that were of interest to Rainwater (such as muons, rapidly decaying particles that are 207 times heavier than electrons, and pi-mesons, or pions, short-lived particles that carry a force binding nuclei together). Rainwater participated in the building of this new accelerator, which began operation in 1950. This started his long-standing connection with the laboratory. His research at the Nevis Cyclotron Laboratory lasted for more than thirty years, with Rainwater being the lab's director from 1951 to 1953 and again from 1956 to 1961.

In 1949 Rainwater began formulating a new theory regarding the shape of atomic nuclei. At the time there were two principal models of the nucleus, the liquid-drop model (which supposed that the nucleus acts like a liquid drop capable of vibrating and changing its shape) and the shell model (which supposed that its protons and neutrons moved in independent concentric orbits resembling a series of onionlike layers or shells). Neither of these models could explain all the experimentally obtained data.

After listening to a talk by Charles H. Townes on the disparities between the predictions of the shell theory and the experimental data, Rainwater came up with a new idea. He proposed that the motion of the nuclear particles could create centrifugal forces within the nucleus that might make what the shell model said should be a spherical shape around the nucleus (which was not borne out by the experimental data) more like an ellipsoid or football. This new hypothesis could explain the discrepancies presented by Townes.

In 1950 Rainwater published his hypothesis in his best-known paper, "Nuclear Energy Level Argument for a Spheroidal Nuclear Model." He convinced the physicist Aage Bohr (with whom he shared an office from 1949 to 1950 at Columbia) that his hypothesis was correct. When Bohr returned to Copenhagen, he and fellow Danish physicist Ben Mottelson developed a comprehensive theory of nuclear behavior and published it in 1952. They used Rainwater's hypothesis to combine aspects of the liquid-drop model and the shell model of the nucleus, proposing that if the outer shell was not filled with all the nucleons (protons and neutrons) it could hold, the surface of the nucleus would act like a drop of liquid that could be deformed into a football-like shape. If the outer shell of the nucleus had its complete number of nucleons, it would appear spherical. Using this new collective model, Mottelson and Bohr confirmed Rainwater's hypothesis in 1953.

Meanwhile, Rainwater had returned to his experimental studies. Working at the Nevis Laboratory with Val L. Fitch, he studied the X rays emanating from muons and determined in 1953 that the size of protons was being overestimated. He also worked on the properties of muons and their interactions with nuclei and generated advanced insight into the behavior of neutrons.

James Rainwater (*center*) is congratulated by Nobel laureates I. I. Rabi (*left*) and Tsung-Dao Lee (*right*) on winning the 1975 Nobel Prize for physics. UPI/CORBIS-BETTMANN

Rainwater, Mottelson, and Bohr shared the 1975 Nobel Prize in physics for their discovery of the connection between the collective motion and the particle motion in atomic nuclei and for the development of the theory of the structure of the atomic nucleus based on this connection. Their work achieved a deep understanding of the atomic nucleus and paved the way for the study and use of nuclear fusion.

Rainwater contributed to numerous professional journals and received many honors during his career, including the Atomic Energy Commission's Ernest Orlando Lawrence Prize for Physics in 1963. He was elected a member of the National Academy of Sciences in 1968, and he was a member of the Institute of Electrical and Electronic Engineers, the New York Academy of Sciences, the American Physical Society, and the American Association of Physics Teachers. He was also a fellow of the American Association for the Advancement of Science and the Optical Society of America and an honorary member of the Royal Swedish Academy of Sciences.

Rainwater's interests included geology, astronomy, and classical music. He retired from Columbia in 1986 and died at St. John's Riverside Hospital in Yonkers.

★

Additional information on Rainwater can be found in Tyler Wasson, ed., *Nobel Prize Winners* (1987); Emily J. McMurray, ed., *Notable Twentieth-Century Scientists* (1995); and *McGraw-Hill's Modern Men of Science,* vol. 1, (1968). An obituary is in the *New York Times* (3 June 1986).

MARIA PACHECO

RAY, Gordon Norton (*b.* 8 September 1915 in New York City; *d.* 15 December 1986 in New York City), scholar, book and manuscript collector, educator, and administrator who headed the Guggenheim Foundation from 1963 to 1985.

The only child of Jesse Gordon Ray, a businessman, and Jessie Norton, a housewife, Ray grew up in comfortable circumstances in the Chicago area. In 1932 the family moved to Bloomington, Indiana, where in 1927 Ray's father, on his wife's family land, had founded the Independent Limestone Company, which flourished.

After graduating in 1932 from New Trier High School in the Chicago suburb of Winnetka, Ray attended Indiana University. He earned A.B. and A.M. degrees in French literature in 1936, having been elected to three honor societies, including Phi Beta Kappa. Going on to graduate work in English literature at Harvard University, he held a series of prestigious scholarships there, gaining an M.A. in 1938 and a Ph.D. in 1940. His doctoral dissertation, titled "Thackeray and France," was, in his own words, "actually a preliminary sketch for a biography." The study of this eminent nineteenth-century English author would be a significant part of Ray's scholarship; in the next years he edited the four-volume *Letters and Private Papers of William Makepeace Thackeray* (1945–1946), described by the noted bibliographer G. Thomas Tanselle as "a model of documentary editing"; wrote a well-received two-volume biography (1955–1958); authored an important monograph on Thackeray's fiction, *The Buried Life* (1952), wrote seminal articles and essays on Thackeray; and provided introductions to his works (including the 1952 Modern Library edition of *The History of Henry Esmond, Esq.*).

Ray became an instructor in the English department of Harvard University in 1940, held Guggenheim Fellowships in 1941 and 1942, and in December 1942 joined the U.S. Navy. On active service until March 1946, he rose to the rank of lieutenant, serving both as a staff and a line officer. His tour of duty included two and a half years on carriers in the Pacific theater of operations. He served as a fighter director and radar officer. Ray won seven battle stars, and his unit earned a presidential citation.

After World War II a third Guggenheim Fellowship enabled Ray to do research in England before taking up a professorship in the English department at the University of Illinois in the fall of 1946. While becoming prominent as a Thackeray scholar, he also served as chair of the English department (1950–1957) and as vice president and provost of the university (1957–1960). In addition, he served as a member of the U.S. commission in the United Kingdom that helped establish the Fulbright program (1948–1949), as a visiting professor at New York University (1952–1953), and as a Guggenheim fellow for the fourth time (1956–1957). In 1954 he began a seventeen-year tenure as general editor of the Riverside Series at Houghton Mifflin, overseeing the re-publication of some eighty literary classics.

In the late 1940s Ray became serious about book and manuscript collecting, and began his annual summer buying trips to Europe. Many of his collecting activities were underwritten by his father's profitable limestone company. Described subsequently as "legendary," these trips enabled Ray to build extensive, noteworthy collections of English and French literature (both manuscript and printed material), and during his stay at the University of Illinois to enhance its holdings as well. Major acquisitions by Illinois that Ray facilitated included the archives of two important nineteenth- and early-twentieth-century English publishers, a library of some eight thousand volumes of twentieth-century English literature (described by Ray as "better in poetry than . . . fiction and better in fiction than . . . other prose"), and the H. G. Wells papers (some sixty thousand letters to and from Wells and various manuscripts). Ray drew on the Wells material for a variety of important articles and books, including an edition of Wells's *The Desert Daisy* (1957), *Henry James and H. G. Wells* (1958), a comparative study coauthored by James scholar Leon Edel, and *H. G. Wells and Rebecca West* (1974), an account of their love affair.

Ray became associate secretary general of the Guggenheim Foundation in 1960, and three years later became its chief administrative officer (only the second in the organization's history). He served until 1985, when he became president emeritus. Ray diligently and thoughtfully fur-

Gordon N. Ray. GUGGENHEIM MEMORIAL FOUNDATION

thered the foundation's policy of "research excellence in individual achievement," administering the awarding of some $96 million to more than eight thousand fellows. Starting in 1962 he also served as a professor in the English department of New York University, becoming professor emeritus in 1980. There he was active in directing dissertations and taught popular courses in Victorian literature. In addition, in 1976 Ray had taken over his father's limestone business, serving as president until his death.

Over the years, what became his dominant collecting interests (English nineteenth-century illustrated books, and French illustrated books and bindings from 1700 through the 1930s) resulted in two important exhibitions at the prestigious Morgan Library in New York City. Drawing almost exclusively on his collections (which subsequently were left to the Morgan), these exhibitions benefited from Ray's comprehensive catalogs, *The Illustrator and the Book in England from 1790 to 1914* (1976) and *The Art of the French Book, 1700 to 1914* (2 vols., 1982), both works with formal bibliographical descriptions by Thomas V. Lange. The five Lyall lectures Ray gave at Oxford in May 1985 allowed him to add what he called "a small sequel" on French art deco books.

During his Guggenheim years, Ray was a widely admired public intellectual. He spoke at celebrations, commencements, conferences, dedications, and numerous other functions on an eclectic array of subjects, including the rare-book trade, educational goals, the role of libraries, and various literary topics. He served on more than three dozen boards and committees, often in an executive capacity (including chairman of the Smithsonian, 1970–1985; president of the Grolier Club, 1965–1969; and treasurer of the American Council of Learned Societies, 1973–1985). For more than a decade Ray served as chairman of the Friends of the Columbia University Library, the organization that administers the famous Bancroft Prizes in American history. His honors included election to the American Academy of Arts and Sciences (1962) and the Roxburghe Club (1982), as well as the Sir Thomas More Medal of the University of San Francisco for book collecting. Despite failing health, in his last few years Ray, who never married and had no children, remained active. He died in his home of a heart attack. His remains are buried alongside his parents' grave in Bloomington, Indiana.

Ray's contributions to the study of literature and of illustrated books remain significant. His many fine accomplishments and all of his efforts were marked by a general good sense and wisdom that supported learning. Although extremely professional in all his many endeavors, Ray never lost his humanity.

★

Ray's papers, except for material relating to the Guggenheim Foundation, are at the Morgan Library in New York City, which also houses the manuscripts, drawings, and thousands of books he collected. His correspondence while at the Guggenheim Foundation is at the foundation's archives in New York City. The best account of Ray's life is G. Thomas Tanselle's introduction to Gordon N. Ray, *Books As a Way of Life: Essays by Gordon N. Ray* (1988). An obituary is in the *New York Times* (16 Dec. 1986). See also *A Memorial Tribute to Gordon N. Ray 1915–1986* (Pierpont Morgan Library, 1987).

Daniel J. Leab

RAY, John Alvin ("Johnnie") (*b.* 10 January 1927 in Polk Station, Oregon; *d.* 24 February 1990 in Los Angeles, California), singer, songwriter, and showman whose uninhibited, emotional performance style in songs such as "Cry" (1951) heralded the rock-and-roll era.

The second child of Elmer Ray and Hazel Simkins, Ray and his sister, Alma, were raised on the family farm. Both parents were musical: Elmer played the fiddle at local dances; Hazel played piano and organ for the church. This background in country music and gospel was evident in Ray's later musical style. At age three, Ray startled his family by playing "Rock of Ages" on an old pump organ. When the farm failed during the Great Depression, the family moved into the town of Dallas, Oregon, where Elmer got a job at a lumber mill.

Johnnie Ray. Archive Photos

Ray's parents realized that he had talent and sent him for lessons to "Uncle" Will Caldwell, organist at Dallas' First Christian Church. Although Ray could play anything he heard once, he was not inclined to do the exercises required for a disciplined study of the piano. Caldwell attempted to instruct Ray in classical music, and he was not pleased with his student's jazz improvisations. For Ray, who was left-handed, playing boogie-woogie came naturally. When he was six years old, he was playing organ for Sunday school and accompanying Alma on the piano when she sang at local elementary schools.

Years later, Ray recalled that every summer, from age seven until he was twelve or thirteen, he went to a farm several miles away to pick hops. "It was hot, hard work and I hated it, except for Saturday nights when they'd give me pennies to sing and play." At this time show business became an obsession with Ray, who decided that he was not going to be a farmer or a laborer. He was going to be a movie star, he said, "like Clark Gable or Tarzan."

During the summer of 1940 Ray suffered an accident that had a lasting effect. While roughhousing with friends, Ray was dropped on his head. He suffered both a concussion and the loss of 50 percent hearing in his left ear, but he never informed his parents of the accident. Unable to hear properly, his schoolwork suffered and he lost his confidence. His musical ability was not affected, however. In the fall of 1941 Ray got his first hearing aid.

When Ray's family moved to Portland, Oregon, during World War II, he enrolled at Franklin High School, where he appeared in high school plays. He also wrote music and played piano and sang at the YMCA and the Starlight Club, which sponsored youth dances every weekend. In addition, he became a regular on *Uncle Nate's Stars of Tomorrow,* a radio show in Portland where singer and film star Jane Powell also got her start in show business.

After graduating from high school in 1945, Ray got his first professional job, singing "Look for the Silver Lining" in a production number at Portland's Four Star Theater, a burlesque house. His next job was at an after-hours bar in Portland, as a piano player and singer.

When the war ended, the family moved to Salem, Oregon, where Ray worked at the Oregon Pulp and Paper Mill as a relief man on the night shift. Nearly every weekend, he drove to Portland to take whatever performing jobs he could find. After his twenty-second birthday he went to Hollywood, hoping to get work in the movies. His first job, however, was not in film but at a Beverly Boulevard nightspot, playing piano for $7.50 a night. Ray later said that he wasn't "setting out to be a singer, I wanted to be an actor, but the only way I could stay in show business was to sing and play the piano." This first job was short-lived, and he played for tips at a variety of places until he settled in at the Yacht Club, an establishment in south central Los Angeles. Unfortunately, this job, which paid $40 a week, did not last. Ray's excessive emotionalism, loudness, and almost spastic physical movements in performance put people off. He then worked as a soda jerk, a car hop, and a bellboy.

In 1949 Ray discovered that he was bisexual, began to drink heavily, and almost starved to death. "I remember stealing lemons for breakfast once. It was not a pretty year," he later recalled. By the end of the year he gave up on Hollywood and returned to Portland, where he worked a series of jobs and continued with his hobby of writing songs. In total, he wrote 184 songs; most were never published. Early in 1950 Ray wrote "The Little White Cloud That Cried," a song that reflected his unhappiness. Through some friends from his Yacht Club days, he got a two-week booking in Ashtabula, Ohio, for $150 a week. Ray had to borrow bus fare from his father, but he was on his way. Although his overt sexuality and his wailing cries and tears made his performances a startling display of raw emotion, the public was beginning to respond favorably.

Ray's next significant engagement was in early 1951 at Detroit's Flame Showbar, the Midwest's leading showcase for black jazz, rhythm-and-blues, and variety artists. He auditioned and was told, "the louder you sing, boy, the better." Ray was quickly accepted. The white singer who sounded and performed black was a success. Ray was befriended by singer LaVern Baker, who helped him refine his style, which already had much in common with rhythm-and-blues "shouting."

In April 1951 he signed with Danny Kessler, a talent scout who heard him at the Flame, to record four sides for Okeh Records, a subsidiary of Columbia specializing in black music. Only two songs were released, "Whiskey and Gin" and "Tell the Lady I Said Goodbye," both written by Ray. Before "Whiskey and Gin" was released in July, Ray was arrested in Detroit for soliciting men. He pled guilty and paid the $25 fine. Ray continued working at various clubs, often spending his entire salary on drinks, but his record was reaching beyond the black audience at which it was targeted. White fans began calling the radio stations asking for more Johnnie Ray. By the end of September he was being booked into clubs for $1,750 a week and getting national attention.

It was Ray's recording of "Cry" that made him into a superstar. Recorded for Columbia, it became the number-one pop record by Christmas of 1951, with Ray's "The Little White Cloud That Cried" at number two. This was the first time in the history of *Billboard* magazine that both sides of a single disk held these spots. In the first two weeks of 1952, "Cry" sold 200,000 copies. After Ray appeared on Ed Sullivan's television program *Toast of the Town,* another 480,000 copies were sold in a matter of days. Eventually, the record sold more than 25 million copies worldwide and became Ray's signature song. By April 1952 Ray was playing the Copacabana in New York City, and when he sang "Cry" *Billboard* reported that "it was hard to say who screamed more—Ray or the customers." "Cry" was followed by other successful records: "(Here Am I) Broken Hearted" (1951), which also went gold; "Please Mr. Sun" (1952); and "Walkin' My Baby Back Home" (1952).

On 25 May 1952 Ray married Marilyn Morrison (Carol Elizabeth Morrison), daughter of Charlie Morrison, owner of the Macombo Club in Los Angeles. The marriage was pushed by Marilyn and by Ray's publicist, who hoped to squash rumors of Ray's homosexuality. Ray was separated from Marilyn within a year, and they were divorced in 1954. In 1952 Ray was doing five grueling shows a day at the Paramount in New York City, playing to huge crowds. His drinking escapades were described as equally spectacular.

In March 1953 Ray made his European debut by playing three weeks at the London Palladium and causing near riots. His popularity in Great Britain would outlast his fame in the United States (he was also a huge success in Australia). That summer he went to Hollywood to start shooting *There's No Business Like Show Business* (1954) with Ethel Merman, Dan Dailey, Mitzi Gaynor, Donald O'Connor, and Marilyn Monroe. Finally realizing his dream of being an actor, Ray played the sensitive son who left the family vaudeville act to become a priest. His rendition of "Alexander's Ragtime Band" was restrained by Ray's standards.

Throughout 1955 Ray toured continually. In 1956 he did many television guest-star appearances. His only dramatic role came in a segment of *General Electric Theater* entitled "The Big Shot," in which he played an up-and-coming crooner named Johnnie Pulaski. In the spring of 1956 he appeared as a mystery guest on the television quiz show *What's My Line,* where he met the columnist Dorothy Kilgallen. Previously, in her column "The Voice of Broadway," Kilgallen had pronounced him "endsville," but they fell passionately in love, and their affair survived a series of Ray's concurrent male lovers.

In January 1956 Ray recorded "Just Walking in the Rain," which sold a million copies, his first gold record in years, and revived his popularity. Yet 1957 saw a string of flops. A January 1958 operation to restore his hearing was unsuccessful; a second operation eradicated what remained of the hearing in his left ear and diminished hearing in his right ear by almost 60 percent. Also in 1958, Ray starred on the short-lived *Johnnie Ray Show* on radio and appeared on *The Dick Clark Show* on television and in rock-and-roll impresario Alan Freed's "Christmas Jubilee of Stars" at the Loews' State Theater in New York City. But in 1959 Ray was arrested in Detroit again, this time for soliciting an undercover male policeman. This time it was front-page news. Kilgallen used her numerous contacts, and Ray was acquitted. Bad press, poor performances because of drunkenness, and a lack of hit records resulted in the end of his connection with Columbia records in 1960.

The exhausted Ray was hospitalized with tuberculosis and spent months recuperating. He returned to work in November 1960 at Basin Street East in New York City to favorable reviews. By mid-1963, however, he was again hospitalized, close to death, with cirrhosis and malnutrition. Both his career and his health hit bottom. Although he had sufficiently recovered by the summer of 1964 and had renounced alcohol, his money troubles were escalating. Poor financial management resulted in tax problems with the Internal Revenue Service. Ray went to Spain accompanied by his lover Bill Franklin, and returned to New York in September to an engagement at the Latin Quarter which the *New Yorker* magazine called a "good show." Shortly thereafter, Ray moved to the West Coast, jumping from club to club, trying to pay back taxes.

From 1969 to his final engagement in 1989, Ray played a series of small clubs and nostalgia dates in the United States while continuing to headline in Great Britain. He started to drink again, and his health continued to fail. Ray died of liver failure at Cedars-Sinai Medical Center and was buried in Forest Lawn Memorial Park.

Singer Tony Bennett, who played with Ray during the early days, described him as "a visual performer . . . the first to charge an audience. He had to rip the curtain down . . . or jump on the piano because he just couldn't stay cool enough not to." With his tears and histrionics Ray was the first popular singer to break with the smooth image of the crooners. Ray had many critics and many names: the Weeper, the Nabob of Sob, the Prince of Wails, the Howling Success. Some questioned his ability as a singer, and Ray himself stated, "I don't have a voice, I've got a style."

★

The Margaret Herrick Library at the Academy of Motion Picture Arts and Sciences in Beverly Hills has an extensive clippings file on Ray. Jonny Whiteside, *Cry: The Johnnie Ray Story* (1994), the only biography of Ray, includes an extensive bibliography. There is a collection of essays and other material edited by Ray Sonin, *The Johnnie Ray Story* (1955). Nik Cohn in *Rock from the Beginning* (1969) focuses on Ray's performance antics, while George Simon's essay "Johnnie Ray" in his *The Best of the Music Makers* (1979) includes an assessment of his style. Contemporary articles show how his audiences reacted to Ray: " 'Mr. Emotion,' " *Newsweek* (21 Jan. 1952); "Like Mossadegh," *Time* (21 Jan. 1952); "Again—Shrieks and Swoons," *Life* (24 Mar. 1952); "Friends of the Weeper," *New Yorker* (7 June 1952); and "Humility at the Hip," *Time* (14 Nov. 1955), which describes Ray's impact on London. Articles that include biographical information include Robert Sylvester, "Million-Dollar Teardrop," *Saturday Evening Post* (26 July 1952); Jerome Beatty, "Who's Crying Now?" *American Magazine* 154 (Aug. 1952); and Booton Herndon, "Why Johnnie Ray Cries," *Coronet* 33 (Dec. 1952). Obituaries are in the *New York Times* (26 Feb. 1990) and *Variety* (14 Mar. 1990).

MARCIA B. DINNEEN

REED, Donna (*b.* 27 January 1921 near Denison, Iowa; *d.* 14 January 1986 in Beverly Hills, California), Academy Award–winning actress who starred in more than forty films and a long-running television show, portraying primarily an image of the wholesome wife and mother throughout her career; she is perhaps best known for starring opposite Jimmy Stewart in *It's a Wonderful Life* (1946).

Born Donna Belle Mullenger on a 140-acre Iowa farm, Reed, the oldest of the five children of farmer William R. Mullenger and schoolteacher Hazel Mullenger, grew up in an isolated environment. In high school she was shy until a teacher suggested that she read Dale Carnegie's *How to Win Friends and Influence People* and try drama. She followed his advice and in her last two years of high school performed in school plays and won several beauty contests. Reed wanted to be a teacher, but the Great Depression limited her educational plans. An aunt in California wrote her about Los Angeles City College, which had low tuition and offered business courses. Reed moved to Los Angeles, arriving in 1938 with $68, and lived with her aunt while

Donna Reed, *c.* 1950s. ARCHIVE PHOTOS

taking courses in hopes of getting a position as a secretary. Her stunning appearance contributed to her popularity, and in her second year of college she was elected campus queen. On the day her photograph appeared in the *Los Angeles Times,* she was asked to audition for three Hollywood studios.

Reed decided to finish college before pursuing a film career. After graduating, she did a screen test for MGM because it was the movie company most familiar to her. She received a $75-a-week contract and moved to the Hollywood Studio Club on Lodi Place; at the prompting of MGM executives, she changed her name to Donna Reed. Her first film was *The Get-Away* (1941) and she made four films in the first year of her career. While making her earliest movies Reed practiced her shorthand regularly in case her acting career fell through. Reed married William J. Tuttle, a makeup man, on 30 January 1943; the couple divorced in 1944. They had no children. On 15 June 1945 Reed married producer Anthony Owen. In 1946 the couple adopted a daughter, Penny Jane, and the following year they adopted a son, Tony junior. Physicians had told Owen that he could not father children, but they were proven wrong in 1949 when Reed gave birth to a son, Timothy. The couple also had a daughter, Mary Anne, in 1957.

Reed's first acting opportunities were "nice-girl" supporting roles, but in 1945 she performed in two films, *The Picture of Dorian Gray* and *They Were Expendable,* which earned her critical attention. Starring roles followed, but mainly in minor films. In 1946 she was cast as Jimmy Stewart's wife in *It's a Wonderful Life,* directed by Frank Capra, a film that initially failed at the box office but has since become a perennial holiday favorite on television. Her subsequent lack of major roles caused her to leave MGM for Paramount and then Columbia. In 1953 Columbia boss Harry Cohn wanted Reed for the role of Alma, a prostitute, in *From Here to Eternity* (1953), directed by Fred Zinnemann, who had directed Reed in his first film, *Eyes in the Night*, in 1942. Initially, Zinnemann felt that Reed was not right for the part, but after three screen tests he was persuaded to cast her. The role, though a sanitized Hollywood depiction of a prostitute, nevertheless marked a change in the type of character Reed had previously portrayed. She won the Academy Award for best supporting actress for her work in the film. Reed felt that studio executives disapproved of her change in image and punished her by offering her only bland roles after *From Here to Eternity.* Her last starring role in a feature film was in *The Whole Truth* in 1958.

That year, Reed moved to television to star in *The Donna Reed Show,* produced by her husband, Tony Owen. Reed played the wife of a small-town pediatrician on the series, which premiered on ABC on 24 September 1958. The show was successful and ran until 1966. Reed's role as the woman who overcomes the everyday problems of upper-middle-class life established her as an icon of American motherhood. After 1966 Reed essentially retired from show business, traveling and taking up photography. She was, however, politically active. Although a lifelong Republican, she cofounded the organization Another Mother for Peace in 1967 to protest the war in Vietnam. She was also an activist for women's rights in the 1970s. In 1971 she and Tony Owen divorced. Reed subsequently married a retired military officer, Colonel Grover Asmus, on 30 August 1974. Their marriage, which lasted to Reed's death, was childless.

In 1984 Reed returned to television, assuming the role of Miss Ellie on the CBS series *Dallas,* when Barbara Bel Geddes left the show due to illness. Although Reed portrayed a different, more elegant Miss Ellie from that depicted by Bel Geddes, she was accepted by fans, and ratings for the series continued to be strong. Reed's contract was renewed for two years, but Bel Geddes recovered and the role was returned to her the next year, necessitating Reed's firing. Reed filed a $7.5 million lawsuit and accepted a $1 million settlement for breach of contract. In December 1985 Reed entered Cedars-Sinai Medical Center in Beverly Hills, California, for treatment of an ulcer. She was diagnosed with pancreatic cancer and the following year she died of the disease at her one-floor, Spanish-style home in Beverly

Hills. She was buried at Westwood Memorial Cemetery in Beverly Hills.

Donna Reed is best remembered as the quintessential American wife and mother in films and television. A radiant beauty, she often portrayed characters with a quiet reserve. Although she tried to move beyond the wholesome image, and despite winning an Oscar for portraying a prostitute, she continues to be best known for her roles in *It's a Wonderful Life* and *The Donna Reed Show.* Sadly, her return to acting ended on a sour note, but television reruns continue to keep alive her image as a strong and compassionate wife and mother.

★

Brenda Scott Royce, *Donna Reed: A Bio-Bibliography* (1990), the only book-length work on the actress, contains a short biography, a complete listing of Reed's film and television appearances, and a bibliography of reviews of her work. Entries on Reed appear in David Thomson, ed., *The Biographical Dictionary of Film* (1976), and James Vinson, ed., *The International Directory of Films and Filmmakers,* vol. 3, *Actors and Actresses* (1986). Obituaries are in the *New York Times* (15 Jan. 1986) and *Variety* (22 Jan. 1986).

ANDREW S. TOMKO

REISCHAUER, Edwin Oldfather (*b.* 15 October 1910 in Tokyo, Japan; *d.* 1 September 1990 in La Jolla, California), scholar and diplomat who was the foremost American expert on East Asia during the postwar years and who, as U.S. ambassador to Japan in the 1960s, helped forge closer links between the United States and Japan.

Reischauer was the son of August Karl Reischauer and Helen Sidwell Oldfather, who were American Presbyterian missionaries in Japan. He lived in that country until 1928, when he went to the United States to attend Oberlin College in Ohio. His childhood experiences had given him a solid grasp of the Japanese language and a sympathetic attitude toward Asian nationalism. While at Oberlin, Reischauer majored in history and participated in sports. After graduating in 1931 he received a graduate fellowship to study at Harvard, which had one of the few East Asian programs in the United States at the time. After receiving his M.A. degree in 1932, Reischauer did postgraduate work in Paris, Tokyo, Kyoto, and China. He married Adrienne Danton, a graduate student in art history, on 5 July 1935. They had three children, Ann, Robert, and Joan. Reischauer received his Ph.D. in Far Eastern languages from Harvard in 1938. Also that year, he became an instructor at Harvard, beginning a long and productive collaboration with John K. Fairbank, the foremost China scholar of the period. Beginning in 1939 they taught the first survey of modern East Asia at Harvard, and eventually cowrote the mammoth textbook *East Asia: Tradition and Transformation* (1978), which dominated the field for years.

Edwin O. Reischauer, *c.* 1963. ARCHIVE PHOTOS

Reischauer and Fairbank began their careers with only mild interest in contemporary Asian politics, but events from 1937 to 1941 pulled them into the orbit of U.S. military commanders and diplomats who needed the advice of experts knowledgeable about the region. Reischauer spent the summer of 1941 working for the Far East division of the Department of State. By the summer of 1942 the United States was at war, and the need for Reischauer's language skills was urgent. He spent the summer training military translators whose intelligence work saved Allied lives during the Pacific campaign against Japan. Reischauer's contributions led to his being commissioned as a major in the U.S. Army and placed in charge of a unit that analyzed intercepted Japanese messages in Washington, D.C. The unit became especially busy after January 1944, when the first complete Japanese Army code book fell into Allied hands. During the last year of the war, Reischauer participated in Department of State discussions focusing on postwar planning. Reischauer generally refrained from commenting about American wartime policies toward Japan, but he blasted the Allied demand for Japan's unconditional surrender in discussions with personal friends, while giving credit to the diplomats who modified the demand so that it was acceptable to the prosurrender faction in Japan.

Reischauer received his discharge in November 1945 and returned to Harvard to begin what he called the golden years of his academic career. His professional success was accompanied by personal tragedy. His wife, Adrienne, who had suffered from diphtheria as a child and who had a series of heart attacks beginning in 1951, died on 17 January 1955. Shortly thereafter, Reischauer renewed his acquaintance with Haru Matsukata, with whom he had gone to school as a child. They were married on 4 February 1956.

Reischauer helped build one of the best East Asian studies programs in the United States. Although he later expressed disgust at the treatment of the "China Hands" (diplomats who had served in China for decades) by the Truman and Eisenhower administrations, he kept a low political profile and focused on the academic world. Despite portraying himself as "an intellectual loner," Reischauer successfully led the Harvard-Yenching Institute of Oriental Studies through a period of limited resources and managed to teach regularly. Many former graduate students of Reischauer's obtained faculty positions at elite research institutions. His publishing career continued at a brisk pace, and he interacted with colleagues in fields such as art, literature, and economics.

In 1961 Reischauer returned to government service when President John F. Kennedy appointed him ambassador to Japan. The timing was crucial; the United States had just been humiliated by the tumult in Japan that took place prior to the renewal of the Japanese-American Security Treaty in 1960. As ambassador from 1961 to 1966, Reischauer made strides in reestablishing good relations between the two nations. One persistent irritation of Reischauer's was the coverage he received in the Japanese media for defending American policies in Asia, which he perceived as sensational and partisan. An assassination attempt on Reischauer on 24 March 1964 left him with a twenty-inch scar and lingering health problems. He left Japan to return to teaching in 1966, missing the most acrimonious events in American-Japanese relations revolving around the Vietnam War.

Back at Harvard, Reischauer struggled with the political movements surging across the campus. He later commented that his service on the faculty council from 1970 to 1972 was especially difficult as academic colleagues became politically divided. Reischauer retired from Harvard in 1980 but continued his research and was featured in the controversy over American nuclear weapons in Japanese ports when he admitted in 1981 that he knew about nuclear-armed navy ships docking in Japan in the 1960s in violation of the Security Treaty. Reischauer died of complications from hepatitis that he had contracted from a blood transfusion.

Few scholars have dominated a field of history the way Reischauer dominated the study of modern Japan. By training a generation of scholars, his influence spanned several decades. In addition, his service in war and diplomacy had lasting effects on the relations between two diverse nations.

★

Reischauer spoke candidly of his professional and personal life in his autobiography, *My Life Between Japan and America* (1986). His colleague John K. Fairbank gave an assessment of Reischauer in *Chinabound: A Fifty-Year Memoir* (1982). An obituary is in the *New York Times* (2 Sept. 1990).

MICHAEL POLLEY

RICH, Bernard ("Buddy") (*b.* 30 June 1917 in Brooklyn, New York; *d.* 2 April 1987 in Los Angeles, California), jazz drummer and bandleader whose explosive style made him one of the preeminent musicians of the Swing Era.

Born in the Sheepshead Bay area of Brooklyn, Bernard Rich was one of four children of Jewish parents who worked in vaudeville as the team of Wilson and Rich. He began drumming when he was eighteen months old and was soon after pressed into service in the song-and-dance routine of his parents. "Baby Traps, the Boy Wonder" played Broadway at age four, his place in the family act growing as his drumming technique improved. "By the time I was fifteen," he later told the jazz writer Whitney

Buddy Rich, 1949. ARCHIVE PHOTOS

Balliett, "I was making a thousand dollars a week. I was the second-highest-paid kid star, after Jackie Coogan." Rich had tutors until he was fourteen years old, but as a drummer he was largely self taught.

By the 1930s Rich had grown interested in the more serious jazz drumming of Chick Webb, Gene Krupa, and Tony Briglia. At Brooklyn's Crystal Club in 1937 he met the drummer Henry Adler and bassist Artie Shapiro, who were amazed by his technique and showmanship and recommended him for his first ensemble job, with the bandleader Joe Marsala at the Hickory House in Manhattan. Now Rich was commuting to gigs from his parents' Brooklyn house and making $66 per week. He could not yet read music but instead would memorize whole band charts after one or two listenings. Rich furthered his reputation drumming at Dickie Wells's club uptown, then in January 1939 he went to work for Artie Shaw's big band, with whom he performed for his first film, *The Dancing Co-ed.* Later that year, after Shaw stalked huffily off the Pennsylvania Hotel bandstand all the way to Mexico, Rich left the Shaw band to begin his famous stint with Tommy Dorsey, giving the Dorsey band's rhythm section a distinctive new drive and suffering ably through the ballads when he had to play softly. (Rich and Frank Sinatra roomed together for two years while they were with Dorsey, and the two became lifelong friends.) Rich won the *Down Beat* magazine readers' poll for 1941, 1942, and 1944.

In 1942 Rich enlisted in the Marine Corps, serving as a judo instructor and combat rifleman, although he never saw action overseas. After the war Rich formed his own band, but as the swing sound popularity began to wane, and with the great expense of jazz orchestras in general, he was forced to disband after two years. Rich felt that press stories about the astonishing playing of Duke Ellington's young drummer, Louis Bellson—on a trap set with two bass drums—were a challenge to his own preeminence. He fended it off in 1949 by playing a full solo at the Paramount Theater using two bass drums and no hands. In August 1952, Buddy and Marie Rich married; they had one child.

Although he could play ballads and was adept with brushes, his aggressive brilliance in up-tempo numbers could expose undercompetent rhythm players. Rich was not humble and never one for suffering fools, and through the years he settled many arguments with fellow musicians in parking lots and damaged hotel rooms. Rich sported a stocky figure whose hangdog grimace behind the drums was almost as much a signature as his driving playing style. Any band—except perhaps Count Basie's (with whom he sat in through the years)—kept the stormy Rich on a tether. He needed his own orchestra, organized around the hard-driving Rich sound and temperament. Before the bebop movement of the mid-1940s he was one of the marquee white jazz players most respected by black jazz musicians, more than Gene Krupa, Benny Goodman, or Dave Tough. The emerging tension between his swing style and that of the sparer, more tuneful and pensive Charlie Parker–era drummers was perfectly illustrated in his two-day battle with Max Roach in the spring of 1959, recorded as *Rich Versus Roach: A Battle of Bands and Drums.* These amazing sessions include the spectacular "Figure Eights," in which the two men trade eight-bar percussion riffs in an unaccompanied drum dialogue for four and a half minutes. That same year, Rich suffered his first heart attack.

Among other engagements, Rich played for Harry James in the late 1950s and early 1960s, when his $1,500-per-week salary got him into the *Guinness Book of World Records* as the world's highest-paid orchestral musician. However, he gave up the honor and his drum chair in the James band in the mid-1960s to again try bandleading himself. In the midst of rock's British Invasion he established his new sixteen-piece jazz orchestra, the Buddy Rich Big Band, which proved his longest-lived and was known, among other numbers, for its powerfully arranged *West Side Story* medley. In 1974 he opened a small club in Manhattan, Buddy's Place. A quadruple-bypass operation in early 1980s slowed the drummer somewhat; in January 1987 Rich suffered a stroke, and in March the UCLA Medical Center found he had multiple brain tumors. After a few recuperative weeks with friends and family, he died on 2 April. Riding in the elevator to his final operation, Rich was asked if he was allergic to anything. "Country and western music," the jazz master answered gruffly. Sinatra gave the eulogy at his funeral in Westwood, California; Rich's quiet drum set sat before the casket. He was buried in Westwood.

In the 1940s Rich was almost peerless among big-band drummers for his speed, big bass drum sound, and crisp ferocity on the snare. Rich made the drums high drama, and his remarkable coordination and quickness around the drum set were such that in 1947 he played a convincing concert at Harlem's Apollo Theater with his left arm hanging injured in a sling. Not every band could stand up to his explosive playing, but for nearly forty years he remained one of the great musicians of the swing era.

★

For overviews on Rich's life and career, see Whitney Balliett, *American Musicians: 56 Portraits in Jazz* (1986), and Burt Korall, *Drummin' Men: The Heartbeat of Jazz* (1990). An obituary is in the *New York Times* (3 Apr. 1987).

NATHAN WARD

RICHARDS, Paul Rapier (*b.* 21 November 1908 in Waxahachie, Texas; *d.* 4 May 1986 in Waxahachie, Texas), baseball player and manager who was an executive in major league baseball for over five decades.

Paul Richards. NATIONAL BASEBALL HALL OF FAME LIBRARY, COOPERSTOWN, N.Y.

Richards's father, Jesse T. Richards, a teacher, and his mother, Stella McGowan, a housewife, encouraged their son's early passion for baseball. Richards, an only child, later claimed that it was not true that he decided to become a big league manager when he was in the third grade. "I decided to manage when I found out I wasn't going to be a .300 hitter," he recalled, "and I found that out pretty early." The tall, taciturn Texan with the cool green eyes, skinny neck, and squared jaw became an East Texas legend while playing third base and pitching for his high school team. Waxahachie won sixty-five consecutive games and three successive state championships. The ambidextrous Richards added to his legend by leading his team to a doubleheader victory, pitching right-handed to right-handed batters and left-handed to left-handed batters.

Richards began his six-year minor league apprenticeship as an infielder with Pittsfield of the Eastern Shore League in 1926. By the time he reached the Brooklyn Dodgers at the end of the 1932 season, he had converted to catching. He quickly developed a reputation as a student of the game, dedicating himself to building the confidence of his pitcher, while outdueling the enemy batter and opposing manager. Richards had a fascination for the mental part of the game. "Winning baseball requires strong-hearted, intelligent pitchers," he observed, "and the proper knowledge of strategy, a phase of the game too often neglected." Richards was convinced that baseball games were won and lost not simply by the best players, but by teams that put their talents to best use.

Richards married Margie Marie McDonald in 1932, the year he moved to the big leagues. They had two daughters, Lou Redith and Paula Del. Richards realized that caring for his family required more than he was earning as a marginal major leaguer. He closed 1935 as a part-time catcher for Connie Mack's last-place Philadelphia Athletics, his third team in four years. Richards was an excellent defensive catcher but had never hit higher than .245 in any big league season. Most teams, however, could find a roster spot for a skilled catcher who knew how to handle pitchers. But Richards decided to return to the minors at the beginning of the 1936 season as a player, coach, and later manager of the Atlanta Crackers of the Southern Association. The Crackers finished first twice and second once during Richards's five years at the helm, including remarkable ninety-nine-, ninety-three-, and ninety-one-win seasons, establishing his growing reputation as a highly skilled skipper who got the most out of his players.

Steve O'Neill, new manager of the fifth-place Detroit Tigers, brought Richards back to the majors at the start of the 1943 season to help develop the team's young pitching staff. Richards's on-field leadership and off-the-field care and feeding of Paul "Dizzy" Trout helped transform the staff ace from an eighteen-game loser to a league-leading twenty-game winner. Virgil Trucks posted a career-high sixteen wins and veteran Tommy Bridges had his best season in three years for the improving Bengals. Richards's major achievement the following year was helping to transform Hal Newhouser, a seventeen-game loser in 1943, into a league-leading twenty-nine-game winner in 1944. The Tigers leaped to second in the standings. The year 1945 capped the three-year rebuilding process. Richards made the *Sporting News* Major League All-Star Team and his Tigers won the American League pennant. They played the Chicago Cubs in the World Series. Richards helped win the seventh and deciding game with a two-run double that highlighted a series in which he had six RBIs.

Richards's eight-year big league playing career ended in 1946. During three years as player-manager of Buffalo, the International League team went from sixth to first in the standings. A year managing Seattle of the Pacific Coast League led General Manager Frank Lane to name Richards manager of the Chicago White Sox for the 1951 season. In an era dominated by the powerful New York Yankees, Richards helped transform the Sox from a dull, sixth-place also-ran into a pennant-contending group of hustlers and overachievers, the sport's most exciting team. The baseball world christened them "the Go-Go White Sox." Over four years ending in 1954, Richards increased the team's seasonal win total by thirty-one games, improving its winning percentage to .628, the highest for any White Sox team since the disbanding of the scandal-ridden "Black Sox," who had thrown the World Series in 1919.

Richards built his White Sox on pitching, speed, defense, heads-up play, and aggressive teamwork. Staff ace Billy Pierce, who had come under Richards's influence while an eighteen-year-old rookie with the 1945 Tigers, never met anyone who knew so much about pitching. "He taught our pitchers the slip pitch, which is actually a change-up curve, and he taught me the slider. He would actually teach baseball, and not many managers can do that." Eddie Robinson, the Sox's slugging first baseman who later worked with Richards for Houston, Atlanta, and Texas, considered him one of the great minds of the game. Leo Durocher thought there wasn't anyone with "a greater understanding of the game." It made a conversation with the wily Richards "a postgraduate course" in the "strategy, tactics, and opportunism" that made the game worth playing and watching.

At the end of the 1954 season Richards left the White Sox to take over the American League's perennial doormat, the Baltimore Orioles (the St. Louis Browns through 1953). As field manager and general manager he had complete control over baseball operations. His $50,000 salary was a record for its day and pleased the money-minded Richards as much as the prestige. His seven years with the Orioles saw the development of Baltimore's famous "kiddie corps," a pitching staff of Steve Barber, Chuck Estrada, Jack Fisher, and Milt Pappas, none of whom were older than twenty-three in 1961, when the Orioles won a franchise-record ninety-five games. Richards's success with Baltimore led to his selection as manager of the year by Associated Press and United Press International in 1960. His innovations with the Orioles included a machine that pitched batting practice, a special catcher's mitt to handle knuckleballs, and the practice of switching pitchers to the infield while a reliever faced one batter.

For the third time in his career Richards could not resist building a team from the ground floor. In 1961 he was named general manager of the Houston Colt 45s, an expansion team in the National League. In their inaugural season in 1962, Houston beat out the Chicago Cubs and the expansion New York Mets, and began developing future stars in Hall of Famer Joe Morgan, Jimmy Wynn, Rusty Staub, Larry Dierker, and Dave Giusti. Richards returned to Atlanta and served as vice president of baseball operations for the Braves between 1967 and 1972. During this time he earned the enmity of Atlanta stars Joe Torre and Ralph Garr for being a tough contract negotiator. For four years Richards was out of baseball. He indulged in newspaper publishing and sportswriting in his native Texas and kept a daily appointment at Waxahachie's eighteen-hole golf course.

In 1976, at the age of sixty-seven, Richards reluctantly returned to manage the White Sox as a favor to team owner Bill Veeck, a longtime friend. The team responded by reeling off a ten-game winning streak in an otherwise forgettable year. Richards served as the White Sox director of player development through 1980, once again building a staff of young pitchers who would propel Chicago to the 1983 Western Division championship. Richards could never leave the game he loved. Returning to Texas, he served as consultant for the American League Texas Rangers, and was working in that capacity when he died of a heart attack on the thirteenth hole at the Waxahachie Country Club. He is buried in Hillcrest Cemetery in Waxahachie, and in 1996 Paul Richards Park was dedicated to his memory by the people of his hometown.

Called "the thinking man's manager," Richards was widely considered his generation's greatest teacher of baseball. Hall of Fame writer Jerome Holtzman captured the sentiment of many in baseball when he noted that Richards's "busy and fertile brain possessed more baseball knowledge than anyone since Branch Rickey." A book by Richards, *Modern Baseball Strategy,* first published in 1955, became a wide-selling hit on how to play and watch the national pastime. The secret of Richards's success, veteran hurler Saul Rogovin remembered, was that "he conned all of us into thinking we were better than we were." The Wizard of Waxahachie prepared his men to win, Rogovin observed, and made them confident that they couldn't lose.

★

In addition to the manuscript collections of Richards's daughter, Paula Del Richards, in Reno, Nevada, the front offices of the Chicago White Sox, Baltimore Orioles, and Houston Astros hold substantial files on Richards's many contributions to those franchises. A file of Richards's columns is available through the *Waxahachie* (Texas) *Light.* David L. Porter, ed., *Biographical Dictionary of American Sports, 1989–1992: Supplement for Baseball, Football, Basketball, and Other Sports* (1992), contains a biographical sketch. His career as a player is chronicled in *The Baseball Encyclopedia* (1976). Jerome Holtzman, "Richards Put Excitement into Sox," *Chicago Tribune* (6 May 1986), is a tribute. Obituaries are in the *Chicago Tribune, Chicago Sun-Times,* and *Baltimore Sun* (all 5 May 1986).

BRUCE J. EVENSEN

RICKOVER, Hyman George (*b.* 27 January 1900 in Makow, Russian Poland; *d.* 8 July 1986 in Arlington, Virginia), four-star admiral who, as head of the Nuclear Power Division in the U.S. Navy's Bureau of Ships, was responsible for production of the first atomic-powered warships.

Admiral Hyman Rickover. ARCHIVE PHOTOS

Abraham R. Rickover, a poor Jewish tailor, emigrated to New York City in 1904, and in 1906 his wife, Ruckal Unger, a homemaker, along with son Hyman and daughter Fanny, joined him there. They soon moved to Chicago. Another daughter, Gitel ("Augusta"), was born in 1908. Although he worked long hours for Western Union, at John Marshall High School, Rickover excelled in German, physics, and drawing. Entering the U.S. Naval Academy in 1918, he was hazed as a bookworm and as a Jew. A lone wolf who shunned athletics and socializing, he graduated 116th out of the 539 graduates in the class of 1922. Only five feet, six inches tall, thin, wiry, iron-fisted, a tireless worker, and lightning-quick in making decisions, he was no diplomat who followed protocol, but he got the job done.

While assigned to a destroyer and battleship, Rickover forwent shore leave in order to take Naval War College correspondence courses. In 1928 and 1929 he attended the navy's Postgraduate School, in Annapolis, Maryland, and then obtained an M.A. degree in electrical engineering at the Columbia University School of Engineering. In these schools he learned engineering analysis. In New York he met and in 1931 married Ruth D. Masters. A son, Albert Masters, his only child, was born in 1940. While serving as the electrical officer of a battleship, Rickover requested duty on a small ship as a way to quicker command and was detailed to a submarine. After schooling at the Submarine School in New London, he served in the SS-9 and SS-48. He not only improved their machinery while taking additional correspondence courses, but he put out a battery fire, saved an enlisted man from drowning, and translated Admiral Hermann Bauer's *Das Unterseeboot*.

Yet he did not fit in; he remained an intellectual loner. A fitness assessment by the captain of the SS-48 prevented him from obtaining a submarine command. After serving in the Office of the Inspector of Materials at the Philadelphia Navy Yard from 1933 to 1935, where he learned a significant amount from private industry, he became the assistant engineering officer of the battleship *New Mexico* and helped the vessel win the coveted "E" for engineering efficiency for three years. His only ship command, as of 1 July 1937, when he became a lieutenant commander, was of a Bird-class minesweeper on the Asiatic Station, which he used to repatriate Americans from Shanghai and Tsingtao, China, during the Sino-Japanese War. After September 1937, when he became an engineering-duty-only officer, command afloat was no longer available to him.

In June 1939 Rickover became second man in the Electrical Section of the Bureau of Ships. Convinced that a European war was imminent, he studied reports on damaged British ships and produced electrical equipment that could better withstand bomb, depth-charge, and torpedo damage. He also produced smaller, lighter, and more compact equipment; improved an infrared signaling system; and invented an antimagnetic mine device. A commander (1 January 1942) quickly promoted to captain in wartime (26 June 1943), he ordered that the electrical plants of the damaged battleships *California* and *West Virginia* be repaired at Pearl Harbor rather than being towed to the mainland. In three months in 1944 he had a crew straighten out disarray at the Bureau of Ships fleet spares establishment at Mechanicsburg, Pennsylvania. His request for sea duty was approved, and in late 1944 he began supervising the building of a naval base at Okinawa, Japan, only to have it destroyed by a typhoon in October 1945. He then expedited ways of mothballing ships stored on the Pacific Coast.

Rickover's involvement with atomic energy for ship propulsion began when Rear Admiral Earle Mills, deputy chief of the Bureau of Ships (later under other names), ordered him in May 1946 to a laboratory of the Atomic Energy Commission (AEC, later also under other names, now the Department of Energy) at Oak Ridge, Tennessee. There Rickover learned all that was in the navy's files about nuclear fission, and he determined to build an atomic-powered submarine even though the navy first wanted nuclear power for aircraft carriers. It would take him six years to achieve his goal, in part because the AEC, under civilian control, concentrated on producing atomic bombs rather than propulsion plants. General Electric and the Westinghouse Corporation planned to build large atomic-powered propulsion plants, and Captain Albert G. Mumma, chief of the Nuclear Power Branch of the Bureau of Ships, refused to support Rickover's desire for smaller plants. Rickover believed that Mumma and the corporations erred in thinking that scientific theory was more important than engineering; he contended that 95 percent of the problems to be solved in providing atomic propulsion were engineering problems. At Oak Ridge, he put together a Naval Group, insisting that it work the twelve-, fourteen-, and sixteen-hour days he did and often disregarding his superiors, because he believed efficiency to be more important than rank. His group nicknamed him O^2, reducing Old Man to Old One, then to O times O, or O squared. One either liked Rickover or hated him for his rejection of middle-ground mediocrity.

After the Naval Group had studied nuclear reactor progress throughout the United States, the physicist Edward Teller, at Los Alamos, asked Rickover what was being done about the submarine he wanted. Interested in helping Rickover with the nuclear ship propulsion system, Teller then wrote to Admiral Mills, who assigned the group to other duties but kept Rickover as his special assistant on nuclear matters. In his new billet Rickover set out to convince the government, the navy, and the AEC to support a nuclear ship propulsion program. His first step was to write a letter to the chief of naval operations, Admiral Chester W. Nimitz. On 5 December 1947, the old submariner gave Rickover his support. Secretary of the Navy James V. Forrestal approved and ordered the Bureau of Ships to follow through. Admiral Mills wrote to the AEC requesting its cooperation in producing an atomic-powered submarine, but the commission pigeonholed the letter. At a symposium on underwater warfare Mills lashed the commission in a speech written by Rickover. If the commission did not move, Mills said, the navy would—alone.

After months of fighting, Rickover won. Previously, as a staff aide to Mills, Rickover had had no authority. On 6 July 1948 Mills appointed Rickover as the Bureau of Ships liaison with the AEC, and therefore head of the navy's nuclear propulsion program. On 4 August 1948 Rickover formed a Nuclear Power Division in the Bureau of Ships. Mills furnished him $3 million, and Rickover and his group, now in Washington, worked more sixteen-hour days. He also convinced the AEC to establish a special school at the Massachusetts Institute of Technology to train nuclear engineers. He interviewed its prospective attendees, indeed all who wished to enter the nuclear program. These meetings gained him additional fame or disrepute, as they became legendary for their invective, unfairness, and personal destructiveness as Rickover sought to learn not what men knew, but how they thought. Jimmy Carter, Annapolis class of 1948, grew to love him, whereas Elmo Zumwalt, interviewed as a commander, remarked that he was "greasy."

In any event, Rickover's group lectured Westinghouse on how to solve the engineering problems involved in nuclear propulsion. While Westinghouse went to work and the Bureau of Ships designed what would become the first atomic-powered submarine, the *Nautilus,* Rickover had a mock-up of the vessel built in the desert near Arco, Idaho, and another at the Electric Boat Company yard in Groton, Connecticut. On 14 June 1952, after years of cajoling, browbeating, and often showing disrespect for his uniformed superiors, Rickover had the keel laid for the world's first nuclear-powered ship. One estimate put it as fifty times as effective as a snorkel submarine, which in turn was sixteen times as effective as the U-boat of World War II. It revolutionized naval warfare. By demanding zero defects and firing those unable to meet this standard, Rickover succeeded in beating the Soviets at producing a nuclear boat. Yet the navy, which said it had other captains better suited for promotion to the very few openings for rear admiral, passed him over in 1951 and 1952, which meant that Rickover would be forced to retire in 1953. By issuing the requirement that one engineering-duty-only officer must be qualified in nuclear ship propulsion, Secretary of the Navy Robert B. Anderson enabled Rickover's promotion to rear admiral on 1 July 1953. Raised to vice admiral in 1964, Congress forced his further promotion to full admiral in December 1973.

In its sea trials in January 1955 the *Nautilus* set new records for submerged voyages at high sustained speeds. By 1957 nuclear power was being applied to submarines and surface ships via a pressurized-water reactor and to the civilian power plant at Shippingport, Pennsylvania. If not the darling of the navy, Admiral Rickover certainly was that of Congress, to which he proved deferential and which greatly helped him in his battles with his navy superiors, the Pentagon's systems analysts, the director of defense engineering, the secretary of defense, the director of the budget, and even occasionally the president.

In 1956 Rickover created the Plant Apparatus Department, near Pittsburgh, and in 1959 the Machinery Apparatus Operations, in Schenectady, New York, to handle procurement for reactor plant components already developed. Personnel training proceeded first at a nuclear power school, then at various land prototypes. Rickover or his representatives oversaw construction work at seven shipyards. In 1959 Rickover visited the Soviet Union and reported on the less advanced state of Soviet nuclear power systems.

Among Rickover's new high-speed submarines was the *Thresher* (SSN-593), which would be tested at new depths and which would begin its sea trials in 1960. Tragically, the *Thresher* was lost with all hands on board on 10 April 1963, as was the *Scorpion* in 1979. But they were the only two of his 121 nuclear-powered boats that sank, and no evidence pointed to failure of their reactors. Rickover strongly stressed improved training, quality control measures, and safety. As he put it, "Doing the job right the first time was a lot cheaper than going back and doing it over."

Meanwhile, the nuclear-powered carrier *Enterprise,* cruiser *Long Beach,* and destroyer *Bainbridge* (built from 1957 to 1959) circumnavigated the globe without logistic support—that is, without delivery to the ships of fuels, supplies, water, or food. The *Enterprise* especially proved its value during the Cuban blockade of late 1962, the Arab oil embargo of 1973, and the Vietnam War. Yet Secretary of Defense Robert S. McNamara accepted the conclusions of his systems analysts and delayed the building of more major nuclear-powered surface ships until forced to do so by Congress and the administration. In 1967 Congress mandated that in the future all major surface ships would be nuclear powered. The rule was suspended by President Jimmy Carter in the late 1970s. In the name of security Rickover vetoed sharing sensitive nuclear data with foreign nations.

Rickover had strong and controversial views on the subject of education. Among his most important publications on this issue are *Swiss Schools and Ours: Why Their's Are Better* (1962); and *American Education, A National Failure: The Problem of Our Schools and What Can Be Learned from England* (1963). He also wrote *Liberty, Science, and Law* (1969) and *Nuclear Warships and the Navy's Future* (1974). "Leadership," an article illuminating his views on management, was published in *U.S. Naval Institute Proceedings* (January 1981).

A widower since 1972, Rickover married Eleonore Ann Bednoweiz of the Navy Nurse Corps on 19 January 1974. He retired in 1982. He had survived two heart attacks in the 1970s. Another heart attack, in July 1985, followed his being censured for having received gifts from the General Dynamics Corporation, an accusation he denied. He died on 8 July 1986 and was buried with honors at the National Cemetery in Arlington, Virginia.

Iconoclast and perfectionist, Rickover can justifiably be called the father of the nuclear navy. Among his many awards were the Legion of Merit, the Congressional Gold Medal, the Distinguished Service Cross, the Presidential Medal of Freedom, and the Enrico Fermi Award.

★

Norman Polmar and Thomas B. Allen, *Rickover* (1982), is a long biography backed by the U.S. Naval Institute but written without Rickover's cooperation. Francis Duncan and Richard G. Hewlett, *Nuclear Navy 1947–1962* (1962), covers Rickover's relations with the AEC, as does Glenn T. Seaborg, with William R. Corliss, *Man and the Atom: Building a New World Through Atomic Technology* (1971). Norman Polmar, *The Death of the Thresher* (1964), examines the loss of that vessel and Rickover's ties with the AEC. Francis Duncan, *Rickover and the Nuclear Navy: The Discipline of Technology* (1990), is a history of technology, not a biography of Rickover. Theodore Rockwell, *The Rickover Effect: How One Man Made a Difference* (1992), evaluates Rickover's influence. William J. Crowe, Jr., with David Chanoff, *The Line of Fire: From Washington to the Gulf: Politics and Battles of the New Military* (1993), includes an excellent account of Rickover's interviewing method. Character sketches are Edward L. Beach, "Life with Rickover: Stormy Duty in the Silent Service," *Washington Post* (27 May 1977), and "Admiral Rickover, Sixty-three Years in Uniform," *Dolphin* (2 Feb. 1982). An obituary is in the *New York Times* (9 July 1986).

PAOLO E. COLETTA

RITT, Martin (*b.* 2 March 1914 in New York City; *d.* 8 December 1990 in Santa Monica, California), director, producer, and actor who was honored for making films, such as *Hud* (1963) and *Norma Rae* (1979), that investigate moral choices and reflect concern for economically and racially oppressed people.

Ritt grew up on the Lower East Side of Manhattan and in the Bronx. His parents, Morris Ritt and Rose Lass, were Jewish immigrants. His father owned an employment agency in New York City, the Morris Agency. His mother became a talent agent after Martin and his sister were born.

Martin Ritt on the set of *Pete and Tillie.* ARCHIVE PHOTOS

Martin graduated from DeWitt Clinton High School in the Bronx and Elon College in North Carolina, where he was a football player and a boxer. He studied law at St. John's University in New York City, but dropped out without earning a degree.

Ritt began his career as an actor in the late 1930s with the Group Theatre in New York City, where he met and befriended the director Elia Kazan. As Ritt remembered in a 1986 interview, "I was lucky enough to be around the Group Theatre, which was probably the single greatest group of theater intellectuals that ever existed together as a cohesive unit." He acted in *Golden Boy* (1937) and other socially conscious Depression-era plays. On 25 September 1940 Ritt married Adele Wolfe, a dancer; they remained together for the rest of his life, and adopted two children, one of whom, Martina Werner, became a film producer.

During World War II, Ritt served in the Army Air Forces, where he continued to act, appearing in the service's stage (1943) and film (1944) drama *Winged Victory.* After the war he acted in live television plays but increasingly focused his career on directing. Among the New York stage productions he directed were *Set My People Free* (1948), *A View from the Bridge* (1955), and *A Very Special Baby* (1956).

Ritt had started working in television in the late 1940s. He appeared in more than 150 teleplays, directed an additional 100 shows before 1951, and won a Peabody Award for his work. He was a flourishing director and actor in the early days of live television, until he was blacklisted for a previous Communist party affiliation. In 1951 Ritt was dismissed from his position at CBS for his assumed communist links, a victim of Senator Joseph McCarthy and the House Un-American Activities Committee. Ritt never worked in the television industry again. During the five years he was blacklisted, Ritt eked out a living by teaching at the Actors Studio in New York City. Fortunately, producer David Susskind defied the blacklist by hiring Ritt to direct the film drama *Edge of the City* (1957). Starring John Cassavetes and Sidney Poitier, *Edge of the City* was a powerfully realistic waterfront drama that centered on an interracial friendship. The film was a critical success, and after its release Ritt directed solely for Hollywood films. He later told the story of his blacklisting from television in the comedy *The Front* (1976), which starred Woody Allen.

Ritt went to Hollywood relatively late in life, being nearly forty, but he eventually directed over twenty-five films. *Hud,* released in 1963, was a tough-minded drama focusing on the problem of ethical choices. The following year the film brought him an Academy Award for best director. In 1966 he received a British Academy Award for best British film for *The Spy Who Came In from the Cold* (1965). Ritt had been especially attentive to racial themes, from his first picture, *Edge of the City,* to *Sounder* (1972); to labor questions, in *The Molly Maguires* (1970) and *Norma Rae* (1979); and to material of diverse literary origin, in *The Long Hot Summer* (1958) and *Hemingway's Adventures of a Young Man* (1962). During a 1974 interview Ritt acknowledged that "the stage director is the third man on the totem pole—the writer and star are much more important. . . . It doesn't compare with directing a film where you're it."

Ritt achieved his greatest commercial success with *Norma Rae,* a film based on the account of a young southern woman, played by Sally Field, struggling to unionize her coworkers at a textile factory. As he said in an interview with *Film Comment* in 1986, "Implicit in all of my films is a very strong and deep feeling for the minorities, the disenfranchised, the dispossessed, be they Blacks, Mexicans, Jews, or working people." Toward the end of his career Ritt directed *Murphy's Romance* (1985) and *Stanley and Iris* (1990). He also resumed acting, appearing in such films as *The End of the Game* (1976) and *The Slugger's Wife* (1985).

A self-described agnostic, Ritt styled himself as a member of the working class, dressing in trademark navy and brown striped baggy coveralls. For Ritt, the jumpsuit was an unspoken statement of his impatience with tie-wearing respectability. He was a private man who thought of moviemaking as a job, "the only one I ever wanted." He was loyal to his friends, who tended to be longtime associates and collaborators. His alliance with the husband-and-wife writing team of Irving Ravetch and Harriet Frank, Jr., was one of the longest and most creative in film history.

A resident of Pacific Palisades, Ritt was a short, squat man who enjoyed horses and the racetrack. He died in Santa Monica Hospital Center in California of heart disease at the age of seventy-six.

An old-style radical, Ritt had a strong and determined social conscience. He gained prominence for creating films that championed the oppressed and downtrodden, and at the time of his death he was hailed as the United States' greatest maker of social films. For Ritt, movies were about people; his quietly revolutionary pictures made statements through casting and character development, and he never distanced himself from his material with obtrusive, self-consciously artistic camera work. As a result, viewers of Ritt's pictures do not merely glimpse a foreign world but inhabit it, and in so doing their emotions as well as their minds are engaged.

★

Carlton Jackson, *Picking Up the Tab: The Life and Movies of Martin Ritt* (1994), is an excellently researched book that includes film reviews, fan mail, interviews, and correspondence related to Ritt's films and career. John Wakeman, ed., *World Film Directors,* vol. 2, *1945–1985* (1988), contains an essay on Ritt. Patrick McGilligan, "Ritt Large: 1950's Hollywood Blacklist, Interview with M. Ritt," *Film Comment* 22 (Jan./Feb. 1986): 38–46, is a discussion of Ritt's directorial career. Julia Cameron, "True Ritt," *American Film* 15 (Nov. 1989): 42–48, discusses his accomplishments as a director and his blacklisting from television in the 1950s. Thomas O'Connor, "Martin Ritt: Human Relationships and Moral Choices Fuel His Movies," *New York Times* (12 Jan. 1986), is a conversation with Ritt focusing on his concern with the human condition. Lyn Goldfarb and Anatoli Ilyashov, "Working Class Hero: An Interview with Martin Ritt," *Cineaste* 18, no. 4 (1991): 20–23, is an interview conducted in 1985 that focused on Ritt's treatment of labor issues. Michele Willens, "Director Martin Ritt," *Premiere* 3, no. 7 (Mar. 1990): 50, profiles Ritt at the age of seventy-five. A tribute is Charles Champlin, "A Salute to a Scrappy Hollywood Warrior," *Los Angeles Times* (11 Dec. 1990). Obituaries are in the *Boston Globe,* the *Chicago Tribune,* and the *Los Angeles Times* (9 Dec. 1990), the *Washington Post* (10 Dec. 1990), the *Guardian* and the *New York Times* (11 Dec. 1990), and *Time* (24 Dec. 1990).

KAREN LYNN SVENNINGSEN

ROBINSON, Ray ("Sugar Ray") (*b.* 3 May 1921 in Detroit, Michigan; *d.* 12 April 1989 in Culver City, California), boxer who held the world welterweight title for five years and won the world middleweight title five times.

The youngest of three children of Walker Smith, a construction worker, and Leila Hurst, a seamstress, Robinson was born Walker Smith, Jr., in the Black Bottom section of Detroit. As a child he showed a flair for fisticuffs and frequented the Brewster Center Gym, where he watched older boys box and began a lifelong friendship with local hero and future heavyweight champion Joe Louis. The Smiths' marriage was marred by arguments and financial strain, and in 1927 Leila Smith separated from her husband. In 1932 she moved with her three children to New York City, where they lived for a year in Hell's Kitchen at 419 West 53d Street before settling into a three-room flat on Manhattan Avenue and 119th Street in Harlem.

Smith supported her family by working as a seamstress for $12 a week. Her son graduated from Cooper Junior High School and took dance lessons at the Roy Scott Studios. He helped supplement the family income by working at a neighborhood grocery, dancing outside Times Square theaters for change, and selling driftwood that he collected along the Hudson River.

At age thirteen the future "Sugar" Ray Robinson was boxing in Police Athletic League contests and later began training at the Salem-Crescent Gym on 129th Street and Seventh Avenue. There he met the trainer George Gainford, who eventually became his manager. The youngster often accompanied Gainford and other amateur boxers to out-of-town bouts called "bootleg" fights for which the winners were surreptitiously paid $10. On one trip to Kingston, New York, a flyweight was needed and Walker Smith, Jr., eager to earn some money, volunteered. But at age fifteen he was too young to hold the required Amateur Athletic Union card so Gainford passed him the AAU card of another boxer, Ray Robinson. "Robinson" won the decision and continued boxing under that name. Following another bout in Watertown, New York, Jack Case, a local sportswriter, remarked to Gainford that Robinson was a really sweet fighter. A woman at ringside added that he was sweet as sugar. The next day Case's article referred to the fighter as "Sugar" Ray Robinson and the name stuck.

In 1937 Robinson's adolescent romance with a young girl named Marjorie Joseph resulted in a pregnancy. Robinson married her so that the child could have his name, but their marriage was annulled three months later. Soon afterward he left DeWitt Clinton High School to pursue a brilliant amateur career. He engaged in eighty-five bouts and won the featherweight championship in the 1939 Golden Gloves and the lightweight championship in 1940.

Robinson made his professional debut later that year at Madison Square Garden, knocking out Joe Echeverria in the second round. He remained undefeated in his first forty fights. In 1942 Robinson had the first of six brutal clashes with "Raging Bull" Jake LaMotta. Robinson won their first encounter, but in a rematch on 5 February 1943 in Detroit

Sugar Ray Robinson. ARCHIVE PHOTOS

the bull gored the stylish matador and Robinson suffered his first defeat.

On 27 February 1943 Robinson was inducted into the army and joined heavyweight champion Joe Louis and other boxers on exhibition tours of military bases. On 29 May 1943 he married Edna Mae Holly, a former showgirl; they had one son. On the night of 29 March 1944 the boxing troupe was preparing to sail from Brooklyn for an overseas tour when Robinson disappeared. He later claimed that he had suffered a bout of amnesia after falling down a staircase and remembered nothing until he awoke in Halloran Hospital on Staten Island a week later. On 3 June 1944 he received an honorable discharge as sergeant.

Robinson returned to the ring and continued to rampage through the welterweight and middleweight ranks. On 19 December 1946 he easily decisioned Tommy Bell in New York City to win the welterweight title. In Robinsin's first defense, held in Cleveland on 24 June 1947, his opponent Jimmy Doyle suffered a brain injury after an eight-round knockout and died the next day. A troubled Robinson donated part of the earnings from his next two fights to establish a trust fund for Doyle's mother. He defended the title four more times in the next four years.

Handsome and suave, Robinson was as flamboyant outside the ring as he was within it. A sleek five feet, eleven inches, he favored sharp suits and drove a flamingo-pink Cadillac. He was also a shrewd businessman who negotiated his own contracts and never settled for less than he felt he deserved. He owned a popular Harlem nightclub, Sugar Ray's, a dry-cleaning store, a lingerie boutique (run by Edna Mae), and a barber shop. He was also a habitual spendthrift and ladies' man. In late 1950 Robinson embarked on a whirlwind tour of Europe with an entourage that included a valet, secretary, barber, and golf pro. In twenty-nine days he won five bouts, four by knockout.

Upon his return, Robinson challenged then middleweight champion LaMotta. On 14 February 1951 in Chicago, Robinson stopped a battered and defenseless LaMotta in thirteen rounds and won the middleweight crown for the first of five times. Robinson again traveled to Europe, this time bringing the flamingo-pink Cadillac that had become his trademark. He had six nontitle bouts in twenty-two days. On 10 July 1951 Robinson lost his middleweight title in a stunning upset to black British challenger Randy Turpin in London but regained it by stopping Turpin in a rematch on 12 September 1951 in New York City. Robinson successfully defended his title twice in early 1952. On 25 June 1952 Robinson, seeking a title in a third division, challenged light-heavyweight champion Joey Maxim. The temperature at ringside in Yankee Stadium was more than 100 degrees. Robinson was ahead on points before being overcome by the sweltering heat. Maxim won when Robinson was unable to answer the bell for the fourteenth round.

On 18 December 1952 Robinson announced his retirement to become an entertainer and tap dancer. The demise of his Harlem business ventures and unpaid taxes, however, forced his return to boxing in 1954. After several bouts, Robinson knocked out champion Carl ("Bobo") Olson in the second round on 9 December 1955 and won the middleweight title for a third time. The Internal Revenue Service, however, was on hand to place a lien on Robinson's earnings for unpaid taxes. On 2 January 1957 he lost the championship to Gene Fullmer, a hard-hitting Mormon, on a decision in New York. Four months later, on 1 May in Chicago, Robinson knocked out Fullmer in the fifth round and became the first fighter to win the middleweight crown four times. Robinson next lost his title on a split decision to welterweight champion Carmen Basilio in a blood-spattered bout on 23 September 1957 in Yankee Stadium. But in the grueling rematch in Chicago Stadium on 25 March 1958 Robinson decisioned Basilio and won the title for a fifth and final time.

As negotiations for a third battle with Basilio dragged on into 1959, Robinson defended his title against New England champion Paul Pender, who defeated him on 22 January 1960 in the Boston Garden. Robinson also lost the rematch on 10 June 1960. He fought Fullmer to a draw later that year, and on 4 March 1961 lost a decision to Fullmer in a final bid to regain the middleweight crown.

Robinson's career was now in decline. In 1963 Edna Mae obtained a Mexican divorce. Robinson then married longtime companion Mildred Wiggins Bruce on 25 May 1965. Robinson continued fighting well past his prime in a number of uninspired bouts. After an embarrassing loss to lackluster Joey Archer on 10 November 1965, Robinson retired at age forty-four. On 10 December 1965 he bid farewell from the ring in Madison Square Garden and was presented with a trophy inscribed to "The World's Greatest Fighter."

Robinson and his wife moved to Los Angeles. He appeared in several movies and on television programs and in 1969 helped found the Sugar Ray Robinson Youth Foundation to help underprivileged children. During his last years, he suffered from Alzheimer's disease and diabetes. He died of heart disease in the Brotman Medical Center. On 19 April 1989 more than 2,000 mourners, including the Reverend Jesse Jackson, then–heavyweight champion Mike Tyson, and Elizabeth Taylor, attended his memorial service at the West Angeles Church of God in Christ in Los Angeles. His remains are interred in Inglewood Park Cemetery in Inglewood, California, beside those of Mildred.

Sugar Ray Robinson's colorful career spanned twenty-five years. His final record was 202 bouts, 175 won, 19 lost, 6 draws, 2 no-contests, and 109 knockouts. He held the welterweight title for five years (1946–1951) and won the middleweight title an amazing five times, defeating the best middleweights in an era renowned for its middleweight talent. To his brutal craft Robinson brought a sullen art that had never been seen before and rarely has been since. His style spoke of a natural elegance and grace, swiftness of fist and foot, and an uncanny defensive ability. He also possessed a warrior's courage and knockout power in either fist. Generations of fighters were influenced by his flamboyant style and ring acumen, most notably Muhammad Ali and "Sugar" Ray Leonard. Robinson was elected to the Boxing Hall of Fame in 1967 and to the International Boxing Hall of Fame in 1990. Sugar Ray Robinson was arguably the best fighter "pound-for-pound" ever to enter the ring.

★

The Paul Magriel Boxing Collection on the history and literature of pugilism and the L. S. Alexander Gumby Collection, both in the Special Collections Division in Butler Library at Columbia University in New York City, contain papers relating to the boxer and his career. Sugar Ray Robinson with Dave Anderson, *Sugar Ray: The Sugar Ray Robinson Story* (1970), is the definitive account of the boxer's life and career. Gene Schoor, *Sugar Ray Robinson* (1951), provides a short account of his life through 1951. Obituaries are in the *New York Times* and the *Los Angeles Times* (both 13 Apr. 1989). The video *Sugar Ray Robinson: Pound for Pound* (1982) highlights the boxer's career from amateur bouts to retirement.

MICHAEL MCLEAN

Robert Rodale with several of his company's publications, 1990. UPI/CORBIS-BETTMANN

RODALE, Robert (*b.* 27 March 1930 in New York City; *d.* 20 September 1990 in Moscow, Russia), writer and publisher whose books and magazines promoted fitness, healthy living, and sustainable organic approaches to agriculture.

Rodale was the son of Jerome Irving (J. I.) Rodale, a publisher and editor, and Anna (Andrews) Rodale, a homemaker. He had two sisters. Although born in New York City, Rodale's father had a keen interest in the science of agriculture. While working as an auditor for the Internal Revenue Service in Pittsburgh in the late 1930s, he became acquainted with British organic farming research, and he bought an abandoned farm in Emmaus, Pennsylvania, which provided a place for his experiments with organic practices. In 1942 he entered the publishing business with the magazine *Organic Gardening and Farming.*

Robert Rodale grew up in this environment of passionate commitment to organic gardening and farming practices and to improving people's lives spreading these ideas. He attended public schools before attending Lehigh University from 1947 to 1952, where he studied English and journalism. His name first appeared on the masthead of *Organic Gardening and Farming* as staff photographer when he was nineteen. On 23 June 1951 he married Ardath Harter; they had five children. After leaving college without taking a degree, Rodale joined his father at Rodale Press, which had added *Prevention* magazine in 1950. A few years later the press began publishing *New Farm.* In 1960 Rodale took over from his father as editor and publisher of *Organic Gardening and Farming.*

Rodale's diverse interests and talents strengthened and reinforced each other. At six feet tall and 160 pounds, Rodale, who was bearded for much of his adult life, was physically fit and athletic. An avid shooter, he was a member of the 1968 U.S. Olympic skeet-shooting team. While at the Mexico City Olympics he became interested in bicycling. This interest led to an expansion of Rodale Press to include new magazines dealing with fitness: *Bicycling, Runner's World, Backpacker,* and *Men's Health.* His books, which included *The Challenge of Earthworm Research* (1961), *The Basic Book of Organic Gardening* (1971), *Sane Living in a Mad World* (1972), and *The Best Health Ideas I Know* (1974), reflected his diverse interests. He also wrote "Trap and Skeet Department" for *Outdoor Life* and the syndicated column "Organic Living."

In addition to his publishing career, Rodale was active in promoting research in the fields of public health and agriculture. His interest in cycling led to his development of pedal-powered machines for Third World farmers, including grain mills, hoes, and garden cultivators. The Prevention Index, an annual survey investigating changes in preventive health behavior in the United States, was his creation. His father founded the Rodale Institute, originally called the Soil and Health Institute, as a nonprofit means of providing financial support for scientific research. In his later years Robert Rodale devoted much of his time to promoting the goals of the institute. Under his leadership the institute grew and flourished. In addition to the 305-acre main research farm in Pennsylvania, the institute's properties grew to include research stations and demonstration areas around the world. Rodale traveled extensively, helping to establish research and education centers in many countries. His final trip was to Moscow to establish *Novii Fermer,* a Russian-language edition of *New Farm.* It was one more effort to bring environmentally sound and sustainable agriculture to the world. He was killed, along with his Russian partner, his driver, and a translator, when his car collided with a bus as he was returning to the airport. He was buried in Emmaus.

While he shared his father's passion for activism and organic practices, Rodale developed a shrewd business sense. When the company added *Bicycling,* the magazine's circulation was about 50,000. By the time of his death circulation had grown to nearly 400,000. The press successfully employed a direct-marketing strategy to promote both its periodicals and books. Rodale's contrarian instincts led him to seek middle-aged and elderly readers for many of his publications. In 1990, for example, the majority of subscribers to *Prevention* were more than fifty years of age. The Rodale Press list of publications grew, but there was always a unity within the diversity. The magazines presented different aspects of a coherent worldview to varied audiences. With Rodale becoming chairman and chief executive in 1971, after his father's death, the family business developed into a publishing empire.

Although he was head of a $240 million-a-year business, Rodale was unpretentious. He bicycled to work from his modest house and waited in line with his employees in the cafeteria. His office door was almost always open and his private space so unassuming that a new employee once wandered in and lay down on the couch while Rodale was at lunch, mistaking it for an employee lounge. A generous man, about a year before his death he provided a $250,000 loan to a New York City bookstore in danger of closing because he wanted to help preserve a business that spread new ideas. Rodale was also an activist at the local, national, and international levels. Acting on his interest in bicycling, he sponsored the construction of the Lehigh County Velodrome in 1975 and was instrumental in bringing the junior world championships there in 1978. He initiated efforts to make states more self-sufficient in food production, promoting projects to shift demand to locally produced foods. He received a 1984 presidential "World Without Hunger" award for his international nutritional work.

Robert Rodale saw himself as a revolutionary. In 1970 he wrote: "Revolutions don't always start with a bang. A seed is planted, an idea begins to take shape, and gradually people see that their life is being remolded by irresistible revolutionary forces." Rodale planted many seeds around the world in his efforts to revolutionize world agriculture. His legacy may be best stated in his own words. In one of his editorials about his father, he wrote: "His voice in my head trails off. I can't hear the words, but I get the message. And the message is, 'Get back to work. There's plenty more to do.' "

★

Rodale's papers, photographs, and recordings are held by Rodale Press and the Rodale Institute. Of the many tributes published following his death, John Wiley, "Phenomena, Comment, and Notes," *Smithsonian* (Dec. 1990), places Rodale within a context of contemporary visionaries. "Robert Rodale: A Retrospective" *Organic Gardening* (Dec. 1990), assesses his legacy and includes numerous photographs and quotations from his writings. Mark Bricklin, "Personal Memories of *Prevention*'s Editor-in-Chief," *Prevention* (Dec. 1990), provides personal and amusing anecdotes illuminating Rodale's personality. Obituaries are in the *New York Times* (21 Sept. 1990), *Newsweek* (1 Oct. 1990), and *Publisher's Weekly* (5 Oct. 1990), as well as the December 1990 issues of Rodale's *Bicycling, Organic Gardening, Prevention,* and *Runner's World. A World of Sense: The Life Journey of Bob Rodale* (1994) is a video biography by Rodale Productions that examines his beliefs and accomplishments. A U.S. Department of Agriculture video, "Oral History Interview with Mr. Robert Rodale" (1989), discusses the work of Rodale and his father, organic farming, and agricultural innovations.

KEN LUEBBERING

ROGERS, Carl Ransom (*b.* 8 January 1902 in Oak Park, Illinois; *d.* 4 February 1987 in La Jolla, California), psychologist whose theories of "client-centered" psychotherapy and humanistic psychology had a major impact on counseling, psychotherapy, and education and helped inspire the encounter-group movement of the 1960s.

Carl Rogers was the fourth of six children of Walter A. Rogers, a successful civil engineer, and Julia (Cushing) Rogers. His parents, while affectionate, held strict, conservative Protestant views that they instilled in their children. Dancing, card playing, and theatergoing were forbidden, as was association with those who engaged in such activi-

Carl Ransom Rogers. CORBIS-BETTMANN

ties. Rogers later recalled that even carbonated beverages had a faintly sinful aroma for him.

When Rogers was twelve, the family moved to a farm near Chicago, where his father put into practice scientific methods of agriculture. The children were encouraged to raise their own chickens and livestock, and Rogers also collected and bred night-flying moths. He came to see this experience as his first introduction to the use of science to solve problems. He graduated from Naperville (Illinois) High School in 1919 and entered the University of Wisconsin the following year, intending to major in agriculture. He soon decided to prepare for the ministry instead, and in 1922 he was one of ten young Americans chosen to take part in a world conference of Christian students held in Peking (Beijing), China. During the long sea voyage and visit to Asia, his religious views shifted dramatically away from the thinking of his parents.

In 1924 Rogers graduated from the University of Wisconsin with a B.A. degree and election to Phi Beta Kappa. Shortly afterward, on 28 August 1924, he married Helen Martha Elliott, his fellow student and childhood sweetheart. They had two children, a son and a daughter. The newlyweds moved to New York City, where Rogers enrolled at Union Theological Seminary, known as a stronghold of liberal Protestantism. His father tried to forestall this move by offering to pay all the couple's expenses if Rogers would instead attend the much more conservative Princeton Seminary, but Rogers refused.

During two years at Union, Rogers discovered a deep interest in psychology that led him to transfer in 1926 to Columbia University Teachers College. There he came under the influence of the philosopher John Dewey and the child clinical psychologist Leta Hollingworth. He received his M.A. in psychology in 1928 and his Ph.D. in clinical psychology in 1931, both from Columbia. His dissertation research was embodied in his first book, *Measuring Personality Adjustment in Children* (1931).

In 1928, while still a doctoral student, Rogers joined the staff of the child study department of the Society for the Prevention of Cruelty to Children in Rochester, New York. He became director of the agency in 1930 and remained there for ten years. During this time he began to develop his approach of relying on the client or patient to determine the direction of therapy, an approach he described between 1935 and 1940 in lectures at the University of Rochester and in *The Clinical Treatment of the Problem Child* (1939).

In 1940 Rogers accepted a professorship of psychology at Ohio State University. His interactions with intellectually probing graduate students led him to state his increasingly unorthodox views on psychotherapy more explicitly in his book *Counseling and Psychotherapy* (1942). Rogers maintained that through a relationship with an accepting, empathetic therapist, individuals are capable of resolving their own problems and developing the insights needed to reshape their own lives. This nondirective or client-centered approach represented a sharp break from the analytic tradition of Freudian therapy.

In 1945 Rogers moved to the University of Chicago, where he was both a professor and the founder of the counseling center. There he put into practice the then radical idea of conducting empirical research on the process and effectiveness of psychotherapy. He reported some of the results of this research in *Psychotherapy and Personality Change* (1954) and further explained his methods and their application to education and administration in *Client-Centered Therapy* (1951).

Rogers was invited back to his alma mater, the University of Wisconsin, as visiting professor in 1957. He ended up staying as a member of the permanent faculty until 1963, when he left college teaching. While at Wisconsin, he published a biographical essay and collection of his papers, *On Becoming a Person* (1961). This book, his most popular, became the bible of the humanistic psychology movement. This movement maintained that people have within themselves the resources they need for self-discovery and personal growth. The role of the therapist is not to take charge of the client's life but to help the client realize his or her own ability to make important choices.

In 1963 Rogers became a founder of the Center for Studies of the Person in La Jolla, California. The center's guiding spirit, he remained there as a resident fellow for the rest of his life. His activities included leading seminars and workshops around the world, and he took a particular interest and pride in working to bring together people from conflicting groups in such trouble spots as Northern Ireland, Central America, and South Africa. His later books included *Becoming Partners: Marriage and Its Alternatives* (1972), *Carl Rogers on Personal Power* (1977), *A Way of Being* (1980), and *Freedom to Learn* (1983).

Among his many honors, Rogers received the Distinguished Scientific Contribution Award and the first Distinguished Professional Contribution Award of the American Psychological Association. He also served as president of the American Psychological Association (1946–1947). He was a fellow of the American Academy of Arts and Sciences. Rogers died of a heart attack in La Jolla, California, following hip surgery. His remains were cremated.

Classically American in both his belief in human potential and his determination to find practical ways of helping people develop that potential, Rogers took counseling and psychotherapy out of the European-style consulting room and made them an accepted feature of everyday life.

★

The Carl Rogers Collection of manuscripts and personal papers is at the University of California at Santa Barbara. His autobiographical essay, "This Is Me," forms a section of *On Becoming a Person* (1961). The most comprehensive biographies are Howard Kirschenbaum, *On Becoming Carl Rogers* (1979); and David Cohen, *Carl Rogers: A Critical Biography* (1997). On his theory and practice, see Barry A. Farber, Debora C. Brink, and Patricia M. Raskin, eds., *The Psychotherapy of Carl Rogers: Cases and Commentary* (1996). An obituary is in the *New York Times* (6 Feb. 1987).

IAN MCMAHAN

ROONEY, Arthur Joseph (*b.* 27 January 1901 in Coultersville, Pennsylvania; *d.* 25 August 1988 in Pittsburgh, Pennsylvania), owner and founder of the Pittsburgh Steelers of the National Football League, the first team to win four Super Bowl championships.

Art Rooney with the "game ball" after winning the AFC Central Division championship, 1972. UPI/CORBIS-BETTMANN

The eldest of nine children of Daniel Rooney, a saloon keeper, and Margaret Murray, a homemaker, Arthur moved to Pittsburgh with his family when he was two years old. They lived above a saloon in close proximity to Exposition Field, the present site of Three Rivers Stadium, where the Pittsburgh Pirates played baseball. Rooney grew up loving all sports, but baseball was his first love. The red-headed youngster, who was only five feet, seven inches tall and of medium build, attracted much attention with his athletic exploits. In 1920 he earned a place on the U.S. Olympic boxing team and won Amateur Athletic Union championships in the welterweight and middleweight classes. The famed coach Knute Rockne tried to entice him to Notre Dame to play football, but the young man chose to attend Georgetown University in Washington, D.C., to play baseball. He was a pitcher but also a feared batsman at Georgetown, where he earned a B.C.S. in 1920, and then at Duquesne University in Pittsburgh and Indiana State Normal School of Pennsylvania.

From 1921 to 1925 Rooney played minor league baseball in Wheeling, West Virginia, where he batted .372. An injured throwing arm forced him to decline major league offers from the Boston Red Sox and the Chicago Cubs. He then tried playing semiprofessional football for the Canton Bulldogs before fielding his own teams, among them the P. J. Rooneys, the North Side Majestics, and the Hope Harveys, between 1926 and 1932. In 1928 Rooney began staging boxing promotions, which he continued in haphazard fashion for many years. He also cultivated a lifelong interest in horse racing. In 1930 he became involved in breeding racehorses, and he often bet successfully at various tracks. His biggest coup reportedly was in 1936 or 1937, when he bet $500 at the Empire City Raceway on a 14–1 longshot and ended the day with more than $100,000 in winnings. He went to Saratoga Raceway the following day and parlayed his winnings into $380,000.

In the meantime, Rooney had married Kathleen McNulty on 10 June 1931; they had five sons. Two years after his marriage, allegedly using money won at the track, Rooney purchased the fifth franchise issued by the embryonic National Football League in 1933, naming the team the Pittsburgh Pirates after the successful professional baseball team in town. The struggle to attract fans was such that "home" games were played in Louisville, Kentucky; Canton, Ohio; and even New Orleans. During the Great Depression, Rooney often had to rely on horse winnings to meet his football payroll. Up until World War II Rooney's team had never turned a profit, with revenues constricted by low attendance and interminable losing seasons. The lack of profit might also have resulted from the owner's inattention; Rooney seemed to treat the team as a hobby, and he paid his players more than the prevailing wage. In 1938 "the Chief" signed All-American Byron ("Whizzer") White to a $15,800 contract, making him the highest-paid player in the league. White, who earned more than the entire team of the previous year, went on to become a justice on the U.S. Supreme Court.

In 1940 Rooney renamed his team the Steelers. Six years later he hired Jock Sutherland, the famous coach and disciplinarian from the University of Pittsburgh. Sutherland represented a dramatic change from the Steelers 1937 player-coach, Johnny Blood, a renowned bon vivant who once failed to show up for a game because he had not realized it was scheduled. Things did not change, however. To the fans in Pittsburgh it was "SOS," the Same Old Steelers. The team's offices were located in a downtown hotel, and all financial records were kept in a personal black notebook. For years Rooney relied solely on handshakes for contracts, and he was always uncomfortable around lawyers. The Steelers started to make money as public interest in professional football grew in the 1950s, but the fans were unhappy about the loss of local talent, such as Joe Schmidt, Johnny Unitas, and Joe Namath, to other teams.

In 1969 Rooney selected Chuck Noll as the fourteenth head coach of the Steelers. After winning the opening game that season, the team returned to form and lost the next thirteen games. Rooney's policy, however, was never to interfere with the coach. This paid off in the 1970s as a legendary team was quietly built with fortuitous college draft choices, such as Terry Bradshaw, Franco Harris, Joe Greene, Dwight White, Jack Ham, Jack Lambert, and John Stallworth. These players formed the nucleus of the famed Steeler dynasty. The team first made it to the playoffs in 1973 and then proceeded to win Super Bowl championships in 1975, 1976, 1979, and 1980. After forty years of being lucky at horse betting, Rooney finally got lucky in football.

When he died in Mercy Hospital in Pittsburgh, eight days after suffering a stroke in his Three Rivers Stadium office, Art Rooney was the beloved patriarch of the National Football League. Besides being one of the most popular figures in all of sports, Rooney was a rarity in that a feeling of genuine affection existed between him and his players. He treated them more like sons than employees. He invariably traveled with the team and visited in the locker room after every game. Before the advent of unions, Rooney would often represent the interests of players at league meetings. He always took an interest in their personal lives. While Rocky Bleier, a running back injured in combat in Vietnam, was recovering in a hospital from shrapnel wounds, Rooney would constantly visit, send him postcards, or telephone. When Bleier's injuries prevented him from returning to full form, and Coach Noll cut him from the squad, "the Chief" had him placed on the injured reserve list. After intense rehabilitation Bleier returned to the Steelers and contributed handsomely to their impressive string of championships.

Art Rooney, inducted into the Professional Football Hall of Fame in 1964, died a multimillionaire. In addition to the Steelers, which had an estimated worth of more than $140 million at the time of his death, he owned Yonkers Raceway, the William Penn Raceway, the Pompano Raceway, and a horse-breeding farm in Maryland. His generosity was legendary. He loved giving to orphanages and to Irish causes, and he was a big contributor to Catholic missions in China, where his brother Dan served as a missionary priest.

★

There is no biography of Rooney. His former office at Three Rivers Stadium has been transformed into a library containing much information about Rooney and the Steelers. An intimate look at Art Rooney is in Roy Blount, Jr., *About Three Bricks Shy of a Load* (1974). Much of the story concerning the forty losing years can be gleaned from Ray Didinger, *Pittsburgh Steelers* (1974). The winning years are chronicled in Jim O'Brien, *Doing It Right: The Steelers of Three Rivers and Four Super Bowls Share Their Secrets for Success* (1991). A very personal perspective can be gained from Rocky Bleier, "Unforgettable Art Rooney," *Reader's Digest* (Nov. 1989). An obituary is in the *New York Times* (26 Aug. 1988).

FRANCIS R. MCBRIDE

ROUSH, Edd J. (*b.* 8 May 1893 in Oakland City, Indiana; *d.* 21 March 1988 in Bradenton, Florida), baseball player who had a notable career with the Cincinnati Reds (1916–1926, 1931).

Edd and his twin brother, Fred, were the only children of William C. Roush, a dairy farmer, semiprofessional baseball

Edd Roush. COURTESY OF THE NATIONAL BASEBALL HALL OF FAME, COOPERSTOWN, N.Y.

player, and telephone lineman, and Laura (Herrington) Roush, a homemaker. When they were born, Edd got an extra "d," and both boys received the middle name of "J" to represent their grandfathers, Joseph and Jerry. Thus, from birth Edd was already "the game's greatest individualist," as Reds manager Pat Moran would later call him.

Despite his natural abilities Edd did not dream of a baseball career. He and his brother went directly from eighth grade to Oakland City Baptist College. Sensing a lack of academic interest in the boys, the president of the school asked them if they had come to study or play basketball. They chose the wrong answer and were thrown out. Returning to his father's dairy farm, Roush was motivated to find outside interests. As he said, "I just had to get away from them damn cows."

Roush started playing for the Oakland City Walk-Overs in 1909, at the age of sixteen. A regular player did not show up and someone suggested, "Why not put that Roush kid in?" In 1911 he learned that some players were paid $5 per game. The manager wouldn't pay him, so he took his talents to Princeton, Indiana, twelve miles away. The switch caused "quite a ruckus" when Princeton came to Oakland City to play.

Roush possessed grace, speed, power, savvy, and aggressiveness. He was left-handed, both throwing and batting, but since he could not find a leftie's glove as a youngster he threw right-handed. He did not have a left-hander's glove until he started professional ball with Evansville of the Kitty League in 1912.

Roush played nine games with the Chicago White Sox in 1913 before being optioned to Lincoln, Nebraska. On 27 April 1914 he married his boyhood sweetheart, Essie Mae Swallow. They had one daughter, Mary. Also in 1914 Roush played for Indianapolis of the new Federal League, then played for Newark, New Jersey, in 1915. When the Federal League collapsed after the 1915 season, he was sold to the New York Giants and their famous manager, John J. McGraw.

Roush did not like McGraw for many reasons, including his "vicious" tongue. The main problem, though, was what Roush saw as the manager's "meddling." McGraw looked at Roush's forty-eight-ounce bat, the heaviest ever used in the majors, and told his new outfielder that it was too big for him. "What kind of league is this," Roush snapped, "where a manager tells a player what kind of bat to use?" "Where did you ever hit .300?," McGraw retorted. "Every league I've played in," said Roush, "and I'll do it in this one, too."

Using his big bat, Roush was true to his word, compiling a lifetime average of .325 over eighteen seasons, winning National League batting titles in 1917 and 1919, and hitting over .350 in 1921, 1922, and 1923. Overall, he had 2,376 base hits, scored 1,099 runs, and batted in 981. He struck out only 260 times in his eighteen seasons.

McGraw traded the upstart Roush to Cincinnati, where he played from 1916 through 1926, and again in 1931. Realizing his mistake, McGraw tried to get him back, and finally did, from 1927 through 1930.

Often called "Big Edd," he was actually only five feet, eleven inches and 170 pounds. Batting in the "cleanup" spot, in the era of the loosely wound "dead" ball, shifting his feet with every pitch, he used his short, heavy, thick-handled bat to hit to all fields. Possessing great speed, he did not have to hit home runs to be effective. He hit 182 triples, 152 of them as a Red, still the Reds team record. Of his sixty-eight career home runs, twenty-nine were inside the park. He had 268 stolen bases.

Roush's fielding was as natural as his hitting. He knew immediately where a batted ball would go and could run to that spot, looking up only at the last moment. "Oh, what a beautiful and graceful outfielder that man was! The more I played next to him the more I realized his greatness," recalled Rube Bressler. Similarly, Heinie Groh remembered: "Eddie used to take care of the whole outfield, not just center field. He was far and away the best outfielder I ever saw."

Roush was always in shape to play. Immensely popular with players and fans, he was often in trouble with management due to disputes over salary and his dislike of spring training. He held out half the 1922 season in a salary dispute and did not sign until August. In his first game, he got three hits and batted .352 for the season overall. He initially refused to play for McGraw when traded back to the Giants in 1927, and did not sign his contract until the season started. He went to the ballpark, played six innings, and got two hits. "I just didn't see any point to spring training," he said, "so I'd hold out on my contract every year until the week before the season started." He missed all of 1930 because of a salary dispute.

Roush was as noted for his competitive spirit as for his skills. He always claimed that the Reds would have beaten the White Sox in the 1919 World Series even if the "Black Sox" players, led by "Shoeless Joe" Jackson, had tried to win instead of accepting money from gamblers to "throw" the Series. That was his only World Series, but he holds one Series record: thirty-four plate appearances without a strikeout.

In 1962 Roush was elected to the Baseball Hall of Fame. In 1969 he was voted the greatest Reds player and in 1975 was picked by baseball writer Joe Reichler as the best center fielder of the era from 1900 to 1940.

After retirement the Roushes lived comfortably through Edd's investments, on Main Street in Oakland City half of each year, and in Bradenton, Florida, the rest of the year. Ironically, well into his sixties, he would go out to the spring training camp at Bradenton, put on a uniform, and hit line drives. In retirement Roush also liked to hunt and fish. He died at the Bradenton ballpark of a heart attack at age ninety-four, and his body was taken out through center field. Burial was at Montgomery Cemetery in Oakland City.

★

Lee Allen, *The Cincinnati Reds* (1948), is the original source for much of the printed material about Roush. Eliot Asinof, *Eight Men Out: The Black Sox and the 1919 World Series* (1963), contains many references to Roush's play in the Series. Lawrence S. Ritter, *The Glory of Their Times: The Story of the Early Days of Baseball Told by the Men Who Played It* (1966), includes twelve pages of Edd's own memories, plus photos, making it the best Roush source. Harold Seymour, *Baseball: The Golden Age* (1971), contains more direct references to Roush than any other printed source, save Ritter. Joe Reichler, ed., *The Game and the Glory* (1976), cites Roush as the best center fielder of the 1900–1940 era and as the most popular Reds player in a 1969 poll. Donald Honig, *The Cincinnati Reds: An Illustrated History* (1992), contains excellent photographs but no new information about Roush. An obituary is in the *New York Times* (22 Mar. 1988).

JOHN ROBERT MCFARLAND

ROWAN, Dan Hale (*b.* 2 July 1922 in Beggs, Oklahoma; *d.* 22 September 1987 in Englewood, Florida), the straight man in the comedy team of Rowan and Martin, hosts of the hit television program *Laugh-In,* which aired on the National Broadcasting Company from 1968 to 1973.

Dan Rowan was the only child of John and Clella (Hale) Rowan, itinerant carnival workers whose jobs kept them traveling throughout the Midwest and the South. The couple died under mysterious circumstances when Rowan was a young child, and he was raised at the McClelland Home for Children in Pueblo, Colorado. Attending public schools while growing up in the orphanage, he won letters in football and track and was elected president of the senior class at Central High in 1940.

Hoping for a career as a screenwriter, Rowan moved to Los Angeles immediately following graduation. He found work as a mail clerk at Paramount Pictures while attempting to hone his writing skills. With the outbreak of World War II, he enlisted in the Army Air Corps and was accepted to flight school despite a relatively meager educational background. He saw combat as a fighter pilot in the South Pacific, achieving the rank of captain with the Fifth Air Force.

Returning to Los Angeles, he used GI Bill benefits to take courses in acting and writing at both the University of California, Los Angeles, and the University of Southern California. Unable to find work in the movie industry, he borrowed money and became the coproprietor of an automobile dealership. Just as it appeared that his show business aspirations had been stymied, Rowan was introduced to another would-be performer, Dick Martin, a radio comedy writer, who was supporting himself principally as a bartender. The two found an easy synergy both as writers and performers, with Rowan playing the tall, sophisticated mustachioed straight man to Martin's goofy jester.

The pair developed a nightclub act that they took on the cabaret circuit in southern California. Typical sketches included Rowan as a prissy Shakespearean actor being heckled by the drunken Martin; Rowan as a pedantic biology professor attempting to explain "the birds and the bees" to dim-bulb Martin; and Rowan as a military strategist trying to explain the battle plan to a soldier more interested in getting home in one piece than winning the war. Rowan and Martin were among the first generation of nightclub comics to make fun of television, doing send-ups of Westerns and soap operas. Much of the repertoire they developed during the early 1950s would serve them well in later years.

Dan Rowan. ARCHIVE PHOTOS

Although Rowan had indeed found his way back into show business, the team was moderately successful during its early years, managing to gain bookings at only marginal venues. Their prospects began to improve in 1956, when the powerful newspaperman Walter Winchell reviewed the team's act favorably in his nationally syndicated column. In 1958 they made a motion picture, *Once Upon a Horse,* for Universal. Working with director Hal Kanter, Rowan and Martin slapped together several of their old nightclub Western routines, producing a kind of pale parody of Nicholas Ray's cult classic, *Johnny Guitar*. The picture gained little notice from the critics or the public, and the team's option was not picked up by the studio. A later effort at the movies, *The Maltese Bippy* (1969), also failed.

The team's big break came in television. Dean Martin, who was starring in one of the few remaining successful comedy-variety programs on network television, invited them to host a summer replacement for his prime-time show in 1966. To the surprise of everyone, it was the highest-rated program on television that summer, which led NBC executives to approach Rowan and Martin about a permanent vehicle. Offered their choice of a situation comedy or a variety format, Rowan and Martin balked at both. With the counterculture of the 1960s in full swing, they held out for a "pure comedy" format that would allow them to satirize the issues and styles of the day, freed of both the narrative constraints of situation comedy and the musical obligations of a variety show.

Although there had been some "pure comedy" on early television (notably the work of Ernie Kovacs), prime-time formulas had largely calcified by the late 1960s and there was little on the air that deviated from the two dominant genres. The producer George Schlatter, who had been trying unsuccessfully to sell an all-out comedy show to the networks for years, hooked up with Rowan and Martin as executive producer, helping them to develop a vehicle. Ed Friendly, a former NBC programming executive, joined the company and used his connections to get the program a shot on the schedule.

After airing as a one-shot special on NBC on 9 September 1967, *Rowan and Martin's Laugh-In* premiered as a midseason replacement on 22 January 1968. The hour-long show consisted of scores of quickly blacked-out one-liners, casually mixing politically and socially conscious jokes with sexual innuendo and pure physical slapstick. There was nothing else like it on the air; a typical fifty-three-minute episode contained upward of 250 jokes. Celebrities from Richard Nixon to John Wayne to Johnny Carson made cameo appearances. *Laugh-In* was an enormous success, finishing as the highest-rated program on American television during two of its five seasons. Rowan and Martin won an Emmy Award in 1969 as costars of the best variety show. Among the many regulars who achieved celebrity status on the program were Goldie Hawn, Lily Tomlin, Jo Anne Worley, Arte Johnson, Henry Gibson, Ruth Buzzi, Judy Carne, and Richard Dawson.

Rowan took a more active role in the production of *Laugh-In* than Martin. He is credited with adding a good deal of the show's political humor, much of it directed against Vietnam War hawks and segregationists opposed to the civil rights movement. A political maverick, the comedian participated actively in the presidential campaigns of Republican Nelson Rockefeller in 1964 and Democrat Eugene McCarthy in 1968. When questioned by the *New York Times* about the show's groundbreaking use of sexual material, he replied, "violent shows do a hell of a lot more damage than a sex joke."

After the cancellation of *Laugh-In* in 1973, Rowan essentially retired from show business, making only a few guest appearances on television series. He was married twice, from 1946 until their divorce in 1960 to Phyllis Mathis, with whom he had three children, Thomas Patrick, Maryann, and Christie; and then to Adriana van Ballegooyen, an Australian model, whom he married on 17 June 1963. She survived him after his death from cancer at his Florida home.

★

Biographical information may be found in Tim Brooks and Earle Marsh, *The Complete Directory to Prime-Time Network and Cable TV Shows, 1946–Present,* 6th ed. (1995). A collection of correspondence between Rowan and his neighbor, the writer John D. MacDonald, was published in 1986 as *A Friendship: The Letters of Dan Rowan and John D. MacDonald, 1967–1974.* On *Laugh-In,* see *Rowan and Martin's Laugh In: The Burbank Edition* (1969), which was compiled from television scripts from spring 1968 to spring 1969. Obituaries are in the *Los Angeles Times* and *New York Times* (both 23 Sept. 1987).

DAVID MARC

RUBELL, Steve (*b.* 1944 in Brooklyn, New York; *d.* 25 July 1989 in New York City), restaurateur, real estate millionaire, and cofounder of the internationally famous Studio 54 discotheque, which was considered the greatest club of its era and the place where celebrities and socialites came to be seen; there Rubell reigned over New York's nightlife at the height of the disco craze.

Steve Rubell's father, Phillip, was a poor rabbi who had fled the persecution of the Soviet Union to the United States. He settled his family in the East Flatbush section of Brooklyn. Phillip was a postal worker and tennis player who taught his children the game. Rubell's mother, Ann, was a high school Latin teacher. The family lived on Union Street in Brooklyn, where Steve shared the only bedroom in the family's small apartment with his brother, Donald. His parents slept in the living room.

Rubell attended Syracuse University on a partial tennis scholarship and earned bachelor's and master's degrees in finance. In 1964, while at Syracuse, Rubell met his best friend and future partner Ian Schrager. Both belonged to Alpha Mu fraternity. Rubell served in the National Guard and in an intelligence unit of the army reserves. After his military service he spent a year in the back office of a Wall Street brokerage firm, developing an antipathy toward that kind of employment. He decided to borrow funds from his father to open a sirloin and salad restaurant in Rockville Centre, Long Island. By 1974, Rubell owned thirteen Steak Lofts in Connecticut, New York, and Florida, as well as part interest in two discotheques, both in Queens, New York.

With his partner Schrager, Rubell opened Studio 54 in a former CBS television studio on West Fifty-fourth Street in Manhattan on 26 April 1977. From the moment it opened, celebrities such as Bianca Jagger, Truman Capote, and Andy Warhol created a new café society in the discotheque. Rubell successfully courted movie and sports stars with his garrulous personality. He often worked as a sentry at the club entrance's velvet rope, admitting celebrities and patrons, while refusing others lined up outside. Rubell's reputation as the New York's nightlife czar earned him prominent mention in *The Andy Warhol Diaries,* a best-seller.

Steve Rubell dances with Bianca Jagger at Studio 54 in New York City, 1978. UPI/CORBIS-BETTMANN

Described as "a pasha of disco," Rubell reigned as the king of New York City's nightlife. On 14 December 1978, thirty Internal Revenue Service agents apprehended Schrager and seized garbage bags full of cash and financial records hidden behind the ceiling panels of Studio 54 along with five ounces of cocaine in the basement. Rubell was arrested that same day. Both partners were indicted for federal income-tax evasion and charged with skimming more than $2.5 million in club receipts over a three-year period. Rubell and Schrager tried to escape prosecution by offering to testify against President Jimmy Carter's chief of staff, Hamilton Jordan, claiming Jordan had used cocaine in their club. That deal went nowhere, and Jordan was never indicted. In November 1979 Rubell and Schrager pleaded guilty to two counts of personal income and corporate tax evasion, and in January 1980 they were sentenced to three and a half years in prison.

A farewell party for Rubell and Schrager was given on 2 February 1980, two nights before they were to be incarcerated. Liza Minnelli sang "New York, New York" in a tribute to the quintessential New Yorkers. Both served eighteen months in the Metropolitan Detention Center in New York City and six months in a minimum-security prison in Alabama. The pair provided information leading to the conviction of four other New York club owners and were paroled to New York City's Phoenix House, a halfway house, in 1982. Schrager, in a *Vanity Fair* interview, stated, "Steve was like the mayor of jail, the same way he was the mayor of Studio 54. It was there that we decided we wanted to go into the hotel business."

In January 1981, while in prison, the partners sold Studio 54 to hotel owner Mark Fleischman. The club closed its doors in 1983. Rubell and Schrager, in exchange for the notes Fleischman owed them from the defunct Studio 54, took control of Fleischman's Executive Hotel on Madison Avenue. They hired avant-garde designers and turned the hotel into the Morgans, which opened in 1984. It turned a profit within a year, thus beginning their multimillion-dollar real estate syndication. The next luxury hotel, the Royalton, followed in 1988. The partners' style was to purchase the depressed properties, renovate them extravagantly, and then reopen them without marquees. Rubell and Schrager also converted, as high-paid consultants, the old Academy of Music in New York City into a fancy nightclub.

Rubell resided in Manhattan on West Fifty-fifth Street in a plush apartment he shared with Bill Hamilton, a design associate who lived with Rubell until his death. Rubell and Schrager also bought a rambling mansion in Southampton, Long Island, New York, a summer getaway where they enjoyed the beach action and were part of the "in crowd."

Rubell died on 26 July 1989 in Beth Israel Medical Center at the age of forty-five from septic shock and hepatitis, presumably caused by AIDS complications. He was buried on Long Island. His black granite tombstone, unveiled a year later, had the simple inscription, "The Quintessential New Yorker."

Rubell rose from a lower-middle-cless background and made his mark in New York City's glamour crowd by being a loquacious entrepreneur who was in the right place at the right time. He created an institution where patrons clamored to be let through the doors in order to party among the decade's "beautiful people" at New York City's most chic and selective nightspot, a late-night mecca of sex, drugs, and flamboyance that was the epicenter and epitome of 1970s fashionable excess.

★

Andy Warhol's *The Andy Warhol Diaries* (1979) offers an insider's look at Studio 54 during its heyday. Articles with information on Rubell include James Barron, "Rubell Created Homes Away from Home for the Trendsetters," *New York Times* (28 July 1989); Michael Gross, "Little Stevie Wonder: The Death and Life of Steve Rubell," *New York* (14 Aug. 1989); Michael Neill, "Steve Rubell, Studio 54 Puckish Ringmaster, Follows His Club into History," *People* (14 Aug. 1989); Douglas Martin, "Nights of Glitz, a Velvet Rope and Memories," *New York Times* (25 July 1990); and Bob Colacello, "Anything Went: Studio 54 Founders," *Vanity Fair* (Mar. 1996). *Fifty-four,* a feature-length motion picture about the nightclub, was directed by Mark Christopher and released in 1998. Obituaries are in the *Boston Globe* (27 July 1989), *New York Times* (27 July 1989), *Washington Post* (27 July 1989), and *Rolling Stone* (7 Sept. 1989).

KAREN LYNN SVENNINGSEN

RUFFING, Charles Herbert ("Red") (*b.* 3 May 1904 in Granville, Illinois; *d.* 17 February 1986 in Mayfield, Ohio), baseball player who, as a pitcher and pinch hitter for the New York Yankees in the 1930s and 1940s, led his team to six World Series championships.

The son of John and Frances Ruffing, German immigrants, Charles Ruffing and his older brother, John junior, grew up 140 miles south of Granville in the coal mining district of Illinois, where their father was a mine foreman in the coal town of Nokomis, which was owned by the Reliance Coal Company. At fifteen, Charles left school to work in the mines and played first base and outfield for the company baseball team managed by his father. He showed power as a hitter, but he suffered a major injury in March 1921, when his left foot was crushed by an empty coal car and he lost four toes. With his running skills curtailed, Ruffing in 1922 began pitching for his mining team and a local semiprofessional squad, earning $15 per game. The following year he signed his first professional contract for $150 a month with Danville, Illinois, in the Three-I League, appearing in thirty-nine games with a record of twelve wins and sixteen losses. The American League Boston Red Sox then purchased Ruffing's contract from Danville for $4,000. The red-haired, hard-throwing right-hander, who was six foot two and 210 pounds, began his major league career in 1924, appearing in eight games, six in relief, with no decision. In July he was sent to Dover, Delaware, in the Eastern Shore League, where he won four games and lost seven in fifteen showings.

Rejoining the Red Sox in 1925, Ruffing stayed in Boston for five seasons, compiling a record of thirty-nine wins and ninety-three losses for the hapless Bosox, who finished last in the American League every year of Ruffing's tenure. In Boston he twice led the league in losses, with twenty-five

"Red" Ruffing. NATIONAL BASEBALL HALL OF FAME LIBRARY, COOPERSTOWN, N.Y.

in 1928 and twenty-two in 1929. After beginning the 1930 season with three losses, Ruffing was traded to the New York Yankees for outfielder Cedric Durst and $50,000. Durst's ineffectiveness brought his retirement at season's end, while Ruffing went on to 231 wins in a distinguished fifteen-year Yankee career.

In New York, Ruffing completed the 1930 campaign with fifteen wins and five losses. Only once over the next twelve seasons did he fail to win at least fourteen games. From 1936 through 1939 Ruffing won eighty-two games as the Yankees won an unprecedented four consecutive World Series championships. Ruffing pitched in seven World Series for New York, six of which the Yankees won. He started ten games, pitched 85⅔ innings, and achieved a 2.63 earned run average (ERA) and a record of seven wins and two losses. The seven World Series victories stood as a record until 1961, when it was topped by another Yankee, Whitey Ford. Ruffing's most famous World Series experience, however, was as a spectator in 1932, when he witnessed teammate Babe Ruth's alleged call of a center-field home run off Chicago Cub pitcher Charlie Root, a feat Ruffing insisted actually happened. Ruffing's own personal Series highlight came in the 1938 postseason classic, when he won the first and fourth games in a four-game sweep of the Cubs. Following the 1934 season, on 6 October, Ruffing married Pauline Mulholland, a childhood sweetheart from Nokomis. They had one son, Charles junior.

Ruffing earned the *Sporting News* Major League All-Star honors in 1937, 1938, and 1939 and appeared in All-Star games in 1934, 1939, and 1940. In his seven innings of work in those games, Ruffing yielded seven runs on thirteen hits and was the losing pitcher in 1940. In two All-Star at-bats he singled once, driving in two runs in 1934. As one of baseball's premier hitting pitchers, Ruffing was a valuable batter, which often led to tensions with team management when Ruffing pointed out his value as a pinch hitter and demanded a higher salary. All-time, he ranks first among pitchers for career runs batted in (273), second for pinch hits (58), and third for home runs (36) and total hits (521). Ruffing's career batting average was .269, with eight seasons above .300 and a 1931 high of .364. Short-lived salary holdouts at the start of the 1932 and 1937 seasons were unsuccessful. Ruffing's highest salary was $22,000 per year after the 1937 season.

Ruffing's twilight years as a player were interrupted by military service in World War II. Although thirty-seven years old, married, and with four missing toes, Ruffing was inducted on 29 December 1942. He played on a number of military baseball teams and was discharged on 5 June 1945. He rejoined the Yankees on 16 July and pitched in eleven games, winning seven and losing three with a 2.89 earned run average, the lowest of his career. The 1946 campaign began with five wins in six decisions and a 1.77 ERA, but a broken ankle ended Ruffing's year. New York released the forty-two-year-old on 20 September. Ruffing signed for 1947 with the Chicago White Sox, but he retired after recording three wins and five losses and injuring a knee.

Ruffing's career accomplishments reflect his reliability and durability. In twenty-two seasons he appeared in 624 games, winning 273 (including 45 shutouts), losing 225, and saving 16 contests. With a career ERA of 3.80, he recorded 1,987 strikeouts, gave up 4,284 hits, and walked 1,541. At retirement, Ruffing held two dubious records: most runs allowed (2,117) and most earned runs (1,833). From 1928 through 1940 Ruffing never pitched fewer than 222 innings per year and, at one time, posted 241 consecutive starts, a record that lasted until 1973. Ruffing was rewarded for these accomplishments with election to the Baseball Hall of Fame in 1967.

With his playing days over, Ruffing remained in baseball as a scout for the Chicago White Sox in 1948, managing Muskegon in the Central League in 1949 and Daytona Beach in the Florida State League in 1950, and scouting for the Cleveland Indians from 1951 through 1959 and the

New York Mets in 1961. He ended his baseball career in 1962 as the Mets' first pitching coach.

In retirement, Ruffing enjoyed bowling, golf, and basketball. He divided his time between homes in Nokomis and Chicago until he moved to Ohio in 1951, when the Indians hired him as a scout. In 1973 Ruffing suffered a stroke that affected his voice, but his speech returned after a second stroke. Skin cancer resulted in operations on his face and chin. Even with these medical difficulties, Ruffing continued to attend the annual Hall of Fame ceremonies in Cooperstown, New York. He died of cancer.

★

Information on Ruffing can be found in Martin Appel and Burt Goldblatt, *Baseball's Best: The Hall of Fame Gallery* (1977); Hal Lebovitz, "A Trip Down Memory Lane with Red Ruffing," *Baseball Digest* (Feb. 1983): 79–84; and Milton Richmond, "Red Ruffing Was a Winner on the Mound and at Bat," *Baseball Digest* (Aug. 1986): 75–78. An obituary is in the *New York Times* (20 Feb. 1986).

DAVID BERNSTEIN

RUSK, Howard Archibald (*b.* 9 April 1901 in Brookfield, Missouri; *d.* 4 November 1989 in New York City), physician who founded the field of rehabilitation medicine.

The only surviving child (an older brother died at birth) of Michael Yost Rusk, a furniture dealer, undertaker, and county clerk, and of Augusta Eastin Shipp Rusk, a homemaker, Rusk graduated from Brookfield High School in 1919. He subsequently earned a bachelor's degree from the University of Missouri (1923) and an M.D. from the University of Pennsylvania medical school (1925). On 20 October 1926 he married Gladys Houx; they had two sons and a daughter. From 1926 to 1942 Rusk practiced internal medicine in St. Louis, building a successful private practice while serving as associate chief of staff at St. Luke's Hospital and as a member of the medical school faculty of Washington University.

Rusk left his practice in August 1942 to become a major in the U.S. Army Air Force medical service, where he began his career in what would become the field of rehabilitation medicine. Driven by the anguish he saw in the wounded airmen who flooded into hospitals under his charge as head of the Army Air Force's Convalescent Training Program, he developed the first comprehensive program of retraining, physical rehabilitation, and care for these men's emotional and psychological needs. The immediate focus of his program was to reduce the patients' convalescent time and return them to active duty, but Rusk also began to address the needs of the disabled patient as a "whole person" who would have to readjust to society after a debilitating injury.

After the war Rusk moved to New York City, where in 1948 he founded the Institute of Physical Medicine and

Howard A. Rusk. ARCHIVE PHOTOS

Rehabilitation at New York University, with the help of more than a million dollars donated by financier Bernard Baruch, whose father, Simon Baruch, had been an early pioneer in some of the practices that coalesced into rehabilitation medicine. Rusk served as the institute's director until 1978, during that time extending the practices of what he dubbed the "third phase of medicine" (following prevention and treatment). The institute developed procedures for disabled patients—often victims of trauma or disease—as well as those born with physical disabilities. Within a short time it was sending many of its patients on to school or employment, after offering them assistance in learning how to adapt the strengths and weaknesses of their physical frames to day-to-day life. One of its earliest partnerships, announced in July 1948, was with the United Mine Workers, to provide rehabilitation and care for the thousands of miners disabled in shaft collapses and other accidents.

Rusk gained a forum for his ideas through his introduction to Arthur Hays Sulzberger, publisher of the *New York Times*. Sulzberger, who suffered from arthritis in his hands, was fascinated by what Rusk's Air Force team had done for those whose more severe disabilities threatened to deprive them of their livelihoods; he offered Rusk a regular column and an associate editorship with the paper. The column appeared from 1946 to 1969 on a weekly basis; at first it was devoted mostly to veterans' issues, but ultimately it branched out to deal with rehabilitation in general as well as other medical topics.

In the late 1940s Rusk began a relationship with the White House that would continue through the tenure of nine presidents. He knew President Harry S. Truman because they both were from Missouri, and Truman began the practice of appointing Rusk to government commissions, committees, and advisory boards. Not all his posts were purely medical in nature; for example, Rusk's wartime experience led President Truman to appoint him on 7 August 1950 as chairman of the Health Resources Advisory Committee of the National Security Resources Board, charged with health problems related to Korean War mobilization. President Dwight Eisenhower detailed him on a medical mission to South Korea in 1953, to advise the U.S. government on medical needs in that war-torn country. Twelve years later President Lyndon Johnson sent him on a similar mission to South Vietnam, with the assignment of coordinating relief programs there. Following a tour of medical facilities in the nation, Rusk's team of physicians concluded that napalm had caused a negligible number of civilian casualties, thereby incurring the enmity of antiwar groups.

In 1955 Rusk's investigations of medical care overseas led him to found the World Rehabilitation Fund, dedicated to training and placing foreign specialists in rehabilitation medicine, and funding artificial limbs and braces for amputees and other nonmobile persons around the world. His experience in Korea in 1953 led him to become active in the American-Korean Foundation, particularly in coordinating shipments of medicines to South Korea. He had made a similar fact-finding tour of Europe in 1949.

In 1946 Rusk founded the world's first comprehensive medical training program in rehabilitation, the Department of Rehabilitation at New York University's medical school, which he headed until 1980. He also organized the Rehabilitation Institute at New York City's Bellevue Hospital. He later served as a consultant on rehabilitation issues for the Veterans' Administration, the United Nations Secretariat, and the New York City Department of Hospitals. In addition Rusk was a member of New York City's Board of Hospitals, and president of both the International Society for the Welfare of Cripples and the International Society for the Rehabilitation of the Disabled.

Rusk devoted attention to many health and public policy matters beyond the realm of rehabilitation. For example, he was an early advocate of enlarging public programs for the country's growing numbers of elderly people, including those affected by senility, and he argued that the mandatory retirement age of sixty-five was counterproductive. In his *New York Times* column he urged creation of a national heart institute, advocated federal funding for cancer research, and pleaded for more humane coverage practices by insurance companies. During his career Rusk wrote numerous tracts on rehabilitation, many in conjunction with Eugene J. Taylor. These include *New Hope for the Handicapped* (1949) and *Living with a Disability* (1953), as well as *Rehabilitation Medicine, Cardiovascular Rehabilitation,* and *Rehabilitation of the Cardiovascular Patient* (all 1958), the latter appearing in numerous editions. In addition, Rusk published his memoirs, *A World to Care For,* in 1972. An earlier effort aimed at a broad audience was *Doing Something for the Disabled,* a pamphlet published in 1953 and written with Mary E. Switzer. The pamphlet, which attempted to put a human face on the estimated 23 million disabled persons in the United States in 1953, related success stories from Rusk's institute.

During Rusk's career there was a shift within the community of the disabled. Initially persons with disabilities were largely unorganized as an interest group, and were essentially invisible to both the public at large and political leaders. By the time of Rusk's death, the disabled, taking the civil rights movements of the 1960s as their model, had organized into both a powerful lobby and a visible force in the United States. Rusk's writings reflect this sea change. At the beginning of his career, he was a lone advocate for what he perceived as a mass of undifferentiated people with numerous disabilities. While he sought political solutions to some of their problems, most notably increased funding for their rehabilitation and retraining, he preferred to speak personally on their behalf to those in positions of power. In his memoirs he described numerous instances in which his personal argument for policy changes or greater funding made the difference. At the heart of his program was a modified Horatio Alger story in which disabled individuals pulled themselves up by their metaphorical bootstraps to remake themselves as better people, able to succeed in the workplace. He therefore argued against industrial pensions for disabled workers or other policies that he feared would undermine their will to rejoin the workforce. From the 1970s on, Rusk noted the usefulness of organized groups for promoting the rights of people with disabilities.

Rusk received honorary degrees from scores of institutions in the United States and overseas, as well as the Distinguished Service Medal, the French Legion of Honor, and numerous other decorations and awards. He was a three-time recipient of the Albert Lasker Award, for work in public health and international rehabilitation, and for medical journalism.

On 4 November 1989 Rusk died of a stroke in New York City. He was buried at Rose Cemetery, in his hometown of Brookfield, Missouri.

Rusk, who is known as the father of rehabilitation medicine, was the first to admit that many of the procedures he and his medical teams developed had their origins in the work of doctors throughout the country at least since the latter decades of the nineteenth century. However, he is credited with developing a holistic concept of care for rehabilitation patients that stressed education, psychological needs, and retraining no less than physical rehabilitation and provision of artificial limbs and assistive technology. Because, for many, rehabilitation medicine and "Dr. Live-Again" were one and the same, Rusk developed a genius for self-promotion, assisted in no small measure by his *New York Times* forum and his numerous appointments. His lasting legacy, however, is the thousands of patients who under his tutelage and care learned how to make a place for themselves in the world.

★

Rusk's personal papers, covering his entire professional career, are in the Western Historical Manuscripts Collection at the University of Missouri, Columbia. His autobiography, *A World to Care For* (1972), is a valuable if often breezy overview of his life and career. A more rigorous treatment of his early career is Orin Lehman's master's thesis, "The Early Life of Howard A. Rusk (1901–1945)" (1973). An obituary is in the *New York Times* (5 Nov. 1989).

MARK SANTANGELO

RUSSELL, Charles Hinton (*b.* 27 December 1903 in Lovelock, Nevada; *d.* 13 September 1989 in Carson City, Nevada), governor of Nevada who helped guide the state's postwar development as a tourist destination and who was instrumental in regulating its gambling industry.

Charles Russell was one of three children of Robert James Russell, a cattle rancher, and Ellen Daisy (Ernst) Russell. When he was nine years old his family moved to a ranch near Deeth, west of the East Humboldt Range in eastern Nevada, where his father managed the Union Land and Livestock Company. Charles attended Deeth's two-room elementary school and then went to Elko County High School, where he was elected student body president. After graduating from high school in 1922, he entered the University of Nevada in Reno in the fall. He was a member of the Lambda Chi Alpha fraternity and received his A.B. degree in 1926.

Russell's first job was as a teacher in the Ruby Valley School south of Deeth. In the fall of 1927 he moved back to the family ranch, but he spent the following summer as a seaman aboard a Pacific Coast freighter. He next worked for a year as a timekeeper at the Nevada Consolidated Copper Company's big open-pit mine in Ruth, Nevada. In May 1929 he became part owner and managing editor of the *Ely Record,* in nearby Ely, where he subsequently served as

Governor Charles Russell testifying before a U.S. Senate Interior subcommittee, 1958. AP/WIDE WORLD PHOTOS

president of the Lions Club, master of the Masonic Lodge, director of the Chamber of Commerce, and president of the Nevada area council of the Boy Scouts of America.

In 1934 he began his political career as a Republican candidate for one of four White Pine County seats in the state assembly, winning by only thirty votes. He was reelected with more comfortable margins in 1936 and 1938. On 19 March 1939 he married Marjorie Ann Guild in Carson City. The Russells had five children: Clark, Virginia, Craig and David (twins), and Todd.

In 1940 Russell was elected White Pine County's state senator. Reelected in 1944, he was for two years president pro tempore of the Nevada senate. From 1946 to 1948 he served as Nevada's one representative to the Eightieth U.S. Congress, where he took pride in supporting the state's agricultural and mining interests. During the second session he presented a bill that would have subsidized Nevada mines, but it died in the House Rules Committee. Defeated for reelection in 1948 by Walter Baring, Russell was appointed the following year to the staff of the Joint Committee on Foreign Economic Cooperation. From his office in Paris, overseeing the expenditure of Marshall Plan funds, Russell traveled throughout Europe, as well as to Turkey, Morocco, and Algeria.

In July 1950 Russell left the federal government, returned to Nevada, and became the Republican party's nominee for governor, campaigning for reorganization of the state government. In November 1950 he was elected, defeating Democrat Vail Pittman. He had a comfortable Republican majority in the Nevada senate, but faced a Democratic assembly. During his first year in office he managed the sale of an inactive state-owned magnesium plant in Henderson for a reported $150 million, a substantial enhancement of the state's financial resources. Russell also introduced centralized budget control and purchasing, promoted tourism as a major Nevada industry, and increased taxes on prosperous contractors who worked for the U.S. Atomic Energy Commission's bomb testing program in southern Nevada. In December 1953 he called a special session of the legislature to appropriate emergency funds for Nevada's schools, seriously overcrowded by the state's rapid growth after World War II.

Russell's most important challenge as governor came early in his second term. After defeating Pittman again in 1954, but still with a Democratic lieutenant governor and a Democratic majority in the assembly, he faced a serious test of the state's control over the gambling industry, in which organized crime was pressing for greater influence. Estes Kefauver of Tennessee was then chairman of a U.S. Senate committee that in 1951 reported in some detail the extent of mob influence in the Las Vegas casinos. The report aroused lively public interest, but congressional response was deftly discouraged by Senator Pat McCarran of Nevada. In the mid-1950s, Hank Greenspun, editor of the *Las Vegas Sun,* implicated Lieutenant Governor Clifford Jones and Marion Hicks, owners of the Thunderbird Hotel and Casino in Las Vegas, in a conspiracy to remove Robbins Cahill, chairman of the Nevada Tax Commission and vigilant enforcer of Nevada gambling laws. Russell was firm in his support of Cahill when in 1955 the tax commission revoked the Thunderbird's gambling license.

Jones and Hicks challenged this action in a rural court, and *Tax Commission* v. *Hicks* was being considered by the state supreme court when, in 1957, Jones and Hicks sponsored a bill in the senate that would remove the tax commission's licensing power. Russell vetoed it, but it had passed both houses with seemingly veto-proof majorities. In the senate, however, he needed only one additional vote to sustain his veto, and in returning the bill he persuaded State Senator Ralph Lattin to vote his conscience and support the veto. It was sustained, and the Nevada state government retained control of the gambling industry. As Russell would later put it, while speaking at the inauguration of Governor Robert List in 1978, "I would say a Nevada governor's biggest job is keeping gambling clean."

During his second term Russell was for three years chairman of the Conference of Western States' Governors, and he spent one year on the executive board of the National Governors' Conference. In 1958 he ran for a third term as governor but was defeated by Democrat Grant Sawyer.

In 1959 Russell returned to Washington, D.C., to represent Nevada's mercury mining industry, but was shortly appointed by President Dwight D. Eisenhower as chief of the Agency for International Development Mission to Paraguay, where he served until November 1962. He was then reassigned to Washington and spent six months at the State Department's Paraguay desk before returning to Nevada as director of development and assistant to the president of the University of Nevada. From 1964 until his retirement in December 1967 he was also director of alumni relations. N. Edd Miller, the president of the university during this period, remembered him as "a kind and thoughtful man, but he could be forceful when necessary."

Russell suffered in his final years from emphysema and died of heart failure in the Carson City hospital. After a memorial service attended by several hundred friends and admirers at St. Peter's Episcopal Church in Carson City, his ashes were buried in Dayton, Nevada.

★

Russell's papers and an oral history are in the Department of Special Collections of the University of Nevada Library in Reno. The Thunderbird Hotel case is concisely described in James W. Hulse, *Forty Years in the Wilderness* (1986). Obituaries are in the *Nevada Appeal, Ely Daily Times,* and *Reno Gazette-Journal* (all 14 Sept. 1989), and *New York Times* (15 Sept. 1989).

DAVID W. HERON

RUSTIN, Bayard Taylor (*b.* 17 March 1912 in West Chester, Pennsylvania; *d.* 24 August 1987 in New York City), pioneer civil rights activist and theoretician best known for his work with Martin Luther King, Jr., and the A. Philip Randolph Institute.

Born out of wedlock to Archie Hopkins and Florence Rustin, a teenager, in 1912 (some reports have 1910), Bayard was adopted by his grandparents and grew up in their household near Philadelphia, alongside his mother and her brothers and sisters. Rustin's grandfather worked as a caterer to support him and his adoptive siblings, while his grandmother, a devout Quaker, exerted a strong influence over the children of the household, especially Bayard. Rustin excelled in both athletics and his studies. By the time of his graduation with honors from West Chester High School in 1932, Rustin had won acclaim as an honor student, debating society and glee club member, and gifted musician and football player. His widespread achievements earned him recognition as class valedictorian.

Rustin first committed his life to "democratic social change" when he experienced discrimination as a high

Bayard Rustin, 1963. ALLAN BAUM/NEW YORK TIMES CO./ARCHIVE PHOTOS

school football star. During his team's visit to Media, Pennsylvania, a local restaurant owner refused to serve the black football players in his establishment. At that point Bayard determined to always resist injustice through peaceful but persistent means. This commitment would lead Rustin into numerous protest, peace, and civil rights organizations and activities throughout his long and active life, including twenty-three arrests as he demonstrated his willingness "to take to the streets" his protest strategies.

After high school, Rustin attended Wilberforce University in Ohio (1932), Cheyney State Teachers College (now Cheyney University, 1934–1936) in Pennsylvania, and City College of New York (1938–1941), failing to take a degree even though he excelled in his studies. Rustin was a member of the Young Communist League (YCL) in New York City from 1938 to 1941. His Quaker and pacifist background attracted him to YCL activities at City College because of the league's stand against war and discrimination. It was there that he received his indoctrination into radical protest causes. He briefly flirted with socialism in the late 1930s, while simultaneously addressing the more mundane needs of life by singing in New York's Café Society Downtown and other Greenwich Village nightclubs, sometimes performing with such notables as Huddie ("Leadbelly") Ledbetter. Years later acquaintances claimed that Rustin could have become another Harry Belafonte had he not gravitated back into political activism in the early 1940s. Living in the highly charged political and intellectual climate of New York in the late 1930s demonstrably thrust Rustin into a left-wing form of political activism that would characterize his public life until his death.

The year 1941 proved pivotal for Rustin. He left the YCL because he felt the league discriminated against blacks, and it became clear to him, after Nazi Germany invaded the Soviet Union in June, that it was more concerned with the fate of the Soviet Union than with discrimination in the United States. He joined the Fellowship of Reconciliation (FOR), a nonviolent antiwar group led by A. J. Muste. Rustin rose to the position of secretary for race relations in FOR and helped organize a splinter organization, the Congress of Racial Equality (CORE). Also in 1941, Rustin emerged as a youth leader in A. Philip Randolph's March on Washington Movement, a planned mass march to force the federal government to guarantee fair hiring practices in America's burgeoning defense industries. Facing a threatened march of 50,000 persons on the nation's capital, President Franklin Roosevelt responded by issuing Executive Order 8802, which created the Fair Employment Practices Committee (FEPC) to oversee nondiscriminatory hiring in defense industries.

During World War II, Rustin embraced a number of pacifist and civil rights causes, including vocally objecting to the internment of Japanese-Americans. He refused military service on the grounds of being a conscientious objector; because he refused to enlist as a noncombatant or report at a civilian work camp, he was jailed from 1944 to 1946. He spent these years in the Ashland Correctional Institute in Kentucky and the Lewisburg Penitentiary in Pennsylvania.

Following his release from prison, Rustin became chair of the Free India Committee, participated in a number of sit-in protests against Britain's rule over India at the British Embassy in Washington, and traveled to India to study the nonviolent techniques and ideology of Mohandas Gandhi, leader of the movement against British rule. In 1947 Rustin participated in the historic Journey of Reconciliation, a CORE-organized challenge to the illegally segregated interstate buses of the American South. This prototype of the 1960s Freedom Rides sparked an incident outside Chapel Hill that resulted in the arrest of Rustin for violating North Carolina's segregation code and his eventually serving thirty days on a chain gang. Shortly thereafter, Rustin became an active participant in A. Philip Randolph's Committee Against Jim Crow in the Military. In the early 1950s Rustin joined George Houser in founding the American Committee on Africa, which, along with FOR and the

American Friends Service Committee, cosponsored a trip by Rustin to Africa in an attempt to unite American pacifists with emerging African independence leaders. In 1953, at the height of the Korean War, Rustin severed ties with FOR and assumed duties as the executive director of the War Resisters League, a position he held for twelve years.

Rustin was a striking figure. Six feet tall, 200 pounds, and known in his advanced years for his distinctive white hair, Rustin was a chain smoker and spoke in a precise, almost scholarly manner. He would regularly put in eighteen-hour workdays. His leadership qualities in FOR and later in the War Resisters League caught the attention of Martin Luther King, Jr., in June 1955. King invited Rustin to Montgomery, Alabama, to help organize and participate in the Montgomery bus boycott from 1955 to 1956. Rustin proved so adept as a civil rights tactician that King insisted he serve as his special assistant from 1955 to 1960. In that capacity Rustin proved instrumental in creating, along with King and other black ministers, the Southern Christian Leadership Conference in 1957.

Rustin continued to organize civil rights activities until his longtime mentor, Randolph, called on him to help organize a second attempted march on Washington, D.C., in 1963. Rustin served as deputy director, chief logistics expert, and coordinator for the resulting March on Washington, which attracted scores of civil rights groups and leaders, as well as more than 200,000 demonstrators, to the capital on 28 August 1963. The following year Rustin gained national attention for directing the New York City school boycott on 3 February. Rustin took a leave of absence from the War Resisters League (which paid him a salary of $71.04 weekly) to direct the school boycott. Almost half of New York City's public school students participated in the one-day protest against the Board of Education's weak integration policies. The boycott proved historically significant in that it served as the forerunner of later protests in New York and also marked the spread of civil rights activities from the South to the North.

By the mid-1960s Rustin had won wide recognition as one of America's most effective protest tacticians. He continued to capture headlines for his exploits as director of the A. Philip Randolph Institute, founded in the spring of 1965 in New York City, and for his fierce advocacy of nonviolent means to achieve racial and social harmony. This stage in his life, however, marked a discernable move by Rustin to emphasize the need for economic power for America's black underclass. Thereafter, he alienated many Black Power militants by arguing for coalitions with white labor and Jewish organizations. By 1975 Rustin had further earned the opprobrium of militant blacks by founding the Organization for Black Americans to Support Israel Committee, intending to reinforce his perceived role as one of the African-American community's chief liaisons to white religious groups. Rustin remained a controversial figure in the African-American community until he died of cardiac arrest in 1987. At the time of his death, Rustin resided in New York City and was active in the leadership of the A. Philip Randolph Institute and in human rights missions at home and abroad. Scotland Farm, the country home of his friends Robert and Joyce Gilmore, near Millerton in upstate New York, was the final resting place for Rustin's cremated remains.

Bayard Rustin's many decades of involvement in and leadership of nonviolent protests reflected the changing currents of American social movements from the 1930s to the 1980s. Although a longtime icon of civil rights and antiwar activity, Rustin evolved as a controversial figure in later life for his stand on coalition politics and for his avowed homosexuality. Nevertheless, Rustin remains an important figure in nonviolent social struggles.

Rustin won numerous awards, including the Thomas Jefferson Award for the Advancement of Democracy from the Council Against Intolerance in America (1948), the Man of the Year award from the Pittsburgh Chapter of the NAACP (1965), the Eleanor Roosevelt Award from the Trade Union Leadership Council of Pittsburgh (1966), the Liberty Bell Award from Howard Law School (1967), and the Stephen Wise Award from the American Jewish Congress (1981). His honorary degrees include an LL.D. from the New School for Social Research (1968), a Litt.D. from Montclair State (1968), and an LL.D. from Brandeis University (1972), as well as other honorary degrees from Columbia University, Clark College, Harvard University, New York University, and Yale University. In 1974 Rustin delivered the Radner lectures at Columbia University, from which evolved his book *Strategies for Freedom: The Changing Patterns of Black Protest* (1976).

★

Bayard Rustin's papers in the Library of Congress are available on microfiche through University Publications of America (1988). *Down the Line: The Collected Writings of Bayard Rustin* (1971), contains the body of Rustin's writings introduced by C. Vann Woodward. *South Africa: Is Peaceful Change Possible?* (1984), with Charles Bloomstein and Walter Naegle, is Rustin's personal insight into how nonviolence could end apartheid in South Africa. Jervis Anderson, *Bayard Rustin: Troubles I've Seen, a Biography* (1997), is a solid scholarly study of Rustin's life and significance. Fred Powledge, *Free At Last?: The Civil Rights Movement and the People Who Made It* (1991), places Rustin within the context of leadership strategies in contemporary civil rights. See also "Picket-Line Organizer Bayard Rustin," *New York Times* (4 Feb. 1964). Obituaries are in the *New York Times* (25 Aug. 1987) and *Black Enterprise* (Nov. 1987).

IRVIN D. SOLOMON

S

SACKLER, Arthur Mitchell (*b.* 22 August 1913 in New York City; *d.* 26 May 1987 in New York City), research psychiatrist, medical publisher, and art collector whose contributions to scholarly institutions supported research in both medicine and art history and significantly enlarged the holdings of American art museums.

One of the three sons of Isaac and Sophie Sackler, Arthur M. Sackler was educated in New York City public schools. He received a B.S. degree from New York University in 1933. In 1935 Sackler married Else Jorgensen; they had two daughters. Sackler put himself through medical school by working for the William Douglas MacAdams medical advertising agency, and earned his M.D. from New York University in 1937.

After serving as a house physician and pediatrician at Lincoln Hospital in the Bronx (1937–1938), Sackler was a resident in psychiatry at Creedmoor State Hospital in Queens Village from 1944 to 1946. After his divorce from Jorgensen, in 1949 Sackler married Marietta Lutze; they had a son and a daughter. That same year Sackler founded the Creedmoor Institute for Psychobiologic Studies, and was its director of research until 1954. Sackler's theories on the physiological causes of mental illness, investigations of histamine biochemotherapy, and hematological studies of psychotic patients were particularly significant. From 1958 to 1985 he directed the Laboratories of Therapeutic Research at the Long Island University College of Pharmacy.

In 1950 Sackler—who never maintained a private practice—served as associate chairman of the International Committee on Research of the first International Congress of Psychiatry; he also was named editor in chief of the *Journal of Clinical and Experimental Psychobiology,* in which capacity he worked until 1962. In 1954 Sackler joined the board of Medical Press, and he became president of Physicians News Service the following year. In 1960 Sackler founded *Medical Tribune,* a biweekly newspaper published in eight languages and distributed in twenty countries. He was honored by the American Medical Association for his role in communications in 1969. Over the years, Sackler wrote some 145 medical papers (some in collaboration with his brothers—also physicians—and other colleagues) on the biochemistry of mental illness. Sackler was also the editor of *Great Physiodynamic Theories in Psychiatry: An Historical Reappraisal* (1956).

Sackler served with the World Health Organization (beginning in 1969), was chairman of the International Association of Social Psychiatry (1970–1980), and was a trustee and research professor of psychiatry at New York Medical College (1967–1972). For his decades of work in the field, he received a special commendation from the American Psychiatric Association in 1982.

Progress in the medical sciences was aided by benefactions from Sackler and his brothers that helped establish the Sackler School of Medicine at Tel Aviv University (1972) and biomedical institutes at New York University

(1980) and Tufts University (1980). The Arthur M. Sackler Sciences Center at Clark University (1985) and the Arthur M. Sackler Center for Health Communications at Tufts (1986) were named in his honor.

An interest in art that began while he was an undergraduate led Sackler, in the mid-1940s, to become a collector. He started with Western European paintings from the Renaissance to the twentieth century, as well as contemporary American art. By the 1950s he had developed a particular interest in Chinese art, initially ceramics, then jades, bronzes, and sculpture; subsequently he acquired Near Eastern and Indian objects. Rather than individual works, he generally purchased entire collections, seeing himself as "more of a curator than a collector." As he put it, "I collect as a biologist. To truly understand a civilization . . . you must have a large enough corpus of data." And for a total historical reconstruction of a society, one must, he believed, preserve not only its masterpieces but also lesser materials.

With this aim Sackler began in the 1960s to provide Columbia University with archaeological specimens—Iranian seals, pottery, and metalwork—for investigation by its graduate art history students. From 1961 to 1974 he was a member of the advisory council of Columbia's Department of Art History and Archaeology. (Concurrently, between 1967 and 1970, he was a senior research associate in anthropology at Columbia.) Sackler's contributions to the scholarly study of Chinese materials began in 1967, when he acquired for the art museum of Princeton University a group of ritual bronzes, followed by a collection of Chinese paintings (masterpieces dating from the fourteenth to the twentieth century) assembled under the guidance of Professor Wen Fong, chairman of the Art and Archaeology Department at Princeton.

Major donations by Sackler led to the Arthur M. Sackler Gallery at the Princeton University Art Museum in 1967; the Sackler Wing of the Metropolitan Museum of Art in 1978; the Arthur M. Sackler Museum at Harvard University in 1985; and the Arthur M. Sackler Gallery of the Smithsonian Institution, which opened on the Mall in Washington, D.C., just months after Sackler's death. Since 1983 Sackler had been closely involved in the planning and construction of this building, designed to hold a collection of some 1,000 of his Chinese, Near Eastern, and South Asian objects. The Chinese bronze vessels, scrolls, and album leaves are considered particularly fine. In the year before his death, ground was broken at Beijing University for an archaeological museum, with facilities for teaching museology, to be constructed with his support.

Sackler's humanitarian concerns (recognized with a Linus Pauling Humanitarian Award in 1985) included an affiliation (1978–1984) with the American Pro Deo Council, part of a worldwide peace organization, and his sponsorship of the International Symposium for Biblical Studies, held at Tokyo in 1979.

Sackler died of a heart attack in 1987 at the age of seventy-three. He was survived by his third wife, the former Jill Lesley Tully. His wide-ranging goals and ideals live on in the work of the Arthur M. Sackler Foundation for the Arts, Sciences, and Humanities, which he set up in 1965 to provide support for projects devoted to the dissemination of ideas and knowledge. Stressing that his benefactions were not to be considered acts of philanthropy—rather, they were his "privilege"—Sackler summed up his lifework by noting that "art and science are two sides of the same coin. Science is a discipline pursued with passion; art is a passion pursued with discipline. At pursuing both, I've had a lot of fun."

★

Sackler's prefaces to two of the several catalogs of his collections—Marilyn Fu and Shen Fu, *Studies in Connoisseurship: Paintings from the Arthur M. Sackler Collection in New York and Princeton* (1973); and *Asian Art in the Arthur M. Sackler Gallery* (1987)—express his aesthetic and humanistic ideals. An article on Sackler in *The Dictionary of Art,* vol. 27 (1996), provides information on his career as a collector. An obituary is in the *New York Times* (27 May 1987).

ELEANOR F. WEDGE

ST. JOHNS, Adela Rogers (*b.* 20 May 1894 in Los Angeles, California; *d.* 10 August 1988 in Arroyo Grande, California), journalist known for her "sob sister" coverage of major stories for the Hearst newspaper syndicate and for her Hollywood connections.

Adela Rogers was one of two children of Earl Rogers, a well-known criminal attorney, and Harriet (Greene) Rogers. Her parents were divorced when she was a child, and her father had additional children by a second wife. She and her mother shared a mutual antipathy, which she later credited for much of her independence, writing in her memoirs, "My mother . . . disliked me so much that, fortunately for me, she had neglected to give me her version of what mothers are supposed to teach their daughters."

Young Adela was raised in large part by her paternal grandparents and grew up adoring her larger-than-life father, visiting his law offices frequently. She attended Hollywood High School but did not graduate. Although she wished at one time to follow her father into the law, he steered her instead into journalism, obtaining a job for her in 1913 at William Randolph Hearst's *San Francisco Examiner*. A year later she was transferred to the *Los Angeles Herald,* where she moved quickly from cub reporter to feature writer.

On 24 December 1914 she married the paper's chief

copy editor, William Ivan ("Ike") St. Johns and added his name to her byline. The pair had two children, Elaine and William, Jr. In 1918 she retired from full-time newspaper work to work at home near her children on magazine articles and short stories. She also wrote a number of novels. The first, *The Sky Rocket* (1925), became a film, as did two others. *Photoplay* magazine editor James R. Quirk hired her during this time to write a series of pieces on Hollywood and its personalities, dubbing St. Johns the "mother confessor of Hollywood." She was a favorite of many film stars throughout her life.

In 1929 she divorced Ike St. Johns and went back to newspaper work for Hearst, becoming one of the first American women to cover sports events. She also reported on a number of prominent trials, most famously the trial in 1935 of Bruno Richard Hauptmann for the kidnapping and murder of the son of aviation hero Charles Lindbergh. Her lead when Hauptmann was found guilty was typical of St. Johns's emotional approach to news stories. Instead of leading with Hauptmann's death sentence, as many of her colleagues did, she began her article with the phrase, "Keep Your Hands Off Our Children." She claimed that this slogan was the message behind the jury's verdict. One of St. Johns's favorite pieces for Hearst during this period was a series on unemployed women of the Great Depression, for which she posed as a woman out of work in Los Angeles. Like much of her journalism, the series was meant to touch hearts and expose injustices.

Adela Rogers St. Johns, 1935. UPI/CORBIS-BETTMANN

St. Johns was married twice after her divorce from her first husband—to Richard Hyland, best known as a college football player (she later claimed to have forgotten his name), and to Francis O'Toole, an airline executive. Neither marriage lasted. She had a son, Richard, by Hyland, who sued her as unfit to raise him; after his mother's victory in court, this son took the name St. Johns. A close friend of her elder son was adopted by the family and known as McCullah St. Johns.

In the mid-1930s St. Johns went to work in Washington, D.C., for Hearst, operating out of the *Washington Herald*'s city room. Among her coups during this period were a series of profiles on the controversial senator Huey Long and dramatic coverage of the 1940 Democratic convention. In the 1940s she retired from newspapers, concentrating again on magazines and novels. She also worked as a script doctor. From time to time, Hearst brought her out of retirement, asking her, for example, to work on a six-part eulogy after the assassination of Mohandas K. Gandhi in 1948.

Her middle years were not happy ones. The alcoholism she had inherited from her father had been exacerbated by the freewheeling lifestyle of the newsroom. In 1940 she made the front pages of a number of national newspapers when she was arrested for stealing a taxicab and going for what was apparently a drunken ride. Her son Bill's death in World War II added to her sorrows. Sometime thereafter, according to her autobiography, she attempted suicide. She would not finally give up drinking until the early 1960s.

In 1962 St. Johns achieved a lifelong dream and published a biography of her beloved father, *Final Verdict*. She went on to write about her own life in *The Honeycomb* (1969) and *Love, Laughter, and Tears: My Hollywood Story* (1978). *No Goodbyes: My Search Into Life Beyond Death* (1981) discussed the beliefs in psychic phenomena she had come to hold following her son's death.

While writing these and other books, St. Johns continued to produce occasional articles. She also taught various journalism courses over the years, beginning with a two-year stint at the University of California, Los Angeles, in the early 1950s. In 1970 one of her favorite presidents, Richard Nixon, awarded her the Medal of Freedom. In 1976 she came of retirement to cover the trial of her former employer's granddaughter Patty Hearst for the Hearst papers. At the time of her death, St. Johns, a minister in the Church of Religious Science, was reportedly working on a book entitled "The Missing Years of Jesus."

Billed as "the world's greatest girl reporter," Adela Rogers St. Johns was often credited as the model for the independent newspaperwoman of Hollywood films. Her appeal was aimed at her readers' hearts, not their heads, and she never tried to divorce her feelings from a story. She suited the frequently persuasive Hearst newspaper style perfectly. Asked late in life whether she was a sob sister, she replied, " 'Sob sister' is a term that was used to describe women writers who saw the emotional angle of a story and made the readers feel what they were feeling. I certainly hope I was one, and a good one too."

★

The Billy Rose Theater Collection of the New York Public Library has a collection of clippings about St. Johns. Most helpful for information about her life is her autobiography, *The Honeycomb* (1969). Also useful is her book about her father, *Final Verdict* (1962). St. Johns was profiled in *Current Biography* in 1976. Her style of writing and personality are briefly sketched in Ishbel Ross, *Ladies of the Press* (1936), and her alcoholism is discussed in Lucy Barry Robe, *Co-Starring: Famous Women and Alcohol* (1986). An interview with St. Johns in *Contemporary Authors* (1983) also touches on this as well as on her attitude toward her journalism. An obituary is in the *New York Times* (11 Aug. 1988).

TINKY "DAKOTA" WEISBLAT

SALT, Waldo (*b.* 18 October 1914 in Chicago, Illinois; *d.* 7 March 1987 in Los Angeles, California), screenwriter who won Academy Awards for *Midnight Cowboy* (1969) and *Coming Home* (1978) after having been blacklisted by Hollywood studios in the 1950s because of his membership in the Communist party.

Waldo Salt testifying before the House Un-American Activities Committee, 1951. UPI/CORBIS-BETTMANN

After graduating from Stanford University at the precocious age of eighteen, Salt first taught English at nearby Menlo Park Junior College and then was hired by Metro-Goldwyn-Mayer studios as a junior screenwriter for B pictures. At MGM he created some original screenplays but was more frequently used as a "script doctor," rewriting and editing dialogue and revising screenplays that had problems. Although his rewrites often changed scripts significantly, most of his work during these years was uncredited by the time it reached the screen. Only two films during his five years at MGM credit Salt as screenwriter: *The Shopworn Angel* (1938), with James Stewart and Margaret Sullavan, and *The Wild Man of Borneo* (1941), a screen adaptation of the play by Herman J. Mankiewicz and Marc Connelly.

As a young man, Salt idolized F. Scott Fitzgerald and Nathanael West. Although he was younger than the two novelists-turned-screenwriters, they respected him, and the three occasionally socialized and dined together. Salt attempted to emulate not only their writing styles, but their lifestyle as well, one of hedonism and self-indulgence. "They were the reigning heroes of Hollywood," Salt later said.

In 1941 Salt was fired from MGM for political reasons. He had been a member of the Communist party since 1939 and was always quite open about his political affiliations. Shortly afterward he was hired by Warner Brothers, where he wrote adaptations of the short story *Humoresque* by Fannie Hurst and the novel *Ethan Frome* by Edith Wharton. Neither script was produced, however, and the studio reassigned both of the projects to other screenwriters for adaptation.

Moving on to Twentieth Century–Fox in 1948, Salt worked on the screenplay of *Rachel and the Stranger* (for which he was uncredited), starring Robert Mitchum, Loretta Young, and William Holden. He next wrote *The Flame and the Arrow* (1950), a costume drama starring Burt Lancaster and Virginia Mayo, for which he did receive credit. Although a light entertainment, the film received positive reviews, mainly as a result of Salt's dialogue.

On 13 April 1951 Salt was called before the House Un-American Activities Committee. Because Salt was a longtime and active member of the Communist party, he feared that he would be imprisoned, but the hearings were called off the day before he was to appear to testify. Even though Salt never testified and was never one of the ten "unfriendly witnesses" who became known as the Hollywood Ten, he nevertheless received some unfavorable publicity and effectively became the "Hollywood Eleventh."

Barred from working in Hollywood and unable to make a living writing screenplays, Salt moved to New York City. For the next decade, he wrote television scripts and commercials in both the United States and Great Britain, but because he could not officially be hired he used the name Mel Davenport or other pseudonyms.

Not until well into the 1960s, when the hysteria of the HUAC hearings abated, did Salt openly try his hand at screenwriting for Hollywood again. He was hired by the British director John Schlesinger, who had read and been impressed by Salt's unproduced script of *Don Quixote* and by his ability to capture the novel's essence even while also heightening its dramatic appeal. Salt's first public assignment was an adaptation of *Midnight Cowboy,* a gritty novel of the streets of New York City by James L. Herlihy. After many years of working anonymously, Salt was finally able to use his own name on the script. Not only did *Midnight Cowboy* win the Academy Award for best picture in 1969 (it was the only X-rated picture ever to do so), but Salt also was awarded an Oscar for best adapted screenplay. *Midnight Cowboy* became an enormous moneymaker and plunged Salt back into the mainstream of Hollywood screenwriting.

Because the HUAC and Hollywood ban had been "lifted," Salt at this time finally received retroactive credit for a screenplay he had written for the film *Taras Bulba* (1962), an adaptation of the Nikolai Gogol novel. Salt went on to write a number of successful screenplays, and for a time he was considered one of the most innovative screenwriters in Hollywood. Following his success with *Midnight Cowboy* came *The Gang That Couldn't Shoot Straight* (1971), *Serpico* (1973), *The Day of the Locust* (1975), and *Coming Home* (1978), a brilliant and bitter antiwar film that was one of the first pictures to deal seriously with the plight of returning Vietnam War veterans. Salt's screenplay for *Coming Home* earned him a second Academy Award for best screenplay.

As the prodigal son in his triumphant return to Hollywood, Salt was given in 1986 the Writers' Guild of America's Laurel Award, a lifetime achievement prize for his estimable and vigorous screenplays. His wife, the poet Eve Merriam, attended the award ceremony with him, as did his two daughters, Jennifer and Deborah, and a grandson.

Wearing granny bifocals, and with long hair and a graying beard, Salt often dressed in a purple leather jacket, a Superman tee shirt, and striped sneakers, giving him the appearance of an aging hippie. Thirty-five years after being banished by Hollywood, he looked upon the McCarthy era with a certain benign irony, especially since he had long ago relinquished his radical philosophy. He could only laugh when he thought of how he and others were accused of inserting communist propaganda into films. As he told the reporter Tom Buckley in an interview in the *New York Times* (7 December 1973): "Can you imagine trying to get Communist propaganda past Louis B. Mayer?"

Salt died of lung cancer at Cedars-Sinai Hospital in Los Angeles, the city where he had made his home.

★

"The Artful Dodges of a Very Hot Screenwriter," a major profile of Waldo Salt, appeared in *New York Magazine* (26 Apr. 1971) when he was at work on the script of *The Gang That Couldn't Shoot Straight*. Obituaries are in the *New York Times* (8 Mar. 1987) and *Variety* (11 Mar. 1987).

FRANK BRADY

SCHAFFNER, Franklin James (*b.* 30 May 1922 in Tokyo, Japan; *d.* 2 July 1989 in Santa Monica, California), Academy Award–winning film director known for his expertise in creating epic films.

Schaffner spent the first six years of his life in Japan with his parents, who were missionaries. After the death of his father, James Schaffner, Franklin and his mother returned to the United States and settled in Lancaster, Pennsylvania, where he attended public schools and McCardy High School. After he graduated from Franklin and Marshall College with a B.A. degree in government and English and a Phi Beta Kappa key, he enlisted in the U.S. Navy. During World War II, as a lieutenant on landing craft and convoys,

Franklin Schaffner. UPI/CORBIS-BETTMANN

he saw action in Africa and, with the Office of Strategic Services, in Sicily, India, Burma, China, Italy, and Normandy.

Upon his return to civilian life, he was accepted at Columbia University Law School, but before beginning his studies he decided against a career as an attorney. He did get to New York City, though not to the university. He first tried his hand as an actor, without much success, and then became involved in the then-new television industry, working behind the camera. During the 1950s he became part of the impressive talent pool of what is now called television's Golden Age. He landed a job with the *March of Time* as an assistant director and then directed sports, news, and public affairs for the Columbia Broadcasting System, where he was given an opportunity to direct half-hour situation comedies.

Working his way up as a director of drama, Schaffner did many episodes for *Studio One, Playhouse 90, Ford Theatre*, and *The DuPont Show of the Week*. His more famous productions included *Twelve Angry Men, The Caine Mutiny Court-Martial*, and Jacqueline Kennedy's *Tour of the White House*. As a result of directing that show, Schaffner became a friend of the First Lady and subsequently worked as President John F. Kennedy's television adviser. Schaffner's success on television was as a result of his realization that it was a visual medium, closer to motion pictures than to the legitimate theater; many early television dramas of the time had the look of being merely filmed plays. Schaffner learned that the camera must break out of an invisible proscenium arch that trapped the television drama. He was awarded several Emmys and Peabody Awards for his work in television. To show his versatility as an artist, in 1960 he directed the Broadway stage production of *Advise and Consent*.

He then went to Los Angeles to direct feature films. His first was *The Stripper* (1963), with Joanne Woodward, based on William Inge's play *The Loss of Roses*; it was the last of the black-and-white CinemaScope pictures. He also did a film version of Gore Vidal's political satire *The Best Man* (1964) and Charlton Heston's medieval adventure *The War Lord* (1965) before directing *Planet of the Apes* (1968), which was a considerable box office success and which spawned a series of sequels. (Schaffner directed only the original.)

With *Patton* (1970) and the films that followed, critics began comparing Schaffner with the British director David Lean (*Bridge on the River Kwai, Lawrence of Arabia*) because of the size, scope, and dramatic power of his films. *Patton,* which won the Academy Award in 1970 for best director, won six other Oscars, including best picture. Schaffner also received the Directors Guild award for the film, which received numerous awards in dozens of other countries. In addition to critical praise, *Patton* appealed to the public, and it became a box office giant. Schaffner's *Nicholas and Alexandra* (1971) was a stirring account of Russia in the days leading to the revolution. *Papillon* (1973), with Steve McQueen and Dustin Hoffman, was based on a harrowing true-life story of a convicted thief and a counterfeiter doomed to a lifetime of banishment on Devil's Island. Schaffner followed that grueling film with a picture of intensity and beauty: *Islands in the Stream* (1977), based on the Ernest Hemingway novel and starring George C. Scott. *The Boys from Brazil* (1978) was a story of international intrigue, scientific cloning, and murder starring Gregory Peck, James Mason, and Laurence Olivier. In all, Schaffner directed only twelve films, but his pictures garnered no fewer than twenty-eight Academy Award nominations.

Over six feet tall, thin, and always conservatively dressed, usually in a three-piece Brooks Brothers suit, Schaffner had a certain inbred reserve. He looked more like a bank or university president than the typical film director. Because of his aristocratic bearing, his formality, and his impeccable manners, most people thought he was British, which he found amusing.

In addition to being an acknowledged master of the "big look" film (*Patton, Nicholas and Alexandra, Papillon*), Schaffner endeared himself to Hollywood studios for his production economy and gained a reputation for bringing films in below budget and within deadlines. Schaffner discounted the idea that he had to work under a certain kind of pressure because he worked on big-budget films. "The devotion and responsibility and expertise are the same," he was quoted as saying, "no matter what the budget."

Colleagues attributed Schaffner's talent to a visual acuity and a thorough preparation for each shot. His ability to elicit precise and often brilliant performances from his casts also added to his renown. Actors such as George C. Scott, Dustin Hoffman, Steve McQueen, Joanne Woodward, Gregory Peck, James Mason, and Laurence Olivier all gave stunning performances in Schaffner films.

Schaffner served as president of the Directors Guild of America from 1987 until a month before his death, when ill health forced him to step down. He died at his home shortly after being released from a hospital where he had been undergoing treatment for lung cancer.

★

Erwin Kim, *Franklin J. Schaffner* (1985), is a full-length study of the films of Franklin J. Schaffner; an in-depth article about Schaffner as *auteur* by David Wilson is in *Sight and Sound* (spring 1966); other articles are in the *New York Herald Tribune* (15 Nov. 1960), *New York Times* (5 Apr. 1964), *New York Post* (20 Apr. 1964), *Show* (Apr. 1970), and *Action* (May–June 1971). Obituaries are in the *New York Times* and the *Los Angeles Times* (both 3 July 1989) and *Variety* and *The Independent* (London) (both 5 July 1989).

FRANK BRADY

SCHIFF, Dorothy (*b.* 11 March 1903 in New York City; *d.* 30 August 1989 in New York City), newspaper publisher and editor who guided the *New York Post* for more than thirty years (1943–1976).

Schiff, born and reared on Fifth Avenue in New York City, was the elder of two children of Mortimer Leo Schiff and Adele A. Neustadt Schiff. Her father was an investment banker and son of Jacob H. Schiff, a noted financier and head of Kuhn, Loeb, and Company. The Schiffs, German Jews who moved in New York's top social circles, in 1904 became the first Jewish couple to be listed in the New York *Social Register*.

Schiff was raised in an elegant apartment that had been a wedding gift to her parents from Jacob Schiff. Summers were spent at Northwood, the home her father built on the north shore of Long Island. Called Dolly by her parents, she lived a life of solid upper-class comfort. She later described herself as a "hyperactive child" who resented the stern discipline of her father and the coldness of her mother. "I thought I must be a stepchild because I was so badly treated. There was no joy in my growing up."

After several years of home tutoring, Schiff was placed in the Brearley School, a fashionable academy for young women in New York City. She graduated in 1920 and then attended Bryn Mawr College for a year. After failing every course, she returned to New York for her debut. Schiff, an attractive young woman of medium height with short brown hair, striking blue eyes, and a trim figure, soon developed a romantic interest in Richard B. H. Hall, a bond salesman. On 17 October 1923 they were married in an Episcopal ceremony at Northwood. They had a son and a daughter. In 1931 Schiff's father died suddenly; her mother died in 1932. "My God, I'm rich . . . at last," Schiff proclaimed. She proceeded to divorce Hall and abandoned plans to join the Episcopal Church. On 21 October 1932 she married George Backer, the son of Eastern European Jewish immigrants, who was a political consultant and writer. They had one daughter.

Until the 1930s Schiff had been a nominal Republican with little interest in politics. Her second husband was a liberal Democrat, and under his influence she soon developed a keen interest in public affairs. In November 1937 Mayor Fiorello LaGuardia appointed her to New York City's Board of Child Welfare. Favorably impressed with the social and economic measures of the New Deal, Schiff became a Democrat and a supporter of President Franklin D. Roosevelt. Through Eleanor Roosevelt she became active in the National Association for the Advancement of Colored People, working with Mary McLeod Bethune, Walter White, and other African-American leaders.

Schiff first met President Roosevelt at his estate in Hyde Park, New York, shortly after his "rendezvous with destiny" speech of 27 June 1936. She became a regular visitor to Hyde Park and, at the president's urging, purchased land and built a house adjoining the Roosevelt residence. In her diary she described Roosevelt as a "strong radiant sun-god" as well as "a snob . . . who liked women who were well-bred." In later years, addressing rumors that she had had an affair with the late president, she insisted that their friendship had been platonic and that Eleanor Roosevelt "was just as good a friend as Mr. Roosevelt."

In 1939 George Backer committed himself to acquiring the *New York Evening Post,* a struggling daily sympathetic to President Roosevelt and his liberal program. Founded in 1801 by Alexander Hamilton, it was the oldest continuously published daily in the United States. Schiff acquired the controlling interest in the newspaper, and Backer became its president and publisher. In the first year, circulation dropped from 250,000 to 190,000 and the paper lost almost $2 million. Fearing that the venture would bankrupt her, Schiff took control and became New York's first woman newspaper publisher in 1943. The format of the paper changed from broadsheet to tabloid. Schiff added new features and many new columns, including her own. Also in 1943 she divorced Backer. On 29 July 1943, she married Theodore Olin Thackrey, the paper's editor and copublisher; they had no children.

In the years that followed, Schiff managed to cut costs and increase circulation. The *Post* became a livelier and more popular newspaper. She added comics, a syndication service, and a European edition. Editorially it remained a consistent champion of liberal causes. Political differences with Thackrey, however, strained their marital relationship. In 1948 the *Post* became the vehicle for public debate between Schiff and her husband over the presidential candidacy of Henry Wallace. Thackrey supported Wallace, whose campaign Schiff considered "Communist controlled." In 1949 the couple divorced.

The 1950s became known as the golden age of the *Post*. In 1949 Schiff had selected James Wechsler as editor and hired dozens of talented reporters and crusading columnists. These included an African-American journalist, Ted Poston, who covered the early civil rights movement. Such powerful individuals as Robert Moses, Walter Winchell, and J. Edgar Hoover became the targets of *Post* investigations. A series of exposés on Senator Joseph McCarthy precipitated a dramatic counterattack by McCarthy and his followers. Vandals smeared red paint on the newspaper's building on West Street, and McCarthy summoned James Wechsler to appear before his Permanent Committee on Investigations. Schiff vigorously defended her editor and emerged with a much enhanced journalistic reputation. During this crisis Schiff received encouragement and support from Rudolf Sonneborn, a Jewish industrialist. On 18

Dorothy Schiff, publisher of the *New York Post,* holds a copy of the paper as it is printed overhead, March 1963. UPI/CORBIS-BETTMANN

August 1953 they were married. They had no children and were divorced in 1974.

During the 1960s Schiff extended her personal control over the *Post,* becoming editor in chief in 1962 and paying increased attention to the business side of the operation. During a protracted New York newspaper strike and lock-out (1962–1963), she broke ranks with other newspaper owners and resumed publication of the *Post* a month before the strike ended, angered that she was being shut out of the negotiations because of her sex and fearing that the paper would not survive a continued stoppage. The *Post* not only survived but witnessed a dwindling of competition when, in 1966, the *New York Daily Mirror* folded and the morning *Herald Tribune* merged with the two major evening papers to form the *World-Journal-Tribune.* Nicknamed the "Widget," this publication disappeared in 1967 and left Schiff's *Post* as the last daily evening paper in New York.

Although the *Post* had a monopoly on the afternoon field after 1967, Schiff remained fearful of going bankrupt and kept a tight rein on costs. She moved the paper from West Street to the *Journal-American* plant on South Street and oversaw its conversion to automated production technology. By the mid-1970s she faced new economic problems. Rising production costs, changes in the reading habits of New Yorkers, and increased competition from suburban newspapers took their toll on the *Post*'s financial health. In December 1976 Schiff sold the *New York Post* to Rupert Murdoch, the controversial Australian publisher whose newspapers were best known for sensationalism. Twelve years later, in 1989, she died of cancer at her New York City apartment.

Dorothy Schiff had a remarkable journalistic career. Almost forty when she gained control of the *New York Post* and lacking experience in the newspaper business, she transformed the paper from a money-losing venture into a profitable and successful enterprise. Under her leadership the *Post* supported liberal causes including civil liberties during the McCarthy period and the early years of the civil rights movement. A determined and often courageous woman, Schiff extended her influence beyond the corporate office to create an instrument of social change.

★

The files on Dorothy Schiff at the *New York Post* provide clippings, photographs, and some information on her career. Extensive excerpts from her diaries are in Jeffrey Potter, *Men, Money, and Magic: The Candid Story of Dorothy Schiff* (1976), the only published biography. For a concise summary of her life, see the obituary in the *New York Times* (31 Aug. 1989). Obituaries also appeared in the *Washington Post* (31 Aug. 1989), the *Los Angeles Times* (31 Aug. 1989), and the *Times* of London (1 Sept. 1989).

KEVIN J. O'KEEFE

SCHOENBRUN, David Franz (*b.* 15 March 1915 in New York City; *d.* 23 May 1988 in New York City), broadcast journalist noted for incisive, authoritative commentary on French history, culture, and politics and recipient of the 1958 Overseas Press Club award for best book on foreign affairs (*As France Goes,* 1957).

Born in the then predominantly German-Jewish section of Harlem in 1915, Schoenbrun was the son of Max Schoenbrun and Lucy (Cassirer) Schoenbrun. He graduated from Townsend Harris Hall High School and the City College of New York, from which he received his B.A. degree in 1934. While a teacher of French language classes at Far Rockaway High School in Queens, New York, Schoenbrun met Dorothy Scher, whom he married on 23 September 1938; they had one daughter, Lucy. In 1941 Schoenbrun answered a Columbia Broadcasting Systems (CBS) advertisement for fast, accurate typists fluent in European languages. Schoenbrun was hired "on the spot" as a shortwave news monitor, responsible for abstracting foreign radio newscasts. "That," wrote Schoenbrun, "was the beginning of the greatest period of my life."

In 1942 Schoenbrun began freelancing for CBS, submitting background and analysis pieces for newscasts. That March the Office of War Information recruited him as an analyst of enemy propaganda and a broadcaster in French to occupied France over the Voice of America. When called up for military service in February 1943, Schoenbrun was sent to officer-training camp for army intelligence. Before he had completed the program, however, orders from General Dwight D. Eisenhower sent Schoenbrun to Algiers, where he directed the Allied Forces newsroom and broadcast a weekly news commentary in both English and French.

David Schoenbrun. UPI/Corbis-Bettmann

This work brought him into close, regular contact with both Eisenhower and Free French president Charles de Gaulle, two contacts that would figure significantly in his later career as a broadcast journalist and writer. It was also in Algiers that Schoenbrun had his first notable meeting with CBS's London correspondent, Edward R. Murrow. Although he was at Allied headquarters to interview Eisenhower, Murrow also asked Schoenbrun to brief him about de Gaulle. Schoenbrun, understandably, was delighted when Murrow told him to "keep in touch."

Because of his "fine reputation for getting along with the French," in August 1944 Schoenbrun was reassigned to Europe as a Seventh Army combat correspondent and intelligence liaison officer. His task was to cover the front line campaign and send daily dispatches telling the story of the battle for France. Schoenbrun fought with French troops, and when the French broke through at Belfort Gap, Schoenbrun became one of the first American soldiers to reach the Rhine.

After his discharge from the U.S. Army in September 1945, Schoenbrun settled in Paris, where he sought work as a foreign correspondent. Because there was no available post for him yet at CBS, Schoenbrun became Paris bureau chief of the Overseas News Agency, "a liberal, democratic group of men and women dedicated to peace, social justice, and exposure of the evil forces in the world that endangered those goals." In January 1946 Murrow began hiring Schoenbrun for special assignments, and in May 1947 Schoenbrun became a full-time correspondent for CBS News.

From 1947 until 1960 Schoenbrun was Paris bureau chief, a position that both exercised and honed his already substantial knowledge of the people and politics of contemporary France. This was a period of intense conflict, and Schoenbrun traveled often to report on France's increasingly fragile relations with its colonies. In May 1954 Schoenbrun was in Vietnam, watching "the last acts of the Indochinese tragedy being played out." When censors refused to let him file a report about the fall of Dien Bien Phu, Schoenbrun sent a cryptic telegram to CBS, enabling the network to announce that "[t]he French-Indochinese war is all but over." CBS was the first news medium to report France's defeat.

In 1952 Schoenbrun was named CBS News correspondent attached to Eisenhower to cover Eisenhower's presidential campaign. When the Republican party voted to ban television cameras from the nomination proceedings, Schoenbrun broadcast outside the closed door, telling his television audience, "we thought you had a right to be there and see and hear the proceedings." Although he never regretted that tactic, the incident alarmed him: "I realized that we were not just covering the political process, we had become a part of the political process. I wondered just how far [television's influence] would go and what effect it would have on American politics and American society."

After the campaign Schoenbrun eagerly returned to Paris, where he felt he could put his knowledge and skills to best use. While there Schoenbrun wrote the award-winning book *As France Goes*, an analysis of modern French civilization. His aim was mutual interpretation of the French and American people. In 1961 he was named chief correspondent and bureau chief in Washington, D.C. Although loath to leave Paris, Schoenbrun accepted the position, seeing in it the dual opportunity "to join those picking up [President Kennedy's] torch" and to "become a national face and name." Eventually Schoenbrun anchored his own news show, *Washington Report with David Schoenbrun*. Although well-received, the program was short-lived, as, indeed, was Schoenbrun's tenure as Washington bureau chief. The exclusive power and prestige he had relished in Paris worked against him in Washington, where he was constantly at odds with fellow correspondents and the producers of CBS News. In 1962, although offered other positions within the network, Schoenbrun decided to resign from CBS. He continued to do analyses and documentaries for various networks, however, and devoted more time to writing and lecturing.

Between 1966 and 1980 he published five works of sociopolitical analysis, drawing upon the expertise gained from his years as a foreign correspondent: *The Three Lives of Charles de Gaulle* (1966); *Vietnam: How We Got In, How to Get Out* (1968); *The New Israelis* (1973); *Triumph in Paris* (1976); and *Soldiers of the Night: The Story of the French Resistance* (1980). In 1968 Schoenbrun became senior lecturer of international affairs at the New School for Social Research, and in 1983 he took the position of news analyst for the newly formed Independent Network News. He held both positions until his death from a heart attack. Schoenbrun is buried in New York City.

"Articulate," "provocative," and "probing" have all been used to describe David Schoenbrun. He strove to become "America's greatest expert on France," and in forty-eight years of journalism, he achieved that goal. And, by virtue of his key role at CBS News, he became a pioneer in television newscasting, proudly growing with CBS as it became "one of the most powerful voices" in America.

★

David Schoenbrun's personal papers (1963–1978) are at the Mass Communications History Center, State Historical Society of Wisconsin, at Madison. While neither book is intended as autobiography, one learns much about Schoenbrun's professional experiences and philosophy in his *America Inside Out: At Home and Abroad from Roosevelt to Reagan* (1984) and *On and Off the Air: An Informal History of CBS News* (1989). Schoenbrun's memories of working with Edward R. Murrow are woven into A. M. Sperber, *Murrow: His Life and Times* (1986), and Joseph E. Persico, *Edward R. Murrow: An American Original* (1988). Gary Paul Gates, *Air Time: The Inside Story of CBS News* (1978), offers an incisive glimpse into Schoenbrun's Washington experience, while Stanley Cloud and Lynne Olson, *The Murrow Boys: Pioneers on the Front Lines of Broadcast Journalism* (1996), profiles the broadcast careers of the Murrow news team and their relationships with CBS. An entry in *Current Biography* (1960) relates Schoenbrun's career from the 1940s to the 1950s, while the obituary in the *New York Times* (24 May 1988) summarizes his later career. The Broadcast Pioneers Oral History project at the University of Maryland includes an interview with Schoenbrun.

MARILYN SAUDER MCLAUGHLIN

SCOTT, (George) Randolph (*b.* 23 January 1898 in Orange County, Virginia; *d.* 2 March 1987 in Los Angeles, California), actor best known for his cowboy roles in films such as *Fort Worth* (1951) and *Ride the High Country* (1962), which made him one of the screen's popular Western heroes.

Randolph Scott (born in 1903 according to some sources, but more likely in 1898) was the only son among the six children of George G. Scott, an executive with a textile firm, and Lucy Crane, a homemaker from a prominent Charlotte, North Carolina, family. Scott spent most of his youth in Charlotte, where he attended private schools and completed his secondary education at Woodberry Forest Prep. He then entered Georgia Tech to play football. A back injury in his junior year caused Scott to give up contact sports, and in 1921 he enrolled at the University of North Carolina (Chapel Hill) to prepare himself for a career in the textile industry. He left the school without having received a degree and then toured Europe before returning to Charlotte to work in an office at his father's firm. Scott grew dissatisfied with his job and decided to pursue acting, a profession that had attracted his interest during his time overseas. He persuaded his father to write a letter of introduction to an acquaintance, Howard Hughes, who helped Scott get work as an extra in one of the last silent Westerns, *Sharp Shooters* (1928), starring George O'Brien.

Despite his good looks, the six-foot-two-inch Scott did so poorly in his screen tests that he had difficulty getting parts. He joined the Pasadena Community Theater (later known as the Pasadena Playhouse) in order to develop his skills as an actor. For two years he ran errands, painted flats, and got an occasional walk-on part. He was about to admit his failure and return to Charlotte when he landed a part in *Under a Virginia Moon* at the Vine Street Theater. Scott subsequently secured roles in several other plays and was asked to sign a standard seven-year beginner's contract with Paramount. He got good reviews as a second lead in *Hot Saturday* (1932), but Paramount already had Gary

Cooper for first-run action films, Buster Crabbe for low-budget action programmers, and Cary Grant, another newcomer, who showed promise for romantic leads. Not sure what to do with Scott, the studio featured him in two Zane Grey Westerns, *Heritage of the Desert* (1933) and *Wild Horse Mesa* (1933), that it had previously filmed as silents. Paramount executives were sufficiently impressed to film seven more Grey Westerns between 1933 and 1935 with Scott in the lead.

By 1935 Scott was considered ready for more demanding parts. On loan to RKO he starred as the romantic lead opposite Irene Dunne in *Roberta* (1935), a musical in which Fred Astaire and Ginger Rogers played the second leads. A year later the roles were reversed in *Follow the Fleet* (1936), with Scott and Harriet Hilliard in supporting parts beside Astaire and Rogers. At Paramount, Scott starred in two big-budget action films: *The Last of the Mohicans* (1936) and *The Texans* (1938), as well as in the musical *High, Wide, and Handsome* (1937).

On 23 March 1936 Scott married Marianna du Pont Somerville, an older woman with ties to the du Pont fortune. The couple, who had no children, separated in 1938, and for several years Scott shared accommodations with Cary Grant, who had been a friend since their earliest days

Randolph Scott. AMERICAN STOCK/ARCHIVE PHOTOS

at Paramount. Before Scott's marriage they had lived in a Hollywood Hills hacienda, and later they shared a Santa Monica beach house.

After his Paramount contract expired in 1938, Scott signed nonexclusive contracts with both Universal and Twentieth Century–Fox. Rumor had it that he was Margaret Mitchell's choice to play Ashley Wilkes in *Gone with the Wind,* but the film's producer, David O. Selznick, showed no interest in considering Scott for the role. Scott, however, kept busy. In *Rebecca of Sunnybrook Farm* (1938) and *Susannah of the Mounties* (1939) he supported Shirley Temple. He had good roles in such popular Westerns as *Jesse James* (1939), *Virginia City* (1940), and *Western Union* (1941), and he played second lead to Cary Grant in the screwball comedy *My Favorite Wife* (1941), which costarred Irene Dunne. Scott also appeared with John Wayne and Marlene Dietrich in *The Spoilers* (1942) and in *Pittsburgh* (1942). His brawls with Wayne were highlights of both films. From 1942 on, Scott, whose old back injury made him unfit for service in World War II, visited military hospitals and South Pacific bases, and also starred in such war dramas as *Corvette K-225* (1943), *Gung Ho!* (1943), and *China Sky* (1945). In 1944 he secured a divorce from his estranged wife and, in March, married Marie Patricia Stillman; they had two children.

After the war, following appearances in such mediocre if not embarrassing fare as *Captain Kidd* (1945), *Home, Sweet Homicide* (1946), and *Christmas Eve* (1947), Scott decided to concentrate on Westerns. Between 1946 and his retirement in 1961 he made over three dozen films in this genre, more than any other actor during this period. A shrewd businessman, Scott entered into two production partnerships, first with Nat Holt and then with Harry Joe Brown, that produced many of his films after 1949. Starring in *Canadian Pacific* (1949), *Colt .45* (1950), and *Fort Worth* (1951), Scott made the *Motion Picture Herald*'s list of the top ten box-office attractions in the years 1949 through 1953. Pleased with the financial success of his association with Scott, Holt remarked: "Scott is a fine actor, no temperament. . . . Customers come to see him knowing exactly what to expect. They are never disappointed."

Scott's films continued to be profitable throughout the 1950s. As television came to occupy the place in entertainment previously held by low-budget series Westerns once made by such performers as Gene Autry, Roy Rogers, Charles Starrett, Allan Lane, and William Boyd, film studios supplemented the work of such major stars as Gary Cooper and John Wayne with modestly budgeted Technicolor Westerns in which Scott, Joel McCrea, Audie Murphy, and Rory Calhoun figured prominently. Such films could fill a bill by themselves and were especially popular in small-town and drive-in theaters. Of these performers Scott was by far the most active. He carved out a special place in film history, especially when he teamed up with directors Budd Boetticher and, at the end, Sam Peckinpah. In his films Scott often portrayed a middle-aged Westerner: alone, unsentimental, determined to do what needed to be done, whether it was avenging the killing of his wife, bringing law to a lawless town, or finding out the truth about the Custer massacre.

Wary of overexposure, Scott declined television work and seemed prepared to retire in 1960 after filming *Comanche Station.* The following year, however, he accepted a part with McCrea, his longtime friend, in Peckinpah's *Ride the High Country.* In this film the two veteran actors played aging former lawmen whose straitened circumstances force them to accept a job guarding and delivering a shipment of gold. Scott's character, Gil Westrum, plans to steal the gold but is thwarted by McCrea's character, Steve Judd. At the end of the film, Westrum helps Judd save the gold from would-be hijackers and promises the mortally wounded Judd that he will deliver the cargo to its rightful owner. Audiences had no doubt he would. The little-publicized Metro-Goldwyn-Mayer offering initially attracted scant attention in the United States, but in Europe, under the title *Guns in the Afternoon,* it was recognized as a superb film. It received major prizes in 1963 at film festivals in Venice and Brussels, as well as an award in Mexico, and it embellished Scott's already secure reputation as one of the legends of the Western. So identified had he become with this genre that his name graced the title of the 1973 hit country song by the Statler Brothers, "Whatever Happened to Randolph Scott?," a nostalgic look back at a bygone era.

Scott retired after *Ride the High Country,* turning to golf for recreation and to his investments in land, oil, and stocks, which had made him a millionaire many times over. He died at his home in the Bel-Air section of Los Angeles after several years of physical decline caused by heart disease and bouts of pneumonia.

★

A folder on Scott is in the Harry Ransom Humanities Center at the University of Texas, Austin. Production files on some of his postwar Warner Brothers Westerns are in the Warner Brothers Collection at the University of Southern California library. The most thorough recounting of Scott's life and career is Jefferson Brim Crow III, *Randolph Scott: The Gentleman from Virginia* (1987), a lavishly illustrated tribute, with a filmography, that is largely an exercise in hero worship and ignores the question that titillated Hollywood gossipmongers during the 1930s: Were Scott and Grant simply friends and housemates, or was their involvement of a more intimate nature? Sources that do address this question are Brendan Gill, "Pursuer and Pursued: The Still Untold Story of Cary Grant," *New Yorker* (2 June 1997), and biographies of Cary Grant: Lee Guthrie, *The Life and Loves of Cary Grant* (1977); Warren G. Harris, *Cary Grant: A Touch of Elegance* (1987); and Charles Higham and Roy Moseley, *Cary Grant: The Lonely Heart* (1989). See also Gerald Clarke, "Cary Grant and Randolph Scott: The Debonair Leading Man and the Western Star in Santa Monica," *Architectural Digest* (Apr. 1996). Lee O. Miller, *The Great Cowboy Stars of Movies and Television* (1979), is pertinent to Scott's career, as are John H. Lenihan, "The Western Heroism of Randolph Scott," in Archie McDonald, ed., *Shooting Stars: Heroes and Heroines of Western Films* (1987); James Robert Parish, *Great Western Stars* (1976); and Gene Ringgold, "Randolph Scott," *Films in Review* (23 Dec. 1972). Christopher H. Scott, Scott's son, is the author of two biographies: *Whatever Happened to Randolph Scott?* (1994) and *In the Footsteps of the Giant: Randolph Scott's Son Remembers His Father* (1996). An obituary is in the *New York Times* (3 Mar. 1987).

LLOYD J. GRAYBAR

SEGRÈ, Emilio Gino (*b.* 1 February 1905 in Tivoli, Italy; *d.* 22 April 1989 in Lafayette, California), scientist and university professor who shared the 1959 Nobel Prize in physics for discovering the antiproton.

Emilio Segrè was one of three sons of Giuseppe Segrè, a manufacturer, and Amelia (Treves) Segrè. He attended the primary school in Tivoli and completed his secondary education at the Liceo Mamiani in Rome in 1922. He then entered the University of Rome, where he studied engineering for five years before switching to physics. He became a close friend and colleague of the renowned physicist Enrico Fermi, and his doctorate in physics (1928) was the first to be awarded under Fermi's sponsorship.

After graduation Segrè served a yearlong tour of duty as a second lieutenant of artillery in the Italian army before returning to the University of Rome as an instructor in physics. In 1930 he was promoted to assistant professor, and two years later he became an associate professor under Fermi. On 2 February 1936 Segrè married Elfriede Spiro, with whom he had one son, Claudio, and two daughters, Amelia and Fausta. Elfriede died in 1970; on 12 February 1972 Segrè married Rosa Mines.

Segrè was appointed professor and chairman of the physics department at the University of Palermo in 1936. That year he also made his first visit to the United States, where he observed the cyclotron at the University of California at Berkeley. The following year, while working at the University of Palermo, Segrè and Carlo Perrier discovered the artificial element technetium. The two professors had investigated some metal pieces of the deflector of the cyclotron from the radiation laboratory at Berkeley, which Segrè had obtained during his visit, and they found traces of the radioactive element 43 in the deflector, which was made of molybdenum.

In 1938 Segrè again found himself at the radiation lab

Emilio Segrè. UPI/CORBIS-BETTMANN

in Berkeley, this time with the intention of studying short-lived isotopes of technetium. Together with Glenn T. Seaborg, Segrè discovered ^{99}Tc and its isomer within a few weeks; eventually they would name the element after a derivative of the Greek adjective meaning "artificial," to commemorate the fact that it was the first artificial element. During this second visit to Berkeley, the Italian government passed anti-Semitic civil service laws, and Segrè, a Jew and longtime opponent of the regime, decided to remain in the United States.

In 1940, working with Dale Corson and Kenneth MacKenzie at Berkeley, Segrè discovered another "new" element called astatine (atomic number 85). In working with Seaborg, Segrè developed a valuable chemical technique for separating nuclear isomers. Subsequently, Segrè was also involved along with his fellow scientists Fermi, J. Robert Oppenheimer, and Joseph W. Kennedy in the discovery of plutonium 239. The discovery became extremely significant because this element was fissionable. Large quantities were synthesized in 1944, and plutonium became the prime source of energy in the atomic bomb. During the war, Segrè, who became an American citizen in 1944, was a group leader in the Los Alamos, New Mexico, laboratory of the Manhattan Project, the secret effort to develop the atomic bomb.

After the war, Segrè returned to Berkeley as a full professor of physics. In the early 1950s he began a collaboration with Owen Chamberlain in an effort to produce and detect a theoretically predicted particle called the antiproton, a negatively charged twin of the positive proton with certain other opposite properties. The great achievement of Segrè, Chamberlain, and their associates was to devise ingenious techniques for detecting and indisputably identifying these rare particles. After accumulating conclusive evidence, the two scientists announced their verification of the existence of antiprotons in 1955.

For their discovery of the antiproton, Segrè and Chamberlain shared the 1959 Nobel Prize in physics. After receiving the award, Segrè continued his work in particle physics at Berkeley until his retirement in 1972. Two years later, his career came full circle when he was appointed professor of nuclear physics at the University of Rome, where in 1975 he became professor emeritus.

Another facet of Segrè was his prominence as an author and editor. In 1952 he became the editor in chief of the *Annual Review of Nuclear Science,* a position that he held until 1977. During this time he edited a text entitled *Experimental Nuclear Physics* (1953); he also wrote *Nuclei and Particles* (1953), *Enrico Fermi, Physicist* (1970), and *From X Rays to Quarks: Modern Physicists and Their Discoveries* (1980). In 1984 he produced a companion book, *From Falling Bodies to Radio Waves: Classical Physicists and Their Discoveries.* His retirement in 1972 was simply the beginning of a new period of writing and publishing and of lecturing in California, Italy, Israel, Great Britain, and elsewhere.

Among the honors bestowed on him were medals from the German Chemical Society and the Accademia Nazionale dei Lincei. He received honorary degrees from the University of Palermo, the University of San Marco in Lima, Peru, and Tel Aviv University. In 1959 he was named a commander of merit of the Republic of Italy. He was a member of the American Academy of Arts and Sciences and the National Academy of Sciences and was also a fellow of the American and Italian physical societies.

Segrè is best summed up by his colleague and friend Owen Chamberlain: "His uncompromising standards of excellence in experimentation were a model I tried to follow and gave me an education in real physics that was unequaled. As his helper, I experienced both his impatience with shortcomings as well as his kindness and sensitivity to human concerns." A lover of nature and the outdoors, the slight yet robust Segrè enjoyed hiking and long walks. He was interested in skiing and mountain climbing in his earlier years, and fishing and mushroom hunting in his later years. He took raft trips in Montana and Oregon to explore the American wilderness.

Segrè died of a heart attack at the age of eighty-four while walking with his wife near his home in Lafayette, California. He is buried in Oakmount Memorial Park in Lafayette.

★

Segrè offers a personal account of his fascinating life in *A Mind Always in Motion: The Autobiography of Emilio Segrè* (1993), which was published posthumously by Rosa M. Segrè. His son, Claudio Segrè, wrote *Atoms, Bombs, and Eskimo Kisses: A Memoir of Father and Son* (1995). Brief biographical articles are in *McGraw-Hill Modern Scientists* (1980) and *Nobel Prize Winners* (1987). Excellent articles are in *Notable Twentieth-Century Scientists* (1995) and *Pioneers of Science: Nobel Prize Winners in Physics* (1980). Posthumous tributes include Owen Chamberlain, "E. Segrè," *Physics Today* 43 (Oct. 1990): 112–114, and Edoardo Amaldi, "Emilio Segrè," *Nature* 339 (25 May 1989): 255.

After Segrè won the Nobel Prize, the following articles appeared: "Nuclear Properties of Antinucleons: Excerpt from Address, December 11, 1959," *Science* 132 (1 July 1959): 9–14; "Name Three Nobelists," *Science Newsletter* 76 (7 Nov. 1959): 303; "1959 Nobelman," *Time* (9 Nov. 1959); and "Nobel Prize," *Scientific American* 201 (Dec. 1959): 78. Obituaries are in the *New York Times* (24 Apr. 1989) and *Washington Post* (25 Apr. 1989).

BEN DIRUSSO

SELZNICK, Irene Mayer (*b.* 2 April 1907 in Brooklyn, New York; *d.* 10 October 1990 in New York City), theatrical producer and writer whose memoir, *A Private View,* chronicled her membership in two Hollywood families (both as the daughter of executive Louis B. Mayer and as the first wife of producer David O. Selznick) and her success in the theater.

Irene Mayer was the younger daughter of Louis B. Mayer, a theater owner, and Margaret (Shenberg) Mayer, a homemaker who worked as a bookkeeper for her husband in the early years of their marriage. The Mayers moved to the suburbs of Boston shortly after Irene's birth.

The dark, quiet Irene attended public schools in Haverhill and Brookline, Massachusetts, until 1918, when the family moved to California, and she went to the private Hollywood School for Girls. She wrote in her autobiography that she and her mother both hoped she would go to college but that her protective father wanted his daughters to stay at home.

As his daughter went through school, Louis B. Mayer progressed from theater owner to movie mogul. In 1924 he became general manager of the newly formed but instantly prestigious Metro-Goldwyn-Mayer (MGM). Irene Mayer grew up with an insider's view of the film industry, yet

Irene Mayer Selznick with her husband, David O. Selznick, 1938. UPI/CORBIS-BETTMANN

Louis B. Mayer would never consider allowing his dutiful daughter to work in that industry. She wrote later of her family, "Four people, four lives that boiled down to one life and that was my father's."

Although they participated in many Hollywood social functions, the teenage Irene and her sister Edith had few dates. In December 1926 Irene was provided with an escort from her father's studio for a New Year's Eve party. David O. Selznick was a rising young executive confident of his eventual success. According to Irene Mayer's later recollections, he was not pleased to be squiring the boss's daughter. Despite this inauspicious introduction, the pair met again soon and began seeing each other regularly. The reserved, conservative Irene was mesmerized by the flamboyant David, who in turn respected his new friend's humor, intelligence, and caution. Their courtship was slow—inhibited by the senior Mayers' insistence that Irene could not even become engaged until her elder sister was married—but the pair were finally wed on 29 April 1930.

Irene Mayer Selznick quickly became a prominent Hollywood hostess. Having sat in on critiques of motion pictures in progress for years, she was able to provide her husband with thoughtful analyses of his films. The couple had two children, Jeffrey in 1932 and Daniel in 1936, but David proved the primary little boy in the family, living extravagantly in a way that increasingly frightened his wife. A gambler in his career as well as with money, he moved from studio to studio before forming his own company, Selznick International Pictures, in 1936. Irene Selznick was listed as an executive on its books but always said she had little to do with its running. The studio produced a string of hits in the late 1930s and early 1940s—although never quite enough to maintain David Selznick's extravagant tastes. Even as he produced his masterpiece, *Gone with the Wind* (1939), his wife saw that he was deteriorating as a person and as a producer, she later wrote. The amphetamines he took to keep up his frantic pace impaired his judgment, and his grand dreams of films became grandiose near nightmares.

Still maintaining her social life, Irene Selznick found various outlets for her frustration with her marriage. She spent several years in analysis and worked for what she later recalled as fulfilling months as a county juvenile probation officer during World War II. Eventually, however, she decided to cut her losses and asked David for a separation. The pair were separated in 1945 and divorced in 1948.

After the separation, Irene Mayer Selznick decided to use the judgment she had cultivated in motion pictures in a related field. Moving to New York City, she formed the Irene M. Selznick Company in 1946, transforming herself into a theatrical producer. Her first play, Arthur Laurents's *Heartsong* (1947), was not a success, though it did attract the attention of playwright Tennessee Williams's agent, and Selznick was chosen to produce that author's *Streetcar Named Desire* (1947). Although the critic Molly Haskell later wrote that it was probably "the hopes of tapping some of that Hollywood money" that led the agent to approach Selznick, the producer proved herself with this play, demonstrating spirit and brilliance in her dealings with Williams, with director Elia Kazan, and with stars Jessica Tandy and Marlon Brando. Selznick went on to produce *Bell, Book, and Candle* (1950), *Flight into Egypt* (1952), *The Chalk Garden* (1955), and *The Complaisant Lover* (1961). She retired from professional life in the 1960s but remained an active figure in New York's cultural and intellectual circles.

In 1983 Selznick published *A Private View,* a memoir that discussed her childhood, her marriage, and her theatrical career. She presented herself as a slightly distanced inside observer of Hollywood, New York, and the personalities she had known. She was particularly eloquent on the subjects of her father and her husband, managing to observe both their faults and their virtues with understanding and compassion. "I see now that I've had three lives," she wrote, "one as the daughter of my father, another as the wife of my husband. The theater furnished me with a third act. I'd have settled for so much less." Selznick died at her home in New York.

Irene Mayer Selznick's theatrical career and carefully worded autobiography could almost convince the historian of the value of dynasties. Her ways of handling her relationships with two powerful American cultural figures, combined with her capacity for analysis and her sense of humor, show her to have been a remarkable public and private person. In a review of *A Private View,* David Thomson wrote, "In the end, this is a book about being a woman in this century, and of how one woman surpassed her family's plans for her. . . . When will American pictures be capable of showing us a woman like this, so attuned to experience, so unimpressed by wasteful intensity?"

★

Irene Mayer Selznick's theatrical papers were given to Boston University. Some of her correspondence with David O. Selznick may also be found in the Selznick archives at the University of Texas at Austin. The best other sources on her life are her own 1983 autobiography and David Thomson's insightful biography of David O. Selznick, *Showman* (1992). The Molly Haskell piece, "Stepping Out from the Shadows," appeared in the *New York Times* on 22 May 1983. Thomson's review of the autobiography, "Irene, and the Critics' Kitchen Sink," is in *Film Comment* (July–Aug. 1983): 70–72.

TINKY "DAKOTA" WEISBLAT

SHAARA, Michael Joseph, Jr. (*b.* 23 June 1929 in Jersey City, New Jersey; *d.* 5 May 1988 in Tallahassee, Florida), winner of the Pulitzer Prize for fiction in 1975 for his Civil War novel, *The Killer Angels* (1974).

Shaara was the second of the three children of Michael Joseph Shaara, political aide to "Boss" Frank Hague, who was mayor of Jersey City for thirty years, and director of personnel for Pan American Airways, and Florence Allene Maxwell. The family name was originally Sciarra, but it was altered by an immigration official when Shaara's father immigrated from Italy in 1900. Michael Shaara developed a passion for writing early in his childhood, when he would lie on the living room floor and compose stories about a character he created named Bobby Brimwell.

After graduating from Lincoln High School in Jersey City in 1946, Shaara joined the U.S. Army and trained in parachute jumping at Fort Bragg, North Carolina, an experience he exploited in his life and writing. In 1947 he was discharged from the army, and he enrolled at Rutgers University. On 16 September 1950 he married Helen Elizabeth Krumwiede, a psychology student at neighboring Douglass College for Women; they had two children. At Rutgers, Shaara attended a talk given by John O'Hara, a

Michael J. Shaara, Jr., *c.* 1975. PHOTO BY DONN DUGHI

writer, and was struck by O'Hara's comment that a writer "should become a doctor or a cop. It will teach you the truth about people." Shaara graduated from Rutgers with a B.S. in 1951. In May of that year, *Astounding* magazine paid him $229.70 for a piece he had written. Shaara took graduate classes at Columbia University in 1952 and at the University of Vermont from 1953 to 1954. He did not complete a graduate degree.

In 1954 Shaara moved to St. Petersburg, Florida, where his parents had retired, and became a police officer. He remained a student of the craft of writing, a facility that stood him well in Florida. He was an intense, driven, and voluble man whose conversations sounded more like stories, with characters, atmosphere, and scenes. He left the police force after a year to concentrate on writing fiction. His first short story appeared the following year in *Galaxy*. At that time, freelance writers were in demand at weekly and monthly magazines, and Shaara was almost seduced into becoming a one-dimensional writer for that genre. Wanting, however, to write a novel, he moved his family to a lakefront house that his parents owned in Inverness, Florida. His wife took a job as a social worker in family service while he wrote. Establishing a pattern of work that was the reverse of normal living, he often wrote through the night, smoking cigarettes and drinking coffee, which, in combination with a careless diet, harmed his health.

Shaara constantly worked on story lines and settings for action. He studied Ernest Hemingway and William Faulkner and criticized how they handled story, characterization, and language. He saw Faulkner as weak on story and Hemingway, with whom he compared himself, as weak on characterization. Describing himself, Shaara stated, "I can't do women well at all." He felt that only William Shakespeare "had it all," and he hoped to write a novel about him.

Always curious, Shaara in 1961 visited Florida State University, where he considered studying opera. His reputation as a writer preceded him, and he was asked to give a talk on writing. After his talk, the university administration offered Shaara a position as writer in residence. That year he became an associate professor, and over the next twelve years he gained a reputation as a superb, engaged teacher and a mentor of creative writing. His students praised him, and he received awards for his teaching. At over six feet tall, with a bent nose, a shock of brown hair, and an ever-present cigarette, he exuded the look and presence of world-wise toughness and was a symbol of the modern literary man to his students.

Even while teaching, Shaara continued to turn out stories for magazines such as *Redbook*, *Playboy*, and the *Saturday Evening Post*. In 1965 Shaara suffered a massive coronary and survived seven minutes without a pulse. Doctors administered electric shock as a last resort, which resuscitated him. He in 1966 related the experience in a story, "The New Lazarus," for the *Saturday Evening Post* and received an award that year from the American Medical Association for his understanding of heart disease. His novel *The Broken Place* was published in 1968. Written in the style of Damon Runyon, it is a story about a valiant soldier who turns to prizefighting. Though often considered autobiographical because it fit Shaara's mystique, the work was the product of his creativity, aided by observations drawn from his military service and from the experiences of his two uncles who had been golden gloves fighters in New Jersey. Despite publication of Shaara's novel and some seventy-five stories during his academic career, the university would not grant him tenure or promotion beyond associate professor because he lacked a graduate degree. Shaara responded that another degree could not teach him anything about writing.

Shaara next began work on his Civil War novel, *The Killer Angels*, a dramatic narrative of the days surrounding the climactic battle of Gettysburg. His research took him to the Gettysburg National Park, where he and his son walked the terrain of the three-day battle that was fought in July 1863. Shaara finished the book in 1971, but his agent could not place it with a publisher. Shaara was furious and went to New York himself to sell his manuscript. David McKay, a small publisher, finally agreed to publish it in 1974. By then, Shaara had gone to Florence, Italy, to work in Florida State University's overseas program and to visit his father's native country. His stay in Florence took a disastrous turn in the fall of 1972 when he crashed a Vespa motorbike and struck his head against a curbstone. His convalescence lasted a year and a half, during which he was unable to teach, write, or coordinate his thoughts and speech. When the university shied from taking responsibility for him, Shaara engaged it in a bitter dispute to gain disability benefits. He prevailed at the end of 1973, but to the detriment of his academic career.

The publication of *The Killer Angels* was not as heartening as he had hoped, since the large eastern newspapers chose not to review it. Embittered, Shaara felt that the cynical East was less interested in heroes than antiheroes or murderers, such as those of *In Cold Blood* (1965) by Truman Capote. Western reviews were kind to Shaara's book, which captured an audience that, because of the Vietnam War, was primed to read of American valor and to revel in the bittersweet battle at Gettysburg. Shaara's work validated the nobility of combat and elevated both the professional soldier and the common man, the latter personified by the real-life protagonist, Joshua Lawrence Chamberlain. Shaara's research had absorbed something of Chamberlain's *The Passing of the Armies* (1974); Douglas Southall Freeman's *Lee's Lieutenants: A Study in Command* (1942–1944); and *The Fremantle Diary* (1954), edited by Walter Lord. Shaara established a historical foundation that allowed him to explore the minds and speech of the military personalities. His work is a leap of genius made even greater in that he did not presume to be a historian.

Shaara's physical problems and his quarrel with the university left him depressed, so in the spring of 1975, he took his father's advice to get away. He was in a hotel in Denver, Colorado, when he was notified that he had won the Pulitzer Prize. Ironically, his champion on the selection committee was Jean Stafford, a native of Colorado celebrated for her distaste for the conventional. The award made Shaara a literary star and a phenomenon that the eastern press found difficult to fathom. He was suddenly in demand for interviews, appearances, promotional tours, and screenwriting assignments. The Turner Cable Network eventually produced the television film *Gettysburg* (1993), based on *The Killer Angels.* This book also became the centerpiece of *The Civil War* (1990), produced by Ken Burns for the Public Broadcasting Service.

Shaara visited South Africa in 1977 and, upon his return, published another novel, *The Herald* (1981), which he dedicated to his father (both of his parents had died in 1978). Displaying Shaara's versatility, *The Herald* is the story of a scientist who, while working on a cure for sickle-cell anemia, discovers a disease that selectively kills genetically weak people. The stresses of this period took a toll on Shaara's domestic life. He and his wife divorced in June 1980, and he moved into his father's old house in Cocoa Beach, Florida. He continued to return to his family in Tallahassee, however, and his son, Jeffrey Shaara, an author in his own right, became his business agent. Michael Shaara was watching television in an upstairs room of the family home on Thomasville Road in Tallahassee when he died of a heart attack. He was mourned by his former students, his colleagues, and other friends and admirers. At his burial in Meadow Wood Memorial Park in Tallahassee, friends read passages from his works.

Shaara was working up to his death. Among his papers, his former wife found a manuscript novel about baseball entitled "Billy Ball." She published it in 1991 with the title *For Love of the Game*. In addition to taking over negotiations for productions based on his father's work, Jeffrey Shaara wrote a different ending for *The Herald* and published it in 1994 as *The Noah Conspiracy*. He also built on his father's research to produce a prequel to the war novel called *Gods and Generals* (1996), which has been favorably compared with *The Killer Angels*. Jeffrey Shaara followed with a sequel, *The Last Full Measure* (1998), which brings the personalities of *The Killer Angels* to the close of the Civil War.

★

Michael Shaara's papers are with his former wife, Helen K. Shaara, in Tallahassee. The introduction to Michael Shaara, *Soldier Boy* (1982), a collection of short stories, includes material pertinent to Shaara's life. The *New York Times* announced his Pulitzer Prize (6 May 1975). An extended profile by Wayne Harris is in the *Florida State University Alumni Magazine* (Oct. 1978) and is reproduced in the *Floridian* (31 Dec. 1978). A tribute is "Missing a Maverick," *Tallahassee Democrat* (2 June 1988), and a review of Shaara's posthumous novel by Gerald Easley is in the *Tallahassee Democrat* (2 June 1988). Obituaries are in the *Tallahassee Democrat* (6 May 1988), the *Tampa Tribune* (8 May 1988), and the *New York Times* (9 May 1988).

JACK J. CARDOSO

SHANNON, William Vincent (*b.* 24 August 1927 in Worcester, Massachusetts; *d.* 27 September 1988 in Boston, Massachusetts), author, journalist, educator, and U.S. ambassador to Ireland who distinguished himself in intellectual and political circles as a thoughtful and moral observer of government and society.

Shannon was one of the five children of Patrick Joseph Shannon, a carpenter who emigrated from Ireland in 1910, and Nora Agnes McNamara, a homemaker. In 1947 he graduated with a B.A. degree from Clark University in Worcester. He received an M.A. degree from Harvard a year later.

William V. Shannon, 1977. NYT PICTURES/NYT PERMISSIONS

Shannon began his journalism career in 1951 as the Washington, D.C., correspondent for the *New York Post.* He was also the paper's bureau chief there from 1951 until 1957. For the next seven years Shannon wrote a national affairs column for the *Post.* In 1964 he joined the *New York Times,* and he was a member of the editorial board for thirteen years. He married Elizabeth McNelly on 5 August 1961; they had three sons.

In 1977 President Jimmy Carter appointed Shannon U.S. ambassador to Ireland. In addition to his ethnic background, Shannon's Washington experience and his scholarly interest in Ireland and Irish America prepared him well for this post. He had written two books on Irish Americans. The first, *The American Irish,* was published in 1964. He researched and wrote it while on sabbatical from the *Times* as a fellow-in-residence at the Center for the Study of Democratic Institutions, in Santa Barbara, California (1961–1962). Shannon wrote *The Heir Apparent: Robert Kennedy and the Struggle for Power* in 1967, the year before Senator Kennedy was killed as he campaigned for the Democratic presidential nomination. Edward Kennedy attributed President John F. Kennedy's warm reception in Ireland in 1963 to the speeches composed for him by Shannon.

Shannon's interest in the relationship between Ireland and the United States persisted throughout his career. While he was ambassador, he helped the historian Kerby Miller in Miller's search for private correspondence and memoirs from emigrants and their families. Miller's research formed the basis for his groundbreaking work on Irish emigration, *Emigrants and Exiles: Ireland and the Irish Exodus to North America* (1985), and he recognized Shannon's contribution in the book's introduction. Shannon served on the board of directors of the American Irish Foundation (1969) and received a gold medal from the American Irish Historical Society in 1979.

In addition to his books on Irish America and Robert Kennedy, Shannon wrote two others. The first was a collaboration with Robert S. Allen, *The Truman Merry-Go-Round* (1950), a series of vignettes about Washington, D.C., during President Harry S. Truman's administration that was described as a "salty view" of the president. *They Could Not Trust the King* (1974) was about President Richard M. Nixon and Watergate.

When he returned from his diplomatic post in Ireland in 1981, Shannon joined the faculty of Boston University, where he taught a course on the American presidency and conducted graduate seminars in journalism. He also resumed his newspaper career, writing on foreign and domestic affairs for the *Boston Globe* until a week before his death.

In 1951 Shannon received the Page One Award for national coverage from the New York Newspaper Guild, and in 1968 and 1976 he received the Edward J. Meeman Award for conservation writing from the Scripps-Howard Foundation. He was an Alicia Patterson Fund traveling fellow in London from 1969 to 1970.

Shannon died of lymphoma in 1988, at the age of sixty-one. He had been living in Brookline, Massachusetts.

Shannon's life and career were marked by his interest in American politics and the presidency, and by his personal and professional ties to Ireland. He distinguished himself in two fields for which the Irish in America became famous—writing and politics. He observed American politics and the presidency at a period in history when the Irish ethnic community reached the zenith of its power and acceptance as an immigrant group—during the candidacy, election, and presidency of John F. Kennedy.

★

Shannon's papers are in the Twentieth Century Archives, Department of Special Collections, at Boston University's Mugar Memorial Library. There is no full-length biography of Shannon. The *New York Times* obituary (29 Sept. 1988) provides a detailed view of his life. A eulogy written by his friend and colleague James Finn is in *Commonweal* (21 Oct. 1988).

LINDA DOWLING ALMEIDA

SHEPLEY, James Robinson (*b.* 16 August 1917 in Harrisburg, Pennsylvania; *d.* 2 November 1988 in Houston, Texas), news journalist who became president and chief operating officer of Time, Inc., and diversified Time's video offerings by purchasing American Television and Communications Corporation and launching Home Box Office as the first national pay-television service.

Shepley was the only child of Charles Laurence Shepley, the editor of the *Harrisburg Daily Patriot*, and Jean (Robinson) Shepley, a homemaker. He attended Camp Hill High School in Camp Hill, Pennsylvania, from 1931 to 1935. An avid reader and outdoorsman, Shepley respected the strength and leadership of his Boy Scout scoutmaster and eventually earned the rank of Eagle Scout. From 1934 to 1935, as his mother lay dying, Shepley threw himself into reporting as a stringer covering the West Shore Twilight League in Camp Hill.

Shepley entered Dickinson College in Carlisle, Pennsylvania, in 1935. In 1936, during his sophomore year, he married Jean Stevens, with whom he had four children. After his spring semester in 1936, Shepley left Dickinson and became a cub staff reporter for the *Pittsburgh Press*. From the *Press* he joined the United Press International newspaper wire service in 1938 as a Pennsylvania legislative correspondent. He achieved some early fame covering the cabinet scandals of George H. Earle, the first Democratic governor elected in that state in the twentieth century. In 1941 Shepley transferred to Washington, D.C., where he was assigned to head the small staff of United Press correspondents covering the U.S. House of Representatives. Ordered to the White House, Shepley covered President Franklin Roosevelt's famous declaration on 7 December 1941 that "this day will live in infamy."

In early 1942 Shepley joined *Time* magazine's Washington bureau as a correspondent. While in Washington he forged friendships with Henry R. Luce, founder and editor in chief of *Time,* and with General George C. Marshall. Aware of potentially newsworthy actions in the Far East, Shepley persuaded *Time* to send him as a war correspondent to India, where he was attached to the 5307th Composite Unit, U.S. Army. Always the wordsmith, Shepley coined the term "Merrill's Marauders" for the famed jungle combat unit led by Brigadier General Frank D. Merrill. In 1944 Shepley was reassigned to General Douglas MacArthur's command, which was then completing its campaign in New Guinea. From there he traveled to France in time to get caught briefly behind German lines in the Battle of the Bulge in December 1944. Throughout his service, Shepley continued to file weekly reports to *Time* magazine.

At the urging of General Marshall, Shepley took a leave of absence from Time, Inc., in early 1945 to accept a commission as a captain in the army, and he served with General Marshall at the Potsdam Conference. Following the victories in Europe and Japan, he collaborated with Marshall to write the official report on the conduct of World War II, probably the first military document to become a best-seller on the *New York Times* list. In October 1945 Shepley accompanied Marshall on his unsuccessful diplomatic mission to China.

Shepley returned to the *Time* Washington bureau in 1946 to serve as bureau chief and senior correspondent until 1952. Supervising a staff of twenty-two correspondents, he wrote weekly articles for *Time* and occasional articles for *Life* and *Fortune.* He remained in close contact with Marshall, who was now secretary of state, and other leading governmental officials. In 1954 Shepley coauthored *The Hydrogen Bomb: The Men, the Menace, the Mechanism* with Clay Blair, the Pentagon correspondent for *Time*. The book is a journalistic report on the publicly unknown nuclear physicist Edward Teller and the development of the nation's thermonuclear arsenal.

In 1952 Shepley moved to the *Time* headquarters in New York City to serve as chief of correspondents. In 1956 he interviewed President Dwight D. Eisenhower's secretary of state, John Foster Dulles, who promoted a policy of

James Shepley. UPI/Corbis-Bettmann

standing firm against Soviet-induced confrontations. Dulles believed his policy would successfully contain the Soviets, and Shepley's interview, which made front-page news, introduced the concept of "brinkmanship" to the world.

Although he protected his private life, Shepley in October 1956 separated from his wife of twenty years, citing irreconcilable differences. At *Time,* he became more involved in administrative work while still writing occasionally for various sections of the magazine. Observing a photo shoot for *Life* magazine, Shepley met the model Yvonne Hudson. They dated for a few months, and in 1957 they married and settled in New York City. The couple had one child. Professionally, in 1957 Shepley became head of the *Time* news service in the United States and Canada.

Shepley took a temporary leave of absence in 1959 to work on Richard Nixon's unsuccessful presidential campaign. When Shepley returned to *Time* in 1960, Luce appointed him the assistant publisher of *Life*. Between 1960 and 1969 Shepley was also publisher of *Fortune* magazine, which was having circulation problems, and publisher of *Time*. His keen intellect and no-nonsense approach won him a reputation as a troubleshooter and a wise administrator; he was nicknamed "Brass Knuckles Shepley."

In 1969 Shepley was elected president and chief operating officer of *Time* magazine. During his tenure, from 1969 through 1980, he launched *Money, Discover,* and *People* magazines, revived *Life* as a monthly after suspending it as a weekly, and bought the Book of the Month Club. With the astronomical growth of television, many high-cost periodicals collapsed. Shepley diversified Time, Inc., by purchasing American Television and Communications Corporation, an early cable television company, and developed Home Box Office. Retiring as president in 1980, Shepley served as chairman and chief executive officer of the *Washington Star* until August 1981, when the board of directors of Time, Inc., closed the *Star* because of financial losses. Shepley continued to enjoy the outdoors and spent his leisure time shooting, fishing, and yachting.

After retiring in 1982 at age sixty-five, in accordance with *Time* policy, Shepley settled in Hartfield, Virginia, with his wife. From 1982 to 1988, he directed his own consulting company, Wilton II, and served as a board member of Hilton Hotels Corporation, the Henley Group, and Temple-Inland, Inc. Shepley was elected chairman and trustee of the South Street Seaport Museum in New York City, and under his leadership the museum succeeded in converting four blocks of lower Manhattan slums into a showplace of historic preservation.

In 1988 doctors at the M. D. Anderson Clinic in Houston discovered polyps on Shepley's vena cava that eventually restricted blood flow to his heart, causing his death. He died in Houston and was buried at Christ Church, Virginia.

Though Shepley could be harsh, rude, and abrupt, his colleagues respected his decisive, accurate reporting and his honest, fair leadership. His unparalleled rise from news correspondent to chief executive at *Time* illustrated to Americans that hard work and a keen mind could propel one to success. Shepley's innovation, Home Box Office, along with the popular publication *People* profoundly changed the course of communications.

★

Shepley's personal papers are held by the Shepley estate. Obituaries are in the *New York Times* (3 Nov. 1988), *Harrisburg Daily News* (3 Nov. 1988), and *Time* (14 Nov. 1988).

JONATHAN A. GATES

SHIMKIN, Leon (*b.* 7 April 1907 in Brooklyn, New York; *d.* 25 May 1988 in New Rochelle, New York), chairman and owner of Simon and Schuster Publishing Company who was known for his innovations in mass production and marketing of paperback books.

Shimkin was the youngest of the six children of Max Shimkin, a real estate dealer, and Fannie (Nickelsberg) Shimkin, a teacher. His parents had emigrated from Lithuania to

Leon Shimkin. ARCHIVE PHOTOS

New York City around 1885. Leon Shimkin attended public schools and graduated from Alexander Hamilton High School in Brooklyn in 1923. Later that year he matriculated at New York University. In the summer of 1924 he worked as a bookkeeper with Boni and Liveright Publishers. He left his position with Boni and Liveright to take another with the new firm of Simon and Schuster. Completing his degree at night, he graduated in 1926 with a bachelor of commercial science degree.

Starting with Simon and Schuster as a bookkeeper, Shimkin rose to business manager in 1925, secretary-treasurer in 1928, and executive vice president in 1944. His financial acumen was seen in a number of innovations. He actively pursued subsidiary rights for books and made Simon and Schuster an early beneficiary of the Hollywood tie-in by selling the rights to the title "Inner Sanctum Mysteries" to a movie studio. He had a keen sense of the needs and desires of the public and recognized early on the appeal of practical guides and inspirational writing. With his prompting, Simon and Schuster in 1936 published *J. K. Lasser's Your Income Tax,* which became an annual guide to income tax preparation, and Dale Carnegie's *How to Win Friends and Influence People* (1937). Both remained in continuous publication by Simon and Schuster for decades.

Shimkin began the 1930s with his marriage to Rebecca Rabinowitz on 17 August 1930. They had two children. He ended the 1930s with the publishing innovation for which he is most widely known, the cofounding of Pocket Books, Inc., in 1939. By the end of the decade, Shimkin was known as the "third S" of Simon and Schuster. At this time, he, his partners, and the publisher Robert de Graff undertook the production and marketing of inexpensive paperbacks on a scale never seen before. "Pocket Books," as they were known, were chosen for publication based on a survey of the public and were carried into all parts of the country through magazine distributors. Sold by grocery stores, gas stations, drug stores, and general stores and priced at twenty-five cents, the books were an instant success. Among the most popular titles were *Pocket Book of Baby and Child Care* (1946) by Dr. Benjamin Spock; *The Merriam-Webster Pocket Dictionary* (1947); and *Tales of the South Pacific* (1947) by James Michener.

With Pocket Books, Shimkin and his partners had developed a way to give people what they wanted at a price they could afford through a convenient, preexisting distribution network. A popular, low-cost series of children's books, Little Golden Books, was introduced shortly thereafter. During the mid-1940s, Shimkin introduced the People's Book Club, which operated through the Sears, Roebuck, and Company catalog. Soon, books were being sold successfully in rural areas without bookstores, a market that booksellers had hitherto been unable to reach. In 1966 John Tebbel wrote in *Saturday Review* that Shimkin believed "that the number of minds reached by a book is a true measure of its quality."

Shimkin continued as executive vice president of Simon and Schuster, of which he had become an equal partner, and he became president of Pocket Books in 1950. Although both companies were acquired by Field Enterprises in 1944, their management remained intact. Through the 1950s and 1960s Shimkin continued at the forefront of an industry increasingly dependent upon the kind of financial skills for which he was always known. In 1950 Bennett Cerf remarked of Shimkin that he was "happiest . . . when he had graphs and business reports spread out before him."

As publishing news moved from newspapers' book review pages to the business section, Shimkin and Max Schuster repurchased Simon and Schuster in 1957. In 1959 Shimkin purchased Pocket Books for himself. The industry was astonished in 1960, when Pocket Books became the first paperback publisher to take its stock public and revealed that the sales figures of the company had been greatly underestimated by its competitors. In 1966 Shimkin purchased Schuster's half-interest in Simon and Schuster and merged that company with Pocket Books. He became chairman of the board and owner of Simon and Schuster, heading a corporation with annual sales in excess of $40 million. In the same year he made a $2 million gift to New York University, where a building is named for him. He took on the role of chief executive officer of Simon and Schuster, Inc., in 1972. In 1975 Shimkin sold his company to Gulf and Western, but he remained active in its operation and served as cochairman emeritus from 1984 until his death.

Shimkin was a longtime resident of Larchmont, Westchester County, New York. He was a trustee of the Committee on Economic Development and took an active interest in a number of Jewish organizations. He died of a heart ailment in New Rochelle, New York, and is buried in Mount Pleasant Cemetery in Hawthorne, New York.

Kenneth C. Davis said of Shimkin that his concentration on publishing as a business rather than an avocation created some resentment. However, "few people inside publishing begrudged Shimkin his financial savvy, and it was soon acknowledged that the way of the shrewd businessman was the track that the publishing business was heading down. . . . The genteel business of publishing . . . was being supplanted by the business school dynamics of go-go growth." The man who claimed that he wanted to match "the creative art of publishing with the science of commerce" led the way in transforming the publishing industry.

★

Shimkin's correspondence is in the J. M. Dent Publishing Company records at the University of North Carolina and in the archives of Simon and Schuster. His correspondence with Theodore Dreiser is in the Theodore Dreiser Papers, University of Pennsylvania, Special Collections. Leon Shimkin and Freeman Lewis, *History of Pocket Books, Inc.* (1955), is the transcript of an interview conducted for the Oral History Research Office of Columbia University. Kenneth C. Davis, *Two-Bit Culture: The Paperbacking of America* (1984), includes extensive coverage of Shimkin's career and impact. Bennett Cerf, "The Third S," *Saturday Review* (11 Feb. 1950), provides a portrait of Shimkin's professional development and private life with a personal tone. "The Glottologist's New Edition," *Time* (8 July 1966), is a business-oriented sketch of Shimkin's recent accomplishments at that time and includes a photograph. John Tebbel, "Leon Shimkin: The Businessman as Publisher," *Saturday Review* (10 Sept. 1966), contains an interview and a discussion of the publisher's achievements in the year in which he became president of Simon and Schuster. An obituary is in the *New York Times* (26 May 1988).

REBECCA MARTIN

SHOCKLEY, William Bradford (*b.* 13 February 1910 in London, England; *d.* 12 August 1989 in Stanford, California), physicist, educator, and amateur geneticist who shared a Nobel Prize for physics for his role in the development of the transistor.

William Shockley, *c.* 1969. UPI/CORBIS-BETTMANN

Shockley was born in London while his American parents, William Hillman Shockley, a mining engineer, and May (Bradford) Shockley, a mineral surveyor, were living there on business assignment. The Shockleys returned to the United States in 1913 and raised their son in Palo Alto, California. Preferring to educate him at home, they did not enroll William in public elementary school until he was eight years old. Shockley later attended Palo Alto Military Academy and then Hollywood High School, from which he graduated in 1927. Both of Shockley's parents encouraged his early scientific interests, as did a neighbor, who was a professor of physics at Stanford University. By the time he was seventeen, Shockley knew that physics would be his career.

Beginning in the fall of 1927, Shockley attended the University of California at Los Angeles for a year. He then went to the California Institute of Technology, where he received a bachelor of science degree in physics in 1932. A teaching fellowship at the Massachusetts Institute of Technology (MIT) followed, along with graduate studies there. While at MIT, Shockley married Jean Alberta Bailey, a teacher, in 1933; they had three children. MIT awarded Shockley a Ph.D. degree in physics in 1936. His doctoral dissertation, "Calculations of Wave Functions for Electrons in Sodium Chloride Crystals," led him into research in solid-state physics and, according to Shockley, was the foundation for his subsequent work with the transistor.

Immediately after receiving his degree, Shockley joined the technical staff at Bell Telephone Laboratories in Murray Hill, New Jersey, despite several other job offers. His choice of Bell Labs was influenced by the opportunity to work with Clinton J. Davisson, a prominent physicist whose research in electron diffraction would later earn him a Nobel Prize. Shockley's first assignment at Bell, after an indoctrination period in vacuum-tube technology, was to develop an electron multiplier, a special kind of vacuum tube that would act as an amplifier. The amplifier was the basic tool in most electronic devices. Vacuum tubes had the desirable qualities of being able to both rectify (create a unidirectional current) and amplify (increase the strength of current). Shockley wanted to find a way around the obvious disadvantages of vacuum tubes—fragility, bulkiness, short life, necessary warm-up time, and high power consumption. In 1939 he proposed a plan for developing solid-state amplifiers as an alternative to vacuum tubes. Shockley was working with materials called semiconductors, which had properties intermediate to conductors and insulators. He already knew semiconductors could rectify, because they had been used for that purpose in the past in crystal radio sets. Although Shockley's experiments were theoretically sound, the basic properties of semiconductors were still largely not understood, and the results were disappointing.

Shockley's research was sidelined in 1940 by military needs associated with World War II. He began working on the electronic design of radar equipment at a Bell Labs field station in New Jersey. From 1942 to 1944 he served as research director of the Antisubmarine Warfare Operations Research Group of the U.S. Navy, and from 1944 to 1945 he acted as a consultant to the Office of the Secretary of War. In 1946 the War Department awarded Shockley the Medal of Merit, the highest civilian decoration of that time.

Meanwhile, in 1945 Shockley returned to Bell Labs as director of solid-state physics research. His team included John Bardeen, a theoretical physicist, and Walter H. Brattain, an experimental physicist. The group resumed Shockley's earlier research on semiconductors. They focused on silicon and germanium, the two simplest and best understood semiconductors of that time. Shockley was still determined to make a solid-state amplifier. He hypothesized that applying an electric field to a semiconductor would control the flow of electrons inside the semiconductor and that the field effect would produce amplification. When his experiments did not yield the expected results, Bardeen suggested that electrons trapped in a surface layer of the semiconductor were preventing the field from penetrating to the interior. The group shifted its research temporarily to a study of surface phenomena and surface states in an effort to better understand the nature of semiconductors.

By December 1947 Bardeen and Brattain had made the first successful semiconductor amplifier. It consisted of a piece of germanium with two closely spaced pieces of gold on one side (point contacts) and a broad tungsten contact on the other side. When an electrical current was fed to one of the gold contacts, it appeared in a greatly amplified form on the other side. The device had transferred current from a low-resistance input to a high-resistance output. The new invention was later named "transistor" because of its important property of *trans*fer re*sist*ance. Almost immediately, Shockley improved on the point-contact transistor by suggesting that the metal contacts be replaced by rectifying junctions between the negative and positive regions within one semiconductor crystal. Shockley proposed that an "n-p-n junction" would work as an amplifier. His 1950 book, *Electrons and Holes in Semiconductors,* was written in part to describe his junction transistor theory. The first reliable junction transistor was built in 1951, and this was the amplifier that was eventually mass produced. The public used transistors for the first time in 1953, in the form of amplifiers in hearing aids. The transistor radio was invented in 1954. By the late 1950s the first transistorized computers were hitting the commercial market.

In 1956 Shockley, Bardeen, and Brattain were corecipients of the Nobel Prize for physics for their research with semiconductors and discovery of the transistor effect. Shockley had clearly been the inspirational leader of the group. During his acceptance speech, Shockley remarked that he did not care whether his research was viewed as pure or applied; to him "it is more important to know if the experiment will yield new and probably enduring knowledge about nature. If it is likely to yield such knowledge, it is . . . good fundamental research."

Shockley left Bell Labs in 1955 to found Shockley Semiconductor Laboratories in Mountain View, California, just outside of Palo Alto. That same year his first marriage ended in divorce, and he married Emily I. Lanning, a psychiatric nurse. Shockley's company, which had started out as a research and development enterprise for transistors and other devices, began manufacturing in 1958 under the name Shockley Transistor Corporation. It was the first of many semiconductor firms in the area outside of Palo Alto that would later be known as Silicon Valley. In time, Shockley proved to be less successful at business than he was at physics. Shockley Transistor Corporation was incorporated into Clevite Transistor in 1960 and went out of business in 1968, three years after Shockley ended his association with the company.

Ten years earlier Shockley had begun to lecture at Stanford University, and in 1963 he was named the first Alexander M. Poniatoff Professor of Engineering and Applied Science. At Stanford, Shockley, who had always been interested in social issues, became focused on the origins of human intelligence, particularly the relationship between intelligence quotient (IQ) and race. He ventured into the field of genetics, a discipline in which he had no background or formal training, and began to expound a theory that the genetic component of a person's intelligence is based on racial identity. He saw blacks as genetically inferior to whites and unable to achieve the latter's intellectual level. He went on to suggest that blacks were reproducing faster than whites and, therefore, were advancing a genetic deterioration of the human population. Shockley formally defined his theory as "retrogressive evolution through the disproportionate reproduction of the genetically disadvantaged" and termed it "dysgenics." He went so far as to suggest that those with low IQs be paid in return for voluntary sterilization.

Shockley seized every opportunity to advance his hypothesis, but he met with severe criticism both from the scientific community and the public at large. His speaking engagements often sparked large protests, and the press condemned him. Shockley remained undeterred. In 1980 he sued the *Atlanta Constitution* for libel for an article it had published that compared his sterilization plan to Adolf Hitler's eugenics program. A jury found that Shockley had been libeled but awarded him just one dollar in damages.

In 1982 Shockley entered the Republican primary, campaigning for a seat in the U.S. Senate. His single-issue platform was a warning about the threat of dysgenics. He finished eighth, receiving 8,064 votes.

Shockley had retired from teaching at Stanford seven years earlier, in 1975, and had been appointed professor emeritus of electrical engineering that same year. He had also retired in 1975 from a decade of consulting for Bell Labs. He died at home of prostate cancer and is buried in Alta Mesa Memorial Park in Palo Alto.

Those who knew him best described Shockley as a reserved man, independent, intellectually honest, direct, and with a sense of humor. Scientifically, he was considered brilliant, perhaps even a genius. His brainchild, the transistor, is, arguably, the most important invention of the twentieth century. Certainly, it revolutionized computer technology, making computers smaller, cheaper, and more reliable. The transistor's use is virtually limitless in communication systems and other electronic devices as well.

Because of his role in the creation of the transistor, Shockley made a significant contribution to mankind. Perhaps it is both unfortunate and fitting that his scientific accomplishments are often overshadowed by the memory of his racial views. Shockley himself regarded his work on race as more important than his discovery of the transistor.

★

Shockley's collected speeches, addresses, and papers are in the San Jose State University Library in San Jose, California. He was interviewed for and is profiled in Shirley Thomas, *Men of Space* (1962), and Robert Slater, *Portraits in Silicon* (1987). The text of his Nobel Lecture and a short biography appear in *Nobel Lectures in Physics, 1942–1962* (1964). Other biographical sources include *Nobel Prize Winners* (1987), *The Nobel Prize Winners: Physics 1938–1967* (1989), and *Notable Twentieth Century Scientists* (1995). Obituaries are in the *New York Times, Los Angeles Times,* and *Washington Post* (all 14 Aug. 1989) and the *Times* of London (16 Aug. 1989).

VICTORIA TAMBORRINO

SHULMAN, Max (*b.* 14 March 1919 in St. Paul, Minnesota; *d.* 28 August 1988 in Hollywood, California), humorous novelist and playwright best known for the popular television show *The Many Loves of Dobie Gillis.*

Shulman was one of two children of Russian-born house painter Abraham Shulman and Bessie Karchmer, a homemaker. Growing up in poverty, he soon saw humor as a way of making his life more bearable. He began to write at age four and wrote for the school newspaper at Central High School in St. Paul, from which he graduated in 1936. At the University of Minnesota, where he majored in journalism, he edited the humor magazine, *Ski-U-Mah,* and

Max Shulman. ARCHIVE PHOTOS

wrote a column for the university's *Minnesota Daily.* This work brought him to the attention of an editor at Doubleday, who invited him to submit a novel. Inspired by the offer, he wrote *Barefoot Boy with Cheek,* a farcical tale of the adventures of a college freshman named Asa Hearthrug, which was published in 1943.

While still an undergraduate, Shulman married Carol Rees on 21 December 1941. They had four children: Daniel, Max, Jr., Peter, and Martha. Upon graduating with an A.B. degree in 1942, Shulman enlisted in the Army Air Forces. He served until 1946, reaching the rank of sergeant, and managed to find the time to write two more humorous novels, *The Feather Merchants* (1944), which dealt with the home front during World War II, and *The Zebra Derby* (1946), which returned to Asa Hearthrug, depicting his problems after leaving military service.

After the war, Shulman diversified. With producer George Abbott, he adapted *Barefoot Boy with Cheek* into a musical that opened on Broadway on 3 April 1947 and ran for more than two years. His short stories were appearing in popular magazines, and in 1950 his fourth novel, *Sleep Till Noon,* was published. The following year he collected eleven stories about a girl-crazed college undergraduate into the book *The Many Loves of Dobie Gillis.* In 1954 he and Robert Paul Smith collaborated on a play, *The Tender Trap,* which ran for more than 100 performances on Broadway and was made into a movie the following year.

At this point Shulman had not outgrown his reputation as an undergraduate writer, popular but inherently limited. His most successful fiction was set in college backgrounds, and it often seemed like little more than a series of gags. He further emphasized this undergraduate identity by writing a humor column sponsored by Marlboro cigarettes that appeared in college newspapers and by assembling the anthology *Max Shulman's Guided Tour of Campus Humor* (1955). His efforts to bring the larger world into his fiction, as in *Sleep Till Noon,* were generally considered less successful.

All this changed in 1957 with the publication of the novel *Rally Round the Flag, Boys!* A few years earlier Shulman had moved to suburban Westport, Connecticut, with his family, and the new novel described the reaction of a town like his to the installation of a military missile base. He intertwined several love stories with a satirical look at the interrelationships of the town's social strata. The book was Shulman's biggest seller ever, and it was made into a movie in 1958. In that year Shulman was one of six Minnesotans honored by having one of the state's many lakes named after them. Shulman remarked that the lake was, like its namesake, small and round. He was, in fact, five feet, six inches tall, weighing 145 pounds, a round-faced man generally described as either handsome or pleasant looking.

In 1959 Shulman's most popular creation, Dobie Gillis, reentered the public consciousness with the publication of the second Gillis collection, *I Was a Teen-Age Dwarf,* and the beginning of the television show entitled *The Many Loves of Dobie Gillis,* which was based on his characters and sometimes used his scripts. The show immediately found an enthusiastic audience and ran until 1963.

In 1964 Shulman published *Anyone Got a Match?,* a humorous novel about a tobacco manufacturer who attempts to divert attention from concerns about the effect of cigarettes on health by generating scare stories about the supposed dangers of food additives. The book did not make the best-seller lists and was a disappointment after *Rally Round the Flag, Boys!* It was followed in 1967 by the musical comedy *How Now, Dow Jones,* which barely lasted through the 1967–1968 season. In 1963 Shulman's wife, Carol, died. The following year Shulman married Mary Gordon, who had a daughter from a previous marriage.

Shulman's last novel, *Potatoes Are Cheaper,* appeared in 1971. A sentimental look back at the 1930s and Shulman's own Jewish background, the book was only moderately successful. His last film was *House Calls* (1978), a romantic comedy about doctors, for which he wrote the screenplay in collaboration with Julius Epstein. It was made into a television series the following year. Shulman died of bone cancer at his Hollywood home.

Max Shulman rarely aimed to be anything more than an entertainer, but he usually was good at that. His first few books often seemed like college humor columns writ large. His later novels were competent and successful popular fiction, with good though hardly outstanding characterization and plotting. As he outgrew the madcap jester pose of his early work, he retained and honed his verbal wit. He was never a biting Swiftian satirist, but he could occasionally surprise with a sharp observation.

Perhaps his most enduring work is the *Dobie Gillis* television series, which was still being rerun in the late 1990s. While his characters—the sexually desperate Dobie, his beatnik sidekick Maynard G. Krebs, his sardonic father and long-suffering mother, and the beautiful but unattainable Thalia Menninger—were very much of the 1950s, they continued to have an archetypal resonance. If the best satire takes the unspoken elements of society and utters them plainly, with only a few subtle and strategically placed exaggerations for maximum destructive effect, the portrayal of Dobie's desperate efforts to attain the money and success that his culture—and ours—promises will bring him love is true satire.

★

Max Shulman, "American Humor: Its Cause and Cure," *Yale Review* 51 (Oct. 1961): 119–124, is Shulman's only serious statement about his own writing and takes the position that humor is inherently a minor art, offering neither social change nor deep psychological insight. Russell W. Nash, "Max Shulman and the Changing Image of Suburbia," *Midcontinent American Studies Journal* 4, no. 1 (1963): 27–38, looks at *Rally Round the Flag, Boys!* as a sociological document, taking the book far more seriously than Shulman ever would. Darrell Y. Hamamoto, "Max Shulman: Television Author," *Journal of Popular Film and Television* 16 (winter 1989): 156–166, considers *Dobie Gillis* as a treatment of 1950s themes of conformity and success. An obituary is in the *New York Times* (29 Aug. 1988).

ARTHUR D. HLAVATY

SIMPSON, Wallis Warfield. *See* Windsor, Wallis Warfield (Simpson), Duchess of.

SIRK, Douglas (*b.* 26 April 1897 in Hamburg, Germany; *d.* 14 January 1987 in Lugano, Switzerland), theater and film director best known for a series of Hollywood melodramas, including *Magnificent Obsession* (1954) and *All That Heaven Allows* (1955), hailed for their trenchant critique of 1950s America.

Sirk, who was known as Hans Detlef Sierck until he emigrated to the United States in 1939, was the son of Danish parents. His father wrote for German and Danish news-

Director Douglas Sirk and actress Lana Turner work on *Imitation of Life,* 1958. AP/WIDE WORLD PHOTOS

papers and worked as a school principal. The family lived in Skagen, Denmark, during Sirk's early childhood, then returned to Hamburg. During World War I, Sirk enrolled in the Naval Academy in Mürwik in order to avoid the draft. He spent the last nine months of the war in Turkey as a commissioned officer. Returning to Germany in 1918, he pursued his education at institutions as diverse as his interests: law at the University of Munich, philosophy at the University of Jena, and art history under Erwin Panofsky at the University of Hamburg. He attended Albert Einstein's lectures on relativity and wrote a book about Gothic architecture. In 1922 Sirk published a German translation of Shakespeare's sonnets, with illustrations by the expressionist painter Joseph Eberz.

To finance his education, Sirk joined his father for a year as a journalist at the *Neue Hamburger Zeitung.* From 1920 to 1922 he also apprenticed in the theater as assistant dramaturge, then dramaturge, at Hamburg's Deutsches Schauspielhaus. His production of Hermann Bossdorf's *Bahnmeister Tod* inspired the Kleins Theater in Chemnitz to offer Sirk the post of director. Sirk then abandoned his university studies and embarked on a prolific theater career.

In 1923 Sirk assumed the post of artistic director of the Schauspielhaus in Bremen. He stayed in Bremen until the autumn of 1929, when he accepted the post of director at the rococo municipal Altes Theater in Leipzig. In both Bremen and Leipzig, barely a classic work for the stage escaped production under Sirk. In Bremen, he directed his translations of Shakespeare's *The Merry Wives of Windsor, The Tempest, Cymbeline,* and *Twelfth Night,* and of Luigi Pirandello's *Six Characters in Search of an Author.* Sirk's renown spread with productions of works by Germany's avant-garde, including Bertolt Brecht, Kurt Weill, Franz Werfel, and Georg Kaiser, and other Europeans including Max Brod, Noël Coward, and George Bernard Shaw. By his own account, Sirk's production of Weill's *Die Dreigroschenoper* (*Threepenny Opera*), was "extremely harsh," and the controversy the production provoked made it enormously successful.

In 1930 Sirk scandalized the Nazi Party with a sympathetic production of Bernhard Blume's banned play *Im Namen des Volkes!* (*In the Name of the People*), about the trial of the anarchists Nicola Sacco and Bartolomeo Vanzetti. After the Nazi Party came to power in January 1933, Sirk infuriated the regime with his Leipzig production of Kaiser and Weill's *Der Silbersee* (*The Silver Lake*). The work's premiere on 18 February 1933, in the theater where the young Goethe saw plays as a student, marked "the occasion when the curtain rang down on the German Stage," Sirk said. *Volkischer Beobachter,* the Nazi Party daily, vilified the authors as "salon Bolshevists" and attacked Sirk. The Berlin premiere was canceled, and Weill fled Germany the next day.

In retrospect, Sirk said, his production had been "absolute suicide," but at the time he considered Hitler and the National Socialists (Nazis) something of a passing phenomenon. The Third Reich's denunciation and criminalization of modernism as "degenerate art" intensified with the bloody purge of June 1934, in which Hitler rid himself of opponents, and as the German theater world nazified, Sirk found himself frequently targeted by the press. Because he refused to drift with the zeitgeist, he suffered the betrayal of colleagues, friends, and even his former wife, Lydia Brinken. Sirk had married Brinken, an actress, in 1925, and their only child, Claus Detlef Sierck, was born that same year. Divorced in 1929, Brinken became a Nazi Party member, Sirk claimed, out of enmity toward his second wife, stage actress Hilde Jary, who was Jewish. To Sirk's dismay, Brinken used Sirk's marriage to a non-Aryan to obtain a court order forbidding him from having contact with his son. Sirk maintained that Brinken then pushed the boy into joining the Hitler Youth and pursuing a film career. For the next decade, Sirk saw his son only in the movies; at one time they worked on adjacent sound stages.

While leftist intellectuals timed their departures, Sirk remained in Germany, hoping to escape with his son even as he feared his sympathies might make such an escape impossible. The mayor of Leipzig, Carl-Friedrich Goerdeler (executed in 1944 for his role in an attempted coup against Hitler), advised Sirk to seek refuge in the film industry. The dictates of commerce and international prestige afforded Universum Film Aktiengesellschaft (UFA)—free from state control until 1937—a measure of independence from the Nazis. Although it was unusual for established theater directors to work in the film industry, Sirk consciously attracted the notice of UFA's moguls with a cinematic staging of *Twelfth Night* in Berlin in 1934. He gained entrée into UFA, where he was assigned three short films that year. Sirk then directed nine films between 1935 and 1937. These melodramas are remarkable for illuminating the constraints and prospects of creativity under the Third Reich.

Sirk's rising box-office clout shielded him from political harassment, garnering him larger budgets and more discretion. In the winter of 1936 he turned his attention to the Brechtian *Zu Neuen Ufern* (1937) and cast Swedish singer-turned-actress Zarah Leander, a recent UFA discovery. The film triumphed at the box office, making Sirk UFA's most influential director and Leander the Third Reich's new hope for eclipsing the popularity of Greta Garbo and Marlene Dietrich. Sirk rushed his next film with Leander, *La Habanera* (1937), into production. His passport had been seized in the early 1930s because he had allegedly smuggled money across the German border, and he needed a new one to film on location in Spain. At UFA's prodding, Nazi officials granted Sirk a visa to film *La Habanera,* which enlarged his chances for escape.

In December 1937, ostensibly en route to scout locations for his next film, *Wilton's Zoo,* Sirk reunited with his wife in Rome. The Nazi government had granted Jary a passport in 1936 to encourage their divorce, and she had promptly fled. SS agents were dispatched with a UFA official to escort Sirk back to Germany. But Sirk feigned illness in a convent hospital, and the Sirks narrowly escaped to Paris via Zurich. In Paris, Sirk declined a written appeal from Josef Goebbels, Nazi minister of propaganda, that he return to Germany.

During his exile in France, Switzerland, and Holland, Sirk directed two films. In 1939 Warner Brothers invited him to remake *Zu Neuen Ufern,* and he emigrated to the United States, where he would later become an American citizen. An agent suggested he change his name to Douglas Sirk.

In 1940 Warner Brothers canceled the project and terminated Sirk's screenwriting contract. Sirk retreated from Hollywood, shunning the German expatriate circle in Santa Monica—Fritz Lang, Thomas Mann, Peter Lorre, Brecht—whom he considered elitists. While his later Hollywood melodramas would skewer American bourgeois respectability, Sirk loved the United States and was fascinated with its myths. The Sirks tried farming chickens in the San Fernando Valley, then alfalfa in Pomona County. Both ventures failed financially, but Sirk recalled this period as one of the happiest in his life.

Sirk directed his first color film, a short documentary about Napa Valley's Christian Brothers winery, in 1941. An agreement he made to manage a light opera company in San Francisco dissolved after the Japanese bombed Pearl Harbor in 1941 and the United States entered World War II. In 1942 the irascible Harry Cohn at Columbia Pictures put Sirk under contract to write screenplays but kept him idle. It was as a freelancer that Sirk shot his debut American feature, *Hitler's Madmen* (1942), which was filmed in one week. Bought and released by Metro-Goldwyn-Mayer, this film depicted the massacres in the small Czech villages of Lidice and Lezaky after Czech agents assassinated SS general Reinhard Heydrich in May 1942. Sirk directed six other films in the 1940s, including *Summer Storm* (1944), *A Scandal in Paris* (1946), and *Shockproof* (1949), from a script by the director Sam Fuller for Columbia. Cohn then released Sirk from his contract, and Sirk returned to Germany from 1949 to 1950, where he searched for work and tried to uncover news of his son, who had died in the German Army, presumably on the Russian front, in 1944. But Sirk found only a dismantled film industry and no details of his son's fate.

Originally offered a contract by Universal-International in 1945 after the release of a *A Scandal in Paris,* Sirk signed with the company in 1950 and began a long association with producers Ross Hunter and Albert Zugsmith. At Universal, as at UFA, Sirk built a strong repertory company of actors, filming quickly and cheaply. His most important films of this period were *Magnificent Obsession* (1954), a remake of John Stahl's earlier film, and *All That Heaven Allows* (1955), both starring Jane Wyman and Rock Hudson. Two more films—*Written on the Wind* (1957) and *Tarnished Angels* (1958), from William Faulkner's novel *Pylon*—starred Rock Hudson and Dorothy Malone. Sirk's

American film career culminated with another Stahl remake, *Imitation of Life* (1959), starring Lana Turner, which cultural critic Michael Stern called the "apotheosis of the American dream." It had the highest gross receipts to date of any Universal-International film, and all five films were among *Variety's* top moneymakers of the 1950s.

Although he considered *Tarnished Angels* to be his finest work, Sirk's most personal film was *A Time to Love and a Time to Die* (1958). Shot on location in Germany and based on Erich Maria Remarque's novel, *A Time to Love and a Time to Die* can be seen as the director's anguished contemplation of his son's last days. It is about a young German soldier on the eastern front who returns home on leave. While there, he falls in love with a former classmate. They marry and share a few days of happiness before he returns to combat against the Red Army and is killed.

In 1959, at the height of his career, illness and dissatisfaction with the studio system brought about Sirk's abrupt departure. After an aborted film project in France about the painter Utrillo, Sirk retired to Switzerland to convalesce. He never worked in Hollywood again. Instead, Sirk reverted to his old name and returned to Hamburg and Munich to stage works by Molière, Schiller, Eugène Ionesco, Shakespeare, and Tennessee Williams from 1963 to 1969.

Throughout the 1970s Sirk taught at the Munich Academy of Film and Television. He was revered by a generation of post–World War II directors, including Bernardo Bertolucci and Rainer Werner Fassbinder, who loosely adapted *All That Heaven Allows* into *Fear Eats the Soul* (1974). Fassbinder also starred in Sirk's best-known Munich short film, *Bourbon Street Blues* (1978), based on *The Lady of Larkspur Lotion,* a one-act play by Tennessee Williams. Late in life Sirk went blind, an irony not lost on the director, in *Magnificent Obsession,* of one of the cinema's great scenes about sightlessness. Sirk reportedly died of cancer.

Critical acclaim eluded Sirk until French film director Jean-Luc Godard championed him in a 1959 review, in the French film journal *Cahiers du Cinéma,* of *A Time to Love and a Time to Die.* An early appreciation by film critic Andrew Sarris and a major retrospective of Sirk's work at the 1972 Edinburgh Film Festival wrested Sirk's career from obscurity. Sirk participated in his rediscovery with interviews and writings that offered insight into his vision and technique.

Criticism of Sirk's American melodramas unveiled both classical references and encoded reactions to the ideological climate of the United States during McCarthyism. Auteurists—those who believe that the director is a movie's primary creative force—valued the ways in which Sirk injected ambiguity and fatalism into the stock situations of scripts. They noted how he masterfully employed antithetical narrative structures to undermine studio-mandated "happy endings."

Some critics sought to contextualize his work in relation to mass culture, arguing that Sirk's transcendental fusion of banal material and a highly wrought visual style anticipated the pop art movement. Other scholars studied Sirk's melodramas for their subversive dissections of gender coding, sexual roles, and racial difference, and for evidence of Sirk's camp sensibility.

★

The essential biographical text on Douglas Sirk remains *Sirk on Sirk: Conversations with Jon Halliday,* originally published in 1971 and reissued in 1997. Michael Stern, *Douglas Sirk* (1979), is a key study of Sirk's American films. Barbara Klinger, *Melodrama and Meaning: History, Culture, and the Films of Douglas Sirk* (1994), provides an interesting analysis of the shifts of critical and theoretical fashion in Sirk studies. Particularly informative entries on Sirk are found in John Wakeman, *World Film Directors,* vol. 1 (1987), and Justin Wintle, *Makers of Modern Culture* (1981). Interviews of Sirk are James Harvey, "Sirkumstantial Evidence," *Film Comment* 14, no. 4 (July–Aug. 1978), and Peter Lehman, "Thinking with the Heart: An Interview with Douglas Sirk," *Wide Screen* 3, no. 4 (1980). *Screen* 12, no. 2 (summer 1971), is a special issue devoted to Sirk, containing enlightening articles on his films by Fred Camper, Jon Halliday, and Paul Willemen. Obituaries are in the *New York Times* (16 Jan. 1987) and *New Republic* (16 Feb. 1987).

WILLIAM STERLING WALKER

SISK, Mildred Elizabeth. *See* Gillars, Mildred Elizabeth Sisk ("Axis Sally").

SKINNER, B(urrhus) F(rederic) (*b.* 20 March 1904 in Susquehanna, Pennsylvania; *d.* 18 August 1990 in Cambridge, Massachusetts), behavioral scientist and popular writer best known for his advocacy of cultural reconstruction through applied behavioral science.

Reared in the small town where his parents, William Arthur Skinner, a corporate attorney, and Grace Madge Burrhus, had grown up, Skinner resented the restrictions of his Presbyterian home in which "what other people might think" was constantly invoked to justify self-repression. But as the elder of two sons, he also enjoyed the support of an adult community that included his four grandparents. He early exhibited the mechanical know-how of his maternal grandfather, a carpentry shop foreman for the Erie Railroad, and found freedom in inventing mechanical gadgets and roaming the countryside with his friends. Skinner excelled across the curriculum during twelve years in the Susquehanna public schools and, like both of his parents, graduated salutatorian of his high school class. The first in his family to attend college, Skinner hoped to become a writer. In 1922, upon the recommendation of a family friend, he entered Hamilton College in Clinton, New York.

B. F. Skinner, 1971. JOYCE DOPKEEN/NEW YORK TIMES CO./ARCHIVE PHOTOS

Skinner was challenged by the relatively worldly college environment, where his intellectual interests commanded little respect in the peer culture of college life. His sense of dislocation was increased by his parents' move to Scranton, Pennsylvania, where William served as counsel for a coal company, and by the sudden death of his younger brother, Edward. He regained confidence during his sophomore year, however, thanks to the friendship of Arthur Percy Saunders, the college dean and chemistry professor who hired Skinner to tutor one of his children and who welcomed him into their culturally sophisticated household where modern ideas and manners stood in sharp contrast to the Victorian strictures and relative social backwardness of the elder Skinners.

Confirmed in his commitment to intellectual achievement by the Saunders circle, Skinner fashioned a persona for himself as a disillusioned intellectual contemptuous of Victorian traditions and contemporary business-oriented values. During the summer of 1925 Skinner attended the Bread Loaf School of English in Vermont, where he met the poet Robert Frost, who encouraged him to pursue the vocation of writer. Skinner's father reluctantly agreed to support his plan to live at home after graduation while attempting to write a novel. After delivering a satirical address in Latin as salutatorian of the Hamilton College class of 1926, Skinner rejoined his parents, but during his "dark year" failed to find a compelling theme for his novel.

While struggling to find a voice as a writer, Skinner encountered writers who embraced a behavioristic philosophy of science. He overcame his disappointment as a failed artist by shaping a new intellectual identity as a disinterested scientist who recognized that human beings, like other products of evolution, are biological machines that do not control their own development but are shaped by the stimuli or "conditioning" provided by their environment. By April 1927, Skinner had tacitly recognized the futility of his experiment in creative writing and was building ship models and working as a day laborer for a gardener until allergies forced him to quit. From June to December 1927 he worked for his father compiling *A Digest of Decisions of the Anthracite Board of Conciliation,* which was privately published in 1928. Influenced by reading and his mentor Saunders, Skinner decided to pursue a Ph.D. in psychology at Harvard and spent eight months in the open atmosphere of Greenwich Village in New York City and in touring Europe before entering Harvard University in September 1928.

At Harvard, Skinner quickly found the laboratory of William Crozier, a maverick professor of general physiology and a leading exponent of the mechanistic conception of life. Members of Crozier's research group thought of themselves as a heroic elite on the frontiers of knowledge, and even novices were given almost complete freedom after a brief apprenticeship. In an environment where status depended upon claims to originality, Skinner used his remarkable mechanical aptitude to design experiments that allowed him to record, predict, and control the behavior of white rats with unprecedented precision. Skinner admired the ideas of the Russian physiologist Ivan Pavlov, whose work became available in English translation in 1927. But while Pavlov worked with surgically prepared digestive glands to study conditioning, Skinner followed Crozier in studying whole organisms and boldly hypothesized that a rigorous science of behavior need not depend on physiology. Rather, his "radical" behaviorism would ignore the internal physiological state of experimental subjects and concentrate only upon observed behavior.

Skinner's tenuous connection to the academic discipline of psychology was strengthened by his discovery of a well-stocked departmental workshop, where he developed the experimental space that became known as "the Skinner box." In contrast to previous students of animal behavior, Skinner learned to depend upon the spontaneous actions of his subjects in his experiments. His subjects controlled the research apparatus, for example, by pushing a lever, which caused their behavior to be "reinforced" by food or some other positive stimulus. Skinner's growing reputation as a brilliant experimenter grew from his ability to invent experimental tools, such as a kymograph, a device that collected data continuously. Because of his mechanical inventiveness, his experiments could continue while he was at home, and he could return at his convenience to collect the data, which demonstrated how behavior was determined by various schedules of reinforcement. He shunned theory and "tinkered" until he found a pattern of behavior that could be shaped by positive reinforcement of actions initiated by the experimental animal.

Encouraged by his discovery of the power of "operant conditioning" to reveal laws of behavior, Skinner announced in his dissertation that all previous work on the psychophysics and physiology of the reflex was irrelevant to the future of behavioral science, which, he argued, had to follow his model of economical description of the behavior of whole organisms. Skinner's audacity aroused the ire of Edwin G. Boring, chairman of the Department of Psychology and author of *A History of Experimental Psychology* (1929), but Boring recognized Skinner's brilliant originality and removed himself from his dissertation committee. Skinner was awarded the M.A. in 1930 and the Ph.D. in 1931. With the support of Crozier and Boring, Skinner was able to continue research at Harvard for five years, as a National Research Council fellow (1931–1933) and as a junior fellow of the Harvard Society of Fellows (1933–1936). While many academic psychologists were embracing humanistic perspectives in the midst of the Great Depression, the New Deal, and the rise of totalitarianism in Europe, Skinner remained self-consciously detached from current events and hard at work developing a new scientific positivism, which he delineated in some two dozen articles and in *The Behavior of Organisms: An Experimental Analysis* (1938).

In the fall of 1936 Skinner assumed a regular academic appointment in psychology at the University of Minnesota. On 1 November 1936, he married Yvonne Blue, a University of Chicago graduate who shared his interest in literature. Skinner's marriage would have important influences on his career as a social inventor and popular writer. Yvonne was reared in an affluent upper-middle class home in which she had no domestic responsibilities. She had little interest in homemaking or in meeting conventional expectations for faculty wives. When daughters were born in 1938 and 1944, Fred Skinner played an unusually large role in child rearing. He invented a mechanical baby tender that provided a controlled climate and reduced the need for diapers. The invention received national attention through a *Ladies' Home Journal* article (October 1945) and aroused critics, who wrongly equated the "aircrib" with the "Skinner box" and created false rumors about the fate of the Skinner children, both of whom, in fact, had happy childhoods and became successful adults. Yvonne's unhappiness with domesticity also helped the brash behavioral scientist to imagine a better society. His utopian novel *Walden Two* (1948) depicted a commune in which behavioral engineering eliminated the drudgery of work for both men and women and erased the constricting barriers between private and community living.

While at Minnesota, Skinner began his work with pigeons, which would be the main subjects in his laboratory for the rest of his career. The shift from white rats to pigeons resulted from his effort to demonstrate the relevance of behavioral science to national defense. In April 1940 Skinner became convinced that he could train pigeons to serve as a missile guidance system that would save the lives of airplane bomber crews. He won the support of the Minneapolis-based General Mills Company for "Project Pigeon" and in 1942 was granted leave from the university to devote full time to the work. In 1943 the National Defense Research Committee provided $25,000 to support Skinner's team of key-peck operant engineers. Although funding was not continued, the project demonstrated the possibility of conditioning complex behaviors in pigeons, and several of the graduate students associated with the project went on to distinguished careers in behavioral science.

In 1945 Skinner moved to Indiana University as chairman of the Department of Psychology, but he spent the fall term of 1947 as William James Lecturer at Harvard, where he presented his ideas on how verbal behavior is shaped by social experience, an argument he fully developed in *Verbal Behavior* (1957). In 1948 Skinner returned to Harvard as professor in the Department of Psychology and found an excellent pulpit for his energetic efforts to promote radical behaviorism as *the* scientific psychology (*Science and Human Behavior,* 1953), a social technology that could revolutionize education (*The Technology of Teaching,* 1968), and the key to human survival in the shadow of nuclear weapons and rapid population growth (*Beyond Freedom and Dignity,* 1971).

Skinner's dead-earnest conviction that the principles revealed by operant science could make a better world aroused a wide range of critics, who resented Skinner's habit of pushing claims for the applicability of his technology of conditioning to the limits of credibility, but by the 1960s he was the best known and most often cited living psychologist. During the last ten years of his tenure at Harvard, from 1964 to 1974, a federal Career Development Award relieved him of all faculty teaching and administrative responsibilities, and he efficiently marshaled his energies for writing and for promotion of applications of behavioral research such as programmed learning machines. Ironically, Skinner, the ascetic positivist, found a mass audience for *Walden Two* among younger people during the cultural revolution of the 1960s, and several communes modeled upon it were established. Thousands of Harvard students watched him condition a pigeon to walk a circle eight in his popular general education courses, and his methods for changing behavior—through careful delineation of goals, breaking learning into sequential steps, shaping responses through immediate positive reinforcement, and constant revision of stimulus and reinforcement schedules in response to changes in behavior—found application in education, medicine, and business.

On 20 September 1971 Skinner achieved the extreme celebrity, for an academic, of a portrait on the cover of *Time* magazine, under the misleading headline, "B. F. Skinner Says We Can't Afford Freedom." In contrast, the Humanist Society named him Humanist of the Year for 1972. He was a complex figure whose faith in social engineering was very much in an American tradition of self-conscious culture building that can be traced back to the Puritan belief in the need to provide an ordered community so that grace would flourish. A connoisseur of creative literature and the arts and a skilled polemicist gifted with clarity in speech and prose, Skinner enjoyed the theater of public debate. His longest published work was a three-volume autobiography of more than 1,300 pages (*Particulars of My Life,* 1976; *The Shaping of Behaviorist,* 1979; *A Matter of Consequences,* 1983). He died of leukemia and maintained an efficient work schedule until his final illness. He is buried in Mount Auburn Cemetery in Cambridge.

★

Skinner's papers are in the Harvard University Archives, Cambridge, Massachusetts. Clark A. Elliott, "The Papers of B. F. Skinner and His Harvard Colleagues: Documenting an Academic Community in Psychology," in Laurence D. Smith and William R. Woodward, eds., *B. F. Skinner and Behaviorism in American Culture* (1996), provides an excellent introduction to Skinner studies. A Skinner bibliography is appended to Daniel N. Wiener's *B. F. Skinner: Benign Anarchist* (1996), but Daniel W. Bjork's *B. F. Skinner: A Life* (1993) provides the best analysis of Skinner's place in U.S. cultural history. An obituary is in the *New York Times* (20 Aug. 1990).

JAMES W. REED

SMITH, C(yrus) R(owlett) (*b.* 9 September 1899 in Minerva, Texas; *d.* 4 April 1990 in Annapolis, Maryland), head of American Airlines and leader in developing commercial aviation in the United States.

The son of Roy Edgerton Smith and Marion (Burck) Smith, C. R. Smith was born on what he once described as "the wrong side of the tracks." His father, a transient worker, traveled with the family throughout Texas and Louisiana before abandoning his wife and seven children when Smith was nine years old. Smith's mother was left to raise the family by teaching school and keeping boarders. Cyrus, the oldest of the children, found part-time work as an office boy for a wealthy cattle baron in Amarillo, Texas, followed by other casual employment before dropping out of high school at age sixteen to became a bookkeeper in a small bank.

In 1919, while working in the franchise-tax department of the office of the Texas secretary of state, Smith decided to resume his formal education and secured special permission to enroll in the School of Business Administration and Law at the University of Texas. While attending the university, he worked part-time as an examiner with the Federal Reserve Bank in Houston.

In 1924 Smith left the university without taking a degree and joined an accounting firm in Dallas as a junior clerk. Two years later, he became assistant treasurer of the Texas-Louisiana Power Company in Fort Worth, Texas. When the utility company purchased Texas Air Transport, Smith became the treasurer, then financial vice president, of the small airline that flew mail along several routes within the state. In 1929 Texas Air Transport merged with Gulf Air Lines to form Southern Air Transport System. The following year, the company was absorbed by the Aviation Corporation (AVCO), a giant conglomerate, and became part of American Airways. Smith, who had decided to pursue a career in aviation and had secured a pilot's license, took charge of the southern division of American Airways. Three years later he supervised the entire system as vice president for operations.

Following the reorganization of the airline industry in the wake of a Senate investigation of alleged monopolistic practices, Smith became president of the renamed American Airlines in October 1934. Under his dynamic leadership, the airline modernized and standardized its equipment, establishing a close relationship with the Douglas Aircraft Corporation that led to the introduction of the highly profitable Douglas Sleeper Transport/DC-3 in 1936. Emphasizing passenger traffic rather than mail contracts, Smith watched passenger-miles rise from 20 million in 1934 to 141 million in 1938. By 1941, American Airlines had become the leading domestic carrier in the nation, carrying one-third of all passengers flown by the industry's twenty certified airlines. Net profits amounted to more than $2 million a year.

On 29 December 1934 Smith married Elizabeth Lewis Manget. The couple had one son, Douglas, but the marriage soon fell apart due to Smith's preoccupation with managing the airline. He never remarried.

Smith took a leave of absence from American Airlines in April 1942 and joined the U. S. Air Corps Ferrying Command as a colonel. Serving as chief of staff and later deputy commander of what became the Air Transport Command in June 1942, Smith supervised the wartime development of a worldwide air transport system. The military appreciated his managerial skills, promoted him to major general, and awarded him the Distinguished Service Medal prior to his retirement in May 1945.

Smith returned to American Airlines as chairman of the board and chief executive officer at its headquarters in New York City. Thanks to creative financing, American was not only able to survive the lean postwar years but also acquired a fleet of modern pressurized Convair 240s and DC-6s. By the early 1950s, the airline was again recording substantial profits. In 1958, at a time when American was carrying 8 million passengers a year, Smith committed the company to an all-jet engine fleet of aircraft at a cost of $440 million. "With the shrewd calculation of a gambler," *Time* magazine noted in November 1958, "the financial sagacity of a banker, and the dedication of a monk, he has propelled American Airlines into first place in the industry and in the process has done more than any man to improve the service and standards of U.S. airlines."

After seeing American safely—and profitably—into the jet age, Smith retired in 1968 and became secretary of commerce in the cabinet of President Lyndon B. Johnson. He left government nine months later and joined the investment firm of Lazard Frères and Company. When American Airlines experienced economic and managerial turmoil in 1973–1974, Smith returned to the airline for six months as unpaid chief executive officer. After directing a cost-cutting program and helping to restore employee morale, Smith again retired. He died of cardiac arrest at the Ginger Cove Life Care Center in Annapolis.

Smith was an avid collector of Western Americana. His Manhattan apartment was filled not only with paintings by Frederic Remington and Charles M. Russell, but also featured an old-time bar, complete with brass railing and spittoons.

A hands-on manager who traveled incessantly throughout American's system, pecking out one-page memos on his portable typewriter, Smith never lost sight of the broader interests of the industry. While devoted to the success of his airline, he was also an indefatigable promoter of commercial aviation and worked to resolve industry-wide problems. An innovative financial and operational trendsetter, Smith set the standards for the airline industry in the United States as it matured into a vital segment of the nation's transportation infrastructure.

★

There is a small collection of Smith's papers at the American Airlines museum at Dallas–Fort Worth Airport, Texas. Smith discusses the early history of American in a Newcomen Society lecture, *"A.A." American Airlines—Since 1926* (1954). Roger E. Bilstein, "C. R. Smith," in William M. Leary, ed., *The Airline Industry* (1992), is a scholarly treatment of Smith's career, while Robert J. Serling, *Eagle: The Story of American Airlines* (1985), relies mainly on oral history sources to trace the evolution of the airline. An obituary is in the *New York Times* (5 Apr. 1990).

WILLIAM M. LEARY

SMITH, Henry Nash (*b.* 29 September 1906 in Dallas, Texas; *d.* 30 May 1986 in Elko, Nevada), historian, literary critic, and pioneer in the American Studies movement, who is best known for his award-winning book *Virgin Land: The American West as Symbol and Myth* (1950).

Henry Nash Smith was one of three children of Loyd Bond Smith, an accountant, and Elizabeth (Nash) Smith, a homemaker. Next door to their Dallas home lived Loyd's sister and her family, and young Henry spent most of his childhood within this close-knit circle of relatives. The family was active in the Disciples of Christ Church, but Henry stopped attending services at age fifteen, preferring to immerse himself in his uncle's set of Harvard Classics. At the age of sixteen Smith entered Southern Methodist University (SMU), where he joined a group of young intellectuals and developed a taste for American literature and popular music. He graduated with a B.A. degree in 1925, spent an academic year as a teaching assistant, and then headed for Harvard University, where he had been accepted to the graduate program in English.

Although the cosmopolitan life of Cambridge, Massachusetts, fascinated him, Smith found Harvard's English department old-fashioned and unsatisfying. He received a master's degree in 1929, but by then he had returned to SMU to accept a position as instructor in English literature and literary criticism. His interest in American literature and culture did not fall by the wayside, however. Under the guidance of Professor John H. McGinnis, Smith became coeditor of the *Southwest Review,* a journal of regional literature and essays. Smith's connection with the *Review* marks the beginning of his long-standing interest in the exploration and definition of a distinctive culture of the American Southwest. While editing essays on the literature, art, and folklore of Texas and the surrounding states, he also wrote book reviews for the *Dallas Morning News* and supported the growth of cultural institutions in his native city.

On 10 April 1936 Smith married Elinor Lucas; they had one son and two daughters. The following year he returned to Harvard as a student in the university's new program in American civilization. The program was one of the first in the field that came to be known as American Studies, developed as an arena for studying all aspects of American culture without regard to traditional disciplinary boundaries. In 1940 Smith received the program's first doctorate.

After a final year at SMU, where he had achieved the rank of associate professor and had established a program in the history of American civilization, in 1941 Smith took

Henry Nash Smith, 1961. ED KIRWAN, BERKELEY, CALIFORNIA

a joint appointment as professor of English and American history at the University of Texas at Austin. There he became involved in disputes between the faculty and the ultraconservative regents, appointees of the governor, who accused faculty members of immorality, subversiveness, and communist sympathies. After a year at the Huntington Library, where he was a fellow for the 1946–1947 academic year, Smith left Texas in 1947 for the University of Minnesota, where he was a professor of English until 1953.

Smith's first book, *Virgin Land: The American West as Symbol and Myth* (1950), was quickly recognized as a seminal work in the study of American culture and brought its author widespread scholarly acclaim. An expansion of Smith's doctoral dissertation, *Virgin Land* explored broad questions about how nineteenth-century Americans conceived of the American West (through both literature and physical encounters with the land) and how their perceptions influenced their actions. The work drew on an uncommonly wide range of sources, from the writings of traditional literary authors such as Thomas Jefferson, James Fenimore Cooper, and Walt Whitman to less-known popular sources, including dime novels, biographies of frontier heroes, and the everyday writings of scientists, traders, and others who traveled through the West. It was the coalescence of these various views, Smith argued, that determined the actions of those who actually settled the Western territories. In 1951 *Virgin Land* was awarded the John H. Dunning Prize of the American Historical Association and the prestigious Bancroft Prize of Columbia University.

In 1953 Smith joined the English department at the University of California at Berkeley, where he remained until his retirement. He was appointed literary editor of Berkeley's Mark Twain papers, a position that determined the course of his scholarship for well over a decade. He edited several annotated collections and critical editions of Twain's writing, including *Mark Twain of the Enterprise* (1957) and *Mark Twain–Howells Letters, 1872–1910* (1960), before publishing his own definitive study of Twain's career, *Mark Twain: The Development of a Writer* (1962). Smith's lectures on the humorist's later work appeared as *Mark Twain's Fable of Progress: Political and Economic Ideas in "A Connecticut Yankee"* (1964).

While deeply engaged in his work on Twain and his obligations as a teacher, Smith remained committed to the larger academic community. He was chair of his department at Berkeley from 1957 to 1960. He served on the board of directors of the American Council of Learned Societies from 1962 to 1967, and on the executive council of the Modern Language Association from 1959 to 1969 (he was elected president of the latter organization for 1968–1969). He maintained a concern with academic freedom and participated in the free-speech movement at Berkeley in 1964, as well as in resistance to the loyalty oath, required of teachers, in 1967.

Smith retired from teaching in 1974 but remained active as a scholar. His last book was a collection of essays, *Democracy and the Novel: Popular Resistance to Classic American Writers* (1978). He continued to publish in academic journals, and had two articles prepared for publication when he died in an automobile accident in Nevada on 30 May 1986.

American Studies grew rapidly after the publication of *Virgin Land,* and Smith's work on the American West stood as a model for a generation of scholars. Through his attention to regionalism and vernacular literature, Smith provided a framework for thinking about American identity—the ways it is created and the forms it takes—and the complex relationship of Americans to the land they inhabit. Perhaps more important, Smith's bold synthesis of historical documents and literary works of diverse genres inspired scholars to reach beyond disciplinary boundaries to create broad conceptual studies of enduring themes in American culture. The topics they pursued extended the scope of American Studies to encompass a great variety of fields, from folklore and popular music to journalism, education, labor, and technology. Their interests and conclusions were diverse, but all maintained Henry Nash Smith's abiding concern with a broadly conceived American culture and the transmission of ideas and ideals within it.

★

The Henry Nash Smith Papers, 1927–1986, at the Bancroft Library, University of California at Berkeley, contain biographical information, research materials related to Smith's doctoral dissertation and published works, conference papers, book reviews, and correspondence with prominent American writers and scholars. In Robert Forrey, "Interviews on American Studies: Henry Nash Smith," in *Amerikastudien-American Studies* 22 (1977): 190–197, Smith discusses the development of his career and his relationship to the American Studies movement. Mary Young, "The West and American Cultural Identity: Old Themes and New Variations," *Western Historical Quarterly* 1 (1970): 137–160, addresses the influence of Smith's work in the historiography of the American West. Richard Bridgman, "The American Studies of Henry Nash Smith," *American Scholar* 56 (spring 1987): 259–268, is a memorial providing an overview of Smith's career, with some personal information and an evaluation of Smith's main concerns as a scholar. Beverly R. Voloshi, ed., *American Literature, Culture, and Ideology: Essays in Memory of Henry Nash Smith* (1990), a collection of academic essays, pays tribute to Smith by reflecting his interest in the relationship between literature and culture. Included are two personal reminiscences and an essay by Smith. An obituary is in the *New York Times* (6 June 1986).

ELIZABETH KRONZEK

SMITH, Kathryn Elizabeth ("Kate") (*b.* 1 May 1907 in Greenville, Virginia; *d.* 17 June 1986 in Raleigh, North Carolina), singer and radio personality best known for popularizing the song "God Bless America" and for helping to cheer millions of listeners during the difficult days of the Great Depression and World War II.

Kate Smith, *c.* 1945. THE NATIONAL ARCHIVES/CORBIS

Kate Smith was the younger of two daughters of William Smith, the owner of a wholesale newspaper and magazine distributorship, and Charlotte (Hanby) Smith. The family was conventional and conservative, but when Smith developed a love for music after the family moved to Washington, D.C., her father initially encouraged her to perform as a singer and dancer. She made her first public appearance in a church choir at the age of four, singing religious songs while holding her hymnal upside down. She also sang for soldiers stationed in the Washington, D.C., area during World War I.

Although Smith became heavyset as a teenager and remained a large woman throughout her life, she was an agile dancer and once won an amateur contest by performing a spirited version of the Charleston. She wanted to pursue a show business career after graduating from high school in 1925, but her father insisted she enroll in the George Washington University School of Nursing. She quit after a year to perform in local vaudeville. The producer A. L. ("Abe") Erlanger spotted her and signed her for his upcoming Broadway revue, *Honeymoon Lane* (1926), starring Eddie Dowling. Smith made her Broadway debut at the Knickerbocker Theater in New York City on 20 September 1926, playing a character named "Tiny Little." It was the first of many humiliations she suffered because of her weight during her few years in the theater. Later that same year, she made her recording debut with Columbia Records and toured nationally in *Hit the Deck,* in which she sang "Hallelujah," written by Vincent Youmans and Leo Robin.

Smith continued to record for Columbia's lower-priced lines until she appeared on the National Broadcasting Company (NBC) program *RKO Radio Hour* in 1929 with the crooner Nick Lucas and the vaudevillians Sophie Tucker and Ted Lewis. Following a successful engagement at the Palace Theater in New York City, she appeared in her first motion picture, a Vitaphone short filmed in Brooklyn titled *Kate Smith—Songbird of the South,* in which she sang two songs, "Carolina Moon" and "Bless You, Sister."

Smith returned to Broadway in 1930 to appear in *Flying High,* starring the comedian Bert Lahr and featuring a score by the team of Buddy DeSylva, Lew Brown, and Ray Henderson. Although the play was a success, she was miserable because of Lahr's cruel jibes both on and off the stage. Her parents urged her to leave show business, but Smith persisted, though she never again appeared on Broadway. During the show's run, she met the record producer Ted Collins, who took over the management of her career and became her close friend. Collins remained her manager on the basis of a handshake until his death.

Collins persuaded the popular bandleader Rudy Vallee to have Smith appear as a guest on his radio show. After guest spots on several programs, Smith got her own production over the airwaves, *Kate Smith Sings,* in March 1931. The program lasted less than two months, but on this show she introduced her theme song, "When the Moon Comes over the Mountain" (music by Harry Woods, lyrics by Smith). By May 1931 the *Kate Smith Show* was being broadcast three evenings per week at 7 P.M. on the Columbia Broadcasting System (CBS), and Smith soon became the most popular female singer on radio. Although this first show ended in 1933, she remained a great success on the air for the next two decades and was once described as "radio's own Statue of Liberty."

Smith's success on radio led to movie roles. In 1932 she appeared as a singer in several Vitaphone shorts and played herself in a Paramount Studios production, *The Big Broadcast*. The next year she starred as a farm girl who helps her neighbors save their land by becoming a radio star in Paramount's unsuccessful feature *Hello Everybody,* which took its title from her familiar radio greeting. Unhappy with Hollywood, she canceled her contract and toured in vaudeville until 1934, when she returned to radio. In 1937 she began the *Kate Smith Hour,* which ran until 1945 on CBS. In 1938 she also began a CBS weekly noontime series, *Kate Smith Speaks,* in which she offered her own down-home philosophy along with a discussion of current events and women's issues. Also that year she wrote the first of two autobiographies, *Living in a Great Big Way*.

Aware of the approaching war in Europe, Smith in 1938 approached the songwriter Irving Berlin for a new patriotic song, and he gave her a number he had written in 1917 but had never published. She introduced "God Bless America" on the *Kate Smith Hour* on 11 November 1938 and sang it on her radio show and in personal appearances for the rest of her life. When she appeared at the White House to sing for King George VI and Queen Elizabeth of England on 8 June 1939, President Franklin Roosevelt introduced her, saying: "Your Majesties, this is America. This is Kate Smith."

During World War II, Smith appeared at numerous U.S. Army camps and raised a record $600 million selling war bonds through her radio appeals. She also appeared as herself in the movie *This Is the Army* (1943), in which she sang "God Bless America." During the 1930s and 1940s her hit records included *The Music Goes Round and Round, The Last Time I Saw Paris, Thanks for the Memories, Did You Ever See a Dream Walking, I'll Walk Alone, The White Cliffs of Dover, A Nightingale Sang in Berkeley Square,* and *I Don't Want to Walk Without You*. Up to that time, no popular singer had ever had more recordings or introduced more new songs. During her career, she made nearly 3,000 recordings and introduced approximately 1,000 songs on her radio show. Nineteen of her recordings sold over a million copies each.

In 1947 Smith left CBS and Columbia Records for the Mutual Network and MGM Records. Three years later she began her own afternoon television show on NBC, the *Kate Smith Variety Hour,* which quickly became the most popular daytime program on television. She ended her radio show in 1954 and withdrew from television that same year for health reasons. She returned to radio and television briefly at the end of the decade, but she mostly spent the remainder of her career doing personal appearances and television guest spots and making recordings. She also wrote a second autobiography, *Upon My Lips a Song* (1960).

On 1 November 1963 Smith appeared in concert at Carnegie Hall in New York City. Collins died in 1964, and that year Smith converted to Roman Catholicism. For the next ten years she continued her television appearances on shows hosted by Dean Martin and Sonny and Cher, starred in television specials, did a few nightclub appearances in a wheelchair, and made recordings. In 1969 she experienced an unusual resurgence in popularity when the Philadelphia Flyers hockey team used her recording of "God Bless America" rather than "The Star-Spangled Banner" before its home games.

Late in 1976 Smith suffered brain damage caused by a diabetic coma and withdrew from performing. Although she emerged in 1982 to receive an Emmy Award for her contributions to television and the Medal of Freedom from President Ronald Reagan, her final decade was a nightmare of ill health and family disputes over her estate. She had a leg amputated in January 1986 and underwent a mastectomy in May 1986.

Smith's interests included antiques, photography, and cooking, and she was an active swimmer, tennis player, skater, and skier. For many years she had a winter home in Arlington, Virginia; a summer retreat in Lake Placid, New York; and an apartment in New York City. Smith never married, but many people thought erroneously that she and Collins were married because of their close association. She died of heart failure in Raleigh, North Carolina, and is buried in Lake Placid, New York.

Although she performed during a period when most successful female singers were slim and considered sexy, Kate Smith had a resounding voice, a bright manner, and a robust friendliness that made her the most popular female singer and radio personality in show business. She seemed to embody the qualities of straightforward honesty, warmth, and love of country that reassured her millions of listeners during the Great Depression and World War II. A beloved public figure for more than thirty years, she made "God Bless America" one of the nation's most beloved songs.

★

Kate Smith, *Living in a Great Big Way* (1938) and *Upon My Lips a Song* (1960), are chatty, straightforward autobiographies. They would have been familiar in style to Smith's radio listeners. Roy Hemming and David Hajdu, *Discovering the Great Singers of Classic Pop* (1991), provides a chapter-long analysis of Smith as an important popular singer. James Robert Parish and Michael R. Pitts, *Hollywood Songsters* (1991), includes a biographical and evaluative essay on Smith. Michael Lasser, "This Is Kate Smith. This Is America," *Radiance* (summer 1996), examines and evaluates Smith's career with an emphasis on her Americanism and her introduction of "God Bless America." Obituaries are in the *New York Times* (18 June 1986), *Time* (30 June 1986), and *Newsweek* (30 June 1986).

MICHAEL LASSER

SMITH, William French (*b.* 26 August 1917 in Wilton, New Hampshire; *d.* 29 October 1990 in Los Angeles, California), lawyer and attorney general of the United States in the Reagan administration.

Smith was the only child of William French Smith, president of the Mexican Telephone and Telegraph Company, and Margaret Dawson, a homemaker. His father died when Smith was six. Smith grew up in Boston and attended Choate High School. He received an A.B. degree from the University of California at Los Angeles in 1939 and an LL.B. degree from Harvard Law School in 1942. After graduation he joined the U.S. Navy and, as a lieutenant, served in the Pacific. He married Marion Hannah on 5 March 1943; they had two children.

In 1946 Smith joined Gibson, Dunn, and Crutcher, one of the largest law firms in Los Angeles. He became a partner in 1951, and later senior partner and head of the firm's labor department. Another partner, Willard Carr, recalled that Smith was very careful and thorough, and developed extraordinary client loyalty. Smith's sense of fairness in his representation of companies in collective bargaining won respect from trade unionists. As a young lawyer he was active in the Republican party "in the speech and debate arenas," but his political involvement gradually declined as his legal career prospered. In 1958 he and Marion were divorced, and on 6 November 1964 he married Jean Webb, who had two children from a previous marriage.

On election night 1964, when President Lyndon B. Johnson defeated Senator Barry Goldwater, the Republican nominee, in a landslide, Smith attended a Republican gathering at the Ambassador Hotel in Los Angeles, where he heard a speech by Ronald Reagan. Smith remarked to his wife, "Everybody here tonight . . . is crying the blues—except for Ronald Reagan. . . . He believes it's only a matter of time before they win national office."

In 1966 Smith became Reagan's personal attorney and helped him win election as governor of California. He was a member of Reagan's "kitchen cabinet," which included Holmes Tuttle, Henry Salvatori, and A. K. Rubel. They organized Reagan's campaign and raised the funds to compete in the Republican primary for governor. Reagan recalled that Smith had a "gift for clear, reasoned thinking, and I came to rely on his advice more and more." After Reagan's election and inauguration as governor, he named Smith to the board of regents of the University of California in 1968. Smith chaired the board from 1970 to 1972 and from 1974 to 1976.

After his inauguration as president in 1981, Reagan appointed Smith attorney general of the United States. Reagan remarked, "It was a source of the greatest comfort for me to have such a friend from home at the cabinet table." Some of Smith's closest assistants in the Justice Department came from his law firm: Myra L. Tankersley, confidential assistant; Kenneth W. Starr, counselor (chief of staff and later independent counsel to investigate President Bill Clinton); and Theodore B. Olson, assistant attorney general and legislative counsel. The associate attorney general was Rudolph Giuliani (later mayor of New York City), and Robert A. McConnell was assistant attorney general for legal af-

Attorney General William French Smith (*left*) speaks with President Ronald Reagan, 1982. RONALD REAGAN LIBRARY/CORBIS

fairs. Tankersley admired Smith's "perfectionism and demanding but respectful nature."

Smith admired Thomas Jefferson and wanted to curtail judicial activism, which he considered a corruption of the small government (and weak judiciary) envisioned by the Founding Fathers. Smith believed that since the 1930s the Supreme Court had engaged in and had fostered judicial policy making under the guise of substantive due process, and that justices had substituted their own policy preferences for those of the public's elected representatives. He and the assistant attorney general for civil rights, William Bradford Reynolds, opposed mandatory busing and racial quotas. On antitrust policy Smith thought "bigness is not necessary badness."

The attempt by Smith to move the judiciary back to its earlier, less powerful role in American life was criticized by liberals in Congress, the courts, universities, and the media. But Smith was supported by Reagan. On Smith's recommendation President Reagan appointed Sandra Day O'Connor, the first woman justice to sit on the Supreme Court.

In 1985 Smith resigned from the Justice Department and returned to his law firm in Los Angeles. He served as chairman of the board of trustees of Reagan's Presidential Foundation, which created the Ronald Reagan Presidential Library and Center for Public Affairs.

Smith was a quiet, discreet man who did not seek publicity. He was never one to waste time, but for relaxation he played tennis and the organ. He served on the board of directors of many companies, the advisory board of the Center for Strategic and International Studies at Georgetown University (1978–1982, 1985–1990), and the advisory council of the School of Government at Harvard University (1977–1990). He was also a trustee of the Henry E. Huntington Library and Art Gallery in San Marino, California (1971–1990). Smith died in Los Angeles of cancer and was buried in Forest Lawn Memorial Park in Glendale, California.

Smith's most important contribution to his country was the role he played in helping Ronald Reagan enter politics. Smith also left another legacy in the men he promoted, who shared his reverence for the rule of law. McConnell, Olson, and Starr said, "Bill never fought for headlines and publicity. He enjoyed the substance of the work, was a voracious reader, heavy questioner, and methodical student of briefing books. . . . He sought the views of others and encouraged free debate. . . . The enduring legacy of Bill Smith is that he now provides the standard by which those of us who served with him will hereafter measure ourselves."

★

Smith's papers are in the Ronald Reagan Presidential Library, Simi Valley, California. William French Smith, *Law and Justice in the Reagan Administration: The Memoirs of an Attorney General* (1991), includes a foreword by Ronald Reagan; an epilogue, "Ronald Reagan: A Thirty-Year Reminiscence"; an appreciation by Robert A. McConnell, Theodore B. Olson, and Kenneth W. Starr; and a revealing chapter, "The (Much Too) Independent Counsel." Other works by Smith include "The New California Fair Employment Practices Act," *California* (Sept. 1959); "The Republic Revisited," *California* (Sept. 1965); and "Corporate Political Contributions—The Law and the Practice," *Los Angeles Bar Bulletin* (Oct. 1966). The U.S. Department of Justice published a microfiche edition of *William French Smith: Major Policy Statements of the Attorney General* (1985). See also U.S. Congress, Senate, Committee on the Judiciary, *Confirmation Hearing on the Nomination of William French Smith to Be Attorney General,* 97th Cong., 1st sess., 15 Jan. 1981. Obituaries are in the *Los Angeles Times, New York Times,* and *Washington Post* (all 30 Oct. 1990.)

RALPH KIRSHNER

SNYDER, Mitch(ell) Darryl (*b.* 1944 in Brooklyn, New York; *d.* 3 or 4 July 1990 in Washington, D.C.), advocate for the homeless who was famous for using hunger strikes and other radical tactics to attract media attention.

Born to a Jewish family, Snyder grew up in Brooklyn and attended Erasmus Hall High School there. He dropped out and was subsequently sent to reform school for breaking into parking meters. Snyder married Ellen Kleinman on 13 October 1963; they had two sons. On occasion Snyder gave impromptu, leftist political speeches in Manhattan's Union Square. The earnings from his job as a vacuum cleaner salesman were insufficient to support his family, and he started cashing bad checks.

In 1969 Snyder left his family and went to California; the following year he and a friend were arrested in Las Vegas, Nevada, for stealing the car they were driving. Snyder was sentenced to three years in the federal prison at Danbury, Connecticut. There he met Daniel and Philip Berrigan, Jesuit priests imprisoned for destroying draft records to protest American involvement in Vietnam. The Berrigan brothers introduced him to radical Christianity, social activism, and nonviolent protest. Snyder completed his full sentence, but not before staging his first hunger strike, to protest the use of "tiger cages" (tiny prison cells) by the United States in Vietnam.

Although his wife had visited him regularly during his prison stay, Snyder never returned to his family after his release in 1973. He had been "called to live a different kind of life," he said, and "you don't argue with God." Snyder moved to Washington, D.C., and joined the Community for Creative Non-Violence (CCNV), a group of idealistic activists who took on the issues of homelessness and American involvement in Vietnam. The CCNV, founded by a former Paulist priest named Edwin Guinan, seemed an appropriate match for Snyder's newfound religious activ-

Mitch Snyder at a rally for the homeless in Washington D.C., March 1990. UPI/CORBIS-BETTMANN

ism. On Christmas Day of that year Snyder was arrested for climbing the White House fence to protest the Vietnam War.

In 1978, while attending Mass at Holy Trinity Catholic Church in Georgetown, Snyder heard the priest praise his work with the poor. Inspired by this praise, he asked the parish for a donation; when refused, he began a hunger strike. The parishioners then agreed to donate the money but reneged on the promise, prompting Snyder to fast again. He was forced to end the strike when the parishioners voted not to donate the money after all.

In 1984 Synder, in conjunction with the CCNV's five-week series of demonstrations entitled "The Harvest of Shame," went on yet another hunger strike. He and the CCNV hoped to gain support for District of Columbia Initiative 17, a proposed law that was to mandate that the city provide shelter for every homeless person in the District. In addition they hoped to force President Ronald Reagan to turn over a vacant federal building in the District of Columbia to the CCNV, to be used as a homeless shelter. Snyder's near-fatal, fifty-one-day hunger strike gained national media attention. Two days before the presidential election Reagan gave in, allocating approximately $6 million for the building's renovation. Initiative 17 passed on 4 November 1984 with 72 percent of the vote, and 425 Second Street, N.W., became a 1,200-bed shelter.

After fifteen years without any communication, Snyder and his former wife, now called Ellen Daly, were reacquainted when she called him after seeing coverage of his fast on the television show *60 Minutes*. As a result Snyder was able to meet his sons, and he maintained contact with Daly until his death.

Snyder's unorthodox methods were criticized both outside and within the CCNV. Some CCNV members questioned his dominance in an organization that purported to be run by consensus. Snyder was also criticized for his refusal to allow U.S. Census workers into the CCNV shelter. He believed that the census would undercount the homeless, and that the incorrect estimates would be used to determine government funding. Some saw Snyder's hunger strikes as bully tactics or emotional blackmail, and his use of the media as manipulative.

In March 1990 the District of Columbia Council amended Initiative 17, cutting the budget for homeless services by $19 million. That spring Snyder announced plans to take time off from the CCNV to stay at a Trappist monastery in Berryville, Virginia, where he hoped to renew his relationship with God. He also announced his engagement to fellow CCNV activist Carol Fennelly, who had worked with him to organize hunger strikes and marches. But the wedding was postponed indefinitely.

On 5 July 1990 Snyder was found hanged in his room in the CCNV shelter. In a handwritten note he cited his recent breakup with Fennelly as the reason for his suicide. Others close to Snyder, however, said additional factors, including the weakening of Initiative 17 and friction within the CCNV, had contributed to his depression. Because Snyder had last been seen on 3 July, and because of the condition of the body when it was found, police estimated that his death occurred on the night of 3 July or sometime on 4 July.

Although his methods were unorthodox and controversial, Snyder's personal dedication to and sacrifice for his cause have been matched by few. The subject of both the

CBS television movie *Samaritan: The Mitch Snyder Story* (1986) and the documentary *Promises to Keep,* nominated for an Academy Award, Snyder tried to bring the issue of homelessness to the attention of the American media and people.

★

News stories about Snyder appear in the *Washington Post* (16 Mar. 1990, 26 Mar. 1990, and 29 Mar. 1990). An obituary is in the *Washington Post* (6 July 1990). Shortly after Snyder's death *Newsweek* and *U.S. News and World Report* (both 16 July 1990) published reflections on Snyder and his work.

LAURA KATHLEEN SMID

SOULE, Gertrude May (*b.* 19 August 1894 in Topsham, Maine; *d.* 11 June 1988 in Canterbury, New Hampshire), religious leader who was one of the last of the Shakers.

Gertrude May was one of the four children of William Alphus Soule, a painter and woodcraftsman who also lobstered, and Estella Curtis Soule, a homemaker. A paternal ancestor had come to America on the *Mayflower.* Along with her younger sister Cora Maude, Gertrude was placed in the custody of the Sabbathday Lake, Maine, Shaker community in June 1906, after the death of her mother and her father's remarriage. The celibate Shakers, who forbade marriage, maintained their numbers by welcoming into their community converts, orphans, and unwanted children such as the Soule sisters. "My father's new wife," Soule once reminisced, "didn't care for my little sister and me, so he left us with the Shakers. When I lived with my stepmother, she made me work as if I were 20 years old. But when I went to the Shakers, I was a real child. I enjoyed it immensely. You could talk to the sisters as if they were your own mother—they were spiritual mothers."

Eldress Gertrude Soule does needlework in the "sisters' shelter" at Shaker Village in Canterbury, New Hampshire, 1978. UPI/CORBIS-BETTMANN

Membership in the United Society of Believers (whose members were called Shakers because of their uncontrolled physical movements during worship, when they claimed that they were seized by the Holy Spirit) had peaked at 6,000 in the 1840s, with nineteen communities in the eastern and midwestern United States. The Shakers envisioned God as both male and female, and viewed their founder, Mother Ann Lee, an English working-class woman who had emigrated to America in 1774 with a small group of followers, as a female revelation of Christ's second coming. Shakers helped the poor and maintained a pacifist stance during war. Their crafts, particularly their furniture and oval-shaped boxes, became prized by collectors. The Shakers were credited with many inventions, such as the circular saw, the flat broom, and the straight clothespin. The men and women lived separately, eschewed sexual relationships, and shared equally in the society's wealth and leadership. (Celibacy released Shakers from the distractions of marriage and parenthood.) Decisions customarily were made by a ministry of two female leaders (eldresses) and two male leaders (elders).

Having acquired a mastery of needlework and a basic foundation in the society's theology, at age twenty-one Soule signed the Shaker covenant, thus becoming a permanent member of the society, and was known as Sister Gertrude Soule until her elevation to the ministry. Sabbathday Lake records indicate that she left the community in April 1925, but archival papers yield no details of her absence. Individuals who knew her late in life believe that Soule remained in New England either as a governess or as a home health care worker. She returned to Sabbathday Lake fifteen years later, in December 1940. In 1957 she was elevated to the ministry and was appointed to the Board of Corporators. As the ranking member of the Maine community, in the early 1960s Eldress Gertrude split with other Shakers over the proposed admission of additional converts. A majority of Sabbathday Lake members wished to expand; the Shakers at Canterbury, New Hampshire, did not, objecting less to growth than to admitting new members to the existing trust structure. Eldress Gertrude, in her fiduciary role, was concerned about the attractions of the Shakers' valuable community property to potential members. She was one of two senior Shakers (with Eldress Emma B.

King) to make the far-reaching decision, in 1965, to close the Shakers' central enrollment covenant. This would have ensured the extinction of the Christian celibate fellowship, had not the Sabbathday Lake Shaker community continued to admit petitioners via a local covenant.

In the late 1950s Theodore Johnson, a graduate of Colby College and Harvard University, as well as a former Episcopalian and Fulbright scholar, took an interest in the Sabbathday Lake community, and entered the community on 28 May 1960. Johnson's liberal education and his talent for cultural preservation gained him wide acceptance as a spokesman for the Maine community, setting the stage for a conflict between the highly educated and charismatic Johnson, who daily was becoming more useful to the community, and Eldress Gertrude, who had been reared by the Shakers and was charged with partial governing responsibility for the central trust. In the end, Eldress Gertrude's doctrinal argument carried the day with other trustees: she declared that it was not suitable for a male candidate to be admitted to the central convenant when all of the Shaker brothers who customarily would have instructed and sponsored him were dead. Brother Delmer Wilson, the last convenanted male member at Sabbathday Lake, had died in 1961 without formally sponsoring Johnson or any other male convert. An interview with Eldress Gertrude in the *Maine Sunday Telegram* quoted her as saying, "We [also] ruled against accepting young women as members because young people do not want to accept the discipline, the rules and regulations which govern our way of life. . . . Young people are interested in and attracted by the Shaker religion and faith, but the discipline of our living is not acceptable to them. We have had bad experiences in some Shaker communities." The eventual acceptance of Johnson and several others into the Sabbathday Lake community, unsanctioned by the central trust but locally approved by the Maine Shakers, triggered an intense reexamination of one of the society's deepest governing principles: Mother Ann Lee's expressed wish to admit any sincere petitioner.

In 1971 eldress Gertrude voluntarily left Sabbathday Lake for the Canterbury, New Hampshire, community, ostensibly to nurse the sick. Eventually she moved there permanently, taking few personal possessions. Now age seventy-seven, Eldress Gertrude plunged into an active life at Canterbury, where she lived with Sister Bertha Lindsay and Sister Ethel Hudson. She served as vice president of the New Hampshire Shakers' nonprofit corporation and museum, and often personally greeted visitors. She once advised a Brazilian engineer on the Shaker art of broommaking, encouraging the launching of a cottage industry for the poor of South America. In her late eighties Eldress Gertrude broke her hip while throwing a Frisbee for Sister Bertha Lindsay's dog. Always interested in medical treatments, at Concord Hospital she requested local anesthesia so that she could observe her operation. In her final years she maintained a voluminous correspondence with relatives including her sister Cora (who left the Shakers to marry), friends, and children she met through educational speaking engagements.

Active in outreach and always interested in the young, Eldress Gertrude addressed the graduating class of Belmont (New Hampshire) High school on the last night of her life. As a result of sitting through the long outdoor ceremony, she contracted a chill. On 11 June 1988 she asked a friend to drive her to the doctor. Shortly thereafter she died peacefully, apparently of heart failure. She was ninety-three years old.

Eldress Gertrude's funeral at Dwelling House Chapel on 14 June was so well attended that loudspeakers had to be rigged outdoors for the overflow crowd. She was buried at Canterbury according to Shaker custom, near a single granite stone inscribed "Shaker" that marks the location of some 400 graves.

Soule was a complex woman who devoted her life to Christian principles and the preservation of Shaker resources, and suppressed a lingering wistfulness over her philosophical differences with the Maine Shakers. Students of Shaker life and culture view the covenental impasse of the 1960s less as a conflict between Eldress Gertrude and Brother Theodore Johnson than as a paradigmatic shift to a leadership that would permit survival of the Shaker's lifestyle and religious practices and enable preservation and development.

★

The personal papers of Eldress Gertrude Soule are at Canterbury Shaker Village archives, folios 11–12. Background material is in Tim Clark, "Shattering the Shaker Image," *Yankee Magazine* (May 1980); Andy Court, "The Lives of the Last Shakers," *Concord Monitor* (27 Dec. 1984); and Stephen J. Stein, *The Shaker Experience in America* (1992). Accounts of Eldress Gertrude's burial and recollections of her life are in the (Laconia, N.H.) *Evening Citizen* (14 June 1988) and the *Boston Globe, Concord Monitor,* and (Manchester, N.H.) *Union Leader* (all 15 June 1988). An obituary is in the *New York Times* (13 June 1988).

DEBORAH AYDT MARINELLI

SOYER, Raphael (*b.* 25 December 1899 in Borisoglebsk, Russia; *d.* 4 November 1987 in New York City), artist who is best known for paintings depicting ordinary New Yorkers in their homes, places of work, and public spaces.

Soyer's father, Abraham Shoer, was a teacher of Hebrew and Jewish history and a writer of short stories; his mother, Bella Shoer, was an embroiderer of towels and tablecloths (Abraham would sometimes draw the designs). Raphael and his twin brother, Moses, who also became an artist,

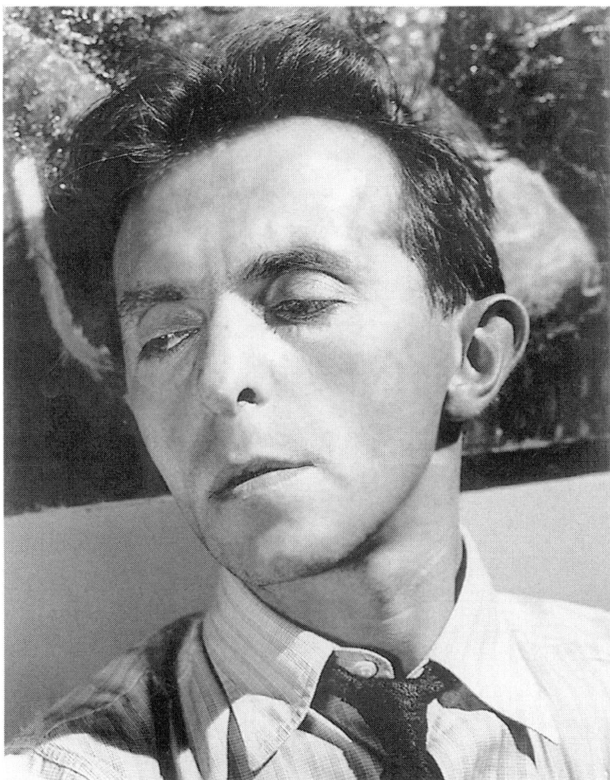

Raphael Soyer, 1940. UPI/CORBIS-BETTMANN

were the eldest of six children. Another brother, Isaac, became a painter as well. The family name was later anglicized as "Soyer." Raphael was encouraged by his parents, in whose library he read the works of Tolstoy, Turgenev, Dostoyevski, and Gogol, and in translation, Dickens and Thackeray. In 1912, because of Abraham's suspected subversive activity, the family was ordered to leave Russia. They traveled to Philadelphia, where they stayed for a few months with relatives, then settled in the borough of the Bronx in New York City. Raphael entered Morris High School but left before graduation, going to work to help contribute to the family income.

Of below-average stature (he was five feet, two inches tall) and exceedingly shy, Soyer drew and painted at home and took night classes in drawing at Cooper Union from 1914 to 1917. In 1918 he entered the National Academy of Design, where he remained for four years. His fellow students included the painters Ben Shahn and Paul Cadmus and the art historian Meyer Schapiro. From December 1920 to January 1921 Soyer also studied with Guy Pène du Bois. In 1927 some of his works appeared in the members' exhibitions of the Whitney Studio Club, and by 1931 Julianna Force, the director of the club, had purchased five of Soyer's paintings and a drawing. Thereafter Soyer was regularly included in the Whitney Museum's annual and biennial exhibitions. The sales from his first one-man show, held in 1929 at the Daniel Gallery in New York City, enabled him to give up his outside jobs and paint full-time.

On 8 February 1931 Soyer married Rebecca Letz; they had one daughter, Mary. In the 1930s he worked in the Graphic Arts Division of the Federal Art Project. He taught at the Art Students League from 1933 through 1942, at the American Artists School for several years after World War II, at the New School for Social Research from 1957 through 1962, and at the National Academy of Design from 1965 to 1967. He lived in New York City for most of the year but spent summers in New England in the late 1920s and 1930s; in Croton-on-Hudson, New York, from 1941 to 1948; in Southampton, New York, from 1949 to 1954; and in Vineland, Maine, from 1957. In the 1960s he made many journeys to Europe, where he went from museum to museum and from country to country, often drawing from the works of the masters.

Soyer's heroes were the great realist painters who concentrated on the human figure: Rembrandt, Degas (whose anti-Semitism disturbed him), and Thomas Eakins. His largest painting, *Homage to Thomas Eakins* (1964–1965, Hirshhorn Museum), loosely based on Ignace Fantin-Latour's *Hommage à Delacroix,* contains, besides himself (shown inconspicuously off to the side), his brother Moses, his daughter, eight of his fellow realist painters, and the writer-curator Lloyd Goodrich seated before Eakins's paintings *Salutat, Gross Clinic,* and *William Rush Carving His Allegorical Figure of the Schuylkill River.*

Soyer was passionately committed to the underdog and an ardent supporter of liberal causes; as a member of the John Reed Club of Artists and Writers he opposed the ascendancy of fascism in Europe in the 1930s, and he initiated publication of the social activist periodical *Reality: A Journal of Artists' Opinions* in the mid-1950s. Consistent with these views, Soyer painted disconsolate, but earnestly responsible, dwellers of New York caught in their struggles for existence: in department stores, in parks, on buses and on the street, and in waiting rooms of train stations (*Waiting Room,* c. 1940, Corcoran Gallery of Art). Sometimes he arranged a variety of types in these elaborate tableaux within his studio, suggesting a cross section of humanity; an example contains fellow artists, friends, and nudes (*My Friends,* 1946, Butler Institute of American Art, Youngstown, Ohio). Singly and in groups Soyer depicted models, derelicts, young would-be dancers, people he would commonly meet on his walks through the streets. While he never directly attacked capitalism or the wealthy, the viewer of his paintings would conclude that here were ordinary folk doing the best they could at their jobs. The art historian Milton W. Brown observed of Soyer that "like Pascin, he transformed the studio picture from an exercise in formal organization into a metaphor for the human condition." In

Soyer's works, the young kept their dream alive as they sought to stave off poverty.

Soyer was also a printmaker. He began about 1917, when he bought a table-model etching press for $25 and set it up in his family's tenement apartment. In 1933 he began to work directly on the stone. His lithographs commonly show one or two young female models, approached sympathetically, posing as seamstresses, mothers, lovers, musicians, or dancers.

Soyer's vision of the city is not the genial, overtly optimistic one of John Sloan and the painters of the Ashcan school, nor is it the stark, harsh vision of acute alienation found in the paintings of Edward Hopper. His paintings depict the warmly lit, gentle melancholy of individuals struggling to make ends meet and keep their relationships intact.

Soyer died of cancer in New York City at the age of eighty-seven.

★

Soyer's *Self-Revealment: A Memoir* (1969) includes diary excerpts of his visits to museums in Germany, Austria, Italy, France, Holland, and Great Britain, as well as memories of life in Russia and observations of his friends and fellow artists. His *Diary of an Artist* (1977) expands on the material of his first book of memoirs. A biography is Lloyd Goodrich, *Raphael Soyer* (1967). On his artistic production see Frank Gettings, *Raphael Soyer: Sixty-five Years of Printmaking* (1982). An obituary is in the *New York Times* (5 Nov. 1987). See also Milton W. Brown's tribute, "He Wore His Heart on His Sleeve," *Artnews* (Feb. 1988).

ABRAHAM A. DAVIDSON

STANWYCK, Barbara (*b.* 16 July 1907 in Brooklyn, New York; *d.* 20 January 1990 in Santa Monica, California), versatile stage, screen, and television actress who made more than eighty films and is remembered for playing tough, clever women in such movies as *The Lady Eve, Ball of Fire*, and *Double Indemnity.*

Stanwyck was born Ruby Stevens, the youngest of five children of Catherine (McGee) Stevens and Byron Stevens, a bricklayer. Both were children of immigrants. In 1910 Catherine died of a fall; two weeks later Byron Stevens ran away to Panama. Ruby and her brother Malcolm boarded with families who took in orphans. The hardship and loneliness of her early life affected Stevens profoundly. Though they lived in separate homes, she and her brother protected each other. Their father died en route from Panama some time before 1914; in 1915 her brother left her to live with an older sister. In school, Ruby had difficulty making friends and little interest in academics. When she was eight, her sister Mildred, who had supported both children from her earnings as a chorus girl, took Ruby on the road for

Barbara Stanwyck, *c.* 1945. © CORBIS

three summers, whetting her desire to be a dancer. From 1919 to 1921 she boarded with the Harold Cohen family—"the first people," she wrote, "ever to brush my hair, to care how I looked. . . . They even tried to stop me from swearing!"

In 1921, just before her fourteenth birthday, Ruby began supporting herself as a department store wrapper, then as a telephone company clerk. Seven months later she sold patterns and later found a typing job with the Remick Music Company in Tin Pan Alley, the legendary music publishing section of Manhattan. A manager there got her a job at the Strand Roof nightclub, where producer Earl Lindsay taught her to dance in a chorus. She had a bit part in the 1922 *Ziegfeld Follies* and in 1923 danced in both *George White's Scandals* and the Shubert revue *Artists and Models*. On 22 May 1924 Stevens opened in Lindsay's *Keep Kool*. Her skit was picked up in September by the Ziegfeld touring company, with whom she performed, among other numbers, the Ziegfeld "Shadowgraph"—a silhouette striptease. The next year she did another Shubert revue, *Gay Paree* (1925).

Through friends, Ruby Stevens met the playwright Willard Mack, who hired her for a bit part as a chorus girl in his new play. Mack built up Stevens's role, giving her an emotional scene begging for the body of an executed man. He coached her intensively and induced her to change her name to Barbara Stanwyck. On 20 October 1926 she opened in *The Noose* to unanimous praise. During the run, Stanwyck won a supporting role in the silent film *Broadway Nights* (1927), her first picture. On stage in September she portrayed the wife of a drunken vaudevillian in George Watter's *Burlesque,* a performance that the critic Alexander Woollcott called "touching and true."

While playing in *The Noose*, Stanwyck had fallen in love with leading man Rex Cherryman, but Cherryman died unexpectedly, and on 26 August 1928 Stanwyck married the actor-comedian Frank Fay. It was his third marriage; the couple had one adopted child. In August 1929 the couple went to California, where Stanwyck was to play in *The Locked Door* for producer Joseph Schenk. In Hollywood Stanwyck found no one like Mack to instruct her in film acting. *The Locked Door* (United Artists, 1929) proved stilted and theatrical. *Mexicali Rose* (Columbia, 1929), in which she played the title role despite her Brooklyn accent, was worse.

For six months Stanwyck did only screen tests. Seeing his wife grow despondent, Fay persuaded director Frank Capra to view a test in which she played a scene from *The Noose.* Capra signed her to star as a party girl in his *Ladies of Leisure* (Columbia, 1930), and he became the mentor Stanwyck needed. Stanwyck's popularity soared. At Warner Brothers she played a canny socialite in *Illicit* (1931), while *Ten Cents a Dance* (Columbia, 1931) and *Night Nurse* (Warners, 1931) showcased her in spunky, unglamorous roles. Her growing popularity strained her marriage; but when she broke her contract to be with Fay, the studio sued and prevailed. They also raised her salary to $50,000 per picture.

On 30 September 1931 Stanwyck returned to work at Columbia. By the end of 1935, she had starred in fourteen films. At Warners for William Wellman she made Edna Ferber's *So Big* (1932)—her first A picture. In *The Bitter Tea of General Yen* (1933) for Capra at Columbia she was daringly in love with a Chinese warlord (Nils Asther), and at RKO for George Stevens she made a memorable *Annie Oakley* (1935).

As his career declined, Fay became periodically drunk and violent. Stanwyck struggled to preserve the illusion of a contented household, and in April 1933 she costarred with Fay in *Tattle Tales,* a revue that traveled to New York City in June. But on New Year's Eve 1935 the couple signed a divorce settlement. The battle for custody of their son—whose relations with both were distant—was protracted and bitter.

The following year friends introduced Stanwyck to actor Robert Taylor. Their romance became so prominent that under studio pressure the couple married, on 14 May 1939. They had no children. After working with Taylor in her first broadcast drama, Stanwyck appeared regularly on the *Lux Radio Theatre*. Her sixteen roles from 1936 to 1943 included performances in *Main Street* and *Wuthering Heights*.

In order to maintain the momentum of her career, Stanwyck searched so diligently for the right scripts that studios put her on suspension for being "too picky." Nevertheless, in her thirties she played her most memorable parts. As *Stella Dallas* (Samuel Goldwyn, 1937) she received her first Academy Award nomination; in *Remember the Night* (Paramount, 1940) for Mitchell Leisen she played a diamond thief; in Preston Sturges's *The Lady Eve* (Paramount, 1941) she practiced her wiles on Henry Fonda, getting her second Academy Award nomination; and in *Ball of Fire* (Samuel Goldwyn, 1942) she was a stripper in a houseful of professors. Other distinguished films included Cecil B. DeMille's *Union Pacific* (Paramount, 1939), Rouben Mamoulian's *Golden Boy* (Columbia, 1939), and Capra's *Meet John Doe* (Warners, 1941). The role usually considered Stanwyck's best came in 1944 when at Paramount she played the predatory Phyllis Dietrichson, who seduces Fred MacMurray into murdering her husband in *Double Indemnity*. It won her a third Academy Award nomination. That same year the Internal Revenue Service proclaimed her the highest-paid woman in the United States.

Her marriage with Taylor was less successful. Stanwyck found his neglect, his attention to other actresses, and his absences difficult to bear. He was away in the U.S. Navy from 1943 to 1945, and he made films in London in 1949 and in Rome in 1950. She followed him to Rome but on their return granted him a divorce on 21 February 1951. That same year she became permanently estranged from her son.

In May 1947 Taylor had begun testifying to the House Un-American Activities Committee, naming colleagues he believed tainted by communism. Stanwyck also embraced anticommunist sentiments but nevertheless worked with artists who were under suspicion. In 1952 she made *Clash by Night* (RKO), Clifford Odets's proletarian drama of adultery, directed by the unofficially blacklisted Fritz Lang.

After *Double Indemnity,* despite cutbacks in studio production, Stanwyck made at least two pictures a year until 1958. A few—like *Clash by Night* and Lewis Milestone's *The Strange Love of Martha Ivers* (Paramount, 1946)—were memorable. *Sorry, Wrong Number* (Paramount, 1948) brought her a fourth Academy Award nomination. After 1957 Stanwyck had no film offers until 1962, when she played the lesbian madam of a bordello in Edward Dmytryk's *Walk on the Wild Side* (Columbia). She made only two more theatrical films, including *Roustabout* (Paramount, 1964), in which she hired Elvis Presley to work in her carnival.

As film offers grew scarce, Stanwyck turned to television. On 10 October 1956 she debuted in her first television drama, a half-hour Western for *Ford Theatre*. She hoped to develop a series based on the lives of frontier women, and in 1958 and 1959 she filmed four episodes of *Zane Grey Theatre*. During the following two years she made the *Barbara Stanwyck Show,* starring in thirty-two half-hour dramas. She won the Emmy for outstanding actress in a series in May 1961.

From 1961 to 1964 she made four episodes of *Wagon Train* and one of *Rawhide*, and she portrayed a missing-persons detective in *The Untouchables*. Then, from 1965 to 1969, she played the matriarch of a family of ranchers in *The Big Valley*. The series renewed her fame; in 1966 she received both an Emmy and the Screen Actors Guild Award. In 1967 and 1968 she was named *Photoplay's* "Most Popular Female Star."

At sixty-seven, suffering from emphysema, she retreated into a carefully guarded private life. In 1982 she emerged to receive an honorary Oscar, and in the following year she played the passionate matriarch in David Wolper's television miniseries *The Thorn Birds*. Despite her difficulty breathing, her performance was among the best of her career and brought her a third Emmy.

In addition to emphysema, Stanwyck now suffered vision loss and spinal deterioration, but she continued to perform and showed up to accept the American Film Institute's Lifetime Achievement Award in 1986. She was hospitalized with pneumonia in 1988 and after recurrent illness died of congestive heart failure complicated by emphysema. Her ashes were scattered over Lone Pine in the California Sierras, where she had filmed on location.

In eighty-four theatrical films and three television series, Barbara Stanwyck portrayed a range of complex women who combined independence with emotional vulnerability. Her forceful, unmannered performances captured these characters convincingly. The same simplicity made her antic comedies disarming and oddly believable. Devoted to her profession, she showed to colleagues—actors and stage crews alike—an understanding and emotional support that sometimes eluded her in personal relationships. Performers with whom she worked, including William Holden, Robert Wagner, and her husband Robert Taylor, acknowledged their debt to her. Colorful and outspoken, she did not cultivate the mystique of other stars but presented herself as a working actress, often performing her own stunts. She was celebrated for her professionalism—always on time, always secure in her lines, always costumed, made up, and ready to work. As one director commented, "There is nothing the least bit phony about her ever. Because she isn't capable of it." Critic David Shipman observed, "She never gave a bad performance—something one feels she would like as an epitaph."

★

The Academy of Motion Picture Arts and Sciences, Beverly Hills, California, maintains an extensive file on Stanwyck. Axel Madsen, *Stanwyck: A Biography* (1994), offers the fullest account of her life and career. Ella Smith's generously illustrated *Starring Miss Barbara Stanwyck,* 2d ed. (1985), is an appreciative survey that quotes extensively from critics and coworkers. Jane Ellen Wayne, *Stanwyck* (1985), adds some sensational scenes to material derived from Al DiOrio's durable *Barbara Stanwyck* (1983). Jerry Vermilye, *Barbara Stanwyck* (1975), in the Pyramid Illustrated History of the Movies, is a concise, pocket-size tour of Stanwyck's life and work. Homer Dickens, *The Films of Barbara Stanwyck* (1984), offers an overview of each film, with cast and credits, plot synopsis, critical response, and notes. There are good short accounts of Stanwyck in David Thomson, *Biographical Dictionary of Film,* 3d ed. (1994), and David Shipman, *The Great Movie Stars: The Golden Years* (1970). Stephen Harvey assessed Stanwyck's movies in *Film Comment* (Mar.–Apr. 1981). Obituaries are in the *Los Angeles Times* (21 Jan. 1990), *New York Times* (22 Jan. 1990), and *Daily Variety* (24 Jan. 1990). Turner Network Television presented a compilation retrospective, "Barbara Stanwyck: Fire and Desire," on 15 April 1992.

ALAN BUSTER

STEBER, Eleanor (*b.* 17 July 1914 in Wheeling, West Virginia; *d.* 3 October 1990 in Langhorne, Pennsylvania), opera singer who was a leading soprano with the Metropolitan Opera Company during the 1940s and 1950s.

Steber was the eldest of the three children of William Charles Steber, a banker, and Ida Nolte Steber, a dramatic soprano who sang at local churches and civic functions, played the organ, and taught piano. Steber spent the first three years of her life above her grandparents' general store in Wheeling. When she was four, the family moved to their own home in Warwood, West Virginia. Steber's mother, her first singing teacher, often sang along with the recordings of Rosa Ponselle as she worked around the house. Also at age four Steber made her musical debut at Trinity Lutheran Church, singing "Buttercups and Daisies." She began piano lessons at age six. Her first stage experiences came when she was a student at Warwood High School. She had the lead in the senior class show, *The Spanish Sweetheart,* but it was not a singing role. Her first professional job as a singer was in 1930, as a member of the quartet of the Second Presbyterian Church in Wheeling, where she later became a soloist.

Following graduation from high school in 1931, Steber attended the Idabel Waggoner School of Dramatic Art in Wheeling. She paid for her acting lessons by playing piano background music for recitations of other students. In the graduation production, *The Nursery Maid of Heaven,* Steber played Mother Superior. More than thirty years later, in 1968, she would play Mother Abbess in *The Sound of Music* at the New York City Center.

In 1933 Steber enrolled at the New England Conservatory of Music in Boston, as a piano major with a singing minor. After the first year, at the urging of her voice teacher, William L. Whitney, she changed her major to singing. Whitney helped Steber win a full scholarship and taught her to sing Mozart. Steber attributed her vocal technique, which was considered flawless, to the training of Whitney, who taught her the bel canto method and how to handle her voice. When Whitney was asked how he had guided Steber, he replied, "It was all there to begin with. I just didn't meddle."

While at the New England Conservatory, Steber worked at different jobs to improve her financial situation. She was a soloist with the Barnstormers, a group that performed short classical works for high schools around Boston; she sang in the choir of the Union Congregational Church in Boston; and she was a soloist at the Eliott Church in Newton, Massachusetts. Steber was hired by the Works Progress Administration Choral Symphony at $19 a week to sing the soprano solos in everything they performed. She sang in two dozen different oratorios and called the job a "priceless experience." In 1936, during her third year at the New England Conservatory, Steber made her opera debut, singing the role of Senta in Richard Wagner's *Der fliegende Hollander,* produced by the WPA Opera Project. She also got a regular job as a featured singer on the *I. J. Fox Fur Trappers Radio Show,* performing light classics and popular songs. She even appeared as a super (extra) in *Die Meistersinger* when the Metropolitan Opera touring company came to Boston.

Eleanor Steber models an outfit for a fashion photo, 1944. UPI/CORBIS-BETTMANN

Steber graduated from the New England Conservatory in 1938. That same year she sang "Pace, pace, mio Dio," an aria from *La forza del destino,* with the Boston Pops Orchestra. In September 1938 she married Edwin L. Bilby, a fellow voice student; they had no children and were divorced in 1954. Meanwhile, Whitney advised Steber that if she wanted to break into opera, she should relocate to New York City and find a first-class vocal coach. In New York, Steber studied with Paul Althouse, formerly a Wagnerian tenor at the Metropolitan Opera. She got a job as soprano soloist in a quartet at the Methodist-Episcopal Church of Saint Paul and Saint Andrew, to which she would return to sing throughout her life. Steber performed on the first broadcast of the *Metropolitan Opera Auditions of the Air* in 1939, singing "Ah, fors e lui" from Verdi's *La Traviata.* She won the finals in 1940 and got a check for $1,000, a silver plaque, and, best of all, a contract with the Metropolitan Opera. Following this success, Steber went on her first concert tour. On 7 December 1940 she made her debut at the Met, singing Sophie in Richard Strauss's *Der Rosenkavalier.* During her first season at the Met, in addition to Sophie she sang Micaela in *Carmen* and, in her words, "a whole slew of Rhine Maidens, Flower Maidens, and Forest Birds." That year she also sang Marguerite in *Faust* in Havana, and was soprano soloist in Mozart's *Requiem* with the New York Philharmonic. On 7 December 1941 Steber was scheduled to make her first radio appearance on the *Coca-Cola Hour,* but the broadcast was preempted because of the bombing of Pearl Harbor.

Steber's career turned a corner during her third season at the Met when Bruno Walter decided to do Mozart's *Le nozze di Figaro* with Ezio Pinza as Figaro and Steber as the Countess. Walter was astounded that an American-trained singer could perform Mozart so well. During the twenty-six years of her association with the Met, Steber sang 404 performances in thirty-three different roles. She was particularly admired for her Mozart and Strauss roles. A highlight during her years at the Met came in 1952, when she sang her first Desdemona in Verdi's *Otello* for the Saturday matinee broadcast performance and that evening sang Fiordiligi in Mozart's *Così fan tutte.*

During her years at the Met, Steber developed and premiered roles for four operas. The first was as Constanza in Mozart's *Die Entführung aus dem Serail,* in 1946; in 1955 she sang Arabella in Richard Strauss's opera of the same name. A classic example of Steber's vocal stamina and ability as a quick learner led to her third premiere role in 1958, when she was asked to learn the role of Vanessa in Samuel

Barber's opera of the same name—only a month before the world premiere. Steber learned the role while singing her regularly scheduled appearances as Donna Anna in the Met's new production of Mozart's *Don Giovanni.* Her fourth premiere role was as Marie in Alban Berg's *Wozzeck* in 1959.

When Steber was removed from the Metropolitan Opera roster in 1962 by manager Rudolph Bing, she was "knocked for a loop," having been totally unprepared for such an abrupt end to her career at the Met. Steber did return to the Met in 1966 to substitute for the ailing Dorothy Kirsten, in the role of Minnie in Giacomo Puccini's *La fanciulla del West.* She had not sung the role in ten years and had less than two days to prepare. When she made her entrance, guns blazing, the audience stood and shouted her name, forcing the orchestra to stop playing. Steber wrote in her autobiography, "It was the greatest single moment of my life." Her final appearance at the Metropolitan Opera was during the gala celebration at the closing of the old opera house in 1966; she sang in the quintet from *Vanessa.*

In addition to performing at the Metropolitan, Steber, who developed a repertoire of fifty-six roles in four languages, sang with a number of other opera companies, both in the United States and in Europe. In 1953 she opened the Bayreuth Festival, singing Elsa in Wagner's *Lohengrin.* She was the first American to sing the role there since Lillian Nordica in 1894.

Steber also sang on the radio and television versions of *The Voice of Firestone* for ten years. She championed American composers, and throughout her career she included a group of American songs in virtually every concert she gave. In 1946 she commissioned Samuel Barber to set the words of James Agee's poem "Knoxville, Summer of 1915" to music. The Boston Symphony Orchestra gave the world premiere of this work in 1948, with Steber singing.

In 1956 Steber began a four-month concert tour of seventeen Middle Eastern and Far Eastern countries as part of the U.S. State Department's cultural exchange program. She gave thirty-three formal concerts and traveled more than 50,000 miles. In Saigon, Vietnam, she met an American military officer, Gordon G. Andrews; they were married on 29 December 1957. In 1959 Steber and Andrews incorporated ST/AND Records. The company recorded Steber as well as the work of young instrumentalists and singers. Her recording *Eleanor Steber at Carnegie Hall* was named the best vocal recording of the year (1958) by the *New York Herald Tribune.* However, the company went bankrupt in 1962. Steber and Andrews were divorced in 1966.

In 1973 Steber sang three "comeback" concerts at Alice Tully Hall in New York City. The concerts were an artistic success, but Steber was disappointed that only a few colleagues from the Met attended and that the media coverage was so poor. That fall she gave another concert, commonly known as the Black Towel Concert, at the Continental Baths, a gay men's health club in the Ansonia Hotel. Steber entered in black towels draped over a flowing peach gown. The event was a media sensation.

In addition to concert work, Steber made over a hundred albums, including five complete operas. She also taught voice. In 1963 she became head of the Vocal Department of the Cleveland Institute of Music, where she remained until 1972. She was artist in residence at the Temple University Music Festival (1967–1972), and in 1971 she began teaching at the Juilliard School. In the 1980s she taught at the Conservatory of Music of Brooklyn College. Steber gave master classes in voice in many different venues until the year of her death. In 1975 she established the Eleanor Steber Foundation to help young singers.

Steber died of congestive heart failure and is buried in Greenwood Cemetery in Wheeling. In her autobiography she wrote: "For me, singing is life! When I am singing, then I am a unified spirit."

★

A primary source of information on Steber is her autobiography, written with Marcia Sloat, *Eleanor Steber: An Autobiography* (1992). See also Judith Buffington et al., *He Loves Me When I Sing: Remembering Eleanor Steber* (1993), a series of tributes by the famous and not-so-famous. Interviews include "The NATS Bulletin Interviews Eleanor Steber," *NATS Bulletin* (1984): 5–7, and Jeannie Williams and Richard Shapp, "A Singers' Roundtable," *Opera Quarterly* (1986): 61–76. See also James Lyons, "Versatility as Well as Dependability Characterizes Eleanor Steber's Career," *Musical America* (Dec. 1952); Emily Coleman, "Non-Prima-Donnaish Prima Donna," *New York Times Magazine* (22 Feb. 1959); Allen Hughes, "Eleanor Steber," *Musical America* (Feb. 1960); Bert Wechsler, "An Anniversary for Eleanor Steber," *Music Journal* 38 (Nov./Dec. 1980); Bruce A. Beatie and Rita V. Beatie, "Eleanor Steber: A Diva in Exile, 1963–1984," *Opera Journal* (1984): 9–18; and Leslie Rubinstein, "Improper Diva," *Opera News* (Oct. 1990). Obituaries are in the *Boston Globe* and the *New York Times* (both 4 Oct. 1990) and in the *Chicago Tribune* (5 Oct. 1990).

MARCIA B. DINNEEN

STEINER, Ralph (*b.* 8 February 1899 in Cleveland, Ohio; *d.* 13 July 1986 in Hanover, New Hampshire), photographer, filmmaker, author, and teacher.

The son of an insurance agent and his wife, both Czech-Jewish immigrants, Steiner grew up in Cleveland, becoming interested in photography in his early teens. By the time he entered Dartmouth College in 1917, he was already planning on pursuing a professional career as a photographer; but finding the atmosphere in Hanover, New Hampshire, decidedly cool to his impressionist/postimpressionist sensibilities, he quickly realized that the most logical major, art, would not be practical. In fact, he got a D grade in the only formal art course he ever took there. Instead, he developed an informal relationship with one "Doc" Griggs, a biology professor and enthusiastic amateur photographer, and spent his four years at college shooting scenes of campus life and nature subsequently published in a volume entitled *Dartmouth* (1922), most of which Steiner later described as "arty beyond belief."

After graduation in 1921, Steiner moved to New York City and enrolled in the school of photography established by the noted "Pictorialist" Clarence White, whose emphasis on design and composition he felt handicapped more than it advanced his development. Initially, however, it was precisely this grounding in photographic technique that commended his work to editors and art directors, enabling him to establish a thriving career as a commercial and editorial photographer by the middle of the decade. But in 1927, as he recalled in his autobiography, he was "pole-axed" on first viewing the work of fellow photographer Paul Strand. "I had never seen prints so rich—with such real texture—and so glorious in tonal value. . . . I was embarrassed by not being able to respond adequately. . . . I realized that I was not yet a craftsman and was inspired by the excellence of Strand's work to do an extensive something about my technique." Coming in 1927, when Steiner was already an established commercial and editorial photographer, this comment was typical of a modesty and a lack of pretension not ordinarily associated with a profession dominated for the most part by such strong-willed and self-certain types as Alfred Stieglitz and Richard Avedon.

The evidence of Strand's influence was already apparent in the well-reviewed exhibition Steiner mounted at the Pynson Gallery in New York City, but it was a 1930 summer fellowship at the Yaddo Colony in Saratoga Springs, New York, that finally freed Steiner from the "straitjacket" of Pictorialism, resulting in some of his most memorable work, including, he later recalled, perhaps the most famous of all his prints. "Late one afternoon, I saw the sun about to go down over the horizon, casting the shadow of a chair on a porch wall. No one . . . ever set a huge, cumbersome 8 x 10 camera and snapped the shutter as fast as I did. Ten seconds later the shadow was gone from the wall." But photography critic and historian John Szarkowski, writing in 1973, suggests Steiner's break with the Pictorialist tradition was perhaps less abrupt than implied by this remembrance. The photograph in question, *American Rural Baroque,* was, Szarkowski conceded, indisputably modern in spirit, almost a "cubist projection" owing to the way the clapboard siding broke the shadow of the wickerwork rocker into overlapping sections in a comical (Saul) "Steinbergian" distortion of reality, and was photographed with a demonstrably Strand-influenced emphasis on tone and texture. But he also noted that this effect was achieved only because the back of the rocker was in contact with the wall and suggested that Steiner might very well have composed the shot by moving the chair, since "it surely could not rock in its present position." In a review of a Steiner retrospective at New York City's Witkin Gallery in 1974, critic Gene Thornton elaborated upon this notion of Steiner as a transitional rather than revolutionary figure by observing that while he "abandoned the soft-focus formalities and romantic subject matter of Pictorialism for the pin-sharp focus and everyday subject matter of Modern Photography, he retained throughout the thirties the formal concerns and high seriousness of Pictorialism."

In the late 1920s and early 1930s, Steiner was part of the radical artistic circle around Harold Clurman and Lee Strasberg that would evolve into the Group Theater. In that circle, he would later claim, he received the education he had failed to get at Dartmouth and his mind and imagination were opened to new possibilities of expression, particularly in the medium of film. In 1929 he made the pioneering "art" film *H_2O*, a prize-winning study of water and sunlight, with the assistance of the composer Aaron Copland, who also scored the work. In 1936 he collaborated with Strand and scriptwriter Pare Lorentz on the seminal documentary film *The Plow That Broke the Plains,* and in 1939 with Willard Van Dyke and Copland on another documentary, *The City*, which ran for two years to great acclaim at the New York World's Fair. Reevaluating *H_2O* fifty years later, the critic Scott Hammen praised the film's "pure abstract beauty," citing Steiner's recruitment of Copland to help edit the final cut as evidence "that he was aware of how close the quality of imagery came to the effect of music and how a visual impression, when intense enough, can almost be an aural one."

Steiner's effort to present film as a "visual adjunct" to music, with performance joined to imagery, Hammen suggests, might have become an accepted art form long before MTV but for the dominance of Hollywood and its determined exclusion of all nonnarrative influences. Even so, Steiner would prove himself sufficiently adept at making narrative films, first with *The Plow That Broke the Plains* and subsequently with *The City* (which *Time* called a million-dollar film made for $50,000) to attract the notice of MGM's Louis B. Mayer, who summoned him to Hollywood upon his discharge from the army in 1945. His years there, however, left him with a profound distaste for meddlesome studio executives and industry politics. "What I wanted," he wrote of his studio career, "was not money so much as to make films on locations—against real backgrounds about real life situations."

Having made neither a great deal of money nor the sort of films he wanted, Steiner returned east five years later only to find himself almost forgotten as a photographer. Luckily, an old admirer of his, Walker Evans, then an editor at *Fortune,* came to his assistance, hiring him to do monthly portraits of heads of corporations, an assignment he carried out with the sense of humor—the CEO of a Geiger counter company, for example, photographed in his three-piece suit seated on a prospector's mule in the middle of the Mojave Desert—that was always a hallmark of his commercial work. He remained active as a teacher, founding the Photographer's Center in New York City in 1962 as a group facility for aspiring young photographers, but otherwise receded from view as a practitioner of the art. From about 1950 to the mid-1970s, in fact, he led what he called "an intermittent creative life: working for a few years at earning money by doing advertising photography; then when my digestion and brains gave out, I'd either make still photographs or films for myself. When the money gave out, I'd go back to advertising." In 1974 the Witkin Gallery retrospective revived interest in him and there followed two well-received published collections of his work, *A Point of View* (1979) and *In Pursuit of Clouds* (1985), as well as an anthology of photographs that he selected and arranged as an antidote to what he considered the tendency of modern photographers to dwell on ugliness, violence, and decay. A series of exhibitions of his work, both past and contemporaneous, was capped in 1986 by "Ralph Steiner—Seven Decades" at the International Photography Center in New York City and, according to the exhibit's curator, Ann Hoy, by long-deserved recognition as "a key figure in winning vanguard status for photography . . . and the last of the American Modernist Photographers."

Judging him solely on the basis of his artistic output, Thornton thought Steiner "a good, though to be perfectly frank not great photographer," and compared to such brilliant contemporaries as Strand, Kertész, the Westons, Adams, and Cartier-Bresson, this may not be an unfair assessment. Indeed, Steiner himself admitted that his outlook may well have been "cramped by the orthodoxies of my day." Even so, one cannot help but be struck by the quiet integrity with which he pursued his craft and the example he set for younger photographers and filmmakers. A writer in *American Photographer* summed up the man shortly before his death: "At 87, Ralph Steiner is old enough to know what he thinks and intelligent enough to change his mind. . . . Whimsical but never casual, chronically allergic to pretension, hero worship and borrowed opinion, Steiner . . . encourages photographers to think more about what they say and less about how they say it." If his legacy is not so striking as an Ansel Adams *Moonrise,* it is no less worthy of celebration.

Steiner was married three times, the last in 1960 to Caroline Neilson. He died of cancer at Mary Hitchcock Hospital in Hanover, New Hampshire, the site of his alma mater, Dartmouth College, where he had the previous year served as a guest curator of an exhibition of his work. He was survived by a daughter, Antonia.

★

Ralph Steiner, *A Point of View* (1978), is, like the man, an understated, often amusing autobiographical memoir, with a helpful introduction by his longtime friend and collaborator Willard Van Dyke. See also the preface by Jacqueline Bass, director of the Hood Museum, to the collection of photographs assembled by Steiner and his wife Caroline and entitled *In Spite of Everything, Yes* (1986), which places Steiner's work as a still photographer in historical context. For appreciations of his pioneering work as a filmmaker, see Joel Zuker, *Ralph Steiner* (1978), and Chuck Kleinhaus, "Ralph Steiner," in Jan-Christopher Horak, *Lovers of Cinema* (1995). Biographical and critical material about Steiner may be found in the *New York Times* (5 Jan. 1930), a review of his Pynson Gallery show; M. F. Agha, "Ralph Steiner," *Creative Art* 10 (Jan. 1934): 34–35; *New York Times* (16 Sept. 1962), on the foundation of the Photographer's Center; John Szarkowski, *Looking at Photographs* (1973), a thoughtful, slightly revisionist analysis of Steiner's *American Rural Baroque*; *New York Times* (13 Oct. 1974), a respectful but only mildly appreciative assessment of Steiner's photographic work by Gene Thornton; Scott Hammen, "Ralph Steiner's H_2O: Simple Significance, Abstract Beauty," *Afterimage* 7 (summer 1979): 10–11, a fiftieth-anniversary reappraisal of Steiner's early film work; *American Photographer* 17 (June 1986): 30–32, a laudatory review of *In Pursuit of Clouds* and a tribute to his long career by Vicki Goldberg; and *American Photographer* (Aug. 1986): 56–63, a portfolio of ten of Steiner's favorite photographs, with his comments on each. An obituary is in the *New York Times* (14 July 1986).

RICHARD B. CALHOUN

STELOFF, (Ida) Frances (*b.* 31 December 1887 in Saratoga Springs, New York; *d.* 15 April 1989 in New York City), independent bookseller and promoter of avant-garde literature.

Steloff was one of four children of Russian immigrants, Gustav Stolov (who later changed his name to Simon Steloff), a dry-goods peddler and itinerant rabbi, and Tobe Metzner, a homemaker who died when Steloff was three and a half. Growing up in Saratoga Springs, a popular pleasure spot for the well-to-do in upstate New York, Steloff had an acute sense of the disparity between her own poverty and the wealth of those frequenting the town's resorts. To help support the family she sold flowers to guests at the large hotels. At one of these hotels she was befriended by a couple who offered to raise and educate her in Boston. An uncomfortable family situation—created by a tense relationship with her stepmother and her father's dire financial circumstances—led to Steloff's moving with this cou-

Frances Steloff at age ninety-eight in her New York City apartment, 1986. AP/WIDE WORLD PHOTOS

ple in July 1900, at the age of twelve, to Roxbury, Massachusetts, and two years later to Wakefield, a town north of Boston. The couple's intentions, however, were not what they initially seemed. Steloff became a virtual servant in their household and acquired formal schooling only through the seventh grade, although she later completed courses in English grammar and commercial math at Roxbury Evening High School. In 1907, at the age of nineteen, she moved to Brooklyn, New York, and found work at Loeser's department store selling corsets. She was later transferred to the book and magazine departments.

After leaving Loeser's, Steloff worked for twelve years at several bookstores in New York City—including Brentano's, Schulte's, and McDevitt-Wilson's—with an intervening two-year stint as assistant to a book buyer for S. Kahn and Son in Washington, D.C. Through her work at these bookshops she learned to locate out-of-print works and identify first editions—skills that proved valuable when she later had her own bookshop. She would purchase unwanted stock from other bookstores, hold on to it (sometimes for decades), and end up with rare first editions of works later regarded as classics.

On New Year's Day, 1920, with $100 in cash and a $100 Liberty Bond, Steloff opened Gotham Book & Art at 128 West Forty-fifth Street in New York City. Its original stock consisted of approximately 100 books drawn from Steloff's personal collection. This shop, in the heart of Manhattan's theater district, catered to local theater people and, after Steloff visited California in 1922, to Hollywood people, for whom she filled orders by mail.

On 17 June 1923 Steloff married David Moss, her partner in Gotham Book & Art. On their four-week honeymoon and book-buying trip they visited London, Leipzig, Vienna, and Paris. In Paris, Steloff met Sylvia Beach, the proprietor of the bookstore Shakespeare and Company and the publisher of James Joyce's *Ulysses.* Shortly after their return to America, Steloff and Moss relocated the shop to 51 West Forty-seventh Street. It was rechristened the Gotham Book Mart and acquired a wrought-iron sign, designed by the cartoonist John Held, Jr., depicting three fishermen in a boat above the words WISE MEN FISH HERE.

In this new location Steloff's shop became a meeting place for the avant-garde. Artists, writers, and intellectuals, including H. L. Mencken, Theodore Dreiser, Marianne Moore, and Henry Miller, gravitated to the place. What drew such an eminent group? Arguably it was Steloff's belief in the value, both economic and literary, of the written word, as well as her support of writers in need. She stocked the works of unproved artists and the little magazines that published their writing, and she loaned money to unrecognized, financially straitened artists. For example, she cosigned a $1,000 loan for Martha Graham that enabled the dancer to make her concert debut in 1926; she loaned $200 to John Dos Passos so he could renew an insurance policy; she made space on the shop's bulletin board for Henry Miller to post appeals for money. This generosity, however, was always accompanied by a shrewd business sense. Steloff earned a reputation among her employees as a demanding and at times intransigent boss. She would find a position in the shop for a writer in need of income—the poets Allen Ginsberg and LeRoi Jones (later known as Amiri Baraka) and the playwright Tennessee Williams all worked at the Gotham at various times—but if an employee did not work out (and rumor has it that Williams lasted less than a day), she would fire him or her immediately.

From the late 1920s through the mid-1930s, Steloff's belief and investment in the avant-garde led to numerous run-ins with the law, thanks to the unflagging efforts of the New York Society for the Suppression of Vice to root out obscenity. In 1928 hundreds of books, including Joyce's *Ulysses,* were seized by a representative of this censorship organization; Moss pleaded guilty to the charges of possessing and selling obscene literature and was fined $250. (To contravene the U.S. ban on importation of Joyce's book, Steloff received pamphlet-sized sections of *Ulysses* from Paris and rebound them herself.) Following the publication in 1930 of the Gotham Book Mart's catalog, which was deemed essential to maintaining the shop's considerable mail-order business, Steloff was summoned to appear before a grand jury on charges of possessing obscene literature; the charges were dismissed. She divorced her husband in 1930; they had no children. In 1936 Steloff was again accused of selling obscene literature—this time for carrying the French writer André Gide's autobiography *If It Die;* the judge, however, determined the book was not obscene. Steloff believed that people should not be told what to read (and, presumably, that she should not be told what to sell).

In 1945 Steloff bought a brownstone at 41 West Forty-seventh Street from Columbia University for $65,000, and the following year moved the Gotham Book Mart to that location. It was there, in 1947, that the James Joyce Society was founded. In 1967 Steloff sold the business to Andreas Brown, a San Diego book appraiser. After her retirement she continued to live in an apartment above the shop and to help out there every day until shortly before her death.

Steloff died of pneumonia, at the age of 101, at the Mount Sinai Medical Center in New York City. She was buried in Saratoga Springs, and a memorial service, held in New York City several weeks after her death, was attended by numerous literati and other artists, all wanting to pay her their respects.

★

A special Gotham Book Mart issue of the *Journal of Modern Literature* 4 (Apr. 1975) contains an introduction by Kathleen Morgan, "Frances Steloff and the Gotham Book Mart," and "In Touch with Genius," Steloff's reminiscences of the Gotham Book Mart and of the many literary personalities with whom she came in contact. Steloff is the lead entry in Lynn Gilbert and Gaylen Moore's *Particular Passions: Talks with Women Who Have Shaped Our Times* (1981), although the nine pages are largely culled from information presented more fully in "In Touch with Genius." Biographies of Steloff include William G. Rogers, *Wise Men Fish Here: The Story of Frances Steloff and the Gotham Book Mart* (1965; repr. 1994); and Herta Hilscher-Wittgenstein, *The Ineffable Frances Steloff: A Photographic Visit* (1976), with comments by Anaïs Nin and Henry Miller. An obituary is in the *New York Times* (16 Apr. 1989). In 1987 Deborah Dickson made the documentary film *Frances Steloff: Memoirs of a Bookseller,* which was nominated for an Academy Award.

INGRID STERNER

STEWART, Leroy Elliott ("Slam") (*b.* 21 September 1914 in Englewood, New Jersey; *d.* 9 December 1987 in Binghamton, New York), jazz bassist who pioneered the technique of humming in unison with solos on string bass.

Stewart was the son of Elliott Edward Stewart and Mary (Harris) Stewart. In childhood he first played violin then switched to the bass. He played with Sonny Marshall and other local groups and spent 1934 to 1935 studying at the Boston Conservatory of Music. In Boston he heard jazz violinist Ray Perry sing an octave below his solo on the violin. Stewart adapted the technique to the bass; while he played a solo with his bow on the strings of his bass, he simultaneously sang one octave higher. The sound, fuller than that of Perry on the violin, soon attracted attention. When not using the bow, Stewart often soloed by slapping the strings. The sound created was a "slam" effect, earning him his nickname from New York City jazz musicians with whom he began playing gigs in 1935. From 1936 to 1937 he played with the Peanuts Holland band in Buffalo, New York, after which he returned to New York City.

"Slam" Stewart. METRONOME COLLECTION/ARCHIVE PHOTOS

In 1937 Stewart met another new arrival at a nightclub in Harlem, the guitar- and vibraphone-playing singer Bulee ("Slim") Gaillard, and together they formed a quartet, Slim and Slam. Backed by piano and drums (later joined by a tenor saxophonist), the two men played and sang rhythmic jazz and novelty tunes, mostly of their own composition. Their first recorded number, in early 1938, became an immediate hit, "Flat Foot Floogie (with a Floy Floy)." Built on a simple riff pattern, it epitomized the small-band jazz found in the clubs on Fifty-second Street (also known as "Swing Street") and became an identifying tune of the Swing Era; a copy of the record was buried with a John Philip Sousa march in a time capsule at the 1939 New York's World's Fair. On this and seventeen other records made by the group in 1938, Stewart played brilliant bass solos with and without his unison singing. The combo broke up early in 1939, with Slam joining the Spirits of Rhythm and Slim leading his own Flat Foot Floogie Boys, which included Slam in gigs and on several recordings until 1942, when Slim was drafted into the U.S. Army. Slim and Slam also performed in the 1941 motion picture *Hellzapoppin'*.

Late in 1940 Stewart formed his own trio to play at Kelly's Stables in New York. He remained on the Fifty-second Street scene for several years, usually at the Three Deuces, whose owner managed him. He appeared in the 1943 film *Stormy Weather* and was part of Art Tatum's trio during 1943 and 1944. After brief periods with the Johnny Guarnieri and Tiny Grimes combos, he spent most of 1945 with the Benny Goodman Sextet and was featured on its recording of "Gotta Be This or That." He played with Goodman in the Broadway show *The Seven Lively Arts* and in 1945 recorded duets with tenor saxophonist Don Byas. Stewart then resumed his own trio with Erroll Garner on the piano, recording again with Tatum in 1946 and the early 1950s. His trio appeared in the 1947 movie *Boy! What a Girl,* and the next year Stewart toured France with Garner.

Stewart's versatility was shared with the xylophonist-vibraphonist Red Norvo and the pianist Teddy Wilson, and during 1944 and 1945 they recorded and performed not only with the Goodman Sextet but also in their own sessions with the new generation of bebop players. During one of these sessions with trumpeter Dizzy Gillespie and alto saxophonist Charlie Parker, Stewart played exceptional solos on "Slam Slam Blues." He also recorded with Gillespie groups.

During the 1950s and 1960s Stewart played with Roy Eldridge, Beryl Booker, and Rose Murphy, including European and Australian tours. On 11 January 1969 Stewart married Claire Louise Wood; they had two children. Also in 1969, he performed classical music with the Lincoln String Quartet, and two years later he began teaching at the State University of New York at Binghamton. He performed with Goodman from 1973 to 1975 and later with guitarist Bucky Pizzarelli. He died of congestive heart failure at his home in Binghamton.

Short and suave, with a thin mustache and (in later life) goatee, Stewart was thought of as cool and steady, and he played with a quiet, wry humor. By his use of the bow and unison humming, Stewart elevated the string bass to an unprecedented level as a solo instrument in jazz even before Jimmy Blanton, who is usually accorded the honor. He remained a favorite bass accompanist for jazz musicians throughout his career.

★

No biography exists of Stewart. His activities in New York are covered in Arnold Shaw, *The Street That Never Slept* (1971), and certain aspects of his career in Gunther Schuller, *The Swing Era* (1989). Representative recordings are preserved in Columbia's *Slim and Slam: The Groove Juice Special,* which covers the years 1938–1942 and includes "Flat Foot Floogie"; and in Sunbeam's *Benny Goodman on V-Disc,* vol. 1, an anthology with the original Columbia recording of "Gotta Be This or That." Also consult Time-Life's *Giants of Jazz: Art Tatum,* for the Tatum Trio sessions in 1944; Time-Life's *Red Norvo,* for the Norvo-Goodman-Gillespie-Parker sessions in 1945; Atlantic's *The Commodore Years: Town Hall Jazz Concert 1945,* for Stewart's concert performances with Norvo, Wilson, and Byas; and Stash's *The Slam Stewart Memorial Album,* for the Bucky Pizzarelli sessions in 1978. An obituary is in the *New York Times,* (11 Dec. 1987). Oral history materials are located at Yale University and the Jazz Oral History Project, Rutgers University.

CLARK G. REYNOLDS

STOESSEL, Walter John, Jr. (*b.* 24 January 1920 in Manhattan, Kansas; *d.* 9 December 1986 in Washington, D.C.), U.S. ambassador to Poland, the Soviet Union, and West Germany and high-level State Department diplomat who made an important contribution to the process that established official relations between the United States and the People's Republic of China.

The oldest of three children, Walter Stoessel was the son of Walter John Stoessel, an insurance agent, and Katherine (Haston) Stoessel. During his childhood, the family also lived in Springfield, Massachusetts, and Beverly Hills, California. He attended Wilbraham Academy in Massachusetts and the Taft School in Watertown, Connecticut, and in 1937 he graduated from Beverly Hills High School in California. Although he was offered a contract at this time by a talent scout from Paramount Film Studios, Stoessel, who was often described as having the looks of a movie star, chose to pursue a career in the Foreign Service. In the fall of 1937 he enrolled at Stanford University to study political science and international affairs. He also studied international law at Lausanne University in Switzerland during the 1939–1940 school year, then graduated from Stanford cum laude with a B.A. degree in 1941.

Stoessel completed the Foreign Service examination the same year and entered the service in early 1942, when he received his first posting as vice consul at the U.S. embassy in Caracas, Venezuela. From 1944 to 1946 he was an ensign in the U.S. Navy and spent some of this period studying the Russian language. This was the only time between 1942 and 1982 that he was not in the Foreign Service. In 1946 Stoessel married Mary Ann Ferrandou; they had three daughters. Also in 1946 he reentered the Foreign Service, and between 1947 and 1952 he served in a number of minor positions in Washington, Moscow, and Germany. In 1949 and 1950 he spent a year of intensive study at Columbia University's Russian Institute, expanding his knowledge of Russian.

Stoessel's first major appointment followed in 1952, when he was appointed chief of the Division of Soviet and East European Affairs at the State Department. Among the international gatherings he attended in this capacity was the 1954 Geneva conference on Southeast Asia. In 1956 he became the special assistant to the presidential adviser on foreign affairs, but during the same year he became political officer at the embassy in Paris, where he remained, with special assignments in Geneva and Germany, until 1959. In between he spent a year at Harvard University's Center for International Affairs (1959–1960) and, as the director of the executive secretariat at the State Department, acted as an adviser to Secretary of State Dean Rusk (1961). He returned to Paris as counselor from 1961 to 1963. From 1963 until 1965 Stoessel, who was by now one of the Foreign Service's experts on the Soviet Union, again served at the embassy in Moscow, this time as deputy chief of mission with the rank of minister. Beginning in 1965 he was the deputy assistant secretary of state for Europe, holding this position until he received his first ambassadorship, to Poland, in June 1968.

In Warsaw, Stoessel, by his own account, had the most unnerving experience of his career. In September 1969 President Richard Nixon personally instructed him to reestablish contact with diplomats from Communist China, contacts that had existed intermittently in the Polish capital since 1955 but had been suspended in January 1968. Nixon was eager to normalize relations with the Chinese government, but for international and domestic political reasons wanted to do so in secret. Stoessel, therefore, had to find an informal setting to pass on his government's message. After failing in this endeavor for three months and receiving three impatient cables from Nixon's national security adviser, Henry Kissinger, Stoessel finally saw an opportunity for communication in early December during a fashion show staged in the Warsaw Palace of Culture by the Yugoslav embassy. Toward the end of the show, Stoessel saw the Chinese chargé d'affaires, Lei Yang, get up to leave. Stoessel later described the encounter:

> I saw him get up and I got up. . . . I was right after him. We went out through the cloak room. I said to him in Polish, "I want to talk to you." He looked scared and made for the stairs that went up. He was running up the stairs, and I was right behind him. And then we came out on a big sort of terrace steps. It was dark. It was snowing. It was cold. There was nobody around. I got him. I said, "I was in Washington recently. I saw the President. I want to tell you the President is very serious about talking with your leaders because we want a better relationship with your country. Please report that and I'll be glad to hear from you." (*New York Times,* 24 September 1982)

Walter Stoessel testifies before the U.S. House of Representatives Foreign Affairs Committee, 1982. UPI/CORBIS-BETTMANN

In this way, the two countries began the process that led to Nixon's historic visit to China in 1972. In the meantime Stoessel returned to Washington to take the position of assistant secretary of state for European affairs in 1972. He served in the position for two years, until Nixon nominated him in 1974 to be ambassador to the Soviet Union, a post that had been vacant for a year after Jacob Beam's resignation in early 1973. Before accepting, Stoessel demanded and received assurances that his role would be more meaningful than that of his predecessor, who habitually had been sidelined and embarrassed by Nixon and Kissinger's secret and exclusive dealings with the Kremlin. Stoessel had the respect of both Kissinger and the Soviet leadership, but he too was unable to halt the deterioration of the East-West détente after 1974. Perhaps the most notorious episode from this assignment was the dispute in 1976 over alleged KGB spying on the U.S. embassy with microwaves. Stoessel contracted leukemia during this time, leading later to speculation as to whether radiation from the microwaves was responsible.

Stoessel nevertheless continued to work, and in 1976 President Gerald Ford nominated him to be ambassador to West Germany. Stoessel remained in Bonn for the entire duration of the administration of President Jimmy Carter, a time when relations between the president and German chancellor Helmut Schmidt were strained. Still, Schmidt in his memoirs characterized Stoessel as an excellent representative of the United States.

By all accounts, Stoessel was a traditional diplomat. Not a creator of policies, he was an official for their skillful implementation. He was able, therefore, to take a position in 1981 under President Ronald Reagan, a politician fiercely critical of the détente policies of the 1960s and 1970s that Stoessel himself had helped carry out. Under Reagan, Stoessel employed his vast experience with the foreign policy process as undersecretary of state for political affairs and as deputy secretary of state. In the latter position, Stoessel presided over the State Department as acting secretary of state during the transition from Alexander Haig's tenure to that of George Shultz.

By 1982 Stoessel was the senior member of the Foreign Service, and that fall he retired. During the following years he undertook several special international assignments. He died in Washington, D.C., of the leukemia he had been diagnosed with during the mid-1970s and was buried at Arlington National Cemetery.

Although he conformed to many stereotypes of a diplomat, Stoessel was no ordinary career Foreign Service officer. Besides being a loyal representative of the policies of the administrations he served, he also became a leading government expert on East-West relations. Over the course of his unusually long career, memorable for its numerous prestigious and often politically sensitive assignments, he earned widespread and singular admiration for his professionalism.

★

Stoessel's papers are at Georgetown University in Washington, D.C. On Stoessel's years as ambassador to Poland, the Soviet Union, and West Germany, see Tad Szulc, *The Illusion of Peace* (1978); Raymond Garthoff, *Détente and Confrontation* (1985); and David Mayers, *The Ambassadors and America's Soviet Policy* (1995). Helmut Schmidt's brief appreciation is in *Men and Powers* (1989). Obituaries are in the *New York Times* and *Washington Post* (both 11 Dec. 1986).

RUUD VAN DIJK

STOKES, Anson Phelps, Jr. (*b.* 11 January 1905 in New Haven, Connecticut; *d.* 7 November 1986 in Brookline, Massachusetts), eleventh bishop of the Protestant Episcopal Diocese of Massachusetts (1956–1962).

Stokes was the eldest of three children of the Reverend Dr. Anson Phelps Stokes and Caroline Green (Mitchell) Stokes. His father's career stretched from Yale University and a family foundation that supported educational and social programs to benefit African Americans to a post at the National Cathedral in Washington, D.C., and ended with a three-volume study entitled *Church and State in the United States* (1950). Stokes, born to privilege, inherited his family's sense of civic duty. His great-great-grandfather Thomas helped to found the London Missionary Society in 1793. His grandfather, also Anson Phelps Stokes, made a fortune in banking. Stokes attended St. Paul's School in Concord, New Hampshire, graduating in 1922. After spending a year at Corpus Christi College at Cambridge, England, he enrolled at Yale, where he majored in history and English. At Yale, Stokes was a member of Skull and Bones and Alpha Delta Phi; he also rowed. After graduating in 1927, he stayed on campus, serving as secretary of the Yale University Christian Association, an organization he had served as president while an undergraduate, and taking classes at Yale Divinity School.

In 1928, influenced by his father and several other members of the clergy, Stokes entered the Episcopal Theological School, located near Harvard University in Cambridge, Massachusetts. After his first year he took a tour of China, Japan, India, the Philippines, Russia, and Palestine. His senior essay dealt with Baron Friedrich von Hugel, a Roman Catholic philosopher. Shortly after graduating with a B.D. degree in 1932, Stokes became a deacon in the Episcopal church. He had a choice of an assistantship at St. Paul's Cathedral in Boston or at St. Mark's Church in Shreveport, Louisiana. His mother recommended going south. Ordained a priest in 1933, Stokes worked actively with Shreveport's African-American population, the YMCA, and the American Red Cross.

From 1937 to 1945 Stokes was rector (chief minister) of Trinity Episcopal Church in Columbus, Ohio, and was involved with the local community chest. On 10 July 1943 he married Hope Procter of Stockbridge, Massachusetts, whose grandfather had been a missionary to the Zulus in South Africa. They had two children. Beginning in 1945, they spent five years in Honolulu, where he served as rector of the parish affiliated with St. Andrew's Cathedral and was appointed to the Governor's Committee on Public Welfare.

In 1950 Stokes was called to become the eighth rector of St. Bartholomew's Episcopal Church in New York City. The Park Avenue parish was large, dynamic, and well-endowed—a perfect position for an activist gentleman in his prime. In 1954 Stokes was elected as one of the eleven directors of the Citizens Housing and Planning Commission of New York City. He also published a biography of Bishop Kinsolving of Brazil in 1954.

Bishop Anson Phelps Stokes, Jr., in Boston, 1963. UPI/CORBIS-BETTMANN

In that same year Stokes was approached to become a candidate for the position of bishop coadjutor of the Episcopal diocese of Massachusetts, which covers the eastern half of the state. Election would automatically guarantee his right to head one of the nation's oldest and wealthiest dioceses, when the Right Reverend Norman Burdett Nash reached retirement age in 1956. Stokes initially declined, preferring to remain at St. Bartholomew's. Nominated anyway, Stokes won on the fifth ballot. He was viewed as a middle-of-the-road Episcopalian who had support from both the evangelical and Anglo-Catholic wings of the church.

Stokes was consecrated a bishop on 4 December 1954 by the Right Reverend Henry Knox Sherrill, who had served as bishop of Massachusetts before becoming the Episcopalians' chief prelate. Stokes's father assisted in the ceremony. Three years later Bishop Stokes enunciated the three ingredients he deemed essential for a strong Christian life—public commitment to Christianity, personal fellowship with God, and the development of bonds of brotherhood with others. Stokes's position was consonant with mainstream views espoused by other moderate bishops, such as Angus Dun and Stephen Bayne, as well as Episcopal publications on ethics.

Stokes became the eleventh bishop of Massachusetts on All Saints Day (1 November) 1956. Organized in 1784, the diocese had approximately 123,000 baptized members; the bishop served as chief pastor to 260 members of the clergy in 200 parishes. Benefiting from a period of postwar prosperity, the diocese grew in size and financial resources during Stokes's years as bishop. Stokes was an able, popular administrator whose tenure was free of scandal and theological controversy. The bishop, nonetheless, did take several stands that irked some members of his flock. During the 1960 presidential campaign, when candidate John F. Kennedy's religion was an issue for some, Stokes joined 165 Roman Catholics in denouncing the "bigotry abroad in the land." Two years later he organized a weeklong program of prayer for Christian unity. Stokes also helped to ensure the election of his successor, John Burgess, the first African American to serve as bishop to a predominantly white diocese.

After his retirement in 1970 Bishop Stokes served on several boards of Episcopal-related private schools and performed society weddings. He maintained memberships in the Century Association and Yale Club in New York City, as well as the country club in Brookline, Massachusetts.

Anson Phelps Stokes, Jr., never achieved the notoriety of such iconoclastic Episcopal bishops as James A. Pike, nor was he an activist like Paul Moore, Jr., who challenged his church to rethink its views on civil rights, women's issues, and gay rights. Stokes's patrician style was more pastoral than patriarchal. He embodied the vital center's concern for tolerance and breadth of vision.

★

Information about Stokes may be found in Mark Duffy, ed., *The Episcopal Diocese of Massachusetts* (1984); David E. Sumner, *The Episcopal Church's History, 1945–1985* (1987); and John Booty, *The Episcopal Church in Crisis* (1988). An obituary is in the *New York Times* (9 Nov. 1986).

W. ANDREW ACHENBAUM

STONE, Irving (*b.* 14 July 1903 in San Francisco, California; *d.* 26 August 1989 in Los Angeles, California), author best known for his immense and meticulously researched biographical novels, including *Lust for Life* (1934), based on the life of Vincent van Gogh, and *The Agony and the Ecstasy* (1961), about Michelangelo.

Stone was born Irving Tennenbaum, the son of Charles Tennenbaum (or Tannenbaum) and Pauline Rosenberg. His parents divorced when Stone was seven years old. His mother put him in the care of his grandmother while she went to work as a department store buyer. At this job, she met another buyer, whose name was Stone. They married, and Irving took the name Stone after he went to live with the couple. His name was legally changed in 1912, on his adoption by his stepfather. Educated at Lowell High School in San Francisco and Manual Arts High School in Los Angeles (graduated 1920), Stone was a bookish boy who regularly attempted to write short stories. Later he said he was heavily influenced by Jack London, who is the subject of Stone's novel *Sailor on Horseback* (1938).

Because Stone's mother wanted her son to become a doctor, in 1920 he entered the University of California at Berkeley, where he eventually chose to study political science rather than medicine. As a student, he supported himself through the performance of music, playing saxophone in a dance band. Stone graduated with a bachelor's degree in 1923 and then enrolled at the University of Southern California, where he was granted a teaching fellowship and took a master's degree in economics in 1924. Having been offered an instructorship in economics at Berkeley, Stone returned there to study for his doctorate but left the university in May 1926 without completing his dissertation. In June of the same year he left the United States for France, determined to pursue a career as a writer.

Stone's early literary efforts were in drama. As a budding playwright, he wrote seventeen full-length plays and thirty-one one-act plays within fifteen months, with little commercial success. Two of his dramas were produced in the United States—*The Dark Mirror* in New York City in 1928 and *The White Life: A Play Based on the Life of Baruch Spinoza* in Jersey City, New Jersey, in 1929—but in France, Stone had already discovered another passion, the art of the Dutch impressionist painter Vincent van Gogh. By chance he had come upon an exhibition of the artist's work at the Rosenberg Galleries in Paris and had been immediately captivated. He later described the encounter as "the single most compelling emotional experience" of his life. Immediately he decided to write a book about van Gogh, although he worried that at twenty-three he was too young and inexperienced a writer for the job. "I thought the story was so big and so great that it should be written by a Thomas Mann, an experienced novelist," Stone later told Roy Newquist in an interview, "but the story of van Gogh and his brother Theo so got into my blood that I found myself dreaming about them at night." Stone knew he had to attempt to write their story: "If I didn't, I would never write anything else."

Irving Stone in a publicity photo for his novel *Adversary in the House*, *c.* 1947. ARCHIVE PHOTOS

Lacking funds to support a large research effort, Stone returned to the United States in 1927 and found work writing mysteries for pulp magazines in New York City, earning a penny a word for his stories. Having decided he needed to return to Europe to, in his words, "go on the trail of van Gogh," he wrote six stories within a week and made enough money to fund a six-month stay in Europe, provided he spent no more than $2 a day. So in 1929 he "literally walked across the face of Europe," following van Gogh's path through Holland, Belgium, and France and gathering information for his book. The result was *Lust for Life,* a huge and unwieldy manuscript that was finished in 1931 but was rejected by seventeen publishers during the next three years.

During this time, Stone published *Pageant of Youth* (1933), a novel about California campus life of which he was not particularly proud. In 1931 he had met Jean Factor, a young editor who helped him cut his massive van Gogh manuscript by about 10 percent. Factor's editing effort proved to be what was needed, and when Stone sent the revised novel to his eighteenth potential publisher, Longman, Green and Co., it was accepted. The final version of *Lust for Life* was published in 1934 and became a best-seller. "Naturally," Stone said of Factor, "we were married." Thereafter, from their marriage in February 1934 on, his wife coresearched and edited all his self-described "overblown" manuscripts down to publishable size. The couple had two children, and apart from extended research trips abroad, the family made its home in Beverly Hills, California.

Stone was a prolific writer who produced novels about a variety of historical subjects. His long list of works includes *The Immortal Wife* (1944), about Jessie Benton Frémont, the wife of the American explorer John C. Frémont; *The Passionate Journey* (1949), a life of the American artist

John Noble; *Love Is Eternal* (1954), an investigation of the marriage between Abraham Lincoln and Mary Todd Lincoln; *The Agony and the Ecstasy* (1961), a tome about Michelangelo that took more than four years to research and write; and *The Passions of the Mind* (1971), based on the life of Sigmund Freud. He also penned several nonfiction biographies and American histories, and he edited collections of the letters of van Gogh and Michelangelo. Asked once to name his favorite genre, Stone offered "bio-history" as a description, defining his work as "bringing history to life in terms of the tremendous human stories that have made that history."

Stone was attracted to subjects whose lives were examples of "great human stories." He wrote about women and men who, he felt, were "on the side of the angels, . . . [who] sought to accomplish something that in some modest way would improve the lot of mankind and make life a little more intelligible, a little more beautiful, a little more peaceable." He was interested in people who had been misunderstood or misrepresented by history, but most importantly, he was attracted to subjects whose lives he would have liked to live, people for whom he could feel "a very genuine affection . . . because I don't have the capacity to get inside the mind or heart or spirit or body of someone I dislike or disapprove of."

Stone's method of getting inside the minds and hearts of his subjects was one of meticulous and exhaustive research, and while some critics offered only lukewarm praise for his novels, almost all noted the painstaking effort behind them. Stone's research took him to the homes of his subjects, to their letters, journals, and published works, as well as to local documentation of their lives and work. He studied and read until he believed he could identify with them accurately enough to be able to bridge the gaps in the existing histories with his own invention. "Even if there were endless documentation it would be impossible to know what a man thought inside his own mind," he said. Therefore, he believed, at some point in the biographical process, the novelist's creative imagination must take over, and Stone made no apologies for combining the factual and the fictional in his work.

Stone received many awards and honors for his writing, including the Christopher Award and the Silver Spur Award from the Western Writers of America in 1957, the Golden Lily of Florence for *The Agony and the Ecstasy* in 1964, and the Author of the Year Award from Book Bank USA in 1976. Critical reception of Stone's work was mixed. Even though his novels were immensely popular, some reviews were damning, such as, "[*The Passions of the Mind*] is more or less an unmitigated disaster, both as a novel and, what is more important, as a popularized portrait or biography of Freud." Other reviews were congratulatory, such as: "Jack London would have applauded the skill and honesty with which his biographer has portrayed him. [*Sailor on Horseback*] is a portrait in full relief, a biography as brave as the life of the man." Generally, however, critics labeled Stone "reliable" and "competent" and often simply wondered whether he allowed his narrative to get too bogged down in the masses of historical details that resulted from his research.

Of the critical reception of his work, Stone said in an interview in 1987: "By and large I have fared extremely well with the press. I have no complaints." Albin Krebs wrote in the *New York Times* obituary that Stone "was indisputably the most successful master of [his] genre." Stone, who was proud of his achievements, wrote:

> I guess that one might say that in 1934, when *Lust for Life* was finally published, the contemporary biographical novel came into a new life of its own. Today it's impossible to pick up any literary magazine without seeing a half-dozen books published very proudly as Biographical Novels. . . . If this is something I launched I'm afraid I succumb to the sin of pride, because I think the biographical novel, honestly and conscientiously done, is important.

Stone wrote biographical fiction for more than fifty years, working well into the 1980s. He died of heart failure in Los Angeles.

★

Roy Newquist, *Counterpoint* (1964), is a collection of literary interviews that offers a strong sense of Stone's own voice. Deborah Straub, ed., *Contemporary Authors*, New Revision Series, vol. 23 (1988), provides an overview of Stone's life, including biographical details, works, awards, and a 1987 interview. Phyllis Carmel Mendelson, ed., *Contemporary Literary Criticism* (1977), offers excerpts of critical commentary on Stone's work. Obituaries are in the *New York Times* and *Los Angeles Times* (both 28 Aug. 1989).

KATE WARNE

STONE, I(sidor) F(einstein) ("Izzy") (*b.* 24 December 1907 in Philadelphia, Pennsylvania; *d.* 18 June 1989 in Boston, Massachusetts), newspaperman best known as a voice of the independent, radical American journalism in the tradition of John Peter Zenger and Thomas Paine.

Born Isidor Feinstein, Stone was the eldest of the four children of Bernard Feinstein, a retailer, and Katy Novack, both Russian-Jewish immigrants. He grew up in Haddonfield, New Jersey, reading precociously and insatiably in literary classics and works of history, politics, and economics, as well as progressive magazines. At age fourteen he published a few issues of his journal *The Progress,* which he distributed personally by bicycle. It supported Woodrow Wilson; "scouts of civilization" such as Plato, Charles Darwin, and

I. F. Stone, 1975. AP/Wide World Photos

Herbert Spencer; and freethinking in religion, although Stone always regarded himself as a proud, if agnostic, Jew. (In 1937, however, he legally changed his name from Feinstein to Stone, arguing that he would influence readers better if seen as "less Jewish.")

Through a chance encounter Stone got a job as the Haddonfield correspondent for liberal publisher J. David Stern's *Camden Evening Courier* while still in high school. The job ruined his academic standing but confirmed his vocation. In 1924 he entered the University of Pennsylvania, where he studied philosophy while working part-time for Philadelphia-area papers; but he dropped out in his junior year, bored with classroom formality. Drawn to socialism as the eventual answer to the world's injustice, Stone remained a Jeffersonian believer in peaceful change through free discussion. If his politics were radical, his personal life was not. On 7 July 1929 he married Esther Roisman, with whom he would have three children and would share a lifelong devoted partnership.

In 1931 Stone joined Stern's *Philadelphia Record* as an editorial writer. Two years later he moved to New York City to fill the same role on Stern's *New York Post,* where he stayed for five years, confronting the twin crises of the 1930s, namely, the Great Depression and the global rise of fascism. Stone's endorsement of the ideology of a "Popular Front"—that is, a coalition of far left and central parties—put him in a typically independent position. On one hand, by supporting the New Deal, he offended communists and socialists who saw Franklin D. Roosevelt's policies as merely postponing the desired collapse of capitalism. On the other, he irked anticommunist liberals by seeking common ground in resisting Hitler between the democracies and the Soviet Union, which at the time he tended to judge as an erring but well-intentioned nation.

Stone left the *New York Post* in 1938 to protest Stern's hardening anticommunist line and joined the staff of the *Nation.* In 1939 he moved to Washington, D.C., as its capital correspondent. He also wrote columns for other left-wing publications, including the New York newspaper *PM,* founded in 1940, whose staff he later joined. Stone supported *PM*'s call for intervention in the European war, and after Japan's bombing of Pearl Harbor in December 1941 he consistently supported America's war effort while urging against the abandonment of democratic principles at home.

In 1946 Stone joined a group of Jewish "displaced persons," survivors of the Holocaust, aboard a vessel that evaded the British blockade and landed them in Palestine, where he remained briefly to file stories. Later that year his reports for *PM* on the exploit got him fired from the *Nation,* which had not been given advance notice of his intentions. After the creation of a secular, democratic Israel in 1948, Stone became its strong supporter but also believed that only a binational state, both Arab and Jewish, would be just and lasting, a stance that alienated other Zionists.

In the 1950s, as the cold war and McCarthyism disrupted the unity of influence of the former antifascist left, Stone's independence lost him contacts and audiences. He opposed the expansionism of the Soviet Union, about which he no longer had illusions, but equally criticized American militarism and global interventions. He supported the free-speech rights of communists and dissenters of every variety. Almost alone he questioned the American claim to be defending South Korea against aggression from North Korea and accused the State Department of complicity in bringing about the Korean War. Under FBI surveillance, Stone briefly considered emigrating to Great Britain or to Israel. He was further discouraged late in 1952, when the *New York Compass* (founded in 1949 as the successor to *PM*) folded, leaving him jobless. But despite these setbacks he started his own four-page newsletter, *I. F. Stone's Weekly.* He signed up 5,300 advance subscribers (including Eleanor Roosevelt and Albert Einstein) at five dollars a year, and published the first issue on 17 January 1953.

Stone published the *Weekly,* with his wife's help, from the Washington home to which they had returned from New York in 1952. It carried Stone's unique personal stamp. Unable and unwilling to play the capital game of cultivating sources, he relied on his ability to read thousands of pages of official documents and, helped by a prodigious memory, to catch the government in contradictions, inconsistencies, and outright falsehoods. The *Weekly* was documented muckraking at its best. The assault on segregation in the 1950s and the Vietnam War in the 1960s gave Stone the opportunity to devote issue after issue to extolling peace and racial and economic justice, and to attack secrecy in government and the arms race. Finding common ground with young idealists in the civil rights and antiwar movements, he tried to unify the Old Left and the New Left without endorsing the countercultural activities of the latter. Renamed *I. F. Stone's Bi-Weekly* in 1967, the newsletter reached a nationwide and foreign circulation of 66,000 by 1971. Stone made a comfortable living and was able to travel abroad in pursuit of stories and to reemerge gradually from isolation. In 1971 he won the George Polk Memorial Award for outstanding reporting.

Stone's frantic pace was exhausting, however, and a brush with a heart attack in 1967 contributed to his decision to close down the *Bi-Weekly* in 1971; its last issue was published on 14 December of that year. In 1972 he took a staff position on the small but influential *New York Review of Books,* from which he resigned in 1976. Thereafter, Stone published essays and reviews in various places, including mainstream papers that once had denounced him. By his mid-seventies he had become a kind of semiofficial gadfly. At the age of eighty he returned to his interest in the sources of the Western intellectual tradition, learned classical Greek, and wrote his final book, *The Trial of Socrates* (1988). Characteristically, it condemned both Socrates' elitist ideas and Athenian justice for suppressing them. Stone died in a Boston hospital in 1989 after cardiac surgery.

Small, bespectacled, and intense, Stone enjoyed fighting the good fight and kept alive the tradition of pugnacious and journalistic crusading at a time when the profession was challenged by an age of "infotainment" and blandness conveyed by corporately owned media giants. And, like other Old Left heroes such as Norman Thomas and A. J. Muste, he sustained a faith in the inevitable triumph of democratic socialism that burned brightly at the twentieth century's start but was sorely beleaguered at its end.

★

Besides *The Trial of Socrates,* Stone's writings include *The Court Disposes* (1937), *Underground to Palestine* (1946), *The Hidden History of the Korean War* (1952), *The Haunted Fifties* (1963), *In a Time of Torment* (1967), *Polemics and Prophecies* (1971), and *The Best of I. F. Stone's Weekly* (1973). Andrew Patner, *I. F. Stone: A Portrait* (1988), is a series of interviews. A full and annotated bibliography of Stone is Robert Cottrell, *Izzy* (1992). See also *I. F. Stone's Weekly,* a documentary film made by Jerry Bruck, Jr., in 1973. An obituary is in the *New York Times* (19 June 1989).

BERNARD A. WEISBERGER

STONEHAM, Horace Charles (*b.* 10 July 1903 in Newark, New Jersey; *d.* 7 January 1990 in Scottsdale, Arizona), owner and general manager of baseball's National League Giants from 1936 until 1976, who moved the team from New York to San Francisco in 1958.

Horace Stoneham was one of two children of Margaret Leonard and Charles A. Stoneham, a "bucket-shop" stockbroker with connections among politicians, sportsmen, and gamblers in New York. In 1919, when Horace was fifteen years old, his father bought the New York Giants baseball team with two partners, one of whom was the legendary Giants manager John McGraw. The Stoneham family moved from Jersey City, New Jersey, to West Eighty-sixth Street in Manhattan shortly thereafter. Stoneham, who went to Catholic grade schools in New Jersey, attended Loyola High School in Manhattan and then several preparatory schools, before graduating from the Pawling School. He attended Fordham University briefly in 1921, receiving no degree. He was an indifferent student but a star athlete in baseball and hockey during his school years.

Horace Stoneham. COURTESY OF THE NATIONAL BASEBALL HALL OF FAME LIBRARY, COOPERSTOWN, N.Y.

After leaving Fordham, Stoneham spent a year working in a California copper mine owned by his father, briefly considering a career as an engineer. Instead, he returned east, taking a job in the Giants ticket office at a salary of $3,500 per year. During the next ten years, he held a number of different jobs in the Giants organization. Stoneham was married in April 1924 to Valleda Pyke; they had two children.

When his father died in 1936, Stoneham took formal possession of the Giants, although he had assumed operational control of the team a year earlier; at thirty-two he was the youngest team owner in the history of the major leagues. At first he deferred to the decisions of his manager, Bill Terry, who had succeeded McGraw in 1932 and who led the Giants to the National League pennant in 1936 and 1937 (they lost the World Series to the Yankees both years). Terry regarded Stoneham as merely a rich kid, but after several years Stoneham began to assert his authority over the team, replacing Terry with Mel Ott in 1942.

Stoneham was a heavy drinker, known for his all-night sessions with friends such as the comedian Jackie Gleason and Toots Shor, at Shor's Manhattan restaurant. Throughout his life, he would try to corral others into late-night baseball-talk and drinking vigils he called "sit-sees." Otherwise, he was a shy and private person. He believed in loyalty above all, and he ran the Giants like a family, an inclination that some regarded as a weakness. He was also known for his generosity and shocked many when he offered Willie Mays a two-year contract for a record $125,000 per year in 1966, because he felt Mays deserved to be the highest-paid player in the game.

Stoneham became an astute judge of baseball talent, and the strong Giants network of farm teams developed players such as Mays and Willie McCovey. Stoneham also became a pioneer in scouting the Caribbean in the 1950s and 1960s, finding future stars like Orlando Cepeda, the Alou brothers, and Juan Marichal.

The Giants were successful again under manager Leo Durocher, hired by Stoneham in 1948. They won the National League pennant in 1951 with the famous Bobby Thomson home run in the third game of a playoff series with the Brooklyn Dodgers, then lost the World Series in six games to the Yankees. In 1954 the Giants won the World Series in four games over favored Cleveland, the only series win in Stoneham's long tenure as Giants owner.

Stoneham first began thinking of moving the team from New York in 1955, citing financial difficulties. The success of the Yankees and Dodgers had eclipsed the Giants' popularity. The Polo Grounds, the team's playing field in northern Manhattan, was deteriorating, and Stoneham deemed alternative sites unsatisfactory. Historians, however, have disputed the financial necessity of the move.

Stoneham's first choice for a move was Minneapolis, where the Giants owned a minor league organization with a new stadium. Instead, in 1957 Stoneham joined Brooklyn Dodger owner Walter O'Malley in announcing a move to the West Coast for the 1958 season. The joint move was meant to keep the long, profitable rivalry between the two teams geographically intact. New Yorkers vilified O'Malley more than Stoneham for the move. The Dodgers went to Los Angeles, while the Giants moved first into San Francisco's minor league Seal Stadium and then in 1960 into the new city-financed Candlestick Park.

As the San Francisco Giants the team fielded competitive teams and drew well during the 1960s. The Giants won the National League pennant in 1962, after a three-game playoff with the Dodgers, reminiscent of the climactic finish of 1951. Again, the Giants lost the World Series to the Yankees, in seven games. Candlestick Park, however, exposed to the fog and chill of the San Francisco Bay area, proved to be unpleasant for both players and spectators, and later owners would struggle for years to develop an alternative venue.

In 1968 the American League Athletics moved to Oakland, across the bay from San Francisco, cutting into the Giants market. This coincided with a period of declining success for the team, although they won the West division in 1971. Attendance fell sharply. Stoneham was blamed for the team's waning fortunes, accused of being a traditionalist who resisted modern promotional techniques. Discouraged, he began looking for a buyer for the team in 1972.

After near-moves to Denver and Toronto, the Giants were sold in 1976 for $8 million to a group of San Francisco investors who pledged to keep the club in the San Francisco Bay area. Stoneham had served as president and principal owner of the Giants for forty years; the team had been in his family for fifty-seven.

Stoneham, who had long been separated from his wife, spent the last thirteen years of his life in retirement near the Giants' spring training complex in Scottsdale, Arizona. He cut his formal ties to the club, but he was frequently seen in the stands at spring training games. He died in a Scottsdale nursing home. He was buried in the St. Francis Cemetery in Phoenix, Arizona.

Horace Stoneham was raised with the Giants. Once it was purchased by his father, the team became his lifelong calling and livelihood. He was devoted to his team and players but moved to the West Coast when he decided that New York was no longer a hospitable environment. It is that act for which he will be principally remembered.

★

Books that make reference to Horace Stoneham include Harvey Frommer, *New York City Baseball, The Last Golden Age: 1947–1957* (1980); Alvin Dark with John Underwood, *When In Doubt, Fire the Manager* (1980), an as-told-to autobiography by the former Giants shortstop and manager; Neil J. Sullivan, *The Dodgers Move*

West (1987), which focuses on the Dodgers but includes information about the Giants as well; and Peter Williams, *When the Giants Were Giants: Bill Terry and the Golden Age of New York Baseball* (1994). The most comprehensive published biography of Stoneham is a magazine article by Robert Shaplen, "The Lonely, Loyal Mr. Stoneham," *Sports Illustrated* (5 May 1958). Stoneham was frequently covered in the sporting press; useful examples include Jack Walsh, "Three's Crowd in New York, Says Stoneham; Horace Blunt About Desire of Giants to Move to Coast," *Sporting News* (24 July 1957); Dan Daniel, "Hail-Fellow Horace Pegged as Perfect Host; Cordial Stoneham Marking Twenty-fifth Year as Chief of Giants; Veteran Exec Saved Club in Trek to Coast," *Sporting News* (12 July 1961); Joe Marcin, "Stonehams' Fifty-seven-Year Link to Giants Broken," *Sporting News* (13 Mar. 1976). Obituaries are in the *New York Times* (9 Jan. 1990) and *Sporting News* (22 Jan. 1990).

SAM STOLOFF

STROUT, Richard Lee (*b.* 14 March 1898 in Cohoes, New York; *d.* 19 August 1990 in Washington, D.C.), political reporter for the *Christian Science Monitor* and author of the *New Republic*'s "TRB from Washington" column for forty years.

Richard Strout, 1977. UPI/CORBIS-BETTMANN

Richard Lee Strout was one of two sons of George Morris Strout, an English teacher who held a Ph.D. from Boston College, and Mary Susan (Lang) Strout, a homemaker who had graduated from Smith College. Soon after Richard's birth the family moved to Brooklyn, New York, where his father taught English at Erasmus Hall High School. After graduating from Erasmus in 1915, Richard enrolled at Dartmouth College, where he joined the Student Training Corps. Two years later the United States entered World War I and Strout joined the army as a second lieutenant, serving for the duration on the faculty of the military school at Norwich University in Northfield, Vermont. After the war he resumed his education at Harvard, where he worked on the *Crimson*, the school newspaper, and graduated with an A.B. degree in 1919.

After college Strout worked his way across the Atlantic Ocean on a grain ship. He arrived in England with a letter of introduction from the political scientist and Harvard professor Harold Laski. Securing a job at the *Sheffield Independent,* Strout served for two years as a reporter and editor. In 1921 he returned to Boston and worked briefly at the *Boston Post* before joining the *Christian Science Monitor.* He also returned to Harvard, earning an M.A. degree in economics and political science in 1923.

The *Monitor* assigned Strout to its Washington, D.C., bureau in 1923, and just after Christmas that year he drove to Washington in his Model T Ford over a windy and snowy three days. He began covering the White House during the administration of Warren Harding, the first of twelve presidents he would cover. He wrote about the Teapot Dome scandal, following it, as he noted years later, "from the very same marble Senate Caucus Room where, half a century later, Senator Ervin heard the Watergate story." These were also the years he began his first family. He married Edith Rittenhouse Mayne on 21 June 1924; they had three children before his wife's death in 1932.

Strout's success in Washington allowed him to write for other prominent publications. In 1936 he wrote a piece lamenting the demise of the Model T and submitted it to the *New Yorker* editor E. B. White. After White had spruced up the piece the two men, under the joint pseudonym Lee Strout White, published it as a book entitled *Farewell to Model T.* On 4 September 1939 Strout married Ernestine Wilke, with whom he had two daughters.

In 1943 Bruce Bliven of the *New Republic,* the nation's leading liberal journal of opinion, asked Strout to take over its flagship political column, "TRB from Washington."

Penned anonymously, the column had been written by a series of reporters since its inception in 1925. Strout accepted the assignment even as he continued to report on politics for the *Monitor*. (The meaning of "TRB" has long been disputed. The most common explanation is the one Bliven gave: that, when he was ferrying the column's first entry from the *New Republic*'s Manhattan offices to its printer in Brooklyn via subway, he realized it had no name. Spying a placard for the old "Brooklyn Rapid Transit" subway line—which became the Brooklyn-Manhattan Transit line in 1923—Bliven reversed the initials and scribbled them down.)

Strout's first column, published 8 March 1943, urged President Franklin Roosevelt to respond to antiwar congressmen with a delineation of specific war aims. Over the next forty years he would address nearly all the great political issues of the day. Immediately after the bombing of Hiroshima in 1945 he recognized the horrible moral dilemmas posed by atomic weaponry; in the aftermath of the war he railed against the willful inaction of Congress. He described the Eisenhower administration as "government by sedative" and called the red-baiting Senator Joseph McCarthy "a mist that carries a lethal contagion." In one frequently reprinted column, Strout, with unsentimental realism, argued that liberals should not mistrust President Lyndon B. Johnson's bold plans for national progress just because "LBJ isn't JFK." He coolly and poignantly described the tragedy of the 1968 Democratic national convention in Chicago and resignedly pointed out Richard Nixon's Machiavellian manipulation of the press.

Bedrock liberal issues—among them economic fairness, public education, racial equality, activist government, and the separation of church and state—always topped his political agenda. More idiosyncratically, Strout argued for reform of the structure of American government (he preferred a European-style parliamentary democracy) and policies to deal with population growth, a concern that led him to conservative positions on immigration.

Strout combined his self-described New Deal liberalism with a tart sense of humor and a "becoming skepticism," as his sometime colleague Alfred Kazin once put it. Strout also reported energetically and sprinkled his columns with acute personal observations. Endowed with an eye for the telling detail, Strout could deftly reveal the character or foibles of the mighty personages he covered through finely worded descriptions of their traits and mannerisms. In his column on the 1959 visit to the United States by the Soviet premier Nikita Khrushchev, he wrote, "I can see him now, acting out in pantomime the can-can dance he saw at Hollywood, giving his heavy posterior a wiggling imitation, and roaring with laughter. . . . Or I can see those little fat eyes narrowed to angry slits and looking out ruthlessly on us—a competitor nation that might be laughing at him and his peasant origin (you could never be sure!)." Strout's commonsense politics, impatience with pretense, and elegant writing won him a wide following; by the end of his career "TRB" was syndicated in some sixty newspapers.

In his later years Strout became known as a dean of Washington reporters and a throwback to an earlier era. Lean and tall with a neatly trimmed white mustache, he looked the part he came to inhabit—the courtly, if crusty, dispenser of wisdom in a city of haste and political turnover. He continued to write his columns on long sheets of white paper and deplored changes that he thought cheapened his trade, such as televised press conferences and the new "staccato literary style [that reflected] an effort . . . to cram too many ideas into 800 words, like the coats bulging in a closet at a cocktail party." Strout modestly disavowed any imputations of greatness; still, colleagues honored him with the National Press Club's Fourth Estate Award in 1975 and a special Pulitzer Prize citation in 1978, among other tributes.

In 1979 Strout published a collection of his columns called *TRB: Views and Perspectives on the Presidency*. Four years later he retired from writing the column. Although he had publicly defined "Strout's Law" as the certain recurrence of scandal every fifty years, from Teapot Dome in 1923 to Watergate in 1973, Michael Kinsley, who took over "TRB," recalled that Strout also applied that label to a different rule: "Sell every piece three times." Strout used to report an article for the *Monitor,* rework it as an opinion column for "TRB," and then try to sell it as a feature elsewhere. Continuing in his final years to live in Washington, D.C., he died in 1990 from complications arising from a fall. He is buried in Washington.

★

Richard L. Strout, *TRB: Views and Perspectives on the Presidency* (1979), includes 200 columns from Strout's forty years on the job, including several that reflect on his career. Robert B. Luce, ed., *The Faces of Five Decades* (1964), and Dorothy Wickenden, ed., *The New Republic Reader* (1994), are anthologies of *New Republic* articles that include some "TRB" columns. A profile of Strout appears in the *New York Times* (4 Apr. 1978). Other helpful articles from the pages of the *New Republic* include Carroll Kilpatrick, "TRB at Eighty" (18 Mar. 1978); "An Irreplaceable Man" (18 Apr. 1983); Richard L. Strout, "TRB Remembered" (10 Dec. 1984); John Patrick Diggins, "*The New Republic* and Its Times" (10 Dec. 1984); Alfred Kazin, "*The New Republic:* A Personal View" (6 Nov. 1989); and the tributes "A Death in the Family" and Michael Kinsley, "Strout's Law" (both 10–17 Sept. 1990). Obituaries also appear in the *Christian Science Monitor* (22 Aug. 1990), *New York Times* (21 and 22 Aug. 1990), and *Washington Post* (21 Aug. 1990).

DAVID GREENBERG

SUBLETT, John William. *See* Bubbles, John Williams.

SULZBERGER, Iphigene Bertha Ochs (*b.* 19 September 1892 in Cincinnati, Ohio; *d.* 26 February 1990 in Stamford, Connecticut), a member of the influential family who owned the *New York Times* and a philanthropist interested in parks, the environment, education, and human rights.

Sulzberger, known to her family as Iffie or If, was the only surviving child of Adolph Simon Ochs, then the owner of the *Chattanooga Times,* and Iphigenia Miriam (Wise) Ochs, a homemaker. In 1896 her father bought the *New York Times,* and in 1904 she laid the cornerstone of Times Tower at Broadway and Forty-second Street. Sulzberger graduated from the Benjamin Dean School in 1910, and four years later from Barnard College with a B.A. degree in economics. While in school she worked at the Henry Street Settlement in lower Manhattan one afternoon a week, and at the Cedar Knoll School, an institution for disturbed children. She entered the Columbia University School of Journalism in 1914 but did not complete the first semester.

On 17 November 1917 Iphigene Ochs married Arthur Hays Sulzberger; they had four children. When her husband became publisher of the *Times* in 1935, Sulzberger was essentially an offstage figure in the newspaper's operations. In the late 1940s she began to work at the paper, initially as a part-timer filling in for staff members on vacation, and then full-time in the promotion department. Her assignment was to attract more women readers. In 1944 she was responsible for a series of articles that showed the public had a low interest and competence in history. As a result of the articles the *Times* won a Pulitzer Prize for meritorious public service and there were changes in curriculum in many states.

Iphigene Ochs Sulzberger and her husband Arthur Sulzberger arrive in Stockholm. UPI/Corbis-Bettmann

Although always concerned about the *Times* and her family, Sulzberger joined many civic and educational groups. A member of the Parks and Playgrounds Association, a volunteer organization dedicated to protecting New York City parks, from 1928, she was its president and chair for twenty-three years and received the annual award of the Parks Council in 1975 for her participation in environmental issues, such as a work-study program in Central Park. The New York Botanical Garden gave her its distinguished service award in 1965. Barnard College presented her with the Distinguished Alumna Award (1972). Sulzberger was a member of the Barnard College board of trustees from 1937 to 1968, when she became a trustee emerita.

Sulzberger received honorary doctorates from Columbia University (1951), the Jewish Theological Seminary (1968), the Hebrew Union College–Jewish Institute of Religion (1973), and Bishop College of Dallas (1978), which at the time was the largest predominantly black private college in the Southwest. She also was the largest single private donor in the history of the United Negro College Fund, giving more than $35,000 a year during 1968–1978. A further honor came when Admiral Richard E. Byrd named Mount Iphigene in Antarctica after her.

Sulzberger also served on the committee for the *Dictionary of American Biography;* on an advisory committee of the Princeton University project for the publication of the papers of Thomas Jefferson; on the board of managers for a home for unwed mothers, Inwood House; on the Jewish Board of Guardians; and on the boards of the New York Child Adoption League and the Girl Scouts.

Sulzberger died of respiratory failure and is buried in the Cemetery of Temple Israel of the City of New York, Hastings-on-Hudson, New York. Her influence on the *New York Times* spanned over half a century and helped to shape "All the News That's Fit to Print."

★

Sulzberger's memoirs, written ("as told to") by her granddaughter Susan W. Dryfoos, have appeared in three versions: *From Iphigene: The Memoirs of Iphigene Ochs Sulzberger* (1979); *Iphigene: Memoirs of Iphigene Ochs Sulzberger of the New York Times Family* (1981); and *Iphigene, My Life and the New York Times: The Memoirs of Iphigene Ochs Sulzberger* (1987). See also Gay Talese, *The Kingdom and the Power* (1966). A front-page obituary is in the *New York Times* (27 Feb. 1990).

Martin Jay Stahl

SUSSKIND, David Howard (*b.* 19 December 1920 in New York City; *d.* 22 February 1987 in New York City), prolific producer of television programs, plays, and films, best known to the public as a controversial talk-show host.

Raised in Brookline, Massachusetts, David Susskind was one of three children of Benjamin Susskind, a sales agent for the Metropolitan Life Insurance Company, and Frances Lear Susskind, a homemaker who had volunteered for military service during World War I. Benjamin Susskind provided a comfortable life for the family and instilled a strong desire for learning in his son. From the time David was eleven years old his father took him to hear scholarly lectures each Sunday. Among the speakers David heard at the Ford Hall Forum in Boston were Harold Laski, Felix Frankfurter, Bertrand Russell, and John Maynard Keynes. In high school Susskind's facile mind allowed him to earn nearly straight As without spending a great deal of time studying. Instead he worked on the school paper, belonged to the debating team, and wrote a weekly column for his hometown newspaper.

After he graduated from Brookline High School in 1938, Susskind enrolled at the University of Wisconsin. In August 1939, after completing his freshman year, eighteen-year-old David Susskind married seventeen-year-old Phyllis Briskin, daughter of a wealthy New York family that owned movie-theater concessions. The couple had three children. In 1940 Susskind transferred to Harvard University to study political science. He hoped to pursue a Ph.D. and someday teach there. He received a B.S. degree in 1942, graduating with honors, then served in the U.S. Navy during World War II as a communications officer in the Pacific. During his military service his career plans changed. Teaching, he came to believe, would be too detached from real life, the ivory tower too cloistered to suit his personality.

David Susskind. ARCHIVE PHOTOS

Upon discharge from the navy in April 1946, Susskind applied for work as a journalist at every newspaper in New York City. Discouraged by the low salaries, however, he took a job with the publicity department of Warner Brothers motion pictures in New York City. A few months later he moved to Universal studios as a senior press agent at double his salary. But the work was still unsatisfying. Recognizing the importance of talent agents in show business, Susskind took a cut in pay and went to work for Century Artists, an agency that represented stars such as Judy Holliday, Burl Ives, and the Andrews Sisters. When the company went out of business Susskind formed a partnership with another agent, Al Levy. With $2,000 borrowed from his father-in-law, Susskind became a partner in Talent Associates, Ltd., formed in 1948. The company handled primarily writers and directors.

Susskind was soon lured away from Talent Associates with a generous offer to become an agent for the Music Corporation of America (MCA). His clients included Dinah Shore, the bandleader Kay Kyser, and the blockbuster comedy team of Dean Martin and Jerry Lewis. At MCA he negotiated contracts, packaged programs, and reassured performers, skills that would be invaluable in the next phase of his career. After three years at MCA, he left in the wake of a bitter dispute, convinced that in show business real control rested with the producer. He rejoined Talent Associates, and in the summer of 1953 he was given the opportunity to fill in for Fred Coe, the outstanding producer of the *Philco Television Playhouse*. While Coe was on a five-week vacation, Susskind filled his shoes admirably.

Soon Susskind was well on his way to becoming a leading television producer. His keen eye for good dramatic material and willingness to take risks were critical qualities. Talent Associates evolved from a talent agency into a company that packaged and produced TV programming, films, and plays. In 1955 Susskind took over production of *Armstrong Circle Theatre*. Formerly a nondescript anthology of half-hour dramas, under Susskind's guidance it gained a unique focus as a collection of dramas based on true stories.

Live television drama and Susskind's work in the genre both reached their pinnacles in 1957. Not a week passed without a Susskind-produced show on the air. In addition to *Armstrong Circle Theatre,* he was producing shows for *Kraft Television Theatre,* the *DuPont Show of the Month,* and occasional specials sponsored by the Rexall drugstore chain.

By the late 1950s the commerce of television production was shifting from New York to Hollywood. Live television drama was being replaced by Westerns and action-adventure series that were produced on film. Susskind's outspoken contempt for the changes in the industry alienated many of Hollywood's biggest stars and power-wielders. He became a self-styled conscience of the medium, declaring that "TV is going down the drain like dirty water."

In 1958 his reputation as an iconoclast was bolstered when he began hosting the syndicated talk show *Open End.* The weekly program was of undetermined length, lasting as long as the host thought the conversation was interesting. *Open End* attracted high-level guests from all fields, and Susskind was an indefatigable interviewer. In May 1960, for instance, he interrogated Vice President Richard Nixon for almost four continuous hours. That same year, when Susskind interviewed Nikita Khrushchev during the latter's visit to the United States, the host was hit with a barrage of criticism for giving the Soviet premier a propaganda platform.

By the time he reached his forties, Susskind's short, coarse, curly hair had started to gray, and the puffy bags under his eyes began to dominate his face. His compact stature gave the impression of stockiness, even though he did not carry excess weight. He was defensive about his height: He stood five feet, seven inches but claimed to be two inches taller.

Although the talk show was his avocation, Susskind continued to be a full-time producer. Among his most critically acclaimed projects in the 1960s were the feature films *A Raisin in the Sun* (1961) and *Requiem for a Heavyweight* (1962), the television series *East Side/West Side,* and a special television presentation of Arthur Miller's *Death of a Salesman.*

In 1966 Susskind, long separated from Phyllis and divorced earlier that year, married the Canadian television personality Joyce Davidson, with whom he had one child. *Open End* was in 1967 retitled the *David Susskind Show* and the format changed to a standard two-hour program that was taped with a studio audience. By then Susskind had become a fixture in American popular culture. His rococo language skills and frequently pugnacious demeanor were the stuff of parody. In the Flintstones' cartoon town of Bedrock, for example, the local TV station carried David Rockkind, a prehistoric talk-show host never at a loss for words.

In the 1970s and 1980s Susskind continued to produce prestige programming, including the miniseries *Eleanor and Franklin* and nine *Hallmark Hall of Fame* specials. He and his second wife were divorced in 1986. Susskind died of heart failure the following year.

In his long career Susskind won twenty-seven Emmy awards and three Peabody awards. He was inducted into the Academy of Television Arts and Sciences Hall of Fame in 1988. In 1990 the Producers Guild of America presented the first David Susskind Lifetime Achievement Award.

Although Susskind is remembered—even by those who loved and admired him—as a difficult man who ruffled many feathers, his true legacy is a remarkable body of work created in an unrelenting quest for excellence. He was embraced by performers, artists, and political figures who respected his commitment to high standards of culture and to the art of conversation. He always believed in the potential of television to uplift a diverse audience of American viewers.

★

The personal and professional papers of David Susskind, including correspondence, scripts, production materials, and clippings, are housed at the State Historical Society of Wisconsin. No full-length biographies of Susskind had been produced by the late 1990s, but many contemporaneous articles examined his career, including Thomas B. Morgan, "David Susskind: Television's Newest Spectacular," *Esquire* (Aug. 1960). For an examination of his contributions in a historical context see two articles by Mary Ann Watson, "*Open End*: A Mirror of the 1960s," *Film and History* 21, nos. 2 and 3 (May and Sept. 1991); and "Continental Rift: David Susskind's Futile Fight to Keep TV Drama in New York," *Television Quarterly* 25, no. 4 (1992): 55–60. An obituary is in the *New York Times* (23 Feb. 1987).

MARY ANN WATSON

SWEENEY, James Johnson (*b.* 30 May 1900 in Brooklyn, New York; *d.* 14 April 1986 in New York City), art museum director and authority on avant-garde art.

Sweeney was the son of Patrick M. Sweeney, an importer of textiles, and Mary Johnson. He studied at Georgetown University, where he majored in literature. He received a B.A. degree in 1922. He continued his study of literature at Jesus College, of Cambridge University (1922–1924).

A large man of athletic build, Sweeney excelled in football, rugby, and track and field. He set shot-put records at both Georgetown and Cambridge. In 1925 he studied at the Sorbonne in Paris, and he spent the following year at the University of Siena in Italy. He married Laura Harden on 17 May 1927; they had five children.

In the late 1920s Sweeney edited the Paris literary magazine *Transition.* He also helped James Joyce edit the manuscript of his "Work in Progress" (which was published as *Finnegans Wake*). Sweeney would later say that he "learned about art from artists," and while in Paris he met and befriended such artists as Alexander Calder and Fernand Léger. During this period he witnessed the high phases of cubism as well as the beginnings of surrealism.

By 1931 Sweeney had returned to the United States, where he worked briefly as the New York art correspondent for the *Chicago Evening Post.* In 1924 he curated an exhibition of twentieth-century painting and sculpture at the University of Chicago. In that year he also published his first book, *Plastic Redirections in Twentieth-Century Painting,* in which he analyzed the development of art from impressionism to surrealism. *Plastic Redirections* helped to establish Sweeney's reputation as a critic supportive of experimental modern art.

During the 1930s Sweeney began his long involvement with the Museum of Modern Art (MOMA). In 1935 he organized the museum's first exhibition of African art. He also edited the catalog, *African Negro Art,* that accompanied the exhibition. From 1935 to 1940 Sweeney lectured at New York University's Institute of Fine Arts.

Sweeney curated several important shows at MOMA that introduced the modern European and American masters to the American public, including an exhibition of the paintings of Joan Miró in 1941 and a show of the sculpture and constructions of Alexander Calder in 1943. He also curated a memorial show of the paintings of Piet Mondrian in 1945. Sweeney held the position of director of painting and sculpture at MOMA from 1945 until 1946, when he resigned from the museum over a dispute concerning his freedom to direct the museum's acquisition program. His resignation caused great controversy. In 1948 he narrated a film on the British sculptor Henry Moore, and in 1950 and 1951 he was visiting scholar at the University of Georgia.

James Johnson Sweeney. NYT PICTURES/NYT PERMISSIONS

In 1952 Sweeney became director of the Solomon R. Guggenheim Museum in New York City. His tenure coincided with the construction of Frank Lloyd Wright's unusual building. He clashed with Wright over several aspects of the plan that he felt would provide an unfavorable environment for exhibiting painting and sculpture. Among the changes that Sweeney pushed for was the use of directed artificial light rather than natural light.

During his years as director Sweeney added some 250 works to the Guggenheim's collection, expanding its range beyond the narrow, nonobjective focus that had characterized the museum upon his arrival. In 1959, with the museum's popularity on the rise, the president and board of trustees of the Guggenheim opted to broaden the public appeal of the museum by directing the general program toward the uninformed viewer. Sweeney resigned, convinced that such a "mass media" approach would undermine the important acquisitional goals of the museum.

In 1961 Sweeney became the director of the Museum of Fine Arts in Houston. Under his guidance the museum's modern, pre-Columbian, and ancient Greek collections were strengthened, and several ambitious exhibitions were arranged, including one on the art of Mexico in 1963. Under his direction the Houston Museum of Fine Arts achieved an international reputation. In 1968 Sweeney resigned over a dispute concerning his role as director.

Following his departure from Houston, Sweeney devoted his energies to writing books: *Joan Miró* (1941), *Eduardo Chillida* (1966), and *Pierre Soulages* (1968). In addition, he edited and wrote many articles for journals and magazines, including *Vogue, House and Garden, Daedalus, Art News,* and *New Republic,* and was an advisory editor for the *Partisan Review* (1948–1963). Sweeney also was an adviser to the Israel Museum of Jerusalem. He died in New York City of complications from a stroke.

Sweeney's critical approach to art was modernist and evolutionary. He said in a 1962 interview in *Artforum:* "All art has to be venturesome, otherwise it's just retreading the same paths." As a curator Sweeney constantly sought the new, looking out for what he called "new nouns." In the exhibitions he arranged, he sought to inspire critical thinking and present works that could serve as "models of order" for a people fragmented and disillusioned by the unlimited industrialism of the twentieth century. Although Sweeney's idealism, with its spiritual overtones, was seldom found in the postmodern criticism of the 1990s, his critical approach to mounting exhibitions set the standard for many high-profile national and international exhibitions.

★

James Johnson Sweeney, *Vision and Image: A Way of Seeing* (1968), is a mature and personal summary of of his critical attitudes. His "Sweeney Setting His American Scene," *Art News* (1950), contains information on his exhibition selection methods; and his "The Artist and the Museum in a Mass Society," *Daedalus* (1960), was written after his resignation from the Guggenheim. See also Campbell Geesin, "Sweeney in Houston," *Art in America* (1962); and Dore Ashton, "Sweeney Revisited," *Studio* (1963). "Man vs. Building," *Time* (1960), outlines Sweeney's disagreements with the Guggenheim. An obituary is in the *New York Times* (15 Apr. 1986).

PETER SUCHECKI

SYMINGTON, (William) Stuart, III (*b.* 26 June 1901 in Amherst, Massachusetts; *d.* 14 December 1988 in New Canaan, Connecticut), business executive, first secretary of the air force, and four-term U.S. senator from Missouri.

Stuart Symington. ARCHIVE PHOTOS

Stuart Symington was one of six children born to William Stuart Symington, Jr., an attorney who had once taught French literature at Stanford University and Amherst College, and Emily Haxall Harrison Symington. (Like his father, Symington seldom used the name William and dropped it altogether when he entered government.) On both sides of his family, Symington's lineage went back to colonial times, and both of his grandfathers served as officers in the Confederate army. Symington's boyhood was spent in Baltimore, where his father practiced law and engaged in a number of business ventures, most of them unsuccessful. Although the Symingtons' finances were always precarious, the family was prominent socially. When Stuart graduated from high school (at Baltimore City College, 1918) he was admitted, after lying about his age, to the army's officer training program and became the youngest second lieutenant in the army. World War I ended, however, before he saw active service.

After being discharged from the army, Symington entered Yale University in 1919, primarily with money supplied by his uncles. He had developed into a handsome six-footer with considerable athletic ability. He was a member of the Yale tennis team and an assistant editor of the *Yale Daily News*. Because of a deficiency in mathematics he left Yale without receiving a degree; in 1945 the university would award him his degree retroactive to the class of 1923.

On 1 March 1924 he married Evelyn Wadsworth, daughter of Senator James Wadsworth of New York, a leading Republican politician, and granddaughter of John Hay, private secretary to Abraham Lincoln and former secretary of state. The couple had two sons, W. Stuart Symington IV and James Wadsworth Symington, the latter of whom became a U.S. congressman from Missouri. Although Symington started out as an iron molder in a manufacturing plant in Rochester, New York, owned by an uncle, he rose rapidly with the aid of his uncles, who put him in one managerial job after another. He developed a reputation as a skilled manager who could turn failed businesses into profitable enterprises. With help from his uncles, in 1913 he acquired the Colonial Radio Company, which became highly profitable. He moved to New York City in 1933 and soon sold the company for a huge profit. In 1935 he became president of Rustless Iron and Steel Company and built it into a successful business that was bought by Armco Steel in 1936, making Symington a millionaire.

From the time of their arrival in New York City the Symingtons moved easily in the upper echelons of New York society. They had money, family background, and good looks. Symington was an accomplished tennis player and a better-than-average golfer. Evelyn Symington (generally known as "Eve"), a ravishing beauty with a lovely voice, sang professionally in some of the city's leading nightclubs. Stuart, who was in the audience almost every night, developed the reputation of being something of a man about town.

In 1938 all of this ended when Symington became president of the Emerson Electric Company and the family relocated to St. Louis. The firm, which manufactured electric fans, had been plagued by labor problems and falling profits, but Symington restored it to profitability and greatly improved labor relations. He integrated the workforce and adopted a revolutionary profit-sharing plan. In the spring of 1941 he secured a government contract to manufacture movable gun turrets for use on bombardment aircraft. He visited England during the height of the Nazi blitz of London to study British designs and returned to develop Emerson into the country's largest producer of gun turrets.

During this time he became acquainted with Senator Harry S. Truman of Missouri, chairman of a committee investigating the war effort. When Truman became president in 1945 he asked Symington to take the chairmanship of the Surplus Property Board.

Holding a series of federal appointments, Symington became known as Harry Truman's troubleshooter. As head of the Surplus Property Administration he established effective procedures for disposing of billions of dollars' worth of surplus property and was especially solicitous of the needs of small business; he was instrumental in breaking the monopoly held by the Aluminum Company of America in the light-metals industry. In 1946 he became assistant secretary of war for air, serving as the War Department's principal civilian representative in the complicated negotiations leading to the unification of the armed services under the Department of Defense.

He was appointed as the first secretary of the air force in 1947 and did much to shape the organization and to establish its identity. He had deep concern for the welfare of air force personnel of all ranks and expedited the branch's integration. He fought hard to increase appropriations for the air force and for the development of its strategic bombardment capacity. He frequently was in public disagreement with President Truman and the secretaries of defense James Forrestal and Louis Johnson. Symington resigned in 1950 because of his failure to secure the kind of appropriations he felt were needed.

He next served as chairman of the National Security Resources Board. He pushed hard for a more aggressive prosecution of the Korean War, an effort that frequently placed him at odds with the rest of the Truman administration. He resigned in 1951 in part over frustration with the war effort. In accepting his resignation Truman asked him to take over the scandal-ridden Reconstruction Finance Corporation. Symington accepted and soon brought about major reforms in the organization.

Although Symington had been a resident of Missouri for only fourteen years, many of which were spent in Washington, D.C., he ran for the U.S. Senate in 1952. Despite the fact that President Truman was committed to his opponent, Symington won the Democratic nomination by a two-to-one margin. In the general election he easily defeated Republican incumbent James M. Kem, as Dwight Eisenhower was narrowly defeating Adlai Stevenson in the presidential race.

During his first term in the Senate he emerged as a major critic of the Eisenhower administration's defense and agricultural policies. He was a member of the committee that conducted the Army-McCarthy hearings and became highly visible as Senator Joseph McCarthy's most vocal antagonist. In 1956 the Democrats of Missouri advanced him as a favorite son for the presidential nomination.

Symington was reelected to the Senate in 1958 and continued his attacks on Eisenhower's defense policies, charging specifically that they had permitted a "missile gap" to develop between the Soviet Union and the United States. Although John F. Kennedy used the missile-gap issue in his 1960 presidential campaign, the charge turned out to have been exaggerated. Symington, too, sought the Democratic presidential nomination that year. However, his strategy, based on the assumption that the principal candidates, Kennedy and Lyndon B. Johnson, would cancel each other's strength and the party would turn to him as a compromise candidate, proved to be unsound. It appeared for a time that Kennedy would offer Symington the vice presidency, but in the end the post went to Johnson.

Initially, Symington strongly supported U.S. efforts in Vietnam, but as the war dragged on he became convinced that the policy of limited war was doomed to failure and in 1967 publicly broke with President Johnson to become a leading opponent of continuing the war. Having easily won reelection in 1964, in 1970 he defeated John C. Danforth by only a narrow margin. During his last years in the Senate he devoted increasing attention to the cause of disarmament. He also played a leading role in the Watergate investigations.

In 1976 he announced that he would not seek reelection to a fifth term. He was seventy-five years old and had had quite enough of politics. Moreover, his wife Evelyn had died in 1972. He remained in Washington, D.C., after his retirement, but on 14 June 1978 he married Ann Hemenway ("Nancy") Watson, widow of the IBM executive Arthur K. Watson, and moved to New Canaan, Connecticut. He died of a heart attack in 1988; his cremated remains were deposited in the Washington National Cathedral.

Stuart Symington was an imposing and powerful figure in the Senate. His principal interests were defense and foreign policy, and he served simultaneously on the Armed Services and Foreign Relations committees, the only person ever to do so. He also served on the Aeronautics and Space Sciences Committee and the Committee on Agriculture and Forestry. Although his interests primarily were national and international, he was exceedingly effective in looking after the needs of his Missouri constituents. He did not think of himself as a liberal, but he acted consistently with the liberal wing of the Democratic party.

★

Symington's senatorial papers are in the Western Historical Manuscripts Collection, University of Missouri, Columbia, Missouri; his papers from service in the Truman administration are in the Harry S. Truman Library, Independence, Missouri. Paul I. Wellman, *Stuart Symington: Portrait of a Man with a Mission* (1960), is a campaign biography by the novelist and historian. Ralph G. Martin and Ed Plaut, *Front Runner, Dark Horse* (1960), is a joint biography of Symington and John F. Kennedy. Edward P. Morgan, "The Missouri Compromise," in Eric Sevareid, ed., *Candidates 1960* (1959), provides a biographical sketch and an estimate of Symington as a presidential candidate. George M. Watson, Jr., *The Office of the Secretary of the Air Force, 1947–1965* (1993), provides an excellent account of Symington's role in the establishment of the air force. Symington was frequently the subject of articles in national periodicals. Among the most useful are: "A Yale Man and a Communist," *Fortune* (Nov. 1943); Bill Davidson, "Mr. Charm of Washington," *Collier's* (15 June 1946); and Hugh Sidey, "Everybody's No. 2," *Time* (9 Nov. 1959). *Congressional Record: Senate* (15, 16, 30 Sept. and 1 Oct. 1976) contains tributes to Senator Symington. Obituaries are in the *New York Times* and *Washington Post* (both 15 Dec. 1988).

JAMES C. OLSON

SZENT-GYÖRGYI, Albert (von Nagyrapolt) (*b.* 16 September 1893 in Budapest, Hungary; *d.* 22 October 1986 in Woods Hole, Massachusetts), biochemist who received the 1937 Nobel Prize in medicine or physiology "for his discoveries in connection with the biological combustion processes, with special reference to Vitamin C and the catalysis of fumaric acid."

Albert Szent-Györgyi was the middle of three sons of an aristocratic Hungarian family. His father, Miklos Szent-Györgyi von Nagyrapolt, was a wealthy landowner and businessman, and his mother's family, the Lenhosseks, included three generations of university scientists. Albert was not close to his brothers, Pal and Imre, nor to his father, who lived apart from the family except for summers on the family's large country estate. Albert was an indifferent student until age sixteen, when he decided on a career in medical research. He published his first papers while still in his teens.

World War I interrupted Szent-Györgyi's medical education. While a medic with the Austro-Hungarian army on the Russian front he was decorated for valor. His experiences shaped his lifelong pacifism. Disgust with the brutality and futility of war and his desire to complete scientific training led him to adopt a drastic but successful strategy. A self-inflicted wound earned him the leave to complete his M.D. at the University of Budapest in 1917.

Albert Szent-Györgyi. UPI/CORBIS-BETTMANN

On 15 September 1917 Szent-Györgyi married Cornelia ("Nelly") Demeny. His young wife was described as beautiful, intelligent, and athletic. A year later daughter Cornelia ("little Nelly") was born. The young couple seemed a close and happy match, enjoying outdoor activities together, and "big Nelly" proved an able laboratory assistant, hostess, and family manager.

During the turbulent postwar years, political instability eroded the family's wealth. Albert's father had died, and his brothers made unwise financial decisions while Albert ignored family matters. He seemed content to support his young family with his modest salary from junior academic positions. Szent-Györgyi's scientific interests had now moved from histology to physiology. He held a series of university appointments in Prague, Berlin, Hamburg, Leyden, Groningen, Cambridge, and Rochester, Minnesota. While his family life suffered, his science did not. He won financial support from the Rockefeller Foundation and growing respect for his inquiries into biochemistry. Completing a fellowship in Cambridge, England, Szent-Györgyi was awarded a Ph.D. in 1927.

The political leadership in Hungary was eager to repatriate a scientist with a growing international reputation. In 1930 Szent-Györgyi accepted an appointment as professor of medical chemistry at the University of Szeged. The hierarchy at the University of Budapest was not yet ready to accept a scientist whose success came more from inspiration and originality than from discipline and tradition. The since-named Albert Szent-Györgyi Medical University of Szeged memorializes the powerful influence of a great mind on an admiring nation.

Szent-Györgyi's varied research interests included Addison's disease and adrenal gland function, vitamin C, vitamin P, and vitamin B_2. His real interests were in fundamental life processes and unifying principles. He began to concentrate on cellular respiration, the process by which all living things break down larger molecules to derive energy. Other research teams around the world were also focusing on energy metabolism, sometimes competitively, and it was widely believed that vitamin C played a key role.

Previous understanding of the role of vitamin C was limited to its dietary role in preventing scurvy. Attempts to isolate it and describe its molecular structure had failed. On a hunch, Szent-Györgyi tested paprika (Hungarian red pepper) for vitamin C content. The concentration was so high that he soon isolated vitamin C (ascorbic acid), described its molecular structure, and supplied it to laboratories around the world. Being first in the competition allowed him to be first in cooperation. There were a few who bitterly contested his place in this race, particularly Charles G. King of the University of Pittsburgh. The Nobel committee, however, unambiguously awarded the prize to Szent-Györgyi.

One of the foremost laboratories in this field became threatened when Hans Krebs, its head in Berlin, became considered an undesirable by the Nazis. Thanks to the recommendation of Szent-Györgyi, Krebs was able to relocate his efforts to Cambridge. Basing subsequent research on Szent-Györgyi's findings, Krebs won the Nobel Prize in 1953 for describing the citric acid cycle (later called the Krebs cycle) and credited Szent-Györgyi for enabling him to do his research.

While 1937 was a high point in Szent-Györgyi's scientific success, the same could not be said for his personal life. His wife, Nelly, felt neglected and sought comfort outside the marriage. Separation followed in 1938. Albert then fell in love with the wife of a fellow scientist whose marriage was breaking up. The two divorces completed, Marta Borbiro Miskolczy became the second Mrs. Szent-Györgyi on 18 October 1941.

The episode with Krebs was only the first major action by Szent-Györgyi against fascism and in support of Jewish colleagues. The University of Szeged was far more hospitable to Jews than the University of Budapest, where there was a pro-Nazi government. While serving a term as university rector in 1940, Szent-Györgyi openly snubbed the Germans. At this time and throughout the war he worked underground to subvert the collaborators and support the resistance.

Szent-Györgyi's research, now concentrating on muscle physiology, maintained a high level of productivity during the war. While the medical implications of muscle research assured the flow of funds, Szent-Györgyi simply wanted to understand the most basic processes of life. Out of his work came the first workable theory of muscle physiology, highlighting the interaction of the protein complex actomyosin, ATP (adenosine triphosphate), and ions.

During World War II, when Hungary was allied with Germany, the Nazis were slow to move against Szent-Györgyi because of his fame and popularity, and his defiance of governmental authority and racist dogma went unchecked for years. Szent-Györgyi undertook a secret mission to Istanbul in 1943 on behalf of anti-Nazi elements in the Hungarian government, seeking outside support to prevent the complete German occupation of Hungary. The mission did not succeed, Szent-Györgyi's role was betrayed, and Hitler personally demanded his arrest. He narrowly escaped an extensive manhunt with the help of the Swedish embassy and Hungarian resisters and eventually reached Moscow.

Upon his triumphal return to Hungary in 1945, Szent-Györgyi was offered the presidency of the nation and declined, but he founded a new National Academy of Sciences. He was appointed to the newly established chair of biochemistry at the University of Budapest and served in the national parliament. His goal was to work toward a reasonable accommodation with the Soviet Union while preserving Hungarian freedom. He observed firsthand, however, that the Russians were as brutal masters as the Germans.

Albert and Marta Szent-Györgyi immigrated to the United States in 1947, facing the difficult task of resuming their life in science with no resources or base of operations. He accepted laboratory space at Woods Hole Marine Biological Laboratory in Massachusetts. Although his efforts to obtain funding were hindered by suspicions about his links to the Soviets and by his speculative approach to research, he was nevertheless able to obtain meat industry funding to establish the Institute for Muscle Research in Woods Hole. Before long the lab was productive, staffed by fellow Hungarians and U.S. scientists. His continued success was recognized by the Lasker Award from the American Heart Association in 1954, the year before he became an American citizen.

The gifted scientist was also a gifted communicator, and he was moved in the 1960s to speak and write on public issues, advocating social justice and opposing the Vietnam War. Writings intended for a general audience included *Science, Ethics, and Politics* (1963) and *The Crazy Ape* (1970). In them he argued for a just and humane society, supported by open inquiry and objective analysis. His rhetorical skills could also be seen in his scientific writings, such as *Chemical Physiology of Contraction in Body and Heart Muscle* (1953) and *The Living State and Cancer* (1978). Arguments were presented in clear, concise, and persuasive language.

Marta Szent-Györgyi died of breast cancer on 13 July 1963, leaving a large void in his life. Albert had been close to his wife and had relied on her help and her role as a stabilizing force. Little Nelly, his daughter, died of breast cancer in 1969. She had remained close to both of her parents, and her visits to Woods Hole had been highlights of Szent-Györgyi's later life. He felt both losses deeply.

In 1971 Szent-Györgyi met Franklin Salisbury, a lawyer, entrepreneur, and advocate for cancer research, and the two formed the National Foundation for Cancer Research. This foundation supported research by raising funds, including donations from the public through direct-mail campaigns. Szent-Györgyi's new research emphasis became cancer and the possible roles played by electrically charged ions in altering the metabolism of cancerous cells.

Marcia Houston, a young, divorced art student, entered Szent-Györgyi's life in 1975. The two were married, and together with Marcia's daughter they formed an unusual and lasting nuclear family. Marcia's care for Albert's welfare and privacy resulted in friction and his alienation from family and friends. Szent-Györgyi became less accessible to his once active social circle, but he seemed content with his new family.

Szent-Györgyi died of kidney failure at age ninety-three. Until the final few weeks of his illness he continued to do experiments daily in his laboratory.

Szent-Györgyi's charismatic personality included mercurial moods, commanding authority, and winning warmth. His spectacularly successful career was shaped by his artistic and intuitive approach to science. He formed speculative theories to prepare his mind for surprises as he examined the results of copious and meticulous experiments. He is remembered for his creativity, his discoveries, and the depth of his knowledge, and also for his charm, wit, and masterly use of language. The Nobel Prize–winning chemist Linus Pauling called him "the most charming scientist in the world."

★

Szent-Györgyi's "Lost in the Twentieth Century," *Annual Review of Biochemistry* 32 (1963): 1–14, is an autobiographical reflection on a career in science and the role of science in the century. Ralph W. Moss, *Free Radical: Albert Szent-Györgyi and the Battle over Vitamin C* (1988), is a biography, illustrated with family photographs, written with Szent-Györgyi's cooperation. Benjamin Kaminer, ed., *Search and Discovery: A Tribute to Albert Szent-Györgyi* (1977), the proceedings of a two-day symposium held at Harvard University for Szent-Györgyi's eighty-second birthday, contains some biographical information. Szent-Györgyi was profiled in *Current Biography Yearbook* (1955) and in Theodore L. Sourkes, ed., *Nobel Prize Winners in Medicine and Physiology, 1901–1965* (1966). An obituary is in the *New York Times* (25 Oct. 1986).

MICHAEL F. HAINES

T

TAUSSIG, Helen Brooke (*b.* 24 May 1898 in Cambridge, Massachusetts; *d.* 21 May 1986 in West Chester, Pennsylvania), pediatric cardiologist who uncovered the cause of pulmonary stenosis, a congenital heart problem, and helped in devising a life-saving surgical procedure to correct it.

Raised in an academic atmosphere, Helen Taussig was the youngest of four children born to Frank William Taussig, a Harvard economics professor, and Edith Guild, one of Radcliffe College's first female students. Although Helen was dyslexic, which made reading difficult, she persevered to achieve good grades. Her interest in the sciences may well have been inspired by her mother, who had studied botany and natural sciences. After her mother's death of tuberculosis when Helen was eleven, Helen grew closer to her father, who taught her the value of compassion and positive thinking.

Helen spent her summers with the family on Cape Cod and in the academic year attended Cambridge School for Girls. In 1917 a blue-eyed, five-foot, ten-inch tall Helen entered Radcliffe, where she played on the tennis and basketball teams. In 1919 she transferred to the University of California at Berkeley and graduated in 1921 with a B.A. degree. When she returned to Cambridge her father encouraged her to enter the new public health program being offered at Harvard University. Because Helen discovered that women were required to have two years of medicine prior to attending and after admittance to the program would not be eligible for degrees, she entered medical school instead.

The medical field was also discriminatory toward women, and Helen had to receive special permission to attend bacteriology and histology classes at Harvard Medical School, where she sat apart from male students. Her professor recognized her potential and encouraged her to transfer to Boston University, where she could earn one year of credit. At Boston University Medical School, which she attended from 1921 to 1924, her hard work and accurate observations caught the attention of the professor of gross anatomy. Upon his suggestion she enrolled in Johns Hopkins Medical School and graduated with her M.D. in 1927.

Although Taussig lost out on the one medical internship open to women, she was fortuitously awarded a cardiology fellowship. She interned in pediatric cardiology from 1928 until she was appointed assistant professor of pediatrics at the Johns Hopkins Hospital in 1930. The following year Dr. Edward Park named her the physician-in-charge of the Pediatric Cardiac Clinic of the Harriet Lane Home, a division of the hospital.

Infant patients came to the clinic with rheumatic fever and an almost always fatal condition called pulmonary stenosis. Challenged by Park to learn about this congenital heart problem, Taussig faced another hurdle when she suddenly suffered an almost complete hearing loss, probably due to an attack of whooping cough, in 1930. Her deafness

Helen Taussig returns by ship to New York City from France, where she received the Legion of Honor for her medical work, 1947. UPI/CORBIS-BETTMANN

prevented her from using a stethoscope, and thenceforth she listened to tiny heart vibrations through the gentle probe of her hands. With the acquisition of a fluoroscope and electrocardiograph, Taussig was able to see certain patterns and similarities, and she found that because of heart defects very little blood circulated through the baby's lungs, where the blood picked up oxygen. Without the oxygen these babies turned a bluish color, often died or suffered brain damage, and were referred to as "blue babies." Taussig thought that if the blood could be rerouted past the heart's defective area through an artificial passage, the blood would be shunted into the lung.

In 1943 Taussig consulted Alfred Blalock, chairman of the Johns Hopkins Department of Surgery. After conferring, Taussig, Blalock, and his assistant, Vivian Thomas, teamed to devise a surgical procedure to create a ductus arteriosus using a subclavian artery that normally went into the arm. After Thomas tried the bypass on 200 dogs, surgery was successfully performed on an eleven-month-old girl on 29 November 1944. More surgeries followed and by 1951, the Blalock-Taussig shunt, as it became known, had been done on 1,037 patients and the mortality rate lessened to under 5 percent.

Taussig was promoted to associate professor of pediatrics at Johns Hopkins in July 1946 and continued studying various anomalies of the heart, especially rheumatic fever. Her research led to *Congenital Malformations of the Heart* (1947), a textbook that became the bible for pediatric cardiologists. New cardiac care centers opened using Blalock-Taussig procedures as a model, and Taussig's success inspired interns to study under her. Throughout the 1950s she taught, researched, and cared for patients. In 1959 she was promoted to a full professor, the first woman at the Johns Hopkins Medical School to hold the position.

In 1962 reports surfaced about infants with severe birth defects born to European women who had used the new drug thalidomide for nausea during pregnancy. Taussig traveled to Germany visiting clinics, questioning mothers and doctors, and seeing infants born without limbs. She reported her findings before a meeting of the American College of Physicians, to the medical community, and in journals. As a result of her investigation, thalidomide was permanently banned for American use.

Taussig retired from Johns Hopkins and the clinic in 1963 but continued to research, write, and commute to the hospital daily. She was the first recipient of the National Foundation of the March of Dimes $40,000 fellowship for scientists, which she used to do a long-term follow-up study of Blalock-Taussig patients. Although Taussig received her first honorary degree from Boston University in 1948, full recognition came slowly. In 1964 President Lyndon B. Johnson presented her with the Medal of Freedom. The following year she was elected the first female president of the American Heart Association, and in 1971 she was made a master of the American College of Physicians. She received more than twenty additional honorary degrees, and her work was published in numerous journals.

Taussig spent her leisure gardening, reading poetry, and sailing during summers on Cape Cod. Her religious affiliation was with the Unitarian church. After moving to Crosslands, a retirement community near Philadelphia, she studied the deformed hearts of birds to find the initial cause of defects. She died as the result of an automobile accident that occurred as she was driving fellow retirees to the election polls and her car was struck. She died within an hour at Chester County Hospital in Philadelphia.

Taussig never married and once remarked that the only children she ever had were "the thousands I've taken care of." To her small patients she was a friend to whom she devoted all of her emotion, observation, and concern. Watching "blue babies" turn pink, she once explained, gave her gratification because she knew she had helped "a child live a more normal life." Taussig's career in medicine was strewn with obstacles and biases, but each detour led her toward the best direction. Taussig's persistence resulted not only in life-saving surgery but also brought her visions of remedies for other heart deficiencies.

★

Helen Brooke Taussig's papers are in the Personal Papers Collection in the Alan Mason Chesney Medical Archives of the Johns Hopkins Medical Institution. Although intended for a young adult audience, a biography by Joyce Baldwin, *To Heal the Heart of a Child* (1992), details Taussig's family life and career. Other works that contain biographical information include Rhoda Truax, *True Adventures of Doctors* (1954); Donald Robinson, *The Miracle Finders: The Stories Behind the Most Important Breakthroughs of Modern Medicine* (1976); Sherwin B. Nuland, "A Triumph of Twentieth-Century Medicine: Helen Taussig and the Blue-Baby Operation," in *Doctors: The Biography of Medicine* (1988); Allen B. Weisse, *Medical Odysseys: The Different and Sometimes Unexpected Pathways to Twentieth-Century Medical Discoveries* (1991); Robert H. Curtis, "Helen Brooke Taussig," in *Medicine* (1993); and Hedda Garza, *Women in Medicine* (1994). An article by E. Kenneth Froslid, "Helen Taussig, M.D.: Savior of Blue Babies," *Today's Health* 46 (Aug. 1968): 48–51, provides a short personal and scientific sketch of Taussig. An interview with Taussig was published in Barbaralee Diamonstein, *Open Secrets: Ninety-four Women in Touch with Our Time* (1972); a videotaped interview by Dr. Helen S. Pittman is in a series "Leaders of American Medicine," National Medical Audiovisual Center in cooperation with Alpha Omega Alpha (1974). Taussig's own narration of her life history is contained in Lynn Gilbert and Gaylen Moore, "Helen B. Taussig," *Particular Passions* (1981). An obituary is in the *New York Times* (22 May 1986).

MARILYN ELIZABETH PERRY

TAYLOR, Maxwell Davenport (*b.* 26 August 1901 in Keytesville, Missouri; *d.* 19 April 1987 in Washington, D.C.), soldier, statesman, and author who formulated the military doctrine of "flexible response," and who served as a key presidential adviser during the administrations of John F. Kennedy and Lyndon B. Johnson.

The only child of John Earle Maxwell Taylor, a lawyer, and Pearle Davenport, Taylor graduated from Northeast High School in Kansas City, Missouri, in 1917. He then took courses in mathematics and science at Kansas City Polytechnic Institute to prepare for admission to the United States Military Academy, which he entered in November 1918. Four years later he graduated fourth in his class with a B.S. degree, and was commissioned a second lieutenant in the Corps of Engineers. On 26 January 1925 Taylor married Lydia Gardner Happer; they had two sons.

Promotion was slow in the peacetime army—Taylor was not promoted to captain until 1935—and in 1926, after two years with the Third Engineers at Schofield Barracks, Hawaii, he transferred to the field artillery in the hope of more

Maxwell Taylor. FROM THE NATIONAL ARCHIVES

interesting duty. After teaching French and Spanish at West Point from 1927 to 1932, he studied for a year at the Artillery School at Fort Sill, Oklahoma, and then attended the Command and General Staff School at Fort Leavenworth, Kansas, from 1933 to 1935.

In the fall of 1935 Taylor was sent to Tokyo, where he studied Japanese and served as assistant military attaché. A minor clash between Japanese and Chinese forces on 7 July 1937 at the Marco Polo Bridge near Peking (Beijing) escalated into a general Sino-Japanese war. Taylor was sent to China as translator and assistant to Colonel Joseph W. ("Vinegar Joe") Stilwell, the U.S. military attaché at Peking, who accompanied the Japanese Army wherever it would permit. Back in Japan, Taylor produced a report entitled "Tactical Doctrine of the Japanese Army." He then returned to the United States to attend the Army War College from 1939 to 1940. After graduation, with the rank of major, he assumed command of the Twelfth Field Artillery Battalion at Fort Sam Houston, Texas, from 1940 to 1941. He was called to Washington, D.C., in July 1941 to join the secretariat of Army Chief of Staff George C. Marshall.

In 1942 Taylor was named chief of staff to Matthew B. Ridgway, commander of the 82d Infantry Division, which later that year was transformed into an airborne unit; thus, as Taylor put it, he became "a paratrooper by accident." Promoted to brigadier general and made commander of the

82nd Airborne's artillery, Taylor saw combat with this unit in both Sicily and Italy in 1943. Italy surrendered in September 1943, and Taylor undertook a mission to Rome to determine whether the city might be seized by an airborne assault before German forces could act to prevent it. When Italian officials refused to cooperate in the effort, Taylor broadcast a message calling off the operation—a decision that later became a matter of some controversy.

In March 1944 Taylor was promoted to major general and given command of the 101st Airborne Division. He parachuted with his unit into Normandy in the predawn hours of D day, 6 June 1944, and captured vital bridges to slow Nazi counterattacks against the invasion beaches. He led his division into the Netherlands in September 1944. He was in Washington when the Germans encircled the 101st at Bastogne in December 1944, during the Battle of the Bulge. He rushed back to his unit and commanded it during the final offensive into Germany in the winter and spring of 1945.

In 1945, with the return of peace, Taylor was named superintendent of the U.S. Military Academy at West Point, where he completely overhauled the curriculum. In 1949 he returned to Germany as commander of American military forces in Berlin. Two years later he was promoted to lieutenant general and assigned to the Army General Staff at the Pentagon. In 1953 he received the fourth star of a full general and was named commander of the U.S. Eighth Army during the final months of the Korean War. He became commander in chief of all American forces in the Far East in 1955.

In June 1955 Taylor was named army chief of staff. However, his opposition to reliance on nuclear weapons to deter communism (the doctrine of "massive retaliation") and his advocacy of a policy of "flexible response"—the ability to respond to limited threats with conventional weapons—led to friction with President Dwight D. Eisenhower.

After retiring from the army in July 1959, Taylor pressed his doctrine of flexible response in *The Uncertain Trumpet* (1960), served as chairman of the board of the Mexican Light and Power Company (1959–1960) until it was bought by the Mexican government, and became president of Lincoln Center for the Performing Arts in New York City (1961).

Following the unsuccessful attempt to invade Cuba at the Bay of Pigs in April 1961, President John F. Kennedy, who had been favorably impressed by the military policies outlined in *The Uncertain Trumpet,* recalled Taylor to duty to study what had gone wrong. After serving as military representative of the president, Taylor was named chairman of the Joint Chiefs of Staff in 1962; his support helped make possible the ratification of the Nuclear Test Ban Treaty of 1963. Taylor was able to advocate his policy of flexible response with presidential backing, and he became increasingly involved in shaping America's Vietnam policy.

Taylor retired from the military again in 1964, when President Lyndon B. Johnson named him ambassador to South Vietnam. He held that post during the months in which the Johnson administration made the fateful decision to Americanize the war in Vietnam. His stint as ambassador ended in 1965, and Taylor served as an adviser during the remainder of Johnson's administration. Although he had initially expressed reservations about the American buildup in Vietnam, he eventually became more hawkish and criticized the media for "sabotaging" the war effort. In 1967 he published *Responsibility and Response,* in which he attempted to place the war in Vietnam in the context of communist "wars of national liberation" as an alternative to direct involvement in the struggle for control of the emerging nations of Latin America, Asia, and Africa.

Although Taylor never again held an official government position, he continued to speak out on national security. When the *New York Times* published the "Pentagon Papers" in June 1971, he condemned the press for irresponsibility. In his memoirs, *Swords and Plowshares* (1972), he continued to defend American policy in Vietnam.

In the wake of the oil crisis of 1973, Taylor advocated the expansion of the National Security Council so that it could deal with all threats to national security—nonmilitary as well as military. He also opposed the passage of the War Powers Act of 1973, on the grounds that it limited the president's power to respond to military emergencies; was alarmed by the creation of an all-volunteer army and the admission of women to West Point; and characterized the MX missile project as a waste of national resources. In *Precarious Security* (1976) he advocated reforming the way in which Defense Department budgets are appropriated, and in testimony before a Senate subcommittee in 1982, he called for the abolition of the Joint Chiefs of Staff and their replacement with a National Military Council to advise future presidents on military strategy.

During the 1980s arthritis made it increasingly difficult for Taylor to get around. In addition he suffered from amyotrophic lateral sclerosis (Lou Gehrig's disease) and grew progressively weaker, eventually losing the ability to speak. In January 1987 he suffered a broken collarbone in a fall and was diagnosed as having pneumonia. Taylor was admitted to Walter Reed Army Medical Center, where he died. He was buried at Arlington National Cemetery.

★

Taylor's papers are at the National Defense University, Fort McNair, Washington, D.C. His memoirs, *Swords and Plowshares* (1972), is a good source on his military career as well as his views on the war in Vietnam. A critical review of the book by Neil Sheehan is in the *New York Times Book Review* (9 Apr. 1972). John M. Taylor, *General Maxwell Taylor: The Sword and the Pen*

(1989), is the only full-length biography of Taylor. The author, Taylor's son, strives to be evenhanded in dealing with controversial aspects of his father's career.

David Halberstam, *The Best and the Brightest* (1972), devotes a good deal of attention to Taylor, painting a somewhat unflattering picture of him. See also Richard Thruelsen and Elliot Arnold, "Secret Mission to Rome: The Complete Story of the Taylor–Gardiner Mission," *Harper's* (Oct. 1944); and Robert S. Gallagher, "Memories of Peace and War: An Exclusive Interview with General Maxwell D. Taylor," *American Heritage* (Apr./May 1981). Obituaries are in the *New York Times* and the *Washington Post* (both 21 Apr. 1987).

ROMAN ROME

TERRY, William Harold ("Memphis Bill") (*b.* 30 October 1898 in Atlanta, Georgia; *d.* 9 January 1989 in Jacksonville, Florida), baseball player, manager, and executive, best known for batting over .400 in a season.

Bill Terry. NATIONAL BASEBALL HALL OF FAME LIBRARY, COOPERSTOWN, N.Y.

Terry was the son of William Thomas Terry, a grain businessman, and Bertha Elizabeth Blackman, a homemaker. He lived with his mother after his parents separated and attended Atlanta schools through the eighth grade. After leaving school, he unloaded freight cars in a railroad yard and pitched for an Atlanta semiprofessional baseball team. He began his professional baseball career as a pitcher with the Newnan team of the Georgia-Alabama League in 1915. The six foot, one inch, 200-pound left-hander hurled the next two seasons for Shreveport of the Texas League.

Terry married Virginia Snead of Memphis, Tennessee, on 18 November 1916; they had four children. Terry, who tended to walk too many batters, left organized baseball in 1917 to give his family greater financial security. He worked until 1922 with the Standard Oil Company of Memphis, pitching and playing outfield for its semipro Polarines team.

In 1922 Tom Watkins, owner of the Memphis Southern Association baseball club, recommended Terry to New York Giants manager John McGraw. McGraw met with Terry on 1 April in Memphis and offered him a tryout with New York. Terry replied that he would play only if the Giants paid him substantially more than he was earning at Standard Oil. Neither the fame and glory of performing for the Giants nor the pride McGraw exhibited in his club's name meant much to the audacious Terry. Three weeks later McGraw offered Terry a $5,000 contract and sent him to Toledo of the American Association. The Giants, more impressed with his hitting ability than his pitching, converted him to a first baseman. Terry batted .336 in 1922 and .377 in 1923 for Toledo, briefly appearing with New York. The Giants won their third consecutive National League pennant in 1923, but Terry was ineligible for the World Series.

Terry shared first base duties with George Kelly in 1924, batting .429 in the World Series against the Washington Senators. He led both clubs in batting with a home run, a triple, two singles, and three walks, but New York lost the seven-game series. Terry batted .325 as regular first baseman in 1925 and in 1927 hit over .300 for the first of ten consecutive seasons, knocking in more than 100 runs for the first of six straight campaigns.

Terry, a scientific hitter, loved to belt low line drives into the power alleys at the Giants home stadium, the Polo Grounds. In 1929 he pasted National League pitching at a .372 clip, making nine hits in a doubleheader on 18 June. The following year he won the National League batting crown with a .401 average, the first of six seasons in which he made more than 200 hits. He tied Lefty O'Doul's National League record for most hits with 254 and fell just three hits short of equaling George Sisler's major league mark, earning the *Sporting News* Most Valuable Player honors.

Terry battled Chick Hafey and Jim Bottomley of the St. Louis Cardinals for the 1931 National League batting title. Hafey edged Terry with a .3488 mark. Terry entered the season finale against the Brooklyn Dodgers batting .3486 and singled in the first inning. His hit would have raised his batting average to .3496, but a fourth-inning downpour prevented the game from becoming an official contest. Terry's hit did not count, and Hafey won the batting crown.

The stubborn, determined Terry frequently held out at spring training for salary increases. He usually won his battles with Giants owner Charles Stoneham, more than doubling his salary from 1925 to 1932. In the latter year Terry belted six home runs in four consecutive games in April and slugged three home runs on 13 August. He batted .350 that season, slugged a career-high twenty-eight home runs, and led the National League with twenty triples. He hit .354 in 1934, but a bad knee limited his playing time and forced his retirement as a player after the 1936 campaign.

Terry stayed with the Giants for a few more years, however. He had been appointed manager on 3 June 1932, and he continued in this role through 1941. McGraw had recommended Terry as his successor even though the autocratic McGraw had clashed with the fiercely independent, confident Terry, and they had not spoken for two years. Terry, a perfectionist with a direct, no-nonsense approach, provided effective leadership, backed his players, and made clever tactical moves and trades. He shrewdly traded veteran Fred Lindstrom and acquired outfielder George Davis, catcher Gus Mancuso, and infielder "Bloody" Ryan.

With Terry as manager, the Giants, benefiting from both his leadership and batting skills, from superb pitching by Carl Hubbell and Hal Schumacher, and from powerful hitting by Mel Ott, rose from sixth place in 1932 to a National League pennant in 1933. They then went on to win the 1933 World Series, defeating the Washington Senators, four games to one. In 1934 and 1935 the Giants frittered away late-season leads. Terry's arrogance may have cost the Giants a pennant in 1934, when he remarked, "Is Brooklyn still in the league?" The Brooklyn Dodgers defeated New York in the final two games of the season and knocked them out of first place. The Giants won National League pennants in 1936 and 1937, but the New York Yankees captured both World Series. Terry's club slipped to third in 1938 and into the second division from 1939 to 1941. Ott replaced Terry as manager in December 1941.

As manager, Terry made few friends among players, fans, or sportswriters. Reporters assailed his blunt, aloof personality and his ultraconservative managerial style that emphasized pitching and defense, often overlooking his abilities as a batter, fielder, and inspirational leader. Terry resented criticism by reporters, believing that baseball writers lacked the competence to second-guess him. The feud with the media delayed Terry's entrance into the National Baseball Hall of Fame until 1954, eighteen years after he first became eligible.

After directing the Giants farm system in 1942, Terry speculated in oil and operated an automobile dealership in Memphis. In 1949 he opened a profitable Buick automobile dealership in Jacksonville, Florida. From 1954 through 1958 he served as president of the South Atlantic League and on the National Baseball Hall of Fame Veterans Committee. He died after a brief illness and was buried in Evergreen Cemetery in Jacksonville.

Terry, a great hitter with determination, intelligence, and imaginativeness, combined the physical power and grace of a natural athlete with a tenacity of purpose. During fourteen major league seasons he batted .341 in 1,721 games and hit over .350 three times. His career batting average was the highest by a left-handed batter to that time. Primarily a singles hitter, he compiled 2,193 hits with 373 doubles, 112 triples, 154 home runs, 1,120 runs scored, and 1,078 RBIs. He possessed good speed for his size, with 56 stolen bases, and led the National League first basemen in fielding percentage four times, double plays three times, putouts and assists five times, and total chances nine times. As Giants manager, Terry compiled 823 wins, 661 losses, and a .555 winning percentage. Under his leadership the team finished in the first division seven times, winning three National League pennants and one World Series.

★

There are Bill Terry files at the National Baseball Library, Cooperstown, New York, and at the *Sporting News,* St. Louis, Missouri. There is no full-length biography of Terry, but his baseball career is reviewed in Tom Meany, *Baseball's Greatest Hitters* (1950); Ira Smith, *Baseball's Famous First Basemen* (1956); and Arnold Hano, *Greatest Giants of Them All* (1967). Gordon Forbes, "Bill Terry, the Strong-Willed Giant," *Sport* 39 (May 1965): 66–67 ff, also looks at his career. Obituaries are in the *New York Times* (10 Jan. 1989), *Jacksonville Times-Union* (10 Jan. 1989), and *Sporting News* (23 Jan. 1989).

DAVID L. PORTER

THOMSON, Virgil Garnett (*b.* 25 November 1896 in Kansas City, Missouri; *d.* 30 September 1989 in New York City), composer, conductor, writer, and music critic.

Thomson was one of two children of Quincy Alfred Thomson, a post office administrator, and Clara May Thomson, a homemaker. Virgil, who attended local public schools, began playing the piano at age five. By the time he was twelve years old he was paid to work as the organist at the Calvary Baptist Church. Because his parents were financially unable to send him away to college, Thomson matriculated with the first class at the Kansas City Polytechnic Institute and Junior College. There he formed a group called the Pansophists, which in May 1916 published a literary magazine called *Pan.* Joining the U.S. Army early in 1917, Thomson studied military aviation at the University of Texas and radio engineering at Columbia University in New York City, leaving the service as a second lieutenant.

Virgil Thomson. OSCAR WHITE/CORBIS

Thanks to a loan from the minister father of a Kansas City classmate, in 1919, at age twenty-two, Thomson matriculated at Harvard. He studied with Archibald T. Davison, who conducted the Harvard Glee Club, and Edward Burlingame Hill, a music historian and composer. At Harvard he also met S. Foster Damon, then a junior instructor in English and only a few years Thomson's senior. Familiar with avant-garde developments in various arts, Damon introduced Thomson to the work of the two people who would become the dominant presences in his creative life—the writer Gertrude Stein and the composer Erik Satie. (Damon played another important part in Thomson's life. When he was a professor at Brown University a decade later, Damon compiled an edition of nineteenth-century American songs that Thomson drew upon again and again for indigenous melodic themes.)

Thomson worked as an assistant instructor at Harvard from 1920 to 1921, before he had completed his degree. At the end of that school year he was invited to accompany the Harvard Glee Club as a pianist on its European tour. When Davison became ill before the first concert in Vienna, Thomson took his place and conducted the group, establishing a competence that he would use again. Thanks to a John Knowles Paine Fellowship (named after Harvard's first professor of music), Thomson spent the following year in Paris, studying organ at the École Normale de Musique with the legendary Nadia Boulanger.

Returning to Harvard in 1922, still short of his undergraduate degree, Thomson worked as an organist at King's Chapel in Boston. Graduating in 1923, he won a Juilliard Fellowship that gave him a year in New York City, mostly studying counterpoint with Rosario Scalero. Returning to Harvard in 1924, Thomson worked again as a teaching assistant. Throughout his years in Cambridge, he made friends with other Harvard men interested in the arts, including Lincoln Kirstein, who later founded the literary magazine *Hound & Horn* (1927–1934) and the School of American Ballet; A. E. ("Chick") Austin, Jr., who for many years directed the Wadsworth Atheneum in Hartford, Connecticut; and the painter Maurice Grosser, who became Thomson's principal companion.

Thomson's career as a writer began in 1924 with H. L. Mencken's invitation to contribute an article on jazz for his *American Mercury,* perhaps the most influential magazine of its time. Thomson, never modest, later claimed this was the first serious discussion of the American musical form to appear in print. Before long, Thomson was making occasional contributions to *Vanity Fair,* the most modish periodical of its time, and *Modern Music,* the most influential professional magazine. In the 1930s he wrote the essays, mostly on informal musical sociology, that were collected as *The State of Music* (1938), which established his literary reputation.

Finding musical prospects in the United States to be limited, Thomson returned to Paris in 1925. Thanks to an introduction to Bernard Faÿ, a French historian who had previously studied at Harvard, Thomson was in turn introduced to many prominent French composers, including Darius Milhaud, Francis Poulenc, and Georges Auric, in addition to the writers Ernest Hemingway, Gertrude Stein, and James Joyce. Stein, more than the others, became Thomson's closest collaborator, providing him with her text "Four Saints in Three Acts," which Thomson turned into one of his best-known operas (1928). Only immediate acquaintances enjoyed Thomson's settings of Stein's obscure language experiments until a group called Friends and Enemies of Modern Music sponsored the first production on 8 February 1934 in Hartford. A *succès d'estime,* the production later had short runs in New York and Chicago.

Following the outbreak of World War II and the fall of France, Thomson in 1940 returned to New York City, where he quickly became the principal music critic of the *New York Herald Tribune,* at that time the second paper (after the *New York Times*) for the city's more cultivated class. Thomson's first review was a salvo announcing that a new critical presence had arrived. Reviewing the New York Philharmonic's opening concert for the season, he judged, "The menu was routine, the playing ditto. Beethoven's *Overture to Egmont* is a classic hors d'oeuvre. Nobody's digestion was ever spoiled by it, and no latecomer has ever lost much by missing it." Not yet done, Thomson continued that the concert "was anything but a memorable experience. The music itself was soggy, the playing dull and brutal." Despite the scathing review by a beginning critic, the *Tribune* retained Thomson for the next fourteen years. After retiring from the newspaper in 1954, Thomson lived as a musical freelance writer and composer, residing in the Chelsea Hotel on West Twenty-third Street for the remainder of his life.

Well-trained and well-disciplined, Thomson was a productive composer for about fifty years. His greatest musical works are two of his operas—*Four Saints in Three Acts* and *The Mother of Us All* (1947), which also used a Gertrude Stein text. The next set of major works were the scores he composed for three films by Pare Lorentz—*The Plow that Broke the Plains* (1936), *The River* (1937), and *Louisiana Story* (1948), for which he won the Pulitzer Prize in music. Whereas the operas reflect Parisian aesthetics, these film scores are very American, often drawing upon the anthology of songs compiled by Damon. Some Thomson fans are attracted to his "portraits," which became his name for short pieces, often composed in a single sitting in the presence of their subjects, who were required to remain quiet. The names of these portrait subjects constitute a pantheon of cultural celebrities.

Thomson composed in other forms as well, if not so notably, producing chamber music, string quartets, ballets, and even symphonies that are still performed and even recorded from time to time. His decision to embrace "popular universality, rather than any set of modernistic doctrines," allowed him to "use the techniques of all ages and all degrees of simplicity or complexity. . . . In so doing he achieved an eclectic illumination of astonishing power of direct communication." The accessibility of his music makes it "postmodern" to some. It is said that the negative turning point in Thomson's life was the failure of his third opera, *Lord Byron,* written between 1961 and 1968 on a commission from New York's Metropolitan Opera, which refused to produce it. As the first informal presentation in 1972 disappointed even his loyal fans, Thomson never tried anything else so grand again.

Thomson continued to write prose through the 1970s and 1980s, publishing essays and producing the short and brilliant *American Music Since 1910* (1971), which, its general title notwithstanding, is a highly personal view of his contemporaries and successors. He joined the *New York Times* music reviewer John Rockwell in compiling *A Virgil Thomson Reader* (1981), which collects some of his best pieces. He gave lectures around the country and in general enjoyed being a celebrity. He was scheduled to speak at a midwestern university when he died of natural causes in 1990, a year after his friend Grosser. He was cremated and his ashes were placed in a family plot in Kansas City.

Thomson, once a combative outsider, saw himself in his later years as an avuncular elder statesman. This new sense of himself was conveyed in his own entry in *American Music Since 1910,* in which he listed his visiting professorships and his commissions, mentioned his association with famous figures in theater, ballet, and opera, and named some of his many honors, including the Pulitzer Prize in music, a gold medal from the National Institute of Arts and Letters, the Brandeis University Award, the David Bispham Medal for American opera, and a special citation from the New York Music Critics Circle. Harvard awarded him an honorary doctorate in 1982, and he received a Kennedy Center award for lifetime achievement in 1983 and a National Medal of the Arts in 1988.

★

Thomson's papers are at the Beinecke Library at Yale University. His autobiography is *Virgil Thomson* (1966). Thomson's other works are *The State of Music* (1938; rev. ed. 1961); *The Art of Judging Music* (1948; repr. 1968); *Music Right and Left* (1951; repr. 1969); and *Music and Words* (1989), which draws upon lectures given in the late 1970s. See also Tim Page and Vanessa Weeks Page, eds., *Selected Letters of Virgil Thomson* (1988); Charles Shere and Margery Teale, *Everbest Ever* (1996), its title being one of Thomson's typical salutations; and Richard Kostelanetz, *Virgil Thomson: American Composers in Their Own Words* (1998), the most recent selection of Thomson's writings. The standard biography is Kathleen Hoover and John Cage, *Virgil Thomson: His Life and Music* (1959; repr. 1977); it includes a chronological list of Thomson's compositions. Anthony Tommasini, *Virgil Thomson: Composer on the Aisle* (1997), draws upon personal friendship for the fullest biography that, uneven, neglects the composer's literary achievements. The Virgil Thomson Foundation in New York City published an informative booklet (1996) with an introduction by Paul Wittke; it lists Thomson's compositions by differing performing forces. See also the entry on Thomson in Nicolas Slonimsky, *Baker's Biographical Dictionary of Musicians,* 8th ed. (1992). An obituary is in the *New York Times* (1 Oct. 1989).

RICHARD KOSTELANETZ

TRAFFICANTE, Santo, Jr. (*b.* 14 November 1914 in Tampa, Florida; *d.* 17 March 1987 in Tampa, Florida), reputed Mafia boss of Tampa, Florida, and one of the key figures in an alleged plot to assassinate Cuban leader Fidel Castro.

Santo Trafficante, Jr., was the favorite among the five sons of Santo Trafficante, Sr., a Sicilian-born immigrant who ruled Tampa's underworld with an iron fist. Santo junior assumed the leadership of numerous Florida Cosa Nostra

Santo Trafficante enters Kew Gardens Criminal Court in New York City, 1966. UPI/CORBIS-BETTMANN

enterprises upon his father's death in 1954. After taking over, he colluded with powerful gangland figures in Chicago, New York, and Cleveland to organize casino gambling operations in Havana, Cuba, with the cooperation of Cuban dictator Fulgencio Batista. Cuba under Batista was a brutal state. Crime syndicate gamblers from the United States paid cash to the dictator for casino concessions; Havana was a wide-open city. Meyer Lansky, Charles ("Lucky") Luciano, and top gangsters from Chicago invested with Trafficante and exerted influence throughout Florida and Cuba. However, when Fidel Castro took over in 1959, he closed the casinos. Trafficante found himself jailed temporarily along with others declared by the new government to be enemies of the Cuban revolution. Eventually he was freed, but he lost all his casino holdings.

In 1963 Trafficante's power and stature in the Mafia were publicly revealed during Senate hearings investigating labor racketeering. Senator John McClellan's Permanent Subcommittee on Investigations heard Tampa police department officials present evidence that Trafficante led a criminal syndicate organization in Tampa. He had also been a delegate to the 1957 meeting in Apalachin in upstate New York, where criminal leaders had gathered to discuss drug operations as well as the assassination of Albert Anastasia, a New York City crime figure. Trafficante was one of the fifty-seven attendees arrested, but charges against him were dropped.

Trafficante played a role in several major criminal intrigues in the course of a career that was remarkably free of jail time. In 1966 Trafficante was one of thirteen people arrested in the borough of Queens in New York City when the police broke up what they believed to be a meeting of Mafia leaders from all over the country. At the time the press dubbed it "Little Apalachin." Not only did he avoid arrest and prosecution over his long career as a mob boss but throughout the dangerous gangland wars in which he participated, Trafficante suffered only an arm wound from a shotgun blast in 1953.

In a 1978 appearance before a House committee looking into the assassinations of Martin Luther King, Jr., and John F. Kennedy, Trafficante said that he participated in an unsuccessful plot arranged by the Central Intelligence Agency (CIA) to assassinate Castro in 1960. Granted immunity from prosecution in return for his testimony, Trafficante claimed that his role in the plot was modest, limited to translating Spanish-language documents and messages. The conspiracy never materialized because one participant after another met death. Trafficante claimed, somewhat disingenuously, that his motives were purely patriotic; he saw himself as helping the United States government. His real motive, however, may have been revenge for losing his casinos under the Castro regime.

Trafficante also denied that he was part of a plot to kill President Kennedy despite rumors, speculation, and spotty evidence that he, Carlos Marcello, Cosa Nostra boss of the Louisiana crime family, and Jimmy Hoffa, head of the International Brotherhood of Teamsters, arranged the murder. The House committee hearings on assassinations revealed that Trafficante, in wiretapped conversations with Marcello and Hoffa, spoke angrily about Attorney General Robert Kennedy's crackdown on mob operations across the country after gangsters had reportedly helped John Kennedy win the 1960 presidential election. Another basis for suspicion was that Trafficante's friend, Hoffa, had been hounded by Robert Kennedy's Justice Department and that Marcello had been illegally deported to Guatemala in 1961.

The book *Mob Lawyer* (1994), by Frank Ragano, who spent three decades as a lawyer representing such organized crime figures as Hoffa, Marcello, and Trafficante, describes a conversation Ragano had with a gravely ill Trafficante shortly before his death. According to Ragano, Trafficante specifically indicated that Marcello and Hoffa were instrumental in arranging the assassination of President Kennedy. Their motives were to neutralize Robert Kennedy by killing his brother; with the president gone, Robert would not long remain in his job as attorney general and harassment by the Justice Department would end. This disclosure seemed credible to some, given the mob's reputed role in the election of the president and the willingness of men like Trafficante to run the risk of deposing Castro.

Trafficante had homes in Tampa and North Miami Beach. He and his wife, Josephine, had two daughters and a son. Trafficante died at the Texas Heart Institute in Houston, where he had gone for heart surgery.

★

For an account of Trafficante's life and his involvement in the plot to kill Castro and President Kennedy, see Frank Ragano and Selwyn Raab, *Mob Lawyer* (1994). For details on Cosa Nostra operations involving Trafficante in gambling, labor racketeering, and narcotics trafficking, consult U.S. Congress, Senate Committee on Governmental Operations, Permanent Subcommittee on Investigations, *Organized Crime: Twenty-five Years After Valachi: Hearings Before the Senate Permanent Subcommittee on Investigations of the Committee on Governmental Affairs* (11, 15, 21, 22, and 29 Apr. 1988), and Robert J. Kelly, Ko-lin Chin, and Rufus Schatzberg, eds., *A Handbook of Organized Crime in the United States* (1994). An obituary is in the *New York Times* (19 Mar. 1987).

ROBERT J. KELLY

TRAPP, Maria von (*b.* 26 January 1905 en route to Vienna, Austria; *d.* 28 March 1987 in Morrisville, Vermont), leader of the Trapp Family Singers, who performed classical and folk music from the 1930s to the 1950s, and author of a memoir that served as the basis for the successful stage and film musical *The Sound of Music*.

Maria Augusta Kutschera was born on a train and raised in the village of Tirol. Her mother, Augusta Rainer Kutschera, died when she was two, and her father, Karl Kutschera, when she was six. She was raised by an appointed guardian who sent her to boarding school in Vienna. A music enthusiast, she joined a youth movement devoted to Austrian folk songs. She had been raised as a socialist and an atheist, but at age eighteen, while attending the State Teachers College for Progressive Education in Vienna, she experienced a religious conversion and became a Catholic. Soon afterward she entered Nonnberg Benedictine Convent in Salzburg to become a nun. Her spirited nature rebelled against the convent's strictures, but of greater concern was her delicate health. It was determined that she would benefit by taking a job outside for a period, and in October 1926 she was sent to become a tutor at the villa of Baron Georg von Trapp, a decorated World War I submarine captain, in nearby Aigen. The baron was a widower with two sons and five daughters, one of whom, Maria, had had scarlet fever and was bedridden. Maria Kutschera was hired initially to tutor her alone but eventually took over management of the house. The baron was engaged to marry a princess, and Kutschera intended to return to Nonnberg after their marriage. But Trapp broke off the engagement and proposed to her instead. She sought advice from the nuns, who told her it was God's will that she marry, and she and Trapp were wed on 26 November 1927. She bore a daughter, Rosmarie, in February 1929 and a second, Eleonore, in May 1931.

In the early 1930s Trapp lost his money, and the family rented out rooms in the villa. They also devoted themselves more frequently to singing classical vocal pieces and folk songs Maria von Trapp remembered from her days with the youth movement. In this they were assisted by their priest, Franz Wasner, who became their bass singer and musical director throughout their career. In August 1936 they were heard by the opera singer Lotte Lehmann, who arranged for them to participate in a choral competition at the Salzburg Festival. They won and soon afterward performed on radio. Heard by the Austrian chancellor, Kurt von Schuschnigg, they were invited to sing with the Vienna Philharmonic Orchestra—their first public concert. They toured Europe beginning in December 1936.

Following the German absorption of Austria in March 1938, the Trapp family found their position increasingly untenable, and, accompanied by Wasner, they escaped across the Alps to Italy in September, then sailed for New York on the promise of an American tour that began in October. It lasted eighteen dates and was canceled when the promoter discovered Maria von Trapp was pregnant; she gave birth to her third child, a boy named Johannes, in early 1939. In March the Trapps were forced to return to Europe when U.S. immigration officials declined to extend their visas. They toured the Scandinavian countries and were able to return to the United States in October, following the beginning of World War II. They were allowed to stay for the war's duration, and they became American citizens in 1948.

After initial difficulties finding an audience, the Trapp Family Singers adapted themselves somewhat, continuing to wear traditional Austrian outfits onstage but expanding their repertoire to include American folk songs and developing greater stagecraft that allowed them to tour successfully throughout the war years, when they frequently appeared as an all-female ensemble because the older boys, Rupert and Werner, were overseas fighting in the United States Army. In 1942 they bought a farm in Stowe, Vermont, where the climate and topography reminded them of Austria. In 1944 they launched a music camp on the site of a disused Civilian Conservation Corps barracks, and they continued to conduct music classes there until the mid-1950s. Georg von Trapp died of cancer on 30 May 1947.

Maria von Trapp wrote a memoir, *The Story of the Trapp Family Singers* (1949), which won the Catholic Writers Guild St. Francis de Sales Golden Book Award as the best nonfiction work of 1950. She followed it with *Yesterday, Today, and Forever* (1952). In the early 1950s the group toured all over the world: South and Central America in 1950; Israel and South Africa in 1953; and Australia and

Maria von Trapp (*seated*) with the Trapp Family Singers. HULTON-DEUTSCH COLLECTION/CORBIS

New Zealand in 1955. By this time, the children had grown up and started their own families, and the group was disbanded after a farewell tour. Their home in Vermont became a popular ski lodge. Maria von Trapp wrote more books, including *A Family on Wheels* (1959, with Ruth Murdoch) and *Maria: My Own Story* (1972). She devoted most of her time to missionary work in the South Pacific. In 1956 she was named Catholic Mother of the Year by the National Catholic Conference on Family Life.

In the late 1950s the Broadway star Mary Martin persuaded Maria von Trapp to allow *The Story of the Trapp Family Singers* to be adapted into a Broadway musical. Martin and her husband, Richard Halliday, produced the show, bringing in Howard Lindsay and Russel Crouse to write the libretto, and Broadway's most successful songwriters, composer Richard Rodgers and lyricist Oscar Hammerstein II, to handle the music. Their story telescoped the romance between the Trapps and the Nazi invasion into a single year, ending with their departure from Austria. Under the title *The Sound of Music*, the show opened on 16 November 1959. It won six Tony Awards, including best musical, and ran 1,443 performances; the cast album sold in the millions. The movie adaptation, shot in Salzburg and starring Julie Andrews, opened on 2 March 1965 and became the highest-grossing film in history up to that time.

In 1967 Maria von Trapp was awarded the Honorary Cross First Class for Science and Art by the Austrian government, in recognition of her efforts to strengthen cultural ties between Austria and the United States. She died of a kidney ailment in 1987 at age eighty-two. She is buried at the Trapp Family Lodge in Stowe, Vermont.

★

Maria von Trapp's own books, especially *The Story of the Trapp Family Singers* (1949), provide biographical information. William Anderson's *The World of the Trapp Family* (1998) is a biography and discography. An obituary is in the *New York Times* (30 Mar. 1987).

WILLIAM J. RUHLMANN

TUCHMAN, Barbara Wertheim (*b.* 30 January 1912 in New York City; *d.* 6 February 1989 in Greenwich, Connecticut), Pulitzer Prize–winning historian whose books ranged in subject from fourteenth-century Europe to twentieth-century China and who upheld the traditional arts of historical narrative and combined them with a cold-eyed realism about the moral prospects of humankind.

Tuchman was one of three daughters of Maurice Wertheim, a prominent New York investment banker, art collector, and philanthropist, and Alma Morgenthau. Her family was very much a part of New York's tight-knit community of accomplished, liberal, assimilated German-American Jews. Her grandfather was the ambassador Henry Morgenthau, Sr., and her uncle, Henry Morgenthau, Jr., was secretary of the

Barbara Tuchman, 1971. UPI/CORBIS-BETTMANN

Treasury during President Franklin D. Roosevelt's administration. Tuchman attended Walden School in New York City. After earning a B.A. degree in history and literature from Radcliffe College in 1933, she took an unpaid job as a research assistant at the liberal Institute of Pacific Relations (IPR), a group that would later come under attack for alleged communist sympathies.

In October 1934 her work took her for a year's stay in Tokyo, as an assistant to the IPR's international secretary, William Lancelot Holland. Her time in Japan deepened what would become her enduring interest in East Asian history and political affairs. It also provided her with a literary apprenticeship, as a contributor to various IPR publications, including *Far Eastern Journal* and *Pacific Affairs.* The apprenticeship continued upon her return to the United States in 1935 at the liberal-leftist *Nation* magazine, of which her father had since become publisher.

Maurice Wertheim was one of the *Nation*'s biggest backers in the early 1930s and counted among his good friends the *Nation* editor and owner Oswald Garrison Villard and Villard's successor as editor, Freda Kirchwey. Wertheim bought the magazine in 1935 to save it from bankruptcy. The following year Barbara Wertheim landed a job there as an editorial assistant. In 1937, armed with *Nation* staff credentials, she set off to cover the Spanish Civil War. Like her father, she had little sympathy for the more determined pro-Soviet leftists at the magazine, but she was a passionate antifascist, and the cause of the Spanish Loyalists, fighting against the forces of Francisco Franco, became the great political commitment of her youth.

Wertheim's weeks in Madrid and Valencia produced only a little published work, but her commentary "What Madrid Reads" was a fine piece that revealed something of an eye for detail and a sensitivity to the continuities of everyday life amid horrifying bloodshed. Staying on in Europe, however, she became involved in various activities against appeasement of the fascists, "what was called by the other side 'premature anti-fascism,'" she remarked years later. In London, where she worked for a weekly bulletin subsidized by the Spanish government, she assembled her first book, *The Lost British Policy: Britain and Spain Since 1700* (1938), which argued for a British role in keeping Adolf Hitler out of Spain. After returning to the United States in 1938, Wertheim collaborated with the *Chicago Tribune* correspondent Jay Allen in compiling a chronology of the war's origins, a work left unfinished.

Franco's triumph, Wertheim later wrote, "replaced my illusions with recognition of realpolitik; it was the beginning of adulthood." She marked that transition in 1939 in the *New Republic* with the article "We Saw Democracy Fail," an angry denunciation of the Western democracies, particularly the part played by American officials and the conservative American press in hastening the downfall of the Loyalists. It was, in many ways, a simplified polemic, as she later came to admit. Still, she observed, no longer could she expect "that the right and rational would win in the end." The journalist's heartbreak would in time become the historian's chief inspiration.

Although Wertheim continued to write for the *Nation* after her father sold it to Kirchwey in 1937, she gradually drifted away from New York journalism. On 18 June 1940 she married Lester R. Tuchman, a New York physician; they had three children and later divorced. During World War II, with her husband overseas in the Medical Corps, Barbara Tuchman worked at the Far East desk of the Office of War Information in New York from 1944 to 1945. Out of that experience would come some of the material for her book on the American general Joseph Stilwell and a recognition of her love for historical research.

After the war she began research on a full-scale piece of history. That book, *Bible and Sword: England and Palestine from the Bronze Age to Balfour* (1956), grew in part out of family interests. At the outbreak of World War I, Henry Morgenthau, Sr., then the U.S. ambassador to Turkey, saved the British colony of Palestine from starvation by arranging for a timely infusion of funds from the American Jewish Committee; Maurice Wertheim, president of the committee, personally delivered the money in a suitcase to Jerusalem. Although it took about ten years to complete *Bible and Sword,* as Tuchman also devoted her time to raising her children, a trio of best-selling books on the World War I era followed in quick succession: *The Zimmerman Telegram* (1958), on America's entry into the war; *The Guns of August* (1962), on the war's causes and outbreak; and *The Proud Tower: A Portrait of the World Before the War, 1890–1914,* on the broader European cultural and political scene. In her late forties, Tuchman suddenly found herself an acclaimed, best-selling author. She received the Pulitzer Prize for general nonfiction for *The Guns of August* in 1963.

Tuchman led what looked like a charmed life: marriage, children, wealth, society, plus the energy and the discipline for an outstanding literary career. Her friend Freda Kirchwey admired how Tuchman, her one-time editorial charge, managed to combine the "immense job" of writing and research "with the complications of children and social life and all the rest." The books kept coming at a steady pace: *Stilwell and the American Experience in China, 1911–1945* (1971), for which she won her second Pulitzer Prize (1972); *Notes from China* (1972); *A Distant Mirror: The Calamitous Fourteenth Century* (1978), on Europe during the bubonic plague and Hundred Years' War; *Practicing History: Selected Essays* (1981); and *The March of Folly: From Troy to Vietnam* (1984), inspired in part by the American involvement in Vietnam. The paradox was that in each of these books, the well-born, fortunate Tuchman, writing from her Park Avenue apartment in New York City or her country home in Cos Cob, Connecticut, examined some of the most atrocious and dispiriting events in history.

In fact, the paradox is fairly easy to resolve if one remembers Tuchman's early days as a writer. Virtually all of her historical writings revolved around a specific kind of drama: how the forces of good rose up, only to be crushed by realpolitik, and then (in some instances) to be transformed into some dictatorial form of radicalism, such as communism. The drama is implicit in *The Guns of August,* explicit in *The Proud Tower*. It is there in the Stilwell book, drawn from Tuchman's days at the IPR and the Office of War Information. It is even there in *A Distant Mirror,* in the bloody suppression of the French *jacquerie,* the revolt of Florence's *popolo minuto,* and the failed uprising of the English peasants. In short, Tuchman made a career out of applying and reapplying the lessons she learned from the fall of the Spanish Loyalists.

Tuchman's success was no less due to her unabashedly traditional narrative style. Her attachment to exact and telling details, her penchant for epigrams, her ability to move fluidly from the specific to the general and back again, all within a carefully plotted narrative, made her seem old-fashioned to some historians but gave her an enormously appreciative general audience. There were, however, drawbacks. At times Tuchman's epigrams verged on the platitudinous, and her unremittingly tragic tone could, at times, be reductionist. Perhaps in order to alleviate some of those problems, Tuchman wrote what would be her final book, *The First Salute: A View of the American Revolution* (1988), detailing an instance in which international power politics for once served, in her eyes, a good cause—American independence.

In her later years, Tuchman stood as an example of how serious scholarship and able writing could be combined in ways that would still attract a huge readership. She took special pride in her presidency of the Society of American Historians (1970–1973), the national organization dedicated to promoting literary excellence in historical work. She was also a popular lecturer, speaking at the Library of Congress, the Army War College, Harvard University, and the Naval War College. Tuchman died of complications following a stroke at her Cos Cob home. *The First Salute* had already been on national best-seller lists for four months. She is buried at Temple of Israel, Mount Hope Cemetery, in Hastings-on-Hudson, New York. A memorial service was held at the main branch of the New York Public Library.

★

Typescripts of Tuchman's books, articles, and speeches are in the Manuscripts and Archives Section of the New York Public Library. For a discussion of her life, see Carolyn See, "Barbara Tuchman," *Kenyon Review* 12 (winter 1990). Her works and methodology are discussed in Kathleen Bowman, *New Women in Social Sciences* (1976), and David Trask, "Popular History and Public History: Tuchman's *The March of Folly,*" *Public History* 7, no. 4 (1985). An obituary is in the *New York Times* (7 Feb. 1989).

SEAN WILENTZ

TUDOR, Antony (*b.* 4 April 1908 in London, England; *d.* 19 April 1987 in New York City), choreographer known as the master of the psychological ballet.

Born William John Cook, one of the two sons of Alfred Robert Cook, a butcher, and Florence Ann (Summers) Cook, Tudor grew up in Finsbury, a working-class neighborhood in London's East End. His artistic and academic aptitudes surfaced early and were encouraged by his parents. His father took him to music shows, his mother tutored him on the piano, and he sang soprano in the church choir until his voice deepened. At fourteen, Tudor was awarded a scholarship to the esteemed Dame Alice Owens' School, where he completed his formal education. A shy, introspective, and sensitive teenager, he often spent his free time reading books about philosophy and religion.

Antony Tudor and Nora Kaye dance the *pas de deux* in the ballet *Pillar of Fire, c.* 1945. HULTON-DEUTSCH COLLECTION/CORBIS

At sixteen Tudor found employment at the Smithfield Meat Market, a giant East End wholesale center. From six in the morning until three in the afternoon, he worked as an errand boy, cashier, and junior clerk. He spent evenings in London's theater district, which offered a spectrum of performances including classical theater, ballet, modern dance, and tableaux vivants. He gravitated toward the ballet, later crediting ballerina Anna Pavlova and Serge Diaghilev's Ballets Russes with his decision to become a dancer and choreographer.

Lured by the stage, at age nineteen Tudor took ballet classes after work with Dame Marie Rambert. Known as the cofounder of the modern British ballet movement (with Dame Ninette de Valois), Rambert formed the Ballet Club in 1929, hiring Tudor as her general assistant; at this time he changed his name to Antony Tudor for professional reasons. He performed with the Ballet Club and also served as stage manager, pianist, electrician, lighting designer, secretary, and accountant. Through his involvement with Rambert, Tudor came into contact with people who would become significant in his life: Frederick Ashton, his contemporary rival; Hugh Laing Skinner (later known as Hugh Laing), his collaborator and romantic partner; and the dancer and choreographer Agnes de Mille. At this time he also studied with Margaret Craske, a specialist in the Cecchetti ballet technique, whom he hired in 1946 to be Ballet Theater's ballet mistress.

Tudor premiered his first ballet, *Cross Gartered,* with the Ballet Club in 1931; it was followed by *Constanza's Lament, Lysistrata, Adam and Eve* (all 1932), and *Atalanta of the East* (1933). He also was an understudy for the Vic-Wells Ballet Company in Frederick Ashton's *Les Rendezvous* (1933) and performed in the Sadler's Wells company's *Nutcracker* (1934).

In 1934 Tudor choreographed the precedent-setting *The Planets,* set to music by Gustav Holst. The piece was composed of episodes, each of which evoked the symbolic meaning of a planet through gesture and movement quality. In the original production Laing played the warlike Mars, costumed in wide red trousers with bands of material wrapped around his bare chest and arms. Describing the solo, the critic John Percival wrote: "Mortal and planet leapt, stamped and groveled in fierce convulsions; everything was extremely contorted and emphatic."

In the next three years Tudor's expressionistic choreography evolved. *Jardin aux Lilas* (1936) portrayed the bittersweet relation of lovers confined by Victorian strictures, and *Dark Elegies* (1937), danced to Mahler's *Kindertotenlieder* (Songs on the Death of Children), expressed grief and mourning. When asked about the source of the latter ballet's scenario, Tudor declined to comment, asserting that "the ultimate importance is that the audience be reached and held in the mood of the work." According to Judith Chazin-Bennahum these dances reflected the maturing of Tudor's method of composition: "He sculpted the dancers' characters in a Stanislavskian way and introduced an intimacy to their understanding by questioning them and teaching them how to listen to the music with an emotional breadth."

Tudor broke with Rambert in 1938 to form the London Ballet company with Laing and de Mille. In 1939 he and Laing moved to New York City to help Lucia Chase and de Mille establish Ballet Theater (later called American Ballet Theater). As the company's resident choreographer for the next ten years, Tudor strove to embody emotional truth in the pantomime of ballet. He often used realistic, bourgeois settings, emphasizing the relevance of the psychological content. *Pillar of Fire* (1942), about the coming of age of a heroine amid the sexual repression and provincialism of a small town, may best exemplify Tudor's quest. Nora Kaye originated the role of Hagar, which catapulted her to fame. As a dramatic dancer Kaye mastered what Anna Kisselgoff called Tudor's "first principle": the dancing *is* the acting. Other works made by Tudor while at Ballet Theater include *Romeo and Juliet* (1942), *Dim Lustre* (1943), *Undertow* (1945), and *Shadow of the Wind* (1948).

Interest in Tudor's expressionistic works waned during the late 1940s, when ballet took a turn toward abstraction led by George Balanchine. In 1949 Tudor left Ballet Theater to stage new works and revivals both in America and abroad. During the 1950s and 1960s he also taught ballet at the Metropolitan Opera Ballet School and later in the Juilliard School's dance division. *Leaves Are Fading* (1975) was the most acclaimed of his later works. His honors include New York City's Handel Medallion, Kennedy Center Honors, and the Capezio Award. He was named choreographer emeritus of American Ballet Theater in 1980. In his later years Tudor studied Zen Buddhism and moved to the Zen Institute in New York City, where he died of a heart attack.

Although Tudor's popularity suffered from the trend toward abstraction in American dance in the postwar years, his legacy endures. He will be remembered for his creation of an expressive idiom that incorporated the language of classical ballet as well as for the nuanced musicality of his movement phrases. Tudor also deserves credit for the realistic ballet that set intimate relationships in an everyday social context. Mikhail Baryshnikov, artistic director of American Ballet Theater at the time of Tudor's death, exclaimed, "We do Tudor's ballets because we must; Tudor is our conscience."

★

Donna Perlmutter, *Shadowplay: The Life of Antony Tudor* (1991), the authorized biography, is based on extensive interviews with Tudor and those in his milieu. Judith Chazin-Bennahum, *The Ballets of Antony Tudor* (1994), balances a biographical portrait of Tudor with descriptions and historiography of his works. For critical perspectives see Arlene Croce, "Sweet Love Remembered," *New Yorker* (13 Aug. 1973); Anna Kisselgoff, "Tudor's Tragic Masterpiece," *New York Times* (1 June 1980), and "Antony Tudor Provides Insights into His Work," *New York Times* (2 May 1982); Arlene Croce, "Zeitgeist," *New Yorker* (6 July 1987); and Tobi Tobias, "Custodial Care," *New York* (11 June 1990). *Ballet Review* (fall 1986) contains the transcription of the tributes to Tudor given at the Capezio Dance Award ceremony, 28 April 1986. An obituary is in the *New York Times* (20 Apr. 1987).

REBEKAH J. KOWAL

U-V

ULLMAN, Al(bert) Conrad (*b.* 9 March 1914 in Great Falls, Montana; *d.* 11 October 1986 in Bethesda, Maryland), congressman (1956–1981) and chairman of the House Ways and Means Committee (1975–1981).

Ullman was the son of Albert C. Ullman, a carpenter and farmer who followed the construction industry, and Julia (Miller) Ullman. During the late 1920s the family moved to eastern Oregon, where Ullman attended public schools. In 1932 he enrolled at Whitman College in Walla Walla, Washington.

After graduating in 1935, having majored in history, Ullman taught in Walla Walla and Port Angeles, Washington, until 1937. Although he enjoyed teaching history and government, he felt a need for further education, so he enrolled at Columbia University and in 1939 obtained a master's degree in public law. In 1941 he married Anita Curfman; they had three children and were divorced in the late 1960s. During World War II he enlisted in the U.S. Navy and served as a communications officer until 1945.

As soon as the war ended, Ullman moved his family to Baker, Oregon, a ranching community, where he became a builder and real estate developer. His interest in history and government involved him in Democratic party politics. In 1956, although President Dwight D. Eisenhower was elected overwhelmingly, Ullman won election to the U.S. House of Representatives, defeating the Republican incumbent, Samuel Coon.

Oregon's Second Congressional District was primarily rural and comprised two-thirds of the state's land area. The voters were mostly farmers, ranchers, timber men, and orchard owners. Having lived in small western towns, Ullman knew the views, concerns, and problems of his constituents, and he represented them very well.

When Ullman first arrived in Washington, he was tutored by House Speaker Sam Rayburn of Texas. Placed on the Ways and Means Committee, he became an expert on the tax laws and policies of the nation. Originally considered a liberal Democrat, Ullman became more conservative during the 1960s as he expressed concern over the costs of President Lyndon Johnson's Great Society programs. Ullman never publicly broke with Johnson on the war in Vietnam, but he constantly worried over increases in taxes to pay for both the war and domestic programs. He supported civil rights, environmental, and education legislation, but his career seemed unspectacular until 1975, when he became chairman of the Ways and Means Committee.

When Ullman assumed the chairmanship, he sponsored a huge tax reduction act designed to shore up the national economy. The $20 billion in tax rebates to American citizens brought considerable national recognition to the Oregon Democrat. However, both interest rates and inflation continued to rise during the late 1970s. Ullman and his committee anguished over the economy as both indicators reached double digits by 1979. Simultaneously, a growing federal deficit and trade deficit offered considerable concern to the committee, which writes all tax legislation.

Ullman concluded that one solution might be a national

Al Ullman, 1980. UPI/CORBIS-BETTMANN

sales tax, an idea he backed in 1979. His own state of Oregon had consistently rejected a sales tax, and had done so by referendum in the 1970s. Ullman could not get Congress or President Jimmy Carter to endorse the concept, and it died in committee. In 1980 Ullman was defeated for reelection by Dennis Smith. He could not withstand the assault on his long service as a demonstration that he "no longer knew Oregon." Ullman also suffered for supporting a national sales tax.

Ullman chose to stay in the nation's capital after his defeat, living there with his second wife, Audrey K. Manuel, whom he had married in 1972. He formed a consulting and lobbying firm and worked there until his death from cancer at age seventy-two. Distinguished by his scraggly eyebrows, full head of lengthy unkempt hair, and 1970s sideburns, Ullman left a lasting impression as a committed public servant whose role was to define national taxation policy.

★

The Albert C. Ullman Collection is in the Special Collections at the University of Oregon, Eugene. Obituaries are in the *New York Times* and the *Portland Oregonian* (12 Oct. 1986).

F. ROSS PETERSON

UNRUH, Jesse Marvin (*b.* 30 September 1922 in Newton, Kansas; *d.* 4 August 1987 in Marina del Rey, California), politician best known for his service as speaker of the California Assembly and state treasurer of California.

Jesse Unruh was the last of five children born to a struggling, illiterate farmer and his poorly educated wife, a seasonal factory hand. Isaac P. Unruh and Nettie (Kessler) Unruh relocated repeatedly during the first ten years of Jesse's life, in central Kansas and then in the Texas panhandle, settling finally as sharecropping cotton farmers near Swenson, Texas. Although she herself attended school only through the third grade, Nettie Unruh recognized early her youngest son's ability and taught him to read before she sent him off to school. As a student, Jesse excelled. His first attempt at college, however, at Wayland Baptist in 1940, was a brief one. Unruh quit, borrowed $50 from his father to spend six weeks in a Dallas trade school, hitchhiked to California, worked for a year at the Douglas Aircraft plant in Santa Monica, drifted back to Swenson and then another aircraft job in Tulsa, and finally enlisted in the U.S. Navy after the Japanese attack on Pearl Harbor in December 1941. He served in the Aleutian Islands.

After the war Unruh returned to California with his young bride, Virginia June Lemon, whom he had married on 2 November 1943; they had five children. He enrolled at the University of Southern California under the GI bill. He majored in economics but also showed an intense interest in government and politics. While still in his senior year, he sought the Democratic nomination for the state assembly from a wealthy west side district of Los Angeles and lost. After graduation he worked at a company that monitored freight car loadings, then tried again for the assembly in 1952 from a blue-collar district in Inglewood. Again, he lost in the Democratic primary, this time to a Republican who had cross-filed for both parties' nominations. Two years later, however, Unruh defeated the same incumbent, first in the Democratic primary and then in the general election.

In Sacramento, the state capital, Unruh demonstrated the appropriateness of his last name, German for "unrest." He found a legislature that was notable for its short sessions, its lack of professional staff, and its domination by lobbyists—and set out to change all of these things. As chair of the Committee on Ways and Means, he obtained an appropriation to support an independent counsel, thereby freeing the committee from its former dependence on information provided by the governor (in this case, fellow Democrat Edmund G. "Pat" Brown). Becoming speaker on his thirty-ninth birthday in 1961, Unruh championed professional staffs for the majority and minority parties of all assembly committees sufficient to conduct research and draft legislation. He subjected the governor's representatives to the same rules that applied to all other lobbyists, denying them the floor privileges they had previously used to round up votes in behalf of the governor's positions. By the time he left the assembly in 1970, the California legislature had been widely recognized as the nation's most effective.

Unruh was a political liberal, albeit of the pragmatic variety. He successfully sponsored bills to limit the interest rates on installment purchases and to require full disclosure of all charges; to ban employment discrimination based on age; to prohibit discrimination based on race in business services and public accommodations; to increase funding for education and recreation; and to establish the California Arts Council. He was an early supporter of John F. Kennedy for president in 1960 and chaired presidential candidate Robert F. Kennedy's California primary victory in 1968.

Unruh, however, could never overcome the hostility of many doctrinaire liberals in his own party. In part, their distrust was a matter of appearance and style. He was a big man, just under six feet tall, who literally carried a lot of weight: when he became speaker he weighed nearly 300 pounds. Although he later reduced his bulk by dieting, he never shook off the nickname "Big Daddy." He was astonishingly plainspoken, shocking people by saying things other politicans only thought. Therefore, this early advocate of public financing of election campaigns told the press, "Money is the mother's milk of politics." He was just as frank about his relationship with lobbyists: "If you can't eat their food, drink their wine, screw their women, take their money, and then vote against them, you've got no business being up here." Unruh's image was severely damaged by a single notorious incident. On 30 July 1963 he locked the Republican minority in the assembly chamber overnight because they would not vote final approval of the state budget. Although a compromise was fashioned the next day, Unruh deprived assembly Republicans of their few committee chairmanships for the next year and a half.

Unruh wanted to run for governor of California in 1966, but Pat Brown sought a third term, only to be soundly defeated by Ronald Reagan. He did not run for the U.S. Senate in 1968 either, because he thought incumbent Republican Thomas H. Kuchel could not be beaten. Kuchel lost in the Republican primary, however, paving the way for Democrat Alan Cranston to win in November. That same year Unruh lost his job as speaker when the Republicans took control of the assembly. Finally, Unruh took on the hopeless task of running against Reagan for governor in 1970. Hamstrung by a limited campaign budget, he staged media events in front of the homes of Reagan's wealthiest contributors and made the election closer than anyone had expected. When he finished third in the race

Jesse Unruh in his office, *c.* 1962. UPI/CORBIS-BETTMANN

for mayor of Los Angeles in 1973, his career appeared to be over, but Unruh bounced back.

Sensing the opportunity created by the Watergate scandal, Unruh ran for state treasurer in 1974 and won easily, as he did again in 1978, 1982, and 1986. He demonstrated anew in this previously obscure office that he knew how to use power to make government work effectively. By the time he died, Unruh had served on fifty-three different boards and commissions and chaired thirty-four of them. Concerned about potential damage to the investments of public pension funds caused by Wall Street raiders seeking "greenmail" (in which companies buy back shares at higher-than-market prices and raiders agree to drop a takeover bid) and by expensive "poison pill" strategies invented by corporate executives to fend them off, he organized the Council of Institutional Investors, a group that could leverage its $100 billion in pension fund capital to demand more attention to the well-being of stockholders. The *Wall Street Journal* called Unruh the "most politically powerful public finance officer outside the U.S. Treasury."

Unruh never lost his knack of saying exactly what he thought. When asked in 1982 whether he was considering another race for the governorship, he replied, "If I were going to run, I'd have to get married, stop drinking, and be nice to reporters, and I don't want to do any of those things." Unruh, whose first marriage had ended in divorce in 1977, did get married again, to Christine Edwards in October 1986, but his principles remained unchanged. At his death after a four-year battle with prostate and bone cancer, he left instructions that his $1.3 million in accumulated campaign funds be used to finance college scholarships and a campaign finance reform initiative.

★

There is no book-length biography of Jesse Unruh. Journalist Lou Cannon covered his years as speaker in *Ronnie and Jessie: A Political Odyssey* (1969), as did former assemblyman James R. Mills in *A Disorderly House: The Brown-Unruh Years in Sacramento* (1987), a memoir both amusing and insightful. Unruh himself, writing as "Assemblyman X," discussed the problem of lobbyists in "This Is How Payola Works in Politics," *Reader's Digest* (Aug. 1960). His service as state treasurer received favorable reviews from Robert Fairbanks, "New Power for an 'Old Statesman': Unruh's $3 Billion Lending Machine," *California Journal* 14 (Feb. 1983): 48–52, and Roger Rapoport, "Jesse Unruh, Guardian Angel on Wall Street," *California Journal* 16 (Aug. 1958): 305–309. Robert Schmidt's obituary, "Jesse Unruh: The Passing of a Political Giant," *California Journal* 18 (Sept. 1987): 435–437, is a balanced summary of his career. An obituary is in the *New York Times* (6 Aug. 1987).

KEITH IAN POLAKOFF

USSACHEVSKY, Vladimir Alexis (*b.* 21 October 1911 in Hailar, Manchuria; *d.* 4 January 1990 in New York City), Russian-born composer who is best known for his achievements in electronic music.

Ussachevsky's father was a career army officer who had seen duty in the Russo-Japanese War in 1905; his mother was a musician and his first piano teacher. Ussachevsky grew up in Manchuria; he was a young child during the Russian Revolution of 1917. In spite of efforts in the new Soviet Union to eradicate traditional religious observance, he received an Orthodox religious education and served as a reader and altar boy. The liturgy of the Russian Orthodox church inspired him throughout his adult life. As a composer, he maintained a strong interest in choral music, writing in what he called a "pseudo-Romantic Russian style." Even after he became famous as an electronic music pioneer, he continued to compose in a style reminiscent of the Russian church, as in the "Missa brevis" (1972) for chorus and brass ensemble.

In 1931 Ussachevsky emigrated to the United States, where he began his formal higher education, earning a B.A. degree at Pomona College in California in 1935. Specializing in composition, he completed an M.A. degree in 1936 and a Ph.D. in 1939 at the Eastman School of Music in Rochester, New York, where Bernard Rogers and Howard Hanson were his teachers. During World War II, Ussachevsky served in Europe with the Office of Strategic Services (forerunner of the Central Intelligence Agency), and he worked for the Department of State immediately following the war. Coming to New York City, he pursued postdoctoral study in composition with Otto Luening at Columbia University, where he soon joined the faculty. In the early 1950s Ussachevsky began experimenting with what composer Edgard Varèse had called "organized sound" in the 1920s. He utilized the relatively new tape-recording technology to create music that consisted of sound events on tape, very much like the sounds being created and recorded by the French radio technologists who developed *musique concrète*. He and Luening collaborated on a number of compositions in which live and recorded sound events generated by each were pieced together to create whole compositions.

In 1957 Ussachevsky joined other artists and scientists at the Bell Laboratories in Murray Hill, New Jersey, in some of the earliest experiments in generating electronic sounds that could be used as the basis for musical compositions. Using Columbia as his base of operations, Ussachevsky joined forces in 1959 with Luening and Princeton University's Milton Babbitt and Roger Sessions to found the Columbia-Princeton Electronic Music Center (later renamed the Columbia University Electronic Music Center). The center's massive synthesizer, which featured vacuum tubes in the days before transistors and microchips, was housed at Prentice Hall near the Columbia campus and was the locus of creative activity throughout the 1960s and 1970s. Students and composers from throughout the United States and all over the world applied for permission to take courses in electronic music or to pursue their own composition projects. Until his retirement from Columbia in 1980, Ussachevsky was the chairman of the committee that ran the center, proposed and taught courses, and selected students each academic year.

Ussachevsky's compositional style was eclectic within the framework of electronic experimentation. He perennially looked for new ways to transform existing instrumental, vocal, and environmental sounds and use them in new works. His "Concerted Piece for Tape Recorder" (1960) and "Of Wood and Brass" (1964–1965) make use of traditional instrumental sounds in what came to be known as "classical studio" compositional technique. The name is derived from the process in which the piece is created by modulating or otherwise altering familiar sounds on tape. In the 1970s Ussachevsky used this technique to create tape tracks that transformed instrumental sounds as a backdrop for live performances by those same or similar instruments. Examples of this technique include "Colloquy" (1976) for solo instruments, orchestra, and tape; "Pentagram" (1980) for oboe and tape; and "Dialogues and Contrasts" (1984) for brass quintet and tape.

Electronic music served as an ideal complement to many avant-garde films. Among Ussachevsky's film credits are *To Catch a Thief* (1955), *No Exit* (1962), and *Duck, Duck* (1970). He also created incidental music and electronic sound effects for plays and radio.

In addition to his work at Columbia University, Ussachevsky served as composer-in-residence in the 1970s at the University of Utah, where he was a regular faculty member (1980–1985) after his retirement. He wrote and lectured extensively on electronic music composition. In 1973 Ussachevsky was recognized by the National Institute of Arts and Letters. He received grants from the National Endowment for the Arts in 1966, 1974, and 1975 and from the National Endowment for the Humanities in 1980. Many of his works were supported by commissions. In May 1992 Ussachevsky's work was celebrated at a festival at the Church of the Good Shepherd and the Cathedral of Saint John the Divine in New York City. These programs included a number of Ussachevsky's choral pieces in the Russian style.

Ussachevsky lived in New York City during his tenure at Columbia, and he returned to the city after his years at the University of Utah. He died in 1990 of a brain tumor at Calvary Hospital in the Bronx. He was married to Elizabeth Denison Kray, who died in 1987. The couple had no children.

Vladimir Ussachevsky's legacy is one of compositional experimentation in the creation of new musical materials. His focus on pure sound as a building block for composition facilitated his own composition and the work of others in the electronic medium.

★

Sources with biographical information about Ussachevsky include C. Wittenberg, "Ussachevsky's Film Music," *American Composers Alliance Bulletin* 11, no. 1 (1963); David Ewen, *American Composers: A Bibliographical Dictionary* (1982); "The Ussachevsky Festival," *New York Times* (30 Mar. 1982); and A. Swan, "Breaking Sound Barriers," *Newsweek* (2 Aug. 1982). An obituary is in the *New York Times* (5 Jan. 1990).

BARBARA L. TISCHLER

VALENTINE, Thomas ("Kid") (*b.* 3 February 1896 in Reserve, Louisiana; *d.* 16 June 1987 in New Orleans, Louisiana), bandleader and trumpeter best known for preserving New Orleans dance-hall jazz and for his role in shaping the Preservation Hall jazz band.

Valentine was born on a small plantation settlement near New Orleans, Louisiana. His education largely consisted of music lessons from his father, Fernand ("Pete") Valentine, an alto saxophone player and instrument custodian for the Picquet Brass Band. By age fourteen Valentine, usually referred to as Kid Thomas, was himself a member of the band. Four years later, in 1914, he formed his own band, Nile. In 1922 Valentine moved to Algiers, Louisiana, west of the Mississippi River. He worked in a livery stable, joined the Elton Theodore Band of Algiers, and as its star attraction became bandleader in 1926. Valentine chose to stay in Algiers, content to be the town's jazz musician. This small but significant distancing from New Orleans made him independent of the developing trends in jazz trumpet playing; as a result, he alone among modern trumpeters was uninfluenced by Louis Armstrong. Valentine and his wife, Maggie, had four children.

In the early 1930s Valentine became associated with dance-hall proprietor Specks Rodriguez, and Valentine's new band, the Algiers Stompers, played in a succession of venues on the west bank of the Mississippi across from New Orleans. The west bank communities of Algiers, Gretna, Marrero, and Westwego were the heart of New Orleans–style dance-hall music. Valentine and the Algiers Stompers built a regular following at Rodriguez's club, Moulin Rouge, in Marrero, Louisiana, and Fireman's Hall in Westwego, Louisiana.

The style of jazz called "dance hall" or "roughhouse" had a motto, "Let joy be unrefined." Valentine's band played crowd-pleasing waltzes, one-steps, fox-trots, and rumbas for its mostly Louisiana French crowd. It worked hard to obtain gigs, including placing Valentine's home address and phone number on a sign to drum up business. The band learned the latest tunes to accommodate requests and even used an old voodoo trick of leaving a trail of raw linseed from the back of a rival club to the site where the Algiers Stompers played. Valentine respected the power of voodoo, and his adopted hometown of Algiers was a center of voodoo activity.

Valentine's trumpet was rhythmic and impressionistic, as it attacked the music and audience. As lead trumpeter, he stated a note forthrightly before exploding into a white-hot succession of notes. Valentine was not so much flamboyant as unique. He employed a slapstick to regulate the rhythm of the band when he was not playing. Valentine would clap the eighteen-inch long, four-inch wide slapstick on the syncopated beats of two and four to keep the band in a driving rhythm. Valentine also used a metal hat as a mute for his trumpet (the hat doubled as a tip receptacle). Valentine played into the metal hat and created a wah-wah effect that electrified audiences.

Valentine's Algiers Stompers were regularly employed at Rodriguez's west bank dance halls from the 1930s into the mid-1950s. By the late 1950s, however, steady music work had died out for them, as for many New Orleans jazz musicians, as the dance-hall generation grew older. Valentine

"Kid" Thomas Valentine performing at Preservation Hall in New Orleans in 1976. AP/WIDE WORLD PHOTOS

supplemented his income by working for the Southern Pacific Railroad and as a house painter. Then, in the early 1960s, Larry Borenstein's art gallery in the French Quarter in New Orleans emerged as a venue for New Orleans jazz veterans. The art gallery at 726 Saint Peter Street, now the world-famous Preservation Hall, was the center of the second wave of jazz revivalism (the first wave took place in the 1940s and 1950s); there Valentine's musical career picked up with renewed vigor. By 1961 Valentine's Algiers Stompers, the most organized of the bands, had become synonymous with Preservation Hall and was often referred to as the Preservation Hall jazz band.

Valentine seldom enjoyed playing with groups other than his own. His band rarely changed, although personnel did vary over time. His regular band included Emanuel Paul, tenor; Louis Nelson, trombone; Joe Butler, bass; and Sammy Penn, drums. Valentine's ways had a charming illogic; when playing a concert in Japan someone reminded him that the two songs he played back-to-back were basically the same tune. Valentine replied brusquely that, "they don't know that, they just speak Japanese."

Until his association with Preservation Hall and his inclusion on the 1964 *Jazzology Poll Winners* album, Valentine toiled in relative obscurity from the world outside of New Orleans jazz. The *New York Times* acclaimed the 1964 album one of the fifty best jazz albums of all time, catapulting Valentine to international attention. Thereafter, Valentine used Preservation Hall as his base and toured the world with his Algiers Stompers, performing in Israel, Australia, Russia, and elsewhere.

Valentine recorded well over fifty albums, the first of them in 1951, and his work eventually made him a household name wherever New Orleans jazz was known. Notable Valentine albums included *Kid Thomas Valentine's Creole Jazz Band* (1957), the *Jazzology Poll Winners* (1964), and *Kid Thomas at Kohlman's Tavern* (1972). The slightly built, dark-walnut-complexioned Valentine continued recording and touring well into his late eighties, while remaining a fixture at Preservation Hall and the annual New Orleans jazz festival. He died from complications from influenza and was buried in New Orleans.

"Kid" Thomas Valentine was a classic New Orleans–style folk musician, not a classically schooled trumpeter. His unique style, his tenacious devotion to New Orleans–style jazz, his longevity, the major role he had in the advent of Preservation Hall, and the inspiration he provided younger jazz musicians made him one of the giants of early New Orleans jazz.

★

There are no biographies or major secondary source materials on Valentine or the dance-hall culture that existed on the west bank across from the center of New Orleans. A vertical file on Valentine is at the Hogan Jazz Archives at Tulane University in New Orleans, and Preservation Hall, 726 Saint Peter Street in the French Quarter, continues to provide information. The most detailed journal article on Valentine was in the July 1987 issue of the *Mississippi Rag*. Primary accounts of Kid Thomas are located in this journal and in journals such as *New Orleans* or in *Down Beat* magazine. An obituary is in the *New Orleans Times-Picayune* (18 June 1987).

JEFFREY BLOODWORTH

VALLEE, Hubert Prior ("Rudy") (*b.* 28 July 1901 in Island Pond, Vermont; *d.* 3 July 1986 in North Hollywood,

California), saxophonist, bandleader, singer, actor, comedian, the first of the "crooners," a top star in radio, and the singing sensation of a generation.

Born the middle of three children of Charles Alphonse Vallee, a pharmacist and proprietor of a Rexall drugstore, and Kathryn Agnes Lynch, Vallee grew up in Westbrook, Maine, where the family moved shortly after his birth. He exhibited an enthusiasm for music from the time he received a snare drum at age eleven and taught himself to play. Although he helped out at his father's drugstore, Vallee did not want to become a druggist; he wanted to be a musician and began serious study of the piano and clarinet. The world of show business also attracted him, and in 1914 he earned his first professional pay, $10, for singing "The Sunshine of Your Smile" at the home of a local paper-mill executive.

Vallee worked part-time as an assistant projectionist at Westbrook's Star Theater, cranking movies by hand. At age fifteen he entered Westbrook High School, but, realizing the industrial arts courses he was taking were not for him, he enlisted in the U.S. Navy. He was stationed in Newport, Rhode Island, as an apprentice seaman until he caught the measles. When the navy realized Vallee was only fifteen, he was sent back to Maine. He enrolled in college preparatory courses and got a part-time job as an usher at the

Rudy Vallee. ARCHIVE PHOTOS

Strand Theater in Portland. There he met an electrician who had a rented saxophone that he was unable to play. Vallee assumed the rental fees and taught himself to play the instrument by hours of practicing in an unoccupied old mill and listening to the records of famed saxophonist Rudy Wiedoeft. Vallee's parents, seeing his enthusiasm, bought Vallee his own saxophone, and by 1918 he was being called "the boy with the singing saxophone." After the former usher-projectionist played a saxophone solo with the Strand Theater Orchestra, he began to get jobs playing at local dances.

Following graduation from high school, Vallee enrolled at the University of Maine in the fall of 1921. He continued to play the saxophone and directed his own band. When he pledged Sigma Alpha Epsilon fraternity, he needed a nickname; because he talked continually about his idol Rudy Wiedoeft, "Rudy" became his name thereafter. During the summer of 1922 Vallee went to New York City to meet Wiedoeft and made his first record, "Japanese Sunset," a saxophone solo, for Columbia. Vallee transferred to Yale College that fall and immediately got a job as a saxophonist with a band that played four or five dates a week. He also played with the student orchestra in the Yale Commons dining hall to get his meals free. The intense hard work that paid his way through college would continue throughout his professional life. In 1924 Vallee took a year off from Yale and went to London to play saxophone with the Havana Band at the Savoy Hotel; he also taught saxophone to more than fifty students. In London, Vallee first heard "My Time Is Your Time," which would later become his signature song.

When Vallee returned from England in June 1925, he got a job with a band in Old Orchard, Maine. He sang romantic songs, for the first time using a megaphone, taken from his baritone saxophone, to amplify his light voice. The megaphone would become part of the Vallee image. Back at Yale, Vallee continued to play band engagements. In his senior year he was leader of the Yale football band. He graduated from Yale in 1927 with a major in Spanish. That summer was spent touring in vaudeville houses with the Yale Collegians, as one of three saxophonists. In the fall he went to New York City with the Vincent Lopez orchestra. His first big break into show business was in January 1928, when Vallee and a group he put together from the Yale Collegians auditioned for the Heigh-Ho Club. Club owner Don Dickerman did not like the voice of the singer Vallee had hired. Rather than lose the chance to play at the club, Vallee grabbed his megaphone and sang "Rain" in his soft, untrained style. When Dickerman said, "That's what I want. You do the singing," it was the beginning of a new style of singing called "crooning" and of Vallee's success.

Radio was a new phenomenon, and WABC wanted to put a "wire" into the Heigh-Ho Club for its first live broadcast. The station did not want to pay an announcer, so Vallee did his own announcing, beginning each broadcast with the cheery phrase "Heigh-ho everybody." That introduction would become part of the Vallee persona. The first broadcast was in February 1928, and Vallee immediately received twelve fan letters. By spring there was a tremendous increase in fan mail, and Vallee and the band, which he renamed the Connecticut Yankees, were on the air twenty times a week. By the fall of 1928 the broadcasts from the Heigh-Ho Club were being carried by WOR, which had a larger audience. When one sponsor offered a free picture of Rudy Vallee, 50,000 fans responded, an indication of how popular he was becoming. Vallee tackled vaudeville when he opened at the 81st Street Theatre; his performance was described as "an explosion in the theatrical world." Vallee next played the Coliseum and then, in April 1929, the Palace Theater, the crowning achievement of a vaudevillian's dreams.

During this time, playing an assortment of theater engagements in addition to appearing at the Heigh-Ho Club and later the Versailles Club (renamed Villa Vallee), the busy Vallee found time to fall in love. In 1928 he met Leonie Cauchois, a recently divorced socialite. They were married five days later; the marriage, which lasted only a few days, was annulled that same year. In the summer of 1929 Vallee left for Hollywood with the Connecticut Yankees to make the film *The Vagabond Lover.* Vallee eventually made a total of forty-four films, but he never again played a leading man. In his 1962 autobiography *My Time,* Vallee described his first movie as a "dud," only shown "in penitentiaries and comfort stations."

Back in New York City, Vallee starred in a nationally broadcast radio show *The Rudy Vallee Show,* also known as *The Fleischmann Hour,* which ran from 24 October 1929 to 28 September 1939. The Thursday night, eight-to-nine time slot was extremely popular (a woman allegedly shot her husband for changing the radio dial during the show). It was the first radio variety show and a venue for new talent, such as Alice Faye, Frances Langford, and Edgar Bergen. The theme song of the show was "My Time Is Your Time." Meanwhile, Vallee continued to play in clubs and theaters. He also wrote original songs, such as "I'm Just a Vagabond Lover" (1929) and "Betty Co-Ed" (1930), and revised, reorchestrated, and recorded hundreds of others. Vallee's versions of the University of Maine's "Stein Song" and Yale's "The Whiffenpoof Song" sold millions of records.

In the spring of 1931 Vallee was grossing $40,000 a week playing the Brooklyn Paramount Theatre, but he felt it was time for a change and took part in the eleventh edition of *George White's Scandals,* a Broadway musical revue. Vallee's impersonation of Maurice Chevalier was a showstopper. Chevalier, after seeing the show, remarked, "He does me better than I do myself." Vallee reprised his role in the 1934 Hollywood film and later played in the 1936 *Scandals.* In July 1931 Vallee married Fay Webb, a minor actress, whom he had met while filming *The Vagabond Lover.* Their divorce in 1936 was a media event. In 1942 he had his best movie role, as John D. Hackensacker III, the richest man in the world, in *Palm Beach Story.* In December 1943 he married Bettejane Greer, a singer and actress; they divorced in 1944.

In the meantime, when the United States entered World War II, Vallee enlisted and from 1942 to 1945 was bandmaster for the Eleventh Naval District Coast Guard Band. The band played at bond rallies, recruiting drives, and more than 500 military bases and hospitals. Until 1943 Vallee continued to star in a thirty-minute radio show, sponsored by Sealtest, that focused on comedy and guest stars and on which he had appeared since 1940, donating his salary to the Coast Guard Welfare Fund. Like *The Fleischmann Hour,* this show was known as *The Rudy Vallee Show.* At the end of the war Vallee went back to radio and continued to make films in Hollywood, including *The Bachelor and the Bobbysoxer* (1947) and *I Remember Mama* (1948). Vallee met Eleanor Kathleen Norris in 1945. She became his fourth wife on 3 September 1949. Vallee had no children.

By the 1950s, the days of radio were over, and although he did some guest-star spots, the tall, blue-eyed, curly-haired Vallee did not like the way he looked on television. He toured nationwide with a one-man show, telling jokes and "outrageously risque" stories and singing his favorites. He returned to Broadway in *How to Succeed in Business Without Really Trying* (1961) as J. B. Biggley, an incompetent corporation president whose hobby was knitting snoods for his golf clubs. Vallee stayed with the show throughout its three-and-a-half-year run and reprised his role in the film version (1967). During the final years of his life he continued his one-man show, *Something Different,* amusing audiences with songs such as "He's Screwing Dolores Del Rio," and he performed at benefits. A week after a successful operation for cancer of the esophagus, Vallee had a stroke. He died at home of a heart attack and is buried with his parents at St. Hyacinth's Cemetery in Westbrook, Maine.

Vallee once said, "I'm a product of radio." Radio made him a star, and Adela Rogers St. Johns reported 20 million people "would recognize that voice anywhere." In the 1930s he was second in popularity on radio only to *Amos 'n' Andy.* Live appearances promoted the crowd hysteria that later singers came to expect. Ceaseless energy, careful study of the art of pleasing an audience, and showmanship characterized Vallee as "America's troubadour."

★

The Rudy Vallee Collection in Thousand Oaks Library, Thousand Oaks, California, includes originals of radio and television scripts from 1929 to 1969, orchestral arrangements, 200 scrapbooks, and correspondence. Vallee wrote three autobiographies: *Vagabond Dreams Come True* (1929), *My Time Is Your Time* (1962), and *Let the Chips Fall* (1975). In addition, see the biography, which is more a tribute than an assessment of a life, by his widow, Eleanor Vallee, *My Vagabond Lover: An Intimate Biography of Rudy Vallee* (1996); the book includes a selected discography and a filmography. Chapters on Vallee covering different aspects of his career are in Alberta Powell Graham, "Rudy Vallee: The Vagabond Lover," in *Strike Up the Band; Bandleaders of Today* (1949); Bill Smith, "Rudy Vallee," in *The Vaudevillians* (1976); and an uncomplimentary assessment in George T. Simon, "Rudy Vallee," in *The Best of the Music Makers* (1979). A four-part series of articles by Adela Rogers St. Johns, "The Private Life of Rudy Vallee," appeared in *Liberty* (7, 14, 21, and 28 Apr. 1934). See also "Vallee Comeback," *Life* (21 Mar. 1949), a review of his opening at Manhattan's Latin Quarter. George Scullin, "How to Succeed in Show Business by Being Rediscovered," *Saturday Evening Post* (23 June 1962), discusses Vallee's success on Broadway. A good indicator of Vallee's personality is Rudy Vallee, "Self-Portrait," *Esquire* (June 1962). Robert S. Gallagher, " 'Heigh-ho, Everybody!,' " *American Heritage* (June 1972), is an interview covering personal and professional aspects of Vallee's life. For Vallee's life in Maine, see C. Stewart Doty, "Rudy Vallee: Franco-American and Man from Maine," *Maine Historical Society Quarterly* 33 (1993): 2–19. An obituary is in the *New York Times* (5 July 1986).

MARCIA B. DINNEEN

VAN ARSDALE, Harry, Jr. (*b.* 23 November 1905 in New York City; *d.* 16 February 1986 in New York City), the most influential labor leader of his time in New York and a nationally known maverick of organized labor.

Van Arsdale was one of two children of Kathryn Plunkett and Harry Van Arsdale, Sr. Literally a child of the labor movement—he was born during a thirty-three-month lockout of electrical workers—Van Arsdale grew up in a poor section of the New York City borough of Manhattan, where he witnessed the erratic working conditions of his father, an electrician journeyman with Local 3 of the International Brotherhood of Electrical Workers (IBEW), which he himself would later head. From a young age Van Arsdale admired his father's labor activism and got his chance early to emulate him. Although he showed promise as a student at Townsend Harris High School, an experimental school for the gifted, Van Arsdale was forced to quit after only two years, at age sixteen, to go to work.

With a father-son hiring hall system typical of building-trades unions, Local 3 was the logical place for Van Arsdale to seek work, but he was initially turned away because of high unemployment. Instead, in 1922, at seventeen, he married Mary Casey, with whom he had four children. (Casey died in 1966, and Van Arsdale later married Madeline Reilly.) In 1925 he succeeded in joining Local 3 and began work in the electrical trade. He had eagerly studied labor history, and his knowledge helped garner him several union staff positions. But the union for which Van Arsdale now worked was ineffective in obtaining employment in a depressed economy, wracked by factionalism to the point of violence, marred by financial irregularities, and, in the 1930s, infiltrated by communists and racketeers.

A precocious and ambitious reformer, Van Arsdale sought control of Local 3 on a platform of purging leftists and gangsters, organizing the electrical industry, and fighting for better wages and steadier employment. At times the battles got rough. He was arrested in 1932 and 1933 on charges of assault in scuffles with opposition unionists. In the first case the charges were dropped; Van Arsdale was convicted in the second case, but the conviction was overturned on appeal. In April 1933 Van Arsdale's group assumed permanent control. In October the union's business manager resigned, and Van Arsdale was appointed to fill the vacancy at twenty-six. He would be elected to that po-

Harry Van Arsdale, Jr., 1962. UPI/CORBIS-BETTMANN

sition for the next twenty-four years. Among his first moves was to reform the local's mismanaged finances.

In contrast to the radical labor leaders of the 1930s, Van Arsdale operated on the assumption that labor and management's interests were essentially the same. "To get more, you must give more" was his mantra. In exchange for higher wages and more benefits, Local 3 would give contractors greater productivity and efficiency and a mentality that was strike-averse. Utilizing this strategy, Van Arsdale won an unusual seven-hour day in 1934 and a six-hour day in 1940. In 1962 he gained an unprecedented twenty-five-hour work week. In each case the construction electricians got overtime at higher rates and avoided a pay cut.

Another strategy Van Arsdale used for empowering Local 3 was to expand the 5,700-member craft union to include industrial factory workers, beginning with switchboard assembly workers in 1933. This endeavor, however, often required direct confrontation, and the tough union boss reemerged. In 1941 Van Arsdale was convicted of inciting a riot while on a picket line; again, the conviction was overturned on appeal. In the end, he prevailed. By the early 1970s, Local 3 would be the largest building-trades local in the country, with 33,000 members and twenty-five divisions.

Despite the strife of industrial organizing, Van Arsdale continued to stress cooperation with employers. When local manufacturers complained that having to pay union wages made them less competitive, Van Arsdale promised that union construction workers would refuse to install any electrical equipment not carrying the Local 3 label. In 1935 this secondary boycott was challenged in court by out-of-town manufacturers. Ten years later, the union won a partial victory at the U.S. Supreme Court, which held that Local 3 could engage in a secondary boycott but could not collude with contractors and manufacturers in doing so. The IBEW was less charitable: in 1950 the international sanctioned Van Arsdale for discriminating against sister locals.

Van Arsdale also worked with industry to establish a wide array of benefits, initially for the union's construction workers. By the 1950s his efforts at "welfare unionism" were well known. Van Arsdale began in 1937 by convincing contractors to pay all social security taxes. But most benefits were won after he and industry representatives established a union-employer entity in 1943 called the Joint Industry Board, which handled everything from work allocation to benefits. The latter included an employer-paid pension, hospitalization, disability, death benefits, and scholarships for union members and their children. Van Arsdale touted worker education, and in 1950 the board purchased a 314-acre estate that was later used as a school for union members. In 1952 the board built a cooperative housing project in the New York City borough of Queens for members.

In the mid-1950s Van Arsdale turned his attention to the labor movement at large. A Democrat, he formed a labor party in 1956 to help reelect Mayor Robert F. Wagner, Jr., and in 1957 he was elected president of the Greater New York Central Trades and Labor Council, which, with his help, became in 1959 the New York City Central Labor Council, an AFL-CIO federation representing nearly 1 million unionists. In these roles he forged close ties with Wagner and New York Governor Nelson Rockefeller and helped to organize hospital workers and taxi drivers and win collective bargaining rights for teachers. Van Arsdale drew national notice in 1962, when, following an eight-day strike, he obtained the twenty-five-hour work week. In exchange, the union agreed to greatly expand its apprenticeship program, another unusual move for a building-trades union. At the urging of civil rights leaders, Van Arsdale used the opportunity to bring hundreds of Puerto Ricans and African Americans into the union's tightly controlled construction division for the first time.

In 1968 Van Arsdale resigned as business manager of Local 3 to become financial secretary of the local and treasurer of the IBEW. In the 1970s he advised New York officials on the city's fiscal crisis. By the mid-1970s, however, his power, along with that of organized labor generally, had waned. In 1985 he announced he was stepping aside from his posts temporarily because of health problems. The following year he died of prostate cancer at his home in Flushing, Queens, in the union's cooperative housing project. He is buried in St. John's Cemetery in Queens.

At his peak in the 1960s, having gained national recognition for the twenty-five-hour week and become a confidant of many New York politicians, Van Arsdale was once dubbed "the unofficial mayor of New York." Although an occasional rabble-rouser, he was above all a masterful power broker who perfected the art of cooperation with industrial and political leaders to obtain impressive and at times unprecedented gains for workers. His commanding, insider leadership style was paternalistic and alienated some unionists; but few questioned his efficacy.

★

The archives of the Joint Industry Board of Local 3, IBEW, contain materials dealing with Van Arsdale but are not open to the public. The "New Yorkers at Work" collection at Tamiment Library, New York University, includes oral histories and other materials on Van Arsdale in his role as president of the New York City Central Labor Council. The Robert F. Wagner Archives at La Guardia Community College in New York City also house collections pertaining to Van Arsdale. There is no published biography of Van Arsdale, but the most extensive treatment of Van Arsdale's life is in George Santiago, "Power and Affiliation Within a Local Trade Union: Local 3 of the International Brotherhood of Electrical Workers" (Ph.D. diss., City University of New York, 1987). Obituaries are in the *New York Times* (17 Feb. 1986), *New*

York Daily News (19 Feb. 1986), and *Los Angeles Times* (25 Feb. 1986).

ANNE KORNHAUSER

VAN HEUSEN, James ("Jimmy") (*b.* 26 January 1913 in Syracuse, New York; *d.* 7 February 1990 in Rancho Mirage, California), songwriter who had a successful Hollywood career; he is best known for hits popularized by Bing Crosby and Frank Sinatra.

Born Edward Chester Babcock, Van Heusen was the second of two sons of Arthur Edward Babcock, a building contractor, and Ida Mae Williams Babcock. Although Babcock played cornet and allowed his son to take piano lessons, and the family was thought to be descended from the American composer Stephen Foster, he insisted that his son put aside music to pursue an academic career. Van Heusen began to write songs as a teenager, but was a dilatory student. In 1928 he was expelled from Syracuse's Central High School for singing a mildly salacious song, "My Canary Has Rings Under His Eyes," in an assembly, and the following year he was thrown out of nearby Cazenovia Seminary.

Van Heusen got his first job at age sixteen as a radio announcer and singer on station WSYR in Syracuse. The station manager of WSYR expressed concern that "Babcock" would sound obscene over the air, and suggested that he adopt a pseudonym based on a popular brand of men's shirts. Van Heusen used the name professionally, but he never legally changed his name, and those who knew him longest called him Chester.

Although his father made him give up the radio job and enroll at Syracuse University to prepare for a business career, Van Heusen found time to study piano, voice, and composition from 1930 until 1932. One of his student friends, and occasionally the lyricist for his early songs, was Jerry Arlen, a neighbor and the brother of composer Harold Arlen. When Arlen invited the team to New York City to contribute to a revue at Harlem's famed Cotton Club, Van Heusen dropped out of college, thereby ending his formal education. Though the revue flopped, one of Van Heusen's songs, "Harlem Hospitality," was published in 1933. Van Heusen was then employed as a waiter and an elevator operator before landing a job as a staff pianist for Jerome H. Remick's music publishing company in 1938. He had been living in a $14-a-week room at the Wellington Hotel and wangling free food from room service.

Van Heusen first began to make a name for himself in 1934, when he published "There's a House in Harlem for Sale." His fortunes improved considerably when he met bandleader Jimmy Dorsey at Remick's in 1938. They collaborated on "It's the Dreamer in Me," which became a hit. Remick then signed Van Heusen to a two-year songwriting contract at $250 per week. At about the same time he began collaborating with bandleader and lyricist Eddie DeLange. In their first year together, they had several hit songs, including "Deep in a Dream" in 1938, and "All This and Heaven Too" and "Heaven Can Wait" in 1939.

They also composed the score for Van Heusen's first Broadway musical, *Swingin' the Dream,* based on Shakespeare's *A Midsummer Night's Dream.* Although it ran for only thirteen performances in 1939, its score included "Darn That Dream," which was made into a hit when Benny Goodman's orchestra recorded it with a vocal by Mildred Bailey. Also that year, Van Heusen wrote the score for Billy Rose's Aquacade at the New York World's Fair, and wrote several songs with lyricist Johnny Mercer, including "I Thought About You." Even though Remick fired him in 1939, Van Heusen already had so many hit songs from radio play that the dismissal had little impact on his career. That year, seven of his songs made the hit parade, two of them—"Heaven Can Wait" and "Imagination"—rising to the number one spot.

At age twenty-seven, Van Heusen signed with Paramount Pictures and met the three people who would have the greatest influence on his career: lyricist Johnny Burke, Bing Crosby, and Frank Sinatra. He and Burke began their thirteen-year collaboration with songs for the movie *Love Thy Neighbor,* starring Jack Benny. In 1940 they also wrote "Polka Dots and Moonbeams," recorded by Frank Sinatra with Tommy Dorsey's orchestra. From then on, Sinatra's recordings of Van Heusen's songs contributed in a major way to their success, just as the songs contributed to Sinatra's.

Impressed by "Imagination," Crosby asked Burke and Van Heusen to write the songs for the first of the "Road" pictures, *Road to Zanzibar,* in 1941. They went on to write songs for *Road to Morocco* (1942), *Road to Utopia* (1945), *Road to Rio* (1947), and *Road to Bali* (1952), starring Crosby, Bob Hope, and Dorothy Lamour. The songs included "Road to Morocco," "Moonlight Becomes You," "Personality," "But Beautiful," "You Don't Have to Know the Language," and "Put It There."

Van Heusen and Burke wrote songs for more than two dozen other Crosby movies, among them "Sunday, Monday, and Always" (*Dixie,* 1943), "Going My Way" and "Swingin' on a Star" (*Going My Way,* 1944), "It Could Happen to You" (*And the Angels Sing,* 1944), "Like Someone in Love" (*Belle of the Yukon,* 1944), "Aren't You Glad You're You" (*The Bells of St. Mary's,* 1946), and "Life Is So Peculiar" (*Mister Music,* 1950). He won the first of his four Oscars for best song for "Swingin' on a Star." He and Sammy Cahn also won, in 1957, for "All the Way," in 1959 for "High Hopes," and in 1963 for "Call Me Irresponsible." Nine other songs, eight of them with Cahn, received Oscar nominations, including "The Second Time Around" (*High*

Jimmy Van Heusen, 1939. UPI/CORBIS-BETTMANN

Time, 1960), "My Kind of Town" (*Robin and the Seven Hoods,* 1964), "Where Love Has Gone" (*Where Love Has Gone,* 1964), and "Thoroughly Modern Millie" (*Thoroughly Modern Millie,* 1967).

During World War II, Van Heusen toured West Coast army camps with Bing Crosby. From 1942 until 1944, he also had a temporary secondary career unrelated to songwriting. He had been avid about flying his own airplane since getting his pilot's license in 1937. Under his own name, he worked as a test pilot for Lockheed in the morning and wrote songs in the afternoon. He kept his creative identity secret from his fellow employees and his airborne activities secret from the studio bosses.

Van Heusen and Burke also wrote two unsuccessful Broadway musicals, *Nelly Bly* in 1946 and *Carnival in Flanders* in 1953, although *Carnival* produced one major song, "Here's That Rainy Day." Other important songs by Van Heusen and Burke include "If You Stub Your Toe on the Moon" (*A Connecticut Yankee in King Arthur's Court,* 1949), "Sunshine Cake" (*Riding High,* 1950), and "Somewhere Along the Way" (1952). In 1944 he and comedian Phil Silvers collaborated on the Sinatra signature song, "Nancy, with the Laughing Face," and he and Burke formed their own music publishing company.

Carnival in Flanders marked the end of Van Heusen and Burke's collaboration because Burke became ill and was unable to work. After a few months of inactivity, Van Heusen composed a few songs under the pseudonym of Arthur Williams and, in 1954, wrote the music for Lena Horne's successful nightclub act. At this time, Crosby introduced Van Heusen to Sammy Cahn, who was dissolving his partnership with composer Jule Styne.

Van Heusen and Cahn established themselves with the title song for the Frank Sinatra movie *The Tender Trap* (1955) and "Love and Marriage" for a TV adaptation of Thornton Wilder's *Our Town,* also starring Sinatra. The latter was Van Heusen's first Emmy-winning song, and both played a pivotal role in restoring Sinatra's career after his popularity dipped earlier in the 1950s. Sinatra eventually recorded seventy-six of Van Heusen and Cahn's songs, including the title songs for such important albums as *Come Fly with Me* (1958), *Only the Lonely* (1958), and *September of My Years* (1965). Van Heusen and Cahn won a second Emmy in 1966 for a TV special of *Jack and the Beanstalk,* starring Gene Kelly. The duo returned to Broadway for the mildly successful *Skyscraper* (1965) and *Walking Happy* (1966). *Skyscraper* was Van Heusen's longest running show, with 248 performances.

Among the movies to which Van Heusen and Cahn contributed songs were *Anything Goes* with Crosby (1956), *Pardners* with Dean Martin and Jerry Lewis (1956), and *Let's Make Love* with Marilyn Monroe (1960). They also wrote nightclub acts for Lena Horne, Nat King Cole, Sammy Davis, Jr., Paul Anka, and Juliet Prowse. "Star," the title song for a 1968 Julie Andrews movie, was his last major song.

Van Heusen and Cahn dissolved their partnership in 1969, when Van Heusen decided to retire. In that same year, at the age of fifty-six, he married Josephine Brock Perlberg, a former singer. They had no children. In 1971 he was one of the initial songwriters elected to the Songwriter's Hall of Fame. He died after a long illness at his home in Rancho Mirage.

Tall, bald, and gregarious, Van Heusen was one of Hollywood's most eligible bachelors for many years. A night owl who rarely began to work before 8 P.M., Van Heusen once said, "I dig chicks, booze, music, and Sinatra—in that order."

Although best known for upbeat songs that lent themselves to the kind of jaunty, wisecracking lyrics favored by both Crosby and Sinatra, Van Heusen also wrote elegantly optimistic romantic ballads. As his success in Hollywood and his relative failure on Broadway also suggest, he was more suited to the writing of individual songs tailored to the styles of specific performers than to the writing of scores whose songs served characters and plots.

★

Alec Wilder, *American Popular Song: The Great Innovators, 1900–1950* (1972), contains the most thoughtful examination of Van Heusen's achievement as a composer. Roy Hemming, *The Melody Lingers On: The Great Songwriters and Their Movie Musicals* (1986), is the most complete and analytic of the few studies of Van Heusen's career. See also David Ewen, *American Songwriters* (1987). An obituary is in the *New York Times* (8 Feb. 1990).

MICHAEL LASSER

VARE, Glenna Collett (*b.* 20 June 1903 in New Haven, Connecticut; *d.* 3 February 1989 in Gulfstream, Florida), leading woman golfer of the 1920s and early 1930s who won the national title a record six times.

The daughter of George H. Collett and Ada (Wilkinson) Collett, Glenna was influenced by the athleticism of her father, a construction worker who was also a skilled cyclist, bowler, and golfer. When Glenna was six, she moved with her parents and her brother Edwin to Providence, Rhode Island. By the age of nine, she had become an excellent swimmer and diver, and she played baseball on her brother's team until she was fourteen. At her mother's suggestion she then tried other sports and began playing tennis.

Glenna's interest in sports changed, however, on accompanying her father to the Metacomet Country Club, where, after hitting some golf balls, she became intrigued with the game. Discouraged at first with her scores, she was coached by a local golf professional and later by Alex Smith, a two-time U.S. Open champion. She dropped out of high school to pursue her sport and won her first golf tournament in 1920 at the age of seventeen. She soon developed the hallmark of her game, long drives, which distinguished her from other golfers of the era. At the age of eighteen, at five-foot-six and 128 pounds, she once drove the ball 307 yards off the tee, the longest distance achieved by a woman golfer to that time.

On the eve of the 1922 U.S. Women's Amateur championship, Vare's fourth appearance in that event, she was favored to win the prestigious title. She overcame pressure from the press and prevailed over four previous American title holders to claim the trophy. On 30 September 1922, the day she won her first national title at the Greenbrier links in White Sulphur Springs, West Virginia, a *New York Times* writer proclaimed her "one of the premier women golfers of all time." The 1922 U.S. Championship marked her third major title of the year, as she had won the North and South Championship and the Eastern women's championship. The teenager's impressive victories in three major tournaments were an indication that she was destined to become one of the greatest women golfers of all time.

Glenna Vare at the Women's Eastern Golf Championship at the Huntington Valley Golf Course, 1935. UPI/CORBIS-BETTMANN

In 1923 and 1924 Vare won the Canadian, Eastern, and North-South Championships. She reclaimed the U.S. Championship at the St. Louis Country Club on 4 October 1925, defeating Alexa Stirling Fraser of Ottawa, Canada, a three-time winner of the event, and shooting a 75 in the final round, producing a new course record. Earlier in the competition, Fraser had carded a 77. Prior to these performances, the lowest score ever made by a woman golfer was 81.

Vare's other victories in 1925 included the Florida, West Coast, and the French Championships. On 15 October

1925 the Providence Board of Alderman adopted a resolution expressing appreciation on behalf of the city's citizens for her achievements in golf, the recognition she brought to the city, and for inspiring young people to participate in sport. The following month she was invited to the White House to be received by President Calvin Coolidge.

In 1928 Vare won her third U.S. Women's Amateur title by the largest margin in the event's history, at the Hot Springs Golf and Tennis Club in Virginia. She successfully defended her national title the following year in Birmingham, Michigan. When in 1930 the national tournament was held on the West Coast for the first time, Vare again retained her title, in Beverly Hills, California. In 1932 she finished second in the national championship. In 1935, in Hopkins, Minnesota, she became the first and only six-time winner of the U.S. Women's Amateur championship.

Continuing into the 1930s, Vare established her reputation as a premier golfer by becoming a multiple winner of prestigious tournaments. In addition to her six U.S. Women's Amateur titles, she won the Canadian Women's Amateur tournament twice, the French Amateur title twice, and the North-South women's tournament six times. Though unable to triumph in the British Ladies Amateur Championship in 1925, 1929, and 1930, she advanced to the final round of that tournament in 1929 and 1930.

In 1931 Glenna married Edwin H. Vare, Jr., a graduate of the University of Pennsylvania. Two years later, on the day after her thirtieth birthday, she gave birth to a daughter, Glenna; a son, Edwin Collett, was born a year later. By the late 1930s, she had left the national golf scene to devote time to her family, but she played locally in Pennsylvania. Later she continued to play in Rhode Island and Florida.

Vare never played professional golf: women's tournaments in her era were amateur events. There was no organized professional women's tour until the 1940s, and the seeds for the Ladies Professional Golf Association (LPGA) were not sown until 1948. Her name nevertheless remains linked to golf. In 1952 the LPGA began recognizing her achievements annually with the Vare Trophy, presented to the player with the lowest average of strokes on the tour. In 1950 she was a charter member of the Women's Golf Hall of Fame, and in 1975 she was inducted into the World Golf Hall of Fame.

When Vare was reigning over the women's game in the 1920s and 1930s, she was revered for her consistent scores, long drives, and pleasant demeanor. Vare had a significant impact on women's golf as a role model and standard-bearer and made an exemplary contribution to the sport as a gracious winner. In her autobiography, *This Life I've Led* (1955), the legendary golfer Babe Didrikson Zaharias wrote that she had developed an interest in golf through newspaper reports heralding the achievements of Vare and Walter Hagen. In a *London Times* tribute following Vare's death from heart failure, Patricia Davies exalted her as the "grande dame of American golf."

★

Collections of pictures, golf periodicals, and memorabilia pertaining to Vare are in the Ralph Miller Golf Library in City of Industry, California; the World Golf Hall of Fame in Ponte Vedra, Florida; and the U.S. Golf Association in Far Hills, New Jersey. Vare, assisted by James M. Neville, wrote *Ladies in the Rough* (1928), a chronology of her early golf career. A biographical account is in Ross Goodner, *Golf's Greatest* (1978). An obituary is in the *New York Times* (6 Feb. 1989).

PAULA D. WELCH

VAUGHAN, Sarah Lois (*b.* 27 March 1924 in Newark, New Jersey; *d.* 4 April 1990 in Los Angeles, California), jazz singer acclaimed for her distinctive voice and imaginative improvisational abilities during a lengthy performing career.

Sarah Lois Vaughan was the only child of Asbury and Ada (Baylor) Vaughan, who had migrated north from Virginia during World War I. Her father was a carpenter who played guitar; her mother was a laundress. She began taking piano lessons at about the age of seven, and by her teens was playing the organ at the First Mount Zion Baptist Church as well as being a soloist in the choir. She initially attended

Sarah Vaughan. FROM THE NATIONAL ARCHIVES

East Side High School, then transferred to Arts High School, which was for gifted students, but dropped out in her junior year. Attracted to jazz and to Newark's nightlife, she was working in clubs as a singer and pianist by the age of fifteen. In October 1942 she competed in the amateur-night contest at the Apollo Theatre in Harlem, winning the $10 prize and a week's booking. That engagement took place in the early spring of 1943, and as a result she was hired as the female singer and second pianist in the jazz big band led by Earl ("Fatha") Hines. She officially joined the orchestra on 4 April 1943, shortly after her nineteenth birthday.

The Hines band was a laboratory for the development of the emerging jazz style of bebop, featuring the genre's progenitors, Dizzy Gillespie and Charlie Parker. Late in 1943 the group's male singer, Billy Eckstine, left, and shortly afterward he formed his own band, taking Gillespie and Parker with him and adding, at various times over the next three years, such jazz innovators as Miles Davis, Fats Navarro, Art Blakey, Dexter Gordon, and Gene Ammons. Vaughan initially stayed with Hines, but she joined the Eckstine orchestra in 1944. On 5 December 1944 she made her recording debut with Eckstine, "I'll Wait and Pray." Soon, however, she left the band to go solo and began performing at the string of jazz clubs located on West Fifty-second Street in New York City. She first recorded under her own name for the Continental label on 31 December 1944, then moved in 1945 to another small record company, Guild.

In October 1945 Vaughan began an extended engagement at Café Society Downtown, a prestigious club in Greenwich Village. There she met trumpeter George Treadwell, who became her personal manager; they were married on 16 September 1946. Meanwhile, she had signed her first recording contract, with Musicraft. With that label she had her first chart hit, "Nature Boy," which reached the Top Ten in July 1948, and her second, "It's Magic," that August. This success earned her a contract with a major record label, Columbia, commencing in January 1949, when she recorded her next hit, "Black Coffee." At Columbia, for which she recorded through 1953, she was made to conform to a more pop style of performing, which resulted in a series of hits. Ten more of her Columbia recordings made the charts through the end of 1952, the most successful of which was "(I Love the Girl) I Love the Guy," which made the Top Ten in September 1950.

Meanwhile, backed by a trio of piano, bass, and drums, Vaughan toured extensively around the United States and, starting in 1951, in Europe. In 1954 the conflict between her desire to record jazz and record companies' need for hits was resolved in a new contract with Mercury Records: she agreed to record pop on Mercury while being allowed to record jazz for the subsidiary EmArcy label. As a result she reached the pop charts with twenty-one songs on Mercury between 1954 and 1960, including the Top Ten hits "Make Yourself Comfortable," "How Important Can It Be?," and "Whatever Lola Wants," all in 1955, and the million-seller "Broken-Hearted Melody" (which earned her first Grammy Award nomination, for best performance by a "Top 40" artist) in July 1959. But she also made more personally satisfying recordings, such as the 1956 album *Sassy* (one of her nicknames), which also sold well enough to chart. (In hindsight, Vaughan's "jazz" and "pop" albums can be difficult to distinguish from each other.)

Vaughan's performing career during the 1950s followed the gradual expansion of jazz in general from the popular low point of the bebop period to the music's emergence into prestigious venues. She appeared at the first Newport Jazz Festival in July 1954 and became a fixture of its annual presentations both in Newport, Rhode Island, and, starting in the 1970s, in New York City. In September 1954 she performed at Carnegie Hall, and the following month she again toured Europe. Whether booked for festivals, concert halls, or nightclubs, she gave hundreds of performances each year.

In 1958 Vaughan divorced George Treadwell. She married Clyde B. Atkins on 4 September 1958, and he became her personal manager. The couple adopted a daughter, Debra Lois, who grew up to become an actress under the name Paris Vaughan. They were divorced in 1962, and Vaughan began living with John ("Preacher") Wells, who took over as her personal manager, a relationship that lasted six years. In April 1960 Vaughan moved to Roulette Records, remaining with the label through 1963, when she returned to Mercury. Despite the quality of some of her 1960s recordings, the marginalization of jazz and pop vocal music in the wake of the rise of rock led to diminished sales, and she stopped recording after January 1967. She continued to perform frequently, however, including extended periods in Nevada hotel-casinos.

In 1970 Vaughan met and began living with Marshall Fisher, who became her personal manager and stayed with her until 1977. She returned to recording with the Mainstream label in 1971. She reached the pop charts with the album *Sarah Vaughan/Michel Legrand* in 1972, and the recording of her concert in Tokyo on 24 September 1973 led to a 1975 Grammy nomination for best jazz vocal performance, for the album *More Sarah Vaughan Live in Japan*. But by then she had left the label and was without a contract again.

In 1974 Vaughan performed at an all-Gershwin concert at the Hollywood Bowl, backed by the Los Angeles Philharmonic Orchestra conducted by Michael Tilson Thomas. This opened a new avenue of appearances for her, as she began to sing with local symphony orchestras around the country. She signed to the jazz label Pablo Records and recorded *How Long Has This Been Going On?* with pianist Oscar Peterson, bassist Ray Brown, drummer Louis Bellson, and guitarist Joe Pass. It brought her third Grammy nomination, for best jazz vocal performance, in 1978. The following year she was again nominated, for the Pablo album *I Love Brazil*, and she earned a fifth nomination in 1980 for the Pablo album *Sarah Vaughan/Duke Ellington Song Book One*.

Vaughan was married for a third time, to trumpeter Waymon Reed, in 1978; they were divorced in 1981. In the 1980s she finally began to win the awards critics claimed she should have received all along. In September 1981 she won an Emmy for outstanding individual achievement—a special class for her performance on the PBS television program *Rhapsody and Song: A Tribute to George Gershwin*. In February 1983 she won a Grammy for best jazz performance, female, for her album *Gershwin Live!*, recorded with Michael Tilson Thomas and the Los Angeles Philharmonic. Her *Crazy and Mixed Up* album was nominated the following year. By now she was making relatively few recordings, often for special events, such as her duet with Barry Manilow, "Blue," for his 1984 album *2 A.M. Paradise Café*, which earned her another Grammy nomination; a version of *South Pacific* with the London Symphony Orchestra in January 1986; and her *Brazilian Romance* album, yet another Grammy nominee, in 1987. Her final recordings were made with Quincy Jones for his *Back on the Block* album in 1989. That year she received her second Grammy, a Lifetime Achievement Award. Diagnosed with lung cancer in the fall of 1989, she died in 1990 at age sixty-six. She is buried in Glendale Cemetary in Belleville, New Jersey.

Sarah Vaughan was rivaled only by Ella Fitzgerald as the most accomplished female jazz singer of the post–World War II era. Possessed of a multioctave range and an extensive knowledge of music (she was also an excellent pianist), she brought unusual gifts to her vocal improvisations. Those very attributes at times led to criticism: some listeners, especially early in her career, complained that her singing was overly embellished and that she sacrificed lyrical comprehension for musical effect. This criticism diminished over the course of her career, however, and as she continued to perform decade after decade, she established herself as a unique vocal interpreter and one of the greatest jazz singers of the century.

★

Leslie Gourse's *Sassy: The Life of Sarah Vaughan* (1993) is the only book-length biography. Discographical information is provided in *Sarah Vaughan: A Discography: The First Forty Years* (1991), compiled by Denis Brown. Martin Williams, in *The Jazz Tradition* (1983), devotes a chapter to Vaughan. An obituary is in the *New York Times* (5 Apr. 1990).

WILLIAM J. RUHLMANN

VAUGHAN, Stevie Ray (*b.* 3 October 1954 in Dallas, Texas; *d.* 27 August 1990 in East Troy, Wisconsin), singer, guitarist, songwriter, record producer, and bandleader.

Vaughan was one of two sons of Jim Vaughan, a laborer, and Martha Vaughan. His older brother, Jimmie, who went on to success with the Fabulous Thunderbirds, was a blues-rock guitarist active in amateur bands while Stevie was in elementary school, and from an early age Stevie was learning guitar chords from Jimmie and listening to his brother's collection of blues records. At age eight Stevie had mastered guitar playing well enough to be accepted as a member of bands organized by much older boys. He had more performing credits when he approached his teen years than most musicians could point to as they approached adulthood.

During his years in junior and senior high school, Vaughan paid scant attention to his class work, focusing his energies and talents on performing professionally with Dallas-based bands. Among the groups that welcomed him from the late 1960s through the early 1970s were the Chantones, Blackbird, and the Night Crawlers. When the chance came for more interesting work outside the Dallas region at the start of the 1970s, Vaughan, now a senior, dropped out of school and moved to Austin, Texas, which would be his home for more than fifteen years.

In 1975 Vaughan joined an Austin-based rhythm-and-blues group, the Cobras, whose reputation grew steadily, ignited at least in part by the intricate string work of its young lead guitarist. Feeling more confident about his audience rapport, Vaughan left the Cobras in 1977 to form his own R&B revue, called Triple Threat. Although there were some rough financial periods, Vaughan kept things going until 1981, when he disbanded the group with a view toward incorporating blues and R&B themes into a more hard-driving rock format.

The avenue he chose was a power-trio concept. For his new venture, Vaughan brought in bass guitarist Tommy Shannon and drummer Chris Layton. The backing twosome was given the name Double Trouble after a song in blues singer Otis Rush's repertoire. Slowly, the group began to pick up a following in Texas among blues-rock fans, to a considerable extent by word of mouth.

As the band's musical peers sang their praises, opportunities arose for Vaughan and Double Trouble to perform in small clubs and as an opening act in places outside Texas. This exposure finally enabled the trio to go overseas to Switzerland in mid-1982 for the annual Montreux Festival. They proceeded to take full advantage of what festival organizers had originally seen as a relatively minor role. As James McBride wrote in *People* magazine, Vaughan "came roaring into the 1982 Montreux festival with a '59 Stratocaster at his hip and two flame-throwing sidekicks he called

Stevie Ray Vaughan in concert, *c.* 1985. KEVIN J. LARKIN/CORBIS-BETTMANN

Double Trouble. He had no record contract, no name, but he reduced the stage to a pile of smoking cinders and, afterward, everyone wanted to know who he was." Most believed at this time it was truly a rags-to-riches story.

Montreux typically lures famous musical personalities and record-industry executives, which augured well for the trio's future. One of the first to respond was the singer David Bowie, who, after seeing the group's virtuoso performance, asked Vaughan to handle lead guitar on his upcoming album, *Let's Dance* (spring 1983); Bowie's debut on a new label (EMI-America), *Let's Dance* would be one of the biggest hits in his career. Meanwhile, the Montreux showcase had brought other offers, including a suggestion by Jackson Browne that Vaughan and his band record an album at his studio in Los Angeles. Negotiations also got under way with Columbia for a contract, an agreement urged on the company by a famed discoverer of new talent, John Hammond, who had been responsible for scouting Aretha Franklin, Bob Dylan, and Bruce Springsteen, among others.

Ranging from updated versions of roots blues to high-powered blues-rock, the debut album by Vaughan and Double Trouble, *Texas Flood* (early 1983), was produced by Hammond and released on the Columbia subsidiary Epic Records. It got on to *Billboard* magazine's Top 40 chart and eventually sold more than 500,000 copies. At the end of 1983 Vaughan and Double Trouble received two Grammy nominations: best rock instrumental (for the song "Rude Mood") and best traditional blues recording. While they did not win any Grammies, Vaughan and Double Trouble did garner top honors in three categories of *Guitar Player* magazine's 1983 readers' poll. *Texas Flood* was named best blues album, and Vaughan headed the lists for best new talent and best electric blues guitarist.

For their second album, *Couldn't Stand the Weather* (summer 1984), Vaughan and his associates brought to bear other influences, including jazz and mainstream rock, on a new version of Jimi Hendrix's "Voodoo Child." The album broke into the top twenty, sold more than 1 million copies, and brought the group a third Grammy nomination.

Vaughan and Double Trouble won their first Grammies in early 1985, not for their album, but for a track on Atlantic Records' *Blues Explosion,* which was voted best traditional blues recording of 1984. Besides Vaughan's group, *Blues Explosion* featured John Hammond, Jr., Sugar Blue, Koko Taylor and the Blues Machine, Luther "Guitar Junior" Johnson, and J. B. Hutto and the New Hawks.

Increasingly, Vaughan was providing original songs to complement his group's versions of blues and R&B numbers written by others. The August 1985 LP *Soul to Soul,* which sold more than 500,000 copies, included his "Empty Arms," "Life Without You," and "Ain't Gone 'n' Give Up on Love." By this time he had reworked Double Trouble to include new member Reese Wynans on keyboards. In the voting for the 1985 Grammy Awards, Vaughan and Double Trouble were best rock instrumental performance finalists for the track "Say What!" from *Soul to Soul.*

In 1986 *Live Alive* was released. Later in the year, after collapsing in Germany, Vaughan entered into rehabilitation in an effort to get his drug problems under control. He cut himself off from dealers and became close again with his mother. He would remain clean and sober for the rest of his life.

In 1987 Vaughan appeared in the movie *Back to the Beach* as himself. He played the song "Pipeline" in a duet with guitarist Dick Dale. Also in 1987, Stevie filed for divorce from Lenora ("Lenny"), whom he had married on 20 December 1979. They had no children.

In 1988, appearing on MTV, Vaughan performed an acoustical set. In the same year his divorce from Lenny became final. In 1989 *In Step,* which would win a Grammy for best contemporary blues recording, was released, and Vaughan toured with another master guitarist, Jeff Beck, which led to an appearance on the television show *Austin City Limits.* Both *Austin City Limits* performances were released years later on a single video entitled *Live from Austin, Texas.* In 1990 Stevie toured with the singer Joe Cocker and finally recorded with brother Jimmie, on *Family Style* (also called *Vaughan Brothers*). That same year, at the ninth annual Austin Awards, Vaughan was named Musician of the Year and Musician of the Decade.

Vaughan died in a helicopter crash after leaving a concert held at Alpine Valley, Wisconsin. He was laid to rest on 31 August 1990 in Laurel Land Cemetery in Oak Cliff, Dallas. Jeff Healy, Dr. John, ZZ Top, Ringo Starr, Stevie Wonder, Jackson Browne, Bonnie Raitt, and Buddy Guy attended the private ceremony. More than 3,000 fans were outside the chapel. Posthumous releases were *Family Style* (1990), *The Sky Is Crying* (1991), *In the Beginning* (1992), and *Greatest Hits* (1995).

Vaughan's meteoric rise from relative obscurity to international fame is best described in a *People* magazine article published in 1984, six years prior to his untimely death: "For a kid who failed music theory in high school, the past two years have been a wild ride from local legend to stardom, from sleeping on club floors to playing Carnegie Hall."

★

Joe Nick Patoski and Bill Crawford, *Stevie Ray Vaughan: Caught in the Crossfire* (1993), and Keri Leigh, *Stevie Ray: Soul to Soul* (1993), are full-length biographies of Vaughan. Magazine articles include those in *Rolling Stone* (4 Oct. 1990), *Variety* (3 Sept. 1990), and *Musician* (June 1991). An obituary is in the *New York Times* (28 Aug. 1990).

MARK SOMMER

VEECK, William Louis, Jr. ("Bill") (*b.* 9 February 1914 in Chicago, Illinois; *d.* 2 January 1986 in Chicago, Illinois), baseball executive best known for his innovative approach to the sport and for having brought the first African-American player into the American League.

Born to William Louis Veeck and Grace Greenwood (DeForest) Veeck, Bill Veeck, Jr., grew up in the world of baseball. His father, following an early career as a journalist, was president of the Chicago Cubs from 1919 to 1933.

Bill Veeck. NATIONAL BASEBALL HALL OF FAME LIBRARY, COOPERSTOWN, N.Y.

Young Bill performed odd jobs at the Cubs' Wrigley Field before attending Phillips Academy in Andover, Massachusetts, and then the Ranch School in Los Alamos, New Mexico, in 1931 and 1932. His undergraduate days at Kenyon College in Ohio were cut short in 1933 by his father's death. For the next eight years, he was treasurer for the Cubs and took extension courses at Northwestern University. In 1935 he married Eleanor Raymond, who, although she came from an affluent family, was a circus performer. The couple had three children together, and divorced in 1949. That same year, Veeck converted to Catholicism—he had been an Episcopalian—and married a Catholic, Mary Frances Ackerman, with whom he had six children.

Veeck's first experience owning a baseball club came in 1941, when he purchased the then minor league Milwaukee Brewers. In order to attract nightshift wartime workers, Veeck organized giveaways and early morning games. Attendance grew, and Veeck, who was named Minor League Executive of the Year, was able to sell the team for a profit in a few years. Like his father, who had experimented with ladies' day games for the Cubs and with allowing radio broadcasts of Cubs games, he was both willing and able to defy tradition. World War II interrupted Veeck's baseball career, and, in December 1943, he joined the Marines. In Bougainville in the South Pacific, his right foot was crushed as the result of the recoil from an antiaircraft gun. In subsequent years he underwent more than two dozen operations on his foot, and eventually his leg had to be amputated above the knee.

In 1943 Veeck tried to buy the Philadelphia Phillies, but was thwarted after he informed Commissioner Kenesaw Mountain Landis that he planned to use African-American players on the team. Had he been successful, Veeck, rather than Branch Rickey, who brought Jackie Robinson to the Brooklyn Dodgers in 1947, would have become the first baseball executive to racially integrate the major leagues. In 1946, Veeck did purchase the Cleveland Indians, who set a major league attendance record in 1948 by drawing more than 2.6 million fans. Previously, no team had drawn more than 2 million patrons in a single season. By giving away ladies' nylon stockings and orchids, setting up a child care center in the stadium, and introducing such attractions as baseball comics, Veeck entertained fans and rewarded them for coming to the ballpark. As he once noted: "A baseball team is a commercial venture, operating for a profit. The idea that you don't have to . . . hustle your product the way General Motors hustles its product is baseball's most pernicious enemy." In 1948 the Indians won the American League pennant for the first time since 1920, and then defeated the Boston Braves in the World Series, bringing Cleveland its first national championship. Meanwhile, Veeck was making history by adding Lary Doby, an African-American, to the team in 1947, thus breaking the league's color line. Veeck received more than 20,000 negative letters as a result, but the following year he hired Satchel Paige, a legendary star pitcher from the Negro Leagues.

In 1951 Veeck, having sold the Indians, bought the St. Louis Browns, one of the weakest teams in the history of major league baseball. That year, Veeck produced his most famous stunt. To the delight of some, but to the consternation of others, he signed and brought to bat Eddie Gaedel, a midget. The next day the league outlawed this type of promotional gimmick. His use of Gaedel also antagonized other team owners, who resented Veeck's outspoken manner, unorthodox ploys, and habitual casual attire (sports shirts without a tie). In 1953 Veeck sold the hapless Browns, who moved to Baltimore the following year.

Veeck remained out of baseball until 1959, when he purchased the Chicago White Sox. Once again he displayed his innovative talents, this time by installing a scoreboard that emitted joyful explosions when team members swatted home runs. He also put the names of the Sox players on their road uniforms. Chicago won the pennant that year, but lost the World Series to the Los Angeles Dodgers. Meanwhile, the amputation of his leg and an operation for a benign brain tumor forced Veeck to take a break from baseball two years later.

Having relocated with his family to Easton, Maryland, after his latest operations, Veeck recuperated and then sought new activities. At different times during the 1960s, he wrote a syndicated newspaper column, undertook public speaking engagements, and published his various reflections, the most notable of which was entitled *Veeck: As in Wreck*. Between 1968 and 1971, he operated the Suffolk Downs racetrack in Boston, and, typically, introduced colorful novelties to a sport steeped in venerable tradition.

A last baseball hurrah came for Bill Veeck in the 1970s. Baseball owners had blocked his attempt to purchase the Baltimore Orioles in 1970, but five years later he put together a group that was able to purchase the Chicago White Sox. As owner of the Sox for the second time, Veeck had less success. Free agency for players, which he had, ironically, championed before it became law, worked to the detriment of his financially pressed team. Only with great difficulty did he manage to sell the White Sox in 1980. He did, however, in 1978 promote Lary Doby to manager, only the second African American (after Frank Robinson) to rise to such a post.

Plagued ever since World War II by serious health problems, Bill Veeck, who regularly smoked four packs of cigarettes daily, developed emphysema and, in 1985, lung cancer. His death in 1986 ended the career of one of baseball's most colorful and exciting personalities, a man who saw the national pastime as both a business and a game. As he noted: "It should be fun, and I hope to make it fun for everyone around here." He is buried in Chicago.

★

Bill Veeck, *Veeck: As in Wreck* (1962), written with Ed Linn, is a witty autobiographical account of a maverick entrepreneur who consistently stepped on the toes of the lords of baseball. Veeck collaborated with Linn on two other books: *The Hustler's Handbook* (1965) recounts interesting baseball anecdotes and developments, while *Thirty Tons a Day* (1972) looks at his brief career as a racetrack operator. The sole biography of Veeck to date is by sportswriter Gerald Eskenazi: *Bill Veeck: A Baseball Legend* (1988), which is a lively and sympathetic, but not entirely uncritical account of Veeck's career. Some useful information on Veeck appears in Jules Tygiel, *Baseball's Great Experiment: Jackie Robinson and His Legacy* (1983), and Charles C. Alexander, *Our Game: An American Baseball History* (1991). An obituary is in the *New York Times* (3 Jan. 1986).

ROBERT MUCCIGROSSO

VON TRAPP, Maria. *See* Trapp, Maria von.

VREELAND, Diana (*b. c.* 1906 in Paris, France; *d.* 22 August 1989 in New York City), a powerful influence on the American fashion scene, first as a legendary fashion editor and later as the creator of spectacular fashion exhibitions at the Metropolitan Museum of Art in New York City.

Diana Vreeland was born in Paris to an American mother, Emily Key Hoffman, and a Scottish father, Frederick Y. Dalziel. She first became aware of the fashion and art world during her early years in Paris, where her parents entertained important figures such as Vaslav Nijinsky, Sergei Diaghilev, Ida Rubenstein, and Vernon and Irene Castle in their home. Diana's privileged childhood included her attendance at the coronation of King George V in London in 1911. She spent summers in Venice, Italy, or in the French resort town of Deauville, among her parents, their friends, and her younger sister, Alexandra.

Prompted by the onset of World War I, the Dalziel family moved in 1914 to New York City, where the sisters attended private school, practiced ballet, and took riding lessons among the upper crust of Manhattan. Diana made her social debut in 1922. In 1924 she met a Yale graduate, banker T. Reed Vreeland, while vacationing at Saratoga, New York. They were married that year and had two sons, Thomas and Frederick. After living in Albany for four years, the young family moved for a short time to London, where Diana ran a lingerie shop. On returning to New York in 1936, Diana Vreeland was invited by Carmel Snow to work for *Harper's Bazaar* magazine. She first wrote a column called "Why Don't You . . . ?," which offered its readership novel beauty and fashion tips as well as lifestyle suggestions. Part of her column's charm was in the willfully fanciful hints that few readers could afford or would have dared to implement in depression-era America. Vreeland recognized early on the importance of whimsy and dream in American popular culture, and she liberally combined fantasy with fashion, creating a mood of optimism despite the surrounding reality. Within a year, she was promoted to fashion editor, working closely with Snow and art director Alexy Brodovitch. During her tenure at *Bazaar,* Vreeland shaped the magazine into the influential monitor of style for which it remains known.

Diana Vreeland, 1980. TOM GATES/ARCHIVE PHOTOS

In 1962 Vreeland left *Harper's Bazaar* to join *Vogue* magazine as associate editor. She quickly moved up the ranks to editor in chief, the position that she held until her departure in 1971. During the 1960s Vreeland's keen eye prevailed over the fashion world; she was taken seriously as a harbinger of the quickly changing fashions of the times. She chose experimental photography for fashion layouts, which proved an immediate success, and when she believed in a fashion tenet, she not only reported on it, but promoted it endlessly, until it took hold. She worked with the legendary photographers of the era: Cecil Beaton, Louise Dahl-Wolfe, and Richard Avedon, collaborating with them to produce the whimsical images for which she became as well known as the photographers themselves.

Vreeland was unique in her own personal style while shaping the American style of her era. Both her Manhattan apartment and her editorial office at *Vogue* were decorated and painted in red. Up to her last days, she maintained her timeless, if strikingly irregular, look: jet-black hair; bright red nail polish and lipstick; rouged cheeks, forehead, and even earlobes. Always fashionably slim and energetic, in the daytime she dressed simply in black, favoring slacks and tunics, then appeared for evening events in elegant gowns by her favorite designers—Givenchy, Saint Laurent, and Grès. She was an early advocate for fitness, and she was able, through her positions as editor, to devote space in her fashion magazines to exercise regimens, as well as to skin care, hair care, and grooming in general.

"Dramatic" is perhaps the best word to describe Vreeland, from her chic appearance to her conversation and writing styles, notable for their hyperbole and inimitability. Her handwritten memos to the *Vogue* staff were circulated, copied, and cherished.

After 1971 Vreeland remained with the *Vogue* staff in the capacity of consulting editor and embarked on a second career as a consultant to the Costume Institute of the Metropolitan Museum of Art. Her first exhibition, in 1973, was "The World of Balenciaga," which detailed the long career of this designer from 1938 to 1972. Among her most memorable exhibitions were "Innovative Designers in Paris" (1974), "American Women of Style" (1975), "The Glory of Russian Costume" (1976), "Vanity Fair" (1977), and "Diaghilev" (1978). In addition to her fondness for European fashion, Vreeland appreciated the multicultural appeal of "ethnic" clothes, and she often highlighted them in her exhibits. Such favorites were Chinese mandarin robes, Russian peasant outfits, and gypsy-style caftans. An extravagant party kicked off each exhibition at the Metropolitan Museum, and these galas soon became major social events in the fashion world.

Vreeland summed up her views of fashion as follows: "Fashion in the final analysis is a social contract. It is a group agreement as to what the new ideal should be. There is always a degree of trial and error. Designers keep proposing something new, but whether their ideas come to fruition depends ultimately on whether the society that counts accepts them or rejects them" (in Joan Nunn, *Costume, 1200–1980,* 1984, p. 175).

Among the many honors bestowed on Vreeland were the Chevalier of the National Order of Merit of France, 1970; Légion d'Honneur, 1976; Lord & Taylor Dorothy Shaver "Rose" Award, 1976; and Parsons School of Design honorary doctor of fine arts degree, 1977. The Italian fashion industry and the Rhode Island School of Design recognized her contribution to fashion, and the Metropolitan Museum of Art began a fund in Diana Vreeland's name to benefit the museum's Costume Institute. She died of a heart attack at Lenox Hill Hospital in Manhattan.

★

Vreeland's autobiography is *D. V.: Give 'Em What They Never Knew They Wanted* (1984). A biography is in Anne Stegemeyer, ed., *Who's Who in Fashion*, 3d ed. (1996). See also Hilton Als, "D. V. on Display," *New Yorker* (22 Sept. 1997). An obituary is in the *New York Times* (23 Aug. 1989).

JENNIFER FARTHING

WALLACE, Irving (*b.* 19 March 1916 in Chicago, Illinois; *d.* 29 June 1990 in Los Angeles, California), best-selling author, screenwriter, and editor.

Irving was born to Alexander Wallace and Bessie (Liss) Wallace, Jewish immigrants from Russia (his father's surname was Wallechinsky until shortened on Ellis Island) who came to the United States as teenagers and met and married in Chicago. When Wallace was one year old the family moved to Kenosha, Wisconsin, where Wallace's father worked in and eventually owned a large general store and where Wallace and his younger sister, Esther, were raised. Wallace sold his first piece of writing, a magazine article, to *Horse and Jockey* for $5 dollars at the age of fifteen. When he was seventeen he sold "Sacrifice Hit," his first short story, to *Challenge* magazine. After graduating from high school in 1934 Wallace went on an expedition with two friends to the jungles of Honduras; he financed the trip by writing articles about his travels for magazines and newspapers back home.

Upon returning to the United States in 1935, Wallace enrolled at the Williams Institute, a small college in Berkeley, California. He stayed for only one semester, however, because, as he recounted, "I was impatient to make a living, hated being constricted in school and unable to smoke my pipe, and I thought I could make it in Hollywood." At the end of 1935 he moved to Los Angeles, and in the following year his father, mother, and sister left Kenosha and joined him.

For the next few years Wallace wrote freelance for various magazines. He also ghostwrote for such celebrities as W. C. Fields, Bob Hope, and Boris Karloff. *Liberty* magazine sent him to Japan and China in 1940 to interview, among others, Japan's foreign minister, Yosuke Matsuoka. The articles he wrote from this trip earned him recognition as a magazine writer of significance. Wallace married Sylvia Kahn, editor and novelist, in Los Angeles on 3 June 1941. She was his main editor throughout his writing career and was the mother of his two children, David Wallechinsky and Amy, both of whom became writers.

In 1942 Wallace joined the U.S. Army Air Forces (he was recruited by Lieutenant Ronald Reagan), and served as a screenwriter in the First Motion Picture Unit and later in the Signal Corps Photographic Center. He was honorably discharged in 1946 as a staff sergeant and returned immediately to magazine freelancing in Los Angeles.

Although by the mid-1950s Wallace's magazine-writing career had begun to flourish (he was writing for the *Saturday Evening Post, Collier's, Cosmopolitan,* and *Reader's Digest*), he decided to focus his efforts on screenwriting and eventually enjoyed success working for movie studios. Among his filmed screenplays were *The West Point Story* (1950), *Gun Fury* (1953), *Bad for Each Other* (1954), *The Burning Hills* (1956), and *Bombers B-52* (1957). After working for approximately ten years in Hollywood, Wallace ended his screenwriting career and devoted himself entirely to writing books, although, interestingly, as Wallace himself noted, "almost every novel I ever wrote sold to movie stu-

Irving Wallace. ARCHIVE PHOTOS

dios." His first three published books, however, were not novels but biographies: *The Fabulous Originals* (1955), *The Square Pegs* (1957), and *The Fabulous Showman: The Life and Times of P. T. Barnum* (1959).

Wallace's first published novel was *The Sins of Philip Fleming* (1959), which went largely unnoticed until Wallace's later success spawned a resurgence in sales. His second novel, and his first best-seller, *The Chapman Report* (1960), examines how a sex survey conducted by a team of sociologists affects the lives of several suburban women. It was on the U.S. best-seller list for thirty weeks and met with comparable success in Europe. Controversy surrounded the novel for its explicit sexual content, and critics found little in it to praise; strife and negative reviews would be associated with most of Wallace's subsequent novels. Also like most of his novels, *The Chapman Report* was made into a movie and went on to become a box-office hit. Despite this success Wallace returned to biography and wrote *The Twenty-Seventh Wife* (1961), the story of Ann Eliza Webb, former wife of Mormon leader Brigham Young and nineteenth-century crusader for the outlawing of polygamy. He then returned to novels and wrote *The Prize* (1962), a fictional portrayal of the Nobel Prize judging process; *The Three Sirens* (1963); and *The Man* (1964), the story of a black man who becomes president of the United States.

By the mid-1960s Wallace was established as a best-selling author, and he continued to write a series of successful novels. *The Word* (1972) is about the discovery of a new Gospel, *The Pigeon Project* (1979) explores the consequences of the creation of a serum that extends human life, and *The Second Lady* (1980) tells the story of a Soviet abduction and replacement of the First Lady of the United States. Other novels from his later life are *The Seven Minutes* (1969), *The Fan Club* (1974), *The R Document* (1976), *The Almighty* (1982), *The Miracle* (1984), *The Seventh Secret* (1986), *The Celestial Bed* (1987), and *The Guest of Honor* (1989).

Interspersed among his novels were Wallace's other nonfiction works: *The Sunday Gentleman* (1965), a collection of his magazine writing; *The Writing of One Novel* (1968), an autobiographical work about his writing process; and *The Nympho and Other Maniacs* (1971), a collective biography of women who refused to conform to the social standards of their time. He also coauthored with his daughter, Amy, *The Two* (1978), a biography of Siamese twins. With his son, David, and later with both David and Amy, he coedited several versions of the extremely popular *The People's Almanac,* beginning in 1975.

As notable as Wallace's popularity, and no doubt one of the causes of it, is the variety of subject matter covered in his works. Wallace never restricted himself to his own experience, but instead followed, as he said, "my desire to listen, to let the imagination run wild, and then to write." He was a tireless researcher in the writing of his sixteen novels and seventeen works of nonfiction, because, he said, he preferred "that a subject be different from anything I've done before."

Although literary critics have not accepted Wallace as a major artist, his contemporaries respected him for the diversity of his work and his ability to tackle social issues. "While, like most novelists, I write novels principally to entertain," Wallace said, "still I choose to make an underlying social statement in my books." This combination enabled him to maintain a large worldwide readership; his works have been translated into twenty-three languages, and at the time of his death, from pancreatic cancer, more than 120 million copies of his works had been sold.

★

Personal and career information can be found in John Leverence, *Irving Wallace: A Writer's Profile* (1974); Charles Moritz, ed., *Current Biography 1979* (1979); Dedria Bryfonski, ed., *Contemporary Authors Autobiography Series,* vol. 1 (1984); and Hal May and James G. Lesniak, eds., *Contemporary Authors,* New Revision Series, vol. 27 (1989). An obituary is in the *New York Times* (30 June 1990).

JAMES P. MILLER

WALLACE, Sippie (*b.* 1 November 1898 in Houston, Texas; *d.* 1 November 1986 in Detroit, Michigan), popular blues singer of the 1920s, who enjoyed a revival of popularity from the late 1960s through the 1970s, influencing a new generation of musicians.

Wallace was born Beulah Belle Thomas, the fourth child in a family that would later grow to thirteen children. Because the wide space between her front teeth forced her to sip everything, she was given the nickname Sippie. Her father, George W. Thomas, Sr., was deacon of the Shiloh Baptist Church; he and her mother, Fanny, ran a household that did not countenance drinking or dancing, so it is ironic that this family produced three children who became prominent in the music world of the 1920s: Sippie, older brother George, Jr., and younger brother Hersal. George, Jr., a composer and musician, changed Sippie's life in 1912, when he moved to the Storyville district of New Orleans in pursuit of his musical career. His sister, whose musical training consisted of singing and playing the organ in their father's church, followed him to New Orleans and fell in love with the world of professional music. She also fell in love with Frank Seals, making an early marriage, lasting roughly from 1914 to 1917, that she later conceded was a mistake. In 1918 she moved back to Houston, where much of her family still lived, although both parents had died.

In Houston, Wallace cut short her high school education and started on the Texas tent show circuit as maid and stage assistant to Madam Dante, a snake dancer with a traveling troupe, the Philip's Reptile Show. Wallace acted in plays, did comic bits, and danced in the chorus. At about this time, Wallace married again, this time to Matthew ("Matt") Wallace, a Houston gambler whose spending habits strained the marriage, which nonetheless lasted until his death in 1936. Wallace's singing ability was soon recognized, and she performed with small bands under the sobriquet "the Texas Nightingale," a lifelong designation. Her brother George again influenced her life in 1923, when he invited her to move to Chicago, where he had become a bandleader and a member of the recording staff of the music division of the W. W. Kimball Company. Wallace arrived with her husband, her niece Hociel, and her brother Hersal, who, even as a young teenager, was an accomplished blues pianist and composer. Wallace and her brothers performed as a trio and composed collaboratively. Their first recordings for Okeh, a so-called race music label (produced for and advertised directly to an African-American audience), "Shorty George," cowritten by George and Sippie, and "Up the Country Blues," were extraordinarily popular, with "Shorty George" selling approximately 100,000 copies. In the mid-1920s, at the peak of her career, Wallace relocated to Detroit with Matt, Hershal, and Hociel; Detroit became Wallace's permanent home.

Sippie Wallace, *c.* 1984. UPI/CORBIS-BETTMANN

In the years between 1923 and 1929 Wallace was a popular recording artist and stage performer, recording with stars like Louis Armstrong, Clarence Williams, and Sidney Bechet and becoming a headliner. Sweet-faced and buxom, she was known for her love of flamboyant dress, often indulging in feather boas and extravagant costumes. A series of personal tragedies, however, subjected her career to blows from which it would not recover for decades. In 1925 her older sister Lillie, who had been a strong influence in Wallace's development as a singer, died; in 1926 her beloved younger brother Hersal died of food poisoning when he was only sixteen; then, in 1928, George, Jr., died after being hit by a streetcar in Chicago. The family members who had buoyed her career were dead, and the Great Depression was under way. In 1929 Wallace recorded four sides for Victor Records but only two were released. Although one of those was the overtly erotic "Mighty Tight Woman," which would be significant in Wallace's return to popularity decades later, the times were not congenial to performers who lacked versatility, and by 1932 Wallace's career seemed over.

For the next several decades Wallace devoted herself to her family and to gospel music. From 1929 she was organist, singer, and church nurse in Detroit's Leland Baptist Church, and from the mid-1930s to the 1970s she served as director of the National Convention of Gospel Choirs and Choruses; she also wrote gospel choral music. She recorded irregularly during this period, doing "Bedroom Blues" for Mercury Records in Chicago in 1945 and later recording for the Fine Arts label (1959) and for Bango (1962) in Detroit. In the 1940s she took into her home the three orphaned daughters of her niece Hociel.

The growing popularity of folk music in the late 1950s and early 1960s swept the blues back into prominence. In 1966, at the urging of fellow Texas blues singer Victoria Spivey, Wallace joined the American Folk Blues Festival touring Europe, demonstrating an apparently undiminished virtuosity of phrasing and authenticity of delivery—the raw "shouting blues," often performed without a microphone, so different from the sophisticated and mellow urban blend of jazz and blues performed by artists such as Alberta Hunter—that thrilled audiences and led to a second career on the folk and blues circuit. Concert recordings and a 1970 recording of old blues standards with Spivey brought Wallace before a new audience. The appreciation of her talents grew further in 1971, when a young white singer, Bonnie Raitt, recorded two of Wallace's songs, "Mighty Tight Woman" and "Women Be Wise, Don't Advertise Your Man," on her debut album and another, "You Got to Know How," on her second album in 1972. In the 1970s and 1980s Wallace toured with Raitt and other artists, although she had suffered a stroke in 1970. The resurgent popularity of the blues was signaled in 1977 and 1980 when Wallace drew packed audiences to New York City's Lincoln Center. Raitt's influence led to a recording contract with Atlantic Records; in 1983 the resultant album, called simply *Sippie,* was nominated for a Grammy Award. The album won the W. C. Handy Award for best blues album of the year in 1984. Wallace continued to perform into her old age and suffered a heart attack while performing in Germany in 1986. She died later that year.

Wallace's music has been characterized as a cross between the "southwestern rolling honky-tonk and Chicago shouting moan," fusing the style of the rural South revival tent with the "true blues shout." In her earliest recordings and performances Wallace's strong voice and unusual timing, vocal shifts, and phrasing placed her in the tradition of Ma Rainey, an acknowledged influence, while setting her apart from many other singers, such as Bessie Smith. The revival of her music in later years demonstrated that both her style—rough and earthy—and her message—female self-assertion, often bawdy—had suddenly come upon times in which their appeal was again fresh, preserving a native American tradition for a new audience.

★

Darlene Clark Hine, ed., *Black Women in America: An Historical Encyclopedia* (1993), includes a biography and analysis of Wallace. Daphne Duval Harrison, "'Up Country . . .' and Still Singing the Blues: Sippie Wallace," in her *Black Pearls: Blues Queens of the 1920s* (1988), offers extensive coverage of Wallace's life and music and includes photographs. *Detroit Free Press Magazine* ran a cover story on Wallace (16 Sept. 1979). An obituary is in the *New York Times* (4 Nov. 1986).

REBECCA MARTIN

WALLIS, Harold Brent ("Hal") (*b.* 14 September 1898[?] in Chicago, Illinois; *d.* 5 October 1986 in Rancho Mirage, California), film producer who, during a career spanning six decades, was the driving force in the production of some of the greatest movies of his generation.

Hal Wallis was the son of Jacob Walinsky, a tailor, and Eva (Blum) Walinsky, both of whom were eastern European Jews; the family name changed to Wallis by 1920. Hal's father, a Russian, developed a gambling habit and abandoned his family when Hal was fourteen, and his mother, a Pole, contracted tuberculosis when Hal was seventeen. Such circumstances forced Wallis to quit McKinley High School at age fourteen and, along with his sisters Minna and Juel, work to support the family. For his mother's health he moved the family to California in 1920, peddling bake ovens to pay the expenses. Wallis's association with the film industry began in 1922 when Minna, a legal secretary, met Jack Warner of Warner Brothers, who offered her a job. She persuaded the influential movie executive to hire her brother to manage the Garrick Theatre, a Warner Brothers property in Los Angeles. Minna later arranged an interview for her brother with Sam Warner at the Warner Brothers studio on Sunset Boulevard and Bronson Avenue in Hollywood.

Wallis was hired as an assistant to the Warner Brothers publicity chief Charley Kurtzman in 1923, and soon became head of the publicity department. After Sam Warner foresaw that sound would dominate the movie industry, Wallis began writing the publicity for *The Jazz Singer* (1927), starring Al Jolson. Using Western Electric's Vitaphone technology to reproduce sound, *The Jazz Singer* opened to record crowds in Manhattan on 6 August 1927. On 24 November 1927 Wallis married Louise Fazenda, an actress; they had one son.

With profits from *The Jazz Singer,* Warner Brothers pur-

Hal Wallis. ARCHIVE PHOTOS

chased First National Studio, naming Wallis production manager. In 1930 Wallis brought W. R. Burnett's 1929 novel, *Little Caesar,* to the screen. Released in 1931 under the same name, the film told the sordid tale of Chicago hoodlums and featured unknown Broadway actor Edward G. Robinson in the leading role. When Darryl F. Zanuck left Warner Brothers for Twentieth Century Productions in 1933, Wallis assumed responsibility for production at the studio. Thus began one of the most profitable and critically acclaimed runs in the period known as the American studio years.

A perfectionist, Wallis brought a sense of realism to films like *I Am a Fugitive from a Chain Gang* (1932) and *Kings Row* (1941). He then added a touch of fantasy to the mix with the Busby Berkeley musicals *Gold Diggers of 1933* (1933) and *Wonder Bar* (1934). Wallis even produced *A Midsummer Night's Dream* (1935) from Shakespeare's play. Instinctively, he knew if a story was worth telling and how to sell it to audiences. And to transform his vision into reality, he gathered together a host of outstanding talent.

Wallis began his tenure as production head by featuring Bette Davis in *Dangerous* (1935); for her role she won an Oscar for best actress. Wallis then persuaded Jack Warner that the genre of biography would make suitable film material during the Great Depression, and Warner Brothers began shooting *The Story of Louis Pasteur* (1936). The studio also released *The Life of Emile Zola* (1937), *Juarez* (1939), *Knute Rockne, All-American* (1940), and *Sergeant York* (1941). When Adolf Hitler pronounced any scientific discovery by a Jew to be "worthless," Wallis rushed into production *Dr. Ehrlich's Magic Bullet* (1940), the story of the Jewish physician who found the cure for syphilis. With the United States teetering on the abyss of war, Wallis finished work on the mystery classic *The Maltese Falcon* (1941), with Humphrey Bogart as detective Sam Spade.

Five days after the Japanese attack on Pearl Harbor in December 1941, Warner Brothers story editor Irene Diamond laid an obscure play called *Everybody Comes to Rick's* on Wallis's desk. He purchased the play, planning to fashion it in the mold of *Algiers* (1938), a dated film set in the North African desert. For the part of the exiled American cabaret owner Rick Blaine, Wallis cast Bogart. He then secured Ingrid Bergman to play Ilsa Lund and Paul Henreid for the role of Czechoslovakian resistance leader Victor Laszlo. Enhancing the dramatic presentation were performances by Claude Rains; Conrad Veidt; Sydney Greenstreet; Peter Lorre; and Dooley Wilson, Blaine's faithful black piano player. Wallis later claimed he had written Bogart's last line: "Louis, I think this is the beginning of a beautiful friendship."

The picture, released as *Casablanca* (1942), benefited from the Allied landing in French North Africa in November 1942, and the Churchill-Roosevelt conference at Casablanca in January 1943. Premiering in blizzard conditions at the Hollywood Theater in New York City on 26 November 1942, the romantic melodrama with the unforgettable love triangle was a smash hit. *Casablanca* won Academy Awards for best screenplay, best director, and best picture in 1943. Other Wallis wartime films included *Yankee Doodle Dandy* (1942), with James Cagney as George M. Cohan, and *This Is the Army* (1943), considered the finest musical of its kind.

Always fashionably dressed and with a suave demeanor, Wallis was of medium stature with a large, tanned face under short hair parted neatly in the middle. His physical appearance was illuminated by a facial expression as radiant as the reflection from the light of a movie projector in a darkened room.

In his autobiography, Wallis claims that a contract dispute and Jack Warner's meddling in the decision-making process contributed to a rift between the two men. At the Academy Awards ceremony in 1943, Warner rushed to the stage to take the Irving Thalberg Award just bestowed on Wallis. Distraught over the snub, Wallis departed Warner

Brothers in 1944, forming Hal Wallis Productions with Joseph Hazen. The prototype of modern film enterprises, Wallis's company contracted with Paramount Pictures to market his pictures that year.

Soon afterward Wallis discovered Shirley MacLaine, Burt Lancaster, and Kirk Douglas on Broadway. While watching television, he noticed Charlton Heston performing in a Shakespearean play and signed him to a contract. At the Copacabana nightclub in New York City, Wallis got caught up in the comedy hysterics of Jerry Lewis and Dean Martin, later showcasing them in *My Friend Irma* (1949). He also signed megastar Elvis Presley, who soon appeared in *Loving You* (1957), *King Creole* (1958), and *Blue Hawaii* (1962). The motifs of the Wallis-Hazen films also reflected the sophistication and complexity of postwar America. Movies like *The Strange Love of Martha Ivers* (1946), *So Evil My Love* (1948), *Sorry Wrong Number* (1948), and *September Affair* (1950) captured the mood of the times.

In 1953 Wallis formed Hal Wallis, Inc., a major independent film company. Traveling to Europe, Wallis persuaded Italian sensation Anna Magnani to portray Serafina in Tennessee Williams's *The Rose Tattoo* (1955). Magnani's performance netted her an Oscar for best actress. Wallis's love of the American West and the art of Frederic Remington found expression in movies such as *Gunfight at the O.K. Corral* (1957); *Last Train from Gun Hill* (1959); *The Sons of Katie Elder* (1965); and *True Grit* (1969), which earned John Wayne an Oscar.

Although Wallis often interpreted historical fact to suit his scripts, his string of successes continued with *Becket* (1964), a Paramount release. The film's leviathan clash of wills, depicted by Richard Burton and Peter O'Toole, preceded Universal's *Anne of the Thousand Days* (1969) and *Mary Queen of Scots* (1971), featuring Glenda Jackson as Elizabeth I and Vanessa Redgrave as her papist nemesis. *Rooster Cogburn* (1975), the sequel to *True Grit,* again starring Wayne and favorite Katharine Hepburn, was Wallis's last film.

Wallis was awarded the Irving Thalberg Award for excellence in motion picture production in 1938 and again in 1943. Of Wallis's 138 films nominated for Oscars in a variety of categories, 32 received Academy Awards. After his appointment as commander of the British Empire during a command performance of *Mary Queen of Scots* in 1971, Queen Elizabeth II shook his hand and stated: "Thank you, Mr. Wallis. We're learning about English history from your films."

Wallis's wife, Louise, died in 1962. The wealthy movie producer married actress Martha Hyer on 31 December 1966, moving to Rancho Mirage, California, where he retired. Wallis died of complications of diabetes and was buried at Forest Lawn Cemetery in Los Angeles.

★

Wallis's personal papers, company memos, and other pertinent documents are in two locations: the Warner Brothers years collection is located in the Warner Brothers Archives at the University of Southern California Library, Los Angeles; the post–Warner Brothers papers can be found at the Center for Motion Picture Study at the Margaret Herrick Library, Beverly Hills, California. Hal Wallis and Charles Higham, *Starmaker: The Autobiography of Hal Wallis* (1980), is a suitable place to begin, but as an historical reference it is difficult to follow. Obituaries are in the *Los Angeles Times* (8 Oct. 1986), *New York Times* (9 Oct. 1986), and *Variety* (15 Oct. 1986).

JEAN W. GRIFFITH, JR.

WALT, Lewis William (*b.* 16 February 1913 near Harveyville, Kansas; *d.* 26 March 1989 in Gulfport, Mississippi), four-star U.S. Marine Corps general best known for his service in Vietnam, where he commanded in the five northernmost provinces of South Vietnam known as I (Eye) Corps.

Walt was born on a farm, one of twelve children of Albert Miller Walt and Estella May Shields. After graduating from high school in Fort Collins, Colorado, he attended Colorado State University, where he received a B.S. degree in chemistry in 1936. While at Colorado State, he was president of the student body and student council, cadet colonel of the Reserve Officers' Training Corps, and captain of the football team and the wrestling team. He enlisted in the Colorado National Guard at the age of seventeen and on graduation from college was commissioned as a second lieutenant in the army reserve. He resigned that commission to accept appointment as a second lieutenant in the U.S. Marine Corps in July 1936.

In April 1937, after finishing marine basic school at Philadelphia, Walt was assigned to the Sixth Marine Regiment in San Diego, California, as a machine gun platoon leader. He was sent to China in August, where he helped to guard the international settlement in Shanghai as part of a contingent of reinforcements during the 1937 crisis in northern China. In February 1938 he returned to San Diego, and in June 1939 he went to Guam, Mariana Islands, where he was promoted to first lieutenant in October 1939. He returned in June 1941 to serve as company commander in the Officer Candidates' Class, Marine Corps Schools, in Quantico, Virginia, where he was promoted to captain in December 1941.

During World War II, Walt volunteered to join the First Marine Raider Battalion, and as commander of Company A he landed on 7 August 1942 in the British Solomon Islands in the assault on Tulagi Island—part of the Guadalcanal campaign. For his gallantry during the landing he was awarded the Silver Star. He subsequently joined the

Fifth Marine Regiment on Guadalcanal as commanding officer of the Second Battalion and was promoted to major in September 1942. In October Walt was wounded in action but continued in combat, and on 22 December he was promoted to lieutenant colonel for distinguished leadership and gallantry in action.

Following hospitalization and training in Australia, Walt led the Second Battalion, Fifth Marines, in the assault at Cape Gloucester, New Britain, in December 1943 and shortly thereafter was assigned as regimental executive officer. On 8 January 1944, the day after the commanding officer of the Third Battalion, Fifth Marines, was wounded, Walt took over command of the battalion in the seemingly fruitless attack on Aogiri Ridge. On 9 January, transporting a 37-millimeter gun, which Walt had insisted on for the assault on the ridge, the battalion proceeded into Japanese machine gun positions through thick jungle. By dusk the forward elements had reached almost to the top of one end of the ridge, on which the Japanese had been ordered to maintain their positions at all costs. After unsuccessfully calling for volunteers to transport the 37-millimeter gun up the ridge, he grabbed the gun himself and pulled both his arms out of their shoulder sockets in the attempt. Thereupon volunteers helped him push the gun up to the top, where it could sweep the ridge and where the marines dug in near the Japanese positions. Starting at 1:15 A.M. the next day, the first of five Japanese counterattacks came. The battle for the ridge was a turning point, and it led to the award of a Navy Cross, the second highest American military decoration, to Walt. The Aogiri Ridge was renamed "Walt's Ridge" by the division commander, Major General Lemuel C. Shepherd, Jr.

Walt left Cape Gloucester in February 1944 and was ordered to the Naval Hospital at Oakland, California, for treatment of wounds and malaria. In June 1944 he married Nancy Mary Sheehan of Northampton, Massachusetts, who was then serving as an officer in the Army Nurse Corps; they had three children and were divorced in 1971. On 27 August of that year, Walt married June B. Jacobsen.

In the same month as his first marriage, Walt returned to the Pacific as regimental executive officer of the Fifth Marines, landing at Peleliu in the southern Palaus Islands, where casualties were extremely high. Beginning on the evening of the first day of the assault, Walt commanded, for a day, a disorganized Third Battalion of the Fifth Marines because its slightly wounded commanding officer had gone to the rear. Walt could not locate even one of the scattered companies of the battalion until dusk, but, accompanied only by a runner at night, he pushed his way through Japanese positions, located each of the units, and directed them into a cohesive defense, thereby salvaging a perilous situation. He earned a second Navy Cross for this action.

Walt returned to the United States in November 1944 and served as the chief of the Officer Candidates' School Tactics Section at the Marine Corps Schools in Quantico, Virginia. After serving at Camp Pendleton in California and on Guam, he returned to the Marine Corps Schools in Quantico in May 1949. While there he entered the senior course of the Amphibious Warfare School. After completing the course in June 1950, he remained at the Marine Corps Schools, first as chief of the Tactics Section and then as executive officer of the basic school. In November 1951 he was promoted to colonel.

In November 1952 Walt was ordered to Korea, where he served in combat with the First Marine Division until August 1953, first as commanding officer of the Fifth Marines and then as assistant chief of staff and chief of staff of the division. He received the Legion of Merit and Bronze Star, both with combat "V," for his Korea service. In August 1953 Walt returned to the Marine Corps Schools in Quantico, where he served as the commanding officer of the Officers' Basic School, with responsibility for training the lieutenants and officer candidates.

In 1957 Walt was transferred to Washington, D.C., and served as assistant director of personnel at Marine Corps headquarters until August 1959, when he entered the National War College in Washington; he completed the course in June 1960. In July 1960 he began a one-year assignment on the Joint Chiefs of Staff, and on its completion he was promoted to brigadier general and became assistant division commander of the Second Marine Division at Camp Lejeune in North Carolina. He returned in September 1962 to the Marine Corps Schools in Quantico as director of the Marine Corps Landing Force Development Center, a post he held until May 1965, when he was promoted to major general.

In June 1965 Walt began his Vietnam service as commander of the III Marine Amphibious Force (III MAF) and Third Marine Division, and he was also chief of naval forces in Vietnam as well as senior adviser to I Corps and I Corps coordinator, Republic of Vietnam. He was operationally under the commander of the U.S. Military Assistance Command, Vietnam (MACV), General William Westmoreland. The Marine Corps had landed in March to protect coastal bases. Walt introduced several civic action programs, defined by the marines as a concern for the social, economic, and political development of the people. Among the programs was project HANDCLASP, which allowed individuals and organizations in the United States to donate material to the navy for shipment to the Marine Corps for distribution in Vietnam. The Marine Corps Reserve also solicited funds for CARE, leading to the formation of MEDCAP, which gave medical help to the Vietnamese and trained medical workers; the funds also supported a school-building program. The participation of public and private aid agencies in I Corps increased dramatically under Walt's leadership. Innovative military programs dealing with the security of surrounding populations were added to the mix. COUNTY FAIR operations involved ARVN (Army, Republic of Vietnam) and marine forces going into villages to give medical aid and entertainment while at the same time securing them. In fall 1965 a village chief's request for protection for rice crops led to the program GOLDEN FLEECE, which used troops to search for hidden caches of confiscated rice and secure the current harvest of the crop. Another military initiative, CAP (Combined Action Program), successfully integrated local Popular Force troops with marines for both civic and military action.

Walt believed that securing the coastal area of greatest population and expanding that security outward over time was the best way to win the war. The strategy favored by General Westmoreland centered on conventional battles with North Vietnamese and Vietcong main force units. While Walt was confident of the marines' ability to come out on top in large-scale warfare, he thought it should take place in the context of the pacification strategy. While in the midst of using his forces for both civic action and conventional warfare, Walt was confronted by a crisis in the South Vietnamese government in spring 1966 brought about by the removal of the local Vietnamese I Corps commanding officer, General Thi, by South Vietnamese Premier Ky. This occurrence led to a period of local chaos known as the "struggle movement," which Walt helped to subdue.

Walt was promoted to lieutenant general on 7 March 1966. He continued his service in Vietnam until June 1967, when he was awarded the Distinguished Service Medal. He was mentioned as a candidate for promotion to commandant of the Marine Corps along with Lieutenant General Victor H. Krulak, but Walt's rivalry with Krulak led President Lyndon B. Johnson to select Lieutenant General Leonard A. Chapman for the post instead. Walt was named assistant commandant on 1 January 1968 and was promoted to four-star rank on 2 June 1969. After his retirement in February 1971, Walt was director of the U.S. Marines Youth Foundation. Walt wrote two books in retirement dealing with national security and lack of U.S. preparedness: *America Faces Defeat* (1972) and *The Eleventh Hour* (1979). He also wrote a book about his Vietnam experience, *Strange War, Strange Strategy* (1970). He died in Gulfport, Mississippi, of cardiac arrest incident to pneumonia and was buried in Quantico National Cemetery.

In Vietnam, Walt was known as the "Big Squad Leader in the Sky," because he spent a lot of time with his troops, traveling by Huey helicopter. He would appear before them in combat boots and fatigues, with the stocky build of a former football player and a crew cut, and talk about how they should be diplomats as well as soldiers and be "one hundred percent human beings."

★

Walt's papers are located in the Marine Corps Historical Center, Washington, D.C. On his World War II service, see Frank O. Hough, *The Campaign on New Britain* (1952) and *The Assault on Peleliu* (1950), both produced by the Historical Branch of the Marine Corps. His service in Korea is covered in *United States Marine Operations in Korea, 1950–1953* (5 vols., 1954–1972), and in Vietnam by three volumes produced by the History and Museums Division at Marine Corps headquarters: Jack Shulimson and Charles M. Johnson, *U.S. Marines in Vietnam: The Landing and the Buildup, 1965* (1978); Jack Shulimson, *U.S. Marines in Vietnam: An Expanding War, 1966* (1982); and Gary L. Telfer et al., *U.S. Marines in Vietnam: Fighting the North Vietnamese, 1967* (1984). Material on Vietnam is also contained in Kenneth J. Clifford, *Progress and Purpose: A Developmental History of the United States Marine Corps, 1900–1970* (1973), and Allen Millett, *Semper Fidelis: The History of the United States Marine Corps* (1980). An interview with General Walt is contained in *U.S. News and World Report* (22 May 1967). Obituaries are in the *New York Times* (28 Mar. 1989) and *Washington Post* (29 Mar. 1989). The Marine Corps Oral History Collection, 1966–1974, at the Marines Corps Historical Center, contains an oral history interview with Walt.

ROBERT T. BRUNS

WANG, An (*b.* 20 February 1920 in Shanghai, China; *d.* 24 March 1990 in Boston, Massachusetts), inventor and industrialist who was a pioneer of the computer age through his invention of magnetic memory cores and was the founder of Wang Laboratories.

The son of Yin Lu, an English teacher who taught at a private elementary school thirty miles outside of Shanghai, and Zen Wan Chien, An Wang (which can be translated as "Peaceful King"), was the oldest boy in a family of five children. Born in the middle of "The Age of Confusion," he grew up against a backdrop of feuding warlords, Japanese brutality, and the corruption that marked the end of the Manchu dynasty. From his earliest years he impressed others with his precocity and unusual determination. Forced by circumstance to enter school as a third grader, Wang, although two years younger than his classmates, quickly became one of the top math students in his class. At the age of sixteen, he entered the Chiao Tung University, a prestigious engineering school, where he once again excelled, graduating at the top of his class despite the chaos and war that swirled around him.

Following graduation in 1941, Wang joined China's war effort against Japan as part of a technical group designing and building radios and transmitters in Kweilin in China's interior. The decision got him safely out of dangerous Shanghai, but the young engineer was disillusioned by the

An Wang, 1979. UPI/CORBIS-BETTMANN

corruption and brutality of the generals of the Nationalist government and jumped at the opportunity to take advantage of a Nationalist government-sponsored program to send engineers to study in the United States.

Armed with knowledge of American society gleaned from books and films like *Gone with the Wind,* Wang and a few fellow technological pilgrims flew "over the hump" (the phrase used to describe trips across the Himalayas) in a DC-3 in April 1945, on the first leg of a trip that would take him by plane, train, and boat to the United States. There, three years later, he would have a moment of inspiration that would have profound effects on the development of computers and launch Wang on a trajectory toward wealth and influence.

Luck as well as talent played a major role in Wang's swift ascent. In part because so many young American men were still in the military, Wang was able to enroll in September 1945 at Harvard University, where once again Wang excelled, earning an M.S. degree in 1946 and his Ph.D. in applied physics in 1948. That same year he met Lorraine Chiu at a function organized for Chinese students and academics. They were married on 10 July 1949 and had three children: Frederick, Courtney, and Juliette. During his lifetime, Wang deprecated the importance of his academic work (although to his death he was always addressed as "Doctor Wang"). He noted that the only lasting value of his graduate education was that the Harvard imprimatur on his doctoral degree later reassured early customers of his company who had discovered that Wang Laboratories was a one-man shop in Boston, owned and operated by a Chinese immigrant.

All of those who came into contact with the deceptively self-deprecating Wang seemed to recognize that he had special gifts. His thesis supervisor, E. Leon Chaffee, gave Wang an introduction to Howard Aiken, one of the pioneers of modern computing, who ran the Harvard Computation Laboratory. Shortly after offering Wang a position as part of a team designing a new generation of computers in 1948, Aiken gave Wang a problem to puzzle out, and just three weeks later, while walking across Harvard Yard, Wang had a flash of insight that was to help enable computers to become the usable, general-purpose tools they are today.

The problem that Aiken had posed for Wang involved the fundamental issue of computer memory. At that time, data storage was a cumbersome process that involved mechanical motion. Then as now, the more memory a computer was able to rapidly access, the more problems it could handle. In 1948 memory was so small that few envisioned that computers would ever deal with more than a very restricted set of problems.

Aiken asked Wang to find a way to record and read magnetically stored information without mechanical motion. It was a devilish problem because at that time there was no way of reading magnetically stored information without changing the flux and destroying the information in the process of reading it. Wang wrote about his flash of insight in his autobiography, *Lessons* (1986): "Like everybody else, I had been so preoccupied with preserving the magnetic flux . . . that I lost sight of the objective. I realized in that moment that it did not matter whether or not I destroyed the information while reading it. With the information I gained from reading the magnetic memory, I could simply rewrite the data immediately afterward." Wang's elegant solution typified his ability to reduce complex problems to simple terms, a talent that served him well as a student, technological innovator, and then later as a businessman.

Wang also invented a cumbersome way of reading a series of his so-called magnetic memory cores. This idea was never widely adopted, but the cores themselves captured the imagination of another great innovator of early computing, Jay W. Forrester, at the Massachusetts Institute of Technology. In 1949 Forrester organized the cores into a grid and devised a way of specifically or randomly (to use common computer parlance) accessing individual cores. Variations on Forrester's configuration of Wang's cores became the model for computer memory for the next twenty years, until silicon-based microchips began to offer far larger memory capacity. Magnetic cores formed the basis of International Business Machine's early mainframe computers, including the famed 360 line, and long after cores faded from hardware, technicians would still refer to the transfer of computer memory as a "core dump."

The invention of magnetic cores gave a great boost to Wang's confidence. While another person might be content to have secured a place in academia, the diminutive and shy Wang quickly revealed a boldness and ambition that would be astonishing in anyone, much less a young immigrant with only an imperfect grasp of English. First, he set about to patent his invention, risking the ire of Aiken, who believed passionately that innovations in computing should remain in the public domain. Then he left the computation laboratory and, on 22 June 1951, founded Wang Laboratories. His assets at that point consisted of little more than his confidence in himself and $600 in savings. His plan was to develop, produce, and market applications using his memory cores and other inventions. In his first year he earned $3,254 in income, surpassing his previous year's income at Harvard, and for the next three decades, until Wang Laboratories stumbled in the mid-1980s, Wang never had a fiscal quarter in which the company's earnings and revenue did not grow. For one ten-year stretch between 1973 and 1983, the company's earnings grew at a rate of 40 percent a year. Wang became a U.S. citizen in 1955.

The true dimensions of Wang's supreme self-confidence and determination became apparent during his five-year battle with the industry giant IBM over the issue of compensation for the licensing of his memory cores. For years the two parties haggled, and IBM lawyers raised questions about the validity of Wang's patent from every conceivable angle. Despite this withering attack, Wang was informed he would receive patents on the great bulk of his claims on 17 May 1955. This would put Wang in a position to virtually dictate terms to IBM, which by then was deeply committed to using his invention. Then, as the deadline for any competing claims loomed, IBM revealed that it had uncovered a challenge to Wang's patent. Faced with the possibility of years of further battles, Wang sued for peace, compromising on a series of issues he had found objectionable and agreeing to accept an offer of $400,000 for his invention, making him a wealthy man in 1956. He went to his grave, however, convinced that IBM had put the other inventor up to the challenge in order to weaken Wang's otherwise impregnable negotiating position. At the time they reached an agreement, IBM was 10,000 times the size of Wang Laboratories.

Wang next showed his versatility as a businessman, when as director, chairman, and chief executive officer of Wang Laboratories, Inc., he negotiated the growth of the company, first as a pioneer in the manufacture of desktop electronic calculators, and then, when he saw that calculators were becoming a commodity, as a maker of office automation equipment. Unlike many inventors who fall in love with technology, Wang always focused on the user of his machines. His company virtually created the word processing industry by producing machines that offered secretaries easy-to-use menus that would guide them through various options.

In 1983, when the company stock price reached $43 a share, Wang's holdings were estimated to be $2.3 billion, and "The Doctor," as he was called, became one of the largest and most visible philanthropists in the Boston area; among the beneficiaries of his wealth were the Wang Institute, Wang Center, and Massachusetts General Hospital. Not long thereafter, however, the founder's fortunes took a turn for the worse as the company found itself badly positioned in a furiously changing marketplace. As problems mounted, Wang was ill-served by some of the very character traits that had earlier enabled his rise in the computing industry: his iron will, his desire for control, and his ego.

Because he had earlier insisted on a public stock offering whose terms guaranteed that voting control of the company would remain in his family, Wang was virtually immune to takeovers or other outside attempts to challenge his leadership of the company. Despite vociferous opposition within the company, he insisted on installing his son, Fred, as his successor, prompting the departure of a number of key executives and distracting the company at a time of rapid change in the computer industry. Indeed, even the user-friendliness that was a hallmark of Wang's philosophy turned out to be a liability because its enabling technologies were so deeply imbedded in the architecture of Wang computer hardware that it was difficult for the company to adapt its business systems to a marketplace that demanded that computers be able to communicate with many different systems.

Instead of seeing the fulfillment of his vision of creating a company that would surpass IBM under the guidance of generations of his family, Wang spent his last months in 1989 and 1990 trying to avoid bankruptcy and, reportedly, beseeching the company's chief executive officer, Richard Miller, not to change the name of the company after he died. Wang died of cancer of the esophagus and was buried in Lincoln, Massachusetts. Two years later Wang Laboratories went bankrupt; it emerged as a much smaller and different company in 1993, no longer pioneering broad applications for business but exploiting narrow profitable niches. Although Wang Laboratories did not become the monument its founder hoped it would be, An Wang's legacy is still rich and varied, ranging from fundamental contributions to the development of the signal industry of the information age to development of a user-friendly approach to technology that all computer manufacturers have embraced.

★

Biographical sources include An Wang, with Eugene Linden, *Lessons: An Autobiography* (1986); Mark L. Goldstein, "An Wang," *Industry Week* 231 (13 Oct. 1986): 55–56; Arthur M. Louis, "Doctor Wang's Toughest Case," *Fortune* 113 (3 Feb. 1986): 106–109; James Fallows, "The Electronics of Revenge," *New York Times Book Review* (26 Oct. 1986); and Alex Beam, "An Wang," *Business Week* (18 Apr. 1990). Obituaries are in the *New York Times* (25 Mar. 1990) and *Electronic Business* 16 (30 Apr. 1990): 31.

EUGENE LINDEN

WARHOL, Andy (*b.* 6 August 1928 in Pittsburgh, Pennsylvania; *d.* 22 February 1987 in New York City), artist, filmmaker, and publisher who was one of the most influential artists in the latter half of the twentieth century and a figure emblematic of both American Pop Art and rags-to-riches fame and fortune.

Born Andrew Warhola, of Carpatho-Rusyn descent, he was the youngest of three children of immigrant parents from the Austro-Hungarian mountain village of Miková, in what is now northeastern Slovakia, near the Polish border. His father, Ondrej Warhola, was a construction worker, and his mother, Julia Zavacky, was a homemaker and naive folk artist. His family regularly attended Saint John Chrysostom Byzantine Catholic Church in Pittsburgh. Canards about his background, actively perpetuated by Warhol, claim he was of Czech descent and Roman Catholic, born sometime between 1929 and 1933 in various locales (including McKeesport, Pennsylvania, and Cleveland, Ohio).

His childhood was marked by crushing poverty during the Great Depression. While his father was away as a laborer and rigger on industrial installation jobs for the Eichleay Corporation, Andy accompanied his mother selling handmade flowers in discarded tin cans door to door. At about age nine he had chorea, which contributed red splotches to his pale, almost albino complexion. While bedridden he made paper cutouts and read comic books. He also helped his mother paint traditional Easter eggs (*pysanka*). Andy had a passion for Hollywood films as well as for celebrity autographs and memorabilia, which he collected as a boy and throughout his life. He had considerable talent sketching portraits. While his brother Paul took photographs by day, Andy learned by age twelve to retouch the portraits at night. During some initial art training at Holmes Elementary School he attended free Saturday art classes from 1937 to 1941 at the Carnegie Institute of Technology. From 1942 to 1945, Andy attended Schenley High School and skipped grade eleven.

In 1945 he was admitted to the Carnegie Institute (now Carnegie Mellon University) and majored in pictorial design at a time when returning GIs, including friend and realist artist Philip Pearlstein, were learning to become art directors or painters. Warhol was self-contained and shy but had a penchant for being outrageous. He almost flunked out after his freshman year but took a remedial summer drawing course, submitting expressive works that illustrated the Oakland area of Pittsburgh. He was reinstated and won a coveted student prize for these drawings, which were exhibited in the art building. For his student work he perfected a blotted-line technique and used overlays of colored construction paper on drawings. Trained in silk-screening, he used that medium in window displays at a downtown department store. During his senior year, in 1949, he submitted to the annual exhibition of the Associated Artists of Pittsburgh an audacious self-portrait, *The Broad Gave Me My Face, but I Can Pick My Own Nose.* Rejected by the jurors, it was shown at a local gallery where the public flocked to see his first controversial show.

Andy moved permanently to New York City after receiving his B.F.A. degree in 1949. His first commercial art commission appropriately illustrated a career ladder of success for the September issue of *Glamour.* Sometime in the early 1950s he changed his name to Warhol, perhaps to avoid having to pay an enormous outstanding telephone bill under his given name; he acquired several nicknames, including "Raggedy Andy" for his calculatedly disheveled clothes. His hair thinned so much that he wore wigs from the mid-1950s. Around 1953 his mother moved to New York and cooked for him in his split-level apartment on Lexington Avenue. (She would live with him until 1971.) A parlor floor became a campy setting glutted with palm trees, a Tiffany lamp, twig furniture, and an ever-growing collection of American folk and funk artifacts. An upper living floor and studio teemed with Siamese cats. In 1960 he bought a town house on upper Lexington Avenue.

During the heyday of illustrated commercial art in the 1950s, Warhol's work appeared in advertisements—including weekly I. Miller shoe ads in the *New York Times*—as

Andy Warhol with his cow wallpaper at a press conference for his 1971 exhibit at the Whitney Museum, New York City. UPI/CORBIS-BETTMANN

well as book covers, record jackets, fashion and entertainment magazines, and window displays at Bonwit Teller and Tiffany and Company. He won numerous awards from the Art Directors Club and the American Institute of Graphic Arts. To maximize commissions he employed assistants, especially Nathan Gluck, to imitate his signature style of a highly decorative, calligraphic blotted-line drawing featuring accidental splotches. He also used his mother's lettering for assignments, and he often used his artist friends to help hand-tint his offset-printed promotional flyers (such as "Happy Greta Garbo Day" of 1953) and booklets ("Wild Raspberries" of 1959) that were given to and avidly collected by clients. As in his later Pop Art, he traced images from various sources, especially *Life* magazine and popular illustrations. After a 1956 world tour with set designer Charles Lisanby, Warhol used Oriental gold-leaf appliqué ("A Gold Book" of 1957). He also underwent cosmetic surgery to improve his bulbous nose and to remove skin blotches. (He alluded to the surgery in his 1963 series *Before and After.*) By the late 1950s he made more than $100,000 annually. Instead of starting his own advertising agency he decided to pursue a fine-art career, financed by commercial art commissions through the mid-1960s.

American Pop Art signaled a radical shift in the notion of what art is or should be, and it became a part of what critics called postmodern art. By 1960 American modern painting was dominated by Abstract Expressionism, with its hermetic drippings and cryptic slashings, thickly globbed all over large canvases. Pop, by contrast, was indebted to Dada artists, especially Marcel Duchamp, who elevated banal objects to the status of art, and to the neo-Dada artists Robert Rauschenberg and Jasper Johns, who both ironically fused popular imagery with abstract designs. In 1960 and 1961, Warhol made paintings, using an opaque projector, based on comic book characters (*Dick Tracy, Superman*) and tabloid advertisements. He approached the art dealer Leo Castelli but was rejected because Castelli felt his paintings were too similar to the comic book works by Roy Lichtenstein, whom Castelli had taken on the week before. Dismayed, Warhol began to create canvases that featured common, mass-produced consumer items, especially *Campbell's Soup Cans,* first exhibited at the Los Angeles Ferus Gallery and then the New York Stable Gallery in 1962.

Employing poet Gerard Malanga as his painting assistant in late 1962, Warhol developed his signature Pop Art style that abandoned the traditional idea of a hand-painted masterpiece. His paintings featured a monumental contemporary iconic image mechanically silk-screened and centered over a brightly colored background or, alternatively, smaller, overlapping images serialized on a large canvas. Warhol's unsigned studio products were produced in an East Forty-seventh Street locale dubbed "The Factory." It was painted silver and covered throughout with silver foil by associate Billy Name, and Warhol wore silver-tinted wigs to match. "I want to be a machine," he quipped to *Art News* interviewer Gene Swenson in November 1963. He adopted an enigmatic, very cool personality that remained passionless and always guarded. His basic self-descriptive qualities were vacuity, plasticity, and surface-orientation. By 1964 he allowed spokesmen, especially art dealer Ivan Karp, to answer questions from the media, which Warhol at once distrusted and courted. During this period his work remained very experimental, expressed in paintings, sculptures, films, books, and multimedia rock presentations.

Warhol's art and films forced viewers to reexperience and reevaluate both the overly familiar and the darkly hidden aspects of American culture, and he did it in a way that shocked but endured. He thematically explored the death of the old Hollywood glamour of airbrushed publicity photos. Marilyn Monroe and Elizabeth Taylor were, for example, monumentally silk-screened at a Max Factorized extreme with ruby-lipsticked lips, perpetual smiles, and overtly heavy eye makeup. *Gold Marilyn* (1962) was a visual pun on her status as a gold mine for Hollywood. The assassination of President John F. Kennedy prompted Warhol to concentrate on a series of close-ups of the widowed Jacqueline, the world's most glamorous woman even in the midst of tragedy. At the same time, he explored the "glamour" of tabloid exploitation of anonymous victims in his *Disaster* series paintings (late 1962–1968). With deadpan irony he rendered the gruesome and grotesque, set against a glisteningly bright background of color: car accidents, suicides, race riots, consumer-product victims, and the electric chair. All of these works were seen after 1964 at the Leo Castelli Gallery.

Warhol was savaged by conservative, modernist critics and editors and later hailed by postmodern cultural critics and theorists such as Jean Baudrillard, Fredric Jameson, and Arthur Danto. Warhol's art confounded Canadian customs officials in 1965, when his *Brillo* series and other box sculptures were declared "nonart" and subject to 20 percent duty. That same year, during the opening of his one-artist show at the Institute of Contemporary Art in Philadelphia, the mob of spectators and media besieged the door, causing the curator, Sam Green, to remove the art from the walls. As a result Warhol and his entourage themselves became "art" as media event. Warhol was commissioned to paint something for the exterior of the New York State Pavilion of the 1964 New York World's Fair, but the work he produced, his *Most Wanted Man* series, was censored by the fair's commissioner, Robert Moses. In 1967 the poet and Warhol's then-lover Alan Midgette impersonated Warhol for a college lecture tour. Warhol perpetuated controversy, invited publicity, and deadpanned candor. In 1966 he took out a *Village Voice* ad proclaiming that he would endorse anything; promoted his Pop paper-dress line, created *Cow* wallpaper and helium-filled *Silver Clouds;* and absurdly announced at his first Paris show that he had "retired" from painting in favor of filmmaking.

By mid-1963 Warhol's first (and silent) films redefined cinema in his experiments with sustained and unedited screen-test portraits and minimal homages to things we think we already know in *Sleep, Eat, Kiss, Haircut,* and *Empire* (in which the Empire State Building is viewed from dusk to dawn). In 1964 these films received the annual Independent Film Award from Jonas Mekas's journal *Film Culture* for "cleansing" and providing "new insight" in cinema as art. By late 1964 Warhol's sound films were being shot statically, consisting of long takes of his "found" personalities or "Superstars" (Ultra Violet, Pope Ondine, Mario Montez, Viva). They improvised amphetamine-driven raptures or read cue cards of scripts by Ronald Tavel (*Harlot, My Hustler, Horse*) that entailed narcissistic exhibitionism, homoerotic encounters, and overt drug abuse. *Chelsea Girls* (1966), which chronicles denizens of a seedy Greenwich Village hotel, was uniquely exhibited with two randomized reels shown simultaneously. By 1967 Chuck Wein, then Paul Morrissey, directed Warhol's films, notably Morrissey's *Trash* (1970), which featured new Superstars (Joe Dallesandro and the transvesitites Holly Woodlawn, Jackie Curtis, and Candy Darling).

From 1966 to 1968, Warhol promoted Lou Reed's Velvet Underground rock group. (The song "Walk on the Wild Side" alludes to a certain "Drella," who is Warhol.) The German singer Nico became part of the group at the behest of Warhol, who produced the group's first album. Pioneering what would become the prototype of multimedia rock concerts in the 1970s, the group performed on a stage where Warhol's films were projected, strobe-light effects filled the auditorium, and whip-dancing Superstars filled out the stage. It was called The Exploding Plastic Inevitable and toured the country. Glam rocker David Bowie and punk groups such as the Ramones were directly influenced, as were the Rolling Stones, whose album *Sticky Fingers* (1970) sported an award-winning cover design by Warhol and included front-and-back close-up photos of Dallesandro's tight-fitting jeans, including an actual, working zipper.

In 1967 Warhol published *Andy Warhol's Index (Book),* which included pull-outs, pop-ups, and a record. His exhibition catalog for the Moderna Museet in Stockholm included Warhol's most often-quoted quip: "In the future everyone will become world famous for fifteen minutes." His incessant activities came to a halt that year when he was critically shot by Valerie Solanas, founder and only member of the Society for Cutting Up Men (SCUM). She told police that he had too much influence over her life. After a long recovery, in 1969 Warhol launched *Interview,* which began as a tabloid film journal and then developed, under editor Bob Colacello, into a trendsetting bible of celebrity chic and haute couture. That year Warhol also published *A, a Novel,* consisting of edited audiotapes of a day in the life of Superstar Ondine.

From 1973 to 1984, Warhol's studio was on Broadway, and the majority of works were commissioned portraits: a cosmeticized *Mao* series and various still-life series (*Hammer and Sickle, Skulls, Gems*). Warhol was living then in a larger town house with an interior designed by his lover Jed Johnson. In 1984 Warhol's studio moved to East Thirty-third Street; projects included an Absolut vodka ad, camouflage self-portraits, and collaborations with Francesco Clemente and Jean-Michel Basquiat. Shortly after the opening of his series *The Last Supper,* shown across the street from the Leonardo da Vinci masterpiece it appropriated, Warhol had routine gall-bladder surgery followed by an unmonitored cardiac arrest. He died on 22 February 1987. In New York there was a celebrity-studded funeral mass at Saint Patrick's Cathedral. In his hometown of Pittsburgh, his family and close associates attended a private funeral, and his burial was in the Warhola family plot in St. John the Baptist Catholic Cemetery, Byzantine Rite, in the Pittsburgh suburb of Bethel Park.

Warhol's estate was conservatively estimated at $220 million. It set up the Andy Warhol Foundation for the Visual Arts, which famously auctioned his effects in New York at Sotheby's in the spring of 1988 (with a boxed set of six volumes for the catalog); authorized a posthumous and controversial diary that alternated tax receipts with caustic remarks; and in 1989 cofounded, with the Carnegie Institute and the Dia Center for the Arts, the Andy Warhol Museum at 117 Sandusky Street in Pittsburgh.

Andy Warhol's legacy also is at the core of postmodernism. He not only dissolved and blended the traditional categories and divisions of art (including painting, sculpture, photography, commercial art, cartoon art, installation art, and media), but he cross-blended and overlaid them into new hybrids. Warhol acutely understood and used the icon-making effects of mass media in art and flouted modernism's reverence for originality. He expanded the notion of the artist-as-entrepreneur to include what he called "Business Art," making possible art boutiques by Keith Haring and others. By becoming a starmaker and art star himself, Warhol changed the role of the artist from mere observer to observer and participant.

★

Andy Warhol's collected and ghosted thoughts are in *The Philosophy of Andy Warhol (From A to B and Back Again)* of 1975; his best-selling social history is *POPism: The Warhol '60s* (1980) with Pat Hackett, who edited the unindexed *The Andy Warhol Diaries* (1989). (An index appeared in an issue of *Fame,* Sept. 1989). Comprehensive studies are Patrick S. Smith's *Andy Warhol's Art and Films* (1986) and David Bourdon's *Warhol* (1989). Interviews with Warhol and his associates from every period are in Patrick S. Smith, *Warhol: Conversations About the Artist* (1988). A fully illustrated retrospective Museum of Modern Art exhibition catalog was edited by Kynaston McShine (1989). The handling of Warhol's estate is examined in Paul Alexander, *Death and Disaster: The Rise of the Warhol Empire and the Race for Andy's Millions* (1994). Obituaries are in the *New York Times* and *Los Angeles Times* (both 23 Feb. 1987).

PATRICK S. SMITH

WARNE, Colston Estey (*b.* 14 August 1900 in Romulus, New York; *d.* 20 May 1987 in Bedford, Massachusetts), consumer advocate and educator who cofounded Consumers Union and served as its president for forty-three years.

Warne, the son of Clinton Arlington Warne and Harriet Ellsworth Estey, developed an interest in banking as a young man. He received a bachelor of arts degree in economics from Cornell University in 1920. That same year,

Colston Warne, 1961. UPI/CORBIS-BETTMANN

on 27 October, he married Frances Lee Corbitt; they had three children. In 1921 Warne obtained a master of arts degree in economics from Cornell. By the time he entered the University of Chicago to work on a doctorate, his interest in banking had lessened. Instead, he studied the labor movement and consumer rights. His doctoral dissertation, dealing with the consumer cooperative movement, led to his Ph.D. in 1925. That year Warne became an associate professor at the University of Denver. He left Denver in 1926 for an associate professorship at the University of Pittsburgh, where his research project exposed the deplorable conditions of mining camp residents. When he presented his findings to a luncheon club, conservative university trustees tried to dismiss him. Warne's interest in civil liberties grew as a result, leading him to chair the Pittsburgh branch of the American Civil Liberties Union from 1927 to 1930.

In 1927 Warne became interested in consumer affairs after reading *Your Money's Worth* by Frederick Schlink and Stuart Chase. When the two authors founded Consumers' Research, Incorporated, in 1928, Warne became a member of its advisory committee. Consumers' Research was the first organization devoted to product testing. Its primary publication, the *Bulletin,* grew from 565 subscriptions in 1928 to 42,000 in 1932. Warne remained actively involved with the rapidly growing organization through the early 1930s.

In 1930 Warne joined the faculty of Amherst College in Massachusetts. Still, he continued to devote attention to Consumers' Research, at a time when its employees were expressing grievances, claiming that certain board members were guilty of mismanagement. A newly formed employees union asked to meet with the board, which fired several workers. A bitter strike ensued in 1935, resulting in a split among the founders of the organization. Warne and others supporting labor during the strike formed a new organization, Consumers Union, in 1936, with Warne as its first president.

Consumers Union grew quickly, but not without opposition from rival consumers' groups and manufacturing companies. Under Warne's direction, Consumers Union continued to test and rate products and devote time to the promotion of consumers' rights. It published its own magazine, *Consumer Reports,* which had about three thousand subscribers in 1936. With the coming of World War II, and especially after the U.S. entry into the war in 1941, the growth of Consumers Union and *Consumer Reports* diminished. This was partly because there was a decrease in the availability of consumer goods due to the priority given to military production, and partly because of the draft, which deprived the organization of several staff members. During the war years Warne and Consumers Union called on the government to teach consumer education in public schools.

After the war Consumers Union underwent a resurgence. Warne, in addition to teaching at Amherst, spent considerable time at Consumers Union headquarters in Mount Vernon, New York. His weekends and holidays were often spent in the laboratory testing products. Test results were reported in *Consumer Reports,* which continued to gain new subscribers.

By the late 1940s Warne had expanded his involvement in the consumer movement. In 1947 he became a member of the Consumer Advisory Committee to the President's Council of Economic Advisers. That year he also rejected an executive order signed by President Harry Truman requiring federal employees to sign an oath of loyalty. Warne stated that "this executive order is so repugnant to the political institutions of our country that I cannot comply with its terms." He then declared, "I am an upstate New York Yankee, I am not a communist." Despite his refusal to sign the oath, Warne remained on the Consumer Advisory Committee until 1951.

In 1939 Consumers Union was the subject of a report to the House Un-American Activities Committee. This report, heavily influenced by rival consumer advocate organizations, claimed there was a link between Consumers Union and the Communist party. Consequently, the committee placed Consumers Union on its list of subversive organizations. In 1953, however, Warne convinced the committee to drop Consumers Union from the list. In 1960 he cofounded the International Organization of Consumers Unions, functioning as its president for ten years. Between 1962 and 1965 he served as a member of the Consumer Advisory Council to the president. In 1970 he retired from Amherst College, remaining as a professor emeritus until his death. Warne retired from Consumers Union in 1979. Warne retained the title of president emeritus until his death. He succumbed to Parkinson's disease at Carleton Willard Village nursing home, where he lived.

Colston Warne was a giant in consumer activism. He elevated a tiny organization into a major force in the consumer field. At the time of his retirement, the organ of Consumers Union, *Consumer Reports,* had a subscription rate that exceeded three million. Under Warne's leadership the organization grew from ten staff members in 1936 to four hundred in 1980.

Warne, a visionary, held his strong proconsumer beliefs throughout his life. Although maintaining a reserved image, he courageously defended his principles and beliefs. He devoted most of his time to the service of others, rarely taking a vacation. Undoubtedly, Warne was one of the most important consumer advocates of the twentieth century. He emulated his nickname, "Mr. Consumer."

★

Norman Isaac Silber, *Test and Protest: The Influence of Consumers Union* (1983), is a narrative look at the history of product testing, with emphasis on the development of Consumers Union. Edward J. Metzen, in the *Journal of Consumer Affairs* (winter 1987): 169–170, presents an excellent tribute to Warne. A Consumers Union press release relating to Warne (20 May 1987) can be found at the Consumers Union Information Center in Yonkers, New York. Obituaries are in the *New York Times* and *Washington Post* (both 21 May 1987).

DANIEL J. PLASTER

WARREN, Robert Penn (*b.* 24 April 1905 in Guthrie, Kentucky; *d.* 15 September 1989 in West Wardsboro, Vermont), one of America's most distinguished men of letters: poet, novelist, short-story writer, dramatist, critic, essayist, biographer, editor, and professor.

Warren was the first of three children born to teacher Anna Ruth Penn and banker-turned-storekeeper Robert Franklin Warren, who came from English stock that included distinguished colonial settlers and veterans of the Revolutionary and Civil Wars. A small child with bright red hair, he grew up in comfortable middle-class houses. Skipping grades and earning straight As, he survived the bullying of envious classmates and graduated from Guthrie High School at age fifteen, then entered the larger Clarksville

Robert Penn Warren. BRYN COLTON; ASSIGNMENTS PHOTOGRAPHERS/ CORBIS

(Tennessee) High School for an additional year. In the spring of 1921, with an appointment to the United States Naval Academy in hand, he was deprived of that longed-for career when his younger brother randomly tossed a huge cinder that landed on his left eye, inflicting a disastrous injury.

That fall Warren entered Vanderbilt University, where he intended to study chemical engineering. He soon switched to the study of literature and came under the influence of such teachers as John Crowe Ransom and Donald Davidson, who were also accomplished poets, and that of another student, Allen Tate, who became a mentor and surrogate older brother. The youngest of the students who, with other poets and teachers, published a magazine of poetry called the *Fugitive,* Warren became passionately devoted to poetry but his schoolwork suffered. Certain that his injured eye was affecting the other, feeling maimed, and depressed over an unrequited love affair, he attempted suicide in 1924. Soon, however, he was publishing melancholy romantic verse in the *Double Dealer.* He graduated in 1925 with honors.

Seeking scholarships, preferably far from home and parental authority, he entered the University of California at Berkeley, where he became a teaching fellow and bohemian student. Soon after his first affair, with a seductive drama student named Carolyn Anspacher, he became involved with another undergraduate who fascinated him, Emma Cinina Brescia, the daughter of a music professor and herself an aspiring writer. He deplored the climate for poetry at Berkeley and attempted unsuccessfully to transfer to Yale. Broadening his range with poems showing both metaphysical influences and ballad models, he published poems in the *New Republic* as well as frequent reviews. In 1927, with his M.A. degree in hand, he accepted a Yale fellowship but found the literary climate there no improvement. Now ruggedly athletic, he was becoming a prodigious swimmer and walker. By the fall of 1928 he had signed a contract for a biography of John Brown and entered New College, Oxford, as a Rhodes scholar.

In June 1929, returning home with eye trouble, he secretly married Brescia before returning to Oxford. *John Brown: The Making of a Martyr* (1929) received mainly favorable notices, and in the spring of the following year he received his B. Litt. Accepting a one-year assistant professorship of English at Southwestern College in Memphis, Tennessee, he formally married Brescia on 12 September 1930. His novelette *Prime Leaf* (1931) drew on his family and on the Kentucky buyer-planter tobacco wars of the early 1900s. With his tremendous energy he continued, despite his heavy teaching load, to write poems and to contribute an essay to *I'll Take My Stand* (1931), the conservative so-called manifesto of the Agrarians, who believed that the agrarian values of the Old South were the best hope not only for the South but for the United States as a whole.

Warren then resumed his manifold but low-paid duties as an acting assistant professor, this time at Vanderbilt. The department head, who had thought him a radical since his student days, gradually reduced his courses. Suffering frequent ill health, Warren underwent removal of his deteriorating left eye in February 1934. With the expansion at Louisiana State University mandated by Governor Huey P. Long and with the recommendation of Cleanth Brooks, his younger friend and fellow student at Vanderbilt and Oxford, he became an LSU assistant professor.

His reputation growing, Warren was asked by LSU president James Monroe Smith to produce a magazine that would be called the *Southern Review.* With Brooks as fellow managing editor and his former student Albert Erskine as business manager, Warren attracted both new and established writers, and in a remarkably short time the *Review* became one of the most influential American literary publications. His *Thirty-six Poems* (1936) enhanced his status. Like Brooks, he had found his students deplorably unprepared, and in 1936 they published *An Approach to Literature,* the first of their collaborations. To counter the impressionistic appreciations of poetry taught in classrooms in place of precise treatments of theme and technique, the two supplied lucid analyses of elements in the poetry, rather than biographical and secondary factual materials. Supplying many examples, their *Understanding Poetry* (1938) became the most influential text of its kind.

After publication of *Night Rider* (1939), a novel of the tobacco wars, Warren spent a Guggenheim Fellowship in Italy and then a visiting professorship at the University of Iowa. He moved to a professorship at the University of Minnesota in 1942 when LSU failed to meet Minnesota's offer. His next novel, *At Heaven's Gate* (1943), was heavily imbued with nineteenth-century Kentucky history. *Selected Poems: 1923–1943,* published in 1944, reinforced his position as a major poet, and in the same year he made his reputation as a narrative poet with "The Ballad of Billie Potts" and took up a one-year appointment as consultant in poetry to the Library of Congress. Meanwhile, Cinina suffered from frequent ill health in their increasingly unhappy marriage.

For years Warren had worked over *Proud Flesh,* a verse play treating politics, power, and ethics and influenced by *Julius Caesar, The Divine Comedy,* and the career of Huey Long. He rewrote it as *All the King's Men* (1946), which received the 1947 Pulitzer Prize in fiction. A story about the drive to power and the confusion of ends and means, the multilevel novel tells of the rise and fall of Governor Willie Stark in a state like Louisiana through the eyes of Stark's assistant and alter ego, Jack Burden. Warren also worked on the screenplay for Columbia Pictures. It won the 1949 Academy Award for best picture and was produced as a play and an opera.

Separated from Cinina upon her psychiatric hospitalization on 15 May 1949, Warren resigned from Minnesota and published *World Enough and Time* (1950), a novel based on a true story of tragic lovers in early nineteenth-century Kentucky. Jeremiah Beaumont is a "young idealist who can't find an object for his idealism." His confused quest involves him in the turmoil of politics before murder and flight lead to his violent death. Familiar Warren motifs such as the search for identity, the omnipresence of original sin, and the flight to the West in search of redemption mark this best-selling novel. In 1950 Warren was elected to the National Institute of Arts and Letters and in 1951 to the American Academy of Arts and Sciences. Always extremely popular in the classroom, he began teaching at Yale as professor of playwriting in fall 1951. At the insistence of Cinina, still hospitalized, he had obtained a divorce in Reno on grounds of cruelty in the summer of 1951. Meanwhile, his relationship with Eleanor Phelps Clark, a writer and a friend of several years, had grown closer.

Now living in New York City, Warren moved in with Clark in April 1952, and on 7 December of that year they were married at her mother's home in Roxbury, Connecticut; they had two children. In August 1953 Warren published *Brother to Dragons: A Tale in Verse and Voices,* set in "No Place" at "Any Time" and whose participants include "R. P. W." and Warren's father. Warren was fascinated by the historical records of the ghastly murder and dismemberment of a family slave, a crime committed by a nephew of Thomas Jefferson with the help of his brother. Brooding over the tragedy's impact upon Jefferson, with his belief in human perfectability, Warren made "R. P. W." Jefferson's antagonist, both finally reaching a kind of resolution with acceptance of the past and hope for the future.

The Warrens bought two ancient barns in Fairfield, Connecticut, rebuilding and expanding them. Theirs was a house for growth, and the almost constant work it required and their frequent entertaining suited the Warrens' energetic and hospitable lifestyles. In 1955 Warren published *Band of Angels,* whose heroine, Amantha Starr, learns upon her father's death that she is part Negro when she is sold into slavery. Her adventures are told against a wide background of the period before, during, and after the Civil War. A film version was released in 1957.

At the end of 1955 Warren resigned from Yale, traveling to Italy with his family. Free from teaching, he wrote current history, essays, and much poetry. A series of magazine articles based on extensive travel and interviews became *Segregation: The Inner Conflict in the South* (1956). For ten years he had published no volume of poems, but with his new marriage and fatherhood he became inspired. *Promises: Poems, 1954–1956* (1957) was dedicated to his children. It is a wide-ranging book that draws on Italy as well as Kentucky and Tennessee and features his grandfather and his memories of the Civil War, as well as the fundamental questions of meaning that obsessed the poet. Using varied metrics and styles as experimental as those in T. S. Eliot's *The Waste Land,* Warren showed that he was going strong in his sixth decade. *Promises* won the National Book Award and the Pulitzer Prize in poetry in 1958.

Elected to the American Academy of Arts and Letters in 1959, Warren wrote history for young readers as well as more fiction. The novel *The Cave* (1959) was suggested by the widely publicized death of a spelunker, and many of its characters are forced to resolve their intimate relationships as they confront the deeper issues of their own identity and philosophic bases for living. *You, Emperors, and Others: Poems, 1957–1960* (1960) recalls Warren's Kentucky childhood as well as his European experiences. Drawing on the ancient world along with early America, he ranged forward to a contemporary wasteland against the brief span of human life and the inevitability of death. He also mined other favorite areas with *The Legacy of the Civil War: Meditations on the Centennial* (1961) and a short novel, *Wilderness: A Tale of the Civil War* (1961).

In January 1962 Warren began a one-term-per-year professorship of English at Yale and then built a vacation home in West Wardsboro, Vermont. During the following eleven years came *Flood: A Romance of Our Time* (1964), *Meet Me in the Green Glen* (1971), and *A Place to Come To* (1977). *Flood* follows a writer who had profitably betrayed his gift of writing for Hollywood. Covering more than twenty years and criticized like others of his novels for melodrama, it teems with characters and events in the writer's attempt to achieve a sense of personal identity and atone for his portion of original sin. (The sins of slavery and segregation figure centrally in Warren's 1965 book of contemporary history prompted by the civil rights crisis, *Who Speaks for the Negro?*) Although *Flood*—about the symbolic federal inundation of a valley—was handled roughly by reviewers, Warren thought it one of his best. *Meet Me in the Green Glen* focuses on country people and involves murder and retribution. *A Place to Come To* is an intensely sexual account of a country boy who achieves academic and professional success only at the cost of an unfulfilled life, until his return to his home place signals the possibility of redemption. The trajectory of the boy's life resembles that of Warren at many points.

Warren published volumes on John Greenleaf Whittier, Herman Melville, and Theodore Dreiser, together with ten more collections of poetry between 1966 and 1985. His verse continued to show extraordinary vigor and lyricism. *Selected Poems: New and Old, 1923–1966* (1966) showed how much he had accomplished in four decades of poetry. Two years later he published *Incarnations: Poems 1966–1968*. *Audubon: A Vision* (1969), *Brother to Dragons: A New Version* (1979), and *Chief Joseph of the Nez Percé* (1983) show his continuing interest in the long narrative poem and the uses of history and its moral issues. He received the National Medal for Literature in 1970 and continued his readings and lectures. His frequent travel was somewhat curtailed by ill health, although his 1973 retirement from Yale gave him more time. *Or Else: Poem/Poems 1968–1974* (1974) was the result of what he called a "seizure" of extended inspiration and composition. *Selected Poems: 1923–1976* (1977) was another example of the way he liked to show work, often as if in a process of frequent summation. For *Now and Then: Poems 1976–1978* (1979) he received his second Pulitzer Prize in poetry, and the flood had not yet ebbed. *Being Here: Poetry 1977–1980* (1980) was followed by his last single volume, *Rumor Verified: Poems 1979–1980* (1980). By the time *Jefferson Davis Gets His Citizenship Back* (1980) was published, Warren's prostate cancer was becoming increasingly debilitating. Among his continuing honors were the American Academy and Institute of Arts and Letters Gold Medal for Poetry in 1985 and his appointment in 1986 as first poet laureate consultant in poetry to the Library of Congress. As a summing up, he published *New and Selected Poems: 1923–1985* (1985). His last three volumes of prose appeared in rapid succession: *A Robert Penn Warren Reader* (1987), *Portrait of a Father* (1988), and *New and Selected Essays* (1989). He died in West Wardsboro, Vermont, and was buried nearby in Stratton.

As poet, novelist, critic, editor, teacher, and commentator upon America past and present, Robert Penn Warren was an outstanding twentieth-century man of letters. In his award-winning poetry he moved from classic, conventional forms to experimental verse and became an eminent literary modernist. Fundamentally a lyricist, he was also one of the few adept practitioners of the demanding form of the extended narrative poem. As critic and influential editor he helped nourish new talent while making a permanent place for himself in the history of the novel as the author of the classic *All the King's Men*. With his colleague Cleanth Brooks, through *Understanding Poetry*, he changed the way poetry was taught in America. His appointment as poet laureate symbolized his leadership in nourishing literary endeavor throughout a long and fruitful career spanning seven decades.

★

Warren's manuscripts and personal papers are in the Beinecke Rare Book and Manuscript Library of Yale University, the Firestone Library of Princeton University, the Kentucky Library of Western Kentucky University, and the Jean and Alexander Heard Library of Vanderbilt University. Autobiographical works include *Portrait of a Father* (1988), with extensive comments on Warren's relationship with other family members as well, and "A Reminiscence," in John Egerton, ed., *Nashville: The Face of Two Centuries* (1979), which treats the Vanderbilt years in some detail. Joseph Blotner, *Robert Penn Warren: A Biography* (1997), is the authorized and definitive biography. For valuable background on the Vanderbilt and Louisiana State University years, see Louis D. Rubin, Jr., *The Wary Fugitives* (1978); Thomas Cutrer, *Parnassus on the Mississippi* (1984); Paul W. Conkin, *Gone with the Ivy: A Biography of Vanderbilt University* (1985); Amy Waldron, *Close Connections: Caroline Gordon and the Southern Renaissance* (1987); and Robert B. Heilman, *The Southern Connection* (1991).

James A. Grimshaw, Jr., *Robert Penn Warren: A Descriptive Bibliography, 1922–1979* (1981), includes a brief foreword by Warren. For criticism of Warren's work, see Victor Strandberg, *The Poetic Vision of Robert Penn Warren* (1977); James H. Justus, *The Achievement of Robert Penn Warren* (1981); Neil Nakadate, ed., *Robert Penn Warren: Critical Perspectives* (1981); Floyd Watkins, *Then and Now: The Personal Past in the Poetry of Robert Penn Warren* (1982); John Burt, *Robert Penn Warren and American Idealism* (1988); Randolph Paul Runyon, *The Braided Dream: Robert Penn Warren's Late Poetry* (1990); Hugh R. Ruppersburg, *Robert Penn Warren and the American Imagination* (1990); and William Bedford Clark, *The American Vision of Robert Penn Warren* (1991).

An obituary is in the *New York Times* (16 Sept. 1989). Forty-four interviews were recorded under the University of Kentucky Robert Penn Warren Oral History Project. Memorabilia are displayed at the Robert Penn Warren birthplace, Guthrie, Kentucky, and the Robert Penn Warren Southern Writers Center, Clarksville, Tennessee.

JOSEPH BLOTNER

WASHINGTON, Harold (*b.* 15 April 1922 in Chicago, Illinois; *d.* 25 November 1987 in Chicago, Illinois), politician who, as a U.S. congressman (1981–1983) and as the first black mayor of Chicago (1983–1987), was a prominent spokesman for civil rights.

Harold Washington was the son of Roy L. Washington, a lawyer and Methodist minister, and Bertha Jones. He grew up on Chicago's South Side. His parents were separated in 1924 and divorced in 1928; Washington's father retained custody of Harold and his three siblings. Harold was sent to Saint Benedict the Moor school, a Catholic and predominantly black boarding school in Milwaukee, Wisconsin, from 1928 until 1932. He did not like the strict regimentation there and ran away from the institution three times, hitch-hiking back to Chicago. He entered Chicago's Forrestville Elementary School in the fall of 1932, and, meanwhile, had his first experience with politics, passing out campaign literature with his father, a Democratic precinct captain in Chicago's Third Ward. Washington attended Du Sable High School from 1936 to 1940 and was an honor student and a top athlete, winning the 120-yard low hurdles in the all-city track meet. Nonetheless, he dropped out his senior year to work for the Civilian Conservation Corps (CCC).

Mayor of Chicago Harold Washington, 1984. JACQUES M. CHENET/CORBIS

Washington worked for the CCC at camps in Stockton, Illinois, and Biteley, Michigan, where he planted trees, built dams, and helped farmers plant crops. As an amateur middleweight boxer in the CCC camps, Washington won sixty of seventy fights. "I was never knocked out or knocked down," he said. "I never got hurt. I was a reasonably good second-rate amateur fighter."

Late in 1940 Washington took a job in the freezer department of Wilson and Company, a meatpacking company in his native Chicago. He married Nancy Dorothy Finch, a high school classmate, in July 1942. They had no children and were divorced in 1951. From 1942 to 1946 Washington served in the Pacific theater in an engineering unit of the Army Air Corps. He spent most of the war years building air strips in an all-black unit under the command of white officers. He was discharged as a sergeant in 1946.

Washington entered Roosevelt University in Chicago in 1946, funding his education with the help of the GI bill. He became politically active as a supporter of Henry A. Wallace's 1948 Progressive party presidential candidacy, which emphasized foreign issues as its platform and advocated the abandonment of the Marshall Plan and the Truman Doctrine. Washington was elected that year as vice president of the Illinois chapter of the National Student Association, and in his senior year he was president of the student body and a teaching assistant in the political science department. After graduating with a B.A. in 1949, he attended Northwestern University Law School, where he received his J.D. in 1952.

Washington joined his father's law practice on Chicago's South Side in 1952, and he became a prominent member of the Cook County Young Democrats. When his father died in 1953, Washington succeeded him as Democratic precinct captain and also inherited his father's position as an assistant corporation counsel to the city of Chicago, where he was assigned to the building, housing, and urban conservation division. Because of his political connections, Washington viewed the job as an entitlement and seldom showed up for work. He left the city job in 1958, and from 1961 until 1965 he was a part-time arbitrator for the Illinois Industrial Commission, where his function was to determine the amount of compensation paid to employees suffering from work-related illness or injury. Washington was a prolabor arbitrator who made decisions promptly and who seldom had a ruling reversed by the full commission.

In 1964 Washington was elected as a state representative from a black-majority South Side district. Reelected five times by overwhelming margins, he became a dependable member of Mayor Richard J. Daley's organization. Washington kept his distance from the Reverend Martin Luther King, Jr., during King's 1966 protest marches in Chicago, and he attended a meeting of black elected officials who denounced King's actions in the city. Washington's stance, however, gradually evolved, as he was among the founders of a black caucus in the state legislature in Springfield, and led a 1969 filibuster to delay appropriations bills until funds were approved for more African Americans in state government. He sponsored a 1965 consumer protection act as well as fair housing legislation, and, in 1973, the first law establishing King's birthday as a state holiday.

As Washington rose to prominence in Springfield, he became less attentive to his private law practice. In 1967 the Chicago Bar Association summoned him to a hearing after five clients complained that he had billed them for unperformed legal services. Washington was unresponsive to the CBA's repeated requests for a written response to the charges and also failed to appear at five scheduled hearings. More than two years after the initial request, Washington acknowledged "negligence." The CBA recommended a five-year suspension. On 21 May 1970 the Illinois Supreme Court suspended his law license "for one year and until further order of the court"; the suspension lasted, in fact, until 1976.

Washington had other problems. On 23 March 1971 he was indicted for failure to file income tax returns from 1964 to 1969. Washington denied this allegation but never produced copies of his tax returns from the period. He pleaded no contest to the charges and was sentenced to forty days in jail and three years' probation. Washington also paid back taxes of $508.05 and a fine of $1,036.68. "I'm not proud of this. But one has to consider whether this kind of mistake is moral turpitude. I don't think it is," he said in 1983.

Elected to the Illinois senate in 1976, Washington joined with seven other independent Democrats in protesting the lack of racial diversity in the senate leadership. The group deadlocked the selection of a senate president for five weeks, ending their opposition to Thomas C. Hynes as senate president only after a black senator had been given a leadership position. After the death of Mayor Daley, Washington ran for mayor in the 1977 special election to fill out the unexpired term. He got only 11 percent of the vote but ran strongly in black areas.

Washington, who gained a higher profile from the mayoral race, was elected to the U.S. House of Representatives in 1980 from the South Side's First District. As a member of the Judiciary Committee, Washington helped to forge the coalition that extended the Voting Rights Act over the opposition of President Ronald Reagan. Washington was elected secretary and a member of the executive committee of the Congressional Black Caucus, where he vigorously opposed Reagan's cuts in social programs and voted against Reagan policies 73 percent of the time, according to *Congressional Quarterly.* He was reelected to a second term in 1982.

Washington, who was by then Chicago's most prominent black political figure, challenged Mayor Jane M. Byrne in the February 1983 Democratic mayoral primary. More than 100,000 new black voters were registered by black activists who had drafted Washington for the race. State's Attorney Richard M. Daley, son of the late mayor, also ran, splitting Byrne's white political base. Washington won the primary with 36 percent, followed by Byrne with 34, and Daley with 30. In a campaign that was bitterly divided along racial lines, he narrowly defeated Republican Bernard Epton in the April general election. "A new day has dawned in Chicago," said Washington, "and it is a bright new day of political freedom."

His four-and-a-half-year administration comprised the most tumultous era in Chicago political history. Washington lost control of the fifty-member City Council to a coalition of white ethnic aldermen led by Edward R. Vrdolyak, the chairman of the Cook County Democratic organization. Vrdolyak's majority blocked many of Washington's appointments to boards and commissions. In 1986 Washington finally won a council majority after special court-ordered elections in redrawn black and Latino wards.

Washington brought more blacks, Hispanics, and women into government than any previous Chicago mayor. He signed a collective bargaining agreement with city workers, pushed through the city's first ethics ordinance, and enacted a freedom of information order to make city records more accessible. Washington disappointed civic leaders by killing the 1992 World's Fair for which Byrne had won international approval. His emphasis was on the city's neighborhoods. He secured a $185 million bond issue for street, sewer, and bridge repairs. Mayor Washington also secured federal funding for a new rapid-transit line. O'Hare airport was expanded and a new $450 million United Airlines terminal was opened. He saved the historic Chicago Theater from destruction and won approval for a $130 million bond to build a new central library in the South Loop that was named for him after his death. Throughout his mayoralty, Washington remained close to his roots on the South Side, and when he moved in 1983 from the Third Ward to a lakefront apartment in the fashionable Hyde Park neighborhood near the University of Chicago, he kept the same phone number so that his old constituents could still contact him.

Washington edged Byrne to win renomination in the 1987 Democratic mayoral primary and easily defeated three white challengers in the general election to become the first two-term mayor since Daley. After Washington's reelection, Vrdolyak quit as Democratic chairman and turned Republican. Washington took control of the Democratic party and slated the first two women and the first two blacks for Cook County executive offices in November 1987. "What this ticket says is that we're about the business of trying to restructure our city," Washington said in his last political speech, "to bring it together."

A week after this speech, Washington died of a massive heart attack in his fifth-floor office at City Hall. He is buried at Oakwood Cemetery in Chicago. "Harold tried to heal wounds and to bridge the gap that separated Chicago, to heal the wounds of racial and ethnic groups," the Reverend B. Herbert Martin, Washington's pastor, said in his eulogy. Senator Edward M. Kennedy called Washington's death "a tragedy for Chicago and for civil rights. He was an outstanding congressman and an outstanding mayor, and the civil rights movement in America has lost one of its greatest and most respected leaders."

★

Washington's papers are in the Harold Washington Library, the main branch of the Chicago Public Library. His early career is chronicled in John Camper, Cheryl Duvall, and John Kass, "The Road to City Hall," *Chicago Tribune Sunday Magazine* (16 Nov. 1986). Books about Washington include Gary Rivlin, *Fire on the Prairie: Chicago's Harold Washington and the Politics of Race* (1992); Melvin G. Holli and Paul M. Green, eds., *The Making of the Mayor: Chicago 1983* (1984), and Melvin G. Holli and Paul M. Green, *Bashing Chicago Traditions: Harold Washington's Last Campaign* (1989). Obituaries are in the *Chicago Sun Times, Chicago Tribune,* and *New York Times* (all 26 Nov. 1987).

STEVE NEAL

WEDEMEYER, Albert Coady (*b.* 9 July 1897 in Omaha, Nebraska; *d.* 17 December 1989 in Fort Belvoir, Virginia), career army officer and business executive.

Wedemeyer was the second of two sons of Margaret Elizabeth Coady and Albert Anthony Wedemeyer, an army bandmaster during the Spanish-American War and later an employee of the Army Quartermaster Depot in Omaha. Wedemeyer graduated from Omaha's Central High School and won an appointment to the United States Military Academy, at West Point, New York, where he earned a B.S. degree in June 1919. His first assignment was at Fort Benning, Georgia, where, according to Wedemeyer, his military career was nearly aborted when he returned from a night in town in an "uninhibited intoxicated condition, irresponsible and noisy." When disciplinary charges were brought against him, he unsuccessfully attempted to resign his commission. Whether because of this youthful indiscretion or simply because of the lack of promotion opportunities in the peacetime army, Wedemeyer would not attain the rank of captain until 1935.

General Albert Wedemeyer with a copy of his book *Wedemeyer Reports,* 1958. AMERICAN STOCK/ARCHIVE PHOTOS

Between 1923 and 1934 First Lieutenant Wedemeyer served in the Philippines, China, and again in the Philippines, with brief stints in the United States between overseas assignments. During his first tour in the Philippines (1923–1925), he married Elizabeth Dade Embick, the daughter of an army officer, on the island of Corregidor on 5 February 1925. The couple had two sons.

Preparation for the role of military strategist that Wedemeyer would assume during World War II began with study at the Command and General Staff School at Fort Leavenworth, Kansas (1934–1936). Meanwhile, in 1935, an exchange agreement had been concluded whereby one U.S. officer would study at the German War College while one German officer would study at U.S. Army schools. Wedemeyer's outstanding performance at the Command and General Staff School, coupled with the fact that he had studied German in high school, gained him this prestigious assignment. At the Kriegsakademie (1936–1938) he became familiar with German strategic theory and met many of the German army's future leaders.

Upon returning to the United States, Wedemeyer wrote about the new mobile warfare strategies being studied at the Kriegsakademie in a report that attracted the attention of General George C. Marshall. In 1940 Marshall, now army chief of staff, appointed Wedemeyer to the War Plans Division of the General Staff. In the summer of 1941, as the possibility of war loomed, President Franklin Roosevelt ordered the army and navy to create a mobilization plan. Wedemeyer worked on the project and helped create the so-called Victory Program.

On 4 December 1941, three days before the Japanese attack on Pearl Harbor, the *Chicago Tribune* published details of this top secret document under the banner headline "F.D.R.'S WAR PLANS!" Perhaps because of his German ancestry, his years at the Kriegsakademie, and his association with members of the isolationist America First Committee, Wedemeyer was investigated as a possible source of the "leak." During questioning by the FBI, Wedemeyer told an agent he was "unequivocally opposed to fascism or any other form of dictatorship," but he "believed bolshevism or communism to be a far greater menace to our country's security than nazism or fascism." This staunchly anticommunist attitude would help shape Wedemeyer's strategic concepts for the European theater as well as his views on postwar China policy.

Cleared of suspicion in connection with the leak, Wedemeyer, who had been promoted to lieutenant colonel in December 1941, was assigned the task of developing strategy for the defeat of Germany. Wedemeyer, who had studied the heartland theory of the British geopolitical thinker Sir Halford MacKinder—the notion that whoever controlled Central Europe would enjoy hegemony on the Continent—became an advocate of a cross-Channel invasion of Europe by the summer of 1943 and accompanied General Marshall on missions to sell the idea to the British. However, the British prime minister Winston Churchill, who favored what Wedemeyer called "periphery pecking," instead convinced Roosevelt to undertake the invasion of North Africa in 1942 and the subsequent invasions of Sicily and Italy in 1943. This, Wedemeyer maintained, wasted resources, postponed the cross-Channel invasion until 6 June 1944, and thereby ensured that the Soviet Union, not the Western Allies, would control the "heartland" of Europe after Germany was defeated.

Wedemeyer suggested in his 1958 memoirs that his advocacy of a cross-Channel invasion may have led to his being "eased out" of Washington. In any case, he was named deputy chief of staff of the Allied Command in Southeast Asia (1943–1944) under Lord Louis Mountbatten of Britain. Wedemeyer, by now a major general, again clashed with British policymakers because of his efforts to get supplies to U.S. forces fighting in China. In October 1944 he replaced General Joseph ("Vinegar Joe") Stilwell as commander of U.S. forces in China and as chief of staff to Generalissimo Chiang Kai-shek.

Wedemeyer was specifically instructed not to involve the United States in the civil strife between Chinese Nationalists and Chinese Communists. Instead, his main task was to encourage Chiang to fight the Japanese as vigorously as possible. After the defeat of Japan in August 1945, Wedemeyer was given responsibility for repatriating Japanese soldiers and civilians in China and for demobilizing his command. Meanwhile, Marshall attempted to mediate between the rival Nationalist and Communist Chinese and sought to create a coalition government. Wedemeyer's opposition to this policy and his advocacy of aid to the Nationalists to forestall a Communist takeover in China opened a rift with Marshall.

In May 1946 Wedemeyer returned to the United States for surgery and to await nomination as ambassador to China. When word of his pending appointment leaked out, the Chinese Communists declared him unacceptable because of his sympathy for Chiang. When President Harry Truman did not go forward with the nomination, Wedemeyer viewed the action as "appeasement." He was given command of the Second Army at Fort Meade, Maryland, but continued his efforts to influence Marshall to change China policy. Nonetheless, in July 1947 Truman sent Wedemeyer on a fact-finding mission to China and Korea. His report, submitted in September 1947, was suppressed by Marshall because Wedemeyer refused to "delete certain specific portions" that ran counter to U.S. policy. The report would become a matter of controversy after the Communist victory in China (1949), which led to angry cries of who "lost" China and the outbreak of the Korean War (June 1950), which critics would blame on Truman's "neglect" of South Korea.

Although Wedemeyer later mused that he might have been mistaken in not immediately resigning and speaking his mind on the situation in China and Korea, he remained in the service and assumed command of the Sixth Army at the Presidio, in San Francisco, California.

After the portions of Wedemeyer's 1947 report dealing with Korea were made public in May 1951 by Senate committees investigating Truman's firing of General Douglas MacArthur from his Korea command, Lieutenant General Wedemeyer announced his intention to retire, and he did so at the end of July. (In July 1954 he was awarded a fourth star in an honorary promotion to general.) His three days of testimony in June 1951 before Congress advocated a hard line in Korea even if it meant war with the Soviet Union. Although his testimony was applauded by critics of Truman's Korea policy, a *New York Times* editorial said it was "confused and unconvincing" and "did no credit to the brilliant intellect of this outstanding officer."

After leaving the army, Wedemeyer moved to New York City to become a vice president and director of Avco Manufacturing Corporation, which he left in 1954 to assume a similar role at Rheems Manufacturing Company. He left Rheems in 1956 due to poor health but continued to serve on the boards of directors of a number of corporations even after he retired to a farm near Boyds, Maryland. In 1989 Wedemeyer, who reportedly suffered from Alzheimer's disease, moved to a retirement center at Fort Belvoir, Virginia, where he died. He was buried with full military honors in Arlington National Cemetery, in Virginia.

★

Wedemeyer's papers are in the Hoover Institution Library, Stanford, California. Wedemeyer's memoirs, *Wedemeyer Reports!* (1958), is a good source on his military career and his views of World War II strategy and U.S. cold war policy, but it is sketchy on his personal life. William Stueck, *The Wedemeyer Mission: American Politics and Foreign Policy during the Cold War* (1984), is the only full treatment of the background and legacy of his 1947 mission to China and Korea. Keith E. Eiler, "The Man Who Planned the Victory: An Interview with Gen. Albert C. Wedemeyer," *American Heritage* 34 (Oct.–Nov. 1983): 36–47, provides an overview of much of Wedemeyer's career, from his early days as a junior officer though his 1947 mission to the Far East. Thomas Fleming, "The Big Leak," *American Heritage* 38 (Dec. 1987): 64–71, contains an account of the unsolved mystery of who leaked to Chesly Manly, Washington correspondent of the *Chicago Tribune,* a verbatim copy of the Victory Program. Fleming absolves Wedemeyer of guilt and suggests that Roosevelt himself may have authorized the leak. Obituaries are in the *New York Times, Washington Post,* and the *Omaha World-Herald* (all 20 Dec. 1989).

ROMAN ROME

WEINBERG, Harry (*b.* 15 August 1908 in Galicia, Austria-Hungary; *d.* 4 November 1990 in Honolulu, Hawaii), businessman, investor, and philanthropist who founded one of America's largest charitable foundations.

Harry Weinberg, *c.* 1939. NYT PERMISSIONS

Weinberg was one of seven children of Joseph Weinberg, a tinsmith and auto mechanic, and Sarah (Kamserman) Weinberg, a homemaker. When he was four the family moved to Baltimore, Maryland, where he attended Samuel F. B. Morse Elementary School. Labeled a "problem child," he left school in the sixth grade, then worked at a number of odd jobs, sold newspapers, and worked for his father's auto body and fender repair shop. In 1931 he married Jeanette Gutman; they had one child.

During the Great Depression of the 1930s, Weinberg established a business buying financially troubled homes in the city and fixing them up for resale. He combined his real estate investments with successful investments in securities, whose price, in the depression, had fallen well below 1920s prices. He sold many of his properties at a large profit after the return of prosperity during and after World War II. He "retired" in 1948 with a net worth of $2 million.

Finding retirement a bore, the still youthful Weinberg began to study *Standard and Poor's* for signs of undervalued stocks. His first major move in his new career was to purchase $100,000 worth of stock in the Baltimore Brick Company. The company's real value, Weinberg discovered, lay in its ownership of vast clay pits in a central section of Baltimore. The land could be developed profitably for shopping centers. With his shares, he obtained a board membership and challenged company management to sell off these land holdings to increase the value of the company's stock. He quietly obtained support from other major stockholders and threatened wide-scale changes in the company's direction. To rid themselves of Weinberg's challenges, management bought his stock for $625,000, a huge profit on his initial investment. Later, this practice would be labeled "greenmail" and would be associated with the maverick financier Carl Icahn and other financial speculators of the 1980s.

Weinberg's next major move was to use the $625,000 to secure a major holding in the Scranton (Pennsylvania) Transit Company. There he maximized the stock's value by raising fares, selling tangible assets such as garages, decreasing service, and depreciating assets where Internal Revenue Service regulations allowed. The profits from this endeavor allowed him to buy a controlling interest in the Honolulu

Rapid Transit Company (HRT), and the profits from that endeavor enabled him in turn to buy control of Dallas Transit Company and New York's Fifth Avenue Coach Lines. By 1962 his transit operations were valued at $100 million.

In the 1960s, Weinberg spent a great deal of time in Hawaii, and he finally moved to Honolulu in 1968. "Honolulu Harry," as his Baltimore associates (including his celebrity attorney Roy Cohn) called him, soon established himself as a brilliant, if often ruthless, business investor. As he had in other cities, he sought out companies with undervalued assets. In Hawaii, these were typically companies with large holdings of agricultural real estate. His targets were such prominent firms as American Factors (sugar, real estate, and shipping); Dillingham Corporation (construction and shipping); American Pacific Group (real estate, insurance, banking, laundry, and a Japanese car franchise); Maui Land and Pine (pineapples and real estate); C. Brewer and Company (agribusiness); and Alexander and Baldwin (agribusiness, shipping, and real estate).

In a series of controversial and well-publicized moves, Weinberg bought large blocks of stock in these companies, thereby driving up the stocks' prices. Demanding a board membership in each company, he then pressured the land-rich companies to sell agricultural land for commercial development. Threatening to sue if his board membership was not allowed, he was typically bought out at huge profits.

In addition, Weinberg made profitable investments in shopping centers, warehouses, and ground leases (the land under dozens of hotels, apartments, office buildings, and condominiums). Given Hawaii's rapid economic growth from the 1960s to the 1980s, and the shortage of land, Weinberg's HRT company profited greatly from reassessing lease rents every ten or twenty-five years. With the rising cost of Hawaiian real estate, particularly in the last half of the 1980s, HRT realized profits exceeding 100 percent in some cases of lease reassessment.

Although Weinberg was not known for his civic-mindedness by the general public, he had quietly started a small charitable foundation in Baltimore in 1959. In addition, he made periodic gifts to the Scranton Jewish Old Age Home, the University of Scranton (which awarded him an honorary doctorate in 1988), Palama Settlement in Hawaii, Baltimore's St. Agnes Hospital, Johns Hopkins Hospital, Sheppard Pratt, Ner Israel Rabbinical College, and Associated Jewish Charities.

In 1983 Weinberg surprised the public by announcing that at his death all his HRT stock (he owned 95 percent of the company) and his personal wealth would be given as a bequest to the Harry and Jeanette Weinberg Foundation. The primary purpose of the foundation was to assist the "poorest of the poor." Weinberg specifically chose to bypass charities that served the relatively well-to-do, such as universities, symphonies, museums, and orchestras. Instead, the foundation would provide a permanent charitable endowment in support of human services, aging services and centers, the homeless, Jewish federated giving programs, and other programs for the economically disadvantaged. Additional support was committed to programs in Israel.

Active in business up until his death from cancer in 1990, Weinberg fulfilled his promise. The Harry and Jeanette Weinberg Foundation became one of the largest in the United States, with assets valued at approximately $1 billion. By 1995, Hawaii's human-services sector had become the recipient of more than $40 million from the foundation, with grants made to the Young Men's Christian Association, the Young Women's Christian Association, the Hawaii Foodbank, the Association for Retarded Citizens, and Hospice Hawaii, among others. Baltimore beneficiaries have included the Salvation Army, the American Red Cross, Meals on Wheels, and the United Way of Central Maryland.

★

Articles on the Weinberg Foundation include "Harry and Jeanette Weinberg Foundation," *Foundation Directory* (1997), and Thomas Jaffe, "Homes for the Homeless," *Forbes* (22 June 1992). See also Mark Cohen, " 'Honolulu' Harry's Last Hurrah," *Honolulu Magazine* (Mar. 1988). Obituaries are in the *New York Times* (6 Nov. 1990), *Time* (19 Nov. 1990), and *U.S. News and World Report* (19 Nov. 1990).

ALFRED L. CASTLE

WEISS, Paul Alfred (*b.* 21 March 1898 in Vienna, Austria; *d.* 8 September 1989 in White Plains, New York), biologist best known for his pioneering work in the theory of cellular development and embryonic organization and in electron microscopy and cinemicrography of the nervous system.

One of two sons of Carl S. Weiss and Rosalie Kohm, Paul Weiss spent his formative years in Vienna. Before entering the University of Vienna, he served in World War I as an officer in the Austro-Hungarian army for three years and was discharged in 1918. Motivated by high school teachers who encouraged both laboratory research and humanistic study, Weiss studied engineering and biological sciences at Vienna. He then decided on advanced study in biology and was awarded a Ph.D. in 1922. His dissertation was "Animal Behavior as Systems Reaction." In his 1967 article "Research in Retrospect," he wrote, "The combination of engineering and life sciences proved to have hybrid vigor, both in conceptual and technical regards." In place of what he called "the antiquated mechanistic doctrine" usually used in the study of organisms, he introduced a "systems" ap-

Paul A. Weiss, 1960. UPI/CORBIS-BETTMANN

proach, which would become a standard tool in physical and behavioral sciences. His work showed that animal behavior did not follow a rigid pattern of cause and effect.

After earning his Ph.D., Weiss became the assistant director of the Biological Research Institute of the Academy of Sciences in Vienna (1922–1929). In 1926 he married Maria Blaschka; they had no children. Also in 1926, on leave from his post at the institute, he took up a Rockefeller Foundation traveling fellowship and began two more years of postgraduate studies at a number of major European research laboratories to acquire wider technical experience. In 1930 Ross Harrison, an outstanding experimental embryologist, invited Weiss to the United States as a Sterling Fellow at Yale University, a post he held for two years. Weiss then moved on to the University of Chicago Department of Zoology, where he taught and conducted research for twenty-one years, from 1933 to 1954, becoming an associate professor in 1935 and a full professor in 1942.

Weiss, who became a U.S. citizen in 1939, had established expertise in regeneration of nervous tissue, and during World War II was the principal investigator for the U.S. government in the search for improved methods of surgical nerve repair. As he wrote later, "The moral obligation of making one's experience available for the mitigation of human suffering became an over-riding commitment." He developed several techniques, such as the sutureless splicing of severed nerves using arterial cuffs (for which he received a merit citation from the U.S. government) and the use of freeze-dried and vacuum-stored nerve stumps, arteries, and corneas for grafting; in essence, he developed the first tissue bank. His methods saved thousands of wounded soldiers from total disability.

From 1947 to 1954 Weiss served as the director of the masters program in the University of Chicago's Division of Biological Sciences. In 1954 he became head of the new Department of Developmental Biology at the Rockefeller Institute in New York City (now Rockefeller University). At Rockefeller he led his department (which he called a "gold plated laboratory") in the research areas of wound healing, cancer, and the development and regeneration of nerve tissue. His pioneering research at Rockefeller established the principle of cellular self-organization, namely, that developing cells mixed randomly from different organs would rebuild themselves into miniature copies of the donor organs without direction from a central source. He also showed that the physical and chemical environment surrounding newly multiplying cells is what determines an embryo's organization and growth.

In 1964, now emeritus professor at Rockefeller, Weiss became dean of the newly formed Graduate School of Biomedical Sciences (which he designed) at the University of Texas at Houston and served in that post for two years. Over the next fourteen years, alternating with his research at Rockefeller University, he held visiting professorships at a number of universities, among them Stanford, the Massachusetts Institute of Technology, New York University, Oxford University, and the University of Frankfurt.

Weiss's interest in the broad problems of the role of science in education, the historical and philosophical foundations of science, the relationships between science and art and science and society, and the use of natural resources led him to serve on the Science Advisory Committee of the President of the United States, as chairman of the Committee of Biology and Agriculture of the National Research Council, on the council of the National Academy of Science, as a consultant to the U.S. State Department, as chief scientific adviser to the Brussels World's Fair, and as chairman of U.S. delegations to the International Council of Scientific Unions and the International Union of Biological Science. He believed that participation in activities such as these not only broadens technical expertise but forces one to make choices and priorities among research projects, fostering concentration on essentiality, creativity, and efficiency.

While he had no formal medical training, Weiss served

as an adviser to medical schools and major hospitals and was awarded two honorary degrees of doctor of medicine and doctor of medicine and surgery. He was the recipient of the nation's highest scientific award, the National Medal of Science. In October 1957 the Ernst Leitz Optical Company awarded him the 500,000th microscope manufactured by them and made him the first American to receive the Leitz award. He also received the Grand Medal Geoffroy Saint-Hilaire from the French government. He served as president of both the Society for Developmental Biology and the International Society for Cell Biologists. He published more than 350 articles and eleven books in the fields of theoretical biology, science organizations, education, research policies, and the relation between science and art. His 1939 text on experimental embryology was the classic in the field, read by all students of embryology for decades.

A courtly gentleman, Weiss wrote poetry, sculptured, and played the violin in his leisure time. He died in the White Plains branch of New York Hospital after a long illness.

Weiss worked on basic problems, both theoretical and experimental, including nerve growth, differentiation, and regeneration; wound healing; and the development, function, and behavior of the nervous system. For more than sixty years he was an influential and supportive teacher, adviser, lecturer, and writer, knowledgeable in many areas, who believed that experience, research, and logic were intertwined and enhanced each other in the promotion of science and humanistic values. His advice to young scientists best sums up his own life's work: "Achievement is marked not so much by what one has learned, but by how one is using that which one has learned, with eyes and mind wide open to the immense range of *terra incognita* in the life sciences and the untapped resources and opportunities for its elucidation and penetration by observation, experiment, and theory."

★

The works of Paul Weiss include *Principles of Development: A Text in Experimental Embryology* (1939), a classic textbook in the field for many years, and "Research in Retrospect," in Giulio Gabbiani, ed., *Reflections on Biologic Research* (1967), an essay on the nature of research and Weiss's philosophical beliefs. Jane Oppenheimer, *Essays in the History of Embryology and Biology* (1967), is a chronological account of important breakthroughs in the field of embryology. See also an interview with Barbara Yuncker in the *New York Post* (14 Mar. 1962). An obituary is in the *New York Times* (12 Sept. 1989).

LESLIE S. JACOBSON

WESCOTT, Glenway (*b.* 11 April 1901 in Kewaskum, Wisconsin; *d.* 22 February 1987 in Rosemont, New Jersey), important expatriate writer of the 1920s and 1930s whose best novels and short fiction explored his midwestern heritage and identity.

Wescott was the eldest of the six children of Bruce Wescott, a farmer, and Josephine Gordon Wescott, a homemaker. He attended the Orchard Grove Country School and the West Bend (Wisconsin) High School (1913–1915) while living with an uncle. His first publication, an essay, appeared in the school magazine. He attended Wanheska High School and published a short story in a school publication in 1915. After graduating in 1917 he entered the University of Chicago, but he withdrew in 1919. That year he met Monroe Wheeler, with whom he established a lifelong intimate relationship.

After leaving the university Wescott worked briefly as a department store clerk and as a companion to the poet and critic Yvor Winters in New Mexico. In 1920 Wheeler published *The Bitterns,* twelve imagistic poems by Wescott, which attracted the interest of the poet Wallace Stevens. In 1921 Wescott and Wheeler made the first of many trips to Europe, where they met many literary luminaries. During the early 1920s Wescott divided his time between New York and Europe, publishing poetry, reviews, and fiction in literary magazines. In 1924 he published *The Apple of the Eye,* his first novel, using Wisconsin regional material; it

Glenway Wescott. ARCHIVE PHOTOS

had evolved from a long short story, "Bad Han." Another short story was selected for *The Best Short Stories of 1924.*

Wescott and Wheeler departed for France in 1925, where they met Jean Cocteau, Pablo Picasso, and Igor Stravinsky. While abroad Wescott worked diligently on his poetry and fiction. He published a book of poems, *Natives of Rock* (1925), and a deluxe edition of his story *Like a Lover* (1926). Wescott's second novel, *The Grandmothers,* appeared in 1927. This best-selling historical family saga, the Harper Prize Novel for 1927, made Wescott a celebrity. He further bolstered his reputation in 1928 with *Goodbye Wisconsin,* a collection of stories. Although he spent nearly a decade in Europe, and was touted along with Hemingway as one of the most acclaimed expatriate writers, Wescott's early fiction remained firmly rooted in the familial and regional material of his midwestern youth.

While in Paris in the late 1920s, Monroe Wheeler formed a partnership with Barbara Harrison, a wealthy Californian, to publish deluxe editions of works by British, European, and American authors. Harrison of Paris published a limited edition of Wescott's *The Babe's Bed,* a collection of stories, in 1930. In 1932 Wescott departed from fiction to publish *Fear and Trembling,* a collection of essays on prewar Germany, and the satirical *A Calendar of Saints for Unbelievers.* Both were poorly received by American critics.

Upon returning to New York City in 1934, Wescott had difficulty regaining his footing as a writer, while Wheeler's career in the arts was launched when he was hired by the Museum of Modern Art to work on exhibitions. Wescott believed his early fame was both a blessing and a burden: "I pretended to be a genius . . . in order to get on in the world; and ever since, it has been as if some god had heard me and somehow condemned me to the uneasy fulfillment of that juvenile bluff and boast."

In 1937 Wescott, Wheeler, and the photographer George Platt Lynes moved to Stone-blossom, a home in New Jersey that was a gift from Barbara Harrison and her husband, Glenway's brother Lloyd. In 1937 Wescott began to keep a journal but did not publish another book until 1940, when his acclaimed novel *Pilgrim Hawk* appeared. Considered to be his finest work, the novel was translated into four languages and was widely anthologized. The critic F. W. Dupee wrote: "Wescott has come through the ordeal of adolescence which proves fatal to so many American writers. . . . His writing is as supple as ever, and has acquired, besides, a certain witty poeticality which may be of French inspiration but which is entirely native in idiom." Also in 1940 Wescott published his ballet libretto, *The Dream of Audubon.* He again enjoyed great critical and commercial success in 1945 with his suspense novel *Apartment in Athens,* set during the German occupation of Greece.

Although he never published another novel, Wescott remained active in the arts. He was elected to the American Academy and Institute of Arts and Letters in 1947 and served as its president from 1957 to 1961. In 1962 he published *Images of Truth,* a collection of essays on Katherine Anne Porter, Colette, Somerset Maugham, Thomas Mann, and other writers, many of whom were his friends. Wescott was elected to the board of trustees of the Museum of Modern Art in 1967. He died at his home some months after suffering a stroke. His diaries, published in 1990, contain frank views on his family, friends, and the New York literary milieu.

Wescott's reputation as one of America's foremost expatriate writers has been eclipsed by his better-known contemporary, Ernest Hemingway. Acclaimed for the beauty of his prose and his technical mastery of various literary forms, Wescott is still considered an important figure in American literature of the mid-twentieth century.

★

Wescott's papers are at Yale University. His journals were published as *Continual Lessons: The Journals of Glenway Wescott 1937–1955,* edited by Robert Phelps (1990). A biography is Sy Myron Kahn, "Glenway Wescott: A Critical and Biographical Study (Ph.D. diss., University of Wisconsin, 1957). See also C. E. Schorer, "The Maturing of Glenway Wescott," *College English* 18 (Mar. 1957): 320–326; Sy Myron Kahn, "Glenway Wescott: A Bibliography," in *Bulletin of Bibliography* 22 (1956–1959): 156–159; William H. Rueckert, *Glenway Wescott* (1965), a critical study; and Ira D. Johnson, *Glenway Wescott: The Paradox of Voice* (1971). An obituary is in the *New York Times* (24 Feb. 1987).

CHRISTINE STENSTROM

WHITE, Jack Edward, Sr. (*b.* 24 July 1921 in Stuart, Florida; *d.* 2 July 1988 in Washington, D.C.), African-American physician whose crusade against cancer led to the founding and his direction of the Howard University Cancer Center.

White was one of sixteen children—six boys and ten girls—born to George White, a farmer, carpenter, and coffin maker, and Emma (Clark) White, a homemaker. He was educated in the public school in Stuart through the eighth grade, but because there was no high school in town, he was sent to live with relatives in South Carolina, where he completed his secondary education at the Seneca Institute. He entered Florida Agricultural and Mechanical University in Tallahassee in 1937 and received his B.A. degree in 1941. He then enrolled in the Howard University College of Medicine in Washington, D.C., where he earned his M.D. degree in 1944. The following year, on 30 September, he married Sara Theodora Williams, a student at the university's Freedmen's School of Nursing in Baltimore. They had five children.

White served his internship in medicine and surgery at

Howard University's Freedmen's Hospital in Washington from 1945 to 1946. He was assistant resident in surgery at the U.S. Marine Hospital in Boston from 1946 to 1947, serving as a first lieutenant, but he developed a peptic ulcer, which halted his military service. He returned to Freedmen's Hospital for a residency in surgery from 1947 to 1948 and was chief resident in general surgery from 1948 to 1949. He then went to the National Cancer Institute's Memorial Hospital for Cancer (later Sloan Kettering) in New York City, as an assistant surgical resident from 1949 to 1950 and as a surgical resident from 1950 to 1951.

Returning to Washington, White joined the faculty at Howard as assistant professor of surgery in 1951, moving with his family to 3809 Seventeenth Street, N.E. The Whites lived there until 1957. In 1958 White became an associate professor and in 1963 professor of surgery. White concurrently directed the Cancer Teaching Project at Howard from 1951 to 1985. In 1972 he was named director of the new Howard University Cancer Center at Freedmen's Hospital. He was named professor of oncology in 1973 and chairman of the Department of Oncology in 1974, maintaining an office at Sixth and Bryant Streets, N.W. The Cancer Center became internationally renowned and, because of White's role in its establishment and funding, was known at his retirement in 1986 as "the house that Jack built."

White became a diplomate of the American Board of Surgery in 1951 and was chosen a fellow of the American College of Surgeons in 1953—the first African American in Washington to be so honored. He also was a member of the Society of Surgical Oncology (1962), the Institute of Medicine, the National Academy of Science (1977), the American Cancer Society, the American Association for the Advancement of Science, the American Medical Society, the D.C. Medical Society, and the National Medical Association. In addition, he served for a time as vice president of the Medico-Chirurgical Society of the District of Columbia and as president of the Southeastern Cancer Research Association. He also was a delegate to the International Union Against Cancer in London (1958), Moscow (1962), and Tokyo (1966). White was a founding member of the American Society of Preventive Oncology, a vice president of the James Ewing Society, and a member of the Alpha Omega Alpha medical honor society.

Florida A&M University honored White with its alumni award for research excellence, and Howard University gave him its medical school student council's faculty award in 1955 and 1965. The Capital Press Club presented White the Pioneer Award in 1978 in recognition of lifetime achievements in cancer research and treatment. Also in 1978, Howard University's School of Medicine gave him its Outstanding Research Award. An annual oncology lecture program in his honor was begun by Howard University in 1983, and in March 1988 he was presented with Howard's Distinguished Alumni Achievement Award for his work in education, surgery, and cancer research.

White's medical papers covered a broad range of cancer research interests, including cancer of the breast, lymphatic organs, and tongue; the epidemiology of the disease; and chemotherapy treatment. His research also delved into peptic ulcers and penetrating trauma of the abdomen.

A short and slender but energetic man, White had dark hair, prominent ears, and a mustache. His intelligence, dynamic personality, and strong convictions made him a formidable battler for the rights of his patients and for better health care for African Americans. Beyond medicine and education, writing, photography, travel, and golf were his strong interests.

The oncologist whose career was a battle against cancer among African Americans died of the disease himself at his home in Washington, D.C. Following a funeral and memorial service at Howard University, he was buried just outside the city in Fort Lincoln Cemetery, Bladensburg, Maryland.

White's life and career are heroic, as well as testament to success through determination, perseverance, and the refinement of talent. Born into a large family with humble beginnings, of a father who was freed from slavery at the age of twelve, he set and achieved lofty goals. He was the first African American to be trained as a cancer surgeon at Memorial Hospital in New York City. His efforts saved many lives and improved and extended many others. He struggled against an entrenched establishment to prove—in more than fifty scientific papers—the differences in the rates at which blacks and whites died of cancer. His efforts, showing this could be substantially reduced if cancer was detected earlier in African-American patients and treatment begun at earlier stages of the disease, resulted in untold lives saved and quality of life improved.

"My life has been characterized by a continuing search for circumstances wherein I could express myself creatively," White once wrote. "There are many things that inhibit the process, but given ability, these can be overcome. I feel also that when you are able to please yourself in any situation, your actions, performance, and behavior will be approved by others."

★

Biographical details about White are in Charles H. Epps, Jr., Davis G. Johnson, and Audrey L. Vaughan, *African-American Medical Pioneers* (1994); and "Obsequies for Jack Edward White, Sr., M.D., F.A.C.S.," obituary and program for the memorial service held by Howard University in Andrew Rankin Memorial Chapel, 7 July 1988. An obituary is in the *Washington Post* (5 July 1988).

CHARLES A. ROND IV

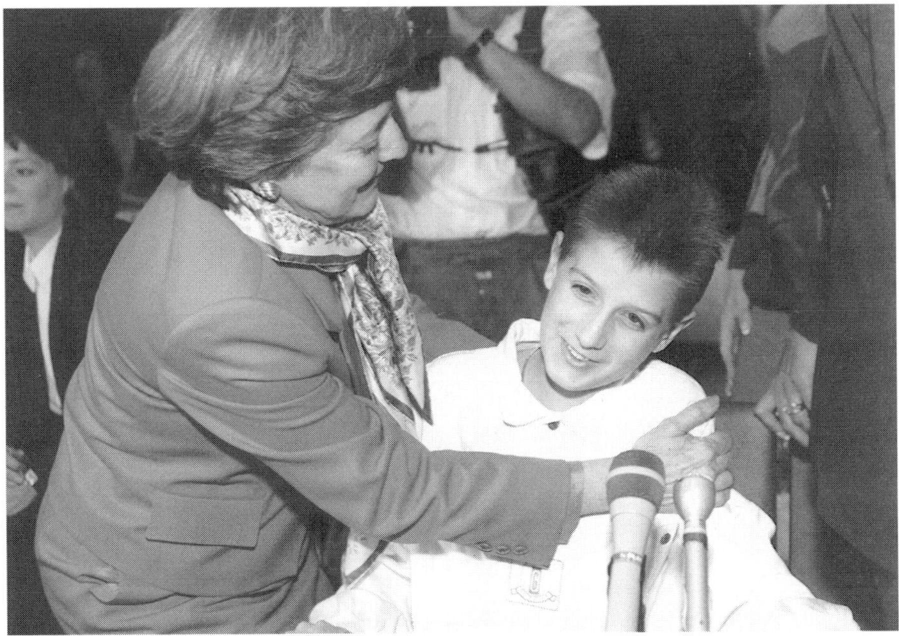

Ryan White is embraced by Dr. Cory Sevaas after his testimony before the Presidential Commission on AIDS about his battle with the disease. REUTERS/NANINE HERTZENBUSCH/ARCHIVE PHOTOS

WHITE, Ryan (*b.* 6 December 1971 in Kokomo, Indiana; *d.* 8 April 1990 in Indianapolis, Indiana), hemophiliac infected with the AIDS virus who taught the nation a lesson in courage and compassion; his clear message helped educate the public that AIDS could not be spread by casual contact.

Ryan White was the elder of two children of Jeanne Hale and Wayne White, who worked at Delco, a division of General Motors. He was born with hemophilia, a serious condition that limits the blood's ability to clot. Ryan was frail as a youngster, thinner and shorter than healthy boys his age, and withdrawn because of his frustration at not being able to keep up with other children. To help control his hemophilia, Jeanne White gave her son regular injections of Factor VIII, a blood product that is made from the clotting factor of blood donated by thousands of people. Factor VIII allowed White and other young hemophiliacs the freedom to suffer the normal cuts and bruises of childhood without excessive risk. Little was known at that time about AIDS, and evidence that the virus that causes AIDS was spread in blood products was not widely accepted by health professionals. Scientists at the Centers for Disease Control in Atlanta were concerned that hemophiliacs receiving Factor VIII should be warned of potential contamination by the AIDS virus, but no public policy changes had been instituted.

When White was thirteen he was admitted to James Whitcomb Riley Hospital, a children's hospital in Indianapolis, Indiana. Dr. Martin Kleiman, who was to care for him in the years ahead, diagnosed *Pneumocystis carinii,* a rare form of pneumonia that is associated with AIDS. White had AIDS, contracted through an injection of Factor VIII. After the shock of this diagnosis, White and his family learned that AIDS could not be spread though casual contact and that no family members had AIDS. They were also reassured that, although the long-term prognosis was bleak, White was likely to have periods of relatively good health when he would be strong enough to participate in the normal life of a teenager.

White was determined not to become an AIDS "victim." He wanted to fight not only the disease itself but also the ignorance and fear surrounding it. The school board in his town of Kokomo voted unanimously to keep him out of school, the one place he wanted to be. He and his family fought the board's decision, and after a nine-month battle he won the right to attend school. The family was harassed, however, and White was called "faggot" and "queer" by people calling in to a local radio show. He became the target of "Ryan White" jokes and was accused of spitting on food and biting people. Obscenities were scribbled in his locker at school. Someone slashed the tires on the family car and pelted it with eggs.

Fear and prejudice finally forced White and his family to leave their hometown. In 1987 he, his mother, and his younger sister (his parents were divorced by this time) left Kokomo and moved twenty-five miles away to Cicero, Indiana, hoping for a new start. They were warmly received by a community that was dedicated to educating the public about AIDS. School personnel at Hamilton Heights High School held informational sessions for students and parents, and White felt accepted by many new friends, a "normal kid" again.

White's situation gained national attention. He attended the American Foundation for AIDS Research (AmFAR) benefit and posed for a poster with celebrities Elizabeth Taylor and Marlo Thomas. He was interviewed by David Hartman on the television show *Good Morning America.* When asked which celebrity he would most like to meet, he said Elton John. After that interview, the singer John contacted him and flew the White family to Disneyland. John became a family friend, offering ongoing support throughout the remainder of White's life. The singer Michael Jackson also became a close friend of White and his family.

Although he went through tough periods of weakness and serious debilitation from AIDS-related health complications, including recurring pneumocystis pneumonia, liver problems, and whooping cough, White maintained a positive attitude. He continued to gain national stature as the young face of AIDS. He wanted to reach other teenagers at risk for contracting the AIDS virus because they experimented with drugs or were sexually active. He could speak directly to the issues on their minds, and they listened to his voice of experience. He did not want sympathy, but he wanted people to understand what he and other AIDS patients were experiencing. By the age of sixteen White had addressed a variety of audiences, millions of viewers of television talk shows, young people watching the science series *3-2-1-CONTACT,* and the President's AIDS Commission (March 1988). He described the pain of the discrimination that he and his family had endured, emphasizing the importance of AIDS education. A television movie, *The Ryan White Story,* was filmed in 1988; White played the part of another young AIDS patient in the film.

When he was not speaking or making public appearances, White tried to live as normally as possible. He went to school dances, got his driver's license, went skateboarding, and cultivated many friendships. He enjoyed life and sought to make the most of it. White's final public appearance was in March 1990, when he was asked to speak at the Athletes and Entertainers for Kids Academy Awards night party in Los Angeles. Feeling ill, he bravely thanked those who had worked for AIDS awareness and education. He met former President Ronald Reagan and Nancy Reagan, but his health was deteriorating, and he rushed back to Indiana and Dr. Kleiman. He was hospitalized immediately with an AIDS-related respiratory infection and died soon after. His funeral drew a crowd of more than 1,500 mourners, including First Lady Barbara Bush, Michael Jackson, and countless other celebrities and friends. Elton John led the congregation in a hymn before playing a song he had written for Ryan, "Skyline Pigeon." The Reverend Raymond Probasco delivered the eulogy. He said that White "helped us to care and to believe that with God's help, nothing is impossible, even for a kid." White was buried at a private service in Cicero, the town that had welcomed him and his family three years before his death. Governor Evan Bayh of Indiana ordered that flags be flown at half-mast to honor White, who taught his state and his nation a lesson in courage.

★

Ryan White and Ann Marie Cunningham, *Ryan White: My Own Story* (1991), is an autobiographical account of White's struggle with AIDS and his public commitment to AIDS education. Cory Ser Vaas, "The Happier Days for Ryan White," *Saturday Evening Post* (Mar. 1988), includes comments from medical researchers working to protect hemophiliacs as well as from ham radio operators who helped White. Jack Freeman, "The Quiet Victories of Ryan White," *People Weekly* (30 May 1988), describes the welcome White and his family received from the people of Cicero, Indiana, and gives details of White's life as he tried to be a normal teenager. Obituaries are in the *New York Times* (9 and 12 Apr. 1990).

GAIL STRANGE THOMPSON

WHITE, Theodore Harold ("Teddy") (*b.* 6 May 1915 in Boston, Massachusetts; *d.* 9 May 1986 in New York City), journalist and author whose books on presidential elections reshaped political reporting in the United States.

White was one of four children of David Vladefsky, a lawyer, and Mary Winkeller White, both of whom were Russian emigrés. His father adopted the name White from a prominent department store. The family lived in the Dorchester section of Boston.

White's family was never well-off. His father worked his way to a law degree but devoted his practice to supporting radical causes and representing poor clients. When he died in 1931, the family went on welfare. After graduation from the Boston Latin School in 1932, White was admitted to Harvard University but could not afford the tuition. He went to work selling newspapers on Boston's streetcars, and with the assistance of a scholarship for newsboys and financial help from the university, he entered Harvard in 1934. While there he majored in history, with an emphasis on Chinese history, was active in liberal causes, and was a leader of the Avukah Society, an organization of Zionist Jewish students. White also helped organize boycotts of German goods as the Nazi regime grew more powerful. At Harvard he was keenly aware of discrimination based on his religion (even the more liberal groups had quotas) and his family's poverty (facilities for day students were poor).

Theodore H. White, 1956. UPI/CORBIS-BETTMANN

John Kenneth Galbraith and John King Fairbank were two of his teachers; Joseph Kennedy, Jr., and Caspar Weinberger were among his classmates. He graduated in 1938 with an A.B. degree.

White received a Frederick Sheldon traveling fellowship and decided to visit China. Before leaving he arranged to submit articles to the *Boston Globe.* He sailed to China by way of the Mediterranean and the Indian Ocean. He earned his first money as a journalist with an article he submitted to the *Globe* on the conflict between Jews and Arabs in Palestine.

White arrived in Hong Kong in March 1939, in the midst of the Sino-Japanese War. He was hired by the Chinese Ministry of Information and went to Chungking, where he spent nine months writing stories for the *Globe,* the *Manchester Guardian,* and the Australian Broadcasting Company. John Hersey, Far Eastern editor of *Time,* recommended White as a stringer for the magazine.

In 1939 White traveled to northwestern China and to the front in Shanxi Province. His subsequent report was the first by a *Time* foreign correspondent to carry a byline. Established as a successful working journalist, he gave up his position with the Chinese government in 1940.

White met Henry R. Luce, editor and publisher of *Time,* in 1941, when Luce visited China. Impressed by White, Luce brought him to New York City to do a series of articles for *Fortune* magazine. After the bombing of Pearl Harbor in December 1941, White returned to Chungking as an accredited war correspondent. His uncensored story on the famine in Honan in 1943 created a stir on both sides of the Pacific and increased the restrictions under which China correspondents labored.

White became increasingly critical of the corruption within the Chinese government; moreover, he disagreed with the strong anticommunism of Whittaker Chambers, *Time*'s foreign editor. White began to spend more time on strictly military coverage, especially of American involvement in the war in China. He was awarded an Air Medal for his performance during combat flights. As he became more acerbic toward *Time* and Chambers, he was ordered to avoid politics and restrict himself to human-interest stories.

In October 1944, when General Joseph ("Vinegar Joe") Stilwell was removed from his command of the Sixth Army in China, White sent his view of the affair to *Time* on the plane that carried Stilwell home. The story was gutted by the time it appeared. Likewise, his sympathetic reporting on the Communist base in Yenan was ignored. An unflattering portrayal of Chiang Kai-shek, which he cabled from Manila, led Luce to order White back to the United States in spring 1946.

In New York, White chafed under *Time*'s anticommunist and pro-Chiang stand. He took a leave of absence while he and Annalee Jacoby worked on the book *Thunder Out of China* (1946). This and his continual support of the "old China hands" soon led White to sever relations with *Time,* which soon began referring to him as a "pinko."

On 29 March 1947 White married Nancy Bean; they had two children. That year Stilwell's widow asked White to edit her husband's papers for publication. The general's testy views, and White's continued criticism of Chiang Kai-shek, made it difficult for him to find work with the mass-circulation journals. The FBI began to construct a file on White at the direct request of J. Edgar Hoover. (As a consequence White's passport was temporarily suspended a few years later.) With employment opportunities so limited, White sailed in June 1948 for Europe as a representative of the independent Overseas News Agency.

White and his family settled in Paris. His major interests were the growth of the Marshall Plan and the beginnings of the European Community. He returned home in 1953 and became a columnist for the *Reporter* but soon found its extreme leftist bias as stifling as the rightist bias of *Time.* In 1955 he joined *Collier's,* where he reported on the Army-McCarthy hearings, the J. Robert Oppenheimer affair, and the northward migration of African Americans.

With the demise of *Collier's* in late 1956, White turned to writing novels. In *The Mountain Road* (1958) he encapsulated a number of incidents that had occurred during the 1944 retreat from the Japanese Ichigo offensive. A gripping story, and well reviewed, it became a selection of book clubs. White's next novel, *The View from the Fortieth Floor* (1960), was a fictionalized account of the death of *Collier's.* Gary Cooper bought the film rights for a reported $85,000, but no film of that title was ever released.

By 1960 White had turned to political reporting. His aim was to analyze the presidential campaign between John F. Kennedy and Richard M. Nixon. He spent time with both men as well as with other candidates during the primary elections. He cast the campaign for the most powerful position in the world almost as a medieval joust. Digging behind the headlines, White created a new way of looking at American politics by highlighting what he felt were the roots of the candidates' political ambitions.

White's manuscript was rejected several times. Few in the publishing business felt that a political book would have a market several months after the election had taken place. When it was published, *The Making of a President* (1961) was a phenomenal success and sold more than 4 million copies. The key was White's intellectual yet visceral style combined with a brilliant narrative. In subsequent elections political reporters tended to follow the lead White had set. Some critics felt that he became too enamored of the Kennedy family, citing as proof his article in *Life* magazine following Kennedy's assassination in 1963 as a perpetuation of the myth of Camelot.

In 1971 White divorced his wife. In March 1974 he married Beatrice Hofstadter, the widow of the American historian Richard Hofstadter. Following President Richard Nixon's resignation in 1974, White wrote *Breach of Faith* (1975), which examined Nixon's political fall.

In *In Search of History* (1978), the first of a planned two-volume memoir, White traced the path of his life as a professional journalist. In 1982 he published *America in Search of Itself,* a study of a nation that had lost its illusions. White was working on the second volume of his memoirs when he died of a stroke in New York City, three days after his seventy-first birthday.

Known for his lucid and dynamic writing, White was a journalist who gave in-depth analyses of the headlines. Trained as a historian, he placed the events and personalities of his time into a historical framework. As a foreign correspondent White made China understandable to American readers. He was passionate and involved, traits he never tried to hide from his audience. He cared about outcomes. His narrative style ensured that his work would not be an ephemeral catalog of passing events but a slice of history in the making.

★

White's personal papers, notes, and correspondence are in the Harvard University Library. His *Fire in the Ashes* (1953) describes the Europe he saw being reborn following World War II. Edward T. Thompson, ed., *Theodore White at Large* (1992), is a collection of many of White's major articles. Joyce Hoffman, *Theodore H. White and Journalism as Illusion* (1995), though generally critical of White as an insider, recognizes the strengths of his work and gives appropriate credit for his reshaping of American journalism. An obituary is in the *New York Times* (17 May 1986).

ART BARBEAU

WILENTZ, David Theodore (*b.* 21 December 1894 in Dvinsk [present-day Daugavpils], Latvia; *d.* 6 July 1988 in Long Branch, New Jersey), lawyer and New Jersey political boss who played an influential role in state and national Democratic party politics.

Wilentz was one of seven children of Nathan Wilentz, a prosperous merchant, and Bertha Crane. The family immigrated to the United States in 1899 and settled in Perth Amboy, New Jersey. Wilentz was naturalized the following year. After graduating from high school he went to work as a reporter at the *Perth Amboy Evening News.* He eventually became the sports editor and also managed a local basketball team. His predecessor as sports editor was Harold G. Hoffman, who became an influential Republican whose political path crossed Wilentz's several times.

While working at the newspaper, Wilentz commuted to Manhattan to attend evening classes at New York Law School. After the United States entered World War I, he enlisted as a private in the U.S. Army; he was discharged in 1918 with a lieutenant's commission. He obtained a law degree in 1919.

Wilentz began his legal practice in Perth Amboy, then the largest city in Middlesex County. He married Lena Goldman on 22 February 1920. They had a daughter and two sons. Wilentz was named city attorney for Perth Amboy in 1923, shortly before the outbreak of two riots protesting attempts of the Ku Klux Klan to organize a chapter in that city. No rioters were prosecuted. After being elected Middlesex County Democratic Committee chairman in 1928, he proceeded to build a coalition of immigrants and blue-collar workers in the county's two largest cities, New Brunswick and Perth Amboy, which resulted in a Democratic sweep of county offices in 1929. Prior to that time, the county had been controlled by the Republican party, led by GOP county chairman Hoffman. Wilentz's electoral victories established a Democratic stranglehold over the county and made him the second most influential Democrat in the state. The state's most powerful boss was Frank Hague, whose control of densely populated Hudson County resulted in the election of A. Harry Moore, Hague's protégé, as governor in 1925, 1931, and 1937.

Governor Moore nominated Wilentz for the position of state attorney general in January 1934; after confirmation by the state senate, Wilentz took his oath of office on 24

New Jersey Attorney General David Wilentz (*left*) and Bronx, New York, Inspector Henry Bruckman at the Hunterdon County Court preparing for the trial of Bruno Richard Hauptmann for kidnapping and murdering the child of Charles Lindbergh. UPI/CORBIS-BETTMANN

January 1934. Several months later he gained international attention for the extradition and prosecution of Bruno Richard Hauptmann for the 1932 kidnapping of Charles A. Lindbergh, Jr., the infant son of the famous aviator. Although Wilentz had no prior experience in criminal law, he led the prosecution team and obtained a guilty verdict. Hauptmann was executed on 3 April 1936, after his plea for clemency was denied by Governor Hoffman, who had been elected Moore's successor in 1934.

In the 1937 gubernatorial election, Hague's candidate, Moore, unexpectedly defeated a strong Republican challenger after Hudson County submitted suspiciously large ballot counts at the last minute. Wilentz refused to respond to the state legislature's charges of voting fraud, and a threatened investigation by the U.S. Senate was stymied after a fire destroyed the Hudson County election records. Governor Moore reappointed Wilentz to a second five-year term as attorney general in 1939.

Governor Moore was succeeded in 1941 by another Democrat, Charles Edison, a former secretary of the navy and the son of the inventor Thomas Edison. Edison's wealth as well as support from "clean government" Republicans in Essex County allowed him to assert independence from Hague. During the ensuing political battles, Wilentz told Edison: "Governor, I hate to do this, but you know how it is," and sided with Hague. Wilentz even initiated a lawsuit challenging the constitutionality of Edison's primary legislative achievement, a restructuring of the taxation of the state's railroads.

During 1940 and 1941 Wilentz vigorously prosecuted the German-American Volksbund, or Bund, a pro-Nazi organization that owned and held rallies at Camp Nordlund in Sussex County. After Bund officials were convicted of violating the state's racial incitement law by giving anti-Semitic speeches at their rallies, Wilentz drafted a bill to revoke the Bund's charter and to dispose of its properties in the state.

When Wilentz's second term expired in 1944, he returned to the private practice of law, as senior partner of Wilentz, Goldman, and Spitzer in Middlesex County. When Jersey City mayor John V. Kenney led a political revolt against Hague in 1950, Wilentz sided with the insurgents and helped oust Hague's supporters from the Democratic National Committee. Wilentz obtained a seat on the National Committee himself, which, combined with his continued role as Middlesex County Democratic chairman, made him one of the most influential politicians in New Jersey during the next two decades.

In 1951 local newspaper reporter Francis T. Field published the novel *McDonough,* a sympathetic portrait of a county boss modeled on Wilentz. Reviewers praised the novel for its realistic portrayal of behind-the-scenes politics, particularly its detailed description of "honest grafting" and "an Irish-Jewish alliance far more common in most big cities than people think."

Referring to Wilentz's power during this period, a lawyer interviewed by *New Jersey Monthly* in 1981 stated: "Middlesex and Wilentz were the same. Wilentz named the judges in Middlesex County, he handled the tax boards. You wanted an assessment changed in any of the towns, you went to the Wilentz law firm. If a Wilentz lawyer was appearing before Judge 'X' in Superior Court in Middlesex

County, you knew damn well you had two strikes against you to go in opposing him."

During the 1950s and 1960s Wilentz was influential in choosing Robert Meyner and Richard Hughes as the successful Democratic candidates for governor. Hughes later recalled: "I relied on Dave for advice and assistance all the time I was governor." In 1965 Wilentz's son Robert was elected to the New Jersey Assembly, and in 1966 his son Warren was nominated as the Democratic candidate for U.S. Senate (he lost to the incumbent Republican Clifford Case).

The election of President Richard M. Nixon, a Republican, in 1968 caused a disruption of Wilentz's political influence, after newly appointed federal prosecutors investigated the influence of organized crime in New Jersey politics. In January 1970 a federal judge released transcripts of tape recordings made by the Federal Bureau of Investigation containing conversations of criminals discussing their links to prominent New Jersey politicians, one describing payoffs directly to Wilentz in exchange for police protection of gambling operations in Middlesex County. Wilentz called the claims "a total fabrication," but, one month later, resigned his position on the Democratic National Committee.

Despite the bribery accusations, Wilentz remained an influential political figure, and his support helped to elect Brendan Byrne as governor in 1973 and 1977. In 1979 Byrne appointed Wilentz's son Robert as chief justice of the New Jersey Supreme Court.

In 1976 Anthony Scaduto published a book which asserted that Hauptmann was not a kidnapper but an innocent man who had been convicted on the basis of evidence fabricated by Wilentz. In 1981 Hauptmann's widow sued Wilentz and the State of New Jersey, seeking to overturn her late husband's conviction. The courts dismissed the lawsuit in 1983.

Wilentz was on the board of directors of both the National State Bank of Elizabeth and the Amerada-Hess Oil Corporation, served as chairman of the board of Breeze Corporations, Inc., and was a trustee of Perth Amboy General Hospital. He died of heart failure on 6 July 1988 and is buried in Beth Israel Cemetery in Woodbridge, New Jersey.

The first influential Jewish politician in New Jersey, Wilentz forged a long-standing alliance of immigrants and blue-collar workers. His control of the Middlesex County Democratic party gave him tremendous influence in New Jersey politics for some sixty years. As a member of the Democratic National Committee, as well as a delegate to every Democratic National Convention from 1940 until 1984, he also exercised an important role in the selection of the national Democratic party's candidates for president and vice president.

★

The Records of Governors Moore, Hoffman, and Edison at the Bureau of Archives and History, New Jersey State Library, Trenton, New Jersey, contain documents concerning Wilentz's work as attorney general. His role in the Lindbergh case is covered in Anthony Scaduto, *Scapegoat: The Lonesome Death of Bruno Richard Hauptmann* (1976); Ludovic H. C. Kennedy, *The Airman and the Carpenter: The Framing of Richard Hauptmann* (1985); Jim Fisher, *The Lindbergh Case* (1987); and Noel Behn, *Lindbergh: The Crime* (1994). The political environment of prewar New Jersey is described in Dayton McKean, *Pressures on the Legislature of New Jersey* (1938). The relationship with bosses Hague and Kenney are mentioned in Dayton McKean, *The Boss: The Hague Machine in Action* (1940; repr. 1967); Richard J. Connors, *A Cycle of Power: The Career of Jersey City Mayor Frank Hague* (1971); Saul Orkin, "New Jersey Democratic Politics, 1949–1953: The Downfall of Boss Frank Hague" (Ph.D. diss., Columbia University, 1971); and William Lemmey, "Boss Kenney of Jersey City," *New Jersey Historical Society* 98 (1980). The Perth Amboy anti-Klan riots are described in Howard B. Furer, "The Perth Amboy Riots of 1923," *New Jersey History* 87 (1969): 211–232. Wilentz's work as attorney general is mentioned in John D. Venable, *Out of the Shadow: The Story of Charles Edison* (1978). His relationship with Governor Hughes is mentioned in Alvin S. Felzenberg, "The Making of a Governor: The Early Political Career of Richard J. Hughes," *New Jersey History* 101 (1983). Reviews of *McDonough* are by Joseph F. Dineen, *Saturday Review of Literature* (26 May 1951) and Warren Moscow, the *New York Times Book Review* (8 July 1951). The allegations and denials of mafia influence are in the *New York Times* (7 and 8 Jan. 1970). Wilentz and his law firm are discussed in Randall Rothenberg, "Superlawyers, Superfirms," *New Jersey Magazine* (Sept. 1981). Obituaries are in the *New York Times* (7 July 1988) and *Time* (18 July 1988).

STEPHEN MARSHALL

WILLIAMS, Edward Bennett (*b.* 31 May 1920 in Hartford, Connecticut; *d.* 13 August 1988 in Washington, D.C.), one of the most prominent and successful trial lawyers of his generation and a powerful insider in the political, social, and sports worlds of Washington.

Williams was the only child of Mary Bennett and Joseph Barnard Williams. His father held a series of modest jobs, including that of a store detective in a Hartford department store. With the onset of the Great Depression he lost that position, and during the 1930s he was often out of work. Edward took odd jobs on a part-time basis to help out. He attended Bulkeley High School in Hartford and then won an academic scholarship to Holy Cross College in Worcester, Massachusetts, where he excelled, graduating summa cum laude in 1941. After the Japanese attack on Pearl Harbor in 1941 and U.S. entry into World War II, Williams

Edward B. Williams. UPI/CORBIS-BETTMANN

enlisted in the Army Air Forces, but was discharged when he failed to graduate from flight school. He began law studies at Georgetown University, from which he graduated in 1944. Later that year he was admitted to the District of Columbia Bar and began his career at the prestigious Washington firm of Hogan and Hartson.

Williams quickly got into the courtroom, defending negligence cases in the lower courts for a local streetcar company. Soon, however, he sought designation as court-appointed counsel for indigents in criminal cases. This step turned out to be pivotal in launching what would become a spectacular career in representing, and regularly obtaining acquittals for, some of the most powerful, notorious, and colorful defendants in the dock of federal and state prosecutions and congressional inquisitions over a span of forty years.

On 3 May 1946 Williams married Dorothy Adair Guider. They had three children. In 1949 he left Hogan and Hartson to start his own law firm. He first became nationally prominent in the early 1950s, when he defended Senator Joseph R. McCarthy of Wisconsin in censure proceedings brought against him in the Senate for abuse of his power as chairman of a subcommittee investigating communist subversives and influence in government, particularly in the Department of the Army. Williams skillfully negotiated a mild rebuke for his client in place of the damaging and rare punishment of censure. On the eve of the dismissal of the censure motion, however, McCarthy inexplicably denounced his senatorial accusers as "unwitting handmaidens" of the Communist party, destroying the resolution that Williams had achieved and ensuring the imposition of the censure. In the aftermath Williams was widely denounced as a fascist by those who detested McCarthy. He was denounced as a communist sympathizer, too, because during this period he also defended Hollywood writers who refused to give testimony to congressional committees investigating alleged communist infiltration of the entertainment industry.

In 1959 Dorothy Williams died. The following year, on 11 June, he married Agnes Anne Neill; they had four children.

During the 1960s the U.S. Supreme Court radically enlarged the rights of defendants in criminal cases, and Williams played a leading advocate's role in the process in the Court on behalf of many of his clients. He was especially effective in getting convictions reversed on the basis of illegal searches and seizures through government use of wiretapping.

Williams's defense in the 1960s of James R. Hoffa, the notorious general president of the International Brotherhood of Teamsters, in Hoffa's epic battles with U.S. attorney general Robert F. Kennedy enlarged Williams's national and controversial reputation as a brilliant courtroom strategist in the service of pariahs widely condemned by the general public. Hoffa was indicted for allegedly taking kickbacks from a Detroit trucking company in 1964, but he escaped conviction when the jury deadlocked. The subject of unrelenting investigation by the Justice Department, he finally went to prison in 1967. Williams's relationship with Hoffa, who was a revered and charismatic rank-and-file leader with irrefutable racketeer connections, was predicated upon the strong professional belief that the massive prosecutorial engines of the government ought not to be loosed upon any citizen when the principle driving the action is that any means, fair or foul, is suitable to ensnare and convict the target.

The New York organized crime figure Frank Costello, facing indictment for tax evasion and hearings on the revocation of his citizenship, was also a client of Williams. It was widely reported at the time that Costello, whose reputation as a brutal mobster was widespread, turned to Williams only reluctantly because he preferred not to associate with the man who had defended McCarthy. It was a prudent choice. Although Costello was convicted of the tax charge, the government's attempts to deport him failed, because Williams got the Supreme Court to endorse his assertion that the Justice Department had misapplied the law in Costello's case.

Williams also represented Adam Clayton Powell, a flamboyant New York congressman, who was tried for but not convicted of tax evasion; John Connolly, President Richard Nixon's secretary of the Treasury, who was acquitted of bribery charges in connection with the approval of federal price supports for milk production; Richard Helms, a former director of the Central Intelligence Agency, who was accused of lying to a congressional committee but pleaded guilty to misdemeanor charges; and Robert G. Baker, President Lyndon Johnson's close confidante and power broker, who was ultimately convicted of fraud and tax evasion. Williams also obtained an inconsequential fine for the Greek shipping magnate Aristotle Onassis, charged with fraud in acquiring surplus U.S. oil tankers.

In the 1970s, when the Watergate investigation reached an ominous stage for President Nixon and his impeachment seemed likely, General Alexander Haig, a senior White House aide (and later secretary of state in the administration of President Ronald Reagan) counseled Nixon to retain Williams. Lacking the wisdom of the mob figure Costello, the president rejected Williams because he was a Democrat.

Williams, who was a longtime adviser to both the Kennedy family and the *Washington Post,* was the founder of the distinguished Washington law firm of Williams and Connolly. The firm, which came into being in 1967, was a successor to the solo practice he had set up in 1949. Williams and his colleagues at the firm were recognized throughout the U.S. legal establishment as having one of the most elite criminal-law practices in the country. The firm's hallmarks were high intelligence, indefatigable preparation, and a resourcefulness that continually astonished prosecutors and judges.

Williams was also an influential figure in national politics. He personally knew and had ready access to every president from John F. Kennedy to Ronald Reagan. His renown as the man to see when legal troubles threatened and his personal relationships with figures at the highest levels of government led to his selection as national treasurer of the Democratic Party—a position he held from 1974 to 1977.

A tall, imposing figure, with wavy hair that reached over the back of his collar, Williams had a third great interest beyond law and politics—sports. He was a part owner of both the Baltimore Orioles basketball team and the Washington Redskins football team, and in 1983 the Orioles won the World Series and the Redskins won the Super Bowl, making Williams the most celebrated man in Washington. Williams died at Georgetown University Hospital after a long battle with colon cancer. He is buried in St. Gabriel's Cemetery in Potomac, Maryland.

Edward Bennett Williams was an extraordinary courtroom lawyer with an almost legendary capacity to charm and persuade juries to understand and resolve cases in his favor. He appeared for some of the most famous clients in the most closely watched trial dramas of his era. He became powerful and respected in Washington and the nation because, in his own words, he was not a lobbyist or a fixer. His political connections never helped him because, he said, "I do most of my work in the goldfish bowl of the courtroom."

★

Edward Bennett Williams, *One Man's Freedom* (1962), is a semiautobiographical work that is principally a commentary on the constitutional, political, and social values in the legal defense of unpopular figures. Robert Pack, *Edward Bennett Williams for the Defense* (1988), is a biography that emphasizes the cases and techniques of a great trial lawyer. Evan Thomas, *The Man to See* (1991), is a full-scale biography that gives equal treatment to Williams's roles as "legendary trial lawyer" and "ultimate insider." See also Irving Younger, *Edward Bennett Williams' Cross Examination of Jake Jacobson in U.S. v. Connally* (1988). Obituaries are in the *Washington Post* and *New York Times* (both 14 Aug. 1988).

KENNETH CONBOY

WILLIAMS, G(erhard) Mennen (*b.* 23 February 1911 in Detroit, Michigan; *d.* 2 February 1988 in Grosse Pointe, Michigan), six-term governor of Michigan and later assistant secretary of state for African affairs and ambassador to the Philippines who was credited with the revitalization of the Democratic party in Michigan after World War II.

Williams was one of three children of Henry Philips Williams and Elma Christina Mennen. The Williams family arrived in Detroit before the Civil War and there began a prosperous food processing industry, offering a line of pickles, relishes, and jellies. His father also developed a successful real estate business. His mother was a granddaughter of Gerhard Mennen, a German immigrant who, while a pharmacist in Hoboken, New Jersey, had developed a baby powder and other toiletries that became the basis of a major fortune. Williams's nickname, "Soapy," was given to him at the age of fourteen by fellow summer campers in reference to this family business.

Williams attended the Detroit University School before enrolling in 1925 in the Salisbury School in Connecticut, where he was an outstanding student. He was particularly moved by his study of England during the industrial revolution and years later stated that the human suffering during industrialization had convinced him to devote his life to helping the underdog. After graduating from Salisbury in 1929, he entered Princeton University, where he was twice elected president of the Young Republican Club before graduating cum laude in 1933. He then entered the University of Michigan Law School with the intention of

G. Mennen Williams. UPI/CORBIS-BETTMANN

pursuing a career in public service. He received his law degree cum laude in 1936, having been elected to the law review. In 1937 he married Nancy Lace Quirk, with whom he had three children. During this period he abandoned the Republican party, becoming a Democrat.

Viewing the federal policies of the New Deal as the best route to a career in public service, Williams began work with the Social Security Advisory Board in Washington, D.C. In 1938 he briefly returned to Michigan as an assistant to Attorney General Raymond Starr, a position he obtained through the influence of his family's attorney, Frank Murphy. When Murphy moved to Washington as U.S. attorney general in 1939, he brought Williams with him. When Murphy was appointed to the U.S. Supreme Court, Williams transferred to the Justice Department's Criminal Division

During World War II, Williams was commissioned in 1941 as an officer in the navy, where he rose to the rank of lieutenant commander. He served in the South Pacific in naval intelligence, winning the Legion of Merit with Combat V. After the war, Williams served briefly as deputy director of the Michigan Office of Price Administration, where he met Hicks Griffiths, his wife Martha Griffiths, and others interested in revitalizing Michigan's Democratic party. Williams's experience with the Michigan Liquor Commission before the war led to his appointment to the Liquor Control Commission by Governor Kim Sigler in 1948. His work in reforming the commission gave him a great deal of public exposure as well as a chance to meet local political leaders all over the state.

In 1948 Williams won the Democratic nomination for governor in a hard-fought primary and went on to win the general election against Sigler by uniting liberal intellectuals and labor, led by Gus Scholle and Walter Reuther of the United Auto Workers. Williams was reelected governor an unprecedented five times.

During Williams's administration, the Mackinac Bridge was built, uniting the two peninsulas of Michigan. For the most part, however, Williams struggled with a state legislature that had not been reapportioned in many years and whose Republican majority frustrated his efforts to deal with population growth. He did obtain passage of a fair employment practices act, increases in both social and mental health services, and highway expansion. As governor, he pushed for a broad range of social programs and more funding for state government to better serve the needs of the working people of Michigan.

Williams's hopes of running for U.S. president in 1960 were a casualty of his struggles with the legislature. After he chose not to run for a seventh term as governor, he was appointed assistant secretary of state for African affairs by President John F. Kennedy. A strong advocate of an "Africa for the Africans" policy, he made thirteen trips to Africa during a period when many black African nations were becoming independent. He also assembled a major collection of African art, which he later donated to the Detroit Institute of Art.

In 1966 Williams returned to Michigan and ran for the U.S. Senate. After winning a bitter primary campaign against Detroit mayor Jerome Cavanagh, he experienced problems with kidney stones that limited his campaigning, and he lost in the general election against Robert Griffin. In 1968 President Lyndon Johnson appointed Williams ambassador to the Philippines. In 1970 he was elected to the first of two eight-year terms on the Michigan state supreme court, on which he served as chief justice from 1983 to 1986. He retired from the court at the end of his second term because the state constitution prohibits justices from seeking reelection after the age of seventy. Williams died of a cerebral hemorrhage and was buried on Mackinac Island in Michigan.

Born to wealth and privilege, Williams applied the policies of the New Deal and political alliance to his home state of Michigan, where the Democratic party had been weak and disorganized for most of the twentieth century. He often referred to his program as a miniature New Deal, expanding education, social services, and civil rights in Michigan as well as building highways to promote continued growth in the state. His alliance with organized labor leaders, especially Walter Reuther of the United Auto Workers, and blacks established the party as an active proponent of social change. His administration and inner political circle included many women at a time when politics was still largely a male preserve. After leaving the governorship, he continued his advocacy of change, as when he called for Africa to be ruled by Africans while white regimes still controlled South Africa and Rhodesia.

★

Williams's papers are in the Michigan Historical Collections, Bentley Historical Library, University of Michigan, which also holds a number of oral histories related to Williams's career. Others important in Williams's career whose papers are also at the Bentley include Helen Washburn Berthelot, Adelaide Hart, Neil Staebler, Margaret Price, Carolyn Sinelli Burns, Tom Downs, Martha Griffiths, John Swainson, and George Romney. The Archives of Urban and Labor Affairs at Wayne State University has extensive manuscript and oral history collections on many individuals involved in Williams's career and Michigan politics. First-hand accounts of his years in Michigan politics include Helen Washburn Berthelot, *Win Some, Lose Some: G. Mennen Williams and the New Democrats* (1995), by the longtime political supporter who managed all of Williams's campaigns from 1954 on; and Neil Staebler, *Out of the Smoke-Filled Room: A Story of Michigan Politics* (1991). William Barry Furlong, "A 'Boy Wonder' Begins to Wonder," *New York Times Magazine* (23 Nov. 1959), discusses Williams's early life and political career. Frank McNaughton, *Mennen Williams of Michigan: Fighter for Progress* (1960), was written while Williams was exploring a run for president. Obituaries are in the *New York Times* and *Detroit News* (both 3 Feb. 1988).

WILLIAM H. MULLIGAN

WILLIAMS, John James (*b.* 17 May 1904 in Bayard, Delaware; *d.* 11 January 1988 in Lewes, Delaware), Republican U.S. senator whose investigations of government wrongdoing and personal standards of high moral conduct earned him the title "conscience of the Senate."

John Williams was one of eleven children of Albert Frank Williams and Annie Eliza (Hudson) Williams, who owned a farm in Sussex County, Delaware. Reared in a devout Methodist home in a conservative rural environment, Williams completed three years of high school in the Frankford, Delaware, public school, which was as much as the school offered but one year short of earning a Delaware high-school diploma. When his hopes of attending college were frustrated by lack of money he went to work as a store clerk. In 1921 he became the junior partner with his brother Harry in a chicken-feed business in Millsboro, Delaware. This proved to be a propitious move because two years later, thanks to the construction of good highways connecting southern Delaware with Philadelphia and New York, local farmers began to raise broilers, and by the end of the decade Sussex County had become a major East Coast poultry supplier.

John J. Williams. COURTESY OF THE UNIVERSITY OF DELAWARE LIBRARY. © HARRIS & GIFFORD, PHOTOGRAPHERS

In 1924 Williams married Elsie E. Steele, a local farmer's daughter, and the couple settled in Millsboro. Following an automobile accident that made it impossible for Elsie to have children, they adopted her youngest sister as their own child. Williams's business prospered and he began buying nearby farm properties. The poultry industry increased dramatically during World War II, bringing hitherto unknown prosperity to Sussex County, but this good fortune was clouded by accusations that Sussex poultry producers were selling through the black market. As head of the poultrymen's association Williams vainly sought to bring attention to U.S. government agents, whom he and other honest farmers suspected of being in collusion with black-market operators. This wartime experience led Williams to enter politics, and, without any previous experience in political office, he won a surprising victory against Senator James M. Tunnell, a respected New Deal Democrat, in the 1946 election that returned Republicans to power in Congress for the first time since 1932.

Capitol watchers expected little from Delaware's freshman senator, but Williams attracted national attention between 1949 and 1951 when he uncovered scandals in Bureau of Internal Revenue offices in several major American cities. The thoroughness of his investigation and his careful avoidance of unsubstantiated accusations earned him the respect of fellow senators and citizens throughout the country.

Williams pursued a conservative political philosophy that was grounded in his rural background and Christian beliefs. He opposed New Deal–era agricultural policies because they created an expensive artificial surplus that aided grain and cotton farmers at the expense of livestock producers and consumers. As a member of the Senate Finance Committee he shared the belief of his Democratic colleague Harry Byrd of Virginia in "pay as you go" federal financing. He opposed tax cuts during times of deficit financing and was a longtime foe of the oil-depletion allowance and other special-interest loopholes in the U.S. tax code. He also criticized policies that allowed a rich man such as the Greek shipping magnate Aristotle Onassis to purchase U.S. government surplus ships at cut-rate prices or Howard Hughes to avoid paying income taxes while he was making large sums from government contracts.

The senator played an important role as a stabilizing influence in Delaware during the civil rights era. In 1954 he quelled unrest in southern Delaware following the Supreme Court's *Brown* v. *Board of Education* decision by calmly noting that there was no recourse to the Court's mandate within the U.S. Constitution. Williams supported the landmark civil rights legislation of 1964 and 1965 but voted against the 1968 civil rights bill because he believed it sacrificed the right of property owners to sell or rent to people of their choice. He also criticized Harlem congressman Adam Clayton Powell Jr. for wasting government money on himself and on ill-conceived community projects.

In 1963 Williams embarked on his most famous investigation when he was made aware of influence peddling by the Senate majority leader's secretary, Robert ("Bobby") Baker. Because Baker had been a close associate of Lyndon B. Johnson, by now the president, the case was fraught with political obstacles, but Williams's investigative tenacity, reputation for honest dealing, knowledge of Senate procedure, and unblemished personal and public life made it possible for him to track down the evidence that sent Baker to jail and showed that the Senate was capable of cleaning up its own scandals.

Williams's independence was challenged during the 1960s when the Justice Department won a major antitrust action against Delaware's largest corporation, the DuPont Company, for its controlling ownership of General Motors Corporation stock. Acting against the views of DuPont Company executives and stockholders, Williams championed a tax remedy for the resulting divestiture that, in his opinion, did justice to both stockholders and to the U.S. Treasury. In 1969 he again demonstrated his independence when he opposed President Richard Nixon's nominee for the Supreme Court, Clement F. Haynsworth, believing that the judge had demonstrated insensitivity to potential conflicts of interest.

Having won four terms in the Senate, Williams chose to retire in 1971. At the same time, he proposed an amendment to the Constitution that, had it been adopted, would have mandated retirement dates for senators and other high government officials. He retired to his home in Millsboro, where he lived as a much-respected citizen until his death from a heart attack. He is buried in Millsboro.

★

The papers of John James Williams, constituting approximately 150 linear feet of material, are housed in the Special Collections Section of the Morris Library at the University of Delaware in Newark, Delaware. A biography of the senator by Carol E. Hoffecker is forthcoming.

CAROL E. HOFFECKER

WILLIAMS, Roy Lee (*b.* 22 March 1915 in Ottumwa, Iowa; *d.* 28 April 1989 in Leeton, Missouri), union leader who served as general president of the International Brotherhood of Teamsters from 1981 to 1983.

The seventh of twelve children, Williams left school after the sixth grade and spent his early years working on his father's truck farm in the Ozark Mountain region south of Springfield, Missouri. He later recalled the poor quality of the land and the hard daily routine of farming. To escape this life, he began driving a truck at the age of sixteen, at first hauling livestock up to Chicago. Eventually he was driving a sleeper truck on a 1,100-mile route between Decatur, Illinois, and Denver, Colorado. In 1938 he joined the Teamsters Union. During World War II, Williams served from 1942 to 1946 in the U.S. Army, fighting in Europe and winning two Bronze Stars. He left military service with the rank of sergeant.

After the war Williams returned to truck driving, but his growing involvement with organized labor led him to make a career as a union official. In the postwar years his fellow drivers at Chief Freight Lines elected him to the post of shop steward, the union's front line representative at the job site. At the same time he became increasingly active in his local union in Kansas City, helping out whenever needed by walking on a picket line or handing out fliers and pamphlets at job sites. In 1949 the union sent him to serve as trustee over a local union in Wichita, Kansas, that had become bankrupt.

During the course of this trusteeship Williams met Jimmy Hoffa, president of the union from 1958 to 1971 but at that time an ambitious Teamster leader based in Detroit.

Roy Williams, 1982. UPI/CORBIS-BETTMANN

As an inexperienced union officer, Williams sought guidance in his role as trustee of the Wichita union by traveling up to Detroit one weekend each month to meet with Hoffa and discuss the issues that had arisen in the Wichita local. Hoffa would answer Williams's questions, and on Sundays, Williams would attend a regular meeting of Hoffa's local union in order to learn by example how to lead the membership. Thirty years later, when describing those sessions, Williams said, "I learned from Hoffa practically everything that I know." In 1952 Williams was appointed trustee over Local 41 in Kansas City. Two years later, as the local's trusteeship was lifted, Hoffa came down and nominated Williams for the post of local union president, an office he would hold until 1981.

Williams steadily moved up the ranks of the national Teamsters organization. He served as president of Joint Council 56, a regional Teamster organization based in Kansas City, from 1956 to 1981. With Hoffa's support he became chairman of the Highway Drivers Council, and later, when that council was folded into the new, fourteen-state Central Conference of Teamsters, Williams became recording secretary of the new organization. In 1961 Hoffa made Williams one of the union's general organizers and assigned him the states of Nebraska, Kansas, and Missouri. Meanwhile, Williams also had strong ties to Frank Fitzsimmons, the man whom Hoffa left in charge of the union after he was jailed in 1967 on jury tampering charges and who replaced him as union president in 1971. The relationship with Fitzsimmons meant that Williams's climb in the organization continued in the 1970s. He became a vice president of the national union in 1971, a post that placed him on the organization's General Executive Board. Fitzsimmons made Williams director of the Central Conference of Teamsters in 1975 and chairman of the union's freight division. With Fitzsimmons, Williams served as co-chairman of the critically important bargaining committee for the National Master Freight Agreement, the contract that covered the union's members in the trucking industry. Eventually, Williams was in a position to become head of the entire union. When Fitzsimmons died in May 1981, shortly before the Teamster regular convention, the General Executive Board selected Williams to serve as interim general president. A few weeks later, delegates at the union's convention elected Williams to a five-year term as general president. He was voted in by an overwhelming margin.

Williams came to power at a difficult moment in the union's history. The Motor Carrier Act of 1980 had effectively deregulated interstate trucking. Ever since the Motor Carrier Act of 1935, the Teamsters had enjoyed the benefits of organizing a limited number of employers in a largely stable business environment. With deregulation, a host of new nonunion companies began undercutting older firms, whose union-set wages and work rules hampered their ability to compete. The effect of deregulation was compounded by an economic recession in 1981 and 1982. Thousands of Teamster members lost their jobs. Indeed, the union itself estimated that between 26 and 32 percent of members working in the trucking industry were unemployed in 1982. To cope with this situation, Williams negotiated in 1982 a new National Master Freight Agreement, which modified the union's work rules and set up a two-tier wage system allowing new employees to be paid at a lower rate.

Although Williams gamely tackled the economic problems confronting the union, his own legal difficulties proved overwhelming. In December 1982 he was convicted in federal court of conspiring to bribe a U.S. senator; the government alleged that he had hoped to stave off trucking deregulation. Sentenced to a ten-year prison term, Williams resigned his office as president of the Teamsters in April 1983. In the years that followed, he steadfastly argued that he was innocent of the bribery charges. Still, he chose to cooperate with government prosecutors in an effort to limit the amount of time he would have to spend in jail. Testifying in major organized crime trials in 1985 and 1987, Williams described how he had long been under the control of Nick Civella, the head of the Kansas City Mafia. Williams's testimony helped the government present a case in

1988 charging that the International Brotherhood of Teamsters was a corrupt organization controlled by organized crime. To resolve a suit filed by government prosecutors under civil provisions of the Organized Crime Control Act of 1970 (popularly known as civil RICO), the Teamsters agreed in 1989 to allow federal monitors to cleanse the union of organized crime figures and to stage the first-ever direct elections for the union's top officers in 1991.

Williams himself did not live to see those elections. Suffering from emphysema and a heart ailment, he died on the small farm in Leeton, Missouri, that he had bought while he served as an official in the Teamsters. He was buried in Leeton. His wife, Clarice, and his two daughters survived him.

★

Williams offered a firsthand account of his career in his testimony at two key trials: *United States* v. *Carl Angelo DeLuna et al.* (1980), U.S. District Court, Western District of Missouri; and *United States* v. *Anthony Salerno et al.* (1985), U.S. District Court, Southern District of New York. Books that offer a useful perspective on the Teamsters Union during Williams's career include: Steven Brill, *The Teamsters* (1978); Dan La Botz, *Rank and File Rebellion: Teamsters for a Democratic Union* (1990); and Charles R. Perry, *Deregulation and the Decline of the Unionized Trucking Industry* (1986). A useful overview of the government's civil RICO suit against the Teamsters is in Kenneth C. Crowe, *Collision: How the Rank and File Took Back the Teamsters Union* (1993). The *New York Times* profiled Williams and the Teamsters in two articles (16 May 1982 and 17 May 1982). Obituaries are in the *Washington Post, New York Times,* and *Kansas City Times* (all 29 Apr. 1989).

DAVID S. WITWER

WILLIAMS, William Appleman (*b.* 12 June 1921 in Atlantic, Iowa; *d.* 5 March 1990 in Waldport, Oregon), historian of U.S. diplomacy whose best-known works include *The Tragedy of American Diplomacy* (1959), *The Contours of American History* (1961), and *The Roots of the Modern American Empire* (1969).

An only child, Williams was raised in Atlantic, a small, farming community along the Rock Island Line, which he later described as a "part of the empire." His father, William Williams, an air force pilot, was killed in March 1929 during war-game exercises in Texas. Upon his death, his widow, Mildrede (Appleman) Williams left her eight-year-old son in the care of her parents while she attended the Iowa State Teachers College. She later returned to Atlantic to teach third grade. In his high school years Williams was an Eagle Scout, a class officer, and something of a local sports star. He also became a drummer in a local jazz band, an early expression of his lifelong love of jazz.

After graduating in 1939, Williams left Iowa to accept a basketball scholarship at Kemper Military Academy in Booneville, Missouri. In 1941 he won an appointment to the United States Naval Academy in Annapolis, Maryland, where he served during his senior year as assistant editor of the academy's *Trident* magazine. While he labored through engineering, he devoured the work of Spinoza, Marx, Freud, and the English socialists G. D. H. Cole and William Morris. When he graduated from Annapolis in 1944, class members voted Williams most likely to serve on the Joint Chiefs of Staff. He received his officer's commission and served fifteen months in the Pacific theater of World War II as an executive officer of an amphibious landing craft. When the war ended, Williams married his high school sweetheart, Emma Jean Preston, in December 1945; they had no children. Williams was next assigned to the navy's flight school in Corpus Christi, Texas. While he loved flying, his military career was cut short when he and his wife published a newsletter for the National Association for the Advancement of Colored People that called for integration and civil rights. By mutual agreement, Williams and the navy parted company—a separation facilitated by a spinal injury. In the spring of 1947 he received a medical discharge from the navy and set out to seek a new profession.

With the help of the GI bill, Williams entered graduate school at the University of Wisconsin in 1947, where he studied with a distinguished cast of progressive professors, including Fred Harvey Harrington, Merrill Jensen, William Best Hesseltine, Howard K. Beale, and Merle Curti. In this nurturing, intellectual environment, Williams extended Frederick Jackson Turner's frontier thesis into the twentieth century to formulate his corporatist thesis, which held that economic expansion has been and continues to be the mainspring of the American political system. When the western frontier closed at the end of the nineteenth century, Williams argued, the United States shifted the locus of expansion outward and aggressively pursued a policy of "open door imperialism." Williams developed his thesis from his study of U.S.–Soviet relations in the 1920s, for which he was awarded a Ph.D. in 1950.

This provocative thesis had a chilling effect on Williams's academic career. With a reputation as a leftist, it was difficult for him to obtain grants and appointments. Over the next few years Williams would be tracked by the Federal Bureau of Investigation, harassed by the Internal Revenue Service, and called before the House Un-American Activities Committee (1962). Meanwhile, he got his first job at Washington and Jefferson College (1950) with the help of Harrington. After one year there Williams went to Ohio State to teach western civilization. When he refused to change a grade for Woody Hayes's star halfback, Williams lost his job. In 1952 he published *American-Russian Relations, 1781–1947,* on which he formulated a critique of U.S. foreign policy that became a central tenet of cold-war revisionism.

With the publication of *American-Russian Relations,* Williams secured a tenure-track appointment at the University of Oregon in 1952, but the book also attracted the attention of critics, some of whom branded him procommunist and effectively killed his chances for tenure at Oregon. Two more books followed in this period. *The Shaping of American Diplomacy* (1956) illustrated how economics shaped foreign policy, while *American Radicals* (1957) featured standard figures from the progressive movement. With his career at Oregon stalled, Williams accepted an offer to fill Harrington's position in diplomatic history at the University of Wisconsin. In 1957 he moved back to Madison with his second wife, Corrinne Croft Hammer (whom he had married in 1956 after a divorce from his first wife), and her son and daughter, whom he adopted. He and Corrinne had three children of their own.

During the Wisconsin period Williams published his three most influential books. *The Tragedy of American Diplomacy* (1959) traced the development of open door imperialism from the 1890s to the cold war; *The Contours of American History* (1961) outlined the phases of capitalism through the whole of American history; and *The Roots of the Modern American Empire* (1969) examined the reasons why the United States had acquired an empire. Moreover, Williams was a popular speaker at socialist rallies, published widely in radical journals, and served as an adviser to the journal *Studies on the Left.* His ideas on American imperialism, cold-war revisionism, and corporate liberalism formed the basis of the Wisconsin school of diplomatic history, whose students included Lloyd Gardner and Walter LaFeber. He teamed with George Mosse and Harvey Goldberg to form a radical trio of professors critical of corporate capitalism.

While his professional life flourished at Wisconsin, his personal life fell apart due to excessive drinking and troubles at home. Hoping that a change in environment would ease personal tensions, Williams accepted a less stressful position at Oregon State University in 1969 where he was able to limit his teaching to undergraduates. In 1971 Corrinne left her family to resume her education, giving Williams sole custody of the children. He married Wendy Margaret Tomlin on 8 December 1973 and settled into a quiet life of teaching and publishing. In 1980 his fellow historians elected him president of the Organization of American Historians. During his presidency Williams worked to expand oral history projects and fought to release government records under the Freedom of Information Act. He died of cancer. His ashes were scattered along the Oregon coast near his home in Waldport.

Although he always denied it, Williams produced a new school of American diplomatic history that revolutionized the field by showing the close relationship between economic expansion and U.S. foreign policy. His concepts of open door imperialism, cold-war revisionism, and corporate liberalism became widely used analytical tools for interpreting the economic and ideological roots of America's international relations. In his reading of American history Williams challenged historians to make history usable. He called upon leaders to acknowledge honestly America's dependence upon empire and to prepare for the harmful social effects of unrestrained capitalism at home and abroad.

★

Paul M. Buhle and Edward Rice-Maximin, *William Appleman Williams: The Tragedy of Empire* (1995), is a full-length biography that traces the development of and influences upon Williams's thought. Lloyd Gardner, ed., *Redefining the Past: Essays in Diplomatic History in Honor of William Appleman Williams* (1986), assesses Williams's influence on diplomatic history. Essays in Paul Buhle, ed., *History and the New Left: Madison, Wisconsin, 1950–1970* (1990), describe the Wisconsin school of diplomatic history. Eugene Genovese, "William Appleman Williams on Marx and America," *Studies on the Left* 6 (Jan.–Feb. 1966): 70–86, explains Williams's position among leftist historians. William Marina, "William Appleman Williams," *Dictionary of Literary Biography,* vol. 17, *Twentieth Century Historians* (1983), is a short essay outlining major works and influence. Gary R. Hess, "After the Tumult: The Wisconsin School's Tribute to William Appleman Williams," *Diplomatic History* 12 (fall 1988): 483–499, places the Wisconsin school in perspective with other schools of diplomatic history. Dina M. Copelman and Barbara Clark Smith, eds., "Excerpts from a Conference to Honor William Appleman Williams," *Radical History Review* 50 (spring 1991): 483–199, reviews Williams's influence as a radical historian.

MARIAN YEATES

WILLIAMS, William B. (*b.* 6 August 1923 in Babylon, New York; *d.* 3 August 1986 in New York City), radio personality best known for his commitment to reviving the popular standards of the 1930s, 1940s, and 1950s.

William Breitbard, who eventually changed his surname to Williams, was born and raised in suburban Babylon, Long Island, east of New York City. He was the younger of two sons of Harry and Sadie (Cener) Breitbard, who owned and ran a dry goods store. Williams studied political science and psychology at Syracuse University (1940–1942). He left college without graduating, served briefly in the U.S. Army during the early part of World War II, and hosted a nightly show on the camp's public-address system. While visiting a friend at WAAT-AM in Newark, New Jersey, after his discharge for medical reasons in 1943, he was informed that the evening disc jockey had been fired for drinking on the job. Bill Williams (as he was known at the time) auditioned

Disc jockey William B. Williams (*right*) plays a song written by Pennsylvania governor Milton Sharp (*left*), 1974. UPI/CORBIS-BETTMANN

and was hired as a staff announcer, and six weeks later he was offered a position at WNEW (AM 1130), an independent radio station in New York City, where he would remain for most of the next forty-two years.

On 25 July 1940, in *RCA Manufacturing Company, Inc.* v. *Whiteman et al.,* the U.S. Court of Appeals, Second Circuit, ruled that playing phonograph records over the radio did not infringe on the rights of the copyright holder. This decision allowed WNEW to legally play records on the air, paving the way for other radio stations as well.

WNEW was home to many of New York's most popular radio personalities, including Gene Rayburn, Jack Lescoulie, Dee Finch, Gene Klavan, Art Ford (*The Milkman's Matinee*), and Martin Block, who had started the *Make Believe Ballroom* program in 1935. The twenty-year-old Bill Williams began his new show, called *The Magic of Music,* with the phrase, "Hello, world," which became his opening line for the rest of his radio career.

In 1947, however, Williams was fired by station manager Bernice Judis after an incident that he later described thusly: "I hosted a combination music/talk show, and one day I was doing the show in very new, very uncomfortable shoes. I took them off, revealing a pair of bright red socks. Well, as my luck would have it, Judis walked into the studio with several advertising clients. It was my last show."

Williams then worked for New York's WNBC, WOR, WOV, and WJZ, before being rehired by WNEW six years later (1953), hosting *Music in a Sentimental Mood* and then *The William B. Williams Show.* When Martin Block left the station in 1954, Art Ford eventually took over his show the *Make Believe Ballroom.* In early 1958, however, management fired Ford and replaced him with Williams. William B. Williams would host the *Make Believe Ballroom* until his death, except for a period when the station changed formats.

WNEW was known for playing standards, the popular music of the 1930s, 1940s, and 1950s, which included the various big bands and vocalists such as Perry Como, Tony Bennett, Lena Horne, Ella Fitzgerald, and, especially, Frank Sinatra. Williams had met Sinatra when the singer was hosting a radio program on WNEW in the early days of his career, and had dubbed him the Chairman of the Board in keeping with the (then) custom of referring to performers by title, such as Benny Goodman, the King of Swing. Very loyal to this music and to these performers, whom he also socialized with, William B., as he was known to his listeners, promised Nat King Cole's widow that he would never let a day go by without playing one of Cole's songs. Williams remained a lifelong friend of Sinatra, who credited the disk jockey with resurrecting his career by continuing to play his music even after it had gone out of fashion. After Williams's death, Sinatra issued a statement saying, "He was the best friend I ever had. He was the best friend anybody could have had."

On 14 February 1960 Williams married Dorothy Macaluso, who was known professionally as Dottie Mack and had hosted a Cincinnati television show. They had one child and, although they eventually separated, they remained close friends.

In 1972 WNEW changed its format to what Williams once jokingly referred to as AOR—"all over the road." As he later recalled, "We were, back then, all over the place and played Donna Summer and Frank Sinatra," alienating our core audience by playing disco and rock and roll. In 1979 Williams revived the *Make Believe Ballroom,* again playing the old standards, and the audience response was overwhelming. The format was back, and the station began using the slogan, "WNEW—Where the Melody Lingers On."

Williams was a longtime member of the Friars Club, which he joined in 1958, becoming prior in 1974 and dean in 1981. Active in charitable work, he hosted scores of fund-raising events and received the Applause Award in 1985 from the Friars Club Foundation, the organization's philanthropic arm. Williams was inducted into the National Broadcasters Hall of Fame in 1981 and was named the

Friars' Man of the Year in 1984, with Frank Sinatra hosting the ceremony.

Williams died at age sixty-two, in Beth Israel Hospital in Manhattan, from leukemia, complicated by chronic anemia and a respiratory ailment, and was buried at Kensico Cemetery in Valhalla, New York. He had been ill more than a year, undergoing surgery for colon cancer and removal of his spleen, which had kept him off the radio for the final five months of his life. Williams's brother, Ric Roman, said in his eulogy, "If a man's proximity to God is reflected in his compassion for his fellow man, my brother is standing next to God." A memorial service held at New's York's Palace Theater a month later was hosted by Sinatra, who asked for (and received) a standing ovation for his old friend.

William B. Williams was known for his smooth, deep voice (familiar to audiences from his many commercial voice-overs), his low-key, relaxed humor and rapport with his audience, and his devotion to the popular repertoire. Universally regarded as a gentleman in an industry that often promotes excess, Williams was famous for his modesty, style, and charm and was referred to as the "dean of communicators" by his colleagues. WNEW-AM was sold in 1992, and its legendary call letters were changed (along with its format) to WBBR—Bloomberg Business Radio.

★

Williams looked back on his career in "A Great Place to Linger On: WNEW D.J. Remembers When," *Variety* (1 Feb. 1984). He was briefly profiled in the early days of his career in William A. Bales, "Ad Libbing's His Stock-in-Trade: Disc Jockey Rides Airwaves on Records and Gift of Gab," *Long Island Press* (8 May 1949), in "William B. Williams: The Man Who Runs the Make Believe Ballroom," *Look* (12 Feb. 1963). The station's early history is covered in Robert G. White, Jr., "Martin Block and WNEW: The Rise of the Recorded Music Radio Format 1934–1954," (Ph.D. diss., Bowling Green State University, 1982), and in *WNEW: Where the Melody Lingers On* (1984), which was published to celebrate the station's fiftieth anniversary. Obituaries are in the *New York Times, Newsday,* and the *Daily News* (4 Aug. 1986) and in *Variety* (6 Aug. 1986). Entertainment critic George Maksian wrote an informative tribute in the *Daily News* (5 Aug. 1986).

JOHN A. DROBNICKI

WILSON, Earl (*b.* 3 May 1907 in Rockford, Ohio; *d.* 16 January 1987 in Yonkers, New York), newspaper columnist who covered show-business nightlife for more than forty years.

Wilson was the son of Arthur Earl Wilson, a farmer and later a real estate broker, and Cloe (Huffman) Wilson, a homemaker. While in high school, Wilson wrote for the weekly *Rockford Press,* and after graduation in 1925, he be-

Earl Wilson. ARCHIVE PHOTOS

came sports editor for $15 a week at the *Piqua Daily Call.* He also attended Heidelberg College and in 1931 received a B.S. degree from Ohio State University. From 1931 to 1935 he worked for newspapers in Columbus and Akron, Ohio, including the *Ohio State Lantern* and the International News Service, and in Washington, D.C., where he wrote headlines for the *Washington Post.*

In 1935 Wilson was offered a $45-per-week job at the *New York Post.* He arrived in New York City in May and lived near Washington Square in lower Manhattan. His early celebrity acquaintances in New York included the writer Dorothy Parker and the Duke and Duchess of Windsor. He also met Rosemary Lyons, a secretary, whom he married on 19 January 1936; they had one son. Rosemary Wilson was referred to as "B.W." (for "Beautiful Wife") in Wilson's columns and in person for the rest of his career.

In 1942 Wilson became the six-times-a-week columnist of "It Happened Last Night" for the *New York Post,* and he was billed as the paper's saloon editor. He began to scour the city's cabarets, bars, and restaurants, looking for items for his column. On his first night on the saloon beat, he wore a dinner jacket, to the amusement of his colleagues, who almost never dressed formally. In 1944 the column was syndicated by United Features, and by the mid-1960s, it was appearing in 175 U.S. newspapers.

Wilson's daily routine included waking late in the morning at his West End Avenue apartment, telephoning news sources, and setting out at eight o'clock in the evening, often accompanied by his wife, for the celebrated nightclubs, most of them located in Midtown Manhattan, including Toots Shor's, the Stork Club (where the number-one gossip columnist, Walter Winchell, who worked for the competing *New York Daily Mirror,* reigned), Sardi's, Lindy's, and the Copacabana. He would return to his apartment at two or three o'clock in the morning and type his column for that day's edition of the *Post.*

Wilson conducted many memorable and historical interviews. In 1945 he interviewed Humphrey Bogart at the 21 Club and learned of his upcoming marriage to the young starlet Lauren Bacall. In 1947, when his interview with Lena Horne, then the most popular African-American entertainer in the United States, appeared in the *Post,* one paper dropped his column, an action indicative of the status accorded African Americans, even famous entertainers, during the 1940s. In 1947 he interviewed mobster Frank Costello, and that same year appeared as himself in the movie *Copacabana,* starring Groucho Marx and Carmen Miranda.

Wilson's columns also chronicled the lives and scandals of Hollywood film stars and studios. He often spent weeks in Hollywood, attending parties and frequenting such clubs as the Brown Derby and Mocambo. He wrote about movie moguls Darryl F. Zanuck and Louis B. Mayer and the "studio couch" casting method for young starlets, and in 1948 he covered the arrest of movie idol Robert Mitchum for smoking marijuana. In 1950 he was asked to squelch rumors of a separation between newly married Elizabeth Taylor and Nicky Hilton, the first of her many husbands. He later reported rumors of romance between Taylor and Eddie Fisher, who was then (1958) married to actress Debbie Reynolds, and he was often sought out for information on the Taylor-Fisher affair by other reporters.

Wilson reported on the rise of Las Vegas hotels and gambling casinos and the competition for big-name entertainers, and he often included the steadily increasing salary figures in his columns. For example, he reported on the opening act in April 1955 of the pianist-entertainer Liberace at the Riviera Hotel for the then unheard-of sum of $50,000 a week. He also became friendly with the mobsters who ran most of the gambling operations in Las Vegas at that time, including Bugsy Siegel, Lucky Luciano, and Meyer Lansky. His Las Vegas columns included accounts of the openings in July 1969 (just under a month apart) at the International Hotel of Barbra Streisand, who had a million-dollar contract, and of Elvis Presley, who had not performed in public for nine years.

During the golden age of television in the 1950s, Wilson was a friend to the great comedians—Milton Berle, who became known as "Mr. Television"; Jack Benny; Jackie Gleason; and Bob Hope—and chronicled their rise and success in the new medium. (Later, in December 1967, Wilson flew with Hope on a tour to entertain U.S. troops in Vietnam, writing that there were "several millions of dollars worth of entertainers aboard.") Wilson even hosted his own television segment in 1957 on the *Tonight Show.*

During the 1960s, Wilson covered the demise of the New York City nightclub scene and the rise of the era of discotheques. He wrote the "obituary" of the Stork Club in his column in 1965. During the disco era, Wilson frequented the top places, including the Peppermint Lounge, where the Twist dance craze was popularized; Shepheard's; and Arthur's, a posh place frequented by such prominent persons as Jacqueline Kennedy. He continued to follow the musical trends and interviewed such rock stars as the Beatles and Mick Jagger and traveled to Nashville for an interview with the country-and-western star Johnny Cash.

Wilson retired from the *New York Post* and the coverage of nightlife in 1983. He moved to Yonkers, New York, and was diagnosed with Parkinson's disease. He was admitted in December 1986 to St. Joseph's Medical Center in Yonkers with pneumonia and died of a stroke a month later.

Wilson's columns from 1942 until his retirement in 1983 constitute a history of show business and a biographical resource on entertainers. From Gloria Swanson and Mae West to Marilyn Monroe and Judy Garland, from Charlie Chaplin and Spencer Tracy to Frank Sinatra (of whom he wrote an unauthorized biography in 1976) and John Travolta, the names in Wilson's columns are a who's who of American celebrities.

★

Back issues of the *New York Post*, and Wilson's columns, are available on microfilm. His columns were often collected in book form, including *I Am Gazing into My Eight-Ball* (1945), *Pike's Peek or Bust* (1946), and *Earl Wilson's New York* (1964). His other accounts of his life amid the entertainment industry are *The Show Business Nobody Knows* (1971), *Show Business Laid Bare* (1974), and *Hot Times: True Tales of Hollywood and Broadway* (1984). An obituary is in the *New York Times* (17 Jan. 1987).

LOUISE B. KETZ

WILSON, Logan (*b.* 6 March 1907 in Huntsville, Texas; *d.* 7 November 1990 in Austin, Texas), university administrator, president of the American Council on Education, and advocate for integration in higher education under whose leadership the University of Texas became the first university system in the South to integrate all its academic programs.

Raised in Huntsville, Texas, the son of Samuel Calhoun Wilson, an educator, and Samuela (Logan) Wilson, a homemaker, Logan Wilson had one brother. He received a bachelor's degree from Sam Houston State College in 1926

Logan Wilson. ARCHIVE PHOTOS

and an M.A. degree in English the next year from the University of Texas. After teaching English for several years at East Texas State College, he began graduate study in sociology at Harvard University in 1932. That same year he married Myra Marshal; they had two children. In 1938 he received an M.A. degree from Harvard and in 1939 a Ph.D. He taught sociology at the University of Maryland (1939–1941) and Tulane University, where he was head of the Sociology Department. In 1944 he became the dean of Tulane's Newcomb College, a position he held until 1951.

Wilson became vice president and provost of the Consolidated University of North Carolina (later the University of North Carolina system) in 1951 but after two years returned to Texas as president of "Main University" (later the University of Texas at Austin). His primary responsibility was to consolidate the numerous campuses into the University of Texas system, and he became its first president in 1953, moving into the position of chancellor in 1960. Wilson's achievements while at the University of Texas included an emphasis on research, on academic quality, and on recruiting a distinguished national faculty. At the same time he played a crucial rule in creating the Texas Commission on Higher Education and in passing a state constitutional amendment that expanded the resource base of the university system. During his tenure African-American students were admitted for the first time. Although university housing remained segregated, all classes and academic programs were integrated. Despite the anger of some alumni and some continuing racial tensions, including an incident in which a black coed studying voice was removed from singing a romantic role with a white male, Wilson worked to promote racial integration throughout the university.

Soon after Wilson took the chancellor's post at Texas, he became president of the American Council on Education and moved to Washington, D.C. As president of the council during a crucial decade (1961–1971), Wilson was one of the most visible and influential national spokespersons on higher education, testifying before the U.S. Congress on numerous occasions and advocating greater federal support for higher education, research, and student financial aid. Wilson retired from the American Council on Education in 1973. He returned to Texas and continued to write, serve on commissions, and advise institutional and legislative leaders on matters related to higher education. He died of lung cancer and was buried in Huntsville.

During his long and distinguished career Wilson received considerable national recognition and was the recipient of more than a dozen honorary degrees. He was also a member of numerous honor and professional societies, including Phi Beta Kappa, Omicron Delta Kappa, and Alpha Kappa Delta.

Wilson was active in many educational and scholarly organizations, including service on the editorial board of the *Journal of Legal and Political Sociology* (1941–1947) and on the council of the American Sociological Society (1951–1952). He served as chair of the Conference of Academic Deans (1949–1951) and as president of the Council of Southern Universities (1953–1954). He was also a member of the Commission on Higher Institutions of the Southern Association of Colleges, the National Commission on Accrediting, and the Association of American Colleges. He served in various capacities on the American Council on Education before becoming its president in 1961.

Wilson also served on the boards of several influential organizations that shaped educational policy in the 1950s and 1960s, including the Educational Testing Service, the Institute of International Education, the Teachers' Insurance and Annuity Association, the Center for Advanced Study in the Behavioral Sciences, and the ERIC Clearinghouse on Higher Education.

In addition to scholarship in the field of sociology, Wilson was a prolific and respected author in the field of higher education. *The Academic Man* (1942) and *Shaping American*

Higher Education (1972) are considered the most influential of his four books. He contributed to many works on higher education, including chapters for numerous books published by the American Council on Education.

Wilson was an influential architect and implementer of the expansion of university systems in North Carolina and Texas and of the integration of academic programs at Texas. In addition, he was a forceful advocate of the importance of higher education and played a role in shaping educational policy from the 1950s through the 1970s.

★

There are three principal sources of information concerning the professional activities of Logan Wilson: the Archives of the University of Texas at Austin; the Archives of the American Council on Education (ACE) in Washington; and the Collection of the Oral History Project of the Barker Texas History Center at the University of Texas at Austin. The Oral History Project tapes include ten hours of Wilson's personal recollections and reflections regarding career, his work at the University of Texas, and his memories of his time spent in Washington at the American Council on Education. The other archives, especially those at ACE, contain extensive material about speeches, legislative testimony, and correspondence with other educators and policymakers. An obituary is in the *New York Times* (9 Nov. 1990).

FREDERIC JACOBS

WILSON, Theodore Shaw ("Teddy") (*b.* 24 November 1912 in Austin, Texas; *d.* 31 July 1986 in New Britain, Connecticut), the most influential jazz pianist of the Swing Era.

Wilson was the younger son of James Augustus Wilson and Pearl Shaw Wilson, teachers at Samuel Houston College. In 1918 the family moved to Alabama, where Wilson's father was head of the English Department at Tuskegee Institute and his mother was librarian. Wilson and his older brother, Gus, took piano lessons in grammar school. Teddy also studied the oboe, clarinet, and violin during his four years at Tuskegee (then a high school; he graduated in 1928), and arranged music for the marching band. His father, who died when Wilson was fourteen, exposed him to opera as well as blues. In 1928 he studied music theory at Talladega College in Alabama, where he developed a love of classical music. While there he listened to records of the stride and jazz pianists Fats Waller and Earl Hines. After a vacation in Detroit, where he heard Fletcher Henderson's and other orchestras, Wilson decided to pursue a career playing jazz piano. He moved to Detroit, where his brother was performing. In 1929 they joined the orchestra of Speed Webb, Wilson on piano and his brother on trombone. Both also were arrangers.

Wilson's piano style, already well formed, was completed when he joined the Milton Senior band in Toledo, Ohio, in mid-1931, replacing Art Tatum, who was switching to solo work. The two men nevertheless established a close musical relationship. Wilson combined the driving styles of Waller, Hines, and Tatum with his own more simplified and subdued approach to jazz piano. Melody and controlled rhythm predominated in his highly individualistic and inventive style, described in terms that reflected his personal character—soft-spoken, subtle, sensitive, clean, tasteful, polished, even-tempered, modest, relaxed. His style proved ideal in ensemble jazz and accompaniment of vocalists, during which Wilson provided not only the rhythmic foundation but also spontaneous, understated solos. He influenced the next generation of jazz pianists—even Tatum, who was inspired to tone down his own style.

Wilson's reputation among jazz musicians spread after the Senior band folded in Chicago late in 1931. Wilson remained there to work with several bands, notably that of Eddie Mallory, and he toured and made his first recordings with Louis Armstrong early in 1933. He arranged music for the Hines orchestra at the Grand Terrace Ballroom and sat in on piano when Hines was on the road. The jazz impresario John Hammond heard Wilson during a radio broadcast from the ballroom in late 1933 and brought him to New York City to play with and arrange for the orchestra of Benny Carter, whose saxophone playing influenced Wilson's style.

In 1934 Wilson joined the Willie Bryant orchestra and began recording with pickup groups, including one led by Benny Goodman in May and one led by Red Norvo in September. Occasional gigs as intermission pianist at the Famous Door on Fifty-second Street ("Swing Street") in New York City led him to leave Bryant early in 1935 to work full-time at the jazz club. With the help of Hammond, Wilson assembled groups of top jazzmen to make records, often with singers, among whom was Billie Holiday. For more than three years, beginning in July 1935, they made recordings that became jazz masterworks.

In June 1935, during a party at the home of Red Norvo and his wife, Mildred Bailey—whom Wilson also accompanied on records—Wilson, Goodman, and an amateur drummer got into a jam session that resulted in the Benny Goodman Trio. The trio made recordings the next month, with Gene Krupa on drums. Wilson continued his busy schedule in New York while the Goodman orchestra went on a nationwide tour that brought them renown.

In April 1936 Goodman invited Wilson to Chicago for a trio performance in concert at the Congress Hotel—an unprecedented public performance by a racially integrated jazz group. It was so successful that Goodman hired Wilson to continue with the trio between sets of the big band. Having broken the color line, Goodman went further by hiring the vibraphonist Lionel Hampton in August for quartet performances. The perfection of both combos playing hot or elegant music epitomized what came to be re-

Teddy Wilson. CORBIS-BETTMANN

garded as chamber jazz, especially because of Wilson's style. This was amply displayed in the 1937 motion picture *Hollywood Hotel.*

Wilson's association with Goodman brought him public acclaim, and more than 400 small band recordings between 1935 and 1940 with other jazz greats enhanced his musical reputation. His creativity reached its peak in 1937, when a session with Norvo, trumpeter Harry James, and a string bass player produced "Just a Mood."

In April 1939 Wilson left Goodman to form a big band, which featured his own arrangements and the tenor saxophonist Ben Webster. The band lasted only a year in the fiercely competitive world of big bands. Wilson then formed a sextet of top sidemen that played at Café Society in New York City between 1940 and 1944. He also played in several film shorts, notably *Boogie Woogie Dream* (1941), and in the feature-length film *Something to Shout About* (1943). Starting in 1944 he appeared regularly on Mildred Bailey's radio program and with Goodman in Cole Porter's Broadway musical *The Seven Lively Arts.*

Although his playing had become less creative by the mid-1940s, it commanded such respect that Wilson added radio work, teaching, and foreign tours to numerous solo and combo recordings. He taught summer courses at the Juilliard School of Music (1945–1952) and the Metropolitan Music School and had private pupils. He was staff pianist for CBS radio beginning in 1946, then led a trio on his own radio program over WNEW (1949–1952) and CBS (1954–1955). Wilson acted and played in the film *The Benny Goodman Story* (1955) and thereafter occasionally rejoined Goodman for concerts, recordings, and tours abroad, including Goodman's visit to the Soviet Union in 1962. He led his own trio at home and in Europe, Australia, Latin America, and Japan, notably at the World's Fair in Brussels (1958). In June 1982 he performed with Goodman and Hampton at Carnegie Hall, forty-six years after his first performance with them. The culmination of Wilson's career was the "Swing Reunion" concert with Benny Carter in March 1985, at Town Hall in New York City.

Wilson's marriages to Irene Armstrong (1931), Janice Carenti (1945), and Blanche Louth (1957) ended in divorce. He married Joan Roberts in 1963. From his four marriages he had five children. He died of cancer in New Britain, Connecticut.

Wilson's controlled playing has been characterized as cool, a major departure from all previous styles that quietly revolutionized jazz piano.

★

A biographical essay on Wilson's music is in Gunther Schuller, *The Swing Era* (1989). A biographical booklet (1981) by George Gelles accompanies the Time-Life Giants of Jazz boxed LP set *Teddy Wilson,* which includes recordings from 1933 to 1976. Interviews with Wilson and his first wife are in Stanley Dance, *The World of Earl Hines* (1977). See also Teddy Wilson, with Arie Lightheart and Humphrey Van Loo, *Teddy Wilson Talks Jazz* (1996). All writings on Benny Goodman include treatments of Wilson, especially James Lincoln Collier, *Benny Goodman and the Swing Era* (1989). An obituary is in the *New York Times* (2 Aug. 1986).

Oral history materials are located at Talladega College and the Jazz Oral History Project, Rutgers University. Numerous Goodman albums include Wilson. His important work with Billie Holiday is found on her Giants of Jazz set and *Billie Holiday: The Golden Years,* a boxed LP set (Columbia). Many Wilson small group recordings from 1936 to 1938 are on the LP *The Teddy Wilson* (CBS). Most of his orchestra's recordings are on *Big Band* (Swing Era). Among collections of his piano solo recordings are the LPs *Piano Solos 1938–1939* (Commodore) and *Striding After Fats* (Black Lion).

CLARK G. REYNOLDS

WINDSOR, Wallis Warfield (Simpson), Duchess of (*b.* 19 June 1896 in Blue Ridge Summit, Pennsylvania; *d.* 24 April 1986 in Paris, France), socialite who became the wife of the duke of Windsor, formerly King Edward VIII of England, who abdicated the British throne in order to marry "the woman I love."

Born Bessie Wallis Warfield, she was the only child of Teackle Wallis Warfield and Alice (Montague) Warfield. Her father, who suffered from tuberculosis, died when Wallis was a small child. Alice Warfield was left poor, so her husband's family offered young Bessie Wallis both money and history: the first Warfield had arrived in Maryland in 1662; Henry M. Warfield, her grandfather, was a director of the Baltimore and Ohio Railroad; her uncle Sol was a banker and railroad executive. The latter paid for her education and her society debut.

Wallis, as she preferred to be called, attended the exclusive Arundell and Oldfields private schools and made her debut at the Baltimore Bachelors' Cotillion in 1914. Some months later she met Lieutenant Earl Winfield Spencer, Jr., while she was vacationing in Florida, and after a whirlwind wartime romance they were married on 8 November 1916. She was able to accompany him to successive postings in Boston, San Diego, and Washington, D.C., but in 1923 Spencer was assigned to Canton, China. Life without duties or a husband was intolerable to Wallis, so she wangled an assignment as a courier, which gave her both purposeful work and passage to China, where she arrived in September 1924. Unfortunately, the trip proved to be a disaster; when Wallis left China a year later, her mission was a fiasco and her marriage lay in ruins. The couple, who had no children, were quietly divorced on 6 December 1927.

Wallis Warfield Simpson on the day she married the former British monarch Edward VIII at Château de Cande, France, 8 June 1937. UPI/CORBIS-BETTMANN

The previous Christmas, Wallis had met Ernest Aldrich Simpson, a married Anglo-American ship broker. Early in 1928 he obtained a divorce, and on 21 July 1928 he and Wallis were married; they had no children. The couple established a popular salon in London, and in June 1931 they were presented at court. Edward, the prince of Wales, was so charmed by the couple that he drove them home in his car. The prince shared many interests with Wallis, from racing to gardening, and a relationship developed. Over the next several years Wallis and Ernest were often the prince's guests, and though rumors circulated privately about Wallis and the prince, the media allowed the affair to remain relatively quiet. However, when King George V died on 20 January 1936, Edward became king. What had been a discreet relationship became a constitutional crisis as Parliament officially noticed the affair and its members condemned it, even to the extent of refusing to vote the king his moneys.

In May the new king introduced Wallis to the prime minister as his "future wife." During August and September the couple toured the eastern Mediterranean, where Edward presented Wallis to King George of Greece, General Kemal Ataturk of Turkey, and President Miklas of Austria. In October, Wallis was granted a divorce from Ernest Simpson; the decree would become final in six months. At the end of November, A. W. F. Blunt, bishop of Bradford, publicly reproached the king for his "need of God's grace." On 3 December stories about the crisis finally appeared in English newspapers and Wallis was forced to leave England. She went to the home of friends who lived near Cannes, France, where she spent the next five months. On 11 December 1936 the crisis reached its resolution: Edward VIII abdicated. The following day he made a speech to the people of England, in which he declared his need for "the help and support of the woman I love." He then left England for Austria, where he was joined by Wallis after her divorce became final on 3 May. On 3 June 1937 they were married. They had no children.

The duke and duchess of Windsor, as the couple was formally titled, lived in exile near Cannes or in Paris until World War II broke out. When the Germans invaded France, they fled to Spain, and thence to the Bahamas, where the duke was named governor in 1940. They remained there through the entire war, visiting the United States several times; during one of these visits, in 1944, the duchess had surgery for stomach cancer. She had surgery again, in 1951, for ovarian cancer. Late in 1945 the duke and duchess sailed back to France, where their possessions had been preserved during the war. Although the royal family still refused to recognize the duchess officially, she was at last allowed to visit England in October 1946—only to have her jewels stolen in a celebrated robbery. A consolation, however, was having been named the best-dressed woman in the world for 1946 in January of that year.

After several years of living on yachts and in rented houses, the duke and duchess settled in Paris, where the duchess established a salon in the grand style. In 1956 she published a memoir, *The Heart Has Its Reasons,* which presented a sanitized version of her life to a wider public, deemphasizing her two divorces and her semisecret business in China, and in January 1961 she published an article, focusing on her husband's treatment by the royal family, in *McCall's* magazine. On 15 March 1965 she finally received her first official acceptance: while attending her husband, who had undergone eye surgery in London, she was recognized by Queen Elizabeth II. Two years later the duke and duchess were invited to attend a ceremony in honor of Queen Mary, where—aside from a scandal when the duchess refused to curtsy to her archenemy, Queen Mother Elizabeth—relations between the couple and the reigning branch of the House of Windsor continued to thaw.

There was little time to enjoy the truce, however. The duke developed a series of ailments, and cancer of the throat proved fatal on 29 May 1972. While Edward lay in state at Windsor Castle, the duchess was allowed to sleep in Buckingham Palace for the first and only time. She lived until 24 April 1986, but her physical and mental condition deteriorated in her later years. Consistent with the decision taken some fifty years before, the duchess was granted no formal state funeral. However, Queen Elizabeth did attend the ceremony, and Wallis's remains were buried next to the duke's in the royal cemetery at Frogmore, not far from Windsor Castle. In death Wallis Warfield Simpson had finally ceased to be a danger to the British monarchy.

★

There are two primary sources of information about the duchess of Windsor: the duchess's memoir, *The Heart Has Its Reasons* (1956); and *Wallis and Edward: Letters 1931–1937,* ed. Michael Bloch (1986). Secondary materials range from the respectful, such as Ralph G. Martin, *The Woman He Loved* (1974), and Lady Diana Mosley, *The Duchess of Windsor* (1980), to the sensational, best represented by Charles Higham, *The Duchess of Windsor: The Secret Life* (1988). An obituary is in the *New York Times* (25 Apr. 1986). In 1996 Prince Edward (as Edward Windsor) researched and narrated the documentary film *Edward on Edward,* which offers a family member's perspective on the duke and duchess of Windsor.

HARTLEY S. SPATT

WOOD, Robert Dennis (*b.* 17 April 1925 in Boise, Idaho; *d.* 20 May 1986 in Santa Monica, California), president of Columbia Broadcasting System (CBS) Television from 1969 to 1976 who helped usher in an era of more realistic television programming.

Robert Wood was the son of Euphrosyne Planck and Raymond Dennis Wood. Raised in Beverly Hills, California, he served in the U.S. Navy during World War II, from 1943 to 1946. In 1949 he graduated from the University of Southern California with a bachelor's degree in business administration and went to work in sales for the local CBS-affiliated station in Los Angeles. In that same year, on 29 October, he married Nancy Harwell; they had two children before their divorce.

During these early years of television, while he worked his way up through the ranks at television stations in Los Angeles, Wood became acquainted with the young actress Mary Tyler Moore. Their paths would cross later. In the meantime, Wood proved an effective executive and was promoted to president of CBS's television stations division in

Robert Wood, 1974. CBS PHOTO ARCHIVE

1967. The job required him to move to New York City, and there he attracted the attention of Frank Stanton, the president of CBS. Worried that executives were out of touch with the affiliated stations that actually carried CBS shows, Stanton recruited Wood to lead the CBS Television Network division in February 1969.

CBS had been number one in television ratings ever since the medium attracted a mass audience in the early 1950s, but there was an underlying weakness to the popularity of its programming. An earlier president, James Aubrey, had installed several "rural" comedies in the 1960s, such as *The Beverly Hillbillies*. Many of the programs had been on the air for years and were losing touch with a younger audience. This combination skewed CBS audiences toward older and more rural viewers, a circumstance that the rival networks pointed out to advertisers, arguing that their younger, more professional viewers were worth more of an advertiser's dollars. Accepting this concept meant targeting programs to the viewers that advertisers wanted rather than to all viewers. In addition to the economic argument, there was also the feeling during the Vietnam War era that television was increasingly irrelevant to the broad cultural changes occurring in the country.

The networks had tried to address this problem, and Wood's first headache as president was over one program that CBS felt had gone too far—*The Smothers Brothers Comedy Hour*. The producer, Tom Smothers, had consistently fought CBS's attempts to eliminate controversial bits from the variety show. The final straw in this ongoing fight may have been Smothers's meeting with sympathetic members of the U.S. Congress. Whatever the final provocation, Wood canceled the show after he had been in the job for only two months. He continued to cancel shows, but these cancellations were for a different reason, to reshape the audience. Older stars such as Jackie Gleason, Red Skelton, and Ed Sullivan were let go. Rural comedies such as *The Beverly Hillbillies, Green Acres, Hee Haw,* and others were dropped.

In June 1970 Wood promoted Fred Silverman to vice president of programming. Silverman would go on to influence programming at all three major networks. CBS's first successful replacement program was *The Mary Tyler Moore Show,* which debuted in September 1970. This was the inaugural effort of Grant Tinker's MTM Productions, a company that soon won a reputation for "quality" television. *The Mary Tyler Moore Show* had the breakthrough premise of a single working woman who was not intent on fulfillment through marriage. In addition, few shows could match *All in the Family,* which debuted in January 1971, in its unblinking look at the beliefs and values of the fictional character of Archie Bunker. He displayed the racial, ethnic resentments and sexist assumptions thought to be typical of lower-class white males. Although the show was intended to poke fun at Bunker, the writing (under the guidance of the producers, Norman Lear and Bud Yorkin) was sufficiently multidimensional that many viewers felt sympathy for Bunker. Despite the controversy surrounding the show and its initial low popularity, Wood had full faith and waited patiently as it developed its audience and won its rating slot (and an Emmy). When it did so, Wood's faith was vindicated and his reputation as an innovator in programming was assured. He continued to buy shows from both MTM and Tandem (Lear and Yorkin). Another memorable acquisition was *M*A*S*H,* the wildly successful sitcom by Larry Gelbart that debuted in 1972 and depicted an army medical unit during the Korean War.

Besides his programming changes, Wood also guided CBS through several regulatory changes, such as the banning of tobacco advertising in 1971 and the limiting of network prime-time programming to three hours. He responded to these and other changes by promoting the switch from sixty-second advertising spots to thirty-second spots. The shorter spots contributed to increased network earnings.

On 27 August 1974 Wood married Laura Rohrer. Two years later he decided to end his successful run as CBS Television president and to return to California. With the longest tenure of any president up to that time, he was able to rest on his laurels. He negotiated an exit contract with CBS in which the network agreed to help his new production company, a "back-end" deal that has since become standard. Soon after his departure CBS lost its number one ranking, due in some part to the rival programming of Wood's onetime protégé, Silverman, who had moved to ABC. Wood finished out his career at Nephi and Metromedia production companies. He served on the board of trustees of his alma mater, the University of Southern California. He died of a heart attack and is buried in the Burbank division of Forest Lawn Cemetery.

Wood's legacy was the realistic situation comedy. Within the cynical milieu of commercial broadcasting, he was an effective promoter of Norman Lear, Grant Tinker, Larry Gelbart, and others who reestablished the potential of television for exploring important issues.

★

Information on Wood's era of innovation at CBS may be found in Sally Bedell, *Up the Tube: Prime-Time TV and the Silverman Years* (1981); Harry Castelman and Walter J. Podrazik, *Watching TV: Four Decades of American Television* (1982); Todd Gitlin, *Inside Prime Time* (1983); and Grant Tinker and Bud Rukeyser, *Tinker in Television: From General Sarnoff to General Electric* (1994). An obituary is in the *New York Times* (22 Apr. 1986).

FREDERICK WASSER

WRIGHT, Sewall (*b.* 21 December 1889 in Melrose, Massachusetts; *d.* 3 March 1988 in Madison, Wisconsin), geneticist who contributed to the understanding of heredity and evolutionary theory during his long and productive career.

Wright was the son of Philip Green Wright, a teacher, and Elizabeth Quincy Sewall, a homemaker; he had two younger brothers. His mother nurtured in him an interest in natural history. Wright's father taught at Lombard College in Galesburg, Illinois, and Wright entered there in 1906. In the summer of 1909 Wright took a year off from studies to work as a surveyor with a railroad company; the experience increased his interest in applied mathematics. On his return to college in 1910, he studied with Wilhelmina Entemann Key, an inspiring biologist. He received a B.S. degree in 1912. With Key's guidance and encouragement, that summer he worked at the Cold Spring Harbor Laboratories in New York. In the fall of 1911 he entered the University of Illinois, where he met William E. Castle, a visiting lecturer in genetics from Harvard University. Wright completed his M.A. degree in 1912 and then went to Harvard that fall to do doctoral work with Castle.

While at Harvard, Wright received a broad exposure to science and developed his special interests. Continuing with Castle's system of studying heredity in guinea pigs, Wright explored the physiology of gene action, the effects of inbreeding, the interactions between genes, and the effects of selection on inherited traits. He received the Sc.D. degree in 1915. The empirical studies of guinea pig genetics and the mathematical interpretation of observable results would occupy much of Wright's career. Early on he developed a quantitative method using path coefficients to calculate the effects of multiple genes as they affect a single trait.

Sewall Wright (*left*) receives an award from the president of Italy, Sandro Pertini, for his work in the science of genetics, 1984. AP/WIDE WORLD PHOTOS

Following graduate school, Wright worked for ten years at the U.S. Department of Agriculture to direct the program in animal breeding and animal husbandry, where he found productive collaboration with the geneticist Guy N. Collins. In 1920 he met Louise Williams, an instructor at Smith College. They were married in 1921 and had three children.

Wright joined the Department of Zoology at the University of Chicago in 1926. His influential ideas carried him rapidly to the top of his profession. He became a member of the American Philosophical Society in 1932 and the National Academy of Sciences in 1934, the year he was also elected president of the Genetics Society of America.

After retiring from Chicago in 1955, Wright continued his scientific investigations on gene interaction and inbreeding in guinea pigs. He became professor emeritus at the University of Wisconsin in 1956 with a minimal teaching load. Between 1968 and 1978 he published *Evolution and the Genetics of Populations* (four volumes). In 1966 President Lyndon B. Johnson awarded him the National Medal of Science, and in 1984 he received the Balzan Price Prize from the Academia Lincel in Italy.

Despite failing eyesight Wright continued his research and correspondence and his habit of long walks. He died in his ninety-ninth year, having just published a response to a criticism of one of his theories.

By showing how gene frequencies can change in populations and by having his theories corroborated by experimentalists like A. H. Sturtevant and T. Dobzhansky, Wright contributed greatly to the new synthesis of evolutionary theory. His name is most closely attached to the concepts of genetic drift and the shifting balance theory of evolution. He believed that the size of effective breeding populations is often quite small, and that random, nonadaptive changes in gene frequencies, migrations, and mutations provide the variability on which natural selection can act. Evolution is then the result of selective pressures, such as predation and ecological changes in climate and food supply. Wright developed quantitative methods to express differential gene frequencies and selective pressures.

★

Wright's correspondence is in the library of the American Philosophical Society in Philadelphia. For a biography of Wright, see William B. Provine, *Sewall Wright and Evolutionary Biology* (1986). For works on genetics and evolutionary theory, see William B. Provine, *The Origins of Theoretical Population Genetics* (1971); Ernst Mayr, *The Growth of Biological Thought* (1982), authored by a collaborator of Wright; and John B. S. Haldane, *The Causes of Evolution* (1990), with an introduction and afterword by Egbert G. Leigh, Jr. An obituary is in the *New York Times* (4 Mar. 1988).

MICHAEL F. HAINES

WYETH, Nathaniel Convers (*b.* 24 October 1911 in Chadds Ford, Pennsylvania; *d.* 4 July 1990 in Glen Cove, Maine), mechanical engineer specializing in plastics who invented the polyester bottle for carbonated beverages and developed several basic manufacturing processes.

Wyeth was the third of five children of Newell Convers ("N. C.") Wyeth, the famous painter and illustrator, and Carolyn Brenneman Bockius. Originally named Newell Convers, Jr., he was renamed at the age of ten after N. C.'s brother Nathaniel. The family was immersed in the art world. Henriette, the oldest child, became an artist and married the painter Peter Hurd. Carolyn was a painter, and Ann, both a composer and an artist, married the painter John W. McCoy. Andrew, the youngest, became the most prominent artist of all the Wyeths. In N. C. Wyeth's depiction of all five of his children in his 1923 mural *The Giant,* at the Westtown School in Westtown, Pennsylvania, the eleven-year-old Nat is second from right.

Like all the Wyeths, Nat had artistic talent. But like Nat's namesake, "Uncle Nat," a General Motors engineer, he turned his natural creativity toward another field, engineering. N. C. supported Nat's choice of a career and advised him against complexity. "Father felt that the simple design was usually best," Nat told interviewer Peter Martin in 1966. But what N. C. taught and practiced in art, Nat had to learn by trial and error in engineering.

Wyeth attended Swarthmore (Pennsylvania) Preparatory School from 1928 to 1931, then enrolled at the University of Pennsylvania, where he served on the student council, played varsity tennis, and boxed. He was a solid but undistinguished student. When he received his B.S. degree in mechanical engineering in 1936, the placement service marked him "average" for dependability, initiative, judgment, thoroughness, accuracy, and speed; and "good" for personality and neatness.

In January 1937 Wyeth married Caroline Ashton Pyle, a daughter of the artist Ellen Bernard Thompson Pyle and niece of N. C.'s teacher, Howard Pyle. They had six children, all boys, five of whom survived to adulthood. The oldest died in the same car-train collision that killed N. C. in 1945. Caroline herself died in an automobile accident in 1973. Wyeth remained a widower until marrying Jean Grady, an administrator at the Hospital of the University of Pennsylvania, in 1984.

After graduation, Wyeth worked briefly as a junior engineer in the engine test lab at the Autocar Company in Ardmore, Pennsylvania. In October 1936 he joined E. I. du Pont de Nemours & Company as a field engineer. DuPont promoted him in 1938 to engineer, in 1945 to section head, and in 1950 to group supervisor. He worked as a project manager from 1955 until 1960, when DuPont made him assistant director of its Engineering Development Laboratory. He was honored as the first DuPont Engineering Fellow in 1963, then as senior engineering fellow in 1974. He retired in 1976.

During his forty years at DuPont, Wyeth was granted twenty-five patents as inventor or coinventor of products, processes, industrial machinery, and automatic systems. His earliest patents, in the 1940s, were for explosives manufacturing processes. By the 1950s he had shifted his research toward synthetic fibers, especially nonwoven fibers. In the late 1950s and early 1960s he teamed with Richard M. Downing and other scientists to discover means of coating wire and other electrical conductors with cellular insulation. In the mid-1960s he helped to develop a process for the continuous extrusion and orientation of plastic tubing, which enabled the Remington Arms Company, a DuPont subsidiary, to begin marketing plastic shotgun shells.

Wyeth's most important invention was the biaxially oriented polyethylene terephthalate bottle, for which he received U.S. Patent 3733309 on 15 May 1973. Known familiarly as the "poly bottle" or the "PET bottle," it had become by the late 1970s a ubiquitous household item, effectively replacing glass as the usual container for soda pop. Several of his subsequent patents (U.S. 3778214, 3849530, 3718229, and 3982877) were for refinements of or improvements to this bottle.

After his retirement, Wyeth was a frequent consultant for DuPont, and he lectured widely, often on the similarities between art and engineering. In these lectures he would recommend counterintuitive, unconventional thinking as the fountainhead of creativity or as the widening of personal horizons. He would advise his audiences to stay dissatisfied with the status quo, to challenge tradition, and to ask constantly whether there might be a better way of doing things. During this time he also pursued his hobby of creating miniature furniture in fine detail, some of which has been displayed at the Brandywine River Museum in Chadds Ford, Pennsylvania.

In 1986 the Society of the Plastics Industry elected him to the Plastics Hall of Fame. In 1990 DuPont gave him its prestigious Lavoisier Award in recognition of his genius in service to technology.

Wyeth was friendly, robust, and cheerful. He was six feet tall, ruggedly handsome, and muscular in his prime, with a winning smile and a charming, never frivolous, presence. A lifelong liberal in both religion and politics, he was an early and vigorous opponent of the Vietnam War. He registered Republican but voted independently. He called himself a Unitarian through the 1930s and 1940s, but later became one of the most active members of the Episcopal Church of the Advent in Kennett Square, Pennsylvania. He "thought globally and acted locally," promoting social welfare in the 1960s and 1970s through his involvement with the Kennett Area Joint Action Committee, the Counterpoint Drug Center in Kennett Square, and the Kennett Area Community Center. He was always a "team player" in the best sense of the term.

Wyeth died of complications from a stroke he had suffered in 1989. His funeral was at the Church of the Advent and his burial in Lafayette Cemetery, Birmingham Township, Pennsylvania.

★

Wyeth's family retains most of his personal papers, and Du Pont holds most of his scientific memorabilia. The alumni files in the archives of the University of Pennsylvania contain a significant amount of information. An interview with Wyeth titled "The Fine Art of Engineering" is in *Design News* 43 (5 Jan. 1987): 53. Newspaper feature stories are in the *Philadelphia Sunday Bulletin Magazine* (3 July 1966), by Peter Martin; the *Kennett News and Advertiser* (20 May 1982), unsigned; the *Philadelphia Inquirer* (17 Mar. 1984), by Gilbert M. Gaul; and the *Allentown (Pennsylvania) Sunday Call* (31 Aug. 1986), by Peter Coy. Obituaries are in the *Wilmington (Delaware) News Journal* (6 July 1990), *New York Times* (7 July 1990), *Chester County (Pennsylvania) Daily Local News* (8 July 1990), and *Plastics News* (16 July 1990).

ERIC V. D. LUFT

Charles E. Wyzanski, Jr., 1937. AP/WIDE WORLD PHOTOS

WYZANSKI, Charles Edward, Jr. (*b.* 27 May 1906 in Boston, Massachusetts; *d.* 3 September 1986 in Boston), lawyer, government official, and judge.

Wyzanski was the son of Charles E. Wyzanski, Sr., and Maude (Joseph) Wyzanski. His father became a prosperous real estate developer who lost much of his money in the Great Depression. Wyzanski's intellectual powers were recognized early; he skipped two grades in the public schools of Brookline, Massachusetts, where he grew up, before attending Phillips Exeter Academy. Because he was too immature for college, he spent an extra year at the academy after graduating. He then attended Harvard College, from which he graduated magna cum laude and as a member of Phi Beta Kappa in 1927.

Inspired by the words of Justice Oliver Wendell Holmes, Jr., who had responded to his letter asking for advice upon his graduation by telling him that "we think more highly of those who are conscious of ulterior ends," Wyzanski attended Harvard Law School. He served on the *Harvard Law Review* and graduated magna cum laude in 1930. He became law clerk to Judge Augustus N. Hand of the U.S. Court of Appeals for the Second Circuit, but he rejected a second clerkship, with Justice Louis D. Brandeis, which Harvard law professor Felix Frankfurter had arranged, in order to practice with the Boston corporate law firm of Ropes and Gray. In the fall of 1932 he served as clerk to Judge Learned Hand, Augustus's cousin on the same court.

Wyzanski returned to practice in Boston in 1933, changed because of the influence of the Hands. He refused to write a brief challenging a state antiinjunction law that he thought was desirable and valid. Frankfurter brought his stand on principle, and the politics it represented, to the attention of President Franklin D. Roosevelt. On his first day in Washington, in May 1933, as a prospective solicitor for the Labor Department, Roosevelt told him at a meeting in the White House, to have on his, the president's, desk the next morning a draft of a bill carrying out the idea that had been discussed. Wyzanski worked all night, and the bill became the legal foundation for the Works Progress Administration and the Public Works Administration. As a result, Roosevelt appointed him solicitor of the Labor Department.

In 1935 Wyzanski moved over to the Justice Department to become a special assistant to the attorney general. He then served, at Roosevelt's request, in the solicitor general's office, preparing cases for the Supreme Court. In 1937 he successfully defended the unemployment insurance provisions of the Social Security Act and the authority of the National Labor Relations Act before the Court. These cases were instrumental in breaking the back of the Court's opposition to federal power. Wyzanski spoke to the justices without notes, but was able to refer to cases by volume and page. After the argument in the social security case, John W. Davis, Wyzanski's opponent and by common agreement the leading appellate lawyer of the time, said, "Never in my palmiest days could I have matched that argument."

Wyzanski argued these cases out of loyalty to the New Deal and despite his strong opposition to Roosevelt's ultimately unsuccessful plan to increase the number of justices on the Supreme Court, which had declared many New Deal laws unconstitutional. When the Court's term was over, he returned to law practice in Boston. In December 1941 Roosevelt nominated him to the federal district court in Boston. The Senate swiftly confirmed him, and Wyzanski took his seat the next month. At the time he was the youngest federal judge ever appointed. In 1943 Wyzanski married Gisela Warburg; they had two children.

Wyzanski came to personify the potential and importance of the trial judge. The judge's "character and personal distinction, open to daily inspection in his courtroom, constitute the guarantees of due process," he wrote. Wyzanski valued the freedom provided by sitting alone, rather than with other judges on a panel. It enabled him to speak to juries and counsel whenever he wished. The person who travels alone gets there the quickest, he said. For this reason Wyzanski refused a seat on the Court of Appeals for the First Circuit in 1959. Over time, through sheer effectiveness and force of personality, he chose his own cases and did not work according to the usual rotation of cases randomly assigned to judges.

In 1953, in *United States* v. *United Shoe Machinery Corporation,* a leading antitrust case, Wyzanski found after a two-year trial that the company used its leases to maintain monopolistic power and ordered its breakup. In 1961, in *United States* v. *Worcester,* he imposed a sentence of probation on a contractor convicted under the income tax laws, on the condition that he name those to whom he paid bribes. Prominent names were mentioned, and critics condemned the process as unfair. In 1973 Wyzanski said he had "long since concluded" that they were right. In 1969, in *United States* v. *Sisson,* Wyzanski ruled that a sincere, but not religious, conscientious objector could not be drafted for combat in Vietnam. His reasoning was that the individual's interest in not killing was more compelling than the country's need for him to be so employed.

Wyzanski's only serious chance for the Supreme Court came in 1952, when Democratic presidential candidate Adlai Stevenson told Wyzanski that if he were elected, he would nominate Wyzanski for the Supreme Court. Starting in 1954 and continuing through the 1960s, Wyzanski was under the care of a psychiatrist for a manic-depressive disorder. In 1971, after serving as chief judge of the Boston court for six years, he took senior status on the bench. Thereafter, he sat with various federal courts across the country.

Wyzanski was very active off the bench, speaking and writing in a steady stream about open-mindedness, fair legal procedures, the democratic tradition, and the human condition. "It is a spirit of reverence for the past which gives our life style and dignity," he said. Wyzanski served as a trustee of the Ford Foundation from 1952 to 1976, and as a member of the Harvard Board of Overseers from 1943 to 1949 and from 1951 to 1957, acting as president from 1953 to 1957. Harvard president Derek Bok called him a "loyal indisciplinable," who engaged in continual critical scrutiny. Wyzanski prized his association with Harvard's Society of Fellows, both for the insights of a new generation of scholars and scientists and for the audience they gave him.

His hobbies were collecting books and art, and Wyzanski made an arresting figure as he walked around American and European cities, browsing art galleries and bookstores while carrying a walking stick, wearing a broad-brimmed hat, and sometimes reading at the same time. He frequently adapted a line by Salvador de Madariaga, "He who is nothing but [a judge], is not even [a judge]." In his later years Wyzanski's quotations from numerous worthies very nearly obscured his own probing and provocative message. His heroes throughout were William James and Learned Hand. Wyzanski retained his intellectual vitality and joy of learning as he grew older and less conventional in his behavior. He died in Beth Israel Hospital in Boston from a sudden cerebral hemorrhage.

Wyzanski gained renown through the power of his mind. He was unusual among trial judges in viewing his most common cases within a broad philosophical framework. He saw law as "the public face radiant with awareness that it is the reflection of men's deepest and noblest ideals." For this to be achieved, judicial review of legislation, especially by the Supreme Court, is necessary. To reduce the Court's comparatively small role, Wyzanski wrote, criticizing Learned Hand's views, "would be greatly to increase the possibility of executive, legislative, or military tyranny, and could hardly promote the kind of democracy in which the Founding Fathers and Judge Hand were interested." Wyzanski's legacy is that of a cultured and cultivated man deeply concerned with expanding individual freedom as part of the current of history.

★

Wyzanski's papers are at the Massachusetts Historical Society and the Harvard Law School Library. He wrote one book, *Whereas: A Judge's Premises* (1965), which consists largely of previously published pieces. Tributes include "In Memoriam: Charles E. Wyzanski Jr.," *Harvard Law Review* (Feb. 1987), originally talks by Derek C. Bok, Stephen Breyer, Paul A. Freund, Carl Kaysen, Edward H. Levi, Anthony Lewis, and Elliot L. Richardson; and Mark L. Wolf, "Few Are Chosen: The Judicial Appointments of Oliver Wendell Holmes, Jr., and Charles Edward Wyzanski, Jr.," *Massachusetts Law Review* (winter 1989). See also "In Memoriam: Charles E. Wyzanski, Jr.," 677 F. Supp. lxix (1987), and "Presentation of the Portrait of Charles E. Wyzanski, Jr.," 937 F. Supp. lxi (1996); Augustus N. Hand, "Introduction" in *Benjamin N. Cardozo Memorial Lectures Delivered Before the Association of the Bar of the City of New York, 1941–1970,* vol. 1. Wyzanski recalled his days at Exeter in "The Phillips Exeter Academy, an Appreciation," in Henry Darcy Curwen, ed., *Exeter Remembered* (1965). Peter Irons, *The New Deal Lawyers* (1982), treats his role in the New Deal; see also Thomas H. Eliot, *Recollections of the New Deal: When the People Mattered* (1992). Wyzanski's letter declining an appointment to the Court of Appeals is in Walter F. Murphy and C. Herman Pritchett, *Court, Judges, and Politics* (1986). Obituaries are in the *Boston Globe* (4 Sept. 1986) and *New York Times* (5 Sept. 1986). A memoir is in the Columbia oral history collection.

ROGER K. NEWMAN

Y-Z

YAMASAKI, Minoru (*b.* 1 December 1912 in Seattle, Washington; *d.* 6 February 1986 in Detroit, Michigan), architect who humanized the glass-and-steel severity of the International Style and is remembered as the designer of New York City's World Trade Center.

Yamasaki was the older of two sons born to Japanese immigrants John Tsunejiro Yamasaki and Hana (Ito) Yamasaki. The family lived in a cold-water tenement until John Yamasaki found a position in the stock department of a large Seattle shoe store. Minoru attended public school with other nisei, or second-generation Japanese-Americans. At Garfield High School, he was an honors student in mathematics and science but had no vocational direction until a visiting uncle, a recent architecture graduate, showed him some drawings. "I almost exploded with excitement when I saw them," he wrote later. "Then and there I decided to become an architect."

Yamasaki studied at the University of Washington, graduating with honors in 1934. During summers he earned money working in an Alaskan salmon cannery, where the brutal conditions instilled in him a chief tenet of his professional life: "a clear understanding that life could be lived more beautifully . . . no matter at how fundamental a level."

After graduation Yamasaki went to New York City, where, unable to find work in architecture, he took a job wrapping dishes for an import company. Studying during evenings at New York University, he took a watercolor course, in which he soon became the instructor. After two years, a fellow student asked Yamasaki to work on a rush job helping to complete the plans for a new state capitol for Oregon. When the firm of Githens and Keally won the competition, Yamasaki was hired as a designer-draftsman.

After a little more than a year, Yamasaki moved to Shreve, Lamb, and Harmon, architects of the Empire State Building. Yamasaki described this as "one of the most fortunate decisions I ever made. . . . From late 1936 to late 1943 I made all types of working drawings, checked shop drawings, and learned a great deal about how to construct a building."

In September 1941 Yamasaki met Teruko Hirashiki, a piano student at Juilliard; they married in December 1941 and had three children. After the attack by the Japanese on Pearl Harbor, when Yamasaki's parents were threatened with internment, he brought them to New York, where he shared with them, along with his younger brother, a one-bedroom apartment.

After getting security clearance, Yamasaki designed and supervised construction of "about ten different building types" for the Sampson Naval Station at Lake Seneca, New York. These two years would be, he wrote, "invaluable experience that helped to prepare me for running my own office." He added to this experience in 1943 working for Harrison, Fouilhoux, and Abramovitz, which he described as a model of a "humane office."

Minoru Yamasaki with his design for the education building at Wayne State University, 1958. UPI/CORBIS-BETTMANN

In 1944, while teaching as an instructor in architectural design at Columbia University, Yamasaki joined Raymond Loewy Associates to explore the field of industrial design. But after a year he concluded that "designing a skin around a machine whose form had already been decided was distasteful."

Yamasaki then became chief designer for Smith, Hinchman, and Grylls in Detroit. With an increase in salary, the Yamasakis expected to purchase a home in a suburban neighborhood, but as nonwhite nisei, they were excluded. The family instead bought a century-old farmhouse in nearby Troy, Michigan, where they lived for twenty-five years.

In 1949 Yamasaki formed a six-year partnership with George Hellmuth and Joseph Leinweber with offices in Detroit and St. Louis. His most distinguished work during this period was the Lambert Terminal of the St. Louis Airport (1953–1956), with its reception hall of thin-shelled concrete vaulting. The design brought Yamasaki prominence and became a prototype for airport terminals. But in 1954, Yamasaki suffered a near-fatal attack of ulcers—a condition he attributed both to overwork and to the pressures of living as a nisei.

"After the airport and my ulcer," he wrote, "I realized there's a danger of an architect getting involved in too many things for the sake of society. He's tempted to forget his real job is beauty." Now in his own firm of Minoru Yamasaki Associates, he designed an American consular office in Kobe, Japan, using the opportunity to travel. Through his studies of architecture in China, India, and Europe, he created a personal vision of delicacy and sculptural ornament—"the play of sun and shadow, a use of texture in materials to give pleasure."

Yamasaki developed the visual effect of a wall dissolving into a softer, fabriclike texture muting structural elements, used notably in the American Concrete Institute in Detroit (1958). Other buildings of the period include the McGregor Conference Center at Wayne State University in Detroit (1958) and the Reynolds Metals Sales Office in Southfield, Michigan (1959). The striking gold-anodized aluminum grilles of the latter prompted its owners to call it "a jewel on stilts." Yamasaki's firm also produced the U.S. Pavilion at New Delhi's Agricultural and Trade Fair (1959), with its multiple gold domes; and the Century 21 World's Fair building complex in Seattle, Washington (1962), sometimes criticized for its decorative Gothic arches.

Yamasaki's popularity strained his personal life. Separated from his wife in 1961, he suffered a recurrence of stomach ulcers. After four surgeries, now in his fifties, he reduced his workload and reunited his family. By the mid-1960s he had built his office staff to eighty employees, primarily to meet the commission for New York City's gargantuan World Trade Center, a project undertaken with Emery Roth and Sons that would take fourteen years to complete.

The World Trade Center (1976) presented problems for which Yamasaki found innovative solutions—the use of exterior walls as the basic cantilever structure and "sky lobbies" that reduced elevator space in the 110-story towers. Critics complained of the height, which seemed out of scale with the New York skyline, but, as Yamasaki wrote, "The buildings went upwards to free the ground space for daily human enjoyment." The Trade Center's five-acre plaza forms an oasis among the crowded buildings of lower Manhattan.

As the Trade Center opened, Yamasaki saw the demolition of an earlier project. The Pruitt-Igoe Public Housing Complex in St. Louis, an award-winning Yamasaki design in 1954, was intentionally destroyed in 1976 because of physical deterioration, vandalism, and crime. Some saw in its demise the end of the modern movement in architecture. Though Yamasaki's design was blamed for its supposed insensitivity to the needs of residents, authorities had truncated most of its humane elements, almost doubling the dwelling units per acre. Yamasaki told an interviewer, "Social ills can't be cured by nice buildings."

In the last ten years of his life Yamasaki designed fifteen major works, including the Performing Arts Center in Tulsa, Oklahoma (1976), the Founder's Hall of the Shiga Prefecture in Japan (1982), and an Islamic Women's Center in Jeddah, Saudi Arabia (1986). He worked nearly to the end, dying of cancer less than a week after entering the hospital. He is buried in Detroit, Michigan.

Minoru Yamasaki's work continues to attract controversy, from both proponents and opponents of modernism. But his 300 designs—and more than eighty-five major buildings—retain their distinctive vision and have proved popular and influential. He is the inheritor of the tradition of architect Ludwig Mies van der Rohe, to which he added a quality of "delight" through the playful use of elements from Indian, European Gothic, and—above all—Japanese design. What some see as deceptive in these elements, others perceive as humane. Yamasaki's mature work was a continuation of principles he summarized in a quotation from Emerson: "Our art saves material by more skillful arrangement and reaches beauty by taking every superfluous ounce that can be spared from a wall and keeping its strength in the poetry of the columns."

★

Yamasaki's *A Life in Architecture* (1979) is a modest, candid memoir with considerable detail about the architect's early years and essays on many of his designs. Muriel Emanuel, *Contemporary Architects,* 3d ed. (1994), contains an excerpt from the memoir, a good bibliography, and a list of Yamasaki's major buildings. V. M. Lampugnani, *Encyclopedia of Twentieth-Century Architecture* (1986), presents a penetrating summary of Yamasaki's work, and Paul Heyer, *Architects on Architecture* (1966), offers a perceptive, longer analysis. H. J. Schmandt and G. D. Wendel of the Center for Urban Problems at St. Louis University have written a sensible, balanced evaluation of what went wrong in *The Pruitt-Igoe Public Housing Complex, 1954–1976* (1976). An obituary is in the *New York Times* (9 Feb. 1986).

ALAN BUSTER

ZACHARIAS, Jerrold Reinach (*b.* 23 January 1905 in Jacksonville, Florida; *d.* 16 July 1986 in Belmont, Massachusetts), atomic physicist and educator who supervised the construction of the first practical atomic clock, the Atomichron, and reformed secondary science teaching.

Zacharias grew up in Jacksonville, Florida, the youngest child in a family that included a natural sister and an adopted brother. His father, Isadore A. Zacharias, a lawyer, and mother, Irma (Kaufman) Zacharias, a violin teacher, raised their children surrounded by music. As a child Zacharias was not musically gifted, so his mother worked with his adopted brother, a child prodigy. His sister, another prospective pianist, offered little companionship. His nurse, Anna Liza Johnson, an illiterate fourteen-year-old black girl, was Zacharias's true companion. Johnson called Zacharias "my boy" and he called her "my real mother." With a household of music, Zacharias said he had to "shut his earlids." As an adult his appreciation for music was rekindled.

Zacharias's first scientific interest was at age four, when his grandfather's chauffeur explained automobile mechanics. At nine he asked abstract questions, such as "How could time have begun?" He practiced science from a mail-order chemistry set. Later he told his mother he liked physics because it smelled better than chemistry. Zacharias once commented that a person could learn more practical physics from a Briggs and Stratton one-cylinder lawn mower engine than any other way.

Between 1918 and 1922 Zacharias was a popular and excellent pupil at Duval High School in Jacksonville. Physics was taught with minimal laboratory work, and Zacharias lost interest. After graduation he entered Columbia College, New York City, in the preengineering program. Despite being "more the raccoon-coat type, than the serious student," as a 1959 *New York Times* article described him, he obtained a B.A. degree in 1926, an A.M. degree in 1927, and a Ph.D. in 1933, all from Columbia.

In 1925, a Columbia graduate student, I. I. Rabi, encouraged Zacharias's interest in physics. Rabi, who would win a Nobel Prize in 1944, became mentor and friend. Also in 1925, Zacharias met his future wife, Leona Hurwitz, a biology major at Barnard College. They were married on 23 June 1927. Mutual interests led to a lifetime respect for the sciences. They had two children, whom they raised in Belmont, Massachusetts, and at a summer home in Buzzard's Bay. Leona Zacharias and I. I. Rabi became the most influential people in Zacharias's life.

Zacharias worked as a tutor at City College of New York from 1929 to 1930, as an instructor and at Hunter College of the City University of New York (1931–1936), and then as an assistant professor at Hunter until 1940. Beginning in 1940, Zacharias conducted research with Rabi in the molecular beam laboratory at the Massachusetts Institute of Technology (MIT). The lab had been set up for the wartime development of radar, and Zacharias soon installed the first microwave radar on a U.S. destroyer. In 1944 he went to Los Alamos to direct the engineering division of the Los Alamos Scientific Laboratory, which developed the atomic bomb. In 1945 Zacharias returned to MIT as a professor of physics. For ten years he directed MIT's Laboratory for Nuclear Science.

Zacharias was described as "a stocky, restless man, with staccato speech spiced with Yiddish phrases, often trailing off without finishing sentences." Sometimes he leaped to a

Jerrold Zacharias (*third from left*) with other members of the Brookhaven National Laboratory of Associated Universities Executive Committee, 1947. UPI/CORBIS-BETTMANN

blackboard and instructed his students, "Look here!" Of physicists in summertime projects he quipped, "Summer studies and some are not."

Zacharias himself took part in a number of summertime projects during his years at MIT. In 1948, for example, he was named associate director of Project Lexington, which studied problems of nuclear-powered flight, and he was awarded a President's Certificate of Merit that year. In 1950 he directed Project Hartwell, which dealt with undersea warfare, and the following year he became associate director of Project Charles, a study of air defense. In the summer of 1952 he initiated and directed a study of the Distant Early Warning system.

In July 1955 Zacharias received the Department of Defense Certificate of Appreciation, the department's highest civilian award. Defense Secretary Charles E. Wilson praised Zacharias's projects, Hartwell and Lamp Light, which showcased his innovative administration of team leadership. In 1956, as an outgrowth of molecular beam research, Zacharias supervised the construction of the first practical atomic clock, a small cesium device called an Atomichron, which oscillated at a constant frequency of 9,192–631,830 megacycles a second. It measured time so exactly that it lost only five seconds every 300 years.

Meanwhile, in 1955 Zacharias had dissolved his relationship with summer studies and resigned as director of the Laboratory of Nuclear Science at MIT. He sent a memo to Dr. James R. Killian, then president of MIT, expressing his concern over the state of high school physics education and his need to do something about it. He wrote, "I've got a lot of experiments to do. . . . Will somebody else do them if I don't? And I said, Yes. . . . In the eye of eternity, the stuff I want to do will get done, but education is a mess." In 1956, largely as a result of Zacharias's prodding, a new Physical Science Study Committee (PSSC) came into being at MIT, with Zacharias in the chair. The result of the committee's work was a completely reorganized and modernized high school physics curriculum reflecting the fact that, as Zacharias said, there had been more changes in physics in the preceding twenty years than in the previous two thousand.

By 1957 eight high schools had adopted the PSSC plan. National acceptance followed. Secondary science teachers presented the curriculum using a fresh approach in a logical and integrated manner. Along with other physicists, Zacharias appeared in some of the approximately sixty films used in the new curriculum. In the inaugural film, on the pressure of light, Zacharias was demonstrator and narrator. A science teacher commented that he enjoyed the film, even though thinking the narrator diffident and shy. In 1960 Zacharias received the Oersted Medal for Notable Contributions to the Teaching of Physics.

Rabi praised Zacharias on his eightieth birthday: "I cannot think of any time in which the world has not been a better place because of Jerrold Reinach Zacharias." Zacharias died at home of heart disease the next year. A memorial service was held at MIT in the October following his death. Biographer Jack S. Goldstein said of Zacharias, "He interacted strongly with the events of his time; his life serves as a window on that time, a particular vantage point from which much of this nation's recent history may be viewed." Zacharias, always the visionary, pictured a future where children could develop scientific curiosity under the watchful eyes of trained teachers. He understood science as something more than ideas hidden away in outdated books. Zacharias envisioned the miracle of young minds grappling with the concept of atoms.

★

Zacharias discusses problem-solving in "Structure of Physical Science," *Science* 125, no. 3245 (1957): 427–428. As the Oersted medalist for 1961, he comments on educational reform in "Team Approach to Education," *American Journal of Physics* 29, no. 6 (1961): 345–349. Francis W. Sears reviews Zacharias's career in the same issue of the *American Journal of Physics*. Daniel J. Kevles, *The Physicists* (1978), identifies Zacharias as a "new physicist." For biographical information, see Jack S. Goldstein, *A Different Sort of Time: The Life of Jerrold R. Zacharias, Scientist, Engineer, Educator* (1992). Zacharias's contributions to atomic physics are in H. Henry Stroke, ed., *The Physical Review: The First Hundred Years* (1994). Profiles are in the *New York Times* (16 Nov. 1959), *Saturday Review* (21 Oct. 1961), and *Time* (1 Feb. 1963).

SANDRA REDMOND PETERS

ZAMBONI, Frank Joseph, Jr. (*b.* 16 September 1901 in Eureka, Utah; *d.* 27 July 1988 in Long Beach, California), entrepreneur and inventor of the Zamboni ice-resurfacing machine.

Zamboni was one of four children of Frank Joseph Zamboni, Sr., and Carmelina (Masoero) Zamboni. He attended grade schools and one year of high school in Eureka before traveling to Chicago, where he attended trade school. In 1922 he moved with his brother Lawrence to Clearwater in southern California to join another brother, George, who owned a garage. The following year he married Norda Chamberlain; they had three children. Frank and Lawrence soon left the auto repair business to start a new company, Service Electric Company, installing water-pumping equipment at local dairies. They subsequently expanded their efforts into the produce industry, building a plant to make block ice that local packing plants could use for transporting their produce across the country.

The demand for block ice began to shrink as refrigeration technology improved, however, and by 1939 the Zambonis were compelled to explore new business opportunities. They decided upon building an ice skating rink, one of the first in the country, under the sunny skies of southern California. The 20,000-square-foot facility, called Iceland, opened in January 1940. Iceland proved to be enormously popular, eventually attracting as many as 150,000 visitors a year. The Zambonis quickly realized that maintaining the 100-by-200-foot rink's ice was a costly, labor-intensive task. First, a tractor pulled a planer to shave the top layer of gouged ice. The shavings were then scooped away, the surface was washed and squeezed clean, and a final spray of water was applied. It typically took five men ninety minutes to complete the task.

Frank Zamboni applied his ingenuity to the problem. Although he endured several false starts, in 1949 he developed a workable ice-resurfacing machine using a war-surplus Jeep engine, the front ends of two surplus army trucks, a series of pulleys, and a wooden bin to catch ice shavings, or "snow." The machine finished the job in fifteen minutes.

At first the machine, dubbed the Model A Zamboni Ice Resurfacer, was only used at Iceland. But after Olympic skater Sonja Henie saw the machine in action while she was rehearsing her Hollywood on Ice Revue at Iceland in 1950, she asked to buy one to take on tour around the United States and Canada. Zamboni hastily gathered the parts for a new machine, placed them on a trailer, and drove the Jeep he would use as the machine's base to Chicago to assemble on site, just in time for the revue. Henie was so pleased with the machine, she bought a second one to go on tour in Europe. As interest in the machine materialized, Zamboni founded the Frank J. Zamboni Company.

Zamboni built and sold fifteen machines from 1950 to 1953, each different, with improvements being made on every one. As ice skating became more and more popular in the United States, demand for Zamboni's resurfacing machine increased. Zamboni said the practice of calling the machine "the Zamboni" was started in Sioux Falls, South Dakota, by an unknown person who shouted out "Let's use the Zamboni." The name stuck. Hockey fans later began greeting the machines, which are used between periods in hockey games, with chants of "Zamboni, Zamboni" when the slow-moving vehicles were driven on to the ice.

The Model E, introduced in 1954, was the first Zamboni to be mass produced. The machine was bought by many rinks across the country, including the Boston Garden. In 1960 six units were used for the Winter Olympics at Squaw Valley, California. Zambonis have been used at almost every Winter Olympics since. Zamboni unveiled the HD Series in 1964. The new machine shed the Jeep chassis used in earlier models and introduced several new features, such as a vertical auger system to convey the snow off the ice and a quick-dumping snow tank. The innovations remained the standard of the industry more than thirty years later.

Although at least a dozen other manufacturers entered the ice-resurfacing business and the entire industry suffered a major disruption during the energy crisis of the 1970s, the Zamboni Company held its leadership position. This was in large part due to Frank's drive to continually improve the product and a commitment to quality derived from the fact that the machine bore his name.

In the 1970s, Monsanto, the manufacturer of Astroturf, asked Zamboni to find a way to remove water from artificial turf on baseball fields. Using a blower and a large vacuum, Zamboni designed the Astro-Zamboni to remove up to 75 percent of the water from the playing surface in forty-five

Frank Zamboni with his Zamboni ice resurfacing machine, 1985. NEAL PRESTON/CORBIS

minutes. He later developed machines to handle artificial turf and to remove painted stripes from artificial playing surfaces. He became less active in the company in the 1980s, handing over its management to his son and grandson.

Zamboni was very active in community affairs, and he played an instrumental role in unifying the towns of Clearwater and Hynes into Paramount in 1948. He was an avid fisherman. He was named to the Ice Skating Institute Hall of Fame in 1965 and received an honorary doctorate from Clarkson University. The North East Ice Skating Managers' Association created the Frank J. Zamboni Hall of Fame in 1988. Zamboni died of a heart attack and is buried in All Souls Cemetery in Long Beach, California.

While the Zamboni machine enjoyed a quirky celebrity status, Zamboni himself was an entrepreneurial inventor who built his own company through hard work, perseverance, and ingenuity. His rise to success coincided with, and contributed to, the rising popularity of ice skating and ice hockey in the United States.

★

Obituaries are in the *Los Angeles Times* and *New York Times* (both 29 July 1988).

ERIK BRUUN

DIRECTORY OF CONTRIBUTORS

ABRAMSON, RUDY
Reston, Virginia
Harriman, W(illiam) Averell
ACHENBAUM, W. ANDREW
University of Michigan
Stokes, Anson Phelps, Jr.
ADAMOWICZ, CATHERINE
Wheaton College
McCree, Wade Hampton, Jr.
AGNEW, BRAD
Northeastern (Oklahoma) State University
Keeler, William Wayne
ALLBRITTON, WILLIAM TODD
Graduate Student, Northeast Louisiana University (Monroe)
Passman, Otto Ernest
ALLEN, HOWARD
Brooklyn College, City University of New York
Hoffmann, Banesh
ALMEIDA, LINDA DOWLING
New York University
Bishop, James Alonzo ("Jim")
Shannon, William Vincent
ANAWALT, SASHA
Los Angeles Weekly
Joffrey, Robert
ANDREWS, TERRY
Freelance Writer, Warrenton, Oreg.
Cousins, Norman
AVERY, GLEN EDWARD
Houghton College
Noyce, Robert Norton
AYDT, RACHEL
Balliett & Fitzgerald, New York City
Piñero, Miguel
BADER-BOREL, PHYLLIS
State University of New York at Albany
Fosse, Robert Louis ("Bob")
BAKER, THERESE DUZINKIEWICZ
Western Kentucky University
Daché, Marie-Louise ("Lilly")
BARBEAU, ART
West Liberty State College
White, Theodore Harold ("Teddy")
BARTEE, ALICE FLEETWOOD
Southwest Missouri State University
Haynsworth, Clement Furman, Jr.
BARTHEL, THOMAS
Herkimer County Community College, N.Y.
Herman, Floyd Caves ("Babe")
BARWICK, DANIEL W.
Alfred State College, Alfred, N.Y.
Daniel, Price
BATINOVICH, KENNETH M.
Engineer, Rancho Palos Verdes, Calif.
Eliade, Mircea
BELL, JOHN L.
Western Carolina University
Gavin, James Maurice
BENSON, KATHLEEN
Museum of the City of New York
Norris, Clarence
BERNSTEIN, DAVID
California State University, Long Beach
Ruffing, Charles Herbert ("Red")
BLOODWORTH, JEFFREY
Instructor of History, Springfield, Mo.
Valentine, Kid Thomas
BLOTNER, JOSEPH
Professor Emeritus, University of Michigan
Warren, Robert Penn
BOSKY, BERNADETTE LYNN
Writer and Teacher, Yonkers, N.Y.
Addams, Charles Samuel

Brady, Frank
St. John's University, New York
Salt, Waldo
Schaffner, Franklin James
Brasel, Ellen O'Connell
Marshall University
Hays, Wayne Levere
Brauch, Patricia
Brooklyn College, City University of New York
Bearden, Romare Howard
Briller, Bert R.
Larchmont, New York
Paley, William Samuel
Browne, William F.
Brooklyn College, City University of New York
Blakey, Arthur ("Art"; Abdullah Ibn Buhaina)
Bruns, Robert T.
Boston College
Lansdale, Edward Geary
Walt, Lewis William
Bruun, Erik
Writer, Great Barrington, Mass.
Baird, William Britton ("Bil")
Peter, Laurence Johnston
Zamboni, Frank Joseph, Jr.
Burns, Charles A.†
State University of New York System Administration
Clifton, Nat(haniel) ("Sweetwater")
Buster, Alan
Harvard-Westlake School, Los Angeles
Stanwyck, Barbara
Yamasaki, Minoru
Byrne, John J.
Montclair State University
Davis, Sammy, Jr.
Calhoun, Richard B.
Editorial Consultant, Merrill Lynch
Flexner, Stuart Berg
Steiner, Ralph
Campbell, Gregg M.
Professor Emeritus, California State University, Sacramento
McCrea, Joel Albert
Cappelletti, J. S.
Songwriter and Writer, New York City
Henson, James Maury ("Jim")
Perls, Laura
Cardoso, Jack J.
State University of New York College at Buffalo
Shaara, Michael Joseph, Jr.
Cardoso, Rosemarie S.
Art Educator and Independent Scholar, Clarence, N.Y.
Loewy, Raymond Fernand
Carleton, Don E.
Center for American History, University of Texas at Austin
Faulk, John Henry
Carp, David M.
Carl Fischer, Inc.
Cugat, Xavier
Daniels, William Boone ("Billy")
Palmieri, Carlos Manuel, Jr. ("Charlie")
Carpenter, Brian
Sterling C. Evans Library, Texas A&M University
Miller, Carl S.
Carroll, John M.
Lamar University
Harmon, Thomas Dudley
Pollard, Frederick Douglass ("Fritz")
Carstensen, Fred
University of Connecticut
Magnin, Cyril
Parks, Henry Green, Jr.
Castle, Alfred L.
The Samuel N. and Mary Castle Foundation
Weinberg, Harry
Chayefsky, Dan
Writer, New York City
Minnelli, Vincente
Chen, Jeffrey H.
Charles Scribner's Sons
Divine (Harris Glenn Milstead)
Jorgensen, Christine
Cherepon, Lois
St. John's University, New York
Ellmann, Richard David
Cheuse, Alan
George Mason University
Malamud, Bernard
Cicarelli, James
Walter E. Heller College of Business Administration, Roosevelt University
Fuller, S. B.
Lekachman, Robert
Cicarelli, Julianne
Early Childhood Educator, Arlington Heights, Ill.
Flesch, Rudolf Franz
Clarke, Peter P.
Herkimer County Community College
Campbell, Joseph
Cobb, Kenneth R.
New York City Municipal Archives
Boudin, Leonard B.
Colby, Ursula Sybille
Russell Sage College (Retired)
Childs, Marquis William
Houseman, John

Coletta, Paolo E.
Professor Emeritus, United States Naval Academy
Anderson, Robert Bernerd
Boyington, Gregory ("Pappy")
Hancock, Joy Bright
Raborn, William Francis, Jr. ("Red")
Rickover, Hyman George
Coll, Blanche D.
Department of Health and Human Services (Retired)
Cohen, Wilbur Joseph
Conboy, Kenneth
Latham and Watkins, New York City
Friendly, Henry Jacob
Medina, Harold Raymond
Williams, Edward Bennett
Craddock, Brian
Writer and Pilot, U.S. Naval Reserves, Burtonsville, Md.
Dodd, Robert Lee ("Bobby")
Cross, Robert D.
Professor Emeritus, University of Virginia
Cremin, Lawrence Arthur
Malone, Dumas
Damon, Allan L.
Horace Greeley High School, Chappaqua, N.Y.
Bingham, Jonathan Brewster ("Jack")
Cowley, (David) Malcolm
Klopfer, Donald Simon
Kraft, Joseph
Davidson, Abraham A.
Tyler School of Art, Temple University
Soyer, Raphael
De Forest, Kellam
De Forest Research Service, Santa Barbara, Calif.
Backus, James Gilmore ("Jim")
Knight, Ted
Decker, Sharon L.
State University of New York Maritime College
Donovan, Hedley Williams
Delbanco, Nicholas
University of Michigan
Malamud, Bernard
Devine, Michael J.
University of Wyoming
Hayes, Wayne Woodrow ("Woody")
Devlin, James E.
State University of New York, Oneonta
Caldwell, Erskine Preston
Diaz, David
Spence School, New York City
Hammer, Armand
Perkins, (Richard) Marlin
Dick, Bernard F.
Farleigh Dickinson University
Martin, Mary Virginia
Dienstag, Eleanor Foa
Author and Journalist, New York City
Heinz, Henry John, II ("Jack")
Dinneen, Marcia B.
Bridgewater State College
University of Massachusetts at Dartmouth
Ray, John Alvin ("Johnnie")
Steber, Eleanor
Vallee, Hubert Prior ("Rudy")
DiRusso, Ben
York College, City University of New York
Segrè, Emilio Gino
Dobson, Melissa A.
Freelance Writer, Newport, R.I.
Broyard, Anatole Paul
Bundy, Theodore Robert ("Ted")
Doenecke, Justus D.
New College of the University of South Florida
Goldman, Eric Frederick
Driver, Julia
Brooklyn College and The Graduate Center of the City University of New York
Hook, Sidney
Drobnicki, John A.
York College Library, City University of New York
Allen, George Herbert
Williams, William B.
Dubal, David
Pianist, New York City
Faculty, Juilliard School of Music
Horowitz, Vladimir
Duff, John B.
Columbia College Chicago
Giamatti, A(ngelo) Bartlett ("Bart")
Dunham, Valerie L.
Ph.D. Candidate, University of New Hampshire
Harlow, Bryce N(athaniel)
Dunning, Jennifer
Dance Critic and Reporter, New York Times
Ailey, Alvin
Ekbladh, David
Columbia University
Norstad, Lauris
Eltscher, Louis R.
Rochester Institute of Technology
Johnson, Clarence Leonard ("Kelly")
Evensen, Bruce J.
DePaul University
Conlan, John Bertrand ("Jocko")
Layne, Robert Lawrence ("Bobby")
Richards, Paul Rapier
Farthing, Jennifer
International Thomson Publishing, New York City
Barthelme, Donald, Jr.

FARTHING, JENNIFER
(Continued)
Ellis, Perry Edwin
Erteszek, Olga Bertram
Vreeland, Diana
FERRELL, ROBERT H.
Indiana University, Bloomington
Collins, J(oseph) Lawton ("Lightning Joe")
FETZER, JAMES
State University of New York Maritime College
Clubb, O(liver) Edmund, II
Haughton, William Robert ("Billy")
Lattimore, Owen
FISCHER, WILLIAM E., JR.
U.S. Air Force
Carpenter, Robert Ruliph Morgan, Jr.
FITZPATRICK, JANE BRODSKY
Stephen B. Luce Library, State University of New York Maritime College
Husted, Marjorie Child
FLEET, SUSAN
Berklee College of Music
Brico, Antonia Louisa
FURLONG, PATRICK J.
Indiana University South Bend
Donner, Frederic Garrett
Halleck, Charles Abraham
GARGAN, WILLIAM M.
Brooklyn College, City University of New York
Carver, Raymond Clevie
Holmes, John Clellon
GATES, JONATHAN A.
Nyack College
Shepley, James Robinson
GELDERMAN, CAROL
University of New Orleans
McCarthy, Mary Therese
GENTILE, RICHARD H.
South Easton, Massachusetts
Conigliaro, Anthony Richard ("Tony")
O'Brien, Lawrence Francis, Jr. ("Larry")
GERBER, BARBARA L.
Brooklyn College, City University of New York
Ciardi, John Anthony
Nagurski, Bronislau ("Bronko")
GILBERT, RICHARD
Ohio University
Harris, Sydney Justin
Hemingway, Mary Welsh
Mannes, Marya
GNEUHS, GEOFFREY B.
Writer, New York City
Manning, Timothy
GONZALEZ, LEROY
Columbia University Graduate School of Business
Alvarez, Luis Walter
GOODSTEIN, JUDITH R.
California Institute of Technology
Beadle, George Wells ("Beets")
GORMAN, ANNA
Fremont Argus
Keeny, Spurgeon Milton ("Sam")
GOULD, KAREN
Independent Scholar, Austin, Tex.
Marble, Alice
GRAFF, HENRY F.
Columbia University
Rabi, I(sidor) I(saac)
GRAYBAR, LLOYD J.
Eastern Kentucky University
Scott, (George) Randolph
GREENBERG, DAVID
Columbia University
Slate Magazine
Strout, Richard Lee
GREENE, KATE
University of Southern Mississippi
Matthews, Burnita Shelton
GREENWALD, RICHARD A.
State University of New York, Morrisville
Bridges, Harry
GRESS, THOMAS G.
Lenexa, Kansas
Nef, John Ulric
GRIFFITH, JEAN W., JR.
Crowder College
Wallis, Harold Brent ("Hal")
GRIMES, ALAN P.
Professor Emeritus, Michigan State University
Harrington, (Edward) Michael
HAINES, MICHAEL F.
Dominican College, Orangeburg, N.Y.
Kraus, Hans Peter
Szent-Györgyi, Albert (von Nagyrapolt)
Wright, Sewall
HANSEN, VAGN K.
High Point University
Miller, William Mosely
HARMOND, RICHARD P.
St. John's University, New York
L'Amour, Louis
Lash, Joseph P.
HASKINS, JAMES
University of Florida
Bubbles, John William

HAUPTMANN, EMILY I.
Western Michigan University
Kohlberg, Lawrence
HAWLEY, ELLIS W.
University of Iowa
Jarvis, Howard Arnold
HERON, DAVID W.
University of California, Santa Cruz
Armour, Richard Willard
Russell, Charles Hinton
HERRINGTON, NANCY J.
Syracuse University
Doisy, Edward Adelbert
HIRSCH, FOSTER
Brooklyn College of the City University of New York
Cagney, James Francis, Jr.
Garbo, Greta
HIRSCHHORN, BERNARD
Historian and Author, New York City
Dangerfield, George
Lord, John Wesley
HLAVATY, ARTHUR D.
Independent Scholar, Yonkers, N.Y.
Shulman, Max
HODGES, GRAHAM RUSSELL
Colgate University
Newton, Huey Percy
HOFFECKER, CAROL E.
University of Delaware
Williams, John James
HOLLAND, MAX
Miller Center for Public Affairs, University of Virginia
McCloy, John Jay
HOOGENBOOM, LYNN
New York Times News Service
Caniff, Milton Arthur
HULSEY, BYRON C.
Woodberry Forest School, Virginia
Bricker, John William
HUNTINGTON, MATTHEW
Syracuse University
Allison, Fran(ces)
HUYGHE, PATRICK
Author and Science Journalist, Putnam Valley, N.Y.
Heinlein, Robert Anson
IRWIN, RAYMOND D.
Ohio State University
Lazarus, Ralph
JACOBS, FREDERIC
American University
Wilson, Logan
JACOBSON, LESLIE S.
Research Foundation, City University of New York
Lipmann, Fritz Albert
Weiss, Paul Alfred
JAŘAB, JOSEF
Central European University, Budapest
Member of Parliament, Czech Republic
Baldwin, James Arthur
JEBSEN, HARRY, JR.
Capital University
Kluszewski, Theodore Bernard ("Ted"; "Big Klu")
JENKINS, EDWARD S.
State University of New York at Buffalo
McNair, Ron(ald) Erwin
JONES, DOUGLAS N.
Graduate Student, Southwest Missouri State University
Lovestone, Jay
KALFATOVIC, MARY
Writer and Librarian, Arlington, Va.
Fain, Sammy
Levine, Joseph Edward
KASS, JUDITH M.
Researcher and Writer, New York City
Bennett, Joan
MacRae, Gordon
KAST, ARI J.
Writer, Astoria, N.Y.
Radner, Gilda
KEANE, TIM
Writer, Mt. Vernon, N.Y.
Duncan, Robert
KELLY, MATTHEW
Writer, Quincy, Mass.
Mohr, Charles Henry
KELLY, ROBERT J.
Brooklyn College and The Graduate School, City University of New York
Provenzano, Anthony ("Tony Pro")
Trafficante, Santo, Jr.
KETZ, LOUISE B.
Louise B. Ketz Literary Agency
Baker, Carlos Heard
Gabel, Hortense Wittstein
Middleton, Drew
Wilson, Earl
KHATUN, SAIYEDA
University of Rhode Island
Janowitz, Morris
KIERNAN, VINCENT
Alexandria, Virginia
Hagen, John Peter

Kirshner, Ralph
Independent Scholar, Chapel Hill, N.C.
Smith, William French
Kornhauser, Anne
Ph.D. Candidate, Columbia University
Hartz, Louis
Van Arsdale, Harry, Jr.
Kostelanetz, Richard
Writer, New York City
Thomson, Virgil Garnett
Kotulak, Thomas D.
Indiana University Southeast
Madden, Ray John
Kowal, Rebekah J.
Ph.D. Candidate, New York University
Tudor, Antony
Kronzek, Elizabeth
Princeton University
Smith, Henry Nash
Kuehl, John†
Professor Emeritus, New York University
Graham, Sheilah
Lagonia, Maria
Rye Free Reading Room, Rye, N.Y.
McCracken, James Eugene
LaHood, Marvin J.
Buffalo State College
Astor, Mary
Haggar, Joseph Marion
Lankevich, George J.
Professor of History Emeritus, City University of New York
Pope, Generoso Paul, Jr.
Larsen, Charles E.
Professor Emeritus, Mills College
Luce, Clare Boothe
Larson, Sylvia B.
Bridgewater State College, Bridgewater, Mass.
Baldwin, Raymond Earl
Cotton, Norris Henry
Hildreth, Horace Augustus
Lasser, Michael
Rochester Democrat and Chronicle
Smith, Kathryn Elizabeth ("Kate")
Van Heusen, James ("Jimmy")
Lauderdale, Kevin
Stanford University
Blanc, Mel(vin) Jerome
Launius, Roger D.
Chief Historian, National Aeronautics and Space Administration
Bergman, Jules Verne
Leab, Daniel J.
Seton Hall University
Ray, Gordon Norton
Leary, William M.
University of Georgia
Smith, C(yrus) R(owlett)
Leiter, Samuel L.
Brooklyn College and The Graduate Center, City University of New York
Davis, Bette
Kaye, Danny
Logan, Joshua Lockwood, III
Ludlam, Charles
Page, Geraldine
Levine, Michael L.
Freelance Writer and Editor, New York City
Barnett, Ross Robert
Levstik, Frank R.
Kentucky Department for Libraries and Archives
Lausche, Frank John
Levy, Sharona A.
Borough of Manhattan Community College, CUNY
Kelman, Wolfe
Prinz, Joachim
Linden, Eugene
Author, Nyack, N.Y.
Contributor, Time Magazine
Wang, An
Lizzio, Joan
Hawley, Pennsylvania
Menninger, Karl Augustus
Lookingbill, Brad
Columbia College, Missouri
Cunliffe, Marcus Falkner
Lord, Tom Forrester
Rice University
Housing Corporation of Greater Houston
Bradshaw, Thornton Frederick ("Brad")
McCarthy, Glenn Herbert
Loughran, James N.
St. Peter's College
Campion, Donald Richard
Lowery, Charles D.
Mississippi State University
Eastland, James Oliver
Luebbering, Ken
Lincoln University of Missouri
Rodale, Robert
Luft, Eric v. d.
State University of New York Health Science Center at Syracuse
Wyeth, Nathaniel Convers
McBride, Carrie C.
Reading Reform Foundation of New York
Attwood, William Hollingsworth
Edwards, Douglas

McBride, Francis R.
Herrick Library, Alfred University
Rooney, Arthur Joseph
McCarthy, Timothy P.
Columbia University
Bailey, Pearl Mae
Maravich, Peter Press ("Pistol Pete")
McCurdy, Sheila
State University of New York Maritime College
Hart, Marion Rice
McDonagh, Don
State University of New York at Purchase
New York University
Bennett, Michael
McDonald, Archie P.
Stephen F. Austin State University
Canutt, Enos Edward ("Yakima")
McDowell, Markus H.
Pepperdine University
Fuller Theological Seminary
Hubbard, L(afayette) Ron(ald)
McFarland, John Robert
Writer and Historian
Roush, Edd J.
McKay, Elizabeth
The New York and Presbyterian Hospital
Hammond, E(dward) Cuyler
McKay, Ellen French
Washington, D.C.
Eaker, Ira Clarence
McKay, Ernest A.†
University of South Carolina at Aiken
Eaker, Ira Clarence
McKay, Stephen
Burlington, Vermont
Eaker, Ira Clarence
Graziano, Rocky
McLaughlin, Marilyn Sauder
Ypsilanti, Michigan
Festinger, Leon
Schoenbrun, David Franz
McLean, Michael
Independent Scholar, New York City
Robinson, Ray ("Sugar Ray")
McMahan, Ian
Brooklyn College, City University of New York
Rogers, Carl Ransom
Magee, Jeffrey
Indiana University
Berlin, Irving
Maloney, Wendy Hall
Brooklyn College, City University of New York
Bauer, Eddie
Bowles, Chester Bliss ("Chet")
Crown, Henry
Marc, David
Newhouse School of Public Relations, Syracuse University
Crawford, (William) Broderick
Gleason, Herbert John ("Jackie")
Rowan, Dan Hale
Marinelli, Deborah Aydt
System Administration, State University of New York
Forbes, Malcolm Stevenson
Soule, Gertrude May
Markgraf, Sarah
Bergen Community College, Paramus, New Jersey
Eldridge, (David) Roy ("Little Jazz")
Persichetti, Vincent Ludwig
Markoe, Lauren
The Patriot Ledger, Quincy, Mass.
McAuliffe, (Sharon) Christa
Marshall, Stephen
Lincoln Park, New Jersey
Arnaz, Desi
Ball, Lucille Désirée
Murchison, Clint(on) Williams, Jr.
Wilentz, David Theodore
Martin, Rebecca
Pace University
Shimkin, Leon
Wallace, Sippie
Mayo, Louise A.
County College of Morris, Randolph, N.J.
Goddard, Paulette
Meckna, Michael
Texas Christian University
Copland, Aaron
Merron, Myrna W.
Mount Dora, Florida
Crawford, Cheryl
Merry, Robert W.
Congressional Quarterly, Inc.
Alsop, Joseph Wright, V
Miller, James P.
ACA Publications, Alexandria, Va.
Wallace, Irving
Miner, Suzanne M.
Fellow, James Madison Memorial Fellowship Foundation
Pritzker, A(bram) N(icholas)
Moberg, Verne
Columbia University
Liberace, Wladziu Valentino
Morgan, Michelle C.
Ph.D. Candidate, Columbia University
Dean, Arthur Hobson

MORRISROE, PATRICIA
Author and Journalist, New York City
Mapplethorpe, Robert
MUCCIGROSSO, ROBERT
Professor Emeritus, Brooklyn College, City College of New York
LeMay, Curtis Emerson
Mumford, Lewis Charles
Veeck, William Louis, Jr. ("Bill")
MULLIGAN, WILLIAM H., JR.
Murray State University
Williams, G(erhard) Mennen
NEAL, STEVE
Chicago Sun-Times
Clark, Joseph Sill, Jr.
Green, Edith Starrett
Ogilvie, Richard Buell
Washington, Harold
NELSON, ALLAN
Caldwell College, Caldwell, N.J.
Cournand, André Frederic
Fredericks, Carlton
Meyner, Robert Baumle
Percy, Walker
NELSON, MARTHA E.
State University of New York College of Agriculture and Technology, Morrisville
Belvin, Harry J. W.
NEWMAN, ROGER K.
School of Law, New York University
Goldberg, Arthur Joseph
Pepper, Claude Denson
Wyzanski, Charles Edward, Jr.
OHL, JOHN KENNEDY
Mesa Community College
Carney, Robert Bostwick
Chase, William Curtis
O'KEEFE, KEVIN J.
Stetson University
Schiff, Dorothy
OLSON, JAMES C.
President Emeritus, University of Missouri
Symington, (William) Stuart, III
OSHINSKY, DAVID M.
Rutgers University
Cohn, Roy Marcus
PACHECO, MARIA
Buffalo State College
Pedersen, Charles John
Rainwater, (Leo) James
PAINO, TROY D.
Winona State University
Daugherty, Hugh ("Duffy")
PARKER, ALISON M.
University of Texas at Arlington
Bowman, Thea Bertha ("Sister Thea")
Koontz, Elizabeth Duncan
Lindsay, Goldie Ina Ruby ("Eldress Bertha")
PARRIS, LAROSE T.
City College of New York
Baker, Ella Josephine
Dolgun, Alexander Michael
PATTERSON, DAVID S.
U.S. Department of State
Labouisse, Henry Richardson
PATTERSON, MARY-MARGARET S.
Journalist, Chevy Chase, Md.
Frederick, Pauline
PERRY, ANNA BEATRICE
Kentucky Historical Society
Bingham, (George) Barry, Sr.
PERRY, LISA R.
Kentucky Historical Society
Dawidowicz, Lucy Schildkret
Negri, Pola
PERRY, MARILYN ELIZABETH
Independent Scholar, Prospect Heights, Ill.
Friend, Charlotte
Libby, Leona Woods Marshall
Taussig, Helen Brooke
PETERS, SANDRA REDMOND
Graduate Student, Southwest Missouri State University
Zacharias, Jerrold Reinach
PETERSON, BARBARA BENNETT
University of Hawaii
Greene, Lorne
Hayworth, Rita
PETERSON, F. ROSS
Utah State University
Ullman, Al(bert) Conrad
PHILLIPPON, DANIEL J.
University of Minnesota, Twin Cities
Abbey, Edward Paul
PHILLIPS, ROBERT
University of Houston
Bacon, Ernst
Mizener, Arthur Moore
PIOUS, RICHARD M.
Barnard College and The Graduate Faculties, Columbia University
Adams, (Llewellyn) Sherman
Mitchell, John Newton
PLASTER, DAN
Graduate Student, Southwest Missouri State University
Warne, Colston Estey

POLAKOFF, KEITH IAN
California State University, Long Beach
Bible, Alan Harvey
Unruh, Jesse Marvin
POLLAK, RICHARD
Contributing Editor, The Nation
Bettelheim, Bruno
POLLEY, MICHAEL
Columbia College (Missouri)
Reischauer, Edwin Oldfather
POMPER, GERALD M.
Rutgers University
Javits, Jacob Koppel
POMPER, MILES A.
Washington, D.C.
Lubell, Samuel
PORTER, DAVID L.
William Penn College
Blaik, Earl Henry ("Red")
Cunningham, Glenn V.
Hubbell, Carl Owen
Terry, William Harold ("Memphis Bill")
POTTER, BARRETT G.
State University of New York College of Technology, Alfred
Gordon, Dexter Keith
POWERS, RICHARD GID
College of Staten Island and The Graduate Center, City University of New York
Casey, William Joseph
PRICHARD, JAMES M.
Archivist, Kentucky State Archives
Carradine, John
PUGH, WILLIAM WHITE TISON
University of Oregon, Eugene
Fidler, James Marion ("Jimmy")
REDMAN, NICK
Santa Monica, California
Marvin, Lee
REED, BRADLEY F.
Writer, Rochester, N.Y.
Carvel, Thomas Andrew
Meeker, Ralph
REED, JAMES W.
Rutgers University
Skinner, B(urrhus) F(rederic)
REGUER, SARA
Brooklyn College, City University of New York
Baron, Salo Wittmayer
Kahane, Meir
REYNOLDS, CLARK G.
College of Charleston
Davison, William Edward ("Wild Bill")
Goodman, Benjamin David ("Benny")
Stewart, Leroy Elliott ("Slam")
Wilson, Theodore Shaw ("Teddy")
RIGGS, CHRISTOPHER K.
University of Colorado at Boulder
Allott, Gordon Llewellyn
ROBERSON, GLORIA GRANT
Adelphi University
Pendleton, Clarence Mclane, Jr.
ROCCO, JOHN
Queens College, City University of New York
Baker, Chesney Henry ("Chet")
ROME, ROMAN
State University of New York Maritime College
Lemnitzer, Lyman Louis
Taylor, Maxwell Davenport
Wedemeyer, Albert Coady
ROND, CHARLES A., IV
Computer Consultant, Center for Earthquake Research and Information, University of Memphis
Northrop, John Howard
White, Jack Edward, Sr.
ROREX, P. DALE
Seiwa College
Folsom, James
Licklider, J(oseph) C(arl) R(obnett)
Matsunaga, Spark Masayuki ("Sparkie")
ROSEN, JEFFREY S.
Spotswood (New Jersey) High School
Greenberg, Henry Benjamin ("Hank")
Hammond, John Henry, Jr.
Orbison, Roy Kelton
ROSENOF, THEODORE
Mercy College, Dobbs Ferry, N.Y.
Means, Gardiner Coit
RUHLMANN, WILLIAM J.
Writer, New York City
Arlen, Harold
Lerner, Alan Jay
Loewe, Frederick
Trapp, Maria von
Vaughan, Sarah Lois
SANTANGELO, MARK
George Washington University
Rusk, Howard Archibald
SAPIENZA, MADELINE
Independent Scholar, Washington, D.C.
Bolet, Jorge
Dorati, Antal
LeRoy, Mervyn
Milanov, Zinka
SCATES, SHELBY
Seattle, Washington
Magnuson, Warren Grant

SCHRAG, ZACHARY M.
Ph.D. Candidate, Columbia University
Bechtel, Stephen Davison, Sr.
SCHWAB, JENNIFER D.
Marion (Arkansas) Ledger
Halston (Roy Halston Frowick)
SENNETT, TED
Author, Closter, N.J.
Arden, Eve
Astaire, Fred
Bolger, Ray(mond) Wallace
Gardner, Ava Lavinia
Grant, Cary
Lanchester, Elsa
Mamoulian, Rouben Zachary
Preston, Robert
SEYEDIAN, MOJTABA
State University of New York, College at Fredonia
Bernhard, Arnold
SHANE, CAROL TONER
Artist, Sioux City, Iowa
Eames, Ray
Kent, Corita
SHISHIN, ALEX
Akashi City, Hyogo Prefecture, Japan
Goodman, Percival
SHOR, RACHEL
York College, City University of New York
Presser, Jackie
SHREEFTER, KAREN
Writer and Editor, Great Barrington, Mass.
Milland, Ray
SIRVET, ENE
Former Editor, The Papers of John Jay, Columbia University
Morris, Richard B(randon)
SMALL, MELVIN
Wayne State University
Goulding, Ray(mond) Walter
Lichine, Alexis
SMID, LAURA KATHLEEN
Charles Scribner's Sons
Snyder, Mitch(ell) Darryl
SMITH, ANDREW
University of New Mexico
Preminger, Otto Ludwig
SMITH, PATRICK
Wichita State University
Warhol, Andy
SMITH, WALTER R.
Corning Community College
Houghton, Arthur Amory, Jr.
SMITH, WHITNEY
The Commercial Appeal, Memphis, Tenn.
Kaye, Sammy

SNEH, ITAI
Ph.D. Candidate, Columbia University
Hickerson, John Dewey
Jessup, Philip C(aryl)
Perlmutter, Nathan
SNYDER, RACHEL
Independent Scholar, Boulder, Colo.
Childress, Alvin
Fredericks, Sara
SOBEL, ROBERT
Hofstra University
Busch, August Anheuser, Jr. ("Gussie")
Little, Royal
SOLOMON, IRVIN D.
Florida Gulf Coast University
Abernathy, Ralph David
Rustin, Bayard Taylor
SOLON, LEONARD R.
Physicist and Educator, Fort Pierce, Fla.
Brattain, Walter Houser
Feynman, Richard Phillips
Hofstadter, Robert
Livingston, M(ilton) Stanley
SOMMER, MARK
Stevens' Institute of Technology, Hoboken, N.J.
Angleton, James Jesus
Gilford, Jack
Vaughan, Stevie Ray
SPATT, HARTLEY S.
State University of New York Maritime College
Bunshaft, Gordon
MacDonald, John Dann
Windsor, Wallis Warfield (Simpson), Duchess of
STAHL, MARTIN JAY
Empire State College, State University of New York
Hobson, Laura Kean Zametkin
Sulzberger, Iphigene Bertha Ochs
STEIN, JUDITH
Graduate School and City College of the City University of New York
Abel, I(orwith) W(ilbur) ("Abe")
STENSTROM, CHRISTINE
LaGuardia Community College, City University of New York
Wescott, Glenway
STERLING, KEIR B.
Command Historian, U.S. Army Combined Arms Support Command
Landon, Alf(red) Mossman
STERNER, INGRID
Writer, New York City
Steloff, (Ida) Frances

Stertz, Stephen A.
Dowling College
Mercy College
Huie, William Bradford
Stoloff, Sam
Cornell University
Jackson, Travis Calvin ("Stonewall")
Stoneham, Horace
Stringer-Hye, Richard
Librarian, Vanderbilt University
Isherwood, Christopher William
Suchecki, Peter C.
Maine College of Art
Basquiat, Jean-Michel
Haring, Keith Allen
Sweeney, James Johnson
Sumbera, Michael W.
Brooklyn College, City University of New York
Bernstein, Leonard
Svenningsen, Karen Lynn
College of Staten Island, City University of New York
Hassenfeld, Stephen David
Hoving, Walter
Mack, Walter Staunton, Jr.
Ritt, Martin
Rubell, Steve
Swain, Craig A.
Graduate Student, Southwest Missouri State University
Collbohm, Franklin Rudolph
Sweet, James Stouder
Writer and Editor, Silver Spring, Md.
Martin, John Bartlow
Tamborrino, Victoria
St. John's University, New York
Shockley, William Bradford
Tapper, Jonathan
Brockton Enterprise, Boston
Crothers, Benjamin Sherman ("Scatman")
Tassinari, Edward J.
Writer, Scarsdale, N.Y.
Martin, Alfred Manuel, Jr. ("Billy")
Taylor, Durahn
Columbia University
Drake, St. Clair
Taylor, Jon E.
National Park Service
Albright, Horace Marden
Blaisdell, Thomas Charles, Jr.
Thomas, Theodore N.
Silver Spring (Md.) Church of Christ
Armstrong, Herbert W.
Gillars, Mildred Elizabeth Sisk ("Axis Sally")

Thompson, Gail Strange
Falmouth, Maine
White, Ryan
Thompson, Gerald†
University of Toledo
Huston, John
Tischler, Barbara L.
Horace Mann School
Hoffman, Abbott ("Abbie")
Ussachevsky, Vladimir
Tomasino, Adriana C.
Ph.D. Candidate, Graduate School and University Center, City University of New York
MacCorquodale, Donald William ("Mac")
Tomko, Andrew S.
Bergen Community College
Reed, Donna
Trask, Roger R.
Historical Office, Office of the Secretary of Defense (Retired)
Lovett, Robert Abercrombie
Tucker, David M.
University of Memphis
Johnson, Wallace Edward
Turgeon, Lynn
Hofstra University
Burns, Arthur Frank
Heller, Walter Wolfgang
Keyserling, Leon Hirsch
Turner, Elizabeth Hutton
Phillips Collection
O'Keeffe, Georgia Totto
Turtell, Stephen
Brooklyn College, City University of New York
Johnson, Eleanor Murdock
Killian, James Rhyne, Jr.
Van Dijk, Ruud
Ohio University
Stoessel, Walter John, Jr.
VanDoren, Sandra Shaffer
Archivist, Balch Institute for Ethnic Studies, Philadelphia
Bruhn, Erik Belton Evers
Chase, Lucia Hosmer
Hartdegen, Stephen Joseph
Venturella, Karen M.
Sprague Library, Montclair State University
Asch, Moses ("Moe")
Bender, Lauretta
Voigt, John
Berklee College of Music
Evans, Gil
Feldman, Morton
Von Winbush, Samuel
State University of New York at Westbury
Mulliken, Robert Sanderson

WAGLEY, STEPHEN
Charles Scribner's Sons
Day, Dennis
WALKER, WILLIAM STERLING
Stults and Balber, New York City
Sirk, Douglas
WARD, NATHAN
Library Journal
Rich, Bernard ("Buddy")
WARNE, KATE
Stanford University Press
Stone, Irving
WASSER, FREDERICK
School of Journalism, Columbia University
Berlin, Richard Emmett
Wood, Robert Dennis
WASSER, HENRY
Academy for Humanities and Sciences, City University of New York
Brewster, Kingman, Jr.
Keppel, Francis
WATSON, MARY ANN
Eastern Michigan University
Susskind, David Howard
WATTEL, HAROLD L.
Hofstra University
Henderson, Leon
Mitchell, (John) Broadus
WEDGE, ELEANOR F.
Freelance Writer and Editor, New York City
DeGaetani, Jan
Sackler, Arthur Mitchell
WEIGOLD, MARILYN E.
Pace University, Pleasantville, N.Y.
Baldrige, (Howard) Malcolm
WEINSTEIN, HONORA RAPHAEL
Brooklyn College, City University of New York
Heifetz, Jascha
WEISBERGER, BERNARD A.
American Heritage
Stone, I(sidor) F(einstein) ("Izzy")
WEISBLAT, LEIGH BULLARD
Independent Art Historian, New York City
De Kooning, Elaine Marie Catherine
Janis, Sidney
Nevelson, Louise
WEISBLAT, TINKY "DAKOTA"
Independent Scholar, Hawley, Mass.
Dunne, Irene Marie
St. Johns, Adela Rogers
Selznick, Irene Mayer
WELCH, PAULA D.
University of Florida
Vare, Glenna Collett
WIENER, JONATHAN
Oxford University Press
Herman, Woody
WILENTZ, SEAN
Princeton University
Tuchman, Barbara Wertheim
WILES, TIMOTHY J.
National Baseball Hall of Fame Library, Cooperstown, N.Y.
Johnson, William Julius ("Judy")
Lyons, Theodore Amar ("Ted")
WITWER, DAVID S.
Lycoming College
Williams, Roy Lee
WONG, AMY AN MEI B.
Nassau Community College
Haughton, Daniel Jeremiah
YEATES, MARIAN
Salt Lake City, Utah
Williams, William Appleman
ZADROZNY, MARK
New York City
Ford, Henry, II ("Hank the Deuce")
Noguchi, Isamu

OCCUPATIONS INDEX, VOLUMES 1–2

See also the Alphabetical List of Subjects beginning on p. 957.

ALPHABETICAL LIST OF SUBJECTS, VOLUMES 1–2

See also the Occupations Index beginning on p. 937.